Biography Almanac

Biography Almanac

A comprehensive reference guide to more than 23,000 famous and infamous newsmakers from Biblical times to the present as found in over 300 readily available biographical sources.

SECOND EDITION

Volume 1

Biographies

Edited by Susan L. Stetler

Gale Research Company • Book Tower
Detroit, Michigan 48226

Editor: Susan L. Stetler

Assistant Editors: Marie Browne, Amy F. Lucas, and Christine Tomassini

Editorial Assistants: Brian Dooms, Nancy Franklin, Laura Hooper, Doris Lewandowski, Evabelle MacKay, Viola Ndenga, Annette Novallo, and Joan Walsh

Special thanks to Elaine Cybulski, Marie Evans, Kim Jones, John Krol, Elizabeth Mulligan, Eric Sarkissian, and Marc Sarkissian

Production Supervisor: Carol Blanchard

Cover Design: Art Chartow

Computerized photocomposition by
Computer Composition Corporation
Madison Heights, Michigan

ISSN 0738-0097
ISBN 0-8103-1632-3 (Volume 1)
ISBN 0-8103-1633-1 (Volume 2)
ISBN 0-8103-1634-X (set)

Contents

Introduction

If the ordinary person wants information about a word, it is easy to find a compact dictionary to supply it. If what's needed is a common fact about a state, a foreign country, a list of the tallest buildings or longest rivers, there are general almanacs to provide the information.

But if the question concerns a personality—especially a contemporary personality—outside such traditional fields as scholarship, government, and the military, the basic facts are much harder to come by.

For example, botanist Addison Brown, clergyman Arthur Judson Brown, chemist Crum Brown, mathematician Ernest William Brown, essayist John Brown, and electrical engineer Sidney George Brown (all of limited interest today and all long dead) can be found in several common sources.

But if brief information is needed on such contemporary people as ballerina Leslie Browne, civil rights activist H. Rap Brown, singer Jackson Browne, test tube baby Louise Joy Brown, or governor John Y. Brown, the search is likely to be a long and tedious one without the help of *Biography Almanac.*

Biography Almanac is a biographical directory to famous people. What is fame? It has neither limitations nor definitions, standard nor rule. Fame thrives as a result of genius or eccentricity, accident or purpose. The person who has "made it" in television, or in the theatre, or in science, sports, business, government, religion, or industry is the prominent person that *Biography Almanac* lists.

Quick Identifications for 23,000 Famous Persons

This edition of *Biography Almanac* contains over 23,000 names. It includes all entries from the first edition and the supplement, many of which have been updated due to death or increased prominence. The last death added to the file was Tennessee Williams on February 24, 1983. The second edition also contains approximately 500 new names, many of whom have become well known since the publication of the supplement. For example, the interest in small computers and video games has made Steven Jobs and Stephen Wozniak, the co-founders of the Apple Computer, and Toro Iwatani, the inventor of the video game "Pac-Man," important newsmakers. The birth, in the summer of 1982, of Prince William of Wales made him an instant celebrity.

Quick identifications sufficient for many needs can be found immediately in

Biography Almanac. The same listing, however, will also direct the user to more detailed information through citations to over 300 widely available biographical dictionaries, thus short-circuiting prolonged searches which might in the end fail to turn up needed information. (A complete list of the biographical dictionaries cited is given in the bibliographical section of this book.)

Clarification

Some readers mistakenly believe that *Biography Almanac* is a substitute for Gale's *Biography and Genealogy Master Index (BGMI).* Actually, the two publications are essentially different types of research tools.

BGMI is an *index* to all names in over 350 different biographical dictionaries, representing over 700 editions and volumes. *BGMI* is a comprehensive and time-saving tool for accessing a wide variety of biographical dictionaries. On the other hand, *Biography Almanac* is *itself* a biographical dictionary. It lists selected people who "have made news." It provides self-contained biographical information on that group of people as well as citations to biographical sources that may be useful to the reader.

New Features

There are several important new features in this edition of *Biography Almanac.*

The most important new feature is the volume of indexes which is being published for the first time. It contains three indexes of interest to the researcher and the trivia buff. There are two chronological indexes: one by year; the other by date. The index by year lists, in alphabetical order, first everyone in *Biography Almanac* who was born on a specific year, month, and day, then everyone in the book who died on that date. For instance, both John Adams and Thomas Jefferson died in 1826 and both died on July 4.

July 4, 1826
b. Foster, Stephen Collins
d. Adams, John
d. Jefferson, Thomas

The second chronological index lists all *Biography Almanac* entrants who were born or died in a specific month on a specific day. The year of birth or death appears after the entrant's name in chronological order. For example, this index lists 55 people who were born on July 4 and 32 people who died on July 4.

July 4
b. Landers, Ann 1918
b. Van Buren, Abigail 1918
b. Garraty, John Arthur 1920
b. Saint, Eva Marie 1924
b. Simon, (Marvin) Neil 1927
b. Boyd, Stephen 1928
b. Lollobrigida, Gina 1928
b. Steinbrenner, George Michael, III 1930
b. Hudson, Joseph Lowthian, Jr. 1931

The third index is the geographic index, enabling the user to find everyone who was born or who died in a specific location. The index is divided into three general sections: the United States, Canada, and Foreign. The United States is further broken down by state and then by city within the state; Canada is broken down by province and city; and Foreign is in alphabetical order by country. Below each city are the names of those people listed in *Biography Almanac* who were either born or who died in that location, followed by the birth or death date. Under New York, New York, for example, Norman Rockwell is listed with his birthdate, Feb. 3, 1894, and Nelson Rockefeller is listed with his deathdate, Jan. 26, 1979. Rockwell also appears under Stockbridge, Massachusetts, with his deathdate and Rockefeller appears under Bar Harbor, Maine, with his birthdate.

MASSACHUSETTS
Stockbridge
Bowker, R(ichard) R(ogers)
d. Nov 12, 1933
Field, Cyrus West b. Nov 30, 1819
French, Daniel Chester d. Oct 7, 1931
Hopkins, Mark b. Feb 4, 1802
Niebuhr, Reinhold d. Jun 1, 1971
Rockwell, Norman d. Nov 8, 1978
Sedgwick, Catherine Maria b. Dec 28, 1789

MAINE
Bar Harbor
Ralston, Esther b. 1902
Rockefeller, Nelson A(ldrich) b. Jul 8, 1908

The second new feature is the addition to about 5,000 of the entries of a "one-line" descriptor which more fully identifies the person or highlights an important detail of the person's life. For example, Sylvester W. Graham is listed as a reformer and a food faddist, but his one-line descriptor describes him as the inventor of the graham cracker; Tony Hulman is a business and sports executive, but his one-line descriptor says he was also the first man who said "Gentlemen, start your engines" at the Indianapolis 500; Sidney Poitier, the actor, was the first black to win an Oscar for best actor; and, at age 22, Wayne Gretzky has already broken 29 National Hockey League records. Future editions of *Biography Almanac* will include more one-line descriptors, for it is felt that these descriptions help to make the book a better reference for quick identifications.

Reading a Citation

The citation gives the person's name as he or she is most popularly known; his or her pseudonym, real name, or group affiliation in brackets; nicknames or other types of identification in quotation marks; nationality; occupation, career, or best-known activity; one-line description; dates and places of birth and death; and alphabetically arranged codes for biographical reference sources which provide further information about the individual.

Habib, Philip Charles
American. Diplomat
Ambassador to Korea, 1971-74; special Middle East envoy, 1981--.
b. Feb 25, 1920 in Brooklyn, New York
Source: *BioIn 11; CurBio 81; FarE&A 78, 79; Int WW 78; PolProf J; USBiR 74; WhoAm 74, 76, 78, 80, 82; WhoAmP 75, 77, 79, WhoGov 72, 75, 77; WhoWor 74, 76*

Hanna, William Denby
[Hanna and Barbera]
American Cartoonist
Producer of cartoons, including *Yogi Bear, The Flintstones.*
b. Jul 14, 1910 in Melrose, New Mexico
Source: *FilmgC; IntMPA 82; OxFilm; WhoAm 74, 76, 78, 80, 82; WorEFlm*

Hamill, Dorothy
[Mrs. Dean Martin, Jr.]
American Figure Skater
Won gold medal, 1976 Olympics.
b. 1956 in Greenwich, Connecticut
Source: *BioIn 10, 11; BkPepl; CurBio 76; WhoAm 80, 82*

Each person is entered under his or her best known name. The last name is followed by the diminutive, the familiar, or the shortened form of the first name with the full name in parenthesis. Jim Henson is entered Henson, Jim (James Murray). J.B. Priestley is entered Priestley, J(ohn) B(oynton).

When it is apparent that a person was known widely or exclusively by a nickname, we have so indicated by placing this name in quotation marks in the position normally occupied by the Christian name. Moses, "Grandma" (Anna Mary Robertson) and Corea, "Chick" (Armando) are examples.

Pseudonyms, real names, or a woman's married name may appear in brackets in the second line. If the person is a member of a group, the group name also appears in the second line in brackets.

Landon, Michael
[Eugene Michael Orowitz]

Livingstone, Mary
[Mrs. Jack Benny]

Lowe, Nick
[Rockpile]

Other forms of nicknames, whether they are forms of address or descriptive in nature, will appear in quotation marks in either the second or third line.

Cobb Ty(rus Raymond)
"The Georgia Peach"

Chaney, Lon (Alonso)
"Man of a Thousand Faces"

Cannon, Dyan
[Samille Diane Frissen]
"Frosty"

If a group is listed as a main entry, the individual members are listed in brackets.

> **Eagles, The**
> [Don Felder; Glenn Frey; Don Henley; Bernie Leadon; Randy Meiser; Tim Schmidt; Joe Walsh]
> American Rock Group
> Sold over 40 million albums; *The Long Run,* 1979 double plantinum.
> Source: *BkPepl; EacPR&S; IlEncRk*

Codes and Lists of Titles Indexed

Codes for the biographical sources indexed, along with complete bibliographic information on the titles of the volumes referred to by the codes, are given in the Key to Publication Codes following this introduction.

A special word is needed here about one indexed source which is itself an index: *Biography Index* has been included because it is a rich source of leads to obituaries, magazine articles, and other types of published information concerning persons on whom information is often not available elsewhere.

Editorial Practices

Biography Almanac attempts to list each person under his or her most popular name and also to give the reader as much individual information as possible. If, for example, one were to look up rock and roll pioneer Bill Haley, one would find his full name given as William John Clifford, Jr. In looking up Carol Bayer-Sager, the songwriter, one would discover her also to be Mrs. Burt Bacharach. And George Brett, the baseball player, is nicknamed "Mulletthead." However, if one were to look up Patti Davis under her real name—Patricia Reagan—one would find a "see" reference, sending the user to Davis, Patti, the name by which she is most commonly known.

It is necessary to point out that the cross references in *Biography Almanac* are not examples of standard library practice. A cross reference was included only when it was believed that a user would look under that name to guide him to the main entry. For example, a cross reference appears at Clemens, Samuel Langhorne, sending the reader to Twain, Mark because it is possible that a user could look him up under both names. On the other hand, no one would look up John Wayne under his real name, Marion Michael Morrison, so there is not a cross reference. However, the name Marion Michael Morrison appears in John Wayne's entry as additional information to the user.

Biography Almanac follows the standard alphabetizing rules used by the Library of Congress with the exception of *Mac* and *Mc,* which are interfiled alphabetically. Searchers should look under all possible variant listings for a name with prefixes or suffixes, Spanish names which may be listed under either part of the surname, or names transliterated from non-Roman alphabets.

Suggestions Are Welcome

While we believe *Biography Almanac* 2nd edition to be a valuable reference tool, as well as an improved product over its predecesors, we also realize that a work of this nature can never be complete. People make news every day and we try our best to keep abreast of all such happenings. We hope, though, that you, the user, will also help and send in candidates for future editions.

Key to Abbreviations

AB Alberta
ABA American Basketball Association
ABC American Broadcasting Corporation
ACDA Arms Control and Disarmament Agency
ACLU American Civil Liberties Union
Af Africa
AFB Air Force Base
Afg Afghanistan
AFL American Federation of Labor, American Football League
AFSCME American Federation of State, County, and Municipal Employees
AIM American Indian Movement
AK Alaska
AL Alabama, American League
Alg Algeria
AP Associated Press
Apr April
AR Arkansas
Arg Argentina
Arm Armenia
ASPCA American Society for the Prevention of Cruelty to Animals
ASPCC American Society for the Prevention of Cruelty to Children
Assn. Association
Ast Australia
AT&T American Telephone and Telegraph
Aug August
Aus Austria
AWCTU American Women's Christian Temperance Union
AZ Arizona
b. Born
BBC British Broadcasting Corporation
BC British Columbia
Bel Belgium
Boh Bohemia
Bol Bolivia
Brz Brazil
Bul Bulgaria
BWI British West Indies
c. Century
CA California
Cam Cameroon
Can Canada
Capt. Captain
CBO Congressional Budget Office
CBS Columbia Broadcasting System
Cey Ceylon
Chl Chile
Chn China
CIA Central Intelligence Agency
CIO Congress of Industrial Organizations
CMA Country Music Association
Cmb Cambodia
CO Colorado
Co. Company, County
Col Colombia
Com. Committee
CORE Committee (or Congress) on Racial Equality
Corp. Corporation
CT Connecticut
Ctr. Center
Cub Cuba
d. Died
DC District of Columbia
DE Delaware
Dec December
Dept. Department
Dist. District
dj disc jockey
Dom Dominican Republic
E East, Eastern
Ecu Ecuador
Egy Egypt
Eng England
ERA Earned Run Average, Equal Rights Amendment
ESP Extra Sensory Perception
Eth Ethiopia
Exec. Executive
FAA Federal Aviation Administration
FBI Federal Bureau of Investigation

FCC	Federal Communications Commission
FDA	Food and Drug Administration
FDR	Franklin Delano Roosevelt
Feb	February
Fin	Finland
FL	Florida
fl.	Flourished
Fr	France
Ft.	Fort
FWI	French West Indies
GA	Georgia
GE	General Electric
Ger	Germany
GM	General Manager, General Motors
GOP	Grand Old Party (Republican)
Govt.	Government
Gr	Greece
Gr.	Great
Gua	Guatemala
Hai	Haiti
HEW	Health, Education, and Welfare
HI	Hawaii
hrs.	Hours
Hts.	Heights
HUD	Housing and Urban Development
Hun	Hungary
IA	Iowa
IBM	International Business Machines
Ice	Iceland
ID	Idaho
Ido	Indonesia
IL	Illinois
ILA	International Longshoremen's Association
ILGWU	International Ladies Garment Workers Union
ILWU	International Longshoremen's and Warehousemen's Union
IN	Indiana
Inc.	Incorporated
Ind	India
INLA	Irish National Liberation Army
IOC	International Olympic Committee
IRA	Irish Republic Army
Ire	Ireland
IRS	Internal Revenue Service
Is.	Island
Isr	Israel
It	Italy
IWW	Industrial Workers of the World
Jam	Jamaica
Jan	January
Jap	Japan
Jct.	Junction
Jor	Jordan
Jul	July
Jun	June
KC	Kansas City
Ken	Kenya
Kor	Korea
KS	Kansas
KY	Kentucky
LA	Los Angeles, Louisiana
Lao	Laos
Leb	Lebanon
Lib	Liberia
Lit	Lithuania
LPGA	Ladies Professional Golf Association
Lt.	Lieutenant
Ltd.	Limited
Lux	Luxembourg
MA	Massachusetts
Mad	Madagascar
Mag	Magazine
Mar	March
MB	Manitoba
MCA	Music Corporation of America
MCI	Microwave Communications In
MD	Maryland
ME	Maine
Mex	Mexico
MGM	Metro-Goldwyn-Mayer
MI	Michigan
mins.	minutes
MIT	Massachusetts Institute of Technology
ML	Major League(s)
MN	Minnesota
Mnc	Monaco
MO	Missouri
Mor	Morocco
mos.	Months
MP	Member of Parliament, Militar Police
MS	Mississippi
MT	Montana
Mt.	Mount, Mountain
Mvmt.	Movement
MVP	Most Valuable Player
N	North, Northern
NAACP	National Association for the Advancement of Colored People
NASA	National Aeronautics and Spac Administration

Nat.	National
NATO	North Atlantic Treaty Organization
NB	New Brunswick
NBA	National Basketball Association
NBC	National Broadcasting Corporation
NC	North Carolina
NCAA	National Collegiate Athletic Association
ND	North Dakota
NE	Nebraska
Net	Netherlands
NF	Newfoundland, Not Found
NFL	National Football League
NH	New Hampshire
NHL	National Hockey League
Nic	Nicaragua
Nig	Nigeria
NJ	New Jersey
NL	National League
NM	New Mexico
Nor	Norway
Nov	November
NOW	National Organization for Women
NRA	National Recovery Administration
NS	Nova Scotia
NT	Northwest Territories
NV	Nevada
NY	New York
NZ	New Zealand
Oct	October
OH	Ohio
OK	Oklahoma
OMB	Office of Management and Budget
ON	Ontario
OR	Oregon
p.	Page
PA	Pennsylvania
Pac.	Pacific
Pak	Pakistan
Pal	Palestine
Pan	Panama
Par	Paraguay
PATCO	Professional Air Traffic Controllers Organization
PBA	Professional Bowlers Association
PBS	Public Broadcasting System
PE	Prince Edward Island
Per	Peru
PGA	Professional Golfers Association
Phi	Philippines
PLO	Palestine Liberation Organization
Pol	Poland
Por	Portugal
POW	Prisoner of War
PQ	Quebec
PR	Puerto Rico
Pres.	President
Prov.	Province
Prs	Persia
Pru	Prussia
Pt.	Point, Port
Pte.	Pointe
RBI	Runs Batted In
RCA	Radio Corporation of America
Repub.	Republic
Rev.	Reverend
RI	Rhode Island
RIF	Reading is Fundamental
Rpds.	Rapids
Rus	Russia
S	South, Southern
SALT	Strategic Arms Limination Talks
SC	South Carolina
SCLC	Southern Christian Leadership Conference
Sct	Scotland
SD	South Dakota
secs.	seconds
Sep	September
SI	Sports Illustrated
SK	Saskatchewan
SLA	Symbionese Liberation Army
SNCC	Student Nonviolent Coordinating Committee
Sp	Spain
Sprgs.	Springs
Sq.	Square
St.	Saint, Sainte
Sud	Sudan
Sum.	Summit
SUNY	State University of New York
Sur	Surinam
Swe	Sweden
Swi	Switzerland
Syr	Syria
TB	Tuberculosis
TD	Touchdown
Terr.	Territory
Tha	Thailand
TN	Tennessee
tr.	Translated
Tur	Turkey

Twp.	Township	Vil.	Village
TX	Texas	VT	Vermont
U	University	W	West, Western
UAW	United Auto Workers	WA	Washington
UFO	Unidentified Flying Object	WBA	World Boxing Association
Ugn	Uganda	WBC	World Boxing Council
UK	United Kingdom	WFL	World Football League
Ukr	Ukraine	WI	Wisconsin
UMW	United Mine Workers	W In	West Indies
UN	United Nations	WV	West Virginia
US	United States	WW	World War
USC	University of Southern California	WY	Wyoming
USFL	United States Football League	yds.	Yards
USSR	Union of Soviet Socialist Republic	YMCA	Young Men's Christian Association
UT	Utah	YWCA	Young Women's Christian Association
VA	Virginia, Veteran's Administration	yrs.	Years
Ven	Venezuela	YT	Yukon Territory
Vie	Vietnam	Yug	Yugoslavia

Bibliographic Key to Publication Codes for Use in Locating Sources

Code	***Book Indexed***
AfSS	*Africa South of the Sahara.* London: Europa Publications Ltd., 1978, 1979, 1980, 1981, 1982. Distributed by Gale Research Co., Detroit, Michigan.
AfSS 78	1978-1979 edition
AfSS 79	1979-1980 edition
AfSS 80	1980-1981 edition
AfSS 81	1981-1982 edition
AfSS 82	1982-1983 edition
	Biographies are found in the "Who's Who in Africa South of the Sahara" section at the back of each volume.
AfrA	*African Authors: A Companion to Black African Writing.* Volume 1: 1300-1973. By Donald E. Herdeck. Washington, D.C.: Black Orpheus Press, 1973.
AfroAA	*Afro-American Artists: A Bio-Bibliographical Directory.* Compiled and edited by Theresa Dickason Cederholm. Boston: Trustees of the Boston Public Library, 1973.
Alli	Allibone, S. Austin. *A Critical Dictionary of English Literature and British and American Authors Living and Deceased from the Earliest Accounts to the Latter Half of the Nineteenth Century.* Containing over 46,000 articles (authors) with 40 indexes of subjects. Three volumes. Philadelphia: J.B. Lippincott & Co., 1858-1871. Reprint. Detroit: Gale Research Co., 1965.
Alli SUP	*A Supplement to Allibone's Critical Dictionary of English Literature and British and American Authors.* Containing over 37,000 articles (authors) and enumerating over 93,000 titles. Two volumes. By John Foster Kirk. Philadelphia: J.B. Lippincott & Co., 1891. Reprint. Detroit: Gale Research Co., 1965.
AlmAP	*The Almanac of American Politics.* The senators, the representatives, the governors--their records, states, and districts. By Michael

Barone, Grant Ujifusa, and Douglas Matthews. New York: E.P. Dutton, 1977, 1979.

AlmAP 78 1978 edition, 1977
AlmAP 80 1980 edition, 1979

Use the "Names Index" at the back of each volume to locate biographies.

AlmAP 82 *The Almanac of American Politics 1982.* The president, the senators, the representatives, the governors: their records and election results, their states and districts. By Michael Barone and Grant Ujifusa. Washington, D.C.: Barone & Co., 1981.

Use the "Index of Persons" which begins on page 1245 to locate biographies.

AmArch 70 *American Architects Directory.* Third edition. Edited by John F. Gane. Published under the sponsorship of American Institute of Architects. New York: R.R. Bowker Co., 1970.

AmAu *American Authors, 1600-1900: A Biographical Dictionary of American Literature.* Edited by Stanley J. Kunitz and Howard Haycraft. New York: H.W. Wilson Co., 1938.

AmAu&B *American Authors and Books, 1640 to the Present Day.* Third revised edition. By W.J. Burke and Will D. Howe. Revised by Irving Weiss and Anne Weiss. New York: Crown Publishers, Inc., 1972.

AmBench 79 *The American Bench: Judges of the Nation.* Second edition. Edited by Mary Reincke and Nancy Lichterman. Minneapolis: Reginald Bishop Forster & Associates, Inc., 1979.

Use the "Name Index" at the front of the volume to locate biographies.

AmBi *American Biographies.* By Wheeler Preston. New York: Harper & Brothers Publishers, 1940. Reprint. Detroit: Gale Research Co., 1974.

AmCath 80 *The American Catholic Who's Who.* Volume 23, 1980-1981. Edited by Joy Anderson. Washington, D.C.: National Catholic News Service, 1979.

AmEA 74 American Economic Association. *Directory of Members, 1974.* Edited by Rendigs Fels. Published as Volume 64, Number 5, October, 1974 of *The American Economic Review.*

AmEnS *The American Encyclopedia of Soccer.* Edited by Zander Hollander. New York: Everest House Publishers, 1980.

AmLY *The American Literary Yearbook.* A biographical and bibliographical dictionary of living North American authors; a record of contemporary literary activity; an authors' manual and students' text book. Volume 1, 1919. Edited by Hamilton Traub. Henning, Minnesota: Paul Traub, Publisher, 1919. Reprint. Detroit: Gale Research Co., 1968.

AmLY "Biographical and Bibliographical Dictionary of Living North American Authors" begins on page 57
AmLY X "Pen-names and Pseudonyms" begins on page 49

AmM&WS *American Men and Women of Science.* Edited by Jaques Cattell Press. New York: R.R. Bowker Co., 1971-1973, 1976-1978, 1979, 1982.

AmM&WS 73P Physical & Biological Sciences, 12th edition, 1971-1973
AmM&WS 73S Social & Behavioral Sciences, 12th edition, 1973
AmM&WS 76P Physical & Biological Sciences, 13th edition, 1976
AmM&WS 78S Social & Behavioral Sciences, 13th edition, 1978
AmM&WS 79P Physical & Biological Sciences, 14th edition, 1979
AmM&WS 82P Physical & Biological Sciences, 15th edition, 1982

AmNov *American Novelists of Today.* By Harry R. Warfel. New York: American Book Co., 1951. Reprint. Westport, Connecticut: Greenwood Press, 1976.

The "Index of Married Names and Pseudonyms," indicated in this index by the code *X*, begins on page 477.

AmPS *American Popular Songs from the Revolutionary War to the Present.* Edited by David Ewen. New York: Random House, 1966.

AmPS "American Popular Songs" begins on page 1
AmPS A "All-Time Best-Selling Popular Recordings" begins on page 485
AmPS B "Some American Performers of the Past and Present" begins on page 499

AmSCAP 66 *The ASCAP Biographical Dictionary of Composers, Authors and Publishers.* Third edition, 1966. Compiled and edited by The Lynn Farnol Group, Inc. New York: American Society of Composers, Authors, and Publishers, 1966.

AmSCAP 80 *ASCAP Biographical Dictionary.* Fourth edition. Compiled for the American Society of Composers, Authors and Publishers by Jaques Cattell Press. New York: R.R. Bowker Co., 1980.

AmWom *American Women.* A revised edition of *Woman of the Century,* 1,500 biographies with over 1,400 portraits; a comprehensive encyclopedia of the lives and achievements of American women during the nineteenth century. Two volumes. Edited by Frances E. Willard and

Mary A. Livermore. New York: Mast, Crowell & Kirkpatrick, 1897. Reprint. Detroit: Gale Research Co., 1973.

AmWomWr *American Women Writers: A Critical Reference Guide from Colonial Times to the Present.* Four volumes. Edited by Lina Mainiero. New York: Frederick Ungar Publishing Co., 1979-1982. Distributed by Gale Research Co., Detroit, Michigan.

AmWr *American Writers: A Collection of Literary Biographies.* Four volumes and supplement. Edited by Leonard Unger. New York: Charles Scribner's Sons, 1974, 1979. Originally published as the *University of Minnesota Pamphlets on American Writers.*

AmWr Volumes 1-4, 1974
AmWr SUP Supplement 1, 1979

AnObit *The Annual Obituary.* New York: St. Martin's Press, 1981, 1982.

AnObit 1980 *1980.* Edited by Roland Turner, 1981.
AnObit 1981 *1981.* Edited by Janet Podell, 1982.

Use the "Alphabetical Index of Entrants," at the front of each volume to locate biographies.

AnCL *Anthology of Children's Literature.* Fourth edition. Edited by Edna Johnson, Evelyn R. Sickels, and Frances Clarke Sayers. Boston: Houghton Mifflin Co., 1970.

Biographies begin on page 1217.

AnMV 1926 *Anthology of Magazine Verse for 1926 and Yearbook of American Poetry.* Edited by William Stanley Braithwaite. New York: G. Sully, 1926. Reprint. Granger Index Reprint Series. Freeport, New York: Books for Libraries Press, 1972.

The "Biographical Dictionary of Poets in the United States" section begins on page 3 of part IV.

AntBDN *The Antique Buyer's Dictionary of Names.* By A.W. Coysh. Newton Abbot, Devon, England: David & Charles, 1970.

AntBDN A "Art Nouveau" begins on page 13
AntBDN B "Book Illustrations and Prints" begins on page 23
AntBDN C "Bronzes" begins on page 48
AntBDN D "Clocks and Barometers" begins on page 59
AntBDN E "Fashion Plates" begins on page 81
AntBDN F "Firearms" begins on page 86
AntBDN G "Furniture" begins on page 98
AntBDN H "Glass" begins on page 123
AntBDN I "Maps, Charts, and Globes" begins on page 137
AntBDN J "Miniatures" begins on page 148
AntBDN K "Musical Instruments" begins on page 170

AntBDN L	"Netsuke" begins on page 179
AntBDN M	"Pottery and Porcelain" begins on page 185
AntBDN N	"Sheffield Plate" begins on page 224
AntBDN O	"Silhouettes or Profiles" begins on page 231
AntBDN P	"Silk Pictures, Portraits, and Bookmarks" begins on page 243
AntBDN Q	"Silver" begins on page 250

ApCAB *Appleton's Cyclopaedia of American Biography*. Six volumes. Edited by James Grant Wilson and John Fiske. New York: D. Appleton & Co., 1888-1889. Reprint. Detroit: Gale Research Co., 1968.

ApCAB SUP *Appleton's Cyclopaedia of American Biography*. Volume seven, Supplement. Edited by James Grant Wilson. New York: D. Appleton & Co., 1901. Reprint. Detroit: Gale Research Co., 1968.

ApCAB X *A Supplement to Appleton's Cyclopaedia of American Biography*. Six volumes. Originally published as *The Cyclopaedia of American Biography, Supplementary Edition.* Edited by L.E. Dearborn. New York: Press Association Compilers, Inc., 1918-1931.

ArizL *Arizona in Literature: A Collection of the Best Writings of Arizona Authors from Early Spanish Days to the Present Time.* By Mary G. Boyer. Glendale, California: Arthur H. Clark Co., 1935. Reprint. Ann Arbor: Gryphon Books, 1971.

Use the Index, beginning on page 569, to locate biographies.

ArtsAmW *Artists of the American West: A Biographical Dictionary.* By Doris Ostrander Dawdy. Chicago: Swallow Press, Inc., 1974.

AsBiEn *Asimov's Biographical Encyclopedia of Science and Technology.* The lives and achievements of 1,195 great scientists from ancient times to the present, chronologically arranged. New revised edition. By Isaac Asimov. New York: Avon, 1976.

Use the "Alphabetic List of Biographical Entries" at the front of the book to locate biographies.

AtlBL *Atlantic Brief Lives: A Biographical Companion to the Arts.* Edited by Louis Kronenberger. Boston: Little, Brown & Co., 1971.

ASpks *The Author Speaks: Selected "PW" Interviews, 1967-1976.* By *Publishers Weekly* editors and contributors. New York: R.R. Bowker Co., 1977.

Au&ICB	*Authors and Illustrators of Children's Books: Writings on Their Lives and Works.* By Miriam Hoffman and Eva Samuels. New York: R.R. Bowker Co., 1972.
Au&Wr 71	*The Author's and Writer's Who's Who.* Sixth edition. Darien, Connecticut: Hafner Publishing Co., Inc., 1971.
AuBYP	*Authors of Books for Young People.* By Martha E. Ward and Dorothy A. Marquardt. Metuchen, New Jersey: Scarecrow Press Inc., 1971, 1979.
AuBYP	Second edition, 1971
AuBYP SUP	Supplement to the second edition, 1979
AuBYP SUPA	Addendum to the Supplement begins on page 301
AuNews	*Authors in the News.* A compilation of news stories and feature articles from American newspapers and magazines covering writers and other members of the communications media. Two volumes. Edited by Barbara Nykoruk. Detroit: Gale Research Co., 1976.
AuNews 1	Volume 1
AuNews 2	Volume 2
AutoN 79	*Automotive News.* 1979 Market Data Book Issue, April 25, 1979. The "Who's Who in the Auto Industry" section begins on page 130.
Baker 78	*Baker's Biographical Dictionary of Musicians.* Sixth edition. Revised by Nicolas Slonimsky. New York: Schirmer Books, 1978.
BaseEn 82	*The Baseball Encyclopedia: The Complete and Official Record of Major League Baseball.* Fifth edition. Edited by Joseph L. Reichler. New York: Macmillan Publishing Co., Inc., 1982.
BestMus	*The Best Musicals: From Show Boat to A Chorus Line.* Revised edition. By Arthur Jackson. New York: Crown Publishers, Inc., 1979. Biographies are found in the "Who's Who of Show and Film Music" section beginning on page 135.
BbD	*The Bibliophile Dictionary.* A biographical record of the great authors, with bibliographical notices of their principal works from the beginning of history. Originally published as Volumes 29 and 30 of *The Bibliophile Library of Literature, Art, and Rare Manuscripts.* Compiled and arranged by Nathan Haskell Dole, Forrest Morgan, and Caroline Ticknor. New York and London: International Bibliophile Society, 1904. Reprint. Detroit: Gale Research Co., 1966.

BbtC *Bibliotheca Canadensis; or, A Manual of Canadian Literature.* By Henry J. Morgan. Ottawa: G.E. Desbarats, 1867. Reprint. Detroit: Gale Research Co., 1968.

BiAUS *Biographical Annals of the Civil Government of the United States, during Its First Century.* From original and official sources. By Charles Lanman. Washington, D.C.: James Anglim, Publisher, 1876. Reprint. Detroit: Gale Research Co., 1976.

The "Additional Facts" section, indicated in this index by the code *SUP*, begins on page 633.

BiB *Biographia Britannica Literaria; or, Biography of Literary Characters of Great Britain and Ireland, Arranged in Chronological Order.* Two volumes. By Thomas Wright. London: John W. Parker, 1842, 1846. Reprint. Detroit: Gale Research Co., 1968.

BiB N Anglo-Norman Period, 1846
BiB S Anglo-Saxon Period, 1842

Use the Index at back of each volume to locate biographies.

BiCAW *The Biographical Cyclopaedia of American Women.* Two volumes. Volume 1: Compiled under the supervision of Mabel Ward Cameron. New York: Halvord Publishing Co., Inc., 1924. Volume 2: Compiled under the supervision of Erma Conkling Lee. New York: Franklin W. Lee Publishing Corp., 1925. Reprint (both volumes). Detroit: Gale Research Co., 1974.

Use the Index at the back of Volume 2 to locate biographies.

BiDAmEd *Biographical Dictionary of American Educators.* Three volumes. Edited by John F. Ohles. Westport, Connecticut: Greenwood Press, 1978.

BiDAmLL *Biographical Dictionary of American Labor Leaders.* Edited by Gary M. Fink. Westport, Connecticut: Greenwood Press, 1974.

BiDAmM *Biographical Dictionary of American Music.* By Charles Eugene Claghorn. West Nyack, New York: Parker Publishing Co., Inc., 1973.

BiDAmS *Biographical Dictionary of American Science, the Seventeenth through the Nineteenth Centuries.* By Clark A. Elliott. Westport, Connecticut: Greenwood Press, 1979.

BiD&SB *Biographical Dictionary and Synopsis of Books Ancient and Modern.* Edited by Charles Dudley Warner. Akron, Ohio: Werner Co., 1902. Reprint. Detroit: Gale Research Co., 1965.

BiDConf *Biographical Dictionary of the Confederacy.* By Jon L. Wakelyn. Westport, Connecticut: Greenwood Press, 1977.

BiDFedJ *Biographical Dictionary of the Federal Judiciary.* Compiled by Harold Chase, Samuel Krislov, Keith O. Boyum, and Jerry N. Clark. Detroit: Gale Research Co., 1976.

BiDFilm *A Biographical Dictionary of Film.* By David Thomson. New York: William Morrow & Co., Inc., 1976, 1981.

BiDFilm First edition, 1976
BiDFilm 81 Second edition, 1981

BiDLA *A Biographical Dictionary of the Living Authors of Great Britain and Ireland.* Comprising literary memoirs and anecdotes of their lives; and a chronological register of their publications, with the number of editions printed; including notices of some foreign writers whose works have been occasionally published in England. London: Printed for Henry Colburn, Public Library, Conduit Street, Hanover Square, 1816. Reprint. Detroit: Gale Research Co., 1966.

The "Supplement of Additions and Corrections," indicated in this index by the code *SUP*, begins on page 407.

BiDPara *Biographical Dictionary of Parapsychology, with Directory and Glossary, 1964-1966.* New York: Garrett Publications, Helix Press, 1964.

BiDSA *Biographical Dictionary of Southern Authors.* Originally published as *Library of Southern Literature, Volume 15, Biographical Dictionary of Authors.* Compiled by Lucian Lamar Knight. Atlanta: Martin & Hoyt Co., 1929. Reprint. Detroit: Gale Research Co., 1978.

BiDrAC *Biographical Directory of the American Congress 1774-1971.* The Continental Congress (September 5, 1774 to October 21, 1788) and The Congress of the United States (From the first through the ninety-first Congress March 4, 1789, to January 3, 1971, inclusive), Washington, D.C.: United States Government Printing Office, 1971.

Biographies begin on page 487.

BiDrAPA 77 *Biographical Directory of the Fellows and Members of the American Psychiatric Association.* Compiled by Jaques Cattell Press. New York: R.R. Bowker Co., 1977.

BiDrGov *Biographical Directory of the Governors of the United States, 1789-1978.* Four volumes. Edited by Robert Sobel and John Raimo.

Westport, Connecticut: Microform Review, Inc., Meckler Books, 1978.

Use the Index at the back of each volume to locate biographies.

BiDrLUS 70 *A Biographical Directory of Librarians in the United States and Canada.* Fifth edition. Edited by Lee Ash. Chicago: American Library Association, 1970.

BiDrUSE *Biographical Directory of the United States Executive Branch 1774-1971.* Edited by Robert Sobel. Westport, Connecticut: Greenwood Publishing Co., 1971.

BiE&WWA *The Biographical Encyclopaedia and Who's Who of the American Theatre.* Edited by Walter Rigdon. New York: James H. Heineman, Inc., 1966. Revised edition published as *Notable Names in the American Theatre.*(See below.)

The "Biographical Who's Who" section begins on page 227.

BiHiMed *A Biographical History of Medicine: Excerpts and Essays on the Men and Their Work.* By John H. Talbott. New York: Grune & Stratton, 1970.

Use the "Name Index," beginning on page 1193, to locate biographies.

BioIn *Biography Index.* A cumulative index to biographical material in books and magazines. New York: H.W. Wilson Co., 1949-1983.

BioIn 1 Volume 1: January, 1946-July, 1949; 1949
BioIn 2 Volume 2: January, 1949-August, 1952; 1953
BioIn 3 Volume 3: September, 1952-August, 1955; 1956
BioIn 4 Volume 4: September, 1955-August, 1958; 1960
BioIn 5 Volume 5: September, 1958-August, 1961; 1962
BioIn 6 Volume 6: September, 1961-August, 1964; 1965
BioIn 7 Volume 7: September, 1964-August, 1967; 1968
BioIn 8 Volume 8: September, 1967-August, 1970; 1971
BioIn 9 Volume 9: September, 1970-August, 1973; 1974
BioIn 10 Volume 10: September, 1973-August, 1976; 1977
BioIn 11 Volume 11: September, 1976-August, 1979; 1980
BioIn 12 Volume 12: September, 1979-August, 1982: 1983

BioNews *Biography News.* A compilation of news stories and feature articles from American news media covering personalities of national interest in all fields. Edited by Frank E. Bair. Detroit: Gale Research Co., 1974-1975.

BioNews 74 Volume 1, Numbers 1-12, 1974
BioNews 75 Volume 2, Number 1, January-February 1975

BlkAmWP *Black American Writers Past and Present: A Biographical and Bibliographical Dictionary.* Two volumes. By Theressa Gunnels Rush, Carol Fairbanks Myers, and Esther Spring Arata. Metuchen, New Jersey: Scarecrow Press, Inc., 1975.

Blood *Bloodletters and Badmen.* By Jay Robert Nash. New York: M. Evans & Co., Inc., 1973.

BlueB 76 *The Blue Book: Leaders of the English-Speaking World.* 1976 edition. London: St. James Press; New York: St. Martin's Press, 1976. Republished in two volumes by Gale Research Co., Detroit, Michigan, 1979.

BluesWW *Blues Who's Who: A Biographical Dictionary of Blues Singers.* By Sheldon Harris. New Rochelle, New York: Arlington House Publishers, 1979.

BkC *The Book of Catholic Authors: Informal Self-Portraits of Famous Modern Catholic Writers.* Edited by Walter Romig. Detroit: Walter Romig & Co., 1942-?

- ***BkC 1*** First series, 1942
- ***BkC 2*** Second series, 1943
- ***BkC 3*** Third series, 1945
- ***BkC 4*** Fourth series (n.d.)
- ***BkC 5*** Fifth series (n.d.)
- ***BkC 6*** Sixth series (n.d.)

BkCL *A Book of Children's Literature.* Third edition. Edited by Lillian Hollowell. New York: Holt, Rinehart & Winston, Inc., 1966.

Biographies begin on page 553.

BkIE *Book Illustrators in Eighteenth-Century England.* By Hanns Hammelmann. Edited and completed by T.S.R. Boase. New Haven, Connecticut: Yale University Press (for The Paul Mellon Centre for Studies in British Art, London), 1975.

BkPepl *The Book of People.* By Christopher P. Anderson. New York: Perigee Books, 1981.

BkP *Books Are by People: Interviews with 104 Authors and Illustrators of Books for Young Children.* Edited by Lee Bennett Hopkins. New York: Citation Press, 1969.

BnBkM 80 *Britannica Book of Music.* Edited by Benjamin Hadley. Garden City, New York: Doubleday & Co., Inc., 1980.

BnEnAmA *The Britannica Encyclopedia of American Art*. Chicago: Encyclopaedia Britannica Educational Corp., 1973. World Book Trade Distribution by Simon & Schuster, New York.

Br&AmS *British and American Sporting Authors: Their Writings and Biographies*. By A. Henry Higginson. London: Hutchinson & Co., Ltd., 1951.

Use the Index to locate biographies.

BrAu *British Authors before 1800: A Biographical Dictionary*. Edited by Stanley J. Kunitz and Howard Haycraft. New York: H.W. Wilson Co., 1952.

BrAu 19 *British Authors of the Nineteenth Century*. Edited by Stanley J. Kunitz. New York: H.W. Wilson Co., 1936.

BrWr *British Writers*. Edited under the auspices of the British Council, Ian Scott-Kilvert, General Editor. New York: Charles Scribner's Sons, 1979, 1981.

BrWr 1 Volume 1: William Langland to The English Bible, 1979
BrWr 2 Volume 2: Thomas Middleton to George Farquhar, 1979
BrWr 3 Volume 3: Daniel Defoe to The Gothic Novel, 1980
BrWr 4 Volume 4: William Wordsworth to Robert Browning, 1981

Use the "List of Subjects" at the front of each volume to locate biographies.

BusPN *Business People in the News*. A compilation of news stories and feature articles from American newspapers and magazines covering people in industry, finance, and labor. Volume 1. Edited by Barbara Nykoruk. Detroit: Gale Research Co., 1976.

Cald 1938 *Caldecott Medal Books: 1938-1957*. With the artist's acceptance papers and related material chiefly from the *Horn Book Magazine*. Horn Book Papers, Volume II. Edited by Bertha Mahony Miller and Elinor Whitney Field. Boston: Horn Book, Inc., 1957.

CaW *Canada Writes!* The members' book of the Writers' Union of Canada. Edited by K.A. Hamilton. Toronto: Writer's Union of Canada, 1977.

The "Additional Members" section, indicated in this index by the code *A*, begins on page 387.

CanNov *Canadian Novelists, 1920-1945*. By Clara Thomas. Toronto: Longmans, Green & Co., 1946. Reprint. Folcroft, Pennsylvania: Folcroft Library Editions, 1970.

CanWW 70 — *The Canadian Who's Who.* A biographical dictionary of notable living men and women. Volume 12, 1970-1972. Toronto: Who's Who Canadian Publications, 1972.

CanWW — *Canadian Who's Who.* Edited by Kieran Simpson. Toronto: University of Toronto Press, 1979, 1980, 1981.

- *CanWW 79* — Volume XIV, 1979
- *CanWW 80* — Volume XV, 1980
- *CanWW 81* — Volume XVI, 1981

CanWr — *Canadian Writers: A Biographical Dictionary.* New edition, revised and enlarged. Edited by Guy Sylvestre, Brandon Conron, and Carl F. Klinck. Toronto: Ryerson Press, 1966.

CarSB — *The Carolyn Sherwin Bailey Historical Collection of Children's Books: A Catalogue.* Edited and compiled by Dorothy R. Davis. New Haven, Connecticut: Southern Connecticut State College, 1966.

Not in strict alphabetic sequence. There is no index.

CasWL — *Cassell's Encyclopaedia of World Literature.* Edited by S.H. Steinberg in two volumes. Revised and enlarged in three volumes by J. Buchanan-Brown. New York: William Morrow & Co., Inc., 1973.

Biographies are found in Volumes 2 and 3.

CathA — *Catholic Authors: Contemporary Biographical Sketches.* Edited by Matthew Hoehn. Newark, New Jersey: St. Mary's Abbey, 1948, 1952. First volume reprint. Detroit: Gale Research Co., 1981.

- *CathA 1930* — First volume: 1930-1947, 1948
- *CathA 1952* — Second volume, 1952

CelCen — *Celebrities of the Century.* Being a dictionary of men and women of the nineteenth century. Two volumes. Edited by Lloyd C. Sanders. London: Cassell & Co., Ltd., 1887. Reprint. Ann Arbor: Gryphon Books, 1971.

CelR — *Celebrity Register.* Third edition. Edited by Earl Blackwell. New York: Simon & Schuster, 1973.

Chambr — *Chambers's Cyclopaedia of English Literature.* A history critical and biographical of authors in the English tongue from the earliest times till the present day with specimens of their writings. Three volumes. Edited by David Patrick, revised by J. Liddell Geddie. Philadelphia: J.B. Lippincott, Co., 1938. Reprint. Detroit: Gale Research Co., 1978.

- *Chambr 1* — Volume 1: 7th-17th century

Chambr 2	Volume 2: 18th century
Chambr 3	Volume 3: 19th-20th century

Use the Index at the back of each volume to locate biographies.

ChPo *Childhood in Poetry.* A catalogue, with biographical and critical annotations, of the books of English and American poets comprising the Shaw Childhood in Poetry Collection in the Library of the Florida State University, with lists of the poems that relate to childhood, notes, and index. By John Mackay Shaw. Detroit: Gale Research Co., 1967, 1972, 1976, 1980.

ChPo	Original Volumes, 1967
ChPo S1	First Supplement, 1972
ChPo S2	Second Supplement, 1976
ChPo S3	Third Supplement, 1980

ChLR *Children's Literature Review.* Excerpts from reviews, criticism, and commentary on books for children and young people. Detroit: Gale Research Co., 1976-1982.

ChLR 1	Volume 1, 1976
ChLR 2	Volume 2, 1976
ChLR 3	Volume 3, 1978
ChLR 4	Volume 4, 1982

CivR 74 *Civil Rights: A Current Guide to the People, Organizations, and Events.* A CBS News Reference Book. Second edition. By Joan Martin Burke. New York: R.R. Bowker Co., 1974.

Biographies begin on page 21.

CivWDc *Civil War Dictionary.* By Mark Mayo Boatner, III. New York: David McKay Co., Inc., 1959.

ClbCR *Colombo's Canadian References.* By John Robert Colombo. New York: Oxford University Press, 1976.

ClDMEL *Columbia Dictionary of Modern European Literature.* Edited by Horatio Smith. New York: Columbia University Press, 1947. Second edition, fully revised and enlarged. Edited by Jean-Albert Bede and William B. Edgerton, 1980.

ClDMEL	First edition, 1947
ClDMEL 80	Second edition, 1980

CmCal *A Companion to California.* By James D. Hart. New York: Oxford University Press, 1978.

CmMov *A Companion to the Movies: From 1903 to the Present Day.* A guide to the leading players, directors, screenwriters, composers, cameramen and other artistes who have worked in the English-speaking cinema over the last 70 years. By Roy Pickard. New York: Hippocrene Books, Inc., 1972.

Use the "Who's Who Index" at the back of the book to locate biographies.

CmOp *A Companion to the Opera.* By Robin May. New York: Hippocrene Books, Inc., 1977.

Use the "Selective Index: I-People," beginning on page 349, to locate biographies.

CmpEPM *The Complete Encyclopedia of Popular Music and Jazz, 1900-1950.* Three volumes. By Roger D. Kinkle. New Rochelle, New York: Arlington House Publishers, 1974.

Biographies are located in Volumes 2 and 3.

CnDAL *Concise Dictionary of American Literature.* Edited by Robert Fulton Richards. New York: Philosophical Library, Inc., 1955. Reprint. New York: Greenwood Press, 1969.

CnE&AP *The Concise Encyclopedia of English and American Poets and Poetry.* Edited by Stephen Spender and Donald Hall. New York: Hawthorne Books, Inc., 1963.

CnMD *The Concise Encyclopedia of Modern Drama.* By Siegfried Melchinger. Translated by George Wellwarth. Edited by Henry Popkin. New York: Horizon Press, 1964.

Biographies begin on page 159. The "Additional Entries" section, indicated in this index by the code *SUP,* begins on page 287.

CnMWL *The Concise Encyclopedia of Modern World Literature.* Edited by Geoffrey Grigson. London: Hutchinson & Co., Ltd., 1963.

Biographies begin on page 29.

CnThe *A Concise Encyclopedia of the Theatre.* By Robin May. Reading, Berkshire, England: Osprey Publishing Ltd., 1974.

Use the Index at the back of the book to locate biographies.

CnOxB *The Concise Oxford Dictionary of Ballet.* By Horst Koegler. London: Oxford University Press, 1977.

CnOxOp 79 *The Concise Oxford Dictionary of Opera.* Second edition. By Harold Rosenthal and John Warrack. New York: Oxford University Press, 1979.

CngDr — *Congressional Directory*. Washington, D.C.: United States Government Printing Office, 1974, 1977, 1978, 1979, 1981.

CngDr 74 — 93rd Congress, 2nd Session, 1974
CngDr 77 — 95th Congress, 1st Session, 1977
CngDr 78 — *Supplement*, 95th Congress, 2nd Session, 1978
CngDr 79 — 96th Congress, 1st Session, 1979
CngDr 81 — 97th Congress, 1st Session, 1981

Use the "Name (Individual) Index" at the back of each volume to locate biographies.

ConAmA — *Contemporary American Authors: A Critical Survey and 219 Bio-Bibliographies*. By Fred B. Millett. New York: Harcourt, Brace & World, Inc., 1940. Reprint. New York: AMS Press, Inc., 1970.

ConAmC — *Contemporary American Composers: A Biographical Dictionary*. Compiled by E. Ruth Anderson. Boston: G.K. Hall & Co., 1976.

ConAmL — *Contemporary American Literature: Bibliographies and Study Outlines*. By John Matthews Manly and Edith Rickert. Revised by Fred B. Millett. New York: Harcourt, Brace, 1929. Reprint. New York: Haskell House Publishers Ltd., 1974.

Biographies begin on page 101.

ConAmTC — *Contemporary American Theater Critics: A Directory and Anthology of Their Works*. Compiled by M.E. Comtois and Lynn F. Miller. Metuchen, New Jersey: Scarecrow Press, Inc., 1977.

ConArch — *Contemporary Architects*. Edited by Muriel Emanuel. New York: St. Martin's Press, 1980.

ConArt — *Contemporary Artists*. Edited by Colin Naylor and Genesis P-Orridge. London: St. James Press; New York: St. Martin's Press, 1977. Distributed by Gale Research Co., Detroit, Michigan.

ConAu — *Contemporary Authors*. A bio-bibliographical guide to current writers in fiction, general nonfiction, poetry, journalism, drama, motion pictures, television, and other fields. Detroit: Gale Research Co., 1967-1982.

ConAu 1R — Volumes 1-4, 1st revision, 1967
ConAu 5R — Volumes 5-8, 1st revision, 1969
ConAu 9R — Volumes 9-12, 1st revision, 1974
ConAu 13R — Volumes 13-16, 1st revision, 1975
ConAu 17R — Volumes 17-20, 1st revision, 1976
ConAu 21R — Volumes 21-24, 1st revision, 1977
ConAu 25R — Volumes 25-28, 1st revision, 1977

ConAu 29R	Volumes 29-32, 1st revision, 1978
ConAu 33R	Volumes 33-36, 1st revision, 1978
ConAu 37R	Volumes 37-40, 1st revision, 1979
ConAu 41R	Volumes 41-44, 1st revision, 1979
ConAu 45	Volumes 45-48, 1974
ConAu 49	Volumes 49-52, 1975
ConAu 53	Volumes 53-56, 1975
ConAu 57	Volumes 57-60, 1976
ConAu 61	Volumes 61-64, 1976
ConAu 65	Volumes 65-68, 1977
ConAu 69	Volumes 69-72, 1978
ConAu 73	Volumes 73-76, 1978
ConAu 77	Volumes 77-80, 1979
ConAu 81	Volumes 81-84, 1979
ConAu 85	Volumes 85-88, 1980
ConAu 89	Volumes 89-92, 1980
ConAu 93	Volumes 93-96, 1980
ConAu 97	Volumes 97-100, 1981
ConAu 101	Volume 101, 1981
ConAu 102	Volume 102, 1981
ConAu 103	Volume 103, 1982
ConAu 104	Volume 104, 1982
ConAu 105	Volume 105, 1982
ConAu 106	Volume 106, 1982
ConAu X	This code refers to pseudonyms entries which appear only as cro references in the cumulative index in *Contemporary Authors.*

ConAu NR — *Contemporary Authors, New Revision Series.* A bio-bibliographical guide to current writers in fiction, general nonfiction, poetry, journalism, drama, motion pictures, television, and other fields. Detroit: Gale Research Co., 1981, 1982.

ConAu 1NR	Volume 1, 1981
ConAu 2NR	Volume 2, 1981
ConAu 3NR	Volume 3, 1981
ConAu 4NR	Volume 4, 1981
ConAu 5NR	Volume 5, 1982
ConAu 6NR	Volume 6, 1982
ConAu 7NR	Volume 7, 1982

ConAu P- — *Contemporary Authors, Permanent Series.* A bio-bibliographical guide to current authors and their works. Detroit: Gale Research Co., 1975-1978.

ConAu P-1	Volume 1, 1975
ConAu P-2	Volume 2, 1978

ConDr — *Contemporary Dramatists.* Edited by James Vinson. London: St. James Press; New York: St. Martin's Press, 1973, 1977.

ConDr 73	First edition, 1973

ConDr 77 Second edition, 1977, "Contemporary Dramatists" begins on page 9
ConDr 77A Second edition, "Screen Writers" begins on page 893
ConDr 77B Second edition, "Radio Writers" begins on page 903
ConDr 77C Second edition, "Television Writers" begins on page 915
ConDr 77D Second edition, "Musical Librettists" begins on page 925
ConDr 77E Second edition, "The Theatre of the Mixed Means" begins on page 941
ConDr 77F Second edition, Appendix begins on page 969

ConICB *Contemporary Illustrators of Children's Books.* Compiled by Bertha E. Mahony and Elinor Whitney. Boston: Bookshop for Boys and Girls, Women's Educational and Industrial Union, 1930. Reprint. Detroit: Gale Research Co., 1978.

ConLC *Contemporary Literary Criticism.* Excerpts from criticism of the works of today's novelists, poets, playwrights, short story writers, filmmakers, screenwriters, and other creative writers. Detroit: Gale Research Co., 1973- 1982.

ConLC 1 Volume 1, 1973
ConLC 2 Volume 2, 1974
ConLC 3 Volume 3, 1975
ConLC 4 Volume 4, 1975
ConLC 5 Volume 5, 1976
ConLC 6 Volume 6, 1976
ConLC 7 Volume 7, 1977
ConLC 8 Volume 8, 1978
ConLC 9 Volume 9, 1978
ConLC 10 Volume 10, 1979
ConLC 11 Volume 11, 1979
ConLC 12 Volume 12, 1980
ConLC 13 Volume 13, 1980
ConLC 14 Volume 14, 1980
ConLC 15 Volume 15, 1980
ConLC 16 Volume 16, 1981
ConLC 17 Volume 17, 1981
ConLC 18 Volume 18, 1981
ConLC 19 Volume 19, 1981
ConLC 20 Volume 20, 1982
ConLC 21 Volume 21, 1982

ConLCrt *Contemporary Literary Critics.* By Elmer Borklund. London: St. James Press; New York: St. Martin's Press, 1977.

ConLCrt 82 *Contemporary Literary Critics.* Second edition. By Elmer Borklund. Detroit: Gale Research Co., 1982.

ConMuA 80 *Contemporary Music Almanac, 1980/81.* By Ronald Zalkind. New York: Macmillan Publishing Co., Schirmer Books, 1980.

ConNov — *Contemporary Novelists.* Edited by James Vinson. London: St. James Press; New York: St. Martin's Press, 1972, 1976, 1982.

ConNov 72 — First edition, 1972
ConNov 76 — Second edition, 1976
ConNov 82 — Third edition, 1982

Deceased novelists are listed in the Appendix at the end of the second and third editions.

ConP — *Contemporary Poets.* London: St. James Press; New York: St. Martin's Press, 1970, 1975, 1980.

ConP 70 — First edition. Edited by Rosalie Murphy, 1970.
ConP 75 — Second edition. Edited by James Vinson, 1975.
ConP 80 — Third edition. Edited by James Vinson, 1980.

Deceased poets are listed in the Appendix at the end of each volume.

ConSFA — *Contemporary Science Fiction Authors.* First edition. Compiled and edited by R. Reginald. New York: Arno Press, 1975. Previously published as *Stella Nova: The Contemporary Science Fiction Authors.* Los Angeles: Unicorn & Son, Publishers, 1970.

Conv — *Conversations.* Conversations series. Detroit: Gale Research Co., 1977-1978.

Conv 1 — Volume 1: *Conversations with Writers*, 1977
Conv 2 — Volume 2: *Conversations with Jazz Musicians*, 1977
Conv 3 — Volume 3: *Conversations with Writers II*, 1978

CorpD — *Corpus Delicti of Mystery Fiction: A Guide to the Body of the Case.* By Linda Herman and Beth Stiel. Metuchen, New Jersey: Scarecrow Press, Inc., 1974.

Biographies begin on page 31.

CounME 74 — *The Country Music Encyclopedia.* By Melvin Shestack. New York: Thomas Y. Crowell Co., 1974.

CreCan — *Creative Canada: A Biographical Dictionary of Twentieth-Century Creative and Performing Artists.* Compiled by the Reference Division, McPherson Library, University of Victoria, B.C. Toronto: University of Toronto Press, 1971, 1972.

CreCan 1 — Volume 1, 1971
CreCan 2 — Volume 2, 1972

CrtT — *The Critical Temper: A Survey of Modern Criticism on English and American Literature from the Beginnings to the Twentieth Century.* Four volumes. Edited by Martin Tucker. A Library of Literary

Criticism. New York: Frederick Ungar Publishing Co., 1969, 1979.

CrtT 1 Volume 1: *From Old English to Shakespeare*, 1969

CrtT 2 Volume 2: *From Milton to Romantic Literature*, 1969

CrtT 3 Volume 3: *Victorian Literature and American Literature*, 1969

CrtT 4 Volume 4: *Supplement*, 1979

Authors are listed alphabetically within each period or division of literature.

CroCAP *Crowell's Handbook of Contemporary American Poetry*. By Karl Malkoff. New York: Thomas Y. Crowell Co., 1973.

Biographies begin on page 43.

CroCD *Crowell's Handbook of Contemporary Drama*. By Michael Anderson, et al. New York: Thomas Y. Crowell Co., 1971.

CroE&S *Crowell's Handbook of Elizabethan and Stuart Literature*. By James E. Ruoff. New York: Thomas Y. Crowell Co., 1975.

CurBio *Current Biography Yearbook*. New York: H.W. Wilson Co., 1940-1983.

Number after the source code indicates the year covered by the yearbook.

CyAL *Cyclopaedia of American Literature*. Embracing personal and critical notices of authors, and selections from their writings, from the earliest period to the present day, with portraits, autographs, and other illustrations. Two volumes. By Evert A. Duyckinck and George L. Duyckinck. Philadelphia: William Rutter & Co., 1875. Reprint. Detroit: Gale Research Co., 1965.

Use the Index at the back of Volume 2 to locate biographies.

CyEd *A Cyclopedia of Education*. Five volumes. Edited by Paul Monroe. New York: Macmillan Co., 1911. Reprint. Detroit: Gale Research Co., 1968.

CyWA *Cyclopedia of World Authors*. Edited by Frank N. Magill. New York: Harper & Row Publishers, 1958. Also published as *Masterplots Cyclopedia of World Authors*.

DcAmArt *Dictionary of American Art*. By Matthew Baigell. New York: Harper & Row Publishers, 1979.

DcAmAu *A Dictionary of American Authors*. Fifth edition, revised and enlarged. By Oscar Fay Adams. New York: Houghton Mifflin Co., 1904. Reprint. Detroit: Gale Research Co., 1969.

Biographies are found in the "Dictionary of American Authors" section beginning on page 1 and in the "Supplement" beginning on page 441.

DcAmB *Dictionary of American Biography*. 20 volumes and 6 supplements. Edited under the auspices of the American Council of Learned Societies. New York: Charles Scribner's Sons, 1928-1936, 1944, 1958, 1973, 1974, 1977, 1980.

DcAmB	Volumes 1-20, 1928-1936
DcAmB S1	Supplement 1, 1944
DcAmB S2	Supplement 2, 1958
DcAmB S3	Supplement 3, 1973
DcAmB S4	Supplement 4, 1974
DcAmB S5	Supplement 5, 1977
DcAmB S6	Supplement 6, 1980

DcAmDH *Dictionary of American Diplomatic History*. By John E. Findling. Westport, Connecticut: Greenwood Press, 1980.

DcAmLiB *Dictionary of American Library Biography*. Edited by Bohdan S. Wynar. Littleton, Colorado: Libraries Unlimited, Inc., 1978.

DcAmReB *Dictionary of American Religious Biography*. By Henry Warner Bowden. Westport, Connecticut: Greenwood Press, 1977.

DcAmSR *Dictionary of American Social Reform*. By Louis Filler. New York: Philosophical Library, 1963.

DcBiA *A Dictionary of Biographies of Authors Represented in the Authors Digest Series*. With a supplemental list of later titles and a supplementary biographical section. Edited by Rossiter Johnson. New York: Authors Press, 1927. Reprint. Detroit: Gale Research Co., 1974.

The "Biographies of Authors" section begins on page 3 and the "Biographies of Authors Whose Works are in Volume XVIII" begins on page 437.

DcBiPP *A Dictionary of Biography, Past and Present*. Containing the chief events in the lives of eminent persons of all ages and nations. Preceded by the biographies and genealogies of the chief representatives of the royal houses of the world. Edited by Benjamin Vincent. Haydn Series. London: Ward, Lock, & Co., 1877. Reprint. Detroit, Gale Research Co., 1974.

DcBrBI *The Dictionary of British Book Illustrators and Caricaturists, 1800-1914*. With introductory chapters on the rise and progress of the art.

By Simon Houfe. Woodbridge, Suffolk, England: Baron Publishing (for The Antique Collectors' Club), 1978.

Biographies begin on page 213.

DcBrWA *The Dictionary of British Watercolour Artists up to 1920.* By H.L. Mallalieu. Woodbridge, Suffolk, England: Baron Publishing (for The Antique Collectors' Club), 1976.

DcCathB *Dictionary of Catholic Biography.* By John J. Delaney and James Edward Tobin. Garden City, New York: Doubleday & Co., Inc., 1961.

DcCAA *A Dictionary of Contemporary American Artists.* By Paul Cummings. London: St. James Press; New York: St. Martin's Press, 1971, 1977.

DcCAA 71 Second edition, 1971
DcCAA 77 Third edition, 1977

DcCLAA *A Dictionary of Contemporary Latin American Authors.* Compiled by David William Foster. Tempe, Arizona: Center for Latin American Studies, Arizona State University, 1975.

DcCM *Dictionary of Contemporary Music.* Edited by John Vinton. New York: E.P. Dutton & Co., Inc., 1974.

This book ignores prefixes in filing surnames.

DcEnA *A Dictionary of English Authors, Biographical and Bibliographical.* Being a compendious account of the lives and writings of upwards of 800 British and American writers from the year 1400 to the present time. New edition, revised with an appendix bringing the whole up to date and including a large amount of new matter. By R. Farquharson Sharp. London: Kegan Paul, Trench, Trubner & Co., Ltd., 1904. Reprint. Detroit: Gale Research Co., 1978.

The Appendix, indicated in this index by the code *AP*, begins on page 311.

DcEnL *Dictionary of English Literature: Being a Comprehensive Guide to English Authors and Their Works.* Second edition. By W. Davenport Adams. London: Cassell Petter & Galpin (n.d.). Reprint. Detroit: Gale Research Co., 1966.

DcEuL *A Dictionary of European Literature.* Designed as a companion to English studies. Second, revised edition. By Laurie Magnus. London: George Routledge & Sons, Ltd.; New York: E.P. Dutton & Co., 1927. Reprint. Detroit: Gale Research Co., 1974.

The Appendix begins on page 595.

DcFM — *Dictionary of Film Makers.* By Georges Sadoul. Translated, edited, and updated by Peter Morris. Berkeley and Los Angeles: University of California Press, 1972. Originally published as *Dictionnaire des Cineastes,* 1965.

DcInB — *Dictionary of Indian Biography.* By C.E. Buckland. London: Swan Sonnenschein & Co., Ltd, 1906. Reprint. Detroit: Gale Research Co., 1968.

DcInv — *Dictionary of Inventions and Discoveries.* Edited by E.F. Carter. Stevenage, Herts, England: Robin Clark Ltd., 1978.

DcIrB — *A Dictionary of Irish Biography.* By Henry Boylan. New York: Barnes & Noble Books, 1978.

DcIrW — *Dictionary of Irish Writers.* By Brian Cleeve. Cork, Ireland: Mercier Press, 1967, 1969, 1971.

- ***DcIrW 1*** — Volume 1: Fiction, 1967
- ***DcIrW 2*** — Volume 2: Non-fiction, 1969
- ***DcIrW 3*** — Volume 3: Writers in the Irish Language, 1971

DcLB — *Dictionary of Literary Biography.* Detroit: Gale Research Co., 1978-1982.

- ***DcLB 1*** — Volume 1: *The American Renaissance in New England.* Edited by Joel Myerson, 1978.
- ***DcLB 2*** — Volume 2: *American Novelists since World War II.* Edited by Jeffrey Helterman and Richard Layman, 1978.
- ***DcLB 3*** — Volume 3: *Antebellum Writers in New York and the South.* Edited by Joel Myerson, 1979.
- ***DcLB 4*** — Volume 4: *American Writers in Paris, 1920-1939.* Edited by Karen Lane Rood, 1980.
- ***DcLB 5*** — Volume 5: *American Poets since World War II.* Two Volumes. Edited by Donald J. Greiner, 1980.
- ***DcLB 6*** — Volume 6: *American Novelists since World War II.* Second series. Edited by James E. Kibler, Jr., 1980.
- ***DcLB 7*** — Volume 7: *Twentieth-Century American Dramatists.* Two volumes. Edited by John MacNicholas, 1981.
- ***DcLB 8*** — Volume 8: *Twentieth-Century American Science-Fiction Writers.* Two volumes. Edited by David Cowart and Thomas L. Wymer, 1981.
- ***DcLB 9*** — Volume 9: *American Novelists, 1910-1945.* Three volumes. Edited by James J. Martine, 1981.
- ***DcLB 10*** — Volume 10: *Modern British Dramatists, 1900-1945.* Two volumes. Edited by Stanley Weintraub, 1982.
- ***DcLB 11*** — Volume 11: *American Humorists, 1800-1950.* Two volumes. Edited by Stanley Trachtenberg, 1982.
- ***DcLB 12*** — Volume 12: *American Realists and Naturalists.* Edited by Donald Pizer and Earl N. Harbert, 1982.

DcLEL — *A Dictionary of Literature in the English Language.* Compiled and edited by Robin Myers. Oxford: Pergamon Press, Inc., 1970, 1978

- *DcLEL* — *From Chaucer to 1940*, 1970
- *DcLEL 1940* — *From 1940 to 1970*, 1978

DcNiCA — *Dictionary of 19th Century Antiques and Later Objets d'Art.* By George Savage. London: Barrie & Jenkins Ltd., 1978.

DcNAA — *A Dictionary of North American Authors Deceased before 1950.* Compiled by W. Stewart Wallace. Toronto: Ryerson Press, 1951. Reprint. Detroit: Gale Research Co., 1968.

DcOrL — *Dictionary of Oriental Literatures.* Three volumes. Jaroslav Prusek, general editor. New York: Basic Books, Inc., 1974.

- *DcOrL 1* — Volume 1: East Asia. Edited by Zbigniew Slupski.
- *DcOrL 2* — Volume 2: South and South-East Asia. Edited by Dusan Zbavitel.
- *DcOrL 3* — Volume 3: West Asia and North Africa. Edited by Jiri Becka.

DcPol — *A Dictionary of Politics.* Revised edition. Edited by Walter Laqueur. New York: Macmillan Publishing Co., Free Press, 1973.

DcRusL — *Dictionary of Russian Literature.* By William E. Harkins. New York: Philosophical Library, Inc., 1956. Reprint. Westport, Connecticut: Greenwood Press, 1971.

DcScB — *Dictionary of Scientific Biography.* 14 volumes and supplement. Edited by Charles Coulston Gillispie. New York: Charles Scribner's Sons, 1970-1976, 1978.

- *DcScB* — Volumes 1-14, 1970-1976
- *DcScB S1* — Volume 15, Supplement 1, 1978

DcSpL — *Dictionary of Spanish Literature.* By Maxim Newmark. New York: Philosophical Library, Inc., 1956. Reprint. Totowa, New Jersey: Littlefield, Adams & Co., 1970.

DcVicP — *Dictionary of Victorian Painters.* By Christopher Wood. Suffolk, England: Baron Publishing (for The Antique Collectors' Club), 1971.

DrAF 76 — *A Directory of American Fiction Writers.* 1976 edition. Names and addresses of more than 800 contemporary fiction writers whose work has been published in the United States. New York: Poets & Writers, Inc., 1976.

Use the Index, beginning on page 123, to locate listings.

DrAP 75 — *A Directory of American Poets.* 1975 edition. Names and addresses of more than 1,500 contemporary poets whose work has been published in the United States. New York: Poets & Writers, Inc., 1974.

Use the Index, beginning on page vii, to locate listings.

DrAS — *Directory of American Scholars.* Edited by Jaques Cattell Press. New York: R.R. Bowker Co., 1974, 1978.

- ***DrAS 74H*** — Sixth edition, volume 1: History
- ***DrAS 74E*** — Sixth edition, volume 2: English, Speech, & Drama
- ***DrAS 74F*** — Sixth edition, volume 3: Foreign Languages, Linguistics, & Philology
- ***DrAS 74P*** — Sixth edition, volume 4: Philosophy, Religion, & Law
- ***DrAS 78H*** — Seventh edition, volume 1: History
- ***DrAS 78E*** — Seventh edition, volume 2: English, Speech, & Drama
- ***DrAS 78F*** — Seventh edition, volume 3: Foreign Languages, Linguistics, & Philology
- ***DrAS 78P*** — Seventh edition, volume 4: Philosophy, Religion, & Law

DrBlPA — *Directory of Blacks in the Performing Arts.* By Edward Mapp. Metuchen, New Jersey: Scarecrow Press, Inc., 1978.

DrInf — *The Directory of Infamy: The Best of the Worst.* An illustrated compendium of over 600 of the all-time great crooks. By Jonathon Green. London: Mills & Boon, 1980.

Use the Index to locate biographies.

DrLC 69 — *Directory of Library Consultants.* Edited by John N. Berry, III. New York: R.R. Bowker Co., 1969.

Dis&D — *Disease and Destiny: A Bibliography of Medical References to the Famous.* By Judson Bennett Gilbert. Additions and introduction by Gordon E. Mestler. London: Dawsons of Pall Mall, 1962.

Drake — Drake, Francis S. *Dictionary of American Biography including Men of the Time.* Containing nearly 10,000 notices of persons of both sexes, of native and foreign birth, who have been remarkable, or prominently connected with the arts, sciences, literature, politics, or history, of the American continent. Giving also the pronunciation of many of the foreign and peculiar American names, a key to the assumed names of writers, and a supplement. Boston: James R. Osgood & Co., 1872. Reprint. Detroit: Gale Research Co., 1974.

Dun&B 79 — *Dun and Bradstreet Reference Book of Corporate Managements, 1979-1980.* 13th edition. New York: Dun & Bradstreet, Inc., 1979.

Use the Index to locate biographies.

EarABI *Early American Book Illustrators and Wood Engravers, 1670-1870.* A catalogue of a collection of American books illustrated for the most part with woodcuts and wood engravings in the Princeton University Library with supplement. By Sinclair Hamilton. Princeton, New Jersey: Princeton University Press, 1958, 1968.

EarABI Volume 1: Main Catalogue, 1958
EarABI SUP Volume 2: Supplement, 1968

Ebony *The Ebony Success Library.* Three volumes. By the Editors of *Ebony.* Nashville, Tennessee: Southwestern Co., 1973.

Ebony 1 Volume 1: 1,000 Successful Blacks
Ebony 3 Volume 3: Career Guide

EncAAH *Encyclopedia of American Agricultural History.* By Edward L. Schapsmeier and Frederick H. Schapsmeier. Westport, Connecticut: Greenwood Press, 1975.

EncAB-A *Encyclopedia of American Biography.* New Series. 40 volumes. New York and West Palm Beach: The American Historical Society, 1934-1970.

Entries are not alphabetic. The page number of the beginning of the biography falls after the volume number.

EncAB-H *Encyclopedia of American Biography.* Edited by John A. Garraty. New York: Harper & Row, Publishers, 1974.

EncACr *The Encyclopedia of American Crime.* By Carl Sifakis. New York: Facts on File, Inc., 1982.

EncE 75 *Encyclopedia of Espionage.* New edition. By Ronald Seth. London: New English Library, 1975.

EncFCWM 69 *Encyclopedia of Folk, Country and Western Music.* By Irwin Stambler and Grelun Landon. New York: St. Martin's Press, 1969.

EncJzS 70 *The Encyclopedia of Jazz in the Seventies.* By Leonard Feather and Ira Gitler. New York: Horizon Press, 1976.

EncLatA *Encyclopedia of Latin America.* Edited by Helen Delpar. New York: McGraw- Hill Book Co., 1974.

EncMA *Encyclopedia of Modern Architecture.* Edited by Wolfgang Pehnt. New York: Harry N. Abrams, Inc., Publishers, 1964.

Biographies begin on page 28.

EncMT *Encyclopaedia of the Musical Theatre.* By Stanley Green. New York: Dodd, Mead & Co., 1976.

EncMys *Encyclopedia of Mystery and Detection.* By Chris Steinbrunner and Otto Penzler. New York: McGraw-Hill Book Co., 1976.

EncO&P *Encyclopedia of Occultism and Parapsychology.* A compendium of information on the occult sciences, magic, demonology, superstitions, spiritism, mysticism, metaphysics, physical science, and parapsychology, with biographical and bibliographical notes and comprehensive indexes. Two volumes and supplements. Edited by Leslie Shepard. Detroit: Gale Research Co., 1978, 1980, 1981.

EncO&P 78 Main volumes, 1978
EncO&P 78 S1 Occultism Update, Issue Number 1, 1978
EncO&P 80 Occultism Update, Issue Number 2, 1980
EncO&P 81 Occultism Update, Issue Numbers 3-4, 1981

EncOp *The Encyclopedia of Opera.* Edited by Leslie Orrey. London: Pitman Publishing, Ltd., 1976.

EncPR&S *Encyclopedia of Pop, Rock, and Soul.* By Irwin Stambler. London: St. James Press and New York: St. Martin's Press, 1974.

EncSF *The Encyclopedia of Science Fiction: An Illustrated A to Z.* By Peter Nicholls. London: Grenada Publishing Ltd., 1979.

EncSoA *Encyclopedia of Southern Africa.* Sixth edition. Compiled and edited by Eric Rosenthal. London and New York: Frederick Warne & Co., Ltd., 1973.

EncSoH *Encyclopedia of Southern History.* Edited by David C. Roller and Robert W. Twyman. Baton Rouge and London: Louisiana State University Press, 1979.

EncTR *Encyclopedia of the Third Reich.* By Louis L. Snyder. New York: McGraw-Hill Book Co., 1976.

EncWL *Encyclopedia of World Literature in the 20th Century.* Three volumes and supplement. Edited by Wolfgang Bernard Fleischmann. New York: Frederick Ungar Publishing Co., 1967, 1975. An enlarged and updated edition of the Herder *Lexikon der Weltliteratur im 20. Jahrhundert.*

EncWL Volumes 1-3, 1967
EncWL SUP Volume 4, Supplement, 1975

EncWL 81 *Encyclopedia of World Literature in the 20th Century.* Four volumes.

Volume 1: A to D. Edited by Leonard S. Klein. New York: Frederick Ungar Publishing Co., 1981.

Volumes two through four forthcoming.

EncWM *Encyclopedia of World Methodism.* Two volumes. Edited by Nolan B. Harmon. Nashville: United Methodist Publishing House, 1974.

EncWT *The Encyclopedia of World Theater.* Translated by Estella Schmid, edited by Martin Esslin. New York: Charles Scribner's Sons, 1977. Based on *Friedrichs Theaterlexikon,* by Karl Groning and Werner Kliess.

Ent *The Entertainers.* Edited by Clive Unger-Hamilton. New York: St. Martin's Press, 1980.

Use the "Index of Entries," beginning on page 306, to locate biographies.

EuAu *European Authors, 1000-1900: A Biographical Dictionary of European Literature.* Edited by Stanley J. Kunitz and Vineta Colby. New York: H.W. Wilson Co., 1967.

EvEuW *Everyman's Dictionary of European Writers.* By W.N. Hargreaves-Mawdsley. London: J.M. Dent & Sons Ltd.; New York: E.P. Dutton & Co., Inc., 1968.

EvLB *Everyman's Dictionary of Literary Biography, English and American.* Revised edition. Compiled after John W. Cousin by D.C. Browning. London: J.M. Dent & Sons Ltd; New York: E.P. Dutton & Co., Inc., 1960.

FairDF *Fairchild's Dictionary of Fashion.* By Charlotte Calasibetta. New York: Fairchild Publications, Inc., 1975.

Biographies are located in the "Fashion Designers" section beginning on page 547.

FairDF ENG England Section begins on page 548
FairDF FIN Finland Section begins on page 553
FairDF FRA France Section begins on page 554
FairDF IRE Ireland Section begins on page 577
FairDF ITA Italy Section begins on page 578
FairDF JAP Japan Section begins on page 583
FairDF SPA Spain Section begins on page 584
FairDF US United States Section begins on page 585

FamA&A *Famous Actors and Actresses on the American Stage: Documents of American Theater History.* Two volumes. By William C. Young. New York: R.R. Bowker Co., 1975.

FamAIYP *Famous Author-Illustrators for Young People.* By Norah Smaridge. New York: Dodd, Mead & Co., 1973.

FamAYP *Famous Authors for Young People.* By Ramon P. Coffman and Nathan G. Goodman. New York: Dodd, Mead & Co., 1943.

FamSYP *Famous Storytellers for Young People.* By Laura Benet. New York: Dodd, Mead & Co., 1968.

FanAl *The Fantasy Almanac.* By Jeff Rovin. New York: E.P. Dutton, 1979.

FarE&A *The Far East and Australasia: A Survey and Directory of Asia and the Pacific.* London: Europa Publications Ltd., 1978, 1979, 1980, 1981. Distributed by Gale Research Co., Detroit, Michigan.

FarE&A 78 1978-79 edition
FarE&A 79 1979-80 edition
FarE&A 79A Wade-Giles/Pinyin spellings of Chinese names begins on page 1155.
FarE&A 80 1980-81 edition
FarE&A 80A Wade-Giles/Pinyin spellings of Chinese names begins on page 1174.
FarE&A 81 1981-82 edition

Biographies are found in the "Who's Who in the Far East and Australasia" section at the back of each volume.

FemPA *The Female Poets of America.* With portraits, biographical notices, and specimens of their writings. Seventh edition, revised. By Thomas Buchanan Read. Philadelphia: E.H. Butler & Co., 1857. Reprint. Detroit: Gale Research Co., 1978.

FilmEn *The Film Encyclopedia.* By Ephraim Katz. New York: Thomas Y. Crowell, 1979.

Film *Filmarama.* Compiled by John Stewart. Metuchen, New Jersey: Scarecrow Press, Inc., 1975, 1977.

Film 1 Volume 1: *The Formidable Years, 1893-1919,* 1975
Film 2 Volume 2: *The Flaming Years, 1920-1929,* 1977

FilmgC *The Filmgoer's Companion.* Fourth edition. By Leslie Halliwell. New York: Hill & Wang, 1974. Seventh edition published as *Halliwell's Filmgoer's Companion.* (See below.)

FootReg *The Football Register.* 1981 edition. Edited by Howard M. Balzar. St. Louis: The Sporting News, 1981.

ForWC 70 *Foremost Women in Communications.* A biographical reference work on accomplished women in broadcasting, publishing, advertising, public relations, and allied professions. New York: Foremost Americans Publishing Corp., in association with R.R. Bowker Co., 1970.

ForYSC *Forty Years of Screen Credits, 1929-1969.* Two volumes. Compiled by John T. Weaver. Metuchen, New Jersey: Scarecrow Press, Inc., 1970.

Entries begin on page 57.

FourBJA *Fourth Book of Junior Authors and Illustrators.* Edited by Doris DeMontreville and Elizabeth D. Crawford. New York: H.W. Wilson Co., 1978.

Funs *The Funsters.* By James Robert Parish and William T. Leonard. New Rochelle, New York: Arlington House Publishers, 1979.

GolEC *Golombek's Encyclopedia of Chess.* Edited by Harry Golombek. New York: Crown Publishers, Inc., 1977.

GoodHs *The Good Housekeeping Woman's Almanac.* Edited by Barbara McDowell and Hana Umlauf. New York: Newspaper Enterprise Association, Inc., 1977.

Use the Index beginning on page 562 to locate biographies.

Grk&L *Greek and Latin Authors, 800 B.C.-A.D. 1000.* By Michael Grant. New York: H.W. Wilson Co., 1980.

HalFC 80 *Halliwell's Filmgoer's Companion.* Seventh edition. By Leslie Halliwell. New York: Granada Publishing Ltd., 1980. Fourth edition published as *The Filmgoer's Companion.* (See above.)

HarEnUS *Harper's Encyclopaedia of United States History: From 458 A.D. to 1915.* New edition entirely revised and enlarged. 10 volumes. By Benson John Lossing. New York and London: Harper & Brothers Publishers, 1915. Reprint. Detroit: Gale Research Co., 1974.

HerW *Her Way: Biographies of Women for Young People.* By Mary-Ellen Kulkin. Chicago: American Library Association, 1976.

HisEWW *Historical Encyclopedia of World War II.* Edited by Marcel Baudot, Henri Bernard, Hendrik Brugmans, Michael R.D. Foot, and Hans-Adolf Jacobsen. New York: Facts On File, Inc., 1980. Originally published as *Encyclopedie de la Guerre 1939-1945.* Paris and Tournai: Editions Casterman, 1977.

HocReg *The Hockey Register.* 1981-82 edition. Edited by Latty Wigge. St. Louis: The Sporting News, 1981.

HolCA *Hollywood Character Actors.* By James Robert Parish. Westport, Connecticut: Arlington House Publishers, 1978.

HolP *Hollywood Players.* New Rochelle, New York: Arlington House Publishers, 1976.

- ***HolP 30*** *The Thirties.* Edited by James Robert Parish and William T. Leonard.
- ***HolP 40*** *The Forties.* Edited by James Robert Parish and Lennard DeCarl.

HsB&A *The House of Beadle and Adams and Its Dime and Nickel Novels: The Story of a Vanished Literature.* Two volumes and supplement. By Albert Johannsen. Norman, Oklahoma: University of Oklahoma Press, 1950, 1962.

- ***HsB&A*** Volumes 1-2, 1950. Biographies are found in volume 2.
- ***HsB&A SUP*** Volume 3, Supplement, Addenda, Corrigenda, 1962

IlBEAAW *The Illustrated Biographical Encyclopedia of Artists of the American West.* By Peggy and Harold Samuels. Garden City, New York: Doubleday & Co., Inc., 1976.

IlDcG *Illustrated Dictionary of Glass.* 2,442 entries, including definitions of wares, materials, processes, forms, and decorative styles, and entries on principal glassmakers, decorators, and designers, from antiquity to the present. By Harold Newman. London: Thames & Hudson, Ltd., 1977.

IlDirFS *The Illustrated Directory of Film Stars.* By David Quinlan. New York; Hippocrene Books, Inc., 1981.

IlEncCM *The Illustrated Encyclopedia of Country Music.* By Fred Dellar, Roy Thompson, and Douglas B. Green. New York: Harmony Books, 1977.

IlEncJ *The Illustrated Encyclopedia of Jazz.* By Brian Case and Stan Britt. New York: Harmony Books, 1978.

IlEncR *The Illustrated Encyclopedia of Rock.* Revised edition. Compiled by Nick Logan and Bob Woffinden. New York: Harmony Books, 1977?

IlWWBF *The Illustrated Who's Who in British Films.* By Denis Gifford. London: Anchor Press, Ltd., 1978.

IlsBYP *Illustrators of Books for Young People.* Second edition. By Martha E. Ward and Dorothy A. Marquardt. Metuchen, New Jersey: Scarecrow Press, Inc., 1975.

IlsCB *Illustrators of Children's Books.* Boston: Horn Book, Inc., 1947, 1958, 1968, 1978.

IlsCB 1744 *1744-1945.* Compiled by Bertha E. Mahony, Louise Payson Latimer, and Beulah Folmsbee, 1947. Biographies begin on page 267.

IlsCB 1946 *1946-1956.* Compiled by Ruth Hill Viguers, Marcia Dalphin, and Bertha Mahony Miller, 1958. Biographies begin on page 62.

IlsCB 1957 *1957-1966.* Compiled by Lee Kingman, Joanna Foster, and Ruth Giles Lontoft, 1968. Biographies begin on page 70.

IlsCB 1967 *1967-1976.* Compiled by Lee Kingman, Grace Allen Hogarth, and Harriet Quimby, 1978. Biographies begin on page 93.

InB&W *In Black and White.* A guide to magazine articles, newspaper articles, and books concerning more than 15,000 Black individuals and groups. Third edition. Two volumes. Edited by Mary Mace Spradling. Detroit: Gale Research Co., 1980.

InSci *Index to Scientists of the World from Ancient to Modern Times: Biographies and Portraits.* By Norma Olin Ireland. Boston: F.W. Faxon Co., Inc., 1962.

InWom *Index to Women of the World from Ancient to Modern Times: Biographies and Portraits.* By Norma Olin Ireland. Westwood, Massachusetts: F.W. Faxon Co., Inc., 1970.

IndAu 1816 *Indiana Authors and Their Books, 1816-1916.* Biographical sketches of authors who published during the first century of Indiana statehood with lists of their books. Compiled by R.E. Banta. Crawfordsville, Indiana: Wabash College, 1949.

IndAu 1917 *Indiana Authors and Their Books, 1917-1966.* A continuation of *Indiana Authors and Their Books, 1816-1916*, and containing additional names from the earlier period. Compiled by Donald E. Thompson. Crawfordsville, Indiana: Wabash College, 1974.

IndAu 1967 *Indiana Authors and Their Books, 1967-1980.* Also containing additional names from the beginnings of Indiana statehood with an index to the three volumes. Compiled by Donald E. Thompson. Crawfordsville, Indiana: Wabash College, 1981.

IntAu&W 76 — *The International Authors and Writers Who's Who.* Seventh edition, 1976. Edited by Ernest Kay. Cambridge, England: Melrose Press, 1976.

IntAu&W 76	Biographical Section
IntAu&W 76A	Addendum begins on page 641
IntAu&W 76X	"Pseudonyms of Included Authors" begins on page 645

IntAu&W 77 — *The International Authors and Writers Who's Who.* Edited by Adrian Gaster. Cambridge, England: International Biographical Centre, 1977, 1982. 1982 edition is combined with *International Who's Who in Poetry.*

IntAu&W 77	Eight Edition, 1977, Biogaphical Section
IntAu&W 77X	"Pseudonyms of Included Authors" begins on page 1131
IntAu&W 82	Ninth Edition, 1982, Biographical Section
IntAu&W 82X	"Pseudonyms of Included Authors" begins on page 719

IntMPA — *International Motion Picture Almanac.* Edited by Richard Gertner. New York: Quigley Publishing Co., Inc., 1975, 1976, 1977, 1978, 1979, 1980, 1981, 1982.

IntMPA 75	1975 edition
IntMPA 76	1976 edition
IntMPA 77	1977 edition
IntMPA 78	1978 edition
IntMPA 79	1979 edition
IntMPA 80	1980 edition
IntMAP 81	1981 edition
IntMAP 82	1982 edition

Biographies are found in the "Who's Who in Motion Pictures and Television" section in each volume. The listings are identical to those found in *The International Television Almanac.*

IntWW — *The International Who's Who.* London: Europa Publications Ltd., 1974, 1975, 1976, 1977, 1978, 1979, 1980, 1981, 1982. Distributed by Gale Research Co., Detroit, Michigan.

IntWW 74	38th edition, 1974-75
IntWW 75	39th edition, 1975-76
IntWW 76	40th edition, 1976-77
IntWW 77	41st edition, 1977-78
IntWW 78	42nd edition, 1978-79
IntWW 79	43rd edition, 1979-80
IntWW 80	44th edition, 1980-81
IntWW 81	45th edition, 1981-82
IntWW 82	46th edition, 1982-83

IntWWP 77 — *International Who's Who in Poetry*. Edited by Ernest Kay. Cambridge, England: International Biographical Centre, 1977, 1982. 1982 edition is combined with *International Authors and Writers Who's Who*.

- *IntWWP 77* — Fifth Edition, 1977, biographical section
- *IntWWP 77A* — Addendum begins on page 470
- *IntWWP 77X* — "Pseudonyms and Pen Names of Included Authors" begins on page 702
- *IntWWP 82* — Sixth Edition, 1982, biographical section
- *IntWWP 82X* — "Pseudonyms of Included Poets" begins on page 1035

IntYB — *The International Year Book and Statesmen's Who's Who*. West Sussex, England: Kelly's Directories Ltd., 1978, 1979, 1980, 1981. Distributed by Gale Research Co., Detroit, Michigan.

- *IntYB 78* — 26th edition, 1978
- *IntYB 79* — 27th edition, 1979
- *IntYB 80* — 28th edition, 1980
- *IntYB 81* — 29th edition, 1981
- *IntYB 82* — 30th edition, 1982

Biographies are found in Part 3 of each volume.

JoeFr — *Joe Franklin's Encyclopedia of Comedians*. Secaucus, New Jersey: Citadel Press, 1979.

JohnWil — *John Willis' Screen World*. 1981, Volume 32. New York: Crown Publishers, Inc., 1981.

JBA 34 — *The Junior Book of Authors*. An introduction to the lives of writers and illustrators for younger readers from Lewis Carroll and Louisa Alcott to the present day. First edition. Edited by Stanley J. Kunitz and Howard Haycraft. New York: H.W. Wilson Co., 1934.

JBA 51 — *The Junior Book of Authors*. Second edition, revised. Edited by Stanley J. Kunitz and Howard Haycraft. New York: H.W. Wilson Co., 1951.

LEduc 74 — *Leaders in Education*. Fifth edition. Edited by Jaques Cattell Press. New York: R.R. Bowker Co., 1974.

LElec — *Leaders in Electronics*. New York: McGraw-Hill Book Co., 1979.

Title page reads: McGraw-Hill's Leaders in Electronics.

LibW — *Liberty's Women*. Edited by Robert McHenry. Springfield, Massachusetts: G. & C. Merriam Co., Publishers, 1980.

LilREn 78 — *Lillian Roxon's Rock Encyclopedia.* Compiled by Ed Naha. New York: Grosset & Dunlap, 1978.

LinLib L — *The Lincoln Library of Language Arts.* Third edition. Two volumes. Columbus, Ohio: Frontier Press Co., 1978.

Biographies start on page 345 of Volume 1 and are continued in Volume 2. The "Pen Names" section, indicated in this index by the code *LP*, begins on page 331.

LinLib S — *The Lincoln Library of Social Studies.* Eighth edition. Three volumes. Columbus, Ohio: Frontier Press Co., 1978.

Biographies begin on page 865 of Volume 3.

LivgBAA — *Living Black American Authors: A Biographical Directory.* By Ann Allen Shockley and Sue P. Chandler. New York: R.R. Bowker Co., 1973.

LivgFWS — *The Living Female Writers of the South.* Edited by Mary T. Tardy. Philadelphia: Claxton, Remsen & Haffelfinger, 1872. Reprint. Detroit: Gale Research Co., 1978.

LongCEL — *Longman Companion to English Literature.* Second edition. By Christopher Gillie. London: Longman Group Ltd., 1977. Also published as *A Companion to British Literature.* Detroit: Grand River Books, 1980.

LongCTC — *Longman Companion to Twentieth Century Literature.* By A.C. Ward. London: Longman Group Ltd., 1970.

LookW — *Look for the Woman.* A narrative encyclopedia of female poisoners, kidnappers, thieves, extortionists, terrorists, swindlers and spies from Elizabethan times to the present. By Jay Robert Nash. New York: M. Evans & Co., Inc., 1981.

LuthC 75 — *Lutheran Cyclopedia.* Revised edition. Edited by Erwin L. Lueker. St. Louis and London: Concordia Publishing House, 1975.

MGM — *The MGM Stock Company: The Golden Era.* By James Robert Parish and Ronald L. Bowers. New Rochelle, New York: Arlington House, 1973.

MacDCB 78 — *The Macmillan Dictionary of Canadian Biography.* Edited by W. Stewart Wallace. Fourth edition, revised, enlarged, and updated by W.A. McKay. Toronto: Macmillan of Canada, 1978.

McGDA *McGraw-Hill Dictionary of Art.* Five volumes. Edited by Bernard S. Meyers. New York: McGraw-Hill Book Co., 1969.

McGEWB *The McGraw-Hill Encyclopedia of World Biography.* An international reference work in 12 volumes including an index. New York: McGraw-Hill Book Co., 1973.

McGEWD *McGraw-Hill Encyclopedia of World Drama.* An international reference work in four volumes. New York: McGraw-Hill Book Co., 1972.

McGMS 80 *McGraw-Hill Modern Scientists and Engineers.* Three volumes. New York: McGraw-Hill Book Co., 1980. Previous edition published as *McGraw-Hill Modern Men of Science.*

MedHR *Medal of Honor Recipients, 1863-1978.* Prepared by the Committee on Veterans' Affairs, United States Senate. 96th Congress, 1st Session, Senate Committee Print No. 3. Washington, D.C.: United States Government Printing Office, 1979.

Use the "Medal of Honor Alphabetical Index," beginning on page 1023, to locate biographies.

MnBBF *The Men behind Boys' Fiction.* By W.O.G. Lofts and D.J. Adley. London: Howard Baker Publishers Ltd., 1970.

The Addendum, indicated in this index by the code *A,* begins on page 339.

MidE *The Middle East and North Africa.* London: Europa Publications Ltd., 1978, 1979, 1980, 1981. Distributed by Gale Research Co., Detroit, Michigan.

MidE 78 25th edition, 1978-79
MidE 79 26th edition, 1979-80
MidE 80 27th edition, 1980-81
MidE 81 28th edition, 1981-82
MidE 82 29th edition, 1982-83

Biographies are found in the "Who's Who in the Middle East and North Africa" section at the end of each volume.

MnnWr *Minnesota Writers: A Collection of Autobiographical Stories by Minnesota Prose Writers.* Edited and annotated by Carmen Nelson Richards. Minneapolis: T.S. Denison & Co., Inc., 1961.

Use the Table of Contents to locate biographies.

ModAL *Modern American Literature.* Fourth enlarged edition. Four volumes. Compiled and edited by Dorothy Nyren Curley, Maurice Kramer, and Elaine Fialka Kramer. A Library of Literary Criticism. New York: Frederick Ungar Publishing Co., 1969, 1976.

ModAL Volumes 1-3, 1969
ModAL SUP Volume 4, Supplement, 1976

ModBlW *Modern Black Writers.* Compiled and edited by Michael Popkin. A Library of Literary Criticism. New York: Frederick Ungar Publishing Co., 1978.

ModBrL *Modern British Literature.* Four volumes. A Library of Literary Criticism. New York: Frederick Ungar Publishing Co., 1966, 1975.

ModBrL Volumes 1-3. Compiled and edited by Ruth Z. Temple and Martin Tucker, 1966.
ModBrL SUP Volume 4, Supplement. Compiled and edited by Martin Tucker and Rita Stein, 1975.

ModCmwL *Modern Commonwealth Literature.* Compiled and edited by John H. Ferres and Martin Tucker. A Library of Literary Criticism. New York: Frederick Ungar Publishing Co., 1977.

ModFrL *Modern French Literature.* Two volumes. Compiled and edited by Debra Popkin and Michael Popkin. A Library of Literary Criticism. New York: Frederick Ungar Publishing Co., 1977.

ModGL *Modern German Literature.* Two volumes. Compiled and edited by Agnes Korner Domandi. A Library of Literary Criticism. New York: Frederick Ungar Publishing Co., 1972.

ModLAL *Modern Latin American Literature.* Two volumes. Compiled and edited by David William Foster and Virginia Ramos Foster. A Library of Literary Criticism. New York: Frederick Ungar Publishing Co., 1975.

ModRL *Modern Romance Literatures.* Compiled and edited by Dorothy Nyren Curley and Arthur Curley. A Library of Literary Criticism. New York: Frederick Ungar Publishing Co., 1967.

ModSL *Modern Slavic Literatures.* Two volumes. A Library of Literary Criticism. New York: Frederick Ungar Publishing Co., 1972, 1976.

ModSL 1 Volume 1: *Russian Literature.* Compiled and edited by Vasa D. Mihailovich, 1972.
ModSL 2 Volume 2: *Bulgarian, Czechoslovak, Polish, Ukrainian and Yugoslav Literatures.* Compiled and edited by Vasa D. Mihailovich, Igor Hajek, Zbrigniew Folejewski, Bogdan Czaykowski, Leo D. Rudnytzky, and Thomas Butler, 1976.

Use the alphabetic listing of authors included on page vii to locate biographies.

ModWD *Modern World Drama: An Encyclopedia.* By Myron Matlaw. New York: E.P. Dutton & Co., Inc., 1972.

MorBMP *More Books by More People: Interviews with Sixty-Five Authors of Books for Children.* By Lee Bennett Hopkins. New York: Citation Press, 1974.

MorJA *More Junior Authors.* Edited by Muriel Fuller. New York: H.W. Wilson Co., 1963.

MotPP *Motion Picture Performers: A Bibliography of Magazine and Periodical Articles, 1900-1969.* Compiled by Mel Schuster. Metuchen, New Jersey: Scarecrow Press, Inc., 1971.

MouLC *Moulton's Library of Literary Criticism of English and American Authors: Through the Beginning of the Twentieth Century.* Four volumes. Abridged, revised, and with additions by Martin Tucker. New York: Frederick Ungar Publishing Co., 1966.

MouLC 1 Volume 1: The Beginnings to the Seventeenth Century
MouLC 2 Volume 2: Neo-Classicism to the Romantic Period
MouLC 3 Volume 3: The Romantic Period to the Victorian Age
MouLC 4 Volume 4: The Mid-Nineteenth Century to Edwardianism

Use the alphabetic listings at the beginning of each volume to locate biographies.

MovMk *The Movie Makers.* By Sol Chaneles and Albert Wolsky. Secaucus, New Jersey: Derbibooks Inc., 1974.

The "Directors" section begins on page 506.

MugS *Mug Shots: Who's Who in the New Earth.* By Jay Acton, Alan LeMond, and Parker Hodges. New York: World Publishing Co., 1972.

MusMk *The Music Makers.* Edited by Clive Unger-Hamilton. New York: Harry N. Abrams, Inc., 1979.

Use the "Alphabetical List of Entries" at the front of the book to locate biographies.

MusSN *Musicians since 1900: Performers in Concert and Opera.* Compiled and edited by David Ewen. New York: H.W. Wilson Co., 1978.

NamesHP *Names in the History of Psychology: A Biographical Sourcebook.* By Leonard Zusne. Washington, D.C.: Hemisphere Publishing Corp.,

1975. Distributed by John Wiley & Sons, Halstead Press, New York.

Use the "Alphabetic List of Names," beginning on page ix, to locate biographies.

NatCAB *The National Cyclopaedia of American Biography.* 61 volumes. New York and Clifton, New Jersey: James T. White & Co., 1892-1982. Reprint. Volumes 1- 50. Ann Arbor: University Microfilms, 1967-1971.

Number after the source code indicates volume number. Use the index at the back of each volume to locate biographies.

NatPD *National Playwrights Directory.* Edited by Phyllis Johnson Kaye. Waterford, Connecticut: The O'Neill Theater Center, 1977, 1981. Distributed by Gale Research Co., Detroit, Michigan.

NatPD First Edition, 1977
NatPD 81 Second Edition, 1981

NegAl 76 *Negro Almanac: A Reference Work on the Afro American.* Third edition. Edited by Harry A. Ploski and Warren Mann, II. New York: Bellwether Co., 1976.

Use the Index to locate biographies.

NewC *The New Century Handbook of English Literature.* Revised edition. Edited by Clarence L. Barnhart with the assistance of William D. Halsey. New York: Appleton-Century-Crofts, 1967.

NewCol 75 *New Columbia Encyclopedia.* Edited by William H. Harris and Judith S. Levey. New York and London: Columbia University Press, 1975.

NewCBMT *New Complete Book of the American Musical Theater.* By David Ewen. New York: Holt, Rinehart & Winston, 1970.

Biographies are found in the "Librettists, Lyricists and Composers" section beginning on page 607.

NewEOp 71 *The New Encyclopedia of the Opera.* By David Ewen. New York: Hill & Wang, 1971.

NewGrD 80 *The New Grove Dictionary of Music and Musicians.* Edited by Stanley Sadie. 20 volumes. London: Macmillan Publishers, Ltd., 1980. Distributed by Grove's Dictionaries of Music, Inc., Washington, D.C.

NewWmR *New Women in Rock.* Edited by Liz Thomson. New York: Delilah Books, 1982.

NewYHSD *The New-York Historical Society's Dictionary of Artists in America, 1564-1860.* By George C. Groce and David H. Wallace. New Haven, Connecticut: Yale University Press, 1957.

NewYTBE *The New York Times Biographical Edition: A Compilation of Current Biographical Information of General Interest.* New York: Arno Press, 1970-1973. Continued by *The New York Times Biographical Service.* (See below.)

NewYTBE 70 Volume 1, Numbers 1-12, 1970
NewYTBE 71 Volume 2, Numbers 1-12, 1971
NewYTBE 72 Volume 3, Numbers 1-12, 1972
NewYTBE 73 Volume 4, Numbers 1-12, 1973

NewYTBS *The New York Times Biographical Service: A Compilation of Current Biographical Information of General Interest.* New York: Arno Press, 1974-1982. A continuation of *The New York Times Biographical Edition.* (See above.)

NewYTBS 74 Volume 5, Numbers 1-12, 1974
NewYTBS 75 Volume 6, Numbers 1-12, 1975
NewYTBS 76 Volume 7, Numbers 1-12, 1976
NewYTBS 77 Volume 8, Numbers 1-12, 1977
NewYTBS 78 Volume 9, Numbers 1-12, 1978
NewYTBS 79 Volume 10, Numbers 1-12, 1979
NewYTBS 80 Volume 11, Numbers 1-12, 1980
NewYTBS 81 Volume 12, Numbers 1-12, 1981
NewTYBS 82 Volume 13, Numbers 1-13, 1982
NewTYBS 83 Volume 14, Numbers, 1-3, 1983

Use the Annual Index to locate entries.

NewYTET *The New York Times Encyclopedia of Television.* By Les Brown. New York: New York Times Book Co., Inc., 1977.

NewbC *Newbery and Caldecott Medal Books.* With acceptance papers, biographies, and related material chiefly from the *Horn Book Magazine.* Edited by Lee Kingman. Boston: Horn Book, Inc., 1965, 1975.

NewbC 1956 *1956-1965,* 1965
NewbC 1966 *1966-1975,* 1975

Newb 1922 *Newbery Medal Books, 1922-1955.* With their authors' acceptance papers and related material chiefly from the *Horn Book Magazine.* Horn Book Papers, Volume 1. Edited by Bertha Mahony Miller and Elinor Whitney Field. Boston: Horn Book, Inc., 1955.

NotAW *Notable American Women, 1607-1950: A Biographical Dictionary.* Three volumes. Edited by Edward T. James. Cambridge, Massachusetts: Harvard University Press, Belknap Press, 1971.

NotAW MOD *Notable American Women, The Modern Period: A Biographical Dictionary*. Edited by Barbara Sicherman and Carol Hurn Green. Cambridge, Massachusetts: Harvard University Press, Belkhap Press, 1980.

NotNAT *Notable Names in the American Theatre*. Clifton, New Jersey: James T. White & Co., 1976. First edition published as *The Biographical Encyclopaedia and Who's Who of the American Theatre*. (See above.)

NotNAT "Notable Names in the American Theatre" section begins on page 489
NotNAT A "Biographical Bibliography" begins on page 309
NotNAT B "Necrology" begins on page 343

This book often alphabetizes by titles of address, e.g.: Dr., Mrs., and Sir.

Novels *Novels and Novelists: A Guide to the World of Fiction*. Edited by Martin Seymour-Smith. New York: St. Martin's Press, 1980.

Biographies are located in the "Novelists: an Alphabetical Guide" section beginning on page 87.

ObitOF 79 *Obituaries on File*. Two volumes. Compiled by Felice Levy. New York: Facts on File, 1979.

ObitT *Obituaries from the Times*. Compiled by Frank C. Roberts. Reading, England: Newspaper Archive Developments Ltd., 1978, 1979. Distributed by Meckler Books, Westport, Connecticut.

ObitT 1951 *1951-1960*, 1979
ObitT 1971 *1971-1975*, 1978

OfEnT United States Tennis Association. *Official Encyclopedia of Tennis*. Revised and updated. Edited by Bill Shannon. New York: Harper & Row, 1979.

OfNBA *Official NBA Register*. Edited by Matt Winick. St. Louis: The Sporting News, 1981.

OhA&B *Ohio Authors and Their Books: Biographical Data and Selective Bibliographies for Ohio Authors, Native and Resident, 1796-1950*. Edited by William Coyle. Cleveland and New York: World Publishing Co., 1962.

OxAmH *The Oxford Companion to American History*. By Thomas H. Johnson. New York: Oxford University Press, 1966.

OxAmL *The Oxford Companion to American Literature*. Fourth edition. By James D. Hart. New York: Oxford University Press, 1965.

OxArt — *The Oxford Companion to Art.* Edited by Harold Osborne. Oxford: Oxford University Press, Clarendon Press, 1970.

OxCan — *The Oxford Companion to Canadian History and Literature.* Toronto: Oxford University Press, 1968, 1973.

- *OxCan* — Original volume, corrected. By Norah Story, 1968.
- *OxCan SUP* — Supplement. Edited by William Toye, 1973.

OxDecA — *The Oxford Companion to the Decorative Arts.* Edited by Harold Osborne. Oxford: Clarendon Press, 1975.

OxEng — *The Oxford Companion to English Literature.* Compiled and edited by Sir Paul Harvey. Fourth edition, revised by Dorothy Eagle. New York: Oxford University Press, 1967.

OxFilm — *The Oxford Companion to Film.* Edited by Liz-Anne Bawden. New York: Oxford University Press, 1976.

OxFr — *The Oxford Companion to French Literature.* Corrected edition. Compiled and edited by Sir Paul Harvey and J.E. Heseltine. Oxford: Clarendon Press, 1966.

OxGer — *The Oxford Companion to German Literature.* By Henry Garland and Mary Garland. Oxford: Clarendon Press, 1976.

OxLaw — *The Oxford Companion to Law.* By David M. Walker. Oxford: Oxford University Press, Clarendon Press, 1980.

OxMus — *The Oxford Companion to Music.* By Percy A. Scholes. 10th edition (corrected). Edited by John Owen Ward. London: Oxford University Press, 1974.

OxShips — *The Oxford Companion to Ships and the Sea.* Edited by Peter Kemp. London: Oxford University Press, 1976.

OxSpan — *The Oxford Companion to Spanish Literature.* Edited by Philip Ward. Oxford: Clarendon Press, 1978.

OxThe — *The Oxford Companion to the Theatre.* Third edition. Edited by Phyllis Hartnoll. London: Oxford University Press, 1967.

Pen — *The Penguin Companion to World Literature.* New York: McGraw-Hill Book Co., 1969, 1971.

- *Pen AM* — *The Penguin Companion to American Literature.* Edited by Malcolm Bradbury, Eric Mottram, and Jean Franco, 1971.

Biographies are found in the "U.S.A." and "Latin America" sections.

Pen CL *The Penguin Companion to Classical, Oriental, and African Literature.* Edited by D.M. Lang and D.R. Dudley, 1969.
Biographies are found in the "Classical," "Byzantine," "Oriental," and "African" sections.

Pen ENG *The Penguin Companion to English Literature.* Edited by David Daiches, 1971.

Pen EUR *The Penguin Companion to European Literature.* Edited by Anthony Thorlby, 1969.

PhDcTCA 77 *Phaidon Dictionary of Twentieth-Century Art.* Second edition. Oxford: Phaidon Press Ltd.; New York: E.P. Dutton, 1977.

PiP *The Pied Pipers: Interviews with the Influential Creators of Children's Literature.* By Justin Wintle and Emma Fisher. New York: Paddington Press Ltd., 1974.

Use the Table of Contents to locate biographies.

PlP&P *Plays, Players, and Playwrights: An Illustrated History of the Theatre.* By Marion Geisinger. Updated by Peggy Marks. New York: Hart Publishing Co., Inc., 1975.

Use the Index, beginning on page 575, to locate biographies in the main section of the book. A Supplemental Index to the last chapter "The Theatre of the Seventies" begins on page 797, and is indicated in this index by the code *A*.

PoChrch *The Poets of the Church: A Series of Biographical Sketches of Hymn-Writers with Notes on Their Hymns.* By Edwin F. Hatfield. New York: Anson D.F. Randolph & Co., 1884. Reprint. Detroit: Gale Research Co., 1978.

PoIre *The Poets of Ireland: A Biographical and Bibliographical Dictionary of Irish Writers of English Verse.* By D.J. O'Donoghue. Dublin: Hodges Figgis & Co., Ltd.; London: Henry Frowde, Oxford University Press, 1912. Reprint. Detroit: Gale Research Co., 1968.

"The Poets of Ireland" section begins on page 5. The Appendices begin on page 495.

PoLE *The Poets Laureate of England.* Being a history of the office of poet laureate, biographical notices of its holders, and a collection of the satires, epigrams, and lampoons directed against them. By Walter Hamilton. London: Elliot Stock, 1879. Reprint. Detroit: Gale Research Co., 1968.

Use the Index to locate biographies.

Po&Wr 77 *The Poets & Writers, Inc. 1977 Supplement.* A complete update to *A Directory of American Poets* (1975) and *A Directory of American Fiction Writers* (1976). New York: Poets & Writers, Inc., 1977.

Use the Index to locate biographies.

PolProf *Political Profiles.* New York: Facts on File, Inc., 1976-1979.

- ***PolProf E*** *The Eisenhower Years.* Edited by Eleanora W. Schoenbaum, 1977.
- ***PolProf J*** *The Johnson Years.* Edited by Nelson Lichtenstein, 1976.
- ***PolProf K*** *The Kennedy Years.* Edited by Nelson Lichtenstein, 1976.
- ***PolProf NF*** *The Nixon/Ford Years.* Edited by Eleanora W. Schoenebaum, 1979.
- ***PolProf T*** *The Truman Years.* Edited by Eleanora W. Schoenebaum, 1978.

Pseud *Pseudonyms of Authors, Including Anonyms and Initialisms.* By John Edward Haynes. New York: John Edward Haynes, 1882. Reprint. Detroit: Gale Research Co., 1969.

The Addenda, indicated in this index by the code *A*, begins on page 104. Pseudonyms are given exactly as written by the author and are filed under the first letter of the pseudonym including the articles "a," "an," and "the."

PseudN *Pseudonyms and Nicknames Dictionary.* Second edition. Edited by Jennifer Mossman. Detroit: Gale Research Co., 1982.

PueRA *Puerto Rican Authors: A Biobibliographic Handbook.* By Marnesba D. Hill and Harold B. Schleifer. Translation of entries into Spanish by Daniel Maratos. Metuchen, New Jersey: Scarecrow Press, Inc., 1974.

RAdv 1 *The Reader's Adviser: A Layman's Guide to Literature.* 12th edition. Volume 1: *The Best in American and British Fiction, Poetry, Essays, Literary Biography, Bibliography, and Reference.* Edited by Sarah L. Prakken. New York: R.R. Bowker Co., 1974.

Use the "Author Index," beginning on page 741, to locate biographies and bibliographies.

RComWL *The Reader's Companion to World Literature.* Second edition. Revised and updated by Lillian Herlands Hornstein, Leon Edel, and Horst Frenz. New York and Scarborough, Ontario: New American Library, 1973.

REn *The Reader's Encyclopedia.* Second edition. By William Rose Benet. New York: Thomas Y. Crowell Co., 1965.

REnAL *The Reader's Encyclopedia of American Literature.* By Max J. Herzberg. New York: Thomas Y. Crowell Co., 1962.

REnAW *The Reader's Encyclopedia of the American West.* Edited by Howard R. Lamar. New York: Thomas Y. Crowell Co., 1977.

REnWD *The Reader's Encyclopedia of World Drama.* Edited by John Gassner and Edward Quinn. New York: Thomas Y. Crowell Co., 1969.

RGAfL *A Reader's Guide to African Literature.* Compiled and edited by Hans M. Zell and Helene Silver. New York: Africana Publishing Corp., 1971.

Biographies begin on page 113.

RkOn *Rock On: The Illustrated Encyclopedia of Rock n' Roll.* By Norm N. Nite. New York: Thomas Y. Crowell Co., 1974, 1978.

RkOn Volume 1: *The Solid Gold Years,* 1974
RkOn 2 Volume 2: *The Modern Years: 1964-Present,* 1978
RkOn 2A Volume 2: Appendix begins on page 543

Rk 100 *Rock 100.* By David Dalton and Lenny Kaye. New York: Grosset & Dunlap, 1977.

ScF&FL *Science Fiction and Fantasy Literature.* A checklist, 1700-1974, with *Contemporary Science Fiction Authors II.* By R. Reginald. Detroit: Gale Research Co., 1979.

ScF&FL 1 Volume 1: "Author Index" begins on page 3
ScF&FL 1A Volume 1: Addendum begins on page 581
ScF&FL 2 Volume 2: *Contemporary Science Fiction Authors II*

SelBAA *Selected Black American Authors: An Illustrated Bio-Bibliography.* Compiled by James A. Page. Boston: G.K. Hall & Co., 1977.

SenS *A Sense of Story: Essays on Contemporary Writers for Children.* By John Rowe Townsend. London: Longman Group Ltd., 1971.

SixAP *Sixty American Poets, 1896-1944.* Revised edition. Selected, with preface and critical notes by Allen Tate. Washington, D.C.: Library of Congress, 1954. Reprint. Detroit: Gale Research Co., 1969.

SmATA *Something about the Author.* Facts and pictures about authors and illustrators of books for young people. Edited by Anne Commire. Detroit: Gale Research Co., 1971-1982.

SmATA 1 Volume 1, 1971
SmATA 2 Volume 2, 1971

SmATA 3	Volume 3, 1972
SmATA 4	Volume 4, 1973
SmATA 5	Volume 5, 1973
SmATA 6	Volume 6, 1974
SmATA 7	Volume 7, 1975
SmATA 8	Volume 8, 1976
SmATA 9	Volume 9, 1976
SmATA 10	Volume 10, 1976
SmATA 11	Volume 11, 1977
SmATA 12	Volume 12, 1977
SmATA 13	Volume 13, 1978
SmATA 14	Volume 14, 1978
SmATA 15	Volume 15, 1979
SmATA 16	Volume 16, 1979
SmATA 17	Volume 17, 1979
SmATA 18	Volume 18, 1980
SmATA 19	Volume 19, 1980
SmATA 20	Volume 20, 1980
SmATA 21	Volume 21, 1980
SmATA 22	Volume 22, 1981
SmATA 23	Volume 23, 1981
SmATA 24	Volume 24, 1981
SmATA 25	Volume 25, 1981
SmATA 26	Volume 26, 1982
SmATA 27	Volume 27, 1982
SmATA 28	Volume 28, 1982
SmATA X	This code refers to pseudonyms entries which appear only as cross references in the cumulative index in *Something about the Author.*

St&PR 75 *Standard and Poor's Register of Corporations, Directors and Executives.* Three volumes. Volume 2: *Directors and Executives.* New York: Standard & Poor's Corp., 1975.

Str&VC *Story and Verse for Children.* Third edition. By Miriam Blanton Huber. New York: Macmillan Co., 1965.

Biographies begin on page 793.

TexWr *Texas Writers of Today.* By Florence Elberta Barns. Dallas: Tardy Publishing Co., 1935. Reprint. Ann Arbor: Gryphon Books, 1971.

ThFT *They Had Faces Then: Super Stars, Stars and Starlets of the 1930's.* By John Springer and Jack Hamilton. Secaucus, New Jersey: Citadel Press, 1974.

ThrBJA *Third Book of Junior Authors.* Edited by Doris DeMontreville and Donna Hill. New York: H.W. Wilson Co., 1972.

TwCA *Twentieth Century Authors: A Biographical Dictionary of Modern Literature.* New York: H.W. Wilson Co., 1942, 1955.

- ***TwCA*** Original volume. Edited by Stanley J. Kunitz and Howard Haycraft, 1942.
- ***TwCA SUP*** First supplement. Edited by Stanley J. Kunitz, 1955.

TwCBDA *The Twentieth Century Biographical Dictionary of Notable Americans.* Brief biographies of authors, administrators, clergymen, commanders, editors, engineers, jurists, merchants, officials, philanthropists, scientists, statesmen, and others who are making American history. 10 volumes. Edited by Rossiter Johnson. Boston: The Biographical Society, 1904. Reprint. Detroit: Gale Research Co., 1968.

TwCCW *Twentieth-Century Children's Writers.* Edited by D.L. Kirkpatrick. New York: St. Martin's Press, 1978.

TwCCr&M *Twentieth-Century Crime and Mystery Writers.* Edited by John M. Reilly. New York: St. Martin's Press, 1980.

TwCLC *Twentieth-Century Literary Criticism.* Excerpts from criticism of the works of novelists, poets, playwrights, short story writers, and other creative writers who lived between 1900 and 1960, from the first published critical appraisals to current evaluations. Detroit: Gale Research Co., 1978-1982.

- ***TwCLC 1*** Volume 1, 1978
- ***TwCLC 2*** Volume 2, 1979
- ***TwCLC 3*** Volume 3, 1980
- ***TwCLC 4*** Volume 4, 1981
- ***TwCLC 5*** Volume 5, 1981
- ***TwCLC 6*** Volume 6, 1982

TwCW *Twentieth Century Writing: A Reader's Guide to Contemporary Literature.* Edited by Kenneth Richardson. Levittown, New York: Transatlantic Arts, Inc., 1971.

TwYS *Twenty Years of Silents, 1908-1928.* Compiled by John T. Weaver. Metuchen, New Jersey: Scarecrow Press, Inc., 1971.

- ***TwYS*** "The Players" begins on page 27
- ***TwYS A*** "Directors" begins on page 407
- ***TwYS B*** "Producers" begins on page 502

USBiR 74 United States. Department of State. *The Biographic Register, July, 1974.* Washington, D.C.: United States Government Printing Office, 1974.

Vers *The Versatiles.* A study of supporting character actors and actresses in the American motion picture, 1930-1955. By Alfred E. Twomey and

Arthur F. McClure. South Brunswick, New Jersey and New York: A.S. Barnes & Co.; London: Thomas Yoseloff Ltd., 1969.

Vers A "Biographical Section" begins on page 25
Vers B "Non-Biographical Section" begins on page 249

Ward *1977 Ward's Who's Who among U.S. Motor Vehicle Manufacturers.* Detroit: Ward's Communications, Inc., 1977.

Ward 77 "U.S. Big Four Biographical Section" begins on page 61
Ward 77A "The Independent Truck, Off-Highway and Farm Vehicle Manufacturers" begins on page 335
Ward 77B "The Importers" begins on page 355
Ward 77C "The United Auto Workers" begins on page 371
Ward 77D "Government Agencies" begins on page 372
Ward 77E "Auto Associations" begins on page 376
Ward 77F "The Automotive Press" begins on page 387
Ward 77G "Where Are They Now?" begins on page 404
Ward 77H "Automotive Suppliers' Section" begins on page 449

WebAB *Webster's American Biographies.* Edited by Charles Van Doren. Springfield, Massachusetts: G. & C. Merriam Co., 1974, 1979.

WebAB 74 1974 edition
WebAB 79 1979 edition

WebAMB *Webster's American Military Biographies.* Springfield, Massachusetts: G. & C. Merriam Co., 1978.

WebBD 80 *Webster's Biographical Dictionary.* Springfield, Massachusetts: G. & C. Merriam Co., Publishers, 1980.

WebE&AL *Webster's New World Companion to English and American Literature.* Edited by Arthur Pollard. New York: World Publishing Co., 1973.

What *Whatever Became of . . .?* By Richard Lamparski. New York: Crown Publishers, Inc., 1967-1974.

What 1 Volume One, 1967
What 2 Second Series, 1968
What 3 Third Series, 1970
What 4 Fourth Series, 1973
What 5 Fifth Series, 1974

Also printed in a paperback edition by Ace Books.

WhDW *Who Did What.* The lives and achievements of the 5000 men and women -- leaders of nations, saints and sinners, artists and scientists -- who shaped our world. Edited by Gerald Howat. New York: Crown Publishers, Inc., 1974.

WhAm HS *Who Was Who in America, Historical Volume, 1607-1896.* A component volume of *Who's Who in American History.* Revised edition. Chicago: Marquis Who's Who, Inc., 1967.

The Addendum, indicated in this index by the code *A*, begins on page 677.

WhAm 1 *Who Was Who in America, Volume one, 1897-1942.* A component volume of *Who's Who in American History.* Chicago: A.N. Marquis Co., 1943.

WhAm 2 *Who Was Who in America, Volume two, 1943-1950.* A component volume of *Who's Who in American History.* Chicago: Marquis Who's Who, Inc., 1966.

WhAm 3 *Who Was Who in America, Volume three, 1951-1960.* A component of *Who's Who in American History.* Chicago: Marquis Who's Who, Inc., 1966.

The Addendum, indicated in this index by the code *A*, begins on page 952.

WhAm 4 *Who Was Who in America with World Notables, Volume four, 1961-1968.* A component volume of *Who's Who in American History.* Chicago: Marquis- Who's Who, Inc., 1968.

The Addendum, indicated in this index by the code *A*, begins on page 1049.

WhAm 5 *Who Was Who in America with World Notables, Volume five, 1969-1973.* Chicago: Marquis Who's Who, Inc., 1973.

WhAm 6 *Who Was Who in America with World Notables, Volume six, 1974-1976.* Chicago: Marquis Who's Who, Inc., 1976.

WhoAm 7 *Who Was Who in America with World Notables, Volume seven, 1977-1981.* Chicago: Marquis Who's Who, Inc., 1981.

WhAmP *Who Was Who in American Politics.* A biographical dictionary of over 4,000 men and women who contributed to the United States political scene from colonial days up to and including the immediate past. By Don and Inez Morris. New York: Hawthorn Books, Inc., Publishers, 1974.

WhE&EA *Who Was Who among English and European Authors, 1931-1949.* Based on entries which first appeared in *The Author's and Writer's Who's Who and Reference Guide,* originally compiled by Edward Martell and L.G. Pine, and in *Who's Who among Living Authors of Older Nations,* originally compiled by Alberta Lawrence. Three volumes. Gale Composite Biographical Dictionary Series, Number 2. Detroit: Gale Research Co., 1978.

WhFla *Who Was Who in Florida.* Written and compiled by Henry S. Marks. Huntsville, Alabama: Strode Publishers, 1973.

WhJnl *Who Was Who in Journalism, 1925-1928.* A consolidation of all material appearing in the 1928 edition of *Who's Who in Journalism,* with Unduplicated Biographical Entries from the 1925 Edition of *Who's Who in Journalism,* originally compiled by M.N. Ask (1925 and 1928 editions) and S. Gershanek (1925 edition). Gale Composite Biographical Dictionary Series, Number 4. Detroit: Gale Research Co., 1978.

WhLit *Who Was Who in Literature, 1906-1934.* Based on entries that first appeared in *Literary Yearbook* (1906-1913), *Literary Yearbook and Author's Who's Who* (1914-1917), *Literary Yearbook* (1920-1922), and *Who's Who in Literature* (1924-1934). Two volumes. Gale Composite Biographical Dictionary Series, Number 5. Detroit: Gale Research Co., 1979.

WhNAA *Who Was Who among North American Authors, 1921-1939.* Compiled from *Who's Who among North American Authors,* Volumes 1-7, 1921-1939. Two volumes. Gale Composite Biographical Dictionary Series, Number 1. Detroit: Gale Research Co., 1976.

WhScrn *Who Was Who on Screen.* By Evelyn Mack Truitt. New York: R.R. Bowker Co., 1974, 1977.

- ***WhScrn 74*** First edition, 1974
- ***WhScrn 77*** Second edition, 1977

WhThe *Who Was Who in the Theatre, 1912-1976.* A biographical dictionary of actors, actresses, directors, playwrights, and producers of the English-speaking theatre. Compiled from *Who's Who in the Theatre,* Volumes 1-15, 1912-1972. Four volumes. Gale Composite Biographical Dictionary Series, Number 3. Detroit: Gale Research Co., 1978.

WhWW-II *Who Was Who in World War II.* Edited by John Keegan. London: Arms & Armour Press, 1978.

Who *Who's Who.* An annual biographical dictionary. New York: St. Martin's Press; London: Adam & Charles Black Ltd., 1974, 1975, 1976, 1977, 1978, 1979, 1982.

- ***Who 74*** 126th Year of Issue, 1974-1975
- ***Who 75*** 127th Year of Issue, 1975-1976
- ***Who 76*** 128th Year of Issue, 1976-1977

Who 77	129th Year of Issue, 1977-1978
Who 78	130th Year of Issue, 1978
Who 79	131st Year of Issue, 1979-1980
Who 80	132nd Year of Issue, 1980-1981
Who 81	133rd Year of Issue, 1981-1982
Who 82	134th Year of Issue, 1982-1983

WhoAdv 72 *Who's Who in Advertising.* Second edition. Edited by Robert S. Morgan. Rye, New York: Redfield Publishing Co., 1972.

Biographies are found in the "U.S. Advertising Executives" section beginning on page 1, "Canadian Advertising Executives" section beginning on page 585, and in the "Addendum" beginning on page 637.

WhoAdv 80 *Who's Who in Advertising.* Third edition. Edited by Catherine Quinn Serie. Monroe, New York: Redfield Publishing Co., Inc., 1980

WhoAm *Who's Who in America.* Chicago: Marquis Who's Who, Inc., 1974, 1976, 1978, 1980, 1982.

WhoAm 74	38th edition, 1974-1975
WhoAm 76	39th edition, 1976-1977
WhoAm 78	40th edition, 1978-1979
WhoAm 80	41st edition, 1980-1981
WhoAm 82	42nd edition, 1982-1983

WhoAmA *Who's Who in American Art.* Edited by Jaques Cattell Press. New York and London: R.R. Bowker Co., 1973, 1976, 1978, 1980, 1982.

WhoAmA 73	1973 edition
WhoAmA 76	1976 edition
WhoAmA 78	1978 edition
WhoAmA 80	1980 edition
WhoAmA 82	1982 editon

WhoAmJ 80 *Who's Who in American Jewry.* Incorporating *The Directory of American Jewish Institutions.* Los Angeles: Standard Who's Who, 1980.

WhoAmL *Who's Who in American Law.* Chicago: Marquis Who's Who, Inc., 1978, 1979.

WhoAmL 78	First edition, 1978
WhoAmL 79	Second edition, 1979

WhoAmP *Who's Who in American Politics.* Edited by Jaques Cattell Press. New York: R.R. Bowker Co., 1973, 1975, 1977, 1979, 1981.

WhoAmP 73	Fourth edition, 1973-1974
WhoAmP 75	Fifth edition, 1975-1976
WhoAmP 77	Sixth edition, 1977-1978

WhoAmP 79 Seventh edition, 1979-1980
WhoAmP 81 Eighth edition, 1981-1982

Biographies in the seventh edition are divided by geographical areas. Use the Index to locate biographies.

WhoAmW *Who's Who of American Women.* Chicago: Marquis Who's Who, Inc., 1958, 1961, 1963, 1965, 1967, 1969, 1971, 1973, 1975, 1978, 1979, 1981.

WhoAmW 58 First edition, 1958-1959
WhoAmW 61 Second edition, 1961-1962
WhoAmW 64 Third edition, 1964-1965
WhoAmW 66 Fourth edition, 1966-1967
WhoAmW 68 Fifth edition, 1968-1969
WhoAmW 70 Sixth edition, 1970-1971
WhoAmW 72 Seventh edition, 1972-1973
WhoAmW 74 Eighth edition, 1974-1975
WhoAmW 75 Ninth edition, 1975-1976
WhoAmW 77 Tenth edition, 1977-1978
WhoAmW 79 Eleventh edition, 1979-1980
WhoAMW 81 Twelfth edition, 1981-1982

WhoArch *Who's Who in Architecture from 1400 to the Present Day.* Edited by J.M. Richards. London: Weidenfeld & Nicolson Ltd., 1977.

WhoArt 80 *Who's Who in Art.* 19th edition. Hants, England: Art Trade Press, Ltd., 1980. Distributed by Gale Research Co., Detroit, Michigan.

WhoAtom 77 *Who's Who in Atoms.* Sixth edition. Edited by Ann Pernet. Guernsey, British Isles: Francis Hodgson, 1977.

WhoBbl 73 *Who's Who in Basketball.* By Ronald L. Mendell. New Rochelle, New York: Arlington House, 1973.

WhoBlA *Who's Who among Black Americans.* Northbrook, Illinois: Who's Who among Black Americans, Inc., 1976, 1978.

WhoBlA 75 First edition, 1975-1976
WhoBlA 77 Second edition, 1977-1978
WhoBLA 80 Third edition, 1980-1981

WhoBox 74 *Who's Who in Boxing.* By Bob Burrill. New Rochelle, New York: Arlington House, 1974.

WhoCan *Who's Who in Canada.* An illustrated biographical record of men and women of the time. Toronto: International Press Ltd., 1973, 1975, 1977, 1980.

WhoCan 73 1973-1974 edition

WhoCan 75 1975-1976 edition
WhoCan 77 1977-1978 edition
WhoCan 80 1980-1981 edition

Use the Index at the front of each volume to locate biographies.

WhoChL *The Who's Who of Children's Literature.* Compiled and edited by Brian Doyle. New York: Schocken Books, 1968.

Biographies are found in "The Authors" section beginning on page 1 and "The Illustrators" section beginning on page 303.

WhoColR *Who's Who of the Colored Race.* A general biographical dictionary of men and women of African descent. Volume one. Edited by Frank Lincoln Mather. Chicago: 1915. Reprint. Detroit: Gale Research Co., 1976.

WhoCon 73 *Who's Who in Consulting.* A reference guide to professional personnel engaged in consultation for business, industry, and government. Second edition. Edited by Paul Wasserman. Detroit: Gale Research Co., 1973.

WhoE *Who's Who in the East.* Chicago: Marquis Who's Who, Inc., 1974, 1975, 1977, 1979, 1981.

WhoE 74 14th edition, 1974-1975
WhoE 75 15th edition, 1975-1976
WhoE 77 16th edition, 1977-1978
WhoE 79 17th edition, 1979-1980
WhoE 81 18th edition, 1981-1982

WhoFash *Who's Who in Fashion.* By Anne Stegemeyer. New York: Fairchild Publications, 1980.

WhoF&I *Who's Who in Finance and Industry.* Chicago: Marquis Who's Who, Inc., 1974, 1975, 1977, 1979, 1981.

WhoF&I 74 18th edition, 1974-1975
WhoF&I 75 19th edition, 1975-1976
WhoF&I 77 20th edition, 1977-1978
WhoF&I 79 21st edition, 1979-1980
WhoF&I 81 22nd edition, 1981-1982

WhoFtbl 74 *Who's Who in Football.* By Ronald L. Mendell and Timothy B. Phares. New Rochelle, New York: Arlington House, 1974.

WhoFr 79 *Who's Who in France: Qui est Qui en France.* 14th edition, 1979-1980. Dictionnaire biographique de personnalites francaises vivant en France, dans les territoires d'Outre-Mer ou a l'etranger et de personnalites etrangeres residant en France. Paris: Editions Jacques Lafitte, 1979.

WhoGolf *Who's Who in Golf.* By Len Elliott and Barbara Kelly. New Rochelle, New York: Arlington House Publishers, 1976.

WhoGov *Who's Who in Government.* Chicago: Marquis Who's Who, Inc., 1972, 1975, 1977.

- ***WhoGov 72*** First edition, 1972-1973
- ***WhoGov 75*** Second edition, 1975-1976
- ***WhoGov 77*** Third edition, 1977

WhoGrA *Who's Who in Graphic Art.* An illustrated book of reference to the world's leading graphic designers, illustrators, typographers and cartoonists. Edited by Walter Amsutz. First edition. Zurich: Amstutz & Herdeg Graphis Press, 1962.

Use the Index, beginning on page 576, to locate biographies.

WhoHcky 73 *Who's Who in Hockey.* By Harry C. Kariher. New Rochelle, New York: Arlington House, 1973.

WhoHol *Who's Who in Hollywood, 1900-1976.* By David Ragan. New Rochelle, New York: Arlington House, 1976.

- ***WhoHol A*** "Living Players" begins on page 11
- ***WhoHol B*** "Late Players (1900-1974)" begins on page 539
- ***WhoHol C*** "Players Who Died in 1975 and 1976" begins on page 845

WhoHr&F *Who's Who in Horror and Fantasy Fiction.* By Mike Ashley. London: Elm Tree Books Ltd., 1977.

WhoHrs 80 *Who's Who of the Horrors and Other Fantasy Films.* The international personality encyclopedia of the fantastic film. First edition. By David J. Hogan. San Diego and New York: A.S. Barnes & Co., Inc.; London: Tantivy Press, 1980.

WhoIns *Who's Who in Insurance.* Englewood, New Jersey: Underwriter Printing & Publishing Co., 1975, 1976, 1977, 1978, 1979, 1980, 1981, 1982.

- ***WhoIns 75*** 1975 edition
- ***WhoIns 76*** 1976 edition
- ***WhoIns 77*** 1977 edition
- ***WhoIns 78*** 1978 edition
- ***WhoIns 79*** 1979 edition
- ***WhoIns 80*** 1980 edition
- ***WhoIns 81*** 1981 edition
- ***WhoIns 82*** 1982 edition

WhoJazz 72 *Who's Who of Jazz: Storyville to Swing Street.* By John Chilton. Philadelphia: Chilton Book Co., 1972.

WhoLab 76 *Who's Who in Labor*. New York: Arno Press, 1976.

WhoLA *Who's Who among Living Authors of Older Nations*. Covering the literary activities of living authors and writers of all countries of the world except the United States of America, Canada, Mexico, Alaska, Hawaii, Newfoundland, the Philippine Islands, the West Indies, and Central America. These countries are covered by our *Who's Who among North American Authors*. Volume 1, 1931-1932. Edited by A. Lawrence. Los Angeles: Golden Syndicate Publishing Co., 1931. Reprint. Gale Research Co., 1966.

WhoMW *Who's Who in the Midwest*. Chicago: Marquis Who's Who, Inc., 1974, 1976, 1978, 1980.

WhoMW 74 14th edition, 1974-1975
WhoMW 76 15th edition, 1976-1977
WhoMW 78 16th edition, 1978-1979
WhoMW 80 17th edition, 1980-1981

WhoMilH 76 *Who's Who in Military History: From 1453 to the Present Day*. By John Keegan and Andrew Wheatcroft. New York: William Morrow & Co., Inc., 1976.

WhoModH *Who's Who in Modern History 1860-1980*. By Alan Palmer. New York: Holt, Rinehart, & Winston, 1980.

WhoMus 72 *Who's Who in Music and Musicians' International Directory*. Sixth edition. New York: Hafner Publishing Co., Inc., 1972. Later editions published as *International Who's Who in Music and Musician's Directory*.

WhoOcn 78 *Who's Who in Ocean and Freshwater Science*. First edition. Edited by Allen Varley. Essex, England: Longman Group Ltd., Francis Hodgson, 1978. Distributed by Gale Research Co., Detroit, Michigan.

WhoOp 76 *Who's Who in Opera*. An international biographical directory of singers, conductors, directors, designers, and administrators. Also including profiles of 101 opera companies. Edited by Maria F. Rich. New York: Arno Press, 1976.

WhoPNW *Who's Who among Pacific Northwest Authors*. Second edition. Edited by Frances Valentine Wright. Missoula, Montana: Pacific Northwest Library Association, Reference Division, 1969.

Biographies are arranged alphabetically by state. Use the Index, beginning on page 103, to locate citations.

WhoPolA *Who's Who in Polish America.* A biographical directory of Polish-American leaders and distinguished Poles resident in the Americas. Third edition. Edited by Francis Bolek. New York: Harbinger House, 1943. Reprint. The American Immigration Collection - Series II. New York: Arno Press and The New York Times, 1970.

WhoProB 73 *Who's Who in Professional Baseball.* By Gene Karst and Martin J. Jones, Jr. New Rochelle, New York: Arlington House, 1973.

WhoPubR *Who's Who in Public Relations (International).* Edited by Adrian A. Paradis. Meriden, New Hampshire: PR Publishing Co., Inc., 1972, 1976.

WhoPubR 72 Fourth edition, 1972
WhoPubR 76 Fifth edition, 1976

WhoRel *Who's Who in Religion.* Chicago: Marquis Who's Who, Inc., 1975, 1977.

WhoRel 75 First edition, 1975-1976
WhoRel 77 Second edition, 1977

WhoRock 81 *Who's Who in Rock.* By Michael Bane. New York: Facts on File, Inc., 1981.

WhoSciF *Who's Who in Science Fiction.* By Brian Ash. London: Elm Tree Books Ltd., 1976.

WhoSocC 78 *Who's Who in the Socialist Countries.* A biographical encyclopedia of 10,000 leading personalities in 16 communist countries. First edition. Edited by Borys Lewytzkyj and Juliusz Stroynowski. New York: K.G. Saur Publishing Inc., 1978. Distributed by Gale Research Co., Detroit, Michigan.

WhoS&SW *Who's Who in the South and Southwest.* Chicago: Marquis Who's Who, Inc., 1973, 1975, 1976, 1978, 1980, 1982.

WhoS&SW 73 13th edition, 1973-1974
WhoS&SW 75 14th edition, 1975-1976
WhoS&SW 76 15th edition, 1976-1977
WhoS&SW 78 16th edition, 1978-1979
WhoS&SW 80 17th edition, 1980-1981
WhoS&SW 82 18th edition, 1982-1983

WhoSpyF *Who's Who in Spy Fiction.* By Donald McCormick. London: Elm Tree Books Ltd., 1977.

WhoStg 1906 *Who's Who on the Stage.* The dramatic reference book and biographical dictionary of the theatre, containing records of the careers of actors, actresses, managers, and playwrights of the American stage. Edited by Walter Browne and F.A. Austin. New York: Walter Browne & F.A. Austin, 1906.

Some entries are not in alphabetic sequence.

WhoStg 1908 *Who's Who on the Stage, 1908.* The dramatic reference book and biographical dictionary of the theatre, containing careers of actors, actresses, managers, and playwrights of the American stage. Edited by Walter Browne and E. DeRoy Koch. New York: B.W. Dodge & Co., 1908.

Some entries are not in alphabetic sequence.

WhoThe *Who's Who in the Theatre: A Biographical Record of the Contemporary Stage.* London: Pitman Publishing Ltd.; Detroit: Gale Research Co., 1972, 1977, 1981.

WhoThe 72 15th edition, compiled by John Parker, 1972.
WhoThe 77 16th edition, edited by Ian Herbert, 1977.
WhoThe 81 17th edition, edited by Ian Herbert, 1981.

WhoTr&F 73 *Who's Who in Track and Field.* By Reid M. Hanley. New Rochelle, New York: Arlington House, 1973.

WhoTwCL *Who's Who in Twentieth Century Literature.* By Martin Seymour-Smith. New York: Holt, Rinehart & Winston, 1976.

WhoUN 75 *Who's Who in the United Nations and Related Agencies.* New York: Arno Press, 1975.

WhoWest *Who's Who in the West.* Chicago: Marquis Who's Who, Inc., 1974, 1976, 1978, 1980, 1982.

WhoWest 74 14th edition, 1974-1975
WhoWest 76 15th edition, 1976-1977
WhoWest 78 16th edition, 1978-1979
WhoWest 80 17th edition, 1980-1981
WhoWest 82 18th edition, 1982-1983

WhoWor *Who's Who in the World.* Chicago: Marquis Who's Who, Inc., 1973, 1976, 1978, 1980.

WhoWor 74 Second edition, 1974-1975
WhoWor 76 Third edition, 1976-1977
WhoWor 78 Fourth edition, 1978-1979
WhoWor 80 Fifth edition, 1980-1981
WhoWor 82 Sixth edition, 1982-1983

WhoWorJ 72 *Who's Who in World Jewry: A Biographical Dictionary of Outstanding Jews.* Edited by I.J. Carmin Karpman. New York: Pitman Publishing Corp., Inc., 1972.

WhoWorJ 78 — *Who's Who in World Jewry: A Biographical Dictionary of Outstanding Jews.* Edited by I.J. Carmin Karpman. Tel-Aviv, Israel: Olive Books of Israel, 1978.

WisWr — *Wisconsin Writers: Sketches and Studies.* By William A. Titus. Chicago: 1930. Reprint. Detroit: Gale Research Co., 1974.

Use the Table of Contents to locate biographies.

WomAch — *Women of Achievement: Thirty-Five Centuries of History.* By Susan Raven and Alison Weir. New York: Harmony Books, 1981.

WomA — *Women Artists: An Historical, Contemporary, and Feminist Bibliography.* By Donna G. Bachmann and Sherry Piland. Metuchen, New Jersey: Scarecrow Press, Inc., 1978.

Use the Table of Contents to locate biographies which begin on page 47. The Addenda, indicated in this index by the code *A*, begins on page 322.

WomPO 76 — *Women in Public Office: A Biographical Directory and Statistical Analysis.* Compiled by The Center for the American Woman and Politics. New York: R.R. Bowker Co., 1976.

Use the "Name Index" to locate citations.

WomPO 78 — *Women in Public Office: A Biographical Directory and Statistical Analysis.* Second edition. Compiled by Center for the American Woman and Politics. Metuchen, New Jersey: Scarecrow Press, Inc., 1978.

Use the "Name Index" to locate citations.

WomWMM — *Women Who Make Movies.* Cinema Study Series. By Sharon Smith. New York: Hopkinson & Blake, 1975.

- *WomWMM* — "Overview" Section. Biographies can be located through the index beginning on page 299
- *WomWMM A* — "The New Filmmakers" begins on page 145
- *WomWMM B* — "Directory" begins on page 221

WomWWA 14 — *Woman's Who's Who of America.* A biographical dictionary of contemporary women of the United States and Canada, 1914-1915. Edited by John William Leonard. New York: American Commonwealth Co., 1914. Reprint. Detroit: Gale Research Co., 1976.

The "Addenda and Corrections" and "Deaths During Printing" sections, indicated in this index by the code *A*, begin on page 29.

WorAl *The World Almanac Book of Who.* Edited by Hana Umlauf Lane. New York: World Almanac Publications, 1980.

Use the Name Index, beginning on page 326, to locate biographies.

WorAu *World Authors.* A companion volume to *Twentieth Century Authors.* Edited by John Wakeman. New York: H.W. Wilson Co., 1975, 1980.

WorAu 1950-1970, 1975
WorAu 1970 1970-1975, 1980

WorDWW *World Defence Who's Who.* Edited by Paul Martell and Grace P. Hayes. London: Macdonald & Jane's, 1974.

WorECar *The World Encyclopedia of Cartoons.* Two volumes. Edited by Maurice Horn. Detroit: Gale Research Co., 1980. Published in association with Chelsea House Publishers, New York and London.

WorECom *The World Encyclopedia of Comics.* Two volumes. Edited by Maurice Horn. New York: Chelsea House Publishers, 1976.

Biographies begin on page 65.

WorEFlm *The World Encyclopedia of the Film.* Edited by John M. Smith and Tim Cawkwell. New York: A. & W. Visual Library, 1972.

WorFshn *World of Fashion: People, Places, Resources.* By Eleanor Lambert. New York: R.R. Bowker Co., 1976.

Use the "Name Index," beginning on page 351, to locate biographies.

WrDr *The Writers Directory.* London: St. James Press; New York: St. Martin's Press, 1976, 1979.

WrDr 76 1976-1978 edition
WrDr 80 1980-1982 edition

WrDr 82 *The Writers Directory 1982-1984.* Detroit: Gale Research Co., 1981.

YABC *Yesterday's Authors of Books for Children.* Facts and pictures about authors and illustrators of books for young people, from early times to 1960. Edited by Anne Commire. Detroit: Gale Research Co., 1977-1978.

YABC 1 Volume 1, 1977
YABC 2 Volume 2, 1978
YABC X This code refers to pseudonym entries which appear only as cross references in the cumulative index to *Yesterday's Authors of Books for Children.*

Biography Almanac

A

Aadland, Beverly
American. Actress, Dancer, Singer
b. 1944
Source: *What 1; WhoHol A*

Aalto, (Hugo) Alvar Henrik
Finnish. Architect
Redesigned Finnish cities damaged during WW II.
b. Feb 3, 1898 in Kuortane, Finland
d. May 11, 1976 in Helsinki, Finland
Source: *ConAu 65; CurBio 48, 76; EncMA; IntWW 74, 75, 76, 77; LinLib S; McGDA; McGEWB; NewYTBS 76; OxDecA; WhAm 7; WhoArch*

Aames, Willie
American. Actor
Played Tommy Bradford on TV series "Eight is Enough."
b. Jul 15, 1960 in Newport Beach, California
Source: *BioIn 12*

Aardema, Verna Norberg
[Verna Norberg Aardema Vugteveen]
American. Author
b. Jun 6, 1911 in New Era, Michigan
Source: *AuBYP SUP; ConAu 5R, 3NR; PseudN; SmATA 4; WhoAmW 68; WrDr 76, 80, 82*

Aaron
First Jewish Priest
Brother of Moses; founded Hebrew priesthood.
Source: *WebBD 80*

Aaron, Chester Norman
American. Author, Educator
b. May 9, 1923 in Butler, Pennsylvania
Source: *AuBYP SUP; ConAu 21R; SmATA 9; WhoWest 74*

Aaron, Hank (Henry Louis)
"Hammerin' Henry"; "The Hammer"
American. Baseball Player
Hit 755 career home runs; Hall of Fame, 1982.
b. Feb 5, 1934 in Mobile, Alabama
Source: *BioNews 74; CelR 73; ConAu 104; CurBio 58; EbonySL 1; NewYTBE 72, 73; NewYTBS 74, 75, 76; PseudN; WebAB; WhoAm 74, 76, 78, 80, 82; WhoBlA 75, 77, 80; WhoProB 73*

Abarbanel, Judah
Spanish. Philosopher, Poet
b. 1460? in Lisbon, Portugal
d. 1535? in Naples, Italy.
Source: *CasWL; EuAu; OxSpan*

ABBA
[Benny Andersson; Annifrid Lyngstad-Fredriksson; Agetha Ulvaeus;Bjorn Ulvaeus]
Swedish. Rock Group
Has outsold every other recording group except The Beatles.
Source: *BkPepl; ConMuA 80; IlEncRk; LilREn 78; RkOn; WhoRock 81*

Abbado, Claudio
Italian. Symphony Conductor
b. Jun 26, 1933 in Milan, Italy
Source: *Baker 78; BnBkM 80; CmOp; CurBio 73; IntWW 74, 75, 76, 77, 78; MusMk; MusSN; NewEOp 71; NewGrD 80; NewYTBE 73; Who 74; WhoAm 82; WhoMus 72; WhoOp 76; WhoWor 74*

Abbas, Khwaja Ahmad
Indian. Author, Filmmaker
b. Jul 6, 1914 in Panipat, India
Source: *ConAu 57; DcFM; DcLEL; DcOrL 2; FilmEn; IntAu&W 76, 77; WhE&EA; WorEFlm*

Abbe, Cleveland
American. Meteorologist
First official weather forecaster of US government.
b. Dec 3, 1838 in New York, New York
d. Oct 28, 1916 in Chevy Chase, Maryland
Source: *AmBi; ApCAB; ApCAB X; AsBiEn; BbD; BiDAmS; BiD&SB; DcAmAu; DcAmB; DcNAA; DcScB; NatCAB 8; OhA&B; TwCBDA; WebAB, 79; WhAm 1*

Abbey, Edwin Austin
American. Artist
Best known work mural series "The Quest for the Holy Grail," Boston Public Library.
b. Apr 1, 1852 in Philadelphia, Pennsylvania
d. Aug 1, 1911 in London, England
Source: *AmBi; AntBDN B; ApCAB; ApCAB X; BnEnAmA; DcAmArt; DcAmB; DcBrBI; DcBrWA; DcVicP; LinLib L, S; McGDA; NatCAB; OxAmL; TwCBDA; WebAB 79; WhAm 1*

Abbey, Henry Eugene
American. Theatre Manager
b. Jun 27, 1846 in Akron, Ohio
d. Oct 17, 1896 in New York, New York
Source: *ApCAB X; BiDAmM; DcAmB; NewEOp 71; OxThe; TwCBDA; WhAm H*

Abbot, Charles Greeley
American. Astrophysicist
b. May 31, 1872 in Wilton, New Hampshire
d. Dec 17, 1973 in Riverdale, Maryland
Source: *ApCAB X; ConAu 45, 77; NewYTBE 73; WhAm 6; WhNAA; Who 74*

Abbott, Berenice
American. Photographer
b. Jul 17, 1898 in Springfield, Ohio
Source: *AmAu&B; BnEnAmA; CurBio 42; GoodHS; InWom; WhoAm 82; WhoAmW 58, 64; WomArt*

Abbott, "Bud" (William A)
[Abbott and Costello]
American. Comedian
Starred in over 35 films with partner, Lou Costello.
b. Oct 2, 1900 in Asbury Park, New Jersey
d. Apr 24, 1974 in Woodland Hills, California
Source: *CmMov; CurBio 41, 74; FilmgC; ForYSC; Funs; HalFC 80; JoeFr; MotPP; MovMk; NewYTBS 74; NotNAT B; OxFilm; PseudN; What 1; WhAm 6; WhScrn 77; WhoHol B*

Abbott, George Francis
American. Director, Dramatist
Directed several plays on Broadway, including *A Tree Grows in Brooklyn.*
b. Jun 25, 1887 in Forestville, New York
Source: *BestMus; BiDAmM; BiE&WWA; BioNews 74; CelR 73; CnMD; ConAu 93; ConDr 73, 77; CurBio 40, 65; EncMT; EncWT; Ent; FilmEn; FilmgC; HalFC 80; IntAu&W 77; McGEWD; ModWD; NewCBMT; NotNAT A; OxThe; PlP&P; WhoAm 74, 76, 78, 80, 82; WhoThe 72, 77; WorEFlm; WrDr 76, 80, 82*

Abbott, Grace
American. Social Reformer
b. Nov 17, 1878 in Grand Island, Nebraska
d. Jun 19, 1939 in Chicago, Illinois
Source: *ApCAB X; DcAmB S2; DcNAA; EncAB-H; InWom; LibW; NatCAB 29; NotAW; WebAB; WhAm 1; WhAmP; WomWWA 14A*

Abbott, (Rufus) Jack Henry
[Jack Eastman, pseud.]
American. Author, Murderer
Wrote *In the Belly of the Beast: Letters from Prison,* 1981.
b. Jan 21, 1944 in Oscoda, Michigan
Source: *BioIn 12; PseudN*

Abbott, Lyman
"Benauly"; "Laicus"
American. Religious Leader, Editor
Editor, *Harper's Magazine, The Outlook.*
b. Dec 18, 1835 in Roxbury, Massachusetts
d. Oct 22, 1922 in New York, New York
Source: *Alli, SUP; AmAu&B; AmBi; AmLY; ApCAB; BbD; BiD&SB; CyAl 2; DcAmAu; DcAmB; DcAmReB; DcEnL; DcNAA; Drake; LinLib L, S; McGEWB; NatCAB 1; OxAmL; PseudN; REn; REnAL; TwCA, SUP; TwCBDA; WebAB; WhAm 1; WhAmP*

Abbott and Costello
[Abbott, Bud; Costello, Lou]
American. Comedy Team
Source: *FilmEn; ForYSC; Funs; JoeFr; MotPP*

Abd al-Karim al-Karmi
see: Abu Salma

Abdallah, Ahmed
Sudanese. President of Comoros
b. 1919
Source: *AfSS 79*

Abdnor, James S
American. Senator
b. Feb 13, 1923 in Kennebec, South Dakota
Source: *AlmAP 78, 80; CngDr 74, 77, 79; WhoAm 74, 76, 78, 80, 82; WhoGov 75, 77; WhoMW 74, 76, 78*

Abdul, Raoul
American. Poet
b. Nov 7, 1929 in Cleveland, Ohio
Source: *ConAu 29R; DcBlPA; SelBAA; SmATA 12; WhoBlA 75, 77; WhoE 77, 79*

Abdul-Jabbar, Kareem
[(Ferdinand) Lew(is) Alcindor, Jr.]
American. Basketball Player
Stands 7'2"; NBA MVP, 1971, 1972, 1974, 1976, 1977, 1980.
b. Apr 16, 1947 in New York, New York
Source: *BkPepl; CelR 73; NewYTBS 74, 76; OfNBA; PseudN; WhoAm 76, 78, 80, 82; WhoBlA 75, 75, 77, 80*

Abdullah, Sheik Mohammad
"Lion of Kashmir"
Indian. Political Leader
Struggled to free country from political domination of India.
b. Dec 5, 1905 in Soura, Kashmir
d. Sep 8, 1982 in Srinagar, Kashmir
Source: *CurBio 52, 83; FarE&A 80; IntWW 79, 80, 81; NewYTBS 82*

Abdullah Ibn Hussein
Jordanian. King
b. 1882 in Mecca, Saudi Arabia
d. Jul 20, 1951 in Jerusalem, Israel
Source: *CurBio 48, 51; NewCol 75*

A'Becket, Thomas
[Saint Thomas a'Becket; Thomas Becket; Thomas of Canterbury]
English. Archbishop, Saint
Killed in his own cathedral; canonized 1173.
b. 1118
d. 1170
Source: *Alli; BiD&SB; NewC*

A'Beckett, Gilbert Abbott
English. Editor, Humorist, Dramatist
Friend of Dickens, Thackeray; little known today; writings too topical.
b. Feb 17, 1811 in London, England
d. Aug 30, 1856 in Boulogne, France
Source: *Alli; BbD; BiD&SB; BrAu 19; CasWL; Chambr 3; DcEnA; DcEnL; EvLB; NewC; OxEng*

Abednego
see: Shadrach

Abel
Biblical Character
Son of Adam and Eve; killed by brother Cain.
Source: *BioIn 10; NewCol 75*

Abel, Alan Wilson
American. Physical Chemist, Editor
b. Mar 7, 1939 in Wilkinsburg, Pennsylvania
Source: *AmM&WS 73P, 76P, 79P; WhoMW 74, 76, 78*

Abel, Elie
Canadian. Broadcast Journalist, Educator
Won George Foster Peabody award for outstanding radio news, 1968.
b. Oct 17, 1920 in Montreal, PQ
Source: *CanWW 79, 82; ConAu 61; LEduc 74; WhoAm 74, 76, 78, 80, 82; WhoE 74; WhoWor 74, 76; WhoWorJ 72*

Abel, I(orwith) W(ilbur)
"Abe"
American. Labor Union Official
President, United Steelworkers of America, 1965-77.
b. Aug 11, 1908 in Magnolia, Ohio
Source: *BiDAmLL; BioNews 74; BusPN; CurBio 65; IntWW 74, 75; NewYTBE 71; PolProf J; PolProf NF; PseudN; WhoAm 76, 78; WhoF&I 75; WhoGov 72, 75; WhoLab 76; WhoWor 74*

Abel, Rudolf Ivanovich
[Martin Collins; Emil R Goldfus; Andrew Kayotis; Mark, aliases]
Russian. Intelligence Agent
b. 1902 in Saint Petersburg, Russia
d. Nov 15, 1971 in Moscow, U.S.S.R.
Source: *BioIn 4, 5, 6, 8, 9, 10; NewYTBE 71; PseudN*

Abel, Sid(ney Gerald)
"Ole Bootnose"
Canadian. Hockey Player, Broadcaster
Center on Production Line with Gordie Howe, Ted Lindsay; Hall of Fame, 1969.
b. Feb 22, 1918 in Melville, SK
Source: *PseudN; WhoHcky 73*

Abel, Walter Charles
American. Actor
Has appeared in over 80 films.
b. Jun 6, 1898 in Saint Paul, Minnesota
Source: *BiE&WWA; FilmEn; FilmgC; ForYSC; HalFC 80; HolCA; IntMPA 75, 76, 77, 78, 79, 80, 81; MotPP; MovMk; NotNAT; Vers B; WhoAm 74, 76, 78, 80, 82; WhoHol A; WhoThe 72, 77, 81*

Abelard, Pierre
French. Author, Theologian
Condemned for heresy, 1141.
b. 1079 in Pallet, France
d. Apr 21, 1142 in Chalon-sur-Saone, France
Source: *BbD; BiD&SB; CasWL; CyWA; DcEuL; DcScB; EuAu; EvEuW; LinLib L, S; LongCEL; McGEWB; NewC; OxEng; OxFr; Pen EUR; RComWL; REn*

Abercrombie, Lascelles
"The Georgian Laureate"
English. Author
b. Jan 9, 1881 in Cheshire, England
d. Oct 27, 1938 in London, England
Source: *Chambr 3; DcLEL; EncWL; EvLB; LinLib L; LongCTC; ModBrL; NewC; OxEng; Pen ENG; PseudN; REn; TwCA, SUP; TwCW; WebE&AL; WhE&EA; WhLit; WhThe; WhoLA*

Aberle, John Wayne
American. Author, Educator
b. Aug 12, 1919 in Lodi, California
Source: *AmM&WS 73S, 78S; ConAu 1R; WhoWest 76*

Abernathy, Ralph David
American. Clergyman, Civil Rights Leader
Replaced Martin Luther King as president of SCLC, 1968-77.
b. Mar 11, 1926 in Linden, Alabama
Source: *BioNews 74; CelR 73; CivR 74; CurBio 68; EbonySL 1; IntWW 74, 75, 76, 77, 78; LinLib S; PolProf E; PolProf J; PolProf K; PolProf NF; WhoAm 74, 76, 78, 80, 82; WhoBlA 75, 77, 80; WhoRel 75, 77; WhoS&SW 73; WhoWor 74, 78*

Abernethy, Robert Gordon
American. Journalist, Editor
b. Nov 5, 1927 in Geneva, Switzerland
Source: *ConAu 21R; SmATA 5; WhoAm 74, 76, 78, 80*

Abish, Walter
American. Author
b. Dec 24, 1931 in Vienna, Austria
Source: *ConAu 101; DrAF 76; DrAP 75; IntAu&W 77*

Ableman, Paul
English. Author, Dramatist
b. Jun 13, 1927 in Leeds, England
Source: *ConAu 61; ConDr 73, 77; ConNov 72, 76; DcLEL 1940; EncSF; IntAu&W 76, 77; ScF&FL 1, 2; WrDr 76, 80, 82*

Abourezk, James George
American. Lawyer, Politician
Senator from SD, 1973-77.
b. Feb 24, 1931 in Woods, South Dakota
Source: *AlmAP 78; CngDr 74, 77; IntWW 74, 75, 76, 77, 78; WhoAm 76, 78, 80, 82; WhoAmL 79; WhoAmP 73, 75, 77, 79; WhoGov 72, 75, 77; WhoMW 74, 76, 78; WhoWor 78*

Abplanalp, Robert H
American. Inventor
Friend of Richard Nixon; invented aerosol valve, 1949.
b. 1923 in New York, New York
Source: *NewYTBE 73; PolProf NF*

Abraham
Patriarch, Biblical Character
Source: *REn*

Abraham, Claude Kurt
American. Author, Professor
b. Dec 13, 1931 in Lorsch, Germany
Source: *ConAu 25R; DrAS 74F; WhoS&SW 73; WhoWorJ 72; WrDr 76*

Abrahams, Harold
British. Track Athlete
Subject of film *Chariots of Fire,* 1982.
b. 1900
d. Jan 14, 1978 in London, England
Source: *BioIn 9, 10*

Abrahams, Jim
American. Motion Picture Director, Author
b. 1944
Source: *BioIn 12; NewYTBS 80*

Abram, Morris Berthold
American. Civil Rights Leader, Lawyer
First head of Peace Corps Legal Department, 1961.
b. Jun 19, 1918 in Fitzgerald, Georgia
Source: *CurBio 65; WhoAm 74, 76, 78, 80, 82; WhoAmP 73; WhoE 74; WhoWor 74; WhoWorJ 72*

Abramovitz, Max
American. Architect
b. May 23, 1908 in Chicago, Illinois
Source: *IntWW 74; WhoAm 74, 76, 78, 80, 82; WhoAmA 73; WhoE 74; WhoWor 74; WhoWorJ 72*

Abrams, Creighton Williams
American. Army Officer
Commanding General, US forces in Vietnam, 1968-72.
b. Sep 15, 1914 in Springfield, Massachusetts
d. Sep 4, 1974 in Washington, DC
Source: *CelR 73; CurBio 68, 74; IntWW 74; NewCol 75; NewYTBS 74; WhAm 6; WhoAm 74*

Abrams, Harry Nathan
English. Publisher
b. Dec 8, 1904 in London, England
d. Nov 25, 1979 in New York, New York
Source: *AmAu&B; BioIn 2, 4, 5, 7, 9, 10; ConAu 93; CurBio 58, 80; WhAm 7; WhoAm 74; WhoAmA 73; WhoWorJ 72*

Abramson, Harold A(lexander)
American. Medical Researcher, Psychiatrist
b. Nov 27, 1899 in New York, New York
d. Sep 29, 1980 in Cold Spring Harbor, New York
Source: *AnObit 1980; BiDrAPA 77; WhoAm 74, 76, 78, 80; WhoWor 74, 76, 78*

Abravanel, Isaac
Portuguese. Theologian
b. 1437 in Lisbon, Portugal
d. 1508 in Venice, Italy
Source: *CasWL; DcEuL; Pen EUR*

Abravanel, Maurice
Turkish. Conductor, Musical Director
b. Jan 6, 1903 in Salonica, Greece
Source: *BiE&WWA; NotNAT; WhoAm 74, 76, 78, 80, 82; WhoWest 74*

Abruzzi, Luigi Amedeo
Italian. Explorer, Mountain Climber
b. 1873
d. 1933
Source: *NewCol 75*

Abse, Dannie
Welsh. Author
b. Sep 22, 1923 in Cardiff, Wales
Source: *Au&Wr 71; ChPo S1; ConAu 53, 4NR; ConDr 73; ConLC 7; ConNov 76; ConP 70, 75; DrAP 75; ModBrL SUP; WorAu; WrDr 76*

Abu Bakr
Arabian. First Caliph of Islam
b. 573 in Mecca, Arabia
d. 634
Source: *McGEWB; NewCol 75; WebBD 80*

"Abu Daoud"
[Muhammad Daoud Audeh; Tarik Shakir Mahdi]
Palestinian. Terrorist
b. 1937
Source: *BioIn 11; PseudN*

Abu Salma, pseud.
[Abd al-Karim al-Karmi]
Palestinian. Poet
b. 1906 in Tulkarm City, Palestine
d. Sep 13, 1980 in Washington, DC
Source: *AnObit 1980*

Abzug, Bella Savitsky
"Battling Bella"
American. Lawyer, Former Congresswoman
First Jewish congresswoman; wide-brimmed hats are trademark.
b. Jul 24, 1920 in New York, New York
Source: *BioNews 75; CelR 73; CngDr 74; ConAu 104; CurBio 71; NewYTBE 71; WhoAm 74, 76, 78, 80, 82; WhoAmP 73; WhoAmW 77; WhoE 74; WhoGov 72; WomPO 76*

AC-DC
[Mark Evans; Phil Rudd; Bon Scott; Cliff Williams; Angus Young; Malcolm Young]
Australian. Rock Group
Source: *ConMuA 80; WhoRock 81*

Ace
[Fran Byrne; Parul Carrack; Tex Comer; Phil Harris; Alan King]
English. Rock Group
Source: *RkOn 2; WhoRock 81*

Ace, Goodman
[Easy Aces]
American. Radio-TV Writer
b. Jan 15, 1899 in Kansas City, Missouri
d. Mar 25, 1982 in New York, New York
Source: *CelR 73; ConAu 61; CurBio 48; NewYTBS 82; NewYTET*

Ace, Jane Sherwood
[Easy Aces]
American. Radio Actress
b. Oct 12, 1905 in Kansas City, Missouri
d. Nov 11, 1974 in New York, New York
Source: *CurBio 48, 75; InWom; NewYTBS 74; WhScrn 77*

Ace, Johnny
[Johnny Marshall Alexander, Jr.]
American. Singer
b. Jun 9, 1929 in Memphis, Tennessee
d. Dec 25, 1954 in Houston, Texas
Source: *BiDAmM; RkOn 2; WhoRock 81*

Achab
[Ahad]
Seventh King of Israel
d. 853
Source: *Chambr 1; WebBD 80*

Achard, Marcel
[Marcel Auguste Ferreol]
French. Dramatist, Director
b. Jul 5, 1900 in Foyles Lyon, France
d. Sep 4, 1974 in Paris, France
Source: *BiE&WWA; CasWL; ClDMEL; CnMD; ConAu 53, 93; EncWL; EvEuW; McGEWD; ModWD; OxFr; REn; Who 74*

Achebe, Chinua
[Albert Chinualumogu]
Nigerian. Author
Received Nigerian National Trophy, 1960.
b. Nov 16, 1930 in Ogidi, Nigeria
Source: *AfrA; Au&Wr 71; CasWL; ConAu 1R, 6NR; ConLC 1, 3, 5, 7, 11; ConNov 72, 76; EncWL; IntWW 74; LongCTC; Pen CL, ENG; PseudN; RGAfL; TwCW; WebE&AL; Who 74; WhoTwCL; WhoWor 74; WorAu; WrDr 76*

Acheson, Dean Gooderham
American. Secretary of State
Won Pulitzer Prize, 1970; primary creator of NATO.
b. Apr 11, 1893 in Middletown, Connecticut
d. Oct 12, 1971 in Sandy Springs, Maryland
Source: *AmAu&B; BiDrUSE; ConAu 25R, 33R; ConAu P-2; EncAB-H; ObitOF 79; REnAL; WebAB; WhAm 5*

Ackerman, Bettye
American. Actress
b. Feb 28, 1928 in Cottageville, South Carolina
Source: *FilmgC; IntMPA 77, 78, 79, 80, 81, 82; WhoHol A*

Ackerman, Carl William
American. Journalist
b. Jan 16, 1890 in Richmond, Indiana
d. Oct 9, 1970 in New York, New York
Source: *AmAu&B; ConAu 29R, 73; CurBio 45, 70; IndAu 1917; NewYTBE 70; WhAm 5*

Ackerman, Forest J
[Dr. Acula; Jacques DeForest Erman; Alden Lorraine; Hubert George Wells; Weaver Wright, pseuds.]
American. Editor, Collector
b. Nov 24, 1916 in Los Angeles, California
Source: *ConAu 102; EncSF; FanAl; PseudN; ScF&FL 1, 2; WhoSciF*

Ackerman, Harry S
American. Motion Picture Executive
b. Nov 17, 1912 in Albany, New York
Source: *IntMPA 77, 78, 79, 80, 81, 82; St&PR 75; WhoAm 74, 76, 78, 80, 82*

Ackerman, Robert Allan
American. Motion Picture Director
b. 1945
Source: *BioIn 12*

Ackland, Joss
English. Actor
b. Feb 29, 1928 in London, England
Source: *FilmEn; FilmgC; WhoThe 77, 81*

Acton, John Emerich Edward Dalberg-Acton, Baron
English. Historian
Planned, wrote first chapter of *The Cambridge Modern History*.
b. Jan 10, 1834 in Naples, Italy
d. Jul 19, 1902 in Tegernsee, Bavaria
Source: *Alli SUP; AtlBL; DcEnA, AP; DcEuL; DcLEL; EvLB; OxEng; Pen ENG*

Acuff, Roy
"The King of Country Music"
American. Singer
Sold over 30 million records; Country Music Hall of Fame, 1962.
b. Sep 15, 1903 in Maynardsville, Tennessee
Source: *EncFCWM 69; PseudN; WhoAm 80, 82*

Adair, Frank E(arl)
American. Surgeon
b. Apr 9, 1887 in Beverly, Ohio
d. Dec 31, 1981 in Bedford, New York
Source: *BioIn 1; CurBio 46, 82; IntWW 76, 77, 78; WhoAm 74, 76*

Adair, "Red" (Paul Neal)
American. Oil Well Technician
b. 1916?
Source: *BioIn 11; PseudN*

Adam
Biblical Character
Source: *BioIn 9, 10; NewCol 75*

Adam, Adolphe Charles
French. Opera Composer
b. Jul 24, 1803 in Paris, France
d. May 3, 1856 in Paris, France
Source: *NewEOp 71*

Adam, Juliette Lamber
[Juliette Lamber; La Messine; Comte Paul Vasili, pseuds.]
French. Author
b. 1836
d. 1936
Source: *BiD&SB; InWom; OxFr; PseudN; REn*

Adam, Robert
Scottish. Architect, Furniture Designer
b. Jul 3, 1728 in Kirkcaldy, Scotland
d. Mar 3, 1792 in London, England
Source: *Alli; AtlBL; NewC*

Adam Ant
see: Ant, Adam

Adamany, David Walter
American. University Administrator
b. Sep 23, 1936 in Jonesville, Wisconsin
Source: *AmM&WS 73S; WhoAm 82; WhoMW 74*

Adamic, Louis
American. Author, Sociologist
Wrote *The Native's Return,* 1934.
b. Mar 23, 1899 in Blato, Dalmatia
d. Sep 4, 1951 in Riegelsville, Pennsylvania
Source: *AmAu&B; CnDAL; ConAmA; CurBio 40, 51; DcAmB S5; DcLEL; OxAmL; REn; REnAL; TwCA, SUP; WhAm 3*

Adamle, Mike (Michael David)
American. Broadcast Journalist
b. Oct 4, 1949 in Euclid, Ohio
Source: *WhoAm 82; WhoFtbl 74*

Adamov, Arthur
Russian. Author, Dramatist
b. Aug 23, 1908 in Kislovodsk, Russia
d. Mar 16, 1970 in Paris, France
Source: *CasWL; CnMD; CnThe; ConAu 17R, 25R; ConAu P-2; ConLC 4; EncWL; McGEWD; ModRL; ModWD; Pen EUR; REnWD; WorAu*

Adamowski, Timothee
Polish. Musician
b. Mar 24, 1858 in Warsaw, Poland
d. Apr 18, 1943 in Boston, Massachusetts
Source: *CurBio 43; WebBD 80*

Adams, Abigail Smith
[Mrs. John Adams; Diana; Portia]
American. Author
Letters provide vivid source of American social history.
b. Nov 11, 1744 in Weymouth, Massachusetts
d. Oct 28, 1818 in Quincy, Massachusetts
Source: *Alli; AmAu; AmAu&B; AmBi; AmWom; ApCAB; BbD; BiCAW; BiD&SB; CyAL 1; DcAmAu; DcAmB; DcNAA; Drake; HerW; InWom; NotAW; OxAmL; PseudN; REn; REnAL; TwCBDA; WebAB; WhAm H; WhAmP*

Adams, Alice Dana
Religious Author
b. 1864
d. Mar 1934
Source: *DcNAA; WomWWA 14*

Adams, Alvan Leigh
American. Basketball Player
b. Jul 29, 1954 in Lawrence, Kansas
Source: *BioIn 10; OfNBA*

Adams, Ansel Easton
American. Photographer
Work includes National Park photo essays.
b. Feb 20, 1902 in San Francisco, California
Source: *AuNews 1; BioNews 74; ConAu 21R; WebAB; WhoAm 74, 76, 78, 80, 82*

Adams, Brock(man)
American. Lawyer, Government Official
Secretary of Transportation, 1977-79.
b. Jan 13, 1927 in Atlanta, Georgia
Source: *BiDrAC; CngDr 74; WhoAm 74, 76, 78, 80, 82; WhoAmP 73; WhoGov 72; WhoWest 74*

Adams, Brooke
American. Actress
b. Feb 8, 1949 in New York, New York
Source: *BioIn 11; IntMPA 82; WhoAm 82*

Adams, Brooks
American. Historian
b. Jun 24, 1848 in Quincy, Massachusetts
d. Feb 13, 1927 in Boston, Massachusetts
Source: *Alli SUP; AmAu; AmAu&B; AmBi; ApCAB; BiD&SB; DcAmAu; DcAmB; DcNAA; EncAB-H; OxAmL; Pen AM; REnAL; TwCBDA; WebAB; WhAm 1*

Adams, Charles Francis, Sr.
American. Diplomat
b. Aug 18, 1807 in Boston, Massachusetts
d. Nov 21, 1886 in Boston, Massachusetts
Source: *Alli, SUP; AmAu&B; AmBi; ApCAB; BbD; BiD&SB; BiDrAC; ChPo S1; CyAl 2; DcAmAu; DcAmB; DcNAA; EncAB-H; OxAmL; TwCBDA; WebAB; WhAm H*

Adams, Charles Francis, Jr.
American. Historian, Lawyer
b. May 27, 1835 in Boston, Massachusetts
d. Mar 20, 1915
Source: *AmAu; AmAu&B; BbD; BiD&SB; DcAmAu; EncAB-H; OxAmL; REn; REnAL; WebAB; WhAm 1*

Adams, Don
[Donald James Yarmy]
American. Actor, Comedian
Played Maxwell Smart on TV series "Get Smart," 1965-70.
b. Apr 19, 1927 in New York, New York
Source: *WhoAm 74, 76, 78, 80, 82*

Adams, Douglas Noel
British. Author
Book *The Hitchhiker's Guide to the Galaxy* made into British TV series, now on PBS.
b. 1952
Source: *WrDr 82*

Adams, Edie
[Elizabeth Edith Enke]
American. Singer, Actress
Wife of Ernie Kovacs; appeared in *It's a Mad, Mad, Mad, Mad World.*
b. Apr 16, 1929 in Kingston, Pennsylvania
Source: *BiE&WWA; FilmgC; ForWC 70; IntMPA 75, 76, 77, 78, 79, 80, 81, 82; MotPP; MovMk; NotNAT; PseudN; WhoAm 74, 76, 78, 80, 82; WhoHol A; WhoThe 77*

Adams, Edwin
American. Actor
b. Feb 3, 1834 in Medford, Massachusetts
d. Oct 25, 1877 in Philadelphia, Pennsylvania
Source: *FamA&A; NotNAT; OxThe*

Adams, Eve Bertrand
American. Government Official
b. Sep 10, 1908 in Wonder, Nevada
Source: *BioIn 6; CurBio 62; WhoAm 80, 82; WhoAmP 73; WhoAmW 74*

Adams, Franklin P(ierce)
"F.P.A."
American. Journalist, Humorist
Best known for columns appearing in NY *Herald-Tribune.*
b. Nov 15, 1881 in Chicago, Illinois
d. Mar 23, 1960 in New York, New York
Source: *AmAu&B; ChPo, S1; CnDAL; ConAmA; ConAu 93; CurBio 41, 60; OxAmL; PseudN; REn; REnAL; TwCA, SUP; WebAB; WhAm 3A; WhNAA*

Adams, Harriet Stratemeyer
[Victor Appleton, III; Carolyn Keene, pseuds.]
American. Children's Author
Wrote Nancy Drew, Hardy Boys; continued series begun by father, Edward Stratemeyer.
b. 1893? in Newark, New Jersey
d. Mar 27, 1982 in Pottersville, New Jersey
Source: *AmAu&B; AmWomWr; AuNews 2; ConAu 81; EncMys; EncSF; NewYTBS 82; PseudN; SmATA 1; WhoAm 78, 82*

Adams, Henry Brooks
American. Historian, Author
Introduced seminar teaching in US; wrote nine-volume history of US.
b. Feb 16, 1838 in Boston, Massachusetts
d. Mar 27, 1918 in Washington, DC
Source: *Alli SUP; AmAu; AmAu&B; AmBi; AmWr; ApCAB; AtlBL; BbD; BiD&SB; CasWL; CnDAL; CyWA; DcAmAu; DcAmB; DcBiA; DcLEL; DcNAA; EncAB-H; EvLB; LongCTC; ModAL, SUP; OxAmL; OxEng; Pen AM; RAdv 1; RComWL; REn; REnAL; TwCBDA; TwCW; WebAB; WebE&AL; WhAm 1; WhAmP; WhoTwCL*

Adams, Jack (John James)
"Jovial Jawn"
Canadian. Hockey Player, Coach
With Detroit Red Wings, 1927-62; won seven Stanley Cups; Hall of Fame, 1959.
b. Jun 14, 1895 in Fort William, ON
d. May 1, 1968 in Detroit, Michigan
Source: *BioIn 3, 8, 10; ObitOF 79; WhoHcky 73*

Adams, James Truslow
American. Historian, Author
b. Oct 18, 1878 in Brooklyn, New York
d. May 18, 1949 in Westport, Connecticut
Source: *AmAu&B; ConAmA; CurBio 41, 49; DcAmB S4; DcLEL; DcNAA; EvLB; OxAmL; REn; REnAL; TwCA, SUP; WebAB; WhAm 2; WhNAA*

Adams, Joey
[Joseph Abramowitz]
American. Comedian, Author
b. Jan 6, 1911 in Brooklyn, New York
Source: *CelR 73; ConAu 49, 1NR; PseudN; WhoAm 74, 76, 78, 80, 82; WhoE 74; WhoWor 74; WhoWorJ 72*

Adams, John
"The Atlas of Independence"
American. 2nd US President
Signed Declaration of Independence, 1776.
b. Oct 30, 1735 in Braintree, Massachusetts
d. Jul 4, 1826 in Quincy, Massachusetts
Source: *Alli; AmAu&B; AmBi; ApCAB; BbD; BiD&SB; BiDLA SUP; BiDrAC; BiDrUSE; ChPo S1; CyAL 1; CyWA; DcAmAu; DcAmB; DcNAA; Drake; EncAB-H; EvLB; OxAmL; PseudN; REn; REnAL; TwCBDA; WebAB; WhAm H; WhAmP*

Adams, John
American. Actor
b. 1874 in Worcester, Massachusetts
d. Jun 3, 1925 in New York, New York
Source: *WhScrn 74*

Adams, John Couch
English. Astronomer
b. Jun 5, 1819
d. Jun 21, 1892
Source: *BioIn 1, 5, 11; McGEWB; NewCol 75*

Adams, John Hanly
American. Author, Editor
b. Nov 2, 1918 in Sikeston, Missouri
Source: *WhoAm 74, 76, 78, 80, 82; WhoF&I 74*

Adams, John Quincy
"The Accidental President"; "Old Man Eloquent"; "Publicola"; "The Second John"
American. 6th US President
Secretary of State, 1817-25; catalyst behind Monroe Doctrine, 1823.
b. Jul 11, 1767 in Braintree, Massachusetts
d. Feb 23, 1848
Source: *AmAu&B; ApCAB; BiAuS; BiDLA; BiDrUSE; CyAL 1; DcLEL; OxAmL; PseudN; REn; WhAm H; WhAmP*

Adams, Julie
[Betty May Adams]
American. Actress
b. 1928 in Waterloo, Iowa
Source: *FilmgC; IntMPA 75, 76, 77, 78, 79, 80, 81, 82; PseudN*

Adams, Leonie Fuller
American. Author
b. Dec 9, 1899 in Brooklyn, New York
Source: *AmAu&B; Au&Wr 71; ChPo, S1; CnE&AP; CnMWL; ConAmA; ConAu P-1; ConP 70, 75; DcLEL; DrAP 75; DrAS 74E; IntWW 74; ModAL; OxAmL; REn; REnAL; SixAP; TwCA SUP; TwCW; WhoAm 74; WhoWor 74; WrDr 76*

Adams, Louisa Catherine
American. Wife of John Quincy Adams
b. 1775
d. 1852
Source: *AmBi; BiCAW; HerW; InWom; NotAW*

Adams, Mason
American. Actor
b. Feb 26, 1919 in New York, New York
Source: *What 4; WhoAm 82*

Adams, Maud
[Maud Wikstrom]
Swedish. Actress, Model
b. 1945? in Lulea, Sweden
Source: *BioIn 10; FilmEn; WhoHol A*

Adams, Maude
[Maude Kiskadden]
American. Actress
b. Nov 11, 1872 in Salt Lake City, Utah
d. Jul 17, 1953 in Tannersville, New York
Source: *DcAmB S5; FamA&A; InWom; OxAmL; OxThe; REnAL; TwCBDA; WebAB; WhAm 3; WhoStg 1906, 1908; WomWWA 14*

Adams, Nick
[Nicholas Adamschock]
American. Actor
b. Jul 10, 1931 in Nanticoke, Pennsylvania
d. Feb 5, 1968 in Beverly Hills, California
Source: *FilmgC; MovMk; PseudN; WhScrn 74, 77; WhoHol B*

Adams, Richard
English. Author
b. May 9, 1920 in Newbury, England
Source: *AuNews 1, 2; ConAu 49, 3NR; ConLC 4, 5, 18; PiP; SmATA 7; WhoAm 82; WrDr 76*

Adams, Samuel
"Alfred"; "The American Cato"; "The Cromwell of New England"; "The Father of America"
American. Revolutionary, Statesman
Force behind Boston Tea Party, 1773; signed Declaration of Independence.
b. Sep 27, 1722 in Boston, Massachusetts
d. Oct 2, 1803 in Boston, Massachusetts
Source: *Alli; AmAu; AmAu&B; AmBi; ApCAB; BiAuS; BiDrAC; DcAmAu; DcAmB; DcNAA; Drake; EncAB-H; OxAmL; PseudN; REn; REnAL; TwCBDA; WebAB; WhAm H; WhAmP*

Adams, Samuel Hopkins
[Warner Fabian, pseud.]
American. Author, Journalist
b. Jan 26, 1871 in Dunkirk, New York
d. Nov 15, 1958 in Beaufort, South Carolina
Source: *AmAu&B; AmLY; AmNov; AuBYP; CnDAL; EncMys; OxAmL; PseudN; REn; TwCA, SUP; WhAm 3*

Adams, Sherman Llewellyn
American. Former Governor
b. Jan 8, 1899 in East Dover, Vermont
Source: *AmAu&B; BiDrAC; CurBio 52; IntWW 74; Who 74; WhoAm 74, 76, 78, 80, 82; WhoAmP 73*

Adams, Walter Sydney
American. Astronomer
b. Dec 20, 1876 in Antioch, Turkey
d. May 11, 1956 in Pasadena, California
Source: *WebAB; WhAm 3; WhNAA*

Adams, William
"Anjin Sama"; "Mr. Pilot"
English. Navigator
First Englishman to visit Japan, 1600; remained there until death.
b. 1564 in England
d. 1620 in Japan
Source: *NewCol 75*

Adamson, George
Kenyan. Animal Expert
Established Kora Reserve wild animal sanctuary, Kenya; husband of Joy Adamson.
b. 1906 in India
Source: *BioIn 8, 9*

Adamson, Joy-Friederike Victoria
[Mrs. George Adamson]
Kenyan. Author, Animal Expert
Best known work, *Born Free,* 1960; filmed, 1966.
b. Jan 20, 1910 in Troppau, Silesia
d. Jan 3, 1980 in Shaba, Kenya
Source: *Au&Wr 71; ConAu 69, 93; ConLC 17; CurBio 72, 80; InWom; SmATA 11; Who 74; WhoAm 74*

Addams, Charles Samuel
American. Cartoonist
Created "The Addams Family" cartoons, TV series, 1964-66.
b. Jan 7, 1912 in Westfield, New Jersey
Source: *AmAu&B; CelR 73; ConAu 61; CurBio 54; IntWW 74; WebAB; WhoAm 74, 76, 78, 80, 82; WhoAmA 73; WhoWor 74; WrDr 76*

Addams, Dawn
English. Actress
b. Sep 21, 1930 in Felixstowe, England
Source: *FilmgC; InWom; IntMPA 75, 76, 77, 78, 79, 80, 81, 82; OxFilm; WhoThe 77*

Addams, Jane
American. Social Worker, Suffragette
Organized Hull House, Chicago, 1889; won Nobel Peace Prize, 1931.
b. Sep 6, 1860 in Cedarville, Illinois
d. May 21, 1935 in Chicago, Illinois
Source: *AmAu&B; AmBi; AmLY; DcAmAu; DcAmB S1; DcLEL; DcNAA; EncAB-H; HerW; InWom; NotAW; OxAmL; REn; REnAL; WebAB; WhAm 1; WhAmP; WhNAA*

Adderley, "Cannonball" (Julian Edwin)
American. Musician
b. Sep 9, 1928 in Tampa, Florida
d. Aug 8, 1975 in Gary, Indiana
Source: *CelR 73; CurBio 61; PseudN; WhAm 6; WhoAm 74*

Addinsell, Richard
English. Composer
b. Jan 13, 1904 in Oxford, England
d. Nov 15, 1977 in London, England
Source: *BiE&WWA; FilmgC; IntMPA 75, 76, 77; NotNAT; OxFilm; Who 74; WhoMus 72; WhoThe 77*

Addison, Adele
American. Opera Singer
b. Jul 24, 1925 in New York, New York
Source: *WhoBlA 75; WhoWor 74*

Addison, John
English. Composer
b. Mar 16, 1920 in West Cobham, England
Source: *Baker 78; CmMov; FilmEn; FilmgC; IntMPA 81; NotNAT A; OxFilm; OxMus*

Addison, Joseph
"Atticus"; "Clio"; "The English Atticus"; "A Literary Machiavel"
English. Essayist, Poet
Prominent in Whig Party; buried in Westminster Abbey.
b. May 1, 1672 in Milston, England
d. Jun 17, 1719 in London, England
Source: *Alli; AtlBL; BbD; BiD&SB; BrAu; CasWL; Chambr 2; ChPo, S1, S2; CrtT 2; CyWA; DcEnA; DcEnL; DcEuL; DcLEL; EvLB; McGEWD; MouLC 2; NewC; OxEng; OxThe; Pen ENG; PoChrch; RAdv 1; PseudN; RComWL; REn; WebE&AL*

Addison, Thomas
English. Physician
b. 1793
d. 1860
Source: *Alli SUP*

Addonizio, Hugh Joseph
American. Former Mayor of Newark
b. Jan 31, 1914 in Newark, New Jersey
d. Feb 2, 1981 in Red Bank, New Jersey
Source: *BiDrAC; BioIn 8, 9; NewYTBE 70; NewYTBS 81; PolProf J; PolProf NF; WhAmP*

Addotta, Kip
American. Comedian
Source: *NF*

Addy, Wesley
American. Actor
b. Aug 4, 1913 in Omaha, Nebraska
Source: *BiE&WWA; NotNAT; WhoAm 74; WhoThe 77*

Ade, George
American. Humorist, Dramatist
Humorous fables published as *Fables in Slang,* 1899.
b. Feb 9, 1866 in Kentland, Indiana
d. May 16, 1944 in Brookville, Indiana
Source: *AmAu&B; AmLY; BbD; BiD&SB; CasWL; Chambr 3; ChPo, S1; CnDAL; ConAmL; CurBio 44; DcAmAu; DcAmB S3; DcNAA; EvLB; IndAu 1816; McGEWD; ModWD; NewCBMT; OxAmL; OxThe; Pen AM; REn; REnAL; TwCA, SUP; TwCBDA; TwCW; WebAB; WhAm 2; WhNAA; WhoStg 1906, 1908*

Adenauer, Konrad
German. Politician
First Chancellor of Federal German Republic, 1949-63.
b. Jan 5, 1876 in Cologne, Germany
d. Apr 19, 1967 in Rhondorf, Germany (West)
Source: *CurBio 49, 58, 67; OxGer; REn; WhAm 4*

Adjani, Isabelle
French. Actress
Source: *WhoHol A*

Adler, Alfred
Austrian. Author, Psychoanalyst
b. Feb 7, 1870 in Vienna, Austria
d. May 28, 1937
Source: *LongCTC; OxGer; REn; TwCA, SUP; WhAm HA, 4; WhoLA*

Adler, "Buddy" (Maurice)
American. Motion Picture Producer
b. Jun 22, 1909 in New York, New York
d. Jul 12, 1960 in Hollywood, California
Source: *DcFM; FilmgC; PseudN; WhAm 4; WorEFlm*

Adler, Cyrus
American. Religious Leader, Educator
b. Sep 13, 1863 in Van Buren, Alaska
d. Apr 7, 1940 in Philadelphia, Pennsylvania
Source: *AmAu&B; AmBi; ApCAB SUP; DcAmAu; DcAmB S2; DcNAA; TwCBDA; WebAB; WhAm 1*

Adler, David
American. Architect
b. Jan 3, 1883 in Milwaukee, Wisconsin
d. Sep 27, 1949
Source: *BioIn 9; WhAm 3*

Adler, Felix
American. Educator, Reformer
b. Aug 13, 1851 in Alzey, Germany
d. Apr 24, 1933 in New York, New York
Source: *Alli SUP; AmAu&B; AmBi; ApCAB; BbD; BiD&SB; DcAmAu; DcAmB S1; DcNAA; REn; REnAL; TwCA, SUP; TwCBDA; WebAB; WhAm 1; WhAmP; WhNAA*

Adler, Irving
[Robert Irving, pseud.]
American. Children's Author
b. 1913 in New York, New York
Source: *AmAu&B; Au&Wr 71; AuBYP; ConAu 5R, 2NR; PseudN; SmATA 1; ThrBJA*

Adler, Jacob Pavlovitch
"The Great Eagle"
American. Actor
b. 1855 in Russia
d. Apr 1, 1926 in New York, New York
Source: *PseudN; WhScrn 77; WhoHol B*

Adler, Julius Ochs
American. Publisher
b. Dec 3, 1892 in Chattanooga, Tennessee
d. Oct 3, 1955 in New York, New York
Source: *AmAu&B; CurBio 58, 55, 56; WhAm 3*

Adler, Kurt Herbert
Austrian. Conductor, Opera Impresario
b. Apr 2, 1905 in Vienna, Austria
Source: *CurBio 79; ConAu 3NR; IntWW 74; WhoAm 74; WhoWest 74; WhoWor 74; WhoWorJ 72*

Adler, Larry (Lawrence Cecil)
American. Musician, Actor, Composer
Has appeared in night clubs, concerts as soloist on harmonica.
b. Feb 10, 1914 in Baltimore, Maryland
Source: *BiE&WWA; FilmgC; NotNAT; Who 74; WhoHol A; WhoMus 72*

Adler, Lou
American. Record Producer
b. 1935
Source: *BioIn 9, 11; IlEncRk*

Adler, Luther (Lutha)
American. Actor, Director
b. May 4, 1903 in New York, New York
Source: *BiE&WWA; FilmgC; IntMPA 77, 78, 79, 80, 81, 82; MovMk; NotNAT; PseudN; Vers B; WhoAm 74; WhoThe 77; WhoWor 74*

Adler, Mortimer Jerome
American. Author, Philosopher
b. Dec 28, 1902 in New York, New York
Source: *ConAu 65; CurBio 40, 52; DrAS 74P; OxAmL; REnAL; TwCA SUP; WebAB; WhNAA; WhoAm 82; WhoWor 74*

Adler, Peter Herman
American. Conductor
b. Dec 2, 1899 in Jablonec, Czechoslovakia
Source: *WhoAm 74, 76, 78, 80, 82*

Adler, Polly
American. Madam, House of Prostitution
Wrote *A House is not a Home,* 1953.
b. 1900 in Poland
d. Jun 1962
Source: *AmAu&B; Au&Wr 71; BioIn 3, 6; InWom*

Adler, Richard
American. Composer, Author
Composed musical score for *Damn Yankees,* 1955.
b. Aug 3, 1921 in New York, New York
Source: *AmSCAP 66; BiE&WWA; EncMT; NotNAT; WhoAm 74, 76, 78, 80, 82; WhoGov 72; WhoThe 77; WhoWor 74*

Adler, Stella
American. Actress
b. 1902 in New York, New York
Source: *BiE&WWA; FilmgC; NotNAT; PlP&P; WhoHol A; WhoThe 77*

Adolfo
[Adolfo Sardina]
American. Fashion Designer
b. Feb 15, 1933 in Cardones, Cuba
Source: *CurBio 72; PseudN; WhoAm 82; WorFshn*

Adonis, Joe
[Joe Adone; Giuseppe Doto]
"Joey A"
Italian. Underworld Leader
b. Nov 22, 1902 in Montemarano, Italy
d. Nov 26, 1971 in Aucona, Italy
Source: *NewYTBE 71; PseudN*

Adoree, Renee
[Jeanne de la Fonte]
French. Actress, Circus Performer
b. Sep 30, 1898 in Lille, France
d. Oct 5, 1933 in Tujunga, California
Source: *BiDFilm; FilmgC; InWom; MovMk; PseudN; TwYS; WhScrn 74, 77; WhoHol B; WorEFlm*

Adrian
[Gilbert Adrain Greenburgh]
American. Fashion Designer
b. Mar 3, 1903 in Naugatauk, Connecticut
d. Sep 14, 1959 in Hollywood, California
Source: *DcFM; FilmgC; PseudN; WorFshn*

Aerosmith
[Tom Hamilton; Joey Kramer; Steve Tyler; Brad Whitford]
American. Rock Band
Source: *BkPepl; IlEncRk*

Aeschylus
"The Father of Greek Drama"; "The Father of Greek Tragedy"; "The Father of Tragedy"; "The Founder of the Greek Drama"
Greek. Poet
Wrote *Prometheus Bound*; died from impact of tortoise dropped on head by eagle.
b. 524?BC in Eleusis, Greece
d. 456?BC in Sicily, Italy
Source: *AtlBL; BbD; BiD&SB; CasWL; CnThe; CyWA; DcEnL; McGEWD; NewC; OxEng; Pen CL; PseudN; RComWL; REn; REnWD*

Aesop
Greek. Author
Semi-legendary figure; hundreds of fables attributed to him.
b. 620?BC
d. 560?BC
Source: *AnCL; AtlBL; BiD&SB; CarSB; CasWL; ChPo, S1, S2; CyWA; DcEnL; NewC; OxEng; Pen CL; RComWL; REn; WhoChL*

Aga Khan III
[Aga Sultan Sir Mahomed Shah]
Indian. Leader, Statesman
b. 1877 in Bombay, India
d. 1957
Source: *NewCol 75; PseudN*

Aga Khan IV
[Shah Karim]
Head of Ismaili Mohammedans
b. Dec 13, 1936 in Geneva, Switzerland
Source: *IntWW 74; WebBD 80; Who 74; WhoWor 74*

Aga Khan, Sadruddin, Prince
Pakistani. Diplomat
b. 1932
Source: *BioIn 10*

Agam, Yaacov
[Yaacov Gibstein]
Israeli. Artist
b. May 11, 1928 in Rishon Letzion, Palestine
Source: *BioIn 7, 8, 11; ConArt; CurBio 81; IntWW 75, 76, 77, 78; McGDA; MidE 78, 79; WhoWor 74*

Agar, Herbert Sebastian
American. Diplomat, Author, Economist
Founded Freedom House, 1941, to stimulate international cooperation.
b. Sep 29, 1897 in New Rochelle, New York
d. Nov 24, 1980 in Sussex, England
Source: *AmAu&B; Au&Wr 71; ConAu 65, 102; IntWW 74; OxAmL; REnAL; TwCA, SUP; Who 74; WhoWor 74*

Agar, John
American. Actor
b. Jan 31, 1921 in Chicago, Illinois
Source: *FilmgC; IntMPA 75, 76, 77, 78, 79, 80, 81, 82; MotPP; WhoHol A*

Agassiz, (Jean) Louis (Rodolphe)
American. Author, Naturalist, Educator
b. May 28, 1807 in Motier, Switzerland
d. Dec 12, 1873 in Cambridge, Massachusetts
Source: *Alli, SUP; AmAu; AmAu&B; AmBi; BbD; BiD&SB; DcAmAu; DcAmB; DcEnL; EncAB-H; OxAmL; OxCan; Pen AM; REn; REnAL; TwCBDA; WebAB; WhAm H*

Agate, James Evershed
English. Drama Critic, Author
b. Sep 9, 1877 in Manchester, England
d. Jun 6, 1947 in London, England
Source: *ChPo S1; DcLEL; EvLB; LongCTC; ModBrL; NewC; OxThe; Pen ENG; REn; TwCA, SUP; TwCW*

Agathocles
Greek. Tyrant of Syracuse
b. 361BC in Thermae, Sicily
d. 289BC in Syracuse, Sicily
Source: *REn*

Agca, Mehmet Ali
[Faruk Ozgun]
Turkish. Terrorist
Convicted of attempting to assassinate Pope John Paul II, May, 1981.
b. 1958 in Malatya Hekinhan, Turkey
Source: *NewYTBS 81; PseudN*

Agee, James Rufus
American. Author, Poet
Won Pulitzer Prize, 1958, for *A Death in the Family.*
b. Nov 27, 1909 in Knoxville, Tennessee
d. May 16, 1955 in New York, New York
Source: *AmAu&B; AmWr; AuNews 1; CasWL; EncWL; FilmgC; ModAL, SUP; OxAmL; OxFilm; Pen AM; RAdv 1; REn; REnAL; SixAP; TwCA SUP; TwCW; WebAB; WebE&AL; WhAm 4; WhoTwCL; WorEFlm*

Agee, Joel
American. Author, Editor
b. 1940
Source: *ConAu 105; NewYTBS 81*

Agee, Philip
American. Former CIA Agent, Author
Wrote CIA exposes: *Inside the Company: CIA Diary,* 1975.
b. Jul 19, 1935 in Tacoma Park, Florida
Source: *ConAu 104; NewYTBS 74*

Agee, William McReynolds
American. Corporation Executive
Chief executive, Bendix Corp. 1977-83; husband of Mary Cunningham.
b. Jan 5, 1938 in Boise, Idaho
Source: *AutoN 79; BioIn 11; Dun&B 79; NewYTBS 82; WhoAm 74, 76, 78, 80, 82; WhoF&I 74, 75, 77, 79; WhoWor 76, 78*

Ager, Milton
American. Composer
b. Oct 6, 1893 in Chicago, Illinois
d. May 6, 1979 in Los Angeles, California
Source: *AmPS; AmSCAP 66; Baker 78; BiDAmM; BioIn 4, 6; CmpEPM; NewYTBS 79*

Agha, Mehemed Fehmy
Russian. Art Director
b. Mar 11, 1896 in Nicolaieff, Russia
d. May 27, 1978
Source: *WhAm 7; WhoAm 74, 76, 78*

Agle, "Nan" (Anna Bradford Hayden)
American. Children's Author
b. Apr 13, 1905 in Baltimore, Maryland
Source: *AuBYP; ConAu 1R, 3NR; PseudN; SmATA 3; WrDr 76*

Agnelli, Giovanni
Italian. Automotive Industrialist
Chairman, FIAT, Italy's largest private business.
b. Mar 12, 1921 in Turin, Italy
Source: *CurBio 72; IntWW 74; Who 74; WhoF&I 74; WhoWor 74*

Agnew, Peter
see: Nazareth

Agnew, Spiro Theodore
American. Former Vice-President
Resigned Oct 10, 1973, pleading nolo contendere to income tax evasion charge.
b. Nov 9, 1918 in Baltimore, Maryland
Source: *BiDrAC; BiDrUSE; BioNews 74; CelR 73; CurBio 68; EncAB-H; IntWW 74; WebAB; WhAmP; Who 74; WhoAm 74, 76, 78, 80, 82; WhoAmP 73; WhoGov 72; WhoS&SW 73; WhoWor 74*

Agnon, S(hmuel) Y(osef)
[Shmuel Yosef Czaczkes]
Israeli. Author
b. 1888 in Buczacz, Galicia
d. Feb 17, 1970 in Rehovot, Israel
Source: *CasWL; ConAu 17R, 25R; ConAu P-2; ConLC 4, 8, 14; EncWL; Pen EUR; PseudN; RComWL; WhAm 5; WorAu*

Agostini, Peter
American. Sculptor
b. Feb 13, 1913 in New York, New York
Source: *BioIn 4, 6; BnEnAmA; DcAmArt; DcCAA 71, 77; WhoAm 74, 76; WhoAmA 73, 76, 78*

Agostino di Duccio
Italian. Sculptor
b. 1418 in Florence, Italy
d. 1481 in Florence, Italy
Source: *BioIn 1; NewCol 75*

Agpaoa, Antonio
Philippine. Healer, Psychic Surgeon
b. 1940?
Source: *BioIn 10*

Agricola, Georgius
[Georg Bauer]
German. Father of Mineralogy
b. Apr 20, 1494 in Eisleben, Germany
d. Sep 22, 1566 in Berlin, Germany
Source: *OxGer; Pen EUR; PseudN*

Agrippa (von Nettlesheim), Heinrich Cornelius
"The Omniscious Doctor"
German. Theologian, Occultist
b. Sep 14, 1486 in Cologne, Germany
d. Feb 18, 1535 in Grenoble, France
Source: *BiD&SB; DcEnL; EvEuW; OxEng; PseudN*

Agrippa, Marcus Vipsanius
Roman. Statesman, General
b. 63BC
d. 12BC
Source: *Pen CL*

Agrippina
Roman. Empress, Nero's Mother
b. 16
d. 59
Source: *REn*

Agronsky, Martin Zama
American. Radio, TV News Analyst
b. Jan 12, 1915 in Philadelphia, Pennsylvania
Source: *AuNews 2; WhoAm 74; WhoS&SW 73; WhoWor 74*

Agt, Andries A M van
Dutch. Politician
b. Feb 2, 1931
Source: *IntWW 74*

Aguilar, Grace
Spanish. Author
b. Jun 2, 1816 in London, England
d. Sep 16, 1847 in Frankfurt, Germany
Source: *Alli; BbD; BiD&SB; BrAu 19; Chambr 3; ChPo S2; DcBiA; DcEnL; DcEuL; DcLEL; EvLB; InWom; NewC*

Aguilar, Jeronimo de
Spanish. Conquistador
d. 1526
Source: *BioIn 9*

Aguinaldo, Emilio
Philippine. General
b. Mar 22, 1869 in Cavite, Philippines
d. Feb 6, 1964 in Manila, Philippines
Source: *WhAm HA, 4*

Aguirre, Mark
American. Basketball Player
b. Dec 10, 1959 in Chicago, Illinois
Source: *BioIn 11; OfNBA*

Agutter, Jenny
English. Actress
b. 1952
Source: *FilmgC*

Ahad
see: Achab

Ahaseurus
see: Xerxes I, King

Ahearn, Jacques Joseph d' Amboise
see: D'Amboise, Jacques

Ahern, Thomas Leo, Jr.
[The Hostages]
American. Former Hostage in Iran
b. 1932? in Falls Church, Virginia
Source: *BioIn 12; NewYTBS 81*

Aherne, Brian
English. Actor
b. May 2, 1902 in King's Norton, England
Source: *BiE&WWA; CurBio 60; FilmgC; IntMPA 75, 76, 77, 78, 79, 80, 81, 82; MotPP; MovMk; NotNAT; OxFilm; WhoHol A; WhoThe 77*

Ahidjo, Ahmadou
Cameroonian. President
b. Aug 1924 in Garoua, Cameroon
Source: *IntWW 74; WhoGov 72; WhoWor 74*

Ahmed, Fakhruddin Ali
Indian. President
b. May 13, 1905 in Delhi, India
d. Feb 11, 1977 in New Delhi, India
Source: *IntWW 74; WhoWor 74*

Aichinger, Helga
Austrian. Children's Author
b. Nov 27, 1937 in Linz, Austria
Source: *ConAu 25R; IlsBYP; SmATA 4*

Aiken, Conrad Potter
[Samuel Jeake, Jr., pseud.]
American. Poet, Critic
Won Pulitzer Prize, 1930, for *Selected Poems.*
b. Aug 5, 1889 in Savannah, Georgia
d. Aug 17, 1973 in Savannah, Georgia
Source: *AmAu&B; AmLY, X; AmWr; AnCL; AuBYP; CasWL; Chambr 3; ChPo, S1, S2; CnDAL; CnE&AP; CnMD; CnMWL; ConAmA; ConAmL; ConAu 5R, 45, 4NR; ConLC 1, 3, 5, 10; ConNov 72; ConP 70; CurBio 70, 73; DcLEL; EncWL; EvLB; LongCTC; ModAL, SUP; ModWD; OxAmL; OxEng; Pen AM; PseudN; RAdv 1; REn; REnAL; SixAP; SmATA 3; TwCA, SUP; TwCW; WebAB; WebE&AL; WhAm 6; WhNAA; WhoAm 74; WhoTwCL*

Aiken, George David
American. Agriculturist, Politician
Governor of VT, 1937-40; Senator, 1941-74.
b. Aug 20, 1892 in Dummerston, Vermont
Source: *AmAu&B; BiDrAC; BioNews 74; CelR 73; CngDr 74; CurBio 47; IntWW 74, 75; PolProf E; PolProf J; PolProf K; PolProf NF; PolProf T; WhE&EA; WhoAm 74, 76; WhoAmP 73, 75, 77; WhoE 74, 75; WhoGov 72, 75; WhoWor 74*

Aiken, Howard Hathaway
American. Professor, Mathematician
Invented world's largest digital calculator--Mark I computer, 1944.
b. Mar 8, 1900 in Hoboken, New Jersey
d. Mar 14, 1973
Source: *BioIn 1, 7, 9, 10; CurBio 47, 73; NewYTBE 73; WhAm 5*

Ailey, Alvin
American. Dancer, Choreographer
b. Jan 5, 1931 in Rogers, Texas
Source: *BiE&WWA; CelR 73; CurBio 68; NotNAT; WhoAm 74, 76, 78, 80, 82; WhoBlA 75; WhoE 74; WhoHol A*

Aiken, Joan Delano
[Nicholas Dee; Rosie Lee, pseuds.]
English. Author
b. Sep 4, 1924 in Rye, England
Source: *Au&Wr 71; AuBYP; ChlLR 1; ConAu 9R, 4NR; IntAu&W 76; PiP; PseudN; ScF&FL 1; SenS; SmATA 2; ThrBJA; TwCCW 78; WhoHrs 80; WrDr 76, 80*

Aimee, Anouk
[Francoise Sorya]
French. Actress
b. Apr 27, 1934 in Paris, France
Source: *BiDFilm; FilmgC; IntMPA 75, 76, 77, 78, 79, 80, 81, 82; MovMk; OxFilm; PseudN; WhoHol A; WorEFlm*

Ainge, Dan(iel Rae)
American. Baseball and Basketball Player
b. Mar 17, 1959 in Eugene, Oregon
Source: *BaseEn; NewYTBS 81*

Ainsworth, W(illiam) H(arrison)
[Cheviot Tichborne, pseud.]
English. Poet, Dramatist, Essayist
b. Feb 4, 1805 in Manchester, England
d. Jan 3, 1882 in Reigate, England
Source: *BbD; BiD&SB; BrAu 19; CasWL; Chambr 3; CyWA; DcBiA; DcEnA; DcEnL; Pen; PseudN; REn*

Air Supply
[Ralph Cooper; Frank Elser-Smith; Rex Goh; David Green; Russell Hitchcock; David Moyse; Graham Russell]
Australian. Rock Group
Hits include "Even the Nights are Better," 1982.
Source: *NF*

Aitken, Hugh
American. Composer
b. Sep 7, 1924 in New York, New York
Source: *AmSCAP 66*

Aitken, Robert
American. Sculptor
b. May 8, 1878 in San Francisco, California
d. Jan 3, 1949 in New York, New York
Source: *WhAm 2*

Aitken, William Maxwell
see: Beaverbrook, William Maxwell Aitken, Baron

Akbar
[Jalalud din Muhammad]
"The Great"
Arabian. Emperor of Hindustan
b. 1542 in Umarkot, Pakistan
d. 1605
Source: *NewC; PseudN*

Akeley, Carl Ethan
American. Naturalist, Curator
b. May 19, 1864 in Orleans County, New York
d. Nov 17, 1926 in Mount Mikeno, Africa
Source: *AmAu&B; AmBi; DcAmB; DcNAA; REnAL; WebAB; WhAm 1*

Akhenaton
see: Ikhnaton, Pharaoh

Akhmatova, Anna, pseud.
[Anna Andreyevna Gorenko]
Russian. Author, Poet
b. Jun 11, 1888 in Odessa, Russia
d. Mar 5, 1966 in Moscow, U.S.S.R.
Source: *AtlBL; CasWL; ClDMEL; ConAu 25R; ConAu P-1; ConLC 11; EncWL; InWom; LongCTC; ModSL 1; Pen EUR; REn; TwCW; WhoTwCL*

Akihito, (Togusama)
Japanese. Crown Prince
b. Dec 23, 1933
Source: *BioIn 1, 2, 3, 5; CurBio 59*

Akins, Claude
American. Actor
b. May 25, 1918 in Nelson, Georgia
Source: *FilmgC; IntMPA 77, 78, 79, 80, 81, 82; Vers A; WhoAm 82; WhoHol A*

Akins, Virgil
American. Boxer
b. Mar 10, 1928 in Saint Louis, Missouri
Source: *WhoBox 74*

Akins, Zoe
American. Poet, Dramatist
b. Oct 30, 1886 in Humansville, Missouri
d. Oct 29, 1958 in Los Angeles, California
Source: *AmAu&B; ChPo; CnDAL; CnMD; ConAmA; ConAmL; DcLEL; FilmgC; InWom; McGEWD; ModWD; OxAmL; OxThe; REn; REnAL; TwCA, SUP; WhAm 3*

Aksakov, Sergei Timofeyevich
Russian. Author
b. Sep 20, 1791 in Ufa, Russia
d. Apr 30, 1859 in Moscow, Russia
Source: *BbD; BiD&SB; CasWL; DcEuL; DcRusL; EuAu; EvEuW; OxEng; Pen EUR; REn*

Alain, pseud.
[Emil Auguste Chartier]
French. Essayist, Philosopher
b. 1868 in Montagne, France
d. 1951 in Le Vesinet, France
Source: *AmAu&B; CasWL; ClDMEL; EncWL; EuAu; EvEuW; IlsBYP; IlsCB 1957; OxFr; Pen EUR; PseudN; REn*

Alain-Fournier, pseud.
[Henri Alban Fournier]
French. Author
b. 1886
d. 1914
Source: *AtlBL; CasWL; ClDMEL; CnMWL; CyWA; EncWL; EvEuW; LongCTC; ModRL; Pen EUR; REn; TwCW; WhoTwCL*

Alabama
[Jeff Cook; Teddy Gentry; Mark Herndon; Randy Owen]
American. Country Music Group
Won 1982 Entertainer of the Year award from CMA; 1983 Grammy.
Source: *NF*

Alajalov, Constantin
American. Artist, Illustrator
b. Nov 18, 1900 in Rostov, Russia
Source: *CurBio 42; IlsBYP; IlsCB 1744, 1946; WhoAm 74, 76, 78, 80, 82; WhoAmA 73*

Alanbrooke, Alan Francis Brooke, 1st Viscount
Irish. General
Chief of imperial general staff for Winston Churchill, 1941-46.
b. Jul 23, 1883 in Fermanagh, Ireland
d. Jun 17, 1963 in Hampshire, England
Source: *CurBio 41, 63; NewCol 75*

Alarcon, Pedro Antonio de
Spanish. Author
b. Mar 10, 1833 in Guadix, Spain
d. Jul 20, 1891 in Madrid, Spain
Source: *BiD&SB; CasWL; ClDMEL; CyWA; EuAu; EvEuW; Pen EUR; REn*

Alarcon y Mendoza, Juan Ruiz de
Spanish. Dramatist
b. 1580 in Taxco, Mexico
d. Aug 4, 1639 in Madrid, Spain
Source: *ApCAB; BbD; BiD&SB; EvEuW; REn*

Alaric I
Visigothic Ruler
b. 370
d. 410
Source: *BioIn 4, 5, 9; NewCol 75; WebBD 80*

Alba, Duke of
see: Toledo, Fernando Alvarez de

Alba, Maria del Pilar
Spanish. Mistress of Goya
b. 1762
d. 1802
Source: *BioIn 4, 5, 9*

Albanese, Licia
Italian. Opera Singer
b. Jul 22, 1913 in Bari, Italy
Source: *CurBio 46; InWom; WhoAm 74, 76, 78, 80, 82; WhoMus 72; WhoWor 74*

Albee, Edward Franklin, III
American. Author, Dramatist
Won Pulitzer Prize, 1967, for *A Delicate Balance.*
b. Mar 12, 1928 in Washington, DC
Source: *AmAu&B; AmWr; AuNews 1; BiE&WWA; CasWL; CelR 73; CnMD; CnThe; ConAu 5R; ConLC 1, 2, 3, 5, 9, 11, 13; CroCD; EncAB-H; EncWL; FilmgC; IntWW 74; LongCTC; McGEWD; ModAL, SUP; ModWD; NatPD; NotNAT; OxAmL; OxThe; Pen AM; RComWL; REn; REnAL; REnWD; TwCW; WebAB; WebE&AL; Who 74; WhoAm 74, 76, 78, 80, 82; WhoThe 77; WhoTwCL; WhoWor 74; WorAu*

Albeniz, Isaac
Spanish. Pianist, Composer
b. May 29, 1860 in Comprodon, Spain
d. Jun 16, 1909 in Cambo, Spain
Source: *AtlBL*

Alberghetti, Anna Maria
American. Singer, Actress
As child, sang for GI's in Italy; debut at Carnegie Hall age 13.
b. May 15, 1936 in Pasaro, Italy
Source: *BiE&WWA; CurBio 55; FilmgC; InWom; IntMPA 75, 76, 77, 78, 79, 80, 81, 82; MotPP; MovMk; NotNAT; WhoAm 74; WhoHol A*

Albers, Josef
American. Artist, Teacher
Best known for series of paintings, "Homage to the Squares."
b. Mar 19, 1888 in Bottrop, Germany
d. Mar 25, 1976 in New Haven, Connecticut
Source: *AmAu&B; ConAu 1R, 65, 3NR; CurBio 62, 76; DcCAA 71; IntWW 74; NewYTBE 71; WebAB; WhoAm 74; WhoAmA 73; WhoE 74; WhoWor 74*

Albert I
[Albert Leopold]
Belgian. King
b. Apr 8, 1875
d. Feb 17, 1934
Source: *Alli; PoIre*

Albert Frederick Arthur George
see: George VI

Albert, Prince
[Albert Alexandre Louis Pierre Grimaldi]
Monacan. Heir to Throne
Son of Prince Rainier and Princess Grace.
b. Mar 14, 1958
Source: *BioIn 6, 12*

Albert, Prince Consort
German. Husband of Queen Victoria
b. Aug 26, 1819 in Rosenau, Germany
d. Dec 13, 1861
Source: *Alli SUP; ChPo S1; McGEWB; NewC; REn*

Albert, Carl Bert
American. Former Congressman
Majority Leader, 1962-71; Speaker of the House, 1971-76.
b. May 10, 1908 in McAlester, Oklahoma
Source: *BiDrAC; CelR 73; CngDr 74; CurBio 57; IntWW 74, 75, 76, 77, 78; NewYTBE 71, 73; PolProf E; PolProf J; PolProf K; PolProf NF; WebAB; Who 74; WhoAm 74, 76, 78; WhoAmP 73, 75, 77, 79; WhoGov 72, 75, 77; WhoS&SW 73, 75, 76; WhoWor 74*

Albert, Eddie
[Edward Albert Heimberger]
American. Actor
Starred in TV series "Green Acres," 1965-71.
b. Apr 22, 1908 in Rock Island, Illinois
Source: *BiE&WWA; BkPepl; CelR 73; CurBio 54; EncMT; FilmgC; HolP 30; IntMPA 75, 76, 77, 78, 79, 80, 81, 82; MotPP; MovMk; NotNAT; PlP&P; PseudN; WhoAm 74, 76, 78, 80, 82; WhoHol A; WhoThe 77*

Albert, Edward
American. Actor, Photographer
Son of Eddie Albert; starred in *Butterflies are Free* with Goldie Hawn.
b. Feb 20, 1951 in Los Angeles, California
Source: *BkPepl; CelR 73; IntMPA 75, 76, 77, 78, 79, 80, 81, 82; WhoAm 74, 76, 78, 80, 82*

Albert, Eugene d'
see: D'Albert, Eugene

Alberti, Leon Battista
Italian. Artist
b. Feb 14, 1404
d. Apr 25, 1472
Source: *AtlBL; BiD&SB; CasWL; DcEuL; EuAu; EvEuW; OxEng; Pen EUR; REn*

Albertson, Frank
American. Actor
b. Feb 2, 1909 in Fergus Falls, Minnesota
d. Feb 29, 1964 in Santa Monica, California
Source: *FilmgC; MovMk; Vers A; WhScrn 74, 77; WhoHol B*

Albertson, Jack
American. Actor
Won Oscar, 1968, for *The Subject was Roses;* Emmy, 1976, for "Chico and the Man."
b. Jun 16, 1910 in Malden, Massachusetts
d. Nov 25, 1981 in Hollywood, California
Source: *CurBio 76, 82; FilmgC; IntMPA 75, 76, 77, 78, 79, 80, 81; MovMk; NewYTBE 72, 73; NewYTBS 81; NotNAT; WhoAm 76, 78, 80, 82; WhoHol A; WhoThe 77*

"Albertus Magnus"
[Albert, Count of Bollstadt; Albrecht von Koln]
"Doctor Universalis"; "The Great"; "Le Petit Albert"
German. Philosopher
Paraphrased Aristotle's works; canonized, 1932.
b. 1193 in Lauingen, Germany
d. Nov 15, 1280 in Cologne, Germany
Source: *BbD; BiD&SB; CasWL; DcEnL; DcEuL; EuAu; EvEuW; NewC; OxEng; OxGer; Pen EUR; PseudN; REn*

Albinoni, Tommaso
Italian. Composer, Violinist
b. 1671 in Venice, Italy
d. 1750 in Venice, Italy
Source: *OxMus; WebBD 80*

Albrand, Martha pseud.
[Katrin Hollnd; Heidi Huberta, other pseuds.; Heidi Huberta Freybe, given name; Mrs. Sydney J Lamon]
American. Author
b. Sep 8, 1914 in Rostock, Germany
d. Jun 24, 1981 in New York, New York
Source: *AmAu&B; AmNov; AnObit 1981; Au&Wr 71; ConAu 13R; EncMys; InWom; IntAu&W 76; TwCA SUP; WhoAm 74, 76, 78, 80, 82; WhoAmW 58, 61, 64, 66, 68, 70, 72, 74; WhoE 74; WhoSpyF; WhoWor 78*

Albright, Lola
American. Actress
b. Jul 20, 1924 in Akron, Ohio
Source: *FilmgC; IntMPA 75, 76, 77, 78, 79, 80, 81, 82; MotPP; MovMk; WhoAm 82; WhoHol A*

Albright, Malvin Marr
[Zsissly]
American. Artist
b. Feb 20, 1897 in Chicago, Illinois
Source: *McGDA; WhoAm 74, 76, 78, 80, 82; WhoAmA 73, 76, 78; WhoWor 76, 78*

Albright, Tenley Emma
American. Figure Skater
Won gold medal, 1956 Olympics.
b. Jul 18, 1935 in Newton Centre, Massachusetts
Source: *CurBio 56; InWom; WhoAmW 77*

Albright, William Foxwell
American. Archaeologist
b. May 24, 1891 in Coquimbo, Chile
d. Sep 19, 1971 in Baltimore, Maryland
Source: *AmAu&B; ConAu 33R; CurBio 55; EncAB-H; NewYTBE 71; WebAB; WhAm 5*

Albuquerque, Affonso de
"The Great"; "The Mars of Portugal"; "The Portuguese Mars"
Portuguese. Governor of India
b. 1453
d. 1515
Source: *BioIn 9; PseudN*

Alcibiades
Greek. Athenian Statesman
b. 450?BC
d. 404?BC
Source: *DcEnL; REn*

Alcindor, Lew
see: Abdul-Jabbar, Kareem

Alcock, Sir John William
English. Aviator
b. 1892 in Manchester, England
d. Jun 14, 1919
Source: *WebBD 80*

Alcott, Amos Bronson
American. Transcendentalist, Educator
Friend of Emerson, Thoreau; founded Concord School of Philosophy, 1879.
b. Nov 29, 1799 in Wolcott, Connecticut
d. Mar 4, 1888 in Boston, Massachusetts
Source: *Alli, SUP; AmAu; AmAu&B; AmBi; ApCAB; BbD; BiD&SB; CasWL; Chambr 3; ChPo, S2; CnDAL; CyAl 2; DcAmAu; DcAmB; DcLEL; DcNAA; Drake; EvLB; OxAmL; Pen AM; REn; REnAL; TwCBDA; WebAB; WhAm H*

Alcott, Amy
American. Golfer
b. Feb 22, 1956 in Kansas City, Missouri
Source: *BioIn 10; WhoAm 82; WhoGolf*

Alcott, Louisa May
American. Author
Her early life in New England described in *Little Women,* 1869.
b. Nov 29, 1832 in Germantown, Pennsylvania
d. Mar 6, 1888 in Boston, Massachusetts
Source: *Alli SUP; AmAu; AmAu&B; AmBi; AmWom; ApCAB; AtlBL; AuBYP; BbD; BiD&SB; CarSB; CasWL; Chambr 3; ChlLR 1; ChPo; CnDAL; CrtT 3; CyAl 2; CyWA; DcAmAu; DcAmB; DcBiA; DcEnL; DcLEL; DcNAA; EncAB-H; EvLB; FamAYP; FilmgC; HerW; InWom; JBA 34; MouLC 4; NotAW; OxAmL; OxEng; Pen AM; REn; REnAL; Str&VC; TwCBDA; WebAB; WhAm H; WhoChL; YABC 1*

Alcuin
[Albinus]
"Ealhwine"; "Flaccus"
Anglo-Saxon. Theologian, Scholar
b. 735
d. 804
Source: *Alli; BbD; BiB S; BiD&SB; BrAu; CasWL; Chambr 1; DcEnL; EvLB; NewC; OxEng; OxFr; OxGer; Pen ENG, EUR; PseudN; REn*

Alda, Alan
[Alphonso d'Abruzzo]
American. Actor, Writer
Played Hawkeye on "MASH"; movie roles in *Paper Lion, Four Seasons.*
b. Jan 28, 1936 in New York, New York
Source: *BiE&WWA; BioNews 74; BkPepl; ConAu 103; IntMPA 75, 76, 77, 78, 79, 80, 81, 82; MotPP; MovMk; NewYTBS 74; NotNAT; PseudN; WhoAm 82; WhoHol A; WhoThe 77*

Alda, Frances
[Frances Davis]
New Zealander. Opera Singer
b. May 31, 1883 in Christchurch, New Zealand
d. Sep 18, 1952 in Venice, Italy
Source: *InWom; PseudN*

Alda, Robert
[Alphonso Giovanni Giusseppi Roberto d'Abruzzo]
American. Actor
Father of Alan Alda; won Tony Award, 1950, for *Guys and Dolls.*
b. Feb 26, 1914 in New York, New York
Source: *BiE&WWA; FilmgC; HolP 40; IntMPA 75, 76, 77, 78, 79, 80, 81, 82; MotPP; MovMk; NotNAT; PlP&P; PseudN; WhoHol A; WhoThe 77*

Alden, Henry M
American. Journalist
b. Nov 11, 1836 in Mount Tabor, Vermont
d. Oct 7, 1919
Source: *Alli SUP; AmAu; AmAu&B; AmBi; ApCAB; BbD; BiD&SB; CnDAL; DcAmAu; DcAmB; DcNAA; OxAmL; REnAL; TwCBDA; WhAm 1*

Alden, John
English. Pilgrim on Mayflower
Founder of Duxbury, MA; last surviving male member of Mayflower Company.
b. 1599 in England
d. Sep 12, 1687 in Duxbury, Massachusetts
Source: *AmBi; ApCAB; DcAmB; Drake; LinLib L, S; NatCAB 10; NewCol 75; OxAmL; REn; REnAL; TwCBDA; WebAB; WhAm H*

Alden, Priscilla Mullens
[Mrs. John Alden]
English. Pilgrim on Mayflower
Married Alden, 1623; romance subject of poem, "The Courtship of Miles Standish."
b. 1604 in Surrey, England
d. 1680 in Duxbury, Massachusetts
Source: *AmBi; InWom; LibW; NotAW*

Alder, Kurt
German. Chemist
b. Jul 10, 1902 in Germany
d. Jun 20, 1958
Source: *BioIn 2, 3, 4, 5, 6; WhAm 3*

Aldington, Richard
English. Author
One of leaders of Imagists poetry movement, 1910-18.
b. Jul 8, 1892 in Hampshire, England
d. Jul 27, 1962 in Sury-en-Vaux, France
Source: *CasWL; Chambr 3; ChPo, S1, S2, S3; ConAu 85; CyWA; DcLEL; EncWL; EvLB; LinLib L, S; LongCTC; ModBrL; NewC; NewCol 75; OxEng; Pen ENG; REn; TwCA, SUP; TwCW; WebE&AL; WhAm 4*

Aldiss, Brian Wilson
[Jael Cracken; Arch Mendicant; Peter Pica; John Runciman; C C Shackleton, pseuds.]
English. Author, Critic
b. Aug 18, 1925 in Dereham, England
Source: *Au&Wr 71; ConAu 5R, 5NR; ConLC 5, 14; ConNov 72, 76; IntWW 74; PseudN; SmATA 2; TwCW; Who 74; WhoWor 74; WrDr 76*

Aldrich, Bess Streeter
[Margaret Dean Stevens, pseud.]
American. Author
b. Feb 17, 1881 in Cedar Falls, Iowa
d. Aug 3, 1954 in Lincoln, Nebraska
Source: *AmAu&B; AmNov; InWom; OxAmL; PseudN; REn; REnAL; TwCA, SUP; WhAm 3; WhNAA*

Aldrich, Nelson Wilmarth
American. Statesman
Senator, 1881-1911; expert on tariff, currency legislation.
b. Nov 6, 1841 in Foster, Rhode Island
d. Apr 16, 1915 in New York, New York
Source: *AmBi; ApCAB; ApCAB X; BiDrAC; DcAmB; EncAAH; McGEWB; NatCAB 10, 25; NewCol 75; TwCBDA; WebAB; WhAm 1; WhAmP*

Aldrich, Robert
American. Motion Picture Director, Producer
Directed motion pictures *The Dirty Dozen, The Longest Yard.*
b. 1918 in Cranston, Rhode Island
Source: *BiDFilm; CmMov; DcFM; FilmgC; IntMPA 75, 76, 77, 78, 79, 80, 81, 82; IntWW 74, 75, 76, 77, 78; MovMk; OxFilm; WhoAm 74, 76, 78, 80, 82; WhoWest 78; WhoWor 78; WorEFlm*

Aldrich, Thomas Bailey
American. Author, Journalist
b. Nov 11, 1836 in Portsmouth, New Hampshire
d. Mar 19, 1907 in Boston, Massachusetts
Source: *Alli, SUP; AmAu; AmAu&B; AmBi; ApCAB; BbD; BiD&SB; CarSB; CasWL; Chambr 3; ChPo, S1, S2; CnDAL; CyAl 2; CyWA; DcAmAu; DcAmB; DcBiA; DcEnA AP; DcEnL; DcLEL; DcNAA; Drake; EncMys; EvLB; JBA 34; OxAmL; OxEng; Pen AM; REn; REnAL; TwCBDA; WebAB; WhAm 1*

Aldrich, Winthrop Williams
American. Banker
b. Nov 2, 1885 in Providence, Rhode Island
d. Feb 25, 1974 in New York, New York
Source: *CurBio 40, 53, 74; NewYTBS 74; WhAm 6; Who 74; WhoAm 74*

Aldridge, Ira Frederick
"The African Roscius"; "The African Tragedian"
American. Actor
b. 1805 in New York, New York
d. Aug 10, 1867 in Lodz, Poland
Source: *DcAmB; Drake; OxThe; PseudN; WebAB; WhAm H*

Aldridge, Tommy
see: Black Oak Arkansas

Aldrin, Edwin E(ugene), Jr.
"Buzz"
American. Businessman, Former Astronaut
Second man to walk on moon, Jul 20, 1969.
b. Jan 20, 1930 in Montclair, New Jersey
Source: *AmM&WS 73P; BioNews 74; CelR 73; IntWW 74; NewYTBE 71; PseudN; Who 74; WhoAm 74, 76, 78, 80, 82; WhoWor 74*

Aleichem, Shalom, pseud.
[Solomon J Rabinowitz]
Russian. Author, Humorist
b. Feb 18, 1859
d. May 13, 1916
Source: *AmAu&B; AtlBL; LongCTC; OxThe; PseudN; REn; REnAL; TwCA, SUP*

Aleixandre, Vicente
Spanish. Poet
Surrealist poet; won Nobel Prize, 1977.
b. Apr 26, 1898 in Seville, Spain
Source: *CasWL; ConAu 85; ConLC 9; CurBio 78; EncWL; IntAu&W 76, 77; IntWW 74, 75, 76, 77, 78; IntWWP 77; Pen EUR; REn; WhoWor 74, 78; WorAu*

Alekhine, Alexander
French. Chess Player
b. Nov 1, 1892 in Russia
d. Mar 24, 1946 in Lisbon, Portugal
Source: *CurBio 46*

Aleman, Miguel
Mexican. Former President
b. 1902 in Sayula, Mexico
Source: *CurBio 46; IntWW 74*

Alembert, Jean le Rond d'
"Anaxagoras"; Le Chancelier du Parnasse"; "The Father of FrenchPhilosophy"; "The Mazarin of Letters"
French. Mathematician, Philosopher
Co-editor *Encyclopedie;* principle of mechanics known as "D'Alembert's Principle."
b. Nov 16, 1717 in Paris, France
d. Oct 29, 1783 in Paris, France
Source: *Baker 78; BbD; BiD&SB; CasWL; DcScB; EuAu; EvEuW; LinLib L; McGEWB; NewCol 75; OxFr; OxMus; Pen EUR; REn*

Alessandro, Victor Nicholas
American. Conductor
b. Nov 27, 1915 in Waco, Texas
d. Nov 27, 1976 in San Antonio, Texas
Source: *Baker 78; BioIn 4, 8, 11; IntWW 74, 75, 76, 77; NewEOp 71; NewYTBS 76; WhAm 7; WhoAm 74, 76; WhoOp 76; WhoS&SW 73, 75, 76*

Alexander I
[Aleksandr Pavlovich]
"The Northern Telemaque"
Russian. Czar
b. 1777
d. 1825
Source: *BioIn 10; PseudN; WebBD 80*

Alexander II
Russian. Czar
b. 1818 in Moscow, Russia
d. Mar 13, 1881 in Saint Petersburg, Russia
Source: *BioIn 10; WebBD 80; WhoModH*

Alexander VI
[Rodrigo Lanzol y Borja]
"The Worst Pope"
Spanish. Pope
Pope, 1492-1503; father of Cesare and Lucrezia Borgia.
b. 1431 in Valencia, Spain
d. 1503
Source: *BioIn 10; McGEWB; NewCol 75; WebBD 80*

Alexander of Hales
"Doctor Doctorum"; Doctor Irrefragabilis"; "Fons Vitae"; The Fountain of Life"; "The Irrefragable Doctor"
English. Scholastic Philosopher
b. 1175
d. 1245
Source: *BiD&SB; DcEnL; NewC; OxEng; PseudN; REn*

Alexander of Tunis, Harold Rupert Leofric George Alexander, Earl
English. General
Commander in charge of British army evacuation from Dunkirk during WW II.
b. Dec 10, 1891 in Northern Ireland
d. Jun 16, 1969 in Slough, England
Source: *CurBio 42, 69; McGEWB; NewCol 75; WhoMilH 76*

Alexander the Great
[Alexander III]
"The Conqueror of the World"; "The Emathian Conqueror; "Macedonia's Madman"
Macedonian. King
Forged largest Western empire of ancient world from Greece to N India.
b. 356BC in Pella, Macedonia
d. Jun 13, 323BC in Babylon
Source: *DcEuL; FilmgC; LinLib L, S; LongCEL; McGEWB; NewC; NewCol 75; OxSpan; Pen CL; REn*

Alexander, Ben (Nicholas Benton)
American. Actor
b. May 26, 1911 in Garfield, Nevada
d. Jul 5, 1969 in Hollywood, California
Source: *Film 1; FilmgC; MovMk; PseudN; TwYS; WhScrn 74, 77*

Alexander, Clifford L, Jr.
American. Lawyer, Former Govt. Official
b. Sep 21, 1933 in New York, New York
Source: *BioNews 74; WhoAm 74, 76, 78, 80, 82; WhoAmP 73; WhoBlA 75*

Alexander, Cris
American. Actor, Photographer
b. Jan 14, 1920 in Tulsa, Oklahoma
Source: *BiE&WWA; NotNAT*

Alexander, Denise
American. Actress, Photographic Journalist
On TV soap opera "General Hospital."
b. Nov 11, 1945 in New York, New York
Source: *ConAu 45; WhoAm 78, 80, 82*

Alexander, Donald Crichton
American. Lawyer, Government Official
IRS commissioner, 1973-77.
b. May 22, 1921 in Pine Bluff, Arkansas
Source: *CurBio 74; IntWW 77, 78; WhoAm 74, 76, 78, 80, 82; WhoAmP 77, 79; WhoGov 75, 77*

Alexander, Frances Laura
American. Children's Author
b. Mar 12, 1888 in Blanco, Texas
Source: *AnCL; ConAu 25R; SmATA 4; TexWr; WrDr 76*

Alexander, Grover Cleveland
"Alex"; "Alex the Great"; "Buck"; "Dode"; "Old Pete"; "Pete"
American. Baseball Player
Won 373 games as pitcher; Hall of Fame, 1938.
b. Feb 26, 1887 in Saint Paul, Nebraska
d. Nov 4, 1950 in Saint Paul, Nebraska
Source: *BaseEn; DcAmB S4; NewCol 75; WhoProB 73*

Alexander, Jane
[Jane Quigley]
American. Actress
Won Tony for *Great White Hope;* played Eleanor Roosevelt on TV.
b. Oct 28, 1939 in Boston, Massachusetts
Source: *BkPepl; CurBio 77; IntMPA 82; NotNAT; PlP&P A; WhoAm 74, 76, 78, 80, 82; WhoAmW 72, 74, 77; WhoHol A; WhoThe 77, 81*

Alexander, Katherine
American. Actress
b. Sep 22, 1901 in Fort Smith, Arkansas
Source: *BiE&WWA; FilmgC; MovMk; NotNAT; PlP&P; ThFT*

Alexander, Lloyd Chudley
American. Children's Author
b. Jan 30, 1924 in Philadelphia, Pennsylvania
Source: *AnCL; Au&Wr 71; AuBYP; ChlLR 1; ConAu 1R, 1NR; PiP; SmATA 3; ThrBJA; WhoAm 74, 76, 78, 80, 82; WhoE 74*

Alexander, Ronald
American. Dramatist, Actor
b. Feb 16, 1917 in West New York, New Jersey
Source: *BiE&WWA; NotNAT*

Alexander, Shana
American. Author, Lecturer
Commentator, CBS "60 Minutes," 1975-79.
b. Oct 6, 1925 in New York, New York
Source: *ConAu 61; ForWC 70; St&PR 75; WhoAm 74, 76, 78, 80, 82; WhoAmW 72, 74, 77, 79; WhoF&I 74; WrDr 76, 80*

Alexander, Sue
American. Author
b. Aug 20, 1933 in Tucson, Arizona
Source: *ConAu 53, 4NR; SmATA 12*

Alexander, William
"Lord Stirling"
American. Army Officer
b. 1726 in New York, New York
d. Jan 15, 1783 in Albany, New York
Source: *AmBi; ApCAB; BioIn 8; DcAmB; Drake; NatCAB 1; NewCol 75; TwCBDA; WebAMB; WhAm H; WhAmP*

Alexanderson, Ernst Frederik Werner
American. Inventor, Engineer
Granted over 320 patents; invented color television receiver.
b. Jan 25, 1878 in Uppsala, Sweden
d. May 14, 1975 in Schenectady, New York
Source: *CurBio 55; WebAB; WhAm 6*

Alexandra Feodorovna
[Alix Victoria Helene Luise Beatrix]
Russian. Czarina
b. 1872
d. Jul 16, 1918 in Ekaterinburg, U.S.S.R.
Source: *InWom; PseudN*

Alexandre
[Louis Albert Alexandre Raimon]
French. Hairstylist
b. 1922
Source: *PseudN; WorFshn*

Alexandrov, Grigori
[Grigori Mormonenko]
Russian. Motion Picture Director
b. 1903
Source: *DcFM; FilmgC; OxFilm; WorEFlm*

Alexius Comnenus
[Alexius I]
Byzantine. Emperor
b. 1048
d. 1118
Source: *REn*

Alfieri, Vittorio
Italian. Artist, Dramatist
b. Jan 16, 1749 in Asti, Italy
d. Oct 8, 1803 in Florence, Italy
Source: *AtlBL; BbD; BiD&SB; CasWL; CnThe; DcEnL; DcEuL; EuAu; EvEuW; McGEWD; OxEng; OxThe; Pen EUR; RComWL; REn; REnWD*

Alfonso XIII
Spanish. King
b. 1886
d. Feb 28, 1941 in Rome, Italy
Source: *CurBio 41*

Alfred the Great
English. King
b. 849
d. 901
Source: *Alli; BbD; BiD&SB; CrtT 1; REn*

Alfred, William
American. Dramatist, Educator
b. Aug 16, 1922 in New York, New York
Source: *ConAu 13R; ConDr 73; CroCD; DrAS 74E; McGEWD; ModAL; NotNAT; WhoAm 74, 76, 78, 80, 82; WorAu; WrDr 76*

Algazel
see: Ghazzali, Abu-Hamid al

Alger, Horatio
American. Author, Clergyman
Wrote over 100 rags-to-riches stories for boys.
b. Jan 13, 1832 in Revere, Massachusetts
d. Jul 18, 1899 in Natick, Massachusetts
Source: *Alli SUP; AmAu; AmAu&B; AmBi; ApCAB; BbD; BiD&SB; CarSB; CasWL; ChPo, S1, S2; CnDAL; CyAl 2; DcAmAu; DcAmB; DcNAA; Drake; EncAB-H; EvLB; OxAmL; Pen AM; REn; REnAL; TwCBDA; WebAB; WebE&AL; WhAm 1; WhoChL*

Algren, Nelson
[Nelson Algren Abraham]
"Poet of the Chicago Slums"
American. Author
Realistic novels include *The Man with the Golden Arm,* 1949.
b. Mar 28, 1909 in Detroit, Michigan
d. May 9, 1981 in Sag Harbor, New York
Source: *AmAu&B; AmNov; BioIn 2, 4, 5, 7, 8, 10; CasWL; CnDAL; CnMWL; ConAu 13R, 103; ConLC 4, 10; ConNov 72, 76; DcLEL; DrAF 76; EncWL; FilmgC; IntAu&W 76, 77; LinLib L; ModAL, SUP; OxAmL; Pen AM; PseudN; RAdv 1; REn; REnAL; TwCA SUP; TwCW; WebE&AL; WhoAm 74, 76; WhoTwCL; WhoWor 74; WrDr 76, 80*

Ali
"The Lion of God"; "The Rugged Lion"
Arabian. Caliph, Islam Convert
b. 600?
d. 661 in Al Kufa, Iraq
Source: *NewCol 75; PseudN; WebBD 80*

Ali, Ahmed
Indian. Author
b. Jul 1, 1908 in Delhi, India
Source: *Au&Wr 71; CasWL; ConAu 25R; ConNov 72, 76; WrDr 76*

Ali, Muhammad
[Cassius (Marcellus, Jr.) Clay]
American. Boxer
First heavyweight boxer ever to hold title three times.
b. Jan 17, 1942 in Louisville, Kentucky
Source: *BioNews 74; BkPepl; CurBio 63; EncAB-H; NewYTBE 71, 72, 73; NewYTBS 74; PseudN; WebAB; WhoAm 74, 76, 78, 80, 82; WhoBlA 75; WhoBox 74*

Ali Pasha
"The Lion of Janina"
Turkish. Governor of Albania
b. 1741 in Tepeleni, Albania
d. 1822
Source: *BioIn 8; PseudN; WebBD 80*

Alice (Mary Victoria Augusta Pauline), Princess
[Countess of Athlone]
English. Member of Royal Family, Author
b. Feb 25, 1883 in Windsor, England
d. Jan 3, 1981 in London, England
Source: *AnObit 1981; BioIn 7, 11; ConAu 103; NewYTBS 81; Who 74*

Alinsky, Saul David
American. Radical Activist
b. Jan 30, 1909 in Chicago, Illinois
d. Jun 12, 1972 in Carmel, California
Source: *AmAu&B; ConAu 37R; CurBio 68, 72; NewYTBE 72; WebAB; WhAm 5*

Alioto, Joseph Lawrence
American. Lawyer, Politician
Mayor of San Francisco, 1968-76.
b. Feb 12, 1916 in San Francisco, California
Source: *CurBio 69; IntWW 74; WhoAm 74, 76, 78, 80; WhoGov 72; WhoWest 74*

Alison, Archibald
Scottish. Episcopal Minister, Author
b. 1757
d. May 17, 1839 in Edinburgh, Scotland
Source: *Alli; BiD&SB; BiDLA, SUP; Chambr 2; DcEnL; EvLB*

Allan, Elizabeth
English. Actress
b. Apr 9, 1908 in Skegness, England
Source: *FilmEn; FilmgC; ThFT; WhoHol A; WhoThe 77*

Allard, Sydney
English. Industrialist
b. 1910
d. 1966
Source: *BioIn 7*

Allbritton, Louise
American. Actress
b. 1920 in Oklahoma City, Oklahoma
Source: *FilmgC; HolP 40; MotPP; WhoHol A*

Allegret, Yves
[Yves Champlain, pseud.]
French. Motion Picture Director
Success directing films starring wife, Simone Signoret, 1940's.
b. Oct 13, 1907 in Paris, France
Source: *BiDFilm; DcFM; FilmEn; MovMk; OxFilm; WorEFlm*

Allegri, Gregorio
Italian. Composer
b. 1582
d. 1652
Source: *WebBD 80*

Allen, Arthur Augustus
American. Ornithologist
b. Dec 28, 1885 in Buffalo, New York
d. Jan 17, 1964
Source: *AmAu&B; ConAu 1R; CurBio 61, 64; WhAm 4*

Allen, Arthur Bruce
English. Educator
b. Feb 12, 1903 in Westgate, England
Source: *Au&Wr 71; ConAu 25R*

Allen, Byron
American. Comedian
Stars in TV series "Real People."
b. 1961?
Source: *BioIn 12*

Allen, Dennis R
Media Personality
Source: *NewYTBE 71*

Allen, Duane
see: Oak Ridge Boys, The

Allen, Elizabeth
[Elizabeth Ellen Gillease]
American. Actress, Singer
Nominated for Tony, 1962, for *The Gay Life.*
b. Jan 25, 1934 in Jersey City, New Jersey
Source: *BiE&WWA; FilmgC; NotNAT; PseudN; WhoAm 74; WhoThe 77*

Allen, Ethan
American. Revolutionary Commander
Leader of Green Mountain Boys, 1770.
b. Jan 21, 1738 in Litchfield, Connecticut
d. Feb 11, 1789 in Burlington, Vermont
Source: *Alli; AmAu&B; AmBi; ApCAB; BbD; BbtC; BiD&SB; CyAL 1; DcAmAu; DcAmB; DcNAA; Drake; OxAmL; REn; REnAL; TwCBDA; WebAB; WhAm H; WhAmP*

Allen, Florence Ellinwood
American. Judge
b. Mar 23, 1884 in Salt Lake City, Utah
d. Sep 12, 1966 in Waite Hill, Ohio
Source: *CurBio 41, 63, 66; InWom; OhA&B; WhAm 4*

Allen, Forest Clare
"Phog"
American. Basketball Coach
b. Nov 18, 1885 in Jamesport, Missouri
d. Sep 16, 1974 in Lawrence, Kansas
Source: *BioIn 4, 9, 10; NewYTBS 74; WhoBbl 73*

Allen, Fred
American. Radio Comedian
b. May 31, 1894 in Cambridge, Massachusetts
d. Mar 17, 1956 in New York, New York
Source: *ChPo; CurBio 41, 56; EncMT; FilmgC; OxFilm; REnAL; WebAB; WhAm 3; WhScrn 74, 77; WhoHol B*

Allen, Mrs. Fred
see: Hoffa, Portland

Allen, Frederick Lewis
American. Journalist, Historian
b. Jul 5, 1890 in Boston, Massachusetts
d. Feb 13, 1954 in New York, New York
Source: *AmAu&B; CnDAL; DcAmB S5; OxAmL; REn; REnAL; TwCA, SUP; WebAB; WhAm 3*

Allen, George
"Ice Cream"
American. Football Coach, Broadcaster
b. Apr 29, 1922 in Detroit, Michigan
Source: *CelR 73; PseudN; WhoAm 74, 76, 78, 80, 82; WhoS&SW 73*

Allen, Gracie Ethel Cecil Rosaline
[Mrs. George Burns; Burns and Allen]
American. Comedienne
With husband, starred in "Burns and Allen Show," 1922-58.
b. Jul 26, 1906 in San Francisco, California
d. Aug 27, 1964 in Hollywood, California
Source: *CurBio 40, 51, 64; FilmgC; InWom; MotPP; MovMk; ThFT; WhAm 4; WhScrn 74, 77; WhoHol B*

Allen, Henry Tureman
American. General, Explorer
b. Apr 13, 1859 in Sharpsburg, Kentucky
d. Aug 30, 1930 in Buena Vista Spring, Pennsylvania
Source: *AmBi; DcAmB S1; DcNAA; WhAm 1; WhNAA*

Allen, Hervey (William Hervey)
American. Author, Poet
Wrote *Israfel,* biography of Edgar Allan Poe, 1926.
b. Dec 8, 1889 in Pittsburgh, Pennsylvania
d. Dec 28, 1949 in Miami, Florida
Source: *AmAu&B; AmNov; AnMV 1926; Chambr 3; ChPo, S1, S2; CnDAL; ConAmA; ConAmL; CyWA; DcAmB S4; DcLEL; DcNAA; EncWL; LongCTC; OxAmL; Pen AM; REn; REnAL; TwCA, SUP; TwCW; WhAm 2; WhNAA*

Allen, Irwin
American. Director, Producer, Writer
Won Oscar, 1952, for *The Sea Around Us,* based on Rachel Carson's book.
b. Jun 12, 1916 in New York, New York
Source: *CmMov; FilmgC; IntMPA 75, 76, 77, 78, 79, 80, 81, 82; NewYTBS 74; NewYTET; WhoAm 74, 78, 80, 82*

Allen, Ivan, Jr.
American. Mayor, Business Executive
b. Mar 15, 1911 in Atlanta, Georgia
Source: *CelR 73; St&PR 75; WhoAm 74, 76, 78, 80, 82; WhoS&SW 73; WhoWor 74*

Allen, Jack
American. Author, Educator
b. Jun 18, 1914 in Prestonsburg, Kentucky
Source: *ConAu 9R, 4NR; DrAS 74H; LEduc 74; WhoAm 74, 76, 78, 80, 82*

Allen, James Lane
American. Author
b. Dec 21, 1849 in Lexington, Kentucky
d. Feb 18, 1925
Source: *AmAu; AmAu&B; AmBi; AmLY; BbD; BiD&SB; BiDSA; CarSB; CasWL; ChPo S1, S2; CnDAL; ConAmL; DcAmAu; DcAmB; DcBiA; DcLEL; DcNAA; LongCTC; OxAmL; REn; REnAL; TwCBDA; WhAm 1*

Allen, Jay Presson
American. Screenwriter, Author
b. Mar 3, 1922 in San Angelo, Texas
Source: *ConAu 73; McGEWD; NotNAT; WhoAm 82; WomWMM A*

Allen, John
American. Dentist, Inventor
Patented false teeth made of porcelain with platium base, 1851.
b. Nov 4, 1810 in Broome County, New York
d. Mar 8, 1892 in Plainfield, New Jersey
Source: *DcAmB; WebAB; WhAm H*

Allen, Karen
American. Actress
Appeared in movies *Animal House, Raiders of the Lost Ark.*
b. 1952 in Carrollton, Illinois
Source: *IntMPA 82*

Allen, Larry
American. Journalist
b. Oct 19, 1908 in Mount Savag, Maryland
Source: *AmEA 74; CurBio 42*

Allen, Leslie
American. Tennis Player
Ranked 26th by Women's Tennis Assn., 1981, highest for black female.
b. Mar 12, 1957
Source: *NewYTBS 81*

Allen, Lisa Marie
American. Figure Skater
b. 1960?
Source: *BioIn 12*

Allen, Lucius
American. Basketball Player
b. Sep 26, 1947 in Kansas City, Kansas
Source: *WhoAm 74; WhoBbl 73*

Allen, Macon B
American. Lawyer, Judge
b. 1816
d. 1894
Source: *BioIn 10*

Allen, Marcus
American. Football Player
Won Heisman Trophy, 1981; rushed for 2,342 yds. as senior at USC.
b. Mar 26, 1960 in San Diego, California
Source: *BioIn 12*

Allen, Maria
American. Revolutionary Patriot
Source: *InWom*

Allen, Mel
[Melvin Allen Israel]
American. Sportscaster
National Sportswriters and Broadcasters Hall of Fame, 1972.
b. Feb 14, 1913 in Birmingham, Alabama
Source: *AuBYP; CurBio 50; IntMPA 75, 76, 77, 78, 79, 80, 81, 82; WhoAm 74, 76, 78; WhoWorJ 72*

Allen, Nancy
[Mrs. Brian DePalma]
American. Actress
Appeared in movies *Blowout, Dressed to Kill.*
b. Jun 24, 1950 in New York, New York
Source: *IntMPA 82*

Allen, "Red" (Henry James, Jr.)
American. Jazz Musician
b. Jan 7, 1908 in New Orleans, Louisiana
d. Apr 17, 1967 in New York, New York
Source: *PseudN; WhoJazz 72*

Allen, Rex E, Sr.
"Arizona Cowboy"
American. Actor, Singer
b. Dec 31, 1924 in Wilcox, Arizona
Source: *BiDAmM; BioIn 8, 11; CmpEPM; EncFCWM 69; FilmgC; IntMPA 75, 76, 77, 78, 79, 80, 81; RkOn; WhoAm 82; WhoHol A; WhoRock 81*

Allen, Richard
American. Religious Leader, Bishop
b. Feb 14, 1760 in Philadelphia, Pennsylvania
d. Mar 26, 1831 in Philadelphia, Pennsylvania
Source: *AmBi; ApCAB; BlkAW; DcAmB; EncAB-H; WebAB; WhAm H*

Allen, Richard Vincent
American. Former National Security Advisor
b. Jan 1, 1936 in Collingswood, New Jersey
Source: *ConAu 21R; WhoAm 82; WhoAmP 73, 75, 77, 79*

Allen, Richie (Richard Anthony)
American. Baseball Player
Rookie of the Year, 1964; MVP, AL, 1972.
b. Mar 8, 1942 in Wampum, Pennsylvania
Source: *BaseEn; WhoAm 74; WhoBlA 75; WhoMW 74; WhoProB 73*

Allen, Rick
see: Box Tops, The

Allen, Rick
see: Def Leppard

Allen, Robert Sharon
American. Author, Journalist
b. Jul 14, 1900 in Latonia, Kentucky
d. Feb 23, 1981 in Washington, DC
Source: *AmAu&B; BioIn 1; ConAu 57, 103; CurBio 41, 81; LinLib L; NewYTBS 81; REnAL; WhoAm 74, 76, 78, 80; WhoWor 74*

Allen, Ross
American. Herpetologist
b. 1908?
d. May 17, 1981 in Gainesville, Florida
Source: *BioIn 2; NewYTBS 81*

Allen, Steve (Stephen Valentine)
[William Christopher Stevens, pseud.]
American. Entertainer, Composer, Author
Has written over 2,000 songs including, "This Could Be the Start of Something Big."
b. Dec 26, 1921 in New York, New York
Source: *AmAu&B; AmSCAP 66; BiE&WWA; BioNews 75; CelR 73; ConAu 25R; CurBio 51; FilmgC; IntMPA 75, 76, 77, 78, 79, 80, 81, 82; PseudN; REnAL; WebAB; WhoHol A; WrDr 76*

Allen, Verden
see: Mott (the Hoople)

Allen, Vivian Beaumont
American. Philanthropist
d. Oct 10, 1962 in New York, New York
Source: *InWom; PlP&P*

Allen, Walter
English. Author
b. Feb 23, 1911 in Birmingham, England
Source: *Au&Wr 71; ConAu 61; ConNov 72, 76; DcLEL; LongCTC; ModBrL; NewC; Pen ENG; TwCW; WhoTwCL; WorAu; WrDr 76*

Allen, William McPherson
American. Aircraft Manufacturer
President, chairman, Boeing Co., 1945-72.
b. Sep 1, 1900 in Lolo, Montana
Source: *CurBio 53; IntWW 74; St&PR 75; WhoAm 82; WhoF&I 74; WhoWest 74; WhoWor 74*

Allen, Woody
[Allen Stewart Konigsburg]
American. Actor, Writer, Producer
Won four Oscars, including best picture, director, for *Annie Hall,* 1978.
b. Dec 1, 1935 in Brooklyn, New York
Source: *AmAu&B; BkPepl; CelR 73; ConAu 33R; CurBio 66; FilmgC; IntMPA 75, 76, 77, 78, 79, 80, 81, 82; MovMk; NewYTBE 73; NotNAT; PseudN; WhoAm 74, 76, 78, 80, 82; WhoHol A; WhoThe 77; WrDr 76*

Allen of Hurtwood, Lady
[Marjory Gill Allen]
English. Author, Landscape Architect
b. May 10, 1897 in London, England
Source: *ConAu P-1; PseudN; Who 74*

Allenby, Edmund Hynman Allenby, Viscount
English. World War I Field Marshal
b. Apr 23, 1861 in Nottinghamshire, England
d. May 14, 1936
Source: *BioIn 1, 2, 6, 7, 10, 11; McGEWB; WhoMilH 76*

Allende, Salvador
Chilean. President
Led first govt. in power through free elections, 1970; violently overthrown, 1973.
b. Jul 26, 1908 in Valparaiso, Chile
d. Sep 11, 1973 in Santiago, Chile
Source: *CurBio 71, 73; NewYTBE 70; WhoGov 72; WhoWor 74*

Allers, Franz
Czech. Conductor
b. Aug 6, 1905 in Karlsbad, Czechoslovakia
Source: *BiE&WWA; CelR 73; NotNAT; WhoAm 74, 76, 78, 80, 82; WhoMus 72; WhoWor 74*

Allgood, Sara
Irish. Actress
b. Oct 31, 1883 in Dublin, Ireland
d. Sep 13, 1950 in Woodland Hills, California
Source: *FilmgC; InWom; MotPP; MovMk; OxThe; PlP&P; Vers A; WhScrn 74, 77; WhoHol B*

Allingham, Margery
[Margery Louise Allingham Carter]
English. Author
b. May 20, 1904 in London, England
d. Jun 30, 1966 in Essex, England
Source: *ConAu 5R, 25R, 4NR; DcLEL; EncMys; EvLB; LongCTC; MnBBF; NewC; PseudN; TwCA, SUP; TwCW*

Allingham, William
Irish. Poet
"Poet of little things and little moments."--William Butler Yeats.
b. Mar 19, 1824 in Ballyshannon, Ireland
d. Nov 18, 1889 in Hampstead, England
Source: *Alli SUP; AnCL; BbD; BiD&SB; BrAu 19; CasWL; Chambr 3; ChPo, S1, S2; DcEnL; DcLEL; EvLB; NewC; Pen ENG; Polre; REn; Str&VC; WebE&AL*

Allison, Bob (William Robert)
American. Baseball Player
b. Jul 11, 1934 in Raytown, Missouri
Source: *BaseEn; BioIn 9, 11*

Allison, Bobby (Robert Arthur)
American. Auto Racer
b. Dec 3, 1937 in Hueytown, Alabama
Source: *BioIn 10, 11*

Allison, Clay
American. Outlaw
"Fast gun," who killed at least 15 other gunmen in NM area, 1870's.
b. 1840 in Tennessee
d. 1877
Source: *BioIn 8, 9, 11; Blood*

Allison, Fran(ces)
American. Actress
Part of "Kukla, Fran, and Ollie," TV show, 1947-57.
b. 1924 in LaPorrete City, Iowa
Source: *InWom; IntMPA 75, 76, 77, 78, 79, 80, 81, 82; WhoAm 74*

Allison, Samuel King
American. Nuclear Physicist
b. Nov 13, 1900 in Chicago, Illinois
d. Sep 15, 1965
Source: *BioIn 7; WhAm 4*

Allman, Duane (Howard Duane)
[Allman Brothers Band]
"Skydog"
American. Singer
b. Nov 20, 1946 in Nashville, Tennessee
d. Oct 29, 1971 in Macon, Georgia
Source: *BioIn 11; IlEncRk; PseudN*

Allman, Gregg (Gregory Lenoir)
[Allman Brothers Band]
American. Singer, Musician
b. Dec 7, 1947 in Nashville, Tennessee
Source: *BioIn 10, 11; BkPepl; IlEncRk; WhoAm 82*

Allman Brothers Band
[Duane Allman; Gregg Allman; Dicky Betts; "Jaimoe" (Jai Johnny) Johanson; Chuck Leavell; (Raymond) Berry Oakley; "Butch" (Claude Hudson) Trucks;Lamar Williams]
American. Rock Group
Source: *IlEncRk; RkOn*

Allon, Yigal
[Yigal Paicovich]
Israeli. General, Statesman
b. Oct 10, 1918 in Kfar Tabor, Palestine
d. Feb 2, 1980 in Asulla, Israel
Source: *ConAu 73, 97; IntWW 74; NewYTBE 71; PseudN; WhoWor 74; WhoWorJ 72*

Allport, Gordon
American. Analyst
b. Nov 11, 1897 in Montezuma, Indiana
d. Oct 9, 1967 in Cambridge, Massachusetts
Source: *AmAu&B; ConAu 1R, 25R; CurBio 60, 67; IndAu 1917; REnAL; WebAB; WhAm 4, 5; WhoE 74*

Allsop, Kenneth
English. Author, Journalist
b. Jan 29, 1920 in Yorkshire, England
d. May 23, 1973 in West Milton, England
Source: *Au&Wr 71; ConAu 1R, 6NR; SmATA 17; WhoWor 74; WorAu*

Allston, Washington
American. Artist, Poet
Part of Romantic school with Coleridge, Wordsworth.
b. Nov 5, 1779 in Georgetown County, South Carolina
d. Jul 9, 1843 in Cambridgeport, Massachusetts
Source: *AmAu; AmAu&B; AmBi; ApCAB; BbD; BiD&SB; BiDLA; BiDSA; BnEnAmA; CasWL; Chambr 3; ChPo, S1; CnDAL; CyAl 2; DcAmArt; DcAmAu; DcAmB; DcEnL; DcLB 1; DcNAA; Drake; EvLB; McGDA; McGEWB; NatCAB 5; NewYHSD; OxAmL; Pen AM; EncMT; TwCBDA; WebAB; WhAm H*

Ally, Carl Joseph
American. Advertising Executive
b. Mar 31, 1924 in Detroit, Michigan
Source: *WhoAdv 72; WhoAm 74, 76, 78, 80, 82*

Allyn, Stanley Charles
American. Manufacturer
b. Jul 20, 1891 in Madison, Wisconsin
d. Oct 31, 1970 in Greenwich, Connecticut
Source: *CurBio 56, 70; NewYTBE 70; WhAm 5*

Allyson, June
[Ella Geisman]
American. Actress
Movie roles projected image of cheerful wholesomeness.
b. Oct 7, 1917 in Lucerne, New York
Source: *BiDFilm; CmpEPM; CurBio 52; FilmgC; IntMPA 76, 77, 78, 79, 80, 81, 82; MGM; MotPP; MovMk; WhoAm 74, 76, 78, 80, 82; WhoAmW 58, 61, 64, 66, 68, 70, 72, 74; WhoHol A; WorEFlm*

Alma-Tadema, Sir Lawrence
English. Artist
b. Jan 8, 1836 in Dronrijp, Netherlands
d. Jun 25, 1912
Source: *BioIn 10; WebBD 80*

Almeida, Antonio Alves de
French. Conductor
b. Jan 20, 1928 in Neuilly, France
Source: *WhoWor 74*

Almeida, Laurindo
Spanish. Musician, Composer
b. Sep 2, 1917 in Sao Paulo, Brazil
Source: *AmSCAP 66; WhoAm 74, 76, 78, 80, 82; WhoWor 74*

Almond, Gabriel Abraham
American. Author, Educator
b. Jan 12, 1911 in Rock Island, Illinois
Source: *AmM&WS 73S; ConAu 101; IntWW 74; WhoAm 74, 76, 78, 80, 82*

Almond, Paul
Canadian. Motion Picture Producer, Director
b. Apr 26, 1931 in Montreal, PQ
Source: *BioIn 10; CanWW 70, 79; ConAu 73; CreCan 2; FilmgC; IntMPA 75, 76, 77, 78, 79, 80, 81; WhoAm 82; WhoAmA 76, 78; WhoE 79*

Alonso, Alicia
Cuban. Ballerina
b. 1921 in Havana, Cuba
Source: *CurBio 55; InWom; WhoWor 74*

Alou, Felipe Rojas
"Panque"
Dominican. Baseball Player
One of three brothers who all played in Giants outfield at same time, 1963.
b. May 12, 1935 in Haina, Dominican Republic
Source: *BaseEn; PseudN; WhoAm 74; WhoProB 73*

Alou, Jesus Maria Rojas
"Jay"
Dominican. Baseball Player
Collected six hits in one game, Jul 10, 1964.
b. Mar 24, 1943 in Haina, Dominican Republic
Source: *BaseEn; PseudN; WhoAm 74; WhoProB 73*

Alou, Matty (Mateo Rojas)
Dominican. Baseball Player
Won NL batting title, 1966, with brother Felipe second.
b. Dec 22, 1938 in Haina, Dominican Republic
Source: *BaseEn; PseudN; WhoProB 73*

Alpert, Herb
[Tiajuana Brass]
American. Musician, Band Leader
Co-founder, president, A & M Records.
b. Mar 31, 1935 in Los Angeles, California
Source: *BiDAmM; BioNews 74; CelR 73; CurBio 67; NewYTBS 74; RkOn, 2; WhoAm 74, 76, 78, 80, 82; WhoHol A*

Alpert, Hollis
American. Movie Critic
b. Sep 24, 1916 in Herkimer, New York
Source: *AmAu&B; ConAu 1R; WhoAm 74, 76, 78, 80, 82*

Alphand, Herve
French. Economist, Diplomat
b. May 31, 1907
Source: *CurBio 51; IntWW 74; Who 74*

Alsop, Joseph Wright, Jr.
American. Journalist, Author
b. Oct 11, 1910 in Avon, Connecticut
Source: *AmAu&B; CelR 73; CurBio 52; IntWW 74; NewYTBE 71; NewYTBS 74; REn; REnAL; WhoAm 74, 76, 78, 80, 82; WhoS&SW 73; WhoWor 74; WorAu*

Alsop, Stewart Johonnot Oliver
American. Journalist
b. May 17, 1914 in Avon, Connecticut
d. May 26, 1974 in Washington, DC
Source: *CelR 73; ConAu 49, 89; CurBio 52, 74; IntWW 74; NewYTBS 74; REn; WhAm 6; WhoAm 74; WhoS&SW 73; WorAu*

Alston, Theodosia Burr
American. Daughter of Aaron Burr
Sailing to NY to join father when ship *Patriot* was lost in Atlantic.
b. 1783 in Albany, New York
d. 1813
Source: *AmBi; DcAmB; InWom; NotAW*

Alston, Walter Emmons
"Smokey"
American. Former Baseball Manager
Manager, Brooklyn Dodgers, LA Dodgers, 1954-76.
b. Dec 1, 1911 in Venice, Ohio
Source: *CelR 73; CurBio 54; NewYTBS 74; PseudN; WhoAm 74, 76, 78, 80, 82; WhoProB 73*

Altdorfer, Albrecht
German. Artist, Architect
b. 1480
d. Feb 12, 1538
Source: *AtlBL; OxGer*

Alter, Hobie (Hobart, Jr.)
American. Nautical Designer
Designed "Hobie Cat" sailboat.
b. 1934? in Capistrano Beach, California
Source: *BioIn 10*

Altgeld, John Peter
American. Governor of Illinois
b. Dec 30, 1847 in Nassau, Germany
d. Mar 12, 1902 in Joliet, Illinois
Source: *Alli SUP; AmAu&B; AmBi; DcAmAu; DcAmB; EncAB-H; OhA&B; OxAmL; REnAL; TwCBDA; WebAB; WhAm 1; WhAmP*

Althouse, Paul Shearer
American. Opera Singer
b. Dec 2, 1889 in Reading, Pennsylvania
d. Feb 6, 1954 in New York, New York
Source: *WhAm 3*

Altman, Benjamin
American. Merchant, Art Collector
b. Jul 12, 1840 in New York, New York
d. Oct 7, 1913 in New York, New York
Source: *AmBi; DcAmB; NewYTBE 70; WebAB; WhAm HA, 4*

Altman, Robert B
American. Motion Picture Director, Producer
Director motion picture *MASH*, TV series "Bonanza."
b. Feb 20, 1925 in Kansas City, Missouri
Source: *BiDFilm; BkPepl; CelR 73; ConAu 73; ConLC 16; CurBio 74; FilmgC; IntMPA 75, 76, 77, 78, 79, 80, 81, 82; MovMk; NewYTBE 71; OxFilm; WhoAm 82*

Altrock, Nick (Nicholas)
American. Baseball Player
Pitcher, coach with Washington Senators known for clowning antics.
b. Sep 15, 1876 in Cincinnati, Ohio
d. Jan 20, 1965 in Washington, DC
Source: *BaseEn; WhoProB 73*

Aluko, Timothy Mofolorunso
Nigerian. Author
b. Jun 14, 1918 in Ilesha, Nigeria
Source: *AfrA; Au&Wr 71; CasWL; ConAu 65; ConNov 72, 76; Pen CL; RGAfL; TwCW; WebE&AL; WrDr 76*

Alva, Duke of
see: Toledo, Fernando Alvarez de

Alvarado, Pedro de
Spanish. Conquistador
b. 1486 in Badajoz, Spain
d. 1541 in Nochistlan, Mexico
Source: *AmBi; ApCAB; Drake*

Alvardo, Trini(dad)
American. Actress
b. 1967 in New York, New York
Source: *NewYTBS 79*

Alvarez, Alfred
English. Poet, Critic
b. Aug 5, 1929 in London, England
Source: *Au&Wr 71; ConAu 1R, 3NR; ConLC 5, 13; ConP 70, 75; ModBrL SUP; REn; Who 74; WhoWor 74; WorAu; WrDr 76*

Alvarez, Luis Walter
American. Physicist
b. Jun 13, 1911 in San Francisco, California
Source: *IntWW 74; WebAB; Who 74; WhoAm 74, 76, 78, 80, 82*

Alvarez, Walter Clement
American. Physician, Author, Journalist
Authority on digestive tract; had syndicated newspaper column.
b. Jul 22, 1884 in San Francisco, California
d. Jun 18, 1978 in San Francisco, California
Source: *AmAu&B; AmM&WS 73P; ConAu 61; CurBio 53, 78; DrAP 75; MnnWr; WhNAA; WhoAm 74; WhoWor 74*

Alvarez de Cienfuegos, Nicasio
see: Cienfuegos, Nicasio Alvarez de

Alvary, Lorenzo
Hungarian. Opera Singer
b. Feb 20, 1909 in Hungary
Source: *WhoAm 74, 76, 78, 80, 82; WhoMus 72; WhoWor 74*

Alvary, Max
German. Opera Singer
b. May 3, 1856 in Dusseldorf, Germany
d. Nov 7, 1898 in Gross-Tabarz, Germany
Source: *BioIn 1; WebBD 80*

Alworth, Lance Dwight
"Bambi"
American. Football Player
Only player to gain over 1,000 yds. receiving in seven consecutive seasons.
b. Aug 3, 1940 in Houston, Texas
Source: *PseudN; WhoFtbl 74*

Amado, Jorge
Brazilian. Author
b. Oct 8, 1912 in Bahia, Brazil
Source: *CasWL; CelR 73; ConAu 77; ConLC 13; CyWA; EncWL; IntWW 74; Pen AM; REn; TwCW; WhoWor 74; WorAu*

Amalrik, Andrei Alekseyevich
Russian. Human Rights Advocate, Author
b. May 12, 1938 in Moscow, U.S.S.R.
d. Nov 11, 1980 in Guadalajara, Spain
Source: *AnObit 1980; BioIn 8, 9, 10, 11; ConAu 102; CurBio 74, 81; NewYTBE 73*

Amara, Lucine
[Lucine Tockqui Armaganian]
American. Opera Singer
b. Mar 1, 1927 in Hartford, Connecticut
Source: *InWom; PseudN; WhoAm 74, 76, 78, 80, 82; WhoAmW 77; WhoMus 72; WhoWor 74*

Amati
Italian. Family of Violinmakers
Source: *BioIn 2*

Amato, Pasquale
Italian. Opera Singer
b. Mar 21, 1878 in Naples, Italy
d. Aug 12, 1942 in New York, New York
Source: *CurBio 42; WhAm 2; WhoHol B*

Amaya, Victor
American. Tennis Player
b. Jul 2, 1954 in Holland, Michigan
Source: *BioIn 12*

Ambers, Lou
[Luigi d'Ambrosio]
"Herkimer Hurricane"
American. Boxer
b. Nov 8, 1913 in Herkimer, New York
Source: *PseudN; WhoBox 74*

Ambler, Eric
[Eliot Reed, pseud.]
English. Author
Encompassed left-wing philosophy into spy and suspense novels.
b. Jun 28, 1909 in London, England
Source: *AmAu&B; Au&Wr 71; CnMWL; ConAu 9R; ConLC 4, 6, 9; ConNov 76; DcLEL; EncMys; FilmgC; LongCTC; NewC; OxFilm; PseudN; REn; TwCA SUP; TwCW; Who 74; WhoWor 74; WrDr 76*

Amboy Dukes, The
[Greg Arma; Cliff Davies; Rusty Day; Steve Farmer; Rob Grange; Viic Mastrianni; Ted Nugent; Dave Palmer; Derek St. Holmes; Andy Solomon]
American. Rock Group
Source: *BiDAmM; ConMuA 80; WhoRock 81*

Ambrose, Saint
Italian. Bishop of Milan
b. 340 in Trier, Italy
d. 397
Source: *BiD&SB; CasWL; NewC; OxEng; Pen CL; PoChrch; REn*

Ameche, Don
[Dominic Felix Amici]
American. Actor
Starred in over 40 films, including musical version of *The Three Musketeers,* 1939.
b. May 31, 1908 in Kenosha, Wisconsin
Source: *CmMov; CurBio 65; EncMT; FilmgC; IntMPA 75, 76, 77, 78, 79, 80, 81, 82; MotPP; MovMk; OxFilm; PseudN; WhoHol A; WhoThe 77*

Ameche, Jim
American. Radio Announcer, Actor
Brother of Don Ameche; portrayed Jack Armstrong on radio, 1930's.
b. 1915
d. Feb 4, 1983 in Tucson, Arizona
Source: *NF*

Ameling, Elly
Dutch. Opera Singer
b. Feb 8, 1938 in Rotterdam, Netherlands
Source: *NewYTBS 74; WhoAm 82; WhoMus 72; WhoWor 74*

Amen, Irving
American. Artist
b. Jul 25, 1918 in New York, New York
Source: *DcCAA 71; WhoAm 74, 76, 78, 80, 82; WhoAmA 73; WhoWor 74; WhoWorJ 72*

Amenhotep IV
see: Ikhnaton, Pharaoh

Amerasinghe, Hamilton Shirley
Sri Lankan. Diplomat, Government Official
b. Mar 18, 1913 in Colombo, Ceylon
d. Dec 4, 1980 in New York, New York
Source: *BioIn 9, 11; CurBio 77, 81; FarE&A 78, 79; IntWW 74, 75, 76, 77, 78; IntYB 78, 79; NewYTBS 76; WhoWor 74, 76, 78*

America
[Gerry Beckley; Dewey Bunnell; Daniel Peek]
American. Rock Group
First million selling record, "A Horse with No Name," 1972.
Source: *EncPR&S; IlEncRk*

Amery, Julian
English. Politican
b. Mar 27, 1919 in London, England
Source: *ConAu 61; IntWW 74; Who 74; WhoWor 74*

Ames, Amyas
American. Investment Banker
b. Jun 15, 1906 in Sharon, Massachusetts
Source: *CurBio 72; NewYTBE 70; St&PR 75; WhoAm 74*

Ames, Ed(mund Dantes)
[The Ames Brothers; Ed Urick]
American. Singer, Actor
b. Jul 9, 1927 in Boston, Massachusetts
Source: *BioIn 8; PseudN; RkOn; WhoAm 82*

Ames, Elinor
American. Newspaper Editor
b. in Ticonderoga, New York
Source: *ForWC 70; InWom; WhNAA; WhoAmW 77*

Ames, Joseph
English. Bibliographer
b. Jan 23, 1689
d. Oct 7, 1759
Source: *Alli; DcEnL*

Ames, Leon
[Leon Wycoff]
American. Actor
b. Jan 20, 1903 in Portland, Indiana
Source: *BiE&WWA; FilmgC; IntMPA 75, 76, 77, 78, 79, 80, 81, 82; MovMk; NotNAT; PseudN; Vers B; WhoHol A*

Ames, Louise Bates
American. Psychologist
b. Oct 29, 1908 in Portland, Maine
Source: *AmAu&B; AmM&WS 73S; ConAu 1R, 3NR; CurBio 56; InWom; LEduc 74; WhoAm 74, 76, 78, 80, 82; WhoAmW 77*

Ames, Nancy
American. Singer
b. 1937 in Washington, DC
Source: *BioIn 6, 7*

Ames, Oakes
American. Congressman
b. Jan 10, 1804 in Easton, Massachusetts
d. May 8, 1873 in Easton, Massachusetts
Source: *AmBi; ApCAB; BiAuS; BiDrAC; DcAmB; TwCBDA; WebAB; WhAm H; WhAmP*

Ames Brothers, The
[Ed, Gene, Joe, and Vic Ames; given name Urick]
American. Singing Group
Source: *PseudN*

Amfiteatrof, Daniele
Russian. Conductor, Composer
b. Oct 29, 1901 in Saint Petersburg, Russia
Source: *AmSCAP 66; FilmgC; IntMPA 77, 78, 79, 80, 81, 82; OxFilm; WorEFlm*

Amherst, Jeffrey
English. General
b. Jan 29, 1717 in Riverhead, England
d. Aug 31, 1797
Source: *AmBi; Drake; McGEWB; NewC; OxCan*

Amicis, Edmond de
Italian. Artist
b. 1846
d. 1908
Source: *WebBD 80*

Amies, Hardy
English. Fashion Designer
b. Jul 17, 1909 in London, England
Source: *CelR 73; CurBio 62; IntWW 74; NewYTBE 73; WhoWor 74; WorFshn*

Amin, Idi
[Idi Amin Dada Oumee]
"Big Daddy"; The Wild Man of Africa"
Ugandan. Former President
Term in office marred by torture, murder of suspected dissidents.
b. 1925 in Koboko, Uganda
Source: *BioNews 74; BkPepl; CurBio 73; IntWW 74; NewYTBE 71, 72; PseudN; WhoGov 72; WhoWor 74*

Amis, Kingsley William
[Robert Markham, pseud.]
"Angry Young Man"
English. Author
Satirical novelist; several produced as movies, including *Lucky Jim,* 1954.
b. Apr 16, 1922 in London, England
Source: *Au&Wr 71; AuNews 2; CasWL; CnMWL; ConAu 9R; ConLC 1, 2, 3, 5, 8, 13; ConNov 72, 76; ConP 70, 75; EncMys; EncWL; FilmgC; IntWW 74; LongCTC; ModBrL, SUP; NewC; Pen ENG; PseudN; RAdv 1; REn; TwCW; WebE&AL; Who 74; WhoAm 74, 76, 78, 80, 82; WhoTwCL; WorAu; WrDr 76*

Amis, Martin
English. Author
b. Aug 25, 1949 in Oxford, England
Source: *BioIn 10; ConAu 65; ConLC 4, 9; WrDr 80*

Ammann, Othmar Hermann
German. Bridge Designer, Engineer
Planned, constructed George Washington Bridge, Golden Gate Bridge.
b. Mar 26, 1876 in Schaffhausen, Switzerland
d. Sep 22, 1965
Source: *BioIn 3, 5, 6, 7, 9, 11; CurBio 63, 65; LinLib L; NatCAB 52; WhAm 4*

Ammons, Albert
American. Jazz Musician
b. 1907 in Chicago, Illinois
d. Dec 2, 1949 in Chicago, Illinois
Source: *CmpEPM; WhoJazz 72*

Ammons, "Jug" (Eugene)
American. Musician
b. Apr 14, 1925 in Chicago, Illinois
d. Aug 6, 1974 in Chicago, Illinois
Source: *BioIn 10; PseudN*

Amory, Cleveland
American. Social Historian, Author
Freelance writer since 1943; president, The Fund for Animals.
b. Sep 2, 1917 in Nahant, Massachusetts
Source: *AmAu&B; AuNews 1; BkPepl; ConAu 69; REnAL; TwCA SUP; WhoAm 74, 76, 78, 80, 82; WhoWor 74; WrDr 76*

Amos
Prophet
b. 750
Source: *BioIn 9; WebBD 80*

Amos, John
American. Actor
Played Kunte Kinte in TV mini-series "Roots."
b. in Newark, New Jersey
Source: *BioNews 74; WhoAm 82; WhoHol A*

Amos 'n Andy
see: Correll, Charles J; Gosden, Freeman F

Amos, Wally
"Famous Amos"
American. Cookie Entrepreneur
b. 1936 in Nutley, New Jersey
Source: *BkPepl; NewYTBS 75*

Ampere, Andre Marie
French. Scientist
b. Jan 22, 1775 in Lyons, France
d. Jun 10, 1836
Source: *OxFr; REn*

Amram, David Werner, III
American. Musician, Conductor
Composer, NY Shakespeare Festival, 1956-57.
b. Nov 17, 1930 in Philadelphia, Pennsylvania
Source: *BiE&WWA; BioNews 74; ConAu 29R; CurBio 69; DcCM; NotNAT; WhoAm 74, 76, 78, 80, 82*

Amsberry, Bob
American. TV Personality
Source: *BioIn 4*

Amsterdam, Morey
American. Actor, Comedian
Starred in "The Dick Van Dyke Show"; cellist with orchestras.
b. Dec 14, 1914 in Chicago, Illinois
Source: *AmSCAP 66; IntMPA 75, 76, 77, 78, 79, 80, 81, 82; WhoAm 74, 76, 78, 80, 82*

Amundsen, Roald Engelbregt
Norwegian. Polar Explorer
b. Jul 16, 1872 in Borge, Norway
d. Jun 18, 1928
Source: *OxCan; REn*

Anacreon
"The Teian Muse"
Greek. Lyric Poet
b. 572?BC in Teos, Asia Minor
d. 488?BC
Source: *AtlBL; BbD; BiD&SB; CasWL; DcEuL; NewC; OxEng; Pen CL; PseudN; RComWL*

Anand, Mulk Raj
[Narad Muni, pseud.]
Indian. Author
b. Dec 12, 1905 in Peshawar, India
Source: *Au&Wr 71; CasWL; ConAu 65; ConNov 76; DcOrL 2; IntWW 74; Pen ENG; PseudN; REn; WebE&AL; WhoWor 74; WorAu; WrDr 76*

Anastasis, Romanovna
see: Romanov, Anastasia

Anastasia, Albert
"Lord High Executioner"; "Mad Hatter"
American. Mafia Chief, Murderer
b. 1903
d. Oct 25, 1957 in New York, New York
Source: *BioIn 4, 11; Blood; PseudN*

Anaxagoras
Greek. Philosopher
Disproved doctrine that things may have arisen by chance.
b. 500BC
d. 428BC
Source: *BbD; BiD&SB; CasWL; Pen CL; REn*

Anaximander
Greek. Astronomer, Philosopher
First to write philosophy in Greek prose; invented sun dial.
b. 611BC
d. 547BC
Source: *BbD; BiD&SB; CasWL; Pen CL; REn*

Anaximenes of Miletus
Greek. Philosopher
b. 570?BC
d. 500?BC
Source: *DcScB; WebBD 80*

Ancerl, Karel
Czech. Conductor
b. Apr 11, 1908 in Tucapy, Czechoslovakia
d. Jul 3, 1973 in Toronto, ON
Source: *CanWW 70; NewYTBE 73; WhAm 6; WhoMus 72; WhoWor 74*

Anda, Geza
Hungarian. Concert Pianist
b. Nov 19, 1921 in Budapest, Hungary
d. Jun 13, 1976 in Zurich, Switzerland
Source: *IntWW 74; Who 74; WhoMus 72; WhoWor 74*

Anders, Merry
American. Actress
Co-starred in TV series "How to Marry a Millionaire."
b. 1932
Source: *FilmgC; InWom; MotPP*

Anders, William Alison
American. Astronaut
Lunar module pilot on first voyage to moon, Apollo 8, Dec 1968.
b. Oct 17, 1933 in Hong Kong, China
Source: *CurBio 69; IntWW 74; WhoAm 74; WhoGov 72; WhoS&SW 73; WhoWor 74*

Andersen, Anna
Model
Source: *NF*

Andersen, Eric
American. Folk Singer, Composer
b. Feb 14, 1943 in Pittsburgh, Pennsylvania
Source: *WhoAdv 72; WhoAm 74, 76, 78, 80, 82*

Andersen, Hans Christian
"The Danish Lafontaine"
Danish. Author, Poet
His 168 fairy tales all have autobiographical quality.
b. Apr 2, 1805 in Odense, Denmark
d. Aug 4, 1875 in Copenhagen, Denmark
Source: *AnCL; AtlBL; AuBYP; BbD; BiD&SB; CarSB; CasWL; ChPo, S1, S2; CyWA; DcBiA; DcEnL; DcEuL; EuAu; EvEuW; FamAYP; FamSYP; FilmgC; JBA 34, 51; NewC; OxEng; Pen EUR; PseudN; RComWL; REn; Str&VC; WhoChL; YABC 1*

Andersen, Ib Steen
Danish. Ballet Dancer
b. Dec 14, 1954 in Copenhagen, Denmark
Source: *BioIn 11; WhoAm 82*

Andersen, Lale
German. Singer
b. 1913
d. Aug 29, 1972 in Vienna, Austria
Source: *NewYTBE 72; OxGer*

Anderson, Bibi
see: Andersson Bibi

Anderson, Bill
"The Pat Boone of Country Music";
"Whispering Bill"
American. Singer, Songwriter
b. Nov 1, 1937 in Columbia, South Carolina
Source: *BioIn 9, 11; EncFCWM 69; PseudN; WhoRock 81*

Anderson, Carl David
American. Scientist
b. Sep 3, 1905 in New York, New York
Source: *IntWW 74; WebAB; Who 74; WhoAm 74, 76, 78, 80, 82; WhoWor 74*

Anderson, Carl Thomas
American. Cartoonist
b. Feb 14, 1865 in Madison, Wisconsin
d. Nov 4, 1948 in Madison, Wisconsin
Source: *AmAu&B; WhAm 2*

Anderson, "Cat" (William Alonzo)
American. Composer, Musician
b. Sep 12, 1916 in Greenville, South Carolina
d. Apr 30, 1981 in Norwalk, California
Source: *AmSCAP 66, 80; BiDAmM; CmpEPM; EncJzS 70; NewYTBS 81; WhoJazz 72*

Anderson, C(larence) W(illiam)
American. Children's Author
Wrote and illustrated *Billy and Blaze* series, 1936-70.
b. Apr 12, 1891 in Wahoo, Nebraska
d. Mar 26, 1971
Source: *AuBYP; BkP; ConAu 29R, 73; IlsCB 1744, 1946, 1957; JBA 51; PseudN; SmATA 11; Str&VC; ThrBJA*

Anderson, Clint(on Presba)
American. Statesman, Senator
b. Oct 23, 1895 in Centerville, South Dakota
d. Nov 11, 1975 in Albuquerque, New Mexico
Source: *BiDrAC; BiDrUSE; CurBio 45; IntWW 74; St&PR 75; WhAm 6; Who 74; WhoAm 74; WhoAmP 73; WhoGov 72; WhoS&SW 73; WhoWor 74*

Anderson, Daryl
American. Actor
Played Animal in TV series "Lou Grant," 1977-82.
b. Jul 1, 1951 in Seattle, Washington
Source: *BioIn 12; WhoAm 82*

Anderson, Donny
American. Football Player
b. May 16, 1943 in Borger, Texas
Source: *WhoFtbl 74*

Anderson, Douglas Dorland
American. Archaeologist
b. Jun 1, 1936 in Olympia, Washington
Source: *AmM&WS 73S*

Anderson, Eddie
"Rochester"
American. Actor
b. Sep 8, 1905 in Oakland, California
d. Feb 28, 1977 in Los Angeles, California
Source: *FilmgC; IntMPA 75, 76, 77, 78, 79, 80, 81, 82; MotPP; MovMk; WhoHol A*

Anderson, Elizabeth Garrett
English. Physician, Pioneer
b. 1836 in England
d. 1917
Source: *Alli SUP; InWom*

Anderson, Eugenie Moore
American. Diplomat
b. May 26, 1909 in Adair, Iowa
Source: *InWom; IntWW 74, 75, 76, 77, 78; WhoAm 74, 76, 78; WhoAmP 73, 75, 77, 79*

Anderson, George Everett
American. Diplomat
b. Aug 20, 1869 in Bloomington, Illinois
d. Mar 17, 1940
Source: *CurBio 40; WhAm 1*

Anderson, Gerry
English. Television Producer
b. 1929 in Hampstead, England
Source: *EncSF; FanAl; IntMPA 81*

Anderson, Gilbert M
[Max Aaronson]
"Broncho Billy"
American. Actor
b. Mar 21, 1882 in Little Rock, Arkansas
d. Jan 20, 1971 in South Pasadena, California
Source: *Film 1; MotPP; NewYTBE 71; OxFilm; PseudN; WhScrn 74, 77; WorEFlm*

Anderson, Harriet
see: Andersson, Harriet

Anderson, Ian
[Jethro Tull]
English. Rock Musician
b. Aug 10, 1947 in Blackpool, England
Source: *BioIn 11; BkPepl; WhoAm 80, 82*

Anderson, Ivie
American. Jazz Singer
b. 1904 in Gilroy, California
d. Dec 28, 1949 in Los Angeles, California
Source: *WhScrn 77; WhoJazz 72*

Anderson, Jack Northman
American. Journalist
Has written syndicated column, "Washington-Merry-Go-Round" since 1969.
b. Oct 19, 1922 in Long Beach, California
Source: *AuNews 1; BioNews 74; CelR 73; ConAu 57; CurBio 72; WhoAm 74, 76, 78, 80, 82; WhoS&SW 73; WhoWor 74; WrDr 76*

Anderson, Jack Zuinglius
American. Politician, Presidential Aide
Congressman, 1939-53; Eisenhower's administrative assistant, 1956-61.
b. 1904? in Oakland, California
d. Feb 9, 1981 in Hollister, California
Source: *NewYTBS 81; WhoAmP 73, 75, 77, 79*

Anderson, John Bayard
American. Politician, Former Congressman
Independent Party presidential candidate, 1980.
b. Feb 15, 1922 in Rockford, Illinois
Source: *ConAu 33R; CurBio 79; PseudN; WhoAm 82*

Anderson, John Murray
English. Theatrical and Film Director
b. 1886 in Saint John's, NF
d. Jan 30, 1954 in New York, New York
Source: *AmSCAP 66; EncMT; WhAm 3*

Anderson, Dame Judith
[Frances Margaret Anderson-Anderson]
Australian. Actress
First Australian-born actress invested as Dame Commander, 1960.
b. Jan 10, 1898 in Adelaide, Australia
Source: *BiE&WWA; CelR 73; CurBio 41, 61; FamA&A; FilmgC; InWom; IntMPA 75, 76, 77, 78, 79, 80, 81, 82; IntWW 74; MotPP; MovMk; NotNAT; OxFilm; OxThe; PseudN; Who 74; WhoAm 74; WhoHol A; WhoThe 77; WhoWor 74*

Anderson, Ken(neth Allan)
American. Football Player
b. Feb 15, 1949 in Batavia, Illinois
Source: *BioIn 10; WhoFtbl 74*

Anderson, Leila W
American. Youth Leader
Source: *BioIn 3, 5*

Anderson, Leroy
American. Composer, Conductor
b. Jun 29, 1908 in Cambridge, Massachusetts
d. May 18, 1975 in Woodbury, Connecticut
Source: *AmSCAP 66; BiE&WWA; NotNAT; WhAm 6; WhoAm 74; WhoE 74; WhoMus 72*

Anderson, Lindsay Gordon
English. Motion Picture Director, Critic
Prime mover in Free Cinema movement of 1950's.
b. Apr 17, 1923 in Bangalore, India
Source: *BiDFilm; DcFM; FilmgC; IntMPA 75, 76, 77, 78, 79, 80, 81, 82; IntWW 74; MovMk; NewYTBE 73; NotNAT; OxFilm; Who 74; WhoThe 77; WhoWor 74; WorEFlm*

Anderson, Loni
American. Actress
Played Jennifer on TV series "WKRP in Cincinnati."
b. Aug 5, 1946? in Saint Paul, Minnesota
Source: *WhoAm 80, 82*

Anderson, Lynn
American. Singer
Named best female vocalist, Academy of Country-Western Music, 1968.
b. Oct 26, 1947 in Grand Forks, North Dakota
Source: *WhoAm 74*

Anderson, Margaret
American. Editor
b. 1893 in Indianapolis, Indiana
d. Oct 18, 1973 in LeCannet, France
Source: *AmAu&B; ConAu 45; IndAu 1917; REnAL; WebAB*

Anderson, Marian
American. Singer
Congressional gold medal, 1978; named Woman of Decade, 1980.
b. Feb 17, 1902 in Philadelphia, Pennsylvania
Source: *CelR 73; EncAB-H; HerW; InWom; REn; WebAB; WhoAm 74, 76, 78, 80, 82; WhoBlA 75; WhoMus 72*

Anderson, Mary Antoinette
"Our Mary"
American. Actress
b. Jul 28, 1859 in Sacramento, California
d. May 29, 1940 in Broadway, England
Source: *BbD; BiD&SB; DcAmAu; DcAmB S2; FamA&A; NotAW; OxThe; PseudN; WhAm HA, 4*

Anderson, Max
American. Balloonist
b. 1934?
Source: *BioIn 11*

Anderson, Maxwell
American. Author, Dramatist
b. Dec 15, 1888 in Atlantic, Pennsylvania
d. Feb 28, 1959 in Stamford, Connecticut
Source: *AmAu&B; AmSCAP 66; CasWL; CnDAL; CnMD; CnThe; ConAmA; ConAmL; CroCD; CurBio 42, 53, 59; CyWA; DcLEL; EncAB-H; EncMT; EncWL; EvLB; FilmgC; LongCTC; McGEWD; ModAL; ModWD; NewCBMT; OxAmL; OxThe; Pen AM; PlP&P; REn; REnAL; REnWD; TwCA, SUP; TwCW; WebAB; WebE&AL; WhAm 3; WorEFlm*

Anderson, Melissa Sue
American. Actress
Played Mary Ingalls on TV series, "Little House on the Prairie," 1973-81.
b. Sep 26, 1962 in Berkeley, California
Source: *BioIn 10, 11; IntMPA 82*

Anderson, Michael
English. Motion Picture Director
Directed *Around the World in 80 Days,* 1956.
b. Jan 30, 1920 in London, England
Source: *BiDFilm; CmMov; FilmgC; IntMPA 75, 76, 77, 78, 79, 80, 81, 82; MovMk; WhoAm 82; WorEFlm*

Anderson, Michael, Jr.
English. Actor
Starred in TV series "The Monroes," 1966-67.
b. Aug 6, 1943 in London, England
Source: *FilmgC; IntMPA 75, 76, 77, 78, 79, 80, 81, 82; WhoHol A*

Anderson, O(ttis) J(erome)
American. Football Player
b. Jan 19, 1957 in West Palm Beach, Florida
Source: *FootReg*

Anderson, Peggy
American. Author
Wrote *Nurse,* 1978, adapted into TV series starring Michael Learned.
b. 1938
Source: *ConAu 93; NewYTBS 79; WrDr 76, 80*

Anderson, Philip Warren
American. Physicist
b. Dec 13, 1923 in Indianapolis, Indiana
Source: *AmM&WS 73P; IntWW 74; Who 74; WhoAm 82; WhoE 74; WhoWor 74*

Anderson, Rich
see: Tubes, The

Anderson, Richard Norman
American. Actor
b. Aug 8, 1926 in Long Beach, New Jersey
Source: *BiE&WWA; FilmgC; IntMPA 82; NotNAT; MovMk; NotNAT; WhoAm 82*

Anderson, Robert
American. Confederate General
b. Jun 14, 1805 in Louisville, Kentucky
d. Oct 27, 1871
Source: *Alli SUP; AmBi; ApCAB; DcAmB; DcNAA; Drake; TwCBDA; WhAm H*

Anderson, Robert Orville
American. Corporation Executive
President, Honda Oil & Gas, 1941-63; chief executive, Atlantic Richfield.
b. Apr 13, 1917 in Chicago, Illinois
Source: *CurBio 82; IntWW 74; St&PR 75; WhoAm 74, 76, 78, 80, 82; WhoAmP 73; WhoF&I 74; WhoGov 72*

Anderson, Robert Woodruff
American. Dramatist, Screenwriter
b. Apr 28, 1917 in New York, New York
Source: *AmAu&B; AuNews 1; BiE&WWA; CelR 73; CnMD; ConAu 21R; Who 74; WhoAm 82; WhoThe 77; WhoWor 74; WorAu; WrDr 76*

Anderson, Sherwood
American. Author, Poet
Wrote *Winesburg, Ohio,* 1919.
b. Sep 13, 1879 in Camden, Connecticut
d. Mar 8, 1941 in Colon, Panama
Source: *AmAu&B; AmWr; AtlBL; CasWL; Chambr 3; CnDAL; CnMWL; ConAmA; ConAmL; CyWA; DcAmB S3; DcLEL; DcNAA; EncWL; EvLB; LongCTC; ModAL, SUP; OhA&B; OxAmL; OxEng; Pen AM; RAdv 1; REn; REnAL; TwCA, SUP; TwCW; WebAB; WebE&AL; WhAm 1; WhNAA; WhoTwCL*

Anderson, "Sparky" (George Lee)
American. Baseball Manager
Manager, Cincinnati Reds 1970-78; Detroit Tigers 1979--.
b. Feb 2, 1934 in Bridgewater, South Dakota
Source: *BaseEn; CurBio 77; PseudN; WhoAm 74, 76, 78, 80, 82; WhoProB 73*

Anderson, Vernon Ellsworth
American. Author, Educator
b. Jun 15, 1908 in Atwater, Minnesota
Source: *ConAu 1R, 5NR; WhoAm 74; WrDr 76*

Anderson, Warner
American. Actor
b. Mar 10, 1911 in Brooklyn, New York
d. Aug 26, 1976 in Santa Monica, California
Source: *FilmgC; IntMPA 75, 76, 77; MotPP; MovMk; WhoHol A*

Anderson, Wendell Richard
American. Former Governor, Senator
b. Feb 1, 1933 in Saint Paul, Minnesota
Source: *BioNews 74; IntWW 74; WhoAm 74; WhoAmP 73; WhoGov 72; WhoMW 74*

Anderson, William
"Bloody Bill"
American. Outlaw, Murderer
d. Oct 1864 in Ray County, Missouri
Source: *Blood*

Anderson, William Robert
American. Corporation Executive
b. Jun 17, 1921 in Bakerville, Tennessee
Source: *BiDrAC; ConAu 5R, 5R; WhoAm 76, 78, 80, 82; WhoAmP 73; WhoGov 72; WhoS&SW 73*

Andersson, Benny
[ABBA]
Swedish. Singer, Musician
b. Dec 16, 1946 in Stockholm, Sweden
Source: *NF*

Andersson, Bibi
[Birgitta Andersson]
Swedish. Actress
b. Nov 11, 1935 in Stockholm, Sweden
Source: *BiDFilm; CelR 73; FilmgC; IntMPA 77, 78, 79, 80, 81, 82; IntWW 74; MotPP; MovMk; OxFilm; WhoHol A; WhoWor 74; WorEFlm*

Andersson, Harriet
Swedish. Actress
Ingmar Bergman wrote script *Monika,* 1952 especially for her.
b. Jan 14, 1932 in Stockholm, Sweden
Source: *BiDFilm; FilmgC; IntWW 74; OxFilm; WhoHol A; WhoWor 74; WorEFlm*

Andes, "Keith" (John Charles)
American. Actor
b. Jul 12, 1920 in Ocean City, New Jersey
Source: *BiE&WWA; FilmgC; IntMPA 75, 76, 77, 78, 79, 80, 81, 82; MotPP; NotNAT; PseudN; WhoHol A*

Andrassy, Gyula
Hungarian. Statesman
b. Mar 3, 1823 in Kassa, Hungary
d. Feb 18, 1890 in Volosca, Hungary
Source: *McGEWB; WebBD 80*

Andre, John
English. Spy
b. 1751 in London, England
d. Oct 2, 1780 in Tappan, New York
Source: *Alli; AmBi; ApCAB; Drake; OxAmL; REn; TwCBDA; WhAm H*

Andre, Pierre
Radio Announcer
Source: *NF*

Andrea da Pontedera
see: Pisano, Andrea

Andreas-Salome, Lou
German. Philosopher
b. 1861
d. 1937
Source: *InWom; OxGer; WhoLA*

Andree, Salomon August
Swedish. Polar Explorer
b. Oct 18, 1854 in Grenna, Sweden
d. 1897
Source: *McGEWB; NewCol 75; WebBD 80*

Andreotti, Giulio
Italian. Premier
b. Jan 14, 1919 in Rome, Italy
Source: *IntWW 74; NewYTBE 70, 72; WhoWor 74*

Andresen, Ivar
Norwegian. Opera Singer
b. Jul 17, 1896 in Oslo, Norway
d. Nov 26, 1940 in Stockholm, Sweden
Source: *NewEOp 71*

Andress, Ursula
Swiss. Actress
First wife of John Derek; movies include *Dr. No,* 1962.
b. Mar 19, 1936 in Bern, Switzerland
Source: *BiDFilm; CelR 73; FilmgC; IntMPA 75, 76, 77, 78, 79, 80, 81, 82; MotPP; MovMk; OxFilm; WhoHol A; WorEFlm*

Andretti, Mario Gabriel
American. Auto Racer
Won Indianapolis 500, 1969.
b. Feb 28, 1940 in Montona Trieste, Italy
Source: *CelR 73; CurBio 68; WebAB; WhoAm 74, 76, 78, 80, 82*

Andrew, Prince
"Randy Andy"
English. Member of British Royal Family
Second son of Queen Elizabeth; fought in Faulkland Islands War, 1982.
b. Feb 19, 1960 in London, England
Source: *BioIn 10; PseudN*

Andrew, Prince of Russia
[Andrew Romanov]
Russian. Prince
b. 1897 in Saint Petersburg, Russia
d. May 8, 1981 in Teynham, England
Source: *NewYTBS 81*

Andrew, Saint
Apostle
d. 70?AD in Patrae, Greece
Source: *REn*

Andrews, Anthony
English. Actor
Starred in TV movies *Brideshead Revisited, Ivanhoe.*
b. Jan 12, 1948 in London, England
Source: *NewYTBS 82*

Andrews, Bert
American. Journalist
b. Jun 2, 1901 in Colorado Springs, Colorado
d. Aug 21, 1953 in Denver, Colorado
Source: *CurBio 48, 53; DcAmB S5; WhAm 3*

Andrews, Bob
see: Graham Parker and the Rumour

Andrews, Charles McLean
American. Historian
b. Feb 22, 1863 in Wethersfield, Connecticut
d. Sep 9, 1943 in New Haven, Connecticut
Source: *BioIn 2, 4, 8; DcAmB S3; McGEWB; WebAB; WhAm 2*

Andrews, Dana
[Carver Dana Andrews]
American. Actor
Brother of Steve Forrest; starred in *The Ox-Bow Incident,* 1943.
b. Jan 1, 1909 in Collins, Mississippi
Source: *BiDFilm; BiE&WWA; CmMov; FilmgC; IntMPA 75, 76, 77, 78, 79, 80, 81, 82; MotPP; MovMk; OxFilm; PseudN; WhoHol A; WorEFlm*

Andrews, Eamonn
Irish. Radio and TV Commentator
b. Dec 19, 1922 in Dublin, Ireland
Source: *IntMPA 75, 76, 77, 78, 79, 80, 81, 82; IntWW 74; Who 74; WhoWor 74*

Andrews, Edward
American. Actor
b. Oct 9, 1915 in Griffin, Georgia
Source: *FilmgC; IntMPA 75, 76, 77, 78, 79, 80, 81, 82; MotPP; NotNAT; WhoHol A*

Andrews, Harry
English. Actor
b. Nov 10, 1911 in Tonbridge, England
Source: *CmMov; FilmgC; IntMPA 75, 76, 77, 78, 79, 80, 81, 82; MotPP; MovMk; WhoHol A; WhoThe 77*

Andrews, J(ames) S(ydney)
Irish. Author
b. Dec 14, 1934 in Belfast, Northern Ireland
Source: *Au&Wr 71; ConAu 29R; PseudN; SmATA 4*

Andrews, John Albion
American. Statesman, Governor
b. May 31, 1813 in Windham, Maine
d. Oct 30, 1867 in Boston, Massachusetts
Source: *WebAB*

Andrews, Julie
[Mrs. Blake Edwards; Julia Elizabeth Wells]
English. Singer, Actress
Won Oscar, 1964, for *Mary Poppins.*
b. Oct 1, 1935 in Walton-on-Thames, England
Source: *BiDFilm; BiE&WWA; BkPepl; CelR 73; CmMov; ConAu 37R; EncMT; FamA&A; FilmgC; InWom; IntMPA 75, 76, 77, 78, 79, 80, 81, 82; IntWW 74; MotPP; MovMk; NotNAT; OxFilm; PlP&P; PseudN; SmATA 7; Who 82; WhoAm 74, 76, 78, 80, 82; WhoHol A; WhoThe 77; WhoWor 74; WorEFlm; WrDr 76*

Andrews, LaVerne
[Andrews Sisters]
American. Singer
b. Jul 6, 1915 in Minneapolis, Minnesota
d. May 8, 1967 in Brentwood, California
Source: *FilmgC; InWom; MotPP; WhScrn 74, 77; WhoHol B*

Andrews, Mark N
American. Senator
b. May 19, 1926 in Fargo, North Dakota
Source: *AlmAP 78, 80; BiDrAC; CngDr 74, 77, 78; WhoAm 74, 76, 78, 80; WhoAmP 73, 75, 77, 79; WhoGov 72, 75, 77; WhoMW 74, 76, 78*

Andrews, Mary Raymond Shipman
American. Author
b. 1860
d. Aug 2, 1936
Source: *AmAu&B; ChPo; ConAmL; DcNAA; InWom; JBA 34; NotAW; REnAL; TwCA; WhAm 1; WhNAA*

Andrews, Maxine
[Andrews Sisters]
American. Singer
b. Jan 3, 1918 in Minneapolis, Minnesota
Source: *FilmgC; InWom*

Andrews, Patti (Patricia)
[Andrews Sisters]
American. Singer
b. Feb 16, 1920 in Minneapolis, Minnesota
Source: *InWom; WhoHol A*

Andrews, Roy Chapman
American. Zoologist, Explorer
Discovered fossil fields yielding unknown plant and animal life.
b. Jan 26, 1884 in Beloit, Wisconsin
d. Mar 11, 1960 in Carmel, California
Source: *AmAu&B; ApCAB X; AsBiEn; AuBYP; CurBio 41, 53, 60; DcAmB S6; EvLB; LinLib L, S; McGEWB; NatCAB; NewCol 75; REnAL; SmATA 19; TwCA, SUP; WebAB; WhAm 3A; WhLit; WhNAA*

Andrews, Tige
[Tiger Androwaous]
American. Actor
b. Mar 19, 1923? in Brooklyn, New York
Source: *FilmgC; PseudN; WhoAm 82; WhoHol A*

Andrews, V(irginia) C
American. Author
Wrote *Flowers in the Attic,* 1979, *Petals in the Wind,* 1980.
b. Jun 6, 1924? in Portsmouth, Virginia
Source: *ConAu 97*

Andrews, Wayne
[Montagu O'Reilly, pseud.]
American. Author, Educator
b. Sep 5, 1913 in Kenilworth, Illinois
Source: *AmAu&B; ConAu 9R, 3NR; DrAS 74H, 78H; IntAu&W 76; PseudN; WhoAm 74, 76, 78, 80, 82*

Andrews Sisters
[LaVerne Andrews; Maxine Andrews; Patti Andrews]
American. Singing Group
Source: *FilmEn*

Andreyev, Leonid Nikolayevich
[James Lynch, pseud.]
"The Edgar Allan Poe of Russian Literature"
Russian. Author
b. Jun 18, 1871 in Orel, Russia
d. Sep 12, 1919 in Helsinki, Finland
Source: *CasWL; ClDMEL; CnMD; CnThe; CyWA; DcRusL; EncWL; EncWT; EvEuW; LinLib S; LongCTC; McGEWD; ModSL; NewCol 75; NewEOp 71; NotNAT B; Pen EUR; PlP&P; REn; REnWD; TwCA, SUP; TwCLC; TwCW; WhoHr&F*

Andric, Ivo
Yugoslav. Author
b. 1892
d. Mar 13, 1975 in Belgrade, Yugoslavia
Source: *Au&Wr 71; CasWL; ClDMEL; ConAu 57, 81; ConLC 8; CurBio 62; EncWL; EvEuW; IntWW 74; ModSL 2; Pen EUR; REn; TwCW; WhAm 6; Who 74; WhoTwCL; WhoWor 74; WorAu*

Androcles
Roman. Slave
Source: *NewC; REn*

Andropov, Yuri Vladimirovich
Russian. Politician
General Secretary, Communist Party, after death of Brezhnev, 1982; former head of KGB.
b. Jun 15, 1914 in Nagutskaia, Russia
Source: *IntWW 74, 75, 76, 77, 78, 79, 80, 81; WhoSocC 78; WhoWor 74*

Andrus, Cecil D(ale)
American. Business Executive
Secretary of Interior, 1977-81.
b. Aug 25, 1931 in Hood River, Oregon
Source: *CngDr 77, 79; CurBio 77; IntWW 74, 75, 76, 77, 78, 79, 79, 80, 81; WhoAm 74, 76, 78, 80, 82; WhoAmP 73, 75, 77, 79; WhoE 77, 79; WhoGov 72, 75, 77; WhoWest 74, 76, 78; WhoWor 78*

Andrzejewski, Jerzy
[George Andrzeyevski, pseud.]
Polish. Author
b. 1909 in Warsaw, Poland
Source: *CasWL; ConAu 25R; EncWL; IntWW 74; ModSL 2; Pen EUR; PseudN; TwCW; WhoTwCL; WhoWor 74*

Anello, John David
American. Conductor
b. 1909 in Milwaukee, Wisconsin
Source: *WhoAm 74, 76, 78, 80, 82*

Angel, Heather
American. Actress
b. Feb 9, 1909 in Oxford, England
Source: *FilmgC; InWom; IntMPA 75, 76, 77, 78, 79, 80, 81, 82; MovMk; ThFT; WhoHol A; WhoThe 77*

Angela Merici, Saint
Italian. Founder of Ursulines
b. 1474?
d. 1540
Source: *WebBD 80*

Angeles, Victoria de los
Spanish. Opera Singer
b. Nov 1, 1923 in Barcelona, Spain
Source: *CurBio 55; InWom; IntWW 74; Who 74; WhoAmW 77; WhoMus 72*

Angeli, Pier
[Anna Maria Pierangeli]
Italian. Actress
Twin sister of Marisa Pavan; most roles were fragile, innocent heroines.
b. Jun 19, 1933 in Sardinia, Italy
d. Sep 10, 1971 in Beverly Hills, California
Source: *FilmEn; FilmgC; InWom; MGM; MotPP; MovMk; NewYTBE 71; WhAm 5; WhScrn 74, 77; WhoAmW 64, 66, 68; WhoHol B*

Angelico, Fra
[Guido di Pietro; Giovanni da Fiesole]
Italian. Artist
b. 1387 in Vicchio, Italy
d. Mar 18, 1455 in Rome, Italy
Source: *AtlBL; PseudN; REn*

Angell, James Burrill
American. Educator, Diplomat
b. Jan 7, 1829 in Scituate, Rhode Island
d. Apr 1, 1916 in Ann Arbor, Michigan
Source: *Alli SUP; AmAu&B; AmBi; ApCAB; BbD; BiD&SB; CyAL 1, 2; DcAmAu; DcAmB; DcNAA; EncAB-H; TwCBDA; WebAB; WhAm 1; WhAmP*

Angell, James Rowland
American. Educator
b. May 8, 1869 in Burlington, Virginia
d. Mar 4, 1949 in Hamden, Connecticut
Source: *AmAu&B; CurBio 40, 49; DcAmB S4; DcNAA; WhAm 2; WhNAA*

Angell, Sir Norman
English. Author, Publicist
b. Dec 26, 1874 in Holbeach, England
d. Oct 7, 1967 in Surrey, England
Source: *ConAu P-1; CurBio 48, 67; DcLEL; EvLB; LongCTC; NewC; OxEng; TwCA, SUP; WhAm 4, 5; WhoLA*

Angell, Roger
American. Author, Editor
Fiction editor, contributor, *New York Magazine,* 1956--; author, *The Summer Game,* 1972.
b. Sep 19, 1920 in New York, New York
Source: *ConAu 57; DrAF 76; WhoAm 74, 76, 78, 80, 82*

Angelo, Frank
American. Journalist
b. Sep 6, 1914 in Detroit, Michigan
Source: *ConAu 53, 4NR; WhoAm 74, 76, 78, 80, 82*

Angelo, Giorgio di Sant
see: DiSant'Angelo, Giorgio

Angelou, Maya Marguerita
American. Actress, Author, Journalist
Wrote *I Know Why the Caged Bird Sings,* 1970 (autobiographical).
b. Apr 4, 1928 in Saint Louis, Missouri
Source: *AmWomWr; BlkAW; ConAu 65; ConLC 12; CurBio 74; DrAP 75; DcBlPA; EbonySL 1; HerW; LivgBAA; NewYTBE 72; NotNAT A; SelBAA; WhoAm 74, 76, 78, 80, 82; WhoAmW 72, 79; WhoBlA 77; WomWMM; WrDr 76, 80*

Anger, Kenneth
American. Motion Picture Director
b. 1932 in Santa Monica, California
Source: *DcFM; FilmgC; OxFilm; WhoAm 82; WorEFlm*

Angle, Edward Hartley
American. Orthodonist
b. Jun 1, 1855 in Herrick, Pennsylvania
d. Aug 11, 1930
Source: *WhAm 1*

Anglim, Philip
American. Actor
b. Feb 11, 1952 in San Francisco, California
Source: *WhoThe 81*

Anglin, Margaret Mary
Canadian. Actress
b. Apr 3, 1876 in Ottawa, ON
d. Jan 7, 1958 in Toronto, ON
Source: *BiCAW; FamA&A; InWom; OxThe; WhAm 5; WhoStg 1906, 1908*

Anglund, Joan Walsh
American. Author, Illustrator
b. Jan 3, 1926 in Hinsdale, Illinois
Source: *AmAu&B; Au&Wr 71; AuBYP; ChILR 1; ChPo S1, S2; ConAu 5R; FamAIYP; SmATA 2; ThrBJA; WhoAm 74*

Angoff, Charles
American. Author, Editor
b. Apr 22, 1902 in Minsk, Russia
d. May 3, 1979 in New York, New York
Source: *AmAu&B; Au&Wr 71; ConAu 5R, 85; CurBio 55, 79; DrAP 75; DrAS 74E; 78E; IntAu&W 76, 77; IntWWP 77; NewYTBS 79; REnAL; ScF&FL 1, 2; WhE&EA; WhNAA; WhoAm 74, 76, 78; WhoWor 74; WhoWorJ 72; WrDr 76, 80*

Angott, Sammy (Samuel Engotti)
American. Boxer
b. Jan 17, 1915 in Washington, Pennsylvania
Source: *WhoBox 74*

Angrist, Stanley Wolff
American. Children's Author
b. Jun 3, 1933 in Dallas, Texas
Source: *AmM&WS 73P; ConAu 25R; SmATA 4*

Angstrom, Anders Jonas
Swedish. Astronomer, Physicist
Noted for his study of light, especially spectrum analysis.
b. Aug 13, 1814 in Logdo, Sweden
d. Jun 21, 1874 in Uppsala, Sweden
Source: *AsBiEn; BioIn 3, 7; DcScB; LinLib S; NewCol 75; WebBD 80*

Anhalt, Edward
[Andrew Holt, pseud.]
American. Screenwriter
b. Mar 28, 1914 in New York, New York
Source: *BioIn 7, 9; ConAu 85; FilmEn; FilmgC; IntMPA 81; PseudN*

Anievas, Augustin
American. Musician
b. Nov 6, 1934 in New York, New York
Source: *WhoAm 74*

Animals, The
[Eric Burdon; Bryan Chandler; Barry Jenkins; Alan Price; Dave Rowberry; John Steel; Hilton Valentine]
English. Rock Group
Source: *EncPR&S; IlEncRk; RkOn*

Animuccia, Giovanni
Italian. Composer
b. 1500
d. 1571
Source: *BioIn 4; WebBD 80*

Anka, Paul
Canadian. Singer, Songwriter
Compositions include "Diana" and "My Way;" has 15 gold records.
b. Jul 30, 1941 in Ottawa, ON
Source: *AmPS A, B; Baker 78; BiDAmM; CanWW 79, 82; CelR 73; CreCan 2; CurBio 64; FilmgC; MotPP; RkOn, 2; WhoAm 74, 76, 78, 80, 82*

Ankers, Evelyn
British. Actress
b. Aug 17, 1918 in Valparaiso, Chile
Source: *FilmEn; FilmgC; IntMPA 75, 76, 77, 78, 79, 80, 81, 82; MotPP; MovMk; WhoHol A*

Ann-Margaret
[Ann-Margaret Olsson; Mrs. Roger Smith]
American. Dancer, Actress
Nominated for Oscars for *Carnal Knowledge,* 1971; *Tommy,* 1975.
b. Apr 28, 1941 in Stockholm, Sweden
Source: *BiDFilm; BioNews 75; BkPepl; CelR 73; CurBio 75; FilmEn; FilmgC; GoodHS; InWom; IntMPA 75, 76, 77, 78, 79, 80, 81, 82; MotPP; MovMk; OxFilm; RkOn; WhoAm 74, 76, 78, 80, 82; WhoAmW 66, 68, 72, 74; WhoHol A*

Annabella
[Suzanne Georgette Charpentier]
French. Actress
b. Jul 14, 1912 in Paris, France
Source: *FilmgC; InWom; MotPP; MovMk; ThFT; WhoHol A; WhoThe 77; WorEFlm*

Annabella (Myant Myant Aye)
see: Bow Wow Wow

Anne
English. Queen
b. Feb 6, 1665
d. Aug 1, 1714
Source: *InWom; NewC*

Anne Boleyn
see: Boleyn, Anne

Anne of Bohemia
English. Queen
b. 1366
d. 1394
Source: *InWom; NewC*

Ann of Cleves
German. 4th Wife of Henry VIII
Protestant princess, married Henry VIII Jan 1540; divorced Jul 1540.
b. 1515 in Cleves, Germany
d. 1557 in England
Source: *BioIn 1, 4, 7, 10; InWom; LinLib S; NewC; NewCol 75; REn*

Anne, Princess
[Anne Elizabeth Alice Louise; Mrs. Mark Phillips]
English. Daughter of Queen Elizabeth II
Accomplished horsewoman; represented England in 1976 Olympics.
b. Aug 15, 1950 in London, England
Source: *CurBio 73; IntWW 76, 77, 78, 79, 80, 81; NewCol 75; NewYTBE 70, 73*

Annenberg, Walter Hubert
American. Publisher, Former Ambassador
Publishes *TV Guide;* Ambassador to UK, 1969-75.
b. Mar 13, 1908 in Milwaukee, Wisconsin
Source: *BioNews 74; CelR 73; CurBio 70; IntWW 74, 75, 76, 77, 78, 79, 79, 80, 81; IntYB 78, 79; NewYTBS 74; NewYTET; St&PR 75; USBiR 74; Who 74; WhoAm 74, 76, 78, 80, 82; WhoAmP 73, 75, 77, 79; WhoE 74, 75, 77; WhoGov 72; WhoWor 74, 76, 78; WhoWorJ 72*

Annigoni, Pietro
Italian. Artist
b. Jun 7, 1910 in Milan, Italy
Source: *Au&Wr 71; IntWW 74; Who 74; WhoWor 74*

Annis, Francesca
English. Actress
b. 1944 in London, England
Source: *FilmEn; FilmgC; HalFC 80; NewYTBS 79*

Anouilh, Jean Marie Lucienpierre
French. Dramatist
Best known plays *Antigone* and *Becket* (filmed, 1964).
b. Jun 23, 1910 in Bordeaux, France
Source: *Au&Wr 71; BiE&WWA; CasWL; CnMD; CnMWL; CnThe; ConAu 17R; ConLC 1, 3, 8, 13; CroCD; CurBio 54; CyWA; DcFM; EncWL; EncWT; EvEuW; FilmEn; FilmgC; IntAu&W 76, 77; IntWW 74, 75, 76, 77, 78, 79, 80, 81; LinLib L, S; LongCTC; McGEWB; McGEWD; ModFrL; ModRL; ModWD; NotNAT; OxEng; OxFilm; OxFr; OxThe; Pen; PlP&P; RComWL; REn; REnWD; TwCA SUP; TwCW; Who 74; WhoThe 72, 77, 81; WhoTwCL; WhoWor 74; WorEFlm*

Anquetil, Jacques
French. Cyclist
b. 1934?
Source: *BioIn 6*

Ansara, Michael George
American. Actor
Played Cochise in "Broken Arrow" TV series, 1956-60.
b. Apr 15, 1922 in Lowell, Massachusetts
Source: *FilmEn; FilmgC; IntMPA 75, 76, 77, 78, 79, 80, 81, 82; MotPP; WhoAm 74, 76, 78, 80, 82; WhoHol A*

Anselm, Saint
Italian. Founder of Scholasticism
b. 1033
d. 1109
Source: *Alli; BiB; CasWL; DcEnL; NewC; OxEng*

Ansermet, Ernest Alexandre
Swiss. Conductor
b. Nov 11, 1883 in Vevey, Switzerland
d. Feb 20, 1969 in Geneva, Switzerland
Source: *CurBio 49, 69; WhAm 5*

Anslinger, Harry Jacob
American. Statesman
b. May 20, 1892 in Altoona, Pennsylvania
d. Nov 14, 1975
Source: *ConAu 61; ConAu P-1; WhAm 6*

Anson, "Cap" (Adrian Constantine)
American. Baseball Player, Manager
Played 27 years; amassed more than 3,500 hits; Hall of Fame, 1939.
b. Apr 17, 1851 in Marshalltown, Iowa
d. Apr 14, 1922 in Chicago, Illinois
Source: *BaseEn; DcAmB; NewCol 75; WebAB; WhAm HA, 4; WhoProB 73*

Anson, George, Baron
English. Admiral
b. 1697
d. 1762
Source: *Alli; DcEnL*

Anson, Jay
American. Scriptwriter, Author
Wrote *The Amnityville Horror,* 1977, adapted to film, 1979.
b. 1924 in New York, New York
d. Mar 12, 1980 in Palo Alto, California
Source: *ConAu 81, 97*

Anson, Robert Sam
American. Journalist
b. 1945?
Source: *BioIn 9*

Anspach, Susan
American. Actress
b. 1944 in New York, New York
Source: *MovMk; WhoAm 82; WhoHol A*

Ant, Adam
[Stewart Goddard; Adam and the Ants]
English. Rock Singer
b. Nov 3, 1954 in London, England
Source: *IlEncRk*

Antes, Horst
German. Artist
b. Oct 28, 1936 in Heppenheim, Germany
Source: *ConArt; IntWW 76, 77, 78*

Antheil, George
American. Opera Composer
b. Jul 8, 1900 in Trenton, New Jersey
d. Feb 12, 1959 in New York, New York
Source: *AmSCAP 66; CurBio 54, 59; DcCM; DcFM; REnAL; WhAm 3; WorEFlm*

Anthony of Padua, Saint
French. Franciscan Monk
b. 1195 in Lisbon, Portugal
d. 1231
Source: *REn*

Anthony, Saint
Father of Christian Monastics
b. 251
d. 350
Source: *NewCol 75; REn; WebBD 80*

Anthony, C L
see: Smith, Dodie, pseud.

Anthony, Earl
American. Author, Activist
Source: *BlkAW; LivgBAA*

Anthony, Earl
American. Bowler
Bowler of year, 1974, 1975, 1976.
b. Apr 27, 1938 in Kent, Washington
Source: *BioIn 11*

Anthony, Edward
American. Publisher, Author
b. Aug 4, 1895 in New York, New York
d. Aug 16, 1971 in Gloucester, Massachusetts
Source: *AmAu&B; AuBYP; BkCL; ChPo; ConAu 33R, 73; REnAL; SmATA 21; WhAm 5*

Anthony, Evelyn, pseud.
[Evelyn Bridget Ward-Thomas]
English. Author
b. Jul 3, 1928 in London, England
Source: *Au&Wr 71; ConAu 9R, 5NR; WrDr 76*

Anthony, John J(ason)
American. Radio and TV Counselor
b. Sep 1, 1898 in New York, New York
d. Jul 16, 1970 in San Francisco, California
Source: *CurBio 42, 70; NewYTBE 70; WhoHol B*

Anthony, Joseph
American. Journalist, Editor
b. 1897 in New York, New York
Source: *AmAu&B; ChPo, S1, S2; WhoHol A*

Anthony, Marc
see: Antony, Marc

Anthony, Michael
see: Van Halen

Anthony, Ray
[Raymond Antonini]
American. Band Leader
Co-composed novelty hit, "The Bunny Hop."
b. Jan 20, 1922 in Bentleyville, Pennsylvania
Source: *CmpEPM; WhoHol A*

Anthony, Susan Brownell
American. Reformer, Suffragette
Organized Daughters of Temperance, first women's temperance assn.
b. Feb 15, 1820 in Adams, Massachusetts
d. Mar 13, 1906 in Rochester, New York
Source: *AmBi; AmWom; AmWomWr; ApCAB; BbD; DcAmB; DcNAA; Drake; EncAB-H; HerW; InWom; LibW; LinLib L, S; McGEWB; NatCAB 4; NewCol 75; NotAW; OxAmL; REn; TwCBDA; WebAB; WhAm 1; WhAmP*

Anthony, Tony
American. Actor
b. Oct 16, 1937 in Clarksburg, West Virginia
Source: *FilmgC; IntMPA 75, 76, 77, 78, 79, 80, 81, 82; WhoBox 74*

Anthony and the Imperials
see: Little Anthony and the Imperials

Antin, Mary
American. Author
b. 1881 in Polotsk, Russia
d. May 15, 1949 in Suffern, New York
Source: *AmAu&B; DcAmAu; DcAmB S4; DcNAA; InWom; NotAW; OxAmL; REn; TwCA, SUP; WebAB; WhAm 6; WhNAA*

Antiphon
Greek. Author, Orator
b. 480BC
d. 411BC
Source: *CasWL; Pen CL; REn*

Antisthenes
Greek. Philosopher
b. 444BC
d. 371BC
Source: *WebBD 80*

Anton, Susan
American. Actress, Singer
b. 1950? in Yucaipa, California
Source: *BioIn 11, 12; WhoAm 82*

Antonelli, Giacomo
Italian. Statesman
b. 1806
d. 1876
Source: *WebBD 80*

Antonelli, John(ny August)
American. Baseball Player
b. Apr 12, 1930 in Rochester, New York
Source: *BaseEn; WhoProB 73*

Antonelli, Laura
Italian. Actress
b. in Pola, Italy
Source: *NewYTBS 79*

Antonello da Messina
Italian. Artist
b. 1430 in Messina, Sicily
d. Feb 15, 1479 in Messina, Sicily
Source: *AtlBL; REn*

Antonescu, Ion
Romanian. General, Premier
b. 1882 in Transylvania, Hungary
d. Jun 1, 1946
Source: *CurBio 40, 46*

Antoninus Pius
Roman. Emperor
b. 86 in Lanuvium, Italy
d. 161
Source: *NewC*

Antonioni, Michelangelo
Italian. Motion Picture Director
b. Sep 29, 1912 in Ferrara, Italy
Source: *BiDFilm; ConAu 73; CurBio 64; DcFM; FilmgC; IntMPA 75, 76, 77, 78, 79, 80, 81, 82; IntWW 74; MovMk; OxFilm; Who 74; WhoWor 74; WorEFlm*

Antony, Marc
[Marcus Antonius; Marc Anthony]
Roman. General, Orator
b. 83?BC
d. 30BC
Source: *BioIn 1, 2, 5, 6, 7; REn; WebBD 80*

Anuszkiewicz, Richard Joseph
American. Artist
b. May 23, 1930 in Erie, Pennsylvania
Source: *BnEnAmA; ConArt; CurBio 78; DcAmArt; DcCAA 71, 77; McGDA; WhoAm 74, 76, 78, 80, 82; WhoAmA 73, 76, 78*

Anza, Juan Bautista de
Spanish. Explorer
b. 1735 in Fronteras, Mexico
d. 1788 in Arizpe, Mexico
Source: *AmBi; DcAmB; OxAmL; REnAL; WebAB; WhAm H*

Aoki, Hiroaki
"Rocky"
American. Restaurateur, Wrestler
b. 1938
Source: *NF*

Aoki, Isao
Japanese. Golfer
First Japanese golfer to win PGA tournament, 1983 Hawaiian Open.
b. Aug 31, 1942 in Abiko, Japan
Source: *BioIn 12*

"Apache Kid"
American. Murderer, Robber
b. 1868?
d. 1894? in Tucson, Arizona
Source: *BioIn 1, 3, 4, 5; Blood*

Aparicio, Luis Ernesto
Venezuelan. Baseball Player
Shortstop; led AL in stolen bases, 1956-64.
b. Apr 29, 1934 in Maracaibo, Venezuela
Source: *BaseEn; WhoAm 74; WhoE 74; WhoProB 73*

Apelles
Greek. Artist
b. in Ionia, Asia Minor
Source: *NewC*

Apgar, Virginia
American. Anesthetist
b. 1909
d. Aug 7, 1974 in Tenafly, New Jersey
Source: *BioIn 5, 8, 9, 10*

Apicius, Marcus Gavius
Roman. Epicure
Source: *CasWL*

Apollinaire, Guillaume
[Guillaume Kostrowitsky]
French. Author, Poet
b. Aug 26, 1880 in Rome, Italy
d. Nov 10, 1918
Source: *AtlBL; CasWL; ClDMEL; CnMD; CnMWL; EncWL; EvEuW; LongCTC; McGEWD; ModRL; ModWD; OxEng; OxFr; Pen EUR; RComWL; REn; REnWD; TwCA, SUP; TwCW; WhoTwCL*

Apollinaris Sidonius, Gaius Sollius
Early Christian Prelate
b. 430
d. 487
Source: *WebBD 80*

Apollonius of Perga
"Great Geometer"
Greek. Mathematician
Influenced development of analytic geometry.
b. 262?BC
d. 200?BC
Source: *DcScB; LinLib L; McGEWB; WebBD 80*

Apostoli, Fred
American. Boxer
b. Feb 2, 1914
Source: *WhoBox 74*

Appel, James Ziegler
American. Physician
b. May 15, 1907 in Lancaster, Pennsylvania
d. Aug 31, 1981 in Lancaster, Pennsylvania
Source: *CurBio 66, 81; NewYTBS 81; WhoAm 74, 76, 78*

Appel, Karel Christian
Dutch. Artist
b. Apr 25, 1921 in Amsterdam, Netherlands
Source: *ConArt; CurBio 61; IntWW 74, 75, 76, 77, 78; McGDA; Who 74; WhoAmA 73, 76, 78; WhoWor 74*

Appert, Francois Nicolas
French. Chef
Invented method of canning food in corked jars.
b. Nov 17, 1749
d. 1841
Source: *BioIn 3, 4, 10, 12; NewCol 75*

Appice, Carmine
see: Vanilla Fudge

Apple, Max Isaac
American. Author
b. Oct 22, 1941 in Grand Rapids, Michigan
Source: *ConAu 81; ConLC 9; DrAF 76; DrAS 74; NewYTBS 81*

Appleseed, Johnny
[John Chapman]
American. Pioneer, Planter, Mystic
Traveled west from PA to IN for 50 yrs., preaching, distributing apple seeds.
b. Sep 26, 1774 in Springfield, Massachusetts
d. Mar 11, 1847 in Allen County, Indiana
Source: *AmAu&B; AmBi; DcAmB; REn; WebAB; WhAm H*

Appleton, Daniel
American. Publisher
b. Dec 10, 1785 in Haverhill, Massachusetts
d. Mar 27, 1849
Source: *AmAu&B; AmBi; ApCAB; DcAmB; Drake; TwCBDA; WhAm H*

Appleton, William Henry
American. Publisher
b. Jan 27, 1814 in Haverhill, Massachusetts
d. Oct 19, 1899
Source: *AmAu&B; DcAmB; TwCBDA; WhAm H, 1*

Appling, Luke (Lucius Benjamin)
"Old Aches and Pains"
American. Baseball Player
Voted greatest White Sox player of all time; Hall of Fame, 1964.
b. Apr 2, 1907 in High Point, North Carolina
Source: *BaseEn; WhoProB 73*

April Wine
[Myles Goodwin; Brian Greenway; Steve Lang; Jerry Mercer; Gary Moffet]
Canadian. Rock Group
Source: *IlEncRk; WhoRock 81*

Apter, David Ernest
American. Author, Educator
b. Dec 18, 1924 in New York, New York
Source: *AmM&WS 73S; ConAu 1R, 3NR; WhoAm 74; WrDr 76*

Aptheker, Herbert
American. Author, Historian
b. Jul 31, 1915 in Brooklyn, New York
Source: *AmAu&B; ConAu 5R; DrAS 74H; WhoAm 74, 76, 78, 80, 82; WhoWor 74; WhoWorJ 72*

Apuleius, Lucius
Roman. Satirist
b. 125 in Madavros, Numidia
d. 200
Source: *AtlBL; BbD; BiD&SB; CasWL*

Aquinas, Thomas, Saint
Italian. Theologian, Philosopher
Synthesis of theology, philosophy known as Thomism; wrote *Summa Theologica*.
b. 1225 in Roccasecca, Italy
d. Mar 7, 1274 in Fossannova, Italy
Source: *BbD; BiD&SB; CasWL; CyWA; DcEuL; EuAu; EvEuW; NewC; OxEng; OxFr; Pen EUR; RComWL; REn*

Arafat, Yasir
Palestinian. Leader of PLO
Described as chief of state to a stateless people.
b. 1929 in Jerusalem, Palestine
Source: *CurBio 71; IntWW 79, 80; MidE 80; NewYTBE 70; NewYTBS 74*

Argo, Dominique Francois Jean
French. Physicist
b. Feb 26, 1786
d. Oct 2, 1853
Source: *BioIn 3; NewCol 75*

Aragon, Louis
French. Poet
One of founders of French Surrealism, 1924.
b. Oct 3, 1897 in Paris, France
d. Dec 24, 1982 in Paris, France
Source: *CasWL; ClDMEL; ConLC 3; EncWL; EvEuW; IntWW 74; LongCTC; ModRL; ModWD; OxEng; OxFr; Pen EUR; REn; TwCA, SUP; TwCW; Who 74; WhoTwCL; WhoWor 74*

Arama, Greg
see: Amboy Dukes, The

Aramburu, Pedro Eugenio
Argentine. Statesman
b. May 21, 1903 in Buenos Aires, Argentina
d. Jul 16, 1970 in Timote, Argentina
Source: *CurBio 57, 70; NewYTBE 70; WhAm 5*

Arbour, Al(ger)
Canadian. Hockey Player, Coach
Won three straight Stanley Cups as coach of NY Islanders.
b. Nov 1, 1932 in Sudbury, ON
Source: *WhoHcky 73*

Arbuckle, "Fatty" (Roscoe Conkling)
[William B Goodrich, pseud.]
American. Comic, Silent Film Director
Involved in famous Hollywood manslaughter scandal, 1921.
b. Mar 24, 1887 in Smith Center, Kansas
d. Jun 29, 1933 in Los Angeles, California
Source: *BiDFilm; Film 1; FilmgC; MotPP; MovMk; OxFilm; TwYS; WhAm 1; WhScrn 74, 77; WhoHol B; WorEFlm*

Arbus, Diane
American. Photographer
b. Mar 14, 1923 in New York, New York
d. Jul 26, 1971 in New York, New York
Source: *NewYTBE 72; WhAm 5*

Arbuzov, Aleksandr
Russian. Chemist
b. 1877
d. Jan 22, 1968 in Kalzan, U.S.S.R.
Source: *BioIn 8*

Arcaro, (George) Eddie (Edward)
American. Journalist, Former Jockey
First jockey to win horseracing's triple crown twice.
b. Feb 19, 1916 in Cincinnati, Ohio
Source: *CelR 73; CurBio 58; WebAB; WhoAm 82*

Archer, Anne
American. Actress
b. 1948? in Los Angeles, California
Source: *IntMPA 81; WhoHol A*

Archer, Jules
American. Author
b. Jan 27, 1915 in New York, New York
Source: *AuBYP; ConAu 9R; ConLC 12; SmATA 4*

Archibald, Joseph Stopford
American. Cartoonist
b. Sep 2, 1898 in Newington, New Hampshire
Source: *ConAu 9R, 5NR; SmATA 3*

Archibald, Nate (Nathaniel)
"Tiny"
American. Basketball Player
Led NBA in scoring, assists, 1973.
b. Apr 18, 1948 in Bronx, New York
Source: *CelR 73; NewYTBE 72, 73; WhoAm 74, 76, 78, 80, 82; WhoBbl 73*

Archimedes
Greek. Mathematician
Found gold content of Hiero's crown by measuring displacement in water.
b. 287?BC
d. 212BC
Source: *CasWL; DcEnL; NewC; Pen CL; REn*

Archipenko, Alexander Porfirievich
American. Artist
b. 1887 in Kiev, Russia
d. Feb 25, 1964 in New York, New York
Source: *CurBio 53, 64; DcCAA 71; REn; WhAm 4*

Arden, Elizabeth
[Florence Nightingale Graham]
American. Cosmetic Manufacturer
Pioneered advertising of beauty aids.
b. Dec 31, 1884 in Woodbridge, ON
d. Oct 18, 1966 in New York, New York
Source: *CurBio 57, 66; InWom; WebAB; WhAm 4*

Arden, Eve
[Eunice Quedens]
American. Actress
Starred in "Our Miss Brooks" on radio and TV, 1948-56.
b. Apr 30, 1912 in Mill Valley, California
Source: *BiE&WWA; CmMov; EncMT; FilmgC; InWom; IntMPA 77, 78, 79, 80, 81, 82; MovMk; NotNAT; ThFT; WhoAm 74, 76, 78, 80, 82; WhoThe 77*

Arden, John
English. Dramatist
Is placed with or above Osborne, Pinter in brilliance, importance to generation.
b. Oct 26, 1930 in Barnsley, England
Source: *Au&Wr 71; CasWL; CnMD; CnThe; ConAu 17R; ConDr 73; ConLC 6, 13, 15; CroCD; IntWW 74; LongCTC; McGEWD; ModBrL SUP; ModWD; NewC; NotNAT; OxThe; Pen ENG; REnWD; TwCW; WebE&AL; Who 74; WhoThe 77; WhoTwCL; WhoWor 74; WorAu; WrDr 76*

Arditi, Luigi
Italian. Opera Composer, Conductor
b. Jul 22, 1822 in Crescentino, Italy
d. May 1, 1903 in Hove, England
Source: *WebBD 80*

Ardizzone, Edward Jeffrey Irving
English. Author, Illustrator
Illustrated more than 120 books; official war artist, 1940-45.
b. Oct 16, 1900 in Haiphong, Indonesia
d. Nov 8, 1979 in London, England
Source: *Au&ICB; Au&Wr 71; AuBYP; ConAu 5R, 89; IlsCB 1946, 1957; IntWW 74; LongCTC; MorJA; PiP; SmATA 1; WhoChL; WhoWor 74*

Ardon, Mordecai
[Max Bronstein]
Israeli. Artist
b. Jul 13, 1896 in Tuchnow, Poland
Source: *ConArt; IntWW 74, 75, 76, 77; PseudN; WhoWor 74*

Ardrey, Robert
American. Scientist, Author
Studied with Thornton Wilder, 1930-35; novels focus on human evolution.
b. Oct 16, 1908 in Chicago, Illinois
d. Jan 14, 1980 in Kalk Bay, South Africa
Source: *AmAu&B; BiE&WWA; BlkAW; CnMD; ConAu 33R, 93; ConDr 73; ModWD; NotNAT; TwCA SUP; WhoAm 74; WhoWor 74; WorEFlm; WrDr 76*

Arellano, Juan de
Spanish. Artist
b. 1614 in Sontorcaz, Spain
d. 1676 in Madrid, Spain
Source: *McGDA*

Arendt, Hannah
German. Author, Philosopher, Historian
b. Oct 14, 1906 in Hannover, Germany
d. Dec 4, 1975 in New York, New York
Source: *AmAu&B; CelR 73; ConAu 21R, 61; InWom; IntWW 74; Pen AM; REn; WebAB; WhAm 6; WhoAm 74; WhoWor 74; WhoWorJ 72; WorAu; WrDr 76*

Aretino, Pietro
Italian. Author
b. Apr 20, 1492 in Arezzo, Italy
d. Oct 21, 1556 in Venice, Italy
Source: *AtlBL; BiD&SB; CasWL; CnThe; CyWA; DcEuL; EuAu; EvEuW; McGEWD; NewC; OxEng; OxThe; Pen EUR; REn; REnWD*

Argelander, Friedrich Wilhelm August
German. Astronomer
b. Mar 22, 1799 in Memel, Prussia
d. Feb 17, 1875 in Bonn, Prussia
Source: *AsBiEn; DcScB; NewCol 75; WebBD 80*

Argent, Rod
see: Argent

Argent
[Rod Argent; Robert Henrit; Jim Rodford; John Verity]
English. Rock Group
Source: *ConMuA 80; LilREn 78; RkOn 2; WhoRock 81*

Argentinita
[Lopez Encarmacion]
Spanish. Dancer
b. Mar 25, 1905 in Buenos Aires, Argentina
d. Sep 24, 1945
Source: *InWom*

Argerich, Martha
Argentine. Musician
b. 1941
Source: *BioIn 7, 8, 9; WhoMus 72*

Arguello, Alexis
Nicaraguan. Boxer
b. Apr 12, 1952 in Managua, Nicaragua
Source: *BioIn 11*

Arias, Roberto Emilio
Panamanian. Lawyer, Editor, Diplomat
b. 1918
Source: *BioIn 5, 6, 7; IntWW 74, 75, 76, 77, 78; Who 74; WhoWor 74*

Arieti, Silvano
American. Psychoanalyst, Author
b. Jun 28, 1914 in Pisa, Italy
d. Aug 7, 1981 in New York, New York
Source: *AmM&WS 79P; ConAu 21R, 104; NewYTBS 81; WhoAm 80*

Ariosto, Ludovico
Italian. Poet
b. Sep 8, 1474
d. Jul 6, 1533 in Ferrara, Italy
Source: *AtlBL; BbD; BiD&SB; CasWL; CyWA; DcEuL; EuAu; McGEWD; NewC; OxEng; Pen EUR; RComWL*

Arisman, Marshall
American. Artist, Illustrator
b. 1939? in Jamestown, New York
Source: *NF*

Aristophanes
Greek. Author, Dramatist
Master comic poet of ancient world; wrote 40 plays, 11 survived.
b. 448BC
d. 385BC
Source: *AtlBL; BbD; BiD&SB; CasWL; CnThe; CyWA; DcEnL; McGEWD; NewC; OxEng; Pen CL; RComWL; REn; REnWD*

Aristotle
Greek. Author, Philosopher
Member Plato's Academy, 367-347 BC; created Logic, the science of reasoning.
b. 384BC
d. 322BC
Source: *AtlBL; BbD; BiD&SB; CasWL; CnThe; CyWA; DcEnL; DcEuL; NewC; OxEng; OxThe; Pen CL; RComWL; REn; REnWD*

Arius
Liberian. Theologian
b. 256
d. 336
Source: *REn*

Arizin, Paul
"Pitchin' Paul"
American. Basketball Player
Scored career total of 16,266 points.
b. Apr 9, 1928 in Philadelphia, Pennsylvania
Source: *BioIn 2, 9; WhoBbl 73*

Arkin, Alan Wolf
American. Actor, Motion Picture Director
Won Tony Award, 1963, for *Enter Laughing.*
b. Mar 26, 1934 in New York, New York
Source: *AmSCAP 66; BiE&WWA; BkPepl; CelR 73; EncFCWM 69; FilmgC; IntMPA 75, 76, 77, 78, 79, 80, 81, 82; MovMk; NotNAT; WhoAm 74, 76, 78, 80, 82; WhoThe 77; WhoWor 74*

Arkwright, Sir Richard
English. Inventor
Patented spinning frame, 1769, which increased cloth production.
b. Dec 23, 1732 in Preston, England
d. Aug 3, 1792 in Nottinghamshire, England
Source: *McGEWB; NewCol 75*

Arledge, Roone Pinckney
American. TV Executive
President, ABC News, ABC Sports; changed sports with slow-stop action, split-screens.
b. Jul 8, 1931 in Forest Hills, New York
Source: *WhoAm 74, 76, 78, 80, 82*

Arlen, Harold
American. Songwriter
Won Oscar, 1939, for best song, "Over the Rainbow," from *The Wizard of Oz.*
b. Feb 15, 1905 in Buffalo, New York
Source: *AmSCAP 66; BiE&WWA; CelR 73; CurBio 55; EncMT; FilmgC; IntMPA 75, 76, 77, 78, 79, 80, 81, 82; NewCBMT; NotNAT; OxFilm; PlP&P; WebAB; WhoAm 74; WhoThe 77; WhoWor 74*

Arlen, Michael
English. Author
b. Nov 16, 1895 in Roustchouk, Bulgaria
d. Jun 25, 1956 in New York, New York
Source: *DcLEL; EncMys; EvLB; LongCTC; ModBrL; Pen ENG; REn; TwCA, SUP; TwCW; WhAm 3*

Arlen, Richard
[Richard Cornelius van Mattimore]
American. Actor
b. Sep 1, 1899 in Charlottesville, Virginia
d. Mar 28, 1976 in North Hollywood, California
Source: *FilmEn; FilmgC; IntMPA 75; MovMk; TwYS*

Arletty
[Arlette-Leonie Bathiat]
French. Actress
b. May 15, 1898 in Courbevoie, France
Source: *BiDFilm; FilmgC; InWom; MovMk; OxFilm; WhoHol A; WorEFlm*

Arliss, George
[George Augustus Andrews]
English. Actor
b. Apr 10, 1868 in London, England
d. Feb 5, 1946 in London, England
Source: *DcAmB S4; FamA&A; FilmEn; FilmgC; MovMk; NewC; OxFilm; OxThe; TwYS; WhAm 2; WhScrn 74, 77; WorEFlm*

Armani, Giorgio
Italian. Fashion Designer
Founded Giorgio Armani Co, 1975.
b. 1934? in Piacenza, Italy
Source: *BioIn 12; CurBio 83; WhoAm 82*

Armatrading, Joan
British. Singer, Songwriter
Acoustic-based album, *Joan Armatrading,* best seller in England, 1976.
b. Dec 9, 1950 in Saint Kitts, West Indies
Source: *IlEncRk; NewWmR*

Armendariz, Pedro
Mexican. Actor
Starred in over 75 films.
b. May 9, 1912 in Mexico City, Mexico
d. Jun 18, 1963 in Los Angeles, California
Source: *FilmEn; Film 2; MotPP; MovMk; NotNAT B; WhScrn 74, 77; WorEFlm*

Armetta, Henry
Italian. Actor
b. Jul 4, 1888 in Palermo, Sicily
d. Oct 21, 1945 in San Diego, California
Source: *CurBio 45; FilmgC; MovMk; TwYS; Vers A; WhScrn 74, 77; WhoHol B*

Arminius, Jacobus
Dutch. Theologian
b. Oct 10, 1560 in Oudewater, Netherlands
d. Oct 19, 1609 in Leiden, Netherlands
Source: *NewC*

Armitage, Kenneth
English. Sculptor
Bronze abstracts noted for suggestions of liberty, movement.
b. Jul 18, 1916 in Leeds, England
Source: *CurBio 57; IntWW 74; Who 74; WhoWor 74*

Armour, Jenner
Dominican. President
Source: *NF*

Armour, Norman
American. Diplomat
Career foreign service officer, serving in a dozen countries.
b. Oct 4, 1887 in Brighton, England
d. Sep 27, 1982 in New York, New York
Source: *CurBio 45, 82; DcAmDH; NewYTBS 82; PolProf E; PolProf T*

Armour, Philip Danforth
American. Businessman
Started Armour and Co., major meat packer; estimated worth $50 million at death.
b. May 16, 1832 in Stockbridge, New York
d. Jan 29, 1901 in Pasadena, California
Source: *AmBi; ApCAB SUP; DcAmB; NewCol 75; TwCBDA; WebAB*

Armour, Richard Willard
American. Author, Educator
b. Jul 15, 1906 in San Pedro, California
Source: *AmAu&B; AnCL; Au&Wr 71; AuBYP; ChPo, S1, S2; ConAu 1R, 4NR; REnAL; SmATA 14; WhoAm 82; WrDr 76*

Armstrong, Anne Legendre
[Mrs. Tobin Armstrong]
American. Educator, Government Official
Ambassador to UK, 1976-77.
b. Dec 27, 1927 in New Orleans, Louisiana
Source: *AmM&WS 73S; BioNews 74; CelR 73; ConAu 13R; NewYTBE 72, 73; WhoAm 74, 76, 78, 80, 82; WhoAmP 73; WhoS&SW 73*

Armstrong, Bess (Elizabeth Key)
American. Actress
b. Dec 11, 1953 in Baltimore, Maryland
Source: *BioIn 11*

Armstrong, Charlotte
American. Author
b. May 2, 1905 in Vulcan, Michigan
d. Jul 18, 1969 in Glendale, California
Source: *AmAu&B; ConAu 1R, 25R, 3NR; CurBio 46, 69; EncMys; InWom; WhAm 5; WorAu*

Armstrong, Edwin Howard
American. Inventor, Electrical Engineer
Constructed first FM radio station, 1937, in Alpine, NJ.
b. Dec 18, 1891 in New York, New York
d. Feb 1, 1954
Source: *CurBio 40, 54; DcAmB S5; WebAB; WhAm 3*

Armstrong, Garner Ted
American. Evangelist
b. 1930 in Eugene, Oregon
Source: *BkPepl; WhoRel 75*

Armstrong, George Edward
Canadian. Hockey Player
Center, Toronto, 1949-71; Hall of Fame, 1975.
b. Jul 6, 1930 in Skead, ON
Source: *WhoHcky 73*

Armstrong, Hamilton Fish
American. Journalist
b. Apr 7, 1893 in New York, New York
d. Apr 24, 1973 in Manhattan, New York
Source: *AmAu&B; ConAu 41R, 93; CurBio 48, 73; TwCA, SUP; WhAm 5; WhNAA; WhoWor 74*

Armstrong, Harry
American. Composer
b. Jul 22, 1879 in Somerville, Massachusetts
d. Feb 28, 1951 in Bronx, New York
Source: *AmSCAP 66; CurBio 51*

Armstrong, Henry
"Homicide Hank"
American. Boxer, Evangelist
b. Dec 12, 1912 in Columbus, Mississippi
Source: *WhoBox 74*

Armstrong, Lil(lian Hardin)
American. Jazz Musician
Suffered fatal heart attack in concert honoring ex-husband, Louis Armstrong.
b. Feb 3, 1902 in Memphis, Tennessee
d. Aug 27, 1971 in Chicago, Illinois
Source: *CmpEPM; WhoJazz 72*

Armstrong, Louis Daniel
"Satchmo"
American. Musician, Band Leader
Called world's greatest trumpeter; introduced "scat" singing.
b. Jul 4, 1900 in New Orleans, Louisiana
d. Jul 6, 1971 in New York, New York
Source: *AmSCAP 66; ConAu 29R; CurBio 44, 66, 71; FilmgC; MovMk; NewCol 75; NewYTBE 70, 71; WebAB; WhAm 5; WhScrn 74, 77; WhoHol B; WhoJazz 72*

Armstrong, Neil Alden
American. Businessman, Former Astronaut
First man to walk on moon, Jul 20, 1969.
b. Aug 5, 1930 in Wapakoneta, Ohio
Source: *AmM&WS 73P; CelR 73; CurBio 79; IntWW 74; WebAB; Who 74; WhoAm 74, 76, 78, 80, 82; WhoGov 72; WhoMW 74; WhoS&SW 73; WhoWor 74*

Armstrong, Otis
American. Football Player
b. Nov 11, 1950 in Chicago, Illinois
Source: *WhoFtbl 74*

Armstrong, Robert
American. Actor
Starred in *King Kong,* 1933 as hunter who brings ape to civilization.
b. Nov 20, 1896 in Saginaw, Michigan
d. Apr 20, 1973 in Santa Monica, California
Source: *FilmEn; FilmgC; HolP 30; MovMk; TwYS; Vers B; WhScrn 77; WhoHol B*

Armstrong, William Howard
American. Author, Educator
b. Sep 14, 1914 in Lexington, Virginia
Source: *AuBYP; AuNews 1; ChlLR 1; ConAu 21R; MorBMP; SmATA 4; ThrBJA; WhoAm 74, 76, 78, 80, 82; WhoE 74; WrDr 76*

Armstrong, William L
American. Senator
b. Mar 16, 1937 in Fremont, Nebraska
Source: *AlmAP 78, 80; BioIn 9; CngDr 74, 77, 79; WhoAm 74, 76, 78, 80, 82; WhoGov 75, 77; WhoWest 74, 76, 78*

Armstrong-Jones, Antony Charles Robert
[Earl of Snowden]
English. Photographer
b. Mar 7, 1930 in London, England
Source: *BioIn 5, 6, 7, 8, 9, 10, 11; CurBio 60; WhoWor 74, 76, 78; WorFshn*

Arnaud, Georges d'
Dutch. Philosopher
b. 1711
d. 1765
Source: *McGEWD*

Arnaz, Desi
[Desiderio Alberto Arnaz de Acha, III]
American. Band Leader, Actor
Formed Desilu Productions with Lucille Ball, 1950.
b. Mar 2, 1917 in Santiago, Cuba
Source: *CurBio 52; FilmEn; FilmgC; IntMPA 76, 77, 78, 79, 80, 81, 82; WhoAm 74; WhoHol A*

Arnaz, Desi, Jr.
American. Actor
Sang with rock group, Dino, Desi, and Billy.
b. Jan 19, 1953 in Los Angeles, California
Source: *IntMPA 75, 76, 77, 78, 79, 80, 81, 82; WhoHol A*

Arnaz, Lucie Desiree
[Mrs. Lawrence Luckinbill]
American. Actress, Singer
Starred *The Jazz Singer,* 1980; *They're Playing Our Song* on Broadway.
b. Jul 17, 1951 in Hollywood, California
Source: *BioIn 9; WhoAm 82*

Arndt, Adolf
German. Jurist, Legislator
b. 1904
d. 1974
Source: *BioIn 10*

Arness, James
American. Actor
Starred in TV series "Gunsmoke," 1955-75; brother of Peter Graves.
b. May 26, 1923 in Minneapolis, Minnesota
Source: *CelR 73; CurBio 73; FilmEn; FilmgC; IntMPA 76, 77, 78, 79, 80, 81, 82; MotPP; MovMk; WhoAm 74, 76, 78, 80, 82; WhoHol A*

Arnett, Judd
American. Journalist
b. Nov 11, 1911 in Russell, Kentucky
Source: *WhoAm 74*

Arno, Peter
[Curtis Arnoux Peters]
American. Cartoonist
b. Jan 8, 1904 in New York, New York
d. Feb 22, 1968 in Port Chester, New York
Source: *AmAu&B; ConAu 25R, 73; CurBio 52, 68; LongCTC; WebAB; WhAm 4*

Arnold, Benedict
American. Army Officer, Traitor
Sensitive to slightest criticism; offered military information to British, 1779.
b. Jan 14, 1741 in Norwich, Connecticut
d. Jun 14, 1801 in London, England
Source: *AmBi; ApCAB; DcAmB; Drake; EncAB-H; OxAmL; OxCan; REn; REnAL; TwCBDA; WebAB; WhAm H*

Arnold, Carroll Clyde
American. Author, Teacher
b. Apr 29, 1912 in Lake Park, Iowa
Source: *DrAS 74E; WhoAm 74*

Arnold, Danny
[Arnold Rothman]
American. TV, Motion Picture Producer
President, Four D Productions, 1958--; produced "Barney Miller," 1973-81.
b. Jan 23, 1925 in New York, New York
Source: *IntMPA 75, 76, 77, 78, 79, 80, 81; NewYTET; WhoAm 78, 80, 82*

Arnold, Eddy
"The Tennessee Plowboy"
American. Singer
Country Music Hall of Fame, 1966; entertainer of year, 1967.
b. May 15, 1918 in Henderson, Tennessee
Source: *CelR 73; CurBio 70; EncFCWM 69; IntMPA 75, 76, 77, 78, 79, 80, 81, 82; WhoAm 74, 76, 78, 80, 82*

Arnold, Edward
[Gunter Edward Arnold Schneider]
American. Actor
Starred in *Diamond Jim,* 1935; *Sutter's Gold,* 1936.
b. Feb 18, 1890 in New York, New York
d. Apr 26, 1956 in San Fernando, California
Source: *Film 1; FilmgC; MovMk; Vers A; WhAm 3; WhScrn 74, 77*

Arnold, Edwin
English. Orientalist
b. 1832
d. 1904
Source: *Alli, SUP; BbD; BiD&SB; BrAu 19; Chambr 3; ChPo, S1, S2; DcEnA, AP; DcEnL; DcEuL; DcLEL; EvLB; LongCTC; NewC; OxEng; REn*

Arnold, Harvey Dalton
see: Outlaws, The

Arnold, Henry Harley
"Hap"
American. Military Leader
First general of Air Force, 1949; used air power as weapon during WW II.
b. Jun 25, 1886 in Gladwyne, Pennsylvania
d. Jan 15, 1950 in Sonoma, California
Source: *AmAu&B; CurBio 42, 50; DcAmB S4; WebAB; WhAm 2*

Arnold, James
see: Four Lads, The

Arnold, Sir Malcolm
English. Composer
b. Oct 21, 1921 in Northampton, England
Source: *CmMov; DcCM; FilmgC; IntWW 74; OxFilm; Who 74; WhoMus 72; WhoWor 74; WorEFlm*

Arnold, Matthew
English. Author, Poet, Critic
Wrote *Empedocles on Etna and Other Poems,* 1852; poetry professor, Oxford, 1857-67.
b. Dec 24, 1822 in Laleham, England
d. Apr 15, 1888 in Liverpool, England
Source: *Alli, SUP; AtlBL; BbD; BiD&SB; BrAu 19; CasWL, ; ChPo, S1, S2; CnE&AP; CrtT 3; CyWA; DcEnA, AP; DcEnL; DcEuL; DcLEL; EvLB; MouLC 4; NewC; OxAmL; OxEng; OxThe; Pen ENG; RAdv 1; RComWL; REn; REnAL; WebE&AL*

Arnold, Oren
American. Children's Author
b. Jul 20, 1900 in Minden, Texas
Source: *ConAu 5R, 2NR; SmATA 4*

Arnold, Thomas
English. Educator
Developed modern British schools with introduction of math, modern language.
b. Jun 13, 1795 in Cowles, Isle of Wight
d. Jun 12, 1842 in Rugby, England
Source: *Alli; BbD; BiD&SB; BrAu 19; CasWL; ChPo; DcEnA; DcEnL; DcEuL; DcLEL; EvLB; NewC; OxEng; Pen ENG; REn*

Arnold, Thurman Wesley
American. Lawyer
b. Jun 2, 1891 in Laramie, Wyoming
d. Nov 7, 1969 in Alexandria, Virginia
Source: *AmAu&B; ConAu P-1; CurBio 40, 69; REnAL; TwCA SUP; WebAB; WhAm 5*

Arnot, Robert Burns
American. Physician, Musician, Sportsman
b. Feb 23, 1948 in Boston, Massachusetts
Source: *BioIn 12*

Arnoux, Rene
Auto Racer
Source: *NF*

Arnstein, Bobbie
American. Hugh Hefner's Secretary
b. 1940
d. Jan 1975 in Chicago, Illinois
Source: *BioIn 10*

Aroldingen, Karin von
[Karin Awny Hannelore Reinbold von Aroldingen und Eltzingen]
German. Dancer
With New York City Ballet, 1962--.
b. Jul 9, 1941 in Greiz, Germany
Source: *CurBio 83*

Aronson, Boris
American. Scenic Designer
b. Oct 15, 1900 in Kiev, Russia
Source: *BiE&WWA; CelR 73; NotNAT; OxThe; PlP&P; WhoAm 74; WhoAmA 73; WhoThe 77; WhoWor 74; WhoWorJ 72*

Arp, Hans
[Jean Arp]
French. Author, Sculptor
Representative of Dadaist movement; wrote *Dreams and Projects,* 1952.
b. Sep 16, 1887 in Strasbourg, France
d. Jun 7, 1966 in Basel, Switzerland
Source: *AtlBL; CasWL; ConAu 25R, 81; CurBio 54, 66; EncWL; ModGL; OxGer; Pen EUR; REn; WhAm 4; WhoTwCL*

Arquette, Cliff
[Charley Weaver]
American. Actor
Best remembered for appearances on game show "Hollywood Squares."
b. Dec 28, 1905 in Toledo, Ohio
d. Sep 23, 1974 in Burbank, California
Source: *AmAu&B; AmSCAP 66; ConAu 53; CurBio 61, 74; NewYTBS 74; WhScrn 77; WhoHol B*

Arrabal, Fernando
Moroccan. Author, Poet, Dramatist
b. Aug 11, 1932 in Melilla, Morocco
Source: *CasWL; CnMD; CnThe; ConLC 2, 9, 18; CroCD; CurBio 72; EncWL; McGEWD 1; ModWD; NewYTBE 70, 72; Pen EUR; REnWD; TwCW; WhoAm 74; WhoThe 77; WhoWor 74; WorAu*

Arran, Arthur Kattendyke
English. Journalist, Politician
b. Jul 5, 1910
Source: *Who 74*

Arrau, Claudio
Chilean. Musician
b. Feb 6, 1903 in Chillan, Chile
Source: *CelR 73; CurBio 42; IntWW 74; Who 74; WhoAm 82; WhoMus 72; WhoWor 74*

Arrhenius, Svante August
Swedish. Chemist
b. Feb 19, 1859 in Uppsala, Sweden
d. Oct 2, 1927
Source: *NewCol 75; WebBD 80*

Arriaga, Juan Crisostomo
Spanish. Composer
b. Jan 27, 1806 in Bilbao, Spain
d. Jan 17, 1826 in Paris, France
Source: *Baker 78; BioIn 7*

Arriola, Gus
Mexican. Comic Strip Artist
b. Jul 23, 1917 in Florence, Arizona
Source: *WhoAm 82; WorECom*

Arroyo, Martina
American. Opera Singer
Leading soprano, Metropolitan Opera, NY.
b. Feb 2, 1940 in New York, New York
Source: *CurBio 71; NewYTBE 72; WhoAm 74, 76, 78, 80, 82; WhoBlA 75; WhoMus 72; WhoWor 74*

Artaud, Antonin
French. Actor, Director, Poet
Closely identified with "Theater of Cruelty"; died in insane asylum.
b. Sep 4, 1896 in Marseilles, France
d. Mar 4, 1948 in Paris, France
Source: *CasWL; CnThe; ConAu 104; CroCD; EncWL; EvEuW; LongCTC; McGEWD; ModRL; ModWD; OxFilm; OxThe; Pen EUR; REn; REnWD; TwCW; WhScrn 77; WhoTwCL; WorAu; WorEFlm*

Artemisia
Persian. Queen to Mausolus
d. 350?BC
Source: *InWom*

Arthur, King
British. Legendary King
Source: *BioIn 10; WebBD 80*

Arthur, Beatrice
[Bernice Frankel]
American. Actress
Starred in TV series "Maude," 1972-78.
b. May 13, 1926 in New York, New York
Source: *BiE&WWA; BkPepl; CelR 73; CurBio 73; EncMT; IntMPA 75, 76, 77, 78, 79, 80, 81, 82; MotPP; NotNAT; WhoAm 74, 76, 78, 80, 82; WhoAmW 77; WhoThe 77*

Arthur, Chester Alan
American. 21st US President
Succeeded James Garfield, 1881; supported civil service reform.
b. Oct 5, 1829 in Fairfield, Vermont
d. Nov 18, 1886 in New York, New York
Source: *AmBi; ApCAB; BiDrAC; BiDrUSE; DcAmB; EncAB-H; OxAmL; REnAL; TwCBDA; WebAB; WhAm H; WhAmP*

Arthur, Jean
[Gladys Georgianna Greene]
American. Actress
b. Oct 17, 1908 in New York, New York
Source: *BiDFilm; BiE&WWA; CmMov; CurBio 45; FilmgC; InWom; IntMPA 75, 76, 77, 78, 79, 80, 81, 82; MovMk; NewYTBE 72; NotNAT; OxFilm; ThFT; TwYS; WhoHol A; WhoThe 77; WorEFlm*

Arthur, Joseph Charles
American. Botanist
b. Jan 11, 1850 in Lowville, New York
d. Apr 30, 1942 in Brook, Indiana
Source: *BioIn 2, 6; CurBio 42; DcAmB S3; WhAm 2*

Artsybashev, Mikhail Petrovich
Russian. Author, Dramatist
Believed in only two realities--sex and death.
b. Oct 18, 1878 in Kharkov, Russia
d. Mar 3, 1927 in Warsaw, Poland
Source: *BioIn 1, 5; CasWL; ClDMEL; CnMD; CyWA; DcRusL; EncWL; EvEuW; ModWD; REn; TwCA, SUP*

Artzybasheff, Boris Mikhailovich
American. Author, Illustrator
b. May 25, 1899 in Kharkov, Russia
d. Jul 16, 1965
Source: *AmAu&B; AnCL; AuBYP; ChPo S2; ConICB; CurBio 45, 65; IlsCB 1744; JBA 34, 51; SmATA 14; Str&VC 4; WhAm 4; WhoGrA*

Arundel, Honor Morfydd
Welsh. Author
Books deal with emotional problems of adolescence.
b. Aug 15, 1919 in Wales
d. Jun 8, 1973 in Hume-by-Kelso, Scotland
Source: *Au&Wr 71; ConAu 21R, 41R; ConAu P-2; ConLC 17; SmATA 4, 24*

Arutumian, Rouben Ter
see: Ter-Arutumian, Rouben

Arvey, Jacob Meyer
American. Political Leader
b. Nov 3, 1895 in Chicago, Illinois
d. Aug 25, 1977 in Chicago, Illinois
Source: *BioIn 1, 2, 3, 9, 11; NewYTBS 77; WhAm 7; WhoAm 74, 76, 78*

Arzner, Dorothy
American. Motion Picture Director
b. Jan 3, 1900 in San Francisco, California
d. Oct 1, 1979 in La Quinta, California
Source: *BioIn 3, 10, 11; DcFM; FilmgC; IntMPA 75, 76, 77, 78, 79; OxFilm; TwYS; WhoAmW 61; WomWMM*

Asbury, Francis
American. Religious Leader
First bishop of Methodist Episcopal Church consecrated in America.
b. Aug 20, 1745 in Staffordshire, England
d. Mar 31, 1816 in Spotsylvania, Virginia
Source: *AmAu&B; AmBi; ApCAB; BiDSA; DcAmB; DcNAA; OxAmL; REnAL; TwCBDA; WebAB; WhAm H*

Ascari, Alberto
Italian. Auto Racer
b. 1918
d. 1955
Source: *BioIn 3*

Asch, Sholem
Polish. Dramatist, Author
Novels of Jewish life are classics in Yiddish literature.
b. Nov 1, 1880 in Kutno, Poland
d. Jul 10, 1957 in London, England
Source: *AmAu&B; AmNov; CasWL; ClDMEL; CnDAL; CnMD; CnThe; CyWA; LongCTC; McGEWD; ModWD; OxAmL; Pen AM; REn; REnAL; REnWD; TwCA, SUP; TwCW; WhAm 3; WhoLA*

Ascoli, Max
Italian. Educator, Author, Editor
b. Jun 25, 1898 in Ferrara, Italy
d. Jan 1, 1978 in New York, New York
Source: *AmAu&B; BioIn 1, 3, 11; ConAu 77; CurBio 54, 78; LinLib L; NewYTBS 78; WhAm 7; WhoAm 74, 76, 78*

Asencio, Diego Cortes
American. Diplomat-Hostage in Colombia
b. Jul 15, 1931 in Nijar, Spain
Source: *WhoAm 80*

Ash, Mary Kay Wagner
American. Cosmetics Company Executive
Founder, chairman, Mary Kay Cosmetics, 1963--based in Dallas, TX.
b. in Hot Wells, Texas
Source: *BusPN; St&PR 75; WhoAm 80, 82; WhoAmW 74, 77*

Ash, Roy Lawrence
"Human Computer"
American. Corporation Executive
Co-founder Litton Industries, 1953; director, OMB, 1972.
b. Oct 20, 1918 in Los Angeles, California
Source: *CelR 73; CurBio 68; IntWW 74; NewYTBE 71, 72; NewYTBS 74; WhoAm 74, 76, 78, 80, 82; WhoAmP 73; WhoF&I 74; WhoWor 74*

Ashbery, John Lawrence
American. Author
b. Jul 28, 1927 in Rochester, New York
Source: *AmAu&B; ConLC 2, 3, 4, 6, 9, 13, 15; ConP 70, 75; CroCAP; DrAP 75; ModAL SUP; Pen AM; RAdv 1; WebE&AL; WhoAm 74, 76, 78, 80, 82; WorAu; WrDr 76*

Ashbrook, John Milan
American. Businessman, Politician
Elected senator from OH, 1960; owned newspaper *The Johnston Independent*.
b. Sep 21, 1928 in Johnston, Ohio
d. Apr 24, 1982 in Newark, Ohio
Source: *BiDrAC; CngDr 74, 77, 79; CurBio 73, 82; NewYTBS 82; WhoAm 74, 76, 78, 80, 82; WhoAmP 73, 75, 77, 79; WhoGov 72, 75, 77; WhoMW 74, 76, 78*

Ashburn, Don Richie
"Whitey"
American. Baseball Player
Played 731 consecutive games, 1950-54.
b. Mar 19, 1927 in Tilden, Nebraska
Source: *BaseEn; BioIn 2, 3, 4, 5, 6, 8; WhoProB 73*

Ashby, Hal
American. Motion Picture Director
Directed *Shampoo,* 1975; *Coming Home,* 1978.
b. 1936 in Ogden, Utah
Source: *BioIn 10; FilmEn; FilmgC; IntMPA 81; WhoAm 80, 82*

Ashcroft, Dame Peggy
English. Actress
b. Dec 22, 1907 in Croydon, England
Source: *BiE&WWA; CurBio 63; FilmEn; FilmgC; IntWW 74; NewC; NotNAT; OxThe; PIP&P; Who 74; WhoHol A; WhoThe 77; WhoWor 74*

Ashe, Arthur
American. Tennis Player
First black player to win men's single title at Wimbledon, 1975.
b. Jul 20, 1943 in Richmond, Virginia
Source: *BioNews 74; BkPepl; ConAu 65; CurBio 66; WebAB; WhoAm 74, 76, 78, 80, 82; WhoBlA 75; WhoS&SW 73*

Ashe, Geoffrey Thomas
English. Author
b. Mar 29, 1923 in London, England
Source: *Au&Wr 71; SmATA 17; WhoWor 74; WrDr 76*

Asher, Peter
see: Peter and Gordon

Ashford, Daisy
English. Author
b. 1881 in Petersham, England
d. Jan 15, 1972 in Norwich, England
Source: *CarSB; ConAu 33R; DcLEL; EvLB; LongCTC; NewYTBE 72; Pen ENG; REn; SmATA 10; WhoChL*

Ashford, Emmett Littleton
American. Baseball Umpire
b. Nov 13, 1916 in Los Angeles, California
d. 1980 in Marina del Rey, California
Source: *BioIn 3, 7, 11, 12; WhoProB 73*

Ashford, Evelyn
[Mrs. Ray Washington]
American. Track Athlete
b. Apr 15, 1957 in Shreveport, Louisiana
Source: *BioIn 12*

Ashford, Nickolas
American. Singer, Songwriter
Wrote song "Ain't No Mountain High Enough," recorded by The Supremes.
b. May 4, 1942 in Fairfield, South Carolina
Source: *AmSCAP 80; BioIn 10, 11; WhoAm 82*

Ashkenasi, Shmuel
Israeli. Musician
b. 1941
Source: *BioIn 7*

Ashkenazy, Vladimir Davidovich
Russian. Musician
b. Jul 6, 1937 in Gorki, U.S.S.R.
Source: *BioNews 75; CurBio 67; IntWW 74; NewYTBE 72; Who 74; WhoAm 82; WhoMus 72; WhoWor 74*

Ashley, Elizabeth
[Elizabeth Ann Cole]
American. Actress
Won Tony Award, 1962; films include *The Carpet Baggers,* 1963.
b. Aug 30, 1941? in Ocala, Florida
Source: *BiE&WWA; FilmgC; IntMPA 77, 78, 79, 80, 81, 82; MovMk; NewYTBS 74; NotNAT; WhoAm 74, 76, 78, 80, 82; WhoHol A; WhoThe 77*

Ashley, Laura
Welsh. Designer
b. 1926? in Wales
Source: *WorFshn*

Ashley, Merrill
[Linda Merrill]
American. Ballerina
b. 1950 in Saint Paul, Minnesota
Source: *BioIn 11; CurBio 81; NewYTBS 81; WhoAm 82*

Ashley, Thomas William Ludlow
"Lud"
American. Congressman
b. Jan 11, 1923 in Toledo, Ohio
Source: *AlmAP 78, 80; BiDrAC; CngDr 74, 77, 79; CurBio 79; NewYTBS 77; PolProf J; PolProf NF; WhoAm 74, 76, 78, 80; WhoAmP 73, 75, 77, 79; WhoGov 72, 75, 77; WhoMW 74, 76, 78*

Ashley, William Henry
American. Fur Trapper, Public Official
Instituted trappers rendezvous, 1824; congressman, 1831-37.
b. Mar 26, 1778 in Powhatan County, Virginia
d. Mar 26, 1838 in Boonville, Missouri
Source: *AmBi; ApCAB; BiAuS; BiDrAC; DcAmB; Drake; EncAB-H; McGEWB; NewCol 75; OxAmL; REnAW; TwCBDA; WebAB; WhAm H; WhAmP*

Ashman, Matthew
see: Bow Wow Wow

Ashmore, Harry Scott
American. Editor, Author
b. Jul 27, 1916 in Greenville, South Carolina
Source: *AmAu&B; ConAu 17R; CurBio 58; WhoAm 74, 76, 78, 80, 82; WhoWest 74; WhoWor 74*

Ashton, Sir Frederick
English. Choreographer, Dancer
b. Sep 17, 1906 in Guayaquil, Ecuador
Source: *CurBio 51; IntWW 74; NewYTBE 70; Who 74; WhoMus 72; WhoThe 77; WhoWor 74*

Ashton-Warner, Sylvia
New Zealander. Author, Teacher
b. Dec 17, 1908 in Stratford, New Zealand
Source: *ConAu 69; ConNov 76; LongCTC; Pen ENG; RAdv 1; TwCW; WorAu; WrDr 76*

Asia
[Geoffrey Downes; Steve Howe; Carl Palmer; John Wetton]
British. Rock Group
Source: *NF*

Asimov, Isaac
[Paul French, pseud.]
American. Author, Biochemist
Author of over 200 books; coined term "robotics."
b. Jan 2, 1920 in Petrovichi, U.S.S.R.
Source: *AmAu&B; AmM&WS 73P, 76P, 79P; AsBiEn; Au&Wr 71; AuBYP; CasWL; CelR 73; ConAu 1R, 2NR; ConLC 3, 9; ConNov 72, 76; ConSFA; DcLEL 1940; DrAF 76; EncMys; EncSF; IntAu&W; IntWW 77, 78, 79, 80, 81; LinLib L, S; LongCTC; NewCol 75; Pen AM; REn; REnAL; ScF&FL 1, 2; SmATA 1; ThrBJA; TwCW; WebAB; WebE&AL; WhoAm 74, 76, 78, 80, 82; WhoE 74; WhoSciF; WhoWor 74, 76, 78; WorAu; WrDr 76, 80*

Askew, Reubin O'Donovan
American. Government Official
b. Sep 11, 1928 in Muskogee, Oklahoma
Source: *BioNews 74; CurBio 73; IntWW 74; NewYTBE 72; WhoAm 74, 76, 78, 80, 82; WhoAmP 73; WhoGov 72*

Asner, Ed(ward)
American. Actor
President, Screen Actors Guild, 1981--; has won six Emmys.
b. Nov 15, 1929 in Kansas City, Missouri
Source: *BkPepl; CurBio 78; FilmgC; IntMPA 77, 78, 79, 80, 81, 82; NewYTBE 73; WhoAm 74, 76, 78, 80, 82; WhoHol A*

Asoka the Great
Indian. King of Magadha
b. 300BC
d. 232BC
Source:

Asplund, Erik Gunnar
Swedish. Architect
b. 1885 in Stockholm, Sweden
d. 1940
Source: *NewCol 75*

Asquith, Anthony
English. Motion Picture Director
Directed *The Importance of Being Earnest,* 1952.
b. Nov 9, 1902 in London, England
d. Feb 20, 1968 in London, England
Source: *BiDFilm; CmMov; DcFM; FilmEn; MovMk; OxFilm; WhAm 5; WhScrn 74, 77; WorEFlm*

Asquith, Herbert
English. Author, Poet
b. Mar 11, 1881
d. Aug 5, 1947 in Bath, England
Source: *BkCL; ChPo, S1, S2; LongCTC; NewC; Str&VC; WhoLA*

Asquith, Herbert Henry
see: Oxford and Asquith, Henry Herbert Asquith, Earl

Assad, Hafez al
Syrian. President
Minister of Defense, 1966-70; led coup d'etat that made him president, 1971.
b. 1928 in Qardaha, Syria
Source: *CurBio 75; IntWW 74, 75, 76, 77, 78, 79, 80, 81; IntYB 79; MidE 78, 79; NewCol 75; NewYTBE 70; NewYTBS 77; WhoGov 72; WhoWor 74, 76, 78*

Assagioli, Roberto
Italian. Psychiatrist, Author
b. 1893
d. Aug 23, 1974
Source: *BiDPara; ConAu 53*

Assante, Armand
American. Actor
Played Michael Moretti in TV mini-series "Rage of Angels," 1983.
b. Oct 4, 1949 in New York, New York
Source: *BioIn 11*

Assis Chateaubriand, Francisco de
Brazilian. Journalist
Owned syndicate of newspapers, magazines in Brazil.
b. Apr 10, 1891 in Umbuzeiro, Brazil
d. 1968
Source: *BioIn 1, 2, 3, 4, 5, 6, 7, 8; CurBio 57*

Assisi, Francis of, Saint
see: Francis of Assisi, Saint

Association, The
[Gary Alexander; Ted Bluechel; Brian Cole; Russ Giguere; Terry Kirkman; Jim Yester]
American. Singing Group
Gold records for "Cherish," 1966; "Windy," 1967; "Never My Love," 1967.
Source: *BiDAmM; EncPR&S; RkOn*

Astaire, Adele
[Adele Austerlitz]
American. Dancer
Dancing partner, 1916-32, of brother Fred.
b. Sep 10, 1898 in Omaha, Nebraska
d. Jan 25, 1981 in Scottsdale, Arizona
Source: *AmPS; BiE&WWA; CmpEPM; EncMT; Film 1; InWom; NotNAT; PlP&P; WhThe*

Astaire, Fred
[Frederick Austerlitz]
American. Actor, Dancer, Singer
Has won nine Emmys; Lifetime Achievement Award, American Film Institute, 1981.
b. May 10, 1899 in Omaha, Nebraska
Source: *AmPS B; AmSCAP 66; BiDFilm; BiE&WWA; BkPepl; CelR 73; CmMov; CmpEPM; CurBio 45, 64; EncMT; EncWT; Film 1; IntMPA 75, 76, 77, 78, 79, 80, 81, 82; LinLib S; MGM; MotPP; MovMk; NewCol 75; NewYTBE 73; NewYTBS 79; NewYTET; NotNAT; OxFilm; PlP&P; WebAB; WhThe; Who 74; WhoAm 74, 76, 78, 80, 82; WhoHol A; WhoMus 72; WhoWor 74, 78; WorEFlm*

Asther, Nils
Swedish. Actor
b. Jan 17, 1901 in Malmo, Sweden
d. Oct 13, 1981 in Stockholm, Sweden
Source: *FilmEn; FilmgC; MotPP; MovMk; TwYS; WhoHol A*

Astin, John Allen
American. Actor, Director, Writer
Played Gomez Addams on "The Addams Family," 1964-66; married to Patty Duke.
b. Mar 30, 1930 in Baltimore, Maryland
Source: *BioNews 74; FilmgC; IntMPA 75, 76, 77, 78, 79, 80, 81, 82; WhoAm 74, 76, 78, 80, 82; WhoHol A*

Astor, John Jacob
American. Fur Trader, Financier
Chartered American Fur Company; wealthiest man in US at his death.
b. Jul 17, 1763 in Heidelberg, Germany
d. Mar 29, 1848 in New York, New York
Source: *AmBi; ApCAB; DcAmB; Drake; EncAB-H; OxAmL; LinLib S; MacDCB 78; McGEWB; NatCAB 8; NewCol 75; OxAmL; OxCan; REn; REnAL; REnAW; TwCBDA; WebAB; WhAm H*

Astor, Mary
[Lucille Vasconcellos Langhanke]
American. Actress
Played Brigid O'Shaughnessy in *The Maltese Falcon* opposite Bogart.
b. May 3, 1906 in Quincy, Illinois
Source: *AmAu&B; BiDFilm; BiE&WWA; CelR 73; ConAu 5R; CurBio 61; Film 2; FilmgC; InWom; IntMPA 75, 76, 77, 78, 79, 80, 81, 82; MGM; MotPP; MovMk; NotNAT A; OxFilm; ThFT; TwYS; WhoAmW 64, 66, 68, 70, 72, 74; WhoHol A; WorEFlm*

Astor, Nancy Witcher (Langhorne) Astor, Viscountess
[Mrs. William Waldorf Astor]
English. Political Leader
First woman to sit in House of Commons, 1919-45.
b. May 19, 1879 in Greenwood, Virginia
d. May 2, 1964 in Lincoln, England
Source: *CurBio 40, 64; InWom; LinLib L, S; NewCol 75; WhAm 4*

Astor, Vincent
American. Financier
b. Nov 15, 1891 in New York, New York
d. Feb 3, 1959 in New York, New York
Source: *WhAm 3; WhAmP*

Astor, William Waldorf Astor, Viscount
British. Financier
Founded *Pall Mall Magazine;* British subject, 1899, viscount, 1917.
b. Mar 31, 1848 in New York, New York
d. Jan 18, 1919 in Brighton, England
Source: *AmAu; AmAu&B; AmBi; BbD; BiD&SB; CyAl 2; DcAmAu; DcAmB; DcBiA; DcNAA; LinLib L, S; NatCAB 8; TwCBDA; WhAm 1*

Astrid
Norwegian. Princess
b. 1932
Source: *InWom*

Asturias, Miguel Angel
Guatemalan. Author, Diplomat
b. Oct 19, 1899 in Guatemala City, Guatemala
d. Jun 9, 1974 in Madrid, Spain
Source: *CasWL; ConAu 25R, 49; ConAu P-2; ConLC 3, 8, 13; CurBio 68, 74; EncWL; IntWW 74; NewYTBS 74; Pen AM; TwCW; WhAm 6; Who 74; WhoTwCL; WhoWor 74; WorAu*

Atahualpa
Peruvian. Last King of Incas
b. 1500
d. Aug 29, 1533
Source: *ApCAB; Drake; McGEWB; REn*

Ataturk, Kemal
[Mustafa Kemal]
Turkish. President
b. 1880 in Salonika, Turkey
d. Nov 10, 1938
Source: *BioIn 10; NewCol 75; WebBD 80*

Atchison, David R
American. Senator
b. Aug 11, 1807 in Frogtown, Kentucky
d. Jun 26, 1886 in Gower, Missouri
Source: *ApCAB; BiDrAC; DcAmB; TwCBDA*

Atget, Eugene
French. Photographer
b. 1855
d. 1927 in Paris, France
Source: *BioIn 11; NewYTBS 81*

Athenagoras I
Greek. Archbishop of Constantinople
b. Mar 25, 1886 in Vassilikon, Greece
d. Jul 6, 1972
Source: *CurBio 49, 72; NewYTBE 72; WhoWor 74*

Atherton, Alfred LeRoy, Jr.
American. Government Official
Joined foreign service, 1947; ambassador to Egypt, 1979--.
b. Nov 22, 1921 in Pittsburgh, Pennsylvania
Source: *MidE 79; NewYTBS 77; USBiR 74; WhoAm 74, 76, 78, 80, 82; WhoAmP 75, 77, 79; WhoGov 72, 75, 77*

Atherton, Gertrude Franklin
American. Author
b. Oct 30, 1857 in San Francisco, California
d. Jun 14, 1948 in San Francisco, California
Source: *Alli SUP; AmAu&B; AmWomWr; ApCAB SUP; BbD; BiD&SB; CasWL; Chambr 3; CnDAL; ConAmA; ConAmL; CurBio 40, 48; DcAmB S4; DcEnA; DcLEL; DcNAA; EncSF; EvLB; InWom; LibW; LinLib L, S; LongCTC; NatCAB 10, 36; NotAW; OxAmL; OxEng; Pen; RAdv 1; REn; REnAL; REnAW; ScF&FL 1; TwCA, SUP; TwCLC; WhAm 2; WhE&EA; WhLit; WhNAA; WhoHr&F; WomWWA 14*

Atherton, William
[William Atherton Knight, II]
American. Actor
b. Jul 30, 1947 in New Haven, Connecticut
Source: *WhoHol A; WhoThe 81*

Athlone, Countess of
see: Alice, Princess

Atkins, Chet (Chester B)
"Mr. Guitar"
American. Musician, Record Co. Executive
Vice-president, country division, RCA records; has won several Grammys.
b. Jun 20, 1924 in Luttrell, Tennessee
Source: *BiDAmM; BioNews 75; CelR 73; CurBio 75; EncFCWM 69; NewYTBS 74; WhoAm 74, 76, 78, 80, 82*

Atkins, Christopher
American. Actor
Co-starred with Brooke Shields in *The Blue Lagoon,* 1980.
b. Feb 1961 in Rye, New York
Source: *BioIn 12*

Atkins, Susan Denise
American. Murderer, Member of Manson Cult
Convicted, with Charles Manson, of Tate-LaBianca murders; sentenced to death.
b. 1948
Source: *BioIn 8, 9, 10, 11*

Atkinson, (Justin) Brooks
American. Drama Critic, Journalist
b. Nov 28, 1894 in Melrose, Massachusetts
Source: *AmAu&B; BiE&WWA; CelR 73; ConAu 61; CurBio 42, 61; IntWW 74; NewYTBE 73; NotNAT; OxAmL; OxThe; REnAL; TwCA, SUP; WebAB; WhNAA; Who 74; WhoAm 74, 76, 78, 80, 82; WrDr 76*

Atkinson, Ted
American. Jockey
Source: *NewYTBE 73*

Atkinson, Ti-Grace
American. Feminist
b. 1939
Source: *BioIn 8, 9*

Atlanta Rhythm Section
[Barry Bailey; J R Cobb; Dean Daugherty; Paul Goddard; Ronnie Hammond; Robert Nix]
American. Rock Group
Source: *IlEncRk; RkOn*

Atlas, Charles
[Angelo Siciliano]
American. Physical Fitness Specialist
Developed dynamic tension method of body-building.
b. Oct 30, 1894 in Acri, Italy
d. Dec 23, 1972 in Long Beach, New York
Source: *WebAB*

Attenborough, David Frederick
British. Author, Naturalist
b. May 8, 1926 in London, England
Source: *Au&Wr 71; ConAu 1R; IntAu&W 77; IntWW 75, 76, 77, 78; Who 74; WhoWor 76, 78; WrDr 76, 80*

Attenborough, Sir Richard Samuel
English. Actor, Producer, Director
b. Aug 29, 1923 in Cambridge, England
Source: *BiDFilm; CelR 73; CmMov; FilmgC; IntMPA 75, 76, 77, 78, 79, 80, 81, 82; IntWW 74; MotPP; MovMk; OxFilm; Who 74; WhoAm 74, 76, 78, 80, 82; WhoHol A; WhoThe 77; WhoWor 74; WorEFlm*

Atterbury, Grosvenor
American. Architect
b. Jul 7, 1869 in Detroit, Michigan
d. Oct 18, 1956 in Long Island, New York
Source: *BioIn 3, 4; BnEnAmA; DcAmB S6; WhAm 3*

Attila
"Scourge of God"
King of the Huns
Known for his cruelty and ruthlessness.
b. 406
d. 453
Source: *NewC; OxGer; REn*

Attlee, Clement Richard Attlee, Earl
English. Labour Party Leader
b. Jan 3, 1883 in London, England
d. Oct 8, 1967 in London, England
Source: *CurBio 40, 47, 67; LongCTC*

Attucks, Crispus
American. Revolutionary Patriot
First colonist to be killed at Boston Massacre, March 5, 1770.
b. 1723
d. Mar 5, 1770 in Boston, Massachusetts
Source: *ApCAB; DcAmB; Drake; REn; TwCBDA; WebAB; WhAm H*

Attwood, William
American. Publisher, Journalist
b. Jul 14, 1919 in Paris, France
Source: *AmAu&B; ConAu 21R; CurBio 68; IntWW 74; WhoAm 74, 76, 78, 80, 82; WhoF&I 74*

Atwater, Edith
American. Actress
b. Apr 22, 1911 in Chicago, Illinois
Source: *BiE&WWA; NotNAT; WhoHol A; WhoThe 77*

Atwill, Lionel
English. Actor
b. Mar 1, 1885 in Croydon, England
d. Apr 22, 1946 in Hollywood, California
Source: *CmMov; CurBio 46; Film 1; FilmgC; MotPP; MovMk; REn; Vers A; WhAm 2; WhScrn 74, 77; WhoHol B*

Atwood, Angela
[S(ymbionese) L(iberation) A(rmy)]
American. Revolutionary
b. 1948?
d. May 24, 1974 in Los Angeles, California
Source: *BioIn 10; NewYTBS 74*

Atwood, Margaret Killam
Canadian. Author, Poet
Canadian wilderness plays large part in her writings.
b. Nov 18, 1939 in Ottawa, ON
Source: *Au&Wr 71; CanWW 82; ConAu 49, 3NR; ConLC 2, 3, 4, 8, 13, 15; ConNov 76; ConP 70, 75; DrAF 76; DrAP 75; OxCan, SUP; WhoAm 74; WrDr 76*

Auber, Daniel Francois Esprit
French. Opera Composer
b. Jan 19, 1782 in Caen, France
d. May 12, 1871 in Paris, France
Source: *AtlBL; OxFr; REn*

Auberjonois, Rene
American. Actor
b. Jun 1, 1940 in New York, New York
Source: *FilmEn; FilmgC; NotNAT; WhoAm 80, 82; WhoThe 77, 81*

Aubrey, James Thomas, Jr.
American. Broadcasting, Movie Executive
b. Dec 14, 1918 in LaSalle, Illinois
Source: *CelR 73; CurBio 72; IntMPA 75, 76, 77, 78, 79, 80, 81, 82; WhoAm 74; WhoF&I 74*

Aubrey, John
English. Author, Antiquary
b. Mar 12, 1626 in Easton Pierce, England
d. Jun 1697 in Oxford, England
Source: *Alli; AtlBL; BrAu; CasWL; Chambr 1; CroE&S; DcEnA; DcEnL; DcLEL; EvLB; MouLC 1; NewC; OxEng; Pen ENG; REn; WebE&AL*

Auchincloss, Hugh D
American. Businessman
Stepfather of Jacqueline Onassis.
b. 1897
d. Nov 20, 1976 in Washington, DC
Source: *St&PR 75*

Auchincloss, Louis
[Andrew Lee, pseud.]
American. Lawyer, Author
Wrote over 30 books, including *The Indifferent Children,* 1947.
b. Sep 27, 1917 in Lawrence, New York
Source: *AmAu&B; Au&Wr 71; CelR 73; ConAu 1R; ConLC 4, 6, 9, 18; ConNov 72, 76; CurBio 54; DrAF 76; IntWW 74; ModAL, SUP; OxAmL; Pen AM; RAdv 1; REn; REnAL; TwCW; WebE&AL; Who 74; WhoAm 74, 76, 78, 80, 82; WhoWor 74; WorAu; WrDr 76*

Auchinleck, Sir Claude
"The Auk"
British. Field Marshal
b. Jun 21, 1884 in Aldershot, England
d. Mar 23, 1981 in Marrakech, Morocco
Source: *AnObit 1981; NewYTBS 81; PseudN; Who 74; WhoWor 74, 76, 78*

Auden, W(ystan) H(ugh)
English. Poet, Critic, Dramatist
Described as "versatile, vigorous, and technically facile poet."
b. Feb 21, 1907 in York, England
d. Sep 28, 1973 in Vienna, Austria
Source: *AmAu&B; AmSCAP 66; Au&Wr 71; BiE&WWA; CasWL; CelR 73; Chambr 3; ChPo, S1, S2; CnE&AP; CnMD; CnMWL; ConAu 9R, 45, 5NR; ConDr 73; ConLC 1, 2, 3, 4, 6, 9, 11, 14; ConP 75; CurBio 73; CyWA; DcLEL; EncWL; EvLB; LongCTC; McGEWD; ModAL, SUP; ModBrL, SUP; ModWD; NewC; NewYTBE 71, 72, 73; OxAmL; OxEng; Pen ENG; PlP&P; RAdv 1; RComWL; REn; REnAL; TwCA, SUP; TwCW; WebE&AL; WhoTwCL*

Audiberti, Jacques
French. Author
b. 1899
d. Jul 10, 1965 in Paris, France
Source: *CasWL; ClDMEL; CnMD; CnThe; ConAu 25R; CroCD; EncWL; EvEuW; McGEWD; ModWD; OxFr; OxThe; Pen EUR; REn; WorAu*

Audran, Stephane
[Mrs. Claude Chabrol]
French. Actress
b. 1939 in Versailles, France
Source: *FilmEn; FilmgC; IntMPA 81; OxFilm; WhoHol A*

Audubon, John James
American. Author, Ornithologist, Artist
Bird drawings called masterpieces; sometimes not scientifically accurate.
b. Apr 26, 1785 in Haiti
d. Jan 27, 1851 in New York, New York
Source: *AfroAA; Alli; AmAu; AmAu&B; AmBi; AtlBL; BbD; BiD&SB; BiDSA; CnDAL; CyAL 1; DcAmAu; DcAmB; DcLEL; DcNAA; EncAB-H; MouLC 3; OhA&B; OxAmL; OxCan; OxEng; Pen AM; REn; REnAL; WebAB; WhAm H*

Auel, Jean Marie
American. Author
Wrote *The Clan of the Cave Bear,* 1980, *The Valley of Horses,* 1982.
b. Feb 18, 1936 in Chicago, Illinois
Source: *BioIn 12; ConAu 103; NewYTBS 80*

Auer, Leopold
Hungarian. Musician, Teacher
b. Jun 7, 1845 in Vesprem, Hungary
d. Jul 15, 1930 in Loschwitz, Germany
Source: *AmSCAP 66; WhAm 1*

Auer, Mischa
[Mischa Ounskowski]
Russian. Actor, Comic
b. Nov 17, 1905 in Saint Petersburg, Russia
d. Mar 5, 1967 in Rome, Italy
Source: *FilmEn; FilmgC; MovMk; TwYS; Vers A; WhScrn 74, 77; WhoHol B*

Auerbach, "Red" (Arnold Jacob)
American. Basketball Coach
Coach of year, 1965; career record 1,037-548; Hall of Fame, 1968.
b. Sep 20, 1917 in Brooklyn, New York
Source: *CelR 73; ConAu 17R; CurBio 69; WhoAm 74, 76, 78, 80, 82; WhoBbl 73; WhoE 74*

Auerbach-Levy, William
American. Artist
b. Feb 14, 1889 in Brest-Litovsk, Russia
d. Jun 29, 1964
Source: *CurBio 48, 64; NatCAB 51; WhAm 4*

Auger, Brian
English. Rock Musician
b. 1939 in London, England
Source: *ConMuA 80; EncJzS 70; WhoRock 81*

August, Jan
[Jan Augustoff]
American. Musician, Band Leader
b. 1912? in New York, New York
d. Jan 18, 1976 in New York, New York
Source: *BioIn 10; CmpEPM; NewYTBS 76*

Augustine, Saint
[Aurelius Augustinus]
Roman. Christian Philosopher
Writings established foundations for medieval catholicism, protestantism.
b. 354 in Agaste, Numidia
d. 430 in Hippo, Numidia
Source: *AtlBL; BbD; BiD&SB; CasWL; CyWA; NewC; OxEng; Pen CL; RComWL; REn*

Augustus
[Octavius Caesar]
Roman. First Roman Emperor
Returned Rome to constitutional rule after death of Caesar, 44BC.
b. Sep 23, 63BC in Rome, Italy
d. Aug 19, 14BC
Source: *AtlBL; BbD; BiD&SB; CasWL; CyWA; NewC; Pen CL; RComWL; REn*

Augustus II
[Frederick Augustine I]
Polish. King
b. May 12, 1670 in Dresden, Germany
d. Feb 1, 1733
Source: *WebBD 80*

Augustyn, Frank Joseph
Canadian. Ballet Dancer
b. Jan 27, 1953 in Hamilton, ON
Source: *BioIn 9; WhoAm 78, 80, 82*

Aulaire, Edgar Parin d'
American. Author, Illustrator
b. Sep 30, 1898 in Munich, Germany
Source: *AnCL; ConAu 49; CurBio 40; JBA 51; SmATA 5*

Aulaire, Ingri Mortenson d'
American. Author, Illustrator
b. Dec 27, 1904 in Kongsberg, Norway
d. Oct 24, 1980 in Wilton, Connecticut
Source: *AnCL; ConAu 49, 102; InWom; JBA 34, 51; SmATA 5, 24*

Ault, George Christian
American. Artist
b. Oct 11, 1891 in Cleveland, Ohio
d. Dec 30, 1948 in Woodside, New York
Source: *BioIn 4, 11; DcAmArt; DcCAA 71, 77; IlBEAAW; McGDA; NatCAB 40*

Aumont, Jean-Pierre
[Jean-Pierre Salomons]
French. Actor, Author
Brother of Francois Villiers; wrote *Sun and Shadow,* 1976 (autobiography).
b. Jan 5, 1909 in Paris, France
Source: *BiE&WWA; ConAu 29R; FilmgC; IntMPA 75, 76, 77, 78, 79, 80, 81, 82; MotPP; MovMk; NotNAT; WhoAm 74, 76, 78, 80, 82; WhoHol A; WhoThe 77*

Aurangzeb
Indian. Emperor
Last Mogul emperor of India, 1658-1707; contributed to collapse of empire.
b. Oct 24, 1618 in Dohad, India
d. Feb 20, 1707
Source: *LinLib S; McGEWB; NewCol 75*

Auric, Georges
French. Composer, Opera Manager
b. Feb 15, 1899 in Lodeve, France
Source: *DcFM; FilmgC; IntWW 74; OxFilm; REn; Who 74; WhoWor 74; WorEFlm*

Auriol, Jacqueline Douet
French. Aviatrix
First woman test pilot; second woman to break sound barrier.
b. Nov 5, 1917 in Challans, France
Source: *CurBio 53; HerW; InWom; WhoWor 74*

Auriol, Vincent
French. President
First president of Fourth Republic, 1947-54; leader of Socialist Party.
b. Aug 25, 1884 in Revel, France
d. Jan 1, 1966 in Paris, France
Source: *CurBio 47, 66; WhAm 4*

Auslander, Joseph
American. Author
b. Oct 11, 1897 in Philadelphia, Pennsylvania
d. Jun 22, 1965 in Coral Gables, Florida
Source: *AmAu&B; ChPo, S1; CnDAL; OxAmL; REn; REnAL; TwCA, SUP; WhNAA*

Austen, Jane
English. Author
Wrote *Pride and Prejudice,* 1813.
b. Dec 16, 1775 in Steventon, England
d. Jul 18, 1817 in Winchester, England
Source: *Alli; AtlBL; BbD; BiD&SB; BrAu 19; CasWL; Chambr 2; CrtT 2; CyWA; DcBiA; DcEnA; DcEnL; DcEuL; DcLEL; EvLB; HerW; InWom; MouLC 2; NewC; OxEng; Pen ENG; RAdv 1; RComWL; REn; WebE&AL*

Austin, Saint
[Saint Augustine (of Canterbury)]
Italian. Archbishop
d. 605
Source: *NewCol 75; WebBD 80*

Austin, Alfred
English. Poet
b. May 30, 1835 in Headingley, England
d. Jun 2, 1913 in Ashford, England
Source: *Alli SUP; BbD; BiD&SB; BrAu 19; Chambr 3; ChPo, S1, S2; DcEnA, AP; DcEnL; DcEuL; DcLEL; EvLB; LongCTC; NewC; OxEng; Pen ENG; TwCW*

Austin, Gene
American. Actor, Songwriter
b. Jun 24, 1900
d. Jan 24, 1972 in Palm Springs, California
Source: *AmSCAP 66; NewYTBE 72; WhScrn 77; WhoHol B*

Austin, Herbert
English. Auto Manufacturer
b. Nov 8, 1866 in Missenden, England
d. May 23, 1941 in Bromsgrove, England
Source: *BioIn 12; WebBD 80*

Austin, James Clayton
American. Author
b. Nov 27, 1923 in Kansas City, Missouri
Source: *ConAu 13R; DrAS 74E*

Austin, John Langshaw
English. Philosopher
b. Mar 26, 1911
d. Feb 8, 1960
Source: *LongCTC; OxEng; WhAm 4*

Austin, John Paul
American. Soft Drink Executive
Chairman, 1970-81; president, 1962-81 of Coca-Cola Co.
b. Feb 14, 1915 in LaGrange, Georgia
Source: *CelR 73; St&PR 75; WhoAm 74, 76, 78, 80, 82; WhoF&I 74; WhoS&SW 73*

Austin, Mary Hunter
American. Author
b. Sep 9, 1868 in Carlinville, Illinois
d. Aug 13, 1934 in Santa Fe, New Mexico
Source: *AmAu&B; AmBi; AmLY; AnCL; BiCAW; BkCL; ChPo, S1, S2; CnDAL; ConAmA; ConAmL; DcAmAu; DcLEL; DcNAA; InWom; NotAW; OxAmL; REnAL; Str&VC; TwCA, SUP; WebAB; WhAm 1; WhNAA*

Austin, Stephen Fuller
American. Texas Colonizer
Established Austin, TX, 1822, first American settlement in TX.
b. Nov 3, 1793 in Austinville, Virginia
d. Dec 27, 1836 in Austin, Texas
Source: *AmAu&B; AmBi; ApCAB; DcAmB; Drake; EncAB-H; REnAL; TwCBDA; WebAB; WhAm H; WhAmP*

Austin, Tracy Ann
American. Tennis Player
Youngest player to crack million dollar prize money barrier.
b. Dec 12, 1962 in Rolling Hills, California
Source: *BioIn 10; BkPepl; WhoAm 82*

Austin, Warren R
American. Statesman
b. Nov 12, 1877 in Highgate, Vermont
d. Dec 25, 1962
Source: *BiDrAC; CurBio 44, 63; WhAm 4; WhAmP*

Austral, Florence Wilson
Australian. Opera Singer
b. Apr 26, 1894 in Melbourne, Australia
d. May 15, 1968 in Sydney, Australia
Source: *InWom*

Autori, Franco
Italian. Conductor
b. Nov 29, 1903 in Naples, Italy
Source: *WhoAm 74*

Autry, (Orvon) Gene
American. Actor, Singer, Broadcasting Exec.
Owner, California Angels, pro baseball team.
b. Sep 29, 1907 in Tioga, Texas
Source: *AmSCAP 66; CmMov; CurBio 47; EncFCWM 69; FilmgC; IntMPA 75, 76, 77, 78, 79, 80, 81, 82; MotPP; MovMk; OxFilm; WhoAm 74, 76, 78, 80, 82; WhoHol A; WhoProB 73; WorEFlm*

Avakian, George
American. Jazz Writer, Critic
b. Mar 15, 1919 in Amavir, U.S.S.R.
Source: *WhoWor 74*

Avallone, Michael Angelo, Jr.
American. Author
b. Oct 27, 1924 in New York, New York
Source: *Au&Wr 71; ConAu 5R, 4NR; EncMys; WhoAm 82; WrDr 76*

Avalon, Frankie
[Francis Thomas Avalone]
American. Actor, Singer
Teen idol in 1960's; starred with Annette Funicello in *Beach* movies.
b. Sep 18, 1940 in Philadelphia, Pennsylvania
Source: *FilmgC; IntMPA 75, 76, 77, 78, 79, 80, 81, 82; MotPP; MovMk; WhoHol A*

Avedon, Doe
American. Actress
b. 1925 in Old Westbury, New York
Source: *InWom; IntMPA 75, 76, 77; WhoHol A*

Avedon, Richard
American. Fashion Photographer
b. May 15, 1923 in New York, New York
Source: *CelR 73; CurBio 75; IntWW 74; WhoAm 74, 76, 78, 80, 82; WhoWor 74; WorFshn*

Average White Band
[Roger Ball; Malcolm Duncan; Steven Ferrone; Alan Gorrie; Onnie M]
English. Rock Band
Source: *IlEncRk; RkOn*

Averback, Hy
American. Motion Picture Director, Producer
b. 1925
Source: *FilmEn; FilmgC*

Averroes
Spanish. Philosopher
b. 1126 in Cordova, Spain
d. 1198
Source: *BbD; BiD&SB; CasWL; DcEuL; DcOrL 3; EuAu; EvEuW; OxEng; REn*

Avery, Milton C
American. Artist
b. Mar 7, 1893 in Altmar, New York
d. Jan 3, 1965 in New York, New York
Source: *CurBio 58, 65; DcCAA 71; WhAm 4*

Avery, Sewell
American. Retailer
Served on board of Montgomery Ward, 1931-56.
b. Nov 4, 1874 in Saginaw, Michigan
d. Oct 31, 1960 in Chicago, Illinois
Source: *CurBio 44, 61*

Avery, "Tex" (Frederick Bean)
American. Animator
One of the creators of Bugs Bunny.
b. Feb 26, 1908 in Taylor, Texas
d. Aug 27, 1980 in Burbank, California
Source: *AnObit 1980; BioIn 11; FilmEn; FilmgC; PseudN; WorEFlm*

Avicenna (Ibn Sina)
Arabian. Physician, Philosopher
His *Canon of Medicine* studied for centuries in European universities.
b. 980 in Afshana, Arabia
d. Jun 1037
Source: *BiD&SB; CasWL; DcOrL 3; OxEng; Pen CL; REn*

Avila, Bobby (Roberto Francisco Gonzalez)
Mexican. Baseball Player
Won AL batting title, 1954.
b. Apr 2, 1924 in Vera Cruz, Mexico
Source: *BaseEn; WhoProB 73*

Avirett, John Williams, II
American. Lawyer
b. May 13, 1902 in Cumberland, Maryland
Source: *WhoAm 74, 76, 78, 80, 82*

Avogadro, Amedeo, Conte di Quaregna
Italian. Physicist
b. Jun 9, 1776 in Turin, Italy
d. Jul 9, 1856 in Turin, Italy
Source: *AsBiEn; McGEWB; NewCol 75*

Avon, Robert Anthony Eden, Earl
see: Eden, Anthony

Awtrey, Dennis
American. Basketball Player
Member, NBA championship team, Seattle Supersonics, 1979.
b. Feb 22, 1948 in Hollywood, California
Source: *OfNBA; WhoBbl 73*

Axelrod, George
American. Dramatist
Wrote plays *The Seven Year Itch* and *Breakfast at Tiffany's.*
b. Jun 9, 1922 in New York, New York
Source: *AmAu&B; BiDFilm; BiE&WWA; CmMov; CnMD; ConAu 65; ConDr 73; FilmgC; IntMPA 75, 76, 77, 78, 79, 80, 81, 82; McGEWD; ModAL; NotNAT; OxFilm; WhoAm 74; WorAu; WorEFlm; WrDr 76*

Axelson, Kenneth Strong
American. Corporation Executive
b. Jul 31, 1922 in Chicago, Illinois
Source: *St&PR 75; WhoAm 74; WhoF&I 74; WhoWor 74*

"Axis Sally"
[Mildred Elizabeth Gillars]
American. Traitor
b. 1900
Source: *BioIn 9*

Axton, Hoyt Wayne
American. Singer, Songwriter
b. Mar 25, 1938 in Duncan, Oklahoma
Source: *RkOn 2; WhoAm 76, 78, 80, 82*

Ayala, Pero Lopez de
Spanish. Poet, Historian, Statesman
b. 1332 in Victoria, Spain
d. 1407
Source: *BbD; BiD&SB; CasWL; DcEuL; DcSpL; EuAu; EvEuW; Pen EUR; REn*

Ayars, James Sterling
American. Children's Author
b. Nov 17, 1898 in Wilmette, Illinois
Source: *AuBYP; ConAu 5R, 2NR; SmATA 4; WhoMW 74; WrDr 76*

Ayckbourn, Alan
English. Dramatist
b. Apr 12, 1939 in London, England
Source: *ConAu 21R; ConLC 5, 18; CurBio 80; IntWW 79*

Ayer, Alfred Jules
English. Author, Philosopher
b. Oct 29, 1910 in London, England
Source: *ConAu 5R, 5NR; DcLEL; IntWW 74; LongCTC; OxEng; REn; Who 74; WhoWor 74; WorAu; WrDr 76*

Ayer, Francis Wayland
American. Advertising Pioneer
b. Feb 4, 1848 in Lee, Massachusetts
d. Mar 5, 1923 in Camden, New Jersey
Source: *AmBi; DcAmB; WebAB*

Ayesha
2nd Wife of Mohammad
b. 614
d. 678
Source: *NewCol 75*

Aykroyd, Dan(iel Edward)
Canadian. Actor, Comedian, Writer
Star of "Saturday Night Live"; won Emmy, 1976.
b. Jul 1, 1952 in Ottawa, ON
Source: *BioIn 12; WhoAm 80, 82*

Aylward, Gladys
English. Missionary
b. 1902 in England
d. Jan 3, 1970 in Taipei, Taiwan
Source: *BioIn 2, 4, 5, 6, 7, 8, 9, 10, 11; InWom; ObitOF 79*

Aymar, Gordon Christian
American. Artist, Art Director
b. Jul 24, 1893 in East Orange, New Jersey
Source: *Au&Wr 71; ConAu 5R; WhoAm 74; WhoAmA 73; WrDr 76*

Ayme, Marcel
French. Author
b. Mar 28, 1902 in Joigny, France
d. Oct 14, 1967 in Paris, France
Source: *BiE&WWA; CasWL; ClDMEL; CnMD; CnThe; ConAu 89; ConLC 11; EncWL; EvEuW; LongCTC; McGEWD; ModRL; ModWD; OxFr; Pen EUR; REn; TwCA SUP; TwCW; WhAm 4A*

Ayres, Agnes
[Agnes Hinkle]
American. Silent Film Actress
Starred with Rudolph Valentino in *The Shiek,* 1921.
b. Sep 4, 1898 in Carbondale, Illinois
d. Dec 25, 1940 in Los Angeles, California
Source: *CurBio 41; Film 1; FilmgC; InWom; MotPP; TwYS; WhScrn 74, 77; WhoHol B*

Ayres, Lew
American. Actor, Comedian
b. Dec 28, 1908 in Minneapolis, Minnesota
Source: *BiDFilm; FilmEn; IntMPA 75, 76, 77, 78, 79, 80, 81, 82; MovMk; OxFilm; WhoAm 82; WhoHol A; WorEFlm*

Ayub Khan, Mohammad
Pakistani. President
b. May 14, 1907 in Rehana, Pakistan
d. Apr 19, 1974
Source: *ConAu 25R; ConAu P-2; CurBio 59, 74; Who 74; WhoWor 74*

Azikiwe, Nnamdi
[Zik Azikiwe]
"Father of Modern Nigerian Nationalism"
Nigerian. Former President
b. Nov 16, 1904 in Zungeri, Nigeria
Source: *CurBio 57; IntWW 78; IntYB 79; McGEWB; PseudN; WhoModH; WhoWor 74*

Aziz, Philip John Andrew Ferris
Canadian. Artist
b. Apr 15, 1923 in Saint Thomas, ON
Source: *CanWW 70, 79; WhoWor 74*

Aznavour, Charles
[Shahnour Varenagh Aznavourian]
French. Singer, Actor
b. May 22, 1924 in Paris, France
Source: *CelR 73; CurBio 68; FilmEn; IntWW 74; MovMk; OxFilm; WhoHol A; WhoWor 74; WorEFlm*

Azuela, Mariano
Mexican. Author
b. Jan 1, 1873 in Logos de Morena, Mexico
d. Mar 1, 1952 in Mexico City, Mexico
Source: *CasWL; ConAu 104; CyWA; DcSpL; Pen AM; REn; TwCW; WhNAA; WorAu*

B

Ba'al Shem Tov, Israel
Polish. Founder of Modern Hasidism
b. 1700 in Okopy, Russia
d. 1760
Source: *CasWL*

Baader, Andreas
German. Terrorist, Revolutionary
b. 1943 in Munich, Germany
d. Oct 18, 1977 in Stuttgart, Germany (West)
Source: *BioIn 9, 10, 11; WhoModH*

Babashoff, Shirley
American. Swimmer
Won gold medals in swimming relay, 1972, 1976 Olympics.
b. Jan 31, 1957 in Whittier, California
Source: *BioIn 10; GoodHS*

Babb, Howard Selden
American. Author
b. May 14, 1924 in Portland, Maine
Source: *ConAu 13R; DrAS 74E; WhoAm 74*

Babbage, Charles
English. Mathematician, Inventor
Tried to perfect mechanical calculating machine, foreshadowing computer.
b. Dec 26, 1792 in Totnes, England
d. Oct 18, 1871 in London, England
Source: *Alli SUP; AsBiEn; BiD&SB; BioIn 1, 2, 4, 5, 6, 7, 8, 9, 10; BrAu; CelCen; DcBiPP; DcEnL; DcScB; Dis&D; InSci; LinLib; McGEWB; NewCol 75; OxMus; WorAl*

Babbitt, Benjamin Talbot
American. Soap Manufacturer, Inventor
Made one of first baking powders; obtained over 100 patents, several for soap.
b. 1809 in Westmoreland, New York
d. Oct 20, 1889 in New York, New York
Source: *DcAmB; NatCAB 8; WhAm H*

Babbitt, Bruce Edward
American. Governor
Governor of AZ, 1977--; has written two books on AZ art, culture.
b. Jun 27, 1938 in Los Angeles, California
Source: *AlmAP 80; BiDrGov; BioIn 11; ConAu 97; NewYTBS 78, 79; WhoAm 82; WhoAmP 79; WhoWest 78, 80*

Babbitt, Irving
American. Author
b. Aug 2, 1865 in Dayton, Ohio
d. Jul 15, 1933 in Cambridge, Massachusetts
Source: *AmAu&B; AmBi; AmLY; CasWL; CnDAL; ConAmA; ConAmL; DcAmB S1; DcLEL; DcNAA; EncAB-H; LongCTC; ModAL; OhA&B; OxAmL; OxEng; Pen AM; REn; REnAL; TwCA, SUP; WebAB; WebE&AL; WhAm 1; WhoTwCL*

Babbitt, Milton Byron
American. Composer
b. May 10, 1916 in Philadelphia, Pennsylvania
Source: *CurBio 62; DcCM; WebAB; WhoAm 74, 76, 78, 80, 82; WhoMus 72; WhoWor 74*

Babcock, Harold Delos
American. Astronomer
b. Jan 24, 1882 in Edgerton, Wisconsin
d. Apr 8, 1968
Source: *BioIn 8, 11; WhAm 5*

Babcock, Stephen Moulton
American. Agricultural Chemist
b. Oct 22, 1843 in Bridgewater, New York
d. Jul 2, 1931
Source: *BioIn 1, 2, 3, 5, 6*

Babel, Isaac Emmanuelovich
Russian. Author
b. 1894 in Odessa, Russia
d. 1941 in Siberia, U.S.S.R.
Source: *AtlBL; CasWL; ClDMEL; CnMD; CnMWL; DcRusL; EncWL; EvEuW; LinLib L, S; LongCTC; McGEWB; McGEWD; ModSL 1; ModWD; Pen EUR; REn; TwCA, SUP; TwCW; WhoTwCL*

Baber
Founder of Mogul Empire
b. 1482
d. 1530
Source: *NewC; WebBD 80*

Babeuf, Francois Noel
French. Revolutionary
b. Nov 25, 1760 in Saint-Quentin, France
d. Apr 27, 1797
Source: *BiD&SB; McGEWB; OxFr; REn*

Babilonia, Tai Reina
American. Figure Skater
Failed in bid for Olympic gold medal, 1980, when partner Randy Gardner was injured.
b. Sep 22, 1960 in Sherman Oaks, California
Source: *BioIn 12; NewYTBS 79*

Babin, Victor
[Vronsky and Babin]
American. Pianist
Formed two-piano team with wife Vitya Vronsky, 1933.
b. Dec 12, 1908 in Moscow, Russia
d. Mar 1, 1972 in Cleveland, Ohio
Source: *AmSCAP 66, 80; Baker 78; BiDAmM; NewYTBE 72; WhoMus 72; WhoWorJ 72, 78*

Babiuch, Edward
Polish. Premier
b. Dec 28, 1927 in Katowice Voivodship, Poland
Source: *IntWW 74, 75, 76, 77, 78; WhoSocC 78; WhoWor 74, 76, 78*

"Baby LeRoy"
[LeRoy Winebrenner]
American. Child Actor
Appeared in films with W C Fields.
b. May 12, 1932 in Los Angeles, California
Source: *FilmEn; MotPP; WhoHol A*

Babys, The
[Tony Brock; Jonathan Cain; Mike Corby; Ricky Phillips; Wally Stocker; John Waite]
English. Rock Group
Source: *ConMuA 80; RkOn 2; WhoRock 81*

Bacall, Lauren
[Betty Joan Perske]
American. Actress, Author
Married Humphrey Bogart, 1945; won Tonys, 1970, 1981, for *Applause* and *Woman of the Year.*
b. Sep 16, 1924 in New York, New York
Source: *BiDFilm; BiE&WWA; BlueB 76; BkPepl; CelR 73; CmMov; ConAu 93; CurBio 70; EncMT; FilmgC; GoodHS; InWom; IntMPA 75, 76, 77, 78, 79, 80, 81, 82; IntWW 74, 75, 76, 77, 78, 79, 80, 81; MotPP; MovMk; NewYTBE 70; NewYTBS 79, 80; NotNAT; OxFilm; WhoAm 74, 76, 78, 80, 82; WhoAmW 58, 61, 64, 66, 68, 70, 72, 74, 79; WhoHol A; WhoThe 72, 77, 81; WhoWor 74, 78; WorEFlm*

Bacardi
Spanish. Family of Distillers
Source: *WebBD 80*

Baccaloni, Salvatore
Italian. Opera Singer
b. Apr 14, 1900 in Rome, Italy
d. Dec 31, 1969 in New York, New York
Source: *CurBio 44, 70; FilmgC; NewYTBE 70; WhAm 5; WhScrn 74, 77; WhoHol B*

Bacchelli, Riccardo
Italian. Author
b. Apr 19, 1891 in Bologna, Italy
Source: *CasWL; ClDMEL; CnMD; ConAu 29R; CyWA; EncWL; EvEuW; IntWW 74; ModRL; Pen EUR; REn; TwCW; WhoWor 74; WorAu*

Bach, Barbara
[Barbara Goldbach; Mrs. Ringo Starr]
American. Actress
Married Ringo Starr, 1981, after starring together in movie *Caveman.*
b. 1949 in New York, New York
Source: *BioIn 11*

Bach, Bert Coates
American. Author
b. Dec 14, 1936 in Jenkins, Kentucky
Source: *ConAu 25R; DrAS 74E*

Bach, Carl Philipp Emanuel
German. Composer
b. Mar 8, 1714 in Weimar, Germany
d. Dec 15, 1788 in Hamburg, Germany
Source: *AtlBL*

Bach, Catherine
[Catherine Bachman]
American. Actress
Plays Daisy Duke on TV series "The Dukes of Hazzard," 1979--.
b. Mar 1, 1954 in Warren, Ohio
Source: *BioIn 12*

Bach, Johann Christian
German. Composer, Organist
b. Sep 3, 1735 in Leipzig, Germany
d. Jan 1, 1782 in London, England
Source: *AtlBL*

Bach, Johann Sebastian
German. Composer, Organist
Composed church, vocal, instrumental music, including "Goldberg Variations."
b. Mar 21, 1685 in Eisenach, Germany
d. Jul 28, 1750 in Leipzig, Germany
Source: *AtlBL; Baker 78; DcBiPP; Dis&D; LinLib S; LuthC 75; McGEWB; NewC; NewCol 75; OxGer; OxMus; REn; WorAl*

Bach, Richard David
American. Author
Wrote allegorical novel *Jonathan Livingston Seagull;* filmed, 1973.
b. Jun 23, 1936 in Oak Park, Illinois
Source: *AuNews 1; BioNews 74; ConLC 14; CurBio 73; EncO&P 78S1; Novels; ScF&FL 1, 2; SmATA 13; WhoAm 76, 78, 80; WrDr 76, 80*

Bach, Wilhelm Friedemann
German. Composer, Organist
b. 1710 in Weimar, Germany
d. 1784 in Berlin, Germany
Source: *OxMus*

Bacharach, Bert(ram Mark)
American. Journalist, Author
"Now See Here!" column syndicated, 1959; father of Burt Bacharach.
b. Mar 10, 1898 in Philadelphia, Pennsylvania
Source: *CelR 73; CurBio 57*

Bacharach, Burt
American. Composer, Musician
Won Oscar, 1970, for "Raindrops Keep Fallin' on My Head"; marriages to Angie Dickinson, Carole Bayer-Sager.
b. May 12, 1929 in Kansas City, Missouri
Source: *AmPS; AmSCAP 66, 80; Baker 78; BiDAmM; BlueB 76; BkPepl; CelR 73; CurBio 70; EncMT; FilmgC; NewCol 75; NewCBMT; NewYTBE 72; NotNAT; WebAB 79; WhoAm 74, 76, 78, 80, 82; WorAl*

Bachauer, Gina
Greek. Musician
b. May 21, 1913 in Athens, Greece
d. Aug 22, 1976 in Athens, Greece
Source: *CelR 73; CurBio 54; InWom; IntWW 74; Who 74; WhoMus 72; WhoWor 74*

Bache, Harold L
American. Businessman, Philanthropist
b. Jun 17, 1894 in New York, New York
d. Mar 14, 1968 in New York, New York
Source: *CurBio 59; WhAm 5*

Bache, Jules
American. Financier
b. Nov 9, 1861 in New York, New York
d. Mar 24, 1944 in Palm Beach, Florida
Source: *CurBio 44; DcAmB S3; WhAm 2*

Bacheller, Irving
American. Author
Wrote *Eben Holden,* 1900.
b. Aug 12, 1859 in Pierpont, New York
d. Feb 24, 1950 in White Plains, New York
Source: *AmAu&B; BiD&SB; Chambr 3; ChPo, S1, S2; ConAmL; DcAmAu; DcAmB S4; DcBiA; DcLEL; JBA 34; OxAmL; REn; TwCA SUP; WhAm 2; WhNAA*

Bachman, John
American. Naturalist, Minister
b. Feb 4, 1790 in Rhinebeck, New York
d. Feb 24, 1874
Source: *BioIn 2*

Bachman-Turner Overdrive
[Chad Allen; Randy Bachman; Robin Bachman; Timothy Bachman; Jim Clench; Blair Thornton; C F Turner]
Canadian. Rock Group
Source: *IlEncRk*

Bachrach, Fabian
Photographer
b. 1881
d. Jul 24, 1963 in Boston, Massachusetts
Source: *BioIn 6*

Backe, John David
American. Former TV Executive
President, CBS, Inc, 1976-80.
b. Jul 5, 1932 in Akron, Ohio
Source: *BioIn 11; CurBio 78; Dun&B 79; IntWW 77, 78, 79, 80, 81; NewYTBS 76, 77; St&PR 75; WhoAm 74, 76, 78, 80, 82; WhoE 74, 79; WhoF&I 74, 79*

Backhaus, Wilhelm
German. Musician
b. Mar 26, 1884 in Leipzig, Germany
d. Jul 5, 1969 in Villach, Austria
Source: *WhAm 5*

Backus, Isaac
American. Clergyman
b. Jan 9, 1724 in Norwich, Connecticut
d. Nov 20, 1806 in Middleborough, Connecticut
Source: *Alli; AmBi; ApCAB; BioIn 2, 3, 4, 6, 8, 9, 10; DcAmAu; DcAmB; DcAmReB; DcNAA; Drake; McGEWB; NatCAB 7; OxAmL; TwCBDA; WebAB 79; WhAm H*

Backus, Jim (James Gilmore)
American. Actor, Author
Voice of cartoon character, Mr. Magoo.
b. Feb 25, 1913 in Cleveland, Ohio
Source: *CelR 73; FilmEn; FilmgC; IntMPA 76, 77, 78, 79, 80, 81, 82; MotPP; MovMk; WhoAm 74; WhoHol A*

Backus, John
Source: *AmM&WS 79P; IntWW 77, 78; WhoAm 76, 78, 80, 82*

Baclanova, Olga
Russian. Actress
b. 1899 in Moscow, Russia
d. Sep 6, 1974 in Vevey, Switzerland
Source: *FilmEn; FilmgC; NewYTBS 74; ThFT; TwYS; WhScrn 77; WhoHol B*

Bacon, Sir Francis
English. Author, Philosopher
Wrote *Novum Organum,* on systematic analysis of knowledge, 1620.
b. Jan 22, 1561 in London, England
d. Apr 9, 1626 in Highgate, England
Source: *Alli; AsBiEn; AtlBL; BbD; BiD&SB; BrAu; BrWr; CasWL; Chambr 1; ChPo, S2; CroE&S; CrtT 1, 4; CyEd; CyWA; DcBiPP; DcEnA; DcEnL; DcEuL; DcLEL; DcScB; Dis&D; EncSF; EvLB; LinLib L, S; LongCEL; LuthC 75; McGEWB; MouLC 1; NamesHP; NewC; NewCol 75; OxEng; Pen ENG; RAdv 1; RComWL; REn; WebE&AL*

Bacon, Francis
English. Artist
b. Oct 28, 1910 in Dublin, Ireland
Source: *IntWW 74; Who 74; WhoWor 74*

Bacon, Frank
American. Actor
b. Jan 16, 1864 in Marysville, California
d. Nov 19, 1922 in Chicago, Illinois
Source: *AmAu&B; AmBi; DcAmB; DcNAA; Film 1; ModWD; OxThe; REn; REnAL; WhAm 1; WhScrn 74, 77; WhoHol B*

Bacon, Henry
American. Architect
b. Nov 28, 1866 in Watseka, Illinois
d. Feb 16, 1924 in New York, New York
Source: *AmBi; DcAmB; WhAm 1*

Bacon, Peggy
American. Illustrator
b. May 2, 1895 in Ridgefield, Connecticut
Source: *AmAu&B; ChPo; ConAu 25R; ConAu P-2; ConICB; CurBio 40; IlsBYP; IlsCB 1744, 1946, 1957; InWom; OxAmL; REnAL; SmATA 2; Str&VC; WhoAm 74, 76, 78, 80, 82; WhoAmA 73*

Bacon, Roger
English. Philosopher, Scientist
b. 1214
d. 1294
Source: *Alli; BbD; BiD&SB; BrAu; CasWL; Chambr 1; DcEnL; DcEuL; EvLB; NewC; OxEng; Pen ENG; REn*

Bacon, Virginia Murray
American. Patron of the Arts
b. 1892? in New York, New York
d. Feb 25, 1980 in Washington, DC
Source: *WhoAmW 58*

Bad Company
[Boz Burrell; Simon Kirke; Michael Ralphs; Paul Rodgers]
English. Rock Group
Source: *IlEncRk*

Baddeley, Angela
English. Actress
b. Jul 4, 1900 in London, England
d. Feb 22, 1976 in Essex, England
Source: *FilmgC; InWom; PlP&P; Who 74; WhoThe 77*

Baddeley, Hermione Clinton
English. Actress, Comedienne
Played Mrs. Bridges, the cook, in TV series "Upstairs, Downstairs."
b. Nov 13, 1906 in Broseley, England
Source: *BiE&WWA; EncMT; FilmgC; InWom; IntMPA 75, 76, 77, 78, 79, 80, 81, 82; MotPP; MovMk; Who 74; WhoAm 82; WhoHol A; WhoThe 77*

Badanjek, John "Bee"
see: Mitch Ryder and the Detroit Wheels

Baden-Powell, Lady Olave St. Claire
English. Organizer of Girl Scouts
Founded International Girl Scout Movement, 1909; wrote *Training Girls as Guides,* 1917.
b. Feb 22, 1889 in Chesterfield, England
d. Jun 26, 1977
Source: *CurBio 46; IntWW 74; Who 74; WhoWor 74*

Baden-Powell, Robert Stephenson Smyth Baden-Powell, Baron
English. Founder of English Boy Scouts
Conceived idea for Boy Scouts when he took group of English boys camping, 1908.
b. Feb 22, 1857
d. Jan 8, 1941 in Nyeri, Kenya
Source: *Alli; CurBio 41; LongCTC; MnBBF; SmATA 16; WhoChL; WhoLA*

Bader, Sir Douglas Robert Steuart
"The Chap with the Tin Legs"
British. Air Force Officer
Legless pilot who shot down at least 22 German planes during WW II.
b. Feb 21, 1910
d. Sep 5, 1982 in London, England
Source: *BioIn 3, 7; NewYTBS 82; WhWW-II; Who 74, 75, 76, 77, 78, 79, 80, 81, 82*

Badfinger
[Tom Evans; Mike Gibbons; Ronald Griffiths; Peter Ham; Joey Molland]
English. Rock Group
Source: *ConMuA 80; RkOn 2; WhoRock 81*

Badillo, Herman
American. Politician
b. Aug 21, 1929 in Caguas, Puerto Rico
Source: *CngDr 74; ConAu 85; CurBio 71; IntWW 74; NewYTBE 73; WhoAm 74, 76, 78, 80, 82; WhoAmP 73; WhoE 74; WhoGov 72*

Badoglio, Pietro
Italian. Field Marshall
b. Sep 28, 1871 in Montferrato, Italy
d. Oct 31, 1956
Source: *CurBio 40, 57*

Badura-Skoda, Paul
Austrian. Musician
b. Jan 15, 1927 in Munich, Germany
Source: *IntWW 74; WhoAm 74, 76, 78, 80, 82; WhoMus 72; WhoWor 74*

Baedeker, Karl
German. Publisher
b. 1801
d. 1859
Source: *NewC; REn*

Baekeland, Leo Hendrick
American. Chemist, Inventor
b. Nov 14, 1863 in Ghent, Belgium
d. Feb 23, 1944 in Beacon, New York
Source: *CurBio 44; DcAmB S3; WebAB; WhAm 2*

Baer, "Bugs" (Arthur)
American. Journalist
b. 1886 in Philadelphia, Pennsylvania
d. May 17, 1969 in New York, New York
Source: *REnAL; St&PR 75; WebAB; WhScrn 77; WhoHol B*

Baer, Max
American. Boxer, Actor
Won heavyweight title, 1934; starred in *The Prizefighter and the Lady.*
b. Feb 11, 1909 in Omaha, Nebraska
d. Nov 21, 1959 in Hollywood, California
Source: *FilmgC; WhScrn 74, 77; WhoBox 74; WhoHol B*

Baer, Max, Jr.
American. Actor, Producer, Director, Author
Played Jethro on "The Beverly Hillbillies," 1962-71.
b. Dec 4, 1937 in Oakland, California
Source: *WhoAm 82; WhoHol A*

Baez, Joan
American. Singer, Political Activist
Founder, 1965; vice-president, Resource Center for Non-Violence, Santa Cruz, CA.
b. Jan 9, 1941 in New York, New York
Source: *BioNews 74; BkPepl; CelR 73; ConAu 21R; CurBio 63; EncFCWM 69; InWom; NewYTBE 72; WebAB; WhoAm 74, 76, 78, 80, 82; WhoWest 74; WhoWor 74*

Baeza, Braulio
Panamanian. Jockey
b. 1940
Source: *BioIn 10*

Baffin, William
English. Navigator
Expeditions in search of the Northwest Passage led to dicovery of Baffin Bay, 1612-14.
b. 1584? in England
d. Jan 23, 1622 in Qishm, Persia
Source: *Alli; ApCAB; BiD&SB; DcEnL; Drake; NewC; OxCan*

Bagaza, Jean-Baptiste
Burundian. President
b. Aug 29, 1946
Source: *IntWW 78; WhoWor 78*

Bagdasarian, Ross S
see: Seville, David

Bagdikian, Ben H
American. Author
b. Jun 30, 1920 in Marash, Turkey
Source: *AmAu&B; ConAu 13R, 6NR; WhoAm 74; WhoS&SW 73; WhoWor 74; WrDr 76*

Bagehot, Walter
English. Author
b. Feb 23, 1826 in Langport, England
d. Mar 24, 1877 in Langport, England
Source: *Alli SUP; AtlBL; BbD; BiD&SB; BrAu 19; CasWL; Chambr 3; CrtT 3; DcEnA; DcEnL; DcEuL; DcLEL; EvLB; NewC; OxEng; Pen ENG; REn; WebE&AL*

Bagnold, Enid
[Lady Jones]
English. Author, Dramatist
b. Oct 27, 1889 in Rochester, England
d. Mar 31, 1981 in London, England
Source: *AuBYP; BiE&WWA; BioIn 2, 4, 6, 7, 8, 9, 10; CnMD; ConAu 5R, 103, 5NR; ConDr 73, 77; ConNov 76; CurBio 64, 81; DcLEL; EncWT; EvLB; FourBJA; InWom; IntAu&W 76, 77; IntWW 78; LinLib L; LongCTC; ModWD; NewC; NotNAT, A; PlP&P; REn; SmATA 1; TwCA, SUP; TwCW; WhE&EA; Who 74; WhoAmW 66, 68, 70, 72, 74; WhoChL; WhoThe 72, 77; WhoWor 74, 76, 78; WrDr 76, 80*

Bagration, Petr
Russian. Hero of Napoleonic Wars
b. 1765 in Kizlar, Russia
d. Sep 24, 1812 in Borodino, Russia
Source: *NewCol 75; WhoMilH 76*

Baha'u'llah
[Husayn Ali]
Persian. Founder of Baha'i Religion
b. 1817 in Teheran, Persia
d. 1892
Source: *BioIn 10; WebBD 80*

Bailar, Benjamin Franklin
American. Government Official
Postmaster General, 1975-78.
b. Apr 21, 1934 in Champaign, Illinois
Source: *St&PR 75; WhoAm 80, 82*

Bailey, Alice
English. Occultist
b. 1880
d. 1949
Source: *BioIn 10*

Bailey, Charles Waldo, II
American. Newspaper Editor
b. Apr 28, 1929 in Boston, Massachusetts
Source: *ConAu 1R, 1NR; WhoAm 74, 76, 78, 80, 82; WrDr 75*

Bailey, F(rancis) Lee
American. Lawyer
Defense lawyer in Patty Hearst trial.
b. Jun 10, 1933 in Waltham, Massachusetts
Source: *ConAu 89; WhoAm 74, 76, 78, 80, 82; WhoE 74*

Bailey, Henry Christopher
English. Author
b. Feb 1, 1878 in London, England
d. 1961
Source: *EvLB; LongCTC; NewC; TwCA, SUP; WhoLA*

Bailey, Jack
American. Radio, TV Host
d. Feb 1, 1980 in Santa Monica, California
Source: *BioIn 4, 12*

Bailey, James Anthony
[Barnum and Bailey]
American. Circus Owner
Founded "Greatest Show on Earth"; later merged with P T Barnum, 1881.
b. Jul 4, 1847 in Detroit, Michigan
d. 1906 in Mount Vernon, New York
Source: *Alli, SUP; DcAmB; TwCBDA; WhAm 1*

Bailey, Kay
American. Public Official
b. 1944
Source: *WomPO 76*

Bailey, Martin Jean
American. Author
b. Oct 17, 1927 in Taft, California
Source: *AmEA 74; AmM&WS 73*

Bailey, Mildred
American. Singer
b. Feb 27, 1907 in Tekoa, Washington
d. Dec 12, 1951 in New York, New York
Source: *DcAmB S5; WhoJazz 72*

Bailey, Pearl Mae
American. Singer, Actress
Special Tony award, 1967, for *Hello, Dolly;* Entertainer of the year, 1967.
b. Mar 29, 1918 in Newport News, Virginia
Source: *AmSCAP 66; BiE&WWA; CelR 73; ConAu 61; CurBio 55, 69; EncMT; FilmgC; HerW; InWom; IntMPA 75, 76, 77, 78, 79, 80, 81, 82; LivgBAA; MotPP; MovMk; NewYTBE 71; NotNAT; WhoAm 74, 76, 78, 80, 82; WhoAmW 77; WhoBlA 75; WhoHol A; WhoThe 77; WhoWor 74*

Bailey, Raymond
American. Actor
b. 1904 in San Francisco, California
d. Apr 15, 1980 in Irvine, California
Source: *FilmgC; WhoHol A*

Baillie, Hugh
American. Journalist
b. Oct 23, 1890 in Brooklyn, New York
d. Mar 1, 1966 in La Jolla, California
Source: *ConAu 89; CurBio 46, 66; WhAm 4*

Bain, Barbara
[Mrs. Martin Landau]
American. Actress
Starred in TV series "Mission Impossible"; "Space 1999."
b. Sep 13, 1932 in Chicago, Illinois
Source: *WhoAm 74, 76, 78, 80, 82; WhoAmW 74*

Bain, Conrad Stafford
Canadian. Actor
Starred in TV series "Maude," 1971-78; founded Actors Federal Credit Union, 1962.
b. Feb 4, 1923 in Lethbridge, ON
Source: *BiE&WWA; NotNAT; WhoAm 82; WhoHol A; WhoThe 77*

Bainbridge, Beryl
English. Author
b. Nov 21, 1933 in Liverpool, England
Source: *ConAu 21R; ConLC 4, 5, 8, 10, 14; ConNov 76; IntAu&W 76, 77; WorAu 1970; WrDr 76, 80*

Bainbridge, William
American. Naval Officer
b. May 7, 1774 in Princeton, New Jersey
d. Jul 27, 1833 in Philadelphia, Pennsylvania
Source: *Alli, SUP; AmBi; ApCAB; DcAmB; Drake; TwCBDA; WebAB; WhAm H*

Baines, Harold Douglass
American. Baseball Player
b. Mar 15, 1959 in Saint Michaels, Maryland
Source: *BaseEn*

Bainter, Fay Okell
American. Actress
b. Dec 7, 1891 in Los Angeles, California
d. Apr 16, 1968 in Hollywood, California
Source: *BiE&WWA; FilmgC; InWom; MotPP; MovMk; ThFT; WhAm 5; WhScrn 74, 77; WhoHol B*

Baio, Scott Anthony
American. Actor
Plays Chachi on TV series "Happy Days," 1974-; "Joanie Loves Chachi," 1982.
b. Sep 22, 1961 in Brooklyn, New York
Source: *BioIn 12*

Baird, Bil (William Britton)
American. Puppeteer
Founded Bil and Cora Baird Puppet Theatre, Greenwich Village, 1966.
b. Aug 15, 1904 in Grand Island, Nebraska
Source: *BiE&WWA; BioNews 74; CelR 73; ChPo S2; CurBio 54*

Baird, Cora Eisenberg
[Mrs. Bil Baird]
American. Puppeteer
Puppets appeared in movie *The Sound of Music,* 1965.
b. Jan 26, 1912 in New York, New York
d. Dec 7, 1967 in New York, New York
Source: *BiE&WWA; CurBio 54, 68; InWom; WhAm 5; WhScrn 74, 77*

Baird, Irwin Lewis
American. Scientist
b. Mar 11, 1925 in Saint Joseph, Missouri
Source: *AmM&WS 73P*

Baird, John Logie
Scottish. Engineer
b. Aug 13, 1888 in Helensburgh, Scotland
d. Jun 14, 1946
Source: *BioIn 1, 2, 3, 4, 5, 6, 7, 8, 9, 10, 11; NewCol 75; WebBD 80; WhoModH*

Baird, Spencer Fullerton
American. Scientist, Physician, Engineer
b. Feb 3, 1823 in Reading, Pennsylvania
d. Aug 19, 1887 in Woods Hole, Massachusetts
Source: *Alli, SUP; AmBi; ApCAB; BiAuS; BiD&SB; CyAl 2; DcAmAu; DcAmB; DcEnL; DcNAA; Drake; TwCBDA; WebAB; WhAm H*

Bairnsfather, Bruce
English. Soldier, Artist, Cartoonist
b. 1888 in India
d. Sep 29, 1959 in Norton, England
Source: *ChPo S1; LongCTC*

Bakeless, John Edwin
American. Author, Editor
b. Dec 30, 1894 in Carlisle, Pennsylvania
d. Aug 8, 1978
Source: *AmAu&B; Au&Wr 71; AuBYP; BioIn 4, 7, 11; ConAu 5R, 5NR; DrAS 74E; IntAu&W 76; REnAL; SmATA 9; TwCA, SUP; WhAm 7; WhE&EA; WhNAA; WhoAm 74, 76, 78; WhoWor 74; WrDr 76*

Baker, Blanche
American. Actress
b. Dec 20, 1956 in New York, New York
Source: *BioIn 12*

Baker, Belle
American. Singer
b. 1895 in New York, New York
d. Apr 29, 1957 in Los Angeles, California
Source: *InWom; WhScrn 74, 77; WhoHol B*

Baker, Bill (William)
[United States Olympic Hockey Team-1980]
American. Hockey Player
b. Nov 29, 1956 in Grand Rapids, Minnesota
Source: *HocReg*

Baker, Bobby (Robert Gene)
American. Former Government Official
b. 1927
Source: *BioIn 6, 7, 8, 9, 10*

Baker, Bonnie
American. Singer
b. 1918
Source: *InWom*

Baker, Buddy
American. Auto Racer
b. 1941?
Source: *BioIn 10, 11, 12*

Baker, Carlos Heard
American. Author
b. May 5, 1909 in Biddeford, Maine
Source: *AmAu&B; ConAu 5R, 3NR; DrAS 74E; IntWW 74; REnAL; WhNAA; WhoAm 74; WhoWor 74; WorAu; WrDr 76*

Baker, Carroll
American. Actress
Nominated for best actress Oscar in *Baby Doll,* 1956.
b. May 28, 1935 in Johnstown, Pennsylvania
Source: *BiDFilm; BiE&WWA; FilmgC; InWom; IntMPA 75, 76, 77, 78, 79, 80, 81, 82; MotPP; MovMk; OxFilm; WhoAm 74; WhoHol A; WorEFlm*

Baker, Charlotte
American. Author
b. Aug 31, 1910 in Nacogdoches, Texas
Source: *AuBYP; ConAu 21R; IlsCB 1946; SmATA 2*

Baker, Chet
American. Musician
b. Dec 23, 1929 in Yale, Oklahoma
Source: *BiDAmM*

Baker, Diane
American. Actress
b. 1938 in Hollywood, California
Source: *FilmgC· MotPP; MovMk; WhoHol A*

Baker, Dorothy Dodds
American. Author
b. Apr 21, 1907 in Missoula, Montana
d. Jun 18, 1968 in Terra Bella, California
Source: *BioIn 2, 4, 8, 10; ConAu 1R; CurBio 43, 68*

Baker, Elbert Hall, II
American. Newspaper Publisher
b. Jul 18, 1910 in Quincy, Massachusetts
Source: *St&PR 75; WhoAdv 72; WhoAm 74; WhoF&I 74; WhoWest 74*

Baker, George
American. Cartoonist
b. May 22, 1915 in Lowell, Massachusetts
d. May 8, 1975 in Los Angeles, California
Source: *AmAu&B; ConAu 57, 93; CurBio 44; WebAB; WhAm 6*

Baker, "Ginger" (Peter)
[Blind Faith; Cream]
English. Rock Musician
b. Aug 19, 1940 in Lewisham, England
Source: *BioIn 8, 9, 10; EncPR&S; IlEncRk; RkOn*

Baker, Gladys Elizabeth
American. Educator
b. Jul 22, 1908 in Iowa City, Iowa
Source: *AmM&WS 73P; WhoAm 74*

Baker, Howard Henry Jr.
American. Senator
Ran for Republican presidential nomination, 1980; Senator from Tennessee, 1966--.
b. Nov 15, 1925 in Huntsville, Tennessee
Source: *BiDrAC; CngDr 74; CurBio 74; IntWW 74; NewYTBE 73; WhoAm 74, 76, 78, 80, 82; WhoGov 72; WhoS&SW 73*

Baker, James Addison, III
American. Presidential Advisor
b. Apr 28, 1930 in Houston, Texas
Source: *BioIn 10, 11; CurBio 82; NewYTBS 81; WhoAm 82*

Baker, Janet Abbott
English. Singer
b. Aug 21, 1933 in York, England
Source: *CurBio 71; IntWW 74; Who 74; WhoAm 82; WhoMus 72; WhoWor 74*

Baker, Joe Don
American. Actor
Best known for role in movie *Walking Tall,* 1973.
b. Feb 12, 1936 in Groesbeck, Texas
Source: *BioIn 10; IntMPA 77, 78, 79, 80, 81, 82; WhoAm 78, 80, 82; WhoHol A*

Baker, Josephine
American. Singer
b. Jun 3, 1906 in Saint Louis, Missouri
d. Apr 12, 1975 in Paris, France
Source: *BiE&WWA; CelR 73; CurBio 64; InWom; IntWW 74; OxFilm; WebAB; WhAm 6; WhScrn 77; WhoAm 74; WhoThe 77; WhoWor 74*

Baker, Julius
American. Musician
b. Sep 23, 1915 in Cleveland, Ohio
Source: *WhoAm 74, 76, 78, 80, 82*

Baker, Kenny
American. Actor, Singer
b. Sep 30, 1912 in Monrovia, California
Source: *BiE&WWA; FilmgC; WhoHol A*

Baker, Laura Nelson
American. Author
b. Jan 7, 1911 in Humboldt, Iowa
Source: *Au&Wr 71; AuBYP; ConAu 5R, 5NR; ForWC 70; MnnWr; SmATA 3; WrDr 76*

Baker, Phil
American. Comedian, Composer
b. Aug 24, 1896 in Philadelphia, Pennsylvania
d. Nov 30, 1963 in Copenhagen, Denmark
Source: *AmSCAP 66; CurBio 46, 64; WhAm 4; WhScrn 74, 77; WhoHol B*

Baker, Rachel
American. Children's Author
b. Mar 1, 1904 in Chernigov, Russia
d. Jul 7, 1978
Source: *AuBYP; BkCL; ConAu 5R, 103; MorJA; SmATA 2*

Baker, Ray Stannard
[David Grayson, pseud.]
American. Author
Won Pulitzer Prize for *Woodrow Wilson: Life and Letters,* 1940.
b. Apr 17, 1870 in Lansing, Michigan
d. Jul 12, 1946 in Amherst, Massachusetts
Source: *AmAu&B; AmLY; CarSB; ChPo S2; ConAmL; CurBio 40, 46; DcAmAu; DcAmB S4; DcLEL; DcNAA; EncAB-H; EvLB; LongCTC; OxAmL; REn; REnAL; TwCA, SUP; TwCW; WebAB; WhAm 2; WhNAA; WisWr*

Baker, Rick
American. Make-up Artist
b. 1950 in New York
Source: *FanAl*

Baker, Russell Wayne
American. Journalist, Author
b. Aug 14, 1925 in Loudoun County, Virginia
Source: *AmAu&B; BioIn 12; ConAu 57; CurBio 80; WhoAm 74, 76, 78, 80, 82; WhoS&SW 73*

Baker, Samm Sinclair
American. Author
b. Jul 29, 1909 in Paterson, New Jersey
Source: *ConAu 5R, 3NR; SmATA 12*

Baker, "Shorty" (Harold)
American. Jazz Musician
b. May 26, 1914 in Saint Louis, Missouri
Source: *AmSCAP 66; WhoJazz 72*

Baker, Stanley
Welsh. Actor
b. Feb 28, 1928 in Glamorgan, Wales
d. Jun 28, 1976 in Malaga, Spain
Source: *BiDFilm; CmMov; FilmgC; IntMPA 75; MotPP; MovMk; OxFilm; Who 74; WhoHol A; WorEFlm*

Bakewell, William
American. Actor
b. 1908 in Hollywood, California
Source: *MovMk; TwYS; WhoHol A*

Bakey, Michael Ellis de
see: DeBakey, Michael Ellis

Bakhtiar, Shahpur
Iranian. Former Prime Minister
Leader of Bakhtiaris, Iran's oldest and largest tribe.
b. 1916?
Source: *BioIn 11, 12*

Bakke, Allan Paul
American. Medical Student
Subject of controversial reverse discrimination case, 1978.
b. 1940
Source: *BioIn 11*

Bakker, Jim (James Orsen)
American. Clergyman, Television Evangelist
b. Jan 2, 1939 in Muskegon, Michigan
Source: *BioIn 11; WhoAm 82*

Bakr, Ahmad Hasan al
Iraqi. President
b. 1914 in Tikrit, Iraq
Source: *IntWW 74; WhoGov 72; WhoWor 74*

Bakshi, Ralph
American. Animated Cartoon Producer
Produced, directed animated version of Tolkien's *Lord of the Rings,* 1978.
b. Oct 26, 1938 in Haifa, Palestine
Source: *CurBio 79; NewYTBE 73, 74; WhoAm 78*

Bakunin, Mikhail Aleksandrovich
Russian. Anarchist, Author
b. May 18, 1814 in Tver, Russia
d. Jul 13, 1876 in Bern, Switzerland
Source: *CasWL; DcRusL; EuAu; REn*

Balaban, Barney
American. Motion Picture Executive
b. Jun 8, 1887 in Chicago, Illinois
d. Mar 7, 1971
Source: *CurBio 46, 71; FilmgC; NewYTBE 71; WhAm 5; WorEFlm*

Balaban, Emanuel
American. Conductor
b. Jan 27, 1895 in Brooklyn, New York
d. May 1973
Source: *BioIn 9; WhAm 5*

Balaguer, Joaquin
Dominican. Diplomat
b. Sep 1, 1907 in Villa Bisono, Dominican Republic
Source: *IntWW 74; NewYTBE 70; WhoGov 72; WhoWor 74*

Balakireff, Mili Alekseyevich
Russian. Composer
b. Jan 2, 1837 in Nizhni-Novgorod, Russia
d. May 28, 1910 in Saint Petersburg, Russia
Source: *BioIn 1; OxMus*

Balanchine, George
"Mr. B"
American. Dancer, Choreographer
Co-founded Ballet Society, now NY City Ballet, 1946--.
b. Jan 9, 1904 in Saint Petersburg, Russia
Source: *BiE&WWA; CelR 73; CurBio 42, 54; EncAB-H; EncMT; IntWW 74; NewYTBE 72; NewYTBS 74; PlP&P; WebAB; Who 82; WhoAm 74; WhoThe 77; WhoWor 74*

Balbo, Italo
Italian. Government Official
b. Jun 6, 1896
d. Jun 28, 1940 in Tobruk, Libya
Source: *CurBio 40; WhWW-II*

Balboa, Vasco Nunez de
Spanish. Explorer
Discovered the Pacific Ocean, 1513; beheaded on false charges of treason.
b. 1475 in Jerez Caballeros, Spain
d. 1517 in Aela, Panama
Source: *ApCAB; Drake; NewC; REn; WhAm H*

Balch, Emily G
American. Social Reformer
Shared 1946 Nobel Peace Prize with John R Mott.
b. Jan 8, 1867 in Jamaica Plain, Massachusetts
d. Jan 9, 1961 in Cambridge, Massachusetts
Source: *CurBio 47, 61; InWom; WebAB; WhAm 4; WomWWA 14*

Balchen, Bernt
American. Pilot
b. Oct 23, 1899 in Tveit Topdal, Norway
d. Oct 17, 1973 in Mount Kisco, New York
Source: *ConAu 45; CurBio 49, 73; NewYTBE 73; WhAm 6; WhoAm 74; WhoWor 74*

Balchin, Nigel Marlin
English. Author
b. Dec 3, 1908 in Wiltshire, England
d. May 17, 1970 in London, England
Source: *ConAu 29R, 97; DcLEL; EvLB; LongCTC; ModBrL; Pen ENG; REn; TwCA SUP; TwCW*

Bald, Kenneth
American. Cartoonist
b. 1920 in New York, New York
Source: *WorECom*

Balderston, John Lloyd
American. Dramatist
b. Oct 22, 1889 in Philadelphia, Pennsylvania
d. Mar 8, 1954 in Beverly Hills, California
Source: *AmAu&B; CnMD; FilmgC; LongCTC; McGEWD; ModWD; WhAm 3; WhNAA*

Baldovinetti, Alesso
Italian. Artist
b. 1425
d. 1499
Source: *NewCol 75*

Baldrige, Letitia
American. Author
b. in Miami Beach, Florida
Source: *ConAu 25R; ForWC 70; WhoAm 82; WhoE 74; WhoF&I 74*

Baldrige, (Howard) Malcolm, Jr.
"Mac"
American. Secretary of Commerce
b. Oct 4, 1922 in Omaha, Nebraska
Source: *CurBio 82; Dun&B 79; NewYTBS 81; PseudN; St&PR 75; WhoAm 74, 76, 78, 80, 82; WhoAmP 73, 75, 77, 79; WhoE 74; WhoF&I 74, 75, 77; WhoWor 74*

Baldung(-Grien), Hans
[Hans Gruen]
German. Artist
b. 1484?
d. 1545 in Strasbourg, France
Source: *BioIn 5, 11; McGDA; NewCol 75; PseudN*

Baldwin, Adam
American. Actor
b. 1962 in Chicago, Illinois
Source: *BioIn 12; NewYTBS 80*

Baldwin, Billy
American. Interior Decorator
b. May 30, 1904 in Rowland Park, Maryland
Source: *CelR 73*

Baldwin, Faith
American. Author
b. Oct 1, 1893 in New Rochelle, New York
d. Mar 19, 1978 in Norwalk, Connecticut
Source: *AmAu&B; AmNov; AuNews 1; BioNews 74; ChPo; ConAu 5R; ForWC 70; InWom; LongCTC; NewYTBE 73; OxAmL; REn; REnAL; TwCA, SUP; WhNAA; WhoAm 74; WhoAmW 77; WrDr 76*

Baldwin, Hanson Weightman
American. Journalist
b. Mar 22, 1903 in Baltimore, Maryland
Source: *AmAu&B; Au&Wr 71; ConAu 61; CurBio 42; LongCTC; REnAL; TwCA SUP; WhoAm 74*

Baldwin, James Arthur
American. Author
Wrote *Go Tell It on the Mountain,* 1953 (autobiographical).
b. Aug 2, 1924 in New York, New York
Source: *AmAu&B; BlkAW; CasWL; CelR 73; ConAu 1R, 3NR; ConDr 73; ConLC 1, 2, 3, 4, 5, 8, 13, 15, 17; ConNov 72, 76; CroCD; EncWL; LivgBAA; LongCTC; McGEWD; ModAL, SUP; ModWD; NotNAT; OxAmL; Pen AM; RAdv 1; REn; REnAL; SmATA 9; TwCW; WebAB; WebE&AL; Who 74; WhoAm 74, 76, 78, 80, 82; WhoBlA 75, 80; WhoE 74; WhoTwCL; WhoWor 74; WorAu; WrDr 76*

Baldwin, Matthias William
American. Industrialist, Philanthropist
b. Dec 10, 1795 in Elizabethtown, Pennsylvania
d. Sep 7, 1866 in Philadelphia, Pennsylvania
Source: *NewCol 75; WhAm H*

Baldwin, Robert
Canadian. Statesman
b. May 12, 1804 in Toronto, ON
d. Dec 9, 1858 in Spadina, ON
Source: *ApCAB; OxCan*

Baldwin, Roger Nash
American. Founder of ACLU
b. Jan 21, 1884 in Wellesley, Massachusetts
d. Aug 26, 1981 in Ridgewood, New Jersey
Source: *AmM&WS 73S, 78S; BioIn 2, 3, 6, 10, 11; BioNews 74; CelR 73; CurBio 40, 81; NewYTBS 81; PolProf T; WhoAm 74, 76, 78, 80; WhoWor 74*

Baldwin of Bewdley, Stanley Baldwin, Earl
English. Statesman
b. Aug 3, 1867 in Bewdley, England
d. Dec 14, 1947 in Ast Pey, England
Source: *NewC; REn*

Balenciaga, Cristobal
Spanish. Fashion Designer
b. Jan 21, 1895 in Guetaria, Spain
d. Mar 23, 1972 in Javea, Spain
Source: *CurBio 54; NewYTBE 72; WhAm 5; WorFshn*

Balewa, Abubakar
Nigerian. Prime Minister
b. Dec 12, 1912 in Bauchi, Nigeria
d. Jan 15, 1966 in Lagos, Nigeria
Source: *BioIn 8; WhAm 4*

Balfour, Arthur James Balfour, Earl
English. Statesman
b. Jul 25, 1848 in East Lothian, Scotland
d. Mar 19, 1930
Source: *Alli SUP; BbD; BiD&SB; BiDPara; DcLEL; EvLB; NewC; OxEng; TwCA, SUP*

Balin, Ina
[Ina Rosenberg]
American. Actress
b. Nov 12, 1937 in Brooklyn, New York
Source: *BiE&WWA; FilmgC; InWom; IntMPA 75, 76, 77, 78, 79, 80, 81; MotPP; PseudN; WhoAmW 72, 74; WhoHol A*

Balin, Marty
[Martyn Jerel Buchwald; Jefferson Airplane]
American. Singer, Songwriter
b. Jan 30, 1943 in Cincinnati, Ohio
Source: *BioIn 9; WhoAm 82*

Ball, Edward
American. Estate Manager
b. Mar 21, 1888 in Tidewater, Virginia
d. Jun 24, 1981 in New Orleans, Louisiana
Source: *BioIn 3, 4, 5, 9, 10, 11, 12; Dun&B 79; NewYTBS 81*

Ball, Ernest
American. Composer
b. Jul 22, 1878 in Cleveland, Ohio
d. May 3, 1927 in Santa Ana, California
Source: *AmSCAP 66*

Ball, George Wildman
American. Lawyer, Government Official
b. Dec 21, 1909 in Des Moines, Iowa
Source: *ConAu 73; CurBio 62; IntWW 74; WhoAm 74, 76, 78, 80, 82; WhoAmP 73; WhoWor 74*

Ball, John Dudley
American. Author
b. Jul 8, 1911 in Schenectady, New York
Source: *AmAu&B; ConAu 5R, 3NR; WhoAm 80, 82; WrDr 80*

Ball, Lucille
[Mrs. Gary Morton]
American. Actress, Comedienne
Starred in "I Love Lucy," 1951-60 with ex-husband Desi Arnaz.
b. Aug 6, 1911 in Jamestown, New York
Source: *BiDFilm; BiE&WWA; BioNews 74; BkPepl; CelR 73; CmMov; CurBio 52; EncMT; FilmgC; HerW; InWom; IntMPA 75, 76, 77, 78, 79, 80, 81, 82; IntWW 74; MotPP; MovMk; NewYTBE 73; OxFilm; ThFT; WebAB; WhoAm 74, 76, 78, 80, 82; WhoHol A; WhoWor 74; WorEFlm*

Ball, Thomas
American. Sculptor
b. Jun 3, 1819 in Charlestown, Massachusetts
d. 1911 in Montclair, New Jersey
Source: *AmBi; ApCAB; BioIn 7, 9, 11; DcAmB; DcNAA; Drake; TwCBDA; WhAm 1*

Balla, Giacomo
Italian. Painter, Educator
b. Jul 18, 1871 in Turin, Italy
d. Mar 1, 1958 in Rome, Italy
Source: *ConArt; McGDA; McGEWB*

Ballantine, Ian
American. Publisher
One of the first to produce hardcover, paperback editions simultaneously.
b. Feb 15, 1916 in New York, New York
Source: *BioIn 3, 11; CurBio 54; WhoAm 78, 80, 82*

Ballantrae, Lord
[Bernard Edward Fergusson]
English. Author, Government Official
b. May 6, 1911 in London, England
d. Nov 28, 1980 in London, England
Source: *AnObit 1980; IntWW 78, 79*

Ballard, Florence
[The Supremes]
American. Singer
Member of original Supremes; grew up with Diana Ross in Detroit projects.
b. Jun 30, 1943 in Detroit, Michigan
d. Feb 22, 1976 in Detroit, Michigan
Source: *BioIn 10; EncPR&S*

Ballard, Hank
American. Singer
b. Nov 18, 1936 in Detroit, Michigan
Source: *EncPR&S; IlEncRk; Rk100*

Ballard, Kaye
[Catherine Gloria Balotta]
American. Singer, Actress
Starred in TV series, "The Mothers-in-Law," 1967-69.
b. Nov 20, 1926 in Cleveland, Ohio
Source: *BiE&WWA; CelR 73; CurBio 69; EncMT; FilmgC; NotNAT; WhoAm 74, 76, 78, 80, 82; WhoHol A; WhoThe 77*

Ballesteros, Seve(riano)
Spanish. Golfer
At 23, was youngest golfer ever to win Masters Tournament, 1980.
b. Apr 9, 1957 in Pedrena, Spain
Source: *BioIn 11, 12; CurBio 80*

Ballinger, (Violet) Margaret (Livingstone)
[Margaret Hodgson, pseud.]
South African. Author, Politician
b. Jan 11, 1894 in Glasgow, Scotland
d. Feb 7, 1980 in Cape Province, South Africa
Source: *AnObit 1980; ConAu 61; PseudN; WhE&EA*

Ballou, Maturin Murray
American. Author, Editor
b. Apr 14, 1820 in Boston, Massachusetts
d. Mar 27, 1895
Source: *Alli, SUP; AmAu; AmAu&B; ApCAB; BbD; BiD&SB; DcAmAu; DcAmB; DcNAA; Drake; OxAmL; WhAm H*

Balmain, Pierre Alexandre
French. Fashion Designer
b. May 18, 1914 in Saint Jean de Maurienne, France
d. Jun 29, 1982 in Paris, France
Source: *CelR 73; CurBio 54, 82; IntWW 74, 75, 76, 77, 78; NewYTBS 82; Who 74; WhoWor 74, 74, 78; WorFshn*

Balopoulos, Michael
Greek. Political Leader
b. 1920?
d. Mar 3, 1978 in Athens, Greece
Source: *BioIn 11*

Balsam, Artur
Polish. Musician
b. Feb 8, 1906 in Warsaw, Poland
Source: *WhoAm 82; WhoMus 72*

Balsam, Martin Henry
American. Actor
Won 1964 Oscar, for *A Thousand Clowns;* starred in "Archie Bunker's Place."
b. Nov 4, 1919 in New York, New York
Source: *BiE&WWA; CelR 73; FilmgC; IntMPA 75, 76, 77, 78, 79, 80, 81, 82; MotPP; MovMk; NotNAT; WhoAm 74, 76, 78, 80, 82; WhoHol A; WhoThe 77*

Baltard, Victor
French. Architect
b. 1805 in Paris, France
d. 1874
Source: *McGDA; WhoArch*

Balthus
[Comte Balthazar Klossowski de Rola]
French. Artist
b. Feb 29, 1908 in Paris, France
Source: *ConArt; CurBio 79; IntWW 74, 75, 76, 77, 78; McGDA; PseudN; WhoWor 74*

Baltimore, George Calvert, Baron
English. Colonizer
Founded MD, 1632.
b. 1580 in Kipling, England
d. Apr 15, 1632 in London, England
Source: *Alli, SUP; AmBi; DcAmB; Drake; OxCan; TwCBDA; WebAB; WhAm H*

Balukas, Jean
American. Billiards Player
b. Jun 28, 1959 in Brooklyn, New York
Source: *BioIn 11; GoodHS; NewYTBS 74; WhoAm 82*

Balzac, Honore de
French. Dramatist, Author
b. May 20, 1799 in Tours, France
d. Aug 18, 1850 in Paris, France
Source: *AtlBL; BbD; BiD&SB; CasWL; ChPo S2; CyWA; DcBiA; DcEuL; EncMys; EuAu; EvEuW; McGEWD; NewC; OxEng; OxFr; OxThe; Pen EUR; RComWL; REn*

Bamberger, George Irvin
American. Baseball Manager
Spent 10 years as pitching coach of Baltimore Orioles; now manages the NY Mets.
b. Aug 1, 1925 in Staten Island, New York
Source: *BioIn 12; NewYTBS 81; WhoProB 73*

Bamberger, Julian Maas
American. Business Executive
b. Feb 9, 1889 in Salt Lake City, Utah
d. Jun 23, 1967 in Salt Lake City, Utah
Source: *BioIn 10; NatCAB 54*

Bamberger, Louis
American. Merchant, Philanthropist
b. May 15, 1855 in Baltimore, Maryland
d. May 11, 1944 in South Orange, New Jersey
Source: *DcAmB S3; WhAm 2*

Bampton, Rose
American. Opera Singer
b. Nov 28, 1909 in Cleveland, Ohio
Source: *CurBio 40; InWom*

Bancroft, Anne
[Annemarie Italiano; Mrs. Mel Brooks]
American. Actress
Won 1962 Oscar for *The Miracle Worker;* played Mrs. Robinson in *The Graduate,* 1967.
b. Sep 17, 1931 in New York, New York
Source: *BiDFilm; BiE&WWA; BkPepl; CelR 73; FilmgC; InWom; IntMPA 75, 76, 77, 78, 79, 80, 81, 82; IntWW 78; MovMk; NotNAT; OxFr; WhoAm 74, 76, 78, 80, 82; WhoAmW 77; WhoThe 77; WhoWor 74; WorEFlm*

Bancroft, George
"Father of American History"
American. Author, Historian, Diplomat
Wrote 10-volume *History of the US,* 1834-1874.
b. Oct 3, 1800 in Worcester, Massachusetts
d. Jan 17, 1891 in Washington, DC
Source: *Alli, SUP; AmAu; AmAu&B; AmBi; ApCAB; BbD; BiAuS; BiD&SB; BiDrUSE; ChPo; CyAl 2; DcAmAu; DcAmB; DcEnA AP; DcEnL; DcLEL; DcNAA; Drake; EncAB-H; EvLB; OxAmL; OxEng; Pen AM; REn; REnAL; TwCBDA; WebAB; WebE&AL; WhAm H; WhAmP*

Bancroft, George
American. Actor
b. Sep 30, 1882 in Philadelphia, Pennsylvania
d. Oct 2, 1956 in Santa Monica, California
Source: *CmMov; FilmgC; MovMk; TwYS; Vers A; WhScrn 74, 77; WorEFlm*

Band, The
[Rick Danko; Levon Helm; Garth Hudson; Richard Manuel; Robbie Robertson]
American. Rock Group
Source: *EncPR&S; IlEncRk; Rk100*

Banda, Hastings Kamuzu
Malawian. President
b. 1906
Source: *CurBio 63; IntWW 74; NewYTBE 71; Who 74; WhoGov 72; WhoWor 74*

Bandaranaike, Sirimavo
Sri Lankan. Politician
b. Apr 17, 1916 in Kandy, Ceylon
Source: *CurBio 61; InWom; IntWW 74; NewYTBE 70; WhoWor 74*

Bandello, Matteo
[Matthew Bandello]
"A Prose Ariosto"
Italian. Author, Poet
b. 1485 in Castelnuovo Scrivia, Italy
d. 1561 in Bassens, France
Source: *BbD; BiD&SB; BioIn 7; CasWL; CroE&S; DcEuL; EuAu; EvEuW; NewC; NewCol 75; OxEng; OxFr; Pen EUR; PseudN; REn*

Bandy, Moe
American. Singer
b. 1944? in Meridian, Mississippi
Source: *IlEncCM; WhoAm 82*

Banghart, Kenneth
Radio Commentator
Source: *NF*

Bangor, Edward Henry H Ward, Viscount
English. Journalist
b. Nov 5, 1905
Source: *Who 74*

Bangs, Lester
American. Rock Critic, Author
b. Dec 1948
d. Apr 30, 1982 in New York, New York
Source: *ConAu 106; NewYTBS 82*

Bani-Sadr, Abolhassan
Iranian. Former President
First president elected in Iran's 2,500 year history, 1980; divested of power by Khomeini, 1981.
b. 1933 in Hamadan Province, Iran
Source: *CurBio 81; IntWW 80; NewYTBS 79*

Baniszewski, Gertrude Wright
American. Murderer
b. 1929 in Indiana
Source: *Blood*

Bankhead, Tallulah Brockman
American. Actress
Starred in plays *The Little Foxes,* 1939; *The Skin of Our Teeth,* 1943.
b. Jan 31, 1903 in Huntsville, Alabama
d. Dec 12, 1968 in New York, New York
Source: *BiDFilm; BiE&WWA; CurBio 41, 53, 69; FamA&A; Film 1; FilmgC; InWom; MotPP; MovMk; OxFilm; PlP&P; ThFT; WebAB; WhAm 5; WhScrn 74, 77; WhoHol B; WorEFlm*

Bankhead, William Brockman
American. Congressman
b. Apr 12, 1874 in Moscow, Alabama
d. Sep 15, 1940 in Bethesda, Maryland
Source: *BiDrAC; CurBio 40; DcAmB S2; WebAB; WhAm 1; WhAmP*

Banks, Ernie (Ernest)
American. Former Baseball Player
Shortstop with Chicago Cubs, 1953-71; Hall of Fame, 1977.
b. Jan 31, 1931 in Dallas, Texas
Source: *BaseEn; CurBio 59; WhoAm 74, 76, 78, 80; WhoBlA 75; WhoProB 73*

Banks, Leslie
English. Actor, Motion Picture Director
b. Jun 9, 1890 in Liverpool, England
d. Apr 21, 1952 in London, England
Source: *FilmgC; MovMk; OxThe; WhScrn 74, 77; WhoHol B*

Banks, Monty (Montague)
[Mario Bianchi]
Italian. Actor, Motion Picture Director
Married to Gracie Fields; appeared in *A Bell for Adono,* 1961.
b. 1897 in Casene, Italy
d. Jan 7, 1950 in Arona, Italy
Source: *FilmgC; TwYS; WhScrn 74, 77; WhoHol B*

Banks, Tony
see: Genesis

Banky, Vilma
American. Actress
b. 1903 in Budapest, Hungary
Source: *FilmgC; InWom; MotPP; MovMk; ThFT; TwYS; WhoHol A; WorEFlm*

Banneker, Benjamin
American. Mathematician, Inventor
b. Nov 9, 1731 in Elliot's Mills, Maryland
d. Oct 1806 in Baltimore, Maryland
Source: *ApCAB; DcAmAu; Drake; EncAB-H; WebAB; WhAm H; WhAmP*

Bannen, Ian
Scottish. Actor
b. Jun 29, 1928 in Airdrie, Scotland
Source: *FilmEn; FilmgC; IntMPA 80, 81; MotPP; MovMk; WhoThe 77, 81*

Banner, James Morril, Jr.
American. Author
b. May 3, 1935 in New York, New York
Source: *ConAu 49; DrAS 74H*

Bannerman, Francis
American. Gun Merchant
b. 1851
d. 1918
Source: *BioIn 3, 10*

Banning, Kendall
American. Author
b. Sep 20, 1879 in New York, New York
d. Dec 27, 1944
Source: *AmAu&B; AnMV 1926; ChPo, S2; CurBio 45; DcNAA; WhAm 2; WhNAA*

Banning, Margaret Culkin
American. Author
b. Mar 18, 1891 in Buffalo, New York
d. Jan 4, 1982 in Tryon, North Carolina
Source: *AmAu&B; AmNov; BiCAW; BkC 6; ConAu 5R, 4NR; CurBio 40, 82; MnnWr; OxAmL; TwCA, SUP; WhNAA; WhoAm 74, 76, 78, 80, 82; WhoAmW 77, 79; WhoWor 74; WrDr 80*

Bannister, Constance
American. Photographer
b. Feb 11, 1919 in Ashland, Tennessee
Source: *CurBio 55; InWom; NewYTBE 72; WhoAm 74*

Bannister, Edward M
American. Artist
b. 1833 in Saint Andrews, NB
d. 1901 in Providence, Rhode Island
Source: *AfroAA; WhAm 4*

Bannister, Roger
English. Track Athlete, Physician
First to run mile under four minutes, 1954.
b. Mar 23, 1929 in Harrow, England
Source: *Au&Wr 71; CurBio 56; Who 74; WhoTr&F 73; WhoWor 74; WrDr 76*

Bannon, Jim
American. Actor
b. 1911
Source: *BioIn 4, 8; FilmgC; WhoHol A*

Banting, Sir Frederick Grant
Canadian. Research Physician
b. Nov 4, 1891
d. Feb 21, 1941 in Newfoundland, Canada
Source: *CurBio 41; LongCTC*

Bantock, Sir Granville
English. Composer, Conductor
b. Aug 7, 1868 in London, England
d. Oct 16, 1946 in London, England
Source: *BioIn 3, 4, 5, 8, 9, 10; CurBio 46*

Banton, Travis
American. Designer
b. 1874 in New York, New York
d. 1958
Source: *WorFshn*

Banzer-Suarez, Hugo
Bolivian. Government Official
President of Bolivia, 1971-78; overthrown in coup, Jul, 1978.
b. Jul 10, 1926 in Santa Cruz, Bolivia
Source: *CurBio 73; IntWW 74; NewYTBE 71; WhoWor 74*

Bar-Ilian, David Jacob
Israeli. Musician
b. Feb 7, 1930 in Haifa, Palestine
Source: *WhoAm 82; WhoMus 72*

Bar Kokhba, Simon
Hebrew. Revolutionary
d. 135
Source: *BioIn 3, 6, 9; WebBD 80*

Bara, Theda
[Theodosia Goodman]
American. Actress
Known for silent screen vamp roles, 1914-19, such as Salome and Cleopatra.
b. Jul 20, 1890 in Cincinnati, Ohio
d. Apr 7, 1955 in Los Angeles, California
Source: *BiDFilm; DcAmB S5; Film 1; FilmgC; InWom; MotPP; MovMk; OxFilm; TwYS; WebAB; WhAm 3; WhScrn 74, 77; WhoHol B; WorEFlm*

Barabbas
Biblical Character
Source: *NewCol 75; WebBD 80*

Baraka, Imamu Amiri
see: Jones, Leroi

Barbaja, Domenica
Italian. Opera Singer
b. 1778 in Milan, Italy
d. Oct 16, 1841 in Posilipo, Italy
Source: *NewEOp 71*

Barbarelli, Giorgio
see: Giorgione, I

Barbarossa, Dave
see: Bow Wow Wow

Barbeau, Adrienne
[Mrs. John Carpenter]
American. Actress
Starred in TV series "Maude," 1972-78; in movie *The Fog,* 1980.
b. 1945?
Source: *BioIn 12*

Barber, Bernard
American. Author, Educator
b. Jan 29, 1918 in Boston, Massachusetts
Source: *AmAu&B; AmM&WS 73; ConAu 65; WhoAm 74*

Barber, Bill (William Charles)
Canadian. Hockey Player
b. Jul 11, 1952 in Callender, ON
Source: *HocReg*

Barber, "Red" (Walter Lanier)
American. Sportscaster
b. Feb 17, 1908 in Columbus, Mississippi
Source: *BioNews 74; CurBio 43*

Barber, Samuel
American. Composer
b. Mar 9, 1910 in West Chester, Pennsylvania
Source: *AmSCAP 66; ConAu 103; DcCM; IntWW 74; OxAmL; WebAB; Who 74; WhoAm 74; WhoMus 72; WhoWor 74*

Barbera, Joseph Roland
[Hanna and Barbera]
American. Cartoonist
Co-produced "Tom and Jerry," "Yogi Bear," "The Flintstones," etc.
b. 1911 in New York, New York
Source: *OxFilm; WhoAm 78; WorEFlm*

Barbie, Klaus
[Klaus Altmann, alais]
"The Butcher of Lyon"
German. Nazi Leader
Captain of Gestapo, Lyon, France, 1942-44; accused of crimes against humanity; extradited to France, 1983.
b. 1914? in Germany
Source: *BioIn 9*

Barbier, Jules
French. Opera Librettist
b. Mar 8, 1825 in Paris, France
d. Jan 16, 1901 in Paris, France
Source: *BiD&SB*

Barbieri, Fedora
Italian. Opera Singer
b. Jun 4, 1920 in Trieste, Italy
Source: *CurBio 57; InWom; IntWW 74; WhoMus 72; WhoWor 74*

Barbirolli, Sir John
English. Conductor
b. Dec 2, 1899 in London, England
d. Jul 28, 1970 in London, England
Source: *CurBio 40, 70; NewYTBE 70; WhAm 5*

Barbour, John
Canadian. Comedian, Writer
b. Apr 24, in Toronto, ON
Source: *WhoAm 80, 82*

Barbour, Walworth
American. Diplomat
US ambassador to Israel, 1961-73.
b. Jun 4, 1908 in Massachusetts
d. Jul 21, 1982 in Gloucester, Massachusetts
Source: *IntWW 74, 75; IntYB 78, 79, 80, 81; Who 74, 82; WhoAmP 73, 75, 77, 79, 81; WhoWor 74*

Barcelo, Carlos Romero
Puerto Rican. Governor of Puerto Rico
b. 1932?
Source: *BioIn 11*

Bardeen, John
American. Physicist
Invented transistor, which won Nobel Prize for Physics, 1956.
b. May 23, 1908 in Madison, Wisconsin
Source: *AmM&WS 73P; CurBio 57; IntWW 74; WebAB; Who 74; WhoAm 74, 76, 78, 80, 82; WhoMW 74; WhoWor 74*

Bardis, Panos Demetrios
Greek. Sociologist, Author
b. Sep 24, 1924 in Lefcohorion, Greece
Source: *AmM&WS 73S; ConAu 25R; WhoAm 74, 76, 78, 80, 82; WhoWor 74; WrDr 76*

Bardot, Brigitte
French. Actress
Married to Roger Vadim when he directed her in *And God Created Woman,* 1956.
b. Sep 28, 1934 in Paris, France
Source: *BiDFilm; BkPepl; CelR 73; CurBio 60; FilmgC; InWom; IntMPA 75, 76, 77, 78, 79, 80, 81, 82; IntWW 74; MotPP; MovMk; OxFilm; WhoHol A; WhoWor 74; WorEFlm*

Barenboim, Daniel
Israeli. Musician, Conductor
b. Nov 15, 1942 in Buenos Aires, Argentina
Source: *CelR 73; CurBio 69; IntWW 74; Who 74; WhoAm 82; WhoMus 72; WhoWor 74; WhoWorJ 72*

Barents, Willem
Dutch. Explorer
b. in Terschelling, Netherlands
d. Jun 1597
Source: *McGEWB; NewCol 75; WebBD 80*

Barentzen, Patrick de
see: DeBarentzen, Patrick

Bares, Basile
American. Musician
b. 1845 in New Orleans, Louisiana
d. 1902 in New Orleans, Louisiana
Source: *BiDAmM*

Barger, Floyd
American. Editor
b. Oct 26, 1906 in Boardman, Ohio
d. Aug 1975
Source: *WhAm 6; WhoAm 74; WhoE 74; WhoF&I 74*

Bargone, Frederic Charles Pierre Edouard
see: Farrere, Claude, pseud.

Bari, Lynn
[Marjorie Bitzer]
American. Actress
b. 1919 in Roanoke, Virginia
Source: *FilmgC; HolP 30; IntMPA 75, 76, 77, 78, 79, 80, 81, 82; MotPP; MovMk; WhoHol A*

Baring, Maurice
English. Author
b. Apr 27, 1874 in London, England
d. Dec 14, 1945 in Inverness-Shire, England
Source: *BkC 4; CasWL; CathA 1930; ChPo, S1, S2; DcLEL; EncWL; EvLB; LongCTC; ModBrL; NewC; OxEng; REn; TwCA, SUP; TwCW; WebE&AL; WhAm 5*

Baring-Gould, Sabine
English. Author, Essayist, Hymnist
Wrote words to hymns, "Onward Christian Soldiers"; "Now the Day is Over."
b. Jan 28, 1834 in Exeter, England
d. Jan 2, 1924
Source: *BbD; BiD&SB; BrAu 19; CarSB; Chambr 3; ChPo, S1; DcBiA; DcEnA, AP; DcEnL; DcLEL; EvLB; LongCTC; NewC; OxEng; Pen ENG; WebE&AL*

Barker, Bernard L
American. Watergate Burglar
Source: *BioIn 10, 11; NewYTBS 74*

Barker, Bob (Robert William)
American. TV Personality
Hosted game shows, "Truth or Consequences"; "The Price is Right."
b. Dec 12, 1923 in Darrington, Washington
Source: *BioIn 4, 10; WhoAm 82*

Barker, Cliff
[Fabulous Five]
American. Basketball Player
b. Jan 15, 1921 in Yorktown, Indiana
Source: *WhoBbl 73*

Barker, "Doc" (Arthur)
American. Murderer, Bank Robber
b. 1899 in Aurora, Missouri
d. Jun 13, 1939 in Alcatraz, California
Source: *BioIn 1; Blood*

Barker, Fred
American. Murderer, Bank Robber
b. 1902 in Aurora, Missouri
d. Jan 16, 1935 in Oklawaha, Florida
Source: *Blood*

Barker, George Granville
English. Author
b. Feb 26, 1913 in Loughton, England
Source: *Au&Wr 71; CasWL; ChPo S2; CnE&AP; CnMWL; ConAu 9R; ConLC 8; ConP 75; DcLEL; DrAF 76; DrAP 75; EncWL; IntWW 74; LongCTC; ModBrL, SUP; NewC; OxEng; Pen ENG; REn; TwCA SUP; TwCW; WebE&AL; Who 74; WhoTwCL; WhoWor 74; WrDr 76*

Barker, Harley Granville
see: Granville-Barker, Harley

Barker, Herman
American. Murderer, Bank Robber
b. 1894 in Aurora, Missouri
d. Sep 19, 1927 in Newton, Kansas
Source: *Blood*

Barker, Len (Leonard Harold, II)
American. Baseball Player
Pitched perfect game, May 15, 1981.
b. Jul 7, 1955 in Fort Knox, Kentucky
Source: *BaseEn; BioIn 12*

Barker, Lex
American. Actor
b. May 8, 1919 in Rye, New York
d. Apr 11, 1973 in New York, New York
Source: *FilmgC; MotPP; MovMk; WhScrn 77; WhoHol B*

Barker, Lloyd
American. Murderer, Bank Robber
b. 1896 in Aurora, Missouri
d. 1949 in Colorado
Source: *Blood*

Barker, "Ma" (Arizona Donnie Clark)
"Kate"
American. Criminal Gangleader
Planned bank robberies with sons; ran hideout in OK for escaped convicts.
b. 1872 in Springfield, Missouri
d. Jan 16, 1935 in Oklawaha, Florida
Source: *Blood*

Barker, Ronnie
English. Actor, Comedian
b. Sep 25, 1929 in Bedford, England
Source: *FilmgC; WhoThe 77, 81*

Barker, Sue
English. Tennis Player
b. Apr 19, 1956
Source: *BioIn 11*

Barkin, Ben
American. Businessman
b. Jun 4, 1915 in Milwaukee, Wisconsin
Source: *WhoAm 74; WhoF&I 74; WhoPubR 72*

Barkley, Alben William
American. Politician
Vice-president under Harry S Truman; congressman, 1912-26.
b. Nov 24, 1877 in Graves County, Kentucky
d. Apr 30, 1956 in Lexington, Virginia
Source: *BiDrAC; BiDrUSE; CurBio 41, 49, 56; WebAB; WhAm 3; WhAmP*

Barlach, Ernst
German. Sculptor
b. Jan 2, 1870 in Holstein, Germany
d. Jan 24, 1938 in Gustrow, Germany
Source: *CasWL; ClDMEL; CnMD; EncWL; EvEuW; McGEWD; ModGL; ModWD; OxGer; Pen EUR; REn*

Barlow, Howard
American. Conductor
b. May 1, 1892 in Plain City, Ohio
d. Jan 31, 1972 in Portland, Oregon
Source: *AmSCAP 66; CurBio 40, 54, 72; NewYTBE 72; WhAm 5*

Barlow, Joel
American. Political Writer, Diplomat
Friend of Thomas Paine; best known poem *The Hasty-Pudding,* 1793.
b. Mar 24, 1754 in Redding, Connecticut
d. Dec 24, 1812 in Zarnowiec, Poland
Source: *Alli; AmAu; AmAu&B; AmBi; ApCAB; BiD&SB; CasWL; Chambr 3; ChPo; CnDAL; CyAL 1; DcAmAu; DcAmB; DcEnL; DcLEL; DcNAA; EncAB-H; EvLB; OxAmL; OxEng; Pen AM; PoChrch; REn; REnAL; TwCBDA; WebAB; WebE&AL; WhAm H; WhAmP*

Barnaby, Ralph S
American. Author, Artist, Engineer
b. Jan 21, 1893 in Meadville, Pennsylvania
Source: *ConAu 61; SmATA 9*

Barnard, Christiaan Neethling
South African. Heart Surgeon
Performed first human heart transplant, Dec 3, 1967.
b. Oct 8, 1922 in Beaufort West, South Africa
Source: *CelR 73; ConAu 61; CurBio 68; IntWW 74; Who 74; WhoWor 74*

Barnard, Frederick Augustus Porter
American. Educator
President, Columbia U, 1864-89; founded Barnard College to extend education to women.
b. May 5, 1809 in Sheffield, Massachusetts
d. Apr 27, 1889 in New York, New York
Source: *McGEWB; WebAB; WhAm H*

Barnard, George Grey
American. Sculptor
b. May 24, 1863 in Belle Fonte, Pennsylvania
d. Apr 24, 1938 in New York, New York
Source: *AmBi; ApCAB SUP; DcAmB S2; OxAmL; REnAL; WebAB; WhAm 1*

Barnard, Henry
American. Educator
First US Commissioner of Education, 1867-70.
b. Jan 24, 1811 in Hartford, Connecticut
d. Jul 5, 1900 in Hartford, Connecticut
Source: *Alli, SUP; AmAu; AmBi; ApCAB; BbD; BiAuS; BiD&SB; CyAL 1, 2; DcAmAu; DcAmB; DcNAA; Drake; EncAB-H; TwCBDA; WebAB; WhAm H*

Barnardo, Thomas John
Irish. Social Reformer
b. Jul 4, 1845 in Dublin, Ireland
d. Sep 19, 1905 in Surbiton, Ireland
Source: *ChPo S1; DcIrB; LongCTC; NewC; NewCol 75*

Barnes, Billy
American. Lyricist, Composer, Singer
b. Jan 27, 1927 in Los Angeles, California
Source: *BiE&WWA; NotNAT*

Barnes, Binnie
English. Actress
b. Mar 25, 1906 in London, England
Source: *FilmgC; HolP 30; MotPP; MovMk; ThFT; WhoHol A; WhoThe 77*

Barnes, Clair Cortland
[The Hostages]
American. Former Hostage in Iran
Source: *NewYTBS 81*

Barnes, Clive Alexander
English. Journalist, Critic
b. May 13, 1927 in London, England
Source: *AmAu&B; AuNews 2; ConAu 77; CurBio 72; IntWW 74; NotNAT; WhoAm 74, 76, 78, 80, 82; WhoE 74; WhoThe 77*

Barnes, Djuna
American. Author, Journalist
Writings influenced by James Joyce and T S Eliot; novel *Nightwood,* 1936.
b. Jun 12, 1892 in Cornwall, New York
d. Jun 18, 1982 in New York, New York
Source: *AmAu&B; AmWomWr; Au&Wr 71; CasWL; CnMD; ConAu 13R; ConDr 73, 77; ConLC 3, 4, 8, 11; ConNov 72, 76; DcLB 4; DcLEL; EncWL; IntAu&W 76, 77; LinLib L; LongCTC; ModAL, SUP; NewYTBS 82; OxAmL; Pen AM; RAdv 1; REn; REnAL; TwCA, SUP; TwCW; WhoAm 74, 76, 78; WhoAmW 66, 68, 70, 72, 74; WhoTwCL; WhoWor 74; WrDr 76, 80*

Barnes, Edward Larrabee
American. Architect
b. Apr 22, 1915 in Chicago, Illinois
Source: *AmArch 70; BioIn 4, 5, 9; BnEnAmA; IntWW 74, 75, 76, 77, 78; McGDA; WhoAm 74, 76, 78, 80, 82; WhoWor 74*

Barnes, Leonard John
English. Author
b. Jul 21, 1895 in London, England
Source: *ConAu 29R; ConAu P-2*

Barnes, Margaret Ayer
American. Author, Critic
b. Apr 8, 1886 in Chicago, Illinois
d. Oct 26, 1967
Source: *AmAu&B; ConAmA; ConAu 25R; DcLEL; InWom; OxAmL; REnAL; TwCA, SUP; WhAm 4; WhNAA; WomWWA 14*

Barnes, Marvin
"Bad News"
American. Basketball Player
b. Jul 27, 1952 in Providence, Rhode Island
Source: *WhoBbl 73*

Barnet, Charlie (Charles Daly)
American. Band Leader
b. Oct 26, 1913 in New York, New York
Source: *WhoJazz 72*

Barnet, Sylvan M, Jr.
American. Author, Educator
b. Dec 11, 1926 in Brooklyn, New York
Source: *ConAu 1R, 4NR; DrAS 74E; WhoAm 74; WhoPubR 72*

Barnet, Will
American. Artist, Educator
b. May 25, 1911 in Beverly, Massachusetts
Source: *DcAmArt; DcCAA 71, 77; WhoAm 74, 76, 78, 80, 82; WhoAmA 73, 76, 78; WhoE 74*

Barnetson, Lord William Denholm
[Lord Barnetson of Crowborough]
British. Journalist
b. Mar 21, 1917 in Edinburgh, Scotland
d. Mar 12, 1981 in London, England
Source: *Au&Wr 71; BioIn 11; IntAu&W 76, 77; IntWW 76, 77, 78; IntYB 78; NewYTBS 81; Who 74; WhoF&I 74, 75, 77, 79; WhoWor 74, 76, 78*

Barnett, Claude A
American. Business Executive
b. Sep 16, 1889 in Sanford, Florida
d. Aug 2, 1967 in Chicago, Illinois
Source: *WhAm 4, 5; St&PR 75*

Barnett, Marvin Robert
American. Charities Executive
b. Oct 31, 1916 in Jacksonville, Florida
Source: *WhoAm 82; WhoE 74*

Barnhart, Clarence Lewis
American. Lexicographer
Co-editor, *The World Book Dictionary,* 1976.
b. Dec 30, 1900 in Plattsburg, Missouri
Source: *AmAu&B; ConAu 13R; CurBio 54; DrAS 74F; WhoAm 74, 76, 78, 80, 82; WhoWor 74*

Barnum, P(hineas) T(aylor)
[Barnum and Bailey]
American. Circus Owner
Opened "The Greatest Show on Earth," 1871; mayor of Bridgeport, CT, 1875.
b. Jul 5, 1810 in Bethel, Connecticut
d. Apr 7, 1891 in Philadelphia, Pennsylvania
Source: *Alli, SUP; AmAu&B; AmBi; ApCAB; BbD; BiD&SB; DcAmAu; DcAmB; DcNAA; Drake; EncAB-H; MnBBF; NewCol 75; OxAmL; OxThe; REn; REnAL; TwCBDA; WebAB; WhAm H*

Barnum and Bailey
see: Bailey, James Anthony; Barnum, P(hineas) T(aylor)

Barolini, Antonio
American. Author
b. May 29, 1910 in Vicenza, Italy
Source: *ConAu 1R, 1NR*

Baron, Samuel
American. Musician
b. Apr 27, 1925 in Brooklyn, New York
Source: *WhoAm 74, 76, 78, 80; WhoWor 74; WhoWorJ 72*

Barr, Alfred Hamilton, Jr.
"The Pope"
American. Art Scholar
b. Jan 28, 1902 in Detroit, Michigan
d. Aug 15, 1981 in Salisbury, Connecticut
Source: *AmAu&B; BioIn 3, 5, 6, 7, 8, 9; ConAu 49; CurBio 61, 81; IntWW 74, 75, 76, 77, 78; LinLib L; NewYTBS 81; PseudN; WhE&EA; Who 74; WhoAm 74, 76, 78; WhoAmA 73, 76, 78*

Barr, George
American. Author
b. Nov 11, 1907 in Brooklyn, New York
Source: *AmAu&B; AuBYP; ConAu 1R, 1NR; SmATA 2*

Barr, Stringfellow
American. Author, Professor
b. Jan 15, 1897 in Suffolk, Virginia
d. Feb 3, 1982 in Alexandria, Virginia
Source: *ConAu 1R, 1NR; CurBio 40, 82; DrAS 74H; IntWW 78, 79; LinLib L, S; NewYTBS 82; OxAmL; REnAL; TwCA SUP; WhoAm 74, 76, 78, 80; WhoWor 74*

Barraclough, Geoffrey
English. Author, Educator
b. May 10, 1908
Source: *ConAu 101; Who 74; WhoWor 74; WorAu*

Barras, Paul Francois Jean Nicolas, Comte de
French. Revolutionary Politician
Took part in overthrow of Robespierre, 1794.
b. Jun 30, 1755
d. Jan 29, 1829
Source: *DcBiPP; DcInB; Dis&D; LinLib S; McGEWB; OxFr; WhDW*

Barrault, Jean-Louis
French. Actor, Stage Director
b. Sep 8, 1910 in Vesinet, France
Source: *BiE&WWA; FilmgC; MovMk; OxFilm; OxThe; WorEFlm*

Barre, Raymond
French. Government Official
Prime Minister, 1976--.
b. Apr 12, 1924 in Saint-Denis, France
Source: *CurBio 77; IntWW 74, 75, 76, 77, 78, 79, 80, 81; IntYB 78, 79, 80, 81; NewYTBS 76; WhoWor 74, 76, 78; WorAl*

Barres, Maurice
French. Author
b. Sep 22, 1862 in Charmes-sur-Moselle, France
d. Dec 4, 1923 in Paris, France
Source: *BiD&SB; CasWL; ClDMEL; EvEuW; LongCTC; NewC; OxEng; OxFr; Pen EUR*

Barrett, Edward Ware
American. Educator, Editor
b. Jul 3, 1910 in Birmingham, Alabama
Source: *CurBio 47; DrAS 74E; IntWW 74; LEduc 74; St&PR 75; WhoAm 74; WhoE 74; WrDr '76*

Barrett, Rona
[Mrs. William A Trowbridge]
American. Gossip Columnist
Began column, 1960; first daily syndicated TV news segment for Metromedia, 1969.
b. Oct 8, 1936 in New York, New York
Source: *AuNews 1; BkPepl; ConAu 103; GoodHS; IntMPA 78, 79, 80, 81, 82*

Barrett, Stan
American. Stuntman
b. 1944 in Saint Louis, Missouri
Source: *BioIn 12*

Barrett, "Syd" (Roger Keith)
[Pink Floyd]
English. Rock Singer, Songwriter
b. Jan 1946 in Cambridge, England
Source: *ConMuA 80; IlEncRk*

Barrett, Sir William
English. Physicist
b. Feb 10, 1844 in Jamaica
d. May 26, 1925 in London, England
Source: *BiDPara*

Barrie, Barbara
American. Actress
b. May 23, 1931 in Chicago, Illinois
Source: *NotNAT; WhoAm 82; WhoHol A; WhoThe 77*

Barrie, Sir James Matthew
Scottish. Dramatist, Author
Wrote *Peter Pan; or, The Boy Who Would Not Grow Up,* 1904.
b. May 9, 1860 in Kirriemuir, Scotland
d. Jun 19, 1937 in London, England
Source: *Alli SUP; AtlBL; BbD; BiD&SB; CarSB; CasWL; Chambr 3; ChPo, S1, S2; CnMD; CnThe; CyWA; DcBiA; DcEnA, AP; DcLEL; EncWL; EvLB; FamAYP; JBA 34; LongCTC; McGEWD; ModBrL; ModWD; NewC; NewCol 75; OxEng; OxThe; Pen ENG; RAdv 1; REn; REnWD; TwCA, SUP; TwCW; WebE&AL; WhScrn 77; WhoChL; WhoStg 1906, 1908; WhoTwCL; YABC 1*

Barrie, Mona
English. Actress
b. Dec 18, 1909 in London, England
Source: *FilmgC; IntMPA 75, 76, 77, 78, 79, 80, 81, 82; MovMk*

Barrie, Wendy
English. Actress
b. Apr 18, 1913 in London, England
d. Feb 2, 1978 in Englewood, New Jersey
Source: *FilmgC; InWom; IntMPA 75, 76, 77; MotPP; MovMk; ThFT; WhoHol A*

Barrios, Francisco Javier
Mexican. Baseball Player
Pitcher, Chicago White Sox, 1974-81.
b. Jun 10, 1953 in Hermosillo, Mexico
d. Apr 9, 1982 in Hermosillo, Mexico
Source: *BaseEn*

Barris, Chuck
American. TV Entertainer, Producer
Created, produced "The Dating Game," 1965-73; "The Newlywed Game," 1966-74.
b. Jun 2, 1929 in Philadelphia, Pennsylvania
Source: *BioNews 74; NewYTET; WhoAm 78, 80, 82; WrDr 76, 80*

Barron, Clarence Walker
American. Editor, Publicist
b. Jul 2, 1855 in Boston, Massachusetts
d. Oct 2, 1928 in Battle Creek, Michigan
Source: *AmBi; DcAmB S1; DcNAA; WebAB; WhAm 1*

Barrow, Clyde
[Bonnie and Clyde]
American. Murderer, Bank Robber
Met Bonnie Parker, 1930; 25 bullets found in body after killed by posse.
b. Mar 24, 1909 in Telice, Texas
d. May 23, 1934 in Louisiana
Source: *BioIn 8, 9; Blood; DrInt; EncACr; REnAW; WorAl*

Barrow, Ed(ward Grant)
American. Baseball Executive
NY Yankees, business manager, 1921-39, president, 1939-45; Hall of Fame, 1953.
b. May 10, 1868 in Springfield, Illinois
d. Dec 15, 1953 in Port Chester, New York
Source: *DcAmB S5; WhoProB 73*

Barrow, Errol Walton
Prime Minister of Barbados
b. Jan 21, 1920 in Saint Lucy, Barbados
Source: *CurBio 68; IntWW 74; Who 74; WhoGov 72; WhoWor 74*

Barrows, (Ruth) Marjorie
American. Author
b. in Chicago, Illinois
Source: *AmAu&B; AuBYP; BioIn 2, 7; ChPo, S1; ConAu P-2; WhoAm 82*

Barry, Daniel
American. Cartoonist
b. Jul 11, 1923 in Long Beach, New Jersey
Source: *WorECom*

Barry, Donald
[Donald Barry de Acosta]
"Red"
American. Actor
b. 1912 in Houston, Texas
d. Jul 17, 1980 in North Hollywood, California
Source: *BioIn 8; FilmgC; IntMPA 75, 76, 77, 78, 79; MotPP; PseudN; WhoHol A*

Barry, Gene
[Eugene Klass]
American. Actor
Starred in TV series "Bat Masterson," "Burke's Law," "Name of the Game."
b. Jun 4, 1922 in New York, New York
Source: *FilmgC; IntMPA 75, 76, 77, 78, 79, 80, 81, 82; MotPP; WhoAm 74, 76, 78, 80, 82; WhoHol A*

Barry, Jack
American. TV Game Show Host, Producer
Producer, "The Joker's Wild," "Tic Tac Dough."
b. Mar 20, 1918 in Lindenhurst, New York
Source: *IntMPA 75, 76, 77, 78, 79, 80, 81, 82; NewYTET; WhoAm 80, 82*

Barry, James Miranda
Scottish. Physician
b. 1795
d. 1865
Source: *BioIn 5, 8, 9, 10, 11; InWom*

Barry, John
American. Naval Officer
b. 1745 in Tacumshane, Ireland
d. Sep 13, 1803 in Philadelphia, Pennsylvania
Source: *AmBi; ApCAB; DcAmB; Drake; TwCBDA; WebAB; WhAm H*

Barry, John
English. Composer
b. Nov 3, 1933 in York, England
Source: *BioIn 7; EncMT; FilmEn; IntMPA 81; OxFilm; WhoMus 72; WhoWor 74; WorEFlm*

Barry, Philip
American. Dramatist
Wrote *The Philadelphia Story;* filmed, 1940 with Katharine Hepburn, Cary Grant.
b. Jun 18, 1896 in Rochester, New York
d. Dec 3, 1949 in New York, New York
Source: *AmAu&B; CasWL; CathA 1930; CnDAL; CnMD; CnThe; ConAmA; DcLEL; DcNAA; EvLB; FilmgC; LongCTC; McGEWD; ModAL; ModWD; NewCol 75; OxAmL; OxThe; Pen AM; REn; REnAL; REnWD; TwCA, SUP; TwCW; WebE&AL; WhAm 2; DcAmB S4*

Barry, Rick (Richard Francis, III)
American. Basketball Player, Broadcaster
Rookie of the Year, 1965; leading scorer, 1966, 1968.
b. Mar 28, 1944 in Elizabeth, New Jersey
Source: *CelR 73; CmCal; CurBio 71; WhoAm 80, 82; WhoBbl 73; WorAl*

Barry, Tom
Irish. Military Tactician
b. Jul 1, 1897 in Rosscarberry, Ireland
d. Jul 2, 1980 in Cork, Ireland
Source: *AnObit 1980; DcIrW 2*

Barrymore, Diana
American. Actress
b. Mar 3, 1922 in New York, New York
d. Jan 25, 1960 in New York, New York
Source: *FilmgC; HolP 40; InWom; MotPP; WhScrn 74, 77; WhoHol B*

Barrymore, Drew
American. Actress
Granddaughter of John Barrymore; Gertie in *ET,* 1982.
b. 1975
Source: *NF*

Barrymore, Elaine Barrie
American. Actress
Source: *BioIn 7; InWom*

Barrymore, Ethel Blythe
"First lady of the American theatre"
American. Actress
Won 1944 Oscar for *None But the Lonely Heart.*
b. Aug 15, 1879 in Philadelphia, Pennsylvania
d. Jun 18, 1959 in Hollywood, California
Source: *CurBio 41, 59; FamA&A; FilmEn; Film 1; FilmgC; HerW; InWom; MotPP; MovMk; OxFilm; OxThe; PlP&P; ThFT; TwYS; WebAB; WhAm 3; WhScrn 74, 77; WhoHol B; WhoStg 1906, 1908; WomWWA 14; WorEFlm*

Barrymore, John Blythe
American. Actor
Known as "great profile" for matinee idol looks; played Richard III, Hamlet on stage.
b. Feb 15, 1882 in Philadelphia, Pennsylvania
d. May 29, 1942 in Hollywood, California
Source: *BiDFilm; CmMov; CurBio 42; DcAmB S3; EncAB-H; FamA&A; FilmEn; Film 1; FilmgC; LongCTC; MotPP; MovMk; OxFilm; OxThe; PlP&P; TwYS; WebAB; WhAm 2; WhScrn 74, 77; WhoHol B; WorEFlm*

Barrymore, John Blythe Drew, Jr.
American. Actor
Son of John Barrymore, Dolores Costello; father of Drew Barrymore.
b. Jun 4, 1932 in Beverly Hills, California
Source: *BioNews 74; FilmEn; FilmgC; IntMPA 75, 76, 77, 78, 79, 80, 81, 82; MotPP; WhoHol A*

Barrymore, Lionel Blythe
American. Actor
Won 1931 Oscar for *Free Soul;* known as composer in later years.
b. Apr 28, 1878 in Philadelphia, Pennsylvania
d. Nov 15, 1954 in Van Nuys, California
Source: *AmSCAP 66; BiDFilm; CurBio 43, 55; DcAmB S5; FamA&A; Film 1; FilmgC; LongCTC; MotPP; MovMk; OxFilm; OxThe; PlP&P; TwYS; WebAB; WhAm 3; WhScrn 74, 77; WhoHol B; WorEFlm*

Barrymore, Maurice
[Herbert Blythe]
English. Actor
Father of Lionel, Ethel, John Barrymore; known as "royal family" of American stage.
b. 1847 in Fort Agra, India
d. Mar 26, 1905 in Amityville, New York
Source: *AmBi; ApCAB SUP; DcAmB; FamA&A; LongCTC; OxThe; PlP&P; WebAB; WhAm 1*

Bart, Jean
French. Privateer
b. Oct 21, 1651
d. Apr 27, 1702
Source: *NewCol 75; WebBD 80*

Bart, Lionel
English. Composer
b. Aug 1, 1930 in London, England
Source: *ConAu 65; EncMT; FilmgC; IntWW 74; NotNAT; Who 74; WhoThe 77; WhoWor 74*

Barth, Belle
[Belle Salzman]
American. Actress
b. Apr 27, 1911 in New York, New York
d. 1971 in Miami Beach, Florida
Source: *WhoHol B*

Barth, Heinrich
German. Explorer, Author
b. 1821 in Hamburg, Germany
d. 1865
Source: *Alli SUP; McGEWB*

Barth, John Simmons
American. Author
Won National Book Award in Fiction, 1973.
b. May 27, 1930 in Cambridge, Maryland
Source: *AmAu&B; AmWr; Au&Wr 71; AuNews 1, 2; CasWL; ConAu 1R, 5NR; ConLC 1, 2, 3, 5, 7, 9, 10, 14; ConNov 72, 76; CurBio 69; DrAF 76; DrAS 74E; EncWL; IntWW 74; ModAL, SUP; OxAmL; Pen AM; RAdv 1; TwCW; WebAB; WebE&AL; WhoAm 74, 76, 78, 80, 82; WhoTwCL; WhoWor 74; WorAu; WrDr 76*

Barth, Karl
Swiss. Theologian
b. May 10, 1886 in Basel, Switzerland
d. Dec 9, 1966 in Basel, Switzerland
Source: *ConAu 25R; CurBio 62, 69; LongCTC; OxGer; TwCA SUP; WhAm 5*

Barth, Roland
American. Author
b. May 18, 1937 in Boston, Massachusetts
Source: *ConAu 45, 1NR*

Barthe, Richmond
American. Sculptor
b. Jan 28, 1901 in Bay St. Louis, Mississippi
Source: *AfroAA; CurBio 40; WhoAm 74; WhoBlA 75; WhoWor 74*

Barthelme, Donald
American. Author
b. Apr 7, 1931 in Philadelphia, Pennsylvania
Source: *AmAu&B; CelR 73; ConAu 21R; ConLC 1, 2, 3, 5, 6, 8, 13; ConNov 76; DrAF 76; ModAL SUP; Pen AM; RAdv 1; SmATA 7; WorAu; WrDr 76*

Barthelmess, Richard
American. Actor
b. May 9, 1895 in New York, New York
d. Aug 17, 1963 in Southampton, New York
Source: *BiDFilm; FilmgC; MotPP; MovMk; OxFilm; TwYS; WhAm 4; WhScrn 74, 77; WhoHol B; WorEFlm*

Barthes, Roland
French. Literary Critic
b. Nov 12, 1915 in Cherbourg, France
d. Mar 25, 1980 in Paris, France
Source: *BioIn 10, 11; ConAu 97; CurBio 79, 80; WhoWor 74*

Bartholdi, Frederic Auguste
French. Artist
b. Apr 2, 1834 in Colmar, France
d. Oct 4, 1904
Source: *ApCAB; REn; TwCBDA*

Bartholomew, Saint
Apostle
Source: *NewC; REn*

Bartholomew, Freddie
American. Actor
Child actor known for first starring part, in *David Copperield,* 1935.
b. Mar 24, 1924 in London, England
Source: *BiDFilm; IntMPA 75, 76, 77, 78, 79, 80, 81, 82; MotPP; MovMk; OxFilm; WhoHol A; WorEFlm*

Bartkowicz, Peaches
American. Tennis Player
b. Apr 4, 1949 in Hamtramck, Michigan
Source: *BioIn 11*

Bartkowski, Steve(n Joseph)
American. Football Player
b. Nov 12, 1952 in Des Moines, Iowa
Source: *BioIn 12; FootReg; NewYTBS 80*

Bartlett, Charles Leffingwell
American. Journalist
b. Aug 14, 1921 in Chicago, Illinois
Source: *ConAu 29R; WhoAm 74, 76, 78, 80, 82; WhoS&SW 73*

Bartlett, John
American. Lexicographer, Publisher
First edition of Bartlett's *Familiar Quotations* published 1855.
b. Jun 14, 1820 in Plymouth, Massachusetts
d. Dec 3, 1905 in Cambridge, Massachusetts
Source: *Alli, SUP; AmAu; AmAu&B; AmBi; ApCAB; BiD&SB; ChPo; CnDAL; DcAmAu; DcAmB; DcNAA; EvLB; LongCTC; OxAmL; REn; REnAL; TwCBDA; WebAB; WhAm 1*

Bartlett, John Russell
American. Historian, Bibliographer
b. Oct 23, 1805 in Providence, Rhode Island
d. May 28, 1886 in Providence, Rhode Island
Source: *Alli, SUP; AmAu; AmAu&B; AmBi; ApCAB; ArizL; BiAuS; BiD&SB; WhAm H*

Bartlett, John Sherren
American. Newspaper Editor
b. 1790 in Dorsetshire, England
d. Aug 23, 1863 in Middletown Point, New Jersey
Source: *ApCAB; DcAmB; Drake; WhAm H*

Bartlett, Josiah
American. Physician, Lawyer
b. Nov 21, 1729 in Amesbury, Massachusetts
d. May 19, 1795 in Kingston, Massachusetts
Source: *AmBi; ApCAB; BiAuS; BiDrAC; DcAmB; Drake; TwCBDA; WhAm H; WhAmP*

Bartlett, Paul Wayland
American. Sculptor
b. 1865 in New Haven, Connecticut
d. Sep 20, 1925
Source: *AmBi; DcAmB; TwCBDA; WhAm 1*

Bartlett, Robert Abram
American. Explorer
Commanded Robert E Peary's ship on expedition that reached North Pole, 1908-9.
b. Aug 15, 1875 in Brigus, NF
d. Apr 28, 1946 in New York, New York
Source: *AmAu&B; CurBio 46; DcNAA; WebAB; WhAm 2*

Bartlett, Vernon
English. Author, Politician
b. Apr 30, 1894 in Westbury, England
Source: *Au&Wr 71; ConAu 61; IntWW 74; LongCTC; NewC; TwCA, SUP; Who 74; WhoLA; WrDr 76*

Bartok, Bela
Hungarian. Composer
b. Mar 25, 1881 in Nagyszentmiklos, Hungary
d. Sep 29, 1945 in New York, New York
Source: *AmSCAP 66; AtlBL; CurBio 40, 45; WhAm 4*

Bartok, Eva
British. Actress
b. Jun 18, 1929 in Budapest, Hungary
Source: *FilmgC; InWom; IntWW 74; WhoHol A*

Bartolommeo, Fra
Italian. Artist, Architect
b. Mar 28, 1475
d. Oct 31, 1517 in Florence, Italy
Source: *AtlBL; NewCol 75*

Barton, Bruce
American. Author, Advertising Executive
b. Aug 5, 1886 in Robbins, Tennessee
d. Jul 5, 1967 in New York, New York
Source: *AmAu&B; BiDrAC; CurBio 61, 67; EncAB-H; OhA&B; WebAB; WhAm 4; WhAmP; WhNAA*

Barton, Clara Harlowe
"Angel of the Battlefield"
American. Teacher, Social Reformer
Organized American National Red Cross, 1891; president until 1904.
b. Dec 25, 1821 in Oxford, Massachusetts
d. Apr 12, 1912 in Glen Echo, Maryland
Source: *AmAu&B; AmBi; DcAmB; DcNAA; EncAB-H; HerW; InWom; NewCol 75; NotAW; REn; REnAL; WebAB; WhAm 1*

Barton, Derek Harold Richard
English. Chemist
b. Sep 8, 1918 in Gravesend, England
Source: *BioIn 1, 3, 4, 6, 8, 9; IntWW 74; Who 74; WhoWor 74*

Barton, George
American. Author, Historian
b. Jan 22, 1866 in Philadelphia, Pennsylvania
d. Mar 16, 1940
Source: *AmAu&B; CathA 1930; CurBio 40; DcNAA; WhAm 1*

Barton, James
American. Actor
b. Nov 1, 1890 in Gloucester, New Jersey
d. Feb 19, 1962 in Mineola, New York
Source: *EncMT; FilmgC; MotPP; MovMk; Vers B; WhScrn 74, 77; WhoHol B*

Bartos, Karl
see: Kraftwerk

Bartram, John
American. Botanist
b. Mar 23, 1699 in Chester County, Pennsylvania
d. Sep 22, 1777 in Kingsessing, Pennsylvania
Source: *AmBi; ApCAB; BioIn 2, 3, 6, 7, 8, 10, 11; DcAmB; DcScB; Drake; EncAAH; McGEWB; NatCAB 7; WebAB*

Bartram, William
American. Naturalist
b. Feb 9, 1739 in Kingsessing, Pennsylvania
d. Jul 22, 1823 in Philadelphia, Pennsylvania
Source: *Alli; AmAu; AmAu&B; AmBi; ApCAB; BiDLA; BiDSA; CasWL; CyAL 1; DcAmAu; DcAmB; DcLEL; DcNAA; Drake; OxAmL; OxEng; Pen AM; REn; REnAL; TwCBDA; WebAB; WhAm H*

Baruch, Andre
French. Announcer, Commentator
b. in Paris, France
Source: *IntMPA 75, 76, 77, 78, 79, 80, 81, 82*

Baruch, Bernard Mannes
American. Businessman, Statesman
b. Aug 19, 1870 in Camden, South Carolina
d. Jun 20, 1965 in New York, New York
Source: *AmAu&B; CurBio 41, 50, 65; EncAB-H; REn; REnAL; WebAB; WhAm 4; WhAmP*

Barylli, Walter
Austrian. Musician
b. 1921 in Vienna, Austria
Source: *WhoMus 72*

Baryshnikov, Mikhail
"Misha"
Russian. Ballet Dancer, Director
Defected to West, Jun 30, 1974; director of American Ballet Theatre, 1980--.
b. Jan 28, 1948 in Riga, U.S.S.R.
Source: *BioNews 75; BkPepl; CurBio 75; NewYTBS 74; Who 82; WhoAm 82*

Barzin, Leon
Belgian. Conductor
b. Nov 27, 1900 in Brussels, Belgium
Source: *CurBio 51; NewYTBE 70; WhoMus 72; WhoWor 74*

Barzini, Luigi
Italian. Author
b. Dec 21, 1908 in Milan, Italy
Source: *ConAu 13R; CurBio 51; IntWW 74; WhoWor 74; WorAu*

Barzun, Jacques Martin
American. Author, Educator, Historian
Advocated liberal arts studies rather than vocational courses.
b. Nov 30, 1907 in Creteil, France
Source: *AmAu&B; Au&Wr 71; CelR 73; ConAu 61; CurBio 64; DrAS 74H; EncMys; IntWW 74; NewCol 75; OxAmL; RAdv 1; REn; REnAL; TwCA, SUP; WebAB; Who 74; WhoAm 74, 76, 78, 80, 82; WhoAmA 73; WhoMus 72; WhoWor 74; WrDr 76*

Basehart, Richard
American. Actor
Won 1956 Oscar for *Moby Dick*.
b. Aug 31, 1914 in Zanesville, Ohio
Source: *BiE&WWA; FilmgC; IntMPA 75, 76, 77, 78, 79, 80, 81, 82; OxFilm; WhoAm 74, 76, 78, 80, 82; WhoHol A*

Basho
Japanese. Poet, Writer
Zen Buddhist haiku master.
b. 1644 in Ueno, Iga, Japan
d. Nov 28, 1694 in Osaka, Japan
Source: *CasWL; DcOrL 1; Pen CL; REn*

Basie, "Count" (William)
American. Jazz Musician, Band Leader
Received Kennedy Center Honors medal, 1981; band leader, 1936--.
b. Aug 21, 1904 in Red Bank, New Jersey
Source: *AmSCAP 66; BioNews 74; CelR 73; CurBio 42; WebAB; WhoAm 74, 76, 78, 80, 82; WhoBlA 75; WhoWor 74*

Basil (the Great)
Greek. Church Statesman, Author
b. 330 in Caesarea, Cappadocia
d. Jan 1, 379
Source: *CasWL; Pen CL*

Baskerville, John
English. Printer, Type Designer
b. Jan 28, 1706
d. Jan 8, 1775
Source: *NewC*

Baskin, Leonard
American. Sculptor
b. Aug 15, 1922 in New Brunswick, New Jersey
Source: *CurBio 64; DcCAA 71; WebAB; WhoAm 74; WhoAmA 73; WhoGrA; WhoWor 74*

Baskin, Wade
American. Author, Educator
b. Jul 27, 1924 in Harmony, Arkansas
Source: *ConAu 25R; ConAu P-2; WhoS&SW 73*

Bass, Alfie
English. Actor
b. 1921 in London, England
Source: *FilmgC; WhoHol A*

Bass, Sam
American. Outlaw
Robber of stage coaches, trains, banks; also owned a whorehouse.
b. Jul 21, 1851 in Mitchell, Indiana
d. Jul 21, 1878 in Round Rock, Texas
Source: *BioIn 4, 5, 8, 11; DcAmB; NewCol 75; REnAW; WebAB; WhAm H*

Bass, Saul
American. Motion Picture Director, Producer
b. May 8, 1920 in New York, New York
Source: *DcFM; FilmgC; IntMPA 75, 76, 77, 78, 79, 80, 81, 82; OxFilm; WhoAm 74; WhoGrA; WhoWor 74; WhoWorJ 72; WorEFlm*

Bassey, Shirley
Welsh. Singer
Sang title song from James Bond film *Goldfinger,* 1964.
b. Jan 8, 1937 in Cardiff, Wales
Source: *CelR 73; FilmgC; WhoAm 82*

Bastianini, Ettore
Italian. Opera Singer
b. 1923 in Siena, Italy
d. Jan 25, 1967 in Sirmione, Italy
Source: *WhAm 4*

Basualto, Neftali Ricardo Reyes
see: Neruda, Pablo, pseud.

Batchelor, Clarence Daniel
American. Cartoonist
b. Apr 1, 1888 in Osage City, Kansas
d. Sep 5, 1977 in Deep River, Connecticut
Source: *ConAu 73; WhAm 7; WhoAm 74, 76; WhoAmA 76, 78*

Bate, Walter Jackson
American. Educator, Author
b. May 23, 1918 in Mankato, Minnesota
Source: *AmAu&B; ConAu 5R; DrAS 74E; OxAmL; Who 74; WhoAm 74, 76, 78, 80, 82; WorAu*

Bateman, Mary
"Yorkshire Witch"
English. Murderer
b. 1768 in Aisenby, England
d. Mar 20, 1809
Source: *LookW*

Bates, Alan Arthur
English. Actor
Starred in films *King of Hearts,* 1967; *An Unmarried Woman,* 1978.
b. Feb 17, 1934 in Derbyshire, England
Source: *BiE&WWA; BkPepl; CelR 73; CurBio 69; FilmgC; IntMPA 77, 78, 79, 80, 81, 82; IntWW 74; MovMk; NotNAT; Who 74; WhoAm 82; WhoHol A; WhoThe 77; WhoWor 74*

Bates, Arlo
American. Author, Poet
b. 1850 in East Machias, Maine
d. Aug 24, 1918 in Boston, Massachusetts
Source: *Alli SUP; AmAu; AmAu&B; BbD; BiD&SB; CarSB; ChPo; DcAmAu; DcBiA; DcNAA; OxAmL*

Bates, Florence
American. Actress
b. Apr 15, 1888 in San Antonio, Texas
d. Jan 31, 1954 in Burbank, California
Source: *FilmgC; MotPP; MovMk; Vers A; WhScrn 74, 77; WhoHol B*

Bates, H(erbert) E(rnest)
English. Author
b. May 16, 1905 in Rushden, England
d. Jan 25, 1974
Source: *Au&Wr 71; CasWL; ChPo, S1; ConAu 45, 93; CurBio 44, 74; DcLEL; EncWL; EvLB; LongCTC; ModBrL; NewC; Pen ENG; REn; TwCA, SUP; TwCW; WhAm 6; Who 74; WhoWor 74*

Bates, Katherine Lee
American. Poet, Educator
b. Aug 12, 1859 in Falmouth, Massachusetts
d. Mar 28, 1929 in Wellesley, Massachusetts
Source: *DcAmB S1; HerW; WomWWA 14*

Bates, Mary Elizabeth
American. Surgeon, Reformer
b. Feb 25, 1861 in Manitowoc, Wisconsin
d. 1954
Source: *InWom; WhAm 4; WomWWA 14*

Bates, "Peg Leg" (Clayton)
American. Dancer
b. 1907
Source: *BioIn 1, 10*

Bates, Ted (Theodore Lewis)
American. Advertising Executive
b. Sep 11, 1901 in New Haven, Connecticut
d. May 1972
Source: *NewYTBE 72; WhAm 5; WhoAdv 72*

Bates, William Horatio
American. Physician
b. 1860 in New York, New York
d. Jul 10, 1931
Source: *DcNAA*

Bateson, Gregory
American. Author, Behavorial Scientist
b. May 9, 1904 in Cambridge, England
d. Jul 4, 1980 in San Francisco, California
Source: *AmAu&B; AmM&WS 73S; ConAu 41R, 101*

Bateson, William
British. Biologist, Founded Genetics
Pioneer in genetics; formulated theories on evolution of vertebrates.
b. Aug 8, 1861
d. 1926
Source: *AsBiEn; BioIn 10; DcScB; WebBD 80*

Bathory, Elizabeth
"The Blood Countess"
Hungarian. Murderer
b. 1560
d. 1614
Source: *BioIn 4, 9; FanAl; InWom; LookW*

Bathsheba
Biblical Character
b. 1040BC
d. 1015BC
Source: *InWom*

Batista y Zaldivar, Fulgencio
Cuban. President
Dictator who came to power, 1952; overthrown by Fidel Castro, 1959.
b. Jan 16, 1901 in Banes, Cuba
d. Aug 6, 1973 in Guadalmina, Spain
Source: *BioIn 1, 2, 3, 4, 5, 6, 8, 10; CurBio 52, 73; NewYTBE 73*

Battelle, Phyllis Marie
American. Journalist
b. Jan 4, 1922 in Dayton, Ohio
Source: *ConAu 77; ForWC 70; InWom; WhoAm 74*

Batten, William Milfred
American. Businessman
Chairman, chief executive, NY Stock Exchange, 1976--.
b. Jun 4, 1909 in Reedy, West Virginia
Source: *IntWW 74, 75, 76, 77, 78, 79, 80; NewYTBS 76; St&PR 75; WhoAm 74; WhoE 74; WhoF&I 74, 75, 77, 79, 81*

Battistini, Mattia
Italian. Opera Singer
b. Feb 27, 1856 in Rome, Italy
d. Nov 7, 1928 in Collebaccaro, Italy
Source: *NewEOp 71*

Battles, Cliff(ord Franklin)
American. Football Player
b. May 1, 1910 in Akron, Ohio
d. Apr 27, 1981 in Clearwater, Florida
Source: *BioIn 6, 8, 9; WhoFtbl 74*

Batu Khan
Mongolian. Leader of Golden Horde
d. 1255
Source: *NewCol 75*

Baucus, Max Sieben
American. Senator
b. Dec 11, 1941 in Helena, Montana
Source: *AlmAP 78, 80; CngDr 77, 79; WhoAm 76, 78, 80, 82; WhoAmP 75, 77, 79; WhoGov 75, 77; WhoWest 78*

Baudelaire, Charles Pierre
French. Poet
Best known poems contained in *Les Fleurs du Mal*, 1857.
b. Apr 9, 1821 in Paris, France
d. Aug 31, 1867 in Paris, France
Source: *AtlBL; BbD; BiD&SB; CasWL; ClDMEL; CyWA; DcEuL; EuAu; EvEuW; NewC; OxEng; OxFr; Pen EUR; REn*

Baudo, Serge
French. Conductor
b. Jul 16, 1927 in Marseilles, France
Source: *WhoWor 74*

Baudouin, Albert Charles
Belgian. King
b. Sep 7, 1930 in Brussels, Belgium
Source: *IntWW 74; WhoWor 74*

Bauer, Hank (Henry Albert)
American. Baseball Player, Manager
Managed Baltimore Orioles to world championship, 1966.
b. Jul 31, 1922 in East St. Louis, Illinois
Source: *BaseEn; CurBio 67; WhoProB 73*

Bauer, Harold
English. Musician
b. Apr 28, 1873 in London, England
d. Mar 12, 1951 in Miami, Florida
Source: *AmSCAP 66; DcAmB S5; WhAm 3*

Bauer, Helen
American. Author
b. Aug 14, 1900 in DeQueen, Arkansas
Source: *ConAu 5R; ForWC 70; SmATA 2*

Bauer, Royal Daniel Michael
American. Author
b. Oct 25, 1889 in Union, Missouri
Source: *AmM&WS 73; ConAu 33R*

Bauersfeld, Walther
German. Inventor, Engineer
b. 1879
d. Oct 28, 1959 in Heidenheim, Germany (West)
Source: *BioIn 3, 5*

Baugh, Albert Croll
American. Author, Medieval Scholar
b. Feb 26, 1891 in Philadelphia, Pennsylvania
d. Mar 21, 1981 in Philadelphia, Pennsylvania
Source: *AmAu&B; BioIn 3; ConAu 103; DrAS 78E; LinLib L; NewYTBS 81; WhoAm 74, 76, 78, 80; WhE&EA; WhoWor 78*

Baugh, Sammy (Samuel Adrian)
American. Football Player, Coach
Quarterback, Washington Redskins, 1937-52; Hall of Fame, 1963.
b. Mar 17, 1914 in Temple, Texas
Source: *WebAB; WhoFtbl 74; WorAl*

Baum, Kurt
Czech. Opera Singer
b. Mar 15, 1908 in Prague, Czechoslovakia
Source: *BioIn 2, 4, 5; CurBio 56; WhoWor 74*

Baum, (Lyman) Frank
American. Author, Journalist
Wrote *The Wizard of Oz,* 1900.
b. May 15, 1856 in Chittenango, New York
d. May 6, 1919 in Hollywood, California
Source: *AmAu&B; AmBi; AuBYP; CarSB; ChPo, S2; CnDAL; DcAmAu; DcAmB; DcNAA; FamSYP; LongCTC; OxAmL; Pen AM; REn; REnAL; ThrBJA; TwCA; WebAB; WhoChL; WhoStg 1906, 1908*

Baum, Vicki
Austrian. Author
b. Jan 24, 1888 in Vienna, Austria
d. Aug 29, 1960 in Hollywood, California
Source: *AmAu&B; AmNov; CasWL; ConAu 93; CyWA; EvEuW; LongCTC; OxGer; TwCA, SUP; TwCW; WhAm 4; WhoLA*

Baumeister, Willi
German. Artist
b. Jan 22, 1889 in Stuttgart, Germany
d. Aug 31, 1955 in Stuttgart, Germany (West)
Source: *ConArt; McGDA*

Baunsgaard, Hilmar
Danish. Prime Minister
b. Feb 26, 1920
Source: *IntWW 74; WhoWor 74*

Bausch, Edward
American. Optical Instruments Inventor
With Henry Lomb, began Vulcanite Optical Instrument Co., 1866.
b. Sep 26, 1854 in Rochester, New York
d. Jul 30, 1944 in Rochester, New York
Source: *CurBio 44; DcAmB S3; DcNAA; WhAm 2*

Bavier, Frances
American. Actress
Played Aunt Bea in TV series "The Andy Griffith Show," 1960-69.
b. 1905 in New York, New York
Source: *WhoHol A*

Bawden, Nina Mary Mabey
[Nina Mary Mabey Kark]
English. Author
b. Jan 19, 1925 in London, England
Source: *Au&Wr 71; AuBYP SUP; BioIn 10, 11; ChILR 2; ConAu 21R; ConNov 76; FourBJA; IntAu&W 76, 77; SmATA 4; TwCCW 78; WrDr 76, 80*

Bax, Sir Arnold Edward Trevor
English. Composer, Author
b. Nov 8, 1883 in Streatham, England
d. Oct 3, 1953 in Cork, Ireland
Source: *CurBio 43, 54; DcCM; LongCTC*

Baxt, George
American. Author
b. Jun 11, 1923 in Brooklyn, New York
Source: *ConAu 21R*

Baxter, Anne
American. Actress
Won 1947 Oscar for *The Razor's Edge.*
b. May 7, 1923 in Michigan City, Indiana
Source: *BiDFilm; BiE&WWA; CelR 73; CurBio 72; FilmgC; InWom; IntMPA 75, 76, 77, 78, 79, 80, 81, 82; MotPP; MovMk; NotNAT; WhoAm 74, 76, 78, 80, 82; WhoThe 77; WorEFlm*

Baxter, Frank Condie
American. Educator
Won seven Emmys for TV show "Shakespeare on TV."
b. May 4, 1896 in Newbold, New Jersey
d. Jan 20, 1982 in San Marino, California
Source: *CurBio 55; WhoAm 74, 76, 78*

Baxter, James Phinney
American. Educator
b. Feb 15, 1893 in Portland, Maine
d. Jun 17, 1974 in Williamstown, Massachusetts
Source: *AmAu&B; ConAu 57, 65; CurBio 47; OxAmL; TwCA SUP; WhAm 6; WhoWor 74*

Baxter, Keith
Welsh. Actor
b. Apr 29, 1935 in Newport, Wales
Source: *BiE&WWA; IntMPA 75, 76, 77, 78, 79, 80, 81, 82; NotNAT; WhoHol A; WhoThe 77*

Baxter, Les
American. Band Leader
b. Mar 14, 1922 in Mexia, Texas
Source: *AmSCAP 66*

Baxter, Warner
American. Actor
b. Mar 29, 1891 in Columbus, Ohio
d. May 7, 1951 in Beverly Hills, California
Source: *BiDFilm; CmMov; Film 1; FilmgC; MotPP; MovMk; OxFilm; TwYS; WhAm 3; WhScrn 74, 77; WhoHol B; WorEFlm*

Baxter-Birney, Meredith
[Mrs. David Birney]
American. Actress
Starred in TV series "Bridget Loves Bernie," 1971-72; "Family," 1976-80.
b. Jun 21, 1947? in Los Angeles, California
Source: *BioIn 9; NewYTBE 72; WhoAm 82*

Bay City Rollers
[Eric Faulkner; Alan Longmuir; Derek Longmuir; Leslie McKeown; St]
Scottish. Rock Group
Source: *BkPepl; IlEncRk*

Bayard, Pierre du Terrail
French. Soldier
b. 1473
d. Apr 30, 1524
Source: *OxFr; REn*

Bayes, Nora
[Dora Goldberg]
American. Singer, Actress
b. Jan 10, 1880 in Los Angeles, California
d. Mar 19, 1928 in New York, New York
Source: *EncMT; FilmgC; InWom; NotAW; WebAB*

Bayes, Ronald
American. Author
b. Jul 19, 1932 in Freewater, Oregon
Source: *ConAu 25R; DrAS 74E; WhoS&SW 73*

Bayh, Birch Evans, Jr.
American. Lawyer, Politician
Senator from IN, 1962-81.
b. Jan 22, 1928 in Terre Haute, Indiana
Source: *BiDrAC; CelR 73; CngDr 74; ConAu 41R; CurBio 65; IntWW 74; NewYTBE 70; WhoAm 74, 76, 78, 80, 82; WhoAmP 73; WhoGov 72; WhoMW 74; WhoWor 74*

Bayle, Pierre
French. Philosopher, Critic
b. Nov 18, 1647
d. Dec 28, 1706
Source: *BbD; BiD&SB; CasWL; DcEnL; DcEuL; EuAu; EvEuW; NewC; OxEng; OxFr; Pen EUR; REn*

Baylis, Lilian Mary
English. Theatrical Manager
b. May 9, 1874 in London, England
d. Nov 25, 1937
Source: *BioIn 1, 2, 3, 4, 6, 10; CnThe; EncWT; LongCTC; NotNAT A; OxMus; OxThe; WhThe*

Baylor, Elgin
American. Basketball Player
NBA Rookie of Year, 1959; scored 71 points in one game, 1960.
b. Sep 16, 1934 in Washington, DC
Source: *NewYTBE 71; WhoBbl 73*

Bayne, Beverly
American. Actress
Played Juliet in first American film version of *Romeo and Juliet,* 1915.
b. 1895
d. Aug 29, 1982 in Scottsdale, Arizona
Source: *Film 1; MotPP; TwYS; WhoHol A*

Bazin, Rene
French. Author
b. Dec 26, 1853 in Angers, France
d. Jul 21, 1932
Source: *CathA 1930; CIDMEL; DcBiA; EvEuW; LongCTC; OxFr; Pen EUR; REn; TwCA, SUP*

Baziotes, William
American. Artist
b. Jun 11, 1912 in Pittsburgh, Pennsylvania
d. Jun 5, 1963 in New York, New York
Source: *DcCAA 71; WhAm 4*

Bazna, Elyesa
[Cicero]
German. Spy
b. 1904
d. 1970 in Munich, Germany (West)
Source: *BioIn 1; NewYTBE 70; WhWW-II*

Beach, Alfred Ely
American. Journalist, Inventor
Built demonstration pneumatic passenger subway under Broadway in NY, 1868.
b. Sep 1, 1826 in Springfield, Massachusetts
d. Jan 1, 1896 in New York, New York
Source: *DcAmB; NatCAB 8; TwCBDA; WebAB; WhAm H*

Beach, Mrs. H H A
[Amy Marcy Cheney]
American. Composer
b. Sep 5, 1867 in Henniker, New Hampshire
d. Dec 27, 1944 in New York, New York
Source: *AmSCAP 66; AmWom; Baker 78; CurBio 45; DcAmB S3; NatCAB 15; TwCBDA*

Beach, Joseph Warren
American. Critic, Author
b. Jan 14, 1880 in Gloversville, New York
d. Aug 13, 1957 in Minneapolis, Minnesota
Source: *AmAu&B; AmLY; CnDAL; OxAmL; TwCA SUP; WhAm 3*

Beach, Rex Ellingwood
American. Author
b. Dec 1, 1877 in Atwood, Michigan
d. Dec 7, 1949 in Sebring, Florida
Source: *AmAu&B; CyWA; DcAmB S4; DcLEL; DcNAA; EvLB; LongCTC; OxAmL; REnAL; TwCA, SUP; TwCW; TwYS; WhAm 2; WhNAA*

Beach, Sylvia
American. Bookseller, Publisher
Printed James Joyce's *Ulysses,* 1919, when no other publisher could be found.
b. 1887 in Baltimore, Maryland
d. Oct 6, 1962 in Paris, France
Source: *CasWL; LongCTC; Pen AM; REnAL*

Beach Boys, The
[Al Jardine; Bruce Johnson; Mike Love; Brian Wilson; Carl Wilson; Dennis Wilson]
American. Rock Group
Created "California Sound" or "Surf Music" of early 1960's.
Source: *BkPepl; EncPR&S; IlEncRk; Rk100*

Beaconsfield, Benjamin Disraeli, Earl
see: Disraeli, Benjamin

Beadle, William
American. Murderer
Slaughtered his family, then killed himself.
d. Dec 11, 1873 in Weathersfield, Connecticut
Source: *Blood*

Beal, John
[J Alexander Bliedung]
American. Actor
b. Aug 19, 1909 in Joplin, Missouri
Source: *BiE&WWA; FilmgC; HolP 30; IntMPA 75, 76, 77, 78, 79, 80, 81, 82; MovMk; NotNAT; WhoHol A; WhoThe 77*

Beale, Betty
[Mrs. George Graeber]
American. Journalist
b. 1912 in Washington, DC
Source: *CelR 73; ForWC 70; InWom; WhoAm 74, 76, 78, 80, 82; WhoS&SW 73*

Bealer, Alex W
American. Children's Author
b. Mar 6, 1921 in Valdosta, Georgia
d. Mar 17, 1980 in Atlanta, Georgia
Source: *ConAu 45, 97, 2NR; SmATA 8*

Beall, Lester Thomas
American. Designer, Illustrator
b. Mar 14, 1903 in Kansas City, Missouri
d. Jun 20, 1969
Source: *CurBio 49, 69; WhoAmA 73; WhoGrA*

Beals, Carleton
American. Author
Wrote extensively about South and Latin America.
b. Nov 13, 1893 in Medicine Lodge, Kansas
d. Jun 26, 1979 in Middletown, Connecticut
Source: *AmAu&B; AuBYP; ConAu 1R, 3NR; CurBio 41, 79; DcLEL; IntAu&W 76, 77; IntWW 75, 76, 77, 78; NewYTBS 79; OxAmL; REnAL; ScF&FL 1, 2; SmATA 12; TwCA, SUP; WhoAm 76, 78; WhoWor 74; WrDr 76, 80*

Beals, Ralph Leon
American. Anthropologist, Author
b. Jul 19, 1901 in Pasadena, California
Source: *AmAu&B; AmM&WS 73S; ConAu 25R; WhoAm 74*

Beame, Abraham David
American. Former Mayor
First Jew ever elected mayor of NY City, 1974-77.
b. Mar 20, 1906 in London, England
Source: *CurBio 74; NewYTBE 73; NewYTBS 74; WhoAm 74, 76, 78, 80, 82; WhoE 74*

Bean, Alan L
American. Astronaut
Lunar module pilot on Apollo 12 flight to moon, 1969.
b. Mar 15, 1932 in Wheeler, Texas
Source: *IntWW 74; NewYTBE 73; WhoAm 74, 76, 78, 80, 82; WhoS&SW 73*

Bean, Andy
American. Golfer
b. Mar 13, 1953 in Lafayette, Georgia
Source: *BioIn 11, 12*

Bean, L(eon) L(eonwood)
American. Retailing, Manufacturing Exec.
b. 1872 in Greenwood, Maine
d. Feb 5, 1967
Source: *BioIn 1, 5, 7; WhAm 4*

Bean, Judge Roy
American. Frontier Lawman
Called "law west of the Pecos"; held court in own saloon.
b. 1825 in Mason County, Kentucky
d. Mar 16, 1903 in Langtry, Texas
Source: *FilmgC; WebAB*

Bean, Orson
[Dallas Frederick Burrows]
American. Actor, Comedian
b. Jul 22, 1928 in Burlington, Vermont
Source: *ConAu 77; CurBio 67; MotPP; NotNAT; WhoAm 74, 76, 78, 80, 82; WhoHol A; WhoThe 77; WhoWor 74*

Beard, Charles Austin
American. Historian, Educator
b. Nov 27, 1874 in Knightstown, Indiana
d. Sep 1, 1948 in New Haven, Connecticut
Source: *AmAu&B; ConAmA; DcAmB S4; DcLEL; DcNAA; EncAB-H; EvLB; IndAu 1816; LongCTC; OxAmL; Pen AM; REnAL; TwCA, SUP; WebAB; WebE&AL; WhAm 2*

Beard, Daniel Carter
American. Artist
Founded Boy Scouts of America, 1910; only recipient of Golden Eagle Medal.
b. Jun 21, 1850 in Cincinnati, Ohio
d. Jun 11, 1941 in Suffern, New York
Source: *AfroAA; Alli SUP; AmAu&B; AmLY; BiD&SB; CarSB; ChPo; CurBio 41; DcAmAu; DcAmB S3; DcNAA; JBA 34; OhA&B; OxAmL; REnAL; TwCA, SUP; TwCBDA; WebAB; WhAm 1; WhNAA*

Beard, Dita
American. Lobbyist
b. 1918
Source: *BioIn 9, 10, 11*

Beard, Frank
see: ZZ Top

Beard, George Miller
American. Scientist, Physician, Engineer
b. May 8, 1839 in Montville, Connecticut
d. Jan 23, 1883 in New York, New York
Source: *Alli SUP; AmBi; ApCAB; BbD; BiD&SB; DcAmAu; DcAmB; DcNAA; TwCBDA; WhAm H*

Beard, James Andrews
American. Chef, Author
b. May 5, 1903 in Portland, Oregon
Source: *AmAu&B; CelR 73; CurBio 64; WhoAm 74, 76, 78, 80, 82; WrDr 76*

Beard, Mary Ritter
American. Historian
b. Aug 5, 1876 in Indianapolis, Indiana
d. Aug 14, 1958 in Phoenix, Arizona
Source: *AmAu&B; CurBio 41, 58; DcAmB S4; DcLEL; DcNAA; InWom; IndAu 1816; OxAmL; REnAL; TwCA, SUP; WhAm 3; WhNAA*

Beard, Matthew
[Our Gang]
"Stymie"
American. Actor
b. Jan 1, 1925 in Los Angeles, California
d. Jan 8, 1981 in Los Angeles, California
Source: *BioIn 10; DcBlPA; PseudN; WhoHol A*

Beard, Myron Gould
American. Airline Pioneer
First airplane pilot to fly DC-3, 1935; helped to develop Boeing 707.
b. Nov 13, 1896 in Foochow, China
d. Dec 1974 in Northport, New York
Source: *NewYTBS 74*

Beard, Ralph
[Fabulous Five]
American. Basketball Player
b. Dec 1, 1927 in Hardingburg, Kentucky
Source: *BioIn 2, 10; WhoBbl 73*

Bearden, Romare Howard
American. Artist
b. Sep 2, 1914 in Charlotte, North Carolina
Source: *AfroAA; BioIn 8, 9, 10, 11; CurBio 72; DcAmArt; DcCAA 71, 77; McGEWB; WhoAm 74, 76, 78, 80, 82; WhoAmA 76, 78; WhoWor 74*

Beardsley, Aubrey Vincent
English. Illustrator
Best known for sensual, often macabre black and white illustrations.
b. Aug 21, 1872 in Brighton, England
d. Mar 16, 1898 in Merton, England
Source: *AtlBL; BrAu 19; ChPo, S2; DcLEL; NewC; REn; WebE&AL*

Beatles, The
[George Harrison; John Lennon; Paul McCartney; Ringo Starr]
English. Rock Group
"I Want to Hold Your Hand," 1963, sold over 12 million copies; have sold over 400 million records.
Source: *EncPR&S; FilmgC; IlEncRk; MotPP; MovMk; NewCol 75; NewYTBS 75; OxFilm; RkOn 2; Rk100; WhoRock 81; WorEFlm*

Beaton, Sir Cecil Walter Hardy
English. Photographer, Designer
b. Jan 14, 1904 in London, England
d. Jan 18, 1980 in Wiltshire, England
Source: *Au&Wr 71; BiE&WWA; ConAu 81; CurBio 44, 62; IntWW 74; LongCTC; NewC; NotNAT; OxFilm; Who 74; WhoThe 77; WhoWor 74; WorEFlm; WorFshn; WrDr 76*

Beatrix
[Beatrix Wilhelmina Armgard]
Dutch. Queen of the Netherlands
Invested as Queen, April 30, 1980.
b. Jan 31, 1938 in Soestdijk, Netherlands
Source: *BioIn 2, 3, 5, 7, 10, 11; InWom; NewCol 75; WhoWor 74*

Beatty, Clyde
American. Animal Trainer, Performer
b. Jun 10, 1905 in Chillicothe, Ohio
d. Jul 19, 1965 in Ventura, California
Source: *BioIn 2, 6, 7, 8; WhScrn 74, 77; WhoHol B*

Beatty, David Beatty, Earl
English. Admiral
b. 1871 in Nantwich, England
d. 1936
Source: *BioIn 2, 6, 11; NewCol 75; WebBD 80; WhoMilH 76; WhoModH*

Beatty, Morgan
American. Journalist, Commentator
b. Sep 6, 1902 in Little Rock, Arkansas
d. Jul 4, 1975 in Antigua Island
Source: *ConAu 61; WhAm 6*

Beatty, Ned
American. Actor
b. Jul 6, 1937 in Louisville, Kentucky
Source: *FilmEn; IntMPA 81; WhoAm 80, 82; WhoHol A*

Beatty, Robert
Canadian. Actor
b. Oct 9, 1909 in Hamilton, ON
Source: *CanWW 70; FilmgC; IntMPA 77, 78, 79, 80, 81, 82; MovMk; WhoThe 77*

Beatty, Warren
[Warren Beaty]
American. Actor, Director, Producer
Won Oscar for *Reds,* 1981.
b. Mar 30, 1937 in Richmond, Virginia
Source: *BiDFilm; BiE&WWA; BkPepl; CelR 73; CurBio 62; FilmgC; IntMPA 75, 76, 77, 78, 79, 80, 81, 82; MotPP; MovMk; NewYTBS 74; OxFilm; WhoAm 74, 76, 78, 80, 82; WhoE 74; WhoHol A; WhoWor 74; WorEFlm*

Beauchamp, Pierre
French. Dancer, Choreographer
b. 1636
d. 1705
Source: *BioIn 10*

Beauharnais, Josephine de
see: Josephine

Beaumarchais, Pierre Augustin
French. Dramatist
b. Jan 24, 1732 in Paris, France
d. May 18, 1799 in Paris, France
Source: *ApCAB; AtlBL; BbD; BiD&SB; CasWL; CnThe; CyWA; DcEuL; Drake; EuAu; EvEuW; McGEWD; NewC; OxEng; OxFr; OxThe; Pen EUR; RComWL; REn; REnWD*

Beaumont, Francis
English. Dramatist
Collaborated with John Fletcher on about 50 tragicomedies.
b. 1584 in Grace-Dieu, England
d. Mar 6, 1616
Source: *Alli; BiD&SB; BrAu; CasWL; Chambr 1; ChPo, S1, S2; CnE&AP; CnThe; CroE&S; CrtT 1; DcEnA; DcEnL; DcEuL; DcLEL; EvLB; McGEWD; MouLC 1; NewC; OxEng; OxThe; Pen ENG; REnWD; WebE&AL*

Beaumont, Hugh
American. Actor
Played Ward Cleaver in "Leave it to Beaver" TV series, 1957-63.
b. Feb 16, 1909 in Lawrence, Kansas
d. May 14, 1982 in Munich, Germany (West)
Source: *FilmgC; IntMPA 75, 76, 77, 78, 79, 80, 81, 82; NewYTBS 82; WhoHol A*

Beaumont, William
American. Physician
b. Nov 21, 1785 in Lebanon, Connecticut
d. Apr 25, 1853 in Saint Louis, Missouri
Source: *AmBi; DcAmB; DcNAA; Drake; EncAB-H; WebAB; WhAm H*

Beaupre, Don(ald William)
Canadian. Hockey Player
b. Sep 19, 1961 in Kitchener, ON
Source: *HocReg*

Beauregard, Pierre Gustav Toutant
American. Confederate General
b. May 28, 1818 in Saint Bernard, Louisiana
d. Feb 20, 1893 in New Orleans, Louisiana
Source: *Alli SUP; AmBi; ApCAB; BiDConf; BiDSA; DcAmAu; DcAmB; DcNAA; EncAB-H; TwCBDA; WebAB; WhAm H*

Beauvoir, Simone de
French. Author
Proponent of Existentialism;wrote *The Second Sex.*
b. Jan 9, 1908 in Paris, France
Source: *CasWL; CelR 73; CnMWL; ConLC 1, 2, 4, 8, 14; CurBio 73; EncWL; EvEuW; InWom; LongCTC; ModRL; NewYTBE 71; NewYTBS 74; OxEng; OxFr; Pen EUR; REn; TwCA SUP; TwCW; Who 82; WhoTwCL; WhoWor 74*

Beaux, Cecelia
American. Artist
b. 1863 in Philadelphia, Pennsylvania
d. Sep 17, 1942 in Gloucester, Massachusetts
Source: *BioIn 2, 4, 7, 8, 10; DcAmB S3; NatCAB 40; NewCol 75; NotAW; WhAm 2; WomWWA 14*

Beaux Arts Trio, The
[Isadore Cohen; Bernard Green; Menahem Pressler]
Musicians
Source: *NF*

Beaverbrook, William Maxwell Aitken, Baron
English. Publisher, Statesman
Author *Politicians and the War 1914-16,* 1928; *Men and Power: 1917-18,* 1956.
b. May 25, 1879 in Maple, ON
d. Jun 9, 1964 in Surrey, England
Source: *BioIn 1, 2, 3, 4, 5, 6, 7, 8, 9; ConAu 89, 103; CurBio 40, 64; LinLib L, S; LongCTC; NewCol 75; WhE&EA; WhLit; WhWW-II*

Beavers, Louise
American. Actress
b. 1898 in Cincinnati, Ohio
d. Oct 26, 1962 in Hollywood, California
Source: *FilmgC; HolP 30; MotPP; MovMk; ThFT; Vers A; WhScrn 74, 77; WhoHol B*

Becaud, Gilbert
French. Singer
b. Oct 24, 1927 in Toulon, France
Source: *WhoHol A; WhoWor 74*

Beccaria, Cesare
Italian. Explorer, Political Leader
Argued against capital punishment in *Essay on Crimes and Punishment,* 1767.
b. Mar 15, 1738 in Milan, Italy
d. Nov 28, 1794 in Milan, Italy
Source: *BioIn 1, 4, 6, 9, 10; CasWL; DcEuL; EvEuW; LinLib; McGEWB; NewCol 75; OxFr; Pen EUR; REn*

Bechet, Sidney
American. Jazz Musician
b. May 14, 1897 in New Orleans, Louisiana
d. May 14, 1959 in Paris, France
Source: *EncAB-H; WhAm 3, 4; WhoJazz 72*

Bechi, Gino
Italian. Opera Singer
b. 1913 in Florence, Italy
Source: *WhoMus 72*

Bechtel, Stephen Davison
American. Business Executive, Engineer
Senior director of Bechtel Group.
b. Sep 24, 1900 in Aurora, Indiana
Source: *BioIn 2, 3, 4, 5, 10, 11; CurBio 57; IntWW 74, 75, 76, 77, 78; IntYB 78, 79; St&PR 75; WhoAm 74, 76, 78, 80, 82; WhoCan 73, 75, 77; WhoF&I 74, 75, 77; WhoWest 74, 76, 76; WhoWor 74, 76, 78*

Bechtel, Steve (Stephen Davison, Jr.)
American. Corporation Executive
Chairman, Bechtel Group, Inc., 1980--.
b. May 10, 1925 in Oakland, California
Source: *St&PR 75; WhoAm 74, 76, 78, 80, 82; WhoCan 73, 75, 77; WhoF&I 74, 75, 77, 79; WhoWest 74, 76, 78*

Beck, Billy de
see: DeBeck, Billy

Beck, C(harles) C(larence)
American. Cartoonist
b. Jun 8, 1910 in Zumbrota, Minnesota
Source: *WorECom*

Beck, David
American. Labor Union Official
President of Teamsters Union, 1952-57.
b. 1894 in Stockton, California
Source: *BioIn 1, 2, 3, 4, 5, 6, 8, 11, 12*

Beck, Jeff
[Yardbirds]
English. Rock Musician
b. Jun 24, 1944 in Surrey, England
Source: *BioIn 11; EncPR&S; IlEncRk*

Beck, Julian
American. Dramatist, Actor
b. May 31, 1925 in New York, New York
Source: *CelR 73; ConAu 102; NotNAT; PlP&P; WhoAm 82; WhoThe 77*

Beck, Marilyn
American. Journalist, Editor
b. Dec 17, 1928 in Chicago, Illinois
Source: *ConAu 65; ForWC 70; WhoAm 82; WhoAmW 77*

Beck, Martin
American. Theatrical Manager
b. 1869
d. Nov 16, 1940 in New York, New York
Source: *CurBio 41; WhAm 4*

Beck, Michael
American. Actor
b. 1948 in Horseshoe Lake, Arkansas
Source: *IntMPA 82*

Beck, Simone (Simca)
French. Chef, Author
b. 1905
Source: *BioIn 12*

Becker, Carl Lotus
American. Historian
b. Sep 7, 1873 in Waterloo, Iowa
d. Apr 10, 1945 in Ithaca, New York
Source: *AmAu&B; DcAmB S3; DcLEL; DcNAA; OxAmL; REn; REnAL; TwCA SUP; WebAB; WhAm 2; WhNAA*

Becker, Jacques
French. Motion Picture Director
b. 1906 in Paris, France
d. 1960 in Paris, France
Source: *BiDFilm; DcFM; FilmgC; OxFilm; WhScrn 77; WorEFlm*

Becker, Stephen David
American. Author
b. Mar 31, 1927 in Mount Vernon, New York
Source: *AmAu&B; ConAu 5R, 3NR; ConNov 76; DrAF 76; WhoAm 74; WhoWorJ 72; WrDr 76*

Becket, Saint Thomas a'
see: A'Becket, Thomas

Beckett, Samuel Barclay
Irish. Author, Dramatist
Won Obie awards for best new play, 1958, *Endgame,* and 1964, *Play.*
b. Apr 13, 1906 in Dublin, Ireland
Source: *Au&Wr 71; BiE&WWA; CasWL; CelR 73; CnMD; CnMWL; CnThe; ConAu 5R; ConDr 73; ConLC 1, 2, 3, 4, 6; ConNov 72, 76; ConP 70; CroCD; CurBio 70; CyWA; DcLEL; EncWL; EvEuW; IntWW 74; LongCTC; McGEWD; ModBrL, SUP; ModRL; ModWD; NewC; NewYTBE 72; NotNAT; OxEng; OxThe; Pen ENG, EUR; PlP&P; RComWL; REn; REnWD; TwCA SUP; TwCW; WebE&AL; Who 74; WhoAm 82; WhoThe 77; WhoTwCL; WhoWor 74; WrDr 76*

Beckford, William
English. Author
b. Sep 29, 1759 in Fonthill, England
d. May 2, 1844 in Bath, England
Source: *Alli; AtlBL; BbD; BiD&SB; BiDLA; BrAu 19; CasWL; Chambr 2; CyWA; DcBiA; DcEnA; DcEnL; DcLEL; EvLB; NewC; OxEng; OxFr; Pen ENG; REn; WebE&AL*

Beckman, Johnny
"The Babe Ruth of Basketball"; "Becky"
American. Basketball Player
b. Oct 22, 1895 in New York, New York
d. Jun 22, 1968 in Miami, Florida
Source: *BioIn 8; WhoBbl 73*

Beckmann, Max
German. Artist
b. Feb 12, 1884 in Leipzig, Germany
d. Dec 12, 1950 in New York, New York
Source: *AtlBL; OxGer; WhAm 4*

Becknell, William
American. Explorer
Established trading route known as Santa Fe Trail, 1822.
b. 1796 in Amherst County, Virginia
d. Apr 30, 1865
Source: *DcAmB; McGEWB; WebAB; WhAm H*

Beckwourth, James Pierson
American. Frontiersman
b. Apr 26, 1798 in Virginia
d. 1867 in Denver, Colorado
Source: *BioIn 3, 4, 5, 6, 7, 8, 9, 10, 11; WhAm H*

Becquerel, Antoine-Cesar
French. Physicist
b. Mar 7, 1788 in Loiret, France
d. Jan 18, 1878 in Paris, France
Source: *DcScB; LinLib S*

Becquerel, Antoine Henri
French. Physicist
Discovered radioactivity, 1896; won Nobel Prize, 1903.
b. Dec 15, 1852 in Paris, France
d. Aug 25, 1908 in Le Croisic, France
Source: *BioIn 2, 3, 4, 5, 9; McGEWB; NewCol 75*

Bede the Venerable
English. Scholar, Theologian
b. 673 in Northumbria, England
d. 735 in Jarrow, England
Source: *AtlBL; BbD; BiB S; BiD&SB; BrAu; CasWL; CrtT 1; DcEnL; DcEuL; EvLB; NewC; OxEng; OxFr; Pen ENG; REn*

Bedelia, Bonnie
American. Actress
b. Mar 25, 1948 in New York, New York
Source: *FilmgC; NotNAT; WhoAm 82; WhoHol A*

Bedford, Brian
English. Actor
Won Tony, 1971, for *School for Wives.*
b. Feb 16, 1935 in Morley, England
Source: *BiE&WWA; CelR 73; FilmgC; MotPP; NewYTBE 71; NotNAT; PlP&P; WhoAm 82; WhoHol A; WhoThe 77*

Bedford, Sybille
German. Author
b. 1911 in Charlottenburg, Germany
Source: *Au&Wr 71; ConNov 72, 76; ModBrL; NewC; RAdv 1; WhoWor 74; WorAu; WrDr 76*

Bee, Clair Francis
"Hillbilly"
American. Basketball Coach
b. Mar 2, 1900 in Grafton, West Virginia
Source: *BioIn 2, 8, 9; NewYTBS 81; PseudN; WhoBbl 73*

Bee Gees, The
[Barry Gibb; Maurice Gibb; Robin Gibb]
English. Rock Group
Soundtrack album *Saturday Night Fever,* 1977, sold over 15 million copies; first triple platinum album.
Source: *BkPepl; EncPR&S; IlEncRk; Rk100; WhoRock 81*

Beebe, Burdetta Faye
American. Children's Author
b. Feb 4, 1920 in Marshall, Oklahoma
Source: *ConAu 1R, 3NR; SmATA 1; WrDr 76*

Beebe, (Charles) William
American. Ornithologist, Explorer
Set world deep-sea diving record in bathysphere, 3,028 feet, 1934.
b. Jul 29, 1877 in Brooklyn, New York
d. Jun 4, 1962 in Trinidad
Source: *AmAu&B; ConAmA; ConAmL; ConAu 73; CurBio 41, 62; DcLEL; EvLB; OxAmL; REnAL; SmATA 19; Str&VC; TwCA, SUP; WebAB; WhAm 4; WhNAA*

Beebe, Lucius Morris
American. Journalist, Author
b. Dec 9, 1902 in Wakefield, Massachusetts
d. Feb 4, 1966 in San Mateo, California
Source: *AmAu&B; ChPo; ConAu 25R; CurBio 40, 66; REn; REnAL; WebAB; WhAm 4*

Beech, Walter Herschel
American. Aircraft Manufacturer
Founded Beech Aircraft Co., 1932.
b. Jan 30, 1891 in Pulaski, Tennessee
d. Nov 29, 1950 in Wichita, Kansas
Source: *BioIn 1, 2, 4; NatCAB 39; WhAm 3*

Beecham, Justin, pseud.
see: Wintle, Justin Beecham

Beecham, Sir Thomas
English. Conductor, Impresario
b. Apr 29, 1879 in Saint Helens, England
d. Mar 8, 1961 in London, England
Source: *CurBio 41, 51, 61; LongCTC; REn; WhAm 4*

Beecher, Henry Ward
American. Clergyman, Author, Orator
b. Jun 24, 1813 in Litchfield, Connecticut
d. Mar 8, 1887 in Brooklyn, New York
Source: *Alli, SUP; AmAu; AmAu&B; AmBi; ApCAB; BbD; BiD&SB; CasWL; Chambr 3; CyAL 1, 2; DcAmAu; DcAmB; DcBiA; DcEnL; DcNAA; EncAB-H; EvLB; OhA&B; OxAmL; OxEng; Pen AM; REn; REnAL; TwCBDA; WebAB; WhAm H; WhAmP*

Beecher, Janet
American. Actress
b. 1887 in Jefferson City, Missouri
d. Aug 6, 1955 in Washington, Connecticut
Source: *FilmgC; MotPP; MovMk; ThFT; WhScrn 74, 77; WhoHol B*

Beemer, Brace
American. Actor
Original radio voice of the Lone Ranger.
b. 1903
d. Mar 1, 1965 in Oxford, Michigan
Source: *BioIn 7*

Beene, Geoffrey
American. Fashion Designer
b. Aug 30, 1927 in Haynesville, Louisiana
Source: *CelR 73; WhoAm 74, 76, 78, 80, 82; WhoE 74; WorFshn*

Beerbohm, Sir (Henry) Max(imilian)
English. Critic, Caricaturist, Essayist
Drama critic for *Saturday Review,* succeeding George Bernard Shaw, 1898.
b. Aug 24, 1872 in London, England
d. May 20, 1956 in Rapallo, Italy
Source: *AtlBL; CasWL; Chambr 3; ChPo S1; CnMD; CnMWL; CyWA; DcLEL; EvLB; LongCTC; ModBrL, SUP; ModWD; NewC; OxEng; OxThe; Pen ENG; RAdv 1; REn; TwCA, SUP; TwCW; WebE&AL; WhAm 3*

Beers, Clifford Whittingham
American. Mental Hygienist, Author
b. Mar 30, 1876 in New Haven, Connecticut
d. Jul 9, 1943
Source: *BioIn 1, 2, 3, 6; WhAm 2*

Beers, Victor Gilbert
American. Editor
b. May 6, 1928 in Sidell, Illinois
Source: *ConAu 1NR; SmATA 9; WhoMW 74*

Beery, Noah
American. Actor
Silent screen's best loved villain; father of Noah Beery, Jr.
b. Jan 17, 1884 in Kansas City, Missouri
d. Apr 1, 1946 in Beverly Hills, California
Source: *CmMov; Film 1; FilmgC; MovMk; OxFilm; TwYS; Vers B; WhScrn 74; WhoHol B*

Beery, Noah, Jr.
American. Actor
Played Rocky, James Garner's father, in "The Rockford Files."
b. Aug 10, 1916 in New York, New York
Source: *FilmgC; IntMPA 75, 76, 77, 78, 79, 80, 81, 82; MovMk; Vers B; WhoAm 82; WhoHol B*

Beery, Wallace
American. Actor
Starred in over 200 films; won Oscar, 1931, for *The Champ.*
b. Apr 1, 1886 in Kansas City, Missouri
d. Apr 15, 1949 in Beverly Hills, California
Source: *BiDFilm; CmMov; DcAmB S4; Film 1; FilmgC; MovMk; OxFilm; TwYS; WebAB; WhAm 2; WhScrn 74, 77; WhoHol B; WorEFlm*

Beesley, H(orace) Brent
"Dr. Doom"
American. Government Official
Director of Federal Savings and Loan Insurance Corp.
b. Jan 30, 1946 in Salt Lake City, Utah
Source: *BioIn 12; WhoAmL 79*

Beeson, Jack Hamilton
American. Composer
b. Jul 15, 1921 in Muncie, Indiana
Source: *AmSCAP 66; DcCM; WhoAm 74, 76, 78, 80, 82; WhoWor 74*

Beethoven, Ludwig van
German. Composer
Became totally deaf, 1817; *Ninth Symphony* composed 1817-23.
b. Oct 16, 1770 in Bonn, Germany
d. Mar 26, 1827 in Vienna, Austria
Source: *AtlBL; Baker 78; BbD; BiD&SB; BioIn 5, 6, 7, 8, 9, 10, 11; LinLib L, S; McGEWB; NewC; NewCol 75; NewEOp 71; OxGer; OxMus; REn*

Beeton, Isabella Mary Mayson
English. Author
b. Mar 14, 1836 in London, England
d. Feb 6, 1865
Source: *Alli SUP; BioIn 1, 2, 8, 11; EvLB; InWom; OxEng*

Begelman, David
American. Motion Picture Executive
b. Aug 26, 1921 in New York, New York
Source: *BioIn 11; IntMPA 80, 81, 82*

Begin, Menachem
Israeli. Prime Minister
Commanded terrorist group Irgun, 1943-48; elected Prime Minister, 1977.
b. Aug 16, 1913 in Brest-Litovsk, Poland
Source: *BioIn 1, 4, 11; BkPepl; CurBio 77; IntWW 74, 75, 76, 77, 78; IntYB 78, 79; MidE; NewYTBE 70; NewYTBS 77; Who 82; WhoWor 74, 78; WhoWorJ 72*

Begle, Edward G
American. Mathematician
b. Nov 27, 1914 in Saginaw, Michigan
d. Mar 2, 1978 in Palo Alto, California
Source: *AmM&WS 73P; LEduc 74; WhoAm 74*

Begley, Ed
American. Actor
Won Oscar, 1964, for *The Unsinkable Molly Brown.*
b. Mar 25, 1901 in Hartford, Connecticut
d. Apr 28, 1970 in Hollywood, California
Source: *BiE&WWA; CurBio 56, 70; FilmgC; MotPP; MovMk; NewYTBE 70; Vers A; WhAm 5; WhScrn 74, 77; WhoHol B*

Behan, Brendan
Irish. Dramatist, Author
b. Feb 9, 1923 in Dublin, Ireland
d. Mar 20, 1964 in Dublin, Ireland
Source: *BiE&WWA; CasWL; CnMD; CnThe; ConAu 73; ConLC 1, 8, 11, 15; CroCD; CurBio 61, 64; EncWL; LongCTC; McGEWD; ModBrL, SUP; ModWD; NewC; Pen ENG; PlP&P; REn; REnWD; TwCW; WebE&AL; WhAm 4; WhoTwCL; WorAu*

Beheshti, Mohammad, Ayatollah
Iranian. Chief Justice
b. 1929 in Isfahan, Iran
d. Jun 28, 1981 in Teheran, Iran
Source: *BioIn 12*

Behn, Aphra
English. Author, Dramatist
b. 1640
d. Apr 16, 1689 in London, England
Source: *Alli; AtlBL; BbD; BiD&SB; BrAu; CasWL; Chambr 2; ChPo; CyWA; DcBiA; DcEnA; DcEnL; DcEuL; EvLB; InWom; McGEWD; MouLC 1; NewC; OxEng; OxThe; Pen ENG; REn; WebE&AL*

Behn, Harry
American. Children's Author
b. Sep 24, 1898 in Yavapai County, Arizona
d. Sep 4, 1973
Source: *AnCL; ArizL; AuBYP; BkCL; ChPo, S1, S2; ConAu 5R, 53, 5NR; IlsCB 1946, 1957; MorBMP; MorJA; SmATA 2; Str&VC*

Behn, Noel
American. Author, Motion Picture Producer
b. Jan 6, 1928 in Chicago, Illinois
Source: *BiE&WWA; NotNAT*

Behring, Emil Adolph von
German. Physiologist, Immunologist
b. Mar 15, 1854
d. Mar 31, 1917
Source: *BioIn 3, 6, 9, 10; NewCol 75*

Behrman, S(amuel) N(athaniel)
American. Author, Dramatist, Screenwriter
Wrote screenplay *Quo Vadis*, 1951; novel *The Burning Glass*, 1968.
b. Jun 9, 1893 in Worcester, Massachusetts
d. Aug 9, 1973 in New York, New York
Source: *AmAu&B; Au&Wr 71; BiE&WWA; CasWL; CmMov; CnDAL; CnMD; CnThe; ConAmA; ConAu 45; ConAu P-1; ConDr 73; CroCD; CurBio 43, 73; DcLEL; FilmgC; LongCTC; McGEWD; ModAL; ModWD; NewYTBE 72, 73; OxThe; OxAmL; Pen AM; REn; REnAL; REnWD; TwCA, SUP; WebE&AL; WhAm 6; WhoAm 74; WhoWor 74; WhoWorJ 72*

Beiderbecke, "Bix" (Leon Bismark)
American. Jazz Musician
Composed "In a Mist"; recognized postumously as one of greatest jazz musicians.
b. Mar 10, 1903 in Davenport, Iowa
d. Aug 7, 1931 in New York, New York
Source: *Baker 78; BiDAmM; BioIn 1, 4, 5, 7, 9, 10; CmpEPM; IlEncJ; NewCol 75; WebAB; WhAm 4; WhoJazz 72*

Beilenson, Edna Rudolph
[Elisabeth Deane, pseud.]
American. Publisher, Printer
b. Jun 16, 1909 in New York, New York
d. Feb 28, 1981 in New York, New York
Source: *AmAu&B; BioIn 1, 2; ConAu 85, 103; NewYTBS 81; PseudN; WhoAm 74, 76, 78; WhoAmW 58, 61, 64, 66, 68, 70, 72, 74; WhoWor 74*

Bein, Albert
Romanian. Dramatist
b. May 18, 1902 in Kishinev, Romania
Source: *BiE&WWA; CnMD; ModWD; NotNAT; OxAmL*

Beinum, Eduard van
Dutch. Conductor
b. Sep 3, 1900 in Arnheim, Netherlands
d. Apr 13, 1959
Source: *BioIn 2, 3, 4, 5, 11; CurBio 55, 59*

Bejart, Maurice
French. Choreographer
b. Jan 1, 1927 in Marseilles, France
Source: *CurBio 71; IntWW 74*

Bekhterev, Vladimir Mikhailovich
Russian. Scientist
b. 1857
d. 1927
Source: *BioIn 11; WebBD 80*

Bel Geddes, Barbara
see: Geddes, Barbara Bel

Bel Geddes, Norman
see: Geddes, Norman Bel

Belafonte, Harry (Harold George, Jr.)
American. Singer, Actor
Won Emmy, 1950, for TV special "Tonight with Belafonte."
b. Mar 1, 1927 in New York, New York
Source: *AmPS A, B; AmSCAP 66; Baker 78; BiDAmM; BiE&WWA; BioIn 3, 4, 5, 6, 7, 8, 9, 10; BlueB 76; CelR 73; CivR 74; CurBio 56; DcBlPA; EbonySL; EncFCWM 69; FilmgC; IntMPA 75, 76, 77, 78, 79, 80, 81; MotPP; MovMk; NewYTBE 72; OxFilm; RkOn; WhoAm 74, 76, 78, 80, 82; WhoBlA 75, 77; WhoHol A; WhoWor 74, 78; WorAl*

Belaney, (Archibald) George Stansfeld
see: Grey Owl, pseud.

Belasco, David
American. Dramatist, Producer
Proponent of naturalism in stage settings and effects.
b. Jul 25, 1859 in San Francisco, California
d. May 14, 1931 in New York, New York
Source: *AmAu&B; AmBi; ApCAB SUP; CasWL; Chambr 3; CnDAL; CnThe; DcAmAu; DcAmB S1; DcLEL; DcNAA; EncAB-H; EvLB; Film 1; LongCTC; McGEWD; ModAL; ModWD; OxAmL; OxThe; PlP&P; REn; REnAL; REnWD; TwCA, SUP; TwCBDA; TwCW; WebAB; WhAm 1; WhNAA; WhoStg 1906, 1908*

Belaunde-Terry, Fernando
Peruvian. Architect, Politician
President of Peru, 1963-68, July, 1980--.
b. Oct 17, 1912 in Lima, Peru
Source: *CurBio 65; DcPol; EncLatA; IntWW 74, 75, 76, 77, 78, 79, 80, 81; NewCol 75; NewYTBS 80; WhoWor 74*

Belbenoit, Rene
French. Devil's Island Escapee
b. 1889
d. Feb 26, 1959 in Lucerne Valley, California
Source: *BioIn 1, 5*

Belinsky, "Bo" (Robert)
American. Baseball Player
b. Dec 7, 1936 in New York, New York
Source: *BaseEn; BioIn 6, 9, 10; WhoProB 73*

Belinsky, Vissarion
Russian. Author
b. May 30, 1811 in Sveaborg, Finland
d. May 26, 1848 in Saint Petersburg, Russia
Source: *BiD&SB; CasWL; DcRusL; EuAu; EvEuW; Pen EUR; REn*

Belisarius
Byzantine. General under Justlan I
b. 505
d. 565
Source: *NewC; REn*

Belisha, Leslie Hore
see: Hore-Belisha, Leslie

Beliveau, Jean Marc
"Le Gros Bill"
Canadian. Hockey Player
Center, Montreal, 1951-71; scored 507 goals; Hall of Fame, 1972.
b. Aug 31, 1931 in Three Rivers, PQ
Source: *CanWW 82; WhoHcky 73; WorAl*

Belk, William E
[The Hostages]
American. Former Hostage in Iran
b. 1938? in Winnsboro, South Carolina
Source: *NewYTBS 81*

Belknap, William Worth
American. Civil War General
Secretary of War, 1869-76; resigned after bribery scandal.
b. Sep 22, 1829 in Newburgh, New York
d. Oct 13, 1890 in Washington, DC
Source: *AmBi; ApCAB; BiDrUSE; BioIn 7, 10; DcAmB; NatCAB 4; TwCBDA; WhAm H*

Bell, Alexander Graham
American. Inventor
Invented telephone, 1876; Bell Telephone Co. organized, 1877.
b. Mar 3, 1847 in Edinburgh, Scotland
d. Aug 2, 1922 in Baddeck, NS
Source: *AmBi; AmLY; ApCAB; DcAmB; DcNAA; EncAB-H; LongCTC; REnAL; TwCBDA; WebAB; WhAm 1*

Bell, Amir
see: Kool and the Gang

Bell, Arthur Donald
American. Author, Psychologist
b. Jul 17, 1920 in Vancouver, Washington
Source: *AmM&WS 73S; WhoAm 74, 76, 78, 80, 82*

Bell, "Buddy" (David Gus)
American. Baseball Player
b. Aug 27, 1951 in Pittsburgh, Pennsylvania
Source: *BaseEn; BioIn 11; WhoProB 73*

Bell, Charles
Scottish. Surgeon, Anatomist
First to describe paralysis of facial nerve--Bell's palsy.
b. Nov 1774 in Edinburgh, Scotland
d. Apr 28, 1842 in Hollow Park, England
Source: *BiHiMed; BioIn 1, 3, 4, 5, 7, 8, 9; CelCen; DcBiPP; DcBrWA; DcScB; InSci; NamesHP; WhDW*

Bell, Clive
English. Art Critic
b. Sep 16, 1881 in East Shefford, England
d. Sep 18, 1964 in London, England
Source: *DcLEL; LongCTC; ModBrL; NewC; OxEng; Pen ENG; REn; TwCA, SUP*

Bell, "Cool Papa" (James Thomas)
American. Baseball Player
Known for speed; Satchel Paige said, "He could turn out the light and jump in bed before the room got dark."
b. May 17, 1903 in Starkville, Mississippi
Source: *BioIn 10, 11*

Bell, Daniel
American. Sociologist
b. May 10, 1919 in New York, New York
Source: *AmAu&B; AmEA 74; AmM&WS 73S; ConAu 1R, 4NR; CurBio 73; WhoAm 74, 76, 78, 80, 82; WhoWor 74; WhoWorJ 72*

Bell, Earl
American. Track Athlete
b. Aug 25, 1955
Source: *BioIn 12*

Bell, Eric
see: Thin Lizzy

Bell, Griffin Boyette
American. Lawyer
US attorney general, 1977-79.
b. Oct 31, 1918 in Americus, Georgia
Source: *BiDFedJ; CngDr 77, 79; CurBio 77; IntWW 77, 78, 79, 80, 81; NewYTBS 76; WhoAm 74, 76, 78, 80, 82; WhoAmL 78, 79; WhoAmP 77, 79; WhoE 77, 79; WhoGov 72, 75, 77; WhoS&SW 76, 78*

Bell, Herbert A
American. Inventor
Founded firm that eventually became Packard Bell Electronics.
b. 1890 in Rock Valley, Iowa
d. Jan 31, 1970 in New York, New York
Source: *NewYTBE 70*

Bell, Joseph
Scottish. Surgeon, Medical Instructor
b. 1837
d. 1911
Source: *Alli SUP; LongCTC*

Bell, "Kool" (Robert)
see: Kool and the Gang

Bell, Lawrence Dale
American. Founder of Bell Aircraft
b. Apr 5, 1894 in Mentone, Indiana
d. Oct 20, 1956 in Buffalo, New York
Source: *CurBio 42, 57; WhAm 3*

Bell, Ricky Lynn
American. Football Player
b. Apr 8, 1955 in Houston, Texas
Source: *BioIn 10, 11*

Bell, Ronald
see: Kool and the Gang

Bell, Steve (Stephen Scott)
American. Broadcast Journalist
b. Dec 9, 1935 in Oskaloosa, Iowa
Source: *ConAu 65; WhoAm 82*

Bell, Terrel Howard
"Ted"
American. Government Official
Secretary, Department of Education, 1981--.
b. Nov 11, 1921 in Lava Hot Springs, Idaho
Source: *BioIn 10, 11; LEduc 74; NewYTBS 81; PseudN; WhoAm 76, 78, 80, 82; WhoAmP 75, 77, 79; WhoGov 75, 77*

Bell, Tom
English. Actor
b. 1932 in Liverpool, England
Source: *FilmEn; FilmgC; IntMPA 81*

Bell, William Holden
American. Spy, Engineer
b. 1920?
Source: *BioIn 12*

Bellairs, John
American. Author
b. Jan 17, 1938 in Marshall, Michigan
Source: *ConAu 25R; SmATA 2; WrDr 76; WhoE 74*

Bellamy, Edward
American. Author, Social Reformer
Wrote *Looking Backward, 2000-1887,* 1888.
b. Mar 26, 1850 in Chicopee Falls, Massachusetts
d. May 22, 1898 in Chicopee Falls, Massachusetts
Source: *Alli SUP; AmAu; AmAu&B; AmBi; ApCAB SUP; BbD; BiD&SB; CasWL; CnDAL; CyWA; DcAmB; DcBiA; DcEnA AP; DcLEL; DcNAA; EncAB-H; EvLB; MouLC 4; OxAmL; OxEng; Pen AM; RAdv 1; REn; REnAL; TwCBDA; WebAB; WebE&AL; WhAm H; WhAmP*

Bellamy, Ralph
American. Actor
Won Tony, 1958, for *Sunrise at Campobello;* founded Screen Actors Guild.
b. Jun 17, 1904 in Chicago, Illinois
Source: *BiE&WWA; CelR 73; ConAu 101; CurBio 51; Film 2; FilmgC; HolP 30; IntMPA 75, 76, 77, 78, 79, 80, 81, 82; MotPP; MovMk; NotNAT; WhThe; WhoAm 74, 76, 78, 80, 82; WhoHol A; WorAl*

Bellamy Brothers, The
[David and Howard Bellamy]
American. Singing Duo
Source: *RkOn 2; WhoRock 81*

Bellanca, Giuseppe Mario
Italian. Founder of Bellanca Aircraft
b. 1886
d. Dec 26, 1960 in New York, New York
Source: *BioIn 3, 5, 9, 11*

Beller, Kathleen
American. Actress
b. 1957 in New York, New York
Source: *JohnWil 81*

Belli, Melvin Mouron
"The King of Torts"
American. Lawyer, Lecturer, Author
Has defended such well-known people as Lenny Bruce and Jack Ruby.
b. Jul 29, 1907 in Sonora, California
Source: *ConAu 104; CurBio 79; WhoAm 76, 78, 80, 82; WhoAmL 78, 79; WhoWest 74, 76, 78; WhoWor 74; WorAl*

Bellincioni, Gemma
Italian. Opera Singer
b. Aug 17, 1864 in Monza, Italy
d. Apr 23, 1950 in Naples, Italy
Source: *BioIn 2, 11; InWom*

Bellinghausen, Fabian Gottlieb von
Russian. Admiral, Explorer
b. 1778
d. 1852
Source: *BioIn 1*

Bellini, Gentile
Italian. Artist
b. 1429 in Venice, Italy
d. Feb 23, 1507 in Venice, Italy
Source: *AtlBL; BioIn 1, 5, 6; LinLib S; McGDA*

Bellini, Giovanni
Italian. Artist, Architect
Founded Venetian school; teacher of Giorgione and Titian.
b. 1430 in Venice, Italy
d. Nov 29, 1516 in Venice, Italy
Source: *AtlBL; DcBiPP; DcCathB; LinLib S; McGDA; McGEWB; OxArt; REn; WorAl*

Bellini, Jacopo
Italian. Artist
b. 1400?
d. 1470?
Source: *BioIn 1, 5, 9; McGDA*

Bellini, Vincenzo
Italian. Opera Composer
b. Nov 3, 1801 in Catania, Sicily
d. Sep 23, 1835 in Puteaux, France
Source: *AtlBL; REn*

Bellison, Simeon
American. Musician
b. Dec 4, 1883 in Moscow, Russia
d. May 4, 1953 in New York, New York
Source: *Baker 78*

Bellman, Carl Michael
Swedish. Poet
b. Feb 4, 1740
d. Feb 11, 1795
Source: *BbD; BiD&SB; CasWL; DcEuL; EuAu; EvEuW; Pen EUR*

Belloc, (Joseph) Hilaire (Pierre), pseud.
English. Author
Wrote from Roman Catholic viewpoint; founded *New Witness* newspaper with G K Chesterton.
b. Jul 27, 1870 in Saint Cloud, France
d. Jul 16, 1953 in Guildford, England
Source: *AnCL; AtlBL; AuBYP; BkC 5; CarSB; CasWL; CathA 1930; Chambr 3; ChPo, S1, S2; CnE&AP; CnMWL; CyWA; DcLEL; EvLB; LongCTC; ModBrL, SUP; NewC; OxEng; Pen ENG; RAdv 1; REn; TwCA, SUP; TwCW; WebE&AL; WhAm 3; WhoChL; WhoLA; YABC 1*

Bellotto, Bernardo
Italian. Artist
b. 1720 in Venice, Italy
d. 1780 in Warsaw, Poland
Source: *AtlBL; McGDA; OxGer*

Bellow, Saul
American. Author
Won Pulitzer Prize, 1976, for *Humboldt's Gift*.
b. Jul 10, 1915 in Lachine, PQ
Source: *AmAu&B; AmNov; AmWr; AuNews 2; BkPepl; CasWL; CelR 73; CnMWL; ConAu 5R; ConDr 73; ConLC 1, 2, 3, 6, 8, 10, 13, 15; ConNov 72, 76; CroCD; CurBio 65; DrAF 76; DrAS 74E; EncAB-H; EncWL; IntWW 74; LongCTC; ModAL, SUP; NewYTBE 71; NewYTBS 76; NotNAT; OxAmL; Pen AM; RAdv 1; REn; REnAL; TwCA SUP; TwCW; WebAB; WebE&AL; Who 82; WhoAm 74, 76, 78, 80, 82; WhoTwCL; WhoWor 74; WhoWorJ 72; WrDr 76, 80*

Bellows, Brian
Canadian. Hockey Player
Prized rookie drafted by Minnesota North Stars, 1982.
b. Sep 1, 1964 in Saint Catherines, ON
Source: *NF*

Bellows, George Wesley
American. Artist, Lithographer
b. Aug 12, 1882 in Columbus, Ohio
d. Jan 8, 1925 in New York, New York
Source: *AmBi; AtlBL; DcAmB; EncAB-H; OxAmL; REn; WebAB; WhAm 1*

Belluschi, Pietro
American. Architect
b. Aug 18, 1899 in Ancona, Italy
Source: *AmArch 70; CurBio 59; IntWW 74; WhoAm 74, 76, 78, 80, 82; WhoWor 74*

Belmondo, Jean-Paul
French. Actor
b. Apr 9, 1933 in Neuilly, France
Source: *BiDFilm; CelR 73; CurBio 65; FilmgC; IntMPA 75, 76, 77, 78, 79, 80, 81, 82; IntWW 74; MotPP; MovMk; WhoHol A; WhoWor 74; WorEFlm*

Belmont, August
[August Shoenberg]
American. Banker
b. Dec 8, 1816 in Alzey, Germany
d. Nov 24, 1890 in New York, New York
Source: *AmBi; ApCAB; BiAuS; DcAmB; DcNAA; EncAB-H; TwCBDA; WebAB; WhAm H; WhAmP*

Belmont, August, Jr.
American. Banker
b. Feb 18, 1853 in New York, New York
d. Dec 10, 1924
Source: *ApCAB SUP; WhAm 1*

Belmont, Mrs. August (Eleanor Robson)
American. Actress, Philanthropist
b. Dec 13, 1879 in Wigan, England
d. Oct 24, 1979 in New York, New York
Source: *ConAu 97; CurBio 44, 80; WhoAmW 58, 61, 68; WomWWA 14*

Belmont, Martin
see: Graham Parker and the Rumour

Belote, Melissa
American. Swimmer
Won three gold medals, 1972 Olympics.
b. Oct 16, 1956 in Washington, DC
Source: *BioIn 10*

Beltrami, Eugenio
Italian. Mathematician
b. 1835
d. 1899
Source: *NewCol 75; WebBD 80*

Belushi, John
"The Black Rhino"
American. Actor, Comedian, Writer
Starred in *Animal House, The Blues Brothers;* died of drug overdose.
b. Jan 24, 1949 in Chicago, Illinois
d. Mar 5, 1982 in Hollywood, California
Source: *CurBio 80, 82; NewYTBS 82; PseudN; WhoAm 80, 82*

Bely, Andrey, pseud.
[Boris Nikolayevich Bugayev]
Russian. Poet
b. Oct 14, 1880 in Moscow, Russia
d. Jan 8, 1934 in Moscow, U.S.S.R.
Source: *CasWL; ClDMEL; CnMWL; DcRusL; EncWL; EvEuW; ModSL 1; Pen EUR; REn; WhoTwCL; WorAu*

Bemelmans, Ludwig
American. Author, Illustrator, Humorist
Wrote *Madeline* series of stories for children, 1953-62.
b. Apr 27, 1898 in Tirol, Austria
d. Oct 1, 1962 in New York, New York
Source: *AmAu&B; AmNov; Au&ICB; AuBYP; Cald 1938; ChPo, S1, S2; CnDAL; ConAu 73; CurBio 41, 62; DcLEL; EncWL; IlsBYP; IlsCB 1744, 1946, 1957; LongCTC; MorJA; OxAmL; Pen AM; REn; REnAL; SmATA 15; TwCA, SUP; TwCW; WhAm 4; WhoChL; WhoGrA*

Bemis, Samuel Flagg
American. Historian, Author
b. Oct 20, 1891 in Worcester, Massachusetts
d. Sep 26, 1973 in Bridgeport, Connecticut
Source: *AmAu&B; ConAu 45; CurBio 50, 73; DcLEL; NewYTBE 73; OxAmL; OxCan; REnAL; TwCA, SUP; WebAB; WhAm 6; WhNAA; WhoWor 74*

Ben Barka, Mehdi
Moroccan. Political Leader
b. 1920
d. 1965
Source: *BioIn 5, 7, 10*

Ben Bella, Ahmed
Algerian. Revolutionary, Former Premier
b. Dec 1916 in Marnia, Algeria
Source: *BioIn 6, 7, 8, 11; CurBio 63*

Ben-Elissar, Eliahu
Israeli. Diplomat
First Israeli ambassador to Arab country--Egypt--, 1980--.
b. 1932 in Poland
Source: *BioIn 11; NewYTBS 77, 80*

Ben-Gal, Avigdor
Israeli. General
b. 1936
Source: *BioIn 11*

Ben-Gurion, David
[David Grun]
Israeli. Political Leader
Emigrated to Palestine, 1906; Israel's first Prime Minister, 1948-53.
b. Oct 16, 1886 in Plonsk, Poland
d. Dec 1, 1973 in Tel Aviv, Israel
Source: *ConAu 45, 101; CurBio 47, 57, 74; LinLib S; McGEWB; NewCol 75; NewYTBE 71, 73; WhAm 6; WhWW-II; Who 74; WhoWor 74; WhoWorJ 72*

Ben-Yehuda, Eliezer
[Eliezer Perelman]
Israeli. Scholar
b. Jan 7, 1858 in Luzhky, Russia
d. Dec 16, 1922 in Jerusalem, Palestine
Source: *CasWL; EuAu; Pen CL, EUR*

Benaderet, Bea
American. Actress
Played the mother on TV series "Petticoat Junction," 1963-68.
b. Apr 4, 1906 in New York, New York
d. Oct 13, 1968 in Los Angeles, California
Source: *WhScrn 74, 77; WhoHol B*

Benarde, Melvin Albert
American. Author, Environmentalist
b. Jun 15, 1923 in Brooklyn, New York
Source: *AmM&WS 73P; ConAu 25R; WhoAm 82; WhoE 74; WrDr 76*

Benary-Isbert, Margot
American. Author
b. Dec 2, 1899 in Saarbrucken, Germany
Source: *AnCL; AuBYP; ConAu 5R, 89, 4NR; ConLC 12; MorJA; SmATA 2, 21*

Benatar, Pat
[Patricia Andrzejewski; Mrs. Neil Geraldo]
American. Rock Singer
b. 1952 in Brooklyn, New York
Source: *IlEncRk; NewWmR; WhoRock 81*

Benavente y Martinez, Jacinto
Spanish. Dramatist
b. Aug 12, 1866 in Madrid, Spain
d. Jul 14, 1954 in Madrid, Spain
Source: *CasWL; CathA 1930; ClDMEL; CnMD; CurBio 53, 54; McGEWD; ModWD; Pen EUR; REn*

Bench, Johnny Lee
"Hands"
American. Baseball Player
Catcher, infielder, Cincinnati Reds, 1967--; MVP 1976 World Series.
b. Dec 7, 1947 in Oklahoma City, Oklahoma
Source: *BaseEn; BioNews 74; BkPepl; CelR 73; CurBio 71; NewYTBE 70; WhoAm 74, 76, 78, 80, 82; WhoProB 73*

Benchley, Nathaniel Goddard
American. Author
b. Nov 13, 1915 in Newton, Massachusetts
d. Dec 14, 1981 in Boston, Massachusetts
Source: *AmAu&B; Au&Wr 71; AuBYP SUP; BiE&WWA; BioIn 3, 4, 9, 10, 11; CelR 73; ConAu 1R, 2NR; CurBio 53, 82; FourBJA; NewYTBS 81; NotNAT; ScF&FL 1A; SmATA 3; TwCCW 78; WhoAm 74, 76, 78, 80; WhoWor 74; WorAu; WrDr 76*

Benchley, Peter Bradford
American. Author, Journalist
Author *Jaws,* 1974, *The Deep,* 1976, *The Island,* 1979.
b. May 8, 1940 in New York, New York
Source: *AuNews 2; BkPepl; ConAu 17R; ConLC 4, 8; CurBio 76; IntAu&W 76, 77; NewYTBS 79; SmATA 3; WhoAm 78, 80, 82*

Benchley, Robert Charles
[Guy Fawkes, pseud.]
American. Author, Humorist
Author *Chips Off the Old Benchley,* 1949; won Oscar, 1935, for *How to Sleep.*
b. Sep 15, 1889 in Worcester, Massachusetts
d. Nov 21, 1945 in New York, New York
Source: *AmAu&B; ChPo; ConAmA; CurBio 41, 46; DcAmB S3; DcLEL; DcNAA; EvLB; FilmgC; LongCTC; ModAL; MovMk; NotNAT A, B; ObitOF 79; OxAmL; OxFilm; OxThe; Pen AM; PlP&P; RAdv 1; REn; REnAL; TwCA, SUP; TwCLC; TwCW; WebAB; WhAm 2; WhScrn 74, 77; WhoHol B; WorEFlm*

Bender, Hans
German. Psychic Investigator
b. 1907
Source: *BiDPara; ModGL; OxGer; WhoWor 74*

Bendick, Jeanne
American. Author, Illustrator
b. Feb 25, 1919 in New York, New York
Source: *AuBYP; BkP; ConAu 5R, 2NR; IlsCB 1946, 1957; MorJA; SmATA 2*

Bendix, Vincent
American. Inventor, Manufacturer
Invented Bendix drive, making self-starting cars practical.
b. Aug 12, 1882 in Moline, Illinois
d. Mar 27, 1945 in New York, New York
Source: *CurBio 45; DcAmB S3; WebAB; WhAm 2*

Bendix, William
American. Actor
Played the father on radio and TV series, "Life of Riley."
b. Jan 14, 1906 in New York, New York
d. Dec 14, 1964 in Los Angeles, California
Source: *BiE&WWA; CmMov; CurBio 48, 65; FilmgC; HolP 40; MotPP; MovMk; OxFilm; WhAm 4; WhScrn 74, 77; WhoHol B; WorEFlm*

Benedict, Dirk
[Dirk Niewoehner]
American. Actor, Singer
b. Mar 1, 1945 in Helena, Montana
Source: *IntMPA 75, 76, 77, 78, 79, 80, 81, 82; WhoAm 82; WhoHol A*

Benedict, Ruth Fulton
American. Anthropologist
b. Jun 5, 1887 in New York, New York
d. Sep 17, 1948 in New York, New York
Source: *AmAu&B; CurBio 41, 48; DcAmB S4; DcNAA; EncAB-H; InWom; NotAW; REnAL; TwCA SUP; WebAB; WhAm 2*

Benedict, Saint
Italian. Founder of Monasticism
b. 480?
d. Mar 21, 547
Source: *McGEWB*

Benedictos I
[Vassilios Papadopoulos]
Turkish. Patriarch of Jerusalem
b. 1892 in Brusa, Asia Minor
d. Dec 10, 1980 in Jerusalem, Israel
Source: *AnObit 1980; WhoWor 74*

Benedictus, David
English. Director, Dramatist
b. Sep 16, 1938 in London, England
Source: *Au&Wr 71; ConNov 72, 76; NewC; WrDr 76*

Benediktsson, Bjarni
Icelandic. Prime Minister
b. 1908
d. Jul 10, 1970 in Thingvalla, Iceland
Source: *BioIn 9*

Benefield, Barry
American. Author
b. in Jefferson, Texas
Source: *AmAu&B; AmNov; ConAmL; OxAmL; REnAL; TexWr; TwCA, SUP*

Beneke, Tex
American. Singer, Band Leader
Led Glenn Miller Orchestra after Miller's death.
b. Feb 12, 1914 in Fort Worth, Texas
Source: *BioIn 2; CmpEPM*

Benelli, Giovanni, Cardinal
"The Kissinger"
Italian. Roman Catholic Prelate
Archbishop of Florence; advisor to Pope Paul VI.
b. May 21, 1921 in Pistoria, Italy
d. Oct 26, 1982 in Florence, Italy
Source: *BioIn 8, 11; CurBio 77; IntWW 78, 79, 80, 81; NewYTBE 70; NewYTBS 82; WhoWor 78*

Benes, Eduard
Czech. Statesman
b. May 28, 1884 in Kozlany, Czechoslovakia
d. Sep 3, 1948 in Usti, Czechoslovakia
Source: *CurBio 42, 48; REn; WhAm 2*

Benet, Brenda
[Brenda Benet Nelson]
American. Actress
b. Aug 14, 1945 in Los Angeles, California
d. Apr 7, 1982 in Los Angeles, California
Source: *NewYTBS 82; WhoHol A*

Benet, Stephen Vincent
American. Author, Poet
Won Pulitzer Prizes for poetry, 1929, 1943.
b. Jul 22, 1898 in Bethlehem, Pennsylvania
d. Mar 13, 1943 in New York, New York
Source: *Alli SUP; AmAu&B; AnCL; ApCAB; BiDSA; BkCL; CasWL; Chambr 3; ChPo, S1, S2; CnDAL; CnE&AP; CnMWL; ConAmA; ConAmL; CurBio 43; CyWA; DcAmB S3; DcLEL; DcNAA; Drake; EncWL; EvLB; ModAL; OxAmL; OxEng; Pen AM; RAdv 1; REn; REnAL; SixAP; TwCA, SUP; TwCBDA; TwCW; WebAB; WebE&AL; WhAm 2; WhNAA; WhoTwCL; YABC 1*

Benet, William Rose
American. Author, Journalist
Won Pulitzer Prize, 1941, for *The Dust Which is God,* autobiographical verse.
b. Feb 2, 1886 in Fort Hamilton, New York
d. May 4, 1950 in New York, New York
Source: *AmAu&B; ChPo, S1, S2; CnDAL; ConAmA; ConAmL; DcAmB S4; DcLEL; LongCTC; OxAmL; OxEng; Pen AM; REn; REnAL; TwCA, SUP; WebAB; WhAm 3; WhNAA*

Benirschke, Rolf Joachim
American Football Player
b. Feb 7, 1955 in Boston, Massachusetts
Source: *BioIn 12; NewYTBS 82*

Benjamin of Tudela
Jewish Traveler, Author
b. 1130 in Tudela, Spain
d. 1173
Source: *CasWL; NewC; NewCol 75; OxEng*

Benjamin, Adam, Jr.
American. Politician
Congressman from IN, 1977-82.
b. Aug 6, 1935 in Gary, Indiana
d. Sep 7, 1982 in Washington, DC
Source: *AlmAP 78, 80; CngDr 77, 79, 81; WhoAm 78, 80, 82; WhoAmL 79; WhoAmP 73, 75, 77, 79; WhoGov 75, 77*

Benjamin, Arthur
Australian. Opera Composer
b. Sep 18, 1893 in Sydney, Australia
d. Apr 10, 1960 in London, England
Source: *BioIn 2, 4, 5, 6, 8; NewEOp 71*

Benjamin, Asher
American. Architect
b. Jun 15, 1773 in Greenfield, Massachusetts
d. Jul 26, 1845 in Springfield, Massachusetts
Source: *DcAmB; DcNAA; WebAB; WhAm H*

Benjamin, Judah Philip
American. Lawyer, Statesman
b. Aug 11, 1811 in Saint Thomas, British West Indies
d. May 8, 1884 in Paris, France
Source: *Alli SUP; AmBi; ApCAB; BiD&SB; BiDConf; BiDSA; BiDrAC; DcAmAu; DcAmB; DcNAA; TwCBDA; WebAB; WhAm H; WhAmP*

Benjamin, Nigel
see: Mott (the Hoople)

Benjamin, Richard
American. Actor
Starred in movie *Goodbye Columbus,* 1969; husband of Paula Prentiss.
b. May 22, 1938 in New York, New York
Source: *BkPepl; CelR 73; FilmgC; IntMPA 75, 76, 77, 78, 79, 80, 81, 82; MovMk; NewYTBE 71; WhoAm 82; WhoHol A*

Benko, Paul Charles
French. Chess Player
b. Jul 15, 1928 in Amiens, France
Source: *WhoAm 80, 82*

Benn, Anthony
British. Business Executive
b. Oct 7, 1912
Source: *Who 78*

Benn, Tony (Anthony Wedgwood)
English. Statesman
Member of Parliament in Labour Party since 1950.
b. Apr 3, 1925 in London, England
Source: *BlueB 76; CurBio 65, 82; DcPol; IntWW 74, 75, 76, 77, 78, 79, 80, 81; IntYB 78, 79, 80, 81; Who 74; WhoWor 74, 76, 78; WrDr 80*

Bennet, Richard Dyer
see: Dyer-Bennet, Richard

Bennett, Arnold
English. Author
b. May 27, 1867 in Staffordshire, England
d. Mar 27, 1931
Source: *AtlBL; Chambr 3; CnMD; CnMWL; CyWA; DcBiA; DcLEL; EncMys; EncWL; FilmgC; LongCTC; McGEWD; ModBrL, SUP; ModWD; NewC; OxEng; OxThe; Pen ENG; RAdv 1; REn; TwCA, SUP; TwCW; WebE&AL; WhoTwCL*

Bennett, Constance
American. Actress
b. 1905 in New York, New York
d. Jul 4, 1965 in Fort Dix, New Jersey
Source: *BiDFilm; BiE&WWA; FilmgC; InWom; MotPP; MovMk; OxFilm; ThFT; TwYS; WhAm 4; WhScrn 74, 77; WhoHol B; WomWMM; WorEFlm*

Bennett, Floyd
American. Aviator
b. Oct 25, 1890 in Warrensburg, New York
d. Apr 25, 1928 in Quebec, Canada
Source: *AmBi; DcAmB; WebAB; WhoWest 74*

Bennett, Hal
American. Author
b. Sep 29, 1936 in Detroit, Michigan
Source: *BlkAW; ConAu 41R; ConLC 5; DrAF 76; LivgBAA*

Bennett, Harry Herbert
American. Auto Executive
b. Jan 17, 1892 in Ann Arbor, Michigan
d. Jan 4, 1979 in California
Source: *BioIn 2, 6*

Bennett, Hugh Hammond
American. Soil Scientist
b. Apr 15, 1881 in Wadesboro, North Carolina
d. Jul 7, 1960 in Burlington, North Carolina
Source: *BioIn 1, 2, 3, 4, 5, 6, 7, 8; CurBio 46, 60; WhAm 4*

Bennett, Hywel
Welsh. Actor
b. Apr 8, 1944 in Garnant, Wales
Source: *FilmEn; FilmgC; WhoHol A; WhoThe 77, 81*

Bennett, James Gordon
American. Newspaper Editor, Publisher
Founded NY *Herald* with $500.00 capital.
b. 1795 in Keith, Scotland
d. Jun 1, 1872 in New York, New York
Source: *AmAu&B; AmBi; ApCAB; DcAmB; EncAB-H; OxAmL; REn; REnAL; TwCBDA; WebAB; WhAm H; WhAmP*

Bennett, James Gordon, Jr.
American. Author, Publisher
Financed Morton Stanley's expedition to find David Livingstone.
b. May 10, 1841 in New York, New York
d. May 14, 1918 in Bealieu, France
Source: *AmAu&B; AmBi; ApCAB; DcAmB; EncAB-H; TwCBDA; WebAB; WhAm 1*

Bennett, Joan
[Mrs. Walter Wanger]
American. Actress
Appeared in over 40 movies and TV series "Dark Shadows."
b. Feb 27, 1910 in Palisades, New Jersey
Source: *BiDFilm; BiE&WWA; CelR 73; CmMov; FilmgC; InWom; IntMPA 75, 76, 77, 78, 79, 80, 81, 82; MotPP; MovMk; OxFilm; ThFT; Who 74; WhoAm 74, 76, 78, 80, 82; WhoE 74; WhoHol A; WhoThe 77; WorEFlm*

Bennett, John
American. Author, Illustrator
b. May 17, 1865 in Chillicothe, Ohio
d. Dec 28, 1956 in Charleston, South Carolina
Source: *AmAu&B; BiDLA; BiDSA; BlkAW; CarSB; ChPo, S1; ConICB; DcAmAu; IlsCB 1744; JBA 34, 51; MnBBF; OhA&B; OxAmL; REnAL; WhAm 3; YABC 1*

Bennett, John Charles
American. Army Officer
b. Dec 6, 1923 in Washington, DC
d. May 4, 1980 in Anchorage, Alaska
Source: *WhoAm 74, 76, 78, 80; WhoE 74*

Bennett, Lerone, Jr.
American. Author, Historian, Editor
b. Oct 17, 1928 in Clarksdale, Mississippi
Source: *BlkAW; ConAu 45, 2NR; WhoAm 74, 76, 78, 80, 82; WhoMW 74*

Bennett, Michael
[Michael Bennett DiFiglia]
American. Choreographer
Won two Tonys, Pulitzer Prize for conceiving, directing, choreographing *A Chorus Line.*
b. Apr 8, 1943 in Buffalo, New York
Source: *CurBio 81; EncMT; NotNAT; WhoAm 82; WhoThe 77*

Bennett, Richard
American. Actor, Motion Picture Producer
b. 1873 in Cass County, Indiana
d. Oct 22, 1944 in Los Angeles, California
Source: *CurBio 44; DcAmB S3; FamA&A; Film 1; FilmgC; TwYS; Vers A; WhAm 2; WhScrn 74, 77; WhoHol B; WhoStg 1908*

Bennett, Robert Russell
American. Composer
b. Jun 15, 1894 in Kansas City, Missouri
d. Aug 18, 1981 in New York, New York
Source: *Baker 78; BiDAmM; BiE&WWA; BioIn 1, 2, 3, 8, 9; CelR 73; CurBio 42, 62, 81; DcCM; NewYTBS 81; NotNAT; OxMus; WhoAm 74, 76, 78, 80; WhoMus 72*

Bennett, Tony
[Joe Bari; Anthony Dominick Benedetto]
"The Singer's Singer"
American. Singer
Biggest hit "I Left My Heart in San Francisco," 1963.
b. Aug 3, 1926 in New York, New York
Source: *AmPS; BiDAmM; BkPepl; CelR 73; CmpEPM; CurBio 65; EncJzS 70; RkOn; WhoAm 74, 76, 78, 80, 82; WhoHol A*

Benny, Jack
[Benjamin Kubelsky]
American. Comedian
Famous for his stinginess; starred in "The Jack Benny Program," 1950-64.
b. Feb 14, 1894 in Waukegan, Illinois
d. Dec 26, 1974 in Los Angeles, California
Source: *BiDFilm; BioNews 74, 75; CelR 73; CurBio 41, 63, 75; FilmgC; IntMPA 75; IntWW 74; MotPP; MovMk; NewYTBE 70; NewYTBS 74; OxFilm; PlP&P; WebAB; WhAm 6; WhScrn 77; WhoAm 74; WhoHol B; WhoWor 74; WhoWorJ 72; WorEFlm*

Benny, Mrs. Jack
see: Livingstone, Mary

Benso di Cavour, Camillo
see: Cavour, Camillo Benso, Conte Di

Benson, Arthur Christopher
English. Author
b. Apr 24, 1862 in Wellington, England
d. Jun 17, 1925
Source: *Alli SUP; Chambr 3; ChPo, S1, S2; DcEnA AP; DcEuL; DcLEL; EvLB; LongCTC; NewC; Pen ENG; REn; TwCA*

Benson, Edward Frederic
English. Author
b. Jul 24, 1867 in Berkshire, England
d. Feb 29, 1940
Source: *BbD; BiD&SB; Chambr 3; CurBio 40; DcEnA AP; DcLEL; EvLB; LongCTC; MnBBF; ModBrL; NewC; OxEng; Pen ENG; TwCA; TwCW*

Benson, Ezra Taft
American. Former Government Official
Secretary of Agriculture, 1953-61.
b. Sep 3, 1899 in Whitney, Idaho
Source: *BiDrUSE; BioIn 3, 4, 5, 9, 10, 11; EncAAH; IntWW 75, 76, 77, 78; LinLib S; NewCol 75; PolProf E; WhoAm 74, 76, 78; WhoRel 75; WhoWor 74*

Benson, Frank Weston
American. Artist
b. Mar 24, 1862 in Salem, Massachusetts
d. Nov 14, 1951 in Salem, Massachusetts
Source: *BnEnAmA; DcAmArt; DcAmB S5; LinLib S; McGDA; NatCAB 13, 41; WhAm 3; WhoAmA 78*

Benson, George
American. Singer, Musician
Won three Grammys, 1977, including record of year, for "This Masquerade."
b. Mar 22, 1943 in Pittsburgh, Pennsylvania
Source: *BiDAmM; BioIn 11; BkPepl; DcBlPA; EncJzS 70; IlEncJ; RkOn; WhoAm 78, 80, 82; WhoBlA 77*

Benson, Renaldo
[The Four Tops]
American. Musician, Singer
b. 1947 in Detroit, Michigan
Source: *NF*

Benson, Robby
[Robin Segal]
American. Actor
Starred in movies *One on One; Ice Castles; The Chosen.*
b. Jan 21, 1957 in Dallas, Texas
Source: *BioIn 10; BkPepl; FilmEn; IntMPA 78, 79, 80, 81, 82; NewYTBS 77; WhoHol A*

Benson, Sally
American. Author
b. Sep 3, 1900 in Saint Louis, Missouri
d. Jul 19, 1972 in Woodland Hills, California
Source: *AmAu&B; BiE&WWA; CnDAL; ConAu 37R; ConAu P-1; CurBio 41, 72; InWom; NewYTBE 72; OxAmL; REn; REnAL; SmATA 1; TwCA SUP; WhAm 5; WomWMM*

Bentham, Jeremy
English. Author, Jurist, Philosopher
Wrote *An Introduction to the Principles of Morals and Legislation,* 1789.
b. Feb 15, 1748 in London, England
d. Jun 6, 1832 in London, England
Source: *Alli; AtlBL; BbD; BiD&SB; BiDLA; BrAu 19; CasWL; Chambr 2; DcEnA; DcEnL; DcEuL; DcLEL; EvLB; NewC; OxEng; Pen ENG; REn; WebE&AL*

Bentinck, William Henry Cavendish, Lord
British. Statesman
b. 1774
d. 1839
Source: *BiDLA; BioIn 2, 4, 10, 11; NewCol 75; WebBD 80*

Bentley, Alvin Morell
American. Diplomat, Congressman
b. Aug 30, 1918 in Portland, Maine
d. Apr 10, 1969 in Owosso, Michigan
Source: *BiDrAC; WhAm 5; WhAmP*

Bentley, Edmund Clerihew
English. Author, Journalist
b. Jul 10, 1875 in London, England
d. Mar 30, 1956 in London, England
Source: *ChPo, S2; DcLEL; EncMys; EvLB; LongCTC; NewC; OxEng; REn; TwCA, SUP; TwCW*

Bentley, Elizabeth Terrill
American. Spy
b. 1908?
d. Dec 3, 1963 in New Haven, Connecticut
Source: *BioIn 1, 2, 3, 6; InWom; ObitOF*

Bentley, Eric
American. Author, Drama Critic
b. Sep 14, 1916 in Lancashire, England
Source: *AmAu&B; AmSCAP 66; Au&Wr 71; BiE&WWA; CelR 73; ConAu 5R; NewC; NotNAT; REnAL; TwCA SUP; WhoAm 74, 76, 78, 80, 82; WhoThe 77; WhoWor 74; WrDr 76*

Bentley, John
English. Actor
b. Dec 2, 1916 in Warwickshire, England
Source: *BiDLA; FilmgC; IntMPA 75, 76, 77, 78, 79, 80, 81, 82; WhoHol A*

Bentley, John
see: Squeeze

Bentley, Max (Maxwell Herbert Lloyd)
Canadian. Hockey Player
NHL scoring champion, 1946, 1947; Hall of Fame, 1966.
b. Mar 1, 1920 in Delisle, SK
Source: *WhoHcky 73*

Bentley, Richard
English. Author
b. Jan 27, 1662 in Oulton, England
d. Jul 14, 1742
Source: *Alli; BiD&SB; BrAu; CasWL; DcEnA; DcEnL; DcEuL; EvLB; NewC; OxEng; Pen ENG; REn*

Bentley, Walter Owen
English. Auto Designer, Manufacturer
b. Sep 16, 1888 in London, England
d. Aug 13, 1971 in Woking, England
Source: *BioIn 5, 6, 8, 9, 10*

Benton, Brook
American. Singer
Wrote "Boll Weevil Song," 1961.
b. Sep 19, 1931 in Camden, South Carolina
Source: *BioIn 6, 11; EncPR&S*

Benton, Nelson
Broadcast Journalist
Source: *NF*

Benton, Thomas Hart
"Old Bullion"
American. Political Leader
Senator from MO, 1820-50; father-in-law of John C Fremont.
b. Mar 14, 1782 in Hillsboro, North Carolina
d. Apr 10, 1858 in Washington, DC
Source: *Alli; AmAu&B; AmBi; ApCAB; BbD; BiAuS; BiD&SB; BiDSA; BiDrAC; CyAL 1; DcAmAu; DcAmB; DcNAA; Drake; EncAB-H; LinLib S; McGEWB; NatCAB 4; NewCol 75; REn; REnAW; REnAL; TwCBDA; WebAB; WhAm H; WhAmP*

Benton, Thomas Hart
American. Artist
Paintings depicted life in Midwest and South; style called Regionalism.
b. Apr 15, 1889 in Neosho, Missouri
d. Jan 19, 1975 in Kansas City, Missouri
Source: *BioIn 1, 2, 3, 4, 5, 6, 7, 8, 9, 10, 11; AmAu&B; ArtsAmW; BnEnAmA; CelR 73; ConAu 53, 93; CurBio 40, 75; DcAmArt; DcCAA 71; EncAAH; EncAB-H; IlBEAAW; IlsCB 1744, 1946; IntWW 74, 75; LinLib S; McGDA; McGEWB; NewCol 75; NewYTBS 75; ObitOF 79; OxAmL; REn; REnAL; WebAB; WhAm 6; WhoAm 74; WhoAmA 73, 76, 78; WhoWor 74*

Benton, William
American. Publisher, Diplomat, Senator
b. Apr 1, 1900 in Minneapolis, Minnesota
d. Mar 18, 1973 in New York, New York
Source: *AmAu&B; BiDrAC; ConAu 41R; ConAu P-1; CurBio 73; St&PR 75; WebAB; WhAm 5; WhAmP; WhoAmA 73; WhoF&I 74*

Bentsen, Lloyd Millard, Jr.
American. Senator, Judge
b. Feb 11, 1921 in Mission, Texas
Source: *BiDrAC; BioNews 74, 75; CngDr 74; CurBio 73; IntWW 74; WhoAm 74, 76, 78, 80, 82; WhoAmP 73; WhoGov 72*

Bentyne, Cheryl
see: Manhattan Transfer

Benz, Carl Friedrich
German. Automotive Pioneer
Built first car powered by internal combustion engine, 1885; forerunner of Mercedes-Benz.
b. Nov 26, 1844 in Karlsruhe, Germany
d. 1929
Source: *BioIn 10; NewCol 75; WebBD 80*

Benzell, Mimi
American. Opera Singer
b. 1924 in Bridgeport, Connecticut
d. Dec 23, 1970 in Manhasset, New York
Source: *BiE&WWA; InWom; NewYTBE 70*

Beranger, Pierre Jean de
French. Poet
b. Aug 19, 1780 in Paris, France
d. Jul 16, 1857
Source: *BbD; BiD&SB; ChPo, S1, S2; DcEuL; EuAu; EvEuW; OxEng; OxFr; Pen EUR; REn*

Berberian, Cathy
[Mrs. Luciano Berio]
American. Opera Singer, Comedienne
b. in Attleboro, Massachusetts
Source: *WhoAm 74, 76, 78, 80, 82; WhoMus 72; WhoWor 74*

Bercovici, Konrad
American. Author
b. Jun 22, 1882 in Braila, Romania
d. Dec 27, 1961 in New York, New York
Source: *AmAu&B; AmNov; CnDAL; ConAmL; DcLEL; OxAmL; REnAL; TwCA, SUP; WhAm 4; WhNAA*

Berdyayev, Nikolay A
Russian. Theologian, Philosopher
b. Mar 19, 1874 in Kiev, Russia
d. Mar 4, 1948 in Paris, France
Source: *CasWL; ClDMEL; DcRusL; EncWL; EvEuW; LongCTC; REn; TwCA, SUP*

Beregovoy, Georgi
Russian. Cosmonaut
b. 1921
Source: *BioIn 10*

Berengar of Tours
French. Theologian
b. 1000
d. 1088
Source: *NewCol 75*

Berenson, Bernard
American. Art Critic, Author
b. Jun 26, 1865 in Vilnius, Lithuania
d. Oct 6, 1959 in Settignano, Italy
Source: *AmAu&B; CasWL; EncAB-H; LongCTC; OxAmL; OxEng; Pen AM; REn; REnAL; TwCA SUP; WebAB; WhAm 3*

Berenson, Marisa
American. Model, Actress
Grandniece of Bernard Berenson; starred in *Barry Lyndon,* 1975.
b. Feb 15, 1948 in New York, New York
Source: *BkPepl; FilmEn; MovMk; WhoHol A*

Berenson, "Red" (Gordon Arthur)
Canadian. Hockey Player, Coach
One of seven NHL players to score six goals in one game, Nov 7, 1968.
b. Dec 8, 1941 in Regina, SK
Source: *BioIn 8, 9, 10, 11; WhoHcky 73*

Beresford, Harry
English. Actor, Author
b. 1864 in London, England
d. Oct 4, 1944 in Los Angeles, California
Source: *WhAm 2; WhScrn 74, 77; WhoHol B*

Berg, Alban
Austrian. Composer
b. Feb 9, 1885 in Vienna, Austria
d. Dec 24, 1935 in Vienna, Austria
Source: *AtlBL; DcCM; OxGer; WhAm 4*

Berg, Gertrude
American. Actress
b. Oct 3, 1899 in Harlem, New York
d. Sep 14, 1966 in New York, New York
Source: *BiE&WWA; CurBio 41, 60, 66; FilmgC; InWom; WhAm 4; WhScrn 74, 77; WhoHol B*

Berg, Patty (Patricia Jane)
American. Golfer
Has won 83 golf tournaments; first president of LPGA.
b. Feb 13, 1918 in Minneapolis, Minnesota
Source: *CurBio 40; InWom; WhoGolf*

Berg, Paul
American. Biochemist, Nobel Prize Winner
b. Jun 30, 1926 in New York, New York
Source: *AmM&WS 73P, 76P, 79P; BioIn 5, 12; IntWW 74, 75, 76, 77, 78; WhoAm 74, 76, 78, 80, 82*

Berganza, Teresa
Spanish. Opera Singer
b. Mar 16, 1935 in Madrid, Spain
Source: *InWom; IntWW 74; Who 74; WhoAm 82; WhoMus 72; WhoWor 74*

Bergen, Candice
[Mrs. Louis Malle]
American. Actress, Photojournalist
Daughter of Edgar Bergen; starred in *Starting Over,* 1979, *Rich and Famous,* 1981.
b. May 9, 1946 in Beverly Hills, California
Source: *BkPepl; CelR 73; FilmgC; IntMPA 75, 76, 77, 78, 79, 80, 81, 82; MotPP; MovMk; NewYTBE 71; WhoAm 74, 76, 78, 80, 82; WhoHol A*

Bergen, Edgar John
[Edgar John Bergren]
American. Ventriloquist, Comedian
Created dummy Charlie McCarthy; they starred in *A Letter of Introduction,* 1938.
b. Feb 16, 1903 in Chicago, Illinois
d. Sep 30, 1978 in Las Vegas, Nevada
Source: *CurBio 45; FilmgC; MotPP; WebAB; WhoHol A*

Bergen, John Joseph
American. Financier, Industrialist
b. Aug 7, 1896 in Pottsville, Pennsylvania
d. Dec 11, 1980 in Cuernavaca, Mexico
Source: *CurBio 61, 81*

Bergen, Polly
American. Actress, Singer, Cosmetician
Starred in *A Guide for the Married Man,* 1967; founded cosmetic firm.
b. Jul 14, 1930 in Knoxville, Tennessee
Source: *BiE&WWA; CelR 73; ConAu 57; ForWC 70; InWom; IntMPA 77, 78, 79, 80, 81, 82; NotNAT; WhoAm 82*

Berger, Al
see: Southside Johnny and the Asbury Jukes

Berger, Arthur
American. Composer
b. May 15, 1912 in New York, New York
Source: *DcCM; WhoAm 74; WhoWor 74*

Berger, David
Israeli. Murdered Olympic Team Member
b. 1944
d. Sep 5, 1972 in Munich, Germany (West)
Source: *BioIn 9*

Berger, Erna
German. Opera Singer, Teacher
b. Oct 19, 1900 in Dresden, Germany
Source: *InWom*

Berger, Helmut
[Helmut Steinberger]
Austrian. Actor
b. May 29, 1944 in Salzburg, Austria
Source: *FilmEn; FilmgC; IntMPA 81; WhoHol A*

Berger, John
English. Author, Art Critic
b. Nov 5, 1926 in London, England
Source: *ConLC 2; ConNov 72, 76; ModBrL; Who 74; WrDr 76*

Berger, Marilyn
American. Broadcast Journalist
Chief White House correspondent, NBC-TV, 1976-77.
b. Aug 23, 1935 in New York, New York
Source: *BioIn 11; ConAu 101; WhoAm 78, 80, 82*

Berger, Melvin H
American. Author
b. Aug 23, 1927 in Brooklyn, New York
Source: *AuBYP; ConAu 5R, 4NR; ConLC 12; SmATA 5*

Berger, Meyer
American. Journalist
b. Sep 1, 1898 in New York, New York
d. Feb 8, 1959 in New York, New York
Source: *AmAu&B; CurBio 43, 59; WhAm 3*

Berger, Raoul
American. Lawyer, Educator
b. Jan 4, 1901 in Russia
Source: *NewYTBE 73; WhoAm 74*

Berger, Samuel David
American. Diplomat
b. Dec 6, 1911 in Gloversville, New York
d. Feb 12, 1980 in Washington, DC
Source: *AnObit 1980; IntWW 74, 75, 76, 77, 78, 79, 80, 81; USBiR 74; WhoGov 72, 75*

Berger, Senta
Austrian. Actress
b. 1941 in Vienna, Austria
Source: *FilmgC; MotPP; WhoHol A*

Berger, Terry
American. Author
b. Aug 11, 1933 in New York, New York
Source: *ConAu 37R; SmATA 8; WrDr 76*

Berger, Thomas Louis
American. Author
b. Jul 20, 1924 in Cincinnati, Ohio
Source: *AmAu&B; ConAu 1R, 5NR; ConLC 3, 5, 8, 11, 18; ConNov 76; DrAF 76; ModAL SUP; Pen AM; RAdv 1; WebE&AL; WhoAm 82; WorAu; WrDr 76*

Berger, Victor L
American. Socialist Leader
b. Feb 28, 1860 in Nieder-Rehbach, Romania
d. Aug 7, 1929 in Milwaukee, Wisconsin
Source: *AmBi; BiDrAC; DcAmB S1; DcNAA; EncAB-H; WebAB; WhAm 1; WhAmP*

Bergerac, Jacques
French. Actor
Appeared in *Gigi;* president, Paris branch of Revlon since 1972.
b. May 26, 1927 in Biarritz, France
Source: *IntMPA 75, 76, 77, 78, 79, 80, 81, 82; MotPP; WhoHol A*

Bergerac, Michel C
American. Cosmetics Executive
b. Feb 13, 1932 in Biarritz, France
Source: *BusPN; WhoAm 82; WhoF&I 74*

Bergeron, Victor J
American. Restaurateur
Founder, owner worldwide "Trader Vic" restaurant chain.
b. 1903 in California
Source: *BioNews 74; BusPN; WhoAm 74, 76, 78, 80, 82; WhoWor 74*

Bergey, Bill
American. Football Player
b. Feb 9, 1945 in South Dayton, Ohio
Source: *WhoFtbl 74*

Bergh, Henry
American. Humanitarian, Reformer
Founder ASPCA; co-founder, with Elbridge T Gerry, of ASPCC.
b. Aug 29, 1811 in New York, New York
d. Mar 12, 1888 in New York, New York
Source: *AmBi; BioIn 1, 3, 4, 8; DcAmB; WebAB; WhAm H*

Bergland, Bob Selmer
American. Government Official
b. Jul 22, 1928 in Roseau, Minnesota
Source: *CngDr 74; WhoAm 74; WhoAmP 73; WhoGov 72; WhoMW 74*

Bergman, Alan
American. Lyricist
b. Sep 11, 1925 in Brooklyn, New York
Source: *AmSCAP 66, 80; BioIn 10; WhoAm 74, 76, 78, 80, 82*

Bergman, Ingmar
[Ernest Ingmar Bergman]
Swedish. Motion Picture Director, Producer
Films include *The Seventh Seal, Wild Strawberries,* both 1957.
b. Jul 14, 1918 in Uppsala, Sweden
Source: *BiDFilm; BkPepl; ConAu 81; ConLC 16; CurBio 60; DcFM; IntMPA 75, 76, 77, 78, 79, 80, 81, 82; IntWW 74; MovMk; NewYTBE 72, 73; OxFilm; OxThe; PlP&P A; REn; Who 82; WhoAm 82; WhoWor 74; WorEFlm*

Bergman, Ingrid
Swedish. Actress
b. Aug 29, 1915 in Stockholm, Sweden
d. Aug 29, 1982 in London, England
Source: *BiDFilm; BiE&WWA; BkPepl; CelR 73; CmMov; CurBio 40, 65, 82; FilmgC; GoodHS; IntMPA 75, 76, 77, 78, 79, 80, 81, 82; IntWW 74, 75, 76, 77, 78, 79, 80, 81, 82; MotPP; MovMk; NewYTBE 71; NewYTBS 75, 82; NotNAT; OxFilm; PlP&P; ThFT; Who 82; WhoAm 74, 76, 78, 80, 82; WhoAmW 58, 64, 66, 68, 70, 72, 74; WhoHol A; WhoThe 72, 77, 81; WhoWor 74, 76; WorEFlm*

Bergman, Jules Verne
American. Broadcast Journalist
b. Mar 21, 1929 in New York, New York
Source: *WhoAm 80, 82*

Bergman, Marilyn Keith
[Mrs. Alan Bergman]
American. Lyricist
b. Nov 10, 1929 in Brooklyn, New York
Source: *AmSCAP 66, 80; BioIn 10; WhoAm 76, 78, 80, 82; WhoAmW 74*

Bergmann, Carl
German. Opera Conductor
b. Apr 11, 1821 in Ebersbach, Germany
d. Aug 16, 1876 in New York, New York
Source: *AmBi; ApCAB; DcAmB; WhAm H*

Bergmoser, J Paul
American. Former President of Chrysler Corp
b. May 23, 1916 in Detroit, Michigan
Source: *Dun&B 79*

Bergner, Elisabeth
Austrian. Actress
b. Aug 22, 1900 in Vienna, Austria
Source: *BiE&WWA; FilmgC; InWom; MovMk; NotNAT; OxFilm; ThFT; Who 74; WhoHol A; WhoThe 77; WorEFlm*

Bergonzi, Carlo
Italian. Opera Singer
b. Jul 13, 1924 in Polesine, Italy
Source: *IntWW 74; WhoMus 72; WhoWor 74*

Bergson, Henri Louis
French. Author, Philosopher
b. Oct 18, 1859 in Paris, France
d. Jan 3, 1941 in Paris, France
Source: *AtlBL; BiDPara; CasWL; ClDMEL; CurBio 41; EncWL; EvEuW; LongCTC; NewC; OxEng; OxFr; Pen EUR; RComWL; REn; TwCA, SUP; TwCW; WhoTwCL*

Beria, Lavrenti Pavlovich
Russian. Communist Leader
b. Mar 29, 1899 in Georgia, Russia
d. Dec 23, 1953
Source: *BioIn 1, 2, 3, 6, 8, 9, 10; CurBio 42, 54*

Berigan, "Bunny" (Rowland Bernart)
American. Musician, Band Leader
b. Nov 2, 1909 in Hilbert, Wisconsin
d. Jun 2, 1942 in New York, New York
Source: *CurBio 42; WhoJazz 72*

Bering, Vitus Jonassen
Danish. Navigator
b. 1680 in Horsens, Denmark
d. Dec 19, 1741 in Bering Island
Source: *ApCAB; OxCan; WhAm H*

Berini, Bianca
Italian. Opera Singer
b. in Trieste, Italy
Source: *WhoOp 76*

Berio, Luciano
Italian. Composer, Conductor
b. Oct 24, 1925 in Oniglia, Italy
Source: *CurBio 71; DcCM; IntWW 74; WhoAm 74, 76, 78, 78, 80; WhoMus 72; WhoWor 74*

Berkeley, "Busby" (William Berkeley Enos)
American. Director, Choreographer
Came out of retirement, 1971, to supervise revival of *No No Nanette.*
b. Nov 29, 1895 in Los Angeles, California
d. Mar 14, 1976 in Palm Springs, California
Source: *BiDFilm; BiE&WWA; CmMov; CurBio 71; DcFM; EncMT; FilmgC; IntMPA 75; MovMk; OxFilm; WebAB; WhoAm 74; WorEFlm; WhAm 6; WhoThe 77*

Berkeley, George
Irish. Author, Philosopher
Wrote *Principals of Human Knowledge,* 1710.
b. Mar 12, 1685 in Ireland
d. Jan 14, 1753 in Oxford, England
Source: *Alli; ApCAB; BbD; BiD&SB; BrAu; CasWL; ChPo, S1; CyAL 1; DcEnA; DcEnL; DcEuL; DcLEL; Drake; EvLB; NewC; OxAmL; OxEng; Pen ENG; PoIre; REn; TwCBDA; WebE&AL*

Berkman, Alexander
Anarchist, Magazine Publisher
b. Nov 21, 1870 in Vilna, Russia
d. Jun 28, 1936 in Nice, France
Source: *DcAmB S2; DcNAA; WhAm 4*

Berkow, Ira
American. Journalist, Author
b. Jan 7, 1940 in Chicago, Illinois
Source: *BioIn 10; ConAu 97*

Berkowitz, Bernard
American. Psychoanalyst, Author
b. 1909
Source: *AuNews 1; BioIn 10, 11*

Berkowitz, David
"Son of Sam"
American. Murderer
Killed six people in NY City, Jul, 1976-Aug, 1977.
b. Jun 1, 1953
Source: *BioIn 11*

Berlage, Hendrik Petrus
Dutch. Architect
b. 1856 in Amsterdam, Netherlands
d. 1934 in The Hague, Netherlands
Source: *BioIn 4, 10; EncMA; McGDA; NewCol 75; WebBD 80; WhoArch*

Berle, Adolf Augustus, Jr.
American. Lawyer, Diplomat
b. Jan 29, 1895 in Boston, Massachusetts
d. Feb 17, 1971 in New York, New York
Source: *AmAu&B; ConAu 25R, 29R; ConAu P-2; CurBio 40, 61, 71; EncAB-H; NewYTBE 71; WhAm 5*

Berle, Milton
[Milton Berlinger]
"Uncle Miltie"
American. Actor, Comedian
Appeared in *The Muppet Movie,* 1979; starred in "The Milton Berle Show," 1948-56.
b. Jul 12, 1908 in New York, New York
Source: *AmAu&B; AmSCAP 66; AuNews 1; BiE&WWA; BioNews 75; ConAu 77; CurBio 49; EncMT; Film 1; FilmgC; IntMPA 75, 76, 77, 78, 79, 80, 81, 82; MovMk; NotNAT; PlP&P; TwYS; WebAB; WhoAm 74, 76, 78, 80, 82; WhoHol A; WhoThe 77; WhoWor 74*

Berlenbach, Paul
American. Boxer
b. Feb 18, 1901 in New York, New York
Source: *WhoBox 74*

Berlin, Irving
[Israel Baline]
American. Composer
Wrote "Alexander's Ragtime Band," "Heat Wave," "White Christmas."
b. May 11, 1888 in Temun, Russia
Source: *AmSCAP 66; BiE&WWA; CelR 73; CmMov; ConAu 25R; CurBio 42, 63; DcFM; EncAB-H; EncMT; FilmgC; IntMPA 75, 76, 78, 79, 80, 81, 82; IntWW 74; McGEWD; NewCBMT; NotNAT; OxAmL; OxFilm; PlP&P; REn; REnAL; St&PR 75; WebAB; Who 82; WhoAm 74, 76, 78, 80, 82; WhoMus 72; WhoThe 77; WhoWor 74; WhoWorJ 72*

Berlin, Sir Isaiah
English. Author
b. Jun 6, 1909 in Riga, Russia
Source: *ConAu 85; CurBio 64; IntWW 74; LongCTC; Who 74; WhoWor 74; WorAu*

Berlin, Richard E
American. Corporation Executive
b. Jan 18, 1894 in Omaha, Nebraska
Source: *St&PR 75; WhoAm 74; WhoE 74; WhoF&I 74; WhoWest 74*

Berliner, Emile
American. Inventor
Invented microphone, 1877, gramaphone, 1887.
b. May 20, 1851 in Hannover, Germany
d. Aug 3, 1929 in Washington, DC
Source: *AmBi; ApCAB; DcAmB S1; DcNAA; WebAB; WhAm 1; WhNAA*

Berlinger, Warren
American. Actor
b. Aug 31, 1937 in Brooklyn, New York
Source: *BiE&WWA; FilmgC; IntMPA 75, 76, 77, 78, 79, 80, 81, 82; MotPP; NotNAT; WhoAm 74, 76, 78, 80, 82; WhoHol A; WhoThe 77*

Berlioz, Louis Hector
French. Composer
b. Dec 11, 1803 in La Cote, France
d. Mar 8, 1869 in Paris, France
Source: *AtlBL; BbD; BiD&SB; OxFr; REn*

Berlitz, Charles Frambach
American. Author, Linguist
Founded Berlitz Schools of Languages, 1934; wrote over 23 *Berlitz Method Books*.
b. Nov 22, 1913 in New York, New York
Source: *AmAu&B; ConAu 5R; CurBio 57; WhoAm 74, 76, 78, 80, 82; WhoWor 74*

Berman, Emile Zola
American. Lawyer
b. Nov 2, 1903 in New York, New York
d. Jul 3, 1981 in New York, New York
Source: *BioIn 4, 7, 8, 9; CurBio 72, 81; NewYTBS 81; WhoAm 74, 76*

Berman, Eugene
American. Artist, Designer
b. Nov 4, 1899 in Saint Petersburg, Russia
d. Dec 14, 1972 in Rome, Italy
Source: *BnEnAmA; ConArt; CurBio 65, 73; DcCAA 71, 77; EncWT; McGDA; WhAm 5; WhoAmA 78*

Berman, Lazar
Russian. Musician
b. Feb 26, 1930 in Leningrad, U.S.S.R.
Source: *BioIn 10, 11; CurBio 77; WhoAm 82*

Berman, Morton
American. Editor
Co-edited *Eight Great Tragedies*, 1957; *Eight Great Comedies*, 1958.
b. Mar 21, 1924 in Syracuse, New York
Source: *ConAu 5R, 2NR; DrAS 74E; WhoAm 74*

Berman, Pandro Samuel
American. Motion Picture Producer
b. Mar 28, 1905 in Pittsburgh, Pennsylvania
Source: *FilmgC; IntMPA 75, 76, 77, 78, 79, 80, 81, 82; WhoAm 82; WorEFlm*

Berman, Shelley
American. Comedian
b. Feb 3, 1926 in Chicago, Illinois
Source: *BiE&WWA; FilmgC; WhoAm 74; WhoWor 74*

Berman, Susan
American. Author
b. May 18, 1945 in Minneapolis, Minnesota
Source: *ConAu 65*

Bermudez, Juan de
Spanish. Navigator, Discovered Bermuda
Source: *ApCAB*

Bern, Paul
[Paul Levy]
American. Motion Picture Director
b. Dec 3, 1889 in Wandsbek, Germany
d. Sep 4, 1932 in Beverly Hills, California
Source: *BioIn 11; FilmEn; FilmgC; PseudN; WhAm 1; WhScrn 74, 77*

Bernacchi, Antonio
Italian. Opera Singer
b. Jun 23, 1685 in Bologna, Italy
d. Mar 1756 in Bologna, Italy
Source: *NewEOp 71*

Bernadette of Lourdes
[Bernadette Soubirous]
French. Canonized Peasant Girl
Site of visions, spring in Lourdes, said to have healing properties.
b. 1844 in Lourdes, France
d. 1879
Source: *HerW; InWom; REn*

Bernadotte, Folke, Count
Swedish: Diplomat
b. Jan 2, 1895 in Stockholm, Sweden
d. Sep 17, 1948 in Jerusalem, Israel
Source: *BioIn 1, 2, 3, 4, 10; CurBio 45, 48*

Bernanos, Georges
French. Author
b. May 5, 1888 in Paris, France
d. Jul 5, 1948 in Paris, France
Source: *CyWA; EncWL; OxFr*

Bernard of Clairvaux, Saint
French. Churchman, Mystic
b. 1090 in Fontaines-les-Dijon, France
d. Aug 20, 1153 in Clairvaux, France
Source: *BbD; BiD&SB; CasWL; EuAu; EvEuW; NewC; Pen EUR; PoChrch; REn*

Bernard of Cluny
French. Monk, Author
b. 1100
d. 1156
Source: *BiD&SB; CasWL; NewC; Pen EUR; REn*

Bernard, Andrew Milroy
[Andrew Milroy Fleming-Bernard]
"Master Bernard, the Blind Poet"
British. Poet Laureate
Poet laureate to Henry VII, Henry VIII.
b. in Toulose, France
d. 1523?
Source: *Alli; DcEnL; PoLE*

Bernard, Claude
French. Experimental Physiologist
b. 1813 in Saint-Julien, France
d. Feb 10, 1878
Source: *DcEuL; OxFr*

Bernard, Sam
[Samuel Barnet]
English. Actor
b. 1863 in Birmingham, England
d. May 16, 1927
Source: *Film 1; WhAm 1; WhScrn 74, 77; WhoHol B; WhoStg 1908*

Bernardi, Hershel
American. Actor, Singer
b. Oct 30, 1923 in New York, New York
Source: *BioIn 7; CelR 73; FilmgC; NotNAT; WhoAm 82; WhoHol A*

Bernardin, Joseph Louis
American. Cardinal
Head of Chicago diosese after death of Cardinal Cody, 1982.
b. Apr 2, 1928 in Columbia, South Carolina
Source: *BioIn 10, 11; CurBio 82; NewYTBS 74, 82; WhoAm 74, 76, 78, 80, 82; WhoMW 76, 78*

Bernardine of Siena, Saint
Italian. Preacher
b. 1380
d. 1444
Source: *BioIn 1, 3, 4, 5, 6; NewCol 75*

Bernardone, Giovanni
see: Francis of Assisi, Saint

Bernays, Edward L
American. Publicist
b. Nov 22, 1891 in Vienna, Austria
Source: *AmAu&B; ConAu 17R; CurBio 42, 60; REnAL; WhNAA; WhoAm 74, 76, 78, 80, 82; WhoPubR 72; WhoWor 74; WhoWorJ 72; WrDr 76*

Bernbach, William
American. Advertising Executive
Founded Doyle Dane Bernbach, 10th largest ad agency in US.
b. Aug 13, 1911 in Bronx, New York
d. Oct 1, 1982 in New York, New York
Source: *CurBio 67, 82; Dun&B 79; NewYTBS 82; WhoAm 74, 76, 78, 80, 82; WhoE 77, 79; WhoF&I 74, 75, 77, 79*

Berndt, Walter
American. Cartoonist
b. Nov 22, 1899 in Brooklyn, New York
Source: *ConAu 89; WorECom*

Berne, Eric Lennard
American. Psychiatrist, Author
b. May 10, 1910 in Montreal, PQ
d. Jul 15, 1970 in Monterey, California
Source: *AmAu&B; ConAu 5R, 25R, 4NR; WhAm 5*

Bernhard, Prince
[Bernhard Leopold Friedrich Eberhard Julius Kurt Karl Gottfried Peter]
German. Consort of Queen Juliana
Married Juliana on Jan 7, 1937.
b. Jun 29, 1911 in Jena, Germany
Source: *BioIn 1, 2, 3, 4, 5, 6, 10, 11; CurBio 50; WebBD 80*

Bernhard, Lucian
American. Type Designer, Graphic Artist
b. 1883 in Germany
d. 1972
Source: *WhoGrA*

Bernhardt, Sarah
[Rosine Bernard]
"The Devine Sarah"
French. Actress
Known for roles in *L'Aiglon, Hamlet;* starred in silent film *Queen Elizabeth,* 1912.
b. Oct 23, 1844 in Paris, France
d. Mar 26, 1923 in Paris, France
Source: *FamA&A; Film 1; FilmgC; HerW; InWom; LongCTC; NewC; NewCol 75; OxFilm; OxFr; OxThe; PlP&P; TwYS; WhAm 1; WhScrn 74, 77; WhoHol B; WhoStg 1906, 1908; WorEFlm*

Bernie, Ben
American. Comedian, Musician
b. May 30, 1891 in New York, New York
d. Oct 20, 1943 in Beverly Hills, California
Source: *AmSCAP 66; CurBio 41, 43; WhAm 2; WhScrn 74, 77; WhoHol B*

Bernini, Giovanni Lorenzo
Italian. Sculptor, Architect
b. Dec 7, 1598 in Naples, Italy
d. Nov 28, 1680 in Rome, Italy
Source: *AtlBL; OxThe*

Bernoulli, David
Swiss. Mathematician
b. Feb 8, 1700 in Groningen, Netherlands
d. Mar 17, 1782 in Basel, Switzerland
Source: *AsBiEn; BioIn 2, 3, 4; DcScB; McGEWB*

Bernstein, Carl
American. Journalist, Author
With Bob Woodward wrote account of Watergate break-in, cover-up, *All the President's Men.*
b. Feb 14, 1944 in Washington, DC
Source: *AuNews 1; BioNews 74; BkPepl; ConAu 81; CurBio 76; WhoAm 74, 76, 78, 80, 82; WorAl; WrDr 80*

Bernstein, Eduard
German. Socialist Critic
b. Jan 6, 1850 in Berlin, Germany
d. 1932
Source: *BioIn 11; McGEWB; REn; WhoModH*

Bernstein, Elmer
American. Composer, Conductor
b. Apr 4, 1922 in New York, New York
Source: *AmSCAP 66; CelR 73; CmMov; DcFM; FilmgC; IntMPA 75, 76, 77, 78, 79, 80, 81, 82; OxFilm; WhoAm 74, 76, 78, 80, 82; WhoWest 74; WhoWor 74; WorEFlm*

Bernstein, Felicia Montealegre
[Mrs. Leonard Bernstein]
American. Actress
b. 1921
d. 1978
Source: *BioIn 5, 10, 11*

Bernstein, Jay
American. Talent Agent
b. 1937? in Oklahoma City, Oklahoma
Source: *BioIn 12*

Bernstein, Leonard
American. Composer, Conductor, Musician
Wrote *West Side Story;* won Emmy for "Young People's Concerts."
b. Aug 25, 1918 in Lawrence, Massachusetts
Source: *AmAu&B; AmPS; AmSCAP 66, 80; Baker 78; BiDAmM; BiE&WWA; CelR 73; CmpEPM; ConAu 1R, 2NR; CurBio 44, 60; DcCM; EncAB-H; EncMT; EncWT; FilmgC; IntAu&W 77; IntWW 74, 75, 76, 77, 78, 79, 80, 81; LinLib L, S; McGEWB; McGEWD; NewCBMT; NewEOp 71; NewYTET; NotNAT; OxAmL; OxFilm; OxMus; PlP&P; REn; REnAL; WebAB, 79; WhoAm 74, 76, 78, 80, 82; WhoE 74, 79; WhoMus 72; WhoOp 76; WhoThe 72, 77; WhoWor 74, 76, 78; WhoWorJ 72, 78; WorAl; WorEFlm; WrDr 80*

Bernstein, Sid(ney Ralph)
American. Editor
b. Jan 29, 1907 in Chicago, Illinois
Source: *WhoAdv 72; WhoAm 74, 76, 78, 80, 82; WhoF&I 74; WhoWorJ 72*

Bernstein, Theodore Menline
American. Journalist
b. Nov 17, 1904 in New York, New York
d. Jun 27, 1979 in New York, New York
Source: *ConAu 1R, 3NR; NewYTBS 79; SmATA 12; WhAm 7; WhNAA; WhoAm 74, 76, 78; WhoWorJ 72*

Beroff, Michel
French. Musician
b. 1950 in Epinal, France
Source: *WhoMus 72*

Berra, "Yogi" (Lawrence Peter)
American. Baseball Player, Manager, Coach
Catcher, NY Yankees, 1946-63; Hall of Fame, 1972.
b. May 12, 1925 in Saint Louis, Missouri
Source: *BaseEn; BioNews 74; BlueB 76; CelR 73; CurBio 52; NewYTBE 72, 73; NewYTBS 75; WebAB, 79; WhoAm 74, 76, 78, 80, 82; WhoE 74; WhoProB 73; WorAl*

Berrigan, Daniel J
American. Poet, Political Activist
Ordained Catholic priest, 1952; convicted of destroying draft records, 1968.
b. May 9, 1921 in Virginia, Minnesota
Source: *AmAu&B; ASpks; CelR 73; ConAu 33R; ConLC 4; ConP 70, 75, 80; CurBio 70; DrAP 75; IntWWP 77; LinLib L; MugS; PolProf J; PolProf NF; WhoAm 74, 76, 78, 80, 82; WhoRel 77; WrDr 76, 80*

Berrigan, Elizabeth McAlister
[Mrs. Philip Berrigan]
American. Educator
b. 1939
Source: *BioIn 9, 10, 11*

Berrigan, Philip Francis
American. Author, Political Activist
Ordained Catholic priest, 1950, married, 1969; co-founded Catholic Peace Fellowship.
b. Oct 5, 1923 in Minneapolis, Minnesota
Source: *AmAu&B; BioNews 74; CelR 73; ConAu 13R; WhoAm 74, 76, 78, 80, 82*

Berry, Bob (Robert Victor)
Canadian. Hockey Player, Coach
Coach, Montreal Canadiens, 1981--.
b. Nov 29, 1943 in Montreal, PQ
Source: *WhoHcky 73*

Berry, "Chu" (Leon)
American. Jazz Musician
b. Sep 13, 1910 in Wheeling, West Virginia
d. Oct 31, 1941 in Conneaut, Ohio
Source: *WhoJazz 72*

Berry, Chuck (Charles Edward Anderson)
American. Singer, Musician, Songwriter
Wrote songs "Roll Over Beethoven"; "Johnny B Goode."
b. Jan 15, 1926 in San Jose, California
Source: *Baker 78; BiDAmM; BluesWW; CurBio 77; DcBlPA; RkOn; WebAB, 79; WhoAm 74, 76, 78, 80, 82; WhoBlA 75, 77; WorAl*

Berry, Jim
American. Editorial Cartoonist
b. Jan 16, 1932 in Chicago, Illinois
Source: *ConAu 25R; WorECom*

Berry, Ken
American. Actor, Singer, Dancer
Starred in TV series "F-Troop," 1965-67 and "Mayberry RFD," 1968-71.
b. in Moline, Illinois
Source: *FilmgC; WhoAm 80, 82; WhoHol A*

Berry, Martha McChesney
American. Educator
b. 1866 in Rome, Georgia
d. Feb 27, 1942 in Mount Berry, Georgia
Source: *CurBio 40, 42; DcAmB S3; HerW; InWom; NotAW; WhAm 2; WomWWA 14*

Berry, Raymond
American. Football Player, Coach
b. Feb 27, 1933 in Corpus Christi, Texas
Source: *BioIn 5, 6, 7, 8, 9, 10, 11; WhoFtbl 74*

Berry, Walter
Austrian. Opera Singer
b. Apr 8, 1929 in Vienna, Austria
Source: *IntWW 74; WhoAm 82; WhoWor 74*

Berry, Wendell
American. Poet, Educator
b. Aug 5, 1934 in Henry County, Kentucky
Source: *ConAu 73; ConLC 4, 6; ConP 70, 75; DrAF 76; DrAP 75; Pen AM; RAdv 1; WhoAm 74, 76, 78, 80, 82; WhoS&SW 73; WrDr 76*

Berryer, Pierre Antoine
French. Lawyer
b. Jan 4, 1790
d. Nov 29, 1868
Source: *DcEuL*

Berryman, Clifford Kennedy
American. Editorial Cartoonist
b. Apr 2, 1869 in Versailles, Kentucky
d. Dec 11, 1949 in Washington, DC
Source: *BioIn 1, 2, 4; DcAmB S4; NatCAB 39; WhAm 2; WhoAmA 78*

Berryman, John
American. Author, Poet
Won Pulitzer Prize, 1964, for *77 Dream Songs*.
b. Oct 25, 1914 in McAlester, Oklahoma
d. Jan 7, 1972 in Minneapolis, Minnesota
Source: *AmAu&B; AmWr; Au&Wr 71; CasWL; CnE&AP; ConAu 33R; ConAu P-1; ConLC 1, 2, 3, 4, 617, 10, 13; ConP 70, 75; CroCAP; CurBio 69, 72; EncWL; ModAL, SUP; NewYTBE 72; OxAmL; Pen AM; RAdv 1; REn; REnAL; TwCA SUP; WebAB; WebE&AL; WhAm 5; WhoTwCL*

Berthollet, Claude Louis, Comte
French. Chemist
b. 1748
d. 1822
Source: *BioIn 1, 6; NewCol 75*

Bertillon, Alphonse
French. Anthropologist, Criminologist
b. 1853
d. 1914
Source: *LongCTC; OxFr*

Bertinelli, Valerie
[Mrs. Eddie Van Halen]
American. Actress
Plays Barbara Cooper Royer on TV series "One Day at a Time," 1975--.
b. Apr 23, 1960 in Wilmington, Delaware
Source: *BioIn 11, 12*

Bertini, Gary
Israeli. Conductor
b. May 1, 1927 in Bessarabia, U.S.S.R.
Source: *Baker 78; MidE 78, 79; WhoMus 72; WhoOp 76; WhoWor 74, 76; WhoWorJ 72*

Bertoia, Harry
American. Artist, Designer
b. Mar 10, 1915 in San Lorenzo, Italy
d. Nov 6, 1978 in Barto, Pennsylvania
Source: *ConArt; DcAmArt; DcCAA 71, 77; McGDA; NewYTBS 78; WhAm 7; WhoAm 74, 76, 78; WhoAmA 73, 76, 78; WhoWor 74*

Bertolucci, Bernardo
Italian. Motion Picture Director
b. Mar 16, 1940 in Parma, Italy
Source: *BiDFilm; CelR 73; ConLC 16; CurBio 74; DcFM; IntWW 74; MovMk; OxFilm; WhoAm 82; WorEFlm*

Berton, Pierre
Canadian. Author, Journalist
b. Jul 12, 1920 in Whitehorse, YT
Source: *Au&Wr 71; CanWW 70; CanWr; ConAu 1R; OxCan, SUP; WhoAm 82; WhoE 74; WrDr 76*

Berwind, Charles G
American. Founder of Big Brothers
b. 1894?
d. 1972
Source: *BioIn 9*

Berzelius, Jons Jacob, Baron
Swedish. Chemist
b. Aug 29, 1779 in Vaversunda, Sweden
d. Aug 7, 1848
Source: *BioIn 1, 3, 6, 7, 8, 9, 10, 11; McGEWB; NewCol 75*

Besant, Annie Wood
English. Social Reformer, Author
Early advocate of birth control and sex education.
b. Oct 1, 1847 in London, England
d. Sep 20, 1933 in Advar, India
Source: *Alli SUP; Chambr 3; DcLEL; EvLB; InWom; LongCTC; NewC; REn; TwCA, SUP; WhoLA*

Besant, Sir Walter
English. Author, Social Reformer
Wrote *All Sorts and Conditions of Men;* founded Society of Authors, 1884.
b. Aug 14, 1836 in Portsmouth, England
d. Jun 9, 1901 in London, England
Source: *Alli SUP; BbD; BiD&SB; BrAu 19; CasWL; Chambr 3; DcBiA; DcEnA, AP; DcEuL; DcLEL; EvLB; HsB&A; MouLC 4; NewC; OxEng; Pen ENG; REn; WebE&AL*

Bessell, Ted
American. Actor
Played Donald Hollinger on TV series "That Girl," 1966-71.
b. 1936 in Flushing, New York
Source: *WhoHol A*

Bessemer, Sir Henry
English. Engineer, Inventor
Invented industrial process for manufacturing steel from molten pig iron.
b. Jan 19, 1813 in Charlton, England
d. Mar 15, 1898 in London, England
Source: *BioIn 1, 2, 3, 4, 5, 6, 7, 11; NewCol 75; WebBD 80*

Bessie, Alvah
American. Author
b. Jun 4, 1904 in New York, New York
Source: *AmAu&B; AmNov; ConAmA; ConAu 5R, 2NR; TwCA, SUP; WhNAA; WrDr 76*

Best, Charles Herbert
Canadian. Physiologist
With F G Banting, discovered use of insulin in treatment of diabetes, 1921.
b. Feb 27, 1899 in West Pembroke, Maine
d. Mar 31, 1978 in Toronto, ON
Source: *AmM&WS 73P; Au&Wr 71; CanWW 70; ConAu 45; CurBio 57; IntWW 74; NewCol 75; Who 74; WhoAm 74; WhoCan 73; WhoWor 74; WrDr 76*

Best, Edna
English. Actress
b. Mar 3, 1900 in Hove, England
d. Sep 18, 1974 in Geneva, Switzerland
Source: *BiE&WWA; CurBio 54, 74; FilmgC; InWom; NewYTBS 74; ThFT; WhScrn 77; Who 74; WhoHol B*

Best, George
Irish. Soccer Player
b. May 22, 1946 in Belfast, Northern Ireland
Source: *BioIn 8, 9, 10, 11*

Best, Oswald Herbert
English. Author
b. Mar 25, 1894 in Chester, England
Source: *AmAu&B; AmNov; AuBYP; ConAu 25R; ConAu P-2; JBA 34, 51; SmATA 2*

Best, Peter
English. Original Member of the Beatles
Replaced by Ringo Starr as drummer for The Beatles, 1962.
b. 1941? in Liverpool, England
Source: *NF*

Betancourt, Romulo
Venezuelan. Statesman
b. Feb 22, 1908 in Guatire, Venezuela
d. Sep 28, 1981 in New York, New York
Source: *BioIn 1, 5, 6; CurBio 60, 81; IntWW 74, 75, 76, 76, 78; McGEWB; NewCol 75; NewYTBS 81; WhoWor 74*

Betaneur, Belisario
Colombian. President
b. 1923 in Amaga, Colombia
Source: *IntWW 81*

Bethe, Hans Albrecht
German. Physicist, Nuclear Advisor
b. Jul 2, 1906 in Strassburg, Germany
Source: *AmM&WS 73P; CurBio 40, 50; IntWW 74; WebAB; Who 74; WhoAm 74, 76, 78, 80, 82; WhoE 74; WhoWor 74*

Bethune, Mary McLeod
American. Educator
b. Jul 10, 1875 in Mayesville, South Carolina
d. May 18, 1955 in Daytona Beach, Florida
Source: *CurBio 42, 55; DcAmB S5; EncAB-H; HerW; InWom; WebAB; WhAm 3; WhAmP*

Bethune, Norman
Canadian. Surgeon
b. 1890 in Gravenhurst, ON
d. Nov 12, 1939 in China
Source: *BioIn 3, 10, 11; ClbCR; MacDCB 78*

Bethune, Thomas Greene
"Blind Tom"
American. Musician
b. 1849 in Georgia
d. 1908 in New York
Source: *BioIn 4, 8, 9, 10; OxMus*

Betjeman, Sir John
English. Poet
Named poet laureate, 1972; autobiography, *Summoned by Bells,* 1960, in verse.
b. Aug 28, 1906 in Highgate, England
Source: *Au&Wr 71; CasWL; ChPo, S1, S2; CnE&AP; CnMWL; ConLC 2, 6, 10; ConP 70, 75; DcLEL; EvLB; IntWW 74; LongCTC; ModBrL, SUP; NewC; NewCol 75; OxEng; Pen ENG; RAdv 1; REn; TwCA SUP; TwCW; WebE&AL; Who 74; WhoTwCL; WhoWor 74; WrDr 76*

Bettelheim, Bruno
Austrian. Psychologist, Author
b. Aug 28, 1903 in Vienna, Austria
Source: *AmAu&B; AmM&WS 73S; ConAu 81; CurBio 61; IntWW 74; LEduc 74; WebAB; WhoAm 74, 76, 78, 80, 82; WhoWor 74; WhoWorJ 72*

Bettenhausen, Tony (Melvin E.)
American. Automobile Racer
b. Sep 12, 1916 in Tinley Park, Illinois
d. 1961 in Indianapolis, Indiana
Source: *BioIn 2, 5, 11*

Betterton, Thomas
English. Actor
b. Aug 1635 in London, England
d. Apr 27, 1710 in London, England
Source: *Alli; BrAu; CasWL; DcEnL; DcLEL; NewC; OxEng; OxThe; REn*

Bettger, Lyle
American. Actor
b. Feb 13, 1915 in Philadelphia, Pennsylvania
Source: *FilmgC; IntMPA 75, 76, 77, 78, 79, 80, 81, 82; WhoHol A*

Betti, Ugo
Italian. Dramatist
b. Feb 4, 1892 in Camerino, Italy
d. Jun 9, 1953 in Rome, Italy
Source: *CasWL; ClDMEL; CnMD; CnMWL; CnThe; EncWL; EvEuW; LongCTC; McGEWD; ModRL; ModWD; OxEng; OxThe; Pen EUR; REnWD; TwCW; WhAm 4; WorAu*

Bettina
[Simone Micheline Bodin]
French. Model
b. 1925
Source: *BioIn 4, 7, 10*

Bettis, Valerie
American. Actress, Choreographer, Dancer
b. Dec 20, 1919 in Houston, Texas
d. Sep 26, 1982 in New York, New York
Source: *BiE&WWA; CurBio 53, 82; NewYTBS 82; NotNAT; WhoAm 74, 76, 78, 80, 82; WhoAmW 64, 66, 68, 70, 72, 74; WhoHol A; WhoThe 72, 77, 81*

Bettmann, Otto Ludwig
German. Picture Archivist, Historian
b. Oct 15, 1903 in Leipzig, Germany
Source: *BioIn 5, 6, 10; ConAu 17R; WhoAm 78, 80, 82*

Betz, Pauline
American. Tennis Player
b. 1919
Source: *InWom*

Beutel, Bill (William Charles)
American. Broadcast Journalist
b. Dec 12, 1930 in Cleveland, Ohio
Source: *ConAu 101; WhoAm 80, 82*

Beuys, Joseph
German. Artist
b. May 12, 1921 in Krefeld, Germany
Source: *BioIn 12; CurBio 80; IntWW 79*

Bevan, Aneurin
British. Political Leader
b. Nov 15, 1897 in Tredagar, Wales
d. Jul 6, 1970 in Chesham, England
Source: *CurBio 43, 60*

Beveridge, Albert Jeremiah
American. Politician, Historian
b. Oct 6, 1862 in Highland County, Ohio
d. Apr 27, 1927 in Indianapolis, Indiana
Source: *AmAu&B; AmBi; ApCAB SUP; BiDrAC; DcAmAu; DcAmB; DcNAA; EncAB-H; IndAu 1816; OhA&B; OxAmL; REn; REnAL; TwCA, SUP; TwCBDA; WebAB; WhAm 1; WhAmP*

Beveridge, Lord William Henry
British. Economist
b. Mar 5, 1879 in Rangpur, Bengal
d. Mar 16, 1963 in Oxford, England
Source: *BioIn 3, 6, 7, 11; CurBio 43, 63; McGEWB; ObitOF 79; WhAm 4; WhoModH*

Bevin, Ernest
English. Labor Party Leader
b. Mar 9, 1881 in Winsford, England
d. Apr 14, 1951 in London, England
Source: *CurBio 40, 49, 51; WhAm 3*

Bewick, Thomas
English. Illustrator, Wood Engraver
b. Aug 12, 1753 in Cherryburn, England
d. Nov 8, 1828 in Gateshead, England
Source: *Alli; BkIE; CarSB; ChPo, S1, S2; DcLEL; NewC; Str&VC; WhoChL*

Bey, Turhan
Turkish. Actor
b. Mar 30, 1920 in Vienna, Austria
Source: *FilmgC; HolP 40; IntMPA 75, 76, 77, 78, 79, 80, 81, 82; MotPP; MovMk; WhoHol A*

Beyle, Marie Henri
see: Stendhal, pseud.

Beymer, (George) Richard
American. Actor
b. Feb 21, 1939 in Avoco, Iowa
Source: *FilmgC; IntMPA 75, 76, 77, 78, 79, 80, 81, 82; MotPP; WhoHol A*

Bhave, Acharya Vinoba
Indian. Nonviolent Revolutionary
Disciple of Gandhi; crusader for social reforms.
b. Sep 11, 1895 in Gagoda, India
d. Nov 15, 1982 in Paunar, India
Source: *CurBio 53, 83; FarE&A 78, 79, 80; IntWW 74, 75, 76, 77, 78, 79, 80, 81; McGEWB; NewYTBS 82; WhDW; WhoWor 74*

Bhumibol, Adulyadej
[Rama IX, King]
Thai. Ruler
b. Dec 5, 1927 in Cambridge, Massachusetts
Source: *CurBio 50; IntWW 74; WhoWor 74*

Bhutto, (Zulfikar) Ali (Khan)
Pakistani. President
Wrote *The Myth of Independence,* study of Pakistan's role in international diplomacy.
b. Jan 5, 1928 in Larkana, Pakistan
d. Apr 4, 1979 in Rawalpirdi, Pakistan
Source: *ConAu 53; CurBio 72; IntWW 74; NewYTBE 71, 72; NewYTBS 79; Who 74; WhoAm 74; WhoGov 72; WhoWor 74*

Biaggi, Mario
American. Congressman
b. Oct 26, 1917 in New York, New York
Source: *BiDrAC; CngDr 74; NewYTBE 73; WhoAm 74, 76, 78, 80, 82; WhoAmP 73; WhoE 74; WhoGov 72*

Bialik, Chaim Nachman
Israeli. Poet
b. Jan 9, 1873 in Rady, Russia
d. Jul 4, 1934 in Tel Aviv, Palestine
Source: *CasWL; Pen CL; WorAu*

Biba
[Barbara Hulanicki]
English. Designer
b. in Poland
Source: *WorFshn*

Bibb, Leon
American. Singer
b. 1935 in Louisville, Kentucky
Source: *EncFCWM 69*

Bibby, Henry
American. Basketball Player
b. Nov 24, 1949 in Franklinton, North Carolina
Source: *WhoBbl 73*

Bibby, Thomas Geoffrey
English. Archaeologist
b. Oct 14, 1917 in Heversham, England
Source: *Au&Wr 71; ConAu 1R; IntAu&W 77; WhoWor 76*

Bible, Frances Lillian
American. Opera Singer
b. Jan 26, in Sacets Harbor, New York
Source: *NewEOp 71; WhoAm 82*

Bichat, Marie Francois Xavier
French. Scientist
Founded the science of histology, the study of tissue.
b. Nov 11, 1771 in Thoirette, France
d. Jul 22, 1802 in Paris, France
Source: *AsBiEn; BiHiMed; BioIn 5, 9; CelCen; DcBiPP; DcScB; InSci; McGEWB; NamesHP; WhDW*

Bickerman, Elias Joseph
American. Historian, Educator
b. Jul 1, 1897 in Russia
d. 1981 in Tel Aviv, Israel
Source: *ConAu 25R, 104; DrAS 74H; WhoAm 76, 78, 80, 82; WhoWorJ 72; WrDr 76*

Bickford, Charles
American. Actor
b. Jan 1, 1889 in Cambridge, Massachusetts
d. Nov 9, 1967 in Boston, Massachusetts
Source: *BiDFilm; BiE&WWA; FilmgC; HolP 30; MotPP; MovMk; OxFilm; WhScrn 74, 77; WhoHol B; WorEFlm*

Bickler, Dave
see: Survivor

Bidault, Georges
French. Politician
Opposed Algeria's independence from France; in exile, 1963-67.
b. Oct 5, 1899 in Moulins, France
d. Jan 27, 1983 in Cambo-les-Bains, France
Source: *CurBio 45; IntWW 74, 75, 76, 77, 78, 79, 80, 81; LinLib S; Who 74; WhoWor 74*

Biddle, Anthony
American. Statesman
b. Dec 17, 1896 in Philadelphia, Pennsylvania
d. Nov 13, 1961 in Washington, DC
Source: *CurBio 41, 62*

Biddle, Francis Beverley
American. Lawyer, Attorney General
b. May 9, 1886 in Paris, France
d. Oct 4, 1968 in Hyannis, Massachusetts
Source: *AmAu&B; BiDrUSE; ConAu 5R, 103; CurBio 41, 68; WhAm 5*

Biddle, George
American. Artist, Author
b. Jan 24, 1885 in Philadelphia, Pennsylvania
d. Nov 6, 1973 in New York
Source: *AmAu&B; ConAu 45; CurBio 42, 74; DcCAA 71; NewYTBE 73; WhAm 6; WhoAm 74; WhoAmA 73*

Biddle, John
English. Founder of Unitarianism
Wrote *Twelve Arguments* against doctrine of Trinity; jailed many times for writings.
b. 1615 in England
d. 1662 in London, England
Source: *Alli; DcEnL; NewCol 75*

Biddle, Nicholas
American. Statesman, Banker
b. Jan 8, 1786 in Philadelphia, Pennsylvania
d. Feb 27, 1844 in Philadelphia, Pennsylvania
Source: *Alli; AmAu; AmAu&B; AmBi; ApCAB; BiAuS; BiD&SB; CyAL 1; DcAmAu; DcAmB; DcNAA; Drake; EncAB-H; OxAmL; REn; TwCBDA; WebAB; WhAm H; WhAmP*

Biden, Joseph Robinette, Jr.
American. Senator, Lawyer
b. Nov 20, 1942 in Scranton, Pennsylvania
Source: *BioIn 9, 10, 11; WhoAm 82*

Bieber, Phil
American. Horse Owner, Trainer
b. 1900?
d. Feb 22, 1981 in Coral Gables, Florida
Source: *NewYTBS 81*

Biebuyck, Daniel Prosper
Belgian. Anthropologist, Author
b. Oct 1, 1925 in Deinze, Belgium
Source: *AmM&WS 73S; ConAu 25R; WhoAm 74, 76, 78, 80, 82; WrDr 76*

Biellmann, Denise
Swiss. Figure Skater
Source: *BioIn 12*

Bierce, Ambrose Gwinett
American. Author, Journalist
Disappeared in Mexico covering revolution led by Pancho Villa.
b. Jun 24, 1842 in Meigs County, Ohio
d. 1914? in Mexico
Source: *AmAu; AmAu&B; AmBi; AmWr; ApCAB SUP; AtlBL; CasWL; Chambr 3; ChPo, S1; CnDAL; CrtT 3; CyWA; DcAmAu; DcAmB; DcLEL; DcNAA; EncAB-H; EncMys; EvLB; LongCTC; ModAL, SUP; OhA&B; OxAmL; OxEng; Pen AM; RAdv 1; REn; REnAL; WebAB; WebE&AL; WhAm HA, 4*

Bierstadt, Albert
American. Artist
b. Jan 7, 1830 in Dusseldorf, Germany
d. Feb 18, 1902 in New York, New York
Source: *AmBi; ApCAB; DcAmB; Drake; EarABI; EncAB-H; OxAmL; TwCBDA; WebAB; WhAm 1*

Big Bopper, The
[J P Richardson]
American. Singer, Disc Jockey
Big hit "Chantilly Lace," 1958; killed with Buddy Holly, Ritchie Valens in plane crash.
b. Oct 24, 1930 in Sabine Pass, Texas
d. Feb 3, 1959 in Fargo, North Dakota
Source: *BiDAmM; ConMuA 80; RkOn*

Big Brother and the Holding Company
[Peter Albin; Sam Andrew; David Getz; James Gurley; Janis Joplin]
American. Rock Group
Source: *EncPR&S; IlEncRk*

Bigard, Albany Barney Leon
American. Musician
b. Mar 3, 1906 in New Orleans, Louisiana
d. Jun 27, 1980 in Culver City, California
Source: *BioIn 10; CmpEPM; EncJzS 70; IlEncJ; WhAm 7; WhoAm 74, 76, 78, 80; WhoBlA 75, 77; WhoJazz 72*

Bigelow, Erastus Brigham
American. Inventor, Manufacturer
Invented power loom; co-founder, MIT, 1861.
b. Apr 2, 1814 in West Boylston, Massachusetts
d. Dec 6, 1879 in Boston, Massachusetts
Source: *Alli SUP; ApCAB; DcAmAu; DcAmB; DcNAA; TwCBDA; WebAB; WhAm H*

Bigelow, Henry Bryant
American. Zoologist
b. Oct 3, 1879 in Boston, Massachusetts
d. Dec 11, 1967 in Concord, Massachusetts
Source: *BioIn 5, 8, 11; WhAm 4A*

Biggers, Earl Derr
American. Author
b. Aug 26, 1884 in Warren, Ohio
d. Apr 5, 1933
Source: *AmAu&B; ChPo S1; DcAmB S1; DcNAA; EncMys; EvLB; FilmgC; MnBBF; OhA&B; OxAmL; Pen AM; REn; REnAL; TwCA; TwCW; WhAm 1; WhNAA*

Biggs, Edward George Power
American. Musician
b. Mar 29, 1906 in Westcliff, England
d. Mar 10, 1977 in Boston, Massachusetts
Source: *IntWW 74; WhoAm 74; WhoMus 72*

Biggs, Ronald Arthur
"The Great Train Robber"
British. Thief
b. 1929?
Source: *BioIn 8, 9, 10*

Bigley, Elizabeth
see: Chadwick, Cassie L

Bignone, Reynaldo Benito Antonio
Argentine. President
b. Jan 21, 1928 in Moron, Argentina
Source: *NewYTBS 82*

Bijedic, Dzemal
Yugoslav. Premier
b. 1917 in Mostar, Yugoslavia
d. 1977
Source: *IntWW 74*

Bikel, Theodore
American. Actor, Singer
Starred in *The Defiant Ones, My Fair Lady, The Russians are Coming.*
b. May 2, 1924 in Vienna, Austria
Source: *BioNews 74; ConAu 1R, 1NR; CurBio 60; EncFCWM 69; FilmgC; MotPP; MovMk; NotNAT; WhoAm 74, 76, 78, 80, 82; WhoE 74; WhoHol A; WhoThe 77; WhoWor 74; WhoWorJ 72*

Biko, Steven
South African. Political Activist
Died while in custody of South African security police.
b. 1947 in Pretoria, South Africa
d. Sep 12, 1977 in South Africa
Source: *BioIn 11*

Bilandic, Michael Anthony
American. Lawyer, Former Mayor of Chicago
Succeeded Richard Daley, 1976; lost re-election bid to Jane Byrne, 1979.
b. Feb 13, 1923 in Chicago, Illinois
Source: *BioIn 11; CurBio 79; WhoAm 82*

Bilbo, Theodore Gilmore
American. Senator
b. Oct 13, 1877 in Poplarville, Mississippi
d. Aug 21, 1947 in New Orleans, Louisiana
Source: *BiDrAC; CurBio 43, 47; DcAmB S4; WebAB; WhAm 2; WhAmP*

Biletnikoff, Fred(erick)
American. Football Player
Leading NFL pass receiver, 1968.
b. Feb 23, 1943 in Erie, Pennsylvania
Source: *WhoAm 74; WhoFtbl 74*

Bill, Tony
American. Actor, Producer
b. 1940 in San Diego, California
Source: *BioIn 10; FilmEn; FilmgC; IntMPA 81; WhoAm 80, 82; WhoHol A*

Billings, John Shaw
American. Editor
b. May 11, 1898 in Beech Island, South Carolina
d. Aug 25, 1975 in Augusta, Georgia
Source: *ConAu 104; WhAm 6*

Billings, Josh, pseud.
[Henry Wheeler Shaw]
American. Author
b. Apr 21, 1818 in Lanesboro, Massachusetts
d. Oct 14, 1885 in Monterey, California
Source: *AmAu; AmAu&B; ApCAB; BiD&SB; CasWL; CnDAL; DcAmAu; DcAmB; DcEnL; DcLEL; DcNAA; EvLB; OhA&B; OxAmL; OxEng; Pen AM; REn; REnAL; TwCBDA; WebAB; WhAm H*

Billingsley, Sherman
American. Night Club Owner
Owned Stork Club, 1929-65; hosted "The Stork Club" TV show, 1950-53.
b. Mar 10, 1900 in Enid, Oklahoma
d. Oct 4, 1966 in New York, New York
Source: *CurBio 46, 66; ObitOF 79; WhAm 4*

Billington, John
American. Murderer
d. 1630
Source: *Blood*

Billington, Ray Allen
American. Historian
b. Sep 28, 1903 in Bay City, Michigan
d. Mar 7, 1981 in San Marino, California
Source: *AmAu&B; Au&Wr 71*

Billroth, A C Theodor
German. Surgeon
b. Apr 26, 1829
d. Feb 6, 1894
Source: *BioIn 1, 3, 4, 5, 9, 11*

"Billy the Kid"
[William H Bonney]
American. Outlaw
Killed 21 men; sentenced to hang for murder of Sheriff Jim Brady.
b. Nov 23, 1859 in New York, New York
d. Jul 15, 1881 in Fort Sumner, New Mexico
Source: *DcAmB; NewCol 75; OxFilm; REnAL; WebAB; WhAm H*

Bilon, Michael Patrick
American. Actor
Played title role in *ET;* was 2 feet, 10 inches tall.
b. 1947? in Youngstown, Ohio
d. Jan 27, 1983 in Youngstown, Ohio
Source: *NF*

Bing, Dave
American. Basketball Player
Averaged over 20 points per game in career, 1967-78.
b. Nov 29, 1943 in Washington, DC
Source: *BioIn 8, 10; WhoBbl 73; WhoBlA 75*

Bing, Sir Rudolf
Austrian. Opera Manager, Educator
Managerial director, Metropolitan Opera of NY, 1950-72.
b. Jan 9, 1902 in Vienna, Austria
Source: *CelR 73; CurBio 50; IntWW 74; NewYTBE 71, 72, 73; REn; Who 74; WhoAm 74, 76, 78, 80, 82; WhoMus 72; WhoWor 74*

Bingham, George Caleb
American. Artist
b. Mar 20, 1811 in Augusta County, Virginia
d. Jul 7, 1879 in Kansas City, Missouri
Source: *AtlBL; DcAmB; EncAB-H; OxAmL; REn; WebAB; WhAm H; WhAmP*

Bingham, Hiram
American. Explorer, Statesman
b. Nov 19, 1875 in Honolulu, Hawaii
d. Jun 6, 1956 in Washington, DC
Source: *CurBio 51, 56; WhAm 3*

Bingham, Jonathan Brewster
American. Congressman
b. Apr 24, 1914 in New Haven, Connecticut
Source: *BiDrAC; CngDr 74; ConAu 33R; CurBio 54; IntWW 74; WhoAm 74, 76, 78, 80, 82; WhoAmP 73; WhoE 74; WhoGov 72*

Binh, Nguyen-thi, Madame
see: Nguyen thi Binh, Madame

Binns, Archie
American. Author
b. Jul 30, 1899 in Port Ludlow, Washington
d. Jun 28, 1971
Source: *AmAu&B; ConAu 73; OxAmL; REnAL; TwCA, SUP; WhAm 5; WhoPNW*

Binns, Joseph Patterson
American. Hotel Executive
b. Jun 28, 1905 in Winona, Ohio
d. Nov 23, 1980 in Indian Creek Island, Florida
Source: *BioIn 3, 6; CurBio 54, 81*

Binswanger, Ludwig
Swiss. Psychiatrist
b. Apr 13, 1881 in Kreuzlingen, Switzerland
d. 1966
Source: *WhoWor 74*

Binyon, Laurence
English. Poet, Critic
b. Aug 10, 1869 in Lancaster, England
d. Mar 10, 1942 in Streatley, England
Source: *CasWL; Chambr 3; ChPo, S1, S2; CnE&AP; LongCTC; ModBrL; NewC; OxEng; REn; TwCA, SUP; TwCW; WebE&AL; WhoLA*

Biossat, Bruce
American. Journalist
b. 1910
d. May 27, 1974 in Washington, DC
Source: *BioIn 10; ConAu 104; WhAm 6*

Biow, Milton H
American. Advertising Executive
b. Jul 24, 1892 in New York, New York
d. Feb 1, 1976 in New York, New York
Source: *WhAm 6*

Bioy-Casares, Adolfo
Argentine. Author
b. Sep 15, 1914 in Buenos Aires, Argentina
Source: *ConAu 29R; ConLC 4, 8, 13; DcCLAA; Pen AM; WhoWor 74*

Birch, John
American. Intelligence Officer
b. May 28, 1918 in Landour, India
d. Aug 25, 1945 in Shuchow, China
Source: *BioIn 5*

Birch, Stephen
American. Mining Executive
b. Mar 24, 1872 in New York, New York
d. Dec 29, 1940
Source: *NatCAB 15, 41; WhAm 1*

Bird, Junius Bouton
American. Anthropologist
b. Sep 21, 1907 in Rye, New York
d. Apr 2, 1982 in Bronx, New York
Source: *AmM&WS 73S, 76P; NewYTBS 82*

Bird, Larry Joe
American. Basketball Player
Forward, Boston Celtics, 1980--; NBA Rookie of Year, 1980.
b. Dec 7, 1956 in French Lick, Indiana
Source: *BioIn 12; CurBio 82*

Birdseye, Clarence Frank
American. Inventor
Developed frozen food process; founded General Foods Corp.
b. Dec 9, 1886 in Brooklyn, New York
d. Oct 7, 1956 in New York, New York
Source: *CurBio 46, 56; WhAm 3*

Birdsong, Otis Lee
American. Basketball Player
b. Dec 9, 1955 in Winter Haven, Florida
Source: *BioIn 12; NewYTBS 81; OfNBA*

Birdwell, Russell
American. Public Relations Counselor
b. Oct 17, 1903 in Coleman, Texas
d. Dec 15, 1977 in Oxnard, California
Source: *CurBio 46, 78; ScF&FL 1; WhoWest 74*

Birendra bir Bikram, Shah dev
Indian. King of Nepal
b. Dec 28, 1945 in Kathmandu, Nepal
Source: *IntWW 74; WhoWor 74*

Biriukov, Pavel Ivanovich
Russian. Author, Pacifist
b. 1860
d. 1931
Source: *BioIn 10*

Birmingham, Stephen
American. Author
Wrote *Jacqueline Bouvier Kennedy Onassis,* 1978, *Duchess,* 1981.
b. May 28, 1931 in Hartford, Connecticut
Source: *AmAu&B; Au&Wr 71; AuNews 1; ConAu 49, 2NR; CurBio 74; WhoAm 74, 76, 78, 80, 82; WrDr 76, 80, 82*

Birney, (Alfred) Earle
Canadian. Poet, Author, Critic
Wrote *David and Other Poems,* 1942, *Turvey,* 1949, and *Trial of a City,* 1952.
b. May 13, 1904 in Calgary, AB
Source: *Au&Wr 71; CanWW 82; CanWr; CasWL; ConAu 1R, 5NR; ConLC 1, 4, 6, 11; ConNov 72, 76; ConP 70, 75; CreCan 1; DcLEL; DrAS 74E; LongCTC; OxCan, SUP; Pen ENG; TwCW; WebE&AL; WhoAm 82*

Birney, David
American. Actor
Married to Meredith Baxter; starred in "Bridgette Loves Bernie," "St. Elsewhere."
b. Apr 23, 1940 in Washington, DC
Source: *IntMPA 82; NotNAT; WhoHol A*

Birnie, William Alfred Hart
American. Editor, Journalist
b. Aug 4, 1910 in Springfield, Massachusetts
d. Sep 19, 1979 in Rockport, Massachusetts
Source: *CurBio 52, 79; WhoAm 74, 76, 78*

Biro, Val
English. Illustrator
b. Oct 6, 1921 in Budapest, Hungary
Source: *Au&Wr 71; ConAu 25R; IlsBYP; IlsCB 1957; SmATA 1*

Birrell, Augustine
English. Author, Statesman
b. Jan 19, 1850 in Wavertree, England
d. Nov 20, 1933 in London, England
Source: *Alli SUP; BiD&SB; Chambr 3; ChPo, S1; DcEnA AP; DcLEL; EvLB; LongCTC; NewC; OxEng; Pen ENG; REn; TwCA, SUP; TwCW*

Birtles, Beeb
see: Little River Band, The

Bishop, Billy (William Avery)
"Hell's Handmaiden"
Canadian. Air Marshal
Shot down 72 enemy aircraft in WW I.
b. Feb 8, 1894 in Owen Sound, ON
d. Sep 11, 1956 in Palm Beach, Florida
Source: *BioIn 4, 5, 7, 8; CurBio 41; MacDCB 78; ObitOF 79; WhoMilH 76*

Bishop, Elizabeth
American. Poet
Won Pulitzer Prize for *North and South-A Gold Spring,* 1955.
b. Feb 8, 1911 in Worcester, Massachusetts
d. Oct 6, 1979 in Boston, Massachusetts
Source: *AmAu&B; Au&Wr 71; CelR 73; ChPo, S1; CnE&AP; ConAu 5R, 89; ConLC 1, 4, 9, 13, 15; ConP 70, 75; CroCAP; DrAP 75; EncWL; IntWW 74; ModAL, SUP; NewCol 75; OxAmL; Pen AM; RAdv 1; REn; REnAL; TwCA SUP; TwCW; WebE&AL; WhoAm 74; WhoE 74; WhoWor 74; WrDr 76*

Bishop, Elvin
American. Rock Musician
b. Oct 21, 1942 in Tulsa, Oklahoma
Source: *EncPR&S; RkOn*

Bishop, Hazel
American. Cosmetics Manufacturer
Introduced first non-smear, long-lasting lipstick.
b. Aug 17, 1906 in Hoboken, New Jersey
Source: *CurBio 57; InWom*

Bishop, Jim (James Alonzo)
American. Author, Journalist
Wrote *The Day Kennedy Was Shot,* 1968.
b. Nov 21, 1907 in Jersey City, New Jersey
Source: *AmAu&B; AuNews 1, 2; CelR 73; ConAu 21R; CurBio 69; DrAP 75; REnAL; WhoAm 74, 76, 78, 80, 82; WhoS&SW 73; WhoWor 74*

Bishop, Joey
[Joseph Abraham Gottlieb]
American. Comedian
Starred in TV series "The Joey Bishop Show," 1961-69.
b. Feb 3, 1918 in Bronx, New York
Source: *CelR 73; CurBio 62; FilmgC; WhoAm 74, 76, 78, 80, 82; WhoHol A; WhoWor 74*

Bishop, Julie
American. Actress
b. Aug 30, 1917 in Denver, Colorado
Source: *FilmgC; IntMPA 75, 76, 77, 78, 79, 80, 81, 82; MotPP; MovMk; WhoAmW 77; WhoHol A*

Bishop, Stephen
American. Rock Composer, Singer
Hit songs include "On and On," "Save it for a Rainy Day."
b. 1952 in San Diego, California
Source: *BioIn 11; RkOn; WhoAm 82*

Bismarck, Otto von
"The Iron Chancellor"
German. Statesman
b. Apr 1, 1815 in Schonhausen, Germany
d. Jul 30, 1898 in Friedrichsruh, Germany
Source: *BbD; BiD&SB; NewC; OxGer; REn*

Bissell, Richard
American. Author
b. Jun 27, 1913 in Dubuque, Iowa
d. May 4, 1977 in Dubuque, Iowa
Source: *AmAu&B; Au&Wr 71; ConAu 1R, 69; NotNAT; REnAL; WhoAm 74; WorAu; WrDr 76*

Bisset, Jacqueline
English. Actress
Starred in movies *The Deep* with Nick Nolte, *Rich and Famous* with Candice Bergen.
b. Sep 13, 1944? in Weybridge, England
Source: *BioNews 74; BkPepl; CelR 73; CurBio 77; FilmgC; IntMPA 75, 76, 77, 78, 79, 80, 81, 82; MovMk; WhoAm 82; WhoHol A*

Bitter, Karl Theodore
American. Sculptor
b. Dec 6, 1867 in Vienna, Austria
d. Apr 10, 1915 in New York, New York
Source: *AmBi; DcAmB; TwCBDA; WebAB; WhAm 1*

Bixby, Bill
American. Actor
Starred in TV series "My Favorite Martian," "The Incredible Hulk."
b. Jan 22, 1934 in San Francisco, California
Source: *IntMPA 75, 76, 77, 78, 79, 80, 81, 82; WhoAm 82; WhoHol A*

Biyidi, Alexandre
French. Author
b. Jun 30, 1932 in Mbalmayo, Cameroon
Source: *AfrA; Pen CL*

Bizet, Georges
French. Composer
Wrote opera *Carmen,* 1875.
b. Oct 25, 1838 in Paris, France
d. Jun 3, 1875 in Bougival, France
Source: *AtlBL; WhDW; WorAl*

Bjorn-Larsen, Knut
American. Developed the Garterless Girdle
b. 1923 in Norway
Source: *BioIn 12*

Bjoerling, Jussi
Swedish. Opera Singer
b. Feb 2, 1911 in Stora Tuna, Sweden
d. Sep 9, 1960 in Siar Oe, Sweden
Source: *CurBio 47, 60; WhAm 4*

Bjornson, Bjornstjerne
Norwegian. Poet, Social Leader
b. Dec 8, 1832 in Kvikne, Norway
d. Apr 26, 1910 in Paris, France
Source: *AtlBL; BbD; BiD&SB; CasWL; ChPo S1; ClDMEL; CnMD; CnThe; CyWA; DcBiA; DcEuL; EuAu; EvEuW; LongCTC; McGEWD; ModWD; Pen EUR; REn; REnWD*

Black, Frank
American. Composer, Musician
b. Nov 28, 1896 in Philadelphia, Pennsylvania
Source: *AmSCAP 66*

Black, Hugo LaFayette
American. Supreme Court Justice
Member of Klu Klux Klan, mid-1920's; served on Supreme Court 34 yrs.
b. Feb 27, 1886 in Harlan, Alabama
d. Sep 25, 1971 in Bethesda, Maryland
Source: *BiDrAC; ConAu 33R; CurBic 41, 64, 71; EncAB-H; NewYTBE 71; WebAB; WhAm 5; WhAmP*

Black, Jay
see: Jay and the Americans

Black, Joseph
Scottish. Chemist, Physicist
b. Apr 16, 1728 in Bordeaux, France
d. Nov 10, 1799 in Edinburgh, Scotland
Source: *Alli*

Black, Karen
American. Actress
Appeared in films *Five Easy Pieces, Nashville, Easy Rider.*
b. Jul 1, 1942 in Park Ridge, Illinois
Source: *BkPepl; CelR 73; CurBio 76; FilmgC; IntMPA 75, 76, 77, 78, 79, 80, 81, 82; MovMk; WhoAm 74, 76, 78, 80, 82; WhoHol A*

Black, Shirley Temple
[Mrs. Charles A Black]
American. Actress, Diplomat
Began acting at age four, won Oscar at age six; US ambassador to Ghana, 1974-76.
b. Apr 23, 1928 in Santa Monica, California
Source: *BiDFilm; BkPepl; CelR 73; CmMov; CurBio 70; FilmgC; InWom; IntWW 74; MotPP; MovMk; OxFilm; ThFT; WebAB; WhoAm 74, 76, 78, 80, 82; WhoAmP 73; WhoAmW 77; WhoHol A; WhoWor 74*

Black, Walter J
American. Publisher
b. May 12, 1893 in Brooklyn, New York
d. Apr 16, 1958 in Roslyn, New York
Source: *WhAm 3*

Black, Winifred
American. Journalist
b. 1863
d. 1936
Source: *BioIn 8, 10*

Black Eagle
see: Julian, Hubert Fauntleroy

Black Hawk
[Ma-Ka-Tae-Mish-Kia-Kiak]
American Indian. Sauk Chief
b. 1767 in Sauk Village, Illinois
d. Oct 3, 1838 in Keokuk, Iowa
Source: *AmBi; ApCAB; DcAmB; Drake; TwCBDA; WebAB; WhAm H*

Black Oak Arkansas
[Tommy Aldridge; Pat Daugherty; Jimmy Henderson; Stan "Goober" Knight; Jim "Dandy" Mangrum; Ricky Reynolds]
American. Rock Group
Source: *RkOn 2; WhoRock 81*

"Blackbeard"
[Edward Teach]
English. Pirate
Privateer during War of Spanish Succession, 1701-14; became pirate at end of war.
b. 1680 in Bristol, England
d. Nov 22, 1718 in Ocracoke Island, North Carolina
Source: *NewCol 75; OxAmL; REn; REnAL; WhAm H*

Black Sabbath
[Terry "Geezer" Butler; Ronnie Dio; Anthony Iommi; (John) "Ozzie" Osbourne; William Ward]
English. Rock Group
Source: *ConMuA 80; LilREn 78; RkOn 2; WhoRock 81*

Blackburn, "Jack" (Charles Henry)
American. Boxer, Trainer
Retired as boxer, 1923; became trainer of Joe Louis.
b. 1883 in Versailles, Kentucky
d. Apr 24, 1942 in Chicago, Illinois
Source: *InB&W 80; WhoBox 74*

Blackett, Patrick Maynard Stuart
English. Scientist, Engineer, Physicist
b. Nov 18, 1897 in London, England
d. Jul 13, 1974 in London, England
Source: *ConAu 49; IntWW 74; WhAm 6; Who 74; WhoWor 74*

Blackie, William
American. Business Executive
b. May 1, 1906 in Glasgow, Scotland
Source: *BioIn 9, 11; IntWW 74, 75, 76, 77, 78; IntYB 78, 79; St&PR 75; WhoAm 74; WhoF&I 74, 75*

Blackman, Honor
English. Actress
b. Aug 22, 1926 in London, England
Source: *IntMPA 75, 76, 77, 78, 79, 80, 81, 82; MotPP; WhoHol A; WhoThe 77; WhoWor 74*

Blackmer, Sidney
American. Actor
b. Jul 13, 1896 in Salisbury, North Carolina
d. Oct 5, 1973 in New York, New York
Source: *FilmgC; MovMk; NewYTBE 73; Vers A; WhScrn 77; WhoAm 74; WhoHol B*

Blackmore, Richard Doddridge
English. Author
b. Jun 7, 1825 in Longworth, England
d. Jan 20, 1900 in Teddington, England
Source: *Alli SUP; BbD; BiD&SB; BrAu 19; Chambr 3; ChPo, S1, S2; CyWA; DcBiA; DcEnA, AP; DcEnL; DcEuL; DcLEL; EvLB; JBA 34; MouLC 4; NewC; OxEng; Pen ENG; REn; WebE&AL*

Blackmore, Ritchie
[Deep Purple; Ritchie Blackmore's Rainbow]
English. Rock Musician
b. Apr 14, 1945 in Weston-Super-Mare, England
Source: *ConMuA 80; WhoRock 81*

Blackmun, Harry Andrew
American. Supreme Court Justice
Moderate/conservative; appointed by Richard Nixon, 1970.
b. Nov 12, 1908 in Nashville, Illinois
Source: *CelR 73; CurBio 70; DrAS 74P; IntWW 74; WebAB; Who 74; WhoAm 74, 76, 78, 80, 82; WhoAmP 73; WhoGov 72; WhoS&SW 73*

Blackmur, Richard Palmer
American. Poet, Educator, Critic
b. Jan 21, 1904 in Springfield, Massachusetts
d. Feb 2, 1965 in Princeton, New Jersey
Source: *AmAu&B; CasWL; CnDAL; ConAu 25R; ConAu P-1; ConLC 2; DcLEL; EncWL; EvLB; LongCTC; ModAL, SUP; OxAmL; Pen AM; RAdv 1; REn; REnAL; SixAP; TwCA, SUP; TwCW; WebE&AL; WhAm 4*

Blackstone, Harry
[Henri Bouton]
American. Magician
b. 1885
d. Nov 16, 1965 in Hollywood, California
Source: *BioIn 2, 5, 7*

Blackstone, Sir William
English. Jurist, Author
b. Jul 10, 1723 in London, England
d. Feb 14, 1780 in London, England
Source: *Alli; AtlBL; BiD&SB; BrAu; CasWL; Chambr 2; DcEnA; DcEnL; EvLB; NewC; OxEng; REn*

Blackton, Jay S
American. Conductor
b. Mar 25, 1909 in New York, New York
Source: *AmSCAP 66; BiE&WWA; NotNAT*

Blackwell, Mr. (Richard)
American. Fashion Designer, Critic
Famous for his yearly list of "worst dressed" women in world.
b. in Brooklyn, New York
Source: *WorFshn*

Blackwell, Antoinette Louisa
American. Abolitionist, Feminist, Minister
First woman ordained minister in US, 1853; wrote *The Making of the Universe,* 1914.
b. 1825 in Henrietta, New York
d. 1921
Source: *BbD; BiD&SB; BioIn 2, 3, 4, 5, 6, 9, 11; DcAmB; DcNAA; NewCol 75*

Blackwell, Sir Basil Henry
British. Bookseller, Publisher
b. 1889
Source: *BioIn 9*

Blackwell, Betsy Talbot
American. Magazine Editor
Editor-in-chief, *Mademoiselle* magazine, 1937-71.
b. in New York, New York
Source: *AmAu&B; BioIn 3, 5, 8; CurBio 54; ForWC 70; NewYTBE 70; WhoAm 74; WhoAmW 74; WorFshn*

Blackwell, Earl
American. Author, Publisher
b. May 3, 1913 in Atlanta, Georgia
Source: *BiE&WWA; CelR 73; CurBio 60; NotNAT; WhoAm 74, 76, 78, 80, 82; WhoWor 74*

Blackwell, Elizabeth
American. Physician, Author
First woman to receive MD in modern times, 1849; practiced in NY, 1850-67.
b. Feb 3, 1821 in Bristol, England
d. May 31, 1910 in Hastings, England
Source: *Alli, SUP; AmWom; ApCAB; BiD&SB; DcAmAu; DcAmB; DcNAA; Drake; EncAB-H; HerW; InWom; NotAW; OhA&B; TwCBDA; WebAB; WhAm 1*

Blackwood, Algernon
English. Author
b. 1869 in Kent, England
d. Dec 10, 1951 in London, England
Source: *Chambr 3; ChPo, S1; DcLEL; EncMys; EvLB; LongCTC; NewC; Pen ENG; REn; TwCA, SUP; TwCW*

Blaiberg, Philip
South African. Dentist
First heart transplant patient, 1967; survived 20 months.
b. 1909
d. 1969
Source: *BioIn 8*

Blaik, "Red" (Earl Henry)
American. Football Coach, Businessman
Football coach, US Military Academy, 1927-34; chairman Blaik Oil Co., 1960--.
b. Feb 15, 1897 in Detroit, Michigan
Source: *CurBio 45; St&PR 75; WhoAm 74, 76, 78, 80, 82; WhoFtbl 74*

Blaikie, William
American. Author, Athlete, Lawyer
b. 1843 in New York, New York
d. Dec 6, 1904 in New York, New York
Source: *Alli SUP; BiD&SB; DcAmAu; DcNAA*

Blaine, James Gillespie
American. Statesman
Founded Republican Party; nominated for president, 1884.
b. Jan 31, 1830 in West Brownsville, Pennsylvania
d. Jan 27, 1893 in Washington, DC
Source: *Alli SUP; AmAu&B; AmBi; BbD; BiD&SB; BiDrUSE; DcAmAu; DcAmB; DcNAA; DcSpL; EncAB-H; OxAmL; REn; REnAL; TwCBDA; WebAB; WhAm H, 5; WhAmP; WrDr 76*

Blaine, Vivian
[Vivian S Stapleton]
American. Actress
b. Nov 21, 1924? in Newark, New Jersey
Source: *BiE&WWA; EncMT; FilmgC; HolP 40; InWom; IntMPA 75, 76, 77, 78, 79, 80, 81, 82; MotPP; NotNAT; WhoAm 74, 76, 78, 80, 82; WhoHol A; WhoThe 77*

Blair, Betsy
[Betsy Boger]
American. Actress
b. Dec 11, 1923 in Cliffside Park, New Jersey
Source: *BiE&WWA; FilmgC; IntMPA 75, 76, 77, 78, 79, 80, 81, 82; MotPP; OxFilm; WhoHol A*

Blair, Clay, Jr.
American. Author, Editor
b. May 1, 1925 in Lexington, Virginia
Source: *AmAu&B; AuNews 2; ConAu 77; IntWW 74; WhoAm 82*

Blair, David
English. Ballet Dancer
b. Jul 27, 1932 in Halifax, England
d. Apr 1, 1976 in London, England
Source: *Alli SUP; BioIn 4, 5, 6, 10, 11; CurBio 61, 76; NewYTBS 77; WhWW-II; Who 74; WhoWor 74*

Blair, Eric Arthur
see: Orwell, George, pseud.

Blair, Francis Preston
American. Soldier, Statesman
b. Feb 10, 1821 in Lexington, Kentucky
d. Jul 8, 1875 in Saint Louis, Missouri
Source: *BiDSA; BioIn 1, 3, 7*

Blair, Frank
American. Television Commentator
b. May 30, 1915 in Yemassee, South Carolina
Source: *CelR 73; Ward 77; WhoAm 74*

Blair, James
Scottish. Clergyman, College Founder
b. 1655 in Scotland
d. Apr 18, 1743
Source: *McGEWB; WebAB; WhAm H*

Blair, Janet
[Martha Jane Lofferty]
American. Actress
Appeared in *Three Girls about Town,* 1941; *My Sister Eileen,* 1942.
b. Apr 23, 1921 in Altoona, Pennsylvania
Source: *BiE&WWA; FilmgC; HolP 40; InWom; IntMPA 75, 76, 77, 78, 79, 80, 81, 82; MotPP; MovMk; WhoAm 74; WhoHol A*

Blair, June
American. Actress
b. 1937
Source: *WhoHol A*

Blair, Linda Denise
American. Actress
Played the possessed girl in *The Exorist,* 1973.
b. Jan 22, 1959 in Saint Louis, Missouri
Source: *BkPepl; IntMPA 82; WhoAm 78, 80, 82; WhoHol A*

Blair, Montgomery
American. Statesman
b. May 10, 1813 in Franklin County, Kentucky
d. Jul 27, 1883 in Silver Spring, Maryland
Source: *AmBi; ApCAB; BiAuS; BiDrUSE; DcAmB; Drake; TwCBDA; WebAB; WhAm H; WhAmP*

Blaisdell, George G
"Mr. Zippo"
American. Businessman
b. 1895
d. 1978 in Miami Beach, Florida
Source: *BioIn 7, 11; PseudN; St&PR 75*

Blaise, Saint
Religious Figure
d. 316?
Source: *BioIn 3, 4, 5, 7, 8, 9*

Blake, Amanda
[Beverly Louise Neill]
American. Actress
Played Miss Kitty on TV series "Gunsmoke," 1955-75.
b. Feb 20, 1931 in Buffalo, New York
Source: *CelR 73; FilmgC; InWom; IntMPA 75, 76, 77, 78, 79, 80, 81, 82; WhoAm 74; WhoHol A*

Blake, Eubie (James Hubert)
American. Pianist, Composer
Best known songs, "I'm Just Wild About Harry," and "Memories of You."
b. Feb 7, 1883 in Baltimore, Maryland
d. Feb 12, 1983 in Brooklyn, New York
Source: *AmSCAP 66; BiDAmM; BioIn 8, 9, 10, 11; CmpEPM; CurBio 74; DcBlPA; EbonySL 1; EncJzS 70; EncMT; IlEncJ; InB&W 80; WhoAm 74, 76, 78, 80, 82; WhoBlA 75, 77; WhoJazz 72*

Blake, Eugene Carson
American. Clergyman
b. Nov 7, 1906 in Saint Louis, Missouri
Source: *CelR 73; DrAS 74P; IntWW 74; Who 74; WhoAm 74; WhoE 74; WhoRel 75; WhoWor 74*

Blake, Florence G
American. Nurse
b. 1907
Source: *BioIn 1, 4, 11*

Blake, Quentin
English. Children's Author, Illustrator
b. Dec 16, 1932 in England
Source: *ChPo S1; ConAu 25R; IlsBYP; IlsCB 1957; SmATA 9*

Blake, Robert
English. Admiral
b. 1599
d. Aug 7, 1657
Source: *NewCol 75; WhoMilH 76*

Blake, Robert
[Michael Gubitosi; Our Gang]
American. Actor
Starred in TV series "Baretta," 1974-78; won Emmy, 1975.
b. Sep 18, 1938 in Nutley, New Jersey
Source: *BkPepl; FilmgC; IntMPA 75, 76, 77, 78, 79, 80, 81, 82; MovMk; WhoAm 74; WhoHol A*

Blake, William
English. Poet, Artist, Mystic
Wrote *Songs of Innocence,* 1789; engraved and published own poetry.
b. Sep 28, 1757 in London, England
d. Jul 12, 1827
Source: *Alli; AnCL; AtlBL; BbD; BiD&SB; BiDLA; BkIE; BrAu 19; CarSB; CasWL; Chambr 2; ChPo, S1, S2; CnE&AP; CrtT 2; CyWA; DcEnA, AP; DcEnL; DcEuL; DcLEL; EvLB; MouLC 3; NewC; OxEng; Pen ENG; RAdv 1; RComWL; REn; Str&VC; WebE&AL*

Blakeley, Ronee
American. Actress, Singer
Screen debut in *Nashville,* 1975; received Oscar nomination.
b. 1946 in Stanley, Idaho
Source: *FilmEn*

Blakelock, Ralph Albert
American. Artist
b. Oct 15, 1847 in New York, New York
d. Aug 9, 1919 in Elizabethtown, New York
Source: *AmBi; ApCAB, X; ArtsAmW; BioIn 1, 3, 4, 6, 7, 8, 9; BnEnAmA; DcAmArt; DcAmB; IlBEAAW; LinLib; McGDA; McGEWB; NatCAB 15; WebAB; WhAm 1*

Blakely, Colin
Irish. Actor
b. Sep 23, 1930 in Bangor, Northern Ireland
Source: *CnThe; FilmEn; FilmgC; WhoThe 77, 81*

Blakely, Susan
American. Actress
b. in West Germany
Source: *IntMPA 77; WhoHol A*

Blakey, Art
American. Jazz Musician
b. Oct 11, 1919 in Pittsburgh, Pennsylvania
Source: *WhoAm 74; WhoBlA 75*

Blalock, Alfred
American. Surgeon
b. Apr 5, 1899 in Culloden, Georgia
d. Sep 15, 1964 in Baltimore, Maryland
Source: *BioIn 1, 2, 3, 5, 7, 11; CurBio 46, 64*

Blalock, Jane
American. Golfer
b. Sep 19, 1945 in Portsmouth, New Hampshire
Source: *BioIn 11; WhoGolf*

Blanc, (Jean Joseph Charles) Louis
French. Socialist Leader
b. 1811 in Madrid, Spain
d. 1882
Source: *OxFr; REn*

Blanc, Mel(vin Jerome)
American. Actor, Voice Specialist
Voice of many cartoon characters: Bugs Bunny, Porky Pig, Daffy Duck.
b. May 30, 1908 in San Francisco, California
Source: *WhoAm 74*

Blanchard, "Doc" (Felix Anthony)
American. Football Player, Coach
Fullback, US Military Academy; scored 19 touchdowns, won Heisman Trophy, 1945.
b. Dec 11, 1924 in Bishopville, South Carolina
Source: *CurBio 46; WhoFtbl 74; WhoHol A*

Blanchard, Francois
French. Balloonist
Credited with first balloon crossing of English Channel, first ascents in US.
b. Jul 4, 1753
d. 1809
Source: *NewCol 75*

Blanchard, James J
American. Governor of Michigan
Supported legislation to bail out Chrysler Corp.; elected governor, 1982.
b. Aug 8, 1942 in Detroit, Michigan
Source: *CngDr 81; WhoAm 80, 82; WhoMW 80*

Blanchard, Thomas
American. Inventor
Invented lathe for automatic duplication of pattern in large quantities.
b. Jun 24, 1788 in Sutton, Massachusetts
d. Apr 16, 1864 in Boston, Massachusetts
Source: *AmBi; ApCAB; DcAmB; Drake; NatCAB 6; TwCBDA; WebAB; WhAm H*

Bland, Richard Parks
American. Statesman
b. Aug 19, 1835 in Hartford, Kentucky
d. 1899
Source: *AmBi; ApCAB; BiAuS; BiDSA; BiDrAC; DcAmB; TwCBDA; WhAm 1; WhAmP*

Blanda, George Frederick
American. Football Player
Quarterback and place kicker, 1949-75; scored record 2,002 points.
b. Sep 27, 1927 in Youngwood, Pennsylvania
Source: *CmCal; CurBio 72; WebAB, 79; WhoAm 74; WhoFtbl 74; WorAl*

Blanding, Sarah Gibson
American. Educator
b. Nov 22, 1898 in Lexington, Kentucky
Source: *BioIn 1, 4, 6, 7; IntWW 74; WhoAm 74; WhoAmW 74*

Blane, Sally
[Elizabeth Jane Young]
American. Actress
b. 1910 in Salida, Colorado
Source: *FilmgC; MovMk; ThFT; TwYS; WhoHol A*

Blankers-Koen, Fanny
Dutch. Track Athlete
b. Apr 7, 1946 in Amsterdam, Netherlands
Source: *InWom; WhoTr&F 73*

Blanqui, Louis Auguste
French. Revolutionary
Participated in French Revolution, downfall of Napoleon III.
b. Feb 1, 1805 in Ruget, France
d. Jan 1, 1881
Source: *BioIn 7, 9; CelCen; DcBiPP; McGEWD; OxFr; REn; WhDW*

Blanton, Jimmy
American. Jazz Musician
b. 1921 in Saint Louis, Missouri
d. Jul 30, 1942 in Los Angeles, California
Source: *WhoJazz 72*

Blanton, (Leonard) Ray
American. Governor of Tennessee
b. Apr 10, 1930 in Hardin County, Tennessee
Source: *BiDrAC; WhoGov 72; WhoS&SW 73*

Blasco-Ibanez, Vicente
Spanish. Author
b. 1867 in Valencia, Spain
d. 1928 in Riviera, France
Source: *CasWL; ClDMEL; CyWA; DcSpL; EncWL; EvEuW; LongCTC; ModRL; OxEng; Pen EUR; REn; TwCA, SUP; TwCW*

Blashfield, Edwin Howland
American. Artist
b. Dec 15, 1848 in New York, New York
d. Oct 12, 1936
Source: *AmAu&B; AmBi; ApCAB; ChPo; DcAmAu; DcAmB S2; DcNAA; TwCBDA; WhAm 1*

Blasingame, Francis James Levi
American. Educator, Physician
b. Jan 17, 1907 in Hot Springs, Arkansas
Source: *WhoAm 74, 76, 78, 80, 82*

Blass, Bill
American. Fashion Designer
Designer of apparel, home furnishings, cars, chocolates.
b. Jun 22, 1922 in Fort Wayne, Indiana
Source: *CelR 73; CurBio 66; NewYTBS 80; WhoAm 74, 76, 78, 80, 82; WhoE 74, 75, 77; WhoF&I 74; WorAl; WorFshn*

Blassingale, Wyatt Rainey
American. Author
b. Feb 6, 1909 in Demopolis, Alabama
Source: *AuBYP; ConAu 1R; SmATA 1; WrDr 76*

Blatch, Harriot Eaton Stanton
American. Feminist, Lecturer
b. Jan 20, 1856 in Seneca Falls, New York
d. Nov 20, 1940 in Greenwich, Connecticut
Source: *BiCAW; CurBio 41; DcAmB S2; DcNAA; NotAW; OxAmL; WhAm 1; WhAmP; WhNAA; WomWWA 14*

Blatchford, Joseph Hoffer
American. Government Official
Director of Peace Corps, 1969-71.
b. Jun 7, 1934 in Milwaukee, Wisconsin
Source: *CurBio 71; IntWW 74; NewYTBE 71; WhoAm 74; WhoAmP 73; WhoGov 72*

Blatchford, Samuel
American. Supreme Court Justice
b. Mar 9, 1820 in New York, New York
d. Jul 7, 1893 in Newport, Rhode Island
Source: *Alli SUP; ApCAB; BiAuS; DcAmB; DcNAA; TwCBDA; WebAB; WhAm H*

Blatty, William Peter
American. Author
Wrote *The Exorcist*, on the best seller list 55 weeks.
b. Jan 7, 1928 in New York, New York
Source: *ConAu 5R; ConLC 2; CurBio 74; FilmgC; IntMPA 75, 76, 77, 78, 79, 80, 81, 82; WhoAm 82; WrDr 76*

Blavatsky, Helena Petrovna
Russian. Founded Theosophical Society
Society promotes Eastern studies; day of death is celebrated as White Lotus Day.
b. Jul 30, 1831 in Ekaterinoslav, Russia
d. May 8, 1891 in London, England
Source: *Alli SUP; AmAu&B; AmBi; BbD; BiD&SB; DcAmAu; DcAmB; NewC; NotAW; OxAmL; REn; TwCBDA; WhAm H*

Blech, Leo
German. Conductor, Composer
b. Apr 21, 1871 in Aiz-la-Chapelle, Germany
d. Aug 24, 1958 in Berlin, Germany
Source: *NewEOp 71; WebBD 80*

Bledsoe, Jules
American. Actor, Composer, Singer
b. Dec 29, 1898
d. Jul 14, 1943 in Hollywood, California
Source: *CurBio 43; WhScrn 74, 77*

Bleeker, Sonia
[Sonia Bleeker Zim]
Russian. Children's Author
b. Nov 28, 1909 in Starchevicvhi, Russia
d. Nov 13, 1971
Source: *BkP; ConAu 1R, 33R, 3NR; ForWC 70; MorJA; SmATA 2*

Blegen, Judith Eyer
American. Opera Singer
b. Apr 27, 1941 in Missoula, Montana
Source: *NewYTBS 74; WhoAm 78, 80, 82; WhoOp 76*

Bleiberg, Robert Marvin
American. Publisher, Editor
Publisher, editorial director, *Barron's National Business and Financial Weekly*.
b. Jun 21, 1924 in Brooklyn, New York
Source: *BlueB 76; WhoAm 74, 76, 78, 80, 82; WhoF&I 74*

Bleier, "Rocky" (Robert Patrick)
American. Football Player
Lost part of right foot in Vietnam; returned to play for Pittsburgh Steelers.
b. Mar 5, 1946 in Appleton, Wisconsin
Source: *ConAu 85; NewYTBS 74, 75, 80; WhoAm 78, 80*

Bleriot, Louis
French. Aviator, Engineer
b. Jul 1, 1872 in Cambrai, France
d. Aug 2, 1936
Source: *WebBD 80*

Bleyer, Archie
Music Arranger
Source: *NF*

Bligh, Captain William
English. Naval Officer
Captain, HMS *Bounty* when mutiny occurred; cast adrift for 4,000 miles.
b. Sep 9, 1754 in Plymouth, England
d. Dec 7, 1817 in London, England
Source: *Alli; BiDLA; McGEWB; NewC; REn; WorAl*

Blind Faith
["Ginger" Baker; Eric Clapton; Rick Grech; Stevie Winwood]
English. Rock Group
Source: *ConMuA 80; IlEncRk; LilREn 78; WhoRock 81*

Blinn, Holbrook
American. Actor, Producer
b. 1872 in San Francisco, California
d. Jun 24, 1928 in Croton, New York
Source: *Film 1, 2; MotPP; NotNAT B; TwYS; WhScrn 74, 77; WhThe; WhoHol B; WhoStg 1906*

Blish, James Benjamin
American. Author
b. May 23, 1921 in East Orange, New Jersey
d. Jul 30, 1975
Source: *AmAu&B; Au&Wr 71; ConAu 1R, 57, 3NR; ConLC 14; ConNov 76; WorAu; WrDr 76*

Bliss, Anthony Addison
American. Metropolitan Opera Director
b. Apr 19, 1913 in New York, New York
Source: *BiE&WWA; CurBio 79; IntWW 75, 76, 77, 78; NewYTBS 81; WhoAm 74, 76, 78, 80, 82; WhoE 77, 79; WhoOp 76*

Bliss, Sir Arthur
English. Composer
b. Aug 2, 1891 in London, England
d. Mar 27, 1975 in London, England
Source: *DcCM; FilmgC; IntWW 74; WhAm 6; Who 74; WhoMus 72; WhoWor 74*

Bliss, Ray C(harles)
American. Political Leader
Chairman, GOP, 1966-68; credited with rebuilding party after defeat of Goldwater, 1964.
b. Dec 16, 1907 in Akron, Ohio
d. Aug 6, 1981 in Akron, Ohio
Source: *BioIn 6, 7, 8; CurBio 66, 81; IntWW 74, 75, 76, 77, 78; NewYTBS 81; WhoAm 74, 76, 78, 80, 82; WhoAmP 73, 75, 77, 79; WhoWor 74, 76, 78*

Bliss, Robert Woods
American. Diplomat
b. 1875
d. Apr 19, 1962 in New York
Source: *BioIn 6, 7; St&PR 75*

Bliss, Tasker H
American. Military Leader
b. Dec 31, 1853 in Lewisburg, Pennsylvania
d. Nov 9, 1930 in Washington, DC
Source: *AmBi; DcAmB S1; WebAB; WhAm 1*

Blitzstein, Marc
American. Composer, Author
b. Mar 2, 1905 in Philadelphia, Pennsylvania
d. Jan 22, 1964 in Martinique
Source: *AmAu&B; AmSCAP 66; BiE&WWA; CnMD; CurBio 40, 64; DcCM; EncMT; McGEWD; ModWD; NewCBMT; OxAmL; PlP&P; REn; REnAL; WebAB; WhAm 4*

Bliven, Bruce
American. Author
b. Jul 27, 1889 in Emmetsburg, Iowa
d. May 27, 1977 in Palo Alto, California
Source: *AmAu&B; AuBYP; ConAu 37R, 69; CurBio 41; IntWW 74; TwCA, SUP; Who 74; WhoAm 74; WhoWest 74; WrDr 76*

Blixen, Karen Christentze, Baroness
[Pierre Andrezel; Isak Dinesen, pseuds.]
Danish. Author
b. Apr 17, 1885 in Rungsted, Denmark
d. Sep 7, 1962 in Rungsted, Denmark
Source: *CasWL; ConAu 25R; ConAu P-2; LongCTC; Pen ENG, EUR; REn; TwCA, SUP; WhoTwCL*

Bloch, Alexander
American. Conductor
b. Jul 11, 1881 in Selma, Alabama
Source: *WhAm 1; WhoMus 72; WhoWorJ 72*

Bloch, Claude Charles
American. Military Leader
b. Jul 12, 1878 in Woodbury, Kentucky
d. Oct 6, 1967 in Washington, DC
Source: *CurBio 42, 67; WhAm 4A*

Bloch, Ernest
American. Composer
Founded Cleveland Institute of Music; director, 1920-25.
b. Jul 24, 1880 in Geneva, Switzerland
d. Jul 15, 1959 in Portland, Oregon
Source: *AmSCAP 66; AtlBL; CurBio 53, 59; DcCM; OxAmL; REn; WebAB; WhAm 3*

Bloch, Felix
Swiss. Physicist, Educator
b. Oct 23, 1905 in Zurich, Switzerland
Source: *IntWW 74; Who 74; WhoAm 74, 76, 78, 80, 82; WhoWorJ 72*

Bloch, Raymond A
American. Band Leader, Arranger
b. Aug 3, 1902 in Alsace-Lorraine, Germany
d. Mar 29, 1982 in Miami, Florida
Source: *AmSCAP 66, 80; BiDAmM; CmpEPM; NewYTBS 82*

Bloch, Robert Albert
[Tarleton Fiske; Nathan Hindin; Collier Young, pseuds.]
American. Author, Screenwriter
b. Apr 5, 1917 in Chicago, Illinois
Source: *AmAu&B; ConAu 5R, 5NR; EncMys; EncSF; FanAl; IntMPA 81; PseudN; SmATA 12; WhoSciF*

Block, Herbert Lawrence
see: Herblock

Block, John Rusling
American. Secretary of Agriculture
b. Feb 15, 1935 in Galesburg, Illinois
Source: *CurBio 82; WhoAm 82*

Block, Joseph L
American. Businessman
b. 1902
d. 1976
Source: *BioIn 2, 5, 6, 8, 11*

Block, Martin
Radio Announcer
b. 1903
d. Sep 19, 1967 in Englewood, New Jersey
Source: *BioIn 8*

Blocker, Dan
American. Actor
Played Hoss Cartwright on TV series "Bonanza," 1959-72.
b. 1927 in Bowie, Texas
d. May 13, 1972 in Inglewood, California
Source: *FilmgC; NewYTBE 72; WhAm 5; WhScrn 77; WhoHol B*

Blodgett, Katherine Burr
American. Physicist
b. Jan 10, 1898 in Schenectady, New York
d. Dec 10, 1979 in Schenectady, New York
Source: *InWom; NewYTBS 79; WhAm 7; WhoAmW 58*

Blofeld, John
American. Author
b. Apr 2, 1913 in London, England
Source: *Au&Wr 71; ConAu 53, 4NR; WrDr 76*

Blok, Aleksandr Aleksandrovich
Russian. Author
b. Nov 28, 1880 in Saint Petersburg, Russia
d. Sep 7, 1921 in Petrograd, U.S.S.R.
Source: *AtlBL; CasWL; ChPo S1; ClDMEL; CnMD; CnMWL; DcRusL; EncWL; EvEuW; LongCTC; McGEWD; ModSL 1; ModWD; OxEng; Pen EUR; REn; TwCA, SUP; TwCW; WhoTwCL*

Blondell, Joan
American. Actress
Starred TV series "Here Come the Brides"; married to Dick Powell, Mike Todd.
b. Aug 30, 1912 in New York, New York
d. Dec 25, 1979 in Santa Monica, California
Source: *BiDFilm; BiE&WWA; CelR 73; FilmgC; ForWC 70; InWom; IntMPA 75, 76, 77; MotPP; MovMk; NewYTBE 72; NotNAT; OxFilm; ThFT; WhoAm 74; WhoAmW 77; WhoHol A; WhoThe 77; WorEFlm*

Blondie
[Clem Burke; Jimmy Destri; Nigel Harrison; Deborah Harry; Frank Infante; Chris Stein]
American. Rock Group
Source: *ConMuA 80; WhoRock 81*

Blondin, Jean Francois Gravelet
French. Acrobat
b. 1824
d. 1897
Source: *BioIn 1, 3, 4, 5, 6, 9*

Blood, Ernest A
"Gray Thatched Wizard"; "Prof"
American. Basketball Coach
Won-loss record 1295-165.
b. Oct 4, 1872 in Manchester, New Hampshire
d. Feb 5, 1955 in New Smyrna, Florida
Source: *BioIn 3, 9; WhoBbl 73*

Blood, Thomas
Irish. Adventurer
b. 1618 in Ireland
d. Aug 24, 1680
Source: *NewC*

Blood, Sweat and Tears
[Dave Bargeron; David Clayton-Thomas; Bobby Colomby; Steve Fieldeer; Jerry Fisher; Dick Halligan; Jeff Hyman; Steve Katz; Al Kooper; Fred Lipsius; Tom Malone; Lou Marini, Jr., Lew Soloff; Georg Wadenius; Larry Willis]
American. Rock Band
Group formed 1968; hit singles "Spinning Wheel," "And When I Die."
Source: *BiDAmM; EncPR&S; IlEncRk; RkOn*

"Bloody Mary"
see: Mary I

Bloom, Claire
English. Actress
Best known for Chaplin film *Limelight,* 1952; former wife of Rod Steiger.
b. Feb 15, 1931 in London, England
Source: *BiDFilm; BiE&WWA; CelR 73; CurBio 56; FilmEn; FilmgC; IntMPA 76, 77, 78, 79, 80, 81, 82; IntWW 80, 81; MotPP; MovMk; NewYTBE 71; NotNAT; OxFilm; Who 82; WhoAm 74, 76, 78, 80, 82; WhoHol A; WhoThe 77; WhoWor 74; WorAl; WorEFlm*

Bloom, Eric
see: Blue Oyster Cult

Bloom, Harry
South African. Author
b. 1913? in South Africa
d. Jul 28, 1981 in Canterbury, England
Source: *ConAu 104; TwCW*

Bloom, Julius
American. Director of Carnegie Hall
b. Sep 23, 1912 in Brooklyn, New York
Source: *BioIn 9; WhoAm 78, 80, 82*

Bloom, Mickey (Milton)
American. Musician, Composer
b. Aug 26, 1906 in Brooklyn, New York
Source: *AmSCAP 66; WhoJazz 72*

Bloom, Murray Teigh
American. Author
b. May 19, 1916 in New York, New York
Source: *ConAu 17R; WhoAm 74, 76, 78, 80, 82; WhoE 74; WrDr 76*

Bloom, Paul Lawrence
American. Former Government Official
b. May 14, 1939 in Norfolk, Virginia
Source: *BioIn 12; NewYTBS 81*

Bloom, Ursula
English. Author
b. in Chelmsford, England
Source: *Au&Wr 71; BioIn 3, 5, 6, 7, 8, 11; ConAu 25R; NewC; Who 74; WhoWor 74*

Bloomer, Amelia Jenks
American. Social Reformer
Advocate of women's rights, dress reform; led to costume called "bloomers."
b. May 27, 1818 in Homer, New York
d. Dec 30, 1894 in Council Bluffs, Iowa
Source: *AmBi; AmWom; ApCAB; DcAmAu; DcAmB; InWom; NotAW; OxAmL; REnAL; TwCBDA; WebAB; WhAm H; WhAmP*

Bloomfield, Mike (Michael)
American. Musician, Singer
b. Jul 28, 1944 in Chicago, Illinois
d. Feb 15, 1981 in San Francisco, California
Source: *AnObit 1981; BluesWW; EncPR&S; WhoAm 74*

Bloomgarden, Kermit
American. Motion Picture Producer
b. Dec 15, 1904 in Brooklyn, New York
d. Sep 20, 1976 in New York, New York
Source: *BiE&WWA; WhoAm 74; WhoThe 77; WhoWor 74*

Bloomingdale, Alfred
American. Corporation Executive
Launched Diners' Club credit card co., 1950.
b. Apr 15, 1916 in New York, New York
d. Aug 20, 1982 in Santa Monica, California
Source: *CelR 73; IntYB 78, 79; NewYTBS 82; WhoAm 74, 76, 78, 80, 82; WhoF&I 74*

Bloomingdale, Joseph Bernard
American. Merchant
Co-founded Bloomingdale's Dept. Store, 1872.
b. Dec 22, 1842 in New York, New York
d. Nov 21, 1904 in New York, New York
Source: *NatCAB 2, 30; WorAl*

Bloomingdale, Samuel
American. Retail Executive
b. Jun 17, 1873 in New York, New York
d. May 10, 1968 in New York
Source: *WhAm 5*

Bloor, "Mother" Ella Reeve
American. Feminist
Organized women to vote in school elections; foremost American woman communist.
b. Jul 8, 1862 in Staten Island, New York
d. Aug 10, 1951 in Richlandtown, Pennsylvania
Source: *BiDAmLL; BioIn 2, 3; DcAmB S5; LibW*

Blore, Eric
American. Actor
b. Dec 23, 1887 in London, England
d. Mar 2, 1959 in Hollywood, California
Source: *FilmgC; MovMk; Vers A; WhScrn 74, 77*

Blotta, Anthony
Italian. Fashion Designer
b. in Italy
d. Sep 11, 1971 in New York
Source: *NewYTBE 71*

Blough, Glenn Orlando
American. Author, Educator
b. Sep 5, 1907 in Edmore, Michigan
Source: *AmAu&B; AuBYP; ConAu P-1; LEduc 74; MorJA; SmATA 1; WhoAm 74, 76, 78, 80, 82*

Blough, Roger M
American. Lawyer, Businessman
b. Jan 19, 1904 in Riverside, Pennsylvania
Source: *IntWW 74; Who 74; WhoAm 74, 76, 78, 80, 82; WhoWor 74*

Blount, Charles
English. Author, Deist
b. Apr 27, 1654 in Upper Holloway, England
d. Aug 1693
Source: *Alli; BrAu; CasWL; DcEnL; NewC*

Blount, Winton Malcolm
American. Businessman, Public Official
b. Feb 1, 1921 in Union Springs, Alabama
Source: *BiDrUSE; CurBio 69; IntWW 74; NewYTBE 71; St&PR 75; WhoAm 74, 76, 78, 80, 82; WhoAmP 73; WhoS&SW 73*

Bloustein, Edward J
American. Author, Educator
b. Jan 20, 1925 in New York, New York
Source: *ConAu 41R; CurBio 65; DrAS 74P; LEduc 74; NewYTBE 71; WhoAm 74, 76, 78, 80, 82; WhoE 74; WhoWorJ 72*

Bloy, Leon Marie
French. Author
b. Jul 11, 1846 in Perigueux, France
d. Nov 3, 1917 in Bourg-la-Reine, France
Source: *CasWL; ClDMEL; EncWL; EuAu; EvEuW; OxFr; Pen EUR; REn*

Blucher, Gebhard Leberecht von
Russian. Field Marshall
b. Dec 16, 1742 in Rostock, Germany
d. Sep 12, 1819 in Schlesian, Germany
Source: *McGEWB; OxGer; WhoMilH 76*

Blucker, Robert Olof
[The Hostages]
American. Former Hostage in Iran
b. Oct 21, 1927 in North Little Rock, Arkansas
Source: *BioIn 12; NewYTBS 81; USBiR 74*

Blue, Ben
Canadian. Comedian, Dancer
Starred in Vaudeville, 1916; appeared in film *It's a Mad, Mad, Mad, Mad World,* 1963.
b. Sep 12, 1901 in Montreal, PQ
d. Mar 7, 1975 in Los Angeles, California
Source: *FilmgC; IntMPA 75; MovMk; WhScrn 77*

Blue, Monte
American. Actor, Screenwriter
b. Jan 11, 1890 in Indianapolis, Indiana
d. Feb 18, 1963 in Milwaukee, Wisconsin
Source: *Film 1; FilmgC; MotPP; MovMk; TwYS; Vers A; WhScrn 74, 77; WhoHol B*

Blue, Vida Rochelle
American. Baseball Player
Fifth pitcher to win Cy Young Award and MVP in same year, 1971.
b. Jul 28, 1949 in Mansfield, Louisiana
Source: *BaseEn; CelR 73; CurBio 72; NewYTBE 71; NewYTBS 74; WhoAm 74, 76, 78, 80, 82; WhoBlA 75; WhoProB 73*

Blue Oyster Cult
[Eric Bloom; Albert Bouchard; Joe Bouchard; Allen Lanier; Donald"Buck Dharma" Roeser]
American. Rock Group
Source: *ConMuA 80; LilREn 78; WhoRock 81*

Bluford, Guion, Jr.
American. Astronaut
First black American assigned to orbital mission, space shuttle Challenger, 1983.
b. Nov 22, 1942 in Philadelphia, Pennsylvania
Source: *WhoBlA 75, 77*

Bluhdorn, Charles G
American. Corporation Executive
Founder, board chairman, Gulf & Western Industries, Inc., 1958-83.
b. Sep 20, 1926 in Vienna, Austria
d. Feb 19, 1983
Source: *IntWW 74, 75, 76, 77, 78, 79, 80, 81; St&PR 75; WhoAm 74, 76, 78, 80, 82; WhoE 74; WhoF&I 74; WhoWor 74*

Blum, Leon
French. Statesman
b. Apr 9, 1872 in Paris, France
d. Mar 30, 1950 in Versailles, France
Source: *ClDMEL; CurBio 40, 50; OxFr; REn; WhAm 2*

Blume, Judy Sussman
American. Author
Wrote *Are You There God? It's Me Margaret,* 1970; *Wifey,* 1978.
b. Feb 12, 1938 in Elizabeth, New Jersey
Source: *ChlLR 2; ConAu 29R; CurBio 80; PiP; SmATA 2; WhoAm 80, 82; WrDr 76*

Blume, Peter
American. Artist
b. Oct 27, 1906 in Russia
Source: *BnEnAmA; CurBio 56; DcAmArt; DcCAA 71, 77; IntWW 74, 75, 76, 77, 78; McGDA; WhoAm 74, 76, 78, 80, 82; WhoAmA 73, 76, 78; WhoE 74*

Blumenbach, Johann Friedrich
German. Physiologist
Published in German *Handbook of Natural History.*
b. May 11, 1752 in Gotha, Germany
d. Jan 22, 1840 in Gottingen, Germany
Source: *CelCen; DcBiPP; DcScB SUP; Dis&D; InSci; LinLib L, S*

Blumenfeld, Isadore
"Kid Cann"
American. Criminal, Bootlegger
b. 1901 in Minneapolis, Minnesota
d. 1981 in New York, New York
Source: *BioIn 12*

Blumenthal, Monica David
American. Psychiatrist
b. Sep 1, 1930 in Tubingen, Germany
d. Mar 16, 1981 in Pittsburgh, Pennsylvania
Source: *AmM&WS 73P, 76P, 79P; BiDrAPA 77; ConAu 73, 103; NewYTBS 81; WhoAmW 74*

Blumenthal, W Michael
American. Corporation Executive
Secretary of Treasury, 1977-79.
b. Jan 3, 1926 in Berlin, Germany
Source: *AmEA 74; BusPN; IntWW 74; NewYTBE 72; St&PR 75; WhoAm 82; WhoF&I 74*

Blunden, Edmund Charles
English. Poet, Critic
Named to Oxford's poetry chair, 1966; author *War Poets, 1914-18,* 1962.
b. Nov 1, 1896 in London, England
d. Jan 20, 1974 in Sudbury, England
Source: *Au&Wr 71; CasWL; Chambr 3; ChPo, S1, S2; CnE&AP; ConAu 17R, 45; ConAu P-2; ConLC 2; ConP 70, 75; DcLEL; EncWL; EvLB; LongCTC; ModBrL, SUP; NewC; OxEng; Pen ENG; RAdv 1; REn; TwCA, SUP; TwCW; WebE&AL; WhoTwCL*

Blunstone, Colin
[The Zombies]
English. Musician
b. Jun 24, 1945 in Hatfield, England
Source: *NF*

Blunt, Wilfrid Scawen
English. Author
b. Aug 14, 1840 in Crawley, England
d. Sep 10, 1922 in London, England
Source: *Alli SUP; BbD; BiD&SB; BrAu 19; Chambr 3; DcEnA, AP; EvLB; ModBrL; NewC; OxEng; Pen ENG; REn; WebE&AL*

Bly, Nellie, pseud.
[Elizabeth Cochrane Seaman]
American. Journalist
b. May 5, 1867 in Cochrane's Mill, Pennsylvania
d. Jan 27, 1922 in New York, New York
Source: *AmAu; AmAu&B; CnDAL; DcAmB; DcNAA; HerW; InWom; NotAW; OxAmL; REn; REnAL; WebAB; WhAm HA, 4*

Bly, Robert Elwood
American. Author
b. Dec 23, 1926 in Madison, Minnesota
Source: *AmAu&B; ConAu 5R; ConLC 1, 2, 5; ConP 70, 75; CroCAP; DrAP 75; ModAL SUP; Pen AM; RAdv 1; WebE&AL; WhoAm 74, 76, 78, 80, 82; WhoTwCL; WhoWor 74; WorAu; WrDr 76*

Blyden, Larry
[Ivan Lawrence Blieden]
American. Actor
b. Jun 23, 1925 in Houston, Texas
d. Jun 6, 1975 in Morocco
Source: *BiE&WWA; IntMPA 75; NotNAT; WhAm 6; WhScrn 77; WhoAm 74; WhoThe 77*

Blyleven, Bert (Rikalbert)
Dutch. Baseball Player
b. Apr 6, 1951 in Zeist, Netherlands
Source: *BaseEn; NewYTBS 81; PseudN*

Blyth, Ann Marie
American. Actress
b. Aug 16, 1928 in Mount Kisco, New York
Source: *FilmgC; HolP 40; IntMPA 75, 76, 77, 78, 79, 80, 81, 82; MotPP; MovMk; WhoAm 74; WhoHol A; WomWMM*

Blyth, Chay
British. Author, Paratrooper
b. 1940
Source: *BioIn 8, 9; IntAu&W 76; WrDr 76, 80*

Blythe, Betty
American. Actress
b. Sep 1, 1893 in Los Angeles, California
d. Apr 7, 1972 in Woodland Hills, California
Source: *BioIn 9; FilmgC; MovMk; WhScrn 77*

Blythe, David Gilmour
American. Artist
b. May 9, 1815 in East Liverpool, Ohio
d. May 15, 1865 in East Liverpool, Ohio
Source: *BioIn 1, 2, 6, 10; BnEnAmA; DcAmArt; McGDA; NewYHSD; WhAm H*

Blyton, Carey
English. Author, Composer
b. Mar 14, 1932 in Beckenham, England
Source: *ChPo S2; ConAu 49; SmATA 9; WhoMus 72*

Blyton, Enid Mary
English. Author
b. Aug 11, 1897 in East Dulwich, England
d. Nov 28, 1968
Source: *AuBYP; ChPo, S1, S2; ConAu 25R, 77; LongCTC; TwCCW 78; WhoChL*

Boadicea
[Boudicca]
Queen of the Iceni
d. 62
Source: *InWom; NewC*

Board, Lillian
English. Track Athlete
b. 1948
d. Dec 26, 1970 in Munich, Germany (West)
Source: *BioIn 9, 11; NewYTBE 70*

Boas, Franz
American. Anthropologist
b. Jul 9, 1858 in Minden, Germany
d. Dec 21, 1942 in New York, New York
Source: *AmAu&B; AmLY; CurBio 40, 43; DcAmAu; DcAmB S3; DcNAA; EncAB-H; OxAmL; OxCan, SUP; REnAL; TwCA SUP; WebAB; WhAm 2; WhNAA*

Bob and Ray
see: Elliott, Bob; Goulding, Ray

Bobbs, William Conrad
American. Book Publisher
b. Jan 25, 1861 in Montgomery, Ohio
d. Feb 11, 1926
Source: *LinLib L; WhAm 1*

Boccaccio, Giovanni
Italian. Author
b. 1313 in Florence, Italy
d. Dec 21, 1375 in Certaldo, Italy
Source: *AtlBL; BbD; BiD&SB; CasWL; CyWA; DcBiA; DcEnL; DcEuL; EuAu; EvEuW; NewC; OxEng; Pen EUR; RComWL; REn*

Boccherini, Luigi
Italian. Composer
b. Feb 19, 1743 in Lucca, Italy
d. May 28, 1805 in Madrid, Spain
Source: *OxMus*

Boccioni, Umberto
Italian. Artist
b. 1882
d. 1916
Source: *OxArt*

Bochner, Hart
Canadian. Actor
b. 1956 in Toronto, ON
Source: *BioIn 11; JohnWil 82*

Bochner, Lloyd
Canadian. Actor
b. 1924 in Toronto, ON
Source: *FilmgC; WhoHol A*

Bock, Jerry (Jerrold Lewis)
American. Composer
b. Nov 23, 1928 in New Haven, Connecticut
Source: *BiE&WWA; CelR 73; EncMT; IntWW 74; NewCBMT; NotNAT; WhoAm 74, 76, 78, 80, 82; WhoThe 77; WhoWor 74*

Bocklin, Arnold
Swiss. Artist
b. Oct 16, 1827 in Basel, Switzerland
d. Jan 16, 1901 in Domenico, Italy
Source: *AtlBL; OxGer*

Bocuse, Paul
French. Chef, Restauranteur
b. Feb 11, 1926 in Collonges, France
Source: *BioIn 7, 8, 9, 10; BioNews 74; NewYTBE 72; WhoFr 79*

Bodanzky, Artur
American. Conductor
b. Dec 16, 1887 in Vienna, Austria
d. Nov 23, 1939 in New York, New York
Source: *CurBio 40; DcAmB S2; WhAm 1*

Bode, Carl
American. Author, Educator
b. Mar 14, 1911 in Milwaukee, Wisconsin
Source: *AmAu&B; Au&Wr 71; ConAu 1R, 3NR; DrAS 74E; WhoAm 74, 76, 78, 80, 82; WhoWor 74; WrDr 76*

Bode, Vaughn
American. Cartoonist
b. 1941
Source: *BioIn 10*

Bodenheim, Maxwell
American. Author, Poet
b. May 23, 1893 in Hermanville, Mississippi
d. Feb 6, 1954 in New York, New York
Source: *AmAu&B; CnDAL; ConAmL; DcLEL; ModAL; OxAmL; Pen AM; REn; REnAL; TwCA, SUP; WebAB; WhAm 3*

Bodley, Sir Thomas
English. Diplomat
b. 1545 in Exeter, England
d. Jan 28, 1613 in London, England
Source: *Alli; CasWL; ChPo; CroE&S; DcEuL; DcLEL; EvLB; NewC*

Bodmer, Johann Jakob
Swiss. Critic, Poet
b. Jul 19, 1698 in Greifensee, Switzerland
d. Jan 2, 1783 in Zurich, Switzerland
Source: *BiD&SB; CasWL; DcEuL; EuAu; EvEuW; OxGer; Pen EUR; REn*

Bodmer, Karl
Swiss. Artist, Explorer
Toured America, 1832-34, painting landscapes, Great Plains Indians.
b. Feb 6, 1809 in Riesbach, Switzerland
d. Oct 30, 1893 in Babizon, France
Source: *ApCAB; WhAm H*

Bodnar, Andrew
see: Graham Parker and the Rumour

Bodoni, Giambattista
Italian. Designer, Typographer
b. 1740
d. 1813
Source: *WebBD 80*

Bodsworth, Charles Frederick
Canadian. Naturalist, Author
b. Oct 11, 1918 in Port Burwell, PQ
Source: *ConAu 1R, 3NR; WhoAm 82*

Boehm, Edward M
American. Sculptor
b. Aug 21, 1913 in Baltimore, Maryland
d. Jan 29, 1969 in Trenton, New Jersey
Source: *WhAm 5*

Boehm, Eric Hartzell
American. Publishing Executive
b. Jul 15, 1918 in Hof, Germany
Source: *ConAu 13R; DrAS 74H; WhoAm 74, 76, 78, 80, 82*

Boehm, Helen Francesca Stefanie Franzolin
[Mrs. Edward Marshall Boehm]
American. Business Executive
b. 1922? in Brooklyn, New York
Source: *NewYTBS 76, 77*

Boehm, Karl
see: Bohm, Karl

Boehme, Jakob
German. Mystic
b. 1575 in Gorlitz, Prussia
d. 1624
Source: *REn*

Boeing, William Edward
American. Airplane Manufacturer
Founded Boeing Aircraft, 1916, United Aircraft and Transport, 1928.
b. Oct 1, 1881 in Detroit, Michigan
d. Sep 28, 1956 in Seattle, Washington
Source: *WhAm 3*

Boerhaave, Herman
Dutch. Physician
b. Dec 31, 1668
d. Sep 23, 1738
Source: *BioIn 4, 5, 6, 8, 9, 10*

Boethius
Roman. Philosopher
b. 475
d. 524
Source: *NewCol 75; WebBD 80*

Boettiger, John Roosevelt
American. Author, Newspaperman
b. Mar 25, 1900 in Chicago, Illinois
d. Oct 31, 1950 in New York, New York
Source: *WhAm 3*

Boeynants, Paul Vanden
Belgian. Prime Minister
b. May 22, 1919
Source: *IntWW 74*

Bofill, Angela
American. Singer, Songwriter
Album *Something About You* was in top five on jazz charts.
b. 1955? in New York, New York
Source: *BioIn 12*

Bogan, Louise
American. Poet, Critic
Wrote *Body of This Death,* 1923; *Achievement in American Poetry, 1900-1950,* 1950.
b. Aug 11, 1897 in Livermore Falls, Maine
d. Feb 4, 1970 in New York, New York
Source: *AmAu&B; AuBYP; ChPo; CnDAL; CnE&AP; ConAmA; ConAu 25R, 73; ConLC 4; ConP 70; DcLEL; EncWL; InWom; ModAL, SUP; NewYTBE 70; OxAmL; Pen AM; RAdv 1; REn; REnAL; SixAP; TwCA, SUP; TwCW; WhAm 5*

Bogarde, Dirk
[Derek Niven van den Bogaerde]
English. Actor, Author
Won British Academy Award for *The Servant,* 1963 and *Darling,* 1965.
b. Mar 29, 1921 in London, England
Source: *BiDFilm; CelR 73; CmMov; ConAu 77; CurBio 67; FilmgC; IntMPA 75, 76, 77, 78, 79, 80, 81, 82; IntWW 74; MotPP; MovMk; OxFilm; Who 82; WhoHol A; WhoThe 77; WhoWor 74; WorEFlm*

Bogart, Humphrey de Forest
"Bogey"
American. Actor
Starred in *Casablanca,* 1942; won Oscar for *The African Queen,* 1951.
b. Dec 25, 1899 in New York, New York
d. Jan 14, 1957 in Los Angeles, California
Source: *BiDFilm; CmMov; CurBio 42, 57; FilmgC; MotPP; MovMk; OxFilm; WebAB; WhAm 3; WhScrn 74, 77; WhoHol B; WorEFlm*

Bogart, Leo
American. Author, Sociologist
b. Sep 23, 1921
Source: *AmM&WS 73; ConAu 41R; WhoE 74*

Bogart, Neil
American. Business Executive, Film Producer
Founder, 1974, president, Casablanca Record and Film Works.
b. Feb 3, 1943 in Brooklyn, New York
d. May 8, 1982 in Los Angeles, California
Source: *BioIn 12; IntMPA 79, 80, 81, 82; WhoAm 78, 80, 82*

Bogatja, Vinto
Yugoslav. Ski Jumper
Epitomizes "agony of defeat" for ABC's "Wide World of Sports."
Source: *NF*

Bogdanovich, Peter
American. Motion Picture Director, Producer
Won NY Film Critics Award, best screenplay for *The Last Picture Show,* 1971.
b. Jul 30, 1939 in Kingston, New York
Source: *BiDFilm; BioNews 74; CelR 73; ConAu 5R; CurBio 72; IntMPA 75, 76, 77, 78, 79, 80, 81, 82; MovMk; WhoAm 74, 76, 78, 80, 82; WrDr 76*

Bogert, Tim
[Vanilla Fudge]
American. Singer, Musician
b. Aug 1944 in Manhattan, New York
Source: *NF*

Boggs, Lindy
[Mrs. Hale Boggs]
American. Congresswoman
b. Mar 13, 1916 in Brunswick, Louisiana
Source: *NewYTBE 71; WomPO 76*

Boggs, Thomas
see: Box Tops, The

Boggs, (Thomas) Hale
American. Politician
Congressman, 1941-43, 1947-72; lost in plane crash in AK.
b. Feb 15, 1914 in Long Beach, Mississippi
d. Oct 1972 in Alaska
Source: *BiDrAC; CurBio 58; NewYTBE 71; WhAm 5; WhAmP; WhoGov 72; WhoS&SW 73*

Bogner, Willi
German. Skiwear Designer
Source: *WorFshn*

Bohan, Marc
French. Fashion Designer
Chief designer, artistic director at Christian Dior since 1960.
b. Aug 22, 1926 in Paris, France
Source: *BioNews 74; CelR 73; CurBio 65; IntWW 74; WhoAm 74, 76, 78, 80, 82; WhoWor 74; WorFshn*

Bohlen, Charles Eustis
American. Diplomat
b. Aug 30, 1904 in Clayton, New York
d. Jan 2, 1974 in Washington, DC
Source: *CurBio 48, 60, 74; EncAB-H; NewYTBS 74; WhAm 6; Who 74; WhoAm 74; WhoAmP 73*

Bohm, Karl
[Karl Boehm]
Austrian. Conductor
b. Aug 28, 1894 in Graz, Austria
d. Aug 14, 1981 in Salzburg, Austria
Source: *Baker 78; BioIn 4, 6, 7, 8, 9, 10; CelR 73; CurBio 68, 81; IntWW 74, 75, 76, 77, 78; MusSN; NewEOp 71; NewYTBE 72; NewYTBS 81; WhoAm 74, 76, 78, 80, 82; WhoMus 72; WhoOp 76; WhoWor 74*

Bohm von Bawerk, Eugene
Austrian. Economist
b. 1851
d. 1914
Source: *BioIn 2, 8*

Bohme, Jacob
see: Boehme, Jakob

Bohr, Niels Henrik David
Danish. Physicist
b. Oct 7, 1885 in Copenhagen, Denmark
d. Nov 18, 1962 in Copenhagen, Denmark
Source: *CurBio 45, 63; OxEng; WhAm 4*

Bohrod, Aaron
American. Artist
b. Nov 21, 1907 in Chicago, Illinois
Source: *ConAu 25R; CurBio 55; DcCAA 71; WhoAm 74, 76, 78, 80, 82; WhoAmA 73; WhoWor 74; WhoWorJ 72*

Boiardo, Matteo Maria
Italian. Poet
b. 1441 in Scandiano, Italy
d. 1494 in Reggio Emilia, Italy
Source: *CasWL; CyWA; DcEnL; DcEuL; EuAu; EvEuW; OxEng; Pen EUR; RComWL; REn*

Boieldieu, Francois Adrien
French. Composer
b. Dec 16, 1775 in Rouen, France
d. Oct 8, 1834 in Jarcy, France
Source: *OxFr*

Boileau(-Despreaux), Nicolas
French. Author, Poet, Critic
b. Nov 1, 1636 in Paris, France
d. Mar 13, 1711
Source: *AtlBL; BbD; BiD&SB; CasWL; CyWA; DcEuL; EuAu; EvEuW; OxEng; OxFr; OxThe; Pen EUR; RComWL; REn*

Bois, Guy Pene du
see: DeBois, Guy Pene

Bois, William Edward du
see: DuBois, William Edward Burghardt

Boit, Mike
American. Track Athlete
Source: *NF*

Boito, Arrigo
Italian. Composer, Librettist
b. Feb 24, 1842 in Padua, Italy
d. Jun 10, 1918 in Milan, Italy
Source: *AtlBL; BiD&SB; CasWL; ClDMEL; EuAu; EvEuW; OxThe; Pen EUR; REn*

Boivin, Leo Joseph
Canadian. Hockey Player
Defenseman, 1958-70; played for five NHL teams.
b. Aug 2, 1932 in Prescott, ON
Source: *WhoHcky 73*

Bojangles
see: Robinson, Bill

Bojer, Johan
Norwegian. Author
b. Mar 6, 1872 in Orkesdalsoren, Norway
d. Jul 3, 1959
Source: *CasWL; ClDMEL; CyWA; DcBiA; EncWL; EvEuW; LongCTC; OxAmL; Pen EUR; REn; REnAL; TwCA, SUP; WhAm 3; WhoLA*

Bok, Derek Curtis
American. Educator, University President
b. Mar 22, 1930 in Bryn Mawr, Pennsylvania
Source: *CelR 73; CurBio 71; DrAS 74P; IntWW 74; LEduc 74; Who 74; WhoAm 74, 76, 78, 80, 82; WhoE 74*

Bok, Edward William
American. Editor, Author
b. Oct 9, 1863 in Den Helder, Netherlands
d. Jan 9, 1930 in Lake Wales, Florida
Source: *Alli SUP; AmAu&B; AmBi; BiD&SB; DcAmAu; DcAmB S1; DcLEL; DcNAA; EncAB-H; OxAmL; REn; REnAL; TwCA, SUP; WebAB; WhAm 1; WhAmP; WhNAA*

Bok, Hannes Vajn
[Dolbokov, joint pseud.]
American. Artist, Author
b. Jul 2, 1914 in Minnesota
d. Apr 11, 1964 in New York
Source: *EncSF; FanAl; PseudN; ScF&FL 1; WhoHr&F; WhoSciF*

Bokassa I
African. Former Central Africa Emperor
b. Feb 21, 1921 in Boubangui, Africa
Source: *BioIn 10, 11*

Bolan, Marc
[Mark Feld; T. Rex]
English. Rock Musician
b. May 8, 1947? in London, England
d. Sep 16, 1977 in London, England
Source: *BioIn 9, 11; ObitOF 79; PseudN; WhoRock 81*

Boland, Mary
American. Actress
b. Jan 28, 1880 in Philadelphia, Pennsylvania
d. Jun 23, 1965 in New York, New York
Source: *BiE&WWA; EncMT; Film 1; FilmgC; InWom; MovMk; ThFT; TwYS; Vers A; WhAm 4; WhScrn 74, 77*

Bolcom, William Elden
American. Composer, Musician
b. May 26, 1938 in Seattle, Washington
Source: *DcCM; WhoAm 74; WhoE 74*

Bolden, "Buddy" (Charles)
American. Jazz Musician
b. 1868 in New Orleans, Louisiana
d. Nov 4, 1931 in New Orleans, Louisiana
Source: *WebAB; WhAm HA, 4; WhoJazz 72*

Boles, John
American. Actor
b. Oct 18, 1895 in Greenville, Texas
d. Feb 27, 1969 in San Angelo, Texas
Source: *EncMT; FilmgC; HolP 30; MovMk; TwYS; WhAm 5; WhScrn 74, 77; WhoHol B*

Boles, Paul Darcy
American. Author
b. Mar 5, 1919 in Auburn, Idaho
Source: *ConAu 9R, 4NR; CurBio 56; IndAu 1917; SmATA 9; WhoS&SW 73*

Bolet, Jorge
Cuban. Musician
b. Nov 15, 1914 in Havana, Cuba
Source: *Baker 78; BioIn 3, 4, 10; MusSN; NewYTBE 73; WhoAm 76, 78; WhoMus 72*

Boley, Forrest Irving
American. Educator, Physicist, Author
b. Nov 27, 1925 in Fort Madison, Iowa
Source: *AmM&WS 73; BioIn 9; WhoAm 74, 76, 78, 80, 82*

Boleyn, Anne
English. 2nd Wife of Henry VIII
Mother of Elizabeth I; marriage voided by Church of Eng, May 17, 1536.
b. 1507
d. May 19, 1536 in London, England
Source: *InWom; NewC; NewCol 75; REn*

Bolger, Ray
American. Actor, Dancer
Played the Scarecrow in *The Wizard of Oz,* 1939.
b. Jan 10, 1904 in Boston, Massachusetts
Source: *BiE&WWA; CmMov; CurBio 42; EncMT; FilmgC; IntMPA 75, 76, 77, 78, 79, 80, 81, 82; MovMk; NotNAT; WhoAm 74, 76, 78, 80, 82; WhoThe 77; WhoWor 74*

Bolger, William Frederick
American. Postmaster General
Joined postal service, 1941; Postmaster General, 1978.
b. Mar 13, 1923 in Waterbury, Connecticut
Source: *CurBio 79; WhoAm 82*

Bolingbroke, Henry
see: Henry IV

Bolingbroke, Henry St. John, Viscount
English. Statesman, Author
b. Oct 1, 1678 in London, England
d. Dec 12, 1751 in Battersea, England
Source: *Alli; BbD; BiD&SB; BiDLA; BrAu; CasWL; Chambr 2; DcEnA; DcEnL; DcLEL*

Bolinger, Dwight Lemerton
American. Author
b. Aug 18, 1907 in Topeka, Kansas
Source: *ConAu 13R; DcSpL; WrDr 76*

Bolitho, Henry Hector
New Zealander. Author
b. May 28, 1897 in New Zealand
d. 1974
Source: *Au&Wr 71; ConAu 53; ConAu P-1; DcLEL; EvLB; IntWW 74; LongCTC; NewC; Pen ENG; TwCA, SUP; Who 74; WhoWor 74*

Bolitho, William
[William Bolitho Ryall]
Author, Journalist
b. 1890 in Capetown, South Africa
d. Jun 2, 1930 in Avignon, France
Source: *DcLEL; LongCTC; NewC; TwCA*

Bolivar, Simon
"El Libertador"
Venezuelan. Revolutionary, Statesman
Led armies against Spanish in S America; resulted in creation of six nations.
b. 1783 in Caracas, Venezuela
d. Dec 17, 1830 in Santa Marta, Colombia
Source: *ApCAB; BioIn 1, 2, 3, 4, 5, 6, 7, 8, 9, 10, 11; CasWL; DcSpL; Drake; LinLib S; McGEWB; NewCol 75; Pen AM; REn; WhAm H; WhoMilH 76*

Boll, Heinrich
German. Author
b. Dec 21, 1917 in Cologne, Germany
Source: *CasWL; CelR 73; ConAu 21R; ConLC 2, 3, 6; CurBio 72; EncWL; EvEuW; IntWW 74; ModGL; NewYTBE 72; NewYTBS 74; OxGer; Pen EUR; REn; TwCW; Who 74; WhoAm 82; WhoTwCL; WhoWor 74; WorAu*

Boller, Paul F, Jr.
American. Author
b. Dec 31, 1916 in Spring Lake, New Jersey
Source: *ConAu 1R; DrAS 74H*

Bolles, Don F
American. Journalist
Investigative reporter for *Arizona Republic;* killed in a car bomb explosion.
b. 1928 in Milwaukee, Wisconsin
d. Jun 13, 1976 in Phoenix, Arizona
Source: *BioIn 10; ConAu 65, 73; ObitOF 79*

Bolotowsky, Ilya
American. Artist, Sculptor
b. Jul 1, 1907 in Saint Petersburg, Russia
d. Nov 21, 1981 in New York, New York
Source: *BioIn 8, 9, 10, 11; BnEnAmA; ConArt; CurBio 75, 82; DcAmArt; DcCAA 77; NewYTBS 81; WhoAm 78, 80; WhoAmA 78; WhoWorJ 72*

Bolt, Carol
Canadian. Dramatist
b. Aug 25, 1941 in Winnipeg, MB
Source: *ConAu 101; ConDr 77; OxCan SUP; WrDr 80*

Bolt, Robert
English. Author
b. Aug 15, 1924 in Manchester, England
Source: *BiE&WWA; CasWL; CelR 73; CnThe; ConAu 17R; ConDr 73; ConLC 14; CroCD; IntMPA 77, 78, 79, 80, 81, 82; McGEWD; ModWD; NewC; NotNAT; OxThe; Pen ENG; REnWD; TwCW; WebE&AL; WhoThe 77; WhoWor 74; WorAu; WorEFlm; WrDr 76*

Bolt, Tommy (Thomas)
American. Golfer
b. Mar 31, 1918 in Haworth, Oklahoma
Source: *BioIn 5, 6, 11; WhoGolf*

Bolton, Frances Payne
American. Politician
b. Mar 29, 1885 in Cleveland, Ohio
d. Mar 9, 1977 in Lyndhurst, Ohio
Source: *BioIn 1, 2, 3, 4, 6, 8, 9, 11; WhoAm 74; WhoAmP 73; WhoAmW 74*

Bolton, Guy Reginald
English. Dramatist
b. Nov 23, 1884 in Brozbourne, England
d. Sep 5, 1979 in Goring, England
Source: *AmAu&B; AmSCAP 66; BioIn 3, 5; ConAu 5R, 89; ConDr 77; LongCTC; IntAu&W 76, 77; ModWD; Who 74; WhoThe 72, 77, 81*

Bolton, Isabel
[Mary Britten Miller]
American. Author
b. Aug 6, 1883 in New London, Connecticut
d. Apr 13, 1975 in New York, New York
Source: *AmAu&B; AmNov; ConAu 1R, 57; InWom; LongCTC; TwCA SUP*

Bombeck, Erma Louise
[Mrs. William Bombeck]
American. Journalist, Author
Wrote *Just Wait Till You Have Children of Your Own,* 1971.
b. Feb 21, 1927 in Dayton, Ohio
Source: *AuNews 1; ConAu 21R; CurBio 79; ForWC 70; LibW; WhoAm 76, 78, 80, 82; WhoAmW 72, 74, 79; WrDr 80*

Bomberg, Dave (David)
English. Artist
b. 1890
d. 1957
Source: *BioIn 1, 5, 8, 11*

Bomhard, Moritz
German. Conductor
b. Jun 19, 1912 in Berlin, Germany
Source: *BioIn 7; WhoAm 74*

Bonanno, Joseph
"Joe Bananas"
American. Racketeer
b. 1904
Source: *BioIn 9*

Bonaparte, Charles Louis Napoleon
see: Napoleon III

Bonaparte, Elizabeth Patterson
American. Wife of Jerome Bonaparte
b. Feb 6, 1785 in Baltimore, Maryland
d. Apr 4, 1879
Source: *AmAu&B; BioIn 1, 2, 4, 6, 11*

Bonaparte, Francois Charles Joseph
[L'Aiglon; Napoleon II]
French. Son of Napoleon Bonaparte
b. 1811 in Paris, France
d. 1832 in Austria
Source: *BioIn 1, 2, 5, 6; NewCol 75; WebBD 80*

Bonaparte, Joseph
American. King of Spain
b. Jan 7, 1768 in Corte, Corsica
d. Jul 28, 1844 in Florence, Italy
Source: *ApCAB*

Bonaparte, Louis Lucien
French. Statesman
b. 1813 in Mangrove, England
d. 1891
Source: *Alli SUP*

Bonaparte, Lucien
French. Statesman
b. 1775
d. 1840 in Italy
Source: *WebBD 80*

Bonaparte, Maria Letizis
French. Mother of Napoleon I
b. 1750
d. 1836
Source: *BioIn 6, 8, 10, 11; ChPo*

Bonaparte, Napoleon
see: Napoleon I

Bonatti, Walter
Italian. Author, Mountain Climber
b. 1930
Source: *BioIn 7, 10; WrDr 76*

Bonavena, Oscar
Argentine. Boxer
b. Sep 25, 1942 in Buenos Aires, Argentina
d. May 22, 1976
Source: *NewYTBE 72; WhoBox 74*

Bonaventure, Saint
Italian. Scholastic Theologian
b. 1221
d. 1274
Source: *REn*

Bonci, Alessandro
Italian. Opera Singer
b. Feb 10, 1870 in Cesena, Italy
d. Aug 8, 1940 in Vitterba, Italy
Source: *CurBio 40; WhAm 5*

Boncour, Joseph Paul
see: Paul-Boncour, Joseph

Bond, Carrie Jacobs
American. Composer, Author
b. Aug 11, 1862 in Janesville, Wisconsin
d. Dec 28, 1946 in Los Angeles, California
Source: *AmAu&B; AmSCAP 66; ChPo; DcAmB S4; DcNAA; InWom; NotAW; REnAL; WhAm 2; WhNAA; WisWr; WomWWA 14*

Bond, Edward
English. Dramatist
b. Jul 18, 1934 in London, England
Source: *CnThe; ConAu 25R; ConDr 73, 77; ConLC 4, 6, 13; CroCD; CurBio 78; DcLEL 1940; EncWT; IntAu&W 76, 77; LinLib L; ModBrL SUP; NotNAT; PlP&P A; WebE&AL; Who 74; WhoThe 72, 77; WhoTwCL; WorAu 1970; WrDr 76, 80*

Bond, George Foote
"Papa Topside"
American. Physician
Medical officer, Sealab missions, 1964-69; tested human endurance undersea.
b. 1915
d. Jan 1983 in Charlotte, North Carolina
Source: *BioIn 3, 8*

Bond, Julian
American. Legislator, Civil Rights Leader
Co-founded Student Nonviolent Coordinating Committee (SNCC), 1960.
b. Jan 14, 1940 in Nashville, Tennessee
Source: *CelR 73; ConAu 49; CurBio 69; LivgBAA; NewYTBE 70; WebAB; WhoAm 74, 76, 78, 80, 82; WhoAmP 73; WhoBlA 75; WhoS&SW 73; WhoWor 74*

Bond, Sheila
American. Actress
b. Mar 16, 1928 in New York, New York
Source: *BiE&WWA; NotNAT; WhoHol A; WhoThe 77*

Bond, Sudie
American. Actress
b. Jul 13, 1928 in Louisville, Kentucky
Source: *BiE&WWA; NotNAT; WhoAm 82; WhoHol A; WhoThe 77*

Bond, Tommy
[Our Gang]
"Butch"
American. Actor
Source: *WhoHol A*

Bond, Victoria
American. Composer, Conductor
b. May 6, 1950 in Los Angeles, California
Source: *WhoAm 80, 82*

Bond, Ward
American. Actor
Appeared in over 200 films; starred in TV series "Wagon Train," 1957-61.
b. Apr 9, 1904 in Denver, Colorado
d. Nov 5, 1960 in Dallas, Texas
Source: *CmMov; FilmgC; MotPP; MovMk; OxFilm; WhScrn 74, 77; WhoHol B*

Bondarchuk, Sergei
Russian. Motion Picture Director
b. Sep 25, 1922 in Byelozerka, U.S.S.R.
Source: *DcFM; IntWW 74; OxFilm; WhoHol A; WhoWor 74; WorEFlm*

Bondi, Beulah
American. Actress
b. May 3, 1892 in Chicago, Illinois
Source: *BiE&WWA; FilmgC; IntMPA 75, 76, 77; MotPP; MovMk; NotNAT; ThFT; Vers A; WhoHol A; WhoThe 77*

Bondi, Sir Hermann
English. Mathematician
b. Nov 1, 1919 in Vienna, Austria
Source: *BioIn 3; IntWW 74; Who 74; WhoWor 74*

Bonds, Gary U S
[Gary Anderson]
American. Singer, Songwriter
b. Jun 6, 1939 in Jacksonville, Florida
Source: *EncPR&S; PseudN; RkOn; WhoRock 81*

Bondurant, Bob (Robert L)
American. Auto Racer, Educator
b. 1933
Source: *BioIn 11*

Bonelli, Richard
[Richard Bunn]
American. Opera Singer
b. Feb 6, 1894 in Port Byron, New York
d. Jun 7, 1980 in Los Angeles, California
Source: *Baker 78; BioIn 4, 9, 10; MusSN; NewEOp 71; PseudN; WebBD 80*

Bonerz, Peter
American. Actor, Director
b. Aug 6, 1938 in Portsmouth, New Hampshire
Source: *WhoAm 74, 76, 78, 80, 82; WhoHol A*

Boness, Arthur James, Jr.
American. Author, Financier
b. Apr 18, 1928 in Milwaukee, Wisconsin
Source: *AmM&WS 73; ConAu 37R; WrDr 80*

Bonestell, Chesley
American. Illustrator
b. 1888 in San Francisco, California
Source: *BioIn 11; EncSF; FanAl*

Bonfanti, Jim
see: Raspberries, The

Bongo, El Hadj Omar
Gabonese. President
b. Dec 30, 1935 in Franceville, Gabon
Source: *IntWW 74*

Bonham, Frank
American. Author
b. Feb 25, 1914 in Los Angeles, California
Source: *AuBYP; ConAu 9R, 4NR; ConLC 12; MorBMP; SmATA 1; ThrBJA*

Bonham, John Henry
[Led Zeppelin]
English. Rock Musician
b. May 31, 1949 in Redditch, England
d. Sep 25, 1980 in Windsor, England
Source: *WhoAm 80*

Bonheur, (Marie) Rosa
French. Artist
b. 1822
d. 1899
Source: *HerW; InWom*

Bonhoeffer, Dietrich
German. Theologian
b. Feb 4, 1906 in Breslau, Germany
d. Apr 9, 1945
Source: *OxGer; WorAu*

Boni, Albert
American. Book Publisher
b. Oct 21, 1892 in New York, New York
d. Jul 31, 1981 in Ormond Beach, Florida
Source: *AmAu&B; ConAu 65, 104; LinLib L; NewYTBS 81; St&PR 75; WhoAm 74, 76, 78, 80; WhoWor 76; WhoWorJ 72*

Boniface, Saint
English. Missionary
b. 680?
d. 755
Source: *Alli; BiB; BiD&SB; CasWL; DcEnL; NewC; OxGer*

Bonifacio, Jose
Brazilian. Statesman, Scientist
b. 1763
d. 1838
Source: *NewCol 75*

Bonington, Richard Parkes
English. Artist
b. Oct 25, 1802 in Arnold, England
d. Sep 23, 1828 in London, England
Source: *AtlBL; BioIn 1, 3, 4, 5, 6, 10, 11*

Bonnard, Pierre
French. Artist
b. Oct 30, 1867 in Fontenay, France
d. Jan 23, 1947 in LeCannet, France
Source: *AtlBL*

Bonner, Frank
American. Actor
Played Herb Tarlek on TV series "WKRP in Cincinnati."
b. Feb 28, 1942 in Little Rock, Arkansas
Source: *WhoAm 80, 82*

Bonner, Robert
American. Financial Executive
b. Sep 26, 1942 in Philadelphia, Pennsylvania
Source: *WhoF&I 77*

Bonnet, Georges
French. Politician
b. Jul 23, 1889 in Bassillac, France
d. Jun 4, 1973 in Paris, France
Source: *NewYTBE 73*

Bonnet, Stede
English. Pirate
d. 1718
Source: *BioIn 4, 5*

Bonneville, Benjamin
American. Army Officer
b. Apr 14, 1796 in Paris, France
d. Jun 12, 1878 in Fort Smith, Arkansas
Source: *OxAmL; WebAB; WebBD 80*

Bonney, William H
see: "Billy the Kid"

Bonnie & Clyde
see: Barrow, Clyde; Parker, Bonnie

Bonnier, Joe (Joachim)
Swedish. Auto Racer
b. 1930
d. Jun 11, 1972
Source: *BioIn 6, 7, 9, 10*

Bonny, Anne
[Anne Bonney]
English. Pirate
b. 1700
d. 1720
Source: *BioIn 1, 3, 4, 5, 6, 7, 10, 11; GoodHS; InWom*

Bono, Chastity
American. Daughter of Sonny and Cher
b. Mar 4, 1969 in Los Angeles, California
Source: *NF*

Bono, Cher
see: Cher

Bono, "Sonny" (Salvatore)
[Sonny and Cher]
American. Singer, Actor
Wrote songs "I Got You, Babe," "The Beat Goes On," recorded with wife, Cher.
b. Feb 16, 1940 in Detroit, Michigan
Source: *BioNews 74; CelR 73; CurBio 74; IntMPA 75, 76, 77, 78, 79, 80, 81, 82; WhoAm 74, 76, 78, 80, 82; WhoHol A*

Bonoff, Karla
American. Singer
b. 1951?
Source: *BioIn 11*

Bononcini, Giovanni Battista
Italian. Composer
b. Jul 18, 1670 in Modena, Italy
d. Jul 9, 1747 in Vienna, Austria
Source: *NewEOp 71; OxMus; WebBD 80*

Bonsal, Stephen
American. Journalist
b. Mar 29, 1865 in Baltimore, Maryland
d. Jun 8, 1951 in Washington, DC
Source: *AmAu&B; BiD&SB; BiDSA; CurBio 45, 51; DcAmAu; DcAmB S5; OxAmL; REnAL; TwCA SUP; WhAm 3*

Bonsall, Joe
see: Oak Ridge Boys, The

Bontemps, Arna Wendell
American. Author
Leader, "Harlem Renaissance" movement, 1920's; wrote *Black Thunder,* 1936.
b. Oct 13, 1902 in Alexandria, Louisiana
d. Jun 4, 1973 in Nashville, Tennessee
Source: *AmAu&B; AmNov; AnMV 1926; Au&Wr 71; AuBYP; BkCL; BlkAW; ChPo S1; ConAu 1R, 41R, 4NR; ConLC 1, 18; ConP 70; CurBio 46, 73; JBA 51; MorBMP; NewYTBE 73; OxAmL; REnAL; SmATA 2; Str&VC; WebE&AL; WhAm 5; WhoAm 74; WhoBlA 75; WhoWor 74*

Bonynge, Richard
Australian. Opera Conductor
b. 1930 in Sydney, Australia
Source: *WhoMus 72; WhoWor 74*

Booker T and the Mg's
[Steve Cropper; Donald Dunn; Al Jackson, Jr; Booker T Jones; Bobby Manuel; Carson Whitsett]
American. Rock Group
Source: *EncPR&S; IlEncRk*

Bookout, John Frank, Jr.
American. President of Shell Oil Co.
b. Dec 31, 1922 in Shreveport, Louisiana
Source: *CanWW 70; Dun&B 79; NewYTBS 76; St&PR 75; WhoAm 74, 76, 78, 80, 82; WhoCan 73; WhoF&I 79; WhoS&SW 78*

Bookspan, Martin
American. Music Critic, Commentator
b. Jul 30, 1926 in Boston, Massachusetts
Source: *ConAu 41R; WhoE 74; WhoWorJ 72*

Boole, Mrs. Ella Alexander
American. Prohibitionist
b. Jul 26, 1858 in Van Wert, Ohio
d. Mar 13, 1952 in New York
Source: *BioIn 2, 3; OhA&B*

Boolootian, Richard Andrew
American. Author, Physical Scientist
b. Oct 17, 1927 in Fresno, California
Source: *AmM&WS 73P*

Boomtown Rats
[Pete Briquette; Gerry Cott; Johnny Fingers; Bob Geldof; Simon Grove; Garry Roberts]
Irish. Rock Group
Took name from gang in Woody Guthrie's song "Bound for Glory."
Source: *ConMuA 80; IlEncRk; WhoRock 81*

Boone, Daniel
American. Pioneer Scout
Established Boonesboro, first settlement in KY, 1775.
b. Nov 2, 1734 in Reading, Pennsylvania
d. Sep 26, 1820 in Saint Charles County, Missouri
Source: *Alli; AmAu&B; AmBi; ApCAB; BiDSA; DcAmB; Drake; EncAB-H; FilmgC; REn; REnAL; TwCBDA; WebAB; WhAm H; WhAmP*

Boone, Debby (Deborah Ann)
[Mrs. Gabriel Ferrer]
American. Singer
Daughter of Pat Boone; platinum record for "You Light Up My Life," 1977.
b. Sep 22, 1956 in Hackensack, New Jersey
Source: *BioIn 11; BkPepl; WhoAm 80, 82*

Boone, "Pat" (Charles Eugene)
American. Singer, Actor, Author
Noted for clean cut image, white buck shoes; starred in *April Love,* 1957.
b. Jun 1, 1934 in Jacksonville, Florida
Source: *AmAu&B; AmSCAP 66; BkPepl; ConAu 1R, 2NR; CurBio 79; FilmgC; IntMPA 75, 76, 77, 78, 79, 80, 81, 82; MotPP; MovMk; SmATA 7; WhoAm 74, 76, 78, 80, 82; WhoHol A; WhoRel 75; WrDr 76*

Boone, Rebecca B
American. Wife of Daniel Boone
b. 1739
d. 1813
Source: *BioIn 7*

Boone, Richard
American. Actor
Starred in TV series "Medic," 1954-56, "Have Gun Will Travel," 1957-63.
b. Jun 18, 1917 in Los Angeles, California
Source: *BiE&WWA; CelR 73; CmMov; CurBio 64; FilmgC; IntMPA 75, 76, 77; MotPP; MovMk; NewYTBE 72; WhoHol A*

Boorman, John
English. Motion Picture Director
b. Jan 18, 1933 in Shepperton, England
Source: *DcFM; EncSF; FilmEn; IntMPA 81; OxFilm; WhoAm 82; WorEFlm*

Boorstin, Daniel Joseph
American. Author, Government Official
Won Pulitzer Prize, 1974, for *Americans: The Democratic Experience.*
b. Oct 1, 1914 in Atlanta, Georgia
Source: *AmAu&B; ConAu 1R, 1NR; CurBio 68; Who 82; WhoAm 74, 76, 78, 80, 82; WhoGov 72; WhoS&SW 73; WhoWorJ 72; WorAu*

Boosey, Leslie Arthur
British. Music Executive
b. Jul 26, 1887
Source: *Who 74; WhoMus 72*

Booth, "Albie" (Albert James, Jr.)
American. Football Player, Coach
b. Feb 1, 1908 in New Haven, Connecticut
d. Mar 1, 1959 in New York, New York
Source: *WhoFtbl 74*

Booth, Catherine Mumford
English. Evangelist
b. 1829
d. 1890
Source: *Alli; BioIn 1, 4, 5, 8, 10, 11*

Booth, Edwin Thomas
American. Actor
b. Nov 13, 1833 in Bel Air, Maryland
d. Jun 7, 1893 in New York, New York
Source: *DcAmB; OxAmL; OxThe; REn; REnAL; TwCBDA; WebAB; WhAm H*

Booth, Evangeline Cory
English. Humanitarian
Commander, Salvation Army operations, London, 1888; US operations, 1904.
b. Dec 25, 1865 in London, England
d. Jul 17, 1950 in Hartsdale, New York
Source: *BiCAW; CurBio 41, 50; DcAmB S4; HerW; InWom; NotAW; WhAm 3; WomWWA 14*

Booth, George
American. Cartoonist
b. Jun 28, 1926 in Cainsville, Missouri
Source: *WhoAm 82; WorECar*

Booth, George Gough
American. Editor
b. Sep 24, 1864 in Toronto, ON
d. Apr 11, 1949 in Detroit, Michigan
Source: *BioIn 1, 2, 7; WhAm 2*

Booth, Hubert Cecil
English. Inventor
Invented the vacuum cleaner, 1901.
b. 1871
d. Jan 14, 1955 in Croydon, England
Source: *BioIn 3*

Booth, John Wilkes
American. Actor, Assassin
Shakespearean actor; shot, killed Lincoln at Ford's Theatre, Apr 14, 1865.
b. 1838 in Hartford City, Maryland
d. Apr 26, 1865 in Virginia
Source: *AmBi; DcAmB; Drake; EncAB-H; FamA&A; OxAmL; OxThe; PlP&P; REn; REnAL; TwCBDA; WebAB; WhAm H; WhAmP*

Booth, Junius Brutus
English. Actor
b. May 1, 1796 in London, England
d. Nov 30, 1852
Source: *AmBi; ApCAB; DcAmB; Drake; FamA&A; OxAmL; OxThe; REn; REnAL; TwCBDA; WebAB; WhAm H*

Booth, Shirley
American. Actress
Played Hazel in TV series, 1961-66; won Emmy, 1963.
b. Aug 30, 1907 in New York, New York
Source: *BiE&WWA; CelR 73; CurBio 42, 53; EncMT; FilmgC; InWom; IntMPA 75, 76, 77, 78, 79, 80, 81, 82; MotPP; MovMk; NotNAT; PlP&P; WhoAm 74, 76, 78, 80, 82; WhoHol A; WhoThe 77; WorEFlm; WhoWor 74; WhoHol A; WhoThe 77*

Booth, William
English. Minister, Humanitarian
Started Christian Mission in E London, 1865, became Salvation Army, 1878.
b. Apr 10, 1829 in Nottinghamshire, England
d. Aug 20, 1912 in London, England
Source: *Alli SUP; LongCTC; NewC; REn*

Boothby, Robert John
Scottish. Politician
b. 1900 in Edinburgh, Scotland
Source: *BioIn 1, 3, 4, 7, 11; IntWW 74; Who 74*

Boothe, Powers
American. Actor
Portrayed Rev. Jim Jones in TV movie *Guyana Tragedy: The Story of Jim Jones.*
b. Jun 1, 1949 in Snyder, Texas
Source: *NewYTBS 79*

Boothroyd, John Basil
English. Author
b. Mar 4, 1910 in Worksop, England
Source: *AuBYP; ConAu 33R; WrDr 76*

Booz, Paul E
American. Economist
b. 1914?
d. 1971
Source: *BioIn 9; NewYTBE 71*

Borah, William E
American. Senator
b. Jun 29, 1865 in Fairfield, Illinois
d. Jan 19, 1940 in Washington, DC
Source: *AmBi; BiDrAC; DcAmB S2; DcNAA; EncAB-H; REn; WebAB; WhAm 1; WhAmP*

Borbon y Borbon, Prince Juan Carlos
see: Juan Carlos I

Borch, Fred J
American. Businessman
b. Apr 28, 1910 in Brooklyn, New York
Source: *BioIn 6, 9; IntWW 74; St&PR 75; WhoAm 74; WhoE 74; WhoF&I 74; WhoWor 74*

Bordeaux, Henry
French. Author
b. Jan 29, 1870 in Thonon, France
d. 1963
Source: *CasWL; CathA 1930; ClDMEL; EncWL; EvEuW; LongCTC; OxFr; REn; TwCA, SUP*

Borden, Gail
American. Inventor
Patented evaporated milk, 1856.
b. Nov 9, 1801 in Norwich, New York
d. Jan 11, 1874 in Borden, Texas
Source: *AmBi; ApCAB; DcAmB; NewCol 75; TwCBDA; WebAB; WhAm H*

Borden, Lizzie Andrew
American. Alleged Murderer
Arrested for murdering father, stepmother, Aug 4, 1892; acquitted, 1893.
b. Jul 19, 1860 in Fall River, Massachusetts
d. Jun 1, 1927 in Fall River, Massachusetts
Source: *DcAmB S1; NotAW; OxAmL; REn; REnAL; WebAB; WhAm HA, 4*

Borden, Robert Laird
Canadian. Prime Minister
b. Jun 26, 1854 in Grand Pre, NS
d. Jun 10, 1937 in Ottawa, ON
Source: *DcNAA; OxCan; WhNAA; WhoPubR 72*

Bordes, Francois
[Francois Carsac, pseud.]
French. Archaeologist
b. 1919
d. Apr 30, 1981 in Tucson, Arizona
Source: *ConAu 103; NewYTBS 81*

Bordet, Jules Jean Baptiste Vincent
Belgian. Scientist
b. Jun 13, 1870 in Soighies, Belgium
d. Apr 6, 1961 in Brussels, Belgium
Source: *WhAm 4*

Bordoni, Faustina
[Faustina Bordoni Hasse]
Italian. Opera Singer
b. 1700
d. Nov 4, 1781 in Venice, Italy
Source: *InWom*

Bordoni, Irene
American. Actress
b. 1893 in Ajaccio, Corsica
d. Mar 19, 1953 in New York, New York
Source: *EncMT; InWom; WhScrn 74, 77; WhoHol B*

Borduas, Paul-Emile
Canadian. Artist
b. Nov 1, 1905 in Saint Hilaire, PQ
d. Feb 22, 1960 in Paris, France
Source: *BioIn 3, 4, 5, 7, 11; ConArt; CreCan 1; MacDCB 78; McGDA; OxCan, SUP*

Borel d'Hauterive, Petrus
French. Poet, Author
b. Jun 28, 1809 in Lyons, France
d. Jul 14, 1859 in Mostaganem, Algeria
Source: *BiD&SB; CasWL; EuAu; EvEuW; OxFr; Pen EUR*

Boren, David Lyle
American. Senator, Former Governor
b. Apr 21, 1941 in Washington, DC
Source: *BioIn 10, 12; WhoAm 78, 80, 82*

Borg, Bjorn
Swedish. Tennis Player
Won Wimbledon championships, 1976-80; retired, 1983.
b. Jun 6, 1956 in Sodertalje, Sweden
Source: *BkPepl; CurBio 74; Who 82; WhoAm 78; WhoWor 78*

Borg, Kim
Finnish. Opera Singer
b. Aug 7, 1919 in Helsinki, Finland
Source: *IntWW 74; WhoMus 72; WhoWor 74*

Borg, Veda Ann
American. Actress
b. Jan 15, 1915 in Boston, Massachusetts
d. Aug 16, 1973 in Hollywood, California
Source: *FilmgC; MotPP; MovMk; ThFT; Vers A; WhScrn 77; WhoHol B*

Borge, Victor
American. Pianist, Comedian
Combines music with humor to create musical satire.
b. Jan 3, 1909 in Copenhagen, Denmark
Source: *AmSCAP 66; BiE&WWA; BioNews 74; CelR 73; CurBio 46; IntMPA 75, 76, 77, 78, 79, 80, 81, 82; IntWW 74; NotNAT; WhoAm 74; WhoHol A; WhoMus 72; WhoWor 74; WrDr 76*

Borges, Jorge Luis
Argentine. Author
Leader, "Ultraismo" literary movement, combining surrealism, imagism.
b. Aug 24, 1899 in Buenos Aires, Argentina
Source: *CasWL; CelR 73; ConAu 21R; ConLC 1, 2, 3, 4, 6, 8, 9, 10, 13; CurBio 70; DcCLAA; DcSpL; EncWL; IntWW 74; NewYTBE 71; Pen AM; REn; TwCW; Who 74; WhoTwCL; WhoWor 74; WorAu*

Borghese, Maria Paolina
French. Sister of Napoleon I
b. 1780
d. 1825
Source: *BioIn 1, 2, 7, 9, 10, 11*

Borgia, Cesare
Italian. Despot, Military Leader
Said to be prototype for Machiavelli's *The Prince.*
b. 1475 in Rome, Italy
d. Mar 12, 1507 in Navarre, France
Source: *FilmgC; McGEWB; NewC*

Borgia, Lucrezia
Italian. Dutchess of Ferrara
Unfairly known as poisoner and participant in family plots.
b. 1480
d. Mar 12, 1519
Source: *InWom; NewC*

Borglum, Gutzon
American. Sculptor
b. Mar 25, 1867 in Bear Lake, Idaho
d. Mar 6, 1941 in Chicago, Illinois
Source: *CurBio 41; OxAmL; REn; REnAL; WebAB; WhAm 1*

Borglum, Solon Hannibal
American. Sculptor
b. Dec 22, 1868 in Ogden, Utah
d. Jan 31, 1922
Source: *DcAmB; WhAm 1*

Borgmann, "Benny" (Bernhard)
American. Basketball Player
b. Nov 21, 1899 in Haledon, New Jersey
d. Nov 11, 1978
Source: *WhoBbl 73*

Borgnine, Ernest
American. Actor
Starred in TV series "McHale's Navy," 1962-66; won Oscar, 1955, for *Marty.*
b. Jan 24, 1917 in Hamden, Connecticut
Source: *BiDFilm; CelR 73; CurBio 56; FilmgC; IntMPA 75, 76, 77, 78, 79, 80, 81, 82; IntWW 74; MotPP; MovMk; NewYTBE 73; OxFilm; WhoAm 74, 76, 78, 80, 82; WhoHol A; WhoWor 74; WorEFlm*

Bori, Lucrezia
Spanish. Opera Singer
b. Dec 24, 1888 in Valencia, Spain
d. May 14, 1960 in New York, New York
Source: *InWom; WhAm 4*

Bork, Robert Heron
American. Lawyer, Judge
b. Mar 1, 1927 in Pittsburgh, Pennsylvania
Source: *BioIn 10; DrAS 78P; IntWW 78; WhoAm 80, 82; WhoGov 77*

Borkh, Inge
German. Opera Singer
b. May 26, 1921 in Mannheim, Germany
Source: *InWom; IntWW 74; WhoMus 72; WhoWor 74*

Borland, Hal
American. Author
b. May 14, 1900 in Sterling, Nebraska
d. Feb 22, 1978 in Sharon, Connecticut
Source: *AmAu&B; Au&Wr 71; ConAu 1R, 77; REnAL; SmATA 5; WhoAm 74; WhoWor 74; WorAu*

Borlaug, Norman Ernest
American. Agriculturalist
b. Mar 25, 1914 in Cresco, Iowa
Source: *AmM&WS 73P; CelR 73; CurBio 71; EncAB-H; IntWW 74; NewYTBE 70; WebAB; Who 74; WhoAm 74, 76, 78, 80, 82; WhoWor 74*

Borman, Frank
American. Astronaut, Airline Executive
Space flights 1965 on Gemini 7; 1968 on Apollo 8, first flight around moon.
b. Mar 14, 1928 in Gary, Indiana
Source: *IntWW 74; WhoAm 74, 76, 78, 80, 82; WhoS&SW 73; WhoWor 74*

Bormann, Martin Ludwig
German. Nazi Leader
Pronounced dead, 1973, when skeleton was found near Hitler's bunker.
b. 1900
d. 1945
Source: *BioNews 75; NewYTBE 73*

Born, Ernest Alexander
American. Architect
b. 1898 in San Francisco, California
Source: *WhoAm 74*

Born, Max
German. Engineer, Naturalist
b. Dec 11, 1882 in Breslau, Germany
d. Jan 5, 1970 in Goettingen, Germany (West)
Source: *ConAu 5R, 25R; NewYTBE 70; WhAm 5*

Borodin, Alexander Profirevich
Russian. Composer
b. Nov 11, 1833 in Saint Petersburg, Russia
d. Feb 7, 1887 in Saint Petersburg, Russia
Source: *AtlBL; REn*

Boros, Julius Nicholas
American. Golfer
Won US Open, 1963, PGA, 1968; Hall of Fame, 1974.
b. Mar 3, 1920 in Fairfield, Connecticut
Source: *WhoGolf*

Borotra, Jean Robert
[The Four Musketeers]
"Bounding Basque"
French. Tennis Player
b. Aug 13, 1898 in Barritz, France
Source: *IntWW 74; WhoWor 74*

Borromeo, Carlo, Saint
Italian. Ecclesiastic, Nobleman
b. 1538
d. 1584
Source: *BioIn 1, 2, 3, 4, 5, 6, 7, 8, 9, 11*

Borromini, Francesco
Italian. Architect
b. Sep 25, 1559 in Bissone, Italy
d. Aug 3, 1677 in Rome, Italy
Source: *AtlBL*

Borrow, George Henry
English. Author
b. Jul 5, 1803 in East Dereham, England
d. Jul 26, 1881 in Oulton, England
Source: *Alli, SUP; AtlBL; BbD; BiD&SB; BrAu 19; CasWL; Chambr 3; CyWA; DcBiA; DcEnA; DcEnL; DcEuL; DcLEL; EvLB; MouLC 3; NewC; OxEng; Pen ENG; REn; WebE&AL*

Bortoluzzi, Paolo
Italian. Ballet Dancer
b. May 17, 1938 in Genoa, Italy
Source: *IntWW 74*

Borzage, Frank
American. Motion Picture Director
b. Apr 23, 1893 in Salt Lake City, Utah
d. Jun 19, 1962 in Hollywood, California
Source: *BiDFilm; CmMov; DcFM; FilmgC; MovMk; OxFilm; TwYS; WhAm 4; WhScrn 74, 77; WhoHol B; WorEFlm*

Bosanquet, Bernard
English. Philosopher
b. 1848
d. 1923
Source: *Alli SUP; LongCTC*

Bosch, Carl
German. Engineer
b. 1874
d. 1940
Source: *BioIn 3, 6*

Bosch, Hieronymus
[Hieronymus VanAeken]
Dutch. Artist
b. 1450 in Hertogenbosch, Netherlands
d. 1516
Source: *AtlBL; REn*

Bosch, Juan
Dominican. Author, Politician
b. Jun 30, 1909 in Dominican Republic
Source: *CurBio 63; DcCLAA; IntWW 74; NewYTBE 70*

Boschwitz, Rudy
American. Senator
b. 1930 in Berlin, Germany
Source: *BioIn 11, 12; WhoAm 82*

Boscovich, Ruggiero Giuseppe
Italian. Mathematician, Physicist
b. 1711 in Ragusa, Dalmatia
d. 1787
Source: *WebBD 80*

Bose, Subhas Chandra
Indian. Politician
b. 1897
d. Aug 19, 1945
Source: *BioIn 1, 2, 3, 5, 7, 8, 9, 11*

Bosin, Blackbear
American Indian. Artist, Designer
b. Jun 5, 1921 in Anadarko, Oklahoma
Source: *WhoAmA 73, 76, 78*

Bosley, Harold A
American. Clergyman, Author
b. Feb 19, 1907 in Burchard, Nebraska
d. Jan 21, 1975
Source: *AmAu&B; ConAu 49, 53; DrAS 74P; WhoAm 74; WhoRel 75; WhoWor 74*

Bosley, Tom
American. Actor
Star of TV series "Happy Days,"1974--; won Tony for role in *Fiorello,* 1959.
b. Oct 1, 1927 in Chicago, Illinois
Source: *BiE&WWA; FilmgC; IntMPA 82; NotNAT; WhoAm 74, 76, 78, 80, 82; WhoHol A; WhoThe 77; WhoWor 74*

Bossuet, Jacques Benigne
French. Pulpit Orator, Author
b. Sep 27, 1627 in Dijon, France
d. Apr 12, 1704 in Paris, France
Source: *AtlBL; BbD; BiD&SB; CasWL; DcEuL; EuAu; EvEuW; OxEng; OxFr; Pen EUR; REn*

Bossy, Mike (Michael)
Canadian. Hockey Player
Scored 53 goals as rookie in 1977-78, an NHL record.
b. Jan 22, 1957 in Montreal, PQ
Source: *BioIn 11, 12; WhoAm 82*

Bostock, Lyman Wesley
American. Baseball Player
Died tragically after being shot by estranged husband of friend.
b. Nov 22, 1950 in Birmingham, Alabama
d. Sep 24, 1978 in Gary, Indiana
Source: *BaseEn; BioIn 11*

Boston
[Brad Delp; Barry Goudreau; Sib Hashian; Tom Scholz; Fran Sheehan]
American. Rock Group
Source: *RkOn*

Boston, Ralph
American. Track Athlete
b. May 9, 1939 in Laurel, Mississippi
Source: *BioIn 5, 6, 8, 9*

"Boston Strangler"
see: DeSalvo, Albert

Bostwick, Barry
American. Actor
b. 1946? in San Mateo, California
Source: *BioIn 12*

Bosustow, Stephen
Canadian. Motion Picture Producer
b. Nov 6, 1911 in Victoria, BC
Source: *CurBio 58; DcFM; FilmgC; IntMPA 75, 76, 77; OxFilm; WhoWest 74; WorEFlm*

Boswell, Charles Albert
American. Golfer
A 13-time champion of US Blind Golfers Assn.
b. Dec 22, 1916 in Birmingham, Alabama
Source: *BioIn 1, 3, 11; WhoGolf*

Boswell, Connee
[Boswell Sisters]
American. Singer, Actress
b. Dec 3, 1912 in New Orleans, Louisiana
d. Oct 11, 1976 in New York, New York
Source: *AmSCAP 66; InWom; WhoHol A; WhoJazz 72*

Boswell, James
Scottish. Lawyer, Biographer
Wrote *Life of Johnson*, 1791, best known biography in English language.
b. Oct 18, 1740 in Edinburgh, Scotland
d. May 19, 1795 in London, England
Source: *Alli; AtlBL; BbD; BiD&SB; BrAu; CasWL; Chambr 2; ChPo S2; CrtT 2; CyWA; DcEnA; DcEnL; DcEuL; DcLEL; EvLB; IlsCB 1957; LongCTC; MnBBF; MouLC 2; NewC; OxEng; Pen ENG; RAdv 1; RComWL; REn; WebE&AL*

Boswell, John
American. Author, Medievalist
b. 1947?
Source: *NF*

Boswell, Martha
[Boswell Sisters]
American. Singer
b. 1905
d. Jul 2, 1958 in Peekskill, New York
Source: *InWom; WhScrn 74, 77; WhoHol B*

Boswell, Vet
[Boswell Sisters]
American. Singer
Source: *InWom; WhoHol A*

Bosworth, Barry
American. Statesman
Source: *NF*

Bosworth, Hobart van Zandt
American. Actor
b. Aug 11, 1867 in Marietta, Ohio
d. Dec 30, 1943 in Glendale, California
Source: *CurBio 44; Film 1; FilmgC; MotPP; MovMk; TwYS; WhAm 2; WhScrn 74, 77; WhoHol B*

Botero (Angulo), Fernando
Colombian. Artist
b. Apr 19, 1932 in Medellin, Colombia
Source: *BioIn 12; CurBio 80; IntWW 79*

Botha, Louis
South African. General, Politician
Prime Minister, 1978--.
b. Sep 27, 1862 in Honigfontein, South Africa
d. Aug 27, 1919 in Pretoria, South Africa
Source: *BioIn 1; McGEWB; WhoMilH 76; WhoModH*

Botha, Pieter Willem
South African. Prime Minister
b. Jan 12, 1916 in Paul Roux, South Africa
Source: *CurBio 79; IntWW 74*

Bothwell, James Hepburn
Scottish. Nobleman
b. 1536
d. 1578
Source: *BioIn 1, 7, 9, 10, 11*

Bothwell, Jean
American. Children's Author
b. in Winside, Nebraska
Source: *ConAu 1R, 3NR; CurBio 46; InWom; JBA 51; SmATA 2*

Bottel, Helen Alfea
American. Journalist
b. Mar 13, 1914 in Beaumont, California
Source: *ConAu 25R; ForWC 70; WhoAm 82; WhoAmW 77; WrDr 76*

Bottger, Johann Friedrich
German. Chemist
Originated Dresden china; established porcelain works, Meissen, Germany.
b. Feb 4, 1682
d. Mar 13, 1719
Source: *BioIn 1, 3, 4, 11*

Botticelli, Sandro
[Alessandrodi Mariano dei Filipipi]
Italian. Artist
Favorite artist, protege of Medici family; best known work "The Birth of Venus."
b. 1444 in Florence, Italy
d. May 17, 1510 in Florence, Italy
Source: *AtlBL; DcCathB; Dis&D; McGDA; McGEWB; NewC; NewCol 75; OxArt; REn; WhDW; WorAl*

Bottome, Phyllis, pseud.
[Mrs. Ernan Forbes-Dennis]
English. Author
b. 1884
d. Aug 23, 1963 in Hampstead, England
Source: *BioIn 1, 3, 4, 6, 8; ConAu 93; REn*

Bottomley, Gordon
English. Dramatist, Poet
b. Feb 20, 1874 in Keighley, England
d. Aug 25, 1948 in Oare, England
Source: *BioIn 3, 4, 5, 7; CasWL; NewC; OxThe; Pen ENG; REn; TwCA, SUP*

Bottoms, Joseph
American. Actor
Film debut, 1974, in *The Dove.*
b. Apr 22, 1954 in Santa Barbara, California
Source: *IntMPA 75, 76, 77, 78, 79, 80, 81, 82; WhoHol A*

Bottoms, Sam
American. Actor
b. 1960 in Santa Barbara, California
Source: *WhoHol A*

Bottoms, Timothy
American. Actor
In movie *The Last Picture Show,* 1971.
b. Aug 30, 1951 in Santa Barbara, California
Source: *FilmgC; IntMPA 75, 76, 77, 78, 79, 80, 81, 82; MovMk; WhoAm 80, 82; WhoHol A; WorAl*

Botvinnik, Mikhail Moiseevich
Russian. Chess Player
b. Aug 17, 1911 in Leningrad, Russia
Source: *CurBio 65; IntWW 74; Who 74; WhoWor 74*

Bouchard, Albert
see: Blue Oyster Cult

Bouchard, Joe
see: Blue Oyster Cult

Boucher, Francois
French. Artist
b. Sep 29, 1703 in Paris, France
d. May 30, 1770 in Paris, France
Source: *AtlBL; OxFr; OxThe; REn*

Bouchet, Edward Alexander
American. Educator
b. Sep 15, 1852 in New Haven, Connecticut
d. 1918
Source: *BioIn 8; WhoColR*

Boucicault, Dion
American. Author
b. Dec 26, 1820 in Dublin, Ireland
d. Sep 18, 1890 in New York, New York
Source: *AmAu&B; ApCAB; BbD; BiD&SB; BrAu 19; CasWL; Chambr 3; ChPo S1; CnThe; DcAmB; DcEnL; EvLB; HsB&A; McGEWD; MouLC 4; NewC; OxAmL; OxEng; Pen AM, ENG; PlP&P; PoIre; REn; REnAL; REnWD; TwCBDA; WebAB; WhAm H*

Boudicca
see: Boadicea

Boudin, Eugene Louis
French. Artist
b. Jul 12, 1824 in Honfleur, France
d. Aug 8, 1898 in Deauville, France
Source: *AtlBL; OxFr*

Boudin, Kathy (Katherine)
American. Revolutionary
Involved in bomb factory explosion, 1970; captured after armored car robbery, 1981.
b. May 13, 1942 in New York, New York
Source: *BioIn 11*

Boudreau, Lou(is)
American. Baseball Player
Shortstop, Cleveland Indians, 1938-50; Hall of Fame, 1970.
b. Jul 17, 1917 in Harvey, Illinois
Source: *BaseEn; CurBio 42; WhoProB 73*

Bougainville, Louis Antoine de
French. Navigator
b. Nov 12, 1729 in Paris, France
d. Aug 31, 1811
Source: *ApCAB; BbtC; Drake; McGEWB; OxCan; OxFr*

Bouillon, Godfrey de
see: Godfrey of Bouillon

Boulanger, Georges Ernest Jean Marie
French. Soldier, Politician
b. 1837 in Rennes, France
d. 1891 in Brussels, Belgium
Source: *OxFr; REn*

Boulanger, Nadia Juliette
French. Composer, Conductor, Teacher
b. Sep 16, 1887 in Paris, France
d. Oct 22, 1979 in Paris, France
Source: *Baker 78; CurBio 62, 80; DcCM; GoodHS; InWom; IntWW 75, 76, 77, 78; LinLib S; NewYTBS 79; REn; Who 74; WhoAmW 61, 64, 66, 68, 70, 72, 74; WhoMus 72; WhoWor 74*

Boulding, Kenneth Ewart
American. Economist, Author, Educator
b. Jan 18, 1910 in Liverpool, England
Source: *AmAu&B; AmEA 74; AmM&WS 73S; ConAu 5R; CurBio 65; IntWW 74; WhoAm 74, 76, 78, 80, 82; WhoWest 74*

Boulez, Pierre
French. Composer, Conductor
b. Mar 26, 1925 in Montbrison, France
Source: *CelR 73; CurBio 69; DcCM; IntWW 74; NewYTBE 71, 73; REn; Who 74; WhoAm 74, 76, 78, 80, 82; WhoMus 72; WhoWor 74*

Boullioun, E(rnest) H(erman, Jr.)
"Tex"
American. Aerospace Executive
With Boeing since 1940; president, 1972--.
b. Nov 3, 1918 in Little Rock, Arkansas
Source: *NewYTBS 81; WhoAm 74, 76, 78; WhoF&I 74, 75, 77*

Boulle, Pierre Francois Marie-Louis
French. Author
b. Feb 20, 1912 in Avignon, France
Source: *Au&Wr 71; CasWL; ConAu 9R; REn; TwCW; WorAu*

Boult, Sir Adrian Cedric
English. Musician, Conductor
Conducted at coronations of King George VI, Queen Elizabeth II.
b. Apr 8, 1889 in Chester, England
d. Feb 23, 1983 in Tunbridge Wells, England
Source: *Au&Wr 71; CurBio 46, 83; IntWW 74, 75, 76, 77, 78, 79, 80, 81; Who 82; WhoMus 72; WhoWor 74*

Boulting, Roy
English. Motion Picture Director
b. Nov 21, 1913 in Bray, England
Source: *BiDFilm; CmMov; DcFM; FilmEn; FilmgC; IntMPA 75, 76, 77, 78, 79, 80, 81; IntWW 75, 76, 77, 78; OxFilm; Who 74; WhoWor 74, 76, 78; WorEFlm*

Boulton, Matthew
English. Manufacturer, Engineer
Built steam engines with James Watt; invented steel inlay process.
b. Sep 3, 1728
d. 1809
Source: *BioIn 10; WebBD 80*

Boumedienne, Houari
Algerian. President
b. Aug 23, 1932 in Clauzel, Algeria
d. Dec 27, 1978 in Algiers, Algeria
Source: *CurBio 71; IntWW 74; WhoGov 72*

Bouquet, Henry
British. Army Officer
b. 1719 in Rolle, Switzerland
d. Sep 2, 1765 in Pensacola, Florida
Source: *AmBi; ApCAB; BioIn 5, 9, 10; DcAmB; Drake; MacDCB 78; NatCAB 20; NewCol 75; REnAW; WebAMB; WhAm H; WhoMilH 76*

Bourassa, Henri
Canadian. Author, Politician
b. Sep 1, 1868 in Montreal, PQ
d. Aug 31, 1952 in Montreal, PQ
Source: *AmLY; CanWr; OxCan*

Bourget, Paul
French. Author, Critic
b. Sep 2, 1852 in Amiens, France
d. Dec 25, 1935 in Paris, France
Source: *BbD; BiD&SB; CasWL; CathA 1930; ClDMEL; CyWA; DcBiA; EncWL; EvEuW; LongCTC; OxEng; OxFr; Pen EUR; REn; TwCA, SUP*

Bourgholtzer, Frank
American. Broadcast Journalist
b. Oct 26, 1919 in New York, New York
Source: *ConAu 25R; WhoAm 82; WhoWest 74*

Bourguiba, Habib Ben Ali
Tunisian. President
b. Aug 3, 1903 in Monastir, Tunisia
Source: *CurBio 55; IntWW 74; WhoWor 74*

Bourjaily, Vance
American. Author
Gained prominence in generation of young writers after WW II.
b. Sep 17, 1922 in Cleveland, Ohio
Source: *AmAu&B; ASpks; Au&Wr 71; ConAu 1R, 2NR; ConLC 8; ConNov 72, 76; Conv; DcLB 2; DcLEL 1940; DrAF 76; IntAu&W 76, 77; IntWW 77, 78, 79, 80; LinLib L; ModAL; OhA&B; OxAmL; Pen AM; REn; REnAL; WhoAm 74, 76, 78, 80, 82; WhoWor 74, 76; WorAu; WrDr 76, 80*

Bourque, Ray
Canadian. Hockey Player
b. Dec 28, 1960 in Montreal, PQ
Source: *BioIn 12*

Boussac, Marcel
"Cotton King of France"
French. Textile Executive
Made cotton airplane fabric during WW I; later used as fashion fabric.
b. Apr 17, 1889 in Chateauroux, France
d. Mar 31, 1980 in Montargis, France
Source: *AnObit 1980; BioIn 2, 3, 5, 11; NewYTBE 71; NewYTBS 80; Who 74; WhoWor 74*

Boussingault, Jean
French. Chemist
b. 1802
d. 1887
Source: *BioIn 1, 2, 3, 5, 6, 7; NewCol 75*

Bouton, Jim (James Alan)
"Bulldog"
American. Baseball Player, Author
Pitcher, NY Yankees, 1962-68; author *Ball Four,* 1970.
b. Mar 8, 1939 in Newark, New Jersey
Source: *BaseEn; CelR 73; ConAu 89; CurBio 71; NewYTBE 70; WhoAm 76, 78, 80, 82; WhoE 74, 75; WhoProB 73; WorAl*

Bouts, Dierick C
Dutch. Artist
b. 1420 in Haarlem, Netherlands
d. 1475
Source: *OxArt*

Boutwell, George Sewell
American. Politician
b. Jan 23, 1818 in Brookline, Massachusetts
d. Feb 27, 1905
Source: *BioIn 8, 10, 11*

Bova, Ben(jamin William)
American. Author, Editor
b. Nov 8, 1932 in Philadelphia, Pennsylvania
Source: *ConAu 5R; SmATA 6; WhoAm 74, 76, 78, 80, 82; WhoE 74*

Bovet, Daniele
Italian. Pharmacologist
b. Mar 23, 1907 in Neuchatel, Switzerland
Source: *BioIn 4, 5, 6; CurBio 58*

Bow, Clara
American. Actress
Starred in Roaring 20's silent films; symbol of flapper age.
b. Aug 6, 1905 in New York, New York
d. Sep 27, 1965 in Los Angeles, California
Source: *BiDFilm; FilmgC; InWom; MotPP; MovMk; OxFilm; ThFT; TwYS; WebAB; WhScrn 74, 77; WhoHol B; WomWMM; WorEFlm*

Bow Wow Wow
[Annabella (Myant Myant Aye); Matthew Ashman; Dave Barbarossa; Leroy Gorman]
British. Rock Group
New Wave band put together by Malcolm McLaren, former manager of Sex Pistols.
Source: *IlEncRk; NewWmR*

Bowa, Larry (Lawrence Robert)
American. Baseball Player
Shortstop, Philadelphia, 1970--.
b. Dec 6, 1945 in Sacramento, California
Source: *BaseEn; BioIn 11; WhoProB 73; WorAl*

Bowditch, Nathaniel
American. Astronomer, Mathematician
b. Mar 26, 1773 in Salem, Massachusetts
d. Mar 16, 1838 in Boston, Massachusetts
Source: *Alli; AmAu; AmBi; ApCAB; BiDAmS; BioIn 1, 2, 3, 4, 5, 6, 7, 8; CyAL 1; DcAmAu; DcAmB; DcNAA; DcScB; Drake; EncAB-A; LinLib S; McGEWB; NatCAB 6; OxAmL; REnAL; TwCBDA; WebAB; WhAm H*

Bowdler, Thomas
English. Editor
b. Jul 11, 1754 in Ashley, England
d. Feb 24, 1825 in Rhyddings, England
Source: *Alli; BiDLA, SUP; BrAu; CasWL; Chambr 2; DcEnL; DcLEL; EvLB; NewC; OxEng*

Bowdoin, James
American. Merchant, Revolutionary Leader
Governor of MA, 1785-87; Bowdoin College founded in his honor, 1794.
b. Aug 7, 1726 in Boston, Massachusetts
d. Nov 6, 1790 in Boston, Massachusetts
Source: *Alli; AmAu&B; AmBi; ApCAB; BiAuS; CyAL 1; DcAmB; Drake; TwCBDA; WebAB; WhAm H*

Bowell, Sir Mackenzie
Canadian. Statesman
b. Dec 27, 1823
d. Dec 11, 1917
Source: *ApCAB; OxCan*

Bowen, Billy
[Ink Spots]
American. Singer
Ink Spots one of first black groups to break color barrier over airwaves.
b. 1909 in Birmingham, Alabama
d. Sep 27, 1982 in New York, New York
Source: *NF*

Bowen, Catherine Drinker
American. Author
b. Jan 1, 1897 in Haverford, Pennsylvania
d. Nov 1, 1973 in Haverford, Pennsylvania
Source: *AmAu&B; ConAu 5R, 45; CurBio 44, 73; InWom; NewYTBE 73; OxAmL; REn; REnAL; SmATA 7; TwCA SUP; WhAm 6; Who 74; WhoAm 74; WhoGov 72; WhoWor 74*

Bowen, Elizabeth Dorothea Cole
Irish. Author
Wrote *The Heat of the Day,* 1949; noted for sensitive use of language, character.
b. Jun 7, 1899 in Dublin, Ireland
d. Feb 22, 1973 in London, England
Source: *Au&Wr 71; AuBYP; CasWL; ConAu 17R, 41R; ConAu P-2; ConLC 1, 3, 6, 11, 15; ConNov 72; CyWA; DcLEL; EncWL; EvLB; LongCTC; ModBrL, SUP; NewC; OxEng; Pen ENG; RAdv 1; REn; TwCA, SUP; TwCW; WebE&AL; WhAm 5; WhoTwCL*

Bowen, Otis Ray
American. Physician, Politician
Governor of IN, 1973-81.
b. Feb 26, 1918 in Rochester, Indiana
Source: *BioIn 9; WhoAm 78, 80, 82*

Bower, Roger
American. Radio Announcer, TV Producer
b. Jan 8, 1904 in New York, New York
Source: *IntMPA 75, 76, 77*

Bowers, Claude Gernade
American. Historian
b. Nov 20, 1878? in Hamilton County, Indiana
d. Jan 21, 1958 in New York, New York
Source: *AmAu&B; CurBio 41, 58; EncAB-H; IndAu 1816; OxAmL; REn; REnAL; TwCA, SUP; WhAm 3*

Bowes, "Major" (Edward)
American. Broadcasting MC
b. Jun 14, 1874 in San Francisco, California
d. Jun 13, 1946 in New York, New York
Source: *ChPo S2; CurBio 41, 46; DcAmB S4; WhAm 2; WhScrn 77; WhoHol B*

Bowie, David
[David Robert Hayward-Jones]
English. Singer, Songwriter, Actor
Starred in movie *The Man Who Fell to Earth,* 1976.
b. Jan 8, 1947 in London, England
Source: *BioNews 74; BkPepl; RkOn; WhoAm 78, 80, 82; WhoHol A*

Bowie, James
American. Soldier, Inventor
Alleged inventor of Bowie knife; killed at Alamo.
b. 1796 in Burke County, Georgia
d. Mar 6, 1836 in The Alamo, Texas
Source: *AmBi; ApCAB; DcAmB; TwCBDA; WebAB; WhAm H*

Bowie, Norman Ernest
American. Author
b. Jun 6, 1942 in Biddeford, Maine
Source: *ConAu 33R; DrAS 74P; WhoAm 74, 76, 78, 80, 82; WhoE 74; WrDr 76*

Bowie, Walter
American. Lawyer, Spy
b. 1837
d. 1864
Source: *BioIn 3, 6*

Bowker, Albert Hosmer
American. Educator
b. Sep 8, 1919 in Winchendon, Massachusetts
Source: *AmM&WS 73P; CurBio 66; LEduc 74; NewYTBE 71; WhoAm 74, 76, 78, 80, 82; WhoWest 74*

Bowker, R(ichard) R(ogers)
American. Publisher, Editor, Author
Founded R R Bowker Co., 1872; co-founder *Library Journal,* 1876.
b. Sep 4, 1848 in Salem, Massachusetts
d. Nov 12, 1933 in Stockbridge, Massachusetts
Source: *Alli SUP; AmAu&B; BbD; BiD&SB; DcAmAu; DcAmB S1; DcNAA; WebAB; WhAm 1; WhNAA*

Bowles, Chester Bliss
American. Diplomat, Economist, Author
b. Apr 5, 1901 in Springfield, Massachusetts
Source: *AmAu&B; Au&Wr 71; BiDrAC; ConAu 69; CurBio 43, 57; IntWW 74; REnAL; Who 74; WhoAm 74; WhoAmP 73; WhoWor 74*

Bowles, Jane Sydney
American. Author
b. Feb 22, 1917 in New York, New York
d. May 4, 1973 in Malaga, Spain
Source: *AmWomWr; Au&Wr 71; BiE&WWA; BioIn 3, 7, 9, 10; ConAu 41R; ConAu P-2; ConLC 3; ConNov 72; DcLEL 1940; ModAL; NewYTBE 73; Pen AM; WhoTwCL; WorAu*

Bowles, Paul
American. Composer, Author
b. Dec 30, 1910 in New York, New York
Source: *AmAu&B; AmSCAP 66; Au&Wr 71; BiE&WWA; ConAu 1R; ConLC 1, 2; ConNov 72, 76; DrAF 76; IntWW 74; ModAL, SUP; NotNAT; OxAmL; Pen AM; RAdv 1; REnAL; TwCA SUP; TwCW; WhoAm 74, 76, 78, 80, 82; WhoE 74; WhoTwCL; WhoWor 74; WrDr 76*

Bowles, Samuel, II
American. Journalist
b. Feb 9, 1826 in Springfield, Massachusetts
d. Jan 16, 1878 in Springfield, Massachusetts
Source: *Alli SUP; AmAu&B; AmBi; BbD; BbtC; BiD&SB; DcAmAu; DcAmB; DcNAA; OxAmL; REnAL; TwCBDA; WebAB; WhAm H*

Bowles, William Augustus
American. Adventurer
b. 1763
d. 1802
Source: *BioIn 7, 8, 9*

Bowling, Roger
American. Songwriter
Wrote songs "Lucille" and "Coward of the County."
b. 1944?
d. Dec 25, 1982 in Clayton, Georgia
Source: *NF*

Bowman, Lee
American. Actor
b. Dec 26, 1914 in Cincinnati, Ohio
Source: *BiE&WWA; IntMPA 75, 76, 77; MovMk; WhoHol A*

Bowman, Scotty (William Scott)
Canadian. Hockey Player, Coach
Coach, Montreal Canadiens, 1973-79; won four Stanley Cups.
b. Sep 18, 1933 in Montreal, PQ
Source: *WhoAm 82; WhoHcky 73*

Bowra, Sir Maurice
English. Classicist
b. 1898
d. 1971
Source: *BioIn 4, 7, 9*

Bowser, Betty Ann
American. Broadcast Journalist
b. 1944 in Norfolk, Virginia
Source: *ForWC 70; WhoAm 82*

Box Tops, The
[Rick Allen; Thomas Boggs; Alex Chilton; Harold Cloud; William Cunningham; John Evans; Swain Scharfer; Daniel Smythe]
American. Rock Group
Source: *ConMuA 80; RkOn 2; WhoRock 81*

Boxleitner, Bruce
American. Actor
b. 1951? in Elgin, Illinois
Source: *BioIn 11*

Boyce, Christopher John
[Anthony Lester]
"Falcon"
American. Spy
Arrested for selling top secret documents to Soviet agents.
b. 1953? in Palos Verdes, California
Source: *BioIn 11; NewYTBS 77; PseudN*

Boyce, Westray Battle
American. Government Official
b. Aug 1901 in Rocky Mount, North Carolina
d. Jan 31, 1972 in Washington, DC
Source: *BioIn 9; CurBio 45, 72*

Boyce, William
English. Organist, Composer
b. 1710 in London, England
d. Feb 7, 1779 in Kensington, England
Source: *BioIn 9; OxMus; WebBD 80*

Boycott, Charles Cunningham
English. Land Agent
b. 1832
d. 1897
Source: *BioIn 10; WebBD 80*

Boyd, Belle
American. Spy, Actress
Confederate spy, 1861-62.
b. May 8, 1843 in Martinsburg, Virginia
d. Jun 11, 1900 in Kilbourne, Wisconsin
Source: *Alli SUP; AmAu&B; AmBi; DcAmB; DcNAA; HerW; InWom; NotAW; WhAm H*

Boyd, Bill
American. Country Singer
b. 1911 in Fannin County, Texas
Source: *EncFCWM 69*

Boyd, Julian Parks
American. Historian, Editor
Wrote *The Papers of Thomas Jefferson,* a complete written record of Jefferson.
b. Nov 3, 1903 in Converse, South Carolina
d. May 21, 1980 in Princeton, New Jersey
Source: *AmAu&B; BioIn 10, 11; ConAu 65, 97; CurBio 76, 80; DrAS 74H, 78H; REnAL; WhoAm 74, 76, 78; WhoE 74*

Boyd, Liona Maria
Canadian. Musician
b. 1949 in London, ON
Source: *BioIn 11; WhoAm 80, 82*

Boyd, Louise Arner
American. Arctic Explorer
First woman to successfully fly over N Pole, 1955.
b. Sep 16, 1887 in San Rafael, California
d. Sep 14, 1972 in San Francisco, California
Source: *BioIn 1, 5, 7, 9; CurBio 60, 72*

Boyd, Malcolm
American. Author, Clergyman
Involved in civil, gay rights; archives at Boston U.
b. Jun 8, 1923 in Buffalo, New York
Source: *AmAu&B; AmM&WS 73P; CelR 73; ConAu 5R, 4NR; WhoAm 74, 76, 78, 80, 82; WhoE 74; WhoRel 75; WhoWor 74; WrDr 76*

Boyd, Stephen
American. Actor
Played Messala in *Ben Hur,* 1959.
b. Jul 4, 1928 in Belfast, Northern Ireland
d. Jun 2, 1977 in Los Angeles, California
Source: *CmMov; CurBio 61; FilmgC; IntMPA 75, 76, 77; MotPP; MovMk; WhoAm 74; WhoHol A; WorEFlm*

Boyd, William (Bill)
"Hopalong Cassidy"
American. Actor
Best known as Hopalong Cassidy, a character he played 66 times, 1935-48.
b. Jun 5, 1898 in Cambridge, Ohio
d. Sep 12, 1972 in South Laguna, California
Source: *CmMov; CurBio 50, 72; Film 1; FilmgC; MovMk; OxFilm; WhAm 5; WhScrn 77; WhoHol B*

Boyd-Orr, John Boyd Orr, Baron
Scottish. Agriculturalist
b. Sep 23, 1880 in Kilmaurs, Scotland
d. Jun 25, 1971
Source: *CurBio 46, 71*

Boyer, Charles
French. Actor
Starred in movies *Algiers,* 1938, *Gaslight,* 1944.
b. Aug 28, 1899 in Figeac, France
d. Aug 26, 1978 in Phoenix, Arizona
Source: *BiDFilm; BiE&WWA; CelR 73; CmMov; CurBio 43, 78; FilmgC; IntMPA 75, 76, 77; MotPP; MovMk; OxFilm; WhoAm 74; WhoHol A; WhoThe 77; WhoWor 74; WorEFlm*

Boyer, Harold R
American. Businessman
b. Feb 25, 1899 in Springfield, Ohio
Source: *BioIn 2, 3; CurBio 52*

Boyer, Herbert Wayne
American. Biochemist
b. Jul 10, 1936 in Pittsburgh, Pennsylvania
Source: *AmM&WS 73P, 76P, 79P; WhoAm 78, 80, 82*

Boyer, Ken(ton Lloyd)
American. Baseball Player
Won five gold gloves; NL MVP, 1964.
b. May 20, 1931 in Liberty, Missouri
d. Sep 7, 1982 in Saint Louis, Missouri
Source: *BaseEn; CurBio 66, 82; NewYTBS 82; WhoProB 73*

Boyington, "Pappy" (Gregory)
American. Pilot
b. 1912 in Coeur d'Alene, Idaho
Source: *AmAu&B*

Boyle, Harold Vincent
American. Journalist
b. Feb 21, 1911 in Kansas City, Missouri
d. Apr 1, 1974 in New York, New York
Source: *ConAu 89, 101; CurBio 45; WhAm 6; WhoAm 74; WhoWor 74*

Boyle, Jack
"Boston Blackie"
American. Author
Source: *EncMys*

Boyle, Kay
American. Author
b. Feb 19, 1903 in Saint Paul, Minnesota
Source: *AmAu&B; AmNov; CasWL; CnDAL; ConAmA; ConAu 17R; ConLC 1, 5; ConNov 72, 76; ConP 70, 75; DcLEL; DrAF 76; DrAP 75; EncWL; ForWC 70; InWom; LongCTC; ModAL; OxAmL; Pen AM; RAdv 1; REn; REnAL; TwCA, SUP; Who 74; WhoAm 74, 76, 78, 80, 82; WhoTwCL; WhoWor 74; WrDr 76*

Boyle, Peter
American. Actor
b. 1933 in Philadelphia, Pennsylvania
Source: *FilmgC; IntMPA 75, 76, 77, 78, 79, 80, 81, 82; NewYTBE 70; WhoAm 82; WhoHol A*

Boyle, Robert
Irish. Scientist
b. 1627 in Lismore Castle, Ireland
d. Dec 30, 1691 in London, England
Source: *Alli; CasWL; CyAL 1; DcEnL; EvLB; REn*

Boyle, Tony (William Anthony)
American. Labor Union Official
President, UMW, 1963-72; convicted of 1969 murders of rival Joseph Yablonski and family.
b. Dec 1, 1904 in Bald Butte, Montana
Source: *NewYTBE 72; WhoS&SW 73*

Boylesve, Rene
French. Author
b. 1867
d. 1926
Source: *BioIn 1, 4, 5*

Bozeman, John M
American. Pioneer
b. 1835 in Georgia
d. Apr 20, 1867 in Yellowstone River, Montana
Source: *AmBi; WebAB; WhAm H*

Brabham, Jack
Australian. Auto Racer
b. 1926
Source: *BioIn 7, 8, 9, 10*

Brace, Charles Loring
American. Social Worker
b. 1826
d. 1890
Source: *BioIn 4, 6*

Brace, Gerald Warner
American. Author, Educator
b. Sep 23, 1901 in Islip, New York
d. Jul 20, 1978 in Blue Hill, Maine
Source: *AmAu&B; AmNov; Au&Wr 71; ConAu 13R, 81; CurBio 47, 78; DrAS 74E, 78E; NewYTBS 78; REnAL; TwCA SUP; WhoAm 74, 76, 78; WrDr 76*

Bracey, John Henry, Jr.
American. Author
b. Jul 17, 1941 in Chicago, Illinois
Source: *ConAu 29R; LivgBAA*

Bracken, Eddie (Edward Vincent)
American. Actor, Director, Singer, Artist
b. Feb 7, 1920 in New York, New York
Source: *BiE&WWA; BioNews 74; BusPN; CurBio 44; FilmgC; HolP 40; IntMPA 75, 76, 77, 78, 79, 80, 81, 82; MotPP; MovMk; NewYTBE 71; NotNAT; WhoAm 74, 76, 78, 80, 82; WhoHol A; WhoThe 77*

Brackman, Robert
American. Artist
b. Sep 25, 1898 in Odessa, Russia
d. Jul 16, 1980 in New London, Connecticut
Source: *CurBio 53, 80; DcCAA 71, 77; McGDA; WhoAm 74, 76, 78, 80; WhoAmA 73, 76, 78; WhoE 74*

Bradbury, Malcolm
English. Author
b. Sep 7, 1932 in Sheffield, England
Source: *Au&Wr 71; ConAu 1R; ConNov 72, 76; ConP 70; ModBrL, SUP; NewC; TwCW; WrDr 76*

Bradbury, Ray Douglas
American. Author
Has written over 1,000 science fiction stories.
b. Aug 22, 1920 in Waukegan, Illinois
Source: *AmAu&B; Au&Wr 71; AuNews 1, 2; BioNews 74; CasWL; CelR 73; CmMov; CnMWL; ConAu 1R, 2NR; ConLC 1, 3, 10, 15; ConNov 72, 76; CurBio 53, 82; DrAF 76; FilmgC; LongCTC; OxAmL; Pen AM; REn; REnAL; SmATA 11; TwCA SUP; TwCW; WebAB; Who 82; WhoAm 74, 76, 78, 80, 82; WhoWor 74; WorEFlm; WrDr 76, 80*

Braddock, Edward
English. Military Commander
b. 1695
d. Jul 13, 1755 in Fort Duquesne, Pennsylvania
Source: *AmBi; ApCAB; DcAmB; OxCan; REn; TwCBDA; WhAm H*

Braddock, James J
"Cinderella Man"
American. Boxer
b. Dec 6, 1905 in New York, New York
d. 1974 in North Bergen, New Jersey
Source: *BioNews 75; NewYTBS 74*

Brademas, John
American. Educator, Former Congressman
b. Mar 2, 1927 in Mishawaka, Indiana
Source: *AlmAP 78, 80; BiDrAC; BioIn 5, 6, 7, 10, 11; CngDr 74, 77, 79; CurBio 77; NewYTBS 81; PolProf J; PolProf NF; WhoAm 74, 76, 78; WhoAmP 73, 75, 77, 79; WhoGov 72, 75, 77; WhoMW 74, 76, 78; WhoWor 78*

Braden, Anne
American. Author, Editor
b. 1924
Source: *BioIn 8*

Braden, Spruille
American. Diplomat
b. Mar 13, 1894 in Elkhorn, Montana
d. Jan 10, 1978 in Los Angeles, California
Source: *CurBio 45; WhoAm 74; WhoWor 74*

Bradford, Gamaliel
American. Biographer
b. Oct 9, 1863 in Boston, Massachusetts
d. Apr 11, 1932
Source: *AmAu&B; AmBi; AmLY; AnMV 1926; CasWL; CnDAL; ConAmA; ConAmL; DcAmB S1; DcLEL; DcNAA; OxAmL; REnAL; TwCA, SUP; WhAm 1; WhNAA*

Bradford, Roark
American. Author
b. Aug 21, 1896 in Lauderdale City, Tennessee
d. Nov 13, 1948 in New Orleans, Louisiana
Source: *AmAu&B; AmSCAP 66; ChPo; CnDAL; DcNAA; LongCTC; OxAmL; REn; REnAL; TwCA, SUP; WhAm 2*

Bradford, William
American. Governor of Plymouth Colony
Landed at Plymouth Rock, Dec, 1620; reelected governor 30 times.
b. 1590 in Austerfield, England
d. May 9, 1657 in Plymouth, Massachusetts
Source: *Alli, SUP; AmAu; AmAu&B; AmBi; ApCAB; BbD; BiD&SB; BiDLA; CasWL; CyAL 1; DcAmAu; DcAmB; DcLEL; DcNAA; Drake; EncAB-H; EvLB; MouLC 1; OxAmL; Pen AM; REn; REnAL; TwCBDA; WebAB; WebE&AL; WhAm H; WhAmP*

Bradham, Caleb D
American. Pharmacist
Invented Pepsi-Cola, 1890's to rival Coke.
b. in New Bern, North Carolina
Source: *NF*

Bradlee, Ben(jamin Crowninshield)
American. Journalist, Editor
Washington *Post*, vice-president, executive editor, 1968--.
b. Aug 26, 1921 in Boston, Massachusetts
Source: *AuNews 2; ConAu 61; WhoAm 74, 76, 78, 80, 82; WhoS&SW 73; WhoWor 74*

Bradley, Bill (William)
American. Football Player
b. Jan 24, 1947 in Palestine, Texas
Source: *WhoFtbl 74*

Bradley, Bill (William Warren)
American. Senator, Ex-Basketball Player
Forward, NY Knicks, 1967-77; senator from NJ, 1979--.
b. Jul 28, 1943 in Crystal City, Missouri
Source: *CelR 73; CurBio 65, 82; WhoAm 82; WhoBbl 73*

Bradley, David Henry, Jr.
American. Author
b. Sep 7, 1950 in Bedford, Pennsylvania
Source: *BioIn 10, 11; ConAu 104; NewYTBS 81*

Bradley, Ed
American. Broadcast Journalist
Co-anchorman "60 Minutes," replacing Dan Rather, 1981--.
b. 1941? in Pennsylvania
Source: *WhoAm 80, 82*

Bradley, Henry
English. Philologist
b. 1845
d. 1923
Source: *Alli, SUP; DcLEL; EvLB; LongCTC; NewC; OxEng*

Bradley, James
English. Astronomer
b. Mar 1693 in Shireborn, England
d. Jul 13, 1762
Source: *Alli; BiAuS*

Bradley, Joseph P
American. Supreme Court Justice
b. Mar 14, 1813 in Berne, New York
d. Jan 22, 1892 in Washington, DC
Source: *ApCAB; BiAuS; DcAmB; DcNAA; Drake; TwCBDA; WebAB; WhAm H*

Bradley, Milton
American. Manufacturer, Publisher
First game, "The Checkered Game of Life" led to success of Milton Bradley Co.
b. Nov 8, 1836 in Vienna, Maine
d. May 30, 1911 in Springfield, Massachusetts
Source: *AmAu&B; DcAmB; DcNAA; WebAB; WhAm 1*

Bradley, Omar Nelson
"The GI's General"
American. General
Last five-star general; first permanent chairman Joint Chiefs of Staff, 1949-53.
b. Feb 12, 1893 in Clark, Missouri
d. Apr 8, 1981 in New York, New York
Source: *BioIn 1, 2, 3, 4, 6, 8, 9, 10, 11; ConAu 103; CurBio 43, 81; EncAB-A; IntWW 74, 75, 76, 77, 78; LinLib S; McGEWB; NewYTBS 81; PolProf T; PseudN; St&PR 75; WebAB; WebAMB; WhWW-II; Who 74; WhoAm 74, 76, 78, 80; WhoWor 74, 78; WorDWW*

Bradley, Tom (Thomas)
American. Politician
First black mayor of predominantly white city--Los Angeles--since 1973.
b. Dec 29, 1917 in Calvert, Texas
Source: *CurBio 73; NewYTBE 73; NewYTBS 74; WhoAm 74, 76, 78, 80, 82; WhoAmP 73; WhoWest 74*

Bradley, Will
[Wilbur Schwichtenberg]
American. Musician, Band Leader
b. Jul 12, 1912 in Newton, New Jersey
Source: *BioIn 9*

Bradshaw, Benjamin
American. Bookseller
b. 1749
d. 1779
Source: *BioIn 10*

Bradshaw, George
English. Printer
b. 1801
d. 1853
Source: *BioIn 1*

Bradshaw, Terry Paxton
American. Football Player
Quarterback, Pittsburgh Steelers, 1970--; also country, western singer.
b. Sep 2, 1948 in Shreveport, Louisiana
Source: *CelR 73; WhoAm 74, 76, 78, 80, 82; WhoFtbl 74*

Bradstreet, Anne
American. Poet
Produced first significant literary work in Colonial New England.
b. 1612 in Northampton, England
d. Sep 16, 1672 in Andover, Massachusetts
Source: *Alli; AmAu; AmAu&B; AmBi; ApCAB; BiD&SB; CasWL; ChPo, S2; CnDAL; CnE&AP; CyAL 1; DcAmAu; DcAmB; DcEnL; DcLEL; DcNAA; Drake; EvLB; HerW; InWom; NotAW; OxAmL; OxEng; Pen; RAdv 1; REn; REnAL; TwCBDA; WebAB; WebE&AL; WhAm H*

Brady, Alice
American. Actress
b. Nov 2, 1893 in New York, New York
d. Oct 28, 1939 in New York, New York
Source: *AmBi; DcAmB S2; Film 1; FilmgC; InWom; MotPP; MovMk; NotAW; OxThe; ThFT; TwYS; Vers A; WebAB; WhAm 1; WhScrn 74, 77; WhoHol B*

Brady, "Diamond Jim" (James Buchanan)
American. Financier
Jewelry collection valued at $2 million.
b. Aug 12, 1856 in New York, New York
d. Apr 13, 1917 in Atlantic City, New Jersey
Source: *AmBi; WebAB; WhAm 4*

Brady, James
American. Editor, Publisher
b. Nov 15, 1928 in Brooklyn, New York
Source: *CelR 73; ConAu 101*

Brady, James Scott
"The Bear"
American. Presidential Press Secretary
Shot during Reagan assassination attempt, 1981.
b. Aug 29, 1940 in Centralia, Illinois
Source: *NewYTBS 81; PseudN*

Brady, Mathew B
American. Photographer
Compiled pictorial record of Civil War.
b. 1823? in Warren County, New York
d. Jan 15, 1896 in New York, New York
Source: *AmAu&B; AmBi; DcAmB; EncAB-H; OxAmL; REn; REnAL; WebAB*

Brady, Pat
American. Actor, Singer
b. Dec 31, 1914 in Toledo, Ohio
d. Feb 27, 1972 in Green Mountain Falls, Colorado
Source: *NewYTBE 72; WhScrn 77; WhoHol B*

Brady, Scott
[Gerard Kenneth Tierney]
American. Actor
b. Sep 13, 1924 in Brooklyn, New York
Source: *FilmgC; HolP 40; IntMPA 75, 76, 77, 78, 79, 80, 81, 82; MotPP; WhoAm 74, 76, 78, 80, 82; WhoHol A*

Brady, William Aloysius
American. Actor, Motion Picture Producer
b. Jun 19, 1863 in San Francisco, California
d. Jan 6, 1950 in New York, New York
Source: *DcAmB S4; OxThe; WebAB; WhAm 2*

Braff, Ruby
American. Jazz Musician
b. Mar 16, 1927 in Boston, Massachusetts
Source: *BioIn 10*

Bragg, Braxton
American. Confederate General
Commander-in-chief, Confederate Army, 1864-65.
b. Mar 22, 1817 in Warrenton, North Carolina
d. Sep 27, 1876 in Galveston, Texas
Source: *AmBi; ApCAB; BiDConf; DcAmB; TwCBDA; WebAB; WhAm H*

Bragg, Donald
American. Track Athlete
b. 1935
Source: *BioIn 9, 10*

Bragg, Sir Lawrence
English. Physicist
b. 1890
d. Jul 1, 1971 in London, England
Source: *BioIn 3, 9, 10*

Bragg, Melvyn
English. Author, Broadcaster
b. Oct 6, 1939 in Carlisle, England
Source: *ConAu 57; ConNov 72, 76; Who 74; WrDr 76*

Brahe, Tyge
Danish. Astronomer
b. Dec 14, 1546
d. Oct 24, 1601
Source: *BioIn 10*

Brahms, Johannes
German. Composer, Pianist
"Brahm's Lullaby" part of song cycle "Weigenlied," officially called Opus 49, no. 4.
b. May 7, 1833 in Hamburg, Germany
d. Apr 3, 1897 in Vienna, Austria
Source: *AtlBL; NewC; OxGer; REn*

Braid, James
"Big Jim"; "Great Triumvirate"
Scottish. Golfer
b. 1870 in Fifeshire, Scotland
d. Nov 27, 1950 in London, England
Source: *BioIn 2, 3; WhoGolf*

Braille, Louis
French. Teacher of the Blind
Blinded at age 3; devised system of raised-point writing.
b. Jan 14, 1809 in Coupvray, France
d. Jan 6, 1852
Source: *OxFr; REn*

Brailowsky, Alexander
American. Musician
b. Feb 16, 1896 in Kiev, Russia
d. Apr 25, 1976 in New York, New York
Source: *CurBio 56; WhoAm 74; WhoMus 72; WhoWor 74*

Brain, Aubrey
English. Musician
b. Jul 12, 1893 in London, England
d. Sep 21, 1955 in London, England
Source: *Baker 78*

Brain, Dennis
English. Musician
b. May 17, 1921 in London, England
d. Sep 1, 1957 in Hatfield, England
Source: *Baker 78*

Braine, John
English. Author
b. Apr 13, 1922 in Yorkshire, England
Source: *Au&Wr 71; CasWL; ConAu 1R; ConLC 1, 3; ConNov 72, 76; LongCTC; ModBrL, SUP; NewC; Pen ENG; RAdv 1; REn; TwCW; WebE&AL; Who 74; WorAu; WrDr 76; WhoWor 74*

Braithwaite, William Stanley
American. Critic, Poet
b. Dec 6, 1878 in Boston, Massachusetts
d. Jun 8, 1962
Source: *AmAu&B; BlkAW; ChPo, S1, S2; OxAmL; REn; REnAL; TwCA*

Brakhage, Stan
American. Author, Motion Picture Producer
b. Jan 14, 1933 in Kansas City, Missouri
Source: *AmAu&B; ConAu 41R; DcFM; OxFilm; WhoAm 74; WorEFlm; WrDr 76*

Braly, Malcolm
American. Author
Wrote novel and screenplay *On the Yard,* filmed in 1979.
b. Jul 16, 1925 in Portland, Oregon
d. Apr 7, 1980 in Baltimore, Maryland
Source: *BioIn 8, 10, 11, 12; ConAu 21R, 97*

Bramah, Joseph
English. Inventor
Patented hydraulic press, called Bramah press, 1795.
b. Apr 13, 1749
d. Dec 9, 1814
Source: *BioIn 2, 7, 8*

Bramante, Donata d'Agnolo
Italian. Architect
b. 1444 in Urbino, Italy
d. Mar 11, 1514
Source: *NewCol 75*

Brambell, Wilfrid
Irish. Actor
b. 1912 in Dublin, Ireland
Source: *FilmgC; IntMPA 75, 76, 77, 78, 79, 80, 81, 82; WhoThe 72, 77*

Bramlett, Delaney
see: Delaney and Bonnie

Branca, Ralph Theodore Joseph
"Hawk"
American. Baseball Player
b. Jan 6, 1926 in Mount Vernon, New York
Source: *BaseEn; WhoProB 73*

Brancusi, Constantin
Romanian. Sculptor
b. Feb 21, 1876 in Pestisanigorj, Romania
d. Mar 16, 1957 in Paris, France
Source: *AtlBL; CurBio 55, 57; REn; WhAm 3*

Brand, Jack
Canadian. Soccer Player
b. Aug 4, 1953 in Braunschweig, Germany (West)
Source: *AmEnS; BioIn 12*

Brand, Max, pseud.
[Frederick Schiller Faust]
American. Author
b. May 29, 1892 in Seattle, Washington
d. May 12, 1944 in Italy
Source: *AmAu&B; CurBio 44; DcAmB S3; DcLEL; DcNAA; EncMys; FilmgC; LongCTC; MnBBF; REn; REnAL; TwCA, SUP; WebAB*

Brand, Neville
American. Actor
b. Aug 13, 1921 in Kewanee, Illinois
Source: *FilmgC; IntMPA 75, 76, 77, 78, 79, 80, 81, 82; MotPP; WhoAm 74, 76, 78, 80, 82; WhoHol A*

Brand, Oscar
Canadian. Singer, Author
b. Feb 7, 1920 in Winnipeg, MB
Source: *AmAu&B; AuBYP; ConAu 1R, 4NR; CurBio 62; EncFCWM 69; NatPD; NotNAT; WhoAm 74, 76, 78, 80, 82; WhoWor 74; WhoWorJ 72; WrDr 76*

Brand, Stewart
American. Ecologist, Author, Editor
b. Dec 14, 1938 in Rockford, Illinois
Source: *AuNews 1; ConAu 81; WhoAm 74, 76, 78, 80, 82*

Brand, Vance DeVoe
American. Astronaut
Crew member, joint US/USSR space mission, 1973-75.
b. May 9, 1931 in Longmont, Colorado
Source: *IntWW 74; WhoAm 74, 76, 78, 80, 82; WhoF&I 74; WhoGov 72; WhoS&SW 73*

Brandeis, Louis Dembitz
American. Supreme Court Justice
b. Nov 13, 1856 in Louisville, Kentucky
d. Oct 5, 1941 in Washington, DC
Source: *CurBio 41; DcAmB S3; DcNAA; EncAB-H; OxAmL; REn; REnAL; WebAB; WhAm 1; WhNAA*

Brandes, Gèorg Morris Cohen
German. Literary Critic, Historian
b. Feb 4, 1842 in Copenhagen, Denmark
d. Feb 19, 1927 in Berlin, Germany
Source: *BbD; BiD&SB; CasWL; ClDMEL; DcEuL; EncWL; EvEuW; LongCTC; OxGer; OxThe; Pen EUR; REn; TwCA, SUP; TwCW*

Brando, Marlon
American. Actor
Won Oscars, 1954, for *On the Waterfront;* 1972, for *The Godfather.*
b. Apr 3, 1924 in Omaha, Nebraska
Source: *BiDFilm; BiE&WWA; BkPepl; CelR 73; CurBio 52, 74; FilmgC; IntMPA 75, 76, 77, 78, 79, 80, 81, 82; IntWW 74; MotPP; MovMk; OxFilm; PlP&P; WebAB; Who 82; WhoAm 74, 76, 78, 80, 82; WhoHol A; WhoWor 74; WorEFlm*

Brandon, Brumsic, Jr.
American. Artist, Author
b. Apr 10, 1927 in Washington, DC
Source: *AfroAA; ConAu 61; SmATA 9; WhoAm 82; WhoBlA 75*

Brandon, Henry Oscar
American. Author, Editor
b. Mar 9, 1916
Source: *BioIn 8; ConAu 49; IntWW 76; Who 74; WhoAm 74; WhoS&SW 73*

Brandt, Bill
English. Photographer
b. 1904 in London, England
Source: *BioIn 10, 11; CurBio 81*

Brandt, Willy
German. Former Chancellor, Mayor
Won Nobel Peace Prize, 1971, for peace efforts between USSR and W Germany.
b. Dec 18, 1913 in Luebeck, Germany
Source: *ConAu 85; CurBio 58, 73; IntWW 74; NewYTBE 71; Who 74; WhoGov 72; WhoWor 74*

Brangwyn, Sir Frank
English. Artist
b. May 13, 1867 in Bruges, Belgium
d. Jun 11, 1956
Source: *BioIn 7; ChPo; WhAm 3*

Braniff, Thomas Elmer
American. Airline Executive
Founded Braniff International Airways.
b. Dec 6, 1883 in Salina, Kansas
d. Jan 9, 1954
Source: *BioIn 2, 3, 4; CurBio 52, 54; WhAm 3*

Branley, Franklyn Mansfield
American. Educator, Author
b. Jun 5, 1915 in New Rochelle, New York
Source: *AmM&WS 73P; Au&Wr 71; AuBYP; BkP; ConAu 33R; MorJA; SmATA 4; WhoAm 74*

Brann, William Cowper
American. Journalist, Editor
b. Jan 4, 1855 in Humboldt, Illinois
d. Apr 2, 1898 in Waco, Texas
Source: *AmAu; AmAu&B; DcAmB S1; DcNAA; OxAmL; REnAL; WhAm H*

Brannan, Samuel
American. Pioneer
Published San Francisco's first newspaper, *The California Star*, 1847.
b. Mar 2, 1819 in Saco, Maine
d. May 5, 1889 in Escondido, California
Source: *AmBi; ApCAB; DcAmB; NewCol 75; TwCBDA; WebAB; WhAm H; WhAmP*

Branner, Martin Michael
American. Cartoonist
b. Dec 28, 1888 in New York, New York
d. May 19, 1970 in New London, Connecticut
Source: *NewYTBE 70; WhAm 5*

Brannigan, Bill
American. Author
b. Jan 12, 1936 in Long Island, New York
Source: *ConAu 65*

Brannigan, Owen
English. Actor, Singer
b. 1909 in Annitsford, England
d. May 9, 1973 in Newcastle, England
Source: *WhScrn 77; WhoMus 72*

Brant, Alice Dayrell
[Helena Morley]
Brazilian. Diarist
b. 1880?
Source: *BioIn 4*

Brant, Joseph
[Thayendanegea]
American Indian. Mohawk Chief
b. 1742 in Ohio
d. Nov 24, 1807 in Wellington Square, ON
Source: *Alli; AmBi; ApCAB; BbtC; DcAmB; OxAmL; OxCan; REn; REnAL; TwCBDA; WebAB; WhAm H*

Branzell, Karin
Swedish. Opera Singer
b. Sep 24, 1891 in Stockholm, Sweden
d. Dec 15, 1974 in Altadena, California
Source: *CurBio 46, 75; NewYTBS 74; WhAm 6*

Braque, Georges
French. Artist
Founded Cubism with Picasso, 1907; developed the collage, 1911.
b. May 13, 1882 in Argenteuil, France
d. Aug 31, 1963 in Paris, France
Source: *CurBio 49, 63; REn; WhAm 4; WhoGrA*

Brasch, Rudolph
German. Rabbi, Author
b. Nov 6, 1912 in Berlin, Germany
Source: *Au&Wr 71; ConAu 21R; WhoWor 74; WhoWorJ 72; WrDr 76*

Brasher, Rex
American. Ornithologist, Artist, Author
b. Jul 31, 1869 in Brooklyn, New York
d. Feb 29, 1960 in Kent, Connecticut
Source: *WhAm 5; WhNAA*

Brashler, William
American. Author
b. Aug 11, 1947 in Grand Rapids, Michigan
Source: *ConAu 45, 2NR*

Braslau, Sophie
American. Opera Singer
b. Aug 16, 1892 in New York, New York
d. Dec 22, 1935 in New York, New York
Source: *DcAmB S1; NotAW; WhAm 1*

Brassai
[Gyula Halasz]
French. Photographer
b. 1899
Source: *BioIn 10*

Brasselle, Keefe
[John J Brasselli]
American. Actor, Producer
b. Feb 7, 1923 in Lorain, Ohio
d. Jul 7, 1981 in Downey, California
Source: *AmSCAP 66; BioIn 8; FilmgC; IntMPA 75, 76, 77, 78, 79, 80, 81; MotPP; NewYTET; PseudN; WhoHol A*

Brassens, Georges
French. Singer, Poet
b. Oct 22, 1921 in Sete, France
d. Oct 30, 1981 in Sete, France
Source: *BioIn 7, 8, 9; IntWW 75, 76, 77, 78; WhoMus 72*

Bratkowski, Zeke (Edmund R)
American. Football Player
b. Oct 20, 1931 in Danville, Illinois
Source: *WhoFtbl 74*

Brattain, Walter Houser
American. Physicist
b. Feb 10, 1902 in Amoy, China
Source: *AmM&WS 73P; CurBio 57; IntWW 74; WebAB; Who 74; WhoAm 74, 76, 78, 80, 82; WhoWor 74*

Bratteli, Trygve Martin
Norwegian. Journalist, Politician
b. Jan 11, 1910 in Notteroy, Norway
Source: *IntWW 74; NewYTBE 71; WhoWor 74*

Brauchitsch, Heinrich Alfred
German. Military Officer
b. Oct 4, 1881 in Berlin, Germany
d. Oct 18, 1948
Source: *CurBio 40, 48*

Brauer, Jerald Carl
American. Educator, Historian
b. Sep 16, 1921 in Fond du Lac, Wisconsin
Source: *AmAu&B; ConAu 33R; DrAS 74P; IntWW 74; WhoAm 74, 76, 78, 80, 82; WhoWor 74; WrDr 76*

Brauer, Max Julius Friedrich
German. Mayor
b. 1887
d. Feb 1, 1973 in Bonn, Germany (West)
Source: *NewYTBE 73*

Braun, Eva
German. Wife of Adolf Hitler
Married Hitler a few days before their suicides.
b. Feb 6, 1912
d. Apr 30, 1945 in Berlin, Germany
Source: *BioIn 10*

Braun, Karl Ferdinand
German. Physicist
b. Jun 6, 1850 in Fulda, Germany
d. Apr 20, 1918 in New York, New York
Source: *AsBiEn; BioIn 1, 2, 3*

Braun, Otto
German. Communist Leader
b. 1901
d. Aug 15, 1974 in Berlin, Germany (West)
Source: *NewYTBS 74*

Brautigan, Richard
American. Author, Poet
b. 1935 in Tacoma, Washington
Source: *AmAu&B; CelR 73; ConAu 53; ConLC 1, 3, 5, 9, 12; ConNov 72, 76; ConP 70; DrAF 76; DrAP 75; ModAL SUP; Pen AM; WhoAm 82; WrDr 76*

Brawley, Benjamin Griffith
American. Clergyman, Educator
b. Apr 22, 1882 in Columbia, South Carolina
d. Feb 1, 1939 in Washington, DC
Source: *AmAu&B; AmLY; BlkAW; DcNAA; REnAL; TwCA, SUP; WhNAA*

Braxton, Carter
American. Continental Congressman
b. Sep 10, 1736 in Newington, Virginia
d. Oct 10, 1797 in Richmond, Virginia
Source: *AmBi; ApCAB; BiAuS; BiDrAC; DcAmB; Drake; TwCBDA; WhAm H; WhAmP*

Bray, Charles William, III
American. Government Official
Deputy director, US Information Agency, 1977-81; ambassador to Senegal, 1981--.
b. Oct 24, 1933 in New York, New York
Source: *NewYTBE 70; USBiR 74; WhoAm 82*

Brayman, Harold
American. Educator, Journalist
b. Mar 10, 1900 in Middleburgh, New York
Source: *ConAu 25R, 73; WhoAm 74, 76, 78, 80, 82; WhoE 74; WhoF&I 74; WhoPubR 72*

Brayton, Matthew
American. Indian Captive
b. Apr 7, 1818 in Sandusky County, Ohio
d. 1862
Source: *BioIn 8, 11; OhA&B*

Brazelton, T(homas) Berry
American. Pediatrician, Author
Researcher in child development; wrote *On Becoming a Family*.
b. May 10, 1918 in Waco, Texas
Source: *ConAu 97; WhoAm 74, 76, 78, 80, 82*

Brazle, Al(pha Eugene)
"Cotton"
American. Baseball Player
b. Oct 19, 1914 in Loyal, Oklahoma
d. Oct 24, 1973 in Grand Junction, Colorado
Source: *BaseEn; NewYTBE 73*

Brazzi, Rossano
Italian. Actor
b. Sep 18, 1916 in Bologna, Italy
Source: *CmMov; CurBio 61; FilmgC; IntMPA 75, 76, 77, 78, 79, 80, 81, 82; MotPP; MovMk; WhoHol A*

Bread
[Mike Botts; David Gates; James Gordon; James Grifin; Larry Knechtel; Robb Royer]
American. Singing Group
Hit songs include "If," "Diary," "Make It with You."
Source: *IlEncRk*

Bream, Julian
English. Musician
b. Jul 15, 1933 in London, England
Source: *IntWW 74; Who 74; WhoAm 82; WhoMus 72; WhoWor 74*

Breasted, James Henry
American. Archaeologist, Historian
b. Aug 27, 1865 in Rockford, Illinois
d. Dec 2, 1933 in New York, New York
Source: *AmAu&B; AmBi; AmLY; DcAmB S1; DcLEL; DcNAA; EvLB; LongCTC; OxAmL; REn; REnAL; TwCA, SUP; WebAB; WhAm 1; WhNAA*

Brecheen, Harry David
"The Cat"
American. Baseball Player
First left-handed pitcher to win three World Series games, 1946.
b. Oct 14, 1914 in Broken Bow, Oklahoma
Source: *BaseEn; BioIn 1, 2; WhoProB 73*

Brecht, Bertolt Eugene Friedrich
German. Poet, Dramatist
Wrote *The Three Penny Opera,* 1928.
b. Feb 10, 1898 in Augsburg, Germany
d. Aug 14, 1956 in Berlin, Germany (East)
Source: *AtlBL; CasWL; ClDMEL; CnMD; CnMWL; CnThe; CroCD; CyWA; DcFM; EncWL; EvEuW; FilmgC; LongCTC; McGEWD; ModGL; ModWD; OxEng; OxFilm; OxGer; OxThe; Pen EUR; RComWL; REn; REnWD; TwCA, SUP; TwCW; WhAm HA; WhoTwCL; WorEFlm*

Breck, John Henry
American. Businessman
Founded Breck, Inc., 1929.
b. Jun 5, 1877 in Holyoke, Massachusetts
d. Feb 16, 1965 in Springfield, Massachusetts
Source: *WhAm 4*

Breckinridge, John
American. Statesman
b. Dec 2, 1760 in Augusta County, Virginia
d. Dec 14, 1806 in Lexington, Kentucky
Source: *BiDSA; BioIn 3, 8, 10*

Breckinridge, John Cabell
American. Lawyer, Statesman, General
b. Jan 21, 1821 in Lexington, Kentucky
d. May 17, 1875 in Lexington, Kentucky
Source: *AmBi; ApCAB; BiAuS; BiDConf; BiDSA; BiDrAC; BiDrUSE; DcAmB; Drake; EncAB-H; TwCBDA; WebAB; WhAmP*

Breckinridge, Mary
American. Nurse
b. 1881
d. 1965
Source: *BioIn 2, 3, 7, 8, 9, 11*

Breckinridge, Sophonisba Preston
American. Social Reformer
First woman admitted to Bar in KY, 1897.
b. Apr 1, 1866 in Lexington, Kentucky
d. Jul 30, 1948
Source: *BiDAmEd; DcAmB S4; EncAB-H; NatCAB; NotAW; WhAm 2; WomWWA 14A*

Breech, Ernest Robert
American. Industrialist
b. Feb 24, 1897 in Lebanon, Missouri
d. Jul 3, 1978 in Royal Oak, Michigan
Source: *BioIn 2, 3, 4, 5, 7, 8, 11; CurBio 55; Who 74; WhoAm 74; WhoF&I 74*

Breedlove, (Norman) Craig
American. Auto Racer
b. Mar 23, 1938 in Costa Mesa, California
Source: *BioIn 6, 7, 8, 9, 10*

Breese, Edmund
American. Actor, Dramatist
b. Jun 18, 1871 in Brooklyn, New York
d. Apr 6, 1936 in New York, New York
Source: *Film 1; TwYS; WhAm 1; WhScrn 74, 77; WhoHol B; WhoStg 1906, 1908*

Breger, Dave
American. Cartoonist, Illustrator
b. 1908 in Chicago, Illinois
d. Jan 16, 1970 in South Nyack, New York
Source: *NewYTBE 70*

Brel, Jacques
Belgian. Songwriter
b. Apr 8, 1929 in Brussels, Belgium
d. Oct 9, 1978 in Bobigny, France
Source: *CelR 73; CurBio 71; WhoE 74; WhoHol A; WhoWor 74*

Bremer, Arthur Herman
American. Attempted Assassin
Shot George Wallace, May 5, 1972 in Lowell, MD.
b. Aug 21, 1950 in Milwaukee, Wisconsin
Source: *NewYTBE 72*

Brendan of Clonfert, Saint
Irish. Monk
b. 484 in Tralee, Ireland
d. 577
Source: *BioIn 1, 2, 3, 4, 5, 6, 7, 8, 10; NewC; OxFr*

Brendel, Alfred
Austrian. Musician
b. Jan 5, 1931 in Wisenberg, Austria
Source: *IntWW 74; Who 74; WhoMus 72; WhoWor 74*

Brendel, El
American. Actor, Comedian
b. Mar 25, 1890 in Philadelphia, Pennsylvania
d. Apr 9, 1964 in Hollywood, California
Source: *FilmgC; MovMk; TwYS; Vers A; WhScrn 74, 77; WhoHol B*

Breneman, Tom
American. Actor
b. 1902
d. Apr 28, 1948 in Encino, California
Source: *BioIn 1; WhScrn 74, 77; WhoHol B*

Brennan, Eileen Regina
American. Actress
Starred in movie, TV series *Private Benjamin.*
b. Sep 3, 1937? in Los Angeles, California
Source: *BiE&WWA; IntMPA 75, 76, 77, 78, 79, 80, 81, 82; NotNAT; WhoAm 82; WhoHol A*

Brennan, Peter Joseph
American. Government Official
Secretary of Labor, 1973-74.
b. May 24, 1918 in New York, New York
Source: *BioNews 74; BusPN; CelR 73; CngDr 74; CurBio 73; IntWW 74; NewYTBE 72; WhoAm 74; WhoAmP 73*

Brennan, Walter Andrew
American. Actor
First actor to win three Oscars, 1936, 1938, 1940.
b. Jul 25, 1894 in Lynn, Massachusetts
d. Sep 22, 1974 in Oxnard, California
Source: *BiDFilm; BioNews 74; CelR 73; CmMov; CurBio 41, 74; FilmgC; IntMPA 75; MotPP; MovMk; NewYTBS 74; OxFilm; TwYS; Vers A; WhAm 6; WhScrn 77; WhoAm 74; WhoHol B; WhoWor 74; WorEFlm*

Brennan, William Joseph
American. Supreme Court Justice
Liberal; appointed by Dwight Eisenhower, 1956.
b. Apr 25, 1906 in Newark, New Jersey
Source: *CelR 73; CngDr 74; CurBio 57; DrAS 74P; IntWW 74; WebAB; Who 74; WhoAm 74, 76, 78, 80, 82; WhoAmP 73; WhoGov 72; WhoS&SW 73*

Brenner, Barbara Johnes
American. Author
b. Jun 26, 1925 in Brooklyn, New York
Source: *AuBYP; ConAu 9R; ForWC 70; SmATA 4*

Brenner, David
American. Comedian
Nightclub performer; named Las Vegas entertainer of year, 1977.
b. Feb 4, 1945 in Philadelphia, Pennsylvania
Source: *BioIn 10, 11; WhoAm 78, 80, 82*

Brent, Evelyn
American. Actress
b. Oct 20, 1899 in Tampa, Florida
d. Jun 7, 1975 in Los Angeles, California
Source: *Film 1; FilmgC; MotPP; MovMk; ThFT; TwYS; WhScrn 77*

Brent, George
American. Actor
b. Mar 15, 1904 in Dublin, Ireland
d. 1979 in Solana Beach, California
Source: *CmMov; FilmgC; IntMPA 75, 76, 77; MotPP; MovMk; WhoHol A*

Brent, Margaret
American. Feminist
First woman landowner in MD.
b. 1600 in Gloucester, England
d. 1671
Source: *BiCAW; DcAmB; WhAm H; WhAmP*

Brent, Romney
Actor, Dramatist, Director
b. Jan 26, 1902 in Saltillo, Mexico
d. Sep 24, 1976
Source: *BiE&WWA; FilmgC; NotNAT; PlP&P; WhoHol A; WhoThe 72, 81*

Brentano, Clemens Maria
German. Dramatist, Author, Poet
b. Sep 8, 1778 in Ehrenbrehstein, Germany
d. Jul 28, 1842
Source: *BbD; BiD&SB; CasWL; ChPo S1; DcEuL; EuAu; EvEuW; OxGer; Pen EUR; REn*

Bresler, Jerry
American. Composer, Author
b. May 29, 1912 in Chicago, Illinois
Source: *AmSCAP 66; FilmgC; IntMPA 75, 76, 77; WorEFlm*

Breslin, Jimmy
American. Author, Journalist
Wrote, *The Gang that Couldn't Shoot Straight,* 1969, filmed, 1971.
b. Oct 17, 1930 in Jamaica, New York
Source: *AmAu&B; AuNews 1; CelR 73; ConLC 4; CurBio 73; WhoAm 74, 76, 78, 80, 82; WhoE 74; WhoWor 74; WrDr 76, 80*

Bresnaham, Roger Phillip
"The Duke of Tralee"
American. Baseball Player
Catcher, 1897-1915; Hall of Fame, 1945.
b. Jun 11, 1879 in Toledo, Ohio
d. Dec 4, 1944 in Toledo, Ohio
Source: *BaseEn; BioIn 3, 7, 8, 10; WhoProB 73*

Bresson, Henri Cartier
see: Cartier-Bresson, Henri

Bresson, Robert
French. Motion Picture Director
b. Sep 25, 1907 in Bromont-Lamothe, France
Source: *BiDFilm; CurBio 71; DcFM; FilmgC; MovMk; OxFilm; Who 74; WorEFlm*

Breton, Andre
French. Poet
Founded Surrealist movement, 1924; wrote *Surrealist of Manifesto.*
b. Feb 18, 1896 in Normandy, France
d. Sep 28, 1966 in Paris, France
Source: *AtlBL; CasWL; ClDMEL; ConAu 25R; ConAu P-2; ConLC 2, 9, 15; EncWL; EvEuW; LongCTC; ModRL; ModWD; OxFr; Pen EUR; RComWL; REn; REnWD; TwCA SUP; TwCW; WhAm 4; WhoTwCL*

Breton, Jules Adolphe
French. Artist, Author
b. 1827 in Calais, France
d. 1906
Source: *LinLib L, S*

Bretonneau, Pierre
French. Epidemiologist
b. Apr 3, 1778
d. Feb 18, 1862
Source: *BioIn 9*

Brett, George Howard
"Mulletthead"
American. Baseball Player
Infielder, KC Royals, 1973--; won batting title, 1976, 1980.
b. May 15, 1953 in Glendale, West Virginia
Source: *BaseEn; BioIn 10, 11, 12; CurBio 81; WhoAm 78, 80, 82*

Brett, Jeremy
[Jeremy Huggins]
English. Actor
b. Nov 3, 1935 in Berkswell, England
Source: *FilmgC; WhoHol A; WhoThe 77*

Brett, Ken(neth Alvin)
American. Baseball Player
b. Sep 18, 1948 in Brooklyn, New York
Source: *BaseEn*

Brett, Simon Anthony Lee
English. Author
b. Oct 28, 1945 in Worcester, England
Source: *ConAu 69; TwCCr&M*

Bretz, Jerry Harlen
American. Geologist
b. Sep 1882 in Ionia County, Michigan
d. Feb 3, 1981 in Homewood, Illinois
Source: *NewYTBS 81; WhNAA*

Breuer, Marcel Lajos
American. Designer, Architect
b. May 22, 1902 in Pecs, Hungary
d. Jul 1, 1981 in New York, New York
Source: *AmArch 70; BioIn 1, 2, 4, 5, 6, 7, 8, 9, 10, 11; BnEnAmA; CelR 73; ConAu 5R, 104, 5NR; CurBio 41, 60, 81; DcNiCA; EncMA; IntAu&W 76; IntWW 74, 75, 76, 77, 78; McGDA; McGEWB; NewYTBS 81; OxDecA; PlP&P; WhoArch; WhoWor 74*

Breuil, Henri Abbe
French. Cataloger
b. 1877
d. 1961
Source: *LongCTC*

Brewer, David Josiah
American. Supreme Court Justice
b. Jun 20, 1837 in Smyrna, Turkey
d. Mar 28, 1910 in Washington, DC
Source: *AmBi; ApCAB; DcAmAu; DcAmB; DcNAA; TwCBDA; WebAB; WhAm 1*

Brewer, Ebenezer
English. Clergyman, Educator
b. May 2, 1810 in London, England
d. Mar 6, 1897
Source: *Alli, SUP; BiD&SB; ChPo; DcEnL; EvLB; NewC*

Brewer, Jim
"Papa"
American. Basketball Player
b. Dec 3, 1951 in Maywood, Illinois
Source: *WhoBbl 73*

Brewer, Theresa
American. Singer, Actress
b. May 7, 1931 in Toledo, Ohio
Source: *InWom*

Brewer and Shipley
[Michael Brewer; Thomas Shipley]
American. Folk Singers
Source: *RkOn*

Brewster, Sir David
Scottish. Philosopher, Scientist
b. Dec 11, 1781 in Jedburgh, Scotland
d. Feb 10, 1868
Source: *Alli; BiDLA; BioIn 1, 4, 8; BrAu 19; CasWL; Chambr 3; DcEnA; DcEnL; EvLB*

Brewster, Kingman, Jr.
American. Educator, Lawyer
b. Jun 17, 1919 in Longmeadow, Massachusetts
Source: *CelR 73; CurBio 64; DrAS 74P; EncAB-H; IntWW 74; LEduc 74; NewYTBE 70; Who 74; WhoAm 74, 76, 78, 80, 82; WhoE 74; WhoWor 74*

Brewster, Owen
American. Politician
b. Feb 22, 1888 in Dexter, Maine
d. Dec 25, 1961 in Brookline, Massachusetts
Source: *BioIn 1, 3, 6; CurBio 47, 62*

Brewster, William
English. Colonial Leader
b. 1566 in Nottinghamshire, England
d. Apr 10, 1644 in Plymouth, Massachusetts
Source: *Alli; AmBi; ApCAB; BiDLA; DcAmB; Drake; TwCBDA; WebAB; WhAm H; WhAmP*

Brezhnev, Leonid Ilyich
Russian. Communist Leader
b. Dec 19, 1906 in Kamenskoye, Russia
d. Nov 10, 1982 in Moscow, U.S.S.R.
Source: *BioNews 74; CurBio 78, 83; DcPol; IntWW 74, 75, 76, 77, 78, 79, 80, 81; IntYB 78, 79, 80, 81; LinLib S; McGEWB; NewYTBE 71, 72, 73; WhDW; Who 74, 82; WhoWor 74, 76, 78; WorAl*

Brian Boru
Irish. King, National Hero
b. 926
d. Apr 23, 1014 in Clontarf, Ireland
Source: *NewC; REn*

Brian, David
American. Actor
b. Aug 5, 1914 in New York, New York
Source: *FilmgC; IntMPA 75, 76, 77, 78, 79, 80, 81, 82; MotPP; WhoHol A*

Brian, Donald
American. Actor, Singer
b. Feb 17, 1875 in Saint John's, NF
d. Dec 22, 1948 in Great Neck, New York
Source: *EncMT; Film 1; WhAm 2; WhScrn 74, 77; WhoHol B; WhoStg 1908*

Brian, Marcel
French. Author
b. Nov 21, 1895 in Marseilles, France
Source: *Au&Wr 71; IntWW 74; WhoWor 74*

Briand, Aristide
French. Statesman
b. Mar 28, 1862 in Nantes, France
d. Mar 7, 1932 in Paris, France
Source: *BioIn 11; McGEWB*

Briand, Rena
Canadian. Journalist, Author
b. Nov 12, 1935
Source: *ConAu 29R; WrDr 76*

Brice, Fanny
[Fanny Borach]
"Baby Snooks"
American. Actress, Singer
Movies *Funny Girl*, 1968, *Funny Lady*, 1975, depict her life.
b. Oct 29, 1891 in New York, New York
d. May 29, 1951 in Beverly Hills, California
Source: *CurBio 46, 51; DcAmB S5; EncMT; FamA&A; FilmgC; InWom; MovMk; OxFilm; PlP&P; ThFT; WhAm 3; WhScrn 74, 77; WhoHol B*

Bricker, John William
American. Politician, Lawyer
b. Sep 6, 1893 in Madison County, Ohio
Source: *BiDrAC; CurBio 43, 56; St&PR 75; Who 74; WhoAm 74, 76, 78, 80, 82; WhoAmP 73*

Bricklin, Malcolm N
American. Corporation Executive
b. Mar 9, 1939 in Philadelphia, Pennsylvania
Source: *BusPN; WhoF&I 74*

Brickman, Morrie
American. Cartoonist
b. Jul 24, 1917 in Chicago, Illinois
Source: *WhoAm 78, 80, 82*

Brico, Antonia
American. Symphony Conductor
b. Jun 26, 1902 in Rotterdam, Netherlands
Source: *CurBio 48; InWom; WhoAm 74, 76, 78, 80, 82*

Bridge, Frank
English. Composer, Conductor
b. Feb 26, 1879 in Brighton, England
d. Jan 11, 1941 in London, England
Source: *CurBio 41; DcCM*

Bridger, James
American. Fur Trapper
b. Mar 11, 1804 in Richmond, Virginia
d. Jul 17, 1881 in Kansas City, Missouri
Source: *AmBi; DcAmB; OxAmL; REnAL; WebAB; WhAm H*

Bridges, "Beau" (Lloyd Vernet, III)
American. Actor
b. Dec 9, 1941 in Los Angeles, California
Source: *BkPepl; CelR 73; FilmgC; IntMPA 75, 76, 77, 78, 79, 80, 81, 82; MovMk; NewYTBE 70; WhoAm 82; WhoHol A*

Bridges, Gil
see: Rare Earth

Bridges, Harry Renton
American. Labor Union Official
Organized ILWU, 1937; allegedly involved with Communist Party.
b. Jul 29, 1901 in Melbourne, Australia
Source: *CelR 73; CurBio 40, 50; EncAB-H; NewYTBE 72; WebAB; WhoAm 74; WhoWest 74; WhoWor 74*

Bridges, James
American. Director, Screenwriter
b. Feb 3, in Little Rock, Arkansas
Source: *FilmEn; IntMPA 81; WhoAm 82*

Bridges, Jeff
American. Actor
b. Dec 4, 1949 in Los Angeles, California
Source: *BkPepl; FilmgC; IntMPA 75, 76, 77, 78, 79, 80, 81, 82; MovMk; WhoHol A*

Bridges, Lloyd
American. Actor
Starred in TV series "Sea Hunt."
b. Jan 15, 1913 in San Leandro, California
Source: *CelR 73; DrAS 74E; FilmgC; IntMPA 75, 76, 77, 78, 79, 80, 81, 82; MotPP; MovMk; WhoAm 74, 76, 78, 80, 82; WhoHol A*

Bridges, Robert Seymour
English. Author, Poet
b. Oct 23, 1844 in Walmer, England
d. Apr 21, 1930 in Chilswell, England
Source: *Alli SUP; AnCL; AtlBL; CasWL; ChPo, S1, S2; CnE&AP; DcEnA, AP; DcLEL; EncWL; EvLB; LongCTC; ModBrL; NewC; OxEng; Pen ENG; REn; TwCA, SUP; TwCW; WebE&AL; WhoTwCL*

Bridges, Styles
American. Senator
b. Sep 9, 1898 in West Pembroke, Maine
d. Nov 26, 1961 in Concord, New Hampshire
Source: *WhAm 4*

Bridges, Todd
American. Actor
b. May 1965
Source: *BioIn 12*

Bridges, Tommy (Thomas Jefferson Davis)
American. Baseball Player
Pitcher, Detroit Tigers, 1930-46.
b. Dec 28, 1906 in Gordonsville, Tennessee
d. Apr 19, 1968 in Nashville, Tennessee
Source: *BaseEn; BioIn 3, 8; WhoProB 73*

Bridgetower, George Augustus
Polish. Musician
b. 1780
d. 1860
Source: *BioIn 1, 6, 8*

Bridgewater, Dee Dee
American. Singer, Actress
b. May 27, 1950 in Memphis, Tennessee
Source: *BioIn 10; WhoAm 82*

Bridgman, Frederic Arthur
American. Artist
b. Nov 10, 1847 in Tuskegee, Alabama
d. Jan 13, 1927 in Rouen, France
Source: *AmBi; BiDSA; DcAmAu; DcAmB; DcNAA; WhAm 1*

Bridgman, Laura Dewey
American. Subject of Educational Experiment
First successfully taught blind deaf-mute.
b. Dec 21, 1829 in Hanover, New Hampshire
d. May 24, 1889 in Boston, Massachusetts
Source: *AmBi; AmWom; ApCAB; DcAmB; Drake; InWom; LibW; NatCAB 2; NotAW; TwCBDA; WebAB, 79; WhAm H*

Bridgman, Percy Williams
American. Scientist, Physician, Engineer
b. Apr 21, 1882 in Cambridge, Massachusetts
d. Aug 20, 1961 in Randolph, New Hampshire
Source: *AmAu&B; WebAB; WhAm 4; WhNAA*

Bridie, James, pseud.
[Osborne Henry Mavor]
Scottish. Dramatist
b. Jan 3, 1888 in Glasgow, Scotland
d. Jan 29, 1951 in Edinburgh, Scotland
Source: *LongCTC; McGEWD; ModBrL; ModWD; Pen ENG; REn; REnWD; WhoTwCL; WorAu; OxThe*

Brieux, Eugene
French. Dramatist
b. Jan 19, 1858 in Paris, France
d. Dec 7, 1932 in Nice, France
Source: *CasWL; EvEuW; McGEWD; ModWD; NewC; OxEng; Pen EUR; REn; REnWD; TwCA, SUP*

Briggs, Austin Eugene
American. Artist, Illustrator
b. Sep 8, 1908 in Humboldt, Minnesota
d. Oct 13, 1973 in Paris, France
Source: *NewYTBE 73; WhAm 6; WhoAm 74; WhoAmA 73*

Brigati, Eddie
see: Rascals, The

Briggs, Clare
American. Cartoonist
b. Aug 5, 1875 in Reedsburgh, Wisconsin
d. Jan 3, 1930 in New York, New York
Source: *ChPo, S1; DcAmB S1; WhAm 1*

Briggs, David
see: Little River Band, The

Briggs, Ellis Ormsbee
American. Diplomat
US Ambassador, 1945-62; wrote *Shots Heard Around the World,* 1957.
b. Dec 1, 1899 in Watertown, Massachusetts
d. Feb 21, 1976
Source: *BioIn 4, 7, 10, 11; CurBio 65, 76; IntWW 74; WhoAm 74; WhoE 74; WhoWor 74*

Briggs, Walter Owen, Jr.
American. Baseball Executive
Owner Detroit Tigers; stadium previously known as Briggs Stadium.
b. Jan 20, 1912 in Detroit, Michigan
d. Jul 3, 1970 in Detroit, Michigan
Source: *NewYTBE 70; WhAm 5*

Bright, John
English. Member of Parliament, Author
b. Nov 16, 1811 in Greenbank, England
d. Mar 27, 1889 in Greenbank, England
Source: *Alli SUP; BbD; BiD&SB; Chambr 3; NewC; REn*

Bright, Richard
English. Physician
b. Sep 28, 1789 in Bristol, England
d. Dec 16, 1858
Source: *Alli, SUP; BioIn 4, 5, 7, 9*

Brigid of Kildare
Irish. Patron Saint
b. 453?
d. 523?
Source: *BioIn 1, 2, 3, 5, 7, 8, 11; NewC*

Briles, Nelson Kelley
"Nellie"
American. Baseball Player
b. Aug 5, 1943 in Dorris, California
Source: *BaseEn; NewYTBE 71; WhoAm 74; WhoProB 73*

Briley, Alex
see: Village People, The

Brill, Abraham Arden
American. Psychiatrist
b. Oct 12, 1874 in Kanczuga, Austria
d. Mar 2, 1948 in New York, New York
Source: *AmAu&B; DcAmB S4; DcNAA; REnAL; TwCA SUP; WhAm 2; WhNAA*

Brill, Marty (Martin)
American. Football Player, Coach
b. 1905
d. May 1, 1973 in Los Angeles, California
Source: *NewYTBE 73; WhoFtbl 74*

Brillat-Savarin, Jean Anthelme
French. Author
b. Apr 1, 1755 in Bellay, France
d. Feb 2, 1826 in Paris, France
Source: *ApCAB; AtlBL; BbD; BiD&SB; CasWL; EuAu; EvEuW; NewC; OxEng; OxFr; REn*

Brimmer, Andrew Felton
American. Economist, Government Official
b. Sep 13, 1926 in Newellton, Louisiana
Source: *AmEA 74; AmM&WS 73S; CurBio 68; IntWW 74; NewYTBE 73; WhoAm 74, 76, 78, 80, 82; WhoAmP 73; WhoBlA 75; WhoGov 72; WhoS&SW 73*

Brinckerhoff, Burt
American. Actor, Director, Producer
b. Oct 25, 1936 in Pittsburgh, Pennsylvania
Source: *BiE&WWA; NotNAT*

Brindle, Melbourne
American. Artist, Illustrator
b. 1904
Source: *BioIn 9*

Brindley, James
English. Engineer
b. 1716
d. 1772
Source: *Alli; BioIn 2, 4, 5, 6, 7, 8, 9, 10*

Brinegar, Claude Stout
American. Government Official
Secretary of Transportation, 1973-75.
b. Dec 16, 1926 in Rockport, California
Source: *AmM&WS 73S; CngDr 74; NewYTBE 72; WhoAm 74, 76, 78, 80, 82; WhoAmP 73; WhoF&I 74; WhoWor 74*

Brinig, Myron
American. Author
b. Dec 22, 1900 in Minneapolis, Minnesota
Source: *AmAu&B; AmNov; OxAmL; REnAL; TwCA, SUP*

Brink, Carol Ryrie
American. Author
b. Dec 28, 1895 in Moscow, Idaho
d. Aug 15, 1981 in La Jolla, California
Source: *AmAu&B; AmWr; AnCL; Au&Wr 71; AuBYP; ConAu 1R, 104, 3NR; CurBio 46, 81; InWom; IntAu&W 76, 77; JBA 51; LinLib L; MnnWr; MorBMP; Newb 1922; REnAL; ScF&FL 1, 2; SmATA 1; Str&VC; TwCCW 78; WhE&EA; WhoAm 74, 76, 78, 80; WhoAmW 58, 64, 66, 68, 70, 72, 74; WhoPNW; WrDr 76, 80*

Brinkley, Christie
American. Model, Actress
b. 1954?
Source: *BioIn 12*

Brinkley, David McClure
American. Broadcast Journalist
Co-anchor, with Chet Huntley, 1958-70.
b. Jul 10, 1920 in Wilmington, North Carolina
Source: *BkPepl; ConAu 97; CurBio 60; IntMPA 77, 78, 79, 80, 81, 82; WhoAm 74, 76, 78, 80, 82; WhoS&SW 73; WhoWor 74*

Brinkley, John Romulus
American. Charlatan
b. 1886
d. May 26, 1942
Source: *BioIn 5, 8, 11; CurBio 42*

Brinkley, Nell
American. Illustrator
b. 1888
d. Oct 21, 1944
Source: *BioIn 1, 10; CurBio 44*

Brinsmead, Hesba Fay
Australian. Author
b. Mar 15, 1922 in New South Wales, Australia
Source: *ConAu 21R; SenS; SmATA 18; WrDr 76*

Brinton, Clarence Crane
American. Author, Educator, Historian
b. Feb 2, 1898 in Winsted, Connecticut
d. Sep 7, 1968
Source: *AmAu&B; BioIn 5, 8; ConAu 5R, 25R; CurBio 58, 68; REn; REnAL*

Brinton, Daniel Garrison
American. Anthropologist, Author
b. May 13, 1837 in Thornbury, Pennsylvania
d. Jul 31, 1899
Source: *Alli SUP; AmAu; AmAu&B; BiD&SB; CyAL 1; DcAmAu; DcNAA; OxAmL*

Brioni, Gaetano Savini, Marquis
Italian. Fashion Designer
b. Sep 10, 1909 in Termi, Italy
Source: *WhoAm 82; WorFshn*

Briquette, Pete
see: Boomtown Rats

Brisbane, Albert
American. Social Reformer, Author
Wrote *Social Destiny of Man,* 1840.
b. Aug 2, 1809 in Batavia, New York
d. May 1, 1890 in Richmond, Virginia
Source: *AmAu; AmAu&B; AmBi; DcAmB; DcNAA; OxAmL; REnAL; WebAB; WhAm H*

Brisbane, Arthur
American. Journalist
b. Dec 12, 1864 in Buffalo, New York
d. Dec 25, 1936 in New York, New York
Source: *AmAu&B; AmBi; DcAmB S2; DcNAA; OxAmL; REnAL; TwCA; WebAB; WhAm 1*

Briscoe, Dolph
American. Politician
b. Apr 23, 1923 in Uvalde, Texas
Source: *WhoAm 74; WhoAmP 73*

Briscoe, Robert
Irish. Public Official
b. Sep 25, 1894 in Dublin, Ireland
d. May 30, 1969
Source: *BioIn 4, 5, 8; CurBio 57, 69*

Brisebois, Danielle
American. Actress
Plays Stephanie on TV series "Archie Bunker's Place," 1981--.
b. Jun 28, 1969 in Brooklyn, New York
Source: *BioIn 12*

Brissie, Lou (Leland Victor, Jr.)
American. Baseball Player
Pitcher, 1947-53; played with brace, artifical left leg as result of WW II injuries.
b. Jun 5, 1924 in Anderson, South Carolina
Source: *BaseEn; BioIn 1, 8; WhoProB 73*

Brisson, Frederick
Danish. Motion Picture Producer
b. Mar 17, 1917 in Copenhagen, Denmark
Source: *BiE&WWA; CelR 73; FilmgC; IntMPA 75, 76, 77, 78, 79, 80, 81, 82; NotNAT; WhoAm 74, 76, 78, 80, 82; WhoThe 77*

Britain, Radie
American. Composer, Author
b. Mar 17, 1903 in Amarillo, Texas
Source: *AmSCAP 66; Baker 78; BiDAmM; BioIn 1, 3; InWom; WhoAm 74, 76, 78, 80, 82; WhoAmW 64, 66, 68, 70, 72, 74, 77; WhoMus 72*

Britt, May
Swedish. Actress
Starred in *The Blue Angel,* 1959; former wife of Sammy Davis, Jr.
b. 1933 in Lidingo, Sweden
Source: *FilmEn; FilmgC; InWom; MotPP; WhoHol A*

Britt, Steuart Henderson
American. Psychologist
b. Jun 17, 1907 in Fulton, Missouri
d. Mar 15, 1979 in Evanston, Illinois
Source: *AmM&WS 73S, 78S; ConAu 1R, 85, 2NR; WhAm 7; WhoAm 74, 76, 78; WhoCan 73; WhoF&I 74, 75, 77, 79; WhoMW 74, 76, 78; WhoWor 74, 76, 78*

Brittain, Sir Harry Ernest
English. Newspaper Publisher
b. Dec 24, 1873
d. Jul 9, 1974
Source: *Au&Wr 71; NewYTBS 74; Who 74*

Brittain, Vera Mary
English. Author
b. 1896 in Newcastle, England
d. Mar 29, 1970
Source: *ConAu 25R; ConAu P-1; DcLEL; EvLB; LongCTC; NewC; NewYTBE 70; Pen; REn; TwCA; TwCW*

Brittany, Morgan
[Suzanne Cupito; Mrs. Jack Gill]
American. Actress
Plays Kathryn Wentworth on TV series "Dallas," 1981--.
b. 1950? in California
Source: *NF*

Britten, (Edward) Benjamin
English. Composer
b. Nov 22, 1913 in Lowestoft, England
d. Dec 4, 1976 in Aldeburgh, England
Source: *CelR 73; ChPo S2; CurBio 42, 61; DcCM; IntWW 74; OxFilm; Who 74; WhoMus 72*

Britton, Barbara
American. Actress
b. 1919 in Long Beach, California
d. Jan 18, 1980 in New York, New York
Source: *FilmgC; HolP 40; InWom; IntMPA 75, 76, 77; MotPP; MovMk; WhoHol A*

Britton, Edgar Clay
American. Chemist
b. Sep 25, 1891 in Rockville, Indiana
d. Jul 31, 1962
Source: *BioIn 1, 2, 3, 4, 6, 9*

Britz, Jerilyn
American. Golfer
b. Jan 1, 1943 in Minneapolis, Minnesota
Source: *BioIn 12*

Broad, Shepard
American. Banker, Developer
b. 1906
Source: *BioNews 74; BusPN; St&PR 75*

Broadbent, J(ohn) Edward
Canadian. Government Official
MP, 1968--; wrote *The Liberal Rip-Off,* 1970.
b. Mar 21, 1936 in Oshawa, ON
Source: *BioIn 11; CanWW 82; WhoAm 82; WhoCan 77*

Broadbent, Eleanor
[Eleanora Cisneros]
American. Opera Singer
b. Nov 1, 1878 in New York, New York
d. Feb 3, 1934 in New York, New York
Source: *InWom; NotAW*

Brock, Alice May
American. Author, Restaurateur
Owner, "Alice's Restaurant"; the Alice in Arlo Guthrie's song.
b. Feb 28, 1941
Source: *ConAu 41R; NewYTBE 73; WhoAm 74, 76, 78, 80, 82*

Brock, Bill (William Emerson)
American. Senator
b. Nov 23, 1930 in Chattanooga, Tennessee
Source: *BiDrAC; CngDr 74; CurBio 71; WhoAmP 73; WhoGov 72; WhoS&SW 73*

Brock, Lou(is Clark)
American. Baseball Player
Outfielder, St. Louis, 1964-79; leds major leagues with 938 stolen bases.
b. Jun 18, 1939 in El Dorado, Arkansas
Source: *BaseEn; CurBio 75; NewYTBE 72, 73; WhoAm 74, 76, 78; WhoBlA 75, 77; WhoProB 73; WorAl*

Brock, Tony
see: Babys, The

Brod, Max
Israeli. Author
b. May 27, 1884 in Prague, Czechoslovakia
d. Dec 20, 1968 in Tel Aviv, Israel
Source: *CasWL; ConAu 5R, 25R; EncWL; EvEuW; LongCTC; McGEWD; ModGL; OxGer; Pen EUR; REn; TwCA, SUP; WhoLA*

Broda, "Turk" (Walter)
Canadian. Hockey Player
Goalie, Toronto Maple Leafs, 1936-52; Hall of Fame, 1967.
b. May 15, 1914 in Brandon, MB
d. Oct 17, 1972 in Toronto, ON
Source: *NewYTBE 72; WhoHcky 73*

Broderick, Helen
American. Actress
b. 1891 in Philadelphia, Pennsylvania
d. Sep 25, 1959 in Beverly Hills, California
Source: *EncMT; FilmgC; MotPP; MovMk; ThFT; Vers A; WhScrn 74, 77; WhoHol B*

Broderick, James Joseph
American. Actor
Played the father on TV series "Family," 1976-81.
b. Mar 7, 1929? in Charlestown, New Hampshire
d. Nov 1, 1982 in New Haven, Connecticut
Source: *IntMPA 79, 80, 81, 82; NewYTBS 82; NotNAT; WhoAm 82; WhoHol A*

Brodie, Fawn McKay
American. Author
b. Sep 15, 1915 in Ogden, Utah
d. Jan 10, 1981 in Santa Monica, California
Source: *Au&Wr 71; BioIn 1; ConAu 17R, 102; DrAS 74H, 78H; ForWC 70; NewYTBS 81; WhoAm 78, 80; WhoAmW 70, 72, 74, 77*

Brodie, John Riley
American. Football Player, Sportscaster
Quarterback, San Francisco 49ers, 1957-73; with NBC Sports, 1974--.
b. Aug 14, 1935 in San Francisco, California
Source: *NewYTBE 71; WhoAm 74, 76, 78, 80, 82; WhoFtbl 74*

Brodie, Steve
American. Actor
b. 1919 in El Dorado, Kansas
Source: *FilmgC; WhoHol A*

Brodie, William
Scottish. Clergyman, Thief
b. 1741 in Edinburgh, Scotland
d. 1788
Source: *BioIn 10*

Brodovitch, Alexey
American. Artist, Designer
b. 1898 in Russia
d. Apr 15, 1971 in Lethor, France
Source: *NewYTBE 71*

Brodsky, Joseph Alexandrovich
[Iosif Alexandrovich Brodsky]
American. Author, Poet
b. May 24, 1940 in Leningrad, U.S.S.R.
Source: *AuNews 1; ConAu 41R; CurBio 82; NewYTBE 72; WhoAm 82*

Brogan, Sir Denis William
Scottish. Author, Political Scientist
b. Aug 11, 1900 in Glasgow, Scotland
d. Jan 5, 1974 in Cambridge, England
Source: *ConAu 45, 97; DcLEL; EvLB; LongCTC; NewC; NewYTBS 74; TwCA SUP; WhAm 6; Who 74*

Brokaw, Tom (Thomas John)
American. Broadcast Journalist
Host, "The Today Show," 1976-82; co-anchor, "NBC Nightly News," 1982--.
b. Feb 6, 1940 in Webster, South Dakota
Source: *BioIn 10; BkPepl; IntMPA 78, 79, 80, 81, 82; WhoAm 78, 80, 82*

Brokenshire, Norman
Canadian. Radio Announcer
b. Jun 10, 1898 in Murcheson, ON
d. May 4, 1965 in Hauppauge, New York
Source: *CurBio 50, 65; WhAm 4*

Brolin, James
American. Actor
Played Dr. Steven Kiley on "Marcus Welby, MD," 1969-76; won Emmy, 1969.
b. Jul 18, 1941 in Los Angeles, California
Source: *FilmgC; IntMPA 75, 76, 77, 78, 79, 80, 81, 82; MovMk; WhoAm 78, 80, 82; WhoHol A; WorAl*

Bromberg, Edward
American. Actor
b. 1904
d. 1951
Source: *MotPP*

Bromfield, John
[Farron Bromfield]
American. Actor
b. Jun 11, 1922 in South Bend, Indiana
Source: *FilmgC; IntMPA 75, 76, 77, 78, 79, 80, 81, 82; MotPP; WhoHol A*

Bromfield, Louis
American. Author
b. Dec 27, 1896 in Mansfield, Ohio
d. Mar 18, 1956 in Columbus, Ohio
Source: *AmAu&B; AmNov; CnDAL; ConAmA; ConAmL; CurBio 44, 56; CyWA; DcBiA; DcLEL; EncWL; EvLB; LongCTC; OhA&B; OxAmL; Pen AM; REn; REnAL; TwCA, SUP; TwCW; WebAB; WhAm 3; WhNAA*

Bron, Eleanor
English. Actress
b. 1934 in Stanmore, England
Source: *FilmEn; FilmgC; IntMPA 75, 76, 77, 78, 79, 80, 81; WhoAmW 72, 74; WhoHol A; WhoThe 77, 81; WhoWor 74*

"Broncho Billy"
see: Anderson, Gilbert M

Bronck, Jonas
Danish. Pioneer in America
d. 1643?
Source: *BioIn 2*

Broneer, Oscar Theodore
American. Archaeologist
b. Dec 28, 1894 in Backebo, Sweden
Source: *BioIn 8, 9; DrAS 74F; WhoAm 74*

Bronfman, Edgar Miles
Canadian. Distillery Executive
Chief executive, chairman, Seagram Co., Ltd.
b. Jun 20, 1929 in Montreal, PQ
Source: *CanWW 79, 82; CurBio 74; Dun&B 79; IntWW 74, 75, 76, 77, 78, 79, 80, 81; St&PR 75; WhoAm 74, 76, 78, 80, 82; WhoCan 73, 75, 77; WhoF&I 74; WhoGov 72; WhoWor 74, 76, 78*

Bronfman, Samuel
Canadian. Distillery Executive
At death, Seagrams was world's largest distiller; sales exceeded $1.3 billion.
b. Mar 4, 1891 in Brandon, MB
d. Jul 10, 1971 in Montreal, PQ
Source: *MacDCB 78; NatCAB 56; NewYTBE 71; WhAm 5; WhoWorJ 72*

Bronfman, Samuel
Canadian. Kidnap Victim
Heir to Seagrams fortune; kidnapped, 1975.
b. 1954
Source: *BioIn 10*

Bronk, Detlev Wulf
American. Biologist
Founded biophysics; pioneered use of electro-microscopy to monitor human nerve network.
b. Aug 13, 1897 in New York, New York
d. Nov 17, 1975 in New York, New York
Source: *AmM&WS 73P, 76P; BlueB 76; CurBio 49, 76; InSci; IntWW 74, 75, 76; McGMS 80; NewYTBS 75; WebAB, 79; WhAm 6; Who 74; WhoAm 74, 76; WhoAtom 77; WhoWor 74, 76; WorAl*

Bronowski, Jacob
English. Mathematician, Author
b. Jan 18, 1908 in Poland
d. Aug 22, 1974 in East Hampton, New York
Source: *AmAu&B; AnCL; ConAu 1R, 53; DcLEL; IntWW 74; NewYTBS 74; WhAm 6; Who 74; WhoAm 74; WhoWor 74; WorAu*

Bronson, Betty
American. Actress
b. Nov 17, 1906 in Trenton, New Jersey
d. Oct 21, 1971 in Pasadena, California
Source: *FilmgC; InWom; MotPP; MovMk; NewYTBE 71; ThFT; TwYS; WhScrn 74, 77; WhoHol B*

Bronson, Charles
[Charles Buchinsky]
American. Actor
Starred in *The Dirty Dozen,* 1967, *Death Wish,* 1974.
b. Oct 3, 1922? in Ehrenfeld, Pennsylvania
Source: *BioNews 74; BkPepl; CelR 73; CurBio 75; IntMPA 75, 76, 77, 78, 79, 80, 81, 82; MovMk; NewYTBS 74; WhoAm 76, 78, 80, 82; WhoHol A*

Bronstein, David
Russian. Chess Player
b. 1925
Source: *BioIn 4*

Bronte, Anne
[Acton Bell, pseud.]
English. Author
Sister of Charlotte and Emily; wrote *Agnes Grey,* 1847.
b. Mar 25, 1820 in Thornton, England
d. May 26, 1849 in Scarborough, England
Source: *BbD; BiD&SB; BrAu 19; CasWL; Chambr 3; ChPo, S1; CyWA; DcBiA; DcEnA, AP; DcEnL; DcEuL; DcLEL; EvLB; HerW; InWom; OxEng; Pen ENG; RAdv 1; WebE&AL*

Bronte, Charlotte
[Currer Bell, pseud.; Mrs. Arthur Bell Nicholls]
English. Author
Most successful of sisters; wrote *Jane Eyre,* 1847.
b. Apr 21, 1816 in Thornton, England
d. Mar 31, 1855 in Haworth, England
Source: *Alli; AtlBL; BbD; BiD&SB; BrAu 19; CasWL; Chambr 3; ChPo, S1, S2; CrtT 3; CyWA; DcBiA; DcEnA, AP; DcEnL; DcEuL; DcLEL; EvLB; FilmgC; HerW; HsB&A; InWom; MouLC 3; OxEng; Pen ENG; RAdv 1; RComWL; WebE&AL*

Bronte, Emily Jane
[Ellis Bell, pseud.]
English. Author
Wrote *Wuthering Heights,* 1848.
b. Aug 20, 1818 in Thornton, England
d. Dec 19, 1848 in Haworth, England
Source: *AtlBL; BbD; BiD&SB; BrAu 19; CasWL; Chambr 3; ChPo, S1, S2; CnE&AP; CrtT 3; CyWA; DcBiA; DcEnA, AP; DcEnL; DcEuL; DcLEL; EvLB; FilmgC; HerW; InWom; MouLC 3; OxEng; Pen ENG; RAdv 1; RComWL; WebE&AL*

Bronte, Patrick Branwell
English. Poet
b. 1817
d. Sep 26, 1848
Source: *BioIn 1, 2, 5, 6, 9, 10, 11; ChPo S1; DcEuL; PoIre*

Bronzino II
Italian. Artist
b. Nov 17, 1503 in Montecelli, Italy
d. Nov 23, 1572
Source: *AtlBL; REn*

Brook, Alexander
American. Artist
b. Jul 14, 1898 in Brooklyn, New York
d. Feb 26, 1980 in Sag Harbor, New York
Source: *CurBio 41, 80; DcCAA 71; IntWW 74; WhoAm 74; WhoAmA 73*

Brook, Clive
English. Actor
b. Jun 1, 1887 in London, England
d. Nov 18, 1974 in London, England
Source: *BiDFilm; FilmgC; MotPP; MovMk; NewYTBS 74; TwYS; WhAm 6; WhScrn 77; Who 74; WhoHol B; WorEFlm*

Brook, Peter
English. Theatrical Director
b. Mar 21, 1925 in London, England
Source: *Au&Wr 71; BiDFilm; BiE&WWA; CelR 73; CroCD; CurBio 61; DcFM; FilmgC; IntWW 74; MovMk; NotNAT; OxFilm; OxThe; Who 74; WhoMus 72; WhoThe 77; WhoWor 74; WorEFlm*

Brooke, Sir Alan Francis
see: Alanbrooke, Alan Francis Brooke, 1st Viscount

Brooke, Edward William
American. Lawyer
Senator from MA, 1967-79.
b. Oct 26, 1919 in Washington, DC
Source: *AlmAP; BiDrAC; CngDr 74, 77; CurBio 67; EbonySL 1; InB&W 80; IntWW 74, 75, 76, 77, 78, 79, 80; PolProf J; PolProf NF; SelBAA; WhoAm 74, 76, 78, 80, 82; WhoAmP 73, 75, 77, 79; WhoBlA 75, 77; WhoE 74, 75, 77, 79; WhoGov 72, 75, 77; WhoWor 74, 76, 78*

Brooke, Hillary
[Beatrice Peterson]
Actress
b. 1916
Source: *FilmgC; IntMPA 75; MovMk; WhoHol A*

Brooke, Sir James
British. 1st Rajah of Sarawak
b. Apr 29, 1803 in Benares, India
d. Jun 11, 1868 in England
Source: *Alli, SUP; McGEWB*

Brooke, Rupert Chawner
English. Poet
Wrote romantic, patriotic poetry during early part of WW I.
b. Aug 3, 1887 in Rugby, England
d. Apr 23, 1915 in Scyros, Greece
Source: *AtlBL; CasWL; Chambr 3; ChPo, S2; CnE&AP; CnMWL; DcEuL; DcLEL; EncWL; EvLB; LongCTC; ModBrL, SUP; NewC; OxCan; OxEng; Pen ENG; RAdv 1; REn; TwCA, SUP; TwCW; WebE&AL; WhoTwCL*

Brookings, Robert Somers
American. Merchant, Philanthropist
b. Jan 22, 1850 in Cecil County, Maryland
d. Nov 15, 1932 in Washington, DC
Source: *AmBi; DcAmB S1; DcNAA; WebAB; WhAm 1*

Brooks, Albert
American. Comedian, Actor, Writer
b. Jul 22, 1947 in Los Angeles, California
Source: *BioIn 10; WhoAm 82*

Brooks, Angie Elizabeth
Liberian. Diplomat
Member, UN General Assembly, 1954--; first African woman president, 1969.
b. Aug 24, 1928 in Virginia, Liberia
Source: *CurBio 70; InB&W 80; IntWW 74, 75; WhoAmW 72, 74; WhoUN 75*

Brooks, Charlie, Jr.
American. Murderer
First to be executed by lethal injection.
b. 1942?
d. Dec 7, 1982 in Huntsville, Texas
Source: *NF*

Brooks, Cleanth
American. Author, Critic
b. Oct 16, 1906 in Murray, Kentucky
Source: *AmAu&B; CasWL; ConAu 17R; DcLEL; DrAS 74E; IntWW 74; LongCTC; ModAL; OxAmL; Pen AM; RAdv 1; REn; REnAL; TwCA SUP; Who 74; WhoAm 74; WhoTwCL; WhoWor 74; WrDr 76*

Brooks, David Owen
American. Mass Murderer
Accused of mass murders of 27 young boys in TX, 1973.
b. 1955
Source: *BioIn 10*

Brooks, Donald Marc
American. Fashion Designer
Designed costumes for movie *The Bell Jar,* 1979.
b. Jan 10, 1928 in New York, New York
Source: *BiE&WWA; CelR 73; CurBio 72; NotNAT; WhoAm 74, 76, 78, 80, 82; WhoFash; WorFshn*

Brooks, Foster
American. Comedian, Actor
Source: *NF*

Brooks, Geraldine
American. Actress
b. Oct 29, 1925 in New York, New York
d. Jun 19, 1977 in Riverhead, New York
Source: *BiE&WWA; FilmgC; HolP 40; InWom; IntMPA 75, 76, 77; ForWC 70*

Brooks, Gwendolyn
American. Author, Poet
First black woman to win Pulitzer Prize for poetry, 1950, for *Annie Allen.*
b. Jun 7, 1917 in Topeka, Kansas
Source: *AmAu&B; AuNews 1; BioNews 74; BkCL; BlkAW; CasWL; CelR 73; ChPo, S1, S2; ConAu 1R, 1NR; ConLC 1, 2, 4, 5, 15; ConP 70, 75; CroCAP; CurBio 50; DrAP 75; EncAB-H; InWom; IntWW 74; LivgBAA; ModAL, SUP; OxAmL; Pen AM; RAdv 1; REnAL; SmATA 6; TwCA SUP; WebAB; WhoAm 74, 76, 78, 80, 82; WhoAmW 77; WhoWor 74; WrDr 76*

Brooks, Herb(ert Paul)
American. Hockey Coach
Coach, US Olympic team, 1980; NY Rangers, 1981--.
b. Aug 5, 1937 in Saint Paul, Minnesota
Source: *WhoAm 80, 82*

Brooks, Jack Bascom
American. Congressman
b. Dec 18, 1922 in Crowley, Louisiana
Source: *BiDrAC; BioIn 10, 11; WhoAm 74, 76, 78, 80, 82; WhoGov 72, 75, 77*

Brooks, Lela
Canadian. Figure Skater
b. 1908
Source: *BioIn 10*

Brooks, Louise
American. Actress
b. 1906 in Cherryvale, Kansas
Source: *BiDFilm; FilmgC; MovMk; OxFilm; ThFT; TwYS; WhoHol A; WorEFlm*

Brooks, Mel
[Melvyn Kaminsky]
American. Actor, Author, Producer, Director
Writer, director *Blazing Saddles*, 1974, *Young Frankenstein*, 1975.
b. 1928 in New York, New York
Source: *BiE&WWA; BkPepl; CurBio 74; FilmgC; IntMPA 76, 77, 78, 79, 80, 81, 82; MovMk; Who 82; WhoAm 74, 76, 78, 80, 82*

Brooks, Phillips
American. Episcopal Bishop, Author
b. Dec 13, 1835 in Boston, Massachusetts
d. Jan 23, 1893 in Boston, Massachusetts
Source: *Alli SUP; AmAu&B; AmBi; AnCL; ApCAB; BbD; BiD&SB; Chambr 3; ChPo, S1, S2; DcAmAu; DcAmB; DcNAA; Drake; OxAmL; REnAL; TwCBDA; WebAB; WhAm H*

Brooks, Richard
American. Motion Picture Director
b. May 18, 1912 in Philadelphia, Pennsylvania
Source: *AmAu&B; AmNov; BiDFilm; CelR 73; ConAu 73; ConDr 73, 77A; DcFM; FilmgC; IntAu&W 76, 77; IntMPA 75, 76, 77, 78, 79, 80, 81; IntWW 74, 75, 76, 77, 78; MovMk; OxFilm; WhoAm 74, 76, 78, 80, 82; WhoWor 74; WorEFlm*

Brooks, Van Wyck
American. Author, Editor, Translator
b. Feb 16, 1886 in Plainfield, New Jersey
d. May 2, 1963 in Bridgewater, Connecticut
Source: *AmAu&B; AmLY; AmWr; AtlBL; CasWL; Chambr 3; CnDAL; ConAmA; ConAmL; ConAu 1R, 1R; CurBio 41, 60, 63; DcLEL; EvLB; LongCTC; ModAL; OxAmL; Pen AM; RAdv 1; REn; REnAL; TwCA, SUP; TwCW; WebE&AL; WhNAA*

Brooks, William Keith
American. Zoologist
b. Mar 25, 1848 in Cleveland, Ohio
d. Nov 12, 1908 in Baltimore, Maryland
Source: *Alli SUP; DcAmAu; DcNAA; OhA&B*

Broonzy, "Big Bill"
American. Singer, Musician
b. Jun 26, 1893 in Scott, Mississippi
d. Aug 14, 1958 in Chicago, Illinois
Source: *EncFCWM 69*

Brophy, Brigid
English. Author
b. Jun 12, 1929 in London, England
Source: *Au&Wr 71; CasWL; ConAu 5R; ConDr 73; ConLC 6; ConNov 72, 76; IntWW 74; LongCTC; ModBrL, SUP; NewC; TwCW; Who 74; WhoTwCL; WhoWor 74; WorAu; WrDr 76*

Brophy, Catherine Mary
American. Golfer
b. 1885
d. 1974
Source: *BioIn 10*

Brophy, John
English. Miner, Labor Leader
Exponent of public ownership of mines; wrote *A Miner's Life*, 1964.
b. Nov 6, 1883 in Lancaster, England
d. Feb 19, 1963
Source: *BioIn 7*

Brosio, Manilo Giovanni
Italian. Diplomat
b. Jul 10, 1897 in Turin, Italy
d. Mar 14, 1980 in Turin, Italy
Source: *BioIn 4; CurBio 55, 82; IntWW 74, 75, 76, 77, 78, 79; NewYTBS 80; WhAm 7; Who 74; WhoWor 74*

Brosnan, Jim (James Patrick)
"Professor"
American. Baseball Player, Sportswriter
b. Oct 24, 1929 in Cincinnati, Ohio
Source: *BaseEn; ConAu 1R; CurBio 64; WhoMW 74; WhoProB 73*

Broten, Neal
[United States Olympic Hockey Team-1980]
American. Hockey Player
b. Nov 29, 1959 in Roseau, Minnesota
Source: *HocReg*

Brothers, Joyce Diane Bauer
[Mrs. Milton Brothers]
American. Psychologist, Author
Only woman to win $64,000 on "The $64,000 Question," 1955-56.
b. Oct 20, 1928 in New York, New York
Source: *AuNews 1; BioNews 74; BkPepl; ConAu 25R; CurBio 71; ForWC 70; InWom; WhoAm 74, 76, 78, 80, 82; WhoAmW 77; WhoWor 74; WhoWorJ 72*

Brothers Johnson, The
[George Johnson; Louis Johnson]
American. Music Group
Source: *RkOn*

Brough, Louise Althea
American. Tennis Player
U.S. women's singles champion, 1947.
b. Mar 11, 1923 in Oklahoma City, Oklahoma
Source: *BioIn 1, 9; CurBio 48*

Broun, Heywood Hale
American. Author, Broadcaster
b. Mar 10, 1918 in New York, New York
Source: *BiE&WWA; BioNews 74; ConAu 17R; NotNAT; WhoAm 82*

Broun, (Matthew) Heywood (Campbell)
American. Journalist
b. Dec 7, 1888 in Brooklyn, New York
d. Dec 18, 1939 in New York, New York
Source: *AmAu&B; AmBi; CathA 1930; ConAmA; CurBio 40; DcAmB S2; DcLEL; DcNAA; OxAmL; PlP&P; REn; REnAL; TwCA, SUP; WebAB; WhAm 1*

Brousse, Amy Elizabeth Thorpe
"Cynthia"
American. Allied Spy in WW II
b. 1910 in Minneapolis, Minnesota
d. 1963 in France
Source: *BioIn 6, 7*

Brouthers, "Dan" (Dennis Joseph)
"Big Dan"
American. Baseball Player
First baseman, 1879-96, 1904; Hall of Fame, 1945.
b. May 8, 1858 in Sylvan Lake, New York
d. Aug 3, 1932 in East Orange, New Jersey
Source: *BaseEn; WhoProB 73*

Brouwer, Adriaen C
Flemish. Artist
b. 1606 in Oudenaarde, Belgium
d. Jan 1638 in Antwerp, Belgium
Source: *AtlBL*

Browder, Earl Russell
American. Communist Leader
b. May 20, 1891 in Wichita, Kansas
d. Jun 27, 1973 in Princeton, New Jersey
Source: *ConAu 45; CurBio 44, 73; EncAB-H; NewYTBE 73; WebAB; WhAm 5; WhAmP*

Brown, A Roy
Canadian. Shot down the "Red Baron" in WW I
b. 1893 in Carleton Place, ON
d. Mar 9, 1944 in Stouffville, ON
Source: *ClbCR; ObitOF 79*

Brown, Barnum
American. Paleontologist
b. Feb 12, 1873
d. Feb 5, 1963
Source: *BioIn 2, 6, 7, 8*

Brown, Blair
American. Actress
b. 1948 in Washington, DC
Source: *NewYTBS 81*

Brown, Bryan
Australian. Actor
b. 1947? in Sydney, Australia
Source: *BioIn 12*

Brown, Charles Brockden
American. Author
b. Jan 17, 1771 in Philadelphia, Pennsylvania
d. Feb 22, 1810 in Philadelphia, Pennsylvania
Source: *Alli; AmAu; AmAu&B; AmBi; ApCAB; AtlBL; BbD; BiD&SB; CasWL; Chambr 3; CnDAL; CrtT 3; CyAL 1; CyWA; DcAmAu; DcAmB; DcEnL; DcLEL; DcNAA; Drake; EncMys; EvLB; MouLC 2; OxAmL; OxEng; Pen AM; RAdv 1; REn; REnAL; TwCBDA; WebAB; WebE&AL; WhAm H*

Brown, Charles Lee
American. Businessman
With AT&T and affiliates, 1946--, chairman, 1979--.
b. Aug 23, 1921 in Richmond, Virginia
Source: *BioIn 11; WhoAm 78, 80, 82*

Brown, Christy
Irish. Author, Poet
Wrote with only useable limb--left foot: *Down All the Days,* 1970.
b. Jun 5, 1932 in Dublin, Ireland
d. Sep 6, 1981 in Parbrook, England
Source: *AnObit 1981; BioIn 8, 9, 10; ConAu 104; DcIrW 2; NewYTBE 70, 71; WrDr 76, 80*

Brown, Clarence
American. Motion Picture Director
b. May 10, 1890 in Clinton, Massachusetts
Source: *BiDFilm; CmMov; DcFM; FilmgC; IntMPA 75, 76, 77, 78, 79, 80, 81, 82; MovMk; OxFilm; TwYS*

Brown, Danny Joe
see: Molly Hatchet

Brown, Dean
American. Photographer
b. 1936
d. Jul 10, 1973
Source: *BioIn 10*

Brown, Drew
American. Boxing Trainer
b. 1928
Source: *BioIn 9*

Brown, Eddy
American. Musician
b. 1895 in Chicago, Illinois
d. Jun 17, 1974
Source: *NewYTBS 74*

Brown, Edmund Gerald
see: Brown, Pat

Brown, Edmund Gerald, Jr.
see: Brown, Jerry

Brown, Edward Gerald
see: Brown, Ned

Brown, (Elford Cornelious) Kelly (Kingman)
American. Actor, Dancer
b. Sep 24, 1928 in Maysville, Kentucky
d. Mar 13, 1981 in Phoenix, Arizona
Source: *BiE&WWA; NewYTBS 81; NotNAT*

Brown, Ford Maddox
English. Artist
b. 1821 in Calais, France
d. 1893
Source: *REn*

Brown, Frank Arthur, Jr.
American. Biologist, Educator
b. Aug 30, 1908 in Beverly, Massachusetts
Source: *AmM&WS 73P; WhoAm 74, 76, 78, 80, 82*

Brown, George
see: Kool and the Gang

Brown, George Mackay
Scottish. Poet, Author
b. Oct 17, 1921 in Stromness, Scotland
Source: *CasWL; ChPo S2; ConAu 21R; ConLC 5; ConNov 72, 76; ConP 70, 75; WrDr 76*

Brown, George Scratchley
American. General
b. Aug 17, 1918 in Montclair, New Jersey
d. Dec 5, 1978 in Washington, DC
Source: *BioIn 10, 11*

Brown, Georgia
English. Actress
b. Oct 21, 1933 in London, England
Source: *BiE&WWA; FilmgC; NotNAT; WhoHol A; WhoThe 77*

Brown, H(ubert) Rap
[Jamiel Abdul Al-Amin]
American. Black Leader, Minister
Chairman, SNCC, 1967; converted to Islam while serving prison term.
b. Oct 4, 1943 in Baton Rouge, Louisiana
Source: *LivgBAA; WhoBlA 77, 80*

Brown, Harold
American. Businessman
Secretary of Defense, 1977-81.
b. Sep 19, 1927 in New York, New York
Source: *AmM&WS 73P; CurBio 61; IntWW 74; LEduc 74; WhoAm 74, 76, 78, 80, 82; WhoWest 74; WhoWor 74*

Brown, Helen Gurley
American. Author, Editor
Editor *Cosmopolitan* magazine, 1965--.
b. Feb 18, 1922 in Green Forest, Arkansas
Source: *AmAu&B; CelR 73; ConAu 5R; CurBio 69; ForWC 70; InWom; WhoAm 74, 76, 78, 80, 82; WhoAmW 77; WhoE 74; WhoWor 74; WrDr 76*

Brown, Henry Billings
American. Supreme Court Justice
b. Mar 2, 1836 in South Lee, Massachusetts
d. Sep 4, 1913 in Bronxville, New York
Source: *BioIn 2, 5; WebAB; WhAm 1*

Brown, Henry Kirke
American. Sculptor
b. Feb 24, 1814 in Leyden, Massachusetts
d. Jul 10, 1886
Source: *BioIn 5, 7, 8, 9*

Brown, Jacob Jennings
American. Military Leader
b. May 9, 1775 in Bucks County, Pennsylvania
d. Feb 24, 1828 in Washington, DC
Source: *AmBi; ApCAB; BiAuS; DcAmB; Drake; TwCBDA; WebAB; WhAm H*

Brown, James
American. Publisher
With Charles Little, formed Little, Brown and Co., 1837.
b. May 19, 1800 in Acton, Massachusetts
d. Mar 10, 1855
Source: *AmAu&B; ApCAB; DcAmB; TwCBDA; WhAm H*

Brown, James
"Mister Dynamite"; "Soul Brother Number One"
American. Singer
Has 38 gold records in 20 years; won Grammy, 1965.
b. May 3, 1934 in Augusta, Georgia
Source: *CelR 73; WebAB; WhoBlA 75, 80; WhoE 74*

Brown, Jerry (Edmund Gerald, Jr.)
American. Politician
Son of Pat Brown; governor of CA, 1975-82.
b. Apr 7, 1938 in San Francisco, California
Source: *BioNews 74; BkPepl; CurBio 75; WhoAm 82; WhoAmP 73; WhoGov 72*

Brown, Jim (James Nathaniel)
American. Actor, Football Player
Running back, Cleveland, 1957-65; all-time NFL rusher with 15, 459 yds.
b. Feb 17, 1936 in Saint Simons Island, Georgia
Source: *BioNews 74; CelR 73; FilmgC; IntMPA 75, 76, 77, 78, 79, 80, 81, 82; MotPP; MovMk; NewYTBE 73; WhoAm 74, 76, 78, 80, 82; WhoBlA 75; WhoHol A*

Brown, Jim Ed (James Edward)
American. Singer
b. Apr 1, 1934 in Sparkman, Arkansas
Source: *EncFCWM 69; WhoAm 82*

Brown, Joe Evan
American. Comedian, Actor
b. Jul 28, 1892 in Holgate, Ohio
d. Jul 17, 1973 in Brentwood, California
Source: *BiE&WWA; CurBio 45, 73; EncMT; FilmgC; MotPP; MovMk; NewYTBE 73; OhA&B; OxFilm; WhAm 5; WhScrn 77; WhoAm 74; WhoHol B*

Brown, John
"Old Brown of Osawatomie"
American. Abolitionist
Convicted of treason and hanged; subject of song "John Brown's Body."
b. May 9, 1800 in Torrington, Connecticut
d. Dec 2, 1859 in Charles Town, West Virginia
Source: *AmBi; ApCAB; DcAmB; Drake; EncAB-H; OxAmL; REn; REnAL; TwCBDA; WebAB; WhAm H; WhAmP*

Brown, John Carter
American. Art Museum Director
b. Oct 8, 1934 in Providence, Rhode Island
Source: *WhoAm 74, 76, 78, 80, 82; WhoAmA 73; WhoGov 72; WhoS&SW 73*

Brown, John Mason
American. Critic, Lecturer
b. Jul 3, 1900 in Louisville, Kentucky
d. Mar 16, 1969 in New York, New York
Source: *AmAu&B; CnDAL; ConAu 9R, 25R; LongCTC; OxAmL; OxThe; Pen AM; REnAL; TwCA, SUP*

Brown, John Young, Jr.
American. Businessman, Politician
Chairman, Kentucky Fried Chicken, 1971-74; governor of KY, 1980--.
b. 1933 in Lexington, Kentucky
Source: *WhoAm 82; WhoF&I 74; WhoS&SW 73*

Brown, Johnny Mack
American. Football Player, Actor
b. Sep 1, 1904 in Dothan, Alabama
d. Nov 14, 1974 in Woodland Hills, California
Source: *CmMov; NewYTBS 74; TwYS; WhScrn 77; WhoHol A, B*

Brown, Lancelot
"Capability"
English. Landscape Architect
Founded modern "English style" landscapes.
b. 1715 in Harle-Kirk, England
d. Feb 6, 1783 in London, England
Source: *AtlBL; NewC*

Brown, Larry
American. Basketball Coach
b. 1940?
Source: *BioIn 11*

Brown, Larry
American. Football Player
b. Sep 19, 1947 in Clairton, Pennsylvania
Source: *CurBio 73; NewYTBE 70; WhoBbl 73*

Brown, Lawrence
American. Composer, Pianist
b. 1893
d. Dec 25, 1972
Source: *BioIn 9*

Brown, Les
American. Band Leader
b. Mar 12, 1912 in Reinerton, Pennsylvania
Source: *AmSCAP 66*

Brown, Lew
American. Songwriter
Songs include "Button Up Your Overcoat," "Beer Barrel Polka."
b. Dec 10, 1893 in Odessa, Russia
d. Feb 5, 1958 in New York, New York
Source: *AmSCAP 66; EncMT; NewCBMT; WhAm 3; WhoHol A*

Brown, Louise Joy
English. First Test Tube Baby
b. Jul 25, 1978 in Oldham, England
Source: *BioIn 11; BkPepl*

Brown, Mace
American. Professional Killer
b. 1943
Source: *BioIn 9*

Brown, Marcia
American. Author, Artist
b. Jul 13, 1918 in Rochester, New York
Source: *AmAu&B; AnCL; AuBYP; BkP; Cald 1938; ChPo, S2; ConAu 41R; FamAIYP; IlsBYP; IlsCB 1946, 1957; MorJA; SmATA 7; WhoAm 74, 76, 78, 80, 82*

Brown, Margaret Wise
American. Author
b. May 23, 1910 in New York, New York
d. Nov 13, 1952 in Nice, France
Source: *AmSCAP 66; Au&ICB; AuBYP; ChPo, S1; DcAmB S5; JBA 51; REnAL; WhAm 3*

Brown, Mordecai
"Three-Finger Brown"
American. Baseball Player
Farm accident injured fingers, helped make curve ball more effective.
b. Oct 19, 1876 in Byesville, Indiana
d. Feb 14, 1948 in Terre Haute, Indiana
Source: *BaseEn; WhoProB 73*

Brown, Nacio Herb
American. Songwriter
b. Feb 22, 1896 in Deming, New Mexico
d. Sep 28, 1964 in San Francisco, California
Source: *AmSCAP 66; FilmgC*

Brown, Nathan
American. Educator
b. Nov 24, 1912 in Zemplan, Hungary
d. Mar 5, 1981 in Tarrytown, New York
Source: *NewYTBS 81; WhoE 75, 77; WhoWorJ 72*

Brown, Ned (Edward Gerald)
American. Journalist
b. 1881
d. Apr 25, 1976
Source: *BioIn 10*

Brown, Oliver
see: K C and the Sunshine Band

Brown, Oscar, Jr.
American. Author, Entertainer
b. Oct 10, 1926 in Chicago, Illinois
Source: *WhoAm 74, 76, 78, 80, 82; WhoBlA 75; WhoWor 74*

Brown, Pamela
English. Actress
b. Jul 8, 1917 in London, England
d. Sep 18, 1975 in London, England
Source: *BiE&WWA; FilmgC; InWom; OxFilm; WhScrn 77*

Brown, Pamela Beatrice
English. Author, Actress
b. Dec 31, 1924 in Colchester, England
Source: *Au&Wr 71; AuBYP; ConAu 13R; IntMPA 75; SmATA 5; WhoChL*

Brown, Pat (Edmund Gerald)
American. Lawyer, Politician
Father of Jerry Brown; governor of CA, 1959-66.
b. Apr 21, 1905 in San Francisco, California
Source: *CurBio 60; IntWW 74; WhoAm 74, 76, 78, 80, 82; WhoAmP 73*

Brown, Paul
American. Football Coach
Coach, Cleveland Browns, 1946-62, Cincinnati Bengals, 1968-76.
b. Jul 9, 1908 in Norwalk, Ohio
Source: *WhoAm 74, 76, 78, 80, 82; WhoFtbl 74*

Brown, Peter
English. Singer
b. 1940 in London, England
Source: *IlEncRk*

Brown, Robert
English. Botanist
b. Dec 21, 1773 in Montrose, Scotland
d. Jun 10, 1858 in London, England
Source: *AsBiEn; BioIn 2, 3, 4, 5; BrAu 19; DcScB; LinLib S; NewCol 75*

Brown, Roger
American. Basketball Player
b. May 22, 1942 in Brooklyn, New York
Source: *WhoBbl 73*

Brown, "Rooky" (William)
American. Basketball Player
Played with Harlem Globetrotters, 1947-58.
b. 1924
d. May 23, 1971
Source: *BioIn 9*

Brown, Rosemary
English. Psychic
Wrote *Unfinished Symphonies: Voices from the Beyond*, 1971.
Source: *BioIn 10*

Brown, Samuel W, Jr.
American. Government Official
b. Jul 27, 1943 in Council Bluffs, Iowa
Source: *BioIn 11; WhoAm 78*

Brown, "Sonny" (William)
American. Composer
b. 1928 in Cincinnati, Ohio
Source: *BioIn 9*

Brown, "Tarzan" (Ellison)
American. Track Athlete
b. 1914
d. Aug 23, 1975
Source: *BioIn 10*

Brown, Tom
American. Actor
b. Jan 6, 1913 in New York, New York
Source: *FilmgC; IntMPA 75, 76, 77, 78, 79, 80, 81, 82; MovMk; TwYS; Vers B; WhoHol A*

Brown, Toni
American. Rock Musician
Source: *BiDAmM; BioIn 10*

Brown, Vanessa
American. Actress, Author, Artist
b. Mar 24, 1928 in Vienna, Austria
Source: *FilmgC; InWom; WhoAmW 77; WhoHol A*

Brown, Walter Augustine
American. Executive
Organized Boston Celtics basketball team.
b. Feb 10, 1905 in Hopkinton, Massachusetts
d. Sep 7, 1964 in Boston, Massachusetts
Source: *EncAB-A 37; WhoBbl 73*

Brown, William
American. Author
b. Dec 1, 1765
d. Sep 2, 1793
Source: *BioIn 9*

Brown, William Wells
American. Author, Reformer
b. 1815 in Lexington, Kentucky
d. Nov 6, 1884 in Chelsea, Massachusetts
Source: *AmAu; AmAu&B; BlkAW; DcAmB; DcNAA; EncAB-H; REnAL; WhAm H; WhAmP*

Browne, Coral Edith
Australian. Actress
b. Jul 23, 1913 in Melbourne, Australia
Source: *BiE&WWA; CurBio 59; FilmgC; InWom; MotPP; MovMk; NotNAT; Who 74; WhoHol A; WhoThe 77*

Browne, Dik
American. Cartoonist
Created "Hi and Lois," 1954; "Hagar the Horrible,"1973.
b. Aug 11, 1917 in New York, New York
Source: *AuNews 1; WhoAm 82*

Browne, Jackson
American. Singer, Songwriter
Hit single "Doctor My Eyes," 1971, gold album *The Pretender,* 1976.
b. Oct 9, 1950 in Heidelberg, Germany (West)
Source: *BioIn 9, 11; BkPepl; EncPR&S; IlEncRk; RkOn; WhoAm 82; WhoRock 81*

Browne, Leslie
American. Ballerina, Actress
b. Jun 29, 1957 in New York, New York
Source: *BioIn 11; NewYTBS 77; WhoAm 80, 82*

Browne, Patsy
American. Gambler, Bookmaker
b. 1907
Source: *BioIn 10*

Browne, "Phiz" (Hablot Knight)
English. Artist, Illustrator
b. Jun 15, 1815 in Kensington, England
d. Jul 8, 1882 in West Brighton, England
Source: *ChPo, S1, S2; HsB&A; NewC*

Browne, Walter Shawn
American. Chess Player, Journalist
b. Jan 10, 1949 in Sydney, Australia
Source: *BioNews 74; WhoAm 82*

Brownell, Herbert, Jr.
American. Lawyer, Government Official
Managed Thomas Dewey's presidential campaigns; attorney general, 1953-57.
b. Feb 20, 1904 in Peru, Nebraska
Source: *BiDrUSE; CurBio 44, 54; IntWW 74; WhoAm 74, 76, 78, 80, 82; WhoAmP 73; WhoWor 74*

Brownwell, Samuel Miller
American. Educator, Government Official
b. Apr 3, 1900 in Peru, Nebraska
Source: *BioIn 3, 4, 5, 6, 7; CurBio 54*

Browning, "Daddy"
American. Playboy
Source: *NF*

Browning, Elizabeth Barrett
[Mrs. Robert Browning]
English. Poet
Wrote *Sonnets from the Portuguese,* 1850, her own love story in verse.
b. Mar 6, 1806 in Coxhoe Hall, England
d. Jun 30, 1861 in Florence, Italy
Source: *Alli, SUP; AtlBL; BbD; BiD&SB; BrAu 19; CasWL; Chambr 3; ChPo, S1, S2; CnE&AP; CrtT 3; CyWA; DcEnA AP; DcEnL; DcEuL; DcLEL; EvLB; InWom; MouLC 3; NewC; OxEng; Pen ENG; RAdv 1; RComWL; REn; WebE&AL; HerW*

Browning, Sir Frederick A(rthur) M(ontague) "Boy"
British. Army Officer
b. Dec 20, 1896
d. Mar 14, 1965 in Cornwall, England
Source: *BioIn 7; CurBio 43, 65; ObitOF 79; PseudN; WhWW-II*

Browning, James Louis
American. Government Official
b. Dec 8, 1932 in Globe, Arizona
Source: *WhoGov 72*

Browning, John
American. Musician
b. May 23, 1933 in Denver, Colorado
Source: *CurBio 69; WhoAm 82; WhoMus 72*

Browning, John Moses
American. Inventor, Firearms Designer
Developed automatic rifles, pistols, and the machine gun.
b. Jan 21, 1855 in Ogden, Utah
d. Nov 26, 1926 in Liege, Belgium
Source: *AmBi; DcAmB; WebAB; WhAm 1*

Browning, Norma Lee
[Mrs. Russell Joynerogg]
American. Journalist
b. Nov 24, 1914 in Spickard, Missouri
Source: *AmAu&B; ConAu 61; WhoAm 82*

Browning, Robert
English. Poet
Married Elizabeth Barrett, 1846; wrote *Pippa Passes,* 1841.
b. May 7, 1812 in London, England
d. Dec 12, 1889 in Venice, Italy
Source: *Alli, SUP; AnCL; AtlBL; BiD&SB; BrAu 19; CasWL; Chambr 3; ChPo, S1, S2; CnE&AP; CnThe; CrtT 3; CyWA; DcEnA, AP; DcEnL; DcEuL; DcLEL; EvLB; McGEWD; MouLC 4; NewC; OxEng; OxThe; Pen ENG; RAdv 1; RComWL; REn; REnWD; Str&VC; WebE&AL; YABC 1*

Browning, Tod
American. Motion Picture Director
b. Jul 12, 1882 in Louisville, Kentucky
d. Oct 6, 1962 in Santa Monica, California
Source: *BiDFilm; DcFM; FilmEn; MovMk; ObitOF 79; OxFilm; WhScrn 74; WorEFlm*

Brownlee, John
Australian. Opera Singer
b. Jan 7, 1901 in Geelong, Australia
d. Jan 10, 1969 in New York, New York
Source: *BiE&WWA*

Brownmiller, Susan
American. Author, Feminist
b. Feb 15, 1935 in Brooklyn, New York
Source: *BioIn 10, 11, 12; ConAu 103; CurBio 78*

Brownson, Orestes Augustus
American. Author, Clergyman
b. Sep 16, 1803 in Stockbridge, Vermont
d. Apr 17, 1876 in Detroit, Michigan
Source: *Alli, SUP; AmAu; AmAu&B; AmBi; ApCAB; BbD; BiD&SB; CasWL; CyAl 2; DcAmAu; DcAmB; DcEnL; DcLEL; DcNAA; OxAmL; Pen AM; REn; REnAL; TwCBDA; WebAB; WebE&AL; WhAm H*

Broyhill, Joel Thomas
American. Congressman
b. Nov 4, 1919 in Hopewell, Georgia
Source: *BiDrAC; BioNews 74; CurBio 74; CngDr 74; WhoAm 74; WhoAmP 73; WhoGov 72; WhoS&SW 73*

Broz, Josip
see: Tito

Brubeck, Dave (David Warren)
American. Jazz Musician
Leader, Dave Brubeck Quartet 1951-1967.
b. Dec 6, 1920 in Concord, California
Source: *CelR 73; CurBio 56; IntWW 74; WebAB; Who 74; WhoAm 74, 76, 78, 80, 82; WhoE 74; WhoWor 74*

Bruce, Ailsa Mellon
American. Philanthropist
b. Jun 28, 1901 in Pittsburgh, Pennsylvania
d. Aug 25, 1969 in New York, New York
Source: *BioIn 8, 10; NatCAB 55*

Bruce, Carol
American. Actress, Singer
b. Nov 15, 1919 in Great Neck, New York
Source: *BiE&WWA; NotNAT; WhoHol A; WhoThe 77*

Bruce, David Kirkpatrick Estes
American. Diplomat
Head of US diplomatic office in Peking, China, 1973-74; U.S. Ambassador to NATO, 1974-76.
b. Feb 12, 1898 in Baltimore, Maryland
d. Dec 4, 1978 in Washington, DC
Source: *CurBio 49, 61; NewYTBE 70, 73; IntWW 74; USBiR 74; WhoAm 74; WhoWor 74*

Bruce, Jack
[Cream]
Scottish. Rock Musician
b. May 14, 1943 in Glasgow, Scotland
Source: *EncPR&S; IlEncRk*

Bruce, Lenny
American. Author, Comedian
Charged with obscenity for using four-letter words in act; Dustin Hoffman starred in *Lenny,* 1974.
b. 1925 in Mineola, New York
d. Aug 3, 1966 in Hollywood, California
Source: *AmAu&B; ConAu 25R, 89; NewYTBE 71; WhAm 4; WhScrn 77*

Bruce, Nigel
American. Actor
b. Feb 4, 1895 in Ensenada, Mexico
d. Oct 8, 1953 in Santa Monica, California
Source: *CmMov; FilmgC; MotPP; MovMk; Vers A; WhScrn 74, 77; WhoHol B*

Bruce, Robert
see: Robert I

Bruce, Virginia
[Helen Virginia Briggs]
American. Actress
b. 1910 in Minneapolis, Minnesota
d. Feb 24, 1982 in Woodland Hills, California
Source: *Film 2; FilmgC; MGM; MotPP; MovMk; NewYTBS 82; PseudN; ThFT; WhoHol A*

Bruch, Max
German. Conductor, Teacher, Composer
b. Jan 6, 1838 in Cologne, Germany
d. Oct 2, 1920 in Friedenau, Germany
Source: *NewEOp 71; OxMus*

Bruckner, Anton
Austrian. Composer, Organist
b. Sep 4, 1824 in Ausfelden, Austria
d. Oct 11, 1896 in Vienna, Austria
Source: *AtlBL; OxGer; REn*

Bruegel, Pieter, (The Elder)
[Pieter Breughel or Brueghel]
Flemish. Artist
b. 1525
d. Sep 5, 1569 in Brussels, Belgium
Source: *AtlBL; REn*

Brughel, Jan
[Jan Breughel or Brueghel]
Flemish. Artist
b. 1568 in Brussels, Belgium
d. 1625
Source: *BioIn 6; OxArt*

Brugnon, Jacques
[The Four Musketeers]
"Toto"
French. Tennis Player
b. May 11, 1895 in Paris, France
d. Mar 20, 1978 in Paris, France
Source: *BioIn 11*

Bruhn, Erik Belton Evers
Danish. Ballet Dancer, Producer
b. Oct 3, 1928 in Copenhagen, Denmark
Source: *CelR 73; CurBio 59; IntWW 74; NewYTBE 72; Who 74; WhoAm 82; WhoWor 74*

Brumidi, Constantino
Italian. Artist
b. Jul 26, 1805 in Rome, Italy
d. Feb 19, 1880 in Washington, DC
Source: *BioIn 2, 3, 4, 7, 8; DcAmB; WhAm H*

Brummell, "Beau" (George Bryan)
English. Dandy, Gambler
Set fashion standards for English society: trousers instead of breeches.
b. Jun 7, 1778 in London, England
d. Mar 31, 1840 in Caen, France
Source: *LinLib L, S; NewC; NewCol 75; WebBD 80*

Brundage, Avery
American. Olympic Official
President, IOC, 1952-72.
b. Sep 28, 1887 in Detroit, Michigan
d. May 8, 1975 in Gavmisch, Germany (West)
Source: *CelR 73; CurBio 48; IntWW 74; NewYTBE 72; St&PR 75; WebAB; WhAm 6; Who 74; WhoAm 74; WhoAmA 73; WhoTr&F 73; WhoWor 74*

Brundage, John Herbert
see: Herbert, John, pseud.

Brundtland, Gro Harlem
"The Green Goddess"
Norwegian. Former Prime Minister
b. Apr 20, 1939 in Oslo, Norway
Source: *CurBio 81; IntWW 75, 76, 77, 78; NewYTBS 81; PseudN; WhoWor 78*

Brunel, Isambard Kingdom
English. Engineer
b. Apr 9, 1806 in Portsmouth, England
d. Sep 15, 1859 in London, England
Source: *BioIn 1, 2, 3, 4, 5, 6, 7, 8, 9, 10, 11; McGEWB*

Brunelleschi, Filippo
Italian. Architect, Sculptor
b. 1377 in Florence, Italy
d. Apr 16, 1446 in Florence, Italy
Source: *AtlBL; OxThe; REn*

Brunhart, Hans
Liechtenstein. Politician
b. Mar 28, 1945 in Liechtenstein
Source: *IntWW 79*

Brunhoff, Jean de
French. Children's Author, Illustrator
b. 1899 in France
d. Oct 16, 1937 in Switzerland
Source: *AuBYP; BioIn 1, 2, 5, 6, 7, 8; IlsCB 1946; JBA 51; WhoChL*

Brunhoff, Laurent de
French. Author, Illustrator
Continues "Barbar" children's books his father originated.
b. Aug 30, 1925 in Paris, France
Source: *AuBYP; ConAu 73; IlsCB 1946, 1957; MorJA; NewYTBE 72; PiP; SmATA 24; WhoChL*

Bruning, Heinrich
German. Economist
b. 1885
d. 1970
Source: *BioIn 3, 8, 9; NewYTBE 70; OxGer*

Brunis, George
American. Jazz Musician
b. Feb 6, 1902 in New Orleans, Louisiana
d. Nov 19, 1974 in Chicago, Illinois
Source: *WhoAm 74*

Brunler, Oscar
English. Physician, Scientist
b. 1894
d. Aug 1, 1952 in Santa Barbara, California
Source: *BioIn 3*

Brunner, Emil
Swiss. Theologian
b. Dec 23, 1889
d. Apr 6, 1966 in Zurich, Switzerland
Source: *TwCA SUP*

Bruno, Giordano
Italian. Philosopher
b. 1548 in Nola, Italy
d. Feb 17, 1600 in Rome, Italy
Source: *BiD&SB; CasWL; DcEuL; EuAu; EvEuW; McGEWD; OxThe; Pen EUR; RComWL; REn; REnWD*

Brunton, Paul
English. Journalist
b. 1898
Source: *Au&Wr 71*

Brush, George
American. Artist
b. Sep 28, 1855
d. Apr 24, 1941
Source: *BioIn 3, 9; CurBio 41*

Brustein, Robert Sanford
American. Educator, Author
b. Apr 21, 1927 in New York, New York
Source: *AmAu&B; Au&Wr 71; BiE&WWA; CelR 73; ConAu 9R; LEduc 74; NotNAT; WhoAm 74, 76, 78, 80, 82; WhoE 74; WhoThe 77; WhoWor 74; WorAu*

Brutus, Dennis Vincent
African. Poet, Educator
b. Nov 28, 1924 in Salisbury, Rhodesia
Source: *CasWL; ConAu 49, 2NR; ConP 70, 75; DrAS 74E; IntWW 74; Pen CL; RGAfL; TwCW; WhoAm 82; WrDr 76*

Brutus, Marcus Junius
Roman. Politician, Conspirator
Principal assassin, with Cassius, of Julius Caesar, 44BC.
b. 85BC
d. 42BC
Source: *NewC; REn*

Bryan, Dora
[Mrs. William Lawton]
English. Actress
b. Feb 7, 1924 in Southport, England
Source: *EncMT; IntMPA 75; Who 74; WhoThe 72, 77*

Bryan, William Jennings
"The Great Commoner"
American. Lawyer, Political Leader
Secretary of State, 1913-15; presidential candidate, 1896, 1900, 1908.
b. Mar 19, 1860 in Salem, Ohio
d. Jul 26, 1925 in Dayton, Ohio
Source: *AmAu&B; AmBi; ApCAB SUP; BiDrAC; BiDrUSE; DcAmAu; DcAmB; DcNAA; EncAB-H; OxAmL; REn; REnAL; TwCBDA; WebAB; WhAm 1; WhAmP*

Bryant, Anita
American. Singer
Lost contract promoting orange juice due to views on homosexuals.
b. Mar 25, 1940 in Barnsdale, Oklahoma
Source: *BkPepl; ConAu 85; WhoAm 74, 76, 78, 80, 82*

Bryant, "Bear" (Paul William)
"The Titan of Tuscaloosa"
American. Football Coach, Athletic Director
With U of Alabama, 1944-82; winningest coach in history of college football.
b. Sep 11, 1913 in Kingsland, Arkansas
d. Jan 26, 1983 in Tuscaloosa, Alabama
Source: *BioNews 75; CurBio 80; WhoAm 74, 76, 78, 80, 82; WhoFtbl 74; WhoS&SW 73*

Bryant, Felice
American. Songwriter
b. Aug 7, 1925 in Milwaukee, Wisconsin
Source: *BioIn 9; EncFCWM 69*

Bryant, Lane
[Lena Himmelstein]
American. Retailer
Founded Lane Bryant clothing stores, circa 1904.
b. Dec 1, 1879 in Lithuania
d. Sep 26, 1951
Source: *BioIn 1, 2, 3, 7; NatCAB 47*

Bryant, Louise Stevens
American. Public Health Leader
b. Sep 19, 1885 in Paris, France
d. Aug 29, 1956 in New York
Source: *BioIn 4, 6; WhAm 3; WomWWA 14*

Bryant, William Cullen
American. Poet, Editor
Best known poem *Thanatopsis,* 1811; editor NY *Evening Post,* 1829-78.
b. Nov 3, 1794 in Cummington, Massachusetts
d. Jun 12, 1878 in New York, New York
Source: *Alli, SUP; AmAu; AmAu&B; AmBi; ApCAB; AtlBL; BbD; BiD&SB; CarSB; CasWL; Chambr 3; ChPo, S1, S2; CnDAL; CnE&AP; CrtT 3; CyAL 1; CyWA; DcAmAu; DcAmB; DcEnL; DcLEL; DcNAA; EncAB-H; EvLB; MouLC 3; OxAmL; OxEng; Pen AM; PoChrch; RAdv 1; REn; REnAL; Str&VC; TwCBDA; WebAB; WebE&AL; WhAm H*

Bryce, James Bryce, Viscount
British. Politician, Historian, Lawyer
b. May 10, 1838 in Belfast, Northern Ireland
d. Jan 22, 1922 in Sidmouth, England
Source: *Alli SUP; BbD; BiD&SB; BrAu 19; DcEnA, AP; EvLB; LongCTC; NewC; OxAmL; OxEng; Pen AM, ENG; REn; WhAm 1*

Brymer, Jack
English. Musician
b. Jan 27, 1915 in South Shields, England
Source: *IntWW 74; Who 74; WhoMus 72; WhoWor 74*

Brynner, Yul
American. Actor
Won Tony, 1951, Oscar, 1956, for role in *The King and I.*
b. Jul 11, 1917 in Sakhalin, Russia
Source: *BiDFilm; CelR 73; CurBio 56; EncMT; FilmgC; IntMPA 75, 76, 77, 78, 79, 80, 81, 82; IntWW 74; MotPP; MovMk; OxFilm; PlP&P; Who 74; WhoAm 74, 76, 78, 80, 82; WhoHol A; WhoWor 74; WorEFlm*

Bryson, Wally
see: Raspberries, The

Brzezinski, Zbigniew Kazimierz
American. Author, Educator, Businessman
Advisor to Jimmy Carter on national security affairs, 1977-81.
b. Mar 28, 1928 in Warsaw, Poland
Source: *AmAu&B; AmM&WS 73S; ConAu 1R, 5NR; CurBio 70; WhoAm 74, 76, 78, 80, 82; WhoWor 74*

Bubbles, John
[John Sublett; Buck and Bubbles]
American. Tap Dancer
In Vaudville, 1920's-30's; appeared in *Porgy and Bess,* 1935.
b. 1902 in Louisville, Kentucky
Source: *AmPS B; DcBlPA; PlP&P*

Buber, Martin
Israeli. Philosopher, Author
b. Feb 8, 1878 in Vienna, Austria
d. Jun 13, 1965 in Jerusalem, Israel
Source: *ConAu 25R; CurBio 53, 65; EncWL; ModGL; OxGer; REn; TwCA SUP; WhAm 4; WhoTwCL*

Buchalter, "Lepke" (Louis)
American. Racketeer, Murderer
Number one labor racketeer; led professional "hit" squad, 1930's.
b. 1897 in Manhattan, New York
d. Mar 4, 1944 in Sing Sing, New York
Source: *Blood*

Buchan, Sir John
[Baron Tweedsmuir]
Canadian. Author, Governor-General
b. Aug 26, 1875 in Perth, Scotland
d. Feb 11, 1940 in Montreal, PQ
Source: *CasWL; ChPo, S1, S2; CnMWL; CurBio 40; CyWA; DcLEL; EncMys; EvLB; JBA 34; LongCTC; MnBBF; ModBrL; NewC; OxCan; OxEng; Pen ENG; REn; TwCA, SUP; TwCW; WebE&AL*

Buchanan, Angela Marie
"Bay"
American. Treasurer of the United States
b. 1948 in Washington, DC
Source: *BioIn 12; WhoAm 82*

Buchanan, Edgar
[J J Jackson]
American. Actor
Played Uncle Joe on TV series "Petticoat Junction," 1963-70.
b. Mar 20, 1903 in Humansville, Missouri
d. 1979 in Palm Desert, California
Source: *CmMov; FilmgC; IntMPA 75, 76, 77; MotPP; MovMk; WhoHol A*

Buchanan, Jack
Scottish. Comedian, Actor
b. Apr 2, 1891 in Glasgow, Scotland
d. Oct 20, 1957 in London, England
Source: *EncMT; Film 1; FilmgC; MotPP; OxFilm; WhScrn 74, 77; WhoHol B*

Buchanan, James
American. 15th US President
Opposed slavery in principle, but defended it under Constitution.
b. Apr 23, 1791 in Mercersburg, Pennsylvania
d. Jun 1, 1868 in Lancaster, Pennsylvania
Source: *Alli SUP; AmAu&B; AmBi; ApCAB; BiAuS; BiDrAC; BiDrUSE; DcAmAu; DcAmB; Drake; EncAB-H; OxAmL; REnAL; TwCBDA; WebAB; WhAm H; WhAmP*

Buchanan, Pat
American. Admiral
b. 1888
d. 1950
Source: *BioIn 2*

Buchanan, Patrick Joseph
American. Journalist
Assistant to Richard Nixon, 1966-73; wrote *The New Majority*, 1973.
b. Nov 2, 1938 in Washington, DC
Source: *WhoAm 74, 76, 78, 80, 82; WhoAmP 73; WhoGov 72; WhoS&SW 73*

Bucher, Lloyd Mark
American. Naval Officer
Commander, USS *Pueblo*, seized by N Korea, 1968.
b. Sep 1, 1927 in Pocatello, Idaho
Source: *BioIn 9; PolProf NF*

Buchholz, Francis
see: Scorpions

Buchholz, Horst
German. Actor
b. Dec 4, 1933 in Berlin, Germany
Source: *BiE&WWA; CurBio 60; FilmgC; IntMPA 75, 76, 77, 78, 79, 80, 81, 82; MotPP; MovMk; WhoHol A; WorEFlm*

Buchman, Frank Nathan Daniel
American. Clergyman
b. Jun 4, 1878 in Pennsburg, Pennsylvania
d. Aug 7, 1961
Source: *AmAu&B; BioIn 1, 2, 4, 5, 6, 9, 10; CurBio 40, 61; LongCTC*

Buchner, Ludwig
German. Philosopher
b. 1824
d. 1899
Source: *BiD&SB; OxGer*

Buchwald, Art
American. Journalist, Author, Humorist
Column syndicated in over 550 newspapers; wrote *The Buchwald Stops Here*, 1978.
b. Oct 20, 1925 in Mount Vernon, New York
Source: *AmAu&B; AuNews 1; BioNews 74; CelR 73; ConAu 5R; CurBio 60; IntWW 74; NewYTBE 72; Pen AM; SmATA 10; Who 82; WhoAm 74, 76, 78, 80, 82; WhoS&SW 73; WhoWor 74; WorAu; WrDr 76*

Buck, Frank
American. Animal Trainer
b. Mar 17, 1884 in Gainesville, Texas
d. Mar 25, 1950 in Houston, Texas
Source: *AmAu&B; CurBio 43, 50; FilmgC; MnBBF; REnAL; WebAB; WhScrn 74, 77; WhoHol B*

Buck, Gene
American. Songwriter, Artist, Producer
b. Aug 8, 1886 in Detroit, Michigan
d. Feb 24, 1957 in Manhasset, New York
Source: *AmAu&B; AmSCAP 66; CurBio 41, 57; EncMT; NewCBMT; REnAL*

Buck, Paul Herman
American. Author, Educator
b. Sep 25, 1899 in Columbus, Ohio
d. Dec 23, 1978 in Cambridge, Massachusetts
Source: *AmAu&B; BioIn 3, 4; ConAu 81; CurBio 55; DrAS 74H, 78H; OhA&B; OxAmL; TwCA, SUP; WhAm 7; WhoAm 74, 76; WhoWor 74, 76*

Buck, Pearl S(ydenstricker)
American. Author
Won Pulitzer Prize, 1932, Nobel Prize, 1938; wrote *The Good Earth*, 1930.
b. Jun 26, 1892 in Hillsboro, West Virginia
d. Mar 6, 1973 in Danby, Vermont
Source: *AmAu&B; AmNov; Au&Wr 71; AuBYP; AuNews 1; BiE&WWA; CasWL; CnDAL; ConAmA; ConAu 1R, 41R, 1NR; ConLC 7, 11, 18; ConNov 72; CurBio 56, 73; CyWA; DcLEL; EncWL; EvLB; FilmgC; HerW; InWom; LongCTC; ModAL; NewYTBE 73; OxAmL; Pen AM; REn; REnAL; SmATA 1; TwCA, SUP; TwCW; WebAB; WhAm 5; WhNAA*

Buckingham, Lindsey
[Fleetwood Mac]
American. Rock Musician
b. Oct 3, 1947 in Palo Alto, California
Source: *WhoAm 80, 82*

Buckinghams, The
[Nick Fortune; Carl Giamarese; Marty Grebb; Jon Paulos; Denny Tufano]
American. Rock Group
Source: *BiDAmM; LilREn 78; RkOn 2; WhoRock 81*

Buckland, William
English. Geologist
b. Mar 12, 1784 in Axminster, England
d. Aug 14, 1856 in Islip, England
Source: *Alli; DcEnL; DcScB*

Buckley, Betty
American. Actress
Played Abby Bradford on TV series "Eight is Enough."
b. Jul 3, 1947 in Big Spring, Texas
Source: *BioIn 12*

Buckley, Charles Anthony
American. Congressman
b. Jun 23, 1890 in New York, New York
d. Jan 22, 1967 in New York, New York
Source: *BiDrAC; WhAm 4; WhAmP*

Buckley, Emerson
American. Conductor
b. Apr 14, 1916 in New York, New York
Source: *WhoAm 74, 76, 78, 80, 82; WhoS&SW 73*

Buckley, James Lane
American. Senator, Author
Senator from NY, 1971-77; wrote *If Men were Angels*, 1975.
b. Mar 9, 1923 in New York, New York
Source: *CelR 73; CngDr 74; ConAu 61; CurBio 71; IntWW 74; WhoAm 74, 76, 78, 80, 82; WhoAmP 73; WhoE 74; WhoGov 72*

Buckley, Tim
American. Singer, Songwriter
b. Feb 17, 1947 in Washington, DC
d. Jun 29, 1975 in Santa Monica, California
Source: *BioIn 10; EncPR&S; IlEncRk; WhoAm 74*

Buckley, William F(rank), Jr.
American. Editor, Author
Editor, *National Review* magazine, 1955--;wrote *Atlantic High*, 1982.
b. Nov 24, 1925 in New York, New York
Source: *AmAu&B; AuNews 1; ConAu 1R, 1NR; ConLC 7, 18; CurBio 62, 82; IntWW 74; St&PR 75; WebAB; WhoAm 74, 76, 78, 80, 82; WhoAmP 73; WhoE 74; WhoF&I 74; WhoGov 72; WhoWor 74; WorAu; WrDr 76*

Buckmaster, Henrietta, pseud.
[Henrietta Henkle; H H Stephens]
American. Author, Journalist
b. 1909 in Cleveland, Ohio
Source: *AmNov; Au&Wr 71; ConAu 9R; CurBio 46; SmATA 6; WorAu*

Buckner, Bill (William Joseph)
"Billy"; "Buck"
American. Baseball Player
b. Dec 14, 1949 in Vallejo, California
Source: *BaseEn; NewYTBS 81; PseudN; WhoAm 82*

Buckner, Simon, Jr.
American. Military Leader, Politician
b. Jul 18, 1886 in Munfordville, Kentucky
d. Jun 18, 1945 in Okinawa, Japan
Source: *CurBio 42, 45; DcAmB S3; WebAB; WhAm 2*

Buckner, Simon B
American. Military Leader
Confederate general, 1864; governor of Kentucky, 1887-91.
b. Apr 1, 1823 in Hart County, Kentucky
d. Jan 8, 1914
Source: *AmBi; ApCAB; DcAmB; TwCBDA; WebAB; WhAm 1*

Bucyk, John Paul
"The Chief"
Canadian. Hockey Player
Left wing, 1955-78; in fourth place for career points.
b. May 12, 1935 in Edmonton, AB
Source: *BioIn 9, 10; WhoHcky 73*

Budd, Julie
American. Singer
b. 1944 in Brooklyn, New York
Source: *BioIn 9*

Budd, Ralph
American. Railroad Executive
b. Aug 20, 1879 in Waterloo, Iowa
d. Feb 2, 1962
Source: *REnAW; WhAm 4*

Buddha
[Gautama Buddha]
Indian. Founder of Buddhism
Renounced world at age 29 to search for solution to human suffering.
b. 563BC in Kapilavastu, India
d. 483BC in Kusinagara, India
Source: *NewC; NewCol 75; RComWL*

Budenz, Louis Francis
American. Educator
b. Jul 17, 1891 in Indianapolis, Indiana
d. Apr 27, 1972
Source: *AmAu&B; BkC 6; CathA 1952; CurBio 51, 72*

Budge, Ernest Alfred
English. Egyptologist, Author
b. 1857
d. 1934
Source: *Alli SUP; BiD&SB*

Budge, (John) Don(ald)
American. Tennis Player
Won "grand slam" of tennis, 1938; Hall of Fame, 1964.
b. Jun 13, 1915 in Oakland, California
Source: *WebAB*

Buechner, Frederick
American. Author, Educator
b. Jul 11, 1926 in New York, New York
Source: *AmAu&B; ConAu 13R; ConLC 2, 4, 6; ConNov 72, 76; DrAF 76; ModAL, SUP; OxAmL; TwCW; WhoAm 82; WorAu; WrDr 76*

Bueno, Maria Ester Audion
Brazilian. Tennis Player
b. 1940 in Sao Paulo, Brazil
Source: *CurBio 65; InWom*

Bufano, Beniamino
American. Artist
b. 1898
d. 1970
Source: *BioIn 2, 5, 6, 9, 10, 11; NewYTBE 70*

"Buffalo Bill"
see: Cody, "Buffalo Bill" (William Frederick)

"Buffalo" Bob
[Bob Smith]
American. Entertainer
Creator, star TV show "Howdy Doody," 1947-60.
b. Nov 27, 1917 in Buffalo, New York
Source: *WhoAm 76*

Buffalo Springfield
[Richie Furay; Dewey Martin; Jim Messina; Bruce Palmer; Stephen Stills; Neil Young]
American. Rock Group
Source: *BiDAmM; ConMuA 80; LilREn 78; RkOn 2; WhoRock 81*

Buffet, Bernard
French. Artist
b. Jul 10, 1928 in Paris, France
Source: *CurBio 59; IntWW 74; Who 74; WhoGrA*

Buffet, Jimmy
[Jimmy Buffett]
American. Singer, Songwriter
Hit single "Margaritaville," 1977.
b. Dec 25, 1946 in Pascagoula, Mississippi
Source: *IlEncRk; RkOn; WhoAm 82*

Buffin, Terry
see: Mott (the Hoople)

Buffon, Georges Louis Leclerc
French. Naturalist
b. Sep 7, 1707 in Montbard, France
d. Apr 16, 1788 in Paris, France
Source: *AtlBL; BbD; BiD&SB; CasWL; DcEuL; EuAu; EvEuW; OxEng; OxFr; Pen EUR; REn*

Bufman, Zev
Israeli. Motion Picture Producer
b. Oct 11, 1930 in Tel Aviv, Palestine
Source: *BiE&WWA; WhoAm 82; WhoThe 77*

Buford, Don(ald Alvin)
American. Baseball Player
b. Feb 2, 1937 in Linden, Texas
Source: *BaseEn; WhoProB 73*

Buford, John
American. Military Leader
b. Mar 4, 1826 in Woodford County, Kentucky
d. Dec 16, 1863 in Washington, DC
Source: *AmBi; ApCAB; DcAmB; Drake; TwCBDA; WhAm H*

Bugatti, Ettore
Italian. Engineer, Auto Manufacturer
b. 1881 in Milan, Italy
d. 1947
Source: *BioIn 10*

Bugatti, Jean
Italian. Automobile Executive
b. 1909
Source: *BioIn 10*

Bugayev, Boris Nikolayevich
see: Bely, Andrei, pseud.

Bugbee, Emma
American. Journalist, Suffragist
b. 1888? in Shippensburg, Pennsylvania
d. Oct 6, 1981 in Warwick, Rhode Island
Source: *AuBYP; BioIn 7, 10; InWom; NewYTBS 81*

Bugliosi, Vincent T
American. Lawyer, Author
Prosecutor in Manson family murder trials; wrote *Helter-Skelter,* 1974.
b. Aug 18, 1934 in Hibbing, Minnesota
Source: *ConAu 73; WhoAm 82*

Buick, David Dunbar
American. Auto Manufacturer
Formed Buick Co., 1902; built first car, 1903.
b. Sep 17, 1854 in Arbroth, Scotland
d. Mar 6, 1929 in Detroit, Michigan
Source: *NatCAB 34; WebBD 80*

Buitoni, Giovanni
Italian. Food Executive
b. Nov 6, 1891 in Perugia, Italy
d. Jan 13, 1979 in Rome, Italy
Source: *CurBio 62, 79; NewYTBS 79; St&PR 75*

Bujold, Genevieve
Canadian. Actress
b. Jul 1, 1942 in Montreal, PQ
Source: *CanWW 70; CelR 73; CreCan 1; FilmgC; IntMPA 75, 76, 77, 78, 79, 80, 81, 82; WhoAm 82; WhoHol A*

Buketoff, Igor
American. Conductor
b. May 29, 1915 in Hartford, Connecticut
Source: *WhoAm 74, 76, 78, 80, 82; WhoMus 72; WhoWor 74*

Bukharin, Nikolai Ivanovich
Russian. Communist Leader, Editor
b. 1888 in Moscow, Russia
d. Mar 1938
Source: *McGEWB; REn*

Bukharov, Alexandr Semyonovich
Russian. Politician
b. 1912
Source: *IntWW 74*

Bukovsky, Vladimir
Russian. Dissident
b. Dec 30, 1942 in Moscow, U.S.S.R.
Source: *CurBio 78; DcPol; IntWW 78, 79, 80, 81; NewYTBS 76, 77*

Bulfinch, Charles
American. Architect
b. Aug 8, 1763 in Boston, Massachusetts
d. Apr 15, 1844 in Boston, Massachusetts
Source: *AmBi; ApCAB; AtlBL; BiAuS; DcAmB; Drake; EncAB-H; OxAmL; REnAL; TwCBDA; WebAB; WhAm H*

Bulfinch, Thomas
American. Historian, Mythologist
b. Jul 15, 1796 in Newton, Massachusetts
d. May 27, 1867 in Boston, Massachusetts
Source: *Alli, SUP; AmAu; AmAu&B; AmBi; ApCAB; BiD&SB; CarSB; ChPo; DcAmAu; DcAmB; DcNAA; Drake; OxAmL; REn; REnAL; WebAB; WhAm H*

Bulgakov, Mikhail
Russian. Author
b. 1891 in Kiev, Russia
d. 1940 in Moscow, U.S.S.R.
Source: *CasWL; ClDMEL; CnMD; CnThe; DcRusL; EncWL; EvEuW; McGEWD; ModSL 1; ModWD; Pen EUR; REn; REnWD; TwCW; WhoTwCL; WorAu*

Bulganin, Nikolai Aleksandrovich
Russian. Premier
b. Jun 11, 1895 in Gorky, Russia
d. Feb 24, 1975 in Moscow, U.S.S.R.
Source: *CurBio 55; IntWW 74; WhAm 6; Who 74; WhoWor 74*

Bulgari, Constantine
Italian. Jeweler
d. 1973
Source: *WorFshn*

Bulgari, Giorgio
Italian. Jeweler
Source: *WorFshn*

Bulifant, Joyce
American. Actress
Source: *WhoHol A*

Bulkeley, Morgan
American. Baseball Executive
First president of NL, 1876; Hall of Fame, 1937.
b. Dec 26, 1837 in East Haddam, Connecticut
d. Nov 6, 1922 in Hartford, Connecticut
Source: *ApCAB; BiDrAC; BiDrGov; BioIn 3, 7, 9; DcAmB; NatCAB 10; TwCBDA; WhAm 1; WhAmP; WhoProB 73*

Bull, John
English. Organist, Composer
b. 1563 in Somerset, England
d. Mar 12, 1622 in Antwerp, Belgium
Source: *Alli; NewC*

Bull, Odd
Norwegian. UN Official
Chief of staff, UN truce supervision, Palestine, 1963-70.
b. Jun 28, 1907 in Oslo, Norway
Source: *ConAu 81; CurBio 68; IntWW 74, 75, 76, 77, 78, 79, 80, 81; NewYTBE 70; WhoUN 75; WhoWor 74, 76, 78*

Bull, Ole Bornemann
Norwegian. Musician
b. Feb 5, 1810 in Bergen, Norway
d. Aug 17, 1880 in Lysoe, Norway
Source: *ApCAB; Drake; OxAmL; OxThe; REnAL; TwCBDA*

Bull, Peter
English. Actor, Author
b. Mar 21, 1912 in London, England
Source: *Au&Wr 71; BiE&WWA; ConAu 25R; FilmgC; MotPP; NotNAT A; PlP&P; WhoHol A*

Bullard, Dexter M
American. Psychiatrist, Medical Director
b. Aug 14, 1898 in Waukesha, Wisconsin
d. Oct 5, 1981 in Rockville, Maryland
Source: *AmM&WS 73P; BiDrAPA 77; NewYTBS 81*

Bullard, Sir Edward Crisp
English. Geophysicist
b. Sep 21, 1907 in Norwich, England
d. Apr 3, 1980 in La Jolla, California
Source: *CurBio 54, 80*

Bullard, Robert Lee
American. Military Leader
b. Jan 15, 1861 in Youngsboro, Alabama
d. Sep 11, 1947 in New York, New York
Source: *DcAmB S4; DcNAA; WhAm 2; WhNAA*

Bullins, Ed
American. Author, Dramatist, Producer
b. Jul 25, 1935 in Philadelphia, Pennsylvania
Source: *BlkAW; ConAu 49; ConDr 73; ConLC 1, 5; CroCD; LivgBAA; ModAL SUP; NotNAT; PlP&P A; WhoAm 74, 76, 78, 80, 82; WhoBlA 75; WhoE 74; WhoThe 77; WrDr 76*

Bullitt, William C
American. Statesman
b. Jan 25, 1891 in Philadelphia, Pennsylvania
d. Feb 15, 1967 in Neuilly, France
Source: *ConAu 89; CurBio 40, 67; REn; REnAL; WhAm 4*

Bullock, Alain Louis Charles
English. Author, Educator
b. Dec 13, 1914 in England
Source: *Au&Wr 71; ConAu 1R; LongCTC; WhoWor 74*

Bulow, Bernhard H M
German. Chancellor
b. May 3, 1849 in Altona, Germany
d. Oct 28, 1929 in Rome, Italy
Source: *OxGer*

Bulow, Hans Guido von
see: VonBulow, Hans Guido

Bultmann, Rudolf
German. Theologian
b. Aug 20, 1884 in Wiefelstede, Germany
d. Jul 30, 1976 in Marburg, Germany (West)
Source: *ConAu 5R, 65; CurBio 72; IntWW 74; OxGer; WhoWor 74; WorAu*

Bulwer-Lytton, Edward George
see: Lytton, Edward George Earle Lytton, Bulwer-Lytton Baron

Bulwer-Lytton, Edward Robert
see: Lytton, Edward Robert Bulwer-Lytton, Earl

Bumbry, Grace Ann Jaeckel
American. Opera Singer
b. Jan 4, 1937 in Saint Louis, Missouri
Source: *CelR 73; CurBio 64; InWom; IntWW 74; Who 74; WhoAm 74, 76, 78, 80, 82; WhoBlA 75; WhoMus 72; WhoWor 74*

Bumpers, Dale Leon
American. Politician
Governor of AR, 1970-74; US senator, 1975--.
b. Aug 12, 1925 in Charleston, Arkansas
Source: *AlmAP 78, 80; CngDr 77, 79, 81; CurBio 79; IntWW 74, 75, 76, 77, 78, 79, 80, 81; WhoAm 82; WhoS&SW 73, 75, 76, 78; WorAl*

Bunce, Alan
American. Actor
b. 1904 in Westfield, New Jersey
d. Apr 27, 1965 in New York, New York
Source: *BiE&WWA; WhScrn 74, 77; WhoHol B*

Bunche, Ralph Johnson
American. UN Official
Won Nobel Peace Prize for UN work, 1950.
b. Aug 7, 1904 in Detroit, Michigan
d. Dec 9, 1971 in New York, New York
Source: *ConAu 33R; CurBio 48, 72; EncAB-H; LinLib L, S; McGEWB; NatCAB 57; NewYTBE 71; PolProf E; PolProf J; PolProf K; PolProf T; REnAL; SelBAA; WebAB; WhAm 5; WorAl*

Bundy, McGeorge
American. Educator
Special assistant to Presidents Kennedy, Johnson on national securty affairs.
b. Mar 30, 1919 in Boston, Massachusetts
Source: *AmM&WS 73S, 78S; CelR 73; CurBio 62; EncAB-H; IntWW 74, 75, 76, 77, 78, 79, 80; LEduc 74; LinLib L, S; NewYTBS 79; PolProf J; PolProf K; PolProf NF; WhoAm 78, 80, 82; WhoWor 74, 78*

Bundy, Ted
[Theodore Robert Cowell]
American. Murderer
Convicted of two sorority house murders in FL, 1978; sentenced to death.
b. Nov 24, 1946 in Burlington, Vermont
Source: *BioIn 11; NewYTBS 78*

Bundy, William Putnam
American. Government Official, Lawyer
b. Sep 24, 1917 in Washington, DC
Source: *BioIn 5, 6, 7, 9, 11; CelR 73; CurBio 64; IntWW 74; WhoAm 74, 76, 78, 80, 82; WhoAmP 73; WhoE 74*

Bunge, Bettina
German. Tennis Player
b. Jun 13, 1963 in Adliswick, Switzerland
Source: *NF*

Bunin, Ivan Alekseevich
Russian. Author
b. Oct 10, 1870 in Voronezh, Russia
d. Nov 8, 1953 in Paris, France
Source: *CasWL; ClDMEL; CnMWL; CyWA; DcRusL; EncWL; EvEuW; LongCTC; ModSL 1; Pen EUR; REn; TwCA, SUP; TwCW; WhoLA; WhoTwCL*

Bunker, Chang and Eng
see: Chang and Eng

Bunker, Ellsworth
American. Diplomat
Ambassador to Vietnam, 1967-73; chief negotiator, Panama Canal Treaties, 1973-78.
b. May 11, 1894 in Yonkers, New York
Source: *CurBio 54, 78; IntWW 74, 75, 76, 77, 78, 79, 80, 81; PolProf J; PolProf NF; USBiR 74; WhoAm 74, 76, 78, 80; WhoAmP 73, 75, 77, 79; WhoGov 72, 75, 77; WhoWor 74, 76, 78*

Bunner, Henry Cuyler
American. Journalist
b. Aug 3, 1855 in Oswego, New York
d. May 11, 1896 in Nutley, New Jersey
Source: *Alli SUP; AmAu; AmAu&B; AmBi; ApCAB SUP; BbD; BiD&SB; Chambr 3; ChPo, S1, S2; CnDAL; DcAmAu; DcAmB; DcLEL; DcNAA; EvLB; OxAmL; REn; REnAL; TwCBDA; WhAm H*

Bunning, Jim (James Paul David)
American. Baseball Player
Pitcher; won 224 games in career; pitched perfect game against NY Mets, 1964.
b. Oct 23, 1931 in Southgate, Kentucky
Source: *BaseEn; WhoProB 73*

Bunny, John
American. Actor
b. Sep 21, 1863 in New York, New York
d. Apr 26, 1915 in Brooklyn, New York
Source: *Film 1; FilmgC; MotPP; TwYS; WhScrn 77; WhoHol B*

Bunsen, Robert Wilhelm Eberhard
German. Chemist, Inventor
Developed, improved laboratory equipment, including Bunsen burner.
b. Mar 31, 1811 in Goettingen, Germany
d. Aug 16, 1899 in Heidelberg, Germany
Source: *AsBiEn; DcInv; Dis&D; InSci; LinLib S; NewCol 75; OxGer; REn*

Bunting, Basil
English. Poet
Greatest popularity in 1960's as leader of British literary avant-garde.
b. 1900 in Northumberland, England
Source: *BioIn 11; ConAu 53, 7NR; ConLC 10; ConP 70, 75; ModBrL SUP; Who 74; WhoTwCL; WhoWor 74; WorAu; WrDr 76, 76*

Bunting, Mary Ingraham
American. Educator
b. Jul 10, 1910 in Brooklyn, New York
Source: *AmM&WS 73P, 76P, 79P; CurBio 67; WhoAm 74, 76, 78; WhoAmW 58, 61, 64, 66, 68, 70, 72, 74, 77, 79; WhoE 74; WhoWor 74*

Bunuel, Luis
Mexican. Motion Picture Director
b. Feb 22, 1900 in Calanda, Spain
Source: *BiDFilm; CelR 73; CurBio 65; DcFM; FilmgC; IntMPA 75, 76, 77, 78, 79, 80, 81, 82; IntWW 74; MovMk; OxFilm; Who 74; WhoS&SW 73; WhoWor 74; WorEFlm*

Bunyan, John
English. Preacher, Author
b. Nov 1628 in Elstow, England
d. Aug 31, 1688 in London, England
Source: *Alli; AtlBL; BbD; BiD&SB; BrAu; CarSB; CasWL; Chambr 1; ChPo, S1, S2; CroE&S; CrtT 2; CyWA; DcEnA; DcEnL; DcEuL; DcLEL; EvLB; MouLC 1; NewC; OxEng; Pen ENG; RAdv 1; RComWL; REn; WebE&AL*

Bunzel, Ruth L
American. Anthropologist, Author
Source: *InWom*

Buoniconti, Nick
American. Football Player
b. Dec 15, 1940 in Springfield, Massachusetts
Source: *NewYTBE 72*

Buono, Victor
American. Actor
b. 1939 in San Diego, California
d. Jan 1, 1982 in Apple Valley, California
Source: *FilmEn; FilmgC; IntMPA 75, 77, 78, 79, 80, 81; MotPP; MovMk; NewYTBS 82; WhoHol A*

Burbage, James
English. Actor
b. 1530
d. 1597
Source: *BioIn 11*

Burbage, Richard
English. Actor
b. 1567
d. 1619
Source: *NewC; OxThe; PlP&P; REn*

Burbank, Luther
American. Horticulturist
Experimented with and developed many new plant varieties.
b. Mar 7, 1849 in Lancaster, Massachusetts
d. Apr 11, 1926 in Santa Rosa, California
Source: *AmBi; ApCAB X; AsBiEn; DcAmB; DcNAA; EncAAH; EncAB-H; LinLib L, S; McGEWB; NatCAB 11, 33; REn; WebAB, 79; WhAm 1*

Burberry, Thomas
English. Fashion Designer
b. 1835
d. 1889
Source: *WorFshn*

Burch, Dean
American. Lawyer, Government Official
Chairman, FCC, 1969-74; senior advisor Reagan-Bush campaign, 1980.
b. Dec 20, 1927 in Enid, Oklahoma
Source: *BioNews 74; CelR 73; IntWW 74, 75, 76, 77, 78, 79, 80, 81; NewYTET; PolProf J; PolProf NF; WhoAm 74, 76, 78, 80, 82; WhoAmP 73, 75, 77, 79; WhoGov 72; WhoS&SW 73*

Burch, Robert Joseph
American. Author
b. Jun 26, 1925 in Inman, Georgia
Source: *AuBYP; ConAu 5R, 2NR; MorBMP 1; SmATA 1; ThrBJA; WrDr 76*

Burchard, John Ely
American. Architectural Historian
b. Dec 8, 1898 in Marshall, Minnesota
d. Dec 25, 1975 in Boston, Massachusetts
Source: *AmAu&B; BioIn 10; ConAu 1R; DrAS 74H; NewYTBS 75; ObitOF 79; WhAm 6; WhoAm 74, 76; WhoWor 74*

Burchfield, Charles
American. Artist
b. Apr 9, 1893 in Ashtabula, Ohio
d. Jan 10, 1967 in Gardenville, New York
Source: *CurBio 42, 61, 67; DcCAA 71; WebAB; WhAm 4*

Burck, Jacob
American. Editorial Cartoonist
Created daily editorial cartoon in Chicago *Sun Times;* won Pulitzer Prize, 1941.
b. Jan 10, 1904 in Poland
d. May 11, 1982 in Chicago, Illinois
Source: *WhoAm 74, 76, 78; WhoAmA 76, 78*

Burckhardt, Carl Jacob
Swiss. Diplomat, Historian
b. Sep 10, 1891 in Basel, Switzerland
d. Mar 3, 1974 in Vinzel, Switzerland
Source: *ConAu 49, 93; EncWL; NewYTBS 74; OxGer*

Burden, Ian
see: Human League

Burden, (Shirley) Carter, (Jr.)
American. Lawyer, Publisher
b. Aug 25, 1941 in Los Angeles, California
Source: *CelR 73; WhoAm 82; WhoAmA 73*

Burdette, (Selva) Lew(is, Jr.)
American. Baseball Player
b. Nov 22, 1926 in Nitro, West Virginia
Source: *BaseEn; WhoProB 73*

Burdick, Eugene
American. Author
b. Dec 12, 1918 in Sheldon, Louisiana
d. Jul 26, 1965
Source: *AmAu&B; ConAu 5R, 25R; SmATA 22; TwCW; WorAu*

Burdick, Quentin Northrop
American. Senator
b. Jun 19, 1908 in Munich, North Dakota
Source: *AlmAP 78, 80; BiDrAC; BioIn 5, 6, 9, 10; CngDr 74, 77, 79; CurBio 63; EncAAH; IntWW 74, 75, 76, 77, 78; PolProf J; PolProf K; WhoAm 74, 76, 78, 80, 82; WhoAmP 73, 75, 77, 79; WhoGov 72, 75, 77; WhoMW 74, 76, 78*

Burdon, Eric
[The Animals]
English. Rock Singer
b. Apr 5, 1941 in Walker-on-Tyne, England
Source: *EncPR&S; IlEncRk*

Burger, Carl
American. Author, Illustrator
b. Jun 18, 1888 in Maryville, Tennessee
d. Dec 1967
Source: *BioIn 8, 11; ConAu 21R; ConAu P-2; IlsCB 1957; SmATA 9*

Burger, Warren Earl
American. Supreme Court Justice
Conservative; appointed chief justice by Richard Nixon, 1969.
b. Sep 17, 1907 in Saint Paul, Minnesota
Source: *CelR 73; CngDr 74; CurBio 69; DrAS 74P; IntWW 74; NewYTBE 70; WebAB; Who 74; WhoAm 74, 76, 78, 80, 82; WhoGov 72; WhoS&SW 73; WhoWor 74*

Burgess, Anthony
English. Author, Journalist
b. Feb 25, 1917 in Manchester, England
Source: *Alli; Au&Wr 71; AuNews 1; CasWL; CelR 73; ConAu 1R, 2NR; ConLC 1, 2, 4, 5, 8, 10, 13, 15; ConNov 72, 76; CurBio 72; DrAF 76; EncWL; IntWW 74; LongCTC; ModBrL, SUP; NewC; Pen ENG; RAdv 1; TwCW; WebE&AL; Who 74; WhoAm 82; WhoTwCL; WhoWor 74; WorAu; WrDr 76*

Burgess, (Frank) Gelett
American. Author
Humorist whose best known poem was *The Purple Cow.*
b. Jan 30, 1866 in Boston, Massachusetts
d. Sep 18, 1951 in Carmel, California
Source: *AmAu&B; AmLY; AnMV 1926; BiD&SB; ChPo, S1; CnDAL; ConAmL; ConICB; DcAmAu; EncMys; EvLB; IlsCB 1744, 1946; LongCTC; OxAmL; REn; REnAL; TwCA, SUP; TwCW; WebAB; WhAm 3; WhNAA*

Burgess, Guy Francis de Moncy
English. Traitor
b. 1911
d. 1963
Source: *BioIn 2, 3, 4, 5, 6, 8, 9, 11; EncE 75*

Burgess, Paul
see: 10 CC

Burgess, "Smoky" (Forrest Harrill)
American. Baseball Player
Catcher, 1949-67; set record with 145 pinch hits in career.
b. Feb 6, 1927 in Caroleen, North Carolina
Source: *BaseEn; BioIn 8, 10; WhoProB 73*

Burgess, Thornton Waldo
American. Author, Journalist
Best known for nature and animal stories for children.
b. Jan 14, 1874 in Sandwich, Massachusetts
d. Jun 7, 1965 in Hampden, Massachusetts
Source: *AmAu&B; AuBYP; CarSB; ConAu 73; JBA 34, 51; OxAmL; REn; REnAL; SmATA 17; WhAm 4; WhNAA; WhoChL*

Burghley, William Cecil, Baron
English. Statesman
b. 1520
d. 1598
Source: *NewC; REn*

Burghoff, Gary
American. Actor
Played Radar in motion picture and TV series, *MASH.*
b. May 24, 1934 in Bristol, Connecticut
Source: *WhoAm 82; WhoHol A*

Burgin, Richard
Polish. Conductor
b. Oct 11, 1892 in Warsaw, Poland
Source: *WhoAm 74*

Burgoyne, John
English. General, Dramatist
b. 1723
d. Jun 4, 1792 in London, England
Source: *Alli; AmBi; BbtC; BrAu; ChPo; DcEnL; DcLEL; NewC; OxAmL; OxEng; REn; REnAL; WhAm H*

Burke, Arleigh Albert
American. Former Navy Chief of Staff
b. Oct 19, 1901 in Boulder, Colorado
Source: *CurBio 55; IntWW 74; St&PR 75; Who 74; WhoAm 74; WhoWor 74*

Burke, "Billie" (Mary William Ethelberg Appleton)
[Mrs. Flo Ziegfeld]
American. Actress
Played Glinda, the Good Witch, in *The Wizard of Oz,* 1939.
b. Aug 7, 1886 in Washington, DC
d. May 14, 1970 in Los Angeles, California
Source: *BiE&WWA; Film 1; FilmgC; InWom; MotPP; MovMk; NewYTBE 70; OxFilm; ThFT; TwYS; Vers B; WhAm 5; WhScrn 74, 77; WhoHol B; WhoStg 1906, 1908; WomWWA 14*

Burke, Clem
see: Blondie

Burke, Edmund
British. Statesman, Orator, Author
Member House of Commons, 1766-94; against taxation of American colonies.
b. Jan 12, 1729 in Dublin, Ireland
d. Jul 9, 1797
Source: *Alli; ApCAB; AtlBL; BbD; BiD&SB; BrAu; CasWL; Chambr 2; CyWA; DcEnA; DcEnL; DcEuL; DcLEL; Drake; EvLB; MouLC 2; NewC; OxAmL; OxEng; Pen ENG; PoIre; REn; WebE&AL; WhAm H*

Burke, John
Irish. Genealogist
b. 1787 in Ireland
d. 1848
Source: *Alli, SUP; DcEnL; NewC; PoIre*

Burke, Johnny
American. Composer
b. Oct 3, 1908 in Antioch, California
d. Feb 25, 1964 in New York, New York
Source: *AmSCAP 66; BiE&WWA; FilmgC*

Burke, Kenneth
American. Literary Critic, Author
b. May 5, 1897 in Pittsburgh, Pennsylvania
Source: *AmAu&B; AmWr; Au&Wr 71; CasWL; CnDAL; ConAmA; ConAu 5R; ConLC 2; ConNov 72, 76; ConP 70, 75; DcLEL; DrAS 74E; EvLB; IntWW 74; ModAL, SUP; OxAmL; Pen AM; RAdv 1; REn; REnAL; TwCA, SUP; WebE&AL; WhoAm 74, 76, 78, 80, 82; WhoTwCL; WrDr 76*

Burke, Paul
American. Actor
b. Jul 21, 1926 in New Orleans, Louisiana
Source: *FilmgC; IntMPA 75, 76, 77, 78, 79, 80, 81, 82*

Burke, William
[Burke and Hare]
Irish. Murderer
b. 1792 in Orrery, Ireland
d. Jan 28, 1829 in Edinburgh, Scotland
Source: *BioIn 1, 4, 8, 10; DcIrB*

Burke, Yvonne Brathwaite Watson
[Mrs. William A Burke]
American. Lawyer, Former Congresswoman
First black woman elected to CA General Assembly, 1967.
b. Oct 5, 1932 in Los Angeles, California
Source: *BioNews 74; CngDr 74; WhoAm 74, 76, 78, 80, 82; WhoAmP 73; WhoAmW 77; WhoBlA 75; WhoWest 74*

Burke and Hare
see: Burke, William; Hare, William

Burkett, Jesse Cail
"The Crab"
American. Baseball Player
Hit .400 or better three times, 1895, 1896, 1900.
b. Feb 12, 1870 in Wheeling, West Virginia
d. May 27, 1953 in Worcester, Massachusetts
Source: *BaseEn; BioIn 3, 7; WhoProB 73*

Burleigh, Harry Thacker
American. Singer, Composer
b. Dec 2, 1866 in Erie, Pennsylvania
d. Sep 12, 1949 in Stamford, Connecticut
Source: *AmSCAP 66; CurBio 41, 49; WebAB; WhAm 2*

Burlington, Richard Boyle, Earl
British. Architect, Art Patron
b. 1694
d. 1753
Source: *BioIn 6, 11; WhoArch*

Burman, Ben Lucien
American. Journalist, Author
b. Dec 12, 1895 in Covington, Kentucky
Source: *AmAu&B; AmNov; Au&Wr 71; ConAu 5R; OxAmL; REnAL; SmATA 6; TwCA, SUP; WhNAA; WhoAm 74; WhoWor 74; WrDr 76*

Burne-Jones, Edward
English. Artist
b. Aug 23, 1833 in Birmingham, England
d. Jun 17, 1898 in London, England
Source: *AtlBL; ChPo, S2; NewC; REn*

Burnett, Carol
[Mrs. Joe Hamilton]
American. Actress, Comedienne, Singer
Won $1.6 million libel suit against *National Enquirer*, 1981.
b. Apr 26, 1936 in San Antonio, Texas
Source: *BiE&WWA; BioNews 74; BkPepl; CelR 73; CurBio 62; EncMT; FilmgC; ForWC 70; InWom; IntMPA 75, 76, 77, 78, 79, 80, 81, 82; NewYTBE 73; WhoAm 74, 76, 78, 80, 82; WhoHol A; WhoThe 77; WhoWor 74*

Burnett, Frances Eliza Hodgson
American. Author
b. Nov 24, 1849 in Manchester, England
d. Oct 29, 1924 in Plandome, New York
Source: *Alli SUP; AmAu&B; AmBi; AmWom; ApCAB; AuBYP; BbD; BiD&SB; BiDSA; CarSB; Chambr 3; ChPo, S2; ConAmL; DcAmAu; DcAmB; DcBiA; DcLEL; DcNAA; EvLB; FamSYP; HerW; InWom; JBA 34; LongCTC; NotAW; OxAmL; OxEng; Pen AM, ENG; PlP&P; REn; REnAL; TwCA, SUP; TwCBDA; WhAm 1; WhoChL; WhoStg 1906, 1908; WomWWA 14*

Burnett, Ivy Compton
see: Compton-Burnett, Dame Ivy

Burnett, Leo
American. Advertising Executive
b. Oct 21, 1891 in Saint John's, Michigan
d. Jun 7, 1971 in Lake Zurich, Illinois
Source: *NewYTBE 71; WhAm 5, 6; WhoMW 74*

Burnett, Whit
American. Author, Editor
b. Aug 14, 1899 in Salt Lake City, Utah
d. Apr 22, 1973 in Norwalk, Connecticut
Source: *AmAu&B; ConAu 13R, 41R; ConAu P-2; CurBio 41, 73; REnAL; TwCA, SUP; WhAm 5; WhoAm 74*

Burnett, W(illiam) R(iley)
[James Updyke, pseud.]
American. Author
b. Nov 25, 1899 in Springfield, Ohio
d. Apr 25, 1982 in Santa Monica, California
Source: *AmAu&B; AmNov; CnDAL; ConAmA; ConAu 5R; DcLEL; EncMys; LongCTC; NewYTBS 82; OxAmL; Pen AM; PseudN; REn; REnAL; TwCA, SUP; TwCW; WhNAA; WhoAm 74, 76, 78, 80, 82; WhoWor 74*

Burnette, "Smiley" (Lester Alvin)
American. Actor
b. Mar 18, 1911 in Summun, Illinois
d. Feb 16, 1967 in Los Angeles, California
Source: *FilmgC; MotPP; WhScrn 74, 77; WhoHol B*

Burney, Charles
English. Organist, Musicologist
b. Apr 7, 1726 in Shrewsbury, England
d. Apr 12, 1814 in Chelsea, England
Source: *Alli, SUP; BiD&SB; BiDLA, SUP; CasWL; DcEnA; DcEnL; DcEuL; DcLEL; OxEng*

Burney, Fanny (Frances)
[Madame d'Arblay]
English. Author, Diarist
b. Jun 13, 1752 in Norfolk, England
d. Jan 6, 1840 in London, England
Source: *AtlBL; BrAu 19; CasWL; Chambr 2; CyWA; EvLB; InWom; NewC; Pen ENG; RAdv 1; REn*

Burnham, Daniel H
American. Architect
b. Sep 4, 1846 in Henderson, New York
d. Jun 1, 1912 in Heidelberg, Germany
Source: *AmBi; ApCAB SUP; DcAmB; EncAB-H; TwCBDA; WebAB; WhAm 1, 4*

Burnham, (Linden) Forbes (Sampson)
Guinean. Prime Minister
b. Feb 20, 1923 in Kitty, Guyana
Source: *BioIn 7, 8, 9; CurBio 66; IntWW 74; Who 74; WhoGov 72; WhoWor 74*

Burns, Arthur F
American. Economist, Educator
Wrote *Reflections of an Economic Policy Maker*, 1978.
b. Apr 27, 1904 in Stanislau, Austria
Source: *AmAu&B; AmEA 74; AmM&WS 73S; CelR 73; ConAu 13R; CurBio 53; IntWW 74; WebAB; Who 74; WhoAm 74; WhoAmP 73; WhoGov 72; WhoS&SW 73; WhoWorJ 72; WrDr 76*

Burns, Bob
"Bazooka"
American. Actor
b. Aug 2, 1893 in Van Buren, Alaska
d. Feb 2, 1956 in San Fernando, California
Source: *FilmgC; WhAm 3; WhScrn 74, 77; WhoHol B*

Burns, David
American. Actor
b. Jun 22, 1902 in New York, New York
d. Mar 12, 1971 in Philadelphia, Pennsylvania
Source: *BiE&WWA; EncMT; FilmgC; NewYTBE 71; WhAm 5; WhScrn 74, 77; WhoHol B*

Burns, George
[Nathan Birnbaum]
American. Comedian, Actor
Won Oscar, 1975, for *The Sunshine Boys.*
b. Jan 20, 1896 in New York, New York
Source: *CelR 73; CurBio 51; FilmgC; IntMPA 75, 76, 77, 78, 79, 80, 81, 82; MotPP; MovMk; WhoAm 74, 76, 78, 80, 82; WhoHol A; WhoWor 74*

Burns, Jack
American. Comedian
Source: *BioIn 10*

Burns, John Horne
American. Author
b. Oct 7, 1916 in Andover, Massachusetts
d. Aug 10, 1953 in Leghorn, Italy
Source: *AmAu&B; AmNov; EvLB; ModAL; OxAmL; Pen AM; REn; REnAL; TwCA SUP; TwCW; WebE&AL; WhAm 4*

Burns, Robert
[Bard of Ayrshire]
Scottish. Poet
Wrote songs "Auld Lang Syne" and "Comin' thro' the Rye."
b. Jul 21, 1759 in Alloway, Scotland
d. Jan 21, 1796 in Dumfroes, Scotland
Source: *Alli; AtlBL; BiD&SB; BiDLA; BrAu; CasWL; Chambr 2; ChPo, S1, S2; CnE&AP; CrtT 2; CyWA; DcEnA, AP; DcEnL; DcEuL; DcLEL; EvLB; FamAYP; MouLC 2; NewC; OxEng; Pen ENG; RAdv 1; RComWL; REn; WebE&AL*

Burns, Tommy
[Noah Brusso]
Canadian. Boxer
b. Jun 17, 1881 in Hanover, ON
d. May 10, 1955 in Vancouver, BC
Source: *WhoBox 74*

Burns, William John
American. Detective
b. Oct 19, 1861 in Baltimore, Maryland
d. Apr 14, 1932
Source: *DcAmB S1; DcNAA; OhA&B; WhAm 1; WhScrn 77*

Burns and Allen
see: Allen, Gracie; Burns, George

Burnshaw, Stanley
American. Author
b. Jun 20, 1906 in New York, New York
Source: *AmAu&B; AnMV 1926; ConAu 9R; ConLC 3; ConP 70, 75; DrAP 75; REnAL; WhoAm 74, 76, 78, 80, 82; WorAu; WrDr 76*

Burnside, Ambrose Everett
American. Army Commander
b. May 23, 1824 in Liberty, Indiana
d. Sep 13, 1881 in Bristol, Rhode Island
Source: *AmBi; ApCAB; BiAuS; BiDrAC; DcAmB; Drake; IndAu 1917; TwCBDA; WebAB; WhAm H; WhAmP*

Burpee, David
American. Horticulturist
Plant breeder who created, introduced new flowers and vegetables.
b. Apr 5, 1893 in Philadelphia, Pennsylvania
d. Jun 24, 1980 in Doylestown, Pennsylvania
Source: *CurBio 55; St&PR 75; WhoAm 74*

Burpee, W(ashington) Atlee
American. Horticulturist
b. Apr 5, 1858 in Sheffiel, NB
d. Nov 26, 1915
Source: *NatCAB 6; WebBD 80; WhAm 1*

Burr, Aaron
American. Vice-President, Lawyer
b. Feb 6, 1756 in Newark, New Jersey
d. Sep 14, 1836 in New York, New York
Source: *Alli; AmAu&B; AmBi; ApCAB; BiAuS; BiDrAC; BiDrUSE; DcAmB; DcNAA; Drake; EncAB-H; OxAmL; REn; REnAL; TwCBDA; WebAB; WhAm H; WhAmP*

Burr, Clive
see: Iron Maiden

Burr, Henry
American. Singer
b. Jan 15, 1882
d. Apr 6, 1941 in Chicago, Illinois
Source: *CurBio 41*

Burr, Raymond William Stacey
American. Actor
Starred in TV series "Perry Mason," 1957-65; "Ironside," 1967-75.
b. May 21, 1917 in New Westminster, BC
Source: *BioNews 75; CurBio 61; FilmgC; IntMPA 75, 76, 77, 78, 79, 80, 81, 82; MotPP; MovMk; WhoAm 74, 76, 78, 80, 82; WhoWor 74; WorEFlm*

Burrenchobay, Dayendranath
Mauritian. Governor General
b. Mar 24, 1919
Source: *IntWW 78*

Burroughs, Edgar Rice
American. Author, Cartoonist
Wrote *Tarzan* series; have sold more than 35 million copies.
b. Sep 1, 1875 in Chicago, Illinois
d. Mar 10, 1950 in Los Angeles, California
Source: *AmAu&B; AmLY; DcAmB S4; EvLB; FilmgC; LongCTC; MnBBF; OxAmL; Pen AM; REn; REnAL; TwCA, SUP; TwCW; WebAB; WhAm 2*

Burroughs, John
American. Author, Naturalist
b. Apr 3, 1837 in Roxbury, New York
d. Mar 25, 1921
Source: *Alli, SUP; AmAu; AmAu&B; AmBi; AmLY; AnCL; ApCAB; BbD; BiD&SB; CarSB; Chambr 3; ChPo; ConAmL; DcAmAu; DcAmB; DcEnA AP; DcLEL; DcNAA; EvLB; JBA 34; OxAmL; Pen AM; REn; REnAL; TwCBDA; WebAB; WhAm 1*

Burroughs, William S(eward)
American. Author
b. Feb 5, 1914 in Saint Louis, Missouri
Source: *AmAu&B; Au&Wr 71; AuNews 2; CasWL; CelR 73; ConAu 9R; ConLC 1, 2, 5, 15; ConNov 72, 76; CurBio 71; DrAF 76; EncWL; IntWW 74; ModAL, SUP; OxAmL; Pen AM; RAdv 1; REn; REnAL; TwCW; WebAB; WebE&AL; WhoAm 74, 76, 78, 80, 82; WhoTwCL; WhoWor 74; WorAu; WrDr 76*

Burroughs, William Seward
American. Inventor
Developed practical calculator, 1891.
b. Jan 28, 1855 in Auburn, New York
d. Sep 14, 1898 in Citronelle, Alabama
Source: *DcAmB S1; WebAB; WhAm H*

Burrows, Abe (Abram S)
American. Humorist, Dramatist
Won Pulitzer Prize, 1961, for *How to Succeed in Business Without Really Trying.*
b. Dec 18, 1910 in New York, New York
Source: *AmAu&B; AmSCAP 66; BiE&WWA; CelR 73; ChPo S1; ConDr 73; CurBio 51; EncMT; FilmgC; ModWD; NewCBMT; NotNAT; OxAmL; WhoAm 74, 76, 78, 80, 82; WhoThe 77; WhoWor 74; WhoWorJ 72; WrDr 76*

Burstyn, Ellen
[Edna Rae Gillooly]
American. Actress
Won Oscar, 1974, for *Alice Doesn't Live Here Anymore.*
b. Dec 7, 1932 in Detroit, Michigan
Source: *BkPepl; IntMPA 75, 76, 77, 78, 79, 80, 81, 82; MovMk; NewYTBE 72; WhoAm 82; WhoHol A; WomWMM*

Burt, Maxwell Struthers
American. Author
b. Oct 18, 1882 in Baltimore, Maryland
d. Aug 28, 1954 in Jackson, Wyoming
Source: *ChPo, S2; TwCA, SUP*

Burt, Richard
American. Journalist
Source: *BioIn 12*

Burtin, Will
American. Designer, Model Builder
b. Jan 27, 1908 in Cologne, Germany
d. Jan 18, 1972 in New York, New York
Source: *NewYTBE 72; WhoGrA; WhAm 5*

Burton, Isabel Arundel
English. Traveler, Author
b. 1831
d. 1896
Source: *Alli SUP; BioIn 3, 6, 8, 10; DcEuL; NewC*

Burton, LeVar(dis Robert Martyn, Jr.)
American. Actor
Played Kunta Kinte in TV series "Roots."
b. Feb 16, 1957 in Landstuhl, Germany (West)
Source: *BioIn 11; IntMPA 82; WhoAm 82*

Burton, Michael
American. Swimmer
Only swimmer to win gold medal in 1,500 meters freestyle in two succesive Olympics, 1968, 1972.
b. Jul 3, 1947 in Des Moines, Iowa
Source: *WorDWW*

Burton, Nelson, Jr.
American. Bowler
b. 1942?
Source: *BioIn 11*

Burton, Phillip
American. Congressman
b. Jun 1, 1926 in Cincinnati, Ohio
Source: *BioIn 10, 11; NewYTBS 75; PolProf J; WhoAm 82*

Burton, Richard
[Richard Jenkins]
Welsh. Actor
Won Tony, 1961, for *Camelot;* nominated for seven Oscars.
b. Nov 10, 1925 in Pontrhydfen, Wales
Source: *BiDFilm; BiE&WWA; BioNews 74; BkPepl; CelR 73; CmMov; CurBio 60; EncMT; FilmgC; IntMPA 75, 76, 77, 78, 79, 80, 81, 82; IntWW 74; MotPP; MovMk; NewC; NewYTBE 73; NotNAT; OxFilm; Who 82; WhoAm 74, 76, 78, 80, 82; WhoHol A; WhoThe 77; WhoWor 74; WorEFlm*

Burton, Sir Richard Francis
English. Author, Explorer, Orientalist
Discovered Lake Tanganyika, 1858.
b. Mar 19, 1821 in Hertfordshire, England
d. Oct 20, 1890 in Trieste, Italy
Source: *AtlBL; BrAu 19; DcEnA, AP; DcEnL; DcEuL; DcLEL; EvLB; MouLC 4; PoIre; REn*

Burton, Robert
English. Author
b. Feb 8, 1577 in Lindley, England
d. Jan 25, 1640 in Oxford, England
Source: *Alli; AtlBL; BrAu; CasWL; CyWA; EvLB; NewC; OxEng; Pen ENG; RAdv 1; REn*

Burton, Virginia Lee
American. Author, Illustrator
b. Aug 30, 1909 in Newton Centre, Massachusetts
d. Oct 15, 1968
Source: *AmAu&B; Au&ICB; AuBYP; Cald 1938; ConAu 13R, 25R; ConAu P-1; CurBio 43, 68; IlsCB 1957; JBA 51; SmATA 2*

Busbee, George Dekle
American. Politician
Governor of GA, 1975-82.
b. Aug 7, 1927 in Vienna, Georgia
Source: *BioNews 74; WhoAm 82; WhoAmP 73*

Busby, Sir Matthew
English. Soccer Player, Manager
b. 1909
Source: *BioIn 8, 9, 10; Who 74*

Busch, Adolphus
German. Businessman
b. 1842 in Mainz, Germany
d. 1913
Source: *NatCAB 12*

Busch, August Anheuser, Jr.
American. Brewer, Baseball Executive
Chief executive, Anheuser-Busch; president, St. Louis Cardinals baseball team.
b. Mar 28, 1899 in Saint Louis, Missouri
Source: *CurBio 73; IntWW 74; St&PR 75; WhoAm 74, 76, 78, 80, 82; WhoF&I 74; WhoProB 73*

Busch, Fritz
German. Conductor
b. Mar 13, 1890 in Siegen, Germany
d. Sep 14, 1951 in London, England
Source: *CurBio 46, 51; WhAm 3*

Busch, Wilhelm
German. Poet, Artist
b. Apr 15, 1832 in Hannover, Germany
d. Jan 9, 1908 in Mechtshausen, Germany
Source: *BiD&SB; CasWL; ChPo, S1, S2; ClDMEL; EuAu; EvEuW; OxGer; Pen EUR; REn*

Buse, Don
American. Basketball Player
b. Aug 10, 1950 in Holland, Indiana
Source: *BioIn 11; WhoBbl 73*

Busey, Gary
American. Actor, Musician
b. 1944 in Goose Creek, Texas
Source: *BioIn 11; WhoAm 82*

Bush, Alan
English. Composer, Conductor
b. Dec 22, 1900 in London, England
Source: *BioIn 3, 6, 7; IntWW 74; Who 74; WhoMus 72; WhoWor 74*

Bush, Barbara Pierce
American. Wife of George Bush
b. Jun 8, 1925 in Rye, New York
Source: *NewYTBS 81; WhoAm 82*

Bush, George Herbert Walker
American. Vice-President
Ambassador to UN, 1971-72; CIA director, 1976-77.
b. Jun 12, 1924 in Milton, Massachusetts
Source: *BiDrAC; BioNews 74; CelR 73; CurBio 72; IntWW 74; NewYTBE 70, 71, 72; NewYTBS 74; Who 74; WhoAm 74, 76, 78, 80, 82; WhoAmP 73; WhoGov 72*

Bush, Kate
English. Singer, Songwriter
b. Jul 30, 1958 in Kent, England
Source: *IlEncRk; NewWmR*

Bush, Vannevar
American. Electrical Engineer
b. Mar 11, 1890 in Everett, Massachusetts
d. Jun 28, 1974 in Belmont, Massachusetts
Source: *AmAu&B; CelR 73; ConAu 53; CurBio 40, 47, 74; EncAB-H; IntWW 74; NewYTBS 74; REnAL; St&PR 75; WebAB; WhAm 6; WhNAA; Who 74; WhoAm 74*

Bush-Brown, Albert
American. Author, University Administrator
b. Jan 2, 1926 in West Hartford, Connecticut
Source: *BioIn 6; DrAS 74H, 78H; WhoAm 74, 76, 78, 80; WhoAmA 73, 76, 78; WhoWor 74*

Bushell, Anthony
English. Actor
b. May 19, 1904 in Kent, England
Source: *FilmgC; WhoHol A; WhoThe 77*

Bushkin, Joe (Joseph)
American. Jazz Musician
b. Nov 6, 1916 in New York, New York
Source: *AmSCAP 66; WhoAm 74; WhoJazz 72*

Bushman, Francis X(avier)
American. Actor
b. Jan 10, 1883 in Baltimore, Maryland
d. Aug 23, 1966 in Pacific Palisades, California
Source: *Film 1; FilmgC; MotPP; MovMk; OxFilm; TwYS; WebAB; WhAm 4; WhScrn 74, 77; WhoHol B*

Bushmiller, Ernie (Ernest Paul)
American. Cartoonist
Created comic strip "Nancy."
b. Aug 23, 1905 in New York, New York
d. Aug 15, 1982 in Stamford, Connecticut
Source: *AuNews 1; ConAu 29R; WhoAm 74, 76, 78, 80, 82; WhoAmA 73, 76, 78; WorECom*

Bushnell, David
American. Inventor
Built man-propelled submarine boat, 1775; originated submarine warfare.
b. 1742 in Saybrook, Connecticut
d. 1824 in Warrenton, Georgia
Source: *ApCAB; DcAmB; TwCBDA; WebAB; WhAm H*

Bushnell, Horace
American. Religious Leader
b. Apr 14, 1802 in Bantam, Connecticut
d. Feb 17, 1876 in Hartford, Connecticut
Source: *AmAu&B; BbD; BiD&SB; CyAl 2; DcAmAu; DcEnL; DcLEL; DcNAA; OxAmL; WebAB*

Bushnell, Nolan Kay
American. Electronics Executive
Chairman, Atari, 1972; created "Pong" 1971, first coin-operated video game.
b. Feb 5, 1943 in Ogden, Utah
Source: *BioIn 12; WhoWest 78*

Busia, Kofi A
Ghanaian. Prime Minister
b. Jul 11, 1913
d. Aug 28, 1978 in Oxford, England
Source: *AfrA; IntWW 74; Who 74; WhoGov 72; WhoWor 74*

Busoni, Ferruccio Benvenuto
Italian. Pianist, Composer
b. Apr 1, 1866 in Empoli, Italy
d. Jul 27, 1924 in Berlin, Germany
Source: *AtlBL; DcCM*

Buss, Jerry Hatten
American. Real Estate and Sports Executive
Owner, LA Kings and Lakers, sports teams.
b. Jan 27, 1933 in Salt Lake City, Utah
Source: *NewYTBS 79; WhoAm 80, 82*

Busse, Henry
American. Jazz Musician
b. May 19, 1894 in Magdeburg, Germany
d. Apr 23, 1955 in Memphis, Tennessee
Source: *AmSCAP 66*

Busseri, Frank
see: Four Lads, The

Bustamante, William Alexander
Jamaican. Prime Minister
b. Feb 24, 1884
d. Aug 6, 1977 in Irish Town, Jamaica
Source: *BioIn 11; IntWW 74*

Butala, Tony
[The Letterman]
American. Singer
b. in Sharon, Pennsylvania
Source: *NF*

Butcher, Willard C(arlisle)
American. Banker
b. Oct 25, 1926 in Bronxville, New York
Source: *BioIn 12; CurBio 80; IntWW 79; WhoAm 80, 82*

Butkus, Dick (Richard J)
American. Football Player, Actor
Linebacker, Chicago Bears, 1965-73; Hall of Fame, 1979.
b. Dec 9, 1942 in Chicago, Illinois
Source: *CelR 73; NewYTBS 74; WhoAm 74, 76, 78, 80, 82*

Butler, Benjamin Franklin
American. General, Congressman
b. Nov 5, 1818 in Deerfield, New Hampshire
d. Jan 11, 1893 in Washington, DC
Source: *AmBi; ApCAB; BiAuS; BiDrAC; DcAmAu; DcAmB; DcNAA; Drake; EncAB-H; TwCBDA; WebAB; WhAm H; WhAmP*

Butler, John
American. Choreographer, Dancer
b. Sep 29, 1920 in Memphis, Tennessee
Source: *BiE&WWA; WhoAm 74; WhoMus 72; WhoWor 74*

Butler, Joseph
English. Philosopher, Theologian
b. May 18, 1692 in Wantage, England
d. Jun 16, 1752 in Bath, England
Source: *BiD&SB; BrAu; Chambr 2; DcEnA; DcEnL; DcEuL; EvLB; NewC; OxEng; Pen ENG; REn*

Butler, Matthew Calbraith
American. Soldier, Statesman
b. Mar 8, 1836 in Greenville, South Carolina
d. Apr 14, 1909 in Columbia, South Carolina
Source: *BiDSA; BioIn 5*

Butler, Michael
American. Businessman
b. Nov 26, 1926 in Chicago, Illinois
Source: *BioIn 8, 9; CelR 73; IntWW 74; WhoAm 74, 76, 78, 80, 82; WhoWor 74*

Butler, Nicholas Murray
American. Educator
b. Apr 2, 1862 in Elizabeth, New Jersey
d. Dec 4, 1947 in New York, New York
Source: *Alli SUP; AmAu&B; ChPo S2; CurBio 40, 47; DcAmAu; DcAmB S4; DcNAA; EncAB-H; OxAmL; REnAL; TwCBDA; WebAB; WhAm 2; WhNAA*

Butler, Paul
American. Industrialist
b. Jun 23, 1892 in Chicago, Illinois
d. Jun 24, 1981 in Oak Brook, Illinois
Source: *BioIn 6; NewYTBS 81; WhoF&I 74, 75*

Butler, Samuel
English. Poet
b. Feb 14, 1612 in Worcestershire, England
d. Sep 25, 1680 in London, England
Source: *Alli; AtlBL; BbD; BiD&SB; BrAu; CasWL; ChPo, S1; CnE&AP; CrtT 2; CyWA; DcEnA; DcEnL; DcEuL; DcLEL; EvLB; MouLC 1; NewC; OxEng; Pen ENG; REn; WebE&AL*

Butler, Samuel
English. Author
b. Dec 4, 1835 in Nottinghamshire, England
d. Jun 18, 1902 in London, England
Source: *AtlBL; BrAu 19; CnMWL; CrtT 3; DcEnA, AP; EvLB; ModBrL; NewC; OxEng; Pen ENG*

Butler, Terry "Geezer"
see: Black Sabbath

Butler of Saffron Walden, Richard Austen, Baron
British. Statesman
b. Dec 9, 1902 in Attock Serai, India
d. Mar 9, 1982 in Great Yeldham, England
Source: *BioIn 7, 8, 9, 10; CurBio 44, 82; IntWW 74, 76, 77, 78; IntYB 78, 79; Who 74; WhoWor 74, 78; WrDr 76, 80*

Butor, Michel
French. Author
b. Sep 14, 1926 in Mans-en-Baroeul, France
Source: *Au&Wr 71; CasWL; ConAu 9R; ConLC 1, 3; EncWL; EvEuW; IntWW 74; ModRL; Pen EUR; REn; TwCW; WhoTwCL; WorAu; WhoWor 74*

Buttenheim, Edgar Joseph
American. Publisher
b. Oct 16, 1882 in Jersey City, New Jersey
d. Nov 23, 1964
Source: *WhAm 4*

Butterfield, Alexander Porter
American. Government Official
Assistant to Richard Nixon, 1969-73; FAA administrator, 1973-75.
b. Apr 6, 1926 in Pensacola, Florida
Source: *NewYTBE 73; WhoAm 74, 76, 78, 80, 82; WhoAmP 73; WhoS&SW 73*

Butterfield, Billy
American. Jazz Musician
b. Jan 14, 1917 in Middletown, Ohio
Source: *WhoJazz 72*

Butterfield, Sir Herbert
English. Author
b. Oct 7, 1900 in Oxenhope, England
Source: *BioIn 4, 5; ConAu 1R; IntWW 74; Who 74; WhoWor 74*

Butterfield, Lyman Henry
American. Historian
Edited the 20 volume *Adams Papers.*
b. Aug 8, 1909 in Lyndonville, New York
d. Apr 25, 1982 in Boston, Massachusetts
Source: *AmAu&B; DrAS 74H, 78H; NewYTBS 82; WhoAm 74, 76, 78, 80*

Butterfield, Roger Place
American. Historian, Journalist
b. Jul 29, 1907 in Lyndonville, New York
d. Jan 31, 1981 in Hartwick, New York
Source: *AmAu&B; BioIn 1; ConAu P-1; CurBio 48; REnAL*

Butterfield, William
English. Architect, Dcsigner
b. 1814 in London, England
d. 1900
Source: *BioIn 9, 11; DcNiCA; McGDA; WhoArch*

Butterick, Ebenezer
American. Tailor
Invented standardized paper patterns for clothes; first marketed, 1863.
b. May 29, 1826 in Sterling, Massachusetts
d. Mar 31, 1903
Source: *AmBi; DcAmB; WhAm H*

Butterworth, Charles
American. Actor
b. Jul 26, 1897 in South Bend, Indiana
d. Jun 14, 1946 in Los Angeles, California
Source: *CurBio 46; FilmgC; MotPP; MovMk; Vers A; WhScrn 74, 77; WhoHol B*

Buttigieg, Anton
Maltese. President
b. Feb 19, 1912 in Gozo, Malta
Source: *IntWW 74; WhoWor 74*

Button, Dick (Richard Totten)
American. Skater, Sportscaster
Won gold medal in figure skating, 1948, 1952 Olympics.
b. Jul 18, 1929 in Englewood, New Jersey
Source: *BiE&WWA; CelR 73; ConAu 9R; CurBio 49; WhoAm 82; WhoHol A*

Buttons, Red
[Aaron Chwatt]
American. Comedian, Actor
Won Oscar, 1957, for *Sayonara.*
b. Feb 5, 1919 in New York, New York
Source: *AmSCAP 66; CurBio 58; FilmgC; IntMPA 75, 76, 77, 78, 79, 80, 81, 82; MotPP; MovMk; WhoAm 74, 76, 78, 80, 82; WhoHol A; WhoWor 74*

Buttram, Pat
American. Actor
Source: *WhoHol A*

Buttrick, George Arthur
American. Clergyman, Author
b. Mar 23, 1892 in Seaham Harbour, England
d. Jan 23, 1980 in Louisville, Kentucky
Source: *AmAu&B; Au&Wr 71; ConAu 61, 93; WhoAm 74*

Butts, Alfred Mosher
American. Architect
Invented word game "Scrabble," 1933.
b. Apr 13, 1899 in Poughkeepsie, New York
Source: *BioIn 3; CurBio 54*

Butz, Earl Lauer
American. Government Official
Secretary of Agriculture, 1971-76; sentenced to five years in prison for tax evasion, 1981.
b. Jul 3, 1909 in Noble County, Indiana
Source: *AmM&WS 73S; CngDr 74; CurBio 72; IndAu 1917; IntWW 74; NewYTBE 71, 72; USBiR 74; WhoAm 74; WhoAmP 73; WhoGov 72*

Buxtehude, Dietrich
Danish. Organist, Composer
b. 1637 in Elsinore, Denmark
d. May 9, 1707 in Lubeck, Germany
Source: *AtlBL*

Buzhardt, J Fred
American. Watergate Lawyer
Special counsel to Richard Nixon, 1973-74.
b. 1924
d. Dec 16, 1978 in Hilton Head Island, South Carolina
Source: *WhoAmP 73*

Buzzell, Eddie
American. Actor, Motion Picture Director
b. Nov 13, 1907 in Brooklyn, New York
Source: *WhoHol A*

Buzzi, Ruth Ann
[Mrs. Basil Keko]
American. Actress, Comedienne
Best known for appearances in TV series "Laugh In."
b. Jul 24, 1936 in Westerly, Rhode Island
Source: *CelR 73; IntMPA 82; WhoAm 82*

Byars, Betsy
American. Children's Author
b. Aug 7, 1928 in Charlotte, North Carolina
Source: *AuBYP; ChlLR 1; ConAu 33R; MorBMP; SmATA 4; ThrBJA*

Byers, William Newton
American. Editor, Surveyor
b. Feb 22, 1831 in Madison County, Ohio
d. Mar 25, 1903
Source: *Alli SUP; BioIn 8; DcNAA; OhA&B*

Byington, Spring
American. Actress
Starred in TV series "December Bride," 1954-59.
b. Oct 17, 1893 in Colorado Springs, Colorado
d. Sep 7, 1971 in Hollywood, California
Source: *BiE&WWA; CurBio 56, 71; FilmgC; InWom; MotPP; MovMk; NewYTBE 71; ThFT; Vers A; WhAm 5; WhScrn 74, 77; WhoHol B*

Byner, John
American. Comedian
Source: *NF*

Byng, George
British. Naval Explorer
b. 1663
d. 1733
Source: *Alli*

Bynner, Harold Witter
American. Author, Traveler
b. Aug 10, 1881 in Brooklyn, New York
d. Jun 1, 1968 in Santa Fe, New Mexico
Source: *ChPo, S1; ConAu 25R, 4NR*

Byrd, Charlie (Charles Lee)
American. Jazz Musician
b. Sep 16, 1925 in Chuckatuck, Virginia
Source: *BioNews 74; CurBio 67*

Byrd, Donald
American. Jazz Musician
b. Dec 9, 1932 in Detroit, Michigan
Source: *WhoAm 74; WhoWor 74*

Byrd, Harry Flood
American. Statesman, Journalist
b. Jun 10, 1887 in Martinsburg, West Virginia
d. Oct 20, 1966
Source: *BiDrAC; WhAm 4; WhAmP*

Byrd, Harry Flood, Jr.
American. Journalist, Senator
b. Dec 20, 1914 in Winchester, Virginia
Source: *BiDrAC; CngDr 74; IntWW 74; WhoAm 74, 76, 78, 80, 82; WhoAmP 73; WhoGov 72; WhoS&SW 73*

Byrd, Henry
"Professor Longhair"
American. Composer, Musician
b. Dec 19, 1918 in Bogalusa, Louisiana
d. Jan 30, 1980 in New Orleans, Louisiana
Source: *AnObit 1980*

Byrd, Richard Evelyn
American. Lawyer, Politician
b. Aug 13, 1860 in Austin, Texas
d. Oct 23, 1925
Source: *WhAm 1*

Byrd, Richard Evelyn
American. Explorer
First man to fly over N Pole, 1925, and S Pole, 1929.
b. Oct 25, 1888 in Winchester, Virginia
d. Mar 11, 1957 in Boston, Massachusetts
Source: *AsBiEn; CurBio 42, 56, 57; EncAB-H; NatCAB 46; WebAB; WebAMB; WhAm 3*

Byrd, Robert Carlyle
American. Senator
Majority leader in Senate, 1977-79; minority leader, 1980--.
b. Nov 20, 1917 in North Wilkesboro, North Carolina
Source: *BiDrAC; CngDr 74; CurBio 60; IntWW 74; NewYTBE 70, 71; WhoAm 74, 76, 78, 80, 82; WhoAmP 73; WhoE 74; WhoGov 72*

Byrd, William
English. Organist, Composer, Songwriter
b. 1542 in London, England
d. Jul 4, 1623 in London, England
Source: *Alli; AtlBL; BiDSA; BrAu; Chambr 3; BrAu; ChPo, S1; CroE&S; OxEng; REn*

Byrds, The
[Skip Battin; Michael Clark; Gene Clarke; David Crosby; Chris Hillman; Kevin Kelly; Roger McGuinn; Gram Parsons]
American. Rock Group
Source: *EncPR&S; IlEncRk; Rk100*

Byrne, Brendan
American. Government Official
Governor of NJ, 1974-82.
b. Dec 28, 1908 in New York, New York
Source: *CurBio 74; NewYTBE 73; St&PR 75; WhoAm 74, 76, 78, 80, 82; WhoF&I 74; WhoPubR 72; WhoWor 74*

Byrne, David
see: Talking Heads, The

Byrne, Fran
see: Ace

Byrne, Jane Margaret Burke
[Mrs. Jay McMullen]
American. Mayor
Democratic mayor of Chicago, 1979-83.
b. May 24, 1934 in Chicago, Illinois
Source: *BioIn 11, 12; CurBio 80; WhoAm 80, 82; WhoAmP 77; WhoGov 77*

Byrnes, Edd
American. Actor
b. Jul 30, 1933 in New York, New York
Source: *FilmgC; WhoHol A*

Byrnes, Eugene F
[Gene Burns]
American. Cartoonist
b. 1889 in New York, New York
d. Jul 26, 1974
Source: *ConAu 49*

Byrnes, James Francis
American. Statesman
b. May 2, 1879 in Charleston, South Carolina
d. Apr 9, 1972 in Columbia, South Carolina
Source: *AmAu&B; BiDrAC; BiDrUSE; CurBio 41, 51, 72; EncAB-H; NewYTBE 72; WebAB; WhAm 5; WhAmP*

Byron, Anne Isabella (Milbanke)
[Baroness Byron]
English. Wife of Lord Byron
b. 1792
d. 1860
Source: *BioIn 4, 6, 8, 9, 10, 11*

Byron, George Gordon Noel Byron, Baron
English. Poet
Writer of Romantic narrative poems, *Childe Harold's Pilgrimage,* 1812.
b. Jan 22, 1788 in London, England
d. Apr 19, 1824 in Missolonghi, Greece
Source: *Alli; AtlBL; BbD; BiD&SB; BiDLA, SUP; BrAu 19; CasWL; Chambr 3; ChPo, S1, S2; CnE&AP; CnThe; CyWA; DcEnA; DcEnL; DcEuL; DcLEL; EvLB; HsB&A; McGEWD; NewC; OxEng; Pen ENG; RAdv 1; RComWL; REn; REnWD; WebE&AL*

C

Caan, James
American. Actor, Motion Picture Director
Starred in *The Godfather,* 1972; TV movie *Brian's Song,* 1971.
b. Mar 26, 1939 in New York, New York
Source: *BkPepl; CelR 73; FilmgC; IntMPA 75, 76, 77, 78, 79, 80, 81, 82; MovMk; NewYTBE 73; WhoAm 82; WhoHol A*

Caballe, Montserrat
Spanish. Opera Singer
b. Apr 12, 1933 in Barcelona, Spain
Source: *CurBio 67; InWom; IntWW 74; NewYTBE 73; Who 74; WhoMus 72; WhoWor 74*

Cabell, Grete
Dutch. Mystic
Source: *NF*

Cabell, James Branch
American. Author
b. Apr 14, 1879 in Richmond, Virginia
d. May 5, 1958 in Richmond, Virginia
Source: *AmAu&B; AmLY; AmNov; BiDSA; CasWL; Chambr 3; CnDAL; CnMWL; ConAmA; ConAmL; CyWA; DcAmAu; DcBiA; DcLEL; EncWL; EvLB; LongCTC; ModAL; OxAmL; OxEng; Pen AM; RAdv 1; REn; REnAL; TwCA, SUP; TwCW; WebAB; WebE&AL; WhAm 3; WhNAA*

Cabeza de Vaca, Alvar Nunez
Spanish. Explorer
Went on Narvaez expedition to FL, 1528; shipwrecked, imprisoned by Indians.
b. 1490 in Spain
d. 1557 in Spain
Source: *BiDSA; Drake; EuAu; McGEWB; OxAmL; REn*

Cable, George Washington
American. Author
b. Oct 12, 1844 in New Orleans, Louisiana
d. Jan 31, 1925 in Saint Petersburg, Florida
Source: *Alli; AmAu; AmAu&B; AmBi; AmLY; ApCAB; AtlBL; BbD; BiD&SB; BiDSA; CasWL; Chambr 3; ChPo, S1; CnDAL; CrtT 3; CyWA; DcAmAu; DcAmB; DcBiA; DcEnA AP; DcLEL; DcNAA; EvLB; OxAmL; OxEng; Pen AM; RAdv 1; REn; REnAL; WebAB; WebE&AL; WhAm 1; WhNAA*

Cable, Mary
American. Author, Editor
b. Jan 24, 1920 in Cleveland, Ohio
Source: *ConAu 25R; DrAF 76; SmATA 9*

Cabot, Bruce
American. Actor
b. Apr 20, 1904 in Carlsbad, New Mexico
d. May 3, 1972 in Woodland Hills, California
Source: *FilmgC; HolP 30; MotPP; MovMk; NewYTBE 72; WhScrn 77*

Cabot, John
[Giovanni Caboto]
Italian. Navigator, Explorer
Conceived notion of sailing westward to Orient; credited with discovery of N America.
b. Jun 24, 1450 in Genoa, Italy
d. 1498
Source: *AmBi; NewC; OxCan; REn; REnAL; WebAB; WhAm H*

Cabot, John Moors
American. Diplomat
b. Dec 11, 1901 in Cambridge, Massachusetts
d. Feb 23, 1981 in Washington, DC
Source: *AmAu&B; BioIn 3, 5, 11; CurBio 53, 81; IntWW 74, 75, 76, 77, 78; IntYB 78, 79; NewYTBS 81; PolProf E; PolProf K; WhoAm 74, 76*

Cabot, Richard C
American. Scientist, Physician, Engineer
b. May 21, 1868 in Brookline, Massachusetts
d. May 8, 1939
Source: *AmAu&B; DcAmB S2; DcNAA; WhAm 1*

Cabot, Sebastian
Italian. Explorer
Son of John Cabot; reached Hudson Bay in attempt to find Northwest Passage, 1509.
b. 1476 in Venice, Italy
d. 1557
Source: *Alli; ApCAB; Drake; NewC; OxCan; REn; TwCBDA; WhAm H*

Cabot, Sebastian
English. Actor
Played Mr. French on TV series "Family Affair," 1966-71.
b. Jul 6, 1918 in London, England
d. Aug 23, 1977 in Victoria, BC
Source: *CelR 73; FilmgC; MotPP; MovMk; WhoHol A*

Cabot, Susan
American. Actress
b. 1927 in Boston, Massachusetts
Source: *FilmgC; WhoHol A*

Cabral, Luis de Almeida
Guinean. Government Official
b. 1931 in Bissau, Guinea-Bisseau
Source: *IntWW 74; NewYTBS 74*

Cabral, Pedro Alvarez
Portuguese. Explorer
Credited with discovery of Brazil, April 24, 1500.
b. 1460?
d. 1526
Source: *ApCAB; Drake*

Cabrillo, Juan Rodriguez
Portuguese. Explorer
Explored CA coast, 1542; discovered San Diego Bay.
b. 1520 in Portugal
d. Jan 3, 1543 in San Miguel Island, California
Source: *DcAmB; McGEWB; REnAW; WhAm H*

Cabrini, Saint Francis Xavier
[Mother Cabrini]
American. Religious Figure
Founded convents, orphanages, hospitals in Europe, US; canonized, 1946.
b. Jul 15, 1850 in Italy
d. Dec 22, 1917 in Chicago, Illinois
Source: *InWom; WebAB*

Caccini, Giulio
Italian. Composer
b. 1546 in Rome, Italy
d. Dec 10, 1618 in Florence, Italy
Source: *REn*

Cacers, Ernest
American. Musician
b. Nov 22, 1911 in Rockport, Texas
d. Jan 10, 1971 in Texas
Source: *BioIn 9; WhoJazz 72*

Cacoyannis, Michael
Greek. Motion Picture Director
b. Jun 11, 1922 in Limassol, Cyprus
Source: *BiDFilm; ConAu 101; CurBio 66; DcFM; FilmgC; IntMPA 75, 76, 77, 78, 79, 80, 81, 82; IntWW 74; MovMk; NotNAT; OxFilm; Who 74; WhoWor 74; WorEFlm*

Cadbury, Sir George Adrian Hayhurst
English. Food Manufacturer
Chairman, Cadbury Schweppes, Ltd. 1974--; knighted, 1977.
b. Apr 15, 1929 in Birmingham, England
Source: *BioIn 7; IntWW 74, 75, 76, 77, 78; WhoWor 74, 76, 78*

Caddell, Pat(rick Hayward)
American. Public Opinion Company Executive
President, Cambridge Survey Research, 1971--; consultant, Jimmy Carter's presidential campaign.
b. May 19, 1950 in Rock Hill, South Carolina
Source: *BioIn 10; WhoAm 80, 82*

Cadillac, Antoine
[Antoine de la Mothe Cadillac]
French. Explorer, Colonial Official
Founded Detroit, Jul 24, 1701.
b. Mar 5, 1658 in Les Laumets, France
d. Oct 15, 1730 in Castelsarrasen, France
Source: *AmBi; ApCAB; DcAmB; OxCan; REnAL; TwCBDA; WebAB; WhAmP*

Cadman, Charles Wakefield
American. Composer
b. Dec 4, 1881 in Johnstown, Pennsylvania
d. Dec 30, 1946 in Los Angeles, California
Source: *AmSCAP 66; DcAmB S4; OxAmL; REnAL; WhAm 2*

Cadmus, Paul
American. Artist
b. Dec 17, 1904 in New York, New York
Source: *BioIn 6; CelR 73; CurBio 42; DcCAA 71; WhoAm 74, 76, 78, 80, 82; WhoAmA 73; WhoE 74*

Cadogan, Sir Alexander George Montague
English. Statesman
b. Nov 25, 1884
d. Jul 9, 1968 in London, England
Source: *CurBio 44, 68*

Cadogan, William
British. General, Diplomat
b. 1676
d. 1726
Source: *NewCol 75*

Cady, (Walter) Harrison
American. Cartoonist, Illustrator
b. 1877 in Gardner, Massachusetts
d. Dec 9, 1970 in New York, New York
Source: *ChPo, S1; IlsCB 1744; NewYTBE 70; SmATA 19; WhNAA*

Caedmon, Saint
Anglo-Saxon. Poet
b. 650 in England
d. 680 in England
Source: *Alli; BbD; BiB S; BiD&SB; BrAu; CasWL; Chambr 1; CrtT 1; DcEnL; EvLB; MouLC 1; NewC; OxEng; Pen ENG; REn; WebE&AL*

Caen, Herb
American. Journalist, Author
b. Apr 3, 1916 in Sacramento, California
Source: *AuNews 1; CelR 73; ConAu 1R, 1NR; WhoAm 74, 76, 78, 80, 82; WhoWor 74*

Caesar, Irving
American. Songwriter
b. Jul 4, 1895 in New York, New York
Source: *AmSCAP 66; Au&Wr 71; BiE&WWA; ChPo; EncMT; IntMPA 75, 76, 77, 78, 79, 80, 81, 82; NewCBMT; NotNAT; REnAL; Who 74; WhoThe 77*

Caesar, Sid
American. Comedian, Actor
b. Sep 8, 1922 in Yonkers, New York
Source: *AmSCAP 66; BiE&WWA; CelR 73; CurBio 51; EncMT; FilmgC; IntMPA 75, 76, 77, 78, 79, 80, 81, 82; MovMk; WhoAm 74, 76, 78, 80, 82; WhoHol A; WhoThe 77; WhoWor 74*

Caetano, Marcello
Portuguese. Premier
b. Aug 17, 1906 in Lisbon, Portugal
d. Oct 26, 1980 in Rio de Janeiro, Brazil
Source: *CurBio 70; IntWW 74; WhoGov 72; WhoWor 74*

Cafritz, Gwen
Hungarian. Actress
b. 1912 in Budapest, Hungary
Source: *InWom*

Cage, John Milton, Jr.
American. Composer, Author
b. Sep 5, 1912 in Los Angeles, California
Source: *AmAu&B; AmSCAP 66; CelR 73; ConAu 13R; ConDr 73; CurBio 61; DcCM; IntWW 74; NewYTBE 72; Pen AM; WhoAm 74, 76, 78, 80, 82; WhoE 74; WhoMus 72; WhoWor 74; WrDr 76*

Cagle, "Red" (Christian Keener)
American. Football Player
b. May 1, 1905 in Deridder, Louisiana
d. Dec 23, 1942 in New York, New York
Source: *WhoFtbl 74*

Cagliostro, Alessandro, Conte di
[Giuseppe Balsamo]
Italian. Magician, Imposter
b. 1743 in Sicily
d. 1795 in Rome, Italy
Source: *BioIn 1, 4, 5, 8, 10; NewC; OxGer; REn*

Cagney, James
American. Actor
Won Oscar, 1942, for *Yankee Doodle Dandy*.
b. Jul 17, 1899 in New York, New York
Source: *BiDFilm; BiE&WWA; BioNews 74; CelR 73; CmMov; CurBio 42; FilmgC; IntMPA 75, 76, 77, 78, 79, 80, 81, 82; MotPP; MovMk; NewYTBS 74; OxFilm; PlP&P; WebAB; WhoAm 74, 76, 78, 80, 82; WhoHol A; WhoThe 77; WhoWor 74; WorEFlm*

Cagney, Jeanne
American. Actress
b. Mar 25, 1919 in New York, New York
Source: *BiE&WWA; FilmgC; IntMPA 75, 76, 77, 78, 79, 80, 81, 82; MotPP; NotNAT; WhoHol A; WhoThe 77*

Cahan, Abraham
Russian. Editor, Author
b. Jul 7, 1860 in Vilna, Russia
d. Aug 31, 1951 in New York, New York
Source: *AmAu&B; BbD; BiD&SB; CasWL; ConAmL; DcAmAu; DcAmB S5; EncWL; ModAL; OxAmL; Pen AM; REn; REnAL; TwCA, SUP; WebAB; WhAm 3; WhNAA*

Cahill, William Thomas
American. Politician
b. Jun 25, 1912 in Philadelphia, Pennsylvania
Source: *BioIn 8, 9, 10; BioNews; CurBio 70; IntWW 74; NewYTBE 72; WhoAm 74; WhoAmP 73; WhoE 74; WhoGov 72*

Cahn, Sammy
American. Songwriter
Won Oscars for "Three Coins in the Fountain," "All the Way."
b. Jun 18, 1913 in New York, New York
Source: *AmSCAP 66; ConAu 85; CurBio 74; EncMT; FilmgC; IntMPA 75, 76, 77, 78, 79, 80, 81, 82; NewCBMT; NewYTBS 74; NotNAT; WhoAm 74, 76, 78, 80, 82; WhoThe 77; WhoWor 74; WhoWorJ 72*

Caidin, Martin
American. Author
b. Sep 14, 1927 in New York, New York
Source: *AmAu&B; AuNews 2; ConAu 1R, 2NR*

Caillie, Rene
French. Explorer
First European to visit and return from Timbuktu.
b. 1799
d. 1838
Source: *NewCol 75*

Cain
Biblical Character
Source: *BioIn 10; NewCol 75*

Cain, James Mallahan
American. Author, Poet
b. Jul 1, 1892 in Annapolis, Maryland
d. Oct 27, 1977 in Hyattsville, Maryland
Source: *AmAu&B; AmNov; AuNews 1; BiE&WWA; CelR 73; CnDAL; CnMWL; ConAu 17R, 73; ConLC 3, 11; ConNov 72, 76; DcLEL; EncMys; FilmgC; LongCTC; ModAL; NotNAT; OxAmL; Pen AM; REn; REnAL; TwCA, SUP; TwCW; WebE&AL; WhNAA; WhoAm 74; WhoWor 74; WrDr 76*

Cain, Jonathan
see: Babys, The; Journey

Cain, Richard H
American. Congressman
b. 1825
d. 1887
Source: *BioIn 5, 6, 8, 9, 10, 11*

Caine, Sir Hall
English. Author
b. May 14, 1853
d. Aug 31, 1931
Source: *Chambr 3; LongCTC; ModBrL; NewC; REn; TwCA, SUP; TwCW*

Caine, Michael
[Michael Joseph Micklewhite]
English. Actor
Films include *Alfie,* 1966; *Beyond the Poseidon Adventure,* 1979.
b. Mar 14, 1933 in London, England
Source: *BiDFilm; BkPepl; CelR 73; CmMov; CurBio 68; FilmgC; IntMPA 75, 76, 77, 78, 79, 80, 81, 82; MotPP; MovMk; OxFilm; Who 82; WhoAm 82; WhoHol A; WhoWor 74; WorEFlm*

Cairncross, Sir Alexander Kirkland
Scottish. Author, Educator, Economist
b. Feb 11, 1911 in Lemahagow, Scotland
Source: *Au&Wr 71; ConAu 61; IntWW 74; Who 74; WhoAm 74, 76, 78, 80, 82; WhoWor 74; WrDr 76*

Caius, John
English. Physician
b. 1510
d. 1573
Source: *Alli; BioIn 1, 2, 3, 7, 9*

Cakobau, Ratu Sir George
Fijian. Politician
b. Nov 6, 1912 in Suva, Fiji
Source: *IntWW 74; Who 74*

"Calamity Jane"
[Martha Jane Canary Burke]
American. Frontierwoman
Friend of "Wild Bill" Hickok; scouted for General Custer.
b. 1852 in Princeton, Missouri
d. Aug 1, 1903 in South Dakota
Source: *AmBi; FilmgC; InWom; NotAW; OxFilm; WebAB*

Calas, Jean
French. Merchant
b. 1698
d. 1762
Source: *BioIn 4, 5, 6; OxFr*

Caldecott, Randolph
English. Artist
Caldecott Medal given annually to outstanding children's book illustrator established 1938.
b. Mar 22, 1846 in Chester, England
d. Feb 12, 1886 in Saint Augustine, Florida
Source: *AnCL; CarSB; ChPo, S1, S2; IlsBYP; JBA 34, 51; SmATA 17; Str&VC; WhoChL*

Calder, Alexander
American. Artist, Engineer
b. Jul 22, 1898 in Philadelphia, Pennsylvania
d. Nov 11, 1976 in New York, New York
Source: *Alli SUP; BioNews 74; CelR 73; ChPo; CurBio 46, 66; DcCAA 71; EncAB-H; IntWW 74; NewYTBE 73; REn; WebAB; Who 74; WhoAm 74; WhoAmA 73; WhoWor 74*

Calder, Nigel David Ritchie
English. Author
b. Dec 2, 1931 in London, England
Source: *Au&Wr 71; ConAu 21R; Who 74; WrDr 76*

Calderon de la Barca, Pedro
Spanish. Dramatist
b. Jan 17, 1600 in Madrid, Spain
d. May 25, 1681 in Madrid, Spain
Source: *AtlBL; BbD; BiD&SB; CasWL; CnThe; CyWA; DcEuL; DcSpL; EuAu; EvEuW; McGEWD; NewC; OxEng; OxThe; Pen EUR; RComWL; REn; REnWD*

Calderone, Mary Steichen
American. Physician
b. Jul 1, 1904 in New York, New York
Source: *AuNews 1; BioIn 8, 10, 11; BioNews; CurBio 67; WhoAm 74; WhoAmW 74; WhoWor 74*

Caldwell, Erskine Preston
American. Author, Journalist
Author *God's Little Acre,* 1933; *The Sacrilege of Alan Kent,* 1976.
b. Dec 17, 1903 in Moreland, Georgia
Source: *AmAu&B; AmNov; AmWr; Au&Wr 71; AuNews 1; BioNews 74; CasWL; CelR 73; CnDAL; ConAmA; ConAu 1R, 2NR; ConLC 1, 8, 14; ConNov 72, 76; CurBio 40; CyWA; DcLEL; DrAF 76; EncWL; EvLB; FilmgC; IntWW 74; LongCTC; ModAL, SUP; OxAmL; Pen AM; PlP&P; RAdv 1; REn; REnAL; TwCA, SUP; TwCW; WebE&AL; WhNAA; Who 74; WhoAm 74, 76, 78, 80, 82; WhoS&SW 73; WhoTwCL; WhoWor 74; WrDr 76*

Caldwell, (Janet Miriam) Taylor
[Mrs. William Robert Prestie]
English. Author
Wrote *Testimony of Two Men,* 1968; *The Captains and the Kings,* 1972.
b. Sep 7, 1900 in Manchester, England
Source: *AmAu&B; AmNov; CelR 73; ConAu 5R, 5NR; ConLC 2; CurBio 40; ForWC 70; InWom; LongCTC; OxAmL; REn; REnAL; TwCA, SUP; Who 82; WhoAm 74, 76, 78, 80, 82; WhoWor 74; WrDr 76*

Caldwell, John Charles
Australian. Demographer, Educator
b. Dec 8, 1928 in Sydney, Australia
Source: *WhoWor 74*

Caldwell, Sarah
American. Opera Official
Conductor/director major US opera companies; founded Opera Co. of Boston, 1957.
b. Mar 6, 1924 in Maryville, Missouri
Source: *BioNews 74; CurBio 73; NewYTBE 72; WhoAm 74, 76, 78, 80, 82; WhoWor 74*

Caldwell, Zoe
Australian. Actress
b. Sep 14, 1933 in Melbourne, Australia
Source: *CelR 73; CurBio 70; NotNAT; PlP&P, A; WhoAm 74; WhoThe 77; WhoWor 74*

Cale, J J
American. Singer, Songwriter
b. in Tulsa, Oklahoma
Source: *ConMuA 80; IlEncRk; WhoRock 81*

Calhern, Louis
[Carl Henry Vogt]
American. Actor
b. Feb 19, 1895 in New York, New York
d. May 12, 1956 in Nara, Japan
Source: *BiDFilm; CurBio 51, 56; FamA&A; FilmgC; MotPP; MovMk; OxFilm; PlP&P; Vers A; WhAm 3; WhScrn 74, 77; WhoHol B*

Calhoun, John Caldwell
American. Lawyer, Orator, Statesman
b. Mar 18, 1782 in Calhoun Mills, South Carolina
d. 1850
Source: *Alli; AmAu; AmAu&B; AmBi; ApCAB; BbD; BiAuS; BiD&SB; BiDSA; BiDrAC; BiDrUSE; CyAL 1; DcAmAu; DcAmB; Drake; EncAB-H; OxAmL; REn; REnAL; TwCBDA; WebAB; WhAm H; WhAmP*

Calhoun, Lee Q
American. Track Athlete
Only man to win gold medal in 110-meter hurdles twice, 1956, 1960 Olympics.
b. Feb 23, 1933 in Laurel, Mississippi
Source: *InB&W 80*

Calhoun, Rory
[Francis Timothy Durgin]
American. Actor, Director, Producer, Writer
b. Aug 8, 1923 in Los Angeles, California
Source: *FilmgC; IntMPA 75, 76, 77, 78, 79, 80, 81, 82; MotPP; MovMk; WhoAm 74, 76, 78, 80, 82; WhoHol A*

Califano, Joseph Anthony, Jr.
American. Lawyer
Secretary, HEW, 1977-81; wrote *The Media and the Law,* 1976.
b. May 15, 1931 in Brooklyn, New York
Source: *ConAu 45; IntWW 74; WhoAm 74, 76, 78, 80, 82; WhoAmP 73; WhoS&SW 73*

Caliguiri, Richard
American. Mayor of Pittsburgh
b. Oct 20, 1931 in Pittsburgh, Pennsylvania
Source: *WhoAm 78, 80, 82; WhoAmP 77, 79; WhoE 79; WhoGov 77*

Caligula
[Gaius Caesar Germanicus]
Roman. Emperor
Succeeded Tiberius as Roman emperor, 37-41; main character in Camus' play *Caligula,* 1944.
b. Aug 31, 12 in Antium, Italy
d. Jan 24, 41 in Rome, Italy
Source: *McGEWB; NewC; REn*

Calisher, Hortense
[Mrs. Curtis Harnack]
American. Author
b. Dec 20, 1911 in New York, New York
Source: *AmAu&B; ConAu 1R, 1NR; ConLC 2, 4, 8; ConNov 72, 76; CurBio 73; DrAF 76; ModAL SUP; NewYTBE 72; OxAmL; Pen AM; TwCW; WhoAm 74, 76, 78, 80, 82; WhoWor 74; WorAu; WrDr 76*

Calkins, Dick
American. Cartoonist
b. 1895
d. 1962
Source: *WorECom*

Calkins, Earnest Elmo
American. Advertising Innovator
b. Mar 25, 1868 in Genesco, Illinois
d. Oct 4, 1964
Source: *AmAu&B; ChPo; REnAL; WhAm 4; WhNAA*

Callaghan, (Leonard) James
English. Government Official
Leader of Labour Party; Prime Minister of England, 1976-79.
b. Mar 27, 1912 in Portsmouth, England
Source: *CurBio 68; IntWW 74, 75, 76, 77, 78; IntYB 78, 79; NewYTBS 76; Who 74, 82; WhoModH; WhoWor 74, 76, 78*

Callaghan, Morley Edward
Canadian. Author
b. 1903 in Toronto, ON
Source: *CanNov; CanWW 70; CanWr; CasWL; CathA 1930; ConAu 9R; ConLC 3; ConNov 72, 76; CreCan 2; DcLEL; EncWL; IntWW 74; LongCTC; NewC; OxAmL; OxCan, SUP; Pen ENG; REn; REnAL; TwCA, SUP; TwCW; WebE&AL; Who 74; WhoAm 74; WhoTwCL; WrDr 76*

Callahan, Daniel
American. Ethicist
b. Jul 19, 1930 in Washington, DC
Source: *WhoAm 74; WhoE 74; WhoWor 74*

Callan, Michael
American. Actor
b. 1935 in Philadelphia, Pennsylvania
Source: *FilmgC; IntMPA 75, 76, 77, 78, 79, 80, 81, 82; MotPP; WhoHol A*

Callas, Charlie
American. Comedian, Actor
b. Dec 20, in Brooklyn, New York
Source: *WhoAm 82; WhoHol A*

Callas, Maria
[Maria Kalogeropoulou; Maria Meneghini]
American. Opera Singer
Career spanned 1938-60; romantically involved with Aristotle Onassis, 1960's.
b. Dec 3, 1923 in New York, New York
d. Sep 16, 1977 in Paris, France
Source: *BioIn 10; BioNews 74; CelR 73; CurBio 56, 77; IntWW 74; NewEOp 71; NewYTBE 71; WebAB; Who 74; WhoAm 74; WhoHol A; WhoMus 72; WhoWor 74*

Callaway, Howard Hollis
American. Business Executive
Secretary of Army, 1973-75.
b. Apr 2, 1927 in Lagrange, Georgia
Source: *BiDrAC; CngDr 74; WhoAm 74, 76, 78, 80, 82; WhoAmP 73; WhoS&SW 73; WhoWor 74*

Calles, Plutarco
Mexican. Statesman
b. Sep 25, 1877
d. Oct 19, 1945 in Mexico City, Mexico
Source: *CurBio 45; WhAm 2*

Calley, William Laws
American. Army Officer
b. 1943
Source: *NewYTBS 74*

Callimachus
Greek. Critic, Poet
b. 305BC
d. 240BC
Source: *AtlBL; BbD; BiD&SB; CasWL; OxEng; Pen CL; REn*

Callis, Joe
see: Human League

Calloway, Cab(ell)
American. Band Leader, Singer
b. Dec 25, 1907 in Rochester, New York
Source: *AmSCAP 66; BioNews 74; CelR 73; CurBio 45; FilmgC; MovMk; WhoAm 74; WhoBlA 75; WhoHol A; WhoJazz 72; WhoThe 77*

Calmer, Ned
American. News Analyst, Author
b. Jul 16, 1907 in Chicago, Illinois
Source: *ConAu 69; WhoAm 74, 76, 78, 80, 82; WhoWor 74*

Calpurnia
Roman. Wife of Julius Caesar
Third wife of Julius Caesar; had prophetic dream of Caesar's assassination.
b. 59BC
Source: *InWom; REn*

Calve, Emma
[Rosa Calvet]
French. Opera Singer
b. Aug 15, 1858 in Decazevelle, France
d. Jan 6, 1942 in Millan, France
Source: *CurBio 42; InWom; WhAm 1, 2; WhoStg 1906, 1908*

Calvert, Bernie
see: Hollies, The

Calvert, Catherine
American. Actress
b. 1891 in Baltimore, Maryland
d. Jan 18, 1971 in Uniondale, New York
Source: *Film 1, 2; TwYS; WhScrn 74, 77; WhThe; WhoHol B*

Calvert, Edward
British. Engraver, Artist
b. 1799
d. 1883
Source: *BioIn 1, 4, 6*

Calvert, George
see: Baltimore, George Calvert, Baron

Calvert, Louis
English. Actor
b. 1859 in Manchester, England
d. Jul 2, 1923 in England
Source: *Film 1; NotNAT B; OxThe; WhScrn 77; WhThe*

Calvert, Phyllis
English. Actress
b. Feb 18, 1915 in London, England
Source: *CmMov; FilmgC; IntMPA 75, 76, 77, 78, 79, 80, 81, 82; MotPP; MovMk; OxFilm; Who 74; WhoHol A; WhoThe 77*

Calvert, "Sunshine" (Melvin)
American. Horse Trainer
Source: *NF*

Calvet, Corinne
[Corinne Dibos]
French. Actress
b. 1925 in Paris, France
Source: *FilmgC; IntMPA 75, 76, 77, 78, 79, 80, 81, 82; MotPP; MovMk; WhoHol A*

Calvin, John
[Jean Chauvin]
French. Theologian, Religious Reformer
Established Calvinism, recognized Bible as only source of knowledge.
b. Jul 10, 1509 in Noyon, France
d. May 27, 1564 in Geneva, Switzerland
Source: *BbD; BiD&SB; NewC; RComWL; REn*

Calvin, Melvin
American. Chemist, Educator
b. Apr 8, 1911 in Saint Paul, Minnesota
Source: *AmM&WS 73; BioIn 3, 4, 5, 6, 8; CurBio 62; IntWW 74; Who 74; WhoAm 74, 76, 78, 80, 82; WhoWor 74*

Calvino, Italo
Italian. Author, Editor
b. Oct 15, 1923 in San Remo, Italy
Source: *BioIn 10, 11; CasWL; ConAu 85; ConLC 5, 8, 11; EncSF; EncWL; IntAu&W 76, 77; IntWW 74, 75, 76, 77, 78; ModRL; NewYTBS 81; Pen EUR; ScF&FL 1; TwCW; WhoTwCL; WhoWor 74, 76, 78; WorAu*

Calvo, Paul McDonald
American. Businessman, Politician
Governor of Guam, 1978--.
b. Jul 25, 1934 in Agana, Guam
Source: *FarE&A 79; WhoAm 82; WhoAmP 77, 79*

Calvo Sotelo (y Bustelo), Leopoldo
Spanish. Businessman, Politician
Prime Minister of Spain, 1981--.
b. Apr 14, 1926 in Madrid, Spain
Source: *CurBio 81; IntWW 76, 77, 78; NewYTBS 81*

Cambaceres, Jean Jacques Regis de
[Duke of Parma]
French. Statesman
Napoleon's chief legal advisor.
b. Oct 18, 1753 in Montpellier, France
d. Mar 8, 1824
Source: *DcBiPP; LinLib S; OxFr; OxLaw*

Cambridge, Godfrey
American. Actor, Comedian
b. Feb 26, 1933 in New York, New York
d. Nov 29, 1976 in Hollywood, California
Source: *CelR 73; CurBio 69; FilmgC; IntMPA 75, 76, 77; MotPP; MovMk; NotNAT; OxFilm; WhoAm 74; WhoBlA 75; WhoHol A*

Camerarius, Rudolf Jakob
German. Botanist
b. 1665
d. 1721
Source: *NewCol 75*

Camerini, Mario
Italian. Motion Picture Director
b. Feb 6, 1895 in Rome, Italy
d. Feb 6, 1981
Source: *AnObit 1981; DcFM; FilmgC; OxFilm; WorEFlm*

Cameron, Eleanor Butler
Canadian. Author
b. Mar 23, 1912 in Winnipeg, MB
Source: *AuBYP; ChlLR 1; ChPo; ConAu 1R, 2NR; SmATA 1; ThrBJA; WhoAm 82*

Cameron, Rod
[Rod Cox]
American. Actor
b. Dec 7, 1912 in Calgary, AB
Source: *CmMov; FilmgC; HolP 40; IntMPA 75, 76, 77, 78, 79, 80, 81, 82; MotPP; WhoHol A*

Camilli, Dolph (Adolph Louis)
American. Baseball Player
b. Apr 23, 1908 in San Francisco, California
Source: *BaseEn; WhoProB 73*

Camnitz, Howie (Samuel Howard)
"Red"
American. Baseball Player
b. Aug 22, 1881 in Covington, Kentucky
d. Mar 2, 1960 in Louisville, Kentucky
Source: *BaseEn; BioIn 5*

Camoes, Luis de
[Luis de Camoens]
Portuguese. Author
b. 1524 in Lisbon, Portugal
d. 1580 in Lisbon, Portugal
Source: *AtlBL; CasWL; EvEuW; Pen EUR; REn; REnWD*

Camp, Hamilton
English. Actor
b. Oct 30, 1934 in England
Source: *WhoHol A*

Camp, Walter Chauncey
"Father of American Football"
American. Author, Football Executive
Developed rules for modern day football; co-founder of Ivy League.
b. Apr 7, 1859 in New Haven, Connecticut
d. Mar 14, 1925 in New York, New York
Source: *AmAu&B; AmLY; BiD&SB; DcAmAu; DcNAA; JBA 34, 51; REnAL; WhNAA; WhoFtbl 74*

Campagnolo, Gitullio
"Campy"
Italian. Bicycle Manufacturer
Designs, makes bicycle parts.
b. 1901? in Italy
d. Feb 1982 in Monselice, Italy
Source: *BioIn 12*

Campanella, Joseph Mario
American. Actor
b. Nov 21, 1927 in New York, New York
Source: *BiE&WWA; FilmgC; NotNAT; WhoAm 82; WhoHol A*

Campanella, Roy
American. Baseball Player
Catcher, Brooklyn Dodgers, 1948-57; paralyzed in car accident, 1958; Hall of Fame, 1969.
b. Nov 19, 1921 in Homestead, Pennsylvania
Source: *BaseEn; CelR 73; CurBio 53; WhoAm 74; WhoBlA 75; WhoProB 73*

Campanella, Tommaso
[Domenico Giovanni]
Italian. Philosopher, Poet
b. Sep 5, 1568 in Stilo, Italy
d. May 21, 1639 in Paris, France
Source: *BbD; BiD&SB; CasWL; DcEuL; EuAu; EvEuW; Pen EUR; REn*

Campaneris, Bert (Dagoberto Blanco)
"Campy"
Cuban. Baseball Player
Shortstop, 1964-81; led AL in stolen bases six times.
b. Mar 9, 1942 in Pueblo Nuevo, Cuba
Source: *BaseEn; WhoProB 73*

Campbell, Clarence Sutherland
Canadian. Hockey Official
President of NHL, 1946-77; Hall of Fame, 1966.
b. Jul 9, 1905 in Fleming, SK
Source: *WhoAm 82; WhoHcky 73*

Campbell, Sir Clifford
English. Former Governor of Jamaica
b. Jun 28, 1892 in Petersfield, England
Source: *Who 74; WhoGov 72; WhoWor 74*

Campbell, Donald
English. Automobile and Boat Racer
Set water and land speed records, 1964; killed in boat crash.
b. Mar 23, 1921 in Surrey, England
d. Jan 4, 1967
Source: *CurBio 64, 67; NewCol 75*

Campbell, Donald Fraser
English. Engineer
b. 1881
d. 1966
Source: *BioIn 7*

Campbell, Donald Guy
American. Journalist, Author
b. Jun 27, 1922 in Brownsburg, Idaho
Source: *ConAu 21R; IndAu 1917; WhoAm 74, 76, 78, 80, 82*

Campbell, Douglas
Scottish. Actor
b. Jun 11, 1922 in Glasgow, Scotland
Source: *BiE&WWA; BioIn 4, 5, 11; CnThe; CreCan 1; NotNAT; WhoAm 74, 76, 78; WhoThe 72, 77*

Campbell, E Simms
American. Cartoonist
b. Jan 2, 1906 in Saint Louis, Missouri
d. Jan 27, 1971
Source: *BioIn 6, 7, 8, 9; ConAu 93; CurBio 41, 71*

Campbell, Earl Christian
American. Football Player
Won Heisman Trophy, 1977; running back, Houston Oilers, 1978--; MVP, 1978, 1979.
b. Mar 29, 1955 in Tyler, Texas
Source: *BioIn 11; WhoAm 82; WorAl*

Campbell, Glen
American. Singer, Musician
Has won five Grammys; hit songs include "By the Time I Get to Phoenix."
b. Mar 22, 1938 in Delight, Arkansas
Source: *BioNews 74; BkPepl; CelR 73; CurBio 69; EncFCWM 69; FilmgC; IntMPA 75, 76, 77, 78, 79, 80, 81, 82; WhoAm 74, 76, 78, 80, 82; WhoHol A; WhoWest 74, 76; WorAl*

Campbell, Gordon Thomas
British. Politician
b. Jun 8, 1921
Source: *IntWW 74; Who 74; WhoWor 74*

Campbell, John W
American. Author, Editor
b. Jun 8, 1910 in Newark, New Jersey
d. Jul 11, 1971 in Mountainside, New Jersey
Source: *ConAu 21R, 29R; ConAu P-2; WorAu*

Campbell, Sir Malcolm
English. Automobile and Boat Racer
First to attain speed of 150 mph on land, 1925.
b. Mar 11, 1885 in Chislehurst, England
d. Jan 1, 1949
Source: *CurBio 47, 49; EncSoA; WhDW; WhE&EA*

Campbell, Mrs. Patrick
[Beatrice Stella Tanner]
English. Actress
b. Feb 9, 1865 in London, England
d. Apr 9, 1940 in Pau, France
Source: *CurBio 40; FamA&A; FilmgC; InWom; LongCTC; NewC; OxCan; OxFilm; OxThe; PlP&P; REn; ThFT; WhAm 1; WhScrn 74, 77; Who 74; WhoHol B; WhoStg 1906, 1908*

Campbell, Roy
English. Author
b. Oct 2, 1901 in Durban, South Africa
d. Apr 22, 1957 in Portugal
Source: *CathA 1930; ChPo; CnE&AP; CnMWL; EncWL; LongCTC; ModBrL, SUP; OxEng; Pen ENG; REn; TwCA, SUP; TwCW; WebE&AL; WhoTwCL*

Campbell, Thomas
Scottish. Poet
b. Aug 27, 1777 in Glasgow, Scotland
d. Jun 15, 1844 in Boulogne, France
Source: *Alli; BbD; BiD&SB; BiDLA; BrAu 19; CasWL; ChPo, S1, S2; CrtT 2; DcEnA, AP; DcEnL; DcEuL; DcLEL; EvLB; MouLC 3; NewC; OxAmL; OxEng; Pen ENG; PoChrch; REn; WebE&AL*

Campbell, Walter Stanley
American. Author
b. Aug 15, 1887 in Severy, Kansas
d. Dec 1957
Source: *AmAu&B; CnDAL; OxAmL; REn; REnAL; TwCA, SUP; WhAm 3; WhNAA*

Campbell, William Edward March
[William March, pseud.]
American. Author
b. Sep 18, 1893 in Mobile, Alabama
d. May 15, 1954 in New Orleans, Louisiana
Source: *AmAu&B; AmNov X; CnDAL; ConAmA; LongCTC; ModAL; OxAmL; REn; REnAL; TwCA SUP*

Campion, Thomas
English. Poet, Critic
b. Feb 12, 1567 in London, England
d. Mar 1, 1620 in London, England
Source: *Alli; AtlBL; BbD; BiD&SB; BrAu; CasWL; Chambr 1; ChPo, S1, S2; CnE&AP; CroE&S; CrtT 1; DcEnL; DcEuL; DcLEL; EvLB; NewC; OxEng; OxThe; Pen ENG; RAdv 1; REn; WebE&AL*

Campo, John(ny)
"The Fat Man"
American. Horse Trainer
b. 1938? in New York, New York
Source: *BioIn 9, 11; NewYTBS 81; PseudN*

Campora, Hector Jose
Argentine. Former President
b. Mar 26, 1909 in Mercedes, Argentina
d. Dec 19, 1980 in Mexico City, Mexico
Source: *BioIn 9, 10, 11; CurBio 73, 81; NewYTBE 72; WhoWor 74*

Camus, Albert
[Bauchart; Albert Mathe, pseuds.; Saetone, joint pseud.]
French. Author, Philosopher
Proponent of absurdism philosophy; major novel *L'Etranger*, 1942.
b. Nov 7, 1913 in Mondovi, Algiers
d. Jan 4, 1960 in Sens, France
Source: *AtlBL; CasWL; ClDMEL; CnMD; CnMWL; CnThe; ConAu 89; ConLC 1, 2, 4; CroCD; CyWA; EncWL; EvEuW; LongCTC; McGEWD; ModRL; ModWD; OxEng; OxFr; OxThe; Pen EUR; RComWL; REn; REnWD; TwCA SUP; TwCW; WhAm 3; WhoTwCL*

Camus, Marcel
French. Motion Picture Director
b. Apr 21, 1912 in Chappes, France
Source: *DcFM; FilmgC; OxFilm; WorEFlm*

Canaday, John Edwin
American. Art Critic, Author
b. Feb 1, 1907 in Fort Scott, Kansas
Source: *AmAu&B; CelR 73; ConAu 13R; CurBio 62; DrAS 74H; EncMys; NewYTBE 72; St&PR 75; WhoAm 74; WhoAmA 73; WhoE 74; WhoWest 74; WorAu*

Canaletto, Antonio
Italian. Artist
b. Oct 18, 1697 in Venice, Italy
d. Apr 20, 1768 in Venice, Italy
Source: *REn*

Canaris, Wilhelm
German. Admiral, Spy
b. Jan 1, 1887 in Aplerbeck, Germany
d. Apr 9, 1945 in Flossenburg, Germany
Source: *BioIn 10; NewCol 75*

Canary, David
American. Actor
b. 1938 in Elwood, Indiana
Source: *WhoHol A*

Canby, Edward Tatnall
American. Choral Director
b. 1912
Source: *ConAmC*

Canby, Henry Seidel
American. Editor, Critic
b. Sep 6, 1878 in Wilmington, Delaware
d. Apr 5, 1961 in Ossining, New York
Source: *AmAu&B; AmLY; CnDAL; ConAmA; ConAmL; ConAu 89; CurBio 42, 61; DcLEL; LongCTC; OxAmL; REn; REnAL; TwCA, SUP; WhAm 4; WhNAA*

Canby, Vincent
American. Journalist, Critic
b. Jul 27, 1924 in Chicago, Illinois
Source: *ConAu 81; ConLC 13; IntMPA 75, 76, 77, 78, 79, 80; WhoAm 80; IntMPA 82; WhoAm 82*

Candela, (Outerino) Felix
Spanish. Architect, Engineer
b. Jan 27, 1910 in Madrid, Spain
Source: *BioIn 10, 11; EncMA; IntWW 74, 75, 76, 77, 78; McGDA; WhoAm 74, 76, 78; WhoArch; WhoS&SW 73, 75; WhoWor 74, 76*

Candler, Asa Griggs
American. Philanthropist, Manufacturer
b. Dec 30, 1851 in Villa Rica, Georgia
d. Mar 12, 1929 in Atlanta, Georgia
Source: *NatCAB 7, 31; WebAB; WhAm 1*

Canetti, Elias
Bulgarian. Author
Won Nobel Prize in Literature, 1981.
b. Jul 25, 1905 in Ruschuk, Bulgaria
Source: *CasWL; CnMD; CnMWL; ConAu 21R; ConLC 3, 14; CroCD; CurBio 83; EncWT; ModGL; NewYTBS 81; OxGer; Pen EUR; WhoWor 74; WorAu*

Canfield, Cass
American. Publisher
b. Apr 26, 1897 in New York, New York
Source: *AmAu&B; BiE&WWA; ConAu 41R; CurBio 54; NewYTBE 71; Who 74; WhoAm 74, 76, 78, 80, 82; WrDr 76*

Canfield, Dorothea Frances
see: Fisher, Dorothy Frances Canfield

Canfield, James Hulme
American. Educator, Librarian
b. Mar 18, 1847 in Delaware County, Delaware
d. Mar 29, 1909
Source: *Alli SUP; DcAmAu; DcNAA; OhA&B*

Canham, Erwin Dain
American. Newspaper Editor, Journalist
b. Feb 3, 1904 in Auburn, Maine
d. Jan 3, 1982 in Agana, Guam
Source: *AmAu&B; ConAu P-1; CurBio 45, 60, 82; IntWW 74, 75, 76, 77, 78; IntYB 78, 79; NewYTBS 82; WhoAm 74, 76, 78, 80; WhoWor 74*

Caniff, Milt(on Arthur)
American. Cartoonist
b. Feb 28, 1907 in Hillsboro, Ohio
Source: *AuNews 1; ConAu 85; CurBio 44; OhA&B; REnAL; WebAB; WhoAm 74, 76, 78, 80, 82; WhoAmA 73; WhoE 74; WhoWor 74*

Caniglia, Maria
Italian. Opera Singer
b. May 5, 1905 in Naples, Italy
d. Apr 15, 1979 in Rome, Italy
Source: *InWom; WhoMus 72*

Cann, Howard Goodsell
American. Basketball Player, Coach
b. Oct 11, 1895 in Bridgeport, Connecticut
Source: *BioIn 9; WhoBbl 73*

Canning, George
English. Statesman
b. Apr 11, 1770 in London, England
d. Aug 8, 1827 in London, England
Source: *Alli; BiD&SB; BrAu 19; CasWL; ChPo; DcEnL; DcEuL; DcLEL; EvLB; NewC; OxEng; PoIre; WhAm H*

Cannizzaro, Stanislao
Italian. Chemist
Devised method of deducing atomic weights of elements based on molecular weight.
b. Jul 13, 1826 in Palermo, Sicily
d. May 10, 1910 in Rome, Italy
Source: *AsBiEn; DcScB; InSci; LinLib S; NewCol 75; WhDW*

Cannon, Annie Jump
American. Astronomer
b. Dec 11, 1863 in Dover, Delaware
d. Apr 13, 1941 in Cambridge, Massachusetts
Source: *BiCAW; DcAmB S3; DcScB; NotAW; WebAB; WhAm 1; WomWWA 14*

Cannon, Dyan
[Samille Diane Friesen]
"Frosty"
American. Actress
Former wife of Cary Grant and mother of his only child, Jennifer.
b. Jan 4, 1938 in Tacoma, Washington
Source: *FilmgC; IntMPA 75, 76, 77, 78, 79, 80, 81, 82; MovMk; WhoAm 74, 76, 78, 80, 82; WhoHol A*

Cannon, Howard Walter
American. Senator
b. Jan 26, 1912 in Saint George, Utah
Source: *AlmAP 78, 80; BiDrAC; BioIn 5, 6, 9, 10; BioNews 75; CngDr 74, 77, 79; CurBio 60; IntWW 74, 75, 76, 77, 78; NewYTBE 73; PolProf E; PolProf J; PolProf K; PolProf NF; WhoAm 74, 76, 78, 80, 82; WhoAmP 73, 75, 77, 79; WhoGov 72, 75, 77; WhoWest 74, 76, 78*

Cannon, Jimmy (James J)
American. Journalist
b. Apr 10, 1909 in New York, New York
d. Dec 5, 1973 in New York, New York
Source: *REnAL; WhAm 6*

Cannon, Joseph Gurney
"Uncle Joe"
American. Congressman
b. May 7, 1836 in New Garden, North Carolina
d. Nov 12, 1926
Source: *AmBi; BiDrAC; DcAmB; EncAB-H; WebAB; WhAm 1; WhAmP*

Cannon, Poppy
[Poppy Cannon White]
American. Home Economist, Journalist
b. 1907 in Capetown, South Africa
d. Apr 2, 1975 in New York, New York
Source: *ConAu 57, 65; ForWC 70; InWom*

Cannon, Walter Bradford
American. Physiologist
b. Oct 19, 1871 in Prairie Chien, Wisconsin
d. Oct 1, 1945
Source: *BioIn 1, 2, 7, 9, 10; CurBio 45; DcNAA; WhNAA*

Canova, Antonio
Italian. Artist
b. Nov 1, 1757 in Passagno, Italy
d. Oct 13, 1822 in Venice, Italy
Source: *AtlBL; BioIn 4, 5, 6, 8, 9, 11*

Canova, Diana
American. Actress
b. 1953
Source: *BioIn 11, 12*

Canova, Judy
American. Singer, Actress, Comedienne
b. Nov 20, 1916 in Jacksonville, Florida
Source: *FilmgC; ForWC 70; InWom; IntMPA 75, 76, 77, 78, 79, 80, 81, 82; MotPP; MovMk; WhoAm 82; WhoHol A*

Cantacuzene, Princess
[Julia Dent Grant]
American. Author
b. Jun 7, 1876 in Washington, DC
d. Oct 5, 1975 in Washington, DC
Source: *AmAu&B; ConAu 61; WhNAA*

Cantinflas
[Mario Moreno]
Mexican. Actor, Comedian
Won Oscar, 1957, for *Around the World in 80 Days.*
b. Aug 12, 1911 in Mexico City, Mexico
Source: *CurBio 53; EncLatA; FilmgC; MotPP; MovMk; OxFilm; WhoHol A; WhoWor 74*

Cantor, Charles
American. Radio Actor
b. 1898
d. Sep 11, 1966 in Hollywood, California
Source: *WhScrn 74, 77; WhoHol B*

Cantor, Eddie
[Edward Israel Itskowitz]
"Izzie"
American. Comedian, Singer
Starred on Broadway in *The Ziegfield Follies;* won special Oscar, 1956.
b. Jan 31, 1892 in New York, New York
d. Oct 10, 1964 in Beverly Hills, California
Source: *AmSCAP 66; BiE&WWA; CurBio 41, 54, 65; EncMT; FilmgC; MotPP; MovMk; OxFilm; PlP&P; TwYS; WebAB; WhAm 4; WhScrn 74, 77; WhoHol B; WorEFlm*

Cantor, Georg
German. Mathematician
b. 1845 in Saint Petersburg, Russia
d. 1918
Source: *NewCol 75; WebBD 80*

Cantrell, Lana
Australian. Singer, Actress
b. Aug 7, 1943 in Sydney, Australia
Source: *CelR 73; WhoAm 82*

Cantrick, Robert
American. Educator
b. Dec 8, 1917 in Monroe, Michigan
Source: *WhoAm 74; WhoE 74*

Cantwell, Robert Emmett
American. Author
b. Jan 31, 1908 in Little Falls, Washington
d. Dec 8, 1978 in New York, New York
Source: *AmAu&B; Au&Wr 71; BioIn 4, 9, 10, 11; ConAu 5R, 81, 4NR; ConNov 72, 76; NewYTBS 78; OxAmL; REnAL; TwCA, SUP; TwCW; WhAm 7; WhE&EA; WhoAm 74, 76, 78; WhoE 74; WrDr 76*

Canute
English. King
b. 995
d. Nov 12, 1035 in Shaftesbury, England
Source: *NewC; REn*

Canzoneri, Tony
American. Boxer
b. Nov 6, 1908 in Slidel, Louisiana
d. Dec 9, 1959 in New York, New York
Source: *BioIn 5; WhoBox 74*

Capa, Cornell
American. Journalist, Photographer
b. Apr 19, 1918 in Budapest, Hungary
Source: *BioIn 10; WhoAm 82*

Capa, Robert
American. Photographer
Killed by exploding mine; photographs in *Images of War,* 1964.
b. 1913 in Budapest, Hungary
d. May 25, 1954 in Thaibinh, Vietnam
Source: *WhAm 4*

Capablanca, Jose Raoul
Cuban. Chess Player
b. 1888 in Havana, Cuba
d. 1942
Source: *NewCol 75*

Capaldi, Jim
[Traffic]
English. Rock Musician
b. Aug 24, 1944 in Evesham, England
Source: *RkOn 2; WhoRock 81*

Capehart, Homer Earl
American. Senator
b. Jun 6, 1897 in Algiers, Indiana
d. Sep 3, 1979 in Indianapolis, Indiana
Source: *BiDrAC; BioIn 1, 3, 6, 9, 11; CurBio 47, 79; IntWW 74; NewYTBS 79; PolProf E; PolProf K; PolProf T; WhoAm 74, 76, 78*

Capek, Karel
Czech. Author
b. 1890 in Bohemia
d. Dec 24, 1938
Source: *CasWL; ClDMEL; CnMD; CnThe; CyWA; EncWL; EvEuW; LongCTC; McGEWD; ModSL 2; ModWD; OxThe; Pen EUR; REn; REnWD; TwCA, SUP; TwCW; WhoTwCL*

Capezio, Salvatore
American. Shoe Designer
Source: *WorFshn*

Caples, John
American. Advertising Executive, Author
b. May 1, 1900 in New York, New York
Source: *AmAu&B; ConAu 25R; WhoAdv 72; WhoAm 74, 76, 78, 80, 82*

Capone, Al(phonse)
"Scarface Al"
American. Gangster
Dominated Chicago crime scene, gang warfare during 1920's.
b. Jan 17, 1899 in Brooklyn, New York
d. Jan 25, 1947 in Miami Beach, Florida
Source: *DcAmB S4; FilmgC; OxFilm; WebAB*

Capone, Teresa
Italian. Mother of Al Capone
b. 1867? in Italy
d. Nov 29, 1952 in Chicago, Illinois
Source: *BioIn 10*

Caponi, Donna
[Donna Caponi Young]
American. Golfer
b. Jan 29, 1945 in Detroit, Michigan
Source: *NewYTBS 81; WhoGolf*

Capote, Truman
American. Author
Wrote *Breakfast at Tiffany's* (filmed, 1961); *In Cold Blood* (filmed, 1968).
b. Sep 30, 1924 in New Orleans, Louisiana
Source: *AmAu&B; AmNov; AmSCAP 66; Au&Wr 71; BiE&WWA; BkPepl; CasWL; CnDAL; CnMD; ConAu 5R; ConDr 73; ConLC 1, 3, 8, 13; ConNov 72, 76; CurBio 51, 68; DrAF 76; EncWL; FilmgC; IntWW 74; LongCTC; ModAL, SUP; ModWD; NewYTBE 71; NotNAT; OxAmL; OxFilm; Pen AM; RAdv 1; REn; REnAL; TwCA SUP; TwCW; WebAB; WebE&AL; Who 82; WhoAm 74, 76, 78, 80, 82; WhoHol A; WhoTwCL; WhoWor 74; WrDr 76*

Capp, Al
[Alfred Gerald Caplin]
American. Cartoonist
Created "Li'l Abner," 1934-77; syndicated in over 900 newspapers.
b. Sep 28, 1909 in New Haven, Connecticut
d. Nov 5, 1979 in Cambridge, Massachusetts
Source: *AmAu&B; ConAu 57, 89; CurBio 47, 80; IntAu&W 77; IntWW 74, 75, 76, 77, 78, 79; LinLib L; NewYTBS 79; REnAL; WebAB, 79; WhoAm 74, 76, 78; WhoWor 74; WorAl; WorECom*

Cappeletti, "Duke" (Gino)
American. Football Player
b. Mar 26, 1934 in Keewatin, Minnesota
Source: *WhoFtbl 74*

Cappelletti, John Raymond
American. Football Player
Won Heisman Trophy, 1973; TV movie *Something for Joey* about cancer-stricken brother.
b. Aug 9, 1952 in Philadelphia, Pennsylvania
Source: *WhoAm 80, 82; WhoFtbl 74*

Capper, Arthur
American. Editor, Publisher, Politician
b. Jul 14, 1865 in Garnett, Kansas
d. Dec 19, 1951 in Topeka, Kansas
Source: *AmAu&B; BiDrAC; CurBio 46, 52; DcAmB S5; WhAm 3; WhAmP; WhNAA*

Cappon, Lester Jesse
American. Historian
b. Sep 18, 1900 in Milwaukee, Wisconsin
d. Aug 24, 1981 in Chicago, Illinois
Source: *AmAu&B; BioIn 8; ConAu 104; DrAS 74H, 78H; WhoAm 74, 76, 78*

Capra, Frank
American. Motion Picture Director, Producer
Won Oscars for *It Happened One Night, Mr. Deeds Goes to Town.*
b. May 18, 1897 in Palermo, Sicily
Source: *BiDFilm; CelR 73; ConAu 61; ConLC 16; CurBio 48; DcFM; FilmgC; IntMPA 75, 76, 77, 78, 79, 80, 81, 82; IntWW 81; MovMk; NewYTBE 71; OxFilm; REnAL; TwYS; WebAB; Who 82; WhoAm 74, 76, 78, 80, 82; WhoWest 74; WhoWor 74, 76, 78; WorAl; WorEFlm*

Captain and Tennille, The
[Daryl Dragon; Toni Tennille]
American. Singing Duo
Won Grammy, 1975, for "Love Will Keep Us Together."
Source: *BkPepl; RkOn*

Captein, Jacques Eliza Jean
African. Clergyman
b. 1745
Source: *BioIn 1, 6, 8*

Capucci, Roberto
Italian. Fashion Designer
Source: *WorFshn*

Capucine
[Germaine Lefebvre]
French. Actress
b. Jan 6, 1935 in Toulon, France
Source: *FilmgC; IntMPA 77, 78, 79, 80, 81, 82; MotPP; MovMk; WhoHol A*

Caputo, Philip Joseph
American. Author, Journalist
Wrote *Rumor of War,* memoir of Vietnam; won Pulitzer Prize, 1972.
b. Jan 10, 1941 in Chicago, Illinois
Source: *ConAu 73; NewYTBS 81; WhoAm 74, 76, 78, 80, 82*

Cara, Irene
American. Actress, Singer
Starred in movie *Fame,* 1980; sang Oscar winning song.
b. Mar 18, 1959 in Bronx, New York
Source: *DcBlPA*

Caracalla, Marcus Aurelius Antonius
Roman. Emperor
b. Apr 4, 186
d. Apr 8, 217
Source: *NewCol 75; WebBD 80*

Caramanlis, Constantinos
see: Karamanlis, Constantine

Caravaggio, Michelangelo da
[Michelangelo Merisi]
Italian. Artist
b. Sep 8, 1569 in Caravaggio, Italy
d. Jul 18, 1609
Source: *AtlBL; McGEWB; REn*

Carawan, Guy
American. Singer, Songwriter
b. Jul 28, 1927 in Los Angeles, California
Source: *ConAu 17R; EncFCWM 69*

Caraway, Hattie Wyatt
American. Politician
First woman senator, 1931-44.
b. Feb 1, 1878 in Bakerville, Tennessee
d. Dec 21, 1950 in Falls Church, Virginia
Source: *BiDrAC; CurBio 45, 51; DcAmB S4; InWom; NotAW; WhAm 3; WhAmP*

Carazo (Odio), Rodrigo
Costa Rican. Former President
President, 1978-82.
b. Dec 27, 1926 in Cartago, Costa Rica
Source: *IntWW 78; IntYB 79; WhoWor 78*

Cardano, Cirolamo
Italian. Philosopher
b. 1501
d. 1576
Source: *BioIn 1, 2, 3, 5, 6, 8; REn*

Cardenas, Lazaro
Mexican. President
b. May 21, 1895 in Jiquilpan, Mexico
d. Oct 19, 1970 in Mexico City, Mexico
Source: *NewYTBE 70; WhAm 5*

Carder, Frederick
English. Glass Craftsman
Co-founded Steuben Glass Works, 1903.
b. 1863 in Brockmoor, England
d. 1963
Source: *BnEnAmA; DcNiCA; IlDcG; OxDecA*

Cardigan, Earl

Cardigan, Earl
British. Crimean War General
b. 1797
d. 1868
Source: *Alli SUP*

Cardin, Pierre
French. Fashion Designer
Founded fashion house, 1949; purchased Paris restaurant, Maxim's, 1981.
b. Jul 7, 1922 in Venice, Italy
Source: *BkPepl; CelR 73; CurBio 65; IntWW 74; WhoAm 74, 76, 78, 80, 82; WhoWor 74; WorFshn*

Cardinale, Claudia
Italian. Actress
Appeared in over 40 films, including *The Pink Panther,* 1963.
b. Apr 15, 1938 in Tunis, Italy
Source: *BiDFilm; FilmgC; IntMPA 75, 76, 77, 78, 79, 80, 81, 82; IntWW 74; MotPP; MovMk; OxFilm; WhoHol A; WhoWor 74; WorEFlm*

Cardozo, Benjamin Nathan
American. Supreme Court Justice
b. May 24, 1870 in New York, New York
d. Jul 9, 1938 in Port Chester, New York
Source: *AmAu&B; AmBi; DcAmB S2; DcLEL; DcNAA; EncAB-H; OxAmL; REn; REnAL; WebAB; WhAm 1; WhNAA*

Cardozo, Francis Louis
American. Educator
b. 1837
d. 1903
Source: *BioIn 10*

Carducci, Giosue
Italian. Poet, Critic
b. Jul 27, 1835 in Val di Castello, Italy
d. Feb 16, 1907 in Bologna, Italy
Source: *AtlBL; BbD; BiD&SB; CasWL; ClDMEL; CyWA; DcEuL; EuAu; EvEuW; LongCTC; NewC; OxEng; Pen EUR; RComWL; REn; WhoTwCL*

Carestini, Giovanni
Italian. Opera Singer
b. 1705 in Filottrano, Italy
d. 1760 in Filottrano, Italy
Source: *NewEOp 71*

Carew, Rod(ney Cline)
American. Baseball Player
Infielder, 1967--; has won seven batting titles.
b. Oct 1, 1945 in Gatun, Panama
Source: *BaseEn; NewYTBS 74; WhoAm 74, 76, 78, 80, 82; WhoProB 73*

Carew, Thomas
English. Poet
First of Cavalier poets; influenced by Donne and Jonson.
b. 1595 in West Wickham, England
d. 1639
Source: *Alli; AtlBL; BbD; BiD&SB; BrAu; CasWL; Chambr 1; ChPo; CnE&AP; CroE&S; CrtT 1; DcEnA AP; DcEnL; DcEuL; DcLEL; EvLB; MouLC 1; NewC; OxEng; Pen ENG; REn; WebE&AL*

Carey, Ernestine Muller Gilbreth
[Mrs. Charles E Carey]
American. Author, Lecturer
b. Apr 5, 1908 in New York, New York
Source: *Au&Wr 71; BioIn 1, 2; ConAu 5R; ConLC 17; CurBio 49; SmATA 2; WhoAm 74, 76, 78, 80, 82; WhoAmW 74; WhoWor 74; WrDr 76*

Carey, Harry
American. Actor
b. Jan 16, 1878 in New York, New York
d. Sep 21, 1947 in Brentwood, California
Source: *CmMov; Film 1; FilmgC; MovMk; TwYS; Vers A; WhScrn 74, 77; WhoHol B; WorEFlm*

Carey, Henry
English. Composer, Poet
b. 1687? in England
d. Oct 4, 1743 in London, England
Source: *BiD&SB; BioIn 3; BrAu; CasWL; DcEnL; DcLEL; EvLB; NewC; OxEng; Pen ENG; REn*

Carey, Hugh Leo
American. Politician
Governor of NY, 1974-81; prevented default by selling bonds.
b. Apr 11, 1919 in Brooklyn, New York
Source: *CngDr 74; CurBio 65; NewYTBS 74; WhoAm 74, 76, 78, 80, 82; WhoAmP 73; WhoE 74; WhoGov 72*

Carey, MacDonald
American. Actor
b. Mar 15, 1914 in Sioux City, Iowa
Source: *BiE&WWA; FilmgC; HolP 40; IntMPA 75, 76, 77, 78, 79, 80, 81, 82; MotPP; MovMk; WhoAm 82; WhoHol A*

Carey, Max George
[Maximilian Carnarius]
"Scoops"
American. Baseball Player
Outfielder, 1910-29; led NL in stolen bases 10 times; Hall of Fame, 1961.
b. Jan 11, 1890 in Terre Haute, Indiana
d. May 30, 1976 in Miami Beach, Florida
Source: *BaseEn; BioIn 1, 3, 6, 7, 10; WhoProB 73*

Carey, Phil
American. Actor
b. Jul 15, 1925 in Hackensack, New Jersey
Source: *FilmgC; IntMPA 75, 76, 77, 78, 79, 80, 81, 82; MotPP*

Carl Gustaf XVI
[Carl Gustaf Folke Hubertus]
Swedish. King
Ascended to throne, Sep 19, 1973, as world's youngest reigning monarch.
b. Apr 30, 1946 in Stockholm, Sweden
Source: *BioIn 10; CurBio 74; IntWW 74; WhoWor 74*

Carle, Eric
American. Artist, Illustrator
b. Jun 25, 1929 in Syracuse, New York
Source: *ChPo S2; ConAu 25R; IlsBYP; SmATA 4; WhoE 74*

Carle, Frankie
American. Pianist, Composer
b. Mar 25, 1903 in Providence, Rhode Island
Source: *AmSCAP 66; WhoHol A*

Carle, Richard
American. Actor
b. Jul 7, 1876 in Somerville, Massachusetts
d. Jun 28, 1941 in North Hollywood, California
Source: *AmAu&B; CurBio 41; FilmgC; MovMk; TwYS; Vers A; WhAm 1; WhScrn 74, 77; WhoHol B; WhoStg 1906, 1908*

Carleton, Will
American. Poet, Journalist, Lecturer
Best known for poems on rural life, including *Farm Legends,* 1875.
b. Oct 21, 1845 in Hudson, Michigan
d. Dec 18, 1912 in Brooklyn, New York
Source: *Alli SUP; AmAu; AmAu&B; AmBi; ApCAB; BbD; BiD&SB; ChPo, S1, S2; CyAl 2; DcAmB; DcNAA; EvLB; OxAmL; REnAL; TwCBDA; WhAm 1*

Carlile, Richard
English. Journalist, Reformer
b. 1790 in Devonshire, England
d. 1843 in London, England
Source: *BioIn 11; BrAu; NewC; NewCol 75; WebBD 80*

Carlin, George
American. Comedian
Created characters, Biff Burns (sportscaster), Al Sleet (hippy dippy weatherman).
b. May 12, 1937 in New York, New York
Source: *BioIn 7, 10, 11; BioNews 75; BkPepl; CurBio 76; WhoHol A*

Carlino, Lewis John
American. Dramatist
b. 1932 in New York, New York
Source: *ConAu 77; IntMPA 75, 76, 77, 78, 79, 80, 81, 82; NotNAT; WrDr 76*

Carlisle, John Griffin
American. Government Official
b. Sep 5, 1835 in Kenton County, Kentucky
d. Jul 31, 1910
Source: *BioIn 7, 10*

Carlisle, Kitty
[Katherine Conn; Mrs, Moss Hart]
American. Actress, Singer
Chairman, NY State Council on Arts; panelist, "To Tell the Truth."
b. Sep 3, 1915 in New Orleans, Louisiana
Source: *BiE&WWA; CelR 73; CurBio 82; EncMT; FilmgC; InWom; NotNAT; ThFT; WhoHol A; WhoThe 77*

Carlisle, Mary
American. Actress
b. 1912
Source: *BioIn 9; FilmgC; MotPP; MovMk; ThFT; WhoHol A*

Carlisle, William
American. Train Robber
b. 1890
Source: *BioIn 1, 6*

"Carlos"
[Ilitch Ramirez Sanchez]
"The Jackal"
Venezuelan. Terrorist
b. 1947? in Venezuela
Source: *BioIn 10, 11; PseudN*

Carlos, Bun E
see: Cheap Trick

Carlos, John
American. Track Athlete
b. Jun 5, 1945 in New York, New York
Source: *BioIn 9, 10, 11; WhoTr&F 73*

Carlota
[Charlotte; Marie Charlotte A V C]
Belgian. Empress of Mexico
Daughter of King Leopold I; wife of Maximilian.
b. 1840
d. 1927
Source: *REn*

Carlsen, Henrik Kurt
American. Sea Captain
b. 1915
Source: *BioIn 2, 3, 5, 7, 8*

Carlson, Chester
American. Inventor, Physicist
Invented photocopying process called xerography, 1940; Xerox made first machine, 1959.
b. Feb 8, 1906 in Seattle, Washington
d. Sep 19, 1968 in New York, New York
Source: *EncAB-H; WebAB; WhAm 5*

Carlson, "Doc" (Harold Clifford)
American. Physician, Basketball Coach
b. Jul 4, 1894 in Murray City, Ohio
d. Nov 1, 1964
Source: *BioIn 7, 9; WhoBbl 73*

Carlson, Earl
American. Physician
b. 1897
Source: *BioIn 3, 8*

Carlson, Edward Elmer
American. Businessman
b. Jun 4, 1911 in Tacoma, Washington
Source: *IntWW 74; St&PR 75; WhoAm 74, 76, 78, 80, 82; WhoF&I 74; WhoMW 74*

Carlson, Evans Fordyce
American. Soldier
Led commando force "Carlson's Raiders"; battle cry was "Gung Ho," during WW II.
b. Feb 26, 1896 in Sidney, New York
d. May 27, 1947 in Mount Hood, Oregon
Source: *CurBio 43, 47; DcAmB S4; DcNAA; WhAm 2*

Carlson, Richard
American. Actor
b. 1912 in Albert Lea, Minnesota
d. Nov 25, 1977 in Encino, California
Source: *FilmgC; IntMPA 75, 76, 77; MotPP; MovMk*

Carlson, Wally (Wallace A)
American. Cartoonist
b. 1894
d. 1969
Source: *WorECom*

Carlson, William Hugh
American. Author
b. Sep 5, 1898 in Waverly, Nebraska
Source: *BiDrLUS 70; ConAu 25R; ConAu P-2; WhoCon 73; WhoPNW*

Carlton, Larry
see: Crusaders, The

Carlton, Steve(n Norman)
"Lefty"
American. Baseball Player
Only major league pitcher to win Cy Young award four times.
b. Dec 22, 1944 in Miami, Florida
Source: *BaseEn; WhoAm 74, 76, 78, 80, 82; WhoProB 73*

Carlucci, Frank Charles, III
American. Deputy Secretary of Defense
b. Oct 18, 1930 in Scranton, Pennsylvania
Source: *CurBio 81; IntWW 75, 76, 77, 78; USBiR 74; WhoAm 76, 78, 80, 82; WhoGov 72, 75, 77; WhoS&SW 73; WhoWor 78*

Carlyle, Randy
Canadian. Hockey Player
b. Apr 19, 1954 in Sudbury, ON
Source: *HocReg*

Carlyle, Thomas
Scottish. Critic, Historian
Influenced by German literature; wrote *The French Revolution*, 1837.
b. Dec 4, 1795 in Ecclefechan, Scotland
d. Feb 4, 1881
Source: *Alli, SUP; AtlBL; BbD; BiD&SB; BrAu 19; CasWL; ChPo, S1, S2; CrtT 3; CyWA; DcEnA; DcEnL; DcEuL; DcLEL; EvLB; FamAYP; MouLC 3; NewC; OxEng; Pen ENG; RAdv 1; RComWL; REn; WebE&AL*

Carman, (William) Bliss
Canadian. Author
b. Apr 15, 1861 in Frederickton, NB
d. Jun 8, 1929 in New Canaan, Connecticut
Source: *BbD; BiD&SB; CanWr; CasWL; Chambr 3; ChPo, S1, S2; CnDAL; ConAmL; CreCan 1; DcAmAu; DcEnA AP; DcLEL; DcNAA; EvLB; LongCTC; OxAmL; OxCan; OxEng; Pen AM, ENG; REn; REnAL; TwCA, SUP; TwCBDA; WebE&AL; WhAm 1; WhNAA*

Carmen, Eric
[The Raspberries]
American. Singer, Musician
Best known song "All By Myself."
b. Aug 11, 1949 in Cleveland, Ohio
Source: *RkOn*

Carmer, Carl Lamson
American. Author
b. Oct 16, 1893 in Cortland, New York
d. Sep 11, 1976 in Bronxville, New York
Source: *AmAu&B; Au&Wr 71; AuBYP; ChPo, S1, S2; ConAu 5R, 69, 4NR; OxAmL; REn; REnAL; Str&VC; TwCA, SUP; WhoAm 74; WhoWor 74*

Carmichael, Franklin
[Group of Seven]
Canadian. Artist
b. 1890 in Orillia, ON
d. Oct 24, 1945 in Toronto, ON
Source: *CreCan 2; MacDCB 78; McGDA*

Carmichael, Harold
American. Football Player
b. Sep 22, 1949 in Jacksonville, Florida
Source: *BioIn 11; WhoFtbl 74*

Carmichael, Hoagy (Hoagland Howard)
American. Songwriter
Wrote "Stardust"; "In the Cool, Cool, Cool of the Evening" (1951 Oscar).
b. Nov 22, 1899 in Bloomington, Indiana
d. Dec 27, 1981 in Rancho Mirage, California
Source: *AmPS; AmSCAP 66, 80; Baker 78; BiDAmM; BioIn 1, 3, 4, 6, 7, 8, 9; CelR 73; CmpEPM; CurBio 41, 82; FilmgC; IndAu 1917; IntMPA 75, 76, 77, 78, 79, 80, 81; MotPP; MovMk; OxFilm; PseudN; WebAB; WhoAm 74, 76, 78, 80; WhoHol A; WhoMus 72; WhoWor 80; WorEFlm*

Carmichael, Ian
English. Actor
b. Jun 18, 1920 in Hull, England
Source: *CmMov; EncMT; FilmgC; IntMPA 75, 76, 77, 78, 79, 80, 81, 82; Who 74; WhoThe 77*

Carmichael, James Vinson
American. Business Executive
b. Oct 2, 1910 in Smyrna, Georgia
d. Nov 28, 1972 in Marietta, Georgia
Source: *BioIn 7; NewYTBE 72; ObitOF 79; WhoS&SW 73*

Carmichael, Stokely
[Kwame Toure]
American. Civil Rights Leader
Responsible for Black Power concept, 1960's.
b. Jun 29, 1941 in Port of Spain, British West Indies
Source: *AmAu&B; ConAu 57; CurBio 70; WhoS&SW 73; WhoWor 74*

Carmines, Al
American. Composer
b. Jul 25, 1937 in Hampton, Virginia
Source: *CurBio 72; NotNAT; WhoThe 77*

Carnap, Rudolf
German. Philosopher, Educator
b. May 18, 1891 in Wuppertal, Germany
d. Sep 14, 1970 in Santa Monica, California
Source: *AmAu&B; ConAu 29R; ConAu P-1; NewYTBE 70; WebAB; WhAm 5; WorAu*

Carne, Judy
English. Actress, Comedienne
Appeared in TV series "Laugh In"; married briefly to Burt Reynolds.
b. 1939 in Northampton, England
Source: *BioIn 8, 11; FilmgC; WhoHol A*

Carne, Marcel
French. Motion Picture Director
b. Aug 18, 1909
Source: *BiDFilm; DcFM; FilmgC; IntWW 74; MovMk; OxFilm; REn; WhoWor 74; WorEFlm*

Carnegie, Andrew
American. Industrialist, Humanitarian
Began as bobbin boy making $1.20 a week; sold Carnegie Steel for $250 million, 1901.
b. Nov 25, 1835 in Dunfermline, Scotland
d. Aug 11, 1919 in Lenox, Massachusetts
Source: *Alli SUP; AmAu&B; AmBi; ApCAB; BbD; BiD&SB; DcAmAu; DcAmB; DcNAA; EncAB-H; LongCTC; OxAmL; Pen AM; REn; REnAL; TwCBDA; WebAB; WhAm 1; WhAmP*

Carnegie, Dale
American. Author, Lecturer
Wrote *How to Win Friends and Influence People,* 1936; has sold over five million copies.
b. Nov 24, 1888 in Maryville, Mississippi
d. Nov 1, 1955 in New York, New York
Source: *CurBio 41, 55; DcAmB S5; LongCTC; Pen AM; REnAL; WebAB; WhAm 3*

Carnegie, Hattie
[Henriette Kannengiser; H C Zanft]
American. Fashion Designer
b. 1889 in Vienna, Austria
d. Feb 22, 1956 in New York, New York
Source: *CurBio 42, 56; InWom; WhAm 3; WorFshn*

Carner, Joanne Gunderson
American. Golfer
b. Mar 4, 1939 in Kirkland, Washington
Source: *GoodHS; WhoAm 82; WhoGolf*

Carnera, Primo
"Ambling Alp"
American. Boxer
b. Oct 26, 1906 in Sequals, Spain
d. Jun 29, 1967 in Sequals, Spain
Source: *WhScrn 77; WhoBox 74; WhoHol B*

Carnes, Kim
American. Singer, Songwriter
Won Grammy, 1981, for "Bette Davis Eyes."
b. 1948 in Hollywood, California
Source: *BioIn 12; NewWmR*

Carnevale, Ben (Bernard L)
American. Basketball Coach
b. Oct 30, 1915 in Raritan, New Jersey
Source: *WhoBbl 73*

Carney, Art
American. Actor
Won Oscar, 1972, for *Harry and Tonto;* won three Emmys for TV series "The Honeymooners."
b. Nov 4, 1918 in Mount Vernon, New York
Source: *BioNews 74; CelR 73; CurBio 58; FilmgC; IntMPA 75, 76, 77, 78, 79, 80, 81, 82; NotNAT; WhoAm 74, 76, 78, 80, 82; WhoHol A; WhoThe 77; WhoWor 74*

Carney, Don
"Uncle Don"
American. Children's Entertainer
b. 1897
d. Jan 14, 1954 in Miami, Florida
Source: *WhScrn 74, 77*

Carney, Harry Howell
American. Jazz Musician
b. Apr 1, 1910 in Boston, Massachusetts
d. Oct 8, 1974 in New York, New York
Source: *NewYTBS 74; WhAm 6; WhScrn 77; WhoAm 74; WhoJazz 72*

Carney, Robert Bostwick
American. Admiral
b. Mar 26, 1895 in Vallejo, California
Source: *CurBio 51; Who 74; WhoS&SW 73*

Carnot, Hippolyte
French. Revolutionary, Statesman
b. 1801
d. 1888
Source: *NewCol 75*

Carnot, Lazare Nicolas
French. Revolutionary Leader
b. 1753
d. 1823 in Magdeburg, Prussia
Source: *BioIn 4, 9; NewCol 75*

Carnovsky, Morris
American. Actor
b. Sep 5, 1897 in Saint Louis, Missouri
Source: *BiE&WWA; FamA&A; FilmgC; IntMPA 75, 76, 77; MotPP; MovMk; NotNAT; PlP&P; WhoAm 74; WhoHol A; WhoThe 77*

Caro, Anthony
English. Sculptor
b. Mar 8, 1924 in London, England
Source: *BioIn 7, 8, 10; ConArt; CurBio 81; IntWW 74, 75, 76, 77, 78; McGDA; McGEWB; Who 74; WhoWor 74, 76, 78*

Caro, Joseph
Spanish. Talmudist
Wrote, *Shulhan'Arukh,* 1565, outlining legal code for Orthodox Jewery.
b. 1488 in Toledo, Spain
d. Mar 24, 1575
Source: *BioIn 2, 3, 6, 7, 11; CasWL; EuAu*

Carol II
Romanian. King
b. 1893 in Sinaia, Romania
d. 1953
Source: *NewCol 75; WebBD 80*

Carol, Martine
French. Actress
b. 1920 in Paris, France
d. Feb 6, 1967 in Monte Carlo, Monaco
Source: *BiDFilm; FilmgC; InWom; MotPP; MovMk; OxFilm; WhScrn 74, 77; WhoHol B; WorEFlm*

Caroline, Princess
[Caroline Louise Marguerite Grimaldi]
Monacan. Daughter of Grace Kelly
b. Jan 23, 1957 in Monte Carlo, Monaco
Source: *BioIn 10; BkPepl*

Caron, Leslie Clare Margaret
French. Actress, Dancer
Starred with Gene Kelly in *An American in Paris,* 1951.
b. Jul 1, 1931 in Paris, France
Source: *BiDFilm; CelR 73; CmMov; CurBio 54; FilmgC; InWom; IntMPA 75, 76, 77, 78, 79, 80, 81, 82; MotPP; MovMk; OxFilm; Who 74; WhoAm 74, 76, 78, 80, 82; WhoHol A; WhoThe 77; WhoWor 74; WorEFlm*

Carot, "Papa"
see: Corot, Jean Baptiste Camille

Carothers, Wallace Hume
American. Chemist
Work in organic chemistry resulted in discovery of synthetic rubber, nylon.
b. Apr 27, 1896 in Burlington, Iowa
d. Apr 29, 1937 in Philadelphia, Pennsylvania
Source: *DcAmB S2; EncAB-H; WebAB; WhAm 1*

Carpaccio, Vittore
Italian. Artist
b. 1465?
d. 1525?
Source: *AtlBL; BioIn 1, 3, 5; REn*

Carpenter, Bobby
American. Hockey Player
b. Jul 13, 1963 in Beverly, Massachusetts
Source: *HocReg; NewYTBS 81*

Carpenter, Edward
English. Poet, Reformer
b. Aug 29, 1844 in Brighton, England
d. Jun 28, 1929 in Guildford, England
Source: *BioIn 2, 9, 10; BrAu 19; EvLB; LongCTC; ModBrL; NewC; Pen ENG; REn; WhoTwCL*

Carpenter, Francis Bicknell
American. Artist
b. Aug 6, 1830 in Homer, New York
d. May 23, 1900
Source: *AmBi; ApCAB; DcAmB S2; Drake; NatCAB 11; NewYHSD; TwCBDA; WhAm 1*

Carpenter, John
American. Motion Picture Director
Films include *Halloween*, 1978, *The Fog*, 1980; married to Adrienne Barbeau.
b. Jan 16, 1948 in Carthage, New York
Source: *BioIn 11; IntMPA 82; WhoAm 82*

Carpenter, John Alden
American. Composer
b. Feb 28, 1876 in Park Ridge, Illinois
d. Apr 26, 1951 in Chicago, Illinois
Source: *AmSCAP 66; ChPo S1; CurBio 47, 51; DcAmB S5; OxAmL; WhAm 3*

Carpenter, Karen Ann
[The Carpenters]
American. Singer
At time of death, The Carpenters had sold over 80 million records.
b. Mar 2, 1950 in New Haven, Connecticut
d. Feb 4, 1983 in Downey, California
Source: *BioIn 10; BkPepl; EncPR&S; WhoAm 78, 80, 82*

Carpenter, Leslie
American. Journalist
b. 1922
d. Jul 24, 1974 in Washington, DC
Source: *WhAm 6; WhoAm 74*

Carpenter, Liz (Elizabeth Sutherland)
American. Journalist
Press secretary, staff director for Lady Bird Johnson, 1963-69.
b. Sep 1, 1920 in Salado, Texas
Source: *ConAu 41R; WhoAm 74; WhoAmP 73*

Carpenter, (Malcolm) Scott
American. Astronaut
One of seven original astronauts; orbited Earth three times, May, 1962.
b. May 1, 1925 in Boulder, Colorado
Source: *CelR 73; CurBio 62; IntWW 74; WhoAm 74; WhoWor 74*

Carpenter, Richard Lynn
[The Carpenters]
American. Singer, Musician, Songwriter
b. Oct 15, 1946 in New Haven, Connecticut
Source: *BioIn 10; BkPepl; EncPR&S; WhoAm 78, 80, 82*

Carpenter, William S, Jr.
American. Football Player, Army Officer
b. Sep 30, 1937 in Springfield, Pennsylvania
Source: *BioIn 7, 8, 9; WhoFtbl 74*

Carpenters, The
[Karen Carpenter; Richard Carpenter]
American. Singing Duo
Hits include "Close to You," 1970, "We've Only Just Begun," 1971.
Source: *BiDAmM; BkPepl; RkOn 2*

Carpentier, Georges
French. Boxer
b. Jan 12, 1894 in Lens, France
d. Oct 27, 1975 in Paris, France
Source: *WhScrn 77; WhoBox 74*

Carpini, Giovanni de Piano
Italian. Monk, Traveler
b. 1180
d. 1252
Source: *NewCol 75*

Carr, Allan
American. Movie Producer, Promoter
Co-producer *Grease*, on Broadway, 1977, motion picture, 1978.
b. May 27, 1941 in Chicago, Illinois
Source: *BioIn 11; WhoAm 82*

Carr, Alexander
American. Actor
b. 1878 in Rumni, Russia
d. Sep 19, 1946 in Los Angeles, California
Source: *BioIn 1; CurBio 46; Film 2; NotNAT; WhScrn 74, 77; WhThe; WhoHol B*

Carr, Austin George
American. Basketball Player
b. Mar 10, 1948 in Washington, DC
Source: *BioIn 9; OfNBA*

Carr, Elizabeth Jordan
American. First Test Tube Baby Born in US
b. Dec 28, 1981 in Norfolk, Virginia
Source: *NF*

Carr, Emily
Canadian. Artist, Author
b. Dec 12, 1871 in Victoria, BC
d. Mar 2, 1945 in Victoria, BC
Source: *BioIn 1, 2, 3, 5, 7, 8, 9, 10, 11; CreCan 1; DcLEL 1940; DcNAA; InWom; LongCTC; MacDCB 78; McGDA; McGEWB; OxCan; REnAL; WomArt, A*

Carr, Gerald Paul
American. Astronaut
Commanded third Skylab manned mission, 1973-74.
b. Aug 22, 1932 in Denver, Colorado
Source: *BioIn 10; WhoAm 82*

Carr, Harold Noflet
American. Businessman
b. Mar 14, 1921 in Kansas City, Kansas
Source: *AmEA 74; St&PR 75; WhoAm 74, 76, 78, 80, 82; WhoF&I 74; WhoS&SW 73*

Carr, John Dickson
American. Author
b. 1905 in Uniontown, Pennsylvania
d. Feb 27, 1977 in Greenville, South Carolina
Source: *AmAu&B; Au&Wr 71; ConAu 49, 69, 3NR; ConLC 3; DcLEL; EncMys; EvLB; LongCTC; NewC; Pen ENG; REn; REnAL; TwCA, SUP; TwCW; WhoAm 74; WhoWor 74*

Carr, Joseph F
American. Football Executive
b. Oct 22, 1880 in Columbus, Ohio
d. May 20, 1939
Source: *BioIn 6, 8; WhoFtbl 74*

Carr, Vikki
[Florencia Bisenta de Casillas]
American. Singer
b. Jul 19, 1941 in El Paso, Texas
Source: *BioIn 10; EncPR&S; WhoAm 76, 78, 80, 82*

Carra, Carlo
Italian. Artist
b. 1881
d. 1966
Source: *BioIn 4, 7*

Carracci, Annibale
Italian. Artist
b. Nov 3, 1560 in Bologna, Italy
d. Jul 15, 1609 in Rome, Italy
Source: *AtlBL; REn*

Carracci, Lodovico
Italian. Artist
b. Apr 21, 1555 in Bologna, Italy
d. Nov 13, 1619 in Bologna, Italy
Source: *AtlBL*

Carrack, Paul
see: Ace

Carradine, David
American. Actor
Son of John Carradine; starred in "Shane," 1966, "Kung Fu," 1972.
b. Oct 8, 1940 in Hollywood, California
Source: *BkPepl; FilmgC; IntMPA 75, 76, 77, 78, 79, 80, 81, 82; MotPP; NewYTBE 73; WhoAm 82; WhoHol A*

Carradine, John Richmond
American. Actor
Father of David, Keith, and Robert Carradine; starred in over 170 films.
b. Feb 5, 1906 in New York, New York
Source: *BiE&WWA; CmMov; FilmgC; IntMPA 75, 76, 77, 78, 79, 80, 81, 82; MotPP; MovMk; OxFilm; Vers A; WhoAm 74, 76, 78, 80, 82; WhoHol A; WhoThe 77; WorEFlm*

Carradine, Keith Ian
American. Actor, Singer
Wrote and sang "I'm Easy," which won Oscar, 1975.
b. Aug 8, 1950 in San Mateo, California
Source: *BkPepl; IntMPA 75, 76, 77, 78, 79, 80, 81, 82; WhoAm 82; WhoHol A*

Carradine, Robert
American. Actor
Starred in *The Big Red One,* 1979.
b. 1954 in Los Angeles, California
Source: *FilmEn; WhoHol A*

Carranza, Venustiano
Mexican. Political Leader
President of Mexico, 1917-20.
b. Dec 29, 1859 in Coahuila, Mexico
d. May 21, 1920 in Tlaxcalantongo, Mexico
Source: *McGEWB; REn*

Carre, Mathilde
German. Spy
b. 1910?
Source: *BioIn 5, 8, 10, 11*

Carrel, Alexis
American. Biologist, Surgeon
b. Jun 28, 1873 in Sainte-Foyles, France
d. Nov 5, 1944
Source: *CurBio 40, 44*

Carrera, Barbara
American. Actress
b. 1945? in Managua, Nicaragua
Source: *BioIn 11; WhoHol A*

Carreras, Jose
Spanish. Opera Singer
b. Dec 5, 1946 in Barcelona, Spain
Source: *BioIn 9; CurBio 79; NewYTBS 78; WhoAm 82; WhoOp 76*

Carrier, Willis H
American. Inventor
Developed first practical air conditioning process, 1911.
b. Nov 26, 1876 in Angola, New York
d. Oct 7, 1950 in New York, New York
Source: *DcAmB S4; WhAm 3*

Carrier-Belleuse, Albert Ernest
French. Sculptor
b. 1824
d. 1887
Source: *BioIn 11*

Carriere, Eugene
French. Artist
b. 1849
d. 1906
Source: *BioIn 2, 4, 8, 9, 11; OxFr*

Carrillo, Leo
American. Actor
b. Aug 6, 1880 in Los Angeles, California
d. Sep 10, 1961 in Santa Monica, California
Source: *FilmgC; MotPP; MovMk; WhScrn 77; WhoHol B*

Carrington, Peter Alexander
English. Politician
Secretary of State for Defense, 1970-74.
b. Jun 6, 1919 in London, England
Source: *BioIn 8, 9; IntWW 74; WhWW-II; WhoWor 74*

Carritt, (Hugh) David Graham
British. Art Historian
b. Apr 15, 1927 in England
d. Aug 3, 1982 in London, England
Source: *BioIn 10; NewYTBS 82; Who 82*

Carroll, Charles
American. Patriot
Member of Continental Congress; signer of Declaration of Independence.
b. Sep 19, 1737 in Annapolis, Maryland
d. Nov 14, 1832 in Baltimore, Maryland
Source: *AmBi; ApCAB; BiAuS; BiDSA; BiDrAC; DcAmB; Drake; TwCBDA; WebAB; WhAm H; WhAmP*

Carroll, Diahann
[Carol Diahann Johnson]
American. Actress, Singer
First black to star in own TV series, "Julia," 1968-69.
b. Jul 17, 1935 in New York, New York
Source: *BiE&WWA; BioNews 74; BkPepl; CelR 73; CurBio 62; EncMT; FilmgC; InWom; MotPP; NotNAT; WhoAm 74, 76, 78, 80, 82; WhoBlA 75; WhoHol A; WhoWor 74; WomWMM*

Carroll, Earl
American. Theatrical Producer
b. Sep 16, 1893 in Pittsburgh, Pennsylvania
d. Jun 17, 1948
Source: *AmAu&B; AmSCAP 66; DcAmB S4; EncMT; OxThe; WhAm 2; WhScrn 77*

Carroll, Gladys Hasty
American. Author
b. Jun 26, 1904 in Rochester, New Hampshire
Source: *AmAu&B; AmNov; ConAu 1R, 5NR; ForWC 70; InWom; OxAmL; REnAL; TwCA, SUP; WhNAA; WhoAm 74, 76, 78, 80, 82; WhoE 74; WhoWor 74; WrDr 76*

Carroll, Jim
American. Poet, Singer
b. Aug 1, 1951 in New York, New York
Source: *ConAu 45; DrAP 75*

Carroll, Joe Barry
American. Basketball Player
b. Jul 24, 1958 in Denver, Colorado
Source: *BioIn 12; OfNBA*

Carroll, John
American. Roman Catholic Prelate
b. Jan 8, 1735 in Upper Marlboro, Maryland
d. Dec 3, 1815 in Baltimore, Maryland
Source: *BioIn 2, 3, 4, 5, 10, 11; McGEWB; WebAB; WhAm H*

Carroll, Leo G
English. Actor
b. Oct 18, 1892 in Weedon, England
d. Oct 16, 1972 in Hollywood, California
Source: *BiE&WWA; CmMov; FilmgC; MotPP; MovMk; NewYTBE 72; Vers A; WhAm 5; WhScrn 77; WhoHol B*

Carroll, Lewis, pseud.
[Charles Lutwidge Dodgson]
English. Author, Mathematician
Wrote *Alice's Adventures in Wonderland,* 1865; *Through the Looking Glass,* 1872.
b. Jan 27, 1832 in Cheshire, England
d. Jan 14, 1898 in Guildford, England
Source: *Alli SUP; AnCL; AtlBL; AuBYP; BbD; BiD&SB; BrAu 19; CasWL; Chambr 3; ChlLR 2; ChPo, S1, S2; CnE&AP; CrtT 3; CyWA; DcEnA; DcEnL; DcEuL; DcLEL; EvLB; FamAYP; FilmgC; JBA 34; NewC; OxEng; Pen ENG; RAdv 1; REn; Str&VC; WebE&AL; WhoChL*

Carroll, Madeleine
English. Actress
b. Feb 26, 1909 in West Bronwich, England
Source: *BiDFilm; BiE&WWA; CurBio 49; FilmgC; InWom; IntMPA 75, 76, 77, 78, 79, 80, 81, 82; MotPP; MovMk; OxFilm; ThFT; Who 74; WhoHol A; WhoThe 77; WorEFlm*

Carroll, Nancy
American. Actress
b. Nov 19, 1906 in New York, New York
d. Aug 6, 1965 in New York, New York
Source: *FilmgC; InWom; MotPP; MovMk; ThFT; TwYS; WhScrn 74, 77; WhoHol B; WomWMM*

Carroll, Pat(ricia Ann Angela Bridgit)
American. Actress, Comedienne
b. May 5, 1927 in Shreveport, Louisiana
Source: *BiE&WWA; BioIn 12; CurBio 80; IntMPA 75, 76, 77, 78, 79, 80, 81, 82; NotNAT; WhoAm 80, 82*

Carroll, Vinnette (Justine)
American. Actress, Theatrical Producer
b. Mar 11, 1922 in New York, New York
Source: *BioIn 10; WhoAm 82; WhoThe 81*

Carruthers, George E
American. Physicist
b. Oct 1, 1940 in Cincinnati, Ohio
Source: *AmM&WS 73P; WhoBlA 75*

Carruthers, John(ny)
Australian. Boxer
b. Jul 5, 1929 in Paddington, Australia
Source: *WhoBox 74*

Cars, The
[Elliot Easton; Greg Hawkes; Ric Ocasek; Ben Orr; David Robinson]
American. Rock Group
Source: *ConMuA 80; WhoRock 81*

Carson, Edward Henry
British. Judge
b. 1854 in Dublin, Ireland
d. Oct 22, 1935
Source: *BioIn 2, 3, 10; WhoModH*

Carson, Jack
American. Actor
b. Oct 27, 1910 in Carman, MB
d. Jan 2, 1963 in Encino, California
Source: *FilmgC; HolP 40; MotPP; MovMk; OxFilm; WhScrn 74, 77; WhoHol B*

Carson, Jeannie
American. Comedienne, Singer
b. 1929 in Yorkshire, England
Source: *BiE&WWA; FilmgC; InWom; IntMPA 75, 76, 77, 78, 79, 80, 81, 82; MotPP; WhoHol A; WhoThe 77*

Carson, Johnny
American. Entertainer
Host of "The Tonight Show," 1962--.
b. Oct 23, 1925 in Corning, Iowa
Source: *BkPepl; CelR 73; CurBio 64, 82; IntMPA 75, 76, 77, 78, 79, 80, 81, 82; WhoAm 74, 76, 78, 80, 82; WhoE 74; WhoWor 74*

Carson, "Kit" (Christopher)
American. Trapper, Scout, Indian Agent
Brigadier general during Civil War; commanded Fort Garland, CO, 1866-67.
b. Dec 24, 1809 in Madison County, Kentucky
d. May 23, 1868 in Fort Lyon, Colorado
Source: *AmBi; ApCAB; DcAmB; Drake; LongCTC; MnBBF; OxAmL; OxFilm; REn; REnAL; TwCBDA; WebAB; WhAm H*

Carson, Mindy
American. Actress, Singer
b. 1927 in New York, New York
Source: *BiE&WWA; InWom*

Carson, Rachel Louise
American. Marine Biologist, Author
Wrote *The Sea Around Us*, 1951; *Silent Spring*, 1962.
b. May 27, 1907 in Springdale, Pennsylvania
d. Apr 14, 1964 in Silver Spring, Maryland
Source: *AmAu&B; ConAu 77; CurBio 51, 64; EncAB-H; EvLB; HerW; InWom; LongCTC; OxAmL; REn; SmATA 23; TwCA SUP; TwCW; WebAB; WhAm 4*

Carstens, Karl Walter
German. President
b. Dec 14, 1914 in Bremen, Germany
Source: *CurBio 80; IntWW 74; WhoWor 78*

Carswell, George Harrold
American. Judge
b. Dec 22, 1919 in Irwinton, Georgia
Source: *WhoAm 74; WhoAmP 73*

Carte, Richard d'Oyly
English. Opera Singer
b. May 3, 1844 in London, England
d. Apr 3, 1901 in London, England
Source: *LongCTC; NewCol 75; NotNAT B; OxThe*

Carter, Amon Giles
American. Publisher
b. Dec 11, 1880 in Crafton, Texas
d. Jun 23, 1955
Source: *BioIn 2, 3, 4, 5, 6; WhAm 3*

Carter, Amy
American. Daughter of Jimmy Carter
b. Oct 19, 1967 in Plains, Georgia
Source: *BioIn 11, 12; InWom*

Carter, Benny (Bennett Lester)
American. Jazz Musician
b. Aug 8, 1907 in New York, New York
Source: *AmSCAP 66; BiDAmM; BioIn 9, 10, 11; CmpEPM; DcBlPA; EncJzS 70; IlEncJ; WhoAm 74, 76, 78, 80; WhoJazz 72*

Carter, Billy
American. Brother of Jimmy Carter
b. Mar 29, 1937 in Plains, Georgia
Source: *BioIn 11, 12; BkPepl*

Carter, Boake
American. Radio Commentator
b. Sep 28, 1898 in Baku, Russia
d. Nov 16, 1944 in Hollywood, California
Source: *CurBio 42, 47; DcAmB S3; DcNAA; WhAm 2; WhScrn 77*

Carter, Carlene
[Mrs. Nick Lowe]
American. Singer, Songwriter
Daughter of June Carter; stepdaughter of Johnny Cash.
b. 1957 in Madisonville, Tennessee
Source: *BioIn 11; NewWmR; WhoRock 81*

Carter, "Chip" (James Earl, III)
American. Son of Jimmy Carter
b. Apr 12, 1950 in Honolulu, Hawaii
Source: *BioIn 11; PseudN; WhoAmP 77, 79*

Carter, Don(ald Jones)
American. Bowler
b. Jul 29, 1926 in Saint Louis, Missouri
Source: *CurBio 63*

Carter, (Donnel) Jeff(rey)
American. Son of Jimmy Carter
b. Aug 18, 1952 in New London, Connecticut
Source: *NewYTBS 81*

Carter, Dorothy Sharp
American. Children's Author
b. Mar 22, 1921 in Chicago, Illinois
Source: *BiDrLUS 70; ConAu 49; SmATA 8; WhoAmW 77*

Carter, Edward William
American. Businessman
b. Jun 29, 1911
Source: *BioIn 2, 8, 9; IntWW 74; LEduc 74; NewYTBE 71; St&PR 75; WhoAm 82; WhoWest 74*

Carter, Elliott Cook Jr.
American. Composer
b. Dec 11, 1908 in New York, New York
Source: *CurBio 60; DcCM; IntWW 74; Who 74; WhoAm 74, 76, 78, 80, 82; WhoE 74; WhoMus 72; WhoWor 74*

Carter, Ernestine Marie
American. Author, Journalist
b. in Washington, DC
Source: *Au&Wr 71; BioIn 9; Who 74; WrDr 76*

Carter, Gary Edmund
American. Baseball Player
b. Apr 8, 1954 in Culver City, California
Source: *BaseEn*

Carter, Howard
English. Egyptologist, Archaelogist
b. 1873
d. 1939
Source: *LongCTC*

Carter, "Hurricane" (Rubin)
American. Boxer
b. 1937
Source: *NewYTBE 72; NewYTBS 74*

Carter, Jack
[Jack Chakrin]
American. Comedian
b. Jun 24, 1923 in Coney Island, New York
Source: *IntMPA 75, 76, 77, 78, 79, 80, 81, 82; WhoHol A*

Carter, Jack (John William)
American. Son of Jimmy Carter
b. Jul 3, 1947 in Portsmouth, Virginia
Source: *NF*

Carter, Jimmy (James Earl, Jr.)
American. 39th US President
Initiated human rights campaign in foreign policy; hostage crisis contributed to defeat, 1980.
b. Oct 1, 1924 in Plains, Georgia
Source: *BkPepl; ConAu 69; CurBio 71; IntWW 74; Who 82; WhoAm 76, 78, 80, 82; WhoAmP 73; WhoGov 72; WhoS&SW 73*

Carter, Jimmy (James W)
American. Boxer
b. Dec 15, 1923 in Aiken, South Carolina
Source: *WhoBox 74*

Carter, John Garnet
American. Businessman
Invented miniature golf, 1928.
b. Feb 9, 1883 in Sweetwater, Tennessee
d. Jul 21, 1954 in Lookout Mountain, Tennessee
Source: *BioIn 9; NatCAB 52*

Carter, June
[The Carter Family; Mrs. Johnny Cash]
American. Singer
Married Johnny Cash, 1968; songs include "He Don't Love Me Anymore."
b. Jun 23, 1929 in Maces Spring, Virginia
Source: *EncFCWM 69; WhoAm 82; WhoHol A*

Carter, Katherine Jones
American. Children's Author
b. Feb 25, 1905 in Greenbackville, Virginia
Source: *ConAu 5R; SmATA 2*

Carter, Mrs. Leslie
American. Actress
b. Jun 10, 1862 in Lexington, Kentucky
d. Nov 12, 1937 in Los Angeles, California
Source: *AmBi; DcAmB S2; FamA&A; Film 1; FilmgC; InWom; NotAW; OxThe; TwYS; WhAm 1; WhScrn 74, 77; WhoHol B*

Carter, Lillian
[Bessie Lillian Gordy]
American. Mother of Jimmy Carter, Nurse
Joined Peace Corps; served in India at age 68.
b. Aug 15, 1898 in Richmond, Georgia
Source: *BioIn 11; BkPepl; CurBio 78; WhoAmW 79*

Carter, Lynda
American. Actress, Singer
Starred in TV series "Wonder Woman," 1977-79.
b. Jul 24, 1951 in Phoenix, Arizona
Source: *BioIn 11; IntMPA 82; WhoAm 80, 82*

Carter, "Mother" Maybelle
[The Carter Family]
American. Singer, Songwriter
b. May 10, 1909 in Nickelsville, Virginia
d. Oct 23, 1978 in Nashville, Tennessee
Source: *BioIn 9, 11; EncFCWM 69*

Carter, Nick, pseud.
see: Coryell, John Russell

Carter, Rosalynn Smith
American. Wife of Jimmy Carter
b. Aug 18, 1927 in Plains, Georgia
Source: *BioIn 11; BkPepl; CurBio 78; WhoAm 80, 82*

Carter, Wilf
"Montana Slim"
Canadian. Singer
b. Dec 12, 1904 in Port Hilford, NS
Source: *EncFCWM 69*

Carter, (William) Hodding, (III)
American. Government Official
b. Apr 7, 1935 in New Orleans, Louisiana
Source: *BioIn 11; CurBio 81; WhoAm 80, 82*

Carter Family, The
[A P Carter; Anita Carter; Helen Carter; June Carter; Maybelle Carter]
American. Country Singing Group
Source: *EncFCWM 69*

Cartier, Claude
American. Jeweler
b. 1925
d. 1975
Source: *BioIn 10*

Cartier, Sir Georges Etienne
Canadian. Statesman, Lawyer
b. Sep 6, 1814
d. May 20, 1873
Source: *BioIn 9, 11*

Cartier, Jacques
French. Navigator, Explorer
Discovered St. Lawrence River and Montreal.
b. Dec 31, 1491 in Saint Malo, France
d. Sep 1, 1557 in Saint Malo, France
Source: *ApCAB; BioIn 1, 2, 4, 5, 6, 8, 9, 11; Drake; McGEWB; OxCan; OxFr; REn; REnAL; WhAm H*

Cartier, Pierre C
American. Jeweler
b. 1878 in France
d. 1964
Source: *BioIn 7*

Cartier-Bresson, Henri
French. Photographer
b. Aug 22, 1908 in Chanteloup, France
Source: *CurBio 47; DcFM; IntWW 74; OxFilm; Who 74; WhoWor 74; WorEFlm*

Cartland, Barbara Hamilton
English. Author, Dramatist
Wrote over 250 books; step-grandmother of Princess Diana of Wales.
b. Jul 9, 1901 in England
Source: *Au&Wr 71; ConAu 9R; LongCTC; NewYTBE 73; TwCW; Who 82; WhoAm 82; WrDr 76*

Cartouche, Louis Dominique
[Louis Dominique Bourguignon]
French. Thief
b. 1693
d. Nov 28, 1721
Source: *BioIn 8*

Cartwright, Alexander Joy, Jr.
American. Sports Pioneer
Orgainzed first recorded baseball game, 1846; Hall of Fame, 1938.
b. Apr 17, 1820 in New York, New York
d. Jul 12, 1892 in Honolulu, Hawaii
Source: *WhAm H; WhoProB 73*

Cartwright, Angela
American. Actress
b. 1952
Source: *ForWC 70; WhoHol A*

Cartwright, Bill (James William)
American. Basketball Player
b. Jul 30, 1957 in Lodi, California
Source: *BioIn 10; OfNBA*

Cartwright, Edmund
English. Clergyman, Inventor
Developed first power loom, 1785-87.
b. Apr 24, 1743 in Nottinghamshire, England
d. Oct 23, 1823
Source: *Alli; BiDLA; DcEnL*

Carty, Rico (Ricardo Adolfo Jacobo)
Dominican. Baseball Player
b. Sep 1, 1939 in San Piedro de Macoris, Dominican Republic
Source: *BaseEn; WhoAm 74; WhoProB 73*

Caruso, Enrico
Italian. Opera Singer
With NY Metropolitan Opera, 1903-20.
b. Feb 5, 1873 in Naples, Italy
d. Aug 2, 1921 in Naples, Italy
Source: *AmBi; ChPo S1; DcAmB; Film 1; FilmgC; NewC; NewYTBE 73; REn; TwYS; WhAm 1; WhScrn 74, 77; WhoHol B*

Carvel, Thomas A
Canadian. Ice Cream Franchiser
Founded Carvel Corp., 1934; owns over 600 retail ice cream stores.
b. 1906 in Bridgeport, Canada
Source: *BusPN; NewYTBE 73; NewYTBS 79*

Carver, George Washington
American. Botanist, Chemist, Educator
Agricultural researcher, 1896-1943; first to make synthetic marble from wood shavings.
b. Jan 5, 1864 in Diamond Grove, Missouri
d. Jan 5, 1943 in Tuskegee, Alabama
Source: *AfroAA; CurBio 40, 43; DcAmB S3; EncAB-H; WebAB; WhAm HA, 2, 4A*

Carver, John
English. Colonial Governor
First governor of Plymouth Colony, 1620-21.
b. 1576 in Nottinghamshire, England
d. Apr 5, 1621 in Plymouth, Massachusetts
Source: *AmBi; ApCAB; DcAmB; Drake; TwCBDA; WhAm H*

Cary, Alice
American. Author
b. Apr 26, 1820 in Cincinnati, Ohio
d. Feb 12, 1871 in New York, New York
Source: *Alli SUP; AmAu; AmAu&B; AmBi; AmWom; ApCAB; BbD; BiD&SB; CarSB; Chambr 3; ChPo, S1; CyAl 2; DcAmAu; DcAmB; DcNAA; Drake; EvLB; InWom; NotAW; OhA&B; OxAmL; TwCBDA; WebAB; WhAm H*

Cary, (Arthur) Joyce (Lunel)
English. Author
b. Dec 7, 1888 in Londonderry, Northern Ireland
d. Mar 29, 1957 in Oxford, England
Source: *CurBio 49, 57; CasWL; CnMWL; ConNov 76; CyWA; DcLEL; EncWL; EvLB; LongCTC; ModBrL, SUP; NewC; OxEng; Pen ENG; RAdv 1; REn; TwCA SUP; WebE&AL; WhAm 3; WhoTwCL*

Cary, Frank Taylor
American. Businessman
IBM, president, 1971--, chairman, 1973--.
b. Dec 14, 1920 in Gooding, Idaho
Source: *BioIn 12; CurBio 80; IntWW 79; WhoAm 80, 82*

Cary, Phoebe
American. Poet
b. Sep 4, 1824 in Cincinnati, Ohio
d. Jul 31, 1871 in New York, New York
Source: *Alli SUP; AmAu; AmAu&B; AmBi; AmWom; ApCAB; BbD; BiD&SB; Chambr 3; ChPo, S1; CyAl 2; DcAmAu; DcAmB; DcNAA; Drake; EvLB; InWom; NotAW; OhA&B; OxAmL; Pen AM; TwCBDA; WebAB; WhAm H*

Carzou, Jean
French. Artist
b. Jan 1, 1907 in Alep, Syria
Source: *WhoWor 74*

Casablancas, John(ny)
American. Modeling Agency Owner
b. Dec 12, 1942 in Manhattan, New York
Source: *NF*

Casadesus, Gaby Lhote
French. Musician
b. Aug 9, 1901 in Marseilles, France
Source: *WhoAmW 74*

Casadesus, Jean
French. Musician
b. Jul 7, 1927 in Paris, France
d. Jan 20, 1972 in Renfrew, ON
Source: *Baker 78; BiDAmM; BioIn 9*

Casadesus, Robert
French. Musician, Composer
b. Apr 7, 1899 in Paris, France
d. Sep 19, 1972 in Paris, France
Source: *CurBio 45, 72; NewYTBE 72; WhAm 5; WhoMus 72*

Casady, Jack
[Jefferson Airplane]
American. Musician, Singer
b. Apr 13, 1944 in Washington, DC
Source: *NF*

Casale, Bob
see: Devo

Casale, Jerry
see: Devo

Casals, Pablo (Pau Carlos Salvador)
Spanish. Cellist, Composer, Conductor
b. Dec 29, 1876 in Vendrell, Spain
d. Oct 22, 1973 in Rio Piedras, Puerto Rico
Source: *AmSCAP 66; ConAu 45, 93; CurBio 50, 64, 73; NewYTBE 73; REn; WhAm 6; WhScrn 77; Who 74; WhoMus 72; WhoWor 74*

Casals, Rosemary
American. Tennis Player
Granddaughter of Pablo Casals.
b. Sep 16, 1948 in San Francisco, California
Source: *BioNews 74; CurBio 74; HerW; WhoAm 82*

Casanova (de Seingalt), Giovanni Giacomo
Italian. Author, Adventurer
b. Apr 2, 1725 in Venice, Italy
d. Jun 4, 1798 in Dux, Bohemia
Source: *RAdv 1; REn*

Casaubon, Isaac
Theologian, Classical Scholar
b. Feb 8, 1559 in Geneva, Switzerland
d. Jul 1, 1614 in London, England
Source: *BbD; DcEuL; NewC; OxEng; OxFr*

Case, Anna
American. Opera Singer, Actress
b. 1889
Source: *Film 1; WhoHol A*

Case, Clifford Philip
American. Lawyer, Former Senator
b. Apr 16, 1904 in Franklin Park, New Jersey
d. Mar 5, 1982 in Washington, DC
Source: *AlmAP 78; BiDrAC; CngDr 74, 77; CurBio 55, 82; IntWW 74, 75, 76, 77, 78; NewYTBS 82; PolProf E; PolProf J; PolProf K; PolProf NF; WhoAm 74, 76, 78, 80, 82; WhoAmP 73, 75, 77, 79; WhoE 74, 75, 77, 79; WhoGov 72, 75, 77; WhoWor 74, 78*

Casement, Roger David
Irish. Diplomat, Rebel
b. Sep 1, 1864 in Dun Laoghaire, Ireland
d. Aug 3, 1916 in London, England
Source: *BioIn 9*

Casewit, Curtis
American. Author
b. Mar 21, 1922 in Mannheim, Germany
Source: *ConAu 13R; SmATA 4*

Casey, Edward Pearce
American. Architect
b. Jun 18, 1864 in Portland, Maine
d. Jan 2, 1940
Source: *NatCAB 36; WebBD 80; WhAm 1*

Casey, H(arry) W(ayne)
see: K C and the Sunshine Band

Casey, Hugh Thomas
American. Baseball Player
b. Oct 14, 1913 in Buckhead, Georgia
d. Jul 3, 1951 in Atlanta, Georgia
Source: *BaseEn; BioIn 3, 7; WhoProB 73*

Casey, William Joseph
American. Lawyer, Author
Ronald Reagan's campaign manager, 1980; director, CIA, 1981--.
b. Mar 13, 1913 in Elmhurst, New York
Source: *CurBio 72; IntWW 74; WhoAm 74, 76, 78, 80, 82*

Cash, Johnny
[Tennessee Three]
"The Man in Black"
American. Singer, Songwriter
Hit songs include "I Walk the Line," 1964; "A Boy Named Sue," 1969.
b. Feb 26, 1932 in Kingsland, Arkansas
Source: *CelR 73; CurBio 69; EncFCWM 69; FilmgC; NewYTBE 73; WebAB; WhoAm 74, 76, 78, 80, 82; WhoHol A; WhoS&SW 73*

Cash, Roseanne
[Mrs. Rodney Crowell]
American. Singer, Daughter of Johnny Cash
b. 1956? in Memphis, Tennessee
Source: *BioIn 12*

Cash, Norman
"Stormin' Norman"
American. Baseball Player
First baseman, 1958-74; won batting title, 1961.
b. Nov 10, 1934 in Justiceburg, Texas
Source: *BaseEn; WhoAm 74; WhoProB 73*

Cashin, Bonnie
American. Fashion Designer
b. 1915 in Oakland, California
Source: *CurBio 70; InWom; WhoAm 74, 76, 78, 80, 82; WhoWor 74; WorFshn*

Casimir, Saint
Polish. Religious Figure
b. 1458
d. 1484
Source: *BioIn 1, 3, 4, 5, 6, 7, 9*

Caslon, William
English. Type Designer
b. Jan 23, 1692 in Cradley, England
d. Jan 23, 1766 in London, England
Source: *NewC*

Caspary, Vera
American. Author, Dramatist
b. Nov 13, 1904 in Chicago, Illinois
Source: *AmAu&B; Au&Wr 71; BiE&WWA; ConAu 13R; EncMys; LongCTC; REnAL; TwCA SUP; WrDr 76*

Casper, Billy (William Earl)
American. Golfer
Winner, US Open, 1959, 1966, Masters, 1970.
b. Jun 24, 1931 in San Diego, California
Source: *CelR 73; CurBio 66; WhoAm 74, 76, 78, 80, 82; WhoGolf*

Cass, Lewis
American. Statesman
b. Oct 9, 1782 in Exeter, New Hampshire
d. Jun 17, 1866 in Detroit, Michigan
Source: *Alli; AmAu&B; AmBi; ApCAB; BiAuS; BiD&SB; BiDrAC; BiDrUSE; CyAL 1; DcAmAu; DcAmB; DcNAA; Drake; EncAB-H; OhA&B; TwCBDA; WebAB; WhAm H; WhAmP*

Cass, Peggy
American. Actress
Starred in TV series "The Hathaways," 1961-62; panelist "To Tell the Truth."
b. May 21, 1925 in Boston, Massachusetts
Source: *BiE&WWA; CelR 73; InWom; MotPP; NotNAT; WhoHol A; WhoThe 77*

Cassady, Neal
American. Author
b. 1936?
d. 1968 in Mexico
Source: *BioIn 11*

Cassandra
see: Connor, Sir William Neil

Cassandre, A(dolphe) M(ouron)
French. Poster Designer
b. Jan 24, 1909 in Kharkov, Russia
d. 1968
Source: *WhoGrA*

Cassatt, Mary
American. Artist
b. May 22, 1844 in Allegheny, Pennsylvania
d. Jun 14, 1926 in Paris, France
Source: *AmBi; AtlBL; DcAmB; EncAB-H; HerW; InWom; NotAW; OxAmL; REn; WebAB; WhAm 1*

Cassavetes, John
American. Actor, Motion Picture Director
Starred in *Rosemary's Baby,* 1976; married to actress Gena Rowlands.
b. Dec 9, 1929 in New York, New York
Source: *BiDFilm; CelR 73; ConAu 85; ConDr 73; CurBio 69; DcFM; FilmgC; IntMPA 75, 76, 77, 78, 79, 80, 81, 82; IntWW 74; MotPP; MovMk; OxFilm; WhoAm 74, 76, 78, 80, 82; WhoHol A; WorEFlm*

Cassidy, Butch
[George Leroy Parker]
American. Outlaw
Bank robber, train robber, 1887-1912.
b. Apr 6, 1867 in Circleville, Utah
d. 1912
Source: *BioIn 10; Blood*

Cassidy, Claudia
American. Drama, Music Critic
b. 1900 in Shawneetown, Illinois
Source: *AmAu&B; BiE&WWA; CelR 73; CurBio 55; InWom; NotNAT; WhoAm 74, 76, 78, 80, 82*

Cassidy, David Bruce
American. Singer, Actor
Son of Jack Cassidy; starred in TV series "The Partridge Family," 1970-74.
b. Apr 12, 1950 in New York, New York
Source: *CelR 73; WhoAm 82*

Cassidy, Harold Gomes
American. Chemist, Educator, Author
b. Oct 17, 1906 in Havana, Cuba
Source: *AmM&WS 73P; ConAu 25R; WhoAm 74, 76, 78, 80, 82*

Cassidy, Hopalong
see: Boyd, William

Cassidy, Jack
American. Actor, Singer, Dancer
b. Mar 5, 1927 in New York, New York
d. Dec 12, 1976 in West Hollywood, California
Source: *BiE&WWA; BioNews 74; EncMT; FilmgC; NotNAT; WhoHol A; WhoThe 77*

Cassidy, Joanna
American. Actress
b. 1946?
Source: *WhoHol A*

Cassidy, Marshall
American. Jockey
b. 1892
d. 1968
Source: *BioIn 8*

Cassidy, Shaun
American. Singer, Actor
b. Sep 27, 1959 in Los Angeles, California
Source: *BioIn 11; BkPepl; WhoAm 82*

Cassill, R(onald) V(erlin)
American. Author
b. May 17, 1919 in Cedar Falls, Iowa
Source: *ConAu 9R; ConLC 4; WhoAm 74, 76, 78, 80, 82*

Cassin, Rene
French. Jurist, Human Rights Advocate
b. Oct 5, 1887 in Bayonne, France
d. Feb 20, 1976 in Paris, France
Source: *IntWW 74; WhAm 6; Who 74; WhoWor 74; WhoWorJ 72*

Cassini, Igor Loiewski
American. Journalist
b. 1913
Source: *BioIn 6*

Cassini, Oleg Lolewski
French. Fashion Designer
Official White House designer for Jacqueline Kennedy, 1961-63.
b. Apr 11, 1913 in Paris, France
Source: *CelR 73; CurBio 61; WhoAm 74, 76, 78, 80, 82; WhoWor 74; WorFshn*

Cassirer, Ernst
German. Philosopher
b. Jul 28, 1874 in Breslau, Prussia
d. Apr 13, 1945 in New York, New York
Source: *DcNAA; Pen EUR; TwCA SUP; WhAm 4; WhoLA*

Cassius
[Caius Cassius Longinus]
"The Last of the Romans"
Roman. General, Politician
d. 42BC
Source: *LinLib S; NewCol 75; PseudN; REn*

Cassou, Jean
French. Author, Critic
b. Jul 9, 1879 in Deusto, France
Source: *CasWL; EncWL; EvEuW; IntWW 74; WhoWor 74*

Castagna, Bruna
Italian. Opera Singer
b. Oct 15, 1908 in Bari, Italy
Source: *InWom*

Castagno, Andrea del
Italian. Artist
b. 1423 in Castagno, Italy
d. Aug 19, 1457 in Florence, Italy
Source: *AtlBL*

Castaneda, Carlos
American. Anthropologist, Author
b. Dec 25, 1931 in Sao Paulo, Brazil
Source: *ConAu 25R; NewYTBE 72; WhoAm 74, 76, 78, 80, 82; WrDr 76*

Castel, Frederic
French. Fur Designer
Source: *WorFshn*

Castellano, Richard
American. Actor, Motion Picture Producer
b. Sep 4, 1934 in New York, New York
Source: *CelR 73; FilmgC; IntMPA 75, 76, 77, 78, 79, 80, 81, 82; WhoAm 82; WhoHol A*

Castello Branco, Humberto
Brazilian. President
b. Sep 20, 1900 in Fortaleza, Brazil
d. Jul 18, 1967
Source: *BioIn 6, 7, 8; CurBio 65, 67*

Castellon, Frederico
American. Artist
b. Sep 14, 1914 in Almeria, Spain
d. Sep 27, 1971 in New York, New York
Source: *BioIn 2, 5, 9; DcCAA 71; IlsCB 1946; NewYTBE 71*

Castelnuovo-Tedesco, Mario
American. Composer
b. Apr 3, 1895 in Florence, Italy
d. Mar 15, 1968 in Hollywood, California
Source: *AmSCAP 66; DcCM; WhAm 5*

Castiglione, Baldassare, Conte
Italian. Diplomat
b. Dec 3, 1478 in Casatico, Italy
d. Feb 2, 1529 in Toledo, Spain
Source: *AtlBL; BbD; BiD&SB; CasWL; CroE&S; DcEuL; EuAu; EvEuW; NewC; OxEng; Pen EUR; RComWL; REn*

Castil-Blaze, Francois-Joseph
French. Author
b. Dec 1, 1784 in Cavaillon, France
d. Dec 11, 1857 in Paris, France
Source: *NewEOp 71*

Castillo, Antonio Canovas del
French. Dress Designer
b. 1908 in Madrid, Spain
Source: *WorFshn*

Castle, Barbara Anne Betts
English. Politician
b. Oct 6, 1911 in Chesterfield, England
Source: *BioIn 2, 7, 8, 9; CurBio 67; IntWW 74; NewYTBE 72; Who 74; WhoWor 74*

Castle, Frederick W
American. General, Aviator
b. 1908
d. 1944
Source: *BioIn 1, 2, 7*

Castle, Irene Foote
American. Ballroom Dancer
b. 1893 in New Rochelle, New York
d. Jan 25, 1969 in Eureka Springs, Arkansas
Source: *EncMT; Film 1; FilmgC; InWom; OxFilm; PlP&P; TwYS; WebAB; WhScrn 74, 77; WhoHol B; WorFshn*

Castle, John
English. Actor
b. Jan 14, 1940 in Croydon, England
Source: *WhoThe 72, 77, 81*

Castle, Peggie
American. Actress
b. Dec 22, 1927 in Appalachia, Virginia
d. Aug 11, 1973 in Hollywood, California
Source: *FilmgC*

Castle, Vernon
[Vernon Blythe]
American. Dancer, Aviator
b. May 2, 1887 in Norwich, England
d. Feb 15, 1918 in Fort Worth, Texas
Source: *DcAmB; DcNAA; EncMT; Film 1; FilmgC; OxFilm; PlP&P; WebAB; WhAm 4; WhScrn 77; WhoHol B*

Castle, William
[William Schloss]
American. Motion Picture Director, Producer
b. Apr 24, 1914 in New York, New York
d. May 31, 1977 in Beverly Hills, California
Source: *BioIn 5, 10, 11; ConAu 69, 77; FanAl; FilmgC; IntMPA 75, 76, 77; PseudN; WhoAm 74, 76, 78; WorEFlm*

Castlereagh, Robert
British. Statesman
b. 1769
d. 1822
Source: *Alli*

Caston, Saul
American. Symphony Conductor
b. Aug 22, 1901 in New York, New York
d. Jul 28, 1970
Source: *BioIn 4, 11; WhAm 5*

Castro (Ruz), Fidel
Cuban. Premier
b. Aug 13, 1926 in Mayari, Cuba
Source: *CurBio 58, 70; IntWW 74; WhoGov 72; WhoHol A; WhoWor 74*

Caswell, Richard
American. Governor, Army Officer
First governor of NC, 1777-79.
b. Aug 3, 1729 in Cecil County, Maryland
d. Nov 10, 1789 in Fayetteville, North Carolina
Source: *ApCAB; BiAuS; DcAmB S2; Drake; NatCAB 4; TwCBDA; WebAB; WhAm H*

Catalani, Alfredo
Italian. Composer
b. Jun 19, 1854 in Lucca, Italy
d. Aug 7, 1893 in Milan, Italy
Source: *NewEOp 71*

Cater, Douglass
American. Author, Editor, Educator
b. Aug 24, 1923 in Montgomery, Alabama
Source: *AmAu&B; BioIn 8; ConAu 1R, 1NR; IntWW 74; WhoAm 74, 76, 78, 80, 82; WhoWor 74; WrDr 76*

Cates, Clifton Bledsoe
American. Military Leader
US Marine, 1917-54; distinguished veteran of WW I and II.
b. Aug 31, 1884 in Tiptonville, Tennessee
d. Jun 6, 1970 in Annapolis, Maryland
Source: *CurBio 50, 70; NewYTBE 70; WhAm 5*

Cather, Willa Sibert
American. Author
b. Dec 7, 1873 in Winchester, Virginia
d. Apr 24, 1947 in New York, New York
Source: *AmAu&B; AmWr; AtlBL; CasWL; Chambr 3; ChPo, S1; CnDAL; ConAmA; ConAmL; CyWA; DcAmB S4; DcBiA; DcLEL; DcNAA; EncAB-H; EncWL; EvLB; HerW; InWom; JBA 34; LongCTC; ModAL, SUP; NotAW; OxAmL; OxCan; OxEng; Pen AM; RAdv 1; RComWL; REn; REnAL; TwCA, SUP; TwCW; WebAB; WebE&AL; WhAm 2; WhNAA; WhoTwCL; WomWWA 14*

Catherall, Arthur
English. Author
b. Jun 2, 1906 in Bolton, England
Source: *Au&Wr 71; AuBYP; ConAu 5R; MnBBF; SmATA 3; WrDr 76*

Catherall, Joanne
see: Human League

Catherine de Medicis
Italian. Monarch
Became Queen of France, 1547; advisor to son Charles IX, 1560-74.
b. Apr 13, 1519 in Florence, Italy
d. Jan 5, 1589 in Blois, France
Source: *BioIn 10; Dis&D; InWom; LinLib S; LuthC 75; McGEWB; NewCol 75; OxFr; OxMus; REn; WebBD 80; WorAl*

Catherine of Alexandria, Saint
Religious Figure
d. 307?
Source: *BioIn 1, 2, 3, 4, 5, 6, 7, 8, 9; NewC*

Catherine of Aragon
English. 1st Wife of Henry VIII
Mother of Mary I; marriage voided, 1533, so Henry could marry Anne Boleyn.
b. Dec 16, 1485 in Alcala, Spain
d. Jan 7, 1536 in Kimbolton, England
Source: *DcCathB; Dis&D; HerW; InWom; LinLib S; NewCol 75; WorAl*

Catherine of Genoa, Saint
Italian. Religious Figure
b. 1447 in Genoa, Italy
d. Sep 14, 1510 in Genoa, Italy
Source: *BioIn 1, 2, 4, 5, 6, 7*

Catherine of Sienna
Italian. Religious Leader
b. 1347
d. 1380
Source: *CasWL; InWom*

Catherine of Valois
French. Queen of Henry V of England
b. 1401
d. 1437
Source: *InWom*

Catherine the Great
[Catherine II; Sophia Augusta Frederike of Anhaltzerbst]
Russian. Czarina
Deposed husband Peter III to rule herself.
b. Apr 21, 1729 in Stettin, Germany
d. Nov 6, 1796
Source: *CasWL; DcEuL; DcRusL; Dis&D; EvEuW; HerW; LinLib L, S; McGEWB; NewCol 75; OxFr; REn; WebBD 80; WhDW; WorAl*

Catherwood, Frederick
English. Artist
b. 1799
d. 1854
Source: *BioIn 10*

Catiline, Lucius
Roman. Statesman
b. 108BC
d. 62BC
Source: *BioIn 4, 7, 8; NewCol 75*

Catledge, Turner
American. Journalist, Editor
b. Mar 17, 1901 in Ackerman, Mississippi
Source: *AmAu&B; AuNews 1; ConAu 57; IntWW 74; NewYTBE 70; Who 74; WhoAm 74; WhoWor 74*

Catlett, "Big Sid" (Sidney)
American. Musician
b. Jan 17, 1910 in Evansville, Idaho
d. Mar 25, 1951 in Chicago, Illinois
Source: *DcAmB S5*

Catlett, Walter
American. Actor
b. Feb 4, 1889 in San Francisco, California
d. Nov 14, 1960 in Woodland Hills, California
Source: *EncMT; FilmgC; MotPP; MovMk; Vers A; WhScrn 74, 77; WhoHol B*

Catlin, George
American. Explorer, Artist
Best known for paintings of Indians, tribal life 1829-38.
b. Jul 26, 1796 in Wilkes-Barre, Pennsylvania
d. Dec 23, 1872 in Jersey City, New Jersey
Source: *Alli SUP; AmAu; AmAu&B; AmBi; ApCAB; AtlBL; BbD; BiD&SB; CasWL; DcAmAu; DcAmB; DcEnL; DcLEL; DcNAA; Drake; EncAB-H; EvLB; OxAmL; REn; REnAL; TwCBDA; WebAB; WhAm H*

Catlin, Sir George Edward Gordon
English. Political Scientist, Educator
b. Jul 29, 1896 in Liverpool, England
d. Feb 8, 1979
Source: *Au&Wr 71; ConAu 13R; IntAu&W 76, 77; IntWW 74, 75, 76, 77, 78; IntYB 78, 79; WhAm 7; WhE&EA; WhNAA; Who 74; WhoAm 74, 76, 78; WhoWor 74, 76; WrDr 76*

Cato
British. Intelligence Agent
b. 1911
d. 1959
Source: *BioIn 10*

Cato, Marcus Porcius Censorius
Roman. Statesman, Historian
b. 234BC in Tusculum, Italy
d. 149BC
Source: *BiD&SB; CasWL; NewC; Pen CL; REn*

Cato, Marcus Porcius Uticensis
Roman. Philosopher
b. 95BC
d. 46BC
Source: *BioIn 1, 3*

Catonsville Nine
American. Peace Activists
Source: *NF*

Catt, Carrie Chapman
American. Feminist
Organized League of Women Voters, 1920.
b. Jan 9, 1859 in Ripon, Wisconsin
d. Mar 9, 1947 in New Rochelle, New York
Source: *AmWom; BiCAW; CurBio 40, 47; DcAmB S4; EncAB-H; InWom; NotAW; WebAB; WhAm 2; WhAmP; WomWWA 14*

Catton, Bruce
American. Author, Journalist
Won Pulitzer Prize, 1954, for *A Stillness at Appomattox.*
b. Oct 9, 1899 in Petoskey, Michigan
d. Aug 28, 1978 in Frankfort, Michigan
Source: *Alli SUP; AmAu&B; AuNews 1; CelR 73; ConAu 5R, 81; CurBio 54; IntWW 74; OxAmL; Pen AM; REn; REnAL; SmATA 2; TwCA SUP; WebAB; Who 74; WhoAm 74; WhoWor 74; WrDr 76*

Catullus, Gaius Valerius
Roman. Poet
Wrote over 100 lyric poems.
b. 84BC in Verona, Italy
d. 54BC
Source: *WebBD 80*

Caudill, Rebecca
[Mrs. James Ayars]
American. Author
b. Feb 2, 1899 in Poor Fork, Kentucky
Source: *AmAu&B; AuBYP; ConAu 5R, 2NR; CurBio 50; ForWC 70; InWom; MorJA; SmATA 1; WhoAm 74, 76, 78, 80, 82; WrDr 76*

Caulfield, Joan
American. Actress
b. Jun 1, 1922 in Orange, New Jersey
Source: *CurBio 54; FilmgC; InWom; IntMPA 75, 76, 77, 78, 79, 80, 81, 82; MotPP; WhoHol A*

Caulfield, Lore
American. Fashion Designer
Source: *NF*

Caulkins, Tracy
American. Swimmer
b. Jan 11, 1963 in Wimona, Minnesota
Source: *BioIn 11*

Causley, Charles Stanley
English. Author
b. Aug 24, 1917 in Launceston, England
Source: *Au&Wr 71; AuBYP; ChPo, S1, S2; CnE&AP; ConAu 9R, 5NR; ConLC 7; ConP 70; LongCTC; NewC; SmATA 3; WebE&AL; Who 74; WhoWor 74; WorAu; WrDr 76*

Cauthen, Steve
American. Jockey
Horses won over $6 million, 1977.
b. May 1, 1961 in Florence, Kentucky
Source: *BioIn 11; BkPepl; CurBio 77; NewYTBS 76, 77, 78, 79, 80, 81; WhoAm 78, 80, 82*

Cavalcanti, Alberto
Brazilian. Motion Picture Director
b. Feb 6, 1897 in Rio de Janeiro, Brazil
Source: *BiDFilm; DcFM; FilmgC; IntMPA 75, 76, 77, 78, 79, 80, 81, 82; MovMk; OxFilm; Who 74; WorEFlm*

Cavaliere, Felix
see: Rascals, The

Cavalieri, Lina
Italian. Opera Singer
b. Dec 25, 1874 in Viterbo, Italy
d. Feb 8, 1944 in Florence, Italy
Source: *Film 1; InWom; TwYS; WhAm 5; WhScrn 77; WhoHol B*

Cavallaro, Carmen
American. Band Leader
b. May 6, 1913 in New York, New York
Source: *AmSCAP 66*

Cavalli, Francesco
Italian. Composer
b. Feb 14, 1602 in Crema, Italy
d. Jan 14, 1676 in Venice, Italy
Source: *NewEOp 71*

Cavanagh, Jerry (Jerome Patrick)
American. Lawyer, Mayor of Detroit
b. Jun 11, 1928 in Detroit, Michigan
d. Nov 27, 1979 in Lexington, Kentucky
Source: *BioIn 6, 7, 8, 11; WhoAm 78*

Cavanaugh, Hobart
American. Actor
b. 1887 in Virginia City, Nevada
d. Apr 27, 1950 in Woodland Hills, California
Source: *FilmgC; MovMk; Vers A; WhScrn 74, 77; WhoHol B*

Cavanna, Betty (Elizabeth Allen)
[Betsy Allen; Elizabeth Headley, pseuds.]
American. Children's Author
Has written books for girls for 30 yrs., including *Going on Sixteen.*
b. Jun 24, 1909 in Camden, New Jersey
Source: *Au&Wr 71; AuBYP; ConAu 9R; ConLC 12; CurBio 50; InWom; IntAu&W 76, 77; MorJA; SmATA 1; TwCCW 78; WhoAmW 58, 61; WrDr 76, 80*

Cavarretta, Phil(ip Joseph)
American. Baseball Player
Outfielder, first baseman, Chicago, 1934-55; won batting title, 1945.
b. Jul 19, 1916 in Chicago, Illinois
Source: *BaseEn; WhoProB 73*

Cavell, Edith
English. Nurse
b. 1865 in Norfolk, England
d. Oct 12, 1915
Source: *BioIn 2, 4, 5, 6, 7, 8, 10, 11; GoodHS; HerW; InWom; LinLib S; LongCTC*

Cavendish, Henry
English. Chemist, Physicist
b. Oct 10, 1731 in Nice, France
d. Mar 10, 1810 in London, England
Source: *Alli; NewC; NewCol 75; WebBD 80*

Cavendish, Thomas
English. Navigator
Third to circumnavigate globe, 1586.
b. 1555? in Suffolk, England
d. Jun 1592
Source: *Alli; BioIn 1, 2, 3, 4, 10; NewC; NewCol 75; OxShips; WebBD 80; Alli; BioIn 1, 2, 3, 4, 10; NewC; NewCol 75; OxShips; Alli; BioIn 1, 2, 3, 4, 10; NewC; NewCol 75; OxShips*

Cavendish, William, Duke of Newcastle
English. Statesman, Author
b. 1592
d. Dec 25, 1676 in London, England
Source: *Alli; BrAu; CasWL; CroE&S; DcEnL*

Cavett, Dick (Richard Alva)
American. Entertainer
Won Emmy, 1972; host of PBS talk show, 1978-- ; author *Cavett,* 1974.
b. Nov 19, 1936 in Gibbon, Nebraska
Source: *BioNews 74; BkPepl; CelR 73; CurBio 70; IntMPA 75, 76, 77, 78, 79, 80, 81, 82; NewYTBS 81; WhoAm 74, 76, 78, 80, 82; WhoE 74*

Cavour, Camillo Benso di
Italian. Statesman
b. Aug 10, 1810 in Turin, Italy
d. Jun 6, 1861 in Turin, Italy
Source: *BiD&SB; NewC; REn*

Cawein, Madison Julius
American. Poet
b. Mar 23, 1865 in Louisville, Kentucky
d. Dec 7, 1914 in Louisville, Kentucky
Source: *AmAu&B; BbD; BiD&SB; BiDSA; DcAmAu; DcEnL; DcNAA; OxAmL; REn; REnAL*

Cawthorn, Joseph
American. Actor
b. Mar 29, 1868 in New York, New York
d. Jan 21, 1949 in Beverly Hills, California
Source: *BioIn 1; WhScrn 77; WhThe; WhoStg 1906, 1908*

Caxton, William
English. Author, Printer
First to print books translated into English, 1475.
b. Aug 13, 1422 in Weald of Kent, England
d. 1491 in Westminster, England
Source: *Alli; BbD; BiD&SB; BrAu; CasWL; Chambr 1; CrtT 1; DcEnA; DcEnL; DcEuL; DcLEL; EvLB; MouLC 1; NewC; OxEng; Pen ENG; REn; WebE&AL*

Cayatte, Andre
French. Motion Picture Director
b. Feb 3, 1909 in Carcassonne, France
Source: *BiDFilm; DcFM; FilmgC; OxFilm; WorEFlm*

Cayce, Edgar
American. Therapist, Clairvoyant
Worked from trances to yield diagnoses, prescriptions for patients.
b. Mar 18, 1877 in Hopkinsville, Kentucky
d. Jan 3, 1945
Source: *BiDPara; EncO&P 78; WhAm 4*

Cayley, Sir George
British. Founder of Aerodynamics
Built first successful glider, 1853.
b. Dec 27, 1773
d. Dec 15, 1857
Source: *Alli; DcInv; InSci; NewCol 75; WhDW*

Cazenove, Christopher
English. Actor
b. Dec 17, 1945 in Winchester, England
Source: *WhoThe 81*

Ceausescu, Nicolae
Romanian. President
b. Jan 26, 1918 in Scornicesti-Olt, Romania
Source: *CurBio 67; IntWW 74; NewYTBE 70; WhoGov 72; WhoWor 74*

Cebotari, Maria
Russian. Opera Singer
b. Feb 10, 1910 in Kishinev, Russia
d. Jun 9, 1949 in Vienna, Austria
Source: *InWom*

Ceccato, Aldo
Italian. Symphony Conductor
b. Feb 18, 1934 in Milan, Italy
Source: *BioNews 74; WhoAm 78; WhoMus 72*

Cecchetti, Enrico
Italian. Dancer, Teacher
b. 1850 in Italy
d. Nov 16, 1928
Source: *BioIn 3, 4, 5, 8, 9; NotNAT B*

Cecchi, Emilio
Italian. Essayist, Critic
b. 1884 in Florence, Italy
d. 1966 in Rome, Italy
Source: *CasWL; ClDMEL; DcFM; EncWL; EvEuW; Pen EUR*

Cecil, Edgar Algernon Robert
English. Statesman, Author
b. Sep 14, 1864 in London, England
d. Nov 24, 1958
Source: *McGEWB; WebBD 80*

Cecil, Edward Christian David Gascoyne
English. Critic, Biographer, Educator
b. Apr 9, 1902
Source: *EvLB; TwCA, SUP*

Cecelia, Saint
Christian Martyr
d. 230 in Rome, Italy
Source: *BioIn 1, 2, 3, 4, 5, 6, 7, 8; NewC; REn*

Cedeno, Cesar
Dominican. Baseball Player
Outfielder, first baseman, Houston Astros; had two doubles in one inning, 1973.
b. Feb 25, 1951 in Santo Domingo, Dominican Republic
Source: *BaseEn; NewYTBE 73; WhoProB 73*

Celebrezze, Anthony Joseph
American. Politician, Judge
b. Sep 4, 1910 in Anzi, Italy
Source: *BiDrUSE; CurBio 63; IntWW 74; WhoAm 74; WhoAmP 73; WhoGov 72; WhoMW 74*

Celeste, Richard F
American. Governor of Ohio
Elected governor, 1982.
b. Nov 11, 1937 in Cleveland, Ohio
Source: *WhoAm 78, 80, 82; WhoAmP 75, 77, 79; WhoGov 75, 77; WhoMW 78*

Celibidache, Sergiu
Romanian. Conductor
b. Jun 28, 1912
Source: *IntWW 74; Who 74; WhoWor 74*

Celine, Louis-Ferdinand
[Louis-Ferdinand Destouches]
French. Author
b. May 27, 1894 in Courbevoie, France
d. Jul 4, 1961 in Meudon, France
Source: *AtlBL; CasWL; ClDMEL; ConAu 85; ConLC 1, 3, 4, 9, 15; CyWA; EncWL; EvEuW; LongCTC; ModRL; OxFr; Pen EUR; REn; TwCA, SUP; TwCW; WhAm 4; WhoTwCL*

Celler, Emanuel
American. Politician
b. May 6, 1888 in Brooklyn, New York
Source: *BiDrAC; CelR 73; CurBio 49, 66; IntWW 74; NewYTBE 72; St&PR 75; WhoAm 74; WhoAmP 73; WhoE 74; WhoGov 72*

Cellini, Benvenuto
Italian. Sculptor, Metalworker
Autobiography *The Life of Benvenuto Cellini,* 1558-66, record of Renaissance life.
b. Nov 1, 1500 in Florence, Italy
d. Feb 14, 1571 in Florence, Italy
Source: *AtlBL; BbD; BiD&SB; CasWL; CyWA; DcEuL; EuAu; EvEuW; NewC; OxEng; OxFr; Pen EUR; RComWL; REn*

Celsius, Anders
Swedish. Astronomer
Invented centigrade temperature scale, 1742.
b. Nov 27, 1701 in Uppsala, Sweden
d. Apr 25, 1744
Source: *WebBD 80*

Cepeda, Orlando
"The Baby Bull"; "Cha-Cha"
Puerto Rican. Baseball Player
b. Sep 17, 1937 in Ponce, Puerto Rico
Source: *BaseEn; CurBio 68; WhoAm 74; WhoProB 73*

Ceresole, Pierre
Swiss. Humanitarian
b. 1879
d. 1945
Source: *BioIn 3, 11*

Cerf, Bennett Alfred
American. Publisher, Journalist
Random House Publishers, founder, 1927, president, 1927-65, chairman, 1965-70.
b. May 25, 1898 in New York, New York
d. Aug 27, 1971 in Mount Kisco, New York
Source: *AmAu&B; AuBYP; BiE&WWA; ConAu 21R, 29R; ConAu P-2; CurBio 41, 58, 71; NewYTBE 71; PlP&P; REn; REnAL; SmATA 7; WebAB; WhAm 5*

Cermak, Anton Joseph
American. Mayor of Chicago
Killed in Miami by bullet intended for Franklin D Roosevelt.
b. May 9, 1873 in Prague, Bohemia
d. Mar 6, 1933 in Miami, Florida
Source: *DcAmB S1; WhAm 1; WhAmP*

Cernan, Eugene Andrew
American. Astronaut, Businessman
In space on Gemini 9, Apollo 10, 17; walked on moon, 1972.
b. Mar 14, 1934 in Chicago, Illinois
Source: *CurBio 73; IntWW 74; WhoAm 74, 76, 78, 80, 82; WhoS&SW 73; WhoWor 74*

Cernik, Oldrich
Czech. Premier
b. Oct 27, 1921 in Ostrava, Czechoslovakia
Source: *IntWW 74; WhoWor 74*

Cerone, Rick (Richard Aldo)
"Spongehead"
American. Baseball Player
b. May 19, 1954 in Newark, New Jersey
Source: *BaseEn*

Cervantes, Alfonso Juan
American. Former Mayor of St. Louis
b. Aug 27, 1929 in Saint Louis, Missouri
Source: *WhoAm 74; WhoAmP 73; WhoGov 72*

Cervantes (Saavedra), Miguel(de)
Spanish. Poet, Dramatist
Began writing *Don Quixote* in prison, 1605; forerunner of modern novel.
b. 1547 in Alcala, Spain
d. Apr 23, 1616 in Madrid, Spain
Source: *AtlBL; BbD; BiD&SB; CasWL; ChPo S2; CnThe; CyWA; DcBiA; DcEuL; DcSpL; EuAu; EvEuW; McGEWD; NewC; OxEng; OxThe; Pen EUR; RComWL; REn; REnWD*

Cesnola, Luigi Palma di
Italian. Archeologist, Soldier
b. Jul 29, 1832 in Rivarola, Italy
d. Nov 20, 1904 in New York, New York
Source: *BbD; BiD&SB; BioIn 7, 9; DcAmAu; DcNAA*

Cessna, Clyde Vernon
American. Airplane Manufacturer
Organized Cessna Aircraft Co.; built cantilever monoplanes, 1928.
b. Dec 5, 1879 in Hawthorne, Iowa
d. Nov 20, 1954 in Rago, Kansas
Source: *NatCAB 41*

Cey, Ron(ald Charles)
"The Penguin"
American. Baseball Player
b. Feb 15, 1948 in Tacoma, Washington
Source: *BaseEn; PseudN; WhoAm 78, 80, 82*

Cezanne, Paul
French. Artist
Post impressionist; influenced Cubism with emphasis on geometric form.
b. Jan 19, 1839 in Aix-en-Provence, France
d. Oct 22, 1906 in Aix-en-Provence, France
Source: *AtlBL; OxFr; REn*

Chaban-Delmas, Jacques
French. Political Leader
b. Mar 7, 1915 in Paris, France
Source: *CurBio 58; IntWW 74; WhoWor 74*

Chabrier, (Alexis) Emmanuel
French. Composer
b. Jan 18, 1841 in Ambert, France
d. Sep 13, 1894 in Paris, France
Source: *AtlBL; OxFr*

Chabrol, Claude
French. Motion Picture Director
b. Jun 24, 1930 in Paris, France
Source: *BiDFilm; ConLC 16; CurBio 75; DcFM; FilmgC; IntMPA 75, 76, 77, 78, 79, 80, 81, 82; IntWW 74; MovMk; NewYTBE 70; OxFilm; WhoWor 74; WorEFlm*

Chace, Marian
American. Therapist, Dancer
b. 1896
d. 1970
Source: *BioIn 9, 11*

Chacksfield, Frank
British. Musical Director
Source: *WhoMus 72*

Chad and Jeremy
[Jeremy Clyde; Chad Stuart]
English. Rock Duo
Source: *BiDAmM; ConMuA 80; LilREn 78; WhoRock 81*

Chadwick, Cassie L
[Elizabeth Bigley]
Canadian. Swindler
b. 1859 in Strathroy, ON
d. 1907
Source: *BioIn 2, 5, 10; LookW; PseudN*

Chadwick, Florence
American. Swimmer
Established a new record for women swimming the English Channel, 1950.
b. Nov 9, 1917 in San Diego, California
Source: *CurBio 50; InWom*

Chadwick, French Ensor
American. Naval Officer
b. Feb 29, 1844 in Morgantown, West Virginia
d. Jan 27, 1919
Source: *AmBi; ApCAB SUP; ApCAB X; DcAmB S2; NatCAB 9; WebBD 80; WhAm 1*

Chadwick, George Whitefield
American. Composer
b. Nov 13, 1854 in Lowell, Massachusetts
d. Apr 7, 1931 in Boston, Massachusetts
Source: *AmBi; ApCAB; DcAmB S1; OxAmL; TwCBDA; WhAm 1*

Chadwick, Henry
American. Journalist, Baseball Organizer
Responsible for rules of baseball; editor, Spaulding's *Official Baseball Guide*.
b. Oct 5, 1824 in Exeter, England
d. Apr 20, 1908 in New York, New York
Source: *Alli SUP; AmAu&B; DcAmAu; DcAmB; DcNAA; HsB&A; WebAB; WhoProB 73*

Chadwick, Sir James
English. Engineer, Scientist, Physician
b. Oct 22, 1891 in Manchester, England
d. Jul 24, 1974 in Cambridge, England
Source: *ConAu 49; CurBio 45, 74; IntWW 74; NewYTBS 74; WhAm 6; Who 74; WhoAm 74; WhoWor 74*

Chadwick, William Owen
English. Historian
b. May 20, 1916 in Bromley, England
Source: *ConAu 1NR; IntWW 74; Who 74; WhoWor 74*

Chafee, John Hubbard
American. Senator
b. Oct 22, 1922 in Providence, Rhode Island
Source: *CurBio 69; IntWW 74; WhoAm 74, 76, 78, 80, 82; WhoAmP 73; WhoE 74*

Chaffee, Roger Bruce
American. Astronaut
Killed in fire with Gus Grissom, Ed White, aboard spacecraft during simulation of Apollo flight.
b. Feb 15, 1935 in Grand Rapids, Michigan
d. Jan 27, 1967 in Cape Canaveral, Florida
Source: *WhAm 4*

Chaffee, Suzy
American. Skier, Businesswoman
Captain, US Olympic Ski Team, 1968; world free style champ, 1971-73.
b. Nov 29, 1946
Source: *BioIn 9; WhoAm 80, 82*

Chaffin, Lillie Dorton
American. Children's Author
b. Feb 1, 1925 in Varney, Kentucky
Source: *ConAu 33R; DrAF 76; ForWC 70; SmATA 4; WrDr 76*

Chagall, Marc
Russian. Artist
Famous works include "Self Portrait with Seven Fingers," "I and My Village."
b. Jul 7, 1887 in Vitebsk, Russia
Source: *CelR 73; CurBio 43, 60; IntWW 74; NewYTBE 73; REn; Who 82; WhoGrA; WhoWor 74*

Chaikin, Joseph
American. Actor, Theatrical Director
b. Sep 16, 1935 in Brooklyn, New York
Source: *BioIn 1, 9, 10, 11; CurBio 81; NotNAT; WhoThe 77, 81; WhoWorJ 72*

Chaikin, Sol Chick
American. Labor Union Official
b. Jan 9, 1918 in New York, New York
Source: *CurBio 79; NewYTBS 75; WhoAm 78, 80, 82; WhoE 77, 79; WhoLab 76*

Chain, Sir Ernest Boris
British. Biochemist, Educator
b. Jun 19, 1906 in Berlin, Germany
d. Sep 14, 1979 in Ireland
Source: *AsBiEn; BioIn 3, 5, 6, 7; CurBio 65, 79; IntWW 75, 76, 77, 78; Who 74; WhoWor 78; WhoWorJ 72*

Chait, Lawrence G
American. Advertising Executive
b. Jun 27, 1917 in Scranton, Pennsylvania
Source: *WhoAdv 72; WhoAm 74, 76, 78, 80, 82; WhoE 74*

Chaka
African. Zulu Chief
b. 1773
d. 1828
Source: *BioIn 1, 4, 6, 7, 8, 9, 10*

Chakiris, George
American. Dancer, Actor
Won Oscar, 1961, for *West Side Story.*
b. Sep 16, 1934 in Norwood, Ohio
Source: *FilmgC; IntMPA 75, 76, 77, 78, 79, 80, 81, 82; MotPP; MovMk; WhoAm 74, 76, 78, 80, 82; WhoHol A*

Chalgrin, Francois
French. Architect
b. 1739 in Paris, France
d. 1811
Source: *McGDA; WhoArch*

Chaliapin, Feodor Ivanovitch
[Feodor Ivanovich Shaliapin]
Russian. Opera Singer
b. Feb 13, 1873 in Kazan, Russia
d. Apr 12, 1938 in Paris, France
Source: *FilmgC; OxFilm; REn; WhAm 1; WhScrn 74, 77; WhoHol B*

Chalk, Oscar Roy
English. Business Executive
b. Jun 7, 1907 in London, England
Source: *WhoAm 78*

Challans, Mary
see: Renault, Mary, pseud.

Chamberlain, Sir Austen
British. Statesman
b. 1863
d. 1937
Source: *BioIn 1, 2, 7, 9, 11; WhE&EA*

Chamberlain, John Rensselear
American. Journalist
b. Oct 28, 1903 in New Haven, Connecticut
Source: *AmAu&B; ConAu 57; CurBio 40; OxAmL; REnAL; TwCA, SUP; WhoAm 74, 76, 78, 80, 82; WhoWor 74*

Chamberlain, Joseph
English. Statesman
b. Jul 8, 1836 in London, England
d. Jul 2, 1914
Source: *Alli SUP*

Chamberlain, Neville
English. Statesman, Prime Minister
Policy of appeasement to Hitler resulted in Munich Pact, 1938.
b. Mar 18, 1869 in Edgbaston, England
d. Nov 9, 1940 in Odiham, England
Source: *CurBio 40; REn; WhoModH*

Chamberlain, Richard
American. Actor
Starred in "Dr. Kildare," "Shogun" on TV.
b. Mar 31, 1935 in Beverly Hills, California
Source: *BioNews 75; BkPepl; CelR 73; FilmgC; IntMPA 75, 76, 77, 78, 79, 80, 81, 82; MotPP; MovMk; WhoHol A; WhoThe 77*

Chamberlain, Samuel
American. Author, Photographer
b. Oct 28, 1895 in Cresco, Iowa
d. Jan 10, 1975 in Marblehead, Massachusetts
Source: *ConAu 53; ConAu P-2; CurBio 54; WhAm 6*

Chamberlain, Wilt(ton Norman)
"Wilt the Stilt"
American. Basketball Player
NBA's leading scorer with 31,419 career points; MVP four times.
b. Aug 21, 1936 in Philadelphia, Pennsylvania
Source: *BkPepl; CelR 73; CurBio 60; NewYTBE 72, 73; WhoBbl 73; WhoBlA 75*

Chamberlin, (B) Guy
American. Football Player, Coach
b. Jan 16, 1894 in Blue Springs, Nebraska
d. Apr 4, 1967
Source: *BioIn 3, 6, 8; WhoFtbl 74*

Chamberlin, Thomas Chrowder
American. Geologist
b. Sep 25, 1843 in Mattoon, Illinois
d. Nov 15, 1928
Source: *ApCAB; NatCAB 11; NewCol 75; WhAm 1*

Chamberlin, William Henry
American. Author, Critic
b. Feb 17, 1897 in Brooklyn, New York
d. Sep 12, 1969
Source: *AmAu&B; ConAu 5R; OxAmL; OxCan; REnAL; TwCA, SUP; WhAm 5*

Chambers, Sir Edmund Kerchever
English. Essayist, Critic
b. Mar 16, 1866 in Berkshire, England
d. Jan 21, 1954 in Devonshire, England
Source: *CasWL; DcLEL; EvLB; LongCTC; NewC; OxEng; Pen ENG; REn; TwCA, SUP*

Chambers, Martin
see: Pretenders, The

Chambers, Sir Paul
English. Businessman, Civil Servant
b. Apr 2, 1904 in London, England
Source: *BioIn 8; IntWW 74; Who 74*

Chambers, Robert
Scottish. Publisher, Author
b. Jul 10, 1802 in Peebles, Scotland
d. Mar 17, 1871 in Saint Andrews, Scotland
Source: *BioIn 2, 5, 10; BrAu 19; CasWL; DcEnA; DcEnL; EvLB*

Chambers, Robert W
American. Author
b. May 26, 1865 in Brooklyn, New York
d. Dec 16, 1933
Source: *AmAu&B; AmBi; ApCAB SUP; BbD; BiD&SB; CarSB; Chambr 3; ChPo, S2; DcAmAu; DcAmB S1; DcBiA; DcLEL; DcNAA; OxAmL; REnAL; TwCA; TwCBDA; WhAm 1*

Chambers, Whittaker
[Jay David Chambers]
American. Editor, Journalist
b. Apr 1, 1901 in Philadelphia, Pennsylvania
d. Jun 9, 1961 in Carroll County, Maryland
Source: *AmAu&B; ConAu 89; LongCTC; WorAu*

Chambers, Sir William
"W C"
British. Architect
b. 1723 in Gothenburg, Sweden
d. Mar 8, 1796 in London, England
Source: *AtlBL; BioIn 2, 3, 7, 8, 9; PseudN*

Chaminade, Cecile
[Louise Stephanie Chaminade]
French. Composer
b. Aug 8, 1861 in Paris, France
d. Apr 18, 1944 in Monte Carlo, Monaco
Source: *CurBio 44; OxMus*

Champion, Gower
American. Choreographer, Dancer
Won Tonys for *Bye Bye Birdie,* 1961, *Hello, Dolly,* 1964, *42nd Street,* 1981.
b. Jun 22, 1921 in Geneva, Illinois
d. Aug 25, 1980 in New York, New York
Source: *BiE&WWA; CelR 73; CmMov; EncMT; FilmgC; IntMPA 75, 76, 77, 78, 79, 80, 81; MotPP; MovMk; NotNAT; WhoAm 74; WhoHol A; WhoThe 77; WhoWor 74; WorEFlm*

Champion, Marge Celeste
[Marjorie Celeste Belcher; Mrs. Gower Champion]
American. Dancer, Actress
b. Sep 2, 1923 in Los Angeles, California
Source: *BiE&WWA; CmMov; FilmgC; InWom; IntMPA 75, 76, 77, 78, 79, 80, 81, 82; MotPP; MovMk; NotNAT; WhoAm 74, 76, 78, 80, 82; WhoHol A*

Champlain, Samuel de
French. Explorer
Founded Quebec, 1608; discovered Lake Champlain, 1609.
b. Jul 3, 1567 in Rochefort, France
d. Dec 25, 1635 in Quebec, Canada
Source: *AmBi; ApCAB; DcAmB; Drake; OxAmL; OxCan; OxFr; REn; REnAL; WebAB; WhAm H*

Champollion, Jean Francois
French. Egyptologist
Deciphered Egyptian hieroglyphics using Rosetta stone.
b. Dec 23, 1790
d. Mar 4, 1832
Source: *BbD; OxFr; REn*

Chance, Frank Leroy
"Peerless Leader"
American. Baseball Player, Manager
First baseman in "Tinker to Evers to Chance" double play combination, 1906-10.
b. Sep 9, 1877 in Fresno, California
d. Sep 15, 1924 in Los Angeles, California
Source: *BaseEn; WhoProB 73*

Chance, (Wilmer) Dean
American. Baseball Player
Pitched six 1-0 winning games to set major league record.
b. Jun 1, 1941 in Wayne, Ohio
Source: *BaseEn; BioIn 7, 8; CurBio 69; WhoProB 73*

Chancellor, John William
American. Broadcast Journalist
Anchorman, "NBC Nightly News," 1970-81; commentator since 1981.
b. Jul 14, 1927 in Chicago, Illinois
Source: *AuNews 1; BioNews 74; CelR 73; CurBio 62; IntMPA 75, 76, 77, 78, 79, 80, 81, 82; WhoAm 74, 76, 78, 80, 82*

Chancellor, Richard
English. Explorer
Negotiated trade agreements between Moscow, England; organized Muscovy Co., 1554.
d. Nov 10, 1556
Source: *BioIn 4, 7; NewC*

Chandler, Colby H
American. Eastman Kodak Co. President
b. 1925
Source: *Dun&B 79; IntWW 77, 78, 79, 80; WhoAm 82; WhoF&I 79*

Chandler, Don
American. Football Player
b. Sep 9, 1934 in Council Bluffs, Iowa
Source: *BioIn 8; WhoFtbl 74*

Chandler, Dorothy Buffum
American. Journalist
b. May 19, 1901 in Lafayette, Illinois
Source: *BioIn 4, 5, 7, 8, 9, 11; CurBio 57; WhoAm 74; WhoAmW 74; WhoWor 74*

Chandler, "Happy" (Albert Benjamin)
American. Lawyer, Former Governor
Governor of KY, 1935-39; 1955-59.
b. Jul 14, 1898 in Corydon, Kentucky
Source: *BiDrAC; WebAB; WhoAm 76, 78, 80, 82; WhoAmP 73; WhoProB 73; WhoS&SW 73*

Chandler, Jeff
[Ira Grossel]
American. Actor, Author
b. Dec 15, 1918 in Brooklyn, New York
d. Jun 17, 1961 in Culver City, California
Source: *AmSCAP 66; BiDFilm; CmMov; FilmgC; MotPP; MovMk; OxFilm; WhScrn 74, 77; WhoHol B; WorEFlm*

Chandler, Norman
American. Newspaper Publisher
b. Jul 23, 1899 in Chicago, Illinois
d. Oct 20, 1973 in Los Angeles, California
Source: *ConAu 89; CurBio 73; WhAm 6; WhoF&I 74; WhoWest 74; WhoWor 74*

Chandler, Otis
American. Newspaper Publisher
b. Nov 23, 1927 in Los Angeles, California
Source: *BioIn 5, 7, 8, 9, 11; CurBio 68; WhoAm 82*

Chandler, Raymond Thornton
American. Author
b. Jul 23, 1888 in Chicago, Illinois
d. Mar 26, 1959 in La Jolla, California
Source: *AmAu&B; CasWL; CnMWL; CurBio 46, 59; DcFM; DcLEL; EncMys; FilmgC; LongCTC; ModAL, SUP; NewYTBE 73; OxAmL; OxEng; OxFilm; Pen AM; REn; REnAL; TwCA SUP; TwCW; WebAB; WebE&AL; WhAm 3; WhoTwCL; WorEFlm*

Chandler, "Spud" (Spurgeon Ferdinand)
American. Baseball Player
AL MVP, 1943; led league with winning percentage of .833, 1943.
b. Sep 12, 1909 in Commerce, Georgia
Source: *BaseEn; WhoProB 73*

Chandos, Oliver Lyttelton
English. Statesman, Industrialist
b. Mar 15, 1893 in London, England
d. Jan 21, 1972
Source: *Au&Wr 71; BioIn 3, 5, 6, 9; CurBio 41, 72*

Chanel, "Coco" (Gabrielle)
French. Fashion Designer
Created Chanel No. 5 perfume, 1924; subject of Broadway musical *Coco.*
b. Aug 19, 1882 in Saumur, France
d. Jan 10, 1971 in Paris, France
Source: *CurBio 54, 71; InWom; NewYTBE 71; WhAm 5; WorFshn*

Chaney, James
American. Civil Rights Organizer
b. 1943
d. 1964
Source: *BioIn 7*

Chaney, Lon (Alonso)
"Man of a Thousand Faces"
American. Actor
Starred in *The Hunchback of Notre Dame,* 1923; *The Phantom of the Opera,* 1925.
b. Apr 1, 1883 in Colorado Springs, Colorado
d. Aug 26, 1930 in Los Angeles, California
Source: *BiDFilm; CmMov; DcAmB S1; Film 1; FilmgC; MotPP; MovMk; OxFilm; TwYS; WebAB; WhAm HA, 4; WhScrn 74, 77; WhoHol B; WorEFlm*

Chaney, Lon, Jr. (Creighton)
American. Actor
Starred in over 100 films, mostly horror; played Lenny in *Of Mice and Men,* 1940.
b. Feb 10, 1905 in Oklahoma City, Oklahoma
d. Jul 12, 1973 in San Clemente, California
Source: *CmMov; FilmgC; MovMk; OxFilm; WhScrn 77; WhoHol B*

Chaney, Norman
[Our Gang]
"Chubby"
American. Child Actor
b. Jan 18, 1918 in Baltimore, Maryland
d. May 30, 1936 in Baltimore, Maryland
Source: *Film 2; PseudN; WhScrn 74, 77*

Chang and Eng
[Chang and Eng Bunker]
American. Original Siamese Twins
Toured carnivals in US, Europe, 1829-54; Chang died first, Eng died of fright two hrs. later.
b. May 11, 1811 in Meklong, Thailand
d. Jan 17, 1874 in Mount Airy, North Carolina
Source: *ApCAB; DcAmB; WebAB; WhAm H*

Chang Tso-Lin
Chinese. General, Warlord of Manchuria
b. 1873
d. Jun 4, 1928
Source: *BioIn 3, 11; NewCol 75; WebBD 80*

Chanin, Henry I
Builder
b. 1893
d. 1973
Source: *NewYTBE 73*

Channing, Carol
[Carol Channing Lowe]
American. Actress
Trademark song, "Diamonds Are a Girl's Best Friend," from *Gentlemen Prefer Blonds.*
b. Jan 31, 1923 in Seattle, Washington
Source: *BiE&WWA; BkPepl; CelR 73; CurBio 64; EncMT; FamA&A; FilmgC; InWom; IntMPA 75, 76, 77, 78, 79, 80, 81, 82; MotPP; NewYTBE 70; NotNAT; WhoAm 74, 76, 78, 80, 82; WhoHol A; WhoThe 77; WhoWor 74*

Channing, Edward
American. Historian
b. Jun 15, 1856 in Dorchester, Massachusetts
d. Jan 7, 1931
Source: *AmBi; ApCAB; DcAmB; McGEWB; NatCAB 13; TwCBDA; WebBD 80; WhAm 1*

Channing, Stockard
American. Actress
b. 1944 in New York, New York
Source: *IntMPA 77, 78, 79, 80, 81, 82; WhoAm 82; WhoHol A*

Channing, Walter
American. Physician
b. Apr 15, 1786 in Newport, Rhode Island
d. Jul 27, 1876 in Boston, Massachusetts
Source: *ApCAB; DcAmB; Drake; TwCBDA; WhAm H*

Channing, William Ellery
American. Clergyman, Abolitionist
b. Apr 7, 1780 in Newport, Rhode Island
d. Oct 2, 1842 in Bennington, Vermont
Source: *Alli; AmAu; AmAu&B; AmBi; ApCAB; BbD; BiD&SB; CasWL; Chambr 3; CnDAL; CyAL 1; DcAmAu; DcAmB; DcEnL; DcNAA; Drake; EncAB-H; EvLB; OxAmL; OxEng; Pen AM; REn; REnAL; TwCBDA; WebAB; WhAm H*

Chantrey, Sir Francis Legatt
English. Artist
b. Apr 7, 1781 in Jordanthorpe, England
d. Nov 25, 1841 in London, England
Source: *BioIn 4; NewC; NewCol 75*

Chanute, Octave
American. Engineer, Aviation Pioneer
b. Feb 18, 1832 in Paris, France
d. Nov 23, 1910 in Chicago, Illinois
Source: *AmBi; DcAmB; DcNAA; TwCBDA; WebAB; WhAm 1*

Chapais, Sir Thomas
Canadian. Journalist, Statesman
b. Mar 23, 1858 in Saint Denis, PQ
d. Jul 15, 1948? in Saint Denis, PQ
Source: *AmLY; BioIn 1; CanWr; DcNAA; OxCan, SUP*

Chao, Yuen Ren
Chinese. Poet
b. Nov 3, 1892 in Tientsin, China
d. Feb 24, 1982 in Cambridge, Massachusetts
Source: *ConAu 21R, 106; ConAu P-2; WhoLA*

Chapin, Dwight Lee
American. Watergate Participant
Organized "dirty tricks" unit to harass Democrats; convicted of perjury, Apr 5, 1974.
b. Dec 2, 1940 in Wichita, Kansas
Source: *WhoAm 82; WhoAmP 73*

Chapin, Harry Foster
American. Singer, Songwriter
Nominated for Grammy, 1974, for "The Cat's in the Cradle."
b. Dec 7, 1942 in New York, New York
d. Jul 16, 1981 in Jericho, New York
Source: *ConAu 104; IlEncRk; LilREn 78; NewYTBS 81; RkOn 2; WhoAm 76, 78, 80; WhoRock 81*

Chapin, James Ormsbee
American. Artist
b. Jul 9, 1887 in West Orange, New Jersey
d. Jul 12, 1975 in Toronto, ON
Source: *CurBio 40, 75; McGDA; WhAm 6*

Chapin, Roy Dikeman
American. Automobile Executive
Director, Hudson Motor Car Co., 1946-54; chairman, American Motors, 1967-78.
b. Sep 21, 1915 in Detroit, Michigan
Source: *IntWW 74; NewYTBS 74; St&PR 75; Ward 77; WhoAm 74; WhoF&I 74; WhoWor 74*

Chapin, Schuyler Garrison
American. Opera Manager
b. Feb 13, 1923 in New York, New York
Source: *CurBio 74; IntWW 74; NewYTBE 73; WhoAm 74; WhoE 74*

Chaplin, Charlie
[Sir Charles Spencer]
English. Actor, Author, Composer
Known for character created in *The Tramp,* 1915; won special Oscar, 1972.
b. Apr 16, 1889 in London, England
d. Dec 25, 1977 in Vevey, Switzerland
Source: *ConAu 73, 81; CurBio 40, 61; DcFM; EncAB-H; Film 1; IntMPA 75, 76, 77; IntWW 74; OxAmL; REn; REnAL; TwYS; WebAB; Who 74; WhoAm 74; WhoThe 77; WhoWor 74*

Chaplin, George
American. Boxer
b. 1950 in Baltimore, Maryland
Source: *NF*

Chaplin, Geraldine
American. Actress
Daughter of Charlie Chaplin; appeared in *Doctor Zhivago, Nashville.*
b. Jul 31, 1944 in Santa Monica, California
Source: *FilmgC; IntMPA 82; MotPP; WhoAm 74; WhoHol A*

Chaplin, Saul
American. Musical Director, Producer
b. Feb 19, 1912 in New York, New York
Source: *AmSCAP 66; CmMov; IntMPA 75, 76, 77, 78, 79, 80, 81, 82; OxFilm*

Chaplin, Sydney
English. Brother of Charlie Chaplin
b. Mar 17, 1885 in Capetown, South Africa
d. Apr 16, 1956 in Nice, France
Source: *BioIn 7; WhScrn 74*

Chaplin, Sydney
American. Actor
b. Mar 30, 1926 in Los Angeles, California
Source: *BiE&WWA; EncMT; FilmgC; MotPP; NotNAT; WhoHol A*

Chaplin, Victoria
American. Daughter of Charlie Chaplin
b. 1952
Source: *BioIn 9*

Chapman, (Anthony) Colin (Bruce)
British. Automobile Designer
Founded Lotus Cars sports car co., 1955.
b. May 19, 1928
d. Dec 16, 1982 in Norfolk, England
Source: *BioIn 7, 8; Who 74, 82*

Chapman, Ceil (Cecilia Mitchell)
American. Fashion Designer
b. Feb 19, 1912 in New York, New York
d. Jul 13, 1979 in Bronx, New York
Source: *InWom; NewYTBS 79; WhAm 7; WhoAmW 58, 61, 64, 66, 68, 70, 72, 74; WorFshn*

Chapman, Christian Addison
American. Diplomat
b. Sep 19, 1921 in Paris, France
Source: *USBiR 74; WhoAm 74, 76, 78, 80, 82; WhoGov 72, 75, 77*

Chapman, Eddie (Edward Arnold)
English. Safecracker, Spy
Source: *BioIn 3, 4*

Chapman, Frank Michler
American. Ornithologist
b. Jun 12, 1864 in Englewood, New Jersey
d. Nov 15, 1945 in New York, New York
Source: *AmAu&B; CurBio 46; DcAmAu; DcNAA; REnAL; TwCA, SUP*

Chapman, George
English. Poet, Dramatist
b. 1560 in Hitchin, England
d. May 12, 1634 in London, England
Source: *Alli, SUP; AtlBL; BbD; BiD&SB; BrAu; CasWL; Chambr 1; ChPo; CnE&AP; CnThe; CroE&S; CrtT 1; CyWA; DcEnA; DcEnL; DcEuL; DcLEL; EvLB; McGEWD; MouLC 1; NewC; OxEng; OxThe; Pen ENG; PlP&P; REn; REnWD; WebE&AL*

Chapman, Gilbert Whipple
American. Businessman, Cultural Leader
b. May 24, 1902 in Woodmere, New York
d. Dec 16, 1979 in Manhattan, New York
Source: *BiE&WWA; CurBio 57, 80; NewYTBS 79; WhoAm 74, 76, 78*

Chapman, Graham
[Monty Python's Flying Circus]
English. Actor, Writer
b. Jan 8, 1941 in Leicester, England
Source: *BioIn 10; WhoAm 82*

Chapman, John
see: Appleseed, Johnny

Chapman, John (Arthur)
American. Drama Critic
b. Jun 25, 1900 in Denver, Colorado
d. Jan 19, 1972 in Westport, Connecticut
Source: *AmAu&B; ConAu 33R; WhAm 5*

Chapman, Leonard F, Jr.
American. Brigadier General
b. Nov 3, 1913 in Key West, Florida
Source: *CurBio 68; WhoGov 72; WhoS&SW 73*

Chapman, Mark David
American. Murderer
Shot, killed John Lennon, Dec 8, 1980.
b. May 10, 1955 in Fort Worth, Texas
Source: *BioIn 12*

Chappell, William
English. Dancer
b. Sep 27, 1908 in Wolverhampton, England
Source: *BioIn 3, 4, 11; Who 74; WhoThe 72, 77*

Chapple, Stanley
English. Symphony Conductor
b. Oct 29, 1900 in London, England
Source: *BioIn 5; Who 74; WhoMus 72*

Char, Rene (Emile)
French. Poet
b. Jun 14, 1907 in L'Isle Sorgue, France
Source: *CasWL; CnMWL; ConAu 13R; EncWL; EvEuW; IntWW 74; ModRL; OxFr; Pen EUR; REn; TwCW; WhoAm 74; WhoTwCL; WhoWor 74; WorAu*

Charboneau, Joe (Joseph)
"Super Joe"
American. Baseball Player
b. Jun 17, 1955 in Belvedere, Illinois
Source: *BaseEn; NewYTBS 81; PseudN*

Charcot, Jean Baptiste Etienne Auguste
French. Explorer, Neurologist
b. Jul 15, 1867 in Neuilly, France
d. Sep 16, 1936 in Iceland
Source: *DcScB; NewCol 75*

Charcot, Jean Martin
French. Physician
b. Nov 29, 1825 in Paris, France
d. Aug 16, 1893
Source: *DcBiPP; McGEWB; WebBD 80*

Chardin, Jean Baptiste Simeon
French. Artist
b. Nov 2, 1699 in Paris, France
d. Dec 6, 1779 in Paris, France
Source: *AtlBL; OxFr; REn*

Chardonnet, Louis Marie
French. Chemist, Inventor
Patented rayon, 1884, first artificial fiber commonly used.
b. May 1, 1839 in Besancon, France
d. Mar 12, 1924 in Paris, France
Source: *AsBiEn*

Chares
Greek. Sculptor
b. 320BC
Source: *NewCol 75; WebBD 80*

Charisse, Cyd
[Tula Ellice Finklea; Mrs. Tony Martin]
American. Dancer, Actress
b. Mar 8, 1923 in Amarillo, Texas
Source: *BiDFilm; CmMov; CurBio 54; FilmgC; InWom; IntMPA 75, 76, 77, 78, 79, 80, 81, 82; MotPP; MovMk; OxFilm; WhoAm 74, 76, 78, 80, 82; WhoHol A; WorEFlm*

Charlemagne
[Charles the Great]
King of the Franks
Conquered, ruled almost all Christian lands of Europe; crowned emperor, 800.
b. Apr 2, 742
d. Jan 28, 814
Source: *DcEuL; DcSpL; NewC; OxFr; OxGer; REn; WebBD 80*

Charles I
English. King
b. Nov 19, 1600
d. Jan 30, 1649
Source: *BioIn 10; DcBiPP; WebBD 80*

Charles II
English. King
b. May 29, 1630
d. 1685
Source: *BioIn 10; DcBiPP; WebBD 80*

Charles V
Holy Roman Emperor
b. Feb 24, 1500 in Ghent, Flanders
d. Sep 21, 1558 in Spain
Source: *BioIn 10; DcBiPP; McGEWB; WebBD 80*

Charles VII
Holy Roman Emperor
b. 1697
d. 1745
Source: *NewCol 75; WebBD 80*

Charles XII
King of Sweden
b. 1682
d. 1718
Source: *NewCol 75; WebBD 80*

Charles Martel
Ruler of Franks
Source: *OxFr; REn*

Charles, Prince
[Charles Philip Arthur George]
English. Heir to British Throne
Invested as Prince of Wales and Earl of Chester, Jul 1, 1969.
b. Nov 14, 1948 in London, England
Source: *BioIn 11; BkPepl; CurBio 69*

Charles the Bald
French. Ruler
b. 823
d. 877
Source: *NewCol 75*

Charles, Ezzard
American. Boxer
Heavyweight champion, 1949-51.
b. Jul 7, 1921 in Lawrenceville, Georgia
d. May 28, 1975 in Chicago, Illinois
Source: *BioNews 74; CurBio 49; WhoBox 74*

Charles, Jacques-Alexandre-Cesar
French. Physicist, Mathematician
b. Nov 12, 1746 in Beaugency, France
d. Apr 7, 1823 in Paris, France
Source: *AsBiEn; BioIn 1, 7; DcScB*

Charles, Ray
[Ray Charles Robinson]
American. Singer, Composer, Musician
Won 10 Grammy awards; appeared in movie *The Blues Brothers.*
b. Sep 23, 1930 in Albany, Georgia
Source: *BioNews 74; BkPepl; CelR 73; CurBio 65; EncAB-H; WhoAm 74, 76, 78, 80, 82; WhoBlA 75; WhoWor 74*

Charleson, Ian
Scottish. Actor
Starred in *Chariots of Fire,* 1981.
b. Aug 11, 1949 in Edinburgh, Scotland
Source: *NewYTBS 81; WhoThe 81*

Charlevoix, Pierre Francis Xavier de
French. Traveler, Author
b. Oct 29, 1682 in Saint Quentin, France
d. Feb 1, 1761 in La Fleche, France
Source: *BiDSA; OxCan*

Charlie Daniels Band, The
[Tom "Bigfoot" Crain; Charlie Daniels; Joe "Taz" DiGregorio; Fred Edwards; Charlie Hatward; Don Murray]
American. Rock Group
Source: *IlEncRk*

Charlip, Remy
American. Dancer, Author, Actor
b. Jan 10, 1929 in Brooklyn, New York
Source: *AuBYP; ChPo S1; ConAu 33R; IlsCB 1946, 1957; SmATA 4; ThrBJA; WrDr 76*

Charlotte Aldegonde E M Wilhelmine
Luxembourg. Grand Duchess
b. Jan 23, 1896
Source: *InWom; IntWW 74*

Charlotte Sophia
English. Wife of George III
b. 1744
d. 1818
Source: *InWom*

Charlton, Manny
see: Nazareth

Charlton, Robert
British. Soccer Player
b. Oct 11, 1937
Source: *Who 74*

Charmoli, Tony
American. Choreographer
b. in Minnesota
Source: *WhoAm 74, 78*

Charney, Nicolas Herman
American. Publisher
b. May 11, 1941 in Saint Paul, Minnesota
Source: *WhoAm 74, 76, 78, 80, 82*

Charoux, Siegfried
British. Sculptor
b. 1896
d. Apr 26, 1967 in London, England
Source: *BioIn 8*

Charpentier, Gustave
French. Composer
b. Jun 25, 1860 in Dieuze, France
d. Feb 18, 1956 in Paris, France
Source: *OxFr; REn*

Charpentier, Marc-Antoine
French. Composer
b. 1634 in Paris, France
d. Feb 24, 1704 in Paris, France
Source: *REn*

Charriere, Henri
"Papillon"
French. Author, Criminal
Murderer sent to Devil's Island, 1931, escaped 1941; played by Steve McQueen in *Papillion,* 1973.
b. 1906
d. Jul 29, 1973 in Madrid, Spain
Source: *ConAu 101; NewYTBE 73; WhScrn 77*

Charron, Pierre
French. Theologian
b. 1541 in Paris, France
d. Nov 16, 1603 in Paris, France
Source: *BioIn 6; CasWL; DcEuL; OxFr; Pen EUR*

Charteris, Leslie
American. Author, Producer
b. May 12, 1907 in Singapore
Source: *AmAu&B; Au&Wr 71; ConAu 5R; EncMys; EvLB; FilmgC; IntMPA 75, 76, 77, 78, 79, 80, 81, 82; IntWW 74; LongCTC; MnBBF; NewC; REn; REnAL; TwCA, SUP; TwCW; Who 74; WhoAm 74, 76, 78, 80, 82; WhoS&SW 73; WrDr 76*

Chartier, Emile Auguste
see: Alain, pseud.

Chase, Charley
American. Comedian
b. Oct 20, 1893 in Baltimore, Maryland
d. Jun 20, 1940 in Hollywood, California
Source: *CurBio 40; MotPP; OxFilm; TwYS; WhScrn 74, 77; WhoHol B; WorEFlm*

Chase, "Chevy" (Cornelius Crane)
American. Actor, Comedian
Starred on "Saturday Night Live"; won Emmy, 1976.
b. Oct 8, 1943 in New York, New York
Source: *BioIn 10; WhoAm 80, 82*

Chase, Chris
American. Author, Actress
Source: *AuNews 1*

Chase, Ilka
American. Author, Actress, Humorist
b. Apr 8, 1905 in New York, New York
d. Feb 15, 1978 in Mexico City, Mexico
Source: *AmAu&B; CelR 73; ConAu 61, 77; CurBio 42; FamA&A; FilmgC; InWom; IntMPA 75, 76, 77; MovMk; NotNAT; REnAL; ThFT; WhoAm 74; WhoHol A; WhoThe 77*

Chase, Mary Coyle
American. Author, Dramatist
Best known for Pulitzer Prize winning play *Harvey*, 1944.
b. Feb 25, 1907 in Denver, Colorado
d. Oct 20, 1981 in Denver, Colorado
Source: *AmAu&B; AmWomWr; AuBYP; BioIn 1, 3, 4, 6, 7, 8, 10; CnDAL; ConAu 73, 77; CurBio 45, 82; DcLEL; EncWT; InWom; LongCTC; McGEWB; ModWD; NewYTBS 81; OxAmL; REn; REnAL; TwCA SUP; WhoAm 74, 76, 78; WhoAmW 58, 64, 66, 68, 70, 72, 74; WrDr 76*

Chase, Mary Ellen
American. Children's Author
b. Feb 24, 1887 in Blue Hill, Maine
d. Jul 28, 1973 in Northampton, Massachusetts
Source: *ConAu 41R; ConAu P-1; CurBio 40, 73; OxAmL; Pen AM; REn; REnAL; SmATA 10; TwCA, SUP; WhAm 5*

Chase, Philander
American. Clergyman
b. Dec 14, 1775 in Cornish, New Hampshire
d. Sep 20, 1852 in Robin's Nest, Illinois
Source: *Alli; AmBi; ApCAB; CyAL 1; DcAmAu; DcAmB; DcNAA; Drake; OhA&B; TwCBDA; WebAB; WhAm H*

Chase, Richard Volney
American. Literary Critic, Educator
b. Oct 12, 1914 in Lakeport, New Hampshire
d. Aug 26, 1962 in Plymouth, Massachusetts
Source: *AmAu&B; BioIn 4, 6, 9; Pen AM; REnAL; TwCA SUP*

Chase, Salmon Portland
American. Supreme Court Justice
b. Jan 13, 1808 in Cornish, New Hampshire
d. May 7, 1873 in Washington, DC
Source: *AmAu&B; AmBi; ApCAB; BbD; BiAuS; BiD&SB; BiDrAC; BiDrUSE; DcAmB; DcNAA; Drake; EncAB-H; OhA&B; TwCBDA; WebAB; WhAm H; WhAmP*

Chase, Samuel
American. Revolutionary Leader
b. Apr 17, 1741 in Somerset County, Missouri
d. Jun 19, 1811 in Baltimore, Maryland
Source: *AmBi; ApCAB; BiAuS; BiDrAC; DcAmB; Drake; TwCBDA; WebAB; WhAm H; WhAmP*

Chase, Stuart
American. Author, Economist
b. Mar 8, 1888 in Somersworth, New Hampshire
Source: *AmAu&B; ChPo S2; ConAmA; CurBio 40; DcLEL; IntWW 74; LongCTC; OxAmL; REn; REnAL; TwCA, SUP; WebAB; WhNAA; Who 74; WhoAm 74; WhoWor 74*

Chase, Sylvia
American. Broadcast Journalist
b. 1942
Source: *BioIn 10; WhoAm 80, 82*

Chase, William Curtis
American. Army Officer
b. Mar 9, 1895 in Providence, Rhode Island
Source: *WebAMB*

Chase, William Merritt
American. Artist
b. Nov 1, 1849 in Williamsburg, Indiana
d. Oct 25, 1916
Source: *AmBi; ApCAB; DcAmB; OxAmL; TwCBDA; WhAm 1*

Chasins, Abram
American. Pianist, Composer
b. Aug 17, 1903 in New York, New York
Source: *AmAu&B; AmSCAP 66; ConAu 37R; CurBio 60; WhoAm 74; WhoMus 72; WhoWorJ 72*

Chataway, Christopher John
English. Journalist, Politician
b. Jan 31, 1931
Source: *BioIn 7; IntWW 74; Who 74; WhoWor 74*

Chateaubriand, Francois Rene de
French. Author, Statesman
b. Sep 4, 1768 in Saint-Malo, France
d. Jul 4, 1848 in Paris, France
Source: *ApCAB; AtlBL; BbD; BiD&SB; BiDLA SUP; CasWL; CyWA; DcBiA; DcEuL; EuAu; EvEuW; NewC; OxAmL; OxEng; OxFr; Pen EUR; RComWL; REn; REnAL*

Chatfield, Alfred E Montacute, Baron
British. Admiral
b. 1873
d. Nov 15, 1967 in London, England
Source: *BioIn 8*

Chatterton, Ruth
American. Actress, Author
b. Dec 24, 1893 in New York, New York
d. Nov 24, 1961 in Norwalk, Connecticut
Source: *AmAu&B; BiDFilm; CmMov; FilmgC; InWom; MotPP; MovMk; ThFT; WhAm 4; WhScrn 74, 77; WhoHol B; WomWMM*

Chatterton, Thomas
English. Poet
Claimed his "Rowley Poems" were copies of 15th c. manuscripts.
b. Nov 20, 1752 in Bristol, England
d. Aug 25, 1770 in Bristol, England
Source: *Alli; AtlBL; BbD; BiD&SB; BrAu; CasWL; Chambr 2; ChPo, ; CnE&AP; CrtT 2; DcEnA; DcEnL; DcEuL; DcLEL; EvLB; MouLC 2; NewC; OxEng; Pen ENG; RComWL; REn; WebE&AL*

Chaucer, Geoffrey
English. Poet
Wrote *The Canterbury Tales;* circa 1387, but never completed.
b. 1340 in London, England
d. Oct 25, 1400 in London, England
Source: *Alli; AnCL; AtlBL; BbD; BiD&SB; BrAu; CasWL; Chambr 1; ChPo, S1, S2; CnE&AP; CrtT 1; CyWA; DcEnA; DcEnL; DcEuL; DcLEL; EvLB; MouLC 1; NewC; OxEng; Pen ENG; PoLE; RAdv 1; RComWL; REn; WebE&AL*

Chaudhuri, Haridas
Indian. Educator, Author
b. May 24, 1913 in Calcutta, India
d. 1975
Source: *ConAu 5R; WhoWest 74*

Chauncey, Isaac
American. Military Leader
b. Feb 20, 1772 in Black Rock, Connecticut
d. Jan 27, 1840 in Washington, DC
Source: *AmBi; ApCAB; DcAmB; Drake; TwCBDA; WhAm H*

Chausson, Ernest
French. Composer
b. Jun 21, 1855 in Paris, France
d. Jun 10, 1899 in Limay, France
Source: *AtlBL; NewCol 75; WebBD 80*

Chautemps, Camille
French. Premier
b. Feb 1, 1885 in Paris, France
d. Jul 1, 1963 in Washington, DC
Source: *WhAm 4*

Chauvire, Yvette
French. Dancer
b. Apr 22, 1917 in Paris, France
Source: *BioIn 1, 2, 3, 4, 5; IntWW 74; Who 74; WhoWor 74*

Chavez, Carlos
Mexican. Composer, Conductor
b. Jun 13, 1899 in Mexico City, Mexico
d. Aug 2, 1978 in Mexico City, Mexico
Source: *AmSCAP 66; CurBio 49; DcCM; IntWW 74; REn; WhoMus 72; WhoS&SW 73; WhoWor 74*

Chavez, Cesar
American. Labor Union Official
Organized National Farm Workers Assn. 1962.
b. Mar 31, 1927 in Yuma, Arizona
Source: *BioNews 74; BkPepl; BusPN; CelR 73; CurBio 69; EncAB-H; WebAB; WhoAm 82; WhoWor 74*

Chavis, Ben
[Wilmington 10]
American. Civil Rights Activist
Source: *BioIn 10*

Chavis, John
American. Clergyman, Educator
b. 1763
d. 1838
Source: *BioIn 1, 2, 7, 9*

Chayefsky, "Paddy" (Sidney)
American. Dramatist
Best known for screenplays *Marty,* 1953; won Oscar, 1976, for *Network.*
b. Jan 29, 1923 in New York, New York
d. Aug 1, 1981 in New York, New York
Source: *AmAu&B; AmSCAP 66; BiE&WWA; AmSCAP 80; BioIn 3, 4, 10, 11, 12; CelR 73; CnMD; CnThe; ConAu 9R, 104; ConDr 73, 77; CroCD; CurBio 57, 81; DcFM; DcLEL 1940; EncSF; EncWT; FilmgC; IntAu&W 76, 77; IntMPA 75, 76, 77, 78, 79; IntWW 74, 75, 76, 77, 78; LinLib L; McGEWD; ModWD; NewYTBS 81; NewYTET; NotNAT; OxAmL; OxFilm; Pen AM; PlP&P; REnAL; WebAB; WhoAm 74, 76, 78, 80; WhoE 74; WhoThe 77; WhoTwCL; WhoWor 74; WorAu; WorEFlm; WrDr 76*

Chayes, Abram J
American. Lawyer, Government Official
b. Jul 18, 1922 in Chicago, Illinois
Source: *BioIn 5, 11; DrAS 74P; IntWW 74; WhoAm 74, 76, 78, 80, 82; WhoWorJ 72*

Cheap Trick
[Bun E Carlos; Rick Nielsen; Tom Petesson; Robin Zander]
American. Rock Group
Source: *ConMuA 80; WhoRock 81*

Checker, Chubby
[Ernest Evans]
American. Rock Musician
Recorded "The Twist," which became dance sensation of early 1960's.
b. Oct 3, 1941 in South Philadelphia, Pennsylvania
Source: *AmSCAP 66; FilmgC; WhoAm 74; WhoBlA 75; WhoHol A*

Cheech and Chong
[Tommy Chong; Cheech Marin]
American. Comedy Group
Source: *EncPR&S*

Cheever, John
American. Author
Won Pulitzer Prize, 1979; noted for subtle, comic style.
b. May 27, 1912 in Quincy, Massachusetts
d. Jun 18, 1982 in Ossining, New York
Source: *AmAu&B; AmWr SUP; CasWL; ConAu 5R, 5NR; ConLC 3, 7, 8, 11; ConNov 72, 76; CurBio 75, 82; DcLB 2; DcLEL 1940; DrAF 76; EncWL; IntAu&W 76, 77; IntWW 74, 75, 76, 77, 78; LinLib L; ModAL, SUP; NewYTBS 78, 79, 82; OxAmL; Pen AM; Po&Wr 77; RAdv 1; REn; REnAL; TwCW; WebE&AL; Who 82; WhoAm 74, 76, 78, 80, 82; WhoTwCL; WhoWor 74, 76, 78; WorAu; WrDr 76, 80*

Chekhov, Anton Pavlovich
Russian. Author, Dramatist
Wrote *Three Sisters,* 1901, *The Cherry Orchard,* 1904.
b. Jan 17, 1860 in Teganrog, Russia
d. Jul 2, 1904 in Badenweiler, Germany
Source: *AtlBL; CasWL; ClDMEL; CnMD; CnThe; CyWA; DcEuL; DcRusL; EncWL; EuAu; EvEuW; McGEWD; ModSL 1; ModWD; NewC; OxEng; OxThe; Pen EUR; PlP&P, A; RComWL; REn; REnWD*

Chekhov, Michael
Russian. Actor, Motion Picture Director
b. Aug 28, 1891 in Leningrad, Russia
d. Sep 30, 1955 in Beverly Hills, California
Source: *FilmgC; MotPP; OxThe; WhScrn 74, 77; WhoHol B*

Chen, Joyce Liao
Restaurateur
b. 1917
Source: *BioIn 9*

Cheney, John Vance
American. Poet, Librarian
b. Dec 29, 1848 in Groveland, New York
d. May 1, 1922 in San Diego, California
Source: *AmAu; AmAu&B; AmLY; BbD; BiD&SB; DcAmAu; DcNAA; OxAmL; REnAL*

Cheney, Sheldon Warren
American. Author, Critic
b. Jun 29, 1886 in Berkeley, California
d. Oct 10, 1980 in Berkeley, California
Source: *AmAu&B; BiE&WWA; BioIn 4; ConAu 102; IntAu&W 76; NotNAT; REnAL; TwCA, SUP; WhE&EA; WhThe; WhoAm 74, 76, 78; WhoAmA 73, 76, 78; WhoWor 74, 76*

Chenier, Marie-Andre de
French. Author, Poet
b. Oct 30, 1762 in Constantinople, Turkey
d. Jul 25, 1794
Source: *AtlBL; BbD; BiD&SB; CasWL; DcEuL; EuAu; EvEuW; OxEng; OxFr; Pen EUR; REn*

Chenier, Phil(ip)
American. Basketball Player
b. Oct 30, 1950 in Berkeley, California
Source: *OfNBA; WhoBbl 73*

Chennault, Anna Chan
[Mrs. Claire Lee Chennault]
Chinese. Lobbyist, Author
b. Jun 23, 1925 in Peking, China
Source: *AmAu&B; ConAu 61; ForWC 70; WhoAm 74, 76, 78, 80, 82; WhoAmP 73; WhoAmW 77; WhoS&SW 73*

Chennault, Claire Lee
American. Aviator
b. Sep 6, 1890 in Commerce, Texas
d. Jul 27, 1958
Source: *AmAu&B; CurBio 42, 58; WhAm 3*

Chenoweth, Dean
"Comeback Kid"
American. Hydroplane Racer
b. 1934? in Xenia, Ohio
d. Jul 31, 1982 in Pasco, Washington
Source: *NF*

Cheops
[Khufu]
Egyptian. Pharoah
Source: *BioIn 2, 3, 7, 10, 11; NewCol 75; WebBD 80*

Cher
[Cher Bono; Cherylynn LaPiere; Cherilyn Sarkisian; Sonny and Cher]
American. Singer
Hits include "Gypsies, Tramps and Thieves"; "Half Breed."
b. May 20, 1946 in El Centro, California
Source: *BkPepl; CelR 73; CurBio 74; HerW; IntMPA 77, 78, 79, 80, 81, 82; WhoAm 74; WhoHol A*

Chermayeff, Ivan
American. Artist, Designer
b. Jun 6, 1932 in London, England
Source: *BioIn 8, 9, 10; IlsCB 1957; WhoAm 74, 76, 78, 80, 82; WhoAmA 73; WhoE 74*

Chermayeff, Serge
American. Author
b. Oct 8, 1900 in Caucasia, Colombia
Source: *ConAu 21R*

Chernenko, Konstantin Ustinovich
Russian. Politician
Member of Politburo; Brezhnev's chief of staff.
b. Sep 24, 1911 in Bolshaya Tes, Russia
Source: *IntWW 78, 79, 80, 81; NewYTBS 78; WhoSocC 78*

Cherniavsky, Josef
Russian. Symphony Conductor, Composer
b. Mar 31, 1895 in Russia
d. Nov 3, 1959 in New York, New York
Source: *AmSCAP 66; BioIn 5*

Chernov, Viktor Mikhailovich
Russian. Journalist
b. 1876
d. Apr 15, 1952 in New York, New York
Source: *WebBD 80*

Cherrington, Ben Mark
American. UN Charter Author, Educator
b. Nov 1, 1885 in Gibbon, Nebraska
d. May 4, 1980 in Denver, Colorado
Source: *BioIn 6; WhoAm 74; WhoWest 74*

Cherry, Don(ald Stewart)
Canadian. Broadcaster, Former Hockey Coach
b. Feb 5, 1934 in Kingston, ON
Source: *BioIn 11; WhoAm 82*

Cherubini, Maria Luigi
Italian. Composer
b. Sep 14, 1760 in Florence, Italy
d. Mar 15, 1842 in Paris, France
Source: *NewEOp 71; WebBD 80*

Cherwell, Frederick Alexander L
English. Physicist
b. 1886 in Sidmouth, England
d. Jul 2, 1957
Source: *BioIn 1, 2, 3, 4, 5, 6, 7, 8; CurBio 52, 57*

Chesbro, "Happy Jack" (John Dwight)
American. Baseball Player
Pitcher, NY Highlanders; won 41 games, 1904, highest total in 20th c.
b. Jun 5, 1874 in North Adams, Massachusetts
d. Nov 6, 1931 in Conway, Massachusetts
Source: *BaseEn; BioIn 3, 7; WhoProB 73*

Chesebrough, Robert Augustus
American. Chemist
b. Jan 9, 1837 in London, England
d. Sep 8, 1933 in Spring Lake, New Jersey
Source: *BioIn 3; TwCBDA; WhAm 1*

Cheshire, Maxine
[Mrs. Bert W Cheshire]
American. Journalist
Reporter, Washington *Post,* 1954-65; columnist LA Times Syndicate since 1965.
b. Apr 5, 1930 in Harlan, Kentucky
Source: *CelR 73; WhoAm 74, 76, 78, 80, 82*

Chesney, Francis Rawdon
British. Soldier, Explorer
b. Mar 16, 1789 in Ireland
d. Jan 30, 1872
Source: *NewCol 75; WebBD 80*

Chessex, Jacques
Swiss. Author
b. Mar 1, 1934 in Payerne, Switzerland
Source: *BioIn 10; ConAu 65*

Chessman, Caryl Whittier
American. Criminal, Author
Lived on Death Row 12 years; Alan Alda played him in movie of his life, 1977.
b. May 27, 1921 in Saint Joseph, Michigan
d. May 2, 1960 in San Quentin, California
Source: *AmAu&B; Blood; ConAu 73; WebAB*

Chesnutt, Charles Waddell
American. Author, Lawyer
b. Jun 20, 1858 in Cleveland, Ohio
d. Nov 15, 1932 in Cleveland, Ohio
Source: *AmAu&B; AmLY; BlkAW; CasWL; CnDAL; CyWA; DcAmAu; DcNAA; OhA&B; OxAmL; TwCA SUP*

Chesterfield, Philip Dormer, Earl
[Philip Dormer Stanhope]
English. Author, Statesman
b. Sep 22, 1694 in London, England
d. Mar 24, 1773 in London, England
Source: *Alli; AtlBL; BbD; BiD&SB; BrAu; CasWL; Chambr 3; CyWA; DcEnA; DcEnL; DcEuL; DcLEL; EvLB; MouLC 2; NewC; OxEng; Pen ENG; REn; WebE&AL*

Chesterton, Gilbert Keith
English. Author, Journalist
b. May 29, 1874 in Kensington, England
d. Jun 14, 1936 in Chiltern Hills, England
Source: *AnCL; AtlBL; BkC 6; CasWL; CathA 1930; Chambr 3; ChPo, S1, S2; DcLEL; EvLB; OxEng; Pen ENG; TwCA, SUP; TwCW; WhoLA*

Chevalier, Maurice Auguste
French. Actor, Singer
b. Sep 12, 1888 in Paris, France
d. Jan 1, 1972 in Paris, France
Source: *BiDFilm; BiE&WWA; CmMov; ConAu 33R; CurBio 48, 69, 72; Film 1; FilmgC; MovMk; OxFilm; OxThe; WhAm 5; WhScrn 77; WhoHol B; WorEFlm*

Chevallier, Gabriel
French. Author
b. May 1895 in Lyons, France
d. 1969
Source: *CasWL; EvEuW; REn; TwCW*

Chevreul, Michel
French. Chemist
b. Aug 31, 1786 in Angers, France
d. Apr 9, 1889 in Paris, France
Source: *BioIn 1, 3, 5, 6, 10; NewCol 75*

Chevrolet, Gaston
Auto Manufacturer
Source: *NF*

Chevrolet, Louis
American. Auto Racer, Designer
Defeated Barney Oldfield in auto race, 1905.
b. 1879 in Switzerland
d. Jun 6, 1941 in Detroit, Michigan
Source: *CurBio 41*

Chew, Peter
American. Horse Racing Authority, Author
b. Apr 5, 1924 in New Rochelle, New York
Source: *ConAu 57*

Chiang, Ching
[Chiang Ching Mao; Ping Lan]
Chinese. Actress, Wife of Mao
b. 1913 in Chucheng, China
Source: *DcOrL 1; WomWMM*

Chang, Ching-Kuo
Chinese. President
b. 1906
Source: *BioIn 1, 3, 4, 6, 7, 8, 9, 10, 11*

Chiang Kai-Shek
Chinese. Nationalist Statesman
b. Oct 31, 1886 in Fenghua, China
d. Apr 5, 1975 in Taipei, Taiwan
Source: *CurBio 40, 53; REn; WhAm 6; Who 74*

Chiang Mei-Ling
[Madame Chiang Kai-Shek; Mayling Soong]
Chinese. Sociologist
b. 1899
Source: *CurBio 40; REn; Who 82*

Chiang, Yee
American. Author, Educator
b. May 19, 1903 in Kiukiang, China
d. Oct 17, 1977 in Peking, China
Source: *ConAu 65, 73; IlsCB 1744, 1946; IntAu&W 77; IntWW 75, 76, 77, 78; LinLib L; LongCTC; NewYTBS 77; TwCA SUP; WhAm 7; Who 74; WhoAm 74, 76, 78; WhoE 75*

Chicago, Judy
[Judy Cohen]
American. Artist, Feminist
b. Jul 20, 1939 in Chicago, Illinois
Source: *BioIn 9, 10; ConArt; ConAu 85; CurBio 81; NewYTBS 79; WhoAm 76, 78, 80, 82; WhoAmA 73, 76, 78, 80; WhoAmW 75, 77, 79; WomWMM B*

Chicago
[Peter Cetera; Donnie Dacus; Laudir DeOliveira; Terry Kath; Robert Lamm; Lee Loughnane; James Pankow Walter Parazaider; Walt Perry; Daniel Seraphine]
American. Rock Group
Formed, 1968 as Chicago Transit Authority; albums have sold over 20 million copies.
Source: *BiDAmM; IlEncRk*

Chicago Seven, The
[Rennie Davis; David Dellinger; John Radford Froines; Tom Hayden; Abbie Hoffman; Jerry Rubin; Lee Weiner]
American. Radicals
Disrupted the 1968 Democratic National Convention in Chicago.
Source: *NF*

Chichester, Sir Francis Charles
English. Cartographer, Yachtsman
b. Sep 17, 1901 in North Devon, England
d. Aug 26, 1972 in Plymouth, England
Source: *Au&Wr 71; ConAu 37R; ConAu P-1; CurBio 67, 72; NewYTBE 72; WhAm 5*

Chickering, Jonas
American. Piano Manufacturer
Built first grand piano with full iron frame in single casting, 1837.
b. Apr 5, 1798 in Mason Village, New Hampshire
d. Dec 8, 1853 in Boston, Massachusetts
Source: *AmBi; ApCAB; DcAmB; Drake; TwCBDA; WhAm H*

Chidsey, Donald Barr
American. Author, Historian
b. May 14, 1902 in Elizabeth, New Jersey
d. 1981 in New London, Connecticut
Source: *AmAu&B; AmNov; BioIn 2, 4, 9; ConAu 5R, 103; REnAL; SmATA 3*

Ch'ien Lung
[Hung-Li]
Chinese. Emperor during Ching Dynasty
b. Sep 25, 1711 in Peking, China
d. Feb 7, 1799 in Peking, China
Source: *BioIn 4, 9, 10; NewCol 75; WebBD 80*

Chikamatsu, Monzaemon
[Sugimori Mobumori]
Japanese. Dramatist
b. 1653 in Eichizen Province, Japan
d. Jan 6, 1725
Source: *McGEWB; NewCol 75*

Child, Julia McWilliams
[Mrs. Paul Child]
American. Food Expert, Author
Star of "The French Chef," 1962--; wrote *Mastering the Art of French Cooking*, 1961.
b. Aug 15, 1912 in Pasadena, California
Source: *AmAu&B; BkPepl; CelR 73; ConAu 41R; CurBio 67; ForWC 70; InWom; WhoAm 74, 76, 78, 80, 82; WhoWor 74*

Child, Lydia Maria
American. Author, Feminist
b. Feb 11, 1802 in Medford, Massachusetts
d. Oct 22, 1880 in Wayland, Massachusetts
Source: *Alli, SUP; AmAu; AmAu&B; AmBi; AmWom; ApCAB; BbD; BiD&SB; CarSB; CasWL; Chambr 3; ChPo, S1, S2; CyAl 2; DcAmAu; DcAmB; DcEnL; DcLEL; DcNAA; Drake; EncAB-H; EvLB; HerW; InWom; NotAW; OxAmL; REnAL; Str&VC; TwCBDA; WebAB; WhAm H*

Childe, Vere Gordon
Australian. Archeologist
b. Apr 14, 1892 in Sydney, Australia
d. Sep 19, 1957 in Mount Victoria, Australia
Source: *BioIn 1, 4, 5; McGEWB*

Childers, (Robert) Erskine
Irish. Author, Rebel
b. Jun 25, 1870 in London, England
d. Nov 24, 1922 in Dublin, Ireland
Source: *DcLEL; EncMys; EvLB; LongCTC; REn; TwCA; TwCW*

Childs
American. Family of Restauranteurs
Source: *WebBD 80*

Childs, George William
American. Publisher
b. May 12, 1829 in Baltimore, Maryland
d. Feb 3, 1894 in Philadelphia, Pennsylvania
Source: *AmAu&B; BbD; BiD&SB; BioIn 4, 8; DcAmAu; DcNAA*

Childs, Marquis William
American. Journalist, Author
b. Mar 17, 1903 in Clinton, Iowa
Source: *AmAu&B; CelR 73; ConAu 61; CurBio 43; IntWW 74; OxAmL; REn; REnAL; TwCA SUP; WhoAm 74, 76, 78, 80, 82; WhoS&SW 73*

Chiles, Lawton Mainor, Jr.
American. Senator
b. Apr 3, 1930 in Lakeland, Florida
Source: *BioNews 74; CngDr 74; CurBio 71; IntWW 74; WhoAm 74, 76, 78, 80, 82; WhoAmP 73; WhoGov 72; WhoS&SW 73*

Chilton, Alex
see: Box Tops, The

Chinaglia, Giorgio
Italian. Soccer Player
b. Jan 24, 1947 in Carrara, Italy
Source: *BioIn 12; NewYTBS 81*

Chinard, Gilbert
French. Professor
b. Oct 17, 1881 in Chatellerault, France
d. Feb 8, 1972
Source: *AmAu&B; NewYTBE 72; OxAmL; WhAm 5; WhNAA*

Chinmoy, Sri
see: Ghose, Sri Chinmoy Kumar

Chippendale, Thomas
English. Cabinetmaker
Catalog, *Gentleman and Cabinet-Maker's Director,* 1754, influenced 18th c. designs.
b. 1718 in Yorkshire, England
d. Nov 1779 in London, England
Source: *Alli; NewC*

Chipperfield, Joseph Eugene
English. Author
b. Apr 20, 1912 in Saint Austell, England
Source: *Au&Wr 71; AuBYP; ConAu 9R; MorJA; SmATA 2*

Chirac, Jacques
French. Prime Minister
b. Nov 29, 1932 in Paris, France
Source: *IntWW 74; WhoWor 74*

Chirico, Giorgio de
Italian. Artist
b. Jul 10, 1888 in Volos, Greece
d. Nov 20, 1978 in Rome, Italy
Source: *ConArt; CurBio 56, 72, 79; LinLib S; McGDA; McGEWB; NewYTBE 70, 72; NewYTBS 78; REn; Who 74*

Chisholm, Jesse
American. Pioneer
b. 1806? in Tennessee
d. Mar 4, 1868 in Blaine City, Oklahoma
Source: *BioIn 5; NatCAB 19; REnAW; WebAB 79*

Chisholm, Shirley Anita St. Hill
American. Congresswoman, Author
b. Nov 30, 1924 in Brooklyn, New York
Source: *AmAu&B; BiDrAC; CelR 73; CngDr 74; ConAu 29R; CurBio 69; HerW; LivgBAA; WhoAm 74, 76, 78, 80, 82; WhoAmP 73; WhoAmW 77; WhoE 74; WhoBlA 75; WhoGov 72; WrDr 76*

Chisum, John Simpson
American. Cattle Rancher
b. Aug 15, 1824 in Hardeman County, Tennessee
d. Dec 23, 1884 in Eureka Springs, Arkansas
Source: *BioIn 4, 7, 11; DcAmB; WebAB*

Chittenden, Thomas
American. Governor
b. Jan 6, 1730 in East Guilford, Connecticut
d. Aug 25, 1797 in Williston, Vermont
Source: *BioIn 1, 6; DcAmB*

Chivers, Stephen Oswald
British. Businessman
b. 1899
Source: *Who 74*

Choate, Rufus
American. Lawyer, Orator, Senator
b. Oct 1, 1799 in Essex County, Massachusetts
d. Jul 15, 1859 in Halifax, NS
Source: *Alli, SUP; AmAu; AmAu&B; AmBi; ApCAB; BbD; BiAuS; BiD&SB; BiDrAC; CyAl 2; DcAmAu; DcAmB; DcNAA; Drake; REnAL; TwCBDA; WebAB; WhAm H; WhAmP*

Chodorov, Edward
American. Author, Director, Producer
b. Apr 17, 1904 in New York, New York
Source: *AmAu&B; BiE&WWA; ConAu 102; CurBio 44; FilmgC; IntMPA 75, 76, 77, 78, 79, 80, 81, 82; ModWD; NotNAT; OxAmL; REnAL; WhoThe 77*

Chodorov, Jerome
American. Dramatist, Director
b. Aug 10, 1911 in New York, New York
Source: *WhoWor 74*

Ch'oe Kyu Ha
Korean. Diplomat
b. Jul 16, 1919 in Kangwon Province, Korea
Source: *WhoWor 74*

Choiseul, Cesar, Comte Du Plessis-Praslin, duc de
French. Soldier
Marshal of France; credited with making confection "pralines."
b. 1598
d. 1675
Source: *NewCol 75*

Chomsky, Marvin
American. Motion Picture Director
b. May 23, 1929 in Bronx, New York
Source: *IntMPA 77, 78, 79, 80, 81, 82; WhoAm 82*

Chomsky, Noam
American. Linguist, Peace Activist
b. Dec 7, 1928 in Philadelphia, Pennsylvania
Source: *AmAu&B; CelR 73; ConAu 17R; CurBio 70; IntWW 74; Pen AM; WebAB; Who 74; WhoWorJ 72; WrDr 76*

Chones, Jim
American. Basketball Player
b. Oct 30, 1949 in Racine, Wisconsin
Source: *NewYTBS 74; WhoBbl 73*

Chopin, Frederic Francois
[Fryderyk Franciszek Chopin]
Polish. Pianist, Composer
b. Feb 22, 1810 in Zelazowa Wola, Poland
d. Oct 17, 1849 in Paris, France
Source: *AtlBL; NewC; OxFr; REn*

Chopin, Kate
American. Author
b. Feb 8, 1851 in Saint Louis, Missouri
d. Aug 22, 1904 in Saint Louis, Missouri
Source: *AmAu; AmAu&B; BbD; BiDSA; CasWL; CnDAL; DcAmAu; DcLEL; DcNAA; ModAL; REnAL*

Chorzempa, Daniel Walter
American. Musician, Composer
b. Dec 7, 1944 in Minneapolis, Minnesota
Source: *IntWW 74, 75, 76, 77, 78; WhoMus 72*

Chotzinoff, Samuel
American. Pianist, Music Critic
b. Jul 4, 1889 in Vitebsk, Russia
d. Feb 9, 1964
Source: *CurBio 40, 64; WhAm 4*

Chou, En-Lai
Chinese. Communist Leader
A founder of Communist party in China; premier, 1949-76.
b. 1898 in Shaohsing, China
d. Jan 8, 1976 in Peking, China
Source: *REn; WhAm 6; Who 74*

Chouteau, Yvonne
American. Dancer
b. 1929 in Fort Worth, Texas
Source: *BioIn 3, 4, 5*

Chretien, Henri
French. Inventor
Invented anamorphic lens used in cinemascope films.
b. Feb 1, 1879 in Paris, France
d. Feb 6, 1956 in Washington, DC
Source: *DcFM; FilmEn; FilmgC; ObitOF 79; OxFilm; WorEFlm*

Chretien de Troyes
French. Poet
b. 1130?
d. 1183
Source: *AtlBL; BbD; BiD&SB; CasWL; CyWA; DcEuL; EuAu; EvEuW; NewC; OxEng; OxFr*

Christ-Janer, Albert
American. Artist, Author, Educator
b. Jun 13, 1910 in Appleton, Wisconsin
d. Dec 12, 1973 in Como, Italy
Source: *AmAu&B; ConAu 45; NewYTBE 73; WhAm 6; WhoAm 74; WhoAmA 73, 76, 78; WhoWor 74*

Christian IV
Danish. King of Denmark and Norway
Reigned as king, 1588-1648.
b. Apr 12, 1577 in Denmark
d. Feb 28, 1648 in Copenhagen, Denmark
Source: *BioIn 3, 8; NewCol 75; WebBD 80*

Christian, Charlie (Charles)
American. Jazz Musician
b. 1919 in Dallas, Texas
d. Mar 2, 1942 in New York, New York
Source: *WhoJazz 72*

Christian, Dave
[United States Olympic Hockey Team-1980]
American. Hockey Player
b. May 12, 1959 in Warroad, Minnesota
Source: *HocReg*

Christian, Fletcher
English. Mutineer
Leader of mutiny on *Bounty*, Apr 1784; founded colony on Pitcairn Island.
b. 1764
d. 1793
Source: *NewC*

Christian, Linda
[Blanca Rosa Welter]
American. Actress
b. Nov 13, 1923 in Tampico, Mexico
Source: *FilmgC; InWom; IntMPA 75, 76, 77, 78, 79, 80, 81, 82; MotPP; WhoHol A*

Christian, Mary Blount
American. Children's Author
b. Feb 20, 1933 in Houston, Texas
Source: *ConAu 45, 1NR; SmATA 9; WrDr 76*

Christian-Jaque
French. Motion Picture Director
b. Sep 4, 1904 in Paris, France
Source: *BiDFilm; DcFM; FilmgC; OxFilm; WorEFlm*

Christians, Mady
American. Actress
b. Jan 19, 1900 in Vienna, Austria
d. Oct 28, 1951 in Norwalk, Connecticut
Source: *CurBio 45, 51; FilmgC; InWom; MovMk; ThFT; WhScrn 74, 77; WhoHol B*

Christiansen, Arthur
English. Editor
b. Jul 27, 1904 in Wallasey, England
d. Sep 27, 1963
Source: *BioIn 1, 5, 6; ConAu 1R; LongCTC*

Christiansen, Olaf
American. Symphony Conductor
b. 1901 in Minneapolis, Minnesota
Source: *WhoMus 72*

Christie, Dame Agatha Mary Clarissa Miller
"Queen of Crime"
English. Author, Dramatist
Created characters of Hercule Poirot, Miss Jane Marple; wrote over 80 books.
b. 1891 in Torquay, England
d. Jan 12, 1976 in Wallingford, England
Source: *Au&Wr 71; AuBYP; AuNews 1, 2; BiE&WWA; BioNews 74; CasWL; CelR 73; CnThe; ConAu 17R, 61; ConDr 73; ConLC 1, 6, 8, 12; ConNov 72, 76; CurBio 40, 64; DcLEL; EncMys; EvLB; IntWW 74; LongCTC; MnBBF; NewC; OxEng; Pen ENG; PlP&P; REn; TwCA, SUP; TwCW; WhAm 6; Who 74; WhoThe 77; WrDr 76*

Christie, Audrey
American. Actress
b. Jun 27, 1912 in Chicago, Illinois
Source: *BiE&WWA; ForWC 70; NotNAT; WhoHol A; WhoThe 77*

Christie, James
English. Auctioneer
b. 1730 in England
d. 1803
Source: *NewC*

Christie, John
English. Clyndebourne Festival Founder
b. Dec 14, 1882 in Clyndebourne, England
d. Jul 4, 1962 in Clyndebourne, England
Source: *LongCTC*

Christie, John Reginald Halliday
"The Strangler of Notting Hill"
English. Murderer
b. 1899?
d. 1953
Source: *BioIn 4, 5, 6*

Christie, Julie
English. Actress
Won Oscar, 1965, for *Darling;* starred in *Doctor Zhivago,* 1965.
b. Apr 14, 1940 in Chukua, India
Source: *BiDFilm; BkPepl; CelR 73; CurBio 66; FilmgC; InWom; IntMPA 75, 76, 77, 78, 79, 80, 81, 82; IntWW 74; MotPP; MovMk; OxFilm; Who 74; WhoAm 82; WhoHol A; WhoWor 74; WorEFlm*

Christina
Swedish. Queen
b. 1626 in Stockholm, Sweden
d. 1689
Source: *DcEuL; InWom; REn*

Christina
Swedish. Princess
b. 1943
Source: *BioIn 10*

Christina
Dutch. Princess
b. Feb 18, 1947 in Soestdijk, Netherlands
Source: *WhoWor 74*

Christo
[Christo Javacheff]
Bulgarian. Artist
Created 24 mile long fabric fence in Sonoma, Marin Counties, CA, 1972-76.
b. Jun 13, 1935 in Gabrovo, Bulgaria
Source: *CurBio 77*

Christoff, Boris
Bulgarian. Opera Singer
b. May 18, 1918 in Sofia, Bulgaria
Source: *IntWW 74; Who 74; WhoMus 72; WhoWor 74*

Christoff, Steve
[United States Olympic Hockey Team-1980]
American. Hockey Player
b. Jan 23, 1958 in Springfield, Illinois
Source: *HocReg*

Christophe, Henri
Haitian. King
b. 1767 in Grenada, West Indies
d. in Haiti
Source: *ApCAB; Drake; REn*

Christopher, Saint
Christian Martyr
Source: *NewC; REn*

Christopher, Dennis
[Dennis Carelli]
American. Actor
b. 1955 in Philadelphia, Pennsylvania
Source: *BioIn 12*

Christopher, Jordan
American. Actor, Musician
b. 1941 in Youngstown, Ohio
Source: *IntMPA 75, 76, 77, 78, 79, 80, 81, 82; MotPP; WhoHol A*

Christopher, Matthew F
American. Children's Author
b. Aug 16, 1917 in Bath, Pennsylvania
Source: *AuBYP; ConAu 1R, 5NR; MorBMP; SmATA 2; WrDr 76*

Christopher, Sybil Burton
[Mrs. Jordan Christopher; Sybil Williams]
Welsh. Actress, Celebrity
First wife of Richard Burton, 1949-63; married Jordan Christopher, 1965.
b. 1928 in Taylorstown, Wales
Source: *BioIn 6, 7*

Christopher, Warren Miner
American. Lawyer, Government Official
Negotiator for release of American hostages in Iran, 1980-81.
b. Oct 27, 1925 in Scranton, North Dakota
Source: *BioIn 11; WhoAm 78, 80, 82*

Christopher, William
American. Actor
b. Oct 20, in Evanston, Illinois
Source: *WhoAm 80, 82*

Christy, Howard Chandler
American. Artist
b. Jan 10, 1873 in Morgan County, Ohio
d. Mar 4, 1952 in New York, New York
Source: *AmAu&B; ChPo, S2; DcAmB S5; IlsCB 1744; WhAm 3*

Christy, June
American. Singer
b. Nov 20, 1925 in Springfield, Illinois
Source: *WhoAmW 74*

Christy, Marian
American. Journalist
b. Nov 9, 1932 in Ridgefield, Connecticut
Source: *ConAu 65; ForWC 70; WhoAm 82; WhoAmW 77*

Chrysler, Walter Percy
American. Auto Manufacturer
President, Buick Motor Co., 1916-19; founded Chrysler Corp., 1925.
b. Apr 2, 1875 in Wamego, Kansas
d. Aug 18, 1940 in Great Neck, New York
Source: *CurBio 40; DcAmB S2; WebAB; WhAm 1*

Chu Te
Chinese. Army Commander
b. 1886 in Szechwan, China
d. Aug 6, 1976 in Peking, China
Source: *WebBD 80*

Chu Yuan-Chang
see: Ming T'ai-Tsu

Chuikov, Vasili Ivanovitch
Russian. Marshal
b. Feb 12, 1900 in Serebryanye Prudy, Russia
d. Mar 18, 1982 in Moscow, U.S.S.R.
Source: *BioIn 1; CurBio 43, 82; IntWW 74, 75; NewYTBS 82; WhoMilH 76; WhoSocC 78*

Chukovsky, Korney Ivanovich
[Nikolai Ivanovich Korneichuk]
Russian. Scholar, Children's Author
b. Mar 31, 1882 in Saint Petersburg, Russia
d. Oct 28, 1969 in Moscow, U.S.S.R.
Source: *AuBYP; CasWL; ChPo S1, S2; ConAu 5R, 25R, 4NR; Pen EUR; SmATA 5; WorAu*

Chukrai, Grigori
Russian. Motion Picture Director
b. 1921 in Melitopol, U.S.S.R.
Source: *DcFM; FilmgC; OxFilm; WorEFlm*

Chun Doo Hwan
Korean. President
b. Jan 23, 1931 in Naechonri, Korea
Source: *CurBio 81; NewYTBS 81*

Chung, Arthur
Guyanese. President
b. Jan 10, 1918 in Demerara, Guyana
Source: *IntWW 74; WhoGov 72; WhoWor 74*

Chung, Connie (Constance Yu-Hwa)
American. Broadcast Journalist
b. Aug 20, 1946 in Washington, DC
Source: *BioIn 10; WhoAm 82*

Chung Hee Park
see: Park, Chung Hee

Chung, Il-Kwon
Korean. Former Prime Minister
b. Nov 21, 1917
Source: *WhoGov 72*

Church, Frank
American. Lawyer, Politician
Senator, 1957-81; chairman foreign relations committee, 1979-81.
b. Jul 25, 1924 in Boise, Idaho
Source: *BiDrAC; CelR 73; CngDr 74; CurBio 58; IntWW 74; WhoAm 74, 76, 78, 80, 82; WhoAmP 73; WhoGov 72; WhoWest 74; WhoWor 74*

Church, Fredrick Edwin
American. Landscape Artist
b. May 4, 1826 in Hartford, Connecticut
d. Apr 7, 1900
Source: *AmBi; ApCAB; BnEnAmA; DcAmB; McGEWB; NatCAB 20; WebAB; WhAm 1*

Church, Sam(uel Morgan, Jr.)
American. Labor Union Official
President, United Mine Workers Union, 1979-82.
b. Sep 20, 1936 in Matewan, West Virginia
Source: *CurBio 81; NewYTBS 79, 81; WhoAm 82*

Church, Sandra
American. Actress
b. Jan 13, 1943 in San Francisco, California
Source: *BiE&WWA; InWom; NotNAT; WhoHol A*

Churchill, Clementine Ogilvy (Hozier) Spencer, Baroness
English. Wife of Winston Churchilll
b. Apr 1, 1885
d. Dec 12, 1977 in London, England
Source: *CurBio 53, 78; InWom*

Churchill, Diana Josephine
English. Actress
b. Aug 21, 1913 in Wembley, England
Source: *FilmgC; Who 74; WhoHol A; WhoThe 77*

Churchill, Jennie Jerome
American. Mother of Winston Churchill
b. 1850 in New York, New York
d. Jun 29, 1921
Source: *AmWom; ApCAB SUP; NotAW; WhAm 1*

Churchill, John
see: Marlborough, John Churchill, Duke

Churchill, May (Beatrice Desmond)
[May Lambert]
"Chicago May"
Swindler
b. 1876 in Sligo, Ireland
d. 1929 in Philadelphia, Pennsylvania
Source: *BioIn 10; LookW*

Churchill, Randolph
English. Son of Winston Churchill
b. May 28, 1911
d. Jun 6, 1968 in London, England
Source: *ConAu 89; CurBio 47, 68; LongCTC*

Churchill, Randolph Henry Spencer, Lord
English. Statesman
b. Feb 13, 1849 in Woodstock, England
d. Jan 24, 1895 in London, England
Source: *Alli SUP*

Churchill, Sarah
[Lady Audley]
"Mule"
English. Singer, Actress, Narrator
b. Oct 7, 1914 in London, England
d. Sep 24, 1982 in London, England
Source: *ChPo S3; CurBio 55, 83; FilmgC; InWom; IntMPA 75, 76, 77, 78, 79, 80, 81, 82; NewYTBS 82; REn; WhoAmW 70; WhoHol A; WhoThe 72, 77, 81*

Churchill, Winston
American. Author
b. 1871 in Saint Louis, Missouri
d. Mar 12, 1947 in Winter Park, Florida
Source: *AmAu&B; ApCAB SUP; BbD; BiD&SB; BiDSA; CarSB; CasWL; CnDAL; ConAmA; ConAmL; CyWA; DcAmAu; DcAmB S4; DcBiA; DcLEL; DcNAA; EvLB; LongCTC; OxAmL; OxEng; Pen AM; REn; REnAL; TwCA SUP; TwCBDA; TwCW; WebE&AL; WhAm 2; WhNAA*

Churchill, Sir Winston Leonard Spencer
English. Statesman, Author
Coined expression "Iron Curtain," 1946, warning against Soviet expansionism.
b. Nov 30, 1874 in Woodstock, England
d. Jan 24, 1965 in London, England
Source: *CasWL; CurBio 53; CyWA; DcLEL; EvLB; LongCTC; NewC; OxEng; REn; TwCA; TwCW*

Chute, Beatrice Joy
American. Author
b. Jan 3, 1913 in Minneapolis, Minnesota
Source: *ConAu 1R; CurBio 50; InWom; SmATA 2; WhoAm 82*

Chute, Marchette Gaylord
American. Author
b. Aug 16, 1909 in Minneapolis, Minnesota
Source: *AmAu&B; Au&Wr 71; AuBYP; BiE&WWA; BkCL; ChPo, S1, S2; ConAu 1R, 5NR; CurBio 50; DrAS 74H; EvLB; InWom; MnnWr; MorJA; NotNAT; RAdv 1; REnAL; SmATA; TwCA SUP; Who 74; WhoAm 74, 76, 78, 80, 82; WrDr 76*

Chuvalo, George
Canadian. Boxer
b. Sep 12, 1937 in Toronto, ON
Source: *WhoBox 74*

Chwast, Seymour
American. Graphic Designer
b. 1931 in New York
Source: *IlsBYP; SmATA 18*

Chylak, Nester
American. Umpire
AL umpire, 1947-72.
b. May 11, 1922 in Olyphant, Pennsylvania
d. Feb 17, 1982 in Dunmore, Pennsylvania
Source: *NewYTBS 82; WhoProB 73*

Ciano (di Cortellazzo), Conte Galeazzo
Italian. Politician
b. Mar 8, 1903 in Livorno, Italy
d. Jan 11, 1944
Source: *CurBio 40, 44*

Ciardi, John
American. Poet, Author
b. Jun 24, 1916 in Boston, Massachusetts
Source: *AmAu&B; AuBYP; BkCL; BkP; CasWL; CelR 73; ChPo, , S2; CnDAL; ConAu 5R, 5NR; ConLC 10; ConP 70, 75; CurBio 67; DrAP 75; DrAS 74E; ModAL; OxAmL; Pen AM; RAdv 1; REn; REnAL; SmATA 1; Str&VC; ThrBJA; TwCA SUP; WebAB; WebE&AL; WhoAm 74, 76, 78, 80, 82; WhoE 74; WhoWor 74; WrDr 76*

Cibber, Colley
English. Author, Actor, Dramatist
Poet laureate, 1730; ridiculed in Alexander Pope's *The Dunciad.*
b. Nov 6, 1671 in London, England
d. Dec 12, 1757 in London, England
Source: *Alli; BbD; BiD&SB; BrAu; CasWL; Chambr 2; ChPo; CnThe; CrtT 2; CyWA, ; DcEnA; DcEnL; DcEuL; DcLEL; EvLB; McGEWD; NewC; OxEng; OxThe; Pen ENG; PlP&P; REn; REnWD; WebE&AL*

Cicero, Marcus Tullius
Roman. Orator, Statesman, Philosopher
b. 106BC in Arpino, Italy
d. 43BC in Formia, Italy
Source: *AtlBL; BbD; BiD&SB; CasWL; CyWA; DcEuL; NewC; OxEng; Pen CL; RComWL; REn*

Cicotte, Eddie (Edward V)
American. Baseball Player
b. Jun 19, 1894 in Detroit, Michigan
d. May 5, 1969 in Detroit, Michigan
Source: *BaseEn; WhoProB 73*

Cid, El
[Rodrigo Diaz de Bivar]
Spanish. Soldier, Hero
Conquered, ruled kingdom of Valencia, 1094-99.
b. 1040 in Burgos, Spain
d. 1099
Source: *DcSpL; NewC; RComWL; REn*

Cienfuegos, Nicasio Alvarez de
Spanish. Poet
b. 1761 in Madrid, Spain
d. 1809
Source: *BbD; BiD&SB; DcEuL; EvEuW; Pen EUR*

Cierva, Juan de la
Spanish. Aeronautical Engineer
Invented rotary wing aircraft called autogiro.
b. 1895
d. 1936
Source: *BioIn 1, 4, 8; NewCol 75*

Cigna, Gina
French. Opera Singer
b. Mar 6, 1900 in Paris, France
Source: *InWom*

Cilea, Francesco
Italian. Composer
b. Jul 26, 1866 in Palmi, Italy
d. Nov 20, 1950 in Verazza, Italy
Source: *NewEOp 71*

Cilento, Diane
Australian. Actress
b. 1933 in Brisbane, Australia
Source: *BiE&WWA; FilmgC; IntMPA 75, 76, 77, 78, 79, 80, 81, 82; MotPP; MovMk; NotNAT; WhoHol A; WhoThe 77*

Cimabue, Giovanni
Italian. Artist
b. 1240 in Florence, Italy
d. 1302 in Florence, Italy
Source: *AtlBL; NewC; REn*

Cimarosa, Domenico
Italian. Composer
b. Dec 17, 1749 in Aversa, Italy
d. Jan 11, 1801 in Venice, Italy
Source: *AtlBL*

Cimino, Michael
American. Motion Picture Director, Writer
b. 1943 in New York, New York
Source: *CurBio 81; IntMPA 75, 76, 77, 78, 79, 80, 81; WhoAm 80, 82*

Cinque, Joseph
American. Former Slave, Revolutionary
b. 1811
d. 1852
Source: *BioIn 6, 8, 10*

Cipriani, Amilcare
Italian. Revolutionary
b. 1845 in Rimini, Italy
d. 1918
Source: *WebBD 80*

Cipullo, Aldo Massimo Fabrizio
American. Jewelry Designer
b. Nov 18, 1938 in Naples, Italy
Source: *WhoAm 82; WorFshn*

Cisler, Walker Lee
American. Utilities Executive
b. Oct 8, 1897 in Marietta, Ohio
Source: *AmM&WS 73P; BioNews 74; BusPN; CurBio 55; IntWW 74; St&PR 75; WhoAm 74, 76, 78, 80, 82; WhoF&I 74; WhoMW 74; WhoWor 74*

Cisneros, Henry Gabriel
American. Mayor of San Antonio
b. Jun 11, 1947 in San Antonio, Texas
Source: *WhoAm 82; WhoS&SW 78*

Citroen, Andre Gustave
French. Auto Manufacturer
b. Feb 5, 1878 in Paris, France
d. 1935
Source: *WebBD 80*

Ciulei, Liviu
Romanian. Actor, Architect
b. Jul 7, 1923 in Bucharest, Romania
Source: *DcFM; IntWW 74, 75, 76, 77, 78; WhoSocC 78, 78*

Civiletti, Benjamin R
American. Government Official
US Attorney General, 1979-81.
b. Jul 17, 1935 in Peekskill, New York
Source: *BioIn 11; CurBio 80; IntWW 80; WhoAm 78*

Claflin, Tennessee Celeste
American. Journalist
b. 1846 in Ohio
d. 1923
Source: *DcAmB; InWom; NotAW*

Claiborne, Craig
American. Editor, Author
Food editor NY *Times;* wrote *The New New York Times Cook Book,* 1979.
b. Sep 4, 1920 in Sunflower, Mississippi
Source: *AmAu&B; ConAu 1R, 5NR; CurBio 69; WhoAm 74, 76, 78, 80, 82; WhoE 74*

Claiborne, Liz (Elisabeth)
[Mrs. Arthur Ortenberg]
American. Fashion Designer
President, Liz Claiborne, Inc., 1976--.
b. Mar 31, 1929 in Brussels, Belgium
Source: *WhoAm 80, 82; WhoAmA 80*

Clair, Rene
French. Producer, Author
b. Nov 11, 1898 in Paris, France
d. Mar 15, 1981 in Neuilly, France
Source: *BiDFilm; BioIn 1, 5; ConAu 103; CurBio 41, 81; DcFM; Film 2; FilmgC; IntMPA 75, 76, 77, 78, 79; IntWW 74, 75, 76, 77, 78; MovMk; NewYTBS 81; OxFilm; REn; WhAm 7; Who 74; WhoWor 74; WorEFlm*

Clairborne, William Charles
French. Author, Director, Producer
b. Nov 11, 1898 in Paris, France
d. Mar 15, 1981 in Paris, France
American. Governor
b. 1775 in Sussex County, Virginia
d. Nov 23, 1817 in New Orleans, Louisiana
Source: *AnObit 1981; BiDFilm; BioIn 1, 5, 9; CurBio 41, 81; DcFM; FilmEn; Film 2; FilmgC; IntAu&W 77; IntMPA 75, 76, 77, 78, 79; BioIn 1, 3, 4, 5, 6, 10, 11; NatCAB 10; IntMPA 80, 81; IntWW 74, 75, 76, 77, 78, 79, 80; JohnWil 82; MovMk; NewYTBS 81; OxFilm; REn; WhAm 7; Who 74; WhoWor 74; WorEFlm*

Claire, Ina
[Ina Fagan]
American. Actress
b. Oct 15, 1895 in Washington, DC
Source: *BiE&WWA; CurBio 54; EncMT; FamA&A; Film 1; FilmgC; InWom; MotPP; NotNAT; ThFT; WhoHol A; WhoThe 77*

Clairmont, Claire
English. Friend of Shelley and Byron
b. 1798
d. 1879
Source: *InWom*

Clampett, Bob (Robert)
American. Cartoonist, Filmmaker
Created cartoon characters Tweetie Pie, Porky Pig, Bugs Bunny.
b. May 8, 1910 in San Diego, California
Source: *AuNews 1; WhoAm 82*

Clancy, "King" (Francis Michael)
Canadian. Hockey Player, Executive
Player, coach, vice-president of Toronto Maple Leafs.
b. Feb 25, 1903 in Ottawa, ON
Source: *BioIn 8, 10; WhoHcky 73*

Clapp, Margaret Antoinette
American. Educator, Historian
b. Apr 11, 1910 in East Orange, New Jersey
d. May 3, 1974
Source: *AmAu&B; ConAu 49; CurBio 48, 74; InWom; IntWW 74; NewYTBS 74; OxAmL; REnAL; TwCA SUP; WhAm 6; WhoGov 72*

Clapp, Patricia
American. Children's Author
b. Jun 9, 1912 in Boston, Massachusetts
Source: *ConAu 25R; SmATA 4; WrDr 76*

Clapper, Raymond Lewis
American. Journalist
b. Apr 30, 1892 in La Cygne, Kansas
d. Feb 1944
Source: *AmAu&B; CurBio 40, 44; DcAmB S3; WhAm 2; WhNAA*

Clapton, Eric
[Blind Faith; Eric Clap; Cream; Yardbirds]
English. Rock Musician
Appeared in movie *Tommy,* 1975.
b. Mar 30, 1945 in Ripley, England
Source: *BkPepl; CelR 73; WhoAm 74, 76, 78, 80, 82; WhoRock 81*

Clara Ward and Her Gospel Singers
American. Vocal Group
Source: *NF*

Clare, Saint
Italian. Founded Franciscan Nuns
b. 1193
d. 1253
Source: *NewCol 75*

Clare, John
"Northamptonshire Peasant Poet"
English. Poet
b. Jul 13, 1793 in Helpstone, England
d. May 20, 1864 in Northampton, England
Source: *AtlBL; BrAu 19; CasWL; DcEnL; DcLEL; NewC; OxEng; Pen ENG; REn; WebE&AL*

Clarendon, Edward Hyde, Earl
English. Statesman, Historian
b. Feb 18, 1609 in Wiltshire, England
d. Dec 9, 1674 in Rouen, France
Source: *Alli; AtlBL; BiD&SB; BrAu; CasWL; Chambr 1; DcEnA; DcEnL; DcLEL; EvLB; NewC; OxEng; Pen ENG; REn; WebE&AL*

Clark, Abraham
American. Lawyer, Historian
b. Feb 15, 1726 in Elizabethtown, New Jersey
d. Sep 15, 1794
Source: *NewCol 75*

Clark, Barney B
American. Heart Patient
First recipient of permanent, completely artificial heart, Dec, 1982.
b. Jan 21, 1921 in Provo, Utah
Source: *NF*

Clark, Barrett H
American. Author, Editor
b. Aug 26, 1890 in Toronto, ON
d. Aug 5, 1953 in Briarcliff, New York
Source: *AmAu&B; OxAmL; REnAL; TwCA, SUP; WhAm 3; WhNAA*

Clark, Bennett Champ
American. Lawyer, Politician
b. Jan 8, 1890 in Bowling Green, Missouri
d. Jul 13, 1954 in Gloucester, Massachusetts
Source: *AmAu&B; CurBio 41, 54; DcAmB S5; WhAm 3*

Clark, Bobby
American. Comedian
b. Jun 16, 1888 in Springfield, Ohio
d. Feb 12, 1960 in New York, New York
Source: *CurBio 49, 60; EncMT; FilmgC; WhAm 3; WhScrn 74, 77; WhoHol B*

Clark, "Champ" (James Beauchamp)
American. Politician
b. Mar 7, 1850 in Lawrenceburg, Kentucky
d. Mar 2, 1921 in Washington, DC
Source: *AmBi; BiDrAC; BiDSA; DcAmB; DcNAA; TwCBDA; WebAB; WhAm 1; WhAmP; WhoAm 74*

Clark, Charles Badger
American. Poet
b. Jan 1, 1883 in Albia, Iowa
d. Sep 26, 1957
Source: *AmAu&B; ChPo, S1; DcLEL; REnAL*

Clark, Colin Grant
English. Economist
b. Nov 2, 1905 in Westminster, England
Source: *ConAu 61; IntWW 74, 75, 76, 77, 78, 79, 80, 81; Who 74; WhoWor 74*

Clark, Dane
[Bernard Zanville]
American. Actor
b. Feb 18, 1913 in New York, New York
Source: *FilmgC; HolP 40; IntMPA 75, 76, 77, 78, 79, 80, 81, 82; MotPP; MovMk; WhoAm 74; WhoHol A*

Clark, Dave
[Dave Clark Five]
English. Rock Musician
b. Dec 15, 1942 in London, England
Source: *EncPR&S*

Clark, Dick
American. Entertainer
Host of American Bandstand since 1952.
b. Nov 30, 1929 in Mount Vernon, New York
Source: *BkPepl; CurBio 59; IntMPA 75, 76, 77, 78, 79, 80, 81, 82; IntWW 74; WhoAm 74, 76, 78, 80, 82; WhoHol A*

Clark, "Dutch" (Earl)
American. Football Player, Coach
b. Oct 11, 1906 in Fowler, Colorado
d. Aug 5, 1978
Source: *WhoFtbl 74*

Clark, Fred
American. Actor
b. Mar 9, 1914 in Lincoln, California
d. Dec 5, 1968 in Santa Monica, California
Source: *BiE&WWA; FilmgC; MotPP; MovMk; Vers A; WhAm 5; WhScrn 74, 77; WhoHol B*

Clark, George Rogers
American. Revolutionary Frontier Leader
Assurred colonial control of KY, IL, 1778-79.
b. Nov 19, 1752 in Charlottesville, Virginia
d. Feb 13, 1818 in Indiana
Source: *AmBi; ApCAB; DcAmAu; DcAmB; EncAB-H; OxAmL; REn; REnAL; TwCBDA; WebAB; WhAm H*

Clark, Jack Anthony
American. Baseball Player
b. Nov 10, 1955 in Covina, California
Source: *BaseEn; BioIn 11*

Clark, James
Scottish. Auto Racer
b. Mar 4, 1936 in Kilmany, Scotland
d. Apr 7, 1968 in Hochheim, Germany (West)
Source: *CurBio 65, 68; WhAmP*

Clark, James Beauchamp
see: Clark, "Champ"

Clark, Joe (Charles Joseph)
Canadian. Politician
Prime minister, 1979-80.
b. Jun 5, 1939 in High River, AB
Source: *BioIn 11; IntWW 77; WhoAm 82*

Clark, Joseph Sill
American. Former Senator
b. Oct 21, 1901 in Philadelphia, Pennsylvania
Source: *BiDrAC; CurBio 52; IntWW 74; WhoAm 74, 76, 78, 80, 82*

Clark, Kenneth Bancroft
American. Educator, Psychologist
b. Jul 24, 1914 in Panama Canal Zone
Source: *AmAu&B; CelR 73; ConAu 33R; CurBio 64; LEduc 74; LivgBAA; WebAB; WhoAm 74, 76, 78, 80, 82; WhoBlA 75; WhoGov 72; WhoWor 74*

Clark, Kenneth McKenzie
English. Art Historian, Author
b. Jul 13, 1903 in London, England
Source: *ConAu 93; CurBio 63; IntMPA 75; IntWW 74; Who 74; WhoWor 74*

Clark, Marguerite
American. Actress
b. Feb 22, 1887 in Avondale, Ohio
d. Sep 25, 1940 in New York, New York
Source: *NotNAT B; WhScrn 74, 77*

Clark, Marion L
American. Journalist, Author
b. 1942?
d. Sep 4, 1977 in East Tawas, Michigan
Source: *ConAu 73, 77*

Clark, Mark Wayne
American. Army Officer
b. May 1, 1896 in New York
Source: *CelR 73; CurBio 42; IntWW 74; Who 74; WhoAm 74; WhoGov 72; WhoWor 74*

Clark, Michele
American. Journalist
b. 1943
d. 1972
Source: *BioIn 9*

Clark, Monte
American. Football Player, Coach
b. Jan 24, 1937 in Fillmore, California
Source: *BioIn 11*

Clark, Peggy
American. Theatrical Lighting Designer
b. Sep 30, 1915 in Baltimore, Maryland
Source: *BiE&WWA; NotNAT; WhoAm 74, 76, 78, 80, 82; WhoAmW 77; WhoE 74*

Clark, Petula
English. Singer, Actress
Won Grammys for "Downtown," 1964, "I Know a Place," 1965.
b. Nov 15, 1932 in Epsom, England
Source: *BkPepl; CelR 73; CurBio 70; FilmgC; IntMPA 75, 76, 77, 78, 79, 80, 81, 82; MotPP; MovMk; WhoAm 74, 76, 78, 80, 82; WhoHol A*

Clark, Richard Clarence
American. Politician
b. Sep 14, 1929 in Paris, Iowa
Source: *WhoAmP 73; WhoGov 72*

Clark, Robert Edward
American. Journalist
b. May 14, 1922 in Omaha, Nebraska
Source: *WhoAm 74, 76, 78, 80, 82*

Clark, Roy
American. Singer, Composer, Musician
Named Entertainer of the Year by CMA, 1973.
b. Mar 15, 1933 in Meaherrin, Virginia
Source: *BioNews 74; EncFCWM 69; WhoAm 74, 76, 78, 80, 82; WhoPubR 72*

Clark, Steve
see: Def Leppard

Clark, Susan Nora Goulding
[Mrs. Alex Karras]
Canadian. Actress
Starred with husband in movies *Babe; Jimmy B and Andre; Maid in America.*
b. Mar 8, 1944 in Sarnia, ON
Source: *BioIn 8, 10, 11; FilmEn; FilmgC; IntMPA 75, 76, 77, 78, 79, 80, 81; WhoAm 80, 82; WhoHol A*

Clark, Sydney
American. Author, Lecturer
b. Aug 18, 1890 in Auburndale, Massachusetts
d. Apr 20, 1975
Source: *AmAu&B; Au&Wr 71; ConAu 5R, 57, 4NR; CurBio 56*

Clark, Thomas Dionysius
American. Author, Historian
b. Jul 14, 1903 in Louisville, Mississippi
Source: *AmAu&B; ConAu 5R, 4NR; DrAS 74H; WhNAA; WhoAm 74, 76, 78, 80, 82*

Clark, Tom (Thomas Campbell)
American. Supreme Court Justice
US Attorney General, 1945-49; Supreme Court Justice, 1949-67.
b. Sep 23, 1899 in Dallas, Texas
d. Jun 1977 in New York, New York
Source: *BiDrUSE; CngDr 74; CurBio 45; DrAS 74P; IntWW 74; WebAB; Who 74; WhoAm 74; WhoAmP 73; WhoGov 72*

Clark, Walter van Tilburg
American. Author
b. Aug 3, 1909 in East Oreland, Maine
d. Nov 10, 1971 in Reno, Nevada
Source: *AmAu&B; AmNov; CnDAL; ConAu 9R, 33R; ConNov 72, 76; CyWA; ModAL; NewYTBE 71; OxAmL; Pen AM; RAdv 1; REn; REnAL; SmATA 8; TwCA SUP; WhAm 5*

Clark, William
American. Explorer
With Meriwether Lewis, went on overland expedition to Pacific, 1803.
b. Aug 1, 1770 in Caroline County, Virginia
d. Sep 1, 1838 in Saint Louis, Missouri
Source: *Alli, SUP; AmBi; ApCAB; BiDrAC; DcAmB; OxAmL; REnAL; TwCBDA; WebAB; WhAm H; WhAmP*

Clark, William P(atrick, Jr.)
American. Government Official
National security advisor, 1981--.
b. Oct 23, 1931 in Oxnard, California
Source: *CurBio 82; WhoAm 78, 80, 82*

Clark, (William) Ramsey
American. Former-Attorney General, Lawyer
b. Dec 18, 1927 in Dallas, Texas
Source: *AmAu&B; BiDrUSE; BioNews 74; CelR 73; ConAu 29R; CurBio 67; IntWW 74; NewYTBS 74; Who 74; WhoAm 74; WhoAmP 73; WhoWor 74*

Clarke, Allan
see: Hollies, The

Clarke, Arthur C(harles)
English. Author, Scientist
With Stanley Kubrick, wrote novel, screenplay *2001: A Space Odyssey,* 1968.
b. Dec 16, 1917 in Minehead, England
Source: *Alli; AmM&WS 73P; Au&Wr 71; AuBYP; CelR 73; ConAu 1R, 2NR; ConLC 1, 4, 13, 18; ConNov 72, 76; CurBio 66; EvLB; IntWW 74; LongCTC; NewC; TwCA SUP; TwCW; WebE&AL; Who 82; WhoWor 74; WrDr 76*

Clarke, Austin
Irish. Poet
b. May 9, 1896 in Dublin, Ireland
d. Mar 20, 1974
Source: *CasWL; CnMD SUP; ConAu 49; ConAu P-2; ConLC 6; ConP 70, 75; ModBrL, SUP; NewC; RAdv 1; REn; TwCA SUP; TwCW*

Clarke, Bobby (Robert Earl)
Canadian. Hockey Player
Center, Philadelphia Flyers; MVP 1972, 1973, 1975, 1976.
b. Aug 13, 1949 in Flin Flon, MB
Source: *BioIn 10, 11; WhoHcky 73*

Clarke, Bruce Cooper
American. General
b. Apr 29, 1901 in Adams, New York
Source: *BioIn 3, 4, 5, 9, 10; WhoAm 74*

Clarke, Ellis Emmanuel
Trinidadian. Lawyer, Diplomat
b. Dec 28, 1917 in Trinidad
Source: *IntWW 74; Who 74; WhoGov 72; WhoWor 74*

Clarke, Fred Clifford
"Cap"
American. Baseball Player, Manager
Playing manager on four pennant winning Pittsburgh Pirate teams.
b. Oct 3, 1872 in Winterset, Iowa
d. Aug 14, 1960 in Winfield, Kansas
Source: *BaseEn; BioIn 2, 3, 5, 7; WhoProB 73*

Clarke, Gilmore David
American. Landscape Architect
Chairman, National Commission of Fine Arts, 1937-50.
b. Jul 12, 1892 in New York, New York
d. Aug 6, 1982
Source: *BioIn 9; NewYTBS 82; WhoAm 74, 76, 78, 80, 82*

Clarke, James Alfred
[Rene Clarke]
American. Art Director
b. 1886
d. 1969
Source: *BioIn 8*

Clarke, Jeremiah
English. Composer
b. 1673 in London, England
d. Dec 1, 1701 in London, England
Source: *Alli; Baker 78; OxMus*

Clarke, John
English. Colonial Figure
Co-founder of RI, 1638.
b. Oct 8, 1609 in Westhorpe, England
d. Apr 28, 1676 in Newport, Rhode Island
Source: *AmBi; ApCAB; CyAL 1; DcAmB; Drake; NewCol 75; OxAmL; REnAL; TwCBDA; WhAm H*

Clarke, John Henrik
American. Author
b. Jan 1, 1915 in Union Springs, Alabama
Source: *AmAu&B; AuNews 1; BioIn 10; BlkAW; ConAu 53; LivgBAA; WhoAm 74; WhoE 74*

Clarke, Ron
Australian. Track Athlete
b. Feb 21, 1937 in Melbourne, Australia
Source: *CurBio 71; WhoTr&F 73*

Clarke, Shirley
American. Motion Picture Director
b. Oct 2, 1927 in New York, New York
Source: *DcFM; FilmgC; OxFilm; WhoAm 74; WhoWor 74; WomWMM; WorEFlm*

Clarke, Stanley Marvin
American. Rock Musician, Composer
b. 1951 in Philadelphia, Pennsylvania
Source: *BioIn 11; WhoAm 82*

Clarkson, Adrienne
Canadian. Author, Broadcast Journalist
b. Feb 10, 1939 in Hong Kong, China
Source: *CanWW 70, 79; ConAu 49*

Clarkson, Ewan
English. Author
b. Jan 23, 1929 in England
Source: *ConAu 25R; SmATA 9; WrDr 76*

Clarkson, John Gibson
American. Baseball Player
b. Jul 1, 1861 in Cambridge, Massachusetts
d. Feb 4, 1909 in Cambridge, Massachusetts
Source: *BaseEn; BioIn 7; WhoProB 73*

Clary, Robert
American. Actor
Played LaBeau in TV series "Hogan's Heroes," 1965-71.
b. Mar 1, 1926 in Paris, France
Source: *WhoHol A; BiE&WWA; WhoAm 74, 76, 78, 80, 82*

Clash, The
[Topper Headon; Mick Jones; Paul Simonon; Joe Strummer]
English. Rock Group
Source: *ConMuA 80; IlEncRk; WhoRock 81*

Classen, Willie
American. Boxer
b. Sep 16, 1950 in Santurce, Puerto Rico
d. Nov 28, 1979 in New York, New York
Source: *BioIn 12; NewYTBS 79*

Claude, Georges
French. Chemist, Physicist
Research in liquefying gases led to invention of neon lights.
b. Sep 24, 1870 in Paris, France
d. May 23, 1960 in Saint Cloud, France
Source: *AsBiEn; DcScB; LinLib S; WebBD 80*

Claudel, Paul Louis Charles
French. Author, Diplomat, Poet
b. Aug 6, 1868 in Villenluve, France
d. Feb 23, 1955 in Paris, France
Source: *AtlBL; CasWL; CathA 1930; ClDMEL; CnMD; CnMWL; CnThe; EncWL; EvEuW; LongCTC; McGEWD; ModRL; ModWD; OxEng; OxFr; OxThe; Pen EUR; REn; REnWD; TwCA, SUP; TwCW; WhAm 3; WhNAA; WhoTwCL*

Claudian
Alexandrian. Poet
b. 365
d. 408
Source: *CasWL; NewC; OxEng; Pen CL*

Claudius I
[Tiberius Claudius Nero Germanicus]
Roman. Emperor
b. Aug 1, 10BC
d. Oct 13, 54AD in Rome, Italy
Source: *McGEWB; NewCol 75; WebBD 80*

Claudius, Matthias
German. Poet
b. Aug 15, 1740 in Reinfeld, Germany
d. Jan 21, 1815 in Hamburg, Germany
Source: *BiD&SB; CasWL; ChPo S1; DcEnL; EuAu; EvEuW; OxGer; Pen EUR; REn*

Claus, Hugo
Belgian. Poet, Dramatist
b. Apr 5, 1929
Source: *CasWL; CnMD; EncWL; ModWD*

Clausen, A(lden) W(inship)
American. Banker
President, World Bank, 1981--.
b. Feb 17, 1923 in Hamilton, Illinois
Source: *BioIn 8, 11; Dun&B 79; IntWW 74, 75, 76, 77, 78; PolProf NF; St&PR 75; WhoAm 74, 76, 78, 80, 82; WhoF&I 74, 75, 77, 79; WhoWest 76, 78; WhoWor 74*

Clausewitz, Karl von
Prussian. Author, Military Strategist
b. Jun 1, 1780 in Burg, Prussia
d. 1831
Source: *OxGer*

Clave, Antoni
French. Artist
b. Apr 5, 1913 in Barcelona, Spain
Source: *IntWW 76, 77, 78; McGDA; WhoGrA*

Clavell, James Dumaresq
American. Author
Wrote *Taipan,* 1966, *Shogun,* 1975, *Noble House,* 1981.
b. Oct 10, 1924 in Australia
Source: *ConAu 25R; ConLC 6; CurBio 81; WhoAm 74, 76, 78, 80, 82; WhoWor 74; WorEFlm; WrDr 80*

Clay, Cassius
see: Ali, Muhammad

Clay, Cassius Marcellus
American. Public Official, Abolitionist
b. Oct 19, 1810 in Madison County, Kentucky
d. Jul 22, 1903 in Madison County, Kentucky
Source: *ApCAB; BiD&SB; BiDSA; DcAmAu; DcAmB; DcNAA; Drake; TwCBDA; WebAB; WhAm 1*

Clay, Henry
"The Great Compromiser"
American. Lawyer, Statesman
Secured MO Compromise; Compromise Tariff of 1833; Compromise of 1850.
b. Apr 12, 1777 in Hanover County, Virginia
d. Jun 29, 1852 in Washington, DC
Source: *Alli; AmAu; AmAu&B; AmBi; ApCAB; BbD; BiAuS; BiD&SB; BiDSA; BiDrAC; BiDrUSE; CyAL 1; DcAmAu; DcAmB; DcNAA; Drake; EncAB-H; OxAmL; REn; REnAL; TwCBDA; WebAB; WhAm H; WhAmP*

Clay, Lucius du Bignon
American. Army Officer
b. Apr 23, 1897 in Marietta, Georgia
d. Apr 16, 1978 in Chatham, Massachusetts
Source: *ConAu 77, 81; CurBio 45, 63; IntWW 74; Who 74; WhoAm 74; WhoAmP 73; WhoWor 74*

Clay, William Lacy
American. Congressman
b. Apr 30, 1931 in Saint Louis, Missouri
Source: *BioIn 8, 9, 10; CngDr 74; WhoAm 74, 76, 78, 80, 82; WhoAmP 73; WhoGov 72; WhoMW 74*

Clayburgh, Jill
[Mrs. David Rabe]
American. Actress
Named best actress, Cannes Film Festival, 1978, for *An Unmarried Woman.*
b. Apr 30, 1944 in New York, New York
Source: *CurBio 79; IntMPA 78, 79, 80, 81, 82; NewYTBS 76, 79; WhoAm 80, 82; WhoHol A*

Clayton, Bessie
American. Actress
b. 1885 in Philadelphia, Pennsylvania
d. Jul 16, 1948 in Long Branch, New Jersey
Source: *BioIn 1; NotNAT B*

Clayton, Buck
American. Jazz Musician
b. Nov 12, 1911 in Parsons, Kansas
Source: *AmSCAP 66; WhoJazz 72*

Clayton, Herbert
English. Actor, Producer, Director
b. Dec 1, 1876 in London, England
d. Feb 16, 1931
Source: *NotNAT B; WhThe*

Clayton, Jack
British. Motion Picture Director
b. 1921
Source: *BiDFilm; DcFM; FilmgC; IntMPA 75, 76, 77, 78, 79, 80, 81, 82; IntWW 74; MovMk; OxFilm; Who 74; WhoWor 74; WorEFlm*

Clayton, Jan
American. Actress
Starred in *Hopalong Cassidy;* played the mother in TV series "Lassie."
b. Aug 26, 1925 in Alamogordo, New Mexico
Source: *IntMPA 75, 76, 77, 78, 79, 80, 81, 82; WhoHol A*

Clayton, John Middleton
American. Politician
b. Jul 24, 1796 in Dagsborough, Delaware
d. Nov 9, 1856 in Dover, Delaware
Source: *AmBi; ApCAB; BiAuS; BiDrAC; BiDrUSE; DcAmB; Drake; TwCBDA; WebAB; WhAm H; WhAmP*

Clayton, Lou
[Louis Finkelstein]
American. Actor
b. 1887 in Brooklyn, New York
d. Sep 12, 1950 in Santa Monica, California
Source: *WhScrn 74, 77; WhoHol B*

Cleaveland, Moses
American. Founder of Cleveland
Founded, named Cleaveland, Ohio, 1796; spelling later changed to Cleveland.
b. Jan 29, 1754 in Canterbury, Connecticut
d. Nov 16, 1806 in Canterbury, Connecticut
Source: *AmBi; ApCAB; DcAmB; OhA&B; TwCBDA; WhAm H*

Cleaver, Eldridge
American. Political Activist, Author
Served time in prisons; wrote *Soul on Ice,* 1968; *Soul on Fire,* 1978.
b. Aug 31, 1935 in Little Rock, Arkansas
Source: *AmAu&B; BlkAW; CelR 73; ConAu 21R; CurBio 70; LivgBAA; Pen AM; WebE&AL; WrDr 76*

Cleaver, Vera Allen
[Mrs. William Joseph Cleaver]
American. Author
b. Jan 6, 1919 in Virgil, South Dakota
Source: *BioIn 8; ConAu 73; FourBJA; SmATA 22; WhoAm 78, 80, 82*

Cleaver, William Joseph (Bill)
American. Author
b. Mar 20, 1920 in Hugo, Oklahoma
d. Aug 20, 1981 in Winter Haven, Florida
Source: *ConAu 73, 104; WhoAm 78, 80*

Cleese, John
[Monty Python's Flying Circus]
English. Actor, Writer
b. Oct 27, 1939 in Weston-Super-Mare, England
Source: *BioIn 10; FilmgC*

Cleghorn, Sarah Norcliffe
American. Author
b. Feb 4, 1876 in Norfolk, Virginia
d. Apr 4, 1959 in Philadelphia, Pennsylvania
Source: *AmAu&B; ChPo, S1, S2; InWom; REnAL; TwCA, SUP; WhAm 3; WhNAA; WomWWA 14*

Cleland, John
English. Author, Dramatist
b. 1709
d. Jan 23, 1789
Source: *Alli, SUP; BiDSA; CasWL; NewC; OxEng*

Cleland, (Joseph) Max(well)
American. Government Official
Lost legs, forearm in Vietnam; head, VA, 1977-80.
b. Aug 24, 1942 in Atlanta, Georgia
Source: *CurBio 78; NewYTBS 77; WhoAm 78, 80, 82; WhoAmP 73, 77, 79; WhoGov 77*

Cleland, Thomas Maitland
American. Artist
b. Aug 18, 1880 in Brooklyn, New York
d. Nov 9, 1964
Source: *BioIn 1, 3, 7, 9, 10; WhAm 4; WhoAmA 78*

Clemenceau, Georges Eugene Benjamin
French. Statesman
b. Sep 28, 1841 in Mouilleron, France
d. Nov 24, 1929 in Paris, France
Source: *ClDMEL; REn*

Clemens, Samuel Langhorne
see: Twain, Mark, pseud.

Clement VII
[Giulio DeMedici]
Florentine. Pope
Pope, 1523-34; Henry VIII attempted to divorce Catherine of Aragon during his reign.
b. 1475
d. 1534
Source: *NewCol 75*

Clement, Rene
French. Motion Picture Director
b. Mar 18, 1913
Source: *BiDFilm; DcFM; FilmgC; IntWW 74; MovMk; OxFilm; Who 74; WhoWor 74; WorEFlm*

Clemente, Roberto Walker
Puerto Rican. Baseball Player
b. Aug 18, 1934 in Carolina, Puerto Rico
d. Dec 31, 1972 in San Juan, Puerto Rico
Source: *BaseEn; CurBio 73; NewYTBE 71, 72, 73; WhAm 5; WhoProB 73*

Clementi, Muzio
Italian. Pianist, Composer
b. 1752 in Rome, Italy
d. Mar 10, 1832 in Evesham, England
Source: *NewCol 75*

Clemson, David "Clem"
see: Humble Pie

Cleopatra VII
Macedonian. Queen of Egypt
Mistress of Julius Caesar, Marc Antony; killed herself with asp.
b. 69BC
d. 30BC
Source: *FilmgC; HerW; InWom; NewC; NewCol 75; REn*

Cleva, Fausto
American. Conductor
b. May 17, 1902 in Trieste, Italy
Source: *NewYTBE 71; WhAm 5; WhoMus 72*

Cleve, Joos van
Flemish. Artist
b. 1485
d. 1540 in Antwerp, Belgium
Source: *McGDA*

Cleveland, James Harlan
American. Political Scientist
b. Jan 19, 1918 in New York, New York
Source: *AmM&WS 73; ConAu 1R; CurBio 61; IntWW 74; LEduc 74; WhoAm 74, 76, 78, 80, 82; WhoAmP 73; WhoWest 74; WhoWor 74; WrDr 76*

Cleveland, (Stephen) Grover
American. 22nd and 24th US President
In office, 1885-89; 1893-97; married former ward Frances Folsom in White House, 1886.
b. Mar 18, 1837 in Caldwell, New Jersey
d. Jun 24, 1908 in Princeton, New Jersey
Source: *AmAu&B; AmBi; ApCAB, SUP; BiD&SB; BiDrAC; BiDrUSE; DcAmAu; DcAmB; EncAB-H; OxAmL; REn; REnAL; WebAB; WhAm 1; WhAmP*

Clevenger, Shobal Vail
American. Sculptor, Physician
b. Oct 22, 1812 in Middletown, Ohio
d. Sep 23, 1843
Source: *AmBi; ApCAB; BnEnAmA; DcAmB; Drake; NatCAB 8; NewYHSD; TwCBDA; WhAm H*

Cliburn, Van (Harvey Lavan, Jr.)
American. Pianist
Won first prize, International Tchaikovsky Piano Competition, Moscow, 1958.
b. Jul 12, 1934 in Shreveport, Louisiana
Source: *CelR 73; CurBio 58; IntWW 74; Who 74; WhoAm 74, 76, 78, 80, 82; WhoMus 72; WhoWor 74*

Clifford, Clark McAdams
American. Government Official
Special advisor to presidents Truman, Kennedy, and Johnson.
b. Dec 25, 1906 in Fort Scott, Kansas
Source: *BiDrUSE; CelR 73; CurBio 47, 68; EncAB-H; IntWW 74; NewYTBE 71; Who 74; WhoAm 74, 76, 78, 80, 82; WhoAmP 73; WhoWor 74*

Clifford, Nathan
American. Supreme Court Justice
b. Aug 18, 1803 in Rumney, New Hampshire
d. Jul 25, 1881 in Cornish, Maine
Source: *Alli SUP; AmBi; ApCAB; BiAuS; BiDrAC; BiDrUSE; DcAmAu; DcAmB; Drake; TwCBDA; WebAB; WhAm H; WhAmP*

Clift, Montgomery
American. Actor
b. Oct 17, 1920 in Omaha, Nebraska
d. Jul 23, 1966 in New York, New York
Source: *BiDFilm; BiE&WWA; CmMov; CurBio 54, 66; FilmgC; MotPP; MovMk; OxFilm; WhAm 4; WhScrn 74, 77; WhoHol B; WorEFlm*

Climax Blues Band, The
[Colin Cooper; John Cuffley; Peter Haycock; Derek Holt; Richard Jones; George Newsome; Arthur Wood]
English. Rock Group
Source: *ConMuA 80; IlEncRk; RkOn 2; WhoRock 81*

Cline, Patsy
[Virginia Patterson Hensley]
American. Singer
b. Sep 8, 1932 in Winchester, Virginia
d. Mar 5, 1963 in Camden, Tennessee
Source: *EncFCWM 69*

Clinton, Bill (William Jefferson)
American. Governor of Arkansas
Former governor reelected, 1982.
b. Aug 19, 1946 in Hope, Arkansas
Source: *WhoAm 78, 80, 82; WhoAmL 78, 79; WhoS&SW 78, 80*

Clinton, DeWitt
American. Lawyer, Statesman
b. Mar 2, 1769 in Little Britain, New York
d. Feb 11, 1828 in Albany, New York
Source: *Alli; AmAu&B; AmBi; ApCAB; BiAuS; BiD&SB; BiDrAC; CyAL 1; DcAmAu; DcAmB; DcNAA; Drake; EncAB-H; REnAL; TwCBDA; WebAB; WhAm H; WhAmP*

Clinton, George
American. Lawyer, Vice-President
b. Jul 26, 1739 in Little Britain, New York
d. Apr 20, 1812 in Washington, DC
Source: *AmBi; ApCAB; BiAuS; BiDrAC; BiDrUSE; DcAmB; DcNAA; Drake; EncAB-H; OxAmL; REnAL; TwCBDA; WebAB; WhAm H; WhAmP*

Clinton, Henry
British. Military Officer
b. 1738 in NF
d. Dec 23, 1795 in Gilbraltar
Source: *Alli; AmBi; ApCAB; Drake; OxAmL; REn; REnAL; WhAm H*

Clinton, Larry
American. Band Leader
b. Aug 17, 1909 in Brooklyn, New York
Source: *AmSCAP 66; WhoJazz 72*

Clive, Colin
British. Actor
b. Jan 20, 1900 in Saint Malo, France
d. Jun 25, 1937 in Hollywood, California
Source: *NotNAT B; WhThe*

Clive, Robert
[Baron Clive of Plassey]
English. Colonial Governor
b. Sep 29, 1725 in Styche, England
d. Nov 22, 1774 in London, England
Source: *Alli, ; NewC; REn*

Clodagh
[Clodagh Aubry]
Irish. Designer
b. Oct 8, 1937 in Galway, Ireland
Source: *WorFshn*

Cloete, Stuart
South African. Author
b. Jul 23, 1897 in Paris, France
d. Mar 19, 1976 in Capetown, South Africa
Source: *AmAu&B; CasWL; ConAu 1R; ConNov 72, 76; EncWL; IntWW 74; LongCTC; REn; TwCA, SUP; TwCW; WhNAA; WhoWor 74; WrDr 76*

Clooney, Rosemary
American. Actress, Singer
Hit single "Come On-a My House"; autobiography *This for Remembrance,* 1979.
b. May 23, 1928 in Maysville, Kentucky
Source: *CurBio 57; FilmgC; InWom; WhoAm 74; WhoHol A; WhoMus 72*

Close, Upton, pseud.
see: Hall, Josef Washington

Cloud, Harold
see: Box Tops, The

Clouet, Francois
French. Artist
b. 1510 in Tours, France
d. 1572 in Paris, France
Source: *AtlBL; REn*

Clouet, Jean
French. Artist
b. 1485 in Netherlands
d. 1540 in Paris, France
Source: *AtlBL; BioIn 1, 8, 9, 11*

Clouzot, Henri-George
French. Motion Picture Director
b. Nov 20, 1907
d. Jan 12, 1977 in Paris, France
Source: *BiDFilm; DcFM; FilmgC; IntWW 74; MovMk; OxFilm; WhoWor 74; WorEFlm*

Clurman, Harold Edgar
American. Author, Theatrical Director
b. Sep 18, 1901 in New York, New York
d. Sep 9, 1980 in New York, New York
Source: *AmAu&B; BiE&WWA; ConAu 1R, 101, 2NR; CurBio 59; IntWW 74; NotNAT; OxThe; Pen AM; PlP&P; REnAL; WhoThe 77; WhoWorJ 72; WorEFlm; WrDr 76; WhoWor 74*

Cluytens, Andre
Belgian. Conductor
b. Mar 26, 1905 in Antwerp, Belgium
d. Jun 3, 1967 in Paris, France
Source: *WhAm 4*

Clyde, Andy
American. Actor, Comedian
b. Mar 18, 1892 in Blairgowrie, Scotland
d. May 18, 1967 in Los Angeles, California
Source: *FilmgC; MotPP; TwYS; Vers A; WhScrn 74, 77; WhoHol B*

Clyde, Jeremy
see: Chad and Jeremy

Clymer, George
American. Merchant
b. Mar 16, 1739 in Philadelphia, Pennsylvania
d. Jan 23, 1813 in Mornsville, Pennsylvania
Source: *AmBi; ApCAB; BiAuS; BiDrAC; DcAmB; Drake; TwCBDA; WhAm H; WhAmP*

Coanda, Henri Marie
French. Engineer, Inventor
Designed rudimentary jet plane, 1910.
b. Jun 6, 1885 in Bucharest, Romania
d. Nov 25, 1972
Source: *CurBio 56, 73; NewYTBE 72*

Coasters
[Carl Gardner; Cornelius Gunter; Billy Guy; Adolph Jacobs]
American. Rock Group
Source: *BiDAmM; EncPR&S; IlEncRk; Rk100*

Coates, Albert
English. Conductor, Composer
b. Apr 23, 1882 in Saint Petersburg, Russia
d. Dec 11, 1953 in Capetown, South Africa
Source: *NewEOp 71*

Coates, Edith
English. Singer
Founding member of Covent Garden Opera Co, 1937--.
b. May 31, 1908 in Lincoln, England
d. Jan 7, 1983 in Worthing, England
Source: *BioIn 2, 3, 5; Who 74, 75, 76, 77, 78, 79, 80, 81; WhoMus 72*

Coates, Robert Myron
American. Author, Art Critic
b. Apr 6, 1897 in New Haven, Connecticut
d. Feb 8, 1973 in New York, New York
Source: *AmAu&B; AmNov; Au&Wr 71; CnDAL; ConAu 5R, 41R; ConNov 72; DcLEL; NewYTBE 73; OxAmL; Pen AM; REn; REnAL; TwCA, SUP; WhAm 5; WhoAmA 73*

Coats, James
Scottish. Manufacturer
Organized factory to make thread, 1826; became J P Coats, Ltd., 1890.
b. 1774
d. 1857
Source: *WebBD 80*

Coatsworth, Elizabeth Jane
American. Poet, Children's Author
Won Newbery Award for *The Cat Who Went to Heaven,* 1930.
b. May 31, 1893 in Buffalo, New York
Source: *AmAu&B; AmNov; AnCL; Au&ICB; AuBYP; BkCL; ChlLR 2; ChPo, S1, S2; ConAu 5R, 4NR; InWom; JBA 34, 51; MorBMP; Newb 1922; OxAmL; REnAL; SmATA 2; Str&VC; TwCA, SUP; WhoAm 74, 76, 78, 80, 82; WhoChL; WhoWor 74*

Cobb, Arnett Cleophus
American. Musician
b. Aug 10, 1918 in Houston, Texas
Source: *BioIn 10; WhoJazz 72*

Cobb, Irvin Shrewsbury
American. Journalist, Humorist
b. Jun 23, 1876 in Paducah, Kentucky
d. Mar 10, 1944 in New York, New York
Source: *AmAu&B; ChPo; CnDAL; ConAmL; CurBio 44; DcAmB S3; DcNAA; EncMys; EvLB; Film 1; LongCTC; OxAmL; REn; REnAL; TwCA, SUP; WhAm 2; WhNAA; WhScrn 74, 77; WhoHol B*

Cobb, Jerrie
American. Pilot
b. Mar 5, 1931 in Norman, Oklahoma
Source: *BioIn 7; CurBio 61; WhoAmW 74; WhoS&SW 73*

Cobb, Joe
[Our Gang]
"Fat Joe"; "Wheezer"
American. Actor
b. 1917
Source: *Film 2; TwYS; WhoHol A*

Cobb, Lee J (Leo Jacob)
American. Actor
b. Dec 9, 1911 in New York, New York
d. Feb 11, 1976 in Los Angeles, California
Source: *BiDFilm; BiE&WWA; CelR 73; CmMov; CurBio 60; FamA&A; FilmgC; IntMPA 75; MotPP; MovMk; OxFilm; PlP&P; WhAm 6; WhoAm 74; WorEFlm*

Cobb, Stanley
American. Scientist, Physician, Engineer
b. Dec 10, 1887 in Brookline, Massachusetts
d. Feb 18, 1968 in Cambridge, Massachusetts
Source: *BioIn 4; WhAm 4*

Cobb, Ty(rus Raymond)
"The Georgia Peach"
American. Baseball Player
During 24-year career had .367 batting average, 4,191 hits; won 12 batting titles.
b. Dec 18, 1886 in Narrows, Georgia
d. Jul 17, 1961 in Atlanta, Georgia
Source: *CurBio 51, 61; WebAB; WhAm 4; WhScrn 77; WhoProB 73*

Cobb, Vicki
American. Children's Author, Scientist
b. Aug 19, 1938 in New York, New York
Source: *ChlLR 2; ConAu 33R; SmATA 8; WrDr 76*

Cobb, Will D
American. Songwriter
b. Jul 6, 1876 in Philadelphia, Pennsylvania
d. Jan 20, 1930 in New York, New York
Source: *AmSCAP 66; BioIn 4*

Cobb, William Montague
American. Anatomist
b. Oct 12, 1904 in Washington, DC
Source: *AmM&WS 73; BioIn 2, 7, 11; WhoAm 74, 76, 78, 80, 82*

Cobbett, William
English. Journalist
b. Mar 19, 1762 in Farnham, England
d. Jun 18, 1835
Source: *Alli; AmBi; ApCAB; AtlBL; BbD; BbtC; BiD&SB; BiDLA, SUP; BrAu 19; CarSB; CasWL; Chambr 2; CnDAL; DcAmB; DcEnA; DcEnL; DcEuL; DcLEL; Drake; EvLB; MouLC 3; NewC; OxAmL; OxEng; Pen ENG; REn; WebE&AL; WhAm H; WhAmP*

Cobden, Richard
English. Political Leader
b. Jun 3, 1804 in Sussex, England
d. Apr 2, 1865 in London, England
Source: *Alli, SUP; BiD&SB; BrAu 19; NewC; REn*

Cobleigh, Ira Underwood
American. Author, Economist
b. Dec 25, 1903 in Derby, Connecticut
Source: *WhoE 74*

Coburn, Charles Douville
American. Actor, Manager
b. Jun 19, 1877 in Savannah, Georgia
d. Aug 30, 1961 in New York, New York
Source: *BiDFilm; CurBio 44, 61; FilmgC; MotPP; MovMk; OxFilm; OxThe; Vers A; WhAm 4; WhScrn 74, 77; WhoHol B; WorEFlm*

Coburn, James
American. Actor
Starred in *Our Man Flint,* 1966; *In Like Flint,* 1967.
b. Aug 31, 1928 in Laurel, Nebraska
Source: *BiDFilm; BkPepl; CelR 73; FilmgC; IntMPA 75, 76, 77, 78, 79, 80, 81, 82; MotPP; MovMk; OxFilm; WhoAm 74, 76, 78, 80, 82; WhoHol A; WorEFlm*

Coburn, Julia
American. Fashion Executive, Editor
b. in Kansas City, Missouri
Source: *WhoAm 74*

Coca, Imogene
American. Comedienne, Actress
Appeared with Sid Caesar in "Your Show of Shows," 1950-52; had own show, 1954-55.
b. Nov 19, 1908 in Philadelphia, Pennsylvania
Source: *BiE&WWA; BioNews 74; CurBio 51; EncMT; FilmgC; InWom; IntMPA 75, 76, 77, 78, 79, 80, 81, 82; NotNAT; WhoAm 74, 76, 78, 80, 82; WhoHol A; WhoThe 77; WhoWor 74*

Cochet, Henri
[The Four Musketeers]
French. Tennis Player
b. Dec 14, 1901 in Lyons, France
Source: *BioIn 11*

Cochin, Charles Nicholas
French. Type Designer
b. 1715
d. 1790
Source: *NewCol 75; WebBD 80*

Cochise
American Indian. Apache Chief
Waged war against US Army, 1861-72; agreed to live on reservation.
b. 1815 in Arizona
d. Jun 9, 1874 in Arizona
Source: *FilmgC; NewCol 75; WebAB; WhAm H*

Cochran, Barbara Ann
American. Skier
b. Jan 4, 1951 in Claremont, New Hampshire
Source: *BioIn 10, 11*

Cochran, C(harles) B(lake)
English. Impresario
b. Sep 25, 1872 in Lindfield, England
d. Jan 31, 1951 in London, England
Source: *CurBio 40, 51; EncMT; NotNAT B; ObitOF 79; OxThe; WhThe*

Cochran, Eddie
American. Rock Singer, Composer
b. Oct 3, 1938 in Oklahoma City, Oklahoma
d. Apr 17, 1960 in London, England
Source: *WhScrn 77*

Cochran, Jacqueline
[Mrs. Floyd B Odlum]
American. Aviatrix, Cosmetologist
Organized Women's Air Force Service (WASP), 1943.
b. 1910 in Pensacola, Florida
d. Aug 9, 1980 in Indio, California
Source: *AmAu&B; ConAu 101; CurBio 40, 63, 80; GoodHS; HerW; IntWW 75, 76, 77, 78; LibW; WebAB; WebAMB; WhoAm 76, 78; WhoAmW 58, 64, 66, 68, 70, 72, 74, 75*

Cochran, Steve
American. Actor
b. May 25, 1917 in Eureka, California
d. Jun 15, 1965 in Guatemala
Source: *BiE&WWA; FilmgC; MotPP; HolP 40; MovMk; WhScrn 74, 77; WhoHol B; WorEFlm*

Cochran, Thad
American. Senator
b. Dec 7, 1937 in Pontotoc, Mississippi
Source: *AlmAP 78, 80; CngDr 77, 79; WhoAm 74, 76, 78, 80, 82; WhoGov 77; WhoS&SW 75, 76, 78*

Cochrane, Edward Lull
American. Government Official
b. Mar 18, 1892 in Mare Island, California
d. Nov 14, 1959
Source: *CurBio 51, 60*

Cochrane, Mickey (Gordon Stanley)
"Black Mike"
American. Baseball Player, Manager
Managed Detroit Tigers, 1933-38 to two pennants, 1934, 1935.
b. Apr 6, 1903 in Bridgewater, Massachusetts
d. Jun 28, 1962 in Lake Forest, Illinois
Source: *BaseEn; WhoProB 73*

Cockburn, Alexander
English. Journalist
Source: *BioIn 11*

Cockburn, (Francis) Claud
[James Helvick; Frank Pitcairn, pseud.]
British. Journalist
Publisher of *The Week* newssheet, 1933-46.
b. Apr 12, 1904 in Peking, China
d. Dec 15, 1981 in Cork, Ireland
Source: *Au&Wr 71; NewYTBS 81; Who 74, 82; WorAu*

Cockcroft, Sir John Douglas
English. Scientist, Engineer, Physician
b. May 27, 1897 in York, England
d. Sep 18, 1967 in Cambridge, England
Source: *ConAu 21R; WhAm 4*

Cocker, "Joe" (Robert John)
English. Rock Musician
Recorded "Up Where We Belong" from *An Officer and a Gentleman,* with Jennifer Warnes, 1982.
b. May 20, 1944 in Sheffield, England
Source: *BkPepl; EncPR&S; IlEncRk*

Cockerell, Christopher
English. Engineer
b. Jun 1910 in Cambridge, England
Source: *IntWW 74; Who 74; WhoWor 74*

Cockrell, Ewing
American. Peace Organization Official
Founder, president US Federation of Justice, 1929.
b. May 28, 1874 in Warrensburg, Missouri
d. Jan 21, 1962
Source: *CurBio 51, 62*

Coco, James
American. Actor
Oscar nomination for *Only When I Laugh,* 1981.
b. Mar 21, 1929 in New York, New York
Source: *CelR 73; CurBio 74; FilmgC; IntMPA 75, 76, 77, 78, 79, 80, 81, 82; NewYTBE 70; NotNAT; PlP&P; WhoAm 82; WhoE 74; WhoHol A; WhoThe 77*

Cocteau, Jean
French. Author, Artist, Poet
b. Jul 5, 1889 in Maisons-Lafitte, France
d. Oct 12, 1963 in Paris, France
Source: *AtlBL; BiDFilm; CasWL; ClDMEL; CnMD; CnMWL; CnThe; ConAu 25R; ConAu P-2; ConLC 1, 8, 15, 16; CyWA; DcFM; EncWL; EvEuW; FilmgC; LongCTC; McGEWD; ModRL; ModWD; MovMk; OxEng; OxFilm; OxFr; OxThe; Pen EUR; REn; REnWD; TwCA, SUP; TwCW; WhAm 4; WhScrn 77; WhoGrA; WhoTwCL; WorEFlm*

Codarini, Connie
see: Four Lads, The

Codrington, Sir Edward
British. Admiral
b. 1770
d. 1851
Source: *NewCol 75*

Cody, "Buffalo Bill" (William Frederick)
American. Scout, Showman
Shot bison to feed railroad workers; began Buffalo Bill's Wild West Show, 1883.
b. Jan 26, 1846 in Scout County, Iowa
d. Jan 10, 1917 in Denver, Colorado
Source: *AmAu&B; AmBi; ApCAB; DcAmB; DcNAA; EncAB-H; FilmgC; HsB&A; OxAmL; OxFilm; OxThe; REn; REnAL; TwCBDA; WebAB; WhAm 1; WhScrn 77*

Cody, Iron Eyes
American Indian. Actor
b. Apr 3, 1915 in Oklahoma
Source: *FilmEn; MotPP; WhoAm 76, 78, 80, 82; WhoHol A*

Cody, John Patrick
American. Roman Catholic Cardinal
b. Dec 24, 1907 in Saint Louis, Missouri
d. Apr 25, 1982 in Chicago, Illinois
Source: *BioIn 7, 10, 11; CurBio 65, 82; IntWW 74, 75, 76, 77, 78; NewYTBS 82; WhoAm 74, 76, 78, 80, 82; WhoMW 74, 76, 78; WhoRel 75, 77; WhoWor 74*

Cody, Lew
American. Comedian
b. Feb 22, 1887 in Waterville, Maine
d. May 31, 1934 in Beverly Hills, California
Source: *Film 1; FilmgC; MotPP; MovMk; TwYS; WhScrn 74, 77; WhoHol B*

Coe, Frederick H
American. TV Producer
b. Dec 23, 1914 in Alligator, Mississippi
d. Apr 29, 1979 in Los Angeles, California
Source: *BiE&WWA; ConAu 85; CurBio 59, 79; FilmgC; IntMPA 75, 76, 77, 78, 79; NewYTBS 79; NewYTET; NotNAT; WhoAm 74; WhoThe 77*

Coe, Ralph T(racy)
American. Author, Museum Director
b. Aug 27, 1929 in Cleveland, Ohio
Source: *ConAu 1R, 1NR; DrAS 74H, 78H*

Coe, Sebastian
English. Track Athlete
First to hold world records for fastest mile, 800 meter, and 1,500 meter races.
b. 1957? in Sheffield, England
Source: *NF*

Coen, Jan Pieterszoon
Dutch. Dutch Colonial Governor
b. 1587 in Hoorn, Netherlands
d. Sep 21, 1629
Source: *BioIn 4; McGEWB*

Coeur, Jacques
French. Merchant Prince
b. 1395
d. 1456
Source: *NewCol 75*

Coffin, Charles Albert
American. Business Executive
b. Dec 1844 in Somerset County, Maine
d. Nov 9, 1926 in Portland, Oregon
Source: *DcAmB; WhAm 1*

Coffin, Henry Sloane
American. Clergyman
b. Jan 5, 1877 in New York, New York
d. Nov 25, 1954 in Lakeville, Connecticut
Source: *AmAu&B; CurBio 44, 55; DcAmB S5; WhAm 3*

Coffin, Levi
American. Abolitionist
b. Oct 28, 1798 in New Garden, North Carolina
d. Sep 16, 1877
Source: *BioIn 1, 2, 6, 8, 10; DcNAA; IndAu 1816; McGEWB; OhA&B; WebAB*

Coffin, Robert Peter Tristram
American. Poet, Essayist, Biographer
b. Mar 18, 1892 in Brunswick, Maine
d. Oct 29, 1956 in Raleigh, North Carolina
Source: *AmAu&B; AnMV 1926; ChPo, S1, S2; CnDAL; ConAmA; DcAmB S5; DcLEL; LongCTC; OxAmL; Pen AM; REn; REnAL; Str&VC; TwCA, SUP; WhAm 3; WhNAA*

Coffin, William Sloan
American. Clergyman, Social Activist
b. Jun 1, 1924 in New York, New York
Source: *CurBio 68; WhoAm 74, 76, 78, 80, 82; WhoWor 74*

Coggan, Frederick Donald
English. Archbishop
b. Oct 9, 1909 in London, England
Source: *IntWW 74; WhoAm 74, 76, 78, 80, 82; WhoWor 74*

Coghill, Nevill Henry Kendall Aylmer
English. Chaucer Scholar, Director
b. Apr 19, 1899 in Castletownshend, England
d. Nov 1980 in Cheltenham, England
Source: *ConAu 13R, 102; ConDr 73, 77D; NewC; REn; WhoThe 77, 81*

Coghlan, Charles Francis
Actor, Dramatist
b. 1841 in Paris, France
d. Nov 27, 1899 in Galveston, Texas
Source: *NotNAT B; OxThe; PlP&P*

Coghlan, Eamonn
"Cockie"
Irish. Track Athlete
b. 1953 in Dublin, Ireland
Source: *BioIn 11; NewYTBS 81*

Coghlan, Rose
Actress
b. Mar 18, 1851 in Peterborough, England
d. Apr 2, 1932 in Harrison, New York
Source: *FamA&A; NotNAT B; OxThe; PlP&P; WhScrn 74, 77*

Cohan, George Michael
American. Actor, Dramatist, Producer
b. Jul 3, 1878 in Providence, Rhode Island
d. Nov 5, 1942 in New York, New York
Source: *AmAu&B; AmSCAP 66; CnMD; CurBio 43; DcAmB S3; EncAB-H; EncMT; FamA&A; Film 1; FilmgC; LongCTC; McGEWD; ModWD; NewCBMT; OxThe; PlP&P; REn; REnAL; TwYS; WebAB; WhAm 1; WhScrn 74, 77; WhoHol B; WhoStg 1906, 1908*

Cohan, Josephine
American. Actress
b. 1876 in Providence, Rhode Island
d. Jul 12, 1916 in New York, New York
Source: *NotNAT B*

Cohen, Alexander H
American. Motion Picture Producer
b. Jul 24, 1920 in New York, New York
Source: *BiE&WWA; CelR 73; CurBio 65; EncMT; NotNAT; WhoAm 74, 76, 78, 80, 82; WhoThe 77; WhoWor 74*

Cohen, Benjamin V
American. Lawyer
b. Sep 23, 1894 in Muncie, Indiana
Source: *ConAu P-1; CurBio 41; IndAu 1917; WhoAm 74; WhoWorJ 72*

Cohen, Daniel
American. Author
b. Mar 12, 1936 in Chicago, Illinois
Source: *ConAu 45, 1NR; SmATA 8*

Cohen, Joan Lebold
American. Author
b. Aug 19, 1932 in Highland Park, Illinois
Source: *ConAu 25R; SmATA 4*

Cohen, Leonard
Canadian. Author, Songwriter, Singer
Songs include "Suzanne"; "Hey, That's No Way to Say Goodbye," 1968.
b. Sep 21, 1934 in Montreal, PQ
Source: *CanWW 82; CanWr; CasWL; CelR 73; ConAu 21R; ConLC 3; ConNov 72, 76; ConP 70, 75; OxCan, SUP; WebE&AL; WhoAm 74, 76, 78, 80, 82; WrDr 76*

Cohen, "Mickey" (Meyer)
American. Racketeer
b. 1913
d. 1976
Source: *BioIn 10, 11*

Cohen, Myron
American. Comedian
b. 1902 in Grodno, Poland
Source: *NewYTBE 70*

Cohen, Octavus Roy
American. Author, Journalist
b. Jun 26, 1891 in Charleston, South Carolina
d. Jan 6, 1959 in Los Angeles, California
Source: *AmAu&B; EncMys; OxAmL; REn; REnAL; TwCA, SUP; WhAm 3; WhNAA*

Cohen, Wilbur Joseph
American. Educator, Author
b. Jun 10, 1913 in Milwaukee, Wisconsin
Source: *AmEA 74; AmM&WS 73S; BiDrUSE; ConAu 25R; CurBio 68; IntWW 74; LEduc 74; WhoAm 74, 76, 78, 80, 82; WhoAmP 73; WhoWor 74; WhoWorJ 72*

Cohen, William Sebastian
American. Congressman
b. Aug 28, 1940 in Bangor, Maine
Source: *AlmAP 78, 80; BioIn 10, 11; CurBio 82; PolProf NF; WhoAm 74, 76, 78, 80, 82; WhoAmP 73, 75, 77, 79; WhoE 77, 79; WhoGov 75, 77*

Cohn, Al
American. Jazz Musician, Composer
b. Nov 24, 1925 in Brooklyn, New York
Source: *AmSCAP 66; WhoAm 82*

Cohn, Arthur
American. Composer, Conductor
b. Nov 6, 1910 in Philadelphia, Pennsylvania
Source: *AmSCAP 66; BioIn 1; WhoWorJ 72*

Cohn, Emil Ludwig
see: Ludwig, Emil

Cohn, Ferdinand Julius
Polish. Botanist
b. Jan 24, 1828 in Breslau, Poland
d. Jun 25, 1898 in Breslau, Poland
Source: *AsBiEn; BiHiMed; DcScB*

Cohn, Roy Marcus
American. Lawyer
b. Feb 20, 1927 in New York, New York
Source: *WhoAm 74, 76, 78, 80, 82; WhoE 74; WhoWorJ 72*

Cohn-Bendit, Daniel
French. Anarchist
b. 1945
Source: *BioIn 11*

Coit, Margaret Louise
American. Author
b. May 30, 1922 in Norwich, Connecticut
Source: *AmAu&B; AuBYP; ConAu 1R, 5NR; CurBio 51; DrAS 74H; InWom; OxAmL; REnAL; SmATA 2; TwCA SUP; WhoAm 74, 76, 78, 80, 82*

Coke, Sir Edward
English. Jurist
b. Feb 1, 1552 in Mileham, England
d. Sep 3, 1634 in Stoke Poges, England
Source: *Alli; BrAu; DcEnL; McGEWB; NewC; OxEng*

Colavito, Rocky (Rocco Domenico)
American. Baseball Player
Lead AL in RBI's with 108, 1965.
b. Aug 10, 1933 in New York, New York
Source: *BaseEn; BioIn 5, 6, 7, 9; WhoProB 73*

Colbert, Claudette
[Claudette Chauchoin]
American. Actress
b. Sep 13, 1905 in Paris, France
Source: *BiDFilm; BiE&WWA; BioNews 74; CelR 73; CurBio 45, 64; FilmgC; InWom; IntMPA 75, 76, 77, 78, 79, 80, 81, 82; MotPP; MovMk; OxFilm; PlP&P; ThFT; Who 82; WhoAm 74, 76, 78, 80, 82; WhoHol A; WhoThe 77; WomWMM; WorEFlm*

Colbert, Jean Baptiste
French. Statesman
b. Aug 29, 1619 in Reims, France
d. Sep 6, 1683
Source: *OxFr; REn*

Colbert, Lester Lum
American. Lawyer
b. Jun 13, 1905 in Oakwood, Texas
Source: *BioIn 2, 4, 5; CurBio 51; IntWW 74; WhoAm 74, 76, 78, 80, 82*

Colbran, Isabella
Spanish. Opera Singer
b. Feb 2, 1785 in Madrid, Spain
d. Oct 7, 1845 in Bologna, Italy
Source: *InWom*

Colby, Anita
American. Actress, Model, Editor
b. 1914 in Washington, DC
Source: *AmAu&B; InWom; MotPP; WhoHol A*

Colby, Carroll Burleigh
American. Author, Artist
b. Sep 7, 1904 in Claremont, New Hampshire
d. Oct 31, 1977
Source: *AuBYP; ConAu 1R; MorJA; SmATA 3; WhAm 7; WhoAm 74, 76, 78*

Colby, William Egan
American. Former Government Official
Director, CIA, 1973-76.
b. Jan 4, 1920 in Saint Paul, Minnesota
Source: *CurBio 75; IntWW 74; NewYTBE 73; WhoAm 74, 76, 78, 80, 82; WhoGov 72; WhoS&SW 73; WhoWor 74*

Colden, Cadwallader
Irish. Botanist, Author
b. Feb 7, 1688 in Ireland
d. Sep 28, 1776 in Long Island, New York
Source: *AmAu; AmAu&B; CyAL 1; DcAmAu; DcEnL; DcNAA; OxAmL; OxCan; REnAL*

Cole, Charles Woolsey
American. Educator, Ambassador to Chile
b. Feb 8, 1907 in Montclair, New Jersey
d. Feb 6, 1978 in Los Angeles, California
Source: *AmAu&B; IntWW 74; Who 74; WhoAm 74*

Cole, "Cozy" (William Randolph)
American. Musician
b. Oct 17, 1909 in East Orange, New Jersey
d. Jan 29, 1981 in Columbus, Ohio
Source: *BiDAmM; CmpEPM; DcBlPA; EncJzS 70; IlEncJ; NewYTBS 81; WhAm 7; WhoAm 74; WhoE 74; WhoJazz 72*

Cole, Dennis
American. Actor
b. Jul 19, 1943 in Detroit, Michigan
Source: *WhoHol A*

Cole, Edward Nicholas
American. Auto Executive, Engineer
President, GM, 1967-74.
b. Sep 17, 1909 in Michigan
d. May 2, 1977 in Kalamazoo, Michigan
Source: *BioNews 74; BusPN; CelR 73; CurBio 72; IntWW 74; St&PR 75; Ward 77G; Who 74; WhoAm 74; WhoF&I 74; WhoMW 74*

Cole, George
English. Actor
b. Apr 22, 1925 in London, England
Source: *FilmgC; IntMPA 75, 76, 77, 78, 79, 80, 81, 82; Who 74; WhoHol B; WhoThe 77*

Cole, Jack
American. Choreographer
b. Apr 27, 1914 in New Brunswick, New Jersey
d. Feb 17, 1974 in Los Angeles, California
Source: *BiE&WWA; CmMov; EncMT; FilmgC; NewYTBS 74; WhAm 2; WhScrn 77; WhoAm 74; WhoHol B; WorEFlm*

Cole, Kenneth Reese
American. Presidential Aide, Business Exec.
Special assistant to Nixon, 1969-70; assistant to Ford on domestic affairs, 1974-75.
b. Jan 27, 1938 in New York, New York
Source: *NewYTBS 74; WhoAm 74, 76, 78, 80, 82*

Cole, Michael
American. Actor
b. Jul 3, 1945 in Madison, Wisconsin
Source: *WhoHol A*

Cole, Nat "King" (Nathaniel Adams)
American. Singer, Band Leader, Actor
Best known songs include "Mona Lisa," 1950; "Ramblin' Rose," 1962.
b. Mar 17, 1919 in Montgomery, Alabama
d. Feb 15, 1965 in Santa Monica, California
Source: *AmSCAP 66; CurBio 56, 65; FilmgC; MovMk; WhAm 4; WhScrn 74, 77; WhoHol B; WhoJazz 72*

Cole, Natalie
American. Singer
Won Grammy for best new artist, 1976; debut album *Inseparable.*
b. Feb 6, 1950 in Los Angeles, California
Source: *BioIn 10, 11; BkPepl; WhoAm 80, 82*

Cole, Olivia
American. Actress
b. 1942 in Memphis, Tennessee
Source: *BioIn 11; WhoAm 82*

Cole, Thomas
American. Artist
b. Feb 1, 1801 in Bolton, England
d. Feb 11, 1848 in Catskill, New York
Source: *Alli; AmAu&B; AmBi; ApCAB; CyAl 2; DcAmB; Drake; EncAB-H; OxAmL; TwCBDA; WebAB; WhAm H*

Cole, Timothy
American. Wood Engraver
b. Apr 6, 1852 in London, England
d. May 11, 1931
Source: *BioIn 3, 4, 5; NatCAB 13; WhAm 1; WhNAA*

Cole, Tina
[The King Family]
American. Actress, Singer
b. 1943 in Hollywood, California
Source: *WhoHol A*

Coleman, Cy
[Seymour Kaufman]
American. Songwriter
Wrote song "If My Friends Could See Me Now."
b. Jun 14, 1929 in New York, New York
Source: *AmSCAP 66; BiE&WWA; BioNews 75; CelR 73; EncMT; NewCBMT; NotNAT; WhoAm 74, 76, 78, 80, 82; WhoE 74*

Coleman, Gary
American. Actor
b. Feb 8, 1968 in Zion, Illinois
Source: *BioIn 11*

Coleman, James Samuel
American. Sociologist
b. May 12, 1926 in Bedford, Indiana
Source: *AmM&WS 73S; ConAu 13R, 1NR; CurBio 70; IndAu 1917; IntWW 74; LEduc 74; WhoAm 74, 76, 78, 80, 82; WhoE 74; WhoWor 74*

Coleman, John
American. Meteorologist
Gives national weather report on "Good Morning, America."
b. Nov 15, 1935 in Champaign, Illinois
Source: *NF*

Coleman, Lester L
American. Biochemist
b. Nov 6, 1912 in Maricopa, California
Source: *AmM&WS 73P; WhoMW 74*

Coleman, Lonnie William
American. Author
Wrote *Beulah Land; Look Away, Beulah Land; The Legacy of Beulah Land.*
b. Aug 2, 1920 in Barstow, Georgia
d. Aug 13, 1982 in Savannah, Georgia
Source: *AmAu&B; AmNov; BiE&WWA; ConAu 77; CurBio 58, 82; NewYTBS 82; NotNAT*

Coleman, Ornette
American. Jazz Musician
b. Mar 19, 1930 in Fort Worth, Texas
Source: *AmSCAP 66; CurBio 61; WhoAm 74, 76, 78, 80, 82; WhoBlA 75*

Coleman, William T
American. Lawyer
b. Jul 7, 1920 in Germantown, Pennsylvania
Source: *WhoAm 74, 76, 78, 80, 82; WhoBlA 75*

Coleridge, Hartley
English. Poet, Journalist
b. Sep 19, 1796 in Bristol, England
d. Jan 6, 1849 in Grasmere, England
Source: *BiD&SB; CasWL; Chambr 3; DcEnA; DcEnL; DcEuL; DcLEL; EvLB; NewC; Pen ENG*

Coleridge, Samuel Taylor
English. Author, Poet, Critic
Wrote "The Rime of the Ancient Mariner" and "Kubla Khan."
b. Oct 21, 1772 in Devonshire, England
d. Jul 25, 1834 in London, England
Source: *Alli; AtlBL; BbD; BiD&SB; BiDLA; BrAu 19; CasWL; Chambr 3; ChPo, S1, S2; CnE&AP; CrtT 2; CyWA; DcEnA; DcEnL; DcEuL; DcLEL; EvLB; MouLC 3; NewC; OxEng; OxThe; Pen ENG; RAdv 1; RComWL; REn; WebE&AL*

Coleridge-Taylor, Samuel
English. Composer
b. Aug 15, 1875 in London, England
d. Sep 1, 1912 in Thornton, England
Source: *WhDW*

Coles, Manning, pseud.
[Cyril Coles and Adelaide Frances Oke Manning]
English. Authors
Source: *ConAu 9R; ConAu P-1; EncMys; LongCTC; TwCA SUP*

Coles, William Allan
American. Author
b. Oct 15, 1930 in Boston, Massachusetts
Source: *ConAu 33R; DrAS 74E, 78E*

Colette, pseud.
[Sidonie Gabriellee Colette]
French. Author
b. Jan 28, 1873 in Saint Sauveur, France
d. Aug 3, 1954 in Paris, France
Source: *AtlBL; CasWL; ClDMEL; CnMWL; CyWA; EncWL; EvEuW; LongCTC; ModRL; OxEng; OxFr; Pen EUR; REn; TwCA, SUP; TwCW; WhoTwCL*

Colfax, Schuyler
American. Politician, Vice-President
Vice-President under U S Grant, 1869-73; involvement in scandal ended career.
b. Mar 23, 1823 in New York, New York
d. Jan 13, 1885 in Mankato, Minnesota
Source: *AmBi; ApCAB; BiAuS; BiDrAC; BiDrUSE; DcAmB; Drake; IndAu 1816; TwCBDA; WebAB; WhAm H; WhAmP*

Colgate, William
American. Manufacturer
Began soap making business, 1806; later became Colgate-Palmolive.
b. Jan 25, 1783 in Hollingbourne, England
d. Mar 25, 1857 in New York, New York
Source: *AmBi; ApCAB; DcAmB; TwCBDA; WebAB; WhAm H*

Colicos, John
Canadian. Actor
b. Dec 10, 1928 in Toronto, ON
Source: *CreCan 1; FilmgC; NotNAT; WhoAm 82; WhoThe 77*

Collazo, Oscar
Puerto Rican. Revolutionary
b. 1914
Source: *BioIn 10*

Collett, Glenna
American. Golfer
b. 1903
Source: *BioIn 6, 9, 11*

Collier, Constance
English. Actress
b. Jan 22, 1878 in Windsor, England
d. Apr 25, 1955 in New York, New York
Source: *CurBio 54, 55; DcAmB S5; Film 1; FilmgC; InWom; MotPP; MovMk; NewC; OxThe; PlP&P; REn; ThFT; TwYS A; Vers A; WhScrn 74, 77; WhoHol B*

Collier, John
English. Author
b. May 3, 1901 in London, England
d. Apr 6, 1980 in Pacific Palisades, California
Source: *ConNov 72, 76; DcLEL; EncMys; NewC; REn; TwCA, SUP; WrDr 76*

Collier, William, Sr.
American. Actor, Director, Dramatist
b. Nov 12, 1866 in New York, New York
d. Jan 13, 1944 in Beverly Hills, California
Source: *Film 1; FilmgC; MovMk; WhAm 2; WhScrn 74, 77; WhoHol B; WhoStg 1906, 1908*

Collin, Frank
American. Leader of American Nazi Party
b. 1945?
Source: *BioIn 11*

Collinge, Patricia
Irish. Actress
b. Sep 20, 1894 in Dublin, Ireland
Source: *BiE&WWA; FilmgC; NewYTBS 74; NotNAT B; OxFilm; WhScrn 77; WhThe; WhoAmW 74*

Collingwood, Charles
American. Broadcast Journalist
b. Jun 4, 1917 in Three Rivers, Michigan
Source: *CelR 73; ConAu 29R; CurBio 43; IntWW 74; WhoAm 74, 76, 78, 80, 82; WhoWor 74*

Collingwood, Robin George
English. Philosopher, Archeologist
b. 1889 in Coniston, England
d. Jan 9, 1943
Source: *CasWL; CnMWL; DcLEL; LongCTC; OxEng; Pen ENG; REn; TwCA SUP*

Collins, Dorothy
[Marjorie Chandler]
Canadian. Singer
b. Nov 18, 1926 in Windsor, ON
Source: *InWom; NewYTBE 71; PlP&P A*

Collins, Doug
American. Basketball Player
b. Jul 28, 1951 in Christopher, Illinois
Source: *BioIn 9; WhoBbl 73*

Collins, Eddie (Edward Trowbridge, Sr.)
"Cocky"
American. Baseball Player, Manager
Hall of Fame, 1939; lifetime batting average .333.
b. May 2, 1887 in Millertown, New York
d. Mar 25, 1951 in Boston, Massachusetts
Source: *BaseEn; DcAmB S5; WhoProB 73*

Collins, James Joseph (Jimmy)
American. Baseball Player
b. Jan 16, 1873 in Niagara Falls, New York
d. Mar 6, 1943 in Buffalo, New York
Source: *BaseEn; BioIn 2, 3, 7; WhoProB 73*

Collins, Joan
[Mrs. Ron Kass]
English. Actress
Plays role of Alexis Carrington Colby on TV series "Dynasty."
b. May 23, 1933 in London, England
Source: *FilmgC; InWom; IntMPA 75, 76, 77, 78, 79, 80, 81, 82; MotPP; MovMk; WhoAm 82; WhoHol A*

Collins, Joseph L
American. Army Officer
b. May 1, 1896 in New Orleans, Louisiana
Source: *CurBio 49; IntWW 74; Who 74; WhoAm 74*

Collins, Judy (Judith)
American. Singer
Hits include "Both Sides Now," 1968; "Send in the Clowns," 1975.
b. May 1, 1939 in Seattle, Washington
Source: *CelR 73; CurBio 69; EncFCWM 69; WhoAm 74, 76, 78, 80, 82; WhoAmW 77; WhoWor 74*

Collins, Kelly
American. Sister of Bo Derek
b. 1962?
Source: *NF*

Collins, Larry
American. Author, Journalist
b. Sep 14, 1929 in Hartford, Connecticut
Source: *AmAu&B; CelR 73; WhoAm 74, 76, 78, 80, 82; WhoWor 74*

Collins, Lee
American. Musician
b. Oct 17, 1901 in New Orleans, Louisiana
d. Jul 7, 1960 in Chicago, Illinois
Source: *WhoJazz 72*

Collins, Marva Deloise Nettles
American. Teacher, Education Reformer
Film *Welcome to Success,* 1981 based on her life.
b. Aug 31, 1936 in Monroeville, Alabama
Source: *BioIn 12; WhoAm 82*

Collins, Michael
Irish. Revolutionary
b. 1890 in County Cork, Ireland
d. Aug 22, 1922
Source: *WebBD 80*

Collins, Mike (Michael)
American. Astronaut
Command module pilot, Apollo 11, first US landing on moon, 1969.
b. Oct 31, 1930 in Rome, Italy
Source: *AmM&WS 73P; CelR 73; ConAu 53; IntWW 74; Who 74; WhoAm 74, 76, 78, 80, 82; WhoGov 72; WhoS&SW 73; WhoWor 74*

Collins, Phil
see: Genesis

Collins, Ray
American. Actor
b. 1890 in Sacremento, California
d. Jul 11, 1965 in Santa Monica, California
Source: *FilmgC; MotPP; MovMk; Vers A; WhScrn 74, 77; WhoHol B*

Collins, Stephen
American. Actor
Stars in TV series "Tales of the Gold Monkey," 1982--.
b. Oct 1, 1947 in Des Moines, Iowa
Source: *IntMPA 82*

Collins, Ted
American. Radio, TV Producer
b. Oct 12, 1899 in New York, New York
d. May 27, 1964 in Lake Placid, New York
Source: *NotNAT B*

Collins, Wilkie (William)
English. Author
Mystery novels *The Woman in White,* 1860; *The Moonstone,* 1868.
b. Jan 8, 1824 in London, England
d. Sep 23, 1889 in London, England
Source: *AtlBL; BbD; BiD&SB; BrAu 19; CasWL; Chambr 3; CrtT 3; CyWA; DcBiA; DcEnA; DcEnL; DcEuL; DcLEL; EncMys; EvLB; HsB&A; MnBBF; NewC; Pen ENG; RAdv 1; REn; WebE&AL*

Collins, William
English. Poet
b. Dec 25, 1721 in Chichester, England
d. Jun 12, 1759 in Chichester, England
Source: *Alli; AtlBL; BbD; BiD&SB; BrAu; CasWL; Chambr 2; ChPo, S1; CnE&AP; CrtT 2; DcEnA; DcEnL; DcEuL; DcLEL; EvLB; MouLC 2; NewC; OxEng; Pen ENG; REn; WebE&AL*

Collinsworth, (Anthony) Chris
"Cadillac"
American. Football Player
b. Jan 27, 1959 in Titusville, Florida
Source: *NewYTBS 82*

Collishaw, Raymond
English. World War I Air Ace
b. Nov 22, 1893 in Nonaimo, BC
d. 1977?
Source: *CanWW 70; Who 74*

Collodi, Carlo, pseud.
[Carlo Lorenzini]
Italian. Author
Story *Pinocchio,* first appeared in newspaper, 1880; English translation, 1892.
b. Nov 24, 1826 in Tuscany, Italy
d. Oct 26, 1890 in Florence, Italy
Source: *AnCL; AuBYP; BkCL; CasWL; EuAu; EvEuW; JBA 34, 51; NewCol 75; Str&VC; WhoChL*

Collyer, "Bud" (Clayton)
American. TV Announcer
b. 1908 in New York, New York
d. Sep 8, 1969 in Greenwich, Connecticut
Source: *BioIn 8*

Collyer, Homer Lusk
American. Recluse
b. 1881
d. 1947
Source: *BioIn 1, 3, 4, 8*

Collyer, Langley
American. Recluse
b. 1886
d. 1947
Source: *BioIn 1, 3, 4, 8*

Colman, Norman Jay
American. Government Official
First Secretary of Agriculture, 1889.
b. May 16, 1827 in Otsego County, New York
d. Nov 3, 1911
Source: *AmBi; BiDrUSE; DcAmB; EncAAH; TwCBDA; WhAm 1*

Colman, Ronald
American. Actor
Won Oscar for *A Double Life,* 1948; appeared in *A Tale of Two Cities,* 1936.
b. Feb 9, 1891 in Richmond, England
d. May 19, 1958 in Santa Barbara, California
Source: *BiDFilm; CmMov; CurBio 43, 58; Film 1; FilmgC; MotPP; MovMk; OxFilm; TwYS; WhAm 3; WhScrn 74, 77; WhoHol B; WorEFlm*

Colombo, Emilio
Italian. Political Leader
b. Apr 11, 1920 in Potenza, Italy
Source: *CurBio 71; IntWW 74; WhoWor 74*

Colombo, Joseph Anthony
American. Gangster
b. 1922
d. 1978 in Newburgh, New York
Source: *BioIn 10*

Colonius, Lillian
American. Children's Author
b. Mar 19, 1911 in Irvine, California
Source: *ConAu 25R; SmATA 3*

Colonna, Jerry
American. Comedian, Musician
b. Sep 17, 1905 in Boston, Massachusetts
Source: *AmSCAP 66; FilmgC; MovMk; WhoHol A*

Colonna di Castiglione, Adele
Italian. Artist
b. 1836
d. 1879
Source: *BioIn 10*

Colonne, Edouard
French. Conductor
b. Jul 23, 1838 in Bordeaux, France
d. Mar 28, 1910 in Paris, France
Source: *NewCol 75; OxMus*

Colson, Charles Wendell
American. Watergate Participant
b. Oct 16, 1931 in Boston, Massachusetts
Source: *NewYTBE 73; NewYTBS 74; WhoAm 74, 76, 78, 80, 82; WhoGov 72; WhoS&SW 73*

Colt, Samuel
American. Inventor
Patented revolving breech pistol, 1835; word "Colt" often synonymous with revolver.
b. Jul 19, 1814 in Hartford, Connecticut
d. Jan 10, 1862 in Hartford, Connecticut
Source: *AmBi; ApCAB; DcAmB; Drake; TwCBDA; WebAB; WhAm H*

Colter, Jessi
[Miriam Johnson Jennings; Mrs. Waylon Jennings]
American. Singer
b. May 25, 1947 in Phoenix, Arizona
Source: *BkPepl; RkOn; WhoAm 82*

Colter, John
American. Explorer, Trapper
First white man to explore Teton Mt. Range, 1807.
b. 1775 in Staunton, Virginia
d. Nov 1813 in Dundee, Missouri
Source: *NewCol 75; WhAm H*

Coltrane, "Trane" (John William)
American. Jazz Musician
b. Sep 26, 1926 in Hamlet, North Carolina
d. Jul 17, 1967 in Huntington, New York
Source: *WebAB; WhAm 4*

Colum, Padraic
Irish. Poet, Dramatist, Author
b. Dec 8, 1881 in Langford, Ireland
d. Jan 12, 1972 in New York, New York
Source: *AmAu&B; AmSCAP 66; AnCL; AuBYP; BkC 3; CarSB; CasWL; CathA 1930; ChPo, S1, S2; CnMD; ConAu 33R, 73; ConP 70; DcLEL; EncWL; EvLB; FamSYP; JBA 34, 51; LongCTC; McGEWD; ModBrL, SUP; ModWD; NewC; NewYTBE 71, 72; OxThe; Pen ENG; RAdv 1; REn; REnWD; SmATA 15; Str&VC; TwCA, SUP; TwCW; WebE&AL; WhAm 5*

Columba, Saint
Irish. Missionary
b. 521
d. 597
Source: *NewCol 75*

Columban, Saint
Irish. Missionary, Scholar
b. 543
d. 615 in Bobbia, Italy
Source: *NewC; NewCol 75*

Columbo, Russ
[Ruggerio de Rudolpho Columbo]
American. Actor, Singer
Appeared in *Broadway Through a Keyhole*, 1933.
b. Jan 4, 1908 in Philadelphia, Pennsylvania
d. Sep 2, 1934 in Hollywood, California
Source: *FilmgC; WhScrn 74, 77; WhoHol B*

Columbus, Christopher
[Cristoforo Colombo]
Italian. Explorer
Sailed from Palos, Spain, Aug 3, 1492; sighted land, San Salvador, Oct 12, 1492.
b. 1451 in Genoa, Italy
d. May 20, 1506 in Spain
Source: *CasWL; DcEuL; EncAB-H; EvEuW; NewC; OxAmL; REn; REnAL; WebAB*

Comaneci, Nadia
Romanian. Gymnast
Won three Olympic gold medals, 1976; received seven perfect scores.
b. Nov 12, 1961 in Onesti, Romania
Source: *BioIn 10; BkPepl; NewYTBS 81; WorAl*

Combs, Earle Bryan
"The Kentucky Colonel"
American. Baseball Player
Outfielder, NY Yankees, 1924-35; Hall of Fame, 1970.
b. May 14, 1899 in Pebworth, Kentucky
Source: *BaseEn; WhoProB 73*

Comden, Betty
[Mrs. Steven Kyle]
American. Songwriter
Won Tony, 1970, for *Applause.*
b. May 3, 1915 in New York, New York
Source: *WomWMM; WorEFlm; AmAu&B; AmSCAP 66; BiE&WWA; CelR 73; ConAu 49, 2NR; ConDr 73; CurBio 45; EncMT; FilmgC; InWom; IntMPA 75, 76, 77, 78, 79, 80, 81, 82; NewCBMT; NotNAT; OxFilm; WhoAm 74, 76, 78, 80, 82; WhoThe 77*

Comencini, Luigi
Italian. Motion Picture Director
b. Jun 8, 1916 in Saio, Italy
Source: *DcFM; FilmgC; WorEFlm*

Comenius, Johann Amos
Czech. Theologian, Educator, Mystic
b. Mar 28, 1592 in Unersky, Moravia
d. Nov 15, 1670 in Amsterdam, Netherlands
Source: *BbD; BiD&SB; CarSB; CasWL; ChPo, S1; DcEuL; EuAu; EvEuW; Pen EUR; Str&VC*

Comer, Anjanette
American. Actress
b. Aug 7, 1942 in Dawson, Texas
Source: *FilmEn; FilmgC; MotPP; WhoHol A*

Comer, Tex
see: Ace

Comfort, Alexander
English. Author, Sociologist
b. Feb 10, 1920 in London, England
Source: *ConAu 1R, 1NR; ConNov 72, 76; ConP 70, 75; EncWL; EvLB; IntWW 74; LongCTC; ModBrL; Pen ENG; TwCA SUP; Who 82; WhoAm 82; WhoWor 74; WrDr 76*

Comines, Philippe de
French. Historian, Diplomat
b. 1445 in Renescure, Flanders
d. 1511 in Argentan, France
Source: *BbD; BiD&SB; NewCol 75; OxEng; REn*

Comiskey, Charlie (Charles Albert)
["Commy"; "Old Roman"]
American. Baseball Player, Executive
Purchased franchise that became Chicago White Sox, 1895; Hall of Fame, 1939.
b. Aug 15, 1859 in Chicago, Illinois
d. Oct 26, 1931 in Eagle River, Wisconsin
Source: *BaseEn; WhoProB 73*

Comissiona, Sergiu
Romanian. Conductor
b. Jun 16, 1928 in Bucharest, Romania
Source: *BioNews 74; WhoAm 74, 76, 78, 80, 82; WhoMus 72; WhoWor 74*

Commager, Henry Steele
American. Historian, Educator
b. Oct 25, 1902 in Pittsburgh, Pennsylvania
Source: *AmAu&B; ApCAB; AuBYP; BioNews 74; ChPo S1; ConAu 21R; CurBio 46; DcLEL; DrAS 74H; IntWW 74; OxAmL; Pen AM; REn; REnAL; SmATA 23; TwCA SUP; WebAB; Who 74; WhoAm 74, 76, 78, 80, 82; WhoE 74; WhoWor 74; WrDr 76*

Commander Cody & His Lost Planet Airmen
[Bruce Barlow; Robert Black; Lance Dickerson; William Farlow; George Fayne; Ernest Hager; William Kirchen; Andrew Stein; John Tichy]
American. Rock Group
Source: *IlEncRk*

Commodores, The
[William King; Ronald LaPread; Thomas McClary; Walter "Clyde" Orange; Lionel Richie, Jr.; Milan Williams]
American. Singing Group
Source: *BkPepl; RkOn*

Commoner, Barry
American. Biologist, Politician
b. May 28, 1917 in Brooklyn, New York
Source: *AmAu&B; AmM&WS 73P; CelR 73; CurBio 70; IntWW 74; WhoAm 74, 76, 78, 80, 82; WhoWor 74*

Commons, John Rogers
American. Economist, Labor Historian
b. Oct 13, 1862 in Hollansburg, Ohio
d. May 11, 1945 in Raleigh, North Carolina
Source: *DcAmAu; DcAmB S3; McGEWB; WebAB; WhAm 2*

Como, Perry (Pierino Roland)
American. Singer
First hit "Till the End of Time," 1945; TV show, 1948-63.
b. May 18, 1913 in Canonsburg, Pennsylvania
Source: *AmCath 80; AmPS A, B; BiDAmM; BkPepl; CelR 73; CmpEPM; CurBio 47; FilmgC; IntMPA 75, 76, 77, 78, 79, 80, 81, 82; NewYTET; RkOn; WhoAm 74, 76, 78, 80, 82; WhoHol A; WhoMus 72*

Compton, Ann
American. Broadcast Journalist
b. Jan 19, 1947 in Chicago, Illinois
Source: *BioIn 10; WhoAm 80, 82*

Compton, Arthur Holly
American. Scientist, Physician, Engineer
b. Sep 10, 1892 in Wooster, Ohio
d. Mar 15, 1962 in Berkeley, California
Source: *AmAu&B; CurBio 40, 58, 62; EncAB-H; OhA&B; REnAL; WebAB; WhAm HA, 4*

Compton, Betty
English. Actress, Singer
b. 1907 in Isle of Wight
d. Jul 12, 1944 in New York, New York
Source: *NotNAT B; WhScrn 74, 77; WhoHol B*

Compton, Fay
English. Actress
b. Sep 18, 1894 in London, England
d. Dec 12, 1978
Source: *BiE&WWA; Film 1, 2; NotNAT A; OxThe; PlP&P; Who 74; WhoThe 72*

Compton, Joyce
American. Actress
b. 1907 in Lexington, Kentucky
Source: *IntMPA 75, 76, 77, 78, 79, 80, 81, 82; MotPP; MovMk; ThFT*

Compton, Karl Taylor
American. Physicist
b. Sep 14, 1887 in Wooster, Ohio
d. Jun 22, 1954
Source: *AmAu&B; CurBio 41, 54*

Compton, Wilson Martindale
American. Economist
b. Oct 15, 1890 in Wooster, Ohio
d. Mar 7, 1967
Source: *CurBio 52, 67*

Compton-Burnett, Dame Ivy
English. Author
b. Jun 5, 1892 in London, England
d. Aug 27, 1969 in London, England
Source: *ConAu 1R, 25R, 4NR; ConLC 1, 3, 10, 15; DcLEL; EncWL; EvLB; InWom; LongCTC; ModBrL, SUP; NewC; OxEng; Pen ENG; RAdv 1; REn; TwCA SUP; TwCW; WebE&AL; WhAm 5; WhoTwCL*

Comstock, Anthony
American. Author, Reformer
b. Mar 7, 1844 in New Canaan, Connecticut
d. Sep 21, 1915
Source: *AmAu&B; LongCTC; OxAmL; REnAL*

Comstock, Elizabeth L
English. Religious Leader
b. Oct 30, 1815 in Maidenhead, England
d. Aug 3, 1891 in Union Springs, New York
Source: *DcAmB; InWom; NotAW; WhAm H; WhAmP*

Comstock, Henry Tompkins Paige
American. Prospector
b. 1820 in Trenton, ON
d. Sep 27, 1870 in Bozeman, Montana
Source: *AmBi; DcAmB; WhAm H*

Comte, Auguste
French. Author, Philosopher
b. Jan 19, 1798 in Montpellier, France
d. Sep 5, 1857 in Paris, France
Source: *BbD; BiD&SB; CasWL; DcEuL; EuAu; EvEuW; OxEng; OxFr; REn*

Conacher, Charles, Sr.
Canadian. Hockey Player
b. Dec 10, 1909 in Toronto, ON
d. Dec 30, 1967 in Toronto, ON
Source: *BioIn 2, 8; WhoHcky 73*

Conant, James Bryant
American. Educator, Author, Diplomat
b. Mar 26, 1893 in Dorchester, Massachusetts
d. Feb 11, 1978 in Hanover, New Hampshire
Source: *AmAu&B; ConAu 13R, 77; CurBio 41, 51; EncAB-H; IntWW 74; OxAmL; REnAL; WebAB; Who 74; WhoAm 74; WhoWor 74*

Conaway, Jeff
American. Actor
Starred on Broadway in *Grease;* played Bobby on TV series "Taxi."
b. Oct 5, 1950 in New York, New York
Source: *BioIn 11; IntMPA 82; NewYTBS 78*

Condit, Carl Wilbur
American. Educator
b. Sep 29, 1914 in Cincinnati, Ohio
Source: *ConAu 1R; DrAS 74H, 78H; IntAu&W 76, 77; WhoAm 74, 76, 78, 80, 82; WrDr 76, 80*

Condon, Eddie
American. Band Leader, Musician
b. Nov 16, 1905 in Goodland, Indiana
d. Aug 3, 1973 in New York, New York
Source: *ConAu 45; CurBio 44, 73; NewYTBE 73; WhAm 6; WhoAm 74; WhoE 74; WhoJazz 72; WhoMus 72*

Condon, Edward
American. Scientist, Physicist, Engineer
b. Mar 2, 1902 in Alamogordo, New Mexico
d. Mar 26, 1974 in Boulder, Colorado
Source: *BioNews 74; NewYTBS 74; WebAB; WhAm 6; Who 74; WhoAm 74; WhoWor 74*

Condon, Jackie
[Our Gang]
Actor
b. 1913
Source: *Film 2; TwYS*

Condon, Richard Thomas
American. Author
b. Mar 18, 1915 in New York, New York
Source: *AmAu&B; ConAu 1R, 2NR; ConLC 4, 6; ConNov 72, 76; ModAL, SUP; Pen AM; WhoAm 74, 76, 78, 80, 82; WhoWor 74; WorAu; WrDr 76*

Condorcet, Marie-Jean-Antoine
French. Author
b. Sep 17, 1743 in Ribemont, France
d. Mar 25, 1794 in Bourg-la-Reine, France
Source: *BbD; BiD&SB; CasWL; DcEuL; EuAu; EvEuW; NewC; OxEng; OxFr; REn*

Cone, Fairfax Mastick
American. Advertising Executive
b. Feb 21, 1903 in San Francisco, California
d. Jun 20, 1977 in Carmel, Massachusetts
Source: *CurBio 66; IntWW 74; St&PR 75; WhoAdv 72; WhoAm 74*

Cone, Molly Lamken
American. Children's Author
b. Oct 3, 1918 in Tacoma, Washington
Source: *AuBYP; ConAu 1R; ForWC 70; SmATA 1; ThrBJA; WrDr 76*

Confrey, "Zez" (Edward E)
American. Composer
b. Apr 3, 1895 in Peru, Illinois
d. Nov 22, 1971 in Lakewood, New Jersey
Source: *AmSCAP 66; NewYTBE 71; WhAm 5*

Confucius
[Fu-Tzu Kung]
Chinese. Philosopher
Developed religious system for management of society.
b. 551BC in Lu, China
d. 479BC
Source: *BbD; BiD&SB; CasWL; DcOrL 1; NewC; Pen CL; RComWL; REn*

Conger, Clement Ellis
American. White House Curator
b. Oct 15, 1912 in Rockingham, Virginia
Source: *NewYTBS 77; WhoAm 74, 76, 78, 80, 82; WhoAmA 78; WhoGov 72, 75, 77*

Congreve, Richard
English. Essayist
b. Sep 14, 1818 in Warwickshire, England
d. Jul 5, 1899 in Hampstead, England
Source: *Alli SUP; BiD&SB; BrAu 19; DcEnL; NewC*

Congreve, William
English. Dramatist
Wrote *The Way of the World,* a comedy of manners, 1700.
b. 1670 in Bardsey, England
d. Jan 19, 1729 in London, England
Source: *Alli; AtlBL; BbD; BiD&SB; BiDLA; BrAu; CasWL; Chambr 2; ChPo S1; CnThe; CrtT 2; CyWA; DcEnA, AP; DcEnL; DcEuL; DcLEL; EvLB; McGEWD; MouLC 2; NewC; OxEng; OxThe; Pen ENG; RComWL; REn; REnWD; WebE&AL*

Conigliaro, Tony (Anthony Richard)
American. Baseball Player
Suffered heart attack, January, 1982; in coma five months.
b. Jan 7, 1945 in Revere, Massachusetts
Source: *BaseEn; CurBio 71; NewYTBE 71; WhoProB 73*

Conkle, Ellsworth Prouty
American. Dramatist, Educator
b. Jul 10, 1899 in Peru, Nebraska
Source: *AmAu&B; CnMD; ConAu 65; DrAS 74E; ModWD; OxAmL*

Conklin, Chester
American. Comedian
b. Jan 11, 1888 in Oskaloosa, Iowa
d. Oct 11, 1971 in Hollywood, California
Source: *Film 1; FilmgC; MotPP; MovMk; NewYTBE 71; OxFilm; TwYS; WhScrn 74, 77; WhoHol B*

Conklin, Gladys Plemon
American. Children's Author
b. May 30, 1903 in Harpster, Idaho
Source: *AuBYP; BiDrLUS 70; ConAu 1R, 4NR; ForWC 70; SmATA 2; WhoAmW 77*

Conklin, Peggy
American. Actress
b. Nov 2, 1912 in Dobbs Ferry, New York
Source: *BiE&WWA; NotNAT; ThFT; WhoHol A; WhoThe 77*

Conkling, Roscoe
American. Statesman
b. Oct 30, 1829 in Albany, New York
d. Apr 18, 1888 in New York, New York
Source: *AmBi; ApCAB; BiAuS; BiDrAC; DcAmB; Drake; EncAB-H; REnAL; TwCBDA; WebAB; WhAm H; WhAmP*

Conley, Eugene
American. Opera Singer
b. Mar 12, 1908 in Lynn, Massachusetts
d. Dec 18, 1981 in Denton, Texas
Source: *BioIn 2, 3, 4, 10; CurBio 54, 82; NewYTBS 81; WhoAm 74, 76, 78, 80; WhoWor 76, 78*

Connally, John Bowden, Jr.
American. Lawyer, Politician
Governor of TX, 1963-69; wounded when Kennedy was assassinated.
b. Feb 27, 1917 in Floresville, Texas
Source: *BiDrUSE; BioNews 74; CelR 73; CurBio 61; IntWW 74; Who 74; WhoAm 74, 76, 78, 80, 82; WhoAmP 73; WhoGov 77; WhoS&SW 73*

Connally, Tom (Thomas Terry)
American. Senator
b. Aug 19, 1877 in McLennan County, Texas
d. Oct 28, 1963 in Washington, DC
Source: *AmAu&B; BiDrAC; CurBio 41, 49, 64; WhAm 4; WhAmP*

Connell, Evan S, Jr.
American. Author
b. Aug 17, 1924 in Kansas City, Missouri
Source: *AmAu&B; ConAu 1R, 2NR; ConLC 4, 6; ConNov 72, 76; DrAF 76; ModAL SUP; OxAmL; Pen AM; RAdv 1; REnAL; WhoTwCL; WorAu; WrDr 76; WhoAm 74, 76, 78, 80, 82; WhoWor 74*

Connelly, Marc(us Cook)
American. Dramatist
Won Pulitzer Prize for *The Green Pastures*, 1930.
b. Dec 13, 1890 in McKeesport, Pennsylvania
d. Dec 21, 1980 in New York, New York
Source: *AmAu&B; BiE&WWA; Chambr 3; CnDAL; CnMD; CnThe; ConAmA; ConAmL; ConAu 85, 102; ConDr 73; CurBio 69; DcFM; DcLEL; IntWW 74; LongCTC; McGEWD; ModAL; ModWD; NotNAT; OxAmL; Pen AM; REn; REnAL; REnWD; TwCA, SUP; WebAB; Who 74; WhoAm 74; WhoThe 77; WhoWor 74; WrDr 76*

Connelly, "One-Eyed" (James Leo)
American. Gate Crasher
b. 1879?
d. Dec 20, 1953 in Zion, Illinois
Source: *BioIn 3, 4, 5*

Conner, Nadine
American. Opera Singer
b. Feb 20, 1913 in Compton, California
Source: *CurBio 55; InWom*

Connery, Sean
[Thomas Connery]
Scottish. Actor
Originated film role of James Bond in *Dr. No*, 1962.
b. Aug 25, 1930 in Edinburgh, Scotland
Source: *BiDFilm; BlueB 76; CelR 73; CmMov; CurBio 66; FilmgC; IntMPA 75, 76, 77, 78, 79, 80, 81, 82; IntWW 75, 76, 77, 78, 79, 80, 81; MotPP; MovMk; OxFilm; Who 82; WhoAm 80, 82; WhoHol A; WhoWor 74; WorAl; WorEFlm*

Conniff, Frank
American. Journalist
b. Apr 24, 1914 in Danbury, Connecticut
d. May 25, 1971 in New York, New York
Source: *BioIn 9; ConAu 93; WhAm 5*

Conniff, Ray
American. Band Leader
"Ray Coniff" sound launched with album *S'Wonderful*, 1956.
b. Nov 6, 1916 in Attleboro, Massachusetts
Source: *WhoAm 74, 76, 78, 80, 82; WhoJazz 72*

Connolly, Cyril Vernon
English. Author, Literary Critic
b. Sep 10, 1903 in Coventry, England
d. Nov 26, 1974 in London, England
Source: *CasWL; CnMWL; ConAu 21R, 53; ConAu P-2; ConNov 72; CurBio 47; DcLEL; EncWL; EvLB; IntWW 74; LongCTC; ModBrL; NewC; OxEng; Pen ENG; RAdv 1; REn; TwCA SUP; TwCW; WebE&AL*

Connolly, James B
American. Author
b. 1868 in Boston, Massachusetts
d. Jan 20, 1957
Source: *AmAu&B; AmLY; BkC 3; CathA 1930; REnAL; TwCA, SUP; WebBD 80*

Connolly, Maureen
"Little Mo"
American. Tennis Player
Wimbledon singles champion 1952-54; won Australian, French, and US open, 1953.
b. Sep 17, 1934 in San Diego, California
d. Jun 21, 1969 in Dallas, Texas
Source: *CurBio 51, 69; InWom; NewCol 75; WebAB*

Connolly, Mike
American. Journalist, Commentator
b. Jul 10, 1915 in Chicago, Illinois
d. Nov 1966
Source: *WhAm 4*

Connolly, Sybil
Welsh. Fashion Designer
b. Jan 24, 1921 in Swansea, Wales
Source: *InWom; WhoWor 74; WorFshn*

Connolly, Thomas Henry
American. Baseball Umpire
b. Dec 31, 1870 in Manchester, England
d. Apr 28, 1961 in Natick, Massachusetts
Source: *BioIn 5, 7; WhoProB 73*

Connolly, Walter
American. Actor
b. Apr 8, 1887 in Cincinnati, Ohio
d. May 28, 1940 in Beverly Hills, California
Source: *CurBio 40; FilmgC; MotPP; MovMk; OxFilm; Vers A; WhScrn 74, 77; WhoHol B*

Connor, "Bull" (Theophilus Eugene)
American. Police Commissioner
b. 1897
d. Mar 8, 1973 in Birmingham, Alabama
Source: *BioIn 9*

Connor, Sir William Neil
[Cassandra]
Irish. Journalist
b. 1910 in County Derry, Northern Ireland
d. Apr 6, 1967 in London, England
Source: *ConAu 25R; LongCTC; WhAm 4*

Connors, "Chuck" (Kevin Joseph)
American. Actor
Starred in TV show "The Rifleman," 1957-62.
b. Apr 10, 1921 in New York, New York
Source: *FilmgC; IntMPA 75, 76, 77, 78, 79, 80, 81, 82; MotPP; WhoAm 74, 76, 78, 80, 82; WhoHol A; WhoProB 73*

Connors, Dorsey
American. Journalist
b. in Chicago, Illinois
Source: *ConAu 45; ForWC 70; WhoAm 82; WhoAmW 77*

Connors, Jimmy (James Scott)
American. Tennis Player
Won US Open 1974, 1976, 1978, 1982; won Wimbledon 1974, 1982.
b. Sep 2, 1952 in East St. Louis, Illinois
Source: *BkPepl; NewYTBS 74; WhoAm 80, 82*

Connors, Mike
[Krekor Ohanian]
American. Actor
Starred in TV series "Mannix," 1967-74.
b. Aug 15, 1925 in Fresno, California
Source: *CelR 73; IntMPA 75, 76, 77, 78, 79, 80, 81, 82; MotPP; WhoAm 82; WhoHol A*

Conover, Harry
American. Businessman
b. Aug 29, 1911 in Chicago, Illinois
d. Jul 21, 1965 in New York, New York
Source: *CurBio 49, 65*

Conquest, Robert
English. Author
b. Jul 15, 1917 in Malvern, England
Source: *ConAu 13R; ConNov 72; ConP 70, 75; LongCTC; RAdv 1; TwCW; Who 74; WorAu; WrDr 76*

Conrad, Charles, Jr.
"Pete"
American. Astronaut
Crew member on Gemini V, 1965; Gemini XI, 1966; Apollo 12, 1969; Skylab, 1973.
b. Jun 2, 1930 in Philadelphia, Pennsylvania
Source: *CurBio 65; IntWW 74; NewYTBE 73; WhoAm 74, 76, 78, 80, 82; WhoS&SW 73; WhoWor 74*

Conrad, Con
[Conrad K Dober]
American. Composer, Publisher
b. Jun 18, 1891 in New York, New York
d. Sep 28, 1938 in Van Nuys, California
Source: *AmSCAP 66*

Conrad, Joseph
[Teodor Josef Konrad Koreniowski]
Polish. Author
Wrote *Lord Jim,* 1900; *Heart of Darkness,* 1902; *Victory,* 1915.
b. 1857 in Berdichev, Russia
d. Aug 3, 1924 in Bishopsbourne, England
Source: *AtlBL; BbD; BiD&SB; CasWL; Chambr 3; CnMD; CnMWL; CyWA; DcEnA AP; DcEuL; DcLEL; EncMys; EncWL; EvLB; FilmgC; JBA 34; LongCTC; ModBrL, SUP; ModWD; NewC; OxEng; Pen ENG; RAdv 1; RComWL; REn; TwCA, SUP; TwCW; WebE&AL; WhoTwCL*

Conrad, Michael
American. Actor
Won Emmy for role of Phil Esterhaus in "Hill Street Blues," 1981.
b. Oct 16, 1927? in New York, New York
Source: *WhoHol A*

Conrad, Paul Francis
American. Editorial Cartoonist
b. Jun 27, 1924 in Cedar Rapids, Iowa
Source: *WhoAm 74, 76, 78, 80, 82; WhoWest 74*

Conrad, Robert
[Conrad Robert Falk]
American. Actor
Starred in "Hawaiian Eye," 1959-63; "The Wild, Wild West," 1965-69.
b. Mar 1, 1935 in Chicago, Illinois
Source: *FilmgC; IntMPA 75, 76, 77, 78, 79, 80, 81, 82; WhoAm 74, 76, 78, 80, 82; WhoHol A*

Conrad, William
American. Actor, Director, Producer
Star of "Cannon," 1971-76; "Nero Wolfe," 1981.
b. Sep 27, 1920 in Louisville, Kentucky
Source: *BioNews 74; FilmgC; IntMPA 75, 76, 77, 78, 79, 80, 81, 82; MovMk; WhoAm 82; WhoHol A*

Conreid, Hans
American. Actor
Played Uncle Tonoose on "Make Room for Daddy," 1957-64.
b. 1917 in Baltimore, Maryland
d. Jan 5, 1982 in Burbank, California
Source: *FilmgC; MotPP; MovMk; NewYTBS 82; WhoAm 74, 76, 78, 80; WhoHol A; WhoThe 77*

Conroy, Frank
American. Author
b. Jan 15, 1936 in New York, New York
Source: *AmAu&B; ConAu 77; WhoAm 74*

Conroy, Frank
American. Actor
b. Oct 14, 1890 in Derby, England
d. Feb 4, 1964 in Paramus, New Jersey
Source: *FilmgC; MovMk; NotNAT B; PlP&P; WhScrn 74, 77; WhThe; WhoHol*

Conroy, Jack (John Wesley)
American. Author
b. Dec 5, 1899 in Moberly, Missouri
Source: *AmNov; ConAu 5R, 3NR; ConNov 72, 76; OhA&B; OxAmL; WhNAA; WhoAm 74; WrDr 76*

Considine, Bob (Robert Bernard)
American. Journalist
b. Nov 4, 1906 in Washington, DC
d. Sep 25, 1975 in New York, New York
Source: *AmAu&B; AuNews 2; CathA 1930; CelR 73; ConAu 61; CurBio 47; REnAL; WhAm 6; WhoAm 74; WhoWor 74*

Considine, Tim
American. Actor
b. 1940 in Los Angeles, California
Source: *WhoHol A*

Constable, John
English. Artist
b. Jun 11, 1776 in East Bergholt, England
d. Mar 30, 1837 in London, England
Source: *AtlBL; ChPo S1; NewC; REn*

Constant de Rebeque, (Henri) Benjamin
French. Author
b. Oct 25, 1767 in Lausanne, Switzerland
d. Dec 8, 1830 in Paris, France
Source: *AtlBL; CyWA; Pen EUR*

Constantine I
[Constantine the Great]
Roman. Emperor
b. 280 in Naissus
d. 337
Source: *BioIn 10; NewCol 75; WebBD 80*

Constantine V
Byzantine. Emperor
b. 718
d. 775
Source: *NewCol 75*

Constantine VI
Byzantine. Emperor
b. 770?
d. 820?
Source: *NewCol 75*

Constantine XI
Byzantine. Emperor
d. 1453
Source: *NewCol 75*

Constantine XII
Greek. Former King
Succeeded to throne, 1964; left Greece, 1967; deposed, 1973.
b. Jun 2, 1940 in Athens, Greece
Source: *IntWW 74, 75, 76, 77, 78, 79, 80, 81; NewCol 75*

Constantine, Eddie
American. Actor
b. 1917 in Los Angeles, California
Source: *FilmgC; MotPP; OxFilm; WorEFlm*

Constantine, Michael
American. Actor
b. May 22, 1927 in Reading, Pennsylvania
Source: *BiE&WWA; FilmgC; WhoHol A*

Conte, Richard
American. Actor
b. Mar 24, 1914 in Jersey City, New Jersey
d. Apr 15, 1975 in Los Angeles, California
Source: *CmMov; FilmgC; HolP 40; IntMPA 75; MotPP; MovMk; WhAm 6; WhScrn 77; WhoAm 74; WorEFlm*

Conti, Tom (Thomas Antonio)
Scottish. Actor
Won Tony, 1979, for *Whose Life is it Anyway?*
b. Nov 22, 1941 in Paisley, Scotland
Source: *NewYTBS 79; WhoAm 80, 82; WhoThe 81*

Contino, Dick
American. Musician
b. 1930 in Fresno, California
Source: *WhoHol A*

Converse, Frank
American. Actor
Played Johnny Corso on "NYPD," 1967-69.
b. May 22, 1938 in Saint Louis, Missouri
Source: *IntMPA 77, 78, 79, 80, 81, 82; WhoHol A*

Converse, Frederick Shepherd
American. Composer
b. Jan 5, 1871 in Newton, Massachusetts
d. Jun 8, 1940 in Boston, Massachusetts
Source: *AmSCAP 66; CurBio 40; DcAmB S2; OxAmL; REnAL; WhAm 1*

Convy, Bert
American. Actor
b. Jul 23, 1934 in Saint Louis, Missouri
Source: *BiE&WWA; NotNAT; WhoHol A; WhoThe 77*

Conway, Gary
[Garth Carmody]
American. Motion Picture Executive
b. 1938 in Boston, Massachusetts
Source: *FilmgC; IntMPA 82; WhoAm 74; WhoHol A*

Conway, Jack
American. Actor, Motion Picture Director
b. Jul 17, 1887 in Graceville, Minnesota
d. Oct 11, 1952 in California
Source: *CmMov; DcFM; FilmgC; MovMk; TwYS; WhScrn 74, 77; WhoHol B; WorEFlm*

Conway, Moncure Daniel
American. Clergyman, Author
b. Mar 17, 1832 in Falmouth, Virginia
d. Nov 15, 1907
Source: *AmAu; AmAu&B; DcLEL; OhA&B; OxAmL; Pen AM; REnAL*

Conway, Shirl
[Shirl Conway Larson]
American. Actress, Singer
b. Jun 13, 1916 in Franklinville, New York
Source: *BiE&WWA; InWom; IntMPA 75, 76, 77, 78, 79, 80, 81, 82; NotNAT; WhoHol A*

Conway, Thomas
[Count de Conway]
American. Army Officer
b. Feb 27, 1735 in Ireland
d. 1800
Source: *AmBi; ApCAB; DcAmB; Drake; NatCAB 1; TwCBDA; WebAB; WebAMB; WhAm H*

Conway, "Tim" (Thomas Daniel)
American. Comedian, Actor
In TV series "McHale's Navy," 1962-66; "The Carol Burnett Show," 1975-78.
b. Dec 13, 1933 in Willoughby, Ohio
Source: *CurBio 81; IntMPA 77, 78, 79, 80, 81, 82; WhoHol A*

Conway, Tom
American. Actor
b. 1904 in Saint Petersburg, Russia
d. Apr 22, 1967 in Culver City, California
Source: *FilmgC; HolP 40; MotPP; MovMk; WhScrn 74, 77; WhoHol B*

Cony, Edward Roger
American. Newspaperman
b. Mar 15, 1923 in Augusta, Maine
Source: *WhoAm 74; WhoE 74*

Conyers, John, Jr.
American. Politician
MI congressman, 1964--; wrote *Anatomy of an Undeclared War,* 1972.
b. May 16, 1929 in Detroit, Michigan
Source: *BiDrAC; CngDr 74; CurBio 70; IntWW 74; WhoAm 74, 76, 78, 80, 82; WhoAmP 73; WhoBlA 75; WhoGov 72*

Conze, Edward
English. Author
b. Mar 18, 1904 in London, England
Source: *Au&Wr 71; ConAu 13R*

Conzelman, Jimmy (James Gleason)
American. Football Coach
b. Mar 6, 1898 in Saint Louis, Missouri
d. Jul 31, 1970 in Saint Louis, Missouri
Source: *WhoFtbl 74*

Cooder, Ry(land Peter)
American. Musician
b. Mar 15, 1947 in Los Angeles, California
Source: *BioIn 10, 11; ConMuA 80; EncPR&S; IlEncRk; WhoAm 80, 82; WhoRock 81*

Coogan, Jackie (Jack Leslie)
American. Actor
Issue over control of earnings as child star resulted in CA's Child Actors Bill.
b. Oct 26, 1914 in Los Angeles, California
Source: *Film 1; FilmgC; IntMPA 75, 76, 77, 78, 79, 80, 81, 82; MotPP; MovMk; NewYTBE 72; OxFilm; TwYS; WhoAm 82; WhoHol A*

Cook, Barbara
American. Actress, Singer
b. Oct 25, 1927 in Atlanta, Georgia
Source: *BiE&WWA; CurBio 63; EncMT; InWom; NotNAT; WhoAm 82; WhoThe 77*

Cook, Donald
American. Actor
b. Sep 26, 1901 in Portland, Oregon
d. Oct 1, 1961 in New Haven, Connecticut
Source: *CurBio 54, 61; FilmgC; HolP 30; MotPP; MovMk; WhAm 4; WhScrn 74, 77; WhoHol B*

Cook, Elisha, Jr.
American. Actor
b. Dec 26, 1906 in San Francisco, California
Source: *CmMov; FilmgC; IntMPA 75, 76, 77, 78, 79, 80, 81, 82; MovMk; OxFilm; Vers B; WhoHol A; WhoThe 77; WorEFlm*

Cook, Frederick Albert
American. Explorer, Naturalist
Claimed to have been first to reach N Pole and scale Mt. McKinley.
b. Jun 10, 1865 in Callicoon Depot, New York
d. Aug 5, 1940
Source: *CurBio 40; DcAmAu; DcAmB S2; DcNAA; NewCol 75; OxCan; WhAm 1*

Cook, Greg(ory Lynn)
American. Football Player
b. Nov 20, 1946 in Dayton, Ohio
Source: *BioIn 8; WhoFtbl 74*

Cook, James, Captain
English. Explorer, Navigator
Discovered New Caledonia on South Sea expedition, 1772-75.
b. Oct 28, 1728 in Morton Village, England
d. Feb 14, 1779 in Kealakeua, Hawaii
Source: *Alli, SUP; ApCAB; BbD; BbtC; BrAu; ChPo S2; DcLEL; Drake; NewC; OxCan; OxEng; REn; REnAL; WhAm H*

Cook, Joe
American. Actor
b. 1890 in Evansville, Indiana
d. May 16, 1959 in Clinton Hollows, New York
Source: *EncMT; IndAu 1917; WhScrn 77; WhoHol B*

Cook, Marlow Webster
American. Senator
b. Jul 27, 1926 in Akron, Ohio
Source: *BioNews; CurBio 72; IntWW 74; WhoAm 74; WhoGov 72*

Cook, Michael
Canadian. Dramatist
b. Feb 14, 1933 in London, England
Source: *BioIn 11; ConAu 93; ConDr 77; WhoAm 80, 82; WrDr 80*

Cook, Paul
see: Sex Pistols

Cook, Peter
English. Actor, Producer, Author
b. Nov 17, 1937 in Devonshire, England
Source: *BiE&WWA; FilmgC; NotNAT; WhoHol; WhoThe 77*

Cook, Phil
American. Comedian
b. 1893
d. Sep 18, 1958 in Morristown, New Jersey
Source: *BioIn 5*

Cook, Thomas
English. Travel Agent
b. 1808
d. 1892
Source: *BioIn 10; WebBD 80*

Cooke, (Alfred) Alistair
American. Journalist, Broadcaster
Best known for introductions to "Masterpiece Theatre" on PBS.
b. Nov 20, 1908 in Manchester, England
Source: *AmAu&B; AuNews 1; CelR 73; ConAu 57; CurBio 52, 74; IntMPA 75, 76, 77, 78, 79, 80, 81, 82; IntWW 74; LongCTC; OxAmL; REnAL; TwCA SUP; Who 74; WhoAm 74, 76, 78, 80, 82; WhoWor 74*

Cooke, Christopher M
American. Air Force Officer
Made unauthorized visits to Soviet Embassy working as Titan-missle launch officer.
b. 1956
Source: *BioIn 12*

Cooke, David Coxe
American. Children's Author
b. Jun 7, 1917 in Wilmington, Delaware
Source: *AuBYP; ConAu 1R, 2NR; SmATA 2*

Cooke, Donald
[The Hostages]
American. Former Hostage in Iran
b. 1955? in Long Island, New York
Source: *NewYTBS 81*

Cooke, Hope
[Hope Namgyal]
American. Former Maharani of Sikkim
b. Jun 21, 1940 in San Francisco, California
Source: *CurBio 67; InWom; NewYTBS 74*

Cooke, Jack Kent
American. Business, Sports Executive
b. Sep 25, 1912 in Hamilton, ON
Source: *CanWW 82; NewYTET; St&PR 75; WhoAm 74, 76, 78, 80, 82*

Cooke, Janet
American. Journalist
Won Pulitzer Prize for story on 8 yr. old heroin addict; story was false.
b. 1954? in Toledo, Ohio
Source: *BioIn 12*

Cooke, Jay
American. Banker, Philanthropist
b. Aug 10, 1821 in Sandusky, Ohio
d. Feb 18, 1905 in Ogortz, Pennsylvania
Source: *AmBi; ApCAB; BiAuS; DcAmB; Drake; EncAB-H; TwCBDA; WebAB; WhAm 1, 4*

Cooke, John Esten
American. Author, Historian
b. Nov 3, 1830 in Winchester, Virginia
d. Sep 27, 1886
Source: *AmAu; AmAu&B; CasWL; DcAmAu; OxAmL; REnAL*

Cooke, Rose Terry
American. Author
b. Feb 17, 1827 in Hartford, Connecticut
d. Jul 18, 1892
Source: *AmAu; AmAu&B; DcAmAu; DcNAA; OxAmL; REnAL*

Cooke, Sam
American. Singer, Jazz Musician
b. Jan 22, 1935 in Chicago, Illinois
d. Dec 11, 1964 in Los Angeles, California
Source: *WhoHol B*

Cooke, Terence James
American. Roman Catholic Cardinal
b. Mar 1, 1921 in New York, New York
Source: *CurBio 68; IntWW 74; NewYTBE 73; WhoAm 82; WhoE 74; WhoRel 75*

Cooke, Sir William Fothergil
English. Engineer, Inventor
With Charles Wheatstone, invented electric telegraph, 1845.
b. May 4, 1806
d. Jun 25, 1879
Source: *WebBD 80*

Cooley, Denton Arthur
American. Surgeon, Educator
b. Aug 22, 1920 in Houston, Texas
Source: *AmM&WS 73P; BioIn 8, 9, 10, 11; CelR 73; CurBio 76; WhoAm 74, 76, 78, 80, 82; WhoS&SW 73, 75; WhoWor 74*

Coolidge, Dane
American. Naturalist, Author
b. Mar 24, 1873 in Natick, Massachusetts
d. Aug 8, 1940
Source: *AmAu&B; AmLY; ChPo; CurBio 40; DcNAA; OxAmL; WhNAA*

Coolidge, (John) Calvin
"Silent Cal"
American. 30th US President
Assumed presidency upon death of Harding, Aug 1923; reelected, 1924.
b. Jul 4, 1872 in Plymouth, Vermont
d. Jan 5, 1933 in Northampton, Massachusetts
Source: *AmAu&B; AmBi; BiDrAC; BiDrUSE; DcAmB; DcNAA; EncAB-H; OxAmL; REn; REnAL; WebAB; WhAm 1; WhAmP*

Coolidge, Rita
American. Singer
Ex-wife of Kris Kristofferson; platinum album *Anytime...Anywhere,* 1977.
b. May 1, 1945 in Nashville, Tennessee
Source: *BiDAmM; BioIn 10; BkPepl; EncPR&S; IlEncRk; WhoAm 82*

Coolidge, William David
American. Inventor
Invented X-ray tube; director of research for GE Co., 1932-40.
b. Oct 23, 1873 in Hudson, Massachusetts
d. Feb 3, 1975 in Schenectady, New York
Source: *NewCol 75; WhAm 6; Who 74; WhoAm 78*

Coombs, Charles Ira
American. Children's Author
b. Jun 27, 1914 in Los Angeles, California
Source: *AuBYP; ConAu 5R, 4NR; SmATA 3*

Coon, Carleton Stevens
American. Author, Social Anthropologist
b. Jun 23, 1904 in Wakefield, Massachusetts
d. Jun 3, 1981 in Gloucester, Massachusetts
Source: *AmAu&B; BioIn 4, 5, 10; ConAu 5R, 104, 2NR; CurBio 56, 81; NewYTBS 81; WhoAm 74, 76, 78, 80; WorAu*

Cooney, Barbara
American. Children's Author, Illustrator
b. Aug 6, 1916 in Brooklyn, New York
Source: *AmAu&B; AuBYP; BkP; ConAu 5R, 3NR; IlsBYP; IlsCB 1744, 1946, 1957; InWom; MorJA; SmATA 6; Str&VC; WhoAm 74, 76, 78, 80, 82; WhoAmA 73*

Cooney, Gerry (Gerald Arthur)
American. Boxer
Defeated Ken Norton in 54 seconds, May 11, 1981.
b. Aug 24, 1956 in Brooklyn, New York
Source: *NewYTBS 81, 82*

Cooney, Joan Ganz
American. TV Producer
Executive director, Children's TV Workshop; produces "Sesame Street."
b. Nov 30, 1929 in Phoenix, Arizona
Source: *CelR 73; CurBio 70; ForWC 70; WhoAm 74, 76, 78, 80, 82; WhoAmW 77; WhoE 74*

Coons, Albert Hewett
American. Scientist
b. Jun 28, 1912 in Gloversville, New York
Source: *AmM&WS 73P; CurBio 60; IntWW 74; WhoAm 74; WhoE 74*

Cooper, Alfred Duff
see: Norwich, Alfred Duff Cooper, Viscount

Cooper, Alice
[Vincent Damon Furnier]
American. Rock Singer, Songwriter
Hits include "I'm 18," 1970; "No More Mr. Nice Guy," 1973.
b. Feb 4, 1948 in Detroit, Michigan
Source: *BioNews 74; BkPepl; CelR 73; WhoAm 74, 76, 78, 80, 82*

Cooper, Sir Astley Paston
English. Surgeon, Anatomist
b. Aug 23, 1768
d. Feb 12, 1841
Source: *Alli; BiDLA*

Cooper, Colin
see: Climax Blues Band, The

Cooper, D B
American. Highjacker
Source: *BioIn 12*

Cooper, Diana Manners
see: Norwich, Diana (Manners) Cooper, Viscountess

Cooper, Emil
Russian. Conductor
b. Dec 20, 1877 in Kherson, Russia
d. Nov 19, 1960 in New York, New York
Source: *NewEOp 71*

Cooper, "Gary" (Frank James)
American. Actor
Won Oscars for *Sergeant York,* 1941; *High Noon,* 1952.
b. May 7, 1901 in Helena, Montana
d. May 13, 1961 in Hollywood, California
Source: *BiDFilm; CmMov; CurBio 41, 61; FilmgC; MotPP; MovMk; OxFilm; TwYS; WebAB; WhAm 4; WhScrn 74, 77; WhoHol B; WorEFlm*

Cooper, Dame Gladys
English. Actress
b. Dec 18, 1888 in Lewisham, England
d. Nov 17, 1971 in Henley, England
Source: *BiE&WWA; ConAu 33R; CurBio 56, 72; Film 1; FilmgC; InWom; MotPP; MovMk; NewYTBE 71; Vers A; WhAm 5; WhScrn 74, 77; WhoHol B*

Cooper, Jackie (John, Jr.)
[Our Gang]
American. Actor, Motion Picture Producer
Described life as child star in autobiography *Please Don't Shoot My Dog,* 1981.
b. Sep 15, 1922 in Los Angeles, California
Source: *BiE&WWA; FilmgC; IntMPA 75, 76, 77, 78, 79, 80, 81, 82; MovMk; WhoAm 74, 76, 78, 80, 82*

Cooper, James Fenimore
American. Author
Wrote *Leatherstocking Tales,* 1823-1841.
b. Sep 15, 1789 in Burlington, New Jersey
d. Sep 14, 1851 in Cooperstown, New York
Source: *Alli; AmAu; AmAu&B; AmBi; AmWr; ApCAB; AtlBL; AuBYP; BbD; BiD&SB; CarSB; CasWL; Chambr 3; CnDAL; CrtT 3; CyAL 1; CyWA; DcAmAu; DcAmB; DcBiA; DcEnA; DcEnL; DcLEL; DcNAA; Drake; EncAB-H; EvLB; FilmgC; HsB&A; MnBBF; MouLC 3; OxAmL; OxEng; Pen AM; RAdv 1; RComWL; REn; REnAL; TwCBDA; WebAB; WebE&AL; WhAm H; WhoChL*

Cooper, John Sherman
American. Lawyer, Diplomat
UN delegate 1949-51, 1968, 1981--; former ambassador to India, Nepal, and E Germany.
b. Aug 23, 1901 in Somerset, Kentucky
Source: *BiDrAC; BioNews 74; CurBio 50; IntWW 74; WhoAm 74, 76, 78, 80, 82; WhoAmP 73; WhoGov 72; WhoS&SW 73*

Cooper, Joseph D
American. Government Official
b. May 25, 1917 in Boston, Massachusetts
d. Mar 25, 1975
Source: *AmM&WS 73S; ConAu 5R, 57; CurBio 52; WhAm 6; WhoAm 74; WhoWorJ 72*

Cooper, Kent
American. Journalist
b. Mar 22, 1880 in Columbus, Indiana
d. Jan 31, 1965
Source: *CurBio 44; ConAu 89; CurBio 65*

Cooper, (Leroy) Gordon, Jr.
American. Astronaut
Astronaut on Faith 7, 1963; Gemini V, 1965.
b. Mar 6, 1927 in Shawnee, Oklahoma
Source: *CurBio 63; WhoAm 74, 76, 78, 80, 82; WhoS&SW 73*

Cooper, Melville
American. Actor
b. Oct 15, 1896 in Birmingham, England
d. Mar 29, 1973 in Woodland Hills, California
Source: *BiE&WWA; FilmgC; MovMk; Vers A; WhScrn 77; WhoHol B*

Cooper, Miriam
American. Actress
b. 1894
d. Apr 12, 1976 in Charlottesville, Virginia
Source: *Film 1; TwYS; WhoHol A*

Cooper, Morton Cecil
American. Baseball Player
b. Mar 4, 1914 in Atherton, Missouri
d. Nov 17, 1958 in Little Rock, Arkansas
Source: *BaseEn; WhoProB 73*

Cooper, Peter
American. Businessman, Philanthropist
b. Feb 12, 1791 in New York, New York
d. Apr 4, 1883 in New York, New York
Source: *Alli SUP; AmAu&B; AmBi; ApCAB; BbD; BiD&SB; DcAmAu; DcAmB; DcNAA; Drake; EncAB-H; OxAmL; REn; REnAL; TwCBDA; WebAB; WhAm H*

Cooper, Wilhelmina Behmenburg
American. Model, Agency Owner
b. 1940
d. Mar 1, 1980 in Greenwich, Connecticut
Source: *NF*

Coors, Adolph
German. Brewery Executive
b. 1847 in Germany
d. Jun 5, 1919 in Virginia Beach, Virginia
Source: *NF*

Coors, Joseph
American. Brewery Executive
b. Nov 12, 1917
Source: *BioIn 11*

Coors, William K (Bill)
American. Brewery Executive
Chairman, executive officer, Adolph Coors Co.
b. 1916 in Golden, Colorado
Source: *St&PR 75; WhoAm 78, 80, 82*

Coote, Robert
English. Actor
Played Colonel Pickering in Broadway version of *My Fair Lady,* 1956.
b. Feb 4, 1909 in London, England
d. Nov 25, 1982 in New York, New York
Source: *BiE&WWA; FilmgC; MotPP; MovMk; NotNAT; Vers; WhoHol A; WhoThe 72, 77, 81*

Coots, J Fred
American. Actor
b. May 2, 1897 in Brooklyn, New York
Source: *AmSCAP 66; BiE&WWA; EncMT; NewCBMT; NotNAT*

Coover, Robert
American. Author
b. Feb 4, 1932 in Charles City, Iowa
Source: *ConAu 45, 3NR; ConLC 3, 7, 15; DrAF 76; ModAL SUP; Pen AM; RAdv 1; WhoAm 74, 76, 78, 80, 82; WhoE 74; WrDr 76*

Copeau, Jacques
French. Dramatist
b. 1878 in Paris, France
d. Oct 20, 1949 in Beaune, France
Source: *NotNAT B; OxThe; PlP&P; WhScrn 77; WhThe*

Copeland, Charles Townsend
English. Educator
b. Apr 27, 1860 in Calais, Maine
d. Jul 24, 1952 in Waverly, Massachusetts
Source: *AmAu&B; DcAmB S5; OxAmL; REnAL; WhAm 3; WhNAA*

Copeland, George
American. Musician
b. 1882 in Boston, Massachusetts
d. 1971 in Princeton, New Jersey
Source: *BioIn 9*

Copeland, Jo
American. Fashion Designer
b. 1899 in New York, New York
d. Mar 20, 1982 in New York, New York
Source: *NewYTBS 82; WhoAm 74, 76, 78, 80, 82; WorFshn*

Copeland, Lammot du Pont
American. Businessman
b. May 19, 1905 in Christiana, Delaware
Source: *CurBio 63; IntWW 74; St&PR 75; WhoAm 74, 76, 78, 80, 82; WhoE 74; WhoF&I 74; WhoWor 74*

Copeland, Stewart
see: Police, The

Copernicus, Nicolaus
[Niklas Kopernik]
Polish. Astronomer
Proposed theory that sun was center of universe and all planets revolved around it, 1543.
b. Feb 19, 1473 in Torun, Poland
d. May 24, 1543 in Frauenburg, Poland
Source: *BbD; BiD&SB; NewCol 75*

Copland, Aaron
American. Composer
Ballet scores include *Billy the Kid,* 1938; *Rodeo,* 1942.
b. Nov 14, 1900 in Brooklyn, New York
Source: *AmAu&B; AmSCAP 66; Au&Wr 71; BioNews 74; CelR 73; ConAu 5R; CurBio 40, 51; DcCM; EncAB-H; FilmgC; IntWW 74; NewYTBE 70; OxAmL; OxFilm; REn; REnAL; WebAB; Who 82; WhoAm 74, 76, 78, 80, 82; WhoMus 72; WhoWor 74; WorEFlm*

Copley, John Singleton
American. Artist
b. Jul 3, 1733 in Boston, Massachusetts
d. Sep 9, 1815 in London, England
Source: *AmBi; ApCAB; AtlBL; DcAmB; Drake; EncAB-H; OxAmL; REn; TwCBDA; WebAB; WhAm H*

Coplon, Judith
American. Accused Spy
b. 1921
Source: *InWom*

Coppard, A(lfred) E(dgar)
English. Author, Poet
b. Jan 4, 1878 in Folkestone, England
d. Jan 13, 1957 in London, England
Source: *ChPo, S1, S2; DcLEL; EvLB; LongCTC; ModBrL; NewC; OxEng; Pen ENG; REn; TwCA, SUP; TwCW; WhoChL; WhoTwCL; YABC 1*

Coppee, Francois Edouard Joachim
French. Poet, Dramatist
b. Jan 26, 1842 in Paris, France
d. May 23, 1908 in Paris, France
Source: *BbD; BiD&SB; ClDMEL; CnMD; DcEuL; EuAu; McGEWD; ModWD; OxFr; Pen EUR; REn*

Copperfield, David
[David Kotkin]
American. Magician
b. 1956 in Metuchen, New Jersey
Source: *NF*

Coppola, Carmine
American. Composer, Conductor
b. Jun 11, 1910 in New York, New York
Source: *AmSCAP 66; WhoAm 82*

Coppola, Francis Ford
American. Motion Picture Director
Directed *The Godfather I, II,* 1972, 1974; *Apocalypse Now,* 1979.
b. Apr 7, 1939 in Detroit, Michigan
Source: *BiDFilm; BioNews 75; BkPepl; CelR 73; CurBio 74; FilmgC; IntMPA 75, 76, 77, 78, 79, 80, 81, 82; MovMk; NewYTBS 74; OxFilm; WhoAm 76, 78, 80, 82; WorEFlm*

Coquelin, Benoit Constant
[Coquelin Aine]
French. Actor
b. 1841 in France
d. 1909
Source: *BbD; BiD&SB; WhAm HA, 4; WhoHol B*

Corben, Richard Vance
American. Artist
b. Oct 1, 1940 in Anderson, Missouri
Source: *FanAl; WorECom*

Corbett, James John
"Gentleman Jim"
American. Boxer
Defeated John L Sullivan for heavyweight boxing championship, 1892.
b. Sep 1, 1866 in San Francisco, California
d. Feb 18, 1933 in New York, New York
Source: *AmBi; DcAmB S1; Film 1; WebAB; WhAm HA, 4; WhScrn 74, 77; WhoBox 74; WhoHol B; WhoStg 1906, 1908*

Corbett, (Winfield) Scott
American. Children's Author
Wrote over 60 books, including *Cutlass Island,* 1962.
b. Jul 27, 1913 in Kansas City, Missouri
Source: *Au&Wr 71; AuBYP; ChlLR 1; ConAu 1R; SmATA 2*

Corbett, Young, III
[Ralph Giordano]
Italian. Boxer
b. May 27, 1905 in Naples, Italy
Source: *WhoBox 74*

Corbiere, Tristan
French. Poet
b. Jul 18, 1845 in Morlaix, France
d. Mar 1, 1875 in Morlaix, France
Source: *AtlBL; ClDMEL*

Corby, Ellen
[Ellen Hansen]
American. Actress
Played Grandma on "The Waltons."
b. Jun 3, 1913 in Racine, Wisconsin
Source: *BioIn 10, 11; FilmEn; FilmgC; MovMk; Vers A; WhoAm 76; WhoAmW 72, 74; WhoHol A*

Corby, Mike
see: Babys, The

Corcoran, Thomas Gardiner
"Tommy the Cork"
American. Lawyer, Politician
b. Dec 29, 1900 in Pawtucket, Rhode Island
d. Dec 6, 1981 in Washington, DC
Source: *CurBio 40, 82; NewYTBS 81; WhoAm 74, 76, 78; WhoWor 74*

Corcoran, William Wilson
American. Financier, Philanthropist
b. Dec 27, 1798 in Baltimore, Maryland
d. Feb 24, 1888 in Washington, DC
Source: *AmBi; ApCAB; DcAmB; TwCBDA; WebAB; WhAm H*

Corcos, Lucille
American. Children's Illustrator
b. Sep 21, 1908 in New York, New York
d. Aug 25, 1973
Source: *AmAu&B; AuBYP; ChPo; ConAu 21R; IlsCB 1946, 1957; SmATA 10; WhAm 6; WhoAm 74; WhoAmA 73*

Cord, Alex
[Alexander Viespi]
American. Actor
b. Aug 3, 1931 in Floral Park, New York
Source: *CelR 73; FilmgC; IntMPA 75, 76, 77, 78, 79, 80, 81, 82; MotPP; WhoAm 82; WhoHol A*

Cord, E(rret) L(obban)
American. Automobile Manufacturer
b. 1895 in Warrensburg, Missouri
d. Jan 2, 1974 in Reno, Nevada
Source: *NewYTBS 74*

Corday d'Armount, (Marie Anne) Charlotte
French. Revolutionary, Assassin
Murdered Jean Paul Marat in his bath, Jul 13, 1793; guillotined.
b. Jul 27, 1768 in Saint Saturnin, France
d. Jul 17, 1793 in Paris, France
Source: *InWom; NewCol 75; REn; WebBD 80*

Cordero, Angel Tomas
Puerto Rican. Jockey
b. May 8, 1942 in Santurce, Puerto Rico
Source: *BioIn 10*

Cordes, Eugene Harold
American. Author, Educator
b. Apr 7, 1936 in York, Nebraska
Source: *AmM&WS 73; WhoAm 74; WhoWor 74*

Cordier, Andrew Wellington
American. University Dean
b. Mar 3, 1901 in Canton, Ohio
d. 1974
Source: *CurBio 50; IntWW 74; Who 74; WhoAm 74; WhoE 74; WhoWor 74*

Cordiner, Ralph Jarron
American. Corporation Executive
Chairman, GE, 1958-63.
b. Mar 20, 1900 in Walla Walla, Washington
d. Dec 4, 1973 in Clearwater, Florida
Source: *BioNews 74; BusPN; CurBio 51, 74; NewYTBE 73; WhAm 6; WhoAmP 73*

Cordoba, Francisco Fernandez
Spanish. Soldier, Explorer
b. 1475
d. 1526
Source: *WebBD 80*

Cordobes, El
[Mauel Benetez Perez]
Spanish. Bullfighter
Retired 1972, as Spain's highest paid matador; returned to ring, 1979.
b. 1936 in Palma del Rio, Spain
Source: *BioIn 6, 7, 8*

Cordon, Norman
American. Opera Singer
b. Jan 20, 1904 in Washington, DC
d. Mar 1, 1964 in Chapel Hill, North Carolina
Source: *BioIn 9; NewEOp 71*

Cordtz, Dan
American. Broadcast Journalist
b. May 1, 1927 in Gary, Indiana
Source: *ConAu 73; WhoAm 82*

Corea, "Chick" (Armando)
American. Jazz Musician
Founded group, Return to Forever, 1971; won four Grammys.
b. Jun 12, 1941 in Chelsea, Massachusetts
Source: *WhoAm 74, 76, 78, 80, 82*

Corelli, Arcangelo
Italian. Musician, Composer
b. Feb 17, 1653 in Fusignano, Italy
d. Jan 8, 1713 in Rome, Italy
Source:

Corelli, Franco
Italian. Opera Singer
b. Apr 8, 1923 in Ancona, Italy
Source: *CelR 73; IntWW 74; NewYTBE 70; WhoAm 82*

Corelli, Marie, pseud.
[Mary Mackay]
English. Author
b. 1855 in London, England
d. Apr 21, 1924
Source: *Alli SUP; BbD; BiD&SB; Chambr 3; ChPo, S1; DcBiA; DcEnA AP; DcLEL; EvLB; InWom; LongCTC; ModBrL; NewC; OxEng; Pen ENG; REn; TwCA, SUP; TwCW*

Corena, Fernando
Italian. Opera Singer
b. Dec 22, 1923 in Geneva, Switzerland
Source: *NewEOp 71; WhoAm 82*

Corey, Irwin, Professor
American. Comedian
Source: *WhoHol A*

Corey, Jeff
American. Actor
b. Aug 10, 1914 in New York, New York
Source: *FilmgC; IntMPA 75, 76, 77, 78, 79, 80, 81, 82; Vers B; WhoAm 82; WhoHol A*

Corey, Jill
American. Actress
b. 1935
Source: *InWom*

Corey, Lewis
[Louis C Fraina]
Italian. Author
b. Oct 13, 1894 in Italy
d. Sep 16, 1953
Source: *AmAu&B; OhA&B; OxAmL; TwCA, SUP*

Corey, Wendell
American. Actor
b. Mar 20, 1914 in Dracut, Massachusetts
d. Nov 9, 1968 in Woodland Hills, California
Source: *BiDFilm; BiE&WWA; FilmgC; HolP 40; MotPP; MovMk; WhAm 5; WhScrn 74, 77; WhoHol B; WorEFlm*

Corey, William Ellis
American. Industrialist
b. May 4, 1866 in Braddock, Pennsylvania
d. May 11, 1934
Source: *DcAmB S1; NatCAB 14; WhAm 1*

Cori, Carl Ferdinand
American. Biochemist
Discovered steps in glycogen-glucose conversion known as Cori cycle, 1939.
b. Dec 5, 1896 in Prague, Austria
Source: *AmM&WS 73P; CurBio 47; IntWW 74; WebAB; Who 74; WhoAm 74, 76, 78, 80, 82; WhoWor 74*

Cori, Gerty Theresa
American. Biochemist
b. Aug 15, 1896 in Prague, Austria
d. Oct 26, 1957 in Saint Louis, Missouri
Source: *CurBio 47, 58; InWom; WebAB; WhAm 3*

Corigliano, John
American. Composer, Musician
b. Feb 16, 1938 in New York, New York
Source: *AmSCAP 66; DcCM*

Corinth, Lovis
German. Artist
b. 1858
d. 1925
Source: *BioIn 2, 4, 5, 7, 10; OxGer*

Corio, Ann
American. Actress, Burlesque Queen
b. 1914 in Hartford, Connecticut
Source: *CelR 73; InWom; WhoHol A*

Coriolanus, Gaius
Roman. Soldier
Source: *NewCol 75; WebBD 80*

Corle, Edwin
American. Author
b. May 7, 1906 in Wildwood, New Jersey
d. Jun 11, 1956
Source: *AmAu&B; OxAmL; REnAL; TwCA SUP; WhAm 3; WhNAA*

Corman, Roger William
American. Director, Producer, Author
b. Apr 5, 1926 in Detroit, Michigan
Source: *BiDFilm; BioIn 9, 11; CmMov; DcFM; EncSF; FilmgC; IntMPA 75, 76, 77, 78, 79, 80, 81; OxFilm; WhoAm 74, 76, 78, 80, 82; WhoWor 74, 76, 78, 80; WorEFlm*

Corn, Ira George, Jr.
American. Business Executive
Organized first US pro bridge team, "The Aces," 1968; won three world championships.
b. Aug 22, 1921 in Little Rock, Arkansas
d. Apr 28, 1982 in Dallas, Texas
Source: *ConAu 85; WhoAm 74, 76, 78, 80, 82; WhoF&I 74, 75, 77, 79; WhoS&SW 78; WhoWor 78*

Corneille
[Cornelis Guillaume van Beverloo]
Dutch. Artist
b. 1922 in Liege, Belgium
Source: *ConArt; McGDA*

Corneille, Pierre
French. Dramatist, Poet
b. Jun 6, 1606 in Rouen, France
d. Oct 1, 1684 in Paris, France
Source: *AtlBL; BbD; BiD&SB; CasWL; CnThe; CyWA; DcEuL; EuAu; EvEuW; McGEWD; NewC; OxEng; OxFr; OxThe; Pen EUR; PlP&P; RComWL; REn; REnWD*

Cornelius, Henry
British. Motion Picture Director
b. Aug 18, 1913 in South Africa
d. May 3, 1958 in London, England
Source: *CmMov; DcFM; FilmgC; MovMk; OxFilm*

Cornelius, Peter
German. Composer
b. Dec 24, 1824 in Mainz, Germany
d. Oct 26, 1874 in Mainz, Germany
Source: *Alli; EvEuW*

Cornelius, Peter von
German. Artist
b. 1783
d. 1867
Source: *OxGer; WebBD 80*

Cornell, Don
American. Singer
b. 1921 in New York, New York
Source: *BiDAmM; CmpEPM*

Cornell, Douglas B
American. Journalist
AP White House correspondent for 36 years, beginning 1933.
b. 1907 in Saint Louis, Missouri
d. Feb 20, 1982 in Detroit, Michigan
Source: *BioIn 12; NewYTBS 82*

Cornell, Ezra
American. Business Leader
Founded Western Union Telegraph Co, 1855; Cornell U, 1865.
b. Jan 11, 1807 in Westchester, New York
d. Dec 9, 1874
Source: *AmBi; ApCAB; DcAmB; TwCBDA; WebAB; WhAm H*

Cornell, Joseph
American. Artist
b. Dec 24, 1903 in Nyack, New York
d. Dec 1972
Source: *WhAm 5; WhoAmA 78*

Cornell, Katharine
American. Actress
Played Elizabeth Barrett in *The Barretts of Wimpole Street,* 1931.
b. Feb 16, 1898 in Berlin, Germany
d. Jun 9, 1974 in Vineyard Haven, Massachusetts
Source: *BiE&WWA; BioNews 74; CelR 73; ConAu 49; CurBio 41, 52, 74; FamA&A; HerW; NewYTBS 74; OxAmL; OxThe; PlP&P; WebAB; WhAm 6; WhScrn 77; Who 74; WhoAm 74; WhoHol B; WhoWor 74*

Cornell, Lydia
American. Actress
Plays Sarah Rush on TV series "Too Close for Comfort," 1980--.
b. 1957? in El Paso, Texas
Source: *BioIn 12*

Cornfeld, Bernard
American. Mutual Fund Executive
b. 1927
Source: *NewYTBE 70*

Corning, Erastus
American. Financier, Congressman
b. Dec 14, 1794 in Norwich, Connecticut
d. Apr 9, 1872 in Albany, New York
Source: *AmBi; ApCAB; BiAuS; BiDrAC; BioIn 3, 5; DcAmB; Drake; EncAB-A; EncAB-H; McGEWB; TwCBDA; WhAm H; WhAmP*

Cornish, Gene
see: Rascals, The

Cornwallis, Charles, Marquis
English. General, Colonial Governor
Surrendered to George Washington at Yorktown, 1781.
b. Dec 31, 1738 in London, England
d. Oct 5, 1805 in Ghazipore, India
Source: *Alli; AmBi; ApCAB; Drake; OxAmL; REn; REnAL; WhAm H*

Corona, Juan
American. Mass Murderer
Convicted of murdering 25 migrant workers, 1970-71.
Source: *NewYTBE 71*

Coronado, Francisco Vasquez de
"El Dorado"
Spanish. Explorer
Led Mexico expedition searching for wealth of Seven Cities of Cibola, 1540.
b. Feb 25, 1510 in Salamanca, Spain
d. Nov 12, 1554
Source: *AmBi; ApCAB; DcAmB; REn; REnAL; WebAB; WhAm H*

Corot, Jean Baptiste Camille
"Papa"
French. Artist
b. Jul 16, 1796 in Paris, France
d. Feb 22, 1875 in Paris, France
Source: *AtlBL; NewC; OxFr; REn*

Correggio, Antonio Allegri da
Italian. Artist
Most famous work "The Assumption of the Virgin" in dome of Parma cathedral.
b. Aug 30, 1494 in Italy
d. Mar 5, 1534
Source: *AtlBL; ChPo, S1; REn*

Correll, Charles J
[Amos 'n Andy]
American. Radio Comedian
Andy of Amos 'n Andy comedy team; on radio, 1928-58.
b. Feb 2, 1890 in Peoria, Illinois
d. Sep 26, 1972 in Chicago, Illinois
Source: *WebAB*

Corri, Adrienne
Scottish. Actress
b. Nov 13, 1933 in Glasgow, Scotland
Source: *FilmgC; IntMPA 75, 76, 77, 78, 79, 80, 81, 82; WhoHol A*

Corrigan, Douglas
"Wrong Way"
American. Aviator, Actor
Nicknamed for landing in Ireland after taking off from NY for LA, 1938.
Source: *WhoHol A*

Corrigan, Mairead
Irish. Pacifist
Won Nobel Peace Prize for forming N Ireland Peace Movement, 1976.
b. Jan 27, 1944 in Belfast, Northern Ireland
Source: *BioIn 11*

Corsaro, Frank
American. Actor, Motion Picture Director
b. Dec 22, 1925 in New York, New York
Source: *BiE&WWA; NewYTBE 72; NotNAT; WhoAm 82; WhoThe 77*

Corsi, Jacopo
Italian. Opera Originator
The first operas performed took place at his palace.
b. 1560 in Celano, Italy
d. 1604 in Florence, Italy
Source: *NewEOp 71*

Corso, Gregory
American. Poet
b. Mar 26, 1930 in New York, New York
Source: *AmAu&B; ConAu 5R; ConLC 1, 11; ConP 70, 75; CroCAP; DrAP 75; OxAmL; Pen AM; RAdv 1; REn; REnAL; TwCW; WebE&AL; WhoAm 74, 76, 78, 80, 82; WhoWor 74*

Corson, William R
American. Author
b. 1926
Source: *BioIn 8*

Cort, Bud
American. Actor
Appeared in *MASH*, 1970; *Harold and Maude*, 1971.
b. Mar 29, 1951 in Rye, New York
Source: *FilmgC; MovMk; WhoAm 82; WhoHol A*

Cortazar, Julio
Argentine. Author
b. Aug 26, 1914 in Brussels, Belgium
Source: *CasWL; ConAu 21R; ConLC 2, 3, 5, 10, 13, 15; CurBio 74; DcCLAA; EncWL; IntWW 74; Pen AM; TwCW; WhoTwCL; WorAu*

Cortesa, Valentina
Italian. Actress
b. Jan 1, 1925 in Milan, Italy
Source: *FilmgC; IntMPA 75, 76, 77, 78, 79, 80, 81, 82; MovMk*

Cortez, Hernando
[Hernan Cortes]
Spanish. Conquistador
Conquered Mexico; caused downfall of Aztec empire, 1521.
b. 1485 in Medellin, Spain
d. 1547
Source: *DcEuL; Drake; NewC; OxAmL; REn; REnAL; WhAm H*

Cortez, Ricardo
[Jacob Kranz]
American. Actor
b. 1899 in Vienna, Austria
d. May 28, 1977 in New York, New York
Source: *FilmgC; MotPP; MovMk; WhoHol A*

Cortissoz, Royal
American. Journalist, Author
b. Feb 10, 1869 in Brooklyn, New York
d. Oct 17, 1948 in New York, New York
Source: *AmAu&B; DcAmB S4; DcNAA; TwCA, SUP; WhAm 2*

Corum, Martene Windsor
"Bill"
American. Journalist
b. Jul 20, 1895 in Speed, Missouri
d. Dec 16, 1958 in New York, New York
Source: *WhAm 3*

Corvo, Baron, pseud.
[Frederick William Rolfe]
English. Author
b. Jul 22, 1860 in London, England
d. Oct 26, 1913 in Venice, Italy
Source: *AtlBL; CasWL; ChPo S2; CnMWL; DcLEL; EvLB; LongCTC; ModBrL, SUP; NewC; OxEng; Pen ENG; REn; TwCA, SUP; TwCW*

Corwin, Norman
American. Author, Producer, Director
b. May 3, 1910 in Boston, Massachusetts
Source: *AmAu&B; AmSCAP 66; AuNews 2; BiE&WWA; CnDAL; ConAu 1R; CurBio 40; IntMPA 75, 76, 77, 78, 79, 80, 81, 82; IntWW 74; NotNAT; OxAmL; REnAL; TwCA SUP; WhoAm 74, 76, 78, 80, 82; WhoWor 74; WhoWorJ 72; WrDr 76*

Corwin, Thomas
American. Statesman
b. 1794 in Bourbon County, Kentucky
d. 1865
Source: *DcNAA; NewCol 75; OhA&B*

Coryell, Don(ald David)
American. Football Coach
Head coach, San Diego Chargers, 1978--.
b. Oct 17, 1924 in Seattle, Washington
Source: *FootReg; WhoAm 82*

Coryell, John Russell
[Nick Carter, pseud.]
American. Author
b. 1848?
d. Jul 15, 1924
Source: *AmAu&B; DcNAA; EncMys; OxAmL; REn; REnAL*

Cosby, Bill
American. Actor, Comedian
Starred in "I Spy," 1965-68; "The Bill Cosby Show," 1969-71.
b. Jul 12, 1937 in Philadelphia, Pennsylvania
Source: *BioNews 74; BkPepl; CelR 73; CurBio 67; FilmgC; IntMPA 75, 76, 77, 78, 79, 80, 81, 82; WhoAm 74, 76, 78, 80, 82; WhoBlA 75; WhoHol A; WhoWest 74; WhoWor 74*

Cosell, Howard
[Howard William Cohen]
American. Sportscaster
Sportscaster, ABC, 1956--; host "Saturday Night Live," 1975-76.
b. Mar 25, 1920 in Winston-Salem, North Carolina
Source: *BioNews 74; BkPepl; CelR 73; CurBio 72; IntMPA 82; NewYTBS 74; WhoAm 82; WhoE 74*

Cosgrave, Liam
Irish. Prime Minister
b. Apr 30, 1920 in Dublin, Ireland
Source: *IntWW 74; NewYTBE 73; Who 74; WhoWor 74*

Cosgrave, William Thomas
Irish. Statesman
President, Irish Free State, 1922-32.
b. Jun 6, 1880 in Dublin, Ireland
d. Nov 16, 1965 in Dublin, Ireland
Source: *BioIn 7; DcIrB; LinLib S; NewCol 75; ObitOF 79; WebBD 80; WhAm 4*

Cosgrove, Gordon Dean
American. Pipeline Company Executive
b. Mar 2, 1934 in Oklahoma City, Oklahoma
Source: *WhoAm 74; WhoF&I 74*

Cosimo, Piero di
Italian. Artist, Architect
b. 1462
d. 1521
Source: *REn*

Coslow, Sam
American. Composer
Won Oscar for best two-reel short *Heavenly Music,* 1943.
b. Dec 27, 1905 in New York, New York
d. Apr 2, 1982 in Bronxville, New York
Source: *AmPS; AmSCAP 66, 80; CmpEPM; ConAu 77; IntMPA 75, 76, 77, 78, 79, 80, 81, 82; NewYTBS 82*

Cossart, Ernest
English. Actor
b. Sep 24, 1876 in Cheltenham, England
d. Jan 21, 1951 in New York, New York
Source: *Film 1; FilmgC; NotNAT B; PlP&P; WhScrn 74, 77; WhThe; WhoHol*

Cossiga, Francesco
Italian. Prime Minister
b. Jul 26, 1928 in Sassari, Sardinia
Source: *IntWW 79; NewYTBS 79*

Cossotto, Fiorenza
Italian. Opera Singer
b. Apr 22, 1935 in Crescentino, Italy
Source: *NewYTBE 71; WhoAm 82*

Costa, Lucio
Brazilian. Architect
b. 1902
Source: *IntWW 74*

Costa, Mary
American. Opera Singer
b. 1934 in Knoxville, Tennessee
Source: *WhoAm 74, 76, 78, 80, 82; WhoHol A; WhoWor 74*

Costa, Victor Charles
American. Fashion Designer
President, Victor Costa, Inc., 1973--.
b. Dec 17, 1935 in Houston, Texas
Source: *WhoAm 82; WorFshn*

Costa e Silva, Arthur da
Brazilian. Army Officer, President
b. Oct 3, 1902 in Taquari, Brazil
d. Dec 17, 1969 in Rio de Janeiro, Brazil
Source: *CurBio 67, 70*

Costa-Gavras(, Henri)
[Kostantinos Gavras]
Greek. Motion Picture Director
Won Oscar for *Z,* 1969.
b. 1933 in Athens, Greece
Source: *BioIn 9, 10; CurBio 72; WhoAm 82*

Costa Mendez, Nicanor
Argentine. Former Foreign Minister
b. Oct 30, 1922 in Buenos Aires, Argentina
Source: *IntWW 74; NewYTBS 82*

Costain, Thomas B
American. Author, Journalist
b. May 28, 1885 in Brantford, ON
d. Oct 8, 1965 in New York, New York
Source: *AmAu&B; AmNov; AuBYP; CanWr; ConAu 5R, 25R; CreCan 2; CurBio 53, 65; DcLEL; LongCTC; OxAmL; OxCan; REn; REnAL; TwCA SUP; TwCW; WhAm 4*

Costakis, George
Russian. Art Collector
b. 1911
Source: *BioIn 10*

Costanza, "Midge" (Margaret)
American. Former Presidential Aide
b. Nov 28, 1928 in Leroy, New York
Source: *CurBio 78; WhoAmW 77*

Coste, Dieudonne
French. Pioneer Aviator
b. 1896
d. May 19, 1973
Source: *NewYTBE 73*

Costello, Dolores
American. Actress
b. 1905 in Pittsburgh, Pennsylvania
Source: *Film 1; FilmgC; InWom; MotPP; MovMk; ThFT; TwYS; WhoHol A*

Costello, Elvis
[Declan Patrick McManus]
English. Singer, Songwriter
Best known album, *Armed Forces,* 1979; released *Imperial Bedroom,* 1982.
b. 1954 in London, England
Source: *BioIn 11; WhoAm 82*

Costello, Frank
American. Gambler, Reputed Mobster
b. 1891
d. Feb 18, 1973 in New York, New York
Source: *BioIn 10; NewYTBE 73*

Costello, Helene
American. Actress
b. Jun 21, 1903 in New York, New York
d. Jan 26, 1957 in Los Angeles, California
Source: *Film 1; FilmgC; MotPP; ThFT; TwYS; WhScrn 74, 77; WhoHol B*

Costello, John Aloysius
Irish. Prime Minister
b. Jun 20, 1891 in Dublin, Ireland
d. Jan 5, 1976 in Dublin, Ireland
Source: *CurBio 48; IntWW 74; PoIre; WhAm 6; Who 74*

Costello, Larry
American. Basketball Coach
b. Jul 2, 1931 in Minoa, New York
Source: *BioIn 6; OfNBA; WhoBbl 73*

Costello, Lou
[Abbott and Costello; Louis Francis Cristillo]
American. Actor, Comedian
Stuntman, 1926-28; starred in over 30 films with Abbott.
b. Mar 6, 1908 in Paterson, New Jersey
d. Mar 3, 1959 in Los Angeles, California
Source: *CmMov; CurBio 41, 59; FilmgC; MotPP; MovMk; OxFilm; WhAm 3; WhScrn 74, 77; WhoHol B; WorEFlm*

Costello, Maurice
American. Actor
b. 1877 in Pittsburgh, Pennsylvania
d. Oct 30, 1950 in Hollywood, California
Source: *Film 1; FilmgC; MotPP; TwYS; WhScrn 74, 77; WhoHol B*

Coster, Laurens Janszoon
[Laurens Janszoon Koster]
Dutch. Inventor
Invented moveable type; doubtful evidence that he preceded Gutenberg.
b. 1410 in Haarlem, Netherlands
Source: *NewCol 75; WebBD 80*

Costle, Douglas Michael
American. Government Official
b. Jul 27, 1939 in Long Beach, California
Source: *BioIn 12; CurBio 80; WhoAm 80, 82*

Cote, Gerard
Canadian. Track Athlete
b. 1913
Source: *BioIn 10*

Cothran, Shirley
American. Beauty Queen
Miss America, 1975.
b. 1953
Source: *NewYTBS 74*

Cotman, John S
English. Artist
b. Aug 16, 1782 in Norwich, England
d. Jul 24, 1865 in London, England
Source: *Alli; AtlBL; BiDLA; NewC*

Cotrubas, Ileana
Romanian. Opera Singer
b. Jun 9, 1939 in Galati, Romania
Source: *CurBio 81; IntWW 78; NewYTBS 77; WhoAm 82; WhoMus 72; WhoOp 76*

Cotsworth, Staats
American. Actor, Artist
b. Feb 17, 1908 in Oak Park, Illinois
Source: *BiE&WWA; IntMPA 75, 76, 77; NotNAT; WhoAmA 73; WhoHol A; WhoThe 77*

Cott, Gerry
see: Boomtown Rats

Cott, Nate
American. Engineer
Founded Fly without Fear.
b. 1913
d. Oct 5, 1973 in Lawrence, New York
Source: *BioIn 10; NewYTBE 73*

Cott, Ted
American. Radio, TV Executive, Author
b. Jan 1, 1917 in Poughkeepsie, New York
d. Jun 13, 1973 in New York, New York
Source: *AmAu&B; NewYTBE 73; WhAm 6; WhoPubR 72*

Cottam, Clarence
American. Biologist
b. Jan 1, 1899 in Saint George, Utah
d. Mar 30, 1974 in Corpus Christi, Texas
Source: *BioIn 10; NewYTBS 74; WhoAm 74; WhoWor 74*

Cotten, Joseph
American. Actor
Starred in *Citizen Kane,* 1941; *Journey into Fear,* 1942.
b. May 15, 1905 in Petersburg, Virginia
Source: *BiDFilm; BiE&WWA; BioNews 74; CmMov; CurBio 43; FilmgC; IntMPA 75, 76, 77, 78, 79, 80, 81, 82; MotPP; MovMk; NotNAT; OxFilm; PlP&P; WhoAm 74, 76, 78, 80, 82; WhoHol A; WhoThe 77; WorEFlm*

Cotten, Michael
see: Tubes, The

Cotton, John
American. Religious Leader
b. Dec 4, 1584 in Derby, England
d. Dec 23, 1652 in Boston, Massachusetts
Source: *Alli, SUP; AmAu; AmAu&B; AmBi; ApCAB; BiD&SB; CnDAL; CyAL 1; DcAmAu; DcAmB; DcLEL; DcNAA; Drake; EncAB-H; OxAmL; Pen AM; REn; REnAL; TwCBDA; WebAB; WhAm H*

Cotton, Norris
American. Senator
b. May 11, 1900
Source: *BiDrAC; CngDr 74; CurBio 56; IntWW 74; WhoAm 74; WhoAmP 73; WhoE 74; WhoGov 72*

Cotton, Paul
see: Poco

Cottrell, Alan Howard
English. Scientist
b. Jul 17, 1919 in Birmingham, England
Source: *IntWW 74; Who 74; WhoWor 74*

Coty, Rene
French. Statesman
b. Mar 20, 1882 in Le Havre, France
d. Nov 22, 1962
Source: *CurBio 54, 63; WhAm 4*

Coubertin, Baron Pierre de
French. Revived Olympic Games
b. Jan 1, 1862 in Paris, France
d. 1937 in Geneva, Switzerland
Source: *BioIn 2; WhE&EA; WhLit; WhoLA; WhoModH*

Coue, Emile
French. Psychologist
b. Feb 26, 1857 in Troyes, France
d. Jul 2, 1926 in Nancy, France
Source: *BioIn 3, 7; NewC*

Cougar, John
[John Mellencamp]
American. Singer, Songwriter
Had two number one hits, "Jack and Diane" and "Hurts So Good" from *American Fool,* 1982.
b. 1952? in Seymour, Indiana
Source: *NF*

Coughlin, Father (Charles Edward)
American. Priest, Radio Commentator
Founded National Union for Social Justice, 1934; published *Social Justice,* 1934-42.
b. Oct 25, 1891 in Hamilton, ON
d. Oct 27, 1979 in Bloomfield Hills, Michigan
Source: *ConAu 97; CurBio 40; EncAB-H; NewCol 75; WebAB*

Coulomb, Charles Augustin de
French. Physicist
b. Jun 14, 1736 in Angouleme, France
d. Aug 23, 1806 in Paris, France
Source: *AsBiEn; McGEWB; NewCol 75*

Coulouris, George
English. Actor
b. Oct 1, 1903 in Manchester, England
Source: *BiE&WWA; FilmgC; MovMk; NotNAT; Vers A; WhoHol A; WhoThe 77*

Coulter, John William
Canadian. Dramatist
b. Feb 12, 1888 in Belfast, Northern Ireland
d. Dec 1980 in Toronto, ON
Source: *BioIn 1, 11; CanWW 70, 79; ConAu 5R, 3NR; OxCan, SUP*

Country Joe and the Fish
[Bruce Barthol; David Cohen; Chicken Hirsch; Joseph McDonald; Barry Melton]
American. Country Rock Group
Source: *BiDAmM; Rk100*

Couperin
French. Family of Musicians
Source: *WebBD 80*

Couperin, Francois
[LeGrand Couperin]
French. Musician, Composer
b. Nov 10, 1668 in Paris, France
d. Sep 12, 1733 in Paris, France
Source: *AtlBL; OxFr*

Courbet, Gustave
French. Artist
b. Jun 10, 1819 in Ornans, France
d. Dec 31, 1877 in Vevey, Switzerland
Source: *AtlBL; OxFr; REn*

Courboin, Charles
American. Organist, Music Director
b. 1883
d. Apr 13, 1973
Source: *BioIn 9*

Cournand, Andre Frederic
American. Physiologist
b. Sep 24, 1895 in Paris, France
Source: *AmM&WS 73P; BioIn 4, 5, 6, 11; CurBio 57; IntWW 74; WhoAm 74, 76, 78, 80, 82; WhoWor 74*

Cournos, John
Author
b. Mar 6, 1881 in Russia
d. Aug 29, 1966
Source: *AmAu&B; ConAmL; ConAu 13R; ConAu P-2; DcLEL; LongCTC; OxAmL; REnAL; TwCA, SUP; WhoLA*

Courreges, Andre
French. Fashion Designer
b. Mar 9, 1923 in Pau, France
Source: *CurBio 70; IntWW 74; WhoAm 74; WhoWor 74; WorFshn*

Court, Margaret
[Margaret Smith]
Australian. Tennis Player
Wimbledon champ, 1963-65, 1970; US Open champ, 1962, 1965, 1968-70, 1973.
b. Jul 16, 1942 in Albury, Australia
Source: *BioNews 74; CelR 73; CurBio 73; NewYTBE 70, 71; WhoAm 82; WhoWor 74*

Courtenay, Tom
English. Actor
b. Feb 25, 1937 in Hull, England
Source: *CelR 73; CurBio 64; FilmgC; IntMPA 75, 76, 77, 78, 79, 80, 81, 82; MotPP; MovMk; OxFilm; WhoHol A; WhoThe 77; WhoWor 74; WorEFlm*

Courtneidge, Dame Cicely
British. Actress
b. Apr 1, 1893 in Sydney, Australia
d. Apr 26, 1980 in London, England
Source: *BioIn 3, 9, 10; EncMT; NotNAT A; Who 74, 76, 78; WhoThe 77*

Courtney, Clint(on Dawson)
"Scrap Iron"
American. Baseball Player
Catcher, 1951-61; AL Rookie of Year, 1952.
b. Mar 16, 1927 in Hall Summit, Louisiana
d. Jun 16, 1975 in Rochester, New York
Source: *BaseEn; BioIn 3, 10; WhoProB 73*

Courtright, Timothy Isaiah
American. Marshal
b. 1845
d. 1887
Source: *BioIn 4, 5*

Cousins, Frank
English. Trade Unionist
Former Labour MP; vice-president, International Transport Workers Federation, 1968--.
b. Sep 8, 1904 in Bulwell, England
Source: *BioIn 4, 5, 6, 7, 8, 9; CurBio 60; IntWW 74; Who 74*

Cousins, Margaret
American. Children's Author
b. Jan 26, 1905 in Munday, Texas
Source: *AmAu&B; AuBYP; ConAu 1R, 1NR; ForWC 70; InWom; SmATA 2; TexWr; WhoAm 74, 76, 78, 80, 82; WhoWor 74; WrDr 76*

Cousins, Norman
American. Editor
b. Jun 24, 1912 in Union Hill, New Jersey
Source: *AmAu&B; CelR 73; ChPo; ConAu 17R; CurBio 43; IntWW 74; NewYTBE 71; OxAmL; REn; REnAL; TwCA SUP; WebAB; Who 82; WhoAm 74, 76, 78, 80, 82; WhoE 74; WhoF&I 74; WhoWor 74; WrDr 76*

Cousins, Robin
English. Ice Skater
Won Olympic gold medal in figure skating, 1980.
b. 1957 in Bristol, England
Source: *NewYTBS 79*

Cousteau, Jacques Yves
French. Oceanographer, Author
Leader Calypso expeditions; host TV's "Undersea World of Jacques Cousteau," won Oscar, 1965, for best documentary.
b. Jun 11, 1910 in Sainte Andre de Cubzac, France
Source: *AnCL; AsBiEn; BioNews 74; CelR 73; ConAu 65; DcFM; FilmgC; IntAu&W 77; IntWW 74, 75, 76, 77, 78, 79, 80, 81; LinLib L; OxFilm; OxShips; REn; WhDW; Who 82; WhoAm 80, 82; WhoOcn 78; WhoUN 75; WhoWor 74, 76, 78; WorAl; WorEFlm*

Cousteau, Philippe
French. TV Producer, Oceanographer
b. Dec 30, 1940 in Toulon, France
d. Jun 28, 1979 in Alverca, Portugal
Source: *ConAu 33R, 89*

Cousy, Bob (Robert)
American. Basketball Player
Bill Russell said, "The image of the Celtics is the image of Cousy."
b. Aug 9, 1928 in New York, New York
Source: *CelR 73; CurBio 58; WebAB; WhoAm 74, 76, 78, 80, 82; WhoBbl 73; WorAl*

Couthon, Georges
French. Politician, Lawyer
Paralyzed, he led army that took Lyons from counter-revolutionaries.
b. 1756
d. Jul 28, 1794
Source: *DcBiPP; Dis&D; OxFr*

Couve de Murville, (Jacques) Maurice
French. Premier, Politician
b. Jan 24, 1907 in Reims, France
Source: *IntWW 74; Who 74*

Couzens, James Joseph, Jr.
American. Businessman, Public Official
b. Aug 26, 1876 in Chatham, ON
d. Oct 22, 1936 in Detroit, Michigan
Source: *AmBi; BiDrAC; DcAmB S2; EncAB-A; NatCAB 30; WebAB; WhAm 1; WhAmP*

Covarrubias, Miguel
Mexican. Artist, Caricaturist
b. Feb 4, 1904 in Mexico City, Mexico
d. Feb 6, 1957 in Mexico City, Mexico
Source: *CurBio 40, 57; IlsCB 1744, 1946; REnAL; WhAm 3*

Coveleski, Harry Frank
[Harry Frank Kowalewski]
"The Giant Killer"
American. Baseball Player
Pitcher, 1907-10; 1914-19.
b. Apr 23, 1886 in Shamokin, Pennsylvania
d. Aug 4, 1950 in Shamokin, Pennsylvania
Source: *BaseEn; WhoProB 73*

Coveleski, Stanley Anthony
[Stanislaus Kowalewski]
American. Baseball Player
Had four 20-game seasons with Cleveland, 1918-21; Hall of Fame, 1969.
b. Jul 13, 1890 in Shamokin, Pennsylvania
Source: *BaseEn; WhoProB 73*

Covey, Cyclone
American. Author
b. May 21, 1922 in Guthrie, Oklahoma
Source: *ConAu 21R; DrAS 74H; WhoAm 74, 76, 78, 80, 82; WhoS&SW 73*

Covington, Glen
American. Jazz Musician
Source: *NF*

Covington, Warren
American. Musician, Author, Singer
b. Aug 7, 1921 in Philadelphia, Pennsylvania
Source: *AmSCAP 66; CmpEPM*

Cowan, Jerome
American. Actor
b. Oct 6, 1897 in New York, New York
d. Jan 24, 1972 in Encino, California
Source: *BiE&WWA; FilmgC; MovMk; NewYTBE 72; Vers A; WhScrn 77; WhoHol B*

Cowan, Peter Wilkinshaw
Australian. Author
b. Nov 4, 1914 in Perth, Australia
Source: *ConAu 21R; ConNov 72, 76; WrDr 76*

Coward, Sir Noel Pierce
English. Actor, Dramatist, Composer
Wrote 27 plays, 281 songs; plays include *Private Lives,* 1930; *Blithe Spirit,* 1941.
b. Dec 16, 1899 in London, England
d. Mar 26, 1973 in Kingston, Jamaica
Source: *Au&Wr 71; AuNews 1; BiE&WWA; BioNews 74; CasWL; Chambr 3; ChPo, S2; CnMD; CnThe; ConAu 17R, 41R; ConAu P-2; ConDr 73; ConLC 1, 9; CurBio 41, 62, 73; CyWA; DcFM; DcLEL; EncMT; EncWL; EvLB; FamA&A; Film 1; FilmgC; LongCTC; McGEWD; ModBrL, SUP; ModWD; MovMk; NewC; NewYTBE 70, 73; NewYTBS 74; OxEng; OxFilm; OxThe; Pen ENG; PlP&P; REn; REnWD; TwCA, SUP; TwCW; WebE&AL; WhAm 5; WhScrn 77; WhoHol B; WhoMus 72; WorEFlm*

Cowdrey, Colin
English. Cricket Player
b. Dec 24, 1932
Source: *Who 74*

Cowdry, Edmund Vincent
Canadian. Scientist
Cancer researcher; discovered heartwater.
b. Jul 18, 1888 in MacLeon, AB
d. Jun 25, 1975
Source: *BioIn 1, 10; InSci; WhAm 6; WhoAm 74; WhoWor 74*

Cowell, Henry Dixon
American. Composer, Musician
b. Mar 11, 1897 in Menlo Park, California
d. Dec 10, 1965 in Shady, New York
Source: *DcCM; EncFCWM 69; REnAL; WebAB; WhAm 4; WhNAA*

Cowen, Joshua Lionel
American. Inventor, Industrialist
Invented toy electric train, 1900; headed Lionel Corp., 1945-65.
b. Aug 25, 1880 in New York, New York
d. Sep 8, 1965 in New York, New York
Source: *CurBio 54, 65; WhAm 4*

Cowen, Sir Zelman
Australian. Governor General, Author
b. Oct 7, 1919 in Melbourne, Australia
Source: *Au&Wr 71; BioIn 11; ConAu 1R, 1NR; Who 74; WhoWorJ 72; WrDr 76*

Cowens, Dave
American. Basketball Player
b. Oct 25, 1948 in Newport, Kentucky
Source: *WhoBbl 73*

Cowl, Jane
American. Actress
b. Dec 14, 1884 in Boston, Massachusetts
d. Jun 22, 1950 in Santa Monica, California
Source: *FamA&A; Film 1; FilmgC; NotNAT B; PlP&P; WhScrn 77; WhThe; WhoHol B*

Cowles, Fleur Fenton
American. Editor
b. Feb 13, 1910 in New York, New York
Source: *AmAu&B; Au&Wr 71; AuNews 1; BioNews 74; ConAu 5R, 4NR; CurBio 52; WhoAm 74, 76, 78, 80, 82; WhoWor 74; WrDr 76*

Cowles, Gardner
"Mike"
American. Publisher
Founded *Look Magazine,* 1937; chairman, Cowles Communications, Inc.
b. Jan 31, 1903 in Algona, Iowa
Source: *AmAu&B; CelR 73; CurBio 43; IntWW 74, 75, 76, 77, 78, 79, 80, 81; LinLib L, S; NewYTBE 71; St&PR 75; WebAB, 79; WhoAm 74, 76, 78, 80, 82; WhoAmA 73, 76, 78, 80; WhoF&I 74; WhoWor 74*

Cowles, William Hutchinson, Jr.
American. Publisher
President, Spokane Chronicle Co., 1935-68; Cowles Publishing Co., 1946-70.
b. Jul 23, 1902 in Sands Point, New York
d. Aug 12, 1971 in Spokane, Washington
Source: *BioIn 1, 2, 9, 11; NatCAB 57; WhAm 5*

Cowley, Abraham
English. Poet
b. 1618 in London, England
d. Jul 28, 1667 in Chertsey, England
Source: *Alli; AtlBL; BbD; BiD&SB; BrAu; CasWL; Chambr 1; ChPo, S1; CnE&AP; CroE&S; CrtT 2; CyWA; DcEnA; DcEnL; DcEuL; DcLEL; EvLB; MouLC 1; NewC; OxEng; OxThe; Pen ENG; REn; WebE&AL*

Cowley, Malcolm
American. Author, Literary Critic
b. Aug 24, 1898 in Belsano, Pennsylvania
Source: *AmAu&B; Au&Wr 71; CelR 73; ChPo; CnDAL; ConAu 5R, 3NR; ConP 70, 75; DcLEL; EncWL; IntWW 74; ModAL, SUP; OxAmL; Pen AM; RAdv 1; REn; REnAL; SixAP; TwCA, SUP; WebAB; WhNAA; WhoAm 74, 76, 78, 80, 82; WhoWor 74; WrDr 76*

Cowper, William
English. Poet
Wrote hymn "Oh for a Closer Walk with God," 1779.
b. Nov 15, 1731 in Berkhampstead, England
d. Apr 25, 1800 in Dereham, England
Source: *Alli; AnCL; AtlBL; BbD; BiD&SB; BrAu; CarSB; CasWL; Chambr 2; ChPo, S1, S2; CnE&AP; CrtT 2; CyWA; DcEnA; DcEnL; DcEuL; DcLEL; EvLB; MouLC 2; NewC; OxEng; Pen ENG; PoChrch; RAdv 1; REn; WebE&AL*

Cowsills, The
[Barbara Cowsill; Barry Cowsill; John Cowsill; Paul Cowsill; Richard Cowsill; Robert Cowsill; Susan Cowsill; William Cowsill]
American. Singing Group
Source: *RkOn*

Cox, Archibald
American. Lawyer
Watergate prosecutor fired by Richard Nixon; replaced by Leon Jaworski.
b. May 17, 1912 in Plainfield, New Jersey
Source: *ASpks; BioNews 74; BlueB 76; ConAu 73; CurBio 61; DrAS 78P; IntWW 74, 75, 76, 77, 78, 79, 80, 81; NewYTBE 73; PolProf J; PolProf K; PolProf NF; WhoAm 74, 76, 78, 80, 82; WhoAmL 78, 79; WhoAmP 73, 75, 77, 79; WhoWor 78; WrDr 80*

Cox, Constance
English. Dramatist
b. Oct 25, 1915 in Surrey, England
Source: *Au&Wr 71; ConAu 21R; WhoAmW 77; WhoThe 77; WrDr 76*

Còx, David
English. Artist
b. Apr 29, 1783 in Deritend, England
d. Jun 7, 1859 in Harborne, England
Source: *BioIn 1, 3, 4, 10, 11; NewCol 75; OxArt; WebBD 80*

Cox, Edward Finch
American. Husband of Tricia Nixon, Lawyer
Married Tricia Nixon, Jun 1971.
b. Oct 2, 1946 in Southampton, New York
Source: *BioIn 10; ConAu 29R*

Cox, Gardner
American. Portrait Artist
b. Jan 22, 1906 in Holyoke, Massachusetts
Source: *WhoAm 74, 76, 78, 80, 82; WhoAmA 73*

Cox, Harvey Gallagher, Jr.
American. Theologian, Social Activist
b. May 19, 1929 in Chester County, Pennsylvania
Source: *AmAu&B; AuNews 1; ConAu 77; CurBio 68; WhoAm 74, 76, 78, 80, 82; WhoE 74; WrDr 76*

Cox, Herald Rea
American. Bacteriologist
b. Feb 28, 1907 in Rosedale, Indiana
Source: *WhoAm 74*

Cox, James Middleton, Sr.
American. Political Leader
b. Mar 31, 1870 in Jacksonburg, Ohio
d. Jul 15, 1957 in Dayton, Ohio
Source: *BiDrAC; OhA&B; WhAm 3; WhAmP*

Cox, James Middleton, Jr.
American. Publisher
President, Dayton *Daily News*, Dayton *Journal-Herald*.
b. Jun 27, 1903 in Dayton, Ohio
d. Oct 27, 1974 in Miami, Florida
Source: *BioNews 74; ConAu 89; NewYTBS 74; St&PR 75; WhAm 6; WhoAm 74; WhoMW 74*

Cox, Jean
American. Opera Singer
b. Jan 14, 1922 in Gadsden, Alabama
Source: *BioIn 9*

Cox, John Rogers
American. Artist
b. Mar 24, 1915 in Terre Haute, Indiana
Source: *WhoAm 74, 76, 78; WhoAmA 76, 78*

Cox, Kenyon
American. Artist
b. Oct 27, 1856 in Warren, Ohio
d. Mar 17, 1919
Source: *AmAu&B; AmBi; AmLY; ApCAB; ChPo, S1; DcAmB; DcNAA; OhA&B; TwCBDA; WhAm 1*

Cox, Lynne
American. Swimmer
b. 1958
Source: *BioIn 10*

Cox, Wally (Wallace Maynard)
American. Actor, Comedian
Starred in "Mr. Peepers," 1952-55; regular on "Hollywood Squares."
b. Dec 6, 1924 in Detroit, Michigan
d. Feb 15, 1973 in Los Angeles, California
Source: *ConAu 41R, 97; CurBio 54, 73; NewYTBE 73; WhAm 5; WhScrn 77; WhoHol B*

Cox, William Trevor
see: Trevor, William

Coxe, George Harmon
American. Author
b. Apr 23, 1901 in Oleon, New York
Source: *AmAu&B; ConAu 57; EncMys; MnBBF; REnAL; WhoAm 74, 76, 78, 80, 82; WorAu*

Coxe, Louis Osborne
American. Poet
b. 1918 in Manchester, New Hampshire
Source: *AmAu&B; BiE&WWA; ChPo, S1; ConAu 13R; ConP 70, 75; DrAP 75; McGEWD; NotNAT; OxAmL; WhoAm 74, 76, 78, 80, 82; WhoWor 74; WorAu; WrDr 76*

Coxey, Jacob Sechler
American. Reformer, Social Protester
b. Apr 16, 1854 in Selinsgrove, Pennsylvania
d. May 18, 1951 in Massillon, Ohio
Source: *DcAmB S5; EncAB-H; OhA&B; WebAB; WhAm 3*

Coy, Harold
American. Children's Author
b. Sep 24, 1902 in LaHabra, California
Source: *AuBYP; ConAu 5R, 4NR; SmATA 3; WrDr 76*

Cozzens, James Gould
American. Author
b. Aug 19, 1903 in Chicago, Illinois
d. Aug 9, 1978 in Stuart, Florida
Source: *AmAu&B; AmNov; AmWr; CasWL; ConAu 9R, 81; ConLC 1, 11, 4; ConNov 72, 76; CurBio 49; CyWA; DcLEL; DrAF 76; EncWL; IntWW 74; LongCTC; ModAL; OxAmL; Pen AM; RAdv 1; REn; REnAL; TwCA, SUP; TwCW; WebAB; WebE&AL; Who 74; WhoAm 74; WhoWor 74; WrDr 76*

Crabbe, "Buster" (Larry)
[Clarence Linden]
American. Actor, Swimmer
Won Olympic gold medal, 1932; played Buck Rogers, Flash Gordon in movie serials.
b. Feb 7, 1908 in Oakland, California
Source: *FilmgC; IntMPA 77, 78, 79, 80, 81, 82; MotPP; WhoAm 74, 76, 78, 80, 82; WhoHol A*

Crabbe, George
English. Author
b. Dec 24, 1754 in Aldborough, England
d. Feb 3, 1832 in Trowbridge, England
Source: *Alli; AtlBL; BbD; BiD&SB; BiDLA, SUP; BrAu 19; CasWL; Chambr 2; ChPo, S1, S2; CnE&AP; CrtT 2; CyWA; DcEnA; DcEnL; DcEuL; DcLEL; EvLB; MouLC 3; NewC; OxEng; Pen ENG; PoChrch; RAdv 1; REn; WebE&AL*

Crabtree, Lotta
American. Actress
Began career entertaining in CA mining camps; appeared in *Old Curiosity Shop,* 1867.
b. Nov 7, 1847 in New York, New York
d. Sep 25, 1924 in Boston, Massachusetts
Source: *AmBi; AmWom; ApCAB; CmCal; DcAmB; FamA&A; HerW; InWom; LibW; NewCol 75; NotAW; NotNAT A; OxAmL; TwCBDA; WebAB, 79*

Craddock, "Crash" (Billy)
American. Singer
b. Jun 16, 1940 in Greensboro, North Carolina
Source: *WhoAm 78, 80, 82*

Craft, Ellen
American. Fugitive Slave, Abolitionist
b. 1826 in Clinton, California
d. 1897 in Charleston, South Carolina
Source: *HerW; InWom; NotAW*

Craft, Robert
American. Conductor
b. Oct 20, 1923 in Kingston, New York
Source: *AmAu&B; ConAu 9R; WhoAm 82; WhoMus 72; WhoWor 74; WrDr 76*

Crafts, James Mason
American. Chemist
b. Mar 8, 1839 in Boston, Massachusetts
d. Jun 20, 1917 in Ridgefield, Connecticut
Source: *DcNAA*

Craig, Cleo F
American. Business Executive
b. Apr 6, 1895 in Rich Hill, Missouri
d. Apr 21, 1978 in Ridgewood, New Jersey
Source: *CurBio 51, 78*

Craig, Elijah
American. Baptist Preacher
b. 1743
d. 1800
Source: *ApCAB*

Craig, Elizabeth May
American. Journalist
b. Dec 24, 1889 in Coosaw, South Carolina
d. Jul 15, 1975 in Silver Spring, Maryland
Source: *ConAu 89, 101; CurBio 49, 75; InWom*

Craig, Gordon
English. Stage Designer, Director
b. Jan 16, 1872 in Harpenden, England
d. 1966
Source: *BioIn 7, 8, 9, 10, 11; LongCTC; OxThe; PIP&P; REn; TwCA, SUP*

Craig, Jim
[United States Olympic Hockey Team-1980]
American. Hockey Player
b. May 31, 1957 in North Easton, Massachusetts
Source: *BioIn 12; HocReg; NewYTBS 80*

Craig, May
Irish. Actress
b. 1889 in Ireland
d. Feb 9, 1972 in Dublin, Ireland
Source: *NewYTBE 72; WhScrn 77; WhoHol B*

Craig, Wendy
English. Actress
b. Jun 20, 1930 in Sacriston, England
Source: *FilmgC; WhoHol A; WhoThe 77*

Craig, William
Irish. Politician
b. Dec 2, 1924
Source: *BioIn 9; IntWW 74; Who 74*

Craik, Dinah Maria Mulock
English. Author
b. Apr 20, 1826 in Stoke-on-Trent, England
d. Oct 12, 1887 in Bromley, England
Source: *AnCL; BbD; BiD&SB; BrAu 19; CarSB; CasWL; DcEnA; DcEuL; DcLEL; EvLB; NewC*

Crain, Jeanne
American. Actress
b. May 25, 1925 in Barstow, Georgia
Source: *BiDFilm; CurBio 51; FilmgC; InWom; IntMPA 75, 76, 77, 78, 79, 80, 81, 82; MotPP; MovMk; WhoAm 74; WhoHol A; WorEFlm*

Cram, Ralph Adams
American. Architect
b. Dec 16, 1863 in Hampton Falls, New Hampshire
d. Sep 22, 1942 in Boston, Massachusetts
Source: *AmBi; AmAu&B; AmLY; BiD&SB; DcAmAu; DcAmB S3; DcNAA; OxAmL; REnAL; WebAB; WhAm 2; WhNAA*

Cramer, "Doc" (Roger Maxwell)
"Flit"
American. Baseball Player
Outfielder, 1929-48; had 2,705 hits; batting average .296.
b. Jul 22, 1905 in Beach Haven, New Jersey
Source: *BaseEn; WhoProB 73*

Cramer, Floyd
American. Singer, Musician
b. Oct 27, 1933 in Shreveport, Louisiana
Source: *EncFCWM 69*

Cramer, Johann Baptist
German. Pianist, Composer
b. 1771 in Mannheim, Germany
d. 1858
Source: *BioIn 5, 7; NewCol 75; WebBD 80*

Cramer, Polly
American. Journalist
b. Oct 14, 1903 in Garfield, Kentucky
d. May 13, 1981 in Palm Springs, California
Source: *ForWC 70; WhoAmW 77*

Cramm, Gottfried von, Baron
German. Tennis Player, Socialite
b. 1909
d. Nov 8, 1976 in Cairo, Egypt
Source: *BioIn 11*

Crampton, Bruce Sidney
"Iron Man"
Australian. Golfer
Has won over $1 million; won Vardon Trophy for low score average of 70.576, 1973.
b. Sep 28, 1935 in Sydney, Australia
Source: *WhoAm 74, 76, 78, 80, 82; WhoGolf*

Cranach, Lucas
German. Artist, Designer
b. Oct 4, 1472 in Kronach, Germany
d. Oct 16, 1553 in Weimar, Germany
Source: *AtlBL; REn*

Crandall, Del(mar Wesley)
American. Baseball Player, Manager
Catcher, 1949-1966; hit 15 or more home runs in eight seasons, 1953-60.
b. Mar 5, 1930 in Ontario, California
Source: *BaseEn; BioIn 5, 6, 8; WhoAm 74; WhoProB 73*

Crandall, Prudence
American. Educator, Abolitionist
b. 1803 in Hopkinton, Rhode Island
d. 1889 in Elk Falls, Kansas
Source: *BioIn 5, 6, 7, 9, 10, 11; DcAmB; NewCol 75*

Crane, Bob
American. Actor
Played Colonel Robert Hogan in "Hogan's Heroes," 1965-71.
b. Jul 13, 1928 in Waterbury, Connecticut
d. Jun 29, 1978 in Scottsdale, Arizona
Source: *IntMPA 75, 76, 77; WhoAm 74; WhoHol A*

Crane, Cheryl
American. Daughter of Lana Turner
Killed reputed gangster Johnny Stompanato, Apr 5, 1958.
b. 1944
Source: *What 3*

Crane, Hart
American. Poet
b. Jul 21, 1899 in Garrettsville, Ohio
d. Apr 27, 1932
Source: *LongCTC; ModAL, SUP; OhA&B; OxAmL; OxEng; Pen AM; RAdv 1; REn; REnAL; SixAP; TwCA, SUP; TwCW; WebAB; WebE&AL; WhAm 1; WhoTwCL*

Crane, Les
American. TV Performer
b. 1934 in Long Beach, California
Source: *BioIn 7*

Crane, Nathalia Clara Ruth
American. Poet, Author
b. Aug 11, 1913 in New York, New York
Source: *AmAu&B; ChPo, S1, S2; ConAmL; DcLEL; InWom; OxAmL; REnAL*

Crane, Philip Miller
American. Congressman
b. Nov 3, 1930 in Chicago, Illinois
Source: *BioIn 11, 12; CurBio 80; WhoAm 80, 82*

Crane, Richard O
American. Actor
b. 1918
d. Mar 9, 1969 in California
Source: *WhScrn 74, 77; WhoHol B*

Crane, Roy(ston Campbell)
American. Cartoonist
b. Nov 22, 1901 in Abilene, Texas
d. Jul 7, 1977 in Orlando, Florida
Source: *ConAu 89; WhoAm 74; WhoAmA 73; WhoWor 74*

Crane, Stephen
American. Author, Journalist, Poet
Wrote novels *Maggie: A Girl of the Streets,* 1893; *The Red Badge of Courage,* 1895.
b. Nov 1, 1871 in Newark, New Jersey
d. Jun 5, 1900 in Badenweiler, Germany
Source: *AmAu; AmAu&B; AmBi; AmWr; ApCAB SUP; AtlBL; BbD; BiD&SB; CasWL; Chambr 3; ChPo; CnDAL; CnE&AP; CrtT 3; CyWA; DcAmAu; DcAmB; DcLEL; DcNAA; EncAB-H; EvLB; LongCTC; ModAL; OxAmL; OxEng; Pen AM; RAdv 1; RComWL; REn; REnAL; TwCBDA; WebAB; WebE&AL; WhAm 1*

Crane, Walter
English. Illustrator, Artist
b. Aug 15, 1845 in Liverpool, England
d. Mar 15, 1915 in London, England
Source: *Alli SUP; CarSB; ChPo, S1, S2; IlsBYP; JBA 34, 51; NewC; Str&VC; WhoChL*

Cranko, John
South African. Dancer, Choreographer
b. Aug 15, 1927 in Rustenberg, South Africa
d. Jun 26, 1973
Source: *ConAu 45; CurBio 70, 73; NewYTBE 73; WhoWor 74*

Crankshaw, Edward
British. Author, Journalist
b. Jan 3, 1909 in Woodford, England
Source: *ConAu 25R; LongCTC; TwCA SUP; Who 74; WhoWor 74*

Cranmer, Thomas
English. Author, Archbishop
b. Jul 2, 1489 in Aslacton, England
d. Mar 21, 1556 in Oxford, England
Source: *Alli; BrAu; CasWL; Chambr 1; CroE&S; DcEnL; DcLEL; EvLB; NewC; OxEng; Pen ENG; REn; WebE&AL*

Cranston, Alan MacGregor
American. Senator
Elected to Senate, 1969; declared candidacy for President, 1982.
b. Jun 19, 1914 in Palo Alto, California
Source: *BiDrAC; CngDr 74; CurBio 50, 69; IntWW 74; WhoAm 74, 76, 78, 80, 82; WhoAmP 73; WhoGov 72; WhoWest 74*

Cranston, Toller
Canadian. Figure Skater
b. 1949 in Hamilton Lake, ON
Source: *BioIn 11; CanWW 79; NewYTBS 77*

Crapper, Thomas
English. Engineer
Invented valve and siphon arrangement that made modern flush toilet possible.
b. 1837
d. 1910
Source: *BioIn 8*

Crapsey, Adelaide
American. Poet
b. Sep 9, 1878 in New York, New York
d. Oct 8, 1914 in Saranac Lake, New York
Source: *AmAu&B; ChPo; CnDAL; ConAmL; DcAmB; DcNAA; InWom; NotAW; OxAmL; REn; REnAL; TwCA*

Crashaw, Richard
English. Poet
b. 1613 in London, England
d. Aug 21, 1649 in Loreto, Italy
Source: *Alli; AtlBL; BiD&SB; BrAu; CasWL; Chambr 1; ChPo, S1, S2; CnE&AP; CroE&S; CrtT 1; DcEnA; DcEnL; DcEuL; DcLEL; EvLB; MouLC 1; NewC; OxEng; Pen ENG; RAdv 1; REn; WebE&AL*

Crassus, Marcus Lincinius
Roman. General
b. 115BC
d. Jun 6, 53BC in Carrhae, Mesopotamia
Source: *REn*

Crater, Joseph Force
American. Judge
Disappeared Aug 6, 1930; declared legally dead, Jul 1937.
b. 1889 in Easton, Pennsylvania
d. 1937?
Source: *BioIn 2, 3, 5, 6; WebAB*

Crauste, Michel
French. Rugby Player
b. 1934
Source: *BioIn 9*

Craven, Frank
American. Actor, Director, Dramatist
b. 1878 in Boston, Massachusetts
d. Sep 1, 1945 in Beverly Hills, California
Source: *AmAu&B; CurBio 45; DcAmB S3; FilmgC; MotPP; MovMk; OxThe; Vers A; WhAm 2; WhScrn 74, 77; WhoHol B*

Craven, Thomas
American. Art Critic, Author
Thomas Hart Benton shaped his preferences to American regional art.
b. Jan 6, 1889 in Salina, Kansas
d. Feb 27, 1969
Source: *Alli SUP; AmAu&B; AuBYP; ConAu 97; CurBio 44, 69; REnAL; SmATA 22; TwCA, SUP; WhAm 5*

Cravens, Rupert Thomas
American. Clergyman, Hymn Writer
b. 1911
Source: *BioIn 9*

Crawford, Broderick
American. Actor
b. Dec 9, 1911 in Philadelphia, Pennsylvania
Source: *BiDFilm; BiE&WWA; BioNews 74; CelR 73; CurBio 50; FilmgC; IntMPA 75, 76, 77, 78, 79, 80, 81, 82; MotPP; MovMk; OxFilm; WhoAm 74, 76, 78, 80, 82; WhoHol A; WhoWor 74; WorEFlm*

Crawford, Cheryl
American. Theatrical Producer
b. Sep 24, 1902 in Akron, Ohio
Source: *BiE&WWA; CurBio 45; EncMT; InWom; NotNAT; PlP&P; WhoAm 74, 76, 78, 80, 82; WhoAmW 77; WhoThe 77; WhoWor 74*

Crawford, Christina
American. Author, Daughter of Joan Crawford
Wrote *Mommie Dearest,* 1978; Faye Dunaway starred in movie, 1981.
b. Jun 11, 1939 in Hollywood, California
Source: *BioIn 11; ConAu 85*

Crawford, Francis Marion
Italian. Author, Historian
b. Aug 2, 1854 in Bagni di Lucca, Italy
d. Apr 9, 1909 in Sorrento, Italy
Source: *Alli SUP; AmAu; AmAu&B; AmBi; ApCAB; BbD; BiD&SB; Chambr 3; CnDAL; DcAmAu; DcAmB; DcBiA; DcEnA, AP; DcLEL; DcNAA; EvLB; LongCTC; OxAmL; OxEng; Pen AM; REn; REnAL; TwCBDA; WebAB; WhAm 1*

Crawford, Jack (John Shea)
American. Hockey Player
Defenseman, Boston Bruins, 1938-50; wore helmut because of baldness.
b. Oct 26, 1916 in Dublin, ON
d. Jan 19, 1973 in Cape Cod, Massachusetts
Source: *BioIn 9; WhoHcky 73*

Crawford, James Strickland
American. Jazz Musician
b. Jan 4, 1910 in Memphis, Tennessee
Source: *WhoJazz 72*

Crawford, Jim
American. Boat Racer
b. 1924
Source: *BioIn 10*

Crawford, Joan
[Lucille LeSueur]
American. Actress
Won Oscar for *Mildred Pierce,* 1945.
b. Mar 23, 1908 in San Antonio, Texas
d. May 13, 1977 in New York, New York
Source: *CelR 73; FilmgC; ForWC 70; InWom; IntMPA 75, 76, 77; IntWW 74; MovMk; OxFilm; ThFT; TwYS; WhoAm 74; WhoAmW 77; WhoWest 74; WhoWor 74*

Crawford, John Edmund
American. Child Psychologist, Author
b. Jan 21, 1904 in Pittsburgh, Pennsylvania
d. Oct 12, 1971
Source: *ConAu 17R; ConAu P-2; SmATA 3*

Crawford, Michael Patrick
American. Actor
b. Jan 19, 1942 in Salisbury, England
Source: *FilmgC; IntMPA 75, 76, 77, 78, 79, 80, 81, 82; WhoHol A; WhoThe 77; WhoWor 74*

Crawford, Sam(uel Earl)
"Wahoo Sam"
American. Baseball Player
Outfielder, 1899-1917; only player to lead both leagues in home runs.
b. Apr 18, 1880 in Wahoo, Nebraska
d. Jun 15, 1968 in Hollywood, California
Source: *BaseEn; BioIn 3, 7, 8; WhoProB 73*

Crawford, Thomas
American. Sculptor
b. Mar 22, 1813 in New York, New York
d. Oct 10, 1857 in London, England
Source: *AmBi; ApCAB; BiAuS; DcAmB; Drake; OxAmL; TwCBDA; WhAm H*

Crawford, William Hulfish
American. Editorial Cartoonist
b. Mar 18, 1913 in Hammond, Indiana
d. Jan 6, 1982 in Washington, DC
Source: *WhoAm 74, 76, 78; WhoAmA 73, 76, 78*

Crazy Horse
American Indian. Sioux Chief
b. 1849?
d. Sep 5, 1877 in Camp Robinson, Nebraska
Source: *AmBi; ApCAB; DcAmB; WebAB; WhAm H*

Creach, "Papa" (John)
American. Musician
b. May 17, 1917 in Beaver Falls, Pennsylvania
Source: *BioIn 9; WhoRock 81*

Cream
["Ginger" Baker; Jack Bruce; Eric Clapton]
English. Rock Group
Source: *EncPR&S; IlEncRk; Rk100*

Crean, Robert
American. Dramatist
b. 1923
d. May 6, 1974 in New Rochelle, New York
Source: *NewYTBS 74; WhAm 6*

Creasey, John
English. Author
b. Sep 17, 1908 in Surrey, England
d. Jun 9, 1973 in Salisbury, England
Source: *Au&Wr 71; ConAu 5R, 41R; CurBio 63, 73; EncMys; LongCTC; MnBBF; NewYTBE 73; REn; TwCW; WhAm 6; WorAu*

Creed, Linda
American. Songwriter, Singer
b. 1949
Source: *BioIn 10*

Creedence Clearwater Revival
[Douglas Ray Clifford; Stuart Cook; John Fogerty; Thomas Fogerty]
American. Rock Group
Source: *EncPR&S; IlEncRk*

Creeley, Robert White
American. Author, Poet
b. May 21, 1926 in Arlington, Massachusetts
Source: *AmAu&B; Au&Wr 71; CasWL; ConAu 1R; ConLC 1, 2, 4, 8, 11, 15; ConP 70, 75; CroCAP; DrAF 76; DrAP 75; IntWW 74; ModAL, SUP; Pen AM; RAdv 1; REnAL; WebE&AL; WhoAm 74, 76, 78, 80, 82; WhoTwCL; WhoWor 74; WorAu; WrDr 76*

Cregar, Laird
American. Actor
b. Jul 28, 1916 in Philadelphia, Pennsylvania
d. Dec 8, 1944 in Los Angeles, California
Source: *BiDFilm; CmMov; CurBio 45; FilmgC; HolP 40; MovMk; WhScrn 74, 77; WhoHol B*

Creighton, Edward
American. Pioneer Telegraph Builder
Helped build transcontinental telegraph to Salt Lake City.
b. 1820 in Ohio
d. 1874
Source: *BioIn 3, 5; DcAmB*

Creighton, Fred
Canadian. Hockey Coach
b. Jul 14, 1933
Source: *WhoAm 82*

Creighton, Thomas H(awk)
American. Architect, Author
b. May 19, 1904 in Philadelphia, Pennsylvania
Source: *AmArch 70; AmAu&B; BioIn 1; ConAu 5R; WhoAm 74, 76, 78, 80, 82; WhoWest 74, 76, 78*

Creme, Lol
see: 10 CC

Cremer, Sir William Randal
English. Pacifist
b. Mar 18, 1838 in Fareham, England
d. Jul 22, 1908 in London, England
Source: *BioIn 5, 9, 10, 11; WebBD 80*

Cremieux, Isaac-Adolphe
French. Statesman
b. Apr 30, 1796 in Nimes, France
d. Feb 10, 1880 in Paris, France
Source: *BioIn 11; NewCol 75*

Crenna, Richard
American. Actor
Starred in "Our Miss Brooks," 1952-56; "The Real McCoys," 1957-63.
b. Nov 30, 1927 in Los Angeles, California
Source: *FilmgC; IntMPA 75, 76, 77, 78, 79, 80, 81, 82; MotPP; MovMk; WhoAm 74, 76, 78, 80, 82; WhoHol A*

Crenshaw, Ben
American. Golfer
b. Jan 11, 1952 in Austin, Texas
Source: *BioNews 75; NewYTBE 73; WhoAm 82*

Crescentini, Girolamo
Italian. Opera Singer
b. Feb 2, 1762 in Urbania, Italy
d. Apr 24, 1846 in Naples, Italy
Source: *NewEOp 71*

Crespin, Regine
French. Opera Singer
b. Mar 23, 1927 in Marseilles, France
Source: *IntWW 74; Who 74; WhoAm 74, 76, 78, 80, 82; WhoAmW 77; WhoMus 72; WhoWor 74*

Creston, Paul
American. Composer
b. Oct 10, 1906 in New York, New York
Source: *AmSCAP 66; DcCM; REnAL; WhoAm 74, 76, 78, 80, 82; WhoMus 72; WhoWest 74; WhoWor 74*

Crevecoeur, Michel-Guillaume Jean de
[J Hector St. John, pseud.]
French. Author
b. Jan 31, 1735 in Caen, France
d. Nov 12, 1813 in Sarcelles, France
Source: *AmAu; AmAu&B; CasWL; ChPo; CnDAL; CyWA; DcAmB; DcLEL; DcNAA; EvLB; OxAmL; REn; REnAL; WebAB; WebE&AL; WhAm H*

Crews, Harry Eugene
American. Author
b. Jun 6, 1935 in Almo, Georgia
Source: *AuNews 1; BioIn 8, 10, 11; BioNews 74; ConAu 25R; ConLC 6; DrAF 76; NewYTBS 78; WhoAm 74, 76, 78, 80, 82*

Crews, Laura Hope
American. Actress
b. Dec 12, 1879 in San Francisco, California
d. Nov 13, 1942 in New York, New York
Source: *CurBio 43; Film 1; FilmgC; InWom; MotPP; MovMk; NotAW; ThFT; Vers A; WhScrn 74, 77; WhoHol B; WhoStg 1908*

Crichton, Charles
English. Motion Picture Director
b. Aug 6, 1910 in Wallasey, England
Source: *CmMov; DcFM; FilmgC; IntMPA 75, 76, 77, 78, 79, 80, 81, 82; MovMk; OxFilm; WorEFlm*

Crichton, James
Scottish. Adventurer, Scholar
b. Aug 19, 1560 in Eliock, Scotland
d. Jul 3, 1582 in Mantua, Italy
Source: *Alli; BrAu; NewC; OxEng*

Crichton, Michael
American. Author, Motion Picture Director
b. Oct 23, 1942 in Chicago, Illinois
Source: *AmAu&B; Au&Wr 71; AuNews 2; CelR 73; ConAu 25R; ConLC 2, 6; ConNov 76; FilmgC; IntMPA 75, 76, 77, 78, 79, 80, 81, 82; SmATA 9; WhoAm 82; WrDr 76*

Crichton, Robert
American. Author
b. Jan 29, 1925 in Albuquerque, New Mexico
Source: *AuNews 1; BioNews 74; ConAu 17R; WrDr 76*

Crick, Francis Harry Compton
English. Biologist
b. Jun 8, 1916 in Northampton, England
Source: *CelR 73; IntWW 74; Who 74; WhoWor 74*

Crimmins, Alice
American. Murder Suspect
b. 1938
Source: *BioIn 9, 10*

Crippen, Hawley Harvey
English. Murderer
b. 1862
d. 1910
Source: *BioIn 11*

Crippen, Robert Laurel
American. Astronaut
b. Sep 11, 1937 in Beaumont, Texas
Source: *IntWW 74; WhoAm 82; WhoS&SW 73*

Cripps, Sir Stafford
English. Statesman, Lawyer
b. Apr 24, 1889
d. Apr 21, 1952
Source: *CurBio 40, 48, 52*

Crisler, "Fritz" (Herbert Orin)
American. Football Coach
b. Jan 12, 1899 in Earlville, Illinois
d. Aug 19, 1982 in Ann Arbor, Michigan
Source: *CurBio 48, 82; NewYTBS 82; WhoAm 74; WhoFtbl 74*

Crisp, Donald
American. Actor
b. Apr 18, 1880 in Aberfeldy, Scotland
d. May 26, 1974 in Van Nuys, California
Source: *BiDFilm; CmMov; Film 1; FilmgC; MotPP; MovMk; NewYTBS 74; OxFilm; TwYS; WhAm 6; WhScrn 77; WhoHol B; WorEFlm*

Crispin, Edmund, pseud.
[Robert Bruce Montgomery]
English. Author, Composer
Best known for detective novels featuring Gervase Fen. Montgomery.
b. Oct 2, 1921 in Buckinghamshire, England
d. Sep 15, 1978 in England
Source: *Au&Wr 71; ConAu 104; EncMys; WorAu*

Criss, Charlie (Charles W)
American. Basketball Player
b. Nov 6, 1949 in Valhalla, New York
Source: *BioIn 11; OfNBA*

Criss, Peter
[Kiss]
American. Rock Musician
b. 1947
Source: *BioIn 12; RkOn*

Crist, Judith Klein
American. Motion Picture Critic
b. May 22, 1922 in New York, New York
Source: *AuNews 1; CelR 73; ConAu 81; ForWC 70; IntMPA 75, 76, 77, 78, 79, 80, 81, 82; WhoAm 74, 76, 78, 80, 82; WhoE 74; WhoWorJ 72; WrDr 76*

Cristal, Linda
Argentine. Actress
b. 1936 in Buenos Aires, Argentina
Source: *FilmgC; MotPP; WhoHol A*

Cristofer, Michael
[Michael Procaccino]
American. Dramatist, Actor
b. Jan 22, 1945 in Trenton, New Jersey
Source: *WhoAm 78, 80, 82*

Crittenden, Christopher
American. Historian
b. Dec 1, 1902 in Wake Forest, North Carolina
d. Oct 13, 1969
Source: *AmAu&B; WhAm 5*

Crittenden, John Jordan
American. Attorney General
b. Sep 10, 1787 in Versailles, Kentucky
d. Jul 26, 1863 in Frankfort, Kentucky
Source: *AmBi; ApCAB; BiAuS; BiDSA; BiDrAC; BiDrUSE; DcAmB; Drake; EncAB-H; TwCBDA; WebAB; WhAm H; WhAmP*

Crittendon, Thomas L
American. Union General
b. 1819 in Russellville, Kentucky
d. 1893
Source: *NewCol 75; WhAm H*

Crittenton, Charles Nelson
American. Businessman, Philanthropist
b. Feb 20, 1833 in Henderson, New York
d. Nov 16, 1909 in San Francisco, California
Source: *DcAmB*

Critters
[Don Ciccone; Christopher Darway; Jack Decker; Kenneth Gorka; James Ryan]
American. Rock Group
Source: *BiDAmM*

Crivelli, Carlo
Italian. Artist
b. 1435 in Venice, Italy
d. 1493
Source: *AtlBL*

Croce, Benedetto
Italian. Statesman, Philosopher, Critic
b. Feb 25, 1866 in Pescasseroli, Italy
d. Nov 20, 1952 in Naples, Italy
Source: *AtlBL; CasWL; ClDMEL; CurBio 44, 53; DcEuL; EncWL; EvEuW; LongCTC; NewC; OxEng; Pen EUR; REn; TwCA, SUP; TwCW; WhAm 3; WhoLA*

Croce, Jim
American. Singer, Songwriter
Hits include "Operator," 1972; "Bad Bad Leroy Brown," 1973.
b. Jan 10, 1943 in Philadelphia, Pennsylvania
d. Sep 20, 1973 in Natchitoches, Louisiana
Source: *BioIn 10, 11; BioNews 74; EncPR&S; RkOn*

Crocker, Charles
American. Financier
b. Sep 16, 1822 in Troy, New York
d. Aug 14, 1888 in Monterey, California
Source: *AmBi; ApCAB; BioIn 3; DcAmB; REnAW; TwCBDA; WebAB; WhAm H*

Crockett, Davy (David)
American. Frontiersman
Served as scout under Andrew Jackson during Creek War, 1813-14.
b. Aug 17, 1786 in Greene City, Tennessee
d. Mar 6, 1836 in The Alamo, Texas
Source: *Alli; AmAu&B; AmBi; ApCAB; BiAuS; BiD&SB; BiDrAC; CyWA; DcAmAu; DcAmB; DcNAA; Drake; EncAB-H; FilmgC; OxAmL; OxFilm; Pen AM; REn; REnAL; TwCBDA; WebAB; WhAm H; WhAmP*

Crockett, Ivory
American. Track Athlete
Source: *BioIn 10*

Crockett, James Underwood
American. Author, Horticulturist
b. Oct 9, 1915 in Haverhill, Massachusetts
d. Jul 11, 1979 in Jamaica
Source: *BioIn 11; ConAu 33R, 89*

Croesus
Last King of Lydia
b. 560BC
d. 546BC
Source: *NewC; REn*

Croft, Arthur C
American. Publisher, Labor Mediator
b. May 26, 1890 in Cleveland, Ohio
d. Sep 6, 1975
Source: *BioIn 2, 3; CurBio 52; WhAm 7*

Croft, Michael
English. Theatrical Director
b. Mar 8, 1922 in Oswestry, England
Source: *Au&Wr 71; Who 74; WhoThe 77*

Croft-Cooke, Rupert
English. Author
Detective novels examples of classic British mystery.
b. Jun 20, 1903 in Edenbridge, England
d. 1979 in Bournemouth, England
Source: *Au&Wr 71; CathA 1952; ConAu 9R, 89, 4NR; LongCTC; TwCA, SUP; Who 74; WhoWor 74; WrDr 76*

Crofts, Dash
[Seals and Crofts]
American. Singer, Songwriter
b. 1940 in Cisco, Texas
Source: *BkPepl; WhoAm 82*

Crofts, James
see: Monmouth, James Scott, Duke of

Croker, "Boss" (Richard)
American. Politician
b. Nov 23, 1841 in Clonakilty, Ireland
d. Apr 29, 1922 in New York, New York
Source: *AmBi; DcAmB; WhAm 1*

Croly, Herbert David
American. Journalist
b. Jan 23, 1869 in New York, New York
d. May 17, 1930 in Santa Barbara, California
Source: *AmAu&B; BioIn 1, 2, 3, 5; DcAmB S1; DcNAA; EncAB-H; OxAmL; TwCA; WebBD 80*

Crome, John
English. Artist
b. Dec 22, 1768 in Norwich, England
d. Apr 22, 1821 in Norwich, England
Source: *AtlBL; BioIn 1, 2, 4, 5, 8, 10, 11; NewC*

Cromie, Robert Allen
American. Author, Journalist
b. Feb 28, 1909 in Detroit, Michigan
Source: *AmAu&B; ConAu 1R, 1NR; WhoAm 76, 78, 80, 82; WhoMW 74*

Cromley, Raymond Avolon
American. Journalist
b. Aug 23, 1910 in Tulare, California
Source: *WhoAm 78, 80, 82*

Crompton, Richmal
see: Lamburn, Richard Crompton

Cromwell, Dean Bartlett
American. Track Coach
b. Sep 20, 1879 in Turner, Oregon
d. Aug 3, 1962 in Los Angeles, California
Source: *WhoTr&F 73*

Cromwell, John
American. Director, Actor
Directed *Of Human Bondage,* 1964.
b. Dec 23, 1887 in Toledo, Ohio
d. Sep 26, 1979 in Santa Barbara, California
Source: *BiDFilm; CmMov; ConAu 89; DcFM; FilmgC; MovMk; NatPD; NotNAT; OxFilm; WhoHol A; WhoThe 77; WorEFlm*

Cromwell, Nolan
American. Football Player
b. Jan 30, 1955 in Smith Center, Kansas
Source: *BioIn 12; FootReg*

Cromwell, Oliver
"Old Noll"
English. Lord Protector
Favored execution of Charles I, 1649; became Lord Protector, 1653.
b. Apr 25, 1599 in Huntingdon, England
d. Sep 3, 1658
Source: *Alli; McGEWB; NewC; PlP&P; REn*

Cromwell, Richard
English. Lord Protector
b. 1626
d. 1712
Source: *BioIn 9; NewCol 75*

Cromwell, Thomas
[Earl of Essex]
English. Statesman
b. 1485 in Putney, England
d. Jul 28, 1540 in London, England
Source: *Alli; DcEnL; McGEWB; NewC; REn*

Cronin, A(rchibald) J(oseph)
English. Author, Physician
b. Jul 19, 1896 in Helensburgh, England
d. Jan 6, 1981 in Glion, Switzerland
Source: *Au&Wr 71; CasWL; CathA 1930; Chambr 3; ConAu 1R, 102, 5NR; ConNov 76; CurBio 42, 81; DcLEL; EncWL; EvLB; FilmgC; IntWW 74; LongCTC; ModBrL; NewC; Pen ENG; RAdv 1; REn; TwCA, SUP; TwCW; WhNAA; Who 74; WhoWor 74; WrDr 76*

Cronin, Joe (Joseph Edward)
American. Baseball Player, Executive
Infielder, 1926-1945; president AL, 1959-74; Hall of Fame, 1956.
b. Oct 12, 1906 in San Francisco, California
Source: *BaseEn; BioIn 1, 6, 7, 8, 9, 10; WhoAm 74, 76, 78, 80, 82; WhoProB 73*

Cronin, Kevin
see: REO Speedwagon

Cronkite, Walter Leland, Jr.
"Uncle Walter"
American. Broadcast Journalist
Anchored CBS evening news, 1962-81; host of "Universe" TV series.
b. Nov 4, 1916 in Saint Joseph, Missouri
Source: *AuNews 1, 2; BkPepl; CelR 73; ConAu 69; CurBio 56; IntMPA 75, 76, 77, 78, 79, 80, 81, 82; IntWW 74; WebAB; WhoAm 74, 76, 78, 80, 82; WhoWor 74; WrDr 76*

Cronyn, Hume
Canadian. Actor, Author, Director
b. Jul 18, 1911 in London, ON
Source: *BiE&WWA; CanWW 82; CelR 73; CurBio 56; FilmgC; IntMPA 75, 76, 77, 78, 79, 80, 81, 82; MotPP; MovMk; NewYTBS 74; NotNAT; PlP&P; WhoAm 74, 76, 78, 80, 82; WhoHol A; WhoThe 77; WhoWor 74*

Crook, George
American. General
b. Sep 23, 1829 in Dayton, Ohio
d. Mar 21, 1890 in Chicago, Illinois
Source: *AmBi; ApCAB; DcAmB; Drake; OhA&B; TwCBDA; WebAB; WhAm H*

Crook, William G
American. Health Columnist
b. Sep 13, 1917 in Jackson, Tennessee
Source: *WhoAm 74*

Crookes, Sir William
English. Chemist
b. Jun 17, 1832 in London, England
d. Apr 4, 1919 in London, England
Source: *Alli SUP; BiDPara; McGEWB*

Crooks, Richard Alexander
American. Opera Singer
b. Jun 26, 1900 in Trenton, New Jersey
d. 1972
Source: *BiDAmM; NewEOp 71*

Cropsey, Jasper Francis
American. Artist
b. Feb 18, 1823 in Rossville, New York
d. 1900
Source: *AmBi; ApCAB; BnEnAmA; DcAmArt; DcBrBI; Drake; EarABI; McGDA; NatCAB 1; NewYHSD; TwCBDA; WhAm 1*

Crosby, Alexander L
American. Author, Journalist
b. Jun 10, 1906 in Cantonsville, Maryland
d. Jan 31, 1980 in Quakertown, Pennsylvania
Source: *AuBYP; ConAu 29R, 93; MorBMP; SmATA 2, 23*

Crosby, "Bing" (Harry Lillis)
American. Actor, Singer
Won Oscar for *Going My Way*, 1944; biggest hit "White Christmas," 1942.
b. Mar 2, 1904 in Tacoma, Washington
d. Oct 14, 1977 in Madrid, Spain
Source: *AmSCAP 66; BiDFilm; BioNews 75; CelR 73; ConAu 73; CurBio 41, 53, 78; FilmgC; IntMPA 75, 76, 77; IntWW 74; MotPP; MovMk; NewYTBE 70; OxFilm; WebAB; Who 74; WhoAm 74; WhoHol A; WhoMus 72; WhoProB 73; WhoWor 74; WorEFlm*

Crosby, Bob (George Robert)
American. Band Leader
b. Aug 23, 1913 in Spokane, Washington
Source: *AmSCAP 66; BioIn 2, 3, 4, 5, 9; FilmgC; IntMPA 75, 76, 77, 78, 79, 80, 81, 82; WhoHol A; WhoJazz 72*

Crosby, David
[The Byrds; Crosby, Stills, Nash and Young]
American. Singer, Songwriter
b. Aug 14, 1941 in Los Angeles, California
Source: *BiDAmM; BioIn 9; BkPepl; ConMuA 80; WhoAm 78, 80, 82; WhoRock 81*

Crosby, Enoch
American. Spy
b. 1750
d. 1835
Source: *BioIn 6, 10*

Crosby, Fanny (Frances Jane)
American. Hymn Writer, Poet
Blind from birth; wrote hymn "Safe in the Arms of Jesus."
b. Mar 24, 1820 in Putnam County, New York
d. Feb 12, 1915
Source: *AmAu&B; ChPo; DcAmAu; DcNAA; REnAL; WebE&AL*

Crosby, Harry
American. Publisher, Poet
b. 1898 in Boston, Massachusetts
d. Dec 10, 1929 in New York, New York
Source: *AmAu&B; BioIn 10, 11; DcNAA*

Crosby, Joan Carew
American. Journalist
b. Feb 14, 1933 in Baltimore, Maryland
Source: *ForWC 70; WhoAm 82*

Crosby, John
American. Conductor
b. Jul 12, 1926 in New York, New York
Source: *WhoAm 74, 76, 78, 80, 82; WhoWest 74; WhoWor 74*

Crosby, John Campbell
American. Journalist
b. May 18, 1912 in Milwaukee, Wisconsin
Source: *ConAu 1R, 4NR; IlsBYP; IntWW 74; REnAL; WhoAm 74, 76, 78, 80, 82; WhoWor 74; WrDr 76*

Crosby, Kathryn
[Mrs. Bing Crosby; Kathryn Grandstaff; Kathryn Grant]
American. Actress
b. Nov 25, 1933 in Houston, Texas
Source: *IntMPA 75, 76, 77, 78, 79, 80, 81, 82; NewYTBE 71; WhoAm 74, 76, 78, 80, 82*

Crosby, Mary Frances
American. Actress
b. 1959?
Source: *BioIn 11*

Crosby, Nathaniel
American. Golfer, Son of Bing Crosby
b. 1961
Source: *BioIn 12; NewYTBS 81*

Crosby, Norm
American. Comedian
b. Sep 15, in Boston, Massachusetts
Source: *WhoAm 80, 82*

Crosby, Percy
American. Cartoonist
b. Dec 8, 1930 in Brooklyn, New York
d. Dec 8, 1964 in New York, New York
Source: *WorECom*

Crosby, Stills, Nash, & Young
[David Crosby; Graham Nash; Stephen Stills; Neil Young]
American. Rock Group
Source: *BiDAmM; IlEncRk*

Crosby, Sumner McKnight
American. Art Historian, Educator
b. Jul 29, 1909 in Minneapolis, Minnesota
d. Nov 16, 1982 in Waterbury, Connecticut
Source: *BioIn 8; ConAu 13R; DrAS 74H; NewYTBS 82; WhoAm 74, 76, 78, 80, 82; WhoAmA 73; WhoWor 74*

Crosland, Charles
British. Politician
b. Aug 29, 1918
Source: *Who 74*

Crosley, Powel, Jr.
American. Inventor, Baseball Executive
Marketed first popularly priced radio, 1921; co-owner Cincinnati Reds.
b. Sep 18, 1886 in Cincinnati, Ohio
d. Mar 28, 1961 in Cincinnati, Ohio
Source: *CurBio 47, 61; WhAm 4; WhoProB 73*

Crosman, Henrietta
American. Actress
b. 1861? in Wheeling, West Virginia
d. Oct 31, 1944 in Pelham Manor, New York
Source: *BioIn 3; Film 2; PlP&P; WhScrn 77; WhThe; WhoHol B*

Cross, Ben
English. Actor
b. 1948? in London, England
Source: *BioIn 12; NewYTBS 81, 82*

Cross, Christopher
[Christopher Geppert]
American. Singer, Songwriter
Won Oscar for "Arthur's Song," 1982.
b. 1952 in San Antonio, Texas
Source: *BioIn 12*

Cross, Milton John
American. Opera Radio Announcer
b. Apr 16, 1897 in New York, New York
d. Jan 3, 1975 in New York, New York
Source: *AmAu&B; CelR 73; ConAu 53; CurBio 40, 75; NewYTBE 71; WhAm 6; WhScrn 77; WhoAm 74*

Cross, Wilbur
American. Educator
b. Apr 10, 1862 in Mansfield, Connecticut
d. Oct 5, 1948 in New Haven, Connecticut
Source: *AmAu&B; DcAmAu; DcAmB S4; DcLEL; DcNAA; OxAmL; REnAL; TwCA, SUP; WhAm 2*

Crosse, Rupert
American. Actor
b. 1928
d. Mar 5, 1973 in Nevis, West Indies
Source: *WhScrn 77; WhoHol B*

Crossman, Richard Howard Stafford
English. Statesman, Author
b. Dec 15, 1907 in London, England
d. Apr 5, 1974
Source: *Au&Wr 71; ConAu 49, 61; CurBio 47, 74; NewYTBS 74; REn; Who 74; WhoWor 74; WorAu*

Croter, Vina
see: Delmar, Vina

Crothers, Rachel
American. Dramatist
b. Dec 12, 1878 in Bloomington, Illinois
d. Jul 5, 1958 in Danbury, Connecticut
Source: *AmAu&B; CnDAL; CnMD; CnThe; ConAmA; ConAmL; DcLEL; EncWL; FilmgC; InWom; LongCTC; McGEWD; ModWD; OxAmL; OxThe; REn; REnAL; REnWD; TwCA, SUP; WebAB; WhNAA*

Crothers, "Scatman" (Benjamin Sherman)
American. Actor, Musician, Singer
Starred in TV series "Chico and the Man," 1974-78.
b. May 23, 1910 in Terre Haute, Indiana
Source: *BioIn 10, 11; WhoAm 82; WhoHol A*

Crouch, Marcus
English. Children's Author
b. Feb 12, 1913 in Tohenham, England
Source: *Au&Wr 71; ChPo, S2; ConAu 9R, 5NR; SmATA 4; WhoChL; WrDr 76*

Crouse, Lindsay Ann
American. Actress
b. May 12, 1948 in New York, New York
Source: *IntMPA 78, 79, 80, 81; NewYTBS 81*

Crouse, Russel
American. Journalist, Dramatist
Won Pulitzer Prize for *The State of the Union,* 1945.
b. Feb 20, 1893 in Findlay, Ohio
d. Apr 3, 1966 in New York, New York
Source: *AmAu&B; AuBYP; BiE&WWA; CnDAL; ConAu 25R, 77; CurBio 41, 66; EncMT; McGEWD; ModWD; NewCBMT; OhA&B; OxAmL; REn; REnAL; TwCA SUP; WhAm 4*

Crowe, Sir Colin Tradescant
British. Diplomat
b. Sep 7, 1913 in Yokohama, Japan
Source: *IntWW 74; Who 74; WhoGov 72; WhoWor 74*

Crowell, Luther Childs
American. Inventor
Invented square bottomed grocer's bag, machine to manufacture it, 1872.
b. Sep 7, 1840 in West Dennis, Massachusetts
d. Sep 16, 1903 in Wellfleet, Massachusetts
Source: *DcAmB; NatCAB 13; WhAm 1*

Crowley, Aleister
"The Great Beast"
English. Author, Magician
b. 1875
d. Dec 1, 1947 in Brighton, England
Source: *ChPo S1; LongCTC; REn*

Crowley, James
[Four Horsemen of Notre Dame]
American. Football Player
b. Sep 10, 1902 in Chicago, Illinois
Source: *WhoFtbl 74*

Crowley, Leo T
American. Businessman, Public Official
b. Aug 15, 1889 in Milton Junction, Wisconsin
d. Apr 15, 1972 in Madison, Wisconsin
Source: *CurBio 43, 72; NewYTBE 72; WhAm 5*

Crowley, Pat
American. Actress
b. Sep 17, 1929 in Scranton, Pennsylvania
Source: *BioIn 3; FilmgC; MotPP; WhoAm 82; WhoHol A*

Crowninshield, Francis Welch
[Arthur Loring Bruce]
American. Editor, Publisher
b. Jun 24, 1872 in Paris, France
d. Dec 28, 1947 in New York, New York
Source: *DcAmB S4; DcNAA*

Crowther, (Francis) Bosley
American. Journalist, Film Critic
b. Jul 13, 1905 in Lutherville, Maryland
d. Mar 7, 1981 in Mount Kisco, New York
Source: *BioIn 4, 5, 10; ConAu 65, 103; CurBio 57, 81; IntMPA 75, 76, 77, 78, 79, 80, 81; NewYTBS 81; WhAm 7; WhoWor 74*

Crowther, Samuel Adjai
Nigerian. Bishop
b. 1808 in Ochuga, Nigeria
d. Dec 31, 1891
Source: *BioIn 1, 2, 7, 8, 9, 10, 11*

Crozier, Eric
English. Author, Producer
b. Nov 14, 1914 in London, England
Source: *Au&Wr 71; ChPo S2; LongCTC; Who 74; WhoMus 72*

Crozier, Roger Allan
"The Dodger"
Canadian. Hockey Player
Goalie, 1963-77; rookie of the year, 1965.
b. Mar 16, 1942 in Bracebridge, ON
Source: *WhoHcky 73*

Cruickshank, Andrew John
Scottish. Actor
b. Dec 25, 1907 in Aberdeen, Scotland
Source: *FilmgC; PlP&P; Who 74; WhoHol A; WhoThe 77*

Cruikshank, George
English. Artist, Illustrator
b. Sep 27, 1792 in London, England
d. Feb 1, 1878 in London, England
Source: *Alli; CarSB; ChPo, S1, S2; IlsBYP; NewC; REn; Str&VC*

Cruikshank, Sally
American. Animator
b. in Chatham, New Jersey
Source: *WomWMM B*

Crumb, Robert
American. Cartoonist
b. Aug 30, 1943 in Philadelphia, Pennsylvania
Source: *BioIn 9, 10; ConLC 17; NewYTBE 72*

Crummell, Alexander
American. Missionary
b. Mar 1819 in New York, New York
d. Sep 1898 in Point Pleasant, New Jersey
Source: *AmAu&B; BioIn 3, 4, 6, 8, 10, 11; DcAmAu; DcNAA*

Crump, Bruce
see: Molly Hatchet

Crump, Edward Hull
American. Congressman
b. 1874 in Holly Springs, Mississippi
d. Oct 16, 1954 in Memphis, Tennessee
Source: *BiDrAC; BioNews 74; DcAmB S5; WhAm 3; WhAmP*

Crusaders, The
[Larry Carlton; Witon Felder; Wayne Henderson; "Stix" Hooper; Joe Sample]
American. Jazz Group
Source: *ConMuA 80*

Cruyff, Johan
Dutch. Soccer Player
b. Apr 25, 1947 in Amsterdam, Netherlands
Source: *BioIn 10; CurBio 81*

Cruzen, Richard H
American. Explorer, Naturalist
b. 1896
d. 1970
Source: *BioIn 8*

Cryer, David
American. Actor
b. Mar 8, 1936 in Evanston, Illinois
Source: *NotNAT; WhoThe 77*

Crystal, Billy
American. Actor
b. Mar 14, 1947 in Long Island, New York
Source: *BioIn 11; IntMPA 82; WhoAm 82*

Csonka, Larry Richard
American. Football Player
Running back, Miami Dolphins, 1968-74, 79-80, NY Giants, 1976-79, WFL, 1975.
b. Dec 25, 1946 in Akron, Ohio
Source: *BioNews 75; CelR 73; NewYTBE 73; NewYTBS 74; WhoAm 74, 76, 78, 80, 82*

Cuauhtemoc
Aztec Emperor
b. 1495?
d. 1525
Source: *REn*

Cubert, Joe
see: Mitch Ryder and the Detroit Wheels

Cudahy, Michael
American. Meat Packer, Merchant
Partner with Philip D Armour, 1875-90; established Cudahy Packing Co., Omaha, NE.
b. Dec 7, 1841 in Callan, Ireland
d. 1910
Source: *AmBi; DcAmB; NewCol 75; WhAm 1*

Cuellar, Mike (Miguel Santana)
Cuban. Baseball Player
b. May 8, 1937 in Santa Clara, Cuba
Source: *BaseEn; WhoProB 73*

Cuesta, Juan de la
Spanish. Printer
Source: *BioIn 10*

Cueva de Garoza, Juan de la
Spanish. Dramatist, Poet
b. 1550
d. 1610
Source: *REn*

Cuffe, Paul
American. Seaman, Colonizer
b. Jan 17, 1759 in Cutty Hunk, Massachusetts
d. Sep 9, 1817 in Westport, Massachusetts
Source: *BioIn 4, 6, 7, 8, 9, 10, 11; DcAmB; WhAm H*

Cuffley, John
see: Climax Blues Band, The

Cugat, Xavier
"Rhumba King"
Spanish. Band Leader
b. Jan 1, 1900 in Barcelona, Spain
Source: *CelR 73; CurBio 42; FilmgC; WhoAm 74; WhoHol A*

Cui, Cesar Antonovich
Russian. Composer
b. Jan 18, 1835 in Vilna, Russia
d. Mar 24, 1918 in Saint Petersburg, U.S.S.R.
Source: *NewEOp 71*

Cukor, George Dewey
American. Motion Picture Director
Won 1964 Oscar for *My Fair Lady;* last film *Rich and Famous,* 1981.
b. Jul 7, 1899 in New York, New York
d. Jan 24, 1983 in Los Angeles, California
Source: *BiDFilm; BiE&WWA; CelR 73; CmMov; CurBio 43; DcFM; FilmgC; IntMPA 75, 76, 77, 78, 79, 80; IntWW 74, 75, 76, 77, 78, 79, 80, 81; MovMk; NewYTET; OxFilm; WhoAm 74, 76, 78, 80, 82; WhoWor 74, 78; WhoWorJ 72, 78; WorEFlm*

Culbertson, Ely
American. Bridge Player, Authority
b. Jul 22, 1891 in Verbilao, Romania
d. Dec 27, 1955 in Brattleboro, Vermont
Source: *AmAu&B; CurBio 40, 56; DcAmB S5; WebAB; WhAm 3*

Cullen, Bill (William Lawrence)
American. TV Personality
b. Feb 18, 1920 in Pittsburgh, Pennsylvania
Source: *CurBio 60; IntMPA 75, 76, 77, 78, 79, 80, 81, 82; WhoAm 74, 76, 78, 80, 82*

Cullen, Countee
American. Poet
Wrote *Color,* 1925; *The Black Christ,* 1930.
b. May 30, 1903 in New York, New York
d. Jan 10, 1946 in New York, New York
Source: *AmAu&B; AnCL; AnMV 1926; BlkAW; CasWL; ChPo, S1; ConAmA; ConAmL; CurBio 46; DcLEL; DcNAA; ModAL, SUP; OxAmL; Pen AM; RAdv 1; REn; REnAL; TwCA, SUP; WebE&AL; WhAm 2; WhNAA*

Culliford, "Peyo" (Pierre)
Belgian. Author, Cartoonist
Created the Smurfs, 1957; top children's TV show in US.
b. Jun 25, 1928 in Brussels, Belgium
Source: *WorECom*

Cullum, John
American. Actor
b. Mar 2, 1930 in Knoxville, Tennessee
Source: *EncMT; NotNAT; WhoAm 82; WhoThe 77*

Culp, Robert
American. Actor
Starred in "I Spy," 1965-68; "The Greatest American Hero," 1981--.
b. Aug 13, 1930 in Berkeley, California
Source: *CelR 73; FilmgC; IntMPA 75, 76, 77, 78, 79, 80, 81, 82; MotPP; WhoAm 78, 80, 82; WhoHol A*

Culpeper, Nicholas
English. Herbalist
b. 1616 in London, England
d. 1654
Source: *BrAu*

Culver, John C
American. Senator
b. Aug 8, 1932 in Rochester, Minnesota
Source: *CurBio 79; WhoAm 78, 80, 82*

Cummings, Bob (Robert Orville)
American. Actor
Starred in "Love That Bob," 1954-61; "The Bob Cummings Show," 1961-62; "My Living Doll," 1964-65.
b. Jun 9, 1910 in Joplin, Missouri
Source: *BiE&WWA; CelR 73; CurBio 56; Film 1; FilmgC; IntMPA 75, 76, 77, 78, 79, 80, 81, 82; MotPP; MovMk; WhoAm 74, 76, 78, 80, 82; WhoHol A; WorEFlm*

Cummings, Burton
[Guess Who]
Canadian. Singer, Musician
b. Dec 31, 1947 in Winnipeg, MB
Source: *RkOn*

Cummings, Constance
[Constance Halverstadt]
American. Actress
b. May 15, 1910 in Seattle, Washington
Source: *BiE&WWA; FilmgC; HolP 30; InWom; IntMPA 75, 76, 77, 78, 79, 80, 81, 82; MotPP; MovMk; NotNAT; ThFT; Who 74; WhoAm 80, 82; WhoHol A; WhoThe 77*

Cummings, E(dward) E(stlin)
American. Author, Poet
Wrote of WW I prison camp experiences in *The Enormous Room,* 1922.
b. Oct 14, 1894 in Cambridge, Massachusetts
d. Sep 3, 1962 in North Conway, New Hampshire
Source: *AmAu&B; AmWr; AnCL; AtlBL; AuBYP; CasWL; ChPo; CnDAL; CnE&AP; CnMD; CnMWL; ConAmA; ConAmL; ConAu 73; ConLC 1, 3, 8, 12, 15; EncWL; EvLB; LongCTC; McGEWD; ModAL, SUP; ModWD; OxAmL; OxEng; Pen AM; RAdv 1; REn; REnAL; SixAP; TwCA, SUP; TwCW; WebE&AL; WhoTwCL*

Cummings, Quinn
American. Actress
Nominated for Oscar, 1977, for *The Goodbye Girl.*
b. Aug 13, 1967 in Hollywood, California
Source: *BioIn 11*

Cummins, Peggy
Welsh. Actress
b. Dec 18, 1926 in Prestatyn, Wales
Source: *FilmgC; IntMPA 75, 76, 77, 78, 79, 80, 81, 82; MotPP; WhoHol A; WhoThe 77*

Cunard, Sir Samuel
Canadian. Shipowner
b. Nov 15, 1787 in Halifax, NS
d. Apr 28, 1865 in London, England
Source: *ApCAB*

Cuneo, Ernest
American. Lawyer, Publisher, Author
b. May 27, 1905 in Carlstadt, New Jersey
Source: *WhoAm 78, 80, 82; WhoWor 74*

Cuneo, Terence Tenison
English. Artist
b. Nov 1, 1907
Source: *BioIn 1, 3, 11; Who 74*

Cunha, Euclides da
Brazilian. Author
b. Jan 20, 1866 in Santa Rita, Brazil
d. Aug 15, 1909 in Rio de Janeiro, Brazil
Source: *CasWL*

Cunningham, Sir Alan Gordon
English. General
Commanded forces that liberated Ethiopia from Italian rule, restored Haile Selassie to throne, 1971.
b. May 1, 1887
d. Feb 1983 in Tunbridge Wells, England
Source: *CurBio 46, 83; Who 74*

Cunningham, Billy (William)
"Kangaroo Kid"
American. Basketball Coach
Coach, Philadelphia 76ers.
b. Jun 3, 1943 in Brooklyn, New York
Source: *BioIn 7, 9, 11; OfNBA; WhoAm 82; WhoBbl 73*

Cunningham, E. V. pseud.
see: Fast, Howard

Cunningham, Glenn Clarence
"Kansas Ironman"
American. Track Athlete
Held world record in mile, 1934-37.
b. Aug 4, 1909 in Atlanta, Kansas
Source: *WhoTr&F 73*

Cunningham, Harry Blair
American. Business Executive
b. Jul 23, 1907 in Home Camp, Pennsylvania
Source: *BioIn 11; IntWW 74, 75, 76, 77, 78; St&PR 75; WhoAm 74, 76, 78, 80, 82; WhoF&I 74; WhoWor 78*

Cunningham, Imogen
American. Photographer
b. Apr 12, 1883 in Portland, Oregon
d. Jun 24, 1976 in San Francisco, California
Source: *BioIn 10; ConAu 65*

Cunningham, Mary Elizabeth
[Mrs. William Agee]
American. Business Executive
Vice-president, strategic planning Joseph E Seagram and Sons, 1981--.
b. Sep 1, 1951 in Maine
Source: *BioIn 12*

Cunningham, Merce
American. Dancer, Choreographer
b. Apr 16, 1919 in Centralia, Washington
Source: *ConDr 73; CurBio 66; WhoAm 74, 76, 78, 80, 82; WhoWor 74*

Cunningham, R Walter
American. Astronaut, Corporation Executive
Flew first manned Apollo spacecraft, 1968; founded The Capital Group, 1979--.
b. Mar 16, 1932 in Creston, Iowa
Source: *IntWW 74; WhoAm 74, 76, 78, 80, 82; WhoWor 74*

Cunningham, Sam
American. Football Player
b. Aug 15, 1950 in Santa Barbara, California
Source: *WhoFtbl 74*

Cunningham, William
see: Box Tops, The

Cuomo, Mario Matthew
American. Governor of New York
Defeated Hugh Carey for governor, 1982.
b. Jun 15, 1932 in Queens County, New York
Source: *AmCath 80; WhoAm 78, 80, 82; WhoAmP 75, 77, 79; WhoE 79; WrDr 76, 80*

Cuppy, Will(iam Jacob)
American. Humorist
b. Aug 23, 1884 in Auburn, Indiana
d. Sep 19, 1949 in New York, New York
Source: *AmAu&B; DcAmB S4; DcNAA; IndAu 1816; REnAL; TwCA, SUP; WhAm 2*

Curb, Mike (Michael Charles)
American. Lt. Governor of California
b. Dec 24, 1944 in Savannah, Georgia
Source: *BioIn 9, 10, 11; EncPR&S; WhoAm 78, 80, 82*

Curci, Amelita Galli
see: Galli-Curci, Amelita

Curcio, Renato
Italian. Terrorist
b. 1940?
Source: *BioIn 11*

Curel, Francois de
French. Dramatist
b. Jun 10, 1854 in Metz, France
d. Apr 25, 1928 in Paris, France
Source: *CasWL; ClDMEL; CnMD; EvEuW; McGEWD; ModWD; OxFr; Pen EUR; REn; WhoLA*

Curie, Eve
[Mrs. Henry R Labouisse]
French. Author, Journalist
b. Dec 6, 1904 in Paris, France
Source: *AmAu&B; AnCL; Au&Wr 71; ConAu P-1; CurBio 40; InWom; SmATA 1; Who 74; WhoAm 74, 76, 78, 80, 82; WhoWor 74*

Curie, Irene
see: Joliot-Curie, Irene

Curie, Marie (Marja Sklodowska)
[Mrs. Pierre Curie]
Polish. Chemist, Discovered Radium
Discovered radium, 1898; first person awarded two Nobel Prizes, 1903, 1911.
b. Nov 7, 1867 in Warsaw, Poland
d. Jul 4, 1934 in Valence, France
Source: *HerW; InWom; REn*

Curie, Pierre
French. Chemist, Discovered Radium
Shared Nobel Prize in Physics with wife, 1903.
b. May 15, 1859 in Paris, France
d. Apr 19, 1906 in Paris, France
Source: *OxFr*

Curley, James Michael
American. Political Leader
b. Nov 20, 1874 in Boston, Massachusetts
d. Nov 12, 1958 in Boston, Massachusetts
Source: *BiDrAC; EncAB-H; WebAB; WhAm 3*

Curran, Charles Courtney
American. Artist
b. Feb 13, 1861 in Hartford, Kentucky
d. Nov 9, 1942 in New York, New York
Source: *BioIn 10; CurBio 43; WhAm 2*

Curran, Joseph Edwin
"Big Joe"
American. Labor Leader
Organizer, president of National Maritime Union, 1937-73.
b. Mar 1, 1906 in New York, New York
d. Aug 14, 1981 in Boca Raton, Florida
Source: *BiDAmLL; CurBio 45, 81; NewYTBS 81; PolProf E; PolProf J; PolProf K; PolProf NF; PolProf T; WhoAm 74; WhoWor 74*

Currie, Finlay
Scottish. Actor
b. Jan 20, 1878 in Edinburgh, Scotland
d. May 9, 1968 in Gerrards Cross, England
Source: *CmMov; FilmgC; MotPP; MovMk; Vers A; WhScrn 74, 77; WhoHol B*

Currie, Steven
see: T. Rex

Currier, Nathaniel
[Currier and Ives]
American. Lithographer
Started lithography business, 1835; partnership with James Ives, 1857.
b. Mar 27, 1813 in Roxbury, Massachusetts
d. Nov 20, 1888 in New York, New York
Source: *AmBi; DcAmB; WebAB; WhAm H*

Currier and Ives
see: Currier, Nathaniel; Ives, James Merritt

Curry, John Anthony
English. Figure Skater
Won Olympic gold medal for figure skating, 1976.
b. Sep 9, 1949 in Birmingham, England
Source: *CurBio 79; NewYTBE 71; Who 79; WhoAm 82*

Curry, John Steuart
American. Artist
b. Nov 14, 1897 in Dunavant, Kansas
d. Aug 29, 1946 in Madison, Wisconsin
Source: *CurBio 41, 46; DcAmB S4; DcCAA 71; IlsCB 1744; OxAmL; REn; REnAL; WhAm 2*

Curry, Peggy Simson
American. Author
b. Dec 30, 1912 in Dunure, Scotland
Source: *ConAu 33R; CurBio 58; DrAF 76; InWom; SmATA 8*

Curti, Merle Eugene
American. Historian
b. Sep 15, 1897 in Papillion, Nebraska
Source: *ConAu 5R, 4NR; DrAS 74H; IntWW 74; OxAmL; REnAL; TwCA SUP; WhoAm 74, 76, 78, 80, 82; WhoWor 74*

Curtice, Harlow Herbert
American. Auto Executive
President of GM, 1953-58.
b. Aug 15, 1893 in Eaton Rapids, Michigan
d. Nov 3, 1962 in Flint, Michigan
Source: *CurBio 53, 63; WhAm 4*

Curtin, Andrew Gregg
American. Political Leader
b. Apr 28, 1817 in Bellefonte, Pennsylvania
d. Oct 7, 1894 in Bellefonte, Pennsylvania
Source: *AmBi; ApCAB; BiAuS; BiDrAC; DcAmB; Drake; TwCBDA; WhAm H; WhAmP*

Curtin, Jane
American. Actress, Comedienne
b. Sep 6, 1947 in Cambridge, Massachusetts
Source: *WhoAm 78, 80, 82*

Curtin, John
Australian. Prime Minister
b. Jan 8, 1885 in Creswick, Australia
d. Jul 5, 1945 in Canberra, Australia
Source: *CurBio 41, 45*

Curtin, Phyllis Smith
American. Singer
b. Dec 3, 1927 in Clarksburg, West Virginia
Source: *CurBio 64; InWom; NewYTBE 72; WhoAm 74, 76, 78, 80, 82; WhoAmW 77; WhoMus 72; WhoWor 74*

Curtis, Alan
American. Comedian, Actor
b. Jul 24, 1909 in Chicago, Illinois
d. Feb 1, 1953 in New York, New York
Source: *FilmgC; MotPP; WhScrn 74, 77; WhoHol B*

Curtis, Ann
American. Swimmer
b. 1926
Source: *BioIn 11*

Curtis, Charles
American. Vice-President
Vice-president under Herbert Hoover, 1929-33.
b. Jan 25, 1860 in Topeka, Kansas
d. Feb 8, 1936 in Washington, DC
Source: *Alli; AmBi; BiDLA; BiDrAC; BiDrUSE; DcAmB S2; TwCBDA; WebAB; WhAm 1; WhAmP*

Curtis, Charles Gordon
American. Inventor of Steam Turbine
b. Apr 20, 1860 in Boston, Massachusetts
d. 1953
Source: *NatCAB 42; WhAm 3*

Curtis, Charlotte Murray
American. Newspaper Editor
b. 1930 in Chicago, Illinois
Source: *AuNews 2; CelR 73; ConAu 9R; ForWC 70; WhoAm 74, 76, 78, 80, 82; WhoAmW 77; WhoE 74*

Curtis, Cyrus Hermann Kotszchmar
American. Newspaper Publisher
b. Jun 18, 1850 in Portland, Maine
d. Jun 7, 1933 in Wyncote, Pennsylvania
Source: *AmAu&B; AmBi; DcAmB S1; WebAB; WhAm 1*

Curtis, Edward Sheriff
American. Ethnologist, Photographer
b. Feb 19, 1868 in Madison, Wisconsin
d. Oct 19, 1952 in Los Angeles, California
Source: *AmAu&B; DcAmB S5; WhAm 4*

Curtis, George William
American. Journalist, Author
b. Feb 24, 1824 in Providence, Rhode Island
d. Aug 31, 1892 in Staten Island, New York
Source: *Alli, SUP; AmAu; AmAu&B; AmBi; ApCAB; BbD; BiD&SB; CasWL; Chambr 3; ChPo; CyAl 2; DcAmAu; DcAmB; DcBiA; DcEnL; DcLEL; DcNAA; Drake; EncAB-H; EvLB; OxAmL; REn; REnAL; TwCBDA; WebAB; WhAm H; WhAmP*

Curtis, Isaac
American. Football Player
b. Oct 20, 1950 in Santa Ana, California
Source: *BioIn 11; WhoFtbl 74*

Curtis, Jackie
American. Dramatist, Screenwriter
b. Feb 19, 1947 in Stony Creek, Tennessee
Source: *BioIn 10; ConDr 77; WrDr 76*

Curtis, (James) Mike (Michael)
American. Football Player
b. Mar 27, 1943 in Rockville, Maryland
Source: *WhoFtbl 74*

Curtis, Jamie Lee
American. Actress
Daughter of Tony Curtis and Janet Leigh; starred in *The Fog,* 1981.
b. Nov 22, 1958
Source: *BioIn 11*

Curtis, John Duffield, II
American. Baseball Player
b. Mar 9, 1948 in Newton, Massachusetts
Source: *BaseEn*

Curtis, Ken
American. Actor
b. Jul 2, 1916 in Lamar, Colorado
Source: *IntMPA 75, 76, 77, 78, 79, 80, 81, 82; WhoHol A*

Curtis, Tony
[Bernard Schwartz]
American. Actor
Starred in *The Defiant Ones,* 1958; *Some Like it Hot,* 1959.
b. Jun 3, 1925 in New York, New York
Source: *BiDFilm; CelR 73; ConAu 73; FilmgC; IntMPA 75, 76, 77, 78, 79, 80, 81, 82; MovMk; NewYTBE 70; OxFilm; WhoAm 82; WhoHol A; WorEFlm*

Curtiss, Glenn Hammond
American. Aviation Pioneer, Inventor
Invented seaplane, 1911; established first flying schools.
b. May 21, 1878 in Hammondsport, New York
d. Jul 23, 1930 in Buffalo, New York
Source: *AmBi; DcAmB S1; WebAB; WhAm 1*

Curtiz, Michael
American. Motion Picture Director
b. Dec 24, 1898 in Budapest, Hungary
d. Apr 11, 1962 in Hollywood, California
Source: *BiDFilm; CmMov; DcFM; FilmgC; MovMk; OxFilm; TwYS; WhAm 4; WhScrn 74, 77; WorEFlm*

Curwood, James Oliver
American. Author
b. Jun 12, 1878 in Owosso, Michigan
d. Aug 13, 1927 in Owosso, Michigan
Source: *AmAu&B; DcNAA; LongCTC; MnBBF; OxAmL; OxCan; REnAL; TwCA, SUP; WhNAA*

Curzon, Sir Clifford Michael
English. Musician
b. May 18, 1907 in London, England
d. Sep 1, 1982 in London, England
Source: *Baker 78; CurBio 50, 82; IntWW 74, 75, 76, 77, 78; NewYTBS 82; Who 74; WhoMus 72; WhoWor 74, 74, 78*

Curzon of Kedleston, George Nathaniel Curzon, Marquis
English. Statesman
b. Jan 11, 1859 in Kedleston Hall, England
d. Mar 20, 1925
Source: *ChPo S1; DcEuL; McGEWB; NewC*

Cusack, Cyril
Irish. Actor
b. Nov 26, 1910 in Durban, South Africa
Source: *BiE&WWA; Film 1; FilmgC; IntMPA 75, 76, 77, 78, 79, 80, 81, 82; IntWW 74; MovMk; NotNAT; WhoHol A; WhoThe 77; WhoWor 74*

Cushing, Caleb
American. Jurist, Diplomat
b. Jan 17, 1800 in Salisbury, Massachusetts
d. Jan 2, 1879 in Newburyport, Massachusetts
Source: *Alli; AmAu; AmAu&B; AmBi; ApCAB; BiAuS; BiD&SB; BiDrAC; BiDrUSE; CyAl 2; DcAmAu; DcAmB; DcNAA; Drake; TwCBDA; WebAB; WhAm H; WhAmP*

Cushing, Harvey Williams
American. Neurosurgeon
b. Apr 8, 1869 in Cleveland, Ohio
d. Oct 7, 1939 in New Haven, Connecticut
Source: *AmAu&B; AmBi; DcAmB S2; DcNAA; EncAB-H; LongCTC; OhA&B; OxAmL; REnAL; WebAB; WhAm 1; WhNAA*

Cushing, Peter
English. Actor
b. May 26, 1913 in Surrey, England
Source: *CmMov; FilmgC; IntMPA 75, 76, 77, 78, 79, 80, 81, 82; MotPP; WhoHol A; WhoThe 77*

Cushing, Richard James, Cardinal
American. Roman Catholic Prelate
b. Aug 24, 1895 in Boston, Massachusetts
d. Nov 2, 1970 in Boston, Massachusetts
Source: *CurBio 52, 70; NewYTBE 70; WhAm 5*

Cushing, William Barker
American. Military Leader
b. Nov 4, 1842 in Delafield, Wisconsin
d. Dec 17, 1874 in Washington, DC
Source: *AmBi; ApCAB; DcAmB; Drake; TwCBDA; WebAB; WhAm H*

Cushman, Austin
American. Bakery Executive
b. 1901
d. Jun 12, 1978 in Pasadena, California
Source: *BioIn 11*

Cushman, Charlotte Saunders
American. Actress
b. Jul 23, 1816 in Boston, Massachusetts
d. Feb 17, 1876 in Boston, Massachusetts
Source: *AmBi; AmWom; ApCAB; DcAmB; Drake; FamA&A; FemPA; InWom; NotAW; OxAmL; OxThe; PlP&P; REnAL; TwCBDA; WebAB; WhAm H*

Cushman, Pauline
American. Actress, Spy
b. Jun 10, 1833 in New Orleans, Louisiana
d. Dec 2, 1893 in San Francisco, California
Source: *AmBi; ApCAB; DcAmB; InWom; TwCBDA; WhAm H*

Cushman, Robert Everton, Jr.
American. Marine Corps General
b. Dec 24, 1914 in Saint Paul, Minnesota
Source: *CurBio 72; IntWW 74; NewYTBE 71, 73; WhoAm 74; WhoGov 72; WhoS&SW 73*

Custer, Elizabeth Bacon
American. Author
b. Apr 8, 1842 in Monroe, Michigan
d. Apr 4, 1933 in New York, New York
Source: *AmAu&B; BiD&SB; BioIn 2, 6, 7, 10, 11; DcAmAu; DcNAA; REnAL*

Custer, George Armstrong
American. Army General
Youngest general in Union Army, 1863; killed at Battle of Little Bighorn, 1876.
b. Dec 5, 1839 in New Rumley, Ohio
d. Jun 25, 1876 in Little Big Horn, South Dakota
Source: *Alli SUP; AmBi; ApCAB; DcAmAu; DcAmB; DcNAA; Drake; EncAB-H; FilmgC; OhA&B; OxAmL; OxFilm; REn; TwCBDA; WebAB; WhAm H*

Custin, Mildred
American. Merchandising Executive
b. 1906 in Manchester, New Hampshire
Source: *CurBio 67; InWom; St&PR 75; WhoAm 74, 76, 78, 80, 82; WorFshn*

Cuthbert, Betty
Australian. Track and Field Athlete
b. Apr 20, 1938 in Sydney, Australia
Source: *WhoTr&F 73*

Cutler, Manasseh
American. Clergyman, Scientist
b. May 13, 1742 in Killingly, Connecticut
d. Jul 28, 1823 in Ipswich Hamlet, Massachusetts
Source: *AmBi; ApCAB; BiAuS; BiDAmS; BiDrAC; BioIn 5, 9; DcAmAu; DcAmB; Drake; McGEWB; NatCAB 3; NewCol 75; OhA&B; TwCBDA; WebAB; WhAm H*

Cutpurse, Moll
[Mary Frith]
English. Thief
b. 1589 in London, England
d. 1662 in London, England
Source: *BioIn 4, 8, 11; LookW*

Cuvier, Georges, Baron
French. Zoologist
b. Aug 23, 1769 in Montbeliard, France
d. May 13, 1832 in Paris, France
Source: *AsBiEn; BiD&SB; McGEWB; OxFr; REn*

Cuyler, "Kiki" (Hazen Shirley)
American. Baseball Player
Outfielder, 1921-38; led NL in stolen bases, 1926, 1928-30.
b. Aug 30, 1899 in Harrisville, Michigan
d. Feb 11, 1950 in Ann Arbor, Michigan
Source: *BaseEn; WhoProB 73*

Cuyp, Aelbert
Dutch. Artist
b. 1620 in Dordrecht, Netherlands
d. Nov 1691 in Dordrecht, Netherlands
Source: *AtlBL*

Cuypers, Petrus Josephus Hubertus
Dutch. Architect
b. 1827 in Roermond, Netherlands
d. 1921
Source: *WhoArch*

Cuzzoni, Francesca
Italian. Opera Singer
b. 1700 in Parma, Italy
d. 1770 in Bologna, Italy
Source: *InWom*

Cynewulf
English. Poet
Source: *Alli; BiB S; BrAu; CasWL; Chambr 1; CrtT 1; DcEnL; EvLB; NewC; OxEng; Pen ENG; REn; WebE&AL*

"Cynthia"
see: Brousse, Amy Elizabeth Thorpe

Cyr, Louis
Canadian. Boxer, Strongman
b. 1863
d. 1912
Source: *BioIn 10, 11*

Cyrankiewicz, Josef
Polish. Premier
b. Apr 23, 1911
Source: *WhoGov 72*

Cyrano de Bergerac, Savinien de
French. Poet, Soldier
Life romanticized by Edmond Rostand in *Cyrano de Bergerac,* 1897.
b. Mar 6, 1619
d. Sep 1655
Source: *BiD&SB; CasWL; EuAu; EvEuW; OxFr; Pen EUR; REn*

Cyril of Alexandria
Greek. Ecclesiastical Author
b. 376
d. Jun 27, 444
Source: *BioIn 3, 5, 6; CasWL*

Cyrus the Great
Founder of Persian Empire
b. 600BC
d. 529BC
Source: *REn*

Czerny, Karl
Austrian. Composer, Pianist, Teacher
Beethoven's pupil who wrote widely-used finger exercises.
b. Feb 20, 1791 in Vienna, Austria
d. Jul 15, 1857 in Vienna, Austria
Source: *WebBD 80*

Czolgosz, Leon F
American. President McKinley's Assassin
Shot McKinley at Pan American Expo, Buffalo, NY, Sep 6, 1901; sent to electric chair.
b. 1873 in Detroit, Michigan
d. Oct 29, 1901 in New York
Source: *BioIn 9, 10; Blood; NewCol 75; WebBD 80*

D

Dabney, Virginius
American. Editor, Author
b. Feb 15, 1835 in Gloucester County, Virginia
d. Jun 2, 1894 in New York, New York
Source: *Alli SUP; AmAu; AmAu&B; ApCAB; BiD&SB; BiDSA; DcAmAu; DcAmB; DcNAA; TwCBDA; WhAm H*

Da Castelfranco, Giorgione
see: Giorgione II

Dache, Lilly
American. Milliner, Fashion Designer
b. 1904 in Beigles, France
Source: *CurBio 41; InWom; WhoAm 74; WorFshn*

Da Correggio, Antonio Allegri
see: Correggio, Antonio Allegri da

DaCosta, Morton
American. Producer, Director, Actor
b. Mar 7, 1914 in Philadelphia, Pennsylvania
Source: *BiE&WWA; FilmgC; NotNAT; WhoThe 77; WorEFlm*

Daddario, Emilio Quincy
American. Lawyer, Politician
b. Sep 24, 1918 in Newton Centre, Massachusetts
Source: *BioIn 11; St&PR 75; WhoAm 74; WhoAmP 73; WhoGov 72*

Da Fiesole, Giovanni
see: Fra Angelico

Dafoe, Allan Roy
Canadian. Physician
b. May 29, 1883
d. Jun 2, 1943 in North Bay, ON
Source: *CurBio 43*

DaGama, Vasco
[Gama, Vasco da]
Portuguese. Explorer, Navigator
Led expedition around Africa to India, 1497-99, opening first sea route to Asia.
b. 1460 in Sines, Portugal
d. Dec 24, 1524 in Cochin, India
Source: *NewC; NewCol 75; REn; WebBD 80; WhAm H*

Dagmar
[Virginia Ruth Egnor]
American. Actress
b. 1920? in Huntington, West Virginia
Source: *InWom*

Dagover, Lil (Marta Maria Liletta)
German. Actress
b. Sep 30, 1897 in Madiven, Indonesia
d. Jan 30, 1980 in Munich, Germany (West)
Source: *FilmEn; Film 1, 2; FilmgC; MovMk; OxFilm; WhoHol A; WorEFlm*

Daguerre, Louis Jacques Mande
French. Inventor, Artist
Invented the daguerreotype photograph, 1839.
b. Nov 18, 1787 in Cormeilles en Parisis, France
d. Jul 12, 1851 in Paris, France
Source: *AsBiEn; FilmgC; McGEWB; NewC; OxFr*

Dahl, Arlene
American. Actress
b. Aug 11, 1927 in Minneapolis, Minnesota
Source: *CelR 73; FilmgC; ForWC 70; InWom; IntMPA 75, 76, 77, 78, 79, 80, 81, 82; MotPP; MovMk; WhoAdv 72; WhoAm 74, 76, 78, 80, 82; WhoAmW 77; WhoHol A; WhoWest 74*

Dahl, Roald
Welsh. Author
b. Sep 13, 1916 in Llandaff, Wales
Source: *Au&Wr 71; AuBYP; BioNews 74; ChlLR 1; ConAu 1R; ConLC 1, 6, 18; ConNov 76; DrAF 76; MorBMP; NewC; PiP; RAdv 1; REn; REnAL; SmATA 1; ThrBJA; WhoAm 74; WhoWor 74; WorAu; WrDr 76*

Dahlberg, Edward
American. Author, Critic
b. Jul 22, 1900 in Boston, Massachusetts
d. Feb 27, 1977 in Santa Barbara, California
Source: *AmAu&B; CelR 73; ConAu 9R, 69; ConLC 1, 7, 14; ConNov 72, 76; DrAF 76; ModAL, SUP; OxAmL; Pen AM; TwCA SUP; TwCW; WhoAm 74; WhoWor 74; WrDr 76*

Dahlgren, John Adolph
American. Naval Officer
b. Nov 13, 1809 in Philadelphia, Pennsylvania
d. Jul 12, 1870 in Washington, DC
Source: *Alli SUP; ApCAB; DcAmAu; DcAmB; DcNAA; Drake; TwCBDA; WebAB; WhAm H*

Daiches, David
English. Author
b. Sep 2, 1912 in Sunderland, England
Source: *Au&Wr 71; ChPo S1; ConAu 5R; DcLEL; EvLB; IntWW 74; LongCTC; ModBrL; RAdv 1; REn; TwCA SUP; Who 74; WhoAm 74; WhoWor 74; WrDr 76*

Dailey, Dan
American. Dancer, Actor
b. Dec 14, 1915 in New York, New York
d. Oct 17, 1978 in Hollywood, California
Source: *BiDFilm; CmMov; FilmgC; MotPP; MovMk; WhoHol A; WhoThe 77; WorEFlm*

Dailey, Irene
American. Actress
b. Sep 12, 1920 in New York, New York
Source: *BiE&WWA; NotNAT; WhoAm 82; WhoHol A; WhoThe 77*

Dailey, Janet
American. Author
America's best-selling romance author; has written 60 books since 1976.
b. May 21, 1944 in Storm Lake, Iowa
Source: *ConAu 89; NewYTBS 81*

Daimler, Gottlieb
German. Automotive Engineer, Inventor
Founded Daimler Motor Co., 1890, which produced the Mercedes.
b. Mar 17, 1834 in Wurttemberg, Germany
d. Mar 6, 1900
Source: *NewCol 75; WebBD 80*

Daladier, Edouard
French. Political Leader
b. Jun 18, 1884 in Vancluse, France
d. Oct 10, 1970 in Paris, France
Source: *CurBio 40, 70; NewYTBE 70; REn*

Dalai Lama, the 14th Incarnate
[Gejong Tenzin Gyatsho]
Tibetan. Ruler, Religious Leader
Temporal and religious head of Tibet and all Buddhist sects, now living in India.
b. Jul 6, 1935 in Chhija Nangso, Tibet
Source: *BioIn 5, 6, 8, 11; CurBio 51, 82; FarE&A 78, 79; IntWW 74, 75, 76, 77, 78, 79, 80; WhoWor 74, 76, 78*

D'Albert, Eugene
Scottish. Pianist, Composer
b. Apr 10, 1864 in Glasgow, Scotland
d. Mar 3, 1932 in Riga, U.S.S.R.
Source: *NewEOp 71*

Dale, Alan
American. Musician, Singer
b. Jul 9, 1926 in Brooklyn, New York
Source: *BioIn 8; CmpEPM*

Dale, Carroll W
American. Football Player
b. Apr 24, 1938 in Wise, Virginia
Source: *WhoFtbl 74*

Dale, Clamma Churita
American. Singer
b. Jul 4, 1948 in Chester, Pennsylvania
Source: *CurBio 79; NewYTBS 76; WhoBlA 77*

Dale, Henry Hallett
English. Scientist, Engineer, Physician
b. 1875 in London, England
d. Aug 23, 1968 in Cambridge, England
Source: *Alli SUP; WhAm 5*

Dale, Jim
[James Smith]
English. Actor, Singer, Songwriter
b. Aug 15, 1935 in Rothwell, England
Source: *BioIn 10; FilmEn; WhoAm 82*

Dalen, Nils Gustaf
Swedish. Inventor, Engineer
b. Nov 30, 1869
d. Dec 9, 1937
Source: *BioIn 2, 3*

Daley, Arthur
American. Sportswriter
b. Jul 31, 1904 in New York, New York
d. Jan 3, 1974 in New York, New York
Source: *AmAu&B; ConAu 25R, 45; ConAu P-2; CurBio 56, 74; NewYTBS 74*

Daley, Richard Joseph
American. Mayor
Democratic mayor of Chicago, 1955-76.
b. May 15, 1902 in Chicago, Illinois
d. Dec 20, 1976 in Chicago, Illinois
Source: *CelR 73; CurBio 55; EncAB-H; IntWW 74; WebAB; WhoAm 74; WhoAmP 73; WhoGov 72; WhoMW 74; WhoWor 74*

Dalgleish, Alice
American. Children's Author
b. Oct 7, 1893 in Trinidad
d. Jun 11, 1979 in Woodbury, Connecticut
Source: *AmAu&B; AnCL; AuBYP; ChPo; ConAu 73, 89; JBA 34, 51; SmATA 17; Str&VC; WhNAA*

Dalhousie, James A B R, Marquess
British. Statesman, Colonial Governor
b. 1812
d. 1860
Source: *BioIn 10; NewCol 75*

Dali, Gala
[Mrs. Salvador Dali; Elena Diaranoff]
Model
Wife and muse for over 50 years of surrealist painter Salvador Dali.
b. 1893? in Kazan, Russia
d. Jun 10, 1982 in Gerona, Spain
Source: *BioIn 12; NewYTBS 82*

Dali, Salvador
Spanish. Artist
Leader of Surrealist Movement; best known work "Persistence of Memory," 1931.
b. May 11, 1904 in Figueras, Spain
Source: *AmAu&B; BioNews 74; CelR 73; CurBio 40, 51; FilmgC; IntWW 74; OxFilm; REn; Who 82; WhoAm 74, 76, 78, 80, 82; WhoGrA; WhoWor 74; WorEFlm*

Dalis, Irene
American. Opera Singer
b. Oct 8, 1929 in San Jose, California
Source: *WhoAm 74, 76, 78, 80, 82*

Dall, John
American. Actor
b. 1918
d. Jan 15, 1971 in Beverly Hills, California
Source: *FilmgC; MotPP; MovMk; NewYTBE 71; WhScrn 74, 77; WhoHol B*

Dalla Rizza, Gilda
Italian. Opera Singer
b. Oct 12, 1892 in Verona, Italy
d. Jul 5, 1975
Source: *BioIn 10*

Dallapiccola, Luigi
Italian. Musician, Composer
b. Feb 3, 1904 in Pisino, Yugoslavia
d. Feb 19, 1975 in Florence, Italy
Source: *CurBio 66; DcCM; IntWW 74; WhAm 6; Who 74; WhoMus 72; WhoWor 74*

Dallas, George Mifflin
American. Vice-President
b. Jul 10, 1792 in Philadelphia, Pennsylvania
d. Dec 31, 1864 in Philadelphia, Pennsylvania
Source: *Alli, SUP; AmBi; ApCAB; BiAuS; BiDrAC; BiDrUSE; DcAmAu; DcAmB; DcNAA; Drake; TwCBDA; WebAB; WhAm H; WhAmP*

Dallin, Cyrus
American. Sculptor
b. Nov 22, 1861 in Springville, Vermont
d. Nov 14, 1944 in Boston, Massachusetts
Source: *CurBio 45; DcAmB S3; WhAm 2*

Dalmores, Charles
French. Opera Singer
b. Jan 1, 1871 in Nancy, France
d. Dec 6, 1939 in Hollywood, California
Source: *WhAm 1; WhoStg 1908*

Dalrymple, Jean
American. Theatrical Producer, Director
b. Sep 2, 1910 in Morristown, New Jersey
Source: *BiE&WWA; ConAu 5R; CurBio 53; EncMT; InWom; NotNAT; WhoAm 74, 76, 78, 80, 82; WhoE 74; WhoGov 72; WhoThe 77; WrDr 76*

Dalton, Abby
American. Singer, Actress
Plays Julia Cumson on TV series "Falcon Crest."
b. 1935 in Las Vegas, Nevada
Source: *WhoHol A*

Dalton, Charles
American. Actor
b. Aug 29, 1864
d. Jun 11, 1942 in Stamford, Connecticut
Source: *NotNAT B; WhThe; WhoHol B; WhoStg 1908*

Dalton, Emmett
[Dalton Brothers]
American. Bankrobber, Trainrobber
b. 1871 in Cass County, Missouri
d. Jul 13, 1937 in Los Angeles, California
Source: *Blood*

Dalton, Gratton
[Dalton Brothers]
American. Bankrobber, Trainrobber
b. 1862 in Cass County, Missouri
d. Oct 5, 1892 in Coffeyville, Kansas
Source: *Blood*

Dalton, John
English. Scientist
b. Sep 6, 1766 in Cumberland, England
d. Jul 27, 1844 in Manchester, England
Source: *Alli; BiDLA; BrAu 19*

Dalton, John Call
American. Physiologist
b. Feb 2, 1825 in Chelmsford, Massachusetts
d. 1889
Source: *BioIn 9*

Dalton, Robert
[Dalton Brothers]
American. Bankrobber, Trainrobber
b. 1867 in Cass County, Missouri
d. Oct 5, 1892 in Coffeyville, Kansas
Source: *Blood*

Dalton, Timothy
Welsh. Actor
b. 1944 in Wales
Source: *BioIn 9; FilmEn; FilmgC; WhoHol A*

Dalton, William
[Dalton Brothers]
American. Bankrobber, Trainrobber
b. 1873 in Cass County, Missouri
d. 1893
Source: *Blood*

Daltrey, Roger
[The Who]
English. Rock Singer
Appeared in *Tommy,* 1974, *The Kids are Alright,* 1979.
b. Mar 1, 1945 in Hammersmith, England
Source: *BkPepl; WhoAm 80, 82*

D'Alvarez, Marguerite
English. Opera Singer
b. 1886 in Liverpool, England
d. Oct 18, 1953 in Alassio, Italy
Source: *InWom*

Dalvit, Lewis David, Jr.
American. Symphony Conductor
b. Dec 11, 1925 in Denver, Colorado
Source: *WhoAm 74, 76, 78, 80, 82; WhoS&SW 73*

Daly, Arnold
American. Actor
b. Oct 4, 1875 in Brooklyn, New York
d. Jan 12, 1927 in New York, New York
Source: *Film 1; NotNAT; OxThe; PlP&P; REn; WhScrn 77; WhThe; WhoHol B; WhoStg 1906, 1908*

Daly, Augustin
American. Dramatist
b. Jul 20, 1838 in Plymouth, North Carolina
d. Jun 7, 1899 in Paris, France
Source: *AmAu; AmAu&B; BbD; CnDAL; CnThe; DcNAA; HsB&A; PlP&P; REnAL; REnWD*

Daly, James
American. Actor
Played Dr. Paul Lochner on TV series "Medical Center."
b. Oct 23, 1918 in Wisconsin Rapids, Wisconsin
d. Jul 3, 1978 in Nyack, New York
Source: *BiE&WWA; CurBio 59; FilmgC; IntMPA 75, 76, 77; NotNAT; WhoAm 74; WhoHol A; WhoThe 77*

Daly, John Charles, Jr.
American. TV News Analyst, Host
b. Feb 20, 1914 in Johannesburg, South Africa
Source: *WhoAm 74, 76, 78, 80, 82; WhoE 74*

Daly, Marcus
American. Copper Magnate
b. Dec 5, 1841 in Ballyjamesduff, Ireland
d. Nov 12, 1900 in New York, New York
Source: *AmBi; BioIn 2, 3, 4, 6, 8, 11; DcAmB; McGEWB; REnAW; WebAB*

Daly, Maureen Patricia
Irish. Author
b. Mar 15, 1921 in Ulster, Northern Ireland
Source: *AmAu&B; AmNov; AuBYP; BkC 4; CathA 1930; CurBio 46; InWom; MorJA; REnAL; SmATA 2; WhoAmW 77*

Daly, Thomas Augustine
American. Journalist, Poet
b. May 28, 1871 in Philadelphia, Pennsylvania
d. Oct 4, 1948 in Philadelphia, Pennsylvania
Source: *AmAu&B; AmLY; BkC 1; CnDAL; ConAmL; DcNAA; OxAmL; REn; REnAL; TwCA, SUP*

Dam, (Carl Peter) Henrik
Danish. Biochemist
b. Feb 21, 1895
d. Apr 17, 1976 in Copenhagen, Denmark
Source: *CurBio 49; IntWW 74; Who 74; WhoWor 74*

D'Amato, Alfonse M
American. Senator
b. Aug 1, 1937 in Brooklyn, New York
Source: *AlmAP 82*

D'Amboise, Jacques
[Jacques Joseph d'Amboise Ahearn]
American. Ballet Dancer
b. Jul 28, 1934 in Dedham, Massachusetts
Source: *CelR 73; CurBio 64; WhoAm 74, 76, 78, 80, 82*

Damian, Saint
Religious Figure
d. 303
Source: *BioIn 2, 3, 4, 7*

Damien, Father
[Joseph Damien de Veuster]
Belgian. Missionary
Devoted life to leper colony in Hawaii; died from disease.
b. Jan 3, 1840 in Tremeloo, Belgium
d. Apr 15, 1889 in Molokai, Hawaii
Source: *AmBi; NewC; OxAmL; REn*

Damita, Lily
French. Actress
b. 1906 in Paris, France
Source: *InWom*

Damocles
Courtier
b. 370?BC in Syracuse, Sicily
Source: *NewC*

Damon and Pythias
Pythagorean Philosophers
Noted for their mutual devotion.
Source: *WebBD 80*

Damon, Ralph Shepard
American. Aircraft Executive
b. Jul 6, 1897 in Franklin, New Hampshire
d. Jan 4, 1956
Source: *WhAm 3*

Damon, Stuart
American. Actor
b. Feb 5, 1937 in Brooklyn, New York
Source: *BiE&WWA; FilmgC; NotNAT; WhoThe 72, 77, 81*

Damone, Vic
[Vito Farinola]
American. Singer, Actor
Winner Arthur Godfrey talent show, 1945; starred in *Hell to Eternity*, 1960.
b. Jun 12, 1928 in Brooklyn, New York
Source: *FilmgC; IntMPA 75, 76, 77, 78, 79, 80, 81, 82; WhoAm 74, 76, 78, 80, 82; WhoHol A*

Dampier, William
English. Explorer, Author
Discovered New Britain Islands in Pacific on expedition, 1699-1701.
b. Jun 1652? in East Coker, England
d. Mar 1715 in London, England
Source: *BrAu; Chambr 2; DcLEL; EvLB; NewC; OxEng; Pen ENG; REn*

Damrosch, Frank Heino
American. Musician
b. Jun 22, 1859 in Breslau, Prussia
d. Oct 22, 1937 in New York, New York
Source: *BioIn 1, 2, 4*

Damrosch, Leopold
German. Conductor
b. Oct 22, 1832 in Posen, Germany
d. Feb 15, 1885 in New York, New York
Source: *AmBi; ApCAB; DcAmB; OxAmL; TwCBDA; WebAB; WhAm H*

Damrosch, Walter Johannes
German. Conductor, Composer
b. Jan 30, 1862 in Breslau, Prussia
d. Dec 22, 1950 in New York, New York
Source: *AmSCAP 66; ApCAB; CurBio 44, 51; DcAmB S4; OxAmL; REn; REnAL; TwCBDA; WebAB; WhAm 3; WhScrn 77*

Dana, Bill
"Jose Jimenez"
American. Comedian, Actor, Author
b. Oct 5, 1924 in Quincy, Massachusetts
Source: *AmSCAP 66; WhoAm 82; WhoHol A*

Dana, Charles Anderson
American. Editor
b. Aug 8, 1819 in Hinsdale, New Hampshire
d. Oct 17, 1879 in West Island, New York
Source: *Alli, SUP; AmAu; AmAu&B; AmBi; ApCAB; BbD; BiAuS; BiD&SB; ChPo; CnDAL; DcAmAu; DcAmB; DcNAA; Drake; OxAmL; REn; REnAL; TwCBDA; WebAB; WhAm H, 6*

Dana, James Dwight
American. Geologist
b. 1813 in Utica, New York
d. Apr 14, 1895 in New Haven, Connecticut
Source: *AmAu; BbD; BiD&SB; CyAL 1; DcAmAu; DcNAA; OxAmL; REnAL; WebBD 80*

Dana, Margaret
American. Journalist
b. in Verona, New Jersey
Source: *ForWC 70; WhoAmW 77*

Dana, Richard Henry, Jr.
American. Sailor, Author, Lawyer
Wrote *Two Years Before the Mast,* 1840.
b. Aug 1, 1815 in Cambridge, Massachusetts
d. Jan 6, 1882 in Rome, Italy
Source: *Alli, SUP; AmAu; AmAu&B; AmBi; ApCAB; BbD; BiD&SB; CarSB; CasWL; Chambr 3; CnDAL; CrtT 3; CyAl 2; CyWA; DcAmAu; DcAmB; DcEnL; DcLEL; DcNAA; EncAB-H; EvLB; MouLC 4; OxAmL; OxEng; Pen AM; REn; REnAL; TwCBDA; WebAB; WebE&AL; WhAm H; WhAmP*

Danby, Thomas Osborne
[Earl of Danby]
English. Statesman
b. 1632
d. 1712
Source: *NewCol 75; WebBD 80*

Dancer, Stanley
American. Harness Racer
b. Jul 25, 1927 in New Egypt, New York
Source: *CelR 73; CurBio 73; NewYTBS 74*

Danco, Suzanne
Belgian. Opera Singer
b. Jan 22, 1911 in Brussels, Belgium
Source: *WhoMus 72; WhoWor 74*

Dandridge, Bob (Robert L)
American. Basketball Player
b. Nov 15, 1947 in Richmond, Virginia
Source: *BioIn 11; WhoBbl 73*

Dandridge, Dorothy
American. Singer, Actress
b. 1922? in Cleveland, Ohio
d. Sep 8, 1965 in West Hollywood, California
Source: *FilmgC; MotPP; MovMk; WhAm 4; WhScrn 74, 77; WhoHol B*

Dane, Clemence, pseud.
[Winifred Ashton]
English. Author, Screenwriter
First novel, *Regiment of Women,* 1917.
b. 1888 in Blackheath, England
d. Mar 28, 1965 in London, England
Source: *BiE&WWA; Chambr 3; ConAu 93; DcLEL; EncMys; EvLB; LongCTC; McGEWD; ModBlW; ModWD; NewC*

Dane, Maxwell
American. Advertising Executive
b. Jun 7, 1906 in Cincinnati, Ohio
Source: *St&PR 75; WhoAdv 72; WhoAm 74, 76, 78, 80, 82; WhoWorJ 72*

Danelli, Dino
see: Rascals, The

Danforth, David Charles
"Dauntless Dave"
American. Baseball Player
b. Mar 7, 1890 in Granger, Texas
d. Sep 19, 1970 in Baltimore, Maryland
Source: *BaseEn; NewYTBE 70; WhoProB 73*

Danforth, John Claggett
American. Senator
b. Sep 5, 1936 in Saint Louis, Missouri
Source: *AlmAP 78, 80; BioIn 8, 10; CngDr 77, 79; IntWW 77, 78; WhoAm 74, 76, 78, 80, 82; WhoAmP 73, 75, 77, 79; WhoGov 72, 75, 77; WhoMW 78*

Danforth, William
Actor
b. May 13, 1869
d. Apr 16, 1941
Source: *CurBio 41; WhoHol B*

Danforth, William H
American. Founder of Ralston Purina
b. Sep 10, 1870 in Charleston, Missouri
d. Dec 24, 1952 in Saint Louis, Missouri
Source: *BioIn 1, 4, 5, 9; ObitOF 79; WhAm 3*

D'Angelo, Beverly
American. Actress
b. 1952? in Columbus, Ohio
Source: *IntMPA 81*

Dangerfield, George Bubb
English. Author
b. Oct 28, 1904 in Berkshire, England
Source: *AmAu&B; ConAu 9R; CurBio 53; DrAS 74H; OxAmL; PoIre; WhoAm 74; WhoWest 74; WhoWor 74; WorAu; WrDr 76*

Dangerfield, Rodney
[Jacob Cohen, real name; Jack Roy, pseud.]
American. Comedian
b. Nov 22, 1921 in Babylon, New York
Source: *ConAu 102; WhoHol A*

Daniel
Biblical Character
d. 745BC
Source: *NewCol 75*

Daniel, Clifton, Jr.
American. Journalist
Associate editor, NY *Times,* 1969--; married to Margaret Truman.
b. Sep 19, 1912 in Zebulon, North Carolina
Source: *IntWW 74; WhoE 74; WhoWor 74*

Daniel, Dan(iel)
American. Journalist, Editor
b. 1891
d. Jul 1, 1981 in Pompano Beach, Florida
Source: *NewYTBS 81*

Daniel, Lewis C
American. Artist
b. Oct 23, 1901 in New York, New York
d. Jul 8, 1952
Source: *BioIn 3; ChPo S1; WhAm 3*

Daniel, Samuel
English. Poet
b. 1562? in Taunton, England
d. Oct 14, 1619 in Beckington, England
Source: *Alli; AtlBL; BbD; BiD&SB; BiDLA; BrAu; CasWL; Chambr 1; ChPo, S1; CnE&AP; CroE&S; CrtT 1; DcEnA; DcEnL; DcEuL; DcLEL; EvLB; MouLC 1; NewC; OxEng; Pen ENG; PlP&P; PoLE; REn; REnWD; WebE&AL*

Danielian, Leon
American. Dancer, Choreographer
b. Oct 31, 1920 in New York, New York
Source: *BioIn 3, 10, 11; WhoAm 74, 76, 78, 80, 82; WhoWor 74*

Daniell, Henry
English. Actor
b. Mar 5, 1894 in London, England
d. Oct 31, 1963 in Santa Monica, California
Source: *CmMov; FilmgC; MotPP; MovMk; PlP&P; Vers A; WhScrn 74, 77; WhoHol B*

Daniell, John Frederic
English. Inventor
Developed Daniell's hygrometer, 1820.
b. Mar 12, 1790
d. Mar 13, 1845
Source: *BioIn 2*

Daniels, "Bebe" (Virginia)
American. Actress
b. Jan 14, 1901 in Dallas, Texas
d. Mar 16, 1971 in London, England
Source: *BiDFilm; Film 1; FilmgC; InWom; MotPP; MovMk; NewYTBE 71; OxFilm; ThFT; TwYS; WhScrn 74, 77; WhoHol B; WomWMM*

Daniels, Billy
American. Singer
b. 1914 in Jacksonville, Florida
Source: *WhoHol A*

Daniels, Charlie
[The Charlie Daniels Band]
American. Musician, Songwriter
b. Oct 28, 1936 in Wilmington, North Carolina
Source: *IlEncCM; RkOn 2; WhoAm 80, 82; WhoRock 81*

Daniels, Draper
American. Advertising Executive
b. Aug 12, 1913 in Morris, New York
Source: *ConAu 53; WhoAdv 72; WhoAm 74, 76, 78, 80, 82; WhoF&I 74*

Daniels, Frank
American. Actor
b. 1860 in Dayton, Ohio
d. Jan 12, 1935 in Palm Beach, Florida
Source: *Film 1; PlP&P; WhAm 1; WhScrn 74, 77; WhoHol B; WhoStg 1906, 1908*

Daniels, Jonathan Worth
American. Author
b. Apr 26, 1902 in Raleigh, North Carolina
d. Nov 6, 1981 in Hilton Head Island, South Carolina
Source: *AmAu&B; Au&Wr 71; AuBYP; CnDAL; ConAu 49; CurBio 42, 82; IntAu&W 76; IntYB 78, 79; LinLib L; NewYTBS 81; OxAmL; REn; REnAL; ScF&FL 1, 2; TwCA, SUP; WhoAm 74, 76, 78, 80; WhoAmP 73, 75, 77, 79; WhoS&SW 73; WhoWor 74; WrDr 80*

Daniels, Josephus
American. Journalist, Secretary of Navy
b. May 18, 1862 in Washington, DC
d. Jan 15, 1948
Source: *AmAu&B; BiDSA; BiDrUSE; CurBio 44, 48; DcAmB S4; DcNAA; EncAB-H; OxAmL; REn; REnAL; TwCBDA; WhAmP*

Daniels, Mickey
[Our Gang]
Actor
b. 1914
Source: *Film 2; WhoHol A*

Daniels, William
American. Actor
b. Mar 31, 1927 in Brooklyn, New York
Source: *BiE&WWA; IntMPA 82; NotNAT; WhoAm 74, 76, 78, 80, 82*

Danielson, Gary
American. Football Player
b. Sep 10, 1951 in Detroit, Michigan
Source: *FootReg*

Danilova, Alexandra
American. Ballerina, Choreographer
b. 1906 in Peterhof, Russia
Source: *BiE&WWA; InWom; Who 74; WhoAm 82; WhoAmW 77; WhoThe 77; WhoWor 74*

Dankworth, John Philip William
English. Composer, Conductor
b. Sep 20, 1927 in London, England
Source: *OxFilm; Who 74; WhoMus 72*

Dannay, Frederic
[Daniel Nathan; Ellery Queen, pseud.]
American. Author, Editor
Wrote Ellery Queen mysteries with cousin Manfred B Lee.
b. Oct 20, 1905 in Brooklyn, New York
d. Sep 3, 1982 in White Plains, New York
Source: *AmAu&B; ASpks; AuBYP; ConAu 1R; ConLC 11; CurBio 40, 82; DcLEL; EncMys; EvLB; IntAu&W 76, 77; IntWW 74, 75, 76, 77, 78, 79, 80; NewYTBS 82; Pen AM; REn; ScF&FL 1; TwCA, SUP; TwCCr&M; WebAB; WhoAm 74, 76, 78, 80, 82; WhoWor 74; WrDr 76, 80*

Danner, Blythe Katharine
[Mrs. Bruce W Paltrow]
American. Actress
b. 1943 in Philadelphia, Pennsylvania
Source: *BioIn 10; CurBio 81; IntMPA 75, 76, 77, 78, 79, 80, 81; NewYTBS 81; WhoAm 80, 82; WhoHol A; WhoThe 77, 81*

D'Annunzio, Gabriele
Italian. Poet, Author, Dramatist
b. Mar 12, 1863 in Pescara, Italy
d. Mar 1, 1938 in Vittoriale, Italy
Source: *WebBD 80*

Dante Alighieri
Italian. Poet
b. May 1265 in Florence, Italy
d. Sep 14, 1321 in Ravenna, Italy
Source: *AtlBL; BbD; BiD&SB; BlkAW; CasWL; ChPo; CyWA; DcEnL; DcEuL; EuAu; EvEuW; NewC; OxEng; Pen EUR; RComWL; REn*

Danton, Georges Jacques
French. Revolutionary Leader
b. Oct 28, 1759 in Arcis-sur-Aube, France
d. Apr 5, 1794 in Paris, France
Source: *BioIn 1, 4, 5, 8, 9, 11; DcEuL; NewC; OxFr; OxGer; REn*

Danton, Ray
American. Actor
b. Sep 19, 1931 in New York, New York
Source: *FilmgC; IntMPA 75, 76, 77, 78, 79, 80, 81, 82; WhoHol A; WorEFlm*

Danza, Tony
American. Actor, Boxer
Plays Tony Banta on TV series "Taxi," 1978--.
b. 1953 in New York, New York
Source: *BioIn 12*

DaPonte, Lorenzo
[Emmanuel Conegliano]
Italian. Poet, Librettist for Mozart
b. Mar 10, 1749 in Ceneda, Italy
d. Aug 17, 1838 in New York, New York
Source: *AmAu&B; ApCAB; BiD&SB; CasWL; CyAl 2; DcAmAu; DcAmB; DcNAA; EvEuW; OxGer; REn; REnWD; TwCBDA; WhAm H*

Darby, Kim
[Derby Zerby]
American. Actress
Starred with John Wayne in *True Grit,* 1969.
b. Jul 8, 1948 in Hollywood, California
Source: *FilmgC; IntMPA 75, 76, 77, 78, 79, 80, 81, 82; WhoAm 82; WhoHol A*

Darcel, Denise
American. Singer, Actress
b. Sep 8, 1925 in Paris, France
Source: *FilmgC; InWom; WhoHol A*

D'Arcy, Martin Cyril
English. Roman Catholic Priest, Author
b. Jun 15, 1888 in Bath, England
d. Nov 20, 1976 in London, England
Source: *Au&Wr 71; BioIn 1, 2, 5, 7, 11; CathA 1930; ConAu 5R, 69, 3NR; CurBio 60, 77; IntAu&W 76; IntWW 74, 75, 76, 77; LinLib L; NewYTBS 76; WhAm 7; WhE&EA; Who 74; WhoWor 74, 76*

Darcy, Tom
American. Editorial Cartoonist
b. Jun 7, 1916 in Saint Louis, Missouri
Source: *WhoAm 74*

Darden, Colgate Whitehead
American. Politician
b. Feb 11, 1897 in Franklin, Virginia
d. Jun 9, 1981 in Norfolk, Virginia
Source: *BiDrAC; BioIn 1; CurBio 48; WhoAmP 73, 75, 77*

Dare, Virginia
American. Colonial Figure
First child born in America of English parents.
b. Aug 18, 1587 in Roanoke Island, Virginia
Source: *AmBi; ApCAB; ChPo; DcAmB; Drake; HerW; InWom; NotAW; OxAmL; REn; WebAB; WhAm H*

Dargan, Olive Tilford
American. Poet, Author
b. 1869 in Grayson County, Kentucky
d. Jan 22, 1968
Source: *AmAu&B; AmNov X; BiDSA; ChPo, S2; CnDAL; InWom; OxAmL; REnAL; TwCA, SUP; WhAm 5; WomWWA 14*

Dargomijsky, Alexander
[Alexander Dargomizyhsky]
Russian. Composer
b. Feb 14, 1813 in Tula, Russia
d. Jan 17, 1869 in Saint Petersburg, Russia
Source: *NewEOp 71; OxMus*

Darin, Bobby
[Walden Robert Cassotto]
American. Singer, Actor
Best known song "Mack the Knife"; won two Grammys, 1960.
b. May 14, 1936 in New York, New York
d. Dec 20, 1973 in Hollywood, California
Source: *CurBio 63, 74; MotPP; MovMk; NewYTBE 73; WhAm 6; WhScrn 77; WhoHol B*

Daringer, Helen Fern
American. Children's Author
b. 1892 in Mattoon, Illinois
Source: *ConAu 17R; ConAu P-2; CurBio 51; MorJA; SmATA 1*

Darius I
[Darius the Great]
Peruvian. King
b. 558BC
d. 486BC
Source: *WebBD 80*

Dark, Alvin Ralph
"Blackie"
American. Baseball Player, Manager
Shortstop, 1946-60; rookie of year, 1948.
b. Jan 7, 1923 in Comanche, Oklahoma
Source: *BaseEn; NewYTBS 74; WhoAm 82; WhoProB 73*

Darken, Lawrence Stamper
American. Chemist
b. Sep 18, 1909 in Brooklyn, New York
d. 1978
Source: *AmM&WS 73P; BioIn 8, 11; IntWW 74; WhoAm 74*

Darlan, Jean Francois
French. Government Official
b. Aug 7, 1881 in Nerac, France
d. Dec 24, 1942
Source: *CurBio 41, 43*

Darley, Felix Octavius Carr
American. Illustrator, Author
b. Jun 23, 1822 in Philadelphia, Pennsylvania
d. Mar 27, 1888 in Claymont, Delaware
Source: *AmAu&B; BiD&SB; BioIn 1, 2, 3, 7, 8, 9; CarSB; DcAmAu; DcNAA*

Darling, Erik
[The Weavers]
American. Singer, Musician
b. Sep 25, 1933 in Baltimore, Maryland
Source: *EncFCWM 69*

Darling, Sir Frank Fraser
Scottish. Scientist, Author
Expert in biology, genetics, agriculture.
b. Jun 23, 1903 in Scotland
d. Oct 25, 1979 in Forres, Scotland
Source: *ConAu 61, 89; IntWW 74; OxEng; Who 74*

Darling, Jay Norwood
[J N Ding, pseud.]
American. Political Cartoonist
b. Oct 21, 1876 in Norwood, Michigan
d. Feb 12, 1962 in Des Moines, Iowa
Source: *AmAu&B; ConAu 93; CurBio 42, 62; WhAm 4; WhNAA*

Darling, Joan
[Joan Kugell]
American. Actress, Director
b. Apr 14, 1935 in Boston, Massachusetts
Source: *BiE&WWA; BioIn 11; FilmEn; WhoAm 80; WhoAmW 79; WhoHol A*

Darnell, Linda
American. Actress
Famous for role in *Forever Amber,* 1948.
b. Oct 16, 1921 in Dallas, Texas
d. Apr 12, 1965 in Chicago, Illinois
Source: *BiDFilm; EvEuW; FilmgC; InWom; MotPP; MovMk; ThFT; WhScrn 74, 77; WhoHol B; WorEFlm*

Darnley, Lord Henry Stuart
English. Claimant to Throne
b. 1545
d. 1567
Source: *NewC; REn*

Darren, James
American. Actor, Singer
Starred in *Gidget,* 1959; TV series "The Time Tunnel," 1966-67.
b. Jun 8, 1936 in Philadelphia, Pennsylvania
Source: *FilmgC; IntMPA 75, 77, 78, 79, 80, 81, 82; MotPP; MovMk; WhoHol A*

Darrieux, Danielle
French. Actress
b. May 1, 1917 in Bordeaux, France
Source: *BiDFilm; FilmgC; InWom; IntMPA 75, 76, 77, 78, 79, 80, 81, 82; IntWW 74; MotPP; MovMk; NewYTBE 70; OxFilm; ThFT; WhoHol A; WorEFlm*

Darro, Frankie
American. Actor
b. 1917
Source: *FilmgC; MovMk; Vers B; WhoHol A*

Darrow, Clarence Seward
American. Lawyer
Defense counsel in widely publicized trials, Leopold-Loeb murder, 1924, Scottsboro case, 1932.
b. Apr 18, 1857 in Kinsman, Ohio
d. Mar 13, 1938 in Chicago, Illinois
Source: *AmAu&B; AmBi; DcAmB S2; DcLEL; DcNAA; EncAB-H; FilmgC; OhA&B; OxAmL; REn; REnAL; TwCA, SUP; WebAB; WhAm 1; WhNAA*

Darrow, Henry
American. Actor
b. 1933 in New York, New York
Source: *WhoHol A*

Darrow, Whitney, Jr.
American. Author, Cartoonist
b. Aug 22, 1909 in Princeton, New Jersey
Source: *ConAu 61; SmATA 13*

Dart, Justin Whitlock
American. Business Executive
b. Aug 17, 1907 in Evanston, Illinois
Source: *BioIn 1, 7, 8, 10; CurBio 46; Dun&B 79; IntWW 74, 75, 76, 77, 78, 80; IntYB 78, 79; St&PR 75; WhoAm 74, 76, 78, 80; WhoF&I 74, 75, 77, 81; WhoWest 76; WhoWor 74*

Dart, Raymond Arthur
Australian. Anthropologist
b. Feb 4, 1893 in Toowong, Australia
Source: *Au&Wr 71; BioIn 5, 7; ConAu 13R; ConAu P-1; CurBio 66; IntWW 74; Who 82; WhoWor 74*

Darvas, Lili
American. Actress
b. Apr 10, 1906 in Budapest, Hungary
d. Jul 22, 1974 in New York, New York
Source: *BiE&WWA; NewYTBE 73; NewYTBS 74; NotNAT; WhAm 6; WhScrn 77; WhoAm 74; WhoHol B*

Darvi, Bella
American. Actress
b. Oct 23, 1929 in Sosnowiec, Poland
d. Sep 1971 in Monte Carlo, Monaco
Source: *FilmgC; NewYTBE 71; WhScrn 74, 77; WhoHol B*

Darwell, Jane
[Patti Woodward]
American. Actress
b. Oct 15, 1880 in Palmyra, Missouri
d. Aug 13, 1967 in Woodland Hills, California
Source: *BiDFilm; CurBio 41, 67; Film 1; FilmgC; InWom; MotPP; MovMk; OxFilm; ThFT; TwYS; Vers A; WhScrn 74, 77; WhoHol B; WorEFlm*

Darwin, Charles Robert
English. Author, Naturalist
Notes from cruise on HMS *Beagle,* 1831-36, resulted in book, *Origin of Species,* 1859.
b. Feb 12, 1809 in Shrewsbury, England
d. Apr 19, 1882 in Down, England
Source: *Alli, SUP; ApCAB SUP; AtlBL; BbD; BiD&SB; BrAu 19; CarSB; CasWL; Chambr 3; CyWA; DcEnA, AP; DcEnL; DcEuL; DcLEL; EvLB; MouLC 4; NewC; OxEng; Pen ENG; RComWL; REn; WebE&AL*

Daryush, Elizabeth Bridges
English. Poet
b. Dec 5, 1887 in London, England
d. Apr 7, 1977 in Stockwell, England
Source: *BioIn 11; ConAu 49, 3NR; ConLC 6*

Dash, Samuel
American. Watergate Lawyer
b. Feb 27, 1925 in Camden, New Jersey
Source: *BioNews 74; NewYTBE 73; WhoAm 74, 76, 78, 80, 82*

Dashwood, Elizabeth Monica
English. Author
b. Jun 9, 1890 in Sussex, England
d. Dec 2, 1943 in Cullompton, England
Source: *BioIn 4, 5; NewC; REn; WhoLA*

DaSilva, Howard
American. Actor
b. May 4, 1909 in Cleveland, Ohio
Source: *BiE&WWA; EncMT; FilmgC; IntMPA 75, 77; MovMk; NewYTBS 74; PlP&P; WhoAm 74, 76, 78, 80, 82; WhoHol A; WhoThe 77; WhoWor 74*

Dassault, Marcel
French. Airplane Executive
Manufactured world's best selling jets, Mystere and Mirage.
b. Jan 22, 1892 in Paris, France
Source: *BioIn 4, 7, 8, 9, 11; CurBio 70; IntWW 74; WhoWor 74*

Dassin, Jules
American. Motion Picture Director
b. Dec 12, 1911 in Middletown, Connecticut
Source: *BiDFilm; BiE&WWA; CmMov; ConDr 73; CurBio 71; FilmgC; IntMPA 75, 76, 77, 78, 79, 80, 81, 82; IntWW 74; OxFilm; WhoAm 74, 76, 78, 80, 82; WhoHol A; WhoWor 74; WorEFlm*

Dassler, Adolf
"Adi"
German. Founder of Adidas Company
b. 1901
d. Sep 18, 1978 in Herzogenaurach, Germany (West)
Source: *BioIn 11; ObitOF 79*

Daubeny, Sir Peter Lauderdale
British. Theatrical Director
b. Apr 1921 in Wiesbaden, Germany
d. Aug 6, 1975 in London, England
Source: *BioIn 3, 9, 10; CnThe; ConAu 61; IntWW 74; OxThe; WhThe; Who 74; WhoWor 74*

Daubert, Jake (Jacob Ellsworth)
American. Baseball Player
b. May 15, 1885 in Llewellyn, Pennsylvania
d. Oct 9, 1924 in Cincinnati, Ohio
Source: *BaseEn; BioIn 4; WhoProB 73*

Daubigny, Charles F
French. Artist
b. Feb 15, 1817 in Paris, France
d. Feb 19, 1878 in Auvers, France
Source: *AtlBL*

D'Aubuisson, Roberto
Salvadoran. Politician
Head of ultraright Nationalist Republican Alliance Party.
b. 1944 in Santa Tecla, El Salvador
Source: *NewYTBS 82*

Daudet, Alphonse Marie Leon
French. Author
b. May 13, 1840 in Nimes, France
d. Dec 16, 1897
Source: *AtlBL; BbD; BiD&SB; ChPo, S2; ClDMEL; CyWA; DcBiA; DcEuL; EvEuW; McGEWD; NewC; OxEng; OxFr; Pen EUR; RComWL; REn*

Daudet, Leon
French. Author, Politician
b. Nov 16, 1867
d. Jul 1, 1942
Source: *CasWL; ClDMEL; CurBio 42; EncWL; NewC; OxFr; REn*

Daugherty, Pat
see: Black Oak Arkansas

Daugherty, William J
[The Hostages]
American. Former Hostage in Iran
b. 1948?
Source: *NewYTBS 81*

Daumier, Honore
French. Artist
b. Feb 26, 1808 in Marseilles, France
d. Feb 11, 1879 in Valmondois, France
Source: *AtlBL; OxFr; REn*

Dauphin, Claude Le Grand Maria Eugene
French. Actor
b. Aug 19, 1903 in Corbeil, France
d. Nov 17, 1978 in Paris, France
Source: *BiE&WWA; BioIn 4; FilmgC; IntMPA 75, 76, 77, 78, 79; MotPP; MovMk; NewYTBS 78; NotNAT; ObitOF 79; WhAm 7; WhoHol A; WhoThe 72, 77; WhoWor 74*

Dauss, George August
"Hooks"
American. Baseball Player
b. Sep 22, 1889 in Indianapolis, Indiana
d. Jul 27, 1963 in Saint Louis, Missouri
Source: *BaseEn; WhoProB 73*

Dausset, Jean (Baptiste Gabriel Joachim)
French. Medical Scientist
b. Oct 19, 1916 in Toulouse, France
Source: *CurBio 81*

Dave Clark Five
[Dave Clark; Lenny Davidson; Rick Huxley; Denis Payton; Michael Smith]
English. Singing Group
Source: *EncPR&S; RkOn*

Davenant, William
English. Poet
b. Feb 1606 in Oxford, England
d. Apr 7, 1668 in London, England
Source: *Alli; BbD; BiD&SB; BrAu; CasWL; Chambr 1; ChPo, S1; CnE&AP; CnThe; CroE&S; CyWA; DcEnA; DcEnL; DcEuL; EvLB; McGEWD; NewC; OxEng; OxThe; Pen ENG; PlP&P; REn; REnWD; WebE&AL*

Davenport, Eva
English. Actress
b. 1858 in London, England
d. Sep 26, 1932 in White Plains, New York
Source: *NotNAT B; WhoStg 1906, 1908*

Davenport, Fanny Lily Gypsy
American. Actress
b. Apr 10, 1850 in London, England
d. Sep 26, 1898 in South Duxbury, Massachusetts
Source: *FamA&A; NotNAT B; OxThe*

Davenport, Harry George Bryant
American. Actor
b. Jan 19, 1886 in New York, New York
d. Aug 9, 1949 in Los Angeles, California
Source: *Film 1; FilmgC; MotPP; MovMk; OxThe; Vers A; WhScrn 74, 77; WhoHol B; WhoStg 1906, 1908*

Davenport, Homer Calvin
American. Caricaturist
b. Mar 8, 1867 in Silverton, Oregon
d. May 2, 1912 in New York, New York
Source: *AmAu&B; BioIn 6, 9, 10; DcAmAu; DcNAA; WebBD 80*

Davenport, Marcia
American. Author, Music Critic
b. Jun 9, 1903 in New York, New York
Source: *AmAu&B; AmNov; AuBYP; ConAu 9R; CurBio 44; DcLEL; InWom; LongCTC; OxAmL; REn; REnAL; TwCA SUP; WhoAm 74; WhoWor 74*

Davenport, Nigel
English. Actor
b. May 23, 1928 in Shelford, England
Source: *FilmgC; IntMPA 82; WhoHol A; WhoThe 77*

Davenport, Thomas
American. Inventor
Discovered principle of starting, stopping electric current over wire, 1834.
b. Jul 19, 1802 in Williamstown, Vermont
d. Jul 6, 1851 in Salisbury, Vermont
Source: *AmBi; ApCAB; DcAmB; TwCBDA; WebAB; WhAm H*

Davenport, Willie
American. Olympic Athlete
b. Jun 8, 1943 in Troy, Alabama
Source: *WhoTr&F 73*

DaVerrazano, Giovanni
see: Verrazano, Giovanni da

David, Saint
Patron Saint of Wales
b. 495?
d. 589?
Source: *BioIn 1, 2, 3, 4, 5, 6, 7, 8, 10; NewC; REn*

David
King of Judah and Israel
b. 1000?BC
d. 960?BC
Source: *BiB N; DcOrL 3; NewC*

David, Elizabeth
British. Author
b. 1914
Source: *Au&Wr 71; Who 74*

David, Gerard
Dutch. Artist
b. 1460? in Oudewater, Netherlands
d. Aug 13, 1523 in Bruges, Netherlands
Source: *AtlBL*

David, Hal
American. Lyricist
Former partner of Burt Bacharach; won Oscar, 1969, for "Raindrops Keep Fallin' on My Head."
b. May 25, 1921 in New York, New York
Source: *AmSCAP 66; CelR 73; CurBio 80; EncMT; NotNAT; WhoAm 74, 76, 78, 80, 82*

David, Jacques Louis
French. Artist
b. Aug 30, 1748 in Paris, France
d. Dec 29, 1825 in Brussels, Belgium
Source: *AtlBL; OxFr*

David-Neel, Alexandra
French. Explorer, Author
First European woman to enter forbidden Tibetan capital, Lhasa; author *My Journey to Lhasa.*
b. Oct 24, 1868
d. Sep 8, 1969 in Digne, France
Source: *ConAu 25R*

Davidson, Donald Grady
American. Poet, Critic, Historian
Founded Fugitive School of southern American literature, 1920's.
b. Aug 18, 1893 in Campbellsville, Tennessee
d. Apr 25, 1968 in Nashville, Tennessee
Source: *AmAu&B; ChPo, S1; ConAmA; ConAu 5R, 25R, 4NR; ConLC 2, 13; DcLEL; NewYTBE 71; OxAmL; Pen AM; REnAL; SixAP; TwCA, SUP; WhAm 5; WhNAA*

Davidson, J Brownlee
American. Agricultural Engineer
b. Feb 1880 in Douglas, Nebraska
d. 1957
Source: *BioIn 1, 2, 4, 6, 9; WhNAA*

Davidson, Jo
American. Sculptor
b. Mar 30, 1883 in New York, New York
d. Jan 2, 1952 in Bercheron, France
Source: *CurBio 45, 52; DcAmB S5; OxAmL; REn; REnAL; WebAB; WhAm 3*

Davidson, John
American. Singer, Actor
Starred in *The Happiest Millionaire,* 1967; TV series, "That's Incredible," 1980--.
b. Dec 13, 1941 in Pittsburgh, Pennsylvania
Source: *BkPepl; IntMPA 75, 76, 77, 78, 79, 80, 81, 82; MotPP; WhoAm 74, 76, 78, 80, 82; WhoHol A*

Davie, Alan
Scottish. Poet, Jazz Musician
b. 1920 in Grangemouth, Scotland
Source: *BioIn 4, 7, 8; IntWW 74; Who 74; WhoWor 74*

Davie, Donald
English. Author
b. Jul 17, 1922 in Yorkshire, England
Source: *CasWL; ChPo; ConAu 1R; ConLC 5; ConP 70, 75; LongCTC; ModBrL, SUP; NewC; REn; TwCW; Who 74; WhoAm 74; WhoTwCL; WorAu, ; WrDr 76*

Davies, Arthur Bowen
American. Artist
b. Sep 26, 1862 in Utica, New York
d. Oct 24, 1928 in Florence, Italy
Source: *AmBi; ChPo; DcAmB; OxAmL; WebAB; WhAm 1*

Davies, Cliff
see: Amboy Dukes, The

Davies, Hunter
Scottish. Author
b. Jan 7, 1936 in Renfrew, Scotland
Source: *ConAu 57; WhoWor 74, 76; WrDr 76, 80*

Davies, Joseph Edward
American. Lawyer, Diplomat
b. Nov 29, 1876 in Watertown, Wisconsin
d. May 9, 1958 in Washington, DC
Source: *AmAu&B; CurBio 42, 58; WhAm 3*

Davies, Leslie Purnell
English. Author
b. Oct 20, 1914 in Cheshire, England
Source: *ConAu 21R; WrDr 76*

Davies, Marion
[Marion Douras]
American. Actress
b. Jan 3, 1897 in New York, New York
d. Sep 22, 1961 in Hollywood, California
Source: *BiDFilm; Film 1; FilmgC; MotPP; MovMk; OxFilm; ThFT; TwYS; WhAm 4; WhScrn 74, 77; WhoHol B*

Davies, Peter Maxwell
English. Composer
b. Sep 8, 1934 in Manchester, England
Source: *BioIn 6, 8; CurBio 80; IntWW 79*

Davies, Robert Edris
"Harrisburg Houdini"
American. Basketball Player
b. Jan 15, 1920 in Harrisburg, Pennsylvania
Source: *BioIn 3; WhoBbl 73*

Davies, Robertson
Canadian. Author
Literary figure best known for Deptford trilogy.
b. Aug 28, 1913 in Thamesville, ON
Source: *Au&Wr 71; CaW; CanWW 79; CanWr; CasWL; CnThe; ConAu 33R; ConDr 77; ConLC 2, 7, 13; ConNov 72, 76; CreCan 1; CurBio 75; DcLEL; DrAS 74E, 78E; IntAu&W 76, 77; IntWW 77, 78, 79, 80; LongCTC; McGEWD; ModCmwL; OxCan, SUP; Pen ENG; REnAL; REnWD; TwCW; WhoAm 74, 76, 78, 80, 82; WhoWor 74; WorAu; WrDr 76, 80*

Davies, Rodger Paul
American. Ambassador to Cyprus
b. May 7, 1921 in Berkeley, California
d. Aug 19, 1974 in Nicosia, Cyprus
Source: *WhoAm 74; WhoGov 72*

Davis, Adelle
American. Nutritionist
b. Feb 25, 1904 in Lizion, Indiana
d. May 31, 1974 in Palos Verdes, California
Source: *BioNews 74; CelR 73; ConAu 37R, 49; CurBio 73; NewYTBS 74; REnAL; WhAm 6; WhoAm 74*

Davis, Al
American. Football Club Owner
b. Jul 4, 1929 in Brockton, Massachusetts
Source: *BioIn 6, 8, 10, 11; WhoAm 82; WhoWest 76*

Davis, Alexander Jackson
American. Architect
b. Jul 24, 1803 in New York, New York
d. Jan 14, 1892 in West Orange, New Jersey
Source: *AmBi; ApCAB SUP; DcAmB; DcNAA; EarABI SUP; TwCBDA; WhAm H*

Davis, Angela Yvonne
American. Revolutionary, Author
On FBI's ten most-wanted list, 1970; wrote autobiography, 1974.
b. Jan 26, 1944 in Birmingham, Alabama
Source: *BioIn 8, 9, 10, 11; BioNews 74; BkPepl; CelR 73; ConAu 57; CurBio 72; HerW; NewYTBE 70, 71, 72*

Davis, Anne B
American. Actress
b. May 3, 1926 in Schenectady, New York
Source: *InWom; WhoAm 82; WhoHol A*

Davis, Arthur Vining
American. Real Estate Developer
b. May 30, 1867 in Sharon, Massachusetts
d. Nov 17, 1962 in Miami, Florida
Source: *BioIn 4, 5, 6, 11; WhAm 4*

Davis, Benjamin O, Jr.
American. Air Force General
b. Dec 18, 1912 in Washington, DC
Source: *CurBio 55; NewYTBE 70; WhoAm 74; WhoBlA 75; WhoGov 72; WhoS&SW 73*

Davis, Benjamin Oliver
American. Army Brigadier General
b. Jul 1, 1877 in Washington, DC
d. Nov 26, 1970 in North Chicago, Illinois
Source: *CurBio 42, 71; EncAB-H; NewYTBE 70; WebAB*

Davis, Bette (Ruth Elizabeth)
American. Actress
Won Oscars, 1935, 1938, for *Dangerous; Jezebel.*
b. Apr 5, 1908 in Lowell, Massachusetts
Source: *BiDFilm; BiE&WWA; BioNews 74; BkPepl; CelR 73; CmMov; ConAu 61; CurBio 41, 53; EncMT; FilmgC; InWom; IntMPA 75, 76, 77, 78, 79, 80, 81, 82; IntWW 74; MotPP; MovMk; NewYTBE 70; NotNAT; OxFilm; ThFT; WebAB; Who 74; WhoAm 74, 76, 78, 80, 82; WhoHol A; WhoThe 77; WhoWor 74; WorEFlm*

Davis, Brad
American. Actor
b. 1950 in Florida
Source: *BioIn 11; IntMPA 82*

Davis, Burke
American. Children's Author
b. Jul 24, 1913 in Durham, North Carolina
Source: *AuBYP; ConAu 1R, 4NR; SmATA 4; WhoAm 74, 76, 78, 80, 82; WrDr 76*

Davis, Clifton
American. Actor, Singer, Composer
Wrote gold record song "Never Can Say Goodbye."
b. Oct 4, 1945 in Chicago, Illinois
Source: *WhoBlA 75; WhoHol A*

Davis, Clive Jay
American. Businessman
b. Apr 4, 1932 in Brooklyn, New York
Source: *BioIn 9, 10, 11; BusPN; WhoAm 78, 80, 82*

Davis, Clyde Brion
American. Author
b. May 22, 1894 in Unadilla, Nebraska
d. Jul 19, 1962 in Salisbury, Connecticut
Source: *AmNov; CnDAL; ConAu 5R; OxAmL; REn; REnAL; TwCA, SUP; WhAm 4*

Davis, Colin
English. Conductor
b. Sep 25, 1927 in Weybridge, England
Source: *CurBio 68; IntWW 74; NewYTBE 72; Who 74; WhoMus 72; WhoWor 74*

Davis, David
American. Supreme Court Justice
b. Mar 9, 1815 in Cecil County, Maryland
d. Jun 26, 1886 in Bloomington, Illinois
Source: *ApCAB; BiAuS; BiDrAC; DcAmB; Drake; EncAB-H; TwCBDA; WebAB; WhAm H; WhAmP*

Davis, Dwight Filley
American. Secretary of War
b. Jul 5, 1879 in Saint Louis, Missouri
d. Nov 28, 1945 in Washington, DC
Source: *BiDrUSE; DcAmB S3; WhAm 2*

Davis, Edward Michael
American. Police Chief
b. Nov 15, 1916 in Los Angeles, California
Source: *BioIn 10, 11; WhoWest 74*

Davis, Elmer Holmes
American. Journalist, Radio Commentator
b. Jan 13, 1890 in Aurora, Indiana
d. May 18, 1958 in Washington, DC
Source: *AmAu&B; CurBio 40, 58; EncAB-H; IndAu 1816; OxAmL; REn; REnAL; TwCA, SUP; WebAB; WhAm 3; WhNAA*

Davis, Glenn
"Mr. Outside"
American. Football Player
b. Dec 26, 1924 in Claremont, California
Source: *CurBio 46; WhoFtbl 74*

Davis, Hal Charles
American. Labor Union Official
President, American Federation of Musicians International, 1970--.
b. Feb 27, 1914 in Pittsburgh, Pennsylvania
d. Jan 1, 1978 in New York, New York
Source: *BioIn 11; WhoAm 74*

Davis, Harold Lenoir
American. Author
b. Oct 18, 1896 in Yoncalla, Oregon
d. Oct 31, 1960 in San Antonio, Texas
Source: *AmAu&B; ChPo S1; DcLEL; TwCA, SUP*

Davis, James Curran
American. Congressman
Representative from GA, 1947-63; advocated racial segregation.
b. May 17, 1895 in Franklin, Georgia
d. Dec 28, 1981 in Atlanta, Georgia
Source: *BiDrAC; BioIn 12; CurBio 57, 82; NewYTBS 81; WhAmP; WhoAm 74*

Davis, Janette
American. Singer
Source: *BioIn 3; InWom*

Davis, Jefferson
American. President of Confederacy
Captured, Apr, 1865; confined to Fortress Monroe until May, 1867.
b. Jun 3, 1808 in Christian County, Kentucky
d. Dec 6, 1889 in New Orleans, Louisiana
Source: *Alli SUP; AmAu&B; AmBi; ApCAB; BbD; BiAuS; BiD&SB; BiDConf; BiDSA; BiDrUSE; DcAmAu; DcAmB; Drake; EncAB-H; OxAmL; REn; REnAL; TwCBDA; WebAB; WhAm H; WhAmP*

Davis, Jim
American. Actor
Played Jock Ewing on TV series "Dallas," 1978-81.
b. Aug 26, 1916 in Edgerton, Missouri
d. Apr 26, 1981 in Northridge, California
Source: *BioIn 1, 11; NewYTBS 81; WhoHol A*

Davis, Jim (James Robert)
American. Cartoonist
b. Jul 28, 1945 in Marion, Indiana
Source: *ConAu 85*

Davis, Joan
American. Actress, Comedienne
b. Jun 29, 1907 in Saint Paul, Minnesota
d. May 23, 1961 in Palm Springs, California
Source: *CurBio 45, 61; FilmgC; MotPP; MovMk; ThFT; WhScrn 74, 77; WhoHol B; WhoThe 77*

Davis, Joe
English. Billiards Player
b. 1901
d. Jul 1978
Source: *BioIn 11*

Davis, John
English. Explorer
Discovered entrance to Baffin Bay, 1587; sighted Falkland Islands, 1592.
b. 1550? in Sandridge, England
d. Dec 29, 1605 in Strait of Malacca
Source: *Alli; ApCAB; DcEnL; Drake; EvLB; OxCan*

Davis, John Staige
American. Plastic Surgeon
b. Jan 15, 1872 in Norfolk, Virginia
d. Dec 23, 1946 in Baltimore, Maryland
Source: *BioIn 1, 2; DcNAA; WhAm 2*

Davis, John Williams
American. Politician, Lawyer
b. Apr 13, 1873 in Clarksburg, West Virginia
d. Mar 24, 1955 in New York, New York
Source: *BiDrAC; CurBio 53, 55; DcAmB S5; EncAB-H; WebAB; WhAm 3; WhAmP*

Davis, Judy
Australian. Actress
Starred in *My Brilliant Career,* 1981.
b. 1956?
Source: *BioIn 12*

Davis, Kingsley
American. Sociologist
b. Aug 20, 1908 in Tuxedo, Texas
Source: *AmM&WS 73S; ConAu 13R; IntWW 74; WhoAm 74; WhoWor 74*

Davis, Loyal
American. Neurosurgeon
Father-in-law of President Reagan.
b. Jan 17, 1896 in Galesburg, Illinois
d. Aug 19, 1982 in Scottsdale, Arizona
Source: *AmM&WS 73P, 76P, 79P; NewYTBS 82; WhoAm 74, 76, 78, 80*

Davis, Mac
American. Actor, Singer, Songwriter
Hit song "I Believe in Music," 1972; starred in *North Dallas Forty,* 1979.
b. Jan 21, 1942 in Lubbock, Texas
Source: *BioIn 11, 12; BkPepl; CurBio 80; EncPR&S; IntMPA 82; WhoAm 82*

Davis, Martha
see: Motels, The

Davis, Marvin
American. Oil Wildcatter
b. 1926? in Denver, Colorado
Source: *NewYTBS 81*

Davis, Mary L
American. Children's Author
b. Mar 21, 1935 in Worthington, Minnesota
Source: *ConAu 49; SmATA 9*

Davis, Meyer
American. Orchestra Leader
b. Jan 10, 1895 in Ellicott City, Maryland
d. Apr 5, 1976 in New York, New York
Source: *BiE&WWA; BioNews 75; CelR 73; CurBio 61; WhoAm 74*

Davis, Michael
American. Juggler, Comedian
b. 1953?
Source: *BioIn 12*

Davis, Miles Dewey
American. Jazz Musician, Composer
b. May 25, 1926 in Alton, Illinois
Source: *BioNews 74; CelR 73; CurBio 62; WebAB; WhoAm 74, 76, 78, 80, 82; WhoBlA 75; WhoE 74; WhoMus 72; WhoWor 74*

Davis, Ossie
American. Actor, Dramatist
Wrote, directed, starred in *Purlie Victorious,* 1961.
b. Dec 18, 1917 in Cogdell, Georgia
Source: *AmAu&B; BiE&WWA; BlkAW; CelR 73; ConDr 73; CurBio 69; FilmgC; IntMPA 75, 76, 77, 78, 79, 80, 81, 82; LivgBAA; MotPP; MovMk; NotNAT; PlP&P; WhoAm 82; WhoHol A; WhoThe 77; WhoWor 74; WrDr 76*

Davis, Owen
American. Dramatist
b. Jan 29, 1874 in Portland, Maine
d. Oct 13, 1956 in New York, New York
Source: *AmAu&B; CnDAL; CnMD; McGEWD; ModWD; OxAmL; OxThe; REn; REnAL; TwCA, SUP; WhAm 3*

Davis, Patti
[Patricia Reagan]
American. Ronald Reagan's Daughter, Actress
b. Oct 21, 1952 in Los Angeles, California
Source: *BioIn 12*

Davis, Perscell
"Magic"
American. Boxer
b. 1958? in Los Angeles, California
Source: *NF*

Davis, Phil
American. Cartoonist
b. Mar 4, 1906 in Saint Louis, Missouri
d. Dec 16, 1964
Source: *BioIn 1, 7; WorECom*

Davis, Rennie
[The Chicago 7]
American. Peace Activist
b. May 23, 1941 in Lansing, Michigan
Source: *BioNews 74; WhoAm 74*

Davis, Richard Harding
American. Author, Journalist
Wrote *Gallegher and Other Stories,* 1901.
b. Apr 18, 1864 in Philadelphia, Pennsylvania
d. Apr 11, 1916 in Mount Kisco, New York
Source: *AmAu&B; AmBi; BbD; BiD&SB; CarSB; CasWL; Chambr 3; CnDAL; DcAmAu; DcAmB; DcBiA; DcEnA AP; DcLEL; DcNAA; EncMys; EvLB; JBA 34; LongCTC; OxAmL; Pen AM; REn; REnAL; TwCA, SUP; TwCBDA; WebAB; WebE&AL; WhAm 1; WhoStg 1906, 1908*

Davis, Sam
American. Confederate Scout
b. 1842 in Smyrna, Tennessee
d. Nov 27, 1863
Source: *BioIn 11; WhAm H*

Davis, Sammy, Jr.
American. Actor, Singer, Dancer
Began career at age three; wrote autobiography *Yes, I Can,* 1965.
b. Dec 8, 1925 in New York, New York
Source: *BiE&WWA; BioNews 74; CelR 73; CurBio 56; EncMT; FilmgC; IntMPA 75, 76, 77, 78, 79, 80, 81, 82; MotPP; MovMk; NewYTBE 71, 72; NotNAT; OxFilm; WebAB; WhoAm 74; WhoBlA 75; WhoHol A; WhoThe 77; WhoWor 74*

Davis, Skeeter
American. Singer
b. Dec 30, 1931 in Dry Ridge, Kentucky
Source: *BioIn 9, 11; EncFCWM 69*

Davis, Spencer
[The Spencer Davis Group]
English. Rock Musician
b. Jul 17, 1942 in England
Source: *ConMuA 80; WhoRock 81*

Davis, Stuart
American. Artist
b. Dec 7, 1894 in Philadelphia, Pennsylvania
d. Jun 24, 1964 in New York, New York
Source: *CurBio 40, 64; DcCAA 71; EncAB-H; OxAmL; REn; WebAB; WhAm 4*

Davis, T Cullen
American. Industrialist, Acquitted Murderer
b. 1933?
Source: *BioIn 11*

Davis, "Tobe" (Coller)
American. Fashion Executive
b. 1893? in Milwaukee, Wisconsin
d. Dec 25, 1962
Source: *BioIn 3, 4, 5, 6; CurBio 59, 63; InWom; WhAm 4*

Davis, Tommy (Thomas Herman, Jr.)
American. Baseball Player
b. Mar 21, 1939 in Brooklyn, New York
Source: *BaseEn; BioIn 6, 8, 11; WhoProB 73*

Davis, Walter
American. Track Athlete
b. Jan 5, 1931 in Beaumont, Texas
Source: *BioIn 3, 5*

Davis, "Wild Bill" (William Strethen)
American. Musician
b. Nov 24, 1918 in Glasgow, Missouri
Source: *WhoJazz 72*

Davis, Willie (William Henry)
American. Football, Baseball Player
b. Apr 15, 1940 in Mineral Springs, Arkansas
Source: *WhoAm 74; WhoBlA 75; WhoProB 73*

Davison, Bruce
American. Actor
b. in Philadelphia, Pennsylvania
Source: *BioIn 11; FilmgC; IntMPA 75, 76, 77, 78, 79, 80, 81; WhoHol A*

Davison, Emily Wilding
English. Feminist
d. Jun 4, 1913
Source: *BioIn 11*

Davison, Frederic Ellis
American. Army General
b. Sep 28, 1917 in Washington, DC
Source: *BioIn 8; CurBio 74*

Davison, William
American. Jazz Musician
b. Jan 5, 1906 in Defiance, Ohio
Source: *WhoAm 74; WhoJazz 72*

Davisson, Clinton Joseph
American. Physicist
b. Oct 22, 1881 in Bloomington, Illinois
d. Feb 1, 1958 in Charlottesville, Virginia
Source: *AsBiEn; BioIn 2, 3, 4, 5, 6; DcScB; NewCol 75; WebAB; WhAm 3*

Davitt, Michael
Irish. Revolutionary
b. Mar 25, 1846 in Straide, Ireland
d. May 31, 1906 in Dublin, Ireland
Source: *Alli SUP; NewCol 75; PoIre; WebBD 80*

Davout, Louis Nicholas
[Prince d'Eckmuhl]
French. Military Leader
b. May 10, 1770 in Annoux, France
d. Jun 1, 1823 in Paris, France
Source: *BioIn 9, 10, 11; NewCol 75; OxFr; WebBD 80; WhoMilH 76*

Davy, Sir Humphrey
English. Scientist
Discovered laughing gas, 1799; invented miner's safety lamp, 1815.
b. Dec 17, 1778 in Cornwall, England
d. May 29, 1829 in Geneva, Switzerland
Source: *Alli; BbD; BiD&SB; BiDLA; BrAu 19; Chambr 2; ChPo, S1; DcEnL; EvLB; NewC; OxEng*

Dawber, Pam
American. Actress
Played Mindy on TV series "Mork and Mindy."
b. Oct 18, 1951 in Farmington, Michigan
Source: *BioIn 11, 12; IntMPA 82; WhoAm 80, 82*

Dawes, Charles Gates
American. Lawyer, Statesman
b. Aug 27, 1865 in Marietta, Ohio
d. Apr 23, 1951 in Evanston, Illinois
Source: *AmAu&B; ApCAB SUP; BiDrAC; BiDrUSE; DcAmB S5; EncAB-H; OhA&B; WebAB; WhAm 3; WhAmP*

Dawes, William
American. Revolutionary
b. Apr 6, 1745 in Boston, Massachusetts
d. Feb 25, 1799 in Boston, Massachusetts
Source: *Alli, SUP; AmBi; ApCAB; DcAmB; WhAm H*

Dawkins, Darryl
American. Basketball Player
b. Jan 11, 1957 in Orlando, Florida
Source: *BioIn 11, 12*

Dawn
[Telma Hopkins; Tony Orlando; Joyce Wilson]
American. Vocal Group
Source: *EncPR&S; RkOn*

Dawn, Hazel
American. Actress
b. Mar 23, 1898 in Ogden, Utah
Source: *BiE&WWA; EncMT; Film 1; InWom; MotPP; NotNAT; TwYS; WhoHol A; WhoThe 77*

Dawson, Len (Leonard Ray)
American. Football Player, Sportscaster
b. Jun 20, 1935 in Alliance, Ohio
Source: *BioIn 3, 4, 9, 10; NewYTBE 70; WhoAm 82; WhoFtbl 74*

Dawson, Richard
English. Actor, TV Game Show Host
Played Newkirk on TV series "Hogan's Heroes," 1965-71; host of game show "Family Feud."
b. Nov 20, 1932 in Gosport, England
Source: *WhoAm 78, 80, 82; WhoHol A*

Dawson, William L
American. Congressman
b. Apr 26, 1886 in Albany, Georgia
d. Nov 9, 1970 in Chicago, Illinois
Source: *BiDrAC; CurBio 45, 70; NewYTBE 70; WhAm 5*

Day, Benjamin Henry
American. Publisher
b. Apr 10, 1810 in West Springfield, Massachusetts
d. Dec 21, 1889 in New York, New York
Source: *AmAu&B; DcNAA; NewCol 75; WebBD 80; WhAm H*

Day, Chon
American. Cartoonist
b. Apr 6, 1907 in Chatham, New Jersey
Source: *BioIn 3; WhoAm 82; WhoAmA 73*

Day, Clarence Shepard, Jr.
American. Biographer, Essayist, Humorist
b. Nov 18, 1874 in New York, New York
d. Dec 28, 1935 in New York, New York
Source: *AmAu&B; ChPo, S1; ConAmA; CyWA; DcAmB S1; DcLEL; DcNAA; EvLB; LongCTC; OxAmL; Pen AM; REn; REnAL; TwCA, SUP; TwCW; WebAB; WhAm 1*

Day, Dennis
American. Singer, Actor
b. May 21, 1917 in New York, New York
Source: *FilmgC; MotPP; WhoHol A*

Day, Doris
[Doris VonKappelhoff]
American. Actress, Singer
Starred in *The Pajama Game,* 1957; *Pillow Talk,* 1959.
b. Apr 3, 1924 in Cincinnati, Ohio
Source: *BiDFilm; BioNews 74; BkPepl; CelR 73; CmMov; CurBio 54; FilmgC; InWom; IntMPA 75, 76, 77, 78, 79, 80, 81, 82; MotPP; MovMk; OxFilm; WhoAm 74, 76, 78, 80, 82; WhoHol A; WorEFlm*

Day, Dorothy
American. Editor, Activist
Founded Catholic Workers movement, 1933.
b. Nov 8, 1897 in New York, New York
d. Nov 29, 1980 in New York, New York
Source: *BioNews 74; CathA 1930; CelR 73; ConAu 65, 102; CurBio 62; NewYTBE 72; WebAB; WhoAm 74; WhoE 74*

Day, J(ames) Edward
American. Former Postmaster General
b. Oct 11, 1914 in Jacksonville, Florida
Source: *BiDrUSE; ConAu 17R; CurBio 62; IntWW 74; WhoAm 74, 76, 78, 80, 82; WhoAmP 73*

Day, James Wentworth
English. Author, Publisher
b. Apr 21, 1899 in Exning, England
Source: *ConAu 13R; Who 74*

Day, Joseph Paul
American. Real Estate Developer
b. Sep 22, 1873 in New York, New York
d. Apr 10, 1944 in New York, New York
Source: *BioIn 3; WhAm 3*

Day, Laraine
[Laraine Johnson]
American. Actress
b. Oct 13, 1920 in Roosevelt, Utah
Source: *CurBio 53; FilmgC; InWom; IntMPA 75, 76, 77, 78, 79, 80, 81, 82; MotPP; MovMk; ThFT; WhoHol A*

Day, Ned (Edward Gately)
American. Bowler
b. 1911?
d. Nov 26, 1971 in Milwaukee, Wisconsin
Source: *BioIn 2, 3, 5, 9*

Day, Robin
English. Broadcast Journalist
b. Oct 24, 1923 in London, England
Source: *BioIn 11; IntWW 74; Who 74*

Day, Rusty
see: Amboy Dukes, The

Day, William Rufus
American. Supreme Court Justice
b. Apr 17, 1849 in Ravenna, Ohio
d. Jul 9, 1923 in Mackinac Island, Michigan
Source: *AmBi; ApCAB SUP; BiDrUSE; DcAmB; TwCBDA; WebAB; WhAm 1*

Day-Lewis, Cecil
[Nicholas Blake, pseud.]
British. Poet Laureate
b. Apr 27, 1904 in Ballintogher, Ireland
d. May 22, 1972 in London, England
Source: *Au&Wr 71; CasWL; ChPo, S1; CnE&AP; CnMWL; ConAu 33R; ConAu P-1; ConLC 1, 6, 10; ConNov 72; ConP 70, 75; DcLEL; EncMys; EncWL; LongCTC; ModBrL, SUP; NewC; OxEng; Pen ENG; RAdv 1; REn; TwCA, SUP; TwCW; WebE&AL; WhAm 5; WhoTwCL*

Dayan, Assaf
Israeli. Actor
b. 1945 in Afula, Palestine
Source: *BioIn 8; WhoHol A*

Dayan, Moshe
Israeli. Soldier, Statesman
b. May 20, 1915 in Degania, Palestine
d. Oct 16, 1981 in Tel Aviv, Israel
Source: *BioIn 4, 7, 8, 9, 10, 11; CelR 73; ConAu 21R; CurBio 57, 82; IntAu&W 77; IntWW 74, 75, 76, 77, 78; IntYB 78, 79; LinLib L; McGEWB; MidE 78, 79; NewYTBE 70; NewYTBS 78, 81; WhoMilH 76; WhoWor 74, 78; WhoWorJ 72; WorDWW*

Deacon, John
see: Queen

Deacon, Richard
American. Actor
b. 1923
Source: *FilmgC; MotPP; WhoHol A*

Dean, Alfred Lovill
"Chubby"
American. Baseball Player
b. Aug 24, 1916 in Mount Airy, North Carolina
d. Dec 21, 1970 in Riverside, New Jersey
Source: *BaseEn; BioIn 1; WhoProB 73*

Dean, Basil
English. Actor, Director
b. Sep 27, 1888 in Croydon, England
d. Apr 22, 1978 in London, England
Source: *BioIn 9; ConAu 69; EncWT; Film 2; FilmgC; IntWW 74, 75, 76, 78; ModWD; OxThe; WhThe; WhoWor 74*

Dean, "Daffy" (Paul Dee)
American. Baseball Player
Pitcher, 1934-43; brother of Dizzy Dean.
b. Aug 14, 1913 in Lucas, Arkansas
d. Mar 17, 1981 in Springdale, Arkansas
Source: *BaseEn; BioIn 7; NewYTBS 81; WebAB; WhoProB 73*

Dean, "Dizzy" (Jay Hanna)
American. Baseball Player, Sportscaster
Pitcher who won 30 games, 1934; Hall of Fame, 1953.
b. Jan 16, 1911 in Lucas, Arkansas
d. Jul 17, 1974 in Reno, Nevada
Source: *BaseEn; BioIn 1, 2, 3, 4, 5, 6, 7, 8, 9, 10; BioNews 74; CurBio 51, 74; NewYTBS 74; WebAB; WhoProB 73*

Dean, Gordon Evans
American. Investment Banker
b. Dec 28, 1905 in Seattle, Washington
d. Aug 15, 1958
Source: *CurBio 58; WhAm 3*

Dean, Henry Trendley
American. Dental Surgeon
b. Aug 25, 1893 in Winstanley Park, Illinois
d. May 13, 1962 in Chicago, Illinois
Source: *BioIn 4, 6; CurBio 57, 62*

Dean, James
[James Byron]
American. Actor
Starred in *East of Eden,* 1955, *Rebel Without a Cause,* 1955, *Giant,* 1956.
b. Feb 8, 1931 in Marion, Indiana
d. Sep 30, 1955 in Paso Robles, California
Source: *BiDFilm; FilmgC; MotPP; MovMk; OxFilm; WhAm 4; WhScrn 74, 77; WhoHol B; WorEFlm*

Dean, Jimmy
[Seth Ward]
American. Singer
Best known song "Big Bad John," 1961; chairman, Jimmy Dean Meat Co., 1972--.
b. Aug 10, 1928 in Plainview, Texas
Source: *CurBio 65; EncFCWM 69; IntMPA 77, 78, 79, 80, 81, 82; WhoAm 82; WhoHol A*

Dean, John Gunther
American. Diplomat
b. Feb 24, 1926 in Germany
Source: *BioIn 10; IntWW 74, 75, 76, 77, 78; IntYB 78, 79; MidE 79; USBiR 74; WhoAm 74, 76, 78, 80, 82; WhoAmP 75, 77, 79*

Dean, John Wesley
American. Lawyer
Counsel to Richard Nixon, 1971-73; author *Blind Ambition,* 1976.
b. Oct 14, 1938 in Akron, Ohio
Source: *WhoAm 74; WhoAmP 73; WhoGov 72*

Dean, Laura
American. Choreographer, Composer
b. Dec 3, 1945 in Staten Island, New York
Source: *BioIn 11; WhoAm 80, 82*

Dean, "Man Mountain"
[Frank Simmons Leavitt]
American. Wrestler
b. Jun 30, 1889 in New York, New York
d. May 29, 1953 in Norcross, Georgia
Source: *BioIn 3; WebAB*

Dean, Morton
American. Broadcast Journalist
b. Aug 22, 1935 in Fall River, Massachusetts
Source: *ConAu 69; WhoAm 82*

Dean, Sir Patrick Henry
British. Diplomat
b. Mar 16, 1909 in Berlin, Germany
Source: *CurBio 61; IntWW 74; Who 74; WhoWor 74*

Dean, William Frishe
American. Army Officer
b. Aug 1, 1899 in Carlyle, Illinois
d. Aug 24, 1981 in Berkeley, California
Source: *BioIn 2, 3, 5, 7, 8, 9; CurBio 54, 81; NewYTBS 81; WebAMB*

Deane, Sandy
see: Jay and the Americans

Deane, Silas
American. Colonial Diplomat
b. Dec 24, 1737 in Groton, Connecticut
d. Sep 23, 1789
Source: *ApCAB; BiAuS; BiDrAC; BioIn 2, 5, 10, 11; Drake; EncAB-H; McGEWB; NatCAB 12; TwCBDA; WebAB; WhAm H*

DeAngeli, Marguerite
American. Children's Author
b. Mar 14, 1889 in Lapeer, Michigan
Source: *AmAu&B; Au&ICB; Au&Wr 71; AuBYP; AuNews 2; BkCL; ChlLR 1; ChPo, S1; ConAu 5R, 3NR; ConICB; CurBio 47; HerW; IlsCB 1744, 1946, 1957; InWom; JBA 51; MorBMP; Newb 1922; SmATA 1, 27; WhoAm 74; WhoAmA 73*

Dearden, John Francis, Cardinal
American. Ecclesiastic
b. Oct 15, 1907 in Valley Falls, Rhode Island
Source: *CurBio 69; IntWW 74; WhoAm 78, 80, 82; WhoHol A*

Dearie, Blossom
American. Nightclub Singer
b. Apr 28, 1926 in East Durham, New York
Source: *BioIn 9, 10*

DeBakey, Michael Ellis
American. Surgeon
Implanted first artificial heart in man, 1966.
b. Sep 7, 1908 in Lake Charles, Louisiana
Source: *AmM&WS 73P; CelR 73; CurBio 64; IntWW 74; LEduc 74; NewCol 75; Who 74; WhoAm 74, 76, 78, 80, 82; WhoS&SW 73; WhoWor 74; WrDr 76*

DeBalzac, Honore
see: Balzac, Honore de

DeBanzie, Brenda
English. Actress
b. 1915 in Manchester, England
d. Mar 5, 1981 in Maywards Heath, England
Source: *BiE&WWA; FilmgC; IntMPA 75, 76, 77, 78, 79, 80, 81; JohnWil 82; NotNAT; WhThe; WhoHol A; WhoThe 72*

DeBarentzen, Patrick
Danish. Couturier, Designer
Source: *WorFshn*

DeBartolo, Edward J, Jr.
American. Businessman
Owner, president, San Francisco 49ers football team, 1977--.
b. Nov 6, 1946 in Youngstown, Ohio
Source: *NewYTBE 73; WhoAm 80, 82*

DeBeauvoir, Simone
see: Beauvoir, Simone de

DeBeck, Billy
American. Cartoonist
b. Apr 15, 1890 in Chicago, Illinois
d. Nov 11, 1942 in New York, New York
Source: *WorECom*

Debecker, Luc Jean Francois
Discovered Cave Paintings
Source: *NF*

Debell, Kristine
Actress, Model
Source: *NF*

DeBernardi, Forrest S
American. Basketball Player
b. Mar 3, 1899 in Nevada, Missouri
d. Apr 29, 1970
Source: *BioIn 9; WhoBbl 73*

Deborah
Biblical Character
Source: *DcOrL 3; InWom*

Debost, Michel H
French. Musician
b. 1934 in Paris, France
Source: *WhoMus 72*

Debray, (Jules) Regis
French. Writer, Governmant Official
b. Sep 2, 1940 in Paris, France
Source: *BioIn 10; ConAu 21R; CurBio 82; NewYTBE 70; WhoAm 74*

Debre, Michel Jean Pierre
French. Premier, Statesman
b. Jan 15, 1912 in Paris, France
Source: *BioIn 4, 5, 6, 7; CurBio 59; WhoWor 74*

Debrett, John
English. Publisher
b. 1752
d. 1822
Source: *Alli; BiDLA; NewC; REn*

DeBroca, Philippe Claude Alex
French. Motion Picture Director
b. Mar 15, 1933 in Paris, France
Source: *BiDFilm; DcFM; FilmgC; IntMPA 75, 76, 77, 78, 79, 80, 81, 82; MovMk; OxFilm; WhoWor 74; WorEFlm*

DeBrunhoff, Laurent
see: Brunhoff, Laurent de

Debs, Eugene Victor
American. Socialist Leader; Union Organizer
First president, American Railway Union, 1893; formed Social Democratic Party, 1898.
b. Nov 5, 1855 in Terre Haute, Indiana
d. Oct 20, 1926 in Elmhurst, Illinois
Source: *AmBi; AmLY; DcAmB; DcNAA; EncAB-H; IndAu 1816; OxAmL; REn; REnAL; TwCBDA; WebAB; WhAm 1*

Debus, Kurt Heinrich
American. Space Agency Official
b. Nov 29, 1908 in Frankfurt, Germany
Source: *CurBio 73; IntWW 74; WhoAm 74; WhoGov 72; WhoS&SW 73; WhoWor 74*

Debus, Sigurd Friedrich
German. Terrorist
b. 1943
d. Apr 16, 1981 in Hamburg, Germany (West)
Source: *BioIn 12*

DeBusschere, Dave (David Albert)
"The Buffalo"
American. Basketball Player, Executive
b. Oct 16, 1940 in Detroit, Michigan
Source: *BioIn 7, 10; BioNews 75; CelR 73; CurBio 73; WhoAm 74, 76, 78, 80; WhoBbl 73*

Debussy, Claude Achille
French. Composer
Founded Impressionist School in music; composed "L'Apres-Midi d'un Fanne," 1894.
b. Aug 22, 1862 in Saint Germain, France
d. Mar 25, 1918 in Paris, France
Source: *AtlBL; BioIn 1, 2, 3, 4, 5, 6, 7, 8, 9, 10, 11; DcCM; OxFr; REn*

DeButts, John Dulany
American. Corporate Chairman
b. Apr 10, 1915 in Greensboro, North Carolina
Source: *IntWW 74; St&PR 75; WhoAm 74, 76, 78, 80, 82; WhoE 74; WhoF&I 74*

Debye, Peter Joseph William
American. Physicist
b. Mar 24, 1884 in Maastricht, Netherlands
d. Nov 2, 1966 in Ithaca, New York
Source: *BioIn 2, 3, 4, 6, 7, 8, 9, 11; CurBio 63, 67*

DeCamp, L(yon) Sprague
American. Author
b. Nov 27, 1907 in New York, New York
Source: *AuBYP; ConAu 1R, 1NR; SmATA 9; WhoAm 82; WorAu; WrDr 76*

DeCamp, Rosemary
American. Actress
Wrote children's story, *Here Duke,* 1962.
b. Nov 14, 1910 in Prescott, Arizona
Source: *InWom; IntMPA 75, 76, 77, 78, 79, 80, 81, 82; MotPP; WhoAm 82; WhoHol A*

Decamps, Alexandre Gabriel
French. Artist
b. Mar 3, 1803 in Paris, France
d. Aug 22, 1860 in Fontainebleau, France
Source: *NewCol 75*

DeCarlo, Yvonne
[Peggy Yvonne Middleton]
Canadian. Actress
Played Lily on TV series "The Munsters," 1964-66.
b. Sep 1, 1924 in Vancouver, BC
Source: *BiDFilm; CelR 73; CmMov; FilmgC; InWom; IntMPA 75, 76, 77, 78, 79, 80, 81, 82; MotPP; MovMk; PlP&P A; WhoHol A; WorEFlm*

Decatur, Stephen
American. Naval Officer
b. Jan 5, 1779 in Sinepuxent, Maryland
d. Mar 22, 1820 in Bladensburg, Maryland
Source: *AmBi; ApCAB; DcAmB; Drake; REn; TwCBDA; WebAB; WhAm H*

DeChardin, Pierre Teilhard
see: Teilhard de Chardin, Pierre

De Chavannes, Pierre Cecile Puvis
see: Puvis de Chavannes, Pierre Cecile

Decker, Mary
see: Tabb, Mary Decker

Decker, Thomas
see: Dekker, Thomas

Deckers, Jeanine
Singing Nun
b. 1933
Source: *BioIn 7, 9, 10*

DeConcini, Dennis Webster
American. Senator
b. May 8, 1937 in Tucson, Arizona
Source: *AlmAP 78, 80; CngDr 77, 79; IntWW 77, 78; NewYTBS 78; WhoAm 78, 80, 82; WhoAmL 79; WhoAmP 73, 75, 77, 79; WhoGov 77; WhoWest 74, 76, 78*

DeCordoba, Pedro
American. Actor
b. Sep 28, 1881 in New York, New York
d. Sep 17, 1950 in Sunland, California
Source: *Film 1; FilmgC; MotPP; MovMk; TwYS; WhScrn 74, 77; WhoHol B*

Decoster, Charles Theodore
Belgian. Author
b. Aug 20, 1827 in Munich, Germany
d. May 7, 1879 in Brussels, Belgium
Source: *BbD; BiD&SB; CasWL; ClDMEL; EuAu*

DeCreeft, Jose
American. Sculptor
b. Nov 27, 1884 in Guadalajara, Spain
Source: *CurBio 42; DcCAA 71; WhoAm 74; WhoAmA 73*

DeCrevecoeur, Michel-Guillaume Jean
see: Crevecoeur, Michel-Guillaume Jean de

Decter, Midge
American. Journalist
b. Jul 25, 1927 in Saint Paul, Minnesota
Source: *ConAu 45, 2NR; CurBio 82; WhoAm 76, 78, 80, 82; WhoAmW 77; WhoE 74; WrDr 76*

Dederich, Charles E
American. Founder of Synanon
b. 1913
Source: *BioIn 8, 11*

Dedijer, Vladimir
Yugoslav. Author
b. Feb 2, 1914 in Belgrade, Yugoslavia
Source: *Au&Wr 71; ConAu 1R, 4NR; IntWW 74; Who 74; WhoWor 74*

Dee, Frances
American. Actress
b. 1907 in Los Angeles, California
Source: *FilmgC; HolP 30; MotPP; MovMk; ThFT; WhoHol A; WomWMM*

Dee, Kiki
[Pauline Matthews]
English. Singer
b. Mar 6, 1947 in Bradford, England
Source: *BkPepl; RkOn*

Dee, Ruby
[Mrs. Ossie Davis; Ruby Ann Wallace]
American. Actress
Starred in stage, movie productions of *Raisin in the Sun,* 1959, 1961.
b. Oct 27, 1924 in Cleveland, Ohio
Source: *BiE&WWA; BlkAW; CelR 73; CurBio 70; FilmgC; IntMPA 82; MotPP; MovMk; NewYTBE 70; NotNAT; WhoAm 74, 76, 78, 80, 82; WhoBlA 75; WhoHol A; WhoThe 77; WomWMM*

Dee, Sandra
[Alexandra Zuck]
American. Actress, Singer
Starred in *Gidget,* 1959, *Tammy Tell Me True,* 1961; was married to Bobby Darrin.
b. Apr 23, 1942 in Bayonne, New Jersey
Source: *FilmgC; InWom; IntMPA 75, 76, 77, 78, 79, 80, 81, 82; MotPP; MovMk; WhoHol A*

Deep Purple
[Ritchie Blackmore; Thomas Bolin; David Coverdale; Rod Evans; IanGillan; Roger Glover; Glenn Hughs; Jon Lord; Ian Paige; Nicholas Simper]
American. Rock Group
Source: *EncPR&S; IlEncRk; RkOn*

Deeping, (George) Warwick
English. Author
b. May 28, 1877 in Southend, England
d. Apr 20, 1950 in Weybridge, England
Source: *DcLEL; EvLB; LongCTC; NewC; Pen ENG; REn; TwCA, SUP; TwCW; WhoLA*

DeErdely, Francis (Ferenc)
Hungarian. Artist, Teacher
b. May 3, 1904 in Budapest, Hungary
d. Nov 28, 1959
Source: *DcCAA 71; WhAm 4*

Deere, John
American. Industrialist
Developed, manufactured steel plow, 1837; incorporated Deere and Co., 1868.
b. Feb 7, 1804 in Rutland, Vermont
d. May 17, 1886 in Moline, Illinois
Source: *AmBi; DcAmB; EncAB-H; WebAB; WhAm H*

Deering, William
American. Manufacturer
b. Apr 25, 1826 in Paris, Maine
d. Dec 9, 1913 in Coconut Grove, Florida
Source: *AmBi; DcAmB; TwCBDA; WhAm 1*

Def Leppard
[Rick Allen; Steve Clark; Joe Elliott; Rick Savage; Peter Willis]
British. Rock Group
Heavy metal group from Sheffield, England; named after poster designed by Joe Elliott.
Source: *IlEncRk*

De Falla, Manuel
see: Falla, Manuel de

Defauw, Desire
Belgian. Conductor
b. Sep 5, 1885 in Ghent, Belgium
d. Jul 25, 1960 in Gary, Indiana
Source: *CurBio 40, 60; WhAm 4*

Defeo, Ronald
American. Murderer-Amityville Horror
b. 1951
Source: *BioIn 12*

Defoe, Daniel
English. Author
Wrote *Robinson Crusoe,* 1719, based on adventures of Alexander Selkirk.
b. Apr 26, 1661 in London, England
d. Apr 26, 1731 in London, England
Source: *Alli; AtlBL; BbD; BiD&SB; BrAu; CarSB; CasWL; Chambr 2; ChPo S1; CrtT 2; CyWA; DcBiA; DcEnA; DcEnL; DcEuL; DcLEL; EvLB; FilmgC; HsB&A; MnBBF; MouLC 2; NewC; OxEng; Pen ENG; RAdv 1; RComWL; REn; WebE&AL; WhoChL*

DeFore, Don
American. Actor
b. Aug 25, 1917 in Cedar Rapids, Iowa
Source: *BiE&WWA; FilmgC; MotPP; MovMk; NotNAT; WhoAm 74; WhoHol A*

DeForest, Lee
"Father of the Radio"
American. Inventor
Patented over 300 inventions; developed wireless radio, motion picture sound system.
b. Aug 26, 1873 in Council Bluffs, Iowa
d. Jun 30, 1961 in Hollywood, California
Source: *CurBio 41, 61; EncAB-H; FilmgC; WebAB; WhAm 4; WorEFlm*

DeFranco, Buddy
American. Jazz Musician
b. 1933
Source: *CmpEPM*

DeFrank, Vincent
American. Conductor
b. Jun 18, 1915 in Long Island, New York
Source: *WhoAm 74, 76, 78, 80, 82; WhoS&SW 73*

Defreeze, Donald David
"Cinque"
American. SLA Revolutionary
Leader of terrorist group that kidnapped Patricia Hearst, 1974.
b. 1944
d. May 24, 1974 in Los Angeles, California
Source: *BioIn 10, 11; BioNews 74; NewYTBS 74*

Degas, (Hilaire Germain) Edgar
French. Artist
Impressionist painter whose favorite subjects were ballet dancers, cafe life.
b. Jul 19, 1834 in Paris, France
d. Sep 27, 1917 in Paris, France
Source: *AtlBL; NewC; OxFr; REn; WhAm HA, 4*

DeGasperi, Alcide
see: Gasperi, Alcide de

DeGaulle, Charles Andre Joseph
French. President
Organized Free French Forces in London, Jun, 1940; president of France, 1959-69.
b. Nov 22, 1890 in Lille, France
d. Nov 9, 1970 in Colombey les deux Eglises, France
Source: *BioIn 10; CurBio 40, 49, 60, 70; REn; WhAm 5*

DeGhelderode, Michel
see: Ghelderode, Michel de

DeGivenchy, Hubert
see: Givenchy Hubert de

DeGoncourt, Edmond Louis
see: Goncourt, Edmond Louis Antoine Huot de

DeGoncourt, Jules Alfred Hout
see: Goncourt, Jules Alfred Hout de

DeGraff, Robert F(air)
American. Founder of Pocket Books
b. Jun 9, 1895 in Plainfield, New Jersey
d. Nov 1, 1981 in Mill Neck, New York
Source: *CurBio 43, 82*

DeHartog, Jan
Dutch. Author
b. Apr 22, 1914 in Haarlem, Netherlands
Source: *AmAu&B; CasWL; CnMD; ConAu 1R, 1NR; CurBio 70; EncWL; IntWW 74; NotNAT; TwCA SUP; WhoAm 74, 76, 78, 80, 82; WhoWor 74*

DeHaven, Gloria
American. Actress
b. Jul 23, 1925 in Los Angeles, California
Source: *BiE&WWA; FilmgC; MotPP; MovMk; WhoHol A*

DeHavilland, Geoffrey
English. Airplane Designer
b. Jul 27, 1882
d. May 21, 1965 in London, England
Source: *WhAm 4*

DeHavilland, Olivia
American. Actress
Played Melanie in *Gone With the Wind,* 1939; won Oscars, 1946, 1949.
b. Jul 1, 1916 in Tokyo, Japan
Source: *BiDFilm; BiE&WWA; CelR 73; CmMov; CurBio 66; FilmgC; IntMPA 75, 76, 77; MotPP; MovMk; OxFilm; ThFT; Who 74; WhoAm 74, 76, 78, 80, 82; WhoHol A; WorEFlm*

DeHidalgo, Elvira
see: Hidalgo, Elvira de

Dehmel, Richard
German. Poet
b. Nov 18, 1868 in Germany
d. Feb 8, 1920 in Blankenese, Germany
Source: *CasWL; ClDMEL; EncWL; EuAu; EvEuW; ModGL; OxGer; Pen EUR; REn*

Dehn, Adolf Arthur
American. Artist
b. Nov 22, 1895 in Waterville, Minnesota
d. May 19, 1968 in New York, New York
Source: *CurBio 41, 68; DcCAA 71; WhAm 5*

Dehnert, Henry
"Dutch"
American. Basketball Player
Developed the pivot play.
b. Apr 5, 1898 in New York, New York
d. Apr 20, 1979 in Far Rockaway, New York
Source: *NewYTBS 79; WhoBbl 73*

Deighton, Len
English. Cartoonist, Author
b. Feb 18, 1929 in London, England
Source: *ConAu 9R; ConLC 4, 7; ConNov 72, 76; IntMPA 75, 76, 77; IntWW 74; NewC; TwCW; WhoWor 74; WorAu; WrDr 76*

Deiss, Joseph Jay
American. Author
b. Jan 25, 1915 in Twin Falls, Idaho
Source: *Au&Wr 71; ConAu 33R; SmATA 12; WhoAm 74; WhoWor 74; WrDr 76*

Deitch, Kim
American. Cartoonist
b. 1944
Source: *BioIn 10*

Dejean, Alain
French. Photojournalist
b. 1935?
d. Oct 25, 1981 in Paris, France
Source: *BioIn 12*

DeJong, David Cornel
Dutch. Author
b. Jun 9, 1905 in Blija, Netherlands
d. Sep 5, 1967 in Providence, Rhode Island
Source: *AmAu&B; AmNov; AuBYP; ConAu 5R; CurBio 44, 67; OxAmL; REn; REnAL; SmATA 10; TwCA, SUP; WhAm 4A*

Dejong, Meindert
American. Children's Author
b. Mar 4, 1906 in Wierum, Netherlands
Source: *AnCL; Au&ICB; Au&Wr 71; AuBYP; BkCL; CasWL; ChlLR 1; ConAu 13R; CurBio 52; MorBMP; MorJA; Newb 1922; SenS; SmATA 2; WhoAm 74, 76, 78, 80, 82*

DeJong, Petrus
Dutch. Prime Minister
b. Apr 13, 1915 in Apeldoorn, Netherlands
Source: *WhoGov 72*

Dekker, Albert
American. Actor
b. Dec 20, 1905 in New York, New York
d. May 5, 1968 in Hollywood, California
Source: *BiE&WWA; FilmgC; MotPP; MovMk; Vers B; WhAm 5; WhScrn 74, 77; WhoHol B*

Dekker, Thomas
[Thomas Decker]
English. Dramatist
b. 1572 in London, England
d. 1632 in London, England
Source: *Alli; AtlBL; BbD; BiD&SB; BrAu; CasWL; Chambr 1; ChPo, S1, S2; CnE&AP; CnThe; CroE&S; CrtT 1; CyWA; DcEnA; DcEnL; DcLEL; EvLB; McGEWD; MouLC 1; NewC; OxEng; OxThe; Pen ENG; PlP&P; REn; REnWD; WebE&AL*

DeKnight, Jimmy
[James E Myers]
American. Composer
b. Oct 26, in Philadelphia, Pennsylvania
Source: *AmSCAP 66*

DeKooning, Elaine Marie Catherine Fried
American. Artist, Art Critic
b. Mar 12, 1920 in New York, New York
Source: *CurBio 82; DcCAA 71; WhoAm 74, 76, 78, 80, 82; WhoAmA 73; WhoE 74*

DeKooning, Willem
American. Artist
Abstract Expressionism leader, 1940's; known for distorted portraits of women.
b. Apr 24, 1904 in Rotterdam, New Hampshire
Source: *CelR 73; CurBio 55; DcCAA 71; EncAB-H; IntWW 74; REn; WebAB; WhoAm 74, 76, 78, 80, 82; WhoAmA 73; WhoWor 74*

DeKoven, (Henry Louis) Reginald
American. Composer, Music Critic
b. Apr 3, 1861 in Middletown, Connecticut
d. Jan 16, 1920 in Chicago, Illinois
Source: *AmAu&B; AmBi; AmSCAP 66; ApCAB SUP; DcAmB; EncMT; NewCBMT; OxAmL; REn; REnAL; TwCBDA; WhoStg 1906, 1908*

DeKruif, Paul Henry
American. Bacteriologist, Author
b. Mar 2, 1890 in Zeeland, Michigan
d. Feb 28, 1971 in Holland, Michigan
Source: *AmAu&B; BiE&WWA; ConAu 9R, 29R; CurBio 42, 63, 71; JBA 34; LongCTC; OxAmL; REn; REnAL; SmATA 5; TwCA, SUP; WhAm 5*

Delacorte, George Thomas, Jr.
American. Newspaper, Magazine Publisher
b. Jun 20, 1894 in New York, New York
Source: *CelR 73; CurBio 65; St&PR 75; WhoAm 74, 76, 78, 80, 82; WhoAmA 73; WhoWor 74*

DeLaCova, Carlos Perez
see: Perez de la Cova, Carlos

Delacroix, (Ferdinand Victor) Eugene
French. Artist
b. Apr 26, 1798 in Charenton, France
d. Aug 13, 1863 in Paris, France
Source: *AtlBL; OxFr; REn*

Delahanty, Edward James
"Big Ed"
American. Baseball Player
Only man to lead both leagues in hitting, 1899, 1902; Hall of Fame, 1945.
b. Oct 31, 1867 in Cleveland, Ohio
d. Jul 2, 1903 in Fort Erie, ON
Source: *BaseEn; BioIn 3, 6, 7, 10; WhoProB 73*

Delahanty, Thomas K
American. Police Officer Shot With R Reagan
b. 1935? in Pittsburgh, Pennsylvania
Source: *BioIn 12*

DelaMadrid Hurtado, Miguel
Mexican. President
Elected president, 1982.
b. 1935? in Colima, Mexico
Source: *NF*

Delamare, Delphine
French. Inspiration of Flaubert
b. 1822
d. 1848
Source: *BioIn 4; InWom*

DeLaMare, Walter
English. Author, Poet
b. Apr 25, 1873 in Charlton, England
d. Jun 22, 1956 in Twickenham, England
Source: *AnCL; AtlBL; AuBYP; BkCL; CarSB; CasWL; Chambr 3; ChPo, S1, S2; CnE&AP; CnMWL; CyWA; DcLEL; EncWL; EvLB; JBA 34, 51; LongCTC; ModBrL; NewC; OxEng; Pen ENG; RAdv 1; REn; Str&VC; TwCA, SUP; TwCW; WebE&AL; WhAm 3; WhoChL; WhoTwCL*

Deland, Margaret Wade
American. Author
b. Feb 23, 1857 in Allegheny, Pennsylvania
Source: *AmAu&B; BbD; BiD&SB; Chambr 3; ChPo, S1; ConAmL; CurBio 45; DcAmAu; DcBiA; DcEnL*

DeLanda, Diego
see: Landa, Diego de

Delaney, Jack
Canadian. Boxer
b. Mar 18, 1900 in Saint Francis, PQ
d. Nov 27, 1948 in Katonah, New York
Source: *BioIn 1, 10; WhoBox 74*

Delaney, Shelagh
English. Dramatist
b. 1939 in Salford, England
Source: *BiE&WWA; CnMD; ConAu 17R; ConDr 73; CroCD; CurBio 62; InWom; LongCTC; McGEWD; ModWD; NewC; NotNAT; Pen ENG; PlP&P; REn; TwCW; Who 74; WhoThe 77; WhoWor 74; WorAu; WrDr 76*

Delaney and Bonnie
[Delaney Bramlett; Bonnie Lynn]
American. Rock Duo
Source: *ConMuA 80; LilREn 78; WhoRock 81*

Delannoy, Jean
French. Motion Picture Director
b. Jan 12, 1908 in Noisy, France
Source: *DcFM; FilmgC; IntMPA 75, 76, 77, 78, 79, 80, 81, 82; WorEFlm*

Delano, Isaac O
Nigerian. Author
b. Nov 4, 1904 in Okenla, Nigeria
Source: *ConAu 25R*

Delany, Martin R
American. Author, Social Reformer
b. 1812
d. 1885
Source: *Alli; AmAu; BlkAW; DcNAA; EncAB-H; WebBD 80*

Delany, Samuel Ray, Jr.
American. Author
Helped to make science fiction a respected literary genre.
b. Apr 1, 1942 in New York, New York
Source: *BlkAW; ConAu 81; ConLC 8, 14; ConNov 76; DrAF 76; LivgBAA*

DeLaRamee, Louise
see: Ouida, pseud.

DeLaRenta, Oscar
American. Fashion Designer
Known for lavish evening clothes; won Coty awards, 1967, 1968.
b. Jul 22, 1932 in Santo Domingo, Dominican Republic
Source: *BioNews 74; CelR 73; CurBio 70; WhoAm 74, 76, 78, 80, 82; WorFshn*

Delaroche, Hippolyte
[Paul Delaroche]
French. Artist
b. 1797
d. 1856
Source: *NewCol 75; OxFr*

DeLaRoche, Mazo
Canadian. Author
b. Jan 15, 1885? in Toronto, ON
d. Jul 12, 1961 in Toronto, ON
Source: *CanNov; CanWr; CasWL; Chambr 3; ConAu 85; ConLC 14; CyWA; DcLEL; EvLB; InWom; JBA 34; LongCTC; OxAmL; OxCan; OxEng; Pen ENG; REn; REnAL; TwCA, SUP; TwCW; WhAm 4; WhNAA*

DeLaRochefoucauld, Duc
see: LaRochefoucauld, Francois, Duc de

Delaunay, Robert
French. Artist
b. Apr 12, 1885 in Paris, France
d. Oct 25, 1941 in Montpellier, France
Source: *AtlBL*

Delaunay-Terk, Sonia
French. Artist
b. Nov 14, 1885 in Gradizhsk, Russia
d. Dec 5, 1979 in Paris, France
Source: *BioIn 4, 5, 8, 10, 11, 12; ConArt; CurBio 77, 80; GoodHS; NewYTBS 74; WhoAmW 70, 74; WhoWor 74, 78*

DeLaurentiis, Dino
Italian. Motion Picture Producer
Best known films *Serpico,* 1974, *King Kong,* 1976, *Ragtime,* 1981.
b. Aug 8, 1919 in Torre Annunziata, Italy
Source: *BiDFilm; CmMov; CurBio 65; DcFM; FilmgC; IntMPA 75, 76, 77; IntWW 74; OxFilm; WhoAm 82; WhoWor 74; WorEFlm*

DeLaurentiis, Federico
Italian. Motion Picture Producer
b. 1955?
d. 1981 in Kvichak Bay, Alaska
Source: *BioIn 12*

DeLavallade, Carmen
American. Dancer
b. Mar 6, 1931 in Los Angeles, California
Source: *BiE&WWA; CurBio 67; InWom; NotNAT; WhoAm 74; WhoBlA 75*

DeLaWarr, George
English. Researcher, Author
b. Aug 19, 1904 in Southwick, England
d. Mar 31, 1969
Source: *ConAu P-1*

Delbruck, Max
American. Molecular Geneticist
b. Sep 4, 1906 in Berlin, Germany
d. Mar 9, 1981 in Pasadena, California
Source: *AmM&WS 73P, 76P, 79P; IntWW 74, 75, 76, 77, 78; NewYTBS 81; WebAB; WhAm 7; Who 74; WhoAm 74, 76, 78; WhoWest 78*

Delderfield, Ronald Frederick
English. Author, Dramatist
b. Jun 24, 1912 in London, England
d. Jun 24, 1972 in Sidmouth, England
Source: *Au&Wr 71; ConAu 37R, 73; NewYTBE 72; SmATA 20; WhThe*

Deledda, Grazia
Italian. Author
b. Sep 27, 1875 in Nvoro, Sardinia
d. Aug 16, 1936 in Rome, Italy
Source: *CasWL; ClDMEL; CyWA; EncWL; EvEuW; ModRL; Pen EUR; REn; TwCA, SUP; TwCW; WhoTwCL*

DeLeeuw, Adele Louise
American. Children's Author
b. Aug 12, 1899 in Hamilton, Ohio
Source: *AmAu&B; AuBYP; ConAu 1R, 1NR; JBA 51; OhA&B; SmATA 1; WhNAA; WhoAmW 77; WrDr 76*

DeLenclos, Anne
see: Lenclos, Ninon de

DeLenclos, Ninon
see: Lenclos, Ninon de

DeLeon, Juan Ponce
see: Ponce de Leon, Juan

DeLesseps, Ferdinand Marie
see: Lesseps, Ferdinand Marie de

DelGesu, Guarneri
see: Guarnieri, Giuseppe Antonio

Delibes, Leo
French. Composer
b. Feb 21, 1836 in Paris, France
d. Jan 16, 1891 in Paris, France
Source: *AtlBL; OxFr; REn*

Delilah
Biblical Character
Source: *InWom*

Delius, Frederick
English. Composer
b. Jan 29, 1862 in Bradford, England
d. Jun 10, 1934 in Grez-sur-Loing, France
Source: *AtlBL; DcCM; WhAm HA, 4*

Dell, Floyd
American. Editor, Author, Dramatist
b. Jun 28, 1887 in Barry, Illinois
d. Jul 23, 1969 in Bethesda, Maryland
Source: *AmAu&B; AnMV 1926; CnDAL; ConAmA; ConAu 89; DcLEL; LongCTC; ModAL; OxAmL; Pen AM; REn; REnAL; TwCA, SUP; WebAB; WhAm 5; WhNAA*

Dell, Gabriel
American. Actor
b. Oct 7, 1923 in Barbados, British West Indies
Source: *NewYTBE 72; NotNAT; WhoHol A; WhoThe 77*

DellaCasa, Lisa
[Lisa DellaCase-Debeljevic]
Swiss. Opera Singer
b. Feb 1, 1919 in Burgdorf, Switzerland
Source: *CurBio 56; InWom; IntWW 74; WhoMus 72; WhoWor 74*

DellaChiesa, Vivian
American. Opera Singer
b. Oct 9, 1915? in Chicago, Illinois
Source: *CurBio 43; InWom*

DellaFemina, Jerry
American. Advertising Executive, Author
b. Jul 22, 1936 in Brooklyn, New York
Source: *CelR 73; WhoAdv 72; WhoAm 82*

DellaRobbia, Andrea
Italian. Sculptor
b. 1435 in Florence, Italy
d. 1525
Source: *BioIn 1, 6, 9; NewCol 75*

DellaRobbia, Giovanni
Italian. Sculptor
b. 1469 in Florence, Italy
d. 1529
Source: *AtlBL; BioIn 10; OxDecA; WebBD 80*

DellaRobbia, Luca
Italian. Sculptor
b. 1400 in Florence, Italy
d. Feb 23, 1482 in Florence, Italy
Source: *AtlBL; REn*

Dellenbaugh, Frederick Samuel
American. Artist
b. Sep 13, 1853 in Ohio
d. Jan 29, 1935
Source: *AmAu&B; AmLY; DcAmAu; DcNAA; OhA&B; WhNAA*

Deller, Alfred George
English. Opera Singer
b. May 31, 1912 in Margate, England
d. Jul 16, 1979 in Bologna, Italy
Source: *BioIn 5, 7, 8, 9; Who 74*

Dellinger, David T (Dave)
[The Chicago 7]
American. Author, Editor, Activist
Chairman, National Mobilization Committee to End War in Vietnam, 1967-71.
b. Aug 22, 1915 in Wakefield, Massachusetts
Source: *BioIn 10, 11; ConAu 65; CurBio 76; WhoAm 76, 78, 80, 82*

Dello Joio, Norman Joseph
American. Composer
b. Jan 24, 1913 in New York, New York
Source: *CelR 73; CurBio 57; DcCM; LEduc 74; WebAB; WhoAm 74, 76, 78, 80, 82; WhoMus 72; WhoWor 74*

Dellums, Ronald
American. Politician
b. Nov 24, 1935 in Oakland, California
Source: *CngDr 74; CurBio 72; WhoAm 82; WhoAmP 73; WhoBlA 75; WhoGov 72*

Delmar, Kenny
American. Radio Actor
b. 1911?
Source: *BioIn 1; WhoHol A*

DelMar, Norman Rene
English. Conductor
b. Jul 31, 1919 in London, England
Source: *IntWW 74; Who 74; WhoMus 72*

Delmar, Vina Croter
American. Author
b. Jan 29, 1905 in New York, New York
Source: *AmAu&B; CnDAL; ConAu 65; OxAmL; REnAL; TwCA, SUP*

Delmas, Jacques Chaban
see: Chaban-Delmas, Jacques

DelMonaco, Mario
Italian. Opera Singer
Tenor, most noted for rendition of Verdi's *Otello,* performed 427 times.
b. Jul 27, 1915 in Florence, Italy
d. Oct 16, 1982 in Venice, Italy
Source: *Baker 78; CurBio 57, 83; IntWW 74, 75, 76, 77, 78, 79, 80, 81; NewEOp 71; NewYTBS 82; WhoMus 72*

Delmonico, Lorenzo
Swiss. Restaurateur
With uncles, established Delmonico's Restaurant, NY City, circa 1834.
b. Mar 13, 1813 in Marengo, Switzerland
d. Sep 3, 1881 in Sharon Springs, New York
Source: *DcAmB; WebAB; WhAm H*

Delon, Alain
French. Actor
b. Nov 8, 1935 in Seceaux, France
Source: *BiDFilm; CelR 73; CurBio 64; FilmgC; IntMPA 75, 76, 77, 78, 79, 80, 81, 82; IntWW 74; MovMk; OxFilm; WhoHol A; WhoWor 74; WorEFlm*

DeLong, George Washington
American. Explorer, Naturalist
Died attempting to reach N Pole by way of Bering Strait, 1879-81.
b. Aug 22, 1844 in New York, New York
d. Oct 30, 1881 in Siberia, Russia
Source: *Alli SUP; AmAu&B; AmBi; ApCAB; BbD; BiD&SB; DcAmAu; DcAmB; DcNAA; TwCBDA; WhAm H*

DeLorean, John Zachary
American. Automobile Executive, Author
Chairman, DeLorean Motor Co., 1975--; arrested for smuggling drugs, 1982.
b. Jan 6, 1925 in Detroit, Michigan
Source: *BioNews 74; BusPN; CurBio 76; WhoAm 74, 76, 78, 80, 82; WhoF&I 74*

Deloria, Vine, Jr.
American. Lecturer, Political Activist
b. Mar 26, 1933 in Martin, South Dakota
Source: *AmAu&B; ConAu 53, 5NR; CurBio 74; SmATA 21; WhoAm 74, 76, 78, 80, 82*

DeLosAngeles, Victoria
see: Angeles, Victoria de los

Del Ray, Lester Ramon Alvarez
American. Author
b. Jun 2, 1915 in Saratoga, Minnesota
Source: *AmAu&B; AuBYP; ConAu 65; SmATA 22; WhoAm 80*

DelRio, Dolores
[Dolores Ansunsolo]
Mexican. Actress
b. Aug 3, 1905 in Durango, Mexico
Source: *BiDFilm; CelR 73; Film 1; FilmgC; InWom; IntMPA 75, 76, 77, 78, 79, 80, 81, 82; MovMk; OxFilm; TwYS; WhoHol A; WorEFlm*

DeLuca, Giuseppe
Italian. Opera Singer
b. Dec 29, 1876 in Rome, Italy
d. Aug 27, 1950 in New York, New York
Source: *CurBio 47, 50; DcAmB S4; WhAm 3*

DeLugg, Milton
American. Composer, Author, Conductor
b. Dec 2, 1918 in Los Angeles, California
Source: *AmSCAP 66*

DeLuise, Dom
American. Comedian, Actor
Appeared in films *Blazing Saddles,* 1974, *The End,* 1978.
b. Aug 1, 1933 in Brooklyn, New York
Source: *IntMPA 75, 76, 77, 78, 79, 80, 81, 82; WhoAm 74, 76, 78, 80, 82; WhoHol A*

Delvecchio, Alex
"Fats"
Canadian. Hockey Player, Coach
Center, Detroit Red Wings, 1950-73; Hall of Fame, 1977.
b. Dec 4, 1931 in Fort William, ON
Source: *WhoHcky 73*

DelVerrocchio, Andrea
see: Verrocchio, Andrea del

DeMagalhaes, Fernando
see: Magellan, Ferdinand

DeMalherbe, Francois
see: Malherbe, Francois de

DeManio, Jack
English. Broadcast Journalist
Host, BBC "Today" show, 1958-71.
b. Jan 26, 1914 in London, England
Source: *BioIn 9; ConAu 61; Who 74*

DeMar, Clarence
American. Track Athlete
b. 1888
d. Jun 11, 1958 in Reading, Massachusetts
Source: *BioIn 3, 4, 5, 6, 8*

Demara, Ferdinand Waldo, Jr.
"The Great Imposter"
American. Imposter
b. Dec 12, 1921 in Lawrence, Massachusetts
d. Jun 7, 1982 in Anaheim, California
Source: *BioIn 2, 4, 5, 6; NewYTBS 82*

DeMarco, Tony
American. Actor, Dancer
b. 1898 in Buffalo, New York
d. Nov 14, 1965 in Palm Beach, Florida
Source: *WhScrn 74, 77; WhoHol B*

DeMarco Sisters
[Arlene DeMarco; Gene DeMarco; Gloria DeMarco; Marie DeMarco]
American. Singers
Source: *InWom*

Demarest, William
American. Actor
Appeared in TV series "My Three Sons," 1967-73.
b. Feb 27, 1892 in Saint Paul, Minnesota
Source: *FilmgC; IntMPA 75, 76, 77, 78, 79, 80, 81, 82; MotPP; MovMk; TwYS; Vers A; WhoHol A*

Demaret, Jimmy (James Newton B)
American. Golfer
First to win Masters tournament three times; Hall of Fame, 1960.
b. May 10, 1910 in Houston, Texas
Source: *WhoGolf*

DeMarivaux, Pierre Carlet
see: Marivaux, Pierre Carlet de

DeMaupassant, Henri Rene Albert Guy
see: Maupassant, Henri Rene Albert Guy de

DeMedici, Catherine
see: Catherine de Medicis

DeMedici, Cosimo
see: Medici, Cosimo de

DeMedici, Francesco
see: Medici, Francesco de

DeMedici, Lorenzo
see: Medici, Lorenzo de

DeMedicis, Marie
see: Marie de Medicis

Demetrius I
[Demetrius Poliorcetes]
Macedonian. King
b. 337BC
d. 283BC
Source: *NewCol 75; WebBD 80*

DeMille, Agnes George
[Mrs. Walter Foy Prude]
American. Dancer, Author
Choreographer musicals *Oklahoma,* 1943, *Carousel,* 1945, *Brigadoon,* 1947.
b. 1905 in New York, New York
Source: *AmAu&B; BioNews 74; CelR 73; ConAu 65; CurBio 43; EncMT; HerW; InWom; NotNAT; REnAL; WebAB; Who 74; WhoAm 74, 76, 78, 80, 82; WhoThe 77; WhoWor 74*

DeMille, Cecil Blount
American. Motion Picture Director, Producer
With Jesse Lasky, Samuel Goldwyn, formed Jesse Lasky Feature Play Co., 1913; evolved into Paramount.
b. Aug 12, 1881 in Ashfield, Massachusetts
d. Jan 21, 1959 in Hollywood, California
Source: *AmAu&B; BiDFilm; CmMov; CurBio 42, 59; DcFM; EncAB-H; FilmgC; MovMk; OxFilm; REn; REnAL; TwYS; WebAB; WhAm 3; WhScrn 74, 77; WhoHol B; WomWMM; WorEFlm*

DeMiranda, Francisco
see: Miranda, Francisco de

Demirel, Suleyman
Turkish. Prime Minister
b. Oct 6, 1924 in Islamkoy, Asia Minor
Source: *BioIn 12; CurBio 80; IntWW 74*

Democritus
"The Laughing Philosopher"
Greek. Philosopher
Developed atomic theory: reality consists of atoms and space between them.
b. 460BC in Abdera, Greece
d. 370BC
Source: *CasWL; NewC; Pen CL; REn*

DeMontesquieu, Charles Louis
see: Montesquieu, Charles Louis de

DeMontfort, Simon
see: Montfort, Simon de

DeMoraes, Vinicius
see: Moraes, Vinicius de

DeMoss, Arthur S
American. Insurance Executive
b. Oct 26, 1925 in Albany, New York
Source: *WhoE 74; WhoF&I 74; WhoIns 75*

Demosthenes
Greek. Orator, Statesman
Considered greatest Greek orator; leader of democratic faction, Athens.
b. 384BC in Attica, Greece
d. Oct 322BC in Calavria, Greece
Source: *BbD; BiD&SB; CasWL; CyWA; DcEnL; NewC; OxEng; Pen CL; RComWL; REn*

DeMott, Benjamin Haile
American. Author, Educator
b. Jun 2, 1924 in Rockville Centre, New York
Source: *AmAu&B; ConAu 5R; DrAF 76; DrAS 74E; WhoAm 74, 76, 78, 80, 82; WorAu*

Dempsey, Jack (William Harrison)
American. Boxer
Heavyweight boxing champ, 1917-27, 1931-40; Hall of Fame, 1954.
b. Jan 24, 1895 in Manassa, Colorado
Source: *CelR 73; ConAu 89; CurBio 45; NewYTBE 70, 73; WebAB; WhoAm 74; WhoBox 74; WhoHol A; WhoWor 74*

Dempsey, John Noel
American. Former Governor
b. Jan 3, 1915 in Cahir, Ireland
Source: *CurBio 61; IntWW 74; WhoAm 74; WhoAmP 73*

Dempsey, Sir Miles Christopher
English. Army Officer
b. Dec 15, 1896 in Hoylake, England
d. Jun 6, 1969 in Yattendon, England
Source: *BioIn 1, 8; CurBio 44, 69*

Dempster, Carol
American. Actress
b. 1901 in Duluth, Minnesota
Source: *Film 1; FilmgC; MotPP; TwYS; WhoHol A*

DeMurville, (Jacques) Maurice Couve
see: Couve de Murville, (Jacques) Maurice

Demus, Joreg
Austrian. Musician
b. Dec 2, 1928 in Saint Poelten, Austria
Source: *BioIn 5; IntWW 78; WhoMus 72*

Demuth, Charles
American. Artist
b. Nov 8, 1883 in Lancaster, Pennsylvania
d. Oct 23, 1935 in Lancaster, Pennsylvania
Source: *DcAmB S1; DcCAA 71; EncAB-H; WebAB; WhAm HA, 4*

Demy, Jacques
French. Motion Picture Director
b. Jun 5, 1931 in Pont Chateau, France
Source: *BiDFilm; DcFM; FilmgC; IntWW 74; MovMk; OxFilm; WhoWor 74; WorEFlm*

DeNagybanya, Nicholas Horthy
see: Horthy de Nagybanya, Nicholas

Den Uyl, Joor
Dutch. Politician
b. 1919 in Amsterdam, Netherlands
Source: *IntWW 74*

Dench, Judith Olivia
English. Actress
b. 1934 in York, England
Source: *CnThe; FilmgC; IntMPA 77, 78, 79, 80, 81, 82; Who 74; WhoThe 72*

Denenberg, Herbert S
American. Educator, Lawyer
b. Nov 20, 1929 in Omaha, Nebraska
Source: *BioIn 9, 10, 11; ConAu 37R; WhoAm 82; WrDr 76*

Deneuve, Catherine
[Catherine Dorleac]
French. Actress
Starred in *Mayerling,* 1968; appears in print, TV ads for Chanel No. 5.
b. Oct 22, 1943 in Paris, France
Source: *BiDFilm; BkPepl; CelR 73; FilmgC; IntMPA 75, 76, 77, 78, 79, 80, 81, 82; IntWW 74; MotPP; MovMk; OxFilm; WhoAm 82; WhoHol A; WorEFlm*

Deng Xiaoping
see: Teng Hsiao-Ping

Denikin, Anton Ivanovich
Russian. General
b. 1872
d. Aug 8, 1947 in Ann Arbor, Michigan
Source: *BioIn 1, 5, 10; ObitOF 79; REn; WhoMilH 76*

DeNiro, Robert
American. Actor
Won Oscar, 1981, for *Raging Bull.*
b. Aug 17, 1943 in New York, New York
Source: *BkPepl; IntMPA 75, 76, 77, 78, 79, 80, 81, 82; MovMk; WhoAm 82; WhoHol A*

Denney, Charles Eugene
American. Railway Official
b. Oct 18, 1879 in Washington, DC
d. 1965
Source: *BioIn 1, 2, 7; WhAm 6*

Denning, Richard
American. Actor
b. Mar 27, 1914 in Poughkeepsie, New York
Source: *BioIn 3; FilmgC; MotPP; MovMk; WhoAm 74, 76, 78, 80, 82; WhoHol A*

Dennis, Patrick, pseud.
[Edward Everett Tanner]
American. Author
b. May 18, 1921 in Chicago, Illinois
d. Nov 6, 1976 in New York, New York
Source: *AmAu&B; ConAu 69, 73; CurBio 59; WhoAm 74; WorAu; WrDr 76*

Dennis, Sandy
American. Actress
Won Oscar, 1966, for *Who's Afraid of Virginia Woolf.*
b. Apr 27, 1937 in Hastings, Nebraska
Source: *BiE&WWA; CelR 73; CurBio 69; FilmgC; InWom; IntMPA 75, 76, 77, 78, 79, 80, 81, 82; MotPP; MovMk; NotNAT; WhoAm 74, 76, 78, 80, 82; WhoHol A; WhoThe 77*

Dennison, George
American. Editor, Author
Wrote *Oilers and Sweepers,* 1979.
b. Sep 10, 1925 in Ashburn, Georgia
Source: *AmAu&B; BioIn 10; ConAu 101*

Dennison, Robert Lee
American. Admiral
b. Apr 13, 1901 in Warren, Pennsylvania
d. Mar 14, 1980 in Bethesda, Maryland
Source: *BioIn 5; CurBio 60, 80*

Denny, Ludwell
American. Journalist
b. Nov 18, 1894 in Boonville, Indiana
d. Oct 12, 1970
Source: *AmAu&B; ConAu 29R; IndAu 1917; WhAm 5*

Denny, Reginald Leigh
English. Actor
b. Nov 20, 1891 in Richmond, England
d. Jun 16, 1967 in Surrey, England
Source: *BiE&WWA; Film 1; FilmgC; MotPP; MovMk; TwYS; Vers A; WhAm 4; WhScrn 74, 77; WhoHol B*

Denny-Brown, Derek Ernest
American. Neurologist, Author
b. Jun 1, 1901 in Christchurch, New Zealand
d. Apr 20, 1981 in Cambridge, Massachusetts
Source: *AmM&WS 73P, 76P, 79P; ConAu 103; IntWW 77, 78; NewYTBS 81; WhE&EA; Who 74; WhoAm 74*

Densmore, John
[The Doors]
American. Singer, Musician
b. Dec 1, 1945 in Los Angeles, California
Source: *NF*

Dent, Alan Holmes
Scottish. Author, Critic, Journalist
b. Jan 7, 1905 in Ayrshire, Scotland
d. Dec 1978
Source: *Au&Wr 71; ConAu 9R, 5NR; DcLEL 1940; IntAu&W 76, 77; LongCTC; Who 74; WhoThe 72, 77; WrDr 76*

Dent, "Bucky" (Russell Earl)
American. Baseball Player
b. Nov 25, 1951 in Savannah, Georgia
Source: *BaseEn; NewYTBS 79; WhoAm 82*

Dent, Edward Joseph
English. Opera Impressario, Author
b. Jul 16, 1876 in Ribston, England
d. Aug 22, 1957 in London, England
Source: *Chambr 1; NewEOp 71*

Denton, Jeremiah Andrew, Jr.
American. Senator, Former POW in Vietnam
b. Jul 15, 1924 in Mobile, Alabama
Source: *ConAu 69; CurBio 82; WhoAm 76, 78, 80, 82; WhoGov 77*

Denver, Bob
American. Actor
Starred in "The Many Loves of Doby Gillis," 1959-63; "Gilligan's Island," 1964-67.
b. 1935 in New Rochelle, New York
Source: *FilmgC; WhoHol A*

Denver, James William
American. Territorial Governor
b. Oct 23, 1817 in Winchester, Virginia
d. Aug 9, 1892 in Washington, DC
Source: *AmBi; ApCAB; BiAuS; BiDrAC; DcAmB; Drake; OhA&B; WhAm H; WhAmP*

Denver, John
[Henry John Deutschendorf]
American. Singer, Songwriter, Actor
Sang "Take Me Home Country Road," 1971; appeared in *Oh, God!,* 1977.
b. Dec 31, 1943 in Roswell, New Mexico
Source: *BioNews 74; BkPepl; CurBio 75; WhoAm 82*

DeOrtega, Francisco
see: Ortega, Francisco de

Depailler, Patrick
French. Auto Racer
b. Aug 8, 1944
d. Aug 1, 1980 in Heidelberg, Germany (West)
Source: *BioIn 11*

DePalma, Brian Russell
American. Motion Picture Director
b. Sep 11, 1940 in Newark, New Jersey
Source: *BioIn 10, 11; CurBio 82; FilmgC; IntMPA 77, 78, 79, 80, 81, 82; NewYTBE 73; WhoAm 78, 80, 82*

DePalma, Ralph
American. Auto Racer
b. 1883
d. Mar 31, 1956 in South Pasadena, California
Source: *BioIn 4, 6, 7, 10*

DePaolis, Alessio
Italian. Opera Singer
b. Apr 5, 1893 in Rome, Italy
d. Mar 9, 1964 in New York, New York
Source: *NewEOp 71; WhAm 4*

Depardieu, Gerard
French. Actor
b. Dec 27, 1948 in Chateauroux, France
Source: *BioIn 11; FilmEn; NewYTBS 81; WhoHol A*

DeParis, Wilbur
American. Jazz Musician
b. Sep 20, 1900 in Crawfordsville, Indiana
d. Jan 1973 in New York, New York
Source: *NewYTBE 73; WhAm 5; WhScrn 77; WhoJazz 72*

DePaul, Vincent
see: Vincent de Paul, Saint

Depew, Chauncey M
American. Senator, Philanthropist
b. Apr 23, 1834 in Peekskill, New York
d. Apr 5, 1928 in New York, New York
Source: *AmAu&B; AmBi; ApCAB; BiD&SB; BiDrAC; DcAmAu; DcAmB; DcNAA; REnAL; TwCBDA; WebAB; WhAm 1; WhAmP; WhNAA*

DePriest, Oscar Stanton
American. Congressman
b. 1871 in Florence, Alabama
d. May 12, 1951 in Chicago, Illinois
Source: *BiDrAC; DcAmB S5; WhAm 3; WhAmP*

DePugh, Robert Bolivar
American. Minutemen Organization Founder
b. 1925
Source: *BioIn 9, 11*

DeQuincey, Thomas
English. Author
b. Aug 15, 1785 in Greenheys, England
d. Dec 8, 1859 in Edinburgh, Scotland
Source: *Alli; AtlBL; BbD; BiD&SB; BrAu 19; CasWL; Chambr 3; CrtT 2; CyWA; DcBiA; DcEnA; DcEnL; DcEuL; DcLEL; EvLB; MouLC 3; NewC; OxEng; Pen ENG; RAdv 1; RComWL; REn; WebE&AL*

Derain, Andre
French. Artist
b. Jun 10, 1880 in Chatou, France
d. Sep 10, 1954 in Chambourcy, France
Source: *AtlBL; REn*

Derby, Jane (Jeanette Barr)
American. Costume Designer
b. May 17, 1895 in Rockymount, Virginia
d. Aug 7, 1965
Source: *BioIn 3, 7; WhAm 4*

DeRegniers, Beatrice Schenk
American. Children's Author
b. Aug 16, 1914 in Lafayette, Indiana
Source: *AmAu&B; Au&Wr 71; AuBYP; BkP; ChPo, S1; ConAu 13R; IndAu 1917; MorJA; SmATA 2; WhoAm 74, 76, 78, 80, 82; WhoE 74; WrDr 76*

Derek, Bo
[Mary Cathleen Collins; Mrs. John Derek]
American. Actress
Starred with Dudley Moore in *10,* 1979; fourth wife of John Derek.
b. 1956 in Long Beach, California
Source: *BioIn 12; BkPepl; IntMPA 82*

Derek, John
[Dereck Harris]
American. Actor
Starred in *The Ten Commandments,* 1956; former wives Linda Evans, Ursula Andress.
b. 1926 in Hollywood, California
Source: *CmMov; FilmgC; MotPP; MovMk; WhoHol A; WorEFlm*

DeReszke, Edouard
Polish. Opera Singer
b. Dec 22, 1853 in Warsaw, Poland
d. May 25, 1917 in Garnek, Poland
Source: *WhAm 1*

DeReszke, Jean
[Jan Mieczyslaw]
Polish. Opera Singer
b. Jan 14, 1850 in Warsaw, Poland
d. Apr 3, 1925 in Nice, France
Source: *ApCAB SUP; WhAm 2*

DeRita, Joe
[The Three Stooges]
"Curly Joe"
American. Comedian
Joined The Three Stooges, 1959.
Source: *MotPP; WhoHol A*

DeRivera, Jose
American. Artist, Sculptor
b. Sep 18, 1904 in West Baton Rouge, Louisiana
Source: *BioIn 4, 5; DcCAA 71; WhoAm 82; WhoAmA 73; WhoE 74*

Derleth, August
American. Author
b. Feb 24, 1909 in Sauk City, Wisconsin
d. Jul 4, 1971
Source: *AmAu&B; AmNov; AuBYP; BkC 6; ChPo, S2; CnDAL; ConAu 1R, 29R, 4NR; ConNov 72; DcLEL; EncMys; OxAmL; REn; REnAL; SmATA 5; TwCA, SUP; WhAm 5; WhNAA*

Dern, Bruce MacLeish
American. Actor
Starred with Jane Fonda, Jon Voight in *Coming Home,* 1978.
b. Jun 4, 1936 in Chicago, Illinois
Source: *BkPepl; CurBio 78; IntMPA 75, 76, 77, 78, 79, 80, 81, 82; WhoAm 74, 76, 78, 80, 82; WhoHol A; WorAl*

DeRoburt, Hammer
President of Nauru
b. 1922
Source: *BioIn 10; WhoWor 74*

DeRochemont, Louis
American. Motion Picture Producer
b. Jan 13, 1899 in Chelsea, Massachusetts
d. Dec 23, 1978 in York Harbor, Maine
Source: *CurBio 49; DcFM; FilmgC; IntMPA 75, 76, 77; OxFilm; WhoAm 74; WhoWor 74; WorEFlm*

DeRojas, Fernando
see: Rojas, Fernando de

DeRonsard, Pierre
see: Ronsard, Pierre de

DeRouvroy, Claude Henri
see: Saint-Simon, Claude-Henri de Rouvroy

Derringer, Rick
[Rick Zehringer]
American. Rock Singer, Musician
b. 1947 in Union City, Illinois
Source: *ConMuA 80; RkOn 2; WhoRock 81*

Derwentwater, Amelia Mary Tudor
English. Claimant, Impostor
b. 1830
d. 1880
Source: *BioIn 9*

DeSabata, Victor
Italian. Conductor, Composer
b. Apr 10, 1892 in Trieste, Italy
d. Dec 11, 1967 in Santa Margherita, Italy
Source: *NewEOp 71; OxMus*

DeSade, Marquis
see: Sade, Donatien de

Desai, Morarji Ranchodji
Indian. Political Leader
b. Feb 29, 1896 in Bhadeli, India
Source: *CurBio 58; IntWW 74; NewCol 75*

DeSalvo, Albert
"Boston Strangler"
American. Criminal
Never tried for slayings of 13 women, confessed to psychiatrist; stabbed to death in jail cell.
b. 1931
d. Dec 27, 1973 in Walpole Prison, Massachusetts
Source: *BioIn 7, 10*

DeSanctis, Francesco
Italian. Statesman, Literary Historian
b. Mar 28, 1817 in Morra Irpino, Italy
d. Dec 19, 1883 in Naples, Italy
Source: *BiD&SB; CasWL; ClDMEL; DcEuL; EuAu; EvEuW; Pen EUR; REn*

DeSantis, Giuseppe
Italian. Motion Picture Director
b. Feb 11, 1917 in Fondi, Italy
Source: *DcFM; FilmgC; IntMPA 75, 76, 77, 78, 79, 80, 81, 82; OxFilm; WorEFlm*

DeSapio, Carmine Gerard
American. Politician
b. Dec 10, 1908 in Manhattan, New York
Source: *CurBio 55*

Descartes, Rene
French. Mathematician, Philosopher
b. Mar 31, 1596 in La Haye, France
d. Feb 11, 1650 in Stockholm, Sweden
Source: *BbD; BiD&SB; CasWL; DcEuL; EuAu; EvEuW; NewC; OxEng; OxFr; Pen EUR; REn*

DeScudery, Madeleine
see: Scudery, Madeleine de

DeSegonzac, Andre Dunoyer
see: Dunoyer de Segonzac, Andre

DeSeversky, Alexander Procofieff
[Alexander de Seversky]
American. Aeronautical Engineer
b. Jun 7, 1894 in Tiflis, Russia
d. Aug 24, 1974 in New York, New York
Source: *CelR 73; ConAu 53; CurBio 41, 74; IntWW 74; NewYTBS 74; St&PR 75; WebAB; WhAm 6; Who 74; WhoAm 74; WhoF&I 74*

DeShannon, Jackie
American. Singer, Songwriter
b. Aug 21, 1944 in Hazel, Kentucky
Source: *EncPR&S*

Deshayes, Catherine
"La Voisin"
French. Poisoner
d. Feb 22, 1680 in Paris, France
Source: *LookW*

DeSica, Vittorio
Italian. Actor, Motion Picture Director
b. Jul 7, 1901 in Scra, Italy
d. Nov 13, 1974 in Paris, France
Source: *BiDFilm; DcFM; FilmgC; IntMPA 75; IntWW 74; MovMk; NewYTBE 72; OxFilm; REn; WhAm 6; WhScrn 77; Who 74; WhoAm 74; WhoHol B; WorEFlm*

DeSilhouette, Etienne
see: Silhouette, Etienne de

Desmond, Johnny
[Giovanni Alfredo DeSimone]
American. Singer, Actor
b. Nov 14, 1925 in Detroit, Michigan
Source: *AmSCAP 66; IntMPA 75, 76, 77, 78, 79, 80, 81, 82; WhoHol A*

Desmond, Paul Breitenfeld
American. Musician
b. Nov 25, 1924 in San Francisco, California
d. May 30, 1977 in New York, New York
Source: *WhoAm 74*

Desmond, William
American. Actor
b. May 21, 1878 in Dublin, Ireland
d. Nov 3, 1949 in Los Angeles, California
Source: *Film 1; FilmgC; MotPP; TwYS; WhScrn 74, 77; WhoHol B*

Desmoulins, Camille
French. Pamphleteer, Journalist
b. Mar 2, 1760 in Guise, France
d. Apr 5, 1794 in Paris, France
Source: *DcEuL; EvEuW; OxFr; REn*

Desormiere, Roger
French. Conductor
b. Sep 13, 1898 in Vichy, France
d. Oct 25, 1963 in Paris, France
Source: *NewEOp 71*

DeSoto, Hernando
Spanish. Explorer
First to see and cross Mississippi River, 1539-42.
b. 1500 in Barcarrota, Spain
d. May 21, 1542 in Ferriday, Louisiana
Source: *AmBi; DcAmB; DcCathB; EncSoH; LuthC 75; McGEWB; OxAmH; REn; REnAL; REnAW; WhAm H; WhFla; WorAl*

DesPres, Josquin
[Josse Depres]
Flemish. Composer
b. 1445? in Conde sur l'Escaut, France
d. Aug 27, 1521 in Conde, France
Source: *AtlBL*

Dessalines, Jean J
Haitian. Emperor
b. 1758 in Guinea
d. Oct 17, 1806 in Haiti
Source: *ApCAB; Drake; REn*

Desses, Jean
French. Fashion Designer
b. Aug 6, 1904 in Alexandria, Egypt
d. Aug 2, 1970 in Athens, Greece
Source: *CurBio 56, 70; NewYTBE 70; WhAm 5; WhoFash; WorFshn*

D'Estaing, Charles Henri Hector, Comte
see: Estaing, Charles Henri Hector, Comte d'

D'Estaing, Valery Giscard
see: Giscard d'Estaing, Valery

Destinn, Emmy
[Emmy Kittl]
Czech. Opera Singer
b. Feb 26, 1878 in Prague, Czechoslovakia
d. Jan 28, 1930 in Budejovice, Czechoslovakia
Source: *WhAm 1; WhScrn 77*

Destouches, Louis-Ferdinand
[Louis-Ferdinand Celine]
French. Author
b. May 27, 1894 in Paris, France
d. Jul 4, 1961 in Paris, France
Source: *ConAu 85; ConLC 9, 15; LongCTC; REn; TwCA, SUP*

Destri, Jimmy
see: Blondie

DeSylva, "Buddy" (George Gard)
American. Songwriter, Producer
b. Jan 27, 1896 in New York, New York
d. Jul 11, 1950 in Oak Park, Illinois
Source: *CurBio 43, 50; DcAmB S4; WhAm 3*

Deterding, Sir Henri Wilhelm August
Dutch. Founded Shell Oil Co.
b. 1866
d. 1939 in Germany
Source: *BioIn 4*

DeTocqueville, Alexis, Comte de
see: Tocqueville, Alexis, Comte de

DeToledano, Ralph
see: Toledano, Ralph de

Dett Robert Nanthaniel
American. Composer
b. Oct 11, 1882 in Drummondsville, ON
d. Oct 2, 1943 in Battle Creek, Michigan
Source: *AmAu&B; AmSCAP 66; CurBio 73*

Deukmejan, George
American. Governor of California
Defeated Tom Bradley for governor, 1982.
b. Jun 6, 1928 in Albany, New York
Source: *WhoAm 80, 82; WhoAmL 79; WhoAmP 73, 75, 77, 79; WhoWest 80*

Deutsch, Adolph
American. Composer
b. Oct 20, 1897 in London, England
d. Jan 1, 1980 in Palm Desert, California
Source: *AmSCAP 66; AnObit 1980; BioIn 1; CmpEPM*

Deutsch, Albert
American. Public Health Pioneer
b. Oct 23, 1905 in New York
d. Jun 18, 1961 in Horsham, England
Source: *AmAu&B; BioIn 1, 5; WhAm 4*

Deutsch, Babette
[Mrs. Avrahm Yarmolinsky]
American. Author, Poet
Verse concerned with social problems; first book, *Banners,* 1919.
b. Sep 22, 1895 in New York, New York
d. Nov 13, 1982 in New York, New York
Source: *AmAu&B; AnCL; Au&Wr 71; ChPo, S1, S2; ConAmL; ConAu 1R, 4NR; ConLC 18; ConP 70, 75; DcLEL; DrAP 75; DrAS 74E; EvLB; IntWW 74; LongCTC; MorJA; NewYTBS 82; OxAmL; Pen AM; RAdv 1; REn; REnAL; SmATA 1; TwCA, SUP; TwCW; WhNAA; WhoAm 74; WhoWor 74; WhoWorJ 72; WrDr 76*

Deutsch, Harold C
American. Author
b. Jun 7, 1904 in Milwaukee, Wisconsin
Source: *ConAu 21R; DrAS 74H*

Deutsch, Helene R
American. Psychoanalyst
Wrote *The Psychology of Women,* 1944.
b. Oct 9, 1884 in Przemysl, Austria-Hungary
d. Mar 29, 1982 in Cambridge, Massachusetts
Source: *NewYTBS 78, 82; WorAl*

Deutsch, Karl Wolfgang
American. Political Scientist
b. Jul 12, 1912 in Prague, Czechoslovakia
Source: *AmM&WS 73; ConAu 41R; WhoAm 74, 76, 78, 80, 82; WhoWor 74*

DeVaca, Alvar Nunez Cabeza
see: Cabeza de Vaca, Alvar Nunez

DeValera, Eamon
Irish. Statesman
b. Oct 14, 1882 in New York, New York
d. Aug 30, 1975 in Dublin, Ireland
Source: *ConAu 89; CurBio 40, 51; IntWW 74; REn; WhAm 6; Who 74; WhoGov 72; WhoWor 74*

DeValois, Ninette
British. Choreographer, Author
b. Jun 6, 1898 in Blessington, Ireland
Source: *Au&Wr 71; CurBio 49; IntWW 74; PlP&P; WhThe; Who 74; WhoAmW 74*

Devane, William
American. Actor
b. Sep 5, 1937 in Albany, New York
Source: *IntMPA 82; WhoAm 82; WhoHol A*

DeVega, Lope
see: Lope de Vega

Devereaux, Robert
[Earl of Essex]
English. Courtier
b. Nov 19, 1566
d. Feb 25, 1601
Source: *Alli; NewC*

Devereux, George
Anthropologist, Author
b. Sep 13, 1908 in Lugos, Hungary
Source: *BiDPara; ConAu 69*

Devers, Jacob Loucks
American. Army Officer
b. Sep 8, 1887 in York, Pennsylvania
d. Oct 15, 1979 in Bethesda, Maryland
Source: *CurBio 42; Who 74*

DeVeuster, Joseph Damien
see: Damien, Father

DeVicenzo, Roberto
Argentine. Golfer
b. Apr 14, 1923 in Argentina
Source: *WhoGolf*

DeVigny, Alfred Comte
see: Vigny, Alfred, Comte de

DeVilleneuve, Justin
English. Publicity Agent
b. 1940?
Source: *BioIn 8, 9*

DeVincennes, Sieur
see: Vincennes, Francois Marie Bissot

Devine, Andy
American. Actor
b. Oct 7, 1905 in Flagstaff, Arizona
d. Feb 18, 1977 in Orange, California
Source: *CmMov; FilmgC; IntMPA 75, 76, 77; MotPP; MovMk; OxFilm; TwYS; WhoHol A*

Devine, Dan(iel John)
American. Football Coach
b. Dec 23, 1924 in Augusta, Wisconsin
Source: *WhoAm 74; WhoFtbl 74*

Devine, Michael
[Irish Hunger Strikers]
Irish. Jailed IRA Member
b. 1954? in Londonderry, Northern Ireland
d. Aug 20, 1981 in Belfast, Northern Ireland
Source: *NF*

DeVinne, Theodore Low
American. Typographer, Printer
b. Dec 25, 1828 in Stamford, Connecticut
d. Feb 16, 1914 in New York, New York
Source: *AmAu&B; AmBi; ApCAB; DcAmAu; DcAmB; DcNAA; OxAmL; REn; REnAL; TwCBDA; WebAB; WhAm 1*

DeVita, Vincent Theodore, Jr.
American. Chemotherapist
b. Mar 7, 1935 in Bronx, New York
Source: *AmM&WS 73P, 76P, 79P; WhoAm 78, 80, 82; WhoS&SW 73*

DeVito, Danny Michael
American. Actor
Plays Louis DePalma on TV series "Taxi," 1978--; won Emmy, 1981.
b. Nov 27, 1944 in Neptune, New Jersey
Source: *BioIn 12; IntMPA 82; WhoAm 82*

DeVito, Tommy
[The Four Seasons]
American. Singer, Musician
b. Jun 19, 1935 in Belleville, New Jersey
Source: *NF*

Devlin, Bernadette Josephine
[Bernadette Devlin McAliskey]
Irish. Political Activist
At age 21, youngest woman elected to British Parliament, 1969-74.
b. Apr 23, 1947 in Cookstown, Northern Ireland
Source: *BlueB 76; CelR 73; CurBio 70; HerW; Who 74, 82; WhoAmW 72, 74; WhoWor 74; WorAl*

Devo
[Bob Casale; Jerry Casale; Bob Mothersbaugh; Mark Mothersbaugh; Alan Myers]
American. Rock Group
Source: *ConMuA 80; WhoRock 81*

DeVos, Richard Martin
American. Business Executive
Co-founder, president, Amway Corp.
b. Mar 4, 1926 in Grand Rapids, Michigan
Source: *WhoAdv 80; WhoAm 74, 76, 78, 80, 82; WhoF&I 74, 77; WhoWor 78*

DeVoto, Bernard Augustine
[John August, pseud.]
American. Author, Journalist, Critic
b. Jan 11, 1897 in Ogden, Utah
d. Nov 13, 1955 in New York, New York
Source: *AmAu&B; AmNov; AuNews 1; CnDAL; ConAmA; DcAmB S5; DcLEL; EncWL; LongCTC; ModAL; OxAmL; Pen AM; RAdv 1; REn; REnAL; TwCA, SUP; WebAB; WhAm 3; WhNAA*

DeVries, David Pieterson
Dutch. Colonizer in America
Founded colonies on Staten Island called New Netherlands.
b. 1592 in LaRochelle, France
d. 1655
Source: *ApCAB; DcAmB; WhAm H*

DeVries, Hugo
Dutch. Botanist
b. Feb 16, 1848 in Haarlem, Netherlands
d. May 21, 1935 in Amsterdam, Netherlands
Source: *NewCol 75*

DeVries, Peter
American. Author
b. Feb 27, 1910 in Chicago, Illinois
Source: *AmAu&B; Au&Wr 71; BiE&WWA; CelR 73; CnDAL; ConAu 17R; ConLC 1, 2, 3, 7, 10; ConNov 72, 76; DrAF 76; EncWL; IntWW 74; ModAL, SUP; NotNAT; OxAmL; Pen AM; REnAL; Who 74; WhoAm 74, 76, 78, 80, 82; WhoTwCL; WhoWor 74; WorAu; WrDr 76*

DeVries, William Castle
American. Surgeon
Implanted artificial heart in Barney Clark, 1982.
b. Dec 19, 1943 in Brooklyn, New York
Source: *WhoAm 82*

DeWaart, Edo
Dutch. Conductor
b. Jun 1, 1941 in Amsterdam, Netherlands
Source: *WhoAm 82; WhoWor 74*

Dewaere, Patrick
[Patrick Maurin]
French. Actor
Films include *Beau Pere, Get Out Your Hankerchiefs.*
b. Jan 26, 1947 in Saint-Brieuc, France
d. Jul 16, 1982 in Paris, France
Source: *FilmEn; NewYTBS 82*

Dewey, Charles Schuveldt
American. Government Official
b. Nov 10, 1882 in Cadiz, Ohio
d. Dec 26, 1980 in Washington, DC
Source: *BiDrAC; BioIn 1, 2; CurBio 49, 81; WhoAm 74; WhoGov 72, 75*

Dewey, George
American. Naval Officer
b. Dec 26, 1837 in Montpelier, Vermont
d. Jan 16, 1917 in Washington, DC
Source: *AmBi; ApCAB SUP; DcAmB; DcNAA; EncAB-H; REn; TwCBDA; WebAB; WhAm 1*

Dewey, John
American. Philosopher, Educator
Philosophy "Instrumentalism" says human activity developed by man to solve problems.
b. Oct 20, 1859 in Burlington, Vermont
d. Jun 1, 1952 in New York, New York
Source: *Alli SUP; AmAu&B; CasWL; ConAmA; DcAmAu; DcAmB S5; DcLEL; EncAB-H; EvLB; LongCTC; OxAmL; OxEng; Pen AM; REn; REnAL; TwCA, SUP; WebAB; WebE&AL; WhAm 3; WhNAA; WhoTwCL*

Dewey, Melvil
American. Librarian
b. Dec 10, 1851 in Adams Center, New York
d. Dec 26, 1931 in Lake Placid, Florida
Source: *Alli SUP; AmAu&B; AmBi; AmLY; ApCAB; DcAmAu; DcAmB S1; DcNAA; OxAmL; REn; REnAL; TwCBDA; WebAB; WhAm 1; WhNAA*

Dewey, Thomas Edmund
American. Politician
Ran for president, 1948, against Truman; lost very close race.
b. Mar 24, 1902 in Owosso, Michigan
d. Mar 16, 1971 in Bal Harbour, Florida
Source: *CurBio 40, 71; EncAB-H; NewYTBE 71; WebAB; WhAm 5*

Dewhurst, Colleen
Canadian. Actress
b. Jun 3, 1926 in Montreal, PQ
Source: *BiE&WWA; BioNews 74; CelR 73; CurBio 74; IntMPA 82; MovMk; NotNAT; PlP&P A; WhoAm 74, 76, 78, 80, 82; WhoHol A; WhoThe 77*

DeWilde, Brandon
American. Actor
b. Apr 9, 1942 in New York, New York
d. Jul 6, 1972 in Denver, Colorado
Source: *BiE&WWA; FilmgC; MotPP; MovMk; NewYTBE 72; OxFilm; WhAm 5; WhScrn 77; WhoHol B*

DeWitt, Joyce
American. Actress
Plays Janet Wood on TV series "Three's Company," 1977--.
b. Apr 23, 1949 in Wheeling, West Virginia
Source: *BioIn 11; IntMPA 82; WhoAm 80, 82*

DeWitt, William Orville, Sr.
American. Baseball Executive
Associated with nine pennant-winning teams.
b. Aug 3, 1902 in Saint Louis, Missouri
d. Mar 3, 1982 in Cincinnati, Ohio
Source: *NewYTBS 82; WhoAm 74, 76, 78; WhoF&I 74, 75; WhoMW 74, 76, 78; WhoProB 73*

DeWohl, Louis
[Ludwig Von Wohl-Musciny]
German. Author
b. Jan 24, 1903 in Berlin, Germany
d. Jun 2, 1961 in Lucerne, Switzerland
Source: *BioIn 3, 4, 5, 6; CurBio 55, 61*

DeWolfe, Billy
[Billy Jones]
American. Actor
b. Mar 6, 1907 in Wollaston, Massachusetts
d. Mar 5, 1974 in Los Angeles, California
Source: *BiE&WWA; FilmgC; HolP 40; MotPP; MovMk; NewYTBS 74; Vers B; WhScrn 77; WhoHol B*

DeWolfe, Lady Elsie
see: Mendl, Lady Elsie de Wolfe

Dexter, Al
American. Singer, Songwriter
b. May 4, 1902 in Jacksonville, Texas
Source: *EncFCWM 69*

Dexter, John
English. Motion Picture Director
b. Aug 2, 1925 in Derby, England
Source: *BioIn 9, 10, 11; CnThe; CurBio 76; EncWT; NotNAT; WhoAm 78, 80, 82; WhoOp 76*

Dey, Susan Hallock
American. Model, Actress
b. Dec 10, 1952 in Pekin, Illinois
Source: *IntMPA 82; WhoAm 74; WhoHol A*

DeYoung, Cliff
American. Actor
b. Feb 12, 1945 in Los Angeles, California
Source: *NF*

DeYoung, Michel Harry
American. Newspaper Editor
b. Oct 1, 1849 in Saint Louis, Missouri
d. Feb 15, 1925
Source: *NatCAB 1; WebBD 80; WhAm 1*

Diaghilev, Sergei Pavlovich
Russian. Ballet Producer, Art Critic
b. Mar 19, 1872 in Nizhni-Novgorod, Russia
d. Aug 19, 1929 in Venice, Italy
Source: *DcRusL; REn*

Diamand, Peter
Dutch. Concert Manager
b. Jun 8, 1913
Source: *BioIn 7; IntWW 74; Who 74; WhoWor 74*

Diamond, David
American. Composer
b. Jul 9, 1915 in Rochester, New York
Source: *AmSCAP 66; CurBio 66; DcCM; REnAL; WhoAm 74; WhoE 74; WhoMus 72; WhoWor 74; WhoWorJ 72*

Diamond, I(sidore) A L
American. Scriptwriter
b. Jun 27, 1920 in Unghani, Romania
Source: *CmMov; ConAu 81; IntMPA 76, 77, 78, 79, 80, 81, 82; OxFilm; WhoAm 82; WorEFlm*

Diamond, "Legs" (Jack)
[John Thomas Diamond]
American. Criminal
b. 1896 in Philadelphia, Pennsylvania
d. Dec 18, 1931 in Albany, New York
Source: *Blood*

Diamond, Neil
American. Singer, Songwriter, Actor
Wrote first song at age 15; has 13 consecutive gold albums; latest hit "Heartlight," 1982.
b. Jan 24, 1941 in Brooklyn, New York
Source: *BioNews 74; BkPepl; CelR 73; NewYTBE 72; WhoAm 74, 76, 78, 80, 82*

Diamond, Selma
American. Scriptwriter, TV Personality
Source: *BioIn 6*

Diana, Princess of Wales
[Lady Diana Frances Spencer]
English. Wife of Prince Charles
Married Prince Charles, Jul 29, 1981; several movies depict their romance.
b. Jul 1, 1961 in Sandringham, England
Source: *BioIn 12; CurBio 83; NewYTBS 81; Who 81*

Di'Anno, Paul
see: Iron Maiden

Dias, Bartholomew
[Bartholomew Diaz]
Portuguese. Navigator
First to sail around Cape of Good Hope, 1488; opened passage to India.
b. 1450
d. 1500
Source: *NewCol 75*

Diaz, Justino
Puerto Rican. Opera Singer
b. Jan 29, 1940 in San Juan, Puerto Rico
Source: *WhoAm 74, 76, 78, 80, 82; WorEFlm*

Diaz, Porfirio
[Jose de la Cruz Porfirio]
Mexican. President
b. Sep 15, 1830 in Oaxaca, Mexico
d. Jul 2, 1915 in Paris, France
Source: *ApCAB; REn*

Diaz de Bivar, Rodrigo
see: Cid, El

Diaz de la Pena, Narciso Virgilio
French. Artist
b. 1807 in Bordeaux, France
d. 1876
Source: *NewCol 75*

Diaz Ordaz, Gustavo
Mexican. President
b. Mar 12, 1911 in Puebla, Mexico
d. Jul 15, 1979 in Mexico City, Mexico
Source: *CurBio 65; IntWW 74; WhoAm 74; WhoS&SW 73*

Dibbs, Eddie (Edward George)
American. Tennis Player
b. Feb 23, 1951 in Brooklyn, New York
Source: *BioIn 10; WhoAm 82*

Dibdin, Thomas Frognall
English. Bibliographer
b. 1776 in Calcutta, India
d. Nov 18, 1847 in London, England
Source: *Alli; BiD&SB; BiDLA; ChPo S1; DcEnL; DcEuL; DcLEL; NewC; OxEng*

DiCamerino, Roberta
Italian. Designer, Boutique Owner
b. Dec 8, 1920 in Venice, Italy
Source: *WorFshn*

DiCavour, Camillo Benso
see: Cavour, Camillo Benso di

Dichter, Ernest
American. Psychologist, Researcher
b. Aug 14, 1907 in Vienna, Austria
Source: *AmAu&B; AmM&WS 73S; CelR 73; ConAu 17R; CurBio 61; IntWW 74; WhoAdv 72; WhoAm 74, 76, 78, 80, 82; WhoCon 73; WhoWor 74*

Dichter, Mischa
American. Musician
b. Sep 27, 1945 in Shanghai, China
Source: *WhoAm 78, 80, 82*

Dick, Philip K(indred)
American. Author
b. Dec 16, 1928 in Chicago, Illinois
d. Mar 2, 1982 in Santa Ana, California
Source: *AmAu&B; ConAu 49, 2NR; ConLC 10; ConNov 76; ConSFA; DrAF 76; EncSF; LinLib L; ScF&FL 1, 2; WhoSciF; WrDr 76, 80*

Dickens, Charles John Huffam
English. Author, Dramatist
Wrote *A Christmas Carol,* 1843; novels adapted into over 70 films.
b. Feb 7, 1812 in Portsmouth, England
d. Jun 9, 1870 in Godshill, England
Source: *Alli, SUP; AtlBL; AuBYP; BbD; BiD&SB; BrAu 19; CarSB; CasWL; Chambr 3; ChPo, S1, S2; CrtT 3; CyWA; DcBiA; DcEnA, AP; DcEnL; DcEuL; DcLEL; EncMys; EvLB; FamAYP; FilmgC; HsB&A; JBA 34; MnBBF; MouLC 3; NewC; OxAmL; OxEng; OxFilm; OxThe; Pen AM, ENG; RAdv 1; RComWL; REn; Str&VC; WebE&AL; WhAm H; WhoChL*

Dickens, "Little" Jimmy
American. Singer, Songwriter
b. Dec 19, 1925 in Bolt, West Virginia
Source: *BiDAmM; EncFCWM 69; IlEncCM; RkOn 2*

Dickens, Monica Enid
English. Author
b. May 10, 1915 in London, England
Source: *Au&Wr 71; ConAu 5R, 2NR; ConNov 72, 76; DcLEL; EvLB; ForWC 70; LongCTC; NewC; Pen ENG; REn; SmATA 4; TwCW; Who 74; WorAu; WrDr 76*

Dickerson, Nancy Hanschman
American. Broadcast Journalist
Correspondent, NBC News, 1960-70; wrote *Among Those Present,* 1976.
b. Jan 19, 1930 in Wauwatosa, Wisconsin
Source: *ConAu 69; CurBio 62; ForWC 70; WhoAm 74, 76, 78, 80, 82; WhoAmW 77; WhoS&SW 73*

Dickey, Bill (William Malcolm)
American. Baseball Player
Caught 100 or more games 13 consecutive seasons; Hall of Fame, 1954.
b. Jun 6, 1907 in Bastrop, Louisiana
Source: *BaseEn; WhoProB 73*

Dickey, Herbert Spencer
American. Physician, Explorer
Discovered source of Orinoco River, S America, 1931.
b. Feb 4, 1876 in Highland Falls, New York
d. Oct 28, 1948 in Huigra, Ecuador
Source: *AmAu&B; BioIn 1, 2*

Dickey, James
American. Poet, Critic
Wrote *Deliverance,* 1970; filmed, 1972, starring Burt Reynolds, Jon Voight.
b. Feb 2, 1923 in Atlanta, Georgia
Source: *AmAu&B; AnCL; AuNews 1, 2; CelR 73; ConAu 9R; ConLC 1, 2, 4, 7, 10, 15; ConP 70, 75; CroCAP; CurBio 68; DrAF 76; DrAP 75; DrAS 74E; EncWL; IntWW 74; ModAL, SUP; OxAmL; Pen AM; RAdv 1; WebAB; WebE&AL; WhoAm 74, 76, 78, 80, 82; WhoS&SW 73; WhoTwCL; WhoWor 74; WorAu; WrDr 76*

Dickie, Murray
Scottish. Opera Singer
b. 1924 in Renfrew, Scotland
Source: *WhoMus 72*

Dickinson, Angie
[Angeline Brown]
American. Actress
Starred in TV series "Policewoman," 1974-78; former wife of Burt Bacharach.
b. Sep 30, 1931 in Kulm, North Dakota
Source: *BiDFilm; BkPepl; CelR 73; FilmgC; IntMPA 75, 76, 77, 78, 79, 80, 81, 82; MotPP; MovMk; WhoAm 74, 76, 78, 80, 82; WhoHol A; WorEFlm*

Dickinson, Edwin W
American. Artist
b. Oct 11, 1891 in Seneca Falls, New York
d. Dec 2, 1978 in Cape Cod, Massachusetts
Source: *BioIn 3, 4, 5, 6, 7, 11; CurBio 63, 79; DcCAA 71; NewYTBS 78; WhAm 7; WhoAm 74, 76, 78; WhoAmA 73; WhoWor 74*

Dickinson, Emily Elizabeth
American. Poet
Hardly ever left home after age 30; most poems published after death.
b. Dec 10, 1830 in Amherst, Massachusetts
d. May 15, 1886 in Amherst, Massachusetts
Source: *AmAu; AmAu&B; AmBi; AmWr; AnCL; AtlBL; BiD&SB; CasWL; Chambr 3; ChPo, S1, S2; CnDAL; CnE&AP; CrtT 3; CyWA; DcAmAu; DcAmB; DcLEL; DcNAA; EncAB-H; EvLB; HerW; InWom; ModAL, SUP; NewYTBE 73; NotAW; OxAmL; OxEng; Pen AM; RAdv 1; RComWL; REn; REnAL; Str&VC; TwCBDA; WebAB; WebE&AL; WhAm H*

Dickman, Joseph Theodore
American. Military Leader
b. Oct 6, 1857 in Dayton, Ohio
d. Oct 23, 1927
Source: *AmBi; DcAmB; DcNAA; OhA&B; WhAm 1*

Dickson, Gloria
American. Actress
b. Aug 13, 1916 in Pocatello, Idaho
d. Apr 10, 1945 in Hollywood, California
Source: *MotPP; NotNAT B; ThFT; WhScrn 74, 77; WhoHol B*

Dickson, Gordon Rupert
Canadian. Author
b. Nov 1, 1923 in Edmonton, AB
Source: *ConAu 9R*

Diddley, Bo
American. Rock Musician, Composer
b. Dec 30, 1928 in McCombs, Mississippi
Source: *BiDAmM; EncPR&S; IlEncRk*

Diderot, Denis
French. Editor, Philosopher
Editor, *Encyclopedie,* 1745, an encyclopedia of arts and sciences.
b. Oct 15, 1713 in Langres, France
d. Jul 30, 1784 in Paris, France
Source: *AtlBL; BbD; BiD&SB; CasWL; CnThe; CyWA; DcEuL; EuAu; EvEuW; McGEWD; NewC; OxEng; OxFr; OxThe; Pen EUR; RComWL; REn; REnWD*

Didion, Joan
American. Author, Journalist
b. Dec 5, 1934 in Sacramento, California
Source: *AmAu&B; AuNews 1; ConAu 5R; ConLC 1, 3, 8, 14; ConNov 76; DrAF 76; ModAL SUP; WhoAm 82; WomWMM; WrDr 76*

Dido
[Elissa]
Mythical Queen of Carthage
Source: *BioIn 4, 7; NewCol 75*

DiDonato, Pietro
American. Author
Wrote autobiographical novel *Christ in Concrete,* 1939.
b. Apr 3, 1911 in West Hoboken, New Jersey
Source: *ConAu 101; OxAmL; REnAL; TwCA, SUP*

Didrikson, "Babe" (Mildred)
[Mrs. George Zaharias]
American. Sportswoman
Voted greatest woman athlete of 20th c. by AP, 1949.
b. Jun 26, 1912 in Port Arthur, Texas
d. Sep 27, 1956 in Galveston, Texas
Source: *BioNews 74; CurBio 47, 56; HerW; InWom; WebAB; WhAm 4; WhoTr&F 73*

Didymus
Alexandrian. Philologist, Grammarian
b. 80BC
d. 10BC
Source: *CasWL; NewC; Pen CL*

Diebenkorn, Richard
American. Artist
b. Apr 22, 1922 in Portland, Oregon
Source: *CurBio 71; DcCAA 71; IntWW 74; WhoAm 74, 76, 78, 80, 82; WhoAmA 73; WhoWest 74; WhoWor 74*

Diebold, Alfred John
American. Business Executive
b. 1879
d. 1966
Source: *BioIn 9*

Diederichs, Nicholaas
South African. Political Leader
b. Nov 17, 1904 in Orange Free State, South Africa
d. Aug 21, 1978 in Capetown, South Africa
Source: *BioIn 11; IntWW 74; WhoWor 74*

Diefenbaker, John George
Canadian. Lawyer, Prime Minister
b. Sep 18, 1895 in Grey County, ON
d. Aug 16, 1979 in Ottawa, ON
Source: *CanWW 70; CurBio 57; IntWW 74; OxCan SUP; Who 74; WhoAm 74; WhoCan 73; WhoWor 74*

Diem, Ngo-dinh
see: Ngo dinh Diem

Diemer, Emma Lou
American. Composer, Musician
b. Nov 24, 1927 in Kansas City, Missouri
Source: *AmSCAP 66, 80; BioIn 5; WhoAm 82; WhoAmW 74, 75, 77*

Dierdorf, Dan(iel Lee)
American. Football Player
b. Jun 29, 1949 in Canton, Ohio
Source: *NewYTBS 77*

Dies, Martin, Jr.
American. Lawyer, Congressman
b. Nov 5, 1900 in Colorado, Texas
d. Nov 14, 1972 in Lufkin, Texas
Source: *BiDrAC; CurBio 40, 73; NewYTBE 72; WebAB; WhAm 5; WhAmP*

Diesel, Rudolf
German. Engineer, Inventor
Developed Diesel internal combustion engine, 1892.
b. Mar 18, 1858 in Paris, France
d. Sep 29, 1913
Source: *NewCol 75; OxGer*

Dieskaul, Dietrich Fischer
see: Fischer-Dieskau, Dietrich

Dieterle, William
American. Motion Picture Director
b. Jul 15, 1893 in Ludwigshafen, Germany
d. Dec 9, 1972 in Ottobrunn, Germany (West)
Source: *BiDFilm; CmMov; CurBio 43, 73; DcFM; FilmgC; MovMk; NewYTBE 72; OxFilm; WhAm 5; WhScrn 77; WorEFlm*

Dietrich, Marlene
American. Actress, Singer
Began career as violinist; starred *The Blue Angel, Rancho Notorious.*
b. Dec 27, 1904 in Berlin, Germany
Source: *BiDFilm; CelR 73; CmMov; CurBio 53, 68; FilmgC; InWom; IntMPA 75, 76, 77, 78, 79, 80, 81, 82; IntWW 74; MotPP; MovMk; NewYTBE 72; OxFilm; ThFT; TwYS; Who 74; WhoAm 74, 76, 78, 80, 82; WhoHol A; WhoThe 77; WhoWor 74; WorEFlm*

Dietrich, Noah
American. Aide to Howard Hughes
b. Feb 28, 1889 in Batavia, Wisconsin
d. Feb 15, 1982 in Palm Springs, California
Source: *BioIn 9; ConAu 45; NewYTBS 82*

Dietz, Howard
American. Songwriter
b. Sep 8, 1896 in New York, New York
Source: *AmAu&B; AmSCAP 66; BiE&WWA; CelR 73; ChPo; ConAu 53; ConDr 73; CurBio 65; EncMT; FilmgC; ModWD; NewCBMT; NotNAT; PlP&P; REnAL; WhoAm 74, 76, 78, 80, 82; WhoThe 77*

Difford, Chris
see: Squeeze

Digges, Dudley
Irish. Actor
b. Jun 9, 1880 in Dublin, Ireland
d. Oct 24, 1947 in New York, New York
Source: *DcAmB S4; FamA&A; FilmgC; MovMk; OxThe; WhAm 2; WhScrn 74, 77; WhoHol B*

Diggs, Charles Coles, Jr.
American. Politician
Congressman, 1954-80; convicted of defrauding government in payroll kickback, 1980.
b. Dec 2, 1922 in Detroit, Michigan
Source: *BiDrAC; CngDr 74; CurBio 57; NewYTBE 71; WhoAm 74, 76, 78, 80; WhoAmP 73; WhoBlA 75; WhoGov 72; WhoMW 74*

DiGregorio, Ernie
American. Basketball Player
b. Jan 15, 1951 in North Providence, Rhode Island
Source: *NewYTBE 73; NewYTBS 74; WhoBbl 73*

Dillard, Harrison
American. Track Athlete
b. Jul 8, 1923 in Cleveland, Ohio
Source: *BioIn 1, 2, 8, 9, 10; WhoTr&F 73*

Diller, Phyllis
American. Actress, Comedienne
Known for outrageous appearance, stories about husband, Fang; is also a concert pianist.
b. Jul 17, 1917 in Lima, Ohio
Source: *CelR 73; CurBio 67; FilmgC; InWom; IntMPA 75, 76, 77, 78, 79, 80, 81, 82; MotPP; WhoAm 74, 76, 78, 80, 82; WhoAmW 77; WhoHol A; WhoWor 74*

Dillinger, John
American. Bank Robber, Murderer
Killed by FBI officers in front of Biograph Theater, betrayed by "Lady in Red."
b. Jun 28, 1902 in Indianapolis, Indiana
d. Jul 22, 1934 in Chicago, Illinois
Source: *BioNews 74; DcAmB S1; OxFilm; WebAB*

Dillman, Bradford
American. Actor
b. Apr 13, 1930 in San Francisco, California
Source: *BiE&WWA; CurBio 60; FilmgC; IntMPA 75, 76, 77, 78, 79, 80, 81, 82; MotPP; MovMk; NotNAT; WhoAm 82; WhoHol A*

Dillon, (Clarence) Douglas
American. Investment Banker, Diplomat
b. Aug 21, 1909 in Geneva, Switzerland
Source: *BiDrUSE; CelR 73; WhoAm 74, 76, 78, 80, 82; WhoGov 72*

Dillon, Diane Claire Sorber
[Mrs. Leo Dillon]
American. Author, Illustrator
b. Mar 13, 1933 in Glendale, California
Source: *AuBYP SUP; BioIn 12; EncSF; IlsCB 1967; SmATA 15; WhoAm 78, 80, 82*

Dillon, George
American. Author
b. Nov 12, 1906 in Jacksonville, Florida
d. May 9, 1968 in Charleston, South Carolina
Source: *AmAu&B; ChPo; ConAmA; ConAu 89; DcLEL; OxAmL; REn; REnAL; TwCA, SUP; WhAm 5*

Dillon, Leo
American. Author, Illustrator
b. Mar 2, 1933 in Brooklyn, New York
Source: *AuBYP SUP; BioIn 12; EncSF; IlsCB 1967; SmATA 15*

Dillon, Matt
American. Actor
Played role of bully in *My Bodyguard,* 1980; starred in *Tex,* 1982.
b. 1964? in Larchmont, New York
Source: *JohnWil 81*

Dillon, Melinda
American. Actress
b. Oct 31, 1939 in Hope, Arkansas
Source: *BiE&WWA; BioIn 6, 11; IntMPA 82; NotNAT*

Dillon, William A
American. Songwriter
b. Nov 6, 1877 in Cortland, New York
d. Feb 10, 1966 in Ithaca, New York
Source: *AmSCAP 66; BioIn 4, 7*

DiMaggio, Dom(inic Paul)
"The Little Professor"
American. Baseball Player
b. Feb 12, 1917 in San Francisco, California
Source: *BaseEn; St&PR 75; WhoProB 73*

DiMaggio, Joe (Joseph Paul)
"Joltin' Joe"; "The Yankee Clipper"
American. Baseball Player
Hit safely in record 56 consecutive games, 1941; married Marilyn Monroe, 1954.
b. Nov 24, 1914 in San Francisco, California
Source: *BaseEn; CelR 73; CurBio 41, 51; WebAB; WhoHol A; WhoProB 73*

Dimitrov, Georgi
Bulgarian. Communist Leader, Premier
b. Jun 18, 1882 in Bulgaria
d. Feb 7, 1949 in Sofia, Bulgaria
Source: *CurBio 49; WhAm 3*

Dimmock, Peter
British. Broadcasting Executive
b. Dec 6, 1920
Source: *Au&Wr 71; IntMPA 77, 78, 79, 80, 81, 82; NewYTET*

Di Mucci, Dion
[Dion and the Belmonts]
American. Singer
b. Jul 18, 1939 in Bronx, New York
Source: *EncPR&S*

DiMuro, Lou
American. Umpire
AL umpire, 1963-82.
b. 1932 in New Jersey
d. Jun 6, 1982 in Arlington, Texas
Source: *NewYTBS 82*

D'Indy, Vincent
see: Indy, Paul d'

Dine, Jim
American. Neosurrealist Artist
b. Jun 16, 1935 in Cincinnati, Ohio
Source: *CelR 73; ConDr 73; CurBio 69; DcCAA 71; WhoAm 74; WhoWor 74*

Dinehart, Alan
American. Actor
b. Oct 3, 1890 in Missoula, Montana
d. Jul 17, 1944 in Hollywood, California
Source: *CurBio 44; FilmgC; MovMk; WhAm 2; WhScrn 74, 77; WhoHol B*

Dinesen, Isak, pseud.
see: Blixen, Karen Christentze, Baroness

Ding, J. N. pseud.
see: Darling, Jay Norwood

Dinitz, Simcha
Israeli. Diplomat
b. Jun 23, 1930 in Tel Aviv, Palestine
Source: *IntWW 74; WhoWorJ 72*

Dinkeloo, John Gerard
American. Architect, Engineer
b. Feb 28, 1918 in Holland, Michigan
d. Jun 15, 1981 in Fredericksburg, Virginia
Source: *AmArch 70; NewYTBS 81; WhoAm 74, 76, 78, 80; WhoF&I 75, 77, 79*

Dinwiddie, John Ekin
American. Architect, Educator
b. Oct 27, 1902 in Chicago, Illinois
d. Sep 11, 1959 in New Orleans, Louisiana
Source: *BioIn 7; McGDA; NatCAB 48; WhAm 4*

Dinwiddie, Robert
British. Colonial Governor
b. 1693 in Glasgow, Scotland
d. Jul 27, 1770 in Bristol, England
Source: *BiDSA; BioIn 9, 10; WebBD 80*

Dio, Johnny
Racketeer
Source: *NF*

Dio, Ronnie
see: Black Sabbath

Diocletian
Roman. Emperor
b. 245
d. 313
Source: *NewC; REn*

Diogenes
Greek. Philosopher
Cynic, usually depicted with a lantern in search of an honest man.
b. 412BC in Sinope, Asia Minor
d. 323BC
Source: *AmAu; NewC; PlP&P; PueRA; REn*

Dion and the Belmonts
[Angelo D'Angelo; Dion DiMucci; Carlo Mastangelo; Fred Milano]
American. Vocal Group
Source: *EncPR&S; Rk100*

Dionne, Annette
[Dionne Sisters]
Canadian. Dionne Quintuplet
b. May 28, 1934 in Callander, ON
Source: *BioIn 9, 10*

Dionne, Cecile
[Dionne Sisters]
Canadian. Dionne Quintuplet
b. May 28, 1934 in Callander, ON
Source: *BioIn 9, 10*

Dionne, Emilie
[Dionne Sisters]
Canadian. Dionne Quintuplet
b. May 28, 1934 in Callander, ON
d. Aug 6, 1954 in Saint Agathe, PQ
Source: *WhoHol B*

Dionne, Marcel
"Beaver"
Canadian. Hockey Player
Has more hat tricks (24) than any other active NHL player.
b. Aug 3, 1951 in Drummondville, PQ
Source: *BioIn 10, 11; WhoHcky 73*

Dionne, Marie
[Dionne Sisters]
Canadian. Dionne Quintuplet
b. May 28, 1934 in Callander, ON
d. Feb 27, 1970 in Montreal, PQ
Source: *WhScrn 74, 77; WhoHol B*

Dionne, Yvonne
[Dionne Sisters]
Canadian. Dionne Quintuplet
b. May 28, 1934 in Callander, ON
Source: *BioIn 9, 10*

Dionne Sisters
[Annette Dionne; Cecile Dionne; Emilie Dionne; Marie Dionne; Yvonne Dionne]
Canadian. Quintuplets
b. May 28, 1934 in Callander, ON
Source: *InWom*

Dionysius of Halicarnassus
Greek. Historian
b. 30BC
d. 7BC
Source: *CasWL; NewC; Pen CL*

Dionysius the Elder
Tyrant
b. 430BC
d. 367BC in Syracuse, Sicily
Source: *NewC*

Dior, Christian
French. Fashion Designer
Introduced long hemlines, full skirts; controversial before accepted.
b. Jan 21, 1905 in Granville, France
d. Oct 24, 1957 in Montecatini, Italy
Source: *CurBio 48, 58; WorFshn*

Dioscorides, Pedacius
Greek. Physician, Botanist
Source: *BioIn 7, 9; CasWL; WebBD 80*

Diouf, Abdou
Senegalese. Prime Minister
b. Sep 7, 1935
Source: *IntWW 74; WhoGov 72; WhoWor 74*

Dirac, Paul
English. Mathematician, Physicist
b. Aug 8, 1902 in Bristol, England
Source: *IntWW 74; Who 74; WhoAm 74; WhoWor 74*

Dire Straits
[John Illsley; Dave Knopfler; Mark Knopfler; Pick Withers]
English. Rock Group
Source: *ConMuA 80; WhoRock 81*

Dirks, Rudolph
American. Cartoonist
b. Feb 26, 1877
d. Apr 20, 1968 in New York, New York
Source: *WorECom*

Dirksen, Everett McKinley
American. Senator
Important role in passage of Voting Rights Act, 1965, Fair Housing Act, 1968.
b. Jan 4, 1896 in Pekin, Illinois
d. Sep 7, 1969 in Washington, DC
Source: *BiDrAC; CurBio 41, 57, 69; EncAB-H; WebAB; WhAm 5; WhAmP; WhScrn 77*

DiSalle, Michael Vincent
American. Government Official
b. Jan 6, 1908 in New York, New York
d. Sep 15, 1981 in Pescara, Italy
Source: *BioIn 2, 3, 5, 9; CurBio 51, 81; IntWW 74, 75, 76, 77, 78; NewYTBS 81; PolProf E; PolProf K; PolProf T; WhoAm 74, 76, 78, 80; WhoWor 74*

DiSant'Angelo, Giorgio
American. Fashion Designer
b. May 5, 1936 in Florence, Italy
Source: *CelR 73; WhoAm 74, 76, 78, 80, 82; WorFshn*

Disney, Doris Miles
American. Author
Novel *Do Not Fold, Spindle, or Mutilate* adapted to film, 1971.
b. Dec 22, 1907 in Glastonbury, Connecticut
d. Mar 8, 1976 in Fredericksburg, Virginia
Source: *AmAu&B; AmWomWr; ConAu 65, 3NR; CurBio 54, 76; EncMys; InWom; NewYTBS 76; WhAm 7; WhoAm 74; WhoAmW 58, 64, 66, 68, 70, 72, 74*

Disney, Roy O
American. Motion Picture Executive
b. 1893 in Chicago, Illinois
d. Dec 20, 1971 in Burbank, California
Source: *BioIn 7, 9, 11; NewYTBE 71; WhAm 5*

Disney, Walt(er Elias)
American. Cartoonist, Film Producer
Introduced Mickey Mouse in "Steamboat Willie," 1928; won 29 Oscars.
b. Dec 5, 1901 in Chicago, Illinois
d. Dec 15, 1966 in Los Angeles, California
Source: *ChPo, S1, S2; CurBio 40, 52, 67; DcFM; EncAB-H; FilmgC; LongCTC; OxAmL; OxFilm; REn; REnAL; WebAB; WhoChL; WhoGrA; WorEFlm*

Disraeli, Benjamin
[Benjamin Disraeli Beaconsfield, Earl of]
English. Author, Statesman
b. Dec 21, 1804 in London, England
d. Apr 19, 1881 in London, England
Source: *Alli, SUP; AtlBL; BiD&SB; BrAu 19; CasWL; Chambr 3; CyWA; DcBiA; DcEnA, AP; DcEnL; DcEuL; DcLEL; EvLB; FilmgC; MouLC 3; NewC; OxEng; Pen ENG; RAdv 1; REn; WebE&AL*

D'Israeli, Isaac
English. Author
b. May 11, 1766 in London, England
d. Jan 19, 1848
Source: *Alli; BbD; BiD&SB; BrAu 19; CasWL; Chambr 2; ChPo; DcEnA; DcEnL; DcEuL; DcLEL; EvLB; NewC; OxEng; Pen ENG; REn*

DiStefano, Giuseppe
Italian. Opera Singer
b. Jul 24, 1921 in Catania, Sicily
Source: *IntWW 74*

DiSuvero, Mark
American. Sculptor
Built Tower of Peace, LA, 1966, as protest against Vietnam War.
b. Sep 18, 1933 in Shanghai, China
Source: *BnEnAmA; ConArt; CurBio 79; DcAmArt; DcCAA 71, 77; WhoAm 82*

Ditmars, Raymond Lee
American. Naturalist, Author
b. Jun 20, 1876 in Newark, New Jersey
d. May 12, 1942 in New York, New York
Source: *AmAu&B; AuBYP; CurBio 40, 42; DcAmB S3; DcNAA; JBA 34, 51; REnAL; TwCA, SUP; WhAm 2; WhNAA*

Ditters, Karl
[Karl Ditters von Dittersdorf]
Austrian. Musician, Composer
b. Nov 2, 1739 in Vienna, Austria
d. Dec 24, 1799 in Neuhof, Bohemia
Source: *NewEOp 71; WebBD 80*

Ditzen, Rudolph
see: Fallada, Hans, pseud.

Diver, Jenny
[Mary Jones]
British. Pickpocket
b. 1700?
d. Mar 18, 1740 in London, England
Source: *LookW*

Divine, Arthur Durham
[David Divine; David Rame, pseuds.]
English. Author, Journalist
b. Jul 27, 1904 in Capetown, South Africa
Source: *Au&Wr 71; BioIn 2; ConAu 103; DcLEL; Who 74*

Divine, Father
[George Baker]
American. Religious Leader
b. 1874?
d. Sep 10, 1965 in Philadelphia, Pennsylvania
Source: *BioIn 1, 2, 3, 4, 7, 8, 9, 11; CurBio 44; WebAB*

Dix, Dorothea Lynde
American. Reformer
Instrumental in building state hospitals for the insane.
b. Apr 4, 1802 in Hampden, Maine
d. Jul 17, 1887 in Trenton, New Jersey
Source: *Alli; AmAu; AmAu&B; AmBi; AmWom; ApCAB; BiD&SB; DcAmAu; DcAmB; DcNAA; Drake; EncAB-H; HerW; InWom; NotAW; OxAmL; TwCBDA; WebAB; WhAm H*

Dix, Dorothy, pseud.
[Elizabeth Meriwether Gilmer]
American. Journalist, Author
b. Nov 18, 1870 in Woodstock, Tennessee
d. Dec 16, 1951 in New Orleans, Louisiana
Source: *AmAu&B; BiDSA; CurBio 40, 52; DcAmB S5; InWom; OxAmL; REn; REnAL; WhAm 3, 5; WomWWA 14*

Dix, John Adams
American. Soldier, Statesman
b. Jul 24, 1798 in Boscawen, New Hampshire
d. Apr 21, 1879 in New York, New York
Source: *Alli, SUP; AmBi; ApCAB; BbD; BiAuS; BiD&SB; BiDrAC; BiDrUSE; CyAl 2; DcAmAu; DcAmB; DcNAA; Drake; TwCBDA; WebAB; WhAm H; WhAmP*

Dix, Otto
German. Artist, Draftsman
b. Dec 2, 1891 in Gera, Germany
d. Jun 25, 1969
Source: *BioIn 2, 4, 6, 8; WhAm 5*

Dix, Richard
[Ernest Brimmer]
American. Actor
b. Aug 8, 1895 in Saint Paul, Minnesota
d. Sep 20, 1949 in Los Angeles, California
Source: *BiDFilm; CmMov; Film 1; FilmgC; MotPP; MovMk; TwYS; WhScrn 74, 77; WhoHol B*

Dix, William Shepherd
American. Librarian
b. Nov 19, 1910 in Berryville, Virginia
d. Feb 22, 1978 in Princeton, New Jersey
Source: *BiDrLUS 70; CurBio 69, 78; DrAS 74E; DrLC 69; NewYTBS 78; WhoAm 74, 76, 78*

Dixon, Alan John
American. Senator
b. Jul 7, 1927 in Belleville, Illinois
Source: *WhoAm 78, 80, 82; WhoAmP 73, 75, 77; WhoGov 72, 75, 77; WhoMW 74, 76, 78*

Dixon, Dean
American. Conductor
b. Jan 10, 1915 in New York, New York
d. Nov 3, 1976
Source: *Baker 78; CurBio 43, 77; NewYTBS 76; WhAm 7; WhoAm 74, 76; WhoBlA 75; WhoMus 72*

Dixon, Ivan
American. Actor
b. Apr 6, 1931 in New York, New York
Source: *MovMk; WhoAm 74, 76, 78, 80, 82; WhoBlA 75; WhoHol A*

Dixon, Jean
[Marie Jacques]
American. Actress
b. Jul 14, 1894 in Waterbury, Connecticut
d. Feb 12, 1981 in New York, New York
Source: *AnObit 1981; BiE&WWA; Film 2; NewYTBS 81; NotNAT; ThFT; WhThe; WhoHol A*

Dixon, Jeane Pinckert
American. Clairvoyant, Astrologist
Proponent of ESP; began predicting future at age 8.
b. Jan 5, 1918 in Medford, Wisconsin
Source: *BkPepl; CelR 73; ConAu 65; CurBio 73; WhoAm 78, 80, 82; WhoS&SW 73*

Dixon, Jeremiah
English. Surveyor
d. 1777 in Durham, England
Source: *ApCAB; WebAB*

Dixon, Margaret Rumer Haynes
see: Godden, Rumer, pseud.

Dixon, Mort
American. Songwriter
b. Mar 20, 1892 in New York, New York
d. Mar 23, 1956 in Bronxville, New York
Source: *AmSCAP 66; BioIn 4*

Dixon, Paul Rand
American. Government Official
b. Sep 29, 1913 in Nashville, Tennessee
Source: *CurBio 68; IntWW 74; WhoAm 74, 76, 78, 80, 82; WhoAmP 73; WhoGov 72; WhoS&SW 73*

Dixon, Robert Ellington
American. Admiral
b. 1906?
d. Oct 21, 1981 in Virginia Beach, Virginia
Source: *BioIn 12*

Dixon, Thomas
American. Author, Clergyman
b. Jan 11, 1865 in Shelby, North Carolina
d. Apr 3, 1946 in Raleigh, North Carolina
Source: *AmAu&B; BiD&SB; BiDSA; CasWL; CnDAL; CurBio 46; DcAmAu; DcAmB S4; DcLEL; DcNAA; FilmgC; OxAmL; REnAL; TwCA, SUP; WebE&AL; WhAm 2; WhNAA; WhoStg 1906, 1908*

Djilas, Milovan
Yugoslav. Author, Politician
b. 1911 in Kolasin, Yugoslavia
Source: *Au&Wr 71; CurBio 58; IntWW 74; WhoAm 74; WhoWor 74; WorAu*

Djugashvili, Ekaterina
Russian. Mother of Joseph Stalin
b. 1856
d. 1937
Source: *BioIn 10*

Doak, Bill (William Leopold)
"Spittin' Bill"
American. Baseball Player
b. Jan 28, 1891 in Pittsburgh, Pennsylvania
d. Nov 26, 1954 in Bradenton, Florida
Source: *BaseEn; BioIn 3; WhoProB 73*

Doar, John
American. Lawyer
b. Dec 3, 1921 in Minneapolis, Minnesota
Source: *BioNews 74; NewYTBE 73; NewYTBS 74; WhoAm 78*

Dobbs, Mattiwilda
American. Opera Singer
b. Jul 11, 1925 in Atlanta, Georgia
Source: *CurBio 55; IntWW 74; Who 74; WhoAm 74, 76, 78, 80, 82; WhoBlA 75; WhoMus 72; WhoWor 74*

Dobie, J(ames) Frank
American. Folklorist, Author, Educator
b. Sep 26, 1888 in Live Oak County, Texas
d. Sep 18, 1964 in Austin, Texas
Source: *AmAu&B; ConAu 1R; CurBio 45, 64; DcLEL; OxAmL; REn; REnAL; TexWr; TwCA SUP*

Dobloug, Lisa
Health Farm Owner
b. 1940? in Norway
Source: *NF*

Dobozy, Imre
Hungarian. Author
b. Oct 30, 1917 in Hungary
Source: *IntWW 74*

Dobrovolsky, Georgi
Russian. Cosmonaut
b. 1928? in Odessa, U.S.S.R.
Source: *NewYTBE 71*

Dobrowen, Issai
Russian. Conductor
b. Feb 27, 1893 in Nizhni-Novgorod, Russia
d. Dec 9, 1953 in Oslo, Norway
Source: *NewEOp 71*

Dobrynin, Anatoly Fedorovich
[Anatoliy Federovich Dobrynin]
Russian. Diplomat
Soviet diplomat to US, 1962--.
b. Nov 16, 1919 in Krasnaya Gorka, U.S.S.R.
Source: *BioNews 74; CurBio 62; IntWW 74; WhoGov 72; WhoUN 75; WhoWor 74*

Doby, Larry (Lawrence Eugene)
American. Baseball Player
First black player in AL, with Cleveland Indians, 1947.
b. Dec 13, 1924 in Camden, South Carolina
Source: *BaseEn; BioIn 3, 4, 5, 6, 7, 8, 11; WhoProB 73*

Dobyns, Lloyd Allen, Jr.
American. Broadcast Journalist
Correspondent for NBC; currently on news show "Overnight."
b. Mar 12, 1936 in Newport News, Virginia
Source: *WhoAm 78, 80, 82*

"Doc Middleton"
see: Riley, James

Dockstader, Lew
[George Alfred Clapp]
American. Vaudeville Minstrel
b. 1856 in Hartford, Connecticut
d. 1924 in New York, New York
Source: *DcAmB; OxThe; PlP&P*

Doctorow, E(dgar) L(aurence)
American. Author, Editor
Wrote *Ragtime,* 1976.
b. Jan 6, 1931 in New York, New York
Source: *BioIn 10; ConAu 45, 2NR; ConLC 6, 11, 15, 18*

Dodd, Charles Harold
English. Theologian
b. Apr 7, 1884
d. Sep 22, 1973 in Goring, England
Source: *Au&Wr 71; ConAu 45; NewYTBE 73; WhoLA; WhoWor 74*

Dodd, Christopher John
American. Senator
b. May 27, 1944 in Willimantic, Connecticut
Source: *AlmAP 78, 80; BioIn 10; CngDr 77, 79; WhoAm 78, 80, 82; WhoAmP 75, 77, 79; WhoE 77, 79; WhoGov 75, 77*

Dodd, Ed(ward) Benton
American. Cartoonist
b. Nov 7, 1902 in Lafayette, Georgia
Source: *ConAu 73; SmATA 4; WhoAm 74, 76, 78, 80, 82*

Dodd, Robert Lee (Bobby)
American. Football Coach
b. Oct 11, 1908 in Galax, Virginia
Source: *BioIn 1, 4; WhoFtbl 74*

Dodd, Thomas Joseph
American. Senator
b. May 15, 1907 in Norwich, Connecticut
d. May 24, 1971 in Old Lynne, Connecticut
Source: *BiDrAC; ConAu 29R; CurBio 59, 71; NewYTBE 71; WhAm 5; WhAmP*

Dodds, "Baby" (Warren)
American. Jazz Musician
b. Dec 24, 1898 in New Orleans, Louisiana
d. Feb 14, 1959 in Chicago, Illinois
Source: *WhoJazz 72*

Dodds, Harold Willis
American. Educator, Political Scientist
b. Jun 28, 1889 in Utica, Pennsylvania
d. Oct 25, 1980 in Hightstown, New Jersey
Source: *AmAu&B; CurBio 45; IntWW 74; Who 74; WhoAm 74; WhoGov 72*

Dodds, Johnny
American. Jazz Musician
b. Apr 12, 1892 in New Orleans, Louisiana
d. Aug 8, 1940 in Chicago, Illinois
Source: *WhoJazz 72*

Dodge, Bertha S
American. Children's Author
b. Mar 23, 1902 in Cambridge, Massachusetts
Source: *AuBYP; ConAu 5R, 2NR; SmATA 8; WrDr 76*

Dodge, Grace Hoadley
American. Educator, Philanthropist
President, YWCA, 1906-14.
b. May 21, 1856 in New York, New York
d. Dec 27, 1914 in New York, New York
Source: *AmBi; AmWom; ApCAB, SUP; BiDAmEd; BioIn 8; DcAmB; NatCAB 18; NotAW; WhAm 1; WomWWA 14*

Dodge, Gregg Sherwood
American. Wealthy Socialite
b. 1923
Source: *InWom*

Dodge, Grenville Mellen
American. General, Civil Engineer
b. Apr 12, 1831 in Danvers, Massachusetts
d. Jan 3, 1916
Source: *BioIn 1, 5, 9; DcNAA; WhAm 1*

Dodge, Horace Elgin
American. Automobile Manufacturer
Built first Dodge car, Nov, 1914, Detroit, MI.
b. May 17, 1868 in Niles, Michigan
d. Dec 10, 1920 in Palm Beach, Florida
Source: *NatCAB 19*

Dodge, John Francis
American. Automobile Manufacturer
President, Dodge Brothers Co., established 1901, Detroit, MI.
b. Oct 25, 1864 in Niles, Michigan
d. Jan 4, 1920 in New York, New York
Source: *NatCAB 19*

Dodge, Joseph Morrell
American. Banker, Government Official
b. Nov 18, 1890 in Detroit, Michigan
d. Dec 12, 1964 in Detroit, Michigan
Source: *BioIn 1, 3, 7, 9, 11; WhAm 4*

Dodge, Mary Elizabeth Mapes
American. Author, Editor
b. Jan 26, 1831 in New York, New York
d. Aug 21, 1905 in Onteora Park, New York
Source: *Alli SUP; AmAu; AmBi; BbD; BiD&SB; CarSB; ChPo, S1, S2; DcAmB; DcBiA; DcNAA; FamAYP; FamSYP; InWom; JBA 34; NotAW; OxAmL; REn; REnAL; WebAB; WhoChL*

Dodgson, Charles Lutwidge
see: Carroll, Lewis, pseud.

Doe, Samuel Kanyon
Liberian. Head of State
b. May 6, 1951? in Tuzon, Liberia
Source: *CurBio 81*

Doenitz, Karl C
[Karl C Donitz]
German. World War II Admiral
b. Sep 16, 1891 in Berlin, Germany
d. Dec 24, 1980 in Hamburg, Germany (West)
Source: *AnObit 1981; BioIn 1, 3, 4, 5, 6, 8, 11; CurBio 42, 81*

Doerr, Bobby (Robert Pershing)
American. Baseball Player
b. Apr 7, 1918 in Los Angeles, California
Source: *BaseEn; WhoProB 73*

Doesburg, Theo van
Dutch. Artist
b. 1883
d. 1931
Source: *BioIn 1, 4, 10; WebBD 80*

Doggett, Bill
American. Singer, Musician, Songwriter
b. Feb 6, 1916 in Philadelphia, Pennsylvania
Source: *EncPR&S*

Dohanos, Stevan
American. Illustrator, Artist
b. May 18, 1907 in Lorain, Ohio
Source: *WhoAmA 73*

Doheny, Edward Lawrence
American. Oilman
b. Aug 10, 1856 in Fond du Lac, Wisconsin
d. Sep 8, 1935
Source: *DcAmB S1; NatCAB 29; WhAm 1; WhoAmP 73*

Doherty, Brian
Canadian. Founder of Shaw Festival
b. Feb 3, 1906 in Toronto, ON
d. 1974
Source: *CanWW 70; ClbCR*

Doherty, Kieran
[Irish Hunger Strikers]
Irish. Jailed IRA Member
b. 1956?
d. Aug 2, 1981 in Belfast, Northern Ireland
Source: *BioIn 12*

Doherty, Robert Ernest
American. Engineer, Educator
b. Jan 22, 1885 in Clay City, Illinois
d. Oct 19, 1950 in Scotia, New York
Source: *BioIn 1, 2, 3, 4; CurBio 49, 50*

Dohnanyi, Christoph von
German. Conductor
b. 1929
Source: *BioIn 9*

Dohnanyi, Erno von
[Ernst von Dohnanyi]
Hungarian. Composer, Musician, Conductor
b. Jul 27, 1877 in Presburg, Hungary
d. 1960 in New York, New York
Source: *WhAm 5*

Dohrn, Bernadine Rae
American. Radical Activist
b. Jan 12, 1942 in Chicago, Illinois
Source: *BioIn 9, 10*

Doisy, Edward Adelbert
American. Biochemist
b. Nov 13, 1893 in Hume, Illinois
Source: *AmM&WS 73; CurBio 49; IntWW 74; Who 74; WhoAm 74; WhoWor 74*

Dokes, Michael
American. Boxer
b. Aug 10, 1958 in Akron, Ohio
Source: *NF*

Doktor, Paul Karl
American. Musician
b. 1919 in Vienna, Austria
Source: *WhoAm 82; WhoMus 72*

Dolbier, Maurice
American. Author, Journalist
b. May 5, 1912 in Skowhegan, Maine
Source: *AmAu&B; AuBYP; ConAu 65; CurBio 56; MorJA; WhoAm 74*

Dolby, Ray
American. Inventor
Developed Dolby sound, a noise reduction system, circa 1965.
b. Jan 18, 1933 in Portland, Oregon
Source: *IlEncRk; WhoAm 82*

Dolci, Danilo
Italian. Architect, Social Reformer
Built Borgo di Dio, a refuge for homeless, in Trappeto, Italy, 1953.
b. Jun 28, 1924 in Sesana, Italy
Source: *Au&Wr 71; CurBio 61; IntWW 74; NewYTBE 72; TwCW; Who 74; WhoWor 74; WorAu*

Dole, Bob (Robert Joseph)
American. Senator
b. Jul 22, 1923 in Russell, Kansas
Source: *BiDrAC; CelR 73; CngDr 74; CurBio 72; IntWW 74; NewYTBE 71; WhoAm 74, 76, 78, 80, 82; WhoAmP 73; WhoGov 72; WhoMW 74*

Dole, Elizabeth Hanford
[Mrs. Robert Dole]
American. Secretary of Transportation
Nominated to replace Drew Lewis; first woman to head Transportation Dept.
b. Jul 29, 1936 in Salisbury, North Carolina
Source: *WhoAm 78, 80, 82; WhoGov 77*

Dolenz, Mickey
[The Monkees]
American. Singer
b. Mar 8, 1945 in Los Angeles, California
Source: *NF*

Dolin, Anton
English. Dancer, Choreographer
b. Jul 27, 1904 in Slinfold, England
Source: *CanWW 70; CurBio 46; IntWW 74; Who 74; WhoAm 74, 76, 78, 80, 82; WhoThe 77; WhoWor 74*

Dollar, Robert
American. Shipping Magnate
Founded steamship companies; began first round-the-world passenger service.
b. Mar 20, 1844 in Falkirk, Scotland
d. May 16, 1932 in San Rafael, California
Source: *DcAmB S1; DcNAA; WhAm 1*

Dollard, John
American. Psychologist, Author
b. Aug 29, 1900 in Menasha, Wisconsin
d. Oct 8, 1980 in New Haven, Connecticut
Source: *AmAu&B; AmM&WS 73S, 78S; ConAu 102*

Dollfuss, Engelbert
Austrian. Chancellor
b. Oct 4, 1892 in Texing, Austria
d. Jul 25, 1934
Source: *McGEWB; OxGer; REn*

Dolly, Jenny
[Dolly Sisters]
Hungarian. Dancer, Choreographer
b. Oct 25, 1892 in Budapest, Hungary
d. Jun 1, 1941 in Hollywood, California
Source: *CurBio 41; InWom; WhScrn 74, 77; WhoHol B*

Dolly, Rosie
[Dolly Sisters]
Hungarian. Dancer, Choreographer
b. Oct 25, 1892 in Budapest, Hungary
d. Feb 1, 1970 in New York, New York
Source: *WhScrn 74, 77; WhoHol B*

Domagk, Gerhard
German. Chemist
b. Oct 30, 1895 in Lagow, Germany
d. Apr 24, 1964 in Burberg, Germany
Source: *BioIn 3, 4; CurBio 58, 64*

Domenichino, Il
[Domenico Zampieri]
Italian. Artist
b. Oct 21, 1581 in Bologna, Italy
d. Apr 6, 1641 in Naples, Italy
Source: *AtlBL; WebBD 80*

Domenici, Pete V(ichi)
American. Senator
b. May 7, 1932 in Albuquerque, New Mexico
Source: *AlmAP 78, 80; BioIn 9, 10; CngDr 74, 77, 79; CurBio 82; IntWW 74, 75, 76; NewYTBS 81; WhoAm 80, 82; WhoAmP 73, 75, 77, 79; WhoGov 77; WhoWest 76, 78*

Domgraf-Fassbaender, Willi
German. Opera Singer
b. Feb 19, 1897 in Aachen, Germany
Source: *NewEOp 71*

Domingo, Placido
Spanish. Opera Singer
Tenor, who recorded hit single "Perhaps Love" with John Denver, 1981.
b. Jan 21, 1941 in Madrid, Spain
Source: *CelR 73; CurBio 72; NewYTBE 72; WhoAm 82; WhoE 74; WhoMus 72; WhoWor 74*

Dominguin, Luis Miguel
Spanish. Bullfighter
b. Dec 9, 1926 in Madrid, Spain
Source: *CurBio 72*

Dominic, Saint
[Domingo DeGuzman]
Spanish. Religious Figure
b. 1170
d. 1221
Source: *NewCol 75; REn*

Dominici, Gaston
French. Murderer
b. 1877
d. 1965
Source: *BioIn 3, 4, 10*

Dominick, Peter Hoyt
American. Government Official
b. Jul 7, 1915 in Stamford, Connecticut
d. Mar 18, 1981 in Hobe Sound, Florida
Source: *BioIn 9, 10, 11; CngDr 74; IntWW 74, 75, 76, 77, 78; NewYTBS 81; PolProf J; PolProf K; WhoAm 74, 76, 78; WhoAmP 73, 75, 77; WhoWest 74*

Domino, "Fats" (Antoine)
American. Singer
Best known song "Blueberry Hill," 1956.
b. Feb 26, 1928 in New Orleans, Louisiana
Source: *WhoAm 74*

Donahue, Elinor
American. Actress
Played Betty Anderson in TV series "Father Knows Best," 1954-62.
b. Apr 19, 1937 in Tacoma, Washington
Source: *BioIn 3; WhoAm 82; WhoHol A*

Donahue, Phil(ip John)
American. Television Personality
Host of talk show "Donahue," 1967--; won Emmys, 1977, 1979.
b. Dec 21, 1935 in Cleveland, Ohio
Source: *BioIn 11, 12; BkPepl; CurBio 80; IntMPA 82; WhoAm 78, 80, 82*

Donahue, Sam Koontz
American. Musician
b. Mar 8, 1918 in Detroit, Michigan
Source: *BiDAmM*

Donahue, Troy
[Merle Johnson, Jr.]
American. Actor
Starred in TV series "Hawaiian Eye" and "Surfside 6."
b. Jan 17, 1937 in New York, New York
Source: *FilmgC; IntMPA 75, 76, 77, 78, 79, 80, 81, 82; MotPP; MovMk; WhoHol A*

Donahue, Woolworth
American. Chain Store Heir
b. 1913
d. 1972
Source: *BioIn 9; NewYTBE 72*

Donald, James
Scottish. Actor
b. May 18, 1917 in Aberdeen, Scotland
Source: *FilmgC; IntMPA 75, 76, 77, 78, 79, 80, 81, 82; WhoHol A; WhoThe 77*

Donald, Peter
American. Radio Actor
b. 1918? in Bristol, England
Source: *BioIn 3*

Donaldson, Sam(uel Andrew)
American. Broadcast Journalist
b. Mar 11, 1934 in El Paso, Texas
Source: *BioIn 11; WhoAm 78, 80, 82*

Donaldson, Stephen Reeder
American. Author
b. May 13, 1947 in Cleveland, Ohio
Source: *ConAu 89; WhoAm 82*

Donaldson, Walter
American. Songwriter
b. Feb 15, 1893 in Brooklyn, New York
d. Jul 15, 1947 in Santa Monica, California
Source: *AmSCAP 66; EncMT; NotNAT B*

Donat, Robert
English. Actor
b. Mar 18, 1905 in Manchester, England
d. Jun 9, 1958 in London, England
Source: *BiDFilm; FilmgC; MotPP; MovMk; OxFilm; OxThe; WhAm 3; WhScrn 74, 77; WhoHol B; WorEFlm*

Donatello
[Donatodi Niccolo di Betto Bardi]
Italian. Artist
b. 1386 in Florence, Italy
d. Dec 13, 1466 in Florence, Italy
Source: *AtlBL; REn*

Donath, Helen
American. Opera Singer
b. 1940 in Corpus Christi, Texas
Source: *IntWW 74; WhoMus 72*

Donati, Pino
Italian. Musician, Opera Director
b. 1907
d. 1975
Source: *BioIn 9, 10*

Donegan, Dorothy
American. Musician
b. Apr 6, 1926 in Chicago, Illinois
Source: *WhoAm 74; WhoBlA 75*

Donehue, Vincent J
American. Theatre, Film Director
b. Sep 22, 1922 in Whitehall, New York
d. Jan 17, 1966 in New York, New York
Source: *BiE&WWA; FilmgC; WhAm 4*

Donen, Stanley
American. Motion Picture Director
b. Apr 13, 1924 in Columbia, South Carolina
Source: *BiDFilm; CmMov; DcFM; FilmgC; IntMPA 75, 76, 77, 78, 79, 80, 81, 82; IntWW 74; MovMk; OxFilm; WhoAm 74, 76, 78, 80, 82; WorEFlm*

Dongen, Kees van
[Cornelius Theodorus Dongen]
French. Artist
b. Jan 26, 1877 in Delfshaven, Netherlands
d. May 28, 1968 in Monte Carlo, Monaco
Source: *CurBio 60, 68*

Donitz, Karl C
see: Doenitz, Karl C

Donizetti, Gaetano
Italian. Opera Composer
b. Nov 29, 1797 in Bergamo, Italy
d. Apr 8, 1848 in Bergamo, Italy
Source: *AtlBL; REn*

Donleavy, James Patrick
American. Author, Dramatist
b. Apr 23, 1926 in Brooklyn, New York
Source: *ConAu 9R; ConLC 1, 4, 6, 10; IntWW 74; Who 74; WhoAm 74, 76, 78, 80, 82; WhoWor 74*

Donlevy, Brian
American. Actor
b. Feb 9, 1899 in Portadown, Ireland
d. Apr 5, 1972 in Woodland Hills, California
Source: *BiDFilm; BiE&WWA; FilmgC; MotPP; HolP 30; MovMk; NewYTBE 72; OxFilm; WhScrn 77; WhoHol B*

Donlon, Mary Honor
American. Jurist
b. 1893? in Utica, New York
d. Mar 5, 1977 in Tucson, Arizona
Source: *CurBio 49; WhoAmW 74; WhoGov 72*

Donne, John
English. Poet
Metaphysical poet wrote sonnet, *Death Be Not Proud;* poems neglected until 20th c.
b. 1573 in London, England
d. Mar 31, 1631 in London, England
Source: *Alli; AtlBL; BiD&SB; BrAu; CasWL; Chambr 1; ChPo, S1, S2; CnE&AP; CroE&S; CrtT 1; CyWA; DcEnA, AP; DcEnL; DcEuL; DcLEL; EvLB; MouLC 1; NewC; OxEng; Pen ENG; RAdv 1; RComWL; REn; WebE&AL*

Donnell, Jeff
American. Actress
b. Jul 10, 1921 in South Windham, Maine
Source: *FilmgC; IntMPA 75, 76, 77, 79, 80, 81, 82; MotPP; WhoHol A*

Donnelly, Ignatius
American. Social Reformer, Author
b. Nov 3, 1831 in Philadelphia, Pennsylvania
d. Jan 1, 1901 in Minneapolis, Minnesota
Source: *Alli; AmAu; AmAu&B; AmBi; ApCAB; BbD; BiAuS; BiD&SB; BiDrAC; CasWL; DcAmAu; DcAmB; DcEnA AP; DcLEL; DcNAA; EncAB-H; OxAmL; Pen AM; PoIre; REnAL; TwCBDA; WebAB; WebE&AL; WhAm 1; WhAmP*

Donnelly, Ruth
American. Actress
Films include *Mr. Deeds Goes to Town; The Bells of St. Mary's.*
b. May 17, 1896 in Trenton, New Jersey
d. Nov 17, 1982 in New York, New York
Source: *BiE&WWA; FilmgC; MovMk; NewYTBS 82; NotNAT; ThFT; Vers A; WhoHol A*

Donner, Frederic Garrett
American. Businessman
b. 1902 in Three Oaks, Michigan
Source: *CurBio 59; IntWW 74; St&PR 75; Who 74; WhoGov 72; WhoWor 74*

Donohue, Jack
American. Actor, Dancer, Director
b. Nov 3, 1912 in New York, New York
Source: *BiE&WWA; FilmgC; IntMPA 75, 76, 77, 78, 79, 80, 81, 82; NotNAT; WhoThe 77*

Donovan
[Donovan P Leitch]
Scottish. Singer, Songwriter
Mid-1960's hits included "Sunshine Superman," "Mellow Yellow."
b. Feb 10, 1946 in Glasgow, Scotland
Source: *EncFCWM 69; EncPR&S*

Donovan, Art
American. Football Player
b. Jun 5, 1925 in Bronx, New York
Source: *BioIn 4, 7, 8; WhoFtbl 74*

Donovan, Hedley Williams
American. Journalist
b. May 24, 1914 in Brainerd, Minnesota
Source: *CurBio 65; IntWW 74; Who 74; WhoAm 74, 76, 78, 80, 82; WhoE 74; WhoWor 74*

Donovan, Raymond James
American. Government Official
Secretary of Labor, 1981--.
b. Aug 31, 1930 in Bayonne, New Jersey
Source: *CurBio 82; WhoAm 82*

Donovan, Robert John
American. Journalist
b. Aug 21, 1912 in Buffalo, New York
Source: *AmAu&B; ConAu 1R, 2NR; WhoAm 74, 76, 78, 80, 82; WhoWor 74*

Donovan, William Joseph
"Wild Bill"
American. Lawyer
Founded Office of Strategic Services (OSS); later evolved into CIA.
b. Jan 1, 1883 in Buffalo, New York
d. Feb 8, 1959 in Washington, DC
Source: *CurBio 41, 54, 59; WebAB; WhAm 3*

Doobie Brothers, The
[Jeff Baxter; "Little" John Hartman; Mike Hossack; Tom Johnston;Keith Knudson; Michael McDonald; Tiran Porter; Dave Shogren; Pat Simmons]
American. Rock Group
Source: *EncPR&S; Rk100*

Dooley, Rae
Scottish. Actress
b. 1896 in Glasgow, Scotland
Source: *BioIn 9; EncMT; WhThe*

Dooley, Tom
see: Dula, Thomas

Dooley, Thomas Anthony
American. Medical Missionary
b. Jan 17, 1927 in Saint Louis, Missouri
d. Jan 18, 1961 in New York, New York
Source: *AmAu&B; ConAu 93; CurBio 57, 61; WebAB; WhAm 4A*

Doolittle, Hilda
[H D, pseud.]
American. Author
b. Sep 10, 1886 in Bethlehem, Pennsylvania
d. Sep 27, 1961 in Zurich, Switzerland
Source: *AmAu&B; AtlBL; CasWL; Chambr 3; ChPo S2; CnDAL; ConAmA; ConAmL; ConAu 97; ConLC 3, 14; DcLEL; EncWL; EvLB; InWom; LongCTC; ModAL, SUP; OxAmL; Pen AM; RAdv 1; REn; REnAL; TwCA, SUP; TwCW; WebAB; WebE&AL; WhAm 4; WhoTwCL*

Doolittle, James Harold
American. Aviator, Army Officer
b. Dec 14, 1896 in Alameda, California
Source: *CelR 73; CurBio 42, 57; IntWW 74; St&PR 75; WebAB; Who 74; WhoAm 74, 76, 78, 80, 82*

Doors, The
[John Densmore; Bobby Krieger; Ray Manzarek; Jim Morrison]
American. Rock Group
Source: *EncPR&S; Rk100*

Doppler, Christian Johann
Austrian. Physicist, Mathematician
b. Nov 30, 1803 in Salzburg, Austria
d. Mar 17, 1853 in Venice, Italy
Source: *AsBiEn; WebBD 80*

Dorati, Antal
American. Conductor, Composer
b. Apr 9, 1906 in Budapest, Hungary
Source: *CurBio 48; IntWW 74; Who 74; WhoAm 74, 76, 78, 80, 82; WhoMus 72; WhoS&SW 73; WhoWor 74*

Dore, (Paul) Gustave
French. Artist
b. Jan 6, 1832
d. Jan 23, 1883
Source: *AtlBL; ChPo, S1, S2; IlsBYP; OxFr; REn*

Dorgan, Thomas Aloysius
"Tad"
American. Cartoonist, Journalist
b. Apr 29, 1877 in San Francisco, California
d. 1929
Source: *AmAu&B; DcAmB; WhAm HA, 4; WhAmP*

Doria, Andrea
Italian. Admiral, Statesman
b. Nov 30, 1468
d. Nov 25, 1560
Source: *BioIn 1; NewCol 75; REn; WebBD 80*

Doriot, Georges Frederic
French. Educator, Business Executive
b. Sep 24, 1899 in Paris, France
Source: *BioIn 1, 6, 7; IntWW 75, 76, 77, 78; IntYB 78; St&PR 75; WhoAm 74; WhoF&I 74*

Dorleac, Francoise
French. Actress
b. Mar 21, 1942 in Paris, France
d. Jun 26, 1967 in Nice, France
Source: *BioIn 7, 8; FilmEn; FilmgC; MotPP; ObitOF 79; OxFilm; WhScrn 74, 77; WhoHol B*

Dorman, Isiah
American. Army Interpreter
d. 1876 in Little Big Horn, Montana
Source: *BioIn 1*

Dorman, Maurice
English. Political Leader
b. Aug 7, 1912 in Staffordshire, England
Source: *IntWW 74; Who 74; WhoGov 72; WhoWor 74*

Dornberger, Walter Robert
German. Engineer, Rocket Developer
b. Sep 6, 1895 in Giessen, Germany
d. Jun 1980 in Hamburg, Germany (West)
Source: *BioIn 6, 7; CurBio 65, 80; NewYTBS 80*

Dorne, Albert
American. Illustrator
b. Feb 7, 1904 in New York, New York
d. Dec 15, 1965 in New York, New York
Source: *BioIn 1, 2, 4, 5, 6, 7; WhAm 4*

Dornier, Claude
German. Airplane Manufacturer
Built the DO-X, largest passenger plane at time, 1929.
b. 1884
d. Dec 5, 1969 in Zug, Switzerland
Source: *BioIn 8; WebBD 80*

Dors, Diana
English. Actress
b. Oct 23, 1931 in Swindon, England
Source: *FilmgC; InWom; IntMPA 75, 76, 77, 78, 79, 80, 81, 82; MotPP; MovMk; WhoHol A*

D'Orsay, Fifi
Canadian. Actress
b. 1904 in Montreal, PQ
Source: *FilmgC; MotPP; MovMk; ThFT; WhoHol A*

Doreset, Marion
American. Chemist
b. Dec 14, 1872 in Columbia, Tennessee
Source: *BioIn 7; WhAm 1*

Dorset, Tony (Anthony Drew)
"T D"; "Hawk"
American. Football Player
Won Heisman Trophy, 1976; running back, Dallas Cowboys, 1977--.
b. Apr 7, 1954 in Aliquippa, Pennsylvania
Source: *BioIn 12; CurBio 80; WhoAm 82; WhoFtbl 74*

Dorsey, Bob Rawls
American. Oil Company Executive
Gulf Oil Corp., president, 1965-72, chairman, executive, 1972-76.
b. Aug 27, 1912 in Rockland, Texas
Source: *IntWW 74; NewYTBE 71; St&PR 75; WhoAm 74, 76, 78, 80, 82; WhoE 74; WhoF&I 74*

Dorsey, Jimmy (James)
American. Musician, Band Leader
Played clarinet, saxophone in own band and with brother, Tommy, during Big Band era.
b. Feb 29, 1904 in Shenandoah, Pennsylvania
d. Jun 12, 1957 in New York, New York
Source: *AmSCAP 66; CurBio 42, 57; FilmgC; WhScrn 74, 77; WhoHol B; WhoJazz 72*

Dorsey, Thomas Andrew
"Georgia Tom"; "The Professor"
American. Founder of Gospel Music
Wrote the classic "Precious Lord, Take My Hand".
b. Jul 1, 1900 in Villa Rica, Georgia
Source: *BluesWW; DcBlPA; InB&W 80; WhoAm 74, 76, 78*

Dorsey, Tommy (Thomas Francis)
American. Band Leader
Played trombone, trumpet in own band and with brother, Jimmy, during Big Band era.
b. Nov 19, 1905 in Mahonoy Plains, Pennsylvania
d. Nov 26, 1956 in Greenwich, Connecticut
Source: *CurBio 42, 57; WhAm 3; WhScrn 74, 77; WhoHol B; WhoJazz 72*

DosPassos, John
American. Author
b. Jan 14, 1896 in Chicago, Illinois
d. Sep 28, 1970 in Baltimore, Maryland
Source: *AmAu&B; AmNov; AmWr; AtlBL; Au&Wr 71; BiE&WWA; CasWL; Chambr 3; CnDAL; CnMD; ConAmA; ConAmL; ConAu 29R, 3NR; ConLC 1, 4, 8, 11, 15; CyWA; DcLEL; EncAB-H; EncWL; EvLB; LongCTC; ModAL, SUP; ModWD; OxAmL; OxEng; Pen AM; RAdv 1; REn; REnAL; TwCA, SUP; TwCW; WebAB; WebE&AL; WhAm 5; WhNAA; WhoTwCL*

Dostoyevsky, Fyodor Mikhailovich
[Fyodor Dostoevski; Fedor Dostoevsky; Fyoder Dostoievsky]
Russian. Author
b. Nov 11, 1821 in Saint Petersburg, Russia
d. Feb 9, 1881 in Moscow, Russia
Source: *AtlBL; BbD; BiD&SB; CasWL; ClDMEL; CyWA; DcEuL; DcRusL; EncMys; EuAu; EvEuW; FilmgC; OxEng; Pen EUR*

Dott, Gerard
[The Incredible String Band]
Scottish. Singer, Musician
b. in Edinburgh, Scotland
Source: *NF*

Dou, Gerard
Dutch. Artist
b. Apr 7, 1613 in Leiden, Netherlands
d. Feb 1675 in Leiden, Netherlands
Source: *AtlBL*

Doubleday, Abner
American. Civil War General
Wrongly credited as inventor of baseball.
b. Jun 26, 1819 in Ballston Spa, New York
d. Jan 26, 1893 in Mendham, New Jersey
Source: *Alli SUP; AmBi; ApCAB; DcAmAu; DcAmB; DcNAA; Drake; TwCBDA; WebAB; WhAm H; WhoProB 73*

Doubleday, Frank Nelson
American. Publisher
Founded Doubleday and Co., 1897.
b. Jan 8, 1862 in Brooklyn, New York
d. Jan 30, 1934 in Coconut Grove, Florida
Source: *AmAu&B; DcAmB S1; WebAB; WhAm 1*

Doubleday, Nelson
American. Publisher
Son of Frank Doubleday; founded Nelson Doubleday, Inc., 1910.
b. Jun 16, 1889 in Brooklyn, New York
d. Jan 11, 1949 in Oyster Bay, New York
Source: *DcAmB S4; NatCAB 37; WhAm 2*

Doubleday, Nelson
American. Publisher, Baseball Executive
President, Doubleday and Co., 1959--; majority owner of NY Mets.
b. 1933?
Source: *WhoAm 74, 76, 78, 80, 82*

Doubrovska, Felia
[Felizata Dluzhnevska; Mrs. Pierre Vladimiroff]
Russian. Ballerina, Teacher
b. 1896 in Saint Petersburg, Russia
d. Sep 18, 1981 in New York, New York
Source: *AnObit 1981; BioIn 3, 6, 9, 11; NewYTBS 81*

Doughty, Charles Montagu
English. Poet
b. Aug 19, 1843 in Suffolk, England
d. Jan 30, 1926 in Kent, England
Source: *Alli SUP; AtlBL; BrAu 19; CasWL; Chambr 3; CnE&AP; CyWA; DcLEL; EncWL; NewC; REn*

Doughty, Neal
see: REO Speedwagon

Douglas, Aaron
American. Artist
b. 1899 in Topeka, Kansas
d. Feb 2, 1979 in Nashville, Tennessee
Source: *AfroAA; BioIn 11; DcAmArt; NewYTBS 79*

Douglas, Lord Alfred Bruce
English. Author
b. 1870
d. Mar 20, 1945 in Sussex, England
Source: *CathA 1930; ChPo, S2; DcLEL; EvLB; LongCTC; NewC; OxEng; Pen ENG; REn; WhoLA*

Douglas, Amanda Minnie
American. Children's Author
b. Jul 14, 1837 in New York, New York
d. Jul 18, 1918 in Newark, New Jersey
Source: *Alli SUP; AmAu; AmAu&B; AmWom; ApCAB; BbD; BiD&SB; CarSB; ChPo S1, S2; DcAmAu; DcAmB; DcNAA; InWom; TwCBDA; WhAm 1; WomWWA 14*

Douglas, Cathleen Heffernan
[Mrs. William O Douglas]
American. Lawyer, Conservationist
b. Apr 30, 1943
Source: *WhoAm 74, 76, 78, 80, 82*

Douglas, David
Scottish. Botanist
b. 1798 in Scone, Scotland
d. 1834
Source: *BioIn 1, 2, 3, 4; OxCan*

Douglas, Donald Willis
American. Aircraft Manufacturer
Founded Douglas Aircraft, 1920; produced DC series for commerical airlines.
b. Apr 6, 1892 in Brooklyn, New York
d. Feb 1, 1981 in Palm Springs, California
Source: *BioIn 1, 2, 3, 4, 5, 7, 8, 10, 11; CurBio 41, 50, 81; IntWW 74, 75, 76, 78; McGEWB; NewYTBS 81; WebAMB; Who 74; WhoAm 74; WhoF&I 74*

Douglas, Donna
American. Actress
Played Elly May Clampett in TV series "The Beverly Hillbillies," 1962-71.
b. 1939 in Baywood, Louisiana
Source: *InWom; MotPP; WhoHol A*

Douglas, Emmitt
American. Civil Rights Activist
b. 1926?
d. Mar 25, 1981 in New Roads, Louisiana
Source: *BioIn 12*

Douglas, Helen Mary Gahagan
American. Singer, Congresswoman
b. Nov 25, 1900 in Boonton, New Jersey
d. Jun 28, 1980 in New York, New York
Source: *BiDrAC; ConAu 101; CurBio 44, 80; NewYTBE 71; NotNAT; WhoAm 74; WhoHol A; WhoThe 77*

Douglas, Jack
American. Comedian
b. 1908 in New York, New York
Source: *BioIn 5, 6, 8, 10*

Douglas, Keith Castellain
English. Poet
b. 1920 in Tunbridge Wells, England
d. Jun 1944 in Normandy, France
Source: *BioIn 10; DcLEL 1940; LongCTC; ModBrL SUP; OxEng; Pen ENG; WebE&AL; WhoTwCL; WorAu*

Douglas, Kirk
[Issur Danielovich Demsky]
American. Actor
Has appeared in over 50 films including *Lust for Life,* 1956; *Spartacus,* 1960.
b. Dec 9, 1916 in Amsterdam, New York
Source: *BiDFilm; BiE&WWA; BkPepl; CelR 73; CmMov; CurBio 52; FilmgC; IntMPA 75, 76, 77, 78, 79, 80, 81, 82; IntWW 74; MotPP; MovMk; NotNAT; OxFilm; WhoAm 74, 76, 78, 80, 82; WhoHol A; WhoWor 74; WorEFlm*

Douglas, Laura Virginia O'Hanlon
[Virginia O'Hanlon]
American. Santa Claus Letter Writer
b. 1889
d. 1971 in Valatie, New York
Source: *InWom*

Douglas, Lloyd Cassel
American. Author
b. Aug 27, 1877 in Columbia City, Indiana
d. Feb 13, 1951 in Los Angeles, California
Source: *AmAu&B; AmNov; CyWA; DcAmB S5; EvLB; FilmgC; IndAu 1917; LongCTC; OhA&B; OxAmL; Pen AM; REn; REnAL; TwCA, SUP; TwCW; WebAB; WhAm 3; WhNAA*

Douglas, Melvyn
[Melvin Hesselberg]
American. Actor
Won Oscars, 1963, 1979, for *Hud,* and *Being There.*
b. Apr 5, 1901 in Macon, Georgia
d. Aug 4, 1981 in New York, New York
Source: *BiDFilm; BiE&WWA; BioIn 5, 6, 9, 11; CelR 73; CurBio 42, 81; FamA&A; FilmgC; IntMPA 75, 76, 77, 78, 79, 80, 81; MGM; MotPP; MovMk; NewYTBS 81; NotNAT; OxFilm; WhoAm 74, 76, 78, 80; WhoHol A; WhoThe 72, 77; WorEFlm*

Douglas, Michael Kirk
American. Actor, Motion Picture Producer
Won Oscar, 1975, as producer of *One Flew Over the Cuckoo's Nest.*
b. Sep 25, 1944 in New York, New York
Source: *BkPepl; FilmgC; IntMPA 75, 76, 77, 78, 79, 80, 81, 82; WhoAm 82; WhoHol A; WrDr 76*

Douglas, Mike
[Michael Delaney Dowd, Jr.]
American. TV Host, Singer
Host, "The Mike Douglas Show," 1961--; has won four Emmys.
b. Aug 11, 1925 in Chicago, Illinois
Source: *BioNews 75; BkPepl; CelR 73; CurBio 68; IntMPA 82; WhoAm 74, 76, 78, 80, 82; WhoE 74; WhoHol A*

Douglas, Norman
Scottish. Author
b. Dec 8, 1868 in Aberdeen, Scotland
d. Feb 9, 1952 in Capri, Italy
Source: *AtlBL; CasWL; Chambr 3; ChPo, S1; CnMWL; CyWA; DcLEL; LongCTC; ModBrL; NewC; OxEng; Pen ENG; RAdv 1; REn; TwCA, SUP; TwCW; WebE&AL; WhoTwCL*

Douglas, Paul
American. Actor
b. Apr 11, 1907 in Philadelphia, Pennsylvania
d. Sep 11, 1959 in Hollywood, California
Source: *BiDFilm; FilmgC; MotPP; MovMk; WhScrn 74, 77; WhoHol B; WorEFlm*

Douglas, Paul Howard
American. Economist, Senator
b. May 26, 1892 in Salem, Massachusetts
d. Sep 24, 1976 in Washington, DC
Source: *AmAu&B; AmEA 74; AmM&WS 73S; BiDrAC; ConAu 69; CurBio 49, 76; IntWW 74; WhoAm 74; WhoAmP 73; WhoWor 74*

Douglas, Robert L
American. Basketball Team Owner, Coach
Owner/coach all-black Renaissance Big-Five team, 1922; first black in Hall of Fame.
b. Nov 4, 1884 in Saint Kitts, British West Indies
d. Jul 16, 1979 in New York, New York
Source: *NewYTBS 79; WhoBbl 73*

Douglas, Stephen Arnold
American. Politician
US Senator, 1947-61; lost to Lincoln in 1860 presidential election.
b. Apr 23, 1813 in Brandon, Vermont
d. Jun 3, 1861 in Chicago, Illinois
Source: *AmAu&B; AmBi; ApCAB; BiAuS; BiDrAC; DcAmB; Drake; EncAB-H; OxAmL; REn; REnAL; TwCBDA; WebAB; WhAm H; WhAmP*

Douglas, William Orville
American. Supreme Court Justice
Liberal justice, 1939-75; granted stay of execution to Rosenbergs, 1953.
b. Oct 16, 1898 in Maine, Minnesota
d. Jan 19, 1980 in Washington, DC
Source: *ConAu 9R, 93; CurBio 41, 50, 80; IntWW 74; REn; REnAL; Who 74; WhoAm 74; WhoAmP 73; WhoWor 74; WrDr 76*

Douglas-Home, Alexander Frederick
English. Politician
b. Jul 2, 1903 in London, England
Source: *Alli; CurBio 58; EvLB; IntWW 74; NewYTBE 71; Pen ENG; Who 74; WhoWor 74*

Douglass, Frederick
[Frederick Augustus W Bailey]
American. Lecturer, Author
Escaped slavery, 1838; established *North Star,* 1847.
b. Feb 1817 in Tuckahoe, Maryland
d. Feb 20, 1895 in Anacosta Heights, Maryland
Source: *Alli SUP; AmAu; AmAu&B; AmBi; ApCAB; BbD; BiD&SB; BiDSA; BlkAW; Chambr 3; DcAmAu; DcAmB; DcNAA; Drake; EncAB-H; OxAmL; REn; REnAL; TwCBDA; WebAB; WebE&AL; WhAm H; WhAmP*

Douglass, Lathrop
American. Architect, Urban Planner
b. Sep 5, 1907 in Kansas City, Missouri
d. Jan 21, 1981 in Greenwich, Connecticut
Source: *AmArch 70; BioIn 8; NewYTBS 81; WhoAm 74, 76, 78, 80; WhoF&I 74; WhoWor 74, 76*

Doulton, Sir Henry
English. Potter
b. 1820 in England
d. 1897
Source: *WebBD 80*

Dourif, Brad
American. Actor
b. Mar 18, 1950 in Huntington, West Virginia
Source: *WhoAm 82; WhoHol A*

Dove, Arthur Garfield
American. Artist
b. Aug 2, 1880 in Canandaigua, New York
d. Nov 23, 1946 in Huntington, New York
Source: *AtlBL; BioNews 75; ChPo; DcAmB S4; DcCAA 71; WebAB*

Dovzhenko, Alexander
Russian. Motion Picture Director
b. 1894 in Sosnitsa, Russia
d. 1956
Source: *BiDFilm; DcFM; FilmgC; MovMk; OxFilm; WhScrn 74, 77; WomWMM; WorEFlm*

Dow, Charles Henry
American. Financial Statistician
b. Nov 6, 1851 in Sterling, Connecticut
d. Dec 4, 1902 in Brooklyn, New York
Source: *WebAB*

Dow, Herbert Henry
American. Chemist, Manufacturer
Founded Dow Chemical Co., 1900.
b. Feb 26, 1866 in Belleville, ON
d. Oct 15, 1930 in Rochester, Minnesota
Source: *DcAmB S1; EncAB-H; WebAB; WhAm 1*

Dowding, Baron Hugh C T
British. Air Force Officer
b. Apr 24, 1883
d. Feb 15, 1970 in Kent, England
Source: *CurBio 40, 70*

Dowell, Anthony
English. Dancer
b. Feb 16, 1943 in London, England
Source: *CurBio 71; IntWW 74; NewYTBS 74; Who 74; WhoAm 82; WhoWor 74*

Dowie, John Alexander
Scottish. Evangelist
b. May 25, 1847 in Scotland
d. Mar 9, 1907
Source: *BioIn 2, 5, 8*

Dowland, John
English. Composer
b. Jan 1563 in Dublin, Ireland
d. Apr 7, 1626 in London, England
Source: *Alli; AtlBL; BrAu; ChPo S2; NewC; OxEng; REn*

Dowler, Boyd
American. Football Player
b. Oct 18, 1937 in Rock Springs, Wyoming
Source: *WhoFtbl 74*

Dowling, Dan(iel Blair)
American. Editorial Cartoonist
b. Nov 16, 1906 in O'Neill, Nebraska
Source: *WhoAm 74; WhoAmA 73*

Dowling, Eddie (Edward)
American. Actor, Dramatist, Producer
b. Dec 9, 1894 in Woonsocket, Rhode Island
d. Feb 18, 1976 in Smithfield, Rhode Island
Source: *AmSCAP 66; BiE&WWA; CurBio 46; EncMT; PlP&P; WhAm 6; WhoAm 74; WhoThe 77*

Down, Lesley-Anne
English. Actress
b. Mar 17, 1954 in London, England
Source: *BioIn 10, 11; FilmEn; IntMPA 81, 82*

Downes, Edward Olin Davenport
American. Opera, Symphony Conductor
b. Aug 12, 1911 in Boston, Massachusetts
Source: *DrAS 74H; WhoAm 74, 76, 78, 80, 82; WhoE 74*

Downes, (Edwin) Olin
American. Critic, Author
b. Jan 27, 1886 in Evanston, Illinois
d. Aug 22, 1955 in New York, New York
Source: *AmAu&B; CurBio 43, 55; DcAmB S5; WhAm 3; WhScrn 74, 77*

Downey, Eric
see: Thin Lizzy

Downey, Fairfax Davis
American. Author
b. Nov 28, 1893 in Salt Lake City, Utah
Source: *ConAu 1R, 1NR; CurBio 49; SmATA 3*

Downey, Morton
American. Singer
b. Nov 14, 1902 in Wallingford, Connecticut
Source: *AmSCAP 66; CurBio 49; WhoAm 74, 76, 78, 80, 82; WhoHol A*

Downing, Andrew Jackson
American. Horticulturist, Architect
Authority on landscape gardening and design.
b. Oct 30, 1815 in Newburgh, New York
d. Jul 28, 1852 in New York
Source: *AmAu&B; AmBi; ApCAB; BnEnAmA; DcAmAu; DcAmB; McGDA; McGEWB; NatCAB 11; OxAmH; OxArt; WebAB 79; WhAm H*

Downing, K K
see: Judas Priest

Downs, Hugh
American. TV Personality
b. Feb 14, 1921 in Akron, Ohio
Source: *CelR 73; ConAu 45; CurBio 65; IntMPA 75, 76, 77, 78, 79, 80, 81, 82; WhoAm 74, 76, 78, 80, 82*

Downs, Johnny
American. Actor
b. 1915 in New York, New York
Source: *FilmgC; WhoHol A*

Downs, William Randall, Jr.
American. Broadcast Journalist
b. Aug 17, 1914 in Kansas City, Kansas
d. May 3, 1978 in Bethesda, Maryland
Source: *ConAu 77, 81; WhAm 7; WhoAm 76, 78*

Dowson, Ernest Christopher
English. Author
b. Aug 2, 1867 in Kent, England
d. Feb 23, 1900 in London, England
Source: *AtlBL; BrAu 19; CasWL; Chambr 3; ChPo, S1, S2; CnE&AP; DcLEL; EvLB; MouLC 4; NewC; OxEng; Pen ENG; REn; WebE&AL*

Doxiadis, Constantinos Apostolos
Greek. Architect
b. May 14, 1913 in Stenimochos, Greece
d. Jun 28, 1975 in Athens, Greece
Source: *ConAu 41R, 57; CurBio 64; IntWW 74; WhAm 6; Who 74; WhoWor 74*

Doyle, Sir Arthur Conan
Scottish. Author, Physician
Introduced Sherlock Holmes in *A Study in Scarlet*, 1887.
b. May 22, 1859 in Edinburgh, Scotland
d. Jul 7, 1930 in Crowborough, England
Source: *Alli SUP; AtlBL; AuBYP; BbD; BiD&SB; BiDPara; CarSB; CasWL; Chambr 3; ChPo, S1; CyWA; DcBiA; DcEnA AP; DcLEL; EncMys; EvLB; FilmgC; JBA 34; LongCTC; MnBBF; ModBrL; NewC; OxEng; Pen ENG; PoIre; RAdv 1; REn; TwCA, SUP; TwCW; WebE&AL; WhoChL; WhoTwCL*

Doyle, David
American. Actor
Played John Bosley in TV series "Charlie's Angels."
Source: *WhoHol A*

Dozier, James Lee
American. General
Kidnapped by Red Brigade Terrorists, Dec 17, 1981; rescued by Italian police, Jan 28, 1982.
b. Apr 10, 1931 in Arcadia, Florida
Source: *NewYTBS 82*

Dr. Acula, pseud.
see: Ackerman, Forest J

Drabble, Margaret
English. Author
b. Jun 5, 1939 in Sheffield, England
Source: *Au&Wr 71; ConAu 13R; ConLC 2, 3, 5, 8, 10; ConNov 72, 76; IntWW 74; LongCTC; ModBrL SUP; RAdv 1; TwCW; Who 74; WhoAm 74, 76, 78, 80, 82; WhoTwCL; WrDr 76*

Drachler, Norman
American. Educator
b. May 20, 1912 in Poland
Source: *LEduc 74; WhoAm 74, 76, 78, 80, 82; WhoWorJ 72*

Draco
Greek. Legislator
Responsible for Draconian laws, the first written down in Athens.
d. 650BC
Source: *NewC; REn*

Dracula
[Vlad the Impaler]
Hungarian. Prince
b. 1431
d. 1476
Source: *BioIn 9, 10*

Draddy, Vincent de Paul
American. Sportswear Designer
Source: *WorFshn*

Dragon, Carmen
American. Symphony Conductor
b. Jul 28, 1914 in Antioch, California
Source: *AmSCAP 66; WhoMus 72*

Dragon, Daryl
[The Captain and Tennille]
American. Musician, Songwriter
b. Aug 27, 1942 in Studio City, California
Source: *BkPepl*

Dragonette, Jessica
Indian. Opera Singer
b. Feb 14, 1910? in Calcutta, India
d. Mar 18, 1980 in New York, New York
Source: *InWom; PlP&P; WhoAmW 77; WhoMus 72*

Drake, Alfred
American. Opera Singer
b. Oct 7, 1914 in New York, New York
Source: *BiE&WWA; CelR 73; CurBio 44; EncMT; FamA&A; FilmgC; NotNAT; WhoAm 74; WhoHol A; WhoThe 77; WhoWor 74*

Drake, Betsy
American. Actress
b. 1923 in Paris, France
Source: *FilmgC; MotPP; WhoHol A*

Drake, Edwin Laurentine
American. Petroleum Entrepreneur
Established first producing oil well in US, near Titusville, PA, Aug 27, 1859.
b. Mar 29, 1819 in Greenville, New York
d. Nov 8, 1880 in Bethlehem, Pennsylvania
Source: *AmBi; DcAmB; WebAB; WhAm H*

Drake, Frances
Horoscope Columnist
Source: *NF*

Drake, Sir Francis
English. Admiral, Navigator
First Englishman to circumnavigate globe, 1577-80.
b. 1540 in Devonshire, England
d. Jan 28, 1596 in Portobelo, Panama
Source: *Alli, SUP; ApCAB; Drake; NewC; REn; REnAL; WhAm H*

Drake, Frank Donald
American. Astronomer
Organized search for extra-terrestrial life, called project OZMA, 1960.
b. May 28, 1930 in Chicago, Illinois
Source: *ConAu 17R; CurBio 63; IntWW 74; WhoAm 74, 76, 78, 80, 82; WhoE 74; WhoWor 74*

Drake, Galen
Radio Personality
Source: *NF*

Drake, Joseph Rodman
American. Poet
b. Aug 17, 1795 in New York, New York
d. Sep 21, 1820 in New York, New York
Source: *Alli; AmAu; AmAu&B; AmBi; ApCAB; BbD; BiD&SB; Chambr 3; ChPo, S2; CnDAL; CyAL 1; DcAmAu; DcAmB; DcLEL; DcNAA; Drake; EvLB; OxAmL; Pen AM; REn; REnAL; TwCBDA; WhAm H*

Drake, Stanley
American. Cartoonist
b. Nov 9, 1921 in Brooklyn, New York
Source: *WhoAm 82; WorECom*

Drake, Tom
[Alfred Alderdice]
American. Actor
Appeared in 1940's musicals including *Meet Me in St. Louis.*
b. Aug 5, 1918 in New York, New York
d. Aug 11, 1982 in Torrance, California
Source: *FilmEn; FilmgC; IntMPA 75, 76, 77, 78, 79; MGM; MotPP; MovMk*

Draper, Dorothy Tuckerman
American. Interior Decorator
b. Nov 22, 1889 in New York, New York
d. Mar 10, 1969 in Cleveland, Ohio
Source: *CurBio 41, 69; InWom; WhAm 5*

Draper, Paul
Italian. Dancer
b. Oct 25, 1909 in Florence, Italy
Source: *BiE&WWA; CurBio 44; NotNAT; WhoHol A*

Draper, Ruth
American. Actress
b. Dec 2, 1884 in New York, New York
d. Dec 30, 1956 in New York, New York
Source: *InWom; OxThe; REnAL; WhAm 3*

Drayton, Michael
English. Author
b. 1563 in Warwickshire, England
d. Dec 23, 1631 in London, England
Source: *Alli; AtlBL; BbD; BiD&SB; BrAu; CasWL; Chambr 1; ChPo, S1; CnE&AP; CroE&S; CrtT 1; CyWA; DcEnA; DcEnL; DcEuL; DcLEL; EvLB; McGEWD; MouLC 1; NewC; OxEng; Pen ENG; REn; WebE&AL*

Dreier, Alex
American. Radio, TV Commentator
b. Jun 26, 1916 in Honolulu, Hawaii
Source: *WhoAm 74*

Dreifus, Claudia
American. Journalist
b. Nov 24, 1944
Source: *BioIn 10; ConAu 45, 1NR; ForWC 70*

Dreiser, Theodore
American. Editor, Author
Wrote *Sister Carrie,* 1900, *An American Tragedy,* 1925; books attacked as immoral.
b. Aug 27, 1871 in Terre Haute, Indiana
d. Dec 28, 1945 in Hollywood, California
Source: *AmAu&B; AmLY; AmWr; AtlBL; CasWL; Chambr 3; CnDAL; CnMD; CnMWL; ConAmA; ConAmL; CyWA; DcAmAu; DcAmB S3; DcBiA; DcLEL; DcNAA; EncAB-H; EncMys; EncWL; EvLB; FilmgC; IndAu 1816; LongCTC; ModAL, SUP; ModWD; OxAmL; OxEng; Pen AM; RAdv 1; RComWL; REn; REnAL; TwCA, SUP; TwCW; WebAB; WebE&AL; WhAm 2; WhNAA; WhoTwCL*

Dressen, Charlie (Charles W)
American. Baseball Manager
b. Sep 20, 1898 in Decatur, Illinois
d. Aug 10, 1966 in Detroit, Michigan
Source: *CurBio 51, 66; WhAm 4; WhoFtbl 74; WhoProB 73*

Dresser, Davis
[Brett Halliday, pseud.]
American. Author
b. Jul 31, 1904 in Chicago, Illinois
d. Feb 4, 1977 in Montecito, California
Source: *AmAu&B; ConAu 69, 77; CurBio 69, 77; EncMys; WorAu*

Dresser, Louise
American. Actress
b. Oct 5, 1882 in Evansville, Indiana
d. Apr 24, 1965 in Woodland Hills, California
Source: *FilmgC; InWom; MotPP; MovMk; ThFT; TwYS; WhAm 4; WhScrn 74, 77; WhoHol B*

Dressler, Marie
[Leila Koerber]
Canadian. Actress
b. Nov 9, 1869 in Cobourg, ON
d. Jul 28, 1934 in Santa Barbara, California
Source: *AmAu&B; AmBi; BiDFilm; DcAmB S1; DcNAA; EncMT; Film 1; FilmgC; InWom; MotPP; MovMk; NotAW; OxFilm; OxThe; REn; ThFT; TwYS; WebAB; WhAm 1; WhScrn 74, 77; WhoHol B; WhoStg 1906, 1908; WorEFlm*

Drew, Charles Richard
American. Scientist
b. Jun 3, 1904 in Washington, DC
d. Apr 1, 1950 in Washington, DC
Source: *CurBio 44, 50; DcAmB S4; EncAB-H; WebAB; WhAm 3*

Drew, Daniel
American. Financier
b. Jul 29, 1792
d. Sep 18, 1874
Source: *BioIn 3; WhAm H*

Drew, Elizabeth Brenner
American. Journalist
b. Nov 16, 1935 in Cincinnati, Ohio
Source: *ConAu 104; ForWC 70; WhoAm 74, 76, 78, 80, 82; WhoAmW 77; WhoS&SW 73*

Drew, Ellen
[Terry Ray]
American. Actress
b. Nov 23, 1915 in Kansas City, Missouri
Source: *FilmgC; IntMPA 75, 76, 77, 78, 79, 80, 81, 82; MotPP; MovMk; ThFT; WhoHol A*

Drew, John
American. Actor
b. Nov 13, 1853 in Philadelphia, Pennsylvania
d. Jul 9, 1927 in San Francisco, California
Source: *AmAu&B; AmBi; DcAmB; DcNAA; Film 1; OxThe; TwCBDA; WebAB; WhAm 1*

Drew, John E
American. Basketball Player
b. Sep 30, 1954 in Vredenburgh, Alabama
Source: *BioIn 10; WhoBlA 77*

Drew, Louisa Lane
[Mrs. John Drew]
English. Actress
b. Jan 10, 1820 in London, England
d. Aug 31, 1897 in Larchmont, New York
Source: *AmBi; ApCAB; DcAmB; InWom; NotAW; OxThe; TwCBDA; WhAm H*

Drew, Richard G
American. Engineer
Invented transparent tape, 1930.
b. 1899 in Minnesota
d. Dec 7, 1980 in Santa Barbara, California
Source: *BioIn 1; NewYTBS 80*

Drewry, John Eldridge
American. Author, Educator
b. Jun 4, 1902 in Griffin, Georgia
Source: *AmAu&B; DrAS 74E; WhNAA; WhoAm 74, 76, 78, 80, 82; WrDr 76*

Drexel, Anthony J
American. Banker, Philanthropist
b. Sep 13, 1806 in Philadelphia, Pennsylvania
d. Jun 30, 1893
Source: *AmBi; ApCAB; DcAmB; TwCBDA; WhAm H*

Drexel, Francis Martin
American. Banker
b. Apr 7, 1792 in Dornbirn, Austria
d. Jun 5, 1863 in Philadelphia, Pennsylvania
Source: *ApCAB; DcAmB; WhAm H*

Drexler, Rosalyn
American. Actress
b. Nov 25, 1926 in Bronx, New York
Source: *AmAu&B; ConDr 73; ConLC 2, 6; DrAF 76; ModAL SUP; NewYTBE 71; NotNAT; WhoAm 82; WrDr 76*

Dreyer, Carl Theodore
Danish. Motion Picture Director
b. 1889
d. Mar 28, 1968 in Copenhagen, Denmark
Source: *BiDFilm; DcFM; FilmgC; MovMk; OxFilm; WorEFlm*

Dreyfus, Alfred
French. Army Officer
b. Oct 9, 1859 in Alsace, France
d. Jul 12, 1935
Source: *FilmgC; NewC; OxFilm; REn*

Dreyfus, Hubert L
American. Author
b. Oct 15, 1929 in Terre Haute, Indiana
Source: *ConAu 33R; DrAS 74P; IndAu 1917*

Dreyfus, Jack Jonas
American. Financier, Author
b. 1913 in Alabama
Source: *BioIn 6, 7, 8, 9*

Dreyfuss, Henry
American. Industrial Designer
b. Mar 2, 1904 in New York, New York
d. Oct 5, 1972 in Pasadena, California
Source: *ConAu 37R, 45; CurBio 48, 59, 72; WhAm 5; WhoAdv 72; WhoWorJ 72*

Dreyfuss, Richard Stephan
American. Actor
Starred in *Jaws,* 1975; won Oscar, 1978, for *The Goodbye Girl.*
b. Oct 29, 1947 in Brooklyn, New York
Source: *BkPepl; IntMPA 75, 76, 77, 78, 79, 80, 81, 82; NewYTBS 74; WhoAm 82; WhoHol A*

Drifters, The
[Clyde McPhatter; Billy Pickney; Andrew Thrasher; Gerhart Thrasher]
American. Singing Group
Source: *EncPR&S; IlEncRk; Rk100*

Drinkwater, John
English. Poet, Author, Biographer
b. Jun 1, 1882 in Leytonstone, England
d. Mar 25, 1937 in Kilburn, England
Source: *Alli; BiDLA; CasWL; Chambr 3; ChPo, S1, S2; CnMD; CnThe; DcLEL; EvLB; JBA 34; LongCTC; McGEWD; ModBrL; ModWD; NewC; OxEng; OxThe; Pen ENG; REn; Str&VC; TwCA, SUP; WebE&AL; WhoLA*

Drinkwater, Terry
American. Author
b. May 9, 1936 in Denver, Colorado
Source: *ConAu 69*

Driscoll, Bobby
American. Actor
b. Mar 3, 1936 in Cedar Rapids, Iowa
d. Jan 1968 in New York, New York
Source: *FilmgC; HolP 40; WhScrn 74, 77; WhoHol B*

Dropo, Walt
"Moose"
American. Baseball Player
First baseman, 1949-61; rookie of year, 1950.
b. Jan 30, 1923 in Moosup, Connecticut
Source: *BaseEn; BioIn 1, 2, 3, 4, 5; WhoProB 73*

Droubay, Marc
see: Survivor

Drouet, Bessie Clark
American. Author, Psychic, Artist
b. 1879
d. Aug 27, 1940
Source: *CurBio 40*

Dru, Joanne
[Letitia LaCock]
American. Actress
b. Jan 31, 1923 in Logan, West Virginia
Source: *BiDFilm; CmMov; FilmgC; InWom; IntMPA 75, 76, 77, 78, 79, 80, 81, 82; MotPP; WhoHol A; WorEFlm*

Drucker, Peter
American. Government Official
b. Nov 9, 1909 in Vienna, Austria
Source: *AmAu&B; AmM&WS 73; Au&Wr 71; ConAu 61; CurBio 64; IntWW 74; NewYTBS 74; Who 74; WhoAm 82; WhoWor 74*

Druckman, Jacob Raphael
American. Composer
b. Jun 26, 1928 in Philadelphia, Pennsylvania
Source: *Baker 78; BioIn 9; CurBio 81; DcCM; WhoAm 80, 82*

Drum, Hugh A
American. Military Leader
b. Sep 19, 1879 in Fort Brady, Michigan
d. Oct 3, 1951
Source: *CurBio 41, 51; DcAmB S5; WhAm 3*

Drummond, (James) Roscoe
American. Journalist
b. Jan 13, 1902 in Theresa, New York
Source: *BioIn 2, 3; ConAu 104; CurBio 49; IntAu&W 77; IntWW 74, 75, 76, 77, 78, 79, 80; WhoAm 74, 76, 78, 80, 82; WhoS&SW 73; WhoWor 74*

Drury, Allen Stuart
American. Author
b. Sep 2, 1918 in Houston, Texas
Source: *AmAu&B; CelR 73; ConAu 57; ConNov 72, 76; IntWW 74; OxAmL; REnAL; TwCW; Who 74; WhoAm 74, 76, 78, 80, 82; WhoWor 74; WorAu; WrDr 76*

Drury, James
American. Actor
b. 1934 in New York, New York
Source: *FilmgC; IntMPA 75, 76, 77, 78, 79, 80, 81, 82; MotPP; WhoHol A*

Dryden, John
English. Poet, Dramatist
Poet laureate, 1668-89; best known play *Marriage a la Mode,* 1672.
b. Aug 9, 1631 in North Hamptonshire, England
d. May 1, 1700 in London, England
Source: *Alli; AtlBL; BbD; BiD&SB; BrAu; CasWL; Chambr 1; ChPo, S1; CnE&AP; CnThe; CrtT 2; CyWA; DcEnA; DcEnL; DcEuL; DcLEL; EvLB; McGEWD; MouLC 1; NewC; OxEng; OxThe; Pen ENG; PlP&P; PoChrch; PoLE; RAdv 1; RComWL; REn; REnWD; WebE&AL*

Dryden, Ken(neth Wayne)
Canadian. Hockey Player, Lawyer
Goalie whose 2.24 career goals-against average lowest in league since 1941.
b. Aug 8, 1947 in Islington, ON
Source: *NewYTBE 71; WhoE 74; WhoHcky 73*

Dryden, Spencer
[Jefferson Airplane]
American. Singer, Musician
b. Apr 7, 1943 in New York, New York
Source: *NF*

Dryer, (John) Fred(erick)
American. Football Player, Actor
b. Jul 6, 1946 in Hawthorne, California
Source: *FootReg*

Dryfoos, Orvil E
American. Newspaper Publisher
b. Nov 8, 1912 in New York, New York
d. May 25, 1963 in New York, New York
Source: *CurBio 62, 63; WhAm 4*

Drysdale, Don(ald Scott)
"Big D"
American. Baseball Player, Sportscaster
Pitcher, Brooklyn, LA Dodgers, 1956-69; broadcaster, ABC Sports, 1978--.
b. Jul 23, 1936 in Van Nuys, California
Source: *BaseEn; CmCal; CurBio 65; WhoAm 80, 82; WhoProB 73*

Duarte, Jose Napoleon
Salvadoran. Former President
b. 1926 in San Salvador, El Salvador
Source: *CurBio 81*

DuBarry, Comtesse Jeanne Becu
French. Mistress of Louis XV
b. Aug 19, 1746
d. Dec 7, 1793
Source: *NewC; OxFr*

DuBay, William Bryan
American. Artist, Editor
b. 1948 in San Francisco, California
Source: *FanAl*

Dubcek, Alexander
Czech. Communist Leader
b. Nov 27, 1921 in Uhrovec, Czechoslovakia
Source: *CurBio 68; IntWW 74; WhoWor 74*

Dubin, Al
Swiss. Songwriter
b. Jun 10, 1891 in Zurich, Switzerland
d. Feb 11, 1945 in New York, New York
Source: *AmSCAP 66; BioIn 4, 5; NotNAT B*

Dubinsky, David
American. Labor Leader
President, ILGWU, 1932-66; co-founded American Labor Party, 1936.
b. Feb 22, 1892 in Brest-Litovsk, Poland
d. Sep 17, 1982 in New York, New York
Source: *BiDAmLL; CurBio 42, 57, 83; EncAB-H; IntWW 74, 75, 76, 77, 78; McGEWB; NewYTBS 82; PolProf E; PolProf K; PolProf T; WebAB; WhoAm 76*

DuBois, Guy Pene
American. Artist, Critic
Paintings generally presented the human spectacle.
b. Jan 4, 1884 in Brooklyn, New York
d. Jul 18, 1958 in New York, New York
Source: *AmAu&B; CurBio 46, 58; DcCAA 71; WhAm 3*

DuBois, W(illiam) E(dward) B(urghardt)
American. Author, Reform Leader
b. Feb 23, 1868 in Barrington, Massachusetts
d. Aug 27, 1963 in Accra, Ghana
Source: *BiDSA; BlkAW; CasWL; ConAmL; ConAu 85; ConLC 1, 2, 13; DcAmAu; DcLEL; EncAB-H; LongCTC; OxAmL; Pen AM; REn; REnAL; TwCA, SUP; WebAB; WebE&AL; WhAm 4; WhAmP; WhNAA*

Dubos, Rene Jules
American. Author, Scientist
b. Feb 20, 1901 in Saint-Brice, France
d. Feb 20, 1982 in New York, New York
Source: *AmAu&B; AmM&WS 73P, 76P, 79P; AsBiEn; CelR 73; ConAu 5R; CurBio 52, 73, 82; IntWW 74, 75, 76, 77, 78; McGEWB; NewYTBE 70, 71; NewYTBS 82; WebAB; WhoAm 74, 76, 78, 80; WhoE 74; WhoWor 74; WrDr 80*

Dubs, Adolph
"Spike"
American. Diplomat
b. Aug 4, 1920 in Illinois
d. Feb 14, 1979
Source: *BioIn 11; USBiR 74; WhAm 7; WhoAm 74, 76, 78; WhoGov 72, 75, 77; WhoWor 74, 78*

Dubuffet, Jean
French. Artist
b. Jul 31, 1901 in Le Havre, France
Source: *CurBio 62; IntWW 74; NewYTBE 72; Who 74; WhoWor 74*

Duc de Armand, Jean du Plessis
see: Richelieu, Armand Jean du Plessis, Cardinal

Ducasse, Isidore Lucien
see: Lautreamont, Comte de, pseud.

Duccio di Buoninsegna
Italian. Artist
b. 1278 in Siena, Italy
d. 1319 in Siena, Italy
Source: *AtlBL; REn*

Duchamp, Marcel
French. Artist
b. Jul 28, 1887 in Blainville, France
d. Oct 1, 1968 in Neuilly, France
Source: *AtlBL; CurBio 60, 68; DcCAA 71; REn*

Duchin, Eddie
American. Band Leader, Pianist
Father of Peter Duchin; wrote four books on piano technique.
b. Apr 1, 1909 in Cambridge, Massachusetts
d. Feb 9, 1951 in New York, New York
Source: *CurBio 47, 51; WhScrn 74, 77; WhoHol B*

Duchin, Peter
American. Band Leader, Pianist
b. Jul 28, 1937 in New York, New York
Source: *BioNews 74; BkPepl; CelR 73; WhoAm 74, 76, 78, 80, 82; WhoHol A*

Ducis, Jean Francois
French. Dramatist, Poet
b. Aug 22, 1733 in Versailles, France
d. Mar 31, 1816 in Versailles, France
Source: *BiD&SB; CasWL; DcEuL; EvEuW; OxFr; OxThe*

Duclos, Jacques
French. Communist Leader
b. Oct 2, 1896 in Louey, France
d. Apr 25, 1975 in Paris, France
Source: *CurBio 46; IntWW 74; WhoWor 74*

Ducloux, Walter
Swiss. Conductor, Educator
b. Apr 17, 1913 in Lucerne, Switzerland
Source: *AmSCAP 66; BioIn 6*

Dudley, William
"Bullet Bill"
American. Football Player
b. Dec 24, 1921 in Bluefield, Virginia
Source: *BioIn 3, 7, 8, 9; WhoFtbl 74*

Duel, Peter
American. Actor
b. 1940 in Rochester, New York
d. Dec 31, 1971 in Hollywood, California
Source: *WhScrn 74, 77; WhoHol B*

Duerk, Alene B
American. Admiral
b. Mar 29, 1920 in Defiance, Ohio
Source: *CurBio 73*

Duesenberg, August S
American. Automobile Manufacturer
b. 1879?
d. Jan 18, 1955 in Indianapolis, Indiana
Source: *BioIn 3*

Duesenberg, Frederick S
American. Automobile Manufacturer
Built engine for motorcycles adapted for cars, boats, airplanes, 1913.
b. Dec 6, 1876 in Lippe, Germany
d. 1932
Source: *NatCAB 16; WebBD 80*

Duff, Howard
American. Actor
b. Nov 24, 1917 in Bremerton, Washington
Source: *FilmgC; IntMPA 75, 76, 77, 78, 79, 80, 81, 82; MotPP; MovMk; WhoAm 82; WhoHol A*

Duffey, Joseph Daniel
American. Clergyman, Sociologist
b. 1932
Source: *BioIn 8, 9, 10, 11*

Duffy, Ben (Bernard Cornelius)
American. Advertising Executive
b. Jan 21, 1902 in New York, New York
d. Sep 1, 1972 in Rye, New York
Source: *Au&Wr 71; ConAu 37R; CurBio 52, 72; WhAm 5*

Duffy, Clinton T
American. Prison Warden
Warden at San Quentin, 1940-52; instituted many penal reforms.
b. Aug 24, 1898 in San Quentin, California
d. Oct 11, 1982 in Walnut Creek, California
Source: *BioIn 1, 2; NewYTBS 82*

Duffy, Hugh
American. Baseball Player
b. Nov 26, 1866 in River Point, Rhode Island
d. Oct 19, 1954 in Allston, Massachusetts
Source: *BaseEn; BioIn 3, 7; WhoProB 73*

Duffy, Patrick
American. Actor
Plays Bobby Ewing on TV series "Dallas," 1978--.
b. Mar 17, 1949 in Townsend, Montana
Source: *BioIn 11; IntMPA 82; WhoAm 80, 82*

Dufresne, Charles
French. Artist
b. 1876 in Millemont, France
d. 1938 in Seyne-sur-Mer, France
Source: *McGDA*

Dufy, Raoul
French. Artist
b. Jun 3, 1877 in Le Havre, France
d. Mar 23, 1953 in Forcalquier, France
Source: *AtlBL; CurBio 51, 53; REn; WhAm 3*

Dugan, Alan
American. Author
b. Feb 12, 1923 in Brooklyn, New York
Source: *AmAu&B; ConAu 81; ConLC 2, 6; ConP 70, 75; CroCAP; DrAP 75; ModAL, SUP; OxAmL; Pen AM; RAdv 1; REnAL; WhoAm 74; WhoWor 74; WorAu; WrDr 76*

Duggan, Maurice Noel
New Zealander. Author
b. Nov 25, 1922 in Auckland, New Zealand
d. Jan 1975
Source: *CasWL; ConAu 53, 73; ConNov 72, 76; WebE&AL*

Duguay, Ron
Canadian. Hockey Player
b. Jul 6, 1957 in Sudbury, ON
Source: *HocReg; NewYTBS 82*

Duhamel, Georges
[Denis Thevenin]
French. Author
b. Jun 30, 1884 in Paris, France
d. Apr 13, 1966 in Valmondois, France
Source: *CasWL; ClDMEL; ConAu 25R, 81; ConLC 8; EncWL; EvEuW; LongCTC; ModRL; ModWD; OxFr; Pen EUR; REn; TwCA, SUP; TwCW; WhoTwCL*

Dukakis, Michael S
American. Governor
Governor of MA, re-elected, 1982.
b. Sep 3, 1933 in Brookline, Massachusetts
Source: *BioNews 75*

Dukas, Paul Abraham
French. Composer
b. Oct 1, 1865 in Paris, France
d. May 17, 1935 in Paris, France
Source: *OxFr*

Duke, Angier Biddle
American. Diplomat
b. Nov 30, 1915 in New York, New York
Source: *CelR 73; CurBio 62; IntWW 74; WhoAm 74, 76, 78, 80, 82; WhoAmP 73*

Duke, Benjamin Newton
American. Industralist
b. Apr 27, 1855 in Orange County, North Carolina
d. Jan 8, 1929
Source: *BioIn 10; WhAm 1*

Duke, Charles Moss, Jr.
American. Astronaut
Lunar module pilot, Apollo 16, Apr, 1972.
b. Oct 3, 1935 in Charlotte, North Carolina
Source: *IntWW 74, 75, 76, 77; NewYTBE 72; WhoS&SW 73, 75*

Duke, Doris
American. Heiress
b. Nov 22, 1912 in New York, New York
Source: *CelR 73; InWom*

Duke, James Buchanan
American. Businessman, Philanthropist
Founded American Tobacco Co., 1890; large benefactor of Trinity College, later renamed Duke University.
b. Dec 23, 1856 in Durham, North Carolina
d. Oct 10, 1925 in New York, New York
Source: *AmBi; DcAmB; EncAB-H; WebAB; WhAm 1*

Duke, Patty (Anna Marie)
[Mrs. John Astin]
American. Actress
Won Oscar, 1963, for *The Miracle Worker;* won Emmy, 1979, for "The Miracle Worker."
b. Dec 14, 1946 in New York, New York
Source: *BiE&WWA; BioNews 74; CelR 73; CurBio 63; FilmgC; InWom; IntMPA 75, 76, 77, 78, 79, 80, 81, 82; MotPP; MovMk; NotNAT; WhoAm 74, 76, 78, 80, 82; WhoAmW 66, 68, 70, 72, 74, 79; WhoHol A*

Duke, Vernon
[Vladimir Dukelsky]
American. Composer, Poet, Author
b. Oct 10, 1903 in Pskov, Russia
d. Jan 17, 1969 in Santa Monica, California
Source: *AmSCAP 66; BiE&WWA; ConAu 29R; CurBio 41, 69; DcCM; EncMT; NewCBMT; WhAm 5*

Duke, Wayne
American. Athletic Conference Director
b. Nov 9, 1928 in Burlington, Iowa
Source: *WhoAm 80, 82*

Dukes, David
American. Actor
Played Leslie Slote in TV mini-series, "The Winds of War," 1983.
b. 1946? in San Francisco, California
Source: *NewYTBS 79; WhoAm 82*

Dula, Tom (Thomas)
[Tom Dooley]
American. Murderer
b. 1844
d. 1868
Source: *BioIn 4*

Dull Knife
American Indian. Cheyenne War Chief
b. 1828
d. 1879
Source: *BioIn 4; REnAW*

Dullea, Keir
American. Actor
b. May 30, 1936 in Cleveland, Ohio
Source: *CelR 73; CurBio 70; FilmgC; IntMPA 75, 76, 77, 78, 79, 80, 81, 82; MotPP; MovMk; NotNAT; WhoAm 74, 76, 78, 80, 82; WhoHol A; WhoThe 77*

Dulles, Allen Welsh
American. Lawyer, Diplomat
b. Apr 7, 1893 in Watertown, New York
d. Jan 29, 1969 in Washington, DC
Source: *AmAu&B; ConAu 25R; CurBio 49, 69; WhAm 5*

Dulles, Eleanor Lansing
American. Diplomat, Educator
b. Jun 1, 1895 in Watertown, New York
Source: *AmM&WS 73S; ConAu 9R; CurBio 62; ForWC 70; WhoAm 74, 76, 78, 80, 82; WhoAmW 74; WhoWor 74*

Dulles, John Foster
American. Lawyer, Government Official
Secretary of State, 1953-59; advocated development of nuclear weapons.
b. Feb 25, 1888 in Washington, DC
d. May 24, 1959 in Washington, DC
Source: *AmAu&B; BiDrAC; BiDrUSE; ConAu 1NR; CurBio 44, 53, 59; EncAB-H; WebAB; WhAm 3; WhAmP*

Duluth, Daniel
French. Explorer
Claimed upper Mississippi region and Lake Superior for France, circa 1678.
b. 1636 in Saint Germain, France
d. Feb 27, 1710 in Montreal, PQ
Source: *BioIn 4, 5, 7, 9; DcAmB; NewCol 75; WebBD 80; WhAm H*

Dumas, Alexandre
[Dumas Pere]
French. Author, Dramatist
Best known works *The Three Musketeers,* 1844, *The Count of Monte Cristo,* 1845.
b. Jul 24, 1802 in Villers-Cotterets, France
d. Dec 5, 1870 in Puys, France
Source: *AtlBL; BbD; BiD&SB; CarSB; CasWL; CnThe; CyWA; DcEuL; EuAu; EvEuW; FilmgC; HsB&A; McGEWD; MnBBF; NewC; OxEng; OxFr; Pen EUR; RComWL; REn; REnWD; WhoChL*

Dumas, Alexandre
[Dumas Fils]
French. Author, Dramatist
Play *La Dame aux Camelias,* (Camille), 1852, basis for Verdi's opera, "La Traviata."
b. Jul 27, 1824 in Paris, France
d. Nov 27, 1895 in Paris, France
Source: *AtlBL; BbD; BiD&SB; CasWL; CnThe; CyWA; DcBiA; DcEuL; EuAu; EvEuW; REn*

Dumas, Jean Baptiste Andre
Canadian. Scientist
b. Jun 4, 1925 in Montreal, PQ
Source: *AmM&WS 73P*

DuMaurier, Daphne
[Lady Browning]
English. Author
b. May 13, 1907 in London, England
Source: *Au&Wr 71; BiE&WWA; ConAu 5R; ConLC 6, 11; ConNov 72, 76; CurBio 40; CyWA; DcLEL; EncMys; EvLB; FilmgC; InWom; IntWW 74; LongCTC; ModBrL; NewC; NotNAT; OxThe; Pen ENG; RAdv 1; REn; TwCA, SUP; TwCW; Who 74; WhoThe 77; WhoWor 74; WrDr 76*

DuMaurier, George Louis P B
English. Author, Artist
b. Mar 6, 1834 in Paris, France
d. Oct 8, 1896 in London, England
Source: *BbD; BiD&SB; BrAu 19; CasWL; Chambr 3; ChPo, S2; CyWA; DcBiA; DcEuL; DcLEL; EvLB; MouLC 4; NewC; OxEng; OxThe; Pen ENG; RAdv 1; REn*

DuMaurier, Sir Gerald Hubert
English. Actor, Motion Picture Producer
b. Mar 26, 1873 in London, England
d. Apr 11, 1934 in London, England
Source: *CnThe; Film 2; NewC; NotNAT A, B; OxThe; WhScrn 77; WhThe; WhoHol B*

Dumke, Ralph
American. Actor
b. 1900
d. Jan 4, 1964 in Sherman Oaks, California
Source: *FilmgC; NotNAT B; WhScrn 74, 77; WhoHol B*

Dummar, Melvin
American. Alleged Heir of Howard Hughes
Source: *BioIn 10*

Dumont, Alberto Santos-
see: Santos-Dumont, Alberto

DuMont, Allen Balcom
American. Radio Engineer, TV Pioneer
b. Jan 29, 1901 in Brooklyn, New York
d. Nov 16, 1965 in New York, New York
Source: *CurBio 46, 66; WhAm 4*

Dumont, Margaret
American. Actress
b. 1890 in New York, New York
d. Mar 6, 1965 in Los Angeles, California
Source: *BiDFilm; FilmgC; MotPP; MovMk; OxFilm; ThFT; Vers A; WhScrn 74, 77; WhoHol B; WorEFlm*

Dumont d'Urville, Jules Sebastian Cesar
French. Navigator
Explored Australia, Oceania Islands, 1826-29; discovered Adelie Coast, Antarctica, 1837-40.
b. May 23, 1790 in France
d. May 8, 1842
Source: *CelCen; DcBiPP; Dis&D; NewCol 75; OxShips; WhDW*

DuMotier, Marie Joseph Paul
see: Lafayette, Marie Joseph Paul, Marquis

Dumurq, Charles
[Alain Gauthier; Charles Gurmukh Sabhraj]
French. Thief, Murderer
Subject of book *Serpentine,* by Thomas Thompson.
b. 1944? in Saigon, Vietnam
Source: *BioIn 11*

Dun, Robert Graham
American. Financier
b. 1826 in Chillicothe, Ohio
d. 1900
Source: *DcAmB; WhAm 1*

Dunant, Jean Henri
Swiss. Philanthropist
Founded Red Cross, 1864; shared first Nobel Peace Prize, 1901.
b. May 8, 1828 in Geneva, Switzerland
d. Oct 30, 1910
Source: *WebBD 80*

Dunaway, (Dorothy) Faye
American. Actress
Starred in *Bonnie and Clyde,* 1967; won Oscar, 1976, for *Network.*
b. Jan 14, 1941 in Tallahassee, Florida
Source: *BiDFilm; BkPepl; CelR 73; CurBio 72; FilmgC; InWom; IntMPA 75, 76, 77, 78, 79, 80, 81, 82; MotPP; MovMk; NewYTBS 74; OxFilm; WhoAm 74, 76, 78, 80, 82; WhoAmW 70, 72, 74, 79; WhoHol A; WhoThe 77; WorEFlm*

Dunbar, Aynsley
see: Journey

Dunbar, Paul Laurence
American. Poet, Author
Published 24 volumes of fiction, poetry; poems used Negro folk material, dialect.
b. Jun 27, 1872 in Dayton, Ohio
d. Feb 9, 1906 in Dayton, Ohio
Source: *AmAu; AmAu&B; AmBi; ApCAB SUP; BiD&SB; BkCL; BlkAW; CasWL; Chambr 3; ChPo, S1, S2; CnDAL; DcAmAu; DcAmB; DcNAA; OhA&B; OxAmL; Pen AM; RAdv 1; REn; REnAL; TwCBDA; WebAB; WebE&AL; WhAm 1*

Duncan I
Scottish. King
d. 1040
Source: *NewC*

Duncan, Augustin
American. Actor, Producer
b. Apr 12, 1873 in San Francisco, California
d. Feb 20, 1954 in New York, New York
Source: *BioIn 3, 5; NotNAT B; ObitOF 79; WhThe*

Duncan, Charles William, Jr.
American. Former Government Official
b. Sep 9, 1926 in Houston, Texas
Source: *BioIn 12; CurBio 80; IntWW 79; NewYTBS 79; WhoAm 74, 76, 78, 80, 82; WhoAmP 77, 79; WhoF&I 74; WhoGov 77*

Duncan, David Douglas
American. Photojournalist, Author
b. Jan 23, 1916 in Kansas City, Missouri
Source: *AuNews 1; CurBio 68; WhoAm 74, 76, 78, 80, 82; WhoWor 74*

Duncan, Isadora
American. Dancer
b. May 27, 1878 in San Francisco, California
d. Sep 14, 1927 in Nice, France
Source: *AmAu&B; AmBi; DcAmB; EncAB-H; InWom; NotAW; OxAmL; REn; REnAL; WebAB; WhAm HA, 4*

Duncan, Robert
American. Author
b. Jan 7, 1919 in Oakland, California
Source: *AmAu&B; CasWL; ChPo, S2; ConAu 9R; ConLC 1, 2, 4, 7, 15; ConP 70, 75; CroCAP; DrAP 75; ModAL, SUP; Pen AM; RAdv 1; REn; REnAL; WebE&AL; WhoAm 82; WorAu; WrDr 76*

Duncan, Sandy
American. Actress
Starred as Peter Pan, on Broadway, 1980.
b. Feb 20, 1946 in Tyler, Texas
Source: *BioIn 12; CurBio 80; EncMT; FilmgC; IntMPA 75, 76, 77, 78, 79, 80, 81, 82; WhoAm 82; WhoHol A; WhoThe 77*

Duncan, Todd
American. Singer, Actor, Educator
b. Feb 12, 1903 in Danville, Kentucky
Source: *BiE&WWA; CurBio 42; EncMT; NotNAT; PlP&P; WhoHol A; WhoThe 77*

Duncan, Vivian
American. Actress
b. Jun 17, 1902 in Los Angeles, California
Source: *AmSCAP 66; InWom; WhoHol A; WhoThe 77*

Dundee, Angelo
American. Boxing Trainer, Manager
Trainer of Muhammad Ali since 1964.
b. 1921
Source: *BioNews 74*

Dundee, Johnny
American. Boxer
b. Nov 22, 1893 in Sciacca, Italy
d. Apr 22, 1965 in East Orange, New Jersey
Source: *WhoBox 74*

Dunham, Katherine
American. Dancer, Choreographer
b. Jun 22, 1910 in Chicago, Illinois
Source: *BiE&WWA; BlkAW; ConAu 65; CurBio 41; HerW; InWom; IntWW 74; LivgBAA; NotNAT; REnAL; WebAB; WhoAm 74; WhoBlA 75; WhoE 74; WhoHol A; WhoThe 77; WhoWor 74; WomPO 76*

Dunham, "Sonny" (Elmer Lewis)
American. Musician
b. 1914 in Brockton, Massachusetts
Source: *WhoJazz 72*

Dunhill, Alfred Henry
English. Tobacco Executive
President, Dunhill Tobacco Group; author *The Gentle Art of Smoking,* 1954.
b. 1896
d. Jul 8, 1971 in Sussex, England
Source: *NewYTBE 71*

Duniway, Abigail Jane Scott
American. Feminist, Suffragette
First registered woman voter in Oregon.
b. Oct 22, 1834 in Groveland, Illinois
d. Oct 11, 1915
Source: *Alli SUP; AmAu; AmAu&B; AmBi; AmWom; DcAmB; DcNAA; InWom; NotAW; WhAm 4; WhAmP; WomWWA 14*

Dunlap, William
American. Author
b. Feb 11, 1766 in Perth Amboy, New Jersey
d. Sep 28, 1839 in New York, New York
Source: *Alli; AmAu; AmAu&B; AmBi; ApCAB; BbD; BiDAmM; BiD&SB; BiDLA; BioIn 7, 8, 9, 10; BnEnAmA; CasWL; CnDAL; CnThe; CyAl 2; DcAmArt; DcAmAu; DcAmB; DcNAA; Drake; EncWT; EvLB; McGDA; McGEWB; NatCAB 16; NewYHSD; NotNAT A, B; OxAmL; OxThe; Pen AM; PlP&P; REnAL; REnWD; TwCBDA; WebAB; WebE&AL; WhAm H*

Dunlop, Frank
English. Motion Picture Director
b. Feb 15, 1927 in Leeds, England
Source: *PlP&P A; Who 74; WhoThe 77*

Dunlop, John Boyd
Scottish. Inventor
Patented pneumatic tire, 1888.
b. Feb 5, 1840 in Scotland
d. 1921
Source: *WebBD 80*

Dunlop, John Thomas
American. Economist
b. Jun 5, 1914 in Placerville, California
Source: *AmM&WS 73S; BioIn 2, 8, 9, 10, 11; ConAu 13R; WhoAm 78, 80, 82; WhoE 74*

Dunn, Alan
American. Cartoonist, Artist
b. Aug 11, 1900 in Belmar, New Jersey
d. May 20, 1974 in New York, New York
Source: *AmAu&B; ConAu 33R, 49; ConAu P-2; NewYTBS 74; WhAm 6; WhoAm 74; WhoAmA 73; WhoWor 74*

Dunn, James
American. Actor
b. Nov 2, 1905 in New York, New York
d. Sep 3, 1967 in Santa Monica, California
Source: *BiE&WWA; FilmgC; HolP 30; MotPP; MovMk; WhScrn 74, 77; WhoHol B*

Dunn, Michael
[Gary Neil Miller]
American. Actor
Dwarf actor, whose movie credits include *Ship of Fools,* 1965.
b. Oct 20, 1934 in Shattuck, Oklahoma
d. Aug 29, 1973 in London, England
Source: *BiE&WWA; FilmgC; MotPP; MovMk; NewYTBE 73; WhScrn 77; WhoHol B*

Dunn, Mignon
American. Opera Singer
b. in Memphis, Tennessee
Source: *NewYTBE 73; WhoAm 74, 76, 78, 80, 82*

Dunne, Dominique
American. Actress
Starred in *Poltergeist,* 1982; allegedly strangled by her boyfriend.
b. 1960?
d. Nov 4, 1982 in Los Angeles, California
Source: *NF*

Dunne, Finley Peter
[Mr. Dooley, pseud.]
American. Humorist, Author, Editor
b. Jul 10, 1867 in Chicago, Illinois
d. Apr 24, 1936 in New York, New York
Source: *AmAu&B; AmBi; BiD&SB; CathA 1930; Chambr 3; ConAmL; DcAmAu; DcAmB S2; DcLEL; DcNAA; EncAB-H; EvLB; LongCTC; OxAmL; OxEng; Pen AM; REn; REnAL; TwCA, SUP; WebAB; WhAm 1*

Dunne, Irene
American. Actress
b. Dec 20, 1904 in Louisville, Kentucky
Source: *BiDFilm; BiE&WWA; CmMov; CurBio 45; FilmgC; InWom; IntMPA 75, 76, 77, 78, 79, 80, 81, 82; MotPP; MovMk; OxFilm; ThFT; WhoAm 74; WhoHol A; WhoThe 77; WomWMM; WorEFlm*

Dunne, John Gregory
American. Author
b. May 25, 1932 in Hartford, Connecticut
Source: *AuNews; ConAu 25R*

Dunne, John William
English. Airplane Designer, Philosopher
b. 1875
d. Aug 24, 1949 in London, England
Source: *DcLEL; EvLB; REn*

Dunninger, Joseph
American. Astrologer, Magician
b. Apr 28, 1896 in New York, New York
d. Mar 9, 1975 in Cliffside Park, New Jersey
Source: *CurBio 44; NewYTBS 75; WhAm 6*

Dunnock, Mildred
American. Actress
b. Jan 25, 1906 in Baltimore, Maryland
Source: *BiE&WWA; CurBio 55; FilmgC; InWom; IntMPA 75, 76, 77, 78, 79, 80, 81, 82; MotPP; MovMk; NotNAT; PlP&P; Vers A; WhoAm 74, 76, 78, 80, 82; WhoHol A; WhoThe 77*

Dunoyer de Segonzac, Andre
French. Artist
b. Jul 6, 1884 in France
d. Sep 17, 1974
Source: *ConAu 53; IntWW 74; NewYTBS 74; WhAm 6; Who 74; WhoGrA; WhoWor 74*

Duns Scotus, John
"Subtle Doctor"
Scottish. Scholastic Theologian
Believed in "divine will" rather than "divine intellect."
b. 1266 in Duns, Scotland
d. Nov 8, 1308 in Cologne, Germany
Source: *Alli; NewC; REn*

Dunsany, Edward J M Plunkett, Baron
Irish. Author
b. Jul 24, 1878 in London, England
d. Oct 25, 1957 in Dublin, Ireland
Source: *AtlBL; CasWL; ChPo, S1, S2; CnMD; CnThe; DcLEL; EncMys; EvLB; JBA 34; LongCTC; McGEWD; ModBrL; ModWD; NewC; OxEng; Pen ENG; REn; REnWD; TwCA, SUP; TwCW*

Duong Van Minh
"Big Minh"
Vietnamese. Exiled S Vietnamese General
b. 1916
Source: *BioIn 10*

Dupea, Tatzumbie
American Indian. Actress
b. Jul 26, 1849 in Pine Hills, California
d. Feb 28, 1970 in Los Angeles, California
Source: *ObitOF 79; WhScrn 77*

Duplessis, Marie
French. Courtesan, Model
Source: *InWom; OxFr*

Duplessis, Maurice le Noblet
Canadian. Premier
b. Apr 20, 1890 in Three Rivers, PQ
d. Sep 7, 1959 in Schefferville, PQ
Source: *CurBio 48, 59; ObitOF 79; OxCan; WhAm 3*

DuPont, Clifford Walter
South African. President of Rhodesia
b. Dec 6, 1905 in London, England
d. Jun 28, 1978 in Salisbury, Rhodesia
Source: *IntWW 74; WhoGov 72; WhoWor 74*

DuPont, Eleuthere Irenee
American. Industrialist
b. Jun 24, 1771 in Paris, France
d. Oct 31, 1834
Source: *BioIn 2, 4, 5, 6, 8, 9; REn*

DuPont, Margaret Osborne
American. Tennis Player
b. Mar 4, 1918
Source: *InWom*

DuPont, Pierre Samuel
see: DuPont de Nemours, Pierre Samuel

DuPont, Pierre Samuel, III
American. Business Executive
b. Jan 1, 1911 in Wilmington, Delaware
Source: *WhoAm 74; WhoF&I 74*

DuPont, Pierre Samuel, IV
American. Governor
b. Jan 22, 1935 in Wilmington, Delaware

DuPont de Nemours, Pierre Samuel
French. Economist
b. Sep 14, 1739 in Paris, France
d. Aug 7, 1817 in Delaware
Source: *ApCAB; BiD&SB; McGEWB; OxFr; REn; TwCBDA*

DuPre, Jacqueline
English. Musician
b. Jan 26, 1945 in Oxford, England
Source: *CurBio 70; IntWW 74, 75, 76, 77, 78, 79, 80, 81; Who 74; WhoAm 82; WhoMus 72*

DuPre, Marcel
French. Composer, Musician
b. May 3, 1886 in Rouen, France
d. May 30, 1971 in Meudon, France
Source: *DcCM; NewYTBE 71; WhAm 5*

Dupree, Minnie
American. Actress
b. 1873 in San Francisco, California
d. May 23, 1947 in New York, New York
Source: *BioIn 1; Film 2; FilmgC; NotNAT B; WhScrn 74, 77; WhThe*

DuPrez, Gilbert
French. Tenor, Teacher, Composer
b. Dec 6, 1806 in Paris, France
d. Sep 23, 1896 in Passy, France
Source: *NewEOp 71*

Duran, Roberto
Panamanian. Boxer
b. Jun 16, 1951 in Chorillo, Panama
Source: *BioIn 9, 10, 11; CurBio 80*

Durand, Asher Brown
American. Artist
b. Aug 21, 1796 in Jefferson, New Jersey
d. Sep 17, 1886 in Jefferson, New Jersey
Source: *AmAu&B; AmBi; ApCAB; DcAmB; EarABI; OxAmL; TwCBDA; WebAB; WhAm H*

Durant, (Ida) Ariel (Ethel) Kaufman
[Mrs. William James Durant]
American. Author
b. May 10, 1898 in Proskurov, Russia
d. Oct 25, 1981 in Los Angeles, California
Source: *AmWomWr; AnObit 1981; ASpks; BioIn 10, 11; CelR 73; ConAu 9R, 4NR; NewYTBS 75, 81; WhoAm 74, 76, 78, 80; WhoAmW 66, 68, 70, 72, 74, 75, 77; WhoWest 74, 76; WhoWor 74, 76*

Durant, Thomas Clark
American. Financier, Railroad Official
b. Feb 6, 1820 in Lee, Massachusetts
d. Oct 5, 1885 in North Creek, New York
Source: *AmBi; BioIn 6; DcAmB; McGEWB; REnAW; WebAB; WhAm H*

Durant, William Crapo
American. Auto Manufacturer
b. Dec 8, 1861 in Boston, Massachusetts
d. Mar 18, 1947 in New York, New York
Source: *DcAmB S4; EncAB-H; WebAB; WhAm 2*

Durant, Will(iam James)
American. Historian, Author
b. Nov 5, 1885 in North Adams, Massachusetts
d. Nov 7, 1981 in Los Angeles, California
Source: *AmAu&B; BioIn 3, 4, 6, 7, 8, 9, 10, 11; CelR 73; ConAu 9R, 4NR; CurBio 64, 82; DcLEL; EvLB; IntWW 74, 76, 77, 78; LinLib L, S; LongCTC; NewYTBS 75, 81; OxAmH; REn; REnAL; TwCA, SUP; WebAB; WhNAA; Who 74; WhoAm 74, 76, 78, 80; WhoWest 74, 78; WhoWor 74; CngDr 74; WhoAm 82; WhoAmP 73; WhoE 74; WhoGov 72*

Durante, Francesco
Italian. Composer, Opera Teacher
b. Mar 31, 1684 in Frattamaggiore, Italy
d. Aug 13, 1755 in Naples, Italy
Source: *NewEOp 71*

Durante, Jimmy (James Francis)
American. Comedian, Singer, Pianist
Entertainer for over 60 years; nose was insured for $100,000 with Lloyd's of London.
b. Feb 10, 1893 in New York, New York
d. Jan 29, 1980 in Santa Monica, California
Source: *AmSCAP 66; BiE&WWA; CelR 73; CurBio 46, 80; EncMT; IntMPA 75, 76, 77; MotPP; MovMk; NotNAT; WebAB; WhoAm 74, 76, 78, 80; WhoHol A; WhoThe 77; WhoWor 74*

Duranty, Walter
English. Journalist, Author
b. May 25, 1884 in Liverpool, England
d. Oct 3, 1957 in Orlando, Florida
Source: *AmAu&B; CurBio 43, 58; OxAmL; REnAL; TwCA, SUP; WhAm 3*

Duras, Marguerite, pseud.
[Marguerite Donnadieu]
French. Author
b. Apr 4, 1914 in Saigon, Vietnam
Source: *CasWL; CnMD SUP; CnThe; ConAu 25R; ConLC 3, 6, 11; CroCD; EncWL; EncWT; EvEuW; FilmgC; InWom; IntAu&W 76, 77; IntWW 74, 75, 76, 77, 78; McGEWD; ModFrL; ModRL; ModWD; OxFilm; Pen EUR; REn; REnWD; TwCW; WhoThe 72, 77; WhoTwCL; WomWMM; WorAu; WorEFlm*

Durbin, Deanna
Canadian. Actress
b. Dec 4, 1921 in Winnipeg, MB
Source: *BiDFilm; CmMov; CurBio 41; FilmgC; InWom; MotPP; MovMk; OxFilm; ThFT; WhoHol A; WorEFlm*

Duren, Ryne (Rinold George)
American. Baseball Player
b. Feb 22, 1929 in Cazenovia, Wisconsin
Source: *BaseEn; BioIn 5, 7, 11; WhoProB 73*

Durenberger, David Ferdinand
American. Senator
b. Aug 19, 1934 in Saint Cloud, Minnesota
Source: *AlmAP 80; CngDr 79; St&PR 75; WhoAm 78, 80, 82; WhoAmP 79*

Durer, Albrecht
German. Artist
b. May 21, 1471 in Nuremberg, Germany
d. Apr 6, 1528 in Nuremberg, Germany
Source: *AtlBL; NewC; OxGer; REn*

Durham, Leon
"Bull"
American. Baseball Player
b. Jul 31, 1957 in Cincinnati, Ohio
Source: *BaseEn*

Durkheim, Emile
French. Sociologist
b. Apr 15, 1858 in Epinal, France
d. Nov 15, 1917 in Paris, France
Source: *ClDMEL; OxFr*

Durning, Charles
American. Actor
Co-starred in *Tootsie,* 1982.
b. Feb 28, 1923 in Highland Falls, New York
Source: *IntMPA 82; NotNAT; PlP&P A; WhoAm 82; WhoHol A*

Durocher, Leo Ernest
"The Lip"
American. Baseball Player, Manager
Infielder, 1925-45; coined saying "Nice guys finish last."
b. Jul 27, 1906 in West Springfield, Massachusetts
Source: *BaseEn; CelR 73; CurBio 40, 50; NewYTBE 71; WebAB; WhoAm 82; WhoProB 73*

Durr, Francoise
French. Tennis Player
b. Dec 25, 1942 in Algiers, Algeria
Source: *BioIn 9*

Durrell, Gerald Malcolm
British. Zoologist
b. Jan 7, 1925 in Jamshedpur, India
Source: *Au&Wr 71; AuBYP; ConAu 5R; IntWW 74; LongCTC; NewC; REn; SmATA 8; TwCW; Who 74; WhoWor 74; WorAu; WrDr 76*

Durrell, Lawrence George
[Charles Norden, pseud.]
English. Author
b. Feb 27, 1912 in Darjeeling, India
Source: *Au&Wr 71; CasWL; ChPo; CnE&AP; CnMD; CnMWL; ConAu 9R; ConDr 73; ConLC 1, 4, 6; ConNov 72, 76; ConP 70, 75; CurBio 63; DcLEL; EncWL; EvLB; IntWW 74; LongCTC; ModBrL, SUP; ModWD; NewC; OxEng; Pen ENG; RAdv 1; REn; TwCA SUP; TwCW; WebE&AL; Who 74; WhoTwCL; WhoWor 74; WrDr 76*

Durrenmatt, Friedrich
[Duerrenmatt, Friedrich]
Swiss. Author
b. Jan 5, 1921 in Konolfingen, Switzerland
Source: *Au&Wr 71; BiE&WWA; CasWL; CnMD; CnThe; ConAu 17R; ConLC 1, 4, 8, 11, 15; CroCD; EncWL; EvEuW; IntWW 74; McGEWD; ModGL; ModWD; NotNAT; OxGer; OxThe; Pen EUR; REn; REnWD; TwCW; Who 74; WhoThe 77; WhoTwCL; WhoWor 74; WorAu*

Durrie, George Henry
American. Artist
b. Jun 6, 1820 in Hartford, Connecticut
d. Oct 15, 1863 in New Haven, Connecticut
Source: *BnEnAmA; DcAmArt; McGDA; NewYHSD; WhAm H*

Durslag, Melvin
American. Journalist
b. Apr 29, 1921 in Chicago, Illinois
Source: *WhoAm 74, 76, 78, 80, 82; WhoWest 74*

Duryea, Charles Edgar
"Father of the Automobile"
American. Inventor, Manufacturer
Organized Duryea Motor Wagon Co., 1895; sold first car, 1896.
b. Dec 15, 1862 in Canton, Illinois
d. Sep 28, 1938 in Philadelphia, Pennsylvania
Source: *DcAmB S2; WebAB; WhAm HA, 4*

Duryea, Dan
American. Actor
b. Jan 23, 1907 in White Plains, New York
d. Jun 7, 1968 in Los Angeles, California
Source: *BiDFilm; CmMov; FilmgC; HolP 40; MotPP; MovMk; OxFilm; WhAm 5; WhScrn 74, 77; WhoHol B; WorEFlm*

Duryea, J(ames) Frank
American. Inventor
Designed first successful gasoline-powered car in US; won first auto race, Chicago, 1895.
b. Oct 8, 1869 in Washburn, Illinois
d. Feb 15, 1967 in Saybrook, Connecticut
Source: *BioIn 8; OxAmH*

DuSable, Jean Baptiste
American. Pioneer Trader, Settler
Built first house, opened first trading post on site of modern-day Chicago.
b. 1750
d. Aug 28, 1818 in Saint Charles, Missouri
Source: *WebAB; WhAm H*

Duse, Eleanora
Italian. Actress
b. 1859 in Vigerano, Italy
d. Apr 23, 1924 in Pittsburgh, Pennsylvania
Source: *InWom; WhScrn 74, 77; WhoHol B; WhoStg 1908*

Dussault, Nancy
American. Actress, Singer
Plays Muriel Rush on TV series "Too Close for Comfort," 1980--.
b. Jun 30, 1936 in Pensacola, Florida
Source: *BiE&WWA; BioIn 11; EncMT; NewYTBS 77; NotNAT; WhoThe 72, 77, 81*

Dustin, Hannah
American. Indian Captive
b. 1657
d. 1729?
Source: *BioIn 1, 3; NewCol 75*

Dutton, E(dward) P(ayson)
American. Publisher
Founded E P Dutton publishing house, 1858.
b. Jan 4, 1831 in Keene, New Hampshire
d. Sep 6, 1923
Source: *AmAu&B; ChPo; WhAm 1*

Duvalier, Francois
"Papa Doc"
Haitian. President
b. Apr 14, 1907 in Port-au-Prince, Haiti
d. Apr 21, 1971 in Port-au-Prince, Haiti
Source: *CurBio 58, 71; NewYTBE 71; WhAm 5*

Duvalier, Jean-Claude
"Baby Doc"
Haitian. President
Became "president for life" of Haiti at age 19.
b. Jul 3, 1951 in Port-au-Prince, Haiti
Source: *CurBio 72; IntWW 74; NewYTBE 71; WhoGov 72; WhoWor 74*

Duvall, Robert
American. Actor
b. 1930 in San Diego, California
Source: *FilmgC; IntMPA 75, 76, 77, 78, 79, 80, 81, 82; MovMk; NewYTBE 72; WhoAm 82; WhoHol A*

Duvall, Shelley
American. Actress
Appeared in films *Nashville*, 1975, *Popeye*, 1979.
b. 1949 in Houston, Texas
Source: *BioIn 10, 11; BioNews 74; FilmEn; IntMPA 82; NewYTBS 77; WhoAm 80, 82; WhoHol A*

Duveneck, Frank
American. Artist, Educator
b. Oct 9, 1848 in Covington, Kentucky
d. Jan 3, 1919 in Cincinnati, Ohio
Source: *BioIn 4, 7, 8, 9; OxAmL; REn; WebAB; WhAm 1*

Duveyrier, Anne Honore
[Melesville, pseud.]
French. Dramatist, Librettist
b. Nov 13, 1787 in Paris, France
d. Nov 1865 in Paris, France
Source: *InWom*

Duvivier, Julien
French. Motion Picture Director
b. Oct 8, 1896 in Lille, France
d. Oct 29, 1967 in Paris, France
Source: *BiDFilm; CurBio 43, 68; DcFM; FilmgC; MovMk; OxFilm; WorEFlm*

Duyckinck, Evert Augustus
American. Editor
b. Nov 23, 1816 in New York, New York
d. Aug 13, 1878 in New York, New York
Source: *Alli, SUP; AmAu; AmAu&B; AmBi; ApCAB; BbD; BiD&SB; CyAl 2; DcAmAu; DcAmB; DcEnL; DcNAA; OxAmL; Pen; REnAL; TwCBDA; WhAm H*

Dvorak, Ann
American. Actress
b. Aug 2, 1912 in New York, New York
d. 1979 in Honolulu, Hawaii
Source: *FilmgC; HolP 30; MotPP; MovMk; ThFT; WhoHol A*

Dvorak, Anton
Czech. Composer
b. Sep 8, 1841 in Nalahozeves, Bohemia
d. May 1, 1904 in Prague, Bohemia
Source: *AtlBL; OxAmL; REn; REnAL; WhAm H*

Dwan, Allan
[Joseph Aloysius Dwan]
Canadian. Motion Picture Director
Directed an estimated 1,850 films during career, 1909-61.
b. Apr 3, 1885 in Toronto, ON
d. Dec 21, 1981 in Woodland Hills, California
Source: *AnObit 1981; BiDFilm; BioIn 9, 11; DcFM; FilmgC; IntMPA 75, 76, 77, 78, 79, 80, 81; NewYTBS 81; OxFilm; TwYS A; WhoAm 76; WorEFlm*

Dwiggins, Don
American. Children's Author
b. Nov 15, 1913 in Plainfield, New Jersey
Source: *ConAu 17R; SmATA 4*

Dwiggins, William Addison
American. Type Designer, Illustrator
b. Jun 19, 1880 in Martinsville, Ohio
d. Dec 25, 1956 in Hingham, Massachusetts
Source: *AmAu&B; IlsCB 1744, 1946; OhA&B; OxAmL; REnAL; WhAm 3*

Dwight, Timothy
American. Religious Leader
President, Yale University, 1795-1817.
b. May 14, 1752 in Northampton, Massachusetts
d. Jan 11, 1817 in New Haven, Connecticut
Source: *Alli; AmAu; AmAu&B; AmBi; ApCAB; BiD&SB; BiDLA; CasWL; ChPo, S1; CnDAL; CyAL 1; DcAmAu; DcAmB; DcEnL; DcNAA; Drake; EncAB-H; EvLB; OxAmL; Pen AM; PoChrch; REn; REnAL; TwCBDA; WebAB; WebE&AL; WhAm H*

Dwyer, Cynthia
American. "53rd" Hostage in Iran
b. 1931?
Source: *BioIn 12*

Dwyer, Florence Price
American. Congresswoman
b. Jul 4, 1902 in Reading, Pennsylvania
d. Feb 29, 1976 in Elizabeth, New Jersey
Source: *BiDrAC; InWom; WhoAm 74; WhoAmP 73; WhoE 74; WhoGov 72*

Dyck, Anthony van
Flemish. Artist
b. 1599 in Antwerp, Belgium
d. 1641 in London, England
Source: *McGDA*

Dyer, Charles
English. Author, Actor, Director
b. Jul 17, 1928 in Shrewsbury, England
Source: *Au&Wr 71; BiE&WWA; ConAu 21R; ConDr 73; CroCD; NotNAT; Who 74; WrDr 76*

Dyer, Sir Edward
English. Diplomat, Poet
b. 1545? in Somerset, England
d. May 1607 in London, England
Source: *BiD&SB; BrAu; CasWL; Chambr 1; CnE&AP; CroE&S; DcEuL; EvLB; NewC; OxEng; REn*

Dyer, Wayne
American. Author
Wrote *Your Erroneous Zones,* 1976, *The Sky's the Limit,* 1980.
b. May 10, 1940 in Detroit, Michigan
Source: *ConAu 69; WhoAm 82*

Dyer-Bennet, Richard
American. Singer
b. Oct 6, 1913 in Leicester, England
Source: *CurBio 44; EncFCWM 69; WhoAm 74*

Dykstra, John
American. Businessman
b. Apr 16, 1898 in Steins, Netherlands
Source: *BioIn 5, 6, 9; CurBio 63*

Dylan, Bob
[Robert Zimmerman]
American. Singer, Composer
Songs include "Blowin' in the Wind," 1962; "The Times They are a'Changin," 1964.
b. May 24, 1941 in Hibbing, Minnesota
Source: *AmAu&B; AmSCAP 66; BkPepl; CelR 73; ConAu 41R; ConLC 3, 4, 6; ConP 70, 75; EncAB-H; EncFCWM 69; IntWW 74; WebAB; WhoAm 74, 76, 78, 80, 82; WhoE 74; WhoWor 74; WrDr 76*

Dyson, Freeman John
English. Physicist, Educator
b. Dec 15, 1923 in Crowthorne, England
Source: *BioIn 12; ConAu 89; CurBio 80; WhoAm 82*

Dzerzhinsky, Felix E
Russian. Bolshevik Politician
b. 1877 in Poland
d. 1926
Source: *BioIn 4, 10, 11; McGEWB*

Dzhanibekov, Vladimir Alexandrovich
Russian. Cosmonaut
b. 1942
Source: *BioIn 10*

E

E-Street Band
[Roy Bittan; Clarence Clemons; Danny Federici; Garry Tallent; Steve Van Zandt; Max Weinberg]
American. Rock Band
Back-up band for Bruce Springsteen.
Source: *NF*

Eads, James Buchanan
American. Scientist, Bridge Builder
b. May 23, 1820 in Lawrenceburg, Indiana
d. Mar 8, 1887 in Nassau, Bahamas
Source: *Alli SUP; AmBi; ApCAB; DcAmAu; DcAmB; DcNAA; EncAB-H; IndAu 1917; WebAB; WhAm H*

Eagels, Jeanne
American. Actress
b. 1894 in Kansas City, Missouri
d. Oct 3, 1929 in New York, New York
Source: *AmBi; DcAmB; FamA&A; FilmgC; InWom; NotAW; ThFT; TwYS; WhAm 1; WhScrn 74, 77; WhoHol B*

Eagles, The
[Don Felder; Glenn Frey; Don Henley; Bernie Leadon; Randy Meiser;Tim Schmidt; Joe Walsh]
American. Rock Group
Sold over 40 million albums; *The Long Run,* 1979 double platinum.
Source: *BkPepl; EncPR&S; IlEncRk*

Eagleton, Thomas Francis
American. Senator
George McGovern's running mate, 1972; withdrew due to past history of nervous exhaustion.
b. Sep 4, 1929 in Saint Louis, Missouri
Source: *BiDrAC; BioNews 74; CelR 73; CngDr 74; CurBio 73; IntWW 74; NewYTBE 72; WhoAm 74, 76, 78, 80, 82; WhoAmP 73; WhoGov 72; WhoMW 74*

Eaker, Ira Clarence
American. Aviator, Army Officer
b. Apr 13, 1896 in Field Creek, Texas
Source: *AmAu&B; CurBio 42; WebBD 80; Who 74*

Eakins, Thomas
American. Artist
b. Jul 25, 1844 in Philadelphia, Pennsylvania
d. Jun 25, 1916 in Philadelphia, Pennsylvania
Source: *AmBi; ApCAB; AtlBL; DcAmB; EncAB-H; OxAmL; REn; REnAL; WebAB; WhAm 1*

Eames, Charles
American. Designer
b. Jun 17, 1907 in Saint Louis, Missouri
d. Aug 21, 1978 in Saint Louis, Missouri
Source: *WebAB; WhoAm 74; WhoWor 74; WorEFlm*

Eames, Clare
American. Actress
b. 1896 in Hartford, Connecticut
d. Nov 8, 1930 in London, England
Source: *WhScrn 74, 77; WhoHol B*

Eames, Emma Hayden
American. Opera Singer
b. Aug 13, 1865 in Shanghai, China
d. Jun 13, 1952 in New York, New York
Source: *AmWom; InWom; WebBD 80; WomWWA 14*

Eanes, Antonio Ramalho
Portuguese. President
b. Jan 25, 1935 in Alcains, Portugal
Source: *BioIn 10, 11; CurBio 79*

Earhart, Amelia Mary
American. Aviatrix
First woman to fly solo across Atlantic, 1932.
b. Jul 24, 1898 in Atchison, Kansas
d. 1937?
Source: *AmBi; ChPo; DcAmB S2; DcNAA; HerW; InWom; NotAW; REn; WebAB; WhAm 1; WomWMM*

Earle, Ralph
[Ralph Earl]
American. Artist
b. May 11, 1751 in Shrewsbury, Massachusetts
d. Nov 24, 1801 in Pendleton, South Carolina
Source: *ApCAB; BnEnAmA; DcAmArt; DcAmB; Drake; McGDA; NewYHSD; OxAmL; TwCBDA; WebAB; WhAm H*

Early, James
American. University Administrator
b. Apr 19, 1923 in Worcester, Massachusetts
Source: *ConAu 45; DrAS 74E, 78E; WhoAm 74, 76, 78, 80, 82*

Early, Jubal Anderson
American. Military Leader
b. Nov 3, 1816 in Franklin County, Virginia
d. Mar 2, 1894 in Lynchburg, Tennessee
Source: *Alli SUP; AmBi; BbD; BiD&SB; BiDConf; BiDSA; DcAmAu; DcAmB; DcNAA; TwCBDA; WebAB; WhAm H*

Earp, Morgan
American. Law Officer
b. Apr 24, 1851 in Pella, Iowa
d. Mar 18, 1882 in Tombstone, Arizona
Source: *REnAW*

Earp, Virgil W
American. Law Officer
b. Jul 18, 1843 in Hartford, Kentucky
d. 1905 in Goldfield, Nevada
Source: *REnAW*

Earp, Wyatt Berry Stapp
American. Law Officer
Friend of "Doc" Holliday; portrayed in movies, including *Gunfight at OK Corral,* 1956.
b. Mar 19, 1848 in Monmouth, Illinois
d. Jan 13, 1929 in Los Angeles, California
Source: *BioIn 5, 11; FilmgC; NewCol 75; OxFilm; WebAB; WebBD 80; WhAm H*

Earth, Wind, and Fire
[Philip Bailey; Jessica Cleaves; Larry Dunn; Johnny Graham; RalphJohnson; Al McKay; Fred White; Maurice White; Verdine White; Andrew Woolfolk]
American. Vocal Group
Source: *IlEncRk*

East, John Porter
American. Senator
b. May 5, 1931 in Springfield, Illinois
Source: *AmM&WS 73S, 78S; ConAu 17R; WhoAm 82; WhoAmP 73, 75, 77, 79; WrDr 76, 80*

"Eastern Jewel"
[Yoshiko Kawashima]
Chinese. Spy
b. 1906
d. 1948
Source: *LookW*

Eastlake, Charles Lock
English. Artist
b. Nov 17, 1793 in Plymouth, England
d. Dec 24, 1865 in Pisa, Italy
Source: *Alli, SUP; BiD&SB; DcEnL; NewC; REn*

Eastlake, William
American. Author
b. Jul 14, 1917 in New York, New York
Source: *AmAu&B; Au&Wr 71; ConAu 5R, 5NR; ConLC 8; ConNov 72, 76; DrAF 76; ModAL SUP; OxAmL; Pen AM; REnAL; WhoAm 74, 76, 78, 80, 82; WhoWor 74; WorAu; WrDr 76*

Eastland, James Oliver
American. Senator
b. Nov 28, 1904 in Doddsville, Mississippi
Source: *BiDrAC; CelR 73; CngDr 74; CurBio 49; IntWW 74; NewYTBE 72; WhoAm 74, 76, 78, 80, 82; WhoAmP 73; WhoGov 72; WhoS&SW 73; WhoWor 74*

Eastman, George
American. Inventor, Industralist
Invented roll film, 1884, the Kodak camera, 1888.
b. Jul 12, 1854 in Waterville, New York
d. Mar 14, 1932 in Rochester, New York
Source: *AmBi; DcAmB S1; DcFM; EncAB-H; FilmgC; OxFilm; WebAB; WhAm 1; WorEFlm*

Eastman, Max Forrester
American. Author
b. Jan 4, 1883 in Canandaigua, New York
d. Mar 25, 1969 in Bridgetown, Barbados
Source: *AmAu&B; AmLY; CasWL; ChPo; CnDAL; ConAmA; ConAmL; ConAu 9R, 25R; CurBio 69; DcLEL; LongCTC; OxAmL; Pen AM; REn; REnAL; TwCA, SUP; WebAB; WhAm 5*

Easton, Elliot
see: Cars, The

Easton, Florence Gertrude
English. Opera Singer
b. Oct 25, 1884 in Middlesbrough, England
d. Aug 13, 1955 in New York, New York
Source: *InWom*

Easton, Sheena
[Sheena Shirley Orr]
Scottish. Singer
Sang title song for James Bond film, *For Your Eyes Only*.
b. Apr 27, 1959 in Bellshill, Scotland
Source: *BioIn 12; IlEncRk; NewWmR*

Eastwood, Clint
American. Actor
Starred on TV series "Rawhide," 1959-66; movie *Dirty Harry*, 1971.
b. May 31, 1930 in San Francisco, California
Source: *BiDFilm; BioNews 74; BkPepl; CelR 73; CurBio 71; FilmgC; IntMPA 75, 76, 77, 78, 79, 80, 81, 82; MotPP; MovMk; OxFilm; WhoAm 74, 76, 78, 80, 82; WhoHol A; WorEFlm*

Easy Aces
see: Ace, Goodman; Ace, Jane Sherwood

Eaton, Cyrus Stephen
American. Financier
b. Dec 27, 1883 in Pugwash, NS
d. May 9, 1979 in Northfield, Ohio
Source: *AmAu&B; BioNews 74; BusPN; CanWW 70, 79; CelR 73; CurBio 48, 79; IntWW 75, 76, 77, 78; NewYTBE 73; NewYTBS 79; PolProf E; PolProf K; WhAm 7; WhoAm 76, 78; WhoF&I 75; WhoWor 78*

Eaton, Mary
American. Actress
b. 1901 in Norfolk, Virginia
d. Oct 10, 1948 in Hollywood, California
Source: *BioIn 1; EncMT; Film 2; NotNAT B; WhScrn 74, 77; WhThe; WhoHol B*

Eaton, Shirley
English. Actress
b. 1936 in London, England
Source: *FilmgC; MotPP; WhoHol A*

Eaton, Timothy
Canadian. Merchant
b. 1834
d. Jan 31, 1907
Source: *BioIn 11*

Eban, Abba
[Aubrey Solomon]
Israeli. Diplomat
UN representative, 1949-59; ambassador to US, 1950-59; wrote *Israel in the World*, 1966.
b. Apr 2, 1915 in Capetown, South Africa
Source: *BioNews 75; ConAu 57; CurBio 57; IntWW 74; Who 74; WhoWor 74; WhoWorJ 72*

Ebbets, Charles H
American. Baseball Executive
Owner, Brooklyn Dodgers, early 1900's; built Ebbets Field in Brooklyn.
b. Oct 29, 1859 in New York, New York
d. Apr 18, 1925 in New York, New York
Source: *WhoProB 73*

Eberhard, Johann August
German. Philosopher
b. 1739
d. 1809
Source: *BiD&SB; DcEuL; WebBD 80*

Eberhart, Mignon Good
American. Author
b. Jul 6, 1899 in Nebraska
Source: *AmAu&B; AuNews 2; ConAu 73; EncMys; LongCTC; REnAL; TwCA, SUP; WhNAA; WhoAm 74, 76, 78, 80, 82; WhoWor 74*

Eberhart, Richard
American. Author
b. Apr 5, 1904 in Austin, Minnesota
Source: *AmAu&B; AmWr; BiE&WWA; CasWL; ChPo; CnE&AP; ConAu 2NR; ConLC 1, 3, 11; ConP 70, 75; DcLEL; DrAP 75; DrAS 74E; IntWW 74; LongCTC; ModAL, SUP; NotNAT; OxAmL; Pen AM; RAdv 1; REn; REnAL; SixAP; TwCA SUP; TwCW; WebE&AL; Who 74; WhoAm 74, 76, 78, 80, 82; WhoE 74; WhoTwCL; WhoWor 74; WrDr 76*

Eberle, Irmengarde
American. Author
b. Nov 11, 1898 in San Antonio, Texas
Source: *AmAu&B; AuBYP; BkCL; ConAu 1R, 85, 2NR; InWom; JBA 51; SmATA 2; WhoAm 74; WhoAmW 77; WhoWor 74*

Eberle, Ray
[The Eberle Brothers]
American. Singer
b. Jan 19, 1919 in Hoosick Falls, New York
Source: *CmpEPM*

Eberly, Bob
[Robert Eberle; The Eberle Brothers]
American. Singer, Band Leader
b. Jul 24, 1916 in Mechanicville, New York
d. Nov 17, 1981 in Glen Burnie, Maryland
Source: *BioIn 3, 10; CmpEPM; NewYTBS 81*

Eberstadt, Ferdinand
American. Government Official
b. Jun 19, 1890 in New York, New York
d. Nov 11, 1969
Source: *BioIn 1, 2, 3, 8, 9; CurBio 42, 70*

Ebert, Carl (Anton Charles)
American. Opera Director
b. Feb 20, 1887 in Berlin, Germany
d. May 14, 1980 in Santa Monica, California
Source: *CnOxOp 79; EncOp; EncWT; IntWW 74, 75, 76, 77, 78; NewEOp 71; Who 74*

Ebert, Friedrich
German. President
b. Feb 4, 1871 in Heidelberg, Germany
d. Feb 28, 1925
Source: *NewCol 75; OxGer; REn; WebBD 80*

Ebert, Roger Joseph
American. Motion Picture Critic
Wrote screenplay for *Beyond the Valley of the Dolls*, 1970.
b. Jun 18, 1942 in Urbana, Illinois
Source: *BioIn 8; ConAu 69; WhoAm 82*

Ebing, Richard von Krafft
see: Krafft-Ebing, Richard von

Ebsen, Buddy
[Christian Ebson, Jr.]
American. Actor, Dancer
Starred in TV series "The Beverly Hillbillies," 1962-71, "Barnaby Jones," 1973-79.
b. Apr 2, 1908 in Orlando, Florida
Source: *AmSCAP 66; EncMT; FilmgC; IntMPA 75, 76, 77, 78, 79, 80, 81, 82; MovMk; WhoAm 82; WhoHol A*

Eccles, Sir John Carew
Australian. Scientist
b. Jan 27, 1903 in Melbourne, Australia
Source: *AmM&WS 73P; ConAu 65; CurBio 72; IntWW 74; Who 74; WhoAm 74; WhoWor 74*

Eccles, Marriner Stoddard
American. Economist
b. Sep 9, 1890 in Logan, Utah
d. Dec 18, 1977 in Salt Lake City, Utah
Source: *AmAu&B; CurBio 41, 78; EncAB-H; IntWW 74, 75, 76, 77, 78; IntYB 78; LinLib L, S; NewYTBS 77; PolProf T; WhAm 7; WhoAm 74, 76, 78; WhoF&I 74; WhoWor 74*

Ecevit, Bulent
Turkish. Journalist, Politician
b. May 28, 1925 in Istanbul, Turkey
Source: *BioIn 10, 11; CurBio 75; IntWW 74; NewCol 75; WhoWor 74*

Echegaray, Jose
Spanish. Dramatist
b. Apr 19, 1831 in Madrid, Spain
d. Sep 15, 1916 in Madrid, Spain
Source: *BbD; BiD&SB; CIDMEL; CnMD; DcSpL; McGEWD; ModRL; ModWD; OxThe; Pen EUR; REn; TwCW*

Echeverria Alvarez, Louis
Mexican. Politician
b. Jan 17, 1922 in Mexico City, Mexico
Source: *BioIn 8, 9, 10, 11; BioNews 74; CurBio 72; IntWW 74; NewYTBE 70; WhoGov 72; WhoS&SW 73; WhoWor 74*

Eckener, Hugo
German. Aeronatuical Engineer
Trained German dirigible crews during World War I.
b. 1868
d. Aug 14, 1954 in Friedrichshafen, Germany (West)
Source: *ObitOF 79; WebBD 80*

Eckert, Horst
[Janosch, pseud.]
Polish. Children's Author, Illustrator
b. Mar 11, 1931 in Zaborze, Poland
Source: *ConAu 37R; SmATA 8*

Eckhart, Johannes
German. Philosopher, Mystic
b. 1260 in Hochheim, Germany
d. 1327 in Avignon, France
Source: *CasWL; EuAu; EvEuW; NewC; OxGer; Pen EUR*

Eckstein, Gustav
American. Physiologist, Author
b. Oct 26, 1890 in Cincinnati, Ohio
d. Sep 23, 1981 in Cincinnati, Ohio
Source: *AmAu&B; BioIn 1, 3, 4; ConAu 57, 104; CurBio 42, 81; NewYTBS 81; OhA&B; TwCA SUP; WhE&EA; WhNAA*

Eckstine, Billy
American. Singer
b. Jul 8, 1914 in Pittsburgh, Pennsylvania
Source: *CurBio 52; WhoAm 74, 76, 78, 80, 82; WhoBlA 75; WhoHol A; WhoMus 72*

Economaki, Chris(topher Constantine)
American. Publisher, Broadcast Journalist
b. Oct 15, 1920 in Brooklyn, New York
Source: *WhoAm 76, 78, 80, 82*

Ed, Carl Frank Ludwig
American. Cartoonist
b. Jul 16, 1890 in Moline, Illinois
d. Oct 10, 1959 in Evanston, Illinois
Source: *AmAu&B; WhAm 3*

Eda-Pierre, Christiane
French. Opera Singer
b. in Fort de France, Martinique
Source: *WhoOp 76*

Eddington, Sir Arthur Stanley
English. Astronomer
Translated theories of relativity into lay terms.
b. Dec 28, 1882 in Kendal, England
d. Nov 22, 1944 in Cambridge, England
Source: *Chambr 3; CurBio 41; DcLEL; EvLB; LongCTC; NewC; NewCol 75; OxEng; TwCA, SUP; WhoLA*

Eddy, Duane
American. Musician
b. Apr 26, 1938 in Corning, New York
Source: *EncPR&S*

Eddy, Mary Baker Morse
American. Religious Leader
Founded Christian Science Religious Movement; organized first church, 1879.
b. Jul 16, 1821 in Bow, New Hampshire
d. Dec 3, 1910 in Chestnut Hill, Massachusetts
Source: *Alli SUP; AmAu; AmAu&B; AmBi; BiD&SB; CasWL; ChPo, S1, S2; DcAmAu; DcAmB; DcLEL; DcNAA; EncAB-H; HerW; InWom; LongCTC; NotAW; OxAmL; OxEng; REn; REnAL; TwCBDA; WebAB; WhAm 1*

Eddy, Nelson
American. Singer, Actor
Starred with Jeanette MacDonald in major musicals of the 1930's.
b. Jun 29, 1901 in Providence, Rhode Island
d. Mar 6, 1967 in Miami, Florida
Source: *CmMov; CurBio 43, 67; FilmgC; MotPP; MovMk; OxFilm; WhAm 4; WhScrn 74, 77; WhoHol B*

Eddy, Sherwood
American. Author
b. Jan 11, 1871 in Leavenworth, Kansas
d. Mar 3, 1963 in Jacksonville, Illinois
Source: *OxAmL; REnAL; WhAm 4; WhNAA*

Edel, (Joseph) Leon
American. Author, Journalist
b. Sep 9, 1907 in Pittsburgh, Pennsylvania
Source: *AmAu&B; CanWW 70; ConAu 1R, 1NR; CurBio 63; DrAS 74E; IntWW 74; NewYTBE 72; OxAmL; RAdv 1; REn; Who 74; WhoAm 82; WhoWor 74; WorAu; WrDr 76*

Edelman, Herb
American. Actor
b. 1933 in Brooklyn, New York
Source: *FilmgC; WhoHol A*

Edelmann, Otto
Austrian. Opera Singer
b. Feb 5, 1917 in Brunn, Austria
Source: *IntWW 74; WhoMus 72; WhoWor 74*

Eden, Anthony
[Robert Anthony Eden, Earl of Avon]
English. Prime Minister
b. Jun 21, 1897 in Durham, England
d. Jan 14, 1977 in Alvediston, England
Source: *ConAu 69, 77; CurBio 40, 51; WebBD 80; Who 74*

Eden, Barbara Jean
[Mrs. Charles Fegert]
American. Actress
Starred with Larry Hagman in TV series "I Dream of Jeannie," 1965-69.
b. Aug 23, 1934 in Tucson, Arizona
Source: *FilmgC; MovMk; WhoAm 74, 76, 78, 80, 82; WhoHol A*

Eden, Dorothy
New Zealander. Author
b. Apr 3, 1912 in Canterbury, New Zealand
d. Mar 4, 1982 in London, England
Source: *ConAu 81; WrDr 76, 80*

Eder, Shirley
American. Journalist
Source: *NF*

Ederle, Gertrude Caroline
American. Swimmer
b. Oct 23, 1906 in New York, New York
Source: *InWom; WebAB; WhoHol A*

Edeson, Robert
American. Actor
b. 1868 in New Orleans, Louisiana
d. Mar 24, 1931 in Hollywood, California
Source: *Film 1, 2; NotNAT; OxThe; TwYS; WhScrn 74, 77; WhThe; WhoHol; WhoStg 1906, 1908*

Edgar
[Eadgar]
English. King
b. 943?
d. 975
Source: *BioIn 6, 9; NewCol 75*

Edgar, David
English. Dramatist
b. Feb 26, 1948 in Birmingham, England
Source: *BioIn 10; ConAu 57; ConDr 77; WrDr 76, 80*

Edgell, George Harold
American. Author, Museum Director
b. Mar 4, 1887 in Saint Louis, Missouri
d. Jun 29, 1954 in Newport, New Hampshire
Source: *BioIn 1, 3, 5, 6; NatCAB 45; WhAm 3; WhE&EA; WhLit*

Edgerton, Harold Eugene
American. Engineer
b. Apr 6, 1903 in Fremont, Nebraska
Source: *BioIn 3, 4, 6, 7, 10; WhoAm 82*

Edgeworth, Maria
English. Children's Author
b. Jan 1, 1767 in Bourton Abbots, England
d. May 22, 1849 in Edgeworthstown, Ireland
Source: *Alli; AtlBL; BbD; BiD&SB; BiDLA; BrAu 19; CarSB; CasWL; Chambr 2; ChPo; CrtT 2; CyWA; DcBiA; DcEnA; DcEnL; DcEuL; DcLEL; EvLB; InWom; MouLC 3; NewC; OxEng; Pen ENG; PoIre; RAdv 1; REn; WebE&AL; WhoChL*

Edison, Thomas Alva
American. Inventor
Invented automatic telegraph, phonograph, incandescent light; held over 1,300 patents.
b. Feb 11, 1847 in Milan, Ohio
d. Oct 18, 1931 in West Orange, New Jersey
Source: *AmBi; ApCAB; DcAmB S1; DcFM; EncAB-H; FilmgC; LongCTC; NewCol 75; OxFilm; REn; REnAL; TwCBDA; WebAB; WhAm 1; WorEFlm*

Edmiston, Mark Morton
American. President of Newsweek, Inc.
b. Jul 9, 1943 in Yonkers, New York
Source: *WhoAm 80, 82*

Edmonds, Emma E
American. Nurse, Spy
b. 1841
d. 1898
Source: *BioIn 1, 3, 5, 6, 8, 9*

Edmonds, Walter Dumaux
American. Author
b. Jul 15, 1903 in Boonville, New York
Source: *AmAu&B; AmNov; AuBYP; CnDAL; ConAmA; ConAu 5R, 2NR; CurBio 42; CyWA; DcLEL; ModAL; MorBMP; MorJA; Newb 1922; OxAmL; Pen AM; REn; REnAL; SmATA 1; TwCA, SUP; WhoAm 74, 76, 78, 80, 82; WrDr 76*

Edmonson, Munro Sterling
American. Educator, Anthropologist
b. May 18, 1924 in Nogales, Arizona
Source: *AmM&WS 73S; ConAu 33R; WhoAm 74; WrDr 76*

Edmund, Saint
King of East Anglia
b. 840?
d. 870
Source: *BioIn 1, 2, 3, 4, 5, 6, 7, 8, 9; NewC; NewCol 75*

Edmunds, Dave
[Rockpile]
Welsh. Musician, Producer
Songs include "Crawling from the Wreckage," "Cruel to be Kind."
b. Apr 15, 1944 in Cardiff, Wales
Source: *ConMuA 80; IlEncRk*

Edmunds, George Franklin
American. Lawyer, Politician
b. Feb 1, 1828 in Richmond, Vermont
d. Feb 27, 1919 in Pasadena, California
Source: *BioIn 7; WebAB; WebBD 80; WhAm 1*

Edson, Gus
American. Cartoonist
b. Sep 20, 1901 in Stamford, Connecticut
d. Sep 26, 1966 in Stamford, Connecticut
Source: *BioIn 7; ObitOF 79*

Edward I
English. King
b. 1239 in Westminster, England
d. 1307
Source: *BioIn 10; NewCol 75; WebBD 80*

Edward II
[Edward of Carnarvon]
English. King
b. 1284 in Carnarvon, England
d. 1327
Source: *BioIn 10; NewCol 75; WebBD 80*

Edward III
English. King
b. 1312 in Windsor, England
d. 1377
Source: *BioIn 10; NewCol 75; WebBD 80*

Edward IV
English. King
b. 1442 in Rouen, France
d. 1483 in London, England
Source: *BioIn 10; NewCol 75; WebBD 80*

Edward V
English. King
b. 1470 in Westminster, England
d. 1483? in London, England
Source: *BioIn 10; NewCol 75; WebBD 80*

Edward VI
English. King
b. 1537 in Hampton Court, England
d. 1553 in London, England
Source: *BioIn 10; NewCol 75; WebBD 80*

Edward VII
[Edward Albert]
English. King
b. 1841 in London, England
d. 1910 in London, England
Source: *NewCol 75; WebBD 80; WhoModH*

Edward VIII
[Duke of Windsor]
English. King
Reigned from Jan 20-Dec 10, 1936; abdicated to marry Wallis Simpson, a twice-divorced American.
b. Jun 23, 1894 in Richmond, England
d. May 18, 1972 in Paris, France
Source: *BioIn 10; ConAu 33R; NewCol 75; WhAm 5; WebBD 80*

Edward, Prince
[Edward Antony Richard Louis]
English. Son of Queen Elizabeth II
b. Mar 10, 1964 in London, England
Source: *Who 82*

Edward the Black Prince
English. Son of Edward III
b. 1330 in Woodstock, England
d. 1376 in London, England
Source: *BioIn 1, 3, 5, 6, 7, 8, 9, 11; NewCol 75*

Edward the Confessor
[Eadward]
English. King
b. 1002? in Oxford, England
d. 1066
Source: *NewC; NewCol 75; WebBD 80*

Edwards, Alan
American. Actor
b. Jun 3, 1900 in New York, New York
d. May 8, 1954 in Los Angeles, California
Source: *BioIn 3; Film 2; IntMPA 82; WhScrn 74, 77*

Edwards, Blake
American. Motion Picture Producer, Author
Produced *Pink Panther* film series; husband of Julie Andrews.
b. Jul 26, 1922 in Tulsa, Oklahoma
Source: *ConAu 81; CurBio 83; FilmgC; IntMPA 75, 76, 77, 78, 79, 80, 81, 82; MovMk; OxFilm; WhoAm 74, 76, 78, 80, 82; WorEFlm*

Edwards, Cliff
American. Singer, Actor
b. Jul 14, 1895 in Hannibal, Missouri
d. Jul 17, 1971 in Hollywood, California
Source: *FilmgC; MotPP; MovMk; NewYTBE 71; Vers B; WhScrn 74, 77; WhoHol B*

Edwards, Dennis
[The Temptations]
American. Singer
b. Feb 3, 1943 in Birmingham, Alabama
Source: *NF*

Edwards, Douglas
American. Radio, TV Announcer
b. Jul 14, 1917 in Ada, Oklahoma
Source: *IntMPA 75, 76, 77, 78, 79, 80, 81, 82; Who 74; WhoAm 74, 76, 78, 80, 82*

Edwards, Edwin Washington
American. Governor
b. Aug 7, 1927 in Marksville, Louisiana
Source: *BiDrAC; NewYTBS 74; WhoAm 74, 76, 78, 80, 82; WhoAmP 73; WhoGov 72; WhoS&SW 73*

Edwards, Gus
American. Songwriter
b. Aug 18, 1879 in Hohensaliza, Germany
d. Nov 7, 1945 in Los Angeles, California
Source: *AmAu&B; AmSCAP 66; CurBio 45; REnAL; WhScrn 74, 77; WhoHol B*

Edwards, India
American. Journalist, Politician
b. 1895 in Chicago, Illinois
Source: *BioIn 2, 3, 11; CurBio 49*

Edwards, James Burrows
American. Former Govt. Official
Secretary of Energy, 1981-82.
b. Jun 24, 1927 in Hawthorne, Florida
Source: *CurBio 82; IntWW 78; WhoAm 76, 78, 80, 82; WhoAmP 73, 75, 77, 79; WhoGov 75, 77; WhoS&SW 73, 75, 76, 78*

Edwards, Joan
American. Singer, Songwriter
b. Feb 13, 1919 in New York, New York
d. Aug 27, 1981 in New York, New York
Source: *AmSCAP 66; CmpEPM; CurBio 53, 81; InWom; NewYTBS 81*

Edwards, Jonathan
American. Author, Theologian
b. Oct 5, 1703 in East Windsor, Connecticut
d. Mar 22, 1758 in New Jersey
Source: *Alli; AmAu; AmAu&B; AmBi; AmWr; ApCAB; AtlBL; BbD; BiD&SB; CasWL; CnDAL; CrtT 3; CyAL 1; CyWA; DcAmAu; DcAmB; DcEnL; DcLEL; DcNAA; Drake; EncAB-H; EvLB; MouLC 2; NewC; OxAmL; OxEng; Pen AM; RComWL; REn; REnAL; TwCBDA; WebAB; WebE&AL; WhAm H*

Edwards, Ralph
American. TV Producer
b. Jun 13, 1913 in Marino, California
Source: *BioIn 10; WhoAm 82*

Edwards, Robert Geoffrey
English. Physiologist
b. 1925
Source: *BioIn 11*

Edwards, Sherman
American. Composer, Lyricist
b. Apr 3, 1919 in New York, New York
d. Mar 30, 1981 in New York, New York
Source: *AmSCAP 66; EncMT; WhoAm 74; WhoThe 77*

Edwards, Vince
[Vincent Edward Zoino]
American. Actor
Starred in TV series "Ben Casey," 1961-66.
b. Jul 7, 1928 in Brooklyn, New York
Source: *FilmgC; IntMPA 75, 76, 77; MotPP; MovMk; WhoAm 74; WhoHol A*

Edwards, Willard
American. Journalist
b. Dec 7, 1902 in Chicago, Illinois
Source: *WhoAm 74; WhoS&SW 73*

Edwy
[Eadwig]
English. King
d. 959
Source: *NewC; NewCol 75; WebBD 80*

Efron, Marshall
American. Comedian
b. 1938
Source: *BioIn 10*

Egan, Eddie
"Popeye"
American. New York Police Detective
Source: *BioIn 9*

Egan, Richard
American. Actor
b. Jul 29, 1923 in San Francisco, California
Source: *FilmgC; IntMPA 82; MotPP; MovMk; WhoHol A*

Egan, Richard B
Canadian. Songwriter
b. Nov 14, 1890 in Windsor, ON
d. Nov 13, 1952 in Westport, Connecticut
Source: *AmSCAP 66; BioIn 3, 4, 5*

Egan, Walter Lindsay
American. Singer, Songwriter
b. Jul 12, 1948 in Jamaica, New York
Source: *AmSCAP 80; ConMuA 80*

Eggar, Samantha
English. Actress
b. Mar 5, 1940 in Hampstead, England
Source: *CelR 73; FilmgC; IntMPA 75, 76, 77, 78, 79, 80, 81, 82; MotPP; MovMk; WhoAm 82; WhoHol*

Eggerth, Marta
Hungarian. Actress, Singer
b. Apr 17, 1916? in Budapest, Hungary
Source: *BiE&WWA; CurBio 43; NotNAT; WhoHol A; WhoThe 77*

Eggleston, Edward
American. Author, Clergyman
b. Dec 10, 1837 in Veray, Indiana
d. Sep 4, 1902 in Lake George, New York
Source: *Alli SUP; AmAu; AmAu&B; AmBi; ApCAB; BbD; BiD&SB; CarSB; CasWL; Chambr 3; ChPo, S1; CnDAL; CyAl 2; CyWA; DcAmAu; DcAmB; DcBiA; DcNAA; DcRusL; EvLB; IndAu 1816; JBA 34; OxAmL; OxEng; Pen AM; REn; REnAL; TwCBDA; WebAB; WebE&AL; WhAm 1*

Egk, Werner
German. Composer
b. May 17, 1901 in Auchsensheim, Germany
Source: *DcCM; IntWW 74; WhoMus 72; WhoWor 74*

Eglevsky, Andre
Russian. Ballet Dancer
b. Dec 21, 1917 in Moscow, U.S.S.R.
d. Dec 4, 1977 in Elmira, New York
Source: *CurBio 53; IntWW 74; WhoAm 74*

Ehmke, Howard Jonathan
"Bob"
American. Baseball Player
b. Apr 24, 1894 in Silver Creek, New York
d. Mar 17, 1959 in Philadelphia, Pennsylvania
Source: *BaseEn; BioIn 5, 7, 10; WhoProB 73*

Ehrenburg, Ilya Grigoryevich
[Ilya Ehrenbourg; Ilya Erenburg]
Russian. Author
b. Jan 27, 1891 in Kiev, Russia
d. Aug 31, 1967 in Moscow, U.S.S.R.
Source: *CasWL; ClDMEL; ConAu 25R, 102; ConLC 18; CurBio 66, 67; DcRusL; EncWL; EvEuW; LongCTC; ModSL 1; Pen EUR; REn; TwCA, SUP; TwCW*

Ehricke, Krafft Arnold
American. Engineer
b. Mar 24, 1917 in Berlin, Germany
Source: *AmM&WS 73P; BioIn 4, 5, 6; WhoAm 74, 76, 78, 80, 82*

Ehrlich, Bettina Bauer
Austrian. Artist
b. Mar 19, 1903 in Vienna, Austria
Source: *AuBYP; ConAu P-1; IlsCB 1946, 1957; MorJA; SmATA 1*

Ehrlich, Paul
German. Bacteriologist
b. Feb 12, 1854 in Schlesian, Germany
d. Aug 20, 1915 in Homburg, Prussia
Source: *AsBiEn; DcBiPP; McGEWB*

Ehrlich, Paul
American. Population Biologist
b. May 29, 1932 in Philadelphia, Pennsylvania
Source: *BioIn 9; CurBio 70*

Ehrlichman, John Daniel
American. Government Official
Served 18 months in prison for involvement in Watergate, 1976-78.
b. Mar 20, 1925 in Tacoma, Washington
Source: *ConAu 65; IntWW 74; NewYTBE 70, 73; NewYTBS 74; WhoAm 74, 76, 78, 80, 82; WhoAmP 73; WhoGov 72; WhoS&SW 73*

Ehrling, Sixten
Swedish. Conductor
b. Apr 3, 1918 in Malmo, Sweden
Source: *BioNews 74; WhoAm 74, 76, 78, 80, 82; WhoMus 72; WhoWor 74*

Eichelberger, Dave
American. Golfer
b. Sep 3, 1943 in Waco, Texas
Source: *WhoGolf*

Eichelberger, Robert Lawrence
American. Army General, Author
b. Mar 9, 1886 in Urbana, Ohio
d. Sep 26, 1961 in Asheville, North Carolina
Source: *AmM&WS 73P; CurBio 43, 61; WhAm 4*

Eichenberg, Fritz
English. Illustrator
b. Oct 24, 1901 in Cologne, Germany
Source: *AnCL; ChPo S2; ConAu 57; IlsBYP; IlsCB 1744, 1946, 1957; MorJA; SmATA 9; Str&VC; WhoAm 74; WhoAmA 73; WhoGrA*

Eichendorff, Joseph Karl Benedict
German. Poet
b. Mar 10, 1788 in Ratibor, Silesia
d. Nov 26, 1857 in Neisse, Silesia
Source: *AtlBL; BbD; BiD&SB; DcEuL; EuAu; OxFr; OxGer; Pen; RComWL; REn*

Eichhorn, Lisa
American. Actress
b. 1952? in Reading, Pennsylvania
Source: *IntMPA 81, 82; NewYTBS 79*

Eichmann, (Karl) Adolf
Austrian. Nazi War Criminal
b. 1906
d. May 31, 1962 in Jerusalem, Israel
Source: *NewCol 75; REn; WebBD 80*

Eifert, Virginia Snider
American. Children's Author
b. Jan 23, 1911 in Springfield, Illinois
d. Jun 16, 1966
Source: *AmAu&B; Au&Wr 71; AuBYP; ConAu 1R; SmATA 2; WhAm 4*

Eiffel, Alexandre Gustave
French. Engineer
Designed Eiffel Tower, 1889, framework for Statue of Liberty, 1885.
b. 1832 in Dijon, France
d. Dec 23, 1923
Source: *McGEWB; NewCol 75; WebBD 80*

Eight, The
[Arthur B Davies; William J Glackens; Robert Henri; Ernest Lawson; George Luks; Maurice Pendergast; Everett Shinn; John Sloan]
American. Artists
Established "Ashcan School" of painting, circa 1907.
Source: *NewCol 75; OxArt*

Eikerenkoetter, Frederick Joseph, II
see: Ike, Reverend

Einaudi, Luigi
Italian. President
b. Mar 24, 1874 in Cuneo, Italy
d. Oct 30, 1961
Source: *CurBio 48, 62; NewCol 75; WhAm 4*

Einhorn, David
German. Rabbi
b. Nov 10, 1809 in Dispeck, Bavaria
d. Nov 2, 1879 in New York, New York
Source: *BioIn 2, 4, 5, 7; NatCAB 12; NewCol 75; WhAm H*

Einhorn, Eddie (Edward Martin)
American. Baseball Club Executive
Chief operating officer, Chicago White Sox baseball club.
b. Jan 3, 1936 in Paterson, New Jersey
Source: *NewYTBS 81; WhoAm 78, 80, 82*

Einstein, Albert
American. Physicist
Introduced theories of relativity, 1905, 1915; won Nobel Prize, 1921.
b. Mar 14, 1879 in Ulm, Germany
d. Apr 18, 1955 in Princeton, New Jersey
Source: *AmAu&B; CasWL; CurBio 41, 53, 55; DcAmB S5; DcLEL; EncAB-H; LongCTC; NewYTBE 72; OxAmL; OxEng; REn; REnAL; WebAB; WhAm 3; WhNAA; WhoLA*

Einstein, Alfred
German. Musicologist, Critic, Editor
b. Dec 30, 1880 in Munich, Germany
d. Feb 13, 1952 in El Cerrito, California
Source: *AmAu&B; LongCTC; TwCA SUP; WhAm 3*

Einthoven, Willem
Dutch. Physiologist
b. May 22, 1860 in Semarang, Indonesia
d. Sep 28, 1927 in Leiden, Netherlands
Source: *AsBiEn; BioIn 3, 5, 9; DcScB*

Eisele, Donn Fulton
American. Astronaut, Businessman
Command module pilot, first Apollo voyage, 1968.
b. Jun 23, 1930 in Columbus, Ohio
Source: *USBiR 74; WhoAm 74, 76, 78, 80, 82; WhoS&SW 73; WhoWor 74*

Eiseley, Loren Corey
American. Anthropologist
b. Sep 3, 1907 in Lincoln, Nebraska
d. Jul 9, 1977 in Philadelphia, Pennsylvania
Source: *AmAu&B; AmM&WS 73S; Au&Wr 71; CelR 73; ConAu 1R; CurBio 60; REnAL; WebAB; WhoAm 74; WhoE 74; WhoGov 72; WhoWor 74; WorAu*

Eisenhower, David
American. Author, Lawyer
Grandson of Dwight Eisenhower; presidential retreat "Camp David" named for him.
b. Apr 1, 1947 in West Point, New York
Source: *BioIn 10*

Eisenhower, Dwight David
American. 34th US President
WW II general; sent Federal troops to AR to force compliance with desegregation orders.
b. Oct 14, 1890 in Denison, Texas
d. Mar 28, 1969 in Washington, DC
Source: *AmAu&B; BiDrAC; BiDrUSE; BioNews 74; CurBio 42, 48, 57, 69; EncAB-H; NewYTBE 71; OxAmL; REn; REnAL; WebAB; WhAm 5; WhAmP; WhoFtbl 74*

Eisenhower, John Sheldon Doud
American. Author, Diplomat
b. Aug 3, 1922 in Denver, Colorado
Source: *ConAu 33R; CurBio 69; IntWW 74; WhoAm 74, 76, 78, 80, 82; WhoAmP 73*

Eisenhower, Julie Nixon
[Mrs. David Eisenhower]
American. Daughter of Richard Nixon, Author
Edited *Saturday Evening Post* two years; wrote *Special People.*
b. Jul 5, 1948 in Washington, DC
Source: *BioIn 10, 11; BkPepl; NewYTBE 71; NewYTBS 75*

Eisenhower, Mamie Geneva Doud
American. Wife of Dwight Eisenhower
b. Nov 14, 1896 in Boone, Iowa
d. Nov 1, 1979 in Washington, DC
Source: *BioNews 74; CelR 73; CurBio 53, 80; InWom; WhoAm 74; WhoAmW 77; WhoGov 72; WhoWor 74*

Eisenhower, Milton Stover
American. Educator
b. Sep 15, 1899 in Abilene, Kansas
Source: *CelR 73; CurBio 46; IntWW 74; Who 74; WhoAm 74; WhoAmP 73; WhoE 74; WhoWor 74*

Eisenstaedt, Alfred
Photographer
b. Dec 6, 1898 in Dirschau, Germany
Source: *IntWW 74; WhoAm 82*

Eisenstein, Sergei Mikhailovich
Russian. Motion Picture Director
b. 1898 in Riga, Russia
d. Feb 10, 1948 in Moscow, U.S.S.R.
Source: *BiDFilm; CurBio 46, 48; DcFM; FilmgC; MovMk; NewCol 75; NewYTBE 73; ObitOF 79; OxFilm; REn; WomWMM; WorEFlm*

Eizenstat, Stuart E
American. Government Official
Assistant to Jimmy Carter on domestic affairs and policy, 1977-80.
b. Jan 15, 1943 in Chicago, Illinois
Source: *WhoAm 82; WhoAmP 73*

Ekberg, Anita
Swedish. Actress
b. Sep 29, 1931 in Malmo, Sweden
Source: *FilmgC; InWom; IntMPA 75, 76, 77, 78, 79, 80, 81, 82; MotPP; MovMk; WhoAm 74; WhoHol A; WorEFlm*

Ekland, Britt
Swedish. Actress
b. 1942 in Stockholm, Sweden
Source: *FilmgC; IntMPA 75, 76, 77; WhoHol A*

Elam, Jack
American. Actor
b. Nov 13, 1916 in Phoenix, AZ
Source: *CmMov; FilmgC; IntMPA 82; MotPP; MovMk; WhoAm 82; WhoHol A*

Elazar, David
Israeli. General
b. 1925 in Yugoslavia
d. Apr 15, 1976 in Tel Aviv, Israel
Source: *InWom*

Elder, Lee
American. Golfer
First black to play in Masters tournament, 1975.
b. Jul 14, 1934 in Dallas, Texas
Source: *BioIn 8, 10; CurBio 76; WhoBlA 75, 77; WhoGolf*

Elder, Ruth
American. Actress, Aviatrix
b. 1904
d. Oct 9, 1977 in San Francisco, California
Source: *InWom*

Eldjarn, Kristjan
Icelandic. Politician
President of Iceland, 1968-1980.
b. Dec 6, 1916 in Tjorn, Iceland
d. Sep 13, 1982 in Cleveland, Ohio
Source: *IntWW 74, 75, 76, 77, 78, 79, 80; IntYB 78, 79, 80, 81; NewYTBS 82; WhoGov 72; WhoWor 74, 76, 78*

Eldridge, David Roy
American. Musician, Band Leader
b. 1911
Source: *BioIn 10*

Eldridge, Florence
American. Actress
b. Sep 5, 1901 in New York, New York
Source: *BiE&WWA; CurBio 43; FilmgC; InWom; MotPP; MovMk; NotNAT; ThFT; WhoHol A; WhoThe 77*

Eldridge, Roy
American. Jazz Musician
b. Jan 29, 1911 in Pittsburgh, Pennsylvania
Source: *WhoAm 74, 76, 78, 80, 82; WhoJazz 72*

Eleanor of Aquitaine
[Eleanor of Guienne]
French. Consort of Henry II
b. 1122? in Aquitaine, France
d. Apr 1, 1204
Source: *DcEuL; McGEWB; NewC; REn; NewC*

Electric Light Orchestra
[Michael Alberquerque; Bev Bevan; Michael Edwards; Melvyn Gale; Wilf Gibson; Kelly Groucutt; Mik Kaminski; Jeff Lynne; Hugh MacDowell; Richard Tandy; Colin Walker]
English. Rock Group
Source: *BkPepl; IlEncRk*

Elegant, Robert Sampson
American. Author
b. Mar 7, 1928 in New York, New York
Source: *AmAu&B; BioIn 4, 7, 11; ConAu 1R, 1NR; IntAu&W 76, 77; WhoAm 74, 76, 78, 80, 82; WhoWest 74, 76; WhoWor 74; WrDr 76, 80*

Elgar, Sir Edward William
English. Composer, Conductor, Musician
b. Jun 2, 1857 in Broadheath, England
d. Feb 23, 1934 in London, England
Source: *AtlBL; DcCM; REn*

Eliade, Mircea
American. Theologian
b. Mar 9, 1907 in Bucharest, Romania
Source: *AmAu&B; Au&Wr 71; BiDPara; CasWL; DrAS 74P; EncWL; WhoAm 74, 76, 78, 80, 82; WhoMW 74; WhoWor 74; WorAu*

Elias, Rosalind
American. Opera Singer
b. Mar 13, 1931 in Lowell, Massachusetts
Source: *CelR 73; CurBio 67; InWom; WhoAm 82*

Eliezer, Israel ben
see: Ba,al Shem Tov, Israel

Elijah
Biblical Character
Source: *NewC*

Elijah Ben Solomon
Polish. Jewish Scholar
b. 1720 in Vilna, Poland
d. 1797 in Vilna, Poland
Source: *BioIn 1, 3, 4, 5, 7; EuAu; McGEWB; NewCol 75*

Eliot, Charles William
American. Educator
President, Harvard U, 1869-1909.
b. Mar 20, 1834 in Boston, Massachusetts
d. Aug 22, 1926 in Maine
Source: *Alli SUP; AmAu; AmAu&B; AmBi; ApCAB; BiD&SB; CyAL 1; DcAmAu; DcAmB; DcNAA; EncAB-H; NewCol 75; OxAmL; REn; REnAL; TwCBDA; WebAB; WhAm 1*

Eliot, Earl
see: Mitch Ryder and the Detroit Wheels

Eliot, George, pseud.
[Mary Ann Evans]
English. Author
b. Nov 22, 1819 in Warwickshire, England
d. Dec 22, 1880 in London, England
Source: *Alli SUP; AtlBL; BbD; BiD&SB; BrAu 19; CasWL; Chambr 3; ChPo, S2; CrtT 3; CyWA; DcBiA; DcEnA, AP; DcEnL; DcEuL; DcLEL; EvLB; HerW; HsB&A; InWom; MnBBF; MouLC 3; NewC; OxEng; Pen ENG; RAdv 1; RComWL; REn; WebE&AL*

Eliot, George Fielding
American. Radio Commentator
b. Jun 22, 1894 in Brooklyn, New York
d. Apr 21, 1971 in Torrington, Connecticut
Source: *AmAu&B; ConAu 29R; CurBio 40, 71; MnBBF; REnAL; TwCA, SUP*

Eliot, John
English. Colonist
b. Aug 5, 1604 in Widford, England
d. May 20, 1690 in Roxbury, Massachusetts
Source: *BioIn 1, 2, 3, 4, 5, 6, 7, 8, 10, 11; DcAmB; McGEWB; WebAB; WhAm H*

Eliot, Martha May
American. Government Official, Physician
b. Apr 7, 1891 in Dorchester, Massachusetts
d. Feb 1978 in Cambridge, Massachusetts
Source: *BioIn 1, 2, 4, 5, 7, 11; CurBio 48, 78; IntWW 74*

Eliot, T(homas) S(tearns)
English. Poet, Critic
Wrote *Murder in the Cathedral,* 1935, *The Cocktail Party,* 1950; won Nobel Prize, 1948.
b. Sep 26, 1888 in Saint Louis, Missouri
d. Jan 4, 1965 in London, England
Source: *AmAu&B; AmWr; AnCL; AtlBL; BiE&WWA; CasWL; Chambr 3; ChPo, S1, S2; CnDAL; CnE&AP; CnMD; CnMWL; CnThe; ConAmL; ConAu 5R, 25R; ConLC 1, 2, 3, 6, 9, 10, 13, 15; CroCD; CurBio 62, 65; CyWA; DcLEL; EncWL; EvLB; LongCTC; McGEWD; ModAL, SUP; ModBrL, SUP; ModWD; NewC; OxAmL; OxEng; OxThe; Pen AM, ENG; PlP&P; RAdv 1; RComWL; REn; REnAL; REnWD; SixAP; TwCA, SUP; TwCW; WebE&AL; WhAm 4; WhNAA; WhoChL; WhoTwCL*

Elisofon, Eliot
American. Photographer, Artist
b. Apr 17, 1911 in Manhattan, New York
d. Apr 7, 1973 in New York, New York
Source: *AmAu&B; ConAu 41R; CurBio 72; NewYTBE 73; WhAm 5; WhoAmA 73*

Elizabeth I
English. Queen
Daughter of Henry VIII, Anne Boleyn; ruled Great Britain, N Ireland, 1558-1603.
b. Sep 7, 1533 in Greenwich, England
d. Mar 24, 1603
Source: *BioIn 1, 2, 3, 4, 5, 6, 7, 8, 9, 10; McGEWB; NewCol 75; WebBD 80*

Elizabeth II
[Elizabeth Alexandra Mary]
English. Queen
Succeeded father George VI to throne upon his death, Feb 6, 1952.
b. Apr 21, 1926 in London, England
Source: *BioIn 2, 3, 4, 5, 6, 7, 8, 9, 10; CurBio 44, 55; IntWW 74; NewCol 75; Who 82; WhoAm 82*

Elizabeth, the Queen Mother
[Elizabeth Angela Marguerite]
English. Queen
Wife of King George VI; mother of Queen Elizabeth II, Princess Margaret.
b. Aug 4, 1900 in Hertfordshire, England
Source: *CurBio 81; IntWW 74; NewCol 75; WebBD 80*

Elizabeth of Hungary, Saint
Hungarian. Religious Figure
b. 1207
d. 1231
Source: *BioIn 1, 2, 3, 4, 5, 6, 7, 8, 11; NewCol 75; REn*

Elizondo, Hector
American. Actor
b. Dec 22, 1936 in New York, New York
Source: *IntMPA 77, 78, 79, 80, 81, 82; WhoHol A; WhoThe 77*

Elkin, Benjamin
American. Children's Author
b. Aug 10, 1911 in Baltimore, Maryland
Source: *Alli; Au&Wr 71; AuBYP; ConAu 1R, 4NR; SmATA 3; WhoMW 74; WhoWorJ 72; WrDr 76*

Elkin, Stanley Lawrence
American. Author, Journalist
b. May 11, 1930 in New York, New York
Source: *AmAu&B; ConAu 9R; ConLC 4, 6, 9, 14; ConNov 72, 76; DrAF 76; DrAS 74E; EncWL; Pen AM; WhoAm 74, 76, 78, 80, 82; WrDr 76*

Elkins, Hillard
"Hilly"
American. Actor
b. Oct 18, 1929 in New York, New York
Source: *CelR 73; WhoAm 82; WhoThe 77*

Elkins, Stanley Maurice
American. Historian, Educator
b. Apr 29, 1925 in Boston, Massachusetts
Source: *ConAu 102; DrAS 74H; WhoAm 74, 76, 78, 80, 82*

Ellender, Allen Joseph
American. Senator
b. Sep 24, 1890 in Montegut, Louisiana
d. Jul 27, 1972 in Bethesda, Maryland
Source: *BiDrAC; CurBio 46, 72; NewYTBE 71, 72; WhAm 5; WhAmP; WhoGov 72; WhoS&SW 73*

Ellerbee, Linda
American. Broadcast Journalist
b. Aug 15, 1944 in Bryan, Texas
Source: *WhoAm 82*

Ellery, William
American. Jurist
b. Dec 22, 1727 in Newport, Rhode Island
d. Feb 15, 1820 in Newport, Rhode Island
Source: *AmBi; ApCAB; BiAuS; BiDrAC; DcAmB; Drake; TwCBDA; WhAm H; WhAmP*

Elliman, Yvonne
[Mrs. William Oakes]
American. Singer
Appeared in *Jesus Christ Superstar;* sang "I Don't Know How to Love Him."
b. 1951 in Hawaii
Source: *RkOn; WhoAm 82*

Ellin, Stanley
American. Author
b. Oct 6, 1916 in Brooklyn, New York
Source: *AmAu&B; Au&Wr 71; ConAu 1R, 4NR; EncMys; REnAL; WorAu; WrDr 76*

Ellington, "Duke" (Edward Kennedy)
American. Band Leader, Composer
Wrote over 5,000 original works, including "Satin Doll," "Mood Indigo."
b. Apr 29, 1899 in Washington, DC
d. May 24, 1974 in New York, New York
Source: *AmSCAP 66; BiE&WWA; BioNews 74; CelR 73; ConAu 49, 97; CurBio 41, 70, 74; EncAB-H; FilmgC; NewYTBE 72; NewYTBS 74; WebAB; WhAm 6; WhScrn 77; Who 74; WhoAm 74; WhoE 74; WhoGov 72; WhoJazz 72; WhoMus 72; WhoWor 74*

Ellington, Edward
British. Air Marshal
b. 1877
d. Jun 13, 1967 in London, England
Source: *BioIn 8*

Ellington, Mercer
American. Musician, Band Leader
Son of Duke Ellington; took over orchestra, 1974.
b. Mar 11, 1919 in Washington, DC
Source: *AmSCAP 66; WhoAm 82*

Elliot, Cass
[Ellen Naomi Cohen; Mamas and the Papas]
American. Singer
Solo career, 1967-74; hit song "Dream a Little Dream of Me," 1968.
b. Feb 19, 1943 in Arlington, Virginia
d. Jul 29, 1974 in London, England
Source: *BioNews 74; CelR 73; NewYTBS 74; WhoHol B*

Elliot, Win (Irwin)
American. Radio Performer
b. May 7, 1915 in Chelsea, Massachusetts
Source: *BioIn 1, 2; IntMPA 75*

Elliott, Bob
[Bob and Ray]
American. Comedian
b. Mar 26, 1923 in Boston, Massachusetts
Source: *CelR 73; CurBio 57*

Elliott, Bobby
see: Hollies, The

Elliott, Charles Loring
American. Artist
b. Oct 12, 1812 in Scipio, New York
d. Aug 25, 1868 in Albany, New York
Source: *AmBi; ApCAB; DcAmB; Drake; EarABI; TwCBDA; WhAm H*

Elliott, Denholm
English. Actor
b. May 31, 1922 in London, England
Source: *BiE&WWA; FilmgC; IntMPA 82; WhoHol A*

Elliott, Dennis
see: Foreigner

Elliott, George Paul
American. Author
b. Jun 16, 1918 in Knightstown, Indiana
d. May 3, 1980 in New York, New York
Source: *ConAu 1R, 2NR; ConLC 2; ConNov 72, 76; ConP 70, 75; DrAF 76; DrAP 75; DrAS 74E; IndAu 1917; ModAL, SUP; OxAmL; WhoAm 74; WhoWor 74; WrDr 76*

Elliott, Gertrude
American. Actress
b. 1874 in Rockland, Maine
d. Dec 24, 1950 in Kent, England
Source: *BioIn 2; Film 1; NotNAT A, B; WhScrn 74, 77; WhThe; WhoHol B; WhoStg 1908*

Elliott, Joe
see: Def Leppard

Elliott, "Jumbo" (James Francis)
American. Track Coach
b. Aug 8, 1915 in Philadelphia, Pennsylvania
d. Mar 22, 1981 in Juno Beach, Florida
Source: *BioIn 6, 11; NewYTBS 79, 81; WhoTr&F 73*

Elliott, Maxine
[Jessie D McDermott Goodwin]
American. Actress
b. Feb 5, 1873 in Rockland, Maine
d. Mar 5, 1940 in Juan les Pins, France
Source: *AmBi; CurBio 40; DcAmB S2; FamA&A; Film 1; InWom; NotAW; OxThe; TwYS; WhAm 1; WhScrn 74, 77; WhoHol B; WhoStg 1906, 1908; WomWWA 14*

Elliott, Osborn
American. Journalist, Public Official
b. Oct 25, 1924 in New York, New York
Source: *AmAu&B; ConAu 69; CurBio 78; IntAu&W 77; IntWW 74, 75, 76, 77, 78; NewYTBS 76; St&PR 75; WhoAm 74, 76, 78, 80, 82; WhoE 74; WhoWor 74, 76, 78*

Elliott, Robert B
American. Congressman
b. Aug 11, 1842 in Boston, Massachusetts
d. Aug 9, 1884 in New Orleans, Louisiana
Source: *BioIn 1, 5, 6, 8, 9, 10; WhAm H*

Elliott, Sam
American. Actor
b. 1944 in Sacramento, California
Source: *WhoHol A*

Ellis, Dock Phillip, Jr.
American. Baseball Player
b. Mar 11, 1945 in Los Angeles, California
Source: *BaseEn; WhoProB 73*

Ellis, Harry Bearse
American. Journalist
b. Dec 9, 1921 in Springfield, Massachusetts
Source: *AmAu&B; AuBYP; ConAu 1R, 2NR; SmATA 9; WhoAm 74, 76, 78, 80, 82; WhoWor 74; WrDr 76*

Ellis, (Henry) Havelock
English. Psychologist
b. Feb 2, 1859 in Surrey, England
d. Jul 8, 1939 in Hintlesham, England
Source: *AtlBL; CasWL; ChPo; DcLEL; EvLB; LongCTC; ModBrL; NewC; OxEng; REn; TwCA, SUP; WhoLA*

Ellis, Perry Edwin
American. Fashion Designer
Received Winnie award from Coty American Fashion Critics, 1979.
b. Mar 3, 1940 in Churchland, Virginia
Source: *NewYTBS 82; WhoAm 82; WhoFash*

Ellis, Robin
English. Actor
Lead role in BBC TV series "Poldark", shown on PBS.
b. 1944 in London, England
Source: *BioIn 11; NewYTBS 78*

Ellis, Ruth
Welsh. Murderer
b. 1927 in Rhyl, Wales
d. Jul 13, 1955 in London, England
Source: *BioIn 11; LookW*

Ellis, Stephan
see: Survivor

Ellison, Harlan Jay
American. Author
b. May 27, 1934 in Cleveland, Ohio
Source: *ConAu 5R, 5NR; ConLC 1, 13; DrAF 76; WhoAm 76, 78, 80, 82; WrDr 76*

Ellison, Ralph Waldo
American. Author
b. Mar 1, 1914 in Oklahoma City, Oklahoma
Source: *AmAu&B; BlkAW; CasWL; CnDAL; ConAu 9R; ConLC 1, 3, 11; ConNov 72, 76; CurBio 68; DrAF 76; EncAB-H; EncWL; IntWW 74; LivgBAA; ModAL, SUP; OxAmL; Pen AM; RAdv 1; REn; REnAL; TwCW; WebAB; WebE&AL; WhoAm 74, 76, 78, 80, 82; WhoBlA 75; WhoE 74; WhoGov 72; WhoTwCL; WhoWor 74; WorAu; WrDr 76*

Ellison, Virginia Howell
American. Children's Author
b. Feb 4, 1910 in New York, New York
Source: *BiDrLUS 70; ConAu 33R; SmATA 4; WrDr 76*

Ellsberg, Daniel
American. Author, Economist, Peace Activist
Leaked Penatgon Papers to press, 1971; wrote *Papers on the War*, 1972.
b. Apr 7, 1931 in Chicago, Illinois
Source: *ConAu 69; BioNews 74; CurBio 73; NewYTBE 71; WhoAm 74, 76, 78, 80, 82*

Ellsberg, Edward
American. Admiral, Engineer, Author
b. Nov 21, 1891 in New Haven, Connecticut
Source: *AmAu&B; AmNov; Au&Wr 71; AuBYP; ConAu 5R; CurBio 42; JBA 34, 51; REnAL; SmATA 7; TwCA, SUP; WhoAm 74, 76, 78, 80, 82*

Ellsworth, Lincoln
American. Explorer
First man to cross both Arctic and Antarctic by air.
b. May 12, 1880 in Chicago, Illinois
d. May 26, 1951 in New York, New York
Source: *AmAu&B; DcAmB S5; NewCol 75; WebAB; WebBD 80; WhAm 3*

Elman, Mischa
Russian. Musician
b. Jan 21, 1891 in Talnoye, Russia
d. Apr 5, 1967 in New York, New York
Source: *AmSCAP 66; CurBio 45, 67; WhAm 4*

Elman, Ziggy
[Harry Finkelman]
American. Musician
b. May 26, 1914 in Philadelphia, Pennsylvania
d. Jun 26, 1968 in Los Angeles, California
Source: *WhoHol B; WhoJazz 72*

Elsheimer, Adam
[Adam Tedesco]
German. Artist
b. Mar 18, 1578 in Frankfurt, Germany
d. Dec 1610 in Rome, Italy
Source: *AtlBL; WebBD 80*

Elting, Mary Letha
American. Children's Author
b. Jun 21, 1906 in Creede, Colorado
Source: *AuBYP; ConAu 9R, 4NR; ForWC 70; MorJA; SmATA 2*

Elting, Victor, Jr.
American. Advertising Executive
b. Aug 12, 1905 in Winnetka, Illinois
Source: *WhoF&I 74*

Eltinge, Julian
American. Actor
b. May 14, 1883
d. Mar 7, 1941 in New York, New York
Source: *BioIn 3, 5; CurBio 41; Film 1, 2; FilmgC; ObitOF 79*

Elton, Charles Sutherland
English. Zoologist
b. Mar 29, 1900
Source: *BioIn 8, 9; IntWW 74; Who 74*

Eluard, Paul
[Eugene Grindel]
French. Author
b. Dec 14, 1895 in Saint Denis, France
d. Nov 18, 1952 in Charenton, France
Source: *AtlBL; CasWL; ClDMEL; CnMWL; EncWL; EvEuW; ModRL; OxEng; OxFr; Pen EUR; REn; TwCA SUP; TwCW; WhoTwCL*

Elvira, Pablo
Puerto Rican. Opera Singer
b. Sep 24, 1938 in Santurce, Puerto Rico
Source: *WhoOp 76*

Ely, Joe
American. Musician, Singer
b. 1947 in Lubbock, Texas
Source: *BioIn 12*

Ely, Ron
American. Actor
b. 1938 in Hereford, Texas
Source: *MotPP; WhoHol A*

Elytis, Odysseus
Greek. Poet, Art Critic
b. Nov 2, 1911 in Iraklion, Crete
Source: *BioIn 12; CurBio 80; IntWW 79*

Emanuel, David
English. Fashion Designer
With wife, Elizabeth, designed Princess Diana's wedding dress, 1981.
b. 1953? in England
Source: *NewYTBS 81*

Emanuel, Elizabeth
[Mrs. David Emanuel]
English. Fashion Designer
With husband, David, designed Princess Diana's wedding dress, 1981.
b. 1954?
Source: *NewYTBS 81*

Emanuel the Great
see: Manuel I

Emanuel, James A
American. Author
b. Jun 21, 1921 in Allande, Nebraska
Source: *BlkAW; ConAu 29R; ConP 75; DrAP 75; DrAS 74E; LivgBAA; WrDr 76*

Emanuelli, Enrico
Italian. Author, Journalist
b. 1909
d. 1967
Source: *BioIn 8*

Embry, Wayne
American. Basketball Player, Executive
b. Mar 26, 1937 in Springfield, Ohio
Source: *WhoAm 74, 76, 78, 80, 82; WhoBbl 73*

Emerson, Faye
American. Actress
b. Jul 8, 1917 in Elizabeth, Louisiana
Source: *BiE&WWA; CurBio 51; FilmgC; HolP 40; InWom; MotPP; MovMk; WhoHol A; WhoThe 77*

Emerson, Gladys Anderson
American. Biochemist, Nutritionist
b. Jul 1, 1903 in Caldwell, Kansas
Source: *AmM&WS 73P; BioIn 3, 5, 11; WhoAm 74, 76, 78, 80, 82*

Emerson, Hope
American. Actress
b. Oct 29, 1898 in Hawarden, Iowa
d. Apr 25, 1960 in Hollywood, California
Source: *FilmgC; MotPP; MovMk; Vers A; WhScrn 74, 77; WhoHol B*

Emerson, Lake, and Palmer
[Keith Emerson; Gregory Lake; Carl Palmer]
English. Rock Group
Source: *BkPepl; EncPR&S*

Emerson, Ralph Waldo
American. Essayist, Poet, Philosopher
Friend of Henry Thoreau; wrote essay *Self-Reliance,* 1844.
b. May 25, 1803 in Boston, Massachusetts
d. Apr 27, 1882 in Concord, Massachusetts
Source: *Alli, SUP; AmAu; AmAu&B; AmBi; AmWr; AnCL; ApCAB; AtlBL; BbD; BiD&SB; CasWL; Chambr 3; ChPo, S1; CnDAL; CnE&AP; CrtT 3; CyAl 2; CyWA; DcAmAu; DcAmB; DcEnA, AP; DcEnL; DcLEL; DcNAA; Drake; EncAB-H; EvLB; MouLC 4; OxAmL; OxEng; Pen AM; RAdv 1; RComWL; REn; REnAL; Str&VC; TwCBDA; WebAB; WebE&AL; WhAm H*

Emerson, Roy
Australian. Tennis Player
b. Nov 3, 1936 in Kingsway, Australia
Source: *CurBio 65*

Emery, Anne
American. Author
b. Sep 1, 1907 in Fargo, North Dakota
Source: *BioIn 2, 3, 6, 7, 9; ConAu 1R, 2NR; SmATA 1*

Emin Pasha
[Eduard Schnitzer]
German. Physician, Explorer
Governor of Equatoria, Egyptian Sudan province.
b. Mar 8, 1840 in Oppeln, Prussia
d. 1892 in Stanley Falls, Congo
Source: *BioIn 1, 2, 8, 9, 10; NewCol 75; WebBD 80*

Eminescu, Mihail
Romanian. Poet
b. Dec 20, 1849 in Botosoni, Romania
d. Jun 15, 1889 in Bucharest, Romania
Source: *ClDMEL; EuAu; EvEuW*

Emmet, Robert
Irish. Nationalist
Led uprising in Dublin for independence, 1803.
b. Sep 20, 1728 in Ireland
d. Sep 20, 1803
Source: *McGEWB; NewCol 75; PoIre; REn; WebBD 80*

Emmett, Daniel Decatur
American. Minstrel, Songwriter
b. Oct 29, 1815 in Clinton, Ohio
d. Jun 28, 1904
Source: *AmAu; AmAu&B; BioIn 1, 3, 4, 6, 9; OxAmL; REnAL*

Empedocles
Greek. Philosopher
First to state principles central to theory of physics.
b. 493BC in Acragas, Sicily
d. 433BC
Source: *BbD; BiD&SB; CasWL; NewC; NewCol 75; Pen CL; WebBD 80*

Empson, William
English. Author
b. Sep 27, 1906 in Goole, England
Source: *CasWL; CnE&AP; CnMWL; ConAu 17R; ConLC 3; ConP 70, 75; DcLEL; EncWL; IntWW 74; LongCTC; ModBrL; NewC; OxEng; Pen ENG; RAdv 1; REn; TwCA SUP; TwCW; WebE&AL; Who 74; WhoTwCL; WhoWor 74; WrDr 76*

En-Lai, Chou
see: Chou En-Lai

Ender, Kornelia
[Mrs. Roland Matthes]
German. Swimmer
Won four gold medals, 1976 Olympics; called greatest woman swimmer ever.
b. Oct 25, 1958 in Plauen, Germany (East)
Source: *BioIn 10*

Enders, John Franklin
American. Educator
b. Feb 10, 1897 in West Hartford, Connecticut
Source: *BioIn 3, 4, 5, 6, 8, 11; IntWW 74; Who 74; WhoAm 74; WhoWor 74*

Endo, Shusaku
Japanese. Author
b. Mar 27, 1923 in Tokyo, Japan
Source: *BioIn 8, 11; ConAu 29R; ConLC 7, 14*

Enesco, Georges
[Georges Enescu]
Romanian. Violinist, Composer
b. Aug 7, 1881 in Cordaremi, Romania
d. May 4, 1955 in Paris, France
Source: *NewCol 75; WebBD 80; WhAm 3*

Engel, Georgia Bright
American. Actress
Played Georgette on TV series "The Mary Tyler Moore Show," 1972-77.
b. Jul 28, 1948 in Washington, DC
Source: *WhoAm 80, 82*

Engel, Lehman
American. Author, Conductor
b. Sep 12, 1910 in Jackson, Mississippi
d. Aug 29, 1982 in New York, New York
Source: *AmAu&B; Baker 78; BiE&WWA; BioIn 5, 10; ConAu 41R; DcCM; NewYTBS 82; NotNAT; WhoAm 76, 78, 80, 82; WhoMus 72; WhoWor 74, 76, 78; WhoWorJ 72*

Engelman, Wilfred
American. Opera Singer
b. 1905 in Detroit, Michigan
d. Feb 12, 1978 in Cincinnati, Ohio
Source: *BioIn 11*

Engels, Friedrich
German. Socialist
b. Sep 28, 1820 in Barmen, Germany
d. Aug 5, 1895 in London, England
Source: *McGEWB; OxGer; REn*

Engholm, Sir Basil
British. Director of Film Institute
b. Aug 2, 1912
Source: *Who 74*

England Dan and John Ford Coley
[John Edward Coley; Danny Seals]
American. Singing Group
Source: *RkOn*

Engle, Eloise Katherine
American. Author
b. Apr 12, 1923 in Seattle, Washington
Source: *ConAu 1R, 2NR; ForWC 70; SmATA 9; WrDr 76*

Engle, Joe Henry
American. Astronaut
Crew member aboard second flight of space shuttle Columbia, Nov, 1981.
b. Aug 26, 1932 in Abilene, Kansas
Source: *NewYTBS 81; WhoS&SW 73; WorDWW*

Engle, Paul
American. Author
b. Oct 12, 1908 in Cedar Rapids, Iowa
Source: *AmAu&B; ChPo, S1, S2; CnDAL; ConAmA; ConAu 1R, 5NR; ConP 70, 75; CurBio 42; DcLEL; DrAP 75; DrAS 74E; OxAmL; REnAL; SixAP; WhoAm 74, 76, 78, 80, 82; WhoWor 74; WorAu; WrDr 76*

Englemann, Robert A
[The Hostages]
American. Former Hostage in Iran
b. 1947? in Pasadena, California
Source: *NewYTBS 81*

English, Doug (Lowell Douglas)
American. Football Player
b. Aug 25, 1953 in Dallas, Texas
Source: *FootReg*

Enke, Karin
German. Speed Skater
b. 1962?
Source: *BioIn 12*

Ennis, Del(mer)
American. Baseball Player
b. Jun 8, 1925 in Philadelphia, Pennsylvania
Source: *BaseEn; BioIn 1, 3; WhoProB 73*

Eno, Brian
[Roxy Music]
English. Musician, Producer
Co-founder of rock group Roxy Music, 1971; solo performer since 1973.
b. 1948 in Woodbridge, England
Source: *BioIn 11; IlEncRk; WhoAm 82*

Enoch, Kurt
American. Publisher
Pioneer in paperback publishing with New American Library, Inc., 1947-60.
b. Nov 22, 1895 in Hamburg, Germany
d. Feb 15, 1982 in Puerto Rico
Source: *New YTBS 82; WhoAmJ 80; WhoE 77, 79; WhoWorJ 78*

Enright, Dennis Joseph
English. Author
b. Mar 11, 1920 in Leamington, England
Source: *Au&Wr 71; ChPo S2; ConAu 1R; ConLC 4; ConNov 72, 76; ConP 70, 75; IntWW 74; LongCTC; ModBrL, SUP; NewC; Pen ENG; TwCW; Who 74; WhoTwCL; WhoWor 74; WorAu; WrDr 76*

Enright, Elizabeth
American. Artist, Author
b. Sep 17, 1909 in Oak Park, Illinois
d. Jun 8, 1968
Source: *AmAu&B; AnCL; AuBYP; BkCL; ConAu 25R, 61; CurBio 47, 68; IlsCB 1744, 1946; InWom; JBA 51; Newb 1922; SmATA 9; WhAm 5*

Ensor, James
Belgian. Artist
b. Apr 13, 1860 in Ostend, Belgium
d. Nov 19, 1949 in Ostend, Belgium
Source: *AtlBL; CurBio 43; WhAm 4*

Entremont, Phillippe
French. Musician
b. Jun 7, 1934 in Reims, France
Source: *WhoAm 82; WhoMus 72*

Entwistle, John
[The Who]
English. Rock Musician
b. Sep 10, 1944 in London, England
Source: *WhoAm 80, 82*

Enver Pasha
Turkish. General, Political Leader
b. Nov 23, 1881 in Apana, Turkey
d. Aug 4, 1922 in Bukhara, Turkey
Source: *McGEWB; NewCol 75*

Ephron, Nora
American. Author
b. May 19, 1941 in New York, Norway
Source: *AuNews 2; ConAu 65; ConLC 17; WhoAm 78, 80, 82*

Epictetus
Greek. Philosopher
Stoic philosophy based on indifference to external goods.
b. 55?
d. 135?
Source: *BbD; BiD&SB; CasWL; NewC; Pen CL; RComWL; REn*

Epicurus
Greek. Philosopher
Epicureanism described pleasure as highest, only good; the avoidance of pain.
b. 342BC in Samos, Greece
d. 270BC
Source: *BbD; BiD&SB; CasWL; NewC; OxEng; Pen CL; RComWL; REn*

Eppes, Maria Jefferson
American. Daughter of Thomas Jefferson
b. 1778
d. 1804
Source: *BioIn 1, 3, 6, 7*

Epstein, Alvin
American. Author
b. May 24, 1925 in Bronx, New York
Source: *BiE&WWA; NotNAT; PlP&P; WhoAm 74; WhoThe 77*

Epstein, Brian
English. Manager of The Beatles
Managed The Beatles, 1961-67; died in swimming pool accident.
b. Sep 19, 1934 in Liverpool, England
d. Aug 27, 1967 in London, England
Source: *IlEncRk*

Epstein, Edward Jay
American. Author, Educator
b. Dec 6, 1935 in New York, New York
Source: *ConAu 17R; WhoWorJ 72*

Epstein, Sir Jacob
English. Sculptor
b. Aug 9, 1880 in London, England
d. Aug 9, 1959 in London, England
Source: *AtlBL; CurBio 45, 59; LongCTC; OxAmL; REn; REnAL; WhAm 3*

Erasmus, Desiderius
[Geert Geerts; Gerhard Gerhards]
Dutch. Author, Humanist, Scholar
b. 1466? in Rotterdam, Netherlands
d. Jul 12, 1536 in Basel, Switzerland
Source: *AtlBL; BbD; BiD&SB; CasWL; CroE&S; CyWA; DcEnL; DcEuL; DcSpL; EuAu; EvEuW; NewC; OxEng; OxFr; OxGer; Pen EUR; RComWL; REn*

Eratosthenes
Greek. Scholar
Head of library at Alexandria, 240BC; measured circumference, tilt of Earth.
b. 275?BC in Cyrene, Greece
d. 195?BC
Source: *BioIn 3, 7, 8, 9; CasWL; Pen CL*

Erdman, Paul E
Canadian. Economist, Author
b. May 19, 1932 in Stratford, ON
Source: *AuNews 1; ConAu 61; WhoAm 82; WrDr 76*

Erede, Alberto
Italian. Conductor
b. Nov 8, 1909 in Genoa, Italy
Source: *WhoMus 72*

Erhard, Ludwig
German. Economist, Politician
b. Feb 4, 1897 in Fuerth, Germany
d. May 7, 1977 in Bonn, Germany (West)
Source: *Au&Wr 71; CurBio 50, 64; IntWW 74; Who 74*

Erhard, Werner
[John Paul Rosenberg]
American. Educator
Developed est, 1971, an individual, social transformation technique.
b. Sep 5, 1935 in Philadelphia, Pennsylvania
Source: *BioIn 10; BkPepl; WhoAm 78, 80, 82*

Eric IX
Swedish. King
d. 1161
Source: *BioIn 5; NewCol 75*

Eric the Red
[Eirikr Thorvaldsson]
Norwegian. Navigator
Father of Leif Ericson; discovered, colonized Greenland, 982.
b. 950 in Norway
d. 1000
Source: *ApCAB; NewCol 75; OxCan; REn; WhAm H*

Erickson, Leif
American. Singer, Actor
b. Oct 27, 1911 in Alameda, California
Source: *BiE&WWA; FilmgC; IntMPA 75, 76, 77, 78, 79, 80, 81, 82; MotPP; MovMk; WhoAmP 73; WhoHol A*

Ericson, Leif
Icelandic. Navigator, Explorer
Discovered N American coast, circa 1000, which he named Vinland.
b. 975? in Iceland
Source: *NewC; NewCol 75; PlP&P; REn; REnAL*

Ericsson, John
American. Engineer
Invented ironclad "Monitor" battleship, 1862; began age of modern warshhips.
b. Jul 31, 1803 in Varmland, Sweden
d. Mar 8, 1889 in New York, New York
Source: *Alli SUP; AmBi; ApCAB; BiD&SB; DcAmAu; DcAmB; Drake; TwCBDA; WebAB; WhAm H*

Erigena, John Scotus
Irish. Scholastic Philosopher
b. 810?
d. 891?
Source: *BrAu; DcEnL; EvLB; OxEng*

Erikson, Erik Homburger
American. Psychoanalyst
b. Jun 15, 1902 in Frankfurt, Germany
Source: *AmAu&B; AmM&WS 73S; CelR 73; ConAu 25R; CurBio 71; EncAB-H; IntWW 74; WebAB; WhoAm 74, 76, 78, 80, 82; WhoWor 74; WrDr 76*

Erlander, Tage Fritiof
Swedish. Politician
b. Jun 13, 1901 in Ransater, Sweden
Source: *CurBio 47; IntWW 74*

Erman, Jacques DeForest, pseud.
see: Ackerman, Forest J

Ernst, Kenneth
American. Cartoonist
b. 1918 in Illinois
Source: *WorECom*

Ernst, Max
German. Artist
b. Apr 2, 1891 in Cologne, Germany
d. Apr 1, 1976 in Paris, France
Source: *BioNews 74; CelR 73; ConAu 65; CurBio 42, 61; IntWW 74; REn; Who 74; WhoAm 74*

Ernst, Paul
German. Author, Critic
b. Mar 7, 1866 in Elbingerode, Germany
d. May 13, 1933 in Saint Georgen, Germany
Source: *CasWL; ClDMEL; CnMD; EncWL; EvEuW; McGEWD; ModGL; ModWD; OxGer; Pen EUR; WhoLA*

Errol, Leon
Australian. Actor
b. Jul 3, 1881 in Sydney, Australia
d. Oct 12, 1951 in Los Angeles, California
Source: *DcAmB S5; EncMT; FilmgC; MotPP; MovMk; PlP&P; Vers B; WhScrn 74, 77; WhoHol B*

Erskine, Carl Daniel
"Oisk"
American. Baseball Player
Pitcher, Brooklyn/LA Dodgers, 1948-59; had two no-hitters, 1952, 1956.
b. Dec 13, 1926 in Anderson, Indiana
Source: *BaseEn; WhoProB 73*

Erskine, John
American. Author, Educator
b. Oct 5, 1879 in New York, New York
d. Jun 2, 1951 in New York, New York
Source: *AmAu&B; AmLY; AmNov; ChPo, S1; CnDAL; ConAmA; ConAmL; DcAmB S5; DcLEL; LongCTC; OxAmL; REnAL; TwCA, SUP; WebAB; WhAm 3; WhNAA*

Erte
[Romain DeTirtoff]
Russian. Fashion Designer
b. Nov 23, 1892 in Saint Petersburg, Russia
Source: *CurBio 80; WorFshn*

Ertegun, Ahmet
American. Businessman, Sports Executive
Co-founder, Atlantic Records, 1947; president, NY Cosmos soccer team, 1971--.
b. Jul 31, 1923 in Istanbul, Turkey
Source: *CelR 73; WhoAm 78, 80, 82*

Eruzione, Mike
[United States Olympic Hockey Team-1980]
American. Hockey Player
Captained gold medal winning hockey team; advisor on movie *Miracle on Ice*.
b. Oct 25, 1954 in Boston, Massachusetts
Source: *BioIn 12; NewYTBS 82*

Ervin, Patrick, pseud.
see: Howard, Robert Ervin

Ervin, Sam(uel James, Jr.)
American. Former Senator
Headed Senate committee that investigated Watergate cover-up.
b. Sep 27, 1896 in Morganton, North Carolina
Source: *BioNews 74; CelR 73; CngDr 74; CurBio 55, 73; IntWW 74; NewYTBE 70, 73; WhoAm 74, 76, 78, 80, 82; WhoAmP 73; WhoGov 72; WhoS&SW 73*

Erving, Julius Winfield
"Doctor J"
American. Basketball Player
Forward, Philadelphia 76ers, 1976--; MVP, 1974, 1976, 1981.
b. Feb 22, 1950 in Roosevelt, New York
Source: *BkPepl; CurBio 75; InB&W 80; NegAl 76; NewYTBE 72; NewYTBS 75, 76; WhoAm 78, 80, 82; WhoBbl 73; WhoBlA 77*

Erwin, "Pee Wee" (George)
American. Jazz Musician, Composer
b. May 30, 1913 in Falls City, Nebraska
d. Jun 20, 1981 in Teaneck, New Jersey
Source: *AmSCAP 66; BiDAmM; EncJzS 70; WhoJazz 72*

Erwin, Stuart
American. Comedian, Actor
b. Feb 14, 1902 in Squaw Valley, California
d. Dec 21, 1967 in Beverly Hills, California
Source: *FilmgC; MotPP; MovMk; WhScrn 74, 77; WhoHol B*

Esau
Biblical Character
Source: *BioIn 10; NewCol 75; WebBD 80*

Escher, Maurits Cornelis
Dutch. Artist
b. 1898
d. 1972 in Hilversum, Netherlands
Source: *BioIn 10*

Escobar, Sixto
Puerto Rican. Boxer
b. Mar 23, 1913 in Barceloneta, Puerto Rico
Source: *WhoBox 74*

Escobedo, Danny
American. Criminal
b. 1940
Source: *BioIn 10*

Escoffier, Georges Auguste
French. Chef
b. 1846
d. 1935
Source: *NewCol 75; WebBD 80*

Esenin, Sergei Aleksandrovich
[Sergei Aleksandrovich Yesenin]
Russian. Poet
b. Feb 21, 1895 in Konstantinovo, Russia
d. Dec 28, 1925 in Leningrad, U.S.S.R.
Source: *BioIn 3, 7, 8, 9, 10; CasWL; ClDMEL; CnMWL; EncWL; EvEuW; ModSL 1; REn; TwCW; WhoTwCL*

Eshkol, Levi
Israeli. Prime Minister
b. 1895
d. Feb 26, 1969 in Jerusalem, Israel
Source: *CurBio 63, 69; WhAm 5*

Esmond, Jill
English. Actress
b. 1908 in London, England
Source: *FilmgC; WhoHol A; WhoThe 77*

Espinosa, Al
American. Golfer
b. Mar 24, 1894 in Monterey, California
d. Jan 4, 1957 in San Francisco, California
Source: *BioIn 4; WhoGolf*

Esposito, Joseph
"Diamond Joe"
American. Labor Racketeer, Bootlegger
b. Apr 28, 1872 in Acerra, Italy
d. Mar 21, 1928
Source: *Blood*

Esposito, Phil(ip)
Canadian. Hockey Player
Scored 778 goals in career, second highest in NHL history.
b. Feb 20, 1942 in Sault St. Marie, ON
Source: *CurBio 73; NewYTBS 79, 81; WhoAm 78, 80, 82; WhoHcky 73*

Esposito, Tony (Anthony James)
Canadian. Hockey Player
Goaltender who set modern NHL record for shutouts in season, 15, 1969-70.
b. Apr 23, 1944 in Sault St. Marie, ON
Source: *WhoAm 74, 76, 78, 80, 82; WhoHcky 73*

Essex, David
[David Cook]
English. Singer, Actor
b. Jul 23, 1947 in Plaistow, England
Source: *IntMPA 77, 78, 79, 80, 81, 82; RkOn; WhoHol A*

Essex, Earl of
see: Cromwell, Thomas

Essex, Earl of
see: Devereaux, Robert

Esslin, Martin Julius
British. Author
b. Jun 8, 1918 in Budapest, Hungary
Source: *BiE&WWA; NotNAT; WhThe; Who 74*

Estaing, Charles Henri Hector, Comte d'
French. Naval Officer
b. Nov 28, 1729 in Auvergne, France
d. Apr 28, 1794 in Paris, France
Source: *AmBi; ApCAB; Drake; NewCol 75; WhAm H*

Estes, Billie Sol
American. Financier
b. 1925
Source: *BioIn 10*

Estes, Eleanor Ruth Rosenfeld
American. Children's Author
b. May 9, 1906 in West Haven, Connecticut
Source: *AmAu&B; AmNov; AnCL; AuBYP; BkCL; ChlLR 2; ConAu 1R, 5NR; CurBio 46; IlsCB 1946; InWom; JBA 51; MorBMP; Newb 1922; REnAL; SenS; SmATA 4, 5, 7; Str&VC; WhoAm 74, 76, 78, 80, 82*

Estes, E(lliott) M(arantette)
"Pete"
American. Former President of GM
b. Jan 7, 1916 in Mendon, Michigan
Source: *AmM&WS 79P; AutoN 79; BioNews 74; BusPN; CurBio 79; IntWW 77, 78; Ward 77; WhoAm 74, 76, 78, 80; WhoF&I 77, 79*

Estevanico
Moroccan. Explorer
b. 1500?
d. 1540
Source: *BioIn 1, 8, 9, 10, 11*

Estevez (de Galvez), Luis
American. Fashion Designer
b. Dec 5, 1930 in Havana, Cuba
Source: *WhoAm 82; WorFshn*

Esther
Biblical Character
Source: *InWom*

Estienne, Henri
French. Printer, Scholar
b. 1531? in Paris, France
d. 1598 in Lyons, France
Source: *BioIn 3, 7; CasWL; DcEuL; EuAu; EvEuW; Pen EUR; REn*

Estrada, Erik (Enrique)
American. Actor
Stars in TV series "CHIPs," 1977--.
b. Mar 16, 1949 in New York, New York
Source: *BioIn 11; WhoAm 80, 82*

Ethridge, Mark Foster
American. Newspaper Editor
b. Apr 22, 1896 in Meridian, Mississippi
d. Apr 5, 1981 in Moncure, North Carolina
Source: *BioIn 1, 2; ConAu 103; CurBio 46, 81; IntWW 74, 75, 76, 77, 78; PolProf T; WhoAm 74*

Ethridge, Mark Foster, Jr.
American. Publisher
b. Jul 29, 1924 in New York, New York
Source: *BioIn 1, 2; IntWW 74; WhoAm 74*

Ets, Marie Hall
American. Children's Author
b. Dec 16, 1895 in Milwaukee, Wisconsin
Source: *AnCL; Au&ICB; Au&Wr 71; AuBYP; BkP; ChPo; ConAu 1R, 4NR; FamAIYP; IlsBYP; IlsCB 1744, 1946, 1957; InWom; JBA 51; SmATA 2; Str&VC; WhoAm 82; WhoAmA 73; WrDr 76*

Etting, Ruth
American. Singer
b. Nov 23, 1897 in David City, Nebraska
d. Sep 24, 1978 in Colorado Springs, Colorado
Source: *EncMT; InWom; WhoHol A; WhoThe 77*

Etzioni, Amitai Werner
American. Sociologist
b. Jan 4, 1929 in Cologne, Germany
Source: *AmM&WS 73S; ConAu 1R, 5NR; CurBio 80; WhoAm 74, 76, 78, 80, 82; WhoWorJ 72*

Eucken, Rudolf Christoph
German. Philosopher, Author
b. 1846 in Aurich, Germany
d. 1926 in Jena, Germany
Source: *OxGer*

Euclid
[Eucleides]
Greek. Mathematician
Compiled, arranged geometrical knowledge of his time.
b. 323?BC
d. 283?BC
Source: *CasWL; NewC; OxEng; Pen CL; REn*

Eugenie
[Eugenie Marie de Montijo de Guzman]
French. Empress
Wife of Napoleon III and empress, 1853-71; fashion trendsetter of her time.
b. 1826 in Granada, Spain
d. 1920
Source: *OxFr; REn; WebBD 80*

Eulenspiegel, Till
German. Clown, Jokester
b. 1290 in Kheitlingen, Germany
d. 1350 in Lubeck, Germany
Source: *NewC; REn*

Euler, Leonhard
Swiss. Mathematician, Physicist
b. Apr 15, 1707 in Basel, Switzerland
d. Sep 18, 1783
Source: *NewCol 75*

Euphorion
Greek. Poet, Scholar
b. 276?BC
Source: *CasWL; NewC; OxThe; Pen CL*

Euripides
Greek. Dramatist
Wrote about 90 tragedies, including *Medea, Electra.*
b. 480?BC in Salamis, Greece
d. 406?BC in Pella, Greece
Source: *OxThe; PlP&P*

Eusden, Laurence
English. Poet
b. 1688 in Spofforth, England
d. Sep 27, 1730 in Coningsby, England
Source: *Alli; BiD&SB; BrAu; ChPo; DcEnA; DcEnL; EvLB; NewC; OxEng; Pen ENG; Polre; PoLE*

Eusebius of Caesarea
[Eusebius Pamphili]
Greek. Historian
Bishop of Palestine, 314-339; wrote *Chronicle; Ecclesiastical History.*
b. 264? in Palestine
d. 340?
Source: *BioIn 3, 5, 6, 7, 9; NewC; NewCol 75; REn*

Eustachio, Bartolomeo
Italian. Scientist
Discovered Eustachian tube leading from ear drum to throat.
b. 1510 in San Severino, Italy
d. Aug 1574 in Rome, Italy
Source: *AsBiEn; BiHiMed; BioIn 1, 9; DcBiPP; DcCathB; InSci; LinLib L, S; NewCol 75*

Euwe, Max (Machgielis)
American. Chess Champion, Educator
World chess champ, 1935-37; president, International Chess Federation, 1970-78.
b. May 20, 1901 in Amsterdam, New Hampshire
d. Nov 26, 1981 in Amsterdam, New Hampshire
Source: *GolEC; IntAu&W 77; NewYTBS 81; Who 74, 82; WhoWor 74, 76*

Evans, Bergen Baldwin
American. Lexicographer, Author
b. Sep 19, 1904 in Franklin, Ohio
d. Feb 4, 1978 in Highland Park, Illinois
Source: *AmAu&B; Au&Wr 71; CelR 73; ConAu 5R, 77, 4NR; CurBio 55; DrAS 74E; OhA&B; WhoAm 74; WhoWor 74*

Evans, Bill (William John)
American. Jazz Musician, Composer
b. Aug 16, 1929 in Plainfield, New Jersey
d. Sep 1, 1980 in New York, New York
Source: *BiDAmM; BioIn 6, 9; EncJzS 70; IlEncJ; WhoE 74*

Evans, Bob (Robert L)
American. Restaurant Executive
President, Bob Evans Farms, Inc.
b. Mar 30, 1918 in Sugar Ridge, Ohio
Source: *BusPN; WhoAm 82*

Evans, Bob (Robert)
American. Actor, Motion Picture Producer
Child actor; produced *Chinatown,* 1974, *Urban Cowboy,* 1980.
b. Jun 29, 1930 in New York, New York
Source: *BusPN; CelR 73; FilmgC; IntMPA 75, 76, 77, 78, 79, 80, 81, 82; MotPP; WhoAm 80, 82*

Evans, Charles, Jr.
American. Golfer, Author
b. Jul 18, 1893 in Indianapolis, Indiana
d. Nov 1979 in Chicago, Illinois
Source: *WhoGolf*

Evans, Clifford
American. Archaeologist, Author
b. Jun 13, 1920 in Dallas, Texas
Source: *AmM&WS 73S; BioIn 6; WhoAm 74; WhoGov 72; WhoWor 74*

Evans, Dale
[Mrs. Roy Rogers; Frances Smith]
American. Actress, Evangelist
Starred with husband in TV series "The Roy Rogers Show," 1951-64.
b. Oct 31, 1912 in Uvalde, Texas
Source: *AmAu&B; AmSCAP 66; BioNews 74; ConAu 103; CurBio 56; EncFCWM 69; FilmgC; HolP 40; InWom; MotPP; MovMk; WhoHol A*

Evans, Dame Edith Mary Booth
English. Actress
b. Feb 8, 1888 in London, England
d. Oct 14, 1976 in Kent, England
Source: *BioNews 75; CurBio 56; Film 1; FilmgC; InWom; IntMPA 77, 75; IntWW 74; MotPP; MovMk; NewC; OxFilm; OxThe; PlP&P; Who 74; WhoHol A; WhoThe 77; WorEFlm*

Evans, Sir Geraint Llewellyn
Welsh. Opera Singer
b. Feb 16, 1922 in Pontypridd, Wales
Source: *IntWW 74; Who 74; WhoAm 82; WhoMus 72; WhoWor 74*

Evans, Harold Matthew
English. Author, Editor
b. Jun 28, 1928 in Manchester, England
Source: *BioIn 10; ConAu 41R; Who 74; WhoWor 74; WrDr 76*

Evans, Heloise Cruse
American. Newspaper Columnist
Took over mother's nationally syndicated column "Hints from Heloise," 1977.
b. Apr 15, 1951 in Waco, Texas
Source: *WhoAm 82*

Evans, Herbert McLean
American. Embryologist
b. Sep 23, 1882 in Modesto, California
d. Mar 6, 1971 in Berkeley, California
Source: *CurBio 59, 71; NewYTBE 71*

Evans, Hiram W
American. Musician
b. Oct 3, 1941 in Philadelphia, Pennsylvania
Source: *EncPR&S*

Evans, James Roose
see: Roose-Evans, James

Evans, John
American. Educator, Government Official
b. Mar 9, 1814 in Waynesville, Ohio
d. Jul 3, 1897
Source: *BioIn 6, 8; OhA&B*

Evans, John
see: Box Tops, The

Evans, Madge
American. Actress
b. 1909 in New York, New York
d. Apr 26, 1981 in Oakland, New Jersey
Source: *BiE&WWA; Film 1; FilmgC; MovMk; ThFT; TwYS; WhoHol A*

Evans, Mark
see: AC-DC

Evans, Mary Ann
see: Eliot, George, pseud.

Evans, Maurice
English. Actor, Manager
b. Jun 3, 1901 in Dorchester, England
Source: *BiE&WWA; CurBio 61; EncMT; FamA&A; FilmgC; IntMPA 75, 76, 77, 78, 79, 80, 81, 82; IntWW 74; MovMk; NewC; NotNAT; OxThe; REn; WhoAm 74; WhoThe 77; WhoWor 74*

Evans, Mike (Michael Jonas)
American. Actor
Plays Lionel in TV series "The Jeffersons."
b. Nov 3, 1949 in Salisbury, North Carolina
Source: *WhoAm 82; WhoHol A*

Evans, Oliver
American. Inventor
Constructed first high-pressure steam engine in America, circa 1800.
b. 1755 in New Castle, Delaware
d. Apr 15, 1819 in New York, New York
Source: *Alli; AmBi; ApCAB; DcAmAu; DcAmB; DcNAA; Drake; EncAAH; EncAB-H; LinLib S; McGEWB; NatCAB 6; TwCBDA; WebAB; WhAm H*

Evans, Orrin C
American. Journalist
b. in Steelton, Pennsylvania
d. Aug 7, 1971 in Philadelphia, Pennsylvania
Source: *BioIn 9; NewYTBE 71*

Evans, Richard Louis
American. Journalist
b. Mar 23, 1906 in Salt Lake City, Utah
d. Nov 1, 1971 in Salt Lake City, Utah
Source: *AmAu&B; ConAu 9R; NewYTBE 71; WhAm 5*

Evans, Robley Dunglison
American. Military Leader
b. Aug 18, 1846 in Floyd County, Virginia
d. Jan 3, 1912
Source: *AmAu&B; AmBi; ApCAB SUP; DcAmAu; DcAmB; DcNAA; TwCBDA; WhAm 1*

Evans, Ronald Ellwin
American. Astronaut
Command module pilot, Apollo 17.
b. Nov 10, 1933 in Saint Francis, Kansas
Source: *IntWW 74; WhoS&SW 73*

Evans, Rowland, Jr.
[Evans and Novak]
American. Journalist
b. Apr 28, 1921 in White Marsh, Pennsylvania
Source: *CelR 73; ConAu 25R; WhoAm 74, 76, 78, 80, 82; WhoS&SW 73; WhoWor 74; WrDr 76*

Evans, Timothy
English. Pardoned Murderer
b. 1924
d. Mar 9, 1950 in Pentonville Prison, England
Source: *BioIn 5, 6, 8*

Evans, Tom
see: Badfinger

Evans, Vince(nt Tobias)
American. Football Player
b. Jun 14, 1955 in Greensboro, North Carolina
Source: *FootReg*

Evans, Walker
American. Photographer
b. Nov 3, 1903 in Saint Louis, Missouri
d. Apr 10, 1975 in New Haven, Connecticut
Source: *AmAu&B; ConAu 89; CurBio 71; EncAB-H; WebAB; WhAm 6; WhoAm 74; WhoWor 74*

Evans and Novak
see: Evans, Rowland, Jr.; Novak, Robert

Eve
Biblical Character
Source. *InWom; NewCol 75*

Evelyn, John
English. Author
b. Oct 31, 1620 in Wotton, England
d. Feb 27, 1706 in Wotton, England
Source: *Alli; AtlBL; BbD; BiD&SB; BrAu; CasWL; Chambr 1; CroE&S; CyWA; DcEnA; DcEnL; DcEuL; DcLEL; EvLB; NewC; OxEng; Pen ENG; RAdv 1; REn; WebE&AL*

Evelyn, Judith
American. Actress
b. 1913
d. May 7, 1967 in New York, New York
Source: *BiE&WWA; FilmgC; InWom; MotPP; WhAm 4; WhScrn 74, 77; WhoHol B*

Everett, Chad
[Raymon Lee Cramton]
American. Actor
Best known role Dr. Joe Gannon on TV series "Medical Center," 1969-76.
b. Jun 11, 1937 in South Bend, Indiana
Source: *CelR 73; FilmgC; IntMPA 75, 76, 77, 78, 79, 80, 81, 82; MovMk; WhoAm 74, 76, 78, 80, 82; WhoHol A*

Everett, Edward
American. Clergyman, Statesman
b. Apr 11, 1794 in Dorchester, Massachusetts
d. Jan 15, 1865 in Boston, Massachusetts
Source: *Alli, SUP; AmAu; AmAu&B; AmBi; ApCAB; BbD; BiAuS; BiD&SB; BiDrAC; BiDrUSE; CyAL 1; DcAmAu; DcAmB; DcEnL; DcNAA; Drake; OxAmL; Pen AM; REnAL; TwCBDA; WebAB; WhAm H; WhAmP*

Evergood, Philip Howard
American. Artist
b. Oct 26, 1901 in New York, New York
d. Mar 11, 1973 in Bridgewater, Connecticut
Source: *ConAu 41R; CurBio 44, 60, 73; DcCAA 71; NewYTBE 73; WhAm 5; WhoAmA 73*

Everleigh, Ada
[Everleigh Sisters]
American. Madam, House of Prostitution
b. 1876 in Kentucky
d. Jan 3, 1960 in Roanoke, Virginia
Source: *BioIn 10; LookW*

Everleigh, Minna
[Everleigh Sisters]
American. Madam, House of Prostitution
b. 1878 in Kentucky
d. Sep 16, 1948 in New York, New York
Source: *BioIn 10; LookW*

Everly Brothers
[Don Everly; Phil Everly]
American. Singing Group
Source: *EncFCWM 69; EncPR&S; IlEncRk; Rk100*

Evers, Charles
American. Civil Rights Activist
b. Sep 11, 1923 in Decatur, Mississippi
Source: *CelR 73; CurBio 69; NewYTBE 70; WebAB*

Evers, Jason
American. Actor
b. Jan 2, 1927 in New York, New York
Source: *WhoAm 74; WhoHol A*

Evers, John Joseph
"The Crab"; "The Trojan"
American. Baseball Player
Second baseman in double play combination of Tinker to Evers to Chance.
b. Jul 21, 1881 in Troy, New York
d. Mar 28, 1947 in Albany, New York
Source: *BaseEn; BioIn 1, 3, 7, 10; WhoProB 73*

Evers, Medgar Wiley
American. Civil Rights Activist
b. Jul 2, 1926 in Decatur, Mississippi
d. Jun 12, 1963 in Jackson, Mississippi
Source: *WebAB*

Everson, William Oliver
[Brother Antoninus]
American. Poet
b. Sep 10, 1912 in Sacramento, California
Source: *AmAu&B; ConAu 9R; ConLC 1, 5; ConP 70, 75; DrAP 75; OxAmL; Pen AM; RAdv 1; WhoAm 82; WorAu; WrDr 76*

Evert, Chris(tine Marie)
[Mrs. John Lloyd]
American. Tennis Player
Number one female tennis player, 1974-78; SI athlete of year, 1976.
b. Dec 21, 1954 in Fort Lauderdale, Florida
Source: *BkPepl; CelR 73; CurBio 73; HerW; NewYTBE 72, 73; NewYTBS 74; WhoAm 74, 76, 78, 80, 82*

Evert, Jeanne
American. Tennis Player
Sister of Chris Evert.
b. Oct 5, 1957 in Fort Lauderdale, Florida
Source: *BioIn 10*

Evigan, Greg(ory Ralph)
American. Actor
Starred in TV series "BJ and the Bear," 1979-81.
b. Oct 14, 1953 in South Amboy, New Jersey
Source: *BioIn 12; WhoAm 82*

Evinrude, Ole
American. Inventor, Manufacturer
Built first motor to propel rowboat, 1906; president, Outboard Motors Corp., 1909-34.
b. Apr 19, 1877 in Christiania, Norway
d. Jul 12, 1934 in Milwaukee, Wisconsin
Source: *BioIn 5, 6, 7, 11*

Evins, David
American. Shoe Designer
b. in London, England
Source: *WorFshn*

Evren, Kenan
Turkish. Government Leader
b. 1918
Source: *BioIn 12*

Evtushenko, Evgeniy Alexandrovich
[Yevgeni Alexandrovich Yevtushenko]
Russian. Poet
b. Jul 18, 1933 in Zima, U.S.S.R.
Source: *CasWL; ConLC 1, 3; EncWL; EvEuW; ModSL 1; Pen EUR; REn; WhoTwCL; WorAu*

Ewbank, "Weeb" (Wilbur)
American. Football Coach
Coached NY Jets to AFL's first Super Bowl victory, 1969.
b. May 6, 1907 in Richmond, Indiana
Source: *BioNews 75; CelR 73; WhoAm 74; WhoE 74; WhoFtbl 74*

Ewell, Tom
[Yewell Tompkins]
American. Actor
b. Apr 29, 1909 in Owensboro, Kentucky
Source: *BiE&WWA; CurBio 61; FilmgC; IntMPA 75, 76, 77, 78, 79, 80, 81, 82; MotPP; MovMk; NewYTBE 71; NotNAT; WhoAm 74, 76, 78, 80, 82; WhoHol A; WhoThe 77; WorEFlm*

Ewen, David
American. Author, Musician, Editor
b. Dec 6, 1907 in Lemberg, Austria
Source: *AmAu&B; Au&Wr 71; AuBYP; BiE&WWA; ConAu 1R, 2NR; REnAL; SmATA 4; WhoAm 74, 76, 78, 80, 82; WhoMus 72; WhoS&SW 73; WhoWor 74; WhoWorJ 72; WrDr 76*

Ewen, Frederic
American. Educator, Author
b. Oct 11, 1899 in Lemberg, Austria
Source: *ConAu 73; WhoAm 74; WhoWor 74; WrDr 76*

Ewing, Alfred Cyril
English. Author
b. May 11, 1899 in Leicester, England
Source: *Au&Wr 71; ConAu 5R, 4NR; WhoWor 74*

Ewing, Julianna Horatia
English. Author
b. Aug 3, 1841 in Ecclesfield, England
d. May 13, 1885 in Bath, England
Source: *BbD; BiD&SB; BrAu 19; CarSB; CasWL; DcLEL; EvLB; FamSYP; JBA 34; NewC; OxEng*

Ewing, Patrick
American. Basketball Player
b. 1961? in Kingston, Jamaica
Source: *NewYTBS 82*

Ewing, William Maurice
American. Educator, Scientist
b. May 12, 1906 in Lockney, Texas
Source: *Au&Wr 71; CurBio 53*

Exner, Judith Campbell
American. Friend of John F Kennedy
b. 1934
Source: *BioIn 10*

Exon, J(ohn) James, Jr.
American. Senator
b. Aug 9, 1921 in Geddes, South Dakota
Source: *AlmAP 78, 80; BioIn 10; CngDr 79; IntWW 74, 75, 76, 77, 78, 79, 80; IntYB 79; WhoAm 74, 76, 78, 80, 82; WhoAmP 73, 75, 77, 79; WhoGov 72, 75, 77; WhoMW 74, 76, 78; WhoWor 74, 78*

Eyadema, Gnassingbe
Togolese. President
b. 1935 in Pya, Togo
Source: *BioIn 11; IntWW 74; WhoGov 72; WhoWor 74*

Eysenck, Hans Jurgen
German. Author
b. Mar 14, 1916 in Berlin, Germany
Source: *Au&Wr 71; BioIn 9, 11; ConAu 9R, 4NR; CurBio 72; IntWW 74; Who 74; WhoWor 74; WrDr 76*

Eyskens, Gaston
Belgian. Prime Minister
b. Apr 1, 1905 in Lierre, Belgium
Source: *CurBio 49; IntWW 74; WhoGov 72; WhoWor 74*

Ezekiel
Prophet
Source: *DcOrL 3; REn*

Ezekiel, Moses Jacob
American. Sculptor
b. Oct 28, 1844 in Richmond, Virginia
d. Mar 27, 1917
Source: *AmBi; ApCAB; DcAmB; TwCBDA; WhAm 1*

Ezra
Biblical Character
Source: *BioIn 1, 4, 5, 7; NewCol 75*

F

Faas, Horst
German. Photographer
b. Apr 28, 1933 in Berlin, Germany
Source: *BioIn 8, 9; WhoAm 74; WhoWor 74*

Fabares, Shelley
American. Actress
b. 1942? in Santa Monica, California
Source: *FilmgC; WhoHol A*

Faber, "Red" (Urban Charles)
American. Baseball Player
Pitcher, Chicago White Sox, 1914-33; Hall of Fame, 1964.
b. Sep 6, 1888 in Cascade, Iowa
d. Sep 25, 1976 in Chicago, Illinois
Source: *BaseEn; BioIn 2, 3, 7; WhoProB 73*

Faberge, (Peter) Carl
Russian. Goldsmith, Jeweler
b. 1846
d. 1920
Source: *BioIn 2, 3, 4, 6, 7, 8, 11*

Fabian
[Fabian Forte]
American. Singer, Actor
Teen idol of 1950-60's whose hits included "Turn Me Loose," "Hound Dog Man."
b. Feb 6, 1943 in Philadelphia, Pennsylvania
Source: *FilmgC; IntMPA, , , 75, 76, 77, 78, 79, 80, 81, 82; MotPP; WhoHol A*

Fabian, Robert Honey
English. Detective
b. Jan 31, 1901 in Ladywell, England
d. Jun 14, 1978 in Epsom, England
Source: *BioIn 2, 3, 7, 8, 11; ConAu 77, 81; CurBio 54, 78; NewYTBS 78*

Fabray, Nanette
[Ruby Nanette Fabares]
American. Actress
b. Oct 27, 1920 in San Diego, California
Source: *BiE&WWA; CurBio 56; EncMT; FilmgC; InWom; IntMPA 75, 76, 77, 78, 79, 80, 81, 82; MotPP; NotNAT; WhoAm 74; WhoHol A; WhoThe 77*

Fabre, Jean Henri
French. Author, Scientist
Observed, studied insect behavior; wrote *The Marvels of the Insect World*, 1938.
b. Dec 22, 1823 in Saint Leons, France
d. Oct 11, 1915 in Serigran, France
Source: *AnCL; BioIn 5, 6, 8, 9, 11; JBA 34, 51; LongCTC; OxFr; REn*

Fabri, Zoltan
Hungarian. Motion Pictue Director
b. Oct 15, 1917 in Budapest, Hungary
Source: *DcFM; FilmgC; IntWW 74; OxFilm; WhoWor 74; WorEFlm*

Fabricius, Hieronymus ab Aquapendente
Italian. Surgeon
b. 1537 in Aquapendente, Italy
d. 1619
Source: *BiHiMed; BioIn 1, 7, 9; LinLib S; NewCol 75*

Fabritius, Carel
Dutch. Artist
b. 1622 in Netherlands
d. Oct 12, 1654 in Delft, Netherlands
Source: *AtlBL*

Fabrizi, Aldo
Italian. Actor
b. 1905 in Rome, Italy
Source: *FilmgC; IntMPA 75, 76, 77, 78, 79, 80, 81, 82; MovMk; WhoHol A*

Face, Elroy Leon
American. Baseball Player
b. Feb 20, 1928 in Stephentown, New York
Source: *BaseEn; WhoProB 73*

Factor, Max
American. Cosmetician
Began career as makeup artist; later established own cosmetic co.
b. 1877 in Poland
d. 1938
Source: *BioIn 9*

Fadiman, Clifton Paul
American. Author, Editor
b. May 15, 1904 in Brooklyn, New York
Source: *AmAu&B; CelR 73; ChPo S2; ConAu 61; CurBio 41, 55; IntMPA 77, 75; RAdv 1; REnAL; SmATA 11; TwCA, SUP; WebAB; WhoWest 74*

Fahd ibn Abdul Aziz
Saudi. King
b. 1922 in Riyadh, Arabia
Source: *BioIn 10; CurBio 79; IntWW 75, 76, 77, 78, 79, 80; MidE 78, 79; NewYTBS 75; WhoWor 74*

Fahrenheit, Gabriel Daniel
German. Physicist
Invented mercury thermometer, 1714; developed Fahrenheit temperature scale.
b. May 14, 1686 in Danzig, Germany
d. Sep 16, 1736 in The Hague, Netherlands
Source: *AsBiEn; DcBiPP; DcInv; Dis&D; InSci; LinLib S; McGEWB; REn; WhDW*

Fain, Ferris Roy
"Burrhead"
American. Baseball Player
b. Mar 29, 1922 in San Antonio, Texas
Source: *BaseEn; BioIn 3; WhoProB 73*

Fain, Sammy
American. Singer, Composer, Musician
b. Jun 17, 1902 in New York, New York
Source: *AmSCAP 66; BiE&WWA; EncMT; IntMPA 75, 76, 77, 78, 79, 80, 81, 82; NewCBMT; NotNAT; WhoAm 74*

Fairbank, Janet Ayer
American. Author
b. 1879 in Chicago, Illinois
d. Dec 28, 1951 in Chicago, Illinois
Source: *AmAu&B; InWom; OxAmL; TwCA, SUP; WhAm 3; WhNAA*

Fairbanks, Charles Warren
American. Politician
Served as vice-president under Theodore Roosevelt, 1905-09.
b. May 11, 1852 in Unionville Center, Ohio
d. Jun 4, 1918 in Indianapolis, Indiana
Source: *AmBi; ApCAB; BiDrAC; BiDrUSE; DcAmB; EncWM; NatCAB 11, 14, 39; TwCBDA; WebAB, 79; WhAm 1; WhAmP*

Fairbanks, Chuck (Charles Leo)
American. Football Coach
b. Jun 10, 1933 in Detroit, Michigan
Source: *NewYTBS 74; WhoAm 78, 80, 82; WhoFtbl 74; WhoS&SW 73*

Fairbanks, Douglas
[Douglas Elton Ulman]
American. Actor
b. May 23, 1883 in Denver, Colorado
d. Dec 12, 1939 in Santa Monica, California
Source: *AmBi; BiDFilm; CmMov; CurBio 40; DcAmB S2; Film 1; FilmgC; MotPP; MovMk; OxFilm; TwYS; WebAB; WhAm 1; WhNAA; WhScrn 74, 77; WhoHol B; WorEFlm*

Fairbanks, Douglas, Jr.
[Douglas Elton Ulman, Jr.]
American. Actor, Motion Picture Producer
Appeared in over 75 films; married to Joan Crawford, 1928-33.
b. Dec 9, 1909 in New York, New York
Source: *BiDFilm; BioNews 74; BlueB 76; CelR 73; CmCal; CmMov; CurBio 41, 56; FilmgC; Film 2; IntMPA 75, 76, 77, 78, 79, 80, 81, 82; IntWW 78, 79, 80, 81; IntYB 78, 79, 80, 81; MotPP; MovMk; OxFilm; TwYS; WebAB, 79; Who 74; WhoAm 74, 76, 78, 80, 82; WhoHol A; WhoThe 77; WhoWor 74; WorEFlm*

Fairbanks, Thaddeus
American. Inventor
Developed platform scale, 1831.
b. Jan 17, 1796 in Brinfield, Massachusetts
d. Apr 12, 1886 in Saint Johnsbury, Vermont
Source: *AmBi; ApCAB; DcAmB; NatCAB 10; TwCBDA; WhAm H*

Fairchild, David Grandison
American. Botanist
b. Apr 7, 1869 in East Lansing, Michigan
d. Aug 6, 1954 in Coconut Grove, Florida
Source: *BioIn 1, 2, 3, 5, 6, 8, 10; DcAmB S5; EncAAH; WebAB; WhAm 3*

Fairchild, John Burr
American. Publisher
Has published *Women's Wear Daily* and *Daily News Record* since 1960.
b. Mar 6, 1927 in Newark, New Jersey
Source: *CelR 73; CurBio 71; Dun&B 79; WhoAm 74, 76, 78, 80, 82; WhoE 74; WhoFash; WorFshn*

Fairchild, Louis W
American. Publisher
b. Mar 3, 1901 in Glen Ridge, New Jersey
d. Oct 16, 1981 in Hanover, New Hampshire
Source: *AmAu&B; NewYTBS 81*

Fairchild, Morgan
[Patsy Ann McClenny]
American. Actress
Starred in TV series "Flamingo Road."
b. Feb 3, 1950 in Dallas, Texas
Source: *BioIn 10, 12*

Fairchild, Sherman Mills
American. Inventor
Developed Fairchild aerial camera.
b. Apr 7, 1896 in Oneonta, New York
d. Mar 28, 1971 in New York, New York
Source: *NatCAB 58; NewYTBE 71; WhAm 5*

Fairfax, Beatrice, pseud.
[Marie Manning]
American. Author, Journalist
b. 1878 in Washington, DC
d. Nov 28, 1945 in Allendale, New Jersey
Source: *CurBio 44, 46; DcAmB S3; InWom; NotAW; REnAL*

Fairfax, Thomas
English. General
b. Jan 17, 1612 in Leeds Castle, England
d. Nov 12, 1671 in Winchester, Virginia
Source: *Alli; NewC; Pen ENG; REn*

Fairless, Benjamin F
American. Philanthropist
b. May 3, 1890 in Pigeon Run, Ohio
d. Jan 1, 1962 in Ligonier, Pennsylvania
Source: *CurBio 42, 57, 62; WhAm 4*

Faisal II
Iraqi. King
b. May 2, 1935 in Baghdad, Iraq
d. Jul 14, 1958
Source: *CurBio 55, 58; NewCol 75; WebBD 80*

Faisal, King of Saudi Arabia
[Faisal ibn Abdul Aziz al Saud]
Saudi. King
b. 1905 in Riyadh, Saudi Arabia
d. Mar 25, 1975
Source: *BioIn 10; CurBio 66; Who 74*

Faisal ibn Musaed
Saudi. Prince
b. 1947
d. 1975
Source: *BioIn 10*

Faith, Percy
Canadian. Orchestra Leader
b. Apr 7, 1908 in Toronto, ON
d. Feb 9, 1976 in Los Angeles, California
Source: *AmSCAP 66; CanWW 70; CreCan 1; WhAm 6; WhoAm 74*

Faithfull, Marianne
English. Singer, Actress
Hit with Jagger/Richard song "As Tears Go By," 1964.
b. Dec 29, 1946 in London, England
Source: *ConMuA 80; FilmgC; NewWmR; RkOn 2; WhoHol A; WhoRock 81; WhoThe 72, 77*

Fakir, Abdul
[Four Tops]
American. Singer
b. 1938? in Detroit, Michigan
Source: *NF*

Falana, Lola
American. Actress, Singer, Dancer
Won Theatre World award, 1975; Tony nomination for *Doctor Jazz.*
b. Sep 11, 1943 in Philadelphia, Pennsylvania
Source: *BkPepl; DcBlPA; WhoAm 78, 80, 82; WhoAmW 72; WhoHol A*

Falco, Louis
American. Choreographer, Dancer
b. Aug 2, 1942? in New York, New York
Source: *BioIn 6, 9, 11; WhoAm 78*

Falconetti, Marie
Actress
b. 1901
d. 1946
Source: *Film 2; FilmgC; MotPP; WhoHol B*

Falk, Lee Harrison
American. Cartoonist, Author
b. 1915 in Saint Louis, Missouri
Source: *ConAu 97; WhoAm 78; WorECom*

Falk, Peter
American. Actor
Starred in TV series "Columbo," 1971-78; won Emmy, 1972.
b. Sep 16, 1927 in New York, New York
Source: *BiE&WWA; BioNews 75; BkPepl; CelR 73; CurBio 72; FilmgC; IntMPA 75, 76, 77, 78, 79, 80, 81, 82; MotPP; MovMk; NewYTBE 71; NotNAT; WhoAm 74, 76, 78, 80, 82; WhoHol A; WhoWest 74; WhoWor 74*

Falkenburg, Jinx
[Jinx McCrary]
American. Actress, Journalist
b. Jan 21, 1919 in Barcelona, Spain
Source: *CurBio 53; FilmgC; InWom; WhoHol A*

Falkner, Frank
English. Physician, Journalist
b. Oct 27, 1918 in Hale, England
Source: *AmM&WS 73P*

Falkner, Murry Charles
American. Author
b. Jun 26, 1899 in Ripley, Mississippi
Source: *ConAu 25R*

Fall, Albert Bacon
American. Cabinet Member
b. Nov 26, 1861 in Frankfort, Kentucky
d. Nov 30, 1944 in El Paso, Texas
Source: *BiDrAC; BiDrUSE; CurBio 45; DcAmB S3; EncAB-H; WhAm 2; WhAmP*

Fall, Bernard B
American. Author, Journalist
b. Nov 11, 1926 in Vienna, Austria
d. Feb 21, 1967 in Vietnam
Source: *AmAu&B; ConAu 1R, 25R, 77; ConLC 11; WhAm 4; WorAu*

Falla, Manuel de
Spanish. Composer
b. Nov 23, 1876 in Cadiz, Spain
d. Nov 14, 1946 in Alta Gracia, Argentina
Source: *AtlBL; CurBio 46; DcCM; REn*

Fallaci, Oriana
Italian. Journalist
b. Jun 29, 1930 in Florence, Italy
Source: *NewYTBE 73*

Fallada, Hans, pseud.
[Rudolph Ditzen]
German. Author
b. Jul 21, 1893
d. Feb 6, 1947 in Berlin, Germany
Source: *CasWL; EncWL; EvEuW; LongCTC; ModGL; OxGer; Pen EUR; REn; TwCA, SUP; WhoTwCL*

Falldin, Thorbjorn Nils Olof
Swedish. Former Prime Minister
b. Apr 24, 1926 in Vastby, Sweden
Source: *CurBio 78*

Falls, Joe
American. Sportswriter, Author
b. May 2, 1928 in New York, New York
Source: *ConAu 77*

Falstaff, Sir John
see: Fastolf, Sir John

Falter, John
American. Illustrator
b. Feb 28, 1910 in Plattsmouth, Nebraska
Source: *WhoAmA 73*

Faltskog, Agnetha
[ABBA]
Swedish. Singer
b. Apr 5, 1950 in Stockholm, Sweden
Source: *NF*

Falwell, Jerry
American. Clergyman
Founded Moral Majority, Inc, 1979.
b. Aug 11, 1933 in Lynchburg, Virginia
Source: *BioIn 9, 11; ConAu 102; WhoAm 82*

Famolare, Joseph P
American. Shoe Designer & Manufacturer
b. 1931
Source: *BioIn 12*

"Famous Amos"
see: Amos, Wally

Fanfani, Amintore
Italian. Economist, Politician
b. Feb 6, 1908 in Arezzo, Italy
Source: *CurBio 58; IntWW 74; WhoUN 75; WhoWor 74*

Fangio, Juan Manuel
Argentine. Automobile Racer
b. 1912
Source: *BioIn 4, 5, 6, 7, 8, 9, 10*

Fanon, Frantz
American. Psychoanalyst, Philosopher
b. Jul 20, 1925 in Martinique
d. Dec 6, 1961 in Washington, DC
Source: *ConAu 89; WorAu*

Fantin-Latour, (Ignace) Henri
French. Artist
b. Jan 14, 1836 in Grenoble, France
d. Aug 25, 1904 in Bure, France
Source: *AtlBL; NewCol 75; WebBD 80*

Faraday, Michael
English. Scientist
Developed first dynamo; discovered electromagnetic induction and compound bencene.
b. Sep 22, 1791 in Surrey, England
d. Aug 25, 1867 in Hampton Court, England
Source: *Alli, SUP; BbD; BiD&SB; BrAu 19; Chambr 3; DcEnL; EvLB; NewC; NewCol 75; OxEng; REn*

Farago, Ladislas
Hungarian. Author
b. Sep 21, 1906 in Csuro, Hungary
d. Oct 15, 1980 in New York, New York
Source: *AmAu&B; BioNews 75; CelR 73; ConAu 65, 102; WhoAm 74; WhoWor 74; WhoWorJ 72*

Farah, Pahlevi
see: Pahlevi, Farah

Farah, Robert Norman
American. Apparel Company Executive
Secretary, Farah Manufacturing Co, Inc, 1978--.
b. Aug 5, 1952 in El Paso, Texas
Source: *Dun&B 79; WhoAm 82*

Faralla, Dana (Dorothy W)
American. Children's Author
b. Aug 4, 1909 in Renville, Minnesota
Source: *AmAu&B; AmNov; ConAu 49; InWom; SmATA 9*

Farb, Peter
American. Author, Editor
b. Jul 25, 1929 in New York, New York
d. Apr 8, 1980 in Boston, Massachusetts
Source: *AuBYP SUP; BioIn 11; ConAu 17R, 97; SmATA 12; WorAu*

Farber, Edward Rolke
American. Inventor
Credited with invention of portable strobe light for still cameras.
b. Jul 22, 1914 in Milwaukee, Wisconsin
d. Jan 22, 1982 in Delafield, Wisconsin
Source: *LElec; NewYTBS 82*

Farenthold, Frances T
American. Educator, Political Activist
b. Oct 2, 1926 in Corpus Christi, Texas
Source: *WhoAm 82; WhoAmP 73; WhoAmW 77*

Farentino, James
American. Actor
b. Feb 24, 1938 in Brooklyn, New York
Source: *FilmgC; IntMPA 75, 76, 77, 78, 79, 80, 81, 82; MotPP; NewYTBE 73; WhoAm 74, 76, 78, 80, 82; WhoHol A*

Fargo, Donna
[Yvonne Vaughan]
American. Singer, Songwriter
Hits include "Happiest Girl in the USA" and "Funny Face."
b. Nov 10, 1949 in Mount Airy, North Carolina
Source: *BkPepl; WhoAm 74, 76, 78, 80, 82*

Fargo, William George
American. Businessman
b. May 20, 1818 in Pompey, New York
d. Aug 3, 1881 in Buffalo, New York
Source: *AmBi; ApCAB; DcAmB; TwCBDA; WebAB; WhAm H; WhAmP*

Farina, Richard
American. Author, Singer, Songwriter
Part of folk music scene, 1960's; author *Been Down So Long It Looks Like Up To Me.*
b. 1936 in Brooklyn, New York
d. Apr 30, 1966 in Carmel, California
Source: *AmAu&B; BiDAmM; ConAu 25R, 81; ConLC 9; WhScrn 77*

Farinacci, Roberto
Italian. Fascist Leader
b. 1892
d. 1945
Source: *BioIn 9*

Farinelli
[Carlo Broschi]
Italian. Opera Singer
b. Jan 24, 1705 in Andria, Italy
d. Jul 15, 1782 in Bologna, Italy
Source: *REn*

Farjeon, Eleanor
English. Author
b. Feb 13, 1881 in London, England
d. Jun 5, 1965
Source: *AnCL; AuBYP; BkCL; CasWL; CathA 1952; ChPo, S1, S2; ConAu P-1; DcLEL; HerW; InWom; JBA 34, 51; LongCTC; NewC; SmATA 2; Str&VC; TwCA, SUP; TwCW; WhoChL*

Farley, James A(loysius)
American. Political Leader
b. May 30, 1888 in Grassy Point, New York
d. Jun 9, 1976 in New York, New York
Source: *BiDrUSE; CathA 1952; CelR 73; ConAu 65; CurBio 44; EncAB-H; Film 1; IntWW 74; St&PR 75; TwYS; WebAB; WhoAmP 73; WhoHol B*

Farmer, Arthur Stewart
American. Jazz Musician
b. 1928
Source: *BioIn 7*

Farmer, Don
American. Broadcast Journalist
b. Sep 27, 1938 in Saint Louis, Missouri
Source: *ConAu 65; WhoAm 82*

Farmer, Fannie Merritt
American. Culinery Expert
b. Mar 23, 1857 in Boston, Massachusetts
d. Jan 15, 1915 in Boston, Massachusetts
Source: *AmAu&B; AmBi; DcAmAu; DcAmB; DcNAA; InWom; NotAW; REnAL; WebAB; WhAm 1*

Farmer, Frances
American. Actress
b. Sep 19, 1914 in Seattle, Washington
d. Aug 1, 1970 in Indianapolis, Indiana
Source: *BiDrLUS 70; BioNews 74; FilmgC; HolP 30; MotPP; MovMk; NewYTBE 70; PlP&P; ThFT; WhScrn 74, 77; BioNews 74; FilmgC; HolP 30; MotPP; MovMk; NewYTBE 70; PlP&P; ThFT; WhScrn 74, 77; WhoHol B*

Farmer, James
American. Civil Rights Leader
Founded CORE, 1942.
b. Jan 12, 1920 in Marshall, Texas
Source: *AmAu&B; BlueB 76; CivR 74; CurBio 64; EncSoH; NegAl 76; WhoAm 74, 76, 78, 80, 82; WhoAmP 73, 75, 77, 79; WhoBlA 75, 77; WhoS&SW 73; WhoWor 74, 78*

Farmer, Philip Jose
American. Author
b. Jan 26, 1918 in Terre Haute, Indiana
Source: *AmAu&B; ConAu 1R, 4NR; ConLC 1; IndAu 1917; WhoAm 82*

Farmer, Steve
see: Amboy Dukes, The

Farndon, Pete
see: Pretenders, The

Farnese, Alessandro
Spanish. Duke of Parma
b. Aug 27, 1545
d. Dec 3, 1592
Source: *NewCol 75*

Farnham, Sally James
American. Sculptor
b. 1869 in Ogdensburg, New York
d. Apr 28, 1943
Source: *InWom; WhAm 2*

Farnsworth, Philo Taylor
American. Inventor
Received patents for many inventions relating to television.
b. Aug 19, 1906 in Beaver, Utah
d. Mar 11, 1971 in Salt Lake City, Utah
Source: *BioIn 1, 3, 6, 9, 10; NewCol 75; NewYTBE 71; NewYTET; WebAB, 79; WebBD 80; WhAm 5*

Farnum, Dustin Lancy
American. Actor
b. 1870 in Hampton Beach, Maine
d. Jul 3, 1929 in New York, New York
Source: *DcAmB; Film 1; FilmgC; MotPP; TwYS; WhAm 1; WhScrn 74, 77; WhoHol B; WhoStg 1906, 1908*

Farnum, William
American. Actor
b. Jul 4, 1876 in Boston, Massachusetts
d. Jun 5, 1953 in Los Angeles, California
Source: *Film 1; FilmgC; MotPP; MovMk; TwYS; WhScrn 74, 77; WhoHol B*

Farouk I
Egyptian. King
b. Feb 11, 1920 in Cairo, Egypt
d. Mar 18, 1965 in Rome, Italy
Source: *CurBio 42, 65; NewCol 75*

Farquhar, George
English. Dramatist
b. 1678 in Londonderry, Northern Ireland
d. Apr 29, 1707 in London, England
Source: *Alli; AtlBL; BrAu; CasWL; CnThe; DcEnA; DcEnL; DcLEL; McGEWD; NewC; Pen ENG; REn; REnWD; WebE&AL*

Farquharson, Martha, pseud.
see: Finley, Martha

Farr, Felicia
American. Actress
b. Oct 4, 1932 in Westchester, New York
Source: *FilmgC; IntMPA 75, 76, 77, 78, 79, 80, 81, 82; MotPP; WhoHol A*

Farr, Jamie
[Jameel Farah]
American. Actor
Played Corporal Max Klinger on TV series "MASH."
b. Jul 1, 1936? in Toledo, Ohio
Source: *WhoAm 80, 82; WhoHol A*

Farragut, David Glasgow
American. Admiral
Union naval commander, Civil War; first to receive rank of admiral, 1866.
b. Jul 5, 1801 in Knoxville, Tennessee
d. Aug 14, 1870 in Portsmouth, New Hampshire
Source: *AmBi; ApCAB; CelCen; CivWDc; DcAmB; EncAB-H; EncSoH; HarEnUS; LinLib S; McGEWB; NatCAB 2; OxAmH; OxShips; TwCBDA; WebAB, 79; WebAMB; WhAm H; WhoMilH 76*

Farrar, Geraldine
American. Opera Singer
b. Feb 28, 1882 in Melrose, Massachusetts
d. Mar 11, 1967 in Ridgefield, Connecticut
Source: *AmSCAP 66; Film 1; FilmgC; InWom; REn; TwYS; WhAm 4; WhScrn 74, 77; WhoHol B*

Farrar, John Chipman
American. Publisher, Author
b. Feb 25, 1896 in Burlington, Vermont
d. Nov 6, 1974 in New York, New York
Source: *AmAu&B; ChPo, S1, S2; ConAu 53, 65; REnAL; Str&VC; WhAm 6; WhoAm 74*

Farrell, Carolyn
American. Nun, Former Mayor of Dubuque
b. 1936? in Des Moines, Iowa
Source: *BioIn 12*

Farrell, Charles
American. Actor
b. Aug 6, 1906 in Dublin, Ireland
Source: *IntMPA 75, 76, 77, 78, 79, 80, 81, 82; WhoThe 77*

Farrell, Eileen
American. Opera Singer
b. Feb 13, 1920 in Willimantic, Connecticut
Source: *CelR 73; CurBio 61; InWom; IntWW 74; WebAB; WhoAm 74, 76, 78, 80, 82*

Farrell, Glenda
American. Actress
b. Jun 30, 1904 in Enid, Oklahoma
d. May 1, 1971 in New York, New York
Source: *BiE&WWA; FilmgC; HolP 30; MotPP; MovMk; NewYTBE 71; OxFilm; ThFT; WhAm 5; WhScrn 74, 77; WhoHol B*

Farrell, James Thomas
American. Author, Journalist
b. Feb 27, 1904 in Chicago, Illinois
d. Aug 22, 1979 in New York, New York
Source: *AmAu&B; AmNov; AmWr; CasWL; CnDAL; ConAmA; ConAu 5R; ConLC 1, 4; ConNov 72, 76; CurBio 42; CyWA; DcLEL; DrAF 76; EncAB-H; EncWL; EvLB; IntWW 74; LongCTC; ModAL; NewYTBS 74; OxAmL; Pen AM; RAdv 1; REn; REnAL; TwCA, SUP; TwCW; WebAB; WebE&AL; Who 74; WhoAm 74; WhoWor 74; WrDr 76*

Farrell, Mike
American. Actor
Plays BJ Hunnicutt on TV series "MASH," 1975-83.
b. Feb 6, 1943? in Saint Paul, Minnesota
Source: *WhoAm 78, 80, 82; WhoHol A*

Farrell, Suzanne
American. Ballerina
Principal dancer, NY Ballet, 1965-69, 1975--.
b. Aug 16, 1945 in Cincinnati, Ohio
Source: *CurBio 67; InWom; WhoAm 74, 76, 78, 80, 82; WhoWor 74*

Farrere, Claude, pseud.
[Frederic Charles Pierre Edouard Bargone]
French. Naval Officer, Author
Member of French Academy, 1935; wrote 30 novels, many sea stories.
b. Apr 27, 1876 in Lyons, France
d. Jun 21, 1957 in Paris, France
Source: *CasWL; EncWL; EvEuW; OxFr*

Farrow, George Edward
American. Children's Author
b. 1866
d. 1920
Source: *ChPo, S1, S2; MnBBF; WhoChL*

Farrow, John Villiers
Australian. Author, Motion Picture Director
Father of Mia Farrow; Oscar for best screenplay *Around the World in 80 Days,* 1956.
b. Feb 10, 1906 in Sydney, Australia
d. Jan 28, 1963 in Beverly Hills, California
Source: *AmAu&B; BiDFilm; BkC 5; CathA 1930; CmMov; FilmgC; MovMk; WhAm 4; WhNAA; WorEFlm*

Farrow, Mia Villiers
American. Actress
Starred in TV series "Peyton Place," 1964-67; married to Frank Sinatra, 1967-69.
b. Feb 9, 1945 in Los Angeles, California
Source: *BiDFilm; BkPepl; CelR 73; CurBio 70; FilmgC; IntMPA 75, 76, 77, 78, 79, 80, 81, 82; MotPP; MovMk; NewYTBE 71; Who 82; WhoAm 74, 76, 78, 80, 82; WhoHol A; WhoThe 77; WhoWest 74; WhoWor 74; WorEFlm*

Fascell, Dante Bruno
American. Politician
b. Mar 9, 1917 in Bridgehampton, New York
Source: *BiDrAC; CngDr 74; CurBio 60; WhoAm 74, 76, 78, 80, 82; WhoAmP 73; WhoGov 72; WhoS&SW 73*

Fasch, Johann Friedrich
German. Composer
b. Apr 15, 1688 in Buttelstedt, Germany
d. Dec 5, 1758 in Zerbst, Germany
Source: *Baker 78; BioIn 9; OxMus*

Fass, Bob
American. Singer
b. Jun 29, 1943 in Brooklyn, New York
Source: *BioIn 10*

Fassbinder, Rainer Werner
German. Actor, Author, Director
b. May 31, 1946 in Bad Worishofen, Germany
d. Jun 10, 1982? in Munich, Germany (West)
Source: *BiDFilm; BioIn 9, 11; CurBio 77, 82; IntWW 78; NewYTBS 77, 82; OxFilm; WhoAm 82; WhoWor 78*

Fast, Howard
[E V Cunningham, Walter Ericson, pseuds.]
American. Author
Movies *Spartacus,* 1960; *Mirage,* 1965 based on stories by Fast.
b. Nov 11, 1914 in New York, New York
Source: *AmAu&B; AmNov; AuBYP; CnDAL; ConAu 1R, 1NR; ConNov 72, 76; CurBio 43; DcLEL; IntWW 74; ModAL; OxAmL; Pen AM; REn; REnAL; SmATA 7; TwCA SUP; TwCW; WebE&AL; WhoAm 74, 76, 78, 80, 82; WhoWor 74; WhoWorJ 72; WrDr 76*

Fastolf, Sir John
[Sir John Falstaff]
English. Landowner, Soldier
b. 1378
d. 1459
Source: *NewC; REn*

Fath, Jacques
French. Fashion Designer
b. Sep 12, 1912 in Vincennes, France
d. Nov 13, 1954 in Paris, France
Source: *CurBio 51, 55; WhAm 3; WorFshn*

Fatima
Arabian. Daughter of Mohammed
b. 606 in Mecca, Arabia
d. 632 in Medina, Arabia
Source: *Film 1; InWom; NewC*

Faubus, Orval Eugene
American. Governor, Journalist
b. Jan 7, 1910 in Combs, Arkansas
Source: *CurBio 56; WhoAm 74, 76, 78, 80, 82; WhoAmP 73*

Faulk, John Henry
American. TV and Radio Announcer
b. Aug 21, 1913 in Austin, Texas
Source: *AmAu&B; WhoAm 74; WhoHol A; WhoS&SW 73*

Faulkner, Brian
Irish. Prime Minister of N Ireland
b. Feb 18, 1921 in Belfast, Northern Ireland
Source: *CurBio 72; Who 74; WhoAm 74; WhoWor 74*

Faulkner, Eric
[Bay City Rollers]
Scottish. Musician, Singer
b. Oct 21, 1955 in Edinburgh, Scotland
Source: *BkPepl*

Faulkner, William
American. Author
Wrote *The Sound and the Fury,* 1929; won Nobel Prize, 1949, Pulitzer Prize, 1962.
b. Sep 25, 1897 in New Albany, Mississippi
d. Jul 6, 1962 in Oxford, Mississippi
Source: *AmAu&B; AmNov; AmWr; AtlBL; AuNews 1; BioNews 74; CasWL; Chambr 3; CnDAL; CnMD; CnMWL; ConAmA; ConAu 81; ConLC 1, 3, 6; CroCD; CurBio 51, 62; CyWA; DcFM; DcLEL; EncMys; EncWL; FilmgC; LongCTC; ModAL, SUP; ModWD; OxAmL; OxEng; OxFilm; Pen AM; RAdv 1; RComWL; REn; REnAL; TwCA, SUP; TwCW; WebAB; WebE&AL; WhAm 4; WhoTwCL; WorEFlm*

Fauntroy, Walter E
American. Social Reformer
Congressman, 1971--; chairman Congressional Black Caucus, 1981--.
b. Feb 6, 1933 in Washington, DC
Source: *CngDr 74; NewYTBE 71; WhoAm 74, 76, 78, 80, 82; WhoAmP 73; WhoBlA 75; WhoS&SW 73*

Faure, Elie
French. Art Historian, Critic
b. Apr 4, 1873 in Saint Foy, France
d. Oct 31, 1937 in Paris, France
Source: *CasWL; ClDMEL; OxFilm; TwCA, SUP; WorEFlm*

Faure, Felix
French. President
b. Jan 30, 1841
d. Feb 16, 1899
Source: *NewCol 75*

Faure, Gabriel Urbain
French. Composer, Musician
b. May 12, 1845 in Pamiers, France
d. Nov 4, 1924 in Paris, France
Source: *AtlBL; OxFr; REn*

Fauset, Jessie Redmon
American. Author
b. 1884? in Philadelphia, Pennsylvania
d. Apr 30, 1961
Source: *AmAu&B; BlkAW; InWom; TwCA SUP, SUP*

Faust, Frederick Schiller
[Max Brand, pseud.]
American. Author
b. May 29, 1892 in Seattle, Washington
d. May 12, 1944 in Germany
Source: *AmAu&B; ChPo; CurBio 44; DcAmB S3; DcLEL; DcNAA; EncMys; LongCTC; MnBBF; REn; REnAL; TwCA, SUP; WebAB*

Faust, Gerry (Gerard Anthony, Jr.)
American. Football Coach
Succeeded Dan Devine as football coach at Notre Dame, 1981--.
b. May 21, 1935 in Dayton, Ohio
Source: *NewYTBS 81*

Faust, Johann
[Johann Faustus]
German. Magician, Astrologer
b. 1480 in Knittlingen, Germany
d. 1540
Source: *FilmgC; NewC*

Faust, Lotta
Actress
b. 1881
d. Jan 25, 1910 in New York, New York
Source: *NotNAT B; WhoStg 1908*

Faversham, William Alfred
English. Actor
b. Feb 12, 1868 in London, England
d. Apr 7, 1940 in Bay Shore, New York
Source: *AmBi; CurBio 40; DcAmB S2; FamA&A; Film 1; OxThe; PlP&P; TwYS; WhAm 1; WhScrn 74, 77; WhoHol B; WhoStg 1906, 1908*

Fawcett, Farrah Leni
American. Actress, Model
Starred in "Charlie's Angels," 1976-77; movie *Murder in Texas,* 1982.
b. Feb 2, 1947 in Corpus Christi, Texas
Source: *BioIn 10, 11; IntMPA 78, 79, 80, 81, 82; WhoAm 78, 80, 82*

Fawcett, George
American. Actor
b. Aug 25, 1861 in Alexandria, Virginia
d. Jun 6, 1939 in Nantucket, Massachusetts
Source: *Alli SUP; Film 1; MotPP; MovMk; WhoHol B; TwYS; WhAm 1; WhScrn 74, 77*

Fawcett, Henry
English. Economist
b. Aug 26, 1833 in Salisbury, England
d. Nov 6, 1884
Source: *Alli SUP; BbD; BiD&SB; BioIn 8; BrAu 19; DcEnA; DcEnL; EvLB; LinLib S; NewCol 75*

Fawcett, Dame Millicent Garrett
[Mrs. Henry Fawcett]
English. Feminist
b. 1847 in Adleburgh, England
d. 1929
Source: *Alli SUP; BbD; BiD&SB; BioIn 2, 9; EvLB; NewC; NewCol 75; WhLit; WhoModH*

Fawcett, Wilford Hamilton, Jr.
American. Publisher
b. Aug 1, 1909 in Saint Paul, Minnesota
d. May 28, 1970 in Norwalk, Connecticut
Source: *WhAm 5*

Fawkes, Guy
English. Gunpowder Plot Conspirator
Failed to blow up House of Commons, 1605; Guy Fawkes Day celebrated Nov 5.
b. 1570 in York, England
d. 1606
Source: *NewC*

Fay, Frank
American. Actor
b. Nov 17, 1897 in San Francisco, California
d. Sep 25, 1961 in Santa Monica, California
Source: *BiDFilm; CelR 73; CmMov; FilmgC; InWom; MovMk; OxFilm; ThFT; WorEFlm*

Faye, Alice
[Ann Leppert]
American. Actress, Singer
b. May 5, 1915 in New York, New York
Source: *BiDFilm; CelR 73; CmMov; FilmgC; InWom; MovMk; OxFilm; ThFT; WorEFlm*

Faye, Joey
American. Actor, Comedian
b. Jul 12, 1910 in New York, New York
Source: *BiE&WWA; NotNAT; WhoHol A; WhoThe 77*

Fazenda, Louise
American. Actress
b. Jun 17, 1899 in Lafayette, Indiana
d. Apr 17, 1962 in Beverly Hills, California
Source: *Film 1; FilmgC; MotPP; MovMk; ThFT; TwYS; WhScrn 74, 77; WhoHol B; WorEFlm*

Fearing, Kenneth Flexner
American. Author
b. Jul 28, 1902 in Oak Park, Illinois
d. Jun 26, 1961 in New York, New York
Source: *AmAu&B; AmNov; CnDAL; CnE&AP; ConAmA; ConAu 93; DcLEL; EncMys; ModAL; OxAmL; Pen AM; RAdv 1; REn; REnAL; SixAP; TwCA, SUP; WebAB; WebE&AL; WhAm 4; WhoTwCL*

Fears, Tom (Thomas Jesse)
American. Football Player
b. Dec 3, 1923 in Los Angeles, California
Source: *BioIn 9; WhoFtbl 74*

Feather, Leonard Geoffrey
American. Jazz Historian
b. Sep 13, 1914 in London, England
Source: *AmAu&B; AmSCAP 66; ConAu 61; WhoAm 74, 76, 78, 80, 82; WhoWor 74*

Feather, Victor
English. Trade Union Official
Helped to make Trades Union Congress one of Europe's most powerful unions.
b. Apr 10, 1908 in Bradford, England
d. Jul 28, 1976 in London, England
Source: *BioIn 8, 9, 10, 11; IntWW 74; Who 74; WhoWor 74*

Fedin, Konstantin
Russian. Author
b. Feb 27, 1892 in Saratov, Russia
d. Jul 15, 1977 in Moscow, U.S.S.R.
Source: *CasWL; ClDMEL; ConAu 73, 81; DcRusL; EncWL; EvEuW; IntWW 74; ModSL 1; Pen EUR; REn; TwCW; WhoWor 74; WorAu*

Fedorova, Alexandra
Russian. Ballerina
b. 1884
d. 1972
Source: *NewYTBE 72*

Feiffer, Jules Ralph
American. Cartoonist, Author
b. Jan 26, 1929 in New York, New York
Source: *AmAu&B; Au&Wr 71; CelR 73; CnThe; ConAu 17R; ConDr 73; ConLC 2, 8; CroCD; CurBio 61; FilmgC; IntWW 74; McGEWD; NotNAT; SmATA 8; WhoAm 74, 76, 78, 80, 82; WhoThe 77; WhoWor 74; WhoWorJ 72; WrDr 76*

Feigner, Eddie (Edward)
"King of Softball"; "Golden Arm"
American. Softball Player
b. 1925
Source: *BioIn 6, 9*

Feininger, Andreas Bernhard Lyonel
American. Photographer, Author
b. Dec 27, 1906 in Paris, France
Source: *AmAu&B; BioIn 2, 4; ConAu 85; CurBio 57; LinLib L; WhoAm 74, 76, 78, 80; WhoWor 74, 76*

Feininger, Lyonel
[Charles Adrian Feininger]
American. Artist
b. Jul 17, 1871 in New York, New York
d. Jan 13, 1956
Source: *AtlBL; CurBio 55, 56; DcCAA 71; OxGer; REn; WhAm 3*

Feinstein, Dianne
American. Mayor of San Francisco
Became mayor, 1978, after assassination of George Moscone.
b. Jun 22, 1933 in San Francisco, California
Source: *CurBio 79; WhoAm 80, 82*

Feis, Herbert
American. Author, Economist, Historian
b. Jun 7, 1893 in New York, New York
d. Mar 2, 1972 in Winter Park, Florida
Source: *AmAu&B; Au&Wr 71; ConAu 33R; ConAu P-1; CurBio 61, 72; NewYTBE 72; OxAmL; WhAm 5; WhoWorJ 72; WorAu*

Feld, Eliot
American. Dancer
b. Jul 5, 1942 in Brooklyn, New York
Source: *CurBio 71; NewYTBE 70; NewYTBS 74; WhoAm 74, 76, 78, 80, 82; WhoE 74*

Feld, Fritz
German. Actor
b. Oct 15, 1900 in Berlin, Germany
Source: *FilmgC; IntMPA 75, 76, 77; MovMk; TwYS; Vers A; WhoAm 74, 76, 78, 80, 82; WhoHol A*

Feld, Irvin
American. Circus Producer
b. May 9, 1918 in Hagerstown, Maryland
Source: *CelR 73; CurBio 79; WhoAm 76, 78, 80, 82; WhoWor 78*

Felder, Don(ald William)
[The Eagles]
American. Musician, Singer, Songwriter
b. Sept 21, 1947 in Gainesville, Florida
Source: *WhoAm 82*

Felder, Wilton
see: Crusaders, The

Feldman, Alvin Lindbergh
American. Airline Executive
b. Dec 14, 1927 in New York, New York
d. Aug 9, 1981 in Los Angeles, California
Source: *WhoAm 78, 80*

Feldman, Marty
English. Actor, Director, Writer
Made American film debut in *Young Frankenstein,* 1974.
b. 1933 in London, England
d. Dec 2, 1982 in Mexico City, Mexico
Source: *FilmgC; IntMPA 79, 80, 81, 82; WhoAm 78, 80, 82; WhoHol A; WorAl*

Feldon, Barbara
American. Actress
Best known for role as Agent 99 on TV series "Get Smart," 1965-70.
b. Mar 12, 1941 in Pittsburgh, Pennsylvania
Source: *WhoHol A*

Feldshuh, Tovah
American. Actress
b. Dec 27, 1952 in New York, New York
Source: *BioIn 11; WhoAm 82; WhoThe 81*

Feliciano, Jose
American. Singer, Musician
Blind singer, guitarist; composed theme for TV show "Chico and the Man."
b. Sep 10, 1945 in Larez, Puerto Rico
Source: *CurBio 69; CelR 73; RkOn; WhoAm 74, 76, 78, 80, 82*

Felker, Clay S
American. Journalist
b. Oct 2, 1928 in Saint Louis, Missouri
Source: *ConAu 73; CurBio 75; St&PR 75; WhoAm 74, 76, 78, 80, 82; WhoE 74; WhoF&I 74; WhoWor 74*

Fell, John
English. Clergyman, Scholar
b. Jun 23, 1625 in Longworth, England
d. Jul 10, 1686
Source: *BrAu; DcEnL; NewC; OxEng; REn*

Fell, Norman
American. Actor
b. Mar 24, 1925 in Philadelphia, Pennsylvania
Source: *IntMPA 82; WhoAm 74, 76, 78, 80, 82; WhoHol A*

Feller, Bob (Robert William Andrew)
"Rapid Robert"
American. Baseball Player
Pitcher who won 266 career games, including three no-hitters; Hall of Fame, 1962,
b. Nov 3, 1918 in Van Meter, Iowa
Source: *AuBYP; BaseEn; BioNews 74; CurBio 41; WhoProB 73*

Fellig, Arthur
"Weegee"
American. Photographer
b. 1899
d. 1968
Source: *BioIn 10*

Fellini, Federico
Italian. Screenwriter, Director
Won four Oscars for best foreign film, including *La Dolce Vita,* 1960.
b. Jan 20, 1920 in Rimini, Italy
Source: *BiDFilm; BkPepl; ConAu 65; ConLC 16; CurBio 57; DcFM; FilmgC; IntMPA 75, 76, 77, 78, 79, 80, 81, 82; IntWW 74; MovMk; OxFilm; REn; Who 82; WhoAm 82; WhoWor 74; WomWMM; WorEFlm*

Fellows, Edith
American. Actress, Singer
b. 1923 in Boston, Massachusetts
Source: *FilmgC; ThFT; WhoHol A*

Fels, Samuel Simeon
American. Businessman, Philanthropist
b. Feb 16, 1860 in Yanceyville, North Carolina
d. Jun 23, 1950 in Philadelphia, Pennsylvania
Source: *DcAmB S4; WhAm 3*

Felsenstein, Walter
Austrian. Actor, Director, Producer
b. May 30, 1901 in Vienna, Austria
d. Oct 8, 1975 in Berlin, Germany (East)
Source: *IntWW 74; WhoWor 74*

Felton, Harold W
American. Author
b. Apr 1, 1902 in Neola, Iowa
Source: *AuBYP; ChPo S2; ConAu 1R, 1NR; MorJA; SmATA 1*

Felton, Verna
American. Actress
b. Jul 20, 1890 in Salinas, California
d. Dec 14, 1966 in North Hollywood, California
Source: *FilmgC; Vers B; WhScrn 74, 77; WhoHol B*

Fender, Freddy
[Baldermar Huerta]
American. Singer, Songwriter
Won Grammy, 1977, for "Before the Next Teardrop Falls."
b. Jun 4, 1937 in San Benito, Texas
Source: *BioIn 10; RkOn; WhoAm 78, 80, 82*

Fender, Leo
American. Guitar Manufacturer
Designed solid body electric guitar; helped in development of rock music.
b. 1907
Source: *IlEncRk*

Fendler, Edvard
German. Conductor, Composer
b. Jan 22, 1902 in Leipzig, Germany
Source: *AmSCAP 66*

Fenelon, Fania
[Fanny Goldstein]
French. Author, Singer
TV movie *Playing for Time* based on her life.
b. Sep 2, 1918 in Paris, France
Source: *BioIn 11; ConAu 77; NewYTBS 78*

Fenelon, Francois de Salignac
French. Author, Theologian
b. Aug 6, 1651 in Perigord, France
d. Jan 7, 1715 in Cambrai, France
Source: *AtlBL; BbD; BiD&SB; CasWL; ChPo S1; DcEuL; EuAu; NewC; OxEng; OxFr; Pen EUR; REn*

Fennell, Frederick
American. Conductor, Music Educator
b. 1914 in Cleveland, Ohio
Source: *WhoMus 72*

Fennelly, Parker
American. Radio Performer
Source: *BioIn 11; WhoHol A*

Fenneman, George
American. Radio Announcer
b. Nov 10, 1919 in Peking, China
Source: *IntMPA 75, 76, 77, 78, 79, 80, 81, 82*

Fenollosa, Ernest Francisco
American. Art Historian, Orientalist
b. Feb 18, 1853 in Salem, Massachusetts
d. Sep 21, 1908 in London, England
Source: *AmAu; AmBi; BiDSA; CnDAL; DcAmAu; DcAmB; DcLEL; DcNAA; OxAmL; REn; REnAL; WebAB; WebE&AL; WhAm 1*

Fenten, D X
American. Children's Author
b. Jan 3, 1932 in New York, New York
Source: *ConAu 33R; SmATA 4; WrDr 76*

Fenton, Carroll Lane
American. Author, Illustrator
b. Feb 12, 1900 in Parkersburg, Iowa
d. Nov 16, 1969
Source: *AmAu&B; AuBYP; ConAu 1R, 29R; MorJA; SmATA 5*

Fenton, Leslie
English. Actor, Motion Picture Director
b. 1903 in Liverpool, England
Source: *MovMk*

Fenton, Thomas Trail
American. Journalist
b. Apr 8, 1930 in Baltimore, Maryland
Source: *ConAu 102; WhoAm 74, 76, 78, 80, 82; WhoWor 74*

Fenwick, Millicent Hammond
American. Politician
Congresswoman from NJ, 1975-82; defeated in bid for Seante, 1982.
b. Feb 25, 1910 in New York, New York
Source: *NewYTBS 74; WhoAm 82; WhoAmP 73; WhoAmW 74*

Feoktistov, Konstantin Petrovich
Russian. Cosmonaut, Engineer
b. Feb 7, 1926 in Voronezh, U.S.S.R.
Source: *CurBio 67*

Ferber, Edna
American. Author
b. Aug 15, 1887 in Kalamazoo, Michigan
d. Apr 16, 1968 in New York, New York
Source: *AmAu&B; AmNov; AuNews 1; BiE&WWA; Chambr 3; CnDAL; CnMD; CnThe; ConAmA; ConAmL; ConAu 5R, 25R; ConLC 18; DcLEL; EncWL; EvLB; FilmgC; InWom; LongCTC; McGEWD; ModAL; ModWD; OxAmL; OxThe; Pen AM; PlP&P; REn; REnAL; SmATA 7; TwCA, SUP; TwCW; WebAB; WhAm 5; WhNAA; WisWr*

Ferdinand I
Spanish. Holy Roman Emperor
b. 1503
d. 1564
Source: *BioIn 10; NewCol 75; WebBD 80*

Ferdinand V
Spanish. King
b. Mar 10, 1452 in Sos, Spain
d. Jan 23, 1516 in Madrigalejo, Spain
Source: *BioIn 10; LinLib S; McGEWB; NewCol 75*

Ferdinand
see: Franz Ferdinand

Ferdinand Maximilian Joseph
see: Maximilian

Ferencsik, Janos
Hungarian. Conductor
b. Jan 18, 1907 in Budapest, Hungary
Source: *IntWW 74, 75, 76, 77, 78; WhoOp 76; WhoSocC 78*

Ferguson, Elsie
American. Actress
b. Aug 19, 1885 in New York
d. Nov 15, 1961 in New London, Connecticut
Source: *WhThe; WhoHol B*

Ferguson, Harry George
English. Industrialist
b. Nov 4, 1884 in Dromore, Northern Ireland
d. Oct 25, 1960 in Abbotswood, England
Source: *BioIn 3, 4, 5, 6, 9, 10; CurBio 56, 61; WhAm 4*

Ferguson, Homer
American. Judge, Politician
Senator from MI, 1943-1954.
b. Feb 25, 1888 in Harrison City, Pennsylvania
d. Dec 17, 1982 in Grosse Pointe, Michigan
Source: *BiDrAC; CngDr 74, 77, 79, 81; CurBio 43; IntWW 74, 75, 76, 77, 78, 79, 80, 81; PolProf E; PolProf T; WhoAm 74, 76, 78, 80, 82; WhoAmP 73, 75, 77, 79; WhoGov 72, 75, 77*

Ferguson, Homer Lenoir
American. Shipbuilder
b. Mar 6, 1873 in Waynesville, North Carolina
d. Mar 14, 1952
Source: *NatCAB 17, 40; WhAm 3*

Ferguson, Jimmy
see: Irish Rovers

Ferguson, Joe Carlton, Jr.
American. Football Player
b. Apr 23, 1950 in Alvin, Texas
Source: *FootReg*

Ferguson, John Bowie
Canadian. Hockey Player, Executive
Forward, Montreal, 1963-71; currently general manager, Winnipeg.
b. Sep 5, 1938 in Vancouver, BC
Source: *WhoHcky 73*

Ferguson, Maynard
Canadian. Jazz Musician
Plays trumpet; has sold more records than any band leader since 1940.
b. May 4, 1928 in Verdun, PQ
Source: *BioIn 12; CanWW 82; CurBio 80; WhoAm 76, 78, 80, 82*

Ferguson, Miriam Amanda
American. Governor of Texas
b. Jun 13, 1875 in Bell County, Texas
d. Jun 25, 1961 in Austin, Texas
Source: *WhAm 4*

Fergusson, Bernard Edward
see: Ballantrae, Lord

Fergusson, Francis
American. Author
b. Feb 21, 1904 in Albuquerque, New Mexico
Source: *AmAu&B; ConAu 9R, 3NR; DrAS 74E; NotNAT; REnAL; TwCA SUP; WhoAm 74, 76, 78, 80, 82; WhoWor 74; WrDr 76*

Fergusson, Harvey
American. Author
b. Jan 28, 1890 in Albuquerque, New Mexico
d. Aug 24, 1971
Source: *AmAu&B; AmNov; CnDAL; ConAu 33R; OxAmL; REnAL; TwCA, SUP; WhNAA*

Ferkauf, Eugene
American. Merchant
b. 1921
Source: *BioIn 6, 7*

Ferlinghetti, Lawrence
American. Author, Poet
b. Mar 24, 1919 in Yonkers, New York
Source: *ConAu 5R, 3NR; ConDr 73; ConLC 2, 6; ConP 70, 75; CroCAP; CroCD; DrAP 75; ModAL; OxAmL; Pen AM; RAdv 1; REn; REnAL; TwCW; WebE&AL; WhoAm 82; WhoTwCL; WhoWest 74; WorAu; WrDr 76*

Fermat, Pierre de
French. Mathematician
b. 1601?
d. 1665
Source: *BioIn 2, 5*

Fermi, Enrico
American. Physicist
Discovered uranium fission; won Nobel Prize, 1938; developed atomic bomb, 1942-45.
b. Sep 29, 1901 in Rome, Italy
d. Nov 28, 1954 in Chicago, Illinois
Source: *CurBio 45, 55; DcAmB S5; EncAB-H; WebAB; WhAm 3*

Fernald, John Bailey
American. Motion Picture Director
b. Nov 21, 1905 in California
Source: *OxThe; Who 74; WhoThe 77*

Fernandel
[Fernand Contandin]
French. Actor
b. May 8, 1903 in Marseilles, France
d. Feb 26, 1971 in Paris, France
Source: *FilmgC; MotPP; MovMk; OxFilm; WhAm 5; WhScrn 74, 77; WhoHol B; WorEFlm*

Fernandez-Muro, Jose Antonio
Argentine. Artist
b. Mar 1, 1920
Source: *IntWW 74*

Ferragamo, Vince
American. Football Player
b. Apr 24, 1954 in Torrance, California
Source: *BioIn 12; FootReg*

Ferrante, Arthur
[Ferrante and Teicher]
American. Pianist, Arranger, Composer
b. Sep 7, 1921 in New York, New York
Source: *AmSCAP 66; WhoAm 74*

Ferrante & Teicher
see: Ferrante, Arthur; Teicher, Louis

Ferrari, Enzo
Italian. Automobile Executive
Developed the Ferrari, 1940.
b. Feb 20, 1898 in Modena, Italy
Source: *BusPN; CurBio 67; IntWW 74; Who 74; WhoWor 74*

Ferraris, Galileo
Italian. Explorer, Scientist
Discovered rotary magnetic field, 1885.
b. 1847
d. 1897
Source: *NewCol 75*

Ferre, Maurice Antonio
American. Politician
b. Jun 23, 1935 in Ponce, Puerto Rico
Source: *St&PR 75; WhoAm 74, 76, 78, 80, 82; WhoF&I 74; WhoWor 74*

Ferrell, Conchata Galen
"Chatti"
American. Actress
b. Mar 28, 1943 in Charleston, West Virginia
Source: *BioIn 10; WhoAm 82*

Ferrell, Wes(ley Cheek)
American. Baseball Player, Executive
Holds record for most home runs hit by a pitcher (38).
b. Feb 2, 1908 in Greensboro, North Carolina
d. Dec 9, 1976 in Sarasota, Florida
Source: *BaseEn; BioIn 3, 10, 11; WhoProB 73*

Ferrer, Jose Figueres
see: Figueres Ferrer, Jose

Ferrer, Jose Vicente
American. Actor, Producer, Director
Won 1950 Oscar for *Cyrano de Bergerac.*
b. Jan 8, 1912 in Santurce, Puerto Rico
Source: *BiDFilm; BiE&WWA; CelR 73; CurBio 44; EncMT; FilmgC; IntMPA 75, 76, 77, 78, 79, 80, 81, 82; MotPP; MovMk; NotNAT; OxFilm; Who 74; WhoAm 74, 76, 78, 80, 82; WhoHol A; WhoThe 77; WhoWor 74; WorEFlm*

Ferrer, Mel(chor Gaston)
American. Actor
b. Aug 25, 1917 in Elberon, New Jersey
Source: *BiDFilm; BiE&WWA; FilmgC; IntMPA 75, 76, 77, 78, 79, 80, 81, 82; MotPP; MovMk; NotNAT; OxFilm; WhoHol A; WorEFlm*

Ferrier, David
Scottish. Neurologist
b. 1843
d. 1928
Source: *BioIn 4, 6, 7; WebBD 80*

Ferrier, Jim (James B)
Australian. Golfer
Won first tournament in US, 1944; won PGA, 1947.
b. Feb 24, 1915 in Sydney, Australia
Source: *BioIn 10; WhoGolf*

Ferrier, Henry Eliza
Surinamese. Governor
b. May 12, 1910 in Paramaribo, Surinam
Source: *IntWW 74; WhoWor 74*

Ferrier, Kathleen
English. Opera Singer
b. Apr 22, 1912 in Higher Walter, England
d. Oct 8, 1953 in London, England
Source: *CurBio 51, 53; InWom; WhAm HA, 4*

Ferrigno, Lou
American. Actor
Played the Hulk on TV series "The Incrdible Hulk," 1977-81.
b. Nov 9, 1951 in Brooklyn, New York
Source: *NewYTBS 76*

Ferril, Thomas Hornsby
American. Publisher
b. Jun 23, 1896 in Keeseville, New York
Source: *AmAu&B; ChPo, S1, S2; ConAu 65; ConP 70, 75; OxAmL; REnAL; TwCA SUP; WhoAm 74, 76, 78, 80, 82; WrDr 76*

Ferris, Barbara
English. Actress
b. 1942 in London, England
Source: *FilmgC; NotNAT; WhoHol A; WhoThe 77*

Ferris, George Washington Gale
American. Inventor, Businessman
Invented Ferris Wheel, 1893, for World's Columbian Exposition, Chicago.
b. Feb 14, 1859 in Galesburg, Illinois
d. Nov 22, 1896 in Pittsburgh, Pennsylvania
Source: *ApCAB SUP; DcAmB; WebAB; WhAm H*

Ferry, Bryan
[Roxy Music]
English. Rock Musician
b. Sep 26, 1945 in Durham, England
Source: *BioIn 11; ConMuA 80; WhoAm 82; WhoRock 81*

Fessenden, Reginald Aubrey
Canadian. Inventor
Made first radio broadcast, first two-way telegraphic communication, 1906.
b. Oct 6, 1866 in Bolton, PQ
d. Jul 22, 1932 in Bermuda
Source: *AmBi; DcAmB S1; DcNAA; TwCBDA; WebAB; WhAm 1*

Fessenden, William Pitt
American. Politician
b. Oct 16, 1806 in Boscawen, New Hampshire
d. Sep 8, 1869 in Portland, Maine
Source: *DcAmB; WebAB; WhAm H*

Fetchit, Stepin
[Lincoln Perry]
American. Actor
b. 1892 in Key West, Florida
Source: *BioNews 74; FilmgC; HolP 30; MotPP; MovMk; WhoHol A*

Feti, Domenico
Italian. Artist
b. 1589 in Rome, Italy
d. 1623 in Venice, Italy
Source: *McGDA*

Fetzer, John Earl
American. Baseball and Radio Executive
Owner, Fetzer Broadcasting, 1930; Detroit Tigers baseball club, 1956--.
b. Mar 25, 1901 in Decater, Indiana
Source: *IntMPA 82; WhoAm 78, 80, 82; WhoProB 73*

Feuchtwanger, Lion
German. Author, Dramatist
b. Jul 7, 1884 in Munich, Germany
d. Dec 21, 1958 in Los Angeles, California
Source: *AmAu&B; CasWL; ClDMEL; CnMD; CyWA; EncWL; EvEuW; LongCTC; McGEWD; ModGL; ModWD; OxEng; OxGer; Pen EUR; REn; TwCA, SUP; WhAm 3*

Feuer, Cy
American. Motion Picture Director, Producer
b. Jan 15, 1911 in New York, New York
Source: *BiE&WWA; CelR 73; EncMT; NotNAT; WhoAm 74; WhoThe 77; WhoWor 74*

Feuerbach, Anselm
German. Artist
b. Sep 12, 1829
d. Jan 4, 1880
Source: *NewCol 75; OxArt; OxGer; Pen EUR; REn*

Feuerbach, Ludwig Andreas
German. Philosopher
b. Jul 28, 1804 in Landshut, Germany
d. Sep 13, 1872 in Rechenberg, Germany
Source: *McGEWB; NewCol 75; OxGer; Pen; REn*

Feuerbach, Paul Johann Anseim
German. Jurist
b. 1775
d. 1833
Source: *BiD&SB; DcEuL; NewCol 75*

Feuermann, Emanuel
American. Musician
b. Nov 22, 1902 in Kolomea, Poland
d. May 25, 1942 in New York, New York
Source: *CurBio 42*

Feuillade, Louis
French. Motion Picture Director
b. 1873 in Lunel, France
d. 1925 in Paris, France
Source: *BiDFilm; DcFM; FilmgC; OxFilm; WorEFlm*

Feuillet, Octave
French. Dramatist, Author
b. Jul 11, 1821 in Saint Lo, France
d. Dec 29, 1890 in Paris, France
Source: *CasWL; DcBiA; DcEuL; EuAu; EvEuW; HsB&A; NotNAT B; OxFr*

Fey, Thomas Hossler
American. President of A & W Beverages
b. Sep 17, 1939 in Chicago, Illinois
Source: *WhoAm 82*

Feydeau, Georges
French. Dramatist
b. Dec 8, 1862 in Paris, France
d. Jun 6, 1921 in Rueil-Malmaison, France
Source: *AtlBL; CasWL; CnMD; CnThe; EvEuW; McGEWD; ModWD; OxFr; Pen EUR; TwCW; WorAu*

Feynman, Richard Phillips
American. Physicist
Joint winner of 1965 Nobel Prize in Physics.
b. May 11, 1918 in New York, New York
Source: *AmM&WS 73P, 76P, 79P; AsBiEn; IntWW 74, 75, 76, 77, 78, 79, 80, 81; WebAB; WhoAm 74, 76, 78, 80, 82; WhoWest 78; WhoWor 74*

Fibiger, Johannes Andreas Grib
Danish. Pathologist
b. Apr 23, 1867
d. Jan 30, 1928
Source: *BioIn 3; NewCol 75; WebBD 80*

Fibber McGee & Molly
see: McGee, Fibber; McGee, Molly

Fichte, Johann Gottlieb
German. Philosopher
b. May 19, 1762 in Rammenau, Germany
d. Jan 27, 1814 in Berlin, Germany
Source: *BbD; BiD&SB; DcEuL; EvEuW; NewC; OxEng; OxGer; Pen EUR; REn*

Ficke, Arthur Davidson
American. Poet, Author
b. Nov 10, 1883 in Davenport, Iowa
d. Nov 30, 1945 in Hudson, New York
Source: *AmAu&B; AmLY; ChPo, S1, S2; CnDAL; ConAmL; DcLEL; DcNAA; OxAmL; REn; REnAL; TwCA, SUP; WhAm 2*

Fidler, Jimmy (James M)
American. Journalist, Radio Commentator
b. 1900 in Memphis, Tennessee
Source: *BioIn 9; What 3*

Fidrych, Mark
"The Bird"
American. Baseball Player
Pitcher, Detroit Tigers, 1976-80, who talked to baseball; rookie of year, 1976.
b. Aug 14, 1954 in Worcester, Massachusetts
Source: *BaseEn; BioIn 11; CurBio 78*

Fiedler, Arthur
American. Orchestra Conductor
Conducted Boston Symphony Pops Concerts, 1930-79.
b. Dec 17, 1894 in Boston, Massachusetts
d. Jul 10, 1979 in Brookline, Massachusetts
Source: *BioNews 74; CelR 73; CurBio 45; NewYTBE 72; WebAB; WhoAm 74; WhoWor 74*

Fiedler, Jean(nette Feldman)
American. Children's Author
b. in Pittsburgh, Pennsylvania
Source: *ConAu 17R, 29R; ForWC 70; SmATA 4; WhoAmW 77*

Fiedler, Leslie Aaron
American. Author
b. Mar 8, 1917 in Newark, New Jersey
Source: *AmAu&B; CasWL; CelR 73; ConAu 9R; ConLC 4, 13; ConNov 72, 76; CurBio 70; DrAF 76; DrAS 74E; EncWL; IntWW 74; ModAL SUP; Pen AM; RAdv 1; REnAL; WhoAm 74, 76, 78, 80, 82; WhoE 74; WhoTwCL; WhoWor 74; WhoWorJ 72; WorAu; WrDr 76*

Field, Betty
American. Actress
b. Feb 8, 1918 in Boston, Massachusetts
d. Sep 13, 1973 in Hyannis, Massachusetts
Source: *BiE&WWA; CurBio 59, 73; FilmgC; HolP 40; InWom; MotPP; MovMk; NewYTBE 73; PlP&P; ThFT; WhAm 6; WhScrn 77; WhoE 74; WhoHol B; WhoThe 77; WhoWor 74*

Field, Cyrus West
American. Merchant, Financier
Promoter of first Atlantic cable, 1858, and other oceanic cables.
b. Nov 30, 1819 in Stockbridge, Massachusetts
d. Jul 12, 1892 in New York, New York
Source: *AmBi; ApCAB; DcAmB; Drake; EncAB-H; NewCol 75; TwCBDA; WebAB; WhAm H*

Field, Eugene
American. Poet, Journalist
b. Sep 23, 1850 in Saint Louis, Missouri
d. Nov 4, 1895 in Chicago, Illinois
Source: *Alli SUP; AmAu; AmAu&B; AmBi; AmSCAP 66; ApCAB SUP; AuBYP; BbD; BiD&SB; BiDSA; CarSB; CasWL; Chambr 3; ChPo, S1, S2; CnDAL; DcAmAu; DcAmB; DcLEL; DcNAA; EvLB; JBA 34; OxAmL; OxEng; Pen AM; RAdv 1; REn; REnAL; Str&VC; TwCBDA; WebAB; WhAm H*

Field, John
Irish. Pianist, Composer
b. Jul 26, 1782 in Dublin, Ireland
d. Jan 11, 1837 in Moscow, Russia
Source: *WebBD 80*

Field, Kate
American. Actress, Author
b. Oct 1, 1838 in Saint Louis, Missouri
d. May 19, 1896
Source: *AmAu&B; BbD; BiD&SB; BiDSA; DcAmAu; DcNAA; NotNAT B*

Field, Marshall
American. Merchant, Journalist
Opened Marshall Field Dept. Store, 1881; donated money to Chicago museums.
b. Aug 18, 1834 in Conway, Massachusetts
d. Jan 16, 1906 in New York, New York
Source: *AmBi; ApCAB SUP; DcAmB; EncAB-H; TwCBDA; WebAB; WhAm 1*

Field, Marshall, III
American. Publisher, Philanthropist
Established the Chicago *Sun,* 1941, Field Enterprises, Inc., 1944.
b. Sep 28, 1893 in Chicago, Illinois
d. Nov 8, 1956 in New York, New York
Source: *CurBio 41, 52, 57; WhAm 3*

Field, Marshall, V
American. Newspaper Publisher
Publisher, Chicago *Sun-Times,* 1969-80; chairman Field Enterprises, 1972--.
b. May 13, 1941 in Charlottesville, Virginia
Source: *CelR 73; WhoAm 74, 76, 78, 80, 82; WhoF&I 74; WhoMW 74; WhoWor 74*

Field, Michael
American. Musician
b. Feb 21, 1915 in Manhattan, New York
d. Mar 22, 1971
Source: *BioIn 7, 8, 9; ConAu 29R; NewYTBE 71*

Field, Rachel Lyman
American. Children's Author
b. Sep 19, 1894 in New York, New York
d. Mar 15, 1942 in Beverly Hills, California
Source: *AmAu&B; AnCL; AuBYP; BkCL; CarSB; ChPo, S1, S2; CnDAL; ConAmA; ConICB; CurBio 42; DcNAA; FilmgC; InWom; JBA 34, 51; LongCTC; Newb 1922; NotAW; OxAmL; REnAL; Str&VC; TwCA, SUP; TwCW; WhAm 2*

Field, Ron
American. Choreographer, Director
b. 1934 in Queens, New York
Source: *EncMT; NotNAT; WhoAm 74, 76, 78, 80, 82; WhoE 74; WhoThe 77*

Field, Sally Margaret
American. Actress
Won 1979 Oscar for *Norma Rae;* 1977 Emmy for "Sybil."
b. Nov 6, 1946 in Pasadena, California
Source: *BkPepl; FilmgC; IntMPA 82; WhoAm 74, 76, 78, 80, 82; WhoHol A*

Field, Sid(ney Arthur)
English. Comedian
b. Apr 1, 1904 in Birmingham, England
d. Feb 3, 1950 in Surrey, England
Source: *FilmgC; NotNAT B; WhScrn 74, 77; WhThe; WhoHol B*

Field, Stanley
American. Author, Government Official
b. May 20, 1911 in Ukraine, Russia
Source: *ConAu 21R; WhoS&SW 73*

Field, Stephen Johnson
American. Supreme Court Justice
b. Nov 4, 1816 in Haddam, Connecticut
d. Apr 9, 1899 in Washington, DC
Source: *AmBi; ApCAB; BiAuS; DcAmB; DcNAA; Drake; EncAB-H; OxAmL; TwCBDA; WebAB; WhAm H*

Field, Virginia (Margaret Cynthia)
American. Actress
b. 1917 in London, England
Source: *FilmgC; IntMPA 75, 76, 77, 78, 79, 80, 81, 82; MovMk; ThFT; WhoHol A; WhoThe 77*

Fielding, Fenella Marion
English. Actress
b. Nov 17, 1934 in London, England
Source: *Who 74; WhoThe 77*

Fielding, Gabriel, pseud.
[Alan Gabriel Barnsley]
English. Author, Physician
b. Mar 25, 1916 in Hexham, England
Source: *ConAu 13R; ConNov 72, 76; CurBio 62; ModBrL, SUP; NewC; RAdv 1; Who 74; WhoAm 74, 76, 78, 80, 82; WorAu; WrDr 76*

Fielding, Henry
English. Author, Dramatist
b. Apr 22, 1707 in Sharpham Park, England
d. Oct 8, 1754 in Lisbon, Portugal
Source: *Alli; AtlBL; BbD; BiD&SB; BrAu; CasWL; Chambr 2; ChPo, S1; CnThe; CrtT 2; CyWA; DcBiA; DcEnA; DcEnL; DcEuL; DcLEL; EvLB; McGEWD; MouLC 2; NewC; OxEng; OxThe; Pen ENG; RAdv 1; RComWL; REn; REnWD; WebE&AL*

Fielding, Lewis J
American. Daniel Ellsberg's Psychiatrist
b. Oct 2, 1909 in New York, New York
Source: *BiDrAPA 77*

Fielding, Temple Hornaday
American. Author, Travel Expert
b. Oct 8, 1913 in Bronx, New York
Source: *AmAu&B; CelR 73; ConAu 21R; CurBio 69; WhoAm 74, 76, 78, 80, 82; WhoWor 74*

Fields, Dorothy
American. Songwriter
b. Jul 15, 1905 in Allenhurst, New Jersey
d. Mar 28, 1974 in New York, New York
Source: *AmSCAP 66; BiE&WWA; ConAu 49, 93; ConDr 73; CurBio 58, 74; EncMT; InWom; NewCBMT; NewYTBS 74; WhAm 6; WhScrn 77; WhoAm 74; WhoHol B*

Fields, Gracie
[Grace Stansfield]
English. Comedienne
b. Jan 9, 1898 in Rochdale, England
d. Sep 27, 1979 in Capri, Italy
Source: *CurBio 41; FilmgC; InWom; MotPP; MovMk; OxFilm; OxThe; ThFT; Who 74; WhoHol A; WhoThe 77*

Fields, James T
American. Publisher, Author
b. Dec 31, 1817 in Portsmouth, New Hampshire
d. Apr 24, 1881 in Boston, Massachusetts
Source: *Alli, SUP; AmAu; AmAu&B; AmBi; ApCAB; BbD; BiD&SB; ChPo, S1, S2; CnDAL; CyAl 2; DcAmAu; DcAmB; DcEnL; DcLEL; DcNAA; Drake; OxAmL; REnAL; TwCBDA; WhAm H*

Fields, Joseph
American. Screenwriter, Director
b. Feb 21, 1895 in New York, New York
d. Mar 3, 1966 in Beverly Hills, California
Source: *AmAu&B; CnMD; ConAu 25R; McGEWD; ModWD; NotNAT B; WhThe*

Fields, Lew Maurice
[Weber and Fields]
American. Comedian
b. Jan 1, 1867 in New York, New York
d. Jul 20, 1941 in Beverly Hills, California
Source: *CurBio 41; EncMT; FamA&A; Film 1; TwYS; WhAm 1; WhScrn 74, 77; WhoHol B; WhoStg 1908*

Fields, Shep
[Rippling Rhythm Orchestra]
American. Band Leader
b. Sep 12, 1910 in Brooklyn, New York
d. Feb 23, 1981 in Los Angeles, California
Source: *BiDAmM; BioIn 9; CmpEPM; NewYTBS 81; WhoHol A*

Fields, Stanley
American. Actor
b. 1880 in Allegheny, Pennsylvania
d. Apr 23, 1941 in Los Angeles, California
Source: *MovMk; WhScrn 74, 77; WhoHol B*

Fields, Totie
[Sophie Feldman]
American. Comedienne
b. 1931 in Hartford, Connecticut
d. Aug 2, 1978 in Las Vegas, Nevada
Source: *BioIn 11*

Fields, W C
[William Claude Dukenfield, real name; Charles Bogle, Otis J Criblecoblis, Mahatma Kane Jeeves, pseuds.]
American. Actor
Performed in Ziegfeld Follies, 1915-21; starred in *My Little Chickadee,* 1940.
b. Jan 29, 1880 in Philadelphia, Pennsylvania
d. Dec 25, 1946 in Pasadena, California
Source: *BiDFilm; CmMov; EncMT; FamA&A; Film 1; FilmgC; MotPP; MovMk; OxFilm; PlP&P; TwYS; WebAB; WhAm 2; WhScrn 74, 77; WhoHol B; WorEFlm*

Fiesole, Giovanni da
see: Angelico, Fra

Fifield, Elaine
Australian. Ballerina
b. Oct 28, 1930 in Sydney, Australia
Source: *BioIn 4, 8; WhThe*

Fifth Dimension
[Daniel Beard; William Davis, Jr.; Florence LaRue Gordon; Marilyn McCoo; Lamonte McLemore; Ronald Townson]
American. Singing Group
Hits include "Up, Up and Away," 1967; "Aquarius," 1969.
Source: *BioNews 74; EncPR&S; RkOn*

Figueiredo, Joao Baptista de Oliveira
Brazilian. President
b. Jan 15, 1918 in Rio de Janeiro, Brazil
Source: *BioIn 11; CurBio 80; IntWW 79*

Figueres Ferrer, Jose
Costa Rican. President
b. Sep 25, 1908
Source: *CurBio 53; IntWW 74; NewYTBE 70; WhoGov 72; WhoWor 74*

Filene, Edward Albert
American. Merchant
b. Sep 3, 1860 in Salem, Massachusetts
d. Sep 26, 1937 in Paris, France
Source: *DcAmB S2; DcNAA; WebAB; WhAm 1; WhAmP*

Filene, Lincoln
American. Merchant
b. Apr 5, 1865 in Boston, Massachusetts
d. Aug 27, 1957
Source: *WhAm 3*

Fillmore, Millard
American. 13th US President
Succeeded to presidency upon death of Zachary Taylor, 1850-52.
b. Jan 7, 1800 in Locke, New York
d. Mar 8, 1874 in Buffalo, New York
Source: *AmAu&B; AmBi; ApCAB; BiAuS; BiDrAC; BiDrUSE; DcAmB; Drake; EncAB-H; OxAmL; REnAL; TwCBDA; WebAB; WhAm H; WhAmP*

Finch, Jon
English. Actor
b. 1941 in England
Source: *IntMPA 78, 79, 80, 81, 82*

Finch, Peter
[William Mitchell]
English. Actor
Awarded posthumous 1978 Oscar for *Network*.
b. Sep 28, 1916 in London, England
d. Jan 14, 1977 in Beverly Hills, California
Source: *BiDFilm; CmMov; CurBio 72; FilmgC; IntMPA 75, 76, 77; MotPP; MovMk; OxFilm; Who 74; WhoHol A; WhoThe 77; WhoWor 74; WorEFlm*

Finch, Rick
see: K C and the Sunshine Band

Finch, Robert Hutchison
American. Government Official
Political adviser to Richard Nixon; Secretary of HEW, 1969-70.
b. Oct 9, 1925 in Tempe, Arizona
Source: *BiDrUSE; CurBio 69; IntWW 74; PolProf NF; WhoAm 74; WhoAmP 73; WhoGov 72; WhoS&SW 73; WhoWor 74*

Fine, Larry
[The Three Stooges]
American. Comedian, Actor
b. 1911 in Philadelphia, Pennsylvania
d. Jan 24, 1975 in Woodland Hills, California
Source: *MotPP; WhScrn 77*

Fine, Sidney Albert
American. Social Scientist
b. Sep 18, 1915 in New York, New York
Source: *AmM&WS 73S*

Fine, Sylvia
[Mrs. Danny Kaye]
American. Lyricist, Producer
b. Aug 29, 1893 in New York, New York
Source: *AmSCAP 66; InWom; WhoAm 74, 76, 78, 80, 82*

Fine Arts Quartet, The
[Irving Ilmer; Abram Loft; George Sopkin; Leonard Sorkin]
American. Musicians
Source: *NF*

Fineman, Irving
American. Author
b. Apr 9, 1893 in New York, New York
Source: *AmAu&B; AmNov; Au&Wr 71; ConAu 1R, 5R; OxAmL; REnAL; TwCA, SUP; WhNAA; WhoAm 74; WhoWorJ 72; WrDr 76*

Fingers, Johnny
see: Boomtown Rats

Fingers, Rollie (Roland Glen)
American. Baseball Player
Pitcher who holds major league record for games saved, 272, through 1981.
b. Aug 25, 1946 in Steubenville, Ohio
Source: *BaseEn; BioIn 11; WhoAm 82; WhoProB 73*

Fini, Leonor
Italian. Artist
b. Aug 30, 1918 in Buenos Aires, Argentina
Source: *ConArt; IntWW 74, 75, 76, 77, 78; WomArt, A*

Fink, Mike
American. Frontiersman
Life elaborated by legend; facts difficult to discern.
b. 1720 in Pittsburgh, Pennsylvania
d. 1823?
Source: *CnDAL; NewCol 75; OxAmL; REnAL*

Finlay, Frank
English. Actor
b. Aug 6, 1926 in Farnworth, England
Source: *WhoThe 77*

Finlay, Virgil
American. Illustrator
b. 1914 in Rochester, New York
d. Jan 18, 1971
Source: *EncSF; FanAl; ScF&FL 1; WhoSciF*

Finletter, Thomas Knight
American. Lawyer, Ambassador
b. Nov 11, 1893 in Philadelphia, Pennsylvania
d. Apr 24, 1980 in New York, New York
Source: *AmAu&B; CurBio 48, 80; IntWW 74; WhAm 7; Who 74; WhoAm 74; WhoWor 74*

Finley, Charlie (Charles Oscar)
American. Businessman
Insurance company exec., 1945--; owner, Oakland A's baseball club, 1960-80.
b. Feb 22, 1918 in Birmingham, Alabama
Source: *CelR 73; CurBio 74; NewYTBE 72, 73; WhoAm 74, 76, 78, 80, 82; WhoHcky 73; WhoProB 73*

Finley, John Huston
American. Educator, Philanthropist
b. Oct 19, 1863 in Grand Ridge, Illinois
d. Mar 7, 1940
Source: *Alli SUP; AmAu&B; AmBi; ApCAB; BbD; BiD&SB; BiDSA; ChPo, S1; CurBio 40; DcAmAu; DcAmB S2; DcNAA; IndAu 1816; OhA&B; PoIre; REnAL; TwCBDA; WhAm 1, 2*

Finley, Martha
[Martha Farquaharson, pseud.]
American. Author
b. Apr 26, 1828 in Chillicothe, Ohio
d. Jan 30, 1909
Source: *Alli SUP; AmAu; AmAu&B; BiD&SB; BiDSA; CarSB; CnDAL; DcAmAu; DcNAA; IndAu 1816; OhA&B; OxAmL; REnAL; WhoChL*

Finn, Mickey
see: T. Rex

Finnbogadottir, Vigdis
Icelandic. President
Iceland's first female head of state, 1980--.
b. Apr 15, 1930 in Reykjavik, Iceland
Source: *IntWW 81; NewYTBS 82*

Finney, Albert
English. Actor, Motion Picture Director
Starred in *Tom Jones,* 1963; *Murder on the Orient Express,* 1974.
b. May 9, 1936 in Salford, England
Source: *BiDFilm; BiE&WWA; BkPepl; CelR 73; CurBio 63; FilmgC; IntMPA 75, 76, 77, 78, 79, 80, 81, 82; IntWW 74; MotPP; MovMk; NotNAT; OxFilm; PlP&P; Who 74; WhoHol A; WhoWor 74; WorEFlm*

Finney, Charles Grandison
American. Clergyman, Educator
b. Aug 29, 1792 in Warren, Connecticut
d. Aug 16, 1875 in Oberlin, Ohio
Source: *Alli; AmAu&B; AmBi; ApCAB; BiDAmEd; BioIn 8, 10, 11; DcAmAu; DcAmB; DcAmReB; DcNAA; Drake; EncAAH; EncAB-A; McGEWB; NatCAB 2; OhA&B; REnAW; TwCBDA; WebAB; WhAm H*

Finney, Jack, pseud.
[Walter Braden Finney]
American. Author
b. 1911 in Milwaukee, Wisconsin
Source: *Au&Wr 71; ConSFA; WhoSciF*

Firbank, Ronald
English. Author
b. Jan 17, 1886 in London, England
d. May 21, 1926 in Rome, Italy
Source: *AtlBL; CasWL; CnMWL; DcLEL; EncWL; LongCTC; ModBrL, SUP; NewC; OxEng; Pen ENG; RAdv 1; REn; TwCW; WebE&AL; WhoTwCL*

Firestone, Bert
American. Owner of Filly, Genuine Risk
Source: *NF*

Firestone, Harvey Samuel
American. Manufacturer
Founder, president, Firestone Tire and Rubber Co, Akron, OH, 1900-38.
b. Dec 20, 1868 in Columbus, Ohio
d. Feb 7, 1938 in Miami Beach, Florida
Source: *AmBi; DcAmB S2; DcNAA; OhA&B; WebAB; WhAm 1*

Firestone, Harvey Samuel, Jr.
American. Tire Company Executive
Chairman until 1966, Firestone Tire and Rubber Co; oversaw expansion to worldwide firm.
b. Apr 20, 1898 in Chicago, Illinois
d. Jun 1, 1973 in Akron, Ohio
Source: *CelR 73; ConAu 41R; CurBio 44, 73; NewYTBE 73; OhA&B; WhoF&I 74; WhoWor 74*

Firestone, Idabelle Smith
American. Composer
b. Nov 10, 1874 in Minnesota City, Minnesota
d. Jul 7, 1954 in Akron, Ohio
Source: *AmSCAP 66*

Firkusny, Rudolf
American. Musician
b. Feb 11, 1912 in Napajedla, Czechoslovakia
Source: *IntWW 74; NewYTBE 73; WhoAm 74, 76, 78, 80, 82; WhoMus 72; WhoWor 74*

Firpo, Luis Angel
"Wild Bull of Pampas"
Argentine. Boxer
b. Oct 11, 1896 in Buenos Aires, Argentina
d. Aug 7, 1960 in Buenos Aires, Argentina
Source: *WhoBox 74*

Firth, Peter
English. Actor
b. Oct 27, 1953 in Bradford, England
Source: *FilmEn; IntMPA 81, 81; NewYTBS 74; PlP&P A*

Fischer, Alice
American. Actress
b. Jan 16, 1869 in Terre Haute, Indiana
d. Jun 23, 1947 in New York, New York
Source: *NotNAT B; WhThe; WhoStg 1908*

Fischer, Anton Otto
German. Illustrator
b. Feb 23, 1882 in Munich, Germany
d. Mar 26, 1962
Source: *IlsCB 1744, 1946; WhAm 4*

Fischer, Bobby (Robert James)
American. Chess Player
First American to win world class title, beating Boris Spassky, 1972.
b. Mar 4, 1943 in Chicago, Illinois
Source: *ConAu 103; CurBio 63; IntWW 74; NewYTBE 73; WebAB; WhoAm 74, 76, 78, 80, 82; WhoWor 74*

Fischer, Carl
American. Manufacturer, Music Publisher
b. 1849
d. 1923
Source: *BioIn 9*

Fischer, Emil
German. Chemist
b. Oct 9, 1852
d. Jul 15, 1919
Source: *NewCol 75*

Fischer, Irwin
American. Conductor, Composer
b. Jul 5, 1903 in Iowa City, Iowa
Source: *WhoMW 74*

Fischer, John
American. Journalist, Author
b. Apr 27, 1910 in Texahoma, Oklahoma
d. Aug 18, 1978 in New Haven, Connecticut
Source: *AmAu&B; BiDrLUS 70; ConAu 9R, 81; CurBio 53, 78; IntWW 74, 75, 76, 77, 78; IntYB 78; Who 74; WhoAm 74, 76, 78; WhoWor 74, 74; WrDr 80*

Fischer, Louis
American. Author
b. Feb 29, 1896 in Philadelphia, Pennsylvania
d. Jan 15, 1970 in Hackensack, New Jersey
Source: *AmAu&B; Au&Wr 71; ConAu 25R; ConAu P-1; CurBio 40, 70; REn; REnAL; TwCA SUP; WhoWorJ 72*

Fischer-Dieskau, Dietrich
German. Opera Singer
b. May 28, 1925 in Berlin, Germany
Source: *CelR 73; CurBio 67; IntWW 74; NewYTBE 71; Who 74; WhoAm 74, 76, 78, 80, 82; WhoMus 72; WhoWor 74*

Fischetti, John
American. Editor, Cartoonist
b. Sep 27, 1916 in Brooklyn, New York
d. 1978 in New Haven, Connecticut
Source: *ConAu 102; WhoAm 74; WhoWor 74*

Fish, Albert
[Robert Hayden; Frank Howard; John W Pell; Thomas A Sprague, alaises]
"The Moon Maniac"
American. Mass Murderer
Molested 400 children, killed at least six; practiced cannibalism.
b. 1870 in Washington, DC
d. Jan 16, 1936 in Sing Sing, New York
Source: *Blood*

Fish, Hamilton
American. Statesman
b. Aug 3, 1808 in New York, New York
d. Sep 6, 1893 in Garrison, New York
Source: *AmBi; ApCAB; BiAuS; BiDrAC; BiDrUSE; CurBio 41; DcAmB; Drake; EncAB-H; TwCBDA; WebAB; WhAm H; WhAmP*

Fish, Hamilton, III
American. Congressman
b. Dec 7, 1888 in Garrison, New York
Source: *BiDrAC; WhAmP; WhoFtbl 74*

Fish, Robert Lloyd
[Robert L Pike, pseud.]
American. Author
b. Aug 21, 1912 in Cleveland, Ohio
d. Feb 24, 1981 in Trumbull, Connecticut
Source: *Au&Wr 71; EncMys; ConAu 13R, 103; IntAu&W 76, 77*

Fishback, Margaret
American. Poet
b. Mar 10, 1904 in Washington, DC
Source: *AmAu&B; ChPo, S2; CurBio 41; InWom*

Fishbein, Harry J
American. Bridge Player
b. 1898
d. Feb 19, 1976 in New York
Source: *BioIn 10*

Fishbein, Morris
American. Physician, Editor, Author
b. Jul 22, 1889 in Saint Louis, Missouri
d. Sep 27, 1976 in Chicago, Illinois
Source: *AmAu&B; ConAu 5R, 69, 4NR; CurBio 40; St&PR 75; WebAB; WhNAA; WhoAm 74; WhoWor 74; WhoWorJ 72*

Fisher, Avery
Phonograph Designer
b. 1906?
Source: *BioIn 5, 6, 10, 11*

Fisher, "Bud" (Harry Conway)
American. Cartoonist
Created "Mutt and Jeff" comic strip, 1907.
b. Apr 3, 1885 in Chicago, Illinois
d. Sep 7, 1954 in New York, New York
Source: *AmAu&B; DcAmB S5; WebAB; WhAm 3*

Fisher, Carl
American. Insurance Company Executive
b. Nov 21, 1911 in Newkirk, Oklahoma
Source: *BiE&WWA; St&PR 75; WhoAm 74; WhoIns 75; WhoWor 74*

Fisher, Carrie Frances
American. Actress
Daughter of Debbie Reynolds, Eddie Fisher; in *Star Wars*, 1977; *The Empire Strikes Back*, 1980.
b. Oct 21, 1956 in Beverly Hills, California
Source: *BkPepl; IntMPA 82; WhoAm 78, 80, 82; WhoHol A*

Fisher, Dorothy Frances Canfield
American. Author, Essayist
b. Feb 17, 1879 in Lawrence, Kansas
d. Nov 9, 1958 in Arlington, Vermont
Source: *AmAu&B; AmNov; CarSB; Chambr 3; ChPo, S1, S2; CnDAL; ConAmA; ConAmL; HerW; InWom; LongCTC; ModAL; OhA&B; OxAmL; REn; REnAL; TwCA, SUP; WebAB; WhAm 3; WhNAA; WomWWA 14; YABC 1*

Fisher, Eddie (Edwin Jack)
American. Singer
"O, My Papa," 1953 million-selling hit; married to Debbie Reynolds, Elizabeth Taylor, Connie Stevens.
b. Aug 10, 1928 in Philadelphia, Pennsylvania
Source: *CurBio 54; FilmgC; IntMPA 75, 76, 77, 78, 79, 80, 81, 82; WhoAm 74, 76, 78, 80, 82; WhoHol A*

Fisher, Fred
American. Composer
b. Sep 30, 1875 in Cologne, Germany
d. Jan 14, 1942 in New York, New York
Source: *AmPS; AmSCAP 66; BiDAmM; BioIn 11; CmpEPM; NotNAT B*

Fisher, Gail
American. Actress
Played Peggy Fair in TV series "Mannix," 1968-74.
b. Aug 18, 1935 in Orange, New Jersey
Source: *WhoAm 74; WhoBlA 75*

Fisher, Ham(mond Edward)
American. Cartoonist
b. Sep 24, 1900 in Wilkes-Barre, Pennsylvania
d. Dec 27, 1955 in New York, New York
Source: *AmAu&B; DcAmB S5; WhAm 3*

Fisher, Harry
American. Basketball Palyer, Coach
First paid coach at Columbia U, 1907-16; had 109-46 record.
b. Feb 6, 1882 in New York, New York
d. Dec 29, 1967 in New York, New York
Source: *WhoBbl 73*

Fisher, Irving
American. Economist
b. Feb 27, 1867 in Saugerties, New York
d. Apr 29, 1947 in New York, New York
Source: *AmAu&B; AmLY; ApCAB X; BiDAmEd; BioIn 1, 2, 4, 5, 8, 11; DcAmAu; DcAmB S4; LinLib S; McGEWB; ObitOF 79; TwCBDA; WebAB; WhAm 2; WhNAA*

Fisher, John
English. Clergyman, Author
b. 1469 in Beverley, England
d. Jun 22, 1535 in London, England
Source: *BbD; BrAu; CasWL; DcEnL; EvLB*

Fisher, John Arbuthnot
British. Admiral
b. 1841 in Rambodde, Ceylon
d. 1920
Source: *NewCol 75; WhoModH*

Fisher, Mary Frances Kennedy
[Mary Francis Parrish, pseud.]
American. Author
b. Jul 3, 1908 in Albion, Michigan
Source: *BioIn 1, 2, 6, 9, 11; ConAu 77*

Fisher, Max Martin
American. Corporation Executive
b. Jul 15, 1908 in Pittsburgh, Pennsylvania
Source: *BioIn 9; St&PR 75; WhoAm 74, 76, 78, 80, 82; WhoWorJ 72*

Fisher, Morgan
see: Mott (the Hoople)

Fisher, Terence
English. Motion Picture Director
b. 1904 in London, England
d. Jun 18, 1980 in Twickenham, England
Source: *BiDFilm; CmMov; DcFM; FilmgC; IntMPA 75, 76, 77, 78, 79; WorEFlm*

Fisher, Vardis
American. Author
b. Mar 31, 1895 in Annis, Idaho
d. Jul 9, 1968 in Jerome, Idaho
Source: *AmAu&B; AmNov; Au&Wr 71; CnDAL; ConAmA; ConAu 5R, 25R; ConLC 7; CyWA; DcLEL; LongCTC; ModAL; OxAmL; Pen AM; REn; REnAL; TwCA, SUP; WhAm 5; WhNAA; Who 74*

Fisher, Welthy (Blakesley Honsinger)
American. Missionary, Educator
b. Sep 18, 1879 in Rome, New York
d. Dec 16, 1980 in Southbury, Connecticut
Source: *BioIn 6, 7, 8; CurBio 69, 81; ForWC 70; IntAu&W 77; NewYTBS 74; WhoAmW 58, 61, 68, 70, 72*

Fisk, Carlton Ernest
"Pudge"
American. Baseball Player
Catcher, Boston Red Sox, 1971-80; Chicago White Sox, 1980--.
b. Dec 26, 1947 in Bellows Falls, Vermont
Source: *BaseEn; NewYTBE 73; WhoProB 73*

Fisk, James Brown
American. Physicist, Corporation Executive
b. Aug 30, 1910 in West Warwick, Rhode Island
d. Aug 10, 1981 in Elizabethtown, New York
Source: *AmM&WS 76P, 79P; CurBio 59, 81; IntWW 74, 75, 76, 77, 78; IntYB 78, 79; St&PR 75; Who 74; WhoAm 74, 76, 78; WhoF&I 74*

Fisk, Jim (James)
American. Financier
b. Apr 1, 1834 in Bennington, Vermont
d. Jan 7, 1872 in New York, New York
Source: *AmBi; DcAmB; Drake; EncAB-H; WebAB; WhAm H*

Fiske, Jamie
American. Transplant Patient
Received liver transplant Nov 5, 1982 after father pleaded cause nationally.
b. Nov 25, 1980
Source: *NF*

Fiske, John
American. Historian, Philosopher
b. Mar 30, 1842 in Hartford, Connecticut
d. Jul 4, 1901 in Gloucester, Massachusetts
Source: *Alli SUP; AmAu; AmAu&B; AmBi; ApCAB; BbD; BiD&SB; Chambr 3; DcAmAu; DcAmB; DcLEL; DcNAA; EvLB; OxAmL; OxCan; Pen AM; REnAL; TwCBDA; WebAB; WhAm 1*

Fiske, Minnie
American. Actress
b. 1865 in New Orleans, Louisiana
d. Feb 16, 1932
Source: *AmBi; AmWom; BiDSA; DcAmB S1; FamA&A; InWom; NotAW; OxAmL; OxThe; PlP&P; WebAB; WhAm 1; WhScrn 77; WhoHol B; WhoStg 1906, 1908; WomWWA 14*

Fistoulari, Anatole
English. Conductor
b. Aug 20, 1907
Source: *IntWW 74; Who 74; WhoMus 72; WhoWor 74*

Fitch, Aubrey
American. Naval Officer
b. Jan 11, 1884 in Saint Ignace, Michigan
d. May 22, 1976 in Newcastle, Maine
Source: *CurBio 45*

Fitch, Bill (William C)
American. Basketball Coach
b. May 19, 1934 in Cedar Rapids, Iowa
Source: *OfNBA*

Fitch, James Marston
American. Architect, Author
b. May 8, 1909 in Washington, DC
Source: *AmAu&B; BioIn 10; ConAu 89; WhoAm 74, 76*

Fitch, John
American. Inventor
Built steam boat, 1787; paddlewheeler, 1788.
b. Jan 21, 1743 in Hartford, Connecticut
d. Jul 12, 1798 in Bardstown, Kentucky
Source: *Alli, SUP; AmBi; ApCAB; DcAmB; Drake; EncAB-H; TwCBDA; WebAB; WhAm H*

Fitch, (William) Clyde
American. Dramatist
Author, society-oriented dramas *Barbara Frietchie, Nathan Hale.*
b. May 2, 1865 in Elmira, New York
d. Sep 4, 1909 in Chalons-sur-Marne, France
Source: *AmAu&B; AmBi; DcAmB; DcLEL; McGEWD; ModAL; ModWD; NatCAB 13, 15; NotNAT A, B; OxAmL; Pen AM; REnAL; REnWD; WhAm 1*

Fittipaldi, Emerson
Brazilian. Auto Racer
b. 1946 in Sao Paulo, Brazil
Source: *BioIn 9, 10, 11*

Fitts, Dudley
American. Author, Educator
b. Apr 28, 1903 in Boston, Massachusetts
d. Jul 10, 1968
Source: *AmAu&B; ConAu 25R, 93; ModAL; OxAmL; Pen AM; REnAL; TwCA, SUP; WhAm 5*

Fitzgerald, Barry
[William Joseph Shields]
American. Actor
Won 1944 Oscar for *Going My Way.*
b. Mar 10, 1888 in Dublin, Ireland
d. Jan 4, 1961 in Dublin, Ireland
Source: *BiDFilm; CurBio 45, 61; FilmgC; HolP 40; MotPP; MovMk; OxFilm; PlP&P; WhAm 4; WhScrn 74, 77; WhoHol B*

Fitzgerald, Cissy
English. Actress
b. 1874? in England
d. May 5, 1941 in Ovingdean, England
Source: *CurBio 41; InWom; WhScrn 74, 77; WhoHol B*

Fitzgerald, Edward
English. Author, Poet, Translator
b. Mar 31, 1809 in Bradfield, England
d. Jun 14, 1883 in Merton, England
Source: *Alli SUP; AtlBL; BbD; BiD&SB; BrAu 19; CasWL; ChPo, S1, S2; CnE&AP; CrtT 3; CyWA; DcEnA, AP; DcEuL; DcLEL; Drake; EvLB; MouLC 4; NewC; OxEng; Pen ENG; Polre; RComWL; REn; WebE&AL*

Fitzgerald, Ed(ward)
American. Radio Broadcaster
With wife Pegeen broadcast "The Fitzgerald's" radio show for 44 years.
b. 1893 in Troy, New York
d. Mar 22, 1982 in New York, New York
Source: *CurBio 47; NewYTBS 82*

Fitzgerald, Ella
American. Singer
Began career with Chick Webb Orchestra, 1934; has won eight Grammys.
b. Apr 25, 1918 in Newport News, Virginia
Source: *AmSCAP 66; BkPepl; CelR 73; CurBio 56; EncAB-H; InWom; IntWW 74; WebAB; WhoAm 74, 76, 78, 80, 82; WhoBlA 75; WhoMus 72; WhoWor 74*

Fitzgerald, F(rancis) Scott (Key)
American. Author
Wrote *This Side of Paradise,* 1920; *The Great Gatsby,* 1925.
b. Sep 24, 1896 in Saint Paul, Minnesota
d. Dec 21, 1940 in Hollywood, California
Source: *Alli SUP; AmAu&B; AmWr; AtlBL; AuNews 1; BioNews 74; CasWL; Chambr 3; CnDAL; CnMD; CnMWL; ConAmA; ConAmL; CurBio 41; CyWA; DcAmB S2; DcLEL; DcNAA; EncAB-H; EncMys; EncWL; EvLB; FilmgC; LongCTC; ModAL, SUP; OxAmL; OxEng; OxFilm; Pen AM; RAdv 1; RComWL; REn; REnAL; TwCA, SUP; TwCW; WebAB; WebE&AL; WhAm 1; WhNAA; WhoTwCL; WorEFlm*

FitzGerald, Garret
Irish. Former Prime Minister
b. Feb 9, 1926 in Dublin, Ireland
Source: *IntWW 74, 75, 76, 77, 78, 79; Who 74; WhoWor 78; WrDr 80*

Fitzgerald, Geraldine
American. Actress
b. Nov 24, 1914 in Dublin, Ireland
Source: *BiE&WWA; FilmgC; HolP 40; InWom; IntMPA 75, 76, 77, 78, 79, 80, 81, 82; MotPP; MovMk; NewYTBE 71; NotNAT; PlP&P A; ThFT; WhoAm 82; WhoHol A; WhoThe 77*

Fitzgerlad, John Francis
"Honey Fitz"
American. Businessman, Politician
b. Feb 11, 1863 in Boston, Massachusetts
d. Oct 2, 1950 in Boston, Massachusetts
Source: *DcAmB S4; WhAm 3*

Fitzgerald, Pegeen
American. Radio Commentator
b. Nov 24, 1910 in Norcatur, Kansas
Source: *CurBio 47; ForWC 70; InWom; IntMPA 75, 76, 77, 78, 79, 80, 81, 82*

Fitzgerald, Robert Stuart
American. Author, Translator
b. Oct 12, 1910 in Geneva, New York
Source: *AmAu&B; AmM&WS 73P; ConAu 1R, 1NR; ConP 70, 75; DrAP 75; DrAS 74E; ModAL; OxAmL; Pen AM; REnAL; TwCA SUP; WhoAm 74, 76, 78, 80, 82; WrDr 76*

Fitzgerald, Zelda
[Zelda Sayre]
American. Wife of F Scott Fitzgerald
Wrote *Save Me the Waltz,* 1932; also a ballet dancer and painter.
b. Jul 24, 1900 in Montgomery, Alabama
d. Mar 10, 1948 in Asheville, North Carolina
Source: *AmAu&B; AuNews 1*

Fitz-Gibbon, Bernice Bowles
American. Advertising Executive
Source: *BioIn 1, 5, 7, 8*

Fitzgibbon, (Robert Louis) Constantine
American. Author
b. Jun 8, 1919 in Lenox, Massachusetts
Source: *Au&Wr 71; ConAu 1R, 2NR; IntWW 74; WhoAm 82; WhoWor 74; WorAu; WrDr 76*

Fitzpatrick, Daniel R
American. Cartoonist
b. Mar 5, 1891 in Superior, Wisconsin
d. May 18, 1969 in Saint Louis, Missouri
Source: *ConAu 89; CurBio 41, 69; WebBD 80*

Fitzpatrick, Thomas
American. Explorer, Naturalist
One of great mountain men; spent life opening up West.
b. 1799 in County Cavan, Ireland
d. Feb 7, 1854 in Washington, DC
Source: *AmBi; DcAmB; EncAB-H; OxAmL; WebAB; WhAm H*

Fitzroy, James
see: Monmouth, James Scott, Duke

Fitzsimmons, Bob (Robert Prometheus)
English. Boxer
b. Jun 4, 1862 in Helston, England
d. Oct 22, 1917 in Chicago, Illinois
Source: *AuBYP; DcAmB; DcNAA; Film 1; WebAB; WhoBox 74*

Fitzsimmons, "Cotton" (Lowell)
American. Basketball Coach
b. Oct 7, 1931 in Hannibal, Missouri
Source: *WhoBbl 73*

Fitzsimmons, Frank
American. Labor Union Official
President, Teamsters, 1971-81.
b. Apr 7, 1908 in Jeannette, Pennsylvania
d. May 6, 1981 in San Diego, California
Source: *BiDAmLL; BioIn 9, 10, 11; CelR 73; CurBio 71, 81; IntWW 74, 75, 76, 77, 78; NewYTBE 71; PolProf J; PolProf NF; WhoAm 74, 78, 80; WhoE 79; WhoLab 76; WhoS&SW 73; WhoWor 78*

Fitzsimmons, James E
"Sunny Jim"
American. Horse Trainer
Best known horse trainer of all time; had 2,275 winners totaling over $13 million.
b. Jul 23, 1874 in Brooklyn, New York
d. Mar 11, 1966 in Miami, Florida
Source: *BioIn 4, 5, 6, 7, 10*

Fix, Paul
American. Actor
b. Mar 13, 1902 in Dobbs Ferry, New York
Source: *FilmgC; IntMPA 75, 76, 77, 78, 79, 80, 81, 82; MovMk; Vers B; WhoHol A*

Fixx, James Fuller
American. Author, Editor
b. Apr 23, 1932 in New York, New York
Source: *BioIn 11; ConAu 73; WhoAm 74, 76, 78, 80, 82*

Fizdale, Robert
American. Musician
b. 1920
Source: *BioIn 5, 6, 7*

Flack, Roberta
American. Singer
Grammys for "The First Time Ever I Saw Your Face," 1972; "Killing Me Softly," 1973.
b. Feb 10, 1940 in Black Mountain, North Carolina
Source: *BkPepl; CurBio 73; HerW; WhoAm 74, 76, 78, 80, 82; WhoBlA 75*

Flagg, Ernest
American. Architect
b. Feb 6, 1857 in Brooklyn, New York
d. Apr 10, 1947 in New York, New York
Source: *DcAmB S4; DcNAA; WhAm 2*

Flagg, Fannie
American. Comedienne, Actress
Source: *ForWC 70; WhoHol A*

Flagg, James Montgomery
American. Artist, Author
b. Jun 18, 1877 in Pelham Manor, New York
d. May 27, 1960 in New York, New York
Source: *AmAu&B; ChPo, S2; CurBio 40, 60; Film 1; OxAmL; REnAL; WebAB; WhAm 4; WhScrn 77*

Flagler, Henry Morrison
American. Business Executive
b. Jan 2, 1830 in Hopewell, New York
d. May 20, 1913 in West Palm Beach, Florida
Source: *AmBi; DcAmB; EncAB-H; WebAB; WhAm 1*

Flagstad, Kirsten
Norwegian. Opera Singer
b. Jul 12, 1895 in Oslo, Norway
d. Dec 7, 1962 in Oslo, Norway
Source: *CurBio 47, 63; FilmgC; InWom; REn; WhAm 4; WhScrn 74, 77; WhoHol B*

Flaherty, Robert Joseph
American. Motion Picture Director
b. Feb 16, 1884 in Iron Mountain, Michigan
d. Jul 23, 1951 in Dummerston, Vermont
Source: *AmAu&B; BiDFilm; CurBio 49, 51; DcAmB S5; DcFM; EncAB-H; FilmgC; MovMk; OxCan; OxFilm; REn; WhAm 3; WomWMM; WorEFlm*

Flammarion, Camille
French. Astronomer
Popularized study of astronomy; wrote *The Atmosphere,* 1872.
b. Feb 25, 1842 in Montigny-le-Roi, France
d. 1925
Source: *BbD; BiD&SB; BiDPara; DcEuL*

Flamsteed, John
English. Astronomer
b. Aug 19, 1646 in Denby, England
d. Dec 31, 1719
Source: *Alli; McGEWB*

Flanagan, Edward Joseph, Father
American. Roman Catholic Priest
Founded Father Flanagan's Home for Boys, 1917; became Boys Town, 1922.
b. Jul 13, 1886 in Roscommon, Ireland
d. May 15, 1948 in Berlin, Germany
Source: *DcAmB S4; WebAB; WhAm 2; WhScrn 74, 77; WhoHol B*

Flanagan, Mike (Michael Kendall)
American. Baseball Player
Pitcher, Baltimore Orioles, 1975--; won Cy Young Award, 1979.
b. Dec 16, 1951 in Manchester, New Hampshire
Source: *BaseEn; WhoAm 82*

Flanders, Michael
English. Actor, Author
b. Mar 1, 1922 in London, England
d. Apr 14, 1975 in Wales
Source: *Au&Wr 71; AuBYP; BiE&WWA; ChPo, S1, S2; ConAu 5R, 57, 4NR; CurBio 70; IntWW 74; OxThe; WhAm 6; WhScrn 77; Who 74; WhoMus 72; WhoWor 74*

Flanders, Ralph Edward
American. Senator
b. Sep 28, 1880 in Barnet, Vermont
d. Feb 19, 1970 in Springfield, Vermont
Source: *ConAu P-1; CurBio 48, 70; NewYTBE 70*

Flanders and Swann
see: Flanders, Michael; Swann, Donald Ibrahim

Flannagan, John Bernard
American. Sculptor
b. Apr 7, 1895 in Fargo, North Dakota
d. Jan 6, 1942 in New York, New York
Source: *CurBio 42; DcAmB S3; WebAB*

Flanner, Janet
[Genet, pseud.]
American. Journalist, Author
b. Mar 13, 1892 in Indianapolis, Indiana
d. Jan 7, 1978 in New York, New York
Source: *AmAu&B; ConAu 65, 81; CurBio 43; IndAu 1917; OxAmL; REnAL; WhoAm 74; WhoWor 74; WorAu; WrDr 76*

Flannery, Susan
American. Actress
b. Jul 31, 1943 in Jersey City, New Jersey
Source: *WhoHol A*

Flatt, Lester Raymond
[Flatt and Scruggs]
American. Musician, Singer
Teamed with Earl Scruggs for 25 years; appeared on TV series "The Beverly Hillbillies."
b. Jun 28, 1914 in Overton County, Tennessee
Source: *EncFCWM 69*

Flatt and Scruggs
see: Flatt, Lester; Scruggs, Earl

Flaubert, Gustave
French. Author
b. Dec 12, 1821 in Rouen, France
d. May 8, 1880 in Croisset, France
Source: *AtlBL; BbD; BiD&SB; CasWL; ClDMEL; CyWA; DcBiA; DcEuL; EuAu; EvEuW; NewC; OxEng; OxFr; Pen EUR; RComWL; REn*

Flavin, Martin Archer
American. Author
b. Nov 2, 1883 in San Francisco, California
d. Dec 27, 1967 in Carmel, California
Source: *AmAu&B; AmNov; CnMD; ConAu 5R, 25R; DcLEL; McGEWD; ModWD; OxAmL; REnAL; TwCA, SUP*

Flaxman, John
English. Artist
b. Jul 6, 1755 in York, England
d. Dec 7, 1826 in London, England
Source: *Alli; AtlBL; BiDLA; BkIE; ChPo*

Fleeson, Doris
American. Journalist
b. May 20, 1901 in Sterling, Kansas
d. Aug 1, 1970 in Washington, DC
Source: *ConAu 93; CurBio 59, 70; NewYTBE 70; WhoAmW 74*

Fleetwood Mac
[Lindsey Buckingham; Mick Fleetwood; Christine McVie; John McVie;Stevie Nicks; Bob Welch; Robert Weston]
English. Rock Group
Album *Rumours,* 1977, second biggest selling album of all time.
Source: *EncPR&S; IlEncRk; RkOn*

Fleetwood, Mick
[Fleetwood Mac]
English. Rock Musician
b. Jun 24, 1942 in Cornwall, England
Source: *BioIn 11; BkPepl; WhoAm 80, 82*

Fleischer, Max
American. Cartoonist
b. Jul 19, 1883 in Vienna, Austria
d. Sep 11, 1972 in Los Angeles, California
Source: *DcFM; FilmgC; NewYTBE 72; OxFilm; WorEFlm*

Fleischer, Nat(haniel S)
American. Boxing Editor
b. 1887
d. Jun 25, 1972 in New York, New York
Source: *ConAu 37R; NewYTBE 72; WhoBox 74*

Fleisher, Leon
American. Musician
b. Jul 23, 1928 in San Francisco, California
Source: *BioIn 10; CurBio 71; NewYTBE 70; WhoAm 82; WhoE 74*

Fleischmann, Charles Louis
Yeast Manufacturer
b. Nov 3, 1834 in Budapest, Hungary
d. Dec 10, 1897
Source: *DcAmB; WhAm H*

Fleming, Sir Alexander
Scottish. Bacteriologist
Discovered penicillin by chance, 1928; won Nobel Prize, 1945.
b. Aug 6, 1881 in Lochfield, Scotland
d. Mar 11, 1955 in London, England
Source: *CurBio 44, 55; LongCTC; WhAm 3*

Fleming, Ian
British. Actor
b. Sep 10, 1888 in Melbourne, Australia
d. Jan 1, 1969 in London, England
Source: *FilmgC; WhScrn 74, 77; WhoHol B*

Fleming, Ian Lancaster
English. Author
b. May 28, 1908 in London, England
d. Aug 12, 1964 in Canterbury, England
Source: *AuBYP; ConAu 5R; ConLC 3; CurBio 64; EncMys; FilmgC; LongCTC; NewC; Pen ENG; REn; SmATA 9; TwCW; WhAm 4; Who 74; WorAu*

Fleming, Joan Margaret
English. Author
b. Mar 27, 1908 in Horwich, England
d. Nov 15, 1980 in England
Source: *AnObit 1980; ConAu 81, 102; TwCCr&M; WrDr 80*

Fleming, John Ambrose
British. Physicist
Leader in development of electric light in England.
b. Nov 29, 1849
d. Apr 19, 1945 in London, England
Source: *CurBio 45; NewCol 75*

Fleming, Peggy Gale
American. Figure Skater
Won gold medal, 1968 Olympics.
b. Jul 27, 1948 in San Jose, California
Source: *CelR 73; CurBio 68; HerW; InWom; WhoAm 82*

Fleming, Rhonda
[Marilyn Lewis]
American. Actress
b. Aug 10, 1923 in Los Angeles, California
Source: *BiDFilm; FilmgC; InWom; IntMPA 75, 76, 77, 78, 79, 80, 81, 82; MotPP; MovMk; WhoAm 82; WhoHol A; WorEFlm*

Fleming, Victor
American. Motion Picture Director
b. 1883 in Pasadena, California
d. Jan 6, 1949 in Cottonwood, Arizona
Source: *BiDFilm; DcFM; FilmgC; MovMk; OxFilm; TwYS; WhAm 2; WorEFlm*

Flemming, Arthur Sherwood
American. Government Official
Chairman, US Commission on Civil Rights, 1974-81.
b. Jun 12, 1905 in Kingston, New York
Source: *AmM&WS 73S; BiDrUSE; CurBio 60; IntWW 74; NewYTBE 71; WhoAm 82; WhoAmP 73; WhoGov 72*

Flemming, Bill (William Norman)
American. Sportscaster
b. Sep 3, 1926 in Chicago, Illinois
Source: *NewYTET; WhoAm 82*

Flesch, Karl
Hungarian. Musician, Teacher
b. Oct 9, 1873 in Moson, Hungary
d. Nov 15, 1944 in Lausanne, Switzerland
Source: *CurBio 45*

Flesch, Rudolf
American. Author
b. May 8, 1911 in Vienna, Austria
Source: *ConAu 9R; WhoAm 74; WhoE 74*

Fletcher, Arthur A
American. Government Official
b. Dec 22, 1924 in Phoenix, Arizona
Source: *CurBio 71; NewYTBE 71; WhoAmP 73; WhoE 74; WhoGov 72*

Fletcher, Bramwell
English. Author
b. Feb 20, 1906 in Bradford, England
Source: *BiE&WWA; NotNAT; WhoHol A; WhoThe 77*

Fletcher, Glenn Robert
American. Football Player
b. Dec 5, 1956 in Thibodaux, Louisiana
Source: *BioIn 12*

Fletcher, Grant
American. Conductor, Composer
b. Oct 25, 1913 in Hartsburg, Illinois
Source: *AmSCAP 66*

Fletcher, John
English. Author, Dramatist
b. Dec 20, 1579 in Rye, England
d. Aug 1625 in London, England
Source: *AtlBL; BbD; BiD&SB; BrAu; CasWL; ChPo, S1; CnE&AP; CnThe; CroE&S; CrtT 1; CyWA; DcEnA; DcEnL; DcEuL; DcLEL; EvLB; McGEWD; MouLC 1; NewC; OxEng; OxThe; Pen ENG; REn; REnWD; WebE&AL*

Fletcher, John Gould
American. Poet, Critic
b. Jan 3, 1886 in Little Rock, Arkansas
d. May 20, 1950 in Little Rock, Arkansas
Source: *AmAu&B; AnCL; CasWL; Chambr 3; CnDAL; ConAmA; ConAmL; DcAmB S4; DcLEL; EncWL*

Fletcher, Louise
American. Actress
Won 1975 Oscar for *One Flew Over the Cuckoo's Nest.*
b. 1936 in Birmingham, Alabama
Source: *IntMPA 77; WhoAm 78, 80, 82; WhoHol A*

Fleury, Andre Hercule de
French. Cardinal, Statesman
b. 1653
d. 1743
Source: *NewCol 75; OxFr*

Flexner, Abraham
American. Educator, Author
b. Nov 13, 1866 in Louisville, Kentucky
d. Sep 21, 1959 in Falls Church, Virginia
Source: *AmAu&B; CurBio 41, 59; REnAL; TwCA, SUP*

Flick, Elmer Harrison
American. Baseball Player
Outfielder, 1898-1910; Hall of Fame, 1963.
b. Jan 11, 1876 in Bedford, Ohio
d. Jan 9, 1971 in Bedford, Ohio
Source: *BaseEn; BioIn 6, 7, 9; WhoProB 73*

Flick, Friedrich
German. Industrialist
b. 1883
d. Jul 20, 1972 in Lake Constance, Switzerland
Source: *BioIn 4, 6, 8, 9, 11; NewYTBE 72*

Flinders, Matthew
English. Explorer, Hydrographer
Known for surveying, charting coasts of Australia, Tasmania.
b. Mar 16, 1774 in Donnington, England
d. Jul 19, 1814 in England
Source: *Alli; CelCen; DcBiPP; LinLib L, S; McGEWB; NewCol 75; OxShips*

Flippen, Jay C
American. Actor
b. 1900 in Little Rock, Arkansas
d. Feb 3, 1971 in Hollywood, California
Source: *CmMov; FilmgC; MotPP; MovMk; NewYTBE 71; Vers B; WhScrn 74, 77; WhoHol B*

Flipper, Henry Ossian
American. Soldier
Source: *Alli SUP*

A Flock of Seagulls
[Frank Maudsley; Paul Reynolds; Ali Score; Mike Score]
British. New Wave Band
Hit single, "I Ran," 1982.
Source: *NF*

Flood, Curt(is Charles)
American. Baseball Player
Fought baseball reserve clause, 1970; lawsuit led to new rules on free agency.
b. Jan 18, 1938 in Houston, Texas
Source: *AfroAA; BaseEn; InB&W 80; NewYTBE 70; NewYTBS 81; WhoProB 73*

Flood, Daniel J
American. Politician
b. Nov 26, 1904 in Hazelton, Pennsylvania
Source: *AmAu&B; CngDr 74; WhoAm 74; WhoAmP 73; WhoE 74; WhoGov 72*

Flora, James Royer
American. Author, Illustrator
b. Jan 25, 1914 in Bellefontaine, Ohio
Source: *ConAu 5R, 3NR; IlsBYP; IlsCB 1946; SmATA 1; ThrBJA*

Florey, Howard Walter
British. Scientist, Engineer, Physician
b. Sep 24, 1898 in Adelaide, Australia
d. Feb 21, 1968 in London, England
Source: *CurBio 44, 68; McGEWB; WhAm 5*

Flotow, Friedrich von, Baron
German. Composer
b. Apr 26, 1812 in Teutendorf, Germany
d. Jan 24, 1883 in Darmstadt, Germany
Source: *AtlBL*

Floyd, Carlisle
American. Composer
b. Jun 11, 1926 in Latta, South Carolina
Source: *AmSCAP 66; CurBio 60; WhoAm 74, 76, 78, 80, 82; WhoS&SW 73; WhoWor 74*

Floyd, "Pretty Boy" (Charles Arthur)
American. Criminal
"Public enemy no. 1," 1933; killed in gun battle with FBI's Melvin Purvis.
b. 1904 in Akins, Oklahoma
d. Oct 22, 1934 in East Liverpool, Ohio
Source: *BioIn 8, 9; Blood; DrInt; EncACr*

Floyd, Raymond
American. Golfer
Won Masters tournament, named player of year, 1976.
b. Sep 14, 1942 in Fort Bragg, North Carolina
Source: *NewYTBS 76; WhoAm 74, 76, 78, 80, 82; WhoGolf*

Floyd, William
American. Statesman
Signed Declaration of Independence from NY.
b. Dec 17, 1734 in Brookhaven, New York
d. Aug 4, 1821 in Westernville, New York
Source: *AmBi; ApCAB; BiAuS; BiDrAC; DcAmB; DcNAA; Drake; TwCBDA; WhAm H; WhAmP; WhNAA*

Fluckey, Eugene Bennett
American. Naval Officer
b. Oct 5, 1913 in Washington, DC
Source: *BioIn 7; WhoAm 74*

Flur, Wolfgang
see: Kraftwerk

Flying Burrito Brothers, The
[Chris Ethridge; Chris Hillman; "Sneaky Pete" Kleinow; Gram Parsons]
American. Rock Group
Source: *BiDAmM; ConMuA 80; IlEncCM; IlEncRk; LilREn 78; WhoRock 81*

Flynn, Edward Joseph
American. Politician
b. Sep 22, 1891 in Bronx, New York
d. Aug 18, 1953
Source: *CurBio 40, 53; WhAm 3*

Flynn, Elizabeth Gurley
American. Political Leader
b. Aug 7, 1890 in Concord, New Hampshire
d. Sep 5, 1964 in Moscow, U.S.S.R.
Source: *CurBio 61, 64; InWom*

Flynn, Errol
American. Actor
Starred in *Captain Blood,* 1936; *They Died with Their Boots On,* 1942.
b. Jun 20, 1909 in Tasmania, New Zealand
d. Oct 14, 1959 in Vancouver, BC
Source: *AmAu&B; BiDFilm; CmMov; FilmgC; MotPP; MovMk; OxFilm; WhAm 3; WhScrn 74, 77; WhoHol B; WorEFlm*

Flynn, F M
American. Newspaper Publisher
b. 1903
d. Nov 15, 1974 in Pelham, New York
Source: *NewYTBS 74*

Flynn, Joe
American. Actor
Played Captain Binghamton in TV series "McHale's Navy," 1962-66.
b. Nov 8, 1925 in Youngstown, Ohio
d. Jul 19, 1974 in Los Angeles, California
Source: *NewYTBS 74; WhScrn 77; WhoHol B*

Flynn, Sean
American. Photographer, Actor
Son of Errol Flynn; missing on assignment in Vietnam.
b. 1941
d. 1970?
Source: *BioIn 6, 8, 9, 10; MotPP*

Flynt, Larry Claxton
American. Magazine Publisher
Publishes *Hustler* magazine, 1974--; paralyzed in assassination attempt.
b. Nov 1, 1942 in Magoffin County, Kentucky
Source: *AuNews 2; WhoAm 80, 82*

Foch, Ferdinand, Marshal
French. Military Leader
b. Oct 2, 1851 in Tarbes, France
d. Mar 20, 1929 in Paris, France
Source: *McGEWB; OxFr; REn*

Foch, Nina
American. Actress
b. Apr 20, 1924 in Leiden, Netherlands
Source: *BiE&WWA; FilmgC; HolP 40; InWom; IntMPA 75, 76, 77, 78, 79, 80, 81, 82; MotPP; MovMk; NotNAT; WhoAm 74, 76, 78, 80, 82; WhoHol A; WhoThe 77; WhoWor 74*

Focke, Heinrich
German. Aeronautical Engineer, Designer
b. 1890
d. Feb 25, 1979 in Bremen, Germany (West)
Source: *BioIn 11; NewYTBS 79; WebBD 80*

Fodor, Eugene
American. Editor, Publisher
Began publishing *Fodor's Travel Guides,* 1949.
b. Oct 5, 1905 in Leva, Hungary
Source: *AmAu&B; BioNews 74; ConAu 21R; NewYTBS 74; WhoAm 74, 76, 78, 80, 82; WhoWor 74*

Fodor, Eugene Nicholas
American. Musician
b. Mar 5, 1950 in Denver, Colorado
Source: *Baker 78; BioIn 10; CurBio 76; WhoAm 80, 82*

Foerster, Friedrich Wilhelm
German. Author, Educator
b. Jun 2, 1869 in Berlin, Germany
d. Jan 9, 1966 in Kilchberg, Germany (West)
Source: *BioIn 1, 6, 7; CurBio 62, 66*

Foerster, Norman
American. Author, Educator
b. Apr 14, 1887 in Pittsburgh, Pennsylvania
Source: *AmAu&B; ChPo; CnDAL; ConAmA; ConAu 5R; DcLEL; OxAmL; Pen AM; REnAL; TwCA, SUP; WhNAA*

Fogarty, Anne
American. Fashion Designer
b. Feb 2, 1926 in Pittsburgh, Pennsylvania
d. Jan 15, 1980 in New York, New York
Source: *CurBio 58; InWom; WhoAm 74; WorFshn*

Fogazzaro, Antonio
Italian. Author, Poet
b. Mar 25, 1842 in Vicenza, Italy
d. Mar 7, 1911 in Vicenza, Italy
Source: *BbD; BiD&SB; CasWL; ClDMEL; CyWA; DcBiA; EuAu; EvEuW; LongCTC; McGEWD; ModRL; OxEng; Pen EUR; REn; TwCA, SUP*

Fogelberg, Dan(iel Grayling)
American. Composer, Singer
First hit song "Part of the Plan," 1975; recent hit "Leader of the Band," 1982.
b. Aug 13, 1951 in Peoria, Illinois
Source: *IlEncRk; RkOn; WhoAm 76, 78, 80, 82*

Foghat
[Roger Earl; David Peverett; Rod Price; Anthony Stevens]
British. Rock Group
Source: *IlEncRk; RkOn*

Fokine, Michel
Russian. Choreographer
b. Apr 26, 1880 in Saint Petersburg, Russia
d. Aug 22, 1942 in Yonkers, New York
Source: *BioNews 74; CurBio 42; DcAmB S3; WhAm 2*

Fokker, Anthony Herman Gerard
American. Aircraft Designer
b. Apr 6, 1890 in Kediri, Indonesia
d. Dec 23, 1939 in Alpine, New Jersey
Source: *AmBi; WhAm 1*

Foley, "Red" (Clyde Julian)
American. Singer
Founding father of country music; starred in "Ozark Mountain Jubilee," 1955-61.
b. Jun 17, 1910 in Bluelick, Kentucky
d. Sep 19, 1968 in Fort Wayne, Indiana
Source: *EncFCWM 69; WhScrn 74, 77*

Folger, Henry Clay
American. Industrialist
b. 1857
d. 1930
Source: *DcNAA; NewCol 75; REnAL*

Foligno, Mike (Michael Anthony)
Canadian. Hockey Player
b. Jan 29, 1959 in Sudbury, ON
Source: *HocReg*

Follen, Charles Theodore
German. Author, Abolitionist
b. Sep 4, 1796 in Giessen, Germany
d. Jan 13, 1840
Source: *AmAu&B; CyAL 1; DcAmAu; DcNAA; OxAmL*

Follett, Ken(neth Martin)
[Myles Symon, pseud.]
Welsh. Author
b. Jun 5, 1949 in Cardiff, Wales
Source: *ConAu 81; WhoAm 82; WhoSpyF*

Folon, Jean-Michel
Belgian. Artist
b. Mar 1, 1934 in Uccle, Belgium
Source: *BioIn 8, 11; CurBio 81*

Folsom, Frank M
American. Businessman, Philanthropist
b. May 14, 1894 in Sprague, Washington
d. Jan 22, 1970 in Scarsdale, New York
Source: *CurBio 49, 70; NewYTBE 70*

Folsom, Marion Bayard
American. Government Official
b. Nov 23, 1894 in McRue, Georgia
d. Sep 28, 1976 in Rochester, New York
Source: *BiDrUSE; ConAu 17R; CurBio 50; IntWW 74; WhoAm 74*

Fonck, Rene
French. World War I Flying Ace
Credited with shooting down 75 enemy planes during WW I.
b. 1894
d. Jun 18, 1953 in Paris, France
Source: *WebBD 80*

Fonda, Henry Jaynes
American. Actor
Won 1982 Oscar for last film *On Golden Pond.*
b. May 16, 1905 in Grand Island, Nebraska
d. Aug 12, 1982 in Los Angeles, California
Source: *BiDFilm; BiE&WWA; BkPepl; CelR 73; CmMov; CurBio 48, 74, 82; FilmgC; IntMPA 75, 76, 77, 78, 79, 80, 81, 82; IntWW 74, 75, 76, 77, 78; MotPP; MovMk; NewYTBS 82; NotNAT; OxFilm; PlP&P; WebAB; WhoAm 74, 76, 78, 80, 82; WhoHol A; WhoThe 72, 77, 81; WhoWor 74, 78; WorEFlm*

Fonda, Jane
[Mrs. Tom Hayden]
American. Actress, Political Activist
Oscars for *Klute,* 1971; *Coming Home,* 1978;author *Jane Fonda's Work-Out Book,* 1982.
b. Dec 21, 1937 in New York, New York
Source: *BiDFilm; BiE&WWA; BkPepl; CelR 73; CurBio 64; FilmgC; IntMPA 77, 78, 79, 80, 81, 82; IntWW 74; MotPP; MovMk; NewYTBE 71; NewYTBS 74; NotNAT; OxFilm; WhoAm 74, 76, 78, 80, 82; WhoAmW 77; WhoHol A; WhoThe 77; WomWMM; WorEFlm*

Fonda, Peter
American. Actor
Wrote, co-produced, and starred in *Easy Rider,* 1969.
b. Feb 23, 1939 in New York, New York
Source: *BiDFilm; BkPepl; CelR 73; FilmgC; IntMPA 75, 76, 77, 78, 79, 80, 81, 82; MotPP; MovMk; OxFilm; WhoAm 74, 76, 78, 80, 82; WhoHol A*

Fonda, Shirlee
American. 5th Wife of Henry Fonda
b. 1931? in Aurora, Illinois
Source: *BioIn 10*

Fong, Hiram
American. Attorney, Senator
b. Oct 1, 1907 in Honolulu, Hawaii
Source: *BiDrAC; CelR 73; CngDr 74; CurBio 60; IntWW 74; WhoAm 74, 76, 78, 80, 82; WhoAmP 73; WhoGov 72; WhoWest 74; WhoWor 74*

Fontaine, Frank
"Crazy Guggenheim"
American. Entertainer
b. 1920 in Haverhill, Massachusetts
d. Aug 4, 1978 in Spokane, Washington
Source: *IntMPA 75, 76, 77; WhoHol A*

Fontaine, Jean de la
see: LaFontaine, Jean de

Fontaine, Joan
[Joan de Havilland]
American. Actress
Won 1941 Oscar for *Suspicion;* sister of Olivia de Haviland.
b. Oct 22, 1917 in Tokyo, Japan
Source: *BiDFilm; BiE&WWA; CelR 73; ConAu 81; CurBio 44; FilmgC; ForWC 70; InWom; IntMPA 75, 76, 77, 78, 79, 80, 81, 82; MotPP; MovMk; OxFilm; ThFT; WhoAm 74, 76, 78, 80, 82; WhoE 74; WhoHol A; WomWMM; WorEFlm*

Fontane, Theodor
German. Author
b. Dec 30, 1819 in Neu-Ruppin, Germany
d. Sep 20, 1898 in Berlin, Germany
Source: *CasWL; ClDMEL; CyWA; EuAu; EvEuW; OxGer; Pen; REn*

Fontanne, Lynn
American. Actress
b. Dec 6, 1887 in London, England
Source: *BiE&WWA; CelR 73; CurBio 41; FamA&A; FilmgC; InWom; NotNAT; OxThe; PlP&P; ThFT; WebAB; Who 74; WhoAm 74, 76, 78, 80, 82; WhoAmW 77; WhoHol A; WhoThe 77; WhoWor 74*

Fonteyn, Dame Margot
[Mrs. Roberto de Arias; Margaret Hookham]
English. Ballerina
President, Royal Academy of Dancing, 1954--; first dancer named Dame Commander of British Empire.
b. May 18, 1919 in Reigate, England
Source: *CelR 73; CurBio 49, 72; InWom; IntWW 74; NewYTBE 72; NewYTBS 74; Who 74; WhoAm 82; WhoThe 77; WhoWor 74*

Foot, Michael
English. Journalist, Poltician
b. Jul 13, 1913 in Plymouth, England
Source: *CurBio 50; IntWW 74; Who 74; WhoWor 74; WrDr 76*

Foote, Andrew Hull
American. Military Leader
b. Sep 12, 1806 in New Haven, Connecticut
d. Jun 26, 1863 in New Haven, Connecticut
Source: *Alli; AmBi; ApCAB; DcAmAu; DcAmB; DcNAA; Drake; TwCBDA; WebAB; WhAm H*

Forain, Jean-Louis
French. Artist
b. 1852 in Reims, France
d. 1931 in Paris, France
Source: *McGDA; OxFr*

Foran, Dick
American. Actor
b. Jun 18, 1910 in Flemington, New Jersey
d. Aug 10, 1979
Source: *FilmgC; IntMPA 75, 76, 77; WhoHol A*

Forbes, Bertie Charles
Scottish. Journalist
b. May 14, 1880 in Aberdeen, Scotland
d. May 6, 1954 in New York, New York
Source: *BioIn 7, 8; CurBio 50, 54; WebBD 80*

Forbes, Bryan
English. Screenwriter, Film Director
Directed *The Stepford Wives,* 1974; *International Velvet,* 1978.
b. Jul 22, 1926 in London, England
Source: *BiDFilm; CmMov; ConAu 69; ConDr 73; IntMPA 75, 76, 77, 78, 79, 80, 81, 82; IntWW 74; MovMk; NewYTBE 71; OxFilm; Who 74; WhoAm 82; WhoHol A; WhoThe 77; WhoWor 74; WorEFlm; WrDr 76*

Forbes, Esther
American. Author
b. Jun 28, 1894? in Westboro, Massachusetts
d. Aug 12, 1967 in Worcester, Massachusetts
Source: *AmAu&B; AmNov; AnCL; AuBYP; ChPo S2; ConAu 25R; ConAu P-1; CyWA; DcLEL; InWom; MorJA; Newb 1922; OxAmL; REn; REnAL; SmATA 2; TwCA, SUP*

Forbes, John
British. Army Officer
b. 1710 in Dunfermline, Scotland
d. Mar 11, 1759 in Philadelphia, Pennsylvania
Source: *AmBi; ApCAB; DcAmB; Drake; WhAm H*

Forbes, Kathryn, pseud.
[Kathryn Anderson McLean]
American. Author
b. Mar 20, 1909 in San Francisco, California
d. May 15, 1966 in San Francisco, California
Source: *AmAu&B; ConAu 21R, 25R; ConAu P-2; CurBio 44, 66; InWom; REn; REnAL; SmATA 9*

Forbes, Malcolm Stevenson
American. Publisher, Editor
Publisher, *Forbes* magazine, 1957--; wrote *The Sayings of Chairman Malcolm,* 1978.
b. Aug 19, 1919 in New York, New York
Source: *ConAu 69; CurBio 75; St&PR 75; WhoAm 74, 76, 78, 80, 82; WhoF&I 74; WhoWor 74*

Forbes, Ralph
[Ralph Taylor]
English. Actor
b. Sep 30, 1896 in London, England
d. Mar 31, 1951 in New York, New York
Source: *Film 2; MotPP; TwYS; WhScrn 74, 77; WhThe*

Forbes-Robertson, Sir Johnston
English. Actor, Manager
b. 1853 in London, England
d. Nov 6, 1937 in Saint Margaret's, England
Source: *NewCol 75; WhScrn 77*

Ford, Alexander
Polish. Motion Picture Director
b. Jan 24, 1908
Source: *FilmgC; IntWW 74*

Ford, Anne McDonnell
American. First Wife of Henry Ford II
Source: *BioIn 5*

Ford, Arthur A
American. Medium, Spiritualist
b. 1896
d. 1971
Source: *NewYTBE 71*

Ford, Benson
American. Auto Executive
b. Jul 20, 1919 in Detroit, Michigan
d. Jul 27, 1978 in Cheboygan, Michigan
Source: *CurBio 52, 78; IntWW 74, 75, 76, 77, 78; NewYTBS 78; Ward 77; WhoAm 74, 76, 78; WhoF&I 74*

Ford, Betty (Elizabeth Bloomer)
American. Wife of Gerald Ford
Dancer with Martha Graham Concert Group, 1939-41.
b. Apr 8, 1918 in Chicago, Illinois
Source: *BioNews 74; BkPepl; NewYTBE 73; NewYTBS 74; WhoAm 82; WhoAmW 77*

Ford, Bob (Robert Newton)
"The Dirty Little Coward"
American. Jesse James' Assassin
b. 1860
d. Jun 24, 1892 in Creede, Colorado
Source: *Blood*

Ford, Charlotte
American. Socialite, Designer
Daughter of Henry Ford II.
b. 1941
Source: *BioIn 10*

Ford, Christina
[Maria Christina Vettore Austin Ford]
American. Second Wife of Henry Ford II
b. 1927
Source: *NewYTBE 73*

Ford, Corey
[John Riddell, psued.]
American. Humorist, Author
b. Apr 29, 1902 in New York, New York
d. Jul 27, 1969 in Hanover, New Hampshire
Source: *AmAu&B; ConAu 25R; EncMys; REnAL; WhAm 5; WhNAA*

Ford, Doug
American. Golfer
b. Aug 6, 1922 in West Haven, Connecticut
Source: *BioIn 5, 10*

Ford, Edsel Bryant
American. Auto Executive
Son of Henry Ford; president, Ford Motor Co., 1919-43; the Edsel was named for him.
b. Nov 6, 1893 in Detroit, Michigan
d. May 26, 1943 in Grosse Pointe, Michigan
Source: *DcAmB S3; WhAm 2*

Ford, Edsel Bryant, II
American. Auto Executive
Son of Henry Ford II; has worked for Ford Motor Co. since 1969.
b. 1949
Source: *BioIn 10; BioNews 74; BusPN*

Ford, Eileen
American. Model Agency Executive
b. Mar 25, 1922 in New York, New York
Source: *CurBio 71; WhoAm 74*

Ford, Eleanor Clay
American. Mother of Henry Ford II
b. 1896
d. Oct 19, 1976 in Detroit, Michigan
Source: *InWom*

Ford, Ford Madox
[Ford Madox Hueffer]
English. Author, Poet
b. Dec 17, 1873 in Merton, England
d. Jun 26, 1939 in Deauville, France
Source: *AtlBL; CasWL; Chambr 3; ChPo, S1; CnMWL; CyWA; DcLEL; EncWL; EvLB; LongCTC; ModBrL, SUP; NewC; OxEng; Pen ENG; RAdv 1; REn; REnAL; TwCA, SUP; TwCW; WebE&AL; WhAm HA, 3; WhoTwCL*

Ford, Gerald Rudolph
[Gerald King]
American. 38th US President
President after Nixon resignation, 1974-76; pardoned Nixon, 1974.
b. Jul 14, 1913 in Omaha, Nebraska
Source: *BiDrAC; BioNews 74; BkPepl; CelR 73; CngDr 74; CurBio 61; IntWW 74; NewCol 75; NewYTBE 73; NewYTBS 74; WhoAm 74, 76, 78, 80, 82; WhoAmP 73; WhoFtbl 74; WhoGov 72; WhoMW 74; WhoWor 74*

Ford, Glenn
[Gwyllyn Samuel Newton Ford]
American. Actor
Starred in *Pocketful of Miracles,* 1961, *Superman,* 1978; married to Eleanor Powell, 1943-59.
b. May 1, 1916 in Quebec, Canada
Source: *BiDFilm; CelR 73; CmMov; CurBio 59; FilmgC; IntMPA 76, 76, 77, 78, 79, 80, 81, 82; MotPP; MovMk; OxFilm; WhoAm 74, 76, 78, 80, 82; WhoHol A; WorEFlm*

Ford, Harrison
American. Actor
b. Jul 13, 1942 in Chicago, Illinois
Source: *BioIn 11; IntMPA 82; WhoAm 78, 80, 82*

Ford, Henry
American. Auto Manufacturer
Ford Model T sold over 15 million; signed first union shop contract in auto industry, 1941.
b. Jul 30, 1863 in Greenfield, Michigan
d. Apr 7, 1947 in Dearborn, Michigan
Source: *AmAu&B; CurBio 44, 47; DcAmB S4; EncAB-H; NewCol 75; REn; WebAB; WhAm 2*

Ford, Henry, II
American. Auto Manufacturer
Grandson of Henry Ford; chairman, chief executive, Ford Motor Co., 1960-80.
b. Sep 4, 1917 in Detroit, Michigan
Source: *BusPN; CelR 73; CurBio 46; EncAB-H; IntWW 74; St&PR 75; Ward 77; Who 74; WhoAm 74, 76, 78, 80, 82; WhoF&I 74*

Ford, Jack (John)
American. Son of Gerald Ford
b. 1952?
Source: *BioIn 11*

Ford, John
English. Dramatist
b. 1586 in Ilsington, England
d. 1640?
Source: *Alli; AtlBL; BbD; BiD&SB; BrAu; CasWL; ChPo; CnE&AP; CnThe; CroE&S; CrtT 1; CyWA; DcEnA; DcEnL; EvLB; McGEWD; MouLC 1; NewC; Pen ENG; REn; REnWD; WebE&AL*

Ford, John
[Sean O'Feeney]
American. Motion Picture Director
b. Feb 1, 1895 in Cape Elizabeth, Maine
d. Aug 31, 1973 in Palm Desert, California
Source: *CmMov; ConAu 45; DcFM; EncAB-H; Film 1; FilmgC; MovMk; WebAB; WhAm 6; WhScrn 77; WhoAm 74*

Ford, Kathleen DuRoss
[Kathleen King]
American. 3rd Wife of Henry Ford II
b. Feb 11, 1940 in Belding, Michigan
Source: *BioIn 10, 11, 12*

Ford, Mary
[Les Paul and Mary Ford]
American. Singer, Musician
b. 1924?
d. Sep 30, 1977 in Los Angeles, California
Source: *InWom*

Ford, Mary Litogot
American. Mother of Henry Ford
b. 1839
d. 1876
Source: *BioIn 10*

Ford, Michael
American. Son of Gerald Ford
b. 1950?
Source: *BioIn 10*

Ford, Paul
American. Actor
b. Nov 2, 1901 in Baltimore, Maryland
d. Apr 12, 1976 in Mineola, New York
Source: *BiE&WWA; FilmgC; MotPP; MovMk; NewYTBS 76; NotNAT B; WhAm 7; WhoAm 74, 76; WhoE 74; WhoWor 74*

Ford, Paul Leicester
American. Author, Historian
b. Mar 23, 1865 in Brooklyn, New York
d. May 8, 1902 in New York, New York
Source: *AmAu; AmAu&B; BiD&SB; Chambr 3; CnDAL; DcAmAu; OxAmL; REn; REnAL; WebAB; WhAm 1*

Ford, Phil
[Ford and Hines]
American. Comedian
b. 1902 in Portland, Maine
Source: *Film 1*

Ford, Phil Jackson
American. Basketball Player
b. Feb 9, 1956 in Rocky Mount, North Carolina
Source: *OfNBA*

Ford, Russ(ell William)
Canadian. Baseball Player
b. Apr 25, 1883 in Brandon, MB
d. Jan 24, 1960 in Rockingham, North Carolina
Source: *BaseEn; BioIn 5; WhoProB 73*

Ford, Ruth
American. Actress, Dramatist
b. Jul 1920 in Hazelhurst, Mississippi
Source: *BiE&WWA; CelR 73; InWom; NotNAT; WhoHol A; WhoThe 77*

Ford, "Senator" (Ed)
American. Comedian
b. 1887
d. 1970 in Greenport, New York
Source: *NewYTBE 70*

Ford, Steven
American. Son of Gerald Ford, Actor
b. 1956
Source: *BioIn 10*

Ford, Susan Elizabeth
[Mrs. Charles Vance]
American. Daughter of Gerald Ford
b. 1957
Source: *BioIn 10, 11*

Ford, "Tennessee Ernie" (Ernest J)
American. Singer
Best known song "16 Tons."
b. Feb 13, 1919 in Bristol, Tennessee
Source: *AmSCAP 66; CurBio 58; EncFCWM 69; IntMPA 75, 76, 77, 78, 79, 80, 81, 82; WhoAm 74, 76, 78, 80, 82*

Ford, Wallace
[Samule Jones Grundy]
English. Actor
b. Feb 12, 1899 in Batton, England
d. Jun 11, 1966 in Woodland Hills, California
Source: *BiE&WWA; FilmEn; FilmgC; MovMk; Vers B; WhScrn 74, 77; WhoHol B*

Ford, Wendell Hampton
American. Senator, Former Governor
b. Sep 8, 1924 in Owensboro, Kentucky
Source: *BioNews 75; WhoAm 74, 76, 78, 80, 82; WhoAmP 73; WhoGov 72; WhoS&SW 73*

Ford, "Whitey" (Edward Charles)
"The Chairman of the Board"
American. Baseball Player
Pitcher, NY Yankees, 1950-67; won 10 World Series games; Hall of Fame, 1974.
b. Oct 21, 1928 in New York, New York
Source: *BaseEn; CurBio 62; NewYTBS 74; WhoAm 82; WhoProB 73*

Ford, William Clay
American. Automobile, Football Executive
Brother of Henry Ford II; owner, Detroit Lions football club, 1964--.
b. Mar 14, 1925 in Detroit, Michigan
Source: *BioIn 1, 3, 11; WhoAm 82; WhoFtbl 74*

Ford and Hines
see: Ford, Phil; Hines, Mimi

Foreigner
[Dennis Elliott; Ed Gagliardi; Lou Gramm; Al Greenwood; Mick Jones; Ian McDonald; Rick Wills]
English. Rock Group
Source: *ConMuA 80; IlEncRk; LilREn 78; RkOn 2; WhoRock 81*

Foreman, Carl
American. Motion Picture Producer, Author
b. Jul 23, 1914 in Chicago, Illinois
Source: *BioIn 4, 8, 11; IntMPA 78, 79, 80, 81, 82; WhoAm 78, 80, 82*

Foreman, Carol Lee Tucker
American. Government Official
b. May 3, 1938 in Little Rock, Arkansas
Source: *BioIn 11; WhoAm 78, 80, 82*

Foreman, "Chuck" (Walter Eugene)
American. Football Player
Running back, Minnesota, 1973-80, New England, 1980--; rookie of the year, 1973.
b. Oct 26, 1950 in Frederick, Missouri
Source: *FootReg; WhoAm 78, 80, 82; WhoBlA 77; WhoFtbl 74*

Foreman, Earl
American. Sports Commissioner
Source: *WhoAm 74*

Foreman, George
American. Boxer
Won gold medal, 1968 Olympics; professional heavyweight champ, 1973-74.
b. Jan 10, 1949 in Marshall, Texas
Source: *CelR 73; CurBio 74; NewYTBE 73; NewYTBS 74; WhoAm 74; WhoBlA 75; WhoBox 74*

Foreman, Percy
American. Lawyer
b. Jun 21, 1902 in Polk County, Texas
Source: *WhoS&SW 73*

Forest, Lee de
see: DeForest, Lee

Forester, Cecil Scott
English. Author
Wrote *Horatio Hornblower* series; *The African Queen,* 1935.
b. Aug 27, 1899 in Cairo, Egypt
d. Apr 2, 1966 in Fullerton, California
Source: *AmAu&B; ConAu 25R, 73; CyWA; DcLEL; EncMys; EvLB; LongCTC; MnBBF; ModBrL; NewC; RAdv 1; REn; REnAL; SmATA 13; TwCA, SUP; TwCW; WebE&AL; WhAm 4; WhoChL*

Forman, James Douglas
American. Lawyer, Author
b. Nov 12, 1932 in Mineola, New York
Source: *AuBYP; ConAu 9R; SmATA 8; ThrBJA*

Forman, Milos
Czech. Motion Picture Director
b. Feb 18, 1932 in Caslav, Czechoslovakia
Source: *BiDFilm; CurBio 71; DcFM; FilmgC; IntMPA 77, 78, 79, 80, 81, 82; IntWW 74; MovMk; NewYTBE 71; OxFilm; WhoAm 82; WhoWor 74; WorEFlm*

Forrest, Arthur
Actor
b. 1859 in Bayreuth, Germany
d. May 16, 1933 in New York, New York
Source: *Film 2; NewYTET; NotNAT B; WhoHol B*

Forrest, Edwin
American. Actor
b. Mar 9, 1806 in Philadelphia, Pennsylvania
d. Dec 12, 1872 in Philadelphia, Pennsylvania
Source: *AmBi; ApCAB; DcAmB; Drake; EncAB-H; FamA&A; OxAmL; OxThe; PlP&P; REnAL; TwCBDA; WebAB; WhAm H*

Forrest, Helen
American. Singer
b. 1919?
Source: *BioIn 6, 11; WhoHol A*

Forrest, Nathan Bedford
American. General
b. Jul 13, 1821 in Chapel Hill, Tennessee
d. Oct 29, 1877 in Memphis, Tennessee
Source: *AmBi; ApCAB; BiDConf; DcAmB; TwCBDA; WebAB; WhAm H*

Forrest, Sally
[Katherine Sally Feeney]
American. Actress
b. May 28, 1928 in San Diego, California
Source: *FilmEn; FilmgC; MotPP; WhoHol A*

Forrest, Steve
American. Actor
b. Sep 29, 1925 in Huntsville, Texas
Source: *FilmgC; IntMPA 75, 76, 77, 78, 79, 80, 81, 82; WhoAm 82; WhoHol A*

Forrestal, James Vincent
American. Public Official
b. Feb 15, 1892 in Beacon, New York
d. May 22, 1949 in Bethesda, Maryland
Source: *AmAu&B; BiDrUSE; CurBio 42, 48, 49; DcAmB S4; EncAB-H; WebAB; WhAm 2*

Forrester, Maureen
Canadian. Opera Singer
b. Jul 25, 1931 in Montreal, PQ
Source: *CanWW 82; CreCan 2; CurBio 62; InWom; WhoAm 82; WhoMus 72*

Forssmann, Werner Theodor Otto
German. Surgeon
b. Aug 29, 1904 in Berlin, Germany
d. Jun 1, 1979 in Schopfheim, Germany (West)
Source: *CurBio 57, 79; IntWW 74, 75, 76; NewYTBS 79; Who 74; WhoWor 74, 76*

Forster, E(dward) M(organ)
English. Author
Wrote *A Room with a View,* 1908, *A Passage to India,* 1924.
b. Jan 1, 1879 in London, England
d. Jun 7, 1970 in Coventry, England
Source: *AtlBL; CasWL; Chambr 3; ChPo S2; CnMWL; ConAu 25R; ConAu P-1; ConLC 1, 2, 3, 4, 9, 10, 13, 15; CyWA; DcLEL; EncWL; EvLB; LongCTC; ModBrL, SUP; NewC; OxEng; Pen ENG; RAdv 1; RComWL; REn; TwCA, SUP; TwCW; WebE&AL; WhAm 5; WhoTwCL*

Forster, Robert
American. Actor
b. Jul 13, 1942 in Rochester, New York
Source: *FilmgC; IntMPA 75, 76, 77, 78, 79, 80, 81, 82; NewYTBE 72; WhoHol A*

Forster, William Edward
English. Statesman
b. 1818 in Bradpole, England
d. 1886 in London, England
Source: *NewCol 75*

Forsyth, Frederick
English. Author
b. 1938 in Ashford, England
Source: *ConAu 85; ConLC 2, 5; WhoAm 74; WrDr 76*

Forsythe, John
American. Actor
Plays Blake Carrington on TV series "Dynasty," 1981--.
b. Jan 29, 1918 in Penns Grove, New Jersey
Source: *BiE&WWA; CelR 73; CurBio 73; FilmgC; IntMPA 75, 76, 77, 78, 79, 80, 81, 82; MotPP; MovMk; NotNAT; WhoAm 74, 76, 78, 80, 82; WhoHol A; WhoThe 77; WhoWest 74*

Fort, Charles Hoy
American. Author
b. 1874 in Albany, New York
d. May 3, 1932 in Bronx, New York
Source: *AmAu&B; DcNAA; OxAmL; REnAL; TwCA*

Fortas, Abe
American. Supreme Court Justice
b. Jun 19, 1910 in Memphis, Tennessee
d. Apr 5, 1982 in Washington, DC
Source: *CurBio 66, 82; DrAS 74P; IntWW 74, 75, 76, 77, 78; LinLib L, S; NewYTBS 82; PolProf NF; WebAB; WhoAm 76, 78, 80, 82; WhoAmL 78, 79; WhoAmP 73, 75, 77, 79; WhoS&SW 73*

Forten, James
American. Reformer, Sail Maker
b. Sep 2, 1766
d. Mar 4, 1842
Source: *WhAm H*

Fortmann, Daniel John
American. Football Player
b. Apr 11, 1916 in Pearl River, New York
Source: *BioIn 6, 8; WhoFtbl 74*

Fortune, Nick
see: Buckinghams, The

Fortune, Timothy Thomas
American. Author, Editor
b. Oct 3, 1856 in Marianna, Florida
d. Jun 2, 1928
Source: *AmAu&B; BlkAW; DcNAA; EncAB-H*

Fortuny
[Mariano Fortuny y Madrazo]
Spanish. Fashion Designer
b. 1871 in Granada, Spain
d. 1949
Source: *WhoFash; WorFshn*

Foscolo, (Niccolo) Ugo
Italian. Poet, Patriot
b. 1778 in Zante, Greece
d. Sep 10, 1827 in London, England
Source: *CasWL; EuAu; EvEuW; McGEWD; Pen; REn*

Fosdick, Harry Emerson
American. Clergyman
b. May 24, 1878 in Buffalo, New York
d. Oct 5, 1969 in Bronxville, New York
Source: *AmAu&B; AuBYP; ConAu 25R; CurBio 40, 69; REnAL; TwCA SUP; WebAB; WhNAA*

Fosdick, Raymond Blaine
American. Author, Lawyer
b. Jun 9, 1883 in Buffalo, New York
d. Jul 18, 1972 in Newtown, Connecticut
Source: *AmAu&B; AmLY; ConAu 37R; CurBio 45, 72*

Foss, Joseph Jacob
American. Pilot
b. Apr 17, 1915 in Sioux Falls, South Dakota
Source: *CurBio 55; WhoAmP 73*

Foss, Lukas
German. Composer, Conductor
b. Aug 15, 1922 in Berlin, Germany
Source: *AmSCAP 66; CurBio 66; DcCM; WhoAm 74, 76, 78, 80, 82; WhoE 74; WhoMus 72; WhoWor 74*

Fosse, Bob
American. Choreographer, Director
Won Oscar, 1972, for *Cabaret;* directed *All that Jazz,* 1979.
b. Jun 23, 1927 in Chicago, Illinois
Source: *BiDFilm; BiE&WWA; BkPepl; CelR 73; CmMov; CurBio 72; EncMT; FilmgC; IntMPA 77, 78, 79, 80, 81, 82; MovMk; NotNAT; OxFilm; WhoAm 74, 76, 78, 80, 82; WhoThe 77; WhoWor 74; WorEFlm*

Foster, George Arthur
American. Baseball Player
b. Dec 1, 1949 in Tuscaloosa, Alabama
Source: *BaseEn; BioIn 11; WhoAm 78, 80, 82; WhoBlA 75, 77*

Foster, Hal (Harold Rudolf)
American. Cartoonist
Created "Prince Valiant" comic strip.
b. Aug 16, 1892 in Halifax, NS
d. Jul 25, 1982 in Spring Hill, Florida
Source: *LinLib L; NewYTBS 82; WhoAm 78; WhoAmA 73, 76, 78*

Foster, "Jodie" (Alicia Christian)
American. Actress
Starred in *Taxi Driver,* 1976, *Foxes,* 1980; student at Yale U.
b. Nov 19, 1962 in Los Angeles, California
Source: *BkPepl; CurBio 81; IntMPA 77, 78, 79, 80, 81, 82; NewYTBS 76; WhoAm 78, 80, 82; WhoAmW 79; WhoHol A*

Foster, Joseph C
American. President of Foster Grant Co.
b. Oct 30, 1904 in Providence, Rhode Island
d. Nov 10, 1971 in New York, New York
Source: *BioIn 9, 11; WhAm 6*

Foster, Norman
American. Actor, Director, Producer
b. Dec 13, 1903 in Richmond, Indiana
d. Jul 7, 1976
Source: *BiDFilm; Film 2; FilmgC; MovMk; NewYTET; WhAm 7; WhoAm 76, 78; WhoHol A; WhoThe 72; WorEFlm*

Foster, Paul
American. Dramatist
b. Oct 15, 1931 in Penns Grove, New Jersey
Source: *Au&Wr 71; ConAu 21R; ConDr 73; WhoAm 74; WhoE 74; WhoThe 77; WrDr 76*

Foster, Phil
American. Actor, Comedian
b. Mar 29, 1914 in Brooklyn, New York
Source: *WhoAm 78; WhoHol A*

Foster, "Pops" (George Murphy)
American. Jazz Musician
b. May 19, 1892 in McCall, Louisiana
d. Oct 30, 1969 in San Francisco, California
Source: *WhoJazz 72*

Foster, Preston
American. Actor
b. Aug 24, 1900 in Ocean City, New Jersey
d. Jul 14, 1970 in La Jolla, California
Source: *AmSCAP 66; FilmgC; HolP 30; MotPP; MovMk; NewYTBE 70; WhScrn 74, 77; WhoHol B*

Foster, Stephen Collins
American. Composer, Author
Best known songs "Oh Susannah," 1848, "My Old Kentucky Home," 1853.
b. Jul 4, 1826 in Pittsburgh, Pennsylvania
d. Jul 13, 1864 in New York, New York
Source: *AmAu; AmAu&B; AmBi; ApCAB; AtlBL; BbD; BiD&SB; Chambr 3; ChPo, S1, S2; DcAmAu; DcAmB; DcLEL; DcNAA; EvLB; OxAmL; PoIre; REn; REnAL; TwCBDA; WebAB; WhAm H*

Foster, Susanna
American. Singer, Actress
b. 1924 in Chicago, Illinois
Source: *FilmgC; HolP 40; MotPP; MovMk; WhoHol A*

Foster, William Zebulon
American. Labor Leader, Marxist
b. Feb 25, 1881 in Taunton, Massachusetts
d. Sep 1, 1961 in Moscow, U.S.S.R.
Source: *AmAu&B; CurBio 45, 61; WebAB; WhAm 4*

Foucault, Jean Bernard
French. Physicist
Invented gyroscope, 1852; known for research on speed of light.
b. Sep 18, 1819
d. Feb 11, 1868
Source: *NewCol 75*

Foucault, Michel
French. Author, Philosopher
b. Oct 15, 1926 in Poitiers, France
Source: *BioIn 8; WorAu 1970*

Fouche, Joseph
French. Revolutionary
b. 1759
d. 1820 in Trieste, Italy
Source: *NewCol 75; OxFr; REn*

Fountain, Pete(r Dewey)
American. Jazz Musician
Plays clarinet; member Lawrence Welk Orchestra, 1957-60.
b. Jul 3, 1930 in New Orleans, Louisiana
Source: *WhoAm 74, 76, 78, 80, 82; WhoS&SW 73*

Fouquet, Jean
French. Artist
b. 1420 in Tours, France
d. 1480 in Tours, France
Source: *AtlBL; OxFr; REn*

Fouquet, Nicolas
French. Statesman
b. 1615
d. Mar 23, 1680
Source: *NewCol 75; OxFr; REn*

Fouquier-Tinville, Antoine Quentin
French. Lawyer
Revolutionary tribunal prosecutor; Marie Antoinette was one of his victims.
b. 1746
d. May 8, 1795
Source: *BioIn 2; DcBiPP; Dis&D; OxFr; REn*

Four Chaplains
[George L Fox; Alexander Goode; Clark V Poling; John P Washington]
American. WW II Heroes
Source: *BioIn 3, 4, 5, 7*

Four Lads, The
[James Arnold; Frank Busseri; Connie Codarini; Bernard Toorish]
Canadian. Music Group
Source: *AmPS A, B; RkOn; WhoRock 81*

Four Horsemen of Notre Dame, The
[James Crowley; Elmer Layden; Don Miller; Harry Stuhldreher]
American. Football Players
Source: *NF*

Four Musketeers, The
[Jean Borotra; Jacques Brugnon; Henri Coclet; (Jean-)Rene Lacoste]
French. Tennis Players
Source: *NF*

Four Seasons, The
[Tommy DeVito; Bob Gaudio; Nick Massi; Frankie Valli]
American. Vocal Group
Have sold over 80 million records.
Source: *EncPR&S; IlEncRk; RkOn; Rk100*

Four Tops
[Renaldo Benson; Abdul Fakir; Lawrence Payton; Levi Stubbs]
American. Vocal Group
Source: *BiDAmM; EncPR&S; RkOn*

Fourier, Francois Marie Charles
French. Social Philosopher
b. Apr 7, 1772 in Besancon, France
d. Oct 8, 1837 in Paris, France
Source: *BbD; BiD&SB; CasWL; DcEuL; EuAu; NewC*

Fourier, Jean Baptiste
French. Physicist
b. Mar 21, 1768
d. May 16, 1830
Source: *BiD&SB*

Fourment, Helena
Belgian. Model, Wife of Peter Rubens
b. 1614
Source: *InWom*

Fournier, Henri Alban
see: Alain-Fournier, pseud.

Fournier, Pierre
French. Musician
b. Jun 24, 1906 in Paris, France
Source: *IntWW 74; Who 74; WhoMus 72; WhoWor 74*

Fouts, Dan(iel Francis)
American. Football Player
Quarterback, San Diego Chargers, 1973--.
b. Jun 10, 1951 in San Francisco, California
Source: *BioIn 12; FootReg; WhoAm 82*

Fowler, Gene
American. Journalist, Author
b. Mar 8, 1890 in Denver, Colorado
d. Jul 2, 1960 in Los Angeles, California
Source: *AmAu&B; ConAu 5NR; CurBio 44, 60; REn; REnAL; TwCA, SUP; WhAm 4*

Fowler, Henry Watson
English. Lexicographer, Author
b. 1858
d. Dec 27, 1933 in London, England
Source: *DcLEL; EvLB; NewC; REn; TwCA, SUP*

Fowler, Lydia Folger
American. Pioneer, Author
b. 1822
d. 1879
Source: *BioIn 9; DcAmAu; DcNAA*

Fowles, John
English. Author
b. Mar 31, 1926 in Essex, England
Source: *Au&Wr 71; CelR 73; ConAu 5R; ConLC 1, 2, 3, 4, 6, 9, 10, 15; ConNov 72, 76; EncWL; IntWW 74; ModBrL SUP; NewC; SmATA 22; TwCW; WebE&AL; WhoAm 82; WhoWor 74; WorAu; WrDr 76*

Fowlie, Wallace
American. Educator, Author
b. Nov 8, 1908 in Brookline, Massachusetts
Source: *AmAu&B; BiE&WWA; ConAu 5R; DrAS 74F; ModAL; TwCA SUP; WhoAm 74, 76, 78, 80, 82; WhoS&SW 73*

Fox, Carol
American. Impresario, Opera Producer
b. Jun 15, 1926 in Chicago, Illinois
d. Jul 21, 1981 in Chicago, Illinois
Source: *BioIn 6, 9, 11; CurBio 78, 81; NewYTBS 81; WhoAm 74, 76, 78, 80; WhoAmW 58, 64, 66, 68, 70, 72, 79; WhoMW 74, 76, 78; WhoOp 76; WhoWor 74*

Fox, Charles James
British. Statesman
b. Jan 24, 1749 in London, England
d. Sep 13, 1806 in Chiswick, England
Source: *Alli; BbD; CasWL; ChPo S1, S2; EvLB; NewC; REn*

Fox, Edward
English. Actor
b. Apr 13, 1937 in London, England
Source: *FilmEn; FilmgC; IntMPA 82; MovMk; WhoHol A*

Fox, Fontaine Talbot, Jr.
American. Illustrator, Cartoonist
b. Mar 3, 1884 in Louisville, Kentucky
d. Aug 10, 1964 in Greenwich, Connecticut
Source: *AmAu&B; ChPo; ConAu 89; WhAm 4*

Fox, George
English. Religious Leader
Founded Society of Friends, the Quakers, 1671.
b. Jul 1624 in Leicester, England
d. Jan 13, 1691 in Sussex, England
Source: *Alli; ApCAB; BbD; BiD&SB; BrAu; Chambr 1; DcEuL; DcLEL; EvLB; NewC; OxAmL; OxEng; REn*

Fox, James
English. Actor
b. 1939 in London, England
Source: *FilmgC; IntMPA 75, 76, 77, 78, 79, 80, 81, 82; MovMk*

Fox, John W, Jr.
American. Author
b. Dec 16, 1863 in Stoney Pointe, Kentucky
d. Jul 8, 1919
Source: *AmAu&B; BbD; BiD&SB; BiDSA; CarSB; CnDAL; ConAmL; DcAmAu; DcBiA; DcLEL; DcNAA; EvLB; OxAmL; REn; REnAL; TwCA, SUP; TwCW; WhAm 1*

Fox, Kate
American. Spiritualist
b. 1839 in Bath, NB
d. 1894
Source: *InWom*

Fox, Margaret
American. Spiritualist
Toured US, England with act "Rochester Rapping"; exposed as fake, 1888.
b. Oct 7, 1833 in Bath, NB
d. Mar 8, 1893 in Brooklyn, New York
Source: *Alli SUP; ApCAB; DcAmB; DcNAA; InWom; NotAW; OxAmL; WebAB; WhAm H*

Fox, "Nellie" (Jacob Nelson)
American. Baseball Player
Infielder, 1947-65; went 98 straight games without striking out, 1958.
b. Dec 25, 1927 in Saint Thomas, Pennsylvania
d. Dec 1, 1975 in Baltimore, Maryland
Source: *BaseEn; CurBio 60, 76; WhoProB 73*

Fox, Sonny
American. Author
b. Jun 17, 1925 in Brooklyn, New York
Source: *ConAu 41R*

Fox, Terry (Terrance Stanley)
Canadian. Runner, Cancer Victim
After losing leg to cancer began marathon run across Canada to raise money for research; never completed, but raised $24 million.
b. Jul 28, 1958 in Winnipeg, MB
d. Jun 28, 1981 in New Westminster, BC
Source: *AnObit 1981; NewYTBS 81*

Fox, Uffa
British. Yachtsman, Designer, Author
b. Jan 15, 1898
d. Oct 26, 1972
Source: *ConAu 37R; NewYTBE 72*

Fox, Virgil Keel
American. Musician
b. May 3, 1912 in Princeton, Illinois
d. Oct 25, 1980 in West Palm Beach, Florida
Source: *CurBio 64; NewYTBS 74; WhoAm 74; WhoMus 72; WhoWor 74*

Foxworth, Robert
American. Actor
Plays Chase Gioberti on TV series "Falcon Crest," 1981--.
b. Nov 1, 1941 in Houston, Texas
Source: *IntMPA 77, 78, 79, 80, 81, 82*

Foxx, Jimmy (James Emory)
"The Beast"; "Double X"
American. Baseball Player
Infielder, 1925-44; won AL triple crown, 1933; Hall of Fame, 1951.
b. Oct 22, 1907 in Sudlersville, Maryland
d. Jul 21, 1967 in Miami, Florida
Source: *BaseEn; WebAB; WhoProB 73*

Foxx, Redd
[John Elroy Sanford]
American. Comedian, Actor
Starred as Fred Sanford in TV series "Sanford and Son," 1972-77, 1980.
b. Dec 9, 1922 in Saint Louis, Missouri
Source: *BioNews 74; BkPepl; ConAu 89; CurBio 72; IntMPA 82; NewYTBE 72; WhoAm 74, 76, 78, 80, 82; WhoBlA 75; WhoHol A*

Foy, Eddie
[Edward Fitzgerald]
American. Actor
b. Mar 9, 1856 in New York, New York
d. Feb 16, 1928 in Kansas City, Missouri
Source: *DcAmB; DcNAA; EncMT; Film 1; FilmgC; OxThe; WebAB; WhAm 1; WhScrn 74, 77; WhoHol B*

Foy, Eddie, Jr.
American. Actor, Dancer
b. Feb 4, 1905 in New Rochelle, New York
Source: *BiE&WWA; EncMT; NotNAT; WhoHol A; WhoThe 77*

Foyle, Christina
English. Bookstore Executive
Managing director, W & G Foyle, Ltd., 1963--.
b. Jan 30, 1911 in London, England
Source: *IntWW 74, 75, 76, 77, 78, 79, 80, 81, 82; Who 74; WhoWor 74*

Foyle, Gilbert Samuel
English. Bookstore Executive
Founded W & G Foyle, Ltd. bookstore in London with brother William.
b. Mar 9, 1886 in London, England
d. Oct 28, 1971
Source: *CurBio 54, 72*

Foyt, A(nthony) J(oseph, Jr.)
American. Automobile Racer
Winner, Indianapolis 500, 1961, 1964, 1967, 1977.
b. Jan 16, 1935 in Houston, Texas
Source: *BusPN; CelR 73; CurBio 67; WebAB; WhoAm 74, 76, 78, 80, 82*

Fra Angelico
see: Angelico, Fra

Fracastoro, Gerolamo
Italian. Physician
b. 1478 in Verona, Italy
d. Aug 8, 1553 in Verona, Italy
Source: *CasWL; DcEuL; REn*

Fracci, Carla
Italian. Ballerina
b. Aug 20, 1936 in Milan, Italy
Source: *CurBio 75; WhoAmW 74; WhoWor 74*

Fradon, Dana
American. Cartoonist
b. Apr 14, 1922 in Chicago, Illinois
Source: *WhoAm 78, 80, 82; WhoAmA 76, 78*

Fraenkel, Heinrich
Journalist, Author
b. Sep 28, 1897 in Germany
Source: *ConAu 17R; Who 74; WrDr 76*

Fragonard, Jean Honore
French. Artist, Engraver
b. Apr 5, 1732 in Grasse, France
d. Aug 22, 1806 in Grasse, France
Source: *AtlBL; OxFr; REn*

Frailberg, Selma
American. Child Psychoanalyst
Wrote *The Magic Years.*
b. 1919 in Detroit, Michigan
d. Dec 19, 1981 in San Francisco, California
Source: *NewYTBS 81*

Frampton, Peter
[Humble Pie]
American. Singer, Songwriter
Album *Frampton Comes Alive!* 1976, sold over 12 million copies.
b. Apr 22, 1950 in Beckenham, England
Source: *BkPepl; EncPR&S; IlEncRk; RkOn; WhoAm 82*

Franca, Celia
English. Ballerina, Choreographer
Founded National Ballet of Canada, Toronto, 1951.
b. Jun 25, 1921 in London, England
Source: *CurBio 56; WhoAm 74, 76, 78, 80, 82; WhoAmW 74; WhoWor 74*

Francaix, Jean
French. Composer, Musician
b. May 23, 1912 in Le Mans, France
Source: *NewEOp 71; OxMus*

France, Anatole, pseud.
[Jacques Anatole Thibault]
French. Author, Critic, Poet
Wrote *Penguin Island,* 1908; won Nobel Prize, 1921.
b. Apr 16, 1844 in Paris, France
d. Oct 12, 1924 in Tours, France
Source: *AtlBL; BbD; BiD&SB; CasWL; ClDMEL; CyWA; DcBiA; DcEuL; EncWL; EvEuW; LongCTC; ModRL; NewC; OxEng; OxFr; Pen EUR; RComWL; REn; TwCA, SUP; TwCW; WhoTwCL*

France, Harry Clinton
American. Financial Writer, Lecturer
b. Jul 17, 1890 in Richmondville, New York
d. Jan 18, 1972
Source: *WhAm 5*

France, Pierre Mendes
see: Mendes-France, Pierre

Francesca da Rimini
Italian. Literary Subject, Noblewoman
d. 1285
Source: *InWom; NewC; REn*

Francescatti, Zino Rene
French. Musician
b. Aug 9, 1902 in Marseilles, France
Source: *CurBio 47; IntWW 74; WhoAm 74, 76, 78, 80, 82; WhoMus 72; WhoWor 74*

Francesco de Medici
see: Medici, Francesco de

Franchi, Sergio
Italian. Singer
Source: *BioIn 6, 7; WhoHol A*

Francine, Anne
American. Actress
b. 1917 in Atlantic City, New Jersey
Source: *BiE&WWA; NotNAT; WhoHol A*

Franciosa, Anthony
[Anthony Papaleo]
American. Actor
b. Oct 25, 1928 in New York, New York
Source: *BiE&WWA; BioIn 10; IntMPA 82; WhoAm 74, 76, 78, 80, 82; WhoWor 74*

Francis I
French. King
b. 1494
d. 1547
Source: *BioIn 10; NewCol 75*

Francis, Anne
American. Actress
b. Sep 16, 1930 in Ossining, New York
Source: *FilmgC; IntMPA 75, 76, 77, 78, 79, 80 81, 82; MotPP; MovMk; WhoHol A; WorEFlm; WrDr 76*

Francis, Arlene
[Mrs. Martin Gabel; Arlene Francis Kazanjian]
American. Actress
b. Oct 20, 1908 in Boston, Massachusetts
Source: *BiE&WWA; CelR 73; CurBio 56; FilmgC; ForWC 70; InWom; IntMPA 76, 77, 78, 79, 80, 81, 82; NotNAT; WhoAm 74, 76, 78, 80, 82; WhoAmW 77; WhoHol A; WhoThe 77*

Francis, Connie
[Constance Franconero]
American. Singer
Sang title song, starred in *Where the Boys Are,* 1963.
b. Dec 12, 1938 in Newark, New Jersey
Source: *AmSCAP 66; CurBio 62; FilmgC; InWom; IntMPA 75, 76, 77, 78, 79, 80, 81, 82; MotPP; WhoHol A*

Francis, Dick
Welsh. Author
b. Oct 31, 1920 in Tenby, Wales
Source: *Au&Wr 71; ConAu 5R; ConLC 2; ConNov 76; CurBio 81; EncMys; WhoAm 82*

Francis, Edward
American. Bacteriologist
b. Mar 27, 1872 in Shandon, Ohio
d. 1957
Source: *BioIn 4; WhAm 5*

Francis, Emile Percy
"Cat"
Canadian. Hockey Player, Executive
Goalie, 1946–52; president, general manager, St. Louis Blues, 1978--.
b. Sep 13, 1926 in North Battleford, SK
Source: *CurBio 68; WhoE 74; WhoHcky 73*

Francis, Genie
American. Actress
Played Laura on daytime soap opera "General Hospital," 1977-81.
b. May 26, 1962 in Los Angeles, California
Source: *BioIn 12*

Francis, James Bicheno
"The Father of Modern Hydraulic Engineering"
English. Engineer
Developed hydraulic turbine.
b. May 18, 1815 in Southleigh, England
d. Sep 18, 1892 in Boston, Massachusetts
Source: *Alli; AmBi; ApCAB; DcAmAu; DcAmB; DcNAA; NatCAB 9; TwCBDA*

Francis, Kay
[Katherine Gibbs]
American. Actress
b. Jan 13, 1903 in Oklahoma City, Oklahoma
d. Aug 26, 1968 in New York, New York
Source: *BiDFilm; CmMov; FilmgC; InWom; MotPP; MovMk; OxFilm; ThFT; WhAm 5; WhScrn 74, 77; WhoHol B; WorEFlm*

Francis, Russ(ell Ross)
American. Football Player
b. Apr 3, 1953 in Seattle, Washington
Source: *BioIn 10; WhoAm 82*

Francis, Sam
American. Artist
b. Jul 25, 1923
Source: *IntWW 79; WhoAm 82*

Francis, Thomas, Jr.
American. Scientist, Educator
b. Jul 15, 1900 in Gas City, Indiana
d. Oct 1, 1969
Source: *BioIn 1, 5, 8, 11; WhAm 5*

Francis, Trevor
English. Soccer Player
b. Apr 19, 1954 in Plymouth, England
Source: *AmEnS*

Francis, Wallace
American. Football Player
b. Nov 7, 1951 in Franklin, Louisiana
Source: *WhoBlA 75, 77*

Francis of Assisi, Saint
[Giovanni Bernardone]
Italian. Preacher, Franciscan Founder
b. 1182
d. Oct 3, 1226
Source: *CasWL; EuAu; EvEuW; NewC; RComWL; REn*

Francis Xavier, Saint
Spanish. Missionary, Jesuit Co-Founder
b. 1506 in Pamplona, Spain
d. 1557
Source: *NewC*

Francisco, Peter
American. Revolutionary War Hero
b. 1760?
d. 1831
Source: *BioIn 4, 5, 11*

Franciscus, James Grover
American. Actor
b. Jan 31, 1934 in Clayton, Missouri
Source: *FilmgC; IntMPA 75, 76, 77, 78, 79, 80, 81, 82; MotPP; WhoAm 74, 76, 78, 80, 82; WhoHol A*

Franck, Cesar Auguste
French. Musician, Composer
b. Dec 10, 1822 in Liege, Belgium
d. Nov 8, 1890 in Paris, France
Source: *AtlBL; OxFr; REn*

Franck, James
American. Physicist, Educator
b. Aug 26, 1882 in Hamburg, Germany
d. May 21, 1964
Source: *BioIn 3, 4, 5, 6, 7, 9, 11; CurBio 57, 64*

Franco, Francisco
Spanish. Chief of State
Dictator who overthrew government, in power until death, 1936-75.
b. Dec 4, 1892 in El Ferrol, Spain
d. Nov 20, 1975 in Madrid, Spain
Source: *BioNews 75; CurBio 42, 54; REn*

Francois, Samson
French. Musician
b. May 18, 1924 in Frankfurt, Germany
d. Sep 22, 1970 in Paris, France
Source: *NewYTBE 70; WhAm 5*

Frank, Anne
German. Diarist
Diary depicted life as Jew during WW II.
b. Jun 12, 1929 in Frankfurt, Germany
d. Mar 1945
Source: *HerW; InWom; REn; TwCW*

Frank, Bruno
German. Author
b. Jun 13, 1887 in Stuttgart, Germany
d. Jun 20, 1945 in Beverly Hills, California
Source: *AmAu&B; CIDMEL; CnMD; EncWL; McGEWD; ModGL; ModWD; OxGer; REn; TwCA, SUP*

Frank, Gerold
American. Author
b. 1907 in Cleveland, Ohio
Source: *Au&Wr 71; BioIn 5, 7, 8, 9; WhoAm 82*

Frank, Hans
German. Nazi Leader
b. May 23, 1900
d. Oct 16, 1946 in Nuremberg, Germany
Source: *BioIn 1, 8; CurBio 41, 46; EncTR; ObitOF 79; WhWW-II*

Frank, Jerome David
American. Psychiatrist, Educator, Author
b. May 30, 1909 in New York, New York
Source: *AmM&WS 73S; BioIn 4, 9; ConAu 5R, 3NR; WhoAm 74, 76, 78, 80, 82; WhoE 74, 74; WhoWorJ 72*

Frank, Johann Peter
German. Physician
b. Mar 14, 1745 in Rodalben, Germany
d. Apr 24, 1821 in Vienna, Austria
Source: *BioIn 5, 6, 9, 11; WebBD 80*

Frank, Waldo
American. Author
b. Aug 25, 1889 in Long Branch, New Jersey
d. Jan 9, 1967 in White Plains, New York
Source: *AmAu&B; AmNov; CnDAL; ConAmA; ConAmL; ConAu 25R, 93; CurBio 40, 67; DcLEL; ModAL; OxAmL; Pen AM; REn; REnAL; TwCA, SUP; WhAm 4; WhNAA*

Frankau, Ethel
American. Fashion Director
b. 1886
d. 1971
Source: *BioIn 9; NewYTBE 71*

Frankau, Gilbert
English. Author
b. Apr 21, 1884 in London, England
d. Nov 4, 1952 in Hove, England
Source: *ChPo S1, S2; DcLEL; EncMys; EvLB; LongCTC; NewC; REn; TwCA, SUP; WhoLA*

Frankau, Pamela
English. Author
b. Jan 8, 1908 in London, England
d. Jun 8, 1967 in Hampstead, England
Source: *AmAu&B; CathA 1930; ConAu 25R; DcLEL; EvLB; LongCTC; NewC; Pen ENG; REn; TwCA, SUP; TwCW; WhAm 4*

Frankel, Charles
American. Historian, Philosopher
b. Dec 13, 1917 in New York, New York
d. May 10, 1979 in Bedford Hills, New York
Source: *AmAu&B; BioIn 4, 7; ConAu 5R, 89, 4NR; CurBio 66, 79; DrAS 78P; NewYTBS 79; WhAm 7; WhoAm 74, 76, 78; WhoAmP 73, 75, 77*

Frankel, Emily
American. Dancer, Choreographer
b. in New York, New York
Source: *BioIn 9*

Frankel, Max
American. Journalist
b. Apr 3, 1930 in Gera, Germany
Source: *ConAu 65; WhoAm 74, 76, 78, 80, 82; WhoS&SW 73; WhoWorJ 72*

Franken, Rose
American. Author, Dramatist
b. Dec 28, 1898 in Gainesville, Texas
Source: *AmAu&B; AmNov; Au&Wr 71; BiE&WWA; BioIn 1, 2, 4, 6; CnMD; CurBio 47; TwCA SUP*

Frankenheimer, John
American. Motion Picture Director
b. Feb 19, 1930 in Malba, New York
Source: *BiDFilm; CurBio 64; DcFM; FilmgC; IntMPA 75, 76, 77, 78, 79, 80, 81, 82; MovMk; OxFilm; WhoAm 74, 76, 78, 80, 82; WhoWor 74; WorEFlm*

Frankenstein, Alfred
American. Art Critic, Curator
b. Oct 5, 1906 in Chicago, Illinois
d. Jun 22, 1981 in San Francisco, California
Source: *Baker 78; WhoAm 74, 76, 78, 80; WhoWest 74; WhoWor 74*

Frankenthaler, Helen
[Mrs. Robert Motherwell]
American. Artist
Abstract expressionist; numerous one-woman shows, 1950's--.
b. Dec 12, 1928 in New York, New York
Source: *CelR 73; CurBio 66; DcCAA 71; InWom; IntWW 74; WhoAm 80, 82; WhoAmA 73; WhoWor 74*

Frankfurter, Felix
American. Supreme Court Justice
b. Nov 15, 1882 in Vienna, Austria
d. Feb 22, 1965 in Washington, DC
Source: *AmAu&B; CurBio 41, 57, 65; DcLEL; EncAB-H; OxAmL; REn; REnAL; WebAB; WhAm 4; WhNAA*

Frankl, Viktor E
Austrian. Psychiatrist, Author
b. Mar 26, 1905 in Vienna, Austria
Source: *ConAu 65; WhoAm 74, 76, 78, 80, 82; WhoWor 74; WhoWorJ 72*

Franklin, Aretha
[Mrs. Glynn Turman]
American. Singer
Hits include "Respect," "Baby I Love You," 1967.
b. Mar 25, 1942 in Memphis, Tennessee
Source: *BkPepl; CelR 73; CurBio 68; HerW; InWom; WhoAm 74, 76, 78, 80, 82; WhoBlA 75*

Franklin, Benjamin
[Richard Saunders, pseud.]
American. Statesman, Scientist, Author
Published *Poor Richard's Almanack,* 1732-57; invented lightning rod, bifocal glasses.
b. Jan 17, 1706 in Boston, Massachusetts
d. Apr 17, 1790 in Philadelphia, Pennsylvania
Source: *Alli; AmAu; AmAu&B; AmBi; AmWr; ApCAB; AtlBL; BbD; BiAuS; BiD&SB; BiDrAC; CasWL; ChPo, S1, S2; CnDAL; CrtT 3; CyAL 1; CyWA; DcAmAu; DcAmB; DcEnL; DcLEL; DcNAA; Drake; EncAB-H; EvLB; MouLC 2; NewC; OxAmL; OxEng; Pen AM; RComWL; REn; REnAL; TwCBDA; WebAB; WebE&AL; WhAm H; WhAmP*

Franklin, Bonnie Gail
American. Actress, Dancer
Starred on Broadway in *Applause,* 1970-71; TV series "One Day at a Time," 1975--.
b. Jan 6, 1944 in Santa Monica, California
Source: *WhoAm 78, 80, 82; WhoHol A*

Franklin, Frederic
English. Dancer
b. Jun 13, 1914 in Liverpool, England
Source: *BioIn 3, 10; CurBio 43; WhoAm 74*

Franklin, Irene
American. Actress, Songwriter
b. Jun 13, 1876 in New York, New York
d. Jun 16, 1941 in Englewood, New Jersey
Source: *CurBio 41; NotNAT B; WhScrn 77; WhThe; WhoHol B*

Franklin, John
English. Explorer
Died in search of Northwest Passage, 1845; quest for relics and diaries continues today.
b. Apr 16, 1786 in Spilsby, England
d. Jun 11, 1847 in Arctic Region
Source: *Alli; ApCAB; BrAu 19; Drake; NewC; OxCan; OxEng*

Franklin, Joseph Paul
[James Clayton Vaughan, Jr.]
American. Murderer, Racist
b. 1950?
Source: *BioIn 12*

Franklin, Mel(vin)
[The Temptations]
American. Singer
b. Oct 12, 1942 in Montgomery, Alabama
Source: *NF*

Franklin, Miles, pseud.
[Stella Maria Sarah Franklin]
"Brent of Bin Bin", pseud.
Australian. Author
Best known work is autobiographical *My Brilliant Career,* written at 16.
b. Oct 14, 1879 in Talbingo, Australia
d. Sep 19, 1954 in Sydney, Australia
Source: *CasWL; McGEWB; ModFrL; TwCW*

Franklin, Pamela
English. Actress
b. Feb 4, 1950 in Tokyo, Japan
Source: *FilmgC; IntMPA 75, 76, 77, 78, 79, 80, 81, 82; WhoHol A*

Frankovich, Mike J
American. Motion Picture Producer
b. Sep 29, 1910 in Bisbee, Arizona
Source: *FilmgC; IntMPA 82; WhoAm 82; WhoHol A; WorEFlm*

Franks, Sir Oliver Shewell
English. Government Official
b. Feb 16, 1905 in Birmingham, England
Source: *CurBio 48; IntWW 74; NewC; Who 74; WhoWor 74*

Frantz, Chris
see: Talking Heads, The

Franz Ferdinand
Austrian. Archduke
Political leader whose assassination, 1914, led to outbreak of WW I.
b. Dec 18, 1863 in Graz, Austria
d. Jun 28, 1914 in Sarajevo, Yugoslavia
Source: *BioIn 2, 5, 6, 7, 8, 9, 10; NewCol 75; OxGer; REn; WebBD 80*

Franz Josef II
[Prince of Liechtenstein]
Liechtenstein. Ruler
b. Aug 16, 1906 in Liechtenstein
Source: *IntWW 74*

Franz Joseph I
Austrian. Emperor
b. 1830
d. 1916
Source: *BioIn 2, 3, 6, 7, 8, 10; DcCathB; NewCol 75; OxGer; REn; WebBD 80*

Franz, Arthur
American. Actor
b. Feb 29, 1920 in Perth Amboy, New Jersey
Source: *FilmgC; IntMPA 75, 76, 77; Vers B*

Franz, Eduard
American. Actor
b. Oct 31, 1902 in Milwaukee, Wisconsin
Source: *MotPP; WhoHol A; WhoThe 77*

Frasconi, Antonio
American. Artist, Author
b. Apr 28, 1919 in Montevideo, Uruguay
Source: *AmAu&B; AnCL; ConAu 1NR; CurBio 72; DcCAA 71; ThrBJA; WhoAm 74, 76, 78, 80, 82; WhoAmA 73; WhoE 74; WhoGrA; WhoWor 74*

Fraser, Lady Antonia Pakenham
English. Author
Wrote *Mary Queen of Scots,* 1969; mysteries featuring Jemima Shore.
b. Aug 27, 1932 in London, England
Source: *ConAu 85; CurBio 74; IntWW 74; Who 74; WhoWor 74; WrDr 76*

Fraser, Sir Bruce Austin
[Lord Fraser of North Cape]
"Tubby"
English. Government Official
b. Feb 5, 1888 in Acton, England
d. Feb 12, 1981 in London, England
Source: *AnObit 1981; BioIn 1; CurBio 43, 81; WhWW-II; Who 74*

Fraser, Dawn
Australian. Swimmer
Only swimmer to win Olympic medal in same event three successive Olympics--freestyle in 1956, 1960, 1964.
b. Sep 4, 1937 in Balmain, Australia
Source: *BioIn 7*

Fraser, Donald Mackay
American. Mayor of Minneapolis
b. Feb 20, 1924 in Minneapolis, Minnesota
Source: *AlmAP 78; BiDrAC; CngDr 74, 77; WhoAm 74, 76, 78, 80, 82; WhoAmP 75, 77, 79; WhoGov 72, 75, 77; WhoMW 74, 76, 78*

Fraser, Douglas Andrew
American. Labor Union Official
President, UAW, 1977-83.
b. Dec 18, 1916 in Glasgow, Scotland
Source: *BusPN; Ward 77C; WhoAm 78, 80, 82*

Fraser, George MacDonald
English. Author
b. Apr 2, 1925 in Carlisle, England
Source: *Au&Wr 71; ConAu 45, 2NR; WrDr 76*

Fraser, Gretchen Kunigh
American. Skier
b. 1919
Source: *BioIn 3, 6, 9, 11*

Fraser, James Earle
American. Sculptor
b. Nov 4, 1876 in Winona, Minnesota
d. Oct 11, 1953 in Westport, Connecticut
Source: *CurBio 51, 54; DcAmB S5; WebAB; WhAm 3*

Fraser, John Malcolm
Australian. Prime Minister
b. Mar 21, 1930 in Melbourne, Australia
Source: *IntWW 74; WhoWor 74*

Fratianne, Linda
American. Figure Skater
Won silver medal, 1980 Olympics.
b. Aug 2, 1960 in Los Angeles, California
Source: *BioIn 11, 12*

Fraunhofer, Joseph von
German. Physicist, Optician
b. Mar 6, 1787 in Straubing, Germany
d. Jun 7, 1826 in Munich, Germany
Source: *BioIn 8, 9, 10; WebBD 80; WhDW*

Frawley, Dennis
American. Rock Music Critic
b. Jul 12, 1942 in Minneapolis, Minnesota
Source: *BioIn 10*

Frawley, William
American. Actor
Played Fred Mertz on TV series "I Love Lucy," 1951-60.
b. Feb 26, 1893 in Burlington, Iowa
d. Mar 3, 1966 in Los Angeles, California
Source: *Film 1; FilmgC; MotPP; MovMk; Vers B; WhAm 4; WhScrn 74, 77; WhoHol B*

Frayn, Michael
English. Author
b. Sep 8, 1933 in London, England
Source: *Au&Wr 71; BioIn 10; ConAu 5R; ConDr 73; ConLC 3, 7; ConNov 72, 76; ModBrL; Who 74; WorAu; WrDr 76*

Frazer, Sir James George
Scottish. Anthropologist
b. 1854 in Glasgow, Scotland
d. May 7, 1941 in Cambridge, England
Source: *Alli SUP; AtlBL; CasWL; Chambr 3; DcEnA AP; DcLEL; EvLB; LongCTC; NewC; OxEng; Pen ENG; REn; TwCA, SUP; WebE&AL*

Frazetta, Frank
American. Artist
b. Feb 9, 1928 in Brooklyn, New York
Source: *BioIn 10, 11; EncSF; FanAl; WhoAm 78, 80; WorECom*

Frazier, Brenda Diana Dudd
[Brenda Frazier Kelly Chatfield-Taylor]
American. Heiress, Socialite
b. 1921
d. May 3, 1982 in Boston, Massachusetts
Source: *InWom; NewYTBS 82*

Frazier, Dallas June
American. Singer, Songwriter
b. Oct 27, 1939 in Spiro, Oklahoma
Source: *EncFCWM 69; WhoAm 78, 80, 82*

Frazier, Joe
"Smokin' Joe"
American. Boxer
Won gold medal, 1964 Olympics; pro heavyweight champ, 1970-73.
b. Jan 17, 1944 in Beaufort, South Carolina
Source: *CelR 73; CurBio 71; NewYTBE 70; WhoAm 74, 76, 78, 80, 82; WhoBlA 75; WhoBox 74*

Frazier, Walt Clyde
American. Basketball Player
Forward, NY Knicks, 1967-77, Cleveland Cavaliers, 1977--.
b. Mar 29, 1945 in Atlanta, Georgia
Source: *CelR 73; CurBio 73; NewYTBE 72, 73; NewYTBS 74; WhoAm 74, 76, 78, 80, 82; WhoBbl 73*

Frederic, Harold
American. Author
b. Aug 19, 1856 in Utica, New York
d. Oct 19, 1898 in Henley, England
Source: *AmAu; AmAu&B; AmWr; BbD; BiD&SB; CasWL; Chambr 3; DcAmAu; EvLB; OxAmL; REnAL*

Freberg, Stan
American. Satirist
b. Aug 7, 1926 in Pasadena, California
Source: *AmSCAP 66; WhoAm 74*

Freccia, Massimo
Italian. Conductor
b. Sep 19, 1906 in Florence, Italy
Source: *IntWW 74; WhoAm 74; WhoMus 72; WhoWor 74*

Frederick I
[Frederick Barbarossa]
Holy Roman Emperor
b. 1123?
d. 1190
Source: *BioIn 10; NewCol 75; WebBD 80*

Frederick II
Holy Roman Emperor
b. 1194
d. 1250
Source: *NewCol 75; WebBD 80*

Frederick III
German. Emperor
b. 1831 in Potsdam, Germany
d. Jun 15, 1888 in Berlin, Germany
Source: *BioIn 9; WhoModH*

Frederick IX
Danish. King
b. Mar 11, 1899 in Copenhagen, Denmark
d. 1972
Source: *BioIn 1, 2, 3, 4, 5, 6, 9, 10; NewCol 75; NewYTBE 72; WebBD 80*

Frederick Augustus I
see: Augustus II

Frederick the Great
[Frederick II]
German. King of Prussia
b. 1712 in Berlin, Germany
d. 1786 in Berlin, Germany
Source: *NewC; NewCol 75; OxFr; REn; WebBD 80*

Frederick Louis
English. Prince of Wales
b. Jan 20, 1707 in Hannover, Germany
d. Mar 20, 1751 in London, England
Source: *BioIn 1, 3, 4, 5, 6, 7, 9, 10, 11; NewCol 75; WebBD 80*

Frederick William
see: Friedrich Wilhelm

Frederick William I
Prussian. King
b. Aug 15, 1688 in Berlin, Germany
d. May 31, 1740 in Potsdam, Germany
Source: *BioIn 1, 11; NewCol 75; WebBD 80*

Frederick, Pauline
American. Actress
b. Aug 12, 1885 in Boston, Massachusetts
d. Aug 19, 1938
Source: *AmBi; CurBio 54; Film 1; FilmgC; InWom; MovMk; NotAW; OxFilm; ThFT; TwYS; WhAm 1; WhScrn 74, 77; WhoHol B; WhoStg 1906*

Frederick, Pauline
American. Radio, TV Commentator
b. 1908 in Gallitzen, Pennsylvania
Source: *ConAu 102; CurBio 74; InWom; WhoAm 82; WhoUN 75*

Frederick, Vicki
American. Actress
b. 1954? in Georgia
Source: *NewYTBS 79*

Fredericks, Carlton
American. Nutritionist
b. Oct 23, 1910 in New York, New York
Source: *AuNews 1; BioNews 74; ConAu 53*

Frederika Louise
Greek. Exiled Queen Mother of Greece
b. Apr 18, 1917 in Blankenburg, Germany
d. Feb 6, 1981 in Madrid, Spain
Source: *BioIn 2, 3, 4, 5, 6, 9; CurBio 55, 81; InWom; NewYTBS 81*

Free, World B
[Lloyd Free]
American. Basketball Player
b. Dec 9, 1953 in Atlanta, Georgia
Source: *BioIn 11*

Freed, Alan
American. Disc Jockey, Songwriter
b. Dec 15, 1922 in Johnstown, Pennsylvania
d. Jan 20, 1965 in Palm Springs, California
Source: *WhScrn 77*

Freed, Arthur
American. Songwriter, Film Producer
b. Sep 9, 1894 in Charleston, South Carolina
d. Apr 12, 1973 in Los Angeles, California
Source: *AmSCAP 66; BiDFilm; CmMov; ConAu 41R; DcFM; FilmgC; NewYTBE 73; OxFilm; WhAm 5; WhoWest 74; WorEFlm*

Freed, Bert
American. Actor
b. Nov 3, 1919 in New York, New York
Source: *WhoAm 74, 76, 78, 80, 82; WhoHol A*

Freedman, Gerald
American. Motion Picture Director, Author
b. Jun 25, 1927
Source: *AmSCAP 66; NewYTBE 73; NotNAT; WhoAm 82; WhoThe 77*

Freehan, Bill (William Ashley)
American. Baseball Player
Catcher, Detroit Tigers, 1961-76; AL All-Star team, 1965-73.
b. Nov 29, 1941 in Detroit, Michigan
Source: *BaseEn; WhoAm 74; WhoProB 73*

Freeling, Nicolas
English. Author
b. Mar 3, 1927 in London, England
Source: *ConAu 49, 1NR; ConNov 72, 76; EncMys; TwCW; WorAu*

Freeman, Al, Jr.
American. Actor
Starred in "Hot L Baltimore" and "One Life to Live."
b. Mar 21, 1934 in San Antonio, Texas
Source: *DcBlPA; FilmgC; NotNAT; WhoHol A; WhoThe 77, 81*

Freeman, "Bud" (Lawrence)
American. Musician
b. Apr 13, 1906 in Chicago, Illinois
Source: *AmSCAP 66; WhoAm 74; WhoJazz 72; WhoWor 74*

Freeman, Douglas S
American. Historian, Journalist
b. May 16, 1886 in Lynchburg, Virginia
d. Jun 13, 1953 in Richmond, Virginia
Source: *AmAu&B; CyWA; DcAmB S5; OxAmL; REn; REnAL; TwCA, SUP; WebAB; WhAm 3*

Freeman, Joseph
Author
b. Oct 7, 1897 in Ukraine, Russia
d. Aug 9, 1965
Source: *AmAu&B; AmNov; ConAu 89; OxAmL; TwCA, SUP; WhAm 4*

Freeman, Mary E Wilkins
American. Author
b. Oct 31, 1852 in Randolph, Massachusetts
d. Mar 13, 1930 in Metuchen, New Jersey
Source: *AmAu&B; AmBi; AmLY; CarSB; CasWL; ChPo, S1, S2; CnDAL; ConAmL; DcAmAu; DcAmB; DcEnA AP; DcLEL; DcNAA; InWom; LongCTC; NotAW; OxAmL; OxEng; Pen AM; REn; REnAL; TwCA; WebAB; WhAm 1*

Freeman, Mona
American. Actress
b. Jun 9, 1926 in Baltimore, Maryland
Source: *FilmgC; HolP 40; MovMk; WhoHol A*

Freeman, Orville Lothrop
American. Government Official
b. May 9, 1918 in Minneapolis, Minnesota
Source: *BiDrUSE; CurBio 56; IntWW 74; WhoAm 74, 76, 78, 80, 82; WhoAmP 73; WhoWor 74*

Freeman, R(ichard) Austin
English. Author
b. Apr 11, 1862 in London, England
d. Sep 30, 1943 in Gravesend, England
Source: *BioIn 4, 7, 9, 11; EncMys; EvLB; NewC; REn; TwCA, SUP; TwCCr&M*

Freeman-Mitford, Unity Valkyrie
English. Friend of Hitler
b. 1914
d. May 29, 1948 in Oban, Scotland
Source: *BioIn 11*

Freemantle, Brian Harry
English. Author
b. Jun 10, 1936 in Southampton, England
Source: *ConAu 65; TwCCr&M*

Freer, Charles Lang
American. Art Collector, Industrialist
b. Feb 25, 1856 in Kingston, New York
d. Sep 25, 1919 in New York, New York
Source: *BioIn 4, 5, 9, 11; DcAmB; WhAm 1*

Frei (Montalva), Eduardo
Chilean. Lawyer, Politician
President of Chile, 1964-70.
b. Jan 16, 1911 in Santiago, Chile
d. Jan 22, 1982 in Santiago, Chile
Source: *CurBio 65, 82; IntWW 74, 75, 76, 77, 78, 79, 80; IntYB 78, 79; McGEWB; WhoWor 74*

Freidberg, Jerry
American. Educator
b. 1938 in Brooklyn, New York
Source: *BioIn 10*

Frelich, Phyllis
American. Actress
b. 1944 in Devils Lake, North Dakota
Source: *BioIn 12; NewYTBS 80*

Fremont, John Charles
American. Explorer, Historian
First Republican candidate for US president, 1856.
b. Jan 21, 1813 in Savannah, Georgia
d. Jul 13, 1890 in New York, New York
Source: *Alli, SUP; AmAu; AmAu&B; AmBi; ApCAB; BbD; BiAuS; BiD&SB; BiDSA; BiDrAC; CyAl 2; DcAmAu; DcAmB; DcNAA; Drake; EncAB-H; OxAmL; REn; REnAL; TwCBDA; WebAB; WhAm H; WhAmP*

Fremont-Smith, Frank
American. Scientist, Physician, Engineer
b. Mar 19, 1895 in Saint Augustine, Florida
d. Feb 27, 1974
Source: *NewYTBS 74; WhAm 6; WhoAm 74*

French, Daniel Chester
American. Sculptor
b. Apr 20, 1850 in Exeter, New Hampshire
d. Oct 7, 1931 in Stockbridge, Massachusetts
Source: *AmBi; ApCAB; DcAmB S1; OxAmL; REnAL; TwCBDA; WebAB; WhAm 1*

French, Marilyn
[Mara Solwoska, pseud.]
American. Author
Wrote *The Women's Room,* 1977, *House of Mirth,* 1981.
b. Nov 21, 1929 in New York, New York
Source: *BioIn 11; ConAu 69, 3NR; ConLC 10, 18; WhoAm 82*

Freneau, Philip Morin
American. Poet, Journalist
b. Jan 2, 1752 in New York, New York
d. Dec 18, 1832 in Monmouth County, New Jersey
Source: *Alli; AmAu; AmAu&B; AmBi; ApCAB; AtlBL; BiD&SB; CasWL; Chambr 3; ChPo, S1; CnDAL; CrtT 3; CyAL 1; CyWA; DcAmAu; DcAmB; DcLEL; DcNAA; Drake; EncAB-H; EvLB; MouLC 3; OxAmL; OxEng; Pen AM; REn; REnAL; WebAB; WebE&AL; WhAm H*

Freni, Mirella
Italian. Opera Singer
b. 1936 in Modena, Italy
Source: *IntWW 74; WhoAm 82; WhoMus 72*

Frere, Maurice
Belgian. Banker, Economist
b. 1890
d. 1970
Source: *BioIn 9*

Frescobaldi, Girolamo
Italian. Musician, Composer
b. 1583 in Ferrara, Italy
d. Mar 2, 1644 in Rome, Italy
Source: *AtlBL; NewCol 75; WebBD 80*

Freuchen, Peter
Danish. Author, Explorer
Explored Arctic, 1906-08; wrote *Eskimo,* 1930, *Arctic Adventure,* 1936.
b. Feb 20, 1886
d. Sep 2, 1957 in Anchorage, Alaska
Source: *AuBYP; Pen EUR; TwCA, SUP; WhAm 3*

Freud, Anna
English. Psychoanalyst
Daughter of Sigmund Freud; authority on childhood mental disorders.
b. Dec 3, 1895 in Vienna, Austria
d. Oct 8, 1982 in London, England
Source: *Au&Wr 71; BiDrAPA 77; CurBio 79, 82; IntAu&W 76, 77; IntWW 74, 75, 76, 77, 78; NewYTBS 82; WhoAmW 68, 70, 72, 74; WhoWor 74, 78; WrDr 76, 80*

Freud, Clement Raphael
English. Author
b. Apr 24, 1924
Source: *Who 74*

Freud, Lucian
English. Artist
b. Dec 8, 1922
Source: *IntWW 74; Who 74*

Freud, Martha Bernays
Austrian. Wife of Sigmund Freud
b. 1861?
d. 1951
Source: *BioIn 1, 2, 8*

Freud, Sigmund
Austrian. Psychoanalyst
Developed free association method, 1892-95, psychoanalysis, 1895-1900.
b. May 6, 1856 in Freiberg, Moravia
d. Sep 23, 1939 in London, England
Source: *AtlBL; BiDPara; CasWL; ChPo S2; CyWA; EncWL, ; FilmgC; LongCTC; NewC; OxGer; Pen EUR; RComWL; REn; TwCA, SUP; TwCW; WhAm HA, 4; WhoLA; WhoTwCL*

Frey, Charles N
American. Chemist
b. 1885
Source: *BioIn 1, 2, 3, 9, 11*

Frey, Glenn
[The Eagles]
American. Musician, Songwriter, Singer
Released solo album, *No Fun Aloud,* 1982.
b. Nov 6, 1948 in Detroit, Michigan
Source: *WhoAm 82*

Freydis, Ericsdotter
Icelandic. Explorer
Source: *BioIn 11*

Freyse, William
American. Cartoonist
b. 1899 in Detroit, Michigan
d. Mar 3, 1969 in Tucson, Arizona
Source: *BioIn 8; WorECom*

Frick, Ford Christopher
American. Baseball Executive, Journalist
Baseball commissioner, 1951-65; Hall of Fame, 1970.
b. Dec 19, 1894 in Wawaka, Indiana
d. Apr 8, 1978 in Bronxville, New York
Source: *CurBio 45; WhoAm 74; WhoProB 73*

Frick, Gottlob
German. Opera Singer
b. 1906 in Stuttgart, Germany
Source: *IntWW 74; WhoWor 74*

Frick, Henry Clay
American. Industrialist, Philanthropist
b. Dec 19, 1849 in West Overton, Pennsylvania
d. Dec 2, 1919 in New York, New York
Source: *AmBi; ApCAB SUP; DcAmB; EncAB-H; WebAB; WhAm 1*

Frick, Wilhelm
German. Nazi Leader
b. Mar 3, 1877 in Alsenz, Germany
d. Oct 16, 1946 in Nuremberg, Germany
Source: *BioIn 1; CurBio 42, 46; EncTR; ObitOF 79; WebBD 80; WhWW-II*

Fricsay, Ferenc
Hungarian. Conductor
b. Aug 9, 1914 in Budapest, Hungary
d. Feb 20, 1963 in Basel, Switzerland
Source: *NewEOp 71*

Fried, Alfred Hermann
Austrian. Pacifist
b. Nov 11, 1864 in Vienna, Austria
d. May 6, 1921 in Vienna, Austria
Source: *BioIn 5, 9, 11; NewCol 75; WebBD 80*

Fried, Miriam
Israeli. Musician
b. Sep 9, 1946 in Satu Mare, Romania
Source: *BioIn 11; WhoAm 82; WhoMus 72*

Friedan, Betty Naomi Goldstein
American. Feminist, Author, Journalist
Founded NOW, 1966, president until 1970; wrote *The Feminine Mystique,* 1963.
b. Feb 4, 1921 in Peoria, Illinois
Source: *AmAu&B; BkPepl; ConAu 65; CurBio 70; EncAB-H; ForWC 70; IntWW 74; NewYTBE 70, 71; WebAB; WhoAm 74, 76, 78, 80, 82; WhoAmW 77; WrDr 76*

Friedel, Charles
French. Chemist, Mineralogist
b. Mar 12, 1832 in Strasbourg, France
d. Apr 20, 1899 in Mantauban, France
Source: *BioIn 1; WebBD 80*

Friedkin, William
American. Motion Picture Director
Movies include *The French Connection* (Oscar, 1971), *The Exorcist,* 1973.
b. Aug 29, 1939 in Chicago, Illinois
Source: *BiDFilm; BkPepl; CelR 73; FilmgC; IntMPA 75, 76, 77, 78, 79, 80, 81, 82; MovMk; WhoAm 74, 76, 78, 80, 82; WhoWest 74; WhoWor 74*

Friedman, Bruce Jay
American. Author
b. Apr 26, 1930 in New York, New York
Source: *AmAu&B; ConAu 9R; ConDr 73; ConLC 3, 5; ConNov 72, 76; DrAF 76; McGEWD; ModAL, SUP; NatPD; Pen AM; RAdv 1; WhoAm 74; WorAu; WrDr 76*

Friedman, Herbert
American. Physicist
b. Jun 21, 1916 in New York, New York
Source: *AmM&WS 73P; BioIn 6, 7, 8; CurBio 63; WhoAm 74, 76, 78, 80, 82*

Friedman, Max
[Heavenly Twins]
American. Basketball Player
b. Jul 12, 1889 in New York, New York
Source: *WhoBbl 73*

Friedman, Milton
American. Economist, Journalist
Economics professor, U of Chicago, 1948--; columnist, *Newsweek,* 1966--.
b. Jul 31, 1912 in Brooklyn, New York
Source: *AmAu&B; AmEA 74; AmM&WS 73S; Au&Wr 71; ConAu 1R, 1NR; EncAB-H; IntWW 74; WebAB; Who 74; WhoAm 74, 76, 78, 80, 82; WhoWor 74; WhoWorJ 72; WrDr 76*

Friedman, Ze'ev
Israeli. Murdered Olympic Team Member
b. 1944?
d. Sep 5, 1972 in Munich, Germany (West)
Source: *BioIn 9*

Friedrich Wilhelm
[Frederick William]
German. Elector of Brandenburg
b. 1620
d. 1688
Source: *OxGer*

Friedrich, Caspar David
German. Artist
b. Sep 5, 1774 in Greifswald, Germany
d. May 7, 1840 in Dresden, Germany
Source: *BioIn 6, 9, 10, 11; NewCol 75; OxGer*

Friel, Brian
Irish. Dramatist
b. Jan 9, 1929 in Ireland
Source: *Au&Wr 71; CnThe; ConAu 21R; ConDr 73; ConLC 5; McGEWD; ModBrL SUP; ModWD; NotNAT; REnWD; Who 74; WhoAm 82; WhoThe 77; WhoWor 74; WorAu; WrDr 76*

Friend, Bob (Robert Bartmess)
"Warrior"
American. Baseball Player
b. Nov 24, 1930 in Lafayette, Indiana
Source: *BaseEn; BioIn 4, 5*

Friendly, Ed
American. Television Producer
b. Apr 8, 1922 in New York, New York
Source: *NewYTET; WhoAm 80, 82*

Friendly, Edwin Samson
American. Newspaper Executive
b. Jun 15, 1884 in Elmira, New York
d. Jul 9, 1970
Source: *BioIn 2, 7, 9; CurBio 49, 70; NewYTBE 70; WhNAA*

Friendly, Fred W
American. TV Producer, Broadcaster
b. Oct 30, 1915 in New York, New York
Source: *AmAu&B; ConAu 25R; CurBio 57; IntMPA 75; IntWW 74; WhoAm 74, 76, 78, 80, 82*

Friese-Greene, William Edward
[William Edward Green]
British. Inventor, Photographer
Patented motion picture camera; other devices related to film.
b. Sep 7, 1855 in Bristol, England
d. 1921 in London, England
Source: *BioIn 1, 2, 3, 4, 10; FilmEn; FilmgC; OxFilm; WorEFlm*

Friesz, Othon
French. Artist
b. 1879
d. Jan 11, 1949?
Source: *BioIn 1, 2*

Friganza, Trixie
[Delia O'Callahan]
American. Actress, Singer
b. Nov 29, 1870 in Grenola, Kansas
d. Feb 27, 1955 in Flintridge, California
Source: *TwYS; WhScrn 74, 77; WhoHol B; WhoStg 1908*

Frijid Pink
[Thomas Beaudry; Thomas Harris; Richard Stevers; Gary Thompson; Jon Wearing; Craig Webb; Lawrence Zelanka]
American. Rock Group
Source: *RkOn*

Frimbo, E M, pseud.
see: Whitaker, Rogers E M

Friml, Rudolf
American. Musician, Composer
b. Dec 2, 1879 in Prague, Bohemia
d. Nov 12, 1972 in Hollywood, California
Source: *AmSCAP 66; EncMT; FilmgC; NewCBMT; NewYTBE 72; PlP&P; WebAB; WhAm 5*

Frings, Joseph Richard
German. Cardinal
b. 1887?
d. Dec 17, 1978 in Cologne, Germany (West)
Source: *BioIn 1, 7, 8, 11*

Frings, "Ketti"
[Katherine Hartley]
American. Dramatist, Author
b. 1915 in Columbus, Ohio
d. Feb 11, 1981 in Los Angeles, California
Source: *AmAu&B; AmWomWr; AnObit 1981; BiE&WWA; ConAu 101, 103; CurBio 60, 81; FilmgC; InWom; McGEWD; NatPD; NewYTBS 81; NotNAT; OhA&B; OxAmL; REnAL; ScF&FL 1; WhoAm 74, 76, 78, 80; WhoAmW 58, 64, 68, 70, 72, 74, 75, 77; WhoE 74*

Fripp, Robert
see: King Crimson

Frisch, Frankie (Frank Francis)
"The Fordham Flash"
American. Baseball Player, Manager
Infielder, 1919-37; Hall of Fame, 1947.
b. Sep 9, 1898 in New York, New York
d. Mar 12, 1973 in Wilmington, Delaware
Source: *BaseEn; WhoProB 73*

Frisch, Karl von
German. Zoologist, Ethologist
b. Nov 20, 1886 in Vienna, Austria
Source: *ConAu 85; CurBio 74; IntWW 74; NewYTBE 73; WhoWor 74*

Frisch, Max
Swiss. Author, Architect
b. May 15, 1911 in Zurich, Switzerland
Source: *BiE&WWA; BioNews 74; CasWL; CnMD; CnThe; ConAu 85; ConLC 3, 9, 14, 18; CroCD; CurBio 65; EncWL; EvEuW; IntWW 74; McGEWD; ModGL; ModWD; NotNAT; OxGer; OxThe; Pen EUR; REn; REnWD; TwCW; WhoThe 77; WhoTwCL; WhoWor 74; WorAu*

Frisch, Ragnar
Norwegian. Economist
b. Mar 2, 1895 in Oslo, Norway
d. Jan 31, 1973 in Oslo, Norway
Source: *NewYTBE 73; WhAm 5*

Frisco, Joe
American. Actor
b. 1890 in Milan, Illinois
d. Feb 16, 1958 in Woodland Hills, California
Source: *BioIn 2, 4, 5; NotNAT B; WhScrn 77; WhoHol B*

Fritchey, Clayton
American. Journalist, Political Leader
b. 1905? in Bellefontaine, Ohio
Source: *WhoAm 74*

Fritchie, Barbara
American. Civil War Heroine
Supposedly waved Union flag at Lee's army as it marched through her town, 1862.
b. 1766 in Frederick, Maryland
d. 1862
Source: *NotAW*

Frith, Mary
see: Cutpurse, Moll

Fritzsche, Hans
German. Nazi Leader
b. Apr 21, 1900 in Bochum, Germany
d. Sep 27, 1953 in Cologne, Germany (West)
Source: *BioIn 1, 2, 3; EncTR; ObitOF 79*

Frizon, Maud
[Maud Frison]
French. Shoe Designer
b. 1942? in Paris, France
Source: *BioIn 12*

Frizzell, "Lefty" (William Orville)
American. Singer
b. Mar 31, 1928 in Corsicana, Texas
d. Jul 27, 1975 in Nashville, Tennessee
Source: *EncFCWM 69*

Frobe, Gert
German. Actor
b. 1913
Source: *FilmgC; IntMPA 82; MotPP; MovMk; WhoHol A*

Froben, Johann
German. Scholar, Printer
b. 1460 in Hammelburg, Germany
d. Oct 1527 in Basel, France
Source: *OxGer*

Frobenius, Leo
German. Archaeologist, Anthropologist
b. 1873
d. 1938
Source: *NewCol 75*

Frobisher, Martin
English. Navigator
Made three voyages to New World attempting to discover Northwest Passage, 1576, 1577, 1578.
b. 1535 in Dorcaster, England
d. Nov 22, 1594 in Plymouth, England
Source: *Alli; ApCAB; Drake; NewC; OxCan; REn; WhAm H*

Froebel, Friedrich Wilhelm August
German. Educator
b. Apr 21, 1782 in Oberweissbach, Germany
d. Jun 21, 1852 in Marienthal, Germany
Source: *BbD; BiD&SB; BioIn 1, 3, 4, 6, 8, 11; LongCTC*

Frohman, Charles
American. Impresario, Theater Producer
b. Jun 17, 1860 in Sandusky, Ohio
d. May 7, 1915
Source: *AmBi; DcAmB; EncMT; OxAmL; OxThe; REnAL; WebAB; WhAm 1; WhoStg 1906, 1908*

Frohman, Daniel
American. Theatrical Manager
b. Aug 22, 1851 in Sandusky, Ohio
d. Dec 26, 1940 in New York, New York
Source: *AmAu&B; CurBio 41; DcAmB S2; OhA&B; OxAmL; OxThe; PlP&P; REnAL; TwCBDA; WhAm 1; WhoStg 1906, 1908*

Froines, John
[The Chicago 7]
American. Member of Chicago 7
Source: *BioIn 10*

Froissart, Jean
French. Chronicler, Poet
b. 1338 in Valenciennes, France
d. 1410
Source: *AtlBL; BbD; BiD&SB; CasWL; CyWA; DcEuL; EuAu; EvEuW; NewC; OxEng; OxFr; Pen EUR; REn*

Froman, Jane
American. Actress, Singer
b. 1917 in Saint Louis, Missouri
d. Apr 22, 1980 in Columbia, Missouri
Source: *InWom; WhoHol A*

Fromentin, Eugene
French. Author
b. Oct 24, 1820 in LaRochelle, France
d. Aug 27, 1876 in LaRochelle, France
Source: *BiD&SB; CasWL; CyWA; DcEuL; EuAu; EvEuW; OxFr; Pen EUR*

Fromm, Erich
American. Psychoanalyst
Dealt with problem of how Western man can come to terms with sense of isolation.
b. Mar 23, 1900 in Frankfurt, Germany
d. Mar 18, 1980 in Muralto, Switzerland
Source: *CurBio 67; AmAu&B; AmM&WS 73S; ConAu 73, 97; EncAB-H; Pen AM; REn; REnAL; TwCA SUP; WebAB; WhoAm 74; WhoE 74; WhoS&SW 73; WhoTwCL; WhoWor 74; WrDr 76*

Fromme, Lynette Alice
"Squeaky"
American. Would-Be Assassin
Charles Manson follower, convicted of attempting to assassinate Gerald Ford, 1975.
b. 1949
Source: *BioIn 10; GoodHS*

Frondizi, Arturo
Argentine. Lawyer, Politician
b. Sep 28, 1908 in Argentina
Source: *CurBio 58; IntWW 74; WhoWor 74*

Frontenac, Louis de
French. Political Leader
b. 1620 in Paris, France
d. Nov 28, 1698 in Quebec, Canada
Source: *ApCAB; Drake; OxAmL; OxCan; WhAm H*

Frontiere, Georgia
see: Rosenbloom, Georgia

Frost, Arthur Burdett
American. Illustrator, Humorist
b. Jan 17, 1851 in Philadelphia, Pennsylvania
d. Jun 22, 1928 in Pasadena, California
Source: *AmAu&B; BioIn 2, 3, 4, 5; ChPo, S1, S2; DcAmAu; DcNAA; OxAmL; REnAL; Str&VC*

Frost, David
English. TV Personality, Author
b. Apr 7, 1939 in Tenterden, England
Source: *ConAu 69; CurBio 69; IntMPA 75, 76, 77, 78, 79, 80, 81, 82; IntWW 74; NewYTBE 71; Who 74; WhoAm 82; WhoWor 74*

Frost, John
English. Chartist
b. 1784
d. 1877
Source: *Alli SUP; BioIn 7, 8*

Frost, Robert
American. Poet
Recited poem, *The Gift Outright,* at John F Kennedy's inaugeration, 1961; won four Pulitzer Prizes.
b. Mar 26, 1874 in San Francisco, California
d. Jan 29, 1963 in Boston, Massachusetts
Source: *AmAu&B; AmLY; AmWr; AnCL; AtlBL; CasWL; Chambr 3; ChPo, S1, S2; CnDAL; CnE&AP; CnMWL; ConAmA; ConAmL; ConAu 89; ConLC 1, 3, 4, 9, 10, 13, 15; CurBio 42, 63; CyWA; DcLEL; EncWL; EvLB; LongCTC; ModAL, SUP; NewYTBE 72; NewYTBS 74; OxAmL; OxEng; Pen AM; RAdv 1; RComWL; REn; REnAL; SixAP; SmATA 14; Str&VC; TwCA, SUP; TwCW; WebE&AL; WhAm 4; WhNAA; WhoTwCL*

Fruehauf, Harvey Charles
American. Founder of Truck Trailer Firm
b. Dec 15, 1893 in Grosse Pointe, Michigan
d. Oct 14, 1968
Source: *WhAm 5*

Fruits, George
American. Centenarian
b. 1762
d. Aug 6, 1876 in Alamo, Indiana
Source: *ApCAB*

Frum, Barbara
Canadian. Actress, Broadcaster
b. Sep 8, 1937 in Niagara Falls, New York
Source: *BioIn 10; CanWW 82*

Fry, Charles Burgess
British. Cricket Player
b. 1872
d. 1956
Source: *BioIn 2, 4*

Fry, Christopher
English. Dramatist
Wrote plays *The Lady's not for Burning,* 1949, *Venus Observed,* 1950.
b. Dec 18, 1907 in Bristol, England
Source: *Au&Wr 71; AuBYP; BiE&WWA; CasWL; CnMD; CnMWL; CnThe; ConAu 17R; ConDr 73; ConLC 2, 10, 14; ConP 70, 75; CroCD; CurBio 51; CyWA; DcLEL; EncWL; EvLB; IntWW 74, 75, 76, 77, 78, 79, 80, 81; LongCTC; McGEWD; ModBrL SUP; ModWD; NewC; NotNAT; OxEng; OxThe; Pen ENG; REn; TwCA SUP; TwCW; WebE&AL; Who 74; WhoThe 77; WhoWor 74, 76, 78; WorEFlm; WrDr 76, 80*

Fry, Elizabeth Gurney
English. Prison Reformer, Philanthropist
b. May 21, 1780
d. 1845
Source: *BioIn 2, 5, 6, 7, 8, 9, 10, 11; REn*

Fry, Franklin Clark
American. Clergyman
b. Aug 30, 1900 in Bethlehem, Pennsylvania
d. Jun 6, 1968
Source: *CurBio 46, 68; WebAB; WhAm 5*

Fry, Roger Eliot
English. Artist, Art Critic
b. Dec 14, 1866 in London, England
d. Sep 9, 1934 in London, England
Source: *LongCTC; ModBrL; NewC; OxEng; REn; TwCA, SUP*

Frye, David
American. Comedian
b. 1934 in Brooklyn, New York
Source: *BioIn 10*

Frye, H(erman) Northrop
Canadian. Literary Critic
b. Jul 14, 1912 in Sherbrooke, PQ
Source: *AmAu&B; CanWW 82; CasWL; ConAu 5R; EncWL; NewC; OxCan, SUP; Pen AM, ENG; RAdv 1; WhoCan 73; WorAu; WrDr 76*

Fuchida, Mitsuo
Japanese. Naval Officer, Aviator
b. 1903
d. May 30, 1976 in Kashiwara, Japan
Source: *BioIn 10*

Fuchs, Daniel
American. Author
b. Jun 25, 1909 in New York, New York
Source: *AmAu&B; ConAu 81; ConLC 8; ConNov 72, 76; DrAF 76; ModAL, SUP; OxAmL; Pen AM; REnAL; WebE&AL; WhoTwCL; WrDr 76*

Fuchs, Joseph
American. Muscian
b. Apr 26, 1900 in New York, New York
Source: *CurBio 62; WhoAm 74; WhoWor 74*

Fuchs, Klaus Emil Julius
German. Physicist, Spy
b. 1912 in Russelsheim, Germany
Source: *BioIn 9*

Fuchs, Leo
Polish. Actor, Folksinger
b. May 15, 1911 in Lwow, Poland
Source: *BiE&WWA; IntMPA 82; NotNAT; WhoHol A*

Fuchs, Marta
German. Opera Singer
b. Jan 1, 1898
d. 1974
Source: *BioIn 10; NewEOp 71*

Fuchs, Sir Vivian Ernest
English. Geologist, Explorer
With Sir Edmund Hillary, were first to cross Antarctica overland, 1957-58.
b. Feb 11, 1908 in Kent, England
Source: *ConAu 104; CurBio 58; IntWW 74, 75, 76, 77, 78, 79, 80, 81; Who 74, 82; WhDW; WhoWor 74, 76, 78; WrDr 76, 80*

Fuentes, Carlos
Mexican. Author
b. Nov 11, 1928 in Mexico City, Mexico
Source: *AuNews 2; CasWL; ConAu 69; ConLC 3, 8, 10, 13; CurBio 72; DcCLAA; EncWL; IntWW 74; Pen AM; TwCW; WhoAm 82; WhoTwCL; WhoS&SW 73; WorAu*

Fuertes, Louis Agassiz
American. Ornithologist, Artist
b. Feb 7, 1874 in Ithaca, New York
d. Aug 22, 1927
Source: *AmBi; DcAmB; DcNAA; WhAm 1*

Fuess, Claude Moore
American. Educator, Author
b. Jan 12, 1885 in Waterville, New York
d. Sep 9, 1963
Source: *AmAu&B; OxAmL; REnAL; TwCA, SUP; WhAm 4; WhNAA*

Fugard, Athol Harold
South African. Actor, Director, Dramatist
Writes about apartheid in *Sizwe Banzi is Dead, A Lesson from Aloes.*
b. Jun 11, 1932 in Middleburg, South Africa
Source: *AfSS 79; CasWL; CnThe; ConAu 85; ConDr 73, 77; ConLC 5, 9, 14; CurBio 75; DcLEL 1940; EncWT; IntAu&W 76; IntWW 74, 75, 76, 77, 78, 79, 80; ModCmwL; NewYTBE 70; NotNAT; PlP&P; TwCW; WhoThe 72, 77, 81; WhoTwCL; WhoWor 80; WorAu 1970; WrDr 76, 80*

Fugate, Caril Ann
American. Murderer
Friend of Charles Starkweather allegedly involved in NE murders; spent 18 years in prison.
b. 1943
Source: *BioIn 10; GoodHS*

Fugger, Jacob
[Jacob the Rich]
German. Merchant
b. 1459
d. 1525
Source: *WebBD 80*

Fugs, The
[John Anderson; Lee Crabtree; Pete Kearney; Tuli Kupferberg; Charles Larkey; Vinny Leary; Bob Mason; Ken Pine; Ed Sanders; Peter Stampfield; KenWeaver]
American. Rock Group
Source: *BiDAmM; EncPR&S; IlEncRk; Rk100*

Fukuda, Takeo
Japanese. Prime Minister
b. Jan 14, 1905 in Japan
Source: *CurBio 74; IntWW 74; NewYTBE 71*

Fulbright, James William
American. Former Senator
b. Apr 9, 1905 in Sumner, Missouri
Source: *BiDrAC; ConAu 9R; EncAB-H; WhoAm 74, 76, 78, 80, 82; WhoAmP 73; WhoGov 72; WhoS&SW 73; WhoWor 74*

Fuld, Stanley H
American. Judge
b. Aug 23, 1903 in New York, New York
Source: *WhoAm 74, 76, 78, 80, 82; WhoE 74; WhoGov 72; WhoWorJ 72*

Fulks, Joe
"Jumpin' Joe"
American. Basketball Player
b. Mar 21, 1921 in Marshall County, Kentucky
d. Mar 21, 1976
Source: *BioIn 10; WhoBbl 73*

Fuller, Alfred Carl
American. Manufacturer
Founded Fuller Brush Co., 1910.
b. Jan 13, 1885 in Kings County, NS
d. Dec 4, 1973 in Hartford, Connecticut
Source: *BioNews 74; BusPN; ConAu 45; CurBio 50, 74; NewYTBE 73; WebAB; WhAm 6*

Fuller, "Bucky" (Richard Buckminster)
American. Architect, Author
Developed geodesic dome, circa 1940.
b. Jul 12, 1895 in Milton, Massachusetts
Source: *BlueB 76; CelR 73; ConArch; ConAu 9R; CurBio 60; EncAB-H; EncMA; IntWW 74, 75, 76, 77, 78, 79, 80, 81; McGDA; McGEWB; NewYTBS 75; WebAB, 79; Who 74; WhoAm 74, 76, 78, 80, 82; WhoArch; WhoWor 74; WrDr 80*

Fuller, Edmund
American. Author
b. Mar 3, 1914 in Wilmington, Delaware
Source: *AmAu&B; AuBYP; ChPo S1; ConAu 77; ConNov 72, 76; DrAS 74E; SmATA 21; WorAu; WrDr 76*

Fuller, George
American. Artist
b. 1822
d. 1884
Source: *AmBi; ApCAB; DcAmB; OxAmL; TwCBDA; WhAm H*

Fuller, Henry Blake
American. Author
b. Jan 9, 1857 in Chicago, Illinois
d. Jul 29, 1929 in Chicago, Illinois
Source: *AmAu&B; BbD; BiD&SB; CasWL; CnDAL; ConAmL; DcAmAu; DcLEL; DcNAA; OxAmL; Pen AM*

Fuller, Hoyt William
American. Critic, Editor
b. Sep 10, 1926 in Atlanta, Georgia
d. May 11, 1981 in Atlanta, Georgia
Source: *BlkAW; ConAmTC; ConAu 53, 103; EbonySL 1; LivgBAA; SelBAA; WhoAm 76, 78, 80; WhoBlA 75, 77*

Fuller, Ida
American. First Social Security Recipient
b. Sep 6, 1875 in Ludlow, Vermont
d. Jan 27, 1975 in Brattleboro, Vermont
Source: *BioIn 10; NewYTBS 75*

Fuller, Loie
American. Dancer, Author
b. Jan 22, 1862 in Fullersburg, Illinois
d. Jan 2, 1928
Source: *AmBi; DcAmB; NotAW; WhAm 1*

Fuller, Margaret
[Sarah Margaret Fuller Ossoli]
American. Critic, Social Reformer
b. May 23, 1810 in Cambridge, Massachusetts
d. Jul 19, 1850 in Fire Island, New York
Source: *AmAu; AmAu&B; AmBi; AtlBL; BbD; BiD&SB; ChPo; CnDAL; CrtT 3; DcAmAu; DcAmB; DcLEL; NotAW; OxAmL; OxEng; Pen AM; REn; REnAL; TwCBDA; WebE&AL*

Fuller, Robert
American. Actor
b. Jul 29, 1934
Source: *FilmgC; WhoHol A*

Fuller, Roy Broadbent
English. Author
b. Feb 11, 1912 in Failsworth, England
Source: *Au&Wr 71; CasWL; ChPo S1, S2; CnE&AP; ConAu 5R; ConLC 4; ConNov 72, 76; ConP 70, 75; IntWW 74; LongCTC; ModBrL, SUP; NewC; Pen ENG; RAdv 1; REn; TwCA SUP; TwCW; WebE&AL; Who 74; WhoChL; WhoTwCL; WhoWor 74; WrDr 76*

Fuller, Samuel
American. Director, Screenwriter
b. Aug 12, 1911 in Worcester, Massachusetts
Source: *BiDFilm; BioIn 7, 9, 11; CmMov; DcFM; FilmEn; FilmgC; OxFilm; ScF&FL 1; WhoAm 82; WorEFlm*

Fuller-Maitland, John Alexander
English. Music Critic, Author
b. Apr 7, 1856 in London, England
d. Mar 30, 1936 in Lancashire, England
Source: *Chambr 3; NewC; WhoLA*

Fullerton, (Charles) Gordon
American. Astronaut
Aboard the third flight of space shuttle *Columbia,* Apr, 1982.
b. Oct 11, 1936 in Rochester, New York
Source: *IntWW 74, 75, 76, 77, 78; WhoAm 80, 82; WhoS&SW 73, 75, 76, 78; WorDWW*

Fulton, Maude
American. Actress, Dramatist
b. May 14, 1881 in El Dorado, Kansas
d. Nov 4, 1950 in Los Angeles, California
Source: *BioIn 2; Film 2; NotNAT B; WhScrn 77; WhThe; WhoHol B*

Fulton, Richard Harmon
American. Mayor of Nashville
b. Jan 27, 1927 in Nashville, Tennessee
Source: *BiDrAC; CngDr 74; WhoAm 78, 80, 82; WhoAmP 73, 75, 77, 79; WhoGov 72, 75, 77; WhoS&SW 73, 75, 76, 78*

Fulton, Robert
American. Engineer
First to develop a practical, profitable steamboat, 1807.
b. Nov 14, 1765 in Lancaster County, Pennsylvania
d. Feb 24, 1815 in New York, New York
Source: *Alli; AmBi; ApCAB; BiDLA; DcAmB; DcNAA; Drake; REn; REnAL; TwCBDA; WebAB; WhAm H*

Funicello, Annette
American. Actress, Singer
Disney Mousketeer, 1950's; star of *beach party* films, 1960's.
b. Oct 22, 1942 in Utica, New York
Source: *BiDAmM; FilmgC; InWom; MotPP; WhoHol A*

Funikawa, Gyo
American. Illustrator
b. in Berkeley, California
Source: *BioIn 3, 8, 9; IlsBYP; IlsCB 1957*

Funk, Casimir
American. Biochemist
b. Feb 23, 1884 in Warsaw, Poland
d. Nov 19, 1967 in Albany, New York
Source: *CurBio 45, 68; WebAB; WhAm 4*

Funk, Isaac Kauffman
American. Publisher
Funk and Wagnalls Co. published *Standard Dictionary of the English Language,* 1893.
b. Sep 10, 1839 in Clifton, Ohio
d. Apr 4, 1912 in Montclair, New Jersey
Source: *AmAu&B; DcAmAu; DcAmB; DcNAA; OhA&B; TwCBDA; WebAB; WhAm 1*

Funk, Walther
German. Nazi Leader
Minister of Economics, 1938; responsible for financial leadership of Germany.
b. Aug 18, 1890 in Trakehnen, Prussia (East)
d. May 31, 1960 in Dusseldorf, Germany (West)
Source: *BioIn 1, 3, 5; CurBio 40, 60; EncTR; ObitOF 79*

Funk, Wilfred John
American. Publisher
b. Mar 20, 1883 in Brooklyn, New York
d. Jun 1, 1965 in Montclair, New Jersey
Source: *AmAu&B; ChPo, S2; ConAu 89; CurBio 55, 65; WhAm 4*

Funston, Frederick
American. Military Leader
b. Nov 9, 1865 in New Carlisle, Ohio
d. Feb 19, 1917
Source: *AmBi; ApCAB SUP; DcAmB; DcNAA; OhA&B; TwCBDA; WebAB; WhAm 1*

Funston, George Keith
American. Businessman
b. Oct 12, 1910 in Waterloo, Iowa
Source: *IntWW 74; WhoAm 74*

Funt, Allen
American. Radio, TV Producer
Creator, host of TV series "Candid Camera."
b. Sep 16, 1914 in Brooklyn, New York
Source: *AmSCAP 66; CurBio 66; FilmgC; IntMPA 82; WhoAm 74, 78*

Furay, Richie
[Buffalo Springfield; Poco; The Souther-Hillman-Furay Band]
American. Rock Musician
b. in Ohio
Source: *ConMuA 80; WhoRock 81*

Furie, Sidney J
Canadian. Motion Picture Director
b. Feb 28, 1933 in Toronto, ON
Source: *FilmEn; FilmgC; IntMPA 75, 76, 77, 78, 79; MovMk; OxFilm; WorEFlm*

Furillo, Carl Anthony
"The Reading Rifle"; "Skoonj"
American. Baseball Player
Sued Dodgers for dropping him without pay following injury, won $21,000.
b. Mar 8, 1922 in Stony Creek, Pennsylvania
Source: *BaseEn; WhoProB 73*

Furness, Betty (Elizabeth Mary)
American. Actress, Consumer Advisor
Actress, 1932-37; chairman, president's committee on consumer interests, 1967-69.
b. Jan 3, 1916 in New York, New York
Source: *CelR 73; CurBio 68; ForWC 70; InWom; NewYTET; ThFT; WhoAm 74, 76, 78, 80, 82; WhoAmW 58, 61, 64, 66, 68, 70, 72, 74, 75, 77; WhoE 74; WhoHol A; WhoS&SW 73*

Furstenberg, Diane Halfin von
Fashion Designer, Author
Began designing, 1971; first effort was jersey wrapdress.
b. Dec 31, 1946 in Brussels, Belgium
Source: *BioNews 74; BkPepl; CelR 73; WhoAm 82; WorFshn*

Furstenberg, Egon von
Fashion Designer, Author
b. Jun 29, 1946 in Lausanne, Switzerland
Source: *CelR 73; WhoAm 82*

Furtseva, Ekaterina Alexeyevna
Russian. Minister of Culture
b. Dec 7, 1910 in Vyshni Volochek, Russia
d. Oct 25, 1974 in Moscow, U.S.S.R.
Source: *BioIn 4, 5, 10; BioNews 75; CurBio 56, 74; IntWW 74, 75; NewYTBE 72; NewYTBS 74; WhAm 6; WhoAmW 68, 70, 72, 74; WhoSocC 78; WhoWor 74*

Furtwangler, Wilhelm
German. Conductor
b. Jan 25, 1886 in Berlin, Germany
d. Nov 30, 1954 in Eberstein, Germany (West)
Source: *WhAm 3*

Fuseli, Henry
Swiss. Artist, Author
b. Feb 7, 1741 in Zurich, Switzerland
d. Apr 16, 1825 in London, England
Source: *Alli; AtlBL; BiDLA; BkIE; CasWL; NewC*

Fust, Johann
German. Artist, Bookdealer
b. 1400
d. 1466
Source: *NewC; OxGer*

Futrelle, Jacques
American. Author
b. Apr 9, 1875 in Pike County, Georgia
d. Apr 15, 1912
Source: *AmAu&B; BiDSA; DcNAA; EncMys; TwCA; WhAm 1*

Fyffe, Will
Scottish. Actor
b. 1885 in Dundee, Scotland
d. Dec 14, 1947 in Saint Andrews, Scotland
Source: *FilmgC; OxThe; WhScrn 74; WhoHol B*

Fyodorova, Victoria
Russian. Model, Actress
b. 1945
Source: *BioIn 10, 11*

G

Gabel, Martin
American. Actor
b. Jun 19, 1912 in Philadelphia, Pennsylvania
Source: *BiE&WWA; FilmgC; MovMk; NotNAT; WhoHol A; WhoThe 77*

Gabin, Jean
French. Actor
b. May 17, 1904 in Paris, France
d. Nov 15, 1976 in Neuilly, France
Source: *BiDFilm; CurBio 41, 77; IntMPA 77, 75; IntWW 74; MotPP; MovMk; OxFilm; Who 74; WhoHol A; WhoWor 74; WorEFlm*

Gable, Clark
American. Actor
Won Oscar, 1934, for *It Happened One Night;* played Rhett Butler in *Gone With the Wind,* 1939.
b. Feb 1, 1901 in Cadiz, Ohio
d. Nov 16, 1960 in Hollywood, California
Source: *BiDFilm; CmMov; CurBio 45, 61; FilmgC; MotPP; MovMk; OxFilm; WebAB; WhAm 4; WhScrn 74, 77; WhoHol B; WorEFlm*

Gable, John Clark
American. Son of Clark Gable
b. 1961
Source: *BioIn 6, 9*

Gabo, Naum Pevsner
American. Sculptor, Constructivist
b. Aug 5, 1890 in Briansk, Russia
d. Aug 23, 1977 in Waterbury, Connecticut
Source: *Au&Wr 71; ConAu 33R, 73; ConAu P-2; CurBio 72; DcCAA 71; IntWW 74; WhoAm 74; WhoWor 74*

Gabor, Dennis
British. Electrical Engineer
b. Jun 5, 1900 in Budapest, Hungary
d. Feb 9, 1979 in London, England
Source: *AmM&WS 73P; Au&Wr 71; BioIn 9, 10, 11; ConAu 17R; CurBio 72, 79; IntAu&W 76; IntWW 75, 76, 77, 78; NewYTBE 71; NewYTBS 79; WhoWor 76, 78; WrDr 80*

Gabor, Eva
Hungarian. Actress
Co-starred with Eddie Albert in TV series "Green Acres," 1965-71.
b. Feb 11, 1921 in Budapest, Hungary
Source: *BiE&WWA; BioNews 74; CelR 73; CurBio 68; FilmgC; InWom; MotPP; MovMk; WhoAm 76, 78, 80, 82; WhoAmW 70, 72, 74; WhoHol A; WhoWor 74, 76; WorAl*

Gabor, Jolie
Hungarian. Mother of Gabor Sisters
b. 1896 in Hungary
Source: *BioNews 74; InWom*

Gabor, Magda
Hungarian. Actress
b. 1918 in Hungary
Source: *InWom*

Gabor, Zsa Zsa (Sari)
Hungarian. Actress
Better known for her many husbands than acting career--married eight times.
b. Feb 6, 1919 in Budapest, Hungary
Source: *CelR 73; FilmgC; InWom; IntMPA 75, 76, 77, 78, 79, 80, 81, 82; MotPP; MovMk; WhoAm 74, 76, 78, 80, 82; WhoHol A; WhoWor 74, 76; WorAl*

Gabriel, Ange-Jacques
French. Architect
b. Oct 23, 1698 in Paris, France
d. Jan 4, 1782 in Paris, France
Source: *AtlBL; McGDA; McGEWB; WhoArch*

Gabriel, Peter
[Genesis]
English. Rock Musician
b. May 13, 1950 in England
Source: *ConMuA 80; LilREn 78; WhoRock 81*

Gabriel, Roman, Jr.
American. Football Player
Quarterback, LA Rams, 1962-73, Philadelphia Eagles, 1973-78; MVP, 1969.
b. Aug 5, 1940 in Wilmington, North Carolina
Source: *CurBio 75; WhoAm 74, 76, 78; WhoFtbl 74*

Gabrieli, Giovanni
Italian. Composer, Musician
b. 1557 in Venice, Italy
d. Aug 12, 1612 in Venice, Italy
Source: *AtlBL; NewCol 75; REn; WebBD 80*

Gabrielli, Catarina
Italian. Opera Singer
b. Nov 12, 1730 in Rome, Italy
d. Apr 1796 in Rome, Italy
Source: *WebBD 80*

Gabrilowitsch, Ossip
American. Conductor, Musician
b. Jan 26, 1878 in Saint Petersburg, Russia
d. Sep 14, 1936 in Detroit, Michigan
Source: *AmBi; DcAmB S2; NewCol 75; WebBD 80; WhAm 1*

Gacy, John Wayne, Jr.
American. Mass Murderer
Convicted, 1980, of murders of 33 boys in Chicago area, 1972-78.
b. 1942?
Source: *BioIn 11; EncACr*

Gaddafi, Moamar al-
see: Qadhafi, Mu'ammar al-

Gaddis, William
American. Author
b. 1922 in New York, New York
Source: *AmAu&B; ConAu 17R; ConLC 1, 3, 6; ConNov 72, 76; DrAF 76; ModAL SUP; Pen AM; RAdv 1; WhoAm 74, 76, 78, 80, 82; WorAu; WrDr 76*

Gadsby, Bill (William Alexander)
Canadian. Hockey Player, Coach
Defenseman, 1946-66; Hall of Fame, 1970.
b. Aug 8, 1927 in Calgary, AB
Source: *WhoHcky 73*

Gadsen, James
American. Railroad Executive, Politician
b. May 15, 1788 in Charleston, South Carolina
d. Dec 26, 1858 in Charleston, South Carolina
Source: *BioIn 3; DcAmB; WhAm H*

Gadski, Johanna
German. Opera Singer
b. Jun 15, 1872 in Anclam, Germany
d. Feb 22, 1932 in Berlin, Germany
Source: *InWom; WhAm 1*

Gaedel, Eddie (Edward Carl)
American. Baseball Player, Midget
Batted against Detroit, Aug 9, 1951, in promotional gimmick; walked.
b. Jun 8, 1925 in Chicago, Illinois
d. Jun 18, 1961 in Chicago, Illinois
Source: *BaseEn*

Gag, Wanda
American. Children's Author, Illustrator
b. May 11, 1893 in New Ulm, Minnesota
d. Jun 27, 1946 in New York, New York
Source: *AmAu&B; AnCL; AuBYP; ChPo S2; ConICB; CurBio 42; DcAmB S4; DcNAA; FamAIYP; HerW; IlsCB 1744; JBA 34, 51; REnAL; TwCA, SUP; WhAm 2; YABC 1*

Gagarin, Yuri Alexseyevich
Russian. Cosmonaut
First man to travel in space, Apr 12, 1961.
b. Mar 9, 1934 in Gzhatsk, U.S.S.R.
d. Mar 27, 1968 in Moscow, U.S.S.R.
Source: *AsBiEn; CurBio 61, 68; McGEWB; NewCol 75; WhDW; WhAm 5; WorAl*

Gage, Harlow W
American. Business Executive
b. Feb 6, 1911 in Springfield, Massachusetts
Source: *IntWW 74*

Gage, Robert
American. Art Director, Graphic Designer
b. 1917
Source: *WhoE 74*

Gage, Thomas
English. Army General
b. 1721 in Firle, England
d. Apr 2, 1787 in England
Source: *AmBi; ApCAB; DcAmB; WhAm H; WhAmP*

Gagn, Reynaldo
Venezuelan. Composer, Conductor
b. Aug 9, 1875 in Caracas, Venezuela
d. Jan 28, 1947 in Paris, France
Source: *NewEOp 71*

Gagliardi, Ed
see: Foreigner

Gahagan, Helen Mary
see: Douglas, Helen Mary Gahagan

Gail, Max(well Trowbridge, Jr.)
American. Actor
Played Sergeant Wojehowicz on TV series "Barney Miller," 1975-81.
b. Apr 5, 1943 in Detroit, Michigan
Source: *WhoAm 80, 82*

Gailhard, Pierre
French. Opera Singer, Manager
b. Aug 1, 1848 in Toulouse, France
d. Oct 12, 1918 in Paris, France
Source: *NewEOp 71*

Gaines, Ernest J
American. Author
b. Jan 15, 1933 in Oscar, Louisiana
Source: *AuNews 1; BlkAW; ConAu 9R; ConLC 3; ConNov 72, 76; DrAF 76; LivgBAA; WhoAm 76, 78, 80, 82; WhoBlA 75; WrDr 76*

Gaines, Lee
American. Composer, Singer
b. Apr 21, 1914 in Houston, Texas
Source: *AmSCAP 66*

Gaines, Steve
[Lynyrd Skynard]
American. Rock Musician
b. 1949?
d. Oct 20, 1977 in Mississippi
Source: *BioIn 11*

Gainey, Bob (Robert Michael)
Canadian. Hockey Player
b. Dec 13, 1953 in Peterborough, ON
Source: *HocReg; WhoAm 82*

Gainsborough, Thomas
English. Artist
b. 1727 in Sudbury, England
d. 1788 in London, England
Source: *AtlBL; BkIE; ChPo; NewC; REn*

Gairy, Sir Eric M
West Indian. Government Official
b. 1922 in Grenada, West Indies
Source: *NewYTBS 74; WhoWor 74*

Gaitskell, Hugh Todd Naylor
English. Socialist Leader
b. Apr 9, 1906
d. Jan 18, 1963
Source: *CurBio 50, 63; WhAm 4*

Gaius Caesar Germanicus
see: Caligula

Gajdusek, D(aniel) Carleton
American. Biomedical Scientist
b. Sep 9, 1923 in Yonkers, New York
Source: *AmM&WS 76P, 79P; BioIn 6, 11; CurBio 81; IntWW 76, 78; NewYTBS 76; WhoAm 78, 80, 82; WhoE 77, 79; WhoGov 72; WhoWor 78*

Galamian, Ivan
American. Violin Teacher
b. Jan 23, 1903 in Tabriz, Persia
d. Apr 14, 1981 in New York, New York
Source: *Baker 78; BioIn 8, 9; WhAm 7*

Galamison, Milton
American. Clergyman, City Official
b. Jan 25, 1923 in Philadelphia, Pennsylvania
Source: *BioIn 6, 11; WhoBlA 75; WhoE 74*

Galanos, James
American. Fashion Designer
Very expensive ready-to-wear designer; customers include Nancy Reagan.
b. Sep 20, 1924 in Philadelphia, Pennsylvania
Source: *CelR 73; CurBio 70; WhoAm 74, 76, 78, 80, 82; WorFshn*

Galard, Genevieve
French. Nurse
b. 1925
Source: *BioIn 3, 4, 7*

Galbraith, John Kenneth
American. Economist, Diplomat, Author
Editor, *Fortune* magazine, 1943-48; wrote *The New Industrial State,* 1967.
b. Oct 15, 1908 in Iona Station, ON
Source: *AmAu&B; AmEA 74; AmM&WS 73S; CanWW 70; CelR 73; ConAu 21R; EncAB-H; LongCTC; REnAL; WebAB; Who 74; WhoAm 82; WorAu; WrDr 76*

Galbreath, John Wilmer
American. Baseball Club Owner
b. 1897
Source: *BioIn 4, 5*

Galbreath, Tony (Anthony)
American. Football Player
b. Jan 29, 1954 in Fulton, Missouri
Source: *FootReg; WhoBlA 77*

Galdos, Benito Perez
see: Perez Galdos, Benito

Gale, Zona
American. Author, Journalist
b. Aug 26, 1874 in Portage, Wisconsin
d. Dec 27, 1938 in Chicago, Illinois
Source: *AmAu&B; AmBi; AmLY; AnMV 1926; ChPo, S2; CnDAL; CnMD; ConAmA; ConAmL; DcAmB S2; DcLEL; DcNAA; EvLB; InWom; LongCTC; McGEWD; ModWD; NotAW; OxAmL; Pen AM; REn; REnAL; TwCA, SUP; TwCW; WhAm 1; WhNAA; WisWr*

Galella, Ron
American. Photographer
Famous for his pursuit to photograph Jacqueline Onassis.
b. Jan 10, 1931 in Bronx, New York
Source: *AuNews 1; BioNews 74; ConAu 53; WhoAm 82; WrDr 76*

Galen
Greek. Physician, Author
b. 129 in Pergamum, Greece
d. 199
Source: *CasWL; NewC; NewCol 75; Pen; WebBD 80*

Galento, Tony
"Two Ton"
American. Boxer, Wrestler
b. Mar 10, 1909 in Orange, New Jersey
d. 1979 in Livingston, New Jersey
Source: *WhoBox 74; WhoHol A*

Galgani, Gemma
[Saint Gemmagalgani]
Italian. Saint
b. 1878
d. 1903
Source: *InWom*

Galileo
[Galileo Galilei]
Italian. Mathematician, Astronomer
Constructed first astronomical telescope, 1609; developed scientific method.
b. 1564 in Pisa, Italy
d. Jan 8, 1642
Source: *CasWL; DcEuL; EuAu; EvEuW; NewC; OxEng; Pen EUR; RComWL; REn*

Galili, Israel
Israeli. Politician
b. May 1911 in Brailov, Russia
Source: *IntWW 74; WhoWorJ 72*

Galitzine, Princess Irene
Italian. Fashion Designer, Cosmetician
b. in Tiflis, Italy
Source: *WorFshn*

Gall, Saint
Irish. Missionary
b. 550?
d. 645?
Source: *BioIn 4, 5, 7; WebBD 80*

Gall, Franz Joseph
German. Physician
Founder of now discredited science of phrenology.
b. Mar 9, 1758 in Tiefenbru, Germany
d. Aug 22, 1828 in Montrouge, France
Source: *NewC; OxFr; REn*

Gallagher, Helen
American. Actress
b. 1926 in Brooklyn, New York
Source: *BiE&WWA; CelR 73; EncMT; NewYTBE 71; NotNAT; PIP&P; WhoAm 74, 76, 78, 80, 82; WhoHol A; WhoThe 77*

Gallagher, Mary Barelli
American. Secretary to Jackie Onassis
Source: *BioIn 8*

Gallagher, Richard
American. Actor
b. Jul 28, 1900 in Terre Haute, Indiana
d. May 22, 1955
Source: *BioIn 3, 4, 11*

Gallagher, Rory
Irish. Rock Musician
b. in Ballyshannon, Ireland
Source: *ConMuA 80; IlEncRk; LilREn 78; WhoRock 81*

Gallant, Mavis
Canadian. Author
b. Aug 11, 1922 in Montreal, PQ
Source: *ConAu 69; ConNov 72, 76; DrAF 76; NewC; OxCan, SUP; WhoAm 74, 76, 78, 80, 82; WorAu; WrDr 76*

Gallant, Roy Arthur
American. Children's Author
b. Apr 17, 1924 in Portland, Maine
Source: *AuBYP; ConAu 5R, 4NR; ConLC 17; SmATA 4; WrDr 76*

Gallatin, (Abraham Alfonse) Albert
American. Financier, Statesman
b. Jan 29, 1761 in Geneva, Switzerland
d. Aug 12, 1849 in Astoria, New York
Source: *Alli; AmAu&B; AmBi; ApCAB; BbtC; BiAuS; BiD&SB; BiDrAC; BiDrUSE; CyAL 1; DcAmAu; DcAmB; DcLEL; DcNAA; Drake; EncAB-H; OxAmL; REnAL; TwCBDA; WebAB; WhAm H; WhAmP*

Gallatin, Albert Eugene
American. Art Critic, Collector
b. Jul 23, 1881 in Villanova, Pennsylvania
d. Jun 15, 1952
Source: *AmAu&B; BioIn 1, 2, 3, 5, 11; DcCAA 71*

Gallaudet, Thomas Hopkins
American. Teacher
Established first free school for deaf in US at Hartford, CT, 1917.
b. Dec 10, 1787 in Philadelphia, Pennsylvania
d. Sep 10, 1851 in Hartford, Connecticut
Source: *AmBi; ApCAB; DcAmB; Drake; McGEWB; TwCBDA; WebAB; WhAm H*

Gallegos, Romulo
Venezuelan. Author
b. Aug 2, 1884 in Caracas, Venezuela
d. Apr 4, 1969 in Caracas, Venezuela
Source: *CasWL; CyWA; DcSpL; EncWL; Pen; REn; TwCW*

Gallegos, William
[The Hostages]
American. Former Hostage in Iran
b. 1959?
Source: *BioIn 12; NewYTBS 81*

Gallen, Hugh J
American. Governor of New Hampshire
Governor, 1978-82.
b. Jul 30, 1924 in Portland, Oregon
d. Dec 29, 1982 in Boston, Massachusetts
Source: *AlmAP 80; WhoAm 80, 82; WhoAmP 75, 77, 79; WhoE 79*

Galli-Curci, Amelita
Italian. Opera Singer
b. Nov 18, 1882 in Milan, Italy
d. Nov 26, 1963 in La Jolla, California
Source: *InWom; WhAm 4*

Galli-Marie, Marie Celestine
French. Opera Singer
b. Nov 1840 in Paris, France
d. Sep 22, 1905 in Vence, France
Source: *InWom*

Gallico, Paul William
American. Author, Sportswriter
Wrote *The Snow Goose,* 1941; *The Poseidon Adventure,* 1969.
b. Jul 26, 1897 in New York, New York
d. Jul 15, 1976 in Monaco
Source: *AmAu&B; AmNov; AuNews 1; ConAu 5R, 69; ConLC 2; ConNov 72, 76; CurBio 46; DcLEL; EvLB; FilmgC; IntWW 74; REnAL; SmATA 13; TwCA SUP; TwCW; Who 74; WhoAm 74; WhoWor 74; WrDr 76*

Gallieni, Joseph Simon
French. Marshal
b. 1849
d. 1916
Source: *BioIn 2, 11*

Gallitzin, Demetrius
Russian. Missionary
b. Dec 22, 1770 in The Hague, Netherlands
d. May 6, 1840 in Loretto, Pennsylvania
Source: *BioIn 2, 3, 4, 11*

Gallo, Ernest
American. Vintner
b. 1909
Source: *BusPN*

Gallo, Fortune
Italian. Opera Singer
b. May 9, 1878 in Torremaggiore, Italy
d. Mar 28, 1970 in New York, New York
Source: *CurBio 49, 70; NewYTBE 70; WhAm 5*

Gallo, Frank
American. Artist
b. Jan 13, 1933 in Toledo, Ohio
Source: *BioIn 7, 8, 9; DcCAA 71; WhoAm 74, 76, 78, 80, 82; WhoAmA 73*

Gallo, Julio
American. Vintner
b. 1910
Source: *BusPN*

Galloway, Don
American. Actor
Played Sergeant Ed Brown in TV series "Ironside," 1967-75.
b. Jul 27, 1937 in Brooksville, Kentucky
Source: *WhoAm 82; WhoHol A*

Gallup, George Horace
American. Public Opinion Analsyt
Originated Gallup Poll; founded American Institute of Public Opinion, 1935.
b. Nov 18, 1901 in Jefferson, Iowa
Source: *AmAu&B; AmM&WS 73S; BioNews 74; CelR 73; ConAu 13R; CurBio 40, 52; EncAB-H; IntWW 74; LongCTC; REn; REnAL; WebAB; WhoAm 74, 76, 78, 80, 82; WhoWor 74*

Galois, Evariste
French. Mathematician
b. Oct 25, 1811 in Bourg-la-Reine, France
d. May 31, 1832 in Paris, France
Source: *BioIn 1, 5, 7, 8, 11; NewCol 75; WebBD 80*

Galsworthy, John
[John Sinjohn, pseud.]
English. Author, Dramatist
b. Aug 14, 1867 in Kingston, England
d. Jan 31, 1933 in Hampstead, England
Source: *AtlBL; CasWL; Chambr 3; ChPo, S1, S2; CnMD; CnMWL; CnThe; CyWA; DcBiA; DcLEL; EncWL; EvLB; FilmgC; LongCTC; McGEWD; ModBrL, SUP; ModWD; NewC; OxEng; OxThe; Pen ENG; RAdv 1; RComWL; REn; REnWD; TwCA, SUP; TwCW; WebE&AL; WhoLA; WhoTwCL*

Galt, John
Scottish. Author
b. May 2, 1779 in Irvine, Scotland
d. Apr 11, 1839 in Greenock, Scotland
Source: *BbD; BrAu 19; CasWL; Chambr 3; CyWA; EvLB; NewC; OxCan; OxEng; Pen ENG; WebE&AL*

Galtieri, Leopoldo Fortunato
Argentine. Former President
b. Jul 15, 1926 in Caseros, Argentina
Source: *CurBio 82*

Galton, Sir Francis
English. Scientist, Explorer
Founded modern technique of weather mapping, 1863.
b. Feb 16, 1822 in Birmingham, England
d. Jan 17, 1911 in Haslemere, England
Source: *Alli SUP; BbD; BiD&SB; BrAu 19; Chambr 3; DcEnL; DcLEL; EvLB; LongCTC; NewC*

Galuppi, Baldassare
Italian. Composer
b. Oct 18, 1706 in Burano, Italy
d. Jan 3, 1785 in Venice, Italy
Source: *REn*

Galvani, Luigi
Italian. Physicist, Scientist, Doctor
b. 1737
d. 1798
Source: *NewC*

Galvez, Bernardo de
Spanish. Colonial Administrator
b. Jul 23, 1746? in Macharaviaya, Spain
d. Nov 30, 1786 in Mexico
Source: *AmBi; ApCAB; BioIn 3, 9, 10, 11; DcAmB; Drake; McGEWB; NatCAB 10; NewCol 75; REnAW; WebBD 80; WhAm H*

Galvin, Edward J
Irish. Bishop
b. 1882
d. 1956
Source: *BioIn 7, 8*

Galvin, "Pud" (James Francis)
"Gentle Jeems"; "The Little Steam Engine"
American. Baseball Player
Pitcher, won 46 games in two consecutive seasons, 1883-84; Hall of Fame, 1965.
b. Dec 25, 1856 in Saint Louis, Missouri
d. Mar 7, 1902 in Pittsburgh, Pennsylvania
Source: *BaseEn; BioIn 7, 10; WhoProB 73*

Galway, James
Irish. Musician
b. Dec 8, 1939 in Belfast, Northern Ireland
Source: *BioIn 11, 12; CurBio 80; IntWW 79; WhoAm 80, 82*

Gam, Rita Elenore
American. Actress
b. 1927 in Pittsburgh, Pennsylvania
Source: *BiE&WWA; ConAu 45; FilmgC; ForWC 70; InWom; MotPP; MovMk; NotNAT; PlP&P; WhoAm 74, 76, 78, 80, 82; WhoHol A*

Gama, Vasco da
see: DaGama, Vasco

Gamaliel the Elder
Palestinian. Rabbi
d. 50
Source: *NewC*

Gambetta, Leon
French. Lawyer, Statesman
b. Apr 3, 1838 in Cahors, France
d. Dec 31, 1882
Source: *OxFr; REn; WhoModH*

Gambino, (Don) Carlo
American. Racketeer, Mafia Chief
b. 1902
d. Oct 15, 1976 in Massapequa, New York
Source: *NewYTBE 71*

Gamble, James Norris
American. Manufacturer
Partner in Proctor and Gamble Co.; developed Ivory Soap.
b. Aug 9, 1836 in Cincinnati, Ohio
d. Jul 2, 1932
Source: *WhAm 1*

Gambling, John A
American. Radio Announcer
b. 1930 in New York, New York
Source: *NewYTBE 73*

Gambling, John Bradley
English. Radio Broadcaster
b. Apr 9, 1897 in Norwich, England
d. Nov 21, 1974 in Palm Beach, Florida
Source: *BioIn 2, 10; CurBio 50, 75; NewYTBS 74*

Gamelin, Maurice Gustave
French. General
b. Sep 20, 1872 in Paris, France
d. Apr 18, 1958 in Paris, France
Source: *CurBio 40, 58*

Gance, Abel
French. Motion Picture Director, Writer
b. Oct 25, 1889 in Paris, France
d. Nov 10, 1981 in Paris, France
Source: *BiDFilm; BioIn 10, 11; DcFM; FilmEn; IntWW 78; OxFilm; WhoWor 74; WorEFlm*

Gandhi, Indira Nehru
Indian. Politician
Prime Minister, 1966-77; worked for economic planning, social reform.
b. Nov 19, 1917 in Allahabad, India
Source: *BioNews 74; CurBio 59, 66; HerW; InWom; NewYTBE 71, 72; Who 74; WhoGov 72; WhoWor 74*

Gandhi, Mahatma (Mohandas Karamchand)
Indian. Religious Leader, Lawyer
Leader of Indian nationalist movement against British rule.
b. Oct 2, 1869 in Porbandar, India
d. Jan 30, 1948 in New Delhi, India
Source: *CasWL; CurBio 42, 48; DcLEL; OxEng; Pen CL; REn; WhAm 2*

Gandhi, Sanjay
Indian. Son of Indira Gandhi
b. Dec 14, 1946 in New Delhi, India
d. Jun 23, 1980 in New Delhi, India
Source: *AnObit 1980; BioIn 10; NewYTBS 76*

Gann, Ernest Kellogg
American. Author
b. Oct 13, 1910 in Lincoln, Nebraska
Source: *AmAu&B; AmNov; AuNews; ConAu 1R; TwCW; WhoAm 82; WhoPNW; WorAu; WrDr 76*

Gannett, Deborah Sampson
American. Revolutionary War Heroine
Served in Continental forces, May, 1782-Oct, 1783, disguised as man.
b. Dec 17, 1760 in Plymouth, Massachusetts
d. Apr 29, 1827 in Sharon, Massachusetts
Source: *BioIn 1, 3, 5, 8, 9, 10, 11*

Gannett, Frank Ernest
American. Newspaper Publisher
b. Sep 15, 1876 in Bristol, New York
d. Sep 3, 1957 in Rochester, New York
Source: *AmAu&B; CurBio 45, 58; REnAL; WhAm 3; WhNAA*

Gannett, Lewis Stiles
American. Critic
b. Oct 3, 1891 in Rochester, New York
d. Feb 3, 1966
Source: *AmAu&B; ConAu 89; CurBio 41, 66; REnAL; TwCA, SUP; WhAm 4, 4A*

Gannett, Ruth
American. Children's Author
b. Aug 12, 1923 in New York, New York
Source: *AuBYP; BkCL; ConAu 21R; IlsCB 1946; MorJA; SmATA 3*

Gans, Joe
"Old Master"
American. Boxer
b. Nov 25, 1874 in Philadelphia, Pennsylvania
d. Aug 16, 1910 in Baltimore, Maryland
Source: *WhoBox 74*

Ganz, Rudolph
Swiss. Conductor, Musician, Composer
b. Feb 24, 1877 in Zurich, Switzerland
d. Aug 2, 1972 in Chicago, Illinois
Source: *AmSCAP 66; NewYTBE 72; WhAm 5*

Garagiola, Joe (Joseph Henry)
American. Baseball Player, Sportscaster
Catcher, 1946-54; baseball broadcaster on radio and TV, 1955--.
b. Feb 12, 1926 in Saint Louis, Missouri
Source: *BaseEn; BioNews 74; CelR 73; WhoAm 74, 76, 78, 80, 82; WhoE 74; WhoProB 73*

Garamond, Claude
French. Type Designer
b. 1480
d. 1561
Source: *NewCol 75; WebBD 80*

Garand, John Cantius
American. Engineer, Inventor
Developed Garand semiautomatic rifle (M-1) for US Army, 1930.
b. Jan 1, 1888 in Saint Remi, PQ
d. Feb 16, 1974 in Springfield, Massachusetts
Source: *CurBio 45, 74; NewYTBS 74; WebAB; WhAm 6*

Garavani, Valentino
Italian. Fashion Designer
b. 1932 in Voghera, Italy
Source: *WorFshn*

Garber, Jan
American. Band Leader
b. 1895?
d. Oct 5, 1977 in Shreveport, Louisiana
Source: *BioIn 11*

Garbo, Greta
[Greta Louisa Gustafsson]
Swedish. Actress
Starred in film *Anna Karenina,* 1935; won special Oscar, 1954.
b. Sep 18, 1905 in Stockholm, Sweden
Source: *BiDFilm; BioNews 74; BkPepl; CelR 73; CmMov; CurBio 55; FilmgC; InWom; IntMPA 75, 76, 77, 78, 79, 80, 81, 82; IntWW 74; MotPP; MovMk; OxFilm; ThFT; TwYS; WebAB; Who 74; WhoAm 74, 76, 78, 80, 82; WhoHol A; WorEFlm*

Garcia, Carlos P
Philippine. President
b. Nov 4, 1896 in Philippines
d. Jun 14, 1971 in Manila, Philippines
Source: *CurBio 57, 71; NewYTBE 71; WhAm 5*

Garcia, Damaso Domingo
Dominican. Baseball Player
b. Feb 7, 1957 in Moca, Dominican Republic
Source: *BaseEn*

Garcia, Jerry (Jerome John)
[The Grateful Dead]
American. Musician, Singer
b. Aug 1, 1942 in San Francisco, California
Source: *BiDAmM; BioIn 9, 11; BkPepl; ConMuA 80; WhoAm 82; WhoRock 81*

Garcia, Manuel del Popolo Vincente, I
Spanish. Opera Singer, Composer
b. Jan 22, 1775 in Seville, Spain
d. Jun 2, 1832 in Paris, France
Source: *BiDAmM; NewEOp 71; OxMus*

Garcia, Manuel Patricio Rodriguez, II
Spanish. Opera Singer, Teacher
b. Mar 17, 1805 in Madrid, Spain
d. Jul 1, 1906 in London, England
Source: *NewEOp 71; OxMus*

Garcia, Mike (Edward Miguel)
"The Big Bear"
American. Baseball Player
b. Nov 17, 1923 in San Gabriel, California
Source: *BaseEn; BioIn 3; WhoProB 73*

Garcia Lorca, Federico
Spanish. Poet, Dramatist
b. Jun 5, 1899 in Fuente Vaqueros, Spain
d. Aug 19, 1936 in Fuente Vaqueros, Spain
Source: *AtlBL; CasWL; ClDMEL; CnMD; CnMWL; CnThe; CyWA; DcSpL; EncWL; EvEuW; LongCTC; McGEWD; ModRL; ModWD; OxEng; OxThe; Pen EUR; RComWL; REn; REnWD; TwCA, SUP; TwCW; WhAm 4; WhoTwCL*

Garcia-Marquez, Gabriel
Colombian. Author
Won 1982 Nobel Prize for literature.
b. Mar 6, 1928 in Aracatacca, Colombia
Source: *CasWL; ConAu 33R; ConLC 2, 3, 8, 10, 15; DcCLAA; Pen AM; WorAu*

Gard, Wayne
American. Journalist, Historian
b. Jun 21, 1899 in Brocton, Illinois
Source: *AmAu&B; AnMV 1926; ConAu 1R; TexWr; WhNAA*

Gardella, Kay
American. Broadcaster
b. 1923 in Belleville, New Jersey
Source: *ForWC 70*

Garden, Mary
Scottish. Opera Singer
b. Feb 20, 1874 in Aberdeen, Scotland
d. Jan 4, 1967 in Aberdeen, Scotland
Source: *Film 1; InWom; REn; TwYS; WebAB; WhAm 4; WhScrn 74, 77; WhoHol B*

Gardenia, Vincent
American. Actor
b. Jan 7, 1922 in Naples, Italy
Source: *BiE&WWA; FilmgC; IntMPA 75, 76, 78, 79, 80, 81, 82; NewYTBS 74; NotNAT; PlP&P A; WhoAm 82; WhoHol A; WhoThe 77*

Gardiner, Reginald
English. Actor
b. Feb 27, 1903 in Wimbledon, England
d. Jul 7, 1980 in Westwood, California
Source: *BiE&WWA; BioIn 2, 10; FilmgC; MotPP; MovMk; Vers A; WhoHol A; WhoThe 77*

Gardner, Ava
[Lucy Johnson]
American. Actress
Starred in movie *Show Boat,* 1951; husbands included Mickey Rooney, Artie Shaw, Frank Sinatra.
b. Dec 24, 1922 in Smithfield, North Carolina
Source: *BiDFilm; CelR 73; CurBio 65; FilmEn; FilmgC; IntMPA 75, 76, 77, 78, 79, 80, 81, 82; IntWW 74; MotPP; MovMk; OxFilm; WhoAm 74, 76, 78, 80, 82; WhoHol A; WorEFlm*

Gardner, Ed(ward Francis)
American. Comedian
b. Jun 29, 1905 in Astoria, New York
d. Aug 17, 1963
Source: *CurBio 43, 63; WhScrn 74, 77; WhoHol B*

Gardner, Erle Stanley
[A A Fair, pseud.]
American. Author
b. Jul 17, 1889 in Malden, Massachusetts
d. Mar 11, 1970 in Temecula, California
Source: *AmAu&B; ConAu 5R, 25R; CurBio 44, 70; EncMys; EvLB; FilmgC; LongCTC; MnBBF; NewYTBE 70; OxAmL; Pen AM; REn; REnAL; TwCA, SUP; TwCW; WebAB; WhAm 6; WhNAA*

Gardner, George
Irish. Boxer
b. Mar 17, 1877 in Lisdoonvarna, Ireland
d. Jul 8, 1954 in Chicago, Illinois
Source: *BioIn 3; WhoBox 74*

Gardner, Hy
American. Journalist, Interviewer
b. Dec 2, 1908 in New York, New York
Source: *ConAu 101; WhoAm 74, 76, 78, 80, 82*

Gardner, Isabella
American. Poet
b. Sep 7, 1915 in Newton, Massachusetts
d. Jul 7, 1981 in New York, New York
Source: *AmWomWr; BioIn 10; IntWWP 77; WhoAm 74; WhoAmW 74*

Gardner, Mrs. Jack
[Isabella Stewart]
American. Patron of the Arts
b. 1840
d. 1924
Source: *NotAW*

Gardner, John Champlin, Jr.
American. Author
Wrote *Grendel* and *October Light*.
b. Jul 21, 1933 in Batavia, New York
d. Sep 14, 1982 in Susquehanna, Pennsylvania
Source: *AuBYP SUP; AuNews 1; ConAu 65; ConLC 2, 3, 5, 7, 8, 10; ConNov 76; CurBio 78, 82; DcLB 1; DcLEL 1940; DrAF 76; EncSF; ModAL SUP; NewYTBS 82; RAdv 1; ScF&FL 1; WhoAm 74, 76, 78, 80; WorAu 1970; WrDr 76, 80*

Gardner, John William
American. Former Cabinet Member
Secretary of HEW, 1965-68; wrote *In Common Cause*, 1972.
b. Oct 8, 1912 in Los Angeles, California
Source: *AmAu&B; ConAu 1R, 5R, 4NR; CurBio 56; IntWW 74; Who 74; WhoAm 74, 76, 78, 80, 82; WhoAmP 73; WhoWor 74*

Gardner, Martin
American. Journalist
b. Oct 21, 1914 in Tulsa, Oklahoma
Source: *AmAu&B; AuBYP SUP; BioIn 6, 10; ConAu 73; EncSF; SmATA 16; WhoE 74*

Gardner, Randy
American. Figure Skater
Teamed with Tai Babilonia to win five national championships, 1979 world title.
b. Dec 2, 1958 in Marina del Rey, California
Source: *BioIn 12; NewYTBS 79*

Gardner, Samuel
Russian. Musician
b. Aug 25, 1891 in Elisavetgrad, Russia
Source: *AmSCAP 66; WhoMus 72*

Gareau, Jacqueline
American. Marathon Runner
b. Mar 10, 1953
Source: *BioIn 12*

Garfield, Brian Wynne
American. Author
b. Jan 26, 1939 in New York, New York
Source: *BioIn 10; ConAu 1R; WhoAm 82*

Garfield, James Abram
American. 20th US President
Shot Jul 2, 1881 in Washington railway station by Charles J Guiteau who wanted Chester Arthur president.
b. Nov 19, 1831 in Cuyahoga County, Ohio
d. Sep 19, 1881 in Elberon, New Jersey
Source: *Alli SUP; AmAu&B; AmBi; ApCAB; BiAuS; BiD&SB; BiDrAC; BiDrUSE; DcAmAu; DcAmB; Drake; EncAB-H; OhA&B; OxAmL; REnAL; TwCBDA; WebAB; WhAm H; WhAmP*

Garfield, John
[Julius Garfinkle]
American. Actor
b. Mar 4, 1913 in New York, New York
d. May 21, 1952 in New York, New York
Source: *BiDFilm; CmMov; CurBio 48, 52; DcAmB S5; FilmgC; MotPP; MovMk; OxFilm; PlP&P; WhScrn 74, 77; WhoHol B; WorEFlm*

Garfield, Leon
English. Author
b. Jul 14, 1921 in Brighton, England
Source: *ConAu 17R; ConLC 12; PiP; SenS; SmATA 1; WhoChL; WrDr 76*

Garfield, Lucretia Rudolph
American. Wife of James Garfield
b. Apr 19, 1832 in Hiram, Ohio
d. 1918
Source: *BioIn 2, 3, 5, 6, 7, 8, 9; TwCBDA*

Garfunkel, Art(hur)
[Simon and Garfunkel]
American. Singer, Actor
Best known songs with Paul Simon include "The Sounds of Silence," "Mrs. Robinson."
b. Oct 13, 1942 in Forest Hills, New York
Source: *BkPepl; CelR 73; CurBio 74; FilmgC; IntMPA 75, 76, 77, 78, 79, 80, 81, 82; WhoAm 74, 76, 78, 80, 82*

Gargan, William
American. Actor
b. Jul 17, 1905 in New York, New York
Source: *CurBio 69; FilmgC; HolP 30; IntMPA 75, 76, 77; MotPP; MovMk; WhoHol A; WhoThe 77*

Garibaldi, Guiseppe
Italian. Patriot, Soldier
b. Jul 4, 1807 in Nice, France
d. Jun 2, 1882
Source: *McGEWB; WhAm H*

Garis, Howard Roger
American. Author
Worked for Stratemeyer syndicate; wrote *Uncle Wiggly* series.
b. Apr 25, 1873 in Binghamton, New York
d. Nov 5, 1962 in Amherst, Massachusetts
Source: *AmAu&B; CarSB; ConAu 73; REnAL; SmATA 13; WhAm 4*

Garland, Ailsa
English. Broadcaster
Source: *Au&Wr 71; Who 74*

Garland, Beverly
American. Actress
b. Oct 17, 1929 in Santa Cruz, California
Source: *FilmgC; IntMPA 77, 75; MotPP; MovMk; WhoAm 74, 76, 78, 80, 82; WhoHol A*

Garland, Hamlin
American. Author
b. Sep 14, 1860 in West Salem, Wisconsin
d. Mar 4, 1940 in Los Angeles, California
Source: *AmAu&B; AmBi; AmLY; ApCAB SUP; AtlBL; BbD; BiD&SB; BiDPara; CasWL; Chambr 3; ChPo; CnDAL; ConAmA; ConAmL; CurBio 40; CyWA; DcAmAu; DcAmB S2; DcBiA; DcLEL; DcNAA; EvLB; LongCTC; ModAL; OxAmL; OxCan; OxEng; Pen AM; RAdv 1; REn; REnAL; Str&VC; TwCA, SUP; TwCBDA; WebAB; WebE&AL; WhAm 1; WhNAA; WisWr*

Garland, Judy
[Frances Gumm]
American. Actress, Singer
Played Dorothy in *The Wizard of Oz,* 1939; mother of Liza Minnelli, Lorna Luft.
b. Jun 10, 1922 in Grand Rapids, Minnesota
d. Jun 22, 1969 in London, England
Source: *BiDFilm; CmMov; CurBio 41, 52, 69; FilmgC; InWom; MotPP; MovMk; OxFilm; ThFT; WebAB; WhAm 5; WhScrn 74, 77; WhoHol B; WorEFlm*

Garlits, Don
American. Auto Racer
b. 1932
Source: *BioIn 7, 8, 9, 10, 11*

Garment, Leonard
American. Lawyer, Human Rights Advocate
b. May 11, 1924 in Brooklyn, New York
Source: *NewYTBE 73; WhoAm 74, 76, 78; WhoAmP 73; WhoGov 72; WhoS&SW 73*

Garms, Shirley Rudolph
American. Bowler
b. 1924
Source: *BioIn 6, 9*

Garn, Jake (Edwin Jacob)
American. Senator
b. Oct 12, 1932 in Richfield, Utah
Source: *AlmAP 78, 80; BioIn 10, 11; WhoAm 78, 80, 82; WhoAmP 73; WhoGov 75, 77; WhoWest 74, 76, 78*

Garner, Erroll
American. Musician, Composer
b. Jun 15, 1921 in Pittsburgh, Pennsylvania
d. Jan 2, 1977 in Los Angeles, California
Source: *AmSCAP 66; CelR 73; CurBio 59; WhoAm 74; WhoE 74; WhoBlA 75*

Garner, James
[James Baumgarner]
American. Actor
Starred in "The Rockford Files"; appears in Polaroid commercials with Mariette Hartley.
b. Apr 17, 1928 in Norman, Oklahoma
Source: *BkPepl; CelR 73; CmMov; CurBio 66; FilmgC; IntMPA 75, 76, 77, 78, 79, 80, 81, 82; MotPP; MovMk; NewYTBE 71; WhoAm 74, 76, 78, 80, 82; WhoHol A; WorEFlm*

Garner, John Nance
American. Lawyer, Politician
Served as vice-president under Franklin Roosevelt, 1933-41.
b. Nov 22, 1868 in Blossom Prairie, Texas
d. Nov 7, 1967 in Uvalde, Texas
Source: *BiDrAC; BiDrUSE; EncAB-H; WebAB; WhAm 4; WhAmP*

Garner, Peggy Ann
American. Actress
b. Feb 8, 1931 in Canton, Ohio
Source: *FilmgC; ForWC 70; HolP 40; IntMPA 75, 76, 77; MotPP; MovMk; WhoAm 82; WhoHol A*

Garnet, Henry Highland
American. Abolitionist, Clergyman
b. Dec 23, 1815 in New Market, Maryland
d. Feb 13, 1882 in Monrovia, Liberia
Source: *BioIn 4, 6, 8, 9, 11; DcAmB; WhAm H*

Garnett, Constance
English. Translator
b. 1861
d. Dec 17, 1946 in Edenbridge, England
Source: *DcLEL; LongCTC; NewC; OxEng; Pen ENG; REn*

Garnett, David
[Leda Burke, pseud.]
English. Author
b. Mar 9, 1892 in Brighton, England
d. Feb 17, 1981 in Montucq, France
Source: *Au&Wr 71; BioIn 1, 2, 3, 4, 5, 6, 8; CasWL; ConAu 5R, 103; ConLC 3; ConNov 72, 76; CyWA; DcLEL; EncSF; EncWL; EvLB; IntAu&W 76; IntWW 74, 75, 76, 77, 78; LongCTC; ModBrL; NewC; Pen ENG; REn; ScF&FL 1, 2; TwCA, SUP; TwCW; WhE&EA; WhLit; Who 74; WhoHr&F; WhoLA; WhoWor 74, 76, 78*

Garnett, Eve C R
English. Children's Author, Illustrator
b. in Worcestershire, England
Source: *Au&Wr 71; AuBYP; ConAu 1R; IlsCB 1744, 1946; SmATA 3; WhoChL; WrDr 76*

Garnett, Gale
New Zealander. Actress, Singer
b. Jul 17, 1942 in New Zealand
Source: *RkOn 2; WhoRock 81*

Garnett, Richard
English. Author
b. Feb 27, 1835 in Staffordshire, England
d. Apr 13, 1906 in London, England
Source: *Alli SUP; BbD; BiD&SB; BrAu 19; CasWL; ChPo, S1; DcEnA, AP; DcEnL; DcLEL; EvLB; LongCTC; NewC; OxEng; Pen ENG; REn*

Garr, Teri
American. Actress
Daughter of Eddie Garr; starred in *The Black Stallion,* 1979.
b. Dec 11, 1945 in Hollywood, California
Source: *WhoAm 82; WhoHol A*

Garraty, John Arthur
American. Historian, Educator, Author
b. Jul 4, 1920 in Brooklyn, New York
Source: *BioIn 10; ConAu 1R, 2NR; DrAS 74H; SmATA 23; WhoAm 74; WhoWor 74*

Garrett, Betty
American. Actress
b. May 23, 1919 in Saint Joseph, Missouri
Source: *BiE&WWA; CmMov; FilmgC; IntMPA 75, 76, 77, 78, 79, 80, 81, 82; MotPP; MovMk; NotNAT; WhoAm 82; WhoHol A; WhoThe 77*

Garrett, Eileen Jeanette Lyttle
American. Psychic, Publisher
b. Mar 17, 1893 in Beau Park, Ireland
d. Sep 16, 1970 in Nice, France
Source: *AmAu&B; BiDPara; ConAu 25R; ConAu P-2; NewYTBE 70; WhAm 5*

Garrett, George Palmer, Jr.
American. Author, Educator
b. Jun 11, 1929 in Orlando, Florida
Source: *AmAu&B; ConAu 1R, 1NR; ConNov 72, 76; ConP 70, 75; DrAF 76; DrAP 75; IntMPA 82; OxAmL; RAdv 1; REnAL; WhoAm 74, 76, 78, 80, 82; WhoWor 74; WorAu; WrDr 76*

Garrett, Leif
American. Actor, Singer
b. Nov 8, 1961 in Hollywood, California
Source: *BioIn 11; WhoRock 81*

Garrett, Michael Lockett
American. Football, Baseball Player
b. Apr 12, 1944 in Los Angeles, California
Source: *BioIn 7, 8, 9, 10; WhoFtbl 74*

Garrett, Patrick Floyd
American. Constable
b. 1850
d. 1908
Source: *BioIn 4, 5, 6, 9, 10, 11; DcNAA*

Garrett, Ray, Jr.
American. Government Official
b. Aug 11, 1920 in Chicago, Illinois
d. Feb 3, 1980 in Evanston, Illinois
Source: *BioIn 10; IntWW 75, 76, 77, 78; WhAm 7; WhoAm 74, 76, 78; WhoAmL 79; WhoAmP 75, 77, 79; WhoGov 75*

Garrick, David
English. Actor
b. Feb 19, 1717 in Hereford, England
d. Jan 20, 1779 in London, England
Source: *Alli; BrAu; CasWL; Chambr 2; CrtT 2; DcEnA; DcEnL; DcEuL; DcLEL; EvLB; FilmgC; McGEWD; MouLC 2; NewC; OxEng; OxThe; Pen ENG; REn*

Garrigue, Jean
American. Poet
b. Dec 8, 1914 in Evansville, Indiana
d. Dec 27, 1972 in Boston, Massachusetts
Source: *AmAu&B; BioIn 4, 8, 9; ConAu 5R, 37R; ConLC 2; ConP 70, 75; IndAu 1917; ModAL, SUP; OxAmL; Pen AM; RAdv 1; REnAL; TwCA SUP; WhAm 5*

Garriott, Owen
American. Astronaut, Scientist
Science pilot for second Skylab space mission, Jul-Sep, 1973.
b. Nov 22, 1930 in Enid, Oklahoma
Source: *AmM&WS 73P; IntWW 74; NewYTBE 73; WhoAm 82; WhoGov 72; WhoS&SW 73*

Garrison, Jim C
American. Lawyer
b. Nov 20, 1921 in Denison, Iowa
Source: *WhoAm 74, 78*

Garrison, William Lloyd
American. Abolitionist, Author
b. Dec 12, 1805 in Newburyport, Massachusetts
d. May 24, 1879 in New York, New York
Source: *Alli; AmAu; AmAu&B; AmBi; ApCAB; BiD&SB; Chambr 3; ChPo; DcAmAu; DcAmB; DcEnL; DcLEL; DcNAA; EncAB-H; EvLB; OxAmL; REn; REnAL; TwCBDA; WebAB; WhAm H; WhAmP*

Garroway, Dave Cunningham
American. TV Broadcaster
Original host of "The Today Show," 1952-61.
b. Jul 13, 1913 in Schenectady, New York
d. Jul 21, 1982 in Swarthmore, Pennsylvania
Source: *CurBio 52, 82; IntMPA 75, 76, 77, 78, 79, 80, 81, 82; IntWW 74, 75; NewYTBE 71; NewYTBS 82; NewYTET; WhoAm 74, 76, 78, 80, 82*

Garry, Charles R
American. Lawyer
b. Mar 17, 1909 in Bridgewater, Massachusetts
Source: *BioIn 8, 10, 11; WhoAm 74*

Garson, Greer
American. Actress
Won Oscar, 1942, for *Mrs. Miniver*.
b. Sep 29, 1908? in County Down, Northern Ireland
Source: *BiDFilm; CmMov; CurBio 42; FilmgC; InWom; IntMPA 75, 76, 77, 78, 79, 80, 81, 82; MotPP; MovMk; OxFilm; ThFT; Who 74; WhoAm 74, 76, 78, 80, 82; WhoHol A; WhoThe 77; WorEFlm*

Garst, Roswell
American. Agriculturist, Banker
b. 1898 in Rockford, Illinois
d. Nov 5, 1977 in Carroll, Iowa
Source: *BioIn 5, 6, 7, 10, 11; CurBio 64, 78; EncAAH; NewYTBS 77; ObitOF 79*

Garth, David
American. Political Consultant
b. 1930 in Woodmere, New York
Source: *BioIn 11; CurBio 81; WhoAm 82*

Garver, Kathy
American. Actress
b. 1948 in Long Beach, California
Source: *WhoHol A*

Garvey, Ed(ward Robert)
American. Lawyer, Union Official
Director NFL Players' Assn.; chief negotiator during strike, 1982.
b. Apr 18, 1940 in Burlington, Wisconsin
Source: *WhoAm 82*

Garvey, Marcus Moziah
Jamaican. Political Leader
b. Aug 17, 1887 in Saint Ann's Bay, Jamaica
d. Jun 10, 1940 in London, England
Source: *CurBio 40; DcAmB S2; EncAB-H; WebAB; WhAm HA, 4; WhAmP*

Garvey, Steve Patrick
American. Baseball Player
First baseman, LA Dodgers, 1970-82; signed multi-million dollar contract with San Diego, 1982.
b. Dec 22, 1948 in Tampa, Florida
Source: *BaseEn; WhoAm 82; WhoProB 73*

Garvin, Clifton Canter, Jr.
American. Oil Company Executive
b. Dec 22, 1921 in Portsmouth, Virginia
Source: *CurBio 80; WhoAm 78, 80, 82; WhoF&I 79*

Garwood, Robert Russell
American. Former Marine, POW in Vietnam
b. Dec 22, 1921 in Portsmouth, Virginia
Source: *BioIn 12*

Gary, Elbert H
American. Businessman, Philanthropist
b. Oct 8, 1846 in Wheaton, Illinois
d. Aug 15, 1927 in New York, New York
Source: *AmBi; DcAmB; EncAB-H; WebAB; WhAm 1*

Gary, John
American. Singer
b. Nov 29, 1932 in Watertown, New York
Source: *AmSCAP 66; CurBio 67; WhoAm 74; WhoHol A*

Gary, Romain
French. Author, Diplomat
b. May 8, 1914 in Wilno, Lithuania
d. Dec 2, 1980 in Paris, France
Source: *CasWL; ConAu 102; EncWL; IntWW 74; ModRL; REn; TwCW; Who 74; WhoAm 74; WhoWor 74; WorAu; WorEFlm*

Gary Puckett and the Union Gap
[Dwight Cement; Kerry Chater; Gary Puckett; Paul Wheatbread; Mutha Withem]
American. Vocal, Instrumental Group
Source: *EncPR&S*

Gascoyne, David Emery
English. Poet
b. Oct 10, 1916 in Salisbury, England
Source: *BioIn 10; CnE&AP; ConAu 65; ConP 70; EncWL; LongCTC; ModBrL; Pen ENG; TwCW; WebE&AL; WhoTwCL; WorAu; WrDr 76*

Gaskell, Elizabeth Cleghorn
English. Author
b. Sep 29, 1810 in Chelsea, England
d. Nov 12, 1865 in Alton, England
Source: *Alli SUP; AtlBL; BbD; BiD&SB; BrAu 19; CasWL; CrtT 3; CyWA; DcBiA; DcEnA; DcEuL; DcLEL; EvLB; HsB&A; MouLC 3; NewC; OxEng; Pen ENG; RAdv 1; REn; WebE&AL*

Gaspari, Remo
Italian. Lawyer, Politician
b. 1921 in Gissi, Italy
Source: *IntWW 74*

Gasperi, Alcide de
[DeGasperi, Alcide]
Italian. Statesman, Premier
b. Apr 3, 1881 in Terentino, Italy
d. Aug 19, 1954
Source: *CurBio 46, 54; NewCol 75*

Gass, William H
American. Author
b. Jul 30, 1924 in Fargo, North Dakota
Source: *AmAu&B; Au&Wr 71; ConAu 17R; ConLC 1, 2; ConNov 72, 76; DrAF 76; EncWL; ModAL SUP; Pen AM; RAdv 1; WhoAm 74, 76, 78, 80, 82; WorAu; WrDr 76*

Gasser, Herbert Spencer
American. Physiologist
b. Jul 5, 1888 in Platteville, Wisconsin
d. May 11, 1963
Source: *BioIn 1, 3, 6, 7, 11; CurBio 45, 63; WhAm 4*

Gassman, Vittorio
Italian. Actor, Motion Picture Director
b. Sep 1, 1922 in Genoa, Italy
Source: *BiDFilm; CurBio 64; FilmgC; IntMPA 75, 76, 77; IntWW 74; MotPP; MovMk; WhoAm 82; WhoHol A; WhoWor 74; WorEFlm*

Gassner, John Waldhorn
American. Author
b. Jan 30, 1903 in Sziget, Hungary
d. Apr 2, 1967 in New Haven, Connecticut
Source: *AmAu&B; ConAu 1R, 25R, 3NR; CurBio 47, 67; REnAL; WhAm 4; WhNAA*

Gaston, Arthur George
American. Insurance Company Executive
b. 1892
Source: *BioIn 6, 8, 9, 11*

Gastoni, Lisa
Italian. Actress
b. 1935
Source: *FilmgC*

Gates, David
[Bread]
American. Singer, Songwriter
b. Dec 11, 1940 in Tulsa, Oklahoma
Source: *RkOn 2; WhoRock 81*

Gates, Horatio
American. Revolutionary General
b. Jul 26, 1728 in Malden, England
d. Apr 10, 1806 in New York, New York
Source: *AmBi; ApCAB; DcAmB; Drake; OxAmL; REn; REnAL; TwCBDA; WebAB; WhAm H*

Gates, John Warne
"Bet a Million"
American. Financier, Speculator
b. May 8, 1855 in Turner Junction, Illinois
d. Aug 9, 1911 in Paris, France
Source: *AmBi; BusPN; DcAmB; WebAB; WhAm 1, 4*

Gates, Larry
American. Actor
b. Sep 24, 1915 in Saint Paul, Minnesota
Source: *BiE&WWA; FilmgC; NotNAT; WhoThe 77*

Gates, Thomas S, Jr.
American. Businessman, Statesman
b. Apr 10, 1906 in Philadelphia, Pennsylvania
Source: *BiDrUSE; CurBio 57; IntWW 74; St&PR 75; Who 74; WhoAm 74; WhoAmP 73; WhoE 74*

Gatlin, Larry
American. Singer, Songwriter
b. May 2, 1949 in Odessa, Texas
Source: *BioIn 11; WhoAm 82*

Gatling, Richard Jordan
American. Inventor
Creator of first practical rapid-firing gun, 1862, forerunner of modern machine gun.
b. Sep 12, 1818 in Hertford County, North Carolina
d. Feb 26, 1903 in New York, New York
Source: *AmBi; ApCAB; DcAmB; TwCBDA; WebAB; WhAm 1*

Gatti-Casazza, Giulio
Italian. Opera Manager
b. Feb 3, 1869 in Udine, Italy
d. Sep 2, 1940 in Ferrara, Italy
Source: *CurBio 40; DcAmB S2*

Gaubert, Philippe
French. Musician, Conductor, Composer
b. Jul 4, 1879 in Cahors, France
d. Jul 10, 1941 in Paris, France
Source: *NewEOp 71; OxMus*

Gaud, William Steen, Jr.
American. Lawyer, Government Official
b. Aug 9, 1905 in New York, New York
d. Dec 5, 1977 in Washington, DC
Source: *CurBio 69, 78; IntWW 74, 76, 77, 78; NewYTBS 77; WhAm 7; WhoAm 74, 76, 78; WhoWor 78*

Gaudi y Cornet, Antonio
Spanish. Architect
b. Jun 25, 1852 in Reus, Spain
d. 1926
Source: *BioIn 2, 3, 4, 5, 8, 9, 10; DcBiPP; McGDA; McGEWB; NewCol 75*

Gaudio, Bob
[The Four Seasons]
American. Singer, Musician
b. Nov 17, 1942 in Bronx, New York
Source: *NF*

Gauguin, (Eugene Henri) Paul
French. Artist
Friend of Van Gogh; lived in Tahiti; best known works depict Tahitian natives.
b. Jun 7, 1848 in Paris, France
d. Jun 6, 1903 in Marquesas Islands
Source: *AtlBL; LongCTC; NewC; NewCol 75; OxFr; REn; WebBD 80*

Gaulli, Giovanni Battista
[Il Baciccio]
Italian. Artist
b. 1639
d. 1709
Source: *BioIn 10*

Gault, William Campbell
American. Author
b. Mar 9, 1910 in Milwaukee, Wisconsin
Source: *AuBYP; ConAu 49, 1NR; EncMys; SmATA 8*

Gaunt, William
English. Author, Critic, Artist
b. Jul 5, 1900 in Hull, England
d. May 24, 1980 in London, England
Source: *Au&Wr 71; BioIn 4, 10, 11; ConAu 9R, 97; IntAu&W 76, 77; LongCTC; TwCA SUP; WhE&EA; Who 74; WhoWor 76, 78; WrDr 76, 80*

Gauquelin, Michel
French. Author, Biologist
b. Nov 13, 1928 in Paris, France
Source: *ConAu 57*

Gauss, Karl Friedrich
German. Mathematician
b. Apr 30, 1777 in Brunswick, Germany
d. Feb 23, 1855 in Goettingen, Germany
Source: *AsBiEn; DcBiPP; McGEWB*

Gauthier, Alain
see: Dumurq, Charles

Gautier, Dick
American. Actor
b. Oct 30, 1937 in Los Angeles, California
Source: *AmSCAP 66; FilmgC; WhoAm 82; WhoHol A*

Gautier, (Pierre Jules) Theophile
French. Poet, Author, Critic
b. Aug 31, 1811 in Tarbes, France
d. Oct 23, 1872 in Neuilly, France
Source: *AtlBL; BbD; BiD&SB; CasWL; CyWA; DcBiA; DcEuL; EuAu; EvEuW; NewC; OxEng; OxFr; Pen EUR; RComWL; REn*

Gavilan, Kid
"The Hawk"
Cuban. Boxer
b. Jan 6, 1926 in Camaguey, Cuba
Source: *WhoBox 74*

Gavin, James Maurice
American. Army Officer, Author
b. Mar 22, 1907 in New York, New York
Source: *AmAu&B; ConAu P-1; CurBio 45, 61; IntWW 74; WhoAm 78, 80, 82; WhoF&I 74; WhoWor 74*

Gavin, John
American. Actor
b. Apr 8, 1928 in Los Angeles, California
Source: *CurBio 62; FilmgC; IntMPA 75, 76, 77, 78, 79, 80, 81, 82; MovMk; WhoHol A*

Gaxton, William
American. Actor
b. Dec 2, 1893 in San Francisco, California
d. Feb 2, 1963 in New York, New York
Source: *EncMT; FilmgC; PlP&P; WhScrn 74, 77; WhoHol B*

Gay, John
English. Poet, Dramatist
Friend of Swift and Pope; wrote *Beggar's Opera,* 1728.
b. 1685 in Barnstaple, England
d. Dec 4, 1732 in London, England
Source: *Alli; AtlBL; BiD&SB; BrAu; CarSB; CasWL; Chambr 2; ChPo, S1, S2; CnE&AP; CnThe; CrtT 2; CyWA; DcEnA, AP; DcEnL; DcEuL; DcLEL; EvLB; McGEWD; MouLC 2; NewC; OxEng; OxThe; Pen ENG; REn; REnWD; WebE&AL*

Gay, Peter
American. Author, Educator
b. Jun 20, 1923 in Berlin, Germany
Source: *ConAu 13R; DrAS 74H; WhoAm 74, 76, 78, 80, 82; WhoE 74; WhoWor 74*

Gay-Lussac, Joseph Louis
French. Chemist, Physicist
b. Dec 6, 1778 in St. Leonard, France
d. May 9, 1850 in Paris, France
Source: *AsBiEn; BiHiMed; DcScB; McGEWB; NewCol 75; REn*

Gaye, Marvin
American. Singer
b. Apr 2, 1939 in Washington, DC
Source: *BiDAmM; EncPR&S; IlEncRk; WhoAm 82*

Gayle, Crystal
[Mrs. Vassilios Gatzimos; Brenda Gail Webb]
American. Singer
Won Grammy, 1978; sister of Loretta Lynn.
b. Jan 9, 1951 in Paintsville, Kentucky
Source: *BioIn 11; BkPepl; WhoAm 80, 82*

Gaynor, Gloria
American. Singer
b. Sep 7, 1949 in Newark, New Jersey
Source: *DcBlPA; RkOn 2; WhoRock 81*

Gaynor, Janet
American. Actress
Won first Oscar given, 1928, for *Sunrise;* seriously injured in car accident, 1982.
b. Oct 6, 1906 in Philadelphia, Pennsylvania
Source: *BiDFilm; CmMov; FilmgC; InWom; MotPP; MovMk; OxFilm; ThFT; TwYS; WhoHol A; WorEFlm*

Gaynor, Mitzi
[Francesca Mitzi Marlene de Charney von Gerber]
American. Singer, Dancer
Starred in film version of *South Pacific,* 1958.
b. Sep 4, 1931 in Chicago, Illinois
Source: *CmMov; FilmgC; InWom; IntMPA 75, 76, 77, 78, 79, 80, 81, 82; MotPP; MovMk; OxFilm; WhoAm 74, 76, 78, 80, 82; WhoHol A; WorEFlm*

Gayoom, Maumoon Abdul
Maldivian. Politician
b. Dec 16, 1939
Source: *IntWW 79*

Gazda, Ricky
see: Southside Johnny and the Asbury Jukes

Gazzaniga, Giuseppe
Italian. Composer
b. 1743 in Verona, Italy
d. Feb 1, 1818 in Crema, Italy
Source: *NewEOp 71*

Gazzara, Ben (Biago Anthony)
American. Actor
b. Aug 28, 1930 in New York, New York
Source: *BiDFilm; BiE&WWA; CelR 73; CurBio 67; FilmgC; IntMPA 77, 78, 79, 80, 81, 82; MotPP; MovMk; OxFilm; PlP&P A; WhoAm 74, 76, 78, 80, 82; WhoHol A; WhoThe 77*

Gazzelloni, Severino
Italian. Musician
b. Jan 5, 1919 in Roccasecca, Italy
Source: *WhoMus 72; WhoWor 74*

Gearhart, Daniel F
American. Mercenary
b. 1942?
d. Jul 1976 in Angola
Source: *BioIn 11; NewYTBS 76*

Geary, Anthony
American. Actor
Plays Luke Spencer on TV soap opera "General Hospital."
b. 1948? in Coalville, Utah
Source: *BioIn 12*

Gebert, Ernst
German. Conductor
b. 1901 in Berlin, Germany
d. Nov 22, 1961 in Hollywood, California
Source: *BioIn 6; NotNAT B*

Ged, William
Scottish. Inventor
Invented stereotyping, patented 1725.
b. 1690 in Edinburgh, Scotland
d. 1749
Source: *LinLib L, S*

Gedda, Nicolai
Swedish. Opera Singer
b. Jul 11, 1925 in Stockholm, Sweden
Source: *CurBio 65; IntWW 74; NewYTBE 72; WhoAm 82; WhoMus 72; WhoWor 74*

Geddes, Barbara Bel
American. Actress
Plays Miss Ellie on TV series "Dallas," 1978--.
b. Oct 31, 1922 in New York, New York
Source: *BiE&WWA; CelR 73; CurBio 48; InWom; IntMPA 75; MotPP; OxThe; WhoAm 74, 76, 78, 80, 82; WhoHol A*

Geddes, Norman Bel
American. Scenic Designer
b. Apr 27, 1893 in Adrian, Michigan
d. May 8, 1958 in New York, New York
Source: *CurBio 40, 58; PlP&P; OxThe; REn; REnAL; WebAB; WhAm 3*

Geddes, Sir Patrick
British. Physicist
b. Oct 2, 1854 in Ballater, Scotland
d. Apr 16, 1932 in Montpellier, France
Source: *Alli SUP; BbD; BiD&SB; LongCTC; NewCol 75; TwCA, SUP; WebBD 80; WhoLA*

Geer, Will
American. Actor
Played grandfather on TV series "The Waltons"; won Emmy, 1975.
b. Mar 9, 1902 in Frankfort, Indiana
d. Apr 22, 1978 in Los Angeles, California
Source: *BiE&WWA; FilmgC; IntMPA 75, 76, 77; MovMk; NewYTBE 72; NotNAT; WhoHol A; WhoThe 77*

Geertz, Clifford
American. Anthropologist, Author
b. Aug 23, 1926 in San Francisco, California
Source: *AmM&WS 73S; ConAu 33R; WhoAm 82*

Geeson, Judy
English. Actress
b. Sep 10, 1948 in Arundel, England
Source: *FilmgC; IntMPA 75, 76, 77, 78, 79, 80, 81; MovMk*

Gehlen, Reinhard
"The Doctor"; "Number 30"
German. Espionage Leader
b. Apr 3, 1902 in Erfurt, Germany
d. Jun 8, 1979 in Lake Starnberg, Germany (West)
Source: *BioIn 3, 4, 5, 6, 8, 9, 10; ConAu 89; EncE 75; NewYTBS 79*

Gehrig, (Henry) Lou(is)
"Columbia Lou"; "The Iron Horse"
American. Baseball Player
First baseman, NY Yankees, 1925-39; played in record 2,130 consecutive games.
b. Jun 19, 1903 in New York, New York
d. Jun 2, 1941 in New York, New York
Source: *BaseEn; CurBio 40, 41; DcAmB S3; WebAB; WhAm 4; WhScrn 77; WhoProB 73*

Gehringer, Charlie (Charles Leonard)
American. Baseball Player
Called "mechanical man" because made game look so easy; Hall of Fame, 1949.
b. May 11, 1903 in Fowlerville, Michigan
Source: *BaseEn; WhoProB 73*

Geiberger, Al(len L)
American. Golfer
b. Sep 1, 1937 in Red Bluff, California
Source: *BioIn 7, 10, 11; WhoAm 82; WhoGolf*

Geiger, Abraham
German. Theologian
b. 1810
d. 1874
Source: *BioIn 6; NewCol 75; WebBD 80*

Geiger, Hans (Johannes Wilhelm)
German. Physicist
Invented Geiger counter.
b. Sep 30, 1882 in Germany
d. Sep 24, 1945 in Berlin, Germany
Source: *AsBiEn; NewCol 75; WebBD 80*

Geis, Bernard
American. Editor, Publisher
b. Aug 30, 1909 in Chicago, Illinois
Source: *CurBio 60; WhoAm 74, 76, 78, 80, 82; WhoF&I 74; WhoWor 74; WhoWorJ 72*

Geisel, Ernesto
Brazilian. President
b. Aug 3, 1907 in Rio Grande, Brazil
Source: *BioIn 10, 11; IntWW 74; NewYTBE 73; WhoWor 74*

Geisel, Theodore Seuss
see: Seuss, Doctor, pseud.

Geisler, Jerry Hubert
American. Attorney
b. Jul 6, 1934 in Big Stone Gap, Virginia
Source: *WhoAmP 73; WhoS&SW 73*

Geist, Jacob
American. Chemist
b. Feb 2, 1921 in Bridgeport, Connecticut
Source: *AmM&WS 73P; WhoAm 82*

Gejvall, Nils-Gustaf
Swedish. Osteologist
b. 1915
Source: *BioIn 8*

Gelb, Arthur
American. Journalist, Author
b. Feb 3, 1924 in New York, New York
Source: *BiE&WWA; ConAu 1R; NotNAT; WhoAm 74, 76, 78, 80, 82; WhoE 74*

Gelb, Barbara Stone
American. Author
b. Feb 6, 1926 in New York, New York
Source: *ConAu 1R; NotNAT*

Gelb, Lawrence
American. Founder of Clairol, Inc
b. 1898?
d. Sep 27, 1980 in New York, New York
Source: *NF*

Gelbart, Larry
American. Television Producer
b. Feb 25, 1928 in Chicago, Illinois
Source: *AmAu&B; AmSCAP 66, 80; WhoAm 74, 76, 78, 80, 82; WhoWor 74; WrDr 80*

Gelber, Jack
American. Author, Dramatist
b. Apr 12, 1932 in Chicago, Illinois
Source: *AmAu&B; BiE&WWA; CasWL; ConAu 1R, 2NR; ConDr 73; ConLC 1, 6, 14; CroCD; McGEWD; ModAL; ModWD; NotNAT; Pen AM; REn; REnAL; REnWD; TwCW; WebE&AL; WhoAm 74, 76, 78, 80, 82; WhoE 74; WhoThe 77; WhoWor 74; WorAu; WrDr 76*

Geldof, Bob
[Boomtown Rats]
Irish. Actor, Musician, Singer
Played role of Pink in movie *The Wall.*
Source: *NF*

Gell-Mann, Murray
American. Physicist
b. Sep 15, 1929 in New York, New York
Source: *McGEWB; WebAB; WhoAm 82*

Geller, Bruce
American. TV Writer, Producer
b. Oct 13, 1930 in New York, New York
d. May 21, 1976 in Santa Barbara, California
Source: *AmSCAP 66; ConAu 77; IntMPA 76, 77; WhoAm 74; WhoWorJ 72*

Geller, Uri
Israeli. Psychic, Clairvoyant
Psychic powers include ability to bend metal; start, stop watches mentally.
b. Dec 20, 1946 in Tel Aviv, Palestine
Source: *BioNews 74; ConAu 69*

Gellhorn, Martha Ellis
American. Author, Journalist
b. 1908 in Saint Louis, Missouri
Source: *AmAu&B; AmNov; ConAu 77; ConNov 72, 76; DrAF 76; InWom; IntWW 74; OxAmL; REnAL; TwCA, SUP; WhoAm 74, 76, 78, 80, 82; WrDr 76*

Gellhorn, Peter
German. Director of BBC Chorus
b. Oct 24, 1912 in Breslau, Germany
Source: *Who 74; WhoMus 72*

Gellis, Roberta Leah Jacobs
American. Author
b. Sep 27, 1927 in New York, New York
Source: *ConAu 5R; ForWC 70*

Gelmis, Joseph Stephen
American. Film Critic, Author
b. Sep 28, 1935 in Brooklyn, New York
Source: *ConAu 45; WhoAm 74, 76, 78, 80, 82*

Gemayel, Amin
Lebanese. President
Elected president after assassination of younger brother, 1982.
b. 1942 in Bikfaya, Lebanon
Source: *NewYTBS 82*

Gemayel, Bashir
Lebanese. President-elect
Assassinated in bomb attack before taking office.
b. Nov 10, 1947 in Bikfaya, Lebanon
d. Sep 14, 1982 in Beirut, Lebanon
Source: *NewYTBS 82*

Gemayel, Sheikh Pierre
Lebanese. Politician
Founder of Phalange party.
b. 1905
Source: *IntWW 74, 75, 76, 77, 78; MidE 78, 79; WhoWor 74*

Geminiani, Francesco
Italian. Musician, Composer
b. Feb 5, 1687 in Lucca, Italy
d. Dec 17, 1762 in Dublin, Ireland
Source: *OxMus*

Gemmill, Henry
American. Editor
b. Jun 11, 1917 in Toledo, Ohio
Source: *St&PR 75; WhoAm 74; WhoE 74; WhoS&SW 73*

Genaro, Frankie
[Frank DiGennara]
American. Boxer
b. Aug 26, 1901 in New York
d. 1966
Source: *BioIn 7; WhoBox 74*

Genauer, Emily
American. Art Critic, Author
b. in New York, New York
Source: *InWom; WhoAm 74, 78; WhoAmA 73; WhoAmW 77; WhoGov 72*

Gendron, Maurice
French. Musician
b. Dec 26, 1920 in Nice, France
Source: *WhoMus 72; WhoWor 74*

Geneen, Harold Sydney
American. Businessman
b. Jun 11, 1910 in Bournemouth, England
Source: *CurBio 74; IntWW 74; NewYTBE 72; St&PR 75; WhoAm 74, 76, 78, 80, 82; WhoE 74; WhoF&I 74; WhoWor 74*

Genesis
[Tony Banks; Phil Collins; Peter Gabriel; Steve Hackett; AnthonyPhillips; Michael Rutherford; Chester Thompson]
English. Rock Group
Source: *ConMuA 80; IlEncRk; RkOn 2; WhoRock 81*

Genet, Arthur Samuel
American. Transportation Executive
b. 1909
Source: *BioIn 4, 8*

Genet, Edmond Charles Edouard
"Citizen Genet"
French. Statesman
b. 1763 in Versailles, France
d. 1834
Source: *BioIn 1, 2, 9; NewCol 75; WebBD 80*

Genet, Jean
French. Dramatist
b. Dec 19, 1910 in Paris, France
Source: *BiE&WWA; CasWL; CelR 73; CnMD; CnMWL; ConAu 13R; ConLC 1, 2, 5, 10, 14; CroCD; EncWL; EvEuW; LongCTC; McGEWD; ModRL; ModWD; NotNAT; OxThe; Pen EUR; REn; TwCW; WhoThe 77; WhoTwCL; WhoWor 74; WorAu*

Genet, Louis Rene Fernandat
French. Poet, Dramatist
b. 1884
Source: *BioIn 3, 9*

Genevieve
[G Auger]
French. Singer
b. 1930 in Paris, France
Source: *InWom*

Genevieve, Saint
French. Patron Saint of Paris
b. 422?
d. 512
Source: *NewC; NewCol 75; OxFr; WebBD 80*

Genghis Khan
[Genchiz Khan]
Mongolian. Conqueror
b. 1162 in Lake Baikal, Asia
d. 1227
Source: *NewC; REn; WebBD 80*

Genn, Leo
English. Actor
b. Aug 9, 1905 in London, England
d. Jan 26, 1978 in London, England
Source: *BiE&WWA; FilmgC; IntMPA 77, 75; MovMk; NotNAT; Who 74; WhoHol A; WhoThe 77*

Gennaro, Peter
American. Choreographer
b. 1924 in Metaire, Louisiana
Source: *BiE&WWA; CurBio 64; EncMT; NotNAT; WhoAm 74, 76, 78, 80, 82; WhoWor 74*

Genovese, Kitty
American. Murder Victim
Stabbed, as 38 neighbors watched, but did nothing to help.
b. 1935
d. Mar 13, 1964 in New York, New York
Source: *EncACr*

Genovese, Vito
Italian. Gangster, Mafia Leader
b. Nov 27, 1879
d. Feb 14, 1969
Source: *BioIn 8*

Genscher, Hans-Dietrich
German. Diplomat
b. Mar 21, 1927 in Reideburg, Germany
Source: *BioIn 10; CurBio 75*

Gentele, Goeran
Swedish. Opera Director
b. Sep 10, 1917 in Stockholm, Sweden
d. Jul 18, 1972 in Sardinia, Italy
Source: *CurBio 72; NewYTBE 71, 72; WhoMus 72*

Genthe, Arnold
American. Journalist, Photographer
b. Jan 8, 1869 in Berlin, Germany
d. Aug 8, 1942
Source: *AmAu&B; CurBio 42; DcAmB S3; DcNAA; WhAm 2*

Gentile da Fabriano
Italian. Artist
b. 1370 in Fabriano, Italy
d. 1427 in Rome, Italy
Source: *AtlBL; NewCol 75; REn; WebBD 80*

Gentile, Giovanni
Italian. Philosopher
b. May 30, 1875 in Castelvetrano, Italy
d. Apr 15, 1944 in Florence, Italy
Source: *CasWL; ClDMEL; EvEuW; NewCol 75; WebBD 80*

Gentileschi, Orazio
Italian. Artist
b. 1562
d. 1647
Source: *NewCol 75; WebBD 80*

Gentry, Bobbie
[Roberta Streeter]
American. Singer, Songwriter
Wrote, recorded "Ode to Billy Joe," 1967; won three Grammys, adapted to film, 1976.
b. Jul 27, 1942 in Chicasaw County, Mississippi
Source: *EncFCWM 69; WhoAm 74*

Genung, John Franklin
American. Scholar
b. Jan 27, 1850 in Willseyville, New York
d. Oct 10, 1919
Source: *AmBi; TwCBDA; WebBD 80; WhAm 1*

Geoffrion, "Boom-Boom" (Bernie)
Canadian. Hockey Player
Right wing, 1950-68; Hall of Fame, 1972.
b. Feb 14, 1931 in Montreal, PQ
Source: *WhoHcky 73*

George I
English. King
b. Mar 28, 1660 in Hanover, Prussia
d. Jun 12, 1727 in Germany
Source: *BioIn 10; DcBiPP; NewCol 75; WebBD 80*

George II
English. King
b. Nov 10, 1683 in Prussia
d. Oct 25, 1760 in London, England
Source: *BioIn 10; OxMus; WebBD 80*

George II
Greek. King
b. Jul 20, 1890
d. Apr 1, 1947
Source: *CurBio 43, 47; NewCol 75; WebBD 80*

George III
[George William Frederick]
English. King
b. Jun 4, 1738 in London, England
d. Jan 29, 1820 in Windsor, England
Source: *BioIn 10; DcBiPP; WebBD 80*

George IV
[George Augustus Frederick]
English. King
b. Aug 12, 1762 in London, England
d. Jun 25, 1830 in Windsor, England
Source: *BioIn 10; NewCol 75; WebBD 80*

George V
[George Frederick Ernest Albert]
English. King
b. 1865 in London, England
d. 1936 in London, England
Source: *BioIn 10; DcBiPP; WebBD 80; WhoModH*

George VI
[Albert Frederick Arthur George]
English. King
Ascended to throne, Dec 11, 1936, upon abdication of brother Edward VIII.
b. 1895 in Sandringham, England
d. Feb 6, 1952 in Sandringham, England
Source: *CurBio 52; DcBiPP; WebBD 80; WhoModH*

George, Saint
English. Religious Figure
d. Apr 23, 303AD
Source: *NewC; REn*

George, Bill (William)
American. Football Player
Linebacker, Chicago Bears, 1952-65; Hall of Fame, 1974.
b. Oct 27, 1930 in Waynesburg, Pennsylvania
d. Sep 30, 1982 in Rockford, Illinois
Source: *NewYTBS 82; WhoFtbl 74*

George, Chief Dan
Canadian. Indian Chief, Actor
b. 1899 in North Vancouver, BC
d. Sep 23, 1981 in Vancouver, BC
Source: *BioIn 9; CelR 73; FilmgC; NewYTBE 71; WhoAm 76, 78, 80; WhoHol A*

George, Christopher
American. Actor
b. Feb 25, 1929 in Royal Oak, Michigan
Source: *FilmgC; WhoHol A*

George, Don
American. Composer, Author, Artist
b. Aug 27, 1909 in New York, New York
Source: *AmSCAP 66*

George, Gladys
American. Actress
b. Sep 13, 1904 in Hatton, Maine
d. Dec 8, 1954 in Los Angeles, California
Source: *DcAmB S5; Film 1; FilmgC; MotPP; MovMk; ThFT; TwYS; Vers A; WhScrn 74, 77; WhoHol B*

George, Grace
American. Actress
b. Dec 25, 1879 in New York, New York
d. May 19, 1961 in New York, New York
Source: *FamA&A; InWom; OxThe; WhScrn 74, 77; WhoHol B*

George, Graham Elias
English. Conductor
b. Apr 11, 1912 in Norwich, England
Source: *CanWW 70; WhoAm 78, 80, 82; WrDr 76*

George, Henry, Sr.
American. Author, Economist, Reformer
b. Sep 2, 1839 in Philadelphia, Pennsylvania
d. Oct 29, 1897 in New York, New York
Source: *Alli SUP; AmAu; AmAu&B; AmBi; BbD; BiD&SB; CasWL; DcAmAu; DcAmB; DcLEL; DcNAA; EncAB-H; EvLB; NewC; OxAmL; OxEng; Pen AM; REn; REnAL; TwCBDA; WebAB; WebE&AL; WhAm H; WhAmP*

George, Henry, Jr.
American. Journalist
b. Nov 3, 1862 in Sacramento, California
d. Nov 14, 1916 in New York, New York
Source: *AmAu&B; BiDrAC; DcAmB; DcNAA; WhAm 1; WhAmP*

George, Jean Craighead
American. Artist, Author
b. Jul 2, 1919 in Washington, DC
Source: *AmAu&B; AnCL; Au&Wr 71; AuBYP; ChlLR 1; ConAu 5R; IlsCB 1946; MorBMP; MorJA; SmATA 2; WhoAm 82*

George, Lynda Day
[Mrs. Christopher George]
American. Actress
b. 1946
Source: *WhoAm 82; WhoHol A*

George, Phyllis
[Mrs. John Y Brown, Jr.]
American. Sports Announcer
Miss America, 1971; author *I Love America Diet*, 1982.
b. 1949 in Denton, Texas
Source: *BioIn 9, 10; BkPepl; WhoAm 78, 80, 82*

George, Stefan Anton
German. Poet
b. Dec 12, 1868 in Budesheim, Germany
d. Dec 4, 1933 in Locarno, Switzerland
Source: *AtlBL; CasWL; ChPo; ClDMEL; CnMWL; CyWA; EncWL; EvEuW; LongCTC; ModGL; OxGer; Pen EUR; REn; TwCA, SUP; TwCW; WhoTwCL*

George, Susan
English. Actress
b. Jul 26, 1950 in London, England
Source: *FilmEn; FilmgC; IntMPA 76, 77, 78, 79, 80, 81, 82; MovMk; NewYTBE 72; WhoHol A*

George, Walter Franklin
American. Senator
b. Jan 28, 1878 in Preston, Georgia
d. Aug 4, 1957 in Vienna, Georgia
Source: *ApCAB X; BiDrAC; BioIn 1, 2, 3, 4; CurBio 43, 55, 57; DcAmB S6; LinLib S; ObitOF 79; PolProf E; PolProf T; WhAm 3; WhAmP*

Georges-Picot, Jacques Marie Charles
French. Statesman
b. Dec 16, 1900 in Paris, France
Source: *BioIn 7; IntWW 74, 75, 76, 77, 78; IntYB 78, 79; Who 74; WhoWor 74*

Gerard, Dave
American. Cartoonist
b. Jun 18, 1909 in Crawfordsville, Indiana
Source: *ConAu 53*

Gerard, Francois
French. Artist
b. May 4, 1770 in Rome, Italy
d. Jan 11, 1837 in Paris, France
Source: *AtlBL*

Gerard, Gil
American. Actor
b. Jan 23, 1943 in Little Rock, Arkansas
Source: *WhoAm 80, 82*

Gerasimov, Sergei Appolinarievich
Russian. Motion Picture Director
b. May 21, 1906 in Sverdlovsk, Russia
Source: *BiDFilm; DcFM; FilmgC; IntWW 74; OxFilm; WhoWor 74; WorEFlm*

Geray, Steven
Czech. Actor
b. Nov 10, 1904 in Uzhored, Czechoslovakia
d. Dec 26, 1973
Source: *IntMPA 75, 76, 77; Vers B; WhScrn 77; WhoHol A*

Gerber, Daniel Frank
American. Baby Food Manufacturer
Invented strained baby food process, 1928, to feed own baby.
b. May 6, 1898 in Fremont, Michigan
d. Mar 16, 1974 in Fremont, Michigan
Source: *DcAmB S5; NewYTBS 74; WhAm 6; WhoAm 74; WhoF&I 74; WhoWor 74*

Gere, Richard
American. Actor
b. Aug 29, 1949 in Philadelphia, Pennsylvania
Source: *BioIn 11, 12; CurBio 80; IntMPA 82; WhoAm 80, 82*

Gerhardi, William Alexander
British. Author
b. Nov 21, 1895 in Saint Petersburg, Russia
d. Jul 5, 1977 in London, England
Source: *Au&Wr 71; ConAu 25R, 73; ConLC 5; ConNov 72, 76; LongCTC; ModBrL; NewC; OxEng; REn; TwCA, SUP; TwCW; WrDr 76*

Gerhardt, Paul(us)
German. Poet, Theologian
b. Mar 12, 1607 in Saxony, Germany
d. May 27, 1676 in Lubben, Germany
Source: *BbD; BiD&SB; CasWL; DcEnL; EuAu; EvEuW; OxGer; Pen; PoChrch*

Gericault, Jean Louis Andre Theodore
French. Artist
b. Sep 26, 1791 in Rouen, France
d. Jan 26, 1824 in Paris, France
Source: *AtlBL; McGDA; NewCol 75; OxFr; REn; WebBD 80*

Germain, George Sackville
British. Soldier, Statesman
b. 1716
d. 1785
Source: *BioIn 1, 6, 7, 10; NewCol 75; WebBD 80*

German, Bruce W
[The Hostages]
American. Former Hostage in Iran
b. Mar 31, 1936
Source: *NewYTBS 81; USBiR 74*

Germi, Pietro
Italian. Actor, Motion Picture Director
b. Sep 14, 1904 in Genoa, Italy
d. Dec 5, 1974 in Rome, Italy
Source: *DcFM; FilmgC; IntMPA 75; IntWW 74; MovMk; NewYTBS 74; OxFilm; WhScrn 77; WhoHol B; WorEFlm*

Gernreich, Rudi
American. Fashion Designer
Introduced topless bathing suits, 1974.
b. Aug 8, 1922 in Vienna, Austria
Source: *BioNews 74; CelR 73; CurBio 68; WhoAm 74, 76, 78, 80, 82; WhoWest 74; WhoWor 74; WorFshn*

Gernsback, Hugo
Inventor, Publisher
Received over 80 patents for radio and electronic devices.
b. Aug 16, 1884 in Luxembourg City, Luxemburg
d. Aug 19, 1967 in New York, New York
Source: *AmAu&B; ConAu 93; WebAB; WhAm 4; WhNAA*

Gero, Erno
Hungarian. Government Official
b. Aug 17, 1898 in Budapest, Hungary
d. Mar 12, 1980 in Budapest, Hungary
Source: *BioIn 1, 2; WhoSocC 78*

Gerold, Karl
German. Journalist
b. Aug 29, 1906
d. Feb 28, 1973
Source: *ConAu 41R; NewYTBE 73*

Gerome, Jean Leon
French. Artist
b. 1824 in Vesoul, France
d. 1904
Source: *NewCol 75; WebBD 80*

Geronimo
[Goyathlay]
American Indian. Apache Chieftain
Known for raids before capture, 1888; wrote autobiography *Geronimo's Story of His Life,* 1906.
b. Jun 1829 in Arizona
d. Feb 17, 1909 in Fort Sill, Oklahoma
Source: *AmBi; DcAmB; EncAB-H; FilmgC; REn; REnAL; WebAB; WhAm HA*

Gerould, Gordon Hall
American. Author, Educator
b. Oct 4, 1877 in Goffstown, New Hampshire
d. Jul 27, 1953 in Princeton, New Jersey
Source: *AmAu&B; ChPo; OxAmL; WhAm 3*

Gerritsen, Rinus
see: Golden Earring

Gerry, Elbridge
American. Vice-President
b. Jul 17, 1744 in Marblehead, Massachusetts
d. Nov 23, 1814 in Washington, DC
Source: *AmBi; ApCAB; BiAuS; DcAmB; Drake; EncAB-H; McGEWB; TwCBDA; WebAB; WhAm H*

Gerry, Elbridge Thomas
American. Lawyer, Social Reformer
b. Dec 25, 1837 in New York
d. Feb 18, 1927
Source: *AmBi; ApCAB; DcAmB; TwCBDA; WhAm 1*

Gershwin, George
American. Composer
Wrote folk opera *Porgy and Bess,* 1935; included songs "Summertime," "I Got Plenty o' Nuttin."
b. Sep 26, 1898 in Brooklyn, New York
d. Jul 11, 1937 in Hollywood, California
Source: *AmBi; AmSCAP 66; AtlBL; CmMov; DcAmB S2; DcCM; DcFM; EncAB-H; EncMT; FilmgC; McGEWD; NewCBMT; NewYTBE 73; OxAmL; OxFilm; PlP&P; REn; REnAL; WebAB; WhAm 1*

Gershwin, Ira
American. Lyricist
Brother of George; wrote lyrics for *Porgy and Bess, An American in Paris.*
b. Dec 6, 1896 in New York, New York
Source: *AmAu&B; AmSCAP 66; BiE&WWA; CelR 73; CurBio 56; DcLEL; EncMT; FilmgC; IntMPA 75, 76, 77, 78, 79, 80, 81, 82; NewCBMT; NotNAT; OxAmL; PlP&P; REnAL; WhoAm 74, 76, 78, 80, 82; WhoMus 72; WhoThe 77; WhoWor 74; WhoWorJ 72*

Gerson, Noel Bertram
American. Author
b. Nov 6, 1914 in Chicago, Illinois
Source: *AmAu&B; ConAu 81; SmATA 22; WhoAm 74, 76, 78, 80, 82; WhoE 74; WhoWor 74; WrDr 76*

Gerstenberg, Richard Charles
American. Automobile Executive
Chief executive, GM, 1972-74.
b. Dec 24, 1909 in Little Falls, New York
Source: *BioNews 74; BusPN; IntWW 74; NewYTBE 71; NewYTBS 74; Ward 77; Who 74; WhoAm 74; WhoF&I 74; WhoMW 74*

Gertrude the Great, Saint
German. Religious Figure
b. 1256
d. 1311
Source: *BioIn 2, 3, 4, 5, 6; WebBD 80*

Gerulaitis, Vitas
American. Tennis Player
b. Jul 26, 1954 in Brooklyn, New York
Source: *BioIn 11; WhoAm 82*

Gerussi, Bruno
Canadian. Actor, Broadcaster
b. 1928 in Medicine Hat, AB
Source: *WhThe; WhoThe 72*

Gervasi, Frank
American. Journalist
b. Feb 5, 1908 in Baltimore, Maryland
Source: *AmAu&B; ConAu 13R; ConAu P-1; CurBio 42*

Gervin, George
"The Iceman"
American. Basketball Player
b. Apr 27, 1952 in Detroit, Michigan
Source: *OfNBA; WhoAm 82; WhoBlA 77*

Gesell, Gerhard Alden
American. Judge
b. Jun 16, 1910 in Los Angeles, California
Source: *CngDr 74; WhoAm 74; WhoGov 72; WhoS&SW 73*

Gesualdo, Carlo
Italian. Composer
b. 1560 in Naples, Italy
d. Sep 8, 1613 in Naples, Italy
Source: *AtlBL; REn*

Getty, J(ean) Paul
American. Oil Executive, Millionaire
Getty Oil Co., largest personally controlled oil co.; total wealth over $1 billion.
b. Dec 15, 1892 in Minneapolis, Minnesota
d. Jun 6, 1976 in Surrey, England
Source: *ConAu 65, 69; EncAB-H; WebAB; WhoAm 74; WhoF&I 74; WhoWest 74; WhoWor 74*

Getz, Stan
American. Musician
b. Feb 2, 1927 in Philadelphia, Pennsylvania
Source: *CurBio 71; WhoAm 82; WhoWor 74*

Geva, Tamara
Russian. Choreographer, Dancer
b. 1908 in Leningrad, Russia
Source: *BiE&WWA; EncMT; NotNAT; WhoHol A; WhoThe 77*

Geyer, Georgie Anne
American. Journalist, Author
b. Apr 2, 1935 in Chicago, Illinois
Source: *ConAu 29R; ForWC 70; WhoAm 74, 76, 78, 80, 82; WhoAmW 77; WhoMW 74; WhoWor 74*

Ghazzali, Abu al-
[Algazel]
Arabian. Philosopher
b. 1058
d. 1111
Source: *CasWL; DcOrL 3; WebBD 80*

Ghelderode, Michel de
[Adolphe-Adhemar-Louis-Michel Martens]
Belgian. Dramatist
b. Apr 3, 1898 in Elsene, Belgium
d. Apr 1, 1962 in Brussels, Belgium
Source: *CasWL; CnMD; ConAu 85; ConLC 6; EncWL; McGEWD; ModRL; ModWD; OxThe; Pen EUR; REn; REnWD; TwCW; WhoTwCL; WorAu*

Gheorghiu-Dej, Gheorghe
Romanian. Communist Leader
b. Nov 8, 1901 in Barlad, Romania
d. Mar 19, 1965
Source: *CurBio 58, 65; NewCol 75*

Gherardi, Gherardo
American. Pathologist
b. Jul 1, 1921 in Lucca, Italy
Source: *AmM&WS 73P*

Ghiaurov, Nicolai
Bulgarian. Opera Singer
b. Sep 13, 1929 in Velimgrad, Bulgaria
Source: *IntWW 74; WhoAm 82*

Ghiberti, Lorenzo
Italian. Sculptor
b. 1378 in Florence, Italy
d. Dec 1, 1455 in Florence, Italy
Source: *AtlBL; NewCol 75; WebBD 80*

Ghiringhelli, Antonio
Italian. Theatrical Director
b. 1903 in Brunello, Italy
Source: *IntWW 74*

Ghirlandajo, Domenico
[Domenico di Tommaso Bigordi]
Italian. Artist
b. 1449 in Florence, Italy
d. Jan 11, 1494 in Florence, Italy
Source: *AtlBL*

Ghorbal, Ashraf
Egyptian. Ambassador to United States
b. 1925
Source: *IntWW 77*

Ghormley, Robert Lee
American. Naval Officer
b. Oct 15, 1883 in Portland, Oregon
d. Jun 21, 1958 in Washington, DC
Source: *BioIn 1, 4, 5; CurBio 58; WhAm 3*

Ghose, Sri Chinmoy Kumar
[Sri Chinmoy]
Indian. Author, Poet, Mystic
b. Aug 27, 1931 in Bengal, India
Source: *ConAu 49, 2NR; CurBio 76; NewCol 75*

Ghostley, Alice
American. Actress
b. Aug 14, 1926 in Eve, Missouri
Source: *BiE&WWA; MotPP; NotNAT; WhoAm 82; WhoHol A; WhoThe 77*

Ghotbzadeh, Sadegh
Iranian. Foreign Minister
Executed for plot to kill Khomeini and topple government.
b. 1939?
d. Sep 15, 1982 in Teheran, Iran
Source: *BioIn 11; NewYTBS 82*

Giacalone, Anthony
American. Racketeer
b. 1919
Source: *BioIn 10*

Giacometti, Alberto
Swiss. Sculptor
b. Oct 10, 1901 in Stampa, Switzerland
d. Jan 11, 1966 in Chur, Switzerland
Source: *AtlBL; CurBio 56, 66; REn; WhAm 4*

Giacomin, Eddie (Edward)
Canadian. Hockey Player
Goalie 1965-77; won Vezina Trophy, 1971.
b. Jun 6, 1939 in Sudbury, ON
Source: *CurBio 68; NewYTBE 72; WhoHcky 73*

Giamarese, Carl
see: Buckinghams, The

Giamatti, A(ngelo) Bartlett
American. University President
b. Apr 4, 1938 in Boston, Massachusetts
Source: *CurBio 78; DrAS 78E; NewYTBS 77; WhoAm 78, 80, 82; WhoE 79*

Giancana, Salvatore (Sam)
American. Gangster
b. 1894?
d. 1974 in Oak Park, Illinois
Source: *BioIn 11*

Gianelli, John
American. Basketball Player
b. Jun 10, 1950 in Stockton, California
Source: *NewYTBE 73; NewYTBS 74; WhoBbl 73*

Giannini, Amadeo Peter
American. Banker
b. May 6, 1870 in San Jose, California
d. Jun 3, 1949 in San Mateo, California
Source: *DcAmB S4; WebAB; WhAm 2*

Giannini, Dusolina
American. Opera Singer
b. Dec 19, 1902 in Philadelphia, Pennsylvania
Source: *InWom*

Giannini, Giancarlo
Italian. Actor
b. Aug 1, 1942 in Spezia, Italy
Source: *IntMPA 77; WhoAm 82; WhoHol A*

Giannini, Vittorio
American. Composer
b. Oct 19, 1903 in Philadelphia, Pennsylvania
d. Nov 28, 1966 in New York, New York
Source: *AmSCAP 66; DcCM; WhAm 4*

Giap, Vo Nguyen
Vietnamese. Statesman
b. Sep 1, 1912 in Quangblin, Vietnam
Source: *CurBio 69; IntWW 74; WhoWor 74*

Giardello, Joey
[Carmine Orlando Tilelli]
American. Boxer
b. Jul 16, 1930 in Brooklyn, New York
Source: *BioIn 6, 7, 10; WhoBox 74*

Giardini, Felice de
Italian. Musician
b. 1716
d. 1796
Source: *BioIn 4; WebBD 80*

Giauque, William F(rancis)
American. Chemist, Educator
b. May 12, 1895 in Niagara Falls, ON
d. Mar 29, 1982 in Oakland, California
Source: *AmM&WS 73P, 76P, 79P; AsBiEn; BioIn 2, 3, 6; CurBio 50, 82; IntWW 74, 75, 76, 77, 78; NewCol 75; NewYTBS 82; WebAB; WhoAm 74, 76, 78, 80, 82; WhoWest 78*

Gibb, Andy
English. Singer, Songwriter, Musician
b. Mar 5, 1958 in Manchester, England
Source: *BioIn 11; BkPepl*

Gibb, Barry
[The Bee Gees; Douglas Gibb]
English. Singer, Songwriter
b. Sep 1, 1946 in Manchester, England
Source: *BkPepl; WhoAm 82*

Gibb, Maurice
[The Bee Gees]
English. Singer, Songwriter
b. Dec 22, 1949 in Manchester, England
Source: *BkPepl; WhoAm 82*

Gibb, Robin
[The Bee Gees]
English. Singer, Songwriter
b. Dec 22, 1949 in Manchester, England
Source: *BkPepl; WhoAm 82*

Gibbon, Edward
English. Historian
b. Apr 27, 1737 in Surrey, England
d. Jan 16, 1794
Source: *Alli; AtlBL; BbD; BiD&SB; BrAu; CasWL; Chambr 2; CyWA; DcEnA; DcEnL; DcEuL; DcLEL; EvLB; MouLC 2; NewC; OxEng; Pen ENG; REn; WebE&AL*

Gibbon, Lewis Grassic, pseud.
[James Leslie Mitchell]
Scottish. Author
b. Feb 13, 1901 in Arbuthnott, Scotland
d. Feb 21, 1935 in Welwyn, England
Source: *CasWL; DcLEL; Pen ENG; REn*

Gibbons, Billy
see: ZZ Top

Gibbons, Euell
American. Author, Food Faddist
Lived in Hawaii in thatched hut eating wild food, 1945-47; wrote *Stalking the Good Life,* 1971.
b. Sep 8, 1911 in Clarksville, Texas
d. Dec 29, 1975 in Sunbury, Pennsylvania
Source: *AmAu&B; AuNews 1; BioNews 74; ConAu 25R, 61; ConAu P-2; WhoE 74*

Gibbons, Floyd Phillips
American. Journalist
b. Jul 16, 1887 in Washington, DC
d. Sep 24, 1939 in Saylorsburg, Pennsylvania
Source: *AmAu&B; AmBi; CathA 1930; DcAmB S2; DcNAA; REnAL; TwCA, SUP; WhAm 1*

Gibbons, Grinling
English. Woodcarver, Sculptor
b. Apr 4, 1648 in Rotterdam, Netherlands
d. Aug 3, 1721 in London, England
Source: *AtlBL; WebBD 80*

Gibbons, James, Cardinal
American. Religious Leader
b. Jul 23, 1834 in Baltimore, Maryland
d. Mar 24, 1921 in Baltimore, Maryland
Source: *Alli SUP; AmAu&B; AmBi; ApCAB; BiD&SB; BiDSA; ChPo S1; DcAmAu; DcAmB; DcNAA; EncAB-H; REnAL; TwCBDA; WebAB; WhAm 1*

Gibbons, Mike
see: Badfinger

Gibbons, Orlando
English. Composer, Musician
b. 1583 in Cambridge, England
d. Jun 5, 1625 in Canterbury, England
Source: *Alli; NewC; NewCol 75; WebBD 80*

Gibbons, Stanley
Stamp Dealer
Source: *NF*

Gibbons, Stella Dorethea
English. Author, Poet
b. Jan 5, 1902 in London, England
Source: *Au&Wr 71; Chambr 3; ChPo; ConAu 13R; ConNov 72; IntWW 74; Who 74; WhoWor 74; WrDr 76*

Gibbons, Tom
American. Boxer
b. Mar 22, 1891 in Saint Paul, Minnesota
d. Nov 19, 1960 in Saint Paul, Minnesota
Source: *WhoBox 74*

Gibbs, Anthony
English. Author
b. Mar 9, 1902 in Bolton, England
d. Mar 11, 1975
Source: *ConAu 29R; ConAu P-2; WhoLA*

Gibbs, Charles
American. Pirate
b. 1794
d. 1831
Source: *BioIn 5*

Gibbs, Georgia
American. Singer
b. 1923 in Worcester, Massachusetts
Source: *InWom*

Gibbs, James
Scottish. Architect
b. Dec 23, 1682 in Aberdeen, Scotland
d. Aug 5, 1754 in London, England
Source: *AtlBL; McGDA; McGEWB; WhoArch*

Gibbs, Joe Jackson
American. Football Coach
Coach, Washington Redskins; coach of year, 1982.
b. Nov 25, 1940 in Mocksville, North Carolina
Source: *FootReg; WhoAm 82*

Gibbs, Josiah Willard
American. Scientist, Physician, Engineer
b. Feb 11, 1839 in New Haven, Connecticut
d. Apr 28, 1903 in New Haven, Connecticut
Source: *AmBi; ApCAB; DcAmAu; DcAmB; DcNAA; EncAB-H; OxAmL; REnAL; TwCBDA; WebAB; WhAm 1*

Gibbs, Katherine
American. Business Educator
b. 1865
d. 1934
Source: *BioIn 10*

Gibbs, Terri
American. Singer, Musician
b. 1954
Source: *BioIn 12*

Gibbs, Terry
American. Composer, Conductor
b. Oct 13, 1924 in Brooklyn, New York
Source: *AmSCAP 66*

Gibbs, William Francis
American. Architect
b. Aug 24, 1886 in Philadelphia, Pennsylvania
d. Apr 28, 1967 in New York, New York
Source: *CurBio 44, 67; WhAm 4*

Gibbs, Woolcott
American. Drama Critic
b. 1902
d. Aug 16, 1958 in Ocean Beach, New York
Source: *BioIn 6*

Gibran, Kahlil
Poet, Artist
Finest work *The Prophet* translated into 13 languages.
b. Apr 10, 1883 in Bechari, Lebanon
d. Apr 10, 1931 in New York, New York
Source: *AmAu&B; CasWL; ConAu 104; DcNAA; TwCA, SUP; WebBD 80*

Gibran, Kahlil George
American. Author, Sculptor, Artist
Exhibited paintings, 1949-52, life-sized steel sculpture, 1953--.
b. Nov 29, 1922 in Boston, Massachusetts
Source: *DcCAA 71; WhoAm 74, 76, 78, 80, 82; WhoAmA 73; WhoWor 74*

Gibson, Althea
American. Tennis Player
First black to win Wimbledon, US championships, 1957, 1958.
b. Aug 25, 1927 in Silver, South Carolina
Source: *CurBio 57; HerW; InWom; NewCol 75; WebAB; WhoAm 74, 76, 78, 80, 82; WhoBlA 75*

Gibson, Bob
American. Folk Singer, Musician
b. Nov 16, 1931 in New York, New York
Source: *EncFCWM 69; WhoAm 82*

Gibson, Bob (Robert)
"Hoot"
American. Baseball Player
Pitcher, St. Louis Cardinals, 1959-75; Hall of Fame, 1981.
b. Nov 9, 1935 in Omaha, Nebraska
Source: *BaseEn; BioIn 8, 9, 10, 11; WhoAm 74; WhoBlA 75; WhoProB 73*

Gibson, Charles Dana
American. Illustrator
b. Sep 14, 1867 in Roxbury, Massachusetts
d. Dec 23, 1944 in New York, New York
Source: *AmAu&B; ChPo; CurBio 45; DcAmAu; DcAmB S3; DcNAA; OxAmL; REn; REnAL; TwCBDA; WebAB; WhAm 2; WhScrn 77*

Gibson, Edward George
American. Astronaut
Pilot of third manned Skylab mission; orbited earth 84 days.
b. Nov 8, 1936 in Buffalo, New York
Source: *AmM&WS 73P; WhoAm 74; WhoS&SW 73*

Gibson, Guy
British. Air Force Officer
b. 1918
d. Sep 1944
Source: *BioIn 5, 8; WhWW-II*

Gibson, Henry
American. Actor, Author
b. Sep 21, 1935 in Germantown, Pennsylvania
Source: *IntMPA 82; WhoAm 74, 76, 78, 80, 82; WhoHol A*

Gibson, "Hoot" (Edmund Richard)
American. Actor
b. Aug 6, 1892 in Tememah, Nebraska
d. Aug 23, 1962 in Woodland Hills, California
Source: *Film 1; FilmgC; MotPP; MovMk; OxFilm; TwYS; WhScrn 74; WhoHol B*

Gibson, John
British. Sculptor
b. 1790
d. 1866
Source: *BioIn 6, 9, 10; NewCol 75; WebBD 80*

Gibson, Josh(ua)
American. Baseball Player
Considered finest slugger ever to play in Negro Leagues.
b. Dec 21, 1911 in Buena Vista, Georgia
d. Jan 20, 1947 in Pittsburgh, Pennsylvania
Source: *BioIn 9, 10, 11; DcAmB S4*

Gibson, Kenneth Allen
American. Mayor of Newark
b. May 15, 1932 in Enterprise, Alabama
Source: *CelR 73; CurBio 71; NewYTBE 70; WhoAm 74, 76, 78, 80, 82; WhoAmP 73; WhoBlA 75; WhoE 74; WhoGov 72*

Gibson, Kirk Harold
"Gibby"
American. Baseball Player
b. May 28, 1957 in Pontiac, Michigan
Source: *BaseEn; NewYTBS 82*

Gibson, Mel
American. Actor
Starred in *Gallipoli,* 1981; *The Road Warrior,* 1982; *The Year of Living Dangerously,* 1983.
b. 1956 in Peekskill, New York
Source: *BioIn 12; JohnWil 82*

Gibson, William
American. Dramatist
b. Nov 13, 1914 in New York, New York
Source: *BiE&WWA; CnMD; ConAu 9R; ConDr 73; McGEWD; ModAL; ModWD; NotNAT; Pen AM; REnAL; WhoAm 74, 76, 78, 80, 82; WhoE 74; WhoThe 77; WhoWor 74; WorAu; WrDr 76*

Gidal, Sonia
German. Author
b. Sep 23, 1922 in Berlin, Germany
Source: *Au&Wr 71; AuBYP; ConAu 5R; SmATA 2*

Gidal, Tim
German. Journalist
b. May 18, 1909 in Munich, Germany
Source: *ConAu 5R; SmATA 2*

Gide, Andre Paul Guillaume
French. Author, Critic
b. Nov 22, 1869 in Paris, France
d. Feb 19, 1951 in Paris, France
Source: *AtlBL; CasWL; ClDMEL; CnMD; CnMWL; CyWA; EncWL; EvEuW; LongCTC; ModRL; ModWD; NewC; OxEng; OxFr; OxThe; Pen EUR; RAdv 1; RComWL; REn; REnWD; TwCA, SUP; TwCW; WhAm 3; WhoTwCL*

Gielgud, Sir (Arthur) John
English. Actor, Director, Producer
b. Apr 14, 1904 in London, England
Source: *BiDFilm; BiE&WWA; CelR 73; CurBio 47; FamA&A; FilmgC; IntMPA 75, 76, 77, 78, 79, 80; IntWW 74; MotPP; MovMk; NewC; NewYTBE 70; NotNAT; OxFilm; OxThe; PlP&P; REn; Who 74; WhoAm 82; WhoHol A; WhoThe 77; WhoWor 74*

Gielgud, Val Henry
British. Dramatist
b. Apr 28, 1900
Source: *Au&Wr 71; ConAu 9R, 5NR; EncMys; IntWW 74; MnBBF; NotNAT A; Who 74; WhoLA; WhoWor 74; WrDr 76*

Gierek, Edward
Polish. Politician
b. Jan 6, 1913 in Porabka, Poland
Source: *BioNews 74; CurBio 71; IntWW 74; NewCol 75; NewYTBE 70; WhoWor 74*

Gieseking, Walter Wilhelm
German. Musician
Developed Leimer-Gieseking method of piano study.
b. Nov 5, 1895 in Lyons, France
d. Oct 26, 1956 in London, England
Source: *CurBio 56, 57; NewCol 75; WebBD 80; WhAm 3*

Giesler, Jerry (Harold Lee)
American. Lawyer
b. 1890 in Wilton Junction, Iowa
d. Sep 27, 1962 in Beverly Hills, California
Source: *WhAm 4*

Gifford, Frank (Francis Newton)
American. Football Player, Sportscaster
Hall of Fame, 1977; won Emmy for outstanding sports personality, 1977.
b. Aug 16, 1930 in Santa Monica, California
Source: *CelR 73; CurBio 64; WhoAm 82; WhoFtbl 74; WhoHol A*

Gifford, Walter Sherman
American. Philanthropist
b. Jan 10, 1885 in Salem, Massachusetts
d. May 7, 1966 in New York, New York
Source: *CurBio 45, 66; WhAm 4*

Gigli, Beniamino
Italian. Opera Singer
b. Mar 20, 1890 in Recanati, Italy
d. Nov 30, 1957 in Rome, Italy
Source: *FilmgC; WhScrn 74, 77; WhoHol B*

Gilbert, A(lfred) C(arleton)
American. Business Executive
b. Feb 15, 1884 in Salem, Oregon
d. Jan 24, 1961 in Boston, Massachusetts
Source: *WebAB; WhAm 4; WhoTr&F 73*

Gilbert, Alfred Carlton, Jr.
American. Manufacturer
b. Dec 1, 1919 in New Haven, Connecticut
d. Jun 27, 1964
Source: *WhAm 4*

Gilbert, Billy
American. Actor
b. Sep 12, 1894 in Louisville, Kentucky
d. Sep 23, 1971 in Hollywood, California
Source: *BiE&WWA; Film 1; FilmgC; MovMk; TwYS; WhScrn 74, 77*

Gilbert, Bruce
American. Motion Picture Producer
b. 1948 in Beverly Hills, California
Source: *IntMPA 81*

Gilbert, Cass
American. Architect
b. Nov 24, 1859 in Zanesville, Ohio
d. May 17, 1934 in Brockenhurst, England
Source: *AmBi; DcAmB S1; OxAmL; WebAB; WhAm 1*

Gilbert, Sir Humphrey
English. Navigator, Explorer
Founded first British colony in N America at St. John's, NF, Aug 5, 1583.
b. 1537 in Compton, England
d. Sep 9, 1583
Source: *Alli; CasWL; NewC; NewCol 75; OxAmL; OxCan; OxEng; REn; REnAL; WebBD 80*

Gilbert, John
[John Pringle]
American. Actor
Starred opposite Greta Garbo in several films; talking pictures destroyed career.
b. Jul 10, 1897 in Logan, Utah
d. Jan 9, 1936 in Los Angeles, California
Source: *AmBi; BiDFilm; CmMov; DcAmB S2; Film 1; FilmgC; MovMk; OxFilm; WhAm 1; WhScrn 74, 77; WorEFlm*

Gilbert, Sir Joseph Henry
English. Chemist
b. 1817
d. 1901
Source: *BioIn 1, 4, 6, 7; WebBD 80*

Gilbert, Melissa
American. Actress
Plays Laura Ingalls Wilder in TV series "Little House on the Prairie," 1974--.
b. May 8, 1964 in Los Angeles, California
Source: *BioIn 10; IntMPA 82*

Gilbert, Rod(rique Gabriel)
Canadian. Hockey Player
Skated with Jean Ratelle, Vic Hadfield on GAG (goal a game) Line for NY Rangers.
b. Jul 1, 1941 in Montreal, PQ
Source: *BioIn 8, 10, 11; CurBio 69; WhoAm 82; WhoHcky 73*

Gilbert, William
English. Scientist
b. 1540 in Colchester, England
d. Nov 30, 1603
Source: *Alli; BrAu; DcEnL; NewC; OxEng*

Gilbert, Sir William Schwenck
[Gilbert and Sullivan]
English. Dramatist, Humorist
b. Nov 18, 1836 in London, England
d. May 29, 1911 in Harrow, England
Source: *AtlBL; BrAu 19; ChPo; DcLEL; EvLB; ModWD; PlP&P; REn; REnWD; Str&VC; WebE&AL*

Gilbert and Sullivan
see: Sullivan, Sir Arthur Seymour

Gilbertson, Mildred Geiger
American. Author
b. Jun 9, 1908 in Galena, Illinois
Source: *ConAu 5R, 2NR; ForWC 70; SmATA 2; WrDr 76*

Gilbreth, Frank Bunker, Jr.
American. Author, Journalist
b. Mar 17, 1911 in Plainfield, New Jersey
Source: *AmAu&B; ConAu 9R; CurBio 49; SmATA 2; WhoAm 74, 76, 78, 80, 82; WhoS&SW 73; WhoWor 74*

Gilbreth, Lillian Moller
American. Engineer
b. May 24, 1878 in Oakland, California
d. Jan 2, 1972 in Phoenix, Arizona
Source: *CurBio 40, 51; WebBD 80; WhAm 5*

Gilder, George
American. Economist, Author
b. Nov 29, 1939 in New York, New York
Source: *AuNews 1; ConAu 17R; CurBio 81; WhoAm 82*

Gildersleeve, Virginia Crocheron
American. Educator
b. Oct 3, 1877 in New York, New York
d. Jul 7, 1965 in Centerville, Massachusetts
Source: *AmAu&B; CurBio 41, 65; InWom; NewCol 75; WebBD 80; WhAm 4; WhNAA; WomWWA 14*

Gilels, Emil Grigorevich
Russian. Musician
b. Oct 19, 1916 in Odessa, Russia
Source: *CurBio 56; IntWW 74; WhoAm 82*

Giles, Mike
see: King Crimson

Giles, Warren Crandall
American. Baseball Executive
President, NL, 1951-70.
b. May 28, 1896 in Tiskilwa, Illinois
d. Feb 7, 1979 in Cincinnati, Ohio
Source: *NewYTBS 79; WhAm 7; WhoAm 74, 76, 78; WhoProB 73*

Gilfond, Henry
American. Author
Source: *ConAu 25R; NatPD; SmATA 2*

Gilford, Jack
[Jacob Gellman]
American. Actor
b. Jul 25, 1913 in New York, New York
Source: *BiE&WWA; EncMT; FilmgC; IntMPA 75; MovMk; NotNAT; PlP&P; WhoAm 76, 78, 80; WhoHol A; WhoThe 77*

Gill, Amory Tingle
"Slats"
American. Basketball Coach
b. May 1, 1901 in Salem, Oregon
d. Apr 5, 1966 in Cornwallis, Oregon
Source: *BioIn 6, 9; WhoBbl 73*

Gill, Brendan
American. Drama Critic, Author
b. Sep 4, 1914 in Hartford, Connecticut
Source: *AmAu&B; ConNov 72, 76; DrAF 76; NotNAT; Pen AM; REnAL; TwCA SUP; WhoAm 74, 76, 78, 80, 82; WhoThe 77; WrDr 76*

Gill, Eric
English. Author, Sculptor, Engraver
b. Feb 22, 1882 in Brighton, England
d. Nov 18, 1940
Source: *CurBio 41; BkC 5; CathA 1930; DcLEL; LongCTC; TwCA SUP*

Gill, Jocelyn Ruth
American. Astronomer
b. Oct 29, 1916 in Flagstaff, Arizona
Source: *AmM&WS 73; WhoAm 74; WhoAmW 74; WhoGov 72*

Gilles, D(onald) B(ruce)
American. Dramatist
b. Aug 30, 1947 in Cleveland, Ohio
Source: *NatPD*

Gillespie, "Dizzy" (John Birks)
American. Jazz Musician
Responsible for "be-bop" sound; wrote *To Be or Not...to Bop*, 1979.
b. Oct 21, 1917 in Cheraw, South Carolina
Source: *Alli SUP; AmM&WS 73P; AmSCAP 66; BioNews 74; CelR 73; CurBio 57; NewYTBE 73; WhoAm 74, 76, 78, 80, 82; WhoBlA 75*

Gillespie, George
Scottish. Author, Clergyman
b. 1613
d. 1648
Source: *Alli; EvLB; NewC*

Gillette, Anita
American. Actress, Singer
b. Aug 16, 1936 in Baltimore, Maryland
Source: *BiE&WWA; NotNAT; WhoThe 77*

Gillette, Duane
[The Hostages]
American. Former Hostage in Iran
b. 1957?
Source: *NewYTBS 81*

Gillette, King Camp
American. Inventor
Invented safety razor, 1895.
b. Jan 5, 1855 in Fond du Lac, Wisconsin
d. Jul 9, 1932 in Los Angeles, California
Source: *AmBi; DcAmB S1; DcNAA; WebAB; WhAm 1*

Gillette, William
American. Actor, Dramatist
b. Jul 24, 1855 in Hartford, Connecticut
d. Apr 29, 1937 in Hartford, Connecticut
Source: *AmAu&B; AmBi; ApCAB; BbD; BiD&SB; Chambr 3; DcAmAu; DcAmB S2; DcLEL; DcNAA; FamA&A; Film 1; FilmgC; McGEWD; ModWD; OxAmL; OxThe; PlP&P; REnAL; TwCBDA; TwYS; WebAB; WhAm 1; WhScrn 74, 77; WhoHol B; WhoStg 1906, 1908*

Gilley, Mickey Leroy
American. Musician, Bar Owner
b. Mar 9, 1936 in Natchez, Mississippi
Source: *WhoAm 78, 80, 82; WhoRock 81*

Gilliam, Jim (James William)
"Junior"
American. Baseball Player
b. Oct 17, 1928 in Nashville, Tennessee
d. Oct 8, 1978 in Los Angeles, California
Source: *BaseEn; WhoBlA 75; WhoProB 73*

Gilliam, Joe
American. Football Player
b. Dec 29, 1950 in Charleston, West Virginia
Source: *BioIn 11*

Gilliam, Terry
[Monty Python's Flying Circus]
American. Illustrator, Animator
b. Nov 22, 1940 in Minneapolis, Minnesota
Source: *BioIn 10, 11; WhoAm 82; WorECom*

Gilliatt, Penelope Ann Douglas
English. Drama, Motion Picture Critic
b. Mar 25, 1932 in London, England
Source: *AuNews 2; ConAu 13R; ConLC 2; ConNov 72, 76; DrAF 76; FilmgC; WhoAm 74, 76, 78, 80, 82; WhoE 74; WomWMM; WrDr 76*

Gillies, Clark
Canadian. Hockey Player
b. Apr 7, 1954 in Regina, SK
Source: *HocReg; WhoAm 82*

Gilligan, John Joyce
American. Former Governor of Ohio
b. Mar 22, 1921 in Cincinnati, Ohio
Source: *IntWW 74; WhoAm 74; WhoAmP 73; WhoGov 72; WhoMW 74*

Gillis, Don
American. Opera, Symphony Composer
b. Jun 17, 1912 in Cameron, Missouri
d. Jan 10, 1978 in Columbia, South Carolina
Source: *AmSCAP 66; DcCM; WhoMus 72*

Gillmore, Frank
American. Labor Union Official
Founder, first president Actors Equity Assn., 1929-37.
b. May 14, 1867 in New York, New York
d. Mar 29, 1943 in New York, New York
Source: *CurBio 43; WhAm 2; WhoStg 1906, 1908*

Gillott, Jacky
English. Author, Journalist
b. Sep 24, 1939 in Bromley, England
d. Sep 19, 1980 in Somerset, England
Source: *AnObit 1980; ConAu 102; IntAu&W 77; WrDr 80*

Gillray, James
English. Caricaturist
b. 1757 in London, England
d. Jun 1, 1815 in London, England
Source: *Alli; BkIE; NewC*

Gilman, Daniel Coit
American. Educator
b. Jul 6, 1831 in Norwich, Connecticut
d. Oct 13, 1908 in Norwich, Connecticut
Source: *Alli SUP; AmAu&B; AmBi; ApCAB; BiD&SB; BiDSA; DcAmAu; DcAmB; DcNAA; EncAB-H; OxAmL; REnAL; TwCBDA; WebAB; WhAm 1*

Gilman, Dorothy
[Dorothy Gilman Butters]
American. Author
b. Jun 25, 1923 in New Brunswick, New Jersey
Source: *BioIn 7, 8, 10; ConAu 2NR; SmATA 5; WhoAm 82*

Gilman, Lawrence
American. Music Critic, Journalist
b. Jul 5, 1878 in Flushing, New York
d. Sep 8, 1939 in Franconia, New Hampshire
Source: *AmAu&B; DcAmB S2; DcNAA; REnAL; TwCA, SUP; WhAm 1*

Gilmer, Elizabeth Meriwether
see: Dix, Dorothy, pseud.

Gilmore, Artis
American. Basketball Player
Center, 1972--; has averaged over 1,000 rebounds each season.
b. Sep 21, 1949 in Chipley, Florida
Source: *WhoAm 74, 76, 80, 82; WhoBbl 73; WhoBlA 75, 77; WorAl*

Gilmore, Eddy Lanier King
American. Journalist
b. May 28, 1907 in Selma, Alabama
d. Oct 6, 1967 in London, England
Source: *Au&Wr 71; ConAu 5R; CurBio 47, 67; WhAm 4*

Gilmore, Gary Mark
American. Murderer
First execution, by firing squad, following reinstatement of death penalty.
b. 1941
d. Jan 18, 1977 in Point of Mountain, Utah
Source: *BioIn 11*

Gilmore, Tom
Sheriff
b. 1936?
Source: *BioIn 9*

Gilmore, Virginia
American. Actress
b. Jul 26, 1919 in Del Monte, California
Source: *BiE&WWA; FilmgC; HolP 40; MotPP; MovMk; NotNAT; WhoHol A; WhoThe 77*

Gilpatric, Roswell Leavitt
American. Attorney, Government Official
b. Nov 4, 1906 in Brooklyn, New York
Source: *CurBio 64; WhoAm 74, 76, 78, 80, 82; WhoE 74*

Gilpin, Charles Sidney
American. Actor
b. Nov 20, 1878 in Richmond, Virginia
d. May 6, 1930 in Eldridge Park, New Jersey
Source: *AmBi; DcAmB; FamA&A; OxThe; WebAB; WhAm 1; WhScrn 74, 77; WhoHol B*

Gilroy, Frank D
American. Dramatist
b. Oct 13, 1925 in New York, New York
Source: *AmAu&B; ConAu 81; ConDr 73; CroCD; CurBio 65; DrAF 76; McGEWD; ModWD; NotNAT; OxAmL; WhoAm 74, 76, 78, 80, 82; WhoE 74; WhoThe 77; WhoWor 74; WrDr 76*

Gilruth, Robert Rowe
American. Aeronautical Engineer
b. Oct 8, 1913 in Nashwauk, Minnesota
Source: *AmM&WS 73P; CurBio 63; IntWW 74; WhoAm 82; WhoGov 72; WhoWor 74*

Gilson, Etienne Henry
French. Philosopher, Historian
b. Jun 13, 1884
d. Sep 19, 1978 in Cravant, France
Source: *CathA 1930; ConAu 81, 102; IntWW 74; OxFr; TwCA, SUP; Who 74; WhoWor 74*

Gilstrap, Suzy
American. Actress
b. Jan 1966
Source: *BioIn 12*

Gimbel, Adam
American. Chain Store Merchant
Emigrated to US, 1835; founded dept. store in Philadelphia, 1894.
b. 1815 in Bavaria, Germany
d. 1896
Source: *NewCol 75*

Gimbel, Bernard Feustman
American. Chain Store Merchant
Grandson of Adam Gimbel; president of Gimbel Brothers, 1927-53.
b. Apr 10, 1885 in Vincennes, Indiana
d. Sep 29, 1966
Source: *CurBio 50, 66; NatCAB 53; WhAm 4*

Gimbel, Peter Robin
American. Motion Picture Director, Producer
b. Feb 14, 1928 in New York, New York
Source: *BioIn 11; CelR 73; CurBio 82; WhoAm 76, 78, 80, 82*

Gimbel, Richard
American. Chain Store Merchant
Grandson of Adam Gimbel; curator of aeronautical literature at Yale.
b. Jul 26, 1898 in Atlantic City, New Jersey
d. May 27, 1970 in Munich, Germany (West)
Source: *BioIn 8, 9; NewYTBE 70*

Gimbel, Sophie Haas
"Sophie of Saks Fifth Avenue"
American. Fashion Designer
b. 1898 in Houston, Texas
d. Nov 28, 1981 in New York, New York
Source: *AnObit 1981; InWom; NewYTBS 81; WhoAmW 58, 64, 66, 68, 70, 72, 74; WorFshn*

Gimpel, Jakob
Polish. Musician
b. 1906 in Lwow, Poland
Source: *WhoMus 72*

Ginastera, Alberto
American. Composer
b. Apr 11, 1916 in Buenos Aires, Argentina
Source: *CurBio 71; DcCM; IntWW 74; WhoAm 74; WhoMus 72; WhoWor 74*

Gingold, Hermione Ferdinanda
English. Actress
b. Dec 9, 1897 in London, England
Source: *BiE&WWA; CelR 73; ConAu 5R; CurBio 58; EncMT; FilmgC; InWom; MotPP; MovMk; NotNAT; PlP&P; Who 74; WhoAm 74, 76, 78, 80, 82; WhoHol A; WhoThe 77; WhoWor 74*

Gingrich, Arnold
American. Magazine Editor, Author
b. Dec 5, 1903 in Grand Rapids, Michigan
d. Jul 9, 1976 in Ridgewood, New Jersey
Source: *AmAu&B; Au&Wr 71; CelR 73; ConAu 65, 69; CurBio 61, 78; IntAu&W 76, 77; IntWW 74, 75, 76, 77; NewYTBS 76; REnAL; St&PR 75; WhAm 7; WhNAA; WhoAm 74, 76; WhoWor 74; WorFshn; WrDr 76*

Ginn, Edwin
American. Publisher
b. Feb 14, 1838 in Orland, Maine
d. Jan 21, 1914
Source: *AmAu&B*

Ginott, Haim
American. Author, Child Psychologist
Wrote *Between Parent and Child,* 1965.
b. Aug 5, 1922
d. Nov 4, 1973 in New York, New York
Source: *AmAu&B; ConAu 45; NewYTBE 73; WhAm 6*

Ginsberg, Allen
American. Poet
Associated with "Beat" movement; best known poem *Howl,* 1956.
b. Jun 3, 1926 in Newark, New Jersey
Source: *AmAu&B; AuNews 1; CasWL; ConAu 1R, 2NR; ConLC 1, 2, 3, 4, 6; ConP 70, 75; CroCAP; DrAP 75; EncAB-H; EncWL; IntWW 74, 75, 76, 77, 78, 79, 80, 81; LongCTC; ModAL, SUP; OxAmL; Pen AM; RAdv 1; REn; REnAL; TwCW; WebAB; WebE&AL; WhoAm 74, 76, 78, 80, 82; WhoTwCL; WhoWor 74; WhoWorJ 72; WorAu; WrDr 76*

Ginzburg, Aleksandr
Russian. Dissident, Poet
b. 1936 in Leningrad, U.S.S.R.
Source: *NewYTBS 78, 79; WhoModH*

Ginzburg, Charles Pauson
American. Engineer
b. 1920
Source: *BioIn 9*

Ginzburg, Ralph
American. Publisher, Journalist
b. Oct 28, 1929 in Brooklyn, New York
Source: *Au&Wr 71; ConAu 21R; WhoAm 74, 76, 78, 80, 82; WhoWor 74*

Gioconda, Lisa Gherardini
[Mona Lisa]
Italian. Noblewoman
b. 1479 in Italy
Source: *InWom*

Giolitti, Giovanni
Italian. Statesman
b. 1842 in Mondovi, Italy
d. 1928
Source: *BioIn 8, 10; NewCol 75; WebBD 80; WhoModH*

Giono, Jean
French. Author
b. Mar 30, 1895 in Manosque, France
d. Oct 9, 1970 in Manosque, France
Source: *CasWL; ClDMEL; CnMD; CnMWL; ConAu 29R, 45, 2NR; ConLC 4, 11; CyWA; EncWL; EvEuW; McGEWD; ModRL; ModWD; OxFr; Pen EUR; REn; TwCA, SUP; TwCW; WhoTwCL*

Giordano, Luca
"Fa Presto"
Italian. Artist
b. 1632 in Naples, Italy
d. 1705
Source: *NewCol 75*

Giordano, Umberto
Italian. Composer
b. Aug 27, 1867 in Foggia, Italy
d. Nov 12, 1948 in Milan, Italy
Source: *NewEOp 71; OxMus; WebBD 80*

Giorgio, Francesco di
Italian. Architect, Artist
b. 1439 in Siena, Italy
d. 1502
Source: *NewCol 75*

Giorgione, Il
[Giorgio Barbarelli; Giorgione da Castelfranco]
Italian. Artist
Pupil of Bellini; influenced Titian.
b. 1477
d. 1511
Source: *AtlBL; REn*

Giorno, John
American. Poet
b. Dec 4, 1936 in New York, New York
Source: *BioIn 10; ConAu 33R; ConP 70; DrAP 75*

Giotto di Bondone
Italian. Artist, Architect
b. 1266? in Vespignamo, Italy
d. Jan 8, 1337 in Florence, Italy
Source: *AtlBL; NewC; REn*

Giovanni da Fiesole
see: Angelico, Fra

Giovanni di Paulo
Italian. Artist
b. 1403
d. 1483
Source: *NewCol 75*

Giovanni, Nikki
[Yolande Cornelia, Jr.]
American. Author, Poet
Writings include *My House,* 1972; *The Women and the Men,* 1975.
b. Jun 7, 1943 in Knoxville, Tennessee
Source: *AuNews 1; BlkAW; CelR 73; ChPo S2; ConAu 29R; ConLC 2, 4; ConP 75; CroCAP; DrAP 75; LivgBAA; RAdv 1; WhoAm 74, 76, 78, 80, 82; WhoBlA 75; WrDr 76*

Giovannitti, Arturo
Italian. Poet
b. Jan 7, 1884 in Campobasso, Italy
d. Dec 31, 1959
Source: *AmAu&B; ConAmL; OxAmL; REn; REnAL; TwCA*

Gipp, George
American. Football Player
Ronald Reagan portrayed him in movie *Knute Rockne All American.*
b. Feb 18, 1895 in Lauriam, Michigan
d. Dec 4, 1920
Source: *WhoFtbl 74*

Gipson, Lawrence Henry
American. Historian, Educator
b. Dec 7, 1880 in Greeley, Colorado
d. Sep 26, 1971 in Bethlehem, Pennsylvania
Source: *AmAu&B; ConAu 5R, 33R, 3NR; CurBio 54, 71; NewYTBE 70, 71; OxAmL; OxCan, SUP; WhNAA; WorAu*

Girard, Stephen
French. Philanthropist
b. 1750 in Bordeaux, France
d. 1831
Source: *BioIn 1, 2, 3, 4, 11; WebBD 80*

Girardon, Francois
French. Sculptor
b. Mar 17, 1628 in Troyes, France
d. Sep 1, 1715 in Paris, France
Source: *McGDA; McGEWB; OxFilm*

Girardot, Annie
French. Actress
b. 1931
Source: *FilmgC; IntMPA 75, 76, 77; NewYTBE 72; OxFilm; WhoHol A; WorEFlm*

Giraud, Henri Honore
French. World War II General
b. Jan 18, 1879
d. Mar 11, 1949 in Dijon, France
Source: *CurBio 42, 49*

Giraudoux, Jean
French. Dramatist, Author, Diplomat
b. Oct 29, 1882 in Bellac, France
d. Jan 31, 1944 in Paris, France
Source: *AtlBL; Au&Wr 71; CasWL; ClDMEL; CnMD; CnMWL; CnThe; CurBio 44; CyWA; EncWL; EvEuW; LongCTC; McGEWD; ModRL; ModWD; NewC; OxEng; OxFr; OxThe; Pen EUR; RComWL; REn; REnWD; TwCA, SUP; TwCW; WhoTwCL*

Girdler, Tom Mercer
American. Steel Manufacturer
Chairman, Republic Steel, 1930-56.
b. May 19, 1877 in Clark County, Indiana
d. Feb 4, 1965 in Easton, Maryland
Source: *CurBio 44, 65; IndAu 1917; WhAm 4*

Giroud, Francoise
Swiss. Journalist, Politician
b. Sep 21, 1916 in Geneva, Switzerland
Source: *AuNews 1; ConAu 81; IntWW 74; NewYTBS 74; WhoWor 74; WomWMM*

Giroux, Robert
American. Editor, Publisher
Chairman, Farrar, Straus, and Giroux, Inc, 1973--.
b. Apr 8, 1914 in New Jersey
Source: *AmCath 80; CurBio 82; WhoAm 74, 76, 78, 80, 82; WhoWor 74*

Girtin, Thomas
English. Artist
b. Feb 18, 1775 in Southwark, England
d. Nov 9, 1802 in London, England
Source: *AtlBL; BioIn 1, 3, 10*

Giscard d'Estaing, Valery
French. Politician
President of France, 1974-81.
b. Feb 2, 1926 in Koblenz, Germany
Source: *BioNews 74; CurBio 67, 74; IntWW 74, 75, 76, 77, 78, 79, 80, 81; IntYB 78, 79, 80, 81; LinLib S; NewYTBS 77; Who 74; WhoWor 76, 78; WorAl*

Gish, Dorothy
American. Actress
b. Mar 11, 1898 in Dayton, Ohio
d. Jun 4, 1968 in Rapallo, Italy
Source: *BiE&WWA; CurBio 44, 68; FamA&A; Film 1; FilmgC; InWom; MotPP; MovMk; OxFilm; TwYS; WebAB; WhScrn 74, 77; WhoHol B; WomWMM; WorEFlm*

Gish, Lillian Diana
"The First Lady of the Silent Screen"
American. Actress
Starred in D W Griffith movies *Broken Blossoms*, 1918; *Orphans of the Storm*, 1922.
b. Oct 14, 1896 in Springfield, Ohio
Source: *BiDFilm; BiE&WWA; CelR 73; CmMov; CurBio 44; FamA&A; Film 1; FilmgC; InWom; IntMPA 75, 76, 77, 78, 79, 80, 81, 82; IntWW 74, 75, 76, 77, 78, 79, 80, 81; MotPP; MovMk; NotNAT; OxFilm; PlP&P; REn; ThFT; WebAB; WhoAm 74, 76, 78, 80, 82; WhoHol A; WhoThe 77; WhoWor 74; WomWMM; WorEFlm*

Gissing, George Robert
English. Author
b. Nov 22, 1857 in Wakefield, England
d. Dec 28, 1903 in Saint Jean de Luz, France
Source: *Alli SUP; AtlBL; BbD; BiD&SB; BrAu 19; CasWL; Chambr 3; CyWA; DcEnA AP; DcEuL; DcLEL; EvLB; LongCTC; ModBrL; NewC; OxEng; Pen ENG; RAdv 1; REn; WebE&AL*

Gitlis, Ivry
Israeli. Musician
b. 1927 in Haifa, Palestine
Source: *WhoMus 72*

Gitlow, Benjamin
American. Political Activist
Involved in Socialist, Communist activities.
b. Dec 22, 1891 in Elizabethport, New Jersey
d. Jul 19, 1965
Source: *BioIn 7; WhAm 4*

Giuffre, James Peter
American. Jazz Musician
b. Apr 26, 1921 in Dallas, Texas
Source: *WhoAm 74; WhoE 74*

Giulini, Carlo Maria
Italian. Opera Conductor
b. May 9, 1914 in Basletta, Italy
Source: *IntWW 74; Who 74; WhoAm 74, 76, 78, 80, 82; WhoMus 72*

Giusti, Dave (David John, Jr.)
American. Baseball Player
b. Nov 27, 1939 in Seneca Falls, New York
Source: *BaseEn; WhoProB 73*

Giusti, George
American. Artist, Graphic Designer
b. Oct 10, 1908 in Milan, Italy
Source: *WhoAm 74, 76, 78, 80, 82; WhoAmA 73; WhoGrA*

Giusti, Giuseppe
Italian. Patriot, Author
b. May 12, 1809 in Monsummano, Italy
d. 1850 in Florence, Italy
Source: *BiD&SB; CasWL; DcEuL; EvEuW; Pen EUR; REn*

Givenchy, Hubert de
French. Fashion Designer
b. Feb 21, 1927 in Beauvais, France
Source: *CurBio 55; WhoAm 82*

Givens, Edward Galen
American. Astronaut
b. 1930
d. Jun 6, 1967 in Pearland, Texas
Source: *BioIn 10*

Givot, George
American. Impersonator, Dialectician
b. 1903 in Omaha, Nebraska
Source: *FilmgC; MovMk*

Glackens, William James
American. Artist
b. Mar 13, 1870 in Philadelphia, Pennsylvania
d. May 22, 1938 in Westport, Connecticut
Source: *AmBi; AtlBL; DcAmB S2; DcCAA 71; OxAmL; WebAB; WhAm 1*

Gladstone, William Ewart
English. Statesman, Author
b. Dec 29, 1809 in Liverpool, England
d. May 19, 1898 in Hawarden, England
Source: *Alli, SUP; BbD; BiD&SB; CasWL; Chambr 3; ChPo; DcEnA, AP; DcEnL; EvLB; NewC; OxEng; REn*

Glaisher, James
English. Meterorolgist, Ballonist
b. Apr 7, 1809 in London, England
d. Feb 8, 1903
Source: *BioIn 1, 8; NewCol 75*

Glanzman, Louis S
American. Artist, Illustrator
b. Feb 8, 1922 in Baltimore, Maryland
Source: *IlsBYP; IlsCB 1957*

Glascock, Brian
see: Motels, The

Glaser, Donald Arthur
American. Nuclear Physicist
b. Sep 21, 1926 in Cleveland, Ohio
Source: *BioIn 5, 6; CurBio 61; IntWW 74; WhoAm 74; WhoWest 74; WhoWor 74*

Glaser, Milton
American. Illustrator, Book Designer
b. Jun 26, 1929 in New York, New York
Source: *ChPo S2; ConAu 17R; CurBio 80; IlsBYP; IlsCB 1957; SmATA 11; WhoAm 82*

Glaser, Paul Michael
American. Actor
Played Starsky on TV series "Starsky and Hutch," 1975-79.
b. Mar 25, 1942 in Cambridge, Massachusetts
Source: *BioIn 11; IntMPA 78, 79, 80, 81, 82; WhoAm 78, 80, 82*

Glasgow, Ellen Anderson Gholson
American. Author
b. Apr 22, 1874 in Richmond, Virginia
d. Nov 21, 1945 in Richmond, Virginia
Source: *AmAu&B; AmWr; AtlBL; BiD&SB; BiDSA; CasWL; Chambr 3; ChPo, S1; CnDAL; ConAmA; ConAmL; CurBio 46; CyWA; DcAmAu; DcAmB S3; DcBiA; DcLEL; DcNAA; EncWL; EvLB; InWom; LongCTC; ModAL; NotAW; OxAmL; OxEng; Pen AM; RAdv 1; REn; REnAL; TwCA, SUP; TwCW; WebE&AL; WhNAA*

Glaspell, Susan Keating
American. Author, Dramatist
b. Jul 1, 1882 in Davenport, Iowa
d. Jul 21, 1948
Source: *AmAu&B; AmNov; Chambr 3; CnDAL; CnMD; ConAmA; ConAmL; DcAmB S4; DcLEL; DcNAA; InWom; LongCTC; McGEWD; ModWD; NotAW; OxAmL; OxThe; PlP&P; REn; REnAL; TwCA, SUP; WhAm 2; WhNAA; WomWWA 14*

Glass, Carter
American. Statesman, Senator
b. Jan 4, 1858 in Lynchburg, Virginia
d. May 28, 1946 in Washington, DC
Source: *BiDrAC; BiDrUSE; CurBio 41, 46; DcAmB S4; DcNAA; EncAB-H; WebAB; WhAm 2; WhAmP*

Glass, David Victor
English. Sociologist
b. Jan 2, 1911 in London, England
Source: *Au&Wr 71; BioIn 1; IntWW 74; Who 74*

Glass, Hiram Bentley
American. Biologist
b. Jan 17, 1906 in Laichowfu, China
Source: *AmM&WS 73; BioIn 4; WhoAm 74*

Glass, Philip
American. Musician, Composer
b. Jan 31, 1937 in Baltimore, Maryland
Source: *Baker 78; BioIn 10, 11; CurBio 81; NewYTBS 74; WhoAm 78, 80, 82*

Glass, Ron
American. Actor
Played Ron Harris on "Barney Miller," 1975-82.
b. Jul 10, 1945 in Evansville, Indiana
Source: *BioIn 11; DcBlPA; WhoAm 82*

Glassco, John Stinson
Canadian. Author
b. Dec 15, 1909 in Montreal, PQ
d. Jan 29, 1981 in Montreal, PQ
Source: *CanWW 70; CanWr; CasWL; ConAu 13R, 102; ConNov 72, 76; ConP 70, 75; OxCan, SUP; WrDr 76*

Glasscock, Jack (John Wesley)
"Pebbly Jack"
American. Baseball Player
b. Jul 22, 1859 in Wheeling, West Virginia
d. Feb 24, 1947 in Wheeling, West Virginia
Source: *BaseEn; BioIn 3*

Glasspole, Florizel
Jamaican. Governor General
b. Sep 25, 1909 in Kingston, Jamaica
Source: *IntWW 74; WhoWor 78*

Glazer, David
American. Musician
b. May 7, 1913 in Milwaukee, Wisconsin
Source: *WhoAm 74, 76, 78, 80, 82; WhoWor 74, 76*

Glazer, Nathan
American. Author
b. Feb 25, 1923 in New York, New York
Source: *AmAu&B; AmM&WS 73; ConAu 5R; CurBio 70; IntWW 74; LEduc 74; WhoAm 74, 76, 78, 80, 82; WhoWorJ 72; WrDr 76*

Glazunov, Alexander Constantinovich
Russian. Composer
b. Aug 10, 1865 in Saint Petersburg, Russia
d. Mar 21, 1936 in Paris, France
Source: *AtlBL*

Gleason, Jackie
American. Actor, Comedian
Starred in TV series "The Honeymooners" with Art Carney.
b. Feb 26, 1916 in Brooklyn, New York
Source: *AmSCAP 66; BiE&WWA; CelR 73; CurBio 55; EncMT; FilmgC; IntMPA 75, 76, 77, 78, 79, 80, 81, 82; MovMk; NewYTBE 73; WebAB; WhoAm 74, 76, 78, 80, 82; WhoHol A*

Gleason, James
American. Actor
b. May 23, 1886 in New York, New York
d. Apr 12, 1959 in Woodland Hills, California
Source: *FilmgC; MotPP; MovMk; TwYS; Vers A; WhAm 3; WhScrn 74, 77*

Gleason, Lucille
American. Actress
b. Feb 6, 1888 in Pasadena, California
d. May 13, 1947 in Brentwood, California
Source: *FilmgC; WhScrn 74, 77; WhoHol B*

Gleason, Ralph Joseph
American. Journalist
b. Mar 1, 1917 in New York, New York
d. Jun 3, 1975 in Berkeley, California
Source: *ConAu 61, 65; WhAm 6; WhoWest 74*

Gleason, Thomas W
American. Labor Leader
President, ILA, 1963--; vice-president, AFL-CIO, 1969--.
b. Nov 8, 1900 in New York, New York
Source: *CurBio 65; WhoAm 74, 76, 78, 80, 82*

Gleizes, Albert L
French. Artist
b. 1881 in Creteil, France
d. 1953
Source: *REn*

Glemp, Jozef
Polish. Primate, Cardinal
Elevated to Cardinal, Feb 2, 1983, by Pope John Paul II.
b. Dec 18, 1929 in Inowroclaw, Poland
Source: *BioIn 12; CurBio 82; NewYTBS 82*

Glendenning, Raymond Carl
American. Journalist
b. Sep 25, 1907
Source: *Au&Wr 71; Who 74*

Glendower, Owen
Welsh. Revolutionary
b. 1359
d. 1416
Source: *BioIn 3, 5, 6, 7, 8, 9; NewC*

Glenn, Carroll
American. Violinist
b. 1922?
Source: *InWom*

Glenn, John Herschel, Jr.
American. Astronaut, Senator
First man to orbit Earth, Feb 20, 1962; Senator from OH, 1975--.
b. Jul 18, 1921 in Cambridge, Ohio
Source: *AnCL; BioNews 74; CelR 73; CurBio 62; IntWW 74; NewYTBE 72; WebAB; Who 74; WhoAm 74, 76, 78, 80, 82; WhoS&SW 73; WhoWor 74*

Glenville, Peter
English. Actor, Motion Picture Director
b. Oct 28, 1913 in Hampstead, England
Source: *BiE&WWA; CelR 73; FilmgC; NotNAT; WhoAm 82; WhoThe 77; WorEFlm*

Glickman, Marty
American. Sportscaster
Source: *BioIn 9*

Gliere, Reinhold Moritzovich
Russian. Composer
b. Jan 11, 1875 in Kiev, Russia
d. Jun 23, 1956 in Moscow, U.S.S.R.
Source: *DcCM*

Glinka, Mikhail Ivanovich
Russian. Composer
b. Jun 1, 1804 in Novospaskoi, Russia
d. Feb 15, 1857 in Berlin, Germany
Source: *AtlBL; REn*

Glossop, Peter
American. Opera Singer
b. Jun 6, 1928 in Indianapolis, Indiana
Source: *IntWW 74; Who 74; WhoMus 72; WhoWor 74*

Gloucester, Duke of
see: Henry William Frederick Albert, Prince

Glover, John
American. Revolutionary
Member MA convention to ratify Constitution, 1788.
b. Nov 5, 1753 in Salem, Massachusetts
d. Jan 30, 1797 in Marblehead, Massachusetts
Source: *AmBi; BioIn 5, 8, 9, 11; DcAmB; WebAB; WebBD 80*

Glover, Julian
English. Actor
b. Mar 27, 1935 in London, England
Source: *FilmgC; WhoHol A; WhoThe 72, 77, 81*

Glover, William H
American. Drama Critic
b. May 6, 1911 in New York, New York
Source: *BiE&WWA; NotNAT; WhoAm 74, 76, 78, 80, 82; WhoWor 74*

Glubb, Sir John Bagot
English. Military Officer, Author
b. Apr 16, 1897 in Lancashire, England
Source: *ConAu 9R, 5NR; CurBio 51; IntWW 74; Who 74; WhoWor 74; WrDr 76*

Gluck, Alma
[Reba Fiersohn]
American. Opera Singer
b. May 11, 1884 in Bucharest, Romania
d. Oct 27, 1938 in New York, New York
Source: *AmBi; DcAmB S2; InWom; NotAW; WhAm 1*

Gluck, Christoph Wilibald
German. Opera Composer
b. Jul 2, 1714 in Erasbach, Germany
d. Nov 15, 1787 in Vienna, Austria
Source: *AtlBL; NewC; REn*

Glueck, Nelson
American. Theologian, Archeologist
b. Jun 4, 1900 in Cincinnati, Ohio
d. Feb 12, 1971 in Cincinnati, Ohio
Source: *AmAu&B; ConAu 17R; ConAu P-2; CurBio 48, 69, 71; OhA&B; REnAL; WhAm 5*

Glueck, (Sol) Sheldon
American. Criminologist
b. Aug 15, 1896 in Warsaw, Poland
d. Mar 10, 1980 in Cambridge, Massachusetts
Source: *AmAu&B; BiDrAPA 77; BioIn 4, 6; ConAu 5R, 97; CurBio 57, 80; DrAS 74P, 78P; IntWW 74, 75, 76, 77, 78; WebAB; WhAm 7; WhNAA; WhoAm 74, 76, 78; WhoWor 74, 76, 78*

Glyn, Elinor Sutherland
English. Author
b. Oct 17, 1864 in Channel Islands
d. Sep 23, 1943 in London, England
Source: *CurBio 43; DcLEL; EvLB; Film 2; FilmgC; LongCTC; NewC; OxEng; OxFilm; TwCA; TwCW*

Gneisenau, August Neithardt von
Prussian. Field Marshal
b. 1760
d. 1831
Source: *NewCol 75; WebBD 80*

Go-Go's, The
[Charlotte Caffey; Belinda Carlisle; Gina Schock; Kathy Valentine ; Jane Wiedlin]
American. Rock Group
Hit album *Beauty and the Beat;* single "We Got the Beat."
Source: *NewWmR*

Goalby, Bob
American. Golfer
b. Mar 14, 1931 in Belleville, Illinois
Source: *BioIn 7, 8, 10; WhoGolf*

Gobbi, Tito
Italian. Opera Singer
b. Oct 24, 1915 in Italy
Source: *CurBio 57; IntWW 74; Who 74; WhoAm 82; WhoMus 72; WhoWor 74*

Gobel, George Leslie
"Lonesome George"
American. Comedian
b. May 20, 1919 in Chicago, Illinois
Source: *CurBio 55; EncFCWM 69; FilmgC; WhoAm 74; WhoHol A*

Gobineau, Joseph Arthur, Comte de
French. Author, Philosopher
b. Jul 14, 1816 in Ville d'Avray, France
d. Oct 13, 1882 in Turin, Italy
Source: *BioIn 1, 2, 7, 9; McGEWB*

Goble, Graham
see: Little River Band, The

Godard, Benjamin L P
French. Composer
b. 1849
d. 1895
Source: *BioIn 3*

Godard, Jean Luc
French. Motion Picture Director
b. Dec 3, 1930 in Paris, France
Source: *BiDFilm; CelR 73; CurBio 69; DcFM; FilmgC; IntMPA 82; IntWW 74; MovMk; NewYTBE 70, 75; OxFilm, ; WhoWor 74; WomWMM; WorEFlm*

Goddard, Calvin Hooker
American. Criminologist
b. Oct 30, 1891 in Baltimore, Maryland
d. Feb 22, 1955
Source: *BioIn 3, 4; WhAm 3*

Goddard, George Henry
American. Architect, Surveyor
b. 1817 in Bristol, England
d. 1906 in Berkeley, California
Source: *BioIn 9*

Goddard, Paulette
[Marian Levee]
American. Actress
b. Jun 3, 1911 in Great Neck, New York
Source: *BiDFilm; CelR 73; CmMov; FilmgC; InWom; IntMPA 75, 76, 77, 78, 79, 80, 81, 82; MotPP; MovMk; OxFilm; ThFT; WhoAm 82; WhoHol A; WorEFlm*

Goddard, Robert Hutchings
American. Physicist
Launched first liquid-fueled rocket, 1926.
b. Oct 5, 1882 in Worcester, Massachusetts
d. Aug 10, 1945 in Baltimore, Maryland
Source: *DcAmB S3; EncAB-H; NewCol 75; WebAB; WhAm 2*

Godden, Rumer, pseud.
[Margaret Rumer Haynes Dixon]
English. Author, Poet, Dramatist
TV movie made from *In This House of Brede,* 1975.
b. Dec 10, 1907 in Sussex, England
Source: *AnCL; Au&Wr 71; AuBYP; ChPo, S1, S2; ConAu 5R, 4NR; ConNov 72, 76; DcLEL; FilmgC; InWom; IntWW 74; LongCTC; ModBrL; MorJA; NewC; PiP; RAdv 1; REn; SmATA 3; TwCA, SUP; TwCW; WhoChL; WhoWor 74; WrDr 76*

Godel, Kurt
American. Mathematician
b. Apr 28, 1906 in Bruenn, Czechoslovakia
d. Jan 14, 1978 in Princeton, New Jersey
Source: *AmM&WS 73P; IntWW 74; NewCol 75; Who 74; WhoAm 74; WhoWor 74*

Godey, Louis Antoine
American. Publisher
b. Jun 6, 1804 in New York, New York
d. Nov 29, 1878 in Philadelphia, Pennsylvania
Source: *AmAu; AmAu&B; AmBi; ApCAB; DcAmB; NewCol 75; REn; WebAB; WhAm H; WorFshn*

Godfrey of Bouillon
French. Crusader, Ruler of Jerusalem
b. 1058? in Baisyin Brabant, France
d. Jul 18, 1100 in Jerusalem, Palestine
Source: *DcEuL; NewC; NewCol 75*

Godfrey, Arthur Michael
American. Actor, Singer
b. Aug 31, 1903 in New York, New York
Source: *AmSCAP 66; BioNews 75; CelR 73; CurBio 48; IntMPA 75, 76, 77, 78, 79, 80, 81, 82; WebAB; WhoAm 74, 76, 78, 80, 82; WhoHol A*

Godfrey, Isadore
English. Opera Conductor
b. 1901?
d. Sep 12, 1977 in Sussex, England
Source: *BioIn 11*

Godiva, Lady
[Godgifu]
English. Social Protester
Made legendary ride naked through Coventry to win tax relief for townspeople.
b. 1010
d. 1067
Source: *InWom; NewC; NewCol 75; REn*

Godkin, Edwin Lawrence
American. Journalist
b. Oct 2, 1831 in Wicklow, Ireland
d. May 21, 1902 in England
Source: *Alli SUP; AmAu; AmAu&B; AmBi; BbD; BiD&SB; DcAmAu; DcAmB; DcLEL; DcNAA; EncAB-H; EvLB; OxAmL; REn; REnAL; TwCBDA; WebAB; WhAm 1*

Godley, Devin
see: 10 CC

Godolphin, Sidney
English. Statesman
b. Jun 15, 1645 in England
d. Sep 15, 1712 in London, England
Source: *BioIn 1, 3, 11; McGEWB; WebBD 80*

Godowsky, Leopold
Polish. Musician
b. Feb 13, 1870 in Wilma, Russia
d. Nov 21, 1938
Source: *AmBi; AmSCAP 66; DcAmB S2; WhAm 1; WhoAm 74*

Godoy Alcayaga, Lucila
Chilean. Poet, Educator
b. 1889
d. 1957
Source: *BioIn 1, 2, 4, 6, 9, 10; DcSpL; REn*

Godunov, Alexander
Russian. Ballet Dancer
First Bolshoi Ballet member to defect to US, 1979.
b. Nov 28, 1949 in U.S.S.R.
Source: *BioIn 10, 11; WhoAm 82*

Godunov, Boris Fedorovich
Russian. Czar
b. 1551 in Moscow, Russia
d. Apr 23, 1605
Source: *McGEWB; NewCol 75; REn*

Godwin, Edward William
English. Architect, Designer
b. 1833 in Bristol, England
d. Sep 6, 1886
Source: *NotNAT B; OxDecA; OxThe; WhoArch*

Godwin, Mary Wollstonecraft
English. Author, Feminist
Wrote feminist paper *The Vindication of the Rights of Women,* 1792; mother of Mary Shelley.
b. Apr 27, 1759 in London, England
d. Nov 10, 1797 in London, England
Source: *Alli; AtlBL; BbD; BiD&SB; BrAu; CasWL; Chambr 2; DcEnA; DcEnL; DcEuL; DcLEL; EvLB; InWom; NewC; NewCol 75; OxEng; Pen ENG; REn*

Godwin, William
English. Author
b. Mar 3, 1756
d. Apr 7, 1836 in London, England
Source: *Alli; AtlBL; BbD; BiD&SB; BiDLA, SUP; BrAu 19; CasWL; Chambr 2; CyWA; DcBiA; DcEnA; DcEnL; DcLEL; EncMys; EvLB; MouLC 3; NewC; OxEng; Pen ENG; REn; WebE&AL*

Goebbels, (Paul) Joseph
German. Nazi Propogandist
b. Oct 29, 1897 in Rheydt, Germany
d. May 3, 1945 in Berlin, Germany
Source: *CurBio 41; NewCol 75; OxGer; REn*

Goering, Emmy Sonnemann
German. Second Wife of Hermann Goering
b. 1893?
d. Jun 8, 1973 in Munich, Germany (West)
Source: *EncTR; NewYTBE 73*

Goering, Hermann Wilhelm
German. Nazi War Criminal
Hitler's minister of aviation; founder of Gestapo.
b. Jan 12, 1893 in Rosenheim, Germany
d. Oct 15, 1946 in Nuremberg, Germany
Source: *CurBio 41, 46; OxGer; REn*

Goes, Hugo van der
Flemish. Artist
b. 1440
d. 1482
Source: *AtlBL; REn*

Goethals, George Washington
American. Army Officer, Engineer
b. Jun 29, 1858 in Brooklyn, New York
d. Jan 21, 1928 in New York, New York
Source: *AmBi; DcAmB; DcNAA; EncAB-H; WebAB; WhAm 1*

Goethe, Johann Wolfgang von
German. Poet, Dramatist, Author
Wrote *Faust,* 1770, 1831; *The Sorrows of Werther,* 1774.
b. Aug 28, 1749 in Frankfurt, Germany
d. Mar 22, 1832 in Weimar, Germany
Source: *AtlBL; BbD; BiD&SB; CasWL; ChPo, S1, S2; CnThe; CyWA; DcBiA; DcEnL; DcEuL; EuAu; EvEuW; McGEWD; NewC; OxEng; OxFr; OxGer; OxThe; Pen EUR; RComWL; REn; REnWD*

Goff, Norris
[Lum 'n Abner]
American. Actor
b. 1906
d. Jun 7, 1978 in Palm Desert, California
Source: *WhoHol A*

Goffstein, Marilyn
American. Author
b. Dec 20, 1940 in Saint Paul, Minnesota
Source: *ConAu 21R; SmATA 8; WhoAmW 77*

Gogol, Nikolai Vasilievich
Russian. Author
b. Mar 21, 1809 in Mirgorod, Russia
d. Mar 4, 1852 in Moscow, Russia
Source: *AtlBL; BbD; BiD&SB; CasWL; CnThe; CyWA; DcBiA; DcEuL; DcRusL; EuAu; EvEuW; McGEWD; NewC; OxEng; OxThe; Pen EUR; PlP&P; RComWL; REn; REnWD*

Goheen, Robert Francis
American. Educator, University President
b. Aug 15, 1919 in Vengurla, India
Source: *AmAu&B; Au&Wr 71; CurBio 58; DrAS 74F; IntWW 74; LEduc 74; Who 74; WhoAm 74, 76, 78, 80, 82; WhoE 74; WhoWor 74*

Goizueta, Roberto Crispulo
American. Beverage Company Executive
With Coca-Cola, 1954--; chairman, 1981--.
b. Nov 18, 1931 in Havana, Cuba
Source: *Dun&B 79; WhoAm 76, 78, 80, 82; WhoF&I 74; WhoS&SW 75, 76*

Gola, Tom B
American. Basketball Player
All-American player at LaSalle U for four years.
b. Jan 13, 1933 in Philadelphia, Pennsylvania
Source: *WhoBbl 73*

Golacinski, Alan Bruce
[The Hostages]
American. Former Hostage in Iran
b. Jun 4, 1950 in Austria
Source: *NewYTBS 81; USBiR 74*

Golar, Simeon
American. Government Official
b. 1928
Source: *BioIn 9, 11; NewYTBE 72*

Gold, Andrew
American. Singer
b. Aug 2, 1951 in Burbank, California
Source: *IlEncRk*

Gold, Arthur
Canadian. Musician
b. 1919
Source: *BioIn 7*

Gold, Harry
Spy
b. 1910
d. Aug 28, 1972 in Philadelphia, Pennsylvania
Source: *NewYTBE 72; NewYTBS 74*

Gold, Herbert
American. Author
b. Mar 9, 1924 in Cleveland, Ohio
Source: *AmAu&B; ConAu 9R; ConLC 4; ConNov 72, 76; DrAF 76; ModAL; OxAmL; Pen AM; RAdv 1; REnAL; TwCW; WhoAm 80, 82; WhoWor 74; WhoWorJ 72; WorAu; WrDr 76*

Gold, Michael
[Irwin Granich]
American. Author
b. Apr 12, 1894 in New York, New York
d. May 14, 1967 in Terra Inda, California
Source: *AmAu&B; ConAu 45, 97; ModWD; OxAmL; Pen AM; REn; REnAL; TwCA, SUP; WebE&AL*

Gold Dust Twins
see: McSpaden, Byron; Nelson, (John) Byron

Goldazher, Herbert
Museum Director
Source: *NF*

Goldberg, Arthur Joseph
American. Supreme Court Justice
As labor lawyer, played important role in 1955 merger of AFL and CIO.
b. Aug 8, 1908 in Chicago, Illinois
Source: *AmAu&B; BiDrUSE; CelR 73; ConAu 65; CurBio 49, 61; EncAB-H; IntWW 74; WebAB; Who 74; WhoAm 74, 76, 78, 80, 82; WhoAmP 73; WhoF&I 74; WhoWor 74; WhoWorJ 72*

Goldberg, Ben Zion
American. Journalist
b. Jan 9, 1894 in Olshani, Russia
Source: *WhoWorJ 72*

Goldberg, Bertrand
American. Architect
b. Jul 17, 1913 in Chicago, Illinois
Source: *AmArch 70; BioNews 74; WhoAm 74, 76, 78, 80, 82*

Goldberg, Rube (Reuben Lucius)
American. Cartoonist
Created comic strips "Mike & Ike," "Lucifer Butts"; won Pulitzer Prize, 1948.
b. Jul 4, 1883 in San Francisco, California
d. Dec 7, 1970 in New York, New York
Source: *AmAu&B; AmSCAP 66; ConAu 5R; CurBio 48, 71; NewYTBE 70; WebAB; WhAm 6; WhNAA; WhScrn 77*

Goldberger, Joseph
American. Physician, Researcher
b. Jul 16, 1874 in Austria
d. Jan 17, 1929 in Washington, DC
Source: *AmBi; DcAmB; WebAB; WhAm 1*

Goldblum, Jeff
American. Actor
b. 1952?
Source: *BioIn 11*

Golden, Bill
see: Oak Ridge Boys, The

Golden, Clinton Strong
American. Labor Leader
Vice-president, United Steelworkers of America, 1942-46.
b. Nov 16, 1886 in Pottsville, Pennsylvania
d. Jun 12, 1961
Source: *BioIn 1, 5, 6; CurBio 48, 61; WhAm 4*

Golden, Harry Lewis
American. Author, Editor, Publisher
b. May 6, 1903 in Mikulinsty, Austria-Hungary
d. Oct 2, 1981 in Charlotte, North Carolina
Source: *AmAu&B; AnObit 1981; BioIn 5, 6, 7, 8; CelR 73; ConAu 1R, 104, 2NR; CurBio 59, 81; Pen AM; RAdv 1; REnAL; WhoAm 74, 76, 78, 80; WhoS&SW 73, 75; WhoWor 74, 76; WhoWorJ 72; WorAu*

Golden, John
American. Dramatist, Producer
b. Jun 27, 1874 in New York, New York
d. Jun 17, 1955 in New York, New York
Source: *AmAu&B; AmSCAP 66; CurBio 44, 55; DcAmB S5; OhA&B; PoIre; REnAL; WhAm 3*

Golden, William
American. Art Director, Graphic Designer
b. Mar 31, 1911 in New York, New York
d. Oct 23, 1959 in Stony Pointe, New York
Source: *BiDLA; WhoGrA*

Golden Earring
[Rinus Gerritsen; Barry Hay; George Kooymans; Robert Jan Stips; Cesar Zuiderwijk]
Dutch. Rock Group
Source: *RkOn 2; WhoRock 81*

Goldenson, Leonard Harry
American. Motion Picture Executive
b. Dec 7, 1905 in Scottdale, Pennsylvania
Source: *CelR 73; CurBio 57; IntMPA 75, 76, 77, 78, 79, 80, 81, 82; St&PR 75; WhoAm 74, 76, 78, 80, 82; WhoE 74; WhoF&I 74; WhoGov 72; WhoWor 74*

Goldfinger, Nathaniel
American. AFL-CIO Economist
b. Aug 20, 1916 in New York, New York
d. Jul 22, 1976 in Silver Spring, Maryland
Source: *AmM&WS 73S; WhoAm 74*

Goldhaber, Maurice
American. Physicist
b. Apr 18, 1911 in Lemberg, Austria
Source: *AmM&WS 73; IntWW 74; WhoAm 74, 76, 78, 80, 82*

Golding, William Gerald
English. Author
Best known for allegorical cult novel, *Lord of the Flies,* 1954.
b. Sep 19, 1911 in Cornwall, England
Source: *CasWL; CnMWL; ConAu 5R; ConLC 1, 2, 3, 8, 10, 17; ConNov 72, 76; EncWL; IntWW 74; LongCTC; ModBrL, SUP; ModWD; NewC; Pen ENG; RAdv 1; REn; TwCW; WebE&AL; Who 74; WhoAm 82; WhoTwCL; WhoWor 74; WorAu; WrDr 76*

Goldman, Edwin Franko
American. Band Leader, Composer
b. Jan 1, 1878 in Louisville, Kentucky
d. Feb 21, 1956 in New York, New York
Source: *AmSCAP 66; CurBio 42, 56; WebAB; WhAm 3*

Goldman, Emma
American. Anarchist, Author
b. Jun 27, 1869 in Kaunas, Lithuania
d. May 14, 1940 in Toronto, ON
Source: *AmBi; CurBio 40; DcAmB S2; DcNAA; EncAB-H; HerW; InWom; NewCol 75; NotAW; OxAmL; REnAL; WebAB; WhAm HA, 4; WhAmP*

Goldman, Eric F
American. Author, Historian
b. Jun 17, 1915 in Washington, DC
Source: *AmAu&B; ConAu 5R; CurBio 64; DrAS 74H; IntWW 74; WhoAm 74; WhoWor 74; WhoWorJ 72; WrDr 76*

Goldman, Eric W
American. Business Executive
b. 1958?
Source: *BioIn 12*

Goldman, James
American. Dramatist, Author
b. Jun 30, 1927 in Chicago, Illinois
Source: *AmAu&B; BiE&WWA; ConAu 45, 1NR; ConDr 73; McGEWD; NotNAT; WhoAm 74, 76, 78, 80, 82; WhoE 74; WhoWor 74; WrDr 76*

Goldman, Richard Franko
American. Composer
b. Dec 7, 1910 in New York, New York
d. Jan 19, 1980 in Baltimore, Maryland
Source: *AmAu&B; ConAu 9R, 93, 5NR; LEduc 74; WhoAm 74; WhoWor 74; WrDr 76*

Goldman, William
American. Author, Screenwriter
b. Aug 12, 1931 in Chicago, Illinois
Source: *AmAu&B; ConAu 9R; ConDr 73, 77A; ConNov 72, 76; IntMPA 78, 79, 80, 81; NotNAT; WhoAm 78, 80, 82; WorAu 1970*

Goldmann, Nahum
American. Jewish Scholar, Zionist
b. Jul 10, 1895 in Wisnewo, Poland
d. Aug 29, 1982 in Bad Reichenhall, Germany (West)
Source: *CurBio 57, 82; IntWW 74, 75, 76, 77, 78; MidE; NewYTBE 70; NewYTBS 82; PolProf K; Who 74; WhoRel 75, 77; WhoWor 74, 76, 78; WhoWorJ 72*

Goldmark, Karl
Hungarian. Composer
b. May 18, 1830 in Keszthely, Hungary
d. Jan 2, 1915 in Vienna, Austria
Source: *NewEOp 71; OxMus*

Goldmark, Peter Carl
American. Engineer, Inventor
Developed first practical color television system, 1940.
b. Dec 2, 1906 in Budapest, Hungary
d. Dec 7, 1977 in Westchester County, New York
Source: *AmM&WS 73P; ConAu 73, 77; CurBio 40, 50; IntWW 74; NewYTBE 72; WhoAm 74; WhoWor 74*

Goldner, Orville
American. Producer, Author
b. May 18, 1906 in Toledo, Ohio
Source: *ConAu 53*

Goldoni, Carlo
Italian. Dramatist
b. Feb 25, 1707 in Venice, Italy
d. Jan 6, 1793 in Versailles, France
Source: *AtlBL; BiD&SB; CasWL; CyWA; DcEuL; EuAu; EvEuW; McGEWD; OxEng; OxThe; Pen EUR; RComWL; REn; REnWD*

Goldovsky, Boris
Russian. Opera Conductor, Director
b. Jun 7, 1908 in Moscow, Russia
Source: *CurBio 66; WhoAm 74, 76, 78, 80, 82; WhoMus 72; WhoWor 74*

Goldsand, Robert
American. Musician
b. 1922 in Vienna, Austria
Source: *WhoMus 72*

Goldsboro, Bobby
American. Singer, Songwriter
CMA star of year, 1968; hits include "Honey," "The Straight Life."
b. Jan 11, 1941 in Marianna, Florida
Source: *CelR 73; WhoAm 82*

Goldsborough, Louis M
American. Naval Officer
b. Feb 18, 1805 in Washington, DC
d. Feb 20, 1877 in Washington, DC
Source: *AmBi; DcAmB; NewCol 75; WebAB; WebBD 80; WhAm H*

Goldschmidt, Neil Edward
American. Politician
Secretary of Transportation, 1979-81.
b. Jun 16, 1940 in Eugene, Oregon
Source: *BioIn 12; CurBio 80; NewYTBS 74; WhoAm 76, 78, 80, 82; WhoAmP 77, 79; WhoGov 75, 77*

Goldsmith, Fred Ernest
American. Baseball Player
b. May 15, 1852 in New Haven, Connecticut
d. Mar 28, 1939 in Berkley, Michigan
Source: *BaseEn; WhoProB 73*

Goldsmith, Jerry
American. Songwriter
b. 1930 in Los Angeles, California
Source: *CmMov; FilmgC; IntMPA 75, 76, 77, 78, 79, 80, 81, 82; WhoAm 82; WorEFlm*

Goldsmith, Judith Ann Becker
American. Feminist
President of NOW, 1982--.
b. Nov 26, 1938 in Manitowoc, Wisconsin
Source: *NewYTBS 82*

Goldsmith, Oliver
British. Poet, Dramatist, Author
Wrote *The Vicar of Wakefield,* 1766; *She Stoops to Conquer,* 1773.
b. Nov 10, 1728 in Pallas, Ireland
d. Apr 4, 1774 in London, England
Source: *Alli; AtlBL; BbD; BiD&SB; BrAu; CarSB; CasWL; Chambr 2; ChPo, S1, S2; CnE&AP; CnThe; CrtT 2; CyWA; DcBiA; DcEnA, AP; DcEnL; DcEuL; DcLEL; EvLB; HsB&A; McGEWD; MouLC 2; NewC; OxThe; OxEng; Pen ENG; PlP&P; PoIre; RAdv 1; REn; REnWD; WebE&AL*

Goldwater, Barry Morris
American. Senator, Author
b. Jan 1, 1909 in Phoenix, Arizona
Source: *AmAu&B; BiDrAC; BioNews 74; CelR 73; CngDr 74; ConAu 41R; CurBio 55; EncAB-H; IntWW 74; NewYTBS 74; WebAB; Who 74; WhoAmP 73; WhoGov 72; WhoWest 74; WhoWor 74; WrDr 76; WhoAm 74, 82*

Goldwyn, Samuel
[Samuel Goldfish]
American. Motion Picture Producer
b. Aug 27, 1882 in Warsaw, Poland
d. Jan 31, 1974 in Los Angeles, California
Source: *BiDFilm; BioNews 74; BusPN; CelR 73; CurBio 44; DcFM; FilmgC; NewYTBS 74; OxFilm; REnAL; WebAB; WhAm 6; Who 74; WhoWor 74; WorEFlm*

Golenpaul, Dan
American. Creator of Information Please
b. 1900
d. Feb 13, 1974 in New York, New York
Source: *NewYTBS 74*

Golgi, Camillo
Italian. Neurologist
b. Jul 7, 1843 in Corteno, Italy
d. Jan 21, 1926 in Pavia, Italy
Source: *BioIn 3, 6, 9; WebBD 80*

Goliath
Biblical Character
Source: *NewCol 75; WebBD 80*

Golonka, Arlene
American. Actress
b. Jan 23, 1936 in Chicago, Illinois
Source: *BiE&WWA; NotNAT; WhoHol A*

Golschmann, Vladimir
French. Conductor
b. Dec 26, 1893 in Paris, France
d. Mar 1, 1972 in New York, New York
Source: *CurBio 51, 72; NewYTBE 72; WhAm 5*

Golson, Benny
American. Jazz Musician
b. Jan 25, 1929 in Philadelphia, Pennsylvania
Source: *AmSCAP 66; WhoAm 74*

Goltz, Gene
American. Journalist
b. Apr 30, 1930 in Marquette, Iowa
Source: *WhoAm 74*

Gombrowicz, Witold
American. Author
b. Sep 4, 1904 in Moloszyee, Poland
d. Jul 25, 1969
Source: *CasWL; ConAu 21R, 25R; ConAu P-2; ConLC 4; CroCD; EncWL; McGEWD; ModSL 2; ModWD; NewCol 75; Pen EUR; TwCW; WhAm 5; WhoTwCL; WorAu*

Gomez, "Lefty" (Vernon Louis)
"The Gay Castillion"; "Goofy"
American. Baseball Player
Pitcher, 1930-43; inducted into Hall of Fame, 1972.
b. Nov 26, 1909 in Rodeo, California
Source: *BaseEn; BioIn 1, 2, 3, 5, 8, 9; WhoProB 73*

Gomez, Thomas
American. Actor
b. Jul 10, 1905 in Long Island, New York
d. Jun 18, 1971 in Santa Monica, California
Source: *BiE&WWA; CmMov; FilmgC; MovMk; NewYTBE 71; Vers A; WhScrn 74, 77; WhoHol B*

Gompers, Samuel
American. Labor Leader, Author
Founder, first president of AFL, 1886-1924.
b. Jan 27, 1850 in London, England
d. Dec 13, 1924 in San Antonio, Texas
Source: *AmAu&B; AmBi; DcAmB; DcNAA; EncAB-H; REn; REnAL; WebAB; WhAm 1; WhAmP*

Gomulka, Wladyslaw
Polish. Political Leader
Led Poland's Communist Party, 1956-70.
b. Feb 6, 1905 in Krosno, Poland
d. Sep 1, 1982 in Warsaw, Poland
Source: *CurBio 57, 82; IntWW 74, 75, 76, 77, 78; IntYB 78, 79; LinLib S; McGEWB; NewYTBE 70; NewYTBS 82; WhoSocC 78*

Goncharov, Ivan A
Russian. Author
b. Jun 1812 in Simbirsk, Russia
d. Sep 1891 in Saint Petersburg, Russia
Source: *AtlBL; BiD&SB; CasWL; CyWA; DcEuL; DcRusL; EuAu; EvEuW; Pen EUR; REn*

Goncourt, Edmond Louis Antoine Huot
[Edmond Louis DeGoncourt]
French. Author
b. May 26, 1822 in Nancy, France
d. Jul 16, 1896 in Chamrosay, France
Source: *AtlBL; BbD; BiD&SB; CasWL; ClDMEL; CyWA; DcBiA; DcEuL; EuAu; EvEuW; NewC; OxEng; OxFr; OxThe; Pen EUR; REn*

Goncourt, Jules Alfred Huot de
[Jules Alfred DeGoncourt]
French. Author
b. Dec 17, 1830 in Paris, France
d. Jun 20, 1870 in Paris, France
Source: *BbD; BiD&SB; CasWL; ClDMEL; CyWA; DcEuL; EuAu; EvEuW; OxEng; OxFr; OxThe; Pen EUR; REn*

Gongora y Argote, Don Luis de
Spanish. Poet
b. Jun 11, 1561 in Cordova, Spain
d. May 24, 1627 in Cordova, Spain
Source: *BiD&SB; BioIn 2, 4, 7, 10; CasWL; DcEuL; DcSpL; EuAu; EvEuW; LinLib L; McGEWB; NewCol 75; OxSpan; Pen EUR; REn*

Gonne, Maud MacBride
Irish. Patriot, Philanthropist
b. 1866 in London, England
d. 1953
Source: *BioIn 1, 3, 7, 10, 11; WebBD 80*

Gonzales, "Pancho" (Richard Alonzo)
American. Tennis Player
Eight time World Pro tennis champ; autobiography *Man with a Racket,* 1959.
b. May 9, 1928 in Los Angeles, California
Source: *CelR 73; CurBio 49; WebAB; WhoAm 74, 76, 78, 80, 82*

Gonzalez Marquez, Felipe
Spanish. Political Leader
First Socialist premier since 1936-39 Civil War; elected 1982--.
b. Mar 5, 1942 in Seville, Spain
Source: *BioIn 11; CurBio 78; IntWW 79, 80, 81; NewYTBS 82*

Good, Sandra
American. Manson Cultist
b. 1944
Source: *BioIn 10*

Goodall, Jane
[Baroness VanLawick-Goodall]
English. Anthropologist, Ethnologist
Wrote *In the Shadow of Man,* 1971.
b. Mar 4, 1934 in London, England
Source: *ConAu 45, 2NR; CurBio 67; InWom*

Goodall, John Strickland
English. Artist, Illustrator
b. Jun 7, 1908 in Heacham, England
Source: *ConAu 33R; IlsCB 1946; SmATA 4*

Goodell, Charles Ellsworth
American. Lawyer, Senator
b. Mar 16, 1926 in Jamestown, New York
Source: *BiDrAC; ConAu 81; CurBio 68; IntWW 74; WhoAm 74, 76, 78, 80, 82; WhoAmP 73; WhoE 74*

Goodell, Brian Stuart
American. Swimmer
b. Apr 2, 1959 in Stockton, California
Source: *BioIn 11, 12*

Goodeve, Grant
American. Actor
Played David on "Eight is Enough," 1977-81.
b. 1952? in Windham, Vermont
Source: *NF*

Goodfriend, Lynda
American. Actress
b. Oct 31, 1950
Source: *BioIn 12*

Goodhue, Bertram G
American. Architect
b. Apr 28, 1869 in Pomfret, Connecticut
d. Apr 23, 1924 in New York, New York
Source: *AmBi; ChPo; DcAmAu; DcAmB; DcNAA; OxAmL; WebAB; WhAm 1*

Goodman, Al(fred)
American. Composer, Conductor
b. Aug 12, 1890 in Nikopol, Russia
d. Jan 10, 1972 in New York, New York
Source: *BiE&WWA; AmSCAP 66; NewYTBE 72*

Goodman, Andrew
American. Civil Rights Organizer
b. 1944
d. 1965
Source: *BioIn 7*

Goodman, Benny (Benjamin David)
"King of Swing"
American. Band Leader, Musician
Hits include "Lullaby in Rhythm," "Stompin' at the Savoy."
b. May 30, 1909 in Chicago, Illinois
Source: *AmSCAP 66; BioNews 74; CelR 73; CurBio 42, 62; EncAB-H; FilmgC; IntWW 74; WebAB; WhoAm 74, 76, 78, 80, 82; WhoE 74; WhoHol A; WhoJazz 72; WhoWor 74*

Goodman, Dody
American. Actress, Dancer
b. Oct 28, 1929 in Columbus, Ohio
Source: *BiE&WWA; InWom; NotNAT; WhoAm 82; WhoHol A; WhoThe 77*

Goodman, George Jerome Waldo
[Adam Smith]
American. Author, Editor
b. Aug 10, 1930 in Saint Louis, Missouri
Source: *AmAu&B; ConAu 21R; WhoAm 74, 76, 78, 80, 82*

Goodman, Julian B
American. Broadcasting Executive
b. May 1, 1922 in Glasgow, Kentucky
Source: *CurBio 67; IntMPA 75, 76, 77, 78, 79, 80; IntWW 74; St&PR 75; WhoAm 74, 76, 78, 80, 82; WhoE 74; WhoF&I 74; WhoWor 74*

Goodman, Martin Wise
Canadian. Newspaper Executive
President of Toronto *Star* Newspapers, Ltd., 1978-81.
b. Jan 15, 1935 in Calgary, AB
d. Dec 20, 1981 in Toronto, ON
Source: *WhoAm 78, 80, 82*

Goodman, Mitchell
American. Author
b. Dec 13, 1923 in New York, New York
Source: *Au&Wr 71; ConAu 1R, 4NR; DrAF 76; DrAP 75*

Goodman, Paul
American. Author, Educator
b. Sep 9, 1911 in New York, New York
d. Aug 2, 1972 in North Stratford, New Hampshire
Source: *AmAu&B; ConAu 21R, 37R; ConAu P-2; ConDr 73; ConLC 1, 2, 4; ConNov 72, 76; ConP 70; ModAL SUP; OxAmL; Pen AM; TwCA SUP; WhAm 5*

Goodman, Steve(n Benjamin)
American. Songwriter
b. Jul 25, 1948 in Chicago, Illinois
Source: *ConMuA 80; WhoAm 82; WhoRock 81*

Goodnight, Charles
American. Rancher
b. Mar 5, 1836 in Macoupin County, Illinois
d. Dec 12, 1929
Source: *BioIn 2, 4, 5; WhAm 4*

Goodpaster, Andrew Jackson
American. Army Officer
b. Feb 12, 1915 in Granite City, Illinois
Source: *AmM&WS 73S, 78S; BioIn 3, 8, 9, 11; CurBio 69; IntWW 74, 75, 76, 77, 78; NewYTBS 77; WebAMB; Who 74; WhoAm 74, 76, 78, 80, 82; WhoWor 78; WorDWW*

Goodpasture, Ernest William
American. Pathologist
b. Oct 17, 1886 in Montgomery County, Indiana
d. Sep 20, 1960
Source: *BioIn 1, 3, 5, 6, 7; WhAm 4*

Goodrich, Benjamin Franklin
American. Industrialist
b. Nov 4, 1841 in Ripley, New York
d. Aug 3, 1888 in Manitou Springs, Colorado
Source: *DcAmB; WhAm H*

Goodrich, Gail
American. Basketball Player
b. Apr 23, 1943 in Los Angeles, California
Source: *BioIn 7, 9, 10; WhoAm 74; WhoBbl 73*

Goodrich, Lloyd
American. Author
b. Jul 10, 1897 in Nutley, New Jersey
Source: *ConAu 69; CurBio 67; WhoAm 74, 76, 78, 80, 82; WhoAmA 73; WhoGov 72*

Goodrich, Samuel Griswold
[Peter Parley, pseud.]
American. Journalist
Wrote *The Tales of Peter Parley about America,* 1827.
b. Aug 19, 1793 in Ridgefield, Connecticut
d. May 9, 1860 in New York, New York
Source: *Alli; AmAu; AmAu&B; AmBi; BbD; BbtC; BiD&SB; CarSB; CyAl 2; DcAmAu; DcAmB; DcNAA; Drake; OxAmL; REn; REnAL; TwCBDA; WebAB; WhAm H; WhoChL*

Goodroe, Michael
see: Motels, The

Goodson, Mark
American. TV Producer
Creator, producer game shows, including "What's My Line"; "Password."
b. Jan 24, 1915 in Sacramento, California
Source: *IntMPA 77, 78, 79, 80, 81, 82; WhoAm 74, 76, 78, 80, 82; WhoWor 74*

Goodwin, Bill
American. Actor, Announcer
b. Jul 28, 1910 in San Francisco, California
d. May 9, 1958 in Palm Springs, California
Source: *BioIn 4; WhScrn 77*

Goodwin, Daniel
"Spiderman"
American. Mountaineer, Stuntman
b. Nov 7, 1955
Source: *BioIn 12*

Goodwin, Hannibal Williston
American. Clergyman, Inventor
Invented photographic film; received patent, 1898.
b. Apr 30, 1822 in Taughannock, New York
d. Dec 31, 1900
Source: *WebBD 80; WhAm H*

Goodwin, Myles
see: April Wine

Goodwin, Nat C
American. Actor
b. 1857 in Boston, Massachusetts
d. Jan 31, 1919 in New York
Source: *BioIn 2, 3, 4; WhScrn 74, 77; WhoHol B*

Goodyear, Charles
American. Inventor
Discovered vulcanization process for rubber, 1839; patented, 1844.
b. Dec 29, 1800 in New Haven, Connecticut
d. Jul 1, 1860 in New York, New York
Source: *AmBi; ApCAB; DcAmB; Drake; EncAB-H; NewCol 75; TwCBDA; WebAB; WhAm H*

Goolagong, Evonne
[Mrs. Roger Cawley]
Australian. Tennis Player
Defeated Margaret Court to become fifth youngest Wimbledon singles champ, 1971.
b. Jul 31, 1951 in Barellan, Australia
Source: *BioNews 74; CelR 73; CurBio 71; HerW; NewYTBE 71; WhoWor 74*

Goossens, Sir Eugene
English. Composer, Conductor
b. May 26, 1893 in London, England
d. Jun 13, 1962 in London, England
Source: *CurBio 45, 62; DcCM; NewCol 75; WhAm 4*

Goossens, Leon Jean
English. Musician
b. Jun 12, 1897 in Liverpool, England
Source: *IntWW 74; Who 74; WhoMus 72*

Gopallawa, William
Sri Lankan. Diplomat
b. Sep 16, 1897 in Dullewa, Ceylon
d. Jan 30, 1981 in Colombo, Sri Lanka
Source: *AnObit 1981; FarE&A 78, 79; IntWW 74, 75, 76, 77, 78; IntYB 78, 79; Who 74; WhoGov 72; WhoWor 74, 76, 78*

Gorbanevskaya, Natalya
Russian. Poet, Translator
b. 1936
Source: *BioIn 9*

Gorbatko, Viktor Vasiliyevich
Russian. Cosmonaut
b. Dec 3, 1934 in Ventsy Zarja, U.S.S.R.
Source: *IntWW 74; WhoWor 74*

Gorbatov, Aleksandr Vassil'evich
Russian. General
b. 1891?
d. Dec 7, 1973 in Moscow, U.S.S.R.
Source: *BioIn 7, 10; ConAu 45; NewYTBE 73*

Gorcey, Leo
American. Actor
b. Jun 3, 1915 in New York, New York
d. Jun 2, 1969 in Oakland, California
Source: *FilmgC; MotPP; MovMk; WhScrn 74, 77; WhoHol B*

Gordimer, Nadine
South African. Journalist, Author
b. Nov 20, 1923 in Springs, South Africa
Source: *CasWL; ConAu 5R, 3NR; ConLC 3, 5; ConNov 72, 76; InWom; IntWW 74; NewC; NewCol 75; Pen ENG; TwCW; Who 74; WhoTwCL; WhoWor 74; WorAu; WrDr 76*

Gordon, Bert
American. Actor
b. 1900 in New York, New York
d. Nov 30, 1974 in Duarte, California
Source: *WhScrn 77; WhoHol B*

Gordon, C Henry
American. Actor
b. Jun 17, 1883 in New York, New York
d. Dec 3, 1940 in Los Angeles, California
Source: *CurBio 41; FilmgC; MotPP; MovMk; Vers A; WhScrn 77; WhoHol B*

Gordon, Caroline
American. Author, Critic
b. Oct 6, 1895 in Trenton, Kentucky
d. Apr 11, 1981 in Chiapas, Mexico
Source: *AmAu&B; AmNov; AmWomWr; AmWr; BioIn 2, 3, 4, 5, 7, 8, 9; CasWL; CathA 1952; ConAu 103; ConAu P-1; ConLC 6, 13; ConNov 72, 76; CyWA; DcLB 4; DrAF 76; InWom; IntAu&W 76, 77; ModLAL; OxAmL; Pen AM; RAdv 1; REn; REnAL; ScF&FL 1; TwCA, SUP; WhAm 7; WhE&EA; WhoAm 74, 76, 78; WhoAmW 64, 66, 68, 70, 72, 74; WrDr 76, 80*

Gordon, Charles George
"Chinese"
English. General
b. Jan 28, 1833 in Woolwich, England
d. Jan 26, 1885 in Khartoum, Sudan
Source: *Alli SUP; NewC; NewCol 75; REn*

Gordon, Cyrus Herzel
American. Orientalist, Educator
b. Jun 29, 1908 in Philadelphia, Pennsylvania
Source: *ConAu 1R, 5NR; CurBio 63; DrAS 74F; WhoAm 74, 76, 78, 80, 82; WhoWor 74; WhoWorJ 72; WrDr 76*

Gordon, Gale
[Charles Aldrich, Jr.]
American. Actor
Played Mr. Wilson on "Dennis the Menace," 1962-64; Mr. Mooney on "The Lucy Show," 1968-74.
b. Feb 2, 1906 in New York, New York
Source: *FilmgC; IntMPA 75, 76, 77, 78, 79, 80, 81, 82; MovMk*

Gordon, Jackie
[Mrs. Lou Gordon]
American. Television Personality
b. 1935
Source: *BioIn 10*

Gordon, James
see: Souther-Hillman-Furay Band, The

Gordon, Joe (Joseph Lowell)
"Flash"
American. Baseball Player, Manager
Second baseman, 1938-50; AL MVP, 1942.
b. Feb 18, 1915 in Los Angeles, California
d. Jun 7, 1978 in Sacramento, California
Source: *BaseEn; BioIn 1, 11; WhoProB 73*

Gordon, John Brown
American. Confederate General
b. Feb 6, 1832 in Upson County, Georgia
d. Jan 9, 1904 in Miami, Florida
Source: *AmAu&B; AmBi; ApCAB; BiDConf; BiDSA; BiDrAC; DcAmAu; DcAmB; DcNAA; NewCol 75; TwCBDA; WhAm 1; WhAmP*

Gordon, John F
American. Former President of GM
b. May 15, 1900 in Akron, Ohio
d. Jan 6, 1978 in Royal Oak, Michigan
Source: *IntWW 74; NewYTBS 78*

Gordon, Kitty
English. Actress
b. Apr 22, 1878 in Folkestone, England
d. May 26, 1974 in Brentwood, New York
Source: *BioIn 10; NewYTBS 74; WhThe; WhoHol B*

Gordon, Lou
American. Journalist, TV Commentator
b. 1918
d. May 24, 1977 in Bloomfield Hills, Michigan
Source: *BioIn 8, 10, 11; ConAu 69; NewYTBS 77*

Gordon, Mary Catherine
American. Author
b. Dec 8, 1949 in Far Rockaway, New York
Source: *BioIn 11; ConAu 102; ConLC 13; CurBio 81; WhoAm 82*

Gordon, Max
American. Theatrical Producer
b. Jun 28, 1892 in New York, New York
d. Nov 2, 1978 in New York, New York
Source: *BiE&WWA; CurBio 43; EncMT; NotNAT; WhoAm 74; WhoThe 77*

Gordon, Richard
American. Author
b. Sep 15, 1921
Source: *Au&Wr 71; MnBBF; TwCW; Who 74*

Gordon, Richard Francis, Jr.
American. Astronaut, Football Executive
Crew member on Gemini VIII, XI; Apollo XII; vice-president New Orleans Saints, 1972--.
b. Oct 5, 1929 in Seattle, Washington
Source: *AmM&WS 73P; IntWW 74; WhoAm 74; WhoS&SW 73*

Gordon, Ruth
[Ruth Jones; Mrs. Garson Kanin]
American. Actress, Author
With husband co-wrote *Adam's Rib,* 1952; won Oscar for *Rosemary's Baby,* 1968.
b. Oct 30, 1896 in Wollaston, Massachusetts
Source: *AmAu&B; BiE&WWA; ConAu 81; CurBio 43, 72; Film 1; FilmgC; InWom; IntMPA 75, 76, 77, 78, 79, 80, 81, 82; MovMk; NatPD; NotNAT; OxFilm; WhoAm 74, 76, 78, 80, 82; WhoThe 77; WhoWor 74; WorEFlm*

Gordon, Seton
Author, Photographer
b. 1886
d. Mar 19, 1977
Source: *Who 74; WhoLA*

Gordon, Sid(ney)
American. Baseball Player
b. Aug 13, 1918 in Brooklyn, New York
d. Jun 17, 1975 in New York, New York
Source: *BaseEn; BioIn 10*

Gordon, Steve
American. Author, Motion Picture Director
Author, director of comedy *Arthur,* 1981.
b. 1940? in Toledo, Ohio
d. Nov 27, 1982 in New York, New York
Source: *BioIn 12; NewYTBS 82*

Gordon, Thomas
American. Psychologist, Author
b. Mar 11, 1918 in Paris, Illinois
Source: *AmM&WS 73S; ConAu 29R; WrDr 76*

Gordon, Vera
American. Actress
b. Jun 11, 1886 in Russia
d. May 8, 1948 in Beverly Hills, California
Source: *MovMk; TwYS; WhScrn 74, 77*

Gordon-Walker of Leyton, Patrick Chrestien Gordon-Walker, Baron
English. Politician, Author
b. Apr 7, 1907 in Worthing, England
d. Dec 2, 1980 in London, England
Source: *AnObit 1980; Au&Wr 71; BioIn 6, 7; ConAu 29R; CurBio 66; IntAu&W 76; IntWW 74, 75, 76, 77, 78; IntYB 78, 79; WhE&EA; Who 74; WhoWor 74, 76; WrDr 76*

Gordone, Charles
American. Dramatist, Actor, Director
b. Oct 12, 1925 in Cleveland, Ohio
Source: *AmAu&B; ConAu 93; ConDr 73; ConLC 1, 4; LivgBAA; McGEWD; NotNAT; PlP&P; WhoAm 74, 76, 78, 80, 82; WhoBlA 75; WhoE 74; WhoThe 77; WrDr 76*

Gordy, Berry, Jr.
American. Record, Motion Picture Executive
Founded Motown Records, 1959; signed The Temptations; The Supremes.
b. Nov 28, 1929 in Detroit, Michigan
Source: *CelR 73; IntMPA 77, 78, 79, 80, 81, 82; NewYTBS 74; WhoAm 74, 76, 78, 80, 82; WhoBlA 75*

Gore, Albert Arnold
American. Senator
b. Dec 26, 1907 in Granville, Tennessee
Source: *BiDrAC; CurBio 52; IntWW 74; WhoAm 74, 76, 78, 80, 82; WhoAmP 73; WhoS&SW 73*

Gore, Lesley
American. Singer
b. May 2, 1946 in Tenafly, New Jersey
Source: *WhoHol A*

Goren, Charles Henry
American. Bridge Expert, Journalist
b. Mar 4, 1901 in Philadelphia, Pennsylvania
Source: *AmAu&B; ConAu 69; CurBio 59; WebAB; WhoAm 74, 76, 78, 80, 82; WhoS&SW 73; WhoWor 74*

Gorenko, Anna Andreevna
see: Akhmatova, Anna, pseud.

Gorey, Edward St. John
American. Author, Illustrator
b. Feb 22, 1925 in Chicago, Illinois
Source: *ChPo, S1; ConAu 5R; IlsBYP; IlsCB 1957; WhoAm 82*

Gorgas, William Crawford
American. Military Doctor
b. Oct 3, 1854 in Mobile, Alabama
d. Jul 3, 1920 in London, England
Source: *AmBi; DcAmB; DcNAA; NewCol 75; WebAB; WhAm 1*

Gorham, Jabez
American. Silversmith
b. Feb 18, 1792 in Providence, Rhode Island
d. Mar 24, 1869 in Providence, Rhode Island
Source: *DcAmB; WhAm H*

Gorham, Scott
see: Thin Lizzy

Gorin, Igor
American. Composer, Singer, Actor
b. Oct 26, 1908 in Grodak, Russia
d. Mar 24, 1982 in Tucson, Arizona
Source: *AmSCAP 66, 80; Baker 78; CurBio 42, 82; WhoAm 74*

Goring, "Butch" (Robert Thomas)
Canadian. Hockey Player
b. Oct 22, 1949 in Saint Boniface, MB
Source: *BioIn 12; HocReg; WhoAm 82*

Goring, Hermann Wilhelm
see: Goering, Hermann Wilhelm

Goring, Marius
English. Actor
b. May 23, 1912 in Newport, England
Source: *FilmgC; IntMPA 75, 76, 77, 78, 79, 80, 81, 82; IntWW 74; MotPP; MovMk; PlP&P; Who 74; WhoHol A; WhoThe 77*

Gorky, Arshile
[Vosdanik Adoian]
American. Artist
Abstract expressionist; works include "Dark Green Painting."
b. Oct 25, 1904 in Armenia
d. Jul 3, 1948 in New York, New York
Source: *AtlBL; DcAmB S4; DcCAA 71; NewCol 75; REn; WebAB; WhAm 4*

Gorky, Maxim, pseud.
[Maxim Gorki; Alexie M Peshov; Aleksey Maximovich Pyeshkov]
Russian. Author, Dramatist
Wrote *The Lower Depths*, 1902; *Mother*, 1907; *My Universities*, 1923.
b. Mar 14, 1868 in Nizhni-Novgorod, Russia
d. Jun 18, 1936 in Moscow, U.S.S.R.
Source: *AtlBL; BiD&SB; CasWL; ClDMEL; CnMD; CnMWL; CnThe; CyWA; DcRusL; EncWL; EvEuW; FilmgC; McGEWD; ModSL 1; ModWD; OxEng; OxFilm; OxThe; Pen EUR; PlP&P, A; RComWL; REn; REnWD; TwCA, SUP; TwCW; WhoTwCL*

Gorman, Chester
American. Archaeologist
b. Mar 11, 1938 in Oakland, California
d. Jun 7, 1981 in Sacramento, California
Source: *AnObit 1981; NewYTBS 81*

Gorman, Herbert Sherman
American. Author, Journalist
b. Jan 1, 1893 in Springfield, Massachusetts
d. Oct 28, 1954 in Hughsonville, New York
Source: *AmAu&B; AmNov; ChPo, S1; CurBio 40, 55; OxAmL; REnAL; TwCA, SUP; WhAm 3; WhNAA; WhoAm 82*

Gorman, Leon Arthur
American. Mail Order Company Executive
President of L L Bean.
b. Dec 20, 1934 in Nashua, New Hampshire
Source: *WhoAm 82*

Gorman, Leroy
see: Bow Wow Wow

Gorman, Rudolph Carl
American. Artist
b. 1932
Source: *BioIn 10*

Gorme, Eydie
[Steve and Eydie; Mrs. Steve Lawrence]
American. Singer
b. Aug 16, 1932 in New York, New York
Source: *BioNews 74; BkPepl; CelR 73; CurBio 65; InWom; WhoAm 74*

Gorr, Rita
[Marguerite Geirnaert]
Belgian. Opera Singer
b. Feb 18, 1926 in Ghent, Belgium
Source: *BioIn 6, 7; NewEOp 71; WhoAmW 74; WhoMus 72*

Gorrie, John
American. Inventor, Physician
Granted patent for mechanical refrigeration, 1851.
b. Oct 3, 1803 in Charleston, South Carolina
d. Jun 16, 1855 in Apalachicola, Florida
Source: *BioIn 2, 3, 5, 7, 9; ApCAB SUP; DcAmB; DcNAA; WebAB; WhAm H*

Gorshin, Frank John
American. Actor, Comedian
Played the Riddler on "Batman," 1966-68.
b. Apr 5, 1934 in Pittsburgh, Pennsylvania
Source: *FilmgC; WhoAm 74, 76, 78, 80, 82; WhoHol A*

Gorsuch, Anne McGill
[Mrs. Robert F Burford]
"Ice Queen"
American. Lawyer, EPA Administrator
b. Apr 21, 1942 in Casper, Wyoming
Source: *CurBio 82; WhoAm 82; WhoAmP 77; WhoAmW 79*

Gortner, (Hugh) Marjoe (Ross)
American. Ex-Evangelist, Actor, Singer
b. Jan 14, 1945 in Long Beach, California
Source: *BkPepl; IntMPA 82; WhoAm 82; WhoHol A*

Gorton, John Grey
Australian. Prime Minister
b. Sep 9, 1911 in Melbourne, Australia
Source: *CurBio 68; IntWW 74; NewYTBE 71; Who 74; WhoAm 74; WhoGov 72; WhoWor 74*

Gorton, Samuel
American. Religious Leader
b. 1592 in Gorton, England
d. 1677 in Warwick, Massachusetts
Source: *Alli; AmBi; ApCAB; CyAL 1; DcAmAu; DcAmB; DcNAA; Drake; NewCol 75; OxAmL; REnAL; WhAm H*

Gorton, Slade
American. Senator
b. Jan 8, 1928 in Chicago, Illinois
Source: *WhoAm 74, 76, 78, 80, 82; WhoAmL 78, 79; WhoAmP 73, 75, 77, 79; WhoGov 72, 75, 77; WhoWest 74, 76, 78*

Gosden, Freeman Fisher
[Amos 'n Andy]
American. Radio Comedian
Amos of "Amos 'n Andy" radio show, 1926-58.
b. May 5, 1899 in Richmond, Virginia
d. Dec 10, 1982 in Los Angeles, California
Source: *BioIn 1, 2, 7, 9; CurBio 47; NewYTBE 72; NewYTET; WebAB, 79; WhoHol A; WorAl*

Goslin, "Goose" (Leon Allen)
American. Baseball Player
Outfielder, 1921-38; led AL with 129 RBIs, 1924; Hall of Fame, 1968.
b. Oct 16, 1900 in Salem, New Jersey
d. May 15, 1971 in Bridgeton, New Jersey
Source: *BaseEn; NewYTBE 71; WhoProB 73*

Gossage, "Goose" (Richard Michael)
American. Baseball Player
Pitcher, 1972--; led AL in saves, 1975, 1978, 1980.
b. Jul 5, 1951 in Colorado Springs, Colorado
Source: *BaseEn; BioIn 11, 12; NewYTBS 77; WhoAm 82*

Gosse, Sir Edmund William
English. Author
b. Sep 21, 1849 in London, England
d. May 16, 1928
Source: *Alli SUP; BbD; BiD&SB; CarSB; CasWL; Chambr 3; ChPo, S1, S2; CnMWL; DcEnA, AP; DcEnL; DcLEL; EvLB; LongCTC; ModBrL; NewC; OxEng; Pen ENG; TwCA, SUP; TwCW; WebE&AL*

Gossec, Francois Joseph
French. Composer
b. Jan 17, 1734 in Vergnies, Belgium
d. Feb 16, 1829 in Passy, France
Source: *Baker 78; BioIn 4, 7; NewCol 75; NewEOp 71; OxFr; OxMus*

Gosset, Lou
American. Actor
b. May 27, 1936 in Brooklyn, New York
Source: *BioIn 11; WhoAm 78, 80, 82*

Gossett, D(aniel) Bruce
American. Football Player
b. Nov 9, 1941 in Cecil, Pennsylvania
Source: *WhoFtbl 74*

Gotch, Frank
American. Wrestler
Source: *BioIn 5*

Gottfried, Brian
American. Tennis Player
b. Jan 27, 1952 in Baltimore, Maryland
Source: *BioIn 10, 11; WhoAm 82*

Gottfried, Martin
American. Drama Critic
b. Oct 9, 1933 in New York, New York
Source: *BiE&WWA; ConAu 25R; NotNAT; WhoAm 82*

Gottfried von Strassburg
German. Poet
b. 1170? in Strassburg, Germany
d. 1215?
Source: *BbD; BiD&SB; CasWL; CyWA; DcEuL; EuAu; EvEuW; OxGer; Pen EUR; RComWL; REn*

Gottlieb, Adolph
American. Artist
b. Mar 14, 1903 in New York, New York
d. Mar 4, 1974 in New York, New York
Source: *ConAu 49; CurBio 59, 74; DcCAA 71; EncAB-H; NewYTBS 74; WhAm 6; WhoAm 74; WhoAmA 73; WhoE 74; WhoWor 74; WhoWorJ 72*

Gottlieb, Eddie (Edward)
"The Mogul"
American. Basketball Coach, Executive
Owner/coach, Philadelphia Warriors, 1947-55.
b. Sep 15, 1898 in Kiev, Russia
d. Dec 7, 1979 in Philadelphia, Pennsylvania
Source: *NewYTBS 79; WhoBbl 73*

Gottschalk, Ferdinand
English. Actor
b. 1869 in London, England
d. Oct 10, 1944 in London, England
Source: *MovMk; WhScrn 74, 77*

Gottschalk, Louis Moreau
American. Musician, Composer
b. May 8, 1829 in New Orleans, Louisiana
d. Dec 18, 1869 in Rio de Janeiro, Brazil
Source: *AmBi; ApCAB; DcAmB; Drake; OxAmL; TwCBDA; WebAB; WhAm H*

Gottschalk, Robert
American. Corporation Executive
Founder, president of Panavision, Inc.
b. Mar 12, 1918 in Chicago, Illinois
d. 1982 in Los Angeles, California
Source: *IntMPA 75, 76, 77, 78, 79, 80, 81, 82*

Gottwald, Klement
Czech. Communist Leader
b. Nov 23, 1896 in Dedidocz, Czechoslovakia
d. Mar 14, 1953
Source: *CurBio 48, 53; NewCol 75; WhAm 3*

Goucher, John Franklin
American. Clergyman, Educator
b. Jun 7, 1845 in Waynesburg, Pennsylvania
d. Jul 19, 1922
Source: *AmAu&B; DcNAA*

Goudge, Elizabeth
English. Author
b. Apr 24, 1900 in Wells, England
Source: *AuBYP; ChPo; ConAu 5R, 5NR; CurBio 40; InWom; LongCTC; NewC; REn; SmATA 2; ThrBJA; TwCA, SUP; TwCW; WhoChL; WrDr 76*

Goudy, Frederic William
American. Type Designer
Designer of over 100 different type faces.
b. Mar 8, 1865 in Bloomington, Illinois
d. May 11, 1947 in Marlboro, New York
Source: *AmAu&B; BioIn 1, 2, 3, 5, 9; CurBio 41, 47; DcAmB S4; DcNAA; NewCol 75; OxAmL; REnAL; WebAB, 79; WhAm 2; WhNAA*

Gougelman, Pierre
American. Ocularist
Invented plastic used in manufacture of artificial eyes, 1941.
b. Feb 16, 1877 in Guttenberg, New York
d. Jun 1, 1963 in Thornwood, New York
Source: *BioIn 6, 7; NatCAB 48*

Goulart, Joao
Brazilian. President
b. Mar 1, 1918 in Sao Borja, Brazil
d. Dec 6, 1976
Source: *BioIn 6, 11; CurBio 62, 77; IntWW 74; McGEWB*

Goulart, Ron(ald Joseph)
[Howard Lee; Kenneth Robeson; Frank S Shawn; Con Steffanson, pseuds.]
American. Author
b. Jan 13, 1933 in Berkeley, California
Source: *ConAu 25R; SmATA 6; WhoAm 82; WhoE 74*

Gould, Beatrice Blackmar
American. Editor, Author
b. 1898 in Emmetsburg, Iowa
Source: *AmAu&B; ConAu 25R; ConAu P-2; CurBio 47; IntWW 74; WhoAmW 74*

Gould, Charles Bruce
American. Editor, Author
b. Jul 28, 1898 in Luana, Iowa
Source: *AmAu&B; CurBio 47*

Gould, Chester
American. Cartoonist
b. Nov 20, 1900 in Pawnee, Oklahoma
Source: *ConAu 77; CurBio 71; EncMys; WebAB; WhoAm 74; WhoMW 74*

Gould, Elliott
[Elliott Goldstein]
American. Actor
Starred in *Bob & Carol & Ted & Alice,* 1969; *MASH,* 1970.
b. Aug 29, 1938 in Brooklyn, New York
Source: *BiE&WWA; BioIn 8, 9, 10, 11; BioNews 74; BkPepl; CelR 73; CurBio 71; EncMT; FilmgC; IntMPA 75, 76, 77, 78, 79, 80, 81, 82; MovMk; WhoAm 74, 76, 78, 80, 82; WhoHol A; WhoThe 77*

Gould, George Milbry
American. Physician, Lexicographer
b. Nov 8, 1948 in Auburn, Maine
Source: *AmAu&B; DcAmAu; DcNAA; OhA&B*

Gould, Glenn Herbert
Canadian. Musician, Composer
Retired from performing, 1964 to concentrate on recording.
b. Sep 25, 1932 in Toronto, ON
d. Oct 4, 1982 in Toronto, ON
Source: *Baker 78; CanWW 70, 79; CreCan 2; CurBio 60, 82; IntWW 75, 76, 77, 78; NewYTBS 75, 82; WhoAm 74, 76, 78; WhoMus 72*

Gould, Gordon
American. Physicist
Coined acronym "laser," 1957.
b. Jul 17, 1920 in New York, New York
Source: *AmM&WS 73P, 76P, 79P; WhoAm 80, 82*

Gould, Jack
American. TV Critic
b. 1919 in New York, New York
Source: *NewYTBE 72; WhoE 74*

Gould, Jay (Jason)
American. Financier
Part owner of many railroads, including the Erie and Union Pacific.
b. May 27, 1836 in Roxbury, New York
d. Dec 2, 1892 in New York, New York
Source: *AmBi; BioIn 1, 3, 4, 6, 11; ApCAB; DcAmB; DcNAA; EncAB-H; NewCol 75; TwCBDA; WebAB, 79; WhAm H*

Gould, Laurence McKinley
American. Explorer, Educator
b. Aug 22, 1896 in Lacota, Michigan
Source: *AmM&WS 73P, 76P, 79P; CurBio 78; IntAu&W 77; IntWW 74, 75, 76, 77, 78; WhoAm 74, 76*

Gould, Lois
American. Author
b. 1938
Source: *AmAu&B; ConAu 77; ConLC 4, 10; DrAF 76; WhoAm 82; WrDr 76*

Gould, Morton
American. Composer, Musician
b. Dec 10, 1913 in Richmond Hill, New York
Source: *AmSCAP 66; BiE&WWA; CurBio 45, 68; DcCM; NewCBMT; NotNAT; WhoAm 74, 76, 78, 80, 82; WhoE 74; WhoMus 72; WhoWor 74; WhoWorJ 72*

Gould, Sandra
American. Actress
Source: *WhoHol A*

Gould, Shane
Australian. Swimmer
First woman to win three Olympic gold medals in individual events in world-record times, 1972.
b. Sep 4, 1956 in Brisbane, Australia
Source: *BioIn 9, 10; CelR 73; HerW*

Gould, Stephen Jay
American. Paleontologist, Author
b. Sep 10, 1941 in New York, New York
Source: *AmM&WS 73P, 76P, 79P; ConAu 77; CurBio 82; WhoAm 78, 80, 82*

Goulding, Edmund
American. Motion Picture Director
b. Mar 20, 1891 in London, England
d. Dec 24, 1959 in Hollywood, California
Source: *AmSCAP 66; BiDFilm; DcFM; FilmgC; MovMk; OxFilm; TwYS; WhAm 3; WhScrn 77; WorEFlm*

Goulding, Phil G
American. Management Consultant
b. Mar 28, 1921 in San Francisco, California
Source: *WhoAm 74*

Goulding, Ray
[Bob and Ray]
American. Comedian
b. Mar 20, 1922 in Lowell, Massachusetts
Source: *CelR 73; CurBio 57*

Goulding, Stephen
see: Graham Parker and the Rumour

Gouldman, Graham
see: 10 CC

Goulet, Robert
American. Actor, Singer
Broadway debut in *Camelot,* 1960; won Tony, 1968, for *The Happy Time.*
b. Nov 26, 1933 in Lawrence, Massachusetts
Source: *BiE&WWA; BioIn 6, 10; BioNews 74; CanWW 82; CelR 73; CurBio 62; EncMT; FilmgC; IntMPA 75, 77; NotNAT; WhoAm 74, 76, 78, 80, 82; WhoHol A; WhoThe 77*

Gounod, Charles Francois
French. Composer
b. Jun 17, 1818 in Paris, France
d. Oct 17, 1893 in Paris, France
Source: *AtlBL; NewC; NewCol 75; OxFr; REn*

Govind Singh
Guru of the Sikhs
b. 1666
d. 1708 in Deccan, India
Source: *BioIn 9; WebBD 80*

Gowans, Alan
Canadian. Educator
b. Nov 30, 1923 in Toronto, ON
Source: *AmAu&B; ConAu 1R; DrAS 74H, 78H; WhoAm 74; WhoAmA 73, 76; WhoWor 74, 76*

Gowdy, Curt
American. Sports Commentator
b. Jul 31, 1919 in Green River, Wyoming
Source: *CelR 73; CurBio 67; IntMPA 75, 76, 77, 78, 79, 80, 81, 82; WhoAm 82*

Gowdy, Hank (Henry Morgan)
American. Baseball Player
b. Aug 24, 1889 in Columbus, Ohio
d. Aug 1, 1966 in Columbus, Ohio
Source: *BaseEn; WhoProB 73*

Gowon, Yakubu
Nigerian. Army Officer
b. Oct 19, 1934 in Pankshin, Nigeria
Source: *CurBio 70; IntWW 74; NewCol 75; WhoGov 72; WhoWor 74*

Goya y Lucientes, Francisco Jose de
Spanish. Artist
b. Mar 30, 1746 in Aragon, Spain
d. Apr 18, 1828 in Bordeaux, France
Source: *AtlBL; NewC; NewCol 75; REn*

Goyen, Jan Josephszoon van
Dutch. Artist
b. 1596 in Leiden, Netherlands
d. 1656 in The Hague, Netherlands
Source: *NewCol 75; OxArt*

Goyen, William
American. Author
b. Apr 24, 1915 in Trinity, Texas
Source: *AmAu&B; Au&Wr 71; AuNews 2; ConAu 5R; ConLC 5; ConNov 72, 76; DrAF 76; OxAmL; Pen AM; REnAL; WhoAm 82; WhoE 74; WhoWor 74; WorAu; WrDr 76*

Gozzi, Gaspare
Italian. Author, Composer
b. Dec 4, 1713 in Venice, Italy
d. Dec 27, 1786 in Padua, Italy
Source: *DcEuL; EvEuW; NewCol 75*

Gozzoli, Benozzo
Italian. Artist
b. 1420 in Florence, Italy
d. Oct 4, 1497 in Pistoria, Italy
Source: *AtlBL; NewCol 75; REn*

Grable, Betty
[Elizabeth Grasle]
American. Actress
WW II pin-up girl; married Jackie Coogan, 1937-40, Harry James, 1943-65.
b. Dec 18, 1916 in Saint Louis, Missouri
d. Jul 3, 1973 in Beverly Hills, California
Source: *BiDFilm; CelR 73; CmMov; FilmgC; InWom; MotPP; MovMk; NewYTBE 73; OxFilm; ThFT; WhAm 5; WhScrn 77; WhoHol B; WorEFlm*

Gracchus, Gaius Sempronius
Roman. Statesman
b. 153BC
d. 121BC
Source: *BioIn 1, 4, 7, 8, 11; NewCol 75*

Grace, Princess
see: Kelly, Grace

Grace, William Russell
American. Merchant, Shipowner
b. May 10, 1832 in Queenstown, Ireland
d. Mar 21, 1904 in New York, New York
Source: *Alli SUP; AmBi; DcAmB; NewCol 75; TwCBDA; WebAB; WhAm 1*

Grade, Sir Lew
British. Television Executive
b. Dec 25, 1906 in Tokmak, Russia
Source: *IntMPA 75, 76, 77; IntWW 75, 76, 77, 78; NewYTET; Who 74; WhoAm 82*

Gradishar, Randy Charles
American. Football Player
b. Mar 3, 1952 in Warren, Ohio
Source: *FootReg; WhoAm 80, 82; WhoFtbl 74*

Grady, Don
American. Actor
b. Jun 8, 1944 in San Diego, California
Source: *WhoHol A*

Grady, Henry Woodfin
American. Journalist, Orator
b. May 24, 1850 in Atlanta, Georgia
d. Dec 23, 1889 in Atlanta, Georgia
Source: *AmAu; AmBi; BiDSA; DcAmB; DcLEL; DcNAA; EncAB-H; OxAmL; REnAL; TwCBDA; WebAB; WhAm H*

Graebner, Clark
American. Tennis Player, Businessman
b. Nov 4, 1943 in Lakewood, Ohio
Source: *CurBio 70*

Graf, Herbert
Austrian. Opera Director
b. Apr 10, 1903 in Vienna, Austria
d. Apr 1973 in Geneva, Switzerland
Source: *CurBio 42, 73; NewYTBE 73; WhAm 5; WhoMus 72*

Graff, Henry Franklin
American. Author
b. Aug 11, 1921 in New York, New York
Source: *AmAu&B; ChPo; ConAu 1R, 1NR; DrAS 74H; WhoAm 74, 78, 80, 82*

Graffman, Gary
American. Musician
b. Oct 14, 1928 in New York, New York
Source: *CurBio 70; IntWW 74; NewYTBE 72, 73; WhoAm 74, 76, 78, 80; WhoWor 74*

Graham, Alex
Scottish. Cartoonist
b. 1915 in Glasgow, Scotland
Source: *WhoAm 82; WorECom*

Graham, Barbara
"Bloody Babs"
American. Murderer
b. 1923
d. Jun 3, 1955 in San Quentin, California
Source: *LookW*

Graham, Bill
[Wolfgang Grajonca]
American. Concert Promoter
b. Jan 8, 1931 in Berlin, Germany
Source: *BkPepl; EncPR&S; IlEncRk; WhoAm 82*

Graham, Billy (William Franklin)
American. Evangelist
Wrote *The Seven Deadly Sins,* 1955; *Challenge,* 1969.
b. Nov 7, 1918 in Charlotte, North Carolina
Source: *AmAu&B; BioNews 74; BkPepl; ConAu 9R; CurBio 51, 73; EncAB-H; IntWW 74; WebAB; Who 74; WhoAm 74, 76, 78, 80, 82*

Graham, David B
Australian. Golfer
b. May 23, 1946 in Windsor, Australia
Source: *WhoGolf*

Graham, Evarts Ambrose
American. Surgeon
b. Mar 19, 1883 in Chicago, Illinois
d. Mar 4, 1957
Source: *BioIn 2, 3, 4, 5, 11; CurBio 52, 57; WhAm 3*

Graham, Fred Patterson
American. Journalist
b. Oct 6, 1931 in Little Rock, Arkansas
Source: *ConAu 37R; DrAS 74P; WhoAm 82; WhoHol A*

Graham, Gene
American. Journalist
b. Aug 26, 1924 in Murray, Kentucky
Source: *ConAu 41R; DrAS 74E*

Graham, Katharine Meyer
American. Newspaper Executive
Washington *Post,* president, 1963-73, publisher, 1969, chairman, 1973.
b. Jun 16, 1917 in New York, New York
Source: *AuNews 1; BioNews 74; CelR 73; CurBio 71; ForWC 70; IntWW 74; St&PR 75; WhoAm 74, 76, 78, 80, 82; WhoAmW 77; WhoF&I 74; WhoS&SW 73; WhoWor 74*

Graham, Martha
American. Dancer, Choreographer
b. May 11, 1893 in Pittsburgh, Pennsylvania
Source: *BioNews 74; CelR 73; CurBio 44, 61; EncAB-H; HerW; InWom; IntWW 74; NewYTBE 70, 73; WebAB; Who 74; WhoAm 74, 82; WhoThe 77; WhoWor 74*

Graham, Otto Everett
American. Athletic Director
b. Dec 6, 1921 in Waukegan, Illinois
Source: *WhoAm 74, 76, 78, 80, 82; WhoFtbl 74*

Graham, Ronny
American. Composer
b. Aug 26, 1919 in Philadelphia, Pennsylvania
Source: *AmSCAP 66; BiE&WWA; NotNAT; WhoThe 77*

Graham, Sheilah
American. Journalist
Friend of F Scott Fitzgerald during last years of life; wrote *For Richer, For Poorer,* 1975.
b. 1908 in London, England
Source: *AmAu&B; AuNews 1; BioNews 74; CelR 73; CurBio 69; InWom; WhoAm 74; WrDr 76*

Graham, Stephen
English. Author
b. 1884 in England
d. 1975
Source: *Au&Wr 71; ConAu 93; DcLEL; EvLB; LongCTC; NewC; REn; TwCA SUP; Who 74*

Graham, Sylvester W
American. Reformer, Food Faddist
Developed the graham cracker.
b. Jul 5, 1794 in West Suffield, Connecticut
d. Sep 11, 1851 in Northampton, Massachusetts
Source: *AmBi; ApCAB; DcAmAu; DcAmB; DcNAA; Drake; NewCol 75; TwCBDA; WebAB; WhAm H*

Graham, Thomas
Scottish. Chemist
b. Dec 20, 1805 in Glasgow, Scotland
d. Sep 16, 1869
Source: *AsBiEn; BioIn 6, 8; NewCol 75; WebBD 80*

Graham, Virginia
[Virginia Komiss]
American. Radio, TV Personality
b. Jul 4, 1912 in Chicago, Illinois
Source: *CelR 73; CurBio 56; ForWC 70; InWom; WhoAm 82*

Graham, William Alexander
American. Governor
b. Sep 5, 1804 in Lincoln County, Nebraska
d. Aug 11, 1875 in Saratoga Springs, New York
Source: *AmBi; ApCAB; BioIn 1, 5, 10; DcAmB; Drake; TwCBDA; WhAm H*

Graham, William Sydney
Scottish. Poet
b. 1918 in Greenock, Scotland
Source: *BioIn 10; ConAu 73*

Graham, Winston Mawdesley
American. Author
b. Jun 30, 1910 in Manchester, England
Source: *ConAu 49, 2NR; ConNov 72, 76; CurBio 55; TwCW; Who 74; WrDr 76*

Graham Parker and the Rumour
[Bob Andrews; Martin Blemont; Andrew Bodnar; Stephen Goulding; Graham Parker; Brinsley Schwarz]
English. Rock Group
Source: *IlEncRk*

Grahame, Gloria
[Gloria Grahame Hallward]
American. Actress
b. Nov 28, 1925 in Los Angeles, California
d. Oct 5, 1981 in New York, New York
Source: *BiDFilm; BioIn 1, 11; FilmgC; IntMPA 76, 77, 78, 79, 80, 81, 82; MGM; MotPP; MovMk; WhoAmW 58, 61, 64; WhoHol A; WorEFlm*

Grahame, Kenneth
Scottish. Children's Author
Wrote children's classic *The Wind in the Willows,* 1908.
b. Mar 8, 1859 in Edinburgh, Scotland
d. Jul 6, 1932 in Pangbourne, England
Source: *AnCL; AtlBL; AuBYP; BkCL; CarSB; CasWL; Chambr 3; ChPo, S1; CnMWL; CyWA; DcLEL; EvLB; FamSYP; JBA 34; LongCTC; ModBrL; NewC; OxEng; Pen ENG; REn; Str&VC; TwCA, SUP; TwCW; WhoChL; YABC 1*

Grahame, Margot
English. Actress
b. 1911 in Canterbury, England
Source: *FilmgC; ThFT; WhoHol A; WhoThe 77*

Grainger, Percy Aldridge
American. Musician, Composer
b. Jul 8, 1882 in Melbourne, Australia
d. Feb 20, 1961 in White Plains, New York
Source: *AmSCAP 66; DcCM; NewCol 75; OxAmL; WhAm 4*

Gram, Hans Christian Joachim
Danish. Physician
b. Sep 13, 1853 in Copenhagen, Denmark
d. Nov 14, 1938 in Copenhagen, Denmark
Source: *AsBiEn; BioIn 5; WebBD 80*

Gramatky, Hardie
American. Children's Author, Illustrator
b. Apr 12, 1907 in Dallas, Texas
d. Apr 29, 1979 in Westport, Connecticut
Source: *AmAu&B; AnCL; AuBYP; AuNews 1; BkP; ConAu 1R, 85, 3NR; IlsCB 1957; JBA 51; NewYTBS 79; SmATA 1; Str&VC; TwCCW 78; WhAm 7; WhoAm 74, 76; WhoAmA 73, 76, 78; WhoWor 74; WrDr 80*

Gramm, Lou
see: Foreigner

Granados, Enrique
Spanish. Composer, Musician
b. Jul 27, 1867 in Lerida, Spain
d. Mar 24, 1916
Source: *DcCM; NewCol 75*

Granatelli, Anthony Joseph
American. Former-Auto Racer, Businessman
b. Mar 18, 1923 in Dallas, Texas
Source: *BioIn 8, 9, 10; WhoAm 74*

Grand Funk Railroad
[Donald Brewer; Mark Farner; Craig Frost; Mel Schacher]
American. Rock Group
Source: *EncPR&S*

Grange, "Red" (Harold Edward)
"Galloping Ghost"
American. Football Player
Played for U of IL, 1923-25; scored 6 TDs in game against MI, 1924.
b. Jun 13, 1903 in Forksville, Pennsylvania
Source: *BioIn 2, 3, 4, 5, 6, 7, 8, 9, 10; NewYTBS 74; WebAB; WhoFtbl 74; WhoHol A*

Grange, Rob
see: Amboy Dukes, The

Granger, Farley
American. Actor
b. Jul 1, 1925 in San Jose, California
Source: *BiDFilm; BiE&WWA; FilmgC; HolP 40; IntMPA 75, 76, 77, 78, 79, 80, 81, 82; MovMk; NotNAT; WhoHol A; WorEFlm*

Granger, Lester
American. Civic Leader
b. Sep 16, 1896 in Newport News, Virginia
d. Jan 9, 1976 in Alexandria, Louisiana
Source: *CurBio 46; WhAm 6; WhoAm 74*

Granger, Stewart
[James Lablache Stewart]
American. Actor, Author
Wrote autobiography *Sparks Fly Upward.*
b. May 6, 1913 in London, England
Source: *BiDFilm; CmMov; FilmgC; IntMPA 75, 76, 77, 78, 79, 80, 81, 82; MotPP; MovMk; OxFilm; Who 74; WhoHol A; WhoThe 77; WorEFlm*

Granit, Ragnar Arthur
Finnish. Neurophysiologist
b. Oct 30, 1900 in Finland
Source: *IntWW 74; Who 74; WhoAm 74, 76, 78, 80, 82; WhoWor 74*

Granjon, Robert
French. Type Designer, Engraver
b. 1545
d. 1588
Source: *NewCol 75; WebBD 80*

Grant, Bruce
American. Journalist, Author
b. Apr 17, 1893 in Wichita Falls, Texas
d. Apr 9, 1977
Source: *AuBYP; ConAu 1R, 69; SmATA 5*

Grant, "Bud" (Harold Peter)
American. Football Coach
Coach of Minnesota Vikings, 1967--.
b. May 20, 1927 in Superior, Wisconsin
Source: *BioNews 74; WhoFtbl 74*

Grant, Cary
[Archibald Leach]
American. Actor
Starred in *The Philadelphia Story,* 1940; *North by Northwest,* 1959.
b. Jan 18, 1904 in Bristol, England
Source: *BiDFilm; BkPepl; CelR 73; CmMov; CurBio 41, 65; EncMT; FilmgC; IntMPA 75, 76, 77, 78, 79, 80, 81, 82; IntWW 74; MotPP; MovMk; NewYTBE 73; OxFilm; WebAB; Who 74; WhoAm 74, 76, 78, 80, 82; WhoWor 74; WorEFlm*

Grant, Earl
American. Musician
b. 1930
d. 1970
Source: *NewYTBE 70*

Grant, Gogi
[Audrey Brown]
American. Singer
b. 1936 in Philadelphia, Pennsylvania
Source: *RkOn*

Grant, Gordon
American. Illustrator
b. Jun 7, 1875 in San Francisco, California
d. May 6, 1962 in New York, New York
Source: *AmAu&B; ConAu 102; CurBio 53, 62; IlsCB 1744, 1946; WhAm 4*

Grant, Harry Johnston
American. Newspaper Publisher
b. Sep 15, 1881 in Chillicothe, Missouri
d. Jul 12, 1963 in Milwaukee, Wisconsin
Source: *MnBBF; WhAm 4; WhNAA*

Grant, James
Scottish. Children's Author
b. Aug 1, 1822 in Edinburgh, Scotland
d. May 5, 1887 in Edinburgh, Scotland
Source: *Alli, SUP; BbD; BiD&SB; BrAu 19; DcBiA; DcEnA AP; DcEnL; DcLEL; EvLB; NewC; OxEng*

Grant, Jane
American. Journalist
b. May 29, 1895 in Joplin, Missouri
d. 1972 in Litchfield, Connecticut
Source: *ChPo S2; ConAu 25R, 33R; ConAu P-2; ForWC 70; InWom; NewYTBE 72*

Grant, Lee
[Mrs. Joseph Feury; Lyova Haskell Rosenthal]
American. Actress
Won Emmy for "Peyton Place," 1965; Oscar for *Shampoo,* 1975.
b. Oct 31, 1931 in New York, New York
Source: *BiE&WWA; BkPepl; CurBio 74; FilmgC; IntMPA 75, 76, 77, 78, 79, 80, 81, 82; MotPP; MovMk; NewYTBE 70; NotNAT; WhoAm 74, 76, 78, 80, 82; WhoHol A*

Grant, Michael
English. Author, Educator
b. Nov 21, 1914 in London, England
Source: *Au&Wr 71; ConAu 1R, 4NR; Who 74; WrDr 76*

Grant, Ulysses S(impson)
[Hiram Ulysses Grant]
American. 18th US President
Commander in chief, Union forces during Civil War; president, 1869-77.
b. Apr 27, 1822 in Point Pleasant, Ohio
d. Jul 23, 1885 in Mount McGregor, New York
Source: *Alli SUP; AmAu&B; AmBi; ApCAB; BbD; BiAuS; BiD&SB; BiDrAC; BiDrUSE; DcAmAu; DcAmB; DcNAA; Drake; EncAB-H; OhA&B; OxAmL; REn; REnAL; TwCBDA; WebAB; WhAm H; WhAmP*

Grantham, George
see: Poco

Granville, Bonita
American. Actress, TV Producer
b. 1923 in New York, New York
Source: *FilmgC; HolP 30; MotPP; MovMk; ThFT; WhoHol A*

Granville, Joseph E(nsign)
American. Investment Adviser
b. Aug 20, 1923 in Yonkers, New York
Source: *ConAu 65*

Granville-Barker, Harley
English. Producer, Dramatist
b. Nov 25, 1877 in London, England
d. Aug 31, 1946 in Paris, France
Source: *CasWL; Chambr 3; CnMD; CnThe; CyWA; DcLEL; EvLB; LongCTC; McGEWD; ModBrL; ModWD; NewC; OxEng; Pen ENG; REn; REnWD; TwCA, SUP; TwCW; WebE&AL; WhoLA; WhoTwCL*

Granz, Norman
American. Jazz Musician
b. Aug 6, 1918 in Los Angeles, California
Source: *WhoAm 82; WhoWest 74*

Grapewin, Charley
American. Actor
b. Dec 20, 1875 in Xenia, Ohio
d. Feb 2, 1956 in Corona, California
Source: *FilmgC*

Grappelli, Stephane
French. Jazz Musician
b. Jan 26, 1908 in Paris, France
Source: *BioIn 9; CmpEPM*

Grass, Gunter Wilhelm
German. Author
b. Oct 16, 1927 in Danzig, Germany
Source: *CasWL; CelR 73; CnMD; ConAu 13R; ConLC 1, 2, 4, 6, 11, 15; CroCD; CurBio 64; EncWL; EvEuW; IntWW 74; McGEWD; ModGL; ModWD; OxGer; Pen EUR; REnWD; TwCW; Who 74; WhoWor 74; WorAu*

Grass, John
[Charging Bear]
American Indian. Leader of Sioux Nation
b. 1837
d. May 10, 1918
Source: *DcAmB; WhAm HA, 4*

Grass Roots, The
[Creed Bratton; Rick Coonce; Warren Entner; Robert Grill; Reed Kailing; Joel Larson; Dennis Provisor]
American. Rock Group
Source: *EncPR&S; RkOn*

Grasse, Count Francois Joseph Paul de
French. Admiral
b. Sep 13, 1722 in Bar, France
d. Jan 11, 1788 in Paris, France
Source: *AmBi; OxFr; WhAm H*

Grassi, Giovanni Battista
Italian. Zoologist
b. Mar 27, 1854 in Rovellasca, Italy
d. May 4, 1925 in Rome, Italy
Source: *BioIn 6; DcScB; NewCol 75; WebBD 80*

Grassle, Karen
American. Actress
Played Caroline Ingalls on "Little House on the Prairie", 1973-81.
b. in Berkeley, California
Source: *BioIn 10; WhoAm 82*

Grassley, Charles Ernest
American. Senator
b. Sep 17, 1933 in New Hartford, Iowa
Source: *AlmAP 78, 80; CngDr 77, 79; WhoAm 78, 80, 82; WhoAmP 75, 77, 79; WhoGov 75, 77; WhoMW 76, 78*

Grasso, Ella
[Ella Tambussi]
American. Governor of Connecticut
b. May 10, 1919 in Windsor Locks, Connecticut
d. Feb 5, 1981 in Hartford, Connecticut
Source: *BioNews 74; CngDr 74; InWom; NewYTBS 74; WhoAm 74; WhoAmP 73; WhoAmW 77; WhoE 74; WhoGov 72; WomPO 76*

Grateful Dead, The
[Jerry Garcia; Donna Godchaux; Keith Godchaux; Bill Kreutzmann; Phil Lesh; Ron McKernan; Robert Hall Weir]
American. Rock Group
Source: *BkPepl; EncPR&S; IlEncRk*

Gratian
[Flavius Gratianus]
Roman. Emperor
b. 359
d. 383
Source: *NewCol 75; WebBD 80*

Grattan, Clinton Hartley
American. Author
b. Oct 19, 1902 in Wakefield, Massachusetts
d. Jun 25, 1980 in Austin, Texas
Source: *AmAu&B; ConAu 1R, 101; DrAS 78H; OxAmL; REnAL; TwCA, SUP; WhAm 7; WhE&EA; WhNAA; WhoAm 74, 76, 78; WhoS&SW 73; WrDr 76*

Gratz, Rebecca
American. Philanthropist
b. Mar 4, 1781 in Philadelphia, Pennsylvania
d. Aug 29, 1869
Source: *AmAu&B; BioIn 2, 4, 5, 8, 9, 10; REnAL*

Gratzer, Alan
see: REO Speedwagon

Grau, Shirley Ann
American. Author
b. Jul 8, 1929 in New Orleans, Louisiana
Source: *AmAu&B; AuNews 2; ConAu 1R, 89; ConLC 4; ConNov 72, 76; DrAF 76; InWom; ModAL; OxAmL; Pen AM; REn; REnAL; WhoAm 82; WhoAmW 77, 77; WhoE 74; WhoWor 74; WorAu; WrDr 76*

Grauer, Ben(jamin Franklin)
American. Broadcast Journalist
b. Jun 2, 1908 in New York, New York
d. May 31, 1977 in New York, New York
Source: *ConAu 69; CurBio 41, 59; Film 1; IntMPA 76, 77; NewYTBE 73; WhoAm 74; WhoWor 74; WhoWorJ 72*

Grauman, Sid(ney Patrick)
American. Theater Owner
Owner, Chinese Theater restaurant, famous for footprints of stars.
b. Mar 17, 1879 in Indianapolis
d. Mar 5, 1950 in Hollywood, California
Source: *BioIn 2; NotNAT B; ObitOF 79; WhoHol B*

Gravel, Mike
American. Senator
b. May 13, 1930 in Springfield, Massachusetts
Source: *CelR 73; CngDr 74; ConAu 41R; CurBio 72; IntWW 74; NewYTBE 71; WhoAm 80, 82; WhoAmP 73; WhoGov 72; WhoWest 74; WrDr 76*

Gravely, Samuel L
American. Admiral
b. Jun 4, 1922 in Richmond, Virginia
Source: *NewYTBE 71; WhoAm 74; WhoBlA 75; WhoS&SW 73*

Graves, Harold Nathan
American. Diplomat
b. Jan 20, 1915 in Manila, Philippines
Source: *IntWW 74; WhoAm 74; WhoGov 72*

Graves, John Earl
[The Hostages]
American. Former Hostage in Iran
b. May 16, 1927 in Detroit, Michigan
Source: *NewYTBS 81; USBiR 74; WhoAm 74, 76, 78; WhoGov 72*

Graves, Michael
American. Architect
b. Jul 9, 1934 in Indianapolis, Indiana
Source: *WhoAm 78, 80, 82*

Graves, Morris Cole
American. Artist
b. Aug 28, 1910 in Fox Valley, Oregon
Source: *ConArt; DcAmArt; McGDA; REnAL; WebAB; WhoAm 74, 76, 78, 80, 82; WhoAmA 73, 76, 78*

Graves, Nancy Stevenson
American. Artist, Filmmaker
b. Dec 23, 1940 in Pittsfield, Massachusetts
Source: *BioIn 8, 9, 11; CurBio 81; DcCAA 77; WhoAm 80, 82; WhoAmA 76, 78, 80*

Graves, Peter
English. Actor
b. Oct 21, 1911 in London, England
Source: *FilmgC; IntMPA 77, 75; MotPP; WhoHol A; WhoThe 72*

Graves, Peter
[Peter Aurness]
American. Actor
Played Jim Phelps in "Mission: Impossible," 1967-73; brother of James Arness.
b. Mar 18, 1926 in Minneapolis, Minnesota
Source: *FilmgC; IntMPA 82; MovMk; WhoAm 74, 76, 78, 80, 82*

Graves, Robert Ranke
English. Poet, Novelist, Essayist
Wrote *Good-bye to All That,* 1929; *I, Claudius; Claudius the God* 1934.
b. Jul 26, 1895 in London, England
Source: *Alli; AnCL; Au&Wr 71; AuBYP; BiDLA; CasWL; Chambr 3; ChPo, S1, S2; CnE&AP; CnMWL; ConAu 5R, 5NR; ConLC 1, 2, 6, 11; ConNov 72, 76; ConP 70, 75; CyWA; DcLEL; EncWL; EvLB; IntWW 74; LongCTC; ModBrL, SUP; NewC; OxEng; Pen ENG; RAdv 1; REn; TwCA, SUP; TwCW; WebE&AL; Who 74; WhoTwCL; WhoWor 74; WrDr 76*

Gray, Asa
American. Botanist
b. Nov 18, 1810 in Sauquoit, New York
d. Jan 30, 1888 in Cambridge, Massachusetts
Source: *Alli, SUP; AmAu; AmAu&B; ApCAB; BbD; BiD&SB; CyAl 2; DcAmAu; DcAmB; DcNAA; EncAB-H; OxAmL; REn; REnAL; TwCBDA; WebAB; WhAm H*

Gray, Barry
[Bernard Yaroslaw]
American. Radio Broadcaster
b. Jul 2, 1916 in Atlantic City, New Jersey
Source: *CelR 73; ConAu 61; IntMPA 75, 76, 77; NewYTBE 70; WhoAm 82*

Gray, Cecil
Scottish. Composer
b. May 19, 1895 in Edinburgh, Scotland
d. Sep 9, 1951 in Worthing, England
Source: *Baker 78; BioIn 1, 2; OxMus; WhE&EA*

Gray, Coleen
American. Actress
b. Oct 23, 1922 in Staplehurst, Nebraska
Source: *InWom; IntMPA 75, 76, 77, 78, 79, 80, 81, 82; MotPP; WhoHol A*

Gray, Dolores
American. Actress
b. Jun 7, 1924 in Chicago, Illinois
Source: *BiE&WWA; EncMT; FilmgC; InWom; MotPP; NotNAT; WhoHol A; WhoThe 77*

Gray, Elisha
American. Inventor
b. Aug 2, 1835 in Barnesville, Ohio
d. Jan 21, 1901 in Newtonville, Massachusetts
Source: *Alli SUP; AmBi; ApCAB; DcAmAu; DcAmB; DcNAA; NewCol 75; OhA&B; TwCBDA; WebAB; WhAm 1*

Gray, Gilda
[Maryanna Michalski]
American. Dancer
b. Oct 24, 1901 in Krakow, Poland
d. Dec 22, 1959 in Hollywood, California
Source: *Film 1; FilmgC; InWom; MotPP; TwYS; WhScrn 74, 77; WhoHol B*

Gray, Glen
[Glen Gray Knoblaugh]
American. Band Leader
b. Jun 7, 1906 in Roanoke, Illinois
d. Aug 23, 1963 in Plymouth, Massachusetts
Source: *WhScrn 74, 77; WhoHol B*

Gray, Gordon
American. Government Official
Secretary of Army, 1949-50; held security posts, 1947-77.
b. May 30, 1909 in Baltimore, Maryland
d. Nov 25, 1982 in Washington, DC
Source: *CurBio 49; IntWW 74; NewYTBS 82; Who 74; WhoAm 74, 76, 78, 80, 82; WhoF&I 74; WhoGov 72; WhoS&SW 73*

Gray, Hanna
American. Educator
b. Oct 25, 1930 in Heidelberg, Germany
Source: *DrAS 74H; LEduc 74; WhoAm 82; WhoAmW 77*

Gray, Harold
American. Comic Strip Artist
b. Jan 20, 1894 in Kankakee, Illinois
d. May 9, 1968 in La Jolla, California
Source: *AmAu&B; REnAL; WebAB; WhAm 5; WhNAA*

Gray, Horace
American. Supreme Court Justice
b. Mar 24, 1828 in Boston, Massachusetts
d. Sep 15, 1902 in Washington, DC
Source: *AmBi; ApCAB; DcAmB; NewCol 75; TwCBDA; WebAB; WhAm 1*

Gray, Linda
[Mrs. Ed Thrasher]
American. Actress
Appeared in over 400 TV commercials; plays Sue Ellen Ewing on "Dallas," 1978--.
b. Sep 12, 1941? in Santa Monica, California
Source: *BioIn 12; WhoAm 80, 82*

Gray, Louis Patrick
American. Former FBI Director
b. Jul 18, 1916 in Saint Louis, Missouri
Source: *BioNews 74; IntWW 74; NewYTBE 71; WhoAm 74; WhoWor 74*

Gray, Nicholas Stuart
Scottish. Children's Author
b. Oct 23, 1922 in Scotland
d. Mar 17, 1981 in London, England
Source: *AnObit 1981; ConAu 21R, 103; IntAu&W 76, 77; ScF&FL 1, 2; SmATA 4; TwCCW 78; WhoThe 72, 77; WrDr 76, 80*

Gray, Peter J
[Peter Wyshner]
American. One-armed Baseball Player
b. Mar 6, 1917 in Nanticoke, Pennsylvania
Source: *BioIn 9, 10; WhoProB 73*

Gray, Simon
English. Dramatist
Wrote *Wise Child,* 1968; *Butley,* 1971; *Otherwise Engaged,* 1975.
b. Sep 21, 1936 in Hayling Island, England
Source: *BioIn 10, 11; ConAu 21R; ConDr 73, 77; ConNov 72, 76; EncWT; IntWW 81; NotNAT; OxCan; WhoThe 77*

Gray, Thomas
English. Poet
b. Dec 26, 1716 in London, England
d. Jul 30, 1771 in Cambridge, England
Source: *Alli, SUP; AtlBL; BbD; BiD&SB; BrAu; CasWL; Chambr 2; ChPo, S1, S2; CnE&AP; CrtT 2; CyWA; DcEnA; DcEnL; DcEuL; DcLEL; EvLB; MouLC 2; NewC; OxEng; Pen ENG; RAdv 1; RComWL; REn; WebE&AL*

Graydon, James Weir
American. Engineer, Inventor
b. Jan 18, 1848 in Indianapolis, Indiana
Source: *NatCAB 13; TwCBDA; WhAm 4*

Grayson, Kathryn
[Zelma Hedrick]
American. Actress
Starred in *Show Boat,* 1951; *Kiss Me Kate,* 1953; *The Vagabond King,* 1956.
b. Feb 9, 1923 in Winston-Salem, North Carolina
Source: *CmMov; FilmgC; InWom; IntMPA 75, 76, 77, 78, 79, 80, 81, 82; MotPP; MovMk; WhoAm 74, 76, 78, 80, 82; WhoHol A*

Graziani, Rodolfo
[Marchese DiNeghelli]
Italian. Military Officer
b. Aug 11, 1882 in Frosinone, Italy
d. Jan 11, 1955 in Rome, Italy
Source: *CurBio 41, 55; NewCol 75*

Graziano, Rocky
[Rocko Barbella]
American. Boxer, Actor
Middleweight champ, 1947-48; portrayed by Paul Newman in *Somebody Up There Likes Me,* 1956.
b. Jun 7, 1922 in New York, New York
Source: *CelR 73; WhoBox 74; WhoHol A*

"Great Gildersleeve"
see: Peary, Harold

Greaza, Walter N
American. Actor
b. Jan 1, 1897 in Saint Paul, Minnesota
d. Jun 1, 1973 in New York, New York
Source: *BiE&WWA; NewYTBE 73; WhScrn 77; WhoHol B*

Greb, Harry (Edward Henry)
American. Boxer
b. Jun 6, 1894 in Pittsburgh, Pennsylvania
d. Oct 22, 1926 in New York, New York
Source: *BioIn 1, 4, 6, 7; NewCol 75; WhoBox 74*

Grebb, Marty
see: Buckinghams, The

Grebey, Ray
American. Baseball Executive
b. 1927 in Chicago, Illinois
Source: *BioIn 12*

Grech, Rick
see: Blind Faith

Grechko, Andrei Antonovick
Russian. Government Official
b. Oct 17, 1903 in Golodaevka, Russia
d. Apr 26, 1976 in Moscow, U.S.S.R.
Source: *CurBio 68; IntWW 74; NewCol 75; NewYTBE 71; WhoWor 74*

Greco, El
[Kyriakas Theotokopoulos]
Spanish. Artist
Works include "Assumption of the Virgin," 1577, "Burial of the Count of Orgaz," 1586.
b. 1541 in Candia, Crete
d. Apr 6, 1614 in Toledo, Spain
Source: *AtlBL; NewC; NewCol 75; REn*

Greco, Buddy (Armando)
American. Singer, Composer, Musician
b. Aug 14, 1926 in Philadelphia, Pennsylvania
Source: *AmSCAP 66; BioNews 74*

Greco, Jose
American. Flamenco Dancer, Choreographer
Debut in *Carmen,* 1937; appeared in *Ship of Fools,* 1965.
b. Dec 23, 1918 in Montorio, Italy
Source: *ConAu 85; CurBio 52; WhoAm 74, 76, 78, 80, 82; WhoHol A*

Greco, Juliette
French. Singer
b. 1927 in Paris, France
Source: *FilmgC; WhoHol A*

Greeley, Andrew Moran
American. Author, Priest, Sociologist
b. Feb 5, 1928 in Oak Park, Illinois
Source: *AmM&WS 73S; ConAu 5R; CurBio 72; LEduc 74; WhoAm 74, 76, 78, 80, 82*

Greeley, Horace
American. Journalist, Editor
Founded NY *Tribune,* 1834; popularzed phrase "Go West, young man."
b. Feb 3, 1811 in Amherst, New Hampshire
d. Nov 29, 1872 in Pleasantville, New York
Source: *Alli, SUP; AmAu; AmAu&B; AmBi; ApCAB; BbD; BiAuS; BiD&SB; BiDrAC; CasWL; Chambr 3; ChPo; CnDAL; CyAl 2; DcAmAu; DcAmB; DcEnL; DcNAA; EncAB-H; EvLB; OxAmL; REn; REnAL; TwCBDA; WebAB; WhAm H; WhAmP*

Greely, Adolphus Washington
American. Explorer, Army Officer
Told of polar expedition in *Three Years of Arctic Service,* 1886.
b. Mar 27, 1844 in Newburyport, Massachusetts
d. Oct 20, 1935
Source: *Alli SUP; AmAu&B; AmBi; ApCAB; BiD&SB; DcAmB S1; DcNAA; NewCol 75; OxCan; REnAL; WebAB; WhAm 1*

Green, Abel
American. Author, Editor, Actor
b. Jun 3, 1900 in New York, New York
d. May 10, 1973 in New York, New York
Source: *BiE&WWA; AmSCAP 66; CelR 73; ConAu 41R; NewYTBE 73; WhAm 6; WhScrn 77; WhoAdv 72; WhoAm 74*

Green, Adolph
American. Actor, Composer
b. Dec 2, 1915 in New York, New York
Source: *AmAu&B; AmSCAP 66; CelR 73; CmMov; ConDr 73; CurBio 45; EncMT; FilmgC; IntMPA 75, 76, 77, 78, 79, 80, 81, 82; NewCBMT; NotNAT; OxFilm; WhoAm 74, 76, 78, 80, 82; WhoThe 77; WhoWor 74; WorEFlm*

Green, Al
American. Singer, Songwriter
b. Apr 13, 1946 in Forrest City, Arkansas
Source: *BkPepl; NewYTBE 73; WhoAm 82*

Green, Anne
American. Author
b. Nov 11, 1899 in Savannah, Georgia
Source: *AmAu&B; AmNov; CathA 1952; ConAmA; DcLEL; InWom; LongCTC; OxAmL; REn; REnAL; TwCA, SUP*

Green, Chad
American. Leukemia Victim
Parents took him to Mexico where he was treated with laetrile, not approved in US.
b. 1976?
d. 1979
Source: *BioIn 11, 12*

Green, Constance Windsor McLaughlin
American. Historian, Author
b. Aug 21, 1897 in Ann Arbor, Michigan
d. Dec 5, 1975 in Annapolis, Maryland
Source: *AmAu&B; ConAu 9R, 61; CurBio 63; DrAS 74H; ForWC 70; InWom; OxAmL; WhAm 6; WhoAm 74; WhoWor 74; WrDr 76*

Green, Dallas (George Dallas, Jr.)
American. Baseball Manager, Executive
b. Aug 4, 1934 in Newport, Delaware
Source: *BaseEn; BioIn 12; WhoAm 82*

Green, Elmer Ellsworth
American. Physicist
b. Oct 17, 1917 in La Grande, Oregon
Source: *AmM&WS 73S; ConAu 103*

Green, Gerald
American. Author
b. Apr 8, 1922 in Brooklyn, New York
Source: *AmAu&B; ConAu 13R; WhoAm 74, 76, 78, 80, 82; WhoWor 74; WorAu*

Green, Henry
[Yorke, Henry Vincent]
English. Author
b. Oct 29, 1905 in Tewkesbury, England
d. 1974
Source: *CasWL; CnMWL; ConAu 49, 85; ConNov 72, 76; CyWA; DcLEL; EncWL; EvLB; LongCTC; ModBrL, SUP; NewC; OxEng; Pen ENG; RAdv 1; REn; TwCA SUP; TwCW; WebE&AL; WhoTwCL*

Green, Hetty
[Henrietta Howland Robinson]
"Witch of Wall Street"
American. Financier, Millionaire
b. Nov 21, 1834 in New Bedford, Massachusetts
d. Jul 3, 1916 in New York, New York
Source: *AmBi; BioIn 2, 3, 4, 5, 6, 7, 9; DcAmB; GoodHS; LinLib S; NewCol 75; NotAW; WebAB; WhAm 1*

Green, Hubie (Hubert)
American. Golfer
b. Dec 28, 1946 in Birmingham, Alabama
Source: *BioIn 10, 11; WhoGolf*

Green, Jack
see: T. Rex

Green, Johnny (John W)
American. Conductor, Musician, Composer
b. Oct 10, 1908 in New York, New York
Source: *AmSCAP 66; BiE&WWA; CmMov; FilmgC; IntMPA 75, 76, 77, 78, 79, 80, 81, 82; WhoAm 74, 76, 78, 80, 82; WhoMus 72; WhoWest 74; WhoWor 74*

Green, Julien
American. Author
b. Apr 9, 1900 in Paris, France
Source: *CasWL; ClDMEL; CnMD; CnMWL; ConAu 21R; ConLC 3; EncWL; EvEuW; IntWW 74; McGEWD; OxFr; Pen EUR; REn; REnWD; TwCW; WhoTwCL*

Green, Martyn
English. Actor
b. Apr 22, 1899 in London, England
d. Feb 8, 1975 in Hollywood, California
Source: *BiE&WWA; ConAu 57; CurBio 50; FilmgC; WhScrn 77; WhoThe 77*

Green, Mitzi
American. Actress
b. Oct 22, 1920 in New York, New York
d. May 24, 1969 in Huntington, California
Source: *FilmgC; HolP 30; MotPP; ThFT; WhScrn 74, 77; WhoHol B*

Green, Paul Eliot
American. Dramatist, Screenwriter
b. Mar 17, 1894 in Lillington, North Carolina
d. May 4, 1981 in Chapel Hill, North Carolina
Source: *AmAu&B; AmSCAP 66; Au&Wr 71; AuNews 1; BiE&WWA; BioIn 2, 3, 4, 5, 8, 9, 10; CnDAL; CnMD; CnThe; ConAmA; ConAmL; ConAu 5R, 103, 3NR; ConDr 73; DcLEL; EncWL; EncWT; IntAu&W 76, 77; IntWW 74; LongCTC; McGEWB; ModAL; ModWD; NotNAT; OxAmL; OxThe; Pen AM; REn; REnAL; REnWD; TwCA, SUP; WebAB; WebE&AL; WhE&EA; WhLit; WhNAA; Who 74; WhoAm 74, 76, 78, 80; WhoThe 77; WhoWor 74; WrDr 76*

Green, Paula
American. Advertising Executive
b. Sep 18, 1927 in Hollywood, California
Source: *WhoAm 74, 76, 78, 80, 82; WhoAmW 77*

Green, Robert L
American. Fashion Editor
Source: *WorFshn*

Green, William
American. Labor Leader
Succeeded Samuel Gompers as president of AFL, 1924-52.
b. Mar 3, 1873 in Coschocton, Ohio
d. Nov 21, 1952 in Coschocton, Ohio
Source: *CurBio 42, 53; DcAmB S5; EncAB-H; OhA&B; WebAB; WhAm 3*

Greenaway, Kate (Catherine)
English. Children's Author, Illustrator
b. Mar 17, 1846 in London, England
d. Nov 6, 1901
Source: *AnCL; AuBYP; CarSB; ChPo, S1, S2; FamAIYP; InWom; JBA 34, 51; NewC; OxEng; WhoChL*

Greenberg, Hank (Henry Benjamin)
"Hammerin' Hank"
American. Baseball Player
Led AL in home runs 1935, 1938, 1940, 1946.
b. Jan 1, 1911 in New York, New York
Source: *BaseEn; CurBio 47; WhoAm 74; WhoProB 73*

Greene, Gael
American. Author
b. 1937 in Detroit, Michigan
Source: *ConAu 13R; ConLC 8*

Greene, Graham
English. Author
Wrote *Brighton Rock,* 1938, *The End of the Affair,* 1951.
b. Oct 2, 1904 in Berkhampstead, England
Source: *Au&Wr 71; AuNews 2; BiE&WWA; CasWL; CathA 1930; CelR 73; ChPo S2; CnMD; CnMWL; CnThe; ConAu 13R; ConDr 73; ConLC 1, 3, 6, 9, 14, 18; ConNov 72, 76; CroCD; CyWA; EncMys; EncWL; FilmgC; IntWW 74; LongCTC; McGEWD; ModBrL, SUP; ModWD; NewC; NotNAT; OxEng; OxFilm; OxThe; Pen ENG; RAdv 1; REn; SmATA 20; TwCA, SUP; TwCW; WebE&AL; Who 74; WhoAm 82; WhoChL; WhoThe 77; WhoTwCL; WhoWor 74; WorEFlm; WrDr 76*

Greene, Joseph
"Mean Joe"
American. Football Player
Tackle, Pittsburgh, 1969-81; starred in award-winning Coca-Cola commercial.
b. Sep 24, 1946 in Temple, Texas
Source: *WhoFtbl 74*

Greene, Lorne
American. Actor
Played Ben Cartwright on TV series "Bonanza," 1959-73.
b. Feb 12, 1915 in Ottawa, ON
Source: *BiE&WWA; CanWW 82; CelR 73; CreCan 2; CurBio 67; FilmgC; IntMPA 75, 76, 77, 78, 79, 80, 81, 82; MotPP; MovMk; WhoAm 74, 76, 78, 80, 82; WhoHol A; WhoWor 74*

Greene, Nancy Catherine
Canadian. Skier
b. May 11, 1943 in Ottawa, ON
Source: *BioIn 8, 10; CanWW 79, 82; CurBio 69*

Greene, Nathanael
American. Revolutionary War General
b. Aug 7, 1742 in Potowomut, Rhode Island
d. Jun 19, 1786 in Savannah, Georgia
Source: *AmBi; ApCAB; DcAmB; EncAB-H; TwCBDA; WebAB; WhAm H*

Greene, Richard
English. Actor
b. 1918 in Plymouth, England
Source: *FilmgC; HolP 30; MotPP; MovMk; WhoHol A*

Greene, Ward
American. Author, Journalist
b. Dec 23, 1892 in Asheville, North Carolina
d. Jan 22, 1956
Source: *AmAu&B; AmNov; REnAL; TwCA, SUP; WhAm 3; WhNAA*

Greenfield, Jeff
American. Author
b. Jun 10, 1943 in New York, New York
Source: *ConAu 37R*

Greenglass, David
Spy
b. 1922
Source: *BioIn 4*

Greenhill, Basil
English. Author
b. Feb 26, 1920 in Somerset, England
Source: *Au&Wr 71; ConAu 5R, 2NR; OxCan SUP; Who 74*

Greenough, Horatio
American. Sculptor
b. Sep 6, 1805 in Boston, Massachusetts
d. Dec 18, 1852 in Somerville, Massachusetts
Source: *Alli; AmAu; AmAu&B; AmBi; ApCAB; BiAuS; CyAl 2; DcAmB; DcNAA; Drake; OxAmL; REnAL; TwCBDA; WebAB; WhAm H*

Greenspan, Alan
American. Economist, Government Official
Chairman, Council of Economic Advisers, 1974-77.
b. Mar 6, 1926 in New York, New York
Source: *AmEA 74; AmM&WS 73S; BioNews 74; CurBio 74; St&PR 75; WhoAm 82*

Greenspan, Bud
American. Television Producer, Director
b. 1927
Source: *BioIn 10*

Greenspan, Martin
American. Physicist
b. May 8, 1912 in New York, New York
Source: *WhoAm 74*

Greenspun, Hank (Herman Milton)
American. Newspaper Publisher
b. Aug 27, 1909 in Brooklyn, New York
Source: *AuNews 2; ConAu 21R; ConAu P-2; WhoAm 74, 76, 78, 80, 82; WhoWorJ 72*

Greenspun, Roger
American. Motion Picture Critic
b. 1929 in Bridgeport, Connecticut
Source: *BioIn 10; ConAu 102*

Greenstreet, Sydney Hughes
English. Actor
b. Dec 27, 1879 in Sandwich, England
d. Jan 19, 1954 in Los Angeles, California
Source: *BiDFilm; CmMov; CurBio 43, 54; DcAmB S5; HolP 40; MotPP; OxFilm; Vers A; WhScrn 74, 77; WhoHol B; WorEFlm*

Greenway, Brian
see: April Wine

Greenwood, Al
see: Foreigner

Greenwood, Charlotte
American. Actress
b. Jun 25, 1893 in Philadelphia, Pennsylvania
d. Jan 18, 1978 in Los Angeles, California
Source: *BiE&WWA; EncMT; Film 1; FilmgC; InWom; IntMPA 77, 75; MotPP; MovMk; NotNAT; ThFT; Vers A; WhoHol A; WhoThe 77*

Greenwood, Joan
English. Actress
b. Mar 4, 1921 in London, England
Source: *BiDFilm; BiE&WWA; CurBio 54; FilmgC; InWom; IntMPA 75, 76, 77, 78, 79, 80, 81, 82; MotPP; MovMk; NotNAT; OxFilm; Who 74; WhoHol A; WhoThe 77; WorEFlm*

Greer, Germaine
Australian. Author, Educator
b. Jan 29, 1939 in Melbourne, Australia
Source: *AuNews 1; CelR 73; ConAu 81; CurBio 71; IntWW 74; NewYTBE 71; WhoAm 82; WhoAmW 77; WhoWor 74; WrDr 76*

Greer, Howard
American. Fashion Designer
b. 1896
d. Apr 20, 1974
Source: *NewYTBS 74*

Greer, Jane
American. Actress
b. Sep 9, 1924 in Washington, DC
Source: *FilmgC; IntMPA 77, 75; MotPP; MovMk; WhoAm 82; WhoHol A*

Greer, Michael
American. Interior Decorator
b. Sep 19, 1917 in Monroe, Georgia
d. 1976 in New York, New York
Source: *CelR 73*

Greer, "Sonny" (William Alexander)
American. Musician
Drummer, Duke Ellington Orchestra for over 30 years.
b. Dec 13, 1903 in Long Branch, New Jersey
d. Mar 23, 1982 in New York, New York
Source: *CmpEPM; EncJzS 70; IlEncJ; NewYTBS 82; WhoJazz 72*

Greg, Sir Walter Wilson
English. Bibliographer, Scholar
b. 1875
d. 1959
Source: *DcLEL; OxEng; Pen ENG; REn*

Gregg, Peter
American. Auto Racer
b. May 4, 1940 in New York, New York
d. Dec 15, 1980 in Ponte Vedra Beach, Florida
Source: *BioIn 12*

Gregg, William
American. Industrialist
b. Feb 2, 1800 in Monongahela County, Virginia
d. Sep 13, 1867
Source: *AmBi; BiDConf; DcAmB; EncAB-A; McGEWB; TwCBDA; WebAB*

Gregor, Arthur
American. Poet
b. Nov 18, 1923 in Vienna, Austria
Source: *ConAu 25R; ConP 70, 75; DrAP 75; WhoAm 74, 76, 78, 80, 82; WrDr 76*

Gregory XIII, Pope
[Ugo Boncompagni]
Italian. Created Gregorian Calendar
b. Jan 1, 1502 in Bologna, Italy
d. Apr 10, 1585
Source: *McGEWB; NewCol 75; WebBD 80*

Gregory the Great
[Gregory I, Pope]
Italian. Saint, Pope
b. 540 in Rome, Italy
d. 604
Source: *CasWL; Pen EUR*

Gregory, Bettina Louise
American. Journalist
b. Jun 4, 1946 in New York, New York
Source: *ConAu 69; WhoAm 82*

Gregory, Cynthia Kathleen
[Mrs. John Hemminger]
American. Ballerina
Principal dancer with American Ballet Theatre, 1967--.
b. Jul 8, 1946 in Los Angeles, California
Source: *CurBio 77; WhoAm 82*

Gregory, Dick
American. Comedian, Author, Activist
b. Oct 12, 1932 in Saint Louis, Missouri
Source: *AmAu&B; BioNews 74; CelR 73; ConAu 45; CurBio 62; LivgBAA; WhoAm 74, 76, 78, 80, 82; WhoAmP 73; WhoBlA 75; WhoHol A; WrDr 76*

Gregory, Horace
American. Author, Translator, Teacher
b. Apr 10, 1898 in Milwaukee, Wisconsin
d. Mar 11, 1982 in Shelburne Falls, Massachusetts
Source: *AmAu&B; ChPo S1, S2; CnDAL; ConAmA; ConAu 5R; ConP 70, 75; DcLEL; DrAP 75; LinLib L; NewYTBS 82; OxAmL; Pen AM; RAdv 1; REn; REnAL; SixAP; TwCA, SUP; WhoAm 82; WrDr 76, 80*

Gregory, Lady Isabella Augusta
Irish. Dramatist
b. Mar 15, 1852 in Roxborough, Scotland
d. May 22, 1932
Source: *AtlBL; Chambr 3; ChPo, S2; DcLEL; EvLB; LongCTC; ModBrL, SUP; ModWD; Pen ENG; PlP&P; REn; REnWD; TwCA, SUP; TwCW; WebE&AL; WhoLA*

Gregson, John
English. Actor
b. Mar 15, 1919 in Liverpool, England
d. Jan 8, 1975 in Porlock Weir, England
Source: *CmMov; FilmgC; IntMPA 75; WhScrn 77*

Grene, Majorie
American. Author
b. Dec 13, 1910 in Milwaukee, Wisconsin
Source: *Au&Wr 71; ConAu 13R; DrAS 74P*

Grenville, Richard
English. Naval Officer
b. 1541 in Cornwall, England
d. 1591
Source: *Alli; AmBi; ApCAB; NewC; REn*

Grenfell, Joyce Irene
English. Actress
b. Feb 10, 1910 in London, England
d. Nov 30, 1979 in London, England
Source: *BiE&WWA; ConAu 81, 89; CurBio 58, 80; EncMT; FilmgC; InWom; IntWW 74, 75, 76, 77, 78; IntWWP 77; MotPP; MovMk; NewYTBS 79; NotNAT; OxThe; Who 74; WhoAmW 61, 66, 68, 70, 72, 74; WhoHol A; WhoThe 72, 77; WhoWor 74, 76, 78*

Gres, Alix
French. Fashion Designer
b. 1899?
Source: *CurBio 80; WorFshn*

Grese, Irma
"Angel of Death"; "Belle of Auschwitz"; "Blond Angel of Hell"
German. Nazi War Criminal
b. 1923
d. Dec 13, 1945 in Hamelin, Germany
Source: *BioIn 1, 7; EncTR; InWom; LookW*

Gresham, Thomas
English. Economist, Merchant, Financier
b. 1520
d. Nov 21, 1579
Source: *NewC; NewCol 75; WebBD 80*

Gretchaninov, Aleksandr Tikhonovich
[Aleksandr Tikhonovich Grechaninov]
American. Composer
b. Oct 25, 1864 in Moscow, Russia
d. Jan 3, 1956 in New York, New York
Source: *NewCol 75; NewEOp 71; OxMus; WebBD 80*

Gretry, Andre Ernest Modeste
French. Composer
b. Feb 9, 1741 in Liege, Belgium
d. Sep 24, 1813 in Montmorency, France
Source: *NewCol 75; NewEOp 71; OxMus*

Gretzky, Wayne
"The Great Gretzky"
Canadian. Hockey Player
As of Feb, 1983, holds 29 NHL scoring records; SI sportsman of year, 1982.
b. Jan 26, 1961 in Brantford, ON
Source: *BioIn 11, 12; CanWW 82; CurBio 82; HocReg; NewYTBS 82*

Greuze, Jean-Baptiste
French. Artist
b. Aug 21, 1725 in Tournus, France
d. Mar 21, 1805 in Paris, France
Source: *McGEWB; NewCol 75; OxArt*

Grevillius, Nils
Swedish. Conductor
b. 1893
d. 1970
Source: *BioIn 9*

Grew, Joseph Clark
American. Statesman
b. May 27, 1880 in Boston, Massachusetts
d. May 25, 1965 in Manchester, Massachusetts
Source: *AmAu&B; CurBio 41, 65; EncAB-H; WebAB; WhAm 4; WhNAA*

Grew, Nehemiah
English. Scientist
b. 1641 in Mancetter, England
d. Mar 25, 1712 in London, England
Source: *Alli; NewCol 75; WebBD 80*

Grey, Charles
English. Statesman
b. Mar 13, 1764 in Fallodon, England
d. 1845 in Northumberland, England
Source: *McGEWB; NewCol 75*

Grey of Fallodon, Edward
English. Statesman, Nature-Lover
b. Apr 25, 1862 in London, England
d. Sep 7, 1933
Source: *ChPo; NewC; NewCol 75; TwCA, SUP*

Grey, Lady Jane
English. Queen
Queen for nine days; imprisoned, beheaded by Mary I's troops.
b. Oct 1537 in Bradgate, England
d. Feb 12, 1554 in London, England
Source: *Alli; HerW; InWom; LinLib S; NewCol 75; REn*

Grey, Joel
[Joel Katz]
American. Singer, Actor, Dancer
Won Oscar for *Cabaret,* 1972.
b. Apr 11, 1932 in Cleveland, Ohio
Source: *CelR 73; CurBio 73; EncMT; IntMPA 75, 76, 77, 78, 79, 80, 81, 82; NotNAT; St&PR 75; WhoAm 74, 76, 78, 80, 82; WhoHol A; WhoThe 77; WhoWor 74; WhoAm 74*

Grey, Virginia
American. Actress
b. 1917
Source: *FilmgC; IntMPA 82; MovMk; ThFT; WhoHol A*

Grey, Zane
American. Author
Wrote *Riders of the Purple Sage,* 1912.
b. Jan 31, 1875 in Zanesville, Ohio
d. Oct 23, 1939 in Altadena, California
Source: *AmAu&B; AmBi; ArizL; DcLEL; DcNAA; EvLB; FilmgC; LongCTC; MnBBF; OhA&B; OxAmL; Pen AM; REn; REnAL; TwCA, SUP; TwCW; WebAB; WebE&AL; WhAm 1; WhNAA*

Grey Owl, pseud.
[(Archibald) George Stansfeld Belaney]
English. Naturalist, Author
b. Sep 1888 in Hastings, England
d. Apr 13, 1938 in Prince Albert, SK
Source: *CanWr; CreCan 1; DcLEL; DcNAA; OxCan*

Gribble, Harry Wagstaff Graham
English. Dramatist, Director
b. Mar 27, 1896 in Sevenoaks, England
d. Jan 28, 1981 in New York, New York
Source: *BiE&WWA; ConAu 102; CurBio 45, 81; NewYTBS 81; NotNAT; WhThe*

Grieder, Walter
Swiss. Artist, Graphic Designer
b. Nov 21, 1924 in Basel, Switzerland
Source: *ConAu 41R; SmATA 9*

Grieg, Edvard Hagerup
Norwegian. Composer, Musician
b. Jun 15, 1843 in Bergen, Norway
d. Sep 4, 1907 in Bergen, Norway
Source: *AtlBL; NewCol 75; REn*

Grier, Pamela Suzette
American. Actress
b. May 26, 1949 in Winston-Salem, North Carolina
Source: *BioNews 74; WhoAm 82*

Grier, Robert Cooper
American. Supreme Court Justice
b. Mar 5, 1794 in Cumberland County, Pennsylvania
d. Sep 25, 1870 in Philadelphia, Pennsylvania
Source: *AmBi; ApCAB; DcAmB; Drake; TwCBDA; WebAB; WebBD 80; WhAm H*

Grier, "Rosey" (Roosevelt)
American. Football Player, Actor
Tackle, 1955-66; bodyguard for Robert Kennedy when assassinated.
b. Jul 19, 1932 in Linden, New Jersey
Source: *NewYTBE 70, 73; WhoBlA 75; WhoFtbl 74; WhoHol A*

Griese, Arnold
American. Author
b. Apr 13, 1921 in Lakota, Iowa
Source: *ConAu 49, 1NR; LEduc 74; SmATA 9*

Griese, Bob (Robert Allen)
American. Football Player
Quarterback, Miami Dolphins, 1967-81.
b. Feb 3, 1945 in Evansville, Indiana
Source: *CelR 73; WhoAm 82; WhoFtbl 74*

Grieve, Christopher Murray
see: MacDiarmid, Hugh, pseud.

Griffes, Charles Tomlinson
American. Composer
b. Sep 7, 1884 in Elmira, New York
d. Apr 8, 1920 in Elmira, New York
Source: *NewCol 75; WebBD 80*

Griffin, Archie
American. Football Player
b. Aug 21, 1954 in Columbus, Ohio
Source: *WhoFtbl 74*

Griffin, Bob (Robert Paul)
American. Politician, Lawyer
Senator from MI, 1966-79.
b. Nov 6, 1923 in Detroit, Michigan
Source: *BiDrAC; CngDr 74; CurBio 60; IntWW 74, 75, 76, 77, 78, 79, 80, 81; NewYTBE 72; WhoAm 74, 76, 78, 80, 82; WhoAmP 73; WhoGov 72; WhoMW 74; WhoWor 74*

Griffin, Dale "Buffin"
see: Mott (the Hoople)

Griffin, John Howard
American. Author, Photographer
b. Jun 16, 1920 in Dallas, Texas
d. Sep 9, 1980 in Fort Worth, Texas
Source: *AmAu&B; Au&Wr 71; AuNews 1; ConAu 1R, 101, 2NR; WhoAm 74; WhoRel 75; WhoWor 74; WorAu; WrDr 76*

Griffin, Merv(yn)
American. TV Entertainer
b. Jul 6, 1925 in San Mateo, California
Source: *BkPepl; CelR 73; CurBio 67; IntMPA 75, 76, 77, 78, 79, 80, 81, 82; WhoAm 74, 76, 78, 80, 82; WhoHol A*

Griffis, Stanton
American. Investment Banker, Author
b. May 2, 1887 in Boston, Massachusetts
d. Aug 29, 1974 in New York, New York
Source: *CurBio 44, 74; NewYTBS 74; St&PR 75; WhAm 6; WhoAm 74*

Griffith, Andy (Andrew)
American. Actor
Broadway debut *No Time for Sergeants,* 1955; starred in "Andy Griffith Show," 1960-69.
b. Jun 1, 1926 in Mount Airy, North Carolina
Source: *BiE&WWA; BioNews 74; CelR 73; CurBio 60; FilmgC; IntMPA 75, 76, 77, 78, 79, 80, 81, 82; MotPP; WhoAm 74, 76, 78, 80, 82; WhoHol A*

Griffith, Clark Calvin
"Old Fox"
American. Baseball Player, Executive
Owner, Washington Senators/Minnesota Twins, 1920-55; Hall of Fame, 1946.
b. Nov 20, 1869 in Stringtown, Missouri
d. Oct 27, 1955 in Washington, DC
Source: *BaseEn; BioIn 2, 3, 4, 7; CurBio 50, 56; WhAm 3; WhoProB 73*

Griffith, Corinne
American. Actress
b. 1898 in Texarkana, Arkansas
d. Jul 13, 1979 in Santa Monica, California
Source: *AmSCAP 66; Film 1; FilmgC; MotPP; MovMk; ThFT; TwYS; WhoHol A*

Griffith, Darrell Steven
"Dr. Dunkenstein"
American. Basketball Player
b. Jun 16, 1958 in Louisville, Kentucky
Source: *BioIn 10*

Griffith, D(avid Lewelyn) W(ark)
American. Film Director, Actor
b. Jan 22, 1875 in La Grange, Kentucky
d. Jul 23, 1948 in Los Angeles, California
Source: *BiDFilm; CmMov; DcAmB S4; DcFM; EncAB-H; Film 1; FilmgC; MovMk; OxAmL; OxFilm; REn; REnAL; TwYS; WebAB; WhAm 2; WhScrn 74, 77; WhoHol B; WomWMM; WorEFlm*

Griffith, Emile Alphonse
American. Boxer
b. Feb 3, 1938 in Virgin Islands
Source: *BioIn 6, 7, 10, 11; WhoBox 74*

Griffith, Hugh Emrys
Welsh. Actor
b. May 30, 1912 in Anglesey, Wales
d. May 14, 1980 in London, England
Source: *BiE&WWA; FilmgC; IntMPA 75, 76, 77; MotPP; MovMk; NotNAT; Who 74; WhoHol A; WhoThe 77*

Griffith, Melanie
American. Actress
b. Aug 9, 1957 in New York, New York
Source: *BioIn 10; WhoHol A*

Griffiths, John Willis
American. Naval Architect
b. Oct 6, 1809 in New York, New York
d. Mar 30, 1882 in Brooklyn, New York
Source: *AmBi; ApCAB; DcAmB; Drake; TwCBDA; WebAB; WebAMB; WhAm H*

Griffiths, Martha Wright
[Martha Wright]
American. Politician, Lawyer
Elected MI Lt.-Governor, Nov, 1982.
b. Jan 29, 1912 in Pierce City, Missouri
Source: *BiDrAC; BioNews 74; CngDr 74; CurBio 55; InWom; NewYTBE 70; Ward 77; WhoAm 74, 76, 78; WhoAmP 73; WhoAmW 61, 64, 66, 68, 70, 72, 74, 75; WhoGov 72; WhoMW 74*

Griffiths, Ronald
see: Badfinger

Grigorovich, Yuri Nikolaevich
Russian. Ballet Dancer
b. Jan 1, 1927
Source: *IntWW 74; WhoWor 74*

Grigson, Geoffrey Edward Harvey
English. Author, Poet
b. Mar 2, 1902 in Pelynt, England
Source: *Au&Wr 71; AuBYP; ChPo, S1, S2; ConAu 25R; ConLC 7; ConP 70, 75; DcLEL; EvLB; IntWW 74; LongCTC; ModBrL, SUP; NewC; Pen ENG; REn; TwCA SUP; Who 74; WhoTwCL; WhoWor 74; WrDr 76*

Grillparzer, Franz
Austrian. Dramatist
b. Jan 15, 1791 in Vienna, Austria
d. Jan 21, 1872 in Vienna, Austria
Source: *AtlBL; BbD; BiD&SB; CasWL; CnThe; CyWA; DcEuL; EuAu; EvEuW; McGEWD; OxGer; OxThe; Pen EUR; RComWL; REn; REnWD*

Grimaldi, Princess Grace
see: Kelly, Grace

Grimaldi, Joseph
English. Clown
b. Dec 18, 1779
d. May 31, 1837
Source: *NewC; NewCol 75; OxThe; PlP&P*

Grimaldi, Rainier III
see: Rainier, Prince

Grimes, Burleigh Arland
"Ol' Stubblebeard"
American. Baseball Player
b. Aug 18, 1893 in Clear Lake, Wisconsin
Source: *BaseEn; BioIn 2, 3, 6, 7, 8; WhoProB 73*

Grimes, Tammy Lee
American. Actress, Singer, Dancer
b. Jan 30, 1936 in Lynn, Massachusetts
Source: *BiE&WWA; CelR 73; CurBio 62; EncMT; InWom; MotPP; NotNAT; WhoAm 74, 76, 78, 80, 82; WhoHol A; WhoThe 77; WhoWor 74*

Grimm, Charlie (Charles John)
"Jolly Cholly"
American. Baseball Player, Manager
b. Aug 28, 1899 in Saint Louis, Missouri
Source: *BaseEn; WhoProB 73*

Grimm, Jakob Ludwig Karl
[Grimm Brothers]
German. Philologist, Folklorist
Best known for collection of German folk tales, *Grimm's Fairy Tales,* 1812-15.
b. Jan 4, 1785 in Hanau, Germany
d. Sep 20, 1863 in Berlin, Germany
Source: *AnCL; AtlBL; AuBYP; BbD; BiD&SB; CarSB; CasWL; ChPo; DcEuL; EuAu; EvEuW; FamSYP; NewC; OxEng; OxGer; Pen EUR; REn; Str&VC; WhoChL*

Grimm, Wilhelm Karl
[Grimm Brothers]
German. Philologist, Folklorist
Best known for collection of German folk tales, *Grimm's Fairy Tales,* 1812-15.
b. Feb 24, 1786 in Hanau, Germany
d. Dec 16, 1859 in Berlin, Germany
Source: *AnCL; AtlBL; AuBYP; BiD&SB; CarSB; CasWL; ChPo, S2; DcEuL; EuAu; EvEuW; FamSYP; OxEng; OxGer; Pen EUR; REn; Str&VC*

Grimsby, Roger
American. Journalist
Source: *NF*

Gripe, Maria
Swedish. Author
b. Jul 25, 1923 in Vaxholm, Sweden
Source: *ConAu 29R; SmATA 2*

Gris, Juan
[Jose Victoriano Gonzales]
Spanish. Artist
b. Mar 13, 1887 in Madrid, Spain
d. May 11, 1927 in Paris, France
Source: *AtlBL; NewCol 75*

Grisi, Guilia
Italian. Opera Singer
b. Jul 28, 1811 in Milan, Italy
d. Nov 29, 1869 in Berlin, Germany
Source: *InWom; NewCol 75*

Grissom, Virgil Ivan
"Gus"
American. Astronaut
Third man in space, 1961; killed during simulation of Apollo I launching.
b. Apr 3, 1926 in Mitchell, Indiana
d. Jan 27, 1967 in Cape Canaveral, Florida
Source: *CurBio 65, 67; WhAm 4*

Grist, Reri
American. Opera Singer
b. 1934 in New York, New York
Source: *IntWW 74; NewYTBE 70; WhoAm 74; WhoBlA 75; WhoMus 72; WhoWor 74*

Griswold, A Whitney
American. Educator, Historian
b. Oct 27, 1906 in Morristown, New Jersey
d. Apr 19, 1963 in New Haven, Connecticut
Source: *AmAu&B; CurBio 50, 63; WhAm 4*

Grivas, George Theodorus
Cypriot. Military Leader
b. Mar 23, 1898 in Trikomo, Cyprus
d. Jan 27, 1974 in Limassol, Cyprus
Source: *BioIn 5, 6, 7, 10; CurBio 64, 74; NewCol 75; WhoModH*

Grizzard, George
American. Actor
b. Apr 1, 1928 in Roanoke Rapids, North Carolina
Source: *BiE&WWA; FilmgC; IntMPA 82; NewYTBE 72; NotNAT; PlP&P; WhoAm 74, 76, 78, 80, 82; WhoHol A; WhoThe 77; WhoWor 74*

Groat, Dick (Richard Morrow)
American. Baseball Player
b. Nov 4, 1930 in Swissvale, Pennsylvania
Source: *BaseEn; CurBio 61; WhoBbl 73; WhoProB 73*

Grodin, Charles
American. Actor, Director, Writer
b. Apr 21, 1935 in Pittsburgh, Pennsylvania
Source: *BioIn 9, 11; CelR 73; IntMPA 78, 79, 80, 81; NotNAT; WhoAm 74, 76, 80, 82; WhoHol A; WhoThe 77, 81*

Grofe, Ferde
American. Composer
b. Mar 27, 1892 in New York, New York
d. Apr 3, 1972 in Santa Monica, California
Source: *CurBio 40, 72; NewYTBE 72; WebAB; WhAm 5*

Grogan, Emmett
American. Author
b. Nov 28, 1942 in Brooklyn, New York
Source: *ConAu 41R*

Grogan, Steve
American. Football Player
b. Jul 24, 1958 in San Antonio, Texas
Source: *BioIn 11; WhoAm 82*

Grol, Lini Richards
Dutch. Author, Illustrator
b. Oct 7, 1913 in Nijmegen, Netherlands
Source: *ConAu 61; SmATA 9*

Gromyko, Andrei Andreevich
Russian. Diplomat
Minister, Foreign Affairs, 1957--; member of ruling Politburo, 1973--.
b. Jul 5, 1909 in Starye Gromyky, Russia
Source: *CurBio 43, 58; IntWW 74, 75, 76, 77, 78, 79, 80, 81; IntYB 78, 79, 80, 81; Who 74; WhoSocC 78; WhoWor 74, 76, 78*

Gronchi, Giovanni
Italian. Politician
b. Sep 10, 1887 in Pontedera, Italy
d. Oct 17, 1978 in Rome, Italy
Source: *CurBio 55; IntWW 74; Who 74*

Groom, Bob (Robert)
American. Baseball Player
Pitcher, 1909-18.
b. Sep 12, 1884 in Belleville, Illinois
d. Feb 19, 1948 in Belleville, Illinois
Source: *BaseEn; WhoProB 73*

Grooms, "Red" (Charles Roger)
American. Artist
b. Jun 2, 1937 in Nashville, Tennessee
Source: *BioIn 7, 9, 10; ConArt; CurBio 72; DcAmArt; DcCAA 71, 77; WhoAm 74, 76, 78, 80, 82; WhoAmA 73, 76, 78*

Groote, Gerhard
Dutch. Mystic, Religious Reformer
b. 1340 in Deventer, Netherlands
d. 1384
Source: *NewCol 75; WebBD 80*

Gropius, Walter Adolf
German. Architect, Author
Wrote *The New Architecture and the Bauhaus,* tr. 1935.
b. Apr 18, 1883 in Berlin, Germany
d. Jul 5, 1969 in Boston, Massachusetts
Source: *AmAu&B; AtlBL; ConAu 25R; CurBio 41, 52, 69; NewCol 75; REn; WebAB; WhAm 5*

Gropper, William
American. Artist
b. Dec 3, 1897 in New York, New York
d. Jan 6, 1977 in Manhasset, New York
Source: *AmAu&B; Au&Wr 71; CurBio 40; DcCAA 71; IlsCB 1946; IntWW 74; REnAL; WebAB; Who 74; WhoAm 74; WhoAmA 73; WhoWor 74; WhoWorJ 72*

Groppi, James E
American. Political Activist, Priest
b. 1930 in Milwaukee, Wisconsin
Source: *NewCol 75; NewYTBE 70; WhoMW 74*

Gross, Chaim
American. Artist
b. Mar 17, 1904 in Austria
Source: *AmAu&B; CurBio 41, 66; DcCAA 71; NewYTBS 74; WhoAm 74, 76, 78, 80, 82; WhoAmA 73; WhoWor 74; WhoWorJ 72*

Gross, Courtlandt Sherrington
American. Aircraft Corporation Executive
Co-founded, Lockheed Aircraft Corp.
b. Nov 21, 1904 in Boston, Massachusetts
d. Jul 16, 1982 in Villanova, Pennsylvania
Source: *IntWW 74, 75, 76, 77; NewYTBS 82; St&PR 75; WhoAm 74, 76, 78; WhoE 74; WhoF&I 74*

Gross, Milt
American. Author, Cartoonist
b. Mar 4, 1895 in New York, New York
d. Nov 29, 1953
Source: *AmAu&B; DcAmB S5; REnAL; WhAm 3*

Gross, Robert Ellsworth
American. Airplane Manufacturer
Purchased Lockheed Aircraft Corp., 1932; developed Polaris missile.
b. May 11, 1897 in Boston, Massachusetts
d. Sep 3, 1961
Source: *ObitOF 79; WhAm 4*

Grossinger, Jennie
American. Hotel Owner, Manager
Owner, Grossinger's, a Catskill mountain resort.
b. Jun 16, 1892 in Vienna, Austria
d. Nov 20, 1972 in Sullivan County, New York
Source: *CurBio 56, 73; InWom; NewYTBE 72; WhAm 5*

Grosvenor, Gilbert Hovey
American. Geographer
b. Oct 28, 1875 in Constantinople, Turkey
d. Feb 4, 1966 in Baddeck, NS
Source: *AmAu&B; CurBio 46, 66; REnAL; WebAB; WhAm 4; WhNAA*

Grosvenor, Melville Bell
American. Magazine Publisher, Editor
b. Nov 26, 1901 in Washington, DC
d. Apr 22, 1982 in Miami, Florida
Source: *AmAu&B; AmM&WS 73S, 76P; CelR 73; ConAu 69; CurBio 60, 82; IntWW 78, 79; LinLib L, S; WhoAm 74, 76, 78, 80, 82; WhoGov 72, 75, 77; WhoS&SW 73, 75, 76; WhoWor 74, 76*

Grosz, George Ehrenfried
American. Artist
Violent drawings were social critiques.
b. Jul 26, 1893 in Berlin, Germany
d. Jul 6, 1959 in Berlin, Germany (West)
Source: *AmAu&B; AtlBL; CurBio 42, 59; DcCAA 71; OxGer; REn; WhAm 3; WhoGrA*

Grote, George
English. Historian, Philosopher
b. Nov 17, 1794
d. Jun 18, 1871
Source: *Alli, SUP; BbD; BiD&SB; BrAu 19; Chambr 3; DcEnA; DcEnL; DcEuL; DcLEL; EvLB; NewC; NewCol 75; OxEng; Pen ENG; REn*

Groth, John August
American. Artist, Journalist
b. Feb 26, 1908 in Chicago, Illinois
Source: *ConAu 101; CurBio 43; SmATA 21; WhoAm 74, 76, 78, 80, 82; WhoAmA 73*

Grotius, Hugo
Dutch. Jurist, Statesman
b. Apr 10, 1583 in Delft, Netherlands
d. Aug 28, 1645 in Rostock, Germany
Source: *BbD; BiD&SB; CasWL; DcEuL; EuAu; EvEuW; McGEWB; NewC; NewCol 75; OxEng; REn*

Group of Seven
[Frank Carmichael; Lauren Harris; A(lexander) Y(oung) Jackson; Frank; Arthur Lismer; J(ames) E(dward) H(ervey) MacDonald; F(rederick) H(orseman)Varley]
Canadian. Artists
Source: *ClbCR*

Grove, Sir George
English. Author
b. Aug 13, 1820 in Clapham, England
d. May 18, 1900 in London, England
Source: *Alli SUP; BiD&SB; Chambr 3; DcEnL; NewC; NewCol 75; OxEng; REn; WebBD 80*

Grove, "Lefty" (Robert Moses)
"Mose"
American. Baseball Player
Pitcher, 1925-41; struck out 2,266 batters.
b. Mar 6, 1900 in Lonaconing, Maryland
d. May 22, 1975 in Norwalk, Ohio
Source: *BaseEn; BioIn 2, 3, 4, 6, 7, 8, 9, 10; NewCol 75; WhoProB 73*

Grove, Simon
see: Boomtown Rats

Grove, Sir William Robert
Welsh. Physicist
b. Jul 11, 1811 in Swansea, Wales
d. Aug 2, 1896
Source: *AsBiEn; BioIn 7; DcScB; WebBD 80*

Groves, Sir Charles
English. Composer
b. Mar 10, 1915 in London, England
Source: *IntWW 74, 75, 76, 77, 78; Who 74; WhoMus 72; WhoWor 74, 76, 78*

Groves, Leslie Richard
American. Army General
b. Aug 17, 1896 in Albany, New York
d. Jul 13, 1970 in Washington, DC
Source: *CurBio 45, 70; NewYTBE 70; WhAm 5*

Groza, Alex
[Fabulous Five]
American. Basketball Player
b. Oct 7, 1926 in Martins Ferry, Ohio
Source: *WhoBbl 73*

Gruber, Frank
American. Author
b. Feb 2, 1904 in Elmer, Minnesota
d. Dec 9, 1969
Source: *AmAu&B; ConAu 25R; ConAu P-1; CurBio 41, 70; EncMys; FilmgC*

Gruber, Franz
German. Musician, Choir Director
b. 1787 in Germany
d. 1863
Source: *NewCol 75; WebBD 80*

Grubert, Carl Alfred
American. Cartoonist
b. Sep 10, 1911 in Chicago, Illinois
Source: *WhoAm 74; WhoAmA 73*

Gruelle, Johnny (John Barton)
American. Cartoonist, Author
Created *Raggedy Ann,* 1918, *Raggedy Andy,* 1920 series.
b. Dec 24, 1880 in Arcola, Illinois
d. Jan 9, 1938 in Miami Beach, Florida
Source: *AmAu&B; AmSCAP 66; ChPo; FanAl; IndAu 1816; OhA&B; REnAL*

Gruen, Victor
American. Architect
Specialized in planning, building shopping centers in US.
b. Jul 18, 1903 in Vienna, Austria
d. Feb 16, 1980 in Vienna, Austria
Source: *AmArch 70; AnObit 1980; CurBio 59, 80; EncMA; IntAu&W 77; IntWW 74, 75, 76, 77, 78, 79; McGDA; NewCol 75; NewYTBS 80; WhoWor 74, 76, 78; WrDr 76, 80*

Gruenberg, Louis
American. Composer
b. Aug 3, 1884 in Russia
d. Jun 9, 1964 in Beverly Hills, California
Source: *AmSCAP 66; DcCM; NewCol 75; OxAmL; WhAm 4*

Gruenberg, Sidonie Matsner
American. Author, Educator
Wrote *The Wonderful Story of How You Were Born,* 1952.
b. Jun 10, 1881 in Vienna, Austria
d. Mar 11, 1974 in New York, New York
Source: *BioIn 10; ConAu 49; ConAu P-1*

Gruenther, Alfred Maximillian
American. Army Officer, Businessman
b. Mar 3, 1899 in Platte Center, Nebraska
Source: *CurBio 50; IntWW 74; NewCol 75; Who 74; WhoAm 74; WhoGov 72; WhoWor 74*

Grumman, Leroy Randle
American. Aeronautical Engineer
Began Grumman Aircraft, 1929; receipts today total $1.9 billion.
b. Jan 4, 1895 in Huntington, New York
d. Oct 4, 1982 in Manhasset, New York
Source: *CurBio 45, 83; IntWW 74, 75, 76, 77, 78, 79, 80; NewYTBS 82; WebAB; WhoAm 74; WhoWor 74*

Grunewald, Matthias
[Mathis Gothart Nithart]
German. Artist, Architect, Engineer
b. 1470? in Wurzburg, Germany
d. 1528 in Halle, Germany
Source: *AtlBL; NewCol 75; OxGer; REn*

Grundy, Hugh
[The Zombies]
English. Singer, Musician
b. Mar 6, 1945 in Winchester, England
Source: *NF*

Guadagni, Gaetano
Italian. Opera Singer
b. 1725 in Lodi, Italy
d. Nov 1792 in Padua, Italy
Source: *NewEOp 71*

Guardi, Francesco
Italian. Artist
b. Oct 5, 1712 in Venice, Italy
d. Jan 1, 1793 in Venice, Italy
Source: *AtlBL; NewCol 75; REn*

Guardini, Romano
Italian. Catholic Theologian
b. Feb 17, 1885 in Verona, Italy
d. 1968
Source: *CathA 1930*

Guardino, Harry
American. Actor
b. Dec 23, 1925 in New York, New York
Source: *BiE&WWA; FilmgC; IntMPA 75, 76, 77, 78, 79, 80, 81, 82; MovMk; WhoAm 82*

Guare, John
American. Dramatist
Won 1971 Tony for best musical, *Two Gentlemen of Verona.*
b. Feb 5, 1938 in New York, New York
Source: *CelR 73; ConAu 73; ConDr 73, 77; ConLC 8, 14; CurBio 82; NatPD 81; NotNAT; PlP&P A; WhoAm 74, 76, 78, 80, 82; WhoE 74; WhoThe 77, 81; WorAu 1970; WrDr 76, 80*

Guarnieri, Giuseppe Antonio
[Guarneri DelGesu]
Italian. Violin Maker
b. 1687
d. 1745
Source: *BioIn 10; NewCol 75; WebBD 80*

Guarnieri, Johnny (John A)
American. Jazz Musician
b. Mar 23, 1917 in New York, New York
Source: *AmSCAP 66; WhoJazz 72*

Guarrera, Frank
American. Opera Singer
b. Dec 3, 1923 in Philadelphia, Pennsylvania
Source: *WhoAm 74, 76, 78, 80, 82*

Gubitosi, Mickey
see: Our Gang

Gucci, Aldo
Italian. Leather Goods Designer
b. May 26, 1909 in Florence, Italy
Source: *CelR 73; WhoAm 82; WorFshn*

Guccione, Bob (Robert Charles Joseph Edward Sabatini)
American. Publisher
Founded *Penthouse* magazine, 1965, *Viva,* magazine, 1973.
b. Dec 17, 1930 in Brooklyn, New York
Source: *CelR 73; WhoAm 82*

Guderian, Heinz
German. Tank Theorist
b. 1888
d. 1953
Source: *BioIn 1, 3, 10, 11; EncTR; WhWW-II; WhoMilH 76*

Gueden, Hilde
Austrian. Opera Singer
b. Sep 15, 1917 in Vienna, Austria
Source: *CurBio 55; WhoMus 72; WhoWor 74*

Guenther, Charles John
American. Librarian, Author
b. Apr 29, 1920 in Saint Louis, Missouri
Source: *BiDrLUS 70; ConAu 29R; DrAP 75; WhoAm 74, 76, 78, 80, 82; WrDr 76*

Guerard, Albert Joseph
American. Author, Educator
b. Nov 2, 1914 in Houston, Texas
Source: *AmAu&B; ConAu 1R, 2NR; ConNov 72, 76; DrAF 76; DrAS 74E; OxAmL; TwCA SUP; WhoAm 74, 76, 78, 80, 82; WhoWest 74; WrDr 76*

Guercino
[Giovanni Francesco Barbieri]
Italian. Artist
b. 1591 in Cento, Italy
d. 1666 in Bologna, Italy
Source: *AtlBL; McGDA; McGEWB; NewCol 75; WebBD 80*

Guerin, Jules
American. Artist
b. 1866 in Saint Louis, Missouri
d. Jun 13, 1946 in Neptune, New Jersey
Source: *ChPo; NewCol 75; WhAm 2*

Guerlain, Pierre Francois Pascal
French. Perfume Manufacturer
b. 1798
d. 1864
Source: *WebBD 80*

Guerrero, Pedro
Dominican. Baseball Player
b. Jun 2, 1956 in San Pedro, Dominican Republic
Source: *BaseEn*

Guess Who
[Randy Bachman; Burton Cummings; James Kale; Garry Peterson;]
Canadian. Rock Group
Source: *EncPR&S*

Guest, Edgar A(lbert)
American. Author, Journalist, Poet
Started with Detroit *Free Press,* 1895; hosted radio show, 1931-42.
b. Aug 20, 1881 in Birmingham, England
d. Aug 5, 1959 in Detroit, Michigan
Source: *AmAu&B; ChPo, S1, S2; CnE&AP; CurBio 41, 59; OxAmL; Pen AM; REn; REnAL; WebAB; WhAm 3; WhNAA*

Guest, Judith
American. Author
Wrote *Ordinary People,* 1976; made into Oscar winning movie, 1980.
b. Mar 29, 1936 in Detroit, Michigan
Source: *ConAu 77; ConLC 8; WhoAm 82*

Guevara, Che Ernesto
Argentine. Revolutionary
b. Jun 14, 1928 in Rosario, Argentina
d. Oct 8, 1967 in Bolivia
Source: *CurBio 63, 67*

Guevara Arze, Walter
Bolivian. President
b. 1912
Source: *BioIn 12; IntWW 74; WhoGov 72; WhoWor 74*

Guggenheim, Daniel
American. Financier, Philanthropist
b. 1856 in Philadelphia, Pennsylvania
d. Sep 28, 1930
Source: *AmBi; DcAmB; EncAB-H; NewCol 75; WebAB; WhAm 1*

Guggenheim, Harry Frank
American. Industrialist, Publisher
b. Aug 23, 1890 in West End, New Jersey
d. Jan 22, 1971 in Sands Point, New York
Source: *ConAu 89; CurBio 56, 71; NewCol 75; NewYTBE 71*

Guggenheim, Meyer
American. Industrialist, Philanthropist
b. Feb 1, 1828 in Langnau, Switzerland
d. Mar 15, 1905 in Palm Beach, Florida
Source: *AmBi; DcAmB; WebAB; WebBD 80*

Guggenheim, Peggy Marguerite
American. Art Patron, Socialite
Collected 20th c. art; patron to Jackson Pollock, Robert Motherwell.
b. Aug 26, 1898 in New York, New York
d. Dec 23, 1979 in Venice, Italy
Source: *Au&Wr 71; CelR 73; CurBio 62; InWom; IntWW 74; NewYTBS 74; WhoAm 74; WhoAmA 73; WhoWor 74*

Guggenheim, Solomon Robert
American. Philanthropist
b. Feb 2, 1861 in Philadelphia, Pennsylvania
d. Nov 3, 1949 in Sands Point, New York
Source: *DcAmB S4; NewCol 75; WhAm 2*

Guggenheimer, Minnie
American. Philanthropist, Music Patron
b. Oct 22, 1882 in New York, New York
d. May 23, 1966 in New York, New York
Source: *CurBio 62, 66; WhAm 4*

Gui, Vittorio
Italian. Opera Conductor
b. Sep 14, 1885 in Rome, Italy
d. Oct 16, 1975 in Florence, Italy
Source: *IntWW 74; Who 74; WhoMus 72*

Guicciardini, Francesco
Italian. Historian, Statesman
b. Mar 6, 1483 in Florence, Italy
d. May 1540 in Florence, Italy
Source: *BiD&SB; CasWL; DcEuL; EuAu; EvEuW; NewC; OxEng; Pen EUR; REn*

Guidry, Ron(ald Ames)
American. Baseball Player
Pitcher, NY Yankees, 1975--; won Cy Young Award, 1978.
b. Aug 28, 1950 in Lafayette, Louisiana
Source: *BaseEn; BioIn 11; WhoAm 82*

Guilbert, Yvette
French. Singer
b. 1867 in Paris, France
d. Feb 2, 1944 in Aix-en-Provence, France
Source: *EncWT; Film 2; InWom; NotNAT B; OxThe; WhAm 4; WhThe*

Guillaume, Gunter
German. Spy
Source: *BioIn 10*

Guillaume, Robert
[Robert Peter Williams]
American. Actor
Star of TV series "Benson."
b. Nov 30, 1928 in Saint Louis, Missouri
Source: *BioIn 11; IntMPA 82*

Guillemin, Roger
French. Physiologist
b. Jan 11, 1924 in Dijon, France
Source: *AmM&WS 73P; WhoAm 74, 76, 78, 80, 82*

Guillotin, Joseph Ignace
French. Physician
Proposed all capital punishment be by decapitation; name used for machine, the guillotine.
b. May 28, 1738 in Saintes, France
d. Mar 26, 1814 in Paris, France
Source: *NewC*

Guinan, "Texas" (Mary Louise Cecelia)
American. Actress, Nightclub Performer
b. 1889? in Waco, Texas
d. Nov 5, 1933 in Vancouver, BC
Source: *Film 1; InWom; NotAW; TwYS; WhScrn 74, 77; WhoHol B*

Guiney, Louise
American. Poet, Essayist
b. 1861 in Boston, Massachusetts
d. Nov 2, 1920 in Chipping Camden, England
Source: *AmBi; BioIn 10; DcAmB; WhAm 1*

Guinness, Sir Alec
English. Actor
Played Obi-Wan Kenobi in *Star Wars* ; said "May the force be with you."
b. Apr 2, 1914 in London, England
Source: *BiDFilm; BiE&WWA; BkPepl; CelR 73; CmMov; CurBio 50; FamA&A; FilmgC; IntMPA 75, 76, 77, 78, 79, 80, 81, 82; IntWW 74; MotPP; MovMk; NewC; NewYTBE 72; NotNAT; OxFilm; OxThe; PlP&P; REn; Who 74; WhoAm 82; WhoHol A; WhoThe 77; WhoWor 74; WorEFlm*

Guion, Connie Myers
American. Physician
b. Aug 9, 1882 in Lincolnton, North Carolina
d. Apr 29, 1971
Source: *BioIn 2, 6, 7, 9, 11; CurBio 62*

Guion, David Wendel Fentress
American. Composer, Author, Musician
b. Dec 15, 1892 in Ballinger, Texas
d. Oct 17, 1981 in Dallas, Texas
Source: *AmSCAP 66; BioIn 1, 6, 7; OxAmL*

Guiscard, Robert
see: Robert Guiscard

Guisewite, Cathy Lee
American. Cartoonist
b. Sep 5, 1950 in Dayton, Ohio
Source: *BioIn 11; WhoAm 80, 82*

Guiteau, Charles Julius
American. Murderer
Shot, killed James Garfield, Washington, DC, Jul 2, 1881; hanged.
b. 1844 in Illinois
d. Jun 30, 1882 in Washington, DC
Source: *Alli SUP; WhAm H*

Guiterman, Arthur
American. Author
b. Nov 20, 1871 in Vienna, Austria
d. Jan 11, 1943
Source: *AmAu&B; AmLY; ChPo, S1, S2; CnDAL; DcNAA; EvLB; OxAmL; REn; REnAL; Str&VC; TwCA, SUP; WhAm 2; WhNAA*

Guitry, Sacha
French. Director, Actor, Dramatist
b. Feb 21, 1885 in Saint Petersburg, Russia
d. Jul 24, 1957 in Paris, France
Source: *BiDFilm; CasWL; ClDMEL; CnMD; DcFM; EvEuW; FilmgC; McGEWD; ModWD; MovMk; OxFilm; OxFr; OxThe; Pen EUR; PlP&P; REn; TwCA, SUP; WhScrn 74, 77; WhoHol B; WorEFlm*

Guizot, Francois Pierre
French. Historian, Statesman
b. 1787 in Nimes, France
d. 1874 in Normandy, France
Source: *BbD; DcEuL; EvEuW; NewC; NewCol 75; OxEng; OxFr; REn*

Gulbenkian, Calouste S
Armenian. Art, Oil Magnate
b. 1869
d. Oct 20, 1955 in Lisbon, Portugal
Source: *BioNews 74; BusPN*

Gulbenkian, Nubar Sarkis
Iranian. Financier
b. 1896
d. Jan 10, 1972
Source: *NewYTBE 72*

Gulda, Friedrich
Austrian. Musician
b. 1930
Source: *WhoMus 72*

Gulick, Luther Halsey
American. Educator, Physician
Founded Camp Fire Girls with wife Charlotte, 1910; helped develop basketball.
b. Dec 4, 1865 in Honolulu, Hawaii
d. Aug 13, 1918 in South Casco, Maine
Source: *AmAu&B; AmBi; BiDAmEd; BioIn 5, 9, 10, 11; DcAmB; NatCAB 26; WebAB; WhAm 1; WhoBbl 73*

Gumbel, Bryant Charles
American. Broadcast Journalist
Hosted "NBC Sports," 1975-82; won Emmys 1976, 1977; host, "Today Show," 1982--.
b. Sep 29, 1948 in New Orleans, Louisiana
Source: *WhoAm 82; WhoBlA 77, 80*

Gumbleton, Thomas
American. Bishop
b. 1930
Source: *BioIn 10*

Gumede, Josiah Zion
Zimbabwean. Statesman
b. Sep 19, 1919
Source: *AfSS 79; IntWW 79, 80; WhoWor 80*

Gumilev, Nikolai
Russian. Poet
b. 1886
d. 1921
Source: *NewCol 75*

Gunn, Moses
American. Actor
b. Oct 2, 1929 in Saint Louis, Missouri
Source: *IntMPA 75, 76, 77, 78, 79, 80, 81, 82; WhoAm 74, 76, 78, 80, 82; WhoBlA 75; WhoHol A; WhoThe 77*

Gunn, Thom
English. Poet
b. Aug 29, 1929 in Gravesend, England
Source: *AmAu&B; Au&Wr 71; CasWL; ChPo, S1, S2; ConAu 17R; ConLC 3, 6, 18; ConP 70, 75; DrAP 75; IntWW 74; LongCTC; ModBrL, SUP; Pen ENG; RAdv 1; REn; TwCW; WebE&AL; WhoAm 74, 76, 78, 80, 82; WhoTwCL; WorAu; WrDr 76*

Gunther, John
American. Journalist, Author
Wrote *Inside Europe,* 1936; *Death Be Not Proud,* 1949.
b. Aug 30, 1901 in Chicago, Illinois
d. May 29, 1970 in New York, New York
Source: *AmAu&B; AmNov; AuBYP; ConAu 9R, 25R; CurBio 41, 61, 70; EvLB; LongCTC; NewYTBE 70; OxAmL; Pen AM; REn; REnAL; SmATA 2; TwCA, SUP; WebAB; WhAm 6*

Gunzberg, Nicolas de, Baron
"Nicky"
American. Fashion Editor
b. 1904 in Paris, France
d. Feb 20, 1981 in New York, New York
Source: *NewYTBS 81; WorFshn*

Guptill, Arthur Leighton
American. Publisher, Author
b. Mar 19, 1891 in Gorham, Maine
d. Feb 29, 1956 in Stamford, Connecticut
Source: *CurBio 55, 56; WhAm 3; WhNAA*

Gurdjieff, Georges Ivanovitch
Armenian. Mystic, Author, Explorer
b. 1872
d. Oct 28, 1949 in Paris, France
Source: *BioIn 10*

Gurie, Sigrid
American. Actress
b. 1911 in Brooklyn, New York
d. Aug 14, 1969 in Mexico City, Mexico
Source: *FilmgC; ThFT; WhScrn 74, 77*

Gurion, David Ben
see: Ben-Gurion, David

Gurney, Dan
American. Automobile Racer
b. Apr 13, 1931
Source: *BioNews 74; WhoAm 82*

Gurney, Edward John
American. Politician, Lawyer
b. Jan 12, 1914 in Portland, Maine
Source: *BiDrAC; BioNews 74; CngDr 74; IntWW 74; WhoAm 74, 76, 78, 80, 82; WhoAmP 73; WhoGov 72; WhoS&SW 73*

Gusberg, Saul Bernard
American. Physician, Educator
b. Aug 3, 1913 in Newark, New Jersey
Source: *AmM&WS 73P; WhoAm 78, 80, 82*

Gustaf VI
Swedish. King
b. Nov 11, 1882 in Stockholm, Sweden
d. 1973 in Helsingborg, Sweden
Source: *BioIn 10; ConAu 45; NewCol 75*

Gustafson, John
see: Roxy Music

Gustavus Adolphus
Swedish. King
b. Dec 9, 1594 in Stockholm, Sweden
d. Nov 16, 1632 in Lutzen, Germany
Source: *NewC; NewCol 75; OxGer*

Guston, Philip
Canadian. Artist
b. Jun 27, 1913 in Montreal, PQ
d. Jun 7, 1980 in Woodstock, New York
Source: *CurBio 71; DcCAA 71; NewCol 75; WhAm 7; WhoAm 74; WhoAmA 73; WhoWor 74*

Gutenberg, Johannes
German. Inventor
Believed to be first European to print using moveable type, circa 1454.
b. Feb 23, 1400? in Mainz, Germany
d. Feb 1468?
Source: *NewC; NewCol 75; OxGer; REn*

Gutfreund, Yosef
Israeli. Murdered Olympic Team Member
b. 1931? in Romania
d. Sep 5, 1972 in Munich, Germany (West)
Source: *NF*

Guthrie, A(lfred) B(ertram), Jr.
American. Journalist, Author
b. Jan 13, 1901 in Bedford, Indiana
Source: *AmAu&B; AmNov; CnDAL; ConAu 57; ConNov 72, 76; CyWA; DcLEL; DrAF 76; IndAu 1917; ModAL; OxAmL; REnAL; TwCA SUP; WhoAm 74, 82; WhoPNW; WhoWest 74; WhoWor 74; WrDr 76*

Guthrie, Arlo
American. Singer
Son of Woody Guthrie; best known for hit "Alice's Restaurant," 1969.
b. Jul 10, 1947 in Brooklyn, New York
Source: *AmAu&B; BkPepl; CelR 73; EncFCWM 69; WhoAm 74, 76, 78, 80, 82*

Guthrie, Janet
American. Auto Racer
First woman to qualify and drive in Indianapolis 500, 1977.
b. Mar 7, 1938 in Iowa City, Iowa
Source: *BioIn 10; WhoAm 82*

Guthrie, Samuel
American. Physician
Discovered chloroform, 1831.
b. 1782 in Brimfield, Massachusetts
d. Oct 19, 1848 in Sackets Harbor, New York
Source: *AmBi; ApCAB; AsBiEn; BiDAmS; DcAmB; DcNAA; Drake; LinLib S; NatCAB; NewCol 75; TwCBDA; WhAm H*

Guthrie, Tyrone
English. Theatrical Director
b. Jul 2, 1900 in Tunbridge Wells, England
d. May 15, 1971 in Newbliss, Ireland
Source: *BiE&WWA; CreCan 1; ConAu 29R; CurBio 54, 71; NewC; NewYTBE 71; OxThe; PlP&P; WhoHol B*

Guthrie, Woody (Woodrow Wilson)
American. Singer, Musician
b. Jul 14, 1912 in Okemah, Oklahoma
d. Oct 4, 1967 in New York, New York
Source: *ConAu 93; CurBio 63, 67; EncAB-H; EncFCWM 69; WebAB; WhAm 4*

Guy, Rosa Cuthbert
American. Author
b. Sep 1, 1928 in Trinidad
Source: *BlkAW; ConAu 17R; SmATA 14*

Guy, (William) Ray
American. Football Player
b. Dec 22, 1949 in Swainsboro, Georgia
Source: *BioIn 9, 11; FootReg; WhoFtbl 74*

Guy-Blanche, Alice
French. Motion Picture Director
b. Jul 1, 1873 in Paris, France
d. 1968 in Mahwah, New Jersey
Source: *DcFM; FilmEn; FilmgC; MovMk; OxFilm*

Guyer, Tennyson
American. Congressman
b. Nov 29, 1913 in Findlay, Ohio
d. Apr 12, 1981 in Alexandria, Virginia
Source: *CngDr 74, 77, 79; WhoAm 74, 76, 78, 80; WhoAmP 73, 75, 77, 79; WhoGov 75, 77*

Guyon, Joe
American. Football Player
b. Nov 26, 1892 in Mahnomen, Minnesota
d. Nov 27, 1971
Source: *BioIn 8, 9; WhoFtbl 74*

Guzman, Antonio
[Silvestre Antonio Guzman Fernandez]
Dominican. President
b. Feb 12, 1911 in La Vega, Dominican Republic
d. Jul 4, 1982 in Santo Domingo, Dominican Republic
Source: *BioIn 12; IntWW 80; WhoWor 78, 80*

Guzman, Nuno Beltran de
Spanish. Conquistador
d. 1544
Source: *ApCAB; NewCol 75*

Gwenn, Edmund
Welsh. Actor
b. Sep 26, 1875 in Glamorgan, Wales
d. Sep 6, 1959 in Woodland Hills, California
Source: *BiDFilm; CurBio 43, 59; Film 1; FilmgC; MotPP; MovMk; OxFilm; Vers A; WhScrn 74, 77; WhoHol B*

Gwilym, Mike
Welsh. Actor
b. Mar 5, 1949 in Neath, Wales
Source: *BioIn 11; WhoThe 77, 81*

Gwinnett, Button
American. Revolutionary Patriot
b. 1735 in Gloucester, England
d. May 19, 1777 in Savannah, Georgia
Source: *AmBi; ApCAB; BiAuS; BiDrAC; DcAmB; Drake; TwCBDA; WebAB; WhAm H; WhAmP*

Gwyn, Nell (Eleanor)
English. Actress, Mistress-Charles II
b. 1650 in Hereford, England
d. Nov 13, 1687 in London, England
Source: *InWom; NewC; NotNAT B; REn*

H

Ha-Levi, Judah
[Judah Ha-Levi]
Spanish. Rabbi, Poet
b. 1085
d. 1140
Source: *CasWL*

Haakon VII
Norwegian. King
b. Aug 3, 1872
d. Sep 21, 1957 in Oslo, Norway
Source: *CurBio 40, 57*

Haas, Karl
American. Musician, Music Critic
b. May 15, in Speyer, Germany
Source: *BioNews 74*

Haas, Walter A(braham), Jr.
American. Business Executive
b. Jan 24, 1916 in San Francisco, California
Source: *BioIn 5; WhoAm 74; WhoF&I 74, 75, 77*

Haas, Walter A(braham), Sr.
American. Business Executive
b. 1899 in San Francisco, California
d. Dec 7, 1979 in San Francisco, California
Source: *NewYTBS 79; St&PR 75; WhAm 7; WhoAm 74, 76, 78; WhoF&I 74, 75, 77; WhoWorJ 72*

Habberton, John
American. Author
b. Feb 24, 1842 in Brooklyn, New York
d. Feb 24, 1921
Source: *Alli SUP; AmAu; AmAu&B; AmBi; ApCAB; BbD; BiD&SB; CarSB; Chambr 3; DcAmAu; DcAmB; DcBiA; DcEnL; DcNAA; EvLB; OxAmL; REnAL; TwCBDA; WhAm 1; WhoChL*

Haber, Joyce
[Joyce Haber Cramer]
American. Journalist
b. Dec 28, 1932 in New York, New York
Source: *CelR 73; ConAu 65; IntMPA 76, 77, 78, 79, 80, 81, 82; WhoAm 82*

Habib, Philip Charles
American. Diplomat
Ambassador to Korea, 1971-74; special Middle East envoy, 1981--.
b. Feb 25, 1920 in Brooklyn, New York
Source: *BioIn 11; CurBio 81; FarE&A 78, 79; IntWW 78; PolProf J; USBiR 74; WhoAm 74, 76, 78, 80, 82; WhoAmP 75, 77, 79; WhoGov 72, 75, 77; WhoWor 74, 76*

Habre, Hissein
Chadian. Prime Minister
Source: *BioIn 11*

Habyarimana, Juvenal
Rwandan. President
b. Aug 3, 1937 in Gasiza, Rwanda
Source: *IntWW 74, 75, 76, 77, 78, 79, 80, 81*

Hack, Shelley
American. Model, Actress
Revlon's "Charlie Girl" in TV commercials; "Charlie's Angels," 1979.
b. Jul 6, 1952 in Connecticut
Source: *BioIn 11, 12; IntMPA 82; WhoAm 80, 82*

Hackett, Albert
American. Actor, Author
b. Feb 16, 1900 in New York, New York
Source: *AmAu&B; AuBYP; BiE&WWA; CmMov; CurBio 56; Film 1; FilmgC; ModWD; NotNAT; OxAmL; REnAL; TwYS; WhoAm 74; WorEFlm*

Hackett, Bobby (Robert Leo)
American. Jazz Musician
b. Jan 31, 1915 in Providence, Rhode Island
d. Jun 7, 1976 in Chatham, Massachusetts
Source: *WhoAm 74; WhoJazz 72*

Hackett, Buddy
[Leonard Hacker]
American. Comedian
Starred in *God's Little Acre,* 1958, and *The Love Bug,* 1969.
b. Aug 11, 1924 in New York, New York
Source: *AmSCAP 66; BiE&WWA; CelR 73; CurBio 65; FilmgC; IntMPA 75, 76, 77, 78, 79, 80, 81, 82; MotPP; MovMk; WhoAm 74, 76, 78, 80, 82; WhoHol A*

Hackett, Charles
American. Opera Singer
b. Nov 4, 1889 in Worcester, Massachusetts
d. Jan 1, 1942 in New York, New York
Source: *CurBio 42; WhAm 1*

Hackett, Joan
American. Actress
b. Mar 1, 1942 in New York, New York
Source: *BiE&WWA; FilmgC; ForWC 70; IntMPA 77, 78, 79, 80, 81, 82; MotPP; MovMk; NewYTBE 72; NotNAT; WhoAm 82; WhoHol A*

Hackett, Raymond
American. Actor
b. Jul 15, 1902 in New York, New York
d. Jun 9, 1958 in Hollywood, California
Source: *Film 1; FilmgC; MotPP; WhScrn 74, 77; WhoHol B*

Hackett, Steve
see: Genesis

Hackman, Gene (Eugene Alden)
American. Actor
Won Oscar for *The French Connection,* 1972.
b. Jan 30, 1931 in San Bernardino, California
Source: *BioNews 74; BkPepl; CmMov; CurBio 72; FilmgC; IntMPA 75, 76, 77, 78, 79, 80, 81, 82; MovMk; NewYTBE 71; OxFilm; WhoAm 74, 76, 78, 80, 82; WhoHol A*

Haden, Pat(rick Capper)
American. Football Player, Scholar
b. Jan 23, 1953 in Westbury, New York
Source: *BioIn 11; WhoAm 82*

Hadley, Henry Kimball
American. Composer
b. Dec 20, 1871 in Somerville, Massachusetts
d. Sep 6, 1937 in New York, New York
Source: *AmBi; AmSCAP 66; DcAmB S2; WhAm 1*

Hadley, Reed
American. Actor
b. 1911 in Petralia, Texas
d. Dec 11, 1974 in Los Angeles, California
Source: *FilmgC; Vers B; WhScrn 77; WhoHol B*

Hadrian
[Publius Aelius Hadrianus]
Roman. Emperor
b. 76 in Rome, Italy
d. 138
Source: *CasWL; NewC; Pen CL; REn*

Haeckel, Ernst
German. Zoologist
b. Feb 15, 1834 in Germany
d. Aug 8, 1919
Source: *BioIn 9*

Haenigsen, Harry William
American. Cartoonist
b. Jul 14, 1902 in New York, New York
Source: *AmAu&B; WhoAm 74*

Hafey, "Chick" (Charles James)
American. Baseball Player
b. Feb 12, 1903 in Berkeley, California
d. Jul 5, 1973 in Calistoga, California
Source: *BaseEn; WhoProB 73*

Hafiz, Shams-al-Din Muhammad
Persian. Poet
b. 1320 in Persia
d. 1389
Source: *CasWL; OxEng; Pen CL; RComWL*

Hagan, Cliff
"Lil Abner"
American. Basketball PLayer, Coach
b. Sep 12, 1931 in Owensboro, Kentucky
Source: *WhoBbl 73*

Hagedorn, Hermann
American. Author, Poet
b. Jul 18, 1882 in New York, New York
d. Jul 27, 1964 in Santa Barbara, California
Source: *AmAu&B; AmLY; ChPo, S1, S2; ConAmL; OxAmL; REnAL; TwCA, SUP; WhAm 4*

Hagen, Jean
American. Actress
b. 1924 in Chicago, Illinois
d. 1977 in Woodland Hills, California
Source: *FilmgC; IntMPA 75, 76, 77; MotPP; MovMk; WhoHol A*

Hagen, Uta Thyra
American. Actress
b. Jun 12, 1919 in Goettingen, Germany
Source: *BiE&WWA; CurBio 63; InWom; IntWW 74; NotNAT; PlP&P; WhoAm 74, 76, 78, 80, 82; WhoE 74; WhoHol A; WhoThe 77; WhoWor 74*

Hagen, Walter Charles
"The Haig"
American. Golfer
Won PGA championship five times; British Open four times.
b. Dec 21, 1892 in New York, New York
d. Oct 5, 1969 in Traverse City, Michigan
Source: *NewCol 75; WebAB; WhoGolf*

Hagerty, James Campbell
American. Radio, TV Executive
b. May 9, 1909 in Plattsburg, New York
d. Apr 11, 1981 in Bronxville, New York
Source: *BioIn 3, 4, 5, 6, 8, 11; CurBio 53, 81; IntWW 74, 75, 76, 77, 78; PolProf E; St&PR 75; Who 74; WhoAm 74, 76, 78; WhoF&I 74; WhoWor 74*

Hagg, Gunder
Swedish. Athlete
b. Dec 31, 1918 in Sorbygden, Sweden
Source: *WhoTr&F 73*

Haggard, Sir Henry Rider
English. Author, Lawyer
Wrote *King Solomon's Mines,* 1885; *Allan Quatermain,* and *She,* 1887.
b. Jun 22, 1856 in Norfolk, England
d. May 14, 1925 in London, England
Source: *Alli SUP; BbD; BiD&SB; Chambr 3; CyWA; DcBiA; DcEnA AP; DcEuL; DcLEL; EvLB; LongCTC; MnBBF; ModBrL; NewC; OxEng; Pen ENG; REn; TwCA, SUP; WebE&AL; WhoChL*

Haggard, Merle Ronald
American. Singer
b. Apr 6, 1937 in Bakersfield, California
Source: *CelR 73; EncFCWM 69; WhoAm 74, 76, 78, 80, 82; WhoE 74; WhoHol A; WhoThe 77; WhoWor 74*

Haggart, Bob
[Robert Sherwood]
American. Composer, Musician
b. Mar 13, 1914 in New York, New York
Source: *CmpEPM; WhoJazz 72*

Haggerty, Dan
American. Actor
b. Nov 19, 1941 in Hollywood, California
Source: *BioIn 11; WhoAm 78, 80, 82*

Hagerty, James Campbell
American. Television Executive
b. May 9, 1909 in Plattsburg, New York
d. Apr 11, 1981 in Bronxville, New York
Source: *BioIn 3, 4, 5, 6, 8, 11; CurBio 53, 81; IntWW 74, 75, 76, 77, 78; PolProf E; St&PR 75; Who 74; WhoAm 74, 76, 78; WhoF&I 74; WhoWor 74*

Haggerty, Sandra Clark
American. Journalist
b. Jul 26, 1939 in Oakley, Kansas
Source: *WhoAm 74*

Hagler, Marvelous Marvin
American. Boxer
WBA, WBC middleweight champ, 1980--.
b. May 23, 1952 in Newark, New Jersey
Source: *BioIn 11; NewYTBS 81*

Hagman, Larry
American. Actor
Starred in "I Dream of Jeannie," 1965-68; plays J R Ewing on "Dallas," 1978--.
b. Sep 21, 1931 in Fort Worth, Texas
Source: *BioIn 12; CurBio 80; FilmgC; IntMPA 82; WhoAm 80, 82; WhoHol A*

Hagopian, Louis Thomas
American. Advertising Executive
b. Jun 1, 1925 in Pontiac, Michigan
Source: *WhoAm 74, 76, 78, 80, 82; WhoE 74; WhoF&I 74*

Hague, Frank
American. Politician
b. Jan 17, 1876 in Jersey City, New Jersey
d. Jan 1, 1956 in Jersey City, New Jersey
Source: *WhAm 3*

Hahn, Emily
American. Author
b. Jan 14, 1905 in Saint Louis, Missouri
Source: *AmAu&B; AuBYP; ConAu 1R, 1NR; LongCTC; REnAL; SmATA 3; TwCA SUP; WhNAA; WhoAm 74, 76, 78, 80, 82; WhoAmW 77; WhoE 74; WhoWor 74*

Hahn, Otto
German. Physicist
b. Mar 8, 1879 in Frankfurt, Germany
d. Jul 28, 1968 in Goettingen, Germany (West)
Source: *CurBio 51, 68; REn; WhAm 5*

Hahnemann, (Christian Friedrich) Samuel
German. Founder of Homeopathy
Wrote *Organon of the Rational Art of Healing,* 1810.
b. Apr 10, 1755 in Meissen, Germany
d. Jul 2, 1843
Source: *NewCol 75; WebBD 80*

Haid, Charles
American. Actor
Plays Andy Renko on TV series "Hill Street Blues," 1981--.
b. 1944?
Source: *NF*

Haig, Alexander Meigs, Jr.
American. General, Government Official
Commander in Chief, US European Command, 1974-78; Secretary of State, 1981-82.
b. Dec 2, 1924 in Philadelphia, Pennsylvania
Source: *BioNews 74; CurBio 73; IntWW 74; NewYTBE 71, 73; WhoAm 74, 76, 78, 80, 82; WhoAmP 73; WhoS&SW 73*

Haig, Douglas
Scottish. Field Marshal
b. 1861 in Edinburgh, Scotland
d. 1928
Source: *WebBD 80; WhoModH*

Haigh, Kenneth
English. Actor
b. 1932 in Mexboro, England
Source: *BiE&WWA; NotNAT; PlP&P; WhoHol A; WhoThe 77*

Haile Selassie I
[Lij Tafari Makonnen]
Ethiopian. Emperor
b. Jul 23, 1892
d. Aug 27, 1975 in Addis Ababa, Ethiopia
Source: *BioIn 1, 2, 3, 4, 5, 6, 7, 8, 9, 10, 11; CurBio 41, 54, 75; IntWW 74; Who 74; WhoGov 72; WhoWor 74*

Hailey, Arthur
Canadian. Author
Wrote *Hotel,* 1965; *Airport,* 1968; *Wheels,* 1971.
b. Apr 5, 1920 in Luton, England
Source: *AmAu&B; Au&Wr 71; AuNews 2; CanWW 82; CanWr; ConAu 1R, 2NR; ConLC 5; ConNov 72, 76; CreCan 2; IntWW 74; OxCan; WhoAm 82; WhoE 74; WhoWor 74; WrDr 76*

Haines, Connie
[Yvonne Marie Jamais]
American. Singer
b. 1923
Source: *InWom; WhoHol A*

Haines, Jesse Joseph
"Pop"
American. Baseball Player
b. Jul 22, 1893 in Clayton, Ohio
d. Aug 5, 1978 in Dayton, Ohio
Source: *BaseEn; WhoProB 73*

Haines, Robert Terrel
American. Actor, Motion Picture Director
b. Feb 3, 1870 in Muncie, Indiana
d. May 6, 1943 in New York, New York
Source: *Film 1; TwYS; WhAm 5; WhScrn 74, 77; WhoStg 1906, 1908*

Haines, William
American. Actor, Interior Decorator
b. 1900
d. Nov 26, 1973 in Santa Monica, California
Source: *FilmgC; MotPP; MovMk; TwYS; WhScrn 77; WhoHol B*

Haire, Bill
American. Fashion Designer
b. Sep 30, 1936
Source: *WhoAm 82; WorFshn*

Haise, Fred W
American. Astronaut
Crew member, Apollo 13, 1970; Apollo 16, 1972.
b. Nov 14, 1933 in Biloxi, Mississippi
Source: *AmM&WS 73P; IntWW 74; WhoAm 74, 76, 78, 80, 82; WhoGov 72; WhoS&SW 73*

Haitink, Bernard
Dutch. Symphony Conductor
b. Mar 4, 1929 in Amsterdam, Netherlands
Source: *IntWW 74; Who 74; WhoMus 72; WhoWor 74*

Hakluyt, Richard
English. Geographer
b. 1552
d. Nov 23, 1616 in London, England
Source: *Alli; AnCL; AtlBL; BiD&SB; BiDSA; BrAu; CasWL; Chambr 1; CroE&S; CyWA; DcEnA; DcEnL; DcEuL; DcLEL; EvLB; NewC; OxAmL; OxCan; OxEng; Pen ENG; REn; REnAL; WebE&AL; WhAm H*

Halaby, Lisa
see: Nur el Hussein

Halaby, Najeeb E
American. Airline Executive
President, Halaby International Corp, 1973--.
b. Nov 19, 1915 in Dallas, Texas
Source: *CurBio 61; IntWW 74; Ward 77; WhoAm 74, 76, 78, 80, 82; WhoE 74; WhoF&I 74; WhoWor 74*

Halas, George Stanley
American. Football Coach
b. Feb 2, 1895 in Chicago, Illinois
Source: *CelR 73; EncAB-H; St&PR 75; WebAB; WhoAm 74, 76, 78, 80, 82; WhoFtbl 74*

Halasz, Gyula
see: Brassai

Halasz, Laszlo
Hungarian. Conductor, Opera Manager
b. Jun 6, 1905 in Debrecen, Hungary
Source: *CurBio 49; WhoAm 82*

Halberstam, David
American. Journalist
b. Apr 10, 1934 in New York, New York
Source: *CelR 73; ConAu 69; CurBio 73; WhoAm 74, 76, 78, 80, 82; WhoWor 74; WrDr 76*

Halberstam, Michael Joseph
American. Cardiologist, Author
b. Aug 9, 1932 in Bronx, New York
d. Dec 5, 1980 in Washington, DC
Source: *AmM&WS 79P; ConAu 65, 102; WhAm 7; WhoAm 76, 78, 80*

Haldane, J(ohn) B(urdon) S(anderson)
English. Scientist
Best known for work in genetics; helped develop heart-lung machine.
b. Nov 5, 1892 in Oxford, England
d. Dec 1, 1964 in Bhubaneswar, India
Source: *McGEWB; WebBD 80*

Haldeman, H(arry) R(obert)
American. Watergate Participant
Convicted for involvement in Watergate, 1975; jailed, 1977-78.
b. Oct 27, 1926 in Los Angeles, California
Source: *NewYTBE 72, 73; NewYTBS 74; WhoAm 74, 76, 78, 80, 82; WhoAmP 73; WhoGov 72; WhoS&SW 73; WhoWor 74*

Haldeman-Julius, Emanuel
American. Publisher
b. Jul 30, 1889 in Philadelphia, Pennsylvania
d. Jul 31, 1951 in Girard, Kansas
Source: *DcAmB S5; WebAB*

Hale, Alan
American. Actor
b. Feb 10, 1892 in Washington, DC
d. Jan 22, 1950 in Hollywood, California
Source: *CmMov; Film 1; FilmgC; IntMPA 82; MotPP; MovMk; TwYS; Vers A; WhScrn 74, 77; WhoHol A*

Hale, Alan, Jr.
American. Actor
b. 1918
Source: *FilmgC; IntMPA 75, 76, 77, 78, 79, 80, 81; WhoHol A*

Hale, Barbara
American. Actress
b. Apr 18, 1922 in DeKalb, Illinois
Source: *FilmgC; IntMPA 75, 76, 77, 78, 79, 80, 81, 82; MotPP; MovMk; WhoHol A*

Hale, Edward Everett
American. Clergyman, Author
b. Apr 3, 1822 in Boston, Massachusetts
d. Jun 10, 1909 in Roxbury, Massachusetts
Source: *Alli, SUP; AmAu; AmAu&B; AmBi; ApCAB; BbD; BiD&SB; CarSB; Chambr 3; ChPo, S1, S2; CnDAL; CyAl 2; CyWA; DcAmAu; DcAmB; DcEnL; DcLEL; DcNAA; Drake; EvLB; JBA 34; OxAmL; Pen AM; REn; REnAL; TwCBDA; WebAB; WhAm 1*

Hale, Nancy
American. Author
b. May 6, 1908 in Boston, Massachusetts
Source: *AmAu&B; Au&Wr 71; ConAu 5R; ConNov 72, 76; DrAF 76; InWom; OxAmL; REn; REnAL; TwCA SUP; WhoAm 74, 82; WhoS&SW 73; WhoWor 74; WrDr 76*

Hale, Nathan
American. Revolutionary War Spy
Before hanged, said, "I only regret that I have but one life to lose for my country."
b. Jun 6, 1755 in Coventry, Connecticut
d. Sep 22, 1776 in Long Island, New York
Source: *AmBi; ApCAB; DcAmB; Drake; OxAmL; REn; REnAL; TwCBDA; WebAB; WhAm H*

Hale, Sarah Josepha
American. Journalist, Author
b. Oct 24, 1788 in Newport, New Hampshire
d. Apr 30, 1879
Source: *BioIn 1, 3, 5, 7, 10, 11*

Halevy, Jacques Francois Fromental
[Jacques Francois F Elie Levy]
French. Opera Composer
b. May 27, 1799 in Paris, France
d. Mar 17, 1862 in Nice, France
Source: *NewEOp 71; WebBD 80*

Haley, Alex Palmer
American. Author, Journalist
Won Pulitzer Prize for *Roots,* 1977; adapted into TV mini-series.
b. Aug 11, 1921 in Ithaca, New York
Source: *BkPepl; ConAu 77; ConLC 8, 12; LivgBAA; WhoAm 82; WhoWest 74*

Haley, Bill (William John Clifford, Jr.)
American. Rock and Roll Pioneer
b. Jul 6, 1925 in Highland Park, Michigan
d. Feb 9, 1981 in Harlingen, Texas
Source: *AmSCAP 66; BiDAmM; BioIn 8; LilREn 78; NewYTBS 81; WhoRock 81*

Haley, Jack
American. Actor
Played the Tin Man in *The Wizard of Oz,* 1939.
b. Aug 10, 1900 in Boston, Massachusetts
d. Jun 6, 1979 in Los Angeles, California
Source: *BiE&WWA; EncMT; FilmgC; MovMk; WhoAm 74; WhoHol A; WhoThe 77*

Haley, Jack, Jr.
American. Motion Picture Producer, Director
b. Oct 25, 1933 in Los Angeles, California
Source: *IntMPA 75, 75, 76, 77, 78, 79, 80, 81, 82; WhoAm 82; WhoWest 74*

Halfin, Eliezer
Israeli. Murdered Olympic Team Member
b. 1948? in U.S.S.R.
d. Sep 5, 1972 in Munich, Germany (West)
Source: *BioIn 9*

Halford, Rob
see: Judas Priest

Halifax, Edward Frederick Lindley
English. Statesman
b. Apr 16, 1881
d. Dec 23, 1959 in York, England
Source: *CurBio 40, 60*

Hall, Bruce
see: REO Speedwagon

Hall, Charles Martin
American. Scientist, Physician, Engineer
b. Dec 6, 1863 in Thompson, Ohio
d. Dec 27, 1914 in Niagara Falls, New York
Source: *AmBi; DcAmB; WebAB; WhAm 1*

Hall, David
American. Politician
b. Oct 20, 1930 in Oklahoma City, Oklahoma
Source: *IntWW 74; WhoAm 74; WhoAmP 73; WhoGov 72; WhoS&SW 73*

Hall, Daryl
[Hall and Oates]
American. Singer, Musician
b. 1948?
Source: *NF*

Hall, Donald Andrew
American. Author
b. Sep 20, 1928 in New Haven, Connecticut
Source: *AmAu&B; AuBYP; CnE&AP; ConAu 5R, 2NR; ConLC 1, 13; ConP 70, 75; DrAF 76; DrAP 75; OxAmL; Pen AM; RAdv 1; REn; REnAL; SmATA 23; WhoAm 82; WorAu; WrDr 76*

Hall, Donald Joyce
American. Greeting Card Executive
b. Jul 9, 1928 in Kansas City, Missouri
Source: *BioIn 10; WhoAm 78, 80, 82*

Hall, Glenn
Canadian. Hockey Player
NHL rookie of year, 1956.
b. Oct 3, 1931 in Humboldt, SK
Source: *BioIn 6, 8, 9, 10, 11*

Hall, Granville Stanley
American. Educator, Author
b. Feb 1, 1844 in Ashfield, Massachusetts
d. 1924
Source: *McGEWB; NewCol 75*

Hall, Gus
[Arro Kusta Hallberg]
American. Communist Party Leader
b. Oct 8, 1910 in Iron, Minnesota
Source: *BioNews 74; CurBio 73; WhoAm 78, 80, 82; WhoAmP 73*

Hall, Huntz
American. Actor
b. 1920 in New York, New York
Source: *FilmgC; IntMPA 75, 76, 77; MovMk; WhoHol A*

Hall, Sir James
Scottish. Chemist, Geologist
b. Jan 17, 1761 in Dunglass, Scotland
d. Jun 23, 1832 in Edinburgh, Scotland
Source: *AsBiEn; BioIn 5; DcScB*

Hall, James Norman
American. Author
b. Apr 22, 1887 in Colfax, Iowa
d. Jul 6, 1951 in Papeete, Tahiti
Source: *AmAu&B; AmNov; AuBYP; CyWA; DcAmB S5; DcLEL; JBA 34; MnBBF; OxAmL; Pen AM; REn; REnAL; TwCA, SUP; WhAm 3; WhNAA*

Hall, Jerry
"Tall Hall"
American. Model
b. 1957? in Texas
Source: *BioIn 11*

Hall, Josef Washington
[Upton Close, pseud.]
American. Radio Commentator, Lecturer
Wrote books on Oriental lifestyle.
b. Feb 27, 1894 in Kelso, Washington
d. Nov 13, 1960
Source: *ConAu 89; CurBio 44, 61; WebBD 80*

Hall, Joseph M
[The Hostages]
American. Former Hostage in Iran
b. 1950? in Oklahoma
Source: *NewYTBS 81*

Hall, Joyce Clyde
American. Greeting Card Company Executive
Founded Hallmark Cards, Inc., 1910.
b. Dec 29, 1891 in David City, Nebraska
d. Oct 29, 1982 in Leawood, Kansas
Source: *CelR 73; CurBio 53, 83; NewYTBS 82; WebAB; WhoAm 74, 76, 78, 80, 82; WhoAmA 73; WorAl*

Hall, Juanita
American. Singer, Actress
b. 1913 in Newport, New Jersey
d. Feb 28, 1968 in Keyport, New Jersey
Source: *BiE&WWA; EncMT; FilmgC; InWom; MotPP; WhAm 4; WhScrn 74, 77; WhoHol B*

Hall, Lyman
American. Statesman
b. Apr 12, 1724 in Wallingford, Connecticut
d. Oct 19, 1790 in Burke County, Georgia
Source: *AmBi; ApCAB; BiAuS; BiDrAC; DcAmB; Drake; TwCBDA; WhAm H; WhAmP*

Hall, Manly Palmer
Canadian. Author
b. Mar 18, 1901 in Peterborough, ON
Source: *Au&Wr 71; ConAu 93; WhNAA; WhoWest 74; WrDr 76*

Hall, Monty
Canadian. Game Show Host
Host of "Let's Make a Deal," 1963; "Beat the Clock," 1979.
b. Aug 25, 1924 in Winnipeg, MB
Source: *BioNews 74; CanWW 70, 82; CelR 73; WhoAm 82*

Hall, Sir Peter Reginald Frederick
English. Director
National Theatre Co., director since 1973.
b. Nov 22, 1930 in Bury St. Edmunds, England
Source: *BiE&WWA; CnThe; CroCD; EncWT; FilmgC; IntWW 80; NotNAT A; OxFilm; OxThe; PlP&P; WhoOp 76; WhoThe 72, 77, 81; WhoWor 80; WorEFlm*

Hall, Radclyffe
English. Author, Poet
Wrote *The Well of Loneliness,* 1928, censored for lesbian theme.
b. 1886 in Bournemouth, England
d. Oct 7, 1943 in London, England
Source: *CurBio 43; InWom; LongCTC; ModBrL; NewC; REn; TwCA, SUP; TwCW; WhoLA*

Hall, Tom T
"The Storyteller"
American. Singer, Songwriter
Wrote song "Harper Valley PTA"; sold over 4.5 million copies.
b. May 25, 1936 in Olive Hill, Kentucky
Source: *BioIn 10; ConAu 102; RkOn; WhoAm 78*

Hall and Oates
[Daryl Hall; John Oates]
American. Singing Duo
Hits include "Maneater," 1982.
Source: *IlEncRk; WhoRock 81*

Halle, Sir Charles
English. Musician, Conductor
b. Apr 11, 1819 in Hagen, Germany
d. Oct 25, 1895 in Manchester, England
Source: *OxMus; WebBD 80*

Halleck, Charles Abraham
American. Lawyer, Politician
b. Aug 22, 1900 in Demotte, Indiana
Source: *BiDrAC; CurBio 47; IntWW 74; WhAmP; WhoAm 74, 76, 78, 80, 82*

Halleck, Fritz-Greene
American. Poet
b. Jul 8, 1790 in Guilford, Connecticut
d. Nov 19, 1867 in Guilford, Connecticut
Source: *Alli, SUP; AmAu; AmAu&B; AtlBL; BbD; BiD&SB; CasWL; ChPo, S1, S2; CnDAL; CyAL 1; DcAmAu; DcEnL; DcLEL; DcNAA; EvLB; OxAmL; Pen AM; REn; REnAL*

Halleck, Henry
American. Military Leader
b. Jan 16, 1815 in Westernville, New York
d. Jan 9, 1872 in Louisville, Kentucky
Source: *Alli, SUP; AmBi; ApCAB; DcAmAu; DcAmB; DcNAA; EncAB-H; TwCBDA; WebAB; WhAm H*

Halley, Edmund
English. Astronomer
Predicted comets seen 1531, 1607, 1682 were same; known as Halley's Comet.
b. Nov 8, 1656 in London, England
d. Jan 14, 1742
Source: *Alli; DcEnL; NewC; REn*

Halliburton, Richard
American. Author, Explorer
Wrote *The Royal Road to Romance,* 1925, *The Flying Carpet,* 1932.
b. Jan 9, 1900 in Brownsville, Tennessee
d. Mar 21, 1939
Source: *AmAu&B; AmBi; CnDAL; DcNAA; EvLB; OxAmL; REnAL; TwCA, SUP; WhAm 1; WhNAA*

Halliday, Richard
American. Motion Picture Producer, Author
b. Apr 3, 1905 in Denver, Colorado
d. Mar 3, 1973 in Brasilia, Brazil
Source: *BiE&WWA; ConAu 41R; NewYTBE 73; WhAm 5; WhoE 74*

Hallstein, Walter
German. Diplomat, Statesman
b. Nov 17, 1901 in Mainz, Germany
d. Mar 29, 1982 in Stuttgart, Germany (West)
Source: *CurBio 53, 82; IntWW 74, 75, 76, 77, 78; IntYB 78, 79; NewYTBS 82; Who 74; WhoWor 74, 76, 78*

Hallstrom, Ivar
Swedish. Composer
b. Jun 5, 1826 in Stockholm, Sweden
d. Apr 11, 1901 in Stockholm, Sweden
Source: *NewEOp 71*

Halop, Billy
American. Actor
b. 1920 in New York, New York
d. Nov 9, 1976 in California
Source: *FilmgC; IntMPA 75, 76, 77; WhoHol A*

Halper, Albert
American. Author
b. Aug 3, 1904 in Chicago, Illinois
Source: *AmAu&B; AmNov; Au&Wr 71; CnDAL; ConAmA; ConAu 5R, 3NR; OxAmL; REn; REnAL; TwCA, SUP; WhNAA; WhoAm 74, 82*

Hals, Frans
Dutch. Artist
b. 1580 in Antwerp, Belgium
d. Aug 26, 1666
Source: *AtlBL; McGEWB; REn*

Halsey, William Frederick
"Bull"
American. Admiral
Commanded US 3rd Fleet, 1944-45.
b. Oct 30, 1882 in Elizabeth, New Jersey
d. Aug 16, 1959 in Fishers Island, New Jersey
Source: *CurBio 42, 59; WebAB; WhAm 3*

Halsman, Philippe
American. Photographer
b. May 2, 1906 in Riga, Russia
d. Jun 25, 1979 in New York, New York
Source: *AmAu&B; Au&Wr 71; AuBYP; ConAu 25R, 89; CurBio 60, 79; NewYTBS 79; WhoAm 76, 78; WhoWor 76*

Halsted, Anna Eleanor Roosevelt
[Mrs. James A Halsted]
American. Newspaper Publisher
Daughter of Franklin and Eleanor Roosevelt; wrote children's books.
b. May 3, 1906 in New York, New York
d. Dec 1, 1975 in New York, New York
Source: *ConAu 61; WhoE 74*

Halsted, William Stewart
American. Surgeon
b. Sep 23, 1852 in New York
d. Sep 7, 1922
Source: *AmBi; DcAmB; DcNAA; EncAB-H; WebAB; WhAm 1*

Halston
[Roy Halston Frowick]
American. Fashion Designer
Won Coty Award 1962, 1969, 1971-72; introduced pillbox hat.
b. Apr 23, 1932 in Des Moines, Iowa
Source: *BkPepl; WhoAm 80, 82; WorFshn*

Ham, Greg
see: Men at Work

Ham, Jack
American. Football Player
b. Dec 23, 1948 in Johnstown, Pennsylvania
Source: *BioIn 9; NewYTBE 70; WhoFtbl 74*

Ham, Peter
see: Badfinger

Hambleton, Hugh George
Canadian. Spy, Economist
Convicted of spying for Soviets while working for NATO, 1956-61.
b. May 4, 1922 in Ottawa, ON
Source: *CanWW 81, 82*

Hambro, Leonid
American. Musician
b. Jun 26, 1920 in Chicago, Illinois
Source: *WhoAm 74*

Hamburger, Michael
British. Poet
b. 1924 in Berlin, Germany
Source: *BioIn 10*

Hamel, Veronica
American. Model, Actress
Plays Joyce Davenport on "Hill Street Blues," 1981--.
b. 1948? in Philadelphia, Pennsylvania
Source: *BioIn 12*

Hamen y Leon, Juan van der
Spanish. Artist
b. 1596 in Madrid, Spain
d. 1631 in Madrid, Spain
Source: *McGDA*

Hamer, Fannie Lou Townsend
American. Civil Rights Activist
b. 1917 in Mississippi
d. Mar 1977 in Mound Bayou, Mississippi
Source: *BioIn 6, 7, 9, 11*

Hamer, Robert
English. Motion Picture Director
b. 1911 in Kidderminster, England
d. 1963
Source: *BiDFilm; CmMov; DcFM; FilmgC; MovMk; OxFilm; WorEFlm*

Hamill, Dorothy
[Mrs. Dean Martin, Jr.]
American. Figure Skater
Won gold medal, 1976 Olympics.
b. 1956 in Greenwich, Connecticut
Source: *BioIn 10, 11; BkPepl; CurBio 76; WhoAm 80, 82*

Hamill, Mark
"Motor-Mouth"
American. Actor
Played Luke Skywalker in *Star Wars,* 1977; *The Empire Strikes Back,* 1980.
b. Sep 25, 1952 in Oakland, California
Source: *BkPepl; FilmEn; IntMPA 82; WhoAm 78, 80, 82*

Hamill, "Pete"
[William Hamill]
American. Journalist
Wrote *The Gift,* 1973; *Flesh and Blood,* 1977.
b. Jun 24, 1935 in Brooklyn, New York
Source: *CelR 73; ConAu 25R; ConLC 10; IntMPA 75, 76, 77; WhoAm 82; WomWMM*

Hamilton, Alexander
American. Politician, Author
First US Treasury Secretary, 1789-95; mortally wounded in duel with Aaron Burr.
b. Jan 11, 1757 in Nevis, West Indies
d. Jul 12, 1804
Source: *Alli; AmAu; AmAu&B; AmBi; ApCAB; BbD; BiAuS; BiD&SB; BiDrAC; BiDrUSE; CyAL 1; CyWA; DcAmAu; DcAmB; DcEnL; DcLEL; DcNAA; Drake; EncAB-H; EvLB; OxAmL; REn; REnAL; TwCBDA; WebAB; WhAm H; WhAmP*

Hamilton, Andrew
American. Lawyer
Helped establish freedom of the press in 1735 libel trial.
b. 1676 in Scotland
d. Aug 4, 1741 in Philadelphia, Pennsylvania
Source: *AmBi; ApCAB; DcAmB; NatCAB 13; WhAm H*

Hamilton, Charles Harold St. John
English. Author
b. Aug 8, 1875 in Ealing, England
d. Dec 24, 1961
Source: *BioIn 3, 6, 7, 8, 10; ConAu 73; MnBBF; OxEng; SmATA 13; WhoChL*

Hamilton, Emma
[Emma Lyon]
English. Mistress of Lord Nelson
b. 1761
d. 1815
Source: *Alli; BiDLA; InWom; NewC; REn*

Hamilton, George
American. Actor
Star, producer of *Love at First Bite,* 1979; *Zorro, the Gay Blade,* 1981.
b. Aug 12, 1939 in Memphis, Tennessee
Source: *CelR 73; FilmgC; IntMPA 77, 78, 79, 80, 81, 82; MnBBF; MotPP; MovMk; WhoAm 82; WhoHol A*

Hamilton, Guy
Motion Picture Director
b. 1922
Source: *IntMPA 75*

Hamilton, Sir Ian Standish Monteith
British. World War I General, Author
b. 1853
d. Oct 12, 1947 in London, England
Source: *Alli SUP; ChPo, S1*

Hamilton, Margaret
American. Actress
Played the Wicked Witch of the West in *The Wizard of Oz,* 1939.
b. Sep 12, 1902 in Cleveland, Ohio
Source: *BiE&WWA; FilmgC; ForWC 70; IntMPA 75, 76, 77, 78, 79, 80, 81, 82; MovMk; NotNAT; ThFT; Vers A; WhoHol A; WhoThe 77*

Hamilton, Neil
American. Actor
b. Sep 9, 1899 in Lynn, Massachusetts
Source: *BiE&WWA; FilmgC; MovMk; NotNAT; TwYS; WhoHol A*

Hamilton, Roy
American. Singer
b. Apr 16, 1929 in Leesburg, Georgia
d. Jul 20, 1969 in New Rochelle, New York
Source: *BiDAmM; BioIn 8; DcBlPA; RkOn; WhoRock 81*

Hamilton, Scott
American. Saxophonist
b. 1954 in Providence, Rhode Island
Source: *BioIn 12*

Hamilton, Scott
American. Figure Skater
b. Aug 28, 1958 in Haverford, Pennsylvania
Source: *BioIn 12*

Hamilton, Virginia
American. Author
b. Mar 13, 1936 in Yellow Springs, Ohio
Source: *Au&ICB; AuBYP; AuNews 1; BlkAW; ChlLR 1; ChPo S2; ConAu 25R; MorBMP; SmATA 4; WhoAm 82; WhoAmW 77*

Hamilton, William
American. Cartoonist, Dramatist
b. Jun 2, 1939 in Palo Alto, California
Source: *BioIn 11; ConAu 69; WhoAm 78, 80, 82*

Hamilton, Sir William
Scottish. Philosopher
b. Mar 8, 1788 in Glasgow, Scotland
d. May 6, 1856 in Edinburgh, Scotland
Source: *Alli; BiD&SB; BrAu 19; CasWL; DcEnL; EvLB; NewC; OxEng*

Hamlin, Hannibal
American. Statesman
b. Aug 27, 1809 in Paris Hill, Maine
d. Jul 4, 1891 in Bangor, Maine
Source: *AmBi; ApCAB; BiAuS; BiDrAC; BiDrUSE; DcAmB; Drake; TwCBDA; WebAB; WhAm H; WhAmP*

Hamlin, Harry
American. Actor
Starred in TV mini-series "Studs Lonigan"; films *Movie, Movie* and *Making Love.*
b. 1952 in Pasadena, California
Source: *IntMPA 82; NewYTBS 79*

Hamlin, Talbot Faulkner
American. Author
b. Jun 16, 1889 in New York, New York
d. Oct 7, 1956 in Beaufort, South Carolina
Source: *AmAu&B; CurBio 54, 56, 57; OxAmL; WhAm 3*

Hamlin, Vincent T
American. Cartoonist
b. 1900 in Perry, Iowa
Source: *WorECom*

Hamlisch, Marvin
American. Composer, Musician
Wrote scores for *The Way We Were, The Sting,* 1974; *A Chorus Line,* 1975.
b. Jun 2, 1944 in New York, New York
Source: *AmSCAP 66; BioNews 74; BkPepl; IntMPA 82*

Hammarskjold, Dag
Swedish. Statesman
Secretary General, UN, 1953-61; won Nobel Peace Prize, 1961.
b. Jul 29, 1905 in Jonkoping, Sweden
d. Sep 18, 1961 in Ndola, Rhodesia
Source: *ConAu 77; CurBio 53, 61; REn; WhAm 4; WhoUN 75*

Hammarskjold, Knut Hjalmar L
Swedish. Premier, Chief Justice
b. 1862
d. Oct 12, 1953 in Stockholm, Sweden
Source: *WebBD 80*

Hammer, Armand
American. Financier, Manufacturer
b. May 21, 1898 in New York, New York
Source: *BioNews 74; BusPN; CurBio 73; IntWW 74; NewYTBE 72, 73; St&PR 75; WhoAm 74, 76, 78, 80, 82; WhoF&I 74; WhoWest 74*

Hammer, Jan
[Mahavishnu Orchestra]
Czech. Musician
b. Apr 17, 1948 in Czechoslovakia
Source: *ConMuA 80; EncJzS 70; WhoRock 81*

Hammerstein, Oscar
German. Theatrical Manager, Impresario
b. May 8, 1846 in Berlin, Germany
d. Aug 1, 1919 in New York, New York
Source: *DcAmB; EncMT; OxAmL; WhAm 1; WhoStg 1906, 1908*

Hammerstein, Oscar, II
[Rodgers and Hammerstein]
American. Lyricist
Wrote lyrics for *Oklahoma!,* 1943; *Carousel,* 1945; *South Pacific,* 1949.
b. Jul 12, 1895 in New York, New York
d. Aug 23, 1960 in Doylestown, Pennsylvania
Source: *AmSCAP 66; ConAu 101; CurBio 44, 60; ModWD; OxThe; REn; WebAB; WhAm 4; WhScrn 77*

Hammett, (Samuel) Dashiell
American. Author
Created fictional detective Sam Spade, *The Maltese Falcon*, 1930.
b. May 27, 1894 in Saint Marys, Maryland
d. Jan 10, 1961 in New York, New York
Source: *AmAu&B; AuNews 1; CasWL; CmMov; CnDAL; ConAu 81; ConLC 3, 5, 10; CyWA; DcFM; DcLEL; EncAB-H; EncMys; EvLB; FilmgC; LongCTC; MnBBF; ModAL, SUP; OxAmL; OxEng; OxFilm; Pen AM; REn; REnAL; TwCA, SUP; TwCW; WebAB; WebE&AL; WhAm 4; WhoTwCL; WorEFlm*

Hammon, Jupiter
American. Poet
b. 1720
d. 1800
Source: *AmAu; AmAu&B; BlkAW; DcAmB; DcNAA; OxAmL; REnAL; WhAm H*

Hammond, Bray
American. Author
b. Nov 20, 1886 in Springfield, Missouri
d. Jul 20, 1968 in Thetford, Vermont
Source: *AmAu&B; OxAmL; WhAm 5*

Hammond, John Henry, Jr.
American. Former Recording Company Exec.
b. Dec 15, 1910 in New York, New York
Source: *BioIn 9; CurBio 79; EncJzS 70; WhoAm 78*

Hammond, Laurens
American. Inventor
b. Jan 11, 1895 in Evanston, Illinois
d. Jul 1, 1973 in Cornwall, Connecticut
Source: *NewYTBE 73; WhAm 6; WhoAm 74; WhoMus 72*

Hammond-Innes, Ralph
see: Innes, Hammond, pseud.

Hammurabi
Babylonian. King
Started to build tower of Babel; established written code of law.
b. 1955BC
d. 1913BC
Source: *BioIn 1, 5, 6, 8, 9, 11; NewCol 75; WebBD 80*

Hamner, Earl Henry, Jr.
American. Author
Creator of TV series "The Waltons" and "Falcon Crest."
b. Jul 10, 1923 in Schuyler, Virginia
Source: *AuNews 2; BioIn 10, 11; ConAu 73; ConLC 12; WhoAm 78, 80, 82*

Hampden, John
English. Statesman
b. 1594 in London, England
d. Jun 24, 1643 in Thame, England
Source: *Alli; NewC; REn*

Hampden, Walter
American. Actor
b. Jun 30, 1879 in New York, New York
d. Jun 11, 1955 in Los Angeles, California
Source: *CurBio 53, 55; DcAmB S5; FamA&A; Film 1; FilmgC; MotPP; MovMk; OxThe; REn; REnAL; Vers B; WebAB; WhAm 3; WhScrn 74, 77; WhoHol B; WhoStg 1908*

Hampshire, Susan
English. Actress
b. May 12, 1942 in London, England
Source: *CelR 73; CurBio 74; FilmgC; IntMPA 75, 76, 77, 78, 79, 80, 81, 82; NewYTBE 70; WhoAm 74, 76, 78, 80, 82; WhoHol A; WhoThe 77*

Hampton, Christopher James
British. Dramatist
b. Jan 26, 1946 in Fayal, Azores
Source: *Au&Wr 71; BioIn 11; CnThe; ConAu 25R; ConLC 1, 2, 3, 4, 5, 6; DcLEL 1940; IntAu&W 76; IntWW 78; WhoThe 72, 77; WrDr 80*

Hampton, Fred
American. Revolutionary
b. 1952?
d. 1969
Source: *BioIn 11*

Hampton, Hope
American. Socialite, Actress
b. 1901 in Houston, Texas
d. Jan 2, 1982 in New York, New York
Source: *FilmgC; InWom; MotPP; NewYTBS 82; TwYS; WhoHol A*

Hampton, Lionel
American. Band Leader
Formed orchestra late 1930's; theme song "Flying Home."
b. Apr 12, 1913 in Louisville, Kentucky
Source: *CelR 73; CurBio 71; WhoAm 74, 76, 78, 80, 82; WhoBlA 75; WhoE 74; WhoHol A*

Hampton, Robert Edward
American. Government Official
b. Sep 21, 1922 in Chattanooga, Tennessee
Source: *BioIn 10; WhoAm 78, 80, 82*

Hampton, Wade
American. Confederate General
b. Mar 28, 1818 in Charleston, South Carolina
d. Apr 11, 1902 in Columbia, South Carolina
Source: *AmBi; ApCAB; BiDConf; BiDrAC; DcAmB; Drake; EncAB-H; TwCBDA; WebAB; WhAm 1; WhAmP*

Hamsun, Knut Pederson
[Knut Pedersen]
Norwegian. Author
Won Nobel Prize for Literature, 1920.
b. Aug 4, 1859 in Lom, Norway
d. Feb 19, 1952 in Noerholmen, Norway
Source: *AtlBL; CasWL; ClDMEL; CnMD; CyWA; DcBiA; EncWL; EvEuW; LongCTC; Pen EUR; REn; REnWD; TwCA, SUP; TwCW; WhAm 3, 4; WhoLA; WhoTwCL*

Han, Suyin
Chinese. Author
b. Sep 12, 1917 in Peking, China
Source: *Au&Wr 71; ConAu 17R; InWom; IntWW 74; TwCW; Who 74; WorAu; WrDr 76*

Hancock, Herbie (Herbert Jeffrey)
American. Jazz Musician, Composer
b. Apr 12, 1940 in Chicago, Illinois
Source: *BioNews 74; WhoAm 74, 76, 78, 80, 82; WhoBlA 75; WhoE 74*

Hancock, John
American. Revolutionary Statesman
Said "There, I guess King George will be able to read that," after singing Declaration of Independence, 1776.
b. Jan 12, 1737 in Braintree, Massachusetts
d. Oct 8, 1793 in Quincy, Massachusetts
Source: *Alli; AmBi; ApCAB; BiAuS; BiDrAC; BiDrUSE; DcAmB; Drake; EncAB-H; REn; REnAL; TwCBDA; WebAB; WhAm H; WhAmP*

Hancock, John D
American. Motion Picture Director
b. Feb 12, 1939 in Kansas City, Missouri
Source: *FilmEn; IntMPA 79, 80, 81; MovMk; WhoAm 80, 82*

Hand, Learned
American. Judge
b. Jan 27, 1872 in Albany, New York
d. Aug 18, 1961 in New York, New York
Source: *AmAu&B; CurBio 50, 61; EncAB-H; WebAB; WhAm 4*

Handel, George Frederick
[Georg Friedrich Handel]
German. Composer
Composed 46 operas; best known work *The Messiah*, 1742.
b. Feb 23, 1685
d. Apr 14, 1759 in London, England
Source: *AtlBL; NewC; REn*

Handelman, Stanley Myron
American. Comedian
Source: *NF*

Handlin, Oscar
American. Educator, Historian
b. Mar 29, 1915 in Brooklyn, New York
Source: *Au&Wr 71; ConAu 1R, 5NR; DrAS 74H; OxAmL; REnAL; TwCA SUP; WebAB; Who 74; WhoAm 74, 76, 78, 80, 82; WhoE 74; WhoWor 74; WhoWorJ 72; WrDr 76*

Handwerker, Nathan
American. Restaurant Owner
b. 1890
d. Mar 24, 1974
Source: *NewYTBS 74*

Handy, Thomas Troy
American. Army General
b. Mar 11, 1892 in Spring City, Tennessee
d. Apr 14, 1982 in San Antonio, Texas
Source: *CurBio 51, 82; NewYTBS 82; WebAMB; Who 74*

Handy, W(illiam) C(hristopher)
"Father of the Blues"
American. Composer, Musician
b. Nov 16, 1873 in Florence, Alabama
d. Mar 29, 1958 in New York, New York
Source: *AmAu&B; AmSCAP 66; CurBio 41, 58; EncAB-H; OxAmL; REnAL; WebAB; WhAm 3; WhoJazz 72*

Haney, Carol
American. Choreographer, Dancer
In Broadway musical *Pajama Game*, 1954; choreographer, *Funny Girl*, 1964.
b. Dec 24, 1924 in Bedford, Massachusetts
d. May 10, 1964 in Saddle River, New Jersey
Source: *EncMT; FilmgC; NotNAT B; WhAm 4; WhScrn 74, 77; WhoHol B; WorAl*

Haney, Paul Prichard
American. Journalist
b. Jul 20, 1928 in Akron, Ohio
Source: *BioIn 8; WhoAm 74*

Hanfstaengl, Ernst Franz Sedgwick
"Putzi"
German. Author, Friend of Hitler
b. 1877
d. Nov 6, 1975 in Munich, Germany (West)
Source: *BioIn 9, 10*

Hanks, Nancy
[Nancy Hanks Lincoln]
American. Mother of Abraham Lincoln
b. 1784
d. 1818
Source: *HerW; InWom; WhoAm 82*

Hanks, Nancy
American. Government Official
Chairman, National Endowment for the Arts, 1969-77.
b. Dec 31, 1927 in Miami Beach, Florida
d. Jan 7, 1983 in New York, New York
Source: *CurBio 71; InWom; LibW; PolProf NF; WhoAm 74, 76, 78, 80, 82; WhoAmA 78, 80; WhoAmP 73, 75, 77, 79; WhoAmW 58, 61, 64, 66, 68, 70, 72, 74, 75; WhoGov 72, 75, 77*

Hanley, William
American. Dramatist
b. Oct 22, 1931 in Lorain, Ohio
Source: *BiE&WWA; CnMD SUP; ConAu 41R; ConDr 73; CroCD; DrAF 76; ModWD; NotNAT; WhoAm 74; WhoE 74; WhoThe 77; WrDr 76*

Hanna, Mark (Marcus Alonzo)
American. Businessman, Politician
b. Sep 24, 1837 in New Lisbon, Ohio
d. Feb 15, 1904 in Washington, DC
Source: *AmBi; ApCAB SUP; BiDrAC; DcAmB; EncAB-H; OhA&B; OxAmL; REnAL; TwCBDA; WebAB; WhAm 1*

Hanna, William Denby
[Hanna and Barbera]
American. Cartoonist
Producer of cartoons, including *Yogi Bear, The Flintstones.*
b. Jul 14, 1910 in Melrose, New Mexico
Source: *FilmgC; IntMPA 82; OxFilm; WhoAm 74, 76, 78, 80, 82; WorEFlm*

Hanna and Barbera
see: Barbera, Joseph; Hanna, William

Hannagan, Steve (Stephen Jerome)
American. Press Agent
b. Apr 4, 1899 in Lafayette, Indiana
d. Feb 5, 1953 in Nairobi, Kenya
Source: *CurBio 44, 53; DcAmB S5; WhAm 3*

Hannah
Biblical Character
Source: *InWom*

Hannah, John Allen
"Hog"
American. Football Player
b. Apr 4, 1951 in Canton, Georgia
Source: *BioIn 12; FootReg*

Hannibal
Carthaginian General
b. 247BC
d. 183BC
Source: *REn*

Hansberry, Lorraine
American. Author
b. May 19, 1930 in Chicago, Illinois
d. Jan 2, 1965 in New York, New York
Source: *AmAu&B; AuNews 2; BiE&WWA; BlkAW; CasWL; CnMD SUP; ConAu 25R; CroCD; CurBio 59, 65; InWom; McGEWD; ModAL SUP; ModWD; PlP&P; REnAL; WhAm 4; WorAu*

Hansen, Alvin Harvey
American. Educator
b. Aug 23, 1887 in Viborg, South Dakota
d. Jun 6, 1975 in Alexandria, Virginia
Source: *AmAu&B; ConAu 57; ConAu P-1; CurBio 45; EncAB-H; IntWW 74; WebAB; WhAm 6; Who 74; WhoAm 74*

Hansen, Clifford Peter
American. Senator
b. Oct 16, 1912 in Zenith, Wyoming
Source: *BiDrAC; CngDr 74; IntWW 74; WhoAm 74; WhoAmP 73; WhoGov 72; WhoWest 74*

Hansen, Joseph
[Rose Brock; James Colton; James Coulton, pseuds.]
American. Author
b. Jul 19, 1923 in Aberdeen, South Dakota
Source: *ConAu 29R; IntAu&W 77; TwCCr&M*

Hansen, Patti (Patricia Evina)
American. Model, Actress
b. 1956?
Source: *BioIn 12*

Hanslick, Eduard
Czech. Music Critic
b. Sep 11, 1825 in Prague, Czechoslovakia
d. Aug 6, 1904 in Baden, Austria
Source: *BbD; BiD&SB*

Hanson, Duane Elwood
American. Artist
b. Jan 17, 1925 in Alexandria, Minnesota
Source: *WhoAm 82; WhoAmA 73*

Hanson, Howard Harold
American. Composer, Conductor, Educator
b. Oct 28, 1896 in Wahoo, Nebraska
d. Feb 26, 1981 in Rochester, New York
Source: *AmSCAP 66; Baker 78; BiDAmEd; BiDAmM; BioIn 1, 2, 3, 4, 6, 7, 8, 9, 11; CurBio 41, 66, 81; DcCM; DrAS 74H, 78H; IntWW 74, 75, 76, 77, 78; LinLib S; McGEWB; NewEOp 71; NewYTBS 81; OxAmL; OxMus; WebAB; WhAm 7; WhoAm 74, 76, 78, 80; WhoE 74; WhoMus 72; WhoWor 74, 76, 78*

Hanson, John
American. Colonial Leader
First president of Continental Congress, 1781-82.
b. Apr 13, 1721 in Charles County, Maryland
d. Nov 22, 1783 in Oxon Hill, Maryland
Source: *BioIn 1, 3, 4, 7; NewCol 75; WebAB*

Hanson, Kitty
American. Journalist
b. in Chicago, Illinois
Source: *AmAu&B; WhoAm 74, 76, 78, 80, 82*

Hapgood, Charles Hutchins
American. Cartographer, Author
b. May 17, 1904 in New York, New York
Source: *Au&Wr 71; ConAu 17R*

Hapgood, Norman
American. Magazine Editor, Author
b. Mar 28, 1868 in Chicago, Illinois
d. Apr 29, 1937
Source: *AmAu&B; AmBi; BiD&SB; DcAmAu; DcAmB S2; DcNAA; OxAmL; REnAL; TwCA; WhAm 1*

Harbach, Otto Abels
American. Librettist
b. Aug 18, 1873 in Salt Lake City, Utah
d. Jan 24, 1963 in New York, New York
Source: *AmAu&B; AmSCAP 66; CurBio 50, 63; EncMT; NewCBMT; REnAL; WhAm 4*

Harbison, John Harris
American. Composer
b. Dec 20, 1938 in Orange, New Jersey
Source: *Baker 78; DcCM; WhoAm 80, 82*

Harburg, E(dgar) Y(ipsel)
"Yip"
American. Composer
b. Apr 8, 1896 in New York, New York
d. Mar 5, 1981 in Los Angeles, California
Source: *AmPS; AmSCAP 66; BiDAmM; BiE&WWA; BioIn 5, 8, 9, 10; CelR 73; CmpEPM; ConAu 85, 103; ConDr 73, 77D; CurBio 80, 81; EncMT; IntAu&W 77; NewCBMT; NewYTBS 81; NotNAT; WhAm 7; WhoAm 74, 76, 78, 80; WhoThe 72, 77, 81*

Hardie, James Keir
Scottish. Socialist Labor Leader
b. 1856 in Scotland
d. 1915
Source: *NewCol 75; WebBD 80*

Hardin, Louis Thomas
"Moondog"
Street Musician
b. 1916
Source: *BioIn 3, 11*

Hardin, Tim
American. Songwriter, Singer
b. 1940 in Eugene, Oregon
d. Dec 29, 1980 in Hollywood, California
Source: *AnObit 1980; IlEncRk; WhoRock 81*

Harding, Ann
[Dorothy Walton Gatley]
American. Actress
b. Aug 17, 1904 in Fort Sam Houston, Texas
d. Sep 1, 1981 in Sherman Oaks, California
Source: *BiE&WWA; BioIn 9, 10; Film 2; FilmgC; InWom; IntMPA 77, 78, 79, 80, 81, 82; MotPP; MovMk; NotNAT; OxFilm; ThFT; Who 74; WhoHol A; WhoThe 77*

Harding, Chester
American. Army Officer, Engineer
b. Dec 31, 1866 in Enterprise, Mississippi
d. Nov 11, 1936
Source: *WhAm 1*

Harding, Florence Kling
American. Wife of Warren G Harding
b. Aug 15, 1860 in Marion, Ohio
d. Nov 21, 1924 in Marion, Ohio
Source: *InWom; NotAW*

Harding, Warren G(amaliel)
American. 29th US President
President, 1921-23; administration was marked by many scandals.
b. Nov 2, 1865 in Blooming Grove, Ohio
d. Aug 2, 1923 in San Francisco, California
Source: *AmAu&B; AmBi; BiDrAC; BiDrUSE; DcAmB; DcNAA; EncAB-H; NewYTBE 72; OhA&B; OxAmL; REn; REnAL; St&PR 75; WebAB; WhAm 1; WhAmP*

Hardwick, Billy
American. Bowler
b. 1932
Source: *NewYTBS 74*

Hardwick, Cathy
Fashion Designer
b. 1934?
Source: *BioIn 11*

Hardwick, Elizabeth
American. Author
b. Jul 27, 1916 in Lexington, Kentucky
Source: *AmAu&B; AmWomWr; ConAu 5R; ConLC 13; CurBio 81; IntAu&W 76, 77; WhoAm 74, 76, 78, 80, 82; WhoAmW 66, 68, 70, 72, 74; WorAu; WrDr 76, 80*

Hardwicke, Sir Cedric Webster
English. Actor
b. Feb 19, 1893 in Lye, England
d. Aug 6, 1964 in New York, New York
Source: *BiDFilm; BiE&WWA; CurBio 49, 64; Film 1; FilmgC; LongCTC; MotPP; MovMk; NewC; OxFilm; OxThe; PlP&P; WhAm 4; WhScrn 74, 77; WhoHol B*

Hardy, Oliver
[Laurel and Hardy; Norvell Hardy]
American. Comedian
First film with Laurel, *Putting Pants on Philip,* 1926.
b. Jan 18, 1892 in Atlanta, Georgia
d. Aug 7, 1957 in Hollywood, California
Source: *BiDFilm; CmMov; Film 1; FilmgC; MotPP; MovMk; OxFilm; TwYS; WebAB; WhScrn 74, 77; WhoHol B; WorEFlm*

Hardy, Thomas
English. Author, Poet
Wrote *Far From the Madding Crowd,* 1874; *Tess of the D'Ubervilles,* 1891.
b. Jun 2, 1840 in Dorsetshire, England
d. Jan 11, 1928 in Dorchester, England
Source: *Alli SUP; AnCL; AtlBL; BbD; BiD&SB; BrAu 19; CasWL; Chambr 3; ChPo, S1, S2; CnE&AP; CnMWL; CrtT 3; CyWA; DcBiA; DcEnA, AP; DcEnL; DcEuL; DcLEL; EncWL; EvLB; LongCTC; ModBrL, SUP; ModWD; NewC; OxEng; Pen ENG; RAdv̄ 1; RComWL; REn; TwCW; WebE&AL; WhoChL; WhoLA; WhoTwCL*

Hare, David
English. Dramatist
Plays include *Teeth 'n' Smiles, Knuckle,* and *Plenty.*
b. Jun 5, 1947 in Sussex, England
Source: *BioIn 11; CnThe; ConDr 73, 77; DcLEL 1940; EncWT; IntAu&W 76; NewYTBS 82; WhoAm 82; WhoThe 77; WrDr 76, 80*

Hare, Ernie (Thomas Ernest)
[The Interwoven Pair]
Singer
b. 1883
d. 1939
Source: *BioIn 5*

Hare, James Henry
English. Journalist
b. Oct 3, 1856 in London, England
d. Jun 24, 1946 in Teaneck, New Jersey
Source: *DcAmB S4; WhAm 2*

Hare, William
[Burke and Hare]
Irish. Murderer
b. 1792? in Derry, Northern Ireland
d. 1870
Source: *BioIn 1, 4, 10*

Harewood, George Henry Hubert Lascelles, Earl
English. Music Director, Critic
b. Feb 7, 1923 in Leeds, England
Source: *Au&Wr 71; BioIn 2, 7, 8; CurBio 65*

Hargis, Billy James
American. Evangelist
b. Aug 3, 1925 in Texarkana, Texas
Source: *CelR 73; CurBio 72; WhoAm 82; WhoS&SW 73*

Harkness, Anna M Richardson
American. Philanthropist
b. Oct 25, 1837 in Dalton, Ohio
d. Mar 27, 1926 in New York, New York
Source: *NotAW*

Harkness, Edward Stephen
American. Businessman, Philanthropist
b. Jan 22, 1874 in Cleveland, Ohio
d. Jan 29, 1940
Source: *AmBi; CurBio 40; DcAmB S2; WhAm 1*

Harkness, Rebekah West
American. Philanthropist, Composer
b. Apr 17, 1915 in Saint Louis, Missouri
d. Jun 17, 1982 in New York, New York
Source: *AmSCAP 66, 80; CelR 73; CurBio 74, 82; GoodHS; NewYTBS 82; WhoAm 74, 76, 78, 80, 82; WhoAmW 70, 72, 74, 75, 77, 79; WhoE 74; WhoGov 72, 75, 77*

Harlan, John Marshall
American. Supreme Court Justice
b. Jun 1, 1833 in Boyle County, Kentucky
d. Oct 14, 1911 in Washington, DC
Source: *AmBi; ApCAB; BiDSA; DcAmB; DcNAA; EncAB-H; TwCBDA; WebAB; WhAm 1*

Harlan, John Marshall
American. Supreme Court Justice
b. May 20, 1899 in Chicago, Illinois
d. Dec 29, 1971 in Washington, DC
Source: *ConAu 33R; CurBio 55, 72; WebAB; WhAm 5; WhoS&SW 73*

Harlan, Veit
German. Motion Picture Director
b. 1899 in Berlin, Germany
d. Apr 13, 1964 in Capri, Italy
Source: *FilmgC; WhScrn 77*

Harlech, William David Ormsby-Gore, Baron
British. Diplomat
b. May 20, 1918
Source: *BioIn 7, 8, 11; IntWW 74; Who 74; WhoWor 74*

Harlem Globetrotters
American. Basketball Team
Source: *NF*

Harlow, Jean
[Harlean Carpenter]
American. Actress
Platinum blonde star of *Hells Angels,* 1930; *Dinner at Eight,* 1933.
b. Mar 3, 1911 in Kansas City, Missouri
d. Jun 7, 1937 in Los Angeles, California
Source: *BiDFilm; DcAmB S2; FilmgC; InWom; MotPP; MovMk; NotAW; OxFilm; ThFT; TwYS; WebAB; WhAm HA, 4; WhScrn 74, 77; WhoHol B; WorEFlm*

Harman, Fred
American. Cartoonist
b. Feb 9, 1902 in Saint Joseph, Missouri
d. Jan 2, 1982 in Phoenix, Arizona
Source: *NewYTBS 82; WorECom*

Harman, Hugh
American. Animator
Created *Looney Tunes* and *Merry Melodies* cartoon series.
b. 1903 in Pagosa Springs, Colorado
d. Nov 26, 1982 in Chatsworth, California
Source: *WorECar*

Harman, Jeanne Perkins
American. Author, Journalist
b. Jul 27, 1919 in Baxter Springs, Kansas
Source: *BioIn 10; ConAu 69; ForWC 70*

Harmon, Ernest N
American. Army Officer
b. Feb 26, 1894 in Lowell, Massachusetts
d. Nov 1979 in Vermont
Source: *CurBio 46; NewYTBS 79; WhoAm 74*

Harmon, Mark
American. Actor
Son of Tom Harmon and Elyse Knox; starred on "Flamingo Road."
b. Sep 2, 1951 in Burbank, California
Source: *BioIn 9, 11; IntMPA 82*

Harmon, Tom (Thomas D)
American. Football Player, Sportscaster
Won Heisman Trophy at U of Michigan, 1940; father of Kelly and Mark Harmon.
b. Sep 28, 1919 in Rensselaer, Indiana
Source: *BioIn 3, 8, 9, 10; IndAu 1917; IntMPA 75, 76, 77, 78, 79, 80, 81, 82; WhoFtbl 74; WhoHol A*

Harmsworth, Alfred Charles William, Viscount
see: Northcliffe, Alfred Charles William Harmsworth, Viscount

Harnack, Curtis Arthur
American. Author
b. Jun 27, 1927 in Le Mars, Iowa
Source: *AmAu&B; BioIn 9; ConAu 1R, 2NR; DrAF 76; WrDr 76*

Harnett, William Michael
American. Artist
b. Aug 10, 1848 in County Cork, Ireland
d. Oct 29, 1892 in New York, New York
Source: *WebAB*

Harnick, Sheldon Mayer
American. Lyricist
b. Apr 30, 1924 in Chicago, Illinois
Source: *BiE&WWA; CelR 73; EncMT; IntWW 74; NewCBMT; NotNAT; PlP&P; WhoAm 74, 76, 78, 80, 82; WhoWor 74*

Harnwell, Gaylord Probasco
American. Atomic Physicist, Educator
President, U of Pennsylvania, 1953-70.
b. Sep 29, 1903 in Evanston, Illinois
d. Apr 18, 1982 in Haverford, Pennsylvania
Source: *AmM&WS 73P, 76P, 79P; CurBio 56; NewYTBS 82; WhoAm 74, 76, 78, 80*

Harold II
British. King
b. 1022
d. Oct 15, 1066 in Hastings, England
Source: *BioIn 10; McGEWB; WebBD 80*

Harper, Fletcher
[Harper Brothers]
American. Publisher
b. Jan 31, 1806 in Newton, New York
d. May 29, 1877 in New York, New York
Source: *AmAu&B; WebAB; WhAm H*

Harper, Frances Ellen Watkins
American. Poet
b. 1825
d. 1911
Source: *BioIn 3, 4, 7, 8*

Harper, Heather
[Mrs. Buck]
British. Opera Singer
b. May 8, 1930 in Belfast, Ireland
Source: *IntWW 74; Who 74; WhoAm 82; WhoWor 74*

Harper, James
[Harper Brothers]
American. Publisher
b. Apr 13, 1795 in Newton, New York
d. Mar 27, 1869 in New York, New York
Source: *AmAu&B; WebAB; WhAm H*

Harper, John
[Harper Brothers]
American. Publisher
b. Jan 22, 1797 in Newton, New York
d. Apr 22, 1875 in New York, New York
Source: *WebAB*

Harper, Joseph Wesley
[Harper Brothers]
American. Publisher
b. Dec 25, 1801 in Newton, New York
d. Feb 14, 1870 in New York, New York
Source: *WebAB*

Harper, Valerie
American. Actress
Won four Emmys for role of Rhoda in "The Mary Tyler Moore Show," 1970-74, "Rhoda," 1974-78.
b. Aug 22, 1941 in Suffern, New York
Source: *BioNews 75; BkPepl; CurBio 75; IntMPA 77, 78, 79, 80, 81, 82; NewYTBE 71; NewYTBS 74; WhoAm 82; WhoHol A*

Harper, William Rainey
American. Educator
b. Jul 26, 1846 in New Concord, Ohio
d. Jan 10, 1906 in Chicago, Illinois
Source: *AmAu&B; AmBi; ApCAB; DcAmAu; DcAmB; DcNAA; EncAB-H; OhA&B; REnAL; TwCBDA; WebAB; WhAm 1*

Harpignies, Henri
French. Artist
b. 1819 in Valenciennes, France
d. 1916 in Saint Prive, France
Source: *McGDA; OxFr*

Harrah, Bill (**William Fisk**)
American. Gambler, Nightclub Owner
Founded Harrah's Casino, 1937; Harrah's Tahoe Casino, 1955.
b. Sep 2, 1911 in Pasadena, California
d. Jun 30, 1978 in Rochester, Minnesota
Source: *BioIn 10; WhAm 7; WhoAm 78*

Harrell, Lynn Morris
American. Musician
b. Jan 30, 1944 in New York, New York
Source: *BioIn 10, 11; NewYTBS 77; WhoAm 80, 82*

Harrell, Mack
American. Opera Singer
b. Oct 8, 1909 in Celeste, Texas
d. Jan 29, 1960 in Dallas, Texas
Source: *WhAm 4*

Harrelson, Ken(**neth Smith**)
"Hawk"
American. Baseball Player, Broadcaster
Acquired nickname after breaking nose three times.
b. Sep 4, 1941 in Woodruff, South Carolina
Source: *BaseEn; CurBio 70; WhoProB 73*

Harrigan, Edward
American. Actor, Dramatist
b. Jul 27, 1844 in Logan, Ohio
d. Sep 2, 1911
Source: *AmAu; AmAu&B; BiD&SB; ChPo S2; CnThe; DcAmAu; DcAmB; DcNAA; EncMT; FamA&A; McGEWD; ModWD; OxAmL; OxThe; PlP&P; PoIre; REnAL; REnWD; WhAm 1; WhoStg 1906, 1908*

Harriman, Edward H
American. Businessman, Philanthropist
b. Feb 25, 1848 in Hampstead, New York
d. Sep 9, 1909 in Orange County, New York
Source: *AmBi; DcAmB; EncAB-H; WebAB; WhAm 1*

Harriman, E(dward) Roland (Noel)
American. Financier
b. Dec 24, 1895 in New York, New York
d. Feb 16, 1978 in Arden, New York
Source: *CurBio 51, 78; IntWW 74, 75, 76, 77, 78; IntYB 78; NewYTBS 78; St&PR 75; WhAm 5, 7; WhNAA; WhoAm 74; WhoF&I 74; WhoGov 72*

Harriman, John Walter
American. Economist
b. Jul 8, 1898 in Providence, Rhode Island
d. Oct 23, 1972
Source: *BioIn 9; NewYTBE 72*

Harriman, (William) Averell
American. Former Government Official
b. Nov 15, 1891 in New York, New York
Source: *BiDrUSE; EncAB-H; IntWW 74; St&PR 75; WebAB; Who 74; WhoAm 74, 76, 78, 80, 82*

Harrington, Michael
American. Socialist, Congressman
b. Feb 24, 1928 in Saint Louis, Missouri
Source: *AmAu&B; CelR 73; ConAu 17R; CurBio 69; NewYTBE 72; OxCan; WhoAm 74, 76, 78, 80, 82*

Harrington, Pat
[Daniel Patrick Harrington, Jr.]
American. Actor
Plays Schneider on TV series "One Day at a Time," 1975--.
b. Aug 13, 1929 in New York, New York
Source: *IntMPA 75, 76, 77, 78, 79, 80, 81, 82; WhoAm 82*

Harris, Sir Arthur Travers
English. Military Officer
b. Apr 13, 1892 in Cheltenham, England
Source: *CurBio 42; IntWW 74; Who 74*

Harris, Sir Augustus
English. Opera Singer
b. 1852 in Paris, France
d. Jun 22, 1896 in Folkestone, England
Source: *OxThe*

Harris, Barbara
American. Actress
b. 1935 in Evanston, Illinois
Source: *BiE&WWA; CelR 73; InWom; IntMPA 75, 76, 77, 78, 79, 80, 81, 82; MotPP; NewYTBE 72; WhoAm 74, 76, 78, 80, 82; WhoE 74; WhoHol A; WhoWor 74*

Harris, "Bucky" (Stanley Raymond)
American. Baseball Player, Manager
Infielder, 1919-31; Hall of Fame, 1975.
b. Nov 8, 1896 in Port Jervis, New York
d. Nov 8, 1977 in Bethesda, Maryland
Source: *BaseEn; CurBio 48, 78; WhoProB 73*

Harris, Cliff(ord Allen)
American. Football Player
b. Nov 12, 1948 in Fayetteville, Arkansas
Source: *WhoAm 78, 80*

Harris, Emily Schwartz
[Mrs. William Harris; S(ymbionese) L(iberation) A(rmy)]
American. Revolutionary
b. Feb 11, 1947 in Baltimore, Maryland
Source: *BioIn 10*

Harris, Emmylou
American. Singer
Won Grammys, 1976, 1977; CMA female vocalist of year, 1980.
b. Apr 2, 1948 in Birmingham, Alabama
Source: *BioIn 10; BkPepl; IlEncRk; WhoAm 78, 80, 82*

Harris, Franco
American. Football Player
Running back, Pittsburgh Steelers, 1972--; rookie of year, 1972.
b. Mar 7, 1950 in Mount Holly, New Jersey
Source: *CelR 73; WhoAm 82; WhoFtbl 74*

Harris, Frank
Irish. Author, Journalist
b. Feb 14, 1856 in Galway, Ireland
d. Aug 26, 1931
Source: *AmBi; CnDAL; CnMD; ConAmL; EvLB; LongCTC; ModBrL; NewC; OxAmL; OxEng; Pen ENG; RAdv 1; TwCA, SUP; TwCW; WhAm 1; WhoTwCL*

Harris, Fred Roy
American. Senator
b. Nov 13, 1930 in Walters, Oklahoma
Source: *CurBio 68; IntWW 74; WhoAm 74, 76, 78, 80, 82; WhoAmP 73; WhoGov 72; WhoS&SW 73*

Harris, Harwell Hamilton
American. Architect, Educator
b. Jul 2, 1903 in Redlands, California
Source: *AmArch 70; BioIn 6; CurBio 62; McGDA; WhoAm 74, 76, 78, 80, 82; WhoS&SW 73, 75, 76; WhoWor 74*

Harris, Jean Witt Struven
American. Convicted Murderer
Killed Dr. Herman Tarnower, Mar 10, 1980.
b. 1924
Source: *BioIn 12*

Harris, Jed
American. Theatrical Producer
b. Feb 25, 1900 in Vienna, Austria
d. Nov 1979 in New York, New York
Source: *BiE&WWA; NotNAT; WhoAm 74; WhoThe 77*

Harris, Joel Chandler
American. Author
Editor, Atlanta *Constitution*, 1890-1900; created Uncle Remus character.
b. Dec 9, 1848 in Eatonton, Georgia
d. Jul 3, 1908 in Atlanta, Georgia
Source: *Alli SUP; AmAu; AmAu&B; AmBi; AnCL; ApCAB; AtlBL; AuBYP; BbD; BiD&SB; BiDSA; CarSB; CasWL; Chambr 3; ChPo, S1, S2; CnDAL; CyWA; DcAmAu; DcAmB; DcBiA; DcEnA AP; DcLEL; DcNAA; EncAB-H; EvLB; FamAYP; JBA 34; OxAmL; OxEng; Pen AM; RAdv 1; REn; REnAL; Str&VC; WebAB; WebE&AL; WhAm 1; WhoChL; YABC 1*

Harris, Johnny
American. Murderer
b. 1945?
Source: *BioIn 12*

Harris, Jonathan
American. Actor
b. 1919?
Source: *FilmgC; WhoHol A*

Harris, Julie
American. Actress
Starred in *Member of the Wedding*, 1952; *East of Eden*, 1956.
b. Dec 2, 1925 in Grosse Pointe, Michigan
Source: *BiDFilm; BiE&WWA; BioNews 74; CelR 73; CurBio 56; FilmgC; InWom; IntMPA 75, 76, 77, 78, 79, 80, 81, 82; MotPP; MovMk; NotNAT; OxFilm; PlP&P A; WhoAm 74, 76, 78, 80, 82; WhoHol A; WhoThe 77; WhoWor 74*

Harris, LaDonna Crawford
American. Social Welfare Leader
b. 1931
Source: *NewYTBE 70; WhoAmW 77; WhoS&SW 73*

Harris, Lauren
[Group of Seven]
Canadian. Artist
b. Oct 23, 1885 in Brantford, ON
d. Jan 29, 1970 in Vancouver, BC
Source: *CreCan 2; IlBEAAW; MacDCB 78; McGDA*

Harris, Leonard
American. Critic, Author
b. Sep 27, 1929 in New York, New York
Source: *ConAu 65*

Harris, Louis
American. Public Opinion Pollster
Founded public opinion, marketing research firm, Louis Harris and Associates, Inc., 1956.
b. Jan 6, 1921 in New Haven, Connecticut
Source: *AmM&WS 73S; CelR 73; ConAu 13R; WebAB; WhoAm 74, 76, 78, 80, 82; WhoWor 74*

Harris, Mark
American. Author
b. Nov 19, 1922 in Mount Vernon, New York
Source: *AmAu&B; Au&Wr 71; ConAu 5R; ConNov 72, 76; DrAF 76; DrAS 74E; OxAmL; RAdv 1; WhoAm 74, 76, 78, 80, 82; WhoWor 74; WrDr 76*

Harris, Patricia Roberts
American. Former Government Official
Ambassador to Luxembourg, 1965-67; Secretary of HUD, 1977-79; HEW, 1979-80.
b. May 31, 1924 in Mattoon, Illinois
Source: *CurBio 65; InWom; IntWW 74; WhoAm 74, 76, 78, 80, 82; WhoAmP 73; WhoAmW 77; WhoBlA 75*

Harris, Paul
see: Souther-Hillman-Furay Band, The

Harris, Phil
American. Comedian, Musician
b. Jun 24, 1906 in Linton, Indiana
Source: *FilmgC; IntMPA 75, 76, 77, 78, 79, 80, 81, 82; MotPP; WhoHol A*

Harris, Phil
see: Ace

Harris, Richard
Irish. Actor
Won Grammy for *Jonathan Livingston Seagull,* 1973; Golden Globe for *Camelot,* 1968.
b. Oct 1, 1930 in Limerick, Ireland
Source: *BiDFilm; BkPepl; CelR 73; CurBio 64; FilmgC; IntMPA 75, 76, 77, 78, 79, 80, 81, 82; MotPP; MovMk; NewYTBE 72; OxFilm; WhoAm 82; WhoHol A; WhoThe 77; WhoWor 74; WorEFlm*

Harris, Rosemary
English. Actress
b. Sep 19, 1930 in Ashby, England
Source: *BiE&WWA; CurBio 67; FilmgC; InWom; IntMPA 75, 76, 77, 78, 79, 80, 81, 82; MotPP; NotNAT, ; WhoAm 74, 76, 78; WhoHol A; WhoThe 77; WhoWor 74*

Harris, Roy Ellsworth
American. Composer
b. Feb 12, 1898 in Lincoln County, Oklahoma
d. Oct 1979 in Santa Monica, California
Source: *CurBio 40; DcCM; IntWW 74; OxAmL; REn; REnAL; WebAB; WhoWor 74*

Harris, Sam Henry
American. Theatrical Manager
b. Feb 3, 1872 in New York, New York
d. Jul 3, 1941 in New York, New York
Source: *CurBio 41; DcAmB S5; EncMT; WhAm 1; WhoStg 1906, 1908*

Harris, Steve
see: Iron Maiden

Harris, Sydney J(ustin)
American. Journalist
Writer of syndicated column *Strictly Personal,* 1944--.
b. Sep 14, 1917 in London, England
Source: *AmAu&B; ConAu 61; WhoAm 74, 76, 78, 80, 82; WhoMW 74*

Harris, Willard Palmer (Bill)
American. Jazz Musician
b. Oct 28, 1916 in Philadelphia, Pennsylvania
d. 1973
Source: *WhoJazz 72*

Harris, William
[S(ymbionese) L(iberation) A(rmy)]
American. Revolutionary, SLA Member
b. Jan 22, 1945 in Fort Sill, Oklahoma
Source: *BioIn 10*

Harris, William Bliss
[Amos Pettingill, pseud.]
American. Editor, Author, Horticulturist
b. 1901? in Denver, Colorado
d. Jun 22, 1981 in Falmouth, Massachusetts
Source: *ConAu 104; NewYTBS 81*

Harrison, Benjamin
American. Continental Congressman
b. 1726? in Charles City, Virginia
d. Apr 24, 1791 in Charles City, Virginia
Source: *AmBi; ApCAB; BiDSA; BiDrAC; BioIn 3, 7, 8; Drake; NatCAB 10; TwCBDA; WhAm H; WhAmP*

Harrison, Benjamin
American. 23rd US President
Grover Cleveland had greater popular vote; was elected in electoral college, 1888.
b. Aug 20, 1833 in North Bend, Ohio
d. Mar 13, 1901 in Indianapolis, Indiana
Source: *Alli SUP; AmAu&B; AmBi; ApCAB, SUP; BiD&SB; BiDrUSE; BioIn 1, 2, 3, 4, 5, 6, 7, 8, 9, 10, 11; DcAmAu; DcAmB; DcNAA; EncAB-H; IndAu 1816; OhA&B; OxAmL; REnAL; TwCBDA; WebAB, 79; WhAm 1; WhAmP*

Harrison, Frederic
English. Author
b. Oct 18, 1831 in London, England
d. Jan 14, 1923
Source: *Alli SUP; BiD&SB; BrAu 19; Chambr 3; ChPo S1; DcEnA, AP; DcEnL; DcEuL; DcLEL; EvLB; LongCTC; NewC; OxEng*

Harrison, George
[The Beatles]
English. Singer, Songwriter
First album after break-up of Beatles, *All Things Must Pass,* sold 1.5 million copies in one week.
b. Feb 25, 1943 in Liverpool, England
Source: *BioIn 6, 7, 8, 9, 10, 11; BkPepl; CelR 73; CurBio 66; IntWW 74, 75, 76, 77, 78, 79, 80; MotPP; WhoAm 80, 82; WhoWor 74*

Harrison, Gregory
American. Actor
Plays Gonzo Gates in "Trapper John, MD," 1979--.
b. May 31, 1950 in Avalon, California
Source: *WhoAm 80, 82*

Harrison, Guy Fraser
English. Conductor
b. Nov 6, 1894 in Guildford, England
Source: *WhoE 74*

Harrison, Jerry
see: Talking Heads, The

Harrison, Nigel
see: Blondie

Harrison, Noel
English. Singer, Actor
b. 1934? in London, England
Source: *BioIn 5, 7; WhoHol A*

Harrison, Peter
American. Architect, Merchant
b. Jun 14, 1716 in York, England
d. Apr 30, 1775 in New Haven, Connecticut
Source: *DcAmB; WebAB; WhAm H*

Harrison, Rex
[Reginald Carey]
English. Actor
Won 1957 Tony, 1964 Oscar for role of Henry Higgins in *My Fair Lady.*
b. Mar 5, 1908 in Huyton, England
Source: *BiDFilm; BiE&WWA; CelR 73; CurBio 47; EncMT; FamA&A; FilmgC; IntMPA 75, 76, 77, 78, 78, 79, 80, 81, 82; IntWW 74; MotPP; MovMk; NewC; NotNAT; OxFilm; PlP&P; Who 74; WhoAm 82; WhoHol A; WhoThe 77; WhoWor 74*

Harrison, Wallace Kirkman
American. Architect
b. Sep 28, 1895 in Worcester, Massachusetts
d. Dec 2, 1981 in New York, New York
Source: *BioIn 1, 3, 5, 7; CurBio 47, 82; EncMA; IntWW 74, 75, 76, 77, 78; McGDA; WhoAm 74, 76, 78, 80; WhoArch; WhoWor 74, 78*

Harrison, William Henry
American. 9th US President
President of US, Mar 4-Apr 4, 1841; first president to die in office.
b. Feb 9, 1773 in Charles City, Virginia
d. Apr 4, 1841 in Washington, DC
Source: *Alli; AmAu&B; AmBi; ApCAB; BiAuS; BiDrAC; BiDrUSE; BioIn 1, 2, 3, 4, 5, 6, 7, 8, 9, 10, 11; DcAmB; Drake; EncAB-H; OhA&B; OxAmL; REn; REnAL; TwCBDA; WebAB, 79; WhAm H; WhAmP*

Harroun, Ray
American. Auto Racer, Engineer
b. Jan 12, 1879
d. Jan 19, 1968 in Anderson, Indiana
Source: *BioIn 8*

Harry, Debbie (Deborah Ann)
[Blondie]
American. Rock Singer
Hit songs include "Call Me," 1977; "Heart of Glass," 1981.
b. Jul 11, 1945 in Miami, Florida
Source: *BioIn 11, 12; BkPepl; CurBio 81; NewWmR; WhoAm 82*

Harryhausen, Ray
American. Special Effects Expert
b. Jun 29, 1920 in Los Angeles, California
Source: *CmMov; EncSF; FilmgC; IntMPA 75, 76, 77, 78, 79, 80, 81*

Harsch, Joseph Close
American. Journalist, Commentator
b. May 25, 1905 in Toledo, Ohio
Source: *AmAu&B; Au&Wr 71; CurBio 44; IntWW 74; Who 74; WhoAm 74, 76, 78, 80, 82; WhoWor 74*

Harsh, George
Canadian. Convict, Aviator
d. Jan 25, 1980 in Toronto, ON
Source: *BioIn 9, 12*

Harshaw, Margaret
American. Opera Singer
b. May 12, 1912 in Narbeth, Pennsylvania
Source: *InWom; WhoMus 72*

Hart, Frances Noyes
American. Author
b. Aug 10, 1890 in Silver Spring, Maryland
d. Oct 25, 1943 in New Canaan, Connecticut
Source: *AmAu&B; DcNAA; EncMys; LongCTC; OxAmL; REnAL; TwCA, SUP; WhAm 2; WhNAA*

Hart, Gary
American. Senator
Declared candidate for President, 1984.
b. Nov 28, 1937 in Ottawa, Kansas
Source: *BioIn 10, 11; CurBio 76*

Hart, George Overbury
American. Artist
b. May 10, 1868 in Cairo, Illinois
d. Sep 9, 1933
Source: *DcAmB S1; WhAm 1*

Hart, Jane Briggs
American. Wife of Senator Philip A Hart
Source: *BioIn 10*

Hart, Jeffrey
American. Educator, Author
b. Feb 24, 1930 in New York, New York
Source: *WhoAm 74*

Hart, Jim W
American. Football Player
b. Apr 29, 1944 in Evanston, Illinois
Source: *BioIn 8, 11; WhoAm 82; WhoFtbl 74*

Hart, John
American. Continental Congressman
b. 1711? in Stonington, Connecticut
d. May 11, 1779 in Hopewell, New Jersey
Source: *AmBi; ApCAB; BiAuS; BiDrAC; DcAmB; Drake; TwCBDA; WhAm H; WhAmP*

Hart, John(ny Lewis)
American. Cartoonist
Draws "BC," 1958--; "The Wizard of Id," 1964--.
b. Feb 18, 1931 in Endicott, New York
Source: *AuNews 1; BioNews 74; ConAu 49, 4NR; WhoAm 82*

Hart, Liddell
see: Liddell Hart, Basil

Hart, Lorenz Milton
American. Lyricist
b. May 2, 1895 in New York, New York
d. Nov 22, 1943 in New York, New York
Source: *AmSCAP 66; CurBio 40; DcAmB S3; EncMT; McGEWD; NewCBMT; OxFilm; PlP&P; REnAL; WhAm 4*

Hart, Mickey
[The Grateful Dead]
American. Singer, Musician
b. in New York, New York
Source: *NF*

Hart, Moss
American. Director, Dramatist, Author
b. Oct 24, 1904 in New York, New York
d. Dec 20, 1961 in Palm Springs, California
Source: *AmAu&B; CasWL; CnDAL; CnMD; CnThe; CurBio 40, 60, 62; EncMT; FilmgC; LongCTC; McGEWD; ModWD; NewCBMT; OxAmL; OxThe; Pen AM; PlP&P; REn; REnAL; REnWD; TwCA, SUP; WebAB; WebE&AL; WhAm 4; WorEFlm*

Hart, Pearl
American. Outlaw
d. 1925
Source: *BioIn 3, 11; Blood*

Hart, Philip Aloysius
American. Senator
b. Dec 10, 1912 in Bryn Mawr, Pennsylvania
d. Dec 26, 1976 in Washington, DC
Source: *BiDrAC; CngDr 74; CurBio 59; WhoAm 74; WhoAmP 73; WhoGov 72; WhoMW 74; WhoWor 74*

Hart, William Surrey
American. Actor, Author
b. Dec 6, 1870 in Newburgh, New York
d. Jun 23, 1946 in Newhall, California
Source: *AmAu&B; BiDFilm; CmMov; CurBio 46; Film 1; FilmgC; MnBBF; MotPP; MovMk; OxFilm; TwYS; WebAB; WhAm 2; WhScrn 74, 77; WhoHol B; WorEFlm*

Hartack, Billy (William, Jr.)
American. Jockey
b. Dec 9, 1932 in Colver, Pennsylvania
Source: *BioIn 10*

Harte, (Francis) Bret
American. Author, Journalist
Wrote *The Outcasts of Poker Flat, Tennessee's Partner, Miggles.*
b. Aug 25, 1836 in Albany, New York
d. May 5, 1902 in London, England
Source: *Alli SUP; AmAu; AmAu&B; AmBi; AtlBL; AuBYP; BbD; BiD&SB; BioIn 1, 3, 4, 5, 6, 7, 8, 9, 10, 11; CasWL; Chambr 3; ChPo, S1, S2; CnDAL; CrtT 3; CyAl 2; CyWA; DcAmAu; DcAmB; DcBiA; DcEnA, AP; DcEnL; DcLEL; DcNAA; EvLB; MouLC 4; OxAmL; OxEng; Pen AM; RAdv 1; REn; REnAL; TwCBDA; WebAB; WebE&AL; WhAm 1*

Hartford, George L A
American. Businessman, Philanthropist
b. 1865
d. Sep 23, 1957 in Montclair, New Jersey
Source: *WhAm 3; DcAmB S5*

Hartford, George Huntington
American. Founder of A & P
b. Sep 5, 1833 in Augusta, Maine
d. Aug 29, 1917 in Spring Lake, New Jersey
Source: *DcAmB S5; WhAm HA, 4*

Hartford, Huntington
American. Financier, Art Patron
b. Apr 18, 1911 in New York, New York
Source: *AmAu&B; BiE&WWA; CelR 73; ConAu 17R; CurBio 59; IntWW 74; WhoAm 74, 76, 78, 80, 82; WhoAmA 73; WhoE 74; WhoGov 72*

Hartford, John Cowan
American. Singer, Songwriter
Song "Gentle on My Mind" recorded by over 300 artists, won three Grammys.
b. Dec 30, 1937 in New York, New York
Source: *BiDAmM; BioIn 9; EncFCWM 69; WhoAm 78, 80, 82; WhoRock 81*

Hartke, Vance
American. Senator
b. May 31, 1919 in Stendal, Indiana
Source: *CngDr 74; ConAu 25R; CurBio 60; IndAu 1917; IntWW 74; WhoAm 74; WhoAmP 73; WhoGov 72; WhoWor 74*

Hartley, Fred Lloyd
American. Business Exectuive
b. Jan 16, 1917 in Vancouver, BC
Source: *BioIn 7; WhoAm 78, 80, 82*

Hartley, Leslie Poles
English. Author
b. Dec 30, 1895 in Whittlesea, England
d. Dec 13, 1972 in London, England
Source: *Au&Wr 71; CasWL; ConAu 37R, 45; ConLC 2; ConNov 72, 76; DcLEL; EncWL; EvLB; LongCTC; ModBrL, SUP; NewC; Pen ENG; RAdv 1; REn; TwCA SUP; TwCW; WebE&AL; WhAm 5; WhoTwCL*

Hartley, Mariette
[Mrs. Patrick Boyriven]
American. Actress
Best known for Polaroid commercials with James Garner.
b. Jun 21, 1940 in New York, New York
Source: *WhoAm 80; WhoHol A*

Hartley, Marsden
American. Artist
b. Jan 4, 1877 in Lewiston, Maine
d. Sep 2, 1943 in Ellsworth, Maine
Source: *AtlBL; CurBio 43; DcAmB S3; DcCAA 71; OxAmL; REnAL*

Hartman, David Downs
American. Actor, Talk Show Host
Hosts "Good Morning America" on ABC, 1975-- ; starred in "Lucas Tanner," 1974-75.
b. May 19, 1935 in Pawtucket, Rhode Island
Source: *BkPepl; IntMPA 77, 78, 79, 80, 81, 82; NewYTET; WhoAm 78, 80, 82; WhoHol A*

Hartman, Grace
American. Dancer, Comedienne
b. 1907
d. Aug 8, 1955 in Van Nuys, California
Source: *CurBio 42, 55; InWom; WhScrn 74, 77; WhoHol B*

Hartman, Paul
American. Actor
b. Mar 1, 1904 in San Francisco, California
d. Oct 2, 1973 in Los Angeles, California
Source: *BiE&WWA; CurBio 42, 73; IntMPA 75, 76, 77; MovMk; NewYTBE 73; WhAm 6; WhScrn 77; WhoAm 74; WhoHol B; WhoWorJ 72*

Hartmann, Rudolph
German. Opera Manager, Producer
b. Oct 11, 1900 in Ingolstadt, Germany
Source: *NewEOp 71*

Hartmann, Sadakichi
American. Author
b. Oct 8, 1869 in Nagasaki, Japan
d. Nov 21, 1944 in Saint Petersburg, Florida
Source: *AmAu&B; DcAmAu; DcNAA; OxAmL; REnAL; WhAm 5; WhScrn 77*

Hartnell, Norman Bishop
English. Dress Designer
b. Jun 12, 1901 in London, England
d. Jun 8, 1979 in Windsor, England
Source: *CurBio 53, 79; IntWW 74, 75, 76, 77, 79; NewYTBS 79; Who 74; WhoWor 74, 76, 78*

Hartnett, "Gabby" (Charles Leo)
"Old Tomato Face"
American. Baseball Player, Manager
Catcher, 1922-41; manager, 1938-40; Hall of Fame, 1955.
b. Dec 20, 1900 in Woonsocket, Rhode Island
d. Dec 20, 1972 in Park Ridge, Illinois
Source: *BaseEn; BioIn 1, 7, 8, 9, 10; NewYTBE 72; WhoProB 73*

Hartog, Jan de
see: DeHartog, Jan

Hartung, Hans
French. Artist
b. Sep 21, 1904 in Leipzig, Germany
Source: *ConArt; CurBio 58; IntWW 74, 75, 76, 77, 78; McGDA*

Hartz, James Leroy
American. Broadcast Journalist
b. Feb 3, 1940
Source: *AuNews 2; BioIn 10, 11; BioNews 74; IntMPA 82*

Harun-Ar-Rashid
Caliph of Baghdad
b. 764?
d. 809?
Source: *NewCol 75*

Harunobu, Suzuki
Japanese. Artist, Printer
b. 1718
d. 1770
Source: *BioIn 10; NewCol 75*

Harvard, John
English. Clergyman
Left library, estate money toward founding of new college; named in his honor, 1639.
b. Nov 1607 in London, England
d. Sep 14, 1638 in Charlestown, Massachusetts
Source: *AmBi; ApCAB; CyAL 1; DcAmB; Drake; REn; TwCBDA; WebAB; WhAm H*

Harvey, Anthony
English. Motion Picture Director
b. Jun 3, 1931 in London, England
Source: *FilmgC; IntMPA 75, 76, 77, 78, 79, 80, 81, 82; IntWW 74; WhoAm 82*

Harvey, Frank Laird
English. Author, Actor, Director
b. Aug 11, 1912 in Manchester, England
Source: *Au&Wr 71; ConAu 5R; FilmgC; IntAu&W 77; WhoThe 72, 77*

Harvey, Frederick Henry
American. Restaurateur
b. 1835 in London, England
d. Feb 9, 1901 in Leavenworth, Kansas
Source: *WebAB*

Harvey, George Brinton M
American. Diplomat, Journalist
b. Feb 16, 1864 in Peacham, Vermont
d. Aug 20, 1928
Source: *AmAu&B; AmBi; DcAmB; DcNAA; WhAm 1*

Harvey, Laurence
[Larushke Mischa Skikne]
British. Actor
b. Oct 1, 1928 in Janiskis, Lithuania
d. Nov 25, 1973 in London, England
Source: *BiDFilm; BiE&WWA; BioNews 74; CurBio 61, 74; FilmgC; MotPP; MovMk; NewC; NewYTBE 73; OxFilm; WhAm 6; WhScrn 77; Who 74; WhoHol B; WhoWor 74; WorEFlm*

Harvey, Paul
American. Broadcast Journalist
b. Sep 4, 1918 in Tulsa, Oklahoma
Source: *CelR 73; WhoAm 74, 76, 78, 80, 82*

Harvey, William
English. Physician, Anatomist
b. Apr 1, 1578 in Folkestone, England
d. Jun 3, 1657
Source: *Alli; BrAu; DcEnL; NewC; OxEng; REn*

Harwell, Ernie
American. Baseball Broadcaster
b. Jan 25, 1918 in Atlanta, Georgia
Source: *BioNews 74*

Harwood, John
English. Actor, Motion Picture Director
b. Feb 29, 1876 in London, England
d. Dec 26, 1944
Source: *NotNAT B*

Harwood, Vanessa Clare
Canadian. Dancer
b. 1947 in Cheltenham, England
Source: *WhoAm 78, 80, 82*

Hasani, Ali Nasir Muhammad
Prime Minister of Yemen
b. 1938
Source: *BioIn 11; WhoWor 74*

Hasegawa, Kazuo
Japanese. Actor
b. 1908
Source: *OxFilm*

Hasek, Jaroslav
Czech. Author
b. Apr 24, 1883 in Prague, Czechoslovakia
d. Jan 3, 1923 in Lipnice, Czechoslovakia
Source: *CasWL; ClDMEL; EncWL; EvEuW; LongCTC; ModSL 2; Pen EUR; REn; TwCA, SUP; TwCW; WhoTwCL*

Hashimoto, Ken
American. Scientist
b. Jun 16, 1931 in Niigata, Japan
Source: *AmM&WS 73P*

Haskell, Arnold Lionel
English. Ballet Critic, Historian
b. Jul 19, 1903 in London, England
d. Nov 14, 1980 in Bath, England
Source: *ConAu 5R; IntWW 74, 75, 76, 77, 78; SmATA 6; Who 74; WhoWor 74*

Hasluck, Sir Paul Meernaa
Australian. Governor-General
b. Apr 1, 1905 in Fremantle, Australia
Source: *CurBio 46; IntWW 74; Who 74; WhoGov 72; WhoWor 74*

Hassam, Childe
American. Artist, Etcher
b. Oct 17, 1859 in Dorchester, Massachusetts
d. Aug 27, 1935 in East Hampton, New York
Source: *AmBi; OxAmL; WebAB; WhAm 1*

Hassan II
Moroccan. King
b. Jul 9, 1929
Source: *BioIn 10; IntWW 74; WhoWor 74*

Hasse, Johann Adolph
German. Composer
b. Mar 25, 1699 in Bergedorf, Germany
d. Dec 16, 1783 in Venice, Italy
Source: *NewEOp 71*

Hasselblad, Victor
Swedish. Industrialist
b. 1906
d. Aug 6, 1978 in Gothenburg, Sweden
Source: *WhoWor 74*

Hasselmans, Louis
French. Conductor
b. Jul 25, 1878 in Paris, France
d. Dec 27, 1947 in San Juan, Puerto Rico
Source: *WhAm 3*

Hasso, Signe Eleonora Cecilia
Swedish. Actress, Composer
b. Aug 15, 1915 in Stockholm, Sweden
Source: *BiE&WWA; FilmgC; ForWC 70; HolP 40; MotPP; MovMk; NotNAT; WhoAm 74, 76, 78, 80, 82; WhoE 74; WhoHol A; WhoThe 77*

Hastie, William Henry
American. Educator, Lawyer, Judge
Dean, Harvard Law School, 1939-46; governor, Virgin Islands, 1946-49.
b. Nov 17, 1904 in Knoxville, Tennessee
d. Apr 14, 1976 in East Norriton, Pennsylvania
Source: *CurBio 44, 76; EncAB-H; IntWW 74; WebAB; WhAm 7; WhoE 74; WhoGov 72*

Hastings, Scott
see: Our Gang

Hastings, Thomas
American. Architect
b. Mar 11, 1860 in New York
d. Oct 22, 1929
Source: *AmBi; DcAmB; WhAm 1*

Hastings, Warren
English. Statesman
b. Dec 6, 1732 in Churchill, England
d. Aug 22, 1818
Source: *Alli; BiDLA; NewC; REn*

Hatch, Carl A
American. Lawyer, Politician
b. Nov 27, 1889 in Kirwin, Kansas
d. Sep 15, 1963 in Albuquerque, New Mexico
Source: *BiDrAC; CurBio 44, 63; WhAm 4*

Hatch, Orrin Grant
American. Senator
b. Mar 22, 1934 in Pittsburgh, Pennsylvania
Source: *AlmAP 78, 80; CngDr 77, 79; CurBio 82; IntWW 77, 78; WhoAm 78, 80, 82; WhoAmP 77, 79; WhoGov 77; WhoWest 78*

Hatcher, Mickey (Michael Vaughn, Jr.)
American. Baseball Player
b. Mar 15, 1955 in Cleveland, Ohio
Source: *BaseEn; BioIn 12*

Hatcher, Richard Gordon
American. Mayor of Gary
b. Jul 10, 1933 in Michigan City, Indiana
Source: *CurBio 72; WhoAm 74, 76, 78, 80, 82; WhoAmP 73; WhoBlA 75; WhoGov 72; WhoMW 74*

Hatchett, John F
American. Political Activist
b. 1931?
Source: *BioIn 8*

Hatfield, Hurd
American. Actor
b. 1920 in New York, New York
Source: *BiDFilm; BiE&WWA; FilmgC; IntMPA 75, 76, 77, 78, 79, 80, 81, 82; MotPP; MovMk; NotNAT; WhoHol A*

Hatfield, Mark Odom
American. Senator, Former Governor
Senator from OR, 1967--; wrote *Between a Rock and a Hard Place*. 1977.
b. Jul 12, 1922 in Dallas, Oregon
Source: *BiDrAC; CelR 73; CngDr 74; CurBio 59; IntWW 74; WhoAm 74, 76, 78, 80, 82; WhoAmP 73; WhoGov 72; WhoRel 75; WhoWest 74; WhoWor 74*

Hathaway, Anne
English. Wife of William Shakespeare
b. 1557 in Temple Grafton, England
d. 1623
Source: *InWom; NewC; REn*

Hathaway, Donny
American. Singer, Songwriter
b. 1945? in Saint Louis, Missouri
d. Jan 13, 1979 in New York, New York
Source: *BioIn 11; RkOn*

Hathaway, Henry
American. Motion Picture Director
b. Mar 13, 1898 in Sacramento, California
Source: *BiDFilm; CmMov; DcFM; FilmgC; IntMPA 75, 76, 77, 78, 79, 80, 81, 82; MovMk; OxFilm; WorEFlm*

Hathaway, Sibyl Collings
[Dame of Sark]
British. Author
Seigneur of Sark, 1927-74.
b. Jan 13, 1884
d. Jul 14, 1974 in London, England
Source: *ConAu 1R, 103; InWom; Who 74*

Hathaway, Stanley Knapp
American. Governor
b. Jul 19, 1924 in Osceola, Nebraska
Source: *IntWW 74; WhoAm 74; WhoAmP 73; WhoGov 72; WhoWest 74*

Hathaway, William Dodd
American. Senator
b. Feb 29, 1924 in Cambridge, Massachusetts
Source: *BiDrAC; CngDr 74; IntWW 74; WhoAm 74; WhoAmP 73; WhoE 74; WhoGov 72*

Hatlo, Jimmy
American. Cartoonist
b. Sep 1, 1898 in Providence, Rhode Island
d. Nov 30, 1963 in Carmel, California
Source: *ConAu 93; WhAm 4*

Hatton, Sir Christopher
English. Statesman
b. 1540 in Holdenby, England
d. Nov 20, 1591 in London, England
Source: *Alli; NewC; OxEng*

Hauberg, John Henry
American. Businessman
b. Jun 24, 1916 in Rock Island, Illinois
Source: *St&PR 75; WhoAm 74*

Hauer, Rutger
Dutch. Actor
b. Jan 23, 1944 in Breukelen, Netherlands
Source: *IntMPA 82*

Hauff, Wilhelm
German. Author
b. Nov 29, 1802 in Stuttgart, Germany
d. Nov 18, 1827 in Stuttgart, Germany
Source: *AuBYP; BiD&SB; CasWL; DcBiA; EuAu; EvEuW; OxGer; Pen EUR; REn; WhoChL*

Haug, Hans
Swiss. Opera Composer
b. Jul 27, 1900 in Basel, Switzerland
Source: *NewEOp 71*

Hauge, Gabriel
American. Economist, Banker
b. Mar 7, 1914 in Hawley, Minnesota
d. Jul 24, 1981 in New York, New York
Source: *CurBio 53, 81; IntWW 74, 75, 76, 77, 78; WhoAm 74, 76, 78, 80; WhoE 74, 77, 79; WhoF&I 74, 75, 79; WhoWor 74, 76, 78*

Haughey, Charles James
Irish. Prime Minister
b. Sep 16, 1925 in Castlebar, Ireland
Source: *CurBio 81; IntWW 74, 75, 76, 77, 78, 80; NewYTBS 79; WhoWor 76, 78*

Hauk, Minnie
American. Opera Singer
b. Nov 16, 1851 in New York, New York
d. Feb 6, 1929 in Triebschen, Switzerland
Source: *AmBi; AmWom; DcAmB; InWom; NotAW; WhAm H, 4*

Haupt, Herman
American. Civil Engineer
b. Mar 26, 1817 in Philadelphia, Pennsylvania
d. Dec 14, 1905
Source: *Alli, SUP; AmBi; ApCAB; DcAmAu; DcAmB; DcNAA; TwCBDA; WhAm 1*

Hauptmann, Bruno Richard
German. Kidnapper, Murderer
Kidnapped son of Charles Lindbergh, Mar 1, 1932; convicted, executed for murder.
b. Nov 26, 1900 in Kamenz, Germany
d. Apr 3, 1936 in Trenton, New Jersey
Source: *AmBi; Blood; NewCol 75*

Hauptmann, Gerhart
German. Dramatist
b. Nov 15, 1862 in Obersalzbrunn, Germany
d. Jun 6, 1946 in Schreiberlau, Germany
Source: *AtlBL; BiD&SB; CasWL; ClDMEL; CnMD; CnThe; CurBio 46; CyWA; EncWL; EvEuW; LongCTC; McGEWD; ModGL; ModWD; NewC; OxEng; OxGer; OxThe; Pen EUR; PlP&P; RComWL; REn; REnWD; TwCA, SUP; TwCW; WhAm 2; WhoTwCL*

Hauser, Gayelord
American. Dietitian, Nutritionist
b. May 17, 1895 in Tubingen, Germany
Source: *CelR 73; NewYTBS 74; WhoAm 76, 78, 80, 82*

Hauser, Kaspar
German. Foundling
b. Apr 30, 1812?
d. Dec 17, 1833
Source: *REn*

Hauser, Tim
see: Manhattan Transfer

Haushofer, Karl
German. Nazi Geographer
b. Aug 27, 1869 in Munich, Germany
d. Mar 10, 1946 in Germany
Source: *CurBio 42, 46; REn*

Hauy, Rene Just
French. Mineralogist
b. Feb 28, 1743
d. Jun 3, 1822
Source: *NewCol 75*

Havell, Robert
English. Engraver
b. 1793
d. 1878
Source: *AntBDN B*

Havelock, Henry
British. Army General
b. 1795
d. 1857
Source: *NewCol 75*

Havemeyer, Henry Osborne
American. Art Collector, Businessman
b. Oct 18, 1847 in New York, New York
d. 1907
Source: *AmBi; DcAmB; EncAB-H; WhAm 1*

Havens, Richie
American. Singer, Musician
b. Jan 21, 1941
Source: *BioIn 9; RkOn*

Haver, June
American. Actress
b. 1926 in Rock Island, Illinois
Source: *CmMov; FilmgC; MotPP; MovMk; WhoHol A*

Havighurst, Walter Edwin
American. Children's Author
b. Nov 28, 1901 in Appleton, Wisconsin
Source: *AmAu&B; AmNov; Au&Wr 71; AuBYP; CnDAL; ConAu 1R; DrAS 74E; MorJA; OhA&B; OxAmL; REnAL; SmATA 1; TwCA SUP; WhoAm 74; WrDr 76*

Haviland, Virginia
American. Librarian, Children's Author
b. May 21, 1911 in Rochester, New York
Source: *BiDrLUS 70; ChPo S1, S2; ConAu 17R; SmATA 6; WhoAm 74, 76, 78, 80, 82; WhoAmW 77; WhoS&SW 73*

Havlicek, John
"Hondo"
American. Basketball Player
Scored 25,073 points; set NBA record most games played, 1,188.
b. Apr 8, 1940 in Martins Ferry, Ohio
Source: *BioIn 6, 8, 9, 10, 11; WhoAm 74, 76; WhoBbl 73*

Havoc, June
[June Hovick]
American. Actress
b. Nov 8, 1916 in Seattle, Washington
Source: *BiE&WWA; FilmgC; HolP 40; InWom; IntMPA 75, 76, 77, 78, 79, 80, 81, 82; MotPP; MovMk; WhoHol A; WhoThe 77*

Hawerchuk, Dale
Canadian. Hockey Player
Won Calder Cup, 1981, for NHL rookie of year.
b. Apr 4, 1963 in Toronto, ON
Source: *HocReg*

Hawkes, Greg
see: Cars, The

Hawkes, John Clendennin Burne, Jr.
American. Author
b. Aug 17, 1925 in Stamford, Connecticut
Source: *AmAu&B; ConAu 1R, 2NR; ConDr 73; ConLC 1, 2, 3, 4, 7, 9, 14, 15; ConNov 72, 76; CroCD; DrAF 76; EncWL; IntWW 74; ModAL, SUP; OxAmL; Pen AM; RAdv 1; WebE&AL; WhoAm 74, 76, 78, 80, 82; WhoE 74; WhoTwCL; WhoWor 74; WorAu; WrDr 76*

Hawkins, "Bean" (Coleman)
American. Jazz Musician
b. Nov 21, 1904 in Saint Joseph, Missouri
d. May 19, 1969 in New York, New York
Source: *WhAm 5; WhScrn 77; WhoJazz 72*

Hawkins, Erskine Ramsey
American. Musician, Band Leader
b. Jul 26, 1914 in Birmingham, Alabama
Source: *AmSCAP 66; CurBio 71; WhoJazz 72*

Hawkins, Jack
English. Actor, Motion Picture Producer
b. Sep 14, 1910 in London, England
d. Jul 18, 1973 in London, England
Source: *BiDFilm; CmMov; CurBio 59, 73; FilmgC; MotPP; MovMk; NewYTBE 73; OxFilm; PlP&P; WhAm 5; WhScrn 77; WhoHol B; WorEFlm*

Hawkins, Sir John
[Sir John Hawkyns]
English. Naval Commander
b. 1532 in Plymouth, England
d. Nov 12, 1595
Source: *Alli; NewC; OxEng; REn*

Hawkins, Osie Penman, Jr.
American. Opera Singer
b. Aug 16, 1913 in Phoenix City, Alabama
Source: *WhoAm 74, 76, 78, 80, 82*

Hawkins, Paula
[Mrs. Walter E Hawkins]
American. Senator
b. Jan 24, 1927 in Salt Lake City, Utah
Source: *WhoAm 74, 78, 80, 82; WhoAmW 70, 72, 74, 75, 77, 79; WhoS&SW 78*

Hawks, Howard Winchester
American. Motion Picture Director, Producer
b. May 30, 1896 in Goshen, Indiana
d. Dec 26, 1977 in Palm Springs, California
Source: *BiDFilm; CmMov; CurBio 72; DcFM; FilmgC; IntMPA 75, 76, 77; MovMk; OxFilm; TwYS; WebAB; WhoAm 74; WhoWor 74; WorEFlm*

Hawley, Cameron
American. Author
b. Sep 19, 1905 in Howard, South Dakota
d. Mar 9, 1969 in Marathon, Florida
Source: *AmAu&B; ConAu 1R, 25R; CurBio 57; WhAm 5*

Hawn, Goldie Jean
American. Actress
Won Oscar for *Cactus Flower,* 1969.
b. Nov 21, 1945 in Washington, DC
Source: *BioNews 74; BkPepl; CelR 73; CurBio 71; FilmgC; IntMPA 75, 76, 77, 78, 79, 80, 81, 82; MotPP; MovMk; NewYTBE 73; WhoAm 74, 76, 78, 80, 82; WhoHol A*

Haworth, Jill
English. Actress
b. 1945 in Sussex, England
Source: *FilmgC; MotPP; WhoHol A*

Haworth, Leland John
American. Physicist
b. Jul 11, 1904 in Flint, Michigan
d. Mar 5, 1979 in Port Jefferson, New York
Source: *AmM&WS 73P, 76P, 79P; CurBio 50, 79; IntAu&W 77; IntWW 74, 75, 76, 77, 78; NewYTBS 79; WhAm 7; WhoAm 74, 76, 78; WhoE 74*

Haworth, Mary Robbins
American. Psychologist
b. Jan 31, 1931 in Chicago, Illinois
Source: *AmM&WS 73S*

Hawthorne, Julian
American. Children's Author
b. Jun 22, 1846 in Boston, Massachusetts
d. Jul 14, 1934 in San Francisco, California
Source: *Alli SUP; AmAu&B; AmBi; ApCAB; BbD; BiD&SB; CarSB; Chambr 3; ChPo, S2; DcAmAu; DcAmB S1; DcBiA; DcEnA, AP; DcEnL; DcNAA; EncMys; OxAmL; REnAL; TwCA; TwCBDA; WhAm 1; WhNAA*

Hawthorne, Nathaniel
American. Author
Wrote *The Scarlet Letter,* 1850; *The House of Seven Gables,* 1851.
b. Jul 4, 1804 in Salem, Massachusetts
d. May 19, 1864 in Plymouth, New Hampshire
Source: *Alli, SUP; AmAu; AmAu&B; AmBi; AmWr; ApCAB; AtlBL; BbD; BiAuS; BiD&SB; CarSB; CasWL; Chambr 3; ChPo S1, S2; CnDAL; CrtT 3; CyAl 2; CyWA; DcAmAu; DcAmB; DcBiA; DcEnA, AP; DcEnL; DcLEL; DcNAA; Drake; EncAB-H; EvLB; FamAYP; FilmgC; MouLC 3; OxAmL; OxEng; Pen AM; RAdv 1; RComWL; REn; REnAL; Str&VC; TwCBDA; WebAB; WebE&AL; WhAm H; WhoChL*

Hay, Barry
see: Golden Earring

Hay, Colin
see: Men at Work

Hay, John Milton
American. Statesman, Author
b. Oct 8, 1838 in Salem, Indiana
d. Jul 1, 1905 in Newburg, New Hampshire
Source: *Alli SUP; AmAu; AmAu&B; AmBi; BbD; BiD&SB; BiDrUSE; CasWL; ChPo, S1, S2; DcAmAu; DcAmB; DcBiA; DcNAA; EncAB-H; EvLB; IndAu 1816; OhA&B; OxAmL; Pen AM; REn; REnAL; WebAB; WhAm 1; WhAmP*

Haya de la Torre, Victor Raul
Peruvian. Political Leader
b. Feb 22, 1895 in Trujillo, Peru
d. Aug 2, 1979 in Lima, Peru
Source: *ConAu 89; CurBio 42, 79; DcSpL; IntWW 74, 75, 76, 77, 78; McGEWB; NewCol 75; NewYTBS 79; OxSpan; WhoWor 74*

Hayakawa, S(amuel) I(chiye)
American. Congressman, Educator, Author
b. Jul 18, 1906 in Vancouver, BC
Source: *AmAu&B; AmM&WS 73S; CelR 73; ConAu 13R; CurBio 59; DrAS 74F; IntWW 74; LEduc 74; REn; REnAL; TwCA SUP; WebAB; WhoAm 74, 76, 78, 80, 82; WhoWest 74; WrDr 76*

Hayakawa, Sessue
Japanese. Actor
b. Jun 10, 1890 in Chiba, Japan
d. Nov 23, 1974 in Tokyo, Japan
Source: *BioNews 74; CurBio 62, 74; Film 1; FilmgC; MotPP; MovMk; NewYTBE 73; OxFilm; TwYS; WhAm 6; WhScrn 77; WhoHol B*

Haycock, Peter
see: Climax Blues Band, The

Hayden, Carl Trumball
American. Politician
b. Oct 2, 1877 in Tempe, Arizona
d. Jan 25, 1972 in Mesa, Arizona
Source: *BiDrAC; ConAu 33R; CurBio 51, 72; NewYTBE 72; WhAm 5, 6; WhAmP*

Hayden, Melissa
[Mildred Herman]
Canadian. Ballerina
Dancer, NY City Ballet Co., 1950-73; wrote *M.H.-Off Stage and On,* 1961.
b. Apr 25, 1923 in Toronto, ON
Source: *CanWW 70; CurBio 55; InWom; NewYTBE 73; WhoAm 74; WhoHol A; WhoWor 74*

Hayden, Robert Earl
American. Poet
b. Aug 4, 1913 in Detroit, Michigan
d. Feb 25, 1980 in Ann Arbor, Michigan
Source: *AmAu&B; BlkAW; ChPo S1, S2; ConAu 69, 97; ConLC 5, 9, 14; CroCAP; DcLEL 1940; DrAP 75; LivgBAA; SelBAA; SmATA 19; WhAm 7; WrDr 76, 80*

Hayden, Russell
[Pate Lucid]
"Lucky"
American. Actor
b. Jun 12, 1912 in Chico, California
d. Jun 9, 1981 in Palm Springs, California
Source: *BioIn 8, 10; FilmgC; IntMPA 75, 76, 77, 78, 79, 80, 81; NewYTBS 81; WhoHol A*

Hayden, Sterling
[John Hamilton]
American. Actor, Author
b. Mar 26, 1916 in Montclair, New Jersey
Source: *BiDFilm; FilmgC; HolP 40; IntMPA 75, 76, 77, 78, 79, 80, 81, 82; MotPP; MovMk; OxFilm; WhoAm 82; WhoHol A; WorEFlm*

Hayden, Tom (Thomas Emmett)
[The Chicago 7]
American. Journalist, Activist
Married to actress Jane Fonda.
b. Dec 12, 1940 in Royal Oak, Michigan
Source: *AmAu&B; WhoAm 78, 80, 82*

Haydn, Franz Joseph
Austrian. Composer
Composed *Surprise Symphony,* 1791; influenced work of Beethoven, Mozart.
b. Mar 31, 1732 in Rohrau, Austria
d. May 31, 1809 in Vienna, Austria
Source: *AtlBL; NewCol 75; REn*

Haydn, Hiram Collins
American. Editor, Author
b. Nov 3, 1907 in Cleveland, Ohio
d. Dec 2, 1973 in Vineyard Haven, Massachusetts
Source: *AmAu&B; AmNov; Au&Wr 71; CnDAL; ConAu 45; ConAu P-1; ConNov 72; NewYTBE 73; OhA&B; OxAmL; REnAL; TwCA SUP; WhAm 6; WhoWor 74*

Haydn, Richard
English. Actor, Director
Starred in *Please Don't Eat the Daisies,* 1960; *The Sound of Music,* 1965,
b. 1905 in London, England
Source: *FilmgC; IntMPA 75, 76, 77, 78, 79, 80, 81, 82; MovMk; Vers B; WhoAm 74; WhoHol A; WorEFlm*

Haydock, Eric
see: Hollies, The

Haydon, Julie
American. Actress
b. Jun 10, 1910 in Oak Park, Illinois
Source: *BiE&WWA; NotNAT; PlP&P; ThFT; WhoHol A; WhoThe 77*

Hayek, Friedrich August von
British. Economist, Author
b. May 8, 1899 in Vienna, Austria
Source: *ConAu 93; CurBio 45; IntWW 74; Who 74; WhoAm 74; WhoWor 74*

Hayes, Alfred
American. Author, Dramatist, Poet
b. 1911 in London, England
Source: *AmAu&B; AmNov; ModAL; OxAmL; REn; REnAL; TwCA SUP*

Hayes, Billy
American. Turkish Prison Escapee
Source: *NewYTBE 73*

Hayes, Elvin
American. Basketball Player
Guard, 1968--; NBA leading scorer, 1969.
b. Nov 17, 1945 in Rayville, Louisiana
Source: *WhoAm 82; WhoBbl 73; WhoBlA 75*

Hayes, "Gabby" (George Francis)
American. Actor
b. May 7, 1885 in Wellsville, New York
d. Feb 9, 1969 in Burbank, California
Source: *BiE&WWA; CmMov; FilmgC; MotPP; MovMk; OxFilm; PlP&P; Vers B; WhScrn 74, 77; WhoHol B*

Hayes, Helen
[Mrs. Charles MacArthur; Helen H Brown]
"First Lady of the American Theater"
American. Actress
Won Oscars for *The Sin of Madelon Claudet,* 1931, *Airport,* 1969; adoptive mother of James MacArthur.
b. Oct 10, 1900 in Washington, DC
Source: *BiE&WWA; CelR 73; CurBio 42; FamA&A; Film 1; FilmgC; InWom; IntMPA 75, 76, 77, 78, 79, 80, 81, 82; IntWW 74; MovMk; NotNAT; OxAmL; OxFilm; OxThe; REn; ThFT; WebAB; Who 74; WhoAm 74; WhoAmW 77; WhoE 74; WhoHol A; WhoThe 77; WhoWor 74; WorEFlm*

Hayes, Isaac
American. Musician, Singer, Songwriter
Won Grammy, Oscar for score of *Shaft,* 1971.
b. Aug 20, 1942 in Covington, Tennessee
Source: *BioNews 74; CelR 73; CurBio 72; NewYTBE 72; WhoAm 74, 76, 78, 80, 82; WhoBlA 75; WhoHol A*

Hayes, Patrick J
American. Religious Leader
b. Nov 20, 1867 in New York, New York
d. Sep 4, 1938
Source: *AmBi; DcAmB S2; WhAm 1*

Hayes, Peter Lind
American. Actor, Composer, Author
b. Jun 25, 1915 in San Francisco, California
Source: *AmAu&B; AmSCAP 66; BiE&WWA; CurBio 59; IntMPA 75, 76, 77, 78, 79, 80, 81, 82; NotNAT; WhoAm 74, 76, 78, 80, 82; WhoHol A*

Hayes, Mrs. Peter Lind
see: Healy, Mary

Hayes, Roland
American. Opera Singer
b. Jun 3, 1887 in Curryville, Georgia
d. 1977 in Boston, Massachusetts
Source: *CurBio 42; WebAB; WhoAm 74; WhoBlA 75*

Hayes, Rutherford B(irchard)
American. 19th US President
Won presidency in newly created electoral college by one vote over Samuel J Tilden, 1876.
b. Oct 4, 1822 in Delaware, Ohio
d. Jan 17, 1893 in Fremont, Ohio
Source: *AmAu&B; AmBi; ApCAB; BiAuS; BiDrAC; BiDrUSE; DcAmB; Drake; EncAB-H; OhA&B; OxAmL; REnAL; TwCBDA; WebAB; WhAm H; WhAmP*

Hayes, "Woody" (Wayne Woodrow)
American. Football Coach
Head coach, Ohio State, 1951-79; 238-72-10 record second only to Bear Bryant.
b. Feb 14, 1913 in Clifton, Ohio
Source: *BioNews 75; CelR 73; CurBio 75; NewYTBS 74; WhoAm 78*

Hayman, Richard Warren Joseph
American. Conductor
Founded Manhattan Pops Orchestra, 1963.
b. Mar 27, 1920 in Cambridge, Massachusetts
Source: *AmSCAP 66, 80; CmpEPM*

Hayman, Richard
American. Banker
b. 1925
Source: *St&PR 75*

Haymes, Dick (Richard)
American. Singer
b. Sep 13, 1917 in Buenos Aires, Argentina
d. Mar 28, 1980 in Los Angeles, California
Source: *FilmgC; HolP 40; IntMPA 75, 76, 77; MotPP; WhoHol A*

Haymes, Joe
American. Jazz Musician
b. 1908 in Marshfield, Missouri
Source: *WhoJazz 72*

Haynes, George Edward
American. Civil Rights Leader
b. May 11, 1880 in Pine Bluff, Arkansas
d. Jan 8, 1960
Source: *NatCAB 44; WhAm 3; WhoColR*

Haynes, Lloyd
American. Actor
b. 1934 in South Bend, Indiana
Source: *WhoHol A*

Haynes Dixon, Margaret Rumer
see: Godden, Rumer, pseud.

Haynie, Carol
American. Politician
Source: *WomPO 76*

Haynie, Hugh
American. Editorial Cartoonist
b. Feb 6, 1927 in Reedville, Virginia
Source: *WhoAm 74, 76, 78, 80, 82; WhoS&SW 73*

Haynsworth, Clement Furman, Jr.
American. Judge
b. Oct 30, 1912 in Greenville, South Carolina
Source: *WhoAm 74, 76, 78, 80, 82; WhoAmP 73; WhoGov 72; WhoS&SW 73*

Hays, Brooks
American. Congressman, Author
b. Aug 9, 1898 in Russellville, Arkansas
d. Oct 11, 1981 in Chevy Chase, Maryland
Source: *BioIn 3, 4, 5, 8, 11; ConAu P-1; CurBio 58, 82; IntWW 78; PolProf E; WhoAm 78, 80; WhoWor 78; WrDr 80*

Hays, Lee
[The Weavers]
American. Singer, Songwriter
b. 1914 in Little Rock, Arkansas
d. Aug 26, 1981 in North Tarrytown, New York
Source: *BiDAmM; EncFCWM 69*

Hays, Robert
American. Actor
Starred in *Airplane,* 1980.
b. Jul 24, 1948 in Bethesda, Maryland
Source: *IntMPA 82*

Hays, Wayne Levere
American. Former Congressman
Retired from office after involvement with Elizabeth Ray, 1976.
b. Jun 13, 1911 in Bannock, Ohio
Source: *BiDrAC; BioNews 74; CngDr 74; CurBio 74; WhoAm 74, 76; WhoAmP 73, 75, 77, 79; WhoGov 72, 75; WhoMW 74, 76*

Hays, Will Harrison
American. Statesman, Film Censor
b. Nov 5, 1879 in Sullivan, Indiana
d. Mar 7, 1954 in Sullivan, Indiana
Source: *CurBio 43, 54; DcAmB S5; DcFM; FilmgC; IndAu 1917; OxFilm; WhAm 3; WorEFlm*

Hayton, Lennie (Leonard George)
American. Composer, Conductor
b. Feb 13, 1908 in New York, New York
d. Apr 24, 1971 in Palm Springs, California
Source: *AmSCAP 66; CmMov; NewYTBE 71; WhoJazz 72*

Hayward, Brooke
American. Author, Actress
b. Jul 5, 1937 in Los Angeles, California
Source: *BioIn 11; BkPepl; ConAu 81; NewYTBS 77*

Hayward, Leland
American. Motion Picture Producer, Agent
b. Sep 13, 1902 in Nebraska City, Nebraska
d. Mar 18, 1971 in Yorktown Heights, New York
Source: *BiE&WWA; CurBio 49, 71; EncMT; FilmgC; NewYTBE 71*

Hayward, Louis
American. Actor
b. Mar 19, 1909 in Johannesburg, South Africa
Source: *CmMov; FilmgC; IntMPA 75, 76, 77; MotPP; MovMk; WhoHol A; WorEFlm*

Hayward, Susan
[Edythe Marrener]
American. Actress
Won Oscar for *I Want to Live,* 1958.
b. Jun 30, 1919 in New York, New York
d. Mar 14, 1975 in Beverly Hills, California
Source: *BiDFilm; CmMov; CurBio 53; FilmgC; InWom; IntMPA 75; MotPP; MovMk; OxFilm; ThFT; WhAm 6; WhScrn 77; WhoAm 74; WorEFlm*

Haywood, "Big Bill" (William Dudley)
American. Labor Leader
Helped organize IWW, 1905; convicted of sedition during WW I.
b. Feb 4, 1869 in Salt Lake City, Utah
d. May 18, 1928 in U.S.S.R.
Source: *AmBi; DcAmB; DcNAA; EncAB-H; WebAB; WhAm HA, 4*

Haywood, Spencer
American. Basketball Player
b. Apr 21, 1950 in Silver City, Mississippi
Source: *WhoBbl 73*

Hayworth, Rita
[Margarita Cansino]
American. Actress
Starred in *Gilda,* 1946; husbands included Orson Welles, 1943-47, Dick Haymes, 1953-54.
b. Oct 17, 1918 in New York, New York
Source: *BiDFilm; CelR 73; CmMov; CurBio 60; FilmgC; InWom; IntMPA 75, 76, 77, 78, 79, 80, 81, 82; MotPP; MovMk; OxFilm; ThFT; WhoAm 74, 76, 78, 80, 82; WhoHol A; WomWMM; WorEFlm*

Hazan, Marcella
Italian. Author, Chef
b. 1924?
Source: *BioIn 11; WhoAm 82*

Hazlitt, William
English. Author
Wrote *Characters of Shakespeare's Plays,* 1817; *Lectures on the English Poets,* 1818.
b. Apr 10, 1778 in Maidstone, England
d. Sep 18, 1830 in London, England
Source: *Alli; AtlBL; BiD&SB; BiDLA; BrAu 19; CasWL; Chambr 3; CrtT 2; CyWA; DcEnA, AP; DcEnL; DcEuL; DcLEL; EvLB; MouLC 3; NewC; OxEng; OxThe; Pen ENG; RAdv 1; RComWL; REn; WebE&AL*

Head, Edith
American. Costume Designer
Won eight Oscars; wrote autobiography *Fashion as a Career,* 1966.
b. Oct 28, 1907? in Los Angeles, California
d. Oct 24, 1981 in Los Angeles, California
Source: *BioIn 1, 2, 4, 5, 10; CelR 73; CurBio 45, 82; FilmgC; IntMPA 78, 79, 80, 81, 82; WhoAm 74, 76, 78, 80; WhoAmW 58, 64, 66, 68, 70, 72, 74*

Headon, Topper
see: Clash, The

Healey, Myron
American. Actor
b. 1922 in Petaluma, California
Source: *IntMPA 75, 76, 77, 78, 79, 80, 81, 82; WhoHol A*

Healy, George Peter Alexander
American. Artist
b. Jul 15, 1813 in Boston, Massachusetts
d. Jun 24, 1894 in Chicago, Illinois
Source: *AmBi; ApCAB; DcAmB; DcNAA; Drake; TwCBDA; WhAm H*

Healy, Mary
[Mrs. Peter Lind Hayes]
American. Actress, Singer
b. Apr 14, 1918 in New Orleans, Louisiana
Source: *BiE&WWA; InWom; NotNAT; WhoAm 74, 76, 78, 80, 82; WhoHol A*

Healy, Ted
American. Actor
b. Oct 1, 1896 in Houston, Texas
d. Dec 21, 1937 in Los Angeles, California
Source: *FilmgC; WhScrn 74, 77; WhoHol B*

Heard, Gerald (Henry FitzGerald)
English. Author
b. Oct 6, 1889 in London, England
d. Aug 14, 1971 in Santa Monica, California
Source: *AmAu&B; Au&Wr 71; BiDPara; ConAu 21R, 29R; ConAu P-2; LongCTC; NewC; REn; TwCA, SUP; WhAm 5; Who 74*

Heard, John
American. Actor
b. Mar 7, 1945 in Washington, DC
Source: *BioIn 11; IntMPA 82*

Hearn, Lafcadio
Japanese. Author, Journalist
b. Jun 27, 1850 in Ionian Islands, Greece
d. Sep 26, 1904 in Okubo, Japan
Source: *Alli SUP; AmAu; AmAu&B; AmBi; AnCL; AtlBL; BbD; BiD&SB; BiDSA; CasWL; Chambr 3; ChPo; CnDAL; CrtT 3; CyWA; DcAmAu; DcAmB; DcBiA; DcEuL; DcLEL; DcNAA; EncAB-H; EvLB; ModAL; NewC; OhA&B; OxAmL; OxEng; Pen AM, ENG; PoIre; RAdv 1; REn; REnAL; WebAB; WhAm 1*

Hearne, Samuel
British. Explorer
First man to reach Arctic Ocean overland, 1771-72.
b. 1745
d. 1792
Source: *Alli; ApCAB; BbtC; DcLEL; Drake; OxCan*

Hearns, Thomas (Tommy)
"Detroit Hit Man"; "Motor City Cobra"
American. Boxer
b. Oct 18, 1958 in Detroit, Michigan
Source: *NewYTBS 81*

Hearst, Catherine
American. Mother of Patty Hearst
b. 1918
Source: *WhoAm 78, 80, 82; WomPO 76*

Hearst, Millicent Willson
[Mrs. William Randolph, Sr.]
American. Philanthropist
b. Jul 16, 1882 in New York, New York
d. Dec 6, 1974 in New York, New York
Source: *BioNews 75; InWom; NewYTBS 74*

Hearst, Patty (Patricia Campbell)
[Mrs. Bernard Shaw]
"Tanya"
American. Kidnap Victim, Author
Kidnapped by SLA, Feb 5, 1974; wrote *Every Secret Thing,* 1981.
b. Feb 20, 1954 in San Francisco, California
Source: *BioNews 74; BkPepl; CurBio 82; NewYTBS 74*

Hearst, Randolph Apperson
American. Newspaper Executive
President, Hearst Foundation, 1972--; father of Patty Hearst Shaw.
b. Dec 2, 1915 in New York, New York
Source: *BioNews 74; IntWW 74; NewYTBS 74; WhoAm 74, 76, 78, 80, 82*

Hearst, William Randolph
American. Newspaper Publisher
Movie *Citizen Kane,* 1941, based on his life.
b. Apr 29, 1863 in San Francisco, California
d. Aug 14, 1951 in Beverly Hills, California
Source: *AmAu&B; BiDrAC; DcAmB S5; DcFM; EncAB-H; FilmgC; LongCTC; OxAmL; OxFilm; REn; REnAL; WebAB; WhAm 3; WhAmP; WorEFlm*

Hearst, William Randolph, Jr.
American. Editor, Newspaper Publisher
b. Jan 27, 1908 in New York, New York
Source: *AmAu&B; CelR 73; CurBio 55; IntWW 74; St&PR 75; Who 74; WhoAm 74, 76, 78, 80, 82*

Hearst, William Randolph, III
American. Newspaper Executive
b. 1949
Source: *BioIn 10*

Heart
[Mike Derosier; Roger Fisher; Steve Fossen; Howard Lesse; Ann Wilson; Nancy Wilson]
American. Rock Group
Source: *NewWmR; RkOn*

Heath, Edward Richard George
English. Politician, Prime Minister
b. Jul 9, 1916 in Broadstairs, England
Source: *ConAu 33R; CurBio 62; IntWW 74; NewYTBE 70, 71; Who 74; WhoWor 74*

Heath, Ted
English. Band Leader, Musician
b. 1902 in London, England
d. Nov 18, 1969 in Virginia Water, England
Source: *WhScrn 74, 77; WhoHol B*

Heatherton, Joey
American. Actress, Singer, Dancer
b. Sep 14, 1944 in Rockville Centre, New York
Source: *FilmgC; MotPP; WhoAm 74; WhoHol A*

Heatherton, Ray
American. Actor, Singer
b. Jun 1, 1910 in Jersey City, New Jersey
Source: *BiE&WWA; NotNAT*

Heatter, Gabriel
American. Radio Commentator, Journalist
b. Sep 17, 1890 in New York, New York
d. Mar 30, 1972 in Miami Beach, Florida
Source: *CurBio 41, 72; NewYTBE 72; WebAB; WhScrn 77*

Heavenly Twins
see: Meadows, Earle; Sefton, William

Hebert, F(elix) Edward
American. Congressman, Editor
b. Oct 12, 1901 in New Orleans, Louisiana
d. Dec 29, 1979 in New Orleans, Louisiana
Source: *BiDrAC; CngDr 74; CurBio 51, 80; NewYTBS 79; PolProf E; PolProf J; PolProf K; PolProf NF; PolProf T; WhAm 7; WhoAm 74, 76, 78; WhoAmP 73, 75, 77, 79; WhoGov 72, 75, 77; WhoS&SW 73, 75, 76*

Hebner, Richie (Richard Joseph)
American. Baseball Player
b. Nov 26, 1947 in Brighton, Massachusetts
Source: *BaseEn; WhoProB 73*

Hechinger, Fred Michael
American. Newspaper Editor, Author
b. Jul 7, 1920 in Nuremberg, Germany
Source: *ConAu 77; WhoAm 74, 76, 78, 80, 82; WhoE 74; WhoWorJ 72; WrDr 76*

Hecht, Ben
American. Author, Dramatist
b. Feb 28, 1893 in New York, New York
d. Apr 18, 1964 in New York, New York
Source: *AmAu&B; BiDFilm; CmMov; CnDAL; CnMD; CnThe; ConAmA; ConAu 85; ConLC 8; CurBio 42, 64; DcFM; DcLEL; EncMys; FilmgC; LongCTC; McGEWD; ModWD; OxAmL; OxFilm; Pen AM; REn; REnAL; TwCA, SUP; WebAB; WhAm 4; WhScrn 77; WorEFlm*

Hecht, George Joseph
American. Publisher
Founded *Parents' Magazine; Humpty Dumpty.*
b. Nov 1, 1895 in New York, New York
d. Apr 23, 1980 in New York, New York
Source: *BioIn 1, 2; ConAu 97; CurBio 47, 80; NewYTBS 75, 80; SmATA 22; St&PR 75; WhNAA; WhoAm 74, 76, 78, 80; WhoWorJ 72*

Heck, Barbara Ruckle
"Mother of Methodism"
Irish. Religious Leader
Helped establish first Methodist chapel in America, 1768.
b. 1734 in County Limerick, Ireland
d. Aug 17, 1804 in Augusta, Canada
Source: *ApCAB; DcAmB; InWom; LibW; MacDCB 78; NatCAB 13; NotAW; OxCan; WhAm H*

Heckart, Eileen
American. Actress
b. Mar 29, 1919 in Columbus, Ohio
Source: *BiE&WWA; CelR 73; CurBio 58; FilmgC; InWom; IntMPA 75, 76, 77, 78, 79, 80, 81, 82; MotPP; MovMk, ; NewYTBE 73; NotNAT; PlP&P; WhoAm 74, 76, 78, 80, 82; WhoE 74; WhoHol A; WhoThe 77*

Heckler, Margaret Mary
American. Secretary of HHS
Nominated to succeed Richard Schweiker, 1983.
b. Jun 21, 1931 in Flushing, New York
Source: *BiDrAC; CngDr 74; InWom; WhoAm 74, 76, 78, 80, 82; WhoAmP 73; WhoAmW 77; WhoE 74; WhoGov 72; WomPO 76*

Heckscher, August
American. Author, Journalist
b. Sep 16, 1913 in Huntington, New York
Source: *AmAu&B; Au&Wr 71; BiE&WWA; ConAu 1R; CurBio 41, 58; IntWW 74; WhoAm 74; WhoE 74; WhoGov 72*

Hedberg, Anders
Swedish. Hockey Player
b. Feb 25, 1951? in Ornskoldsvik, Sweden
Source: *BioIn 11*

Hedren, "Tippi" (Natalie Kay)
American. Actress
b. Jan 19, 1935 in New Ulm, Minnesota
Source: *BiDFilm; FilmgC; MotPP; WhoAm 74; WhoHol A*

Heem, Jan Davidsz de
Dutch. Artist
b. 1606 in Utrecht, Belgium
d. 1684? in Antwerp, Belgium
Source: *McGDA*

Heffelfinger, "Pudge" (William Walter)
American. Football Player
Called greatest blocker of all time.
b. Dec 20, 1867 in Minneapolis, Minnesota
d. Apr 2, 1954 in Blessing, Texas
Source: *DcAmB S5; WebAB; WhoFtbl 74*

Heffer, Eric Samuel
British. Author, Statesman
b. 1922
Source: *Who 74*

Heflin, Van Emmett Evan
American. Actor
b. Dec 13, 1910 in Walters, Oklahoma
d. Jul 23, 1971 in Hollywood, California
Source: *BiDFilm; BiE&WWA; CmMov; CurBio 43, 71; FilmgC; MotPP; MovMk; OxFilm; PlP&P; WhAm 5; WhScrn 74, 77; WhoHol B; WorEFlm*

Hefner, Christie
American. Daughter of Hugh Hefner
b. 1953?
Source: *BioIn 10, 11*

Hefner, Hugh Marston
American. Magazine Publisher
Founded *Playboy*, 1953; *VIP*, 1963-75, *Oui*, 1972-81.
b. Apr 9, 1926 in Chicago, Illinois
Source: *AuNews 1; BioNews 74; BkPepl; CelR 73; CurBio 68; IntWW 74; St&PR 75; WebAB; WhoAm 74, 76, 78, 80, 82; WhoF&I 74; WhoMW 74; WhoWor 74*

Hefti, Neal Paul
American. Composer, Music Publisher
b. Oct 29, 1922 in Hastings, Nebraska
Source: *AmSCAP 66; WhoAm 74, 76, 78, 80, 82*

Hegan, Jim (James Edward)
American. Baseball Player, Coach
b. Aug 3, 1920 in Lynn, Massachusetts
Source: *BaseEn; BioIn 2, 4, 5, 8; WhoProB 73*

Hegel, Georg Wilhelm Friedrich
German. Philosopher
b. Aug 27, 1770 in Stuttgart, Germany
d. Nov 14, 1831 in Berlin, Germany
Source: *BbD; BiD&SB; CasWL; DcEuL; EuAu; EvEuW; NewC; OxEng; OxGer; Pen EUR; REn*

Heger, Robert
Alsatian. Opera Conductor, Composer
b. Aug 19, 1886 in Strassburg, Germany
Source: *Who 74; WhoMus 72*

Heggen, Thomas Orls, Jr.
American. Author, Dramatist
b. Dec 23, 1919 in Fort Dodge, Iowa
d. May 19, 1949 in New York, New York
Source: *AmAu&B; BioIn 1, 2, 3, 4, 5, 10; CyWA; OxAmL; Pen AM; REnAL; TwCA SUP*

Heggie, O P
Australian. Actor
b. Nov 17, 1879 in Angaston, Australia
d. Feb 7, 1936 in Los Angeles, California
Source: *FilmgC; MovMk; TwYS; WhScrn 74, 77; WhoHol B*

Heidegger, Martin
German. Author, Philosopher
Writings deal obsessively with term "being."
b. Sep 26, 1889 in Messkirch, Germany
d. May 26, 1976 in Messkirch, Germany (West)
Source: *CasWL; ConAu 65, 81; CurBio 72; IntWW 74; LongCTC; OxGer; REn; TwCA SUP; TwCW; WhAm 6; Who 74*

Heiden, Beth
American. Speed Skater
b. 1959? in Madison, Wisconsin
Source: *BioIn 12*

Heiden, Eric
American. Speed Skater
First person to win five individual Olympic gold medals, 1980.
b. Jun 14, 1958 in Madison, Wisconsin
Source: *BioIn 12; CurBio 80*

Heidt, Horace Murray
American. Band Leader, Radio Personality
b. 1901
Source: *WhoHol A*

Heifetz, Jascha
American. Musician
Debuted at age five; won Grammys, 1961-62, 1964.
b. Feb 2, 1901 in Vilna, Russia
Source: *AmSCAP 66; CelR 73; CurBio 44; IntWW 74; NewYTBE 71; REn; WebAB; Who 74; WhoAm 74, 76, 78, 80, 82; WhoHol A; WhoMus 72; WhoWor 74*

Heilmann, Harry Edwin
"Slug"
American. Baseball Player
Batted .403, 1923; lifetime batting average, .342; Hall of Fame, 1952.
b. Aug 3, 1894 in San Francisco, California
d. Jul 9, 1951 in Detroit, Michigan
Source: *BaseEn; DcAmB S5; WhoProB 73*

Heim, Jacques
French. Fashion Designer
b. May 8, 1899 in Paris, France
d. Jan 8, 1967 in Paris, France
Source: *WhAm 4; WorFshn*

Heindorf, Ray
American. Motion Picture Director
b. 1910
d. Feb 3, 1980 in Los Angeles, California
Source: *CmMov; FilmgC; IntMPA 77*

Heine, Heinrich
German. Poet, Critic
b. Dec 13, 1797 in Dusseldorf, Germany
d. Feb 17, 1856 in Paris, France
Source: *AtlBL; BbD; BiD&SB; CasWL; ChPo, S1, S2; CyWA; DcEuL; EuAu; EvEuW; NewC; OxEng; OxFr; OxGer; Pen EUR; RComWL; REn*

Heinemann, Gustav Walter
German. President
b. Jul 23, 1899
Source: *CurBio 69; IntWW 74; WhoGov 72; WhoWor 74*

Heinlein, Robert Anson
American. Author
b. Jul 7, 1907 in Butler, Missouri
Source: *ConAu 1R, 1NR; ConLC 3, 8, 14; ConNov 72, 76; CurBio 55; DrAF 76; MorJA; Pen AM; REnAL; SmATA 9; TwCA SUP; TwCW; WebAB; WebE&AL; WhoAm 74, 76, 78, 80, 82; WrDr 76*

Heinsohn, Tommy
American. Basketball Player
b. 1934
Source: *WhoBbl 73*

Heinz, Henry John
American. Manufacturer
Founded H J Heinz Co., 1876; originated "57 varieties" slogan, 1896.
b. Oct 11, 1844 in Pittsburgh, Pennsylvania
d. May 14, 1919 in Pittsburgh, Pennsylvania
Source: *DcAmB; WebAB; WhAm 1*

Heinz, (Henry) John, (III)
American. Senator
b. Oct 23, 1938 in Pittsburgh, Pennsylvania
Source: *AlmAP 78, 80; BioIn 9, 10; CngDr 74, 77, 79; CurBio 81; IntWW 77, 78; WhoAm 74, 76, 78, 80, 82; WhoAmP 73, 75, 77, 79; WhoE 74, 75, 77, 79; WhoGov 75, 77*

Heisenberg, Werner Karl
German. Physicist
b. Dec 5, 1901 in Wurzburg, Germany
d. Feb 1, 1976 in Munich, Germany (West)
Source: *ConAu 65; CurBio 57; IntWW 74; WhAm 6; Who 74; WhoWor 74*

Heiser, Victor George
American. Physician, Author
b. Feb 5, 1873 in Pennsylvania
d. Feb 27, 1972 in New York, New York
Source: *AmAu&B; ConAu 33R; CurBio 42, 72; NewYTBE 72; WhAm 5; WhNAA*

Heiskell, Andrew
American. Publisher
b. Sep 13, 1915 in Naples, Italy
Source: *AmAu&B; CurBio 66; IntWW 74; St&PR 75; Who 74; WhoAm 74, 76, 78, 80, 82; WhoE 74; WhoF&I 74; WhoWor 74*

Heisman, John William
American. Football Player, Coach
b. Oct 23, 1869 in Cleveland, Ohio
d. 1936
Source: *BioIn 4, 6, 7; WhoFtbl 74*

Heiss, Carol Elizabeth
see: Jenkins, Carol Heiss

Helck, (Clarence) Peter
American. Artist, Illustrator
b. Jun 17, 1893 in New York, New York
Source: *WhoAm 74, 76, 78, 80, 82; WhoAmA 73*

Held, Al
American. Artist
b. Oct 12, 1928 in New York, New York
Source: *BnEnAmA; ConArt; DcAmArt; WhoAm 74, 82; WhoAmA 73, 76, 78*

Held, Anna
American. Actress
First wife of Flo Ziegfeld; starred in *Anna Held,* 1902.
b. Mar 8, 1873 in Paris, France
d. Aug 12, 1918 in New York, New York
Source: *EncMT; FamA&A; Film 1; InWom; NotAW; WhAm 1; WhScrn 77; WhoHol B; WhoStg 1906; WomWWA 14*

Held, John, Jr.
American. Comic Strip Artist
b. Jan 10, 1889 in Salt Lake City, Utah
d. Mar 2, 1958 in Belmar, New Jersey
Source: *AmAu&B; ChPo S1; OxAmL; REnAL; WebAB; WhAm 3*

Heliogabalus
Roman. Emperor
b. 204 in Emesa, Syria
d. 222
Source: *NewC; REn*

Heller, Goldie
American. Artist, Advertising Executive
b. in Salem, Massachusetts
Source: *ForWC 70; WhoAdv 72; WhoAmA 73*

Heller, Joseph
American. Author, Dramatist
Wrote *Catch-22,* 1961; filmed, 1970.
b. May 1, 1923 in Brooklyn, New York
Source: *AmAu&B; AuNews 1; BioNews 74; CasWL; ConAu 5R; ConDr 73; ConLC 1, 3, 5, 8, 11; ConNov 72, 76; CurBio 73; DrAF 76; ModAL, SUP; NotNAT; OxAmL; Pen AM; RAdv 1; TwCW; WebE&AL; WhoAm 74, 76, 78, 80, 82; WhoTwCL; WorAu; WrDr 76*

Heller, Walter Wolfgang
American. Economist, Government Advisor
b. Aug 27, 1915 in Buffalo, New York
Source: *AmEA 74; AmM&WS 73; ConAu 21R; CurBio 61; IntWW 74; WhoAm 74; WhoAmP 73; WhoWor 74; WrDr 76*

Hellerman, Fred
[The Weavers]
American. Singer, Musician, Songwriter
b. May 13, 1927 in New York, New York
Source: *AmSCAP 66; EncFCWM 69; WhoAm 74, 76, 78, 82; WhoE 74*

Hellinger, Mark
American. Journalist
b. Mar 21, 1903 in New York, New York
d. Dec 21, 1947 in Hollywood, California
Source: *AmAu&B; BiDFilm; CmMov; CurBio 47, 48; DcFM; DcNAA; FilmgC; OxFilm; REnAL; WhAm 2; WhScrn 77; WorEFlm*

Hellman, Lillian
American. Dramatist, Author
Wrote *The Little Foxes,* 1939; movie *Julia,* based on *Pentimento,* 1973.
b. Jun 20, 1905 in New Orleans, Louisiana
Source: *AmAu&B; Au&Wr 71; AuNews 1, 2; BiE&WWA; BioNews 74; BkPepl; CasWL; CelR 73; CnDAL; CnMD; CnThe; ConAu 13R; ConDr 73; ConLC 2, 4, 8, 14, 18; CroCD; CurBio 41, 60; CyWA; DcFM; EncAB-H; EncWL; FilmgC; ForWC 70; InWom; IntMPA 75, 76, 77, 78, 79, 80, 81, 82; IntWW 74; LongCTC; McGEWD; ModAL, SUP; ModWD; NatPD; NewYTBE 73; NotNAT; OxAmL; OxFilm; OxThe; Pen AM; PlP&P; REn; REnAL; REnWD; TwCA, SUP; WebAB; WebE&AL; Who 74; WhoAm 74, 76, 78, 80, 82; WhoE 74; WhoThe 77; WhoTwCL; WhoWor 74; WhoWorJ 72; WomWMM; WorEFlm; WrDr 76*

Hellmann, Richard
American. Food Manufacturer
b. 1876
d. 1971
Source: *BioIn 9*

Helmholtz, Herman Ludwig Ferdinand von
German. Physicist, Physiologist
b. Aug 31, 1821 in Potsdam, Germany
d. Sep 8, 1894 in Charlottenburg, Germany
Source: *AsBiEn; BbD; BioIn 1, 4, 7, 9, 11; DcScB; LinLib S; McGEWB; REn*

Helmond, Katherine
American. Actress
b. Jul 5, 1933 in Galveston, Texas
Source: *BioIn 11; WhoAm 82*

Helmore, Tom
English. Actor
b. Jan 4, 1912 in London, England
Source: *BiE&WWA; NotNAT; WhoHol A*

Helms, Chet
American. Theatrical Producer
b. 1942
Source: *BioIn 10*

Helms, Jesse Alexander, Jr.
American. Politician, Journalist
b. Oct 18, 1921 in Monroe, North Carolina
Source: *CngDr 74; IntWW 74; St&PR 75; WhoAm 74, 76, 78, 80, 82; WhoAmP 73*

Helms, Richard McGarrah
American. Government Official
b. Mar 30, 1913 in Saint Davids, Pennsylvania
Source: *CelR 73; CurBio 67; IntWW 74; NewYTBE 71, 73; USBiR 74; WhoAm 74, 76, 78, 80, 82; WhoGov 72; WhoS&SW 73; WhoWor 74*

Helmsley, Harry Brakmann
Realtor
b. 1909
Source: *NewYTBE 73; St&PR 75*

Heloise
[Heloise and Abelard]
French. Abbess
b. 1101?
d. 1164
Source: *InWom; OxFr; REn*

Heloise
[Heloise Bowles Reese]
American. Journalist, Author
Wrote syndicated column, *Hints from Heloise,* 1961-77.
b. May 14, 1919 in Fort Worth, Texas
d. Dec 28, 1977 in San Antonio, Texas
Source: *ConAu 9R, 73; InWom*

Helpmann, Sir Robert Murray
Australian. Ballet Dancer, Actor
b. Apr 9, 1909 in Mount Gambier, Australia
Source: *BiE&WWA; CurBio 50; FilmgC; IntMPA 77, 75; IntWW 74; MovMk; NotNAT; OxThe; PlP&P; Who 74; WhoHol A; WhoThe 77; WhoWor 74*

Hemans, Felicia Dorothea Browne
English. Poet
b. Sep 25, 1793 in Liverpool, England
d. May 16, 1835 in Dublin, Ireland
Source: *Alli; BbD; BiD&SB; BrAu 19; CarSB; CasWL; ChPo S2; DcEnA; DcEnL; DcEuL; DcLEL; EvLB; InWom; NewC; OxEng; PoChrch; REn; WebE&AL*

Hemings, Sally
American. Alleged Mistress of Jefferson
b. 1773
d. 1835
Source: *BioIn 11*

Hemingway, Ernest Miller
American. Journalist, Author
Wrote *A Farewell to Arms,* 1929; *For Whom the Bell Tolls,* 1940.
b. Jul 21, 1899 in Oak Park, Illinois
d. Jul 2, 1961 in Ketchum, Idaho
Source: *AmAu&B; AmNov; AmWr; ArizL; AuNews 2; BioIn 1, 2, 3, 4, 5, 6, 7, 8, 9, 10, 11; CasWL; Chambr 3; ChPo S1, S2; CnDAL; CnMD; CnMWL; ConAmA; ConAu 77; ConLC 1, 3, 6, 8, 10, 13; EncWL; EvLB; FilmgC; LongCTC; ModAL, SUP; ModWD; OxAmL; OxEng; OxFilm; Pen AM; RAdv 1; RComWL; REn; REnAL; TwCA, SUP; TwCW; WebAB, 79; WebE&AL; WhAm 4; WhoTwCL; WorEFlm*

Hemingway, Margaux
[Mrs. Bernardo Foucher]
American. Model, Actress
Granddaughter of Ernest Hemingway; starred in *Lipstick,* 1976.
b. Feb 1955 in Portland, Oregon
Source: *BioIn 10, 11; BkPepl; CurBio 78; WhoAm 80; WhoHol A*

Hemingway, Mariel
American. Actress
Granddaughter of Ernest Hemingway; starred in *Lipstick,* 1976; *Manhattan,* 1979.
b. 1962
Source: *BioIn 11*

Hemingway, Mary Welsh
[Mrs. Ernest Hemingway]
American. Author, Journalist
Wrote *How It Was,* 1976, a chronicle of her life with Ernest Hemingway.
b. Apr 5, 1908 in Walker, Minnesota
Source: *BioIn 7, 8, 9, 11; ConAu 73; CurBio 68; ForWC 70; InWom*

Hemion, Dwight
American. Motion Picture Director, Producer
b. Mar 14, 1926 in New Haven, Connecticut
Source: *NewYTET; WhoAm 78, 80, 82*

Hemmings, David Leslie Edward
[Leslie Edward]
English. Actor
b. Nov 21, 1941 in Guildford, England
Source: *CelR 73; FilmgC; IntMPA 75, 76, 77, 78, 79, 80, 81, 82; MotPP; MovMk; Who 74; WhoAm 74; WhoHol A; WorEFlm*

Hempel, Frieda
German. Opera Singer
b. Jun 26, 1885 in Leipzig, Germany
d. Oct 7, 1955 in Berlin, Germany (West)
Source: *InWom; WhAm 3*

Hemphill, Paul
American. Author
b. Feb 18, 1936 in Birmingham, Alabama
Source: *AuNews 2; BioIn 9, 10, 11; ConAu 49*

Hemsley, Sherman
American. Actor
Plays George Jefferson in "The Jeffersons," 1975--.
b. Feb 1, 1938 in Philadelphia, Pennsylvania
Source: *BioIn 10; WhoAm 80, 82*

Hench, Philip Showalter
American. Scientist, Physician, Engineer
b. Feb 28, 1896 in Pittsburgh, Pennsylvania
d. Mar 30, 1965 in Ocho Rios, Jamaica
Source: *CurBio 50, 65; WebAB; WhAm 4*

Henderson, Arthur
British. Statesman
b. Aug 27, 1893
d. Aug 28, 1968 in London, England
Source: *IntYB 78*

Henderson, Fletcher Hamilton
American. Band Leader
b. Dec 18, 1897 in Cuthbert, Georgia
d. Dec 29, 1952 in New York, New York
Source: *AmSCAP 66; DcAmB S5*

Henderson, Florence
American. Actress, Singer
b. Feb 14, 1934 in Dale, Indiana
Source: *BiE&WWA; CurBio 71; EncMT; InWom; NotNAT; WhoAm 82; WhoHol A; WhoThe 77*

Henderson, "Hollywood" (Thomas)
American. Football Player
b. Mar 1, 1953 in Austin, Texas
Source: *BioIn 11*

Henderson, Jimmy
see: Black Oak Arkansas

Henderson, Leon
American. Economist, Educator
b. Feb 22, 1906 in Baker, Florida
d. Feb 7, 1960 in Gainesville, Florida
Source: *CurBio 40; WhAm 4*

Henderson, Marcia
American. Actress
b. Dec 11, 1934 in Seattle, Washington
Source: *FilmgC; InWom; IntMPA 75, 76, 77, 78, 79, 80, 81, 82*

Henderson, Oran K
Army Officer
Source: *BioIn 9*

Henderson, Ray
American. Songwriter
b. Dec 1, 1896 in Buffalo, New York
d. Dec 31, 1971 in Greenwich, Connecticut
Source: *AmSCAP 66; BiE&WWA; EncMT; NewCBMT; NewYTBE 71*

Henderson, Rickey Henley
American. Baseball Player
Stole a record 130 bases, 1982.
b. Dec 25, 1958 in Chicago, Illinois
Source: *BaseEn*

Henderson, "Skitch" (Cedric)
[Lyle Henderson]
American. Orchestra Leader
b. Jan 27, 1918 in Halstad, Minnesota
Source: *AmSCAP 66; CelR 73; CurBio 66; IntMPA 75, 76, 77, 78, 79, 80, 81, 82; NewYTBE 72; WhoAm 74, 76, 78, 80, 82; WhoMus 72*

Henderson, Vivian Wilson
American. Educator, Labor Economist
b. Feb 10, 1923 in Bristol, Tennessee
d. Jan 25, 1976 in Atlanta, Georgia
Source: *ConAu 61, 65; WhAm 6; WhoAm 74; WhoBlA 75; WhoRel 75*

Henderson, Wayne
see: Crusaders, The

Hendl, Walter
American. Conductor, Composer
b. Jan 12, 1917 in West New York, New Jersey
Source: *CurBio 55; WhoAm 74, 76, 78, 80, 82*

Hendrick, Burton Jesse
American. Biographer, Journalist
b. Dec 28, 1870 in New Haven, Connecticut
d. Mar 23, 1949 in New York, New York
Source: *AmAu&B; ChPo S2; DcAmB S4; DcLEL; OxAmL; REnAL; TwCA, SUP; WhAm 2; WhNAA*

Hendrix, Jimi (James Marshall)
American. Musician, Singer
Hits "Purple Haze," 1967; "Hey Joe," 1967; died of drug overdose.
b. Nov 27, 1942 in Seattle, Washington
d. Sep 18, 1970 in London, England
Source: *BioIn 8, 9, 10, 11; NewYTBE 70; WhAm 5; WhScrn 77; WhoHol B*

Hendrix, Wanda
American. Actress
b. Nov 3, 1928 in Jacksonville, Florida
d. Feb 1, 1981 in Burbank, California
Source: *FilmgC; HolP 40; IntMPA 75, 76, 77, 78, 79; JohnWil 82; MotPP; MovMk; NewYTBS 81; WhoHol A*

Hendry, Ian
English. Actor
b. 1931 in Ipswich, England
Source: *FilmgC; IntMPA 81; WhoHol A*

Henie, Sonja
Norwegian. Figure Skater, Actress
Won Olympic gold medals, 1928, 1932, 1936; starred in *Wintertime,* 1943.
b. Apr 8, 1912 in Oslo, Norway
d. Oct 12, 1969 in Los Angeles, California
Source: *CmMov; CurBio 40, 52, 70; FilmgC; InWom; MotPP; MovMk; BioIn 2, 3, 5, 6, 7, 8, 9, 10, 11; OxFilm; ThFT; WhAm 5; WhScrn 74, 77; WhoHol B*

Henize, Karl Gordon
American. Astronomer, Astronaut
b. Sep 17, 1926 in Cincinnati, Ohio
Source: *IntWW 74; WhoAm 74, 76, 78, 80, 82; WhoS&SW 73; WhoWor 74*

Henkle, Henrietta
[Henrietta Buckmaster, pseud.]
American. Author, Journalist
b. 1909 in Cleveland, Ohio
Source: *AmAu&B; ConAu 69; OhA&B*

Henley, Beth
American. Dramatist
Won Pulitzer Prize, 1981, for *Crimes of the Heart.*
b. May 8, 1952 in Jackson, Mississippi
Source: *NewYTBS 81; NatPD 81*

Henley, Don
[The Eagles]
American. Singer, Musician
Released single, "Dirty Laundry," 1982.
b. Jul 22, 1947 in Gilmer, Texas
Source: *NF*

Henley, William Ernest
English. Author, Poet
b. Aug 23, 1849 in Gloucester, England
d. Jul 1, 1903 in Woking, England
Source: *Alli SUP; AtlBL; BiD&SB; BrAu 19; CasWL; Chambr 3; ChPo, S1, S2; CnE&AP; DcEnA, AP; DcEuL; DcLEL; EvLB; LongCTC; MouLC 4; NewC; OxEng; Pen ENG; REn; WebE&AL*

Hennebique, Francois
French. Builder, Engineer
b. 1842
d. 1921
Source: *BioIn 10*

Hennepin, Louis
French. Explorer, Missionary
Wrote *Description de la Louisiane,* 1682, *Nouveau Voyage,* 1696.
b. Apr 7, 1640? in Ath, Belgium
d. 1701?
Source: *AmBi; ApCAB; BiDSA; DcAmB; Drake; OxAmL; REn; REnAL; WebAB; WhAm H*

Henner, Jean Jacques
French. Artist
b. 1829 in Alsace, France
d. 1905 in Paris, France
Source: *McGDA*

Henner, Marilu
American. Actress
Plays Elaine on TV series "Taxi."
b. Apr 4, 1953 in New York, New York
Source: *BioIn 11*

Henning, Doug(las James)
Canadian. Magician
b. 1947 in Fort Gary, MB
Source: *NewYTBS 74; WhoAm 78, 80, 82*

Henning, Linda Kaye
American. Actress
b. Sep 16, 1944 in Toulca Lake, California
Source: *IntMPA 75, 76, 77; WhoHol A*

Henreid, Paul
[Paul G Julius VonHernreid]
Italian. Actor, Motion Picture Director
b. Jan 10, 1908 in Trieste, Italy
Source: *BiDFilm; CmMov; CurBio 43; FilmgC; IntMPA 75, 76, 77, 78, 79, 80, 81, 82; MotPP; MovMk; OxFilm; WhoAm 74, 76, 78, 80, 82; WhoHol A; WorEFlm*

Henri, Robert
American. Artist
b. Jun 25, 1865 in Cincinnati, Ohio
d. Jul 12, 1929 in New York, New York
Source: *AmBi; AtlBL; DcAmB; DcNAA; EncAB-H; OhA&B; OxAmL; REnAL; WebAB; WhAm 1; WhNAA*

Henrich, Tommy (Thomas David)
"Old Reliable"
American. Baseball Player
b. Feb 20, 1913 in Massillon, Ohio
Source: *BaseEn; NewYTBE 71; WhoProB 73*

Henrit, Robert
see: Argent

Henry I
[Henry Beauclerc]
English. King
b. 1068 in Yorkshire, England
d. Dec 1, 1135 in France
Source: *LinLib S; McGEWB; NewC*

Henry II
English. King
b. 1133
d. 1189
Source: *BioIn 10; WebBD 80; WhDW*

Henry III
English. King
b. 1207
d. 1272
Source: *BioIn 10; OxMus; WebBD 80*

Henry IV
[Henry Bolingbroke]
English. King
b. 1367
d. 1413
Source: *BioIn 10; WebBD 80*

Henry V
English. King
b. 1387
d. 1422
Source: *BioIn 10; WebBD 80*

Henry VI
English. King
b. 1421
d. 1471
Source: *BioIn 10; WebBD 80*

Henry VII
[Henry Tudor]
English. King
b. Jan 28, 1457
d. Apr 21, 1509 in Richmond, England
Source: *NewC*

Henry VIII
English. King
Married Katharine of Aragon, Anne Boleyn, Jane Seymour, Anne of Cleves, Catherine Howard, Catherine Parr.
b. Jun 28, 1491 in Greenwich, England
d. Jan 28, 1547
Source: *BioIn 10; NewCol 75; WebBD 80*

Henry the Navigator
Portuguese. Prince
b. Mar 4, 1394 in Porto, Portugal
d. Nov 13, 1460 in Sagres, Portugal
Source: *AsBiEn; McGEWB; REn*

Henry William Frederick Albert, Prince
[Duke of Gloucester]
English. Military Figure
b. Mar 31, 1900 in Sandringham, England
d. Jun 9, 1974
Source: *IntWW 74; NewYTBS 74*

Henry, Buck
[Buck and Bubbles]
American. Actor, Author
b. Dec 9, 1930 in New York, New York
Source: *ConAu 77; ConDr 73; FilmgC; IntMPA 75, 76, 77, 78, 79, 80, 81, 82; NewYTBE 70; WhoAm 82; WhoHol A*

Henry, Charlotte
American. Actress
b. Mar 3, 1913 in Charlotte, New York
d. Apr 1980 in San Diego, California
Source: *FilmEn; FilmgC; WhoHol A*

Henry, Edward Lamson
American. Artist
b. Jan 12, 1841 in Charleston, South Carolina
d. May 9, 1919 in New York, New York
Source: *AmBi; ApCAB; ApCAB X; BnEnAmA; DcAmArt; DcAmB; McGDA; NatCAB 5; NewYHSD; TwCBDA; WhAm 1*

Henry, Sir Edward Richard
British. Fingerprint Expert
b. 1850
d. 1931
Source: *BioIn 2, 5, 6, 9*

Henry, Joseph
American. Inventor, Physicist
Invented electromagnetic telegraph, basis for commercial telegraphic system.
b. Dec 17, 1797 in Albany, New York
d. May 13, 1878 in Washington, DC
Source: *Alli, SUP; AmBi; ApCAB; BiAuS; DcAmAu; DcAmB; DcNAA; Drake; EncAB-H; NewCol 75; OxAmL; REnAL; WebAB; WhAm H*

Henry, Martha
[Martha Buhs]
American. Actress
b. Feb 17, 1938 in Detroit, Michigan
Source: *NotNAT A*

Henry, O, pseud.
[William Sydney Porter]
American. Author, Journalist
Wrote short stories *The Ransom of Red Chief, Gift of the Magi.*
b. Sep 11, 1862 in Greensboro, North Carolina
d. Jun 5, 1910 in New York, New York
Source: *AmAu&B; AmBi; AtlBL; BiDSA; CasWL; Chambr 3; ChPo; CnDAL; CyWA; DcAmB; DcLEL; DcNAA; EncMys; EncWL; EvLB; FilmgC; LongCTC; ModAL; OhA&B; OxAmL; OxEng; Pen AM; RAdv 1; REn; REnAL; TwCA, SUP; TwCW; WebAB; WebE&AL; WhAm 1; WhoTwCL*

Henry, Pat
American. Motion Picture Director
b. Feb 10, 1935 in Portland, Oregon
Source: *BiE&WWA*

Henry, Pat
[Patrick Henry Scarnato]
American. Comedian
b. Aug 28, 1923
d. Feb 18, 1982 in Las Vegas, Nevada
Source: *BioIn 12*

Henry, Patrick
American. Revolutionary Leader
Said "If this be treason, make the most of it," "Give me liberty or give me death."
b. May 29, 1736 in Hanover County, Virginia
d. Jun 6, 1799 in Charlotte County, Virginia
Source: *Alli; AmAu; AmAu&B; AmBi; ApCAB; BbD; BiAuS; BiD&SB; BiDSA; BiDrAC; DcAmAu; DcAmB; Drake; EncAB-H; OxAmL; REn; REnAL; TwCBDA; WebAB; WhAm H; WhAmP*

Henry, William M
American. Journalist
b. Aug 21, 1890 in San Francisco, California
d. Apr 13, 1970 in Chatsworth, California
Source: *ConAu 89; WhAm 5*

Henson, Jim (James Maury)
American. Creator of the Muppets
Big Bird, Kermit, Cookie Monster first seen on *Sesame Street,* 1969; *The Muppet Show* premiered 1976.
b. Sep 24, 1936 in Greenville, Kansas
Source: *CurBio 77; IntMPA 82; WhoAm 82*

Henson, Josiah
American. Slave, Clergyman
Prototype of Uncle Tom in *Uncle Tom's Cabin.*
b. Jun 15, 1789 in Charles County, Maryland
d. May 15, 1883 in Dresden, ON
Source: *AmAu; AmAu&B; AmBi; ApCAB; DcAmB; DcNAA; MacDCB 78; McGEWB; OxAmL; OxCan; REnAL; WhAm H*

Henson, Matthew Alexander
American. Explorer
Accompanied Robert Peary expedition to N Pole, 1909.
b. 1866
d. Mar 9, 1955 in New York, New York
Source: *BioIn 1, 2, 3, 4, 6, 7, 8, 9, 10, 11; DcAmB S5*

Hentoff, Nat(han Irving)
American. Music Critic, Journalist
b. Jun 10, 1925 in Boston, Massachusetts
Source: *AmAu&B; AuBYP; ChlLR 1; ConAu 1R, 5NR; REnAL; ThrBJA; WhoAm 74, 76, 78, 80, 82; WhoE 74; WhoWor 74; WrDr 76*

Henty, George Alfred
English. Children's Author
b. Dec 8, 1832 in Trumpington, England
d. Nov 16, 1902 in Weymouth, England
Source: *Alli SUP; BbD; BiD&SB; BrAu 19; CarSB; CasWL; Chambr 3; DcLEL; EvLB; JBA 34; LongCTC; MnBBF; NewC; OxEng; Pen ENG; WhoChL*

Henze, Hans Werner
German. Composer
b. Jul 1, 1926 in Gutersloh, Germany
Source: *CurBio 66; DcCM; IntWW 74; NewYTBE 72; OxGer; Who 74; WhoAm 74; WhoMus 72; WhoWor 74*

Hepbron, George
American. Basketball Referee
Wrote *How to Play Basketball,* 1904; considered first handbook on game.
b. Aug 27, 1863 in Still Pond, Maryland
d. Apr 30, 1946 in Newark, New Jersey
Source: *WhoBbl 73*

Hepburn, Audrey
[Mrs. Andrea Dotti; Edda Hepburn]
American. Actress
Won Oscar for *Roman Holiday,* 1953; starred in *My Fair Lady,* 1964.
b. May 4, 1929 in Brussels, Belgium
Source: *BiDFilm; BiE&WWA; BkPepl; CelR 73; CurBio 54; FilmgC; InWom; IntMPA 75, 76, 77; IntWW 74; MotPP; MovMk; NotNAT; OxFilm; Who 74; WhoAm 74, 76, 78, 80, 82; WhoHol A; WorEFlm*

Hepburn, Katharine
American. Actress
Has won four Oscars for best actress in 50-year career.
b. Nov 9, 1909 in Hartford, Connecticut
Source: *BiDFilm; BiE&WWA; BioNews 74; BkPepl; CelR 73; CmMov; CurBio 42, 69; EncMT; FamA&A; FilmgC; InWom; IntMPA 75, 76, 77, 78, 79, 80, 81, 82; IntWW 74; MotPP; MovMk; NewYTBE 73; NotNAT; OxFilm; PlP&P; ThFT; WebAB; Who 74; WhoAm 74, 76, 78, 80, 82; WhoHol A; WhoThe 77; WhoWor 74; WomWMM*

Hepplewhite, George
English. Cabinet Maker
d. 1786
Source: *WebBD 80*

Hepworth, Barbara
English. Sculptor
b. Jan 10, 1903 in Wakefield, England
d. May 20, 1975 in Saint Ives, England
Source: *CurBio 57; InWom; IntWW 74; WhAm 6; Who 74; WhoWor 74*

Heraclitus of Ephesus
[The Weeping Philosopher]
Greek. Philosopher
b. 535?BC
d. 475?BC
Source: *NewCol 75; WebBD 80*

Herbert, Sir Alan Patrick
English. Author, Statesman
MP, 1935-50; wrote *Secret Battle,* 1919.
b. Sep 24, 1890 in London, England
d. Nov 11, 1971 in London, England
Source: *Au&Wr 71; ChPo, S1, S2; ConAu 33R, 97; DcLEL; EvLB; LongCTC; ModBrL; NewC; Pen ENG; REn; TwCA, SUP; TwCW*

Herbert, Anthony B
American. General
b. 1930
Source: *BioIn 9*

Herbert, Evelyn
American. Actress
b. 1898 in Philadelphia, Pennsylvania
Source: *Au&Wr 71; EncMT; WhoThe 77*

Herbert, Frank
American. Author
b. Oct 8, 1920 in Tacoma, Washington
Source: *ConAu 53, 5NR; ConLC 12; SmATA 9; WhoAm 74, 76, 78, 80, 82; WrDr 76*

Herbert, George
English. Author
b. Apr 3, 1593 in Montgomery, England
d. Mar 9, 1633 in Bremerton, England
Source: *Alli; AtlBL; BbD; BiD&SB; BrAu; CasWL; ChPo, S1, S2; CnE&AP; CroE&S; CrtT 1; CyWA; DcEnA; DcEnL; DcEuL; DcLEL; EvLB; MouLC 1; NewC; OxEng; Pen ENG; RAdv 1; REn; WebE&AL*

Herbert, George Edward
[Earl of Canarvon]
English. Egyptologist, Archaeologist
b. 1866
d. 1923
Source: *WebBD 80*

Herbert, Henry
American. Actor
b. 1879
d. Feb 20, 1947 in Flushing, New York
Source: *Film 1; WhScrn 74, 77*

Herbert, Hugh
American. Actor
b. Aug 10, 1887 in Binghamton, New York
d. Mar 13, 1951 in Hollywood, California
Source: *FilmgC; MovMk; Vers A; WhScrn 74, 77; WhoHol B*

Herbert, John, pseud.
[John Herbert Brundage]
Canadian. Dramatist, Director
b. Oct 13, 1926 in Toronto, ON
Source: *ClbCR; ConDr 73, 77; WrDr 80*

Herbert, Victor
American. Conductor, Composer
Composed *Babes in Toyland,* 1903; *The Red Mill,* 1906.
b. Feb 1, 1859 in Dublin, Ireland
d. May 27, 1924 in New York, New York
Source: *AmBi; AmSCAP 66; DcAmB; EncMT; McGEWD; NewCBMT; OxAmL; REn; REnAL; TwCBDA; WebAB; WhAm 1; WhoStg 1906, 1908*

Herblock
[Herbert Lawrence Block]
American. Editorial Cartoonist
Cartoonist, Washington *Post,* 1946--; won Pulitzer Prizes, 1942, 1954, 1979.
b. Oct 3, 1909 in Chicago, Illinois
Source: *AmAu&B; CurBio 54; EncAB-H; WebAB; WhoAm 74, 76, 78, 80, 82; WhoS&SW 73; WhoWor 74*

Herbst, Josephine Frey
American. Author
b. Mar 5, 1897 in Sioux City, Iowa
d. Jan 28, 1969 in New York, New York
Source: *AmAu&B; AmNov; ConAmA; ConAu 5R, 25R; InWom; OxAmL; REn; REnAL; TwCA, SUP; WebE&AL; WhAm 5; WhNAA*

Herder, Johann G von
German. Poet, Critic
b. Aug 25, 1744 in Mohrungen, Germany
d. Dec 18, 1803 in Weimar, Germany
Source: *AtlBL; BbD; BiD&SB; CasWL; ChPo S1; DcEuL; EuAu; EvEuW; NewC; OxEng; OxGer; Pen EUR; RComWL; REn*

Hereward the Wake
Anglo-Saxon. Revolutionary
d. 1070?
Source: *NewCol 75; WebBD 80*

Hergesheimer, Joseph
American. Author
b. Feb 15, 1880 in Philadelphia, Pennsylvania
d. Apr 25, 1954 in Sea Isle City, New Jersey
Source: *AmAu&B; CasWL; Chambr 3; CnDAL; ConAmA; ConAmL; CyWA; DcAmB S5; DcBiA; DcLEL; EvLB; LongCTC; OxAmL; OxEng; Pen AM; REn; REnAL; TwCA, SUP; TwCW; WhAm 3; WhNAA*

Herkimer, Nicholas
American. Military Leader
b. Nov 10, 1728 in Herkimer, New York
d. Aug 19, 1777 in Little Falls, New York
Source: *AmBi; ApCAB; DcAmB; Drake; TwCBDA; WhAm H*

Herlie, Eileen
Scottish. Actress
b. Mar 8, 1920 in Glasgow, Scotland
Source: *BiE&WWA; FilmgC; MovMk; NotNAT; Who 74; WhoHol A; WhoThe 77*

Herlihy, James Leo
American. Author
b. Feb 27, 1927 in Detroit, Michigan
Source: *AmAu&B; Au&Wr 71; CelR 73; ConAu 1R, 2NR; ConDr 73; ConLC 6; ConNov 72, 76; CurBio 61; DrAF 76; NotNAT; WhoAm 74; WhoE 74; WhoWor 74; WorAu; WrDr 76*

Herman, "Babe" (Floyd Caves)
American. Baseball Player
b. Jun 26, 1903 in Buffalo, New York
Source: *BaseEn; BioIn 1, 2, 3, 5, 6, 8, 9; NewYTBS 79; WhoProB 73*

Herman, George
American. Broadcast Journalist
b. Jan 14, 1920 in New York, New York
Source: *WhoAm 74, 76, 78, 80, 82*

Herman, Jerry
American. Songwriter
b. Jul 10, 1933 in New York, New York
Source: *AmSCAP 66; BiE&WWA; CelR 73; CurBio 65; EncMT; NewCBMT; NotNAT; PlP&P; WhoAm 74, 76, 78, 80, 82; WhoE 74; WhoThe 77*

Herman, Woody (Woodrow Charles)
American. Band Leader, Musician
b. May 16, 1913 in Milwaukee, Wisconsin
Source: *AmSCAP 66; BioNews 74; CurBio 73; WhoAm 74, 76, 78, 80, 82; WhoHol A; WhoJazz 72; WhoMus 72; WhoWest 74*

Hermann, Bernard
American. Conductor
b. 1911
d. 1975
Source: *BioIn 10*

Herman's Hermits
[Karl Greene; Keith Hopwood; Derek Leckenby; Peter Noone; Barry Whitwam]
English. Rock Group
Source: *EncPR&S; IlEncRk*

Hermening, Kevin Jay
[The Hostages]
American. Former Hostage in Iran
b. 1960? in Milwaukee, Wisconsin
Source: *BioIn 12; NewYTBS 81*

Hermes, Thierry
French. Leather Goods Designer
Source: *WorFshn*

Hernandez, Keith
American. Baseball Player
b. Oct 20, 1953 in San Francisco, California
Source: *BaseEn; WhoAm 80, 82*

Herod Antipas
Tetrarch of Galilee and Peraea
b. 4BC
d. 39AD
Source: *REn*

Herod the Great
King of Judea
b. 73BC
d. 4BC
Source: *NewC; REn*

Herodotus
Greek. Historian
b. 485?BC in Halicarnassus, Asia
d. 425?BC in Thurii, Italy
Source: *AtlBL; BbD; BiD&SB; CasWL; CyWA; DcEnL; DcEuL; NewC; OxEng; Pen CL; RComWL; REn*

Herold, Louis Joseph Ferdinand
French. Composer
b. Jan 28, 1791 in Paris, France
d. Jan 19, 1833 in Les Ternes, France
Source: *NewEOp 71*

Heron, Mike
British. Rock Musician
Source: *IlEncRk*

Herrera Campins, Luis
Venezuelan. President
b. May 4, 1925 in Acarigua, Venezuela
Source: *CurBio 80; NewYTBS 78*

Herrera, Omar Torrijos
see: Torrijos Herrera, Omar

Herrick, Elinore M
American. Business Executive
b. Jun 15, 1895 in New York, New York
d. Oct 11, 1964
Source: *CurBio 47, 65; InWom; WhAm 4*

Herrick, Robert
English. Author, Poet
b. Aug 24, 1591 in London, England
d. Oct 1674 in Dean Prior, England
Source: *Alli; AnCL; AtlBL; BbD; BiD&SB; BrAu; CasWL; Chambr 1; ChPo, S1, S2; CnE&AP; CroE&S; CrtT 1; CyWA; DcEnA; DcEnL; DcEuL; DcLEL; EvLB; LongCTC; MouLC 1; NewC; OxEng; Pen ENG; RAdv 1; REn; WebE&AL*

Herridge, Robert T
American. Author, Television Producer
Created CBS program "Camera Three."
b. 1918? in West Orange, New Jersey
d. Aug 14, 1981 in Woodstock, New York
Source: *AnObit 1981; BioIn 5, 12; NewYTBS 81*

Herriman, George
American. Comic Strip Creator
b. Aug 22, 1880 in New Orleans, Louisiana
d. Apr 25, 1944 in Hollywood, California
Source: *ChPo; DcAmB S3; REnAL; WebAB*

Herriot, Edouard
French. Statesman
b. Jul 5, 1872 in Troyes, France
d. Mar 26, 1957 in Lyons, France
Source: *CurBio 46, 57; REn; WhAm 3*

Herriot, James, pseud.
[James Wight]
Scottish. Veterinarian, Author
Wrote *All Creatures Great and Small,* 1972; *All Things Bright and Beautiful,* 1974.
b. Oct 3, 1916 in Glasgow, Scotland
Source: *BioIn 10, 11; ConAu 77; St&PR 75; WrDr 76*

Herrmann, Bernard
American. Composer
b. Jun 29, 1911 in New York, New York
d. Dec 24, 1975 in Los Angeles, California
Source: *Baker 78; BiDAmM; BioIn 1, 2, 3, 10, 11; CmMov; CmpEPM; DcFM; FanAl; IntMPA 76; NewYTBS 75; OxFilm; OxMus; WhAm 6*

Herschel, Sir John Frederick William
English. Astronomer
b. Mar 7, 1792 in Slough, England
d. May 11, 1871 in Collingwood, England
Source: *Alli, SUP; BiD&SB; BrAu 19; Chambr 3; DcEnL; EvLB; NewC*

Herschel, William
German. Astronomer
b. Nov 15, 1738 in Hannover, Germany
d. Aug 25, 1822 in Slough, England
Source: *Alli; NewC; REn*

Hersey, John Richard
American. Author, Journalist
Wrote *A Bell for Adano,* 1944; *Hiroshima,* 1946.
b. Jun 17, 1914 in Tientsin, China
Source: *AmAu&B; AmNov; CasWL; CelR 73; CnDAL; ConAu 17R; ConLC 1, 2; ConNov 72, 76; CurBio 44; CyWA; DrAF 76; DrAS 74E; IntWW 74; LongCTC; ModAL; OxAmL; Pen AM; RAdv 1; REn; REnAL; TwCA SUP; WebAB; Who 74; WhoAm 74, 76, 78, 80, 82; WhoE 74; WhoWor 74; WrDr 76*

Hersh, Seymour
American. Journalist
b. Apr 8, 1937 in Chicago, Illinois
Source: *AmAu&B; AuNews 1; ConAu 73; WhoAm 74, 76, 78, 80, 82*

Hershey, Lenore
American. Editor
b. Mar 20, 1920 in New York, New York
Source: *WhoAm 74, 76, 78, 80, 82*

Hershey, Lewis Blaine
American. Army Officer
b. Sep 12, 1893 in Steuben City, Indiana
d. 1977 in Angola, Indiana
Source: *CurBio 41, 51; IntWW 74; WhoAm 74; WhoAmP 73; WhoGov 72; WhoS&SW 73*

Hershey, Milton Snavely
American. Candy Manufacturer
Founded Hersey Chocolate Co., 1903.
b. Sep 13, 1857 in Dauphin City, Pennsylvania
d. Oct 13, 1945 in Hershey, Pennsylvania
Source: *CurBio 45; DcAmB S3; WebAB; WhAm 2*

Hershfield, Harry
American. Cartoonist, Humorist
b. Oct 13, 1885 in Cedar Rapids, Iowa
d. Dec 15, 1974 in New York, New York
Source: *ConAu 53; NewYTBS 74; WhScrn 77*

Hersholt, Jean
Danish. Actor
b. Jul 12, 1886 in Copenhagen, Denmark
d. Jun 2, 1956 in Beverly Hills, California
Source: *ChPo; CurBio 44, 56; Film 1; FilmgC; MotPP; MovMk; TwYS; WhAm 3; WhScrn 74, 77; WhoHol B; WorEFlm*

Herter, Christian Archibald
American. Diplomat, Editor
b. Mar 28, 1895 in Paris, France
d. Dec 30, 1966 in Washington, DC
Source: *BiDrAC; BiDrUSE; CurBio 47, 58, 67; DcAmB; DcNAA; WhAm H, 1, 4; WhAmP*

Hertz, Alfred
German. Conductor
b. Jul 15, 1872 in Frankfurt, Germany
d. Apr 17, 1942 in San Francisco, California
Source: *CurBio 42; DcAmB S3; WhAm 2*

Hertz, Heinrich Rudolph
German. Discovered Radio Waves
Hertz unit of frequency named after him.
b. Feb 22, 1857 in Hamburg, Germany
d. Jan 1, 1894
Source: *AsBiEn; McGEWB; NewCol 75; REn*

Hertz, John Daniel
American. Founder of Car Rental Agency
Founded Yellow Cab Co., 1915; Hertz Drive-Ur-Self Corp., 1924.
b. Apr 10, 1879 in Ruttka, Austria
d. Oct 8, 1961 in Los Angeles, California
Source: *BioIn 4, 6; ObitOF 79; WhAm 4*

Hertzberg, Arthur
American. Author, Rabbi
b. Jun 9, 1921 in Lubaczow, Poland
Source: *ConAu 17R; NewYTBE 72; WhoAm 74, 76, 78, 80, 82*

Herzen, Aleksandr
Russian. Author
b. 1812
d. 1870
Source: *NewCol 75*

Herzl, Theodor
"Father of Modern Zionism"
Hungarian. Founder of Zionism, Author
Supported creation of national Jewish state in *Der Judenstaat,* 1896.
b. May 2, 1860 in Budapest, Hungary
d. Jul 3, 1904
Source: *EuAu; NewCol 75; OxGer*

Herzog, Chaim
Israeli. Ambassador to US
b. Sep 17, 1918 in Belfast, Northern Ireland
Source: *WhoWorJ 72*

Herzog, Emile Salomon, pseud.
see: Maurois, Andre

Herzog, Werner
[Werner H Stipetic]
German. Motion Picture Director
b. 1942 in Munich, Germany
Source: *BioIn 11; CurBio 78*

Hesburgh, Theodore Martin
American. Author, Educator
President of U of Notre Dame.
b. May 25, 1917 in Syracuse, New York
Source: *CelR 73; ConAu 13R; CurBio 55, 82; DrAS 74P; IndAu 1917; IntWW 74; LEduc 74; NewYTBE 71; WhoAm 74, 76, 78, 80, 82; WhoGov 72; WhoMW 74; WhoWor 74*

Heschel, Abraham Joshua
Polish. Rabbi
First Jewish scholar on staff of Union Theological Seminary.
b. 1907 in Warsaw, Poland
d. Dec 23, 1972 in New York, New York
Source: *ConAu 5R, 37R, 4NR; CurBio 70, 73; NewYTBE 72; WhAm 5; WhoE 74*

Heseltine, Phillip Arnold
[Peter Warlock, pseud.]
English. Composer, Author
b. Oct 30, 1894 in London, England
d. Dec 17, 1930 in London, England
Source: *Baker 78; BioIn 4, 11; OxMus*

Hesiod
Greek. Poet
Wrote *Works and Days, Theogony, The Shield of Heracles.*
d. in Orchomenus, Greece
Source: *AtlBL; BbD; BiD&SB; CasWL; CyWA; NewC; OxEng; Pen CL; RComWL; REn*

Hesketh, Thomas Alexander Fermor, Baron
English. Car Racing Sponsor
b. Oct 28, 1950
Source: *Who 74*

Hess, Myra
English. Musician
b. Feb 25, 1890 in London, England
d. Dec 26, 1965
Source: *CurBio 43, 66; InWom; WhAm 4*

Hess, Rudolf
German. Nazi Leader
Sentenced at Nuremberg trials to life imprisonment; only prisoner in Soandau Prison.
b. 1894 in Alexandria, Egypt
Source: *CurBio 41; NewYTBS 74; OxGer; REn*

Hess, Sol
American. Cartoonist
b. Oct 14, 1872 in Northville, Illinois
d. Dec 31, 1941 in Chicago, Illinois
Source: *WorECom*

Hess, Victor Francis
American. Scientist, Physician, Engineer
b. Jun 24, 1883 in Waldstein, Austria
d. Dec 17, 1964 in Mount Vernon, New York
Source: *CurBio 63, 65; WhAm 4*

Hesse, Don
American. Editor, Cartoonist
b. Feb 20, 1918 in Belleville, Illinois
Source: *WhoAm 74; WhoAmA 73*

Hesse, Eva
German. Artist
b. Jan 11, 1936 in Hamburg, Germany
d. May 29, 1970 in New York, New York
Source: *BioIn 8, 9, 10, 11; ConArt; DcAmArt; DcCAA 77; NewYTBE 70*

Hesse, Hermann
Swiss. Author
b. Jul 2, 1877 in Claw, Germany
d. Aug 9, 1962 in Montagnola, Switzerland
Source: *AtlBL; CasWL; ConAu 17R; ConAu P-2; ConLC 1, 2, 3, 6, 11, 17; CurBio 62; CyWA; EncWL; EvEuW; ModGL; OxGer; Pen EUR; RComWL; REn; TwCA, SUP; TwCW; WhAm 4; WhoTwCL*

Hesselius, John
American. Artist
b. 1728 in Philadelphia, Pennsylvania
d. Apr 9, 1778 in Bellefield, Maryland
Source: *BnEnAmA; DcAmArt; DcAmB; McGDA; NatCAB 23; NewYHSD; WhAm H*

Hesseman, Howard
American. Actor
b. Feb 27, 1940 in Lebanon, Ohio
Source: *BioIn 12; WhoAm 80, 82*

Heston, Charlton
American. Actor
Won Oscar for *Ben Hur,* 1959; president, Screen Actors Guild, 1966-71.
b. Oct 4, 1922 in Evanston, Illinois
Source: *BiDFilm; BiE&WWA; BkPepl; CelR 73; CmMov; CurBio 57; FilmgC; IntMPA 75, 76, 77, 78, 79, 80, 81, 82; IntWW 74; MotPP; MovMk; OxFilm; Who 74; WhoAm 74, 76, 78, 80, 82; WhoGov 72; WhoHol A; WhoThe 77; WhoWest 74; WhoWor 74; WorEFlm*

Hevesy, George de
Hungarian. Chemist
Won Nobel Prize, 1943.
b. Aug 1, 1885 in Budapest, Hungary
d. Jul 5, 1966
Source: *BioIn 2, 3, 5, 6, 7, 8; CurBio 59, 66*

Hewes, Henry
American. Drama Critic
b. Apr 9, 1917 in Boston, Massachusetts
Source: *AmAu&B; BiE&WWA; ConAu 13R; NotNAT; OxThe; WhoAm 74, 76, 78, 80, 82; WhoThe 77; WhoWor 74*

Hewes, Joseph
American. Merchant
b. Jan 23, 1730 in Kingston, New Jersey
d. Nov 10, 1779 in Philadelphia, Pennsylvania
Source: *AmBi; ApCAB; BiAuS; BiDrAC; DcAmB; Drake; TwCBDA; WhAm H; WhAmP*

Hewish, Antony
English. Scientist
Discovered pulsars; won Nobel Prize, 1974.
b. May 11, 1924 in Fowey, England
Source: *IntWW 74; Who 74*

Hewitt, Abram Stevens
American. Politician, Steelmaker
b. Jul 31, 1822 in Haverstraw, New York
d. 1903
Source: *AmBi; ApCAB; BiAuS; BiDrAC; DcAmB; EncAB-H; McGEWB; NatCAB 3; WebAB; WhAm 1, 4*

Hewitt, Henry Kent
American. Naval Officer
b. Feb 11, 1887 in Hackensack, New Jersey
d. Sep 15, 1972 in Middlebury, Vermont
Source: *BioIn 1, 9, 11; CurBio 43, 72*

Hewitt, Martin
American. Actor
b. Feb 19, 1958 in San Jose, California
Source: *BioIn 12*

Heydrich, Reinhard
"The Hangman of Europe"
German. Nazi Leader
b. Mar 9, 1904 in Halle, Germany
d. Jun 4, 1942 in Lidice, Czechoslovakia
Source: *BioIn 1, 5, 6, 8, 9, 10; CurBio 42; NewCol 75; WebBD 80*

Heyer, Georgette
English. Author
b. Dec 16, 1902 in London, England
d. Jul 4, 1974 in London, England
Source: *ConAu 49, 93; DcLEL; EncMys; LongCTC; NewC; NewYTBS 74; REn; TwCA, SUP; TwCW; WhAm 6; Who 74; WhoAm 74; WhoWor 74*

Heyerdahl, Thor
Norwegian. Anthropologist, Explorer
Wrote *Kon-Tiki*, 1950; *Aku-Aku: The Secret of Easter Island*, 1958.
b. Oct 6, 1914 in Larvik, Norway
Source: *CelR 73; ConAu 5R, 5NR; CurBio 47, 72; IntWW 74; LongCTC; SmATA 2; TwCA SUP; TwCW; Who 74; WhoAm 82; WhoWor 74; WrDr 76*

Heym, Stefan
German. Author
b. Apr 10, 1913 in Chemnitz, Germany
Source: *AmAu&B; AmNov; ConAu 9R, 4NR; CurBio 43; ModGL; OxGer; Pen EUR; REnAL; TwCA SUP*

Heyse, Paul Johann
German. Author
b. Mar 15, 1830 in Berlin, Germany
d. 1914 in Munich, Germany
Source: *BioIn 1, 5, 7; CasWL; ClDMEL; EuAu; EvEuW; NotNAT B; OxGer; Pen EUR; REn*

Heyward, DuBose
American. Author
b. Aug 31, 1885 in Charleston, South Carolina
d. Jun 16, 1940 in Tryon, North Carolina
Source: *AmAu&B; AmSCAP 66; ChPo; CnDAL; CnMD; ConAmA; ConAmL; CurBio 40; CyWA; DcAmB S2; DcLEL; DcNAA; EvLB; LongCTC; McGEWD; ModAL; ModWD; OxAmL; Pen AM; PlP&P; REn; REnAL; TwCA, SUP; TwCW; WebAB; WhAm 1*

Heyward, Thomas, Jr.
American. Lawyer, Farmer
b. Jul 28, 1746 in Saint Helena's, South Carolina
d. Mar 6, 1809 in Saint Luke's, South Carolina
Source: *AmBi; ApCAB; BiAuS; BiDrAC; DcAmB; TwCBDA; WhAm H; WhAmP*

Heywood, Anne
English. Actress
b. Dec 11, 1937 in Birmingham, England
Source: *FilmgC; IntMPA 75, 76, 77, 78, 79, 80, 81, 82; WhoAm 74; WhoHol A*

Heywood, Eddie
American. Musician, Composer
b. Dec 4, 1915 in Atlanta, Georgia
Source: *BioIn 10; CmpEPM; WhoJazz 72*

Heywood, Thomas
English. Dramatist
b. 1574 in Lincoln, England
d. Aug 1641 in London, England
Source: *Alli; AtlBL; BbD; BiD&SB; BrAu; CasWL; Chambr 1; ChPo; CnThe; CroE&S; CrtT 1; CyWA; DcEnA; DcEnL; DcEuL; DcLEL; EvLB; McGEWD; MouLC 1; NewC; OxEng; OxThe; Pen ENG; REn; REnWD; WebE&AL*

Hiawatha
American Indian. Legendary Chief
Subject of Henry Wadsworth Longfellow's *Song of Hiawatha*, 1855.
b. 1530
Source: *NewCol 75; OxAmL; WebAB*

Hibbard, Edna
American. Actress, Comedienne
b. 1895 in California
d. Dec 26, 1942 in New York, New York
Source: *CurBio 43; NotNAT B; WhScrn 74, 77; WhThe; WhoHol B*

Hibbert, Eleanor Alice Burford
[Philippa Carr; Elbur Ford; Victoria Holt; Kathleen Kellow; Jean Paidy; Ellalice Tate, pseuds.]
English. Author
b. 1906 in London, England
Source: *AmAu&B; ConAu 17R; ConLC 7; EncMys; SmATA 2; TwCW; Who 74; WhoAm 74, 76, 78, 80, 82; WhoAmW 77; WorAu; WrDr 76*

Hibbler, Al
American. Singer
b. Aug 16, 1915 in Little Rock, Arkansas
Source: *BioIn 4, 10; CmpEPM*

Hibbs, Ben
American. Journalist
b. Jul 23, 1901 in Fintana, Kansas
d. Mar 29, 1975 in Penn Valley, Pennsylvania
Source: *AmAu&B; CurBio 46; IntWW 74; WhAm 6; WhoAm 74*

Hickel, Walter Joseph
American. Government Official
Secretary of Interior, 1969-70.
b. Aug 18, 1919 in Claflin, Kansas
Source: *BiDrUSE; ConAu 41R; CurBio 69; IntWW 74; WhoAm 74, 76, 78, 80, 82; WhoAmP 73; WhoWor 74*

Hickenlooper, Bourke B
American. Statesman
b. Jul 21, 1896 in Blockton, Iowa
d. Sep 4, 1971 in Shelter Island, New York
Source: *BiDrAC; CurBio 47, 71; NewYTBE 71; WhAm 5; WhAmP*

Hickey, Margaret A
American. Editor
b. Mar 14, 1902 in Kansas City, Missouri
Source: *BioIn 7; WhoAm 74, 76, 78, 80, 82; WhoWor 74*

Hickey, William
English. Lawyer, Traveler
b. 1749 in Westminster, England
d. 1830
Source: *BioIn 6, 8, 10; DcLEL; OxEng; Pen ENG*

Hickman, Darryl
American. Actor
b. Jul 28, 1931 in Los Angeles, California
Source: *BiE&WWA; FilmgC; IntMPA 75, 76, 77, 78, 79, 80, 81, 82; MovMk; WhoHol A*

Hickman, Dwayne
American. Actor
Starred in "The Many Loves of Dobie Gillis," 1959-63.
b. 1934 in Los Angeles, California
Source: *FilmgC; MotPP; MovMk; WhoHol A*

Hickman, Herman Michael, Jr.
American. Football Player
b. Oct 1, 1911 in Johnson City, Tennessee
d. Apr 25, 1958 in Washington, DC
Source: *BioIn 2, 3, 4, 5, 6; WhoFtbl 74*

Hickock, Richard Eugene
American. Murderer
b. 1931
d. Apr 14, 1965
Source: *BioIn 7; Blood*

Hickok, Lorena A
American. Author, Journalist
b. 1892 in East Troy, Wisconsin
d. May 3, 1968 in Rhinebeck, New York
Source: *BioIn 7, 8, 10; SmATA 20*

Hickok, "Wild Bill" (James Butler)
American. Scout, US Marshall
Toured with Buffalo Bill, 1872-73; killed while playing poker.
b. May 27, 1837 in Troy Grove, Illinois
d. Aug 2, 1876 in Deadwood, South Dakota
Source: *DcAmB; FilmgC; OxAmL; REn; REnAL; WebAB*

Hicks, Beatrice Alice
American. Management Consultant
b. Jan 2, 1919 in Orange, New Jersey
d. Oct 21, 1979
Source: *AmM&WS 79P; BioIn 3, 4; CurBio 57; InWom; WhAm 7; WhoAm 76, 78; WhoAmW 58, 61, 64, 66, 68, 70, 72; WhoF&I 74; WhoWor 74*

Hicks, David Nightingale
English. Interior Designer
b. Mar 25, 1929 in Essex, England
Source: *WhoWor 78*

Hicks, Edward
American. Artist
b. Apr 4, 1780 in Attleboro, Pennsylvania
d. Aug 23, 1849 in Newtown, Pennsylvania
Source: *REn; WebAB; WhAm H*

Hicks, Elias
American. Religious Leader
b. Mar 19, 1748 in Hempstead Township, New York
d. Feb 27, 1830 in Jericho, New York
Source: *Alli; AmAu&B; AmBi; ApCAB; BbD; BiD&SB; DcAmAu; DcAmB; DcNAA; Drake; OxAmL; REnAL; TwCBDA; WebAB; WhAm H*

Hicks, Granville
American. Author
b. Sep 9, 1901 in Exeter, New Hampshire
d. Jun 18, 1982 in Franklin Park, New Jersey
Source: *AmAu&B; AmNov; CnDAL; ConAmA; ConAu 9R; ConLCrt; ConNov 72, 76; CurBio 42, 82; DcLEL; IntAu&W 76, 77; IntWW 74, 75, 76, 77, 78; NewYTBS 82; OxAmL; Pen AM; RAdv 1; REn; REnAL; ScF&FL 1; TwCA, SUP; WhLit; WhoAm 74, 76, 78; WhoWor 74, 76, 78; WrDr 76, 80*

Hicks, Louise Day
American. Politician
b. Oct 16, 1923 in Boston, Massachusetts
Source: *CurBio 74; WhoAm 74; WhoAmP 73; WhoE 74; WhoGov 72*

Hicks, Peggy Glanville-
Australian. Opera Singer
b. Dec 29, 1912 in Melbourne, Australia
Source: *DcCM; WhoAm 74, 76, 78, 80, 82*

Hicks, Tony
see: Hollies, The

Hidalgo, Elvira de
Spanish. Opera Singer, Teacher
b. 1882 in Barcelona, Spain
Source: *InWom*

Hidalgo y Costilla, Miguel
Mexican. National Hero, Priest
b. May 8, 1753 in Guanajuato, Mexico
d. Jul 30, 1811 in Chihuahua, Mexico
Source: *ApCAB; REn*

Higginbotham, "Jack" (Jay C)
American. Musician
b. May 11, 1906 in Atlanta, Georgia
d. May 26, 1973 in New York, New York
Source: *WhAm 6*

Higgins, Andrew J
American. Shipbuilder
b. Aug 28, 1886 in Columbus, Nebraska
d. Aug 1, 1952 in New Orleans, Louisiana
Source: *CurBio 43, 52; DcAmB S5; WhAm 3*

Higgins, Bertie (Elbert)
American. Singer, Songwriter
Recorded hit single, "Key Largo," 1982.
b. 1945?
Source: *NF*

Higgins, George V
American. Author
b. Nov 13, 1939 in Brockton, Massachusetts
Source: *ConAu 77; ConLC 4, 7, 10, 18; ConNov 76; DrAF 76; WhoAm 82; WrDr 76*

Higgins, Joe
American. Actor
b. 1913
Source: *BioIn 9; WhoHol A*

Higgins, Marguerite
American. Journalist
Helped to liberate Buchenwald, Dachau concentration camps during WW II.
b. Sep 3, 1920 in Hong Kong, China
d. Jan 3, 1966 in Washington, DC
Source: *AmAu&B; ConAu 5R, 25R; CurBio 51, 66; InWom; WhAm 4*

Higginson, Thomas Wentworth
American. Clergyman, Author
b. Dec 22, 1823 in Cambridge, Massachusetts
d. May 9, 1911
Source: *AmAu; AmAu&B; BbD; BiD&SB; CasWL; Chambr 3; CnDAL; CyAl 2; DcLEL; DcNAA; REn*

Highet, Gilbert Arthur
American. Author, Educator, Critic
b. Jun 22, 1906 in Glasgow, Scotland
d. Jan 20, 1978 in New York, New York
Source: *AmAu&B; Au&Wr 71; CelR 73; ChPo S2; ConAu 1R; CurBio 64; DrAS 74F; IntWW 74; LongCTC; NewC; NewYTBE 72; RAdv 1; REnAL; TwCA SUP; Who 74; WhoAm 74; WhoWor 74; WrDr 76*

Highsmith, Patricia
American. Author
b. Jan 12, 1921 in Fort Worth, Texas
Source: *ConAu 1R, 1NR; ConLC 2, 4, 14; ConNov 72, 76; EncMys; Who 74; WhoTwCL; WorAu; WrDr 76*

Hightower, Florence Josephine Cole
American. Children's Author
b. Jun 9, 1916 in Boston, Massachusetts
d. Mar 6, 1981 in Boston, Massachusetts
Source: *AuBYP; ConAu 1R, 103; SmATA 4; WhoAmW 72, 74, 75*

Hightower, Rosella
American. Dancer
b. 1920
Source: *BioIn 1, 3, 4, 9, 11*

Hightower, Stephanie
American. Track Athlete
b. Jul 19, 1958
Source: *BioIn 12*

Hilbert, Egon
Austrian. Opera Manager, Director
b. 1899 in Austria
d. Jan 18, 1968 in Vienna, Austria
Source: *NewEOp 71*

Hildebrand, Adolf von
German. Artist
b. 1847
d. 1921
Source: *BioIn 9; NewCol 75*

Hildegarde, Loretta Sell
American. Singer
b. Feb 1, 1906 in Adell, Wisconsin
Source: *CurBio 44; InWom*

Hildegard of Bingen, Saint
"Sybil of the Rhine"
German. Religious Figure
b. 1098
d. Sep 17, 1179
Source: *BioIn 4, 5, 11; CasWL*

Hill, Ambrose Powell
American. Military Leader
b. Nov 9, 1825 in Culpeper, Virginia
d. Apr 2, 1865 in Petersburg, Virginia
Source: *AmBi; ApCAB; BiDConf; DcAmB; Drake; TwCBDA; WebAB; WhAm H*

Hill, Archibald Vivian
English. Physiologist
b. Sep 26, 1886? in Bristol, England
d. 1977
Source: *BioIn 1, 2, 3, 6, 11; DcLEL; IntWW 74; Who 74; WhoLA*

Hill, Arthur
Canadian. Actor
b. Aug 1, 1922 in Melfort, SK
Source: *BiE&WWA; FilmgC; IntMPA 75, 76, 77, 78, 79, 80, 81, 82; MotPP; NotNAT; NewYTBE 71; NotNAT; WhoAm 74, 76, 78, 80, 82; WhoHol A; WhoThe 77*

Hill, Benny (Benjamin)
English. Comedian
Best known in US for TV series "The Benny Hill Show."
b. Jan 21, 1925 in Southampton, England
Source: *FilmgC; IntMPA 75, 76, 77, 78, 79, 80, 81, 82; WhoHol A*

Hill, Calvin
American. Football Player
b. Jan 2, 1947 in Baltimore, Maryland
Source: *WhoAm 74; WhoBlA 75; WhoFtbl 74*

Hill, "Chippie" (Bertha)
American. Jazz Musician
b. 1905? in Charleston, South Carolina
d. May 7, 1950 in New York, New York
Source: *CmpEPM; WhoJazz 72*

Hill, Dan
Canadian. Singer, Musician
b. Jun 3, 1954 in Toronto, ON
Source: *BioIn 11; RkOn*

Hill, Dave
American. Golfer
b. May 20, 1937 in Jackson, Michigan
Source: *BioIn 10; WhoGolf*

Hill, Dusty
see: ZZ Top

Hill, Geoffrey
English. Poet
b. Jun 18, 1932 in Bromsgrove, England
Source: *BioIn 7; ConAu 81; ConLC 5, 8, 18*

Hill, George Roy
American. Actor, Motion Picture Director
b. Dec 20, 1922 in Minneapolis, Minnesota
Source: *BiDFilm; BiE&WWA; FilmgC; IntMPA 75, 76, 77, 78, 79, 80, 81, 82; MovMk; NotNAT; OxFilm; WhoAm 78, 80, 82; WhoThe 77; WorEFlm*

Hill, George Washington
American. Tobacco Executive
b. Oct 22, 1884 in Philadelphia, Pennsylvania
d. Sep 13, 1946 in Matapedia, PQ
Source: *CurBio 46; DcAmB S4; WebAB; WhAm 2*

Hill, Graham
English. Auto Racer
b. Feb 15, 1929 in London, England
d. Nov 30, 1975 in London, England
Source: *BioNews 74; CurBio 73; Who 74*

Hill, Herbert
American. Public Official
Labor director, NAACP, 1948--; wrote *Anger and Beyond,* 1966.
b. Jan 24, 1924 in New York, New York
Source: *BioIn 9, 11; ConAu 65; CurBio 70*

Hill, Howard
American. Archer, Actor
b. 1899
d. Feb 4, 1975 in Birmingham, Alabama
Source: *BioIn 10; WhScrn 77*

Hill, Ian
see: Judas Priest

Hill, James Jerome
Canadian. Railroad Executive
b. Sep 16, 1838 in Guelph, ON
d. May 29, 1916 in Saint Paul, Minnesota
Source: *BioIn 1, 2, 3, 4, 5, 8, 9, 10, 11; WebAB; WhAm 1*

Hill, Jimmy (James William Thomas)
English. Sportscaster
b. 1928
Source: *BioIn 11; Who 74*

Hill, Joe, pseud.
[Joseph Hillstrom]
American. Labor Organizer, Songwriter
b. Oct 7, 1879 in Sweden
d. Nov 19, 1915 in Salt Lake City, Utah
Source: *BioIn 1, 2, 3, 7, 8, 9, 11; WebAB; WhAm HA, 4*

Hill, Sir Rowland
English. Postal Reformer
b. Dec 3, 1795 in Kidderminster, England
d. Aug 27, 1879 in Hampstead, England
Source: *Alli; NewC; OxEng*

Hill, Steven
American. Actor
Source: *FilmgC; MotPP; WhoHol A*

Hill, Thomas
English. Artist
b. Sep 11, 1829 in Birmingham, England
d. 1908 in Raymond, California
Source: *ApCAB; ArtsAmW; DcAmArt; DcAmB; Drake; EarABI; IlBEAAW; NatCAB 3; NewYHSD; REnAW; WhAm 1*

Hill, Virginia
"The Flamingo"
American. Actress, Mob Associate
b. Aug 26, 1916 in Lipscomb, Alabama
d. Mar 25, 1966 in Salzburg, Austria
Source: *BioIn 2, 3, 7; LookW; WhScrn 77; WhoHol B*

Hillary, Sir Edmund Percival
New Zealander. Explorer, Mountain Climber
With Tenzing Norkay was first to reach summit of Mt. Everest, 1953.
b. Jul 20, 1919 in Auckland, New Zealand
Source: *Au&Wr 71; CurBio 54; IntWW 74; LongCTC; Who 74; WhoWor 74; WrDr 76*

Hillel
Jewish Scholar
d. 9
Source: *NewCol 75; WebBD 80*

Hillenkoetter, Roscoe H(enry)
American. Business Executive
First director of CIA, 1947-50.
b. May 8, 1897 in Saint Louis, Missouri
d. Jun 18, 1982 in New York, New York
Source: *BioIn 12; CurBio 50, 82; NewYTBS 82; PolProf T; WebAMB; WhoAm 74, 76, 78, 80, 82*

Hiller, Arthur
American. Motion Picture Director
b. Nov 22, 1923 in Edmonton, AB
Source: *BiDFilm; CanWW 70; FilmgC; IntMPA 75, 76, 77, 78, 79, 80, 81, 82; MovMk; WhoAm 74, 76, 78, 80, 82*

Hiller, Johann Adam
Prussian. Composer
b. Dec 25, 1728 in Wendisch-Ossig, Prussia
d. Jun 16, 1804 in Leipzig, Germany
Source: *OxGer*

Hiller, John Frederick
American. Baseball Player
Pitcher, Detroit, 1967-80; suffered heart attack, Jan 1971; returned to game, Jul 1972.
b. Apr 8, 1943 in Scarborough, ON
Source: *BaseEn; BioIn 9, 10, 11; WhoProB 73*

Hiller, Wendy
English. Actress
b. Aug 15, 1912 in Bramhall, England
Source: *BiE&WWA; CurBio 41; FilmgC; InWom; IntMPA 75, 76, 77, 78, 79, 80, 81, 82; MotPP; MovMk; NotNAT; OxFilm; ThFT; Who 74; WhoAm 82; WhoAmW 77; WhoHol A; WhoThe 77*

Hillerman, John Benedict
American. Actor
Plays Jonathan Higgins on "Magnum, P.I."
b. Dec 20, 1932 in Denison, Texas
Source: *WhoAm 82; WhoHol A*

Hillerman, Tony
American. Author
b. May 27, 1925 in Sacred Heart, Oklahoma
Source: *BioIn 8; ConAu 29R; SmATA 6; TwCCr&M*

Hillery, Patrick John
Irish. President
President of the Republic of Ireland, 1976--.
b. May 2, 1923 in Miltown-Malbay, Ireland
Source: *IntWW 74; NewYTBE 70; WhoWor 74*

Hilliard, Nicholas
English. Miniaturist
b. 1537
d. 1619
Source: *NewCol 75*

Hilliard, Robert C
American. Actor
b. May 28, 1857 in New York, New York
d. Jun 6, 1927 in New York, New York
Source: *NotNAT A, B; WhoStg 1906, 1908*

Hillier, James
Canadian. Research Physicist
b. Aug 22, 1915 in Brantford, ON
Source: *AmM&WS 73P; BioIn 3, 5, 10; CanWW 70, 82; St&PR 75; WhoAm 74; WhoF&I 74*

Hillis, Margaret
American. Conductor, Musician
b. Oct 1, 1921 in Kokomo, Indiana
Source: *Baker 78; BioIn 4, 6, 10, 11; WhoAm 78, 80, 82; WhoAmW 79; WhoWor 78*

Hillman, Chris
[The Byrds; The Flying Burrito Brothers; The Souther-Hillman-Furay Band]
American. Rock Musician
b. Dec 4, 1942 in Los Angeles, California
Source: *ConMuA 80; WhoRock 81*

Hillman, Sidney
American. Labor Leader
President, Amalgamated Clothing Workers of America, 1914-46; vice-president, CIO, 1935-40.
b. Mar 23, 1887 in Zagare, Lithuania
d. Jul 10, 1946 in Long Island, New York
Source: *CurBio 40, 46; DcAmB S4; EncAB-H; WebAB; WhAm 2*

Hillquit, Morris
American. Socialist Leader
b. Aug 1, 1869 in Riga, Russia
d. Oct 7, 1933
Source: *AmLY; BioIn 1, 2, 6, 7, 11; DcNAA; REnAL; WhAm 1*

Hills, Argentina
American. Publisher
b. 1922 in Pola, Italy
Source: *WhoAmW 77; WhoS&SW 73*

Hills, Carla Anderson
American. Government Official
Secretary of HUD, 1975-77.
b. Jan 3, 1934 in Los Angeles, California
Source: *WhoAmW 77*

Hills, Lee
American. Newspaper Publisher
b. May 28, 1906 in Granville, North Dakota
Source: *ConAu 101; St&PR 75; WhoAm 74, 76, 78, 80, 82; WhoMW 74; WhoS&SW 73; WhoWor 74*

Hills, Roderick M
American. Attorney
b. Mar 9, 1931 in Seattle, Washington
Source: *WhoAm 74, 76, 78, 80, 82*

Hillyer, Robert
American. Poet, Author, Educator
b. Jun 3, 1895 in East Orange, New Jersey
d. Dec 24, 1961 in Wilmington, Delaware
Source: *AmAu&B; ChPo, S1, S2; CnDAL; CnE&AP; ConAmA; ConAu 89; CurBio 40, 62; DcLEL; OxAmL; Pen AM; REn; REnAL; TwCA, SUP; WhAm 4; WhNAA*

Hilsberg, Alexander
Polish. Conductor, Musician
b. Apr 24, 1900 in Warsaw, Poland
d. Aug 10, 1961 in Camden, Maine
Source: *CurBio 53, 61; WhAm 4*

Hilton, Conrad Nicholson
American. Hotel Proprietor
Formed Hilton Hotel Corp., 1946; wrote autobiography, *Be My Guest,* 1957.
b. Dec 25, 1887 in San Antonio, New Mexico
d. Jan 3, 1979 in Santa Monica, California
Source: *CelR 73; IntWW 74; St&PR 75; WebAB; Who 74; WhoAm 74; WhoF&I 74; WhoWor 74*

Hilton, Daisy
[The Hilton Sisters]
English. Siamese Twin Vaudeville Act
b. Feb 5, 1908? in Brighton, England
d. Jan 4, 1969 in Charlotte, North Carolina
Source: *WhScrn 77*

Hilton, James
English. Author
b. Sep 9, 1900 in Lancashire, England
d. Dec 20, 1954 in Long Beach, California
Source: *ChPo S1; CurBio 42, 55; CyWA; DcLEL; EncMys; EvLB; FilmgC; LongCTC; MnBBF; ModBrL; NewC; Pen ENG; REn; REnAL; TwCA, SUP; TwCW; WhAm 3*

Hilton, Violet
[The Hilton Sisters]
English. Siamese Twin Vaudeville Act
b. Feb 5, 1908? in Brighton, England
d. Jan 4, 1969 in Charlotte, North Carolina
Source: *WhScrn 77*

Hilton, William Barron
American. Hotel Executive
b. 1927
Source: *BioIn 8, 10, 11; BusPN*

Himes, Chester Bomar
American. Author
b. Jul 29, 1909 in Jefferson City, Missouri
Source: *AmAu&B; AmNov; BlkAW; ConAu 25R; ConLC 2, 4, 7, 18; ConNov 72, 76; DrAF 76; EncWL; LivgBAA; ModAL, SUP; OhA&B; Pen AM; RAdv 1; WebE&AL; WhoAm 74, 82; WhoBlA 75; WorAu; WrDr 76*

Himmler, Heinrich
German. Nazi Head of Gestapo
b. Nov 7, 1900 in Munich, Germany
d. May 23, 1945 in Luneburg, Germany
Source: *CurBio 41, 45; NewCol 75; OxGer; REn; WebBD 80*

Hinckley, John Warnock, Jr.
American. Attempted Assassin
Acquitted, 1982, by reason of insanity for shooting Ronald Reagan, Mar 30, 1981.
b. May 29, 1955 in Ardmore, Oklahoma
Source: *BioIn 12; NewYTBS 81*

Hinde, Thomas
English. Author
b. Mar 26, 1926 in Felixstowe, England
Source: *ConAu 5R, 4NR; ConLC 6; ConNov 72, 76; ModBrL SUP; NewC; TwCW; Who 74; WorAu; WrDr 76*

Hindemith, Paul
German. Musician, Composer
b. Nov 16, 1895 in Hanau, Germany
d. Dec 28, 1963 in Frankfurt, Germany (West)
Source: *AtlBL; CurBio 41, 64; DcCM; OxGer; REn; WhAm 4*

Hindenburg, Paul von
German. General, President
b. Oct 2, 1847 in Posen, Prussia
d. Aug 2, 1934 in Neudeck, Germany
Source: *BioIn 10; McGEWB; NewCol 75; WebBD 80*

Hinds, Alfred George
English. Burglar
b. 1917
Source: *BioIn 6*

Hines, Duncan
American. Gastronomist, Author
b. Mar 26, 1880 in Bowling Green, Kentucky
d. Mar 15, 1959 in Bowling Green, Kentucky
Source: *BioIn 1, 3, 4, 5, 6; CurBio 46, 59; WebAB; WhAm 3*

Hines, "Fatha" (Earl Kenneth)
American. Jazz Musician
b. Dec 28, 1905 in Duquesne, Pennsylvania
Source: *AmSCAP 66; CurBio 67; EncAB-H; WhoAm 74, 76, 78, 80, 82; WhoJazz 72*

Hines, Gregory Oliver
American. Dancer, Actor
b. Feb 14, 1946 in New York, New York
Source: *NewYTBS 78; WhoAm 82*

Hines, Jerome
American. Opera Singer
b. Nov 9, 1921 in Hollywood, California
Source: *BioNews 75; CurBio 63; WhoAm 74, 76, 78, 80, 82; WhoMus 72*

Hines, John Elbridge
American. Episcopal Bishop
b. Oct 3, 1910 in Seneca, South Carolina
Source: *CurBio 68; IntWW 74; WhoAm 74; WhoRel 75; WhoWor 74*

Hines, Mimi
[Ford and Hines]
Canadian. Comedienne
b. 1933 in Vancouver, BC
Source: *BioNews 74*

Hingle, Pat
American. Actor
b. Jul 19, 1924 in Denver, Colorado
Source: *BiE&WWA; CurBio 65; FilmgC; IntMPA 75, 76, 77, 78, 79, 80, 81, 82; MotPP; MovMk; NotNAT; WhoAm 74, 76, 78, 80, 82; WhoE 74; WhoHol A; WhoThe 77*

Hinkle, Paul
"Tony"
American. Basketball Coach
Coach, Butler U, 1927-42; 1946-70.
b. Dec 19, 1899 in Logansport, Indiana
Source: *WhoBbl 73*

Hinrichs, Gustav
German. Conductor
b. Dec 10, 1850 in Mecklenburg, Germany
d. Mar 26, 1942 in Mountain Lakes, New Jersey
Source: *CurBio 42*

Hinshelwood, Sir Cyril
English. Scientist, Engineer, Physician
b. Jun 19, 1897 in London, England
d. Oct 9, 1967 in London, England
Source: *CurBio 57, 67; WhAm 4, 5*

Hinton, Sir Christopher
English. Engineer
b. May 12, 1901 in Tisbury, England
Source: *BioIn 3, 4, 6, 7; CurBio 57; WhoWor 74*

Hinton, S(usan) E(loise)
American. Author
Writes books for teenagers: *The Outsiders; That Was Then, This is Now.*
b. 1948 in Tulsa, Oklahoma
Source: *BioIn 12; ChlLR 3; ConAu 81; SmATA 19; TwCCW 78; WhoAm 82; WrDr 80*

Hinton, William Arthur
American. Mechanical Engineer
b. Aug 31, 1908 in Dacula, Georgia
Source: *AmM&WS 73P*

Hinton, William Augustus
American. Physician
b. Dec 15, 1883 in Chicago, Illinois
d. Aug 8, 1959 in Canton, Massachusetts
Source: *BioIn 1, 2, 5, 11; ObitOF 79; SelBAA*

Hipparchus
Greek. Astronomer
b. 160?BC
d. 125?BC
Source: *BioIn 3, 7, 8; CasWL; Pen CL*

Hipple, Eric Ellsworth
American. Football Player
b. Sep 16, 1957 in Lubbock, Texas
Source: *FootReg*

Hippocrates
Greek. Physician
Hippocratic oath cannot be directly credited to him, but represents his ideals, principles.
b. 460BC in Island of Cos
d. 377BC
Source: *CasWL; NewC; OxEng; Pen CL; REn*

Hiraoka, Kimitake
see: Mishima, Yukio, pseud.

Hires, Charles E
American. Soft Drink Manufacturer
Invented, manufactured root beer, 1876.
b. Aug 19, 1851 in Roadstown, New Jersey
d. Jul 31, 1937 in Haverford, Pennsylvania
Source: *DcAmB S2; WebAB; WhAm HA, 4*

Hirohito
Japanese. Emperor
b. Apr 29, 1901 in Tokyo, Japan
Source: *REn*

Hiroshige, Ando
Japanese. Artist
b. 1797
d. 1858
Source: *BioIn 10; NewCol 75; WebBD 80*

Hirsch, "Crazylegs" (Elroy)
American. Football Player
Played for LA Rams, 1949-57; athletic director, U of Wisconsin, 1969--.
b. Jun 17, 1923 in Wausau, Wisconsin
Source: *BioIn 3, 7, 8, 9; WhoAm 82; WhoFtbl 74; WhoHol A*

Hirsch, Joseph
American. Artist
b. Apr 25, 1910 in Philadelphia, Pennsylvania
d. Sep 21, 1981 in New York, New York
Source: *BioIn 1, 4, 6, 9; ChPo S1; DcAmArt; DcCAA 71; McGDA; WhoAm 74, 76, 78, 80; WhoAmA 73, 76, 78*

Hirsch, Judd
American. Actor
Plays Alex on TV series "Taxi," 1978--.
b. Mar 15, 1935 in New York, New York
Source: *IntMPA 82; WhoAm 78, 80, 82*

Hirsch, Robert
French. Actor
Source: *FilmgC*

Hirsch, Samson Raphael
German. Theologian
b. 1808
d. 1888
Source: *BioIn 3, 5, 10*

Hirschfeld, Al(bert)
American. Cartoonist, Artist
b. Jun 21, 1903 in Saint Louis, Missouri
Source: *AmAu&B; BiE&WWA; CelR 73; ConAu 1R, 2NR; CurBio 71; NotNAT; WhoAm 74, 76, 78, 80, 82; WhoAmA 73; WhoWorJ 72*

Hirschmann, Ira Arthur
American. Business Executive
b. Jul 7, 1906 in Baltimore, Maryland
Source: *WhoAm 74; WhoWorJ 72*

Hirshfield, Morris
American. Artist
b. Apr 10, 1872 in Russia-Poland
d. 1946
Source: *BioIn 1, 2; CurBio 43*

Hirshhorn, Joseph
American. Promoter, Art Collector
b. Aug 11, 1899 in Russia
d. Aug 31, 1981 in Washington, DC
Source: *BioIn 3, 4, 5, 6, 7, 8, 9, 10; CanWW 70; WhoAmA 73, 76, 78; WhoE 74*

Hirt, Al
American. Jazz Musician
Plays trumpet; hits include "Bourbon Street," 1961; "Cotton Candy," 1964.
b. Nov 7, 1922 in New Orleans, Louisiana
Source: *CurBio 67; IntMPA 75, 76, 77, 78, 79, 80, 81, 82; WhoAm 74; WhoS&SW 73*

Hiss, Alger
American. Public Official, Lawyer
b. Nov 11, 1904 in Baltimore, Maryland
Source: *Au&Wr 71; ConAu 33R; CurBio 47; EncAB-H; WebAB; Who 74*

Hitch, Charles Johnston
American. University President
b. Jan 9, 1910 in Boonville, Missouri
Source: *AmEA 74; BioIn 5, 7, 8, 9, 11; CurBio 70; WhoAm 82*

Hitchcock, Sir Alfred Joseph
English. Motion Picture Director
Directed suspense thrillers *North by Northwest,* 1959, *Psycho,* 1960; won Oscar, 1940, for *Rebecca.*
b. Aug 13, 1899 in London, England
d. Apr 29, 1980 in Beverly Hills, California
Source: *Au&Wr 71; BiDFilm; BioNews 74; CelR 73; CmMov; ConAu 97; ConLC 16; CurBio 41, 60; DcFM; EncMys; FilmgC; IntMPA 75, 76, 77; IntWW 74; MovMk; NewC; NewYTBE 72; NewYTBS 74; OxFilm; REnAL; WebAB; Who 74; WhoAm 74; WhoWest 74; WhoWor 74; WorEFlm*

Hitchcock, Henry Russell
American. Architectural Historian
b. Jun 3, 1903 in Boston, Massachusetts
Source: *BioIn 3, 6, 9; IntAu&W 77; IntWW 74, 75, 76, 77, 78; Who 74; WhoAm 74, 76, 78, 80, 82; WhoAmA 73, 76, 78; WhoWor 74*

Hitchcock, Lambert
American. Cabinetmaker
b. 1795 in Cheshire, Connecticut
d. 1852
Source: *BioIn 3, 9; NewCol 75*

Hitchcock, Raymond
American. Actor
b. 1865 in Auburn, New York
d. Dec 24, 1929 in Beverly Hills, California
Source: *DcAmB; EncMT; Film 1; MotPP; TwYS; WhScrn 74, 77; WhoHol B; WhoStg 1906*

Hitchcock, Thomas, Jr.
American. Polo Player
b. Feb 11, 1900 in Aiken, South Carolina
d. Apr 19, 1944 in Salisbury, England
Source: *CurBio 44; DcAmB S3; WebAB*

Hite, Robert Ernest, Jr.
[Canned Heat]
"The Bear"
American. Singer
b. Jan 26, 1943 in Torrance, California
d. Apr 1981 in Los Angeles, California
Source: *WhoAm 74; WhoWor 74*

Hite, Shere
American. Author
Wrote *The Hite Report: A Nationwide Study of Female Sexuality,* 1976; *The Hite Report on Male Sexuality,* 1981.
b. Nov 2, 1942 in Saint Joseph, Missouri
Source: *BioIn 11; ConAu 81; WhoAm 78, 80, 82*

Hitler, Adolf
[Adolf Schickelgruber]
German. Fuhrer of Nazi Party
His invasion of Poland, 1939, started WW II.
b. Apr 20, 1889 in Branau, Austria
d. Apr 30, 1945 in Berlin, Germany
Source: *BioIn 1, 2, 3, 4, 5, 6, 7, 8, 9, 10, 11, 12; CurBio 42, 57; FilmgC; NewYTBE 72, 73; OxEng; OxGer; REn; WhAm 4*

Hitotsubashi
[Yoshinobu]
Japanese. Last of Shoguns
b. 1837
d. 1902
Source: *WebBD 80*

Hluber, Dave
see: Molly Hatchet

Ho, Don
American. Singer
b. 1930 in Kakaako, Hawaii
Source: *WhoAm 74; WhoWor 74*

Ho Chi Minh
[Nguyen That Thank]
Vietnamese. Communist Leader
Founder, first president, N Vietnam, 1954-69.
b. May 19, 1890 in Kim Lien, Vietnam
d. Sep 3, 1969 in Hanoi, Vietnam (North)
Source: *CurBio 49, 66, 69; DcOrL 2*

Hoare, Sir Samuel John Gurney
English. Diplomat
b. Feb 24, 1880
d. May 7, 1959 in London, England
Source: *CurBio 40, 59*

Hoban, James
American. Architect
b. 1762 in Callan, Ireland
d. Dec 8, 1831 in Washington, DC
Source: *AmBi; BiAuS; DcAmB; OxAmL; WebAB; WhAm H*

Hoban, Russell
American. Artist, Author
b. Feb 4, 1925 in Lansdale, Pennsylvania
Source: *AuBYP; ChPo S1, S2; ConAu 5R; SmATA 1; ThrBJA; WhoAm 82; WrDr 76*

Hobart, Alice Tisdale Nourse
American. Author
b. Jan 28, 1882 in Lockport, New York
d. Mar 14, 1967 in Oakland, California
Source: *AmAu&B; AmNov; ConAu 5R, 25R; InWom; REnAL; TwCA, SUP; WhAm 4; WhNAA*

Hobart, Garret Augustus
American. Vice-President
Served as vice-president under William McKinley, 1897-99.
b. Jun 3, 1844 in Long Branch, New Jersey
d. Nov 21, 1899 in Paterson, New Jersey
Source: *BioIn 1, 4, 7, 8, 9, 10; WebAB; WhAm 1*

Hobart, Rose
American. Actress
b. May 1, 1906 in New York, New York
Source: *BiE&WWA; FilmgC; ForWC 70; MovMk; NotNAT; ThFT; WhoHol A; WhoThe 77*

Hobbema, Meindert
Dutch. Artist
b. Oct 31, 1638 in Netherlands
d. Dec 7, 1709 in Netherlands
Source: *AtlBL; REn*

Hobbes, Thomas
English. Author, Philosopher
Father of modern analytical philosophy; best known work *Leviathan,* 1651.
b. Apr 5, 1588 in Malmesbury, England
d. Dec 4, 1679 in Hardwick, England
Source: *Alli; AtlBL; BiD&SB; BrAu; CasWL; Chambr 1; CroE&S; CrtT 2; CyWA; DcEnA; DcEnL; DcEuL; DcLEL; EvLB; MouLC 1; NewC; OxEng; Pen ENG; RComWL; REn; WebE&AL*

Hobbs, Leland Stanford
American. Military Leader
b. Feb 24, 1892 in Gloucester, Massachusetts
d. Mar 1966
Source: *BioIn 3, 7; WhAm 4*

Hobbs, Leonard Sinclair
American. Aircraft Engineer, Businessman
b. Dec 20, 1896 in Carbon, Wyoming
d. Nov 1, 1977 in Hartford, Connecticut
Source: *CurBio 54, 78; NewYTBS 77*

Hobbs, Peter
American. Actor
Source: *WhoHol A*

Hobby, Oveta Culp
American. Government Official
b. Jan 11, 1905 in Killeen, Texas
Source: *BiDrUSE; ConAu 81; CurBio 42, 53; ForWC 70; IntWW 74; St&PR 75; TexWr; WhoAm 74; WhoAmP 73; WhoAmW 77; WhoS&SW 73; WhoWor 74*

Hobson, Harold
English. Drama Critic
b. Aug 4, 1904 in Rotherham, England
Source: *BiE&WWA; ConAu 81; CroCD; LongCTC; NotNAT; Who 74; WhoThe 77*

Hobson, John Atkinson
English. Economist
b. Jul 6, 1858 in Derby, England
d. Apr 1, 1940 in London, England
Source: *CurBio 40; NewC*

Hobson, Laura Zametkin
American. Author
b. 1900 in New York, New York
Source: *AmAu&B; AmNov; ConAu 17R; ConLC 7; ConNov 72, 76; CurBio 47; InWom; REn; REnAL; TwCA SUP; WhoAm 74, 76, 78, 80, 82; WhoAmW 77; WrDr 76*

Hobson, Richmond Pearson
American. Military Leader
b. Aug 17, 1870 in Greensboro, Alabama
d. Mar 16, 1937
Source: *AmAu&B; AmBi; ApCAB SUP; BiDSA; BiDrAC; DcAmAu; DcAmB S2; DcNAA; TwCBDA; WhAm 1*

Hobson, Thomas
English. Liveryman, Innkeeper
b. 1544
d. Jan 1, 1631
Source: *Alli; NewC*

Hobson, Valerie Babette
British. Actress
b. 1917
Source: *BioIn 9; FilmgC; MovMk; OxFilm; ThFT; Who 74; WhoHol A*

Hochhuth, Rolf
German. Author, Dramatist
b. Apr 1, 1931 in Germany
Source: *CasWL; CnMD; CnThe; ConAu 5R; ConLC 4, 11, 18; IntWW 74; CroCD; EncWL; IntWW 74; ModGL; ModWD; NotNAT; OxGer; Pen EUR; REnWD; TwCW; WhoThe 77; WhoWor 74; WorAu*

Hochoy, Sir Solomon
West Indian. Governor
b. Apr 20, 1905 in Jamaica
Source: *IntWW 74; Who 74; WhoGov 72; WhoWor 74*

Hocking, William Ernest
American. Educator
b. Aug 1, 1873 in Cleveland, Ohio
d. Jun 12, 1966 in Madison, New Hampshire
Source: *AmAu&B; ConAu P-1; CurBio 62, 66; OhA&B; OxAmL; REnAL; TwCA SUP; WebAB; WhAm 4; WhNAA*

Hockney, David
English. Artist
b. Jul 9, 1937 in Bradford, England
Source: *BioIn 7, 9, 10, 11, 12; IntWW 79; WhoAm 80*

Hodge, Frederick Webb
English. Ethnologist
b. Jan 5, 1864 in Plymouth, England
d. Sep 28, 1956 in Santa Fe, New Mexico
Source: *AmAu&B; AmLY; ApCAB SUP; DcAmAu; OxAmL; OxCan; REnAL; TwCBDA; WhAm 3*

Hodges, Courtney
American. Military Leader
b. Jan 5, 1887 in Perry, Georgia
d. Jan 16, 1966 in San Antonio, Texas
Source: *CurBio 41, 66; WhAm 4*

Hodges, Eddie
American. Actor
b. 1947
Source: *BiE&WWA; BioIn 4, 5; MotPP; WhoHol A*

Hodges, Gil(bert Raymond)
American. Baseball Player
First baseman, 1943-63; manager NY Mets, 1968-71.
b. Apr 4, 1924 in Princeton, Indiana
d. Apr 2, 1972 in West Palm Beach, Florida
Source: *BaseEn; CurBio 62, 72; NewYTBE 72; WhAm 5; WhoProB 73*

Hodges, Johnny
American. Jazz Musician
b. Jul 25, 1906 in Cambridge, Massachusetts
d. May 11, 1970 in New York, New York
Source: *AmSCAP 66; NewYTBE 70; WhAm 5; WhoJazz 72*

Hodges, Luther Hartwell
American. Government Official
b. Mar 9, 1898 in Pittsylvania, Virginia
d. Oct 6, 1974 in Chapel Hill, North Carolina
Source: *BiDrUSE; ConAu 53; CurBio 56, 74; IntWW 74; WhAm 6; WhoAm 74; WhoAmP 73; WhoF&I 74*

Hodges, Russ
American. Sportscaster
b. 1909 in Dayton, Tennessee
d. Apr 20, 1971 in Mill Valley, California
Source: *NewYTBE 71; WhoHol B*

Hodgkin, Alan Lloyd
English. Biophysicist
b. Feb 5, 1914
Source: *BioIn 2, 5, 6; WhoWor 74*

Hodgson, James Day
American. Government Official
Secretary of Labor, 1970-73; ambassador to Japan, 1974-77.
b. Dec 3, 1915 in Dawson, Minnesota
Source: *BioIn 9, 10; USBiR 74; WhoAm 74, 76, 78, 80, 82; WhoAmP 73; WhoF&I 74; WhoGov 72; WhoS&SW 73*

Hodgson, Richard Sargeant
American. Author
b. Oct 18, 1924 in Breckenridge, Minnesota
Source: *ConAu 13R*

Hodiak, John
American. Actor
b. Apr 16, 1914 in Pittsburgh, Pennsylvania
d. Oct 19, 1955 in Tarzana, California
Source: *CmMov; FilmgC; HolP 40; MotPP; MovMk; WhScrn 74, 77; WhoHol B*

Hodler, Ferdinand
Source: *McGDA; McGEWB*

Hodo, David
see: Village People, The

Hoe, Richard March
American. Inventor
Developed Hoe rotary press, which improved speed of printing, 1846-47.
b. Sep 12, 1812 in New York, New York
d. Jun 7, 1886 in Florence, Italy
Source: *AmBi; ApCAB; DcAmB; OxAmL; TwCBDA; WebAB; WhAm H*

Hoesslin, Franz von
German. Conductor
b. Dec 31, 1885 in Munich, Germany
d. Sep 28, 1946 in Site, Germany
Source: *NewEOp 71*

Hofer, Andreas
Austrian. Patriot
b. Nov 22, 1767 in Saint Leonhard, Austria
d. Feb 20, 1810 in Mantua, Italy
Source: *NewC; OxGer*

Hofer, Karl
German. Artist
b. 1878 in Karlsruhe, Germany
d. Apr 3, 1955 in Berlin, Germany (West)
Source: *McGDA; ObitOF 79*

Hoff, Sydney
American. Illustrator, Author
b. Sep 4, 1912 in New York, New York
Source: *AmAu&B; ChPo S1; ConAu 5R, 4NR; IlsCB 1957; SmATA 9; ThrBJA; WhoAm 74, 76, 78, 80, 82; WhoWor 74; WhoWorJ 72*

Hoffa, Jimmy (James Riddle)
American. Labor Union Leader
President, Teamsters, 1957-71; believed killed same day abducted from MI restaurant.
b. Feb 14, 1913 in Brazil, Indiana
d. Jul 30, 1975? in Detroit, Michigan
Source: *CelR 73; CurBio 72; IntWW 74; NewYTBE 71, 72; WebAB; WhoAm 74; WhoWor 74*

Hoffa, Portland
[Mrs. Fred Allen]
American. Radio Actress
b. 1910
Source: *InWom*

Hoffenstein, Samuel Goodman
American. Poet, Humorist
b. Oct 8, 1890 in Lithuania
d. Oct 6, 1947 in Hollywood, California
Source: *AmAu&B; BioIn 1, 4, 8; DcNAA; REnAL; TwCA, SUP*

Hoffer, Eric
American. Author, Longshoreman
b. Jul 25, 1902 in New York, New York
Source: *CelR 73; ConAu 13R; CurBio 65; RAdv 1; WebAB; WhoAm 74, 76, 78, 80, 82; WorAu; WrDr 76*

Hoffer, George Nissley
American. Botanist
b. 1887
d. 1963
Source: *BioIn 6*

Hoffman, Abbie (Abbott)
[Spiro Igloo; The Chicago 7]
American. Author, Social Activist
Wrote *Revolution for the Hell of It,* 1968; *Woodstock Nation,* 1969.
b. Nov 30, 1936 in Worcester, Massachusetts
Source: *AmAu&B; CelR 73; ConAu 21R; CurBio 81; NewYTBE 70; WhoE 74*

Hoffman, Al
American. Composer, Author
b. Sep 25, 1902 in Minsk, Russia
d. Jul 21, 1960 in New York, New York
Source: *AmSCAP 66; BiDAmM; BioIn 5; CmpEPM*

Hoffman, Anna M Rosenberg Lederer
American. Government Official, Lawyer
b. Jun 19, 1902 in Budapest, Hungary
Source: *Who 74; WhoWorJ 72*

Hoffman, Charles Fenno
American. Poet
b. Feb 7, 1806 in New York, New York
d. Jun 7, 1884 in Harrisburg, Pennsylvania
Source: *Alli; AmAu; AmAu&B; AmBi; ApCAB; BiD&SB; CasWL; ChPo; CnDAL; CyAl 2; DcAmAu; DcAmB; DcBiA; DcEnL; DcLEL; DcNAA; Drake; EvLB; OxAmL; Pen AM; REnAL; TwCBDA; WhAm H*

Hoffman, Dustin
American. Actor
Starred in *The Graduate,* 1967; *Kramer vs. Kramer,* 1979; *Tootsie,* 1982.
b. Aug 8, 1937 in Los Angeles, California
Source: *BkPepl; CelR 73; CurBio 69; FilmgC; IntMPA 75, 76, 77, 78, 79, 80, 81, 82; MotPP; MovMk; OxFilm; WhoAm 74, 76, 78, 80, 82; WhoHol A*

Hoffman, Irwin
American. Orchestra Conductor
b. Nov 26, 1924 in New York, New York
Source: *WhoAm 74, 76, 78, 80, 82; WhoMus 72; WhoS&SW 73; WhoWor 74*

Hoffman, Julius Jennings
American. Judge
b. Jul 7, 1895 in Chicago, Illinois
Source: *WhoAm 74, 76, 78, 80, 82; WhoGov 72*

Hoffman, Malvina
American. Sculptor
b. Jun 15, 1887 in New York, New York
d. Jul 10, 1966 in New York, New York
Source: *AmAu&B; CurBio 40, 66; InWom; REnAL; WhAm 4*

Hoffman, Paul Gray
American. UN Official, Auto Executive
b. Apr 26, 1891 in Chicago, Illinois
d. Oct 8, 1974 in New York, New York
Source: *CurBio 46, 74; IntWW 74; NewYTBE 71; NewYTBS 74; WhAm 6; Who 74; WhoAm 74; WhoWor 74*

Hoffmann, Ernst Theodor Amadeus
German. Author
b. Jan 24, 1776 in Konigsberg, Germany
d. Jun 25, 1822 in Berlin, Germany
Source: *BbD; EvEuW; Pen EUR*

Hoffmann, Jan
German. Figure Skater
Source: *BioIn 12*

Hofheinz, Roy Mark
American. Business Executive
Built Houston Astrodome, opened 1965; world's first covered stadium.
b. Apr 10, 1912 in Beaumont, Texas
d. Nov 21, 1982 in Houston, Texas
Source: *CelR 73; NewYTBS 82; WhoAm 74, 76; WhoProB 73; WhoS&SW 73, 75*

Hofmann, Albert
Swiss. Chemist
b. Feb 27, 1933 in Uznach, Switzerland
Source: *AmM&WS 73P*

Hofmann, Hans
German. Artist
His paintings inspired Abstract Expressionism movement.
b. Mar 21, 1880 in Weissenburg, Germany
d. Feb 17, 1966 in New York, New York
Source: *CurBio 58, 66; DcCAA 71; REn; WebAB; WhAm 4*

Hofmann, Josef
American. Musician
b. Jan 20, 1876 in Krakow, Poland
d. Feb 16, 1957 in Los Angeles, California
Source: *BioIn 2, 4, 7, 9, 11; WhAm 3*

Hofmannsthal, Hugo Hoffmann
Austrian. Poet, Dramatist
b. Feb 1, 1874 in Vienna, Austria
d. Jul 15, 1929 in Vienna, Austria
Source: *AtlBL; CasWL; ClDMEL; CnMD; CnMWL; CnThe; EncWL; EvEuW; McGEWD; ModGL; ModWD; NewC; OxEng; OxGer; OxThe; Pen EUR; REn; REnWD; TwCA, SUP; TwCW*

Hofsiss, Jack Bernard
American. Motion Picture Director
b. Sep 28, 1950 in Brooklyn, New York
Source: *WhoAm 80*

Hofstadter, Richard
American. Historian
b. Aug 6, 1916 in Buffalo, New York
d. Oct 24, 1970 in New York, New York
Source: *AmAu&B; ConAu 1R, 29R, 4NR; CurBio 56, 70; EncAB-H; OxAmL; Pen AM; REn; REnAL; WebAB; WhAm 5; WorAu*

Hofstadter, Robert
American. Physicist, Educator
b. Feb 5, 1915 in New York, New York
Source: *AmM&WS 73P; BioIn 6; IntWW 74; Who 74; WhoAm 74, 76, 78, 80, 82; WhoWor 74*

Hogan, Ben (William Benjamin)
American. Golfer
PGA Hall of Fame, 1953; wrote *Power Golf,* 1948.
b. Aug 13, 1912 in Dublin, Texas
Source: *CelR 73; CurBio 48; WhoAm 78, 80, 82; WhoGolf*

Hogarth, Burne
American. Cartoonist
Created, drew "Tarzan," 1937-50; president, Pendragon Press, 1975-79.
b. Nov 25, 1911 in Chicago, Illinois
Source: *WorECom*

Hogarth, William
English. Artist, Engraver
b. Nov 10, 1697 in London, England
d. Oct 26, 1764 in London, England
Source: *Alli; AtlBL; BkIE; ChPo; NewC; REn*

Hoge, James Fulton, Jr.
American. Newspaper Editor
b. Dec 25, 1936 in New York, New York
Source: *BioIn 8, 10, 11; WhoAm 78, 80, 82*

Hogg, Ima
American. Philanthropist
b. Jul 10, 1882
d. Aug 19, 1975 in London, England
Source: *BioIn 10*

Hogg, James
Scottish. Author
b. 1770 in Ettrick, Scotland
d. Nov 21, 1835 in Yarrow, Scotland
Source: *Alli; AtlBL; BbD; BiD&SB; BiDLA, SUP; BrAu 19; CasWL; ChPo, S1, S2; DcEnA; DcEnL; DcEuL; DcLEL; EvLB; MouLC 3; NewC; OxEng; Pen ENG; REn; WebE&AL*

Hogrogian, Nonny
American. Illustrator
b. May 7, 1932 in New York, New York
Source: *AuBYP; BkP; ChlLR 2; ConAu 45, 2NR; IlsBYP; IlsCB 1957; SmATA 7; ThrBJA; WhoAm 74; WhoE 74*

Hohman, Donald
[The Hostages]
American. Former Hostage in Iran
b. 1943? in Yuba City, California
Source: *NewYTBS 81*

Hohner, Karl
German. Harmonica Manufacturer
b. 1892
d. 1971
Source: *BioIn 9*

Hoke, Henry Reed
American. Author, Editor
b. 1894
d. 1970
Source: *BioIn 9*

Hokinson, Helen
American. Cartoonist
b. 1899 in Mendota, Illinois
d. Nov 1, 1949 in Washington, DC
Source: *DcAmB S4; InWom; NotAW; WebAB*

Hokusai
Japanese. Wood Engraver
b. 1760 in Yedo, Japan
d. 1849
Source: *REn*

Holabird, William
American. Architect
b. Sep 11, 1854 in Amenia Union, New York
d. Jul 19, 1923 in Evanston, Illinois
Source: *DcAmB; WebAB; WhAm 1*

Holbein, Hans, the Elder
German. Artist, Sculptor, Architect
b. 1460
d. 1524
Source: *NewCol 75*

Holbein, Hans, the Younger
German. Artist
b. 1497 in Augsburg, Germany
d. 1543 in London, England
Source: *AtlBL; NewC; OxGer; REn*

Holbrook, Hal (Harold Rowe, Jr.)
American. Actor
Won Tony, NY Drama Critics citation for *Mark Twain Tonight*, 1966.
b. Feb 17, 1925 in Cleveland, Ohio
Source: *BiE&WWA; BioNews 74; CelR 73; CurBio 61; FilmgC; IntMPA 75, 76, 77, 78, 79, 80, 81, 82; MotPP; NewYTBE 73; NotNAT; WhoAm 74, 76, 78, 80, 82; WhoHol A; WhoThe 77*

Holbrook, Stewart Hall
American. Author, Journalist
b. Aug 22, 1893 in Newport, Vermont
d. Sep 3, 1964 in Portland, Oregon
Source: *AmAu&B; AuBYP; ConAu P-1; OxAmL; REnAL; SmATA 2; ThrBJA; TwCA SUP; WhAm 4; WhNAA; WhoPNW*

Holbrooke, Josef
English. Composer
b. Jul 5, 1878 in Croydon, England
d. Aug 5, 1958 in London, England
Source: *NewEOp 71*

Holden, Fay
[Fay Hammerton]
English. Actress
b. Sep 26, 1895 in Birmingham, England
d. Jun 23, 1973 in Los Angeles, California
Source: *FilmgC; MotPP; MovMk; NewYTBE 73; ThFT; Vers A; WhScrn 77; WhoHol B*

Holden, William
[William Franklin Beedle, Jr.]
American. Actor
b. Apr 17, 1918 in O'Fallon, Illinois
d. Nov 12, 1981? in Santa Monica, California
Source: *BiDFilm; BioIn 2, 3, 4, 5, 6, 7, 8, 10, 11; BkPepl; CelR 73; CmMov; CurBio 54, 82; FilmgC; IntMPA 75, 76, 77, 78, 79, 80, 81, 82; MotPP; MovMk; OxFilm; WhoAm 74, 76, 78, 80; WhoHol A; WorEFlm*

Holder, Geoffrey
Actor
b. Sep 1, 1930 in Trinidad
Source: *AfroAA; BiE&WWA; BlkAW; CurBio 57; NotNAT; PlP&P A; WhoAm 74, 76, 78, 80, 82; WhoBlA 75; WhoHol A; WhoThe 77*

Holderlin, Johann C F
German. Poet
b. Feb 20, 1770 in Lauffen, Germany
d. Jul 7, 1843 in Tubingen, Germany
Source: *CasWL; EvEuW*

Holdren, Judd Clifton
American. Actor
b. Oct 16, 1915 in Iowa
d. Mar 11, 1974 in Los Angeles, California
Source: *WhScrn 77; WhoHol B*

Holiday, Billie
[Eleanora Fagan]
"Lady Day"
American. Singer
Autobiography, *Lady Sings the Blues,* 1956, inspired film, 1972.
b. Apr 7, 1915 in Baltimore, Maryland
d. Jul 17, 1959 in New York, New York
Source: *InWom; NewYTBE 72; WebAB; WhoHol B; WhoJazz 72*

Holifield, Chet
American. Congressman
b. Dec 3, 1903 in Mayfield, Kentucky
Source: *BioIn 4, 5, 7, 10; CurBio 55; WhoAm 74; WhoAmP 73; WhoGov 72; WhoWest 74*

Holinshed, Raphael
English. Chronicler
d. 1580?
Source: *AtlBL; BbD; BiD&SB; BrAu; CasWL; CroE&S; DcEnA; DcEnL; NewC; OxEng; REn*

Holladay, Terry Ann
American. Tennis Player
b. Nov 28, 1955 in Charlotte, North Carolina
Source: *OfEnT*

Holland, Dave
see: Judas Priest

Holland, Jerome Heartwell
American. Government Official
Ambassador to Sweden, 1970-72; chairman, American Red Cross, 1979--.
b. Jan 9, 1916 in Auburn, New York
Source: *BioIn 6, 8, 9; WhoAm 74, 76, 78, 80, 82; WhoGov 72*

Holland, John Philip
American. Inventor
Developed first submarine used by US Navy, 1900.
b. Feb 24, 1841 in Liscannor, Ireland
d. Aug 12, 1914 in Newark, New Jersey
Source: *BioIn 3, 5, 6, 7; WebAB*

Holland, Leland James
[The Hostages]
American. Former Hostage in Iran
b. 1928? in Shullsburg, Wisconsin
Source: *BioIn 12; NewYTBS 81*

Holland, Steve
see: Molly Hatchet

Hollander, John
American. Author
b. Oct 28, 1929 in New York, New York
Source: *AmAu&B; AuBYP; ChPo, S1; ConAu 1R, 1NR; ConLC 2, 5, 8, 14; ConP 70; DrAP 75; DrAS 74E; OxAmL; Pen AM; REnAL; SmATA 13; WhoAm 74, 76, 78, 80, 82; WhoE 74; WhoTwCL; WorAu; WrDr 76*

Hollander, Xaviera
Dutch. Author, Former Call Girl
b. 1943?
Source: *BioIn 10, 12*

Holliday, "Doc" (John Henry)
American. Gunman, Gambler, Dentist
Friend of Wyatt Earp.
b. 1851 in Griffin, Georgia
d. Nov 8, 1887 in Glenwood Springs, Colorado
Source: *BioIn 3, 4, 11; OxFilm; REnAW*

Holliday, Judy
[Judith Tuvim]
American. Actress
Won Oscar, 1950, for *Born Yesterday.*
b. Jun 21, 1922 in New York, New York
d. Jun 7, 1965 in New York, New York
Source: *BiDFilm; BiE&WWA; CmMov; CurBio 51, 65; EncMT; FilmgC; InWom; MotPP; MovMk; OxFilm; WhAm 4; WhScrn 74, 77; WhoHol B; WorEFlm*

Holliday, Polly Dean
American. Actress
Starred in TV series "Alice," 1976-80; in own series "Flo," 1981.
b. Jul 2, 1937 in Jasper, Alabama
Source: *WhoAm 80, 82*

Hollies, The
[Bernie Calvert; Allan Clarke; Bobby Elliott; Eric Haydock; TonyHicks; Graham Nash; Terry Sylvester]
English. Rock Group
Source: *ConMuA 80; IlEncRk; LilREn 78; RkOn 2; WhoRock 81*

Holliger, Heinz
Swiss. Musician
b. May 21, 1939 in Langenthal, Switzerland
Source: *Baker 78; DcCM; IntWW 77, 78; WhoMus 72*

Holliman, Earl
American. Actor
Starred, with Angie Dickinson, in TV series "Police Woman," 1974-78.
b. Sep 11, 1936 in Delhi, Louisiana
Source: *FilmgC; IntMPA 75, 76, 77, 78, 79, 80, 81, 82; MotPP; WhoAm 82; WhoHol A*

Hollings, Ernest Frederick
"Fritz"
American. Senator
b. Jan 1, 1922 in Charleston, South Carolina
Source: *AlmAP 78, 80; BiDrAC; BioIn 4, 8, 9, 10; CngDr 74, 77, 79; CurBio 82; IntWW 75, 76, 77, 78; PolProf K; WhoAm 74, 76, 78, 80, 82; WhoAmP 73, 75, 77, 79; WhoGov 72, 75, 77*

Hollister, Paul Merrick
American. Advertising Executive, Author
b. 1890 in New York, New York
d. 1970
Source: *NewYTBE 70; WhoAmA 73*

Holloman, "Bobo" (Alva Lee)
American. Baseball Player
b. Mar 27, 1924 in Thomaston, Georgia
Source: *BaseEn; BioIn 3, 10; WhoProB 73*

Holloway, Emory
American. Author, Educator
b. Mar 16, 1885 in Marshall, Missouri
d. Jul 30, 1977 in Bethlehem, Pennsylvania
Source: *AmAu&B; ConAu 49, 73; DrAS 74E; OxAmL; REnAL; TwCA, SUP; WhNAA*

Holloway, Stanley
English. Actor
Played Eliza Doolittle's father in *My Fair Lady*.
b. Oct 1, 1890 in London, England
d. Jan 30, 1982 in Littlehampton, England
Source: *AmPS B; BiE&WWA; BioIn 4, 6, 8; CurBio 63, 82; EncMT; EncWT; Film 2; IntMPA 75, 76, 77, 78, 79, 80, 81, 82; MovMk; NewC; NewYTBS 82; NotNAT; Who 74; WhoThe 72, 77*

Holloway, Sterling
American. Actor
b. 1905 in Cedartown, Georgia
Source: *BiE&WWA; FilmgC; IntMPA 75, 76, 77, 78, 79, 80, 81, 82; MotPP; MovMk; NotNAT; PlP&P; Vers B; WhoAm 82; WhoHol A*

Hollowood, Albert Bernard
English. Editor, Economist
b. Jun 3, 1910 in Burslem, England
d. Mar 28, 1981 in Guildford, England
Source: *ConAu 9R, 103; IntWW 74, 75, 76, 77, 78; WhAm 7; Who 74; WrDr 80*

Holly, "Buddy" (Charles Hardin)
American. Singer, Songwriter
b. Sep 7, 1936 in Lubbock, Texas
d. Feb 2, 1958 in Fargo, North Dakota
Source: *BioIn 9, 10, 11; WhAm 4*

Holly, James Theodore
American. Clergyman
b. Oct 3, 1829 in Washington, DC
d. 1911
Source: *BioIn 5, 9; WhAm 1*

Hollyer, Samuel
English. Engraver
b. Feb 24, 1826 in Landon, England
d. 1919
Source: *DcAmB; WhAm 4*

Hollywood Ten
[Alvah Bessie; Herbert Biberman; lester Cole; Edward Dmytryk; Ring Lardner, Jr.; John Howard Lawson; Albert Maltz; Samuel Ornitz; Adrian Scott; Dalton Trumbo]
American. Blacklisted Group of Writers
Source: *NF*

Holm, Celeste
American. Actress
b. Apr 29, 1919 in New York, New York
Source: *BiE&WWA; CurBio 44; EncMT; FilmgC; HolP 40; InWom; IntMPA 75, 76, 77, 78, 79, 80, 81; MotPP; MovMk; NotNAT; OxFilm; WhoAm 74, 76, 78, 80, 82; WhoHol A; WhoThe 77*

Holm, Eleanor
American. Swimmer, Actress
Played Jane in *Tarzan's Revenge,* 1938; married to Billy Rose 14 years.
b. Dec 6, 1913
Source: *InWom; WhoHol A*

Holm, Ian
[Ian Holm Cuthbert]
English. Actor
b. Sep 12, 1931 in Goodmayes, England
Source: *FilmEn; FilmgC; WhoHol A; WhoThe 72, 77, 81; WhoWor 74*

Holman, Bill
American. Comic Strip Creator
b. 1903 in Crawfordsville, Indiana
Source: *WorECom*

Holman, Eugene
American. Petroleum Executive
b. May 2, 1895 in San Angelo, Texas
d. Aug 12, 1962 in New York, New York
Source: *BioIn 1, 2, 5, 6; CurBio 48, 62*

Holman, Libby
American. Singer, Actress
b. 1906 in Cincinnati, Ohio
d. Jun 18, 1971 in Stamford, Connecticut
Source: *BiE&WWA; EncMT; InWom; NewYTBE 71; PlP&P; WhScrn 77; WhoHol B*

Holman, Nat
"Mister Basketball"
American. Basketball Player, Coach
b. Oct 18, 1896 in New York, New York
Source: *WhoBbl 73; WhoWorJ 72*

Holme, Constance
English. Author
b. 1881 in Milnthorpe, England
d. 1955
Source: *DcLEL; EvLB; LongCTC; OxEng; TwCA, SUP*

Holmes, Anna Marie
Canadian. Dancer
b. Apr 17, 1943 in Mission City, BC
Source: *CreCan 1*

Holmes, Burton
American. Motion Picture Producer
b. Jan 8, 1870 in Chicago, Illinois
d. Jul 22, 1958 in Hollywood, California
Source: *CurBio 44, 58; WhAm 3; WhNAA; WhScrn 74, 77; WhoHol B*

Holmes, David
Canadian. Dancer
Source: *BioIn 8; CreCan 2*

Holmes, John Clennon
American. Author
b. Mar 12, 1926 in Holyoke, Massachusetts
Source: *AmAu&B; ConAu 9R, 4NR; ConNov 72, 76; DrAF 76; OxAmL; Pen AM; WhoAm 74, 76, 78, 80, 82; WhoE 74; WrDr 76*

Holmes, John Haynes
American. Clergyman, Social Activist
b. Nov 9, 1879 in Philadelphia, Pennsylvania
d. Apr 3, 1964 in New York, New York
Source: *AmAu&B; AmLY; ChPo S1; ConAu 89; CurBio 41, 64; REnAL; TwCA SUP; WhAm 4; WhNAA*

Holmes, Larry
American. Boxer
WBC heavyweight champ, 1978--.
b. Nov 3, 1949 in Cuthbert, Georgia
Source: *BioIn 11, 12; CurBio 81; WhoAm 82*

Holmes, Oliver Wendell
American. Poet, Author, Essayist
First dean, Harvard Medical School, 1847-53; wrote *Elsie Venner,* 1861.
b. Aug 29, 1809 in Cambridge, Massachusetts
d. Oct 7, 1894 in Boston, Massachusetts
Source: *Alli, SUP; AmAu; AmAu&B; AmBi; ApCAB; AtlBL; BbD; BiD&SB; CasWL; Chambr 3; ChPo, S1, S2; CnDAL; CrtT 3; CyAl 2; CyWA; DcAmAu; DcAmB; DcBiA; DcEnA; DcEnL; DcLEL; DcNAA; Drake; EncAB-H; EvLB; MouLC 4; OxAmL; OxEng; Pen AM; PoChrch; RAdv 1; REn; REnAL; Str&VC; TwCBDA; WebAB; WebE&AL; WhAm H*

Holmes, Oliver Wendell, Jr.
"The Great Dissenter"
American. Supreme Court Justice
Published Lowell lectures on common law, 1881; Supreme Court Justice, 1902-32.
b. Mar 8, 1841 in Boston, Massachusetts
d. Mar 6, 1935 in Washington, DC
Source: *AmAu&B; AmBi; AtlBL; DcAmAu; DcAmB S1; DcNAA; OxAmL; WebAB*

Holmes, Rupert
American. Singer, Songwriter
Wrote, recorded "Escape," "Him," "Answering Machine."
b. Feb 24, 1947 in Cheshire, England
Source: *BioIn 12; NewYTBS 75; WhoAm 82*

Holmes, Taylor
American. Actor
b. 1878 in Newark, New Jersey
d. Sep 30, 1959 in Hollywood, California
Source: *Film 1; FilmgC; MotPP; MovMk; TwYS; Vers A; WhScrn 74, 77; WhoHol B*

Holst, Gustav
English. Musician, Composer
b. Sep 21, 1874 in Cheltenham, England
d. May 25, 1934 in London, England
Source: *DcCM*

Holt, Derek
see: Climax Blues Band, The

Holt, Harold Edward
Australian. Prime Minister
b. Aug 5, 1908 in Sydney, Australia
d. Dec 17, 1967 in Port Philip Bay, Australia
Source: *BioIn 7, 8, 9; CurBio 66, 68*

Holt, Henry
American. Publisher
b. Jan 3, 1840 in Baltimore, Maryland
d. Feb 13, 1926
Source: *Alli SUP; AmAu&B; AmBi; BiDPara; DcAmAu; DcAmB; DcNAA; MnBBF; TwCBDA; WhAm 1*

Holt, Ivan Lee
American. Clergyman
b. Jan 9, 1886 in De Witt, Arkansas
d. Jan 12, 1967
Source: *BioIn 1, 7; WhAm 4*

Holt, Jack
American. Actor
b. May 31, 1888 in Winchester, Virginia
d. Jan 18, 1951 in Los Angeles, California
Source: *Film 1; FilmgC; MovMk; TwYS; WhScrn 74, 77; WhoHol B*

Holt, John
American. Educator, Author
b. Apr 14, 1923 in New York, New York
Source: *ConAu 69*

Holt, Tim
American. Actor
b. Feb 5, 1918 in Beverly Hills, California
d. Feb 15, 1973 in Shawnee, Oklahoma
Source: *FilmgC; HolP 40; MotPP; MovMk; NewYTBE 73; WhScrn 77; WhoHol B*

Holtz, Lou
American. Actor
b. Apr 11, 1898 in San Francisco, California
Source: *BiE&WWA; EncMT; NotNAT; WhoThe 77*

Holtzman, Elizabeth
American. Politician
Congresswoman from NY, 1974-80.
b. Aug 11, 1941 in Brooklyn, New York
Source: *BioNews 74; CngDr 74; CurBio 73; NewYTBE 72; WhoAm 74; WhoAmP 73; WhoAmW 77; WomPO 76*

Holtzmann, Fanny E
American. Lawyer
b. 1903
Source: *BioIn 11; InWom*

Holyoake, Keith Jacka
New Zealander. Prime Minister
b. Feb 11, 1904 in New Zealand
Source: *CurBio 63; IntWW 74; Who 74; WhoGov 72; WhoWor 74*

Holzer, Jane
"Baby Jane"
American. Fashion Model, Actress
b. 1941?
Source: *BioIn 8; WhoAmW 74*

Holzman, William
American. Basketball Coach
Coach of NY Knicks.
b. Aug 10, 1920 in New York, New York
Source: *OfNBA; WhoBbl 73*

Home, Daniel Douglas
English. Psychic, Medium
b. Mar 20, 1833 in Scotland
d. Jun 21, 1886 in Auteuil, France
Source: *Alli SUP; AmBi; ApCAB; BiDPara; Drake; NewC; OxEng; REn*

Homeier, "Skip" (George Vincent)
American. Actor
b. Oct 5, 1930 in Chicago, Illinois
Source: *FilmgC; IntMPA 75, 76, 77, 78, 79, 80, 81, 82; WhoHol A*

Homer
Greek. Author
Credited with writing *The Iliad* and *The Odyssey,* poems on which subsequent epic literature evolved.
b. 750BC
Source: *AtlBL; BbD; BiD&SB; CasWL; ChPo; CyWA; DcBiA; DcEnL; DcEuL; NewC; OxEng; Pen CL; PlP&P; RComWL*

Homer, Louise
American. Opera Singer
b. Apr 28, 1871 in Sewickley, Pennsylvania
d. May 6, 1947 in Winter Park, Illinois
Source: *DcAmB S4; InWom; NotAW; WhAm 2; WomWWA 14*

Homer, Sidney
American. Composer
b. Dec 9, 1864 in Boston, Massachusetts
d. Jul 10, 1953 in Winter Park, Florida
Source: *AmSCAP 66; OxAmL; REnAL; WhAm 3*

Homer, Winslow
American. Artist
Excelled in watercolors of seascapes, including *Breaking Storm, Maine Coast.*
b. Feb 24, 1836 in Boston, Massachusetts
d. Sep 29, 1910 in Prouts Neck, Maine
Source: *AmBi; ApCAB; AtlBL; ChPo, S1, S2; DcAmB; EarABI, SUP; EncAB-H; OxAmL; REn; REnAL; TwCBDA; WebAB; WhAm 1*

Homolka, Oscar
Austrian. Actor
b. Aug 12, 1903 in Vienna, Austria
d. Jan 27, 1978 in Sussex, England
Source: *BiDFilm; BiE&WWA; MovMk; NotNAT; OxFilm*

Honda, Soichiro
Japanese. Business Executive
Started producing motorcycles, 1948; president, Honda Motor Co., 1973--.
b. Nov 17, 1906 in Iwata Gun, Japan
Source: *FarE&A 78, 79, 80; IntWW 74, 75, 76, 77, 78, 79, 80, 81; NewYTBS 77; WhoF&I 74; WhoWor 74, 78*

Honecker, Erich
German. Politician
b. Aug 25, 1912 in Wiebelskirchen, Germany
Source: *BioIn 9, 10; CurBio 72; IntWW 74; NewYTBE 71; WhoWor 74*

Honegger, Arthur
[Les Six]
French. Composer
b. Mar 10, 1892 in Le Havre, France
d. Nov 27, 1955 in Paris, France
Source: *AtlBL; CurBio 41, 56; DcCM; DcFM; FilmgC; OxFilm; REn; WhAm 4; WorEFlm*

Honeyman-Scott, James (Jimmy)
[The Pretenders]
English. Musician
b. Nov 4, 1956 in Hereford, England
d. Jun 16, 1982 in London, England
Source: *NF*

Honeywell, Mark Charles
American. Inventor, Manufacturer
Honeywell Heating Speciality Co. improved hot water heating systems controls, 1906.
b. Dec 29, 1874 in Wabash, Indiana
d. Sep 13, 1964 in Indianapolis, Indiana
Source: *BioIn 7, 9; NatCAB 52; WhAm 4*

Hooch, Pieter de
Dutch. Artist
b. Dec 20, 1629? in Rotterdam, Netherlands
d. 1683?
Source: *AtlBL; NewCol 75*

Hood, Darla Jean
[Our Gang]
American. Actress
b. 1933 in Leedey, Oklahoma
d. Jun 1979 in Canoga Park, California
Source: *BioIn 8, 10; NewYTBS 79; WhoHol A*

Hood, Frederick Emmart
American. Yacht Designer
b. 1927 in Marblehead, Massachusetts
Source: *NewYTBS 74*

Hood, John Bell
American. Confederate General
b. Jun 1, 1831 in Bath County, Georgia
d. Aug 30, 1879 in New Orleans, Georgia
Source: *Alli SUP; AmBi; ApCAB; BiDConf; BiDSA; DcAmAu; DcAmB; DcNAA; TwCBDA; WebAB; WhAm H*

Hood, Raymond Matthewson
American. Architect
b. Mar 29, 1881 in Pawtucket, Rhode Island
d. Aug 14, 1934
Source: *AmBi; DcAmB S1; WhAm 1*

Hood, Thomas
English. Author
b. May 23, 1799 in London, England
d. May 3, 1845 in London, England
Source: *Alli; AnCL; AtlBL; BbD; BiD&SB; Br&AmS; BrAu 19; CarSB; CasWL; Chambr 3; ChPo, S1, S2; CnE&AP; CrtT 2; DcEnA; DcEnL; DcEuL; DcLEL; EvLB; MouLC 3; NewC; OxEng; Pen ENG; REn; Str&VC; WebE&AL*

Hook, Sidney
American. Philosopher, Author
b. Dec 20, 1902 in New York, New York
Source: *AmAu&B; CelR 73; ConAu 9R; DrAS 74P; IntWW 74; LEduc 74; REnAL; TwCA SUP; WhoAm 74, 76, 78, 80, 82; WhoWorJ 72*

Hooke, Robert
British. Scientist, Philosopher
b. Jul 18, 1635 in Isle of Wight
d. Mar 3, 1705 in London, England
Source: *Alli; DcEnL; McGEWB*

Hooker, Brian
American. Dramatist, Librettist
b. Nov 2, 1880 in New York, New York
d. Dec 28, 1946 in New London, Connecticut
Source: *AmSCAP 66; ChPo, S1; DcNAA; EncMT; OxAmL; REn; REnAL; WhAm 2*

Hooker, John Lee
American. Singer
b. Aug 22, 1917 in Clarksdale, Mississippi
Source: *EncFCWM 69; WhoAm 74; WhoBlA 75*

Hooker, Joseph
"Fighting Joe"
American. Military Leader
Union general in Civil War; commanded Army of the Potomac, 1862-63.
b. Nov 13, 1814 in Hadley, Massachusetts
d. Oct 31, 1879 in Garden City, New York
Source: *AmBi; ApCAB; DcAmB; TwCBDA; WebAB; WhAm H*

Hooker, Richard
English. Theologian
b. Mar 1554 in Heavitree, England
d. Nov 2, 1600 in Bishopsbourne, England
Source: *Alli; BbD; BiD&SB; BrAu; CasWL; Chambr 1; CroE&S; CrtT 1; DcEnA; DcEnL; DcEuL; DcLEL; EvLB; NewC; OxEng; Pen ENG; REn; WebE&AL*

Hooker, Thomas
English. Clergyman
Emigrated to MA, 1633; founded Hartford, CT, 1636.
b. 1586 in Marfield, England
d. Jul 19, 1647 in Hartford, Connecticut
Source: *DcAmB; EncAB-H; McGEWB; WebAB; WhAm H*

Hooks, Benjamin Lawson
American. NAACP Official
b. Jan 31, 1925 in Memphis, Tennessee
Source: *BioNews 74; CivR 74; CurBio 78; EbonySL 1; NewYTBE 72; NewYTET; NewYTBS 76, 79; WhoAm 78, 80, 82; WhoAmP 77, 79; WhoBlA 75*

Hooks, Robert
American. Actor
b. Apr 18, 1937 in Washington, DC
Source: *CurBio 70; FilmgC; NotNAT; PlP&P A; WhoAm 74, 76, 78, 80, 82; WhoBlA 75; WhoHol A; WhoThe 77*

Hooper, "Stix"
see: Crusaders, The

Hooper, William
American. Lawyer
b. Jun 17, 1742 in Boston, Massachusetts
d. Oct 14, 1790 in Hillsboro, North Carolina
Source: *AmBi; ApCAB; BiAuS; BiDrAC; DcAmB; Drake; TwCBDA; WhAm H; WhAmP*

Hooton, Earnest Albert
American. Anthropologist
b. Nov 20, 1887 in Clemansville, Wisconsin
d. May 3, 1954 in Cambridge, Massachusetts
Source: *AmAu&B; CurBio 40, 54; DcAmB S5; REnAL; TwCA, SUP; WebAB; WhAm 3*

Hoover, Herbert Clark
American. 31st US President
Administration dominated by Great Depression; Herbert Hoover Library dedicated in hometown, 1962.
b. Aug 10, 1874 in West Branch, Iowa
d. Oct 20, 1964 in New York, New York
Source: *AmAu&B; AmLY; BiDrAC; BiDrUSE; ConAu 89; CurBio 43; EncAB-H; OxAmL; REn; REnAL; WebAB; WhAmP; WhNAA*

Hoover, J(ohn) Edgar
American. Government Official
Director of FBI, 1924-72; established fingerprint file, crime lab.
b. Jan 1, 1895 in Washington, DC
d. May 2, 1972 in Washington, DC
Source: *AmAu&B; ConAu 1R, 33R, 2NR; CurBio 40, 50, 72; EncAB-H; WebAB; WhAm 5; WhScrn 77*

Hoover, Lou Henry
American. Wife of Herbert Hoover
b. 1875? in Waterloo, Iowa
d. Jan 7, 1944
Source: *BioIn 2, 3, 5, 6, 7, 8, 9, 11; CurBio 44*

"Hopalong Cassidy"
see: Boyd, William (Bill)

Hope, Anthony
English. Author
b. Feb 7, 1863 in London, England
d. Jul 8, 1933 in Tadworth, England
Source: *BiD&SB; Chambr 3; CyWA; DcBiA; DcEnA AP; DcLEL; EvLB; FilmgC; LongCTC; ModBrL; NewC; OxEng; Pen ENG; REn; TwCA, SUP; TwCW; WhoChL*

Hope, Bob (Leslie Townes)
American. Comedian, Actor
Made annual trips to entertain American troops, 1940-72; won four special Oscars.
b. May 29, 1903 in Eltham, England
Source: *AmAu&B; BiDFilm; BiE&WWA; BkPepl; CelR 73; ConAu 101; CurBio 41, 53; EncMT; FilmgC; IntMPA 75, 76, 77, 78, 79, 80, 81, 82; IntWW 80; MotPP; MovMk; NewYTBE 71; OhA&B; OxFilm; WebAB; Who 74; WhoAm 74, 76, 78, 80, 82; WhoHol A; WhoThe 77; WhoWor 74*

Hopf, Hans
German. Opera Singer
b. Aug 2, 1916 in Nuremberg, Germany
Source: *WhoMus 72*

Hopkin, Mary
Welsh. Singer
Discovered by the Beatles; best known song "Those Were the Days," 1968.
b. May 3, 1950 in Ystradgynlais, Wales
Source: *WhoAm 74*

Hopkins, Anthony
Welsh. Actor
b. Dec 31, 1937 in Port Talbot, Wales
Source: *BioIn 12; CurBio 80; IntMPA 82; PlP&P; Who 74; WhoAm 80, 82; WhoHol A; WhoThe 77*

Hopkins, Arthur
American. Motion Picture Director, Producer
b. Oct 4, 1878 in Cleveland, Ohio
d. Mar 22, 1950 in New York, New York
Source: *AmAu&B; NotNAT A, B; OhA&B; REn; REnAL; WhThe*

Hopkins, Bo
American. Actor
b. Feb 2, in Greenwood, South Carolina
Source: *FilmEn; IntMPA 79, 80, 81, 82; WhoHol A*

Hopkins, Claude
American. Musician
b. Aug 3, 1903 in Washington, DC
Source: *AmSCAP 66; WhoJazz 72*

Hopkins, Sir Fredrick
English. Biochemist
b. Jun 30, 1861 in Eastbourne, England
d. May 16, 1947 in Cambridge, England
Source: *McGEWB; NewCol 75*

Hopkins, Gerard Manley
English. Poet
b. Jun 11, 1844 in Stratford, England
d. Jun 8, 1889 in Dublin, Ireland
Source: *AnCL; AtlBL; BrAu 19; CasWL; Chambr 3; ChPo, S1, S2; CnE&AP; CnMWL; CrtT 3; CyWA; DcLEL; EvLB; LongCTC; ModBrL, SUP; NewC; OxEng; Pen ENG; RAdv 1; RComWL; REn; WebE&AL; WhoTwCL*

Hopkins, Harry Lloyd
American. Presidential Aide
b. Aug 17, 1890 in Sioux City, Iowa
d. Jan 29, 1946 in New York, New York
Source: *BiDrUSE; CurBio 41, 46; DcAmB S4; EncAB-H; WebAB; WhAm 2; WhAmP*

Hopkins, Johns
American. Financier, Philanthropist
Bequeathed $7 million for founding of Johns Hopkins U and Johns Hopkins Hospital.
b. May 19, 1795 in Anne Arundel, Maryland
d. Dec 24, 1873 in Baltimore, Maryland
Source: *AmBi; ApCAB; DcAmB; TwCBDA; WhAm H*

Hopkins, "Lightnin'" (Sam)
American. Singer, Musician
b. Mar 15, 1912 in Leon County, Texas
d. Jan 30, 1982 in Houston, Texas
Source: *BiDAmM; BluesWW; EncFCWM 69; IlEncJ; NewYTBS 82; WhoAm 82*

Hopkins, Mark
American. Educator, College President
Professor of philosophy, 1830-87; president of Williams College, 1836-72.
b. Feb 4, 1802 in Stockbridge, Massachusetts
d. Jun 17, 1887 in Williamstown, Massachusetts
Source: *Alli, SUP; AmAu; AmAu&B; AmBi; ApCAB; BbD; BiD&SB; CyAL 1; DcAmAu; DcAmB; DcNAA; OxAmL; REnAL; TwCBDA; WebAB; WhAm H*

Hopkins, Miriam
American. Actress
b. Oct 18, 1902 in Bainbridge, Georgia
d. Oct 9, 1972 in New York, New York
Source: *BiDFilm; BiE&WWA; FilmgC; InWom; MotPP; MovMk; NewYTBE 72; OxFilm; ThFT; WhAm 5; WhScrn 77; WhoHol B; WorEFlm*

Hopkins, Stephen
American. Merchant, Judge
b. Mar 7, 1707 in Providence, Rhode Island
d. Jul 13, 1785 in Providence, Rhode Island
Source: *Alli; AmBi; ApCAB; BiAuS; BiDrAC; DcAmAu; DcAmB; DcNAA; Drake; OxAmL; REnAL; TwCBDA; WhAm H; WhAmP*

Hopkinson, Francis
American. Revolutionary Patriot, Poet
b. Sep 21, 1737 in Philadelphia, Pennsylvania
d. May 9, 1791 in Philadelphia, Pennsylvania
Source: *Alli; AmAu; AmAu&B; AmBi; ApCAB; BbD; BiD&SB; BiDrAC; CasWL; ChPo, S1; CnDAL; CyAL 1; DcAmAu; DcAmB; DcLEL; DcNAA; EvLB; OxAmL; Pen AM; REn; REnAL; TwCBDA; WebAB; WhAm H; WhAmP*

Hoppe, Arthur Watterson
American. Journalist
b. Apr 23, 1925 in Honolulu, Hawaii
Source: *AmAu&B; ConAu 5R, 3NR; WhoAm 74, 76, 78, 80, 82; WhoWest 74; WrDr 76*

Hoppe, Willie (William F)
American. Billiards Player
b. Oct 11, 1887 in New York, New York
d. Feb 1, 1959 in Miami, Florida
Source: *CurBio 47, 59; WebAB*

Hopper, Dennis
American. Actor, Motion Picture Director
Appeared in *Rebel without a Cause,* 1957; starred in *Easy Rider,* 1969.
b. May 17, 1936 in Dodge City, Kansas
Source: *CelR 73; FilmgC; IntMPA 75, 76, 77, 78, 79, 80, 81, 82; MotPP; MovMk; NewYTBE 70; WhoAm 74, 76, 78, 80, 82; WhoHol A*

Hopper, Edna Wallace
American. Actress
b. Jan 17, 1864 in San Francisco, California
d. Dec 14, 1959 in New York, New York
Source: *InWom; WhAm 3; WhScrn 74, 77; WhoStg 1906, 1908*

Hopper, Edward
American. Artist
b. Jul 22, 1882 in Nyack, New York
d. May 15, 1967 in New York, New York
Source: *AtlBL; CurBio 50, 67; DcCAA 71; EncAB-H; REn; WebAB; WhAm 4*

Hopper, Hedda
[Elda Furry]
American. Journalist, Actress
Began 28-year career as Hollywood gossip columnist, 1938; famous for her hats.
b. Jun 2, 1890 in Hollidaysburg, Pennsylvania
d. Feb 1, 1966 in Hollywood, California
Source: *AmAu&B; ConAu 89; CurBio 42, 66; Film 1; InWom; MovMk; OxFilm; ThFT; TwYS; WebAB; WhAm 4; WhScrn 74, 77; WhoHol B; WorEFlm*

Hopper, William
American. Actor
b. Jan 26, 1915 in New York, New York
d. Mar 6, 1970 in Palm Springs, California
Source: *FilmgC; WhScrn 74, 77; WhoHol B*

Hopper, (William) De Wolfe
American. Actor
b. Mar 30, 1858 in New York, New York
d. Sep 23, 1935 in Kansas City, Missouri
Source: *AmAu&B; DcNAA; Film 1; WebAB; WhoStg 1906, 1908*

Hoppner, John
English. Artist
b. Apr 4, 1758 in London, England
d. Jan 23, 1810
Source: *AtlBL; NewCol 75*

Hopwood, Avery
American. Dramatist
b. May 28, 1882 in Cleveland, Ohio
d. Jul 1, 1928 in Juan les Pins, France
Source: *AmAu&B; CnDAL; DcNAA; EncMys; McGEWD; ModWD; OhA&B; OxAmL; REnAL*

Horace
[Quintus Horatius Flaccus]
Roman. Poet, Satirist
b. Dec 8, 65BC in Venosa, Lucania
d. Nov 27, 8AD
Source: *AtlBL; BbD; BiD&SB; CasWL; ChPo; CyWA; DcEnL; DcEuL; NewC; OxEng; Pen CL; RComWL; REn; WebBD 80*

Hordern, Michael
English. Actor
b. Oct 3, 1911 in Berkhampstead, England
Source: *CnThe; FilmEn; FilmgC; IntMPA 79, 80, 81; MovMk; WhoHol A; WhoThe 72, 77*

Hore-Belisha, Leslie, Baron
English. Political Leader, Lawyer
b. Sep 7, 1893 in Kilburn, England
d. Feb 16, 1957 in Reims, France
Source: *CurBio 41, 57*

Horenstein, Jascha
Russian. Conductor, Composer
b. May 6, 1899 in Kiev, Russia
d. Apr 2, 1973 in London, England
Source: *NewYTBE 73; WhAm 5; WhoMus 72*

Horgan, Paul
American. Author
b. Aug 1, 1903 in Buffalo, New York
Source: *AmAu&B; AmNov; Au&Wr 71; AuBYP; CathA 1930; ChPo; CnDAL; ConAu 13R; ConLC 9; ConNov 72, 76; DcLEL; DrAF 76; DrAS 74H; IlsCB 1744; OxAmL; REnAL; TwCA SUP; WhNAA; WhoAm 74, 76, 78, 80, 82; WhoE 74; WhoGov 72; WhoWor 74; WrDr 76*

Horikoshi, Jiro
Japanese. Aeronautical Engineer
Designed the Zero fighter plane used during World War II.
b. 1904?
d. Jan 11, 1982 in Tokyo, Japan
Source: *NewYTBS 82*

Horlick, Alexander James
British. Manufacturer
b. Oct 3, 1873 in Racine, Wisconsin
d. Jun 6, 1950
Source: *BioIn 2, 4, 5; WhAm 3*

Horlick, William
American. Industrialist
b. Feb 23, 1846 in Gloucester, England
d. Sep 25, 1936
Source: *BioIn 4, 5; WhAm 1*

Hormel, George Albert
American. Meat Packer
Founder, president George A Hormel & Co., 1892-1928; produced first canned hams in US.
b. Dec 4, 1860 in Buffalo, New York
d. Jun 5, 1946 in Los Angeles, California
Source: *DcAmB S4; WhAm 2*

Horn, Alfred Aloysius, pseud.
[Alfred Aloysius Smith]
"Trader"
English. Adventurer, Author
b. 1854? in Lancashire, England
d. Jun 26, 1927 in Whitstable, England
Source: *IlBEAAW; LongCTC; TwCA, SUP*

Horn, Paul Joseph
American. Musician
b. Mar 17, 1930 in New York, New York
Source: *AmSCAP 66; WhoAm 74; WhoWest 74*

Horn, Tom
American. Lawman, Murderer
Hired by WY Cattleman's Assn. to eliminate small ranchers, rustlers; hung for murder.
b. 1860 in Memphis, Missouri
d. Nov 20, 1903 in Cheyenne, Wyoming
Source: *BioIn 1, 6, 7, 10, 11; Blood; DcAmB; EncACr; REnAW*

Hornby, Leslie
see: Twiggy

Horne, Josh L
American. Editor, Publisher
b. Dec 21, 1887 in Whitakers, North Carolina
d. Mar 15, 1974 in Rocky Mount, North Carolina
Source: *St&PR 75; WhoAm 74; WhAm 6*

Horne, Lena
American. Singer
Known for song "Stormy Weather"; starred on Broadway in *Lena Horne: The Lady and Her Music.*
b. Jun 30, 1917 in Brooklyn, New York
Source: *BiE&WWA; BkPepl; CelR 73; CurBio 44; EncMT; FilmgC; InWom; IntMPA 75, 76, 77, 78, 79, 80, 81, 82; MotPP; MovMk; NewYTBE 71; NotNAT; WhoAm 74, 76, 78, 80, 82; WhoBlA 75; WhoHol A*

Horne, Marilyn
American. Opera Singer
b. Jan 16, 1934 in Bradford, Pennsylvania
Source: *CelR 73; CurBio 67; InWom; IntWW 74; NewYTBE 70, 71; WhoAm 74, 76, 78, 80, 82; WhoAmW 77; WhoE 74; WhoMus 72; WhoWor 74*

Horner, Bob (James Robert)
American. Baseball Player
b. Aug 6, 1957 in Junction City, Kansas
Source: *BaseEn*

Horner, Matina Souretis
American. Educator, College President
President, Radcliffe College, 1972--.
b. Jul 28, 1939 in Boston, Massachusetts
Source: *AmM&WS 78S; CurBio 73; GoodHS; LEduc 74; WhoAm 74, 76, 78, 80, 82; WhoAmW 74, 75, 79; WhoE 74, 75, 77, 79*

Horney, Karen Danielson
American. Psychoanalyst
Founded, 1941, became dean of American Institute of Psychoanalysis.
b. Sep 16, 1885 in Hamburg, Germany
d. Dec 4, 1952 in New York, New York
Source: *AmAu&B; CurBio 41, 53; DcAmB S5; InWom; NewYTBE 73; TwCA SUP; WhAm 3*

Hornsby, Rogers
"Rajah"
American. Baseball Player, Manager
Had .358 lifetime batting average; Hall of Fame, 1942.
b. Apr 27, 1896 in Winters, Texas
d. Jan 5, 1963 in Chicago, Illinois
Source: *BaseEn; CurBio 52, 63; NewYTBE 73; WebAB; WhAm 4; WhoProB 73*

Hornung, Ernest William
English. Author
b. Jun 7, 1866 in Middlesbrough, England
d. Mar 22, 1921 in Saint Jean de Luz, France
Source: *BbD; BiD&SB; Chambr 3; DcLEL; EncMys; EvLB; LongCTC; MnBBF; NewC; REn; TwCA, SUP; TwCW*

Hornung, Paul Vernon
"The Golden Boy"
American. Football Player, Coach
Runner, placekicker, Green Bay Packers, 1957-66; suspended, 1963, with Alex Karras for gambling.
b. Dec 23, 1935 in Louisville, Kentucky
Source: *CurBio 63; WhoFtbl 74*

Horovitz, Israel
American. Dramatist
b. Mar 31, 1939 in Wakefield, Massachusetts
Source: *CelR 73; ConAu 33R; ConDr 73; CroCD; DrAF 76; DrAP 75; ModAL SUP; NatPD; NotNAT; WhoAm 74, 76, 78, 80, 82; WrDr 76*

Horowitz, Vladimir
American. Musician
Pianist; won 15 Grammys for best classical performance.
b. Oct 1, 1904 in Kiev, Russia
Source: *BioNews 74; CelR 73; CurBio 43, 66; IntWW 74; NewYTBS 74; Who 74; WhoAm 74, 76, 78, 80, 82; WhoMus 72; WhoWor 74, 76, 78*

Horrocks, Sir Brian Gwynne
British. Army Officer
b. Sep 7, 1895 in Rainkhet, India
Source: *BioIn 5, 10, 11; CurBio 45; IntWW 74, 75, 76, 77, 78; WhWW-II; Who 74; WhoWor 74, 76, 78; WrDr 76, 80*

Horrocks, Jeremiah
[Jeremiah Horrox]
English. Astronomer
b. 1617?
d. 1641
Source: *BioIn 8; NewCol 75*

Horsbrugh, Florence
Scottish. Statesman
b. 1889 in Edinburgh, Scotland
d. Dec 6, 1969 in Edinburgh, Scotland
Source: *BioIn 8; CurBio 52, 70*

Horstmann, Dorothy Millicent
American. Physician
b. Jul 2, 1911 in Spokane, Washington
Source: *AmM&WS 73P; WhoAm 74, 76, 78, 80, 82; WhoAmW 74*

Horthy de Nagybanya, Nicholas
[Miklos von Nagybanya]
Hungarian. Admiral, Political Leader
b. Jun 18, 1868 in Kenderes, Hungary
d. Mar 9, 1957
Source: *BioIn 1, 4; CurBio 40, 57*

Horton, Edward Everett
American. Actor
b. Sep 29, 1886 in New York, New York
d. Sep 29, 1970 in Encino, California
Source: *BiE&WWA; CurBio 46, 70; FilmgC; MotPP; MovMk; NewYTBE 70; OxFilm; TwYS; Vers A; WhAm 5; WhScrn 74, 77; WhoHol B; WorEFlm*

Horton, Johnny
American. Singer
b. Apr 30, 1927 in Tyler, Texas
d. Nov 5, 1960 in Austin, Texas
Source: *BiDAmM; EncFCWM 69; ObitOF 79; RkOn; WhoRock 81*

Horton, Robert
American. Actor
b. Jul 29, 1924 in Los Angeles, California
Source: *FilmgC; IntMPA 75, 76, 77, 78, 79, 80, 81, 82; MotPP; WhoE 74; WhoHol A; WhoThe 77; WhoWest 74*

Horton, Tim (Miles Gilbert)
Canadian. Hockey Player
b. Jan 12, 1930 in Cochrane, ON
d. Feb 21, 1974 in Saint Catherines, ON
Source: *BioIn 10; WhoHcky 73*

Horton, Willie (William Wattison)
American. Baseball Player
b. Oct 18, 1942 in Arno, Virginia
Source: *BaseEn; BioIn 8, 9; WhoProB 73*

Hosea
Biblical Prophet
Source: *DcOrL 3*

Hosein, Arthur
English. Murderer
b. 1936
Source: *BioIn 9*

Hosein, Nizamoden
English. Murderer
b. 1948
Source: *BioIn 9*

Hosking, Eric J
English. Ornithologist
b. Oct 2, 1909
Source: *Who 74*

Hoskins, Allen Clayton
[Our Gang]
"Farina"
American. Actor
b. Aug 9, 1920 in Chelsea, Massachusetts
d. Jul 26, 1980 in Oakland, California
Source: *DcBlPA; WhoHol A*

Hosmer, Craig
American. Lawyer, Politician
Representative from California, 1953-1975.
b. May 16, 1915 in Borea, California
d. Oct 11, 1982
Source: *BiDrAC; CngDr 74; CurBio 58; NewYTBS 82; WhoAm 76, 78, 80, 82; WhoAmP 73, 75, 77, 79; WhoGov 72, 75; WhoS&SW 76*

Hosmer, Harriet Goodhue
American. Sculptor
b. Oct 9, 1830 in Watertown, Massachusetts
d. Feb 21, 1908 in Watertown, Massachusetts
Source: *AmBi; AmWom; ApCAB; DcAmB; Drake; InWom; NotAW; TwCBDA; WhAm 1*

Hostages, The
[Thomas Leo Ahern, Jr.; Clair Cortland Barnes; William E Belk; Robert Olof Blucker; Donald Cooke; William J Daugherty; Robert A Englemann; William Gallegos; Bruce W German; Duane Gillette; Alan Bruce Golacinski; John Earl Graves; Joseph M Hall; Kevin Jay Hermening; Donald Hohman; Leland James Holland; Michael Howland; Charles A Jones, Jr.; Malcolm Kalp; Moorehead Cowell Kennedy, Jr.; William Francis Keough, Jr.; Steven William Kirtley; Kathryn L Koob; Frederick Lee Kupke; (Lowell) Bruce Laingen; Steven Lauterbach; Gary Earl Lee; Paul Edward Lewis; John William Limbert, Jr.; James Michael Lopez; Johnny McKeel; Michael John Metrinko; Jerry J Miele; Michael E Moeller; Bert C Moore; Richard H Morefield; Paul M Needham, Jr.; Robert C Ode; Gregory A Persinger; Jerry Plotkin; Richard I Queen; Regis Ragan; David Roeder; Barry Rosen; William Blackburn Royer, Jr.; Thomas E Schaefer; Charles Wesly Scott; Donald A Sharer; Rodney Virgil Sickmann; Joseph Subic, Jr.; Elizabeth Ann Swift; Victor Lloyd Tomseth; Phillip R Ward]
Americans. Held Captive in Iran
Source: *NewYTBS 81*

Hotchkiss, Benjamin Berkeley
American. Inventor
b. Oct 1, 1826 in Watertown, Connecticut
d. Feb 14, 1885 in Paris, France
Source: *AmBi; ApCAB; DcAmB; TwCBDA; WhAm H*

Hotchner, Aaron Edward
American. Author, Biographer
b. Jun 28, 1920 in Saint Louis, Missouri
Source: *AmAu&B; WhoAm 74; WhoE 74; WhoWor 74*

Hottelot, Richard C(urt)
American. Journalist
b. Sep 22, 1917 in New York, New York
Source: *WhoAm 74*

Hotter, Hans
German. Opera Singer
b. Jan 19, 1909 in Offenbach-am-Main, Germany
Source: *Baker 78; IntWW 74, 75, 76, 77, 78; NewEOp 71; Who 74; WhoMus 72; WhoWor 74*

Houdin, Jean Eugene Robert
French. Magician, Conjurer
Houdini named himself after Houdin.
b. 1805 in Blois, France
d. 1871
Source: *NewCol 75; WebBD 80*

Houdini, Harry
[Ehrich Weiss]
American. Magician, Escape Artist
Famous for his escape from bonds, many of which have not been duplicated.
b. Apr 6, 1874 in Appleton, Wisconsin
d. Oct 31, 1926 in Detroit, Michigan
Source: *AmBi; DcAmB; DcNAA; Film 1; FilmgC; OxFilm; TwYS; WebAB; WhAm 1; WhScrn 74, 77; WhoHol B*

Houdon, Jean Antoine
French. Sculptor
b. Mar 20, 1741 in Versailles, France
d. Jul 15, 1828 in Paris, France
Source: *ApCAB; AtlBL; Drake; OxFr; REn*

Houghton, Amory
American. Glass Manufacturer, Ambassador
b. Jul 27, 1899 in Corning, New York
d. Feb 21, 1981 in Charleston, South Carolina
Source: *BioIn 1, 4, 6, 7, 11; CurBio 47, 81; IntWW 74, 75, 76, 77, 78; IntYB 78, 79; WhoAm 74, 76, 78, 80; WhoF&I 74, 75, 77, 79*

Houghton, Henry Oscar
American. Publisher
b. Apr 30, 1823 in Sutton, Vermont
d. Aug 25, 1895 in North Andover, Massachusetts
Source: *AmAu&B; AmBi; ApCAB; DcAmB; TwCBDA; WhAm H*

Houghton, Katharine
American. Actress
b. Mar 10, 1945 in Hartford, Connecticut
Source: *FilmgC; WhoAm 74, 76, 78, 80, 82; WhoHol A*

Houk, Ralph George
"Major"
American. Baseball Player, Manager
Manager, NY Yankees, 1961-63, 1966-73, Detroit, 1974-78, Boston, 1981--.
b. Aug 9, 1919 in Lawrence, Kansas
Source: *BaseEn; CelR 73; CurBio 62; WhoAm 74, 76, 78, 80, 82; WhoE 74; WhoProB 73*

Houle, Rejean
Canadian. Hockey Player
b. Oct 25, 1949 in Rouyn Noranda, PQ
Source: *WhoHcky 73*

Hoult, Norah
Irish. Author, Journalist
b. Sep 20, 1898 in Dublin, Ireland
Source: *LongCTC; TwCA, SUP; Who 74; WhoTwCL*

Hounsfield, Godfrey Newbold
English. Scientist
b. Aug 28, 1919 in Newark, England
Source: *BioIn 12; CurBio 80*

Houphouet-Boigny, Felix
African. Politician
b. Oct 18, 1905 in Ivory Coast
Source: *CurBio 58; IntWW 74*

Housden, Steve
see: Little River Band, The

House, Edward Mandell
American. Diplomat, Presidential Aide
b. Jul 26, 1858 in Houston, Texas
d. Mar 28, 1938 in New York, New York
Source: *AmAu&B; AmBi; DcAmB S2; DcNAA; EncAB-H; OxAmL; TexWr; WebAB; WhAm 1; WhAmP*

Household, Geoffrey
English. Author
b. Nov 30, 1900 in Bristol, England
Source: *ConAu 77; ConNov 72, 76; EncMys; LongCTC; NewC; SmATA 14; TwCA, SUP; Who 74; WhoSpyF; WhoWor 74, 76*

Houseman, John
[John Haussmann]
American. Actor, Director, Producer
Won Oscar, 1973, for *The Paper Chase;* recreated role in TV series.
b. Sep 22, 1902 in Bucharest, Romania
Source: *BiDFilm; BiE&WWA; CelR 73; CurBio 59; FilmgC; IntMPA 75, 76, 77, 78, 79, 80, 81, 82; NotNAT; PlP&P; WhoAm 74, 76, 78, 80, 82; WhoHol A; WhoThe 77; WhoWor 74; WorEFlm*

Housman, A(lfred) E(dward)
English. Poet, Classical Scholar
b. Mar 26, 1859 in Fockbury, England
d. Apr 30, 1936 in Cambridge, England
Source: *AnCL; AtlBL; CasWL; Chambr 3; ChPo, S1, S2; CnE&AP; CnMWL; CyWA; DcLEL; EncWL; EvLB; LongCTC; ModBrL, SUP; NewC; OxEng; Pen ENG; RAdv 1; RComWL; REn; Str&VC; TwCA, SUP; TwCW; WebE&AL; WhoLA; WhoTwCL*

Housman, Laurence
English. Author, Dramatist
b. Jul 18, 1865 in Bromsgrove, England
d. Feb 20, 1959 in Somerset, England
Source: *Chambr 3; ChPo, S1, S2; CnMD; DcEnA AP; DcLEL; EvLB; IlsCB 1744; JBA 34; LongCTC; McGEWD; ModBrL; ModWD; NewC; OxEng; OxThe; Pen ENG; REn; TwCA, SUP; WhAm 3; WhoLA*

Houssay, Bernardo Alberto
Argentine. Physiologist, Educator
b. Apr 10, 1887 in Buenos Aires, Argentina
d. Sep 21, 1971 in Buenos Aires, Argentina
Source: *CurBio 48, 71; NewYTBE 71; WhAm 5*

Houston, Charles Hamilton
American. Lawyer, Minority Rights Leader
b. Sep 3, 1895 in Washington, DC
d. Apr 22, 1950 in Washington, DC
Source: *BioIn 1, 2, 3, 7, 8, 11; CurBio 48, 50*

Houston, Ken(neth R)
American. Football Player
b. Nov 12, 1944 in Lufkin, Texas
Source: *WhoAm 82; WhoFtbl 74*

Houston, Sam(uel)
American. Army Officer, Statesman
First president of Republic of Texas, 1836-38, 1841-44.
b. Mar 2, 1793 in Lexington, Virginia
d. Jul 26, 1863 in Huntsville, Texas
Source: *AmBi; ApCAB; BiDrAC; DcAmB; Drake; WebAB; WhAm H; WhAmP*

Hovey, Richard
American. Poet
b. May 4, 1864 in Normal, Illinois
d. Feb 24, 1900
Source: *AmAu; AmAu&B; AmBi; ApCAB SUP; BbD; BiD&SB; Chambr 3; ChPo, S1, S2; CnDAL; DcAmAu; DcAmB; DcLEL; DcNAA; OxAmL; Pen AM; REn; REnAL; TwCBDA; WhAm 1*

Hoveyda, Amir Abbas
Iranian. Prime Minister
b. Feb 18, 1919 in Teheran, Persia
d. Apr 7, 1979 in Teheran, Iran
Source: *CurBio 71, 79; IntWW 74, 75, 76, 77, 78; WhoWor 76, 78*

Hovhaness, Alan
American. Composer
b. Mar 8, 1911 in Somerville, Massachusetts
Source: *CurBio 65; DcCM; WhoAm 74, 76, 78, 80, 82; WhoWor 74*

Hoving, Thomas Pearsall Field
American. Art Historian
b. Jan 15, 1931 in New York, New York
Source: *ConAu 101; CurBio 67; IntWW 74; Who 74; WhoAm 74, 76, 78, 80, 82; WhoAmA 73; WhoE 74*

Hoving, Walter
American. Business Executive
b. Dec 2, 1897 in Stockholm, Sweden
Source: *CelR 73; CurBio 46; St&PR 75; WhoAm 74, 76, 78, 80, 82; WhoWor 74*

Howar, Barbara
American. Journalist, Author
b. Sep 27, 1934 in Nashville, Tennessee
Source: *AuNews 1, 2; ConAu 89; WhoAm 78, 80, 82; WrDr 76*

Howard, Anthony
British. Editor
b. Feb 12, 1934
Source: *Who 74; WhoAm 76; WhoWor 76*

Howard, Bronson Crocker
American. Dramatist
b. Oct 7, 1842 in Detroit, Michigan
d. Aug 4, 1908 in Avon, New Jersey
Source: *AmAu&B; CnThe; EncWT; McGEWD; ModWD; OxAmL; OxThe; REnAL; REnWD; WhAm 1*

Howard, Catherine
English. 5th Wife of Henry VIII
b. 1520
d. 1542
Source: *BioIn 1, 3, 4, 6, 7, 9; OxGer*

Howard, Clint
American. Actor
b. Apr 20, 1959 in Burbank, California
Source: *WhoHol A*

Howard, Cordelia
American. Actress
b. Feb 1, 1848 in Providence, Rhode Island
d. Aug 10, 1941 in Belmont, Massachusetts
Source: *BioIn 4, 5; CurBio 41; NotNAT B*

Howard, "Curly" (Jerry)
[The Three Stooges]
American. Comedian
b. 1906 in Brooklyn, New York
d. Jan 19, 1952 in San Gabriel, California
Source: *MotPP; WhoHol B*

Howard, Sir Ebenezer
English. Urban Planner
b. 1850
d. 1928
Source: *BioIn 8, 9, 10; NewCol 75*

Howard, Eddy
American. Band Leader, Songwriter, Actor
b. Sep 12, 1909 in Woodland, California
d. May 23, 1963 in Palm Desert, California
Source: *AmSCAP 66; WhAm 4; WhScrn 74, 77; WhoHol B*

Howard, Elston Gene
"Ellie"
American. Baseball Player
Catcher, outfielder, 1955-68; first black coach in AL, 1969.
b. Feb 23, 1929 in Saint Louis, Missouri
d. Dec 14, 1980 in New York, New York
Source: *BaseEn; BioNews 74; CurBio 64, 81; WhoAm 74; WhoBlA 75; WhoProB 73*

Howard, Eugene
American. Comedian, Actor
b. 1881 in Neustadt, Germany
d. Aug 1, 1965 in New York, New York
Source: *BiE&WWA; WhScrn 74, 77; WhoHol B*

Howard, Frank Oliver
"The Capital Punisher"; "Hondo"
American. Baseball Player
b. Aug 8, 1936 in Columbus, Ohio
Source: *BaseEn; CurBio 72; WhoProB 73*

Howard, Jane Temple
American. Journalist, Author
b. May 4, 1935 in Springfield, Illinois
Source: *BioNews 74; ConAu 29R; WrDr 76*

Howard, Joseph Edgar
American. Entertainer, Songwriter
Wrote songs "Hello, My Baby" and "I Wonder Who's Kissing Her Now."
b. Feb 12, 1878 in New York, New York
d. May 19, 1961 in Chicago, Illinois
Source: *AmPS; AmSCAP 66; BiDAmM; CmpEPM; NotNAT B*

Howard, Ken
American. Actor, Singer
b. Mar 28, 1944 in El Centro, California
Source: *NotNAT; WhoAm 82; WhoE 74; WhoHol A; WhoThe 77*

Howard, Leslie
[Leslie Stainer]
English. Actor
Played Ashley Wilkes in *Gone with the Wind,* 1939.
b. Apr 3, 1893 in London, England
d. Jun 2, 1943 in Bay of Biscay
Source: *BiDFilm; CmMov; DcAmB S3; FamA&A; Film 1; FilmgC; MovMk; OxFilm; REn; WhAm 2; WhScrn 74, 77; WhoHol B; WorEFlm*

Howard, Moe
[The Three Stooges]
American. Comedian
b. Jun 19, 1897 in Brooklyn, New York
d. May 24, 1975 in Hollywood, California
Source: *MotPP; WhScrn 77*

Howard, Oliver Otis
American. Army Officer
b. Nov 8, 1830 in Leeds, Maine
d. Oct 26, 1909 in Burlington, Vermont
Source: *Alli SUP; AmAu&B; BiD&SB; DcAmAu; DcNAA; WebAB*

Howard, Robert Ervin
[Patrick Ervin, pseud.]
American. Author
b. Jan 22, 1906 in Peaster, Texas
d. Jun 12, 1936 in Cross Plains, Texas
Source: *BioIn 11; EncSF; FanAl; ScF&FL 1; WhNAA; WhoHr&F; WhoSciF*

Howard, Ron
American. Actor, Motion Picture Director
Played Opie on "The Andy Griffith Show," 1960-68, Richie Cunningham on "Happy Days," 1974-80.
b. Mar 1, 1954 in Duncan, Oklahoma
Source: *BkPepl; IntMPA 75, 76, 77, 78, 79, 80, 81, 82; WhoAm 78, 80, 82; WhoHol A*

Howard, Roy Wilson
American. Journalist
b. Jan 1, 1883 in Gano, Ohio
d. Nov 20, 1964 in New York, New York
Source: *AmAu&B; CurBio 40, 65; WebAB; WhAm 4; WhNAA*

Howard, "Shemp" (Samuel)
[The Three Stooges]
American. Comedian
b. Mar 17, 1900 in New York, New York
d. Nov 22, 1955 in Hollywood, California
Source: *FilmgC; MotPP; WhoHol B*

Howard, Sidney Coe
American. Dramatist, Journalist
b. Jun 26, 1891 in Oakland, California
d. Aug 23, 1939 in Tyringham, Massachusetts
Source: *AmAu&B; AmBi; CasWL; CnDAL; CnMD; CnThe; ConAmA; ConAmL; DcAmB S2; DcLEL; DcNAA; LongCTC; McGEWD; ModAL; ModWD; OxAmL; OxThe; Pen AM; REn; REnAL; REnWD; TwCA, SUP; WebAB; WebE&AL; WhAm 1*

Howard, Susan
[Jeri Lynn Mooney]
American. Actress
Plays Donna Culver Krebs on TV series "Dallas."
b. 1941 in Marshall, Texas
Source: *BioIn 10*

Howard, Tom
British. Actor
b. 1886 in Ireland
d. Feb 27, 1955 in Long Branch, New Jersey
Source: *WhScrn 74, 77; WhoHol B*

Howard, Trevor Wallace
English. Actor
b. Sep 29, 1916 in Kent, England
Source: *BiDFilm; CelR 73; CmMov; FilmgC; IntMPA 75, 76, 77, 78, 79, 80, 81, 82; IntWW 74; MovMk; OxFilm; Who 74; WhoThe 77; WhoWor 74; WorEFlm*

Howard, Willie
American. Comedian
b. 1886 in Germany
d. Jan 14, 1949 in New York, New York
Source: *DcAmB S4; EncMT; WhAm 3; WhScrn 74, 77*

Howatch, Susan
American. Author
b. Jul 14, 1940 in Leatherhead, England
Source: *AuNews 1; ConAu 45; WrDr 76*

Howe, Clarence Decatur
Canadian. Politician, Economist
b. Jan 15, 1886 in Waltham, Massachusetts
d. Dec 31, 1960 in Montreal, PQ
Source: *BioIn 1, 2, 3, 4, 5, 6, 8; CurBio 45, 61*

Howe, Edmund Perry
American. Journalist
b. Dec 14, 1896 in Montpelier, Vermont
Source: *WhJnl*

Howe, Elias
American. Inventor
Patented first sewing machine, 1846.
b. Jul 9, 1819 in Spencer, Massachusetts
d. Oct 3, 1867 in Brooklyn, New York
Source: *AmBi; ApCAB; DcAmB; Drake; EncAB-H; TwCBDA; WebAB; WhAm H*

Howe, Gordie (Gordon)
American. Hockey Player
Played 26 seasons, 801 goals, 1049 assists, all NHL records.
b. Mar 31, 1928 in Saskatoon, SK
Source: *BioNews 74; CanWW 82; CurBio 62; NewYTBS 74; NewYTBE 73; WhoAm 74, 76, 78, 80, 82; WhoHcky 73*

Howe, Harold, II
American. Educator
b. Aug 17, 1918 in Hartford, Connecticut
Source: *BioIn 7, 8, 9; CurBio 67; IntWW 74; NewYTBE 70; WhoAm 82*

Howe, Irving
American. Author, Editor, Critic
b. Jun 11, 1920 in New York, New York
Source: *AmAu&B; ConAu 9R; DrAS 74E; ModAL; RAdv 1; REnAL; TwCA SUP; WhoAm 74, 76, 78, 80, 82; WhoWor 74; WhoWorJ 72*

Howe, James Wong
American. Cinematographer
b. Aug 28, 1899 in Kwangtung, China
d. Jul 12, 1976 in Hollywood, California
Source: *CurBio 43; DcFM; FilmgC; IntMPA 75; OxFilm; WhoAm 74; WhoWor 74; WorEFlm*

Howe, Julia Ward
American. Author, Social Reformer
Wrote words to "Battle Hymn of the Republic," 1861.
b. May 27, 1819 in New York, New York
d. Oct 17, 1910 in Newport, Rhode Island
Source: *Alli, SUP; AmAu; AmAu&B; AmBi; AmWom; ApCAB; BbD; BiCAW; BiD&SB; Chambr 3; ChPo, S1, S2; CnDAL; CyAl 2; DcAmAu; DcAmB; DcEnL; DcLEL; DcNAA; Drake; EncAB-H; EvLB; FemPA; HerW; InWom; NotAW; OxAmL; OxEng; Pen AM; REn; REnAL; TwCBDA; WebAB; WebE&AL; WhAm 1; WhAmP*

Howe, Mark De Wolfe
American. Historian, Lawyer
b. May 22, 1906 in Boston, Massachusetts
d. Feb 28, 1967 in Cambridge, Massachusetts
Source: *AmAu&B; ConAu 89; WhAm 4; WhNAA*

Howe, Oscar
American. Artist
b. May 13, 1915 in Joe Creek, South Dakota
Source: *BioIn 9; WhoAm 82; WhoAmA 73*

Howe, Quincy
American. Editor, Broadcaster
b. Aug 17, 1900 in Boston, Massachusetts
d. Feb 17, 1977 in New York, New York
Source: *AmAu&B; ConAu 49, 69; CurBio 40; EncMT; IntMPA 75, 76, 77; IntWW 74; WhoAm 74*

Howe, Richard
British. Admiral
b. Mar 19, 1725
d. Aug 5, 1799
Source: *Alli; ApCAB; Drake*

Howe, Sir (Richard Edward) Geoffrey
Welsh. Government Official
b. Dec 20, 1926 in Port Talbot, Wales
Source: *CurBio 80; IntWW 74, 75, 76, 77, 78, 79, 80; IntYB 78, 79; NewYTBS 79; Who 74, 80; WhoWor 74, 78*

Howe, Samuel Gridley
American. Humanitarian, Social Reformer
b. Nov 10, 1802 in Boston, Massachusetts
d. Jan 9, 1876 in Boston, Massachusetts
Source: *Alli; AmAu; AmAu&B; AmBi; ApCAB; DcAmAu; DcAmB; DcNAA; Drake; EncAB-H; OxAmL; REn; REnAL; TwCBDA; WebAB; WhAm H*

Howe, Syd(ney Harris)
Canadian. Hockey Player
b. Sep 28, 1911 in Ottawa, ON
Source: *WhoHcky 73*

Howe, William, Viscount
English. General
b. Aug 10, 1729 in London, England
d. Jul 12, 1814
Source: *Alli; AmBi; ApCAB; Drake; OxAmL; WhAm H*

Howell, Clark
American. Journalist, Editor
b. Sep 21, 1863 in Barnwell County, South Carolina
d. Nov 14, 1936 in Atlanta, Georgia
Source: *AmBi; BiDSA; DcAmB S2; DcNAA; WhAm 1; WhAmP*

Howell, Harry (Henry Vernon)
Canadian. Hockey Player
b. Dec 28, 1932 in Hamilton, ON
Source: *WhoHcky 73*

Howells, Anne Elizabeth
English. Opera Singer
b. Jan 12, 1941 in Southport, England
Source: *IntWW 78; Who 74; WhoMus 72; WhoOp 76*

Howells, William Dean
American. Author, Editor
Wrote *A Modern Instance,* 1882, *The Rise of Silas Lapham,* 1885.
b. Mar 1, 1837 in Martins Ferry, Ohio
d. May 10, 1920 in New York, New York
Source: *Alli SUP; AmAu; AmAu&B; AmBi; AmWr; AtlBL; BbD; BiD&SB; CarSB; CasWL; Chambr 3; ChPo, S1, S2; CnDAL; CrtT 3; CyAl 2; CyWA; DcAmAu; DcAmB; DcBiA; DcEnA, AP; DcEnL; DcLEL; DcNAA; EncAB-H; EncWL; EvLB; McGEWD; ModAL, SUP; ModWD; OhA&B; OxAmL; OxEng; Pen AM; RAdv 1; RComWL; REn; REnAL; WebAB; WebE&AL*

Howes, Sally Ann
English. Actress, Singer
b. Jul 20, 1934 in London, England
Source: *BiE&WWA; EncMT; FilmgC; InWom; MotPP; MovMk; NotNAT; Who 74; WhoHol A; WhoThe 77*

Howland, Alfred Cornelius
American. Artist
b. Feb 12, 1838 in Walpole, New Hampshire
d. 1909 in Pasadena, California
Source: *ApCAB; DcAmB; EarABI; NatCAB 7; NewYHSD; TwCBDA; WhAm 1*

Howland, Michael
[The Hostages]
American. Former Hostage in Iran
b. 1947?
Source: *BioIn 12; NewYTBS 81*

Howlin' Wolf
[Chester Burnett]
American. Singer, Songwriter
b. Jun 10, 1910 in West Point, Mississippi
d. Jan 10, 1976 in Chicago, Illinois
Source: *EncPR&S*

Howser, Dick (Richard Dalton)
American. Baseball Player, Manager
b. May 14, 1937 in Miami, Florida
Source: *BaseEn; BioIn 12; WhoAm 82*

Hoxha, Enver
Albanian. Dictator
b. Oct 16, 1908 in Gjinokaster, Albania
Source: *CurBio 50; IntWW 74; WhoWor 74*

Hoyle, Edmond
English. Expert on Games
Codified rules of many card games; saying "according to Hoyle" has come to mean "by highest authority."
b. 1672
d. Aug 29, 1769 in London, England
Source: *Alli; BiD&SB; BrAu; NewC; OxEng*

Hoyle, Fred
English. Author, Astronomer
Wrote *Nature of the Universe,* 1951, including the Steady State Theory, that universe is steadily expanding.
b. Jun 24, 1915 in Bingley, England
Source: *Au&Wr 71; BioIn 4, 5, 6, 10; ConAu 5R, 3NR, 3NR; ConNov 72; TwCW; WhoWor 74; WorAu; WrDr 76*

Hoyt, (Edwin) Palmer
American. Newspaper Publisher
b. Mar 10, 1897 in Roseville, Illinois
d. Jun 25, 1979 in Denver, Colorado
Source: *ConAu 89; CurBio 43, 79; NewYTBS 79*

Hrushevsky, Mykhailo
Ukrainian. Historian, Statesman
b. 1866
d. 1934
Source: *NewCol 75*

Hruska, Roman Lee
American. Senator
b. Aug 16, 1904 in David City, Nebraska
Source: *BiDrAC; CngDr 74; CurBio 56; IntWW 74; WhoAm 74, 76, 78, 80, 82; WhoAmP 73; WhoGov 72; WhoMW 74; WhoWor 74*

Hua, Kuo-Feng
Chinese. Politician, Statesman
b. 1919
Source: *BioIn 10, 11; IntWW 74*

Hubay, Jeno
Hungarian. Musician, Composer
b. Sep 14, 1858 in Budapest, Hungary
d. Mar 12, 1937 in Vienna, Austria
Source: *NewEOp 71*

Hubbard, Cal (Robert Calvin)
American. Football Player
b. Oct 11, 1900 in Keytesville, Missouri
Source: *BioIn 6, 8, 11; WhoFtbl 74*

Hubbard, Elbert Green
[Fra Elbertus]
American. Author, Publisher, Biographer
b. Jun 19, 1856 in Bloomington, Illinois
d. May 7, 1915
Source: *AmAu&B; AmBi; BbD; BiD&SB; ChPo S2; CnDAL; DcAmAu; DcAmB; DcLEL; DcNAA; EvLB; OxAmL; REn; REnAL; TwCA, SUP*

Hubbard, Kin (Frank McKinney)
American. Humorist, Journalist
b. Sep 1, 1868 in Bellefontaine, Ohio
d. Dec 26, 1930 in Indianapolis, Indiana
Source: *BioIn 2, 6; DcNAA; IndAu 1816; OhA&B; OxAmL; TwCA, SUP; WebAB; WhNAA*

Hubbard, Lafayette Ronald
American. Religious Leader
Founded religious movement Scientology, 1950's; author of over 200 books, novels.
b. Mar 13, 1911 in Tilden, Nebraska
Source: *Au&Wr 71; WhoAm 80, 82; WhoS&SW 73; WrDr 76*

Hubbard, Orville Liscum
American. Politician
Mayor of Dearborn, MI, 1941-77; holder national record for full-time mayor.
b. Apr 2, 1903 in Union City, Michigan
d. Dec 16, 1982 in Detroit, Michigan
Source: *BioIn 2, 5, 7, 8; WhoAm 74, 76, 78; WhoAmP 73, 75, 77, 79; WhoGov 72, 75, 77; WhoMW 76, 78*

Hubbell, Carl Owen
"King Carl"; "The Meal Ticket"
American. Baseball Player
Pitcher, NY, 1928-43; won at least 20 games per season, 1933-37; Hall of Fame, 1947.
b. Jun 22, 1903 in Carthage, Missouri
Source: *BaseEn; WhoProB 73*

Hubble, Edwin Powell
American. Astronomer
b. Nov 20, 1889 in Marshfield, Missouri
d. Sep 28, 1953 in San Marino, California
Source: *DcAmB S5; REnAL; WebAB; WhAm 3*

Huberman, Bronislaw
Austrian. Musician
b. Dec 19, 1882 in Czestochowa, Poland
d. Jun 16, 1947 in Nant Corsier, Switzerland
Source: *CurBio 41, 47*

Hubert
Saint
b. 655?
d. 727
Source: *BioIn 2, 3, 4, 5, 10, 11*

Hubley, Season
[Mrs. Kurt Russell]
American. Actress
b. 1951
Source: *BioIn 11; WhoHol A*

Huddleston, (Ernest Urban) Trevor
English. Anglican Bishop
b. Jun 15, 1913 in Bedford, England
Source: *BioIn 4, 6, 7, 8, 9, 10; CurBio 63; WrDr 76*

Huddleston, Walter Darlington
American. Politician
b. 1924
Source: *BioIn 9, 10, 11; WhoAm 82*

Hudson, Henry
English. Navigator
Made several attempts to find Northwest Passage; first white man to go up Hudson River, 1609, which was named for him.
b. Sep 12, 1575?
d. Jun 23, 1611?
Source: *Alli; AmBi; ApCAB; DcAmB; Drake; EncAB-H; OxCan; REn; REnAL; TwCBDA; WebAB; WhAm H*

Hudson, Joseph Lowthian
English. Businessman
Founded J L Hudson, 1881; president, 1891-1912.
b. Oct 17, 1846 in Newcastle, England
d. Jul 15, 1912 in Worthing, England
Source: *NatCAB 47; WhAm 1*

Hudson, Joseph Lowthian, Jr.
American. Businessman
b. Jul 4, 1931 in Buffalo, New York
Source: *St&PR 75; WhoAm 74, 76, 78, 80, 82; WhoF&I 74*

Hudson, Lou
American. Basketball Player
b. Jul 11, 1944 in Greensboro, North Carolina
Source: *WhoBbl 73*

Hudson, Rochelle
American. Actress
b. Mar 6, 1915 in Oklahoma City, Oklahoma
d. Jan 17, 1972 in Palm Desert, California
Source: *FilmgC; InWom; MotPP; MovMk; NewYTBE 72; ThFT; WhScrn 77; WhoHol B*

Hudson, Rock
[Roy Scherer-Fitzgerald]
American. Actor
Starred in *Giant,* 1958; in TV series "McMillan and Wife," 1971-76.
b. Nov 17, 1925 in Winnetka, Illinois
Source: *BiDFilm; BkPepl; CelR 73; CmMov; CurBio 61; FilmgC; IntMPA 75, 76, 77, 78, 79, 80, 81, 82; MotPP; MovMk; OxFilm; WhoAm 74, 76, 78, 80, 82; WhoHol A; WhoWest 74; WhoWor 74; WorEFlm*

Hudson, William Henry
English. Author, Naturalist
Wrote *Green Mansions,* 1904, *The Book of a Naturalist,* 1919.
b. Aug 4, 1841 in Quilmes, Argentina
d. Aug 18, 1922 in London, England
Source: *Alli SUP; AnCL; AtlBL; CarSB; CasWL; Chambr 3; ChPo S1, S2; CyWA; DcBiA; DcEuL; DcLEL; EvLB; LongCTC; ModBrL; NewC; OxEng; Pen ENG; RAdv 1; REn; TwCA, SUP; TwCW; WebE&AL*

Huebner, Clarence R
American. Army Officer
b. Nov 24, 1888 in Bushton, Kansas
d. Sep 23, 1972 in Washington, DC
Source: *CurBio 49, 72; NewYTBE 72; WhAm 5*

Huerta, Dolores Hernandez
Labor Leader
b. 1930
Source: *BioIn 10*

Huey Lewis and the News
[Mario Cipollina; Johnny Colla; Bill Gibson; Chris Hayes; Sean Hopper; Huey (Hugh Cregg) Lewis]
American. Rock Group
Source: *NF*

Huff, Sam (Robert Lee)
American. Football Player
b. Oct 4, 1934 in Edna Gas, West Virginia
Source: *WhoFtbl 74*

Huffman, David
American. Actor
b. May 10, 1945 in Berwyn, Illinois
Source: *NewYTBS 78*

Hufstedler, Shirley (Ann) M(ount)
American. Judge, Government Official
First Secretary of Education, Carter administration, 1979-81.
b. Aug 24, 1925 in Denver, Colorado
Source: *AmAu&B; BioIn 12; CurBio 80; GoodHS; NewYTBS 79; WhoAm 74, 76, 78, 80, 82; WhoAmL 79; WhoAmW 58, 61, 64, 66, 68, 70, 72, 75, 77, 79; WhoGov 72, 77; WhoWest 74, 76, 78*

Hugel, Max
American. Businessman
b. 1925 in Brooklyn, New York
Source: *BioIn 2, 12; St&PR 75*

Huggins, Charles Brenton
Canadian. Surgeon, Researcher
b. Sep 22, 1901 in Halifax, NS
Source: *AmM&WS 73P; CanWW 82; CurBio 65; IntWW 74; WebAB; Who 74; WhoAm 74, 76, 78, 80, 82*

Huggins, Miller James
"Hug"; "The Mighty Mite"
American. Baseball Player, Manager
b. Mar 17, 1879 in Cincinnati, Ohio
d. Sep 25, 1929 in New York, New York
Source: *BaseEn; DcAmB; WhAm H, 4; WhoProB 73*

Hugh Capet
French. King
b. 938
d. 996
Source: *NewCol 75*

Hughan, Jessie Wallace
American. Author, Political Activist
b. Dec 25, 1876 in Brooklyn, New York
d. 1955
Source: *InWom; WhAm 5; WhNAA; WomWWA 14*

Hughes, Arthur
English. Artist, Illustrator
b. 1832 in London, England
d. 1915
Source: *BioIn 1, 5, 6, 8; WhoChL*

Hughes, Barnard
American. Actor
b. Jul 16, 1915 in Bedford Hills, New York
Source: *NotNAT; WhoAm 82; WhoHol A; WhoThe 77*

Hughes, Charles Evans
American. Supreme Court Justice
b. Apr 11, 1862 in Glens Falls, New York
d. Aug 27, 1948 in Osterville, Massachusetts
Source: *AmAu&B; BiDrUSE; CurBio 41, 48; DcAmB S4; DcNAA; EncAB-H; REn; REnAL; WebAB; WhAm 2; WhAmP*

Hughes, Emmet John
American. Author, Journalist
Columnist, *Newsweek,* 1963-68; speechwriter for Dwight Eisenhower and Nelson Rockefeller.
b. Dec 26, 1920 in Newark, New Jersey
d. Sep 20, 1982 in Princeton, New Jersey
Source: *AmAu&B; ConAu 69; CurBio 64, 82; PolProf E; WhoAm 74, 76, 78; WhoWor 74, 76*

Hughes, Francis
[Irish Hunger Strikers]
Irish. Jailed IRA Member
b. 1955? in Bellaghy, Northern Ireland
d. May 12, 1981 in Belfast, Northern Ireland
Source: *BioIn 12*

Hughes, Glenn M
see: Village People, The

Hughes, Howard Robard
American. Aviator, Industrialist
b. Dec 24, 1905 in Houston, Texas
d. Apr 5, 1976 in Houston, Texas
Source: *BiDFilm; CelR 73; CurBio 41; DcFM; EncAB-H; FilmgC; IntMPA 75; IntWW 74; OxFilm; WebAB; WhAm 6; WhoAm 74; WhoF&I 74; WhoWor 74; WorEFlm*

Hughes, (James) Langston
American. Poet, Author, Journalist
Expressed Negro view of America in *Shakespeare in Harlem,* 1942.
b. Feb 1, 1902 in Joplin, Missouri
d. May 22, 1967 in New York, New York
Source: *AmAu&B; AmSCAP 66; AnCL; AuBYP; BiE&WWA; BkCL; BlkAW; CnDAL; CnMD; ConAmA; ConAu 1R, 25R, 1NR; ConLC 1, 5, 10, 15; CroCD; CurBio 40, 67; DcLEL; EncAB-H; EncWL; LongCTC; McGEWD; ModAL, SUP; ModWD; OxAmL; Pen AM; RAdv 1; REn; REnAL; SixAP; SmATA 4; Str&VC; TwCA, SUP; WebAB; WebE&AL; WhAm 4; WhoTwCL*

Hughes, Mary Beth
American. Actress
b. 1919
Source: *FilmgC; MovMk; WhoHol A*

Hughes, Richard Arthur Warren
Welsh. Author, Dramatist
b. Apr 19, 1900 in Weybridge, England
d. Apr 28, 1976 in Merioneth, Wales
Source: *Au&Wr 71; CasWL; ChPo, S2; ConAu 5R; ConLC 1; ConNov 72, 76; CyWA; DcLEL; EncWL; EvLB; LongCTC; ModBrL, SUP; NewC; OxEng; Pen ENG; RAdv 1; REn; SmATA 8; TwCA, SUP; TwCW; WhoChL; WhoLA; WhoTwCL; WrDr 76*

Hughes, Robert Studley Forrest
Australian. Art Critic, Author
b. Jul 28, 1938 in Sydney, Australia
Source: *WhoAm 80*

Hughes, Rupert
American. Author
b. Jan 31, 1872 in Lancaster, Missouri
d. Sep 9, 1956 in Los Angeles, California
Source: *AmAu&B; AmSCAP 66; AnMV 1926; ChPo, S1, S2; ConAmL; DcAmAu; OhA&B; OxAmL; REnAL; TwCA, SUP; TwYS; WhAm 3; WhNAA; WhScrn 77*

Hughes, Ted
English. Poet
b. Aug 17, 1930 in Mytholmroyd, England
Source: *CasWL; ChPo, S1, S2; CnE&AP; ConAu 1R; ConLC 2, 4; ConP 70, 75; EncWL; IntWW 74; LongCTC; ModBrL, SUP; NewC; Pen ENG; RAdv 1; TwCW; WebE&AL; Who 74; WhoAm 82; WhoTwCL; WhoWor 74; WorAu; WrDr 76*

Hughes, Thomas
English. Reformer, Author
b. Oct 20, 1822 in Uffington, England
d. Mar 22, 1896 in Brighton, England
Source: *BrAu 19; CasWL; CyWA; DcEnA; DcLEL; NewC; OxEng; Pen ENG; REn*

Hugo, Adele
French. Daughter of Victor Hugo
b. 1830
d. 1915
Source: *BioIn 11*

Hugo, Victor Marie
French. Dramatist, Author
Best known for *Les Miserables*, 1862.
b. Feb 26, 1802 in Besancon, France
d. May 22, 1885 in Paris, France
Source: *AtlBL; BbD; BiD&SB; CasWL; ChPo, S1, S2; CnThe; CyWA; DcBiA; DcEnL; DcEuL; EncMys; EuAu; EvEuW; HsB&A; McGEWD; MnBBF; NewC; OxEng; OxFr; OxThe; Pen EUR; RComWL; REn; REnWD*

Huie, William Bradford
American. Author, Journalist
b. Nov 13, 1910 in Hartselle, Alabama
Source: *AmAu&B; Au&Wr 71; AuNews 1; ConAu 9R; ConNov 72, 76; REnAL; TwCA SUP; WhoAm 74, 76, 78, 80, 82; WhoS&SW 73; WhoWor 74; WrDr 76*

Huisman, Philippe
French. Art Historian
b. 1924
d. 1970
Source: *BioIn 9, 10*

Hulagu Khan
Mongolian. Ruler
b. 1217
d. 1265
Source: *NewCol 75; WebBD 80*

Hulce, Thomas
American. Actor
b. Dec 6, 1953 in Plymouth, Michigan
Source: *NF*

Hull, Bobby (Robert Martin)
Canadian. Hockey Player, Broadcaster
Scored 672 goals in career, third highest in NHL history.
b. Jan 3, 1939 in Point Anne, ON
Source: *CelR 73; CurBio 66; NewYTBE 73; WhoAm 74, 76, 78, 80, 82; WhoHcky 73; WhoMW 74*

Hull, Cordell
American. Statesman
b. Oct 2, 1871 in Overton County, Tennessee
d. Jul 23, 1955 in Bethesda, Maryland
Source: *BiDrAC; BiDrUSE; CurBio 40, 55; DcAmB S5; EncAB-H; WebAB; WhAm 3; WhAmP*

Hull, Henry
American. Actor
b. 1890 in Louisville, Kentucky
d. Mar 8, 1977 in Cornwall, England
Source: *BiE&WWA; Film 1; FilmgC; IntMPA 75, 76, 77; MotPP; NotNAT; PlP&P; TwYS; Vers A; WhoHol A; WhoThe 77*

Hull, Isaac
American. Military Leader
b. Mar 9, 1773 in Huntington, Connecticut
d. Dec 13, 1843 in Philadelphia, Pennsylvania
Source: *AmBi; ApCAB; DcAmB; REn; TwCBDA; WebAB; WhAm H*

Hull, John Edwin
American. Military Officer
b. May 26, 1895 in Greenfield, Ohio
d. Jun 10, 1975
Source: *BioIn 3, 4, 10; CurBio 54; IntWW 74; WhAm 6*

Hull, Josephine
[Josephine Sherwood]
American. Actress
b. 1884 in Newton, Massachusetts
d. Mar 12, 1957 in New York, New York
Source: *CurBio 53, 57; FilmgC; InWom; MotPP; MovMk; PlP&P; ThFT; Vers B; WhAm 3; WhScrn 74, 77; WhoHol B; WomWWA 14*

Hull, Warren
American. Actor, Singer
b. Jan 17, 1903 in Gasport, New York
d. Sep 21, 1974 in Waterbury, Connecticut
Source: *FilmgC; NewYTBS 74; WhScrn 77; WhoHol B*

Hulman, Tony (Anton), Jr.
American. Business, Sports Executive
President of Indianapolis Speedway who began each race saying "Gentlemen, start your engines."
b. Feb 11, 1901 in Terre Haute, Indiana
d. Oct 27, 1977 in Indianapolis, Indiana
Source: *BioIn 10, 11; St&PR 75*

Hulme, Kathryn Cavarly
American. Author
b. Jan 6, 1900 in San Francisco, California
d. Aug 25, 1981 in Lihue, Hawaii
Source: *BioIn 4, 6, 8; ConAu 104; ConAu P-1; WhoAm 74; WhoAmW 58, 61, 64, 66, 68, 70, 72, 74, 75, 77; WhoWor 74*

Hulme, Thomas Ernest
English. Philosopher
Led anti-Romantic movement called Imagism in early 1900's.
b. Sep 16, 1883 in Endon, England
d. Sep 28, 1917 in Belgium
Source: *BioIn 1, 5, 9, 10; OxEng; Pen ENG; REn*

Human League
[Ian Burden; Joe Callis; Joanne Catherall; Phil Oakey; Susanne Sulley; Adrian Wright]
English. Rock Group
Formed in 1977; hit single, 1982, "Don't You Want Me?" from album *Dare.*
Source: *IlEncRk*

Humbard, Rex
American. Evangelist
b. Aug 13, 1919 in Little Rock, Arkansas
Source: *CurBio 72; NewYTBE 73; WhoAm 82*

Humbert II
[Umberto II]
Italian. Deposed King
b. Sep 15, 1904
Source: *BioIn 1, 5, 8, 10*

Humble Pie
[David "Clem" Clemson; Peter Frampton; Steve Marriott; Gregory Ridley; Jerry Shirley]
English. Rock Group
Source: *ConMuA 80; IlEncRk; LilREn 78; RkOn 2; WhoRock 81*

Humboldt, Alexander, Freiherr von
German. Author, Scientist
b. Sep 14, 1769 in Berlin, Germany
d. May 6, 1859 in Berlin, Germany
Source: *BiD&SB; CasWL; DcEuL; EuAu; NewC; OxEng; OxGer; Pen EUR; REn*

Humboldt, Wilhelm von
German. Statesman, Author
b. Jun 22, 1767 in Potsdam, Germany
d. Apr 8, 1835 in Schloss Tegel, Germany
Source: *BiD&SB; CasWL; DcEuL; EuAu; OxGer; Pen EUR; REn*

Hume, Benita
English. Actress
b. Oct 14, 1906 in London, England
d. Nov 1, 1967 in Egerton, England
Source: *FilmgC; MotPP; MovMk; ThFT; WhScrn 74, 77; WhoHol B*

Hume, David
Scottish. Author, Philosopher, Historian
b. Apr 26, 1711 in Edinburgh, Scotland
d. Aug 25, 1776 in Edinburgh, Scotland
Source: *Alli; AtlBL; BbD; BiD&SB; BrAu; CasWL; Chambr 2; CyWA; DcEnA; DcEnL; DcEuL; DcLEL; EvLB; MouLC 2; NewC; OxEng; Pen ENG; REn; WebE&AL*

Humes, Harold Louis
American. Metallurgical Engineer
b. Jan 31, 1900 in Marquette, Michigan
Source: *WhAm 4*

Humes, Helen
American. Jazz Singer
b. Jun 23, 1913 in Louisville, Kentucky
d. Sep 13, 1981 in Santa Monica, California
Source: *BiDAmM; BioIn 4, 10; CmpEPM; EncJzS 70; WhoJazz 72*

Humes, James Calhoun
American. Lawyer
b. Oct 31, 1934 in Williamsport, Pennsylvania
Source: *ConAu 45; WhoAm 74, 76, 78, 80, 82; WhoGov 72; WhoS&SW 73*

Hummel, Berta
[Sister Maria Innocentia]
German. Artist
b. 1909 in Massing, Bavaria
d. 1946
Source: *BioIn 12*

Hummel, Johann Nepomuk
German. Composer
b. Nov 14, 1778 in Pressburg, Germany
d. Oct 17, 1837 in Weimar, Germany
Source: *OxMus*

Hummel, Lisl
Austrian. Illustrator
b. in Vienna, Austria
Source: *BioIn 1; ChPo; ConICB; IlsCB 1744*

Humperdinck, Engelbert
German. Composer
Wrote opera *Hansel and Gretel,* 1893.
b. Sep 1, 1854 in Siegburg, Germany
d. Sep 27, 1921 in Neustrelitz, Germany
Source: *AtlBL; OxGer; REn*

Humperdinck, Engelbert
[Gerry Dorsey]
English. Singer
Best selling albums *Release Me,* 1968, *A Man Without Love,* 1969.
b. May 3, 1936 in Madras, India
Source: *BkPepl; CelR 73; WhoAm 82; WhoWor 74*

Humphrey, Claude B
American. Football Player
b. Jun 29, 1944 in Memphis, Tennessee
Source: *WhoAm 74; WhoFtbl 74*

Humphrey, Doris
American. Dancer
b. Oct 17, 1895 in Oak Park, Illinois
d. Dec 29, 1958
Source: *CurBio 42, 59; InWom; WhAm 3*

Humphrey, Elliott
American. Animal Trainer
b. 1889 in Saratoga Springs, New York
d. Jun 6, 1981 in Phoenix, Arizona
Source: *NewYTBS 81*

Humphrey, George Magoffin
American. Statesman
b. Mar 8, 1890 in Cheboygan, Michigan
d. Jan 20, 1970 in Cleveland, Ohio
Source: *CurBio 53, 70; NewYTBE 70*

Humphrey, Gordon John
American. Senator
b. Oct 9, 1940 in Bristol, Connecticut
Source: *AlmAP 80; CngDr 79; NewYTBS 78; WhoAm 80, 82; WhoAmP 79; WhoE 79*

Humphrey, Hubert Horatio, Jr.
American. Politician
Mayor of Minneapolis, 1945-48; US senator, 1948-64, 1970-78; vice-president, 1964-68.
b. May 27, 1911 in Wallace, South Dakota
d. Jan 13, 1978 in Waverly, Minnesota
Source: *BiDrAC; BiDrUSE; CelR 73; ConAu 69, 73; CurBio 49, 66; IntWW 74; Who 74; WhoAm 74; WhoGov 72; WhoMW 74; WhoWor 74*

Humphrey, Muriel Fay Buck
[Mrs. Hubert Humphrey]
American. Former Senator
Completed husband's final senate term, 1978-79.
b. Feb 20, 1912 in Huron, South Dakota
Source: *WhoAm 74, 76, 78, 80, 82; WhoMW 74*

Humphreys, Christmas
English. Author, Jurist
b. Feb 15, 1901 in London, England
Source: *Au&Wr 71; ChPo S1, S2; ConAu 77; IntWW 74; Who 74; WhoWor 74*

Humphreys, Joshua
American. Naval Architect
b. Jun 17, 1751 in Delaware County, Delaware
d. Jan 12, 1838 in Haverford, Pennsylvania
Source: *BioIn 3; WebAB*

Humphreys, Noel
English. Physician, Explorer
b. 1883
d. 1966
Source: *BioIn 7*

Humphries, (George) Rolfe
American. Poet
b. Nov 20, 1894 in Philadelphia, Pennsylvania
d. Apr 22, 1969 in Redwood City, California
Source: *BioIn 8; ChPo S1; CnDAL; ConAu 5R, 25R, 3NR; OxAmL; RAdv 1; REnAL; TwCA, SUP; WhAm 5*

Humphries, Stefan
American. Football Player
b. Jan 20, 1962 in Broward, Florida
Source: *BioIn 12*

Hunndertwasser, Friedrich
Austrian. Artist
b. Dec 15, 1928 in Vienna, Austria
Source: *ConArt; IntWW 74, 75, 76, 77, 78; WhoWor 74, 78*

Huneker, James Gibbons
American. Critic, Author
b. Jan 31, 1860 in Philadelphia, Pennsylvania
d. Feb 9, 1921 in New York, New York
Source: *AmAu&B; AmBi; CnDAL; ConAmL; DcAmAu; DcAmB; DcLEL; DcNAA; LongCTC; OxAmL; OxThe; Pen AM; RAdv 1; REn; REnAL; TwCA, SUP; WebAB; WhAm 1*

Hung-Li
see: Ch'ien Lung

Hung Wu
see: Ming T'ai-Tsu

Hunnicutt, Arthur
American. Actor
b. Feb 17, 1911 in Gravelly, Arkansas
Source: *CmMov; FilmgC; IntMPA 75, 76, 77; MovMk; Vers A; WhoHol A*

Hunnicutt, Gayle
American. Actress
b. 1942 in Texas
Source: *FilmgC; IntMPA 82; WhoAm 74; WhoHol A*

Hunsaker, Jerome Clarke
American. Aeronautical Engineer
b. Aug 26, 1886 in Creston, Louisiana
Source: *AmM&WS 73P; CurBio 42; IntWW 74; WebAB; WhoAm 74*

Hunt, E(verette) Howard
American. Watergate Participant, Author
Consultant to Richard Nixon, 1971-72; jailed for involvement in Watergate, 1973-74, 1975-77.
b. Oct 9, 1918 in Hamburg, New York
Source: *AmAu&B; ConAu 45, 2NR; ConLC 3; WhoAm 74, 76, 78, 80, 82*

Hunt, Frazier
"Spike"
American. Journalist
b. Dec 1, 1885 in Rock Island, Illinois
d. Dec 24, 1967 in Newtown, Pennsylvania
Source: *AmAu&B; ConAu 93; WhAm 4*

Hunt, George Wylie Paul
American. Politician, Statesman
b. Nov 1, 1859 in Huntsville, Maryland
d. Dec 24, 1934
Source: *BioIn 1, 6, 8, 10; WhAm 1*

Hunt, H(aroldson) L(afayette)
American. Oil Executive
Billionaire who at height of wealth had a weekly income of over $1 million.
b. Feb 17, 1889 in Vandalia, Illinois
d. Nov 29, 1974 in Dallas, Texas
Source: *BusPN; CelR 73; CurBio 70, 75; EncAB-H; NewYTBS 74; WebAB; WhAm 6; WhoAm 74*

Hunt, James
English. Auto Racer
b. 1947 in Epsom, England
Source: *BioIn 11*

Hunt, Lamar
American. Football Executive
Owner, Kansas City Chiefs, 1959--; founder, first president, AFL, 1959.
b. Aug 2, 1932 in Dallas, Texas
Source: *CelR 73; WhoAm 74, 76, 78, 80, 82; WhoFtbl 74*

Hunt, Leigh
English. Author, Poet
b. Oct 19, 1784 in Southgate, England
d. Aug 28, 1859 in Putney, England
Source: *Alli; AtlBL; BiD&SB; BrAu 19; CnE&AP; CrtT 2; DcEuL; NewC; OxThe; Pen ENG; RAdv 1; REn; WebE&AL*

Hunt, Lois
American. Actress, Singer
b. Nov 26, 1925 in York, Pennsylvania
Source: *WhoAm 74*

Hunt, Marsha
American. Actress
b. Oct 17, 1917 in Chicago, Illinois
Source: *BiE&WWA; FilmgC; IntMPA 75, 76, 77; MotPP; MovMk; NotNAT; ThFT; WhoAm 82; WhoHol A; WhoThe 77*

Hunt, Martita
English. Actress
b. 1900 in Argentina
d. Jun 13, 1969 in London, England
Source: *BiE&WWA; FilmgC; MotPP; MovMk; Vers A; WhScrn 74, 77; WhoHol B*

Hunt, Nelson Bunker
"Bunky"
American. Business Executive
Played prominent role in silver crash of March 27, 1980.
b. Feb 22, 1926 in El Dorado, Texas
Source: *BioIn 10, 11, 12; CurBio 80*

Hunt, Richard Morris
American. Architect
b. Oct 31, 1828 in Brattleboro, Vermont
d. Jul 31, 1896 in Newport, Rhode Island
Source: *Alli SUP; AmBi; ApCAB; DcAmB; Drake; OxAmL; TwCBDA; WebAB; WhAm H*

Hunt, Walter
American. Inventor
Invented the safety pin, fountain pen, and other practical items.
b. Jul 29, 1796 in Martinsburg, New York
d. Jun 8, 1859 in New York, New York
Source: *NatCAB 19; WebAB*

Hunt, (William) Holman
English. Artist
b. Apr 2, 1827 in London, England
d. Sep 7, 1910 in London, England
Source: *AtlBL; BioIn 3, 4, 6, 8, 9, 10, 11; NewCol 75; REn*

Hunt, William Morris
American. Artist
b. Mar 31, 1824 in Brattleboro, Vermont
d. Sep 8, 1879
Source: *AmBi; ApCAB; DcAmB; DcNAA; Drake; OxAmL; TwCBDA; WebAB; WhAm H*

Hunter, Alberta
American. Singer, Songwriter
b. Apr 1, 1897 in Memphis, Tennessee
Source: *AmSCAP 66; WhoJazz 72*

Hunter, Bobby Lee
American. Boxer
b. 1950
Source: *NewYTBE 71*

Hunter, "Catfish" (James Augustus)
American. Baseball Player
Pitched perfect game versus Minnesota, May 8, 1968.
b. Apr 8, 1946 in Hertford, North Carolina
Source: *BaseEn; WhoAm 74, 76, 78, 80, 82; WhoProB 73*

Hunter, Dard
American. Printer, Papermaker
b. Nov 29, 1883 in Steubenville, Ohio
d. Feb 20, 1966
Source: *AmAu&B; ConAu 25R; ConAu P-1; CurBio 60, 66; OhA&B; OxAmL; REnAL; WhNAA*

Hunter, Evan
[Ed McBain, pseud.]
American. Author
b. Oct 15, 1926 in New York, New York
Source: *AmAu&B; AmSCAP 66; AuBYP; ConAu 5R; ConLC 11; CurBio 56; IntWW 74; Pen AM; REn; REnAL; WhoAm 74, 76, 78, 80, 82*

Hunter, Glenn
American. Actor
b. 1897 in Highland, New York
d. Dec 30, 1945 in New York, New York
Source: *CurBio 46; FilmgC; MotPP; TwYS; WhScrn 74, 77; WhoHol B*

Hunter, Ian
South African. Actor, Screenwriter
b. Jun 13, 1900 in Capetown, South Africa
d. Sep 24, 1975 in England
Source: *Film 2; FilmgC; IntMPA 75; MotPP; MovMk; WhScrn 77; WhThe*

Hunter, Ian
[Mott the Hoople]
English. Rock Singer, Musician
b. Jun 3, 1946 in Shrewsbury, England
Source: *ConMuA 80; IlEncRk; LilREn 78; WhoRock 81*

Hunter, "Ivory" Joe
American. Singer
b. 1911 in Kirbyville, Texas
d. Nov 8, 1974 in Memphis, Tennessee
Source: *BiDAmM; EncFCWM 69; RkOn; WhoRock 81*

Hunter, Jeffrey
American. Actor
b. Nov 23, 1926 in New Orleans, Louisiana
d. May 27, 1969 in Van Nuys, California
Source: *BiDFilm; FilmgC; MovMk; WhScrn 74, 77; WhoHol B; WorEFlm*

Hunter, John
English. Surgeon, Anatomist
b. Feb 13, 1728 in Long Calderwood, Scotland
d. Oct 16, 1793 in London, England
Source: *Alli; NewC; OxEng*

Hunter, Kim
[Janet Cole]
American. Actress
b. Nov 12, 1922 in Detroit, Michigan
Source: *BiE&WWA; ConAu 61; CurBio 52; FilmgC; InWom; IntMPA 75, 76, 77, 78, 79, 80, 81, 82; MotPP; MovMk; NotNAT; WhoAm 74, 76, 78, 80, 82; WhoHol A; WhoThe 77; WhoWor 74*

Hunter, Ross
[Martin Fuss]
American. Motion Picture Producer
b. May 6, 1924 in Cleveland, Ohio
Source: *CelR 73; CmMov; CurBio 67; FilmgC; IntMPA 75, 76, 77, 78, 79, 80, 81, 82; MotPP; WhoAm 74, 76, 78, 80, 82; WhoHol A; WhoWor 74; WorEFlm*

Hunter, Tab
[Arthur Gelien]
American. Actor
Made film debut at age 18 with no previous acting experience.
b. Jul 11, 1931 in New York, New York
Source: *FilmgC; IntMPA 75, 76, 77, 78, 79, 80, 81, 82; MotPP; MovMk; WhoHol A*

Hunter, Thomas
Irish. Educator
b. Oct 19, 1831 in Ardglass, Ireland
d. Oct 14, 1915
Source: *DcNAA; WhAm 4*

Hunter, William
Scottish. Surgeon, Scientist
b. 1718
d. 1783
Source: *Alli; BioIn 1, 2, 3, 4, 6, 7, 9, 11; DcEnL; NewC*

Huntington, Collis Potter
American. Railroad Builder
b. Oct 22, 1821 in Harwinton, Connecticut
d. Aug 13, 1900 in Raquette Lake, New York
Source: *NewCol 75; WebAB; WebBD 80*

Huntington, Daniel
American. Artist
b. Oct 14, 1816 in New York, New York
d. 1906
Source: *AmBi; ApCAB; BioIn 7, 11; BnEnAmA; DcAmB; Drake; EarABI; NatCAB 5; TwCBDA; WhAm 1*

Huntington, Henry Edwards
American. Railroad Official, Philanthropist
b. Feb 27, 1850 in Oneonta, New York
d. May 23, 1927 in Philadelphia, Pennsylvania
Source: *AmBi; BioIn 1, 2, 6; DcAmB; LinLib S; WebAB; WhAm 1*

Huntington, Henry S, Jr.
American. Pioneered Organized Nudism
b. 1882 in Gorham, Maine
d. Feb 16, 1981 in Philadelphia, Pennsylvania
Source: *NewYTBS 81*

Huntington, Samuel
American. Jurist
b. Jul 3, 1731 in Windham, Connecticut
d. Jan 5, 1796 in Norwich, Connecticut
Source: *AmBi; ApCAB; BiAuS; BiDrAC; BiDrUSE; DcAmB; Drake; TwCBDA; WhAm H; WhAmP*

Huntley, Chet (Chester Robert)
American. Broadcast Journalist
Teamed with David Brinkley for nightly newscasts, 1956-70; author *The Generous Years,* 1968.
b. Dec 10, 1911 in Cardwell, Montana
d. Mar 20, 1974 in Bozeman, Montana
Source: *AuNews 1; CelR 73; ConAu 49, 97; CurBio 56, 74; NewYTBE 70; NewYTBS 74; WhAm 6; WhScrn 77; WhoAm 74; WhoHol B; WhoWor 74*

Huntley, Joni
American. Track Athlete
b. Aug 4, 1956 in McMinnville, Oregon
Source: *BioIn 11*

Hunyadi, Janos
[John Huniades]
Hungarian. National Hero
b. 1385?
d. 1465
Source: *NewCol 75; WebBD 80*

Huppert, Isabelle
French. Actress
b. Mar 16, 1955 in Paris, France
Source: *BioIn 11; CurBio 81; FilmEn*

Hurd, Peter
American. Artist, Illustrator
b. Feb 22, 1904 in Roswell, New Mexico
Source: *ConICB; CurBio 57; IlsCB 1744; WhoAm 74, 76, 78, 80, 82; WhoAmA 73; WhoWor 74*

Hurkos, Peter
[Peter Van der Hurk]
Dutch. Psychic
b. 1911
Source: *BioIn 6, 9, 11; BioNews 74*

Hurley, Patrick Jay
American. Lawyer, Diplomat
b. Jan 8, 1883 in Oklahoma
d. Jul 30, 1963 in Santa Fe, New Mexico
Source: *BiDrUSE; CurBio 44, 63; WhAm 4*

Hurok, Sol
Russian. Impresario, Author
b. Apr 9, 1888 in Pogar, Russia
d. Mar 5, 1974 in New York, New York
Source: *BiE&WWA; BioNews 74; CelR 73; ConAu 49; NewYTBE 73; NewYTBS 74; WebAB; WhAm 6; Who 74; WhoAm 74; WhoWor 74; WhoWorJ 72*

Hurrell, George
American. Photographer
b. 1904? in Chicago, Illinois
Source: *BioIn 12*

Hurson, Martin
[Irish Hunger Strikers]
Irish. Jailed IRA Member
b. Sep 13, 1954 in Cappagh, Northern Ireland
d. Jul 13, 1981 in Belfast, Northern Ireland
Source: *BioIn 12*

Hurst, Fannie
American. Author
b. Oct 19, 1889 in Hamilton, Ohio
d. Feb 23, 1968 in New York, New York
Source: *AmAu&B; AmLY; AmNov; ChPo; ConAmA; ConAmL; ConAu 25R; ConAu P-1; DcBiA; EvLB; FilmgC; InWom; LongCTC; OhA&B; OxAmL; REn; REnAL; TwCA, SUP; TwCW; WhNAA*

Hurst, George
Scottish. Orchestra Conductor
b. May 20, 1926 in Edinburgh, Scotland
Source: *Who 74; WhoMus 72*

Hurston, Zora Neale
American. Anthropologist, Author
b. Jan 7, 1903 in Eatonville, Florida
d. Jan 28, 1960 in Fort Pierce, Florida
Source: *AmAu&B; AmNov; BlkAW; ConAu 85; ConLC 7; CurBio 42, 60; InWom; OxAmL; REnAL; TwCA, SUP; WhAm 3*

Hurt, John
English. Actor
Starred in *The Elephant Man,* 1980.
b. Jan 22, 1940 in Chesterfield, England
Source: *BioIn 12; CurBio 82; IntMPA 82; WhoAm 82; WhoThe 77, 81*

Hurt, Mississippi John
American. Singer, Musician
b. Mar 8, 1892 in Teoc, Mississippi
d. Nov 2, 1966 in Grenada, Mississippi
Source: *EncFCWM 69*

Hurt, William
American. Actor
Starred in movies *Eyewitness, Altered States,* and *Body Heat.*
b. Mar 20, 1950 in Washington, DC
Source: *IntMPA 82; WhoAm 82*

Hus, Jan
[John Huss]
Czech. Religious Reformer
b. 1369 in Husinec, Czechoslovakia
d. Jul 6, 1415 in Constance, Germany
Source: *CasWL; DcEuL; EuAu; EvEuW; NewC; Pen EUR; REn*

Husak, Gustav
Czech. President
b. Jan 10, 1913 in Bratislava, Czechoslovakia
Source: *BioIn 8, 9, 11; CurBio 71; IntWW 74; NewYTBE 71; WhoWor 74*

Husayn Ali
see: Baha'u'llah

Husch, Gerhard
German. Opera Singer
b. Feb 2, 1901 in Hannover, Germany
Source: *WhoMus 72*

Husing, Ted
American. Sports Announcer
b. Nov 27, 1901 in Bronx, New York
d. Aug 10, 1962 in Pasadena, California
Source: *CurBio 42, 62; WhScrn 77; WhoHol B*

Huskisson, William
English. Statesman
b. 1770 in Worcestershire, England
d. Sep 15, 1830 in England
Source: *Alli; BiDLA*

Husky, Ferlin
American. Singer
b. Dec 3, 1927 in Flat River, Missouri
Source: *EncFCWM 69; WhoAm 74, 76, 78, 80, 82*

Hussain al Takriti, Saddam
[Saddam Husayn al Tikriti]
Iraqi. President
b. Apr 28, 1937 in Tikrit, Iraq
Source: *BioIn 12; IntWW 74; NewYTBS 82*

Hussein (Ibn Talal)
Jordanian. King
b. Nov 14, 1935 in Jordan
Source: *BioIn 2, 3, 4, 5, 6, 7, 8, 9, 10, 11, 12; IntWW 77; WhoWor 78*

Hussein, Saddam
Iraqi. President
Has served as president since 1979.
b. 1937 in Tikrit, Iraq
Source: *IntWW 77, 78, 79, 80; WhoWor 78, 80*

Hussein, Taha
Egyptian. Educator, Author
b. Nov 14, 1889 in Maghagha, Egypt
d. Oct 28, 1973 in Cairo, Egypt
Source: *BioIn 1, 2, 3, 4, 5, 10; ConAu 45; CurBio 53, 73; NewYTBE 73; WhoWor 74*

Husseini, Haj Amin
Palestinian. Political Leader
b. 1893 in Jerusalem, Palestine
d. Jul 4, 1974 in Beirut, Lebanon
Source: *IntWW 74; NewYTBE 71; NewYTBS 74; WhoWor 74*

Husserl, Edmund
German. Philosopher
b. Apr 8, 1859 in Prossnitz, Czechoslovakia
d. Apr 27, 1938
Source: *REn; WorAu*

Hussey, Olivia
English. Actress
Starred as Juliet in screen version of *Romeo and Juliet,* 1969.
b. 1952 in Buenos Aires, Argentina
Source: *FilmgC; MotPP; WhoHol A*

Hussey, Ruth
American. Actress
b. Oct 30, 1915 in Providence, Rhode Island
Source: *BiE&WWA; FilmgC; MotPP; MovMk; NotNAT; ThFT; WhoAm 74, 76, 78, 80, 82; WhoHol A; WhoThe 77*

Huston, John
American. Actor, Director, Writer
Won Oscar, 1948, for *Treasure of the Sierra Madre,* 1948; also directed *The African Queen,* 1952.
b. Aug 5, 1906 in Nevada, Missouri
Source: *BiDFilm; CelR 73; ConAu 73; ConDr 73; DcFM; FilmgC; IntMPA 77, 78, 79, 80, 81, 82; IntWW 74; MovMk; OxFilm; REnAL; WebAB; Who 74; WhoAm 74, 76, 78, 80, 82; WhoWor 74; WorEFlm*

Huston, Walter
American. Actor
b. Apr 6, 1884 in Toronto, ON
d. Apr 7, 1950 in Beverly Hills, California
Source: *BiDFilm; CurBio 49, 50; DcAmB S4; EncMT; FamA&A; FilmgC; MotPP; MovMk; OxFilm; PlP&P; WebAB; WhAm 4; WhScrn 74, 77; WhoHol B; WorEFlm*

Hutcheson, Francis
Scottish. Philosopher
b. Aug 8, 1694 in Saintfield, Northern Ireland
d. 1746
Source: *Alli; BiD&SB; BioIn 3, 7; BrAu; CasWL; Chambr 2; DcEnA*

Hutchins, Bobby
[Our Gang]
"Wheezer"
American. Actor
Source: *Film 2*

Hutchins, Robert Maynard
American. Lawyer, Educator
b. Jan 17, 1899 in Brooklyn, New York
d. May 14, 1977 in Santa Barbara, California
Source: *AmAu&B; CelR 73; ConAu 69; CurBio 40, 54; EncAB-H; IntWW 74; OxAmL; REnAL; WebAB; WhNAA; Who 74; WhoAm 74; WhoWor 74*

Hutchins, Will
American. Actor
b. 1932
Source: *FilmgC; WhoHol A*

Hutchins, William
see: Tyndale, William

Hutchinson, Anne
[Anne Marbury]
English. Religious Leader
Belief in covenant of grace opposed Puritan covenant of works, led to banishment from MA Bay, 1637.
b. 1591 in Alford, England
d. Aug 1643 in Long Island, New York
Source: *AmBi; ApCAB; BiCAW; DcAmB; Drake; EncAB-H; HerW; InWom; NotAW; OxAmL; REn; REnAL; TwCBDA; WebAB; WhAm H; WhAmP*

Hutchinson, Fred(erick Charles)
"Big Bear"
American. Baseball Player, Manager
Pitcher, Detroit Tigers, 1939-1953; manager, Detroit, 1952-54, 1956-64.
b. Aug 12, 1919 in Seattle, Washington
d. Nov 12, 1964 in Bradenton, Florida
Source: *BaseEn; BioIn 6, 7; WhoProB 73*

Hutchinson, Josephine
American. Actress
b. Oct 12, 1916 in Seattle, Washington
Source: *BiE&WWA; NotNAT; WhoThe 77*

Hutchinson, Thomas
English. Loyalist, Governor of MA
b. Sep 9, 1711 in Boston, Massachusetts
d. Jun 3, 1780 in Brompton, England
Source: *Alli; AmAu; AmAu&B; AmBi; ApCAB; CyAL 1; DcAmAu; DcAmB; DcNAA; Drake; EncAB-H; OxAmL; Pen AM; REnAL; TwCBDA; WebAB; WhAm H*

Hutt, William Ian Dewitt
Canadian. Actor, Motion Picture Director
b. May 2, 1920 in Toronto, ON
Source: *CanWW 70, 79; CreCan 1; WhoAm 82; WhoThe 77*

Hutter, Ralf
see: Kraftwerk

Hutton, Addison
American. Quaker Leader, Architect
b. 1834
d. 1916
Source: *BioIn 5, 10*

Hutton, Barbara
American. Heiress
b. Nov 14, 1912 in New York, New York
d. May 11, 1979 in Los Angeles, California
Source: *BioIn 3, 5, 8, 10; CelR 73; InWom; NewYTBS 79; WhAm 7*

Hutton, Betty
[Betty Thornburg]
American. Actress
b. Feb 26, 1921 in Battle Creek, Michigan
Source: *BiE&WWA; CmMov; CurBio 50; FilmgC; InWom; IntMPA 75, 76, 77, 78, 79, 80, 81, 82; MotPP; MovMk; OxFilm; WhoHol A*

Hutton, Edward F
American. Investment Banker
b. 1877 in New York, New York
d. Jul 11, 1962 in Westbury, New York
Source: *BioIn 2, 5, 6; WhAm 4*

Hutton, Ina Ray
American. Band Leader, Singer
b. Mar 3, 1916 in Chicago, Illinois
Source: *WhoJazz 72*

Hutton, James
Scottish. Geologist
b. Jun 3, 1726 in Edinburgh, Scotland
d. Mar 26, 1797
Source: *Alli; BiDLA, SUP; DcEnL; McGEWB*

Hutton, Jim
American. Actor
Starred in films *Where the Boys Are,* 1960; *The Trouble with Angels,* 1966; father of Timothy Hutton.
b. May 31, 1938 in Binghamton, New York
d. Jun 2, 1979 in Los Angeles, California
Source: *FilmgC; IntMPA 77; MotPP; MovMk; WhoHol A*

Hutton, (Mary) Lauren(ce)
American. Model, Actress
b. Nov 17, 1944 in Charleston, South Carolina
Source: *BioIn 11, 12; BioNews 75; BkPepl; IntMPA 82; WhoHol A*

Hutton, Robert
[Robert Winne]
American. Actor
b. Jun 11, 1920 in Kingston, New York
Source: *FilmgC; HolP 40; IntMPA 75, 76, 77, 78, 79, 80, 81, 82; WhoHol A*

Hutton, Timothy James
American. Actor
Won Oscar, 1980, for *Ordinary People,* 1980; starred in *Taps,* 1981.
b. Aug 16, 1960 in Malibu, California
Source: *IntMPA 82*

Huxley, Aldous Leonard
English. Author, Critic
Best known for *Brave New World,* 1932, *Brave New World Revisited,* 1958.
b. Jul 26, 1894 in Godalming, England
d. Nov 22, 1963 in Los Angeles, California
Source: *AmAu&B; AtlBL; BiDPara; CasWL; Chambr 3; ChPo, S1, S2; CnMD; CnMWL; ConAu 85; ConLC 1, 3, 4, 5, 8, 11, 18; CyWA; DcLEL; EncWL; EvLB; LongCTC; ModBrL, SUP; ModWD; NewC; OxEng; Pen ENG; RAdv 1; REn; TwCA, SUP; TwCW; WebE&AL; WhAm 4; WhoTwCL*

Huxley, Andrew Fielding
English. Scientist, Educator
b. Nov 22, 1917 in London, England
Source: *IntWW 74; Who 74; WhoAm 74, 76, 78, 80, 82; WhoWor 74*

Huxley, Elspeth Josceline Grant
English. Author
b. Jul 23, 1907 in London, England
Source: *ConAu 77; DcLEL; EncMys; IntWW 74; LongCTC; TwCW; Who 74; WhoAmW 74; WhoWor 74; WorAu; WrDr 76*

Huxley, Sir Julian Sorell
English. Biologist, Author
b. Jun 22, 1887 in London, England
d. Feb 14, 1975 in London, England
Source: *Au&Wr 71; Chambr 3; ConAu 9R, 57; CurBio 42, 63; DcLEL; EvLB; IntWW 74; LongCTC; NewC; OxEng; OxFilm; Pen ENG; REn; TwCA, SUP; TwCW; WhAm 6; Who 74; WhoLA; WhoUN 75; WhoWor 74*

Huxley, Laura Archera
Italian. Author
b. in Turin, Italy
Source: *AmAu&B; ConAu 13R; NewYTBE 71*

Huxley, Thomas Henry
English. Biologist, Teacher, Author
Defended Darwinism in *Man's Palce in Nature,* 1863.
b. May 4, 1825 in Ealing, England
d. Jun 29, 1895 in Eastbourne, England
Source: *Alli, SUP; AtlBL; BbD; BiD&SB; BrAu 19; CasWL; Chambr 3; ChPo S2; CrtT 3; CyWA; DcEnA, AP; DcEnL; DcEuL; DcLEL; EvLB; MouLC 4; NewC; OxEng; Pen ENG; REn; WebE&AL*

Huxtable, Ada Louise
[Ada Louise Landman]
American. Critic, Editor
b. 1921 in New York, New York
Source: *CelR 73; CurBio 73; WhoAm 74, 76, 78, 80, 82; WhoAmA 73; WhoE 74*

Huygens, Christian
Dutch. Physicist, Astronomer
Discovered rings of Saturn, 1655; developed wave theory of light, 1678.
b. Apr 14, 1629 in The Hague, Netherlands
d. Jun 8, 1695
Source: *AsBiEn; DcEuL; DcScB; McGEWB; NewCol 75; WebBD 80*

Huysmans, Joris Karl
[Charles Marie Georges]
French. Author
b. Feb 5, 1848 in Paris, France
d. May 12, 1907 in Paris, France
Source: *AtlBL; BbD; BiD&SB; CasWL; ClDMEL; CyWA; EncWL; EvEuW; ModRL; OxFr; REn; WhoTwCL*

Hyams, Joe (Joseph)
American. Journalist, Author
b. Jun 6, 1923 in Cambridge, Massachusetts
Source: *AmAu&B; ConAu 17R; WhoAm 82; WrDr 76*

Hyde-White, Wilfrid
English. Actor
b. May 12, 1903 in Glos, England
Source: *BiE&WWA; FilmgC; IntMPA 75, 76, 77; MovMk; NotNAT; OxFilm; Who 74; WhoAm 82; WhoHol A; WhoThe 77*

Hyer, Martha
American. Actress
b. Apr 10, 1926 in Fort Worth, Texas
Source: *FilmgC; IntMPA 75, 76, 77, 78, 79, 80, 81, 82; MotPP; MovMk; WhoAm 82; WhoAmW 77; WhoHol A*

Hyland, Brian
American. Singer
b. Nov 12, 1943 in Woodhaven, New York
Source: *RkOn; WhoRock 81*

Hyland, Diana
American. Actress
Played Joan Bradford on TV series "Eight is Enough"; died after first season.
b. 1936 in Cleveland Heights, Ohio
d. Mar 27, 1977 in Los Angeles, California
Source: *BiE&WWA; WhoAm 74; WhoHol A*

Hyman, Earle
American. Actor
b. Oct 11, 1926 in Rocky Mount, North Carolina
Source: *BiE&WWA; NotNAT; WhoHol A; WhoThe 77*

Hynde, Chrissie
[The Pretenders]
American. Singer, Songwriter
b. 1951? in Akron, Ohio
Source: *BioIn 12*

Hynek, J(oseph) Allen
American. Astronomer
Consultant to US Air Force on UFO's; author *The UFO Experience,* 1951.
b. May 1, 1910 in Chicago, Illinois
Source: *AmM&WS 73P; BioIn 7, 8, 10; CurBio 68; WhoAm 74; WhoWor 74*

Hynes, John B
American. Politician
b. 1898
d. Jan 6, 1970 in Boston, Massachusetts
Source: *NewYTBE 70; WhAm 5*

Hypatia
Alexandrian. Philosopher, Mathematician
d. 415
Source: *NewCol 75*

Hyperides
Greek. Statesman, Orator
b. 389BC
d. 323BC
Source: *CasWL*

Hyslop, James Hervey
American. Philosopher
b. Aug 18, 1854 in Xenia, Ohio
d. Jun 17, 1920
Source: *AmAu&B; AmLY; BiDPara; DcAmAu; DcNAA; OhA&B*

I

Iacocca, Lee (Lido Anthony)
American. Automobile Executive
Chairman, chief executive, Chrysler Corp, 1979--.
b. Oct 15, 1924 in Allentown, Pennsylvania
Source: *BioNews 74; BusPN; CelR 73; CurBio 71; IntWW 74; NewYTBE 71; St&PR 75; Ward 77; WhoAm 74, 76, 78, 80, 82; WhoF&I 74; WhoMW 74, 76, 78; WhoWor 74*

Iakovos, Archbishop
Greek. Orthodox Prelate
b. Jul 29, 1911
Source: *BioIn 9; CurBio 60; WhoAm 82*

Ian, Janis
[Janis Fink]
American. Singer, Songwriter
Won Grammy, 1975, for "At Seventeen."
b. May 7, 1950 in New York, New York
Source: *BioIn 7, 8, 10, 11; BkPepl; EncPR&S; RkOn; WhoAm 82*

Ian and Sylvia
[Sylvia Fricker; Ian Tyson]
Canadian. Singing Duo
Source: *EncFCWM 69*

Iba, Henry P
American. Basketball Coach
b. Aug 6, 1904 in Easton, Missouri
Source: *BioIn 8, 9, 10; WhoBbl 73*

Ibarruri, Dolores
"La Pasionaria"
Spanish. Revolutionary
b. Dec 9, 1895 in Gallarta, Spain
Source: *CurBio 67; InWom*

Ibert, Jacques
French. Composer, Opera Director
b. Aug 15, 1890 in Paris, France
d. Feb 5, 1962 in Paris, France
Source: *DcFM; DcCM; NewCol 75; OxFilm; WhAm 4; WorEFlm*

Ibn Batutah
[Muhammad ibn 'abd Allah]
Arabian. Traveler
b. 1304? in Tangiers, Morocco
d. 1378? in Fez, Morocco
Source: *BiD&SB; NewC; NewCol 75*

Ibn-Saud
Saudi. King
b. 1880 in Riyadh, Saudi Arabia
d. Nov 9, 1953 in Saudi Arabia
Source: *BioIn 1, 2, 3, 4, 7, 11; CurBio 43, 54; NewCol 75; WebBD 80*

Ibsen, Henrik
Norwegian. Dramatist, Author
Depicted 19th c. women in *A Doll's House,* 1879; *Hedda Gabler,* 1890.
b. Mar 20, 1828 in Skien, Norway
d. May 23, 1906 in Christiania, Norway
Source: *AtlBL; BbD; BiD&SB; CasWL; ClDMEL; CnMD; CnThe; CyWA; DcEuL; EncWL; EuAu; EvEuW; LongCTC; McGEWD; ModWD; NewC; OxEng; OxGer; Pen EUR; RComWL; REn; REnWD*

Ichikawa, Fusae
Japanese. Feminist, Politician
Founded Woman's Suffrage League of Japan; elected to Parliament, 1953-71; 1974-81.
b. 1893 in Aichi Prefecture, Japan
d. Feb 11, 1981 in Tokyo, Japan
Source: *AnObit 1981; NewYTBS 81*

Ickes, Harold LeClair
American. Public Official
b. Mar 15, 1874 in Blair County, Pennsylvania
d. Feb 3, 1952 in Washington, DC
Source: *AmAu&B; BiDrUSE; CurBio 41, 52; DcAmB S5; EncAB-H; REnAL; WebAB; WhAm 3*

Idle, Eric
[Monty Python's Flying Circus]
British. Actor, Author
b. Mar 29, 1943
Source: *BioIn 10*

Igoe, "Hype" (Herbert A)
American. Sportswriter, Cartoonist
b. Jun 13, 1885
d. Feb 11, 1954 in New York, New York
Source: *CurBio 45*

Ike, Reverend
[Frederick Joseph Eikerenkoetter II]
American. Evangelist
b. Jun 1, 1935 in Ridgeland, South Carolina
Source: *BioIn 10, 11; BkPepl; EncO&P 78; WhoAm 78*

Ike and Tina Turner
American. Singing Group
Source: *BiDAmM; CelR 73; EncPR&S; IlEncRk; Rk100*

Ikhnaton, Pharaoh
[Akhenaton]
Egyptian. Pharaoh of Ancient Egypt
b. 1372BC
d. 1354BC
Source: *NewC; NewCol 75*

Ileana
Romanian. Princess, Nurse
b. 1904
Source: *InWom*

Ilg, Frances Lillian
American. Author, Physician, Educator
b. Oct 11, 1902 in Oak Park, Illinois
d. Jul 26, 1981 in Manitowish Waters, Wisconsin
Source: *AmAu&B; BioIn 4; ConAu 104; CurBio 56, 81; InWom; NewYTBS 81; WhoAmW 58, 64, 66, 74*

Ilitch, Mike
American. Businessman, Pizza Entrepreneur
Owner, Detroit Red Wings pro hockey team, Little Ceasar's pizza franchises.
b. Jul 20, 1929 in Detroit, Michigan
Source: *NF*

Illich, Ivan
American. Educator, Social Critic
b. Sep 4, 1926 in Vienna, Austria
Source: *AuNews 2; ConAu 53; CurBio 69; WhoAm 74, 76, 78, 80, 82; WhoS&SW 73; WhoWor 74; WrDr 76*

Illingworth, Leslie Gilbert
Cartoonist
b. 1902
Source: *Who 74*

Illsley, John
see: Dire Straits

Ilyushin, Sergei Vladimirovich
Russian. Aircraft Designer
b. Mar 31, 1894 in Diyalora, Russia
d. Feb 9, 1977 in Moscow, U.S.S.R.
Source: *IntWW 74; Who 74; WhoWor 74*

Iman
American. Actress, Model
b. 1955 in Somalia
Source: *BioIn 10, 11*

Imlach, "Punch" (George)
Canadian. Hockey Coach, Executive
Coach, Toronto Maple Leafs, 1958-69; Buffalo Sabres, 1970-71.
b. Mar 15, 1918 in Toronto, ON
Source: *WhoE 74; WhoHcky 73*

Immelmann, Max
German. Aviator
b. 1890
d. Jul 18, 1916
Source: *WebBD 80*

Impellitteri, Vincent R
American. Former Mayor of New York City
b. Feb 4, 1900 in Isnello, Sicily
Source: *CurBio 51*

Ince, Thomas H(arper)
American. Motion Picture Director, Producer
b. Nov 6, 1882 in Newport, Rhode Island
d. Nov 19, 1924 in Beverly Hills, California
Source: *BiDFilm; BioIn 11; CmMov; DcFM; FilmEn; FilmgC; MovMk; OxFilm; TwYS A; WhAm 1; WhScrn 74, 77; WorEFlm*

Incredible String Band, The
[Gerard Dott; Mike Heron; Malcolm LeMaistre; "Licorice" (Christina) McKechnie; Rose Simpson; Robin Williamson]
Scottish. Vocal, Instrumental Group
Source: *EncPR&S; IlEncRk*

Indiana, Robert
American. Artist
Creates art out of words; called designer of trivia.
b. Sep 13, 1928 in New Castle, Indiana
Source: *CelR 73; CurBio 73; DcCAA 71; IntWW 74; WhoAm 74, 76, 78, 80, 82; WhoAmA 73; WhoWor 74*

Indy, Paul d'
[Vincent d'Indy]
French. Composer
b. Mar 27, 1851 in Paris, France
d. Dec 2, 1931 in Paris, France
Source: *AtlBL; OxFr*

Inescort, Frieda
Scottish. Actress
b. 1901 in Edinburgh, Scotland
Source: *FilmgC; MotPP; MovMk; ThFT*

Infante, Frank
see: Blondie

Infeld, Leopold
Polish. Physicist
b. Aug 20, 1898 in Krakow, Poland
d. Jan 16, 1968 in Warsaw, Poland
Source: *BioIn 6, 8; CurBio 63, 68*

Inge, William
American. Dramatist
b. May 3, 1913 in Independence, Kansas
d. Jun 10, 1973 in Hollywood Hills, California
Source: *AmAu&B; BiE&WWA; CnMD; CnThe; ConAu 9R; ConDr 73; ConLC 1, 8; CroCD; CurBio 53, 73; FilmgC; McGEWD; ModAL; ModWD; OxAmL; OxThe; Pen AM; PlP&P; REn; REnAL; REnWD; TwCA SUP; TwCW; WebE&AL; WhAm 5; WhScrn 74; WhoWor 74; WorEFlm*

Inge, William Ralph
English. Religious Leader
b. Jun 6, 1860 in Craike, England
d. Feb 26, 1954 in Wallingford, England
Source: *Alli SUP; Chambr 3; DcLEL; EvLB; LongCTC; NewC; OxEng; TwCA, SUP; WhoLA*

Ingels, Marty
American. Comedian, Actor
b. Mar 9, 1936 in Brooklyn, Michigan
Source: *FilmgC; IntMPA 75, 76, 77, 78, 79, 80, 81, 82; WhoAm 74, 76, 78, 80, 82; WhoHol A*

Ingersoll, Ralph McAllister
American. Journalist, Publisher
b. Dec 8, 1900 in New Haven, Connecticut
Source: *Au&Wr 71; ChPo; ConAu P-1; CurBio 40; IntWW 74; REnAL; TwCA SUP; WhNAA; Who 74; WhoAm 74, 76, 78, 80, 82; WhoE 74*

Ingersoll, Robert Green
American. Lawyer, Agnostic Orator
b. Aug 11, 1833 in Dresden, New York
d. Jul 21, 1899 in New York, New York
Source: *Alli SUP; AmAu; AmAu&B; AmBi; ApCAB; BbD; BiD&SB; DcAmAu; DcAmB; DcNAA; EncAB-H; OxAmL; REn; REnAL; TwCBDA; WebAB; WhAm 1; WhAmP*

Ingersoll, Simon
American. Inventor
b. Mar 3, 1818 in Stanwich, Connecticut
d. Jul 24, 1894
Source: *BioIn 9; WhAm H*

Inghelbrecht, Desire
French. Conductor, Composer
b. Sep 17, 1880 in Paris, France
d. Feb 14, 1965 in Paris, France
Source: *NewEOp 71; OxMus*

Ingold, Christopher
British. Chemist
b. 1893
d. 1970
Source: *BioIn 1, 7, 9*

Ingram, Rex
American. Actor
b. Oct 20, 1895 in Cairo, Illinois
d. Sep 19, 1969 in Los Angeles, California
Source: *BiE&WWA; FilmgC; MovMk; OxFilm; Vers A; WhScrn 74, 77*

Ingres, Jean Auguste Dominique
French. Artist
b. Aug 29, 1780 in Montauban, France
d. Jan 13, 1867 in Paris, France
Source: *AtlBL; NewC; NewCol 75; OxFr; REn*

Ingrid
Danish. Queen
b. 1910
Source: *InWom*

Ingstad, Helge
Norwegian. Author, Explorer
b. Dec 30, 1899 in Meraker, Norway
Source: *ConAu 65; IntWW 74; OxCan; WhoWor 74*

Ink Spots, The
[Billy Bowen; Charlie Fuqua; Orville Jones; Bill Kenny; Herb Kenny; Ivory Watson]
American. Vocal Group
Source: *CmpEPM*

Inman, Bobby Ray
American. Former CIA Official
b. Apr 4, 1931 in Rhonesboro, Texas
Source: *BioIn 11; WhoAm 78, 80, 82; WhoGov 75; WhoS&SW 78*

Inman, Henry
American. Artist
b. Oct 28, 1801 in Utica, New York
d. Jan 17, 1846 in New York, New York
Source: *AmBi; DcAmB; NewCol 75; WebAB; WebBD 80; WhAm H*

Innes, Hammond, pseud.
[Ralph Hammond-Innes]
English. Author
b. Jul 15, 1913 in Horsham, England
Source: *AmAu&B; AuBYP; ConAu 5R, 4NR; ConNov 72, 76; CurBio 54; IntWW 74; LongCTC; REn; TwCW; Who 74; WhoWor 74; WorAu; WrDr 76*

Inness, George
American. Artist
b. May 1, 1825 in Newburgh, New York
d. Aug 3, 1894 in Scotland
Source: *AmBi; ApCAB; AtlBL; DcAmB; Drake; NewCol 75; OxAmL; REn; TwCBDA; WebAB; WhAm H*

Innis, Roy
[Emile Alfredo]
American. Civil Rights Leader
National director, CORE, 1968--.
b. Jun 6, 1934 in Virgin Islands
Source: *CelR 73; CurBio 69; IntWW 74; WhoAm 74, 76, 78, 80, 82; WhoBlA 75; WhoUN 75*

Inonu, Ismet
Turkish. Statesman
b. Sep 24, 1884 in Izmik, Asia Minor
d. Dec 25, 1973 in Ankara, Turkey
Source: *CurBio 41, 64, 74; NewCol 75; NewYTBE 73; WhAm 6; Who 74*

Inouye, Daniel Ken
American. Senator
b. Sep 7, 1924 in Honolulu, Hawaii
Source: *BiDrAC; CelR 73; CngDr 74; ConAu 25R; CurBio 60; IntWW 74; WhoAm 74, 76, 78, 80, 82; WhoAmP 73; WhoGov 72; WhoWest 74; WhoWor 74*

Insull, Samuel
Financier
b. Nov 11, 1859 in London, England
d. Jul 16, 1938 in Paris, France
Source: *AmBi; DcAmB S2; EncAB-H; NewCol 75; WebAB; WhAm 1*

Interwoven Pair, The
see: Hare, Ernie; Jones, Billy

Iommi, Anthony
see: Black Sabbath

Ionesco, Eugene
French. Author, Dramatist
Theater of the absurd; *The Bald Prima Donna,* 1950; *The Rhinoceros,* 1959.
b. Nov 26, 1912 in Slatina, Romania
Source: *BiE&WWA; CasWL; CelR 73; CnMD; CnMWL; CnThe; ConAu 9R; ConLC 1, 4, 6, 9, 11, 15; CroCD; CurBio 59; EncWL; EvEuW; IntWW 74; LongCTC; McGEWD; ModRL; ModWD; NewYTBE 70; NotNAT; OxThe; Pen EUR; PlP&P; RComWL; REn; REnWD; SmATA 7; TwCW; Who 74; WhoAm 74, 76, 78, 80, 82; WhoThe 77; WhoTwCL; WhoWor 74; WorAu*

Ippolitov-Ivanov, Mikhail
Russian. Composer
b. Nov 9, 1859 in Gatchina, Russia
d. Jan 26, 1935 in Moscow, U.S.S.R.
Source: *BioIn 4, 9; NewCol 75*

Iqbal, Mahomed
[Muhammad Iqbal]
Indian. Poet, Philosopher, Leader
b. 1873
d. 1938
Source: *NewCol 75; WebBD 80*

Irani, Merwan S
see: Meher Baba

Iredell, James
American. Supreme Court Justice
b. Oct 5, 1751 in Lewes, England
d. Oct 2, 1799 in Edenton, North Carolina
Source: *AmBi; ApCAB; BioIn 2, 3, 5; Drake; NatCAB 1; NewCol 75*

Ireland, Jill
[Mrs. Charles Bronson]
American. Actress
b. Apr 24, 1936 in London, England
Source: *FilmgC; IntMPA 77, 78, 79, 80, 81, 82; WhoAm 82; WhoHol A*

Ireland, John
English. Composer
b. Aug 13, 1879 in Inglewood, England
d. Jun 12, 1962 in Washington, England
Source: *Baker 78; BioIn 3, 4, 6, 7, 8; DcCM; NewCol 75; WhAm 4*

Ireland, John
Canadian. Actor
b. Jan 30, 1915 in Victoria, BC
Source: *BiE&WWA; CmMov; FilmgC; IntMPA 75, 76, 77, 78, 79, 80, 81, 82; MovMk; NotNAT; OxFilm*

Ireland, William Henry
English. Shakespearean Forger
Wrote two "pseudo-Shakespearian" plays, *Vortigern and Rowena; Henry II.*
b. 1777
d. 1835
Source: *Alli; BiDLA; CasWL; Chambr 2; ChPo; DcEnL; DcLEL; EvLB; NewC; REn*

Irene
[Irene Gibbons]
American. Fashion Designer
b. 1907 in Montana
d. Nov 15, 1962 in Hollywood, California
Source: *FilmgC; InWom; WorFshn*

Irene
Greek. Princess
b. 1942
Source: *BioIn 9*

Irene
Dutch. Princess
b. Aug 5, 1939 in Soestdijk, Netherlands
Source: *WhoWor 74*

Irish, Edward Simmons (Ned)
American. Basketball Promoter
Founded NY Knickerbockers, 1946.
b. May 6, 1905 in Lake George, New York
d. Jan 21, 1982 in Venice, Florida
Source: *NewYTBS 82; WhoAm 74, 76; WhoBbl 73*

Irish Hunger Strikers
[Michael Devine; Kieran Doherty; Francis Hughes; Martin Hurson; Kevin Lynch; Raymond McCreesh; Joe McDonnell; Thomas McIlwee; Patrick O'Hara; Bobby Sands]
Jailed Revolutionaries
Source: *NF*

Irish Rovers
[Jimmy Ferguson; Wilcil McDowell; George Millar; Joe Millar; Will Millar]
Irish. Singing Group
Source: *ClbCR*

Iron Butterfly
[Erik Braun; Ronald Bushy; Lee Dorman; Doug Ingle; Michael Pinera; Lawrence Reinhardt]
American. Rock Group
Source: *EncPR&S; RkOn*

Iron Maiden
[Clive Burr; Paul Di'Anno; Steve Harris; Dave Murray; Adrian Smith; Dennis Stratton]
British. Rock Band
Heavy metal band named after medieval torture device.
Source: *IlEncRk*

Ironside, Christopher
Artist, Designer
b. 1913
Source: *Who 74*

Ironside, William E
Scottish. Army Officer
b. May 6, 1880 in Ironside, Scotland
d. Sep 22, 1959 in London, England
Source: *CurBio 40, 59*

Irvin, Monte (Monford Merrill)
American. Baseball Player
b. Feb 25, 1919 in Columbia, Alabama
Source: *BaseEn; NewYTBE 73*

Irvin, Rea
American. Artist, Art Editor
b. Aug 26, 1881 in San Francisco, California
d. 1972
Source: *ChPo S1; NewYTBE 72; WhAm 5; WhoAmA 73*

Irvin, Robert W
American. Author, Editor
b. Mar 3, 1933 in Highland Park, Michigan
d. Dec 1, 1980 in Chicago, Illinois
Source: *BioIn 9; ConAu 103; Ward 77*

Irving, Clifford Michael
American. Author
Served 17 months in prison for writing false autobiography of Howard Hughes.
b. Nov 5, 1930 in New York, New York
Source: *Au&Wr 71; AuNews 1; BioNews 74; ConAu 1R, 2NR; NewYTBE 72; WrDr 76*

Irving, Edith
[Edith Sommer]
Swiss. Artist
Source: *BioIn 10*

Irving, Edward
Scottish. Mystic
b. Aug 4, 1792 in Annan, Scotland
d. Dec 7, 1834 in Glasgow, Scotland
Source: *Alli; BbD; BrAu 19; Chambr 3; DcEnL; EvLB; NewC; NewCol 75*

Irving, Sir Henry
English. Actor
b. Feb 6, 1838 in Glastonbury, England
d. Oct 13, 1905 in Bradford, England
Source: *FamA&A; NewC; NewCol 75; OxThe; REn; WhAm 1*

Irving, Isabel
American. Actress
b. Feb 28, 1871 in Bridgeport, Connecticut
d. Sep 1, 1944 in Nantucket, Massachusetts
Source: *InWom; WhAm 2; WhoStg 1906, 1908; WomWWA 14*

Irving, John
American. Author
b. Mar 2, 1942 in Exeter, New Hampshire
Source: *ConAu 25R; ConLC 13; WhoAm 82*

Irving, Jules
American. Actor, Producer, Director
b. Apr 13, 1925 in New York, New York
d. Jul 28, 1979 in Reno, Nevada
Source: *BiE&WWA; CurBio 70, 79; NewYTBS 79; NotNAT; PlP&P A; WhAm 7; WhoAm 74; WhoE 75; WhoThe 72, 77*

Irving, Laurence
English. Actor
b. Dec 21, 1871 in London, England
d. May 29, 1914 in Canada
Source: *OxThe*

Irving, Robert Augustine
American. Conductor
b. Aug 28, 1913 in Winchester, England
Source: *Who 74; WhoAm 74, 76, 78, 80, 82; WhoMus 72*

Irving, Washington
[Diedrich Knickerbocker]
American. Author, Diplomat, Historian
Wrote *Rip Van Winkle, Legend of Sleepy Hollow*, 1820.
b. Apr 3, 1783 in New York, New York
d. Nov 28, 1859 in Tarrytown, New York
Source: *Alli; AmAu; AmBi; AmWr; ApCAB; AtlBL; BbD; BiAuS; BiD&SB; CarSB; CasWL; Chambr 3; ChPo, S2; CnDAL; CrtT 3; CyAL 1; CyWA; DcAmAu; DcAmB; DcBiA; DcEnA; DcLEL; DcSpL; Drake; EncAB-H; FamAYP; MouLC 3; OxCan; OxThe; Pen AM; RAdv 1; REn; REnAL; TwCBDA; WebAB; WebE&AL; WhAm H; WhoChL; WisWr*

Irwin, Flo
Canadian. Actress
b. 1859? in Whitby, ON
d. Dec 21, 1930 in Los Angeles, California
Source: *NotNAT B*

Irwin, Hale
American. Golfer
b. Jun 3, 1945 in Joplin, Missouri
Source: *WhoAm 82; WhoGolf*

Irwin, James Benson
American. Astronaut
b. Mar 17, 1930 in Pittsburgh, Pennsylvania
Source: *NewYTBE 71; NewYTBS 74; WhoAm 74, 76, 78, 80, 82; WhoWor 74*

Irwin, Margaret
English. Author
b. 1889 in London, England
d. 1967
Source: *ConAu 93; CurBio 46; DcLEL; LongCTC; TwCA SUP; TwCW; WhoLA*

Irwin, May
Canadian. Actress
b. 1862 in Whitby, ON
d. Oct 22, 1938 in New York, New York
Source: *AmBi; DcAmB S2; FamA&A; Film 1; InWom; MotPP; NotAW; TwYS; WhAm 1; WhoStg 1906, 1908*

Irwin, Wallace
American. Journalist, Humorist
b. Mar 15, 1875 in Oneida, New York
d. Feb 14, 1959 in Southern Pines, North Carolina
Source: *AmAu&B; ChPo S1, S2; CnDAL; ConAmL; DcAmAu; OxAmL; REn; REnAL; Str&VC; TwCA, SUP; WhAm 3; WhScrn 77*

Irwin, Will
American. Journalist
b. Sep 14, 1873 in Oneida, New York
d. Feb 24, 1948 in New York, New York
Source: *AmAu&B; ChPo S1; EncMys; OxAmL; REnAL; WhNAA; WhScrn 77*

Isaac
Biblical Character
Source: *BioIn 10; NewCol 75*

Isabella I
[Isabelala Catolica]
Spanish. Queen of Castle
b. Apr 22, 1451 in Madrigal, Spain
d. Nov 26, 1504 in Medina del Campo, Spain
Source: *InWom; LinLib S; NewCol 75; WebBD 80*

Isabella II
[Maria Isabella Louisa]
Spanish. Queen
b. Oct 10, 1830 in Madrid, Spain
d. Apr 19, 1904 in Paris, France
Source: *BioIn 6, 7; McGEWB; NewCol 75; WebBD 80*

Isaiah
Hebrew. Prophet
fl. 740 century
Source: *DcOrL 3; NewC; NewCol 75*

Isbert, Margot Benary
see: Benary-Isbert, Margot

Ishak, Yusof bin
Singaporean. President
b. Aug 12, 1910
d. Nov 23, 1970 in Singapore
Source: *NewYTBE 70*

Isham, Samuel
American. Artist, Author
b. May 12, 1855 in New York, New York
d. Jun 12, 1914
Source: *AmAu&B; BioIn 2; DcNAA*

Isherwood, Christopher William
American. Author, Dramatist
Play *Caberet,* 1966 was based on his stories *Goodbye to Berlin,* 1935.
b. Aug 26, 1904 in Cheshire, England
Source: *AmAu&B; Au&Wr 71; CasWL; CelR 73; CnMD; CnMWL; ConAu 13R; ConDr 73; ConLC 1, 9, 11, 14; ConNov 72, 76; CurBio 72; DcLEL; DrAF 76; EncWL; EvLB; IntWW 74; LongCTC; McGEWD; ModBrL, SUP; ModWD; NewC; NewYTBE 73; OxAmL; OxEng; Pen ENG; RAdv 1; REn; REnAL; TwCA, SUP; TwCW; WebE&AL; Who 74; WhoAm 74, 76, 78, 80, 82; WhoTwCL; WhoWor 74; WrDr 76*

Isley Brothers
[O'Kelly Isley; Ronald Isley; Rudolph Isley]
American. Vocal Group
Source: *EncPR&S*

Isocrates
Greek. Orator, Teacher
Founded Athenian school of oratory; developed literary form of rhetorical essays.
b. 436BC
d. 338BC
Source: *CasWL; CyEd; DcBiPP; Grk&L; LinLib L, S; LongCEL; McGEWB; NewC; NewCol 75; Pen CL; REn; WhDW*

Israels, Josef
Dutch. Artist
b. 1824 in Groningen, Netherlands
d. 1913
Source: *BioIn 2; NewCol 75; WebBD 80*

Issel, Dan
American. Basketball Player
b. Oct 25, 1948 in Batavia, Illinois
Source: *BioIn 10; WhoAm 82; WhoBbl 73*

Issigonis, Sir Alec Arnold C
British. Engineer
b. 1905
Source: *IntWW 74; Who 74; WhoWor 74*

Istomin, Eugene George
American. Musician
b. Nov 26, 1925 in New York, New York
Source: *IntWW 74; NewYTBE 71; WhoAm 74, 76, 78, 80, 82; WhoMus 72; WhoWor 74*

Ito, Prince Hirobumi
Japanese. Statesman
b. Sep 2, 1841 in Choshu Province, Japan
d. Oct 26, 1909 in Harbin, Manchuria
Source: *NewCol 75; WebBD 80*

Ittner, William Butts
American. Architect
b. Sep 4, 1864 in Saint Louis, Missouri
d. Jan 26, 1936 in Saint Louis, Missouri
Source: *WhAm 1*

Iturbi, Amparo
Spanish. Musician
b. 1899
d. Apr 21, 1969 in Beverly Hills, California
Source: *InWom; WhScrn 77; WhoHol B*

Iturbi, Jose
Spanish. Musician, Conductor, Composer
Appeared in films, 1940's; helped to popularize classical music.
b. Nov 28, 1895 in Valencia, Spain
d. Jun 28, 1980 in Los Angeles, California
Source: *CelR 73; CurBio 43; FilmgC; IntWW 74; MovMk; Who 74; WhoAm 74; WhoHol A; WhoMus 72; WhoWor 74*

Iturbide, Augustin de
[Augustin I]
Mexican. General, Emperor
Won Mexican independence from Spain, 1821; Emperor, 1822-23.
b. Sep 27, 1783 in Valladolid, Mexico
d. Jul 19, 1824
Source: *ApCAB; BioIn 1, 2, 3, 8, 9, 10; CmCal; DcBiPP; EncLatA; HarEnUS; NewCol 75*

Ivan III
"Ivan the Great"
Russian. Czar
b. Jan 22, 1440
d. Oct 27, 1505
Source: *NewCol 75; WebBD 80*

Ivan IV
"Ivan the Terrible"
Russian. Czar
b. Aug 25, 1530
d. Mar 17, 1584
Source: *CasWL; DcRusL; NewCol 75; REn*

Ivanov, Konstantin Konstantinovich
Russian. Conductor
b. May 21, 1907 in Efremov, Russia
Source: *IntWW 74; WhoWor 74*

Ivens, Joris
Dutch. Motion Picture Director
b. Nov 18, 1898 in Nijmegen, Netherlands
Source: *BiDFilm; DcFM; FilmgC; MovMk; OxFilm; WhoWor 74; WorEFlm*

Ives, Burl
[Icle Ivanhoe]
American. Actor, Singer
Won 1959 Oscar for *The Big Country*.
b. Jun 14, 1909 in Hunt, Illinois
Source: *AmAu&B; AmSCAP 66; BiE&WWA; CmMov; ConAu 103; CurBio 46, 60; EncFCWM 69; FilmgC; IntMPA 75, 76, 77, 78, 79, 80, 81, 82; IntWW 74; MovMk; NotNAT; REnAL; WhoAm 74, 76, 78, 80, 82; WhoMus 72; WhoThe 77; WhoWor 74; WorEFlm*

Ives, Charles Edward
American. Composer
b. Oct 20, 1874 in Danbury, Connecticut
d. May 11, 1954 in New York, New York
Source: *AtlBL; BioNews 74; CurBio 47, 54; DcAmB S3; DcCM; EncAB-H; NewCol 75; OxAmL; REn; REnAL; WebAB; WhAm 3*

Ives, Frederic Eugene
American. Inventor
Pioneer in modern photography; developed halftone process of photoengraving.
b. Feb 17, 1856 in Litchfield, Connecticut
d. May 27, 1937 in Philadelphia, Pennsylvania
Source: *AmBi; DcAmB S2; DcNAA; NewCol 75; WebAB; WhAm 1*

Ives, Herbert Eugene
American. Inventor, Physicist
Helped to develop television.
b. Jul 31, 1882 in Philadelphia, Pennsylvania
d. Nov 13, 1953 in Upper Montclair, New Jersey
Source: *NewCol 75; WhAm 3*

Ives, James Merritt
[Currier and Ives]
American. Artist
Partner, from 1857, with Nathaniel Currier, Currier and Ives Lithograph Publishers.
b. Mar 5, 1824 in New York, New York
d. Jan 3, 1895 in Rye, New York
Source: *NewCol 75; WebAB*

Ives, Joseph
American. Clockmaker
b. 1782
d. 1862
Source: *BioIn 1, 2, 9*

Ivogun, Maria
[Ilse VonGunther]
Hungarian. Opera Singer
b. Nov 11, 1891 in Budapest, Hungary
Source: *InWom*

Ivory, James
American. Motion Picture Director
b. Jun 7, 1928 in Berkeley, California
Source: *BioIn 10; CurBio 81; FilmgC; OxFilm*

Iwama, Kazuo
Japanese. Electronics Executive
President, 1976-82; board chairman, 1978-82, Sony Corp.
b. Feb 7, 1919 in Anjo City, Japan
d. Aug 24, 1982 in Tokyo, Japan
Source: *FarE&A 78, 79, 80, 81; IntWW 77, 78, 79, 80, 81; LElec; NewYTBS 82; WhoWor 78*

Iwasaki, Yataro
Japanese. Business Executive
b. 1834
d. 1885
Source: *BioIn 8*

Iwatani, Toro
Japanese. Inventor
Developed video game "Pac-Man."
b. 1955?
Source: *NF*

Iwerks, Ub(be)
American. Animated Cartoonist
b. Mar 24, 1901 in Kansas City, Missouri
d. Jul 8, 1971
Source: *BioIn 9*

Izac, Edouard Victor M
American. Government Official
b. Dec 18, 1891
Source: *BioIn 7; CurBio 45*

J

Jaabari, Mohammed Ali, Sheik
Palestinian. Mayor, Politician
b. 1900 in Jordan
d. May 29, 1980 in Hebron, Israel
Source: *BioIn 12*

Jablonski, Henryk
Polish. Historian, Socialist Leader
b. 1909
Source: *BioIn 10*

Jabotinsky, Vladimir
Russian. Zionist Leader
b. Oct 18, 1880
d. Aug 3, 1940
Source: *CurBio 40*

Jabs, Matthias
see: Scorpions

Jack the Ripper
English. Murderer
Source: *BioIn 9*

Jacklin, Anthony
English. Golfer
b. Jul 7, 1944 in Scunthorpe, England
Source: *BioIn 8, 9, 10; NewYTBE 70; Who 74; WhoGolf*

Jackson, A(lexander) Y(oung)
[Group of Seven]
Canadian. Artist
b. Oct 3, 1882 in Montreal, PQ
d. Apr 6, 1974 in Kleinburg, ON
Source: *BioIn 1, 2, 3, 5, 10; CanWW 70; CreCan 2; MacDCB 78; McGDA; Who 74; WhoAmA 73, 76*

Jackson, Andrew
"Old Hickory"
American. 7th US President
Movement toward popular participation in govt. called Jacksonian democracy.
b. Mar 15, 1767 in Waxhaw, South Carolina
d. Jun 8, 1845 in Nashville, Tennessee
Source: *Alli; AmAu&B; AmBi; ApCAB; BiAuS; BiDSA; BiDrAC; BiDrUSE; DcAmB; Drake; EncAB-H; OxAmL; REn; REnAL; TwCBDA; WebAB; WhAm H; WhAmP*

Jackson, Anne
[Mrs. Eli Wallach]
American. Actress
b. Sep 3, 1926 in Allegheny, Pennsylvania
Source: *BiE&WWA; CurBio 80; FilmgC; InWom; MotPP; MovMk; NotNAT; WhoAm 80, 82; WhoHol A; WhoThe 77*

Jackson, "Aunt" Molly
American. Singer, Union Organizer
b. 1880 in Clay City, Kentucky
d. Sep 1, 1960
Source: *EncFCWM 69*

Jackson, Charles Reginald
American. Author
b. Apr 6, 1903 in Summit, New Jersey
d. Sep 21, 1968 in New York, New York
Source: *AmAu&B; AmNov; ConAu 25R, 101; CyWA; LongCTC; OxAmL; REn; REnAL; TwCA; WhAm 5*

Jackson, Chevalier
American. Scientist
b. Nov 4, 1865 in Greentree, Pennsylvania
d. Aug 16, 1958 in Philadelphia, Pennsylvania
Source: *CurBio 40; WhNAA*

Jackson, Donald
English. Calligrapher, Author
b. in Leigh, England
Source: *BioIn 8*

Jackson, Doris Kenner
see: Shirelles, The

Jackson, George
American. Criminal, Political Theorist
b. 1941
d. 1971
Source: *BioIn 10*

Jackson, Glenda
English. Actress
Won Oscars, 1970, 1973, for *Women in Love; A Touch of Class.*
b. May 9, 1937 in Cheshire, England
Source: *BkPepl; CelR 73; CurBio 71; FilmgC; IntMPA 75, 76, 77, 78, 79, 80, 81, 82; IntWW 74; MovMk; NewYTBE 71; OxFilm; Who 74; WhoAm 82; WhoHol A; WhoThe 77; WhoWor 74*

Jackson, Gordon
Scottish. Actor
b. Dec 19, 1923 in Glasgow, Scotland
Source: *FilmgC; IntMPA 75, 76, 77, 78, 79, 80, 81, 82; WhoThe 77*

Jackson, Helen Hunt
American. Author
b. Oct 18, 1831 in Amherst, Massachusetts
d. Aug 12, 1885 in San Francisco, California
Source: *Alli SUP; AmAu; AmAu&B; AmBi; AmWom; ApCAB; BbD; BiD&SB; CarSB; CasWL; ChPo, S1, S2; CnDAL; DcAmAu; DcAmB; DcBiA; DcLEL; DcNAA; EncAB-H; EvLB; InWom; JBA 34; MouLC 4; NotAW; OxAmL; REn; REnAL; Str&VC; TwCBDA; WebAB; WhAm H*

Jackson, Henry Martin
"Scoop"
American. Senator
b. May 31, 1912 in Everett, Washington
Source: *BiDrAC; BioNews 74; CelR 73; CngDr 74; CurBio 53; IntWW 74; NewYTBE 71; WhoAm 74, 76, 78, 80, 82; WhoAmP 73; WhoGov 72; WhoPNW; WhoWest 74; WhoWor 74*

Jackson, "Hurricane" (Thomas)
American. Boxer
b. Aug 9, 1931 in Sparta, Georgia
d. Feb 14, 1982 in Queens, New York
Source: *NewYTBS 82; WhoBox 74*

Jackson, Jesse
American. Civil Rights Leader
Founder, director, Operation Breadbasket, 1966-71, Operation Push, 1971--.
b. Oct 8, 1941 in Greenville, North Carolina
Source: *BkPepl; CelR 73; CurBio 70; WebAB; WhoAm 74, 76, 78, 80, 82; WhoBlA 75; WhoMW 74; WhoRel 75*

Jackson, Joe (Joseph Jefferson)
"Shoeless Joe"
American. Baseball Player
Banned from baseball for participation in "Black Sox" scandal, 1919 World Series.
b. Jul 16, 1888 in Brandon Mills, South Carolina
d. Dec 5, 1951 in Greenville, South Carolina
Source: *BaseEn; WhoProB 73*

Jackson, John Adams
American. Sculptor
b. Nov 5, 1825 in Bath, Maine
d. Aug 30, 1879 in Pracchia, Italy
Source: *AmBi; ApCAB; DcAmB; TwCBDA; WhAm H*

Jackson, John Hughlings
English. Neurologist
b. Apr 4, 1835 in Yorkshire, England
d. Oct 7, 1911 in London, England
Source: *DcScB; WebBD 80*

Jackson, Kate
[Mrs. David Greenwald]
American. Actress
Starred in "The Rookies," 1972-76; "Charlie's Angels," 1976-79.
b. Oct 29, 1948 in Birmingham, Alabama
Source: *BkPepl; IntMPA 82; WhoAm 82; WhoHol A*

Jackson, Mahalia
American. Gospel Singer
Sang "I Believe," "He's Got the Whole World in His Hands."
b. Oct 26, 1911 in New Orleans, Louisiana
d. Jan 27, 1972 in Evergreen Park, Illinois
Source: *ConAu 33R; CurBio 57, 72; HerW; InWom; NewYTBE 72; WebAB; WhAm 5; WhScrn 77; WhoHol B*

Jackson, Margaret E
American. Physiologist
b. Sep 2, 1928 in Zanesville, Ohio
Source: *AmM&WS 73*

Jackson, Mary Ann
[Our Gang]
American. Actress
b. 1923
Source: *Film 2; TwYS*

Jackson, Maynard Holbrook, Jr.
American. Former Mayor of Atlanta
b. Mar 23, 1938 in Dallas, Texas
Source: *BioNews 74; NewYTBE 73; WhoAm 82; WhoBlA 75; WhoS&SW 73*

Jackson, Michael
[The Jackson Five]
American. Singer, Actor
b. Aug 29, 1958 in Gary, Indiana
Source: *BkPepl; CelR 73; WhoAm 82; WhoBlA 75*

Jackson, Milt(on)
American. Jazz Musician
b. Jan 1, 1923 in Detroit, Michigan
Source: *WhoAm 74, 76, 78, 80, 82; WhoBlA 75*

Jackson, Reggie (Reginald Martinez)
"Mr. October"
American. Baseball Player
Holds AL record for strikeouts; hit three home runs in one World Series game, 1977.
b. May 18, 1946 in Wyncote, Pennsylvania
Source: *BaseEn; BkPepl; CurBio 74; NewYTBE 73; WhoAm 82; WhoProB 73*

Jackson, Robert Houghwout
American. Supreme Court Justice
b. Feb 13, 1892 in Spring Creek, Pennsylvania
d. Oct 9, 1954 in Washington, DC
Source: *BiDrUSE; DcAmB S5; EncAB-H; McGEWB; WebAB; WhAm 3*

Jackson, Shirley
American. Author
Wrote stories dealing with supernatural in everyday setting: *The Lottery,* 1949.
b. Dec 14, 1919 in San Francisco, California
d. Aug 8, 1965 in North Bennington, Vermont
Source: *AmAu&B; AmNov; ConAu 1R, 25R, 4NR; ConLC 11; ConNov 76; LongCTC; ModAL; OxAmL; Pen AM; RAdv 1; REn; REnAL; SmATA 2; TwCA SUP; WhAm 4*

Jackson, "Stonewall" (Thomas Jonathan)
American. Confederate General
Nicknamed at Battle of Bull Run, 1861: "There stands Jackson like a stone wall."
b. Jan 21, 1824 in Clarksburg, Virginia
d. May 10, 1863 in Guinea Station, Virginia
Source: *AmBi; ApCAB; BiDConf; DcAmB; Drake; EncAB-H; REn; REnAL; TwCBDA; WebAB; WhAm H*

Jackson, Travis Calvin
"Stonewall"
American. Baseball Player
b. Nov 2, 1903 in Waldo, Arkansas
Source: *BaseEn; BioIn 8; WhoProB 73*

Jackson, William Henry
American. Artist, Photographer
Best known for photographic record of development of West.
b. Apr 4, 1843 in Keeseville, New York
d. Jun 30, 1942 in New York, New York
Source: *AmAu&B; DcAmB S3; DcNAA; WhAm 2*

Jackson Five, The
[Maureen Brown; Jermaine Jackson; LaToya Jackson; Marlon Jackson; Michael Jackson; Randy Jackson; Jackie Jackson; Tito Jackson]
American. Vocal Group
Source: *EncPR&S; RkOn*

Jackson of Lodsworth, Baroness
see: Ward, Barbara

Jacob
Biblical Character
Source: *NewCol 75; WebBD 80*

Jacob, Francois
French. Geneticist
b. Jun 17, 1920 in Nancy, France
Source: *BioIn 7; CurBio 66; IntWW 74; Who 74; WhoAm 74; WhoWor 74*

Jacob, Max
French. Poet, Artist
b. Jul 11, 1876 in Quimper, France
d. Mar 5, 1944 in Drancy, France
Source: *CasWL; ClDMEL; CnMWL; EncWL; EvEuW; ModRL; OxFr; Pen EUR; REn; WhoTwCL; WorAu*

Jacobi, Derek
English. Actor
b. Oct 22, 1938 in London, England
Source: *WhoThe 77*

Jacobi, Lou
Canadian. Actor
b. Dec 28, 1913 in Toronto, ON
Source: *BiE&WWA; NotNAT; WhoAm 74, 76, 78, 80, 82; WhoThe 77*

Jacobi, Mary Putnam
American. Pioneer Physician
b. Aug 31, 1842 in London, England
d. 1906
Source: *Alli SUP; BiD&SB; DcAmAu; DcNAA; WhAm 1*

Jacobs, Helen Hull
American. Tennis Player, Author
b. Aug 6, 1908 in Globe, Arizona
Source: *AmAu&B; AuBYP; ConAu 9R; InWom; SmATA 12; WhoAm 74, 76, 78, 80, 82; WrDr 76*

Jacobs, Michael S
American. Boxing Promotor
b. Mar 10, 1880 in New York, New York
d. Jan 25, 1953 in New York, New York
Source: *WhoBox 74*

Jacobs, William Wymark
English. Author
b. 1863 in London, England
d. Sep 1, 1943 in London, England
Source: *BbD; BiD&SB; CasWL; Chambr 3; DcBiA; DcEnA AP; DcLEL; EncMys; EvLB; LongCTC; MnBBF; ModBrL; NewC; OxEng; Pen ENG; REn; TwCA, SUP; TwCW; WhoLA*

Jacobsen, Arne
Danish. Architect
b. 1902
d. 1971 in Copenhagen, Denmark
Source: *BioIn 11*

Jacobsen, Jens Peter
Danish. Author
First to translate, introduce Darwin's works to Denmark.
b. Apr 7, 1847 in Thisted, Denmark
d. May 30, 1885 in Thisted, Denmark
Source: *CasWL; ClDMEL; CyWA; DcEuL; EuAu; EvEuW; LinLib L; McGEWB; Pen EUR; REn; WhDW*

Jacobson, Leon Orris
American. Medical Scientist, Professor
b. Dec 16, 1911 in Sims, North Dakota
Source: *AmM&WS 76P; CurBio 62; IntWW 74; LEduc 74; WhoAm 74, 76, 78, 80, 82*

Jacobsson, Ulla
Swedish. Actress
b. 1929? in Gothenburg, Sweden
d. Aug 22, 1982 in Vienna, Austria
Source: *FilmgC; WhoHol A; WorEFlm*

Jacoby, Oswald
Bridge Game Expert
b. 1902
Source: *BioIn 11*

Jacquard, Joseph Marie
French. Inventor
Developed Jacquard loom, 1801, first loom to weave designs in cloth.
b. 1752
d. 1834
Source: *NewCol 75; REn*

Jacquet, Illinois
American. Jazz Musician
b. Oct 31, 1922 in Broussard, Louisiana
Source: *BiDAmM*

Jadlowker, Hermann
Opera Singer
b. Jul 5, 1879 in Riga, Russia
d. May 13, 1953 in Tel Aviv, Israel
Source: *NewEOp 71*

Jaeckel, Richard
American. Actor
b. Oct 26, 1926 in Long Beach, California
Source: *FilmgC; IntMPA 75, 76, 77, 78, 79, 80, 81, 82; MotPP; MovMk; Vers A; WhoHol A*

Jaeger, Andrea
American. Tennis Player
At 14, was youngest player ever to turn pro, 1980.
b. Jun 4, 1965 in Chicago, Illinois
Source: *BioIn 12; NewYTBS 82*

Jaeger, Gustav
English. Sportswear Producer
b. in Stuttgart, Germany
Source: *WorFshn*

Jaegers, Albert
American. Sculptor
b. Mar 28, 1868 in Elberfeld, Germany
d. Jul 22, 1925
Source: *WhAm 1*

Jaffe, Rona
American. Author
Wrote *The Last Chance,* 1976; *Class Reunion,* 1979.
b. Jun 12, 1932 in New York, New York
Source: *AmAu&B; AuNews 1; BioNews 75; ConAu 73; InWom; WhoAm 82; WhoWorJ 72; WrDr 76*

Jaffe, Sam
American. Actor
b. Mar 8, 1893 in New York, New York
Source: *BiE&WWA; IntMPA 82; MotPP; NotNAT; WhoAm 74, 76, 78, 80, 82; WhoHol A; WhoThe 77*

Jaffee, Irving
American. Speed Skater
Won two gold medals, 1932 Olympics.
b. 1907?
d. Mar 20, 1981 in San Diego, California
Source: *NewYTBS 81*

Jagan, Cheddi
Guyanese. Politician
b. Mar 22, 1918 in British Guiana (East)
Source: *CurBio 63; IntWW 74; Who 74*

Jagan, Janet
Guyanese. Politician
b. Oct 20, 1920 in Chicago, Illinois
Source: *IntWW 74; WhoWor 74*

Jagel, Frederick
American. Opera Singer, Teacher
b. Jun 10, 1897 in Brooklyn, New York
d. Jul 5, 1982 in San Francisco, California
Source: *BiDAmM; NewEOp 71; NewYTBS 82*

Jagendorf, Moritz
American. Folklorist, Author
Wrote *Till Ulenspiegel's Merry Pranks,* 1938.
b. Aug 24, 1888 in Czernowitz, Austria
d. Jan 8, 1981 in Ithaca, New York
Source: *AnObit 1981; AnCL; AuBYP; ConAu 5R; IntAu&W 77; MorJA; NewYTBS 81; SmATA 2; WhNAA; WhoAm 78; WrDr 76, 80*

Jaggar, Thomas Augustus
American. Volcanologist, Geologist
b. Jan 24, 1871 in Philadelphia, Pennsylvania
d. Jan 17, 1953
Source: *DcAmAu; DcAmB S5; OhA&B; WhAm 3; WhNAA*

Jagger, Bianca Teresa
[Bianca Perez Morena de Macias]
English. Socialite, Actress
Married to Mick Jagger, 1971-79; youngest member of best-dressed Hall of Fame.
b. 1943 in Managua, Nicaragua
Source: *BioNews 75; BkPepl*

Jagger, Dean
American. Actor
b. Nov 7, 1903 in Columbus Grove, Ohio
Source: *FilmgC; IntMPA 75, 76, 77, 78, 79, 80, 81, 82; MotPP; MovMk; WhoAm 74, 76, 78, 80, 82; WhoHol A; WhoThe 77*

Jagger, Mick (Michael Philip)
[The Rolling Stones]
English. Rock Singer, Musician
Formed Rolling Stones, 1962; hits include "Satisfaction," "Honky Tonk Woman."
b. Jul 26, 1944 in Dartford, England
Source: *BioNews 75; BkPepl; CelR 73; CurBio 72; FilmgC; WhoAm 80, 82; WhoHol A*

Jahoda, Gloria
American. Author
b. Oct 6, 1926 in Chicago, Illinois
d. Jan 13, 1980 in Tallahassee, Florida
Source: *AuNews 1; ConAu 1R, 104, 4NR; ForWC 70; WhoAmW 77; WrDr 76*

Jakes, John
American. Author
Wrote American Bicentennial series: *The Bastard,* 1974; *The Rebels,* 1975, etc.
b. Mar 31, 1932 in Chicago, Illinois
Source: *ConAu 57; OxCan SUP; WhoAm 82*

Jamal, Ahmad
American. Jazz Musician
b. Jul 7, 1930 in Pittsburgh, Pennsylvania
Source: *BioNews 74; WhoBlA 75*

James I
[James VI, King of Scotland]
English. King
b. Jun 19, 1566 in Edinburgh, Scotland
d. Mar 27, 1625 in Theobalds, England
Source: *BioIn 10; CasWL; NewCol 75; WebBD 80*

James I
Scottish. King
b. Jul 1394 in Dunfermline, Scotland
d. Feb 20, 1437 in Perth, Scotland
Source: *BioIn 10; CasWL; NewCol 75; WebBD 80*

James II
English. King
b. 1633
d. Sep 1701 in France
Source: *BioIn 10; McGEWB; WebBD 80*

James the Greater, Saint
[James the Elder, Saint]
Biblical Character
Source: *REn*

James the Less, Saint
Biblical Character
Source: *REn*

James, Art
American. TV Game Show Host
b. Oct 15, in Dearborn, Michigan
d. 1972
Source: *WhoHol B*

James, Daniel, Jr.
"Chappie"
American. Government Official
b. Feb 11, 1920 in Pensacola, Florida
d. Feb 25, 1978 in Colorado Springs, Colorado
Source: *CurBio 76, 78; EbonySL 1; USBiR 74; WebAMB; WhAm 7; WhoAm 76, 78; WhoBlA 75; WhoGov 75, 77; WhoWest 78; WorDWW*

James, Dennis
American. TV Game Show Host
b. 1917 in Jersey City, New Jersey
Source: *IntMPA 75, 76, 77, 78, 79, 80, 81, 82*

James, Edwin
American. Explorer
b. Aug 27, 1797 in Weybridge, Vermont
d. Oct 28, 1861
Source: *Alli; AmAu&B; DcAmAu; DcNAA; REnAL*

James, Frank
American. Outlaw
b. 1843 in Clay County, Missouri
d. 1915
Source: *BioIn 10; Blood*

James, George Payne Rainsford
English. Author
b. Aug 9, 1799 in London, England
d. May 9, 1860 in Venice, Italy
Source: *Alli; BbD; BiD&SB; BrAu 19; CasWL; Chambr 3; ChPo S1; DcBiA; DcEnA; DcEnL; DcEuL; DcLEL; EvLB; HsB&A; MnBBF; NewC; OxEng; WebE&AL*

James, Harry
American. Band Leader
Played trumpet with Benny Goodman; married to Betty Grable, 1943-65.
b. Mar 15, 1916 in Albany, Georgia
Source: *AmSCAP 66; CurBio 43; FilmgC; HolP 40; IntMPA 75, 76, 77, 78, 79, 80, 81, 82; MovMk; WhoHol A*

James, Henry
American. Philosopher
b. Jun 3, 1811 in Albany, New York
d. Dec 18, 1882 in Cambridge, Massachusetts
Source: *Alli SUP; AmAu; AmAu&B; AmBi; ApCAB; BbD; BiD&SB; CyAl 2; DcAmAu; DcAmB; DcNAA; OxAmL; Pen AM; REnAL; TwCBDA; WebAB; WhAm H*

James, Henry
American. Author
Master of psychological novel, stream of consciousness fiction as in *The Turn of the Screw*, 1898.
b. Apr 15, 1843 in New York, New York
d. Feb 28, 1916 in London, England
Source: *AmAu&B; AtlBL; CasWL; CyWA; EncWL; McGEWD; ModAL; ModBrL; ModWD; NewC; WhAm 1*

James, Jesse
American. Outlaw
Robber, with brother, Frank, gang; killed by gang member Robert Ford for reward.
b. Sep 5, 1847 in Centerville, Missouri
d. Apr 3, 1882 in Saint Joseph, Missouri
Source: *AmBi; FilmgC; OxAmL; OxFilm; REn; REnAL*

James, Joni
American. Singer
b. 1930 in Chicago, Illinois
Source: *InWom*

James, Kenny
see: Rare Earth

James, Marquis
American. Author
b. Sep 29, 1891 in Springfield, Missouri
d. Nov 19, 1955
Source: *AmAu&B; DcAmB S5; OxAmL; REnAL; TwCA, SUP; WhAm 3; WhNAA*

James, Philip
American. Composer, Conductor
b. May 17, 1890 in Jersey City, New Jersey
d. Nov 1, 1975 in Southampton, New York
Source: *AmSCAP 66; Baker 78; BioIn 1, 10; WhAm 6, 7; WhoAm 74, 76*

James, P(hyllis) D(orothy)
English. Author
b. Aug 3, 1920 in Oxford, England
Source: *ConAu 21R; ConLC 18; CurBio 80; EncMys*

James, Rick
[James Johnson]
American. Singer
b. 1953? in Buffalo, New York
Source: *BioIn 12; IlEncRk*

James, "Skip" (Nehemiah)
American. Musician, Singer
b. Jun 9, 1902 in Betonia, Mississippi
d. Oct 3, 1969 in Philadelphia, Pennsylvania
Source: *BioIn 7, 8; EncFCWM 69; EncJzS 70; ObitOF 79; WhoRock 81*

James, Sonny
[Jimmy Loden]
"The Southern Gentleman"
American. Singer
b. Mar 1, 1929 in Hackleburg, Alaska
Source: *EncFCWM 69*

James, Will(iam)
American. Author, Illustrator
b. Jun 6, 1892 in Great Falls, Montana
d. Sep 3, 1942 in Hollywood, California
Source: *AuBYP; CurBio 42; DcAmB S3; DcNAA; JBA 34, 51; Newb 1922; OxAmL; REnAL; SmATA 19; TwCA, SUP; WhAm 2; WhNAA*

James, William
American. Psychologist, Philosopher
Exponent of Pragmatism; wrote *The Meaning of Truth*, 1919.
b. Jan 11, 1842 in New York, New York
d. Aug 26, 1910 in Chocorua, New Hampshire
Source: *AmAu; AmAu&B; AmBi; AmWr; ApCAB; AtlBL; BiD&SB; BiDPara; CasWL; CyWA; DcAmAu; DcAmB; DcEuL; DcLEL; DcNAA; EncAB-H; EvLB; LongCTC; ModAL, SUP; NewC; OxAmL; OxEng; Pen AM; RComWL; REn; REnAL; TwCBDA; WebAB; WebE&AL; WhAm 1; WhoTwCL*

James Gang
[Tom Bolin; James Fox; Phil Giallombardo; "Bubba" Keith; Roy Kenner; Dale Peters; Richard Shack; Dom Troiano; Joseph Fidler Walsh; Bob Webb]
American. Rock Group
Source: *EncPR&S; RkOn*

Jameson, House
American. Actor
b. 1902
d. Apr 23, 1971 in Danbury, Connecticut
Source: *BiE&WWA; PlP&P; WhScrn 74, 77; WhoHol B*

Jameson, Margaret Storm
English. Author
b. 1891 in Whitby, England
Source: *ConAu 81; DcLEL; EvLB; LongCTC; ModBrL; NewC; Pen ENG; REn; Who 74*

Jamison, Judith
American. Dancer
b. May 10, 1934 in Philadelphia, Pennsylvania
Source: *BioNews 74; CurBio 73; NewYTBE 72; WhoAm 82; WhoBlA 75*

Jamison, Philip Duane, Jr.
American. Artist
b. Jul 3, 1925 in Philadelphia, Pennsylvania
Source: *WhoAm 74, 76, 78, 80, 82; WhoAmA 73, 76, 78; WhoE 74*

Jammes, Francis
French. Author
b. Dec 2, 1868 in Tournay, France
d. Nov 1, 1938
Source: *CasWL; CathA 1930; ChPo; ClDMEL; EncWL; EvEuW; ModRL; NewC; OxEng; OxFr; Pen*

Jan and Dean
[Jan Berry; Dean Torrance]
American. Singing Duo
Source: *EncPR&S; IlEncRk*

Janacek, Leos
Czech. Composer
b. Jul 3, 1854 in Hukvaldy, Moravia
d. Aug 12, 1928 in Prague, Czechoslovakia
Source: *DcCM*

Janaszak, Steve
[United States Olympic Hockey Team-1980]
American. Hockey Player
b. Jan 7, 1957 in Saint Paul, Minnesota
Source: *HocReg*

Jancso, Miklos
Hungarian. Motion Picture Director
b. Sep 27, 1922
Source: *BiDFilm; DcFM; FilmgC; IntWW 74; OxFilm; WhoWor 74; WorEFlm*

Janeway, Eliot
American. Economist, Author, Lecturer
b. Jan 1, 1913 in New York, New York
Source: *AmAu&B; CurBio 70; IntWW 74; WhoAm 74, 76, 78, 80, 82; WhoWor 74; WrDr 76*

Janeway, Elizabeth
American. Author
b. Oct 7, 1913 in Brooklyn, New York
Source: *AmAu&B; AmNov; Au&Wr 71; AuBYP; AuNews 1; ChPo; ConAu 45, 2NR; CurBio 44; DrAF 76; InWom; REnAL; SmATA 19; TwCA SUP; WhoAm 74, 76, 78, 80, 82; WhoAmW 77; WhoE 74; WhoWor 74*

Janifer, Laurence
American. Author
b. Mar 17, 1933 in Brooklyn, New York
Source: *ConAu 9R, 5NR*

Janigro, Antonio
Italian. Musician, Conductor
b. Jan 21, 1918 in Milan, Italy
Source: *Baker 78*

Janis, Byron
American. Musician
b. Mar 24, 1928 in McKeesport, Pennsylvania
Source: *CelR 73; CurBio 66; WhoAm 74, 76, 78, 80, 82; WhoE 74; WhoMus 72*

Janis, Conrad
American. Actor, Musician
b. Feb 11, 1928 in New York, New York
Source: *BiE&WWA; FilmgC; MotPP; NotNAT; WhoAm 82; WhoAmA 73; WhoHol A; WhoThe 77*

Janis, Elsie
[Elsie Bierbower]
American. Actress
b. Mar 16, 1889 in Columbus, Ohio
d. Feb 26, 1956 in Beverly Hills, California
Source: *AmSCAP 66; EncMT; FamA&A; Film 1; FilmgC; InWom; OhA&B; TwYS; WhAm 3; WhScrn 74, 77; WhoHol B; WhoStg 1906, 1908; WomWWA 14*

Janney, Leon
American. Actor
b. 1917 in Ogden, Utah
d. Oct 28, 1980 in Guadalajara, Mexico
Source: *BiE&WWA; NotNAT; WhoHol A*

Janney, William
American. Actor
b. Feb 15, 1908 in New York, New York
d. Jun 1938 in New York, New York
Source: *Film 2; WhScrn 77*

Jannings, Emil
American. Actor
b. Jul 26, 1886 in Brooklyn, New York
d. Jan 3, 1950 in Lake Wolfgang, Austria
Source: *BiDFilm; Film 1; FilmgC; MotPP; MovMk; OxFilm; REn; TwYS; WhScrn 74, 77; WhoHol B; WorEFlm*

Janosch, pseud.
see: Eckert, Horst

Janov, Arthur
American. Psychologist
b. Aug 21, 1924 in Los Angeles, California
Source: *CurBio 80*

Jansen, Cornelis
Dutch. Roman Catholic Theologian
b. 1585 in Leerdam, Netherlands
d. 1638 in Flanders
Source: *McGEWB; NewCol 75*

Janson, Horst Woldemar
American. Educator, Author
Wrote *History of Art,* 1962; has sold more than two million copies.
b. Oct 4, 1913 in Saint Petersburg, Russia
d. Sep 30, 1982
Source: *AuBYP; ConAu 1R; DrAS 74H, 78H; NewYTBS 82; WhoAm 74, 76, 78, 80; WhoAmA 73, 76, 78, 80; WhoArt 80; WhoWor 74, 76; WrDr 80*

Janssen, David
American. Actor
Starred in TV series "The Fugitive," 1963-67; "Harry-O," 1974-76.
b. Mar 27, 1931 in Naponee, Nebraska
d. Feb 13, 1980 in Malibu Beach, California
Source: *BioNews 74; CurBio 67; FilmgC; IntMPA 75, 76, 77; MotPP; MovMk; WhoAm 74; WhoHol A; WhoWor 74*

Janssen, Herbert
German. Opera Singer
b. Sep 22, 1895 in Cologne, Germany
d. Jun 3, 1965 in New York, New York
Source: *NewEOp 71*

Janssen, Werner
American. Conductor, Composer
b. Jun 1, 1899 in New York, New York
Source: *AmSCAP 66; DcCM; WhoAm 74*

Jardine, Al(lan)
[The Beach Boys]
American. Singer, Musician
b. Sep 3, 1942 in Lima, Ohio
Source: *BioIn 11; BkPepl*

Jarman, Claude, Jr.
American. Actor, Motion Picture Executive
b. Sep 27, 1934 in Nashville, Tennessee
Source: *FilmgC; IntMPA 75, 76, 77; MotPP; MovMk; WhoHol A*

Jarman, John
American. Politician
Congressman from OK, 1951-77; became Republican, 1975.
b. Jul 17, 1915 in Sallisaw, Oklahoma
d. Jan 15, 1982 in Oklahoma City, Oklahoma
Source: *BiDrAC; CngDr 74; WhoAmP 73, 75, 77, 79; WhoGov 72, 75, 77; WhoS&SW 73, 75, 76*

Jaroszewicz, Piotr
Polish. Politician
b. Oct 8, 1909 in Nieswicz, Poland
Source: *IntWW 74; NewYTBE 70; WhoWor 74*

Jarre, Maurice
French. Composer
b. Sep 13, 1924 in Lyons, France
Source: *Baker 78; CmMov; DcFM; FilmEn; FilmgC; IntMPA 75, 76, 77, 78, 79, 80, 81; OxFilm; WorEFlm*

Jarreau, Al
American. Singer
Won Grammys, 1978, 1979, as best jazz vocalist.
b. Mar 12, 1940 in Milwaukee, Wisconsin
Source: *BioIn 11; WhoAm 82*

Jarrell, Randall
American. Author, Poet
b. May 6, 1914 in Nashville, Tennessee
d. Oct 14, 1965 in Chapel Hill, North Carolina
Source: *AmAu&B; AmWr; AnCL; AuBYP; CasWL; ChPo, S1; CnDAL; CnE&AP; ConAu 5R, 25R, 25R; ConLC 1, 2, 6, 9, 13; ConP 75; CroCAP; EncWL; ModAL, SUP; OxAmL; Pen AM; RAdv 1; REn; REnAL; SixAP; SmATA 7; ThrBJA; TwCA SUP; TwCW; WebAB; WebE&AL; WhAm 4; WhoTwCL*

Jarring, Gunnar V
Swedish. Diplomat
b. Oct 12, 1907 in Brunnby, Sweden
Source: *CurBio 57; IntWW 74; NewYTBE 70; Who 74; WhoUN 75; WhoWor 74*

Jarriel, Tom (Thomas Edwin)
American. Broadcast Journalist
b. Dec 29, 1934 in LaGrange, Georgia
Source: *NewYTET; WhoAm 76, 78*

Jarry, Alfred
French. Poet
b. Oct 8, 1873 in Laval, France
d. Nov 1, 1907 in Paris, France
Source: *CasWL; ClDMEL; CnMD; CnThe; EncWL; EuAu; EvEuW; LongCTC; McGEWD; ModRL; ModWD: OxFr; OxThe; Pen EUR; RComWL; REn; REnWD; WhoTwCL*

Jaruzelski, Wojciech Witold
Polish. Premier
b. Jul 6, 1923 in Kurow, Poland
Source: *CurBio 82; IntWW 74, 75, 76, 77, 78; NewYTBS 81; WhoSocC 78; WhoWor 74; WorDWW*

Jarvik, Robert K.
American. Physician
Designed artificial heart Jarvik-7 used in Barney Clark.
b. 1946?
Source: *NF*

Jarvis, Anna
American. Proponent of Mother's Day
Founded Mother's Day to commemorate anniversary of mother's death.
b. May 1, 1864
d. Nov 24, 1948 in West Chester, Pennsylvania
Source: *WomWWA 14*

Jarvis, Howard Arnold
American. Social Reformer
Force behind CA's Proposition 13, which reduced property taxes 57%, 1978.
b. Sep 22, 1902 in Magna, Utah
Source: *BioIn 11; CurBio 79; NewYTBS 78*

Jarvis, John Wesley
American. Artist
b. 1781 in South Shields, England
d. Jan 14, 1839
Source: *BioIn 1, 2, 9; EarABI; WhAm H*

Jason, Rick
American. Actor
b. May 21, 1926 in New York, New York
Source: *FilmgC; IntMPA 75, 76, 77, 78, 79, 80, 81, 82; MotPP; WhoHol A*

Jasper, John J
American. Clergyman
b. 1812
d. 1901
Source: *BioIn 3, 6, 8; REnAL*

Jaspers, Karl
German. Author, Philosopher
b. Feb 23, 1883
d. Feb 26, 1969 in Basel, Switzerland
Source: *CasWL; ConAu 25R; OxGer; REn; TwCA SUP; TwCW*

Jastrow, Robert
American. Author, Astronomer
b. Sep 7, 1925 in New York, New York
Source: *AmM&WS 73P; ConAu 25R; CurBio 73; IntWW 74; WhoAm 74, 76, 78, 80, 82; WhoGov 72; WhoWor 74; WrDr 76*

Jaures, Jean Leon
French. Socialist Leader
Co-founded French Socialist Party, 1905; assassinated by patriotic fanatic.
b. Sep 3, 1859 in Castres, France
d. Jul 31, 1914
Source: *DcAmSR; McGEWB; NewCol 75; OxFr; REn; WhDW; WhoMilH 76*

Javits, Jacob Koppel
American. Senator
b. May 18, 1904 in New York, New York
Source: *AmAu&B; BiDrAC; CelR 73; ConAu 1R, 1NR; CurBio 48, 58; IntWW 74; NewYTBS 74; WhoAm 74, 76, 78, 80, 82; WhoAmP 73; WhoE 74; WhoGov 72; WhoWor 74*

Jawara, Alhaji Dawda Kairaba
Gambian. President
b. May 16, 1924
Source: *IntWW 74; Who 74; WhoGov 72; WhoWor 74*

Jaworski, Leon
American. Prosecutor
Directed Office of Watergate Special Prosecution Force, 1973-74.
b. Sep 19, 1905 in Waco, Texas
d. Dec 9, 1982 in Wimberly, Texas
Source: *ConAu P-1; CurBio 74, 83; IntWW 74, 75, 76, 77, 78, 79, 80, 81; NewYTBE 70, 71, 73; NewYTBS 83; WhoAm 74, 76, 78, 80, 82; WhoAmL 78, 79; WhoAmP 75, 77, 79; WhoGov 75, 77*

Jaworski, Ron(ald Vincent)
"The Polish Rifle"
American. Football Player
b. Mar 23, 1951 in Lackawanna, New York
Source: *BioIn 12; FootReg; WhoAm 82*

Jay, John
American. Supreme Court Justice
First Chief Justice of Supreme Court, 1789-95; wrote five *Federalist* papers.
b. Dec 12, 1745 in New York, New York
d. May 17, 1829 in Bedford, New York
Source: *Alli; AmAu&B; AmBi; ApCAB; BiAuS; BiDrAC; BiDrUSE; CyAL 1; CyWA; DcAmAu; DcAmB; DcNAA; Drake; EncAB-H; OxAmL; REn; REnAL; TwCBDA; WebAB; WhAm H; WhAmP*

Jay, Joseph Richard (Joey)
American. Baseball Player
b. Aug 15, 1935 in Middletown, Connecticut
Source: *BaseEn; BioIn 6*

Jay, Peter
English. Diplomat, Economist
b. Feb 7, 1937 in London, England
Source: *CurBio 78; IntWW 76, 77, 78; IntYB 78, 79; Who 74; WhoWor 76, 78*

Jay and the Americans
[Jay Black; Sandy Deane; Howie Kane; Marty Sander; Kenny Vance]
American. Rock Group
Source: *ConMuA 80; LilREn 78; RkOn; WhoRock 81*

Jayewardene, Junius Richard
Ceylonese. Political Leader
b. Sep 17, 1906 in Colombo, Ceylon
Source: *BioIn 11; IntWW 74*

Jayston, Michael
English. Actor
b. Oct 29, 1936 in Nottinghamshire, England
Source: *FilmgC; WhoHol A; WhoThe 77, 72*

Jean, Grand Duke of Luxembourg
Luxembourg. Ruler
b. Jan 5, 1921 in Colmar, France
Source: *NewCol 75; WebBD 80; WhoWor 74*

Jean Louis
[Jean Louis Berthault]
American. Fashion, Costume Designer
b. 1907 in Paris, France
Source: *WorFshn*

Jeanmaire, Renee Marcelle
"Zizi"
French. Actress, Dancer, Singer
b. 1924 in Paris, France
Source: *CurBio 52; InWom; IntWW 74*

Jeanneret-Gris, Charles Edward
see: LeCorbusier

Jeans, Sir James Hopwood
English. Mathematician, Astronomer
b. Sep 11, 1877 in Lancashire, England
d. Sep 17, 1946
Source: *Chambr 3; CurBio 41, 46; DcLEL; EvLB; LongCTC; NewC; OxEng; TwCA, SUP*

Jeffers, (John) Robinson
American. Poet, Dramatist
b. Jan 10, 1887 in Pittsburgh, Pennsylvania
d. Jan 21, 1962 in Carmel, California
Source: *AmAu&B; AtlBL; CasWL; ChPo S1, S2; CnDAL; CnE&AP; CnMD; CnMWL; ConAmA; ConAmL; ConAu 85; ConLC 2, 3, 11, 15; CyWA; EncWL; LongCTC; McGEWD; ModAL, SUP; ModWD; OxAmL; OxEng; Pen AM; RAdv 1; REn; REnAL; SixAP; TwCA, SUP; TwCW; WebAB; WebE&AL; WhAm 4; WhNAA; WhoTwCL*

Jefferson, Blind Lemon
American. Singer
b. 1897 in Wortham, Texas
d. 1930 in Chicago, Illinois
Source: *BiDAmM*

Jefferson, John Larry
American. Football Player
b. Feb 3, 1956 in Dallas, Texas
Source: *BioIn 12; FootReg; WhoAm 82*

Jefferson, Joseph
American. Actor
b. Feb 20, 1829 in Philadelphia, Pennsylvania
d. 1905
Source: *AmAu&B; AmBi; ApCAB; BbD; BiD&SB; DcAmAu; DcAmB; DcNAA; Drake; FamA&A; Film 1; OxAmL; OxThe; REnAL; REnWD; TwCBDA; WebAB; WhAm 1; WhScrn 77*

Jefferson, Thomas
"Red Fox"
American. 3rd US President
First president inaugurated in Washington, DC, 1801; planned Lewis and Clark Expedition.
b. Apr 13, 1743 in Shadwell, Virginia
d. Jul 4, 1826 in Monticello, Virginia
Source: *Alli; AmAu&B; AmBi; ApCAB; AtlBL; BbD; BiAuS; BiD&SB; BiDSA; BiDrAC; BiDrUSE; CasWL; Chambr 3; CyAL 1; CyWA; DcAmAu; DcAmB; DcLEL; DcNAA; Drake; EncAB-H; EvLB; OxAmL; Pen AM; RComWL; REn; REnAL; TwCBDA; WebAB; WebE&AL; WhAm H; WhAmP*

Jefferson, Thomas
American. Actor
b. 1859
d. Apr 2, 1923 in Hollywood, California
Source: *Film 1; WhScrn 74, 77*

Jefferson Airplane
[Marty Balin; Jack Casady; Joey Covington; Spencer Dryden; Paul Katner; Jorma Kauoknen; Grace Slick]
American. Rock Group
Source: *EncPR&S; IlEncRk*

Jefferson Starship
see: Jefferson Airplane

Jefford, Barbara
English. Actress
b. 1930 in Plymstock, England
Source: *BiE&WWA; FilmgC; NotNAT; Who 74; WhoHol A; WhoThe 77*

Jeffrey, Lord Francis
Scottish. Author
b. 1773 in Edinburgh, Scotland
d. 1850
Source: *Alli; BbD; BiD&SB; BrAu 19; CasWL; Chambr 3; CrtT 2; DcEnA; DcEnL; DcEuL; DcLEL; EvLB; MouLC 3; NewC; OxEng; Pen ENG; WebE&AL*

Jeffreys, Anne
American. Actress
b. Jan 26, 1923 in Goldsboro, North Carolina
Source: *BiE&WWA; FilmgC; InWom; IntMPA 75, 76, 77, 78, 79, 80, 81, 82; MotPP; MovMk; NotNAT; WhoHol A; WhoThe 77*

Jeffreys, Garland
American. Singer, Songwriter
b. 1944 in Brooklyn, New York
Source: *BioIn 11, 12*

Jeffries, Fran
American. Actress
b. 1939 in San Jose, California
Source: *WhoHol A*

Jeffries, James Jackson
"The Boilermaker"
American. Boxer, Actor
b. Apr 15, 1875 in Carroll County, Ohio
d. Mar 3, 1953 in Burbank, California
Source: *DcAmB S5; Film 1; WhScrn 77; WhoPubR 76*

Jeffries, Lionel Charles
English. Actor
b. 1926 in London, England
Source: *FilmgC; IntMPA 75, 76, 77, 78, 79, 80, 81, 82; MovMk; Who 74; WhoHol A; WhoWor 74*

Jehangir
Indian. Emperor
b. 1569
d. 1627
Source: *NewC*

Jellicoe, Ann
English. Dramatist
b. Jul 15, 1927
Source: *ConAu 85; ConDr 73; CroCD; McGEWD; ModWD; NewC; NotNAT; REnWD; TwCW; Who 74; WhoThe 77; WorAu; WrDr 76*

Jellicoe, John
English. Admiral
b. Dec 5, 1859 in Southampton, England
d. Nov 20, 1935
Source: *McGEWB; WhoLA*

Jenkins, Allen
American. Actor
b. 1900 in New York, New York
d. Jul 20, 1974 in Santa Monica, California
Source: *FilmgC; IntMPA 75, 76, 77; MovMk; Vers A*

Jenkins, Carol Elizabeth Heiss
[Carol Heiss]
American. Figure Skater
Won gold medal, 1960 Olympics.
b. Jan 20, 1940 in New York, New York
Source: *CurBio 59; FilmgC; GoodHS; HerW; InWom*

Jenkins, Ferguson Arthur
"Fergie"
Canadian. Baseball Player
Won at least 20 games per season, 1967-72; Cy Young award, 1971.
b. Dec 13, 1943 in Chatham, ON
Source: *BaseEn; NewYTBE 71; WhoAm 74, 76, 78, 80, 82; WhoBlA 75; WhoProB 73*

Jenkins, Gordon
American. Musician
b. May 12, 1910 in Webster Groves, Missouri
Source: *AmSCAP 66*

Jenkins, Hayes Alan
American. Figure Skater
b. Mar 23, 1933 in Akron, Ohio
Source: *CurBio 56*

Jenkins, Newell
American. Conductor
b. Feb 8, 1915 in New Haven, Connecticut
Source: *WhoE 74*

Jenkins, Paul
American. Artist
b. Jul 12, 1923 in Kansas City, Missouri
Source: *BioIn 5, 6, 7; ConArt; DcAmArt; DcCAA 71, 77; WhoAm 74, 76, 78, 80, 82; WhoAmA 73, 76, 78; WhoWor 74, 76*

Jenkins, Ray Howard
American. Lawyer
b. Mar 18, 1897 in Unaka, North Carolina
d. Dec 26, 1980 in Knoxville, Tennessee
Source: *BioIn 3, 7, 8, 9; CurBio 54, 81; WhAm 7; WhoAm 74*

Jenkins, Roy Harris
Welsh. Political Leader
Co-founder, leader of Social Democratic Party in Britain, March, 1981--.
b. Nov 11, 1920 in Abersychan, Wales
Source: *Au&Wr 71; ConAu 9R; CurBio 66, 82; DcLEL 1940; IntAu&W 76, 77; IntWW 74, 75, 76, 77, 78, 79, 80, 81; IntYB 78, 79, 80, 81; OxLaw; Who 74, 82; WhoWor 74, 76, 78; WorAu; WrDr 76, 80*

Jenner, Bruce
American. Track Athlete, Sportscaster
Won gold medal in decathlon, 1976 Olympics.
b. Oct 28, 1949 in Mount Kisco, New York
Source: *BioIn 11; BkPepl; WhoAm 82*

Jenner, Edward
English. Doctor
Discovered process of vaccination for preventing smallpox, 1796.
b. May 17, 1749 in Berkeley, England
d. Jan 24, 1823 in Berkeley, England
Source: *Alli; AsBiEn; BiDLA; DcScB; McGEWB; NewC; NewCol 75; REn*

Jenner, Sir William
English. Scientist, Engineer, Physician
b. 1815 in Chatham, England
d. Dec 7, 1898
Source: *BiHiMed; BioIn 2, 4, 9*

Jenney, Neil
American. Artist
b. 1946
Source: *BioIn 12*

Jenney, William LeBaron
American. Architect
b. Sep 25, 1832 in Fairhaven, Massachusetts
d. Jun 15, 1907 in Los Angeles, California
Source: *AmBi; ApCAB SUP; DcAmB; DcNAA; TwCBDA; WebAB; WhAm 1*

Jennings, Elizabeth
English. Author
b. Jul 18, 1926 in Boston, England
Source: *Au&Wr 71; ChPo, S1, S2; ConAu 61; ConLC 5; ConP 70, 75; LongCTC; ModBrL, SUP; NewC; Pen ENG; RAdv 1; TwCW; WebE&AL; Who 74; WhoTwCL; WorAu; WrDr 76*

Jennings, Gary
American. Author
b. Sep 20, 1928 in Buena Vista, Virginia
Source: *AuBYP; ConAu 5R; SmATA 9*

Jennings, Peter Charles
Canadian. Journalist
b. Jul 29, 1938 in Toronto, ON
Source: *WhoAm 74, 76, 78, 80, 82; WhoE 74*

Jennings, Waylon
American. Singer
b. Jun 15, 1937 in Littlefield, Texas
Source: *BkPepl; CurBio 82; EncFCWM 69; WhoAm 82; WhoHol A*

Jenrette, John Wilson, Jr.
American. Politician
Former Congressman convicted in ABSCAM scandal, Oct, 1980.
b. May 19, 1936 in Conway, South Carolina
Source: *AlmAP 78, 80; CngDr 77, 79; WhoAm 78, 80; WhoAmP 73, 75, 77, 79; WhoGov 75, 77; WhoS&SW 76, 78*

Jenrette, Rita Carpenter
American. Former Wife of John Jenrette
b. 1950?
Source: *NF*

Jens, Salome
American. Actress
b. May 8, 1935 in Milwaukee, Wisconsin
Source: *BiE&WWA; FilmgC; MotPP; NotNAT; WhoHol A; WhoThe 77*

Jensen, Adolph
German. Composer
b. Jan 12, 1837 in Konigsberg, Germany
d. Jan 23, 1879 in Baden-Baden, Germany
Source: *OxMus*

Jensen, Alfred Julio
Artist
b. Dec 11, 1903 in Guatemala City, Guatemala
d. Apr 4, 1981 in Livingston, New Jersey
Source: *BioIn 7, 10; DcCAA 71, 77; WhAm 7; WhoAm 74, 76, 78, 80; WhoAmA 73, 76, 78*

Jensen, Arthur Robert
American. Psychologist, Author
b. Aug 24, 1923 in San Diego, California
Source: *BioIn 8, 9, 10; ConAu 2NR; CurBio 73; WhoAm 82*

Jensen, Jackie (Jack Eugene)
"Golden Boy"
American. Baseball Player
b. Mar 9, 1927 in San Francisco, California
d. Jul 14, 1982 in Charlottesville, Virginia
Source: *BaseEn; CurBio 59, 82; NewYTBS 82*

Jensen, Oliver Ormerod
American. Author
b. Apr 16, 1914 in Ithaca, New York
Source: *ConAu 25R; CurBio 45; DrAS 74H; St&PR 75; WhoAm 74, 76, 78, 80, 82; WhoE 74; WhoWor 74*

Jensen, Virginia Allen
American. Author
b. Sep 21, 1927 in Des Moines, Iowa
Source: *ConAu 45, 1NR; SmATA 8*

Jepsen, Roger William
American. Senator
b. Dec 23, 1928 in Cedar Falls, Iowa
Source: *AlmAP 80; CngDr 79; WhoAm 74, 82; WhoAmP 73, 75, 77, 79; WhoGov 72; WhoMW 74*

Jepson, Helen
American. Opera Singer
b. Nov 25, 1906 in Akron, Ohio
Source: *InWom; WhoHol A*

Jeremiah
Prophet
Source: *DcOrL 3; NewC*

Jergens, Adele
American. Actress
b. 1922 in New York, New York
Source: *FilmgC; IntMPA 75, 76, 77, 78, 79, 80, 81, 82; MotPP; WhoHol A*

Jerger, Alfred
Austrian. Opera Singer
Sang in Solti's recording of *Der Rosenkavalier* at age 80.
b. Jun 9, 1889 in Brunn, Austria
d. Nov 18, 1976 in Vienna, Austria
Source: *NewEOp 71*

Jeritza, Maria
[Mitzi Jedlicka]
American. Opera Singer
b. Oct 6, 1887 in Brunn, Austria
d. Jul 10, 1982 in Orange, New Jersey
Source: *Baker 78; InWom; NewEOp 71; NewYTBS 82; Who 74; WhoAmW 58*

Jerome, Saint
Church Father, Translator
b. 340
d. 420
Source: *CasWL; NewC; OxEng; Pen CL; RComWL; REn*

Jerome, Jerome Klapka
English. Author, Humorist
b. May 2, 1859 in Walsall, England
d. Jun 14, 1927
Source: *Alli SUP; BbD; BiD&SB; CasWL; Chambr 3; CyWA; DcBiA; DcEnA AP; DcLEL; EvLB; LongCTC; McGEWD; MnBBF; ModBrL; ModWD; NewC; OxEng; OxThe; Pen ENG; REn; TwCA; TwCW; WhoStg 1908*

Jerry Murad's Harmonicats
[Al Fiore; Don Les; Jerry Murad]
American. Harmonica Players
Source: *CmpEPM*

Jessel, George Albert
American. Actor
Called "Toastmaster General" for many appearances as MC.
b. Apr 3, 1898 in New York, New York
d. May 24, 1981 in Los Angeles, California
Source: *AmPS B; AmSCAP 66; BiE&WWA; BioIn 1, 2, 3, 5, 7, 8, 10; BioNews 74; CelR 73; CmMov; CmpEPM; ConAu 89, 103; CurBio 43, 81; EncMT; Film 1; FilmgC; IntMPA 75, 76, 77, 78, 79, 80, 81; MovMk; NewYTBS 81; NotNAT; TwYS; WebAB; WhAm 7; Who 74; WhoAm 74, 76, 78, 80; WhoHol A; WhoThe 72, 77; WhoWor 74; WhoWorJ 72*

Jessner, Irene
Austrian. Opera Singer
b. 1909 in Vienna, Austria
Source: *CreCan 1; InWom*

Jessup, Philip C
American. Ambassador
b. Jan 5, 1897 in New York, New York
Source: *AmAu&B; ConAu 77; CurBio 48; IntWW 74; REnAL; WebAB; Who 74; WhoAm 74; WhoWor 74*

Jessup, Richard
American. Author
Wrote *The Cincinnati Kid,* 1964.
b. Jan 1, 1925 in Savannah, Georgia
d. Oct 22, 1982 in Nokomis, Florida
Source: *AmAu&B; NewYTBS 82*

Jesus Christ
Religious Leader
Teacher, founder of Christianity.
b. 4?BC in Bethelehem, Judea
d. 29?AD
Source: *BioIn 1, 2, 3, 4, 5, 6, 7, 8, 9, 10, 11; NewCol 75; REn*

Jethro Tull
[Mick Abrahams; Ian Anderson; Barriemore Barlowe; Martin Barre; Clive Bunker; Glenn Cornick; John Evan; Jeffrey Hammond-Hammond]
English. Rock Group
Source: *EncPR&S; IlEncRk*

Jett, Joan
[Joan Jett and the Blackhearts; Joan Larkin; The Runaways]
American. Singer, Musician
Hit single "I Love Rock 'n Roll," 1982.
b. 1959 in Philadelphia, Pennsylvania
Source: *NewWmR*

Jewett, Henry
American. Actor
b. Jun 4, 1862 in Victoria, Australia
d. Jun 24, 1930 in West Newton, Massachusetts
Source: *NatCAB 22; WhoStg 1906, 1908*

Jewett, Sarah Orne
American. Author
b. Sep 3, 1849 in South Berwick, Maine
d. Jun 24, 1909 in South Berwick, Maine
Source: *Alli SUP; AmAu; AmAu&B; AmBi; AmWr; AmWom; ApCAB; AtlBL; AuBYP; BbD; BiD&SB; CarSB; CasWL; Chambr 3; ChPo, S1, S2; CnDAL; CrtT 3; CyWA; DcAmAu; DcAmB; DcBiA; DcLEL; DcNAA; EvLB; InWom; JBA 34; ModAL; NotAW; OxAmL; OxEng; Pen AM; RAdv 1; REn; REnAL; TwCBDA; WebAB; WebE&AL; WhAm 1*

Jewison, Norman
American. Motion Picture Director
b. Jul 21, 1926 in Toronto, ON
Source: *BiDFilm; CanWW 70, 79; CurBio 79; FilmgC; IntMPA 77, 78, 79, 80, 81, 82; MovMk; NewYTET; OxFilm; WhoAm 74, 76, 78, 80, 82; WorEFlm*

Jezebel
Phoenician Princess
Wife of King Ahab; name is used symbolically for a wicked woman.
fl. 9th century BC
Source: *GoodHS; InWom; LongCEL; NewCol 75; WebBD 80*

Jhabvala, Ruth Prawer
British. Author
b. May 7, 1927 in Cologne, Germany
Source: *ConAu 1R, 2NR; ConLC 4; ConNov 72, 76; NewC; NewYTBE 73; TwCW; WorAu; WrDr 76*

Jillian, Ann
[Mrs. Andy Murcia]
American. Actress
Starred on Broadway in *Sugar Babies;* in TV series "It's a Living," 1980--.
b. 1950? in Los Angeles, California
Source: *BioIn 12*

Jimenez, Juan Ramon
Spanish. Poet
b. Dec 23, 1881 in Monguer, Spain
d. May 29, 1958 in Puerto Rico
Source: *AnCL; AtlBL; CasWL; ClDMEL; CnMWL; CyWA; DcSpL; EncWL; EvEuW; ModRL; Pen EUR; REn; TwCW; WhAm 3; WhoTwCL; WorAu*

Jimenez, Marcos Perez
see: Perez Jimenez, Marcos

"Jimmy the Greek"
[James Snyder; Demetrius George Synodinos]
American. Journalist, Oddsmaker
b. 1923 in Steubenville, Ohio
Source: *BioIn 6, 9, 10, 11; WhoAm 78*

Jinnah, Mahomed Ali
Indian. 1st Governor of Pakistan
b. Dec 25, 1876 in Karachi, Pakistan
d. Sep 11, 1948 in Karachi, Pakistan
Source: *WhAm 2*

Joachim, Joseph
Hungarian. Musician
b. Jun 28, 1831 in Kisstee, Hungary
d. Aug 15, 1907 in Berlin, Germany
Source: *BioIn 1, 2, 4, 8, 9; NewCol 75; WebBD 80*

Joan of Arc
[Jeanne d'Arc]
"Maid of Orleans"
French. Saint, National Heroine
Led troops to victory over English, 1429; tried for heresy, burned at stake.
b. Jan 6, 1412 in Domremy, France
d. May 30, 1431 in Rouen, France
Source: *FilmgC; HerW; InWom; LongCEL; McGEWB; NewC; NewCol 75; OxFr; REn*

Job
Biblical Character
Source: *BioIn 10; NewCol 75; WebBD 80*

Jobert, Michel
French. Diplomat
b. Sep 11, 1921 in Meknes, Morocco
Source: *CurBio 75; IntWW 74; NewYTBS 74; Who 74*

Jobin, Raoul
Canadian. Opera Singer
b. Apr 8, 1906 in Quebec City, PQ
d. Jan 13, 1974 in Quebec City, PQ
Source: *CanWW 70; CreCan 1; WhAm 6*

Jobs, Steven Paul
American. Computer Executive
Chairman, co-founder, Apple Computer, Inc.
b. 1955?
Source: *LElec*

Jobson, Eddie
see: Roxy Music

Jochum, Eugen
German. Conductor
b. Nov 2, 1902 in Babenhausen, Germany
Source: *IntWW 74; WhoMus 72; WhoWor 74*

Joel, Billy (William Martin)
American. Singer, Composer
Won Grammys, 1978, for single "Just the Way You Are," 1979, album *52nd Street*.
b. May 9, 1949 in Hicksville, New York
Source: *BioIn 10, 11; BioNews 74; BkPepl; CurBio 79; IlEncRk; RkOn 2; WhoAm 82*

Joffre, Joseph Jacques Cesaire
French. World War I Marshal
b. Jan 12, 1852 in Rivesaltes, France
d. Jan 13, 1931 in Paris, France
Source: *McGEWB; OxFr; WhoMilH 76*

Joffrey, Robert
[Abdullah Jaffa Bey Khan]
American. Choreographer
Founded Joffrey Ballet Co., 1956--.
b. Dec 24, 1930 in Seattle, Washington
Source: *BioNews 74; CurBio 67; NewYTBE 72; WhoWor 74; WhoAm 74, 76, 78, 80, 82*

Jofre, Eder
Brazilian. Boxer
b. Mar 26, 1936 in Sao Paulo, Brazil
Source: *BioIn 6; WhoBox 74*

Johannesen, Grant
American. Musician
b. 1921 in Salt Lake City, Utah
Source: *BioNews 75; CurBio 61; WhoAm 74; WhoMus 72*

Johanson, Donald Carl
American. Paleoanthropologist
b. Jun 28, 1943 in Chicago, Illinois
Source: *NewYTBS 79; WhoAm 82; WhoMW 76, 78*

Johansson, Ingemar
Swedish. Boxer
b. Sep 22, 1932 in Gothenburg, Sweden
Source: *CurBio 59; WhoHol A; WhoBox 74*

John XXIII, Pope
[Angelo Guiseppe Roncalli]
Italian. Roman Catholic Leader
Pope, 1958-63; convened Second Vatican Council, 1962, to reconsider position of church in modern world.
b. Nov 25, 1881 in Sotto il Monte, Italy
d. Jun 3, 1963 in Rome, Italy
Source: *McGEWB; NewCol 75; WebBD 80; WhDW; WhAm 4*

John, King of England
"John Lackland"
English. Signer of Magna Carta
Son of Henry II; forced by English barons to sign Magna Carta, 1215.
b. Dec 24, 1167 in Oxford, England
d. Oct 29, 1216 in Newark, England
Source: *LinLib S; McGEWB; NewC; NewCol 75; REn*

John of Gaunt
English. Founder of Tudor Line
b. 1340
d. 1399
Source: *NewCol 75; WebBD 80*

John of Salisbury
English. Author
b. 1120 in Salisbury, England
d. Oct 25, 1180
Source: *Alli; BiB N; BrAu; CasWL; DcEnL; DcEuL; EvLB; NewC; OxEng; Pen ENG*

John of the Cross, Saint
[San Juan de la Cruz]
Spanish. Poet
b. Jun 24, 1542 in Avila, Spain
d. Dec 14, 1591 in Penuela, Spain
Source: *AtlBL; CasWL; DcEuL; DcSpL; EuAu; EvEuW; NewC; Pen EUR; RComWL; REn*

John Paul I, Pope
[Albino Luciani]
Italian. Roman Catholic Leader
Pope for 34 days, 1978, before dying of heart attack.
b. Oct 17, 1912 in Belluno, Italy
d. Sep 28, 1978 in Vatican City, Italy
Source: *ConAu 81; CurBio 78; IntWW 79; WhoWor 78*

John Paul II, Pope
[Karol Wojtyla]
Polish. Roman Catholic Leader
Youngest pope elected in 158 yrs.; first non-Italian pope in 455 yrs.
b. May 18, 1920 in Wadowice, Poland
Source: *BioIn 11; BkPepl; CurBio 79*

John III, Sobieski
Polish. King
b. Aug 17, 1624 in Olesko, Poland
d. Jun 17, 1696
Source: *McGEWB; WebBD 80*

John the Baptist
Biblical Character
Source: *BioIn 9; WebBD 80*

John, Augustus Edwin
British. Artist
b. Jan 4, 1878 in Tenby, Wales
d. Oct 31, 1961 in Fordingbridge, England
Source: *AtlBL; ChPo; CurBio 41, 62; OxEng; WhAm 4*

John, Elton
[Reginald Kenneth Dwight]
English. Singer, Songwriter
All albums have gone gold; hits include "Rocket Man," "Blue Eyes."
b. Mar 25, 1947 in Pinner, England
Source: *Baker 78; BioNews 74; BkPepl; CelR 73; CurBio 75; NewYTBE 71; NewYTBS 74; RkOn 2; WhoAm 76, 78, 80, 82; WhoHol A*

John, Gwendolyn Mary
Welsh. Artist
b. 1876 in Haverfordwest, Wales
d. 1939 in Dieppe, France
Source: *ChPo; McGDA; WomArt*

John, John Pico
"Mr. John"
American. Millinery Designer, Couturier
b. Mar 14, 1906 in Florence, Italy
Source: *CurBio 56; WhoAm 74*

John, Tommy (Thomas Edward, Jr.)
American. Baseball Player
Pitcher; left elbow surgically reconstructed, 1974; won 20 games, 1977.
b. May 22, 1943 in Terre Haute, Indiana
Source: *BaseEn; CurBio 81; NewYTBS 77, 78; WhoAm 76, 78, 80, 82; WhoProB 73*

Johns, Glynis
English. Actress
b. Oct 5, 1923 in Pretoria, South Africa
Source: *BiE&WWA; CurBio 73; FilmgC; IntMPA 75, 76, 77, 78, 79, 80, 81, 82; MotPP; MovMk; NewYTBE 73; NotNAT; OxFilm; Who 74; WhoHol A; WhoThe 77*

Johns, Jasper
American. Artist
Pop artist known for using flags, letters, numbers in work.
b. May 15, 1930 in Augusta, Georgia
Source: *CelR 73; CurBio 67; DcCAA 71; EncAB-H; IntWW 74, 75, 76, 77, 78, 79, 80; NewCol 75; WhoAm 74, 76, 78, 80, 82; WhoAmA 73, 76, 78, 80*

Johnson, Alex(ander)
American. Baseball Player
b. Dec 7, 1942 in Helena, Arkansas
Source: *BaseEn; WhoAm 74; WhoProB 73*

Johnson, Amy
English. Aviatrix
b. 1903 in Kingston-upon-Hull, England
d. Jan 5, 1941
Source: *CurBio 41; HerW; InWom; WhoModH*

Johnson, Andrew
American. 17th US President
Succeeded Lincoln, 1865-69; survived impeachment attempt by Congress, 1868.
b. Dec 29, 1808 in Raleigh, North Carolina
d. Jul 31, 1875 in Carter Station, Tennessee
Source: *AmAu&B; AmBi; ApCAB; BiAuS; BiDrAC; BiDrUSE; DcAmB; DcNAA; Drake; EncAB-H; NewCol 75; OxAmL; REn; REnAL; TwCBDA; WebAB; WhAm H; WhAmP*

Johnson, Arte
American. TV Actor, Comedian
b. Jan 20, 1934 in Benton Harbor, Michigan
Source: *WhoAm 82; WhoHol A*

Johnson, Ben
American. Actor
b. 1919? in Pawhuska, Oklahoma
Source: *CmMov; FilmgC; IntMPA 75, 76, 77, 78, 79, 80, 81, 82; MovMk; WhoHol A*

Johnson, Betsey
American. Fashion Designer
b. Aug 10, 1942 in Wethersfield, Connecticut
Source: *WhoAm 82; WorFshn*

Johnson, Beverly
American. Model
b. Oct 13, 1951 in Buffalo, New York
Source: *BioIn 10, 11; WhoBlA 77*

Johnson, Bruce
see: Beach Boys, The

Johnson, "Bunk" (William Geary)
American. Jazz Musician
b. Dec 27, 1879 in New Orleans, Louisiana
d. Jul 7, 1949 in New Iberia, Louisiana
Source: *BiDAmM; WhAm 4; WhoJazz 72*

Johnson, (Byron) Ban(croft)
American. Baseball Executive
b. Jan 8, 1864 in Norwalk, Ohio
d. Mar 18, 1931 in Saint Louis, Missouri
Source: *BioIn 3, 7; DcAmB; WhAm 1; WhoProB 73*

Johnson, Celia
English. Actress
b. Dec 18, 1908 in Richmond, England
d. Apr 25, 1982 in Nettlebed, England
Source: *BiDFilm; CnThe; FilmgC; IntMPA 75, 76, 77, 78, 79, 80, 81, 82; IntWW 74, 75, 76, 77, 78; MotPP; MovMk; NewYTBS 82; OxFilm; PlP&P; WhoHol A; WhoThe 72, 77*

Johnson, Charlie (Charles Wright)
American. Jazz Musician
b. Nov 21, 1891 in Philadelphia, Pennsylvania
d. Dec 13, 1959 in New York, New York
Source: *WhoJazz 72*

Johnson, "Chic" (Harold Ogden)
[Olsen and Johnson]
American. Actor, Comedian
b. Mar 5, 1891? in Chicago, Illinois
d. Feb 1962 in Las Vegas, Nevada
Source: *FilmgC; MovMk; WhScrn 74, 77; WhoHol B*

Johnson, Clarence Leonard
American. Aeronautical Engineer
b. Feb 27, 1910 in Ishpeming, Michigan
Source: *AmM&WS 73P; CurBio 68; WhoAm 74; WhoF&I 74*

Johnson, Cletus Merlin
American. Artist
b. Nov 19, 1941 in Elizabeth, New Jersey
Source: *WhoAm 82; WhoAmA 76, 78, 80*

Johnson, Crockett
[David Johnson Leisk]
American. Children's Author, Illustrator
b. Oct 20, 1906 in New York, New York
d. Jul 11, 1975 in Norwalk, Connecticut
Source: *Au&Wr 71; AuBYP; BkP; ConAu 9R, 57; CurBio 43; IlsCB 1946, 1957; SmATA 1; ThrBJA; WhAm 6; WhoAmA 73*

Johnson, Dennis W
American. Basketball Player
b. Sep 18, 1954 in San Pedro, California
Source: *OfNBA; WhoAm 82*

Johnson, "Dink" (Oliver)
American. Jazz Musician
b. Oct 28, 1892 in New Orleans, Louisiana
d. Nov 29, 1954 in Portland, Oregon
Source: *WhoJazz 72*

Johnson, Earvin
"Magic"
American. Basketball Player
Forward, LA Lakers, 1979--; led Michigan State U to NCAA championship, 1979.
b. Aug 14, 1959 in Lansing, Michigan
Source: *BioIn 12; CurBio 82; OfNBA; WhoAm 82*

Johnson, Eddie
American. Basketball Player
b. Feb 24, 1955 in Ocala, Florida
Source: *BioIn 12; OfNBA*

Johnson, Edward
Canadian. Opera Singer, Manager
b. Aug 22, 1881 in Guelph, ON
d. Apr 20, 1959 in Guelph, ON
Source: *CreCan 2*

Johnson, Evelyn
American. Basketball Player
Sister of Earvin Johnson.
Source: *NF*

Johnson, Gerald White
American. Journalist
b. Aug 6, 1890 in Riverton, North Carolina
d. Mar 23, 1980 in Baltimore, Maryland
Source: *AmAu; AnCL; AuBYP; BioIn 2, 3, 4, 7, 9; CnDAL; ConAu 85, 97; OxAmL; REnAL; SmATA 19; ThrBJA; TwCA SUP; WhAm 7; WhNAA; WhoAm 74, 76, 78; WhoWor 74*

Johnson, Hall
American. Composer, Choir Director
Organized Hall Johnson Choir heard in movie *Lost Horizon.*
b. Mar 12, 1888 in Athens, Georgia
d. Apr 30, 1970 in New York, New York
Source: *AmSCAP 66; BlkAW; CurBio 45, 70; WhScrn 77; WhoHol B*

Johnson, Harold
American. Boxer
b. Aug 9, 1928 in Manayunk, Pennsylvania
Source: *BioIn 9; WhoBox 74*

Johnson, Henry
American. Soldier
b. 1897
d. 1929
Source: *BioIn 4, 8*

Johnson, Herbert Fisk
American. Businessman, Philanthropist
b. Nov 15, 1899 in Racine, Wisconsin
d. Dec 13, 1978 in Racine, Wisconsin
Source: *BioIn 11; IntYB 78; NewYTBS 78; WhAm 7*

Johnson, Hewlett
"Red Dean of Canterbury"
English. Ecclesiastic
b. Jan 25, 1874 in Manchester, England
d. Oct 22, 1966 in Canterbury, England
Source: *CurBio 43, 66; LongCTC; WhAm 4*

Johnson, Hiram W
American. Statesman
b. Sep 2, 1866 in Sacramento, California
d. Aug 6, 1945 in Bethesda, Maryland
Source: *BiDrAC; CurBio 41, 45; DcAmB S3; EncAB-H; WebAB; WhAm 2; WhAmP*

Johnson, Howard Brennan
American. Restaurant Executive
President, director, chairman, Howard Johnson Co., 1964-81.
b. Aug 23, 1932 in Boston, Massachusetts
Source: *BioIn 7, 11; CelR 73; CurBio 66; WhoAm 74, 76, 80, 82; WhoF&I 74; WhoWor 74*

Johnson, Howard Deering
American. Restaurant Executive
Began ice cream business, 1924; first Howard Johnson's opened, 1929 in MA.
b. 1896? in Boston, Massachusetts
d. Jun 20, 1972 in New York, New York
Source: *NewYTBE 72; WebAB; WhAm 5*

Johnson, Hugh S
American. NRA Administrator for FDR
b. Aug 5, 1882 in Fort Scott, Kansas
d. Apr 15, 1942 in Washington, DC
Source: *AmAu&B; CurBio 40, 42; DcAmB S3; DcNAA; EncAB-H; WebAB; WhAm 2*

Johnson, "J J" (James Louis)
American. Jazz Musician
b. Jan 22, 1924 in Indianapolis, Indiana
Source: *WhoAm 74; WhoBlA 75*

Johnson, Jack (John Arthur)
American. Boxer
b. Mar 31, 1878 in Galveston, Texas
d. Jun 10, 1946 in Raleigh, North Carolina
Source: *CurBio 46; DcAmB S4; WebAB; WhAm 2; WhoBox 74*

Johnson, James Price
American. Jazz Musician
b. Feb 1, 1891 in New Brunswick, New Jersey
d. Nov 17, 1955 in New York, New York
Source: *AmSCAP 66; WhoJazz 72*

Johnson, James Ralph
American. Author
b. May 20, 1922 in Fort Payne, Alabama
Source: *AuBYP; ConAu 1R, 2NR; SmATA 1; WrDr 76*

Johnson, James Weldon
American. Author
b. Jun 17, 1871 in Jacksonville, Florida
d. Jun 26, 1938 in Wiscasset, Maine
Source: *AmAu&B; AmBi; CasWL; ConAmA; ConAmL; Pen AM; REn; REnAL; TwCA; WebE&AL; WhAm 1*

Johnson, John Harold
American. Publisher
b. Jan 19, 1918 in Arkansas City, Arkansas
Source: *EncAB-H; WebAB; WhoAm 82; WhoMW 74*

Johnson, Josephine Winslow
American. Author
b. Jan 20, 1910 in Kirkwood, Missouri
Source: *AmAu&B; AmNov; AnMV 1926; ChPo; CnDAL; ConAmA; ConAu 25R; ConNov 72, 76; DcLEL; DrAF 76; ForWC 70; InWom; OxAmL; REnAL; TwCA, SUP; WhNAA; WhoAm 74, 76, 78, 80, 82; WhoMW 74; WrDr 76*

Johnson, Junior
American. Auto Racer
b. 1931 in Ingle Hollow, North Carolina
Source: *BioIn 10*

Johnson, "Lady Bird" (Claudia Alta Taylor)
[Mrs. Lyndon Johnson]
American. Wife of Lyndon Johnson
b. Dec 22, 1912 in Karnack, Texas
Source: *CelR 73; ConAu 89; CurBio 63; InWom; NewYTBE 73; WhoAm 74, 76, 78, 80, 82; WhoAmW 77; WhoGov 72; WhoS&SW 73; WhoWor 74*

Johnson, Luci Baines
American. Daughter of Lyndon Johnson
b. 1947
Source: *BioNews 74; InWom; NewYTBE 71*

Johnson, Lynda Bird
[Mrs. Charles Robb]
American. Daughter of Lyndon Johnson
b. Mar 19, 1943 in Washington, DC
Source: *BioNews 74*

Johnson, Lyndon Baines
American. 36th US President
Domestic achievements overshadowed by Vietnam War; wrote *The Vantage Point,* 1971.
b. Aug 27, 1908 in Stonewall, Texas
d. Jan 22, 1973 in Johnson City, Texas
Source: *AmAu&B; BiDrAC; BiDrUSE; ConAu 41R, 53; CurBio 51, 64, 73; EncAB-H; NewYTBE 71, 73; NewYTBS 74; OxAmL; REn; WebAB; WhAm 5; WhAmP; WhoGov 72; WhoS&SW 73*

Johnson, Lynn-Holly
American. Figure Skater, Actress
Former Ice Capades star; starred in movie *Ice Castles,* 1979.
b. 1959 in Chicago, Illinois
Source: *BioIn 12*

Johnson, Mark
[United States Olympic Hockey Team-1980]
American. Hockey Player
b. Sep 22, 1957 in Madison, Wisconsin
Source: *HocReg*

Johnson, Marques Kevin
American. Basketball Player
b. Feb 8, 1956 in Natchitoches, Louisiana
Source: *OfNBA; WhoAm 80, 82*

Johnson, Martin Elmer
American. Author, Filmmaker, Explorer
Made African, S Seas expeditions, filming vanishing wildlife.
b. Oct 9, 1884 in Rockford, Illinois
d. Jan 13, 1937 in Los Angeles, California
Source: *AmAu&B; AmBi; BioIn 6, 7, 9, 10; DcFM; DcNAA; Film 1; NatCAB 24; REnAL; TwYS; WhAm 1; WhScrn 77*

Johnson, Mordecai Wyatt
American. Educator
b. Jan 12, 1890 in Paris, Texas
d. Sep 10, 1976 in Washington, DC
Source: *CurBio 41*

Johnson, Nicholas
American. Government Official
b. Sep 23, 1934 in Iowa City, Iowa
Source: *AmAu&B; CelR 73; ConAu 29R; CurBio 68; NewYTBE 71; WhoAm 74, 76, 78, 80, 82; WhoGov 72; WhoS&SW 73; WhoWor 74; WrDr 76*

Johnson, Nunnally
American. Director, Scriptwriter
b. Dec 5, 1897 in Columbus, Georgia
d. Mar 25, 1977 in Los Angeles, California
Source: *ConAu 69, 81; CurBio 41, 77; IntMPA 75*

Johnson, Osa Helen Leighty
[Mrs. Martin Johnson]
American. Explorer
Accompanied husband on expeditions; co-author *Safari,* 1928.
b. Mar 14, 1894 in Chanute, Kansas
d. Jan 7, 1953 in New York, New York
Source: *AmAu&B; AuBYP; CurBio 40, 53; DcAmB S5; InWom; REnAL; WhAm 3; WhScrn 77; WomWMM*

Johnson, Pamela Hansford
[Baroness Pamela Hansford Johnson Snow]
English. Author, Critic
b. May 29, 1912 in London, England
d. Jun 18, 1981 in London, England
Source: *Au&Wr 71; BioIn 1, 4, 5; ConAu 1R, 104, 2NR; ConLC 1, 7; ConNov 72, 76; CurBio 48, 81; DcLEL; EncWL; EvLB; InWom; IntAu&W 76, 77; IntWW 74, 75, 76, 77, 78; LongCEL; LongCTC; ModBrL, SUP; NewC; REn; TwCA SUP; TwCW; WebE&AL; Who 74; WhoAmW 66, 68, 70, 72, 74, 75, 77; WhoWor 78; WrDr 76, 80*

Johnson, Phillip Cortelyou
American. Architect, Author
b. Jul 8, 1906 in Cleveland, Ohio
Source: *CurBio 57; WebAB; WhoAm 74, 76, 78, 80, 82*

Johnson, Rafer Lewis
American. Track Athlete
Won silver medal in decathlon, 1956 Olympics; gold medal, 1960 Olympics.
b. Aug 18, 1935 in Hillsboro, Texas
Source: *CelR 73; CurBio 61; FilmgC; WhoAm 82; WhoBlA 75; WhoHol A; WhoTr&F 73*

Johnson, Reverdy
American. Diplomat
b. May 21, 1796 in Annapolis, Maryland
d. Feb 10, 1876 in Annapolis, Maryland
Source: *AmBi; ApCAB; BiAuS; BiDSA; BiDrAC; BiDrUSE; DcAmB; Drake; TwCBDA; WebAB; WhAm H; WhAmP*

Johnson, Richard
English. Actor
b. Jul 30, 1927 in Essex, England
Source: *FilmgC; IntMPA 75, 76, 77, 78, 79, 80, 81, 82; MovMk; WhoThe 77*

Johnson, Robert
see: K C and the Sunshine Band

Johnson, Robert Willard
American. Educator
b. Dec 23, 1921 in Denver, Colorado
Source: *AmM&WS 73S; ConAu 17R; WhoAm 74, 76, 78, 80, 82; WhoCon 73; WrDr 76*

Johnson, Samuel
English. Lexicographer, Critic
Wrote first great critique of Shakespeare, 1765.
b. Oct 18, 1709 in Litchfield, England
d. Dec 13, 1784 in London, England
Source: *Alli; AtlBL; BbD; BiD&SB; BrAu; CasWL; ChPo, S1, S2; CnE&AP; CrtT 2; CyWA; DcBiA; DcEnA, AP; DcEnL; DcEuL; DcLEL; EvLB; MouLC 2; NewC; OxAmL; OxEng; OxThe; Pen ENG; RComWL; REn; WebE&AL*

Johnson, Sonia
American. Excommunicated Mormon Feminist
b. 1936?
Source: *NewYTBS 79*

Johnson, Ural Alexis
American. Ambassador, Diplomat
b. Oct 17, 1908 in Falun, Kansas
Source: *CurBio 55; IntWW 74; USBiR 74; WhoAm 74; WhoAmP 73; WhoGov 72; WhoWor 74*

Johnson, Van
American. Actor
b. Aug 28, 1916 in Newport, Rhode Island
Source: *BiDFilm; BiE&WWA; CelR 73; CmMov; CurBio 45; FilmgC; IntMPA 75, 76, 77, 78, 79, 80, 81, 82; MotPP; MovMk; OxFilm; WhoAm 74, 76, 78, 80, 82; WhoHol A; WhoThe 77; WorEFlm*

Johnson, Virginia E
[Masters and Johnson; Mrs. William H Masters]
American. Psychologist
Researcher in human sexuality; wrote, with husband, *Human Sexual Response,* 1966.
b. Feb 11, 1925 in Springfield, Missouri
Source: *AmAu&B; AuNews 1; ConAu 21R; EncAB-H; NewYTBE 70; WhoAm 74; WhoAmW 77*

Johnson, Walter Perry
"Barney"; "The Big Train"
American. Baseball Player, Manager
Pitcher, 1907-27; holds records for shutouts (113), strikeouts (3,510); Hall of Fame, 1936.
b. Nov 6, 1887 in Humboldt, Kansas
d. Dec 10, 1946 in Washington, DC
Source: *BaseEn; DcAmB S4; WebAB; WhAm HA, 4; WhoProB 73*

Johnson, William
American. Supreme Court Justice
b. Dec 27, 1771 in Charleston, South Carolina
d. Aug 4, 1834 in Brooklyn, New York
Source: *BioIn 2, 3, 5; ApCAB; BiAuS; DcAmB; Drake; NatCAB 2; TwCBDA; WebAB; WhAm H*

Johnson, William
British. Army Officer
b. 1715 in Smithtown, Ireland
d. Jul 11, 1774 in Johnstown, New York
Source: *Alli; AmBi; ApCAB; DcAmB; Drake; EncAB-H; OxAmL; OxCan; REnAL; WebAB; WhAm H*

Johnston, Albert S
American. Military Leader
b. Feb 2, 1803? in Washington, Kentucky
d. Apr 6, 1862 in Shiloh, Tennessee
Source: *AmBi; ApCAB; BiDConf; DcAmB; Drake; NatCAB 29; REnAW; TwCBDA; WebAB; WhAm H; WhoMilH 76*

Johnston, Frank H
[Group of Seven]
Canadian. Artist
b. Jun 19, 1888 in Toronto, ON
d. Jul 10, 1949
Source: *ClbCR; CreCan 1*

Johnston, J Bennett, Jr.
American. Politician
b. Jun 10, 1932 in Shreveport, Louisiana
Source: *CngDr 74; WhoAm 74, 76, 78, 80, 82; WhoAmP 73*

Johnston, Johnny
American. Actor
b. 1916 in Saint Louis, Missouri
Source: *WhoHol A*

Johnston, Joseph Eggleston
American. Military Leader
b. Feb 3, 1807 in Prince Edward, Virginia
d. Feb 21, 1891 in Washington, DC
Source: *Alli SUP; AmBi; BiDConf; BiDSA; BiDrAC; DcAmAu; DcAmB; DcNAA; EncAB-H; TwCBDA; WebAB; WhAm H*

Johnston, Richard Malcolm
American. Author
b. Mar 8, 1822 in Oak Grove, Georgia
d. Sep 23, 1898 in Baltimore, Maryland
Source: *Alli SUP; AmAu; AmAu&B; ApCAB; BiD&SB; BiDSA; DcAmAu; DcAmB; DcBiA; DcLEL; DcNAA; OxAmL; REnAL; TwCBDA; WhAm H*

Johnstone, Jay (John William, Jr.)
American. Baseball Player
b. Nov 20, 1945 in Manchester, Connecticut
Source: *BaseEn*

Jolas, Betsy
American. Composer
b. Aug 5, 1926 in Paris, France
Source: *Baker 78; DcCM; NewYTBE 73*

Joliot-Curie, Irene
French. Physicist
b. Sep 12, 1897 in Paris, France
d. Mar 17, 1956 in Paris, France
Source: *CurBio 40, 56; HerW; InWom; WhAm 3*

Joliot(-Curie), (Jean) Frederic
French. Physicist
b. Mar 19, 1900 in Paris, France
d. Aug 14, 1958
Source: *AsBiEn; BioIn 1, 2, 3, 5, 6, 7, 11, 12; CurBio 58; DcScB; McGEWB; NewCol 75; WhAm 3*

Jolliet, Louis
Canadian. Explorer
First white man, with Jacques Marquette, to travel down Mississippi River, 1673.
b. 1645 in Quebec City, PQ
d. May 1700 in Anticosti Island, PQ
Source: *AmBi; ApCAB; DcAmB; OxCan; REn; WebAB*

Jolson, Al
[Asa Yoelson]
American. Singer
Starred in *The Jazz Singer,* 1927, the first talking film.
b. May 26, 1886? in Sprednik, Lithuania
d. Oct 23, 1950 in San Francisco, California
Source: *AmSCAP 66; BiDFilm; CmMov; CurBio 40, 50; DcAmB S4; EncMT; FamA&A; FilmgC; MotPP; MovMk; NewYTBS 74; OxFilm; PlP&P; WebAB; WhAm 3; WhScrn 74, 77; WhoHol B; WorEFlm*

Jommelli, Niccolo
Italian. Composer
b. Sep 10, 1714 in Aversa, Italy
d. Aug 25, 1774 in Naples, Italy
Source: *NewEOp 71; OxMus*

Jonah
Biblical Character
Source: *WebBD 80*

Jonas, Franz
Austrian. President
b. Oct 4, 1899 in Vienna, Austria
d. Apr 24, 1974 in Vienna, Austria
Source: *NewYTBS 74; WhAm 6; WhoGov 72; WhoWor 74*

Jonathan, Leabua, Chief
Prime Minister of Lesotho
Source: *NewYTBE 70*

Jones, Alan
Australian. Auto Racer
b. Feb 11, 1946 in Melbourne, Australia
Source: *BioIn 12*

Jones, Allan
American. Actor, Singer
b. 1908? in Scranton, Pennsylvania
Source: *FilmgC; HolP 30; MotPP; MovMk; OxFilm; WhoHol A*

Jones, Anissa
American. Actress
Played Buffy in "Family Affair," 1966-71; died of drug overdose.
b. 1958 in West Lafayette, Indiana
d. 1976
Source: *WhoHol A*

Jones, Barry
English. Actor
b. Mar 6, 1893 in Guernsey, England
Source: *BiE&WWA; CurBio 58; FilmgC; IntMPA 75, 76, 77, 78, 79, 80, 81, 82; MovMk; NotNAT; PlP&P; Who 74; WhoHol A; WhoThe 77; WhoWor 74*

Jones, Bert(ram Hays)
American. Football Player
b. Sep 7, 1951 in Ruston, Louisiana
Source: *BioIn 9, 11; NewYTBE 72; WhoAm 78, 80, 82; WhoFtbl 74*

Jones, "Biff" (Lawrence M)
American. Football Coach
b. Oct 8, 1895 in Washington, DC
d. 1980
Source: *BioIn 10; WhoFtbl 74*

Jones, Billy
see: Outlaws, The

Jones, Billy (William Reese)
[The Interwoven Pair]
Singer
b. 1889
d. 1940
Source: *BioIn 5*

Jones, Bob
American. Religious Leader
b. Oct 30, 1883 in Dale County, Alabama
d. Jan 16, 1968
Source: *WhAm 4*

Jones, Bobby (Robert Tyre)
American. Golfer
Biggest name in golf, 1920's; helped to found Masters tournament, 1934.
b. Mar 17, 1902 in Atlanta, Georgia
d. Dec 18, 1971 in Atlanta, Georgia
Source: *WebAB*

Jones, Brian
[The Rolling Stones]
English. Singer, Musician
One of original Rolling Stones; found dead in swimming pool of drug overdose.
b. Feb 26, 1943 in Cheltenham, England
d. Jul 3, 1969 in London, England
Source: *WhAm 5; WhScrn 77*

Jones, Buck
American. Actor
b. Dec 4, 1891 in Vincennes, Indiana
d. Nov 30, 1942 in Boston, Massachusetts
Source: *CmMov; CurBio 43; Film 1; FilmgC; MovMk; OxFilm; TwYS; WhScrn 74, 77; WhoHol B*

Jones, Candy
American. Model, Businesswoman
b. Dec 31, 1925 in Wilkes-Barre, Pennsylvania
Source: *CurBio 61; InWom*

Jones, Carolyn
American. Actress
Played Morticia on TV series "The Addams Family," 1964-66.
b. Apr 28, 1933 in Amarillo, Texas
Source: *CurBio 67; FilmgC; InWom; IntMPA 75, 76, 77, 78, 79, 80, 81, 82; MotPP; MovMk; WhoAm 74, 76, 78, 80, 82; WhoHol A*

Jones, "Casey" (John Luther)
American. Railroad Engineer
Folk hero of songs, ballads; killed in crash of Cannon Ball Express.
b. Mar 14, 1864 in Cayce, Kentucky
d. Apr 30, 1900 in Vaughan, Mississippi
Source: *NewCol 75; WebAB*

Jones, Charles A, Jr.
[The Hostages]
American. Former Hostage in Iran
b. Jul 1, 1940 in Memphis, Tennessee
Source: *BioIn 12; NewYTBS 81*

Jones, Christopher
American. Actor
b. 1941 in Jackson, Tennessee
Source: *FilmgC; WhoHol A*

Jones, Clara Araminta Stanton
American. Librarian
b. May 14, 1913 in Saint Louis, Missouri
Source: *ForWC 70; WhoBlA 75; WhoMW 74*

Jones, David
English. Author, Artist
b. Nov 1, 1895 in Brockley, England
d. Oct 28, 1974 in London, England
Source: *CasWL; CnE&AP; CnMWL; ConAu 9R, 53; ConLC 2, 4, 7, 13; ConP 70; LongCTC; ModBrL, SUP; OxEng; Pen ENG; RAdv 1; REn; TwCW; WhAm 6; Who 74; WhoTwCL; WorAu*

Jones, David Charles
American. General, Government Official
b. Jul 9, 1921 in Aberdeen, South Dakota
Source: *BioIn 10, 11; CurBio 82; WebAMB; WhoAm 82; WorDWW*

Jones, Davy (David)
[The Monkees]
English. Actor, Singer
b. Dec 30, 1946 in Manchester, England
Source: *BioIn 7, 9*

Jones, Dean
American. Actor
b. Jan 25, 1936 in Morgan County, Alabama
Source: *BiE&WWA; FilmgC; IntMPA 75, 76, 77, 78, 79, 80, 81, 82; MotPP; WhoAm 82; WhoHol A*

Jones, Edward Vason
American. Architect
b. Aug 3, 1909 in Albany, Georgia
d. Oct 1, 1980 in Albany, Georgia
Source: *WhAm 7; WhoAm 78*

Jones, Eli Stanley
American. Missionary
b. Jan 1, 1884 in Baltimore, Maryland
d. Jan 26, 1973 in Bareilly, India
Source: *AmAu&B; ConAu 41R, 93; TwCA SUP; WhAm 5, 7; WhNAA*

Jones, George
"The Crown Prince of Country Music"
American. Singer
Named best male vocalist by CMA, 1980, 1981; married to Tammy Wynette, 1968-75.
b. Sep 12, 1931 in Saratoga, Texas
Source: *BiDAmM; BioIn 9, 10; EncFCWM 69; IlEncCM; WhoAm 82; WhoRock 81*

Jones, Glyn
Welsh. Author
b. Feb 28, 1905 in Wales
Source: *CnMWL; ConAu 9R, 3NR; ConNov 72, 76; ConP 70, 75; ModBrL; WorAu; WrDr 76*

Jones, "Gorilla" (William)
American. Boxer
b. May 12, 1906 in Memphis, Tennessee
Source: *BioIn 1; WhoBox 74*

Jones, Grace
Singer
b. in Jamaica
Source: *BioIn 11; NewWmR*

Jones, "Grandpa" (Louis Marshall)
American. Musician, Singer, TV Personality
b. Oct 20, 1913 in Henderson County, Kentucky
Source: *BiDAmM; EncFCWM 69; IlEncCM*

Jones, Gwyneth
Welsh. Opera Singer
b. Nov 7, 1936 in Pontnewynydd, Wales
Source: *IntWW 74; Who 74; WhoAm 82; WhoAmW 77; WhoMus 72; WhoWor 74*

Jones, Henry
American. Actor
b. Aug 1, 1912 in Philadelphia, Pennsylvania
Source: *BiE&WWA; FilmgC; NotNAT; WhoAm 74, 76, 78, 80, 82*

Jones, Howard Mumford
American. Author
b. Apr 16, 1892 in Saginaw, Michigan
d. May 12, 1980 in Cambridge, Massachusetts
Source: *AmAu&B; ChPo S1; ConAu 85, 97; CnDAL; DrAS 74E; IntWW 74; OxAmL; RAdv 1; REnAL; TwCA SUP; WhNAA; WhoAm 74; WhoE 74; WhoWor 74*

Jones, Inigo
English. Architect
b. Jul 15, 1573 in London, England
d. Jun 21, 1652 in London, England
Source: *Alli; AtlBL; CroE&S; DcEnL; NewC; OxThe; REn*

Jones, Isham
American. Band Leader, Songwriter
b. Jan 31, 1894 in Coalton, Ohio
d. Oct 19, 1956 in Hollywood, California
Source: *AmSCAP 66; WhAm 4A; WhoJazz 72*

Jones, Jack
American. Singer
b. Jan 14, 1938 in Beverly Hills, California
Source: *CelR 73*

Jones, James
American. Author
b. Nov 6, 1921 in Robinson, Illinois
d. May 9, 1977 in Southampton, New York
Source: *AmAu&B; AuNews; CasWL; ConAu 1R, 69; ModAL; OxAmL; Pen AM; REnAL; TwCW*

Jones, James Earl
American. Actor
b. Jan 17, 1931 in Arkabutla, Mississippi
Source: *BiE&WWA; BioNews 75; BkPepl; CelR 73; CurBio 69; NotNAT; PlP&P; WhoAm 74; WhoBlA 75; WhoGov 72; WhoThe 77*

Jones, James Robert
American. Congressman
b. May 5, 1939 in Muskogee, Oklahoma
Source: *AlmAP 78, 80; BioIn 8, 11; CngDr 74, 77, 79; NewYTBS 78; WhoAm 74, 76, 78, 80; WhoAmP 73, 75, 77, 79; WhoGov 75, 77; WhoS&SW 76, 78*

Jones, Jenkin Lloyd
American. Editor, Journalist
b. Nov 1, 1911 in Madison, Wisconsin
Source: *ConAu 9R; WhoAm 82; WhoF&I 74; WhoS&SW 73*

Jones, Jennifer
[Phyllis Isley]
American. Actress
Won Oscar, 1943, for *The Song of Bernadette.*
b. Mar 2, 1919 in Tulsa, Oklahoma
Source: *BiDFilm; BiE&WWA; CmMov; CurBio 44; FilmgC; InWom; IntMPA 75, 76, 77, 78, 79, 80, 81, 82; MotPP; MovMk; OxFilm; Who 74; WhoAm 74, 76, 78, 80, 82; WhoHol A; WorEFlm*

Jones, Jesse Holman
American. Cabinet Member
b. Apr 5, 1874 in Robertson County, Tennessee
d. Jun 1, 1956 in Houston, Texas
Source: *BiDrUSE; CurBio 40, 56; EncAB-H; WhAm 3*

Jones, Reverend Jim (James)
American. Religious Leader
Founded People's Temple; led mass suicide of nearly 1,000 followers in Guyana, 1978.
b. May 31, 1931 in Lynn, Indiana
d. Nov 18, 1978 in Jonestown, Guyana
Source: *BioIn 11*

Jones, Jo(nathan)
American. Jazz Musician
b. Oct 7, 1911 in Chicago, Illinois
Source: *AmSCAP 66; WhoJazz 72*

Jones, John Paul
American. Naval Officer
Founded American naval tradition; said "I have not yet begun to fight."
b. Jul 6, 1747 in Kirkcudbright, Scotland
d. Jul 18, 1792 in Paris, France
Source: *AmAu&B; ApCAB; DcAmB; Drake; EncAB-H; OxAmL; REn; REnAL; TwCBDA; WebAB; WhAm H*

Jones, John Paul
[John Baldwin; Led Zeppelin]
English. Rock Musician
b. Jan 3, 1946 in Sidcup, England
Source: *WhoAm 80*

Jones, Jonah
American. Musician
b. 1909 in Louisville, Kentucky
Source: *BioIn 5, 10*

Jones, Joseph John (Joe)
American. Artist
b. Apr 7, 1909 in Saint Louis, Missouri
d. Apr 9, 1963 in Morristown, New Jersey
Source: *McGDA; WhAm 4*

Jones, Kenny
[The Who]
Rock Musician
b. 1948?
Source: *NF*

Jones, Lady
see: Bagnold, Enid

Jones, Leroi
[Imamu Amiri Baraka]
American. Poet, Dramatist
Wrote *Black Magic,* 1969; *It's Nation Time,* 1971.
b. Oct 7, 1934 in Newark, New Jersey
Source: *BlkAW; CasWL; CelR 73; ConAu 21R; ConDr 73; ConLC 1, 2, 3, 5, 10, 14; ConNov 72, 76; ConP 70, 75; CroCAP; CroCD; CurBio 70; DrAP 75; EncWL; LivgBAA; McGEWD; ModAL, SUP; ModWD; NotNAT; OxAmL; Pen AM; PlP&P A; RAdv 1; RComWL; WebAB; WebE&AL; WhoAm 74; WhoBlA 75; WhoE 74; WhoThe 77; WhoTwCL; WhoWor 74; WorAu; WrDr 76*

Jones, Madison Percy, Jr.
American. Author
b. Mar 21, 1925 in Nashville, Tennessee
Source: *Au&Wr 71; ConAu 13R; ConLC 4; ConNov 72, 76; DrAS 74E; WhoAm 74; WrDr 76*

Jones, Mary Harris
"Mother Jones"
American. Labor Leader
b. May 1, 1830 in Cork, Ireland
d. Nov 30, 1930 in Silver Spring, Maryland
Source: *WebAB*

Jones, Mick
see: Clash, The

Jones, Mick
see: Foreigner

Jones, Parnelli (Rufus Parnell)
American. Auto Racer
b. 1933
Source: *BioIn 10*

Jones, Phil(ip Howard)
American. Broadcast Journalist
b. Apr 27, 1937 in Marion, Indiana
Source: *WhoAm 80, 82*

Jones, "Prophet" (James F)
American. Evangelist
b. 1908
d. 1971 in Detroit, Michigan
Source: *BioIn 9; NewYTBE 71*

Jones, Quincy Delight
American. Composer
Has written scores for over 50 films including *In Cold Blood,* 1967; *The Wiz,* 1978.
b. Mar 14, 1933 in Chicago, Illinois
Source: *BioIn 10; IntMPA 82; WhoAm 82*

Jones, R William
American. Basketball Executive
Co-founded International Basketball Federation, 1932.
b. Oct 5, 1906 in Rome, Italy
Source: *BioIn 9; WhoBbl 73*

Jones, Randy (Randall Leo)
American. Baseball Player
b. Jan 12, 1950 in Fullerton, California
Source: *BaseEn; BioIn 10, 11*

Jones, Randy
see: Village People, The

Jones, Richard
see: Climax Blues Band, The

Jones, Richard Lloyd, Jr.
American. Newspaper Executive
President, board chairman of the Tulsa *Tribune*
b. Feb 22, 1909 in Jyack, New York
d. Jan 27, 1982 in Tulsa, Oklahoma
Source: *NewYTBS 82; WhoAm 82; WhoS&SW 73, 75, 76, 78, 80*

Jones, Rickie Lee
American. Singer, Songwriter
Won Grammy, 1980; hit single "Chuck E's in Love."
b. 1955 in Chicago, Illinois
Source: *NewWmR; WhoRock 81*

Jones, Robert Edmond
American. Designer
b. Dec 12, 1887 in Milton, New Hampshire
d. Nov 26, 1954 in Milton, New Hampshire
Source: *CurBio 46, 55; DcAmB S5; OxAmL; OxThe; PlP&P; REn; REnAL; WhAm 3*

Jones, Robert Trent
English. Golf Course Architect
Designed more than 350 of world's most outstanding golf courses.
b. Jun 20, 1906 in Ince, England
Source: *WhoAm 74, 76, 78, 80, 82; WhoE 74; WhoWor 74*

Jones, Sam(uel Pond)
"Sad Sam"
American. Baseball Player
b. Jul 26, 1892 in Barnesville, Ohio
d. Jul 6, 1966 in Barnesville, Ohio
Source: *BaseEn; BioIn 7; WhoProB 73*

Jones, Shirley
[Mrs. Marty Ingels]
American. Actress, Singer
Won Oscar, 1960, for *Elmer Gantry;* starred in "The Partridge Family," 1970-74.
b. Mar 31, 1934 in Smithtown, Pennsylvania
Source: *BiDFilm; BiE&WWA; BioNews 74; CmMov; CurBio 61; FilmgC; InWom; IntMPA 75, 76, 77, 78, 79, 80, 81, 82; MotPP; MovMk; WhoAm 74, 76, 78, 80, 82; WhoHol A; WhoWor 74; WorEFlm*

Jones, "Spike" (Lindsay Armstrong)
American. Band Leader, Musician
b. Dec 14, 1911 in Long Beach, California
d. May 1, 1964 in Los Angeles, California
Source: *AmSCAP 66; FilmgC; WhScrn 74, 77; WhoHol B*

Jones, Steve
see: Sex Pistols

Jones, Terry
[Monty Python's Flying Circus]
Welsh. Actor, Director, Writer
b. Feb 1, 1942 in Colwyn Bay, Wales
Source: *BioIn 10; WhoAm 82*

Jones, Thomas Hudson
American. Sculptor
b. Jul 24, 1892 in Buffalo, New York
d. Nov 4, 1969 in Hyannis, Massachusetts
Source: *WhAm 5*

Jones, Tom
American. Dramatist, Songwriter
b. Feb 17, 1928 in Littlefield, Texas
Source: *AmAu&B; AmSCAP 66; BiE&WWA; ConAu 53; ConDr 73; EncMT; NewCBMT; NotNAT*

Jones, Tom
[Thomas Jones Woodward]
Welsh. Musician, Singer
Hits include "It's Not Unusual," 1964; "What's New Pussycat," 1965.
b. Jun 7, 1940 in Pontypridd, Wales
Source: *BkPepl; CelR 73; WhoAm 82; WhoWor 74*

Jones, Tommy Lee
American. Actor
b. Sep 15, 1946 in San Saba, Texas
Source: *BioIn 11; IntMPA 82; WhoAm 82*

Jones, "Too Tall" (Edward Lee)
American. Football Player, Boxer
b. Feb 23, 1951 in Jackson, Tennessee
Source: *WhoFtbl 74*

Jones, "Toothpick" (Samuel)
"Sad Sam"
American. Baseball Player
b. Dec 14, 1925 in Stewartsville, Ohio
d. Nov 5, 1971 in Morgantown, West Virginia
Source: *BaseEn; BioIn 5, 7; WhoProB 73*

Jones, W D
American. Member of Clyde Barrow Gang
b. 1915
Source: *BioIn 9*

Jones, Weyman
American. Author
b. Feb 6, 1928 in Lima, Ohio
Source: *AuBYP; ConAu 17R; SmATA 4; WhoPubR 72*

Jong, Erica
[Mrs. Jonathan Fast]
American. Author
Wrote *Fear of Flying,* 1973.
b. Mar 26, 1942 in New York, New York
Source: *AuNews 1; BkPepl; ConAu 73; ConLC 4, 6; ConP 75; CroCAP; DrAF 76; DrAP 75; RAdv 1; WomWMM; WrDr 76*

Jongkind, Johan Barthold
Dutch. Artist
b. Jun 3, 1819 in Lattrop, Netherlands
d. Feb 9, 1891 in Cote-Saint-Andre, Netherlands
Source: *AtlBL; McGDA*

Jonson, Ben(jamin)
English. Dramatist, Poet
Master of dramatic satire; wrote *Volpone,* 1606.
b. Jun 11, 1572 in Westminster, England
d. Apr 6, 1637 in Westminster, England
Source: *Alli; AtlBL; BbD; BiD&SB; BrAu; CasWL; Chambr 1; ChPo; CnE&AP; CnThe; CroE&S; CrtT 1; CyWA; DcEnA; DcEnL; DcEuL; DcLEL; EvLB; McGEWD; MouLC 1; NewC; OxEng; OxThe; Pen ENG; PlP&P; PoLE; RAdv 1; RComWL; REn; REnWD; WebE&AL*

Jonsson, John Erik
American. Business Executive
b. Sep 6, 1901 in New York, New York
Source: *AmM&WS 79P; BioIn 5, 6, 7, 10; CurBio 61; IntWW 74, 75, 76, 77; IntYB 78, 79; St&PR 75; WhoAm 74, 76, 78; WhoAmP 73, 75; WhoF&I 74, 77; WhoGov 72; WhoS&SW 73, 75, 76*

Jooss, Kurt
German. Choreographer
b. Jan 12, 1901 in Wasseralfingen, Germany
d. May 22, 1979 in Heilbronn, Germany (West)
Source: *CurBio 76, 79; IntWW 75, 76, 77, 78; NewYTBS 75, 76, 79; OxMus; WhoWor 76, 78*

Joplin, Janis
[Big Brother and the Holding Company]
American. Singer
Hits include "Me and Bobby McGee"; died of drug overdose.
b. Jan 19, 1943 in Port Arthur, Texas
d. Oct 3, 1970 in Hollywood, California
Source: *BioNews 74; CurBio 70; NewYTBE 70; WhAm 5; WhScrn 77; WhoHol B*

Joplin, Scott
American. Musician, Composer
Wrote "The Entertainer," 1902; music revived in score of *The Sting,* 1973.
b. Nov 24, 1868 in Texarkana, Texas
d. Apr 4, 1917 in New York, New York
Source: *AmSCAP 66; BioNews 74; BlkAW; WebAB; WhoJazz 72*

Jorda, Enrique
Spanish. Conductor
b. Mar 24, 1911 in San Sebastian, Spain
Source: *IntWW 74; WhoMus 72; WhoWor 74*

Jordaens, Jacob
Flemish. Artist
b. May 19, 1593 in Antwerp, Belgium
d. Oct 18, 1678 in Antwerp, Belgium
Source: *AtlBL*

Jordan, Barbara C
American. Lawyer, Politician
Congresswoman, 1972-78; wrote *Barbara Jordan-Self Portrait,* 1979.
b. Feb 21, 1936 in Houston, Texas
Source: *CngDr 74; WhoAm 76, 78, 80, 82; WhoAmW 77; WhoBlA 75; WomPO 76*

Jordan, Bobby
American. Leader of the Bowery Boys
b. 1923
d. 1965
Source: *WhoHol B*

Jordan, Don
American. Boxer
b. Jun 22, 1934
Source: *BioIn 10*

Jordan, Hamilton
[William Hamilton Jordan]
"Ham"; "Hannibal Jerkin"
American. Former Presidential Advisor
b. Sep 21, 1944 in Charlotte, North Carolina
Source: *BioIn 10, 11, 12; CurBio 77; PseudN; WhoAm 78, 80, 82; WhoAmP 77; WhoGov 77*

Jordan, June Meyer
[June Meyer, pseud.]
American. Author
b. Jul 9, 1936 in Harlem, New York
Source: *BlkAW; ChPo S1, S2; ConAu 33R; ConLC 5; DrAF 76; DrAP 75; LivgBAA; PseudN; SmATA 4; WhoAmW 77; WrDr 76*

Jordan, Kathy (Kathryn)
American. Tennis Player
b. Dec 3, 1957 in Bryn Mawr, Pennsylvania
Source: *OfEnT*

Jordan, Louis
"King of the Jukeboxes"
American. Musician
b. Jul 8, 1908 in Brinkley, Arkansas
d. Feb 4, 1975 in Los Angeles, California
Source: *PseudN; WhoJazz 72*

Jordan, Taft
American. Musician, Singer
b. Feb 15, 1915 in Florence, South Carolina
Source: *WhoJazz 72*

Jordan, Richard
American. Actor
b. Jul 19, 1938 in New York, New York
Source: *BioIn 11; WhoHol A*

Jordan, Vernon Eulion, Jr.
"The Warrior of Today"
American. Civil Rights Leader
b. Aug 15, 1935 in Atlanta, Georgia
Source: *BioNews 74; BusPN; CurBio 72; PseudN; WhoAm 74, 76, 78, 80, 82; WhoBlA 75; WhoS&SW 73*

Jordy, William H(enry)
American. Educator
b. Aug 31, 1917 in Poughkeepsie, New York
Source: *ConAu 1R; DrAS 74H, 78H; WhoAm 74, 76, 78, 80, 82*

Jorge Blanco, Salvador
Dominican. President
Elected to Presidency, May 1982.
b. Jul 5, 1926 in Santiago, Dominican Republic
Source: *NewYTBS 82*

Jorgensen, Anker Henrik
Danish. Prime Minister
b. Jul 13, 1922 in Copenhagen, Denmark
Source: *CurBio 78*

Jorgensen, Christine
American. Transsexual
Underwent first publicized sex change operation, 1953.
b. May 30, 1926 in New York, New York
Source: *InWom*

Jory, Victor
American. Actor
b. Nov 23, 1902 in Dawson City, Alaska
d. Feb 12, 1982 in Santa Monica, California
Source: *BiE&WWA; FilmgC; HolP 30; IntMPA 75, 76, 77, 78, 79, 80, 81, 82; MotPP; MovMk; NotNAT; Vers A; WhoHol A; WhoThe 77*

Joseph
Biblical Character
Source: *WebBD 80*

Joseph II
"The Hatted King"; "The Kalapos King"; "The Titus of Germany"; "The Unfortunate"
Holy Roman Emperor
b. 1741
d. 1790
Source: *BioIn 9; PseudN; WebBD 80*

Joseph, Chief
[Hinmaton-Yalakit]
"The Napoleon of the Indian Race"
American Indian. Nez Perce Chief
b. 1840 in Wallowa Valley, Washington
d. Sep 21, 1904 in Colville, Washington
Source: *AmBi; DcAmB; PseudN; REnAL; WebAB*

Joseph of Arimathea
Biblical Character
Source: *REn; WebBD 80*

Joseph, Saint
Biblical Character
Source: *REn; WebBD 80*

Joseph, Helen
South African. Author, Political Activist
b. 1906
Source: *BioIn 11*

Joseph, Richard
American. Journalist
b. Apr 24, 1910 in New York, New York
d. Sep 30, 1976
Source: *AmAu&B; CelR 73; ConAu 1R, 69; NewYTBS 76; WhAm 7; WhoAm 74, 76; WhoE 74; WhoWor 76*

Josephine
[Josephine DeBeauharnais]
French. Empress, Wife of Napoleon
b. Jun 24, 1763 in Martinique
d. May 29, 1814 in Malmaison, France
Source: *ApCAB; InWom*

Josephson, Matthew
American. Author
b. Feb 15, 1899 in Brooklyn, New York
d. Mar 13, 1978 in Santa Cruz, California
Source: *AmAu&B; ConAmA; ConAu 77, 81; DcLB 4; NewYTBE 72; NewYTBS 78; OxAmL; Pen AM; REn; REnAL; TwCA, SUP; WhAm 7; WhoAm 74, 76, 78; WhoWor 74; WhoWorJ 72*

Josephus, Flavius
[Joseph Ben Matthias]
"The Greek Livy"
Hebrew. Historian, General
b. 37
d. 95? in Rome, Italy
Source: *AtlBL; BbD; BiD&SB; CasWL; NewC; OxEng; Pen CL; PseudN; RComWL; REn*

Joshua
Biblical Character
Source: *WebBD 80*

Joslyn, Allyn Morgan
American. Actor
b. Jul 21, 1905 in Milford, Pennsylvania
d. Jan 21, 1981 in Woodland Hills, California
Source: *BioIn 10; FilmgC; IntMPA 75, 76, 77, 78, 79, 80, 81; MovMk; Vers A; WhThe; WhoHol A*

Joss, "Addie" (Adrian)
American. Baseball Player
b. Apr 12, 1880 in Juneau, Wisconsin
d. Apr 14, 1911 in Toledo, Ohio
Source: *BaseEn; BioIn 10; PseudN; WhoProB 73*

Joule, James Prescott
English. Physicist
b. Dec 24, 1818 in Salford, England
d. Oct 11, 1889 in Sale, England
Source: *Alli SUP*

Jourard, Marty
see: Motels, The

Jourdan, Louis
[Louis Gendre]
French. Actor
b. Jun 19, 1920 in Marseilles, France
Source: *BiE&WWA; CurBio 67; FilmgC; IntMPA 75, 76, 77, 78, 79, 80, 81, 82; MotPP; MovMk; NotNAT; PseudN; WhoAm 74, 76, 78, 80, 82; WhoHol A*

Journet, Marcel
French. Opera Singer
b. Jul 25, 1870 in Grasse, France
d. Sep 5, 1933 in Vittel, France
Source: *WhAm 1*

Journey
[Jonathan Cain; Aynsley Dunbar; Steve Perry; Gregg Rolie; Neil Schon; Steve Smith; Ross Valory]
American. Rock Group
Source: *ConMuA 80; IlEncRk; LilREn 78; WhoRock 81*

Jouvet, Louis
French. Actor
b. Dec 24, 1887 in Crozon, France
d. Aug 16, 1951 in Paris, France
Source: *BiDFilm; ClDMEL; CurBio 49, 51; EncWL; FilmgC; MovMk; OxFilm; OxFr; OxThe; REn; WhScrn 74, 77; WhoHol B; WorEFlm*

Jouy, Victor (Joseph-Etienne) de
French. Dramatist
b. 1764 in Jouy, France
d. Sep 4, 1846 in Saint Germain en Laye, France
Source: *BbD; BiD&SB; NewEOp 71; OxFr; PseudN*

Jovanovich, William
American. Publisher
b. Feb 6, 1920 in Louisville, Colorado
Source: *IntWW 74; St&PR 75; WhoAm 74, 76, 78, 80, 82*

Joy, Leatrice
[Leatrice Joy Zeidler]
American. Actress
b. 1899
Source: *Film 1; FilmgC; InWom; MotPP; MovMk; PseudN; ThFT; TwYS; WhoHol A*

Joyce, Alice
American. Actress
b. Oct 1, 1890 in Kansas City, Missouri
d. Oct 9, 1955 in Hollywood, California
Source: *Film 1; FilmgC; InWom; MotPP; MovMk; TwYS; WhScrn 74, 77; WhoHol B*

Joyce, Eileen
Australian. Musician
b. Nov 21, 1912 in Zeehan, Tasmania
Source: *InWom; IntWW 74; Who 74; WhoWor 74*

Joyce, Elaine
[Elaine Joyce Pinchot; Mrs. Bobby Van]
American. Actress, Dancer
b. Dec 19, 1945 in Cleveland, Ohio
Source: *WhoHol A*

Joyce, James Augustus Aloysius
Irish. Author, Poet
Wrote *Ulysses,* 1922; banned in US as obscene until 1933.
b. Feb 2, 1882 in Dublin, Ireland
d. Jan 13, 1941 in Zurich, Switzerland
Source: *AtlBL; CasWL; Chambr 3; ChPo, S1; CnMD; CnMWL; CyWA; DcLEL; EncWL; EvLB; LongCTC; McGEWD; ModBrL, SUP; ModWD; NewC; OxEng; Pen ENG; PoIre; RAdv 1; RComWL; REn; TwCA, SUP; TwCW; WebE&AL; WhoTwCL*

Joyce, Peggy Hopkins
[Margaret Upton]
American. Actress
b. 1893 in Norfolk, Virginia
d. Jun 12, 1957 in New York, New York
Source: *InWom; MotPP; PseudN; WhScrn 74, 77; WhoHol B*

Joyce, William
"Lord Haw-Haw"
German. World War II Propagandist
b. 1906
d. Jan 5, 1946 in Wandsworth, England
Source: *BioIn 1, 7; PseudN*

Juan Carlos I
[Prince Juan Carlos Borbon y Borbon]
"Juan Carlos the Brief"
Spanish. King
b. Jan 5, 1938 in Rome, Italy
Source: *BioIn 10; IntWW 74; PseudN*

Juan, Don
[Jaun Matus]
Mexican. Yaqui Sorcerer
Used hallucinogenic drugs to gain power over demonic world.
b. 1891
Source: *BioIn 10*

Juantorena, Alberto
Cuban. Track Athlete
b. 1952
Source: *BioIn 11*

Juarez, Benito Pablo
"The Mexican Washington"; "The Second Washington"
Mexican. President
b. Mar 21, 1806 in Oaxaca, Mexico
d. Jul 18, 1872 in Mexico City, Mexico
Source: *ApCAB; Drake; PseudN; REn; WhAm H*

Juch, Emma
American. Opera Singer, Manager
b. Jul 4, 1863 in Vienna, Austria
d. Mar 6, 1939 in New York, New York
Source: *AmBi; AmWom; InWom; NotAW; WhAm 1; WomWWA 14*

Judah
Biblical Character
Source: *BioIn 10; WebBD 80*

Judah Ha-Levi
see: Ha-Levi, Judah

Judas Iscariot
Biblical Character
Source: *BioIn 10; NewCol 75; WebBD 80*

Judas Priest
[K K Downing; Rob Halford; Ian Hill; Dave Holland; Glenn Tipton]
British. Rock Band
Heavy metal band formed in mid-70's; album, *Screaming for Vengeance,* 1982.
Source: *IlEncRk*

Judd, Winnie Ruth McKinnell
American. Murderer
b. 1905
Source: *BioIn 9*

Jude, Saint
[Saint Thaddeus]
Biblical Character
Source: *REn*

Judith
Biblical Character
Source: *WebBD 80*

Judson, Edward Zane Carroll
[Ned Buntline, pseud.]
American. Adventurer
b. Mar 20, 1823 in Stamford, New York
d. Jul 16, 1886 in Stamford, New York
Source: *Alli SUP; AmAu; AmAu&B; AmBi; ApCAB; DcAmAu; DcAmB; DcNAA; HsB&A; MnBBF; OhA&B; OxAmL; PseudN; REn; REnAL; TwCBDA; WebAB; WhAm H*

Judson, Egbert Putnam
American. Inventor
Developed gentle blasting powder, 1876.
b. Aug 9, 1812 in Syracuse, New York
d. Jan 9, 1893 in San Francisco, California
Source: *DcAmB; WhAm H*

Judson, Emily Chubbock
[Fanny Forester, pseud.]
American. Author
b. Aug 22, 1817 in Eaton, New York
d. Jun 1, 1854 in Hamilton, New York
Source: *Alli; AmAu; AmAu&B; AmBi; ApCAB; BbD; BiD&SB; ChPo, S1, S2; CyAl 2; DcAmAu; DcAmB; DcNAA; Drake; FemPA; InWom; NotAW; PseudN; TwCBDA; WebAB; WhAm H*

Judy, Steven
American. Murderer
Executed by electrocution.
b. 1957? in Indianapolis, Indiana
d. Mar 9, 1981 in Michigan City, Indiana
Source: *NF*

Juilliard, Augustus D
American. Merchant, Music Patron
Donated $12 million toward establishment of Juilliard School of Music.
b. Apr 19, 1836 in Canton, Ohio
d. Apr 25, 1919 in New York, New York
Source: *AmBi; DcAmB; WhAm 1*

Juilliard String Quartet, The
[Claus Adam; Earl Carlyss; Robert Mann; Samuel Rhodes]
American. Musicians
Source: *BiDAmM*

Juin, Alphonse
French. Soldier, Marshal
b. Dec 16, 1888 in Bone, Algeria
d. Jan 27, 1967 in Paris, France
Source: *CurBio 43, 67; WhAm 4*

Jukes, Margaret
Criminal
Source: *NF*

Julia, Raul
[Raul Rafael Carlos Julia y Arcelay]
American. Actor
b. Mar 9, 1940 in San Juan, Puerto Rico
Source: *WhoHol A*

Julian (Flavius Claudius Julianus)
"The Apostate"
Roman. Emperor
General, proclaimed emperor by troops, 361; enemy of Christianity.
b. 331
d. 363
Source: *BioIn 10; PseudN*

Julian, "Doggie" (Alvin T)
American. Basketball Coach
b. Apr 5, 1901 in Reading, Pennsylvania
d. Jul 28, 1967 in Worcester, Massachusetts
Source: *PseudN; WhoBbl 73*

Julian, Hubert Fauntleroy
"Black Eagle"
American. Aviator
b. 1897 in Trinidad
Source: *NewYTBS 74*

Juliana, Queen
Dutch. Former Queen
b. Apr 30, 1909
Source: *BioIn 10; IntWW 74; WebBD 80*

Julius III, Pope
[Giammaria Ciocchi del Monte]
Italian. Roman Catholic Leader
b. 1487
d. 1555
Source: *PseudN; WebBD 80*

Julius Caesar
Roman. General, Statesman
Established Julian calendar, 45BC; month July (Julius) named in honor.
b. Jul 12, 100BC in Rome, Italy
d. Mar 15, 44BC in Rome, Italy
Source: *NewCol 75; WebBD 80*

Jumblatt, Kamal Fouad
Lebanese. Political Leader
b. Jan 6, 1917 in Mukhtara, Lebanon
d. Mar 16, 1977 in Beirut, Lebanon
Source: *IntWW 74*

Jumel, Eliza
[Betsey Bowen; Eliza Brown]
American. Wife of Aaron Burr
b. 1769
d. Jul 16, 1865 in New York, New York
Source: *ApCAB; NotAW; REnAL*

Jump, Gordon
American. Actor
Played Mr. Carlson on "WKRP in Cincinnati," 1978-82.
b. Apr 1, 1927? in Dayton, Ohio
Source: *WhoAm 80, 82*

Jung, Carl Gustav
Swiss. Psychologist, Psychiatrist
Founded analytic psychology; developed introvert, extrovert personality types.
b. Jul 26, 1875 in Basel, Switzerland
d. Jun 6, 1961 in Zurich, Switzerland
Source: *BiDPara; CasWL; CurBio 43, 53, 61; EncWL; LongCTC; OxEng; OxGer; RComWL; REn; TwCA, SUP; WhAm 4; WhoTwCL*

Junior Walker and the All Stars
[Autrey DeWalt, Jr.; James Graves; Vic Thomas; Willie Woods]
American. Musical Group
Source: *RkOn*

Junkers, Hugo
German. Airplane Engineer, Builder
b. 1859
d. 1935
Source: *WebBD 80*

Junot, Philippe
French. Ex-Husband of Princess Caroline
b. 1942
Source: *BioIn 11, 12*

Jurado, Katy
[Maria Christina Jurado Garcia]
Mexican. Actress
b. 1927 in Guadalajara, Mexico
Source: *FilmgC; IntMPA 75, 76, 77, 78, 79, 80, 81, 82; MovMk; OxFilm; PseudN; WhoHol A*

Jurgens, Curt
German. Actor
b. Dec 12, 1915 in Munich, Germany
d. Jun 18, 1982 in Vienna, Austria
Source: *BiDFilm; FilmgC; IntMPA 78, 79, 80, 81, 82; MotPP; MovMk; NewYTBS 77, 82; OxFilm; WhoAm 82; WhoHol A; WorEFlm*

Jurgenson, "Sonny" (Christian Adolph, III)
American. Football Player, Sportscaster
b. Aug 23, 1934 in Wilmington, North Carolina
Source: *PseudN; WhoAm 82; WhoFtbl 74*

Jurinac, Sena
[Srebrenka Jurinac]
Yugoslav. Opera Singer
b. Oct 24, 1921 in Travnik, Yugoslavia
Source: *InWom; IntWW 74; PseudN; Who 74; WhoMus 72; WhoWor 74*

Jussieu, Bernard de
French. Botanist
b. Aug 17, 1699 in Lyons, France
d. Dec 6, 1777? in Paris, France
Source: *OxFr*

Just, Ernest Everett
American. Biologist
Harvard U zoologist noted for study of cellular biology.
b. Aug 14, 1883 in Charleston, South Carolina
d. Oct 27, 1941 in Washington, DC
Source: *BioIn 1, 6, 8, 9, 11; DcAmB S3; DcNAA; ObitOF 79; SelBAA; WebAB; WhAm 1; WhoColR*

Justice, "Choo Choo" (Charles Ronald)
American. Football Player
b. May 18, 1924 in Asheville, North Carolina
Source: *PseudN; WhoFtbl 74*

Justice, James Robertson
British. Actor, Journalist
b. 1905 in Aberdeen, Scotland
d. Jul 2, 1975 in Winchester, England
Source: *FilmgC; MovMk; WhScrn 77*

Justice, William Wayne
American. District Court Judge
b. Feb 25, 1920 in Athens, Texas
Source: *AmBench 79; WhoAm 74, 76, 78, 80, 82; WhoAmL 79; WhoAmP 73; WhoGov 72, 75; WhoS&SW 73*

Justinian I (Flavius Anicius Justinianus)
"The Great"
Byzantine. Emperor of the East
b. 483
d. 565
Source: *BioIn 10; NewCol 75; PseudN; WebBD 80*

Justus, Roy Braxton
American. Editor, Cartoonist
b. May 16, 1901 in Avon, South Dakota
Source: *WhoAm 74, 76, 78, 80, 82; WhoAmA 73*

Jutra, Claude
Canadian. Motion Picture Director
b. Mar 11, 1930 in Montreal, PQ
Source: *BioIn 10; CanWW 79; CreCan 1; DcFM; OxFilm; WorEFlm*

Juvenal (Decimus Junius Juvenalis)
"The Aquinian Sage"; "The Last Poet of Rome"
Roman. Satirist
b. 60 in Aquinum, Italy
d. 140?
Source: *AtlBL; BbD; BiD&SB; CasWL; CyWA; NewC; Pen CL; PseudN; RComWL; REn*

K

K C and the Sunshine Band
[Oliver Brown; H(arry) W(ayne) Casey; Rick Finch; Robert Johnson; Denvil Liptrot; Jerome Smith; Ronnie Smith; James Weaver; Charles Williams]
American. Rock Group
Source: *RkOn 2; WhoRock 81*

Kabalevsky, Dmitri Borisovich
Russian. Composer
b. Dec 30, 1904 in Saint Petersburg, Russia
Source: *DcCM; IntWW 74; WhoMus 72; WhoWor 74*

Kadar, Janos
Hungarian. Politician, Communist Leader
b. May 22, 1912 in Fiume, Hungary
Source: *CurBio 57; IntWW 74; WhoWor 74*

Kael, Pauline
American. Author, Motion Picture Critic
b. Jun 19, 1919 in Sonoma County, California
Source: *AmAu&B; Au&Wr 71; CelR 73; ConAu 45; CurBio 74; ForWC 70; IntMPA 75, 76, 77, 78, 79, 80, 81, 82; OxFilm; WhoAm 74, 76, 78, 80, 82; WhoAmW 77; WrDr 76*

Kaempfert, Bert
German. Singer
b. Oct 16, 1923 in Hamburg, Germany
Source: *EncPR&S*

Kaestner, Erich
see: Kastner, Erich

Kafka, Franz
Austrian. Author, Poet
b. Jul 2, 1883 in Prague, Czechoslovakia
d. Jun 3, 1924 in Kierling, Austria
Source: *AtlBL; CasWL; ClDMEL; CnMD; CnMWL; CyWA; EncWL; EvEuW; LongCTC; ModGL; OxEng; OxGer; Pen EUR; RComWL; REn; TwCA, SUP; TwCW; WhoTwCL*

Kaganovich, Lazar M
Russian. Communist Leader
b. Nov 22, 1893 in Kabany, Russia
Source: *CurBio 42, 55; IntWW 74*

Kagel, Sam
American. Lawyer
Mediator in NFL strike, 1982.
b. Jan 24, 1909 in San Francisco, California
Source: *NewYTBS 82; WhoAm 74, 76, 78; WhoLab 76*

Kahanamoku, Duke
American. Swimmer
b. Aug 24, 1890 in Honolulu, Hawaii
d. Jan 22, 1968 in Honolulu, Hawaii
Source: *WhAm 4A; WhScrn 74, 77; WhoHol B*

Kahane, Meir David
American. Militant Zionist, Rabbi
b. Aug 1, 1932 in Brooklyn, New York
Source: *BioNews 74; CurBio 72; WhoE 74*

Kahles, Charles William
American. Comic Strip Artist
b. Jan 12, 1878 in Lengfurt, Germany
d. Jan 21, 1931
Source: *WorECom*

Kahn, Albert
American. Architect
b. Mar 21, 1869 in Rhaunen, Germany
d. Dec 8, 1942 in Detroit, Michigan
Source: *BioNews 74; CurBio 42; DcAmB S3; WhAm 2*

Kahn, Alfred Edward
American. Presidential Advisor
b. Oct 17, 1917 in Paterson, New Jersey
Source: *AmEA 74; AmM&WS 73S; ConAu 41R; NewYTBS 74; WhoAm 74, 76, 78, 80, 82; WhoE 74; WhoWor 74*

Kahn, Ben
Furrier
b. 1887
d. Feb 5, 1976 in New York, New York
Source: *BioIn 10*

Kahn, Gus
American. Songwriter
b. Nov 6, 1886 in Coblenz, Germany
d. Oct 8, 1941 in Beverly Hills, California
Source: *AmSCAP 66; CurBio 41; EncMT*

Kahn, Louis I
American. Architect
b. Feb 2, 1901 in Oesel, Russia
d. Mar 17, 1974 in New York, New York
Source: *AmArch 70; BioNews 74; CelR 73; ConAu 49; CurBio 64, 74; EncAB-H; NewYTBE 72; NewYTBS 74; WhAm 6; WhoAm 74; WhoE 74; WhoWor 74*

Kahn, Madeline Gail
American. Actress
b. Sep 29, 1942 in Boston, Massachusetts
Source: *BkPepl; IntMPA 75, 76, 77, 78, 79, 80, 81, 82; MovMk; NewYTBS 74; WhoAm 82; WhoHol A*

Kahn, Otto Hermann
American. Banker, Opera Patron
b. Feb 21, 1867 in Mannheim, Germany
d. Mar 29, 1934 in New York, New York
Source: *AmBi; AmLY; DcAmB S1; DcNAA; REnAL; WebAB; WhAm 1*

Kahn, Roger
American. Journalist, Author
Sports editor *Newsweek,* 1956-60; editor *Saturday Evening Post,* 1963-68.
b. Oct 31, 1927 in Brooklyn, New York
Source: *AuBYP; ConAu 25R*

Kai-Shek, Chaing
see: Chiang Kai-Shek

Kai-Shek, Chiang, Madame
see: Chiang Mei-Ling

Kain, Karen Alexandria
Canadian. Ballerina
Principal dancer, National Ballet of Canada, 1971--.
b. Mar 28, 1951 in Hamilton, ON
Source: *BioIn 10, 11; CanWW 79; CurBio 80; WhoAm 80, 82*

Kaiser, Edgar Fosburgh
American. Industrialist
President, chairman, of Kaiser Alumninium & Chemical Corp, Kaiser Steel Corp.
b. Jul 29, 1908 in Spokane, Washington
d. Dec 11, 1981 in San Francisco, California
Source: *CurBio 82; IntWW 74, 75, 75, 77, 78, 79, 80, 81; IntYB 78, 79, 80, 81; NewYTBS 81; WhoAm 74, 76, 78, 80; WhoWest 76, 78*

Kaiser, Georg
German. Dramatist
b. Nov 25, 1878 in Magdeburg, Germany
d. Jun 5, 1945 in Ascona, Switzerland
Source: *CasWL; ClDMEL; CnMD; CnThe; EncWL; EvEuW; LongCTC; McGEWD; ModGL; ModWD; NewC; OxEng; OxGer; OxThe; Pen EUR; REn; REnWD; TwCA, SUP; WhoTwCL*

Kaiser, Henry John
American. Industrialist
b. May 9, 1882 in Canajoharie, New York
d. Aug 24, 1967 in Honolulu, Hawaii
Source: *CurBio 42, 61, 67; EncAB-H; WebAB; WhAm 4A*

Kalakaua, David
King of Hawaiian Islands
b. Nov 16, 1836
d. Jan 30, 1891 in San Francisco, California
Source: *ApCAB*

Kalatozov, Mikhail
[Mikhail Kalatozishvili]
Russian. Motion Picture Director
b. 1903 in Tiflis, Russia
d. Mar 28, 1973 in Moscow, U.S.S.R.
Source: *FilmgC; OxFilm; PseudN; WorEFlm*

Kalb, Bernard
American. Journalist, Author
b. Feb 5, 1922 in New York, New York
Source: *BioIn 12*

Kalb, Johann de
German. Revolutionary War General
b. Jun 29, 1721 in Huttendorf, Bavaria
d. Aug 19, 1780 in Camden, South Carolina
Source: *AmBi; ApCAB; DcAmB; REn; TwCBDA; WebAB; WhAm H*

Kalb, Marvin Leonard
American. News Analyst
b. Jun 9, 1930 in New York, New York
Source: *AmAu&B; ConAu 5R; IntMPA 75, 76, 77, 78, 79, 80, 81, 82; WhoAm 74, 76, 78, 80, 82; WhoTwCL; WhoWor 74*

Kalber, Floyd
American. Broadcast Journalist
b. Dec 23, 1924 in Omaha, Nebraska
Source: *WhoAm 78, 80, 82*

Kalem, Ted
American. Drama Critic
b. Dec 19, 1919 in Malden, Massachusetts
Source: *BiE&WWA*

Kalf, Willem
Dutch. Artist
b. 1619? in Rotterdam, Netherlands
d. 1693 in Amsterdam, Netherlands
Source: *McGDA*

Kaline, Al(bert William)
American. Baseball Player
Collected 3,007 hits in career; Hall of Fame, 1980.
b. Dec 19, 1934 in Baltimore, Maryland
Source: *BaseEn; BioNews 74; CelR 73; CurBio 70; NewYTBE 72; NewYTBS 74, 74; WhoAm 74; WhoProB 73*

Kalinin, Mikhail
Russian. Political Leader
b. Nov 20, 1875 in Upper Troitsa, Russia
d. Jun 3, 1946 in Moscow, U.S.S.R.
Source: *CurBio 42, 46*

Kalish, Max
Polish. Sculptor
Commissioned, 1944, to create bronze statues of WW II personalities.
b. Mar 1, 1891 in Valojen, Poland
d. Mar 18, 1945 in New York, New York
Source: *BioIn 1, 2, 9; NatCab 35; WhAm 2*

Kallen, Horace M
American. Educator, Philosopher
b. Aug 11, 1882 in Barenstadt, Germany
d. Feb 16, 1974 in Palm Beach, Florida
Source: *AmAu&B; ConAu 49, 93; CurBio 53, 74; OxAmL; REnAL; TwCA SUP; WhAm 6; WhNAA*

Kallen, Kitty
American. Singer, Actress
Source: *WhoHol A*

Kalmanoff, Martin
American. Composer, Conductor, Musician
b. May 24, 1920 in Brooklyn, New York
Source: *AmSCAP 66; WhoAm 82; WhoWorJ 72*

Kalmar, Bert
American. Songwriter
b. Feb 16, 1884 in New York, New York
d. Sep 18, 1947 in Los Angeles, California
Source: *AmPS; AmSCAP 66; BiDAmM; BioIn 1, 4; CmpEPM; EncMT; NewCBMT; NotNAT B; ObitOF 79; WhThe*

Kalmbach, Herbert Warren
American. Lawyer, Watergate Participant
b. Oct 19, 1921 in Port Huron, Michigan
Source: *NewYTBE 73; WhoAm 74; WhoWest 74*

Kalmus, Herbert Thomas
American. Inventor
Developed technicolor film; president, Technicolor Inc., 1915-59.
b. Nov 9, 1881 in Chelsea, Massachusetts
d. Jul 11, 1963
Source: *BioIn 1, 2, 6; CurBio 49, 63; WhAm 4*

Kalmus, Natalie
American. Adviser on Technicolor Films
b. 1892
d. Nov 15, 1965 in Boston, Massachusetts
Source: *FilmgC*

Kalp, Malcolm
[The Hostages]
American. Former Hostage in Iran
b. 1939?
Source: *NewYTBS 81*

Kaltenborn, H(ans) V(on)
American. Editor, Radio Commentator
b. Jul 9, 1878 in Milwaukee, Wisconsin
d. Jun 14, 1965 in Brooklyn, New York
Source: *AmAu&B; ConAu 93; CurBio 40, 65; PseudN; REnAL; WebAB; WhAm 4; WhNAA*

Kalthoum, Um
"The Nightingale of the Nile"
Egyptian. Singer
b. 1898 in Tamay-al-Zahirah, Egypt
d. Feb 3, 1975 in Cairo, Egypt
Source: *BioIn 4, 6, 7, 10; NewYTBS 75; ObitOF 79; WhScrn 77*

Kamali, Norma
American. Fashion Designer
b. Jun 27, 1945 in New York, New York
Source: *BioIn 12; WhoAm 82*

Kamehameha I
[Kamehameha the Great]
Hawaiian. First King of Hawaiian Islands
b. 1758? in Kohala, Hawaii
d. May 5, 1819 in Kailua, Hawaii
Source: *BioIn 2, 5, 6, 10, 11; McGEWB; NewCol 75; WhAm H*

Kamen, Martin David
American. Biochemist
b. Aug 27, 1913 in Toronto, ON
Source: *AmM&WS 73P; CanWW 70; IntWW 74; WhoAm 74; WhoWor 74*

Kamen, Milt
American. Comedian, Actor
b. 1924 in Hurleyville, New York
d. Feb 24, 1977 in Beverly Hills, California
Source: *WhoHol A*

Kamenev, Lev Borisovich
[Lev Borisovich Rosenfeld]
Russian. Russian Communist Leader
b. 1883
d. 1936
Source: *PseudN; REn*

Kamerlingh Onnes, Heike
Dutch. Physicist
b. Sep 21, 1853 in Groningen, Netherlands
d. Feb 21, 1926
Source: *NewCol 75; WhDW*

Kaminska, Ida
Russian. Actress
b. Sep 4, 1899 in Odessa, Russia
d. May 21, 1980 in New York, New York
Source: *CurBio 69; FilmgC; IntWW 74; NewYTBE 71; WhoHol A; WhoThe 77*

Kaminsky, Grigorii Naumovich
Russian. Communist Leader
b. 1895
d. 1938
Source: *BioIn 10*

Kaminsky, Max
American. Jazz Musician
b. Sep 7, 1908 in Brockton, Massachusetts
Source: *WhoJazz 72*

Kanaris, Constantine
"The Themistocles of Modern Greece"
Greek. Admiral, Patriot
b. 1790
d. 1887
Source: *NewCol 75*

Kander, John
American. Composer
b. Mar 18, 1927 in Kansas City, Missouri
Source: *BiE&WWA; BioIn 11; EncMT; NewCBMT; NotNAT; WhoAm 74, 76, 78, 80, 82; WhoThe 72, 77, 81*

Kandinsky, Wassily
Russian. Artist
b. Dec 4, 1866 in Moscow, Russia
d. Dec 17, 1944 in Paris, France
Source: *AtlBL; CurBio 45; REn*

Kane, Carol
American. Actress
Plays Simka on TV series, "Taxi"; won Emmy, 1982.
b. Jun 18, 1952 in Cleveland, Ohio
Source: *FilmEn; IntMPA 82; WhoAm 82; WhoHol A*

Kane, Elisha Kent
American. Arctic Explorer, Physician
b. Feb 3, 1820 in Philadelphia, Pennsylvania
d. Feb 16, 1857 in Havana, Cuba
Source: *Alli; AmAu; AmBi; ApCAB; BbD; BiD&SB; CyAl 2; DcAmAu; DcAmB; DcNAA; Drake; EarABI SUP; OxAmL; OxCan; REnAL; TwCBDA; WebAB; WhAm H*

Kane, Helen
[Helen Schroder]
"The Boop Boop a Doop Girl"
American. Singer, Actress
b. Aug 4, 1908 in New York, New York
d. Sep 26, 1966 in Jackson Heights, New York
Source: *EncMT; PseudN; ThFT; WhScrn 74, 77; WhoHol B*

Kane, Henry
American. Author
b. 1918 in New York, New York
Source: *AmAu&B; EncMys*

Kane, Howie
see: Jay and the Americans

Kane, Joseph Nathan
American. Editor
b. Jan 23, 1899 in New York, New York
Source: *BioIn 1*

Kane, Robert Joseph
American. President-US Olympic Committee
b. Apr 24, 1912 in Ithaca, New York
Source: *BioIn 12*

Kang, Sheng
Chinese. Communist Leader
b. 1903 in Shantung, China
Source: *IntWW 74*

Kangaroo, Captain
see: Keeshan, Bob

Kania, Stanislaw
Polish. Government Official
b. Mar 8, 1927 in Wrocanka, Poland
Source: *CurBio 81; IntWW 74, 75, 77, 78, 80; WhoSocC 78*

Kanin, Garson
American. Author, Director
Wrote *Tracy and Hepburn: An Intimate Memoir,* 1971; directed *Funny Girl,* 1964.
b. Nov 24, 1912 in Rochester, New York
Source: *AmAu&B; AmSCAP 66; AuNews 1; BiDFilm; BiE&WWA; BioNews 75; CelR 73; CmMov; CnMD; ConAu 5R; ConDr 73; CurBio 41, 52; DcFM; FilmgC; IntMPA 75, 76, 77, 78, 79, 80, 81, 82; ModWD; MovMk; NatPD; NotNAT; OxAmL; OxFilm; Pen AM; REnAL; WhoAm 74, 76, 78, 80, 82; WhoThe 77; WhoWor 74; WorAu; WorEFlm; WrDr 76*

Kanner, Leo
American. Child Psychologist, Author
b. Jun 13, 1894 in Klekotow, Austria
d. Apr 3, 1981 in Sykesville, Maryland
Source: *BioIn 11; ConAu 17R, 103; WhoAm 74; WhoWor 74; WhoWorJ 72*

Kannon, Jackie
Comedian
b. 1919 in Windsor, ON
d. Feb 1, 1974 in New York, New York
Source: *NewYTBS 74; WhScrn 77; WhoHol B*

Kano, Motonobu
Japanese. Artist
b. 1476
d. 1559
Source: *NewCol 75*

Kant, Immanuel
German. Metaphysician, Philosopher
b. Apr 22, 1724 in Konigsberg, Germany
d. Feb 12, 1804 in Konigsberg, Germany
Source: *BbD; BiD&SB; CasWL; CyWA; DcEuL; EuAu; EvEuW; NewC; OxEng; OxGer; Pen EUR; REn*

Kanter, Hal
[Henry Irving]
American. Writer, Director, Producer
b. Dec 18, 1918 in Savannah, Georgia
Source: *ConAu 81; IntMPA 75, 76, 77, 78, 79, 80, 81, 82; PseudN; WhoAm 82; WorEFlm*

Kantner, Paul
[Jefferson Airplane; Jefferson Starship]
American. Singer, Musician
b. Mar 12, 1942 in San Francisco, California
Source: *BioIn 9; WhoAm 80, 82*

Kantor, Mackinlay
American. Author, Journalist
b. Feb 4, 1904 in Webster City, Iowa
d. Oct 11, 1977 in Sarasota, Florida
Source: *AmAu&B; AmNov; AuBYP; ChPo S1; CnDAL; ConAmA; ConAu 61, 73; ConLC 7; ConNov 72, 76; DcLEL; EncMys; FilmgC; ModAL; OxAmL; Pen AM; REn; REnAL; TwCA, SUP; TwCW; WhoAm 74; WrDr 76*

Kantrowitz, Adrian
American. Heart Surgeon
b. Oct 4, 1918 in New York, New York
Source: *AmM&WS 73P; CurBio 67; IntWW 74; WhoAm 74, 76, 78, 80, 82; WhoE 74; WhoWor 74; WhoWorJ 72*

Kapell, William
American. Musician
b. Sep 20, 1922 in New York, New York
d. Oct 29, 1953 in San Francisco, California
Source: *CurBio 48, 54; WhAm 3*

Kaplan, Gabe (Gabriel)
American. Actor, Comedian
Starred in TV series "Welcome Back, Kotter," 1975-79.
b. Mar 31, 1945 in Brooklyn, New York
Source: *BioIn 10; BkPepl; IntMPA 79, 80, 81, 82; WhoAm 78, 80, 82*

Kaplow, Herbert E
American. Journalist
b. Feb 2, 1927 in New York, New York
Source: *WhoAm 82; WhoWorJ 72*

Kappel, Gertrude
German. Opera Singer
b. Sep 1, 1893 in Halle, Germany
d. Apr 1971 in Munich, Germany (West)
Source: *InWom; NewYTBE 71; WhAm 5*

Kaprow, Allan
American. Artist
b. Aug 23, 1927 in Atlantic City, New Jersey
Source: *DcCAA 71*

Karajan, Herbert von
Austrian. Conductor
b. Apr 5, 1908 in Salzburg, Austria
Source: *CelR 73; CurBio 56; IntWW 74; NewYTBS 74; Who 74*

Karamanlis, Constantine
[Constantinos Caramanlis]
"Costas"
Greek. President
Premier, 1955-63; president, 1980--.
b. Feb 23, 1907 in Prote, Greece
Source: *CurBio 56, 76; IntWW 74, 75, 76, 77, 78, 79, 80, 81; IntYB 78, 79; NewYTBS 74, 80; WhoWor 76, 78*

Kardiner, Abram
American. Psychoanalyst
b. Aug 17, 1891 in New York, New York
d. Jul 20, 1981 in Easton, Connecticut
Source: *AmAu&B; BiDrAPA 77; ConAu 104; NewYTBS 81*

Karfiol, Bernard
American. Artist
b. May 6, 1886 in Budapest, Hungary
d. Aug 16, 1952 in New York, New York
Source: *CurBio 47, 52; DcAmArt; DcAmB S5; DcCAA 71, 77; McGDA; WhAm 3; WhoAmA 78*

Karim, Shah
see: Aga Khan IV

Karloff, Boris
[William Henry Pratt]
English. Actor
In horror films *Frankenstein,* 1931; *The Mummy,* 1933.
b. Nov 23, 1887 in London, England
d. Feb 2, 1969 in Middleton, England
Source: *BiDFilm; BiE&WWA; CmMov; CurBio 41, 69; Film 1; FilmgC; MotPP; MovMk; OxFilm; PseudN; TwYS; WebAB; WhAm 5; WhScrn 74, 77; WhoHol B; WorEFlm*

Karmal, Babrak
Afghan. President
b. 1929
Source: *CurBio 81; IntWW 80; NewYTBS 79*

Karns, Roscoe
American. Comedian
b. Sep 7, 1893 in San Bernardino, California
d. Feb 6, 1970 in Los Angeles, California
Source: *FilmgC; MotPP; MovMk; NewYTBE 70; TwYS; Vers B; WhScrn 74, 77; WhoHol B*

Karp, Lila
American. Sociologist, Author
b. Jun 7, 1933 in New York, New York
Source: *ConAu 25R; DrAF 76; DrAS 74E*

Karpin, Fred Leon
American. Journalist
b. Mar 17, 1913 in New York, New York
Source: *ConAu 13R*

Karpis, Alvin
[Alvin Karpowicz]
"Old Creepy"
Canadian. Criminal
b. 1908 in Montreal, PQ
d. Aug 12, 1979 in Torremolinos, Spain
Source: *Blood; NewYTBS 79; PseudN*

Karpov, Anatoly
Russian. Chess Player
b. May 23, 1951 in Zlatoust, U.S.S.R.
Source: *BioIn 10*

Karras, Alex(ander G)
"The Mad Duck"; "Tippy Toes"
American. Football Player, Actor
Tackle, 1958-62, 1964-70, suspended, 1963, for gambling.
b. Jul 15, 1935 in Gary, Indiana
Source: *BioNews 74; PseudN; WhoAm 74, 76, 78, 80, 82; WhoFtbl 74; WhoHol A*

Karsavina, Tamara
[Tamara Karsavin]
"La Tamara"
Russian. Ballerina
b. 1885
d. May 26, 1978 in London, England
Source: *BioIn 1, 2, 3, 4, 6, 8, 11*

Karsh, Yousuf
Canadian. Photographer, Journalist
Most famous photo of Winston Churchill; wrote *Faces of Our Time,* 1971.
b. Dec 23, 1908 in Mardin, Armenia
Source: *CanWW 82; ConAu 33R; CurBio 52, 80; IntWW 74; NewYTBE 72; Who 74; WhoAm 82; WhoAmA 73; WhoWor 74*

Kasavubu, Joseph
"The Father of Congo Independence"
Congolese. President
b. 1910 in Tshela, Congo
d. Mar 24, 1969 in Boma, Congo
Source: *CurBio 61, 69; PseudN; WhAm 5*

Kasdan, Lawrence Edward
American. Director, Screenwriter
b. Jan 14, 1949 in Miami Beach, Florida
Source: *NewYTBS 81; WhoAm 82*

Kashi, Aliza
American. Actress
b. Apr 5, 1940 in Tel Aviv, Palestine
Source: *WhoAm 74*

Kasper, Herbert
American. Dress, Sportswear Designer
b. Dec 12, 1926 in New York, New York
Source: *PseudN; WhoAm 82; WhoFash; WorFshn*

Kassebaum, Nancy Landon
American. Senator
Daughter of Alf Landon; senator from KS, 1979--.
b. Jul 29, 1932 in Topeka, Kansas
Source: *AlmAP 80; CngDr 79; CurBio 82; NewYTBS 78; WhoAm 80, 82; WhoAmP 79; WomPO 76*

Kassem, Abdul Karim
Iraqi. Politician
b. Nov 21, 1914 in Baghdad, Iraq
d. Feb 9, 1963 in Baghdad, Iraq
Source: *CurBio 59, 63*

Kassorla, Irene Chamie
American. Psychologist, Author
b. Aug 18, 1931 in Los Angeles, California
Source: *BioIn 10; NewYTBS 81; WhoWest 78*

Kasten, Robert W, Jr.
American. Senator
b. Jun 19, 1942 in Milwaukee, Wisconsin
Source: *AlmAP 78; CngDr 77; WhoAm 78, 80; WhoAmP 73, 75, 77, 79; WhoGov 75, 77; WhoMW 76, 78*

Kastner, Erich
[Erich Kaestner]
German. Author, Poet
Wrote *Emil and the Detectives,* 1928; books burned in Germany, 1933.
b. Feb 23, 1899 in Dresden, Germany
d. Jul 29, 1974
Source: *AuBYP; CasWL; ClDMEL; CnMD; ConAu 49, 73; CurBio 64, 74; EncWL; EvEuW; IntWW 74; ModGL; ModWD; SmATA 14; OxGer; Pen EUR; ThrBJA; WhAm 6; Who 74; WhoChL; WhoWor 74; WorAu*

Kasznar, Kurt
[Kurt Serwischer]
Austrian. Actor
b. Aug 13, 1913 in Vienna, Austria
d. Aug 6, 1979 in Santa Monica, California
Source: *BiE&WWA; ConAu 89; FilmgC; IntMPA 77, 78; MotPP; MovMk; NotNAT; PseudN; Vers B; WhoAm 74, 76, 78; WhoHol A; WhoThe 72, 77*

Katims, Milton
American. Musician, Conductor
b. 1909 in Brooklyn, New York
Source: *NewYTBS 74; WhoAm 74, 76, 78, 80, 82; WhoMus 72; WhoWest 74; WhoWor 74*

Katona, George
American. Economist
b. Nov 6, 1901 in Budapest, Hungary
d. Jun 18, 1981 in Berlin, Germany (West)
Source: *AmEA 74; AmM&WS 73S; WhoAm 74, 76, 78, 80; WhoWor 74*

Katt, William
American. Actor
Starred in TV series "The Greatest American Hero."
b. 1955 in Los Angeles, California
Source: *IntMPA 79, 80, 81, 82*

Katzenbach, Nicholas de Belleville
American. Lawyer, Attorney General
b. Jan 17, 1922 in Philadelphia, Pennsylvania
Source: *BiDrUSE; CurBio 65; IntWW 74; St&PR 75; WhoAm 74, 76, 78, 80, 82; WhoAmP 73; WhoF&I 74; WhoWor 74*

Kauff, Benny (Benjamin Michael)
American. Baseball Player
b. Jan 5, 1890 in Pomeroy, Ohio
d. Nov 17, 1961 in Columbus, Ohio
Source: *BaseEn; WhoProB 73*

Kauffer, Edward McKnight
American. Illustrator
b. 1891 in Great Falls, Montana
d. Oct 22, 1954 in New York, New York
Source: *BioIn 1, 3, 4, 8; IlsCB 1744; ObitOF 79*

Kauffman, Ewing Marion
American. Businessman; Baseball Executive
Owner, Marion Labs, 1950--, KC Royals baseball club, 1969--.
b. Sep 21, 1916 in Missouri
Source: *WhoAm 78, 80, 82*

Kauffmann, Angelica
French. Artist
b. 1741
d. 1807
Source: *BkIE; NewCol 75*

Kauffmann, Stanley Jules
[Spranger Barry, pseud.]
American. Critic
b. Apr 24, 1916 in New York, New York
Source: *Au&Wr 71; ConAu 5R; LongCTC; Pen AM; PseudN; WhoAm 74, 76, 78, 80, 82; WhoE 74; WhoWor 74; WorAu; WrDr 76*

Kaufman, Andy
American. Actor, Comedian
Plays Latka on TV series "Taxi," 1978--.
b. Jan 17, 1949 in New York, New York
Source: *BioIn 11; WhoAm 80, 82*

Kaufman, Bel
American. Author, Educator
Wrote *Up the Down Staircase,* 1965.
b. in Berlin, Germany
Source: *AmAu&B; ConAu 13R; DrAF 76; ForWC 70; WhoAm 74, 76, 78, 80, 82; WhoE 74; WhoWor 74; WrDr 76*

Kaufman, Boris
Polish. Cinematographer
b. Aug 24, 1906 in Bialystok, Poland
d. Jun 24, 1980 in New York, New York
Source: *DcFM; FilmgC; IntMPA 75, 76, 77, 78, 79; OxFilm; WorEFlm*

Kaufman, George S(imon)
American. Dramatist, Journalist
b. Nov 16, 1889 in Pittsburgh, Pennsylvania
d. Jun 2, 1961 in New York, New York
Source: *AmAu&B; CasWL; CnDAL; CnMD; CnThe; ConAmA; ConAmL; ConAu 93; CurBio 41, 61; DcLEL; EncMT; EvLB; FilmgC; LongCTC; McGEWD; ModWD; NewCBMT; NewYTBE 72; OxAmL; OxThe; Pen AM; REn; REnAL; REnWD; TwCA, SUP; TwCW; WebAB; WebE&AL; WhAm 4; WorEFlm*

Kaufman, Henry
American. Economist
b. 1927 in Wenings, Germany
Source: *AmEA 74; CurBio 81; NewYTBS 79*

Kaufman, Irving R
American. Judge, Lawyer
b. Jun 24, 1910 in New York, New York
Source: *AmM&WS 73P; ConAu 21R; CurBio 53; NewYTBE 70; WhoAm 74, 76, 78, 80, 82; WhoAmA 73; WhoE 74; WhoF&I 74; WhoGov 72; WhoWorJ 72*

Kaufman, Joseph William
American. Lawyer, Judge
Prosecutor at WW II Nuremburg war crime trials.
b. Mar 27, 1899 in New York, New York
d. Feb 13, 1981 in Washington, DC
Source: *NewYTBS 81; WhoAm 74, 76, 78, 80*

Kaufman, Louis
American. Musician
b. 1905
Source: *WhoMus 72*

Kaufman, Murray
"Murray the K"; "The Fifth Beatle"
American. Disc Jockey
NY dj, 1950's-60's; promoted The Beatles first tour, 1964.
b. Feb 14, 1922 in New York, New York
d. Feb 21, 1982 in Los Angeles, California
Source: *BioIn 8, 10; BioNews 74; NewYTBS 82; PseudN*

Kaufman, Sue
[Sue Kaufman Barondess]
American. Author
b. Aug 7, 1926? in Long Island, New York
d. Jun 25, 1977 in New York, New York
Source: *ConAu 1R, 69, 1NR; ConLC 3; DrAF 76; ForWC 70; PseudN; WhoAm 74; WrDr 76*

Kaunda, Kenneth David
Zambian. President
b. Apr 28, 1924 in Lubwa, Zambia
Source: *CurBio 66; IntWW 74; Who 74; WhoGov 72; WhoWor 74*

Kauokenen, Jorma
[Jefferson Airplane]
American. Singer, Musician
b. Dec 23, 1940 in Washington, DC
Source: *NF*

Kautner, Helmut
German. Screenwriter, Director
b. Mar 25, 1908 in Dusseldorf, Germany
d. Apr 20, 1980 in Castellina, Italy
Source: *AnObit 1980; BiDFilm; DcFM; FilmgC; IntWW 74, 75, 76, 77, 78; WhoWor 74; WorEFlm*

Kavanagh, Patrick
Irish. Poet
b. 1905 in County Monaghan, Ireland
d. Nov 30, 1967 in Dublin, Ireland
Source: *BioIn 9, 10, 11; CasWL; ChPo; ConAu 25R; ConP 75; ModBrL SUP; Pen ENG; REn; TwCW; WhoTwCL; WorAu*

Kavanaugh, Kevin
see: Southside Johnny and the Asbury Jukes

Kawabata, Yasunari
Japanese. Author
b. Jun 11, 1899 in Osaka, Japan
d. Apr 16, 1972 in Zusni, Japan
Source: *CasWL; CnMWL; ConAu 33R, 93; ConLC 2, 5, 9, 18; CurBio 69, 72; DcOrL 1; EncWL; NewYTBE 72; Pen CL; RComWL; REn; WhAm 5; WhoTwCL; WorAu*

Kay, Dianne
American. Actress
Played Nancy Bradford on TV series "Eight is Enough."
b. 1956
Source: *BioIn 12*

Kay, Hershy
American. Composer, Arranger
b. Nov 17, 1919 in Philadelphia, Pennsylvania
d. Dec 2, 1981 in Danbury, Connecticut
Source: *AmSCAP 66, 80; Baker 78; BiDAmM; BiE&WWA; BioIn 10; CurBio 62, 82; NotNAT; WhoAm 74, 76, 78, 80*

Kay, Mary
[Mary Kay Ash]
American. Cosmetics Company Executive
b. in Houston, Texas
Source: *WhoAm 82*

Kaye, Danny
[David Daniel Kaminsky or Kominski]
American. Actor, Comedian
b. Jan 18, 1913 in New York, New York
Source: *BiDFilm; BiE&WWA; CelR 73; CmMov; CurBio 41, 52; EncMT; FilmgC; IntMPA 75, 76, 77, 78, 79, 80, 81, 82; MotPP; MovMk; NewYTBE 70; NotNAT; OxFilm; OxThe; PseudN; WebAB; Who 74; WhoAm 74, 76, 78, 80, 82; WhoHol A; WhoThe 77; WhoUN 75; WhoWor 74; WhoWorJ 72; WorEFlm*

Kaye, Dearwood ("Waldo")
see: Our Gang

Kaye, Mary Margaret Mollie
[Mollie Hamilton; M M Kaye]
English. Author
b. 1909 in Simla, India
Source: *Au&Wr 71; ConAu 89; PseudN*

Kaye, Nora
[Nora Koreff]
American. Ballerina
b. 1920 in New York, New York
Source: *CurBio 53; InWom; PseudN; WhoAm 82*

Kaye, Sammy
American. Band Leader
b. Mar 13, 1913? in Lakewood, Ohio
Source: *AmSCAP 66; WhoAm 74; WhoHol A*

Kaye, Stubby
American. Actor, Comedian
b. Nov 11, 1918 in New York, New York
Source: *BiE&WWA; FilmgC; MotPP; NotNAT; PlP&P; WhoHol A; WhoThe 77*

Kaye-Smith, Sheila
English. Author
b. Feb 4, 1887 in Hastings, England
d. Jan 14, 1956
Source: *BkC 4; CathA 1930; ChPo S1; CyWA; DcLEL; EvLB; InWom; LongCTC; ModBrL; NewC; Pen ENG; REn; TwCA, SUP; TwCW; WhAm 3*

Kayibanda, Gregoire
Rwandan. President
b. May 1, 1924
Source: *IntWW 74; WhoGov 72; WhoWor 74*

Kazan, Elia
[Elia Kazanjoglou]
American. Theatrical, Movie Director
Won 1954 Oscar for *On the Waterfront;* co-founded Actor's Studio, 1947.
b. Sep 7, 1909 in Constantinople, Turkey
Source: *BiDFilm; BiE&WWA; CelR 73; ConAu 21R; ConLC 6; CurBio 48, 72; DcFM; FilmgC; IntMPA 75, 76, 77, 78, 79, 80, 81, 82; IntWW 74; MovMk; NewYTBE 72; NotNAT; OxAmL; OxFilm; OxThe; PlP&P; PseudN; REnAL; WebAB; Who 74; WhoAm 74, 76, 78, 80, 82; WhoE 74; WhoHol A; WhoThe 77; WhoWor 74; WorEFlm; WrDr 76*

Kazan, Lainie
[Lanie Levine]
American. Singer
b. May 16, 1940 in New York, New York
Source: *CelR 73; WhoAm 82; WhoHol A*

Kazantzakis, Nikos
Greek. Author
b. Dec 2, 1883 in Crete
d. Oct 26, 1957 in Freiburg, Germany (West)
Source: *AtlBL; CasWL; CnMD; CurBio 55, 58; EncWL; OxEng; Pen EUR; REn; TwCA SUP; TwCW; WhAm 3, 4A; WhoTwCL*

Kazin, Alfred
American. Critic
b. Jun 5, 1915 in Brooklyn, New York
Source: *AmAu&B; CasWL; CelR 73; ConAu 1R, 1NR; CurBio 66; DrAS 74E; IntWW 74; OxAmL; Pen AM; RAdv 1; REn; REnAL; TwCA SUP; WhoAm 74, 76, 78, 80, 82; WhoWor 74; WhoWorJ 72*

Keach, Stacy, Jr.
American. Actor
b. Jun 2, 1941 in Savannah, Georgia
Source: *CelR 73; CurBio 71; FilmgC; IntMPA 75, 76, 77, 78, 79, 80, 81, 82; MovMk; NewYTBE 72; NotNAT; WhoAm 74, 76, 78, 80, 82; WhoHol A; WhoThe 77*

Kean, Charles John
English. Actor
b. Jan 18, 1811 in Waterford, Ireland
d. Jan 22, 1868 in London, England
Source: *BioIn 10; WebBD 80*

Kean, Edmund
English. Actor
b. Mar 17, 1787 in London, England
d. May 15, 1833
Source: *FamA&A; NewC; OxThe; PlP&P; REn; WhAm H*

Keane, Bil
American. Cartoonist
Creator of the "Family Circus," 1960--.
b. Oct 5, 1922 in Philadelphia, Pennsylvania
Source: *ConAu 33R; SmATA 4; WhoAm 82; WhoAmA 73*

Keane, John B
Irish. Author
b. Jul 21, 1928 in Listowel, Ireland
Source: *ConAu 29R*

Keaney, Frank
American. Basketball Coach
Coach, Rhode Island U, 1921-48; introduced full-court press.
b. Jun 5, 1886 in Boston, Massachusetts
d. Oct 10, 1967
Source: *WhoBbl 73*

Kearns, Doris H
American. Author, Educator
b. Jan 4, 1943 in Rockville Centre, New York
Source: *ConAu 103; WhoE 74*

Kearny, Stephen Watts
American. Soldier
b. Aug 30, 1794 in Newark, New Jersey
d. Oct 31, 1848 in Saint Louis, Missouri
Source: *AmBi; ApCAB; BioIn 2, 6, 7, 8, 9, 11; DcAmB; Drake; McGEWB; NatCAB 13; NewCol 75; REnAW; TwCBDA; WebAB; WebAMB; WhAm H; WhoMilH 76*

Keating, Kenneth B
American. Lawyer, Politician
b. May 18, 1900 in Lima, New York
d. May 5, 1975 in New York, New York
Source: *BiDrAC; CurBio 50; IntWW 74; USBiR 74; WhAm 6; WhoAm 74; WhoAmP 73; WhoE 74; WhoGov 72; WhoWor 74*

Keaton, "Buster" (Joseph Francis)
"The Great Stone Face"
American. Actor, Comedian
Perfected deadpan stare in *The Navigator,* 1924; *The General,* 1927.
b. Oct 4, 1896 in Piqua, Kansas
d. Feb 1, 1966 in Hollywood, California
Source: *BiDFilm; CmMov; DcFM; Film 1; FilmgC; MotPP; MovMk; OxFilm; PseudN; TwYS; WebAB; WhAm 4; WhScrn 74, 77; WhoHol B; WorEFlm*

Keaton, Diane
[Diane Hall]
American. Actress
Won 1977 Oscar for *Annie Hall;* wrote *Reservations,* 1980.
b. Jan 5, 1946 in Los Angeles, California
Source: *BkPepl; FilmgC; IntMPA 77, 78, 79, 80, 81, 82; MovMk; NewYTBE 72; PseudN; WhoAm 82; WhoHol A*

Keats, John
English. Poet
Wrote *Ode on a Grecian Urn, Ode to a Nightingale.*
b. Oct 31, 1795 in London, England
d. Feb 23, 1821 in Rome, Italy
Source: *Alli; AnCL; AtlBL; BiD&SB; BrAu 19; CasWL; Chambr 3; ChPo, S1, S2; CnE&AP; CrtT 2; CyWA; DcEnA; DcEnL; DcEuL; DcLEL; EvLB; MouLC 2; NewC; OxEng; Pen ENG; RAdv 1; RComWL; REn; Str&VC; WebE&AL*

Keble, John
English. Author
b. Apr 25, 1792 in Fairford, England
d. Mar 27, 1866 in Bournemouth, England
Source: *Alli, SUP; BbD; BiD&SB; BrAu 19; CasWL; Chambr 3; ChPo, S1, S2; DcEnA; DcEnL; DcEuL; DcLEL; EvLB; NewC; OxEng; Pen ENG; PoChrch; REn; WebE&AL*

Keel, Howard
[Harold Clifford Keel]
American. Actor, Singer
b. Apr 13, 1919 in Gillespie, Illinois
Source: *BiE&WWA; CmMov; EncMT; IntMPA 82; MovMk; NotNAT; PseudN; WhoAm 74; WhoHol A; WhoThe 77; WorEFlm*

Keeler, Christine
English. Former Call Girl
b. 1941
Source: *BioIn 10*

Keeler, Ruby
[Ethel Hilda Keeler]
American. Dancer, Actress
b. Aug 25, 1909 in Halifax, NS
Source: *BiDFilm; BiE&WWA; CelR 73; CmMov; CurBio 71; EncMT; FilmgC; InWom; MotPP; MovMk; NewYTBE 70, 71; NotNAT; OxFilm; PlP&P; PseudN; ThFT; WhoAm 74, 76, 78, 80, 82; WhoHol A; WhoThe 77*

Keeler, William
American. President of ARCO Oil & Gas Co.
b. 1927
d. Jul 12, 1981 in Dallas, Texas
Source: *Dun&B 79*

Keenan, Frank
American. Actor
b. Apr 8, 1858 in Dubuque, Iowa
d. Feb 24, 1929
Source: *Film 1; MotPP; TwYS; WhAm 1; WhScrn 74, 77; WhoHol B*

Keene, Carolyn, pseud.
see: Adams, Harriet Stratemeyer

Keene, Charles Samuel
English. Artist
b. Aug 10, 1823 in Hornsey, England
d. Jan 4, 1891 in London, England
Source: *ChPo*

Keene, Laura
English. Actress
b. Jul 20, 1820 in London, England
d. Nov 4, 1873 in Montclair, New Jersey
Source: *AmBi; ApCAB; DcAmB; Drake; FamA&A; InWom; NotAW; OxThe; PlP&P; TwCBDA; WebAB; WhAm H*

Keene, Thomas W
American. Actor
b. Oct 26, 1840 in New York, New York
d. Jun 1, 1898 in Tompkinsville, New York
Source: *DcAmB; OxThe; TwCBDA; WhAm H*

Keener, Jefferson Ward
American. Corporation Executive
With BF Goodrich, 1939-74.
b. Aug 6, 1908 in Portersville, Alabama
d. Jan 2, 1981 in Akron, Ohio
Source: *IntWW 74, 75, 76, 77, 78, 79, 80; IntYB 78, 79, 80, 81; NewYTBS 81; St&PR 75; WhoAm 74; WhoF&I 74; WhoWor 74*

Keeshan, Bob
"Captain Kangaroo"
American. TV Personality, Author
Played Clarabell on "The Howdy Doody Show," 1947-52; Captain Kangaroo, 1955-81.
b. Jun 27, 1927 in Lynbrook, New York
Source: *ConAu 5NR; CurBio 65; IntMPA 77, 78, 79, 80, 81, 82; NewYTBE 72; PseudN; WhoAm 74, 76, 78, 80, 82*

Kefauver, Estes
American. Senator
b. Jul 26, 1903 in Madisonville, Tennessee
d. Aug 10, 1963 in Bethesda, Maryland
Source: *AmAu&B; CurBio 49, 63; WhAm 4; WhScrn 77*

Kehoe, Vincent Jeffre-Roux
American. Army Officer
b. 1922
Source: *BioIn 10*

Keilberth, Joseph
German. Conductor
b. Apr 19, 1908 in Karlsruhe, Germany
d. Jul 7, 1968 in Munich, Germany (West)
Source: *WhAm 5*

Keillor, Garrison Edward
American. Writer, Producer
Created radio program "A Prairie Home Companion" about Lake Wobegon, MN.
b. Aug 7, 1942 in Anoka, Minnesota
Source: *WhoMW 76*

Keino, (Hezekiah) Kip(choge)
"The Flying Policeman"
Kenyan. Track Athlete
b. Jan 17, 1940 in Kaptagunyo, Kenya
Source: *CurBio 67; PseudN; WhoTr&F 73*

Keiser, Reinhard
German. Composer, Opera Director
b. Jan 9, 1674 in Teuchern, Germany
d. Sep 12, 1739 in Hamburg, Germany
Source: *NewEOp 71; OxMus*

Keitel, Harvey
American. Actor
b. 1941 in Brooklyn, New York
Source: *IntMPA 77, 78, 79, 80, 81, 82; MovMk; WhoAm 82; WhoHol A*

Keitel, Wilhelm
"Lakaitel"
German. Nazi War Criminal
b. Sep 22, 1882
d. Oct 16, 1946 in Nuremberg, Germany
Source: *CurBio 40, 46; PseudN*

Keith, Benjamin F
American. Vaudeville Performer
b. 1846 in Hillsboro, New Hampshire
d. Mar 26, 1914
Source: *DcAmB; OxThe; WhAm 1; WhoStg 1906, 1908*

Keith, Brian
[Robert Keith, Jr.]
American. Actor
Played Uncle Bill on TV series "Family Affair," 1966-71.
b. Nov 14, 1921 in Bayonne, New Jersey
Source: *FilmgC; IntMPA 77, 78, 79, 80, 81, 82; MotPP; MovMk; PseudN; WhoAm 82; WorEFlm*

Keith, Ian
[Keith Ross]
American. Actor
b. Feb 27, 1899 in Boston, Massachusetts
d. Mar 26, 1960 in New York, New York
Source: *FilmgC; MotPP; MovMk; PseudN; TwYS; WhScrn 74, 77; WhoHol B*

Keith, Minor Cooper
American. Railroad Promoter
b. Jan 19, 1848 in Brooklyn, New York
d. Jun 14, 1929
Source: *AmBi; ApCAB X; BioIn 1, 7; DcAmB; McGEWB; NatCAB 14, 22; NewCol 75; WhAm 1*

Keith, William
American. Artist
b. 1839 in Aberdeen, Scotland
d. 1911 in Berkeley, California
Source: *ArtsAmW; DcAmArt; DcAmB; EarABI, SUP; IlBEAAW; McGDA; NatCAB 13; NewYHSD; REnAW; WhAm 1*

Keker, Samuel J
American. Business Executive
b. 1917
Source: *St&PR 75*

Kekkonen, Urho Kaleva
Finnish. Former President
President, 1956-82.
b. Aug 3, 1900
Source: *CurBio 50; IntWW 74, 75, 76, 77, 78, 79, 80, 81; WhoGov 72; WhoWor 74*

Kell, Reginald George
English. Musician
b. 1918 in Newark, England
Source: *WhoMus 72*

Kelland, Clarence Budington
American. Author
b. Jul 11, 1881 in Portland, Michigan
d. Feb 18, 1964 in Scottsdale, Arizona
Source: *AmAu&B; ConAu 89; OxAmL; REn; REnAL; TwCA, SUP; WhAm 4; WhNAA*

Kellaway, Cecil
American. Actor
b. Aug 22, 1893 in Capetown, South Africa
d. Feb 28, 1973 in Los Angeles, California
Source: *FilmgC; MovMk; NewYTBE 73; Vers A; WhScrn 77; WhoHol B*

Kellems, Vivien
American. Manufacturer, Engineer
b. Jun 7, 1896 in Des Moines, Iowa
d. Jan 25, 1975 in Santa Monica, California
Source: *CurBio 48; InWom; WhAm 6*

Keller, Gottfried
Swiss. Author
b. Jul 19, 1819 in Zurich, Switzerland
d. Jul 16, 1890 in Kilchberg, Switzerland
Source: *BbD; BiD&SB; CasWL; ChPo S2; ClDMEL; CyWA; DcEuL; EuAu; EvEuW; OxGer; Pen EUR; REn*

Keller, Helen Adams
American. Author, Lecturer
How she learned to speak, write despite being blind, deaf told in *The Miracle Worker,* 1962, 1981.
b. Jun 27, 1880 in Tuscumbia, Alabama
d. Jun 1, 1968 in Westport, Connecticut
Source: *AmAu&B; ConAu 89, 101; CurBio 42, 68; DcLEL; HerW; InWom; LongCTC; OxAmL; REn; REnAL; WebAB; WhAm 5; WhNAA; WhoHol B; WomWWA 14*

Keller, Marthe
Swiss. Actress
b. 1946 in Switzerland
Source: *IntMPA 82; WhoAm 82; WhoHol A*

Kellerman, Annette
"The Diving Venus"; "The Million Dollar Mermaid"
Australian. Swimmer, Actress
b. Jul 6, 1888 in Sydney, Australia
d. Oct 30, 1975 in Southport, Australia
Source: *FilmgC; InWom; PseudN; TwYS; WhScrn 77*

Kellerman, Sally
American. Actress
b. Jun 2, 1937 in Long Beach, California
Source: *FilmgC; IntMPA 75, 76, 77, 78, 79, 80, 81, 82; MovMk; WhoAm 74, 76, 78, 80, 82; WhoHol A*

Kelley, Clarence Marion
American. FBI Director
b. Oct 24, 1911 in Kansas City, Missouri
Source: *BioNews 74; CurBio 74; NewYTBE 73; WhoAm 74; WhoAmP 73*

Kelley, DeForrest
American. Actor
b. 1920 in Atlanta, Georgia
Source: *WhoHol A*

Kelley, Frank Joseph
American. State Government Official
b. Dec 31, 1924 in Detroit, Michigan
Source: *WhoAm 74, 76, 78, 80, 82; WhoAmP 73; WhoGov 72; WhoMW 74*

Kelley, Kitty
American. Author
b. Apr 4, 1942 in Spokane, Washington
Source: *BioIn 11; ConAu 81; WhoAm 80, 82*

Kellin, Mike
[Myron Kellin]
American. Actor
b. Apr 26, 1922 in Hartford, Connecticut
Source: *BiE&WWA; NotNAT; PseudN; WhoAm 74, 76, 78, 80, 82; WhoHol A*

Kellogg, Clara Louise
American. Opera Singer, Manager
b. Jul 12, 1842 in Sumterville, South Carolina
d. May 13, 1916 in New Haven, Connecticut
Source: *AmBi; AmWom; ApCAB; DcAmB; DcNAA; Drake; InWom; NotAW; TwCBDA; WhAm 1; WomWWA 14*

Kellogg, Frank Billings
American. Statesman
b. Dec 22, 1856 in Potsdam, New York
d. Dec 21, 1937 in Saint Paul, Minnesota
Source: *AmBi; BiDrAC; BiDrUSE; DcAmB S2; EncAB-H; WebAB; WhAm 1; WhAmP*

Kellogg, Howard
American. Manufacturer
b. Mar 26, 1881 in Buffalo, New York
d. 1969
Source: *WhAm 6*

Kellogg, John Harvey
American. Surgeon, Inventor
Developed grain cereal flakes, late 1800's.
b. Feb 26, 1852 in Battle Creek, Michigan
d. Jan 16, 1943 in Battle Creek, Michigan
Source: *CurBio 44; DcAmB S3; DcNAA; WhAm 2*

Kellogg, Will Keith
American. Businessman
Started Battle Creek Toasted Corn Flake Co., 1906; later became W K Kellogg Co.
b. Apr 7, 1860 in Battle Creek, Michigan
d. Oct 6, 1951 in Battle Creek, Michigan
Source: *DcAmB S5; WebAB; WhAm 3*

Kelly, Colin Purdie
American. Aviator
b. 1915
d. Dec 7, 1941
Source: *BioIn 1, 7*

Kelly, Emmett
"Weary Willie"
American. Clown
Created character of "Weary Willie," 1931.
b. Dec 9, 1898 in Sedan, Kansas
d. Mar 28, 1979 in Sarasota, Florida
Source: *ConAu 85; CurBio 54; FilmgC; WebAB; WhoAm 74; WhoHol A*

Kelly, Gene
[Eugene Curran]
American. Dancer, Actor
Starred in *An American in Paris,* 1951; *Singing in the Rain,* 1952.
b. Aug 23, 1912 in Pittsburgh, Pennsylvania
Source: *BiDFilm; BiE&WWA; BkPepl; CelR 73; CmMov; CurBio 45; EncMT; FilmgC; IntMPA 75, 76, 77, 78, 79, 80, 81, 82; IntWW 74; MotPP; MovMk; NotNAT; OxFilm; PlP&P; WhoAm 74, 76, 78, 80, 82; WhoHol A; WhoThe 77; WorEFlm*

Kelly, George Edward
American. Dramatist
b. Jan 6, 1887 in Philadelphia, Pennsylvania
d. Jun 18, 1974
Source: *AmAu&B; AuNews 1; BiE&WWA; CnDAL; CnMD; ConAmA; ConAmL; ConAu 49; ConDr 73; DcLEL; LongCTC; McGEWD; ModAL; ModWD; OxAmL; OxThe; REn; REnAL; TwCA, SUP; WhAm 6; WomWMM*

Kelly, Grace
[Princess Grace Grimaldi]
American. Actress, Princess of Monaco
Won 1954 Oscar for *The Country Girl;* married Prince Rainier, Apr 18, 1956.
b. Nov 12, 1929 in Philadelphia, Pennsylvania
d. Sep 14, 1982 in Monte Carlo, Monaco
Source: *AmPS; BiDFilm; BiE&WWA; BioNews 74; BkPepl; CelR 73; CmMov; CurBio 55, 77, 82; FilmgC; GoodHS; HerW; InWom; IntMPA 75, 76, 77, 78, 79, 80, 81, 82; IntWW 74, 75, 76, 78; LibW; MotPP; MovMk; NewYTBS 82; NotNAT; OxFilm; WebAB; WhoAm 74, 76, 78, 80, 82; WhoAmW 58, 61, 64, 66, 68, 75, 77, 79; WhoHol A; WhoWor 74, 76, 78; WorEFlm*

Kelly, Jack
American. Actor
b. 1927 in Astoria, New York
Source: *FilmgC; WhoHol A*

Kelly, John Brendan
American. Bricklayer, Olympic Athlete
Father of Princess Grace; won gold medals in sculling, 1920, 1924 Olympics.
b. Oct 4, 1890 in Philadelphia, Pennsylvania
d. Jun 20, 1960 in Philadelphia, Pennsylvania
Source: *BioIn 3, 5; DcAmB S6*

Kelly, "Machine Gun" (George R)
[E W Moore; J C Tichenor]
American. Criminal
Carried machine gun while committing crimes.
b. 1897 in Tennessee
d. 1954 in Alcatraz, California
Source: *BioIn 2, 3; Blood; PseudN*

Kelly, Michael
Irish. Opera Singer
b. Dec 25, 1762 in Dublin, Ireland
d. Oct 9, 1826 in Margate, England
Source: *Alli*

Kelly, Nancy
American. Actress
b. Mar 25, 1921 in Lowell, Massachusetts
Source: *BiE&WWA; CurBio 55; FilmgC; InWom; IntMPA 75, 76, 77, 78, 79, 80, 81, 82; MotPP; MovMk; NotNAT; ThFT; WhoAm 74; WhoHol A; WhoThe 77*

Kelly, Ned (Edward)
Outlaw
b. 1854 in Ireland
d. 1880
Source: *BioIn 2, 4, 6, 7, 8, 9, 10, 11*

Kelly, Orie R
American. Banker
b. Jun 5, 1890 in Butte, Montana
d. Jul 4, 1969
Source: *BioIn 8; WhAm 5*

Kelly, "Patsy" (Sarah Veronica Rose)
American. Comedienne
b. Jan 12, 1910 in Brooklyn, New York
d. Sep 24, 1981 in Hollywood, California
Source: *BioIn 7; CelR 73; EncMT; FilmgC; InWom; MotPP; MovMk; PlP&P; PseudN; ThFT; WhoHol A; WhoThe 77*

Kelly, Paul
American. Actor
b. Aug 9, 1899 in New York, New York
d. Nov 6, 1956 in Los Angeles, California
Source: *Film 1; FilmgC; HolP 30; MovMk; TwYS; WhAm 3; WhScrn 74, 77; WhoHol B*

Kelly, "Shipwreck" (Alvin A)
American. Flagpole Sitter
Spent total of 20,163 hrs. sitting atop flagpoles.
b. May 13, 1893
d. Oct 11, 1952 in New York, New York
Source: *BioIn 3; WebAB*

Kelly, Stephen Eugene
American. Magazine Publisher
b. May 13, 1919 in Brooklyn, New York
d. Apr 6, 1978 in New York, New York
Source: *BioIn 11; NewYTBS 78; WhAm 7; WhoAm 76, 78*

Kelly, Walt
American. Cartoonist
Created comic strip "Pogo," 1943, nationally syndicated, 1949.
b. Aug 25, 1913 in Philadelphia, Pennsylvania
d. Oct 18, 1973 in Hollywood, California
Source: *AmAu&B; AmSCAP 66; CelR 73; ConAu 45, 73; CurBio 56, 73; IlsBYP; NewYTBE 73; REnAL; SmATA 18; WhAm 6; WhoAm 74*

Kelly, Walter C
American. Actor
b. Oct 29, 1873 in Mineville, New York
d. Jan 6, 1939 in Philadelphia, Pennsylvania
Source: *WhScrn 74, 77; WhoHol B*

Kelly, William
American. Inventor
Developed convertor for changing iron into steel, 1857.
b. Aug 21, 1811 in Pittsburgh, Pennsylvania
d. Feb 11, 1888 in Louisville, Kentucky
Source: *AmBi; ApCAB; DcAmB; EncAB-H; TwCBDA; WebAB; WhAm H*

Kelser, Greg(ory)
"Special K"
American. Basketball Player
b. Sep 17, 1957 in Panama City, Florida
Source: *OfNBA; PseudN*

Kelsey, Alice Geer
American. Author
b. Sep 21, 1896 in Danvers, Massachusetts
Source: *AnCL; Au&Wr 71; AuBYP; ConAu 5R; ForWC 70; MorJA; SmATA 1; WrDr 76*

Kelsey, Linda
American. Actress
Played Billie on TV series "Lou Grant," 1977-82.
Source: *WhoAm 82*

Kelton, Pert
American. Actress
b. 1907 in Great Falls, Montana
d. Oct 30, 1968 in Westwood, New York
Source: *BiE&WWA; FilmgC; MovMk; ThFT; WhScrn 74, 77; WhoHol B*

Kelvin, William Thomson, Baron
Irish. Physicist, Mathematician
Evolved theory of electric oscillation which formed basis of wireless telegraphy.
b. Jun 26, 1824 in Belfast, Northern Ireland
d. Dec 17, 1907 in Ayrshire, Scotland
Source: *Alli, SUP; BbD; BiD&SB; BrAu 19; NewC; NewCol 75; OxEng; WhDW*

Kemal, Mustafa
see: Ataturk, Kemal

Kemble, Charles
English. Actor
b. Nov 25, 1775 in Brecknock, Wales
d. Nov 12, 1854 in London, England
Source: *Alli, SUP; ApCAB; BiDLA; DcEuL; FamA&A; NewC; OxThe; PlP&P; REn*

Kemble, Fanny (Frances Anne)
English. Actress, Poet, Dramatist
b. Nov 27, 1809 in London, England
d. Jan 15, 1893 in London, England
Source: *Alli, SUP; AmAu; AmAu&B; AmBi; ApCAB; BiD&SB; BiDSA; BrAu 19; ChPo, S2; DcAmB; DcEnA; DcEnL; DcEuL; DcLEL; FamA&A; InWom; NewC; NotAW; OxAmL; OxEng; OxThe; WhAm H*

Kemble, John Philip
English. Actor
b. Feb 1, 1757 in Prescott, England
d. Feb 26, 1823 in Lausanne, Switzerland
Source: *Alli; BiDLA; DcEuL; NewC; OxThe; PlP&P*

Kemble, Sarah
see: Siddons, Sarah

Kemelman, Harry
American. Author
b. Nov 24, 1908 in Boston, Massachusetts
Source: *AmAu&B; AuNews 1; ConAu 9R; ConLC 2; EncMys; WhoAm 74, 76, 78, 80, 82; WhoWorJ 72; WrDr 76*

Kemp, Hal (James Harold)
American. Actor, Band Leader
b. Mar 27, 1905 in Marion, Alabama
d. Dec 21, 1940 in Madera, California
Source: *CurBio 41; WhScrn 74, 77; WhoHol A; WhoJazz 72*

Kemp, (Harry) Hibbard
American. Author
b. Dec 15, 1883 in Youngstown, Ohio
d. Aug 6, 1960 in Provincetown, Massachusetts
Source: *AmAu&B; ChPo, S2; ConAmL; OhA&B; OxAmL; REn; REnAL; WhAm 4*

Kemp, Jack French
American. Congressman, Football Player
Former pro quarterback; congressman from NY, 1970--.
b. Jul 13, 1935 in Los Angeles, California
Source: *BioIn 6, 9, 10, 11; CngDr 74; CurBio 80; WhoAm 74; WhoAmP 73; WhoE 74; WhoGov 72*

Kemp, Steve(n F)
American. Baseball Player
Outfielder, 1977--; signed multi-million dollar contract with NY Yankees, 1982.
b. Aug 7, 1954 in San Angelo, Texas
Source: *BaseEn*

Kempe, Rudolf
German. Conductor
b. Jun 14, 1910 in Niederpoyritz, Germany
d. May 11, 1976 in Zurich, Switzerland
Source: *IntWW 74; Who 74; WhoMus 72; WhoWor 74*

Kemper, James S(cott)
American. Insurance Executive
b. Nov 18, 1886 in Van Wert, Ohio
d. Sep 17, 1981 in Chicago, Illinois
Source: *BioIn 3, 4, 7; CurBio 41, 81; St&PR 75; WhoAm 74, 76, 78, 80; WhoF&I 74; WhoIns 75, 76, 77, 78, 79, 80*

Kempff, (Wilhelm) Walter Friedrich
German. Musician, Composer
b. Nov 25, 1895 in Juterbog, Germany
Source: *IntWW 74; Who 74; WhoMus 72*

Kempner, Nan
American. Fashion Editor
Source: *ForWC 70*

Kempson, Rachel
English. Actress
b. May 28, 1910 in Dartmouth, England
Source: *CnThe; FilmgC; WhoHol A; WhoThe 72, 77, 81*

Kempton, James Murray, Jr.
American. Author
b. 1945
d. Nov 26, 1971 in Colonial Heights, Virginia
Source: *ConAu 33R; NewYTBE 71*

Kempton, Jean Goldschmidt
American. Author
b. 1946
d. Nov 26, 1971
Source: *ConAu 33R*

Kendal, Felicity
English. Actress
b. Sep 25, 1946 in Olton, England
Source: *WhoThe 77, 81*

Kendal, Madge
English. Actress
b. Mar 15, 1848 in Cleethorpes, England
d. Sep 14, 1935 in Chorley Wood, England
Source: *FamA&A; OxThe; WhoStg 1908*

Kendal, William Hunter
[William Hunter Grimston]
English. Actor
b. Dec 16, 1843 in London, England
d. Nov 6, 1917
Source: *OxThe; PseudN; WhAm 1; WhoStg 1906, 1908*

Kendall, John Walker
American. Scientist
b. Mar 19, 1929 in Bellingham, Washington
Source: *AmM&WS 73P*

Kendall, Kay
[Justine McCarthy]
English. Actress
b. 1926 in Hull, England
d. Sep 6, 1959 in London, England
Source: *BiDFilm; CmMov; FilmgC; MotPP; MovMk; PseudN; WhScrn 74, 77; WhoHol B; WorEFlm*

Kendrick, Pearl Luella
American. Microbiologist
b. Aug 24, 1890 in Wheaton, Illinois
d. Oct 8, 1980 in Grand Rapids, Michigan
Source: *AnObit 1980; WhoAmW 58, 61, 64, 77*

Kendricks, Eddie
[The Temptations]
American. Singer
b. Dec 17, 1940 in Union Springs, Alabama
Source: *WhoBlA 75*

Keniston, Kenneth
American. Educator, Psychologist
b. Jan 6, 1930 in Chicago, Illinois
Source: *AmAu&B; ConAu 25R; WhoAm 74, 76, 78, 80, 82*

Kennan, George Frost
American. Historian, Diplomat
b. Feb 16, 1904 in Milwaukee, Wisconsin
Source: *AmAu&B; ConAu 1R, 2NR; DrAS 74H; EncAB-H; IntWW 74; OxAmL; REnAL; WebAB; Who 74; WhoAm 74, 76, 78, 80, 82; WhoHol A; WhoJazz 72; WhoWor 74; WorAu*

Kennedy, Adrienne
American. Dramatist
b. Sep 13, 1931 in Pittsburgh, Pennsylvania
Source: *ConAu 103; ConDr 73; CroCD; LivgBAA; NotNAT; WhoAm 74, 76, 78, 80, 82; WhoBlA 75; WrDr 76*

Kennedy, Arthur
American. Journalist
b. 1904
d. 1975
Source: *BioIn 10; IntMPA 82; WhoAm 82*

Kennedy, Arthur
American. Actor
b. Feb 17, 1914 in Worcester, Massachusetts
Source: *BiE&WWA; CmMov; FilmgC; HolP 40; IntMPA 75, 77; NotNAT; WhoAm 74; WhoThe 77; WorEFlm*

Kennedy, Caroline
American. Daughter of John F Kennedy
b. Nov 27, 1957
Source: *BioNews 74; NewYTBE 70*

Kennedy, David M
American. Government Official
b. Jul 21, 1905 in Randolph, Utah
Source: *BiDrUSE; CurBio 69; IntWW 74; Who 74; WhoAm 74; WhoAmP 73; WhoGov 72; WhoS&SW 73; WhoWor 74*

Kennedy, Edgar
American. Actor
b. Apr 26, 1890 in Monterey, California
d. Nov 9, 1948 in Woodland Hills, California
Source: *Film 1; FilmgC; MotPP; MovMk; TwYS; Vers A; WhScrn 74, 77; WhoHol B*

Kennedy, Edward Moore
"Ted"
American. Politician
Senator from MA, 1962--.
b. Feb 22, 1932 in Brookline, Massachusetts
Source: *BiDrAC; BkPepl; CelR 73; CngDr 74; CurBio 63; IntWW 74; NewYTBE 70, 71; NewYTBS 74; WebAB; WhoAm 74, 76, 78, 80, 82; WhoAmP 73; WhoE 74; WhoGov 72; WhoWor 74*

Kennedy, Edward Ridgway
American. Published The World Almanac
b. 1923
d. Jun 18, 1975 in Cleveland, Ohio
Source: *BioIn 10*

Kennedy, Ethel Skakel
American. Widow of Robert Kennedy
b. Apr 11, 1928 in Greenwich, Connecticut
Source: *CelR 73; InWom*

Kennedy, Florynce
American. Lawyer, Feminist
b. Feb 11, 1916 in Kansas City, Missouri
Source: *ForWC 70; LivgBAA*

Kennedy, George
American. Actor
Won 1967 Oscar for *Cool Hand Luke.*
b. Feb 18, 1925 in New York, New York
Source: *CmMov; FilmgC; IntMPA 75, 76, 77, 78, 79, 80, 81, 82; MotPP; MovMk; WhoAm 74, 76, 78, 80, 82; WhoHol A; WorEFlm*

Kennedy, Jacqueline Bouvier
see: Onassis, Jacqueline Lee Bouvier Kennedy

Kennedy, Joan Bennett
American. Ex-Wife of Edward Kennedy
b. 1936 in New York, New York
Source: *CelR 73*

Kennedy, John Fitzgerald
"JFK"; "Jack"
American. 35th US President
First Roman Catholic president; won 1957 Pulitzer Prize for *Profiles in Courage.*
b. May 29, 1917 in Brookline, Massachusetts
d. Nov 22, 1963 in Dallas, Texas
Source: *AmAu&B; AnCL; BiDrAC; BiDrUSE; ChPo; ConAu 1R, 1NR; CurBio 50, 61, 64; EncAB-H; OxAmL; PseudN; REn; REnAL; SmATA 11; WebAB; WhAm 4; WhAmP*

Kennedy, John Fitzgerald, Jr.
"John-John"
American. Son of John F Kennedy
b. Nov 25, 1960
Source: *BioIn 10*

Kennedy, John Pendleton
[Mark Littleton, pseud.]
"Solomon Second Thoughts"
American. Author
b. Oct 25, 1795 in Baltimore, Maryland
d. Aug 18, 1870 in Newport, Rhode Island
Source: *AmAu; AmAu&B; AmBi; ApCAB; BbD; BiD&SB; BiDSA; BiDrAC; BiDrUSE; CasWL; PseudN; WhAm H*

Kennedy, Joseph Patrick, Sr.
American. Financier, Diplomat
Ambassador to England, 1938-40; father of Kennedy family.
b. Sep 6, 1888 in Boston, Massachusetts
d. Nov 18, 1969 in Hyannis Port, Massachusetts
Source: *CurBio 40, 70; OxFilm; WhAm 5; WorEFlm*

Kennedy, Joseph Patrick, Jr.
American. Brother of John F Kennedy
TV movie based on his life *Young Joe, the Forgotten Kennedy,* 1978, starred Peter Strauss.
b. 1915
d. 1944
Source: *BioIn 6, 7, 8, 9*

Kennedy, Madge
American. Actress
b. 1892 in Chicago, Illinois
Source: *Film 1; MotPP; TwYS; WhoHol A; WhoThe 77*

Kennedy, Margaret
English. Author
b. Apr 23, 1896 in London, England
d. Jul 31, 1967 in Adderbury, England
Source: *Chambr 3; ChPo S2; ConAu 25R; DcLEL; EvLB; InWom; LongCTC; McGEWD; ModBrL; ModWD; NewC; OxEng; Pen ENG; REn; TwCA, SUP; TwCW; WhAm 4, 6*

Kennedy, Moorehead Cowell, Jr.
[The Hostages]
American. Former Hostage in Iran
b. Nov 5, 1930 in New York
Source: *NewYTBS 81; USBiR 74*

Kennedy, Robert Francis
"Bobby"; "RFK"
American. Lawyer, Senator
US Attorney General, 1961-64; senator, 1964-68.
b. Nov 20, 1925 in Brookline, Massachusetts
d. Jun 6, 1968 in Los Angeles, California
Source: *AmAu&B; BiDrUSE; ConAu 13R, 1NR; CurBio 58, 68; EncAB-H; PseudN; WebAB; WhAm 5; WhAmP*

Kennedy, Rose Fitzgerald
American. Mother of Kennedy Family
b. Jul 22, 1890 in Boston, Massachusetts
Source: *CelR 73; ConAu 53; CurBio 70; HerW; HsB&A; InWom; OhA&B; WhoAm 74, 76, 78, 80, 82; WhoAmW 77*

Kennedy, Tom
American. Actor
b. 1884 in New York, New York
d. Oct 6, 1965 in Woodland Hills, California
Source: *Film 1; TwYS; Vers A; WhScrn 74, 77; WhoHol B*

Kennedy, Walter
American. NBA Commissioner
b. Jun 8, 1912 in Stamford, Connecticut
d. Jun 26, 1977 in Stamford, Connecticut
Source: *WhoBbl 73*

Kennedy, X J, pseud.
[Joseph Charles Kennedy]
American. Author
b. Aug 21, 1929 in Dover, New Jersey
Source: *AmAu&B; ChPo, S2; ConAu 1R; ConP 70, 75; DrAP 75; Pen AM; PseudN; WhoAm 74, 76, 78, 80, 82; WhoWor 74; WorAu; WrDr 76*

Kennerly, David Hume
American. Photographer
Won 1972 Pulitzer Prize for feature photography in Vietnam.
b. Mar 9, 1947 in Roseburg, Oregon
Source: *AuNews 2; ConAu 101; WhoAm 74, 76, 78, 80, 82*

Kenneth
[Kenneth Everette Battelle]
American. Hairdresser
Owner, Kenneth Salons and Products, Inc., NY City, 1962--.
b. Apr 19, 1927 in Syracuse, New York
Source: *PseudN; WhoAm 74, 76, 78, 80, 82; WorFshn*

Kenney, Douglas
American. National Lampoon Magazine Founder
b. Dec 10, 1947 in Cleveland, Ohio
d. Aug 27, 1980 in Kauai Island, Hawaii
Source: *BioIn 12*

Kenney, George Churchill
American. Soldier, Air Force General
b. Aug 6, 1889 in Yarmouth, NS
d. 1974
Source: *BioNews 74; ConAu P-1; CurBio 43; WhoAm 74*

Kenny, Sister Elizabeth
Australian. Nurse
Developed therapy for polio victims, 1933.
b. Sep 20, 1886 in Warrialda, Australia
d. Nov 30, 1952 in Toowoomba, Australia
Source: *CurBio 42, 53; InWom; WhAm 3*

Kenny, Nick
American. Songwriter, Journalist
b. Feb 3, 1895 in Astoria, New York
d. Dec 1, 1975 in Sarasota, Florida
Source: *AmSCAP 66; ChPo, S1; ConAu 89; WhScrn 77*

Kensett, John Frederick
American. Artist
b. Mar 22, 1816 in Cheshire, Connecticut
d. Dec 14, 1872 in New York, New York
Source: *AmBi; ApCAB; DcAmB; Drake; EarABI; TwCBDA; WhAm H*

Kent, Allegra
American. Ballerina
b. Aug 11, 1938 in Santa Monica, California
Source: *CurBio 70; WhoAm 74*

Kent, Arthur Atwater
American. Industrialist
b. 1873
d. Apr 4, 1949 in Bel Air, California
Source: *BioIn 1, 3*

Kent, James
"The American Blackstone"
American. Lawyer
b. Jul 31, 1763 in Fredericksburg, New York
d. Dec 12, 1847 in New York, New York
Source: *Alli; AmAu; AmAu&B; AmBi; ApCAB; BbD; BiAuS; BiD&SB; CyAL 1; DcAmAu; DcAmB; DcEnL; DcNAA; Drake; EncAB-H; OxAmL; PseudN; REnAL; TwCBDA; WebAB; WhAm H*

Kent, Rockwell
[William Hogarth, Jr.]
"RK"
American. Author, Artist
Noted for his stark dramatic lithographs, exotic landscapes.
b. Jun 21, 1882 in Tarrytown, New York
d. Mar 13, 1971 in Plattsburg, New York
Source: *AmAu&B; ConAmA; ConAu 5R, 29R, 4NR; DcCAA 71; IlsBYP; IlsCB 1744; OxAmL; PseudN; REnAL; SmATA 6; TwCA, SUP; WebAB; WhAm 5*

Kent, William
American. Actor
b. 1886
d. Oct 5, 1945 in New York, New York
Source: *WhScrn 74, 77*

Kentner, Louis Philip
English. Musician
b. Jul 19, 1905 in Karwin, Silesia
Source: *IntWW 74; Who 74; WhoMus 72; WhoWor 74*

Kenton, Stan(ley Newcomb)
American. Band Leader
b. Feb 19, 1912 in Wichita, Kansas
d. Aug 25, 1979 in Hollywood, California
Source: *AmSCAP 66; Baker 78; BiDAmM; BioNews 74; CmpEPM; CurBio 79; EncJzS 70; IlEncJ; NewYTBS 79; WhoAm 76, 78; WhoWor 74*

Kenty, Hilmer
American. Boxer
b. Jul 30, 1955 in Austin, Texas
Source: *NF*

Kenyatta, Jomo (Johnstone)
[Johstone Kamau; Kamau wa Ngengi]
"Mzee"
Kenyan. President
b. Oct 20, 1891 in Kenya
d. Aug 22, 1978 in Mombasa, Kenya
Source: *AfSS 78; AfrA; Au&Wr 71; CurBio 53, 74, 78; IntWW 74, 75, 76, 77, 78; IntYB 78; LinLib L, S; McGEWB; NewYTBS 78; PseudN; Who 74; WhoGov 72; WhoWor 74, 76*

Kenyon, (Margaret) Doris
[Margaret Taylor]
American. Actress
b. Sep 5, 1897 in Syracuse, New York
Source: *Film 1; FilmgC; MotPP; MovMk; PseudN; ThFT; TwYS; WhoHol A; WhoThe 77*

Keogan, George
American. Basketball Coach
Coach, Notre Dame U, 1924-43.
b. Mar 8, 1890 in Minnesota Lakes, Minnesota
d. Feb 17, 1943 in South Bend, Indiana
Source: *WhoBbl 73*

Keogh, Eugene James
American. Politician
b. Aug 30, 1907 in Brooklyn, New York
Source: *BiDrAC; St&PR 75; WhoAm 74; WhoAmP 73*

Keogh, James
American. Journalist
b. Oct 29, 1916 in Platte County, Nebraska
Source: *ConAu 45; IntWW 74; USBiR 74; WhoAm 74, 76, 78, 80, 82; WhoE 74; WhoGov 72*

Keokuk
[Kiyo'kaga]
American Indian. Chief
b. 1780 in Rock River, Illinois
d. Jun 1848 in Franklin County, Kansas
Source: *AmBi; ApCAB; DcAmB; WebAB; WhAm H*

Keough, William Francis, Jr.
[The Hostages]
American. Former Hostage in Iran
b. 1931?
Source: *BioIn 12; NewYTBS 81*

Kepler, Johannes
[John Kepler]
"The Father of Modern Astronomy"
German. Astronomer
Described revolutions of planets around sun in Kepler's Laws, 1609.
b. Dec 27, 1571 in Weil der Stadt, Germany
d. Nov 15, 1630 in Regensburg, Germany
Source: *BbD; BiD&SB; NewC; PseudN; REn*

Keppard, Freddie
American. Jazz Musician
b. Feb 15, 1899 in New Orleans, Louisiana
d. Jul 15, 1933 in Chicago, Illinois
Source: *WhoJazz 72*

Keppler, Victor
American. Photographer
b. 1904
Source: *St&PR 75*

Kerby, William Frederick
American. Businessman
b. Jul 28, 1908 in Washington, DC
Source: *IntWW 74; St&PR 75; WhoAm 74; WhoE 74; WhoF&I 74*

Kerekou, Mathieu
Beninese. President
b. Sep 2, 1933 in Dahomey (North)
Source: *IntWW 74; WhoWor 78*

Kerensky, Alexander Fedorovitch
[Aleksandr Kerensky]
Russian. Premier
b. 1881 in Simbirsk, Russia
d. Jun 11, 1970 in New York, New York
Source: *CurBio 66, 70; NewYTBE 70; WhAm 5*

Kerkorian, Kirk
American. Aviator, Airline Executive
b. Jun 6, 1917 in Fresno, California
Source: *BioIn 8; IntMPA 82; WhoAm 82*

Kermode, (John) Frank
English. Educator, Literary Critic
b. Nov 29, 1919 in Isle of Man
Source: *ConAu 1R, 1NR; NewC; Who 74; WhoWor 74; WorAu; WrDr 76*

Kern, Harold G
American. Newspaper Publisher
b. 1899
d. Feb 10, 1976 in Boston, Massachusetts
Source: *WhAm 6*

Kern, Jerome David
American. Composer
b. Jan 17, 1885 in New York, New York
d. Nov 11, 1945 in New York, New York
Source: *AmM&WS 73P; AmSCAP 66; CmMov; CurBio 42, 45; DcAmB S3; EncMT; FilmgC; McGEWD; NewCBMT; OxAmL; OxFilm; PlP&P; REn; REnAL; WebAB; WhAm 2*

Kerner, Otto
American. Governor, Judge
b. Aug 15, 1908 in Chicago, Illinois
d. May 9, 1976 in Chicago, Illinois
Source: *CurBio 61; IntWW 74; NewYTBE 73; WhAm 3, 6; WhoAm 74; WhoGov 72*

Kerouac, Jack
[Jean Louis Lebris de Kerouac; Jean-Louis Incogniteau]
American. Author, Poet
Leader of Beat Movement; wrote *On the Road,* 1957.
b. Mar 12, 1922 in Lowell, Massachusetts
d. Oct 21, 1969 in Saint Petersburg, Florida
Source: *AmAu&B; AuNews 1; CasWL; CnMWL; ConAu 5R, 25R; ConLC 1, 2, 3, 5; ConNov 76; ConP 70; CurBio 59, 69; EncAB-H; EncWL; LongCTC; ModAL, SUP; OxAmL; Pen AM; PseudN; RAdv 1; REn; REnAL; TwCW; WebAB; WebE&AL; WhAm 5; WhoHol B; WhoTwCL; WorAu*

Kerr, Andrew
American. Football Coach
b. Oct 7, 1878 in Cheyenne, Wyoming
d. Mar 1, 1969 in Tucson, Arizona
Source: *WhAm 6; WhoFtbl 74*

Kerr, (Bridget) Jean Collins
American. Author, Humorist
b. Jul 10, 1923 in Scranton, Pennsylvania
Source: *AmAu&B; AmSCAP 66; BiE&WWA; CelR 73; ConAu 5R; CurBio 58; InWom; IntWW 74; NewYTBE 73; NotNAT; OxAmL; WhoAm 74; WhoThe 77; WhoWor 74; WorAu; WrDr 76*

Kerr, Clark
American. Educator
b. May 17, 1911 in Reading, Pennsylvania
Source: *AmAu&B; AmEA 74; AmM&WS 73S; ConAu 45; CurBio 61; EncAB-H; IntWW 74; LEduc 74; NewYTBE 70; Who 74; WhoAm 74, 76, 78, 80, 82; WhoWest 74; WhoWor 74*

Kerr, Deborah Jane
American. Actress
Starred in *From Here to Eternity,* 1953; *Tea and Sympathy,* 1956.
b. Sep 30, 1921 in Helensburgh, Scotland
Source: *BiDFilm; BiE&WWA; CelR 73; CurBio 47; FilmgC; InWom; IntMPA 75, 76, 77, 78, 79, 80, 81, 82; MotPP; MovMk; NotNAT; OxFilm; PlP&P A; PseudN; Who 74; WhoAm 74, 76, 78, 80, 82; WhoHol A; WhoThe 77; WorEFlm*

Kerr, Graham
English. Chef, TV Performer
b. 1933 in London, England
Source: *WhoAm 74*

Kerr, Jean
American. Author, Dramatist
b. Jul 10, 1923 in Scranton, Pennsylvania
Source: *AmAu&B; AmSCAP 66; ConAu 5R; OxAmL; WhoAm 82; WorAu; WrDr 76*

Kerr, John
American. Actor
b. Nov 15, 1931 in New York, New York
Source: *BiE&WWA; FilmgC; IntMPA 82; NotNAT; WhoAm 74, 76, 78, 80, 82; WhoHol A*

Kerr, Orpheus C
[Robert Henry Newell]
American. Author
b. Dec 13, 1836 in New York, New York
d. Jul 1901
Source: *Alli SUP; AmAu; AmAu&B; BbD; BiD&SB; ChPo, S1; CnDAL; DcAmAu; DcEnL; DcLEL; DcNAA; OxAmL; PseudN; REn*

Kerr, Robert Samuel
American. Oil Industrialist, Senator
b. Sep 11, 1896 in Ada, Oklahoma
d. Jan 1, 1963 in Washington, DC
Source: *BiDrAC; WhAm 4; WhAmP*

Kerr, Walter Francis
American. Drama Critic, Author
b. Jul 8, 1913 in Evanston, Illinois
Source: *AmAu&B; AmSCAP 66; Au&Wr 71; BiE&WWA; CelR 73; ConAu 5R; CurBio 53; IntWW 74; NotNAT; OxAmL; REnAL; WhoAm 74, 76, 78, 80, 82; WhoE 74; WhoThe 77; WhoWor 74; WorAu; WrDr 76*

Kerry, John
American. Veterans' Leader
b. 1943
Source: *BioIn 10*

Kershaw, Doug(las James)
American. Singer, Songwriter
b. Jan 24, 1936 in Tel Ridge, Louisiana
Source: *BiDAmM; BioIn 9; ConMuA 80; WhoRock 81*

Kert, Larry
American. Actor
b. Dec 5, 1930 in Los Angeles, California
Source: *BiE&WWA; EncMT; NotNAT; PlP&P A; WhoHol A; WhoThe 77*

Kertesz, Andre
American. Photographer
b. Jul 2, 1894 in Budapest, Hungary
Source: *ConAu 85; WhoAm 74*

Kertesz, Istvan
Hungarian. Conductor
b. Aug 29, 1929 in Budapest, Hungary
d. Apr 17, 1973 in Tel Aviv, Israel
Source: *NewYTBE 73; WhoMus 72; WhoWor 74*

Kerwin, Joseph Peter
American. Astronaut, Physician
Member of Skylab I and II space crews.
b. Feb 19, 1932 in Oak Park, Illinois
Source: *AmM&WS 73P; IntWW 74; NewYTBE 73; WhoAm 74, 76, 78, 80, 82; WhoS&SW 73*

Kerwin, Lance
American. Actor
b. 1960
Source: *BioIn 11*

Kesey, Ken
American. Author
Wrote *One Flew Over the Cuckoo's Nest,* 1962.
b. Sep 17, 1935 in La Hunta, Colorado
Source: *AmAu&B; CasWL; ConAu 1R; ConLC 1, 3, 6, 11; ConNov 72, 76; DrAF 76; EncWL; ModAL SUP; Pen AM; RAdv 1; WebE&AL; WhoAm 74, 76, 78, 80, 82; WhoTwCL; WrDr 76*

Kesselring, Albert
German. Economist
b. Nov 30, 1887
d. Jul 16, 1960 in Bad Nauheim, Germany
Source: *CurBio 42, 60*

Kesselring, Joseph
American. Dramatist, Architect
b. Jun 21, 1902 in New York, New York
d. Feb 1967
Source: *BioIn 10; NatCAB 53; WhAm 4*

Ketcham, Henry King (Hank)
American. Cartoonist
Created comic strip "Dennis the Menace," 1952.
b. Mar 14, 1920 in Seattle, Washington
Source: *AmAu&B; CurBio 56; WhoAm 74, 76, 78, 80, 82; WhoAmA 73; WhoWest 74; WhoWor 74*

Ketchel, Stanley
[Stanislaus Kiecal]
"Cyclone"; "The Michigan Assassin"; "The Montana Wonder"
American. Boxer
b. Sep 14, 1887 in Grand Rapids, Michigan
d. Oct 15, 1910 in New York, New York
Source: *WhoBox 74*

Kettering, Charles Franklin
"Boss"
American. Electrical Engineer
Invented self-starting auto ignition system.
b. Aug 29, 1876 in Loudonville, Ohio
d. Nov 25, 1958 in Dayton, Ohio
Source: *CurBio 40, 51, 59; PseudN; WebAB; WhAm 3*

Key, Francis Scott
American. Composer, Lawyer
Wrote "The Star-Spangled Banner," Sep, 13-14, 1814; adopted by Congress as national anthem, 1931.
b. Aug 1, 1779 in Carroll County, Maryland
d. Jan 11, 1843 in Baltimore, Maryland
Source: *Alli; AmAu; AmAu&B; AmBi; ApCAB; BbD; BiAuS; BiD&SB; BiDSA; ChPo, S2; CnDAL; CyAL 1; DcAmAu; DcAmB; DcLEL; DcNAA; Drake; EncAB-H; EvLB; OxAmL; OxEng; PoChrch; REn; REnAL; TwCBDA; WebAB; WhAm H*

Key, Theodore
American. Cartoonist, Author
b. Aug 25, 1912 in Fresno, California
Source: *ConAu 13R; WhoAm 82*

Keyes, Evelyn
American. Actress
b. 1925 in Port Arthur, Texas
Source: *FilmgC; HolP 40; IntMPA 75, 76, 77, 78, 79, 80, 81, 82; MotPP; MovMk; WhoHol A*

Keyes, Frances Parkinson
American. Author
b. Jul 21, 1885 in Charlottesville, Virginia
d. Jul 3, 1970 in New Orleans, Louisiana
Source: *AmAu&B; AmNov; BiCAW; BkC 5; CathA 1930; CelR 73; ConAu 5R, 25R; EvLB; InWom; LongCTC; Pen AM; REn; TwCA, SUP; TwCW; WhAm 5; WhNAA*

Keyes, Roger
British. Navy Officer
b. 1872
d. Dec 26, 1945 in Buckinghamshire, England
Source: *BioIn 10*

Keylor, Arthur W
American. Publisher
b. 1920?
d. Aug 17, 1981 in Manchester, Vermont
Source: *ConAu 104; Dun&B 79; WhoF&I 74*

Keynes, John Maynard, Baron
English. Economist, Journalist
b. Jun 5, 1883 in Cambridge, England
d. Apr 21, 1946 in London, England
Source: *DcLEL; EvLB; LongCTC; NewC; OxEng; PseudN; REn; TwCA, SUP; WebE&AL; WhAm 2*

Keys, Ancel Benjamin
American. Physiologist, Author
b. Jan 26, 1904 in Colorado Springs, Colorado
Source: *AmM&WS 76P, 79P; BioIn 5, 7; ConAu 61; CurBio 66; WhoWor 74; WrDr 80*

Keyserling, Hermann Alexander
German. Philosopher
b. Jul 20, 1880 in Konno, Russia
d. Apr 26, 1946 in Innsbruck, Austria
Source: *CurBio 46; EvEuW; LongCTC; OxGer; Pen EUR; REn; TwCA, SUP*

Keyserlingk, Robert Wendelin
American. Publishing Executive
b. Nov 2, 1905 in Saint Petersburg, Russia
Source: *CanWW 70; CathA 1952; WhoF&I 74*

Khaalis, Hamaas Abdul
American. Muslim Terrorist
b. 1920
Source: *BioIn 11*

Khachaturian, Aram
[Aram Ilych Khachaturyan]
Russian. Composer
b. Jun 6, 1903 in Tiflis, Russia
d. May 1, 1978 in Moscow, U.S.S.R.
Source: *CurBio 48; DcCM; DcFM; IntWW 74; WhoMus 72*

Khadafy, Muammar
see: Qadhafi, Mu'ammar al-

Khaikin, Boris
Russian. Opera Conductor
b. 1905
d. May 11, 1978 in Moscow, U.S.S.R.
Source: *BioIn 11*

Khalid Ibn Abdul Aziz
Saudi. King
b. 1913 in Riyadh, Saudi Arabia
d. Jun 13, 1982 in Taif, Saudi Arabia
Source: *BioIn 10; CurBio 76, 82; IntWW 75, 76, 77, 78, 79, 80; MidE 78, 79; NewYTBS 75; WhoGov 72; WhoWor 74, 76, 78*

Khalil, Mustafa
Egyptian. Prime Minister
b. 1920
Source: *BioIn 11*

Khama, Seretse M
Botswana. President
b. Jul 1, 1921 in Serowe, Botswana
d. Jul 13, 1980 in Gaborone, Botswana
Source: *CurBio 67; IntWW 74; Who 74; WhoWor 74*

Khambatta, Persis
Indian. Actress
Starred in *Star Trek: The Movie,* 1979; *Nighthawks,* 1982.
b. Oct 2, 1950 in Bombay, India
Source: *BioIn 12; JohnWil 81*

Khan, Ali Akbar
Indian. Musician
b. 1922
Source: *IntWW 74*

Khan, Chaka
[Rufus; Yvette Marie Stevens]
American. Singer, Songwriter
b. 1953 in Chicago, Illinois
Source: *BioIn 10, 11, 12; PseudN*

Khan, Liaquat Ali
[Liaquat Ali Khan]
Pakistani. Moslem Leader
b. Oct 1, 1895 in Karnal, Pakistan
d. Oct 16, 1951
Source: *CurBio 48, 51*

Khan, Princess Yasmin
American. Daughter of Rita Hayworth
b. 1950?
Source: *NewYTBS 78*

Kharitonov, Yevgeni
Russian. Poet, Dramatist
b. 1941?
d. Jun 29, 1981 in Moscow, U.S.S.R.
Source: *BioIn 12; NewYTBS 81*

Kharlamov, Valeri
Russian. Hockey Player
b. 1947?
d. 1981 in U.S.S.R.
Source: *BioIn 12*

Khayyam, Omar
see: Omar Khayyam

Kheel, Theodore Woodrow
American. Lawyer, Labor Mediator
b. May 9, 1914 in New York, New York
Source: *CurBio 64; St&PR 75; WhoAm 74, 76, 78, 80, 82; WhoE 74*

Khomeini, Ayatollah Ruhollah
Iranian. Religious Leader
Leader of Shite Moslems in Iran; supported taking American hostages, 1979.
b. May 17, 1900 in Khomein, Persia
Source: *BioIn 11; BkPepl; CurBio 79*

Khrennikov, Tikhon Nikolaevich
Russian. Composer
b. Jun 10, 1913 in Elets, Russia
Source: *DcCM; IntWW 74; WhoWor 74*

Khrunov, Evgeny
Russian. Cosmonaut
b. Sep 10, 1933
Source: *IntWW 74*

Khrushchev, Nikita Sergeyevich
Russian. Communist Leader
Premier, 1958-64; foreign policy of "peaceful coexistence" in Cold War.
b. Apr 17, 1894 in Kursk, Russia
d. Sep 11, 1971 in Moscow, U.S.S.R.
Source: *ConAu 29R; CurBio 54, 71; REn; WhAm 5*

Khrushchev, Nina Petrovna
Russian. Wife of Nikita Khrushchev
b. 1900
Source: *InWom*

Khufu
see: Cheops

Kiam, Omar
[Alexander Kiam]
American. Fashion Designer
b. 1894 in Monterrey, Mexico
d. Mar 28, 1954 in New York, New York
Source: *CurBio 45, 54; DcAmB S5; WorFshn*

Kiam, Victor Kermit, II
American. Business Executive
President, chief executive, Remington Products, Inc, 1979--.
b. Dec 7, 1926 in New Orleans, Louisiana
Source: *WhoAm 74, 76, 78, 80, 82; WhoF&I 74*

Kibbee, Guy
American. Actor
b. Mar 6, 1882 in El Paso, Texas
d. May 24, 1956 in East Islip, New York
Source: *FilmgC; MotPP; MovMk; Vers A; WhScrn 74, 77; WhoHol B*

Kibbee, Robert Joseph
American. College Administrator
b. Aug 19, 1920 in New York, New York
d. Jun 16, 1982 in New York, New York
Source: *NewYTBE 71; NewYTBS 82; WhoAm 74, 76, 78, 80, 82; WhoE 74, 75, 77, 79*

Kicknosway, Faye
American. Author
b. Dec 16, 1936 in Detroit, Michigan
Source: *ConAu 57*

Kidd, Michael
[Milton Greenwald]
American. Choreographer
b. Aug 12, 1919 in Brooklyn, New York
Source: *BiE&WWA; CelR 73; CmMov; CurBio 60; EncMT; FilmgC; NotNAT; PseudN; WhoAm 74, 76, 78, 80, 82; WhoHol A; WorEFlm*

Kidd, (Captain) William
"The Wizard of the Sea"
Scottish. Pirate
Poe's story *The Gold Bug;* Stevenson's novel *Treasure Island* based on his exploits.
b. 1645 in Greenock, Scotland
d. May 23, 1701 in London, England
Source: *Alli; AmBi; ApCAB; DcAmB; Drake; NewC; OxAmL; PseudN; REn; REnAL; WebAB; WhAm H*

Kidder, Margot
American. Actress
Played Lois Lane in movies *Superman,* 1978; *Superman II,* 1981.
b. Oct 17, 1948 in Yellowknife, NT
Source: *FilmEn; IntMPA 82; WhoAm 82; WhoHol A*

Kiel, Richard
American. Actor
b. in Redford, Michigan
Source: *FilmEn; WhoHol A*

Kiely, Benedict
American. Author
b. Aug 15, 1919 in County Tyrone, Northern Ireland
Source: *Au&Wr 71; CathA 1952; ConAu 1R; ConNov 72, 76; WorAu; WrDr 76*

Kienast Quintuplets
[Abigail, Amy, Gordon, Sara, and Ted Kienast]
Americans.
b. Feb 24, 1970
Source: *BioIn 10*

Kienzle, William Xavier
[Mark Boyle, pseud.]
American. Author, Former Priest
Wrote *The Rosary Murders,* 1979; *Death Wears a Red Hat,* 1980.
b. Sep 11, 1928 in Detroit, Michigan
Source: *BioIn 12; ConAu 93; PseudN*

Kienzl, Wilhelm
Austrian. Composer
b. Jan 17, 1857 in Waizenkircen, Austria
d. Oct 3, 1941 in Vienna, Austria
Source: *NewEOp 71; OxMus*

Kiepura, Jan
American. Journalist
b. May 16, 1902 in Sosnowiec, Poland
d. Aug 15, 1966 in Harrison, New York
Source: *BiE&WWA; CurBio 43, 66; FilmgC; MovMk; OxFilm; WhAm 4; WhScrn 74, 77; WhoHol B*

Kieran, John Francis
"Information Please"
American. Journalist
b. Aug 2, 1892 in New York, New York
d. Dec 10, 1981 in Rockport, Massachusetts
Source: *AmAu&B; AuBYP; BioIn 1, 2, 3, 4, 5, 7, 8; CathA 1930; ConAu 101; CurBio 40, 82; PseudN; REn; REnAL; WhoAm 74, 76, 78; WhoE 74*

Kierkegaard, Soren Aabye
[Soren Aabye Kjerkegaard]
Danish. Philosopher, Author
b. May 5, 1813 in Copenhagen, Denmark
d. Nov 11, 1855 in Copenhagen, Denmark
Source: *AtlBL; BiD&SB; CasWL; CyWA; DcEuL; EuAu; EvEuW; LongCTC; OxEng; OxGer; Pen EUR; RComWL; REn*

Kiernan, Walter
American. Radio Commentator
b. Jan 24, 1902 in New Haven, Connecticut
d. Jan 8, 1978 in Daytona Beach, Florida
Source: *ConAu 73; WhoAm 74*

Kiesinger, Kurt Georg
German. Lawyer, Politician
Chancellor, 1966-69.
b. Apr 6, 1904 in Ebingen, Germany
Source: *CurBio 67; IntWW 74, 75, 76, 77, 78, 79, 80, 81; Who 74; WhoWor 74*

Kiick, Jim (James F)
"Butch Cassidy"
American. Football Player
b. Aug 9, 1946 in Lincoln Park, New Jersey
Source: *BioIn 9; PseudN; WhoFtbl 74*

Kiker, Douglas
American. Journalist
Author of *The Southerner,* 1956, and *Strangers on the Shore,* 1959.
b. Jan 7, 1930 in Griffin, Georgia
Source: *Au&Wr 71; ConAu 65*

Kiki of Montparnasse
see: Prin, Alice

Kilbracken, John Raymond Godley
English. Stockbreeder, Author
b. Oct 17, 1920 in London, England
Source: *Au&Wr 71; ConAu 5R; PseudN; Who 74; WrDr 76*

Kilbride, Percy
American. Actor
b. Jul 16, 1888 in San Francisco, California
d. Dec 11, 1964 in Los Angeles, California
Source: *FilmgC; MotPP; MovMk; Vers A; WhScrn 74, 77; WhoHol B*

Kilenyi, Edward, Sr.
American. Musician, Composer
b. Jan 25, 1884 in Hungary
Source: *AmSCAP 66*

Kiley, Richard
American. Actor, Singer
b. Mar 31, 1922 in Chicago, Illinois
Source: *BiE&WWA; BioNews 75; CelR 73; CurBio 73; EncMT; FilmgC; IntMPA 75, 76, 77, 78, 79, 80, 81, 82; NotNAT; WhoAm 74, 76, 78, 80, 82; WhoAmP 73; WhoHol A; WhoThe 77; WhoWor 74*

Kilgallen, Dorothy
[Mrs. Richard Kollmar]
American. Journalist, TV Personality
Reporter, gossip columnist, NY *Journal-American,* beginning 1930's.
b. Jul 3, 1913 in Chicago, Illinois
d. Nov 8, 1965 in New York, New York
Source: *ConAu 89; CurBio 52, 66; InWom; WhAm 4; WhScrn 74, 77; WhoHol B*

Kilgore, Bernard
American. Journalist
b. Nov 9, 1908
d. Nov 14, 1967 in Princeton, New Jersey
Source: *WhAm 4*

Kilgour, Joseph
Actor
b. 1863 in Ayr, ON
d. Apr 21, 1933 in Bayshore, New York
Source: *Film 1; TwYS; WhScrn 77; WhoHol B*

Kilian, Victor
American. Actor
b. Mar 6, 1898 in Jersey City, New Jersey
d. Mar 11, 1979 in Hollywood, California
Source: *BiE&WWA; BioIn 11; Film 2; FilmgC; IntMPA 75, 76, 77, 78, 79; MovMk; NewYTBS 79; NotNAT; Vers A; WhoHol A*

Killanin, Michael Morris, Lord
Irish. Olympic Committee Official
b. Jul 30, 1914 in London, England
Source: *BioIn 9, 10; ConAu 5NR; CurBio 73; Who 79*

Killebrew, Harmon Clayton
"Killer"
American. Baseball Player
Outfielder-infielder, 1954-75; hit career total of 573 home runs.
b. Jun 29, 1936 in Payette, Idaho
Source: *BaseEn; CurBio 66; PseudN; WhoAm 74; WhoProB 73*

Killian, James Rhyne, Jr.
"The Father of Public Television"
American. Administrator, Advisor
b. Jul 24, 1904 in Blacksburg, South Carolina
Source: *ConAu 97; CurBio 49, 59; IntWW 74; PseudN; St&PR 75; Who 74; WhoAm 74, 76, 78, 80, 82; WhoWor 74*

Killigrew, Thomas
English. Established Drury Lane Theatre
b. 1612 in London, England
d. Nov 19, 1683
Source: *BioIn 2, 3; EncWT; NewCol 75; NotNAT B; OxEng; OxThe*

Killy, Jean-Claude
French. Skier
Won three gold medals, 1968 Olympics.
b. Aug 30, 1943 in Saint Cloud, France
Source: *BioNews 74; CelR 73; CurBio 68; WhoHol A; WhoWor 74*

Kilmer, (Alfred) Joyce
American. Poet, Essayist
Wrote poem *Trees,* 1913; killed in World War I.
b. Dec 6, 1886 in New Brunswick, New Jersey
d. Jul 30, 1918 in Seringes, France
Source: *AmAu&B; AmBi; AmLY; AmSCAP 66; ChPo, S1, S2; CnDAL; ConAmL; DcAmB; DcLEL; DcNAA; EvLB; LongCTC; OxAmL; REn; REnAL; Str&VC; TwCA; WebAB; WhAm 1*

Kilmer, Billy (William O)
"Whiskey"
American. Football Player
b. Sep 5, 1939 in Topeka, Kansas
Source: *PseudN; WhoFtbl 74*

Kilpatrick, James Jackson
American. Journalist
b. Nov 1, 1920 in Oklahoma City, Oklahoma
Source: *AmAu&B; AuNews 1, 2; ConAu 1R; CurBio 80; WhoAm 74, 76, 78, 80, 82; WhoS&SW 73*

Kim, Dae Jung
Korean. Politician
b. 1925
Source: *BioIn 12; NewYTBE 71*

Kim, Duk Koo
Korean. Boxer
Died of brain injuries received in title bout against Ray Mancini, Nov 6, 1982.
b. 1959?
d. Nov 13, 1982 in Las Vegas, Nevada
Source: *NF*

Kim, Il Sung
Korean. Government Official
b. Apr 15, 1912 in Mangyongdae, Korea
Source: *CurBio 51; IntWW 74; NewYTBE 72; WhoGov 72; WhoWor 74*

Kim, Young Sam
Korean. Politician
b. 1928
Source: *BioIn 10*

Kimball, Fiske
American. Museum Director, Architect
b. Dec 8, 1888 in Newton, Massachusetts
d. Aug 14, 1955 in Munich, Germany (West)
Source: *AmAu&B; BioIn 4, 5, 7, 10; DcAmB S5; NatCAB 47; ObitOF 79; WhAm 3*

Kimball, Spencer Woolley
American. Clergyman, Mormon Leader
b. Mar 28, 1895 in Salt Lake City, Utah
Source: *ConAu 45; WhoAm 74, 76, 78, 80, 82; WhoHol A; WhoWor 74*

Kimbrough, Emily
American. Author, Lecturer, Editor
b. Oct 23, 1899 in Muncie, Indiana
Source: *AmAu&B; Au&Wr 71; ConAu 17R; CurBio 44; InWom; IndAu 1917; OxAmL; REnAL; SmATA 2; WhoAm 74, 76, 78, 80, 82; WhoWor 74; WorAu; WrDr 76*

Kimmel, Husband Edward
American. Admiral
b. Feb 26, 1882 in Henderson, Kentucky
d. May 15, 1968 in Groton, Connecticut
Source: *CurBio 42, 68; WhAm 5*

Kindler, Hans
Dutch. Conductor, Musician
b. Jan 8, 1893 in Rotterdam, Netherlands
d. Aug 30, 1949 in Watch Hill, Rhode Island
Source: *CurBio 46, 49; WhAm 2*

Kiner, Ralph McPherran
"Ozark Ike"
American. Baseball Player, Sportscaster
Outfielder, Pittsburgh, 1946-55; Hall of Fame, 1977.
b. Oct 27, 1922 in Santa Rita, New Mexico
Source: *BaseEn; CurBio 54; PseudN; WhoProB 73*

King, Alan
[Irwin Kniberg]
American. Comedian
b. Dec 26, 1927 in New York, New York
Source: *AmAu&B; CelR 73; CurBio 70; FilmgC; IntMPA 75, 76, 77, 78, 79, 80, 81, 82; PseudN; WhoAm 74, 76, 78, 80, 82; WhoHol A*

King, Alan
see: Ace

King, Albert
[Albert Nelson]
American. Musician
b. Apr 25, 1923 in Indianola, Indiana
Source: *EncPR&S; IlEncRk; PseudN*

King, Alberta Christine Williams
American. Wife of M L King, Sr.
b. 1904
d. Jun 30, 1974 in Atlanta, Georgia
Source: *NewYTBS 74*

King, Alexander
American. Author, TV Personality
b. Nov 13, 1900 in Vienna, Austria
d. Nov 16, 1965 in New York, New York
Source: *AmAu&B; REnAL; WhAm 4*

King, B B
"The Beale Street Blues Boy"; "The Blues Boy"; "Bassman of the Blues"; "The Boy from Beale Street"; "King of the Blues"
American. Blues Singer
b. Sep 16, 1925 in Itta Bena, Mississippi
Source: *BioNews 74; CurBio 70; PseudN; WhoAm 74, 76, 78, 80, 82; WhoBlA 75*

King, Ben E
[The Drifters; Benjamin Earl Nelson]
American. Rock Musician
b. Sep 28, 1938 in Henderson, North Carolina
Source: *EncPR&S; PseudN*

King, Billie Jean
[Billie Jean Moffitt]
American. Tennis Player
Co-founder, publisher *WomenSports* magazine, 1974--.
b. Nov 22, 1943 in Long Beach, California
Source: *BioNews 74; BkPepl; CelR 73; ConAu 53; CurBio 67; HerW; InWom; NewYTBE 70; NewYTBS 74; SmATA 12; WhoAm 74, 76, 78, 80, 82*

King, Carole
[Carole Klein]
American. Singer, Songwriter
Won four Grammys, 1972, for album *Tapestry*.
b. Feb 9, 1941 in Brooklyn, New York
Source: *BkPepl; CelR 73; CurBio 74; NewYTBE 70; PseudN; WhoAm 74, 76, 78, 80, 82*

King, Charles
American. Actor
b. Oct 31, 1894 in New York, New York
d. Jan 11, 1944 in London, England
Source: *EncMT; FilmgC; TwYS; WhScrn 74, 77; WisWr*

King, Clarence
American. Geologist
b. Jan 6, 1842 in Newport, Rhode Island
d. Dec 24, 1901 in Phoenix, Arizona
Source: *Alli SUP; AmAu; AmAu&B; AmBi; ApCAB; BiD&SB; DcAmAu; DcAmB; DcNAA; OxAmL; REn; REnAL; TwCBDA; WebAB; WhAm 1*

King, Claude
American. Musician
b. Feb 5, 1933 in Shreveport, Louisiana
Source: *EncFCWM 69*

King, Coretta Scott
American. Widow of M L King, Jr.
b. Apr 27, 1927 in Marion, Alabama
Source: *Au&Wr 71; CelR 73; ConAu 29R; CurBio 69; HerW; LivgBAA; NewYTBE 72; WhoAm 74, 76, 78, 80, 82; WhoAmW 77; WhoBlA 75; WhoS&SW 73; WhoWor 74*

King, Dennis
[Dennis Pratt]
American. Actor
b. Nov 2, 1897 in Coventry, England
d. May 21, 1971 in New York, New York
Source: *BiE&WWA; EncMT; PseudN; WhAm 5; WhScrn 74, 77; WhoHol B*

King, Don
American. Boxing Promoter
b. 1932
Source: *BioIn 10*

King, Ernest Joseph
[Colleen, code name]
American. Admiral
b. Nov 23, 1878 in Lorain, Ohio
d. Jun 25, 1956 in Portsmouth, New Hampshire
Source: *CurBio 42, 56; EncAB-H; PseudN; WebAB; WhAm 3*

King, Francis Henry
[Frank Cauldwell, pseud.]
Swiss. Author
b. Mar 4, 1923 in Adelbosen, Switzerland
Source: *Au&Wr 71; ConAu 1R, 1NR; ConLC 8; ConNov 72, 76; ConP 70; NewC; PseudN; TwCW; Who 74; WhoTwCL; WorAu; WrDr 76*

King, Frank
American. Cartoonist
b. Apr 9, 1883 in Cashon, Wisconsin
d. Jun 24, 1969 in Winter Park, Florida
Source: *WebAB*

King, Henry
American. Motion Picture Director
b. Jan 24, 1896 in Christianburg, Virginia
d. Jun 29, 1982 in Toluca Lake, California
Source: *CmMov; ConAu 89; DcFM; Film 1; FilmgC; IntMPA 75, 76, 77, 78, 79; MovMk; NewYTBS 82; OxFilm; WorEFlm*

King, James Ambros
American. Opera Singer
b. May 22, 1925 in Dodge City, Kansas
Source: *WhoAm 74, 76, 78, 80, 82; WhoMus 72*

King, Martin Luther, Jr.
[Michael Luther King, Jr.]
"The Prince of Peace"
American. Clergyman, Civil Rights Leader
Won Nobel Peace Prize, 1964; wrote *Stride Toward Freedom,* 1958.
b. Jan 15, 1929 in Atlanta, Georgia
d. Apr 4, 1968 in Memphis, Tennessee
Source: *AmAu&B; BlkAW; ConAu 25R; CurBio 57, 65, 68; EncAB-H; NewYTBS 74; OxAmL; PseudN; SmATA 14; WebAB; WhAm 4A; WhAmP*

King, Martin Luther, Sr.
[Michael Luther King, Sr.]
American. Clergyman
b. 1899
Source: *WhoBlA 75*

King, "Micki" (Maxine Joyce)
American. Air Force Officer, Diver
b. 1944
Source: *BioIn 10; PseudN*

King, Morganna
American. Actress
Source: *WhoHol A*

King, Peggy
American. Singer
b. 1931 in Greensburg, Pennsylvania
Source: *InWom; IntMPA 75, 76, 77, 78, 79, 80, 81, 82*

King, Perry
American. Actor
b. Apr 30, 1948 in Alliance, Ohio
Source: *IntMPA 76, 77, 78, 79, 80, 81, 82; WhoHol A*

King, Richard
American. Cattleman
b. Jul 10, 1824 in Orange County, New York
d. Apr 14, 1885 in Corpus Christi, Texas
Source: *DcAmB; WebAB; WhAm H*

King, Rufus
American. Statesman
b. Mar 24, 1755 in Scarboro, Maine
d. Apr 29, 1827 in Jamaica, New York
Source: *AmAu&B; AmBi; ApCAB; BiAuS; BiDrAC; DcAmB; Drake; TwCBDA; WebAB; WhAm H; WhAmP*

King, Stephen Edwin
American. Author
b. Sep 21, 1947 in Portland, Maine
Source: *ConAu 61; ConLC 12; CurBio 81; EncSF; NewYTBS 79; ScF&FL 1, 2; SmATA 9; WhoAm 78, 80, 82; WhoHr&F; WhoS&SW 78*

King, Thomas Starr
American. Author
b. Dec 17, 1824 in New York, New York
d. Mar 4, 1864 in San Francisco, California
Source: *Alli SUP; AmAu&B; AmBi; ApCAB; BbD; BiD&SB; ChPo S1; CyAl 2; DcAmAu; DcAmB; DcNAA; Drake; OxAmL; REnAL; TwCBDA; WhAm H*

King, Walter Woolf
[Walter Woolf]
American. Actor
b. 1899 in San Francisco, California
Source: *FilmgC; PseudN; WhoHol A*

King, Warren Thomas
American. Editor, Cartoonist
b. Jan 3, 1916 in Queens, New York
d. Feb 9, 1978
Source: *WhAm 7; WhoAm 76, 78; WhoAmA 73, 76, 78; WhoE 74; WhoWor 74*

King, Wayne
"The Waltz King"
American. Band Leader
b. Feb 16, 1901 in Savanna, Illinois
Source: *AmSCAP 66; PseudN*

King, William
[The Commodores]
American. Singer
b. 1947 in Birmingham, Alabama
Source: *BkPepl*

King, William Lyon Mackenzie
Canadian. Prime Minister, Statesman
b. Dec 17, 1874 in Berlin, ON
d. Jul 22, 1950 in Kingsmere, ON
Source: *CurBio 40, 50; OxCan; WhAm 3; WhNAA*

King, William Rufus de Vane
American. Vice-President
Elected with Franklin Pierce; took oath of office in Cuba where he went to find cure for TB.
b. Apr 7, 1786 in Sampson County, North Carolina
d. Apr 18, 1853 in Cahaba, Alabama
Source: *Drake; NatCAB 4; WebAB; WhAm H; WhAmP*

King, Yolanda Denise
American. Actress, Daughter of M L King
b. 1955
Source: *BioIn 11*

King Crimson
[Robert Fripp; Mike Giles; Greg Lake; Ian McDonald; Pete Sinfield]
English. Rock Group
Source: *ConMuA 80; LilREn 78; WhoRock 81*

King Sisters
American. Vocal Group
Source: *BiDAmM*

Kinglake, Alexander William
English. Author
b. Aug 5, 1809 in Taunton, England
d. Jan 2, 1891 in London, England
Source: *Alli SUP; BiD&SB; BrAu 19; CasWL; Chambr 3; DcEnA; DcEnL; DcLEL; EvLB; NewC; OxEng; Pen ENG; REn; WebE&AL*

Kingman, Dave (David Arthur)
"Kong"
American. Baseball Player
b. Dec 21, 1948 in Pendleton, Oregon
Source: *BaseEn; BioIn 10, 11; PseudN*

Kingman, Dong M
[Tsang King-Man]
American. Illustrator
b. Apr 1, 1911 in Oakland, California
Source: *CelR 73; CurBio 62; IlsCB 1946; IntMPA 75, 76, 77, 78, 79, 80, 81, 82; WhoAm 74, 76, 78, 80, 82; WhoAmA 73; WhoWor 74*

Kingsbury-Smith, Joseph
American. Journalist
b. Feb 20, 1908 in New York, New York
Source: *IntWW 76; WhoAm 74, 76, 78, 80, 82; WhoWor 74*

Kingsford-Smith, Charles Edward
Australian. Aviator
b. 1897 in Brisbane, Australia
d. 1935
Source: *WebBD 80*

Kingsley, Ben
[Krishna Bhanji]
English. Actor
Played title role in film *Gandhi,* 1982.
b. Dec 31, 1943 in Snaiton, England
Source: *WhoThe 81*

Kingsley, Charles
"CK"; "The Chariot Clergyman"; "The Chartist Parson"
English. Clergyman, Author
b. Jun 12, 1819 in Devonshire, England
d. Jan 23, 1875 in Eversley, England
Source: *Alli, SUP; AnCL; AtlBL; AuBYP; BbD; BiD&SB; Br&AmS; BrAu 19; CarSB; CasWL; Chambr 3; ChPo, S1, S2; CrtT 3; CyWA; DcBiA; DcEnA; DcEnL; DcEuL; DcLEL; EvLB; JBA 34; MouLC 3; NewC; NewYTBE 71; OxEng; Pen ENG; PseudN; RAdv 1; REn; WebE&AL; WhoChL*

Kingsley, Henry
English. Author
b. Jan 2, 1830 in Barnack, England
d. May 24, 1876 in Cuckfield, England
Source: *Alli SUP; BbD; BiD&SB; BrAu 19; CarSB; CasWL; Chambr 3; ChPo S1; CyWA; DcBiA; DcEnA; DcEnL; DcEuL; DcLEL; EvLB; HsB&A; NewC; OxEng; Pen ENG; REn; WebE&AL*

Kingsley, Sidney
[Sidney Kieschner]
American. Dramatist
b. Oct 18, 1906 in New York, New York
Source: *AmAu&B; BiE&WWA; CnDAL; CnMD; CnThe; ConAmA; ConAu 85; ConDr 73; CroCD; CurBio 43; DcLEL; FilmgC; LongCTC; McGEWD; ModAL; ModWD; NotNAT; OxAmL; OxThe; Pen AM; PlP&P; PseudN; REn; REnAL; REnWD; TwCA, SUP; WebE&AL; WhoAm 74, 76, 78, 80, 82; WhoThe 77; WrDr 76*

Kingston, Maxine Hong
American. Author
b. Oct 27, 1940 in Stockton, California
Source: *BioIn 11; ConAu 69; ConLC 12; WhoAm 82*

Kingston Trio, The
[Dave Guard; John Hartford; Nick Reynolds; Bob Shane]
American. Singers
Source: *BiDAmM*

Kinks, The
[Mick Avory; John Beechman; Laurie Brown; David Davies; Raymond Davies; John Gosling; Alan Holmes; Peter Quaife]
English. Rock Group
Source: *EncPR&S; IlEncRk*

Kinmont, Jill
[Mrs. John Boothe]
American. Former Skier, Teacher
Movies *The Other Side of the Mountain,* parts I, II, 1975, 1978, depict her life.
b. 1936
Source: *BioIn 6, 9, 10, 11; HerW*

Kinnell, Galway
American. Author
b. Feb 1, 1927 in Providence, Rhode Island
Source: *AmAu&B; ConAu 9R; ConLC 1, 2, 3, 5, 13; ConP 70, 75; CroCAP; DrAF 76; DrAP 75; ModAL SUP; OxAmL; Pen AM; RAdv 1; WhoAm 74, 76, 78, 80, 82; WhoTwCL; WhoWor 74; WorAu; WrDr 76*

Kinsey, Alfred Charles
American. Sexologist
Founded Institute for Sex Research at Indiana U, 1942.
b. Jun 23, 1894 in Hoboken, New Jersey
d. Aug 25, 1956 in Bloomington, Indiana
Source: *AmAu&B; CurBio 54, 56; EncAB-H; IndAu 1917; REnAL; WebAB; WhAm 3*

Kinski, Nastassia
"Nasti"
German. Actress
Starred in *Tess,* 1981; *Cat People,* 1982.
b. 1961 in Berlin, Germany (West)
Source: *BioIn 11; NewYTBS 81*

Kintner, Robert Edmonds
American. Radio, TV Executive
b. Sep 12, 1909 in Stroudsburg, Pennsylvania
Source: *ConAu 103; CurBio 50*

Kinugasa, Teinousuke
Japanese. Motion Picture Director
b. 1898 in Mie, Japan
Source: *BiDFilm; BioIn 10*

Kipling, Rudyard
English. Author, Poet
Won 1907 Nobel Prize; wrote *The Jungle Book,* 1894; *Just So Stories,* 1902.
b. Dec 30, 1865 in Bombay, India
d. Jan 18, 1936 in Burwash, England
Source: *Alli SUP; AnCL; ApCAB SUP; AtlBL; AuBYP; BbD; BiD&SB; CarSB; CasWL; Chambr 3; ChPo, S1, S2; CnE&AP; CnMWL; CrtT 3; CyWA; DcAmAu; DcBiA; DcEnA, AP; DcEuL; DcLEL; EncWL; EvLB; FamAYP; FamSYP; FilmgC; JBA 34; LongCTC; MnBBF; ModBrL, SUP; NewC; OxAmL; OxCan; OxEng; Pen ENG; RAdv 1; RComWL; REn; Str&VC; TwCA, SUP; TwCW; WebE&AL; WhoChL; WhoLA; WhoTwCL*

Kiplinger, Austin Huntington
American. Publisher
b. Sep 19, 1918 in Washington, DC
Source: *AmAu&B; ConAu 57; St&PR 75; WhoAm 74, 76, 78, 80, 82; WhoS&SW 73; WhoWor 74*

Kiplinger, W(illard) M(onroe)
American. Journalist
b. Jan 8, 1891 in Bellefontaine, Ohio
d. Aug 6, 1967 in Bethesda, Maryland
Source: *AmAu&B; ConAu 89; CurBio 43, 62, 67; LinLib L; ObitOF 79; OhA&B; WhAm 4A*

Kipnis, Alexander
Russian. Opera Singer
b. Feb 1, 1891 in Zhitomir, Russia
d. May 14, 1978 in Westport, Connecticut
Source: *CurBio 43; WhoAm 74; WhoMus 72; WhoWor 74*

Kipnis, Igor
American. Musician
b. Sep 27, 1930 in Berlin, Germany
Source: *WhoAm 74, 76, 78, 80, 82; WhoMus 72; WhoWor 74; WhoWorJ 72*

Kirbo, Charles
American. Lawyer
b. Mar 15, 1917 in Bainbridge, Georgia
Source: *WhoAm 82; WhoAmP 73; WhoS&SW 73*

Kirby, Durward
American. Actor
b. 1912 in Covington, Kentucky
Source: *WhoAm 74; WhoE 74*

Kirby, George
"Big Daddy"
American. Comedian
b. 1923
Source: *BioIn 10; CurBio 77; PseudN; WhoBlA 75*

Kirby, Jack
American. Comic Book Artist
b. Aug 28, 1917 in New York, New York
Source: *EncSF; FanAl; WorECom*

Kirby, John
American. Musician
b. Dec 31, 1908 in Baltimore, Maryland
d. 1952 in Hollywood, California
Source: *WhoJazz 72*

Kirby, Robert Emory
American. Corporation Executive
b. Nov 8, 1918 in Ames, Iowa
Source: *CurBio 79; IntWW 75, 76, 77, 78; WhoAm 76, 78, 80, 82; WhoF&I 74, 79; WhoWor 74, 76, 78*

Kirby, Rollin
American. Cartoonist
b. Sep 4, 1876 in Galva, Illinois
d. May 8, 1952 in New York, New York
Source: *AmAu&B; CurBio 44, 52; DcAmB S5; WhAm 3*

Kirchner, Ernst Ludwig
[L de Marsalle, pseud.]
German. Artist
b. May 6, 1880 in Aschaffenburg, Germany
d. Jun 15, 1938 in Davos, Switzerland
Source: *AtlBL; OxGer; PseudN*

Kirchschlager, Rudolf
Austrian. President
b. Mar 20, 1915 in Austria
Source: *IntWW 74*

Kirk, Claude Roy, Jr.
American. Governor
b. Jan 7, 1926 in San Bernardino, California
Source: *CurBio 67; NewYTBE 70; WhoAmP 73; WhoS&SW 73*

Kirk, Grayson Louis
American. University President
b. Oct 12, 1903 in Jeffersonville, Ohio
Source: *AmAu&B; AmM&WS 73S; CurBio 51; IntWW 74; OhA&B; St&PR 75; Who 74; WhoAm 74, 76, 78, 80, 82; WhoWor 74*

Kirk, Lisa
American. Singer
b. 1925 in Brownsville, Pennsylvania
Source: *InWom; NotNAT; WhoAm 74; WhoThe 77*

Kirk, Phyllis
[Phyllis Kirkegaard]
American. Actress
b. Sep 18, 1930 in Plainfield, New Jersey
Source: *InWom; IntMPA 82; PseudN; WhoAm 74, 76, 78, 80, 82*

Kirk, Russell
American. Journalist
b. Oct 19, 1918 in Plymouth, Michigan
Source: *AmAu&B; Au&Wr 71; AuNews 1; ChPo S2; ConAu 1R, 1NR; CurBio 62; DrAS 74H; WhoAm 74, 76, 78, 80, 82; WhoMW 74; WhoWor 74; WorAu; WrDr 76*

Kirk, Ruth Kratz
American. Author
b. May 7, 1925 in Los Angeles, California
Source: *ConAu 17R; ForWC 70*

Kirkland, Gelsey
American. Ballerina
With American Ballet Theatre, 1974-81.
b. Dec 29, 1952 in Bethlehem, Pennsylvania
Source: *CurBio 75; NewYTBE 70; WhoAm 78, 80, 82*

Kirkland, (Joseph) Lane
American. Labor Union Official
President, AFL-CIO, Nov, 1979--.
b. Mar 12, 1922 in Camden, South Carolina
Source: *BioIn 12; CurBio 80; WhoAm 78, 80, 82*

Kirkpatrick, Jeane Duane Jordan
American. Diplomat
US permanent representative to UN, 1981--.
b. Nov 19, 1926 in Duncan, Oklahoma
Source: *AmM&WS 73S, 78S; ConAu 53; CurBio 81; WhoAm 78, 80, 82; WhoAmW 75, 77, 79*

Kirkpatrick, Ralph
American. Musician
b. Jan 10, 1911 in Leominster, Massachusetts
Source: *ConAu 49; CurBio 71; IntWW 74; WhoAm 74, 76, 78, 80, 82; WhoE 74; WhoMus 72; WhoWor 74*

Kirkus, Virginia
[Virginia Kirkus Glick]
American. Literary Critic, Author
b. Dec 7, 1893 in Meadville, Pennsylvania
d. Sep 10, 1980 in Danbury, Connecticut
Source: *BioIn 12; ConAu 101; CurBio 41, 54; PseudN*

Kirkwood, James
American. Author
b. Aug 22, 1930 in Los Angeles, California
Source: *ConAu 1R, 2NR; ConLC 9; WhoAm 80, 82; WrDr 80*

Kirov, Sergei Mironovich
Russian. Revolutionary Leader
One of Stalin's chief aides.
b. 1886
d. 1934
Source: *BioIn 7, 9, 10, 11; NewCol 75; REn*

Kirshner, Don
American. Rock Publisher, Promoter
b. Apr 17, 1934 in Bronx, New York
Source: *IlEncRk; WhoAm 82*

Kirstein, Lincoln Edward
American. Ballet Impresario
b. May 4, 1907 in Rochester, New York
Source: *AmAu&B; CurBio 52; IntWW 74; Who 74; WhoAm 74, 76, 78, 80, 82; WhoAmA 73; WhoMus 72; WhoWor 74*

Kirsten, Dorothy
American. Opera Singer
b. Jul 6, 1917 in Montclair, New Jersey
Source: *CurBio 48; InWom; WhoAm 74, 76, 78, 80, 82; WhoHol A; WhoMus 72*

Kirtley, Steven William
[The Hostages]
American. Former Hostage in Iran
b. 1958?
Source: *NewYTBS 81*

Kiss
[Peter Criss; Ace Grehley; Gene Simmons; Paul Stanley]
American. Rock Group
Source: *BkPepl; IlEncRk*

Kissinger, Henry Alfred
"The Drone"; "The Flying Peacemaker"; "The Gay Deceiver"; "Henry the K"; "The Iron Stomach"; "Super Kraut"
American. Former Secretary of State
Won Nobel Peace Prize, 1973; wrote *For the Record,* 1981.
b. May 27, 1923 in Fuerth, Germany
Source: *AmAu&B; AmM&WS 73S; BioNews 74; BkPepl; CelR 73; CngDr 74; ConAu 1R, 2NR; CurBio 58, 72; EncAB-H; IntWW 74; NewYTBE 70, 71, 73; USBiR 74; WebAB; Who 74; WhoAm 74, 76, 78, 80, 82; WhoAmP 73; WhoGov 72; WhoS&SW 73; WhoWor 74; WrDr 76*

Kissinger, Nancy Maginnes
American. Wife of Henry Kissinger
b. 1934 in White Plains, New York
Source: *BioNews 74; NewYTBS 74*

Kistiakowsky, George Bogdan
American. Chemist
Leader, explosives division, Los Alamos Project; later opposed nuclear weapons.
b. Nov 18, 1900 in Kiev, Russia
d. Dec 7, 1982 in Cambridge, Massachusetts
Source: *AmM&WS 73P, 76P, 79P; CurBio 60; IntWW 74, 75, 76, 77, 78, 79, 80, 81; PolProf E; Who 74; WhoAm 74, 76; WhoGov 72*

Kistler, Darci
American. Ballerina
b. 1964? in Riverside, California
Source: *BioIn 12*

Kitaj, R(onald) B(rooks)
American. Artist
b. Oct 29, 1932 in Chagrin Falls, Ohio
Source: *BioIn 7, 8, 11; ConArt; CurBio 82; IntWW 78; WhoAm 78, 80, 82; WhoAmA 78*

Kitchener, Horatio Herbert
English. Field Marshall
b. Jun 14, 1850 in Ballylongford, Ireland
d. Jun 5, 1916
Source: *BioIn 10; McGEWB; WebBD 80*

Kitson, Henry Hudson
American. Sculptor
b. Apr 9, 1863 in Huddersfield, New York
d. Jun 26, 1947
Source: *WhAm 2*

Kitson, Theo Alice Ruggles
American. Sculptor
b. 1871 in Brookline, Massachusetts
d. Oct 29, 1932
Source: *InWom; WhAm 1; WomWWA 14*

Kitt, Eartha Mae
American. Singer
b. Jan 16, 1928 in North, South Carolina
Source: *BkPepl; CelR 73; ConAu 77; CurBio 55; FilmgC; InWom; IntMPA 75, 76, 77, 78, 79, 80, 81, 82; LivgBAA; MovMk; NotNAT, ; WhoAm 74, 76, 78, 80, 82; WhoBlA 75; WhoHol A; WhoThe 77*

Kittikachorn, Thanom
Thai. Prime Minister
b. Aug 11, 1911 in Tak, Thailand
Source: *CurBio 69; IntWW 74; WhoGov 72; WhoWor 74*

Kittredge, G(eorge) L(yman)
American. Author
b. Feb 28, 1860 in Boston, Massachusetts
d. Jul 23, 1941 in Barnstable, Massachusetts
Source: *AmAu&B; ChPo; CnDAL; CurBio 41; DcAmB S3; DcLEL; DcNAA; LongCTC; NewC; OxAmL; PseudN; REn; REnAL; TwCA, SUP; WebAB; WhAm 1*

Kiyo'kaga
see: Keokuk

Kjerkegaard, Soren Aabye
see: Kierkegaard, Soren Aabye

Klafsky, Katharina
Hungarian. Opera Singer
b. Sep 19, 1855 in Saint Johann, Hungary
d. Sep 22, 1896 in Hamburg, Germany
Source: *InWom*

Klammer, Franz
Austrian. Skier
b. 1952 in Moaswald, Austria
Source: *BioIn 10*

Klassen, Elmer Theodore
American. Government Official
Appointed first Postmaster General of newly organized postal dept. 1972.
b. Nov 6, 1908 in Hillsboro, Kansas
Source: *CurBio 73; IntWW 74; NewYTBE 71; St&PR 75; WhoAm 74; WhoGov 72; WhoS&SW 73*

Klebe, Giselher
German. Composer
b. Jun 28, 1925 in Mannheim, Germany
Source: *DcCM; IntWW 74; WhoWor 74*

Kleber, Jean Baptiste
French. Revolutionary Leader
b. Mar 9, 1753 in Strasbourg, France
d. Jun 14, 1800 in Cairo, Egypt
Source: *OxFr*

Kleberg, Robert Justus, Jr.
American. Cattle Farmer, Breeder
b. Mar 29, 1896 in Corpus Christi, Texas
d. Oct 13, 1974 in Kingsville, Texas
Source: *IntWW 74; NewYTBS 74; WhAm 6; WhoAm 74; WhoWor 74*

Klee, Paul
Swiss. Artist
Associated with Surrealist and Blaue Reiter schools; produced over 9,000 works.
b. Dec 18, 1879 in Bern, Switzerland
d. Jun 29, 1940 in Muralto, Switzerland
Source: *AtlBL; CurBio 40; OxGer; REn*

Kleiber, Erich
Austrian. Conductor
b. Aug 5, 1890 in Vienna, Austria
d. Jan 27, 1956 in Zurich, Switzerland
Source: *NewEOp 71*

Klein, Allen
American. Motion Picture Producer
b. Dec 18, 1931
Source: *IntMPA 75, 76, 77, 78, 79, 80, 81, 82*

Klein, Anne
American. Fashion Designer
Known for sophisticated sportswear.
b. Aug 3, 1923 in Brooklyn, New York
d. Mar 19, 1974 in New York, New York
Source: *BioNews 74; NewYTBS 74; WorFshn*

Klein, Calvin
American. Fashion Designer
Designer of elegant, modern classics since 1969; jeans caused a sensation.
b. Nov 19, 1942 in New York, New York
Source: *BkPepl; WhoAm 74, 76, 78, 80, 82; WorFshn*

Klein, Chuck (Charles Herbert)
American. Baseball Player
b. Oct 7, 1905 in Indianapolis, Indiana
d. Mar 28, 1958 in Indianapolis, Indiana
Source: *BaseEn; WhoProB 73*

Klein, Herbert George
American. Government Official
b. Apr 1, 1918 in Los Angeles, California
Source: *CurBio 71; IntWW 74; WhoAm 74, 76, 78, 80, 82; WhoAmP 73; WhoGov 72; WhoS&SW 73*

Klein, Robert
American. Comedian
b. Feb 8, 1942 in New York, New York
Source: *WhoAm 78, 80, 82*

Kleindienst, Richard Gordon
American. Former Attorney General
b. Aug 5, 1923 in Winslow, Arizona
Source: *CurBio 72; NewYTBE 72; NewYTBS 74; IntWW 74; Who 74; WhoAm 74, 76, 78, 80, 82; WhoAmP 73; WhoGov 72*

Kleinfield, "Sonny" (Nathan Richard)
American. Journalist, Author
b. Aug 12, 1950 in Paterson, New Jersey
Source: *ConAu 97*

Kleist, Heinrich von
German. Author, Dramatist, Poet
b. Oct 18, 1777 in Frankfurt, Germany
d. Nov 21, 1811 in Wannsee, Germany
Source: *AtlBL; BiD&SB; CasWL; CnThe; CyWA; DcEuL; EuAu; EvEuW; McGEWD; OxGer; OxThe; Pen EUR; RComWL; REn; REnWD*

Klemesrud, Judy Lee
American. Journalist
b. 1939 in Thompson, Iowa
Source: *ConAu 89; ForWC 70*

Klemperer, Otto
German. Conductor, Composer
b. May 14, 1885 in Breslau, Germany
d. Jul 6, 1973 in Zurich, Switzerland
Source: *CurBio 65, 73; NewYTBE 70, 73; WhAm 5; WhoMus 72*

Klemperer, Werner
German. Actor
Played Colonel Klink on TV series "Hogan's Heroes," 1965-71.
b. Mar 22, 1920 in Cologne, Germany
Source: *CelR 73; FilmgC; MotPP; WhoHol A*

Klenau, Paul von
Danish. Composer, Conductor
b. Feb 11, 1883 in Copenhagen, Denmark
d. Aug 31, 1946 in Copenhagen, Denmark
Source: *BioIn 4; OxMus*

Kletzki, Paul
Polish. Conductor
b. Mar 21, 1900 in Lodz, Poland
d. Mar 5, 1973 in Liverpool, England
Source: *NewYTBE 73; WhAm 5; WhoMus 72*

Klien, Walter
Austrian. Musician
b. Nov 27, 1928 in Graz, Austria
Source: *Who 74; WhoMus 72; WhoWor 74*

Klima, Ivan
Czech. Author
b. Sep 14, 1931 in Prague, Czechoslovakia
Source: *ConAu 25R; ModSL 2*

Klimt, Gustav
Austrian. Artist
b. Jul 4, 1862 in Vienna, Austria
d. Feb 6, 1918 in Vienna, Austria
Source: *AtlBL; OxGer*

Kline, Franz Joseph
American. Artist
b. May 23, 1919 in Wilkes-Barre, Pennsylvania
d. May 13, 1962 in New York, New York
Source: *BioIn 3, 4, 5, 6, 7, 8, 10; WebAB*

Kline, Kevin
American. Actor
Starred in *Sophie's Choice,* 1982; *The Pirates of Penzance,* 1983.
b. Oct 24, 1947 in Saint Louis, Missouri
Source: *BioIn 11; NewYTBS 78, 81; WhoThe 81*

Kline, Otis Adelbert
American. Author
b. 1891 in Chicago, Illinois
d. Oct 24, 1946 in New York, New York
Source: *BioIn 1; EncSF; FanAl; WhoHr&F; WhoSciF*

Kling, John Gradwohl
"Noisy"
American. Baseball Player, Manager
b. Nov 13, 1875 in Kansas City, Missouri
d. Jan 31, 1947 in Kansas City, Missouri
Source: *BaseEn; PseudN; WhoProB 73*

Kling, Ken
Cartoonist
Source: *NewYTBE 70*

Klopstock, Friedrich Gottlieb
"The Birmingham Milton"; "The Creator of Biblical Epic Poetry";"The German Milton"; "The Milton of Germany"
German. Poet
b. Jul 2, 1724 in Quedlinburg, Germany
d. Mar 14, 1803 in Hamburg, Germany
Source: *BbD; BiD&SB; CasWL; ChPo; DcEuL; EuAu; EvEuW; McGEWD; NewC; OxEng; OxGer; Pen EUR; PseudN; RComWL; REn*

Klose, Margarete
German. Opera Singer
b. Aug 6, 1905 in Berlin, Germany
d. Dec 14, 1968 in Berlin, Germany (West)
Source: *NewEOp 71*

Klugh, Earl
American. Musician
b. 1953? in Detroit, Michigan
Source: *BioIn 11*

Klugman, Jack
American. Actor
Starred in "The Odd Couple," 1970-75; "Quincy," 1976--.
b. Apr 27, 1922 in Philadelphia, Pennsylvania
Source: *BiE&WWA; BkPepl; FilmgC; IntMPA 75, 76, 77, 78, 79, 80, 81, 82; MotPP; MovMk; NotNAT; WhoAm 82; WhoHol A; WhoThe 77*

Kluszewski, Ted (Theodore Bernard)
"Klu"
American. Baseball Player, Coach
b. Sep 10, 1924 in Argo, Illinois
Source: *BaseEn; PseudN; WhoAm 82; WhoProB 73*

Klutznick, Philip M
American. Former Secretary of Commerce
b. Jul 9, 1907 in Kansas City, Missouri
Source: *WhoAm 74, 76, 78, 80, 82; WhoF&I 74; WhoWorJ 72*

Knack, The
[Berton Averre; Doug Fieger; Bruce Gary; Prescott Niles]
American. Rock Group
Source: *NF*

Knappertsbusch, Hans
German. Conductor
b. Mar 12, 1888 in Elberfeld, Germany
d. Oct 25, 1965 in Munich, Germany (West)
Source: *WhAm 4*

Knaths, (Otto) Karl
American. Artist
b. Oct 21, 1891 in Eau Claire, Wisconsin
d. Mar 9, 1971 in Hyannis, Massachusetts
Source: *BnEnAmA; CurBio 53, 71; DcAmArt; DcCAA 71, 77; McGDA; NewYTBE 71; WhAm 5; WhoAmA 78*

Knauer, Virginia Harrington Wright
American. Government Official
b. Mar 28, 1915 in Philadelphia, Pennsylvania
Source: *BioNews 74; CelR 73; CurBio 70; WhoAm 74, 76, 78, 80, 82; WhoAmP 73; WhoAmW 77; WhoGov 72*

Knebel, Fletcher
American. Author, Journalist
b. Oct 1, 1911 in Dayton, Ohio
Source: *AmAu&B; Au&Wr 71; AuNews 1; BioNews 75; ConAu 1R, 1NR; ConLC 14; ConNov 72, 76; NewYTBS 74; WhoAm 74, 76, 78, 80, 82; WhoE 74; WhoWor 74; WrDr 76*

Kneip, Richard
American. Diplomat, Politician
b. 1933?
Source: *BioIn 10*

Kneller, Sir Godfrey
[Gottfried Kniller]
British. Artist
b. Aug 8, 1646 in Lubeck, Germany
d. Nov 7, 1723 in London, England
Source: *AtlBL; PseudN; REn*

Knerr, H(arold) H
American. Cartoonist
b. 1883 in Bryn Mawr, Pennsylvania
d. Jul 8, 1949 in New York, New York
Source: *WorECom*

Knickerbocker, Diedrich, pseud.
see: Irving, Washington

Knickerbocker, Suzy
[Aileen Mehle; Suzy]
American. Journalist
b. 1919 in El Paso, Texas
Source: *BioIn 10; CelR 73; InWom; PseudN*

Knievel, "Evel" (Robert Craig)
American. Motorcycle Stunt Performer
Attempted sky-cycle jump over Snake River Canyon, ID, 1974.
b. Oct 17, 1938 in Butte, Montana
Source: *BioNews 74; BkPepl; CelR 73; CurBio 72; NewYTBS 74; PseudN; WhoAm 82*

Knight, Arthur
[Arthur Rosenheimer]
American. Motion Picture Critic
b. Sep 3, 1916 in Philadelphia, Pennsylvania
Source: *ConAu 41R, 4NR; IntMPA 76, 77, 78, 79, 80, 81, 82; OxFilm; PseudN; WhoAm 74, 76, 78, 80, 82*

Knight, Billy (William R)
American. Basketball Player
b. Jun 9, 1952 in Braddock, Pennsylvania
Source: *OfNBA; WhoBlA 77*

Knight, Bobby
American. Basketball Coach
b. 1940 in Orville, Ohio
Source: *NewYTBE 71*

Knight, Charles
English. Publisher, Author
b. 1791 in Windsor, England
d. Mar 9, 1873 in Addlestone, England
Source: *Alli, SUP; BbD; BiD&SB; BrAu 19; CasWL; Chambr 3; ChPo; DcEnA; DcEnL; DcLEL; EvLB; NewC; OxEng*

Knight, Frances Gladys
American. Government Official
b. Jul 22, 1905 in Newport, Rhode Island
Source: *CelR 73; CurBio 55; InWom; NewYTBE 71; USBiR 74; WhoAm 74; WhoGov 72; WhoWor 74*

Knight, George Wilson
English. Author
b. Sep 19, 1897 in Sutton, England
Source: *Au&Wr 71; ChPo S1; ConAu 13R; DcLEL; IntWW 74; NewC; Pen ENG; REn; REnAL; TwCA, SUP; Who 74; WhoWor 74; WrDr 76*

Knight, Gladys Maria
[Gladys Knight and the Pips]
American. Singer
Won two Grammys, 1973, for "Midnight Train to Georgia."
b. May 28, 1944 in Atlanta, Georgia
Source: *BkPepl; WhoAm 74, 76, 78, 80, 82; WhoAmW 77; WhoBlA 75*

Knight, John S, III
American. Author, Newspaper Editor
b. Apr 3, 1945 in Columbus, Georgia
d. Dec 7, 1975 in Philadelphia, Pennsylvania
Source: *AuNews 2*

Knight, John Shivley
American. Newspaper Publisher
b. Oct 26, 1894 in Bluefield, West Virginia
d. Jun 16, 1981 in Akron, Ohio
Source: *AuNews 2; BioIn 1, 3, 4, 5, 8, 10, 11; ConAu 93, 103; CurBio 45, 81; IntWW 74, 75, 76, 77, 78; NewYTBS 81; St&PR 75; WhoAm 74, 76, 78; WhoF&I 74, 75; WhoMW 74; WhoS&SW 73, 75, 76, 78; WhoWor 74*

Knight, Phil
American. Founder of Nike, Inc.
b. 1939?
Source: *NF*

Knight, Shirley
American. Actress
b. Jul 5, 1937 in Goessel, Kansas
Source: *BiDFilm; BioIn 8, 10; FilmEn; FilmgC; IntMPA 75, 76, 77, 78, 79, 80, 81; MotPP; MovMk; NewYTBS 74; WhoHol A; WhoThe 77, 81*

Knight, Stan "Goober"
see: Black Oak Arkansas

Knight, Ted
[Tadeus Wladyslaw Konopka]
American. Actor
In TV series "The Mary Tyler Moore Show," 1970-77; "Too Close for Comfort," 1980--.
b. Dec 7, 1923 in Terryville, Connecticut
Source: *BkPepl; IntMPA 82; WhoAm 82; WhoHol A*

Knoetze, Kallie (Nikolaas)
South African. Boxer
b. 1953?
Source: *BioIn 11*

Knopf, Alfred Abraham
American. Publisher
With wife Blanche founded Alfred A Knopf, Inc., 1915.
b. Sep 12, 1892 in New York, New York
Source: *AmAu&B; CelR 73; IntWW 74; REnAL; St&PR 75; WebAB; Who 74; WhoAm 74, 76, 78, 80, 82; WhoWor 74; WhoWorJ 72*

Knopfler, Dave
see: Dire Straits

Knopfler, Mark
see: Dire Straits

Knorr, Nathan Homer
American. Jehovah Witness Official
b. Apr 23, 1905 in Bethlehem, Pennsylvania
d. Jun 15, 1977 in Wallkill, New York
Source: *CurBio 57; WhoAm 74; WhoRel 75; WhoWor 74*

Knote, Heinrich
German. Opera Singer
b. Nov 26, 1870 in Munich, Germany
d. Jan 15, 1953 in Germany (West)
Source: *NewEOp 71*

Knott, Walter
American. Founded Knott's Berry Farm
b. Dec 11, 1889 in San Bernardino, California
d. Dec 3, 1981 in Buena Park, California
Source: *BioIn 4, 6, 7, 9, 10*

Knotts, Don
American. Comedian, Actor
Played Barney Fife on TV series "The Andy Griffith Show," 1960-68.
b. Jul 21, 1924 in Morgantown, West Virginia
Source: *FilmgC; IntMPA 82; MotPP; MovMk; WhoAm 74, 76, 78, 80, 82; WhoHol A*

Knowland, William Fife
American. Senator, Newspaper Publisher
b. Jun 26, 1908 in Alameda, California
d. Feb 23, 1974 in Oakland, California
Source: *BiDrAC; CurBio 47, 74; NewYTBS 74; WhAm 6; Who 74; WhoAmP 73; WhoWest 74; WhoWor 74*

Knowles, James Sheridan
British. Author
b. May 12, 1784 in Cork, Ireland
d. Nov 30, 1862 in Torquay, England
Source: *Alli; BbD; BiD&SB; BrAu 19; CasWL; Chambr 3; ChPo; DcEnA; DcEnL; DcLEL; EvLB; McGEWD; MouLC 3; NewC; OxEng; OxThe; PoIre; REn*

Knowles, John
American. Author
b. Sep 16, 1926 in Fairmont, Washington
Source: *AmAu&B; Au&Wr 71; CasWL; ConAu 17R; ConLC 1, 4, 10; ConNov 72, 76; DrAF 76; RAdv 1; SmATA 8; WhoAm 74, 76, 78, 80, 82; WhoWor 74; WorAu; WrDr 76*

Knowles, Patric
[Reginald Lawrence Knowles]
English. Actor
b. Nov 11, 1911 in Horsforth, England
Source: *FilmgC; IntMPA 75, 76, 77, 78, 79, 80, 81, 82; MovMk; PseudN; WhoHol A; WhoWor 74*

Knowles, Warren Perley
American. Business Executive
b. Aug 19, 1908 in River Falls, Wisconsin
Source: *IntWW 74; WhoAm 74, 76, 78, 80, 82; WhoAmP 73; WhoWor 74*

Knox, Alexander
Canadian. Actor
b. Jan 16, 1907 in Strathroy, ON
Source: *BiE&WWA; CanNov; FilmgC; IntMPA 75, 76, 77, 78, 79, 80, 81, 82; MovMk; NotNAT; WhoAm 74, 76, 78, 80, 82; WhoHol A; WhoThe 72*

Knox, Chuck (Charles Robert)
American. Football Coach
Head coach, LA Rams, 1973-78; Buffalo Bills, 1978--.
b. Apr 27, 1932 in Sewickley, Pennsylvania
Source: *WhoAm 82; WhoFtbl 74*

Knox, E(dmund) G(eorge) V(alpy)
"Evoc"
British. Editor, Journalist
b. 1881
d. Jan 2, 1971 in London, England
Source: *Au&Wr 71; ChPo, S1, S2; ConAu 29R; DcLEL; EvLB; LongCTC; NewC; PseudN; TwCA, SUP*

Knox, Frank
American. Secretary of the Navy
b. Jan 1, 1874 in Boston, Massachusetts
d. Apr 28, 1944 in Washington, DC
Source: *CurBio 40, 44; DcAmB S3*

Knox, Henry
American. Patriot, Revolutionary General
b. Jul 25, 1750 in Boston, Massachusetts
d. Oct 25, 1806 in Thomaston, Maine
Source: *AmBi; ApCAB; BiAuS; BiDrUSE; DcAmB; Drake; TwCBDA; WebAB; WhAm H*

Knox, John
"The Apostle of Presbytery"; "The Apostle of the Scottish Reformers"; "The Reformer of a Kingdom"
Scottish. Religious Leader, Reformer
b. 1505 in Haddington, Scotland
d. Nov 24, 1572 in Edinburgh, Scotland
Source: *Alli; BbD; BiD&SB; BrAu; CasWL; DcEnA; DcEnL; EvLB; NewC; OxEng; Pen ENG; PseudN; RComWL; REn*

Knox, Ronald Arbuthnott
"Hard Knox"
English. Author, Ecclesiastic
b. Feb 17, 1888 in Kibworth, England
d. Aug 24, 1957 in London, England
Source: *BkC 6; CathA 1930; ChPo S2; CurBio 50, 57; DcLEL; EncMys; EvLB; LongCTC; NewC; OxEng; PseudN; TwCA, SUP; TwCW*

Knudsen, Semon Emil
"Bunkie"
American. Automobile Manufacturer
b. Oct 2, 1912 in Buffalo, New York
Source: *BusPN; CurBio 74; IntWW 74; NewYTBS 74; PseudN; St&PR 75; Ward 77A; Who 74; WhoAm 74, 76, 78, 80, 82; WhoF&I 74*

Knudsen, William S
[Signius Wilhelm Paul Knudsen]
American. Industrialist
Helped both Ford, GM become multinational corps.
b. Mar 25, 1879 in Copenhagen, Denmark
d. Apr 27, 1948 in Detroit, Michigan
Source: *CurBio 40, 48; DcAmB S4; EncAB-H; PseudN; WhAm 2*

Kobbe, Gustav
American. Author
b. Mar 4, 1857 in New York, New York
d. Jul 27, 1918 in Babylon, New York
Source: *Alli SUP; AmAu&B; AmLY; BiD&SB; ChPo; DcAmAu; DcAmB; DcNAA; WhAm 1*

Kober, Arthur
Author
b. Aug 25, 1900 in Brody, Austria
d. Jun 12, 1975 in New York, New York
Source: *AmAu&B; Au&Wr 71; BiE&WWA; ConAu 57; ConAu P-1; IntMPA 75; ModWD; OxAmL; REn; REnAL; TwCA, SUP; WhAm 6; WhoAm 74; WhoWorJ 72*

Koch, Bill
American. Skier
b. 1955?
Source: *BioIn 10, 11*

Koch, Ed(ward Irwin)
American. Mayor of New York City
b. Dec 12, 1924 in New York, New York
Source: *BiDrAC; CngDr 74; WhoAm 74, 76, 78, 80, 82; WhoAmP 73; WhoE 74; WhoGov 72*

Koch, Ilse
"Bitch of Buchenwald"; "Red Witch"
German. Nazi War Criminal
b. 1907 in Dresden, Germany
d. 1967
Source: *InWom; LookW; NewYTBE 71*

Koch, John
American. Artist
b. Aug 16, 1909 in Toledo, Ohio
d. Apr 19, 1978 in New York, New York
Source: *BioIn 2, 3, 4, 7, 11; ConArt; CurBio 65, 78; DcCAA 71, 77; NewYTBS 78; ObitOF 79; WhoAm 74, 76, 78; WhoAmA 73, 76, 78*

Koch, Kenneth
American. Author
b. Feb 27, 1925 in Cincinnati, Ohio
Source: *AmAu&B; ChPo S1, S2; ConAu 1R; ConDr 73; ConLC 5, 8; ConP 70, 75; CroCAP; DrAF 76; DrAP 75; DrAS 74E; NewYTBE 70; Pen AM; RAdv 1; WebE&AL; WhoAm 74, 76, 78, 80, 82; WhoWor 74; WorAu; WrDr 76*

Koch, Robert
German. Engineer, Scientist
b. Dec 11, 1843 in Hanover, Prussia
d. May 28, 1910 in Baden-Baden, Germany
Source: *REn*

Kodaly, Zoltan
Hungarian. Composer
b. Dec 16, 1882 in Kecskemet, Hungary
d. Mar 6, 1967 in Budapest, Hungary
Source: *DcCM; WhAm 4*

Koestler, Arthur
Hungarian. Author
b. Sep 5, 1905 in Budapest, Hungary
Source: *Au&Wr 71; CasWL; CnMWL; ConAu 1R, 1NR; ConLC 1, 3, 6, 8, 15; ConNov 72, 76; CurBio 43, 62; CyWA; EncWL; IntWW 74; LongCTC; ModBrL; NewC; NewYTBE 70; OxEng; Pen ENG; REn; TwCA SUP; TwCW; WebE&AL; Who 74; WhoTwCL; WhoWor 74; WhoWorJ 72; WrDr 76*

Kofoed, Jack (John C)
American. Journalist, Commentator
b. Dec 17, 1894 in Philadelphia, Pennsylvania
Source: *ConAu 5R*

Kogan, Leonid Borisovich
Russian. Musician
Refused to play in orchestra which contained a defector.
b. Oct 14, 1924 in Dnepropetrovsk, U.S.S.R.
d. Dec 17, 1982
Source: *Baker 78; IntWW 74, 75, 76, 77, 78, 79, 80, 81; WhoMus 72; WhoSocC 78; WhoWor 74*

Kohl, Helmut Michael
German. Chancellor
Defeated Helmut Schmidt, Sep, 1982.
b. Apr 3, 1930 in Ludwigshafen, Germany
Source: *CurBio 77; IntWW 74, 75, 76, 77, 78, 79, 80, 81; IntYB 78, 79, 80, 81; WhoWor 76, 78*

Kohl, Herbert R
American. Author, Educator
b. 1937?
Source: *AmAu&B; ConAu 65*

Kohler, Fred
American. Actor
b. Apr 20, 1889 in Kansas City, Missouri
d. Oct 28, 1938 in Los Angeles, California
Source: *Film 1; TwYS; WhScrn 74, 77; WhoHol B*

Kohler, Kaufmann
American. Theologian
b. May 10, 1843 in Fuerth, Germany
d. Jan 28, 1926 in New York, New York
Source: *AmAu&B; AmBi; DcAmB; DcNAA; OhA&B; WhAm 1*

Kohler, William R
American. Plumbing Executive
Source: *St&PR 75*

Kohler, Wolfgang
German. Psychologist
b. Jan 21, 1887 in Reval, Russia
d. Jun 11, 1967 in Enfield, New Hampshire
Source: *AmAu&B; TwCA SUP; WhAm 4, 5*

Kohlmeier, Louis Martin, Jr.
American. Journalist
b. Feb 17, 1926 in Saint Louis, Missouri
Source: *ConAu 49; WhoAm 74, 76, 78, 80, 82; WhoS&SW 73*

Kohn, William Roth
American. Artist, Educator
b. Aug 23, 1931 in Saint Louis, Missouri
Source: *WhoAmA 76, 78, 80*

Kohner, Susan
American. Actress
b. Nov 11, 1936 in Los Angeles, California
Source: *BiE&WWA; FilmgC; IntMPA 75, 76, 77, 78, 79, 80, 81, 82; MotPP; NotNAT; WhoHol A*

Kohoutek, Lubos
Czech. Astronomer
b. 1935 in Moravia, Czechoslovakia
Source: *BioNews 74; CurBio 74; NewYTBS 74*

Kohut, Heinz
Austrian. Psychoanalyst
b. May 3, 1913 in Vienna, Austria
d. Oct 8, 1981 in Chicago, Illinois
Source: *AmM&WS 79P; BiDrAPA 77; BioIn 10, 11, 12; ConAu 45, 1NR; NewYTBS 81; WhoAm 78, 80*

Koivisto, Mauno Henrik
"Manu"
Finnish. President
First socialist elected president, Jan, 1982.
b. Nov 25, 1923 in Turku, Finland
Source: *CurBio 82; IntWW 74, 75, 76, 77, 78, 79, 80; IntYB 78, 79, 80, 81; WhoWor 74, 76, 78*

Kokoschka, Oskar
Austrian. Artist, Author
b. Mar 1, 1886 in Austria
d. Feb 22, 1980 in Montreux, Switzerland
Source: *ConArt; ConAu 93; CurBio 56, 80; EncTR; EncWL; EncWT; EvEuW; IntAu&W 76, 77; IntWW 75, 76, 77, 78; McGDA; McGEWD; ModGL; ModWD; OxGer; REn; REnWD; Who 74; WhoGrA; WhoWor 76, 78*

Kolb, Barbara Anne
American. Composer
b. Feb 10, 1939 in Hartford, Connecticut
Source: *BioIn 10, 11; DcCM; WhoE 74, 75*

Kolb, Claudia
American. Swimmer
Won two gold medals, 1968 Olympics.
b. Dec 19, 1949 in Hayward, California
Source: *BioIn 8*

Kolbe, Maximilian
[Maksymilian Kolbe]
Polish. Saint
Catholic priest who chose death in place of condemned prisoner; canonized, 1982.
b. 1894 in Poland
d. Aug 14, 1941 in Auschwitz, Poland
Source: *EncTR; HisEWW; NewYTBE 71; NewYTBS 82*

Kolehmainen, Hannes
Finnish. Track Athlete
b. Dec 9, 1889 in Kuopio, Finland
Source: *WhoTr&F 73*

Kolff, Willem Johan
American. Physician
Developed artifical kidney, 1943.
b. Feb 14, 1911 in Leiden, Netherlands
Source: *AmM&WS 73P, 76P, 79P; IntWW 74, 75, 76, 77, 78, 79, 80, 81; WhoAm 74, 76, 78, 80, 82; WhoWor 74, 76, 78*

Kollek, Teddy (Theodore)
Israeli. Politician, Author
Mayor of Jerusalem since 1965; headed drive to create national museum.
b. May 27, 1911 in Vienna, Austria
Source: *ConAu P-2; CurBio 74; IntWW 74; WhoWor 74*

Kollmar, Richard
American. Theatrical Producer
b. Dec 31, 1910 in Ridgewood, New Jersey
d. Jan 7, 1971 in New York, New York
Source: *ConAu 89; CurBio 71; NewYTBE 71; WhScrn 74; WhoHol B; WhoThe 77*

Kollwitz, Kathe Schmidt
German. Artist
b. Jul 8, 1867 in Konigsberg, Germany
d. Apr 22, 1945 in Dresden, Germany
Source: *AtlBL; HerW; InWom; OxGer; WhAm 4*

Kolodin, Irving
American. Music Critic
b. Feb 22, 1908 in Brooklyn, New York
Source: *AmAu&B; ConAu 93; CurBio 47; REnAL; WhoAm 74, 76, 78, 80, 82; WhoMus 72; WhoWor 74*

Komarov, Vladimir
Russian. Cosmonaut
b. Mar 16, 1927
d. Apr 24, 1967
Source: *WhAm 4*

Komroff, Manuel
American. Author
b. Sep 7, 1890 in New York, New York
d. Dec 10, 1974 in Woodstock, New York
Source: *AmAu&B; AmNov; AuBYP; CnDAL; ConAu 1R, 53, 4NR; OxAmL; REnAL; SmATA 2; TwCA, SUP; WhAm 6; WhoAm 74; WhoWor 74; WrDr 76*

Kondrashin, Kiril Petrovich
Russian. Conductor
b. Feb 21, 1914 in Moscow, Russia
d. Mar 7, 1981 in Amsterdam, Netherlands
Source: *BioIn 11; IntWW 74, 75, 76, 77; WhoMus 72; WhoOp 76; WhoSocC 78; WhoWor 74*

Konetzne, Anni
Austrian. Opera Singer
b. Feb 12, 1902 in Vienna, Austria
d. Jun 9, 1968 in Vienna, Austria
Source: *NewEOp 71*

Konetzni, Hilde
Austrian. Opera Singer
b. Mar 21, 1905 in Vienna, Austria
Source: *WhoMus 72*

Konev, Ivan S
Russian. Field Marshal
b. Dec 27, 1897 in Ladeino, Russia
d. May 21, 1973 in Moscow, U.S.S.R.
Source: *CurBio 43, 56, 73; NewYTBE 73*

Konitz, Lee
American. Jazz Musician
b. 1927
Source: *BioIn 8; CmpEPM*

Konno, Ford
American. Swimmer
b. 1932?
Source: *BioIn 3*

Konoye, Fumimaro, Prince
Japanese. Premier
b. Oct 1891
d. Dec 15, 1945
Source: *CurBio 40, 46*

Konwitschny, Franz
German. Conductor
b. Aug 14, 1901 in Fulnek, Germany
d. Jul 27, 1962 in Belgrade, Yugoslavia
Source: *NewEOp 71*

Konya, Sandor
Hungarian. Opera Singer
b. Sep 23, 1923 in Sarkad, Hungary
Source: *WhoWor 74*

Koo, V(i) K(yuin) Wellington
[Ku Wei-Chun]
Chinese. Statesman, Ambassador
b. 1887 in Shanghai, China
Source: *ConAu 81; CurBio 41; PseudN; REn; Who 74; WhoLA*

Koob, Kathryn L
[The Hostages]
American. Former Hostage in Iran
b. 1939?
Source: *BioIn 12; NewYTBS 81*

Kool and the Gang
[Amir Bell; "Kool" (Robert) Bell; Ronald Bell; George Brown; "Spike" (Robert) Mickens; Charles Smith; J T Taylor; Dennis Thomas ("D T"); Earl Toon, Jr.]
American. Rock Group
Source: *RkOn 2*

Koontz, (Annie) Elizabeth Duncan
[Mrs. Harry Lee Koontz]
"Libby"
American. Educator
b. Jun 3, 1919 in Salisbury, North Carolina
Source: *InWom; LEduc 74; PseudN; WhoAm 74; WhoAmP 73; WhoAmW 77; WhoBlA 75; WhoGov 72; WhoS&SW 73*

Koop, Charles Everett
American. Surgeon
b. Oct 14, 1916 in Brooklyn, New York
Source: *AmM&WS 76P, 79P; WhoAm 76, 78, 80, 82*

Kooper, Al
[Blood, Sweat, and Tears]
American. Musician, Record Producer
b. Feb 5, 1944 in Brooklyn, New York
Source: *LilREn 78; WhoAm 78; WhoRock 81*

Kooymans, George
see: Golden Earring

Kopechne, Mary Jo
American. Secretary
Died in car accident involving Edward Kennedy.
b. Jul 26, 1940
d. Jul 19, 1969 in Chappaquiddick, Massachusetts
Source: *BioIn 8, 9, 10, 11*

Kopell, Bernie (Bernard Morton)
American. Actor
Plays Dr. Adam Bricker on TV series "The Love Boat," 1976--.
b. Jun 21, 1933 in Brooklyn, New York
Source: *WhoAm 80, 82; WhoHol A*

Kopit, Arthur L
American. Dramatist, Architect
b. May 10, 1937 in New York, New York
Source: *AmAu&B; AuNews 1; BiE&WWA; CasWL; CnMD; ConAu 81; ConLC 1, 18; CurBio 72; McGEWD; ModWD; NatPD; NotNAT; OxAmL; Pen AM; REn; WebE&AL; WhoAm 74; WhoThe 77; WorAu; WrDr 76*

Koppel, Ted
American. Broadcast Journalist
Anchorman, ABC News *Nightline,* 1980--.
b. 1940 in Lancashire, England
Source: *ConAu 103; WhoAm 80, 82*

Kops, Bernard
English. Author
b. Nov 28, 1926 in London, England
Source: *BiE&WWA; ChPo; CnMD; ConAu 5R; ConDr 73; ConLC 4; ConNov 72, 76; ConP 70, 75; CroCD; ModBrL SUP; ModWD; NewC; NotNAT; RAdv 1; TwCW; WhoThe 77; WhoWorJ 72; WorAu; WrDr 76*

Korbut, Olga
[Mrs. Leonid Borkevich]
Russian. Gymnast
Won two gold medals, 1972 Olympics.
b. May 16, 1955 in Grodno, U.S.S.R.
Source: *BioNews 74; CurBio 73; HerW; NewYTBE 72*

Korchnoi, Viktor
Russian. Chess Player
b. 1931
Source: *BioIn 10*

Korda, Sir Alexander
[Sandor Kellner; Sandor Korda]
English. Motion Picture Producer
b. Sep 16, 1893 in Turkeve, Hungary
d. Jan 23, 1956 in London, England
Source: *BiDFilm; CurBio 46, 56; DcFM; FilmgC; MovMk; OxFilm; PseudN; WhAm 3; WorEFlm*

Korda, Michael
American. Publishing Executive
b. 1919
d. Dec 24, 1973
Source: *BioIn 10*

Korda, Michael Vincent
American. Publishing Executive
b. Oct 8, 1933 in London, England
Source: *WhoAm 74, 76, 78, 80, 82*

Koren, Edward Benjamin
American. Author
b. Dec 13, 1935 in New York, New York
Source: *ConAu 25R; SmATA 5; WhoAm 82; WhoE 74*

Korff, Baruch
American. Rabbi
b. 1914?
Source: *BioIn 10*

Korin, Ogata
Japanese. Artist
fl. 1658 in Japan
d. 1716
Source: *McGDA; NewCol 75*

Korinetz, Yuri
Russian. Author
b. Jan 14, 1923 in Moscow, U.S.S.R.
Source: *ConAu 61; SmATA 9*

Korjus, Miliza
Polish. Opera Singer
b. 1912 in Warsaw, Poland
d. Aug 26, 1980 in Culver City, California
Source: *BioIn 12; FilmgC; NewYTBS 81; ThFT; WhoHol A; WhoMus 72*

Korman, Harvey Herschel
American. Comedian
Regular on "The Carol Burnett Show," 1967-77; won four Emmys.
b. Feb 15, 1927 in Chicago, Illinois
Source: *CurBio 79; IntMPA 75, 76, 77, 78, 79, 80, 81, 82; WhoAm 74, 76, 78, 80, 82; WhoHol A*

Korngold, Erich Wolfgang
Austrian. Composer
b. May 29, 1897 in Brunn, Austria
d. Nov 29, 1957 in Hollywood, California
Source: *AmSCAP 66; CmMov; CurBio 43, 58; CmMov; FilmgC; OxFilm; WorEFlm*

Kornilov, Lavr Georgyevich
Russian. Anti-Bolshevik General
b. Jul 18, 1870 in Turkistan, Russia
d. Apr 1918
Source: *McGEWB; REn*

Kornman, Mary
[Our Gang]
American. Actress
b. 1917 in Idaho Falls, Idaho
d. Jun 1, 1973 in Glendale, California
Source: *TwYS; WhScrn 77; WhoHol B*

Korolenko, Vladimir Galaktionovich
Russian. Author
b. 1853 in Zhitomir, Russia
d. 1921 in Polatava, U.S.S.R.
Source: *BiD&SB; CasWL; ClDMEL; DcRusL; EncWL; EuAu; EvEuW; ModSL 1; Pen EUR; REn*

Korzybski, Alfred Habdank
American. Semanticist
b. Jul 3, 1879 in Warsaw, Poland
d. Mar 7, 1950 in Sharon, Connecticut
Source: *AmAu&B; REn; REnAL; TwCA SUP; WebAB; WhAm 2*

Kosciuszko, Thaddeus
Polish. Soldier
b. 1746 in Belo, Russia
d. Nov 15, 1817 in Solothurn, Switzerland
Source: *ApCAB; Drake; TwCBDA; WebAB; WhAm H*

Kosinski, Jerzy Nikodem
[Joseph Novak, pseud.]
American. Author
b. Jun 14, 1933 in Lodz, Poland
Source: *AmAu&B; ConAu 17R; ConLC 1, 2, 3, 6; ConNov 72, 76; CurBio 74; DrAF 76; EncWL; ModAL SUP; PseudN; RAdv 1; WhoAm 74, 76, 78, 80, 82; WhoE 74; WhoWor 74; WorAu; WrDr 76*

Kossuth, Lajos
Hungarian. Patriot, Statesman
Principal figure in Hungarian Revolution, 1848.
b. Sep 19, 1802 in Monok, Hungary
d. Mar 20, 1894 in Turin, Italy
Source: *OxGer; Pen EUR; WhAm H*

Kostelanetz, Andre
American. Conductor
b. Dec 22, 1901 in Saint Petersburg, Russia
d. Jan 13, 1980 in Port-au-Prince, Haiti
Source: *CurBio 42; IntWW 74; NewYTBE 72, 73; Who 74; WhoAm 74; WhoMus 72; WhoWor 74*

Kosygin, Aleksei Nikolaevich
Russian. Premier
Led Soviet effort at economic modernization, 1960's.
b. Feb 20, 1904 in Saint Petersburg, Russia
d. Dec 19, 1980 in Moscow, U.S.S.R.
Source: *ConAu 102; CurBio 65; IntWW 74; Who 74; WhoGov 72; WhoWor 74*

Koth, Erika
German. Opera Singer
b. Sep 15, 1927 in Darmstadt, Germany
Source: *WhoMus 72; WhoWor 74*

Kottke, Leo
American. Musician
b. in Athens, Georgia
Source: *IlEncRk*

Kotzebue, August Friedrich Ferdinand von
"The Shakespeare of Germany"
German. Author
b. May 3, 1761 in Weimar, Germany
d. Mar 23, 1819 in Mannheim, Germany
Source: *AtlBL; BbD; BiD&SB; CasWL; CnThe; DcEuL; EuAu; EvEuW; McGEWD; NewC; OxEng; OxFr; OxGer; OxThe; Pen EUR; PseudN; REn; REnWD*

Kotzky, Alex Sylvester
American. Cartoonist
b. Sep 11, 1923 in New York, New York
Source: *WhoAm 74, 76, 78, 80, 82*

Koufax, Sandy (Sanford)
American. Baseball Player, Sportscaster
Youngest player inducted into Hall of Fame, 1971, at age 36.
b. Dec 30, 1935 in Brooklyn, New York
Source: *BaseEn; ConAu 89; CurBio 64; WebAB; WhoAm 74; WhoProB 73*

Kountche, Seyni
Nigerian. President
b. 1931 in Fandou, Niger
Source: *WhoWor 74*

Koussevitzky, Serge Alexandrovich
American. Conductor, Composer
b. Jul 26, 1874 in Vyshni Volochek, Russia
d. Jun 4, 1951 in Boston, Massachusetts
Source: *CurBio 40, 51; DcAmB S5*

Kovacs, Ernie
American. Actor
b. Jan 23, 1919 in Trenton, New Jersey
d. Jan 13, 1962 in Hollywood, California
Source: *AmAu&B; AmSCAP 66; CurBio 58, 62; FilmgC; MotPP; MovMk; WhAm 4; WhScrn 74, 77; WhoHol B*

Kovel, Ralph Mallory
American. Author, Antique Authority
b. Aug 20, 1920 in Milwaukee, Wisconsin
Source: *ConAu 17R; WhoAm 74, 76, 78, 80, 82; WrDr 76*

Kovel, Terry Horvitz
American. Author, Antique Authority
b. Oct 27, 1928 in Cleveland, Ohio
Source: *ConAu 17R; ForWC 70; WhoAm 74, 76, 78, 80, 82; WrDr 76*

Kovic, Ron
American. Author, Soldier
Source: *BioIn 11*

Kozakiewicz, Wladyslaw
Polish. Track Athlete
Source: *NF*

Krafft-Ebing, Richard von
German. Sexologist, Psychiatrist
b. Aug 14, 1840 in Mannheim, Germany
d. Dec 22, 1902 in Mariagru, Austria
Source: *AsBiEn; OxGer; REn*

Kraft, Chris(topher Columbus, Jr.)
American. NASA Administrator
b. Feb 28, 1924 in Phoebus, Virginia
Source: *AmM&WS 73P; CurBio 66; IntWW 74; WhoAm 74; WhoGov 72; WhoWor 74*

Kraft, James Lewis
American. Manufacturer
Invented pasteurizing process for cheese.
b. Dec 11, 1874 in Stevensville, ON
d. Feb 16, 1953 in Chicago, Illinois
Source: *DcAmB S5; WhAm 3*

Kraft, Joseph
American. Journalist, Author
b. Sep 4, 1924 in South Orange, New Jersey
Source: *AmAu&B; ConAu 9R; WhoAm 74, 76, 78, 80, 82; WhoS&SW 73; WrDr 76*

Kraftwerk
[Karl Bartos; Wolfgang Flur; Ralf Hutter; Florian Schneider]
German. Rock Group
Source: *ConMuA 80; WhoRock 81*

Krag, Jens Otto
Danish. Prime Minister
b. Sep 15, 1915 in Randers, Denmark
d. Jun 22, 1978 in Jutland, Denmark
Source: *CurBio 62; IntWW 74; NewYTBE 72; WhoWor 74*

Kramer, Jack
American. Tennis Player
b. Aug 1, 1921 in Las Vegas, Nevada
Source: *BioNews 74; CurBio 47*

Kramer, Stanley E
American. Motion Picture Director, Producer
b. Sep 29, 1913 in New York, New York
Source: *BiDFilm; CelR 73; CurBio 51; DcFM; FilmgC; IntMPA 75, 76, 77, 78, 79, 80, 81, 82; IntWW 74; MovMk; OxFilm; WhoAm 74, 76, 78, 80, 82; WhoWest 74; WhoWor 74; WorEFlm*

Kramm, Joseph
American. Dramatist, Actor
b. Sep 30, 1907 in Philadelphia, Pennsylvania
Source: *AmAu&B; BiE&WWA; CnMD; CurBio 52; ModWD; NotNAT; OxAmL; REn; TwCA SUP; WhoAm 74; WhoE 74; WhoThe 77; WhoWor 74*

Krantz, Hazel Newman
American. Author
b. Jan 29, 1920 in Brooklyn, New York
Source: *ConAu 1R, 1NR; SmATA 12; WrDr 76*

Krantz, Judith
[Judith Tarcher]
American. Author
Wrote *Scruples*, 1978; *Princess Daisy*, 1980; *Mistral's Daughter*, 1982.
b. Jan 9, 1928 in New York, New York
Source: *BioIn 11; ConAu 81; CurBio 82; WhoAm 82*

Krasna, Norman
American. Dramatist, Film Critic
b. Nov 7, 1909 in New York, New York
Source: *AmAu&B; BiDFilm; BiE&WWA; CmMov; CurBio 52; FilmgC; IntMPA 75, 76, 77, 78, 79, 80, 81; McGEWD; NotNAT; OxFilm; WhoAm 74; WhoThe 77; WorEFlm*

Krassner, Paul
American. Editor, Author, Journalist
b. Apr 9, 1932 in Brooklyn, New York
Source: *AmAu&B; ConAu 21R; WhoAm 74*

Kraus, Ernst
German. Opera Singer
b. Jun 8, 1863 in Erlangen, Bavaria
d. Sep 6, 1941 in Worthersee, Austria
Source: *NewEOp 71*

Kraus, Felix von
Austrian. Opera Singer
b. Oct 3, 1870 in Vienna, Austria
d. Oct 30, 1937 in Munich, Germany
Source: *NewEOp 71*

Kraus, Lili
Austrian. Musician, Educator
b. Mar 4, 1908 in Budapest, Hungary
Source: *BioNews 75; NewYTBE 71; WhoAm 74, 76, 78, 80, 82; WhoAmW 77; WhoMus 72*

Krause, Bernie (Bernard Leo)
[The Weavers]
American. Singer, Composer
b. Dec 8, 1938 in Detroit, Michigan
Source: *WhoAm 82*

Krauss, Clemens
Austrian. Conductor
b. Mar 31, 1893 in Vienna, Austria
d. May 16, 1954 in Mexico City, Mexico
Source: *NewEOp 71*

Krauss, Gabrielle
Austrian. Opera Singer
b. Mar 24, 1842 in Vienna, Austria
d. Jan 6, 1906 in Paris, France
Source: *InWom*

Krauss, Ruth Ida
[Mrs. Crockett Johnson]
American. Author
b. 1911 in Baltimore, Maryland
Source: *AmAu&B; Au&ICB; Au&Wr 71; AuBYP; BkP; ConAu 1R, 1NR; ConDr 73; DrAP 75; ForWC 70; MorJA; SmATA 1; WhoAm 74, 76, 78, 80, 82; WrDr 76*

Krauss, Werner
German. Actor
b. 1884 in Gestungshausen, Germany
d. Oct 20, 1959 in Vienna, Austria
Source: *BiDFilm; BioIn 5; EncWT; Film 1, 2; ObitOF 79; OxFilm; OxThe; WhScrn 74, 77; WhThe; WorEFlm*

Kray, Reggie (Reginald)
English. Gangster
b. 1934 in London, England
Source: *BioIn 9, 11*

Kray, Ronnie (Ronald)
English. Gangster
b. 1934 in London, England
Source: *BioIn 9, 11*

Krebs, Sir Hans Adolf
British. Biochemist
Won 1953 Nobel Prize for research on food cycles.
b. Aug 25, 1900 in Hildesheim, Germany
d. Nov 22, 1981 in Oxford, England
Source: *AsBiEn; CurBio 54, 82; IntWW 74, 75, 76, 77, 78, 79, 80, 81; McGEWB; NewYTBS 81; WhoWor 74, 76, 78; WorAl*

Kredel, Fritz
American. Artist, Illustrator
b. Feb 8, 1900
d. Jun 10, 1973 in New York, New York
Source: *ChPo; ConAu 41R; IlsBYP; IlsCB 1744, 1946, 1957; MorJA; SmATA 17; WhoAmA 73*

Kreisler, Fritz
American. Musician
b. Feb 2, 1875 in Vienna, Austria
d. Jan 29, 1962 in New York, New York
Source: *AmSCAP 66; CurBio 44, 62; REn; WebAB; WhAm 4*

Krementz, Jill
American. Photographer, Author
b. Feb 19, 1940 in New York, New York
Source: *AuNews 1, 2; BioNews 75; ConAu 41R; SmATA 17; WhoAm 74, 76, 78, 80, 82*

Krenek, Ernst
American. Composer
b. Aug 23, 1900 in Vienna, Austria
Source: *ConAu 57; CurBio 42; DcCM; IntWW 74; WhoAm 74, 76, 78, 80, 82; WhoMus 72; WhoWor 74*

Krenwinkel, Patricia
American. Member of Manson Cult
b. 1947
Source: *BioIn 9*

Kreps, Juanita Morris
American. Former Government Official
Secretary of Commerce, 1977-79.
b. Jan 11, 1921 in Lynch, Kentucky
Source: *AmEA 74; AmM&WS 73S; WhoAm 74, 76, 78, 80, 82; WhoAmW 77; WhoS&SW 73*

Kresge, Sebastian Spering
American. Founder of S S Kresge
b. Jul 31, 1867 in Bald Mount, Pennsylvania
d. Oct 18, 1966 in Mountainhome, Pennsylvania
Source: *WhAm 4*

Kreskin
[George Joseph Kresge, Jr.]
"The Amazing Kreskin"
American. ESP Expert, Psychic
b. 1935 in Caldwell, New Jersey
Source: *BioIn 10; PseudN*

Kress, Samuel Henry
American. Merchant
Founded Kress dime store chain, 1907.
b. Jul 23, 1863 in Cherryville, Pennsylvania
d. Sep 22, 1955 in New York, New York
Source: *CurBio 55; DcAmB S5; WebAB; WhAm 3*

Kreuger, Ivar
"Match King"
Swedish. Financier, Swindler
b. Mar 2, 1880
d. Mar 12, 1932 in Paris, France
Source: *PseudN; WebBD 80*

Kreuger, Kurt
American. Actor
b. Jul 23, 1917 in Saint Moritz, Switzerland
Source: *FilmgC; IntMPA 75, 76, 77, 78, 79, 80, 81, 82; MotPP; WhoHol A*

Kreutzer, Rodolphe
German. Musician, Composer
b. Nov 16, 1766 in Versailles, France
d. Jan 6, 1831 in Geneva, Switzerland
Source: *NewEOp 71; OxMus; WebBD 80*

Kreutzmann, Bill
[The Grateful Dead]
American. Singer, Musician
b. Jun 7, 1946 in Palo Alto, California
Source: *NF*

Kreymborg, Alfred
American. Dramatist, Poet
b. Dec 10, 1883 in New York, New York
d. Aug 14, 1966 in Milford, Connecticut
Source: *AmAu&B; AmSCAP 66; ChPo, S2; CnDAL; ConAmA; ConAmL; ConAu 25R; LongCTC; ModAL; OxAmL; REnAL; SixAP; TwCA, SUP; WhAm 4*

Krieger, Robby
[The Doors]
American. Singer, Musician
b. Jan 8, 1946 in Los Angeles, California
Source: *NF*

Krigstein, Bernard
American. Artist, Illustrator, Teacher
b. Mar 22, 1919 in New York, New York
Source: *WhoAmA 73*

Krips, Josef
Austrian. Conductor
b. Apr 8, 1902 in Vienna, Austria
d. Oct 12, 1974 in Geneva, Switzerland
Source: *BioNews 75; CurBio 65, 74; IntWW 74; NewYTBS 74; Who 74; WhoMus 72; WhoWor 74*

Krishna Menon, V(engalil) K(rishnan)
Indian. Statesman, Lawyer
b. May 3, 1897
d. Oct 6, 1974
Source: *CurBio 53, 74; IntWW 74; Who 74; WhoWor 74*

Krishnamurti, Jiddu
[Alcyone, pseud.]
Indian. Author, Philosopher
b. May 22, 1895 in Madanapelle, India
Source: *ConAu 61; CurBio 74; DcLEL; PseudN; WhoAm 74, 76, 78, 80, 82*

Kristel, Sylvia
Dutch. Actress
b. Sep 28, 1952 in Utrecht, Netherlands
Source: *BioIn 10; FilmEn; WhoHol A*

Kristofferson, Kris
[Kris Carson]
American. Actor, Singer, Songwriter
Rhodes scholar; wrote song "Help Me Make It Through the Night."
b. Jun 22, 1937 in Brownsville, Texas
Source: *BioNews 74; BkPepl; ConAu 104; CurBio 74; IntMPA 82; MovMk; PseudN; WhoAm 82; WhoHol A*

Kristol, Irving
American. Editor, Author
b. Jan 22, 1920 in New York, New York
Source: *ConAu 25R; CurBio 74; WhoAm 82*

Kroc, Ray Albert
American. Business, Sports Executive
Founded McDonald's, 1955; owner San Diego Padres, 1974--.
b. Oct 5, 1902 in Chicago, Illinois
Source: *BioNews 74; BusPN; CurBio 73; NewYTBS 74; WhoAm 74, 76, 78, 80, 82*

Krock, Arthur
American. Journalist
b. Nov 16, 1886 in Glasgow, Kentucky
d. Apr 12, 1974 in Washington, DC
Source: *AmAu&B; AuNews 1; ConAu 33R, 49; ConAu P-2; CurBio 43, 74; EncAB-H; WhAm 6; WhNAA; WhoAm 74; WhoS&SW 73; WhoWor 74*

Kroeber, Alfred Louis
American. Anthropologist, Author
b. Jun 11, 1876 in Hoboken, New Jersey
d. Oct 5, 1960 in Paris, France
Source: *AmAu&B; WebAB; WhAm 4*

Kroeber, Theodora Kracaw
[Mrs. John Quinn; Theodora Kroeber-Quinn]
American. Author
Mother of author Ursula LeGuin.
b. Mar 24, 1897 in Denver, Colorado
d. Jul 4, 1979 in Berkeley, California
Source: *AmAu&B; ConAu 5R, 89, 5NR; ForWC 70; PseudN; SmATA 1; WrDr 76*

Krofft, Marty
American. Puppeteer, TV Producer
Source: *NewYTET*

Krofft, Sid
American. Puppeteer, TV Producer
Source: *NewYTET*

Kroger, Bernard Henry
American. Businessman
Founded Kroger grocery store chain, 1884.
b. Jan 24, 1860 in Cincinnati, Ohio
d. Jul 21, 1938 in Wianno, Massachusetts
Source: *DcAmB S2; NatCAB 32; WhAm 1*

Krogh, Egil, Jr.
"Bud"
American. Watergate Participant
b. 1939
Source: *BioIn 9, 10; PseudN*

Krol, John
American. Roman Catholic Cardinal
b. Oct 26, 1910 in Cleveland, Ohio
Source: *CurBio 69; IntWW 74; NewYTBE 71; WhoAm 74, 76, 78, 80, 82; WhoE 74; WhoRel 75; WhoWor 74*

Kroll, Leon
American. Artist
b. Dec 6, 1884 in New York, New York
d. Oct 25, 1974 in Gloucester, Massachusetts
Source: *CurBio 43, 74; DcCAA 71; IntWW 74; NewYTBS 74; WhAm 6; WhoAm 74; WhoAmA 73*

Kromm, Bobby
Canadian. Former Hockey Coach
b. 1929? in Calgary, AB
Source: *BioIn 12*

Kronenberger, Louis
American. Author
b. Dec 9, 1904 in Cincinnati, Ohio
d. Apr 30, 1980 in Wellesley, Massachusetts
Source: *AmAu&B; ChPo; ConAu 1R, 97, 2NR; CurBio 44; DrAS 74E; NotNAT; OhA&B; OxAmL; REnAL; TwCA SUP; WhoAm 74; WhoThe 77; WhoWor 74; WhoWorJ 72; WrDr 76*

Kronhausen, Eberhard Wilhelm
German. Psychologist
b. Sep 12, 1915 in Berlin, Germany
Source: *ConAu 9R*

Kronhausen, Phyllis Carmen
American. Psychologist
b. Jan 26, 1929 in Minnesota
Source: *ConAu 9R*

Kronold, Selma
Polish. Opera Singer
b. 1866 in Krakow, Poland
d. Oct 9, 1920 in New York, New York
Source: *InWom; NotAW*

Kropotkin, Peter Alekseyevich, Prince
Russian. Anarchist
b. Nov 26, 1842 in Moscow, Russia
d. Feb 8, 1921 in U.S.S.R.
Source: *BiD&SB; CasWL; ClDMEL; EuAu*

Kruger, Hardy
German. Actor
b. Apr 12, 1928 in Berlin, Germany
Source: *FilmgC; IntMPA 75, 76, 77, 78, 79, 80, 81, 82; WhoHol A; WhoWor 74*

Kruger, Otto
American. Actor
b. Sep 6, 1885 in Toledo, Ohio
d. Sep 6, 1974 in Woodland Hills, California
Source: *BiE&WWA; FilmgC; MotPP; MovMk; NewYTBS 74; PlP&P; Vers; WhAm 6; WhScrn 77; WhoHol B*

Kruger, (Stephanus) Paul(us Johannes)
"Oom Paul"
South African. Statesman
b. 1825 in Colesberg, South Africa
d. 1904 in Switzerland
Source: *NewCol 75; WebBD 80; WhDW*

Krumgold, Joseph
American. Author, Motion Picture Producer
Wrote *And Now Miguel; Onion John.*
b. Apr 9, 1908 in Jersey City, New Jersey
d. Jul 10, 1980 in Hope, New Jersey
Source: *AnObit 1980; AuBYP; BioIn 3, 4, 5, 6, 7, 8, 9; ConAu 9R, 101; ConLC 12; EncMys; SmATA 1; WrDr 80*

Krupa, Gene
American. Band Leader, Musician
b. Jan 15, 1909 in Chicago, Illinois
d. Oct 16, 1973 in Yonkers, New York
Source: *CurBio 47, 73; NewYTBE 73; WhAm 6; WhScrn 77; WhoE 74; WhoHol B; WhoJazz 72; WhoMus 72*

Krupp, Alfred
"The Cannon King"
German. Armaments Manufacturer
Introduced new methods for producing quantities of cast steel.
b. Apr 26, 1812 in Essen, Germany
d. Jul 14, 1887
Source: *NewCol 75*

Krupp von Bohlen und Halbach, Bertha
"Big Bertha"
German. Daughter of Friedrich Krupp
Cannon produced by Krupp Manufacturing during WW II named for her.
b. 1886 in Essen, Germany
d. Sep 21, 1957 in Essen, Germany
Source: *BioIn 4; NewCol 75*

Krutch, Joseph Wood
American. Author, Drama Critic
b. Nov 25, 1893 in Knoxville, Tennessee
d. May 22, 1970 in Tucson, Arizona
Source: *AmAu&B; Au&Wr 71; BiE&WWA; CnDAL; ConAmA; ConAmL; ConAu 1R, 25R, 4NR; CurBio 59, 70; DcLEL; EvLB; OxAmL; OxThe; Pen AM; REn; REnAL; TwCA, SUP; WebAB; WhAm 5; WhNAA*

Krylov, Ivan Andreyevich
Russian. Author
b. Feb 14, 1768 in Moscow, Russia
d. 1844 in Russia
Source: *BiD&SB; CasWL; ChPo S1; DcEuL; DcRusL; EuAu; EvEuW; Pen EUR; REn*

Kubasov, Valery Nikolaevich
Russian. Cosmonaut
b. Jan 7, 1935 in U.S.S.R.
Source: *IntWW 74; WhoWor 74*

Kubek, Tony (Anthony Christopher)
American. Baseball Player, Broadcaster
Shortstop, NY Yankees, 1957-65; broadcaster NBC, 1966--.
b. Oct 12, 1936 in Milwaukee, Wisconsin
Source: *BaseEn; BioIn 4, 6; WhoAm 82; WhoProB 73*

Kubelik, Jan
Czech. Musician
b. Jul 5, 1880 in Michle, Czechoslovakia
d. Dec 5, 1940 in Prague, Czechoslovakia
Source: *CurBio 41; WhAm 1*

Kubelik, Rafael
Czech. Conductor, Composer
b. Jun 29, 1914 in Bychory, Czechoslovakia
Source: *CurBio 51; IntWW 74; NewYTBE 71; Who 74; WhoMus 72; WhoWor 74*

Kubitschek (de Oliveira), Juscelino
Brazilian. Politician
b. Sep 12, 1902 in Diamantina, Brazil
d. Aug 22, 1976 in Rio de Janeiro, Brazil
Source: *CurBio 56; IntWW 74*

Kubla Khan
[Kublai Khan]
Mongolian. Leader of China
b. 1216
d. 1294
Source: *NewCol 75; WebBD 80*

Kubler-Ross, Elisabeth
American. Psychiatrist, Author
b. Jul 8, 1926 in Zurich, Switzerland
Source: *BioIn 12; ConAu 25R; CurBio 80; WhoAm 82*

Kubrick, Stanley
American. Motion Picture Director
Directed *20001: A Space Odyssey*, 1968; *A Clockwork Orange*, 1971.
b. Jul 26, 1928 in New York, New York
Source: *BiDFilm; BkPepl; ConAu 81; ConDr 73; CurBio 63; DcFM; FilmgC; IntMPA 75, 76, 77, 78, 79, 80, 81, 82; IntWW 74; MovMk; OxFilm; WebAB; Who 74; WhoAm 74, 76, 78, 80, 82; WhoWor 74; WomWMM; WorEFlm*

Kucinich, Dennis John
American. Former Mayor of Cleveland
b. Oct 8, 1946 in Cleveland, Ohio
Source: *CurBio 79; WhoAm 78*

Kuerti, Anton
Austrian. Musician
b. 1938 in Vienna, Austria
Source: *BioIn 11; WhoAm 82*

Kuh, Katherine
American. Editor
b. Jul 15, 1904 in Saint Louis, Missouri
Source: *ConAu 13R; WhoAm 76*

Kuhlman, Kathryn
American. Minister
b. 1910 in Concordia, Missouri
d. Feb 20, 1976 in Tulsa, Oklahoma
Source: *ConAu 57, 65; CurBio 74; NewYTBE 72; WhAm 6; WhoRel 75; WrDr 76*

Kuhn, Bowie Kent
American. Lawyer, Baseball Official
Baseball commissioner, 1969-83.
b. Oct 28, 1926 in Tacoma Park, Maryland
Source: *BioNews 74; CelR 73; CurBio 70; St&PR 75; WhoAm 74, 76, 78, 80, 82; WhoE 74; WhoProB 73*

Kuhn, Maggie (Margaret E)
American. Organization Executive
Founded Gray Panthers, 1971--.
b. Aug 3, 1905 in Buffalo, New York
Source: *BioIn 10, 11; CurBio 78; WhoAm 78, 80, 82*

Kuhn, Walt
American. Artist
b. Oct 27, 1880 in New York, New York
d. Jul 13, 1949 in White Plains, New York
Source: *DcAmB S4; DcCAA 71; WhAm 2*

Kuiper, Gerard Peter
American. Astronomer
b. Dec 7, 1905 in Harencarspel, Netherlands
d. Dec 24, 1973 in Mexico City, Mexico
Source: *AmM&WS 73P; ConAu 17R, 45, 2NR; CurBio 59, 74; WhAm 6; Who 74; WhoWor 74*

Kulish, Mykola
Ukrainian. Dramatist
b. 1892 in Kherson, Russia
d. 1942 in Siberia, U.S.S.R.
Source: *DcRusL; ModSL 2; Pen EUR*

Kulp, Nancy
American. Actress
Played Jane Hathaway on "The Beverly Hillbillies," 1962-71.
b. Aug 28, 1921 in Harrisburg, Pennsylvania
Source: *ForWC 70; WhoAm 74, 76, 78, 80, 82; WhoHol A*

Kumin, Maxine Winokur
American. Author
b. Jun 6, 1925 in Philadelphia, Pennsylvania
Source: *AnCL; AuBYP; AuNews 2; ConAu 1R, 1NR; ConLC 5; ConP 75; DrAF 76; DrAP 75; SmATA 12; WhoAm 82; WrDr 76*

Kun, Bela
Hungarian. Communist Dictator
b. 1886
d. 1939
Source: *BioIn 4, 8, 10; NewCol 75*

Kung, Hans
Swiss. Author, Theologian, Educator
b. Mar 19, 1928 in Sursee, Switzerland
Source: *ConAu 53; CurBio 63; OxGer; WhoWor 74*

Kunitz, Stanley Jasspon
[Dilly Tante, pseud.]
American. Author, Poet, Editor
b. Jul 29, 1905 in Worcester, Massachusetts
Source: *AmAu&B; CnE&AP; ConAu 41R; ConLC 6; ConP 70, 75; CurBio 43, 59; DrAP 75; DrAS 74E; IntWW 74; ModAL, SUP; OxAmL; Pen AM; PseudN; RAdv 1; REn; REnAL; WebE&AL; WhoAm 74, 76, 78, 80, 82; WhoTwCL; WhoWor 74; WhoWorJ 72; WorAu; WrDr 76*

Kuniyoshi, Yasuo
American. Artist
b. Sep 1, 1893 in Okayama, Japan
d. May 14, 1953
Source: *CurBio 53; DcCAA 71*

Kunstler, William Moses
American. Lawyer
b. Jul 7, 1919 in New York, New York
Source: *AmAu&B; ConAu 9R, 5NR; CurBio 71; NewYTBE 70; WhoAm 74, 76, 78, 80, 82; WhoE 74; WhoWorJ 72; WrDr 76*

Kunz, George
American. Football Player
b. Jul 5, 1947 in Fort Sheridan, Illinois
Source: *WhoAm 74; WhoFtbl 74*

Kunz, Erich
Austrian. Opera Singer
b. May 20, 1909 in Vienna, Austria
Source: *IntWW 74; WhoWor 74*

Kupchak, Mitch(ell)
American. Basketball Player
b. May 24, 1954 in Hicksville, New York
Source: *BioIn 12; OfNBA*

Kupcinet, Irv
American. Journalist
b. Jul 31, 1912 in Chicago, Illinois
Source: *CelR 73; WhoAm 74, 76, 78, 80, 82; WhoMW 74*

Kupka, Frank
Czech. Artist, Illustrator
b. 1871
d. 1957
Source: *BioIn 4, 5; NewCol 75*

Kupke, Frederick Lee
[The Hostages]
American. Former Hostage in Iran
b. 1948? in Oklahoma
Source: *NewYTBS 81*

Kuprin, Aleksandr Ivanovich
Russian. Author
b. Aug 1870 in Narovchat, Russia
d. Oct 25, 1938 in Leningrad, U.S.S.R.
Source: *CasWL; ConAu 104; DcRusL; EncWL; EvEuW; ModSL 1; Pen EUR; REn; TwCA, SUP; TwCW*

Kuralt, Charles Bishop
American. Broadcast Journalist
CBS News, 1959--; does "On the Road" segments.
b. Sep 10, 1934 in Wilmington, North Carolina
Source: *ConAu 89; IntMPA 82; WhoAm 74, 76, 78, 80, 82*

Kurelek, William
Canadian. Artist, Illustrator
b. Mar 3, 1927 in Whitford, AB
Source: *ConAu 49, 3NR; CreCan 1; SmATA 8; WhoAmA 73*

Kurland, Bob
"Foothills"
American. Basketball Player
First American to play on two Olympic basketball teams, 1948, 1952.
b. Dec 23, 1924 in Saint Louis, Missouri
Source: *WhoBbl 73*

Kurnitz, Harry
American. Dramatist, Screenwriter
b. Jan 5, 1909 in New York, New York
d. Mar 18, 1968 in Los Angeles, California
Source: *BiE&WWA; ConAu 25R; EncMys; FilmgC; WorEFlm*

Kurosawa, Akira
Japanese. Motion Picture Director
b. Mar 23, 1910 in Tokyo, Japan
Source: *BiDFilm; ConAu 101; ConLC 16; IntMPA 82; WhDW*

Kurt, Melanie
Austrian. Opera Singer
b. Jan 8, 1880 in Vienna, Austria
d. Mar 11, 1941 in New York, New York
Source: *InWom*

Kurtz, Efrem
Russian. Conductor
b. Nov 7, 1900 in Saint Petersburg, Russia
d. 1977
Source: *CurBio 46; IntWW 74; WhoMus 72; WhoWorJ 72*

Kurtz, Katherine
American. Author
b. Oct 18, 1944 in Coral Gables, Florida
Source: *ConAu 29R; WrDr 76*

Kurtz, Swoosie
American. Actress
b. Sep 6, in Omaha, Nebraska
Source: *BioIn 11; NewYTBS 81; WhoHol A*

Kurusu, Saburo
Japanese. Diplomat
b. 1888 in Yokohama, Japan
d. Apr 7, 1954 in Tokyo, Japan
Source: *CurBio 42, 54; REn*

Kurz, Selma
Austrian. Opera Singer
b. Nov 15, 1875 in Bielitz, Austria
d. May 10, 1933 in Vienna, Austria
Source: *InWom*

Kutuzov, Mikhail Ilarionovich
Russian. Field Marshal
b. Sep 5, 1745 in Saint Petersburg, Russia
d. Apr 16, 1813 in Bunzlau, Poland
Source: *McGEWB; NewCol 75*

Kuznetsov, Anatoli
[A Anatoli]
Russian. Author
b. Aug 18, 1929 in Kiev, U.S.S.R.
Source: *ConAu 89; IntWW 74; PseudN; WhoWor 74*

Kuznetsov, Vasili Vasilievich
Russian. Politician, Diplomat
b. Feb 13, 1901 in Sofilovka, Russia
Source: *IntWW 74*

Kwan, Nancy
Chinese. Actress
b. 1939 in Hong Kong, China
Source: *FilmgC; InWom; MotPP; MovMk; WhoHol A*

Ky, Nguyen Cao
Vietnamese. Vice-President
b. Sep 8, 1930 in Son Tay, Vietnam
Source: *CurBio 66; IntWW 74*

Kyd, Thomas
English. Dramatist
b. Nov 1558 in London, England
d. 1594 in London, England
Source: *Alli; AtlBL; BiD&SB; BrAu; CasWL; Chambr 1; ChPo; CnE&AP; CnThe; CroE&S; CrtT 1; CyWA; DcEnA; DcEnL; DcEuL; EvLB; McGEWD; MouLC 1; NewC; OxEng; OxThe; Pen ENG; REn; REnWD; WebE&AL*

Kylian, Jiri
Czech. Choreographer, Dancer
b. Mar 21, 1945 in Prague, Czechoslovakia
Source: *BioIn 12; CurBio 82*

Kyne, Peter Bernard
American. Author
b. Oct 12, 1880 in San Francisco, California
d. Nov 25, 1957 in San Francisco, California
Source: *AmAu&B; OxAmL; REnAL; TwCA, SUP; WhAm 3; WhNAA*

Kyprianou, Spyros
Cypriot. President
b. Oct 28, 1932 in Limassol, Cyprus
Source: *CurBio 79*

Kyriakides, Anastasios
Greek. Inventor
b. 1947?
Source: *BioIn 11*

Kyser, "Kay" (James Kern)
American. Musician, Band Leader
b. Jun 18, 1906 in Rocky Mount, North Carolina
Source: *BioNews 74; CurBio 41; FilmgC; PseudN; WhoHol A*

L

La Bara, Fidel
American. Boxer
b. Sep 29, 1905 in New York, New York
Source: *BioIn 10; WhoBox 74*

LaBelle, Patti
American. Singer
b. May 24, 1944 in Philadelphia, Pennsylvania
Source: *BioIn 10*

LaBern, Arthur Joseph
English. Author
b. Feb 28, 1909 in London, England
Source: *TwCCr&M*

Lablache, Luigi
Italian. Opera Singer
b. Dec 6, 1794 in Naples, Italy
d. Jan 23, 1858 in Naples, Italy
Source: *NewEOp 71*

LaBruyere, Jean de
"The Theophrastus of France"
French. Moralist, Satirist
b. Aug 16, 1645 in Paris, France
d. May 10, 1696 in Versailles, France
Source: *AtlBL; BbD; BiD&SB; CasWL; DcEuL; EuAu; EvEuW; OxEng; OxFr; Pen EUR; PseudN; REn*

Lacan, Jacques Marie Emile
French. Psychoanalyst
b. Apr 13, 1901 in Paris, France
d. Sep 9, 1981 in Paris, France
Source: *AnObit 1981; BioIn 11*

Lach, Elmer James
Canadian. Hockey Player
Center, Montreal Canadiens; Hall of Fame, 1966.
b. Jan 22, 1918 in Nokomis, SK
Source: *WhoHcky 73*

Lachaise, Gaston
American. Sculptor
b. Mar 19, 1882 in Paris, France
d. Oct 18, 1935 in New York, New York
Source: *AtlBL; DcAmB S1; DcCAA 71; NewCol 75; REn; WebAB; WhAm 1*

Laclos, (Pierre) Choderlos de
French. Author, General
b. Oct 19, 1741 in Paris, France
d. Nov 5, 1803 in Taranto, Italy
Source: *AtlBL; BiD&SB; CasWL; CyWA; DcEuL; EuAu; EvEuW; OxFr; Pen EUR; REn*

Lacoste, (Jean-) Rene
[The Four Musketeers]
"The Crocodile"
French. Tennis Player
b. Jul 2, 1905 in Paris, France
Source: *NewCol 75*

Lacroix, Georges
French. Illustrator
b. 1945
Source: *BioIn 10*

Ladd, Alan
American. Actor
Appeared in 150 films, including *Shane,* 1954.
b. Sep 3, 1913 in Hot Springs, Arkansas
d. Jan 29, 1964 in Palm Springs, California
Source: *BiDFilm; CmMov; CurBio 43, 64; FilmgC; MotPP; MovMk; OxFilm; WhAm 4; WhScrn 74, 77; WhoHol B; WorEFlm*

Ladd, Alan Walbridge, Jr.
American. Motion Picture Producer
b. Oct 22, 1937 in Los Angeles, California
Source: *BioIn 11; Dun&B 79; FilmEn; IntMPA 76, 77, 78, 79, 80, 81, 82; WhoAm 76, 78, 80, 82*

Ladd, Cheryl
[Cheryl Stoppelmoor; Mrs. Brian Russell]
American. Actress
Played Kris on "Charlie's Angels," 1977-81.
b. Jul 2, 1952 in Huron, South Dakota
Source: *BioIn 11; BkPepl; IntMPA 82; PseudN; WhoAm 82*

Ladd, Diane
[Rose Diane Ladner]
American. Actress
b. Nov 29, 1932 in Meridian, Mississippi
Source: *FilmEn; WhoHol A*

Ladd, George Trumbull
American. Psychologist, Philosopher
b. Jan 19, 1842 in Painesville, Ohio
d. Aug 8, 1921
Source: *Alli SUP; AmAu&B; AmBi; ApCAB; BiD&SB; DcAmAu; DcAmB; DcNAA; NewCol 75; OhA&B; REnAL; TwCBDA; WhAm 1*

Ladd-Franklin, Christine
American. Psychologist, Logician
b. Dec 1, 1847 in Windsor, Connecticut
d. Mar 5, 1930
Source: *AmBi; DcAmB; DcNAA; InWom; NewCol 75; NotAW; TwCBDA; WhAm 1*

Ladewig, Marion
American. Bowler
b. 1914?
Source: *BioIn 2, 9, 11*

Ladnier, Tommy
American. Jazz Musician
b. May 28, 1900 in Mandeville, Louisiana
d. Jun 4, 1939 in New York, New York
Source: *WhoJazz 72*

Laemmle, Carl, Sr.
American. Motion Picture Executive
b. Jan 17, 1867 in Laupheim, Germany
d. Sep 24, 1939 in Hollywood, California
Source: *AmBi; DcAmB S2; DcFM; FilmgC; OxFilm; WebAB; WhAm 1; WorEFlm; WhScrn 74, 77*

Laennec, Rene Theophile Hyacinthe
French. Inventor
Developed the stethoscope.
b. Feb 17, 1781 in Quimper, France
d. Aug 13, 1826 in Kerlouanec, France
Source: *AsBiEn; BiHiMed; BioIn 1; NewCol 75; WebBD 80*

Laessle, Albert
American. Sculptor
b. Mar 28, 1877 in Philadelphia, Pennsylvania
d. Sep 4, 1954
Source: *BioIn 3; WhAm 3*

LaFarge, Christopher Grant
American. Architect
b. Jan 5, 1862 in Newport, Rhode Island
d. Oct 11, 1938
Source: *AmAu&B; AmNov; ChPo; CnDAL; DcAmB S2; OxAmL; REn; REnAL; TwCA, SUP; TwCBDA; WhAm 1*

LaFarge, John
American. Artist
b. Mar 31, 1835 in New York, New York
d. Nov 14, 1910
Source: *AmAu; AmAu&B; AmBi; ApCAB; BbD; BiD&SB; ChPo, S1; DcAmAu; DcAmB; DcNAA; EarABI, SUP; EncAB-H; NewCol 75; OxAmL; TwCBDA; WebAB; WhAm 1*

Lafarge, Marie
[Marie Fortunee Capelle]
French. Murderer
b. 1816 in Picardy, France
d. 1852 in Ussat, France
Source: *BioIn 2, 3, 11; LookW*

LaFarge, Oliver
American. Author
b. Dec 19, 1901 in New York, New York
d. Aug 2, 1963 in Albuquerque, New Mexico
Source: *AmAu&B; AmNov; AuBYP; CnDAL; ConAu 81; CurBio 53, 63; DcLEL; LongCTC; OxAmL; Pen AM; REn; REnAL; TwCA, SUP; WhAm 4; WhNAA*

Lafayette, Marie Joseph Paul, Marquis
French. General, Statesman
b. Sep 6, 1757 in Chavaniac, France
d. May 20, 1834 in Paris, France
Source: *ApCAB; DcAmB; Drake; NewCol 75; OxFr; REn; REnAL; WebAB; WhAm H*

Laffan, William Mackay
American. Newspaper Publisher
b. Jan 22, 1848 in Dublin, Ireland
d. Nov 19, 1909
Source: *AmAu&B; AmBi; DcAmB; DcNAA; WhAm 1*

Laffer, Arthur Betz
American. Economist
b. Aug 14, 1940 in Youngstown, Ohio
Source: *BioIn 11; CurBio 82; WhoAm 80, 82; WhoS&SW 73*

Lafferty, Raphael Aloysius
American. Author
b. Nov 7, 1914 in Neola, Iowa
Source: *Au&Wr 71; ConAu 57*

Laffite, Jean
"The Pirate of the Gulf"
French. Pirate, Smuggler
b. Aug 29, 1780 in Bayonne, France
d. 1825
Source: *AmBi; DcAmB; NewCol 75; OxAmL; PseudN; WebAB; WhAm H*

Lafleur, Guy Damien
"The Flower"
Canadian. Hockey Player
Scored 50 or more goals in six consecutive seasons, 1974-80.
b. Sep 20, 1951 in Thurso, PQ
Source: *BioIn 10, 11; CurBio 80; PseudN; WhoAm 78, 80, 82; WhoHcky 73*

LaFollette, Bronson Cutting
American. Government Official
b. Feb 2, 1936 in Washington, DC
Source: *WhoAm 76, 78, 80, 82*

LaFollette, Robert Marion
American. Politician
b. Jun 14, 1855 in Primrose, Wisconsin
d. Jun 18, 1925 in Washington, DC
Source: *AmBi; BiDrAC; DcAmB; DcNAA; EncAB-H; REn; REnAL; TwCBDA; WebAB; WhAm 1*

LaFontaine, Jean de
French. Author
b. Jul 8, 1621 in Chateau Thierry, France
d. Apr 13, 1695 in Paris, France
Source: *AnCL; AtlBL; BbD; BiD&SB; CasWL; ChPo, S1, S2; CyWA; DcEuL; EuAu; EvEuW; NewC; OxEng; OxFr; Pen EUR; RComWL; REn; WhoChL*

LaFontaine, Sir Louis H
Canadian. Statesman
b. Oct 1807 in Boucherville, PQ
d. Feb 26, 1864 in Montreal, PQ
Source: *ApCAB; BbtC; DcNAA; Drake; OxCan*

Laforgue, Jules
French. Author
b. Aug 16, 1860 in Montevideo, Uruguay
d. Aug 20, 1887 in Paris, France
Source: *AtlBL; CasWL; ClDMEL; DcEuL; EuAu; EvEuW; OxFr; Pen EUR; REn*

Lagerfeld, Karl
German. Fashion Designer
Designer for House of Chloe.
b. Sep 10, 1938 in Hamburg, Germany
Source: *BioNews 74; CurBio 82; FairDF FRA; WhoFash; WorFshn*

Lagerkvist, Par
Swedish. Author
b. May 23, 1891 in Vaxjo, Sweden
d. Jul 11, 1974 in Stockholm, Sweden
Source: *CasWL; ClDMEL; CnMD; CnThe; ConAu 49, 85; ConLC 7, 10, 13; CurBio 52, 74; CyWA; EncWL; EvEuW; IntWW 74; McGEWD; ModWD; NewCol 75; Pen EUR; REn; REnWD; TwCA SUP; TwCW; WhAm 6; Who 74; WhoTwCL; WhoWor 74*

Lagerlof, Selma Ottiliana Lovisa
Swedish. Author
b. Nov 20, 1858 in Marbacka, Sweden
d. Mar 16, 1940 in Marbacka, Sweden
Source: *CarSB; CasWL; ClDMEL; CurBio 40; CyWA; EncWL; EvEuW; InWom; JBA 34; LongCTC; OxFilm; Pen EUR; REn; TwCA, SUP; TwCW; WhoChL; WhoLA; WhoTwCL*

Lagrange, Joseph-Louis
French. Mathematician, Astronomer
b. 1736 in Turin, Italy
d. 1813
Source: *BiD&SB; NewCol 75; OxFr; REn*

LaGuardia, Fiorello Henry
"Little Flower"
American. Mayor, Lawyer
Mayor of NY City, 1934-45; airport named for him.
b. Dec 11, 1882 in New York, New York
d. Sep 20, 1947 in New York, New York
Source: *BiDrAC; CurBio 40, 47; DcAmB S4; EncAB-H; REn; WebAB; WhAm 2; WhAmP*

Laguna, Ismael
Panamanian. Boxer
b. Jun 28, 1943 in Colon, Panama
Source: *BioIn 9; WhoBox 74*

Lahey, Frank Howard
American. Surgeon
b. Jun 1, 1880 in Haverhill, Massachusetts
d. Jun 27, 1953 in Boston, Massachusetts
Source: *CurBio 41, 53; DcAmB S5; WhAm 3*

Lahr, Bert
[Irving Lahrheim]
American. Actor, Comedian
Starred as Cowardly Lion in *The Wizard of Oz,* 1939.
b. Aug 13, 1895 in New York, New York
d. Dec 4, 1967 in New York, New York
Source: *BiE&WWA; CurBio 52, 68; EncMT; FamA&A; FilmgC; MotPP; MovMk; PlP&P; PseudN; WebAB; WhAm 4; WhScrn 74, 77; WhoHol B*

Lahr, John
American. Author, Critic
b. Jul 12, 1941 in Los Angeles, California
Source: *AmAu&B; ConAu 25R; DrAF 76; NotNAT; WhoAm 82; WhoThe 77; WrDr 76*

Laidler, Harry Wellington
American. Author, Economist
b. Feb 18, 1884 in Brooklyn, New York
d. Jul 14, 1970 in New York, New York
Source: *ConAu 5R, 29R, 5NR; CurBio 45, 70; WhAm 5; WhNAA*

Laine, Cleo
[Clementina Dinah Campbell; Mrs. John Dankworth]
English. Singer
b. Oct 28, 1927 in Southall, England
Source: *PseudN; Who 74; WhoMus 72; WhoWor 74*

Laine, Frankie
[Frank Paul LoVecchio]
American. Singer
b. Mar 30, 1913 in Chicago, Illinois
Source: *AmSCAP 66; CurBio 56; FilmgC; PseudN; WhoHol A*

Laing, Alexander Gordon
Scottish. Soldier, Explorer
b. Dec 27, 1793
d. Sep 26, 1826 in Timbuktu, Mali
Source: *BioIn 9; WebBD 80*

Laing, David
Scottish. Editor, Antiquary
b. Apr 20, 1793 in Edinburgh, Scotland
d. Oct 18, 1878 in Portobelo, Panama
Source: *Alli, SUP; BiDLA; BrAu 19; Chambr 3; ChPo; DcEnL; EvLB*

Laing, R(onald) D(avid)
Scottish. Psychiatrist, Author
b. Oct 7, 1927 in Glasgow, Scotland
Source: *CurBio 73; NewYTBE 72; CelR 73; Who 74; WhoAm 74, 76, 78, 80, 82; WrDr 76*

Laingen, (Lowell) Bruce
[The Hostages]
American. Diplomat
Charge d'affaires, Tehran, 1979; held hostage, 1979-81.
b. Aug 6, 1922 in Odin Township, Minnesota
Source: *BioIn 12; NewYTBS 79, 81; USBiR 74; WhoAm 74, 76, 78, 80, 82; WhoGov 72; WhoWor 78*

Laird, Melvin Robert
American. Former Government Official
Secretary of Defense, 1969-73.
b. Sep 1, 1922 in Omaha, Nebraska
Source: *BiDrAC; BiDrUSE; ConAu 65; CurBio 64; IntWW 74; NewYTBE 73; Who 74; WhoAm 74, 76, 78, 80, 82; WhoAmP 73; WhoGov 72; WhoS&SW 73; WhoWor 74*

Laird, Rick
[The Mahavishnu Orchestra]
Irish. Singer, Musician
b. in Dublin, Ireland
Source: *NF*

Lais
Greek. Courtesan
b. in Sicily
Source: *NewC*

Lajoie, Nap(oleon)
"Larry"
American. Baseball Player
Infielder, 1896-1916; Hall of Fame, 1937.
b. Sep 5, 1875 in Woonsocket, Rhode Island
d. Feb 7, 1959 in Daytona Beach, Florida
Source: *BaseEn; WhoProB 73*

Lake, Arthur
[Arthur Silverlake]
American. Actor
b. 1905 in Corbin, Kentucky
Source: *Film 1; FilmgC; IntMPA 75, 76, 77, 78, 79, 80, 81, 82; MovMk; PseudN; TwYS; WhoHol A*

Lake, Greg(ory)
[Emerson, Lake, and Palmer; King Crimson]
English. Singer, Musician
b. Nov 10, 1948 in Bournemouth, England
Source: *NF*

Lake, Simon
American. Engineer, Inventor
Designed submarines and the torpedo-boat used in WW I.
b. Sep 4, 1866 in Pleasantville, New Jersey
d. Jun 23, 1945 in Bridgeport, Connecticut
Source: *ApCAB X; CurBio 45; DcAmB S3; NatCAB 15; WebAB; WebAMB; WhAm 2*

Lake, Veronica
[Constance Frances Marie Ockleman]
American. Actress
Starred in *Samson and Delilah,* 1949.
b. Nov 15, 1919 in Brooklyn, New York
d. Jul 7, 1973 in Burlington, Vermont
Source: *BiDFilm; FilmgC; InWom; MotPP; MovMk; NewYTBE 71, 73; OxFilm; PseudN; WhScrn 77; WhoHol B; WomWMM; WorEFlm*

Laker, Freddie
English. Airlines Executive
b. Aug 6, 1922 in Canterbury, England
Source: *BioIn 10*

LaLanne, Jack
American. Physical Fitness Specialist
b. 1914 in San Francisco, California
Source: *BioIn 5, 10*

Lalique, Rene
French. Jeweler, Glassmaker
b. 1860
d. May 9, 1945 in Paris, France
Source: *BioIn 1, 10*

Lalo, Edouard Victor Antoine
French. Composer
b. Jan 27, 1823 in Lille, France
d. Apr 22, 1892 in Paris, France
Source: *NewCol 75; WebBD 80*

Lamantia, Philip
American. Author
b. Oct 23, 1927 in San Francisco, California
Source: *AmAu&B; ConP 70, 75; DrAP 75; Pen AM; WrDr 76*

Lamar, Joseph Rucker
American. Supreme Court Justice
b. Oct 14, 1857 in Elbert County, Georgia
d. Jan 2, 1916 in Washington, DC
Source: *AmBi; BiDSA; DcAmB; WebAB; WhAm 1*

Lamar, Lucius Q C
American. Senator, Supreme Court Justice
b. Sep 17, 1825 in Eatonton, Georgia
d. Jan 23, 1893 in Vineville, Georgia
Source: *AmBi; ApCAB; BiAuS; BiDConf; BiDrAC; BiDrUSE; DcAmB; TwCBDA; WebAB; WhAm H; WhAmP*

Lamarck, Jean Baptiste Pierre
French. Naturalist
b. Aug 1, 1744 in Bazentin, France
d. Dec 18, 1829 in Paris, France
Source: *BbD; BiD&SB; NewCol 75; OxEng; OxFr; REn*

LaMarr, Barbara
American. Actress
b. Jul 28, 1896
d. Jan 30, 1926 in Altadena, California
Source: *FilmgC; MotPP; MovMk; TwYS; WhScrn 74, 77; WhoHol B*

Lamarr, Hedy
[Hedwig Eva Marie Kiesler; Hedy Kieslerova]
American. Actress
b. Sep 11, 1913 in Vienna, Austria
Source: *BiDFilm; CelR 73; FilmgC; InWom; IntMPA 75, 76, 77, 78, 79, 80, 81, 82; MotPP; MovMk; OxFilm; PseudN; WhoAm 82; WhoHol A; WorEFlm*

Lamartine, Alphonse Marie Louis de Prat de
"The Narcissus of France"
French. Poet, Historian
b. Oct 21, 1790 in Macon, France
d. Mar 1, 1869 in Paris, France
Source: *AtlBL; BbD; BiD&SB; CasWL; DcBiA; DcEuL; EuAu; EvEuW; OxEng; OxFr; Pen EUR; PseudN; RComWL; REn*

La Marsh, Judy Verlyn
Canadian. Government Official, Lawyer
b. Dec 20, 1924 in Chatham, ON
d. Oct 27, 1980 in Toronto, ON
Source: *BioIn 6, 8, 10; ConAu 29R; CurBio 68, 81; IntWW 74, 75, 76, 77, 78; WhoAmW 66, 68, 70, 72, 74; WhoCan 73, 75, 77*

Lamas, Fernando
American. Actor, Director
b. Jan 9, 1925 in Buenos Aires, Argentina
d. Oct 8, 1982 in Los Angeles, California
Source: *BiE&WWA; FilmgC; IntMPA 75, 76, 77, 78, 79, 80, 81, 82; MGM; MotPP; MovMk; NewYTBS 82; WhoHol A; WhoWest 76, 78*

Lamas, Lorenzo
American. Actor
Son of Fernando Lamas and Arlene Dahl; plays Lance Cumson on "Falcon Crest."
b. 1957?
Source: *BioIn 11, 12*

Lamaze, Fernand
Natural Childbirth Advocate
Source: *NF*

Lamb, Lady Caroline Ponsonby
English. Author
b. Nov 13, 1785 in Roehampton, England
d. Jan 24, 1828 in London, England
Source: *Alli; BrAu 19; CasWL; Chambr 2; DcEnL; DcLEL; EvLB; InWom; NewC; OxEng; REn*

Lamb, Charles
[Elia; Upright Telltruth, Esq., pseuds.]
"The Mitre Courtier"
English. Essayist, Author
Wrote *Essays of Elia,* 1820-25; brother of Mary Ann Lamb.
b. Feb 10, 1775 in London, England
d. Dec 27, 1834 in Edmonton, England
Source: *Alli; AtlBL; BbD; BiD&SB; BiDLA; BrAu 19; CarSB; CasWL; Chambr 3; ChPo, S1, S2; CrtT 2; CyWA; DcEnA; DcEnL; DcEuL; DcLEL; EvLB; MouLC 3; NewC; OxEng; OxThe; Pen ENG; PseudN; RAdv 1; RComWL; REn; WebE&AL; WhoChL*

Lamb, Gil
American. Actor
b. Jun 14, 1906 in Minneapolis, Minnesota
Source: *FilmgC; IntMPA 75, 76, 77, 78, 79, 80, 81, 82; WhoHol A*

Lamb, Harold Albert
American. Author
b. Sep 1, 1892 in Alpine, New Jersey
d. Apr 9, 1962 in Rochester, New York
Source: *AmAu&B; AuBYP; ConAu 89, 101; JBA 51; OxAmL; REn; REnAL; TwCA, SUP; WhAm 4; WhNAA*

Lamb, Lawrence Edward
American. Cardiologist
b. Oct 13, 1926 in Fredonia, Kansas
Source: *AmM&WS 73P; ConAu 97; WhoAm 74, 76, 78, 80, 82; WhoS&SW 73*

Lamb, Mary Ann
"MB"
English. Author
In fit of temporary insanity, attacked, wounded father; stabbed, killed mother.
b. 1764 in London, England
d. May 20, 1847 in London, England
Source: *Alli; CarSB; ChPo, S2; DcEnA; DcEnL; DcLEL; NewC; OxEng; PseudN; WhoChL*

Lamb, Peter
South African. Tennis Player
b. 1959
Source: *BioIn 11*

Lambeau, "Curly" (Earl L)
American. Football Player, Coach
Started Green Bay Packers, 1919; Hall of Fame, 1963.
b. Apr 9, 1898 in Green Bay, Wisconsin
d. Jun 1, 1965
Source: *BioIn 6, 7, 8; PseudN; WhoFtbl 74*

Lambert, Constant
English. Composer
b. 1905 in London, England
d. Aug 21, 1951 in London, England
Source: *OxMus*

Lambert, Eleanor
[Mrs. Seymour Berkson]
American. Journalist
b. in Crawfordsville, Indiana
Source: *BioIn 7, 9, 10; BioNews 74; ForWC 70; ConAu 102; WhoAm 82; WorFshn*

Lambert, Jack (John Harold)
American. Football Player
b. Jul 8, 1952 in Mantua, Ohio
Source: *BioIn 11; NewYTBS 76; WhoAm 78, 80, 82*

Lambert, May
see: Churchill, May (Beatrice Desmond)

Lambert, Ward L
"Piggy"
American. Basketball Player, Coach
b. May 28, 1888 in Deadwood, South Dakota
d. Jan 20, 1958 in Lafayette, Indiana
Source: *BioIn 4, 9; PseudN; WhoBbl 73*

Lambsdorff, Otto
German. Cabinet Member, Lawyer
b. Dec 20, 1926 in Aachen, Germany
Source: *CurBio 80; IntWW 79*

Lamburn, Richmal Crompton
[Richmal Crompton, pseud.]
English. Author
b. Nov 15, 1890 in Bury, England
d. Jan 10, 1969
Source: *ConAu 25R; ConAu P-1; LongCTC; NewC; PseudN; SmATA 5; WhoChL*

Lamizana, Sangoule
African. Politician
President, council of ministers, 1967--.
b. 1916 in Dianra Tougan, Upper Volta
Source: *AfSS 78, 79; IntWW 74, 75, 76, 77, 78; NewCol 75; WhoGov 72; WhoWor 74, 76, 78*

Lamm, Richard D
American. Politician
b. Aug 3, 1935 in Madison, Wisconsin
Source: *WhoAm 82; WhoAmP 73*

Lamonica, Daryle Pat
American. Football Player
b. Jul 17, 1941 in Fresno, California
Source: *BioIn 8, 9, 10; WhoFtbl 74*

Lamont, Thomas William
American. Businessman, Philanthropist
b. Sep 30, 1870 in Claverack, New York
d. Feb 2, 1948 in Boca Grande, Florida
Source: *ChPo S1; CurBio 40, 48; DcAmB S4; DcNAA; WhAm 2*

La Motta, Jake (Jacob)
"Bronx Bull"
American. Boxer
Robert DeNiro portrayed him in movie *Raging Bull*, 1981.
b. Jul 10, 1921 in New York, New York
Source: *BioIn 10; PseudN; WhoBox 74*

Lamour, Dorothy
[Dorothy Kaumeyer]
American. Actress, Singer
Best known for "road" films with Bing Crosby and Bob Hope.
b. Dec 10, 1914 in New Orleans, Louisiana
Source: *BiDFilm; BioNews 74; CmMov; FilmgC; InWom; IntMPA 75, 76, 77, 78, 79, 80, 81, 82; MotPP; MovMk; OxFilm; PseudN; ThFT; WhoAm 74; WhoHol A; WorEFlm*

L'Amour, Louis Dearborn
[Tex Burns, pseud.]
American. Author
b. 1908 in Jamestown, North Dakota
Source: *AuNews 1, 2; ConAu 1R, 3NR; CurBio 80; PseudN; WhoAm 74, 76, 78, 80, 82; WrDr 76*

Lamoureux, Charles
French. Conductor
b. Sep 28, 1834 in Bordeaux, France
d. Dec 21, 1899 in Paris, France
Source: *OxFr*

Lampert, Zohra
American. Actress
b. 1936 in New York, New York
Source: *BiE&WWA; ForWC 70; MotPP; NotNAT; WhoAm 74; WhoHol A*

Lamperti, Francesco
Italian. Voice Teacher
b. Mar 11, 1813 in Savona, Italy
d. May 1, 1892 in Como, Italy
Source: *NewEOp 71*

Lampman, Archibald
Canadian. Poet
b. Nov 17, 1861 in Morpeth, ON
d. Feb 10, 1899 in Ottawa, ON
Source: *Alli SUP; BbD; BiD&SB; BrAu 19; CanWr; CasWL; Chambr 3; ChPo, S1, S2; DcLEL; DcNAA; OxAmL; OxCan; OxEng; Pen ENG; REnAL; WebE&AL*

Lampman, Evelyn Sibley
[Lynn Bronson, pseud.]
American. Children's Author
b. Apr 18, 1907 in Dallas, Oregon
d. Jun 13, 1980 in Portland, Oregon
Source: *AuBYP; ConAu 17R, 101; MorJA; PseudN; SmATA 4; WhoAmW 77; WhoPNW*

Lamy, Jean Baptist
American. Archbishop
b. Oct 14, 1814 in Lempdes, France
d. Feb 13, 1888 in Santa Fe, New Mexico
Source: *NewCol 75; WebAB*

Lancaster, Bruce Morgan
American. Diplomat
b. Oct 5, 1923 in Meridian, Mississippi
Source: *WhAm 4; WhoAm 74, 76, 78, 80, 82; WhoGov 72; WhoWor 74*

Lancaster, Burt
[Burton Stephen Lancaster]
American. Actor
Won Oscar, 1960, for *Elmer Gantry*.
b. Nov 2, 1913 in New York, New York
Source: *BiDFilm; BkPepl; CelR 73; CmMov; CurBio 53; FilmgC; IntMPA 75, 76, 77, 78, 79, 80, 81, 82; MotPP; MovMk; OxFilm; WhoAm 74, 76, 78, 80, 82; WhoHol A; WorEFlm*

Lance, (Thomas) Bert(ram)
American. Banker, Government Official
Director, OMB, Jan-Sep, 1977.
b. Jun 3, 1931 in Gainesville, Georgia
Source: *CurBio 77; WhoAm 82; WhoF&I 74; WhoS&SW 73*

Lancetti, Pino
Italian. Fashion Designer
b. 1932 in Perugia, Italy
Source: *WorFshn*

Lanchester, Elsa
[Elizabeth Sullivan]
English. Comedienne, Actress
b. Oct 28, 1902 in Lewisham, England
Source: *BiE&WWA; CelR 73; CurBio 50; FilmgC; IntMPA 75, 76, 77; MotPP; MovMk; NotNAT; OxFilm; PlP&P; PseudN; ThFT; Vers A; Who 74; WhoAm 74, 76, 78, 80, 82; WhoHol A; WhoThe 77; WhoWor 74*

Lancret, Nicolas
French. Artist
b. Jan 22, 1690 in Paris, France
d. Sep 14, 1743 in Paris, France
Source: *AtlBL; NewCol 75; OxFr*

Land, Edwin Herbert
American. Physicist, Inventor
Founded Polaroid Corp., 1937; developed Polaroid lenses, one-step photography.
b. May 7, 1909 in Bridgeport, Connecticut
Source: *AmM&WS 73P; CelR 73; CurBio 53; EncAB-H; IntWW 74; NewYTBE 72; WebAB; Who 74; WhoAm 74, 76, 78, 80, 82; WhoE 74; WhoF&I 74; WhoWor 74*

Landa, Diego de
Spanish. Bishop
b. 1524
d. 1579
Source: *ApCAB*

Landau, Ely A
American. Motion Picture Producer
b. Jan 20, 1920 in New York, New York
Source: *BioIn 10; FilmEn; FilmgC; IntMPA 75, 76, 77, 78, 79, 80, 81; NewYTET; WhoAm 74, 76, 78, 80, 82; WorEFlm*

Landau, Lev Davidovich
Russian. Scientist
b. Jan 22, 1908 in Baku, Russia
d. Apr 2, 1968 in Moscow, U.S.S.R.
Source: *CurBio 63, 68; NewCol 75; WhAm 5*

Landau, Martin
American. Actor
Starred in "Mission Impossible," 1966-69, "Space 1999," 1974-77.
b. 1933 in New York, New York
Source: *FilmgC; IntMPA 75, 76, 77; WhoAm 78; IntMPA 79, 80, 81, 82; MotPP; MovMk; WhoAm 74, 76, 78, 80, 82; WhoHol A; WhoWest 74*

Lander, Richard Lemon
English. Explorer
With brother, John, traced course of Niger River, 1830-31.
b. Feb 8, 1804 in Cornwall, England
d. Feb 16, 1834
Source: *BioIn 6; NewCol 75; WebBD 80*

Landers, Ann
[Esther Pauline Friedman Lederer]
"Eppie"
American. Advice Columnist
Twin sister of Dear Abby; column syndicated in over 1,000 newspapers.
b. Jul 4, 1918 in Sioux City, Iowa
Source: *AmAu&B; BkPepl; ConAu 89; CurBio 57; ForWC 70; InWom; NewYTBS 74; PseudN; WebAB; WhoAm 74, 76, 78, 80, 82; WhoAmW 77; WhoMW 74; WhoWor 74; WhoWorJ 72*

Landers, Audrey
American. Actress
Plays Afton Cooper on TV series "Dallas."
b. 1959?
Source: *NF*

Landers, Harry
American. Actor
b. 1921 in New York, New York
Source: *WhoHol A*

Landers, Judy
American. Actress
b. 1961? in Philadelphia, Pennsylvania
Source: *BioIn 12*

Landesberg, Steve
American. Actor, Comedian
Played Arthur Dietrich on TV series "Barney Miller."
b. in Bronx, New York
Source: *NF*

Landi, Elissa
[Elizabeth Marie Zanardi-Landi]
Italian. Actress
b. Dec 6, 1904 in Venice, Italy
d. Oct 31, 1948 in Kingston, New York
Source: *AmAu&B; DcNAA; FilmgC; HolP 30; InWom; MotPP; MovMk; PseudN; ThFT; WhScrn 74, 77; WhoHol B*

Landis, Carole
[Frances Lillian Mary Ridste]
American. Actress
b. Jan 1, 1919 in Fairchild, Wisconsin
d. Jul 5, 1948 in Brentwood Heights, California
Source: *DcNAA; FilmgC; MotPP; MovMk; PseudN; WhScrn 74, 77; WhoHol B*

Landis, Frederick
American. Judge
b. Jan 17, 1912 in Logansport, Indiana
Source: *CngDr 74; WhoAm 74, 76, 78, 80, 82; WhoAmP 73; WhoGov 72*

Landis, James McCauley
American. Educator, Government Official
b. Sep 25, 1899 in Tokyo, Japan
d. Jul 30, 1964
Source: *BioIn 1, 5, 6, 7, 8, 11; CurBio 42, 64*

Landis, Jessie Royce
[Jessie Royse Medbury]
American. Actress
b. Nov 25, 1904 in Chicago, Illinois
d. Feb 2, 1972 in Danbury, Connecticut
Source: *BiE&WWA; ConAu 33R; FilmgC; ForWC 70; MovMk; NewYTBE 72; PseudN; Vers B; WhAm 5; WhScrn 77; WhoHol B*

Landis, Kenesaw Mountain
American. Jurist, Baseball Commissioner
First commissioner of baseball, 1921-44; worked to keep game honest.
b. Nov 20, 1866 in Millville, Ohio
d. Nov 25, 1944 in Chicago, Illinois
Source: *CurBio 44, 45; DcAmB S3; EncAB-H; WebAB; WhAm 2; WhoProB 73*

Landon, Alf(red Mossman)
American. Businessman, Politician
Opposed, lost overwhelmingly to Franklin Roosevelt, 1936 election.
b. Sep 9, 1887 in West Middlesex, Pennsylvania
Source: *CurBio 44; EncAB-H; WebAB; Who 74; WhoAm 74; WhoAmP 73; WhoWor 74*

Landon, Michael
[Eugene Michael Orowitz]
American. Actor, Director, Scriptwriter
Played Little Joe on TV series "Bonanza," 1959-72.
b. Oct 31, 1937 in Forest Hills, New York
Source: *BioIn 10, 11; CurBio 77; IntMPA 77, 78, 79, 80, 81, 82; MotPP; PseudN; WhoAm 82; WhoHol A*

Landor, Walter Savage
English. Author, Poet
b. Jan 30, 1775 in Warwickshire, England
d. Sep 17, 1864 in Florence, Italy
Source: *Alli, SUP; AtlBL; BiD&SB; BiDLA; BrAu 19; CasWL; Chambr 3; ChPo, S1; CnE&AP; CrtT 2; CyWA; DcEnA, AP; DcEnL; DcEuL; DcLEL; EvLB; MouLC 3; NewC; OxEng; Pen ENG; RAdv 1; REn; WebE&AL*

Landowska, Wanda
Polish. Musician
b. Jul 5, 1877 in Warsaw, Poland
d. Aug 17, 1959 in Lakeville, Connecticut
Source: *CurBio 45, 59; InWom; WhAm 3*

Landreaux, Ken(neth Francis)
American. Baseball Player
b. Dec 22, 1954 in Los Angeles, California
Source: *BaseEn*

Landrieu, "Moon" (Maurice Edwin)
American. Former Government Official
Secretary of HUD, Carter, 1979-81.
b. Jul 23, 1930 in New Orleans, Louisiana
Source: *CurBio 80; WhoAm 74, 76, 78, 80, 82; WhoAmP 73; WhoS&SW 73*

Landru, Henri Desire
French. Murderer
b. 1869
d. 1922
Source: *BioIn 3, 5, 7, 9*

Landry, Tom (Thomas Wade)
American. Football Coach
Head coach, Dallas Cowboys since team's inception, 1960--.
b. Sep 11, 1924 in Mission, Texas
Source: *BioIn 7, 9, 10, 11; CurBio 72; NewYTBE 71; WhoAm 74, 76, 78, 80, 82; WhoS&SW 73*

Landseer, Charles
English. Artist
b. 1799 in London, England
d. 1879
Source: *BioIn 10; DcBrBI; DcVicP*

Landseer, Sir Edwin Henry
English. Artist
b. Mar 7, 1802 in London, England
d. Oct 1, 1873 in London, England
Source: *Alli; AtlBL; ChPo, S1, S2; NewC; REn*

Landsteiner, Karl
Austrian. Pathologist
b. Jul 14, 1868 in Vienna, Austria
d. Jun 26, 1943
Source: *BioIn 3, 5, 6, 8, 11; CurBio 43; NewCol 75*

Landy, John
Australian. Track Athlete
The second man to run mile in less than four minutes
b. Apr 12, 1930 in Melbourne, Australia
Source: *NewCol 75; WhoTr&F 73*

Lane, Abbe
American. Actress, Singer
b. 1932 in Brooklyn, New York
Source: *BioIn 4, 5, 9; InWom; WhoHol A*

Lane, Sir Allen
English. Publisher
Founded Penguin Books, 1935, first British paperback publisher.
b. Sep 21, 1902 in Bristol, England
d. Jul 7, 1970
Source: *BioIn 3, 6, 9; ConAu 29R; CurBio 54, 70*

Lane, Burton
[Burton Levy]
American. Composer
b. Feb 2, 1912 in New York, New York
Source: *AmSCAP 66; BiE&WWA; CurBio 67; EncMT; NewCBMT; NotNAT; PlP&P; PseudN; WhoAm 74, 76, 78, 80, 82; WhoThe 77*

Lane, Edward William
English. Author
b. Sep 17, 1801 in Hereford, England
d. Aug 10, 1876 in Worthing, England
Source: *Alli, SUP; BbD; BiD&SB; BrAu 19; Chambr 3; DcEnL; DcLEL; EvLB; NewC; OxEng*

Lane, "Fitz Hugh" (Nathaniel Rogers)
American. Artist
b. Dec 19, 1804 in Gloucester, Massachusetts
d. Aug 13, 1865
Source: *BnEnAmA; DcAmArt; McGEWB; NewYHSD*

Lane, Kenneth Jay
American. Jewelry Designer
b. Apr 22, 1932 in Detroit, Michigan
Source: *CelR 73; WhoAm 74, 76, 78, 80, 82; WorFshn*

Lane, Lola
[Dorothy Mulligan]
American. Actress, Singer
b. May 21, 1906 in Macy, Indiana
d. Jun 22, 1981 in Santa Barbara, California
Source: *BioIn 10; Film 2; MotPP; NewYTBS 81; PseudN; ThFT; What 4; WhoHol A*

Lane, Louisa
see: Drew, Louisa Lane

Lane, Mark
American. Lawyer
b. Feb 24, 1927 in New York, New York
Source: *BioIn 7, 11; WhoAm 78, 80, 82*

Lane, Priscilla
[Priscilla Mullican]
American. Actress, Singer
b. 1917 in Indianola, Iowa
Source: *MotPP; MovMk; PseudN; ThFT; WhoHol A*

Lane, Rose Wilder
American. Author
Daughter of Laura Ingalls Wilder.
b. Dec 5, 1887 in De Smet, South Dakota
d. Oct 30, 1968 in Danbury, Connecticut
Source: *AmAu&B; BioIn 4, 8; ConAu 102; InWom; REnAL; TwCA, SUP; WhAm 5; WhNAA*

Lane, Rosemary
[Rosemary Mullican]
American. Singer, Actress
b. Apr 4, 1914 in Indianola, Iowa
d. Nov 25, 1974 in Woodland Hills, California
Source: *BiDrLUS 70; MotPP; MovMk; NewYTBS 74; PseudN; ThFT; WhScrn 77; WhoHol B*

Lane, Sara
American. Actress, Singer
b. 1949 in New York, New York
Source: *InWom; OxThe; WhoHol A*

Lang, Andrew
[A Huge Longway]
"A Well Known Author"
Scottish. Author, Poet
b. Mar 31, 1844 in Selkirk, Scotland
d. Jul 20, 1912 in Banchor, Scotland
Source: *AnCL; AuBYP; BbD; BiD&SB; BiDPara; BrAu 19; CarSB; CasWL; Chambr 3; ChPo, S1, S2; DcBiA; DcEnA, AP; DcEuL; DcLEL; EvLB; JBA 34; LongCTC; ModBrL; NewC; OxEng; Pen ENG; PseudN; REn; Str&VC; WebE&AL; WhoChL*

Lang, Daniel
American. Author
b. May 30, 1915 in New York, New York
d. Nov 17, 1981 in New York, New York
Source: *AmAu&B; ConAu 5R, 4NR; WhoAm 74, 76, 78, 80*

Lang, Eddie
[Salvatore Massaro]
American. Jazz Musician
b. Oct 25, 1902 in Philadelphia, Pennsylvania
d. Mar 26, 1933 in New York, New York
Source: *AmSCAP 66; PseudN; WhoJazz 72*

Lang, Fritz
Austrian. Motion Picture Director
b. 1890 in Vienna, Austria
d. Aug 2, 1976 in Los Angeles, California
Source: *ConAu 69, 77; CurBio 43; DcFM; EncMys; FilmgC; IntMPA 75; IntWW 74; MovMk; OxFilm; REn; TwYS; WhoAm 74; WhoWor 74; WomWMM; WorEFlm*

Lang, Harold
English. Actor
b. 1923 in England
d. Nov 16, 1970 in Cairo, Egypt
Source: *BiE&WWA; EncMT; FilmgC; WhScrn 74, 77; WhoHol B*

Lang, Steve
see: April Wine

Langdell, Christopher Columbus
American. Legal Scholar
b. May 22, 1826 in New Boston, New Hampshire
d. Jul 6, 1906 in Cambridge, Massachusetts
Source: *AmBi; ApCAB; BiDAmEd; BioIn 3, 8; DcAmB; NatCAB 6; TwCBDA; WebAB; WhAm 1*

Langdon, Harry
American. Actor
b. Jun 15, 1884 in Council Bluffs, Iowa
d. Dec 22, 1944 in Los Angeles, California
Source: *BiDFilm; CmMov; CurBio 45; DcAmB S3; DcFM; FilmgC; MotPP; MovMk; OxFilm; TwYS; WhScrn 74, 77; WhoHol B; WorEFlm*

Langdon, John
American. Politician
b. Jun 26, 1741 in Portsmouth, New Hampshire
d. Sep 18, 1819 in Portsmouth, New Hampshire
Source: *AmBi; BiDrAC; BioIn 1, 6, 7, 8, 9; DcAmB; NatCAB 1, 11; TwCBDA; WhAm H*

Lange, Dorothea Nutzhorn
American. Photographer
b. 1895 in Hoboken, New Jersey
d. Oct 11, 1965 in San Francisco, California
Source: *BioIn 7, 8, 9, 10, 11; NewCol 75; WebAB; WhAm 4*

Lange, Hans
American. Conductor
b. Feb 14, 1884 in Istanbul, Turkey
d. Aug 13, 1960 in Albuquerque, New Mexico
Source: *BioIn 4, 5; WhAm 4*

Lange, Hope Elise Ross
American. Actress
b. Nov 28, 1933 in Reading Ridge, Connecticut
Source: *FilmgC; InWom; IntMPA 75, 76, 77, 78, 79, 80, 81, 82; MotPP; MovMk; WhoAm 74, 76, 78, 80, 82; WhoHol A*

Lange, Jessica
American. Actress
Starred in movies *King Kong,* 1976, *Tootsie,* 1982.
b. 1952? in Cloquet, Minnesota
Source: *BioIn 11; WhoHol A*

Langella, Frank
American. Actor
b. Jan 1, 1940 in Bayonne, New York
Source: *CurBio 80; FilmgC; IntMPA 82; NewYTBE 70; NotNAT; PlP&P A; WhoAm 80, 82; WhoHol A; WhoThe 77*

Langer, Walter C
American. Psychoanalyst
b. Feb 9, 1899 in Boston, Massachusetts
d. Jul 4, 1981 in Sarasota, Florida
Source: *NewYTBS 81*

Langford, Frances
[Frances Newbern]
American. Singer, Actress
b. Apr 4, 1913 in Lakeland, Florida
Source: *FilmgC; InWom; IntMPA 75, 76, 77, 78, 79, 80, 81, 82; MotPP; PseudN; ThFT; WhoHol A*

Langford, Sam
American. Boxer
b. Mar 4, 1886 in Weymouth, NS
d. Jan 12, 1956 in Cambridge, Massachusetts
Source: *BioIn 4, 10; WhoBox 74*

Langland, William
English. Author
Credited with writing *Piers Plowman,* greatest pre-Chaucerian poem.
b. 1332 in Shropshire, England
d. 1400 in London, England
Source: *AtlBL; BiD&SB; BrAu; CasWL; Chambr 1; CnE&AP; CroE&S; CrtT 1; CyWA; DcEnL; DcEuL; DcLEL; EvLB; MouLC 1; NewC; NewCol 75; OxEng; Pen ENG; RAdv 1; REn; WebE&AL*

Langley, Jane Pickens
American. Singer
b. in Macon, Georgia
Source: *CelR 73; CurBio 49; EncMT; InWom*

Langley, Noel
American. Screenwriter
b. Dec 25, 1911 in Durban, South Africa
d. Nov 4, 1980 in Desert Hot Springs, California
Source: *BioIn 2; BiE&WWA; ConAu 17R, 102; FilmgC; IntAu&W 76; IntMPA 77; NotNAT; ScF&FL 1, 2; WhThe; WhoHr&F; WhoThe 72*

Langley, Samuel Pierpont
American. Astronomer
b. Aug 22, 1834 in Roxbury, Massachusetts
d. Feb 27, 1906 in Aiken, South Carolina
Source: *Alli, SUP; AmBi; ApCAB; DcAmAu; DcAmB; DcNAA; NewCol 75; REnAL; TwCBDA; WebAB; WhAm 1*

Langmuir, Irving
American. Scientist, Physician, Engineer
b. Jan 31, 1881 in Brooklyn, New York
d. Aug 17, 1957 in Schenectady, New York
Source: *CurBio 40, 50, 57; EncAB-H; NewCol 75; WebAB; WhAm 3*

Langner, Nola
American. Author
b. Sep 24, 1930 in New York, New York
Source: *ConAu 37R; IlsBYP; IlsCB 1957; SmATA 8; WhoAmW 77*

Langsdorff, Hans
German. Naval Commander
b. 1890
d. 1939
Source: *WhWW-II*

Langton, Stephen
English. Archbishop of Canterbury
b. 1155
d. Jul 29, 1228
Source: *Alli; NewCol 75; REn*

Langtry, Lillie
[Emilie Charlotte LeBreton]
"The Jersey Lily"
English. Actress
b. 1852 in Isle of Jersey
d. 1929
Source: *BioIn 10; InWom; PseudN; WebBD 80*

Lanier, Allen
see: Blue Oyster Cult

Lanier, Bob (Robert Jerry, Jr.)
"Bob-A-Dob"
American. Basketball Player
Center, 1970--; scoring average of over 20 points per game.
b. Sep 10, 1948 in Buffalo, New York
Source: *NewYTBS 81; WhoAm 82; WhoBbl 73; WhoBlA 77*

Lanier, Sidney
American. Poet, Musician
b. Feb 3, 1842 in Macon, Georgia
d. Sep 7, 1881 in Lynn, North Carolina
Source: *Alli SUP; AmAu; AmAu&B; AmBi; ApCAB; AtlBL; BbD; BiD&SB; BiDSA; CarSB; CasWL; Chambr 3; ChPo, S1, S2; CnDAL; CnE&AP; CrtT 3; CyWA; DcAmAu; DcAmB; DcEnA AP; DcLEL; DcNAA; EvLB; MouLC 3; OxAmL; OxEng; Pen AM; RAdv 1; REn; REnAL; TwCBDA; WebAB; WebE&AL; WhAm H*

Lanin, Lester
American. Band Leader
b. Aug 26, 1911 in Philadelphia, Pennsylvania
Source: *CelR 73; WhoAm 74*

Lansbury, Angela Brigid
[Mrs. Peter Shaw]
American. Actress, Singer
b. Oct 16, 1925 in London, England
Source: *BiDFilm; BiE&WWA; BkPepl; CelR 73; CurBio 67; EncMT; FilmgC; InWom; IntMPA 75, 76, 77, 78, 79, 80, 81, 82; MotPP; MovMk; NewYTBS 74; NotNAT; OxFilm; WhoAm 82; WhoHol A; WhoThe 77*

Lansing, Joi
[Joi Loveland; Joyce Wasmansdoff]
American. Actress
b. 1930 in Salt Lake City, Utah
d. Aug 7, 1972 in Santa Monica, California
Source: *FilmgC; MotPP; NewYTBE 72; PseudN; WhScrn 77; WhoHol B*

Lansing, Robert
[Robert Howell Brown]
American. Secretary of State
b. Oct 17, 1864 in Watertown, New York
d. Oct 30, 1928 in Washington, DC
Source: *AmAu&B; AmBi; AmLY; BiDrUSE; DcAmB; DcNAA; EncAB-H; PseudN; WebAB; WhAm 1; WhNAA*

Lansing, Robert
American. Actor
b. Jun 5, 1929 in San Diego, California
Source: *BiE&WWA; FilmgC; MotPP; NotNAT; WhoAm 82; WhoHol A*

Lansing, Sherry Lee
American. Former Motion Picture Executive
First woman in charge of production at major film studio: 20th Century Fox, 1980-82.
b. Jul 31, 1944 in Chicago, Illinois
Source: *CurBio 81; IntMPA 78, 79, 80, 81, 82; WhoAm 80, 82*

Lansky, Meyer
[Maier Suchowljansky]
"Meyer the Bug"
American. Racketeer
Jailed only once for two-month period on gambling conviction.
b. Jul 4, 1902 in Grodno, Russia
d. Jan 15, 1983 in Miami Beach, Florida
Source: *BioIn 9; Blood; PseudN*

Lanson, "Snooky" (Roy)
American. Singer
b. 1919 in Memphis, Tennessee
Source: *CmpEPM; PseudN; RkOn; What 4*

Lanston, Tolbert
American. Inventor
Patented typesetting machine, 1887.
b. Feb 3, 1844 in Troy, Ohio
d. 1913 in Washington, DC
Source: *AmBi; DcAmB; NatCAB 13; NewCol 75*

Lantz, Walter
American. Cartoonist
Created Woody Woodpecker, 1941.
b. Apr 27, 1900 in New Rochelle, New York
Source: *FilmgC; IntMPA 75, 76, 77, 78, 78, 79, 80, 81, 82; WhoAm 74, 76, 78, 80, 82; WorECar; WorEFlm*

Lanvin, Bernard
French. Fashion Designer
b. Dec 27, 1935 in Neuilly, France
Source: *BusPN; WorFshn*

Lanvin, Jeanne
French. Fashion Designer
b. 1867 in Grasse, France
d. Jul 6, 1946 in Paris, France
Source: *BioIn 1, 5; CurBio 46; InWom; WorFshn*

Lanza, Anthony Joseph
American. Scientist, Physician, Engineer
b. Mar 8, 1884 in New York, New York
d. Mar 23, 1964 in New York, New York
Source: *BioIn 3, 5, 6; WhAm 4*

Lanza, Mario
[Alfredo Arnold Cocozza]
American. Opera Singer, Actor
Tenor; starred in MGM musical *The Great Caruso,* 1951.
b. Jan 31, 1921 in Philadelphia, Pennsylvania
d. Oct 7, 1959 in Rome, Italy
Source: *CmMov; FilmgC; MotPP; MovMk; OxFilm; PseudN; WhAm 3; WhScrn 74, 77; WhoHol B; WorEFlm*

Lao-Tzu
[Lao-Tse; Li Erh]
Chinese. Philosopher
b. 570BC
d. 490BC
Source: *BbD; BiD&SB; CasWL; DcOrL 1; Pen CL; PseudN; RComWL; REn*

Laparra, Raoul
French. Composer
b. May 13, 1876 in Bordeaux, France
d. Apr 4, 1943 in Paris, France
Source: *NewEOp 71; OxMus*

Lapchick, Joseph Bohomiel
American. Basketball Player, Coach
b. Apr 12, 1900 in Yonkers, New York
d. Aug 10, 1970 in Monticello, New York
Source: *BioIn 6, 7, 8, 9, 10; CurBio 65, 70*

Lapidus, Morris
American. Architect
b. Nov 25, 1902 in Odessa, Russia
Source: *ConAu 77; CurBio 66; WhoAm 74, 76, 78, 80, 82; WhoF&I 74; WhoS&SW 73; WhoWor 74; WhoWorJ 72*

Lapidus, Ted
French. Fashion Designer
b. Jun 23, 1929 in Paris, France
Source: *WorFshn*

LaPlace, Pierre-Antoine de
French. Dramatist
b. 1707
d. 1793
Source: *OxFr; WebBD 80*

Laplace, Pierre Simon, Marquis de
French. Astronomer, Mathematician
b. Mar 28, 1749 in Beaumont-en-Auge, France
d. Mar 5, 1827 in Paris, France
Source: *AsBiEn; BbD; BiD&SB; BioIn 1, 2, 3, 4, 8, 11; LinLib S; McGEWB; NewCol 75; OxFr; REn*

LaPlante, Laura
American. Actress
b. Nov 1, 1904 in Saint Louis, Missouri
Source: *FilmgC; InWom; ThFT; TwYS; WhoHol A; WhoThe 77*

Lapotaire, Jane
English. Actress
b. Dec 26, 1944 in Ipswich, England
Source: *WhoThe 72, 77, 81*

Lappe, Francis Moore
American. Nutritionist, Author
b. Feb 10, 1944 in Pendleton, Oregon
Source: *ConAu 37R*

LaRamee, Louise de
see: Ouida, pseud.

LaPread, Ronald
[The Commodores]
American Singer
b. 1948 in Tuskegee, Alabama
Source: *BkPepl*

Larcom, Lucy
American. Poet
b. Mar 5, 1824 in Beverly, Massachusetts
d. Apr 17, 1893 in Boston, Massachusetts
Source: *Alli, SUP; AmAu; AmAu&B; AmBi; AmWom; ApCAB; BiD&SB; Chambr 3; ChPo, S2; DcAmAu; DcAmB; DcLEL; DcNAA; Drake; InWom; NotAW; OxAmL; REnAL; TwCBDA; WhAm H*

Lardner, Dionysius
Irish. Author
b. Apr 3, 1793 in Dublin, Ireland
d. Apr 29, 1859 in Naples, Italy
Source: *Alli; ApCAB; BbD; BiD&SB; BrAu 19; Chambr 3; DcEnL; EvLB; NewC*

Lardner, Ring(gold Wilmer)
American. Author, Humorist
b. Mar 3, 1885 in Niles, Michigan
d. Sep 25, 1933 in East Hampton, New York
Source: *AmAu&B; AmBi; AmSCAP 66; AmWr; AtlBL; CasWL; CnDAL; CnMWL; ConAmA; ConAmL; CyWA; DcLEL; EncWL; LongCTC; ModAL, SUP; OxAmL; Pen AM; PseudN; RAdv 1; REn; REnAL; TwCA, SUP; TwCW; WebAB; WebE&AL; WhNAA; WhoTwCL*

Lardner, Ring Wilmer, Jr.
American. Screenwriter
b. Aug 19, 1915 in Chicago, Illinois
Source: *BioIn 2, 6, 9, 10, 11; ConAu 25R; Conv 1; DrAF 76; FilmEn; IntMPA 75, 76, 77, 78, 79, 80, 81; OxFilm; PolProf T; WhoAm 74, 76, 78, 80, 82*

Laredo, Jaime
Bolivian. Musician
b. Jun 7, 1941 in Cochabamba, Bolivia
Source: *CurBio 67*

Largo Caballero, Francisco
Spanish. Socialist Leader
b. 1869
d. Mar 23, 1946 in Paris, France
Source: *BioIn 1; CurBio 46*

Larkin, Oliver Waterman
American. Author, Educator
b. Aug 17, 1896 in Medford, Massachusetts
d. Dec 17, 1971 in Northampton, Massachusetts
Source: *AmAu&B; Au&Wr 71; ConAu 1R, 29R; CurBio 50, 71; NewYTBE 70; OxAmL; TwCA SUP; WhAm 5*

Larkin, Philip
English. Author, Librarian, Poet
b. Aug 9, 1922 in Coventry, England
Source: *Au&Wr 71; CasWL; ChPo S2; CnE&AP; CnMWL; ConAu 5R; ConLC 3, 5, 8, 9, 13, 18; ConP 70; EncWL; IntWW 74; LongCTC; ModBrL, SUP; NewC; Pen ENG; RAdv 1; REn; TwCW; WebE&AL; Who 74; WhoTwCL; WhoWor 74; WorAu; WrDr 76*

Laroche, Guy
French. Fashion Designer
b. 1923 in LaRochelle, France
Source: *BioIn 9; WorFshn*

LaRochefoucauld, Francois, Duc de
French. Author
b. Sep 15, 1613 in Paris, France
d. Mar 16, 1680 in Paris, France
Source: *AtlBL; BiD&SB; CasWL; CyWA; DcEuL; EuAu; EvEuW; NewC; OxEng; OxFr; Pen EUR; RComWL; REn*

Larocque, Michel
"Bunny"
Canadian. Hockey Player
b. Apr 6, 1952 in Hull, PQ
Source: *HocReg*

LaRocque, Rod
American. Actor
b. Nov 29, 1898 in Chicago, Illinois
d. Oct 15, 1969 in Beverly Hills, California
Source: *Film 1; FilmgC; MotPP; MovMk; TwYS; WhScrn 74, 77; WhoHol B*

LaRosa, Julius
American. Singer
b. Jan 2, 1930 in New York, New York
Source: *BiDAmM; BioIn 4*

LaRose, Rose
American. Burlesque Queen
b. 1913 in Brooklyn, New York
d. Jul 27, 1972 in Toledo, Ohio
Source: *BioIn 9; NewYTBE 72; WomPO 76*

Larouche, Lyndon H, Jr.
American. Labor Party Leader
b. Sep 8, 1922 in Rochester, New Hampshire
Source: *WhoAmP 77, 79*

Larousse, Pierre Athanase
French. Lexicographer, Grammarian
b. Oct 23, 1817 in Toucy, France
d. Jan 3, 1875 in Paris, France
Source: *BiD&SB; EvEuW; NewC; OxEng; OxFr*

Larrieu, Francie
American. Track Athlete
b. Nov 28, 1952 in Palo Alto, California
Source: *BioIn 11*

Larrocha, Alicia de
Spanish. Musician
b. May 23, 1923 in Barcelona, Spain
Source: *CurBio 68; InWom*

Larsen, Don(ald James)
American. Baseball Player
NY Yankee who pitched only perfect game in World Series history, Oct 8, 1956.
b. Aug 7, 1929 in Michigan City, Indiana
Source: *BaseEn; BioIn 4, 5, 7, 10; WhoProB 73*

Larsen, Roy Edward
American. Magazine Publisher
b. Apr 20, 1899 in Boston, Massachusetts
d. Sep 9, 1979 in Fairfield, Connecticut
Source: *ConAu 89; CurBio 50, 79; IntWW 74, 75, 76, 77, 78; NewYTBS 79; Who 74; WhoAm 74, 76; WhoF&I 74, 75, 77, 79; WhoGov 72; WhoWor 74, 78*

Larsen-Todsen, Nanny
Swedish. Opera Singer
b. Aug 2, 1884 in Hagby, Sweden
Source: *BioIn 1, 4; InWom*

Larson, John Augustus
American. Psychiatrist
Invented lie detector, 1921.
b. Dec 11, 1892 in Shelbourne, NS
d. Sep 21, 1965
Source: *AsBiEn; WhAm 4*

Larson, Nicolette
American. Singer
b. 1952?
Source: *BioIn 11*

Lartique, Jacques-Henri
French. Photographer, Artist
b. Jun 13, 1894 in Paris, France
Source: *BioIn 6, 7, 9, 10, 11; ConAu 33R; IntWW 74, 75, 76, 77, 78; NewCol 75; WhoWor 78*

Larue, Frederick Chaney
American. Watergate Participant
b. 1928 in Mississippi
Source: *BioIn 9, 10; NewYTBE 73*

LaRue, Jack
American. Actor
b. 1902 in New York, New York
Source: *FilmgC; MotPP; MovMk; WhoHol A*

LaRussa, Tony (Anthony, Jr.)
American. Baseball Manager, Lawyer
Manager, Chicago White Sox, 1979--.
b. Oct 4, 1944 in Tampa, Florida
Source: *BaseEn; WhoAm 82*

Lary, Frank Strong
"Bulldog"; "Mule"; "Yankee Killer"
American. Baseball Player
Pitcher, Detroit Tigers, 1954-63.
b. Apr 10, 1931 in Northport, Alabama
Source: *BaseEn; BioIn 6; PseudN; WhoProB 73*

LaSalle, Robert Cavelier, Sieur de
French. Explorer
b. 1643 in Rouen, France
d. Mar 19, 1687
Source: *ApCAB; BiDSA; DcAmB; Drake; NewCol 75; REn*

Lasch, Robert
American. Editor
b. Mar 26, 1907 in Lincoln, Nebraska
Source: *ConAu 102; WhoAm 78, 80, 82*

Lasker, Albert Davis
American. Advertising Executive
b. May 1, 1880 in Freiburg, Germany
d. May 30, 1952 in New York, New York
Source: *BioIn 1, 2, 3, 4, 5, 7, 8, 10; DcAmB S5; WebAB; WhAm 3*

Lasker, Edward
American. Chess Player, Author
b. Dec 3, 1885 in Kempen, Germany
d. Mar 23, 1981 in New York, New York
Source: *Au&Wr 71; BioIn 10; ConAu 5R, 103; WhNAA; WhoAm 74, 76; WrDr 76, 80*

Lasker, Emanuel
German. Chess Player
b. Dec 24, 1868
d. Jan 11, 1941 in New York, New York
Source: *CurBio 41*

Lasker, Joe
American. Artist, Illustrator
b. Jun 26, 1919 in Brooklyn, New York
Source: *ConAu 49, 1NR; IlsCB 1957; SmATA 9; WhoAm 82*

Lasker, Mary Woodward
American. Philanthropist
b. Nov 30, 1900 in Watertown, Wisconsin
Source: *CelR 73; CurBio 59; InWom; NewYTBS 74; WhoAm 74, 76, 78, 80, 82; WhoAmW 77; WhoGov 72; WhoWor 74*

Laski, Harold Joseph
English. Socialist Leader
b. Jun 30, 1893 in Manchester, England
d. Mar 24, 1950 in London, England
Source: *CurBio 41, 50; DcLEL; EvLB; LongCTC; NewC; REn; REnAL; TwCA, SUP; WhAm 2*

Lasky, Jesse L
American. Motion Picture Executive
b. Sep 13, 1880 in San Jose, California
d. Jan 13, 1958 in Beverly Hills, California
Source: *BiDFilm; CurBio 47, 58; DcFM; FilmgC; IntMPA 82; OxFilm; WebAB; WhAm 3; WorEFlm*

Lasky, Jesse Louis, Jr.
[Frances Smeed]
American. Author, Screenwriter
b. Sep 19, 1910 in New York, New York
Source: *AmAu&B; AmNov; Au&Wr 71; AuNews 1; CmMov; ConAu 1R, 4NR; DcFM; IntMPA 75, 76, 77; PseudN; REnAL*

Lasky, Victor
American. Journalist, Author
b. Jan 7, 1918 in Liberty, New York
Source: *AmAu&B; AuNews 1; BioNews 75; CelR 73; ConAu 5R; WhoAm 74, 76, 78, 80; WhoE 74; WhoWorJ 72; WrDr 76*

Lasorda, Tom (Thomas Charles)
American. Baseball Player, Manager
LA Dodgers, manager, 1977--.
b. Sep 22, 1927 in Norristown, Pennsylvania
Source: *AmCath 80; BaseEn; BioIn 11; WhoAm 78, 80, 82; WhoWest 80*

Lassale, Jean
French. Opera Singer
b. Dec 14, 1847 in Lyons, France
d. Sep 7, 1909 in Paris, France
Source: *NewEOp 71*

Lassalle, Ferdinand
German. Socialist
Disciple of Karl Marx; founded German Social Democratic Party.
b. Apr 11, 1825 in Breslau, Germany
d. Aug 28, 1864
Source: *BiD&SB; DcEuL; McGEWB; NewCol 75; OxGer; REn*

Lasser, Jacob Kay
American. Accountant, Tax Authority
b. Oct 7, 1896 in Newark, New Jersey
Source: *BioIn 1, 2, 3, 5; CurBio 46, 54*

Lasser, Louise
American. Actress
Starred in "Mary Hartman, Mary Hartman"; was married to Woody Allen.
b. 1940 in New York
Source: *BioIn 10, 11; BkPepl; CurBio 76; IntMPA 82; MovMk; NewYTBE 71; NewYTBS 76; WhoAm 78, 80, 82; WhoHol A*

Lassus, Orlandus de
[Roland Delattre; Orlando di Lasso]
Belgian. Composer
b. 1532 in Mons, Netherlands
d. Jun 14, 1594 in Munich, Germany
Source: *AtlBL; NewCol 75; PseudN; REn*

Lasswell, Fred
American. Cartoonist
b. 1916 in Kennett, Missouri
Source: *BioIn 6; WhoAm 82; WorECom*

Laszlo, Magda
Hungarian. Opera Singer
b. 1919 in Marosvasarhely, Hungary
Source: *NewEOp 71*

Laszlo, Miklos
American. Composer, Dramatist
b. 1904?
d. Apr 19, 1973
Source: *ConAu 41R; NewYTBE 73*

Lateiner, Jacob
American. Musician
b. May 31, 1928 in Havana, Cuba
Source: *WhoAm 74, 76, 78, 80, 82; WhoMus 72; WhoWor 74*

Latham, Jean Lee
[Rose Champion, joint pseud.; Janice Gard; Julian Lee]
American. Author
b. Apr 19, 1902 in Buckhannon, West Virginia
Source: *AmAu&B; Au&Wr 71; AuBYP; AuNews 1; ConAu 5R; ConLC 12; CurBio 56; MorBMP; MorJA; PseudN; SmATA 2; Str&VC; WhoAm 74, 76, 78, 80, 82*

Lathen, Emma, joint pseud.
[Mary J Latis; Martha Hennisart]
American. Authors
Source: *ConLC 2; EncMys; PseudN*

Lathrop, Rose Hawthorne
[Mother Mary Alphonsa]
American. Philanthropist
b. May 20, 1851 in Lenox, Massachusetts
d. Jul 9, 1926 in Hawthorne, New York
Source: *AmAu&B; AmBi; AmWom; ApCAB; BbD; BiD&SB; ChPo, S1; DcAmAu; DcAmB; DcNAA; InWom; NewCol 75; NotAW; REn; REnAL; TwCBDA; WhAm 1*

Latimer, Hugh
"The Apostle of England"
English. Minister, Protestant Martyr
b. 1485 in Thurcaston, England
d. Oct 16, 1555 in Oxford, England
Source: *Alli; BbD; BiD&SB; BrAu; Chambr 1; DcEnL; EvLB; NewC; NewCol 75; OxEng; PseudN; REn; WebE&AL*

Latimer, Lewis Howard
American. Inventor
b. 1848
d. 1928
Source: *BioIn 9, 10; BlkAW*

LaTour, George Dumesnil de
French. Artist
b. 1593 in Vic sur Seille, France
d. Jan 30, 1652 in Luneville, France
Source: *AtlBL; BioIn 10; McGDA; McGEWB; NewCol 75; WhDW*

LaTour D'Auvergne, Theophile de
French. Soldier
b. Nov 23, 1743 in Carhaix, France
d. Jun 27, 1800 in Oberhausen, Bavaria
Source: *NewCol 75*

Latrobe, Benjamin Henry
American. Architect
b. May 1, 1764 in Fulneck, England
d. Sep 3, 1820 in New Orleans, Louisiana
Source: *Alli; AmBi; ApCAB; AtlBL; BiAuS; BiDSA; DcAmB; Drake; EncAB-H; OxAmL; REnAL; TwCBDA; WebAB; WhAm H*

Lattimore, Owen
American. Sinologist, Author
b. Jul 29, 1900 in Washington, DC
Source: *AmAu&B; ConAu 97; CurBio 45, 64; IntWW 74; NewCol 75; OxAmL; REnAL; TwCA SUP; Who 74; WhoAm 74, 76, 78, 80, 82; WhoWor 74*

Lattimore, Richmond Alexander
American. Translator, Educator, Poet
b. May 6, 1906 in Paotingfu, China
Source: *AmAu&B; ConAu 1NR; ConLC 3; ConP 70, 75; DrAS 74F; ModAL, SUP; NotNAT; OxAmL; RAdv 1; REnAL; TwCA SUP; WhoAm 74; WhoWor 74; WrDr 76*

Lattre de Tassigny, Jean de
French. Army Officer
b. Feb 2, 1889 in France
d. Jan 11, 1952
Source: *CurBio 45, 52; WhAm 3*

Lattuada, Felice
Italian. Opera Composer
b. Feb 5, 1882 in Morimondo, Italy
Source: *NewEOp 71*

Latzo, Pete
[Young Clancy]
American. Boxer
b. Aug 1, 1902 in Coloraine, Pennsylvania
d. 1968
Source: *PseudN; WhoBox 74*

Laubenthal, Rudolf
German. Opera Singer
b. Mar 10, 1886 in Dusseldorf, Germany
Source: *NewEOp 71*

Lauck, Chester H
[Lum 'n Abner]
American. Radio Performer
b. 1902
d. Feb 21, 1980 in Hot Springs, Arkansas
Source: *WhoHol A*

Laud, William
[The Hocuspocus"; "The Little Vermin"; "Parva Laus"; "The Urchin"]
English. Archbishop
b. Oct 7, 1573 in Reading, England
d. Jan 10, 1645 in London, England
Source: *Alli; BiD&SB; BrAu; NewC; OxEng; PseudN; REn*

Lauda, Niki (Nikolaus-Andreas)
Austrian. Auto Racer, Author
World champion, Formula 1 Grand Prix, 1975, 1977.
b. Feb 22, 1949 in Vienna, Austria
Source: *BioIn 10, 11; CurBio 80; IntWW 81; NewYTBS 75*

Lauder, Estee
American. Cosmetics Executive
Chairman, Estee Lauder, Inc., 1946--.
b. in Vienna, Austria
Source: *BioIn 9, 10, 11; BioNews 75; BusPN; CelR 73; WhoAm 76, 78, 80, 82; WhoAmW 66, 68, 70, 72, 79, 81*

Lauder, Sir Harry MacLennan
[Harry MacLennan]
"The Laird of the Halls"
Scottish. Singer
b. Aug 4, 1870 in Portobello, Scotland
d. Feb 25, 1950 in Lenarkshire, Scotland
Source: *FilmgC; NewC; OxThe; PseudN; WhAm 4; WhScrn 74, 77; WhoHol B*

Lauderdale, Duke of
see: Maitland, John

Laughlin, James, IV
American. Editor, Poet, Publisher
b. Oct 30, 1914 in Pittsburgh, Pennsylvania
Source: *AmAu&B; BioIn 2, 7, 9; ConAu 21R; ConP 70, 75; CurBio 82; IntWWP 77; REnAL; WhoAm 74, 76, 78, 80, 82; WhoWor 74; WrDr 76, 80*

Laughlin, James Laurence
American. Economist
b. Apr 2, 1850 in Deerfield, Ohio
d. Nov 28, 1933 in Jaffrey, New Hampshire
Source: *Alli SUP; AmBi; ApCAB; BiD&SB; BioIn 8, 11; DcAmAu; DcAmB S1; NatCAB 11, 24; NewCol 75; OhA&B; TwCBDA; WhAm 1*

Laughlin, Tom
[T C Frank, pseud.]
American. Actor, Director, Producer, Writer
Starred in *Billy Jack,* 1971, *The Trial of Billy Jack,* 1974.
b. 1938 in Minneapolis, Minnesota
Source: *BioIn 9, 10; FilmEn; FilmgC; IntMPA 76, 77, 78, 79, 80, 81; WhoHol A*

Laughton, Charles
English. Actor
Won Oscar, 1933, for *The Private Lives of Henry VIII.*
b. Jul 1, 1899 in Scarborough, England
d. Dec 15, 1962 in Los Angeles, California
Source: *BiDFilm; CmMov; CurBio 48, 63; FamA&A; FilmgC; MotPP; MovMk; OxFilm; WhAm 4; WhScrn 74, 77; WhoHol B; WorEFlm*

Laurel, Alicia Bay
American. Author, Illustrator
b. May 14, 1949 in Los Angeles, California
Source: *ConAu 41R; NewYTBE 71*

Laurel, Stan
[Arthur Stanley Jefferson; Laurel and Hardy]
American. Comedian, Actor
Joined with Oliver Hardy, 1926; made over 200 films.
b. Jun 16, 1890 in Ulverston, England
d. Feb 23, 1965 in Santa Monica, California
Source: *BiDFilm; CmMov; Film 1; FilmgC; MotPP; MovMk; OxFilm; PseudN; TwYS; WebAB; WhScrn 74, 77; WhoHol B; WorEFlm*

Laurel and Hardy
see: Hardy, Oliver; Laurel, Stan

Lauren, Ralph
American. Fashion Designer
Head of Polo Fashions, Inc., 1969--.
b. Oct 14, 1939 in New York, New York
Source: *BioIn 10, 11; CurBio 80; WhoAm 82; WhoFash; WorFshn*

Laurence, Margaret Jean
Canadian. Author
b. Jul 18, 1926 in Neepawa, MB
Source: *Au&Wr 71; BioIn 8, 10, 11; CaW; CanWW 70, 79; CanWr; ConAu 5R; ConLC 3, 6, 13; ConNov 72, 76; CreCan 1; IntAu&W 76, 77; ModCmwL; OxCan, SUP; WorAu 1970; WrDr 76, 80*

Laurencin, Marie
French. Artist
b. 1885 in Paris, France
d. 1956 in Paris, France
Source: *McGDA; WomArt*

Laurens, Henry
American. Merchant, Statesman
b. Mar 26, 1724 in Charleston, South Carolina
d. Dec 8, 1792 in Charleston, South Carolina
Source: *AmBi; ApCAB; BiAuS; BiDrAC; BiDrUSE; DcAmB; Drake; EncAB-H; OxAmL; REnAL; TwCBDA; WebAB; WhAm H; WhAmP*

Laurents, Arthur
American. Author, Motion Picture Director
Wrote *The Way We Were,* 1972, *The Turning Point,* 1977, both adapted to film.
b. Jul 14, 1918 in New York, New York
Source: *ConAu 17R; ConDr 73; EncMT; FilmgC; IntMPA 75, 76, 77, 78, 79, 80, 81, 82; McGEWD; NewCBMT; NotNAT; OxAmL; Pen AM; REnAL; TwCA SUP; WhoAm 74, 76, 78, 80, 82; WhoE 74; WhoThe 77; WhoWor 74; WrDr 76*

Lauri-Volpi, Giacoma
Italian. Opera Singer
b. Dec 11, 1894 in Rome, Italy
Source: *BioIn 10; NewEOp 71*

Laurie, Annie
Scottish. Heroine
Subject of song written by man she rejected in marriage.
b. 1682
d. 1764
Source: *InWom; REn*

Laurie, Joe, Jr.
American. Radio Comedian
b. 1892 in New York, New York
d. Apr 29, 1954 in New York, New York
Source: *BioIn 2*

Laurie, Piper
[Rosetta Jacobs]
American. Actress
b. Jan 22, 1932 in Detroit, Michigan
Source: *CmMov; FilmgC; InWom; IntMPA 75, 76, 77, 78, 79, 80, 81, 82; MotPP; MovMk; PseudN; WhoAm 74, 76, 78, 80, 82; WhoHol A; WorEFlm*

Laurier, Sir Wilfrid
Canadian. Prime Minister
First French-Canadian to be Prime Minister, 1896-1911.
b. Nov 20, 1841 in Saint Lin, PQ
d. Feb 17, 1919 in Ottawa, ON
Source: *ApCAB; BioIn 1, 4, 7, 8, 9, 11; LinLib L, S; MacDCB 78; McGEWB; NewCol 75; OxCan*

Lausche, Frank John
American. Politician, Lawyer
b. Nov 14, 1895 in Cleveland, Ohio
Source: *BiDrAC; CurBio 46, 58; WhoAmP 73*

Lauterbach, Steven
[The Hostages]
American. Former Hostage in Iran
b. 1952?
Source: *BioIn 12; NewYTBS 81*

Lautreamont, Comte de, pseud.
[Isidore Lucien Ducasse]
French. Poet
b. Apr 4, 1846 in Montevideo, Uruguay
d. Nov 24, 1870 in Paris, France
Source: *CasWL; NewCol 75; Pen EUR; PseudN; REn*

Laval, Pierre
"Mossbank"
French. Politician, Nazi Collaborator
b. Jun 28, 1883 in Chatelden, France
d. Oct 15, 1945
Source: *BioIn 6, 7, 8; CurBio 40, 45; PseudN; REn*

Lavalle, Paul
American. Conductor, Composer
b. Sep 6, 1908 in Beacon, New York
Source: *AmSCAP 66; IntMPA 75; WhoAm 74*

Laver, James
[Jacques Reval, pseud.]
English. Author, Critic
b. Mar 14, 1899 in Liverpool, England
d. Jun 3, 1975 in London, England
Source: *Au&Wr 71; BiE&WWA; ConAu 1R, 57, 3NR; EvLB; IntWW 74; LongCTC; ModBrL; NewC; OxThe; Pen ENG; PseudN; TwCA, SUP; Who 74; WhoWor 74; WorFshn*

Laver, Rod(ney George)
"Rocket"
Australian. Tennis Player
First player to win double Grand Slam, 1962, 1969.
b. Aug 9, 1938 in Queensland, Australia
Source: *CelR 73; CurBio 63; IntWW 76, 77, 78, 79, 80, 81; NewYTBE 71; NewYTBS 74, 82; WhoAm 78, 80, 82; WhoWor 74, 78*

Laveran, Alphonse
French. Physician
b. Jun 18, 1845
d. May 18, 1922
Source: *AsBiEn; BioIn 3, 4, 6; DcScB; NewCol 75*

Lavery, Sir John
Irish. Artist
b. Mar 1856 in Belfast, Northern Ireland
d. Jan 10, 1941 in Kilmoganny, Ireland
Source: *CurBio 41*

Lavigne, "Kid" (George)
"The Saginaw Kid"
American. Boxer
b. Dec 6, 1869 in Saginaw, Michigan
d. Apr 6, 1936 in Detroit, Michigan
Source: *PseudN; WhoBox 74*

Lavin, Linda
American. Actress
Starred in TV series "Alice," 1976--.
b. Oct 15, 1939 in Portland, Maine
Source: *IntMPA 82; NotNAT; WhoAm 78, 80, 82; WhoAmW 79; WhoHol A; WhoThe 72, 77*

Lavis, Gilson
see: Squeeze

Lavoisier, Antoine Laurent
French. Chemist
b. Aug 1743 in Paris, France
d. May 8, 1794 in Paris, France
Source: *BbD; BiD&SB; NewCol 75; OxFr; REn*

Lavroky, Leonid
Russian. Choreographer
b. 1905
d. 1967
Source: *BioIn 8*

Law, Andrew Bonar
British. Statesman
b. Sep 16, 1858 in Kingston, ON
d. Oct 30, 1923 in London, England
Source: *BioIn 2; NewCol 75*

Law, John Philip
American. Actor
b. Sep 7, 1937 in Hollywood, California
Source: *CelR 73; FilmgC; IntMPA 75, 76, 77, 78, 79, 80, 81, 82; MotPP; WhoAm 82; WhoHol A*

Law, Vernon Sanders
"Deacon"
American. Baseball Player
b. Mar 12, 1930 in Meridian, Iowa
Source: *BaseEn; BioIn 5, 6; CurBio 61; PseudN; WhoProB 73*

Law, William
English. Churchman, Mystic
b. 1686 in King's Cliffe, England
d. 1761 in King's Cliffe, England
Source: *Alli; BrAu; CasWL; Chambr 2; DcEnA; DcEnL; DcEuL; EvLB; NewC; OxEng; REn; WebE&AL*

Lawes, Lewis Edward
American. Criminologist
b. Sep 13, 1883 in Elmira, New York
d. Apr 23, 1947 in Garrison, New York
Source: *AmAu&B; CurBio 41, 47; DcAmB S4; DcNAA; WebAB; WhAm 2; WhNAA; WhScrn 74, 77*

Lawford, Pat(ricia Kennedy)
American. Civic Leader
Sister of John F Kennedy; was married to Peter Lawford.
Source: *NF*

Lawford, Peter
English. Actor
Played Nick Charles in TV series "The Thin Man," 1957-59.
b. Sep 7, 1923 in London, England
Source: *CelR 73; FilmgC; IntMPA 75, 76, 77, 78, 79, 80, 81, 82; MotPP; MovMk; OxFilm; WhoAm 74, 76, 78, 80, 82; WhoHol A; WorEFlm*

Lawrence, Barbara
American. Actress
b. Feb 24, 1930 in Carnegie, Oklahoma
Source: *FilmgC; IntMPA 75, 76, 77, 78, 79, 80, 81, 82; MotPP*

Lawrence, Bill
American. Radio, TV Producer, Director
Source: *NewYTET*

Lawrence, Carol
[Carol Maria Laraia]
American. Singer, Actress
b. Sep 5, 1935 in Melrose Park, Illinois
Source: *BiE&WWA; BioNews 74; CurBio 61; EncMT; InWom; MotPP; PseudN; WhoAm 74; WhoHol A; WhoThe 77*

Lawrence, David
American. Journalist
b. Dec 25, 1888 in Philadelphia, Pennsylvania
d. Feb 11, 1973
Source: *AmAu&B; ConAu 41R, 102; CurBio 43, 73; REnAL; WhAm 5; WhoS&SW 73*

Lawrence, D(avid) H(erbert)
English. Author
Wrote *Lady Chatterley's Lover,* 1928, banned in US, England many years.
b. Sep 11, 1885 in Eastwood, England
d. Mar 2, 1930 in Vence, France
Source: *AtlBL; CnE&AP; CnMWL; CnThe; CyWA; FilmgC; LongCTC; ModBrL, SUP; ModWD; NewC; OxAmL; Pen ENG; RAdv 1; RComWL; REn; REnAL; TwCW; WebE&AL; WebBD 80; WhoTwCL*

Lawrence, Elliot
[Elliot Lawrence Broza]
American. Composer, Conductor
b. Feb 14, 1925 in Philadelphia, Pennsylvania
Source: *AmSCAP 66; BiE&WWA; NotNAT; PseudN*

Lawrence, Ernest Orlando
American. Scientist, Physicist, Engineer
Won Nobel Prize, 1939, for 1930 invention of cyclotron.
b. Aug 8, 1901 in Canton, South Dakota
d. Aug 27, 1958 in Palo Alto, California
Source: *CurBio 40, 52, 58; EncAB-H; NewCol 75; WebAB; WhAm 3*

Lawrence, Frieda
[Frieda von Richthofen]
German. Wife of D H Lawrence
b. 1879
d. 1956
Source: *REn*

Lawrence, Gertrude
[Gertrud Alexandra Dagmar Lawrence Klasen]
English. Actress
b. Jul 4, 1901 in London, England
d. Sep 6, 1952 in New York, New York
Source: *CurBio 40, 52; DcAmB S5; EncMT; FamA&A; FilmgC; InWom; OxFilm; NewC; OxThe; PseudN; ThFT; WhAm 3; WhScrn 74, 77; WhoHol B; WorEFlm*

Lawrence, Sir Henry Montgomery
British. General, Colonial Administrator
b. 1806
d. Jul 1857 in Lucknow, India
Source: *Alli SUP; BioIn 4, 5, 6, 9, 10; NewCol 75; WhoMilH 76*

Lawrence, Jack
American. Composer, Author
b. Apr 7, 1912 in New York, New York
Source: *AmSCAP 66; BiE&WWA*

Lawrence, Jacob
American. Artist
b. Sep 7, 1917 in Atlantic City, New Jersey
Source: *AfroAA; CurBio 65; DcCAA 71; IlsBYP; NewYTBS 74; WhoAm 74, 76, 78, 80, 82; WhoAmA 73; WhoBlA 75; WhoWor 74*

Lawrence, James
American. Naval Officer
b. Oct 1, 1781 in Burlington, New Jersey
d. Jun 1, 1813
Source: *AmBi; ApCAB; DcAmB; Drake; REn; TwCBDA; WebAB; WhAm H*

Lawrence, Jerome
[Jerome Lawrence Schwartz]
American. Composer, Author
b. Jul 14, 1915 in Cleveland, Ohio
Source: *AmAu&B; AmSCAP 66; BiE&WWA; ConAu 41R; ConDr 73; EncMT; ModWD; NotNAT; OhA&B; PseudN; WhoAm 74, 76, 78, 80, 82; WhoThe 77; WhoWor 74; WhoWorJ 72; WrDr 76*

Lawrence, Josephine
American. Author
b. 1897 in Newark, New Jersey
d. Feb 22, 1978 in New York, New York
Source: *AmAu&B; AmNov; ConAu 77; OxAmL; REn; REnAL; WhoAm 74; TwCA, SUP; WhNAA; WhoE 74*

Lawrence, Margaret
American. Actress
b. Aug 2, 1889 in Trenton, New Jersey
d. Jun 9, 1929 in Little Rock, Arkansas
Source: *NotNAT B; WhAm 1*

Lawrence, Marjorie Florence
Australian. Opera Singer
b. Feb 17, 1909 in Deans Marsh, Australia
d. Jan 13, 1979 in Little Rock, Arkansas
Source: *BioNews 74; CurBio 40; InWom; Who 74; WhoMus 72*

Lawrence, Mildred Elwood
American. Author
b. Nov 10, 1907 in Charleston, Illinois
Source: *AuBYP; ConAu 1R, 5NR; CurBio 53; ForWC 70; MorJA; SmATA 3*

Lawrence, Robert
American. Conductor, Critic
b. Mar 18, 1912 in New York, New York
Source: *WhoAm 74; WhoE 74*

Lawrence, Steve
[Sidney Liebowitz]
American. Actor, Singer
b. Jul 8, 1935 in New York, New York
Source: *AmSCAP 66; BiE&WWA; BioNews 74; BkPepl; CelR 73; CurBio 64; EncMT; IntMPA 82; NotNAT; PseudN; WhoAm 74; WhoHol A*

Lawrence, Sir Thomas
"The Wonderul Boy of Devizes"
English. Artist
b. May 4, 1769 in Bristol, England
d. Jan 7, 1830 in London, England
Source: *Alli; BkIE; ChPo, S1; NewC; NewCol 75; PseudN; REn; TwCA SUP*

Lawrence, T(homas) E(dward)
[Thomas Edward Shaw]
"Lawrence of Arabia"
English. Author, Soldier
b. Aug 15, 1888 in Portmadoc, Wales
d. May 19, 1935 in England
Source: *AtlBL; CasWL; Chambr 3; CnMWL; CyWA; DcLEL; EncWL; EvLB; LongCTC; ModBrL; NewC; NewCol 75; OxEng; Pen ENG; PseudN; REn; TwCA, SUP; TwCW; WebE&AL*

Lawrence, Vicki
American. Actress, Singer
Regular on "The Carol Burnett Show"; recorded "The Night the Lights Went Out in Georgia."
b. Mar 26, 1949 in Inglewood, California
Source: *RkOn; WhoAm 78, 80, 82*

Lawrence, William Beach
"An American Citizen"
American. Lawyer
b. Oct 23, 1800 in New York, New York
d. Mar 26, 1881 in New York, New York
Source: *AmBi; ApCAB; BiAuS; BioIn 5; DcAmB; Drake; NewCol 75; PseudN; TwCBDA; WebBD 80; WhAm H*

Lawrie, Lee
American. Sculptor
b. Oct 16, 1877 in Rixdorf, Germany
d. Jan 23, 1961 in Easton, Maryland
Source: *NewCol 75; WhAm 4*

Lawson, Donald Elmer
American. Children's Author, Editor
b. May 20, 1917 in Chicago, Illinois
Source: *AuBYP; ConAu 1R, 2NR; SmATA 9; WhoAm 74, 76, 78, 80, 82; WhoMW 74*

Lawson, John Howard
American. Dramatist
b. Sep 25, 1895 in New York, New York
d. Aug 12, 1977 in San Francisco, California
Source: *AmAu&B; BiE&WWA; CnMD; CnThe; ConAmA; ConAmL; ConAu 73; ConAu P-1; ConDr 73, 77; EncWT; IntMPA 75, 76, 77, 78, 79; McGEWD; ModAL; ModWD; NotNAT; OxAmL; OxFilm; Pen AM; REn; REnAL; TwCA, SUP; WebE&AL; WhE&EA; WhThe; WorEFlm; WrDr 76*

Lawson, Leigh
English. Actor
b. Jul 21, 1945 in Atherston, England
Source: *JohnWil 81*

Lawson, Robert
American. Illustrator, Author
Won Newbery Medal, 1945, for *Rabbit Hill.*
b. Oct 4, 1892 in New York, New York
d. May 26, 1957 in Weston, Connecticut
Source: *AmAu&B; AnCL; Au&ICB; AuBYP; BkCL; Cald 1938; ChlLR 2; ChPo, S2; FamAIYP; IlsBYP; IlsCB 1744, 1946; JBA 51; Newb 1922; Str&VC; WhAm 3*

Lawson, Victor Fremont
American. Editor, Publisher
b. Sep 9, 1850 in Chicago, Illinois
d. Aug 19, 1925
Source: *AmAu&B; AmBi; DcAmB; WhAm 1*

Lawson, "Yank" (John R)
[John R Lausen]
American. Jazz Musician
b. May 3, 1911 in Trenton, Missouri
Source: *PseudN; WhoJazz 72*

Lawton, Henry Ware
American. Military Leader
b. Mar 17, 1843 in Manhattan, Ohio
d. Dec 19, 1899 in Philippines
Source: *AmBi; ApCAB SUP; DcAmB; TwCBDA; WhAm 1*

Laxalt, Paul
American. Lawyer, Senator
b. Aug 2, 1922 in Reno, Nevada
Source: *IntWW 74; WhoAm 74, 76, 78, 80, 82; WhoAmP 73*

Laxness, Halldor Kiljan
[Halldor Kiljan Gudjonsson]
Icelandic. Author, Dramatist
b. Apr 23, 1902 in Reykjavik, Iceland
Source: *CasWL; ConAu 103; CurBio 46; CyWA; EncWL; EvEuW; IntWW 74; NewYTBE 71; Pen EUR; PseudN; REn; TwCA SUP; TwCW; Who 74; WhoTwCL; WhoWor 74*

Lay, Herman Warden
American. Business Executive
Founder, president, Frito-Lay, Inc., 1939-65; chairman, Pepsi Co. Inc., 1965-71.
b. Jun 3, 1909 in Charlotte, North Carolina
d. Dec 6, 1982 in Dallas, Texas
Source: *IntWW 74, 75, 76, 77, 78, 79, 80, 81; WhoAm 74, 76, 78, 80, 82; WhoWor 76, 78*

Layden, Elmer
[Four Horsemen of Notre Dame]
American. Football Player
b. May 4, 1903 in Davenport, Iowa
d. Jun 30, 1973 in Chicago, Illinois
Source: *NewYTBE 73; WhAm 6; WhoFtbl 74*

Laye, Camara
African. Author
b. Jan 1, 1928 in Kouroussa, French Guinea
d. Feb 4, 1980 in Dakar, Senegal
Source: *AfrA; AnObit 1980; BioIn 3, 7, 8, 9, 10; CasWL; ConAu 85; ConLC 4; EncWL; LongCTC; McGEWB; Pen CL; RGAfL; WhoTwCL; WorAu*

Layne, Bobby (Robert Lawrence)
American. Football Player
Quarterback, 1948-62; Hall of Fame, 1967.
b. Dec 19, 1926 in Santa Anna, Texas
Source: *BioIn 3, 7, 8, 9, 10; WhoFtbl 74*

Layton, Larry (Lawrence John)
American. Jonestown Cult Member
b. Jan 1946
Source: *BioIn 11*

Lazar, Irving Paul
"Swifty"
American. Literary Agent
b. Mar 28, 1907 in Stamford, Connecticut
Source: *BiE&WWA; CelR 73; PseudN; WhoAm 82*

Lazarus
Biblical Character
Source: *BioIn 6; NewCol 75*

Lazarus, Emma
American. Poet
b. Jul 22, 1849 in New York, New York
d. Nov 19, 1887 in New York, New York
Source: *Alli SUP; AmAu; AmAu&B; AmBi; AmWom; ApCAB; BbD; BiD&SB; Chambr 3; ChPo, S1; CnDAL; DcAmAu; DcAmB; DcLEL; DcNAA; EvLB; InWom; MouLC 4; NotAW; OxAmL; REn; REnAL; TwCBDA; WebAB; WhAm H*

Lazarus, Charles P
American. Businessman
Founded Toys R Us.
b. 1923?
Source: *BioIn 11*

Lazarus, Mell
[Mell, pseud.]
American. Cartoonist
Draws, writes comics "Miss Peach," 1957--, "Momma," 1970--.
b. May 3, 1927 in Brooklyn, New York
Source: *ConAu 21R; WhoAm 82; WorECom*

Lazear, Jesse William
American. Physician
b. May 2, 1866 in Baltimore, Maryland
d. Sep 25, 1900 in Quemados, Cuba
Source: *AsBiEn; DcAmB; NatCAB; WebBD 80; WhAm H*

Lazzari, Virgilio
Italian. Opera Singer
b. Apr 20, 1887 in Assisi, Italy
d. Oct 4, 1953 in Castel Gandolfo, Italy
Source: *NewEOp 71*

Lazzeri, Tony (Anthony Michael)
"Poosh 'Em Up"
American. Baseball Player
Infielder, NY Yankees, 1925-37; struck out with bases loaded in last game, 1926 World Series.
b. Dec 26, 1903 in San Francisco, California
d. Aug 6, 1946 in San Francisco, California
Source: *BaseEn; CurBio 46; PseudN; WhoProB 73*

Le Duc Tho
Vietnamese. Government Official
b. Oct 14, 1911 in Vietnam
Source: *NewYTBE 73*

Lea, Fanny Heaslip
American. Author, Dramatist
b. Oct 30, 1884 in New Orleans, Louisiana
d. Jan 13, 1955 in New York, New York
Source: *AmAu&B; REnAL; TwCA, SUP; WhAm 3; WhNAA*

Lea, Homer
American. Author, Soldier
b. Nov 17, 1876 in Denver, Colorado
d. Nov 1, 1912 in Los Angeles, California
Source: *AmBi; DcAmB; NatCAB 2; WebAB; WebBD 80; WhAm 1*

Lea, Tom
American. Author, Artist
b. Jul 11, 1907 in El Paso, Texas
Source: *AmAu&B; OxAmL; REnAL; TwCA SUP; WhoAm 74, 76, 78, 80, 82; WhoAmA 73; WhoS&SW 73; WhoWor 74*

Leach, Rick (Richard Max)
American. Baseball Player
b. May 4, 1957 in Ann Arbor, Michigan
Source: *BaseEn*

Leach, Will (Wilford Carson)
American. Motion Picture Director
b. Aug 26, 1934 in Petersburg, Virginia
Source: *BiE&WWA; ConAu 45; NotNAT; WhoAm 74, 76, 78, 80, 82*

Leachman, Cloris
American. Actress
Won Oscar, 1971, for *The Last Picture Show.*
b. Apr 30, 1925 in Des Moines, Iowa
Source: *BioIn 9, 10; BioNews 74; BkPepl; FilmgC; IntMPA 75, 76, 77, 78, 79, 80, 81, 82; MovMk; WhoAm 74, 76, 78, 80, 82*

Leacock, Stephen Butler
Canadian. Humorist, Economist
b. Dec 30, 1869 in Hampshire, England
d. Mar 28, 1944 in Toronto, ON
Source: *CanWr; CasWL; Chambr 3; ConAmL; CreCan 2; CurBio 44; DcLEL; DcNAA; EvLB; LongCTC; NewC; OxAmL; OxCan; OxEng; Pen ENG; RAdv 1; REn; REnAL; TwCA, SUP; TwCW; WebE&AL; WhAm 2; WhNAA*

Leaf, (Wilbur) Munro
[John Calvert; Mun, pseuds.]
American. Humorist, Illustrator
b. Dec 4, 1905 in Hamilton, Maryland
d. Dec 21, 1976 in Garrett Park, Maryland
Source: *AmAu&B; AuBYP; BkP; ConAu 69, 73; LongCTC; PseudN; REnAL; TwCA, SUP; WhAm 7; WhoAm 74, 76; WhoChL*

Leah
Biblical Character
Source: *InWom*

Leahy, Frank
American. Football Coach
b. Aug 27, 1908 in O'Neill, Nebraska
d. Jun 21, 1973 in Portland, Oregon
Source: *CurBio 41, 73; NewYTBE 73; WhAm 5; WhoFtbl 74*

Leahy, Patrick Joseph
American. Senator
b. Mar 31, 1940 in Montpelier, Vermont
Source: *AlmAP 78, 80; CngDr 77, 79; IntWW 75, 76, 77, 78; WhoAm 78, 80, 82; WhoE 77, 79; WhoGov 75, 77*

Leahy, William Daniel
American. Naval Officer
b. May 6, 1875 in Hampton, Iowa
d. Jul 20, 1959 in Bethesda, Maryland
Source: *AmAu&B; CurBio 41, 59; WebAB; WhAm 3*

Leakey, Louis Seymour Bazett
[White Kikuyu]
English. Anthropologist
Discovered fossils in Africa that proved man's evolution began there.
b. Aug 7, 1903 in Kabete, Africa (East)
d. Oct 1, 1972 in London, England
Source: *ConAu 37R, 97; CurBio 66, 72; NewYTBE 72; WhAm 5*

Leakey, Mary Douglas
[Mrs. Louis Leakey]
English. Anthropologist
Discovered fossils in Tanzania; proved man existed four million years earlier than believed.
b. Feb 6, 1913 in London, England
Source: *ConAu 97; Who 74; WhoAm 82*

Leakey, Richard E
Kenyan. Anthropologist
Proved that three forms of humans co-existed; two became extinct, the other evolved into Homo Sapiens.
b. Dec 19, 1944 in Nairobi, Kenya
Source: *ConAu 93; IntWW 74; WhoAm 82*

Lean, David
English. Motion Picture Director
b. Mar 25, 1908 in Croydon, England
Source: *BiDFilm; CelR 73; CurBio 53; DcFM; FilmgC; IntMPA 75, 76, 77, 78, 79, 80, 82; IntWW 74; MovMk; OxFilm; Who 74; WhoWor 74; WorEFlm*

Lear, Edward
English. Artist, Poet
b. May 12, 1812 in Highgate, England
d. Jan 29, 1888 in San Remo, Italy
Source: *AnCL; AtlBL; AuBYP; BiD&SB; BrAu 19; CarSB; CasWL; Chambr 3; ChlLR 1; ChPo, S1, S2; CnE&AP; CrtT 3; DcEnL; DcEuL; DcLEL; EvLB; FamAIYP; JBA 34; MouLC 4; NewC; OxEng; Pen ENG; REn; Str&VC; WebE&AL; WhoChL*

Lear, Evelyn
American. Opera Singer
b. Jan 18, 1931 in New York, New York
Source: *CurBio 73; NewYTBE 72; WhoAm 74, 76, 78, 80, 82; WhoMus 72*

Lear, Norman Milton
American. TV Scriptwriter, Producer
Created TV series, including "All in the Family," 1971.
b. Jul 27, 1922 in New Haven, Connecticut
Source: *BioIn 9, 10, 11; BioNews 74; ConAu 73; CurBio 74; FilmgC; IntMPA 77, 78, 79, 80, 81, 82; WhoAm 74, 76, 78, 80, 82*

Lear, Peter, pseud.
see: Lovesey, Peter Harmer

Lear, William Powell
American. Engineer, Manufacturer
President, Lear Jet Corp., 1963-67, chairman, 1967-69.
b. Jun 26, 1902 in Hannibal, Missouri
d. May 14, 1978 in Reno, Nevada
Source: *AmM&WS 73P; CurBio 66; WebAB; WhoAm 74; WhoWor 74*

Learned, Michael
American. Actress
Played Olivia on "The Waltons," 1972-79; won three Emmys.
b. Apr 9, 1929 in Washington, DC
Source: *BioIn 10; IntMPA 82; WhoAm 82*

Leary, Timothy Francis
American. Drug Cultist, Psychologist
Recorded "Give Peace a Chance," with John Lennon, 1969.
b. Oct 22, 1920 in Springfield, Massachusetts
Source: *AmAu&B; BioIn 7, 8, 9, 10, 11; CelR 73; Pen AM; WhoAm 74, 76, 78, 80, 82*

Leaud, Jean-Pierre
French. Actor
b. 1944 in Paris, France
Source: *BiDFilm; MovMk; OxFilm; WhoHol A; WorEFlm*

Leavis, F(rank) R(aymond)
English. Literary Critic, Author
b. Jul 14, 1895 in Cambridge, England
d. Apr 14, 1978 in Cambridge, England
Source: *Au&Wr 71; CasWL; ConAu 21R, 77; DcLEL; EncWL; EvLB; IntWW 74; LongCTC; ModBrL, SUP; NewC; OxEng; Pen ENG; PseudN; RAdv 1; REn; TwCA SUP; TwCW; WebE&AL; Who 74; WhoTwCL; WhoWor 74; WrDr 76*

Leblanc, Claude
French. Statesman
b. 1669
d. 1728
Source: *BioIn 10*

Leblanc, Maurice
French. Author, Dramatist
b. Dec 19, 1864
d. Nov 6, 1941 in Perpignan, France
Source: *CasWL; CurBio 42; EncMys; EvEuW; LongCTC; MnBBF; OxFr; TwCA*

LeBoutillier, John
"Boot"
American. Former Congressman
b. May 26, 1953 in Glen Cove, New York
Source: *AlmAP 82; WhoAm 82*

Lebowitz, Fran(ces Ann)
American. Author
Wrote *Metropolitan Life Social Studies,* 1978, a book of humorous essays.
b. Oct 27, 1950 in Morristown, New Jersey
Source: *BioIn 11; ConAu 81; ConLC 11; CurBio 82*

Leboyer, Frederick
French. Gentle Birthing Advocate, Poet
Author *Birth without Violence.*
b. 1918 in Paris, France
Source: *CurBio 82; WrDr 80, 82*

Lebrowitz, Barney
see: Levinsky, Battling

Lebrun, Albert
French. President
b. 1871
d. Mar 1950
Source: *BioIn 1; WebBD 80*

Lebrun, Rico (Frederico)
American. Artist
b. Dec 10, 1900 in Naples, Italy
d. May 10, 1964 in Malibu, California
Source: *BnEnAmA; ConArt; CurBio 52, 64; DcAmArt; DcCAA 71, 77; McGDA; WhAm 4; WhoAmA 78*

LeCarre, John, pseud.
[David John Moore Cornwell]
English. Author
Wrote *The Spy Who Came in From the Cold,* 1963.
b. Oct 19, 1931 in Poole, England
Source: *Au&Wr 71; ConAu 5R; ConLC 3, 5; ConNov 72, 76; CurBio 74; EncMys; IntWW 74; NewC; TwCW; Who 74; WhoWor 74; WorAu; WrDr 76*

Lecky, William Edward Hartpole
Irish. Author, Historian
Published essays on Swift, Flood, Grattan, and O'Connell.
b. Mar 26, 1838 in Dublin, Ireland
d. 1903 in London, England
Source: *Alli SUP; BbD; BiD&SB; BrAu 19; CasWL; Chambr 3; DcEnA; DcEnL; DcEuL; DcIrB; DcIrW 2; DcLEL; EvLB; LinLib S; McGEWB; NewC; OxEng; Pen ENG*

LeClear, Thomas
American. Artist
b. Mar 11, 1818 in Oswego, New York
d. Nov 26, 1882 in Rutherford, New Jersey
Source: *ApCAB; DcAmArt; DcAmB; Drake; NatCAB 8; NewYHSD; TwCBDA; WhAm H*

Leclerc, Jacques-Philippe
French. General
b. Nov 28, 1902 in Belloy Saint Leonard, France
d. Nov 28, 1947 in Algeria
Source: *CurBio 44, 47; NewCol 75; WebBD 80*

Leclerc, Marie-Andree
French. Medical Secretary
b. 1945?
Source: *BioIn 11*

LeCorbusier
[Charles Edouard Jeanneret-Gris]
Swiss. Architect
Pioneered use of reinforced concrete; concept of house as "machine for living."
b. Oct 6, 1887 in Switzerland
d. Aug 27, 1965 in Roquebrune, France
Source: *AtlBL; BioIn 1, 2, 3, 4, 5, 6, 7, 8, 9, 10, 11; CurBio 47, 66; REn; TwCA SUP*

Lecouvreur, Adrienne
French. Actress
Changed acting techniques by advocating natural speech, simple manner.
b. 1692
d. Mar 20, 1730
Source: *InWom; OxFr; OxThe; REn*

Led Zeppelin
[John Bonham; John Paul Jones; Jimmy Page; Robert Plant]
English. Rock Group
Source: *BkPepl; EncPR&S; IlEncRk; Rk100*

Ledbetter, Huddie
"King of the 12 String Guitar Players"; "Leadbelly"
American. Folksinger, Musician
b. 1885 in Mooringsport, Louisiana
d. Dec 6, 1949 in New York, New York
Source: *DcAmB S4; EncFCWM 69; PseudN; WebAB; WhAm 4*

Lederer, Francis
[Frantisek or Franz Lederer]
Czech. Actor
b. Nov 6, 1906 in Prague, Czechoslovakia
Source: *BiE&WWA; FilmgC; HolP 30; MotPP; MovMk; NotNAT; PseudN; WhoHol A*

Lederer, William Julius
American. Author
b. Mar 31, 1912 in New York, New York
Source: *AmAu&B; Au&Wr 71; ConAu 1R, 5NR; WhoAm 82; WorAu*

Ledoux, Claude Nicolas
French. Architect
b. Mar 21, 1736 in Dormans, France
d. Nov 19, 1806 in Paris, France
Source: *AtlBL; NewCol 75*

Lee, Andrew Daulton
"Snowman"
American. Spy
b. 1951? in Palos Verdes, California
Source: *BioIn 11; NewYTBS 77*

Lee, Ann
"Ann the Word"; "Mother Ann"
American. Religious Leader
Founded first Shaker settlement in America, in Watervliet, NY, 1776.
b. Feb 29, 1736 in Manchester, England
d. Sep 8, 1784 in Watervliet, New York
Source: *Alli; AmBi; ApCAB; DcAmB; Drake; EncAB-H; InWom; NotAW; OxAmL; PseudN; REn; TwCBDA; WebAB; WhAm H*

Lee, Bernard
English. Actor
b. Jan 10, 1908 in London, England
d. Jan 16, 1981 in London, England
Source: *CmMov; FilmgC; IntMPA 75, 76, 77, 78, 79, 80, 81; NewYTBS 81; WhoHol A; WhoThe 72, 77, 81*

Lee, Beverly
see: Shirelles, The

Lee, Brenda
[Brenda Mae Tarpley]
"Little Miss Dynamite"
American. Singer
Held command performance for Queen Elizabeth, 1964.
b. Dec 11, 1944 in Atlanta, Georgia
Source: *BioIn 4, 6; InWom; PseudN; WhoAm 74, 76, 78, 80, 82; WhoS&SW 73*

Lee, Bruce
[Lee Siu Loong; Lee Yuen Kam]
"The Little Dragon"
American. Kung Fu Expert, Actor
Films include *Enter the Dragon,* 1973.
b. Nov 27, 1940 in San Francisco, California
d. Jul 30, 1973 in Hong Kong, China
Source: *BioIn 10, 11; MovMk; NewYTBE 73; PseudN; WhScrn 77; WhoHol B*

Lee, Canada
[Leonard Lionel Cornelius Canegata]
American. Boxer, Actor
b. May 3, 1907 in New York, New York
d. May 9, 1952 in New York, New York
Source: *CurBio 44, 52; DcAmB S5; FilmgC; MotPP; MovMk; PseudN; Vers A; WhAm 3; WhScrn 74, 77; WhoHol B*

Lee, Charles
American. Revolutionary General, Author
b. 1731 in Dernhall, England
d. Oct 2, 1788 in Philadelphia, Pennsylvania
Source: *Alli; AmAu; AmAu&B; AmBi; ApCAB; DcAmB; Drake; EncAB-H; REnAL; TwCBDA; WebAB; WhAm H*

Lee, Christopher
[Christopher Frank Carandini Lee]
English. Actor
b. May 27, 1922 in London, England
Source: *CmMov; FilmgC; IntMPA 75, 76, 77, 78, 79, 80, 81, 82; MotPP; MovMk; OxFilm; WhoAm 82; WhoHol A*

Lee, Dixie
[Mrs. Bing Crosby; Wilma Winifred Wyatt]
American. Actress
b. Nov 4, 1911 in Harriman, Tennessee
d. Nov 1, 1952 in Holmby Hills, California
Source: *Film 1; PseudN; TwYS; WhScrn 74, 77; WhoHol B*

Lee, Doris Emrick
American. Artist
b. Feb 1, 1905 in Aledo, Illinois
Source: *BnEnAmA; CurBio 54; DcAmArt; IlsCB 1946; InWom; McGDA; WhoAm 74, 76, 78; WhoAmA 73, 76, 78; WhoAmW 58, 64, 66, 68, 70, 72, 74*

Lee, Eugene ("Porky")
see: Our Gang

Lee, Francis Lightfoot
American. Continental Congressman
b. Oct 14, 1734 in Westmoreland, Virginia
d. Jan 11, 1797 in Richmond County, Virginia
Source: *AmBi; ApCAB; BiAuS; BiDrAC; DcAmB; Drake; TwCBDA; WhAm H; WhAmP*

Lee, Gary Earl
[The Hostages]
American. Former Hostage in Iran
b. Feb 4, 1943 in New York, New York
Source: *BioIn 12; NewYTBS 81; USBiR 74*

Lee, Geddy
[Rush]
Canadian. Rock Musician, Singer
b. Jul 29, 1953 in Toronto, ON
Source: *WhoAm 82*

Lee, Gypsy Rose
[Rose Louise Hovick]
American. Strip Tease Artist, Actress
Autobiography *Gyspy,* 1957 basis for Broadway musical, 1959, movie, 1962.
b. Feb 9, 1914 in Seattle, Washington
d. Apr 26, 1970 in Los Angeles, California
Source: *AmAu&B; BiE&WWA; CurBio 43, 70; EncMT; EncMys; FilmgC; InWom; MotPP; MovMk; NewYTBE 70; PseudN; WebAB; WhAm 5; WhScrn 74, 77; WhoHol B; WorEFlm*

Lee, Henry
"Legion Harry"; "Light Horse Harry"
American. Governor of Virginia
b. Jan 29, 1756 in Dunfries, Virginia
d. Mar 25, 1818 in Cumberland Island, Georgia
Source: *Alli; AmAu&B; AmBi; ApCAB; BiAuS; BiDSA; CyAL 1; DcAmAu; DcAmB; DcNAA; Drake; NewC; OxAmL; PseudN; REn; REnAL; TwCBDA; WebAB; WhAm H; WhAmP*

Lee, Jason
American. Missionary
b. Jun 23, 1803 in Stanstead, Vermont
d. Mar 12, 1845 in Stanstead, Vermont
Source: *AmBi; BioIn 1, 3, 8, 9; DcAmB; NatCAB 25; REnAW; WebAB; WhAm H*

Lee, Johnny
American. Singer
Hit song "Looking for Love"; married to Charlene Tilton.
b. 1947?
Source: *BioIn 12*

Lee, Kuan Yew
Chinese. Prime Minister
b. Sep 16, 1923
Source: *IntWW 74; Who 74; WhoGov 72*

Lee, Lila
[Augusta Appel]
American. Actress
b. Jul 25, 1902 in Union Hill, New Jersey
d. Nov 13, 1973 in Saranac Lake, New York
Source: *Film 1; FilmgC; InWom; MotPP; MovMk; PseudN; ThFT; TwYS; WhScrn 77; WhoHol B*

Lee, Louise Harper
American. Civic Worker
b. Apr 3, 1910 in Bainbridge, Georgia
Source: *BiDrLUS 70; WhoAmW 77*

Lee, Manfred B(ennington)
[Manford Lepofsky; Ellery Queen, pseud.]
American. Author
With cousin Frederic Dannay wrote *Ellery Queen* mysteries beginning, 1929.
b. Jan 11, 1905 in Brooklyn, New York
d. Apr 3, 1971 in Roxbury, Connecticut
Source: *AmAu&B; ConAu 1R, 29R, 2NR; CurBio 40; DcLEL; EncMys; LongCTC; ObitT 1971; Pen AM; REn; REnAL; TwCA, SUP; WebAB, 79; WhAm 5*

Lee, Michele
[Michele Lee Dusiak]
American. Actress, Dancer
Plays Karen Fairgate on TV series "Knots Landing."
b. 1942 in Los Angeles, California
Source: *BiE&WWA; FilmgC; NotNAT; PseudN; WhoHol A*

Lee, (Nelle) Harper
American. Author
Won Pulitzer Prize, 1961, for *To Kill a Mockingbird.*
b. Apr 28, 1926 in Monroeville, Alabama
Source: *AmAu&B; ConAu 13R; ConLC 12; DrAF 76; OxAmL; REnAL; SmATA 11; TwCW; WhoAm 82; WorAu*

Lee, Pat Simmons
American. Wife of Former Hostage Gary Lee
b. 1943?
Source: *BioIn 12*

Lee, Peggy
[Norma Delores Egstrom]
American. Singer, Actress
Hits include "Fever," "Is That All There Is?"
b. May 20, 1920 in Jamestown, North Dakota
Source: *CelR 73; CurBio 63; FilmgC; InWom; IntMPA 75, 76, 77, 78, 79, 80, 81, 82; OxFilm; PseudN; WhoAm 74; WhoHol A; WhoWor 74*

Lee, Pinky
[Pincus Leff]
American. Comedian
b. 1916 in Saint Paul, Minnesota
Source: *IntMPA 75, 76, 78, 79, 80, 81, 82; PseudN; WhoHol A*

Lee, Richard Henry
American. Revolutionary Statesman
b. Jan 20, 1732 in Stratford, Virginia
d. Jun 19, 1794 in Chantilly, Virginia
Source: *Alli; AmBi; ApCAB; BiAuS; BiDrAC; BiDrUSE; DcAmB; Drake; EncAB-H; OxAmL; REnAL; TwCBDA; WebAB; WhAm H; WhAmP*

Lee, Robert E(dward)
"The Bayard of the Confederate Army"; "Uncle Robert"
American. Civil War General
Commander-in-chief, Confederate armies, 1865.
b. Jan 19, 1807 in Stratford, Virginia
d. Oct 12, 1870 in Lexington, Virginia
Source: *AmAu&B; AmBi; ApCAB; BiDConf; DcAmB; EncAB-H; OxAmL; PseudN; REn; REnAL; TwCBDA; WebAB; WhAm H*

Lee, Stan
[Stanley Lieber]
American. Comic Book Author, Editor
b. Dec 28, 1922 in New York, New York
Source: *BioIn 9, 11; EncSF; FanAl; WhoAm 78, 80, 82; WorECom*

Lee, Thomas Sim
American. Continental Congressman
b. Oct 29, 1745 in Prince George's County, Maryland
d. Nov 9, 1819 in Frederick County, Maryland
Source: *ApCAB; BiAuS; DcAmB; Drake; TwCBDA; WhAm H*

Lee, Tsung-Dao
American. Physicist
b. Nov 24, 1926 in Shanghai, China
Source: *AmM&WS 73P; CurBio 58; IntWW 74; WebAB; Who 74; WhoAm 74*

Lee, Will
American. Actor, Director
Played Mr. Hooper, the storekeeper, on "Sesame Street", 1969-82.
b. Aug 6, 1908 in Brooklyn, New York
d. Dec 7, 1982 in New York, New York
Source: *BiE&WWA; NotNAT; WhoHol A*

Leech, John
English. Cartoonist, Caricaturist
b. Aug 29, 1817 in London, England
d. Oct 29, 1864 in London, England
Source: *Alli; Br&AmS; ChPo, S2; DcEnL; NewC*

Leech, Margaret Kernoehan
[Mrs. Ralph Pulitzer]
American. Author, Historian
b. Nov 7, 1893 in Newburgh, New York
d. Feb 24, 1974 in New York, New York
Source: *AmAu&B; ConAu 49, 93; CurBio 42, 60, 74; InWom; NewYTBS 74; OxAmL; PseudN; REn; REnAL; TwCA SUP*

Leek, Sybil
[Sybil Falk]
English. Clairvoyant, Witch
Wrote *The Diary of a Witch,* 1968.
b. Feb 22, 1917 in Stoke-on-Trent, England
d. Oct 26, 1982 in Melbourne, Florida
Source: *CelR 73; ConAu 102; EncO&P 78; NewYTBS 82; ScF&FL 1, 2; WhoAm 74, 76, 78, 80, 82; WrDr 76, 80*

Leeuwenhoek, Anton van
Dutch. Naturalist
b. Oct 24, 1632 in Delft, Netherlands
d. Aug 26, 1723
Source: *BioIn 10; NewCol 75; WebBD 80*

Lefebure, Marcel Francois
French. Roman Catholic Archbishop
b. Nov 29, 1905 in Touscoing, France
Source: *CurBio 78*

Lefever, Ernest Warren
American. Educator
b. Nov 12, 1919 in York, Pennsylvania
Source: *AmM&WS 73S, 78S; ConAu 1R, 1NR; WhoAm 82*

Lefkowitz, Louis J
American. Former Attorney General
b. Jul 3, 1904 in New York, New York
Source: *WhoAm 74, 76, 78, 80, 82; WhoAmP 73; WhoE 74; WhoGov 72*

LeGallienne, Eva
American. Actress, Author
b. Jan 11, 1899 in London, England
Source: *AmAu&B; AuBYP; BiE&WWA; ConAu 45; CurBio 42, 55; FamA&A; InWom; IntMPA 82; IntWW 74; NotNAT; OxThe; PlP&P; REn; REnAL; SmATA 9; WebAB; Who 74; WhoAm 74, 76, 78, 80, 82; WhoHol A; WhoThe 77; WhoWor 74*

LeGallienne, Richard
English. Poet, Essayist
b. Jan 20, 1866 in Liverpool, England
d. Sep 14, 1947 in Menton, France
Source: *Alli SUP; AnCL; BbD; BiD&SB; Chambr 3; ChPo, S1, S2; DcAmAu; DcEnA AP; DcLEL; EvLB; LongCTC; MouLC 4; NewC; OxAmL; OxEng; Pen ENG; TwCA, SUP; WebE&AL; WhAm 2; WhNAA*

Legend, Bill
see: T. Rex

Leger, (Marie-Rene) Alexis St. Leger
[St. John Perse]
French. Poet, Diplomat
b. May 31, 1887 in Guadeloupe, French West Indies
d. Sep 20, 1975 in Giens, France
Source: *AnCL; CasWL; ClDMEL; CnMWL; ConAu 13R, 61; ConLC 4; CyWA; EncWL; EvEuW; IntWW 74; OxFr; Pen EUR; PseudN; REn; TwCA, SUP; TwCW; WhAm 6; Who 74; WhoTwCL; WhoWor 74*

Leger, Fernand
French. Artist
b. Feb 4, 1881 in Argentan, France
d. Aug 17, 1955 in Gif-sur-Yvette, France
Source: *AtlBL; CurBio 43, 55; DcFM; OxFilm; REn; WorEFlm*

Leger, Jules
Canadian. Statesman
b. Apr 4, 1913 in Saint Anicet, PQ
d. Nov 22, 1980 in Ottawa, ON
Source: *BioIn 11; CanWW 70, 79; CurBio 76, 81; IntWW 74, 75, 76, 77, 78; IntYB 78, 79; Who 74; WhoAm 76, 78; WhoCan 73, 75, 77; WhoE 75, 77, 79; WhoWor 74, 76, 78*

Legler, Henry Eduard
American. Author, Librarian
b. Jun 22, 1861 in Palermo, Italy
d. Sep 13, 1917
Source: *AmAu&B; DcAmB; DcNAA; WhAm 1*

Legrand, Michel Jean
French. Composer, Conductor
b. Feb 24, 1932 in Paris, France
Source: *BioNews 74; DcFM; FilmgC; IntMPA 75, 76, 77; OxFilm; WhoWor 74; WorEFlm*

LeGuin, Ursula Kroeber
American. Author
Writes science fiction, fantasy; *Left Hand of Darkness,* 1969; *Malafrena,* 1979.
b. Oct 21, 1929 in Berkeley, California
Source: *ConAu 21R; ConLC 8, 13; ConNov 76; CurBio 83; DrAF 76; SmATA 4; WhoAm 74, 76, 78, 80, 82; WrDr 76*

Lehand, "Missy" (Marguerite Alice)
American. Secretary to Franklin Roosevelt
b. 1898?
d. Jul 31, 1944 in London, England
Source: *BioIn 8, 9; InWom*

Lehar, Franz
Hungarian. Composer
b. Apr 30, 1870 in Romorn, Hungary
d. Oct 24, 1948 in Bad Ischl, Austria
Source: *PlP&P; REn; WhoStg 1908*

Lehman, Herbert Henry
American. Philanthropist, Politician
b. Mar 28, 1878 in New York, New York
d. Dec 5, 1963 in New York, New York
Source: *BiDrAC; CurBio 43, 55, 64; WebAB; WhAm 4; WhAmP*

Lehmann, John Frederick
English. Author
b. Jun 2, 1907 in Bourne End, England
Source: *Au&Wr 71; CasWL; ConAu 9R; ConP 70, 75; DcLEL; EvLB; IntWW 74; LongCTC; ModBrL; NewC; OxEng; Pen ENG; REn; TwCA, SUP; TwCW; WebE&AL; Who 74; WhoWor 74; WrDr 76*

Lehmann, Lilli
German. Opera Singer
b. Nov 24, 1848 in Wurzburg, Germany
d. May 17, 1929 in Berlin, Germany
Source: *ApCAB SUP; InWom*

Lehmann, Lotte
American. Opera Singer
b. Feb 27, 1888 in Perlberg, Germany
d. Aug 26, 1976 in Santa Barbara, California
Source: *ConAu 69, 73; CurBio 41, 70; InWom; IntWW 74; REn; Who 74; WhoAm 74; WhoMus 72; WhoWor 74*

Lehmann, Rosamond Nina
English. Author
b. Feb 3, 1901 in London, England
Source: *Au&Wr 71; CasWL; ConAu 77; ConLC 5; ConNov 72, 76; EncWL; LongCTC; ModBrL; RAdv 1; REn; TwCA, SUP; WebE&AL; WhoTwCL; WrDr 76*

Lehmann-Haupt, Christopher
American. Book Critic
b. Jun 14, 1934 in Edinburgh, Scotland
Source: *WhoE 74*

Lehmann-Haupt, Hellmut E
American. Author
b. Oct 4, 1903 in Berlin, Germany
Source: *Au&Wr 71; BiDrLUS 70; ConAu 9R; CurBio 42, 61; DrAS 74H; WhoAm 74*

Lehmbruck, Wilhelm
German. Artist
b. Jan 4, 1881 in Meidereich, Germany
d. Mar 25, 1919 in Berlin, Germany
Source: *AtlBL; BioIn 1, 4, 5, 7, 8, 9*

Lehr, Lew
American. Actor
b. May 14, 1895 in Philadelphia, Pennsylvania
d. Mar 6, 1950 in Brookline, Massachusetts
Source: *WhScrn 74, 77; WhoHol B*

Lehrer, James Charles
American. Broadcast Journalist
b. May 19, 1934 in Wichita, Kansas
Source: *WhoAm 80, 82*

Lehrer, Tom (Thomas Andrew)
American. Songwriter, Mathematician
b. Apr 9, 1928 in New York, New York
Source: *AmAu&B; CurBio 82; Who 74; WhoAm 74, 76, 78, 80, 82; WhoWor 74*

Leiber, Fritz
[Francis Lathrop, pseud.]
American. Author
b. Dec 25, 1910 in Chicago, Illinois
Source: *AmAu&B; ConAu 45; ConNov 76; DrAF 76; PseudN; WhoAm 82; WrDr 76*

Leibniz, Gottfried Wilhelm von
"The First of Philosophers"; "A Living Dictionary"
German. Philosopher, Mathematician
b. Jul 1, 1646 in Leipzig, Germany
d. Nov 14, 1716 in Hannover, Germany
Source: *BbD; BiD&SB; CasWL; DcEuL; EuAu; EvEuW; NewC; OxEng; OxGer; PseudN; REn*

Leibowitz, Rene
French. Composer, Conductor
b. Feb 17, 1913 in Warsaw, Poland
d. Aug 28, 1972 in Paris, France
Source: *ConAu 37R; DcCM; WhAm 5; WhoMus 72*

Leibowitz, Samuel Simon
"Sentencing Sam"
American. Lawyer
b. Aug 14, 1893 in Romania
d. Jan 11, 1978 in New York, New York
Source: *BioIn 2, 3, 4, 5, 6, 9, 11; CurBio 53; PseudN*

Leider, Frida
German. Opera Singer
b. Apr 18, 1888 in Berlin, Germany
d. Jun 4, 1975 in Berlin, Germany (West)
Source: *BioIn 4, 7, 10, 11; ConAu 57; InWom*

Leigh, Janet
[Jeanette Helen Morrison]
American. Actress
Starred in *Psycho,* 1960; mother of actress Jamie Lee Curtis.
b. Jul 6, 1927 in Merced, California
Source: *BiDFilm; FilmgC; InWom; IntMPA 75, 76, 77, 78, 79, 80, 81, 82; MotPP; MovMk; OxFilm; PseudN; WhoAm 74, 76, 78, 80, 82; WhoHol A; WorEFlm*

Leigh, Mitch
[Irwins Michnick]
American. Composer
b. Jan 30, 1928 in Brooklyn, New York
Source: *AmSCAP 66; EncMT; NewCBMT; NotNAT; PseudN; WhoAdv 72; WhoAm 74*

Leigh, Suzanna
English. Actress
b. 1945 in Reading, England
Source: *FilmgC; IntMPA 78, 79,.80, 81, 82; WhoHol C*

Leigh, Vivien
[Vivian Mary Hartley]
English. Actress
Played Scarlett O'Hara in *Gone With the Wind,* 1939.
b. Nov 5, 1913 in Darjeeling, India
d. Jul 7, 1967 in London, England
Source: *BiDFilm; BiE&WWA; CurBio 46, 67; EncMT; FamA&A; FilmgC; InWom; MotPP; MovMk; OxFilm; OxThe; PlP&P; PseudN; ThFT; WhAm 4; WhScrn 74, 77; WhoHol B; WorEFlm*

Leigh Guzman, Jorge Gustavo
Chilean. General
b. Sep 19, 1920
Source: *BioIn 10; IntWW 74*

Leighton, Clare Veronica Hope
English. Illustrator, Author
b. Apr 12, 1900 in London, England
Source: *AmAu&B; ChPo, S1; IlsBYP; IlsCB 1946, 1957; LongCTC; TwCA, SUP; Who 74; WhoAmA 73*

Leighton, Margaret
English. Actress
b. Feb 26, 1922 in Barnt Green, England
d. Jan 13, 1976 in Chichester, England
Source: *BiE&WWA; CurBio 57; FilmgC; InWom; IntMPA 75; MotPP; MovMk; OxThe; PlP&P; Who 74; WhoAm 74; WhAm 6; WhoThe 77; WhoWor 74*

Leinsdorf, Erich
American. Conductor
b. Feb 4, 1912 in Vienna, Austria
Source: *CelR 73; CurBio 40, 63; IntWW 74; Who 74; WhoAm 74, 76, 78, 80, 82; WhoMus 72; WhoWor 74*

Leisk, David Johnson
see: Johnson, Crockett, pseud.

Leitner, Ferdinand
German. Conductor
b. Mar 4, 1912 in Berlin, Germany
Source: *WhoMus 72*

Leitzel, Lillian
[Lillian Alize Elianore Pelikan]
German. Aerialist
b. 1894
d. 1931
Source: *BioIn 4; InWom; NotAW; PseudN*

Leland, Charles Godfrey
[Hans Breitman; Mace Sloper, pseuds.]
American. Author, Journalist
b. Aug 15, 1824 in Philadelphia, Pennsylvania
d. Mar 20, 1903 in Florence, Italy
Source: *Alli, SUP; AmAu; AmAu&B; AmBi; ApCAB; BbD; BiD&SB; CasWL; Chambr 3; ChPo, S1, S2; CyAl 2; DcAmAu; DcAmB; DcEnA, AP; DcEnL; DcNAA; Drake; EvLB; OxAmL; OxEng; Pen AM; PseudN; REn; TwCBDA; WhAm 1*

Leland, Henry Martyn
American. Automobile Manufacturer
Founded Cadillac Motor Co., 1902, Lincoln Motor Co., 1917.
b. Sep 12, 1843 in Danville, Vermont
d. Mar 26, 1932
Source: *WhAm 1*

Leland, Timothy
American. Editor
b. Sep 24, 1937 in Boston, Massachusetts
Source: *ConAu 102; WhoAm 74, 76, 78, 80, 82*

Lelong, Lucien
French. Perfumer, Couturier
b. Oct 11, 1889 in Paris, France
d. May 11, 1958 in Paris, France
Source: *CurBio 55, 58; WhAm 3; WorFshn*

LeLouch, Claude
French. Motion Picture Director
b. Oct 30, 1937 in Paris, France
Source: *BiDFilm; BioNews 74; CurBio 82; DcFM; FilmgC; IntMPA 75, 76, 77, 78, 79, 80, 81, 82; IntWW 74; MovMk; OxFilm; WhoAm 74; WorEFlm*

Lema, Tony (Anthony David)
"Champagne Tony"
American. Golfer
b. Feb 25, 1934 in Oakland, California
d. Jul 24, 1966 in Munster, Indiana
Source: *BioIn 6, 7, 10; PseudN; WhoGolf*

Lemaire, Jacques Gerald
Canadian. Hockey Player
b. Sep 7, 1945 in La Salle, PQ
Source: *WhoHcky 73*

LeMay, Curtis Emerson
American. Air Force Officer
Vice-presidential candidate, Independent Party, with George Wallace, 1968.
b. Nov 15, 1906 in Columbus, Ohio
Source: *CurBio 44, 54; IntWW 74; WebAB; WhoAm 74; WhoWor 74*

Lembeck, Harvey
American. Actor
b. 1923 in New York, New York
d. Jan 5, 1982 in Los Angeles, California
Source: *BiE&WWA; IntMPA 75; NewYTBS 82; WhoAm 74; WhoHol A*

Lemmon, Jack (John Uhler, III)
American. Actor
Won Oscars, 1955, 1971, for *Mister Roberts; Save the Tiger.*
b. Feb 8, 1925 in Boston, Massachusetts
Source: *BiDFilm; BiE&WWA; BkPepl; CelR 73; CmMov; CurBio 61; FilmgC; IntMPA 75, 76, 77, 78, 79, 80, 81, 82; IntWW 74; MotPP; MovMk; OxFilm; WhoAm 74, 76, 78, 80, 82; WhoHol A; WhoWor 74; WorEFlm*

Lemnitz, Tiana
French. Opera Singer
b. Oct 26, 1897 in Metz, France
Source: *InWom*

Lemnitzer, Lyman Louis
American. Army Officer
b. Aug 29, 1899 in Honesdale, Pennsylvania
Source: *CurBio 55; IntWW 74; Who 74; WhoAm 74*

Lemon, Bob (Robert Granville)
American. Baseball Player, Manager
Hall of Fame, 1976; manager, NY Yankees, 1977-79, 1981.
b. Sep 22, 1920 in San Bernardino, California
Source: *BaseEn; NewYTBE 72; WhoAm 82; WhoProB 73*

Lemon, Mark
English. Journalist, Dramatist
Co-founder, *Punch* magazine, editor, 1841-70.
b. Nov 30, 1809 in London, England
d. May 23, 1870 in Cranley, England
Source: *Alli, SUP; BbD; BiD&SB; BrAu 19; CasWL; Chambr 3; ChPo, S1; DcEnA; DcEnL; DcEuL; DcLEL; EvLB; NewC; OxEng; OxThe; REn*

Lemon, "Meadowlark" (Meadow George, III)
"The Clown Prince of Basketball"
American. Basketball Player
Center, Harlem Globetrotters, 1954-78.
b. Apr 25, 1932 in Lexington, South Carolina
Source: *PseudN; WhoAm 82; WhoBbl 73*

Lemoyne, Jean-Baptiste
French. Composer, Conductor
b. Apr 3, 1751 in Eymet, France
d. Dec 30, 1796 in Paris, France
Source: *BioIn 4; NewEOp 71*

Lemoyne, W(illiam) J
American. Actor
b. 1831
d. Nov 6, 1905
Source: *NotNAT B*

Lenclos, Ninon de
[Anne DeLenclos]
French. Courtesan
b. 1620 in Paris, France
d. 1705 in Paris, France
Source: *InWom; Pen EUR*

Lendl, Ivan
Czech. Tennis Player
b. Mar 7, 1960 in Ostrava, Czechoslovakia
Source: *NewYTBS 81, 82*

L'Enfant, Pierre Charles
American. Engineer, Architect, Soldier
b. Aug 2, 1754 in Paris, France
d. Jun 14, 1825 in Maryland
Source: *AmBi; AtlBL; DcAmB; EncAB-H; OxAmL; REnAL; WebAB; WhAm H*

L'Engle, Madeleine
[Madeleine L'Engle Camp; Madeleine Franklin]
American. Author
b. Nov 28, 1918 in New York, New York
Source: *AmAu&B; AmNov; AuBYP; AuNews 2; ChlLR 1; ChPo, S1; ConAu 1R, 3NR; ConLC 12; InWom; MorBMP; MorJA; PiP; PseudN; SenS; SmATA 1; WhoAm 74; WhoAmW 77; WhoE 74; WrDr 76*

Lenglen, Suzanne
"Pavlova of Tennis"
French. Tennis Player
b. 1899 in Compiegne, France
d. Jul 4, 1938 in Paris, France
Source: *InWom; WhScrn 74, 77; WhoHol B*

Lengyel, Emil
American. Author
b. Apr 26, 1895 in Budapest, Hungary
Source: *AmAu&B; AmM&WS 73S; ConAu 9R, 3NR; CurBio 42; DrAS 74H; SmATA 3; TwCA, SUP; WhNAA; WhoAm 74; WhoWor 74*

Lenin, Nikolai
[Vladimir Ilyich Ulyanov]
Russian. Communist Leader, Author
Led Bolsheviks to power, 1917; buried in mausoleum, Red Square, Moscow.
b. Apr 9, 1870 in Simbirsk, Russia
d. Jan 21, 1924 in Gorki, U.S.S.R.
Source: *BioIn 1, 2, 3, 4, 5, 6, 7, 8, 9, 10, 11; CasWL; DcRusL; OxEng; PseudN; REn*

Lennon, Dianne
[Lennon Sisters]
American. Singer
b. Dec 1, 1939? in Los Angeles, California
Source: *BioIn 4, 8, 9*

Lennon, Janet
[Lennon Sisters]
American. Singer
b. Nov 15, 1946 in Culver City, California
Source: *BioIn 8, 9*

Lennon, John Winston
[The Beatles]
English. Singer, Songwriter, Musician
"Love Me Do," 1962 first song written with Paul McCartney; solo career, 1970, included hit "Imagine," 1971.
b. Oct 9, 1940 in Liverpool, England
d. Dec 8, 1980 in New York, New York
Source: *Au&Wr 71; CelR 73; CurBio 65, 81; IntWW 74; MotPP; WhoHol A; WhoWor 74; WrDr 76*

Lennon, Julian (John Charles)
English. Son of John Lennon, Musician
Paul McCartney wrote song "Hey Jude" for him.
b. Apr 8, 1963 in Liverpool, England
Source: *NF*

Lennon, Kathy
[Lennon Sisters]
American. Singer
b. Aug 22, 1942 in Santa Monica, California
Source: *BioIn 8, 9*

Lennon, Peggy
[Lennon Sisters]
American. Singer
b. Apr 8, 1940 in Los Angeles, California
Source: *BioIn 8, 9*

LeNotre, Andre
"The Father of Landscape Gardening"
French. Landscape Architect
b. Mar 12, 1613 in Paris, France
d. Sep 15, 1700 in Paris, France
Source: *AtlBL; OxFr; PseudN*

Lenska, Rula
[Roza-Maria Lubienska]
"The Fair One"
English. Actress
b. 1947
Source: *BioIn 12; PseudN*

Lenski, Lois
American. Author, Illustrator
b. Oct 14, 1893 in Springfield, Ohio
d. Sep 11, 1974 in Tarpon Springs, Florida
Source: *AmAu&B; Au&ICB; Au&Wr 71; AuBYP; BkCL; BkP; CarSB; ChPo, S1, S2; ConAu 53; ConAu P-1; ConICB; FamAIYP; IlsCB 1744, 1946, 1957; JBA 34, 51; Newb 1922; OhA&B; REnAL; SmATA 1; WhAm 6; WhNAA*

Lenya, Lotte
[Karoline Blamauer; Mrs. Kurt Weill]
Austrian. Actress, Singer
Played Jenny in *The Threepenny Opera*, 1928.
b. Oct 18, 1900 in Vienna, Austria
d. Nov 27, 1981 in New York, New York
Source: *BiE&WWA; BioIn 5, 6, 7, 8; CelR 73; CnThe; CurBio 59, 82; EncMT; EncTR; EncWT; FilmgC; InWom; IntWW 74, 75, 76, 77, 78; MotPP; NotNAT; OxFilm; PseudN; WhoAmW 64, 66, 68, 70, 72; WhoHol A; WhoThe 72, 77, 81; WhoWor 74, 78; WorEFlm*

Leo Africanus
Moorish Traveler
b. 1465
d. 1550
Source: *BiD&SB*

Leo, Leonardo
Italian. Composer, Teacher
b. Aug 5, 1694 in San Vito, Italy
d. Oct 31, 1744 in Naples, Italy
Source: *NewEOp 71*

Leonard
[Leonard Lewis]
English. Hair Stylist
Source: *PseudN; WorFshn*

Leonard, Benny
[Benjamin Leiner]
"The Ghetto Wizard"; "The Mama's Boy"
American. Boxer
b. Apr 7, 1896 in New York, New York
d. Apr 18, 1947 in New York, New York
Source: *PseudN; WhoBox 74*

Leonard, Bill (William Augustus, II)
American. CBS News President
b. Apr 9, 1916 in New York, New York
Source: *BioIn 5, 11; WhoAm 74, 76, 78, 80, 82*

Leonard, "Buck" (Walter Fenner)
"The Black Lou Gehrig"
American. Baseball Player
Starred in Negro Leagues; Hall of Fame, 1972.
b. Sep 8, 1907 in Rocky Mount, North Carolina
Source: *PseudN; WhoProB 73*

Leonard, "Dutch" (Hubert Benjamin)
American. Baseball Player
b. Jul 26, 1892 in Lorraine County, Ohio
d. Jul 11, 1952 in Fresno, California
Source: *BaseEn; BioIn 2, 3; PseudN; WhoProB 73*

Leonard, Eddie
[Lemuel Gordon Toney]
American. Actor
b. 1870 in Richmond, Virginia
d. Jul 29, 1941 in New York, New York
Source: *AmSCAP 66; CurBio 41; DcNAA; PseudN; WhScrn 74, 77; WhoHol B*

Leonard, Jack E
[Leonard Lebitsky]
"Fat Jack"
American. Actor
b. Apr 24, 1911 in Chicago, Illinois
d. May 9, 1973 in New York, New York
Source: *NewYTBE 73; PseudN; WhAm 5; WhScrn 77; WhoHol B*

Leonard, John
American. Author
b. Feb 25, 1939 in Washington, DC
Source: *AmAu&B; ConAu 13R; DrAF 76; WhoE 74*

Leonard, Sheldon
[Sheldon Leonard Bershad]
American. TV Producer, Actor
Produced "The Dick Van Dyke Show"; "I Spy."
b. Feb 22, 1907 in New York, New York
Source: *FilmgC; IntMPA 75, 76, 77, 78, 79, 80, 81, 82; MotPP; MovMk; PseudN; Vers A; WhoAm 74, 76, 78, 80, 82; WhoHol A*

Leonard, "Sugar" Ray
[Ray Charles Leonard]
American. Boxer
Won gold medal, 1976 Olympics; retired as welterweight champ, Nov, 1982.
b. May 17, 1956 in Washington, DC
Source: *BioIn 11; PseudN; WhoAm 82*

Leonard, William Ellery
American. Poet
b. Jan 25, 1876 in Plainfield, New Jersey
d. May 2, 1944 in Madison, Wisconsin
Source: *AmAu&B; AmLY; ChPo, S1, S2; CnDAL; ConAmA; ConAmL; DcAmB S3; DcNAA; OxAmL; REn; REnAL; SixAP; TwCA, SUP; WhAm 2; WhNAA; WisWr*

Leonardo da Vinci
Italian. Artist, Musician, Scientist
Greatest paintings *The Last Supper,* 1498; *Mona Lisa,* 1503.
b. Apr 15, 1452 in Vinci, Italy
d. May 2, 1519 in Amboise, France
Source: *AtlBL; BbD; BiD&SB; CasWL; EuAu; NewC; OxEng; OxFr; Pen EUR; REn*

Leoncavallo, Ruggiero
Italian. Opera Composer
b. Mar 8, 1858 in Naples, Italy
d. Aug 9, 1919 in Montecatini, Italy
Source: *AtlBL; REn*

Leone, Giovanni
Italian. Former President
b. Nov 3, 1908 in Pamigliano, Italy
Source: *BioIn 9, 10, 11; CurBio 72; IntWW 74; NewYTBE 71; Who 74; WhoGov 72; WhoWor 74*

Leonetti, Tommy
American. Singer
b. Sep 10, 1929 in North Bergen, New Jersey
d. Sep 15, 1979 in Houston, Texas
Source: *AmSCAP 66*

Leoni, Franco
Italian. Composer
b. Oct 24, 1864 in Milan, Italy
d. Feb 8, 1949 in London, England
Source: *NewEOp 71*

Leonidas I
"The Defender of Thermopylae"
Greek. King of Sparta
d. 480BC in Thermopylae, Greece
Source: *NewC; PseudN*

Leonidoff, Leon
American. Theatrical Producer
b. Jan 2, 1895 in Bender, Romania
Source: *BioIn 2; CurBio 41; IntMPA 75*

Leonov, Alexei Arkhipovich
Russian. Cosmonaut
b. May 30, 1934 in Listvyanka, U.S.S.R.
Source: *BioIn 7, 10; CurBio 65; IntWW 74*

Leonowens, Anna Harriette Crawford
Welsh. Governess
Governess to Rama IV, King of Siam; stories basis of *The King and I.*
b. Nov 5, 1834 in Caenarvon, Wales
d. 1915
Source: *Alli; BbD; BiD&SB; DcAmAu; DcNAA; InWom; WhAm 4*

Leontovich, Eugenie
American. Actress, Motion Picture Director
b. Mar 21, 1900 in Moscow, Russia
Source: *BiE&WWA; FamA&A; FilmgC; NotNAT; WhoHol A; WhoThe 77*

Leopardi, Giacomo
Italian. Poet
b. Jun 29, 1798 in Recanati, Italy
d. Jun 14, 1837 in Naples, Italy
Source: *AtlBL; BbD; BiD&SB; CasWL; DcEuL; EuAu; EvEuW; OxEng; Pen EUR; RComWL; REn*

Leopold III
Belgian. Former King
b. Nov 3, 1901
Source: *CurBio 44; IntWW 74*

Leopold, Nathan Freudenthal
[Morton D Ballard; George Johnson, alaises; William F Lanne; Richard A Lawrence, pseuds.; Leopold and Loeb]
"Babe"
American. Kidnapper, Murderer, Author
Millionaire's son who committed murder, with Richard Loeb, to attempt the "perfect" crime.
b. Nov 19, 1904 in Kenwood, Illinois
d. Aug 28, 1971 in San Juan, Puerto Rico
Source: *Au&Wr 71; Blood; ConAu 17R, 29R; ConAu P-1; NewYTBE 71; PseudN*

Leopold and Loeb
see: Leopold, Nathan F; Loeb, Richard A

Leotard, Jules
French. Trapeze Artist
b. 1830 in Toulouse, France
d. 1870
Source: *BioIn 5; OxThe*

Leppard, Raymond John
English. Conductor
b. Aug 11, 1927 in London, England
Source: *CurBio 80; Who 74; WhoAm 82; WhoMus 72*

Lerman, Leo
American. Author
b. May 23, 1914 in New York, New York
Source: *ConAu 45; WhoAmA 73; WhoWorJ 72*

Lermontov, Mikhail (Michael Jurevich)
Russian. Poet
b. Oct 15, 1814 in Moscow, Russia
d. Jul 27, 1841 in Pyatigorsk, Russia
Source: *AtlBL; BbD; BiD&SB; CasWL; CyWA; DcEuL; DcRusL; EuAu; EvEuW; McGEWD; OxEng; OxThe; Pen EUR; REn*

Lerner, Alan Jay
[Lerner and Loewe]
American. Dramatist, Lyricist
Musicals include *My Fair Lady,* 1956; *Camelot,* 1960.
b. Aug 31, 1918 in New York, New York
Source: *AmAu&B; AmSCAP 66; BiE&WWA; CmMov; ConAu 77; ConDr 73; CurBio 58; EncMT; FilmgC; IntMPA 82; IntWW 74; ModWD; NewCBMT; NotNAT; OxAmL; OxFilm; REnAL; Who 74; WhoAm 74, 76, 78, 80, 82; WhoThe 77; WorEFlm*

Lerner, Max
American. Author, Lecturer, Journalist
b. Dec 20, 1902 in Minsk, Russia
Source: *AmAu&B; AmM&WS 73S; Au&Wr 71; AuNews 1; CelR 73; ConAu 13R; IntWW 74; OxAmL; Pen AM; REnAL; TwCA, SUP; Who 74; WhoAm 74, 76, 78, 80, 82; WhoE 74; WhoWor 74; WhoWorJ 72; WrDr 76*

Lerner and Loewe
see: Lerner, Alan Jay; Loewe, Frederick

LeRoux, Gaston
French. Author
b. May 6, 1868 in Paris, France
d. Apr 15, 1927 in Nice, France
Source: *CasWL; EncMys; LongCTC; OxFr*

Leroux, Xavier
Italian. Composer
b. Oct 11, 1863 in Velletri, Italy
d. Feb 2, 1919 in Paris, France
Source: *NewEOp 71*

Leroy
French. Fashion Designer
b. 1753
d. 1829
Source: *WorFshn*

Leroy, Mervyn
American. Motion Picture Director, Producer
b. Oct 15, 1900 in San Francisco, California
Source: *BiDFilm; CmMov; DcFM; FilmgC; IntMPA 75, 76, 77, 78, 79, 80, 81, 82; MovMk; OxFilm; TwYS; WhoAm 74, 76, 78, 80, 82*

Lert, Ernst
Austrian. Conductor, Stage Director
b. May 12, 1883 in Vienna, Austria
d. Jan 30, 1955 in Baltimore, Maryland
Source: *BiDAmM; NewEOp 71*

Les Six
[George Auric; Louis Durey; Arthur Honegger; Darius Milhaud; Francois Poulenc; Germaine Tailleferre]
French. Composers
Source: *NewEOp 71; OxMus; WebBD 80*

Lesage, Alain Rene
French. Author
b. May 8, 1668 in Sarzeau, France
d. Nov 17, 1747 in Boulogne, France
Source: *AtlBL; BbD; BiD&SB; BioIn 5, 7; CasWL; CnThe; CyWA; DcBiA; DcEuL; EncWT; EuAu; EvEuW; LinLib L, S; McGEWB; McGEWD; NewEOp 71; NotNAT, B; OxCan; OxEng; OxFr; OxSpan; OxThe; Pen EUR; RComWL; REn; REnWD; ScF&FL 1*

Lesage, Jean
Canadian. Statesman
b. Jun 10, 1912 in Montreal, PQ
d. Dec 11, 1980 in Quebec City, PQ
Source: *BioIn 5, 6, 7; CanWW 70, 79; CurBio 61, 81; IntWW 74, 75, 76, 77, 78; IntYB 78, 79; WhoCan 73, 75, 77*

Lescaze, William
American. Architect
b. Mar 27, 1896 in New York, New York
d. Feb 9, 1969 in New York, New York
Source: *CurBio 42, 69*

Lescoulie, Jack
American. TV Announcer
b. Nov 17, 1917 in Sacramento, California
Source: *IntMPA 75; WhoHol A*

Leser, Tina
[Tina Shillard Smith]
American. Fashion Designer
b. Dec 16, 1911 in Philadelphia, Pennsylvania
Source: *CurBio 57; InWom; PseudN; WhoAm 74; WorFshn*

Lesh, Phil
[Grateful Dead]
American. Rock Musician
b. Mar 15, 1940 in Berkeley, California
Source: *CelR 73; EncPR&S; RkOn*

Leskov, Nikolai
Russian. Author
b. Feb 4, 1831 in Gorokhovo, Russia
d. Feb 21, 1895 in Saint Petersburg, Russia
Source: *BbD; BiD&SB; CasWL; DcEuL; DcRusL; EuAu; EvEuW; Pen EUR; REn*

Leslie, Bethel
American. Actress
b. 1930
Source: *FilmgC; WhoHol A*

Leslie, Frank, pseud.
[Henry Carter]
American. Illustrator, Journalist
b. Mar 21, 1821 in Ipswich, England
d. Jan 10, 1880 in New York, New York
Source: *AmAu&B; AmBi; ApCAB; ChPo S2; DcAmB; EncAB-H; OxAmL; PseudN; REnAL; TwCBDA; WebAB; WhAm H*

Leslie, Joan
[Joan Brodell]
American. Actress
b. Jan 26, 1925 in Detroit, Michigan
Source: *FilmgC; HolP 40; InWom; IntMPA 75, 76, 77, 78, 79, 80, 81, 82; MotPP; MovMk; PseudN; WhoHol A*

Leslie, Miriam Florence Folline
American. Publisher, Author
b. 1836 in New Orleans, Louisiana
d. Sep 18, 1914
Source: *Alli SUP; AmAu; AmAu&B; ApCAB; DcAmB; DcNAA; InWom; NotAW; REnAL; TwCBDA; WebAB*

Lesnevich, Gus
"The Russian Lion"
American. Boxer
b. Feb 22, 1915 in Cliffside Park, New Jersey
d. Feb 28, 1964 in Cliffside Park, New Jersey
Source: *BioIn 6; PseudN; WhoBox 74*

Lessard, Mario
Canadian. Hockey Player
b. Jun 25, 1954 in East Broughton, PQ
Source: *HocReg*

Lesseps, Ferdinand Marie de
French. Engineer, Diplomat
b. Nov 19, 1805 in Versailles, France
d. Dec 7, 1894 in La Chanaie, France
Source: *ApCAB; BbD; BiD&SB; OxFr; REn*

Lesser, Sol
American. Motion Picture Producer
b. Feb 17, 1890 in Spokane, Washington
d. Sep 19, 1980 in Hollywood, California
Source: *CmMov; FilmgC; IntMPA 75, 76, 77; OxFilm; WhoAm 74; WhoWor 74; WorEFlm*

Lessing, Doris May
English. Author
b. Oct 22, 1919 in Kermanshah, Persia
Source: *Au&Wr 71; CnMD; ConAu 9R; ConDr 73; ConLC 1, 2, 3, 6, 10, 15; ConNov 72, 76; CroCD; DrAF 76; EncWL; InWom; LongCTC; ModBrL, SUP; ModWD; NewC; Pen ENG; RAdv 1; REn; TwCW; WebE&AL; Who 74; WhoAm 82; WhoTwCL; WhoWor 74; WorAu; WrDr 76*

Lessing, Gotthold Ephraim
"The Aesop of Germany"; "The Father of German Literature"; "The Frederick the Great of Thought"
German. Author
b. Jan 22, 1729 in Kamenz, Germany
d. Feb 15, 1781 in Brunswick, Germany
Source: *AtlBL; BbD; BiD&SB; CasWL; ChPo S1; CnThe; CyWA; DcEuL; EuAu; EvEuW; McGEWD; NewC; OxEng; OxGer; OxThe; Pen EUR; PseudN; RComWL; REn; REnWD*

Lester, Jerry
American. Comedian
b. 1910? in Chicago, Illinois
Source: *WhoHol A*

Lester, Mark
English. Actor
b. 1957? in Richmond, England
Source: *BioIn 10; FilmgC; IntMPA 75, 76, 77, 78, 79, 80, 81, 82; WhoHol A*

Lester, Richard
American. Motion Picture Director
b. Jan 19, 1932 in Philadelphia, Pennsylvania
Source: *BiDFilm; BioNews 75; CelR 73; CurBio 69; DcFM; IntMPA 75, 76, 77, 78, 79, 80, 81, 82; MovMk; OxFilm; Who 74; WhoAm 74, 76, 78, 80, 82; WhoWor 74; WorEFlm*

Lester, Tom
American. Actor
b. 1938 in Jackson, Mississippi
Source: *WhoHol A*

Lesueur, Jean-Francois
French. Composer
b. Feb 15, 1760 in Drucat-Plessiel, France
d. Oct 6, 1837 in Paris, France
Source: *NewEOp 71; OxMus*

Letelier, Orlando
Chilean. Diplomat
b. Apr 13, 1932 in Temuco, Chile
d. Sep 21, 1976 in Washington, DC
Source: *IntWW 74; WhoGov 72; WhoWor 74*

LeTourneau, Robert Gilmour
American. Engineer, Business Executive
b. Nov 30, 1888 in Richmond, Vermont
d. Jun 1, 1969 in Longview, Texas
Source: *WhAm 5*

Letterman, David
American. TV Personality
b. Apr 12, 1947 in Indianapolis, Indiana
Source: *CurBio 80; WhoAm 82*

Lettermen, The
[Tony Butala; Gary Pike; Jim Pike]
American. Vocal Group
Source: *EncPR&S*

Leutze, Emanuel
American. Artist
b. May 24, 1816 in Gumund, Germany
d. Jul 18, 1868 in Washington, DC
Source: *AmBi; ApCAB; BiAuS; DcAmB; Drake; EarABI, SUP; OxAmL; TwCBDA; WebAB; WhAm H*

Lev, Ray
Austrian. Musician
b. May 8, 1912 in Rostov-on-Don, Russia
d. May 20, 1968
Source: *CurBio 49, 68; InWom; WhAm 5*

Leval, Francois de Montmorancy
Canadian. Bishop
b. Apr 30, 1623
d. Mar 6, 1708
Source: *NF*

Levant, Oscar
American. Composer, Musician
b. Dec 27, 1906 in Pittsburgh, Pennsylvania
d. Aug 14, 1972 in Beverly Hills, California
Source: *AmAu&B; AmSCAP 66; CmMov; ConAu 37R; CurBio 40, 52, 72; FilmgC; HolP 40; MotPP; MovMk; NewYTBE 72; REnAL; WhAm 5; WhScrn 77; WhoHol B*

Levasseur, Nicolas Prosper
French. Opera Singer
b. Mar 9, 1791 in Bresles, France
d. Dec 7, 1871 in Paris, France
Source: *NewEOp 71*

Levasseur, Rosalie
French. Opera Singer
b. Oct 8, 1749 in Valenciennes, France
d. May 6, 1826 in Germany
Source: *NewEOp 71*

Leveille, Normand
Canadian. Hockey Player
Hockey career ended when he suffered cerebral hemmorage between periods of game, Oct 23, 1982.
b. Jan 10, 1963 in Montreal, PQ
Source: *HocReg*

Levene, Sam
[Samuel Levine]
American. Actor
b. Aug 28, 1905
d. Dec 29, 1980 in New York, New York
Source: *BiE&WWA; BioNews 74; CelR 73; EncMT; FilmgC; IntMPA 75, 76, 77; MotPP; MovMk; NewYTBE 72; NotNAT; PseudN; Vers B; WhoAm 74; WhoHol A; WhoWor 74*

Levenson, Sam(uel)
American. Humorist
b. Dec 28, 1911 in New York, New York
d. Aug 27, 1980 in Neponsit, New York
Source: *AuNews 1; BioNews 74; CelR 73; ConAu 65, 101; CurBio 59; IntMPA 75, 77; WhoAm 74*

Leventhal, Albert Rice
[Albert Rice, pseud.]
American. Publisher
b. Oct 30, 1907 in New York, New York
d. Jan 4, 1976 in New York, New York
Source: *ConAu 61, 65; WhAm 6; WhoAm 74*

Leverhulme, William Hesketh Lever, Viscount
English. Soap Manufacturer
b. 1851 in Bolton, England
d. 1925
Source: *WhAm 2*

Levertov, Denise
American. Poet
b. Oct 24, 1923 in Ilford, England
Source: *AmAu&B; ConAu 1R, 3NR; ConLC 1, 2, 3, 5, 8, 15; ConP 70, 75; CroCAP; DrAP 75; ModAL, SUP; ModBrL; NewC; OxAmL; Pen AM; RAdv 1; REn; REnAL; WebE&AL; WhoAm 74; WhoE 74; WhoTwCL; WhoWor 74; WorAu; WrDr 76*

Levesque, Rene
"Rene the Red"
Canadian. Government Official
President, Parti Quebecois; wants Quebec to secede from Canada.
b. Aug 24, 1922 in New Carlisle, PQ
Source: *CanWW 82; CurBio 75; NewYTBE 70; OxCan SUP; PseudN; WhoAm 74, 76, 78, 80, 82; WhoE 74; WhoWor 74*

Levi, Edward Hirsch
American. Former Attorney General
b. Jun 26, 1911 in Chicago, Illinois
Source: *ConAu 49, 2NR; CurBio 69; DrAS 74P; LEduc 74; Who 74; WhoAm 74, 76, 78, 80, 82; WhoMW 74; WhoWor 74; WhoWorJ 72; WrDr 76*

Levi, Hermann
German. Conductor
b. Nov 7, 1839 in Giessen, Germany
d. May 13, 1900 in Germany
Source: *NewEOp 71; OxMus*

Levi, Julian Edwin
American. Artist
b. Jun 20, 1900 in New York, New York
d. Feb 28, 1982 in New York, New York
Source: *CurBio 43, 82; DcCAA 71, 77; NewYTBS 82; WhoAmA 73, 76, 78*

Levi-Strauss, Claude
French. Anthropologist
b. Nov 28, 1908 in Brussels, Belgium
Source: *Au&Wr 71; CasWL; ConAu 1R; CurBio 72; EncWL; IntWW 74; Who 74; WhoWor 74; WorAu*

Levin, Bernard
British. Critic, Journalist
Source: *WrDr 80*

Levin, Carl Milton
American. Senator
b. Jun 28, 1934 in Detroit, Michigan
Source: *WhoAm 82; WhoMW 78*

Levin, Harry Tuchman
American. Literary Critic
b. Jul 18, 1912 in Minneapolis, Minnesota
Source: *ConAu 1R, 2NR; DrAS 74E; WhoAm 74, 76, 78, 80, 82*

Levin, Ira
American. Author
b. Aug 27, 1929 in Bronx, New York
Source: *AmAu&B; AmSCAP 66; Au&Wr 71; BiE&WWA; ConAu 21R; ConLC 3, 6; ConNov 72, 76; EncMys; NotNAT; WhoAm 82; WrDr 76*

Levin, Meyer
American. Author
b. Oct 8, 1905 in Chicago, Illinois
d. Jul 9, 1981 in Jerusalem, Israel
Source: *AmAu&B; AmNov; Au&Wr 71; AuNews 1; BiE&WWA; BioIn 2, 4, 7, 10; BioNews 74; CelR 73; CnMD; ConAu 9R, 104; ConLC 7; ConNov 72, 76; CurBio 40, 81; IntAu&W 76, 77; ModAL; NotNAT; OxAmL; Pen AM; REn; REnAL; ScF&FL 1, 2; SmATA 21; TwCA, SUP; WhoAm 74, 76, 78, 80; WhoWorJ 72; WrDr 76, 80*

Levine, Albert Norman
Canadian. Author
b. Oct 22, 1924 in Ottawa, ON
Source: *Au&Wr 71; CanWW 82; CreCan 1*

Levine, Beth
American. Shoe Designer
Source: *WorFshn*

Levine, David
American. Artist, Caricaturist
b. Dec 20, 1926 in Brooklyn, New York
Source: *CurBio 73; IlsCB 1957; WhoAm 82*

Levine, Herbert
American. Shoe Designer
Source: *WorFshn*

Levine, Irving R
American. Broadcast Journalist
b. Aug 26, 1922 in Pawtucket, Rhode Island
Source: *AmAu&B; ConAu 13R; CurBio 59; WhoAm 74, 76, 78, 80, 82; WhoWor 74; WhoWorJ 72*

Levine, Jack
American. Artist
b. Jan 3, 1915 in Boston, Massachusetts
Source: *DcCAA 71; IntWW 74; REn; WebAB; WhoAm 74, 76, 78, 80, 82; WhoAmA 73; WhoWor 74; WhoWorJ 72*

Levine, James
American. Conductor
b. Jun 23, 1943 in Cincinnati, Ohio
Source: *NewYTBE 72; WhoAm 74, 76, 78, 80, 82; WhoE 74; WhoMW 74*

Levine, Joseph E
American. Motion Picture Producer
b. Sep 9, 1905 in Boston, Massachusetts
Source: *BiE&WWA; CelR 73; FilmgC; IntMPA 75, 76, 77, 78, 79, 80, 81, 82; OxFilm; WhoAm 74, 76, 78, 80, 82; WhoWor 74; WorEFlm*

Levine, Philip
[Edgar Poe, pseud.]
American. Author, Poet
b. Jan 10, 1928 in Detroit, Michigan
Source: *ConAu 9R; ConLC 2, 4, 5; ConP 70, 75; CroCAP; DrAP 75; DrAS 74E; PseudN; WhoAm 82; WhoWest 74; WrDr 76*

Levinsky, "Battling"
[Barney Lebrowitz; Barney Williams]
American. Boxer
b. Jun 10, 1891 in Philadelphia, Pennsylvania
d. Feb 12, 1949 in Philadelphia, Pennsylvania
Source: *PseudN; WhoBox 74*

Levitin, Sonia
American. Children's Author
b. Aug 18, 1934 in Berlin, Germany
Source: *ConAu 29R; ConLC 17; SmATA 4*

Levitt, Arthur, Jr.
American. Banker, Government Official
b. Feb 3, 1931 in Brooklyn, New York
d. May 6, 1980 in New York, New York
Source: *St&PR 75; WhoAm 74, 76, 78, 80, 82*

Levitt, William Jaird
American. Builder
b. Feb 11, 1907 in Brooklyn, New York
Source: *CelR 73; CurBio 56; WhoAm 74, 76, 78, 80, 82; WhoF&I 74; WhoWor 74*

Levy, Julien
American. Art Dealer, Author
b. Jan 22, 1906 in New York, New York
d. Feb 10, 1981 in New Haven, Connecticut
Source: *BioIn 11; ConAu 103; NewYTBS 81; WhoAmA 78*

Levy, Leonard Williams
American. Author, Educator
b. Apr 9, 1923 in Toronto, ON
Source: *ConAu 1R, 1NR; WhoAm 76, 78, 80, 82; WhoE 74; WhoWorJ 72*

Levy, Uriah Phillips
American. Naval Officer
b. Apr 22, 1792 in Philadelphia, Pennsylvania
d. Mar 22, 1862 in New York, New York
Source: *Alli SUP; ApCAB; DcAmB; Drake; WebAB; WhAm H*

Levy-Bruhl, Lucien
French. Philosopher
b. Apr 10, 1857 in Paris, France
d. Mar 13, 1939 in Paris, France
Source: *BioIn 9; McGEWB; NewCol 75; OxFr; WorAu 1970*

Lewenthal, Raymond
American. Conductor
b. Aug 29, 1926 in San Antonio, Texas
Source: *NewYTBE 71; WhoMus 72; WhoWor 74*

Lewin, Kurt
American. Psychologist
b. Sep 9, 1890 in Mogilno, Prussia
d. Feb 12, 1947 in Newtonville, Massachusetts
Source: *BioIn 1, 5, 8; DcAmB S4; McGEWB; NewCol 75; WhAm 2*

Lewis, Sir Allen Montgomery
Former Governor of Saint Lucia
b. Oct 26, 1909 in Saint Lucia, West Indies
Source: *WhoWor 78*

Lewis, Anthony
American. Journalist
b. Mar 27, 1927 in New York, New York
Source: *ConAu 9R; CurBio 55; Who 74; WhoAm 74, 76, 78, 80, 82*

Lewis, Boyd de Wolf
American. Editor, Author
b. Aug 18, 1905 in Boston, Massachusetts
Source: *WhoAm 74, 76, 78, 80, 82; WhoWor 74*

Lewis, Cecil Day
see: Day-Lewis, Cecil

Lewis, Charles Bertrand
see: Quad, M pseud.

Lewis, Claude
American. Motion Picture Executive
b. Jul 5, 1926 in Hutchinson, Kansas
Source: *IntMPA 75, 76, 77, 78, 79, 80, 81, 82; WhoBlA 75; WhoE 74; WhoF&I 74*

Lewis, C(live) S(taples)
[N W Clerk; Clive Hamilton, pseuds.]
English. Author
Wrote *Allegory of Love,* 1936, analysis of literary evolution of romantic love.
b. Nov 29, 1898 in Belfast, Northern Ireland
d. Nov 22, 1963 in Heddington, England
Source: *AnCL; Au&ICB; AuBYP; CasWL; ConAu 81; ConLC 1, 3, 6, 14; CurBio 44, 64; DcLEL; EncWL; EvLB; LongCTC; ModBrL, SUP; MorJA; NewC; OxEng; Pen ENG; PseudN; RAdv 1; REn; SmATA 13; TwCA SUP; TwCW; WebE&AL; WhAm 4; WhoChL*

Lewis, Dominic Bevan Wyndham
English. Journalist
b. 1894
d. Nov 23, 1969 in Altea, Spain
Source: *CathA 1930; ChPo S1, S2; ConAu 25R; DcLEL; EvLB; LongCTC; ModBrL; NewC; Pen ENG; REn; TwCA, SUP*

Lewis, Drew (Andrew Lindsay, Jr.)
American. Government Official
Secretary of Transportation, 1981-Feb, 1983.
b. Nov 3, 1931 in Philadelphia, Pennsylvania
Source: *CurBio 82; WhoAm 74, 76, 78, 80, 82; WhoAmP 77, 79*

Lewis, Ed
"Strangler"
American. Wrestler, Actor
b. 1890
d. Sep 7, 1966 in Muskogee, Oklahoma
Source: *BioIn 7; WhScrn 77*

Lewis, Francis
American. Continental Congressman
b. Mar 21, 1713 in Llandaff, Wales
d. Dec 30, 1802 in New York, New York
Source: *AmBi; ApCAB; BiAuS; BiDrAC; DcAmB; Drake; TwCBDA; WhAm H; WhAmP*

Lewis, Fulton, Jr.
American. Broadcast Journalist
b. Apr 30, 1903 in Washington, DC
d. Aug 21, 1966 in Washington, DC
Source: *ConAu 89; CurBio 42, 66; WhAm 4*

Lewis, Henry Jay
American. Conductor
b. Oct 16, 1932 in Los Angeles, California
Source: *CurBio 73; WhoAm 74, 76, 78, 80, 82; WhoBlA 75; WhoE 74; WhoWor 74*

Lewis, James W.
[Robert Richardson, alias]
American. Alleged Extortionist
Accused of extorting Johnson & Johnson during Chicago's Tylenol poisonings, 1982.
b. 1946?
Source: *NF*

Lewis, Janet
[Janet Lewis Winters]
American. Author
b. Aug 17, 1899 in Chicago, Illinois
Source: *AmAu&B; AmNov; AmSCAP 66; Au&Wr 71; ChPo, S1; CnDAL; ConAu P-1; ConNov 72, 76; ForWC 70; InWom; OxAmL; TwCA SUP; WhoAm 74; WrDr 76*

Lewis, Jerry
[Joseph Levitch]
American. Comedian
Telethons for muscular dystrophy have raised over $300 million.
b. Mar 16, 1926 in Newark, New Jersey
Source: *BiDFilm; BkPepl; CelR 73; CmMov; CurBio 62; FilmgC; IntMPA 75, 76, 77, 78, 79, 80, 81, 82; MotPP; MovMk; NewYTBE 72; OxFilm; WhoAm 74, 76, 78, 80, 82; WhoHol A; WorEFlm*

Lewis, Jerry Lee
"Killer"
American. Singer, Musician
Best known recording "Roll Over Beethoven."
b. Sep 29, 1935 in Ferriday, Louisiana
Source: *EncFCWM 69; EncPR&S; IlEncRk; WhoAm 82*

Lewis, Joe E
American. Actor, Comedian
b. Jan 12, 1902 in New York, New York
d. Jun 4, 1971 in New York, New York
Source: *FilmgC; NewYTBE 71; WhScrn 77; WhoHol B*

Lewis, John Aaron
American. Musician
b. May 3, 1920 in LaGrange, Illinois
Source: *CelR 73; WhoAm 74, 76, 78, 80, 82; WhoBlA 75*

Lewis, John Llewellyn
American. Labor Leader
President, UMW, 1920-60.
b. Feb 12, 1880 in Lucas, Iowa
d. Jun 11, 1969 in Washington, DC
Source: *CurBio 42, 69; EncAB-H; WebAB*

Lewis, John Robert
American. Civil Rights Activist
b. Feb 21, 1940 in Troy, Alabama
Source: *CurBio 80*

Lewis, Jordan David
American. Government Official
b. Aug 9, 1937 in Chicago, Illinois
Source: *AmM&WS 73P; WhoAm 74, 76, 78, 80, 82; WhoMW 74*

Lewis, Meade Anderson Lux
American. Musician
b. Sep 5, 1905 in Louisville, Kentucky
d. Jun 7, 1964 in Minneapolis, Minnesota
Source: *AmSCAP 66; WhScrn 74, 77; WhoHol B; WhoJazz 72*

Lewis, Meriwether
American. Explorer
With William Clark, commanded first expedition across America, 1804-06.
b. Aug 18, 1774 in Albemarle County, Virginia
d. Oct 11, 1809 in Nashville, Tennessee
Source: *Alli; AmAu&B; AmBi; ApCAB; BiAuS; BiDSA; CasWL; DcAmB; Drake; EncAB-H; OxAmL; Pen AM; REnAL; TwCBDA; WebAB; WhAm H*

Lewis, Monica
American. Actress
b. May 5, 1925 in Chicago, Illinois
Source: *IntMPA 75, 76, 77, 78, 79, 80, 81, 82; WhoHol A*

Lewis, Oscar
American. Anthropologist, Author
b. Dec 25, 1914 in New York, New York
d. Dec 16, 1970 in New York, New York
Source: *AmAu&B; ConAu 29R; ConAu P-1; CurBio 68, 71; WhAm 5; WorAu*

Lewis, Paul Edward
[The Hostages]
American. Former Hostage in Iran
b. 1957?
Source: *NewYTBS 81*

Lewis, Ramsey Emanuel, Jr.
American. Musician, Composer
b. May 27, 1935 in Chicago, Illinois
Source: *BioIn 7, 10; WhoAm 74, 76, 78, 80, 82; WhoBlA 75*

Lewis, Robert Q
American. Radio, TV Personality
b. Apr 5, 1921 in New York, New York
Source: *BioIn 1, 3; WhoHol A*

Lewis, Rosa
[Rosa Ovenden]
British. Hotelkeeper
b. 1867
d. 1952
Source: *BioIn 3, 6, 7, 11*

Lewis, Shari
[Shari Hurwitz; Mrs. Jeremy Tarcher]
American. Ventriloquist, Author
Starred on TV with puppet Lamb Chop; won five Emmys.
b. Jan 17, 1934 in New York, New York
Source: *ConAu 89; CurBio 58; WhoAm 74, 76, 78, 80, 82*

Lewis, Sinclair
American. Author, Dramatist
First American to win Nobel Prize for Literature, 1930.
b. Feb 7, 1885 in Sauk Centre, Minnesota
d. Jan 10, 1951 in Rome, Italy
Source: *AmAu&B; AmNov; AmWr; AtlBL; CasWL; Chambr 3; ChPo; CnDAL; CnMD; CnMWL; ConAmA; ConAmL; CyWA; DcAmB S5; DcLEL; EncAB-H; EncWL; FilmgC; LongCTC; ModAL, SUP; ModWD; OxAmL; OxEng; Pen AM; RAdv 1; RComWL; REn; REnAL; TwCA, SUP; TwCW; WebAB; WebE&AL; WhAm 3; WhNAA; WhScrn 77; WhoTwCL*

Lewis, Ted
[Theodore Leopold Friedman]
American. Band Leader
b. Jun 9, 1892 in Circleville, Ohio
d. Aug 25, 1971 in New York, New York
Source: *AmSCAP 66; FilmgC; NewYTBE 70, 71; WhAm 5; WhScrn 74, 77; WhoHol B; WhoJazz 72*

Lewis, Ted
"Kid"
English. Boxer
b. Oct 24, 1894 in London, England
d. Oct 20, 1970 in London, England
Source: *BioIn 7, 9; WhoBox 74*

Lewis, Tillie Ehrlich
American. Canning Executive
b. 1901 in Brooklyn, New York
d. Apr 30, 1977 in Stockton, California
Source: *BioIn 2, 3, 9, 10, 11; St&PR 75*

Lewis, Wyndham
English. Author, Artist
b. Nov 18, 1884 in Maine
d. Mar 7, 1957 in London, England
Source: *AtlBL; CasWL; CnE&AP; CnMWL; CyWA; DcLEL; EvLB; LongCTC; ModBrL, SUP; NewC; OxCan; OxEng; Pen ENG; RAdv 1; REn; TwCA, SUP; TwCW; WebE&AL; WhoTwCL*

Lewisohn, Adolph
American. Philanthropist
b. 1849 in Hamburg, Germany
d. Aug 17, 1938 in New York, New York
Source: *ChPo S1; DcAmB S2; WhAm 1*

Lewisohn, Ludwig
English. Author, Artist
b. May 30, 1882 in Berlin, Germany
d. Dec 31, 1955 in Miami Beach, Florida
Source: *BioIn 2, 4, 5, 7, 9, 11*

Lewton, Val Ivan
[Vladimir Leventon]
American. Motion Picture Producer
b. 1904 in Yalta, Russia
d. 1951
Source: *BiDFilm; BioIn 1, 2, 11; DcFM; FanAl; FilmgC; OxFilm; WorEFlm*

Lewyt, Alexander Milton
American. Inventor, Business Executive
b. Dec 31, 1903 in New York, New York
Source: *WhoAm 74, 76, 78, 80, 82; WhoWor 74*

Ley, Robert
German. Nazi Leader
b. Feb 15, 1890 in Niederbreitenbach, Germany
d. Oct 25, 1945 in Nuremberg, Germany
Source: *BioIn 1; CurBio 40, 45; EncTR; LinLib S; ObitOF 79; REn*

Ley, Willy
American. Scientist, Author
b. Oct 2, 1906 in Berlin, Germany
d. Jun 24, 1969 in New York, New York
Source: *AmAu&B; Au&Wr 71; AuBYP; ConAu 9R, 25R; CurBio 41, 53, 69; REnAL; SmATA 2; ThrBJA; TwCA SUP; WhAm 5*

Leyendecker, Joseph Christian
American. Artist
b. Mar 23, 1874 in Montabour, Germany
d. Jul 25, 1951 in New Rochelle, New York
Source: *DcAmB S5; WhAm 3*

L'Hermitte, Leon Augustin
French. Artist
b. 1844 in Mont-Saint-Pere, France
d. 1925 in Paris, France
Source: *McGDA*

Lhevinne, Josef
American. Musician, Teacher
b. Dec 3, 1874 in Moscow, Russia
d. Dec 2, 1944 in New York, New York
Source: *CurBio 45; DcAmB S3; WhAm 2*

Lhevinne, Rosina L
American. Musician, Teacher
b. Mar 29, 1880 in Moscow, Russia
d. Nov 9, 1976 in Glendale, California
Source: *CelR 73; CurBio 61; InWom; NewYTBE 70*

L'Hopital, Michel de
French. Statesman, Jurist
b. 1505
d. Mar 13, 1573
Source: *BiD&SB; CasWL; DcEuL; EuAu; OxFr; REn*

Li Po
[Li T'ai-Pai; Li T'ai Peh; Li T'ai-Po]
Chinese. Poet
b. 701 in Szechwan, China
d. 762
Source: *CasWL; DcOrL 1; Pen CL; RComWL; REn*

Libby, Willard Frank
American. Chemist, Inventor
Won Nobel Prize, 1960, for development of radioactive carbon 14 dating.
b. Dec 17, 1908 in Grand Valley, Colorado
d. Sep 8, 1980 in Los Angeles, California
Source: *AmM&WS 73P; CelR 73; IntWW 74; NewYTBS 80; WebAB, 79; Who 74; WhoAm 74, 76, 78, 80*

Liberace
[Wladziu Valentino Liberace]
"Walter Busterkeys"
American. Musician, Entertainer
b. May 16, 1919 in West Allis, Wisconsin
Source: *AmSCAP 66; BioIn 3, 4, 5, 7, 10, 11; BkPepl; ConAu 89; CurBio 54; FilmgC; IntMPA 77, 78, 79, 80, 81, 82; WhoAm 74, 76, 78, 80, 82; WhoHol A; WhoWor 74*

Liberace, George J
American. Musician
b. Jul 31, 1911 in Menasha, Wisconsin
Source: *AmSCAP 66*

Liberman, Alexander
American. Editor, Artist
b. Sep 4, 1912 in Kiev, Russia
Source: *BioIn 2, 5, 7, 9, 10; BnEnAmA; ConArt; DcCAA 71, 77; NewYTBS 79; WhoAm 80, 82; WhoAmA 73, 76, 78; WhoE 75*

Licavoli, Thomas
American. Criminal
b. 1904
d. Sep 16, 1973 in Columbus, Ohio
Source: *BioIn 8, 10; NewYTBE 73*

Lichine, Alexis
American. Author, Wine Expert
b. Dec 3, 1913 in Moscow, Russia
Source: *Au&Wr 71; ConAu 9R; WhoAm 74; WhoWor 74; WrDr 76*

Lichine, David
Russian. Choreographer
b. Oct 25, 1910 in Rostov-on-Don, Russia
d. Jun 26, 1972 in Los Angeles, California
Source: *NewYTBE 72; WhScrn 77*

Lichtenstein, Roy
American. Artist
Pioneered 1960's Pop Art movement, with comic strip inspired paintings.
b. Oct 27, 1923 in New York, New York
Source: *CelR 73; CurBio 69; DcCAA 71; IntWW 74; WebAB; WhoAm 74, 76, 78, 80, 82; WhoAmA 73*

Lichty, George Maurice
American. Cartoonist
b. May 16, 1905 in Chicago, Illinois
Source: *ConAu 104; WhoAm 76, 78, 80, 82*

Liddell, Eric
"The Flying Scot"
British. Missionary, Track Athlete
Portrayed in the film *Chariots of Fire.*
b. 1902 in China
d. Feb 21, 1945 in Weihsien, China
Source: *BioIn 7, 9*

Liddell Hart, Basil Henry
British. Author
b. Oct 31, 1895 in London, England
d. Jan 29, 1970
Source: *Au&Wr 71; ConAu 89, 103; CurBio 40, 70; DcLEL; EvLB; LongCTC; NewC; TwCA, SUP*

Liddy, G(eorge) Gordon
American. Watergate Participant
b. Nov 30, 1930 in New York, New York
Source: *BioIn 9, 10; NewYTBE 73*

Lidz, Theodore
American. Educator, Psychiatrist
b. Apr 1, 1910 in New York, New York
Source: *AmM&WS 73S; ConAu 29R; WhoAm 74; WhoWorJ 72*

Lie, Trygve Halvdan
Norwegian. Lawyer, Diplomat
b. Jul 16, 1896 in Oslo, Norway
d. Dec 30, 1968 in Geilo, Norway
Source: *CurBio 46, 69; REn; WhoUN 75*

Lieber, Franz
American. Editor, Political Scientist
b. Mar 18, 1800 in Berlin, Germany
d. Oct 2, 1872 in New York, New York
Source: *AmBi; ApCAB; BiDAmEd; BioIn 1, 4, 5, 8, 9; DcAmB; Drake; EncAB-H; NatCAB 5; TwCBDA; WebAB; WebAMB; WhAm H*

Lieberman, Nancy
American. Basketball Player
First woman to be given a try-out with an NBA team.
b. Jul 1, 1958 in Brooklyn, New York
Source: *BioIn 11; NewYTBS 82*

Liebermann, Rolf
Swiss. Composer, Impresario
b. Sep 14, 1910 in Zurich, Switzerland
Source: *CurBio 73; DcCM; IntWW 74; WhoMus 72; WhoWor 74*

Liebig, Justus von
German. Chemist
b. May 12, 1803 in Darmstadt, Germany
d. Apr 18, 1873 in Munich, Germany
Source: *BbD; BiD&SB; OxGer*

Liebknecht, Karl
German. Communist Leader
b. 1871 in Berlin, Germany
d. 1919
Source: *OxGer; REn*

Liebling, Abbot Joseph
American. Journalist
b. Oct 18, 1904 in New York, New York
d. Dec 28, 1963 in New York, New York
Source: *BioIn 1, 2, 4, 5, 6, 8, 10, 11; ConAu 89, 104; TwCA SUP*

Liebling, Estelle
American. Singer, Opera Teacher
b. Apr 21, 1884 in New York, New York
d. Sep 25, 1970 in New York, New York
Source: *AmSCAP 66; InWom; NewEOp 71; NewYTBE 70*

Liebman, Joshua Loth
American. Author
b. Apr 7, 1907 in Hamilton, Ohio
d. Jun 9, 1948
Source: *AmAu&B; CurBio 46, 48; DcAmB S4; DcNAA; OhA&B; REnAL; WhAm 2*

Liebman, Max
American. Director, Producer, Writer
b. Aug 5, 1902 in Vienna, Austria
d. Jul 21, 1981 in New York, New York
Source: *AmSCAP 66; BiE&WWA; BioIn 2, 3; CurBio 53, 81; IntMPA 75, 76, 77, 78, 79, 80, 81, 82; NewYTET; NotNAT; WhoAm 74, 76, 78; WhoWorJ 72*

Liebmann, Philip
American. Advertising Executive
b. Feb 19, 1915 in New York, New York
d. 1972
Source: *NewYTBE 72; WhAm 5*

Liefson, Alex
see: Rush

Lietzke, Bruce
American. Golfer
b. Jul 18, 1951 in Kansas City, Kansas
Source: *BioIn 11*

Lifar, Serge
Russian. Ballet Dancer
b. Apr 2, 1905 in Kiev, Russia
Source: *IntWW 74; Who 74; WhoThe 77; WhoWor 74*

Lifshin, Lyn
American. Author
b. 1942 in Burlington, Vermont
Source: *ConAu 33R; ConP 75; DrAP 75; WrDr 76*

Liggett, Louis Kroh
American. Founder of Liggett Stores
b. Apr 4, 1875 in Detroit, Michigan
d. Jun 5, 1946 in Washington, DC
Source: *CurBio 46; DcAmB S4; WhAm 2*

Light, Enoch Henry
American. Musician
b. Aug 18, 1907 in Canton, Ohio
d. Jul 31, 1978 in New York, New York
Source: *AmSCAP 66; NewYTBS 78; WhoAm 74, 76, 78; WhoF&I 74; WhoWor 74*

Light, Judith
American. Actress
b. 1949?
Source: *BioIn 12*

Lightfoot, Gordon Meredith
Canadian. Singer, Songwriter
Wrote songs "If You Could Read My Mind," 1970, "Sundown," 1974.
b. Nov 17, 1939 in Orillia, ON
Source: *AmSCAP 66; BioIn 8, 10, 11; BioNews 74; BkPepl; CanWW 82; CreCan 2; WhoAm 82*

Lilburne, John
English. Statesman
b. 1614
d. 1657
Source: *BioIn 1, 4, 6, 10, 11; NewCol 75; WebBD 80*

Lilienthal, David Eli
American. Public Administrator
b. Jul 8, 1899 in Morton, Illinois
d. Jan 14, 1981 in New York, New York
Source: *AmAu&B; CelR 73; ConAu 5R, 102, 3NR; CurBio 44; EncAB-H; IntWW 74; WebAB; Who 74; WhoAm 74; WhoWor 74; WhoWorJ 72*

Lilienthal, Otto
German. Engineer, Naturalist
b. 1848
d. 1896
Source: *BioIn 5, 8, 9; NewCol 75*

Liliuokalani, Lydia Kamekeha
Last Hawaiian Monarch
b. Sep 2, 1838 in Honolulu, Hawaii
d. Nov 11, 1917
Source: *AmBi; DcAmAu; HerW; NotAW; WhAm HA, 4*

Lillie, Beatrice
English. Actress, Comedienne
b. May 29, 1898 in Toronto, ON
Source: *CelR 73; CurBio 45, 64; EncMT; FamA&A; FilmgC; IntWW 74; MovMk; ThFT; Who 74; WhoAm 74, 76, 78, 80, 82; WhoHol A; WhoThe 77*

Lilly, Doris
American. Journalist, Author
b. Dec 26, 1926 in Pasadena, California
Source: *BioIn 5; CelR 73; ConAu 29R; InWom; WhoAm 82*

Lilly, Eli
American. Drug Manufacturer
Founded Eli Lilly Pharmaceutical Co.
b. Apr 1, 1885 in Indianapolis, Indiana
d. Jan 24, 1977 in Indianapolis, Indiana
Source: *AmAu&B; ConAu 69; IndAu 1917; WhoAm 74; WhoF&I 74; WhoWor 74*

Lilly, John C
American. Author, Physician
b. Jan 6, 1915 in Saint Paul, Minnesota
Source: *ConAu 1R, 1NR; CurBio 62; WhoAm 74, 76, 78, 80, 82; WhoS&SW 73*

Limann, Hilla
Ghanaian. President
b. Dec 12, 1934? in Gwollu, Ghana
Source: *AfSS 80; CurBio 81; IntWW 80; WhoUN 75*

Limbert, John William, Jr.
[The Hostages]
American. Former Hostage in Iran
b. Mar 10, 1943 in Washington, DC
Source: *NewYTBS 81; USBiR 74*

Limon, Jose Arcadio
American. Choreographer
b. Jan 12, 1908 in Culiacan, Mexico
d. Dec 2, 1972 in Flemington, New Jersey
Source: *CurBio 53, 68, 73; WhAm 5; WhoE 74*

Lin Yu-T'ang
Chinese. Author, Philologist
b. Oct 10, 1895 in Changchow, China
d. Mar 26, 1976 in Hong Kong, China
Source: *AmAu&B; CasWL; ConAu 45, 2NR; CurBio 40; DcLEL; DcOrL 1; LongCTC; REn; REnAL; TwCA, SUP; TwCW; Who 74*

Lin, Maya Ying
American. Student
Designed Vietman War Memorial, Washington, DC, dedicated 1982.
b. 1960 in Athens, Ohio
Source: *NewYTBS 81*

Lin, Piao (Yu-Yung)
Chinese. Marshal, Politician
b. 1908 in Ungkung, China
d. Sep 12, 1971
Source: *CurBio 72; NewYTBS 74; WhAm 5*

Linacre, Thomas
English. Author, Physician
b. 1460 in Canterbury, England
d. Oct 20, 1524 in London, England
Source: *Alli; BrAu; Chambr 1; DcEnL; DcEuL; NewC; OxEng; REn*

Lincoln, Abbey
American. Singer, Actress
b. Aug 6, 1930 in Chicago, Illinois
Source: *BlkAW; CelR 73; WhoAm 74; WhoHol A*

Lincoln, Abraham
American. 16th US President
More written on him than any other American figure.
b. Feb 12, 1809 in Hardin County, Kentucky
d. Apr 15, 1865 in Washington, DC
Source: *AmAu&B; AmBi; ApCAB; AtlBL; BbD; BiAuS; BiD&SB; BiDSA; BiDrAC; BiDrUSE; Chambr 3; ChPo S2; CyWA; DcAmAu; DcAmB; DcLEL; DcNAA; Drake; EncAB-H; EvLB; FilmgC; OxAmL; OxEng; Pen AM; PlP&P; RComWL; REn; REnAL; TwCBDA; WebAB; WebE&AL; WhAm H; WhAmP*

Lincoln, Elmo
American. Actor
b. 1889
d. Jun 27, 1952 in Hollywood, California
Source: *CmMov; Film 1; FilmgC; MovMk; TwYS; WhScrn 74, 77; WhoHol B*

Lincoln, George A
American. Military Leader
b. Jul 20, 1907 in Harbor Beach, Michigan
d. May 24, 1975 in Colorado Springs, Colorado
Source: *AmM&WS 73S; ConAu 1R, 57; NewYTBE 71; WhAm 6; WhoAm 74; WhoAmP 73; WhoGov 72; WhoS&SW 73*

Lincoln, Mary Todd
American. Wife of Abraham Lincoln
Suffered mental instability after husband's death; ruled insane, 1875.
b. Dec 13, 1818 in Lexington, Kentucky
d. Jul 16, 1882 in Springfield, Illinois
Source: *AmBi; AmWom; ApCAB; DcAmB; HerW; InWom; NotAW; REn; REnAL; TwCBDA; WhAm H*

Lincoln, Nancy Hanks
see: Hanks, Nancy

Lincoln, Robert Todd
American. Lawyer, Abraham Lincoln's Son
Secretary of War, 1881-85; minister to Great Britain, 1889-93.
b. Aug 1, 1843 in Springfield, Illinois
d. Jul 26, 1926
Source: *AmBi; ApCAB; BiDrUSE; DcAmB; EncAB-H; TwCBDA; WhAm 1; WhAmP*

Lincoln, Victoria Endicott
American. Author
b. Oct 23, 1904 in Fall River, Massachusetts
d. May 9, 1981 in Baltimore, Maryland
Source: *AmAu&B; ConAu 17R, 104; ConAu P-1; ForWC 70; OhA&B; OxAmL; REnAL; TwCA SUP; WhoAm 74*

Lind, Jakov
Austrian. Author
b. Feb 10, 1927 in Vienna, Austria
Source: *Au&Wr 71; ConAu 9R; ConLC 1, 2, 4; EncWL; ModGL; Pen EUR; WhoWor 74; WorAu*

Lind, Jenny
[Mrs. Otto Goldschmidt]
"Swedish Nightingale"
English. Opera Singer
Toured US, 1850-52, under management of P T Barnum.
b. Oct 6, 1820 in Stockholm, Sweden
d. Nov 2, 1887 in Wynd's Point, England
Source: *AmBi; Film 1; HerW; InWom; WhAm H*

Lindauer, Lois L
American. Founder of Diet Workshop
b. Feb 6, 1934 in Brooklyn, New York
Source: *ConAu 49; WhoAmW 77*

Lindbergh, Anne Spencer Morrow
[Mrs. Charles A Lindbergh]
American. Author
Wrote *Dearly Beloved,* 1962; *Earth Shine,* 1969.
b. 1906 in Englewood, New Jersey
Source: *AmAu&B; AnCL; CelR 73; ChPo; ConAu 17R; CurBio 40; InWom; LongCTC; OxAmL; REn; REnAL; TwCA, SUP; Who 74; WhoAm 76, 78, 80, 82; WhoAmW 77; WhoWor 74; WrDr 76*

Lindbergh, Charles Augustus
American. Congressman
b. 1859 in Stockholm, Sweden
d. 1924
Source: *AmBi; BiDrAC; DcAmB; DcNAA; WhAmP*

Lindbergh, Charles Augustus
"Lucky Lindy"
American. Aviator
Made first solo nonstop trans-Atlantic flight, NY to Paris in *Spirit of St. Louis,* May 21, 1927.
b. Feb 4, 1902 in Detroit, Michigan
d. Aug 26, 1974 in Kipahulu, Hawaii
Source: *AmAu&B; ConAu 53; CurBio 41, 54, 74; OxAmL; REn; REnAL; WhAm 6; WhNAA*

Lindbergh, Charles Augustus
American. Son of Charles and Anne Lindbergh
Kidnapped, murdered by Bruno Hauptmann, who was electrocuted for crime.
b. 1931
d. 1932
Source: *BioIn 9, 10*

Lindbergh, Jon Morrow
American. Oceanographic Executive
b. Aug 16, 1932 in New York
Source: *WhoAm 74*

Linden, Hal
[Harold Lipschitz]
American. Actor
Starred in TV series "Barney Miller," 1975-82.
b. Mar 20, 1931 in Bronx, New York
Source: *BiE&WWA; BkPepl; CelR 73; EncMT; IntMPA 82; NotNAT; WhoAm 82; WhoThe 77*

Linder, Harold Francis
American. Financial Consultant
b. Sep 13, 1900 in Brooklyn, New York
d. Jun 22, 1981 in New York, New York
Source: *BioIn 5; IntWW 74, 75, 76, 77, 78; WhoAm 74, 76, 78, 80; WhoAmP 73, 75, 77, 79*

Lindfors, Viveca
[Elsa Viveca Torstensdotter]
American. Actress
b. Dec 29, 1920 in Uppsala, Sweden
Source: *IntMPA 75, 76, 78, 79, 80, 81, 82; MotPP; MovMk; NotNAT; WhoAm 74, 76, 78, 80, 82; WhoHol A; WhoThe 77; WorEFlm*

Lindgren, Astrid
Swedish. Author
Wrote *Pippi Longstocking* stories for children.
b. Nov 14, 1907 in Vimmerby, Sweden
Source: *Au&ICB; Au&Wr 71; AuBYP; ChlLR 1; ConAu 13R; MorJA; SmATA 2; WhoAmW 77; WhoWor 74*

Lindner, Richard
German. Artist
b. Nov 11, 1901 in Hamburg, Germany
d. Apr 16, 1978 in New York, New York
Source: *BnEnAmA; ConArt; DcCAA 71, 77; McGDA; NewYTBS 78; WhAm 7; WhoAm 76, 78; WhoAmA 76, 78; WhoWor 74; WhoWorJ 72*

Lindsay, Howard
American. Dramatist, Producer, Actor
b. Mar 29, 1889 in Waterford, New York
d. Feb 11, 1968 in New York, New York
Source: *AmAu&B; BiE&WWA; CnThe; ConAu 25R; CurBio 42, 68; EncMT; FilmgC; McGEWD; ModWD; NewCBMT; OxAmL; OxThe; REn; REnAL; TwCA SUP; WhAm 4A; WhScrn 74, 77; WhoHol B*

Lindsay, John Vliet
American. Former Mayor of New York City
b. Nov 24, 1921 in New York, New York
Source: *BiDrAC; BiE&WWA; BioNews 74; ConAu 101; CurBio 62; EncAB-H; IntWW 74; NewYTBE 71, 72, 73, 74; Who 74; WhoAm 74, 76, 78, 80, 82; WhoAmP 73; WhoE 74; WhoGov 72; WhoHol A; WhoWor 74*

Lindsay, Margaret
American. Actress
b. 1910 in Dubuque, Iowa
d. May 8, 1981 in Los Angeles, California
Source: *BioIn 11; FilmgC; HolP 30; MotPP; MovMk; NewYTBS 81; ThFT; WhoHol A*

Lindsay, (Nicholas) Vachel
American. Poet, Author
b. Nov 10, 1879 in Springfield, Illinois
d. Dec 5, 1931 in Springfield, Illinois
Source: *AmAu&B; AmBi; AmLY X; AnCL; AnMV 1926; AtlBL; BkCL; CasWL; Chambr 3; CnDAL; CnE&AP; CnMWL; ConAmA; ConAmL; CyWA; DcAmB; DcNAA; EncWL; EvLB; LongCTC; ModAL; OxAmL; OxEng; Pen AM; RAdv 1; REn; REnAL; SixAP; Str&VC; TwCA, SUP; TwCW; WebAB; WebE&AL; WhAm 1; WhNAA; WhoTwCL*

Lindsay, Ted (Robert Blake Theodore)
Canadian. Hockey Player, Coach
Left wing on Production Line with Sid Abel, Gordie Howe; Hall of Fame, 1966.
b. Jul 29, 1925 in Renfrew, ON
Source: *BioIn 2, 9, 10, 11; WhoAm 78; WhoHcky 73*

Lindsey, Mort
American. Composer, Conductor
b. Mar 21, 1923 in Newark, New Jersey
Source: *AmSCAP 66*

Lindstrom, Pia
American. Journalist
b. Nov 1938 in Stockholm, Sweden
Source: *BioIn 10; CelR 73; WhoAm 78; WhoHol A*

Lindstrom, Fred(erick Charles)
"Lindy"
American. Baseball Player
b. Nov 21, 1905 in Chicago, Illinois
d. Oct 4, 1981 in Chicago, Illinois
Source: *BaseEn; BioIn 8, 11; NewYTBS 75*

Lindtberg, Leopold
Swiss. Motion Picture Director
b. Jun 1, 1902 in Vienna, Austria
Source: *DcFM; FilmgC; IntWW 74; WhoWor 74*

Ling, James J
American. Business Executive
b. 1922 in Hugo, Oklahoma
Source: *CurBio 70; EncAB-H; IntWW 74; St&PR 75; WhoAm 74; WhoF&I 74; WhoS&SW 73; WhoWor 74*

Link, Edwin Albert
American. Inventor, Aviation Executive
b. Jul 26, 1904 in Huntington, Indiana
d. Sep 7, 1981 in Binghamton, New York
Source: *BioIn 3, 7, 8, 9; CurBio 74; IndAu 1917; IntYB 78, 79; St&PR 75; Who 74; WhoAm 74, 76, 78, 80*

Link, Theodore Carl
American. Architect
b. Mar 17, 1850 in Wimpfen, Germany
d. Feb 14, 1923 in Saint Louis, Missouri
Source: *NewYTBS 74; WhAm 4*

Linkletter, Art(hur Gordon)
American. Radio, TV Personality, Author
Star of radio, TV shows "People Are Funny," "House Party."
b. Jul 17, 1912 in Moose Jaw, SK
Source: *AmAu&B; BioNews 75; ConAu 9R, 4NR; CurBio 53; IntMPA 75, 76, 77, 78, 79, 80, 81, 82; St&PR 75; WhoAm 74, 76, 78, 80, 82; WhoHol A; WrDr 76*

Linkletter, Jack
American. Son of Art Linkletter
b. Nov 20, 1937 in San Francisco, California
Source: *BioIn 5*

Links, Marty
Cartoonist
Source: *BioIn 1*

Linn, Bambi
American. Ballet Dancer
b. Apr 26, 1926 in Brooklyn, New York
Source: *BiE&WWA; InWom; NotNAT; WhoHol A; WhoThe 77*

Linnaeus, Carolus
[Linn, Carl von]
Swedish. Botanist
b. May 23, 1707 in Rashult, Sweden
d. Jan 10, 1778 in Uppsala, Sweden
Source: *BbD; BiD&SB; REn*

Linowitz, Sol
American. Diplomat
b. Dec 7, 1913 in Trenton, New Jersey
Source: *BioIn 7, 8, 9; CurBio 67; WhoAm 82*

Linton, Ralph
American. Anthropologist
b. Feb 27, 1893 in Philadelphia, Pennsylvania
d. Dec 24, 1953 in New Haven, Connecticut
Source: *AmAu&B; DcAmB S5; TwCA SUP; WebAB; WhAm 3; WhNAA*

Linton, William James
English. Author, Engraver
b. Dec 7, 1812 in London, England
d. Dec 29, 1897 in New Haven, Connecticut
Source: *Alli SUP; AmAu&B; AmBi; ApCAB; BbD; BiD&SB; BrAu 19; Chambr 3; ChPo, S1, S2; DcAmAu; DcAmB; DcEnL; EarABI, SUP; NewC; REnAL; TwCBDA; WhAm H*

Lionni, Leo
Dutch. Designer, Artist
b. May 5, 1910 in Amsterdam, Netherlands
Source: *AmAu&B; Au&ICB; AuBYP; BkP; ChPo S2; ConAu 53; FamAIYP; IlsCB 1957; SmATA 8; ThrBJA; WhoAm 74, 76, 78, 80, 82; WhoAmA 73; WhoGrA*

Liotard, Jean-Etienne
Swiss. Artist
b. 1702 in Geneva, Switzerland
d. 1789 in Geneva, Switzerland
Source: *McGDA*

Lipatti, Dinu
Romanian. Musician
b. Mar 19, 1917 in Bucharest, Romania
d. Dec 2, 1950 in Chene-Bourg, Switzerland
Source: *DcAmB*

Lipchitz, Jacques
French. Sculptor
b. Aug 22, 1891 in Lithuania
d. May 26, 1973 in New York, New York
Source: *CelR 73; CurBio 48, 62, 73; DcCAA 71; NewYTBE 73; REn; WhAm 5; WhoAmA 73*

Lipinski, Karl
Polish. Musician, Composer
b. Nov 4, 1790 in Radzyn, Poland
d. Dec 16, 1861 in Urlow, Russia
Source: *WebBD 80*

Lipman, Clara
American. Actress
b. Dec 6, 1889 in Chicago, Illinois
d. 1952 in New York, New York
Source: *InWom; WhAm 3; WhoStg 1906, 1908; WhoThe 77; WomWWA 14*

Lippi, Filippino
Italian. Artist, Monk
b. 1459
d. 1504
Source: *DcAmB*

Lippi, Filippo (Lippo), Fra
Italian. Artist
b. 1406 in Florence, Italy
d. Oct 9, 1469 in Spoleto, Italy
Source: *AtlBL; REn*

Lippincott, Joshua Ballinger
American. Publisher
Founded J B Lippincott & Co., 1836.
b. Mar 18, 1813 in Juliustown, New Jersey
d. Jan 5, 1886 in Philadelphia, Pennsylvania
Source: *AmAu&B; AmBi; ApCAB; DcAmB; TwCBDA; WhAm H*

Lippmann, Gabriel
French. Physicist
Developed color photography.
b. 1845 in Hallerich, Luxemburg
d. Jul 13, 1921
Source: *BioIn 3, 5; DcScB; LinLib S; WebBD 80*

Lippmann, Walter
American. Editor, Journalist, Author
Won Pulitzer Prizes, 1958, 1962, for syndicated column, "Today and Tomorrow."
b. Sep 23, 1889 in New York, New York
d. Dec 14, 1974 in New York, New York
Source: *AmAu&B; AuNews 1; BioNews 75; CelR 73; ConAmA; ConAu 9R, 53; CurBio 40, 62; DcLEL; DrAS 74E; EncAB-H; IntWW 74; LongCTC; NewYTBS 74; OxAmL; Pen AM; REn; REnAL; TwCA, SUP; WebAB; WhAm 6; WhNAA; Who 74; WhoAm 74; WhoWor 74*

Lippold, Richard
American. Sculptor, Engineer
b. May 3, 1915 in Milwaukee, Wisconsin
Source: *CelR 73; CurBio 56; DcCAA 71; REn; WhoAm 74, 76, 78, 80, 82; WhoAmA 73; WhoWor 74*

Lipscomb, Eugene
"Big Daddy"
American. Football Player
Defensive tackle, Baltimore Colts, 1956-60.
b. Nov 9, 1931 in Detroit, Michigan
d. May 10, 1963 in Pittsburgh, Pennsylvania
Source: *WhoFtbl 74*

Lipshutz, Robert Jerome
American. Lawyer, Former Public Official
b. Dec 27, 1921 in Atlanta, Georgia
Source: *WhoAm 74, 76, 78, 80, 82; WhoAmP 77, 79; WhoE 77, 79; WhoGov 77*

Lipton, Martha
American. Opera Singer
b. Apr 6, 1915 in New York, New York
Source: *InWom; WhoAm 74, 76, 78, 80, 82; WhoWor 74*

Lipton, Peggy
[Mrs. Quincy Jones]
American. Actress
Starred in TV series "The Mod Squad," 1968-73.
b. Aug 30, 1947 in New York, New York
Source: *BioIn 9; NewYTBE 72; WhoHol A*

Lipton, Sir Thomas Johnstone
Scottish. Merchant, Yachtsman
b. May 10, 1850 in Glasgow, Scotland
d. Oct 2, 1931
Source: *WhAm 3*

Liptrot, Denvil
see: K C and the Sunshine Band

Liquori, Marty (Martin A)
American. Track Athlete
b. Sep 11, 1949 in Montclair, New Jersey
Source: *CelR 73; NewYTBE 70, 72; WhoAm 82; WhoTr&F 73*

Lisagor, Peter Irvin
American. Journalist
b. Aug 5, 1915 in Keystone, West Virginia
d. Dec 10, 1976 in Arlington, Virginia
Source: *ConAu 69; NewYTBS 76; WhAm 7; WhoAm 74; WhoS&SW 73, 76*

Lisi, Virna
Italian. Actress
b. 1937 in Ancona, Italy
Source: *BioIn 7; FilmgC; MotPP; MovMk*

Lismer, Arthur
[Group of Seven]
Canadian. Artist
b. Jun 27, 1885 in Sheffield, England
d. Mar 23, 1969 in Montreal, PQ
Source: *BioIn 1, 2, 3, 4, 6, 11; CreCan 2; McGDA*

List, Emanuel
Austrian. Opera Singer
b. Mar 22, 1891 in Vienna, Austria
d. Jun 21, 1967 in Vienna, Austria
Source: *WhAm 4*

List, Eugene
American. Musician
b. 1921 in Philadelphia, Pennsylvania
Source: *BioIn 1, 2, 3, 4, 5, 7, 10; NewYTBS 74; WhoAm 74, 76, 78, 80, 82; WhoMus 72*

Lister, Joseph
[Baron Lister of Lyme Regis]
English. Surgeon
Founded modern antiseptic surgery, 1865.
b. Apr 5, 1827 in Upton, England
d. Feb 10, 1912 in Walmer, England
Source: *Alli, SUP; BbD; BiD&SB; NewC*

Liston, Emil
"Big Lis"
American. Basketball Coach
Organized National Assn. of Intercollegiate Basketball, 1937.
b. Aug 21, 1890 in Stockton, Missouri
d. Oct 26, 1949 in Baldwin, Kansas
Source: *WhoBbl 73*

Liston, "Sonny" (Charles)
American. Boxer, Actor
Heavyweight champ, 1962-64, lost title to Muhammad Ali.
b. May 8, 1932 in Little Rock, Arkansas
d. Jan 5, 1971 in Las Vegas, Nevada
Source: *NewYTBE 71; WhScrn 77; WhoBox 74*

Liszt, Franz (Ferencz)
Hungarian. Pianist, Composer
b. Oct 22, 1811 in Raiding, Hungary
d. Jul 31, 1886 in Bayreuth, Germany
Source: *AtlBL; BbD; BiD&SB; OxFr; OxGer; REn*

Litolff, Henri Charles
French. Musician, Composer
b. Feb 6, 1818 in London, England
d. Aug 6, 1891 in Paris, France
Source: *OxMus*

Little, Charles Coffin
American. Publisher
b. Jul 25, 1799 in Kennebunk, Maine
d. Aug 9, 1869
Source: *AmAu&B; ApCAB; DcAmB; TwCBDA; WhAm H*

Little, Cleavon Jake
American. Actor
b. Jun 1, 1939 in Chickasha, Oklahoma
Source: *MovMk; NotNAT; PlP&P A; WhoAm 74, 76, 78, 80, 82; WhoBlA 75; WhoHol A; WhoThe 77*

Little, Edward Herman
American. Colgate-Palmolive Co. Executive
b. 1881 in Charlotte, North Carolina
d. Jul 12, 1981 in Memphis, Tennessee
Source: *BioIn 4, 5; NewYTBS 81; St&PR 75*

Little, (Flora) Jean
Author
b. Jan 2, 1932 in Taiwan
Source: *AuBYP; ChPo S2; ConAu 25R; OxCan SUP; SmATA 2*

Little, Joan
American. Prisoner, Rape Victim
While in prison, murdered jailer who raped her.
b. 1954
Source: *BioIn 10, 11*

Little, "Little Jack"
[John Leonard]
American. Band Leader
b. May 28, 1900 in London, England
d. Apr 9, 1956 in Hollywood, California
Source: *AmSCAP 66; WhScrn 74, 77; WhoHol B*

Little, Lou(is)
American. Football Coach
b. Dec 6, 1893 in Leominster, Massachusetts
d. May 28, 1979 in Delray Beach, Florida
Source: *BioIn 1, 4, 5, 10; CurBio 45, 79; NewCol 75; NewYTBS 79*

Little, Malcomb
see: Malcomb X

Little, Rich(ard Caruthers)
Canadian. Impressionist
Can now do 160 impressions.
b. Nov 26, 1938 in Ottawa, ON
Source: *BioNews 74; WhoAm 80, 82*

Little, Royal
American. Business Executive
b. Mar 1, 1896 in Wakefield, Massachusetts
Source: *WhoAm 74, 76, 78, 80, 82*

Little, (William) Lawson, Jr.
American. Golfer
b. Jun 23, 1910 in Newport, Rhode Island
d. Feb 1, 1968 in Pebble Beach, California
Source: *BioIn 6; CurBio 40; WhoGolf*

Little Anthony and the Imperials
[Clarence Collins; Anthony Gourdine; Sam Strain; Ernest Wright]
American. Vocal Group
Source: *EncPR&S*

"Little Esther"
[Esther Phillips]
American. Singer
b. Dec 23, 1935 in Houston, Texas
Source: *BluesWW; RkOn; WhoRock 81*

"Little Eva"
[Eva Narcissus Boyd]
American. Singer
b. 1944 in North Carolina
Source: *AmPS A; RkOn; WhoRock 81*

Little Rascals, The
see: Our Gang

"Little Richard"
[Richard Penniman]
American. Singer, Songwriter
b. Dec 25, 1935 in Macon, Georgia
Source: *EncPR&S*

Little River Band, The
[Beeb Birtles; David Briggs; Graham Goble; Steve Housden; GeorgeMcArdle; Wayne Nelson; Derek Pellicci; Glenn Shorrock]
Australian. Rock Group
Source: *RkOn 2; WhoRock 81*

"Little Tich"
[Harry Relp]
English. Comedian
b. 1868 in England
d. Feb 10, 1928 in London, England
Source: *EncWT; NotNAT B; OxThe*

Littledale, Freya Lota
American. Author
b. in New York, New York
Source: *ConAu 25R; SmATA 2; WhoAmW 77; WrDr 76*

Littler, Gene (Eugene Alex)
American. Golfer
Has won 29 PGA events.
b. Jul 21, 1930 in San Diego, California
Source: *BioIn 3, 4, 5, 6, 7, 9, 11; CurBio 56; WhoAm 82; WhoGolf*

Littlewood, Joan
English. Theatrical Director
b. 1916 in London, England
Source: *BiE&WWA; CroCD; FilmgC; IntWW 74; LongCTC; OxFilm; OxThe; PlP&P; Who 74; WhoAm 74; WhoThe 77; WhoWor 74; WomWMM*

Litton, Charles
American. Businessman, Philanthropist
b. 1903
d. Nov 14, 1972 in Carson City, Nevada
Source: *AmM&WS 73P; NewYTBE 72*

Litvak, Anatole
French. Motion Picture Director
b. May 21, 1902 in Kiev, Russia
d. Dec 15, 1974 in Neuilly, France
Source: *BiDFilm; CmMov; DcFM; FilmgC; IntWW 74; MovMk; NewYTBS 74; OxFilm; WhScrn 77; WorEFlm*

Litvinne, Felia
Russian. Opera Singer
b. Oct 11, 1860 in Saint Petersburg, Russia
d. Oct 12, 1936 in Paris, France
Source: *InWom*

Litvinoff, Emanuel
English. Author
b. Jun 30, 1915 in London, England
Source: *ConNov 72, 76; ConP 70; NewC; WrDr 76*

Litvinov, Maxim
Russian. Revolutionary, Statesman
b. Jul 17, 1871 in Bialystok, Russia
d. Dec 31, 1951 in Moscow, U.S.S.R.
Source: *CurBio 41, 52*

Liu Shao-Ch'i
Chinese. Communist Leader
b. 1898? in Hunan, China
d. Oct 1974?
Source: *CurBio 57, 74; NewYTBS 74; WhAm 6*

Liut, Mike (Michael)
Canadian. Hockey Player
b. Jan 7, 1956 in Weston, ON
Source: *BioIn 12; HocReg*

Liuzzo, Viola
American. Civil Rights Activist
Assassinated while driving marchers from Montgomery to Selma, AL.
b. 1925 in California, Pennsylvania
d. Mar 25, 1965 in Selma, Alabama
Source: *BioIn 7; WhoAmW 66*

Liveright, Horace Brisbin
American. Publisher, Theatrical Producer
b. Dec 10, 1886 in Osceola Mills, Pennsylvania
d. Sep 24, 1933
Source: *DcAmB S1; OxThe; WhAm 1*

Livermore, Mary Ashton Rice
American. Journalist
b. Dec 19, 1820 in Boston, Massachusetts
d. May 23, 1905 in Melrose, Massachusetts
Source: *Alli SUP; AmAu; AmAu&B; AmBi; AmWom; ApCAB; BbD; BiD&SB; ChPo S1; DcAmAu; DcAmB; DcNAA; Drake; InWom; NotAW; TwCBDA; WebAB; WhAm 1*

Livesey, Roger
Welsh. Actor
b. Jun 25, 1906 in Barry, Wales
d. Feb 5, 1976
Source: *FilmgC; IntMPA 75; MovMk; PlP&P; Who 74; WhoThe 77*

Livingston, Barry
American. Actor
b. 1953 in Los Angeles, California
Source: *WhoHol A*

Livingston, Edward
American. Jurist, Statesman
b. May 26, 1764 in Columbia County, New York
d. May 23, 1836 in Rhinebeck, New York
Source: *Alli; AmAu; AmBi; ApCAB; BiAuS; BiDSA; BiDrAC; BiDrUSE; CyAL 1; DcAmAu; DcAmB; DcNAA; Drake; TwCBDA; WebAB; WhAm H; WhAmP*

Livingston, J(oseph) A(rnold)
American. Economist
b. Feb 10, 1905 in New York, New York
Source: *AmEA 74; ConAu 1R; Ward 77; WhoAm 74, 76, 78, 80, 82; WhoE 74*

Livingston, Philip
American. Continental Congressman
b. Jan 15, 1716 in Albany, New York
d. Jun 12, 1778 in New York, New York
Source: *AmBi; ApCAB; BiAuS; BiDrAC; BioIn 3, 7, 8, 9; DcAmB; Drake; NatCAB 3; TwCBDA; WhAm H*

Livingston, Robert R
American. Diplomat
b. Nov 27, 1746 in New York, New York
d. Feb 26, 1813 in Clermont, New York
Source: *Alli; AmBi; ApCAB; BiAuS; BiDrAC; DcAmAu; DcAmB; DcNAA; Drake; EncAB-H; TwCBDA; WebAB; WhAm H; WhAmP*

Livingston, Stanley
American. Actor
Played Chip on TV series, "My Three Sons," 1960-72.
b. Nov 24, 1950 in Los Angeles, California
Source: *WhoHol A*

Livingstone, David
Scottish. Missionary, Explorer
Discovered Victoria Falls, 1855; Henry Stanley found him, 1871, saying "Dr. Livingstone, I presume."
b. Mar 19, 1813 in Lanarkshire, Scotland
d. May 1, 1873 in Ilala, Zambia
Source: *Alli, SUP; BbD; BiD&SB; BrAu 19; CasWL; Chambr 3; DcEnA; DcEnL; DcLEL; EvLB; NewC; OxEng; REn*

Livingstone, Mary
[Mrs. Jack Benny]
American. Radio Comedienne
b. 1908 in Seattle, Washington
Source: *InWom; WhoHol A*

Livius Andronicus
"Father of the Roman Theatre"
Roman. Poet, Dramatist
b. 284?BC in Tarentum, Italy
d. 204?BC
Source: *CasWL; NewCol 75; OxThe; Pen CL; PlP&P; REn*

Livy
Roman. Historian
b. 59BC in Patavium, Italy
d. 17AD in Patavium, Italy
Source: *AtlBL; BbD; BiD&SB; CasWL; DcEnL; NewC; OxEng; Pen CL; RComWL; REn*

Ljungberg, Gota
Swedish. Opera Singer
b. Oct 4, 1893 in Sundsvall, Sweden
d. Jun 28, 1955 in Lidingo, Sweden
Source: *InWom*

Lleras Restrepo, Carlos
Colombian. Former President
b. Apr 12, 1908 in Bogota, Colombia
Source: *CurBio 70; IntWW 74; WhoWor 74*

Lleshi, Haxhi
Albanian. Politician
b. 1913 in Albania
Source: *IntWW 74; WhoWor 74*

Llewelyn-Davies, Richard
British. Architect, City Planner
b. Dec 24, 1912
d. Oct 26, 1981 in London, England
Source: *Au&Wr 71; ConAu 13R; IntWW 74, 75, 76, 77, 78; Who 74; WhoWor 74, 76, 78*

Llewellyn Lloyd, Richard David Vivian
[Richard Llewellyn, pseud.]
Welsh. Author, Dramatist
b. 1907 in Saint David's, Wales
Source: *ConAu 53; CurBio 40; CyWA; DcLEL; EvLB; LongCTC; NewC; RAdv 1; REn; SmATA 11; TwCA, SUP; TwCW; Who 74; WhoWor 74; WrDr 76*

Lloyd, Christopher
American. Actor
Plays Jim on TV series "Taxi."
b. Oct 22, 1938 in Stamford, Connecticut
Source: *BioIn 11; WhoAm 82*

Lloyd, Frank
American. Motion Picture Director
b. Feb 1889 in Glasgow, Scotland
d. Aug 10, 1960 in Santa Monica, California
Source: *BiDFilm; CmMov; DcFM; Film 1; FilmgC; MovMk; NewYTBE 73; OxFilm; TwYS; WhScrn 74, 77; WhoHol B; WorEFlm*

Lloyd, Harold
American. Comedian, Actor
b. Apr 20, 1893 in Burchard, Nebraska
d. Mar 8, 1971 in Hollywood, California
Source: *BiDFilm; CmMov; CurBio 49, 71; DcFM; Film 1; FilmgC; MotPP; MovMk; NewYTBE 71; OxFilm; TwYS; WebAB; WhAm 5; WhScrn 74, 77; WhoHol B; WorEFlm*

Lloyd, John
English. Tennis Player
Married Chris Evert, Apr 17, 1979.
b. Aug 27, 1954
Source: *BioIn 11*

Lloyd, (John) Selwyn Brooke
English. Politician
b. Jul 28, 1904 in Liverpool, England
Source: *CurBio 52; IntWW 74; Who 74; WhoWor 74*

Lloyd, Lewis Kevin
"Black Magic"
American. Basketball Player
b. Feb 22, 1959 in Philadelphia, Pennsylvania
Source: *OfNBA*

Lloyd, Marie
[Matilda Alice Wood]
English. Entertainer
b. Feb 12, 1870 in London, England
d. Oct 7, 1922 in London, England
Source: *InWom; NotNAT B; OxThe; PlP&P; WhThe*

Lloyd George of Dwyfor, David Lloyd George, Earl
English. Statesman
b. Jan 7, 1863 in Manchester, England
d. Mar 26, 1945 in Llanystumdwy, Wales
Source: *Chambr 3; CurBio 44, 45; NewCol 75; REn*

Locatelli, Pietro
Italian. Violinist, Composer
b. Sep 3, 1693 in Bergamo, Italy
d. Mar 30, 1764 in Amsterdam, Netherlands
Source: *WebBD 80*

Locke, Alain Leroy
American. Philosopher
b. Sep 13, 1886 in Philadelphia, Pennsylvania
d. Jun 1954
Source: *AmAu&B; BlkAW; CurBio 44, 54; DcAmB S5; EncAB-H; REnAL; TwCA, SUP; WebAB; WhAm 3; WhNAA*

Locke, Bobbie
South African. Golfer
b. Nov 20, 1917 in Germiston, Transvaal, South Africa
Source: *Who 74*

Locke, David Ross
[Petroleum V Nasby, pseud.]
American. Journalist
b. Sep 20, 1833 in Vestal, New York
d. Feb 15, 1888 in Toledo, Ohio
Source: *Alli SUP; AmAu; AmAu&B; AmBi; ApCAB; BbD; BiD&SB; CasWL; ChPo S2; CnDAL; CyAl 2; DcAmAu; DcAmB; DcLEL; DcNAA; Drake; EvLB; OhA&B; OxAmL; Pen AM; REn; REnAL; TwCBDA; WebAB; WhAm H; WhAmP*

Locke, John
English. Philosopher
Political theories greatly influenced writers of US Constitution.
b. Aug 29, 1632 in Somerset, England
d. Oct 28, 1704 in Oates, England
Source: *Alli; AtlBL; BbD; BiD&SB; BrAu; CasWL; Chambr 2; ChPo S2; CyWA; DcEnA; DcEnL; DcEuL; DcLEL; EvLB; MouLC 1; NewC; OxEng; Pen ENG; RComWL; REn; REnAL; WebE&AL; WhAm H*

Locke, Richard Adams
English. Journalist
b. Sep 22, 1800 in East Brent, England
d. Feb 16, 1871 in New York, New York
Source: *Alli; AmAu; AmAu&B; ApCAB; DcAmAu; DcAmB; DcNAA; OxAmL; WhAm H*

Locke, Sondra
American. Actress
Starred with Clint Eastwood in *Any Which Way You Can,* 1980.
b. May 28, 1947 in Shelbyville, Tennessee
Source: *WhoAm 82; WhoHol A*

Locke, William John
English. Author
b. Mar 20, 1863 in Barbados
d. May 15, 1930
Source: *Chambr 3; EvLB; LongCTC; NewC; OxEng; REn; TwCA; TwCW*

Lockhart, Calvin
American. Actor
b. 1936 in Bahamas
Source: *BioNews 74; FilmgC; NewYTBE 70; WhoHol A*

Lockhart, Gene (Eugene)
American. Actor
b. Jul 18, 1891 in London, ON
d. Mar 31, 1957 in Santa Monica, California
Source: *AmSCAP 66; CurBio 50, 57; FilmgC; MotPP; MovMk; Vers A; WhAm 3; WhScrn 74, 77; WhoHol B*

Lockhart, June
American. Actress
Starred in TV series "Lassie," 1958-64, "Lost in Space," 1965-68.
b. Jun 25, 1925 in New York, New York
Source: *BiE&WWA; FilmgC; InWom; IntMPA 75, 76, 77; MotPP; MovMk; NotNAT; WhoAm 82; WhoAmW 77; WhoHol A*

Lockhart, (Sir Robert Hamilton) Bruce
Scottish. Author, Diplomat
b. 1887 in Fifeshire, Scotland
d. Feb 27, 1970 in Brighton, England
Source: *Au&Wr 71; ConAu 89; DcLEL; EvLB; LongCTC; TwCA, SUP*

Lockridge, Frances Louise
American. Author
b. 1896? in Kansas City, Missouri
d. Feb 17, 1963
Source: *AmAu&B; ConAu 93; EncMys; REnAL; TwCA, SUP; WhAm 4*

Lockridge, Richard
American. Author
b. Sep 26, 1898 in Saint Joseph, Missouri
d. Jun 19, 1982 in Tryon, North Carolina
Source: *AmAu&B; ConAu 85; CurBio 40, 82; EncMys; NewYTBS 82; REnAL; ScF&FL 1; TwCA, SUP; TwCCr&M; WhThe; WhoAm 74, 76, 78*

Lockridge, Ross Franklin, Jr.
American. Author
b. Apr 25, 1914 in Bloomington, Indiana
d. Mar 6, 1948
Source: *AmAu&B; CyWA; DcNAA; IndAu 1917; ModAL; OxAmL; Pen AM; REnAL; TwCA SUP*

Lockwood, Belva Ann Bennett
American. Social Reformer, Lawyer
One of most effective advocates of women's rights.
b. Oct 24, 1830 in Royalton, New York
d. May 19, 1917 in Washington, DC
Source: *AmBi; AmWom; ApCAB; BioIn 1, 4, 5, 6, 9, 10, 11; DcAmB; NatCAB 2; NotAW; TwCBDA; WebAB; WhAm 1*

Lockwood, Margaret Mary
[Margaret Day]
American. Actress
b. Sep 15, 1916 in Karachi, India
Source: *CmMov; CurBio 48; FilmgC; InWom; IntMPA 75, 76, 77, 78, 79, 80, 81, 82; MotPP; MovMk; OxFilm; ThFT; Who 74; WhoHol A; WhoThe 77; WomPO 76; WorEFlm*

Loden, Barbara Ann
American. Actress
b. Jul 8, 1937 in Marion, North Carolina
d. Sep 5, 1980 in New York, New York
Source: *AnObit 1980; BiDFilm; BiE&WWA; CelR 73; IntMPA 75, 76, 77; NotNAT; OxFilm; WhAm 7; WhoHol A; WomWMM*

Loder, John
English. Actor
b. 1898 in London, England
Source: *FilmgC; MotPP; MovMk; WhoHol A*

Lodge, Henry Cabot
American. Historian, Statesman
b. May 12, 1850 in Boston, Massachusetts
d. Nov 9, 1924 in Boston, Massachusetts
Source: *Alli SUP; AmAu; AmAu&B; AmBi; ApCAB; BbD; BiD&SB; BiDrAC; Br&AmS; Chambr 3; ChPo S1; DcAmAu; DcAmB; DcNAA; EncAB-H; OxAmL; REnAL; TwCBDA; WebAB; WhAm 1; WhAmP; WhoAm 82*

Lodge, Henry Cabot, Jr.
American. Politician, Diplomat
US delegate to UN, 1953-60; vice-presidential candidate, 1960.
b. Jul 5, 1902 in Nahant, Massachusetts
Source: *CelR 73; ConAu 53; CurBio 43, 54; IntWW 74; WebAB; Who 74; WhoAm 74; WhoWor 74*

Lodge, Sir Oliver Joseph
English. Scientist
b. Jun 12, 1851 in Penkhull, England
d. Aug 22, 1940 in Amesbury, England
Source: *Alli SUP; BiDPara; Chambr 3; ChPo S1; CurBio 40; DcLEL; EvLB; LongCTC; NewC; OxEng; TwCA, SUP; WhoLA*

Loeb, Gerald Martin
American. Stockbroker, Author
b. Jul 24, 1899 in San Francisco, California
d. 1974 in San Francisco, California
Source: *ConAu 49; ConAu P-1*

Loeb, James
American. Banker, Philanthropist
b. Aug 6, 1867 in New York, New York
d. May 28, 1933 in Murnau, Germany
Source: *AmBi; DcAmB S1; REnAL; WebAB; WhAm 1*

Loeb, Richard A
[Leopold and Loeb]
American. Kidnapper, Murderer
With Nathan Leopold, committed "crime of century"; saved from death by Clarence Darrow.
b. 1907 in Chicago, Illinois
d. Jan 1936 in Stateville, Illinois
Source: *BioIn 10; Blood*

Loeb, William
American. Businessman
b. Oct 9, 1866 in Albany, New York
d. Sep 19, 1937
Source: *AmBi; WhAm 1*

Loeb, William
American. Journalist, Publisher
b. Dec 26, 1905 in Manchester, New Hampshire
d. Sep 13, 1981 in Burlington, Massachusetts
Source: *BioIn 4, 6, 8, 9, 10, 11; ConAu 93, 104; CurBio 74, 81; PolProf J; PolProf K; PolProf NF; St&PR 75; WhoAm 74, 76, 78; WhoE 74*

Loeffler, Charles Martin Tornov
American. Violinist, Composer
b. Jan 30, 1861 in Muhlhausen, Germany
d. May 20, 1935 in Medfield, Massachusetts
Source: *AmBi; DcAmB S1; DcNAA; WhAm 1*

Loeffler, Kenneth D
American. Basketball Coach
b. Apr 14, 1902 in Beaver Falls, Pennsylvania
d. Jan 1, 1974 in Rumson, New Jersey
Source: *BioIn 9, 10; WhoBbl 73*

Loeser, Katinka
[Mrs. Peter DeVries]
American. Author
b. Jul 2, 1913 in Ottumwa, Iowa
Source: *ConAu 17R; DrAF 76; ForWC 70; WhoAmW 74*

Loesser, Frank
American. Composer
Wrote Broadway musicals *Guys and Dolls,* 1951, *Most Happy Fella,* 1956.
b. Jun 29, 1910 in New York, New York
d. Jul 28, 1969 in New York, New York
Source: *AmSCAP 66; BiE&WWA; CurBio 46, 69; EncMT; FilmgC; NewCBMT; OxAmL; PlP&P; WebAB; WhAm 6; WhScrn 74, 77; WhoHol B*

Loew, Arthur M
American. Business Executive
b. Oct 5, 1897 in New York, New York
Source: *IntMPA 75, 76, 77; St&PR 75; WhoAm 74*

Loew, Marcus
American. Theatre Owner, Film Producer
b. 1870 in New York, New York
d. Sep 5, 1927 in New York, New York
Source: *DcAmB; DcFM; FilmgC; OxFilm; WhAm 1; WorEFlm*

Loewe, Frederick
[Lerner and Loewe]
"Fritz"
Austrian. Composer, Musician
With Alan Lerner wrote musicals *My Fair Lady,* 1956; *Camelot,* 1960.
b. Jun 10, 1904 in Vienna, Austria
Source: *AmSCAP 66; BiE&WWA; CelR 73; CurBio 58; EncMT; FilmgC; IntMPA 77, 78, 79, 80, 81, 82; IntWW 74; NewCBMT; OxAmL; PlP&P; REnAL; Who 74; WhoAm 74, 76, 78, 80, 82; WhoThe 77; WhoWor 74*

Loewy, Raymond Fernand
American. Industrial Designer
b. Nov 5, 1893 in Paris, France
Source: *CelR 73; CurBio 41, 53; IntWW 74; WebAB; Who 74; WhoAm 74, 76, 78, 80, 82; WhoWor 74*

Lofgren, Nils
American. Rock Musician
b. 1954?
Source: *AmSCAP 80; ConMuA 80; IlEncRk; LilREn 78; WhoRock 81*

Lofting, Hugh
American. Author
Wrote *Doctor Doolittle* series for children.
b. Jan 14, 1886 in Maidenhead, England
d. Sep 26, 1947
Source: *AmAu&B; AnCL; AuBYP; ChPo, S1; ConICB; DcLEL; DcNAA; EvLB; IlsCB 1744; JBA 34, 51; LongCTC; Newb 1922; REn; REnAL; Str&VC; TwCA, SUP; WhAm 2; WhNAA; WhoChL*

Lofts, Norah Robinson
English. Author
b. Aug 27, 1904 in Shipdham, England
Source: *Au&Wr 71; AuNews 2; ConAu 5R; LongCTC; SmATA 8; TwCA, SUP; WhNAA; Who 74; WhoAm 74; WrDr 76*

Loftus, Cissie
[Marie Cecilia McCarthy]
Scottish. Actress
b. Oct 26, 1876 in Glasgow, Scotland
d. Jul 12, 1943 in New York, New York
Source: *CurBio 40, 43; NotAW; OxThe; REn*

Logan, Daniel
American. Scientist
b. Oct 14, 1936 in San Angelo, Texas
Source: *AmM&WS 73S; ConAu 25R*

Logan, Ella
[Ella Allan]
Scottish. Actress
b. Mar 6, 1913 in Glasgow, Scotland
d. May 1, 1969 in San Mateo, California
Source: *BiE&WWA; EncMT; InWom; MotPP; WhScrn 74, 77; WhoHol B*

Logan, John
[John Burton Logan]
American. Poet
b. Jan 23, 1923 in Red Oak, Iowa
Source: *AmAu&B; ConAu 77; ConP 70, 75; CroCAP; DrAF 76; DrAP 75; OxAmL; Pen AM; RAdv 1; WhoAm 82; WorAu; WrDr 76*

Logan, John Alexander
American. Soldier, Politician
b. Feb 9, 1826 in Murphysboro, Illinois
d. Dec 26, 1886 in Washington, DC
Source: *AmBi; ApCAB; BiAuS; BiDrAC; BioIn 3, 7; DcAmB; Drake; NatCAB 4, 27; TwCBDA; WebAB; WebAMB; WhAm H*

Logan, Josh(ua Lockwood)
American. Author, Producer, Director
b. Oct 5, 1908 in Texarkana, Texas
Source: *AmAu&B; AuNews 1; BiDFilm; BiE&WWA; CelR 73; CmMov; ConAu 89; DcFM; EncMT; FilmgC; IntMPA 77, 78, 79, 80, 81, 82; IntWW 74; ModWD; MovMk; NewCBMT; NotNAT; OxFilm; WhoAm 74, 76, 78, 80, 82; WhoThe 77; WhoWor 74; WorEFlm*

Loggins, Kenny (Kenneth Clarke)
[Loggins and Messina]
American. Singer, Musician, Songwriter
b. Jan 7, 1948 in Everett, Washington
Source: *BioIn 11; BkPepl; WhoAm 80, 82*

Loggins and Messina
[Kenny Loggins; Jim Messina]
American. Rock Group
Source: *EncPR&S; IlEncRk*

Logroscino, Nicola
Italian. Composer
b. Oct 1698 in Bitonto, Italy
d. 1765 in Palermo, Sicily
Source: *NewEOp 71*

Lohse, Otto
German. Conductor
b. Sep 21, 1859 in Dresden, Germany
d. May 5, 1925 in Baden-Baden, Germany
Source: *NewEOp 71*

Lolich, Mickey (Michael Stephen)
American. Baseball Player
Last pitcher to win three games in one World Series, 1968.
b. Sep 12, 1940 in Portland, Oregon
Source: *BaseEn; NewYTBE 72; WhoAm 74, 76, 78, 80, 82; WhoProB 73*

Lollobrigida, Gina
Italian. Actress
b. Jul 4, 1928 in Subiaco, Italy
Source: *BiDFilm; FilmgC; InWom; IntMPA 75, 76, 77, 78, 79, 80, 81, 82; MotPP; MovMk; OxFilm; WhoHol A; WhoWor 74; WorEFlm*

Lom, Herbert
[Herbert C Angelo Kuchacevich]
Czech. Actor
b. 1917 in Prague, Czechoslovakia
Source: *CmMov; FilmgC; IntMPA 75, 76, 77, 78, 79, 80, 81, 82; MotPP; MovMk; WhoHol A*

Lomax, Alan
American. Folk Song Collector
b. Jan 15, 1915 in Austin, Texas
Source: *AmAu&B; Au&Wr 71; ConAu 1R; CurBio 41; EncFCWM 69; IntWW 74; REnAL; TexWr; TwCA SUP; WhoAm 74; WhoWor 74*

Lomax, John Avery
American. Folklorist
b. Sep 23, 1867 in Goodman, Mississippi
d. Jan 26, 1948 in Greenville, Mississippi
Source: *AmAu&B; BiDSA; ChPo; CnDAL; DcAmB S4; DcNAA; EncFCWM 69; OxAmL; REn; REnAL; Str&VC; TexWr; TwCA SUP; WebAB; WhAm 2; WhNAA*

Lomax, Louis
American. Author
b. Aug 6, 1922 in Valdosta, Georgia
d. Jul 1970 in Santa Rosa, New Mexico
Source: *AmAu&B; ConAu 25R; ConAu P-2; NewYTBE 70; WhAm 5; WhScrn 77*

Lombard, Alain
French. Conductor
b. Oct 4, 1940 in Paris, France
Source: *WhoS&SW 73*

Lombard, Carole
[Jane Alice Peters]
American. Actress
Was married to Clark Gable at time of death in plane crash.
b. Oct 6, 1909 in Fort Wayne, Indiana
d. Jan 16, 1942 in Las Vegas, Nevada
Source: *BiDFilm; CurBio 42; DcAmB S3; FilmgC; InWom; MotPP; MovMk; NotAW; OxFilm; ThFT; TwYS; WhAm 1; WhScrn 74, 77; WhoHol B; WorEFlm*

Lombard, Peter
Italian. Theologian
b. 1100? in Novara, Italy
d. 1160? in Paris, France
Source: *NewC; OxEng; REn*

Lombardi, Ernie (Ernesto Natali)
"Bocci"; "Schnozz"
American. Baseball Player
b. Apr 6, 1908 in Oakland, California
d. Sep 26, 1977 in Santa Cruz, California
Source: *BaseEn; WhoProB 73*

Lombardi, Vince(nt Thomas)
American. Football Coach
Trophy given to Super Bowl winning team named after him.
b. Jun 11, 1913 in New York, New York
d. Sep 4, 1970 in Washington, DC
Source: *CurBio 63, 70; NewYTBE 70; WebAB; WhAm 5; WhoFtbl 74*

Lombardo, Carmen
Canadian. Songwriter, Singer
b. Jul 16, 1903 in London, ON
d. Apr 17, 1971 in North Miami, Florida
Source: *AmSCAP 66; NewYTBE 71; WhScrn 74, 77; WhoHol B*

Lombardo, Guy Albert
Canadian. Band Leader
Known for New Year's Eve performances with band, The Royal Canadians.
b. Jun 19, 1902 in London, ON
d. Nov 5, 1977 in Houston, Texas
Source: *BiE&WWA; CanWW 70; CelR 73; CreCan 1; CurBio 46, 75; NewYTBE 71; NotNAT; WebAB; WhoAm 74; WhoWor 74*

Lombroso, Cesare
Italian. Criminologist, Physician
b. Nov 6, 1836 in Venice, Italy
d. Oct 19, 1909 in Turin, Italy
Source: *McGEWB; NewCol 75*

Lomonosov, Mikhail
Russian. Scientist
b. Nov 8, 1711 in Denisovka, Russia
d. Apr 4, 1765 in Saint Petersburg, Russia
Source: *BbD; BiD&SB; CasWL; DcEuL; DcRusL; EuAu; EvEuW; Pen EUR; REn*

Lonborg, Jim (James Reynold)
American. Baseball Player
b. Apr 16, 1942 in Santa Maria, California
Source: *BaseEn; BioIn 8, 10; WhoProB 73*

London, George
[George Burnson]
Canadian. Opera Singer
b. May 30, 1920 in Montreal, PQ
Source: *BioNews 74; CreCan 1; CurBio 53; NewYTBE 71; WhoAm 74, 76, 78, 80, 82; WhoGov 72; WhoMus 72; WhoS&SW 73; WhoWor 74; WhoWorJ 72*

London, Jack (John Griffith)
American. Author
Wrote *The Call of the Wild,* 1903.
b. Jan 12, 1876 in San Francisco, California
d. Nov 22, 1916 in Glen Ellen, California
Source: *AmAu&B; AmBi; AmWr; AtlBL; AuBYP; AuNews 2; BiD&SB; CarSB; CasWL; Chambr 3; CnDAL; ConAmL; CyWA; DcAmAu; DcAmB; DcBiA; DcLEL; DcNAA; EncAB-H; EncMys; EncWL; FamAYP; FilmgC; JBA 34; LongCTC; MnBBF; ModAL, SUP; OxAmL; OxCan; OxEng; Pen AM; RAdv 1; RComWL; REn; REnAL; Str&VC; TwCA, SUP; TwCW; WebAB; WebE&AL; WhAm 1; WhoTwCL*

London, Julie
[Julie Peck]
American. Singer, Actress
b. Sep 26, 1926 in Santa Rosa, California
Source: *AmSCAP 66; CurBio 60; FilmgC; InWom; IntMPA 75, 76, 77, 78, 79, 80, 81, 82; MotPP; MovMk; WhoAm 74; WhoHol A*

Londos, Jim
Greek. Wrestler
b. 1895?
d. 1975
Source: *BioIn 10*

Lone Ranger
see: Beemer, Bruce

Long, Crawford Williamson
American. Scientist, Physician, Engineer
b. Nov 1, 1815 in Danielsville, Georgia
d. Jun 16, 1878 in Athens, Georgia
Source: *AmBi; ApCAB; BiDSA; DcAmB; TwCBDA; WebAB; WhAm H*

Long, Earl Kemp
American. Politician, Governor
b. Aug 26, 1895 in Winnfield, Louisiana
d. Sep 5, 1960 in Alexandria, Louisiana
Source: *CurBio 50, 60; WhAm 4*

Long, Huey Pierce
American. Governor, Politician
b. Aug 30, 1893 in Winnfield, Louisiana
d. Sep 10, 1935 in Baton Rouge, Louisiana
Source: *AmBi; BiDrAC; DcAmB S1; DcNAA; EncAB-H; LongCTC; OxAmL; OxFilm; REn; REnAL; WebAB; WhAm 1; WhAmP*

Long, John Luther
American. Author, Dramatist
b. Jan 1, 1861 in Pennsylvania
d. Oct 31, 1927
Source: *AmBi; BioIn 7, 10, 11; DcAmB; WhAm 1*

Long, Richard
American. Actor
b. Dec 17, 1927 in Chicago, Illinois
d. Dec 22, 1974 in Los Angeles, California
Source: *FilmgC; IntMPA 75; MotPP; MovMk; WhScrn 77; WhoHol B*

Long, (Richard) Dale
American. Baseball Player
b. Feb 6, 1926 in Springfield, Missouri
Source: *BaseEn; BioIn 4, 10; WhoProB 73*

Long, Russell Billiu
American. Senator
b. Nov 3, 1918 in Shreveport, Louisiana
Source: *BiDrAC; CelR 73; CngDr 74; CurBio 51, 65; IntWW 74; WhoAm 74, 76, 78, 80, 82; WhoAmP 73; WhoGov 72; WhoS&SW 73*

Long, Scott
American. Editor, Cartoonist
b. Feb 24, 1917 in Evanston, Illinois
Source: *WhoAm 74, 76, 78, 80, 82*

Long, Stephen H
American. Explorer, Naturalist
Led expeditions to Rocky Mts., 1820; Long's Peak named after him.
b. Dec 30, 1784 in Hopkinton, New Hampshire
d. Sep 4, 1864 in Alton, Illinois
Source: *Alli; AmAu&B; AmBi; ApCAB; BiAuS; DcAmB; DcNAA; Drake; TwCBDA; WhAm H*

Longden, Johnny
American. Jockey
b. 1910
Source: *BioIn 10*

Longet, Claudine Georgette
French. Actress, Singer
Was married to Andy Williams; accused of shooting lover, Spider Sabich.
b. Jan 29, 1942 in Paris, France
Source: *BioNews 74; BkPepl; WhoAm 74; WhoHol A*

Longfellow, Henry Wadsworth
American. Poet
First American to have memorial bust placed in Westminster Abbey.
b. Feb 27, 1807 in Portland, Maine
d. Mar 24, 1882 in Cambridge, Massachusetts
Source: *Alli, SUP; AmAu; AmAu&B; AmBi; AmWr; AnCL; ApCAB; AtlBL; AuBYP; BbD; BiD&SB; CasWL; Chambr 3; ChPo, S1, S2; CnDAL; CnE&AP; CrtT 3; CyAl 2; CyWA; DcAmAu; DcAmB; DcBiA; DcEnA; DcEnL; DcLEL; DcNAA; DcSpL; EncAB-H; EvLB; FamAYP; MouLC 4; OxAmL; OxEng; Pen AM; RAdv 1; RComWL; REn; REnAL; Str&VC; TwCBDA; WebAB; WebE&AL; WhAm H*

Longley, James Bernard
American. Governor of Maine
b. Apr 22, 1924 in Lewiston, Maine
d. Aug 16, 1980 in Lewiston, Maine
Source: *BioNews 74; NewYTBS 74*

Longmuir, Alan
[Bay City Rollers]
Scottish. Singer, Musician
b. Jun 20, 1950 in Edinburgh, Scotland
Source: *BkPepl*

Longmuir, Derek
[Bay City Rollers]
Scottish. Singer, Musician
b. Mar 19, 1955 in Edinburgh, Scotland
Source: *BkPepl*

Longstreet, James
American. Confederate General
b. Jan 8, 1821 in Edgefield District, South Carolina
d. Jan 2, 1904 in Gainesville, Georgia
Source: *AmAu&B; AmBi; ApCAB; BiDConf; BiDSA; DcAmAu; DcAmB; DcNAA; EncAB-H; REnAL; TwCBDA; WebAB; WhAm 1*

Longus
Greek. Author
fl. 3rd century BC in Greece
Source: *BbD; BiD&SB; CasWL; CyWA; OxEng; RComWL*

Longworth, Alice Roosevelt
American. Author, Social Leader
Daughter of Theodore Roosevelt; noted for caustic remarks.
b. Feb 12, 1884 in Long Island, New York
d. Feb 20, 1980 in Washington, DC
Source: *AmAu&B; CelR 73; ChPo; ConAu 93; CurBio 43; InWom; NewYTBS 74*

Lonsberry, (David) Ross
Canadian. Hockey Player
b. Feb 7, 1947 in Humboldt, SK
Source: *WhoHcky 73*

Lonsdale, Gordon Arnold
[Konon Trafimovich Molody]
Russian. Spy
b. 1922
d. Oct 9, 1970 in Moscow, U.S.S.R.
Source: *BioIn 7, 8, 9, 11; EncE 75; NewYTBE 70; ObitOF 79*

Lonsdale, (Leonard) Frederick
English. Dramatist
b. Feb 5, 1881 in Isle of Jersey
d. Apr 4, 1954 in London, England
Source: *BioIn 2, 3, 4; CnMD; CnThe; DcLEL; EncWT; McGEWD; ModWD; NotNAT B; ObitOF 79; OxThe; REn; WhThe*

Loomis, Mahion
American. Inventor
b. Jul 21, 1826 in Oppenheim, New York
d. Oct 13, 1886 in Terre Alta, West Virginia
Source: *WhAm H*

Loos, Anita
American. Author, Dramatist
Wrote *Gentlemen Prefer Blondes,* 1925.
b. Apr 26, 1893 in Sisson, California
d. Aug 18, 1981 in New York, New York
Source: *AmAu&B; ASpks; Au&Wr 71; AuNews 1; BiE&WWA; BioIn 1, 2, 3, 4, 5, 6, 7, 9, 10, 11; ConAu 21R, 104; ConNov 76; Conv 3; CurBio 74, 81; DcLEL; EvLB; FilmgC; GoodHS; InWom; IntAu&W 76, 77; IntMPA 78, 79, 80, 81, 82; IntWW 74, 75, 76, 77, 78; LibW; LongCTC; NewYTBE 73; NotNAT, A; OxAmL; Pen AM; REn; REnAL; TwCA, SUP; TwCW; WhE&EA; WhLit; WhoAm 74, 76, 78, 80; WhoAmW 58, 61, 64, 66, 70, 72, 74; WhoThe 72, 77; WhoWor 78; WomWMM; WorEFlm; WrDr 76, 80*

Lopat, Ed(mund Walter)
[Edmund Walter Lopatynski]
"Steady Eddie"
American. Baseball Player
b. Jun 21, 1918 in New York, New York
Source: *BaseEn; BioIn 2, 3, 4, 11; WhoProB 73*

Lope de Vega
[Lope Felix de Vega Carpio]
Spanish. Dramatist, Poet
b. 1562 in Madrid, Spain
d. 1635 in Madrid, Spain
Source: *BiD&SB; Pen EUR*

Loper, Don
American. Costume Designer
b. 1906 in Toledo, Ohio
d. Nov 22, 1972 in Santa Monica, California
Source: *NewYTBE 72; WhAm 5; WhScrn 77; WhoHol B*

Lopes, Davey (David Earl)
American. Baseball Player
b. May 3, 1946 in Providence, Rhode Island
Source: *BaseEn; WhoAm 76, 78, 80, 82; WhoBlA 77*

Lopez, Al(fonso Ramon)
American. Baseball Player
Catcher, 1928-47; Hall of Fame, 1977.
b. Aug 20, 1908 in Tampa, Florida
Source: *BaseEn; BioIn 2, 3, 4, 5, 6, 7, 8; CurBio 60; WhoProB 73*

Lopez, Encarnacion
see: Argentinita

Lopez, James Michael (Jimmy)
[The Hostages]
American. Former Hostage in Iran
b. 1959?
Source: *BioIn 12; NewYTBS 81*

Lopez, Nancy
[Mrs. Ray Knight]
American. Golfer
Won unprecedented five consecutive LPGA tournaments, 1978.
b. Jan 6, 1957 in Torrance, California
Source: *BioIn 10, 11*

Lopez, Trini(dad, III)
American. Singer
b. May 15, 1937 in Dallas, Texas
Source: *CelR 73; CurBio 68; WhoAm 74, 76, 78, 80, 82; WhoHol A*

Lopez, Vincent
American. Band Leader
b. Dec 30, 1895 in New York, New York
d. Sep 20, 1975 in Miami Beach, Florida
Source: *AmSCAP 66; ConAu 61; CurBio 60; WhScrn 77*

Lopez Bravo, Gregorio
[Gregorio Lopez-Bravo de Castro]
Spanish. Diplomat
b. Dec 19, 1923 in Madrid, Spain
Source: *CurBio 71; IntWW 74; WhoWor 74*

Lopez de Ayala, Pero
Spanish. Statesman, Author, Historian
b. 1332 in Victoria, Spain
d. 1407 in Calahorra, Spain
Source: *CasWL; DcSpL; EuAu; EvEuW; Pen EUR; REn*

Lopez de Legaspi, Miguel
Spanish. Conquerer of Philippines
b. 1510
d. 1572
Source: *ApCAB; WebBD 80*

Lopez Mateos, Adolfo
Mexican. President
b. May 26, 1910 in Atizapan de Zaragoza, Mexico
d. Sep 22, 1969 in Mexico City, Mexico
Source: *CurBio 59, 69; WhAm 5*

Lopez Portillo, Jose
Mexican. President
b. Jul 16, 1920 in Mexico City, Mexico
Source: *BioIn 10, 11; CurBio 77; WhoAm 78, 80, 82; WhoWor 78*

Lopez-Portillo y Rojas, Jose
Mexican. Author, Social Reformer
b. May 26, 1850 in Guadalajara, Mexico
d. May 22, 1923 in Mexico City, Mexico
Source: *AmLY; CasWL; DcSpL; Pen AM*

Lopokova, Lydia Vasilievna
[Mrs. John Maynard Keynes]
Russian. Ballerina
b. Oct 21, 1892 in Saint Petersburg, Russia
d. Jun 8, 1981 in Seaford, England
Source: *AnObit 1981; BioIn 3, 6; InWom; WhThe*

Lor, Denise
American. Singer
Source: *InWom*

Lord, Jack
American. Actor
Produced, starred in TV series "Hawaii Five-O."
b. Dec 30, 1930 in New York, New York
Source: *CelR 73; FilmgC; IntMPA 75, 76, 77, 78, 79, 80, 81, 82; MotPP; MovMk; WhoAm 74, 76, 78, 80, 82; WhoHol A; WhoWor 74*

Lord, James Lawrence
American. Public Relations Executive
b. Jun 20, 1915 in Peoria, Illinois
Source: *WhoPubR 72*

Lord, Marjorie
American. Actress
b. 1921
Source: *FilmgC; InWom; MovMk; WhoHol A*

Lord, Mary Pillsbury
American. Diplomat
b. Nov 14, 1904 in Minneapolis, Minnesota
d. Aug 1978 in New York, New York
Source: *BioIn 2, 3, 11; CurBio 52*

Lord, Pauline
American. Actress
b. 1890 in Hanford, California
d. Oct 11, 1950 in Alamogordo, New Mexico
Source: *DcAmB S4; FamA&A; FilmgC; InWom; NotAW; ThFT; WhAm 3; WhScrn 74, 77*

Lord, Phillips H
American. Radio Producer, Author, Actor
b. Jul 13, 1902 in Hartford, Vermont
d. Oct 19, 1975 in Ellsworth, Maine
Source: *AmAu&B; ConAu 5NR; REnAL; WhAm 6; WhScrn 77*

Loren, Sophia
[Sophia Lazarro; Sofia Scicolone; Mrs. Carlo Ponti]
Italian. Actress
Won Oscar, 1961, for *Two Women;* autobiography, *Sophia: Living and Loving,* 1979.
b. Sep 20, 1934 in Rome, Italy
Source: *BiDFilm; BkPepl; CelR 73; CmMov; CurBio 59; FilmgC; InWom; IntMPA 75, 76, 77, 78, 79, 80, 81, 82; IntWW 74; MotPP; MovMk; NewYTBE 70; OxFilm; WhoAm 82; WhoHol A; WhoWor 74; WorEFlm*

Lorengar, Pilar
[Pilar Lorenca Garcia]
Spanish. Opera Singer
b. Jan 16, 1933 in Zaragoza, Spain
Source: *CelR 73*

Lorentz, Hendrick Antoon
Dutch. Physicist
b. Jul 18, 1853 in Aarnhem, Netherlands
d. Feb 4, 1928
Source: *AsBiEn; BioIn 3; DcScB; McGEWB; NewCol 75; WebBD 80*

Lorenz, Max
German. Opera Singer
b. May 17, 1901 in Dusseldorf, Germany
d. Jan 11, 1975 in Salzburg, Austria
Source: *WhoMus 72*

Lorenzetti, Ambrogio
Italian. Artist
b. 1265?
d. 1348
Source: *REn*

Lorenzo de Medici
see: Medici, Lorenzo de

Lorillard, Louis
American. Tobacco Company Owner
Source: *NF*

Lorillard, Pierre
American. Merchant, Horse Breeder
b. Oct 13, 1833 in New York, New York
d. Jul 7, 1901 in New York, New York
Source: *DcAmB; WhAm H*

Loring, Eugene
[LeRoy Kerpestein]
American. Dancer, Choreographer
Wrote ballet "Billy the Kid," 1938.
b. 1914 in Milwaukee, Wisconsin
d. Aug 30, 1982 in Kingston, New York
Source: *BiE&WWA; CurBio 72, 82; NewYTBS 82; WhoHol A*

Loring, Gloria Jean
American. Singer, Actress
Star of TV soap opera "Days of Our Lives," 1980--.
b. Dec 10, 1946 in New York, New York
Source: *WhoAm 74, 76, 78, 80, 82*

Lorjou, Bernard Joseph Pierre
French. Artist
b. Sep 9, 1908 in Blois, France
Source: *McGDA; WhoWor 74*

Lorne, Marion
American. Actress
b. Aug 12, 1888 in Philadelphia, Pennsylvania
d. May 9, 1968 in New York, New York
Source: *BiE&WWA; FilmgC; InWom; MotPP; WhAm 5; WhScrn 74, 77; WhoHol B*

Lorrain, Claude Gellee
French. Artist
b. 1600 in Chamagne, France
d. Nov 21, 1682 in Rome, Italy
Source: *AtlBL; NewC; REn*

Lorraine, Alden, pseud.
see: Ackerman, Forest J

Lorre, Peter
[Laszlo Loewenstein]
American. Actor
Appeared in *The Maltese Falcon,* 1941.
b. Jun 26, 1904 in Rosenberg, Hungary
d. Mar 24, 1964 in Hollywood, California
Source: *BiDFilm; CmMov; FilmgC; MotPP; MovMk; OxFilm; Vers A; WhAm 4; WhScrn 74, 77; WhoHol B; WorEFlm*

Lorring, Joan
American. Actress
b. 1931 in Hong Kong, China
Source: *BiE&WWA; FilmgC; MotPP; MovMk; NotNAT; WhoHol A*

Lortz, Richard
American. Author, Dramatist
b. Jan 13, 1930 in New York, New York
d. Nov 5, 1980 in New York, New York
Source: *ConAu 57, 102*

Lortzing, Gustav Albert
German. Composer
b. Oct 23, 1801 in Berlin, Germany
d. Jan 21, 1851 in Berlin, Germany
Source: *NewEOp 71*

Losch, Tilly
Austrian. Dancer, Artist
b. Nov 15, 1902 in Vienna, Austria
d. Dec 24, 1975 in New York, New York
Source: *CurBio 44; EncMT; WhScrn 77*

Losey, Joseph
American. Film, Theatre Director
b. Jan 14, 1909 in La Crosse, Wisconsin
Source: *BiDFilm; CelR 73; CurBio 69; DcFM; FilmgC; IntMPA 75, 76, 77, 78, 79, 80, 81, 82; IntWW 74; MovMk; OxFilm; Who 74; WhoAm 74, 76, 78, 80, 82; WhoWor 74; WorEFlm*

Losonczi, Pal
Hungarian. President
b. Sep 18, 1919 in Bolho, Hungary
Source: *IntWW 74*

Lossing, Benson John
American. Author, Editor
b. Feb 12, 1813 in Beekman, New York
d. Jun 3, 1891 in Dover Plains, New York
Source: *Alli, SUP; AmAu; AmAu&B; AmBi; ApCAB; BbD; BiD&SB; ChPo; CyAl 2; DcAmAu; DcAmB; DcNAA; Drake; EarABI, SUP; TwCBDA; WhAm H*

Lot
Biblical Character
Source: *WebBD 80*

Lothrop, Harriet Mulford Stone
[Margaret Sidney, pseud.]
American. Children's Author
b. Jun 22, 1844 in New Haven, Connecticut
d. Aug 2, 1924
Source: *Alli SUP; AmAu; AmAu&B; BbD; BiD&SB; CarSB; ChPo; CnDAL; DcAmAu; DcNAA; OxAmL*

Loti, Pierre
French. Author
b. Jan 14, 1850 in Rochefort, France
d. Jun 10, 1923 in Hendaye, France
Source: *AtlBL; BbD; BiD&SB; CasWL; ClDMEL; CyWA; DcBiA; DcEuL; EncWL; EvEuW; LongCTC; OxEng; OxFr; Pen EUR; REn; TwCA, SUP*

Lotto, Lorenzo
Italian. Artist
b. 1480 in Venice, Italy
d. Sep 1, 1556 in Loreto, Italy
Source: *AtlBL; McGDA; McGEWB; REn*

Louden, Dorothy
American. Actress
b. Sep 17, 1933 in Boston, Massachusetts
Source: *NotNAT; WhoThe 77*

Lougheed, Peter
Canadian. Politician
b. Jul 26, 1928 in Calgary, AB
Source: *CurBio 79; WhoAm 82*

Loughran, Tommy
American. Boxer
Light-heavyweight champion, 1927-29.
b. Nov 29, 1902 in Philadelphia, Pennsylvania
d. Jul 7, 1982 in Hollidaysburg, Pennsylvania
Source: *BioIn 10, 11; NewYTBS 82; WhoBox 74*

Louis I
King of France and Germany
b. 778
d. Jun 20, 840
Source: *BioIn 9; DcBiPP; OxFr; WebBD 80*

Louis IX
[Saint Louis]
French. King
b. Apr 25, 1215 in Poissy, France
d. Aug 25, 1270 in Tunis, Tunisia
Source: *DcBiPP; OxFr; WebBD 80*

Louis XIV
"The Sun King"
French. King
b. Sep 16, 1638 in Saint-Germain, France
d. Sep 1, 1715
Source: *BioIn 10; DcBiPP; McGEWB; OxFr; WebBD 80*

Louis XV
French. King
b. Feb 15, 1710 in Versailles, France
d. May 10, 1774
Source: *DcBiPP; OxFr*

Louis XVI
French. King
b. Aug 23, 1754 in Versailles, France
d. Jan 21, 1793
Source: *BioIn 10; DcBiPP; OxFr; WebBD 80*

Louis Napoleon
French. Prince Imperial
b. 1856
d. 1879
Source: *BioIn 5, 9, 10, 11*

Louis Phillippe
French. King
b. Oct 6, 1773 in Paris, France
d. Aug 26, 1850 in London, England
Source: *BioIn 10; DcBiPP; WebBD 80*

Louis, Jean
French. Costume Designer
b. Oct 5, 1907 in Paris, France
Source: *CelR 73; IntMPA 75, 76, 77, 78, 79, 80, 81, 82; WorFshn*

Louis, Joe
[Joseph Louis Barrow]
"The Brown Bomber"
American. Boxer
Youngest boxer to win heavyweight championship, 1937; retired undefeated, 1949.
b. May 13, 1914 in Lexington, Alabama
d. Apr 12, 1981 in Las Vegas, Nevada
Source: *BioIn 1, 2, 3, 4, 5, 6, 7, 8, 9, 10, 11; CelR 73; ConAu 103; CurBio 40, 81; EncAB-A; McGEWB; NewCol 75; NewYTBS 79, 81; WebAB; WhoAm 74, 76, 78, 80; WhoBlA 75, 77; WhoBox 74*

Louis, Morris
[Morris Louis Bernstein]
American. Artist
b. Nov 28, 1912 in Baltimore, Maryland
d. Sep 7, 1962 in Washington, DC
Source: *BnEnAmA; ConArt; DcAmArt; DcCAA 71, 77; McGDA; WhAm 1*

Louise, Anita
[Louise Fremault]
American. Actress
b. Jan 9, 1917 in New York, New York
d. Apr 25, 1970 in West Los Angeles, California
Source: *FilmgC; HolP 30; MotPP; MovMk; NewYTBE 70; ThFT; WhScrn 74, 77; WhoHol B*

Louise, Tina
[Tina Blacker]
American. Actress
Played Ginger on TV series "Gilligan's Island," 1964-66.
b. Feb 11, 1937 in New York, New York
Source: *BiE&WWA; FilmgC; InWom; IntMPA 75, 76, 77, 78, 79, 80, 81, 82; MotPP; WhoHol A*

Louise Boulanger
French. Dressmaker
b. 1900
Source: *WorFshn*

Lousma, Jack
American. Astronaut
b. Feb 29, 1936 in Grand Rapids, Michigan
Source: *NewYTBE 73*

Louys, Pierre
French. Poet, Author
b. Dec 10, 1870 in Ghent, Belgium
d. Jun 4, 1925 in Paris, France
Source: *AtlBL; CasWL; ClDMEL; EncWL; EvEuW; IntWW 74; LongCTC; OxFr; REn; TwCA, SUP; WhoTwCL*

Love, Bessie
[Juanita Horton]
American. Actress
b. Sep 10, 1898 in Midland, Texas
Source: *BiE&WWA; Film 1, 2; FilmgC; IntMPA 75, 76, 77, 78, 79, 80, 81; MotPP; MovMk; NotNAT; OxFilm; ThFT; WhoHol A; WhoThe 72, 77, 81*

Love, George Hutchinson
American. Corporation Executive
b. Sep 4, 1900 in Johnstown, Pennsylvania
Source: *CurBio 50; IntWW 74; St&PR 75; WhoAm 74; WhoF&I 74*

Love, Mike
[The Beach Boys]
American. Singer, Musician
Lead vocalist for The Beach Boys, 1961--.
b. Mar 15, 1941 in Los Angeles, California
Source: *BkPepl; EncPR&S; IlEncRk; LilREn 78; RkOn*

Lovecraft, H(oward) P(hillips)
American. Author
b. Aug 20, 1890 in Providence, Rhode Island
d. Mar 15, 1937 in Providence, Rhode Island
Source: *AmAu&B; ChPo, S2; OxAmL; REnAL; TwCA SUP; WebAB*

Lovejoy, Clarence Earle
American. Author, Educational Consultant
b. 1894 in Waterville, Maine
d. 1974 in Red Bank, New Jersey
Source: *AmAu&B; Au&Wr 71; ConAu 5R, 45; NewYTBS 74; WhAm 6; WhNAA*

Lovejoy, Elijah P
American. Journalist, Abolitionist
b. Nov 9, 1802 in Albion, Maine
d. Nov 7, 1837 in Alton, Illinois
Source: *AmAu; AmBi; ApCAB; DcAmB; Drake; EncAB-H; OxAmL; REnAL; TwCBDA; WebAB; WhAm H; WhAmP*

Lovejoy, Frank
American. Actor
b. Mar 28, 1914 in New York, New York
d. Oct 2, 1962 in New York, New York
Source: *FilmgC; MotPP; MovMk; WhScrn 74, 77; WhoHol B*

Lovelace, Linda
[Linda Boreman Marciano]
American. Actress, Author
Source: *WhoHol A*

Lovelace, Richard
English. Poet
b. 1618 in Kent, England
d. 1658 in London, England
Source: *Alli; AtlBL; BiD&SB; BrAu; CasWL; Chambr 1; ChPo; CnE&AP; CroE&S; CyWA; DcEnA; DcEnL; DcEuL; DcLEL; EvLB; MouLC 1; NewC; OxEng; Pen ENG; REn; WebE&AL*

Lovelace, William Randolph, II
American. NASA Official
b. Dec 30, 1907 in Springfield, Missouri
d. Dec 12, 1965
Source: *BioIn 6, 7, 9; NatCAB 53; WhAm 4*

Lovell, Jim (James A, Jr.)
American. Astronaut
Flew Gemini 7, 12, Apollo 8, 13 space missions.
b. Mar 25, 1928 in Cleveland, Ohio
Source: *CurBio 59; IntWW 74; WhoAm 74, 76, 78, 80, 82; WhoGov 72; WhoS&SW 73; WhoWor 74*

Lovesey, Peter Harmer
[Peter Lear, pseud.]
English. Author
b. Sep 10, 1936 in Whitton, England
Source: *ConAu 41R; EncMys; IntAu&W 77; TwCCr&M; WrDr 76, 80*

Lovett, Robert A
American. Government Official
b. Sep 14, 1895 in Huntsville, Texas
Source: *BiDrUSE; CurBio 42, 51; IntWW 74; St&PR 75; Who 74; WhoAm 74; WhoAmP 73*

Lovin' Spoonful
[John Boone; Joe Butler; John Sebastian; Zal Yanovsky]
American. Rock Group
Source: *EncPR&S; IlEncRk*

Low, Sir David
English. Cartoonist, Caricaturist
b. Apr 7, 1891 in Dunedin, New Zealand
d. Sep 11, 1963 in London, England
Source: *ConAu 89; CurBio 40, 63; LongCTC; WhAm 4; WhoGrA*

Low, Juliette
[Juliette Gordon]
American. Organization Founder
Founded Girl Guides in US, 1912; name changed to Girl Scouts, 1913.
b. Oct 31, 1860 in Savannah, Georgia
d. Jan 18, 1927 in Savannah, Georgia
Source: *BioNews 74; DcAmB; HerW; InWom; NotAW; WebAB; WhAm HA, 4*

Lowe, Edmund Dante
American. Actor
b. Mar 3, 1892 in San Jose, California
d. Apr 21, 1971 in Woodland Hills, California
Source: *Film 1; FilmgC; MotPP; MovMk; NewYTBE 71; TwYS; WhScrn 74, 77; WhoHol B*

Lowe, Jack Warren
[Whittemore and Lowe]
American. Musician
b. Dec 25, 1917 in Aurora, Colorado
Source: *CurBio 54; WhoAm 74; WhoMus 72*

Lowe, Nick
[Rockpile]
English. Rock Singer, Musician
b. in England
Source: *ConMuA 80; WhoRock 81*

Lowell, Amy
American. Poet, Critic
b. Feb 9, 1874 in Brookline, Massachusetts
d. Feb 9, 1925 in Brookline, Massachusetts
Source: *Alli SUP; AmAu&B; AmBi; AmLY; AmWr; AtlBL; CasWL; Chambr 3; ChPo, S1; CnDAL; CnE&AP; ConAmA; ConAmL; DcAmB; DcLEL; DcNAA; EncAB-H; EvLB; InWom; LongCTC; ModAL; NotAW; OxAmL; OxEng; Pen AM; RAdv 1; REn; REnAL; SixAP; Str&VC; TwCA, SUP; TwCW; WebAB; WebE&AL; WhAm 1*

Lowell, Francis Cabot
American. Industrialist
b. Apr 7, 1775 in Newburyport, Massachusetts
d. Aug 10, 1817 in Boston, Massachusetts
Source: *AmBi; ApCAB; BioIn 2, 8, 10, 11; DcAmB; Drake; EncAB-A; McGEWB; NatCAB 7; NewCol 75; TwCBDA; WebAB; WhAm H*

Lowell, James Russell
American. Poet, Essayist, Diplomat
b. Feb 22, 1819 in Cambridge, Massachusetts
d. Aug 12, 1891 in Cambridge, Massachusetts
Source: *Alli, SUP; AmAu; AmAu&B; AmBi; ApCAB; AtlBL; BbD; BiD&SB; CasWL; Chambr 3; ChPo, S1, S2; CnDAL; CnE&AP; CrtT 3; CyAl 2; CyWA; DcAmAu; DcAmB; DcEnA, AP; DcEnL; DcLEL; DcNAA; DcSpL; EncAB-H; EvLB; MouLC 4; OxAmL; OxEng; Pen AM; RAdv 1; REn; REnAL; Str&VC; TwCBDA; WebAB; WebE&AL; WhAm H*

Lowell, John
American. Continental Congressman, Judge
b. Jun 17, 1743 in Newburyport, Massachusetts
d. May 6, 1802 in Roxbury, Massachusetts
Source: *AmBi; ApCAB; BiDrAC; BioIn 8; DcAmB; Drake; NewCol 75; TwCBDA; WebBD 80; WhAm H*

Lowell, Percival
American. Astronomer
Established Lowell Observatory, Flagstaff, AZ, 1894.
b. Mar 13, 1855 in Boston, Massachusetts
d. Nov 13, 1916 in Flagstaff, Arizona
Source: *Alli SUP; AmAu&B; AmBi; ApCAB SUP; ArizL; BiD&SB; DcAmAu; DcAmB; DcNAA; REnAL; TwCBDA; WebAB; WhAm 1*

Lowell, Robert Trail Spence, Jr.
American. Poet, Dramatist
b. Mar 1, 1917 in Boston, Massachusetts
d. Sep 12, 1977 in New York, New York
Source: *AmAu&B; AmWr; CasWL; CelR 73; ChPo; CnDAL; CnE&AP; CnMWL; CnThe; ConAu 9R, 73; ConDr 73; ConLC 1, 2, 3, 4, 5, 8, 9, 11, 15; ConP 70, 75; CroCAP; CroCD; CurBio 47, 72; DrAP 75; EncAB-H; EncWL; EvLB; IntWW 74; ModAL, SUP; ModWD; NotNAT; OxAmL; Pen AM; RAdv 1; RComWL; REn; REnAL; TwCA SUP; TwCW; WebAB; WebE&AL; Who 74; WhoAm 74; WhoTwCL; WhoWor 74; WrDr 76*

Lowenfels, Walter
American. Author
b. May 10, 1897 in New York, New York
d. Jul 7, 1976 in Tarrytown, New York
Source: *AmAu&B; AuBYP SUP; ConAu 1R, 65, 3NR; ConP 75; DcLB 4; DrAP 75; IntAu&W 76; IntWWP 77; Pen AM; RAdv 1; WhAm 7; WhoAm 74; WrDr 76*

Lowenstein, Allard Kenneth
American. Lawyer
b. Jan 16, 1929 in Newark, New Jersey
d. Mar 14, 1980 in New York, New York
Source: *BiDrAC; CurBio 71, 80; NewYTBE 72; PolProf J; PolProf NF; WhAm 7; WhoAm 74, 76, 78; WhoAmP 73, 75, 77, 79; WhoGov 75*

Lowery, Joseph E
American. Civil Rights Leader, Clergyman
Co-founded, SCLC; president, 1977--.
b. 1925? in Alabama
Source: *CurBio 82; InB&W 80; WhoAm 78, 80, 82; WhoBlA 77, 80; WhoRel 77*

Lowery, "Nick" (Gerald Lowery)
"Nick the Kick"
American. Football Player
b. May 27, 1956 in Munich, Germany (West)
Source: *BioIn 12; FootReg*

Lowery, Robert O
American. City Official
b. Apr 20, 1916 in Buffalo, New York
Source: *WhoE 74*

Lowndes, Marie Adelaide Belloc
English. Author
b. 1868
d. Nov 11, 1947 in Eversley, England
Source: *CathA 1930; DcLEL; EncMys; EvLB; REn; TwCA, SUP*

Lowry, Clarence Malcolm
English. Author, Poet
b. Jul 28, 1909 in Liverpool, England
d. Jun 1957 in Sussex, England
Source: *CreCan 1*

Lowry, Judith Ives
American. Actress
b. Jul 27, 1890 in Morristown, New Jersey
d. Nov 29, 1976 in New York, New York
Source: *WhoHol A*

Loy, Myrna
[Myrna Williams]
American. Actress
Played Nora Charles in *The Thin Man* film series.
b. Aug 2, 1905 in Helena, Montana
Source: *BiDFilm; CelR 73; CmMov; CurBio 50; FilmgC; InWom; IntMPA 75, 76, 77, 78, 79, 80, 81, 82; MotPP; MovMk; OxFilm; ThFT; TwYS; WhoAm 74, 76, 78, 80, 82; WhoHol A; WorEFlm*

Loyola, Ignatius de, Saint
[Inigo do Onez y Loyola; Saint Ignacio de Loyola]
Spanish. Founder of Jesuits
b. 1491 in Loyola, Spain
d. Jul 31, 1556 in Rome, Italy
Source: *CasWL; DcSpL; EuAu; EvEuW; NewC; REn*

Lu, Yu
Chinese. Poet
b. 1125 in Shan-Yin, China
d. 1210
Source: *CasWL; DcOrL 1*

Lualdi, Adriano
Italian. Opera Composer
b. Mar 22, 1887 in Larino, Italy
Source: *NewEOp 71*

Lubalin, Herbert Frederick
American. Graphics Designer
b. May 17, 1918 in New York, New York
d. May 24, 1981
Source: *WhAm 7; WhoAm 78, 80, 82; WhoGrA*

Lubbock, Francis Richard
American. Governor of Texas
b. Oct 16, 1815 in Beaufort, South Carolina
d. 1905
Source: *ApCAB; BiDConf; DcAmB; DcNAA; TwCBDA; WhAm 1*

Lubbock, Percy
English. Literary Critic, Essayist
b. Jun 4, 1879 in London, England
d. 1965
Source: *ConAu 85; DcLEL; EvLB; LongCTC; ModBrL; NewC; OxEng; REn; TwCA, SUP; TwCW*

Lubin, Germaine
French. Opera Singer
b. Feb 1, 1890 in Paris, France
Source: *InWom; NewEOp 71*

Lubitsch, Ernst
American. Motion Picture Director
b. Jan 28, 1892 in Berlin, Germany
d. Nov 30, 1947 in Los Angeles, California
Source: *BiDFilm; CmMov; DcAmB S4; DcFM; FilmgC; MovMk; OxFilm; TwYS; WhAm 2; WhScrn 74, 77; WhoHol B; WorEFlm*

Lubke, Heinrich
German. President of West Germany
b. Oct 11, 1894 in Enkhausen, Germany
d. Apr 6, 1972 in Bonn, Germany (West)
Source: *CurBio 60, 72; NewYTBE 72*

Luboff, Norman
American. Composer, Conductor
b. Apr 14, 1917 in Chicago, Illinois
Source: *AmSCAP 66; WhoAm 74, 76, 78, 80, 82*

Luboshutz, Pierre
Musician, Composer
b. Jun 22, 1894 in Odessa, Russia
d. Apr 18, 1971 in Rockport, Maine
Source: *AmSCAP 66; NewYTBE 71*

Lubovitch, Lar
American. Dancer, Choreographer
b. in Chicago, Illinois
Source: *BioIn 9, 11; WhoAm 78, 80, 82*

Lucan
[Marcus Annaeus Lucanus]
Roman. Poet, Author
Wrote epic *Pharsalia;* conspired against Nero.
b. Jun 3, 39 in Cordova, Spain
d. Jun 30, 65 in Rome, Italy
Source: *BbD; BiD&SB; CasWL; NewC; OxEng; Pen CL; RComWL; REn*

Lucasvan Leyden
[Lucas Hugensz]
Dutch. Artist
b. 1494 in Leiden, Netherlands
d. 1533 in Leiden, Netherlands
Source: *AtlBL*

Lucas, George
American. Motion Picture Director
Directed *Star Wars, The Empire Strikes Back, American Graffiti.*
b. May 14, 1944 in Modesto, California
Source: *BkPepl; ConAu 77; ConLC 16; IntMPA 75, 76, 77, 78, 79, 80, 81, 82; MovMk; WhoAm 76, 78, 80, 82*

Lucas, Jerry
American. Basketball Player
NBA Rookie of year, 1964; scored 14,053 career points.
b. Mar 30, 1940 in Middletown, Ohio
Source: *CurBio 72; NewYTBE 72; WhoBbl 73*

Lucas, Jim Griffing
American. Journalist
b. Jun 22, 1914 in Checotah, Oklahoma
d. Jun 21, 1970 in Washington, DC
Source: *ConAu 104; NewYTBE 70; WhAm 5; WhoS&SW 73*

Lucas, Maurice
American. Basketball Player
b. Feb 18, 1952 in Pittsburgh, Pennsylvania
Source: *BioIn 11; WhoBlA 77*

Lucas, Nick
"The Singing Troubadour"
American. Entertainer
Starred in vaudeville; hit song, "Tiptoe Through the Tulips with Me", 1929.
b. Aug 22, 1897 in Newark, New Jersey
d. Jul 28, 1982 in Colorado Springs, Colorado
Source: *CmpEPM; Film 2; WhoHol A*

Lucas, Scott Wike
American. Government Official
b. Feb 19, 1892 in Chandlerville, Illinois
d. Feb 22, 1968
Source: *BioIn 1, 2, 8, 11; CurBio 47, 68*

Lucas Garcia, Fernando Romeo
Guatemalan. President
Source: *BioIn 11*

Lucca, Pauline
Austrian. Opera Singer
b. Apr 25, 1841 in Vienna, Austria
d. Feb 28, 1908 in Vienna, Austria
Source: *InWom*

Lucchese, Thomas
"Three-Finger Brown"
American. Gangster
b. 1903
d. 1967
Source: *Blood*

Luce, Charles (Franklin)
American. Utilities Executive
b. Sep 29, 1917 in Platteville, Wisconsin
Source: *CurBio 58; IntWW 74; NewYTBS 74; WhoAm 74, 76, 78, 80, 82; WhoE 74; WhoF&I 74; WhoGov 72*

Luce, Clare Boothe
American. Author, Journalist, Dramatist
US Congresswoman, 1943-47; ambassador to Italy, 1953-57.
b. Apr 10, 1903 in New York, New York
Source: *AmAu&B; Au&Wr 71; BiDrAC; BiE&WWA; CelR 73; ConAu 45; CurBio 42, 53; InWom; IntWW 74; LongCTC; McGEWD; ModWD; NotNAT; OxAmL; REn; REnAL; Who 74; TwCA, SUP; WebAB; WhoAm 74, 76, 78, 80, 82; WhoAmP 73; WhoAmW 77; WhoWor 74; WomWMM*

Luce, Don(ald Harold)
Canadian. Hockey Player
b. Oct 2, 1948 in London, ON
Source: *WhoHcky 73*

Luce, Henry Robinson
American. Editor, Publisher
b. Apr 3, 1898 in Shantung, China
d. Feb 28, 1967 in Phoenix, Arizona
Source: *AmAu&B; ConAu 89, 104; CurBio 41, 61, 67; EncAB-H; REn; REnAL; WebAB; WhAm 4*

Lucey, Patrick Joseph
American. Politician
b. Mar 21, 1918 in La Crosse, Wisconsin
Source: *IntWW 74; WhoAm 74; WhoAmP 73; WhoGov 72; WhoMW 74*

Lucian
Greek. Author
b. 125? in Samosato, Syria
d. 200? in Egypt
Source: *AtlBL; BbD; BiD&SB; CasWL; CyWA; NewC; OxEng; Pen CL; RComWL; REn*

Luciano, "Lucky" (Charles)
[Salvatore Luciana]
American. Criminal
Established national crime syndicate, 1930's; deported, 1946.
b. Nov 24, 1897 in Palermo, Sicily
d. Jan 26, 1962 in Naples, Italy
Source: *BioIn 1, 2, 3, 6, 7, 9, 11; Blood; EncACr*

Luciano, Ron(ald Michael)
American. Baseball Umpire, Author
Former pro football player; author *The Umpire Strikes Back,* 1982.
b. Jun 28, 1937 in Binghamton, New York
Source: *BioIn 11; WhoAm 80, 82*

Lucile
[Lady Duff-Gordon]
English. Designer
b. 1864 in England
d. 1935
Source: *WorFshn*

Lucilius
Roman. Poet
b. 180AD in Campania, Italy
d. 102?
Source: *NewCol 75*

Lucioni, Luigi
American. Artist
b. Nov 4, 1900 in Malnate, Italy
Source: *CurBio 43; WhoAm 74, 76, 78, 80, 82*

Luckenbach, Edgar Frederick, Jr.
American. Shipping Executive
b. May 17, 1925 in New York, New York
d. Aug 9, 1974 in New York, New York
Source: *WhoAm 74; WhoF&I 74*

Luckman, Charles
American. Architect, Business Executive
b. May 16, 1909 in Kansas City, Missouri
Source: *AmArch 70; CurBio 47; WhoAm 74, 76, 78, 80, 82; WhoF&I 74; WhoWor 74*

Luckman, Sid(ney)
American. Football Player
b. Nov 21, 1916 in Brooklyn, New York
Source: *BioIn 1, 2, 3, 4, 5, 6, 7, 8, 9, 10; WhoFtbl 74*

Luckner, Felix von, Count
German. Naval Officer
b. 1881
d. 1966
Source: *NewCol 75; WebBD 80*

Lucretius
Roman. Poet
b. 99BC
d. 55BC
Source: *AtlBL; NewC; OxEng; Pen CL; RComWL; REn*

Lucullus, Lucius Licinius
[Ponticus, Lucius Licinius Lucullus]
Roman. General, Patron of Learning
b. 110BC
d. 57BC
Source: *NewC; REn*

Ludd, Ned
"King Ludd"
English. Revolutionary
Source: *WebBD 80*

Ludden, Allen Ellsworth
American. Game Show Host, Producer
Hosted game show "Password," 1961-80; married to Betty White.
b. Oct 5, 1918 in Mineral Point, Wisconsin
d. Jun 9, 1981 in Los Angeles, California
Source: *NewYTET; WhoAm 76, 78, 80*

Luddy, Barbara
American. Actress
Source: *What 4; WhoHol A*

Ludendorff, Erich Friedrich Wilhelm
German. General, Politician
b. Apr 9, 1865 in Kruszewnia, Prussia
d. Dec 20, 1937 in Munich, Germany
Source: *McGEWB; OxGer; REn*

Ludikar, Pavel
Czech. Opera Singer, Manager
b. Mar 3, 1882 in Prague, Czechoslovakia
Source: *NewEOp 71*

Ludington, Sybil
[Mrs. Edward Ogden]
American. Revolutionary Heroine
Warned countryside of attack on Danbury, CT, 1777.
b. Apr 5, 1761 in Fredericksburg, New York
d. Feb 26, 1839 in Unadilla, New York
Source: *BioIn 2, 4, 4, 5, 10; InWom; LibW; WebAB; WebAMB*

Ludlow, Fitz Hugh
American. Author
b. Sep 11, 1836 in New York, New York
d. Sep 12, 1870 in Geneva, Switzerland
Source: *AmBi; TwCBDA; WhAm H*

Ludlum, Robert
American. Author
b. May 25, 1927 in New York, New York
Source: *BiE&WWA; ConAu 33R; CurBio 82; NotNAT; WhoAm 82; WrDr 76*

Ludwig II
[Louis II]
Bavarian. King
b. 1845
d. 1886 in Lake Starnberg, Bavaria
Source: *BioIn 3, 4, 5, 7, 8, 9, 11; DcNiCA; NewCol 75*

Ludwig, Christa
German. Opera Singer
b. Mar 16, 1924 in Berlin, Germany
Source: *CelR 73; CurBio 71; IntWW 74; NewYTBE 71; Who 74; WhoAm 82; WhoAmW 70; WhoWor 74*

Ludwig, Daniel Keith
American. Business Executive
b. Jun 24, 1897 in South Haven, Michigan
Source: *BioIn 4, 6, 9, 10, 11; BioNews 74; BusPN; CurBio 79; NewYTBS 76; WhoAm 74, 76, 78*

Ludwig, Emil
[Emil Ludwig Cohn]
German. Author
b. Jan 25, 1881 in Breslau, Germany
d. Sep 17, 1948 in Ascona, Switzerland
Source: *EvEuW; LongCTC; OxGer; TwCA, SUP; WhAm 2; WhoLA*

Ludwig, Leopold
Austrian. Conductor
b. Jan 12, 1908 in Witfowitz, Austria
d. 1979 in Luneberg, Germany (West)
Source: *NewEOp 71*

Luft, Lorna
[Mrs. Jake Hooker]
American. Singer
Daughter of Judy Garland and Sid Luft.
b. 1952
Source: *BioNews 74; NewYTBE 72*

Lugar, Richard Green
American. Senator
b. Apr 4, 1932 in Indianapolis, Indiana
Source: *CurBio 77; WhoAm 82*

Lugosi, Bela
[Bela Blasko]
American. Actor
Starred in horror film *Dracula,* 1930.
b. Oct 20, 1882 in Lugos, Hungary
d. Sep 16, 1956 in Hollywood, California
Source: *CmMov; Film 1; FilmgC; MotPP; MovMk; TwYS; WebAB; WhScrn 74, 77; WhoHol B*

Luhan, Mabel Dodge
American. Author
b. Feb 26, 1879 in Buffalo, New York
d. Aug 13, 1962
Source: *AmAu&B; CnDAL; ConAmA; CurBio 40, 62; InWom; LongCTC; OxAmL; Pen AM; REn; REnAL; TwCA, SUP; WhAm 4; WhNAA*

Luini, Bernardino
Italian. Artist
b. 1480 in Luino, Italy
d. 1532
Source: *NewCol 75; OxArt*

Luisetti, Angelo Enrico
"Hank"
American. Basketball Player
Introduced one-handed shot.
b. Jun 16, 1916 in San Francisco, California
Source: *BioIn 6, 9, 10; CmCal; WhoBbl 73*

Lujack, John(ny)
American. Football Player
b. Jan 4, 1925 in Connellsville, Pennsylvania
Source: *CurBio 47; WhoFtbl 74*

Lukas, J Anthony
American. Author
b. Apr 25, 1933 in New York, New York
Source: *AmAu&B; ConAu 49, 2NR; WhoAm 74, 76, 78, 80, 82*

Lukas, Paul
American. Actor
b. May 26, 1894 in Budapest, Hungary
d. Aug 15, 1971 in Tangiers, Morocco
Source: *BiDFilm; BiE&WWA; CurBio 42, 71; Film 1; FilmgC; HolP 30; MotPP; MovMk; NewYTBE 71; OxFilm; TwYS; WhAm 5; WhScrn 74, 77; WhoHol B; WorEFlm*

Luke, Saint
Biblical Character
Source: *NewC; REn*

Luke, Keye
American. Actor, Artist
b. 1904 in Canton, China
Source: *IntMPA 77, 78, 79, 80, 81, 82; MovMk; Vers A; WhoHol A*

Lukeman, Henry A
American. Sculptor
b. 1871 in Richmond, Virginia
d. 1935
Source: *AmBi; DcAmB S1*

Luks, George Benjamin
American. Artist
b. Aug 13, 1867 in Williamsport, Pennsylvania
d. Oct 29, 1933
Source: *AmBi; DcAmB S1; OxAmL; REnAL; WhAm 1*

Lully, Jean-Baptiste
[Giovanni Battista Lulli]
French. Composer
Founded Paris Opera, 1672, and French National Opera.
b. Nov 28, 1632 in Florence, Italy
d. Mar 22, 1687 in Paris, France
Source: *AtlBL; Baker 78; McGEWB; NewC; NewCol 75; NewEOp 71; OxFr; OxMus; REn; WhDW*

Lulu
[Marie McDonald McLaughlin]
Scottish. Singer, Actress
b. Nov 3, 1948 in Glasgow, Scotland
Source: *FilmgC; WhoHol A*

Lumet, Sidney
American. Motion Picture Director
b. Jun 25, 1924 in Philadelphia, Pennsylvania
Source: *BiDFilm; BiE&WWA; CelR 73; CurBio 67; DcFM; FilmgC; IntMPA 75, 76, 77, 78, 79, 80, 81, 82; IntWW 74; MovMk; NewYTBS 74; NotNAT; OxFilm; WhoAm 74, 76, 78, 80, 82; WhoHol A; WhoWor 74; WorEFlm*

Lumiere, Auguste
French. Photographer
b. Oct 19, 1862 in Besancon, France
d. Apr 10, 1954 in Lyons, France
Source: *BiDFilm; DcFM; FilmEn; Film 1; OxFilm; OxFr; WorEFlm*

Lumiere, Louis
French. Photographer
b. Oct 5, 1864 in Besancon, France
d. Jun 6, 1948 in Bandol, France
Source: *BiDFilm; DcFM; FilmEn; FilmgC; OxFilm; OxFr; TwYS; WorEFlm*

Lumley, Harry
"Apple Cheeks"
Canadian. Hockey Player
b. Nov 11, 1926 in Owen Sound, ON
Source: *WhoHcky 73*

Lummis, Charles Fletcher
American. Author, Explorer
b. 1859 in Lynn, Massachusetts
d. Nov 25, 1928
Source: *AmAu&B; AmBi; AmLY; ApCAB SUP; BiD&SB; ChPo; DcAmAu; DcAmB; DcNAA; OhA&B; OxAmL; TwCBDA; WhAm 1; WhNAA*

Lum 'n Abner
see: Goff, Norris; Lauck, Chester

Lumumba, Patrice Emergy
Congolese. Premier
b. Jul 2, 1925 in Oualua, Congo
d. Jan 18, 1961 in Elisabethville, Congo
Source: *CurBio 60, 61; McGEWB*

Lunardi, Vincenzo
Italian. Balloonist
b. Jan 11, 1759
d. Jul 31, 1806
Source: *BioIn 5, 7*

Lunceford, Jimmy (James Melvin)
American. Jazz Musician
b. Jun 6, 1902 in Fulton, Mississippi
d. Jul 13, 1947 in Seaside, Oregon
Source: *AmSCAP 66; DcAmB S4; WhScrn 77*

Lund, Art
American. Actor
b. 1920 in Salt Lake City, Utah
Source: *BiE&WWA; NotNAT; WhoHol A; WhoThe 77*

Lund, John
American. Actor
b. 1913 in Rochester, New York
Source: *FilmgC; HolP 40; MotPP; MovMk; NewYTBE 71; Who 74; WhoHol A*

Lundigan, William
American. Actor
b. Jun 12, 1914 in Syracuse, New York
d. Dec 21, 1975 in Los Angeles, California
Source: *FilmgC; IntMPA 75; MotPP; MovMk; WhAm 6; WhScrn 77*

Lunn, Janet
American. Children's Author
b. Dec 28, 1928 in Dallas, Texas
Source: *ConAu 33R; OxCan SUP; SmATA 4*

Luns, Joseph Marie Antoine Hubert
Dutch. Politician, Diplomat
Secretary-general, NATO, 1971--.
b. Aug 28, 1911 in Rotterdam, Netherlands
Source: *CurBio 58, 82; IntWW 74, 75, 76, 77, 78, 79, 80, 81; IntYB 78, 79; NewYTBE 71; Who 74; WhoWor 74, 78*

Lunt, Alfred
American. Actor
b. Aug 19, 1892 in Milwaukee, Wisconsin
d. Aug 2, 1977 in Chicago, Illinois
Source: *BiE&WWA; CelR 73; CurBio 41; FamA&A; FilmgC; IntWW 74; NotNAT; OxAmL; OxThe; PlP&P; REn; TwYS; WebAB; Who 74; WhoAm 74; WhoHol A; WhoThe 77; WhoWor 74*

Lupescu, Magda (Elena)
Romanian. Mistress of King Carol
b. 1896
d. Jun 29, 1977 in Estoril, Portugal
Source: *CurBio 40; InWom*

Lupino, Ida
American. Actress
b. Feb 4, 1918 in London, England
Source: *BiDFilm; CurBio 43; FilmgC; InWom; IntMPA 75, 76, 77, 78, 79, 80, 81, 82; MotPP; MovMk; NewYTBE 72; OxFilm; ThFT; WhoAm 74, 76, 78, 80, 82; WhoHol A; WomWMM; WorEFlm*

Lupino, Stanley
English. Actor, Dramatist, Producer
b. Jun 17, 1896 in London, England
d. Jun 10, 1942 in London, England
Source: *CurBio 42; EncMT; FilmgC; NewC; OxThe; WhScrn 74, 77; WhoHol B*

LuPone, Patti
American. Actress
Won Tony, 1980, for *Evita.*
b. Apr 21, 1949 in Northport, New York
Source: *WhoAm 80, 82; WhoThe 81*

Lupu, Radu
Romanian. Musician
b. Nov 30, 1945 in Galati, Romania
Source: *BioIn 7; IntWW 74, 75, 76, 77, 78; Who 74; WhoAm 80, 82; WhoMus 72; WhoWor 78*

Luque, Dolf (Adolfo)
"The Pride of Havana"
Cuban. Baseball Player
b. Aug 4, 1890 in Havana, Cuba
d. Jul 3, 1957 in Havana, Cuba
Source: *BaseEn; BioIn 3, 4; WhoProB 73*

Lurcat, Jean Marie
French. Artist
b. Jul 1, 1892 in Bruyeres, France
d. Jan 6, 1966 in Saint-Paul-de-Vence, France
Source: *CurBio 48, 66; McGDA; ObitOF 79; WhAm 4; WhoGrA*

Lurie, Alison
American. Author
b. Sep 3, 1926 in Chicago, Illinois
Source: *BioIn 10; ConAu 1R, 4NR; ConLC 4, 5; ConNov 72, 76; DcLB 2; DrAF 76; IntAu&W 76, 77; WhoAm 80, 82; WorAu 1970; WrDr 76, 80*

Lurie, Jane
American. Filmmaker
Source: *WomWMM*

Lurton, Horace Harmon
American. Supreme Court Justice
b. Feb 26, 1844 in Newport, Kentucky
d. Apr 1914 in Atlantic City, New Jersey
Source: *AmBi; ApCAB SUP; DcAmB; TwCBDA; WebAB; WhAm 1*

Lustig, Alvin
American. Graphic Designer
b. Feb 8, 1915 in Denver, Colorado
d. Dec 4, 1955
Source: *WhAm 3*

Luther, Martin
German. Religious Reformer
Led Protestant Reformation, 1517; Lutheran religion named for him.
b. Nov 10, 1483 in Eisleben, Germany
d. Feb 18, 1546
Source: *AnCL; BbD; BiD&SB; CasWL; ChPo, S1; DcEuL; EuAu; EvEuW; NewC; OxEng; OxGer; Pen EUR; PoChrch; RComWL; REn*

Luthuli, Albert John
South African. Zulu Leader
b. 1898 in Rhodesia
d. Jul 21, 1967 in Groutville, South Africa
Source: *BioIn 8*

Lutoslawski, Witold
Polish. Composer
b. 1913
Source: *BioIn 8*

Lutz, Bob
American. Tennis Player
b. 1947
Source: *BioIn 9, 10*

Luxemburg, Rosa
German. Socialist Leader
b. 1870 in Zamosc, Poland
d. Jan 15, 1919 in Berlin, Germany
Source: *McGEWB; OxGer; REn*

Luzinski, Greg(ory Michael)
"The Bull"
American. Baseball Player
b. Nov 22, 1950 in Chicago, Illinois
Source: *BaseEn; BioIn 10, 11; WhoAm 82*

Lyautey, Louis Hubert Gonzalve
French. Administrator of Morocco
b. Nov 17, 1854 in Nancy, France
d. Jul 27, 1934 in Thorey, France
Source: *McGEWB; NewCol 75*

Lydon, James (Jimmy)
American. Actor
b. May 30, 1923 in Harrington, New Jersey
Source: *FilmgC; IntMPA 75, 76, 77, 78, 79, 80, 81, 82; MovMk; WhoHol A*

Lyell, Sir Charles
Scottish. Geologist
b. Nov 14, 1797 in Kinnordy, Scotland
d. Feb 22, 1875 in London, England
Source: *Alli, SUP; ApCAB; BbD; BbtC; BiD&SB; BrAu 19; CasWL; Chambr 3; DcEnL; Drake; EvLB; OxCan; OxEng; REnAL*

Lyendecker, Joseph Cristian
American. Artist
Source: *NF*

Lyle, Katie Letcher
American. Author
b. May 12, 1938 in Peking, China
Source: *ConAu 49; SmATA 8*

Lyle, "Sparky" (Albert Walter)
American. Baseball Player
Won Cy Young Award, 1977; author *The Bronx Zoo,* 1979.
b. Jul 22, 1944 in DuBois, Pennsylvania
Source: *BaseEn; CurBio 78; WhoAm 82; WhoProB 73*

Lyly, John
English. Author
b. 1554 in Weald, England
d. 1606 in London, England
Source: *BiD&SB; BrAu; CasWL; Chambr 1; ChPo; CnE&AP; CnThe; CroE&S; CrtT 1; CyWA; DcEnA, AP; DcEnL; DcEuL; DcLEL; EvLB; McGEWD; MouLC 1; NewC; OxEng; OxThe; Pen ENG; REn; REnWD; WebE&AL*

Lyman, Abe
American. Band Leader
b. Aug 4, 1897 in Chicago, Illinois
d. Oct 23, 1957 in Beverly Hills, California
Source: *AmSCAP 66; WhScrn 74, 77; WhoHol B*

Lyman, William Roy
"Link"
American. Football Player
b. Nov 30, 1898 in Table Rock, Nebraska
Source: *WhoFtbl 74*

Lympany, Moura
English. Musician
b. Aug 18, 1916 in Saltash, England
Source: *IntWW 74, 75, 76, 77, 78; Who 74; WhoMus 72; WhoWor 74*

Lynch, Benny
Scottish. Boxer
b. Aug 6, 1946 in Glasgow, Scotland
Source: *BioIn 7; WhoBox 74*

Lynch, David
[The Platters]
American. Singer
b. 1930 in Saint Louis, Missouri
d. Jan 2, 1981 in Long Beach, California
Source: *BioIn 12*

Lynch, Joe
American. Boxer
b. Nov 30, 1898 in New York, New York
d. Aug 1, 1965 in Brooklyn, New York
Source: *BioIn 7; WhoBox 74*

Lynch, John
Irish. Prime Minister
b. Aug 15, 1917
Source: *Who 74*

Lynch, Kevin
[Irish Hunger Strikers]
Irish. Jailed IRA Member
b. 1956? in Dungiven, Northern Ireland
d. Aug 1, 1981 in Belfast, Northern Ireland
Source: *NF*

Lynch, Thomas, Jr.
American. Continental Congressman
b. Aug 5, 1749 in Winyaw, South Carolina
d. 1779
Source: *AmBi; ApCAB; BiAuS; BiDrAC; DcAmB; Drake; TwCBDA; WhAm H; WhAmP*

Lynd, Helen Merrell
American. Sociologist, Author, Educator
Wrote *Middletown* and *Middletown in Transition,* studies of small-town America.
b. 1896 in LaGrange, Illinois
d. Jan 30, 1982 in Warren, Ohio
Source: *AmWomWr; DrAS 74P, 78P; LinLib L; NewYTBS 82; Pen AM; REnAL; TwCA, SUP; WhoAmW 58, 61, 64, 66, 68, 70*

Lynd, Robert Staughton
American. Sociologist
b. Sep 26, 1892 in New Albany, Indiana
d. Nov 1, 1970 in Warren, Connecticut
Source: *AmAu&B; ConAu 29R; DcLEL; IndAu 1917; LongCTC; OxAmL; Pen AM; REnAL; TwCA, SUP; WebAB; WhAm 5*

Lynde, Paul Edward
American. Comedian, Actor
Known for one-liners as panelist on game show "Hollywood Squares."
b. Jun 13, 1926 in Mount Vernon, Ohio
d. Jan 10, 1982 in Beverly Hills, California
Source: *BiE&WWA; BioNews 75; BkPepl; CurBio 72, 82; EncMT; FilmgC; IntMPA 75, 76, 77, 78, 79, 80, 81, 82; MotPP; MovMk; NewYTBS 82; NotNAT A; WhoAm 80; WhoHol A*

Lynes, Joseph Russell, Jr.
American. Editor, Author
b. Dec 2, 1910 in Barrington, Massachusetts
Source: *ConAu 3NR; WhoAm 74, 76, 78, 80, 82*

Lynley, Carol
American. Actress
b. Feb 13, 1943 in New York, New York
Source: *FilmgC; InWom; MotPP; MovMk; WhoAm 78, 80, 82; WorEFlm*

Lynn, Bonnie
see: Delaney and Bonnie

Lynn, Diana
[Delores Loehr]
American. Actress
b. Oct 7, 1926 in Los Angeles, California
d. Dec 18, 1971 in Los Angeles, California
Source: *BiE&WWA; CurBio 53, 72; FilmgC; InWom; MotPP; MovMk; NewYTBE 71; WhScrn 74, 77; WhoHol B*

Lynn, Fred(ric Michael)
American. Baseball Player
b. Feb 3, 1952 in Chicago, Illinois
Source: *BaseEn; BioIn 10, 11; WhoAm 82*

Lynn, James T
American. Former Secretary of HUD
b. Feb 27, 1927 in Cleveland, Ohio
Source: *BioIn 9, 10; CurBio 73*

Lynn, Janet
[Janet Lynn Nowicki]
American. Figure Skater
Won bronze medal, 1972 Olympics.
b. Apr 6, 1953 in Chicago, Illinois
Source: *BioNews 74; HerW; WhoAm 74, 76, 78, 80, 82; WhoAmW 77*

Lynn, Loretta Webb
[Mrs. Oliver Lynn, Jr.]
American. Singer
Movie *Coal Miner's Daughter,* 1977 was based on her life.
b. Apr 14, 1935 in Butcher Hollow, Kentucky
Source: *BioNews 74; BkPepl; ConAu 81; CurBio 73; EncFCWM 69; NewYTBE 72; WhoAm 74, 76, 78, 80, 82*

Lynne, Jeff
[Electric Light Orchestra]
English. Musician
b. Dec 30, 1947 in Birmingham, England
Source: *BioIn 11; BkPepl; RkOn; WhoAm 82*

Lynott, Phil
see: Thin Lizzy

Lynyrd Skynard
[Robert Burns; Allen Collins; Steve Gaines; Ed King; William Powell; Gary Rossington; Ronnie VanZant; Leon Wilkeson]
American. Rock Group
Source: *IlEncRk*

Lyon, Ben
American. Actor
b. Feb 6, 1901 in Atlanta, Georgia
d. Mar 22, 1979
Source: *BioIn 3, 10, 11; Film 1, 2; FilmgC; MotPP; MovMk; NewYTBS 79; OxFilm; TwYS; WhThe; WhoHol A*

Lyon, Mary
American. Educator
b. Feb 28, 1797 in Buckland, Massachusetts
d. Mar 5, 1849
Source: *AmBi; AmWom; ApCAB; DcAmB; Drake; HerW; InWom; NotAW; TwCBDA; WhAm H*

Lyon, Nathaniel
American. Civil War Soldier
b. Jul 14, 1818 in Ashford, Connecticut
d. Aug 10, 1861 in Wilson's Creek, Missouri
Source: *Alli SUP; AmBi; ApCAB; DcAmB; TwCBDA; WhAm H*

Lyon, "Southside" Johnny
see: Southside Johnny and the Asbury Jukes

Lyons, Dorothy (Marawee)
American. Author
b. Dec 4, 1907 in Fenton, Michigan
Source: *AmAu&B; ConAu 1R; ForWC 70; SmATA 3; WrDr 76*

Lyons, Enid Muriel
Australian. Politician, Author
b. Jul 9, 1897 in Duck River, Tasmania
Source: *ConAu 25R; IntWW 74; Who 74; WhoWor 74; WrDr 76*

Lyons, Eugene
American. Author, Editor
b. Jul 1, 1898 in Uslian, Russia
Source: *AmAu&B; ConAu 9R; CurBio 44; OxAmL; REn; REnAL; TwCA, SUP; WhoAm 74; WhoWor 74; WhoWorJ 72*

Lyons, James
American. Author, Critic
b. 1926 in Peabody, Massachusetts
d. Nov 13, 1973
Source: *BiDLA; BioIn 10; NewYTBE 73*

Lyons, Leonard
American. Journalist
b. Sep 10, 1906 in New York, New York
d. Oct 7, 1976 in New York, New York
Source: *ConAu 69; NewYTBS 74; WhoAm 74; WhoE 74; WhoWorJ 72*

Lyons, Sophie Levy
"Queen of Crime"
American. Swindler
b. Dec 24, 1848 in New York, New York
d. May 8, 1924 in Detroit, Michigan
Source: *LookW*

Lyons, Ted (Theodore Amar)
American. Baseball Player
b. Dec 28, 1900 in Lake Charles, Louisiana
Source: *BaseEn; BioIn 1, 2, 3, 7, 10; WhoProB 73*

Lyot, Bernard Ferdinand
French. Astronomer, Inventor
b. Feb 27, 1897 in Paris, France
d. Apr 2, 1952 in Egypt
Source: *AsBiEn; BioIn 2, 3; DcScB*

Lysenko, Trofim Denisovich
Russian. Geneticist
b. Sep 29, 1898 in Karlovka, Russia
d. Nov 20, 1976 in U.S.S.R.
Source: *IntWW 74; WhoWor 74*

Lysiak, Tom (Thomas James)
Canadian. Hockey Player
b. Apr 22, 1953 in High Prairie, AB
Source: *HocReg*

Lysippus
Greek. Sculptor
fl. 4th century
Source: *NewCol 75*

Lytell, Bert
American. Actor
b. Feb 24, 1885 in New York, New York
d. Sep 28, 1954 in New York, New York
Source: *Film 1; FilmgC; MotPP; MovMk; TwYS; WhAm 3; WhScrn 74, 77; WhoHol B*

Lytle, Andrew Nelson
American. Author, Editor
b. Dec 26, 1902 in Murfreesboro, Tennessee
Source: *AmAu&B; AmNov; ConAu 9R; ConNov 72, 76; CyWA; DrAF 76; OxAmL; Pen AM; RAdv 1; REnAL; WhoAm 74, 76, 78, 80, 82; WorAu; WrDr 76*

Lytton, Edward George Earle Lytton Bulwer-Lytton, Baron
English. Author, Poet
b. May 15, 1803 in London, England
d. Jan 18, 1873 in Torquay, England
Source: *Alli, SUP; AtlBL; BiD&SB; BrAu 19; CasWL; ChPo, S2; CyWA; DcBiA; DcEnA; DcEuL; DcLEL; EvLB; HsB&A; McGEWD; MnBBF; MouLC 3; NewC; Pen ENG; RAdv 1; REn*

Lytton, Edward Robert Bulwer-Lytton, Earl
English. Poet, Diplomat
b. Nov 8, 1831 in London, England
d. Nov 24, 1891 in Paris, France
Source: *NewC*

Lytton, Henry Alfred
English. Actor
b. Jan 3, 1867 in London, England
d. Aug 15, 1936 in London, England
Source: *NotNAT B; WhThe*

M

Ma, Yo-Yo
American. Musician
b. Oct 7, 1955 in Paris, France
Source: *CurBio 82; NewYTBS 79; WhoAm 82*

Maag, Peter
Swiss. Conductor
b. 1919 in Saint Gallen, Switzerland
Source: *WhoMus 72; WhoWor 74*

Maas, Peter
American. Author
b. Jun 27, 1929 in New York, New York
Source: *AmAu&B; ConAu 93; WhoAm 74, 76, 78, 80, 82; WrDr 76*

Maazel, Lorin
American. Conductor
b. Mar 5, 1930 in Paris, France
Source: *CurBio 65; IntWW 74; Who 74; WhoAm 74, 76, 78, 80, 82; WhoMW 74; WhoMus 72; WhoWor 74*

Mabee, (Fred) Carleton
American. Author
b. Dec 25, 1914 in Shanghai, China
Source: *AmAu&B; ConAu 1R; DrAS 74H; OxAmL; OxCan; TwCA SUP; WhoAm 74; WrDr 76*

Mabley, "Moms" (Jackie)
American. Singer, Comedienne
b. Mar 19, 1894 in Brevard, North Carolina
d. May 23, 1975 in White Plains, New York
Source: *BioNews 74; CurBio 75*

Mabuse, Jan de
Flemish. Artist
b. 1478 in Maubeuge, France
d. 1533 in Antwerp, Belgium
Source: *NewCol 75*

Macapagal, Diosdado Pangan
Philippine. Politician
b. Sep 28, 1910 in Lubao, Philippines
Source: *CurBio 62; WhoWor 74*

MacArthur, Arthur
American. Army Officer
b. Jun 2, 1845 in Springfield, Massachusetts
d. Sep 5, 1912 in Milwaukee, Wisconsin
Source: *AmBi; DcAmB S1; TwCBDA; WebAB; WhAm 1*

MacArthur, Charles
American. Dramatist, Director, Actor
b. Nov 5, 1895 in Scranton, Pennsylvania
d. Apr 21, 1956 in New York, New York
Source: *AmAu&B; CnDAL; DcFM; FilmgC; McGEWD; ModWD; OxAmL; OxFilm; REn; REnAL; WhAm 3; WhScrn 74, 77; WorEFlm*

MacArthur, Douglas
American. Army Officer
Accepted Japanese surrender, 1945; dismissed by Truman in Korea, 1951.
b. Jan 26, 1880 in Little Rock, Arkansas
d. Apr 5, 1964 in Washington, DC
Source: *ChPo S1; CurBio 41, 48, 64; EncAB-H; REn; WebAB; WhAm 4*

MacArthur, James
American. Actor
Son of Helen Hayes; starred in TV series "Hawaii Five-O."
b. Dec 8, 1937 in Los Angeles, California
Source: *BiE&WWA; FilmgC; IntMPA 75, 76, 77, 78, 79, 80, 81, 82; MotPP; WhoAm 82; WhoHol A*

MacArthur, John Donald
American. Insurance Executive
b. Mar 6, 1897 in Pittston, Pennsylvania
d. Jan 6, 1978 in West Palm Beach, Florida
Source: *BusPN; NewYTBE 73; St&PR 75; WhoAm 74; WhoF&I 74; WhoIns 75*

Macaulay, Rose
English. Poet, Essayist
b. Aug 1, 1881 in Cambridge, England
d. Oct 30, 1958 in London, England
Source: *Chambr 3; ChPo, S2; CnMWL; DcLEL; EncWL; EvLB; LongCTC; ModBrL; NewC; OxEng; Pen ENG; REn; TwCA, SUP; TwCW; WebE&AL*

Macaulay, Thomas Babington Macaulay, Baron
English. Historian, Essayist, Statesman
b. Oct 25, 1800 in Leicester, England
d. Dec 28, 1859 in Kensington, England
Source: *Alli; AtlBL; BbD; BiD&SB; BrAu 19; CasWL; Chambr 3; ChPo, S1, S2; CrtT 3; CyWA; DcEnA; DcEuL; DcLEL; EvLB; MouLC 3; NewC; OxEng; Pen ENG; RAdv 1; REn; WebE&AL*

Macauley, Ed
"Easy Ed"
American. Basketball Player, Coach
b. Mar 22, 1928 in Saint Louis, Missouri
Source: *WhoBbl 73*

Macbeth
Scottish. King
d. 1057
Source: *NewCol 75; WebBD 80; WhDW*

MacBeth, George Mann
Scottish. Poet, Editor
b. Jan 19, 1932 in Shotts, Scotland
Source: *ConAu 25R; ConLC 2, 5, 9; ConP 70, 75; ModBrL SUP; RAdv 1; SmATA 4; WorAu; WrDr 76*

Maccabees
Family of Jewish Patriots
Source: *NewC; NewCol 75*

MacCameron, Robert L
American. Artist
b. Jan 14, 1866 in Chicago, Illinois
d. Dec 29, 1912 in New York, New York
Source: *DcAmB; WhAm 1*

MacDermot, Galt
Canadian. Composer
b. Dec 19, 1928 in Montreal, PQ
Source: *BiDAmM; CelR 73; EncMT; NotNAT; PlP&P, A; WhoAm 78; WhoThe 77*

MacDiarmid, Hugh, pseud.
[Christopher Murray Grieve]
Scottish. Author
b. Aug 11, 1892 in Langholm, Scotland
d. Sep 9, 1978 in Edinburgh, Scotland
Source: *CasWL; Chambr 3; ChPo S2; CnE&AP; CnMWL; ConAu 5R; ConLC 2, 4, 11; ConP 70, 75; EncWL; IntWW 74; ModBrL, SUP; NewC; Pen ENG; RAdv 1; WebE&AL; WhoTwCL; WhoWor 74; WrDr 76*

MacDonagh, Thomas
Irish. Poet, Patriot
b. 1878 in Cloughjordan, Ireland
d. May 3, 1916 in Dublin, Ireland
Source: *ChPo, S2; EvLB; LongCTC; NewC; PoIre; REn; TwCA; TwCW*

MacDonald, Dwight
American. Critic, Journalist
Wrote *Against the American Grain,* 1963.
b. Mar 24, 1906 in New York, New York
d. Dec 19, 1982 in New York, New York
Source: *AmAu&B; CelR 73; ChPo, S1; ConAu 29R; CurBio 69; DcLEL 1940; LinLib L; ModAL; OxAmL; Pen AM; PolProf J; PolProf T; RAdv 1; WhoAm 74, 76, 78, 80, 82; WhoTwCL; WorAl; WrDr 76, 80*

MacDonald, George
Scottish. Author
b. Dec 10, 1824 in Huntley, Scotland
d. Sep 18, 1905 in Ashstead, England
Source: *Alli, SUP; AuBYP; BbD; BiD&SB; BrAu 19; CarSB; CasWL; Chambr 3; ChPo, S1, S2; DcBiA; DcEnA, AP; DcEnL; DcEuL; DcLEL; EvLB; FamSYP; JBA 34; LongCTC; NewC; OxEng; Pen ENG; REn; WebE&AL; WhoChL*

MacDonald, J(ames) E(dward) H(ervey)
[Group of Seven]
Canadian. Artist
b. May 12, 1873 in Durham, England
d. Nov 26, 1932 in Toronto, ON
Source: *CreCan 2; DcNAA; IlBEAAW; McGDA; OxCan*

MacDonald, James Ramsay
English. Statesman
Formed first Labour govt., 1924; Prime Minister, 1924, 1929-1935.
b. Oct 12, 1866 in Lossiemouth, Scotland
d. Nov 9, 1937
Source: *BioIn 1, 2, 3, 7, 8, 9, 11; ChPo; DcAmSR; DcPol; EncSoA; LinLib L, S; McGEWB; WhLit*

MacDonald, Jeanette
American. Singer, Actress
Soprano, noted for films with Nelson Eddy, 1930's.
b. Jun 18, 1906? in Philadelphia, Pennsylvania
d. Jan 14, 1965 in Houston, Texas
Source: *BiE&WWA; CmMov; EncMT; FilmgC; InWom; MotPP; MovMk; OxFilm; ThFT; WhAm 4; WhScrn 74, 77; WhoHol B; WorEFlm*

MacDonald, John Alexander
Canadian. Statesman
b. Jan 11, 1815 in Glasgow, Scotland
d. Jun 6, 1891 in Ottawa, ON
Source: *Alli; ApCAB; BbtC; Drake; OxCan*

MacDonald, John Dann
American. Author
b. Jul 24, 1916 in Sharon, Pennsylvania
Source: *AmAu&B; ConAu 1R, 1NR; ConLC 3; EncMys; WhoAm 74; WorAu; WrDr 76*

MacDonald, Malcolm John
Scottish. Diplomat
b. Aug 17, 1901 in Lossiemouth, Scotland
d. Jan 11, 1981 in Sevenoaks, England
Source: *Au&Wr 71; BioIn 2, 3, 4, 6, 8; ConAu 9R, 102; CurBio 54, 81; IntAu&W 77; IntWW 74, 75, 76, 77, 78; IntYB 78, 79; NewYTBS 81; OxCan; Who 74; WhoWor 74*

MacDonald, Ross, pseud.
[Kenneth Millar]
American. Author
b. Dec 13, 1915 in Los Gatos, California
Source: *AmAu&B; AmNov; Au&Wr 71; ConAu 9R; ConLC 1, 2, 3, 14; ConNov 72, 76; CurBio 53; EncMys; ModAL, SUP; WhoAm 74; WhoWor 74; WorAu; WrDr 76*

MacDonald-Wright, Stanton
American. Artist
b. Jul 8, 1890 in Charlottesville, Virginia
d. Aug 22, 1973 in Pacific Palisades, California
Source: *ArtsAmW; ConArt; DcAmArt; DcCAA 71, 77; McGDA; NewYTBE 73; WhAm 6; WhoAm 74; WhoAmA 73, 76, 78; WhoWor 74*

MacDonough, Thomas
American. Naval Officer
b. Dec 31, 1783 in New Castle County, Delaware
d. Nov 10, 1825
Source: *AmBi; ApCAB; BioIn 2, 5, 6, 8, 9; DcAmB; Drake; NatCAB 7; NewCol 75; TwCBDA; WebAB; WebAMB; WhAm H*

MacDowell, Edward Alexander
American. Composer, Pianist
b. Dec 18, 1861 in New York, New York
d. Jan 23, 1908 in New York, New York
Source: *AmBi; AmSCAP 66; AtlBL; ChPo S1, S2; DcAmB; DcNAA; EncAB-H; OxAmL; REn; REnAL; WebAB; WhAm 1*

Macfadden, Bernarr Adolphus
[Bernard Adolphus Macfadden]
American. Author, Publisher
b. Aug 16, 1868 in Mill Spring, Missouri
d. Oct 12, 1955 in Jersey City, New Jersey
Source: *AmAu&B; BioIn 1, 2, 3, 4, 6, 10; DcAmAu; DcAmB S5; REnAL; WebAB; WhAm 3; WhNAA; WhScrn 77*

Macfarren, Sir George Alexander
English. Composer
b. Mar 2, 1813 in London, England
d. Oct 31, 1887 in London, England
Source: *Alli SUP; NewC*

MacGrath, Leueen
English. Actress
b. Jul 3, 1914 in London, England
Source: *BiE&WWA; InWom; NotNAT; WhoHol A; WhoThe 77*

MacGraw, Ali
American. Model, Actress
Starred in *Love Story*, 1971; husbands include Robert Evans, Steve McQueen.
b. Apr 1, 1938 in Westchester, New York
Source: *BkPepl; CelR 73; FilmgC; IntMPA 75, 76, 77, 78, 79, 80, 81, 82; MotPP; MovMk; NewYTBE 73; WhoAm 74, 76, 78, 80, 82; WhoHol A*

MacGregor, Clark
American. Government Official
b. Jul 12, 1922 in Minneapolis, Minnesota
Source: *BiDrAC; WhoAm 74, 76, 78, 80, 82; WhoAmP 73; WhoGov 72; WhoS&SW 73*

MacGregor, Ian
American. Chairman of British Steel
b. 1912 in Scotland
Source: *BioIn 11*

MacGregor, Robert
"Rob Roy"
Scottish. Outlaw
b. Mar 7, 1671 in Buchanan, Scotland
d. Dec 28, 1734 in Balquhidder, Scotland
Source: *NewC*

Mach, Ernst
Austrian. Physicist
b. Feb 18, 1838 in Turas, Austria
d. Feb 19, 1916 in Munich, Germany
Source: *NewCol 75; WebBD 80*

Machado, Antonio
Spanish. Author
b. Jul 26, 1875 in Seville, Spain
d. Feb 22, 1939 in Collioure, France
Source: *ClDMEL; CnMWL; McGEWD; ModRL; Pen EUR; REn; TwCW; WhoTwCL; WorAu*

Machado, Manuel
Spanish. Author
b. 1874 in Seville, Spain
d. 1947 in Madrid, Spain
Source: *ClDMEL; McGEWD; Pen EUR; REn*

Machado y Morales, Gerardo
Cuban. President
b. Sep 29, 1871 in Santa Clara, Cuba
d. Mar 29, 1939 in Miami Beach, Florida
Source: *WebBD 80*

Machel, Samora Moises
Mozambican. President
b. 1933 in Gaza, Mozambique
Source: *IntWW 74*

Machen, Arthur
English. Author
b. Mar 3, 1863 in Caerleon, England
d. Dec 15, 1947 in Beaconsfield, England
Source: *Alli SUP; CasWL; CyWA; DcLEL; EncMys; EvLB; LongCTC; ModBrL; NewC; OxEng; Pen ENG; REn; TwCA, SUP; TwCW*

Machiavelli, Niccolo
Italian. Philosopher, Author
Wrote *The Prince,* 1513, outlining pragmatic theory of govt.
b. May 3, 1469 in Florence, Italy
d. Jun 22, 1527 in Florence, Italy
Source: *AtlBL; BiD&SB; CasWL; CnThe; CyWA; DcEuL; EuAu; EvEuW; McGEWD; NewC; OxEng; Pen EUR; RComWL; REn; REnWD*

MacInnes, Helen
American. Author
b. Oct 7, 1907 in Glasgow, Scotland
Source: *AmAu&B; ConAu 1R, 1NR; ConNov 72, 76; CurBio 67; EncMys; ForWC 70; InWom; IntWW 74; NewC; REnAL; SmATA 22; TwCA SUP; Who 74; WhoAm 74, 76, 78, 80, 82; WhoE 74; WrDr 76*

Macintosh, Charles
Scottish. Chemist, Inventor
Developed waterproof fabric used to make raincoats, 1823.
b. Dec 29, 1766
d. Jul 5, 1843
Source: *InSci; NewCol 75; WebBD 80; WhDW*

Mack, Connie
[Cornelius Alexander McGillicuddy]
"The Tall Tactician"
American. Baseball Manager
Owner, manager, Philadelphia A's, 1901-50; won nine pennants; Hall of Fame, 1937.
b. Dec 22, 1862 in East Brookfield, Massachusetts
d. Feb 8, 1956 in Philadelphia, Pennsylvania
Source: *BaseEn; CurBio 44, 56; WebAB; WhAm 3; WhoProB 73*

Mack, Ted
[William E Maguiness]
American. TV Show Host
b. Feb 12, 1904 in Greeley, Colorado
d. Jul 12, 1976 in Tarrytown, New York
Source: *CurBio 51; WhoAm 74*

MacKay, Andrew
see: Roxy Music

Mackay, John Alexander
American. Clergyman, Author, Educator
b. May 17, 1889 in Inverness, Scotland
Source: *Au&Wr 71; DrAS 74P; IntWW 74; Who 74; WhoWor 74*

Mackay, John William
American. Philanthropist, Businessman
b. Nov 28, 1831 in Dublin, Ireland
d. Jul 20, 1902 in London, England
Source: *AmBi; ApCAB; DcAmB; TwCBDA; WhAm 1*

Mackay, Mary
see: Corelli, Marie, pseud.

MacKaye, Percy Wallace
American. Poet, Dramatist
b. Mar 16, 1875 in New York, New York
d. Aug 31, 1956 in Cornish, New Hampshire
Source: *AmAu&B; AnMV 1926; Chambr 3; ChPo, S1, S2; CnDAL; CnMD; CnThe; ConAmA; ConAmL; DcLEL; McGEWD; ModAL; ModWD; OxAmL; OxThe; REn; REnAL; REnWD; Str&VC; TwCA, SUP; WhAm 3; WhNAA; WhoStg 1908*

Macke, August
German. Artist
b. 1887
d. 1914
Source: *OxGer*

MacKellar, William
American. Author
b. Feb 20, 1914 in Glasgow, Scotland
Source: *AuBYP; ConAu 33R; SmATA 4*

Mackendrick, Alexander
American. Motion Picture Director
b. 1912 in Boston, Massachusetts
Source: *BiDFilm; CmMov; DcFM; FilmgC; IntMPA 75, 76, 77; MovMk; OxFilm; WorEFlm*

Mackenzie, Sir Alexander
Scottish. Author, Explorer
Made first overland journey across N America north of Mexico, 1793.
b. 1755 in Lewis, Outer Hebrides Islands
d. Mar 11, 1820 in Mulnain, Scotland
Source: *Alli; ApCAB; BbtC; BiDLA; BrAu 19; DcLEL; NewC; OxAmL; OxCan; REnAL*

Mackenzie, Sir Alexander
Scottish. Composer
b. Aug 22, 1847 in Edinburgh, Scotland
d. Apr 28, 1935 in London, England
Source: *NewEOp 71; OxMus; WebBD 80*

Mackenzie, Sir Compton
English. Author
b. Jan 17, 1883 in West Hartlepool, England
d. Nov 30, 1972 in Edinburgh, Scotland
Source: *Au&Wr 71; CasWL; CathA 1930; Chambr 3; ConAu 21R, 37R; ConNov 72; DcLEL; EncWL; EvLB; LongCTC; ModBrL; NewC; OxEng; Pen ENG; REn; TwCA, SUP; TwCW; WebE&AL; WhoChL; WhoLA; WhoTwCL*

MacKenzie, Gisele
[Marie Marguerite La Fleche]
Canadian. Singer, Actress
b. Jan 10, 1927 in Winnipeg, MB
Source: *AmSCAP 66; CanWW 82; CreCan 2; CurBio 55; InWom; WhoAm 82*

Mackenzie, Henry
Scottish. Author
b. Aug 26, 1745 in Edinburgh, Scotland
d. Jan 14, 1831 in Edinburgh, Scotland
Source: *Alli; BiD&SB; BrAu; CasWL; ChPo S2; CyWA; DcBiA; DcEnA; DcEnL; DcEuL; DcLEL; EvLB; MouLC 3; NewC; OxEng; Pen ENG; REn; WebE&AL*

Mackenzie, William Lyon
Canadian. Statesman
b. Mar 12, 1795 in Dundee, Scotland
d. Aug 28, 1861 in Toronto, ON
Source: *Alli; ApCAB; BbtC; DcLEL; DcNAA; Drake; OxCan*

Mackie, Bob (Robert Gordon)
American. Fashion Designer
Designed clothes for "The Carol Burnett Show," 1967-77; won Emmys, 1969, 1976.
b. Mar 24, 1940 in Monterey Park, California
Source: *BioIn 9, 10, 11; WhoAm 78, 80, 82; WorFshn*

Mackin, Catherine
"Cassie"
American. Broadcast Journalist
First woman to anchor nighttime network newscast.
b. Aug 28, 1939 in Baltimore, Maryland
d. Nov 20, 1982 in Towson, Maryland
Source: *ForWC 70; GoodHS; NewYTBS 82; WhoAm 78; WhoAmW 68; WhoS&SW 73*

Mackinder, Sir Halford John
English. Politician
b. Feb 15, 1861 in Gainsborough, England
d. Mar 6, 1947 in London, England
Source: *WhoLA*

MacLaine, Shirley
[Shirley Beaty; Mrs. Steve Parker]
American. Actress, Dancer
Sister of Warren Beatty; has received five Oscar nominations.
b. Apr 23, 1934 in Richmond, Virginia
Source: *BiDFilm; BkPepl; ConAu 103; CurBio 59; FilmgC; ForWC 70; HerW; InWom; IntMPA 75, 76, 77, 78, 79, 80, 81, 82; IntWW 74; MotPP; MovMk; NewYTBE 71; OxFilm; WhoAm 74, 76, 78, 80, 82; WhoHol A; WhoWor 74; WomWMM; WorEFlm*

MacLane, Barton
American. Actor
b. Dec 25, 1900 in Columbia, South Carolina
d. Jan 1, 1969 in Santa Monica, California
Source: *FilmgC; MotPP; MovMk; Vers A; WhScrn 74, 77; WhoHol B*

MacLean, Alistair
Scottish. Author
b. 1922 in Glasgow, Scotland
Source: *ConAu 57; ConLC 3; IntWW 74; SmATA 23; Who 74; WhoAm 82; WorAu; WrDr 76*

Maclean, Donald Duart
English. Spy for Russians
b. 1913
d. Mar 10, 1983 in Moscow, U.S.S.R.
Source: *BioIn 2,3,4,6,8,11; WhDW*

MacLeish, Archibald
American. Poet, Journalist
Won Pulitzer Prizes, 1932, 1953, 1958.
b. May 7, 1892 in Glencoe, Illinois
d. Apr 20, 1982 in Boston, Massachusetts
Source: *AmAu&B; AmSCAP 66; AmWr; BiE&WWA; CasWL; CelR 73; ChPo, S1, S2, S3; CnDAL; CnE&AP; CnMD; CnMWL; CnThe; ConAmA; ConAu 9R; ConDr 73; ConLC 3; ConP 70, 75; CroCD; CurBio 40, 59, 82; CyWA; DcLEL; EncWL; EvLB; IntWW 74; LongCTC; McGEWB; ModAL, SUP; ModWD; NotNAT; OxAmL; OxEng; OxThe; Pen AM; RAdv 1; REn; REnAL; SixAP; TwCA, SUP; TwCW; WebAB; WebE&AL; WhNAA; Who 74; WhoAm 74, 76, 78, 80, 82; WhoThe 77; WhoWor 74, 78; WrDr 76, 80*

MacLeish, Rod(erick)
American. Journalist, News Commentator
b. Jan 15, 1926 in Bryn Mawr, Pennsylvania
Source: *ConAu 41R; WhoAm 74; WhoS&SW 73*

MacLennan, Hugh
Canadian. Author
b. Mar 20, 1907 in Cape Breton, NS
Source: *Au&Wr 71; CanNov; CanWW 82; CanWr; CasWL; ConAu 5R; ConLC 2, 14; ConNov 72, 76; CreCan 2; EncWL; LongCTC; NewC; OxAmL; OxCan, SUP; Pen ENG; RAdv 1; REn; REnAL; TwCA SUP; TwCW; WebE&AL; Who 74; WhoAm 74, 76, 78, 80, 82; WhoCan 73; WhoWor 74; WrDr 76*

MacLeod, Gavin
American. Actor
Starred in "The Mary Tyler Moore Show," 1970-77, "The Love Boat," 1977--.
b. Feb 28, 1930 in Mount Kisco, New York
Source: *WhoAm 78, 80, 82; WhoHol A*

MacLiammoir, Michael
Irish. Actor, Designer, Director
b. Oct 25, 1899 in Cork, Ireland
d. Mar 6, 1978 in Dublin, Ireland
Source: *McGEWD*

Maclise, Daniel
Irish. Artist
b. 1806
d. 1870
Source: *NewCol 75; WebBD 80*

MacMahon, Aline
American. Actress
b. May 3, 1899 in McKeesport, Pennsylvania
Source: *BiE&WWA; FilmgC; InWom; IntMPA 77, 75; MovMk; NotNAT; ThFT; Vers A; WhoHol A; WhoThe 77*

MacMillan, Daniel
Scottish. Bookseller, Publisher
b. Sep 13, 1813 in Upper Corrie, Scotland
d. Jun 27, 1857 in Cambridge, England
Source: *ChPo, S1; NewC*

MacMillan, Donald Baxter
American. Explorer
Went with Robert Peary on expedition of N Pole, 1908-09.
b. Nov 10, 1874 in Provincetown, Massachusetts
d. Sep 7, 1970 in Provincetown, Massachusetts
Source: *AmAu&B; CurBio 48, 70; OxCan; REnAL; WhAm 6; WhNAA*

MacMillan, Sir Ernest Campbell
Canadian. Conductor
b. Aug 18, 1893 in Mimico, ON
d. May 6, 1973 in Ottawa, ON
Source: *CanWW 70; CreCan 1; CurBio 55, 73; WhAm 5; WhoE 74; WhoMus 72*

MacMillan, Harold
English. Political Leader
b. Feb 10, 1894 in London, England
Source: *CurBio 43, 55; IntWW 74; Who 74; WhoWor 74; WrDr 76*

MacMonnies, Fred W
American. Sculptor
b. Sep 28, 1863 in Brooklyn, New York
d. Mar 22, 1937
Source: *BioIn 8, 11; NewCol 75; WhAm 1*

MacMurray, Fred(erick Martin)
American. Actor
Starred in TV series "My Three Sons," 1960-72.
b. Aug 30, 1908 in Kankakee, Illinois
Source: *BiDFilm; CelR 73; CurBio 67; FilmgC; IntMPA 75, 76, 77, 78, 79, 80, 81, 82; MotPP; MovMk; OxFilm; WhoAm 82; WhoHol A; WhoWor 74; WorEFlm*

MacNee, Patrick
English. Actor
b. Feb 6, 1922
Source: *FilmgC; MotPP; WhoAm 82; WhoHol A*

MacNeice, Louis
Irish. Poet
b. Sep 12, 1907 in Belfast, Northern Ireland
d. Sep 3, 1963 in London, England
Source: *AtlBL; Au&Wr 71; CasWL; CnE&AP; CnMD; CnMWL; ConAu 85; ConLC 1, 4, 10; DcLEL; EncWL; EvLB; LongCTC; ModBrL, SUP; NewC; OxEng; Pen ENG; RAdv 1; REn; TwCA, SUP; TwCW; WebE&AL; WhoTwCL*

MacNeil, Robert Breckenridge Ware
American. Broadcast Journalist
Co-anchor "MacNeil/Lehrer Report," 1975-- on PBS; won Emmy, 1974.
b. Jan 19, 1931 in Montreal, PQ
Source: *Au&Wr 71; CurBio 80; WhoAm 78, 80, 82*

MacNelly, Jeff(rey Kenneth)
American. Cartoonist
Draws comic strip "Shoe"; won Pulitzer Prizes, 1972, 1978.
b. Sep 17, 1947 in New York, New York
Source: *ConAu 102; WhoAm 74, 76, 78, 80; WhoAmA 73, 76, 78*

MacNutt, Father Francis
American. Religious Leader
b. Apr 22, 1925 in Saint Louis, Missouri
Source: *ConAu 73*

MacPhail, Larry (Leland Stanford, Sr.)
American. Baseball Executive
b. Feb 3, 1890 in Cass City, Michigan
d. Oct 1, 1975
Source: *CurBio 45; NewYTBE 72*

MacPhail, Lee (Leland Stanford, Jr.)
American. Baseball Executive
President, AL, 1973--.
b. Oct 25, 1917 in Nashville, Tennessee
Source: *WhoAm 74, 76, 78, 80, 82; WhoProB 73*

Macpherson, James
Scottish. Author
b. Oct 27, 1736 in Ruthven, Scotland
d. Feb 17, 1796 in Ruthven, Scotland
Source: *Alli; BbD; BiD&SB; BrAu; CasWL; Chambr 2; ChPo, S1; CnE&AP; DcEnA; DcEnL; DcEuL; DcLEL; EvLB; MouLC 2; NewC; OxEng; Pen ENG; RComWL; REn; WebE&AL*

MacRae, Carmen
Singer
b. 1922?
Source: *BioIn 8*

MacRae, Elizabeth
American. Actress
Source: *ForWC 70; WhoHol A*

MacRae, Gordon
American. Actor, Singer
b. Mar 12, 1921 in East Orange, New Jersey
Source: *CmMov; FilmgC; IntMPA 75, 76, 77; MovMk; WhoAm 74, 76, 78, 80, 82; WhoHol A*

MacRae, Meredith
[Mrs. Greg Mullavey]
American. Actress
Daughter of Sheila and Gordon MacRae.
b. 1944 in Houston, Texas
Source: *WhoHol A*

MacRae, Sheila
American. Actress, Singer
b. Sep 24, 1923 in London, England
Source: *InWom; WhoAm 74, 76, 78, 80, 82*

Macready, George
American. Actor
b. Aug 29, 1909 in Providence, Rhode Island
d. Jul 2, 1973 in Los Angeles, California
Source: *CmMov; FilmgC; MotPP; MovMk; NewYTBE 73; Vers A; WhScrn 77; WhoHol B*

MacSwiney, Terence
Irish. Hunger Striker, Revolutionary
b. 1879 in Cork, Ireland
d. Oct 24, 1920 in Brixton Prison, England
Source: *BioIn 6, 7; DcIrB; DcIrW 1, 2*

Macy, Anne Sullivan
see: Sullivan, Anne

Macy, Bill
American. Actor
Starred in TV series "Maude."
b. May 18, 1922 in Revere, Massachusetts
Source: *WhoHol A*

Macy, George
American. Publisher
b. May 12, 1900 in New York, New York
d. May 20, 1956 in New York, New York
Source: *AmAu&B; CurBio 54, 56; WhAm 3*

Macy, R(owland) H(ussey)
American. Retailer
b. 1822
d. 1877
Source: *BioIn 7*

Madariaga (y Rojo), Salvador de
Spanish. Author, Philosopher
b. Jul 23, 1886 in Lacoruna, Spain
d. Dec 14, 1978 in Locarno, Switzerland
Source: *CasWL; ClDMEL; ConAu 9R, 81; CurBio 64, 79; DcLEL; DcSpL; EncWL; EvEuW; IntAu&W 77; IntWW 74, 75, 76, 77, 78; LinLib L, S; LongCTC; NewCol 75; NewYTBS 78; OxSpan; REn; TwCA, SUP; TwCW; Who 74; WhoLA*

Madden, Donald
American. Actor
b. Nov 5, 1933 in New York, New York
d. Jan 22, 1983 in Central Islip, New York
Source: *BiE&WWA; NotNAT; WhoThe 77, 81*

Madden, John
American. Sportscaster
Head coach, Oakland Raiders, 1969-79; commentator, CBS Sports, 1979--.
b. 1936 in Austin, New Mexico
Source: *WhoAm 74, 76, 78, 80, 82; WhoFtbl 74*

Maddox, Elliott
American. Baseball Player
b. Dec 21, 1948 in East Orange, New Jersey
Source: *BaseEn; WhoAm 78*

Maddox, Garry Lee
"Buggy Whip"
American. Baseball Player
b. Sep 1, 1949 in Cincinnati, Ohio
Source: *BaseEn; WhoAm 78; WhoBlA 77; WhoProB 73*

Maddox, Gaynor
American. Journalist
b. in San Diego, California
Source: *ConAu 9R*

Maddox, Lester Garfield
American. Politician
b. Sep 30, 1915 in Atlanta, Georgia
Source: *BioNews 74; CelR 73; CurBio 67; IntWW 74; NewYTBS 74; WhoAm 74, 76, 78, 80, 82; WhoGov 72; WhoS&SW 73*

Madeira, Jean
[Jean Browning]
American. Opera Singer
b. Nov 14, 1918 in Centralia, Illinois
d. Jul 10, 1972 in Providence, Rhode Island
Source: *CurBio 63, 72; InWom; NewYTBE 72; WhAm 5; WhoMus 72*

Madero, Francisco Indalecio
Mexican. Revolutionary, President
b. 1873 in Mexico
d. 1913 in Mexico
Source: *REn*

Madison, Dolly Payne Todd
American. Wife of James Madison
Saved important documents when British invaded Washington, 1814.
b. May 20, 1768 in Guilford County, North Carolina
d. Jul 12, 1849 in Montpelier, Virginia
Source: *AmAu&B; AmBi; BioIn 10; DcAmB; HerW; NotAW; OxAmL; REn; REnAL*

Madison, Guy
[Robert Moseley]
American. Actor, Singer
b. Jan 19, 1922 in Bakersfield, California
Source: *FilmgC; IntMPA 75, 76, 77, 78, 79, 80, 81, 82; MotPP; MovMk; WhoHol A*

Madison, Helene
American. Swimmer
b. 1914
d. Nov 25, 1970 in Seattle, Washington
Source: *NewYTBE 70*

Madison, James
American. 4th US President
Wrote 29 *Federalist* papers; called master builder of Constitution.
b. Mar 16, 1751 in Port Conway, Virginia
d. Jun 28, 1836 in Montpelier, Virginia
Source: *Alli; AmAu&B; AmBi; ApCAB; BbD; BiAuS; BiD&SB; BiDSA; BiDrAC; BiDrUSE; CyAL 1; CyWA; DcAmAu; DcLEL; DcNAA; Drake; EncAB-H; OxAmL; REn; REnAL; TwCBDA; WebAB; WhAm H; WhAmP*

Maeght, Aime
French. Art Printer, Dealer
b. Apr 27, 1906 in Hazebrouck, France
d. Sep 5, 1981 in Saint Paul de Vence, France
Source: *AnObit 1981; BioIn 5, 6*

Maestro, Giulio
American. Author
b. May 6, 1942 in New York, New York
Source: *ChPo S2; ConAu 57; IlsBYP; SmATA 8*

Maeterlinck, Maurice
Belgian. Dramatist, Philosopher, Poet
b. Aug 29, 1862 in Ghent, Belgium
d. May 6, 1949 in Nice, France
Source: *AtlBL; BbD; BiD&SB; CasWL; ChPo; ClDMEL; CnMD; CnThe; CyWA; EncWL; EvEuW; LongCTC; McGEWD; ModRL; ModWD; NewC; OxEng; OxFr; OxThe; Pen EUR; RComWL; REn; REnWD; TwCA, SUP; TwCW; WhAm 2; WhoLA; WhoTwCL*

Magee, Harry L
American. Carpet Executive
b. 1901
d. Oct 9, 1972 in Bloomsburg, Pennsylvania
Source: *NewYTBE 72*

Magee, Patrick
Irish. Actor
Won Tony, 1965, for *Marat/Sade.*
b. 1924? in Armagh, Northern Ireland
d. Aug 14, 1982 in London, England
Source: *FilmgC; NewYTBS 82; NotNAT; WhoHol A; WhoThe 72, 77*

Magellan, Ferdinand
[Fernando DeMagalhaes]
Portuguese. Navigator, Explorer
Discovered Philippines, 1521.
b. 1480? in Sabrosa, Portugal
d. Apr 27, 1521 in Philippines
Source: *Drake; NewC; REn; WhAm H*

Magill, Hugh Stewart
American. Educator
b. Dec 5, 1868 in Auburn, Illinois
d. Oct 2, 1958 in Auburn, Illinois
Source: *WhAm 3*

Maginnis, Charles Donagh
Irish. Architect
b. Jan 7, 1867 in Londonderry, Northern Ireland
d. Feb 15, 1955 in Boston, Massachusetts
Source: *BioIn 3, 4, 5, 6; DcAmB S5; NatCAB 43; WhAm 3*

Maginot, Andre
French. Politician
b. Feb 17, 1877 in Paris, France
d. Jan 7, 1932 in Paris, France
Source: *WebBD 80*

Maglie, Sal(vatore Anthony)
"The Barber"
American. Baseball Player
b. Apr 26, 1917 in Niagara Falls, New York
Source: *BaseEn; WhoProB 73*

Magnani, Anna
Italian. Actress
b. Mar 7, 1909 in Alexandria, Egypt
d. Sep 26, 1973 in Rome, Italy
Source: *BiDFilm; CurBio 56, 73; FilmgC; InWom; MotPP; MovMk; NewYTBE 73; OxFilm; PlP&P; WhAm 6; WhScrn 77; WhoHol B; WorEFlm*

Magnante, Charles
American. Composer, Author
b. Dec 5, 1905 in New York, New York
Source: *AmSCAP 66*

Magnasco, Alessandro Lissandrino
Italian. Artist
b. 1667 in Genoa, Italy
d. Mar 12, 1749 in Genoa, Italy
Source: *AtlBL; McGDA; McGEWB*

Magnin, Grover Arnold
American. Chain Store Executive
b. Dec 4, 1885 in San Francisco, California
d. Mar 17, 1969 in San Francisco, California
Source: *BioIn 10; NatCAB 54*

Magnuson, Keith Arlen
Canadian. Hockey Player, Coach
Defenseman, Chicago, 1969-80; author *None Against,* 1973.
b. Apr 27, 1947 in Saskatoon, SK
Source: *WhoAm 82; WhoHcky 73*

Magnuson, Warren Grant
American. Politician
b. Apr 12, 1905 in Moorhead, Minnesota
Source: *BiDrAC; CngDr 74; CurBio 45; IntWW 74; WhoAm 74, 76, 78, 80, 82; WhoAmP 73; WhoGov 72; WhoWor 74*

Magonigle, Harold Van Buren
American. Architect
b. Oct 17, 1867 in Bergen Heights, New Jersey
d. Aug 29, 1935 in Vergennes, Vermont
Source: *ApCAB X; DcAmB S1; DcNAA; NatCAB 15, 27; WhAm 1*

Magritte, Rene
Belgian. Artist
b. Nov 21, 1898
d. Aug 8, 1967 in Brussels, Belgium
Source: *CurBio 66, 67; WhAm 4*

Magruder, Jeb Stuart
American. Watergate Participant
b. Nov 5, 1934 in Staten Island, New York
Source: *NewYTBE 73; WhoAm 74*

Magsaysay, Ramon
Philippine. President
b. Aug 31, 1907 in Iba, Philippines
d. Mar 1957
Source: *CurBio 52, 57; WhAm 3*

Magyar, Gabriel
Hungarian. Musician
b. Dec 5, 1914 in Budapest, Hungary
Source: *WhoAm 76, 78, 80, 82*

Mahan, Alfred Thayer
American. Admiral, Historian
b. Sep 27, 1840 in West Point, New York
d. Dec 1, 1914 in Washington, DC
Source: *Alli SUP; AmAu; AmAu&B; AmBi; ApCAB SUP; BbD; BiD&SB; Chambr 3; DcAmAu; DcAmB; DcEnA AP; DcNAA; EncAB-H; OxAmL; REn; WebAB; WhAm 1*

Mahan, Asa
American. Clergyman, College President
b. Nov 9, 1799 in Vernon, New York
d. Apr 4, 1889 in Eastbourne, England
Source: *BiDAmEd; BioIn 12; DcAmB; WhAm H*

Mahan, Larry
American. Rodeo Rider
b. Nov 21, 1943
Source: *BioIn 7, 8, 9, 10*

Maharaj Ji
Indian. Religious Leader
b. 1957
Source: *BioIn 10*

Maharis, George
American. Actor
b. 1933 in New York, New York
Source: *BiE&WWA; FilmgC; MotPP; MovMk; PlP&P; WhoHol A*

Mahavira
Indian. Founder of Jainism
b. 599BC
d. 527BC
Source: *WebBD 80; WhDW*

Mahavishnu Orchestra, The
[Billy Cogham, Jr.; Jerry Goodman; Jan Hammer; Rick Laird; John McLaughlin]
American. Rock Group
Source: *EncPR&S; IlEncRk*

Mahdi, Mohammed Ahmed
Sudanese. Moslem Leader
b. 1844? in Dongola, Sudan
d. Jun 22, 1885 in Omdurman, Sudan
Source: *WebBD 80*

Maher, George Washington
American. Architect
b. Dec 25, 1864 in Mill Creek, West Virginia
d. Sep 12, 1926
Source: *WhAm 1*

Mahesh
Indian. Hindi Yoga
b. 1911
Source: *BioIn 8, 9, 10*

Mahler, Fritz
Austrian. Conductor
b. Jul 16, 1901 in Vienna, Austria
d. Jun 18, 1973 in New York, New York
Source: *NewYTBE 73; WhAm 6; WhoAm 74; WhoMus 72*

Mahler, Gustav
Austrian. Composer, Conductor
b. Jul 7, 1860 in Kalischt, Bohemia
d. May 18, 1911 in Vienna, Austria
Source: *AmSCAP 66; AtlBL; DcCM; OxGer; REn; WhAm HA, 4*

Mahmud of Ghazni
Arabian. Afghan Emperor, Conqueror
b. 971?
d. 1030
Source: *NewC*

Mahomet
see: Mohammed

Mahone, William
American. Politician
b. Dec 1, 1826 in Southampton County, Virginia
d. Oct 8, 1895 in Washington, DC
Source: *AmBi; ApCAB; BiDConf; BiDrAC; DcAmB; TwCBDA; WhAm H; WhAmP*

Mahoney, David Joseph, Jr.
American. Corporation Executive
Chief executive of Norton Simon Inc, 1970--.
b. May 17, 1923 in New York, New York
Source: *IntWW 74, 75, 76, 77, 78, 79, 80, 81; WhoAm 74, 76, 78, 80, 82; WhoE 77, 79; WhoF&I 75, 77*

Mahoney, James
Canadian. Catholic Bishop
b. Dec 7, 1927 in Saskatoon, SK
Source: *WhoAm 78, 80, 82*

Mahoney, Jock
[James O'Mahoney]
American. Actor
b. Feb 7, 1919 in Chicago, Illinois
Source: *FilmgC; IntMPA 75, 76, 77, 78, 79, 80, 81, 82; MotPP; WhoHol A*

Mahoney, Will
American. Actor
b. 1894?
d. Feb 8, 1966? in Melbourne, Australia
Source: *WhScrn 77; WhoHol B*

Mahovlich, Frank (Francis William)
Canadian. Hockey Player
In 18 NHL seasons, scored 533 goals.
b. Jan 10, 1938 in Timmins, ON
Source: *WhoHcky 73*

Mahovlich, Pete(r Joseph)
Canadian. Hockey Player
b. Oct 10, 1946 in Timmins, ON
Source: *WhoAm 74; WhoHcky 73*

Mahre, Phil(lip)
American. Skier
Won World Cup skiing championship, 1982.
b. May 10, 1957 in Yakima, Washington
Source: *BioIn 11*

Mahre, Steve(n)
American. Skier
b. May 10, 1957 in Yakima, Washington
Source: *BioIn 11*

Maier, Henry W
American. Mayor of Milwaukee
b. Dec 7, 1918 in Dayton, Ohio
Source: *BioIn 9; WhoAm 78, 80, 82*

Mailer, Norman
American. Author
Pearl Harbor attack inspired novel, *The Naked and the Dead.*
b. Jan 31, 1923 in Long Branch, New Jersey
Source: *AmAu&B; AmNov; AmWr; Au&Wr 71; AuNews 2; BioNews 74; BkPepl; CasWL; CelR 73; CnDAL; ConAu 9R; ConLC 1, 2, 3, 4, 5, 8, 11, 14; ConNov 72, 76; CurBio 48, 70; DrAF 76; EncAB-H; EncWL; FilmgC; LongCTC; ModAL, SUP; OxAmL; OxFilm; Pen AM; RAdv 1; REn; REnAL; TwCA SUP; TwCW; WebAB; WebE&AL; Who 74; WhoAm 74, 76, 78, 80, 82; WhoE 74; WhoHol A; WhoTwCL; WhoWor 74; WhoWorJ 72; WrDr 76*

Maillol, Aristide
French. Artist
b. Dec 8, 1861 in Banyuls sur Mer, France
d. Oct 5, 1944 in Banyuls sur Mer, France
Source: *AtlBL; CurBio 42, 44*

Maiman, Theodore
American. Physicist
Developed first working laser, 1960.
b. Jul 11, 1927 in Los Angeles, California
Source: *AmM&WS 79P; AsBiEn; LElec; McGMS 80; WhDW; WhoAm 78, 80, 82*

Maimonides, Moses
Spanish. Philosopher, Rabbi
b. Mar 30, 1135 in Cordova, Spain
d. Dec 13, 1204 in Cairo, Egypt
Source: *BiD&SB; CasWL; EuAu; EvEuW; RComWL*

Main, Marjorie
[Mary Tomlinson Krebs]
American. Actress
b. Feb 24, 1890 in Acton, Illinois
d. Apr 10, 1975 in Los Angeles, California
Source: *CurBio 51; FilmgC; InWom; IntMPA 75; MotPP; MovMk; ThFT; Vers A; WhAm 6; WhScrn 77*

Mainbocher
[Main Rousseau Bocher]
American. Costume Designer
b. Oct 24, 1890 in Chicago, Illinois
d. Dec 27, 1976 in Munich, Germany (West)
Source: *BiE&WWA; CurBio 42, 77; IntWW 74; NewYTBE 71; NewYTBS 76; NotNAT; WorFshn*

Maintenon, Francoise d'Aubigne, Marquise
French. Favorite of Louis XIV
b. 1635
d. 1719
Source: *DcEuL; OxFr; REn*

Maison, Rene
Belgian. Opera Singer
b. Nov 24, 1895 in Traumeries, Belgium
d. Jul 15, 1962 in Mont-Dore, France
Source: *NewEOp 71*

Maitland, John
[Duke of Lauderdale]
Scottish. Statesman
b. May 24, 1616 in Lethington, Scotland
d. Aug 1682 in Tunbridge Wells, England
Source: *WebBD 80*

Major, Clarence
American. Author
b. Dec 31, 1936 in Atlanta, Georgia
Source: *BlkAW; ConAu 25R; ConLC 3; ConP 75; DrAF 76; DrAP 75; LivgBAA; WhoBlA 75; WrDr 76*

Major, Ray
see: Mott (the Hoople)

Majorano, Gaetano
"Caffarelli"
Italian. Opera Singer
b. Apr 12, 1710 in Bitonto, Italy
d. Jan 31, 1783 in Naples, Italy
Source: *NewEOp 71*

Majors, Lee
American. Actor, Motion Picture Producer
Starred in TV series "The Six Million Dollar Man," 1973-78.
b. Apr 23, 1940 in Wyandotte, Michigan
Source: *BkPepl; FilmgC; IntMPA 82; WhoAm 82; WhoHol A*

Makarios III, Archbishop
[Michael Christedoulos Mouskos]
Cypriot. Ecclesiastic, Politician
b. Aug 13, 1913 in Cyprus
d. Aug 2, 1977 in Nicosia, Cyprus
Source: *BioIn 10; CurBio 56*

Makarova, Natalia
Russian. Ballerina
b. Nov 21, 1940 in Leningrad, U.S.S.R.
Source: *CelR 73; CurBio 72; IntWW 74; WhoAm 74, 76, 78, 80, 82*

Makeba, Miriam
South African. Singer
b. Mar 4, 1932 in Prospect Township, South Africa
Source: *AmSCAP 66; CurBio 65; EncFCWM 69; InWom; WhoBlA 75; WhoE 74*

Makem, Tommy
Irish. Singer
b. 1932 in Keady, Ireland
Source: *EncFCWM 69*

Makepeace, Chris
Canadian. Actor
b. 1964 in Toronto, ON
Source: *BioIn 12; JohnWil 81*

Malamud, Bernard
American. Author
b. Apr 26, 1914 in New York, New York
Source: *AmAu&B; Au&Wr 71; CasWL; CelR 73; CnMWL; ConAu 5R; ConLC 1, 2, 3, 5, 8, 9, 11, 18; ConNov 72, 76; DrAF 76; EncWL; IntWW 74; ModAL, SUP; OxAmL; Pen AM; RAdv 1; REn; REnAL; TwCW; WebAB; WebE&AL; Who 74; WhoAm 74, 76, 78, 80, 82; WhoE 74; WhoTwCL; WhoWorJ 72; WorAu; WrDr 76*

Malan, Daniel F
South African. Politician
b. May 22, 1874 in Riebeck, South Africa
d. Feb 7, 1959 in Capetown, South Africa
Source: *CurBio 49, 59; WhAm 3*

Malaparte, Curzio
Italian. Author
b. Jun 9, 1898 in Prado, Italy
d. Jul 19, 1957 in Rome, Italy
Source: *CasWL; ClDMEL; CnMD; EncWL; EvEuW; ModRL; Pen EUR; REn; TwCA SUP; TwCW*

Malbin, Elaine
American. Opera Singer
b. May 24, 1932 in New York, New York
Source: *CurBio 59; InWom; WhoAm 74; WhoWor 74*

Malcolm X
[Malcolm Little]
American. Political Activist
Formed Organizatin for Afro-American Unity, 1964.
b. May 19, 1925 in Omaha, Nebraska
d. Feb 21, 1965 in New York, New York
Source: *AmAu&B; BlkAW; EncAB-H; WebAB; WhAm 4; WhAmP*

Malcolm, George
English. Musician
b. Feb 28, 1917 in London, England
Source: *IntWW 74; Who 74; WhoAm 82; WhoMus 72; WhoWor 74*

Malcuzynski, Witold
Polish. Musician
b. Aug 10, 1914 in Warsaw, Poland
Source: *IntWW 74; WhoMus 72; WhoWor 74*

Malden, Karl
[Mladen Sekulovich]
American. Actor
Won Oscar, 1951, for *A Streetcar Named Desire.*
b. Mar 22, 1913 in Gary, Indiana
Source: *BiDFilm; BiE&WWA; BioNews 74; CelR 73; CmMov; CurBio 57; FilmgC; IntMPA 75, 76, 77, 78, 79, 80, 81; MotPP; MovMk; NotNAT; OxFilm; PlP&P; WhoAm 74, 76, 78, 80, 82; WhoHol A; WhoWor 74; WorEFlm*

Malenkov, Georgi Maximilianovich
Russian. Government Official
b. Jan 8, 1901 in Orenburg, Russia
Source: *CurBio 52; IntWW 74; Who 74*

Malevich, Kasimir Severinovich
Russian. Artist
b. Feb 26, 1878 in Kiev, Russia
d. May 15, 1935 in Leningrad, U.S.S.R.
Source: *ConArt; EncMA; McGDA; McGEWB; WhoArch*

Malherbe, Francois de
French. Author, Poet
b. 1555 in Caen, France
d. Oct 16, 1628 in Paris, France
Source: *BbD; BiD&SB; CasWL; ChPo; DcEuL; EuAu; EvEuW; OxFr; Pen EUR; REn*

Malibran, Maria Felicita
[Maria Felicita Garcia]
Spanish. Opera Singer
b. Mar 24, 1808 in Paris, France
d. Sep 23, 1836 in Manchester, England
Source: *ApCAB; InWom; NewC; OxEng; OxFr; REn*

Malick, Terence (Terry)
[David Whitney, pseud.]
American. Director, Screenwriter
b. Nov 30, 1943 in Waco, Texas
Source: *BioIn 10, 11; ConAu 101; FilmEn; IntMPA 75, 76, 77, 78, 79, 80, 81; MovMk; WhoAm 80, 82*

Malik, Charles Habib
Lebanese. Educator, Statesman
b. Feb 11, 1906 in Bitirram, Lebanon
Source: *ConAu 45; CurBio 48; DrAS 74P; IntWW 74; WhoUN 75; WhoWor 74*

Malik, Yakov Alexandrovich
Russian. Diplomat
b. Feb 11, 1906 in Kharkov, Russia
d. Feb 11, 1980 in Moscow, U.S.S.R.
Source: *IntWW 74; Who 74; WhoAm 74; WhoGov 72; WhoUN 75; WhoWor 74*

Malina, Judith
German. Actress
b. Jun 4, 1926 in Kiel, Germany
Source: *BiE&WWA; NotNAT; PlP&P; WhoAm 82; WhoHol A; WhoThe 77*

Malinovsky, Rodion Y
Russian. Marshal, Minister of Defense
b. Nov 23, 1898 in Odessa, Russia
d. Mar 13, 1967 in Moscow, U.S.S.R.
Source: *CurBio 44, 60, 67; WhAm 4*

Malinowski, Bronislaw
Polish. Anthropologist
b. Apr 7, 1884 in Krakow, Poland
d. May 16, 1942 in New Haven, Connecticut
Source: *CurBio 41, 42; DcNAA; LongCTC; TwCA, SUP; WhAm 2; WhoLA*

Malipiero, Gian Francesco
Italian. Composer
b. Mar 18, 1882 in Venice, Italy
d. Aug 1, 1973 in Treviso, Italy
Source: *ConAu 45; DcCM; NewYTBE 73; WhoMus 72*

Malko, Nicolai
Russian. Conductor
b. May 4, 1888 in Brailov, Russia
d. Jun 1961
Source: *WhAm 4*

Mallarme, Stephane
French. Essayist, Poet, Translator
b. Mar 18, 1842 in Paris, France
d. Sep 9, 1898 in Valvins, France
Source: *AtlBL; CasWL; ClDMEL; CyWA; DcEuL; EuAu; EvEuW; ModRL; NewC; OxEng; OxFr; Pen EUR; RComWL; REn*

Malle, Louis
French. Motion Picture Director
b. 1932 in Thumeries, France
Source: *BiDFilm; DcFM; FilmgC; IntMPA 77, 78, 79, 80, 81, 82; IntWW 74; MovMk; NewYTBE 72; OxFilm; Who 74; WorEFlm*

Mallinckrodt, Edward
American. Chemical Manufacturer
b. Jan 21, 1845 in Saint Louis, Missouri
d. Feb 1, 1928 in Saint Louis, Missouri
Source: *AmBi; DcAmB; WhAm 1*

Mallinger, Mathilde
[Mathilde Lichtenegger]
Croatian. Opera Singer
b. Feb 17, 1847 in Agram, Croatia
d. Apr 19, 1920 in Berlin, Germany
Source: *InWom*

Mallock, William Hurrell
English. Author
b. 1849 in Devonshire, England
d. Apr 5, 1923
Source: *Alli SUP; BbD; BiD&SB; BrAu 19; Chambr 3; DcEnA, AP; DcEnL; DcLEL; LongCTC; NewC; OxEng; Pen ENG; REn*

Mallory, Molla
Finnish. Tennis Player
b. 1892?
d. Nov 22, 1959 in Stockholm, Sweden
Source: *BioIn 5, 11*

Mallory, Stephen R
American. Politician
b. 1812 in Trinidad
d. Nov 19, 1873 in Pensacola, Florida
Source: *AmBi; ApCAB; BiDConf; BiDSA; BiDrAC; DcAmB; TwCBDA; WhAm H; WhAmP*

Malone, Dorothy
[Dorothy Maloney]
American. Actress
b. Jan 30, 1925 in Chicago, Illinois
Source: *BiDFilm; FilmgC; HolP 40; IntMPA 75, 76, 77, 78, 79, 80, 81, 82; MotPP; MovMk; WhoAm 74; WhoHol A; WomPO 76; WorEFlm*

Malone, Dumas
American. Author
b. Jan 10, 1892 in Coldwater, Mississippi
Source: *AmAu&B; ConAu 1R, 2NR; DrAS 74H; IntWW 74; OxAmL; REnAL; TwCA SUP; WhoAm 74, 76, 78, 80, 82; WhoS&SW 73; WhoWor 74; WrDr 76*

Malone, Edmund
Irish. Author
b. Oct 4, 1741 in Dublin, Ireland
d. May 25, 1812 in London, England
Source: *Alli; BbD; BiD&SB; DcEnA; DcEnL; DcEuL; NewC; PoIre; REn*

Malone, Moses
American. Basketball Player
Signed six-year, $13.2 million contract with Philadelphia 76ers, 1982.
b. Mar 23, 1954 in Petersburg, Virginia
Source: *BioIn 12; OfNBA; WhoAm 80, 82*

Malone, Nancy
American. Actress
b. 1935 in New York, New York
Source: *WhoHol A*

Maloney, Dave (David Wilfred)
Canadian. Hockey Player
b. Jul 31, 1956 in Kitchener, ON
Source: *HocReg; NewYTBS 79*

Maloney, Don(ald)
Canadian. Hockey Player
b. Sep 5, 1958 in Lindsay, ON
Source: *HocReg; NewYTBS 79*

Malory, Sir Thomas
English. Author
Wrote *Morte d'Arthur,* source for later versions of King Arthur legend.
d. Mar 12, 1471? in London, England
Source: *Alli; AnCL; AtlBL; BbD; BiD&SB; BrAu; CarSB; CasWL; Chambr 1; CrtT 1; CyWA; DcEnA; DcEnL; DcEuL; DcLEL; EvLB; MouLC 1; NewC; OxEng; Pen ENG; RAdv 1; RComWL; REn; WebE&AL*

Malpighi, Marcello
Italian. Anatomist
b. Mar 10, 1626 in Crevalcore, Italy
d. Nov 30, 1694 in Rome, Italy
Source: *AsBiEn; McGEWB; WebBD 80*

Malraux, Andre
French. Author, Government Official
b. Nov 3, 1901 in Paris, France
d. Nov 23, 1976 in Paris, France
Source: *Au&Wr 71; CasWL; ClDMEL; CnMD; CnMWL; ConAu 21R, 69; ConAu P-2; ConLC 1, 4, 9, 13, 15; CurBio 59; CyWA; DcFM; EncWL; EvEuW; IntWW 74; LongCTC; ModRL; OxEng; OxFilm; OxFr; Pen EUR; REn; TwCA, SUP; TwCW; Who 74; WhoTwCL; WhoWor 74; WorEFlm*

Maltby, Richard E
American. Composer, Conductor
b. Jun 26, 1914 in Chicago, Illinois
Source: *AmSCAP 66*

Maltby, Richard E, Jr.
American. Songwriter
b. Oct 6, 1937 in Ripon, Wisconsin
Source: *AmSCAP 66*

Malthus, Thomas Robert
English. Economist
b. Feb 17, 1766 in Surrey, England
d. Dec 23, 1834 in Bath, England
Source: *Alli; BbD; BiD&SB; BiDLA, SUP; BrAu 19; CasWL; Chambr 2; DcEnA; DcEnL; EvLB; NewC; OxEng; Pen ENG; REn; WebE&AL*

Maltin, Leonard
American. Motion Picture Critic
b. Dec 18, 1950 in New York, New York
Source: *ConAu 29R*

Maltsev, Victor Fyodorovich
Russian. Diplomat, Engineer
b. Jun 12, 1917 in Ukraine, Russia
Source: *IntWW 74; WhoWor 74*

Maltz, Albert
American. Author
b. Oct 8, 1908 in Brooklyn, New York
Source: *AmAu&B; AmNov; Au&Wr 71; BiE&WWA; CnDAL; CnMD; ConAu 41R; ConDr 73; ConNov 76; DcFM; FilmgC; IntMPA 75, 76, 77, 78, 79, 80, 81, 82; ModAL; ModWD; NotNAT; OxAmL; Pen AM; REn; TwCA, SUP; WhoAm 74, 76, 78, 80, 82; WhoWor 74; WhoWorJ 72; WrDr 76*

Mamas and the Papas, The
[Dennis Doherty; Cass Elliot; "Spanky" McFarlane; John Phillips;Mackenzie Phillips; Michelle Gilliam Phillips]
American. Rock Group
Source: *EncPR&S; IlEncRk; Rk100*

Mamet, David
American. Dramatist
b. Nov 30, 1947 in Chicago, Illinois
Source: *BioIn 11; ConAu 81; ConLC 9, 15; CurBio 78; WhoAm 78, 80, 82*

Mamoulian, Rouben
American. Motion Picture Director
b. Oct 8, 1897 in Tiflis, Russia
Source: *BiDFilm; BiE&WWA; CmMov; ConAu 25R; CurBio 49; DcFM; EncMT; FilmgC; IntMPA 75, 76, 77, 78, 79, 80, 81, 82; IntWW 74; MovMk; NotNAT; OxFilm; Who 74; WhoAm 74, 76, 78, 80, 82; WhoThe 77; WhoWor 74; WorEFlm*

Manatt, Charles Taylor
American. Politician
Chairman, Democratic National Committee, 1981--.
b. Jun 9, 1936 in Chicago, Illinois
Source: *IntWW 81; NewYTBS 81; WhoAm 76, 78, 80, 82; WhoAmP 73, 75, 77, 79; WhoF&I 74, 75; WhoWest 76, 78*

Manchester, Melissa Toni
American. Singer, Songwriter
Began career as back-up singer for Bette Midler; hit songs "Midnight Blue"; "Don't Cry Out Loud."
b. Feb 15, 1951 in New York, New York
Source: *BioIn 10; BkPepl; WhoAm 82*

Manchester, William Raymond
American. Author
b. Apr 4, 1922 in Attleboro, Massachusetts
Source: *AmAu&B; Au&Wr 71; AuNews 1; ConAu 1R, 3NR; CurBio 67; IntWW 74; Who 74; WhoAm 74, 76, 78, 80, 82; WhoE 74; WhoWor 74; WorAu; WrDr 76*

Mancinelli, Luigi
Italian. Conductor, Composer
b. Feb 5, 1848 in Orvieto, Italy
d. Feb 2, 1921 in Rome, Italy
Source: *NewEOp 71*

Mancini, Henry
American. Composer
Won Oscars, 1961, 1962, for songs "Moon River" and "Days of Wine and Roses."
b. Apr 16, 1924 in Cleveland, Ohio
Source: *AmSCAP 66; BioNews 74; CelR 73; CmMov; CurBio 64; FilmgC; IntMPA 75, 76, 77, 78, 79, 80, 81, 82; OxFilm; WhoAm 74, 76, 78; WhoWor 74; WorEFlm*

Mancini, Ray
"Boom Boom"
American. Boxer
WBA lightweight champ.
b. Mar 4, 1961 in Youngstown, Ohio
Source: *BioIn 12; NewYTBS 82*

Manco Capac
Legendary Founder of Incas
Source: *WebBD 80*

Mandan, Robert
American. Actor
b. Feb 2, in Clever, Missouri
Source: *WhoAm 78, 80, 82*

Mandel, Marvin
American. Former Governor
b. 1920
Source: *IntWW 74; WhoAm 74; WhoAmP 73; WhoE 74; WhoGov 72*

Mandelbaum, Fredericka
"Marm"
American. Criminal
b. 1818 in New York
d. 1889 in Canada
Source: *NF*

Mandelshtam, Osip Emilyevich
Russian. Author
b. Jan 15, 1891? in Warsaw, Poland
d. Dec 28, 1938? in Vladivostok, U.S.S.R.
Source: *CasWL; ClDMEL; CnMWL; ModSL 1; Pen EUR; REn*

Mandelstam, Nadezhda Yakovlevna
Russian. Author, Philologist
b. Oct 31, 1899 in Sarativ, Russia
Source: *AnObit 1980; BioIn 10; ConAu 102*

Mandeville, Sir John
English. Traveler
b. 1300?
d. 1372
Source: *Alli; BbD; BiD&SB; CasWL; Chambr 1; DcEnA; DcEnL; DcLEL; EvLB; OxEng; WhNAA*

Mandlikova, Hana
Czech. Tennis Player
b. 1963? in Czechoslovakia
Source: *NewYTBS 81*

Mandrell, Barbara Ann
[Mrs. Ken Dudney]
American. Singer
Entertainer of year, 1980.
b. Dec 25, 1948 in Houston, Texas
Source: *BioIn 11; CurBio 82; WhoAm 80, 82*

Maneloveg, Herbert Donald
American. Advertising Executive
b. Jan 25, 1925 in Aliquippa, Pennsylvania
Source: *WhoAdv 72; WhoAm 74*

Manessier, Alfred
French. Artist
b. Dec 5, 1911 in Saint-Ouen, France
Source: *ConArt; ConAu 57; IntWW 74, 75, 76, 77, 78; McGDA; WhoWor 74*

Manet, Edouard
French. Artist
b. Jan 23, 1832 in Paris, France
d. Apr 30, 1883 in Paris, France
Source: *AtlBL; OxFr; REn*

Maney, Richard
American. Press Agent
b. Jun 11, 1892 in Chinook, Michigan
d. Jun 30, 1968 in Norwalk, Connecticut
Source: *BiE&WWA; CurBio 64, 68; REnAL; WhAm 5*

Manfred, Frederick Feikema
[Feike Feikema, pseud.]
American. Author
b. Jan 6, 1912 in Doon, Iowa
Source: *AmAu&B; ConAu 9R, 5NR; ConNov 72, 76; CurBio 50; DrAF 76; MnnWr; OxAmL; REnAL; TwCA SUP; WhoAm 74, 76, 78, 80, 82; WrDr 76*

Mangano, Silvana
Italian. Actress
b. 1930 in Rome, Italy
Source: *BiDFilm; FilmgC; IntMPA 77, 78, 79, 80, 81, 82; MotPP; OxFilm; WorEFlm*

Mangione, Chuck
American. Jazz Musician, Composer
Plays flugelhorn; hit song "Feels So Good," 1978.
b. Nov 29, 1940 in Rochester, New York
Source: *BioIn 11; BkPepl; CurBio 80; WhoAm 80, 82*

Mangrum, Jim "Dandy"
see: Black Oak Arkansas

Mangrum, Lloyd
American. Golfer
b. Aug 1, 1914 in Dallas, Texas
d. Nov 17, 1973 in Apple Valley, California
Source: *CurBio 51, 74; NewYTBE 71, 73*

Manhattan Transfer
[Cheryl Bentyne; Tim Hauser; Laurel Masse; Alan Paul; Janis Siege]
American. Singing Group
Source: *WhoRock 81*

Mani
Persian. Founder of Manichaeism
b. 216?
d. 276?
Source: *CasWL; DcOrL 3; REn*

Manilow, Barry
American. Singer, Songwriter
Wrote commercial jingles, accompanied Bette Midler before first hit, "Mandy," 1975.
b. Jun 17, 1946 in Brooklyn, New York
Source: *BioIn 10, 11; BkPepl; CurBio 78; WhoAm 82*

Manion, Eddie
see: Southside Johnny and the Asbury Jukes

Mankiewicz, Frank Fabian
American. Lawyer, Journalist
b. May 16, 1924 in New York, New York
Source: *WhoAm 74, 76, 78, 80, 82*

Mankiewicz, Joseph Lee
American. Motion Picture Director, Producer
b. Feb 11, 1909 in Wilkes-Barre, Pennsylvania
Source: *BiDFilm; CelR 73; CmMov; ConDr 73; CurBio 49; DcFM; FilmgC; IntMPA 75, 76, 77, 78, 79, 80, 81, 82; IntWW 74; MovMk; OxFilm; REnAL; Who 74; WhoAm 74, 76, 78, 80, 82; WhoWor 74; WhoWorJ 72; WorEFlm*

Mankowitz, Wolf
American. Author
b. Nov 7, 1924 in Whitechapel, England
Source: *ConAu 5R, 5NR; ConDr 73; ConNov 72, 76; FilmgC; IntMPA 75, 76, 77, 78, 79, 80, 81, 82; IntWW 74; LongCTC; NewC; NotNAT; REn; TwCW; Who 74; WhoThe 77; WhoWor 74; WorAu; WrDr 76*

Manley, Joan A Daniels
American. Publisher
b. Sep 23, 1932 in San Luis Obispo, California
Source: *WhoAm 74, 76, 78, 80, 82*

Manley, Michael Norman
Jamaican. Prime Minister
b. Dec 10, 1923 in Kingston, Jamaica
Source: *IntWW 74; Who 74; WhoWor 74*

Mann, Carol Ann
American. Golfer
b. Feb 3, 1941 in Buffalo, New York
Source: *BioIn 7, 8, 10, 11; WhoGolf*

Mann, Erika
German. Author, Actress
b. 1905 in Munich, Germany
d. Aug 27, 1969 in Zurich, Switzerland
Source: *ConAu 25R; CurBio 40, 69; InWom; LongCTC; TwCA, SUP; WhAm 5*

Mann, Heinrich Ludwig
American. Author
b. Mar 27, 1871 in Lubeck, Germany
d. Mar 12, 1950 in Beverly Hills, California
Source: *CasWL; ClDMEL; EncWL; EvEuW; LongCTC; ModGL; ModWD; OxEng; OxGer; Pen EUR; REn; TwCA, SUP; TwCW; WhoLA; WhoTwCL*

Mann, Herbie
[Herbert Jay Solomon]
American. Jazz Musician
b. Apr 16, 1930 in New York, New York
Source: *AmSCAP 66; BioNews 74; NewYTBE 73; WhoAm 74, 76, 78, 80, 82; WhoE 74*

Mann, Horace
American. Educator, Politician
b. May 4, 1796 in Franklin, Massachusetts
d. Aug 2, 1859 in Yellow Springs, Ohio
Source: *Alli; AmAu; AmAu&B; AmBi; ApCAB; BiAuS; BiD&SB; BiDrAC; CyAL 1; DcAmAu; DcAmB; DcNAA; Drake; EncAB-H; OhA&B; OxAmL; REn; REnAL; TwCBDA; WebAB; WhAm H; WhAmP*

Mann, Joseph
Impresario
b. 1893
d. Jun 16, 1973
Source: *NewYTBE 73*

Mann, Klaus
German. Author
b. Nov 18, 1906 in Munich, Germany
d. May 21, 1949 in Pacific Palisades, California
Source: *ClDMEL; CurBio 40, 49; EncWL; LongCTC; ModGL; OxGer; TwCA, SUP; WhAm 3; WhoLA*

Mann, Theodore
American. Actor
b. May 13, 1924 in New York, New York
Source: *BiE&WWA; NotNAT; WhoAm 82; WhoE 74; WhoThe 77; WhoWor 74*

Mann, Thomas
German. Author
Won Nobel Prize, 1929.
b. Jun 6, 1875 in Lubeck, Germany
d. Aug 12, 1955 in Zurich, Switzerland
Source: *AtlBL; CasWL; ClDMEL; CnMWL; CurBio 42, 55; CyWA; EncWL; EvEuW; LongCTC; ModGL; OxEng; OxGer; Pen EUR; RComWL; REn; REnAL; TwCA, SUP; TwCW; WhAm 3; WhoTwCL*

Manne, Shelly (Sheldon)
American. Jazz Musician
b. Jun 11, 1920 in New York, New York
Source: *AmSCAP 66; WhoAm 74, 76, 78, 80, 82; WhoHol A*

Manner, Harold
American. Educator, Biologist
b. Jul 31, 1925 in Brooklyn, New York
Source: *AmM&WS 73P; WhoAm 74*

Mannerheim, Carl Gustav Emil, Baron
Finnish. Field Marshal, President
b. Jun 4, 1867 in Louhissaari, Finland
d. Jan 27, 1951 in Lausanne, Switzerland
Source: *CurBio 40, 51; REn*

Manners, Charles
English. Opera Singer, Impresario
b. Dec 27, 1857 in London, England
d. May 3, 1935 in Dublin, Ireland
Source: *NewEOp 71*

Manners, Dorothy
American. Journalist
b. in Fort Worth, Texas
Source: *CelR 73; WhoAm 74*

Mannes, David
American. Conductor, Musician
b. Feb 16, 1866 in New York, New York
d. Apr 25, 1959 in New York, New York
Source: *WhAm 3*

Mannes, Leopold Damrosch
American. Composer, Musician
b. Dec 6, 1899 in New York, New York
d. Aug 11, 1964 in New York, New York
Source: *WhAm 4*

Mannes, Marya
American. Author, Journalist
b. Nov 14, 1904 in New York, New York
Source: *AmAu&B; ConAu 1R, 3NR; CurBio 59; DrAF 76; ForWC 70; InWom; NewYTBE 71; WorAu; WrDr 76*

Mannheim, Karl
Hungarian. Sociologist, Historian, Educator
b. Mar 27, 1893 in Budapest, Hungary
d. Jan 9, 1947 in London, England
Source: *BioIn 1, 2, 4, 11; EncTR; McGEWB; NewCol 75*

Manning, Archie
American. Football Player
b. May 19, 1949 in Cleveland, Mississippi
Source: *WhoFtbl 74*

Manning, Henry Edward
English. Religious Leader
b. Jul 15, 1808 in Totteridge, England
d. Jan 14, 1892 in London, England
Source: *Alli, SUP; BiD&SB; BrAu 19; CasWL; DcEnL; EvLB; NewC; OxEng*

Manning, Irene
American. Actress, Singer, Author
b. Jul 17, 1918 in Cincinnati, Ohio
Source: *BiE&WWA; FilmgC; MotPP; NotNAT; WhoHol A; WhoThe 77*

Manning, Madeline
American. Track Athlete
b. 1948?
Source: *BioIn 8*

Manning, Maria
[Maria de Roux]
Swiss. Murderer
b. 1825
d. Nov 13, 1849 in London, England
Source: *LookW*

Manning, Marie
see: Fairfax, Beatrice, pseud.

Manning, Olivia
English. Author
b. 1915? in Portsmouth, England
d. Jul 23, 1980 in Isle of Wight
Source: *ConAu 5R, 101; ConNov 72, 76; ModBrL, SUP; NewC; Pen ENG; TwCW; WorAu*

Manns, Sir Augustus
English. Conductor
b. Mar 12, 1825 in Stettin, Germany
d. Mar 2, 1907 in London, England
Source: *OxMus*

Mano, D Keith
American. Actor, Author
b. Feb 12, 1942 in New York, New York
Source: *AmAu&B; Au&Wr 71; ConAu 25R; ConLC 2; DrAF 76; WhoAm 82; WhoE 74*

Manolete
[Manuel Rodriguez y Sanchez]
Spanish. Bullfighter
b. 1917 in Cordova, Spain
d. Aug 28, 1947 in Linares, Spain
Source: *BioIn 1*

Manone, "Wingy" (Joseph)
American. Jazz Musician
b. Feb 13, 1904 in New Orleans, Louisiana
d. Jul 9, 1982 in Las Vegas, Nevada
Source: *AmSCAP 66; BiDAmM; CmpEPM; EncJzS 70; IlEncJ; NewYTBS 82; WhoJazz 72*

Mansart, Francois
[Francois Mansard]
French. Architect
b. Jan 23, 1598 in Paris, France
d. Sep 23, 1666 in Paris, France
Source: *AtlBL; BioIn 10*

Mansart, Jules Hardouin
[Jules Hardouin Mansard]
French. Architect
b. Apr 1645 in Paris, France
d. May 11, 1708 in Marly, France
Source: *AtlBL; OxFr*

Mansfield, Jayne
[Vera Jayne Palmer]
American. Actress
Sex symbol of 1950's; decapitated in auto accident.
b. Apr 19, 1932 in Bryn Mawr, Pennsylvania
d. Jun 29, 1967 in New Orleans, Louisiana
Source: *BiDFilm; FilmgC; InWom; MotPP; MovMk; OxFilm; WhAm 4; WhScrn 74, 77; WhoHol B; WorEFlm*

Mansfield, Katherine
[Kathleen Mansfield Beauchamp; Mrs. John Middleton Murry]
New Zealander. Author
Considered one of founders of modern short story.
b. Oct 14, 1888 in Wellington, New Zealand
d. Jan 9, 1923 in Fontainebleau, France
Source: *AtlBL; CasWL; Chambr 3; ChPo S1; CnMWL; CyWA; DcEuL; DcLEL; EncWL; EvLB; InWom; LongCTC; ModBrL, SUP; NewC; OxEng; Pen ENG; RAdv 1; REn; TwCA, SUP; TwCW; WebE&AL; WhoTwCL*

Mansfield, Michael Joseph
American. Politician
US Senator from MT, 1953-76; ambassador to Japan, 1977--.
b. Mar 16, 1903 in New York, New York
Source: *BiDrAC; CngDr 74; CurBio 52; IntWW 74; WhoAm 74, 76, 78, 80, 82; WhoAmP 73; WhoGov 72; WhoWor 74*

Mansfield, Richard
English. Actor
b. May 24, 1854 in Berlin, Germany
d. Aug 30, 1907 in New London, Connecticut
Source: *AmBi; ApCAB SUP; ChPo; DcAmB; DcNAA; FamA&A; OxAmL; OxThe; REn; REnAL; WebAB; WhAm 1; WhoStg 1906, 1908*

Manship, Paul
American. Sculptor
b. Dec 25, 1885 in Saint Paul, Minnesota
d. Jan 31, 1966 in Massachusetts
Source: *CurBio 40, 66; DcCAA 71; WhAm 4*

Manson, Charles
[No Name Maddox]
American. Murderer, Leader of Cult
In prison for 1969 murders of actress Sharon Tate, eight others.
b. Nov 11, 1934 in Cincinnati, Ohio
Source: *BioIn 10; Blood; BkPepl; NewYTBE 70*

Mansur, Al
Arabian. Founder of Baghdad
b. 712?
d. 775 in Baghdad, Iraq
Source: *WebBD 80*

Mantegna, Andrea
Italian. Artist
b. 1431 in Isola Carturo, Italy
d. Sep 13, 1506 in Mantua, Italy
Source: *AtlBL; McGEWB; REn*

Mantle, Mickey Charles
"The Commerce Comet"
American. Baseball Player
Hit 536 career home runs, record 18 in World Series; Hall of Fame, 1974.
b. Oct 20, 1931 in Spavinaw, Oklahoma
Source: *BaseEn; BioNews 74; CurBio 53; NewYTBS 74; WebAB; WhoAm 74, 76, 78, 80, 82; WhoProB 73*

Mantle, (Robert) Burns
American. Drama Critic, Theatre Analyst
b. Dec 1873 in Watertown, New York
d. Feb 29, 1948 in Long Island, New York
Source: *AmAu&B; CurBio 44, 48; DcAmB S4; DcNAA; OxThe; REnAL; TwCA, SUP; WhAm 2; WhNAA*

Mantovani, Annunzio
Italian. Conductor
b. Nov 5, 1905 in Venice, Italy
d. Mar 30, 1980 in Tunbridge Wells, England
Source: *WhoWor 74*

Manuel I
[Emanuel the Great]
Portuguese. King
b. 1469
d. 1521
Source: *NewCol 75*

Manulis, Martin
American. Motion Picture Producer, Director
b. May 30, 1915 in New York, New York
Source: *IntMPA 75, 76, 77, 78, 79, 80, 81, 82; WhoAm 74, 76, 78, 80, 82; WhoWor 74*

Manuzio, Aldo
[Aldus Teobaldo Manutius]
Italian. Printer, Classical Scholar
b. 1449 in Venice, Italy
d. 1515 in Venice, Italy
Source: *DcEuL; NewC*

Manville, Thomas Franklin
American. Eccentric
b. 1894
d. Oct 8, 1967 in Chappaqua, New York
Source: *BioIn 10*

Manzanera, Phil
see: Roxy Music

Manzarek, Ray
[The Doors]
American. Singer, Musician
Formed group in 1966; keyboard player, 1966-73.
b. Feb 12, 1935 in Chicago, Illinois
Source: *EncPR&S; IlEncRk*

Manzoni, Alessandro (Antonio)
Italian. Author
b. Mar 7, 1785 in Milan, Italy
d. Apr 28, 1873 in Milan, Italy
Source: *AtlBL; BbD; BiD&SB; CasWL; CyWA; DcBiA; DcEuL; EuAu; EvEuW; McGEWD; NewC; OxEng; OxFr; OxThe; Pen EUR; RComWL; REn*

Mao, Chiang Ching
see: Chiang Ching

Mao Tse-Tung
Chinese. Communist Leader, Author
Organized industrial, peasant unions, 1920's; chairman, Chinese Communist Party, 1949-76.
b. Dec 26, 1893 in Shaeshan, China
d. Sep 9, 1976 in Peking, China
Source: *DcOrL 1; IntWW 74; NewYTBE 72; OxEng; REn; WhAm 6*

Mapleson, James Henry
English. Impresario
b. May 4, 1830 in London, England
d. Nov 14, 1901 in London, England
Source: *Alli SUP*

Mara, Wellington T
American. Football Executive
b. 1916?
Source: *BioIn 6, 9, 11; WhoE 74*

Maradona, Diego
Argentine. Soccer Player
b. Oct 30, 1960 in Argentina
Source: *BioIn 12*

Marais, Jean
French. Actor
b. Dec 11, 1913 in Cherbourg, France
Source: *BiDFilm; CurBio 62; FilmgC; IntMPA 75, 76, 77, 78, 79, 80, 81, 82; IntWW 74; MotPP; MovMk; OxFilm; WhoHol A; WhoWor 74; WorEFlm*

Maranville, "Rabbit" (Walter James Vincent)
American. Baseball Player
b. Nov 11, 1891 in Springfield, Massachusetts
d. Jan 5, 1954 in New York, New York
Source: *BaseEn; DcAmB S5; WhoProB 73*

Marat, Jean Paul
French. Politician
b. 1743 in Boudry Neuch, Switzerland
d. Jul 13, 1793
Source: *OxFr; REn*

Maravich, Pete
"Pistol Pete"
American. Basketball Player
Guard, 1970-80; led NBA in scoring, 1977.
b. Jun 28, 1948 in Aliquippa, Pennsylvania
Source: *CelR 73; NewYTBE 70, 71; WhoBbl 73*

Maraziti, Joseph J
American. Former Congressman
b. Jun 15, 1912 in Boonton, New Jersey
Source: *WhoAm 74; WhoAmP 73*

Marble, Alice
American. Tennis Player
b. Sep 28, 1913 in Plumas City, California
Source: *CurBio 40; InWom*

Marc, Franz
German. Artist
b. 1880
d. Mar 4, 1916 in Verdun, France
Source: *OxGer; REn; WebBD 80*

Marc Antony
see: Antony, Marc

Marca-Relli, Conrad
American. Artist
b. Jun 5, 1913 in Boston, Massachusetts
Source: *BnEnAmA; ConArt; CurBio 70; DcAmArt; DcCAA 71, 77; McGDA; WhoAmA 73, 76, 78*

Marcantonio, Vito Anthony
American. Politician
b. Dec 10, 1902 in New York, New York
d. Aug 9, 1954 in New York, New York
Source: *BiDrAC; CurBio 49, 54; DcAmB S5; WhAm 3; WhAmP*

Marceau, Marcel
French. Actor, Pantomimist
World's most famous mime; created character "Bip," 1947.
b. Mar 22, 1923 in Strasbourg, France
Source: *BiE&WWA; ConAu 85; CurBio 57; IntWW 74; NewYTBE 73; NotNAT; OxThe; WhoAm 74, 76, 78, 80, 82; WhoHol A; WhoWor 74; WorEFlm*

Marcel, Gabriel Honore
French. Dramatist, Philosopher
b. Dec 7, 1889 in Paris, France
d. Oct 9, 1973 in Paris, France
Source: *CasWL; CathA 1930; ClDMEL; CnMD; ConAu 45, 102; ConLC 15; EncWL; EvEuW; McGEWD; ModWD; NewYTBE 73; OxFr; Pen EUR; REn; TwCW; WhoWor 74; WorAu*

Marcello, Benedetto
Italian. Composer
b. 1686 in Venice, Italy
d. 1739 in Brescia, Italy
Source: *Baker 78; BioIn 4, 7; OxMus*

March, Fredric
[Frederick McIntyre Bickel]
American. Actor
Won Oscars, 1932, 1946, for *Dr. Jekyll and Mr. Hyde; The Best Years of Our Lives.*
b. Aug 31, 1897 in Racine, Wisconsin
d. Apr 14, 1975 in Los Angeles, California
Source: *BiDFilm; BiE&WWA; CelR 73; CurBio 43; FamA&A; FilmgC; IntMPA 75; IntWW 74; MotPP; MovMk; NewYTBE 73; OxFilm; REn; WhAm 6; WhScrn 77; WhoAm 74; WorEFlm*

March, Hal
American. Actor
b. 1920 in San Francisco, California
d. Jan 11, 1970 in Los Angeles, California
Source: *BiE&WWA; MotPP; NewYTBE 70; WhAm 5; WhScrn 74, 77; WhoHol B*

March, Juan Alberto
Spanish. Financier
b. 1880
d. 1962
Source: *BioIn 1, 2, 5, 6*

Marchand, Nancy
American. Actress
Played Mrs. Pynchon on "Lou Grant," 1977-81; won two Emmys.
b. Jun 19, 1928 in Buffalo, New York
Source: *BiE&WWA; NotNAT; WhoAm 80, 82; WhoHol A; WhoThe 72, 77, 81*

Marchesi, Mathilde de Castrone
German. Voice Teacher
b. Mar 24, 1821 in Frankfurt, Germany
d. Nov 17, 1913 in London, England
Source: *InWom*

Marchesi, Salvatore
Italian. Opera Singer
b. Jan 15, 1822 in Palermo, Sicily
d. Feb 20, 1908 in Paris, France
Source: *NewEOp 71*

Marchetti, Gino
American. Football Player
b. Jan 2, 1927 in Antioch, California
Source: *BioIn 8, 10, 11; WhoFtbl 74*

Marchetti, Victor L
American. Author, Former CIA Agent
b. 1930?
Source: *BioIn 10*

Marchibroda, Ted (Theodore Joseph)
American. Football Coach
b. Mar 15, 1931 in Franklin, Pennsylvania
Source: *WhoFtbl 74*

Marciano, Rocky
[Rocco Francis Marchegiano]
American. Boxer, Actor
Undefeated heavyweight champ, 1952-56; died in plane crash.
b. Sep 1, 1924 in Brockton, Massachusetts
d. Aug 31, 1969 in Des Moines, Iowa
Source: *CurBio 52, 69; WebAB; WhScrn 77; WhoBox 74*

Marcinkus, Paul C
American. Archbishop
President, Vatican Bank, 1971--; involved in monetary scandal.
b. Jan 15, 1922 in Cicero, Illinois
Source: *AmCath 80; WhoAm 80, 82*

Marco Polo
Italian. Traveler, Author
Medieval account of Asian travels was chief source for knowledge of East.
b. 1254 in Venice, Italy
d. Jan 9, 1324 in Venice, Italy
Source: *BbD; BiD&SB; CasWL; CyWA; DcEuL; EuAu; EvEuW; NewC; OxEng; OxGer; Pen EUR; RComWL; REn*

Marconi, Guglielmo
Italian. Physicist
Invented wireless telegraph, 1895.
b. Apr 25, 1874 in Bologna, Italy
d. Jul 20, 1937
Source: *AsBiEn; BioIn 1, 2, 3, 4, 5, 6, 7, 8, 9, 10, 11; DcScB; McGEWB; NewCol 75; OxCan; WebBD 80*

Marcos, Ferdinand Edralin
Philippine. Politician, Lawyer
President of Philippines, 1966--.
b. Sep 11, 1917 in Philippines
Source: *BioIn 7, 8, 9, 10, 11, 12; CurBio 67; IntWW 74; NewYTBE 73; WhoGov 72; WhoWor 74*

Marcos, Imelda Romualdez
Philippine. Wife of Ferdinand Marcos
b. 1931
Source: *BioIn 7, 9, 10, 11; InWom*

Marcoux, Vanni
French. Opera Singer
b. Jun 12, 1877 in Turin, Italy
d. Oct 22, 1962 in Paris, France
Source: *WhAm 6*

Marcum, John Arthur
American. Author
b. Aug 21, 1927 in San Jose, California
Source: *ConAu 25R*

Marcus Aurelius Antoninus
[Marcus Annius Verus]
Roman. Emperor, Philosopher, Author
b. Apr 20, 121 in Rome, Italy
d. Mar 17, 180 in Vindobona, Austria
Source: *AtlBL; BbD; BiD&SB; CasWL; CyWA; NewC; OxEng; Pen CL; REn*

Marcus, David
"Mickey"
American. Army Officer
b. 1901
d. 1948 in Israel
Source: *BioIn 1, 2, 4, 6, 7, 8, 9*

Marcus, Frank
English. Dramatist
b. Jun 30, 1928 in Breslau, Germany
Source: *CnThe; ConAu 45, 2NR; ConDr 73; CroCD; McGEWD; WhoThe 77; WrDr 76*

Marcus, Stanley
American. Retail Executive
Neiman-Marcus founded by father, 1926; chairman, 1977--.
b. Apr 20, 1906 in Dallas, Texas
Source: *BioNews 74; BusPN; CelR 73; ConAu 53; CurBio 49; IntWW 74; WhoAm 74, 76, 78, 80, 82; WhoAmA 73; WhoF&I 74; WhoWor 74; WorFshn; WrDr 76*

Marcuse, Herbert
American. Philosopher
b. Jul 19, 1898 in Berlin, Germany
d. Jul 29, 1979 in Starnberg, Germany (West)
Source: *AmAu&B; ConAu 89; CurBio 69; DrAS 74P; EncAB-H; IntWW 74; Pen AM; WebAB; Who 74; WhoAm 74; WhoWor 74; WorAu; WrDr 76*

Marcy, William Learned
American. Statesman
b. Dec 12, 1786 in Sturbridge, Massachusetts
d. Jul 4, 1857 in Ballston Spa, New York
Source: *AmBi; ApCAB; BiDrAC; BiDrUSE; DcAmB; Drake; EncAB-H; TwCBDA; WebAB; WhAm H; WhAmP*

Mardian, Robert Charles
American. Watergate Participant, Lawyer
b. Oct 23, 1923 in Pasadena, California
Source: *BioIn 9, 10; NewYTBE 70, 73; NewYTBS 74; WhoAm 74; WhoAmP 73*

Marek, Kurt W
[C W Ceram, pseud.]
German. Author
b. Jan 20, 1915 in Berlin, Germany
d. Apr 12, 1972 in Hamburg, Germany (West)
Source: *AmAu&B; ConAu 17R, 33R; ConAu P-2; CurBio 57, 72; NewYTBE 72; REnAL; WhAm 5; WorAu*

Maretzek, Max
Moroccan. Impresario, Conductor
b. Jun 28, 1821 in Brunn,, Moravia
d. May 14, 1897 in Staten Island, New York
Source: *Alli SUP; ApCAB; DcAmAu; DcAmB; DcNAA; WhAm H*

Margaret of Anjou
Consort of Henry VI
b. 1430
d. 1482
Source: *BioIn 1, 4, 5, 6, 9, 11*

Margaret, Princess
[Margaret Rose]
English. Member of Royal Family
Sister of Queen Elizabeth II.
b. Aug 21, 1930 in Glamis, Scotland
Source: *BioIn 1, 2, 3, 4, 5, 6, 7, 8, 9, 10, 11; InWom; IntWW 74; WhoWor 74*

Margo
[Maria Marguerita Boldao y Castillo]
American. Actress
b. May 10, 1918 in Mexico City, Mexico
Source: *FilmgC; IntMPA 77, 78, 79, 80, 81, 82; MotPP; MovMk; NotNAT; ThFT; WhoHol A; WhoThe 77*

Margolies, Marjorie Sue
American. Broadcast Journalist
b. 1943
Source: *BioIn 10*

Margolin, Janet
American. Actress
b. 1943 in New York, New York
Source: *FilmgC; IntMPA 82; MotPP; WhoHol A*

Margolin, Stuart
American. Actor, Motion Picture Director
b. Jan 31, 1940? in Davenport, Iowa
Source: *WhoAm 80; WhoHol A*

Margolius, Sidney Senier
American. Author
b. May 3, 1911 in Perth Amboy, New Jersey
d. Jan 30, 1980 in Roslyn, New York
Source: *ConAu 21R, 93; WhAm 7; WhoE 74*

Margrethe II
Danish. Queen
b. Apr 16, 1940 in Copenhagen, Denmark
Source: *BioIn 3, 4, 5, 7, 8, 9, 10, 11; CurBio 72; InWom; IntWW 74; WhoWor 74*

Marguerite d'Angouleme
French. Queen of Navarre, Author
b. Apr 11, 1492 in Angouleme, France
d. Dec 21, 1549
Source: *BbD; BiD&SB; CasWL; EuAu; InWom; NewC; OxFr*

Maria Theresa
Austrian. Empress, Queen of Hungary
b. May 13, 1717 in Vienna, Austria
d. Nov 29, 1780
Source: *InWom; McGEWB; NewCol 75; REn; WebBD 80*

Mariamne the Hasmonaean
Wife of Herod the Great
Ordered executed by Herod in fit of jealousy.
b. 60?BC
d. 29?BC
Source: *InWom; NewC; OxFr; WebBD 80*

Marichal, Juan Antonio Sanchez
"Manito"; "The Dominican Dandy"
Dominican. Baseball Player
Pitcher, 1960-75.
b. Oct 20, 1938 in Laguana Verde, Dominican Republic
Source: *BaseEn; WhoProB 73*

Marie Alexandra Victoria
English. Queen of Romania, Author
b. 1875 in London, England
d. 1938
Source: *NewCol 75*

Marie Antoinette
Austrian. Wife of Louis XVI
Guillotined for encouraging civil war, betraying her country, 1793.
b. Nov 2, 1755 in Vienna, Austria
d. Oct 16, 1793 in Paris, France
Source: *HerW; InWom; NewCol 75; OxFr; OxGer; REn; WebBD 80*

Marie de Medicis
Italian. Wife of Henry IV of France
b. 1573 in Florence, Italy
d. 1642
Source: *BioIn 9; InWom; OxFr; REn; WebBD 80*

Marie Louise
French. Wife of Napoleon I
b. 1791
d. 1847
Source: *BioIn 9; InWom; NewCol 75; OxGer; WebBD 80*

Marin, John
American. Artist
b. Dec 23, 1872 in Rutherford, New Jersey
d. Oct 1, 1953 in Addison, Maine
Source: *AtlBL; CurBio 49, 53; DcAmB S5; DcCAA 71; EncAB-H; REn; WebAB; WhAm 3*

Marinetti, Filippo Tommaso
Italian. Poet
Founded Futurism; advocate of Fascism.
b. Dec 22, 1876 in Alexandria, Egypt
d. Dec 2, 1944 in Bellagio, Italy
Source: *CasWL; ClDMEL; CnMD; EncWT; McGEWD; ModWD; NewCol 75; OxEng; OxFr; Pen EUR; REn*

Marini, Marino
Italian. Sculptor
b. Feb 27, 1901 in Pistoria, Italy
d. Aug 6, 1980 in Viareggio, Italy
Source: *CurBio 54, 80; IntWW 74, 75, 76, 77, 78; McGDA; McGEWB; NewCol 75; WhoWor 74, 76, 78*

Marinuzzi, Gino
Italian. Conductor, Composer
b. Mar 24, 1882 in Palermo, Sicily
d. Aug 17, 1945 in Milan, Italy
Source: *NewEOp 71*

Mario, Giovanni Matteo
Italian. Opera Singer
b. Oct 17, 1810 in Cagliari, Sardinia
d. Dec 11, 1883 in Rome, Italy
Source: *BioIn 3, 7, 11; NewEOp 71*

Mario, Queena
American. Opera Singer
b. Aug 21, 1896 in Akron, Ohio
d. May 28, 1951 in New York, New York
Source: *BioIn 1, 2, 4; OhA&B; WhAm 3*

Marion, Francis
"Swamp Fox"
American. Revolutionary Commander
b. 1732? in Berkeley County, South Carolina
d. Feb 27, 1795 in Berkeley County, South Carolina
Source: *AmBi; ApCAB; DcAmB; Drake; OxAmL; REn; REnAL; TwCBDA; WebAB; WhAm H*

Marion, "Slats" (Martin Whiteford)
"Mr. Shortstop"; "The Octopus"
American. Baseball Player
b. Dec 1, 1917 in Richburg, South Carolina
Source: *BaseEn; WhoProB 73*

Maris, Roger Eugene
American. Baseball Player
NY Yankee outfielder; hit record 61 home runs, 1961.
b. Sep 10, 1934 in Hibbing, Minnesota
Source: *BaseEn; CurBio 61; WhoHol A; WhoProB 73*

Marisol (Escobar)
Venezuelan. Sculptor
Pop artist, noted for large wooden sculptures.
b. May 22, 1930 in Paris, France
Source: *CelR 73; CurBio 68; InWom*

Maritain, Jacques
French. Philosopher
b. Nov 18, 1882 in Paris, France
d. Feb 12, 1973 in Toulouse, France
Source: *CasWL; CathA 1930; ClDMEL; ConAu 41R, 85; CurBio 42, 73; EvEuW; LongCTC; NewYTBE 71, 73; OxEng; OxFr; REn; REnAL; TwCA, SUP; WhAm 5*

Marivaux, Pierre Carlet de
French. Author
b. Feb 4, 1688 in Paris, France
d. Feb 12, 1763 in Paris, France
Source: *AtlBL; BiD&SB; CasWL; CnThe; CyWA; DcEuL; EuAu; EvEuW; McGEWD; NewC; OxEng; OxFr; Pen EUR; PlP&P; REn; REnWD*

Mark, Saint
Biblical Character
Source: *REn*

Markel, Lester
American. Editor
b. Jan 9, 1894 in New York, New York
d. Oct 23, 1977 in New York, New York
Source: *ConAu 37R, 73; CurBio 52; IntWW 74; WhoAm 74; WhoWorJ 72; WrDr 76*

Marker, Chris
French. Motion Picture Director
b. 1921 in Belleville, France
Source: *BiDFilm; DcFM; FilmgC; OxFilm; WorEFlm*

Markert, Russell
American. Choreographer
b. 1899
Source: *BioIn 8, 9, 10; BioNews 74; NewYTBE 71*

Markevitch, Igor
Russian. Conductor
b. Jul 27, 1912 in Kiev, Russia
Source: *IntWW 74*

Markey, Enid
American. Actress
b. Feb 22, 1886 in Dillon, Colorado
d. Nov 15, 1981 in Bay Shore, New York
Source: *BiE&WWA; BioIn 5; Film 1; MotPP; NotNAT; TwYS; WhoHol A; WhoThe 72, 77*

Markey, Lucille (Parker) Wright
American. Horse Breeder
b. Dec 14, 1896 in Maysville, Kentucky
d. Jul 24, 1982 in Lexington, Kentucky
Source: *NewYTBS 82; WhoAm 74, 76, 78; WhoAmW 64, 66, 68, 70, 72, 75, 77, 79; WhoS&SW 75; WhoWor 74, 76*

Markham, Edwin
American. Poet
b. Apr 23, 1852 in Oregon City, Oregon
d. Mar 7, 1940 in Staten Island, New York
Source: *AmAu&B; AmBi; AmLY; ChPo, S1, S2; CnDAL; ConAmL; CurBio 40; DcAmB S2; DcLEL; DcNAA; EncAB-H; EvLB; LongCTC; ModAL; OxAmL; REn; REnAL; TwCA, SUP; WebAB; WhAm 1; WhNAA*

Markham, Monte
American. Actor
b. Jun 21, 1935 in Monatee, Florida
Source: *FilmgC; IntMPA 78, 79, 80, 81, 82; WhoHol A*

Markham, "Pigmeat" (Dewey M)
American. Comedian
Known for "Here come de judge" skit; appeared on "Laugh-in" TV show.
b. Apr 18, 1904 in Durham, North Carolina
d. Dec 13, 1981 in Bronx, New York
Source: *AnObit 1981; DcBlPA; NewYTBS 81*

Markievicz, Constance Georgine, Countess
[Constance Gore-Booth]
Irish. Revolutionary
b. Feb 4, 1868 in London, England
d. Jul 15, 1927 in Dublin, Ireland
Source: *BioIn 1, 7, 8, 9, 11; DcIrB; InWom; NewCol 75*

Markova, Alicia
English. Ballerina
b. Dec 1, 1910 in London, England
Source: *ConAu 21R; ConAu P-2; CurBio 43; IntWW 74; Who 74; WhoAm 74; WhoThe 77; WhoWor 74*

Marks, Charles
[Smith and Dale]
American. Actor, Comedian
b. 1882 in New York, New York
Source: *BioIn 8; What 2*

Marks, John D
American. Composer, Lyricist
b. Nov 10, 1909 in Mount Vernon, New York
Source: *AmSCAP 66; WhoAm 82*

Marks, Percy
American. Author
b. Sep 9, 1891 in Covelo, California
d. Dec 27, 1956
Source: *AmAu&B; AmNov; OxAmL; REnAL; TwCA, SUP; WhAm 3*

Markus, Robert
American. Journalist
b. Jan 30, 1934 in Chicago, Illinois
Source: *WhoAm 82; WhoMW 74*

Marlborough, John Churchill, Duke
English. General, Statesman
b. 1650 in Devonshire, England
d. Jun 16, 1722 in Windsor, England
Source: *Alli; NewC; REn*

Marlborough, Sarah (Jennings) Churchill, Duchess
English. Wife of John Churchill
b. 1660
d. 1744
Source: *Alli; InWom*

Marley, Bob (Robert Nesta)
[Bob Marley and the Wailers]
Jamaican. Reggae Musician
b. Feb 5, 1945 in Kingston, Jamaica
d. May 11, 1981 in Miami, Florida
Source: *Baker 78; BioIn 10, 11; NewYTBS 77, 81; RkOn 2; WhoRock 81*

Marley, John
American. Actor
b. Oct 17, 1916 in New York, New York
Source: *FilmgC; WhoAm 74; WhoHol A*

Marlowe, Christopher
English. Dramatist, Poet
Established blank verse in drama; wrote *Dr. Faustus,* 1604.
b. Feb 6, 1564 in Canterbury, England
d. May 30, 1593 in Deptford, England
Source: *Alli; AtlBL; BiD&SB; BrAu; CasWL; Chambr 1; ChPo, S1; CnE&AP; CnThe; CroE&S; CrtT 1; CyWA; DcEnA; DcEnL; DcEuL; DcLEL; EvLB; McGEWD; MouLC 1; NewC; OxEng; OxThe; Pen ENG; RComWL; REn; REnWD; WebE&AL*

Marlowe, Derek
English. Author
b. May 21, 1938 in London, England
Source: *ConAu 17R; IntAu&W 76; WrDr 76, 80*

Marlowe, Hugh
[Hugh Hipple]
American. Actor
b. Jan 30, 1914 in Philadelphia, Pennsylvania
d. May 2, 1982 in New York, New York
Source: *BiE&WWA; FilmgC; IntMPA 75, 77; MovMk; NewYTBS 82; NotNAT; WhoHol A; WhoThe 77*

Marlowe, Julia
[Sarah Frances Frost]
American. Actress
b. 1866 in Cumberland, England
d. Nov 12, 1950 in New York, New York
Source: *AmWom; DcAmB S4; FamA&A; InWom; NotAW; OxAmL; OxThe; PlP&P; REn; TwCBDA; WhAm 3; WhoStg 1906, 1908; WomWWA 14*

Marlowe, Marion
American. Singer, Actress
b. Mar 7, 1930 in Saint Louis, Missouri
Source: *BiE&WWA; InWom; WhoAm 74*

Marlowe, Sylvia
[Mrs. Leonid Berman]
American. Musician
b. Sep 26, 1908 in New York, New York
d. Dec 10, 1981 in New York, New York
Source: *InWom; WhoAm 74, 76, 78, 80, 82; WhoAmW 58, 61, 64, 66, 68, 70, 72, 74; WhoWor 74*

Marmontel, Jean Francois
French. Author, Dramatist, Librettist
b. Jul 11, 1723 in Bort, France
d. Dec 31, 1799 in Abloville, France
Source: *BbD; BiD&SB; CasWL; ChPo S1; DcEuL; EuAu; EvEuW; OxFr; OxThe; Pen EUR; REn*

Marot, Clement
Poet
b. 1496 in Cahors, France
d. Sep 10, 1544 in Turin, Italy
Source: *AtlBL; BiD&SB; CasWL; DcEuL; EuAu; EvEuW; NewC; OxEng; OxFr; Pen EUR; REn*

Marquand, John Phillips
American. Author
b. Nov 10, 1893 in Wilmington, Delaware
d. Jul 16, 1960 in Newburyport, Massachusetts
Source: *AmAu&B; AmNov; AmWr; CasWL; CnDAL; ConAu 85; ConLC 2, 10; CyWA; DcLEL; DrAF 76; EncMys; EncWL; EvLB; LongCTC; ModAL; OxAmL; Pen AM; RAdv 1; REn; REnAL; TwCA, SUP; TwCW; WebAB; WebE&AL; WhAm 4*

Marquand, "Rube" (Richard William)
American. Baseball Player
b. Oct 9, 1889 in Cleveland, Ohio
d. Jun 1, 1980 in Baltimore, Maryland
Source: *BaseEn; BioIn 3, 7, 8, 10; WhoProB 73*

Marquet, Albert
French. Artist
b. 1875 in Bordeaux, France
d. 1947 in Paris, France
Source: *McGDA*

Marquette, Jacques, Pere
French. Jesuit Missionary, Explorer
With Louis Jolliet, established existence of waterway from St. Lawrence to Gulf of Mexico.
b. Jun 1, 1637 in Laon, France
d. May 18, 1675 in Ludington, Michigan
Source: *AmBi; DcAmB; Drake; OxAmL; OxCan; REn; WebAB; WhAm H*

Marquis, Albert Nelson
American. Publisher
Founded *Who's Who in America,* 1899.
b. Jan 12, 1854 in Brown County, Ohio
d. Dec 21, 1943 in Evanston, Illinois
Source: *AmAu&B; CurBio 44; DcAmB S5; WhAm 2*

Marquis, Don Robert Perry
[Donald Robert Perry]
American. Journalist, Poet, Dramatist
b. Jul 29, 1878 in Walnut, Illinois
d. Dec 29, 1937 in Forest Hills, New York
Source: *AmAu&B; AmBi; AmLY; BiDSA; CnDAL; CnE&AP; ConAmA; ConAmL; DcAmB S2; DcNAA; LongCTC; ModAL; OxAmL; Pen AM; RAdv 1; REn; REnAL; Str&VC; TwCA, SUP; TwCW; WebAB; WhAm 1; WhNAA*

Marriner, Neville
English. Conductor
b. Apr 15, 1924 in Lincoln, England
Source: *IntWW 74; WhoAm 82; WhoMus 72; WhoWor 74*

Marriott, John Willard
American. Restaurant Executive
Founded Marriott Hotel and Restaurant chain, 1928.
b. Sep 17, 1900 in Marriott, Utah
Source: *Who 74; WhoAm 74, 76, 78, 80, 82*

Marriott, John Willard, Jr.
American. Restaurant Executive
Marriott Corp., chief executive 1972--.
b. Mar 25, 1932 in Washington, DC
Source: *WhoAm 74*

Marriott, Steve
see: Humble Pie

Marryat, Frederick
English. Author
b. Jul 10, 1792 in London, England
d. Aug 9, 1848 in Langham, England
Source: *Alli; ApCAB; AtlBL; BbD; BiD&SB; BrAu 19; CarSB; CasWL; Chambr 3; ChPo; CyWA; DcBiA; DcEnA; DcEnL; DcLEL; Drake; EvLB; HsB&A, SUP; NewC; OxAmL; OxCan; OxEng; Pen ENG; RAdv 1; REn; REnAL; WebE&AL; WhoChL*

Mars, Forrest E
Candy Manufacturer
Source: *BioIn 7*

Marsala, Joe
American. Musician
b. Jan 5, 1907 in Chicago, Illinois
Source: *AmSCAP 66; WhoJazz 72*

Marsala, Marty
American. Jazz Musician
b. Apr 2, 1909 in Chicago, Illinois
Source: *WhoJazz 72*

Marschner, Heinrich
German. Composer
b. Aug 16, 1795 in Zittau, Germany
d. Dec 14, 1861 in Hannover, Germany
Source: *NewEOp 71*

Marsh, Sir Edward
English. Secretary to Churchill
b. Nov 18, 1872
d. 1953
Source: *LongCTC; ModBrL; NewC; OxEng; Pen ENG; WhoLA*

Marsh, Graham B
Australian. Golfer
b. Jan 14, 1944 in Kalgeerlie, Australia
Source: *WhoGolf*

Marsh, Jean
[Jean Lyndsey Torren Marsh]
English. Actress
b. Jul 1, 1934 in London, England
Source: *BioNews 74; CurBio 77; NewYTBS 74; WhoAm 82; WhoHol A*

Marsh, Mae
American. Actress
b. Nov 19, 1895 in Madrid, New Mexico
d. Feb 13, 1968 in Hermosa Beach, California
Source: *BiDFilm; Film 1; FilmgC; MotPP; MovMk; OxFilm; ThFT; TwYS; WhAm 4A; WhScrn 74, 77; WhoHol B; WorEFlm*

Marsh, Dame Ngaio
New Zealander. Author, Theatrical Producer
b. Apr 23, 1899 in Christchurch, New Zealand
d. Feb 18, 1982 in Christchurch, New Zealand
Source: *Au&Wr 71; AuBYP; ConAu 6NR; ConNov 72, 76; CorpD; DcLEL; EncMys; EvLB; FarE&A 78, 79; InWom; IntAu&W 76; IntWW 74, 75, 76, 77, 78; LongCTC; NewC; NewYTBS 82; OxEng; REn; TwCA, SUP; TwCW; WhE&EA; Who 74; WhoAmW 70, 72, 75; WhoWor 74; WrDr 76, 80*

Marsh, Othniel Charles
American. Paleontologist
b. Oct 29, 1831 in Lockport, New York
d. Mar 18, 1899 in New Haven, Connecticut
Source: *AmBi; AsBiEn; DcAmB; DcRusL; EncAB-H; McGEWB; NatCAB; TwCBDA; WebAB; WhAm H*

Marsh, Reginald
American. Artist, Illustrator
b. Mar 14, 1898 in Paris, France
d. Jul 3, 1954 in Bennington, Vermont
Source: *CurBio 41, 54; DcAmB S5; DcCAA 71; IlsBYP; IlsCB 1946; WebAB; WhAm 3*

Marshack, Alexander
Ethnologist, Archeologist
b. 1918
Source: *BioIn 9*

Marshack, Megan
American. Reporter, Secretary
With Nelson Rockefeller at his death.
b. 1953 in Sherman Oaks, California
Source: *BioIn 11*

Marshal, Alan
Australian. Actor
b. Jan 29, 1909 in Sydney, Australia
d. Jul 9, 1961 in Chicago, Illinois
Source: *BioIn 5; FilmgC; MotPP; WhScrn 74, 77; WhoHol B*

Marshall, Brenda
American. Actress
b. 1915 in Philadelphia, Pennsylvania
Source: *FilmgC; MotPP; MovMk; WhoHol A*

Marshall, E G
American. Actor
b. Jun 18, 1910 in Owatonna, Minnesota
Source: *BiE&WWA; CelR 73; FilmgC; IntMPA 75, 76, 77, 78, 79, 80, 81, 82; MotPP; MovMk; NotNAT; PlP&P; WhoAm 74, 76, 78, 80, 82; WhoHol A; WhoThe 77*

Marshall, Esme
American. Model
b. 1961?
Source: *BioIn 12*

Marshall, Frank James
American. Chess Player
b. Aug 10, 1877 in New York, New York
d. Nov 9, 1944 in Jersey City, New Jersey
Source: *DcAmB S3; WhAm 2*

Marshall, Garry
American. TV Producer
b. Nov 13, 1934 in New York, New York
Source: *BioIn 11, 12; WhoAm 82*

Marshall, George Catlett
American. General, Secretary of State
b. Dec 31, 1880 in Uniontown, Pennsylvania
d. Oct 16, 1959 in Washington, DC
Source: *AmAu&B; BiDrUSE; CurBio 40, 47, 59; EncAB-H; REn; WebAB; WhAm 3*

Marshall, Herbert
American. Actor
b. May 23, 1890 in London, England
d. Jan 22, 1966 in Beverly Hills, California
Source: *BiDFilm; FilmgC; MotPP; MovMk; OxFilm; WhAm 4; WhScrn 74, 77; WhoHol B; WorEFlm*

Marshall, John
American. Supreme Court Justice
Fourth chief justice of Supreme Court, 1801-35.
b. Sep 24, 1755 in Germantown, Virginia
d. Jul 6, 1835 in Philadelphia, Pennsylvania
Source: *Alli; AmAu; AmAu&B; AmBi; ApCAB; BiD&SB; BiDLA; BiDSA; BiDrAC; BiDrUSE; CyAL 1; DcAmAu; DcAmB; DcNAA; Drake; EncAB-H; REn; REnAL; TwCBDA; WebAB; WhAm H; WhAmP*

Marshall, Laurence
American. Electronics Expert
b. 1889 in Medford, Massachusetts
d. Nov 5, 1980 in Cambridge, Massachusetts
Source: *BioIn 12; NewYTBS 80*

Marshall, Penny
American. Actress
Plays Laverne in TV series "Laverne and Shirley."
b. Oct 15, 1945 in New York, New York
Source: *BioIn 12; BkPepl; CurBio 80; IntMPA 82; WhoHol A*

Marshall, Peter
[Pierre LaCock]
American. TV Show Host, Actor
b. Mar 30, in Huntington, West Virginia
Source: *IntMPA 82; WhoHol A*

Marshall, Peter
American. Chaplain of the Senate
Senate chaplain, 1947-48; subject of *A Man Called Peter*, written by wife Catherine.
b. May 27, 1902 in Coatbridge, Scotland
d. Jan 25, 1949 in Washington, DC
Source: *CurBio 48, 49; WhAm 2*

Marshall, Ray
[F(reddie) Ray Marshall]
American. Government Official
Secretary of Labor, 1977-81.
b. Aug 22, 1928 in Oak Grove, Louisiana
Source: *AmEA 74; AmM&WS 73S, 78S; BioIn 11; CngDr 77, 79; ConAu 21R; CurBio 77; IntWW 77, 78; NewYTBS 76; WhoAm 78, 80, 82; WhoAmP 77, 79; WhoE 77; WhoF&I 79; WhoGov 77*

Marshall, Robert J
American. Clergyman
b. Aug 26, 1918 in Burlington, Iowa
Source: *BioIn 8, 10; WhoAm 78, 80, 82*

Marshall, S(amuel) L(yman) A(twood)
American. Journalist, General, Author
b. Jul 18, 1900 in Catskill, New York
d. Dec 17, 1977 in El Paso, Texas
Source: *AmAu&B; AuBYP; ConAu 73, 81; CurBio 53; SmATA 21; WhoAm 74; WorAu*

Marshall, (Sarah) Catherine
American. Author
b. Sep 27, 1914 in Johnson City, Tennessee
Source: *ConAu 17R; SmATA 2; WhoAm 82; WrDr 76*

Marshall, Thomas Riley
American. Vice-President
Vice-president, 1913-21; said "What this country needs is a good five-cent cigar."
b. Mar 14, 1854 in North Manchester, Indiana
d. Jun 1, 1925 in Washington, DC
Source: *AmAu&B; AmBi; BiDrAC; BiDrUSE; DcAmB; DcNAA; IndAu 1917; WebAB; WhAm 1; WhAmP*

Marshall, Thurgood
American. Supreme Court Justice
First black appointed to Supreme Court, 1967--.
b. Jul 2, 1908 in Baltimore, Maryland
Source: *CelR 73; CngDr 74; CurBio 54; DrAS 74P; EncAB-H; IntWW 74; WebAB; Who 74; WhoAm 74, 76, 78, 80, 82; WhoAmP 73; WhoBlA 75; WhoGov 72; WhoS&SW 73; WhoWor 74*

Marshall, Tully
American. Actor
b. Apr 13, 1864 in Nevada City, California
d. Mar 10, 1943 in Encino, California
Source: *CurBio 43; Film 1; FilmgC; MotPP; MovMk; TwYS; WhAm 2; WhScrn 74, 77; WhoHol B*

Marshall, William
American. Actor
b. Oct 12, 1917 in Chicago, Illinois
Source: *FilmgC; IntMPA 75, 76, 77, 78, 79, 80, 81, 82*

Marshall, William
American. Actor
b. Aug 19, 1924 in Gary, Indiana
Source: *BiE&WWA; DcBlPA; FilmEn; NotNAT A*

Marshall-Hall, Sir Edward
English. Lawyer
b. 1858
d. 1927
Source: *BioIn 2, 6, 7, 9*

Marshall Tucker Band, The
[Tommy Caldwell; Toy Caldwell; Jerry Eubanks; Doug Gray; George MCorkle; Paul Riddle]
American. Rock Group
Source: *RkOn*

Marston, John
English. Author
b. 1575 in Wardington, England
d. Jun 25, 1634 in London, England
Source: *Alli; AtlBL; BbD; BiD&SB; BrAu; CasWL; Chambr 1; ChPo; CnE&AP; CnThe; CroE&S; CrtT 1; CyWA; DcEnA; DcEnL; DcEuL; DcLEL; EvLB; McGEWD; MouLC 1; NewC; OxEng; OxThe; Pen ENG; REn; REnWD; WebE&AL*

Marston, William Moulton
[Charles Moulton]
American. Psychologist, Cartoonist
b. Mar 9, 1893 in Cliftondale, Massachusetts
d. Mar 2, 1947 in Rye, New York
Source: *DcNAA; WhAm 2; WhNAA*

Martel, Charles
see: Charles Martel

Martell, Vincent
[Vanilla Fudge]
American. Musician
Guitarist with group, 1967-72.
b. Nov 11, 1945 in Bronx, New York
Source: *EncPR&S; IlEncRk; LilREn 78*

Marterie, Ralph
Composer, Conductor
b. Dec 24, 1914 in Naples, Italy
Source: *AmSCAP 66*

Martha and the Vandellas
[Rosalind Ashford; Betty Kelly; Martha Reeves]
American. Vocal Group
Source: *EncPR&S*

Marti, Jose
Cuban. Patriot
b. Jan 28, 1853 in Havana, Cuba
d. May 19, 1895 in Dos Rios, Cuba
Source: *ApCAB SUP; CasWL; DcSpL; Pen AM; REn*

Martial
Roman. Poet
b. 43 in Bilbilis, Spain
d. 104 in Bilbilis, Spain
Source: *AtlBL; BbD; BiD&SB; CasWL; ChPo; CyWA; NewC; OxEng; Pen CL; RComWL; REn*

Martin, "Billy" (Alfred Manuel)
American. Baseball Player, Manager
Wrote *Number 1,* 1980.
b. May 16, 1928 in Berkeley, California
Source: *BaseEn; NewYTBE 72, 73; NewYTBS 74; WhoAm 76, 78, 80, 82; WhoProB 73*

Martin, David Stone
American. Illustrator
b. Jun 13, 1913 in Chicago, Illinois
Source: *IlsBYP; IlsCB 1946; WhoGrA*

Martin, Dean
[Dino Crocetti]
American. Singer, Actor
Teamed with Jerry Lewis in early career, 1948-57.
b. Jun 17, 1917 in Steubenville, Ohio
Source: *BiDFilm; BkPepl; CelR 73; CmMov; CurBio 64; FilmgC; IntMPA 75, 76, 77, 78, 79, 80, 81; MotPP; MovMk; OxFilm; WhoAm 74, 76, 78; WhoHol A; WhoWor 74; WorEFlm*

Martin, Dean Paul (Dino, Jr.)
American. Actor
b. Nov 17, 1953? in California
Source: *WhoHol A*

Martin, Dewey
see: Buffalo Springfield

Martin, Dick
[Rowan and Martin]
American. Comedian
Co-host of "Laugh-In," 1967-73.
b. Jan 30, 1923 in Battle Creek, Michigan
Source: *BioNews 74; CurBio 69; FilmgC; WhoAm 74; WhoHol A*

Martin, Fletcher
American. Artist
b. Apr 29, 1904 in Palisade, Colorado
d. May 30, 1979 in Guanajuato, Mexico
Source: *BioIn 1, 2, 3, 4, 5, 7, 11; CurBio 58, 79; DcCAA 71, 77; IlBEAAW; McGDA; NewYTBS 79; WhoAm 76, 78, 80*

Martin, Frank
Swiss. Composer
b. Sep 15, 1890 in Geneva, Switzerland
d. Nov 21, 1974 in Naarden, Netherlands
Source: *DcCM; IntWW 74; WhAm 6; Who 74; WhoMus 72*

Martin, Freddy
American. Band Leader
b. 1907 in Springfield, Ohio
Source: *WhoHol A*

Martin, Glenn Luther
American. Airplane Manufacturer
Made first over-water flight in US, 1912; constructed B-10 bombers, 1932.
b. Jan 17, 1886 in Macksburg, Iowa
d. Dec 4, 1955 in Baltimore, Maryland
Source: *CurBio 43, 56; DcAmB S5; WebAB; WhAm 3*

Martin, Graham Anderson
American. Diplomat
b. Sep 22, 1912 in Mars Hill, North Carolina
Source: *BioIn 9, 10, 11; WhoAm 78*

Martin, Harold Eugene
American. Newspaper Publisher
b. Oct 4, 1923 in Cullman, Alabama
Source: *WhoAm 74; WhoS&SW 73*

Martin, Harvey
American. Football Player
b. Nov 16, 1950 in Dallas, Texas
Source: *FootReg; WhoBlA 77*

Martin, Homer Dodge
American. Artist
b. Nov 28, 1836 in Albany, New York
d. Feb 12, 1897 in Saint Paul, Minnesota
Source: *AmBi; ApCAB; DcAmB; EarABI; OxAmL; TwCBDA; WebAB; WhAm H*

Martin, James Slattin, Jr.
American. Aeronautical Engineer
b. Jun 21, 1920 in Washington, DC
Source: *CurBio 77*

Martin, Jared
American. Actor
Played Dusty Farlow on "Dallas."
b. Dec 21, 1943 in New York, New York
Source: *WhoHol A*

Martin, Jennifer
American. TV Network Attorney
b. 1947 in Los Angeles, California
Source: *BioIn 12*

Martin, Joseph William, Jr.
American. Politician
b. Nov 3, 1884 in North Attleboro, Massachusetts
d. Mar 6, 1968 in Fort Lauderdale, Florida
Source: *BiDrAC; CurBio 40, 48, 68; WebAB; WhAm 4A; WhAmP*

Martin, Kiel
American. Actor
Plays detective J D LaRue on "Hill Street Blues," 1980--.
b. 1945? in Miami, Florida
Source: *WhoHol A*

Martin, Kingsley
English. Editor, Essayist
b. Jul 28, 1897 in Hertfordshire, England
d. Feb 16, 1969 in Cairo, Egypt
Source: *ConAu 5R, 25R; DcLEL; LongCTC; NewC*

Martin, Mary
American. Actress, Singer
Won Tonys for *Peter Pan,* 1954, *The Sound of Music,* 1959; mother of Larry Hagman.
b. Dec 1, 1914 in Weatherford, Texas
Source: *BiE&WWA; CelR 73; CurBio 44; EncMT; FamA&A; Film 1; FilmgC; InWom; IntMPA 75, 76, 77, 78, 79, 80, 81, 82; MotPP; MovMk; NewYTBE 71; NotNAT; OxFilm; PlP&P; WhoAm 74, 76, 78, 80, 82; WhoHol A; WhoMus 72; WhoThe 77; WhoWor 74*

Martin, Millicent
English. Singer, Actress
b. Jun 8, 1934 in Romford, England
Source: *EncMT; FilmEn; IntMPA 81; WhoThe 77, 81*

Martin, "Pepper" (John Leonard Roosevelt)
"The Wild Hoss of the Osage"
American. Baseball Player
Outfielder, third baseman, St. Louis Cardinals, 1928, 1930-40, 1944.
b. Feb 29, 1904 in Temple, Oklahoma
d. Mar 5, 1965 in McAlester, Oklahoma
Source: *BaseEn; BioIn 3, 6, 7; BioIn 8; WhoProB 73*

Martin, Pete (Thornton)
American. Journalist
b. 1901
d. Oct 13, 1980 in Birchrunville, Pennsylvania
Source: *BiE&WWA*

Martin, "Pit" (Hubert Jacques)
Canadian. Hockey Player, Aviator
b. Dec 9, 1943 in Rouyn Noranda, PQ
Source: *WhoHcky 73*

Martin, Quinn
American. TV Producer
b. May 22, 1922
Source: *NewYTET; WhoAm 82*

Martin, Riccardo
American. Opera Singer
b. Nov 18, 1874 in Hopkinsville, New York
d. Aug 11, 1952 in New York, New York
Source: *NewEOp 71*

Martin, Richard Lionel
Canadian. Hockey Player
b. Jul 26, 1951 in Montreal, PQ
Source: *WhoAm 74; WhoHcky 73*

Martin, Robert Bernard
American. Author, Educator
b. Sep 11, 1918 in LaHarpe, Illinois
Source: *Au&Wr 71; ChPo; ConAu 1R, 2NR; DrAS 74E; WrDr 76*

Martin, Ross
[Martin Rosenblatt]
American. Actor
Played Artemus Gordon on "The Wild, Wild West," 1965-69.
b. Mar 22, 1920 in Gradek, Poland
d. Jul 3, 1981 in Ramona, California
Source: *FilmgC; IntMPA 75, 76, 77, 78, 79; MotPP; WhoAm 74; WhoHol A*

Martin, Steve
American. Comedian, Actor
First gold album, *Let's Get Small;* wrote *Cruel Shoes,* 1980.
b. 1945 in Waco, Texas
Source: *BkPepl; CurBio 78; IntMPA 82; WhoAm 78, 80, 82*

Martin, Strother
American. Actor
b. Mar 26, 1919 in Kokomo, Indiana
d. Aug 1, 1980 in Thousand Oaks, California
Source: *CmMov; FilmgC; IntMPA 75, 77; WhoAm 74; WhoHol A*

Martin, Tony
American. Singer
b. Dec 25, 1913 in San Francisco, California
Source: *AmSCAP 66; FilmgC; IntMPA 75, 76, 77, 78, 79, 80, 81, 82; WhoAm 74, 76, 78, 80, 82*

Martin, William McChesney, Jr.
American. Broker, Government Official
b. Dec 17, 1906 in Saint Louis, Missouri
Source: *CurBio 51; IntWW 74; Who 74; WhoAm 74, 76, 78, 80, 82; WhoS&SW 73; WhoWor 74*

Martin du Gard, Roger
French. Author
b. Mar 23, 1881 in Paris, France
d. Aug 22, 1958 in Belleme, France
Source: *AtlBL; CasWL; ClDMEL; CnMWL; CyWA; EncWL; EvEuW; McGEWD; ModRL; OxEng; OxFr; Pen EUR; REn; TwCA, SUP; TwCW; WhAm 3; WhoTwCL*

Martin y Soler, Vicente
Spanish. Composer
b. Jan 18, 1754 in Valencia, Spain
d. Jan 30, 1806 in Saint Petersburg, Russia
Source: *NewEOp 71*

Martineau, Jean
Canadian. Conductor
b. Oct 6, 1895 in Montreal, PQ
d. 1976
Source: *CanWW 70; WhoCan 73*

Martinelli, Elsa
Italian. Actress
b. 1933 in Rome, Italy
Source: *FilmgC; MotPP; MovMk; WhoHol A; WorEFlm*

Martinelli, Giovanni
American. Opera Singer
b. Oct 22, 1885 in Montagnana, Italy
d. Feb 2, 1969 in New York, New York
Source: *CurBio 45, 69; WhAm 5*

Martinez, Eugenio R
American. Watergate Participant
b. 1922
Source: *BioIn 10*

Martini, Nino
American. Opera Singer
b. Aug 8, 1905 in Verona, Italy
Source: *FilmgC*

Martini, Simone
Italian. Artist
b. 1284? in Siena, Italy
d. 1344 in Avignon, Italy
Source: *AtlBL*

Martino, Al
[Alfred Cini]
American. Actor, Singer, Pianist
b. Nov 7, 1927 in Philadelphia, Pennsylvania
Source: *EncPR&S*

Martinon, Jean
French. Conductor, Composer
b. Jan 10, 1910 in Lyons, France
d. Mar 1, 1976 in Paris, France
Source: *DcCM; IntWW 74; WhAm 6; WhoAm 74; WhoMus 72; WhoWor 74*

Martins, Peter
Danish. Dancer, Choreographer
b. Oct 11, 1946 in Copenhagen, Denmark
Source: *BioIn 8, 10, 11; CurBio 78*

Martinson, Harry Edmund
Swedish. Poet
b. May 6, 1905 in Jamshog, Sweden
d. Feb 11, 1978 in Stockholm, Sweden
Source: *CasWL; ClDMEL; ConAu 77; ConLC 14; EncWL; EvEuW; Pen EUR; TwCW; WhoTwCL; WorAu*

Martinson, Joseph Bertram
Coffee Executive, Art Patron
b. 1911
d. 1970
Source: *BiE&WWA; BioIn 9; NewYTBE 70*

Martinu, Bohuslav
Czech. Composer
b. Dec 8, 1890 in Policka, Czechoslovakia
d. Aug 28, 1959 in Liestal, Switzerland
Source: *AtlBL; CurBio 44, 59; DcCM; WhAm 3*

Marty, Martin
Swiss. Missionary
b. Jan 12, 1834 in Schwyz, Switzerland
d. Sep 19, 1896 in Saint Cloud, Minnesota
Source: *ApCAB; DcAmB; DcNAA; NatCAB 12; WhAm H*

Marusia
Polish. Fashion Designer
Source: *InWom*

Marvell, Andrew
English. Author, Poet
b. Mar 31, 1621 in Winestead, England
d. Aug 18, 1678 in London, England
Source: *Alli; AtlBL; BbD; BiD&SB; BrAu; CanWr; Chambr 1; ChPo, S1, S2; CnE&AP; CroE&S; CrtT 1; CyWA; DcEnA; DcEnL; DcEuL; DcLEL; EvLB; MouLC 1; NewC; OxEng; Pen ENG; RAdv 1; REn; WebE&AL*

Marvin, Lee
American. Actor
Starred in *The Dirty Dozen;* victim of first "palimony" lawsuit.
b. Feb 19, 1924 in New York, New York
Source: *BiDFilm; BkPepl; CelR 73; CmMov; CurBio 66; FilmgC; IntMPA 75, 76, 77, 78, 79, 80, 81, 82; MotPP; MovMk; OxFilm; WhoAm 74, 76, 78, 80, 82; WhoHol A; WhoWor 74; WorEFlm*

Marvin, Michelle Triola
American. Actress, Singer
b. 1932?
Source: *BioIn 11, 12*

Marx, Anne Loewenstein
American. Poet
b. in Bleicherode, Germany
Source: *ConAu 29R; WhoAm 74, 76, 78, 80, 82*

Marx, Barbara
see: Sinatra, Barbara Marx

Marx, "Chico" (Leonard)
[The Marx Brothers]
American. Comedian
Known for outrageous puns, exaggerated accent.
b. Mar 22, 1891 in New York, New York
d. Oct 11, 1961 in Hollywood, California
Source: *CurBio 48, 61; DcFM; EncMT; FamA&A; MotPP; MovMk; OxFilm; WhScrn 74, 77; WhoHol B*

Marx, "Groucho" (Julius)
[The Marx Brothers]
American. Comedian
Famous for ad-lib insults; wrote autobiography *Groucho and Me,* 1959.
b. Oct 2, 1890 in New York, New York
d. Aug 19, 1977 in Los Angeles, California
Source: *BiE&WWA; BioNews 74; CelR 73; ConAu 73, 81; CurBio 48, 73; DcFM; EncMT; FamA&A; IntMPA 75, 77; IntWW 74; MotPP; MovMk; NewYTBE 70, 72; OxFilm; WebAB; WhoHol A; WhoWor 74*

Marx, "Gummo" (Milton)
[The Marx Brothers]
American. Talent Agent, Comedian
Left Marx Brothers early to become business manager for act.
b. 1894 in New York, New York
d. Apr 21, 1977 in Palm Springs, California
Source: *BiE&WWA; BioIn 11*

Marx, "Harpo" (Arthur)
[The Marx Brothers]
American. Comedian
Harp-playing, non-speaking member; autobiography *Harpo Speaks,* 1961.
b. Nov 23, 1893 in New York, New York
d. Sep 28, 1964 in Hollywood, California
Source: *AmSCAP 66; BiE&WWA; CurBio 48, 64; DcFM; EncMT; FamA&A; MotPP; MovMk; OxFilm; WhScrn 74, 77; WhoHol B*

Marx, Karl Heinrich
German. Social Philosopher, Economist
Theorist, modern Socialism, Communism; wrote *Communist Manifesto,* 1848.
b. May 5, 1818 in Treves, Germany
d. Mar 14, 1883 in London, England
Source: *BiD&SB; CasWL; CyWA; EuAu; LongCTC; OxEng; OxFr; OxGer; RComWL; REn; WhAm H*

Marx, Louis
American. Toy Manufacturer
b. 1896
d. Feb 5, 1982 in White Plains, New York
Source: *BioIn 1, 2, 3; NewYTBS 82*

Marx, "Zeppo" (Herbert)
[The Marx Brothers]
American. Comedian
Romantic straight man of act; later a successful agent.
b. Feb 25, 1901 in New York, New York
d. Nov 30, 1979 in Palm Springs, California
Source: *BiE&WWA; EncMT; FamA&A; MovMk; OxFilm; WhoHol A*

Marx Brothers, The
["Chico" (Leonard) Marx; "Groucho" (Julius) Marx; "Gummo" (Milton) Marx; "Harpo" (Arthur) Marx; "Zeppo" (Herbert) Marx]
American. Comedy Team
Starred in *Duck Soup,* 1933; *A Night at the Opera,* 1935.
Source: *MovMk; OxFilm; WorEFlm*

Mary Kay
see: Ash, May Kay Wagner

Mary
English. Queen Consort of George V
b. 1867
d. 1953
Source: *InWom; NewCol 75; WebBD 80*

Mary, Queen of Scots
[Mary Stuart]
Scottish. Monarch
Inherited Scottish throne at age of six days; beheaded by Elizabeth I.
b. Dec 1542 in Linlithgow, Scotland
d. Feb 8, 1587 in Fotheringay Castle, England
Source: *Alli; HerW; InWom; NewC; NewCol 75; OxFr; REn; WebBD 80*

Mary, the Virgin Mother
Mother of Jesus
Source: *BioIn 10; NewCol 75; WebBD 80*

Mary I
[Mary Tudor]
"Bloody Mary"
English. Queen
Daughter of Henry VIII and Katharine of Aragon; first English queen to rule in own right.
b. Feb 18, 1516 in Greenwich Palace, England
d. Nov 17, 1558
Source: *McGEWB; NewC; NewCol 75; REn; WebBD 80*

Mary Magdalene
Biblical Character, Saint
Source: *InWom*

Masaccio
[Tommaso di Giovanni di Simone Cassai]
Italian. Artist
b. Dec 21, 1401 in San Giovanni Valdarno, Italy
d. 1428 in Rome, Italy
Source: *AtlBL; BioIn 1, 2, 3, 4, 5, 7, 8, 11; McGDA; McGEWB; NewCol 75; REn*

Masaryk, Jan Garrigue
Czech. Statesman
b. Sep 14, 1886 in Prague, Czechoslovakia
d. Mar 10, 1948 in Prague, Czechoslovakia
Source: *CurBio 44, 48; WhAm 2*

Masaryk, Tomas Garrigue
Czech. Statesman, Philosopher
b. Mar 7, 1850 in Moravia, Czechoslovakia
d. Sep 14, 1937
Source: *CasWL; ClDMEL; EvEuW; Pen EUR; REn*

Mascagni, Pietro
Italian. Composer
b. Dec 7, 1863 in Leghorn, Italy
d. Aug 2, 1945 in Rome, Italy
Source: *AtlBL; CurBio 45; REn*

Masconi, Willie
American. Billiards Player
b. 1913
Source: *BioIn 10*

Masefield, John
English. Poet, Dramatist, Author
Poet laureate of England, 1930-67.
b. Jun 1, 1878 in Ledbury, England
d. May 12, 1967 in Berkshire, England
Source: *AnCL; AuBYP; Br&AmS; CasWL; Chambr 3; ChPo, S1, S2; CnE&AP; CnMD; CnMWL; ConAu 21R, 25R; ConAu P-2; ConLC 11; DcLEL; EncWL; EvLB; LongCTC; McGEWD; MnBBF; ModBrL, SUP; ModWD; NewC; OxEng; OxThe; Pen ENG; RAdv 1; REn; Str&VC; TwCA, SUP; TwCW; WebE&AL; WhAm 4; WhoChL; WhoTwCL*

Masekela, Hugh Ramapolo
American. Musician
b. Apr 4, 1939 in Witbank, South Africa
Source: *DcBlPA; RkOn 2*

Maserati, Ernesto
Italian. Auto Racer, Industrialist
b. 1898
d. Nov 24, 1975 in Bologna, Italy
Source: *BioIn 10*

Masiello, Alberta
Singer, Music Coach
Source: *BioIn 9, 10*

Masina, Giuletta
Italian. Actress
b. Mar 22, 1921 in Bologna, Italy
Source: *BioIn 4, 5, 7, 11*

Maskelyne, John Nevill
English. Spiritualist
b. 1839
d. 1917
Source: *BioIn 8; NewCol 75; WebBD 80*

Maslow, Abraham
American. Psychologist
b. Apr 1, 1908 in Brooklyn, New York
d. Jun 8, 1970 in Menlo Park, California
Source: *AmAu&B; ConAu 1R, 29R, 4NR; WhAm 5*

Mason, Charles
English. Surveyor, Astronomer
With Jeremiah Dixon, surveyed boundary between PA and MD known as Mason-Dixon Line, 1768.
b. 1730? in England
d. Feb 1787 in Philadelphia, Pennsylvania
Source: *Alli; ApCAB; Drake; NatCAB 10; WebAB; WebBD 80*

Mason, Daniel Gregory
American. Composer, Author
b. Nov 20, 1873 in Brookline, Massachusetts
d. Dec 4, 1953
Source: *AmAu&B; AmSCAP 66; DcAmB S5; OxAmL; REnAL; WhAm 3; WhNAA*

Mason, Dave
[Traffic]
English. Rock Musician
b. May 10, 1946 in Worcester, England
Source: *EncPR&S; IlEncRk; RkOn*

Mason, Francis van Wyck
American. Children's Author
b. Nov 11, 1901 in Boston, Massachusetts
d. Aug 28, 1978 in Bermuda
Source: *ConAu 5R, 81; EncMys; SmATA 3; WhoAm 74*

Mason, George
American. Colonial Leader
b. 1725 in Fairfax County, Virginia
d. Oct 7, 1792 in Gunston Hall, Virginia
Source: *AmBi; ApCAB; BiAuS; BiDSA; BioIn 3, 5, 6, 7, 8, 9, 10, 11; DcAmB; Drake; EncAAH; McGEWB; NatCAB 3; NewCol 75; REnAL; TwCBDA; WebAB; WhAm H*

Mason, Jackie
American. Comedian
b. 1931 in Sheboygan, Wisconsin
Source: *BioIn 10*

Mason, James
English. Actor
Starred in *A Star is Born,* 1955; wrote *Before I Forget,* 1981.
b. May 15, 1909 in Huddersfield, England
Source: *BiDFilm; CelR 73; CmMov; FilmgC; IntMPA 75, 76, 77, 78, 79, 80, 81, 82; MovMk; OxFilm; Who 74; WhoAm 74, 76, 78, 80, 82; WhoHol A; WhoThe 77; WhoWor 74; WorEFlm*

Mason, John Brown
American. Author, Educator
b. Jul 13, 1904 in Berlin, Germany
Source: *AmM&WS 73S; ConAu 49; WhoAm 74*

Mason, John L
American. Inventor
Patented Mason Jar, 1858, used in home canning.
Source: *NF*

Mason, Lowell
American. Composer, Clergyman
b. Jan 8, 1792 in Medfield, Massachusetts
d. Aug 11, 1872 in Orange, New Jersey
Source: *AmBi; ApCAB; BiDAmEd; BioIn 1, 4, 9, 11; DcAmB; Drake; McGEWB; NatCAB 7; TwCBDA; WebAB; WhAm H*

Mason, Marsha
[Mrs. Neil Simon]
American. Actress
Starred in *The Goodbye Girl,* 1977; *Chapter Two,* 1979.
b. Apr 3, 1942 in Saint Louis, Missouri
Source: *CurBio 81; IntMPA 75, 76, 77, 78, 79, 80, 81, 82; MovMk; NotNAT; WhoAm 82; WhoHol A*

Mason, Pamela Helen
English. Actress
b. Mar 10, 1922 in London, England
Source: *IntMPA 75, 76, 77, 78, 79, 80, 81, 82; WhoAm 74, 76, 78, 80, 82; WhoHol A*

Masse, Laurel
see: Manhattan Transfer

Masse, Victor
[Felix-Marie Masse]
French. Composer
b. Mar 7, 1822 in Lorient, France
d. Jul 5, 1884 in Paris, France
Source: *NewEOp 71; OxMus*

Masselos, William
American. Concert Pianist
b. 1920 in Niagara Falls, New York
Source: *CelR 73; NewYTBE 71*

Massenet, Jules Emile Frederic
French. Composer
b. May 12, 1842 in Montaud, France
d. Aug 13, 1912 in Paris, France
Source: *AtlBL; NewCol 75; OxFr; REn; WebBD 80*

Masserman, Jules H(oman)
American. Psychiatrist
b. Mar 10, 1905 in Chudnov, Poland
Source: *ConAu 69; CurBio 80; WhoAm 80, 82*

Massey, D Curtis
American. Singer, Composer, Musician
b. May 3, 1910 in Midland, Texas
Source: *AmSCAP 66*

Massey, Anna
English. Actress
b. Aug 11, 1937 in Thakeham, England
Source: *BiE&WWA; FilmgC; WhoHol A; WhoThe 77*

Massey, Daniel Raymond
English. Actor
b. Oct 10, 1933 in London, England
Source: *BiE&WWA; FilmgC; IntMPA 75, 76, 77; NotNAT; WhoHol A; WhoThe 77*

Massey, Gerald
British. Author
b. May 29, 1828 in Tring, England
d. Oct 12, 1907
Source: *Alli, SUP; BbD; BiD&SB; BrAu 19; Chambr 3; ChPo, S1, S2; DcEnA; DcEnL; DcEuL; DcLEL; EvLB; NewC; REn; WebE&AL*

Massey, Ilona
[Ilona Hajmassy]
American. Actress
b. 1912 in Budapest, Hungary
d. Aug 10, 1974 in Bethesda, Maryland
Source: *FilmgC; InWom; MotPP; MovMk; NewYTBS 74; ThFT; WhScrn 77; WhoHol B*

Massey, James Carlton
American. Architectural Historian
b. Apr 8, 1932 in San Gabriel, California
Source: *WhoS&SW 73*

Massey, Raymond Hart
American. Actor, Producer
Starred in *The Scarlet Pimpernel,* 1934; *How the West Was Won,* 1962.
b. Aug 30, 1896 in Toronto, ON
Source: *BiDFilm; CmMov; ConAu 104; CurBio 46; FamA&A; FilmgC; IntMPA 75, 76, 77, 78, 79, 80, 81, 82; MotPP; MovMk; NotNAT; OxFilm; PlP&P; Who 74; WhoAm 74, 76, 78, 80, 82; WhoThe 77; WhoWor 74; WhoWorJ 72*

Massey, Vincent
Canadian. Diplomat
b. Feb 20, 1887 in Toronto, ON
d. Dec 30, 1967 in London, England
Source: *CanWr; CurBio 51, 68; OxCan; WhAm 4*

Massi, Nick
[Nicholas Macioci; The Four Seasons]
American. Singer, Musician
b. Sep 19, 1935 in Newark, New Jersey
Source: *EncPR&S; LilREn 78; RkOn*

Massine, Leonide Fedorovich
American. Choreographer, Dancer
b. Aug 9, 1896 in Moscow, Russia
d. Mar 16, 1979 in Cologne, Germany (West)
Source: *BioNews 75; ConAu 85, 97; CurBio 40; IntWW 74; NewCol 75; WebBD 80; Who 74; WhoWor 74*

Massinger, Philip
English. Author
b. 1583 in Salisbury, England
d. Mar 1640 in London, England
Source: *Alli; AtlBL; BbD; BiD&SB; BrAu; CasWL; Chambr 1; CnThe; CroE&S; CrtT 1; CyWA; DcEnA; DcEnL; DcEuL; DcLEL; EvLB; McGEWD; MouLC 1; NewC; OxEng; OxThe; Pen ENG; REn; REnWD; WebE&AL*

Massys, Quentin
Flemish. Artist
b. 1466? in Louvain, Belgium
d. 1530
Source: *AtlBL; McGEWB; NewCol 75; WebBD 80*

Masters, Edgar Lee
American. Poet, Dramatist
Wrote *Spoon River Anthology,* 1915.
b. Aug 23, 1869 in Garnett, Kansas
d. Mar 5, 1950 in Philadelphia, Pennsylvania
Source: *AmAu&B; AmLY; AtlBL; CasWL; Chambr 3; ChPo, S1, S2; CnDAL; CnE&AP; CnMWL; ConAmA; ConAmL; CyWA; DcAmB S4; DcLEL; EncWL; EvLB; LongCTC; ModAL; OxAmL; OxEng; Pen AM; RAdv 1; REn; REnAL; SixAP; TwCA, SUP; TwCW; WebAB; WebE&AL; WhAm 2; WhoTwCL*

Masters, John
English. Author
b. Oct 26, 1914 in Calcutta, India
Source: *Au&Wr 71; ConNov 72, 76; LongCTC; ModBrL; REn; TwCA SUP; TwCW; Who 74; WhoAm 82; WhoWor 74; WrDr 76*

Masters, Kelly R
[Zachary Ball, pseud.]
American. Author
b. Jun 16, 1897 in Millgrove, Missouri
Source: *Au&Wr 71; AuBYP; ConAu 1R; CurBio 53; SmATA 3*

Masters, William Howell
[Masters and Johnson]
American. Physician, Sexologist
Author with wife, Virginia Johnson, *Human Sexual Response,* 1966.
b. Dec 27, 1915 in Cleveland, Ohio
Source: *AmM&WS 73P; AuNews 1; BioNews 74; CelR 73; ConAu 21R; CurBio 68; EncAB-H; NewYTBE 70; WhoAm 74, 76, 78, 80, 82; WhoWor 74*

Masters and Johnson
see: Johnson, Virginia E; Masters, William Howell

Masterson, "Bat" (William Barclay)
American. Sheriff, Sportswriter
Marshal of Dodge City, KS; friend of Wyatt Earp.
b. Nov 24, 1853 in Iroquois County, Illinois
d. Oct 25, 1921 in New York, New York
Source: *DcAmB; WebAB; WebBD 80; WhAm HA, 4*

Masterson, Ed
American. Marshal
d. 1878
Source: *BioIn 10*

Masterton, Bill (William)
Canadian. Hockey Player
First player in NHL to die from injuries suffered in game.
b. Aug 16, 1938 in Winnipeg, MB
d. Jan 15, 1968 in Minneapolis, Minnesota
Source: *WhoHcky 73*

Mastrianni, Vic
see: Amboy Dukes, The

Mastroianni, Marcello
Italian. Actor
b. Sep 28, 1924 in Fontana Liri, Italy
Source: *BiDFilm; BkPepl; CelR 73; CurBio 63; FilmgC; IntMPA 75, 76, 77, 78, 79, 80, 81, 82; IntWW 74; MotPP; MovMk; NewYTBE 70; OxFilm; WhoHol A; WorEFlm*

Masur, Harold Q
[Guy Fleming; Edward James, pseuds.]
American. Author
b. Jan 29, 1909 in New York, New York
Source: *ConAu 77; EncMys*

Masur, Kurt
German. Conductor
b. Jul 18, 1927 in Brieg, Germany
Source: *WhoSocC 78*

Mata Hari
[Margaretha Geertruida Macleod]
Dutch. Dancer, Spy
Executed by Germans during WW I for being a double agent.
b. Aug 7, 1876 in Leeuwarden, Netherlands
d. Oct 15, 1917 in Vincennes, France
Source: *BioIn 1, 2, 4, 6, 7, 8, 9, 10, 11; LookW; NewCol 75; WebBD 80*

Materna, Amalia
Austrian. Opera Singer
b. Jul 10, 1844 in Saint Georgen, Austria
d. Jan 18, 1918 in Vienna, Austria
Source: *NewEOp 71*

Mather, Cotton
American. Clergyman, Author
Writings contributed to hysteria of Salem witchcraft trails, 1692.
b. Feb 12, 1663 in Boston, Massachusetts
d. Feb 13, 1728 in Boston, Massachusetts
Source: *Alli; AmAu; AmAu&B; AmBi; ApCAB; AtlBL; BbD; BiD&SB; CasWL; Chambr 3; ChPo; CnDAL; CyAL 1; CyWA; DcAmAu; DcLEL; DcNAA; Drake; EncAB-H; EvLB; MouLC 2; OxAmL; OxEng; Pen AM; REn; REnAL; TwCBDA; WebAB; WebE&AL; WhAm H*

Mather, Increase
American. Clergyman
b. Jun 21, 1639 in Dorchester, Massachusetts
d. Aug 23, 1723 in Boston, Massachusetts
Source: *Alli; AmAu; AmAu&B; AmBi; ApCAB; BbD; BiD&SB; CasWL; Chambr 3; CnDAL; CyAL 1; DcAmAu; DcAmB; DcLEL; DcNAA; Drake; EncAB-H; OxAmL; Pen AM; REn; REnAL; TwCBDA; WebAB; WhAm H*

Mather, Stephen Tyng
American. Conservationist
b. Jul 4, 1867 in San Francisco, California
d. Jan 22, 1930 in Brookline, Massachusetts
Source: *DcAmB; WebAB; WebBD 80; WhAm 1*

Mathers, Jerry
American. Actor, Businessman
Played the Beaver on TV series "Leave it to Beaver," 1957-63.
b. Jun 2, 1948 in Sioux City, Iowa
Source: *BioIn 4, 10; What 4*

Matheson, Murray
Australian. Actor
b. Jul 1, 1912 in Casterton, Australia
Source: *BiE&WWA; FilmgC; NotNAT; WhoAm 74; WhoHol A*

Matheson, Richard Burton
American. Author
b. Feb 20, 1926 in Allendale, New Jersey
Source: *CmMov; ConAu 97; ConSFA; EncSF; FanAl; FilmgC; NewYTET; ScF&FL 1, 2; WhoHrs 80; WhoSciF; WorEFlm*

Matheson, Scott Milne
American. Governor of Utah
b. Jan 9, 1929 in Chicago, Illinois
Source: *WhoAm 78, 80, 82*

Matheson, Tim
American. Actor
b. Dec 31, 1948? in Los Angeles, California
Source: *BioIn 11*

Mathews, Eddie (Edwin Lee, Jr.)
American. Baseball Player
Hit over 30 home runs 10 consecutive years, 1952-62; Hall of Fame, 1978.
b. Oct 13, 1931 in Texarkana, Texas
Source: *BaseEn; WhoAm 78; WhoProB 73*

Mathews, Forrest David
American. Former Cabinet Member
b. Dec 6, 1935 in Grove Hill, Alabama
Source: *LEduc 74; WhoAm 74; WhoS&SW 73*

Mathewson, Christy (Christopher)
"Big Six"
American. Baseball Player
Had 373 career wins; one of first players elected to Hall of Fame, 1936.
b. Aug 12, 1880 in Factoryville, Pennsylvania
d. Oct 7, 1925 in Saranac Lake, New York
Source: *BaseEn; DcAmB; DcNAA; WebAB; WhAm 4; WhScrn 77; WhoProB 73*

Mathias, Bob (Robert Bruce)
American. Track Athlete, Congressman
Won gold medal in decathlon, 1948, 1952 Olympics.
b. Nov 17, 1930 in Tulare, California
Source: *BiDrAC; CurBio 52; NewYTBE 73; WebAB; WhoAm 74; WhoAmP 73; WhoGov 72; WhoTr&F 73*

Mathias, Charles McCurdy, Jr.
American. Senator
b. Jul 24, 1922 in Frederick, Maryland
Source: *BiDrAC; CngDr 74; CurBio 72; IntWW 74; WhoAm 74, 76, 78, 80, 82; WhoAmP 73; WhoE 74; WhoGov 72*

Mathieson, Muir
Scottish. Conductor
b. Jan 24, 1911 in Stirling, Scotland
d. Aug 2, 1975 in Oxford, England
Source: *FilmgC; IntMPA 75; WhScrn 77; WhoMus 72*

Mathis, Buster
American. Boxer
b. 1944?
Source: *BioIn 7, 8, 9; NewYTBE 71*

Mathis, Johnny (John Royce)
American. Singer
Has recorded 76 albums; "Too Much Too Little Too Late" first number one song.
b. Sep 30, 1935 in San Francisco, California
Source: *BioNews 75; BkPepl; CelR 73; CurBio 65; WhoAm 82; WhoWor 74*

Mathison, Richard Randolph
American. Journalist, Author
b. Oct 20, 1919 in Boise, Idaho
Source: *ConAu 1R, 3NR*

Matisse, Henri
French. Artist, Author
b. Dec 31, 1869 in Le Cateau, France
d. Nov 3, 1954 in Nice, France
Source: *AtlBL; CurBio 43, 53, 55; OxFr; REn; WhAm 3, 4*

Matlack, Jon(athan Trumpbour)
American. Baseball Player
b. Jan 19, 1950 in West Chester, Pennsylvania
Source: *BaseEn; NewYTBE 73; WhoProB 73*

Matlock, "Matty" (Julian Clifton)
American. Musician
b. Apr 27, 1909 in Paducah, Kentucky
Source: *AmSCAP 66; WhoJazz 72*

Matson, Oliver G
American. Football Player
b. May 1, 1930 in Trinity, Texas
Source: *WhoFtbl 74*

Matsunaga, Spark Masayuki
American. Senator
b. Oct 8, 1916 in Kauai Island, Hawaii
Source: *WhoAm 78, 80, 82*

Matsushita, Konosuke
Japanese. Industrialist
b. Nov 27, 1894 in Wasa Village, Japan
Source: *IntWW 74; WhoF&I 74; WhoWor 74*

Matta, Roberto Sebastian Antonio Echaurren
Chilean. Artist
b. Nov 11, 1911 in Santiago, Chile
Source: *ConArt; McGDA*

Matteotti, Giacomo
Italian. Socialist Leader
b. 1885 in Fratta Polesine, Italy
d. 1924
Source: *BioIn 2, 6; NewCol 75; WhoModH*

Matteson, Tompkins Harrison
American. Artist
b. May 9, 1813 in Peterboro, New York
d. Feb 2, 1884 in Sherburne, Nevada
Source: *AmBi; ApCAB; DcAmB; Drake; EarABI, SUP; TwCBDA; WhAm H*

Matthau, Walter
American. Actor
Appeared on stage, screen as Oscar Madison in *The Odd Couple.*
b. Nov 1, 1920 in New York, New York
Source: *BiDFilm; BiE&WWA; BioNews 74; BkPepl; CelR 73; CmMov; CurBio 66; FilmgC; IntMPA 75, 76, 77, 78, 79, 80, 81, 82; MotPP; MovMk; NewYTBE 71; NewYTBS 74; NotNAT; OxFilm; WhoAm 74, 76, 78, 80, 82; WhoHol A; WhoThe 77; WhoWor 74; WorEFlm*

Matthes, Roland
German. Swimmer
Won two gold medals, 1968, 1972 Olympics.
b. Nov 17, 1950 in Possneck, Germany (East)
Source: *NF*

Matthew, Saint
Biblical Character
Source: *NewCol 75; REn; WebBD 80*

Matthews, Denis
English. Conductor
b. Feb 27, 1919 in Coventry, England
Source: *IntWW 74; Who 74; WhoMus 72; WhoWor 74*

Matthews, Doris Boozer
American. President of WCTU
b. Aug 18, 1932 in Lexington, South Carolina
Source: *WhoAmW 77; WhoS&SW 73*

Matthias, Corvinus
Hungarian. King
b. 1443
d. 1490
Source: *NewCol 75; WebBD 80*

Matthias, Joseph ben
see: Josephus, Flavius

Matthiessen, Francis Otto
American. Author, Educator
b. Feb 19, 1902 in Pasadena, California
d. Apr 1, 1950
Source: *AmAu&B; CasWL; ChPo S2; DcAmB S4; EvLB; LongCTC; ModAL; OxAmL; Pen AM; REn; REnAL; TwCA, SUP; WhAm 3*

Mattingly, Mack Francis
American. Senator
b. Jan 7, 1931 in Anderson, Indiana
Source: *WhoAm 82; WhoAmP 75, 77, 79*

Mature, Victor
American. Actor
b. Jan 29, 1916 in Louisville, Kentucky
Source: *BiDFilm; CmMov; CurBio 51; FilmgC; IntMPA 75, 76, 77, 78, 79, 80, 81, 82; MotPP; MovMk; NewYTBE 71; OxFilm; WhoHol A; WorEFlm*

Mattus, Reuben
Polish. Created Haagen-Dazs Ice Cream
b. 1914? in Poland
Source: *BioIn 12*

Matuszak, John
American. Football Player
b. Oct 25, 1950 in Oak Creek, Wisconsin
Source: *NewYTBE 73; WhoFtbl 74*

Matzeliger, Jan Ernest
American. Inventor
Patented machine that could make a shoe in one minute, 1883.
b. 1852 in Surinam
d. 1889 in Lynn, Massachusetts
Source: *DcAmB; WebAB*

Matzenauer, Margaret
Hungarian. Opera Singer
b. Jun 1, 1881 in Temesvar, Hungary
d. May 19, 1963 in Van Nuys, California
Source: *BiDAmM; NewEOp 71; WebBD 80*

Mauch, Gene William
"Skip"
American. Baseball Player, Manager
b. Nov 18, 1925 in Salina, Kansas
Source: *BaseEn; CurBio 74; WhoAm 82; WhoProB 73*

Maude, Cyril
American. Actor
b. Apr 24, 1882 in London, England
d. Feb 20, 1951 in Torquay, England
Source: *Film 1; OxThe; REn; TwYS; WhAm 3; WhScrn 74, 77; WhoHol B*

Maugham, Robin (Robert Cecil Romer)
English. Author
b. May 17, 1916 in London, England
d. Mar 13, 1981 in Brighton, England
Source: *ConAu 9R, 103; ConNov 72, 76; NewC; REn; WorAu 1970*

Maugham, William Somerset
English. Author, Dramatist
Wrote *Of Human Bondage,* 1915; *The Razor's Edge,* 1944.
b. Jan 25, 1874 in Paris, France
d. Dec 16, 1965 in Nice, France
Source: *AtlBL; CasWL; Chambr 3; CnMD; CnMWL; CnThe; ConAu 5R, 25R; ConLC 1, 11, 15; CyWA; DcBiA; DcLEL; EncMys; EncWL; EvLB; LongCTC; McGEWD; ModBrL, SUP; ModWD; NewC; OxEng; OxThe; Pen ENG; RAdv 1; REn; REnWD; TwCA, SUP; TwCW; WebE&AL; WhoTwCL*

Mauldin, Bill (William Henry)
American. Cartoonist
b. Oct 29, 1921 in Mountain Park, New Mexico
Source: *AmAu&B; CelR 73; CurBio 45, 64; OxAmL; REnAL; TwCA SUP; WebAB; WhoAm 82; WhoAmA 73; WhoHol A; WhoMW 74*

Maupassant, (Henri Rene Albert) Guy de
French. Author
Wrote *Pierre et Jean,* 1888.
b. Aug 5, 1850 in Normandy, France
d. Jul 6, 1893 in Paris, France
Source: *AtlBL; BiD&SB; ClDMEL; CyWA; DcEuL; EuAu; NewC; OxEng; OxFr; Pen EUR; RComWL; REn*

Maurel, Victor
French. Opera Singer
b. Jun 17, 1848 in Marseilles, France
d. Oct 22, 1923 in New York, New York
Source: *BiDAmM; NewEOp 71*

Maurer, Alfred Henry
American. Artist
b. 1868 in New York, New York
d. 1932
Source: *BnEnAmA; NatCAB 25; NewCol 75*

Maurer, Ion Gheorghe
Romanian. Diplomat
b. Sep 23, 1902 in Bucharest, Romania
Source: *CurBio 71; IntWW 74; WhoWor 74*

Mauriac, Francois
French. Author
b. Oct 11, 1885 in Bordeaux, France
d. Sep 1, 1970 in Paris, France
Source: *AtlBL; CasWL; CathA 1930; ClDMEL; CnMD; CnMWL; ConAu 25R; ConAu P-2; ConLC 4, 9; CyWA; EncWL; EvEuW; LongCTC; McGEWD; ModRL; ModWD; OxEng; OxFr; Pen EUR; RComWL; REn; REnWD; TwCA, SUP; TwCW; WhAm 5; WhoTwCL*

Maurice, Frederick Denison
English. Theologian, Educator
b. Aug 29, 1805 in Lowestoft, England
d. Apr 1, 1872
Source: *Alli; BiD&SB; BrAu 19; CasWL; Chambr 3; DcEnL; DcEuL; EvLB; NewC; Pen ENG; REn*

Maurois, Andre
[Emile Salomon Herzog]
French. Author
Wrote biographies of Shelley, Byron, Disraeli, Washington, etc.
b. Jul 26, 1885 in Elbeuf, France
d. Oct 9, 1967 in Paris, France
Source: *AtlBL; CasWL; ClDMEL; ConAu 21R, 25R; ConAu P-2; EncWL; EvEuW; LongCTC; NewC; OxEng; OxFr; Pen EUR; RAdv 1; REn; TwCA, SUP; TwCW; WhAm 4; WhoLA; WhoTwCL*

Maury, Matthew Fontaine
American. Oceanographer
b. Jan 14, 1806 in Fredericksburg, Virginia
d. Feb 1, 1873 in Lexington, Virginia
Source: *Alli, SUP; AmAu&B; AmBi; ApCAB; BbD; BiAuS; BiD&SB; BiDConf; CyAl 2; DcAmAu; DcAmB; DcNAA; EncAB-H; REnAL; TwCBDA; WebAB; WhAm H*

Maury, Reuben
American. Newspaper Editor
b. Sep 2, 1899 in Butte, Montana
d. Apr 23, 1981 in Norwalk, Connecticut
Source: *BioIn 1, 9; ConAu 103; WhoAm 80*

Mausolus
Persian. King of Caria
d. 353BC
Source: *NewCol 75; WebBD 80*

Maverick, Maury
American. Lawyer, Congressman
b. Oct 23, 1895 in San Antonio, Texas
d. Jun 7, 1954 in San Antonio, Texas
Source: *CurBio 44, 54; DcAmB S5; WhAm 3*

Maverick, Samuel Augustus
American. Cattle Rancher
b. Jul 25, 1803 in Pendleton, South Carolina
d. Sep 2, 1870 in San Antonio, Texas
Source: *BioIn 6; NatCAB 6; TwCBDA; WebAB*

Mavor, Osborne Henry
see: Bridie, James, pseud.

Mawson, Sir Douglas
Australian. Geologist, Explorer
Claimed over two million square miles of Antarctic territory for Australia, 1907-31.
b. May 5, 1882 in Bradford, England
d. Oct 14, 1958 in Adelaide, Australia
Source: *NewCol 75; WebBD 80*

Max, Peter
American. Artist, Designer
b. Oct 19, 1937 in Berlin, Germany
Source: *AmEA 74; BioNews 74; CurBio 71; IlsBYP; WhoAm 74, 76, 78, 80, 82; WhoAmA 73; WhoS&SW 73*

Maxim, Sir Hiram Stevens
English. Inventor
Invented Maxim recoil-operated machine gun.
b. Feb 5, 1840 in Sangerville, Maine
d. Nov 24, 1916 in Streatham, England
Source: *AmBi; ApCAB SUP; DcAmB; TwCBDA; WebAB; WhAm 1*

Maximilian
[Ferdinand Maximilian Joseph]
Austrian. Emperor of Mexico
b. Jul 6, 1832 in Vienna, Austria
d. Jun 19, 1867 in Queretaro, Mexico
Source: *ApCAB; BioIn 1, 2, 4, 5, 6, 7, 8, 9, 10; REn; WebBD 80; WhAm H*

Maximilian I
Holy Roman Emperor
b. 1459
d. 1519
Source: *BioIn 3, 5, 6, 7, 10, 11; NewCol 75; WebBD 80*

Maximilian II
Holy Roman Emperor
b. 1527
d. 1576
Source: *BioIn 6, 8, 10; NewCol 75; WebBD 80*

Maxon, Lou Russell
American. Advertising Executive
b. Jul 28, 1900 in Marietta, Ohio
d. May 15, 1971
Source: *CurBio 43, 71; NewYTBE 71; St&PR 75; WhAm 5*

Maxwell, Elsa
American. Hostess, Journalist
b. May 24, 1883 in Keokuk, Iowa
d. Nov 1, 1963 in New York, New York
Source: *AmSCAP 66; CurBio 43, 64; FilmgC; InWom; WebAB; WhAm 4; WhScrn 77; WhoHol B*

Maxtone Graham, Joyce
see: Struther, Jan, pseud.

Maxwell, James Clerk
Scottish. Mathematician, Physicist
b. Nov 13, 1831 in Edinburgh, Scotland
d. Nov 5, 1879 in Cambridge, England
Source: *Alli SUP; BrAu 19; Chambr 3; ChPo S1; NewC; OxEng*

Maxwell, Marilyn
American. Actress
b. Aug 3, 1921 in Clarinda, Iowa
d. Mar 20, 1972 in Beverly Hills, California
Source: *FilmgC; InWom; MotPP; MovMk; NewYTBE 72; WhScrn 77; WhoHol B*

Maxwell, Vera Huppe
American. Costume Designer
b. Apr 22, 1903 in New York, New York
Source: *BioIn 1, 10; CurBio 77; WhoAm 82; WhoFash*

Maxwell, William
American. Author, Editor
b. Aug 16, 1908 in Lincoln, Illinois
Source: *AmAu&B; AmNov; AuBYP; ConAu 93; ConNov 76; OxAmL; REn; TwCA SUP; WhoAm 74, 76, 78, 80, 82; WhoWor 74; WrDr 76*

May, Billy (E William)
American. Band Leader
b. Nov 10, 1916 in Pittsburgh, Pennsylvania
Source: *WhoAm 74; WhoJazz 72*

May, Brian
[Queen]
English. Singer, Musician
b. Jul 19, 1947 in Hampton, England
Source: *IlEncRk; LilREn 78; RkOn; WhoRock 81*

May, Edna
American. Actress
b. 1879 in Syracuse, New York
d. Jan 1, 1948 in Lausanne, Switzerland
Source: *EncMT; Film 1; InWom; MotPP; WhScrn 74, 77; WhoHol B; WhoStg 1906, 1908*

May, Elaine
American. Actress, Director
b. Apr 21, 1932 in Philadelphia, Pennsylvania
Source: *BiE&WWA; ConDr 73; ConLC 16; CurBio 61; FilmgC; InWom; IntMPA 75, 76, 77, 78, 79, 80, 81, 82; MotPP; NotNAT; PlP&P; WhoAm 74, 76, 78, 80, 82; WhoHol A; WhoThe 77; WhoWor 74; WomWMM; WrDr 76*

May, Karl Friedrich
German. Author
b. Feb 25, 1842 in Chemnitz, Germany
d. Mar 30, 1912 in Radebeul, Germany
Source: *CasWL; ClDMEL; EuAu; EvEuW; OxGer*

May, Marjorie Merriweather
American. Philanthropist
b. Mar 15, 1887 in Springfield, Illinois
d. Oct 12, 1973 in Washington, DC
Source: *BioIn 6, 7, 10, 11; CelR 73; ForWC 70; InWom; WhAm 6; WhoAmW 74*

May, Mortimer
American. Hosiery Manufacturer
b. Dec 20, 1892 in Laconia, New Hampshire
d. May 8, 1974 in Miami Beach, Florida
Source: *WhAm 6; WhoAm 74; WhoF&I 74; WhoS&SW 73; WhoWorJ 72*

May, Morton David
American. Merchant
b. 1914 in Saint Louis, Missouri
Source: *St&PR 75; WhoAm 74; WhoAmA 73; WhoGov 72*

May, Robert Lewis
American. Advertising Executive
b. 1905?
d. Aug 11, 1976 in Evanston, Illinois
Source: *BioIn 1, 2, 5, 7, 11*

May, Rollo
American. Psychoanalyst
Concerned with how to deal with anxiety; wrote *Man's Search for Himself,* 1952.
b. Apr 21, 1909 in Ada, Ohio
Source: *AmAu&B; BioNews 74; CelR 73; CurBio 73; NewYTBE 71; WhoAm 74, 76, 78, 80, 82; WhoE 74*

Mayakovsky, Vladimir
Russian. Poet
b. Jul 19, 1893 in Bagdadi, Russia
d. Aug 14, 1930 in Moscow, U.S.S.R.
Source: *AtlBL; CasWL; ClDMEL; CnMD; CnMWL; CnThe; DcRusL; EncWL; EvEuW; LongCTC; McGEWD; ModSL 1; ModWD; OxEng; OxFilm; OxThe; Pen EUR; PlP&P; REn; REnWD; TwCW; WhoTwCL; WorAu*

Mayall, John Brumwell
American. Jazz Musician
b. Nov 29, 1933 in Manchester, England
Source: *EncPR&S; IlEncRk; NewYTBE 70; RkOn; WhoAm 74, 76, 78, 80, 82*

Maybeck, Bernard Ralph
American. Architect
b. Feb 7, 1862 in New York, New York
d. Mar 2, 1957 in Glendale, California
Source: *BioIn 1, 2, 3, 4, 5, 6, 11; BnEnAmA; DcAmB S6; EncMA; McGDA; NatCAB 43; WhAm 5; WhoArch*

Mayehoff, Eddie
American. Actor
b. Jul 7, 1914 in Baltimore, Maryland
Source: *BiE&WWA; IntMPA 75, 76, 77, 78, 79, 80, 81, 82; NotNAT; WhoHol A*

Mayer, Albert
American. Architect, City Planner
b. Dec 29, 1897 in New York, New York
d. Oct 14, 1981 in New York, New York
Source: *AmArch 70; ConAu 73; IntAu&W 77; IntWW 74, 75, 76, 77, 78; WhoAm 74, 76, 78; WhoWor 74; WhoWorJ 72*

Mayer, Arthur Loeb
"Merchant of Menace"
American. Motion Picture Executive
b. May 28, 1886 in Demopolis, Alabama
d. Apr 14, 1981 in New York, New York
Source: *AmAu&B; BioIn 9, 10, 11; IntMPA 75, 76, 77, 78, 79, 80, 81; NewYTBE 71; NewYTBS 78; WhoAm 74, 76, 78; WhoWorJ 72*

Mayer, Edward Newton, Jr.
American. Author, Advertising Executive
b. 1907
d. Dec 1, 1975 in New York, New York
Source: *BioIn 10, 11; NewYTBS 75*

Mayer, Gene (Eugene)
American. Tennis Player
b. Apr 11, 1956 in New York, New York
Source: *BioIn 12; WhoAm 82*

Mayer, Jean
French. Scientist
b. Feb 19, 1920 in Paris, France
Source: *BioIn 8, 9, 10, 11; CurBio 70; WhoAm 78, 80, 82*

Mayer, L(ouis) B(urt)
American. Motion Picture Producer
Founded Louis B Mayer Pictures Corp., 1918.
b. Jul 4, 1885 in Minsk, Russia
d. Oct 29, 1957 in Santa Monica, California
Source: *BiDFilm; CurBio 43, 58; DcFM; EncAB-H; FilmgC; OxFilm; WebAB; WhAm 3; WomWMM; WorEFlm*

Mayer, Maria Goeppert
German. Physicist
b. Jun 28, 1906 in Kattaivitz, Germany
d. Feb 20, 1972 in La Jolla, California
Source: *BioIn 6, 7, 9, 10, 11; CurBio 64, 72; InWom; ObitOF 79; WebAB; WhAm 5*

Mayer, Martin Prager
American. Author
b. Jan 14, 1928 in New York, New York
Source: *AmAu&B; BioIn 3, 6, 8, 10; ConAu 5R; WhoAm 80; WorAu*

Mayer, Norman D
"Pops"
American. Anti-Nuclear Activist
Held Washington Monument hostage, Dec, 1982.
b. Mar 31, 1916 in El Paso, Texas
d. Dec 8, 1982 in Washington, DC
Source: *NF*

Mayer, Oscar Ferdinand
American. Meat Packer
Founded Oscar Mayer & Brother in Chicago, 1883.
b. Mar 29, 1859 in Bavaria, Germany
d. Mar 11, 1955 in Chicago, Illinois
Source: *BioIn 3, 6; NatCAB 45; WhAm 3*

Mayer, Oscar Gottfried
American. Meat Packer
President, Oscar Mayer Co., 1928-55, chairman, 1955-65.
b. Mar 10, 1888 in Chicago, Illinois
d. Mar 5, 1965
Source: *BioIn 7, 10; WhAm 4*

Mayer, Oscar Gottfried
American. Meat Packer
b. Mar 16, 1914 in Chicago, Illinois
Source: *St&PR 75; WhoAm 74; WhoF&I 74; WhoMW 74; WhoWor 74*

Mayes, Herbert Raymond
American. Editor
b. Aug 11, 1900 in New York, New York
Source: *AmAu&B; ChPo S1; St&PR 75; WhoAm 82*

Mayfield, Curtis
American. Singer, Songwriter
b. Jun 3, 1942 in Chicago, Illinois
Source: *EncPR&S; IlEncRk; Rk100; WhoAm 82*

Mayhew, Richard
American. Artist
b. Apr 3, 1934 in Amityville, New York
Source: *AfroAA; DcCAA 71, 77; WhoAm 74, 76, 78; WhoAmA 73, 76, 78, 80; WhoBlA 77*

Maynard, Ken
American. Actor, Circus Performer
b. Jul 21, 1895 in Vevey, Indiana
d. Mar 23, 1973 in Woodland Hills, California
Source: *FilmgC; MotPP; MovMk; NewYTBE 73; TwYS; WhScrn 77; WhoHol B*

Maynor, Dorothy
American. Singer
b. Sep 3, 1910 in Norfolk, Virginia
Source: *CurBio 40, 51; InWom; WhoAm 74; WhoBlA 75*

Mayo, Charles Horace
American. Surgeon
Co-founded Mayo Clinic, 1915.
b. Jul 19, 1865 in Rochester, Minnesota
d. May 26, 1939 in Chicago, Illinois
Source: *AmBi; DcAmB S2; EncAB-H; WebAB; WhAm 1*

Mayo, Virginia
[Virginia Jones]
American. Actress
b. 1922 in Saint Louis, Missouri
Source: *BiDFilm; FilmgC; IntMPA 75, 76, 77, 78, 79, 80, 81, 82; MotPP; MovMk; WhoHol A; WorEFlm*

Mayo, William James
American. Surgeon
Co-founded Mayo Clinic, 1915.
b. Jun 29, 1861 in LeSueur, Minnesota
d. Jul 28, 1939 in Rochester, Minnesota
Source: *AmBi; DcAmB S2; EncAB-H; WebAB; WhAm 1*

Mayr, Richard
Austrian. Opera Singer
b. Nov 18, 1877 in Henndorf, Austria
d. Dec 1, 1935 in Vienna, Austria
Source: *NewEOp 71; WebBD 80*

Mays, David John
American. Lawyer
b. Nov 22, 1896 in Richmond, Virginia
d. Feb 17, 1971 in Richmond, Virginia
Source: *AmAu&B; NewYTBE 71; OxAmL; WhAm 5*

Mays, Willie Howard, Jr.
"Say Hey"
American. Baseball Player
Hit 660 career home runs; Hall of Fame, 1979; wrote *Born to Play,* 1955.
b. May 6, 1931 in Fairfield, Alabama
Source: *BaseEn; BioNews 74; BlkAW; CelR 73; CurBio 55, 66; NewYTBE 70, 73; NewYTBS 74; WebAB; WhoAm 74; WhoBlA 75; WhoProB 73*

Maytag, Elmer Henry
American. Manufacturer
Maytag Co. produced first washing machine, 1907.
b. Sep 18, 1883 in Newton, Iowa
d. Jul 20, 1940 in Lake Geneva, Wisconsin
Source: *BioIn 9; NatCAB 52*

Mazarin, Jules
French. Cardinal, Statesman
b. Jul 14, 1602 in Pescina, Italy
d. Mar 9, 1661 in Vincennes, France
Source: *NewC; NewCol 75; REn; WebBD 80*

Mazel, Judy
American. Author
b. 1944? in Chicago, Illinois
Source: *NewYTBS 81*

Mazeroski, Bill (William Stanley)
"Maz"
American. Baseball Player
Hit home run in 9th inning of 7th game, 1960 World Series.
b. Sep 5, 1936 in Wheeling, West Virginia
Source: *BaseEn; WhoProB 73*

Mazurki, Mike
American. Actor
b. Dec 25, 1909 in Tarnopal, Austria
Source: *FilmgC; IntMPA 75, 76, 77, 78, 79, 80, 81, 82; Vers A; WhoHol A*

Mazursky, Paul
American. Motion Picture Director
b. Apr 25, 1930 in Brooklyn, New York
Source: *BiDFilm; CelR 73; CurBio 80; FilmgC; IntMPA 75, 76, 77, 78, 79, 80, 81, 82; MovMk; WhoAm 82; WhoHol A*

Mazzilli, Lee Louis
American. Baseball Player
b. Mar 25, 1955 in Brooklyn, New York
Source: *BaseEn; BioIn 12*

Mazzini, Giuseppe
Italian. Revolutionary
b. Jun 22, 1805 in Genoa, Italy
d. Mar 10, 1872 in Pisa, Italy
Source: *CasWL; EuAu; EvEuW; NewC; Pen EUR; REn*

Mboya, Tom (Thomas Joseph)
Kenyan. Nationalist Leader
b. Aug 15, 1930 in Lake Victoria, Kenya
d. Jul 5, 1969 in Nairobi, Kenya
Source: *CurBio 59, 69; NewCol 75*

McAdam, John Loudoun
Scottish. Civil Engineer
b. Sep 21, 1756 in Ayrshire, Scotland
d. Nov 26, 1836 in Scotland
Source: *Drake; WebBD 80*

McAdoo, Bob (Robert)
American. Basketball Player
b. Sep 25, 1951 in Greensboro, North Carolina
Source: *WhoAm 82; WhoBbl 73*

McAdoo, William Gibbs
American. Senator, Cabinet Member
b. Oct 31, 1863 in Marietta, Georgia
d. Feb 1, 1941 in Washington, DC
Source: *BiDrAC; BiDrUSE; DcAmB S3; DcNAA; EncAB-H; WebAB; WhAm 1; WhAmP*

McAliskey, Bernadette Devlin
see: Devlin, Bernadette Josephine

McAlister, Elizabeth
[Mrs. Philip Berrigan]
American. Activist, Former Nun
b. 1939?
Source: *BioIn 9, 10, 11; NewYTBE 71*

McArdle, Andrea
American. Singer, Actress
The original Annie in Broadway musical, *Annie,* 1976.
b. Nov 4, 1963 in Philadelphia, Pennsylvania
Source: *BioIn 11; NewYTBS 77*

McArdle, George
see: Little River Band, The

McArthur, Edwin Douglas
American. Conductor
b. Sep 24, 1907 in Denver, Colorado
Source: *AmSCAP 66; ConAu 17R; WhoMus 72*

McArthur, John
American. Architect
b. May 13, 1823 in Bladenock, Scotland
d. Jan 8, 1890 in Philadelphia, Pennsylvania
Source: *DcAmB; TwCBDA; WhAm H*

McAuliffe, Anthony Clement
American. Army General
b. Jul 2, 1898 in Washington, DC
d. Aug 11, 1975 in Washington, DC
Source: *CurBio 50; WebAB; WhAm 6; WhoAm 74; Who 74*

McAuliffe, Dick (Richard John)
American. Baseball Player
b. Nov 29, 1939 in Hartford, Connecticut
Source: *BaseEn; WhoProB 73*

McAvoy, May
American. Actress
b. 1901 in New York, New York
Source: *Film 1; InWom; MotPP; MovMk; ThFT; TwYS; WhoHol A*

McBride, Floyd Mickey
American. Basketball Player
b. Feb 11, 1902 in Watongo, Oklahoma
Source: *WhoBbl 73*

McBride, Lloyd
American. Labor Union Official
President, US Steelworkers of America.
b. Mar 8, 1916 in Farmington, Missouri
Source: *BioIn 11; CurBio 78; WhoAm 78, 80, 82*

McBride, Mary Margaret
[Martha Deane]
American. Radio Commentator
b. Nov 16, 1899 in Paris, Missouri
d. Apr 7, 1976 in West Shokun, New York
Source: *AmAu&B; ConAu 65, 69; CurBio 41, 54; InWom*

McBride, Patricia
American. Ballerina
b. Aug 23, 1942 in Teaneck, New Jersey
Source: *CurBio 66; InWom; WhoAm 74, 76, 78, 80, 82; WhoHol A*

McBurney, Charles
American. Scientist, Physician, Engineer
b. Feb 17, 1845 in Roxbury, Massachusetts
d. Nov 7, 1913 in Brookline, Massachusetts
Source: *AmBi; DcAmB; WhAm 1*

McCabe, Mary O'Connell
American. Singer
b. Sep 4, 1902 in Mobile, Alabama
d. Dec 24, 1975 in New Haven, Connecticut
Source: *BioIn 10*

McCafferty, Dan
see: Nazareth

McCafferty, Don
American. Football Coach
b. Mar 12, 1921 in Cleveland, Ohio
d. Jul 28, 1974 in Pontiac, Michigan
Source: *NewYTBE 71; NewYTBS 74; WhAm 6; WhoAm 74; WhoE 74*

McCain, John Sidney, Jr.
American. Admiral
b. Jan 17, 1911 in Council Bluffs, Iowa
d. Mar 22, 1981
Source: *BioIn 8, 9, 12; CurBio 70, 81; NewYTBS 81; WhoWor 74*

McCall, Dorothy Lawson
Author
b. 1888
Source: *BioIn 9, 10*

McCall, Thomas Lawson
American. Politician
Environmentalist governor of OR, 1967-74.
b. Mar 22, 1913 in Egypt, Massachusetts
d. Jan 8, 1983 in Portland, Oregon
Source: *BioIn 9, 10, 11; CurBio 74; IntWW 74, 75, 76; PolProf J; PolProf NF; WhoAmP 73, 75, 77, 79; WhoGov 75, 77*

McCallister, Lon
American. Actor
b. Apr 17, 1923 in Los Angeles, California
Source: *FilmgC; HolP 40; MotPP; WhoHol A*

McCallum, David
Scottish. Actor
Played Illya Kuryakin on TV series "The Man from UNCLE," 1964-67.
b. Sep 19, 1933 in Glasgow, Scotland
Source: *FilmgC; IntMPA 75, 76, 77, 78, 79, 80, 81, 82; MotPP; MovMk; NotNAT; OxFilm; WhoAm 74, 76, 78, 80, 82; WhoHol A*

McCambridge, Mercedes
American. Actress
b. Mar 17, 1918 in Joliet, Illinois
Source: *BiE&WWA; CurBio 64; FilmgC; InWom; IntMPA 75, 76, 77, 78, 79, 80, 81, 82; MotPP; MovMk; NotNAT; OxFilm; WhoAm 74, 76, 78, 80, 82; WhoHol A*

McCann, Alfred Watterson
American. Author
b. Jan 7, 1879 in Pittsburgh, Pennsylvania
d. Jan 19, 1931
Source: *DcAmB; DcNAA; WhAm 1*

McCann, Elizabeth (Liz)
American. Motion Picture Producer
b. 1932? in New York, New York
Source: *NewYTBS 81*

McCann, Harrison King
American. Advertising Executive
b. 1880 in Westbrook, Maine
d. 1962
Source: *BioIn 4, 6; WhAm 4*

McCann, Les
American. Musician, Singer
b. Sep 23, 1935 in Lexington, Kentucky
Source: *AmSCAP 66; WhoAm 82*

McCardell, Claire
American. Fashion Designer
b. May 24, 1905 in Frederick, Maryland
d. Mar 22, 1958 in New York, New York
Source: *CurBio 54, 58; InWom; WhAm 3; WorFshn*

McCarey, Leo
American. Motion Picture Director
b. Oct 3, 1898 in Los Angeles, California
d. Jul 5, 1969 in Santa Monica, California
Source: *AmSCAP 66; BiDFilm; CurBio 46, 69; DcFM; FilmgC; MovMk; OxFilm; TwYS; WhAm 5; WorEFlm*

McCartan, Edward
American. Sculptor
b. Aug 16, 1879 in Albany, New York
d. Sep 20, 1947 in New Rochelle, New York
Source: *BioIn 1, 8; WhAm 2*

McCarthy, Clem
American. Horseracing Commentator
b. Sep 9, 1882 in Rochester, New York
d. Jun 4, 1962 in New York, New York
Source: *CurBio 41, 62*

McCarthy, Eugene Joseph
American. Politician
Senator from MN, 1958-70; Democratic presidential candidate, 1968, 1972.
b. Mar 29, 1916 in Watkins, Minnesota
Source: *AmAu&B; BiDrAC; ConAu 1R, 2NR; EncAB-H 74; IntWW 75, 76, 77, 78, 79, 80, 81; IntYB 78, 79, 80, 81; MnnWr; WebAB; Who 74; WhoAm 74, 76, 78, 80, 82; WhoAmP 73, 75, 77, 79; WhoWor 74; WrDr 76*

McCarthy, Glenn Herbert
American. Industrialist
b. 1907
Source: *BioIn 1, 2, 4, 7, 8, 11*

McCarthy, Joe (Joseph Raymond)
American. Senator
Conducted Communist witch hunts in Senate, 1950's.
b. Nov 14, 1908 in Grand Chute, Wisconsin
d. May 2, 1957 in Bethesda, Maryland
Source: *BiDrAC; CurBio 50, 57; EncAB-H; REn; WebAB; WhAm 3; WhAmP*

McCarthy, Joe (Joseph Vincent)
American. Baseball Manager
b. Apr 21, 1887 in Philadelphia, Pennsylvania
d. Jan 13, 1978 in Buffalo, New York
Source: *CurBio 48; WhoProB 73*

McCarthy, J(oseph) P(riestley)
American. Disc Jockey
b. Mar 22, 1934 in Detroit, Michigan
Source: *BioIn 10*

McCarthy, Julia
see: Randolph, Nancy, pseud.

McCarthy, Justin Huntly
English. Author, Historian
b. 1860
d. Mar 21, 1936
Source: *BiD&SB; ChPo, S1; DcEnA AP; EvLB; LongCTC; ModWD; PoIre*

McCarthy, Kevin
American. Actor
b. Feb 15, 1914 in Seattle, Washington
Source: *BiE&WWA; FilmgC; IntMPA 75, 76, 77, 78, 79, 80, 81, 82; MovMk; NotNAT; WhoHol A; WhoThe 77*

McCarthy, Mary
American. Author
b. Jun 21, 1912 in Seattle, Washington
Source: *AmAu&B; AmWr; Au&Wr 71; BiE&WWA; CasWL; CelR 73; ConAu 5R; ConLC 1, 3, 5, 14; ConNov 72, 76; DrAF 76; EncWL; IntWW 74; LongCTC; ModAL, SUP; NotNAT; OxAmL; Pen AM; RAdv 1; REn; REnAL; TwCA SUP; TwCW; WebE&AL; Who 74; WhoAm 74, 76, 78, 80, 82; WhoTwCL; WhoWor 74; WrDr 76*

McCarthy, Timothy
American. Secret Service Agent
Injured during attempt to assassinate Ronald Reagan, Mar, 1981.
b. 1950?
Source: *BioIn 12*

McCartney, (James) Paul
[The Beatles; Wings]
English. Singer, Songwriter
Wrote songs "Yesterday," "Michelle"; has sold 100 million albums, 100 million singles.
b. Jun 18, 1942 in Liverpool, England
Source: *BioIn 10; BioNews 74; BkPepl; CelR 73; CurBio 66; IlWWBF; IntWW 74, 75, 76, 77, 78, 79, 80, 81; MotPP; RkOn 2; WhoAm 78, 80, 82; WhoHol A*

McCartney, Jimmy
see: Mitch Ryder and the Detroit Wheels

McCartney, Linda
[Linda Eastman; Mrs. Paul McCartney; Wings]
American. Musician; Photographer
b. Sep 24, 1942 in New York, New York
Source: *BioIn 9, 10, 11*

McCarty, Mary
American. Actress
b. 1923 in Winfield, Kansas
d. Apr 5, 1980 in Westwood, California
Source: *BioIn 1, 11; WhoHol A; WhoThe 77*

McCay, Winsor
American. Cartoonist
b. Sep 26, 1869 in Spring Lake, Michigan
d. Jul 26, 1934
Source: *WorECom*

McClanahan, Rob
[United States Olympic Hockey Team-1980]
American. Hockey Player
b. Jan 9, 1958 in Saint Paul, Minnesota
Source: *HocReg*

McClanahan, (Eddi-)Rue
American. Actress
Played Vivian on TV series "Maude," 1972-78.
b. Feb 21, in Healdton, Oklahoma
Source: *BioIn 10; WhoAm 78, 80; WhoHol A; WhoThe 77, 81*

McClary, Thomas
American. Singer, Musician
b. 1948 in Florida
Source: *BkPepl*

McClellan, George Brinton
American. Union General
Commanded Army of Potomac, 1861-62; indecisiveness led to Union defeats.
b. Dec 3, 1826 in Philadelphia, Pennsylvania
d. Oct 29, 1885 in Orange, New Jersey
Source: *AmAu&B; AmBi; ApCAB; BiAuS; BiD&SB; DcAmAu; DcAmB; DcNAA; Drake; EncAB-H; REn; REnAL; TwCBDA; WebAB; WhAm H*

McClellan, John Little
American. Senator
b. Feb 25, 1896 in Sheridan, Arkansas
d. Nov 27, 1977 in Little Rock, Arkansas
Source: *BiDrAC; CelR 73; CngDr 74; CurBio 50; IntWW 74; WhoAm 74; WhoAmP 73; WhoGov 72; WhoS&SW 73; WhoWor 74*

McClintic, Guthrie
American. Theatrical Producer
b. Aug 6, 1893 in Seattle, Washington
d. Oct 29, 1961 in Sneden's Landing, New York
Source: *CurBio 43, 62; OxThe; WhAm 4*

McClintock, Barbara
American. Geneticist
b. Jun 16, 1902 in Hartford, Connecticut
Source: *AmM&WS 73P, 76P, 79P; IntWW 74, 75, 76, 77, 78; WhoAmW 58, 64, 66, 68, 70, 72, 75, 77*

McClinton, Delbert
American. Singer
b. 1940 in Lubbock, Texas
Source: *WhoRock 81*

McCloskey, John
American. Clergyman
b. Mar 10, 1810 in Brooklyn, New York
d. Oct 10, 1885 in New York, New York
Source: *AmBi; ApCAB; DcAmB; TwCBDA; WebAB; WhAm H*

McCloskey, Paul Norton, Jr.
American. Congressman
b. Sep 29, 1927 in San Bernardino, California
Source: *BiDrAC; CelR 73; CngDr 74; ConAu 37R; CurBio 74; IntWW 74; NewYTBE 71; WhoAm 74, 76, 78, 80, 82; WhoAmP 73; WhoGov 72*

McCloskey, Robert
American. Author
b. Sep 15, 1914 in Hamilton, Ohio
Source: *AmAu&B; AnCL; Au&ICB; AuBYP; BkP; Cald 1938; ConAu 9R; FamAIYP; IlsBYP; IlsCB 1744, 1946, 1957; JBA 51; OhA&B; REnAL; SmATA 2; Str&VC*

McCloskey, Robert James
American. Diplomat
b. Nov 25, 1922 in Philadelphia, Pennsylvania
Source: *BioIn 10; USBiR 74; WhoAm 74, 76, 78, 80, 82; WhoGov 72; WhoWor 74*

McCloy, John Jay
American. Lawyer, Banker, Diplomat
b. Mar 31, 1895 in Philadelphia, Pennsylvania
Source: *CurBio 47, 61; IntWW 74; St&PR 75; Who 74; WhoAm 74, 76, 78, 80, 82; WhoE 74; WhoF&I 74; WhoWor 74*

McClure, Doug
American. Actor
Played Trampas in TV series "The Virginian," 1962-71.
b. May 11, 1938 in Glendale, California
Source: *MotPP; WhoHol A*

McClure, James A
American. Senator
b. Dec 27, 1924 in Payette, Idaho
Source: *BioIn 9, 10; WhoAm 76, 78, 80, 82*

McClure, Michael
American. Poet, Dramatist
b. Oct 20, 1932 in Marysville, Kansas
Source: *AmAu&B; ConAu 21R; ConDr 73; ConLC 6; ConP 70, 75; CroCAP; DrAF 76; DrAP 75; NatPD; Pen AM; RAdv 1; WhoAm 82; WrDr 76*

McClure, Samuel Sidney
American. Newspaper Editor, Publisher
b. Feb 17, 1857 in Antrim, Northern Ireland
d. Mar 21, 1949 in New York, New York
Source: *AmAu&B; BioIn 1, 2; DcNAA; EncAB-H; REn; REnAL; WebBD 80*

McCluskey, Roger
American. Auto Racer
b. 1930
Source: *BioIn 10*

McCobb, Paul
American. Designer
b. 1917 in Boston, Massachusetts
d. Mar 10, 1969
Source: *CurBio 58, 69; WhAm 5*

McCollum, Elmer Verner
American. Chemist, Nutritionist
b. Mar 3, 1879 in Fort Scott, Kansas
d. Nov 15, 1967
Source: *AsBiEn; BioIn 1, 2, 3, 5, 7, 8, 9, 11; DcScB; EncAB-H; WhAm 4*

McColough, C(harles) Peter
American. Business Executive
Xerox Corp., president, 1966-71, chairman, 1968--.
b. Aug 1, 1922 in Halifax, NS
Source: *BioIn 9; CanWW 70, 79; CurBio 81; Dun&B 79; IntWW 74, 75, 76, 77, 78; IntYB 78, 79; Who 74; WhoAm 74, 76, 78, 80; WhoAmP 73, 75, 79; WhoE 74; WhoF&I 74, 75, 77, 79; WhoWor 74*

McCone, John A
American. Business Executive
b. Jan 4, 1902 in San Francisco, California
Source: *CurBio 59; IntWW 74; Who 74; WhoAm 74; WhoWor 74*

McCoo, Marilyn
[Mrs. Billy Davis, Jr; The Fifth Dimension]
American. Singer, Actress
With Fifth Dimension, 1966-73; co-host of "Solid Gold."
b. Sep 3, 1943 in Jersey City, New Jersey
Source: *EncPR&S; IlEncRk; LilREn 78*

McCord, Andrew King
American. Business Executive
b. Feb 11, 1904 in Blue Island, Illinois
d. Dec 17, 1974 in Pittsburgh, Pennsylvania
Source: *WhAm 6; WhoAm 74*

McCord, David Thompson Watson
American. Poet
b. Nov 15, 1897 in New York, New York
Source: *AmAu&B; BkCL; BkP; ChPo, S1, S2; ConAu 73; OxAmL; REnAL; SmATA 18; Str&VC; ThrBJA; WhNAA; WhoAm 74, 76, 78, 80, 82; WhoWor 74*

McCord, James Walter
American. Watergate Participant
b. 1918
Source: *AuNews 1; BioIn 9, 10, 11; BioNews 74; NewYTBE 73*

McCord, Kent
American. Actor
Starred in TV series "Adam-12," 1968-75.
b. Sep 26, 1942 in Los Angeles, California
Source: *WhoAm 74; WhoHol A*

McCormack, John
American. Opera Singer
b. Jun 14, 1884 in Athlone, Ireland
d. Sep 16, 1945 in Dublin, Ireland
Source: *CurBio 45; FilmgC; REn; WhAm 2; WhScrn 74, 77; WhoHol B*

McCormack, John William
American. Lawyer, Congressman
b. Dec 21, 1891 in Boston, Massachusetts
Source: *BiDrAC; CurBio 43, 62; IntWW 74; WebAB; Who 74; WhoAm 74*

McCormack, Patty
American. Actress
b. Aug 21, 1945 in New York, New York
Source: *BiE&WWA; FilmgC; MotPP; MovMk; NotNAT; WhoHol A*

McCormick, Anne (Elizabeth) O'Hare
American. Journalist
b. 1881 in Yorkshire, England
d. May 29, 1954 in New York, New York
Source: *AmAu&B; CathA 1930; CurBio 40, 54; DcAmB S5; InWom; OhA&B; REn; REnAL; TwCA, SUP; WhAm 3*

McCormick, Bernard
American. Editor, Publisher
Source: *BioIn 10*

McCormick, Cyrus Hall
American. Inventor, Manufacturer
Invented the reaper, 1834.
b. Feb 15, 1809 in Rockbridge County, Virginia
d. May 13, 1884 in Chicago, Illinois
Source: *AmBi; ApCAB X; DcAmB; Drake; EncAB-H; McGEWB; NatCAB 5, 21; TwCBDA; WebAB; WhAm H*

McCormick, Cyrus Hall
American. Manufacturer
Entered family business, International Harvester Co., 1914.
b. Sep 22, 1890 in Chicago, Illinois
d. Mar 30, 1970 in Hartford, Connecticut
Source: *NatCAB 54; WhAm 5*

McCormick, Joseph Medill
American. Journalist, Politician
b. May 16, 1877 in Chicago, Illinois
d. Feb 25, 1925 in Washington, DC
Source: *AmAu&B; AmBi; DcAmB; WhAmP*

McCormick, Myron
American. Actor
b. Feb 8, 1908 in Albany, Indiana
d. Jul 30, 1962 in New York, New York
Source: *CurBio 54, 62; FilmgC; WhAm 4; WhScrn 74, 77; WhoHol B*

McCormick, Patricia Keller
American. Swimmer
b. 1930
Source: *BioIn 3, 4, 9, 11*

McCormick, Robert Rutherford
American. Newspaper Publisher
b. Jul 30, 1880 in Chicago, Illinois
d. Apr 1, 1955 in Wheaton, Illinois
Source: *AmAu&B; CurBio 42, 55; DcAmB S5; REnAL; WebAB; WhAm 3*

McCourt, Dale
Canadian. Hockey Player
b. Jan 26, 1957 in Falconbridge, ON
Source: *BioIn 11; HocReg*

McCovey, Willie Lee
"Stretch"
American. Baseball Player
b. Jan 10, 1938 in Mobile, Alabama
Source: *BaseEn; CurBio 70; WhoAm 74, 76, 78, 80, 82; WhoProB 73*

McCowen, Alec
English. Actor
b. May 26, 1926 in Tunbridge Wells, England
Source: *CelR 73; CurBio 69; FilmgC; MovMk; NotNAT; Who 74; WhoAm 74; WhoHol A; WhoThe 77*

McCoy, Charles
[Norman Selby]
"Kid"
American. Boxer, Actor
b. 1874
d. Apr 18, 1940 in Detroit, Michigan
Source: *WhScrn 77; WhoBox 74*

McCoy, Clyde
American. Jazz Musician
b. Dec 29, 1903 in Ashland, Kentucky
Source: *CmpEPM*

McCoy, Horace
American. Author
b. Apr 14, 1897 in Pegram, Tennessee
d. Dec 17, 1955 in Beverly Hills, California
Source: *AmAu&B; AmNov; OxAmL; REnAL; TexWr; WhNAA; WorAu*

McCoy, Tim
American. Actor
b. Apr 10, 1891 in Saginaw, Michigan
d. Jan 29, 1978 in Nogales, Arizona
Source: *FilmgC; IntMPA 75, 76, 77; MotPP; TwYS; WhoAm 74; WhoHol A*

McCoy, Van
American. Composer, Musician
Source: *BioIn 10*

McCracken, Branch
American. Basketball Player, Coach
Coach, Indiana U, 1939-43, 1947-65; won NCAA titles, 1940, 1953.
b. Jun 9, 1908 in Monrovia, Indiana
d. Jun 4, 1970 in Bloomington, Indiana
Source: *IndAu 1917; NewYTBE 70; WhoBbl 73*

McCracken, James
American. Opera Singer
b. Dec 16, 1926 in Gary, Indiana
Source: *CurBio 63; NewYTBE 72; WhoAm 82; WhoMus 72; WhoWor 74*

McCrae, John
Canadian. Physician, Poet
b. Nov 30, 1872 in Guelph, ON
d. Jan 28, 1918 in Wimereux, France
Source: *CanWr; CasWL; ChPo, S1; CreCan 2; DcLEL; DcNAA; EvLB; LongCTC; NewC; OxAmL; OxCan; REn; REnAL; TwCA*

McCrary, "Tex" (John Reagan)
[Tex and Jinx]
American. Journalist, Commentator
b. 1910 in Calvert, Texas
Source: *IntMPA 75, 76, 77*

McCrea, Joel
American. Actor
b. Nov 5, 1905 in Pasadena, California
Source: *BiDFilm; CmMov; FilmgC; IntMPA 75, 76, 77, 78, 79, 80, 81, 82; MovMk; OxFilm; WhoHol A; WorEFlm*

McCree, Wade Hampton, Jr.
American. Government Official
b. Jul 3, 1920 in Des Moines, Iowa
Source: *BioIn 11; EbonySL 1; NewYTBS 77; WhoAm 74, 76, 78; WhoAmL 79; WhoAmP 77, 79; WhoBlA 75, 77; WhoGov 72, 75, 77; WhoMW 74, 76*

McCreesh, Raymond
[Irish Hunger Strikers]
Irish. Jailed IRA Member
b. 1957 in Camlough, Northern Ireland
d. May 21, 1981 in Belfast, Northern Ireland
Source: *NF*

McCullers, Carson
[Carson Smith]
American. Author
b. Feb 19, 1917 in Columbus, Georgia
d. Sep 29, 1967 in Nyack, New York
Source: *AmAu&B; AmNov; AmWr; CasWL; CnDAL; CnMD; CnMWL; ConAu 5R, 25R; ConLC 1, 4, 10, 12; ConNov 76; CyWA; EncWL; LongCTC; McGEWD; ModAL, SUP; ModWD; OxAmL; Pen AM; RAdv 1; REn; REnAL; TwCA, SUP; TwCW; WebE&AL; WhoTwCL*

McCullin, Donald
English. Photographer
b. Oct 9, 1935 in London, England
Source: *BioIn 6; IntWW 75, 76, 77, 78; WhoWor 78*

McCulloch, Robert P
American. Oilman
b. 1912? in Saint Louis, Missouri
d. Feb 25, 1977 in Los Angeles, California
Source: *BioIn 2, 4, 8, 9, 11; NewYTBS 77; ObitOF 79*

McCullough, Colleen
Australian. Author
Wrote *The Thorn Birds,* 1977.
b. Jun 1, 1937 in Wellington, Australia
Source: *BioIn 11; ConAu 81; CurBio 82; NewYTBS 81*

McCullough, Paul
American. Actor
b. 1883 in Springfield, Ohio
d. Mar 25, 1936 in Boston, Massachusetts
Source: *FilmgC; WhScrn 74, 77; WhoHol B*

McCurdy, Ed
American. Singer
b. Jan 11, 1919 in Willow Hill, Pennsylvania
Source: *AmSCAP 66; EncFCWM 69*

McCutcheon, John Tinney
American. Journalist
b. May 6, 1870 in South Raub, Indiana
d. Jun 10, 1949 in Lake Forest, Illinois
Source: *ChPo, S1, S2; IndAu 1816; REnAL; WebAB; WhAm 2*

McDaniel, Hattie
American. Actress
b. 1898 in Wichita, Kansas
d. Oct 26, 1952 in Hollywood, California
Source: *CurBio 40, 52; DcAmB S5; FilmgC; InWom; MotPP; MovMk; OxFilm; ThFT; Vers A; WhScrn 74, 77; WhoHol B*

McDevitt, Ruth
American. Actress
b. Sep 13, 1895 in Coldwater, Michigan
d. May 27, 1976 in Hollywood, California
Source: *BiE&WWA; NotNAT; WhoAm 74; WhoHol A; WhoThe 77*

McDivitt, Jim (James Alton)
American. Astronaut, Businessman
Flew on Gemini 4, 1965; Apollo 9, 1969.
b. Jun 10, 1929 in Chicago, Illinois
Source: *AmM&WS 73P; CurBio 65; IntWW 77; St&PR 75; WhoAm 74, 76, 78, 80, 82; WhoS&SW 73; WhoWor 74*

McDole, Carol
[Carol Farley]
American. Children's Author
b. Dec 20, 1936 in Ludington, Michigan
Source: *ConAu 21R; SmATA 4; WrDr 76*

McDonald, "Country Joe"
American. Singer, Songwriter, Musician
b. 1942 in El Monte, California
Source: *BioIn 10; EncPR&S; IlEncRk*

McDonald, David John
American. Labor Union Leader
President, United Steelworkers of America, 1952-65.
b. Nov 22, 1902 in Pittsburgh, Pennsylvania
d. Aug 8, 1979 in Palm Springs, California
Source: *BiDAmLL; ConAu 45; CurBio 53, 79; NewYTBS 77; PolProf E; PolProf J; PolProf K; WhoAm 74, 76; WhoLab 76*

McDonald, Garry
[Norman Gunston]
Australian. Actor
b. 1948
Source: *BioIn 10*

McDonald, Harl
American. Composer
b. Jul 27, 1899 in Boulder, Colorado
d. Feb 10, 1955 in Philadelphia, Pennsylvania
Source: *AmSCAP 66; OxAmL; REnAL; WhAm 3*

McDonald, Ian
see: Foreigner; King Crimson

McDonald, Marie
[Mrs. Vic Orsett]
American. Actress
b. 1923 in Burgin, Kentucky
d. Oct 21, 1965 in Hidden Hills, California
Source: *FilmgC; InWom; MotPP; WhScrn 74, 77; WhoHol B*

McDonald, Maurice James
American. Restauranteur
b. 1902?
d. 1971
Source: *BioIn 9, 10; NewYTBE 71*

McDonald, Richard
American. Restauranteur
Source: *BioIn 10*

McDonnell, James Smith
American. Aircraft Manufacturer
Co-founder, McDonnell-Douglas Corp., 1967.
b. Apr 9, 1899 in Denver, Colorado
d. Aug 22, 1980 in Saint Louis, Missouri
Source: *AmM&WS 73P; IntWW 74, 75, 76, 77, 78, 79, 80; NewYTBS 80; WhoAm 74, 76, 78, 80; WhoF&I 74; WhoMW 74; WhoWor 74*

McDonnell, Joe (Joseph)
[Irish Hunger Strikers]
Irish. Jailed IRA Member
b. 1951 in Belfast, Northern Ireland
d. Jul 8, 1981 in Belfast, Northern Ireland
Source: *BioIn 12*

McDonough, Mary
American. Actress
b. May 4, 1961 in Los Angeles, California
Source: *BioIn 12*

McDougall, Alexander
American. General, Pamphleteer
b. 1732 in Islay, Scotland
d. Jun 9, 1786 in New York, New York
Source: *AmBi; BiAuS; BiDrAC; DcAmB; Drake; WhAm H; WhAmP*

McDougald, Gil(bert James)
American. Baseball Player
b. May 19, 1928 in San Francisco, California
Source: *BaseEn; WhoProB 73*

McDougall, Walt(er)
American. Cartoonist
b. Feb 10, 1858 in Newark, New Jersey
d. 1938
Source: *WhAm 4; WorECom*

McDowall, Roddy (Roderick Andrew)
English. Actor
Starred in *My Friend Flicka,* 1943; *Planet of the Apes,* film, TV series.
b. Sep 17, 1928 in London, England
Source: *BiE&WWA; FilmgC; IntMPA 75, 76, 77, 78, 79, 80, 81, 82; MotPP; MovMk; NotNAT; OxFilm; WhoAm 78, 80, 82; WhoHol A; WhoThe 72, 77, 81; WhoWor 74*

McDowell, Ephraim
American. Surgeon
b. Nov 11, 1771 in Rockbridge County, Virginia
d. Jun 25, 1830 in Danville, Kentucky
Source: *ApCAB; BiHiMed; BioIn 1, 3, 4, 5, 6, 8, 9; DcAmB; Drake; NatCAB 5; NewCol 75; REnAW; TwCBDA; WebAB; WhAm H*

McDowell, Frank
American. Plastic Surgeon
b. Jan 30, 1911 in Marshfield, Missouri
Source: *WhoAm 78*

McDowell, Irvin
American. Army Officer
b. Oct 15, 1818 in Columbus, Ohio
d. May 4, 1885 in San Francisco, California
Source: *AmBi; ApCAB; DcAmB; Drake; TwCBDA; WhAm H*

McDowell, Malcolm
English. Actor
b. Jun 13, 1943 in Leeds, England
Source: *CurBio 73; FilmgC; IntMPA 82; MovMk; NewYTBE 72; WhoHol A*

McDowell, Sam(uel Edward)
"Sudden Sam"
American. Baseball Player
b. Sep 21, 1942 in Pittsburgh, Pennsylvania
Source: *BaseEn; WhoProB 73*

McDowell, Wilcil
see: Irish Rovers

McEachin, James Elton
American. Actor
b. 1930 in Pennert, North Carolina
Source: *WhoBlA 75; WhoHol A*

McElhenny, Hugh
"King"
American. Football Player
b. Dec 31, 1928 in Los Angeles, California
Source: *WhoFtbl 74*

McElhone, Eloise
American. Actress
b. 1921
d. Jul 1, 1974 in New York, New York
Source: *BioIn 10*

McElroy, Neil Hosler
American. Chairman of Proctor and Gamble
b. Oct 30, 1904 in Berea, Ohio
d. Nov 30, 1972 in Cincinnati, Ohio
Source: *CurBio 51, 73; NewYTBE 72; WhAm 5*

McEnroe, John Patrick, Jr.
American. Tennis Player
Won US Open, 1979, 1980, Wimbledon, 1981.
b. Feb 16, 1959 in Wiesbaden, Germany (West)
Source: *BioIn 11, 12; CurBio 80; WhoAm 80, 82*

McEntee, Peter Donovan
Governor of Belize
b. Jun 27, 1920
Source: *WhoWor 78*

McFadden, Addie "Micki" Harris
see: Shirelles, The

McFarland, Ernest William
American. Politician
b. Oct 9, 1894 in Earlsboro, Oklahoma
Source: *BiDrAC; CurBio 51; WhoAm 74; WhoAmP 73*

McFarland, "Spanky" (George Emmett)
[Our Gang]
American. Actor
b. 1928 in Fort Worth, Texas
Source: *FilmgC; MovMk; WhoHol A*

McFee, Henry Lee
American. Artist
b. Apr 14, 1886 in Saint Louis, Missouri
d. Mar 19, 1953 in Claremont, California
Source: *BnEnAmA; DcCAA 71, 77; McGDA; ObitOF 79; WhAm 3; WhoAmA 78*

McFee, William
[Morley Punshon, pseud.]
English. Author
b. Jun 15, 1881 in London, England
d. Jul 2, 1966 in New Milford, Connecticut
Source: *AmAu&B; AmNov; CnDAL; ConAmA; CyWA; DcLEL; EvLB; LongCTC; OxAmL; REn; REnAL; TwCA, SUP; TwCW; WhAm 4; WhNAA*

McGarity, (Robert) Lou(is)
American. Jazz Musician
b. Jul 22, 1917 in Athens, Georgia
d. 1971
Source: *NewYTBE 71; WhoJazz 72*

McGavin, Darren
American. Actor
Starred in TV series "The Night Stalker," 1974-75.
b. May 7, 1922 in Spokane, Washington
Source: *BiE&WWA; FilmgC; IntMPA 75, 76, 77, 78, 79, 80, 81, 82; MotPP; MovMk; NotNAT; WhoAm 80, 82; WhoHol A*

McGee, Fibber
[James Edward Jordan; Fibber McGee and Molly]
American. Radio Entertainer, Actor
With wife, formed successful radio team, 1935-56.
b. Nov 16, 1896 in Peoria, Illinois
Source: *CurBio 41; FilmgC; WhoHol A*

McGee, Frank
American. Broadcast Journalist
b. Sep 12, 1921 in Monroe, Louisiana
d. Apr 17, 1975 in New York, New York
Source: *CelR 73; CurBio 64, 74; NewYTBS 74; WhAm 6; WhoAm 74*

McGee, Gale William
American. Historian, Diplomat
b. Mar 17, 1915 in Lincoln, Nebraska
Source: *BiDrAC; CngDr 74; CurBio 61; DrAS 74H; IntWW 74; WhoAm 74, 76, 78, 80, 82; WhoAmP 73; WhoGov 72; WhoWest 74; WhoWor 74*

McGee, Molly
[Marian Driscoll Jordan; Fibber McGee and Molly]
American. Radio Entertainer, Actress
b. Apr 15, 1897 in Peoria, Illinois
d. Apr 7, 1961 in Encino, California
Source: *CurBio 41, 61; InWom; WhAm 4; WhScrn 74, 77; WhoHol B*

McGee, Thomas D'Arcy
Canadian. Editor, Statesman
b. Apr 13, 1825 in Carlingford, Ireland
d. Apr 7, 1868 in Ottawa, ON
Source: *ApCAB; BbtC; BrAu 19; CanWr; ChPo, S1; DcNAA; Drake; NewC; OxCan; PoIre; REn; REnAL; WhAm H*

McGill, James
Canadian. Fur Trader, University Founder
Left bulk of estate to McGill U, founded 1829.
b. Oct 6, 1744 in Glasgow, Scotland
d. Dec 19, 1813 in Montreal, PQ
Source: *ApCAB; Drake; LinLib S; MacDCB 78*

McGill, Ralph Emerson
American. Journalist
b. Feb 5, 1898 in Soddy, Tennessee
d. Feb 3, 1969 in Atlanta, Georgia
Source: *ConAu 5R, 25R; CurBio 47, 69; WhAm 5*

McGill, William James
American. University President
Columbia U, president, 1970-80, president emeritus, 1980--.
b. Feb 27, 1922 in New York, New York
Source: *AmM&WS 73S, 78S; CurBio 71; IntWW 74, 75, 76, 77, 78, 79, 80, 81; WhoAm 74, 76, 78, 80, 82; WhoE 74, 75, 79*

McGinley, Phyllis
American. Poet, Author
b. Mar 21, 1905 in Ontario, Oregon
d. Feb 22, 1978 in New York, New York
Source: *AmAu&B; Au&Wr 71; AuBYP; BkP; CelR 73; ChPo, S1, S2; CnE&AP; CnMWL; ConAu 9R, 77; ConLC 14; ConP 70, 75; CurBio 41, 61; EvLB; InWom; IntWW 74; JBA 51; LongCTC; ModAL; OxAmL; Pen AM; RAdv 1; REn; REnAL; SmATA 2; TwCA SUP; TwCW; WhoAm 74; WhoAmW 77; WhoTwCL; WhoWor 74; WrDr 76*

McGinnis, George
American. Basketball Player
b. Aug 12, 1950 in Indianapolis, Indiana
Source: *WhoAm 74, 76, 78, 80, 82; WhoBbl 73; WhoBlA 75*

McGiver, John
American. Actor
b. Nov 5, 1913 in New York, New York
d. Sep 9, 1975 in West Fulton, New York
Source: *BiE&WWA; FilmgC; MotPP; MovMk; WhoThe 77*

McGivern, William Peter
American. Author
Wrote 23 mystery novels: *The Big Heat*, 1952, *Night of the Juggler*, 1974.
b. Dec 6, 1922 in Chicago, Illinois
d. Nov 18, 1982 in Palm Desert, California
Source: *AmAu&B; ConAu 49; EncMys; NewYTBS 82; WhoAm 80, 82; WorAu*

McGoohan, Patrick
American. Actor
b. Mar 19, 1928 in New York, New York
Source: *IntMPA 75, 76, 77; WhoAm 74, 76, 78, 80, 82; WhoHol A; WhoThe 77*

McGovern, Eleanor Stegeberg
American. Wife of George McGovern
b. 1921
Source: *BioIn 9, 10; NewYTBE 72*

McGovern, Elizabeth
American. Actress
b. 1961 in Evanston, Illinois
Source: *NewYTBS 81*

McGovern, George Stanley
American. Politician
Senator from SD, 1963-81; Democratic presidential candidate, 1972.
b. Jul 19, 1922 in Avon, South Dakota
Source: *BiDrAC; CelR 73; CngDr 74, 77, 79; ConAu 45; CurBio 67; DrAS 74H, 74H; EncAB-H; IntWW 74, 75, 76, 77, 78, 79, 80, 81; NewYTBE 71, 73; WhoAm 74, 76, 78, 80, 82; WhoAmP 73, 75, 77, 79; WhoMW 74, 76, 78, 80; WhoWor 74*

McGovern, Terry (John Terrence)
American. Boxer
b. Mar 9, 1880 in Johnstown, Pennsylvania
d. Feb 26, 1918 in Brooklyn, New York
Source: *WhoBox 74*

McGowan, William
American. Chairman of MCI
b. 1927 in Ashley, Pennsylvania
Source: *BioIn 12; WhoAm 82*

McGraw, Donald Cushing
American. Publisher
McGraw-Hill Publishing Co., president, 1953-56, chairman, 1966-74.
b. May 21, 1897 in Madison, New Jersey
d. Feb 7, 1974 in Boynton Beach, Florida
Source: *BiDrLUS 70; NewYTBS 74; WhAm 6; WhoF&I 74; WhoWor 74*

McGraw, Harold Whittlesey, Sr.
American. Publisher
b. 1890
d. Jul 3, 1970
Source: *BioIn 9; ConAu 29R*

McGraw, John Joseph
"Little Napoleon"
American. Baseball Player, Manager
b. Apr 7, 1873 in Truxton, New York
d. Feb 25, 1934 in New Rochelle, New York
Source: *BaseEn; DcAmB S1; DcNAA; WebAB; WhAm HA; WhoProB 73*

McGraw, "Tug" (Frank Edwin)
American. Baseball Player
b. Aug 30, 1944 in Martinez, California
Source: *BaseEn; NewYTBS 74; WhoProB 73*

McGuffey, William Holmes
American. Educator, Author
b. Sep 23, 1800 in Washington, Pennsylvania
d. May 4, 1873 in Charlottesville, Virginia
Source: *AmAu; AmAu&B; AmBi; ApCAB; ChPo, S1, S2; DcAmB; DcLEL; DcNAA; EncAB-H; OhA&B; OxAmL; Pen AM; REn; REnAL; TwCBDA; WebAB; WhAm H*

McGuinn, Roger
[The Byrds]
American. Rock Musician
b. Jul 13, 1942 in Chicago, Illinois
Source: *ConMuA 80; LilREn 78; WhoRock 81*

McGuire, "Biff" (William J)
American. Actor
b. Oct 25, 1926 in New Haven, Connecticut
Source: *BiE&WWA; NotNAT; WhoHol A; WhoThe 77*

McGuire, Dorothy
American. Actress
b. Jun 14, 1918 in Omaha, Nebraska
Source: *BiDFilm; BiE&WWA; CurBio 41; FilmgC; InWom; IntMPA 75, 76, 77, 78, 79, 80, 81, 82; MotPP; MovMk; NotNAT; OxFilm; WhoAm 82; WhoHol A; WhoThe 77; WorEFlm*

McGuire Sisters
[Christine McGuire; Dorothy McGuire; Phyllis McGuire]
American. Singers
Source: *InWom*

McHale, John Joseph
American. Baseball Player, Executive
President, Montreal Expos, 1968--.
b. Sep 21, 1921 in Detroit, Michigan
Source: *BaseEn; WhoAm 78, 80, 82; WhoProB 73*

McHale, Tom
American. Author
b. 1942? in Scranton, Pennsylvania
d. Mar 30, 1982 in Pembroke Pines, Florida
Source: *AuNews 1; ConAu 77; ConLC 3, 5; ConNov 72, 76; DrAF 76; IntAu&W 76, 77; WrDr 76, 80*

McHenry, Donald Franchot
American. Government Official
b. Oct 13, 1938 in Saint Louis, Missouri
Source: *BioIn 11, 12; CurBio 80; WhoAm 80; WhoAmP 73; WhoGov 72*

McHugh, Frank
American. Actor
b. May 23, 1898 in Homestead, Pennsylvania
d. Sep 11, 1981 in Greenwich, Connecticut
Source: *BiE&WWA; Film 2; FilmgC; IntMPA 75, 76, 77, 78, 79, 80, 81, 82; MotPP; MovMk; NewYTBS 81; NotNAT; Vers A; WhoHol A*

McHugh, Jimmy (James)
American. Songwriter
b. Jul 10, 1894? in Boston, Massachusetts
d. May 23, 1969 in Beverly Hills, California
Source: *AmSCAP 66; BiE&WWA; EncMT; FilmgC; NewCBMT; WhAm 5; WhScrn 74, 77; WhoHol B*

McIlwain, Charles Howard
American. Educator
b. Mar 15, 1871 in Saltzburg, Pennsylvania
d. 1968
Source: *AmAu&B; ConAu 102; OxAmL; TwCA, SUP; WhAm 6; WhNAA; Who 74*

McIlwee, Thomas
[Irish Hunger Strikers]
Irish. Jailed IRA Member
b. 1957 in Bellaghy, Northern Ireland
d. Aug 8, 1981 in Belfast, Northern Ireland
Source: *NF*

McIntire, Carl Thomas
American. Clergyman
b. Oct 4, 1939 in Philadelphia, Pennsylvania
Source: *DrAS 74H; NewYTBE 70*

McIntire, John
American. Actor
b. Jun 27, 1907 in Spokane, Washington
Source: *BiDFilm; FilmgC; IntMPA 77, 78, 79, 80, 81, 82; MotPP; WhoHol A; WorEFlm*

McIntyre, Frank J
Actor
b. 1879
d. Jun 8, 1949 in Ann Arbor, Michigan
Source: *Film 1; MotPP; WhScrn 74, 77; WhoHol B*

McIntyre, Hal (Harold W)
American. Jazz Musician
b. Nov 29, 1914 in Cromwell, Connecticut
d. May 5, 1959 in Hollywood, California
Source: *BioIn 9; CmpEPM*

McIntyre, James
American. Actor
b. 1857 in Kenosha, Wisconsin
d. 1939 in Southampton, New York
Source: *DcAmB S2; WhoStg 1908*

McIntyre, James Francis
American. Roman Catholic Cardinal
b. Jun 25, 1886 in New York, New York
d. Jul 16, 1979 in Los Angeles, California
Source: *CurBio 53; IntWW 74; WebBD 80; Who 74; WhoAm 74*

McIntyre, James Talmadge, Jr.
American. Government Official
b. Dec 17, 1940 in Vidalia, Georgia
Source: *BioIn 11; CurBio 79; WhoAm 78*

McIntyre, John Thomas
American. Author, Dramatist
b. Nov 26, 1871 in Philadelphia, Pennsylvania
d. May 21, 1951 in Philadelphia, Pennsylvania
Source: *AmAu&B; DcAmAu; IntMPA 82; OxAmL; REnAL; TwCA, SUP*

McIntyre, Oscar Odd
American. Journalist
b. Feb 18, 1884 in Plattsburg, Missouri
d. Feb 13, 1938
Source: *AmAu&B; AmBi; DcAmB S2; DcNAA; OhA&B; REnAL; TwCA; WhAm 1; WhNAA*

McKay, David O
American. Religious Leader
b. Sep 8, 1873 in Huntsville, Utah
d. Jan 18, 1970 in Salt Lake City, Utah
Source: *CurBio 51, 70; NewYTBE 70; WhAm 5*

McKay, Jim
[James Kenneth McManus]
American. Sportscaster
Host, ABC's *Wide World of Sports,* 1961--; has won eight Emmys.
b. Sep 24, 1921 in Philadelphia, Pennsylvania
Source: *CurBio 73; WhoAm 74, 76, 78, 80, 82*

McKay, John H
American. Football Coach
Head coach, USC, 1960-76, Tampa Bay, 1976--.
b. Jul 5, 1923 in Everettsville, West Virginia
Source: *BioIn 6, 8, 9, 10; WhoAm 78*

McKay, Scott
American. Actor
b. 1915 in Pleasantville, Iowa
Source: *BiE&WWA; NotNAT; WhoHol A; WhoThe 77*

McKean, Michael
American. Actor
b. 1947?
Source: *BioIn 11*

McKechnie, Donna
American. Dancer, Actress
Won Tony, 1975, for *A Chorus Line.*
b. 1943? in Detroit, Michigan
Source: *WhoHol A; WhoThe 77*

McKeel, Johnny (John D, Jr.)
[The Hostages]
American. Former Hostage in Iran
b. 1954?
Source: *BioIn 12; NewYTBS 81*

McKeen, John Elmer
American. Pharmaceutical Company Executive
b. Jun 4, 1903 in New York, New York
d. Feb 23, 1978 in Palm Beach, Florida
Source: *AmM&WS 73P, 79P; CurBio 61, 78; St&PR 75; WhoAm 74, 76; WhoF&I 74*

McKellen, Ian
English. Actor, Motion Picture Director
b. May 25, 1939 in Burnley, England
Source: *IntWW 78; WhoThe 77, 81; WhoWor 74, 76*

McKelway, St. Clair
American. Author
b. Feb 13, 1905 in Charlotte, North Carolina
d. 1976 in Washington, DC
Source: *AmAu&B; ConAu 5R, 93; WhoAm 74; WhoWor 74*

McKenna, Siobhan
Irish. Actress
b. May 24, 1922 in Belfast, Northern Ireland
Source: *BiE&WWA; CelR 73; CurBio 56; FilmgC; InWom; IntMPA 75, 76, 77, 78, 79, 80, 81, 82; IntWW 74; MotPP; NewC; NotNAT; PlP&P; Who 74; WhoHol A; WhoThe 77; WhoWor 74*

McKenna, Virginia
English. Actress
Played Joy Adamson in *Born Free,* 1965.
b. Jun 7, 1931 in London, England
Source: *FilmgC; InWom; WhoHol A; WhoThe 72, 77, 81*

McKenney, Ruth
American. Author
b. Nov 18, 1911 in Mishawaka, Indiana
d. Jun 25, 1972 in Columbus, Ohio
Source: *AmAu&B; ConAu 37R, 93; CurBio 42, 72; LongCTC; NewYTBE 72; OhA&B; OxAmL; REn; REnAL; TwCA, SUP; WhAm 5*

McKenzie, "Red" (William)
American. Jazz Singer
b. Oct 14, 1907 in Saint Louis, Missouri
d. Feb 7, 1948 in New York, New York
Source: *WhoJazz 72*

McKenzie Brothers, The
[Bob and Doug McKenzie; Rick Moranis; Dave Thomas]
Canadian. Comedians
Source: *BkPepl*

McKeon, Doug
American. Actor
Played Jane Fonda's son in *On Golden Pond.*
b. Jun 10, 1966 in Oakland, New Jersey
Source: *JohnWil 82*

McKeown, Leslie
Scottish. Singer, Musician
b. Nov 12, 1955 in Edinburgh, Scotland
Source: *BkPepl*

McKern, Leo
English. Actor
b. Mar 16, 1920 in Sydney, Australia
Source: *FilmgC; MovMk; WhoHol A; WhoThe 77*

McKernan, Ron
[The Grateful Dead]
"Pigpen"
American. Singer, Musician
b. Sep 8, 1946 in San Bruno, California
d. Mar 8, 1973 in Corte Madera, California
Source: *EncPR&S; IlEncRk*

McKerrow, Amanda
American. Ballerina
Won gold prize, Moscow International Ballet Competition, 1981, highest honor ever given to American.
b. Nov 7, 1964 in New Mexico
Source: *NewYTBS 81*

McKim, Charles Follen
American. Architect
b. Aug 24, 1847 in Chester County, Pennsylvania
d. Sep 14, 1909 in Saint James, New York
Source: *AmBi; ApCAB; DcAmB; OxAmL; TwCBDA; WebAB; WhAm 1*

McKinley, Ray
American. Singer, Musician, Band Leader
b. Jun 18, 1910 in Fort Worth, Texas
Source: *AmSCAP 66; WhoJazz 72*

McKinley, William
American. 25th US President
Held office, 1897-1901; assassinated by anarchist Leon Czolgosz.
b. Jan 29, 1843 in Niles, Ohio
d. Sep 14, 1901 in Buffalo, New York
Source: *AmAu&B; AmBi; ApCAB SUP; BiDrAC; BiDrUSE; DcAmB; EncAB-H; OhA&B; OxAmL; REn; REnAL; TwCBDA; WebAB; WhAm 1; WhAmP*

McKinney, Bill (William)
American. Musician, Band Manager
b. 1894 in Paducah, Kentucky
Source: *WhoJazz 72*

McKissick, Floyd Bixler
American. Lawyer, CORE Executive
b. Mar 9, 1922 in Asheville, North Carolina
Source: *ConAu 49; CurBio 68; IntWW 74; WhoAm 74; WhoBlA 75; WhoWor 74*

McKuen, Rod
American. Poet, Singer
Wrote pop song, "Jean" for film, *The Prime of Miss Jean Brodie.*
b. Apr 23, 1933 in San Francisco, California
Source: *AmAu&B; AuNews 1; BioNews 74; BkPepl; CelR 73; ConAu 41R; ConLC 1, 3; ConP 70; CurBio 70; EncFCWM 69; IntWW 74; NewYTBE 71; WebAB; WhoAm 74, 76, 78, 80, 82; WhoE 74; WhoHol A; WhoWest 74; WrDr 76*

McLaglen, Victor
American. Actor
b. Dec 11, 1886 in Tunbridge Wells, England
d. Nov 7, 1959 in Newport Beach, California
Source: *BiDFilm; CmMov; FilmgC; MotPP; MovMk; OxFilm; TwYS; WhAm 3; WhScrn 74, 77; WhoHol B; WorEFlm*

McLain, Denny (Dennis Dale)
American. Baseball Player
Last pitcher to win 30 games in one season, 1968; won Cy Young Award twice, 1968, 1969.
b. Mar 29, 1944 in Chicago, Illinois
Source: *BaseEn; BioNews 74; CurBio 69; NewYTBE 70, 72; WhoProB 73*

McLane, James Woods
American. Physician
b. Aug 19, 1839 in New York, New York
d. Nov 25, 1912
Source: *WhAm 1*

McLaren, Bruce Leslie
New Zealander. Auto Racer, Manufacturer
b. 1937 in Auckland, New Zealand
d. 1970
Source: *BioIn 7, 8, 9, 10; NewYTBE 70*

McLaren, Norman
Canadian. Motion Picture Director
b. Apr 11, 1914 in Scotland
Source: *CanWW 82; CreCan 1; DcFM; FilmgC; IntWW 74; OxFilm; St&PR 75; WhoAm 74; WhoAmA 73; WhoGrA; WhoWor 74; WorEFlm*

McLarnin, Jimmy
"Baby Face"
Irish. Boxer
b. Dec 17, 1905 in Belfast, Northern Ireland
Source: *WhoBox 74*

McLaughlin, John
[Mahavishnu Orchestra]
English. Singer, Musician
First jazz-rock group to attain fame in both types of music, 1972-74.
b. 1942 in Yorkshire, England
Source: *EncPR&S; IlEncRk; LilREn 78*

McLaughlin, John J
Canadian. Chemist
Patented Canada dry ginger ale, 1907.
d. 1924
Source: *NF*

McLaughlin, John J
American. Former Priest, Educator
b. 1927
Source: *BioIn 9, 10*

McLaughlin, Marya
American. Broadcast Journalist
Source: *BioIn 7*

McLean, Don
American. Singer, Songwriter
Hit songs "American Pie," 1971, "Vincent," 1972.
b. Oct 2, 1945 in New Rochelle, New York
Source: *CurBio 73; EncPR&S; IlEncRk; NewYTBE 72; RkOn; WhoAm 74, 76, 78, 80, 82*

McLean, Evalyn Walsh
American. Washington Hostess
b. Aug 1, 1886 in Denver, Colorado
d. Apr 26, 1947 in Washington, DC
Source: *CurBio 43, 47; InWom; NotAW*

McLean, John Milton
American. Scientist, Physician, Engineer
b. Oct 24, 1909 in New York, New York
d. May 2, 1968
Source: *BbtC; WhAm 5*

McLean, Robert
American. Newspaper Publisher
b. Oct 1, 1891 in Philadelphia, Pennsylvania
d. Dec 5, 1980 in Montecito, California
Source: *BioIn 2; ConAu 103; CurBio 51, 81; IntWW 74; St&PR 75; WhAm 7; WhoE 74, 75; WhoWor 74*

McLerie, Allyn Ann
Canadian. Actress
b. Dec 1, 1926 in Grand Mere, PQ
Source: *BiE&WWA; FilmgC; IntMPA 75, 76, 77, 78, 79, 80, 81, 82; NotNAT; WhoHol A; WhoThe 77*

McLoughlin, John
"Father of Oregon"
American. Fur Trader
b. Oct 19, 1784 in Riviere du Loup, PQ
d. Sep 3, 1857
Source: *AmBi; BioIn 1, 3, 5, 7, 9, 10, 11; DcAmB; MacDCB 78; McGEWB; NewCol 75; NatCAB 6; OxCan; REnAW; WebAB; WhAm H*

McLuhan, (Herbert) Marshall
Canadian. Author, Educator
Mass communications expert; wrote *Understanding Media,* 1964.
b. Jul 21, 1911 in Edmonton, AB
d. Dec 31, 1980 in Toronto, ON
Source: *AmAu&B; CanWW 70; CanWr; CasWL; ConAu 9R, 102; CurBio 67, 81; DrAS 74E; IntWW 74; NewC; OxCan, SUP; Pen AM; WhAm 7; Who 74; WhoAm 74; WhoTwCL; WhoWor 74; WorAu; WrDr 76*

McMahon, Ed(ward Lee)
American. Entertainer
Began on "The Tonight Show" with Johnny Carson, Oct 1, 1962.
b. Mar 6, 1923 in Detroit, Michigan
Source: *BioNews 74; BkPepl; CelR 73; IntMPA 75, 76, 77, 78, 79, 80, 81, 82; WhoAm 74, 76, 78, 80, 82; WhoHol A*

McMahon, Horace
American. Actor
b. 1907 in Norwalk, Connecticut
d. Aug 17, 1971 in Norwalk, Connecticut
Source: *BiE&WWA; MotPP; MovMk; NewYTBE 71; WhScrn 74, 77; WhoHol B*

McMahon, (James O') Brien
American. Senator
b. Oct 6, 1903 in Norwalk, Connecticut
d. Jul 28, 1952 in Washington, DC
Source: *BiDrAC; BioIn 2, 3; CurBio 45, 52; DcAmB S5; NatCAB 40; NewCol 75; ObitOF 79; PolProf T; WhAm 3*

McManaway, James
American. Shakespearian Scholar
b. Aug 24, 1899 in Fayette, Missouri
Source: *WhoAm 78*

McManus, George
American. Comic Strip Artist
b. Jan 23, 1884 in Saint Louis, Missouri
d. Oct 22, 1954 in Santa Monica, California
Source: *DcAmB S5; REnAL; WhAm 3; WhScrn 77*

McMaster, John Bach
American. Historian
b. Jun 29, 1852 in Brooklyn, New York
d. May 24, 1932 in Darien, Connecticut
Source: *AmAu&B; AmBi; ApCAB; BiD&SB; DcAmAu; DcAmB; DcNAA; REn; REnAL; TwCBDA; WebAB; WhAm 1*

McMurtry, Larry
American. Author
b. Jun 3, 1936 in Wichita Falls, Texas
Source: *ConAu 5R; ConNov 76; DrAF 76; EncWL; REnAW; WrDr 76, 80*

McNair, Barbara
American. Singer
b. 1937 in Chicago, Illinois
Source: *BiE&WWA; CurBio 71; WhoAm 74, 76, 78, 80, 82; WhoBlA 75; WhoHol A*

McNair, Robert Evander
American. Former Governor
b. Dec 14, 1923 in Cades, South Carolina
Source: *BioIn 7; WhoAm 78, 80, 82*

McNally, Andrew, III
American. Publisher
Rand-McNally, president, 1948-74, chairman, 1974--.
b. Aug 17, 1909 in Chicago, Illinois
Source: *CurBio 56; St&PR 75; WhoAm 74; WhoF&I 74; WhoMW 74*

McNally, Dave (David Arthur)
American. Baseball Player
b. Oct 31, 1942 in Billings, Montana
Source: *BaseEn; WhoProB 73*

McNally, John Victor
[Johnny Blood]
American. Football Player
b. Nov 27, 1904 in New Richmond, Wisconsin
Source: *BioIn 6, 7, 8, 9, 10; WhoFtbl 74*

McNally, Terrence
American. Dramatist
b. Nov 3, 1939 in Saint Petersburg, Florida
Source: *ConAu 45, 2NR; ConDr 73; ConLC 4; McGEWD; NatPD; NotNAT; WhoAm 74, 76, 78, 80, 82; WhoThe 77; WrDr 76*

McNamara, Margaret Craig
American. Educator, Founder of RIF
b. Aug 22, 1915 in Seattle, Washington
d. Feb 3, 1981 in Washington, DC
Source: *BioIn 11; NewYTBS 81; WhoAmW 66, 77*

McNamara, Robert Strange
American. Banker, Former Cabinet Member
b. Jun 9, 1916 in San Francisco, California
Source: *BiDrUSE; CelR 73; CurBio 61; EncAB-H; IntWW 74; NewYTBE 73; St&PR 75; Ward 77G; Who 74; WhoAm 74, 76, 78, 80, 82; WhoF&I 74; WhoGov 72; WhoWor 74*

McNamee, Graham
American. Broadcaster
b. Jul 10, 1888 in Washington, DC
d. May 9, 1942 in New York, New York
Source: *CurBio 42; DcAmB S3; WhAm 2*

McNary, Charles Linza
American. Statesman
b. Jun 12, 1874 in Salem, Oregon
d. Feb 25, 1944 in Fort Lauderdale, Florida
Source: *BiDrAC; CurBio 40, 44; DcAmB S3; WhAm 2; WhAmP*

McNaughton, F(oye) F(isk)
American. Publisher, Editor
Editor, publisher of Pekin (IL) *Daily Times,* 1927-81.
b. May 15, 1890 in Ray, Indiana
d. Dec 29, 1981 in Effingham, Illinois
Source: *WhJnl; WhoF&I 75, 77*

McNeil, Claudia Mae
American. Actress
b. Aug 13, 1917 in Baltimore, Maryland
Source: *BiE&WWA; InWom; NotNAT; WhoAm 74, 76, 78, 80, 82; WhoBlA 75; WhoHol A; WhoThe 77; WhoWor 74*

McNeil, Neil Venable
American. Journalist
b. Oct 24, 1927 in Houston, Texas
Source: *WhoAm 74*

McNeile, Herman Cyril
[Sapper, pseud.]
English. Author
b. Sep 28, 1888 in Bodmin, England
d. Aug 14, 1937 in Pulborough, England
Source: *DcLEL; EncMys; EvLB; LongCTC; NewC; REn; TwCA, SUP*

McNeill, Don(ald Thomas)
American. Radio Show Host
Hosted *Breakfast Club,* longest running morning show on radio, 1933-68.
b. Dec 3, 1907 in Galena, Illinois
Source: *CurBio 49*

McNeill, Robert Edward, Jr.
American. Banker
b. Jan 20, 1906 in Live Oak, Florida
d. May 4, 1981 in Orlando, Florida
Source: *NewYTBS 81; WhoAm 74, 76*

McNellis, Maggi
[Margaret Eleanor Roche]
American. Radio, TV Personality
b. Jun 1, 1917 in Chicago, Illinois
Source: *CurBio 55; InWom; IntMPA, 75, 76, 77, 78, 79, 80, 81, 82*

McNerney, Walter James
American. Business Executive
b. Jun 8, 1925 in New Haven, Connecticut
Source: *WhoAm 74, 76, 78, 80, 82; WhoMW 74*

McNichol, Jimmy (James Vincent)
American. Actor, Singer
Source: *BioIn 12*

McNichol, Kristy
American. Actress
Won Emmy for role of Buddy in "Family," 1977.
b. Sep 9, 1962 in Los Angeles, California
Source: *BioIn 11, 12; BkPepl; IntMPA 82; WhoAm 80, 82*

McNutt, Paul Vories
American. Government Official
b. Jul 18, 1891 in Franklin, Indiana
d. Mar 24, 1955 in New York, New York
Source: *CurBio 40, 55; DcAmB S5; IndAu 1917; WhAm 3*

McPartland, Jimmy (James Duigald)
American. Jazz Musician, Band Leader
b. Mar 15, 1907 in Chicago, Illinois
Source: *WhoAm 74*

McPartland, Margaret Marian
English. Composer
b. Mar 20, 1918 in Buckinghamshire, England
Source: *WhoAm 74; WhoE 74*

McPhatter, Clyde
[The Drifters]
American. Singer
b. 1933 in Durham, North Carolina
d. Jun 13, 1972 in New York, New York
Source: *EncPR&S*

McPherson, Aimee Semple
American. Evangelist
Founded International Church of Foursquare Gospel, 1918.
b. Oct 9, 1890 in Ingersoll, ON
d. Sep 27, 1944 in Oakland, California
Source: *BioNews 74; CurBio 44; DcAmB S5; InWom; NotAW; WebAB; WhAm HA, 2, 4A*

McPherson, James Birdseye
American. Military Leader
b. Nov 14, 1828 in Green Creek, Ohio
d. Jun 22, 1864
Source: *AmBi; ApCAB; DcAmB; Drake; TwCBDA; WhAm H*

McPherson, Sarah Freedman
American. Artist
b. 1894 in Cleveland, Ohio
d. 1978
Source: *BioIn 12*

McQueen, "Butterfly" (Thelma)
American. Actress
Played Prissy in *Gone With the Wind,* 1939.
b. Jan 7, 1911 in Tampa, Florida
Source: *FilmgC, MotPP; MovMk; NewYTBE 70; ThFT; WhoHol A; WhoThe 77*

McQueen, Steve (Terence Stephen)
American. Actor
Starred in *Bullitt,* 1968; *The Getaway,* 1973.
b. Mar 24, 1930 in Indianapolis, Indiana
d. Nov 7, 1980 in Juarez, Mexico
Source: *BiDFilm; CelR 73; CmMov; CurBio 66; FilmgC; IntMPA 75, 76, 77; IntWW 74; MotPP; MovMk; OxFilm; WhoAm 74; WhoHol A; WhoWor 74; WorEFlm*

McRae, Carmen
American. Singer
b. Apr 8, 1922 in New York, New York
Source: *WhoAm 74, 76, 78, 80, 82; WhoE 74*

McShane, Ian
English. Actor
b. Sep 29, 1942 in Blackburn, England
Source: *FilmgC; WhoHol A; WhoThe 77, 81*

McSpaden, Byron
"Gold Dust Twins"
American. Golfer
b. May 21, 1908 in Rosedale, Kansas
Source: *WhoGolf*

McTear, Houston
American. Track Athlete
b. 1956?
Source: *BioIn 10*

McVie, Christine Perfect
[Fleetwood Mac]
English. Singer, Musician
b. Jul 12, 1943 in England
Source: *WhoAm 80, 82*

McVie, John
[Fleetwood Mac]
English. Rock Musician
b. Nov 26, 1946 in England
Source: *WhoAm 80, 82*

McWhirter, A(lan) Ross
English. Author, Publisher
Editor *The Guinness Book of World Records,* first edition, 1955.
b. Aug 12, 1925 in London, England
d. Nov 27, 1975 in London, England
Source: *ConAu 17R, 61*

McWhirter, Norris Dewar
English. Author, Publisher
Twin brother of Alan; editor *The Guinness Book of World Records,*
b. Aug 12, 1925 in London, England
Source: *Au&Wr 71; ConAu 13R*

McWilliams, Alden
American. Cartoonist
b. 1916 in Greenwich, Connecticut
Source: *WorECom*

McWilliams, Carey
American. Author
b. Dec 13, 1905 in Steamboat Springs, Colorado
d. Jun 27, 1980 in New York, New York
Source: *AmAu&B; ConAu 45, 101, 2NR; CurBio 43; OxAmL; REnAL; TwCA SUP; WhoAm 74; WhoWor 74*

Mead, George Herbert
American. Psychologist
b. Feb 27, 1863 in South Hadley, Massachusetts
d. Apr 26, 1931 in Chicago, Illinois
Source: *DcAmB S1; DcNAA; OhA&B; WebAB; WhAm 1*

Mead, George Houk
American. Business Executive
Organized Mead Corp., 1905.
b. Nov 5, 1877 in Dayton, Ohio
d. Jan 1, 1963 in Dayton, Ohio
Source: *WhAm 4*

Mead, Margaret
[Margaret Beteson]
American. Anthropologist, Author
Studied primitive cultures; wrote *Cooperation and Competition among Primitive Peoples,* 1937.
b. Dec 16, 1901 in Philadelphia, Pennsylvania
d. Nov 15, 1978 in New York, New York
Source: *AmAu&B; AmM&WS 73S; Au&Wr 71; AuBYP; AuNews 1; BioNews 74; CelR 73; ConAu 1R, 4NR; CurBio 40, 51; DcLEL; EncAB-H; EvLB; ForWC 70; HerW; InWom; IntWW 74; LongCTC; NewYTBE 70, 72; OxAmL; Pen AM; REn; REnAL; TwCA, SUP; WebAB; WhNAA; Who 74; WhoAm 74; WhoWor 74; WrDr 76*

Mead, William Rutherford
American. Architect
b. Aug 20, 1846 in Brattleboro, Vermont
d. Jun 20, 1928 in Paris, France
Source: *AmBi; ApCAB X; BioIn 2, 8; DcAmB; LinLib S; NatCAB 23; TwCBDA; WhAm 1; WhoArch*

Meade, George Gordon
American. Military Leader
b. Dec 31, 1815 in Cadiz, Spain
d. Nov 6, 1872 in Philadelphia, Pennsylvania
Source: *AmBi; ApCAB; DcAmB; EncAB-H; TwCBDA; WebAB; WhAm H*

Meade, Julia
American. Actress
b. Dec 17, 1930 in Boston, Massachusetts
Source: *BiE&WWA; CelR 73; InWom; NotNAT; WhoAm 74; WhoE 74; WhoHol A*

Meader, Vaughn
American. Actor
b. 1936
Source: *BioIn 10*

Meadows, Audrey
American. Actress
b. 1924 in Wu Chang, China
Source: *CurBio 58; InWom; MotPP; WhoAm 74, 76, 78, 80, 82; WhoHol A*

Meadows, Earle
"Heavenly Twins"
American. Track Athlete
b. Jun 29, 1913 in Corinth, Mississippi
Source: *WhoTr&F 73*

Meadows, Jayne Cotter
[Mrs. Steve Allen]
American. Actress
b. Sep 27, 1926 in Wu Chang, China
Source: *BiE&WWA; BioNews 75; CurBio 58; InWom; MotPP; WhoAm 74, 76, 78, 80, 82; WhoHol A*

Meagher, Mary T
American. Swimmer
b. 1965?
Source: *BioIn 12*

Means, Marianne Hansen
American. Journalist
b. Jun 13, 1934 in Sioux City, Iowa
Source: *ConAu 9R; ForWC 70; WhoAm 74, 76, 78, 80, 82; WhoS&SW 73*

Means, Russell Charles
American. Indian Rights Activist
Leader of AIM; led 71-day takeover of Wounded Knee, SD, 1973.
b. Nov 10, 1940 in Pine Ridge, South Dakota
Source: *BioIn 10; BioNews 74; CurBio 78*

Meany, George
American. Labor Leader
Participated in merger of AFL-CIO, 1955; president until death.
b. Aug 16, 1894 in New York, New York
d. Jan 10, 1980 in Washington, DC
Source: *BioNews 74; BusPN; ConAu 97; CurBio 42, 54; EncAB-H; IntWW 74; NewYTBE 72; WebAB; Who 74; WhoAm 74; WhoGov 72; WhoS&SW 73; WhoWor 74*

Meara, Anne
[Mrs. Jerry Stiller; Stiller and Meara]
American. Actress, Comedienne
b. 1924 in New York, New York
Source: *BioNews 75; WhoAm 82; WhoHol A*

Mearns, David Chambers
American. Librarian
b. Dec 31, 1899 in Washington, DC
d. May 21, 1981 in Alexandria, Virginia
Source: *AmAu&B; BiDrLUS 70; ConAu 1R; CurBio 61, 81; WhoAm 74, 76*

Mears, Rick Ravon
American. Auto Racer
Won Indianapolis 500, 1979.
b. Dec 3, 1951 in Wichita, Kansas
Source: *BioIn 12; WhoAm 82*

Meat Loaf
[Marvin Lee Aday]
American. Rock Musician, Actor
Sang with Amboy Dukes; weighs 260 pounds.
b. Sep 27, 1947 in Dallas, Texas
Source: *BioIn 11; BkPepl; RkOn*

Mecom, John Whitfield
American. Oilman
b. Jan 13, 1911 in Liberty, Texas
d. Oct 12, 1981 in Houston, Texas
Source: *AnObit 1981; BioIn 4, 7, 11; WhoS&SW 73*

Medary, Milton B
American. Architect
b. Feb 6, 1874 in Philadelphia, Pennsylvania
d. Aug 7, 1929 in Philadelphia, Pennsylvania
Source: *DcAmB; WhAm 1*

Medford, Kay
American. Actress
b. Sep 14, 1920 in New York, New York
d. Apr 10, 1980 in New York, New York
Source: *BiE&WWA; ForWC 70; NotNAT; WhoHol A; WhoThe 77*

Medici, Catherine de
see: Catherine de Medici

Medici, Cosimo de
[Cosimo the Elder]
Italian. Merchant Prince
b. 1389 in Florence, Italy
d. 1464
Source: *BioIn 10; WebBD 80*

Medici, Francesco de
Italian. Grand Duke of Tuscany
b. 1541
d. 1587
Source: *BioIn 10; WebBD 80*

Medici, Lorenzo de
[Lorenzo the Magnificent]
Italian. Poet, Ruler
b. Jan 1, 1449 in Florence, Italy
d. Apr 8, 1492 in Florence, Italy
Source: *BbD; BiD&SB; CasWL; EuAu; EvEuW; Pen EUR*

Medill, Joseph
American. Journalist
b. Apr 6, 1823 in Saint John, NB
d. Mar 16, 1899 in San Antonio, Texas
Source: *AmAu&B; AmBi; ApCAB; DcAmB; OxAmL; TwCBDA; WebAB; WhAm H; WhAmP*

Medina, Ernest L
American. Army Officer
Stood trial for ordering murder of Vietnamese civilians in My Lai, 1968.
b. 1936
Source: *NewYTBE 71*

Medina, Harold Raymond
American. Judge
b. Feb 16, 1888 in New York, New York
Source: *AmAu&B; Au&Wr 71; CurBio 49; WhoAm 74, 76, 78, 80, 82; WhoE 74*

Medina, Patricia
American. Actress
b. 1920 in London, England
Source: *BiE&WWA; BioNews 74; FilmgC; IntMPA 75, 76, 77, 78, 79, 80, 81, 82; MotPP; MovMk; WhoHol A*

Medtner, Nicholas
German. Composer, Musician
b. Dec 24, 1880 in Moscow, Russia
d. Nov 13, 1951 in London, England
Source: *OxMus; WebBD 80*

Medvedev, Zhores Aleksandrovich
Russian. Biologist
b. Nov 14, 1925 in Tiflis, U.S.S.R.
Source: *CurBio 73; IntWW 74; NewYTBE 70, 71, 73*

Medwick, Joseph Michael
"Ducky"
American. Baseball Player
b. Nov 4, 1911 in Carteret, New Jersey
d. Mar 21, 1975 in Saint Petersburg, Florida
Source: *WhoProB 73*

Meegeren, Hans van
Dutch. Artist, Forger
b. 1889
d. 1947
Source: *BioIn 1*

Meek, Donald
Scottish. Actor
b. Jul 14, 1880 in Glasgow, Scotland
d. Nov 18, 1946 in Los Angeles, California
Source: *FilmgC; MotPP; MovMk; Vers A; WhScrn 74, 77; WhoHol B*

Meek, Samuel Williams
American. Advertising Executive
b. Sep 22, 1895 in Nashville, Tennessee
d. Aug 15, 1981 in Greenwich, Connecticut
Source: *BioIn 7; NewYTBS 81; WhoAm 78, 80*

Meeker, Howie (Howard William)
Canadian. Hockey Player, Sportscaster
b. Nov 4, 1924 in Kitchener, ON
Source: *WhoHcky 73*

Meeker, Ralph
American. Actor
b. Nov 21, 1920 in Minneapolis, Minnesota
Source: *BiDFilm; BiE&WWA; CmMov; FilmgC; IntMPA 75, 76, 77, 78, 79, 80, 81, 82; MotPP; MovMk; NotNAT; WhoHol A; WhoThe 77; WorEFlm*

Meer, Jan van der
Dutch. Artist
b. 1628 in Haarlem, Netherlands
d. 1691
Source: *WebBD 80*

Meese, Edwin, III
American. Lawyer, Presidential Advisor
b. Dec 2, 1931 in Oakland, California
Source: *CurBio 81; WhoAm 82*

Meher Baba
[Merwan S Irani]
Indian. Prophet, Religious Leader
b. 1894
d. 1969
Source: *BioIn 10*

Mehta, Ved Parkash
Indian. Author, Journalist
b. Mar 21, 1934 in Lahore, India
Source: *Au&Wr 71; ConAu 1R; NewYTBE 72; Who 74; WhoWor 74; WorAu; WrDr 76*

Mehta, Zubin
Indian. Conductor
Conductor, LA Philharmonic, 1962-78; NY Philharmonic, 1978--.
b. Apr 29, 1936 in Bombay, India
Source: *ConAu 2NR; CurBio 69; IntWW 74; NewYTBE 70; Who 74; WhoAm 74, 76, 78, 80, 82; WhoMus 72; WhoWor 74*

Mehul, Etienne Nicolas
French. Composer
b. Jun 22, 1763 in Givet, France
d. Oct 18, 1817 in Paris, France
Source: *NewCol 75; OxFr; WebBD 80*

Meier-Graefe, Julius
German. Art Critic, Author
b. Jun 10, 1867 in Resitza, Germany
d. Jul 1935
Source: *TwCA; WhoLA*

Meighan, Thomas
American. Actor
b. Apr 9, 1879 in Pittsburgh, Pennsylvania
d. Jul 8, 1936 in Great Neck, New York
Source: *Film 1; FilmgC; MotPP; MovMk; TwYS; WhAm 1; WhScrn 74, 77; WhoHol B*

Meigs, Montgomery Cunningham
American. Army Officer
b. May 3, 1816 in Augusta, Georgia
d. Jan 2, 1892 in Washington, DC
Source: *AmBi; ApCAB; DcAmB; Drake; TwCBDA; WhAm H, 1*

Meiklejohn, Alexander
American. Educator
b. Feb 3, 1872 in Rochdale, England
d. Sep 16, 1964 in Berkeley, California
Source: *AmAu&B; OxAmL; REnAL; WebAB; WhAm 4*

Meiklejohn, William
American. Talent Agent
b. 1902 in Los Angeles, California
d. Apr 26, 1981 in Burbank, California
Source: *NewYTBS 81*

Mein, J Gordon
American. Diplomat
b. 1913
d. Aug 28, 1968
Source: *BioIn 8, 10*

Meine, Klaus
see: Scorpions

Meinhof, Ulrike Marie
German. Terrorist, Revolutionary
Co-leader of Baader-Meinhof Gang, W German terrorists in 1970's.
b. 1934 in Oldenburg, Germany
d. May 9, 1976 in Stuttgart, Germany (West)
Source: *BioIn 10, 11; LookW; WhoModH*

Meir, Golda
[Golda Myerson]
Israeli. Prime Minister
First woman prime minister of Israel, 1969-74; wrote *My Life,* 1975.
b. May 3, 1898 in Kiev, Russia
d. Dec 8, 1978 in Jerusalem, Israel
Source: *ConAu 81, 89; CurBio 70; HerW; InWom; IntWW 74; NewYTBS 74; Who 74; WhoGov 72; WhoWor 74; WhoWorJ 72*

Meisner, Sanford
American. Actor, Motion Picture Director
b. Aug 31, 1905 in New York, New York
Source: *BiE&WWA; NotNAT; PlP&P*

Meisner, Randy
[The Eagles; Poco]
American. Rock Musician, Singer
Bass player with Eagles, 1971-77; left to pursue solo career.
b. Mar 8, 1946 in Scotts Bluff, Nebraska
Source: *AmSCAP 80*

Meissonier, Jean Louis Ernest
French. Artist
b. Feb 21, 1815 in Lyons, France
d. Jan 31, 1891 in Paris, France
Source: *NewC; NewCol 75; WebBD 80*

Meitner, Lise
Austrian. Physicist
b. Nov 7, 1878 in Vienna, Austria
d. Oct 28, 1968 in Cambridge, England
Source: *AsBiEn; BioIn 1, 3, 4, 5, 6, 8, 9, 11; CurBio 45, 68; DcScB; EncTR; GoodHS; HerW; InWom; LinLib S; REn; WhAm 5; WhoAmW 68*

Melachrino, George
Conductor, Actor
b. 1909
d. Jun 18, 1965 in London, England
Source: *WhScrn 74, 77; WhoMus 72*

Melanchthon, Philip Schwarzerd
German. Religious Reformer
b. Feb 16, 1497
d. Apr 19, 1560
Source: *NewCol 75; WebBD 80*

Melanie
[Melanie Safka]
American. Singer
b. Feb 3, 1948 in New York, New York
Source: *EncPR&S; IlEncRk*

Melba, Dame Nellie
[Helen Porter Mitchell Armstrong]
Australian. Opera Singer
b. May 19, 1859 in Melbourne, Australia
d. Feb 23, 1931 in Sydney, Australia
Source: *InWom; LongCTC; NewC; REn; WhAm 1*

Melcher, Frederic Gershon
American. Publisher
b. Apr 12, 1879 in Malden, Massachusetts
d. Mar 9, 1963 in Montclair, New Jersey
Source: *AmAu&B; ChPo, S1, S2; CurBio 45, 63; WhAm 4*

Melcher, John
American. Senator
b. Sep 6, 1924 in Sioux City, Iowa
Source: *BioIn 11; WhoAm 78, 80, 82*

Melchers, Gari
American. Artist
b. Aug 11, 1860 in Detroit, Michigan
d. Nov 30, 1932
Source: *AmBi; DcAmB; WhAm 1*

Melchior, Lauritz
Danish. Opera Singer
b. Mar 20, 1890 in Copenhagen, Denmark
d. Mar 18, 1973 in Santa Monica, California
Source: *CurBio 41, 73; FilmgC; MovMk; NewYTBE 73; WhAm 5; WhScrn 77; WhoHol B; WhoMus 72*

Melies, Georges
French. Cinematographer
b. Dec 8, 1861 in Paris, France
d. 1938
Source: *FilmEn; TwYS; WomWMM*

Melis, Jose
Band Leader
b. Feb 27, 1920 in Havana, Cuba
Source: *AmSCAP 66*

Mell, pseud.
see: Lazarus, Mel

Mellinger, Frederick
American. Fashion Designer
b. 1915?
Source: *BioIn 9, 10*

Mellon, Andrew William
American. Financier, Government Official
Secretary of Treasury, 1921-32; ambassador to Great Britain, 1932-33.
b. Mar 24, 1855 in Pittsburgh, Pennsylvania
d. Aug 26, 1937 in Southampton, New York
Source: *AmBi; BiDrUSE; DcAmB S2; DcNAA; EncAB-H; WebAB; WhAm 1*

Mellon, Paul
American. Business Executive
b. Jun 11, 1907 in Pittsburgh, Pennsylvania
Source: *CelR 73; CurBio 66; IntWW 74; Who 74; WhoAm 74, 76, 78, 80, 82; WhoAmA 73; WhoF&I 74; WhoGov 72; WhoWor 74*

Mellon, Richard King
American. Philanthropist
b. Jun 19, 1899 in Pittsburgh, Pennsylvania
d. Jun 3, 1970 in Pittsburgh, Pennsylvania
Source: *CurBio 65, 70; NewYTBE 70; WhAm 5*

Mellon, William Larimer, Jr.
American. Doctor, Philanthropist
b. 1910 in Pittsburgh, Pennsylvania
Source: *BioIn 3, 4, 5, 6, 7; CurBio 65*

Mellor, Walter
American. Architect
b. Apr 25, 1880 in Philadelphia, Pennsylvania
d. Jan 11, 1940
Source: *CurBio 40; WhAm 1*

Melnick, Daniel
American. Motion Picture Executive
b. Apr 21, 1932 in New York, New York
Source: *WhoAm 78*

Meloy, Francis Edward, Jr.
American. Ambassador to Lebanon
b. Mar 28, 1917 in Washington, DC
d. Jun 16, 1976 in Beirut, Lebanon
Source: *USBiR 74; WhoAm 74; WhoAmP 73; WhoGov 72*

Melrose, William
Scottish. Tea Merchant
Source: *BioIn 10*

Melton, James
American. Opera Singer
b. Jan 2, 1904 in Moultrie, Georgia
d. Apr 21, 1961 in New York, New York
Source: *CurBio 45, 61; FilmgC; WhAm 4; WhScrn 74, 77; WhoHol B*

Meltzer, Bernard C
Journalist
Source: *AmEA 74*

Melville, Herman
American. Author
Wrote *Moby Dick,* 1851.
b. Aug 1, 1819 in New York, New York
d. Sep 28, 1891 in New York, New York
Source: *Alli, SUP; AmAu; AmAu&B; AmBi; AmWr; ApCAB; AtlBL; BbD; BiD&SB; CasWL; Chambr 3; ChPo, S2; CnDAL; CnE&AP; CrtT 3; CyAl 2; CyWA; DcAmAu; DcAmB; DcBiA; DcEnA; DcEnL; DcLEL; DcNAA; EncAB-H; EvLB; MouLC 4; OxAmL; OxEng; Pen AM; RAdv 1; RComWL; REn; REnAL; TwCBDA; WebAB; WebE&AL; WhAm H*

Melville, Jean-Pierre
French. Motion Picture Director
b. 1917 in Paris, France
d. Aug 2, 1973 in Paris, France
Source: *BiDFilm; DcFM; FilmgC; NewYTBE 73; OxFilm; WhoWor 74; WorEFlm*

Melville, Marjorie
American. Catonsville 9 Peace Activist
b. 1929?
Source: *BioIn 9*

Melville, Thomas
American. Catonsville 9 Peace Activist
Source: *BioIn 9*

Memling, Hans
Flemish. Artist
b. 1430 in Seligenstadt, Belgium
d. Aug 11, 1494 in Bruges, Belgium
Source: *AtlBL; NewC; REn*

Men at Work
[Greg Ham; Colin Hay; John Rees; Jerry Speiser; Ron Strykert]
Australian. Rock Group
Album *Business as Usual,* 1982, included hits "Who Can it be Now?" "Down Under."
Source: *NF*

Mencius
[Meng-Tzu]
Chinese. Philosopher
b. 371BC in Shantung, China
d. 289BC
Source: *BbD; BiD&SB; CasWL; DcOrL 1*

Mencken, H(enry) L(ouis)
American. Editor, Satirist
b. Sep 12, 1880 in Baltimore, Maryland
d. Jan 29, 1956 in Baltimore, Maryland
Source: *AmAu&B; AmLY; AmWr; AtlBL; CasWL; Chambr 3; ChPo, S2; CnDAL; CnMWL; ConAmA; ConAmL; CyWA; DcLEL; EncAB-H; EncWL; EvLB; LongCTC; ModAL, SUP; OxAmL; OxEng; Pen AM; RAdv 1; REn; REnAL; TwCA, SUP; TwCW; WebAB; WebE&AL; WhAm 3; WhNAA*

Mendel, Gregor Johann
Austrian. Botanist, Geneticist
Results of experiments with plants form foundation of modern genetics.
b. Jul 22, 1822 in Heinzendorf, Silesia
d. Jan 6, 1884 in Brunn, Bohemia
Source: *AsBiEn; OxGer; REn*

Mendeleev, Dmitri
Russian. Chemist
b. Feb 7, 1834 in Tobolsk, Russia
d. Feb 2, 1907 in Saint Petersburg, Russia
Source: *AsBiEn; McGEWB; WebBD 80*

Mendelsohn, Eric
German. Architect
b. Mar 21, 1887 in Allenskin, Germany
d. Sep 15, 1953 in San Francisco, California
Source: *AtlBL; CurBio 53*

Mendelssohn, Felix
[Felix Mendelssohn-Bartholdy]
German. Composer, Conductor, Musician
Symphonies include *Scottish,* 1830-42; *Reformation,* 1830-32.
b. Feb 3, 1809 in Hamburg, Germany
d. Nov 4, 1847 in Leipzig, Germany
Source: *AtlBL; BbD; BiD&SB; NewC; NewCol 75; OxGer; REn*

Mendes, (Abraham) Catulle
French. Author
b. May 22, 1841 in Bordeaux, France
d. Feb 8, 1909 in Saint Germain, France
Source: *BbD; BiD&SB; CasWL; ChPo; ClDMEL; EuAu; EvEuW; LongCTC; OxFr; Pen EUR; REn*

Mendes, Sergio
Brazilian. Musician, Band Leader
b. Feb 11, 1941 in Niteroi, Brazil
Source: *EncPR&S; RkOn*

Mendes-France, Pierre
French. Statesman
Socialist premier, ended France's war in Indochina.
b. Jan 11, 1907 in Paris, France
d. Oct 18, 1982 in Paris, France
Source: *Au&Wr 71; ConAu 81; CurBio 54, 83; IntWW 74, 75, 76, 77, 78, 79, 80; IntYB 78, 79; LinLib S; NewYTBS 82; WhoWor 74, 78; WhoWorJ 72*

Mendl, Lady Elsie de Wolfe
American. Interior Decorator
b. Dec 20, 1865 in New York, New York
d. Jul 12, 1950 in Versailles, France
Source: *BiCAW; DcAmB S4; InWom; NotAW; WhAm 4; WhoStg 1906, 1908; WomWWA 14*

Menelik II
Ethiopian. Emperor
b. 1844
d. 1913
Source: *NewCol 75*

Menes
King of 1st Egyptian Dynasty
Source: *NewCol 75*

Mengelberg, (Josef) Willem
Dutch. Conductor
b. Mar 28, 1871 in Utrecht, Netherlands
d. Mar 22, 1951 in Zuort, Switzerland
Source: *WebBD 80*

Mengele, Joseph
"The Angel of Extermination"
German. Nazi Official
Doctor at Auschwitz concentration camp; known for medical experimentation.
b. Mar 16, 1911 in Gunzburg, Bavaria
Source: *BioIn 9, 11; EncTR*

Mengistu, Haile Mariam
Ethiopian. Head of State
b. 1937 in Wollamo, Ethiopia
Source: *CurBio 81; IntWW 78, 80*

Mengs, Anton Raphael
German. Artist
b. 1728 in Aussig, Bohemia
d. 1779 in Rome, Italy
Source: *McGDA; McGEWB*

Menjou, Adolphe Jean
American. Actor
b. Feb 8, 1890 in Pittsburgh, Pennsylvania
d. Oct 29, 1963 in Beverly Hills, California
Source: *BiDFilm; CurBio 48, 64; Film 1; FilmgC; MotPP; MovMk; OxFilm; TwYS; WhAm 4; WhScrn 74, 77; WhoHol B; WorEFlm*

Menken, Helen
American. Actress
b. Dec 12, 1901 in New York, New York
d. Mar 27, 1966 in New York, New York
Source: *BiE&WWA; InWom; PlP&P; WhAm 4; WhScrn 74, 77; WhoHol B*

Mennen, William Gerhard
American. Philanthropist
b. Dec 20, 1884 in Newark, New Jersey
d. Feb 17, 1968 in Montclair, New Jersey
Source: *WhAm 4*

Mennin, Peter
American. Composer, Educator
b. May 17, 1923 in Erie, Pennsylvania
Source: *AmSCAP 66; BiE&WWA; CelR 73; CurBio 64; DcCM; IntWW 74; NewYTBE 71; WhoAm 74; WhoE 74; WhoMus 72; WhoWor 74*

Menninger, Karl Augustus
American. Psychiatrist
Wrote *The Human Mind,* 1930; co-founded Menninger Foundation, 1941.
b. Jul 23, 1893 in Topeka, Kansas
Source: *AmAu&B; AmM&WS 73P; Au&Wr 71; CelR 73; ConAu 17R; CurBio 48; IntWW 74; REnAL; TwCA, SUP; WebAB; WhNAA; WhoAm 74, 76, 78, 80, 82; WhoMW 74; WhoWor 74*

Menninger, William C
American. Scientist, Physician, Engineer
b. Oct 15, 1899 in Topeka, Kansas
d. Sep 6, 1966 in Topeka, Kansas
Source: *AmAu&B; ConAu 25R; CurBio 45, 66; REnAL; WhAm 4*

Menotti, Gian Carlo
Italian. Composer
b. Jul 7, 1911 in Cadigliano, Italy
Source: *AmSCAP 66; BiE&WWA; CelR 73; ChPo S2; CurBio 47; DcCM; IntWW 74; McGEWD; NewYTBS 74; NotNAT; OxAmL; REn; REnAL; WebAB; Who 74; WhoAm 74, 76, 78, 80, 82; WhoMus 72; WhoWor 74*

Menuhin, Hephzibah
American. Musician
b. May 20, 1920 in San Francisco, California
d. Jan 1, 1981 in London, England
Source: *Baker 78; BioIn 1; NewYTBS 81; WhoMus 72*

Menuhin, Jeremy
American. Pianist
b. 1951 in San Francisco, California
Source: *NewYTBE 70; WhoMus 72*

Menuhin, Yaltah
American. Pianist
b. in San Francisco, California
Source: *WhoMus 72*

Menuhin, Yehudi
American. Violinist
Child prodigy, debut with San Francisco Symphony at age 7.
b. Apr 22, 1916 in New York, New York
Source: *CelR 73; ConAu 45; CurBio 41, 73; IntWW 74; WebAB; Who 74; WhoAm 74, 76, 78, 80, 82; WhoHol A; WhoMus 72; WhoWor 74*

Menzel, Jiri
Czech. Motion Picture Director
b. 1938
Source: *DcFM; FilmgC; OxFilm; WhoWor 74; WorEFlm*

Menzies, Sir Robert Gordon
Australian. Politician
b. Dec 20, 1894 in Jeparit, Australia
d. May 14, 1978 in Melbourne, Australia
Source: *CurBio 41, 50; IntWW 74*

Mercadante, Saverio
Italian. Composer
b. Sep 1795 in Altamura, Italy
d. Dec 17, 1870 in Naples, Italy
Source: *NewEOp 71*

Mercader, Ramon
[Frank Jacson]
Cuban. Leon Trotsky's Assassin
b. 1914
d. Oct 18, 1978 in Havana, Cuba
Source: *BioIn 4, 5, 6, 11; ObitOF 79*

Mercator, Gerhardus
[Gerhard Kremer]
Flemish. Geographer
b. Mar 5, 1512 in Rupelmonde, Flanders
d. Dec 2, 1594 in Duisburg, Germany
Source: *AsBiEn; McGEWB; NewC; REn*

Mercer, Beryl
American. Actress
b. 1882 in Seville, Spain
d. Jul 28, 1939 in Santa Monica, California
Source: *FilmgC; InWom; MotPP; MovMk; ThFT; WhScrn 74, 77; WhoHol B*

Mercer, David
English. Dramatist, Screenwriter
b. Jun 27, 1928 in Wakefield, England
d. Aug 8, 1980 in Haifa, Israel
Source: *CnThe; ConAu 9R, 102; CroCD; EncWT; Who 74; WhoThe 72, 77; WrDr 76, 80*

Mercer, Henry Chapman
Archeologist
b. 1856
d. 1930
Source: *BioIn 10, 11*

Mercer, Jerry
see: April Wine

Mercer, Johnny
American. Singer, Composer, Songwriter
b. Nov 18, 1909 in Savannah, Georgia
d. Jun 25, 1976 in Bel Air, California
Source: *BiE&WWA; CelR 73; CurBio 48; EncMT; FilmgC; IntMPA 75; WhoAm 74; WhoHol A; WhoThe 77*

Mercer, Lucy Page
see: Rutherfurd, Lucy Page

Mercer, Mabel
English. Singer
b. Jan 1900 in Burton-on-Trent, England
Source: *BioIn 5, 6, 7, 9, 10, 11; CelR 73; CurBio 73*

Merchant, Vivien
[Ada Thomson]
English. Actress
Starred in *The Homecoming,* 1967; written by ex-husband Harold Pinter.
b. Jul 22, 1929 in Manchester, England
d. Oct 3, 1982 in London, England
Source: *FilmgC; MotPP; NewYTBS 82; OxFilm; PlP&P; Who 75, 76, 77, 78, 79, 80, 81, 82; WhoHol A; WhoThe 72, 77, 81*

Mercouri, "Melina" (Maria Amalia)
[Mrs. Jules Dassin]
Greek. Actress, Politician
Starred in *Never on Sunday;* minister, Greek culture,sciences, 1981--.
b. Oct 18, 1925 in Athens, Greece
Source: *BkPepl; CelR 73; CurBio 65; FilmgC; InWom; IntMPA 75, 76, 77, 78, 79, 80, 81, 82; IntWW 74; MotPP; MovMk; NewYTBE 71, 72; OxFilm; WhoAm 74, 76, 78, 80, 82; WhoHol A; WhoWor 74; WorEFlm*

Mercurius, Joannes
[Giovanni Mercurio da Correggio]
Italian. Prophet
Source: *BioIn 10*

Mercury, Freddie
[Frederick Bulsara; Queen]
English. Singer, Musician
Album *We Are the Champions;* included single "Another One Bites the Dust."
b. Sep 8, 1946 in Zanzibar
Source: *BkPepl; IlEncRk; LilREn 78; RkOn; WhoRock 81*

Meredith, Burgess
American. Actor
Starred in *Rocky,* films, 1977, 1979, 1981; plays Dr. Adams on "Gloria," 1982--.
b. Nov 16, 1909 in Cleveland, Ohio
Source: *BiDFilm; BiE&WWA; CurBio 40; FilmgC; HolP 30; IntMPA 75, 76, 77, 78, 79, 80, 81, 82; MotPP; MovMk; NotNAT; OxFilm; PlP&P; WhoAm 74, 76, 78, 80, 82; WhoHol A; WhoWest 74; WhoWor 74; WorEFlm*

Meredith, George
English. Author, Poet
b. Feb 2, 1828 in Portsmouth, England
d. May 18, 1909 in Boxhill, England
Source: *Alli, SUP; AtlBL; BbD; BiD&SB; BrAu 19; CasWL; Chambr 3; ChPo, S1; CnE&AP; CrtT 3; CyWA; DcBiA; DcEnA, AP; DcEnL; DcEuL; DcLEL; EvLB; LongCTC; MouLC 4; NewC; OxEng; Pen ENG; RAdv 1; REn; WebE&AL*

Meredith, James Howard
American. Civil Rights Advocate
b. Jun 25, 1933 in Kosciusko, Mississippi
Source: *WebAB; WhoAm 74, 76, 78, 80, 82; WhoWor 74*

Meredith, (Joseph) Don(ald)
"Dandy Don"
American. Football Player, Sportscaster
Quarterback, Dallas, 1960-69; co-host, "Monday Night Football," 1970-73; 1977--.
b. Apr 10, 1938 in Mount Vernon, Texas
Source: *BioIn 8, 9, 10, 11; NewYTBS 77; WhoAm 76, 78, 80, 82; WhoFtbl 74*

Meredith, Scott
American. Literary Agent
b. Nov 24, 1923 in New York, New York
Source: *BioIn 10; WhoAm 78, 80, 82*

Merejkowski, Dmitri Sergeyevich
[Dmitry Sergeyevich Merezhovsky]
Russian. Author
b. Aug 14, 1865 in Saint Petersburg, Russia
d. Dec 9, 1941 in Paris, France
Source: *CyWA*

Meres, Francis
English. Literary Historian, Critic
b. 1565
d. Jan 29, 1647
Source: *Alli; BrAu; CasWL; Chambr 1; DcEnL; DcEuL; DcLEL; EvLB; NewC; OxEng; Pen ENG; REn*

Mergenthaler, Ottmar
American. Inventor
Invented the linotype, 1884.
b. May 11, 1854 in Hachtel, Germany
d. Oct 28, 1899 in Baltimore, Maryland
Source: *AmBi; DcAmB; EncAB-H; NewCol 75; OxAmL; TwCBDA; WebAB; WhAm H*

Merida, Carlos
Mexican. Artist
b. Dec 2, 1891 in Guatemala City, Guatemala
Source: *CurBio 60; IlsBYP; IlsCB 1946; McGDA; WhoAmA 73, 76, 78; WhoGrA*

Merimee, Prosper
French. Author, Historian, Critic
b. Sep 28, 1803 in Paris, France
d. Sep 23, 1870 in Cannes, France
Source: *AtlBL; BbD; BiD&SB; CasWL; CyWA; DcBiA; DcEuL; EuAu; EvEuW; NewC; OxEng; OxFr; Pen EUR; REn*

Merivale, Philip
English. Actor
b. Nov 2, 1880 in Rehutia, India
d. Mar 13, 1946 in Los Angeles, California
Source: *CurBio 46; FilmgC; PlP&P; REn; WhAm 2; WhScrn 74; WhoHol B*

Meriwether, Lee
American. Actress
Miss America, 1955; co-star of "Barnaby Jones," 1973-80.
b. May 27, 1935 in Los Angeles, California
Source: *WhoAm 78; WhoHol A*

Meriwether, W(ilhelm) Delano
American. Physician, Athlete
b. Apr 23, 1943 in Nashville, Tennessee
Source: *CurBio 78; WhoAm 78, 80, 82; WhoBlA 77*

Merkel, Una
American. Actress
b. Dec 10, 1903 in Covington, Kentucky
Source: *BiE&WWA; FilmgC; IntMPA 75, 76, 77, 78, 79, 80, 81, 82; MotPP; MovMk; NotNAT; ThFT; Vers A; WhoHol A; WhoThe 77*

Merman, Ethel
[Ethel Zimmerman]
American. Singer, Actress
Starred on Broadway in *Annie Get Your Gun,* 1946; *Hello, Dolly,* 1970.
b. Jan 16, 1909 in Astoria, New York
Source: *BiE&WWA; BioNews 75; CelR 73; CmMov; CurBio 41, 55; EncMT; FamA&A; FilmgC; InWom; IntMPA 75, 76, 78, 79, 80, 81, 82; MotPP; MovMk; NotNAT; PlP&P; ThFT; WebAB; WhoAm 74, 76, 78, 80, 82; WhoHol A; WhoThe 77, 81; WhoWor 74*

Mermer, Friedrich Anton
Austrian. Physician
b. 1734
d. 1815
Source: *BioIn 10*

Merola, Gaetano
Italian. Conductor, Opera Director
b. Jan 4, 1881 in Naples, Italy
d. Aug 30, 1953 in San Francisco, California
Source: *WhAm 6*

Merriam, Charles
American. Publisher
b. 1806 in West Brookfield, Massachusetts
d. Jul 9, 1887 in Springfield, Massachusetts
Source: *AmAu&B; ApCAB; DcAmB; TwCBDA; WebAB; WhAm H*

Merriam, Frank Finley
American. Politician
b. Dec 22, 1865 in Delaware County, Iowa
d. Apr 25, 1955 in Long Beach, California
Source: *BioIn 1, 3, 5, 7; NatCAB 42; ObitOF 79; WhAm 3*

Merrick, David
[David Margulois]
American. Theatrical Producer
Plays include *Fanny,* 1954; *Gypsy,* 1958; *Promises, Promises,* 1969.
b. Nov 27, 1912 in Saint Louis, Missouri
Source: *BiE&WWA; BioNews 74; CelR 73; CurBio 61; EncMT; IntMPA 82; IntWW 74; NewYTBE 70, 73; WebAB; WhoAm 74, 76, 78, 80, 82; WhoThe 77; WhoWor 74*

Merrill, Charles Edward
American. Business Executive
b. Oct 19, 1885 in Green Cove, Florida
d. Oct 6, 1956 in Southampton, New York
Source: *CurBio 56; WhAm 3*

Merrill, Dina
[Nedinia Hutton; Mrs. Cliff Robertson]
American. Actress, Heiress
b. Dec 9, 1925 in New York, New York
Source: *CelR 73; FilmgC; InWom; IntMPA 75, 76, 77, 78, 79, 80, 81, 82; MotPP; MovMk; WhoAm 82; WhoAmW 77; WhoHol A*

Merrill, Frank Dow
American. Army Officer
b. Dec 4, 1903
d. Dec 11, 1955 in Fernandina, Florida
Source: *BioIn 1, 4, 6*

Merrill, Gary Franklin
American. Actor
b. Aug 2, 1915 in Hartford, Connecticut
Source: *BiE&WWA; FilmgC; IntMPA 75, 76, 77, 78, 79, 80, 81, 82; MotPP; MovMk; NotNAT; WhoAm 82; WhoHol A*

Merrill, Henry Tindall
"Dick"
American. Pilot
Made first round-trip trans-Atlantic flight, 1936.
b. 1894? in Iuka, Mississippi
d. Nov 30, 1982 in Lake Elsinore, California
Source: *InSci; NewYTBS 82*

Merrill, James
American. Author
b. Mar 3, 1926 in New York, New York
Source: *AmAu&B; ConAu 13R; ConLC 2, 3, 6; ConP 70, 75; CroCAP; CurBio 81; DrAF 76; DrAP 75; ModAL, SUP; OxAmL; Pen AM; REnAL; WhoAm 74, 76, 78, 80, 82; WhoE 74; WhoWor 74; WorAu; WrDr 76*

Merrill, Robert
American. Opera Singer
First American to sing 500 performances at Metropolitan Opera.
b. Jun 4, 1919 in New York, New York
Source: *CelR 73; IntWW 74; WhoAm 74; WhoGov 72; WhoMus 72; WhoWor 74*

Merriman, Nan
American. Opera Singer
b. 1920
Source: *InWom*

Merritt, Abraham
American. Author
b. Jan 20, 1884 in Beverley, New Jersey
d. Aug 30, 1943 in Clearwater, Florida
Source: *AmAu&B; DcNAA; REnAL; WhAm 2; WorAu*

Merton, Thomas
American. Poet, Author
b. Jan 31, 1915 in Prades, France
d. Dec 10, 1968 in Bangkok, Thailand
Source: *AmAu&B; CathA 1930; ConAu 5R, 25R; ConLC 1, 3; LongCTC; ModAL; OxAmL; Pen AM; REnAL; TwCA SUP; WebAB; WhAm 5*

Mertz, Barbara Louise Gross
[Barbara Michaels; Elizabeth Peters, pseuds.]
American. Author
b. Sep 29, 1927 in Canton, Illinois
Source: *Au&Wr 71; BioIn 11; ConAu 21R; DrAS 74H; ScF&FL 1, 2; TwCCr&M; WrDr 76, 80*

Merwin, W(illiam) S(tanley)
American. Poet
b. Sep 30, 1927 in New York, New York
Source: *ConAu 17R; ConLC 1, 2, 3, 5, 8, 13, 18; WhoAm 78, 80, 82; WhoWor 74*

Meshach
see: Shadrach, Meshach and Abednego

Meskill, Thomas J
American. Judge, Former Congressman
b. Jan 30, 1928 in New Britain, Connecticut
Source: *BioIn 10; CurBio 74; WhoAm 78, 80, 82; WhoAmP 79; WhoGov 77*

Mesmer, Franz Anton
German. Physician
b. May 23, 1734 in Baden-Baden, Germany
d. Mar 5, 1815 in Meersburg, Germany
Source: *AsBiEn; BiDPara; McGEWB; OxGer; REn*

Mesple, Mady
French. Opera Singer
Source: *BioIn 9*

Messager, Andre Charles Prosper
French. Composer, Conductor
b. Dec 30, 1853 in Montlucon, France
d. Feb 24, 1929 in Paris, France
Source: *NewEOp 71; OxMus*

Messel, Oliver
English. Designer, Artist
b. Jan 13, 1905 in London, England
d. Jul 14, 1978 in Bridgetown, Barbados
Source: *CnThe; EncWT; NewYTBS 78; NotNAT; ObitOF 79; OxThe; WhoOp 76; WhoThe 77*

Messer, Alfred A
American. Author
b. Oct 29, 1922 in Morristown, New Jersey
Source: *AmM&WS 73P; ConAu 29R*

Messerschmitt, Willy
German. Aviation Engineer
b. Jun 26, 1898 in Augsburg, Germany
d. Sep 15, 1978 in Munich, Germany (West)
Source: *CurBio 40; IntWW 74; WhoWor 74*

Messersmith, Andy (John Alexander)
American. Baseball Player
b. Aug 6, 1945 in Toms River, New Jersey
Source: *BaseEn; NewYTBE 73; WhoProB 73*

Messiaen, Olivier
French. Composer, Musician
b. Dec 10, 1908 in Avignon, France
Source: *DcCM; IntWW 74; WhoMus 72*

Messick, Dale
American. Cartoonist
b. 1906 in South Bend, Indiana
Source: *CurBio 61; InWom; WhoAm 74, 76, 78, 80, 82*

Messick, Henry Hicks
American. Journalist
b. Aug 14, 1922 in Happy Valley, North Carolina
Source: *ConAu 45, 2NR*

Messina, Jim
[Buffalo Springfield; Loggins and Messina; Poco]
American. Singer, Songwriter
b. Dec 5, 1947 in Maywood, California
Source: *BioIn 12*

Messing, Shep
American. Soccer Player
b. Oct 9, 1949 in Bronx, New York
Source: *NewYTBE 72*

Messner, Reinhold
Italian. Mountaineer, Author
First person to reach summit of Mt. Everest without artificial oxygen, May, 1978.
b. Sep 17, 1944 in Bressanone, Italy
Source: *BioIn 12; ConAu 81; CurBio 80*

Mesta, Perle Skirvin
American. Diplomat
Ambassador to Luxembourg, 1949-53; known for parties given for political leaders.
b. Oct 12, 1891 in Sturgis, Michigan
d. Mar 16, 1975 in Oklahoma City, Oklahoma
Source: *BioNews 74; CelR 73; ConAu 57; InWom; WhAm 6; WhoAm 74; WhoWor 74*

Metrinko, Michael John
[The Hostages]
American. Former Hostage in Iran
b. Nov 11, 1946 in Pennsylvania
Source: *BioIn 12; NewYTBS 81; USBiR 74*

Mestrovic, Ivan
American. Sculptor
b. Aug 15, 1883 in Vrpolje, Croatia
d. Jan 16, 1962
Source: *CurBio 40, 62; DcCAA 71; WhAm 4*

Metalious, Grace de Repentigny
American. Author
Wrote *Peyton Place,* 1956; adapted into movie and TV series.
b. Sep 8, 1924 in Manchester, New Hampshire
d. Feb 25, 1964
Source: *AmAu&B; ConAu 21R; ConAu P-2; InWom; LongCTC; TwCW*

Metastasio, Pietro
Italian. Dramatist, Poet, Librettist
b. Jan 3, 1698 in Rome, Italy
d. Apr 12, 1782 in Vienna, Austria
Source: *AtlBL; BiD&SB; CasWL; CnThe; DcEuL; EuAu; EvEuW; McGEWD; NewC; OxEng; Pen EUR; REn; REnWD*

Metaxas, John Ioannis
Greek. General, Dictator
b. Apr 12, 1871 in Cephalonia, Greece
d. Jan 29, 1941 in Athens, Greece
Source: *CurBio 40, 41*

Metcalf, Lee
American. Senator
b. Jan 28, 1911 in Stevensville, Montana
d. Jan 12, 1978 in Helena, Montana
Source: *BiDrAC; CngDr 74; CurBio 70, 78; IntWW 74; WhoAm 74; WhoAmP 73; WhoGov 72*

Metcalf, Willard L
American. Artist
b. Jul 1, 1858 in Lowell, Massachusetts
d. Mar 9, 1925
Source: *AmBi; DcAmB; WhAm 1*

Metcalfe, Ralph H
American. Politician
b. May 30, 1910 in Atlanta, Georgia
d. Oct 10, 1978 in Chicago, Illinois
Source: *CngDr 74; WhoAm 74; WhoAmP 73; WhoBlA 75; WhoGov 72; WhoMW 74; WhoTr&F 73*

Metchnikoff, Elie
Russian. Biologist
b. May 15, 1845 in Ivanovka, Russia
d. Jul 16, 1916
Source: *McGEWB; NewCol 75*

Methuseleh
Biblical Character
Source: *NewCol 75*

Metternich-Winneburg, Clemens
Austrian. Statesman
b. May 15, 1773
d. Jun 11, 1859 in Vienna, Austria
Source: *DcEuL; OxFr*

Metzenbaum, Howard M(orton)
American. Senator
b. Jun 4, 1917 in Cleveland, Ohio
Source: *CurBio 80; St&PR 75; WhoAm 74, 76, 78, 80, 82; WhoAmP 73; WhoMW 74*

Metzinger, Jean
French. Artist
b. 1883 in Nantes, France
d. Nov 3, 1956 in Paris, France
Source: *ConArt; McGDA*

Mew, Charlotte Mary
English. Poet
b. 1869
d. 1928
Source: *BioIn 1, 2, 5, 9*

Meyer, Debbie (Deborah)
American. Swimmer
First to win three gold medals in individual events in one Olympics, 1968.
b. Aug 14, 1952 in Annapolis, Maryland
Source: *BioIn 10*

Meyer, Eugene Brown
American. Chess Player
b. Jun 27, 1952 in Kingston, New York
Source: *WhoAm 78*

Meyer, Joseph
American. Composer
b. Mar 12, 1894 in Modesto, California
Source: *AmPS; AmSCAP 66, 80; BiDAmM; BioIn 11; EncMT*

Meyer, Nicholas
American. Author, Motion Picture Director
b. Dec 24, 1945 in New York, New York
Source: *ConAu 49; IntAu&W 76, 77; WhoAm 76, 78, 80, 82; WrDr 76, 80*

Meyer, Ray(mond Joseph)
American. Basketball Coach
Coach, DePaul U, 1942--; Hall of Fame, 1979.
b. Dec 18, 1913 in Chicago, Illinois
Source: *BioIn 11; WhoAm 78, 80, 82*

Meyer, Russ
American. Motion Picture Director
b. 1922 in Oakland, California
Source: *BioIn 8, 10; FilmEn; FilmgC; IntMPA 75, 76, 77, 78, 79, 80, 81; WhoAm 74, 76, 78, 80, 82; WhoWest 78*

Meyerbeer, Giacomo
[Jakob Liebmann Beer]
German. Opera Composer
b. Sep 5, 1791 in Berlin, Germany
d. May 2, 1864 in Paris, France
Source: *AtlBL; NewC; OxFr; REn*

Meyerhoff, Joseph
American. Philanthropist
b. Apr 8, 1899 in Russia
Source: *WhoAm 78, 80, 82*

Meyerowitz, Jan
German. Opera Composer
b. Apr 23, 1913 in Breslau, Germany
Source: *DcCM*

Meynell, Alice
English. Poet, Essayist
b. 1847 in London, England
d. Nov 27, 1922 in London, England
Source: *Alli SUP; BbD; BiD&SB; Chambr 3; ChPo, S1, S2; CnE&AP; DcEnA, AP; DcEuL; DcLEL; EvLB; LongCTC; ModBrL; NewC; Pen ENG; REn; TwCA, SUP*

Mezzrow, "Mezz" (Milton)
American. Jazz Musician
b. Nov 9, 1899 in Chicago, Illinois
d. Aug 5, 1972 in Paris, France
Source: *ConAu 37R; NewYTBE 72; WhAm 5; WhoJazz 72*

Michael I
Romanian. Former King
b. 1921
Source: *BioIn 10*

Michael, the Archangel
Biblical Character
Source: *BioIn 1, 2, 3, 4, 5, 6, 11; NewCol 75*

Michael, Moina Belle
"The Poppy Lady"
American. Originator of Poppy Day
b. Aug 15, 1869 in Good Hope, Georgia
d. May 10, 1944 in Athens, Georgia
Source: *CurBio 44; InWom; ObitOF 79; WhAm 2*

Michaels, Barbara, pseud.
see: Mertz, Barbara Louise Gross

Michaels, Lorne
Canadian. Producer, Writer
b. Nov 17, in Toronto, ON
Source: *CanWW 82; WhoAm 78*

Michalowski, Kazimierz
Polish. Archaeologist
b. Dec 14, 1901 in Ternopol, Poland
d. Jan 1, 1981 in Warsaw, Poland
Source: *AnObit 1981; IntWW 74, 75, 76, 77, 78; MidE 78, 79; WhoSocC 78; WhoWor 76, 78*

Michals, Duane Steven
American. Photographer
b. Feb 18, 1932 in McKeesport, Pennsylvania
Source: *BioIn 10, 11; CurBio 81; WhoAm 78, 80, 82; WhoAmA 76, 78*

Michaux, Henri
Belgian. Poet, Artist
b. May 24, 1899 in Namur, Belgium
Source: *CasWL; CnMWL; ConAu 85; ConLC 8; EncWL; EvEuW; ModRL; OxFr; Pen EUR; REn; TwCA SUP; TwCW; WhoTwCL*

Michel, F Curtis
American. Astronaut
b. Jun 5, 1934 in La Crosse, Wisconsin
Source: *AmM&WS 73P; WhoAm 74, 76, 78, 80, 82*

Michel, Robert H(enry)
American. Congressman
b. Mar 2, 1923 in Peoria, Illinois
Source: *AlmAP 78, 80; BiDrAC; CngDr 74, 77, 79; CurBio 81; WhoAm 74, 76, 78, 80, 82; WhoAmP 73, 75, 77, 79; WhoGov 72, 75, 77; WhoMW 74, 76, 78*

Michelangeli, Arturo Benedetti
Italian. Musician
b. Jan 5, 1920
Source: *BioIn 9; IntWW 77*

Michelangelo Bounarroti
Italian. Artist, Poet
b. Mar 6, 1475 in Caprese, Italy
d. Feb 18, 1564 in Rome, Italy
Source: *AtlBL; BbD; CasWL; DcEuL; EuAu; EvEuW; OxEng; Pen EUR; REn*

Michelin, Andre
French. Tire Manufacturer
With brother Edouard, first to make rubber tires for motorcars, 1895.
b. 1853
d. 1931
Source: *WebBD 80*

Michelin, Francois
French. Industrialist
b. Jul 3, 1926
Source: *IntWW 74*

Michell, Keith
Australian. Actor
b. 1928 in Adelaide, Australia
Source: *BiE&WWA; EncMT; FilmgC; IntMPA 75, 76, 77, 78, 79, 80, 81, 82; MovMk; NotNAT; Who 74; WhoHol A; WhoThe 77; WhoWor 74*

Michelson, Albert A
American. Scientist, Physician, Engineer
b. Dec 19, 1852 in Strelno, Germany
d. May 9, 1931
Source: *AmBi; ApCAB; DcAmB; DcNAA; EncAB-H; OxAmL; REnAL; WebAB; WhAm 1*

Michener, James A(lbert)
American. Author
Wrote *Tales of the South Pacific,* 1947; *Centennial,* 1974.
b. Feb 3, 1907 in New York, New York
Source: *AmAu&B; AmNov; Au&Wr 71; AuNews 1; BioNews 74; CelR 73; ConAu 5R; ConLC 1, 5, 11; ConNov 72, 76; CurBio 48; DcLEL; FilmgC; IntWW 74; LongCTC; ModAL; NewYTBE 72; OxAmL; Pen AM; PlP&P; RAdv 1; REnAL; TwCA SUP; WebAB; Who 82; WhoAm 74, 76, 78, 80, 82; WhoWor 74; WrDr 76*

Michener, Roland
Canadian. Former Governor General
b. Apr 19, 1900 in Lacombe, AB
Source: *CanWW 82; IntWW 74; Who 74; WhoAm 74, 76, 78, 80, 82; WhoCan 73; WhoGov 72; WhoWor 74*

Mickens, "Spike" (Robert)
see: Kool and the Gang

Middendorf, John William
American. Diplomat
b. Sep 22, 1924 in Baltimore, Maryland
Source: *WhoAm 74; WhoAmP 73; WhoGov 72; WhoWor 74*

Middlecoff, Cary
American. Golfer
b. Jan 6, 1921 in Halls, Tennessee
Source: *CurBio 52*

Middleton, Arthur
American. Continental Congressman
b. Jun 26, 1742 in Charleston, South Carolina
d. Jan 1, 1787 in Goose Creek, South Carolina
Source: *AmBi; ApCAB; BiDSA; BiDrAC; DcAmB; TwCBDA; WhAm H; WhAmP*

Middleton, Christopher
English. Poet, Educator
b. Jun 10, 1926 in Truro, England
Source: *BioIn 8, 10; ConAu 17R; ConLC 13; WhoAm 78, 80, 82*

Middleton, Ray
American. Actor
b. 1907 in Chicago, Illinois
Source: *BiE&WWA; EncMT; FilmgC; IntMPA 75, 76, 77, 78, 79, 80, 81, 82; NotNAT; PlP&P; WhoHol A; WhoThe 77*

Middleton, Thomas
English. Dramatist
b. Apr 18, 1570 in London, England
d. Jul 4, 1627 in Newington Butts, England
Source: *Alli; AtlBL; BbD; BiD&SB; BrAu; CasWL; Chambr 1; ChPo, S2; CnE&AP; CnThe; CroE&S; CrtT 1; CyWA; DcEnA; DcEnL; DcEuL; DcLEL; EvLB; McGEWD; MouLC 1; NewC; OxEng; OxThe; Pen ENG; REn; REnWD; WebE&AL*

Midler, Bette
"The Divine Miss M;" "The last of the tacky ladies"
American. Singer, Actress
Won Emmy for special "Ol' Red Hair is Back," 1978; starred in *The Rose,* 1979.
b. Dec 1, 1944 in Paterson, New Jersey
Source: *BioNews 75; BkPepl; CelR 73; CurBio 73; IntMPA 82; NewWmR; NewYTBE 72, 73; WhoAm 74, 76, 78, 80, 82; WhoHol A*

Miele, Jerry J
[The Hostages]
American. Former Hostage in Iran
b. 1939?
Source: *NewYTBS 81*

Mielziner, Jo
American. Stage Designer
b. Mar 19, 1901 in Paris, France
d. Mar 15, 1976 in New York, New York
Source: *BiE&WWA; ConAu 45, 65; CurBio 46, 76; IntWW 74; NotNAT; OxThe; PlP&P; WhoAm 74; WhoAmA 73; WhoWor 74*

Mies van der Rohe, Ludwig
American. Architect
b. Mar 27, 1886 in Aachen, Germany
d. Aug 18, 1969 in Chicago, Illinois
Source: *AtlBL; CurBio 51, 69; EncAB-H; REn; WebAB; WhAm 5*

Mifflin, George Harrison
American. Publisher
b. May 1, 1845 in Boston, Massachusetts
d. Apr 5, 1921
Source: *AmAu&B; WhAm 1*

Mifune, Toshiro
Actor
b. Apr 1, 1920 in Tsingtao, China
Source: *FilmgC; IntMPA 75, 76, 77, 78, 79, 80, 81, 82; IntWW 74; MotPP; MovMk; OxFilm; WhoHol A; WhoWor 74; WorEFlm*

Mihajlov, Mihajlo
Yugoslav. Dissident, Author
b. Sep 26, 1934 in Pancevo, Yugoslavia
Source: *CurBio 79*

Mihajlovic, Draza
Yugoslav. Soldier
b. 1893 in Ivanjica, Yugoslavia
d. Jul 17, 1946
Source: *NewCol 75; WhoModH*

Miki, Takeo
Japanese. Politician
Prime Minister, 1974-76.
b. Mar 17, 1907 in Tokushima-Ken, Japan
Source: *BioNews 75; IntWW 74, 75, 76, 77, 78, 79, 80, 81; NewYTBS 74; WhoWor 74*

Mikita, Stan
American. Hockey Player
Center, Chicago Black Hawks, 1958-80; NHL MVP, 1968.
b. May 20, 1940 in Sokolce, Czechoslovakia
Source: *CurBio 70; WhoAm 74*

Mikkelsen, Henning Dahl
[Mik, pseud.]
American. Cartoonist
b. Jan 9, 1915 in Skive, Denmark
Source: *WhoAm 78; WorECom*

Mikoyan, Anastas Ivanovich
Russian. Politician
b. Nov 25, 1895 in Sanain, Armenia
d. Oct 22, 1978
Source: *CurBio 55, 79; IntWW 74; Who 74; WhoWor 74*

Mikoyan, Artem I
Russian. Scientist
b. 1905
d. Dec 9, 1970 in Moscow, U.S.S.R.
Source: *BioIn 9*

Mikva, Abner Joseph
American. Lawyer
b. Jan 21, 1926 in Milwaukee, Wisconsin
Source: *BiDrAC; WhoAm 74, 76, 78, 80, 82; WhoAmP 73; WhoGov 72; WhoWorJ 72*

Milano, Fred
[Dion and the Belmonts]
American. Singer
b. Aug 22, 1939
Source: *EncPR&S; IlEncRk; RkOn*

Milanov, Zinka Kunc
Yugoslav. Opera Singer
b. May 17, 1906 in Zagreb, Yugoslavia
Source: *CurBio 44; InWom; WhoMus 72; WhoWor 74*

Milburn, Frank Pierce
American. Architect
b. Dec 12, 1868 in Bowling Green, Kentucky
d. 1926
Source: *NatCAB 12*

Mildenburg, Anna von
Austrian. Opera Singer
b. Nov 29, 1872 in Vienna, Austria
d. Jan 27, 1947 in Vienna, Austria
Source: *InWom*

Milder-Hauptmann, Pauline Anna
Turkish. Opera Singer
b. Dec 13, 1785 in Constantinople, Turkey
d. May 29, 1838 in Berlin, Germany
Source: *InWom*

Mildmay, Audrey
English. Opera Singer
b. Dec 19, 1900 in Hurstmonceaux, England
d. May 31, 1953 in London, England
Source: *NewEOp 71*

Miles, Jackie
American. Comedian
b. 1913 in Kiev, Russia
d. Apr 24, 1968 in Los Angeles, California
Source: *WhoHol B*

Miles, Josephine
American. Educator, Poet
b. Jun 11, 1911 in Chicago, Illinois
Source: *AmAu&B; ConAu 1R, 2NR; ConLC 1, 2; ConP 70, 75; DrAP 75; DrAS 74E; IntWW 74; ModAL; OxAmL; Pen AM; RAdv 1; TwCA SUP; WhoAm 74, 76, 78, 80, 82; WrDr 76*

Miles, Nelson A
American. Soldier, Author, Actor
b. Aug 8, 1839 in Westminster, Massachusetts
d. May 15, 1925 in Washington, DC
Source: *AmAu&B; AmBi; ApCAB; DcAmAu; DcAmB; DcNAA; Drake; TwCBDA; WebAB; WhAm 1; WhScrn 77*

Miles, Sarah
English. Actress
b. Dec 31, 1943 in Igatestone, England
Source: *BiDFilm; BkPepl; CelR 73; FilmgC; IntMPA 75, 76, 77, 78, 79, 80, 81, 82; MotPP; MovMk; WhoHol A; WhoThe 77*

Miles, Sylvia
American. Actress, Comedienne
b. Sep 9, 1932 in New York, New York
Source: *BiE&WWA; CelR 73; NewYTBE 71; NotNAT; WhoHol A*

Miles, Tichi Wilkerson
American. Publisher
b. May 10, 1932 in Los Angeles, California
Source: *WhoAm 78*

Miles, Vera
American. Actress
b. Aug 23, 1930 in Boise City, Oklahoma
Source: *BiDFilm; FilmgC; ForWC 70; IntMPA 75, 76, 77, 78, 79, 80, 81, 82; MotPP; MovMk; WhoAm 78, 80, 82; WhoHol A; WorEFlm*

Milestone, Lewis
American. Motion Picture Director
b. Sep 30, 1895 in Chisinau, Russia
d. Sep 25, 1980 in Los Angeles, California
Source: *BiDFilm; CmMov; DcFM; FilmgC; IntMPA 75, 77; MovMk; OxFilm; TwYS; WorEFlm*

Milford, Penny (Penelope)
American. Actress
b. 1949 in Winnetka, Illinois
Source: *BioIn 12; JohnWil 81*

Milgrim, Sally
American. Fashion Designer
b. Feb 1, 1940
Source: *InWom*

Milhaud, Darius
[Les Six]
French. Composer, Actor
b. Sep 4, 1892 in Aix-en-Provence, France
d. Jun 22, 1974 in Geneva, Switzerland
Source: *BioNews 74; CelR 73; ConAu 49; CurBio 41, 61, 74; DcCM; DcFM; NewYTBS 74; OxFilm; REn; WhAm 6; WhScrn 77; Who 74; WhoMus 72; WhoWor 74; WhoWorJ 72; WorEFlm*

Mill, James
Scottish. Philosopher, Historian
b. Apr 6, 1773 in Northwater Bridge, Scotland
d. Jun 23, 1836 in London, England
Source: *Alli; BbD; BiD&SB; BiDLA; BioIn 1, 6, 7, 8, 9, 10; BrAu 19; CasWL; Chambr 2; DcEnA; DcEnL; DcEuL; DcLEL; EvLB; LinLib L, S; McGEWB; NewC; NewCol 75; OxEng; Pen ENG*

Mill, John Stuart
English. Philosopher, Economist
Wrote *A System of Logic,* 1843; *On Liberty,* 1859.
b. May 20, 1806 in London, England
d. May 8, 1873 in Avignon, France
Source: *Alli, SUP; AtlBL; BbD; BiD&SB; BrAu 19; CasWL; Chambr 3; CrtT 3; CyWA; DcEnA; DcEnL; DcEuL; DcLEL; EvLB; MouLC 3; NewC; OxEng; Pen ENG; REn; WebE&AL*

Millais, Sir John Everett
English. Artist
b. Jun 8, 1829 in Southampton, England
d. Aug 13, 1896 in London, England
Source: *AtlBL; ChPo, S1, S2; NewC; REn*

Milland, Ray(mond Alton)
[Reginald Truscott-Jones]
American. Actor, Motion Picture Director
Won Oscar for *The Lost Weekend,* 1945.
b. Jan 3, 1908 in Neath, Wales
Source: *BiDFilm; CelR 73; CmMov; CurBio 46; FilmgC; IntMPA 75, 76, 77, 78, 79, 80, 81, 82; MotPP; MovMk; NewYTBE 72; OxFilm; WhoAm 78, 80, 82*

Millar, George
see: Irish Rovers

Millar, Jeff(rey) Lynn
American. Journalist, Critic, Cartoonist
b. Jul 10, 1942 in Pasadena, Texas
Source: *BioIn 10; WhoAm 82*

Millar, Joe
see: Irish Rovers

Millar, Kenneth
see: Macdonald, Ross, pseud.

Millar, Margaret Ellis
Canadian. Author
b. Feb 5, 1915 in Kitchener, ON
Source: *AmAu&B; AmNov; Au&Wr 71; CanWW 70; ConAu 13R; ConNov 76; EncMys; REnAL; WhoAm 74, 76, 78, 80, 82; WhoWor 74; WorAu; WrDr 76*

Millar, Will
see: Irish Rovers

Millay, Edna St. Vincent
[Nancy Boyd, pseud.]
American. Author, Poet
Won Pulitzer Prize for *The Ballad of the Harp Weaver,* 1922.
b. Feb 22, 1892 in Rockland, Maine
d. Oct 19, 1950 in Austerlitz, New York
Source: *AmAu&B; AmSCAP 66; AmWr; AtlBL; CasWL; Chambr 3; ChPo, S1, S2; CnDAL; CnE&AP; CnMD; CnMWL; ConAmA; ConAmL; CyWA; DcAmB S4; DcLEL; EncWL; EvLB; HerW; InWom; LongCTC; McGEWD; ModAL; ModWD; NotAW; OxAmL; OxEng; Pen AM; RAdv 1; REn; REnAL; SixAP; Str&VC; TwCA, SUP; TwCW; WebAB; WhAm 3; WhNAA*

Miller, Alfred Jacob
American. Artist
b. Jan 2, 1810 in Baltimore, Maryland
d. Jun 26, 1874 in Baltimore, Maryland
Source: *ApCAB; ArtsAmW; DcAmArt; IlBEAAW; McGDA; NewYHSD; REnAW; WhAm H*

Miller, Ann
[Lucille Ann Collier]
American. Dancer, Actress, Singer
Star of *Sugar Babies,* 1980--.
b. Apr 12, 1923? in Cherino, Texas
Source: *CelR 73; CmMov; CurBio 80; InWom; IntMPA 75, 76, 77, 78, 79, 80, 81, 82; MovMk; ThFT; WhoAm 80, 82; WhoHol A; WhoThe 77; WhoTwCL*

Miller, Arjay Ray
American. Business Executive
b. Mar 4, 1916 in Shelby, Nebraska
Source: *CurBio 67; IntWW 74; St&PR 75; Ward 77, 77G; Who 74; WhoAm 74, 76, 78, 80, 82; WhoF&I 74; WhoWor 74*

Miller, Arnold Ray
American. Labor Union Official
President, UMW, 1972-79.
b. Apr 25, 1923 in Leewood, West Virginia
Source: *BioNews 75; CelR 73; CurBio 74; NewYTBE 72; NewYTBS 74; WhoAm 74*

Miller, Arthur
American. Dramatist
Wrote *Death of a Salesman,* 1949; *The Crucible,* 1953; married Marilyn Monroe, 1956-61.
b. Oct 17, 1915 in New York, New York
Source: *AmAu&B; AmNov; AmWr; Au&Wr 71; AuNews 1; BiE&WWA; CasWL; CelR 73; CnDAL; CnMD; CnMWL; CnThe; ConAu 1R, 2NR; ConDr 73; ConLC 1, 2, 6, 10, 15; CroCD; CurBio 47, 73; CyWA; DcFM; DrAF 76; EncAB-H; EncWL; FilmgC; IntWW 74; LongCTC; McGEWD; ModAL, SUP; ModWD; NotNAT; WebAB; WebE&AL; Who 74; WhoAm 74, 76, 78, 80, 82; WhoThe 77; WhoTwCL; WhoWor 74; WhoWorJ 72; WorEFlm; WrDr 76*

Miller, Caroline
American. Author
b. Aug 26, 1903 in Waycross, Georgia
Source: *AmNov; ChPo; DcLEL; InWom; OxAmL; REnAL; TwCA, SUP*

Miller, Cheryl
American. Actress
b. Feb 4, 1943 in Sherman Oaks, California
Source: *IntMPA 75, 76, 77, 78, 79, 80, 81, 82; WhoHol A*

Miller, Cincinnatus Hiner
see: Miller, Joaquin, pseud.

Miller, Don
[Four Horsemen of Notre Dame]
American. Football Player
b. in Defiance, Ohio
Source: *WhoFtbl 74*

Miller, Dorie
American. World War II Naval Hero
b. 1919
d. 1943
Source: *BioIn 8*

Miller, Elva Ruby Connes
American. Entertainer, Civic Worker
b. 1908? in Joplin, Missouri
Source: *BioIn 8; WhoAmW 74*

Miller, G(eorge) William
American. Government Official
b. Mar 9, 1925 in Sapulpa, Oklahoma
Source: *BioIn 11; CurBio 78; WhoAm 78, 80, 82*

Miller, Gilbert Heron
American. Theatrical Producer
b. Jul 3, 1884 in New York, New York
d. Jan 2, 1969 in New York, New York
Source: *BiE&WWA; CurBio 58, 69; OxThe; PlP&P; WhAm 5*

Miller, Glenn
American. Band Leader
Hits include "In the Mood," "Chattanooga Choo-Choo."
b. Mar 1, 1904 in Clarinda, Iowa
d. Dec 15, 1944?
Source: *AmSCAP 66; CurBio 42; DcAmB S3; FilmgC; WebAB; WhAm 2; WhScrn 74, 77; WhoHol B; WhoJazz 72*

Miller, Henry
American. Author
Books *Tropic of Cancer,* 1934; *Tropic of Capricorn,* 1939 banned in US until 1960's.
b. Dec 26, 1891 in New York, New York
d. Jun 7, 1980 in Pacific Palisades, California
Source: *AmAu&B; AmNov; AmWr; CasWL; CelR 73; CnDAL; CnMWL; ConAu 9R, 97; ConLC 1, 2, 4, 9, 14; ConNov 72, 76; DcLEL; DrAF 76; EncWL; IntWW 74; LongCTC; ModAL, SUP; OxAmL; Pen AM; RAdv 1; REn; REnAL; TwCA, SUP; TwCW; WebE&AL; Who 74; WhoAm 74; WhoTwCL; WhoWor 74; WrDr 76*

Miller, Henry John
American. Actor, Theatrical Manager
b. Feb 1, 1860 in London, England
d. Apr 9, 1926 in New York, New York
Source: *AmBi; DcAmB; FamA&A; WhAm 1*

Miller, Jason
American. Dramatist, Actor
b. Apr 22, 1939 in Scranton, Pennsylvania
Source: *AuNews 1; BioNews 74; CelR 73; ConDr 73; ConLC 2; CurBio 74; IntMPA 75, 76, 77, 78, 79, 80, 81, 82; NatPD; NewYTBE 72; NotNAT; PlP&P A; WhoAm 74, 76, 78, 80, 82; WhoHol A; WhoThe 77; WrDr 76*

Miller, Joan
English. Actress
b. 1910 in Nelson, BC
Source: *WhoHol A; WhoThe 77*

Miller, Joaquin, pseud.
[Cincinnatus Hiner Miller]
American. Poet
b. Sep 8, 1837 in Liberty, Indiana
d. Feb 17, 1913 in Oakland, California
Source: *Alli SUP; AmAu; AmAu&B; AmBi; ApCAB SUP; BbD; BiD&SB; CasWL; Chambr 3; ChPo, S1; CnDAL; CrtT 3; CyAl 2; DcAmAu; DcAmB; DcEnA AP; DcEnL; DcLEL; DcNAA; EvLB; LongCTC; MouLC 4; OxAmL; OxEng; Pen AM; REn; REnAL; Str&VC; TwCBDA; WebAB; WhAm 1*

Miller, Joe
English. Actor
b. 1684
d. 1738
Source: *BioIn 1*

Miller, Johnny Laurence
American. Golfer
Won US Open, 1973; Player of year, 1974.
b. Apr 29, 1947 in San Francisco, California
Source: *BioNews 74; CurBio 74; WhoAm 78, 80, 82*

Miller, Jonathan
English. Actor, Author, Director
b. Jul 21, 1934 in London, England
Source: *BiE&WWA; CurBio 70; FilmgC; IntWW 74; NotNAT; Who 74; WhoHol A; WhoThe 77*

Miller, Linda Kay
American. Ballerina
b. Sep 7, 1953 in Washington, DC
Source: *WhoAm 78*

Miller, Marilyn
American. Actress
Sang "Easter Parade" in *As Thousands Cheer,* 1933.
b. Sep 1, 1898 in Findlay, Ohio
d. Apr 7, 1936 in Evansville, Indiana
Source: *AmBi; EncMT; FilmgC; InWom; MovMk; NotAW; ThFT; WhScrn 74, 77*

Miller, Marvin Julian
American. Baseball Executive
Director, ML Baseball Players' Assn., 1966--.
b. Apr 14, 1917 in New York, New York
Source: *BioIn 10; CurBio 73; WhoAm 78, 80, 82*

Miller, Max
American. Author
b. Feb 9, 1899 in Traverse City, Michigan
d. Dec 27, 1967 in La Jolla, California
Source: *AmAu&B; Au&Wr 71; ConAu 1R, 25R; CurBio 40, 68; NewYTBE 73; REnAL; TwCA, SUP; WhAm 4, 5; WhNAA*

Miller, Merle
American. Author, Journalist
b. May 17, 1919 in Montour, Iowa
Source: *AmAu&B; AmNov; Au&Wr 71; AuNews 1; ConAu 9R, 4NR; REn; REnAL; WhoAm 82; WhoWor 74; WorAu; WrDr 76*

Miller, Mitch(ell William)
American. Conductor
b. Jul 4, 1911 in Rochester, New York
Source: *CelR 73; CurBio 56; WhoAm 74, 76, 78, 80, 82; WhoAmA 73*

Miller, Olive Beaupre
American. Author
b. 1883
d. 1968
Source: *AmAu&B*

Miller, Paul
American. Journalist
b. Sep 28, 1906 in Diamond, Missouri
Source: *BioIn 1, 4, 11; WhoAm 78, 80, 82*

Miller, Perry Gilbert Eddy
American. Historian, Critic
b. Feb 25, 1905 in Chicago, Illinois
d. Dec 9, 1963 in Cambridge, Massachusetts
Source: *AmAu&B; BioIn 3, 4, 6, 7, 8; DcAmB; NewCol 75; Pen AM; REn; REnAL; TwCA SUP; WebAB; WhAm 4*

Miller, Roger Dean
American. Singer, Composer
Hits include "Dang Me," 1964; "King of the Road," 1965; won 11 Grammys, 1965-66.
b. Jan 2, 1936 in Fort Worth, Texas
Source: *EncFCWM 69; WhoAm 74, 76, 78, 80, 82*

Miller, Steve
[The Steve Miller Band]
American. Musician, Singer
b. Oct 5, 1943 in Dallas, Texas
Source: *BkPepl; EncPR&S; IlEncRk; RkOn*

Miller, William Ernest
American. Judge
b. Feb 3, 1908 in Johnson City, Tennessee
d. Apr 12, 1976 in Cincinnati, Ohio
Source: *WhoAm 74; WhoAmP 73; WhoGov 72; WhoS&SW 73*

Miller, William Mosley
"Fish Bait"
American. Congressional Doorkeeper
b. Jul 20, 1909 in Pascagoula, Mississippi
Source: *BioIn 10, 11; BioNews; WhoAmP 73; WhoGov 72*

Milles, Carl
Swedish. Sculptor
b. Jun 23, 1875 in Lagga, Sweden
d. Sep 19, 1955 in Stockholm, Sweden
Source: *CurBio 40, 52, 55; REn; WhAm 3*

Millet, Jean Francois
French. Artist
b. Oct 4, 1814 in Normandy, France
d. Jan 20, 1875 in Barbizon, France
Source: *AtlBL; ChPo; OxFr; REn*

Millett, Kate
[Katherine Murray Millett]
American. Sculptress, Feminist
Author *Sexual Politics,* 1970; member CORE, 1965--.
b. Sep 14, 1934 in Saint Paul, Minnesota
Source: *AmAu&B; AuNews 1; CelR 73; ConAu 73; CurBio 71; ForWC 70; WhoAm 82; WrDr 76*

Milligan, "Spike" (Terence Alan)
British. Actor, Motion Picture Director
b. Apr 16, 1918 in India
Source: *Au&Wr 71; ChPo S1, S2; ConAu 9R; EncWT; FilmgC; IntAu&W 76, 77; Who 74; WhoHol A; WhoThe 72, 77, 81; WrDr 76, 80*

Millikan, Clark Blanchard
American. Educator
b. Aug 23, 1903 in Chicago, Illinois
d. Jan 2, 1966 in Pasadena, California
Source: *AmM&WS 73P; WhAm 4*

Millikan, Robert Andrews
American. Physicist
b. Mar 22, 1868 in Morrison, Illinois
d. Dec 19, 1953 in San Marino, California
Source: *AmAu&B; AmLY; CurBio 40, 52, 54; DcAmB S5; EncAB-H; REnAL; WebAB; WhAm 3; WhNAA*

Milliken, William Grawn
American. Public Official
Governor of MI, 1969-82.
b. Mar 26, 1922 in Traverse City, Michigan
Source: *BioNews 75; IntWW 74; WhoAm 74, 76, 78, 80, 82; WhoAmP 73; WhoGov 72; WhoMW 74*

Millis, Walter
American. Author
b. Mar 16, 1899 in Atlanta, Georgia
d. Mar 17, 1968 in New York, New York
Source: *AmAu&B; ConAu 37R; ConAu P-1; OxAmL; REn; REnAL; TwCA, SUP; WhAm 5*

Mills, Darius Ogden
American. Businessman, Philanthropist
b. Sep 25, 1825 in North Salem, New York
d. Sep 25, 1910
Source: *AmBi; ApCAB; DcAmB; TwCBDA; WhAm 1*

Mills, Donald
[The Mills Brothers]
American. Singer
b. Apr 29, 1915 in Piqua, Ohio
Source: *BioNews 74*

Mills, Donna
American. Actress
Plays Abby Cunningham on "Knots Landing."
b. Dec 11, 1943 in Chicago, Illinois
Source: *BioIn 12; WhoHol A*

Mills, Florence
American. Entertainer
b. Jan 25, 1895 in Washington, DC
d. Nov 1, 1927 in New York, New York
Source: *EncMT; InWom; NotAW; WhoHol B*

Mills, Harry
[The Mills Brothers]
American. Singer
b. Aug 19, 1913 in Piqua, Ohio
d. Jun 28, 1982 in Los Angeles, California
Source: *BioNews 74; NewYTBS 82*

Mills, Hayley
English. Actress
Won Oscar for *Pollyanna,* 1960.
b. Apr 18, 1946 in London, England
Source: *CelR 73; CurBio 63; FilmgC; InWom; IntMPA 75, 76, 77, 78, 79, 80, 81, 82; MotPP; MovMk; WhoHol A; WhoThe 77; WhoWor 74; WorEFlm*

Mills, Herbert
[The Mills Brothers]
American. Singer
b. Apr 2, 1912 in Piqua, Ohio
Source: *BioNews 74*

Mills, John
[The Mills Brothers]
American. Singer
b. Feb 11, 1889 in Bellefonte, Pennsylvania
d. Dec 8, 1967 in Ohio
Source: *WhScrn 77*

Mills, Sir John
English. Actor
Won Oscar for *Ryan's Daughter,* 1970; father of Hayley and Juliet Mills.
b. Feb 22, 1908 in Felixstowe, England
Source: *BiDFilm; BiE&WWA; CelR 73; CmMov; CurBio 63; EncMT; FilmgC; IntMPA 77, 78, 79, 80, 81, 82; IntWW 74; MovMk; WorEFlm*

Mills, Juliet
English. Actress
Starred in "Nanny and the Professor," 1970-71; daughter of John Mills.
b. Nov 21, 1941 in London, England
Source: *BiE&WWA; FilmgC; InWom; MotPP; WhoAm 74; WhoHol A; WhoThe 77; WhoWor 74*

Mills, Ogden Livingston
American. Lawyer, Politician
b. Aug 23, 1884 in Newport, Rhode Island
d. Oct 11, 1937 in New York, New York
Source: *AmBi; BiDrAC; BiDrUSE; DcAmB S2; DcNAA; WhAm 1; WhAmP*

Mills, Robert
American. Architect, Engineer
b. Aug 12, 1781 in Charleston, South Carolina
d. Mar 3, 1855 in Washington, DC
Source: *Alli; AmBi; ApCAB; BiAuS; BiDSA; DcAmAu; DcAmB; DcNAA; Drake; OxAmL; TwCBDA; WebAB; WhAm H*

Mills, Stephanie
[Mrs. Jeffrey Daniels]
American. Singer, Entertainer
b. Mar 22, 1957 in Brooklyn, New York
Source: *BioIn 10; DcBlPA; WhoBlA 77*

Mills, Wilbur Daigh
American. Politician
b. May 24, 1909 in Kensett, Arkansas
Source: *CngDr 74; CurBio 56; IntWW 74; NewYTBE 71; Who 74; WhoAm 74, 76, 78, 80, 82; WhoAmP 73; WhoGov 72; WhoS&SW 73; WhoWor 74*

Mills Brothers, The
[Donald, Harry, Herbert and John Mills]
American. Vocal Group
Source: *DcBiPP*

Milne, A(lan) A(lexander)
English. Author
Wrote *Winnie-the-Pooh,* 1926; *The House at Pooh Corner,* 1928.
b. Jan 18, 1882 in London, England
d. Jan 31, 1956 in Hartfield, England
Source: *AnCL; AuBYP; BkCL; CarSB; CasWL; Chambr 3; ChlLR 1; ChPo, S1, S2; CnMD; DcLEL; EncMys; EvLB; JBA 34, 51; LongCTC; McGEWD; ModBrL; ModWD; NewC; OxEng; Pen ENG; RAdv 1; REn; Str&VC; TwCA, SUP; TwCW; WhAm 3; WhoChL; WhoLA; YABC 1*

Milne, Christopher Robin
English. Author
b. Aug 21, 1920 in London, England
Source: *AuNews 2; ConAu 61; WrDr 76*

Milne, David Brown
Canadian. Artist
b. Jan 1882 in Paisley, ON
d. Dec 26, 1953 in Toronto, ON
Source: *BioIn 1, 2, 3, 10; CreCan 1; McGDA; McGEWB; NewCol 75*

Milne, George
British. Army Officer
b. 1867
d. 1948
Source: *BioIn 1*

Milner, Alfred
British. Statesman
b. Mar 23, 1854 in Giessen, Germany
d. May 13, 1925 in Canterbury, England
Source: *DcEuL; LongCTC*

Milner, Martin Sam
American. Actor
Played Pete Malloy in "Adam-12," 1968-75.
b. Dec 28, 1931 in Detroit, Michigan
Source: *FilmgC; IntMPA 77, 78, 79, 80, 81, 82; MotPP; WhoHol A*

Milnes, Sherrill Eustace
American. Opera Singer
b. Jan 10, 1935 in Downers Grove, Illinois
Source: *CurBio 70; IntWW 74; NewYTBE 72; WhoAm 74, 76, 78, 80, 82; WhoWor 74*

Milosz, Caeslaw
American. Poet, Essayist
b. Jun 30, 1911 in Sateiniai, Lithuania
Source: *CasWL; ConAu 81; ConLC 5, 11; CurBio 81; DrAS 74F, 78F; EncWL; IntWWP 77; ModSL 2; Pen EUR; WhoTwCL; WorAu*

Milsap, Ronnie
American. Singer
Hits include "What Goes on When the Sun Goes Down"; "Stand by Your Woman Man."
b. Jan 16, 1944 in Robinsville, North Carolina
Source: *BioIn 11; WhoAm 78, 80, 82*

Milstein, Nathan
American. Musician
b. Dec 31, 1904 in Odessa, Russia
Source: *CelR 73; CurBio 50; IntWW 74; Who 74; WhoAm 78; WhoMus 72*

Milton, John
English. Poet
Blind poet, wrote *Paradise Lost*, 1667.
b. Dec 9, 1608 in London, England
d. Nov 8, 1674 in London, England
Source: *Alli; AtlBL; BbD; BiD&SB; BrAu; CasWL; ChPo, S1, S2; CnE&AP; CnThe; CroE&S; CrtT 2; CyWA; DcEnA, AP; DcEnL; DcEuL; DcLEL; EvLB; HsB&A; MouLC 1; NewC; OxEng; Pen ENG; PoChrch; RAdv 1; RComWL; REn; REnWD; WebE&AL*

Mimieux, Yvette Carmen M
American. Actress
b. Jan 8, 1939 in Los Angeles, California
Source: *FilmgC; InWom; IntMPA 75, 76, 77, 78, 79, 80, 81, 82; MotPP; MovMk; WhoAm 74; WhoHol A*

Mindszenty, Jozsef, Cardinal
Hungarian. Ecclesiastic
b. Mar 29, 1892 in Hungary
d. Jun 6, 1975 in Vienna, Austria
Source: *ConAu 57; CurBio 57; IntWW 74; NewYTBE 71*

Mineo, Sal
"The Switchblade Kid"
American. Actor, Singer
Oscar nominations for *Rebel Without a Cause*, 1955; *Exodus*, 1960.
b. Jan 10, 1939 in New York, New York
d. Feb 12, 1976 in Los Angeles, California
Source: *FilmgC; IntMPA 75; MotPP; MovMk; WhAm 6*

Miner, Jack (John Thomas)
American. Ornithologist
b. Apr 10, 1865 in Dover Centre, Ohio
d. 1944 in Kingsville, ON
Source: *BioIn 2; DcNAA; MacDCB 78; ObitOF 79; OhA&B; OxCan; WhAm 4; WhNAA*

Miner, Worthington C
American. Theatrical Producer
b. Nov 13, 1900 in Buffalo, New York
Source: *BiE&WWA; CurBio 53; IntMPA 75, 76, 77, 78, 79, 80, 81, 82; NotNAT; WhoAm 74, 76, 78, 80, 82; WhoThe 77*

Minevitch, Borrah
Russian. Harmonica Player, Actor
b. 1903? in Kiev, Russia
d. Jun 25, 1955 in Paris, France
Source: *BioIn 3; WhScrn 74*

Ming, T'ai-Tsu
[Yuan-Chang Chu; Hung Wu]
Chinese. Emperor
b. 1328 in Anhwei Province, China
d. 1398
Source: *BioIn 10; WebBD 80*

Mingus, Charles
American. Musician
b. Apr 22, 1922 in Nogales, Arizona
d. Jan 5, 1979 in Cuernavaca, Mexico
Source: *BiDAmM; CmpEPM; ConAu 85, 93; CurBio 79; EncJzS 70; IlEncJ; NewYTBS 79; WhAm 7; WhoAm 76, 78; WhoBlA 77*

Minguy, Claude
Canadian. Zoo Director
b. Feb 20, 1930 in PQ
Source: *WhoAm 78, 80, 82*

Mink, Patsy Takemoto
American. Politician
b. Dec 6, 1927 in Paia, Hawaii
Source: *BiDrAC; CelR 73; CngDr 74; CurBio 68; InWom; WhoAm 74, 76, 78, 80, 82; WhoAmP 73; WhoAmW 77; WhoGov 72; WomPO 76*

Minnelli, Liza
[Mrs. Mark Gero]
American. Actress, Singer
Daughter of Judy Garland; won Oscar for *Cabaret*, 1972.
b. Mar 12, 1946 in Los Angeles, California
Source: *BiDFilm; BiE&WWA; BkPepl; CelR 73; CurBio 70; FilmgC; IntMPA 75, 76, 77, 78, 79, 80, 81, 82; IntWW 74; MotPP; MovMk; NewYTBE 72; NewYTBS 74; NotNAT; WhoAm 82; WhoHol A; WhoThe 77*

Minnelli, Vincente
American. Motion Picture Director
Won Oscar for *Gigi*, 1958; married Judy Garland, 1945-50.
b. Feb 28, 1913 in Chicago, Illinois
Source: *BiDFilm; CelR 73; CmMov; DcFM; EncMT; FilmgC; IntMPA 75, 76, 77, 78, 79, 80, 81, 82; IntWW 74; MovMk; NotNAT; OxFilm; WhoAm 74, 76, 78, 80, 82; WhoWor 74; WorEFlm*

"Minnesota Fats"
[R Wanderone]
American. Billiards Player
b. 1913 in New York, New York
Source: *BioIn 7, 8*

Minow, Newton Norman
American. Lawyer
b. Jan 17, 1926 in Milwaukee, Wisconsin
Source: *ConAu 13R; CurBio 61; IntWW 74; St&PR 75; WhoAm 74, 76, 78, 80, 82; WhoAmP 73; WhoF&I 74; WhoMW 74; WhoWor 74; WhoWorJ 72; WrDr 76*

Minsky, Abraham Bennett
[The Minsky Brothers]
American. Theatrical Producer
b. 1881
d. Sep 5, 1949 in New York, New York
Source: *BioIn 2, 3*

Minsky, Harold
[The Minsky Brothers]
American. Theatrical Producer
b. 1915?
d. 1977
Source: *BioIn 11*

Minsky, Howard G
American. Motion Picture Executive
Source: *IntMPA 75, 76, 77, 78, 79, 80, 82*

Minton, Sherman
American. Supreme Court Justice
b. Oct 20, 1890 in Georgetown, Indiana
d. Apr 9, 1965 in New Albany, Indiana
Source: *BiDrAC; CurBio 41, 49, 65; WebAB; WhAm 4*

Mintz, Shlomo
Russian. Musician
b. 1958?
Source: *NewYTBE 73*

Minuit, Peter
Dutch. Colonial Leader
b. 1580 in Wesel, Germany
d. Jun 1638
Source: *AmBi; ApCAB; DcAmB; Drake; REn; REnAL; WebAB; WhAm H*

Mirabeau, Honore Gabriel Riquetti
French. Revolutionary, Statesman
b. Mar 9, 1749 in Bignon, France
d. Apr 2, 1791 in Paris, France
Source: *DcEuL; OxFr; REn*

Miranda, Carmen
Brazilian. Singer, Dancer, Actress
b. Feb 9, 1909 in Marco Canavezes, Portugal
d. Aug 5, 1955 in Beverly Hills, California
Source: *CurBio 41, 55; DcAmB S5; FilmgC; InWom; MotPP; MovMk; OxFilm; WhScrn 74, 77; WhoHol B; WorEFlm*

Miranda, Ernesto
American. Criminal
b. 1940?
d. 1976
Source: *BioIn 8, 10*

Miranda, Francisco de
Venezuelan. Soldier, Traveler, Writer
b. 1750 in Caracas, Venezuela
d. Jul 14, 1816 in Cadiz, Spain
Source: *ApCAB; Drake; NewCol 75; REnAL; WhAm H*

Miriam
Biblical Character
Source: *InWom*

Mirisch, Walter Mortimer
American. Motion Picture Director, Producer
b. Nov 8, 1921 in New York, New York
Source: *DcFM; FilmgC; IntMPA 75, 77; WhoAm 74, 76, 78, 80, 82; WhoWor 74*

Miro, Joan
Spanish. Artist
Early masterpiece, *The Farm,* 1922, was puchased by Ernest Hemingway.
b. Apr 20, 1893 in Barcelona, Spain
Source: *CelR 73; CurBio 40, 73; IntWW 74; NewYTBS 74; REn; WhoAm 74; WhoGrA; WhoWor 74*

Mirren, Helen
English. Actress
b. 1946
Source: *WhoHol A; WhoThe 72, 77, 81*

Mischakoff, Mischa
[Mischa Fischberg]
American. Musician
b. Apr 3, 1895 in Proskurov, Russia
d. Feb 1, 1981 in Petoskey, Michigan
Source: *AnObit 1981; Baker 78; BioIn 2, 4, 8; NewYTBS 81; WhoAm 74, 76, 78, 80; WhoWorJ 72*

Mishima, Yukio, pseud.
[Kimitake Hiraoka]
Japanese. Author
b. Jan 14, 1925 in Tokyo, Japan
d. Nov 25, 1970 in Tokyo, Japan
Source: *Au&Wr 71; CasWL; ConAu 29R, 97; ConLC 2, 4, 6; DcOrL 1; EncWL; ModWD; NewYTBE 70; Pen CL; RComWL; REn; WhAm 5; WhScrn 74, 77; WhoTwCL; WorAu*

Mislimov, Shirali
Russian. Peasant, Centenarian
b. 1805?
d. Sep 2, 1973 in Barzavu, U.S.S.R.
Source: *BioIn 10; NewYTBE 73; ObitOF 79*

Mr. Dooley, pseud.
see: Dunne, Finley Peter

Mistinguett
[Jeanne Bourgeois]
French. Entertainer
b. 1875
d. Jan 5, 1956 in Bougival, France
Source: *OxThe*

Mistral, Frederic
French. Poet
b. Sep 8, 1830 in Maillane, France
d. Mar 25, 1914 in Maillane, France
Source: *AtlBL; BbD; BiD&SB; CasWL; ChPo S1; ClDMEL; DcEuL; EuAu; ModRL; NewC; OxEng; OxFr; Pen EUR; REn; TwCW*

Mistral, Gabriela
[Lucila Godoy y Alcayaga]
Chilean. Poet
b. Apr 7, 1899 in Vicuna, Chile
d. Jan 10, 1957 in Paris, France
Source: *AtlBL; CasWL; DcSpL; EncWL; Pen AM; REn; TwCA, SUP; WhoTwCL*

Mitch Ryder and the Detroit Wheels
[John Badenjek; Joe Cubert; Earl Eliot; Jimmy McCartney; Mitch Ryder]
American. Rock Group
Source: *LilREn 78; WhoRock 81*

Mitchel, John Purroy
American. Mayor
Mayor of NY City, 1914-18; noted for civic reforms.
b. Jul 19, 1879 in New York, New York
d. Jul 6, 1918 in Lake Charles, Louisiana
Source: *AmBi; DcAmB; NatCAB 18; WhAm 1*

Mitchell, Arthur
American. Dancer, Choreographer
b. Mar 27, 1934 in New York, New York
Source: *CurBio 66; NewYTBS 74; WhoAm 74, 76, 78, 80, 82; WhoBlA 75; WhoWor 74*

Mitchell, Billy (William)
American. General
b. Dec 29, 1879 in Nice, France
d. Feb 19, 1936 in New York, New York
Source: *AmBi; DcAmB S2; DcNAA; EncAB-H; WebAB; WhAm 1*

Mitchell, Cameron
[Cameron Mizell]
American. Actor
b. Nov 4, 1918 in Dallastown, Pennsylvania
Source: *BiE&WWA; FilmgC; IntMPA 75, 76, 77, 78, 79, 80, 81, 82; MotPP; PlP&P; WhoAm 74, 76, 78, 80, 82; WhoHol A*

Mitchell, Clarence M
American. Diplomat, Civil Rights Leader
b. Mar 8, 1911 in Baltimore, Maryland
Source: *WhoAm 74, 76, 78, 80, 82; WhoS&SW 73*

Mitchell, Edgar Dean
American. Astronaut
b. Sep 17, 1930 in Hereford, Texas
Source: *AmM&WS 73P; ConAu 53; IntWW 74; NewYTBE 71; WhoS&SW 73*

Mitchell, George John
American. Senator
b. Aug 20, 1933 in Waterville, Maine
Source: *AlmAP 78, 80; BioIn 9; WhoAm 78, 80, 82; WhoAmL 79; WhoAmP 73, 75, 77, 79; WhoE 74, 75, 77; WhoGov 77*

Mitchell, Grant
American. Actor
b. Jun 17, 1875 in Columbus, Ohio
d. May 1, 1957 in Los Angeles, California
Source: *FilmgC; MotPP; MovMk; Vers A; WhScrn 74, 77; WhoHol B*

Mitchell, Guy
American. Singer, Actor
b. Feb 22, 1927 in Detroit, Michigan
Source: *FilmgC; IntMPA 75, 76, 77, 78, 79, 80, 81, 82; WhoHol A*

Mitchell, James Leslie
see: Gibbon, Lewis Grassic, pseud.

Mitchell, John
American. Labor Leader
Vice-president, AFL, 1899-1914; wrote *The Wage Earner and His Problems,* 1913.
b. Feb 4, 1870 in Braidwood, Illinois
d. Sep 9, 1919 in New York, New York
Source: *AmBi; DcAmB; EncAB-H; McGEWB; NatCAB 15, 24; WhAm 1*

Mitchell, John Newton
American. Former Attorney General
Attorney General, 1968-72; convicted in Watergate scandal, Jan 1, 1975.
b. Sep 15, 1913 in Detroit, Michigan
Source: *BiDrUSE; CurBio 69; IntWW 74; NewYTBE 73; NewYTBS 74; Who 74; WhoAm 74; WhoAmP 73; WhoS&SW 73*

Mitchell, Joni
[Roberta Joan Anderson]
Canadian. Singer, Songwriter
Wrote, recorded first hit, "Chelsea Morning," 1962.
b. Nov 7, 1943 in McLeod, AB
Source: *BioNews 74; BkPepl; CanWW 82; CelR 73; WhoAm 76, 78, 80, 82; WhoAmW 77*

Mitchell, Margaret
American. Author
Won Pulitzer Prize for her only book *Gone With the Wind,* 1936.
b. Nov 8, 1900 in Atlanta, Georgia
d. Aug 16, 1949 in Atlanta, Georgia
Source: *AmAu&B; CasWL; Chambr 3; CnDAL; CyWA; DcAmB S4; DcLEL; DcNAA; EvLB; FilmgC; InWom; LongCTC; ModAL; NotAW; OxAmL; Pen AM; REn; REnAL; TwCA, SUP; TwCW; WebAB; WebE&AL; WhAm 2; WhNAA*

Mitchell, Maria
American. Astronomer
Discovered comet, 1847; one of original teachers at Vassar College.
b. Aug 1, 1818 in Nantucket, Massachusetts
d. Jun 28, 1889 in Lynn, Massachusetts
Source: *Alli; AmBi; AmWom; ApCAB; CyAl 2; DcAmAu; DcAmB; Drake; EncAB-H; HerW; InWom; NotAW; TwCBDA; WebAB; WhAm H*

Mitchell, Martha Elizabeth Beall
American. Wife of John N Mitchell
Known for calling reporters in middle of night with Washington gossip.
b. Sep 2, 1918 in Pine Bluff, Arkansas
d. May 31, 1976 in New York, New York
Source: *BioNews 74; CelR 73; NewYTBE 70; WhAm 6; WhoAm 74*

Mitchell, Millard
American. Actor
b. 1900 in Havana, Cuba
d. Oct 12, 1953 in Santa Monica, California
Source: *FilmgC; MotPP; WhScrn 74, 77; WhoHol B*

Mitchell, Reginald Joseph
English. Aircraft Designer
b. 1895
d. 1937
Source: *BioIn 2, 3, 4*

Mitchell, Richard
American. Philologist, Grammarian
b. 1906?
Source: *BioIn 11*

Mitchell, Silas Weir
American. Neurologist, Author
b. Feb 15, 1829 in Philadelphia, Pennsylvania
d. Jan 4, 1914 in Philadelphia, Pennsylvania
Source: *Alli SUP; AmAu; AmAu&B; AmBi; ApCAB; BbD; BiD&SB; Chambr 3; ChPo, S1, S2; CnDAL; CyWA; DcAmAu; DcAmB; DcLEL; DcNAA; OxAmL; REn; REnAL; TwCBDA; WebAB; WhAm 1*

Mitchell, Thomas
American. Actor
b. Jul 11, 1892 in Elizabeth, New Jersey
d. Dec 17, 1962 in Beverly Hills, California
Source: *BiDFilm; CmMov; FilmgC; MovMk; OxFilm; Vers A; WhAm 4; WhScrn 74, 77; WhoHol B; WorEFlm*

Mitchell, (William) Chad(bourne)
[Chad Mitchell Trio]
American. Singer
b. Dec 5, 1936 in Portland, Oregon
Source: *WhoAm 74*

Mitchell, William Leroy
American. Automotive Designer
b. Jul 2, 1912 in Cleveland, Ohio
Source: *Ward 77; WhoAm 74*

Mitchell, William Ormond
Canadian. Author
b. Mar 13, 1914 in Weyburn, SK
Source: *CanWW 82; CasWL; ConAu 77; ConNov 72, 76; OxCan; TwCW; WrDr 76*

Mitchelson, Marvin M(orris)
American. Lawyer
Known for palimony trial involving Lee Marvin and Michelle Triola Marvin.
b. May 7, 1928 in Detroit, Michigan
Source: *BioIn 11; WhoAm 80, 82*

Mitchison, Naomi Haldane
Scottish. Author
b. Nov 1, 1897 in Edinburgh, Scotland
Source: *CasWL; Chambr 3; ChPo, S2; ConAu 77; ConNov 72, 76; DcLEL; EvLB; InWom; IntWW 74; LongCTC; ModBrL; NewC; Pen ENG; REn; SmATA 24; TwCA, SUP; Who 74, WhoChL; WhoLA; WhoWor 74; WrDr 76*

Mitchum, Robert
American. Actor
Starred in over 45 films including *Heaven Knows Mr. Allison.*
b. Aug 6, 1917 in Bridgeport, Connecticut
Source: *AmSCAP 66; BiDFilm; BkPepl; CelR 73; CmMov; CurBio 70; FilmgC; IntMPA 75, 76, 77, 78, 79, 80, 81, 82; IntWW 75; MotPP; MovMk; OxFilm; WhoAm 74, 76, 78, 80, 82; WhoHol A; WorEFlm*

Mitford, Jessica
English. Author, Journalist
b. Sep 11, 1917 in Gloucester, England
Source: *AmAu&B; ConAu 1R, 1NR; CurBio 74; NewC; WhoAm 82; WhoWor 74; WorAu; WrDr 76*

Mitford, Nancy Freeman
English. Author
b. Nov 28, 1904 in London, England
d. Jun 30, 1973 in Versailles, France
Source: *Au&Wr 71; ConAu 9R; ConNov 72; DcLEL; EvLB; InWom; LongCTC; ModBrL; NewC; NewYTBE 73; Pen ENG; RAdv 1; REn; TwCA SUP; TwCW; WhAm 6*

Mitropoulos, Dimitri
Greek. Conductor, Composer
b. Feb 18, 1896 in Athens, Greece
d. Nov 2, 1960 in Milan, Italy
Source: *CurBio 41, 52, 61; WhAm 4*

Mitscher, Marc A
American. Military Leader
b. Jan 26, 1887 in Hillsboro, Wisconsin
d. Feb 3, 1947 in Norfolk, Virginia
Source: *CurBio 44, 47; DcAmB S4; WhAm 2*

Mittermaier, Rosi
German. Skier
b. Aug 5, 1950 in Reit im Winkl, Germany (West)
Source: *BioIn 10*

Mitterrand, Francois Maurice
French. President
Defeated Giscard d'Estaing, 1981, ending 23 years of Gaullist rule.
b. Oct 26, 1916 in Jarnac, France
Source: *CurBio 68, 82; IntWW 74; NewYTBS 74; WhoWor 74*

Mix, Tom
American. Actor
Starred in over 400 westerns, usually with his horse, Tony.
b. Jan 6, 1880 in Mix Run, Pennsylvania
d. Oct 12, 1940 in Florence, Arizona
Source: *CmMov; CurBio 40; DcAmB S2; Film 1; FilmgC; MnBBF; MotPP; MovMk; OxFilm; TwYS; WebAB; WhAm 1; WhScrn 74, 77; WhoHol B; WorEFlm*

Mize, John Robert
"Big Cat"
American. Baseball Player
b. Jan 7, 1913 in Demorest, Georgia
Source: *BaseEn; WhoProB 73*

Mizner, Addison
American. Architect
b. 1872 in Benicia, California
d. Feb 5, 1933 in Palm Beach, Florida
Source: *ChPo; DcAmB S1; DcNAA; WebAB*

Mizoguchi, Kenji
Japanese. Motion Picture Director
b. 1898 in Tokyo, Japan
d. 1956
Source: *BiDFilm; DcFM; FilmgC; MovMk; OxFilm; WorEFlm*

Moberg, Vihelm
Swedish. Author
b. Aug 20, 1898 in Algutsboda, Sweden
d. Aug 9, 1973 in Stockholm, Sweden
Source: *CasWL; ClDMEL; ConAu 45, 97; EvEuW; OxEng; WorAu*

Mobius, August Ferdinand
German. Mathematician
b. Nov 17, 1790 in Schulpforte, Germany
d. Sep 26, 1868 in Leipzig, Germany
Source: *AsBiEn; WebBD 80*

Mobley, Mary Ann
[Mrs. Gary Collins]
American. Actress, Singer
Miss America, 1959.
b. 1939
Source: *FilmgC; MotPP; WhoHol A*

Mobutu, Joseph-Desire
[Sese Seko Mobutu]
Congolese. President
b. Oct 14, 1930
Source: *CurBio 66; WhoGov 72; WhoWor 74*

Modern Jazz Quartet, The
[Kenny Clarke; Percy Heath; Milt Jackson; John Lewis]
American. Musical Group
Source: *BiDAmM*

Modernaires, The
[Ralph Brewster; Bill Conway; Hal Dickinson; Chuck Goldstein]
American. Vocal Group
Source: *CmpEPM*

Modigliani, Amedeo
Italian. Artist
b. Jul 12, 1884 in Leghorn, Italy
d. Jan 25, 1920 in Paris, France
Source: *AtlBL*

Modjeska, Helena
[Helena Opid]
Polish. Actress
b. Oct 12, 1840 in Krakow, Poland
d. 1909
Source: *AmBi; AmWom; ApCAB; DcAmB; FamA&A; InWom; NotAW; OxAmL; OxThe; REnAL; WhAm 1; WhoStg 1906, 1908*

Modl, Martha
German. Opera Singer
b. Mar 22, 1912 in Nuremberg, Germany
Source: *InWom; IntWW 74; WhoWor 74*

Moeller, Michael E
[The Hostages]
American. Former Hostage in Iran
b. 1950? in Loup City, Nebraska
Source: *BioIn 12; NewYTBS 81*

Moeller, Philip
American. Dramatist
b. Aug 26, 1880 in New York, New York
d. Nov 23, 1958 in Detroit, Michigan
Source: *AmAu&B; ModWD; OxAmL; PlP&P; REnAL; WhAm 3; WhNAA*

Moerike, Eduard Friedrich
see: Morike, Eduard Friedrich

Moffat, Donald
English. Actor
b. Dec 26, 1930 in Plymouth, England
Source: *BiE&WWA; NotNAT; WhAm 3; WhoAm 74, 76, 78, 80, 82; WhoHol A; WhoThe 77*

Moffet, Gary
see: April Wine

Moffett, Anthony Toby
American. Former Congressman
Resigned congressional seat to run for senate; lost to Lowell Weicker, 1982.
b. Aug 18, 1944 in Holyoke, Massachusetts
Source: *BioIn 10, 11; WhoAm 78, 80, 82*

Moffett, Ken(neth Elwood)
American. Federal Mediator
b. Sep 11, 1931 in Lykens, Pennsylvania
Source: *WhoGov 72, 75*

Moffo, Anna
American. Opera Singer
b. Jun 27, 1934 in Wayne, Pennsylvania
Source: *BioNews 74; CelR 73; CurBio 61; InWom; NewYTBE 72; WhoAm 74, 76, 78, 80, 82; WhoHol A; WhoMus 72*

Mohammed
[Muhammad; Mahomet]
Arabian. Founder of Islam
b. 570 in Mecca, Arabia
d. 632
Source: *NewC; RComWL; REn*

Mohammed V
[Sidi Mohammed Ben Moulay Youssef]
Moroccan. Sultan, King
b. Aug 10, 1910
d. Feb 26, 1961 in Rabat, Morocco
Source: *CurBio 61*

Mohammed Zahir Shah
Afghan. Former King
b. Oct 30, 1914 in Kabul, Afghanistan
Source: *CurBio 56; IntWW 74; WhoWor 74*

Moholy-Nagy, Laszlo
American. Artist
b. Jul 20, 1895 in Bacsbarsod, Hungary
d. Nov 24, 1946 in Chicago, Illinois
Source: *DcAmB S4; OxFilm; WebAB*

Mohs, Friedrich
German. Mineralogist
b. Jan 29, 1773 in Gernrode, Germany
d. Sep 29, 1839 in Agardo, Italy
Source: *AsBiEn; DcScB*

Moi, Daniel
Kenyan. President
b. Sep 1924 in Kuriengwo, Kenya
Source: *CurBio 79; NewYTBS 82*

Moiseiwitsch, Benno
Russian. Musician
b. Feb 22, 1890 in Odessa, Russia
d. Apr 9, 1963 in London, England
Source: *WhAm 4*

Moiseyev, Igor Alexandrovich
Russian. Choreographer, Ballet Director
b. Jan 21, 1906 in Kiev, Russia
Source: *BioNews 74; CurBio 58; WhoWor 74*

Moley, Raymond
American. Journalist
b. Sep 27, 1886 in Berea, Ohio
d. Feb 18, 1975 in Phoenix, Arizona
Source: *AmAu&B; ConAu 61; CurBio 45, 75; OhA&B; REn; REnAL; WhAm 6; WhNAA; WhoAm 74*

Moliere, pseud.
[Jean Baptiste Pouquelin]
French. Dramatist, Actor
Wrote *The School for Wives,* 1662; *The Imaginary Invalid,* 1673.
b. Jan 15, 1622 in Paris, France
d. Feb 17, 1673 in Paris, France
Source: *AtlBL; BbD; BiD&SB; CasWL; ChPo; CnThe; CyWA; DcEnL; DcEuL; EuAu; EvEuW; McGEWD; NewC; OxEng; OxFr; OxThe; Pen EUR; PlP&P, A; RComWL; REn; REnWD*

Molland, Joey
see: Badfinger

Mollenhauer, Emil
American. Musician, Conductor
b. Aug 4, 1855 in Brooklyn, New York
d. Dec 10, 1927 in Boston, Massachusetts
Source: *DcAmB; WhAm 1*

Mollenhoff, Clark Raymond
American. Journalist
b. Apr 16, 1921 in Burnside, Iowa
Source: *AmAu&B; ConAu 17R; CurBio 58; NewYTBE 70; WhoAm 74, 76, 78, 80, 82; WhoWor 74*

Mollet, Guy
French. Socialist Leader
b. Dec 31, 1905 in Orne, France
d. Oct 3, 1975 in Paris, France
Source: *CurBio 50; IntWW 74; WhAm 6; WhoWor 74*

Molly Hatchet
[Danny Joe Brown; Bruce Crump; Dave Hluber; Steve Holland; DuaneRolland; Banner Thomer]
American. Rock Group
Source: *ConMuA 80*

Molnar, Ferenc
Hungarian. Dramatist, Author
b. 1878 in Budapest, Hungary
d. Apr 1, 1952 in New York, New York
Source: *AtlBL; CasWL; ClDMEL; CnMD; CnThe; CyWA; EncWL; EvEuW; LongCTC; McGEWD; ModWD; OxThe; Pen EUR; PlP&P; REn; REnWD; TwCA, SUP; WhAm 3, 4*

Molotov, Viacheslav Mikhailovich
Russian. Government Official
b. Mar 9, 1890 in Kirov District, Russia
Source: *CurBio 40, 54; IntWW 74; NewCol 75; Who 74*

Moltke, Helmuth James, graf von
German. Underground Leader
b. 1906
d. 1945
Source: *BioIn 10*

Moltke, Helmuth Karl Bernhard von
German. Statesman
b. 1800 in Parchim, Germany
d. Oct 26, 1891
Source: *OxGer; REn*

Moltmann, Jurgen
German. Clergyman
b. Apr 8, 1926 in Hamburg, Germany
Source: *WhoWor 74*

Molyneux, Edward H
English. Couturier, Artist
b. Sep 5, 1891 in London, England
d. Mar 23, 1974 in Monte Carlo, Monaco
Source: *CurBio 42, 74; NewYTBS 74; WorFshn*

Mommsen, Theodor
German. Historian
b. Nov 30, 1817 in Garding, Germany
d. Nov 1, 1903 in Charlottenburg, Germany
Source: *BiD&SB; BioIn 3, 7, 9; DcEuL; LinLib L, S; LongCTC; McGEWB; NewC; NewCol 75; OxEng; OxGer; REn*

Mona Lisa
see: Gioconda, Lisa Gherardini

Monaghan, (James) Jay, (IV)
American. Author, Historian
b. Mar 19, 1891 in Philadelphia, Pennsylvania
d. 1981 in Santa Barbara, California
Source: *AmAu&B; BioIn 11; ConAu 41R, 103; DrAS 74H, 78H; REnAL; REnAW*

Mondale, Joan Adams
[Mrs. Walter Mondale]
"Joan of Art"
American. Author, Art Patron
Wrote *Politics in Art,* 1972.
b. Aug 8, 1930 in Eugene, OR
Source: *BioIn 12; ConAu 41R; CurBio 80; WhoAm 80, 82; WhoAmW 77*

Mondale, Walter Frederick
"Fritz"
American. Former Vice-President
MN attorney general, 1960-64; senator, 1964-77; vice-president, 1977-80.
b. Jan 5, 1928 in Ceylon, Minnesota
Source: *BiDrAC; CngDr 74; ConAu 65; CurBio 69; IntWW 74; WhoAm 74, 76, 78, 80, 82; WhoAmP 73; WhoGov 72; WhoMW 74*

Mondello, "Toots" (Nuncio)
American. Jazz Musician
b. 1912 in Boston, Massachusetts
Source: *WhoJazz 72*

Mondrian, Piet(er Cornelis)
Dutch. Artist
Co-founded *De Stijl* magazine, 1917; wrote *Le Neo-Plasticisme,* 1920.
b. Mar 7, 1872 in Amersfoort, Netherlands
d. Feb 1, 1944 in New York, New York
Source: *AtlBL; BioIn 10; CurBio 44; NewCol 75; WhDW*

Monet, Claude
French. Artist
Founded Impressionism; paintings "Haystacks," 1891; "Rouen Cathedral," 1894.
b. Nov 14, 1840 in Paris, France
d. Dec 5, 1926 in Giverny, France
Source: *AtlBL; OxFr; NewCol 75; REn*

Money, Eddie
[Eddie Mahoney]
American. Singer
b. 1949? in Brooklyn, New York
Source: *BioIn 11*

Mongkut
[Rama IV]
King of Siam
b. 1804
d. 1868
Source: *NewCol 75*

Monica, Corbett
American. Actor, Comedian
Source: *NF*

Monicelli, Mario
Italian. Motion Picture Director
b. May 15, 1915 in Rome, Italy
Source: *DcFM; FilmgC; IntMPA 75, 76, 77, 78, 79, 80, 81, 82; IntWW 74; WhoWor 74; WorEFlm*

Moninari-Pradelli, Francesco
Italian. Opera Conductor
b. Jul 4, 1911 in Bologna, Italy
Source: *NewEOp 71*

Moniuszko, Stanislaus
Polish. Composer
b. May 5, 1819 in Ubiel, Poland
d. Jun 4, 1872 in Warsaw, Poland
Source: *NewEOp 71; OxMus*

Monk, Allan James
Canadian. Opera Singer
b. Aug 19, 1942 in Mission City, BC
Source: *EncOp; WhoAm 78, 80, 82; WhoOp 76*

Monk, Julius Withers
American. Motion Picture Director, Producer
b. Nov 10, 1912 in Salisbury, North Carolina
Source: *NewYTBE 70; WhoAm 74, 76, 78, 80, 82; WhoHol A; WhoWor 74*

Monk, Mary
Irish. Poet
b. 1677 in Dublin, Ireland
d. 1715 in Bath, England
Source: *Alli; ChPo; DcEnL; PoIre*

Monk, Thelonius Sphere
American. Composer, Musician
Received International Critics award, outstanding jazz pianist, 1958-60.
b. Oct 10, 1920 in Rocky Mount, North Carolina
d. Feb 17, 1982 in Englewood, New Jersey
Source: *Baker 78; BiDAmM; CelR 73; CmpEPM; CurBio 64, 82; DcBlPA; EncJzS 70; IlEncJ; WhoAm 74, 76, 78, 80; WhoBlA 75, 77; WhoE 74; WhoWor 74*

Monkees, The
[Mickey Dolenz; Davy Jones; Mike Nesmith; Peter Tork]
American. Vocal Group
Hits include "Last Train to Clarksville," 1966; had TV show, 1966-68.
Source: *EncPR&S; IlEncRk; RkOn*

Monmouth, James Scott, Duke
[James Crofts; James Fitzroy]
English. Pretender to Throne
Led unsuccessful uprising against James II; beheaded.
b. Apr 9, 1649 in Rotterdam, Netherlands
d. Jul 25, 1685 in London, England
Source: *REn*

Monnet, Jean (Omer Gabriel)
French. Political Economist, Diplomat
b. Nov 9, 1888 in Cognac, France
d. Mar 16, 1979 in Rambouillet, France
Source: *CurBio 47; IntWW 74; NewYTBS 79; Who 74*

Monnoyer, Jean-Baptiste
French. Artist
b. 1636 in Lille, France
d. 1699 in London, England
Source: *McGDA*

Monod, Jacques
French. Molecular Biochemist
b. Feb 9, 1910 in Paris, France
d. May 31, 1976 in Cannes, France
Source: *ConAu 69; CurBio 71; IntWW 74; Who 74; WhoAm 74; WhoWor 74*

Monro, Harold Edward
English. Author
b. Mar 14, 1879 in Brussels, Belgium
d. Mar 16, 1932 in Broadstairs, England
Source: *AnCL; ChPo, S1, S2; DcLEL; EvLB; LongCTC; ModBrL; NewC; OxEng; Pen ENG; REn; TwCA, SUP; WebE&AL; WhoLA; WhoTwCL*

Monroe, Earl
"The Pearl"
American. Basketball Player
b. Nov 21, 1944 in Philadelphia, Pennsylvania
Source: *NewYTBE 71; NewYTBS 74; WhoBbl 73*

Monroe, Harriet
American. Poet, Editor
b. Dec 23, 1860 in Chicago, Illinois
d. Sep 26, 1936 in Arequipa, Peru
Source: *AmAu&B; AmBi; AmLY; BiD&SB; CasWL; ChPo, S2; CnDAL; ConAmL; DcAmAu; DcAmB S2; DcNAA; EvLB; InWom; LongCTC; NotAW; OxAmL; Pen AM; REn; REnAL; TwCA, SUP; WebAB; WhAm 1; WhNAA; WomWWA 14*

Monroe, James
American. 5th US President
President, 1817-25; responsible for Monroe Doctrine, 1823.
b. Apr 28, 1758 in Westmoreland, Virginia
d. Jul 4, 1831 in New York, New York
Source: *Alli; AmAu&B; AmBi; ApCAB; BiAuS; BiD&SB; BiDLA; BiDSA; BiDrUSE; DcAmAu; DcAmB; DcNAA; Drake; EncAB-H; OxAmL; REnAL; TwCBDA; WebAB; WhAm H; WhAmP*

Monroe, Marilyn
[Norma Jean Baker]
American. Actress
Starred in *Some Like it Hot*, 1959; *The Misfits*, 1961.
b. Jun 1, 1926 in Los Angeles, California
d. Aug 5, 1962 in Hollywood, California
Source: *BiDFilm; CmMov; CurBio 59, 62; FilmgC; InWom; MotPP; MovMk; OxFilm; WebAB; WhAm 4; WhScrn 74, 77; WhoHol B; WorEFlm*

Monroe, Vaughan
American. Singer, Band Leader
b. Oct 7, 1911 in Akron, Ohio
d. May 21, 1973 in Stuart, Florida
Source: *FilmgC; NewYTBE 73*

Monroney, Mike (Aimer Stillwell)
American. Politician
b. Mar 2, 1902 in Oklahoma City, Oklahoma
d. Feb 13, 1980 in Rockville, Maryland
Source: *AnObit 1980; CurBio 51; St&PR 75; WhoAm 74; WhoAmP 73*

Monsarrat, Nicholas John Turney
English. Author
b. Mar 22, 1910 in Liverpool, England
d. Aug 7, 1979 in London, England
Source: *CanWW 70, 79; CanWr; ConAu 3NR; ConNov 72, 76; ConSFA; CurBio 79; DcLEL; EncSF; EvLB; IntAu&W 76, 77; LinLib L; LongCTC; ModBrL; NewYTBS 79; REn; ScF&FL 1; TwCA SUP; TwCW; WhoWor 76, 78; WrDr 76, 80*

Monsigny, Pierre-Alexandre
French. Composer
b. Oct 17, 1729 in Fauquembergue, France
d. Jan 14, 1817 in Paris, France
Source: *NewEOp 71; OxMus*

Montagu, Ashley Montague Francis
English. Anthropologist
b. Jun 28, 1905 in London, England
Source: *AmAu&B; AmM&WS 73S; CelR 73; ConAu 5R, 5NR; TwCA SUP; WebAB; WhoAm 74, 76, 78, 80, 82; WhoE 74; WhoWorJ 72*

Montagu, Lady Mary Wortley
English. Author
b. May 1689 in London, England
d. Aug 21, 1762 in London, England
Source: *Alli; AtlBL; BbD; BiD&SB; BrAu; Chambr 2; ChPo; DcEnA; DcEnL; DcEuL; DcLEL; EvLB; InWom; MouLC 2; NewC; OxEng; Pen ENG; RAdv 1; REn*

Montaigne, Michel Eyquem de
French. Essayist, Courtier
b. Feb 28, 1533 in Bordeaux, France
d. Sep 13, 1592 in Bordeaux, France
Source: *AtlBL; BbD; BiD&SB; CasWL; CroE&S; CyWA; DcEnL; DcEuL; EuAu; EvEuW; NewC; OxEng; OxFr; Pen EUR; RComWL; REn*

Montalban, Carlos
Mexican. Actor
Source: *WhoHol A*

Montalban, Ricardo
Mexican. Actor
Plays Mr. Rourke on "Fantasy Island," 1978--.
b. Nov 25, 1920 in Mexico City, Mexico
Source: *BiE&WWA; FilmgC; IntMPA 75, 76, 77, 78, 79, 80, 81, 82; MotPP; MovMk; WhoAm 82; WhoHol A; WorEFlm*

Montale, Eugenio
Italian. Poet, Critic
Won 1925 Nobel Prize for Literature.
b. Oct 12, 1896 in Genoa, Italy
d. Sep 12, 1981 in Milan, Italy
Source: *BioIn 8, 9, 10, 11; CasWL; ClDMEL; CnMWL; ConAu 17R, 104; ConLC 7, 9, 18; CurBio 76, 81; EncWL; EvEuW; IntWW 74, 75, 76, 77, 78; LinLib L; McGEWB; ModRL; NewCol 75; NewYTBS 75; Pen EUR; REn; TwCW; WhoTwCL; WhoWor 74, 78; WorAu*

Montana, Bob
American. Cartoonist
b. Oct 23, 1920 in Stockton, California
d. Jan 4, 1975 in Meredith, New Hampshire
Source: *ConAu 89; WhAm 6; WhoAm 74; WhoAmA 73; WhoE 74; WhoWor 74*

Montana, "Bull" (Louis)
[Luigi Montagna]
American. Actor
b. May 16, 1887 in Vogliera, Italy
d. Jan 24, 1950 in Los Angeles, California
Source: *Film 1, 2; FilmgC; TwYS; WhScrn 74, 77; WhoHol B*

Montana, Joe (Joseph C, Jr.)
American. Football Player
b. Jun 11, 1956 in Monongahela, Pennsylvania
Source: *FootReg; NewYTBS 81*

Montana, Patsy
American. Singer
b. Oct 30, 1914 in Hot Springs, Arkansas
Source: *AmSCAP 66; EncFCWM 69; InWom; WhoAm 74, 76, 78, 80, 82*

Montand, Yves
[Ivo Livi]
French. Singer, Actor
b. Oct 13, 1921 in Monsummano, Italy
Source: *BiDFilm; CelR 73; CurBio 60; FilmgC; IntMPA 75, 76, 77, 78, 79, 80, 81, 82; IntWW 74; MotPP; MovMk; OxFilm; WhoAm 74; WhoHol A; WhoWor 74; WorEFlm*

Montcalm, Louis Joseph de
French. Military Leader
b. Feb 29, 1712 in Nimes, France
d. Sep 14, 1759 in PQ
Source: *BbtC; Drake; NewCol 75; OxCan; OxFr*

Monte, Toti dal
[Antonietta Meneghelli]
Italian. Opera Singer
b. Jan 27, 1893
d. Jan 26, 1975 in Italy
Source: *BioIn 2, 8, 10*

Montefeltro, Federico da
Italian. Patron of Learning
b. 1422
d. 1482
Source: *REn*

Montefiore, Sir Moses Haim
English. Philanthropist
b. Oct 24, 1784 in Leghorn, Italy
d. Jul 28, 1885 in Ramsgate, England
Source: *NewCol 75; WebBD 80*

Montemezzi, Italo
Italian. Composer
b. Aug 4, 1875 in Vigasio, Italy
d. May 15, 1952 in Verona, Italy
Source: *NewEOp 71; OxMus*

Montenegro, Hugo
American. Musician
b. 1926
d. Feb 6, 1981 in Palm Springs, California
Source: *RkOn 2A*

Montesquieu, Charles Louis de
French. Political Philosopher
b. Jan 18, 1689 in Bordeaux, France
d. Feb 10, 1755 in Paris, France
Source: *AtlBL; BbD; BiD&SB; CasWL; CyWA; DcEuL; EuAu; EvEuW; NewC; OxEng; OxFr; Pen EUR; RComWL; REn*

Montessori, Maria
Italian. Physician, Education Reformer
First Italian woman to receive medical degree, 1894; wrote *The Montessori Method,* 1912.
b. Aug 31, 1870 in Chiaravalle, Italy
d. May 6, 1952 in Noordwijk, Netherlands
Source: *CathA 1930; CurBio 40, 52; InWom; LongCTC; REn*

Monteux, Claude
American. Musician, Conductor
b. Oct 15, 1920 in Brookline, Massachusetts
Source: *WhoAm 74; WhoMus 72*

Monteux, Pierre
American. Orchestra Conductor
b. Apr 4, 1875 in Paris, France
d. Jul 1, 1964 in Hancock, Maine
Source: *CurBio 46, 64; WhAm 4*

Monteverdi, Claudio
Italian. Composer
b. May 1567 in Cremona, Italy
d. Nov 29, 1643 in Venice, Italy
Source: *AtlBL; REn*

Montez, Lola
[Countess of Lansfeld; Marie Dolores Eliza Rosanna Gilbert; LolaMontes]
Irish. Dancer
Mistress of Louis I of Bavaria.
b. 1818 in Limerick, Ireland
d. Jan 17, 1861 in Astoria, New York
Source: *AmAu&B; BioIn 1, 2, 3, 4, 7, 8, 9, 10, 11; DcIrB; DcIrW 2; DcNAA; Drake; FamA&A; FilmgC; GoodHS; InWom; LibW; NewC; NewCol 75; NotAW; NotNAT A, B; OxAmL; OxGer; REnAL; REnAW; WebAB; WhAm H*

Montez, Maria
[Maria Silas]
Spanish. Actress
b. Jun 6, 1918 in Dominican Republic
d. Sep 7, 1951 in Paris, France
Source: *CmMov; FilmgC; MotPP; MovMk; WhScrn 74, 77; WhoHol B; WorEFlm*

Montezuma I
Aztec Emperor
b. 1390
d. 1464
Source: *WebBD 80*

Montezuma II
Aztec Emperor
b. 1480?
d. Jun 1520 in Tenochtitlan, Mexico
Source: *BioIn 10; NewCol 75; WebBD 80*

Montfort, Simon de
English. Military, Political Leader
b. 1208 in Normandy, France
d. Aug 4, 1265 in Evesham, England
Source: *NewCol 75; WebBD 80; WhDW*

Montgolfier, Jacques Etienne
French. Balloonist, Inventor
Invented first practical hot air balloon, 1783.
b. Jan 7, 1745 in Vidalon les Annonay, France
d. Aug 2, 1799 in Serrieres, France
Source: *AsBiEn; DcScB; McGEWB; NewCol 75; WebE&AL; WhDW*

Montgolfier, Joseph Michel
French. Balloonist, Inventor
Invented first practical hot air balloon, 1783.
b. Aug 26, 1740 in Vidalon les Annonay, France
d. Jun 26, 1810 in Balaruc les Bains, France
Source: *AsBiEn; DcScB; McGEWB; OxFr; REn*

Montgomery, Elizabeth
American. Actress
Played Samantha on "Bewitched," 1964-72; daughter of Robert Montgomery.
b. Apr 15, 1933 in Hollywood, California
Source: *FilmgC; InWom; WhoAm 82; WhoHol A*

Montgomery, George
[George Montgomery Letz]
American. Actor
b. Aug 29, 1916 in Brady, Montana
Source: *FilmgC; HolP 40; IntMPA 75, 76, 77, 79, 80, 81, 82; MotPP; MovMk; WhoHol A*

Montgomery, Melba
American. Singer, Songwriter
b. Oct 14, 1938 in Iron City, Tennessee
Source: *EncFCWM 69*

Montgomery, Richard
British. General
b. Dec 2, 1736 in Swords, Ireland
d. Dec 31, 1775 in PQ
Source: *AmBi; ApCAB; DcAmB; Drake; OxCan; TwCBDA; WhAm H*

Montgomery, Robert Henry
[Henry Montgomery, Jr.]
American. Actor, Motion Picture Director
Starred in *Here Comes Mr. Jordan,* 1941; television advisor to Eisenhower.
b. May 21, 1904 in Beacon, New York
d. Sep 27, 1981 in New York, New York
Source: *ApCAB; BiDFilm; BiE&WWA; BioIn 1, 2, 3, 4, 6, 8, 9, 11; CmMov; CurBio 48, 81; Film 2; FilmgC; IntMPA 78, 79, 80, 81, 82; MGM; MotPP; MovMk; NewYTBE 71; NewYTET; NotNAT A; OxFilm; WhoAm 74, 76, 78, 80; WhoE 74; WhoHol A; WhoThe 77; WhoWor 74; WorEFlm*

Montgomery, Ruth Shick
American. Journalist
b. Jun 11, 1912 in Sumner, Illinois
Source: *AuNews 1; ConAu 1R, 2NR; WhoAm 74, 76, 78, 80, 82; WhoAmW 77; WhoWor 74; WrDr 76*

Montgomery, Wes
American. Musician
b. Mar 6, 1925 in Indianapolis, Indiana
d. Jun 15, 1968 in Indianapolis, Indiana
Source: *BiDAmM*

Montgomery of Alamein, Bernard Law Montgomery, Viscount
English. Military Leader
b. Nov 17, 1887 in Moville, Ireland
d. Mar 25, 1976 in Isington, England
Source: *Au&Wr 71; BioIn 1, 2, 3, 4, 5, 6, 7, 8, 9, 10, 11; ConAu 65, 69; CurBio 42, 76; IntWW 74, 75, 76; LinLib L, S; McGEWB; ObitOF 79; WhE&EA; WhWW-II; Who 74; WhoMilH 76; WhoWor 74*

Montor, Henry
American. Philanthropist
Helped found United Jewish Appeal, 1938; founded Israel Bond Organization, 1950.
b. 1906 in NS
d. Apr 15, 1982 in Jerusalem, Israel
Source: *NewYTBS 82*

Montoya, Carlos
American. Musician
b. Dec 13, 1903 in Madrid, Spain
Source: *AmSCAP 66; CelR 73; CurBio 68; NewYTBE 71; USBiR 74; WhoAm 74, 76, 78, 80, 82; WhoE 74; WhoMus 72; WhoWor 74*

Montoya, Joseph Manuel
American. Senator
b. Sep 24, 1915
d. Jun 5, 1978 in Washington, DC
Source: *CngDr 74; IntWW 74; WhoAm 74; WhoAmP 73; WhoGov 72*

Monty Python's Flying Circus
[Graham Chapman; John Cleese; Terry Gilliam; Eric Idle; Terry Jones; Michael Palin]
British. Comedy Team
Source: *NF*

Moody, Dwight Lyman
American. Evangelist
b. Feb 5, 1837 in East Northfield, Massachusetts
d. Dec 22, 1899 in Northfield, Massachusetts
Source: *Alli SUP; AmAu&B; AmBi; ApCAB; BbD; BiD&SB; DcAmAu; DcAmB; DcNAA; EncAB-H; LongCTC; NewYTBE 72; OxAmL; REn; REnAL; TwCBDA; WebAB; WhAm 1*

Moody, Helen Wills
"Miss Poker Face"
American. Tennis Player
US women's singles champ, 1923-25, 1927-29.
b. Oct 6, 1905 in Centerville, California
Source: *InWom; WebAB; Who 74*

Moody, Ron
[Ronald Moodnick]
English. Actor
b. Jan 8, 1924 in London, England
Source: *EncMT; FilmgC; WhoMus 72; WhoThe 77, 81*

Moody, William Vaughn
American. Dramatist, Poet, Educator
b. Jul 8, 1869 in Spencer, Indiana
d. Oct 17, 1910 in Colorado Springs, Colorado
Source: *AmAu&B; AmBi; BiD&SB; CasWL; ChPo, S1; CnDAL; CnThe; DcAmAu; DcAmB; DcLEL; DcNAA; EvLB; IndAu 1816; LongCTC; McGEWD; ModAL; ModWD; OxAmL; OxThe; Pen AM; PlP&P; REn; REnAL; REnWD; TwCA, SUP; TwCBDA; WebAB; WebE&AL; WhAm 1; WhoStg 1908*

Moody Blues
[Graeme Edge; Justin Hayward; Denny Laine; John Lodge; Michael Pinder; Ray Thomas; Clint Warwick]
English. Rock Music Group
Source: *EncPR&S; IlEncRk*

Moog, Robert
American. Inventor
Established R A Moog Co., 1954; created instrument called "The Moog."
b. May 23, 1934 in Flushing, New York
Source: *WhoE 74*

Moon, Keith
[The Who]
English. Rock Musician
b. Aug 23, 1946 in Wembley, England
d. Sep 7, 1978 in London, England
Source: *IlEncRk*

Moon, Sung Myung
Korean. Evangelist
b. 1920
Source: *BioNews 74; NewYTBS 74*

Mooney, Tom (Thomas J)
American. Labor Leader
Convicted of killing 9 persons in bomb explosion; pardoned after 22 years, 1916.
b. 1882?
d. Mar 6, 1942 in San Francisco, California
Source: *CurBio 42*

Moore, Arch Alfred, Jr.
American. Former Governor
b. Apr 16, 1923 in Molinosville, West Virginia
Source: *BiDrAC; IntWW 74; WhoAm 74; WhoAmP 73; WhoE 74; WhoGov 72; WomPO 76*

Moore, Archie
[Archibald Lee Wright]
American. Boxer
b. Dec 13, 1916? in Benoit, Mississippi
Source: *ConAu 33R; CurBio 60; Who 74; WhoBlA 75; WhoBox 74; WhoHol A*

Moore, Bert C
[The Hostages]
American. Former Hostage in Iran
b. Mar 3, 1935 in Kentucky
Source: *NewYTBS 81; USBiR 74; WhoGov 75, 77*

Moore, Brian
Canadian. Author
b. Aug 25, 1921 in Belfast, Northern Ireland
Source: *Au&Wr 71; CanWW 82; CanWr; CasWL; ConAu 1R, 1NR; ConLC 1, 3, 5, 7, 8; ConNov 72, 76; CreCan 2; DrAF 76; ModBrL SUP; NewC; OxCan, SUP; Pen ENG; RAdv 1; REn; REnAL; TwCW; WebE&AL; Who 74; WorAu; WrDr 76*

Moore, Clayton
"The Lone Ranger"
American. Actor
Starred in "The Lone Ranger," 1949-56.
b. Sep 14, 1914 in Chicago, Illinois
Source: *BioIn 8; FilmEn; WhoHol A*

Moore, Clement Clarke
American. Scholar, Poet
Wrote *A Visit from St. Nicholas,* 1823.
b. Jul 15, 1779 in New York, New York
d. Jul 10, 1863 in Newport, Rhode Island
Source: *Alli; AmAu; AmAu&B; AmBi; AnCL; ApCAB; BiD&SB; BkCL; CarSB; ChPo, S1, S2; CnDAL; CyAL 1; DcAmAu; DcAmB; DcLEL; DcNAA; Drake; EvLB; OxAmL; REn; REnAL; Str&VC; TwCBDA; WebAB; WhAm H*

Moore, Colleen
American. Actress
b. Aug 19, 1902 in Port Huron, Michigan
Source: *Film 1; FilmgC; InWom; MotPP; MovMk; NewYTBE 71; ThFT; TwYS; WhoHol A*

Moore, Constance
American. Actress
b. Jan 18, 1922 in Sioux City, Iowa
Source: *FilmgC; ForWC 70; IntMPA 75, 76, 77; MotPP; WhoHol A*

Moore, Dick(ie)
[John Richard Moore, Jr.; Our Gang]
American. Actor, Public Relations Executive
b. Sep 12, 1925 in Los Angeles, California
Source: *Au&Wr 71; ConAu 21R; FilmgC; HolP 30; IntMPA 75, 76, 77, 78, 79, 80, 81, 82; MotPP; MovMk; NotNAT; WhoHol A*

Moore, "Dinty" (James H)
American. Restaurateur
b. 1869
d. Dec 25, 1952 in New York, New York
Source: *BioIn 10*

Moore, Douglas
American. Opera Composer
b. Aug 10, 1893 in Cutchoque, New York
d. Jul 25, 1969 in Greenport, New York
Source: *AmAu&B; AmSCAP 66; ConAu P-1; CurBio 47, 69; DcCM; OxAmL; REn; REnAL; WhAm 5*

Moore, Dudley Stuart John
English. Actor, Musician
Starred in *10* and *Arthur.*
b. Apr 19, 1935 in London, England
Source: *BiE&WWA; CurBio 82; FilmgC; IntMPA 82; NewYTBE 73; NewYTBS 74; NotNAT; WhoAm 82; WhoHol A; WhoThe 77*

Moore, Garry
[Thomas Garrison Morfit]
American. TV Personality
b. Jan 31, 1915 in Baltimore, Maryland
Source: *CelR 73; CurBio 54; IntMPA 77, 78, 79, 80, 81, 82; WhoAm 82; WhoE 74*

Moore, Garry
see: Thin Lizzy

Moore, George Augustus
Irish. Author
b. Feb 24, 1852 in County Mayo, Ireland
d. Jan 21, 1933 in London, England
Source: *Alli, SUP; AtlBL; BbD; BiD&SB; BiDLA; CasWL; Chambr 3; ChPo; CyWA; DcBiA; DcEnA AP; DcLEL; EncWL; EvLB; LongCTC; ModBrL; ModWD; NewC; OxCan; OxEng; OxThe; Pen ENG; PoIre; RAdv 1; REn; REnWD; TwCA, SUP; TwCW; WebE&AL; WhoTwCL*

Moore, George Edward
English. Philosopher
b. Nov 4, 1873 in Surrey, England
d. Oct 24, 1958 in Cambridge, England
Source: *Chambr 3; EvLB; LongCTC; OxEng; REn; TwCA SUP; WhAm 4; WhoLA*

Moore, George Stevens
American. Business Executive
b. Apr 1, 1905 in Hannibal, Missouri
Source: *CurBio 70; IntWW 74; St&PR 75; WhoAm 74; WhoE 74*

Moore, Gerald
English. Musician
b. Jul 30, 1899 in Watford, England
Source: *ConAu 1R, 5NR; CurBio 67; IntWW 74; Who 74; WhoAm 74; WhoMus 72; WrDr 76*

Moore, Grace
American. Singer
Debut at Metropolitan Opera House, 1928; appeared in *New Moon,* 1930.
b. Dec 1, 1901 in Tennessee
d. Jan 26, 1947 in Copenhagen, Denmark
Source: *CurBio 44, 47; DcAmB S4; EncMT; FilmgC; InWom; MovMk; NotAW; OxFilm; PlP&P; REnAL; ThFT; WhAm 2; WhScrn 74, 77; WhoHol B*

Moore, Harry Thornton
American. Author
b. Aug 2, 1908 in Oakland, California
d. Apr 11, 1981 in Carbondale, Illinois
Source: *AmAu&B; Au&Wr 71; BioIn 10; ConAu 5R, 103; DrAS 74E, 78E; IntAu&W 76; Who 74; WhoAm 74, 76, 78, 80; WhoWor 74, 76, 78; WorAu; WrDr 80*

Moore, Henry
English. Sculptor
Best known for sculptures "Reclining Figure," 1929; "Mother and Child," 1931.
b. Jul 30, 1898 in Yorkshire, England
Source: *IntWW 74; REn; Who 74; WhoWor 74*

Moore, Jack
American. Educator, Author
b. Oct 23, 1933 in Newark, New Jersey
Source: *ConAu 33R; DrAS 74E*

Moore, John Bassett
American. Lawyer
b. Dec 3, 1860 in Smyrna, Delaware
d. Nov 12, 1947 in New York, New York
Source: *AmAu&B; ApCAB SUP; BioIn 1; DcAmAu; DcAmB S4; DcNAA; LinLib S; NewCol 75; ObitOF 79; REnAL; TwCBDA; WhAm 2*

Moore, Marianne Craig
American. Poet
b. Nov 15, 1887 in Saint Louis, Missouri
d. Feb 5, 1972 in New York, New York
Source: *AmAu&B; AmWr; AnCL; AnMV 1926; CasWL; ChPo S2; CnDAL; CnE&AP; CnMWL; ConAmA; ConAmL; ConAu 1R, 33R, 3NR; ConLC 1, 2, 4, 8, 10; ConP 70; CurBio 52, 68, 72; DcLEL; EncAB-H; EncWL; EvLB; ForWC 70; InWom; LongCTC; ModAL, SUP; NewYTBE 72; OxAmL; OxEng; Pen AM; RAdv 1; REn; REnAL; SixAP; TwCA, SUP; TwCW; WebAB; WebE&AL; WhAm 5; WhoTwCL*

Moore, Mary Tyler
American. Actress
Star of "Mary Tyler Moore Show," 1970-77; 1981 Oscar nominee, *Ordinary People.*
b. Dec 29, 1936 in Brooklyn, New York
Source: *BkPepl; CelR 73; CurBio 71; FilmgC; InWom; IntMPA 75, 76, 77, 78, 79, 80, 81, 82; MotPP; MovMk; NewYTBS 74; WhoAm 82; WhoHol A*

Moore, Melba
American. Singer, Actress
b. Oct 29, 1945 in New York, New York
Source: *CurBio 73; PlP&P, A; WhoAm 74, 76, 78, 80, 82; WhoBlA 75; WhoHol A*

Moore, Roger George
English. Actor
Starred in "The Saint," 1967-69; movie role as James Bond, Agent 007.
b. Oct 14, 1928 in London, England
Source: *CelR 73; CurBio 75; FilmgC; IntMPA 75, 76, 77, 78, 79, 80, 81, 82; MotPP; MovMk; NewYTBE 70; WhoAm 82; WhoHol A*

Moore, Roy W
American. Chairman of Canada Dry Corp.
b. Feb 27, 1891 in Macon, Georgia
d. Sep 29, 1971 in Bridgeport, Connecticut
Source: *BioIn 4, 9; WhAm 5*

Moore, Sam
see: Sam and Dave

Moore, Sara Jane
American. Attempted Assassin
Tried to kill Gerald Ford, Sep 22, 1975; sentenced to life in prison.
b. Feb 15, 1930 in Charleston, West Virginia
Source: *BioIn 10; LookW*

Moore, Stanford
American. Biochemist
Won Nobel Prize for Chemistry, 1972.
b. Sep 4, 1913 in Chicago, Illinois
d. Aug 23, 1982 in New York, New York
Source: *AmM&WS 73P, 76P, 79P; IntWW 74, 75, 76, 77, 78, 79, 80, 81; NewYTBS 82; WebAB, 79; WhoAm 76, 78, 80, 82; WhoE 77, 79; WhoWor 74; WorAl*

Moore, Terry
[Helen Koford]
American. Actress
b. Jan 1, 1932 in Los Angeles, California
Source: *BusPN; MotPP; FilmgC; InWom; IntMPA 75, 76, 77, 78, 79, 80, 81, 82; WhoHol A*

Moore, Thomas
Irish. Poet
b. May 28, 1779 in Dublin, Ireland
d. Feb 25, 1852 in Bromham, England
Source: *Alli; AtlBL; BbD; BiD&SB; BiDrAC; BrAu 19; CasWL; ChPo, S1, S2; CnE&AP; CrtT 2; CyWA; DcBiA; DcEnA, AP; DcEnL; DcEuL; DcLEL; EvLB; HsB&A; MouLC 3; NewC; OxCan; OxEng; Pen ENG; PoChrch; PoIre; REn; WebE&AL; WhAm H; WhAmP*

Moore, Tom
American. Actor
b. 1885 in County Meath, Ireland
d. Feb 12, 1955 in Santa Monica, California
Source: *Film 1; MotPP; MovMk; TwYS; WhScrn 74, 77; WhoHol B*

Moore, Victor
American. Actor
b. Feb 24, 1876 in Hammonton, New Jersey
d. Jul 23, 1962 in Long Island, New York
Source: *EncMT; Film 1; FilmgC; MotPP; MovMk; PlP&P; TwYS; Vers A; WhAm 4; WhScrn 74, 77; WhoHol B*

Moore, William H
American. Railroad Executive
b. May 8, 1916 in Hazard, Kentucky
Source: *IntWW 74; St&PR 75; WhoE 74; WhoF&I 74; WhoWor 74*

Moorehead, Agnes
American. Actress
Played Endora on "Bewitched," 1964-72.
b. Dec 6, 1906 in Clinton, Massachusetts
d. Apr 20, 1974 in Rochester, Minnesota
Source: *BiDFilm; BiE&WWA; CelR 73; CmMov; ConAu 49; CurBio 52, 72; FilmgC; ForWC 70; InWom; MotPP; MovMk; NewYTBS 74; OxFilm; Vers A; WhAm 6; WhScrn 77; WhoAm 74; WhoHol B; WhoThe 77; WorEFlm*

Moorer, Thomas H(inman)
American. Naval Officer
b. Feb 9, 1912 in Mount Willing, Alabama
Source: *BioIn 8, 9, 10, 11; CurBio 71*

Moraes, Vinicius de
Brazilian. Author
b. 1913
d. 1980 in Rio De Janeiro, Brazil
Source: *ConAu 101; IntWW 74; Pen AM; WhoWor 74*

Morales Bermudez, Francisco
Peruvian. President
b. Oct 4, 1921 in Lima, Peru
Source: *WhoWor 78*

Moran, "Bugs" (George C)
American. Gangster
Committed 26 robberies before age of 21.
b. 1893 in Minnesota
d. Feb 25, 1957 in Leavenworth, Kansas
Source: *Blood; ObitOF 79*

Moran, Edward
American. Artist
b. Aug 19, 1829 in Bolton, England
d. Jun 9, 1901 in New York, New York
Source: *AmBi; ApCAB; DcAmB; EarABI; TwCBDA; WhAm H*

Moran, Erin
American. Actress
Plays Joanie on "Happy Days," 1974--; "Joanie Loves Chachi," 1982.
b. Oct 18, 1961
Source: *WhoHol A*

Moran, George
American. Actor
b. 1882 in Elwood, Kansas
d. Aug 1, 1949 in Oakland, California
Source: *WhScrn 74, 77; WhoHol B*

Moran, Gussie (Gertrude Augusta)
"Gorgeous Gussie"
American. Tennis Player
b. 1923
Source: *BioIn 10*

Moran, Polly
American. Comedienne, Actress
b. Jun 28, 1883 in Chicago, Illinois
d. Jan 25, 1952 in Los Angeles, California
Source: *Film 1; FilmgC; MotPP; MovMk; ThFT; TwYS; WhScrn 74, 77; WhoHol B*

Moran, Thomas
American. Artist
b. Jan 22, 1837 in Bolton, England
d. Aug 25, 1926 in Santa Barbara, California
Source: *AmBi; ApCAB; ChPo; DcAmB; EarABI, SUP; McGEWB; TwCBDA; WhAm HA, 1, 4*

Morandi, Giorgio
Italian. Artist
b. Jul 20, 1890 in Bologna, Italy
d. Jun 18, 1964 in Bologna, Italy
Source: *BioIn 1, 4, 6, 7, 9, 11; ConArt; McGDA; ObitOF 79; WhAm 4*

Morath, Max Edward
American. Entertainer
b. Oct 1, 1926 in Colorado Springs, Colorado
Source: *BioIn 6; CurBio 63; WhoAm 74, 80, 82*

Moravia, Alberto, pseud.
[Alberto Pincherle]
Italian. Author, Journalist
b. Nov 28, 1907 in Italy
Source: *Au&Wr 71; CasWL; ClDMEL; CnMD; CnMWL; ConAu 25R; ConLC 2, 7, 11, 18; CurBio 70; CyWA; EncWL; EvEuW; IntWW 74; LongCTC; ModRL; OxEng; Pen EUR; REn; TwCA SUP; TwCW; Who 74; WhoTwCL; WhoWor 74*

More, Kenneth Gilbert
English. Actor
b. Sep 20, 1914 in Gerrards Cross, England
d. Jul 12, 1982 in London, England
Source: *CmMov; CnThe; FilmgC; IntMPA 75, 76, 77, 78, 79, 80, 81, 82; IntWW 74, 75, 76, 77, 78; NewYTBS 82; Who 74; WhoHol A; WhoThe 72, 77, 81*

More, Paul Elmer
American. Philosopher, Editor, Critic
b. Dec 12, 1864 in Saint Louis, Missouri
d. Mar 9, 1937 in Princeton, New Jersey
Source: *AmAu&B; AmBi; AmLY; BiD&SB; BiDSA; CasWL; Chambr 3; CnDAL; ConAmA; ConAmL; DcAmAu; DcAmB S2; DcLEL; DcNAA; EvLB; LongCTC; ModAL; OxAmL; Pen AM; REn; REnAL; TwCA, SUP; WebAB; WhAm 1; WhNAA*

More, Sir Thomas
English. Author, Statesman
b. Feb 7, 1478 in London, England
d. Jul 6, 1535 in London, England
Source: *Alli; AtlBL; BbD; BiD&SB; BrAu; CasWL; Chambr 1; ChPo, S2; CroE&S; CrtT 1; REn; WebE&AL*

Moreau, Gustave
French. Artist
b. Apr 6, 1826 in Paris, France
d. Apr 18, 1898 in Paris, France
Source: *OxFr*

Moreau, Jeanne
French. Actress
b. Jan 23, 1928 in Paris, France
Source: *BiDFilm; CelR 73; CurBio 66; FilmgC; IntMPA 82; IntWW 74; MotPP; MovMk; OxFilm; Who 74; WhoHol A; WhoWor 74; WorEFlm*

Morefield, Richard H
[The Hostages]
American. Former Hostage in Iran
b. 1930?
Source: *BioIn 12; NewYTBS 81*

Morehouse, Ward
American. Journalist
b. Nov 24, 1899 in Savannah, Georgia
d. Dec 7, 1966 in New York, New York
Source: *AmAu&B; ConAu 25R; CurBio 40, 67; OxThe; REnAL; WhAm 4*

Morello, Joseph A
American. Jazz Musician
b. Jul 17, 1928 in Springfield, Massachusetts
Source: *WhoAm 74*

Morelos y Pavon, Jose M
Mexican. Patriot
b. 1765
d. 1815
Source: *NewCol 75; WebBD 80*

Moreno, Rita
[Mrs. Leonard Gordon; Rosa Dolores Alverio]
American. Actress, Singer
Only woman to win show business' four top awards: Oscar, Grammy, Tony, Emmy.
b. Dec 11, 1931 in Hunacao, Puerto Rico
Source: *CelR 73; FilmgC; InWom; IntMPA 75, 76, 77, 78, 79, 80, 81, 82; MotPP; MovMk; NotNAT; WhoAm 74, 76, 78, 80, 82; WhoAmW 77; WhoHol A; WhoThe 77*

Moretti, Mario
Italian. Red Brigade Terrorist
b. 1946
Source: *BioIn 12*

Morgagni, Giovanni Battista
Italian. Scientist
Founded pathologic anatomy.
b. Feb 25, 1682
d. Dec 6, 1771
Source: *BioIn 7, 9; NewCol 75; WebBD 80*

Morgan, Al(fred Y)
American. Beverage Manufacturer
President, White Rock Corp.
b. Dec 4, 1906 in New York, New York
Source: *WhoAm 74*

Morgan, Arthur
American. Engineer, Educator
b. Jun 20, 1878 in Cincinnati, Ohio
d. Nov 12, 1975 in Xenia, Ohio
Source: *AmAu&B; AmM&WS 73P; Au&Wr 71; ConAu 5R, 61, 3NR; CurBio 56; OhA&B; WhAm 6; WhNAA*

Morgan, Charles Langbridge
English. Author
b. Jan 22, 1894 in Kent, England
d. Feb 6, 1958 in London, England
Source: *CasWL; CnMD; CnThe; CroCD; DcLEL; EvLB; LongCTC; ModBrL; ModWD; NewC; OxEng; OxThe; Pen ENG; REn; TwCA, SUP; TwCW; WebE&AL; WhoLA*

Morgan, Daniel
American. Congressman, Army Officer
b. 1736 in Bucks County, Pennsylvania
d. Jul 6, 1802 in Winchester, Virginia
Source: *Alli; AmBi; ApCAB; BiAuS; BiDrAC; DcAmB; Drake; TwCBDA; WebAB; WhAm H*

Morgan, Dennis
[Stanley Morner]
American. Actor, Singer
b. Dec 10, 1920 in Prentice, Wisconsin
Source: *FilmgC; IntMPA 75, 76, 77, 78, 79, 80, 81, 82; MotPP; MovMk; WhoHol A*

Morgan, Edward P
American. Journalist
b. Jun 23, 1910 in Walla Walla, Washington
Source: *AmAu&B; ConAu P-1; CurBio 51, 64; WhoAm 74, 76, 78, 80, 82; WhoS&SW 73; WhoWor 74*

Morgan, Edwin George
Scottish. Author, Poet
b. Apr 27, 1920 in Glasgow, Scotland
Source: *Au&Wr 71; CasWL; ChPo S2; ConAu 5R; ConP 70, 75; DcLEL 1940; IntWW 77; IntWWP 77; WorAu 1970; WrDr 76, 80*

Morgan, Frank
American. Actor
b. Jul 1, 1890 in New York, New York
d. Sep 18, 1949 in Beverly Hills, California
Source: *EncMT; Film 1; FilmgC; MotPP; MovMk; PlP&P; TwYS; WhAm 3; WhScrn 74, 77; WhoHol B*

Morgan, Frederick
English. Army Officer
b. Feb 5, 1894 in England
d. Mar 20, 1967
Source: *CurBio 46, 67; NewC*

Morgan, Harry
[Harry Bratsburg]
American. Actor
Starred in TV series "Dragnet," 1967-70; "MASH," 1975-83.
b. Apr 10, 1915 in Detroit, Michigan
Source: *FilmgC; IntMPA 75, 76, 77, 78, 79, 80, 81, 82; MotPP; NewYTBE 71; WhoHol A*

Morgan, Helen
American. Singer, Actress
b. 1900 in Danville, Illinois
d. Oct 9, 1941 in Chicago, Illinois
Source: *DcAmB S3; EncMT; FamA&A; FilmgC; NotAW; PlP&P; ThFT; WhScrn 74, 77; WhoHol B*

Morgan, Sir Henry
Welsh. Pirate, Lt. Governor of Jamaica
b. 1635
d. 1688
Source: *Alli; ApCAB; Drake; NewCol 75; OxAmL; REn; REnAL; WebBD 80*

Morgan, Henry
American. Radio, TV Personality
b. Mar 31, 1915 in New York, New York
Source: *CurBio 47; WhoHol A*

Morgan, Jane
American. Singer
b. 1920 in Boston, Massachusetts
Source: *InWom; WhoAm 74*

Morgan, Jaye P
American. Singer
b. Dec 3, 1932 in New York, New York
Source: *InWom; WhoAm 82; WhoHol A*

Morgan, Joe (Joseph Leonard)
American. Baseball Player
b. Sep 19, 1943 in Bonham, Texas
Source: *BaseEn; WhoAm 74, 76, 78, 80, 82; WhoProB 73*

Morgan, J(ohn) P(ierpont)
American. Financier
Formed US Steel Corp., 1901, first billion dollar corp. in world.
b. Apr 17, 1837 in Hartford, Connecticut
d. Mar 31, 1913 in Rome, Italy
Source: *AmBi; ApCAB; DcAmB; EncAB-H; REn; REnAL; TwCBDA; WebAB; WhAm 1*

Morgan, J(ohn) P(ierpont), Jr.
American. Philanthropist
Gave London house to US govt., 1920, for use as embassy.
b. Sep 7, 1867 in Irvington, New York
d. Mar 13, 1943 in New York, New York
Source: *CurBio 43; DcAmB S3; EncAB-H; NewCol 75; WebBD 80; WhAm 2*

Morgan, Marabel
American. Anti-Feminist, Author
b. Jun 25, 1937 in Crestline, Ohio
Source: *AuNews 1; ConAu 49, 2NR; WhoAm 82; WrDr 76*

Morgan, Michele
[Simone Roussel]
French. Actress
b. Feb 29, 1920 in Neuilly, France
Source: *BiDFilm; FilmgC; InWom; IntMPA 75, 76, 77, 78, 79, 80, 81, 82; IntWW 74; MovMk; OxFilm; WhoHol A; WhoWor 74*

Morgan, Ralph
American. Actor
b. Jul 6, 1883 in New York, New York
d. Jun 11, 1956 in New York, New York
Source: *FilmgC; MotPP; MovMk; Vers A; WhScrn 74, 77; WhoHol B*

Morgan, Robert Burren
American. Senator
b. Oct 5, 1925 in Lillington, North Carolina
Source: *BioIn 10; WhoAm 78, 80, 82*

Morgan, Russ
American. Composer, Conductor
b. 1904 in Scranton, Pennsylvania
d. Aug 7, 1969 in Las Vegas, Nevada
Source: *AmSCAP 66; WhScrn 74, 77; WhoHol B; WhoJazz 72*

Morgan, Terence
English. Actor
b. Dec 8, 1921 in London, England
Source: *FilmgC; IntMPA 75, 76, 77, 78, 79, 80, 81, 82; WhoHol A*

Morgan, Thomas H
American. Scientist, Physician, Engineer
b. Sep 25, 1866 in Lexington, Kentucky
d. Dec 4, 1945 in Pasadena, California
Source: *CurBio 46; DcAmAu; DcAmB S3; EncAB-H; NewCol 75; WebAB; WhAm 2*

Morgan, William Wilson
American. Astronomer
b. Jan 3, 1906 in Bethesda, Tennessee
Source: *WhoAm 78, 80, 82*

Morgana, Nina
American. Singer
b. 1895 in Buffalo, New York
Source: *InWom*

Morgenthau, Hans Joachim
American. Political Scientist
b. Feb 17, 1904 in Coburg, Germany
d. Jul 19, 1980 in New York, New York
Source: *AmAu&B; AmM&WS 73S, 78S; BioIn 4, 6, 11; ConAu 9R, 101; CurBio 63, 80; TwCA SUP; WhoAm 74, 76, 78; WhoWor 74; WhoWorJ 72*

Morgenthau, Henry
American. Diplomat
b. Apr 26, 1856 in Mannheim, Germany
d. Nov 25, 1946 in New York, New York
Source: *AmAu&B; DcAmB S4; DcNAA; NewCol 75; WebAB; WebBD 80; WhAm 2; WhNAA*

Morgenthau, Henry, Jr.
American. Government Official
Secretary of Treasury, 1934-45.
b. May 11, 1891 in New York, New York
d. Feb 6, 1967 in Poughkeepsie, New York
Source: *BiDrUSE; CurBio 40, 67; EncAB-H; NewCol 75; WebAB; WebBD 80*

Morgenthau, Robert M
American. Lawyer
b. Jul 31, 1919 in New York, New York
Source: *WhoAm 74, 76, 78, 80, 82; WhoE 74; WhoGov 72; WhoWorJ 72*

Mori, Hanae
Japanese. Fashion, Textile Designer
b. Jan 8, 1926 in Kyoto, Japan
Source: *BioNews 74; WhoFash; WorFshn*

Morial, Ernest Nathan
American. Mayor of New Orleans
b. Oct 9, 1929 in New Orleans, Louisiana
Source: *BioIn 11; NewYTBS 77; WhoAm 76, 78; WhoAmP 73, 79; WhoBlA 75, 77; WhoS&SW 78*

Moriarty, Cathy
American. Actress
Starred in *Raging Bull,* 1981; *Neighbors,* 1982.
b. Nov 29, 1960 in Bronx, New York
Source: *NewYTBS 81*

Moriarty, Michael
American. Actor
Won Emmy, 1978, for "Holocaust."
b. Apr 5, 1942 in Detroit, Michigan
Source: *IntMPA 75, 76, 77, 78, 79, 80, 81, 82; MovMk; NewYTBS 74; NotNAT; PlP&P A; WhoAm 82; WhoHol A; WhoThe 77*

Morike, Eduard Friedrich
German. Poet
b. Sep 8, 1804
d. Jun 4, 1875
Source: *AtlBL; BiD&SB; CasWL; EuAu; EvEuW; OxGer; Pen EUR; RComWL; REn*

Morini, Erica
Austrian. Musician
b. May 26, 1906 in Vienna, Austria
Source: *CurBio 46; InWom; Who 74; WhoAm 74, 76, 78, 80, 82; WhoMus 72; WhoWorJ 72*

Morison, Patricia
American. Actress
b. Mar 19, 1914 in New York, New York
Source: *BiE&WWA; EncMT; FilmgC; HolP 40; InWom; MotPP; NotNAT; ThFT; WhoHol A; WhoThe 77*

Morison, Samuel Eliot
American. Historian
b. Jul 9, 1887 in Boston, Massachusetts
d. May 15, 1976 in Boston, Massachusetts
Source: *AmAu&B; Au&Wr 71; AuBYP; CelR 73; ConAu 1R, 65, 4NR; CurBio 51, 62; DcLEL; DrAS 74H; EncAB-H; IntWW 74; LongCTC; OxAmL; OxCan SUP; Pen AM; REn; REnAL; TwCA SUP; WebAB; Who 74; WhoAm 74; WhoWor 74; WrDr 76*

Morisot, Berthe
French. Artist
b. Jan 14, 1841 in Bourges, France
d. Mar 2, 1895 in Paris, France
Source: *AtlBL; InWom; NewCol 75; WebBD 80*

Morita, Akio
Japanese. Businessman
b. Jan 26, 1921 in Nagoya, Japan
Source: *CurBio 72; IntWW 74; NewYTBE 70; WhoAm 74, 76, 78, 80, 82; WhoF&I 74; WhoWor 74*

Morland, George
English. Artist
b. 1763
d. 1804
Source: *DcBrWA; McGDA; NewC; NewCol 75; WebBD 80*

Morley, Christopher Darlington
American. Author, Journalist
b. May 5, 1890 in Haverford, Pennsylvania
d. Mar 28, 1957 in Roslyn Heights, New York
Source: *AmAu&B; AmNov; CarSB; CasWL; ChPo, S1, S2; CnDAL; ConAmA; ConAmL; DcLEL; EvLB; LongCTC; ModAL; OxAmL; OxEng; Pen AM; REn; REnAL; Str&VC; TwCA, SUP; WhNAA*

Morley, Eric Douglas
English. Impresario
Founded Miss World beauty pageant, 1951.
b. Sep 26, 1918 in London, England
Source: *Who 74, 82; WhoWor 74, 76, 78, 80*

Morley, John
English. Journalist
b. Dec 24, 1838 in Blackburn, England
d. Sep 23, 1923 in London, England
Source: *Alli SUP; BbD; BiD&SB; BrAu 19; CasWL; DcEnA; DcEnL; DcEuL; DcLEL; LongCTC; NewC; OxEng; Pen ENG*

Morley, Robert
English. Actor, Dramatist
Starred in *Pygmalion,* 1937; spokesman for British Airways.
b. May 26, 1908 in Semley, England
Source: *Au&Wr 71; BiE&WWA; CurBio 63; FilmgC; IntMPA 75, 76, 77, 78, 79, 80, 81, 82; IntWW 74; MotPP; MovMk; NotNAT; OxFilm; OxThe; PlP&P; Vers A; Who 74; WhoAm 82; WhoHol A; WhoThe 77; WhoWor 74*

Moro, Aldo
Italian. Politician
Leader, Christian Democratic Party, kidnapped, killed by Red Brigade terrorists.
b. Sep 23, 1916 in Maglie, Italy
d. May 9, 1978 in Rome, Italy
Source: *BioIn 6, 7, 10, 11; CurBio 64, 78; IntWW 74, 75, 76, 77, 78; IntYB 78; NewCol 75; NewYTBS 78; Who 74*

Moroni, Giovanni Battista (Giambattista)
Italian. Artist
b. 1525
d. 1578
Source: *McGDA; NewCol 75; WebBD 80*

Moronobu, Hishikawa
Japanese. Artist
b. 1618
d. 1703
Source: *BioIn 10; NewCol 75; WebBD 80*

Morphy, Paul Charles
American. Chess Player
b. Jun 22, 1837 in New Orleans, Louisiana
d. Jul 10, 1884 in New Orleans, Louisiana
Source: *AmBi; ApCAB; DcAmB; Drake; NewCol 75; WebAB; WebBD 80; WhAm H*

Morrall, Earl E
American. Football Player
b. May 17, 1934 in Muskegon, Michigan
Source: *WhoFtbl 74*

Morrice, James Wilson
Canadian. Artist
b. Aug 10, 1865 in Montreal, PQ
d. Jan 23, 1924 in Tunis, Tunisia
Source: *BioIn 1, 2, 3, 4, 8; CreCan 2; MacDCB 78; McGDA; McGEWB; NewCol 75*

Morrill, Justin Smith
"The Father of the Senate"
American. Politician
b. Apr 14, 1810 in Strafford, Vermont
d. Dec 28, 1898
Source: *BioIn 1, 2, 3, 5, 7, 8; NewCol 75; WebBD 80*

Morris, Chester
American. Actor
b. Feb 16, 1901 in New York, New York
d. Sep 11, 1970 in New Hope, Pennsylvania
Source: *BiE&WWA; Film 1; FilmgC; HolP 30; MovMk; WhAm 5; WhScrn 74, 77; WhoHol B*

Morris, Clara
American. Actress, Author
b. Mar 17, 1848 in Toronto, ON
d. Nov 20, 1925 in New Canaan, Connecticut
Source: *AmAu&B; AmBi; AmWom; ApCAB; BiD&SB; DcAmAu; DcAmB; DcNAA; FamA&A; InWom; NotAW; OhA&B; OxThe; PlP&P; TwCBDA; WhAm 1; WhScrn 74, 77; WhoHol B; WomWWA 14*

Morris, Desmond
English. Zoo Curator, Artist
b. Jan 24, 1928 in Wiltshire, England
Source: *Au&Wr 71; CelR 73; ConAu 45, 2NR; CurBio 74; IntWW 74; SmATA 14; Who 74; WhoAm 74; WhoWor 74; WrDr 76*

Morris, Gouverneur
American. Statesman, Diplomat
b. Jan 31, 1752 in Morrisania, New York
d. Nov 6, 1816 in Morrisania, New York
Source: *Alli; AmAu&B; AmBi; ApCAB; BiAuS; BiD&SB; BiDrAC; CyAL 1; DcAmAu; DcAmB; DcNAA; Drake; EncAB-H; OxAmL; REn; REnAL; TwCBDA; WebAB; WhAm H; WhAmP*

Morris, Greg
American. Actor
Starred in TV series "Mission Impossible," 1966-73.
b. Sep 26, 1934 in Cleveland, Ohio
Source: *WhoAm 82; WhoBlA 75; WhoHol A*

Morris, Howard
American. Actor, Motion Picture Director
b. Sep 4, 1919 in New York, New York
Source: *FilmgC; IntMPA 75, 76, 77, 78, 79, 80, 81, 82; WhoAm 82; WhoHol A*

Morris, Jack (John Scott)
American. Baseball Player
b. May 16, 1956 in Saint Paul, Minnesota
Source: *BaseEn*

Morris, Jan
English. Journalist
b. Oct 2, 1926
Source: *ConAu 53, 1NR; IntWW 74; NewYTBS 74; Who 74; WrDr 76*

Morris, Lewis
American. Continental Congressman
b. Apr 8, 1726 in Morrisania, New York
d. Jan 22, 1796 in Morrisania, New York
Source: *AmBi; ApCAB; BiAuS; BiDrAC; DcAmB; Drake; NewCol 75; TwCBDA; WebBD 80; WhAm H; WhAmP*

Morris, "Mercury" (Eugene)
American. Football Player
Sentenced to 20 years in prison, Jan, 1983, for trafficking cocaine.
b. Jan 5, 1947 in Pittsburgh, Pennsylvania
Source: *WhoFtbl 74*

Morris, Newbold
American. Politician
b. Feb 2, 1902 in New York, New York
d. Mar 30, 1966 in New York, New York
Source: *CurBio 52, 66; WhAm 1, 4*

Morris, Robert
American. Financier, Senator
b. Jan 31, 1734 in Liverpool, England
d. May 7, 1806 in Philadelphia, Pennsylvania
Source: *Alli, SUP; AmBi; ApCAB; BiAuS; BiDLA; BiDrAC; ChPo; CurBio 71; DcAmB; DcNAA; Drake; EncAB-H; REnAL; TwCBDA; WebAB; WhAm H; WhAmP*

Morris, Wayne
American. Actor
b. Feb 17, 1914 in Los Angeles, California
d. Sep 14, 1959 in Oakland, California
Source: *FilmgC; HolP 30; MotPP; MovMk; WhScrn 74, 77; WhoHol B*

Morris, William
English. Author, Poet, Artist
b. Mar 24, 1834 in Watthamstow, England
d. Oct 3, 1896 in London, England
Source: *Alli SUP; AtlBL; BbD; BiD&SB; BrAu 19; CasWL; ChPo, S1, S2; CnE&AP; CrtT 3; DcBiA; DcEnA, AP; DcEnL; DcEuL; EvLB; IntMPA 82; MouLC 4; NewC; OxEng; Pen ENG; RAdv 1; RComWL; REn; Str&VC; WebE&AL; WorFshn*

Morris, William, Jr.
American. Talent Agent
b. Oct 22, 1899 in New York, New York
Source: *WhoAm 78*

Morris, Willie
American. Author, Editor
b. Nov 29, 1934 in Jackson, Mississippi
Source: *ASpks; AuBYP SUP; AuNews 2; BioIn 7, 8, 9, 10, 11; CelR 73; ConAu 17R; CurBio 76; DrAF 76; IntAu&W 77; IntWW 74, 75, 76, 77, 78; WhoAm 74, 76, 78, 80, 82; WhoE 74; WhoWor 74; WrDr 80*

Morris, Wright Marion
American. Author
b. Jan 6, 1910 in Central City, Nebraska
Source: *AmAu&B; AmNov; AmWr; Au&Wr 71; CasWL; ConAu 9R; ConLC 1, 3, 7, 18; ConNov 72, 76; CurBio 82; DrAF 76; EncWL; ModAL, SUP; OxAmL; Pen AM; RAdv 1; REn; REnAL; TwCA SUP; TwCW; WebE&AL; WhoAm 74, 76, 78, 80, 82; WhoTwCL; WhoWor 74; WrDr 76*

Morrison, Cameron
American. Politician
b. Oct 5, 1869 in Richmond County, North Carolina
d. Aug 20, 1953 in Quebec, Canada
Source: *BiDrAC; BioIn 3, 5, 7; WhAm 3*

Morrison, Hobe
American. Drama Critic
b. Mar 24, 1904 in Philadelphia, Pennsylvania
Source: *BiE&WWA; ConAu 77; NotNAT; WhoThe 77*

Morrison, Jim (James Douglas)
[The Doors]
American. Rock Singer
Group name based on phrase by William Blake and study by Aldoux Huxley.
b. Dec 8, 1943 in Melbourne, Florida
d. Jul 3, 1971 in Paris, France
Source: *ConAu 73; NewYTBE 71; WhAm 5; WhScrn 77*

Morrison, Philip
American. Astrophysicist, Educator
b. Nov 7, 1915 in Somerville, New Jersey
Source: *AmM&WS 73P, 76P, 79P; BioIn 5, 7; CurBio 81*

Morrison, Theodore
American. Author
b. Nov 4, 1901 in Concord, New Hampshire
Source: *AmAu&B; ConAu 1R, 1NR; DrAS 74E; OxAmL; REnAL; TwCA SUP; WhoAm 74; WrDr 76*

Morrison, Toni
American. Author
b. Feb 18, 1931 in Lorain, Ohio
Source: *BlkAW; ConAu 29R; ConLC 4; DrAF 76; LivgBAA*

Morrison, Van
Irish. Singer, Songwriter
b. Aug 31, 1945 in Belfast, Northern Ireland
Source: *EncPR&S*

Morrison of Lambeth, Herbert Stanley Morrison, Baron
English. Statesman
b. Jan 3, 1888 in Brixton, England
d. Mar 6, 1965 in London, England
Source: *BioIn 1, 2, 3, 5, 7, 10, 11; ChPo; CurBio 40, 51, 65; NewCol 75; WebBD 80*

Morrow, Buddy
American. Musician
b. Feb 8, 1919 in New Haven, Connecticut
Source: *AmSCAP 66; WhoJazz 72*

Morrow, Dwight Whitney
American. Ambassador to Mexico
b. Jan 11, 1873 in Huntington, West Virginia
d. Oct 5, 1931 in Englewood, New Jersey
Source: *AmBi; BiDrAC; DcAmB; DcNAA; EncAB-H; NewCol 75; WebAB; WebBD 80; WhAm 1*

Morrow, Ken
[United States Olympic Hockey Team-1980]
American. Hockey Player
b. Oct 17, 1956 in Flint, Michigan
Source: *HocReg*

Morrow, Vic
American. Actor
Starred in "Combat," 1962-67; died in helicopter crash making movie.
b. Feb 14, 1932 in New York, New York
d. Jul 23, 1982 in Castaic, California
Source: *FilmEn; FilmgC; IntMPA 75, 76, 77, 78, 79, 80, 81, 82; MotPP; WhoHol A*

Morse, Barry
Canadian. Actor
b. Jun 10, 1918 in London, England
Source: *CanWW 70; CreCan 1; FilmgC; NotNAT; WhoHol A; WhoThe 77*

Morse, Ella Mae
American. Singer
b. Sep 12, 1924 in Mansfield, Texas
Source: *WhoHol A*

Morse, Joseph
American. Financier
b. 1920 in New York, New York
Source: *WhoAm 78*

Morse, Robert Alan
American. Actor
b. May 18, 1931 in Newton, Massachusetts
Source: *BiE&WWA; CelR 73; EncMT; FilmgC; IntMPA 82; NotNAT; WhoAm 82; WhoThe 77*

Morse, Samuel Finley Breese
American. Inventor, Artist
Invented Morse code; founded National Academy of Design.
b. Apr 27, 1791 in Charlestown, Massachusetts
d. Apr 2, 1872 in New York, New York
Source: *Alli, SUP; AmBi; ApCAB; BiD&SB; DcAmAu; DcAmB; DcNAA; EncAB-H; OxAmL; TwCBDA; WebAB; WhAm H*

Morse, Wayne Lyman
American. Politician
b. Oct 20, 1900 in Madison, Wisconsin
d. Jul 22, 1974 in Portland, Oregon
Source: *BiDrAC; BioNews 74; ConAu 49; CurBio 42, 54, 74; EncAB-H; IntWW 74; NewYTBS 74; WhAm 6; WhoAm 74; WhoAmP 73*

Mortada, Saad
Egyptian. Diplomat
b. Jul 1923 in Fayoum, Egypt
Source: *BioIn 4, 12*

Mortimer, Charles Greenough
American. General Foods Corporation Exec.
b. Jul 26, 1900 in Brooklyn, New York
d. Dec 25, 1978 in Orleans, Massachusetts
Source: *BioIn 3, 4, 5, 11; CurBio 55, 79; IntWW 74, 75, 76, 78; ObitOF 79; WhoAm 76; WhoF&I 74*

Morton, Bruce
Journalist
b. 1926
Source: *WrDr 76*

Morton, Craig
American. Football Player
b. Feb 5, 1943 in Flint, Michigan
Source: *CurBio 78*

Morton, Donald Lee
American. Surgeon
b. Sep 12, 1934 in Richwood, West Virginia
Source: *WhoAm 78*

Morton, Frederic
American. Author
b. Oct 5, 1924 in Vienna, Austria
Source: *AmAu&B; AmNov; ConAu 1R, 3NR; ModAL; WhoAm 76, 78, 80, 82; WorAu*

Morton, (Henry) Digby
Irish. Designer
b. Nov 27, 1906 in Dublin, Ireland
Source: *Who 74; WorFshn*

Morton, "Jelly Roll" (Joseph Ferdinand)
American. Jazz Musician, Composer
Innovator of orchestral jazz, early 1900's; composed "London Rag."
b. Sep 20, 1885 in Gulfport, Louisiana
d. Jul 10, 1941 in Los Angeles, California
Source: *DcAmB S3; NewCol 75; WebAB; WhoJazz 72*

Morton, John
American. Continental Congressman
b. 1724 in Ridley Park, Pennsylvania
d. 1777 in Ridley Park, Pennsylvania
Source: *AmBi; ApCAB; BiDrAC; DcAmB; Drake; NewCol 75; TwCBDA; WebBD 80; WhAm H; WhAmP*

Morton, Julius Sterling
American. Journalist, Government Official
Founded Arbor Day; first observed Apr 22, 1872.
b. Apr 22, 1832 in Adams, New York
d. Apr 27, 1902 in Lake Forest, Illinois
Source: *AmBi; ApCAB SUP; BiDrUSE; BioIn 1, 3, 4, 6, 9, 10; DcAmB; DcNAA; EncAAH; NatCAB 6; NewCol 75; REnAW; TwCBDA; WebAB; WhAm 1*

Morton, Rogers Clark Ballard
American. Government Official
Secretary of Interior, 1971-75; Secretary of Commerce, 1975-76.
b. Sep 19, 1914 in Louisville, Kentucky
d. Apr 19, 1979 in Easton, Maryland
Source: *BiDrAC; BiDrUSE; CngDr 74; CurBio 71; IntWW 74; NewYTBE 70; NewYTBS 79; WhoAm 74; WhoAmP 73; WhoGov 72; WhoWor 74*

Morton, Thruston Ballard
American. Politician
b. Aug 19, 1907 in Louisville, Kentucky
d. Aug 14, 1982 in Louisville, Kentucky
Source: *BiDrAC; CurBio 57, 82; IntWW 74, 75, 76, 77, 78; NewYTBS 82; PolProf E; PolProf J; PolProf K; WhoAm 74, 76, 78, 80, 82; WhoF&I 74; WhoS&SW 73*

Morton, William Thomas Green
American. Dentist
First to use ether as anesthetic, 1846.
b. Aug 9, 1819 in Charlton, Massachusetts
d. Jul 15, 1868 in New York, New York
Source: *Alli; AmBi; ApCAB; DcAmB; DcNAA; Drake; NewCol 75; TwCBDA; WebAB; WebBD 80; WhAm H*

Mosby, John Singleton
American. Confederate Officer
b. Dec 6, 1833 in Edgemont, Virginia
d. 1916 in Washington, DC
Source: *Alli SUP; AmBi; ApCAB; BiD&SB; BiDSA; DcAmAu; DcAmB; DcNAA; REn; TwCBDA; WebAB; WhAm 1; WhoS&SW 73*

Moscheles, Ignaz
Czech. Composer, Musician
b. May 30, 1794 in Prague, Czechoslovakia
d. Mar 10, 1870 in Leipzig, Germany
Source: *BioIn 2, 4, 7, 9; NewCol 75, 75*

Moscona, Nicola
Greek. Opera Singer
b. Sep 23, 1907 in Athens, Greece
d. Sep 17, 1975 in Philadelphia, Pennsylvania
Source: *NewYTBS 75; WhAm 6*

Moscone, George Richard
American. Government Official
Mayor of San Francisco, 1976-78; murdered by Daniel White.
b. Nov 24, 1929 in San Francisco, California
d. Nov 27, 1978 in San Francisco, California
Source: *NewYTBS 78; WhAm 7; WhoAmP 73*

Mosconi, Willie (William Joseph)
American. Billiards Player
World pocket billiards champ ten years.
b. Jun 21, 1913 in Philadelphia, Pennsylvania
Source: *BioNews 74; CelR 73; CurBio 63; NewCol 75; WhoAm 82*

Mosel, Tad
American. Dramatist
b. May 1, 1922 in Steubenville, Ohio
Source: *BiE&WWA; CurBio 61; McGEWD; ModWD; NotNAT; OxAmL; REnAL; WhoAm 74, 76, 78, 80, 82; WrDr 76*

Mosenthal, Salomon Hermann von
German. Author, Dramatist, Librettist
b. Jan 14, 1821 in Cassel, Germany
d. Feb 17, 1877 in Vienna, Austria
Source: *BiD&SB; OxGer; WebBD 80*

Moses
Biblical Character
b. 1392?BC in Egypt
d. 1272?BC in Moab, Jordan
Source: *BioIn 1, 2, 3, 4, 5, 6, 7, 8, 9, 10, 11; DcOrL 3; McGEWB; NewCol 75; REn*

Moses, Edwin
American. Track Athlete
b. 1955?
Source: *BioIn 11*

Moses, "Grandma" (Anna Mary Robertson)
American. Artist
Started painting in her late 70's; subjects are rural life, including "Black Horses," 1941.
b. Aug 7, 1860 in Greenwich, New York
d. Dec 13, 1961 in Hoosick Falls, New York
Source: *AuBYP; ChPo; CurBio 49, 62; HerW; InWom; REn; WebAB; WhAm 4*

Moses, Robert
American. Architect, Designer
b. Dec 18, 1888 in New Haven, Connecticut
d. Jul 29, 1981 in West Islip, New York
Source: *BiE&WWA; BioIn 2, 3, 4, 5, 6, 7, 10, 11; ConAu 45, 104; CurBio 40, 54, 81; IntWW 74, 75, 76, 77, 78; LinLib S; NewCol 75; PolProf J; PolProf K; WebAB; WhoAm 74, 76, 78; WhoAmP 73, 75, 77, 79; WhoWorJ 72*

Moshoeshoe II
[Constantine Bereng Seeiso]
King of Lesotho
b. 1938
Source: *NewCol 75*

Mosley, Leonard
English. Journalist
b. 1913 in Manchester, England
Source: *Au&Wr 71; WrDr 76*

Mosley, Sir Oswald Ernald
English. Politician, Activist
b. Dec 12, 1896 in Hickory, Oklahoma
Source: *ConAu 25R, 102; ConAu P-2; CurBio 40; IntWW 74; NewCol 75; WebBD 80; Who 74; WhoWor 74*

Mosley, Zack Terrell
American. Cartoonist
b. Dec 12, 1906 in Hickory, Oklahoma
Source: *WhoAmA 73; WhoAm 74, 76, 78, 80, 82*

Moss, Arnold
American. Actor, Motion Picture Director
b. Jan 28, 1911 in Brooklyn, New York
Source: *BiE&WWA; FilmgC; IntMPA 75, 76, 77, 78, 79, 80, 81, 82; MovMk; NotNAT; Vers A; WhoAm 74; WhoHol A; WhoThe 77*

Moss, Frank Edward
American. Politician
b. Sep 23, 1911 in Salt Lake City, Utah
Source: *BiDrAC; CngDr 74; ConAu 61; CurBio 71; IntWW 74; WhoAm 74; WhoAmP 73; WhoGov 72*

Moss, Geoffrey
American. Cartoonist, Illustrator
b. Jun 30, 1938 in Brooklyn, New York
Source: *BioIn 11; WhoAm 78, 80, 82*

Moss, Jerry (Jerome Sheldon)
American. Record Company Executive
b. 1935 in Brooklyn, New York
Source: *BioIn 9, 11; WhoAm 78, 80, 82*

Moss, Stirling Crauford
English. Auto Racer
b. Sep 17, 1929 in London, England
Source: *Au&Wr 71; ConAu 5R; Who 74; WrDr 76*

Mossadegh, Mohammed
Iranian. Premier
b. 1879? in Teheran, Persia
d. Mar 5, 1967 in Teheran, Iran
Source: *CurBio 51, 67; WhAm 4*

Most, Donny
American. Actor
Played Ralph Malph on TV series "Happy Days."
b. 1952?
Source: *BioIn 12*

Mostel, Zero (Samuel Joel)
American. Actor
Played Tevye in *Fiddler on the Roof;* won three Tonys.
b. Feb 28, 1915 in Brooklyn, New York
d. Sep 8, 1977 in Philadelphia, Pennsylvania
Source: *BiE&WWA; CelR 73; ConAu 89; CurBio 43, 63; EncMT; FamA&A; FilmgC; IntMPA 75, 76, 77; IntWW 74; MotPP; MovMk; NotNAT; PlP&P; WhoAm 74; WhoHol A; WhoThe 77; WhoWor 74*

Moszkowski, Moritz
German. Composer, Musician
b. Aug 23, 1854 in Breslau, Germany
d. Mar 4, 1925 in Paris, France
Source: *OxMus; WebBD 80*

Motels, The
[Davis, Martha; Glascock, Brian; Goodroe, Michael; Jourard, Marty; Perry, Guy]
American. Rock Group
Source: *NewWmR*

Moten, Bennie
American. Jazz Musician
b. Nov 13, 1894 in Kansas City, Missouri
d. Apr 2, 1935 in Kansas City, Missouri
Source: *CmpEPM; WhAm 4; WhoJazz 72*

Mother Teresa
see: Teresa, Mother

Mothers of Invention, The
[Jimmy Carl Black; Ray Collins; Roy Estrada; Bunk Gardner; Don Preston; James Sherwood; Ian Underwood; Frank Zappa]
American. Rock Group
Source: *EncPR&S*

Mothersbaugh, Bob
see: Devo

Mothersbaugh, Mark
see: Devo

Motherwell, Robert Burns
American. Artist
One of founders of Abstract Expressionism, 1940's.
b. Jan 24, 1915 in Aberdeen, Washington
Source: *CelR 73; CurBio 62; DcCAA 71; EncAB-H; IntWW 74; NewCol 75; WhoAm 74, 76, 78, 80, 82; WhoAmA 73; WhoWor 74*

Motley, Arthur Harrison
"Red"
American. Publisher
b. Aug 22, 1900 in Minneapolis, Minnesota
Source: *AuNews 2; BioNews 74; CurBio 61; St&PR 75; WhoAdv 72; WhoAm 74; WhoE 74*

Motley, John L
American. Historian, Diplomat
b. Apr 15, 1814 in Dorchester, Massachusetts
d. May 29, 1877 in Dorsetshire, England
Source: *Alli, SUP; AmAu; AmAu&B; AmBi; ApCAB; BbD; BiAuS; BiD&SB; Chambr 3; CyAl 2; DcAmAu; DcAmB; DcEnA; DcEnL; DcLEL; DcNAA; EvLB; NewCol 75; OxAmL; OxEng; Pen AM; REn; REnAL; TwCBDA; WebAB; WebBD 80; WhAm H*

Motley, Willard Francis
American. Author
b. Jul 14, 1912 in Chicago, Illinois
d. Mar 5, 1965 in Mexico City, Mexico
Source: *AmAu&B; AmNov; BlkAW; OxAmL; Pen AM; REn; REnAL; TwCA SUP; WhAm 4*

Mott, Charles Stewart
American. Industrialist
Founded Mott Foundation, 1926; chairman, US Sugar Corp.
b. Jun 2, 1875 in Newark, New Jersey
d. Feb 18, 1973 in Flint, Michigan
Source: *BusPN; WhAm 5; WhoF&I 74*

Mott, Frank Luther
American. Journalist
b. Apr 4, 1886 in Keokuk County, Iowa
d. Oct 23, 1964
Source: *AmAu&B; ConAu 1R; CurBio 41, 64; NewCol 75; OxAmL; REn; REnAL; TwCA SUP; WebBD 80; WhAm 4; WhNAA*

Mott, Lucretia Coffin
American. Social Reformer
Co-founded women's right movement in US, 1848.
b. Jan 3, 1793 in Nantucket, Massachusetts
d. Nov 11, 1880 in Philadelphia, Pennsylvania
Source: *Alli; AmBi; AmWom; ApCAB; DcAmB; Drake; EncAB-H; HerW; NewCol 75; NotAW; TwCBDA; WebAB; WhAm H*

Mott, Sir Nevill Francis
English. Physicist
b. Sep 30, 1905 in Leeds, England
Source: *Au&Wr 71; IntWW 74; Who 74; WhoWor 74*

Mott, Ruth Rawlings
American. Philanthropist
b. Oct 18, 1901 in El Paso, Texas
Source: *WhoAm 78*

Mott, Stewart Rawlings
American. Philanthropist
Son of Charles Mott; inherited $20 million trust fund; director, US Sugar Corp., 1965--.
b. Dec 4, 1937 in Flint, Michigan
Source: *BusPN; NewYTBE 72; WhoAm 74, 76, 78, 80, 82*

Mott (the Hoople)
[Verden Allen; Nigel Benjamin; Terry Buffin; Morgan Fisher; DaleGriffin ("Buffin"); Ian Hunter; Ray Major; Mick Ralphs; Pete Watts]
English. Rock Group
Source: *ConMuA 80; EncPR&S; IlEncRk; LilREn 78; RkOn 2; WhoRock 81*

Motta, John Richard
American. Basketball Coach
NBA Coach of year, 1970-71.
b. Sep 3, 1931 in Salt Lake City, Utah
Source: *WhoAm 74, 76, 78, 80, 82; WhoE 79*

Mottl, Felix
Austrian. Conductor
b. Aug 24, 1856 in Unter St. Veit, Austria
d. Jul 2, 1911 in Munich, Germany
Source: *NewCol 75; NewEOp 71; OxMus; WebBD 80*

Mottley, John
English. Author
b. 1692 in London, England
d. Oct 3, 1750 in London, England
Source: *Alli; BrAu; DcEnL; DcLEL; NewC; OxEng; WebBD 80*

Mottola, Anthony
American. Musician
b. Apr 18, 1918 in Kearney, New Jersey
Source: *AmSCAP 66*

Mould, Jacob Wrey
English. Architect
b. Aug 8, 1825 in Chislehurst, England
d. Jun 14, 1886 in New York, New York
Source: *ApCAB X; BioIn 8; NatCAB 3; WhAm H*

Moultrie, William
American. General, Governor
b. Dec 4, 1730 in Charleston, South Carolina
d. Sep 27, 1805 in Charleston, South Carolina
Source: *Alli; AmBi; ApCAB; BiAuS; BiDSA; DcAmAu; DcAmB; DcNAA; Drake; NewCol 75; TwCBDA; WebAB; WebBD 80; WhAm H*

Mount, William Sidney
American. Artist
b. Nov 26, 1807 in Setauket, New York
d. Nov 19, 1868 in Setauket, New York
Source: *AmBi; ApCAB; ChPo; DcAmB; Drake; EncAB-H; NewCol 75; TwCBDA; WebAB; WebBD 80; WhAm H*

Mountbatten of Burma, Louis Mountbatten, Earl
English. Naval Officer
Great-grandson of Queen Victoria; killed in bomb explosion credited to IRA.
b. Jun 25, 1900 in Windsor, England
d. Aug 27, 1979 in Mullaghmore, Ireland
Source: *CurBio 42, 79; NewCol 75; WebBD 80; WhWW-II; Who 74; WhoWor 74*

Mowat, Farley
Canadian. Author
b. May 12, 1921 in Belleville, ON
Source: *AmAu&B; AuBYP; CanWW 82; CanWr; CasWL; ConAu 1R, 4NR; CreCan 2; IntWW 74; OxCan, SUP; SmATA 3; ThrBJA; WhoAm 74, 76, 78, 80, 82; WhoCan 73; WhoE 74; WorAu; WrDr 76*

Mowbray, Alan
English. Actor
b. Aug 18, 1897 in London, England
d. Mar 25, 1969 in Hollywood, California
Source: *BiE&WWA; FilmgC; MotPP; MovMk; Vers A; WhScrn 74, 77; WhoHol B*

Mowrer, Edgar Ansel
American. Journalist
b. Mar 8, 1892 in Bloomington, Illinois
d. Mar 2, 1977 in Madeira, Portugal
Source: *AmAu&B; ConAu 69; ConAu P-1; CurBio 41, 62; DrAS 74P; IntWW 74; REnAL; TwCA, SUP; WhNAA; Who 74; WhoAm 74; WhoE 74*

Mowrer, Paul Scott
American. Journalist
b. Jul 14, 1887 in Bloomington, Illinois
d. Apr 5, 1971 in Beaufort, South Carolina
Source: *AmAu&B; ChPo; ConAu 5R, 29R, 4NR; REnAL; WhAm 5; WhNAA*

Moyer, Sheldon
American. Association Executive
b. Dec 11, 1920 in Garrett, Indiana
Source: *WhoAm 74; WhoF&I 74*

Moyers, Bill (William Don)
American. Journalist
b. Jun 5, 1934 in Hugo, Oklahoma
Source: *AuNews 1; ConAu 61; CurBio 66; IntWW 74; Who 74; WhoAm 74, 76, 78, 80, 82; WhoAmP 73; WhoWor 74*

Moyes, Patricia
Irish. Author
b. Jan 19, 1923 in Bray, Ireland
Source: *Au&Wr 71; BiE&WWA; ConAu 17R; EncMys; WrDr 76, 80*

Moynihan, Daniel Patrick
American. Senator, Diplomat
b. Mar 16, 1927 in Tulsa, Oklahoma
Source: *AmAu&B; AmM&WS 73S; CelR 73; ConAu 5R; CurBio 68; IntWW 74; NewYTBS 74; USBiR 74; WhoAm 74, 76, 78, 80, 82; WhoAmP 73; WhoE 74; WhoGov 72; WhoWor 74*

Mozart, (Johann Georg) Leopold
Austrian. Musician, Composer
b. 1719 in Augsburg, Austria
d. 1787 in Salzburg, Austria
Source: *BioIn 9; WebBD 80*

Mozart, Wolfgang Amadeus
Austrian. Composer
Composed over 600 works, including *The Marriage of Figaro,* 1896.
b. Jan 27, 1756 in Salzburg, Austria
d. Dec 5, 1791 in Vienna, Austria
Source: *AtlBL; NewCol 75; OxGer; REn; WebBD 80*

Mravinsky, Eugene
Russian. Conductor
b. 1903 in Saint Petersburg, Russia
Source: *WhoMus 72*

Mubarak, (Muhamed) Hosni
Egyptian. President
Succeeded Anwar Sadat as president, 1981.
b. May 4, 1928 in Kafr-El Meselha, Egypt
Source: *BioIn 11, 12; CurBio 82; IntWW 77, 78, 79, 80; MidE 78, 79; NewYTBS 78; WhoWor 78, 80*

Mucha, Alphonse Marie
Czech. Artist
Specialized in designing posters in art nouveau style.
b. 1860 in Ivancice, Bohemia
d. 1938 in Prague, Czechoslovakia
Source: *AntBDN A; BioIn 7, 9, 10; DcNiCA; NewCol 75; PhDcTCA 77*

Mucha, Jiri
Czech. Author, Journalist
b. Mar 12, 1915 in Prague, Czechoslovakia
Source: *BioIn 8; CasWL; ConAu 21R; ModSL 2; Pen EUR; TwCW; WrDr 76, 80; WhE&EA*

Muck, Karl
German. Conductor
b. Oct 22, 1859 in Darmstadt, Germany
d. Mar 3, 1940 in Stuttgart, Germany
Source: *CurBio 40; WebBD 80*

Muczynski, Robert
American. Composer, Musician
b. Mar 19, 1929 in Chicago, Illinois
Source: *AmSCAP 66; Baker 78; BioIn 7, 9*

Mudd, Roger Harrison
American. Broadcast Journalist
Newscaster, CBS, 1961-80; NBC, 1980--.
b. Feb 9, 1928 in Washington, DC
Source: *CelR 73; WhoAm 74, 76, 78, 80, 82; WhoS&SW 73*

Mudd, Samuel Alexander
American. Physician
Treated broken leg of John Wilkes Booth; convicted as conspirator to assassination plot.
b. Dec 20, 1833
d. 1883
Source: *BioIn 10*

Mudgett, Herman Webster
[Dr. Harry Holmes, alias]
American. Mass Murderer
b. in Gilmantown, New Hampshire
d. May 7, 1896
Source: *BioIn 10; Blood*

Mueller, "Heinie" (Clarence Franklin)
American. Baseball Player
b. Sep 16, 1899 in Creve Coeur, Missouri
d. Jan 23, 1974 in DeSoto, Missouri
Source: *BaseEn; WhoProB 73*

Mueller, Leah Poulos
American. Speed Skater
b. 1952? in Wisconsin
Source: *BioIn 12*

Mueller, Reuben Herbert
American. Bishop
Established National Council of Churches, 1950; president, 1963-1966.
b. Jun 2, 1897 in Saint Paul, Minnesota
d. Jul 5, 1982 in Franklin, Indiana
Source: *CurBio 64, 82; IndAu 1917; IntWW 74, 75, 76, 77, 78, 79, 80, 81; NewYTBS 82; WhoAm 74*

Muenchhausen, Friedrich Ernst von
German. Army Officer
b. 1753
d. 1795
Source: *BioIn 10*

Mugabe, Robert Gabriel
South African. Prime Minister of Zimbabwe
b. Feb 21, 1924 in Kutama, South Africa
Source: *BioIn 11; CurBio 79*

Muggeridge, Malcolm
English. Journalist, Editor, Author
b. Mar 24, 1903 in Sunderstead, England
Source: *Au&Wr 71; AuNews 1; ConAu 101; IntMPA 75, 76, 77, 78, 79, 80, 81, 82; IntWW 74; NewC; Who 74; WhoAm 74, 76, 78, 80, 82; WhoWor 74; WorAu; WrDr 76*

Mugnone, Leopoldo
Italian. Conductor
b. Sep 29, 1858 in Naples, Italy
d. Dec 22, 1941 in Naples, Italy
Source: *NewEOp 71*

Muhammad
see: Mohammed

Muhammad, Elijah
American. Religious Leader
Follower of Wali Farad; leader of Black Muslims, 1934.
b. Oct 10, 1897 in Sandersville, Georgia
d. Feb 25, 1975 in Chicago, Illinois
Source: *CelR 73; CurBio 71; EncAB-H; WebAB; WhoRel 75*

Muhammad, Wallace D
American. Religious Leader
b. Oct 30, 1933 in Detroit, Michigan
Source: *BioIn 10, 11; WhoAm 78, 80, 82*

Muhammad Ali
see: Ali, Muhammad

Muhlenberg, Heinrich Melchior
American. Religious Leader
b. Sep 6, 1711 in Einbech, Germany
d. Oct 7, 1786 in New Providence, Pennsylvania
Source: *McGEWB; NewCol 75*

Muir, Edwin
Scottish. Author, Critic
b. May 15, 1887 in Deerness, Scotland
d. Jan 3, 1959 in Cambridge, England
Source: *AnCL; AtlBL; CasWL; ChPo, S1; CnE&AP; CnMWL; DcLEL; EncWL; EvLB; LongCTC; ModBrL, SUP; NewC; OxEng; Pen ENG; RAdv 1; RComWL; REn; TwCA, SUP; TwCW; WebE&AL; WhoTwCL*

Muir, Jean
American. Actress
b. 1911 in New York, New York
Source: *FilmgC; ThFT; WhoHol A*

Muir, John
American. Naturalist, Author
b. Jul 21, 1838 in Dunbar, Scotland
d. Dec 24, 1914 in Los Angeles, California
Source: *AmAu&B; AmBi; ApCAB SUP; BiD&SB; DcAmAu; DcAmB; DcLEL; DcNAA; EvLB; JBA 34; OxAmL; REn; REnAL; TwCA, SUP; TwCBDA; WebAB; WhAm 1; WisWr*

Muir, Malcolm
American. Publisher
b. Jul 19, 1885 in Glen Ridge, New Jersey
d. Jan 30, 1979 in New York, New York
Source: *AmAu&B; BioIn 3, 8, 11; ConAu 85; CurBio 53, 79; IntWW 74, 75, 76, 77, 78; NewYTBS 79; WhoAm 74, 76, 78*

Muldaur, Diana Charlton
[Mrs. James Mitchell Vickery]
American. Actress
b. Aug 10, 1938 in New York, New York
Source: *FilmgC; IntMPA 75, 76, 77, 78, 79, 80, 81, 82; WhoAm 74, 76, 78, 80, 82; WhoHol A*

Muldaur, Maria
American. Singer
b. Sep 12, 1943 in New York, New York
Source: *NewYTBS 74; RkOn; WhoAm 82*

Muldoon, Robert David
New Zealander. Prime Minister
b. Sep 25, 1921 in Auckland, New Zealand
Source: *IntWW 74; Who 74; WhoWor 74*

Muldowney, Shirley
"Cha Cha"
American. Automobile Racer
b. 1940?
Source: *BioIn 10*

Mulford, Clarence Edward
American. Author
b. Feb 3, 1883 in Streator, Illinois
d. May 10, 1956 in Portland, Maine
Source: *AmAu&B; EvLB; FilmgC; LongCTC; MnBBF; OxAmL; REnAL; TwCA, SUP; WhAm 3; WhNAA*

Mulhall, Jack
American. Actor
b. Oct 7, 1894 in New York
Source: *Film 1; FilmgC; MotPP; MovMk; TwYS; WhoHol A*

Mulhare, Edward
Irish. Actor
b. 1923 in County Cork, Ireland
Source: *BiE&WWA; FilmgC; MotPP; NotNAT; WhoHol A*

Mull, Martin
American. Actor, Comedian
b. 1943 in Chicago, Illinois
Source: *BioNews 74; WhoAm 80, 82*

Mullens, Priscilla
see: Alden, Priscilla Mullens

Muller, Bobby (Robert)
American. Vietnam Veterans of America Head
b. Jul 27, 1945 in Switzerland
Source: *BioIn 12*

Muller, Harold P
American. Football Player
b. Jun 12, 1901 in Dunsmuir, Georgia
d. May 17, 1962
Source: *WhoFtbl 74*

Muller, Hermann Joseph
American. Scientist, Physician, Engineer
b. Dec 21, 1890 in New York, New York
d. Apr 5, 1967 in Indianapolis, Indiana
Source: *TexWr; WebAB; WhAm 4; WhNAA*

Muller, Johannes Peter
German. Scientist
Founded modern science of physiology.
b. Jul 14, 1801 in Koblenz, Prussia
d. Apr 28, 1858 in Berlin, Germany
Source: *AsBiEn; BiHiMed; DcScB; InSci; McGEWD; NamesHP*

Muller, Maria
Bohemian. Opera Singer
b. Jan 29, 1898 in Leitmoritz, Bohemia
d. Mar 13, 1958 in Bayreuth, Germany (West)
Source: *InWom*

Muller-Munk, Peter
Industrial Designer
b. 1904
d. 1967
Source: *BioIn 7, 8*

Mullett, Alfred Bult
American. Architect
b. 1834 in Taunton, England
d. 1890
Source: *McGDA*

Mullgardt, Louis Christian
American. Architect
b. Jan 18, 1866 in Washington, Missouri
d. 1942
Source: *BioIn 4; WhAm 4*

Mulligan, Gerry (Gerald Joseph)
American. Jazz Musician
b. Apr 6, 1927 in New York, New York
Source: *AmSCAP 66; CurBio 60; WhoAm 74, 76, 78, 80, 82; WhoE 74; WhoHol A*

Mulligan, Richard
American. Actor
b. Nov 13, 1932 in Bronx, New York
Source: *FilmgC; WhoAm 74, 76, 78, 80, 82; WhoHol A; WhoThe 77*

Mullin, Willard
American. Sports Cartoonist
b. 1902 in Ohio
d. Dec 21, 1978 in Corpus Christi, Texas
Source: *BioIn 4, 9, 11; ConAu 89; NewYTBE 71; NewYTBS 78; ObitOF 79*

Mulvey, Grant Michael
Canadian. Hockey Player
b. Sep 17, 1956 in Herritt, BC
Source: *HocReg*

Mumford, Lawrence Quincy
American. Librarian
Librarian of Congress, 1954-74.
b. Dec 11, 1903 in Ayden, North Carolina
d. Aug 15, 1982
Source: *BiDrLUS 70; CurBio 54, 83; IntWW 74, 75, 76, 77, 78; LinLib L, S; Who 74; WhoAm 74, 76, 80, 82; WhoGov 72, 75; WhoS&SW 73, 75; WhoWor 74*

Mumford, Lewis
American. Author, Architect
b. Oct 19, 1895 in Flushing, New York
Source: *AmAu&B; Au&Wr 71; CasWL; CelR 73; CnDAL; ConAmA; ConAmL; ConAu 1R, 5NR; CurBio 40, 63; DcLEL; DrAS 74H; EncAB-H; EvLB; IntWW 74; LongCTC; ModAL, SUP; NewYTBE 70; OxAmL; Pen AM; REn; REnAL; TwCA, SUP; WebAB; WebE&AL; Who 74; WhoAm 74, 76, 78, 80, 82; WhoWor 74; WrDr 76*

Mumtaz Mahal
Hindu. Inspiration for Taj Mahal
b. 1593?
d. 1630?
Source: *BioIn 4, 8; NewCol 75*

Muncey, Bill (William)
American. Hydroplane Racer
b. Nov 12, 1928 in Royal Oak, Michigan
d. Oct 18, 1981 in Acapulco, Mexico
Source: *BioIn 6, 9, 10, 11*

Munch, Charles
French. Conductor
b. Sep 26, 1891 in Strasbourg, France
d. Nov 6, 1968 in Richmond, Virginia
Source: *CurBio 47, 68; REnAL*

Munch, Edvard
Norwegian. Artist
b. Dec 12, 1863 in Loyten, Norway
d. Jan 23, 1944 in Oslo, Norway
Source: *AtlBL; CurBio 40, 44; NewCol 75; REn; WebBD 80; WhAm 4*

Munchhausen, Hierony mus Karl Friedrich von, Baron
[Karl Friedrich Hieronymus von Munchausen]
German. Soldier, Raconteur
b. May 11, 1720 in Hannover, Germany
d. Feb 22, 1797
Source: *Alli; BiD&SB; ClDMEL; EncWL; LinLib L, S; LongCEL; OxGer; WebBD 80*

Munchinger, Karl
German. Conductor
b. May 29, 1915 in Stuttgart, Germany
Source: *IntWW 74; WhoMus 72; WhoWor 74*

Muncie, "Chuck" (Henry Vance)
American. Football Player
Running back, New Orleans Saints, 1976-81; San Diego Chargers, 1981--.
b. Mar 17, 1953 in Uniontown, Pennsylvania
Source: *WhoBlA 77, 80*

Mundt, Karl Earl
American. Educator, Senator
b. Jun 3, 1900 in Humboldt, South Dakota
d. Aug 16, 1974 in Washington, DC
Source: *BiDrAC; BioNews 74; CurBio 48, 74; IntWW 74; NewYTBS 74; WhAm 6; WhoAm 74; WhoAmP 73; WhoGov 72; WhoMW 74*

Mundy, Meg
English. Actress
b. in London, England
Source: *BiE&WWA; NewYTBE 73; NotNAT; WhoThe 77*

Muni, Paul
[Muni Weisenfreund]
American. Actor
b. Sep 22, 1895 in Lemberg, Austria
d. Aug 25, 1967 in Montecito, California
Source: *BiDFilm; BiE&WWA; BioNews 74; CurBio 44, 67; FamA&A; FilmgC; MotPP; MovMk; OxFilm; PlP&P; WhScrn 74, 77; WhoHol B; WorEFlm*

Munn, Frank
American. Radio Singer
b. 1894 in Bronx, New York
d. Oct 1, 1953 in New York, New York
Source: *CurBio 44, 53*

Munoz Marin, Luis
Puerto Rican. Governor
b. Feb 18, 1898 in San Juan, Puerto Rico
d. Apr 30, 1980 in San Juan, Puerto Rico
Source: *CurBio 42, 53; PueRA; WebAB; WhNAA; WhoAmP 73; WhoS&SW 73*

Munro, Hector Hugh
see: Saki, pseud.

Munroe, Charles Edward
American. Chemist
b. May 24, 1849 in Cambridge, Massachusetts
d. Dec 7, 1938
Source: *ApCAB; DcAmB S2; DcNAA; TwCBDA; WhAm 1*

Munsel, Patrice
American. Singer
b. May 14, 1925 in Spokane, Washington
Source: *BiE&WWA; CurBio 45; FilmgC; WhoAm 74; WhoE 74; WhoHol A; WhoMus 72*

Munshin, Jules
American. Actor
b. 1915 in New York, New York
d. Feb 19, 1970 in New York, New York
Source: *BiE&WWA; CmMov; FilmgC; MotPP; NewYTBE 70; WhScrn 74, 77; WhoHol B*

Munson, Gorham B(ert)
American. Author, Editor
b. May 26, 1896 in Amityville, New York
d. Aug 15, 1969 in Middletown, Connecticut
Source: *AmAu&B; AuBYP; CnDAL; ConAu P-1; OxAmL; Pen AM; REnAL; TwCA, SUP; WhAm 5*

Munson, Ona
American. Actress
b. Jun 16, 1906 in Portland, Oregon
d. Feb 11, 1955 in New York, New York
Source: *FilmgC; MotPP; MovMk; ThFT; Vers A; WhScrn 74, 77; WhoHol B*

Munson, Thurman Lee
"Squatty"
American. Baseball Player
MVP, 1976; wrote *Thurman Munson: An Autobiography*, 1978; killed in plane crash.
b. Jun 7, 1947 in Akron, Ohio
d. Aug 2, 1979 in Canton, Ohio
Source: *BaseEn; BioIn 11; ConAu 89; CurBio 77, 79; NewYTBS 75, 79; WhoAm 78; WhoProB 73*

Muntz, "Madman" (Earl William)
American. Automobile Dealer
b. 1914
Source: *BioIn 9, 10*

Murasaki, Lady Shikibu
Japanese. Author
b. 978?
d. 1031?
Source: *CasWL; CyWA; DcOrL 1; NewCol 75; Pen CL; REn; WebBD 80*

Murat, Joachim
French. Calvary Leader
b. Mar 25, 1767 in La Baslide-Fortumiere, France
d. Oct 13, 1815
Source: *BioIn 1, 9; LinLib S; McGEWB; NewCol 75; OxFr; REn; REnAL; WhoMilH 76*

Muratore, Lucien
French. Opera Singer
b. Aug 29, 1876 in Marseilles, France
d. Jul 16, 1954 in Paris, France
Source: *WhAm 3; WhScrn 77*

Muratori, Ludovico
Italian. Historian
b. Oct 21, 1672 in Vignola, Italy
d. Jan 23, 1750
Source: *McGEWB; NewCol 75; WebBD 80*

Murcer, Bobby Ray
"Okie"
American. Baseball Player
b. May 20, 1946 in Oklahoma City, Oklahoma
Source: *BaseEn; NewYTBE 73; NewYTBS 74; WhoAm 74; WhoProB 73*

Murchison, Clint(on Williams, Jr.)
American. Football Team Owner
b. 1924
Source: *WhoS&SW 73*

Murchison, Clint(on Williams)
American. Financier
b. 1895 in Athens, Texas
d. Jun 20, 1969 in Athens, Texas
Source: *WhAm 5*

Murchison, Kenneth MacKenzie
American. Architect
b. Sep 29, 1872 in New York, New York
d. Dec 16, 1938
Source: *BioIn 5; NatCAB 42; WhAm 1*

Murdoch, (Jean) Iris
Irish. Author
b. Jul 15, 1919 in Dublin, Ireland
Source: *Au&Wr 71; CasWL; ConAu 13R; ConDr 73; ConLC 1, 2, 3, 4, 6, 8, 11, 15; ConNov 72, 76; CurBio 58, 80; InWom; IntWW 74; LongCTC; ModBrL, SUP; NewC; Pen ENG; PlP&P; RAdv 1; REn; TwCW; WebE&AL; WhoAm 82; WhoTwCL; WhoWor 74; WorAu; WrDr 76*

Murdoch, (Keith) Rupert
Australian. Publisher
b. Mar 11, 1931 in Melbourne, Australia
Source: *IntWW 74; Who 74; WhoAm 82; WhoWor 74*

Murillo, Bartolome Esteban
Spanish. Artist
b. Jan 1, 1618 in Seville, Spain
d. Apr 3, 1682
Source: *AtlBL; ChPo; REn*

Murkowski, Frank Hughes
American. Senator
b. Mar 28, 1933 in Nome, Alaska
Source: *St&PR 75; WhoAm 78, 80, 82; WhoF&I 74, 75, 77*

Murnau, Friedrich W
[Friedrich Wilhelm Plumpe]
German. Motion Picture Director
b. Dec 28, 1899 in Bielefeld, Germany
d. Mar 11, 1931 in California
Source: *BiDFilm; DcFM; FilmEn; MovMk; OxFilm*

Murphy, Audie
American. Actor, Soldier
b. Jun 20, 1924 in Kingston, Texas
d. Jun 1, 1971 in Roanoke, Virginia
Source: *BiDFilm; CmMov; FilmgC; MotPP; MovMk; NewYTBE 71; WebAB; WhScrn 74, 77; WhoHol B; WorEFlm*

Murphy, Calvin
American. Basketball Player
b. May 9, 1948 in Norwalk, Connecticut
Source: *WhoAm 82; WhoBbl 73; WhoBlA 75*

Murphy, Charles
"Stretch"
American. Basketball Player
Hall of Fame, 1960.
b. Apr 10, 1907 in Marion, Indiana
Source: *BioIn 9*

Murphy, Eddie
American. Comedian
Regular on "Saturday Night Live," 1981--.
b. Apr 3, 1961 in Roosevelt, New York
Source: *BioIn 12; NewYTBS 81*

Murphy, Frank
American. Supreme Court Justice
b. Apr 23, 1890 in Harbor Beach, Michigan
d. Jul 17, 1949 in Detroit, Michigan
Source: *BiDrUSE; CurBio 40, 49; DcAmB S4; EncAB-H; NewCol 75; WebAB; WebBD 80; WhAm 2*

Murphy, George Lloyd
American. Actor, Politician
b. Jul 4, 1902 in New Haven, Connecticut
Source: *BiDrAC; CelR 73; ConAu 45; CurBio 65; FilmgC; IntMPA 75, 76, 77, 78, 79, 80, 81, 82; IntWW 74; MotPP; MovMk; WhoAm 74; WhoAmP 73; WorEFlm*

Murphy, Jack R
"Murph the Surf"
American. Jewel Thief
b. May 26, 1937 in Los Angeles, California
Source: *BioNews 74*

Murphy, Jimmy (James Edward)
American. Cartoonist
b. Nov 20, 1891 in Chicago, Illinois
d. Mar 9, 1965 in Beverly Hills, California
Source: *WhAm 4; WhoHol A*

Murphy, John Joseph
"Fireman"; "Grandma"; "Fordham Johnny"
American. Baseball Player
b. Jul 14, 1908 in New York, New York
d. Jan 14, 1970 in New York, New York
Source: *BaseEn; WhoProB 73*

Murphy, John Michael
American. Congressman
b. Aug 3, 1926 in Staten Island, New York
Source: *BioIn 9; WhoAm 78*

Murphy, (John) Reg(inald)
American. Journalist
b. Jan 7, 1934 in Hoschton, Georgia
Source: *ConAu 33R; WhoAm 74; WhoS&SW 73*

Murphy, Patricia
Canadian. Restaurateur
b. 1911 in Newfoundland, Canada
Source: *InWom*

Murphy, Patrick Vincent
American. Business Executive
b. May 12, 1920 in Brooklyn, New York
Source: *CurBio 72; NewYTBE 70, 71; WhoAm 74; WhoE 74*

Murphy, Robert Daniel
American. Statesman
b. Oct 28, 1894 in Milwaukee, Wisconsin
d. Jun 9, 1978 in New York, New York
Source: *ConAu P-1; CurBio 43, 58; IntWW 74; St&PR 75; Who 74; WhoAm 74; WhoWor 74*

Murphy, Rosemary
American. Actress
b. 1927 in Munich, Germany
Source: *BiE&WWA; FilmgC; ForWC 70; NotNAT; WhoAm 74, 76, 78, 80, 82; WhoAmW 77; WhoHol A; WhoThe 77*

Murphy, Thomas Aquinas
American. Auto Executive
GM, vice-chairman, 1972-74, chief executive, 1974--.
b. Dec 10, 1915 in Hornell, New York
Source: *BusPN; IntWW 74; St&PR 75; Ward 77; WhoAm 82; WhoF&I 74*

Murphy, "Turk" (Melvin)
American. Jazz Musician
b. Dec 16, 1915 in Palermo, California
Source: *WhoAm 74*

Murphy, Warren
American. Author
b. Sep 13, 1933 in Jersey City, New Jersey
Source: *ConAu 33R*

"Murray the K"
see: Kauffman, Murray

Murray, Anne
[Mrs. David Langstruth; Morna Anne Murray]
Canadian. Singer
Former physical education teacher; first gold record "Snowbird," 1970.
b. Jun 20, 1945 in Springhill, NS
Source: *BkPepl; CanWW 82; CurBio 82; WhoAm 82*

Murray, Arthur
[Arthur Murray Teichman]
American. Dancer
Began Arthur Murray School of Dancing; over 450 schools throughout US.
b. Apr 4, 1895 in New York, New York
Source: *CurBio 43; WhoAm 74, 76, 78, 80, 82*

Murray, Bill
American. Actor, Comedian, Writer
Appeared in movies *Meatballs,* 1979; *Caddychack,* 1980.
b. Sep 21, 1950 in Evanston, Illinois
Source: *BioIn 11; IntMPA 82; WhoAm 80, 82*

Murray, Dave
see: Iron Maiden

Murray, Don(ald Patrick)
American. Actor
b. Jul 31, 1929 in Hollywood, California
Source: *BiDFilm; BiE&WWA; FilmgC; IntMPA 75, 76, 77, 78, 79, 80, 81, 82; MovMk; WhoAm 82; WorEFlm*

Murray, George
American. Wheelchair Athlete
b. 1948? in Maine
Source: *BioIn 12*

Murray, Jan
[Murray Janofsky]
American. Comedian
b. Oct 4, 1917 in New York, New York
Source: *IntMPA 75, 76, 77, 78, 79, 80, 81, 82; WhoAm 82; WhoHol A*

Murray, Jim
American. Sportswriter
b. 1919
Source: *BioIn 10*

Murray, John
English. Religious Leader
b. Dec 10, 1741 in Alton, England
d. Sep 3, 1815 in Boston, Massachusetts
Source: *Alli; AmAu&B; AmBi; ApCAB; DcAmB; DcNAA; Drake; OxAmL; TwCBDA; WhAm H*

Murray, Katherine
American. Actress, Singer
b. 1894
d. 1974
Source: *BioIn 10*

Murray, Kathryn Hazel
[Mrs. Arthur Murray]
American. Dancer
b. Sep 15, 1906 in Jersey City, New Jersey
Source: *InWom; WhoAm 74, 76, 78, 80, 82*

Murray, Ken
[Don Court]
American. Actor
b. 1903 in New York, New York
Source: *FilmgC; IntMPA 75, 76, 77; WhoHol A*

Murray, Mae
[Marie Koenig]
American. Dancer, Actress
b. Apr 10, 1889 in Portsmouth, Virginia
d. Mar 23, 1965 in Woodland Hills, California
Source: *Film 1; FilmgC; InWom; MotPP; MovMk; OxFilm; ThFT; TwYS; WhScrn 74, 77; WhoHol B*

Murray, Philip
American. Labor Leader
President, United Steelworkers of America, 1942-52.
b. May 25, 1886 in Lanarkshire, Scotland
d. Oct 9, 1952 in San Francisco, California
Source: *CurBio 41, 49, 52; DcAmB S5; EncAB-H; WebAB; WhAm 3*

Murrow, Edward R(oscoe)
American. Broadcast Journalist
TV moderator, "See It Now," 1951-58; director, US Information Agency, 1961-64.
b. Apr 25, 1908 in Greensboro, North Carolina
d. Apr 27, 1965 in Pawling, New York
Source: *ConAu 89, 103; CurBio 42, 53, 65; EncAB-H; REnAL; WebAB; WhAm 4; WhScrn 74, 77; WhoHol A*

Murry, John Middleton
English. Author
b. Aug 6, 1889 in London, England
d. May 13, 1957 in Norfolk, England
Source: *CasWL; ChPo, S1; DcLEL; EvLB; LongCTC; ModBrL; NewC; OxEng; Pen ENG; REn; TwCA SUP; TwCW; WebE&AL; WhAm 3; WhoLA; WhoTwCL*

Murtha, John Patrick
American. Congressman
b. Jun 17, 1932 in Martinsville, West Virginia
Source: *BioIn 10; WhoAm 78, 80, 82*

Musante, Tony
American. Actor
b. Jun 30, 1936 in Bridgeport, Connecticut
Source: *FilmgC; IntMPA 75, 76, 77, 78, 79, 80, 81, 82; WhoHol A*

Musburger, Brent Woody
American. Sportscaster
With CBS Sports, 1974--; hosts "NFL Today."
b. May 26, 1939 in Portland, Oregon
Source: *WhoAm 78, 80, 82*

Musgrave, Thea
Scottish. Composer, Conductor
b. May 27, 1928 in Edinburgh, Scotland
Source: *Baker 78; BioIn 10, 11; CurBio 78; DcCM; IntWW 74, 75, 76, 77, 78; OxMus; Who 74; WhoAm 82; WhoMus 72; WhoWor 74, 76, 78*

Musial, Joe
American. Cartoonist
b. 1905?
d. Jun 6, 1977 in Manhasset, New York
Source: *BioIn 11; ConAu 69*

Musial, Stan(ley Frank)
"Stan the Man"
American. Baseball Player
Collected 3,630 lifetime hits; Hall of Fame, 1969.
b. Nov 21, 1920 in Donora, Pennsylvania
Source: *BaseEn; CurBio 48; WebAB; WhoAm 74, 76, 78, 80, 82; WhoProB 73*

Music, Antonio Zoran
Italian. Artist
b. 1909 in Gorizia, Italy
Source: *McGDA*

Muskie, Edmund Sixtus
American. Government Official
Secretary of State, 1980-81; senator from ME, 1959-80.
b. Mar 28, 1914 in Rumford, Maine
Source: *BiDrAC; CelR 73; CngDr 74; ConAu 49, 2NR; CurBio 55, 68; IntWW 74; NewYTBE 70, 72; Who 74; WhoAm 74, 76, 78, 80, 82; WhoAmP 73; WhoE 74; WhoGov 72; WhoWor 74*

Musset, Alfred de
French. Author
b. Dec 11, 1810 in Paris, France
d. May 2, 1857 in Paris, France
Source: *AtlBL; CnThe; CyWA; DcEuL; EuAu; McGEWD; NewC; OxEng; OxFr; OxThe; Pen EUR; RComWL; REn; REnWD*

Musso, Vido
American. Jazz Musician
b. Jan 17, 1913 in Carrini, Sicily
d. Jan 9, 1982 in Los Angeles, California
Source: *WhoJazz 72*

Mussolini, Benito
"Il Duce"
Italian. Dictator
Founded Italian Fascist Party, 1919; prime minister, 1922-43; allied with Hitler, 1939.
b. Jul 29, 1883 in Dovia, Italy
d. Apr 28, 1945 in Milan, Italy
Source: *CasWL; CurBio 42, 45; EvEuW; REn; WhAm 4; WhoLA*

Mussolini, Rachele Guidi
Italian. Widow of Benito Mussolini
b. 1890
d. Oct 30, 1979 in Carpena di Forli, Italy
Source: *BioIn 7, 10; NewYTBS 79*

Mussolini, Rosa Maltoni
Italian. Mother of Benito Mussolini
b. 1858
d. 1905
Source: *BioIn 10*

Mussorgsky, Modest Petrovich
Russian. Composer
b. Mar 21, 1839 in Karevo, Russia
d. Mar 28, 1881 in Saint Petersburg, Russia
Source: *AtlBL; REn*

Mutesa
Ugandan. King
d. 1884
Source: *NewCol 75*

Muti, Riccardo
Italian. Conductor
b. Jul 28, 1941 in Naples, Italy
Source: *BioIn 9, 11, 12; CurBio 80; Who 74, 79; WhoAm 82*

Muto, Anthony
American. Motion Picture Producer
b. Aug 20, 1903 in New York, New York
d. May 26, 1964
Source: *WhAm 4*

Mutsuhito
Japanese. Emperor
b. 1852 in Kyoto, Japan
d. Jul 1912
Source: *DcBiPP; WhoModH*

Muybridge, Eadweard
[Edward James Muggeridge]
English. Motion Picture Pioneer
b. Apr 9, 1830 in Kingston, England
d. May 8, 1904 in Kingston, England
Source: *AmBi; DcAmB; DcFM; DcNAA; OxAmL; OxFilm; REnAL; WebAB; WhAm H; WorEFlm*

Muzio, Claudia
Italian. Opera Singer
b. Feb 7, 1889 in Pavia, Italy
d. May 24, 1936 in Rome, Italy
Source: *InWom; WhAm 1*

Muzorewa, Abel Tendekai
African. Prime Minister of Zimbabwe
b. Apr 14, 1925 in Umtali, Rhodesia
Source: *AfSS 78, 79; BioIn 9, 11; IntWW 74, 75, 76, 77, 78; NewYTBS 78, 79; WhoWor 74*

Mydans, Carl M
American. Photographer
b. May 20, 1907 in Boston, Massachusetts
Source: *ConAu 97; CurBio 45; WhoAm 74; WhoE 74*

Myer, "Buddy" (Charles Solomon)
American. Baseball Player
b. Mar 16, 1904 in Ellisville, Mississippi
d. Oct 31, 1974 in Baton Rouge, Louisiana
Source: *BaseEn; WhoProB 73*

Myers, Alan
see: Devo

Myers, Garry Cleveland
American. Psychologist
b. Jul 15, 1884 in Sylvan, Pennsylvania
d. Jul 19, 1971
Source: *ConAu 29R; ConAu P-2; OhA&B; WhAm 5; WhNAA*

Myers, James E
see: DeKnight, Jimmy

Myers, Jerome
American. Artist
b. Mar 20, 1867 in Petersburg, Virginia
d. Jun 19, 1940
Source: *AmAu&B; CurBio 40; DcAmB S2; DcNAA; WhAm 1*

Myers, Michael O
American. Congressman
b. May 4, 1943 in Philadelphia, Pennsylvania
Source: *WhoAm 78*

Myers, Russell
American. Cartoonist
b. Oct 9, 1938 in Pittsburg, Kansas
Source: *Ward 77*

Myerson, Bess
American. Entertainer, Government Official
Miss America, 1945; columnist, NY *Daily News,* 1974; co-author *I Love New York Diet,* 1982.
b. 1924 in New York, New York
Source: *BioNews 74; InWom; IntMPA 75, 76, 77, 78, 79, 80, 81, 82; NewYTBE 72; WhoAm 82*

Myrdal, Jan
Swedish. Author
b. Jul 19, 1927 in Stockholm, Sweden
Source: *BioIn 8; IntAu&W 77*

Myrdal, Karl Gunnar
Swedish. Sociologist
b. Dec 6, 1898 in Gustafs, Sweden
Source: *ConAu 9R, 4NR; IntWW 74*

Myricks, Larry
American. Track Athlete
b. Mar 10, 1956
Source: *BioIn 12*

Myron
Greek. Sculptor
b. 400BC
Source: *NewCol 75*

N

Naber, John
American. Swimmer
Won four gold medals, one silver medal, 1976 Olympics.
b. Jan 20, 1956 in Evanston, Illinois
Source: *BioIn 10*

Nabokov, Nicolas
Russian. Composer
b. Apr 4, 1903 in Minsk, Russia
d. Apr 6, 1978 in New York, New York
Source: *ConAu 65, 77; DcCM; WhoAm 74*

Nabokov, Vladimir
[Vladimir Sirin]
American. Author
Wrote *Lolita*, 1955.
b. Apr 23, 1899 in Saint Petersburg, Russia
d. Jul 2, 1977 in Montreux, Switzerland
Source: *AmAu&B; AmNov; AmWr; Au&Wr 71; CasWL; CelR 73; ClDMEL; CnMWL; ConAu 5R, 69; ConLC 1, 2, 3, 6, 8, 11, 15; ConNov 72, 76; ConP 75; DcLEL; DcRusL; DrAF 76; EncWL; EvEuW; IntWW 74; LongCTC; ModAL, SUP; ModSL 1; OxAmL; OxEng; Pen AM; REn; REnAL; TwCA SUP; TwCW; WebE&AL; Who 74; WhoAm 74; WhoTwCL; WhoWor 74; WrDr 76*

Nabors, Jim
American. Singer, Actor
Played Gomer Pyle in "The Andy Griffith Show"; "Gomer Pyle, USMC."
b. Jun 12, 1932 in Sylacauga, Alabama
Source: *BkPepl; CelR 73; CurBio 69; WhoAm 74, 76, 78, 80, 82*

Nachbaur, Franz
German. Opera Singer
b. Mar 25, 1835 in Weiler Giessen, Germany
d. Mar 21, 1902 in Munich, Germany
Source: *NewEOp 71*

Nachman, Gerald Weil
American. Journalist, TV Critic
b. Jan 13, 1938 in Oakland, California
Source: *WhoAm 74, 76, 78, 80, 82*

Nadar, pseud.
[Gaspard-Felix Tournachon]
French. Balloonist, Photographer, Author
b. 1820
d. 1910
Source: *BioIn 4, 5, 7, 10, 11; NewCol 75; OxFr; Pseud*

Nader, George
American. Actor
b. 1921 in Pasadena, California
Source: *FilmgC; IntMPA 75, 76, 77, 78, 79, 80, 81, 82; MotPP; WhoHol A*

Nader, Ralph
American. Lawyer, Author
Investigative reports began with *Unsafe at Any Speed*, 1965.
b. Feb 27, 1934 in Winsted, Connecticut
Source: *AmAu&B; BkPepl; CelR 73; ConAu 77; CurBio 68; IntWW 74; WebAB; Who 74; WhoAm 74, 76, 78, 80, 82; WhoWor 74*

Nadir, Shah
Persian. King
b. 1688 in Khurasan, Persia
d. 1747
Source: *WebBD 80*

Nagako, Empress
Japanese. Consort of Hirohito
b. 1903
Source: *BioIn 9, 10*

Nagel, Conrad
American. Actor
b. Mar 16, 1897 in Keokuk, Iowa
d. Feb 21, 1970 in New York, New York
Source: *BiE&WWA; Film 1; FilmgC; MotPP; MovMk; NewYTBE 70; TwYS; WhAm 5; WhScrn 74, 77; WhoHol B*

Naguib, Mohammed
Egyptian. Premier
b. Feb 20, 1901 in Khartoum, Sudan
Source: *CurBio 52*

Nagurski, "Bronko" (Bronislaw)
American. Football Player
b. Nov 3, 1908 in Rainy River, ON
Source: *NewYTBE 72*

Nagy, Imre
Hungarian. Statesman
b. 1896 in Kaposvar, Hungary
d. Jun 17, 1958
Source: *WhAm 3; WhoModH*

Naipaul, V(idiahar) S(urajprasad)
Author
Wrote *Among the Believers,* 1981.
b. Aug 17, 1932 in Trinidad
Source: *CasWL; ConAu 1R, 1NR; ConLC 4, 7, 9, 13, 18; ConNov 72, 76; EncWL; LongCEL; NewC; Pen ENG; REn; TwCW; WebE&AL; WhoAm 82; WorAu*

Naish, J Carroll
American. Actor
b. Jan 21, 1900 in New York, New York
d. Jan 24, 1973 in La Jolla, California
Source: *BiE&WWA; CurBio 57, 73; FilmgC; MotPP; MovMk; NewYTBE 73; Vers A; WhScrn 77; WhoHol B*

Naismith, James A
American. Physician, Teacher
Invented basketball, 1891, in Springfield, MA.
b. Nov 6, 1861 in Almonte, ON
d. Nov 28, 1939 in Lawrence, Kansas
Source: *DcAmB S2; WebAB; WhAm 1; WhoBbl 73*

Nakasone, Yasuhiro
Japanese. Prime Minister
Succeeded Zenko Suzuki, Nov, 1982.
b. May 27, 1918 in Takasaki, Japan
Source: *FarE&A 78, 79, 80, 81; IntWW 74, 75, 76, 77, 78, 79, 80, 81; NewYTBE 70; NewYTBS 82; WhoWor 74*

Naldi, Nita
[Anita Anne Dooley]
American. Actress
b. Apr 1, 1899 in New York, New York
d. Feb 17, 1961 in New York, New York
Source: *Film 1; FilmgC; MotPP; TwYS; WhScrn 74, 77; WhoHol B*

Namath, Joe (Joseph William)
"Broadway Joe"
American. Football Player, Actor
Passed for record 4,007 yards, 1967; led NY Jets to Super Bowl victory, 1969.
b. May 31, 1943 in Beaver Falls, Pennsylvania
Source: *BkPepl; CelR 73; ConAu 89; CurBio 66; FilmgC; NewYTBE 70, 71, 72, 73; NewYTBS 74; WebAB; WhoAm 74, 76, 78, 80, 82; WhoFtbl 74; WhoHol A*

Nanne, Lou(is Vincent)
American. Hockey Player, Executive
General manager, Minnesota North Stars, 1978--.
b. Jun 2, 1941 in Sault St. Marie, ON
Source: *WhoAm 82; WhoHcky 73*

Nansen, Fridtjof
Norwegian. Explorer, Statesman
Wrote *In Northern Mists,* 1911; won Nobel Peace Prize, 1922.
b. Oct 10, 1861 in Christiania, Norway
d. May 30, 1930 in Lysaker, Norway
Source: *BiD&SB; LongCTC; NewC; OxCan; OxEng; REn*

Nanak
Indian. Religious Figure
b. 1469
d. 1538
Source: *BioIn 4, 5, 8, 9, 11; McGEWB*

Napier, Charles
British. Army Officer
b. 1782
d. 1853
Source: *Alli; BiD&SB; WhoMilH 76*

Napier, Robert Cornelis
British. Army Officer
b. 1810 in Ceylon
d. 1890
Source: *WebBD 80; WhoMilH 76*

Napoleon I
[Napoleon Bonaparte]
French. Emperor
Formed Napoleonic Code, 1804-10; overthrown at Waterloo, 1815.
b. Aug 15, 1769 in Ajaccio, France
d. May 5, 1821 in Saint Helena
Source: *BioIn 10; FilmgC; NewC; REn; WebBD 80; WhDW; WhAm H*

Napoleon III
[Charles Louis Napoleon Bonaparte]
"Napoleon le Petit"
French. Emperor
b. 1808 in Paris, France
d. Jan 9, 1873 in Chislehurst, England
Source: *NewC*

Napravnik, Eduard
Russian. Conductor, Composer
b. Aug 24, 1839 in Beischt, Bohemia
d. Nov 23, 1916 in Saint Petersburg, Russia
Source: *NewEOp 71; OxMus*

Nardini, Tom
American. Actor
b. 1945 in Los Angeles, California
Source: *FilmgC; WhoHol A*

Nash, Florence
American. Actress
b. 1888 in Troy, New York
d. Apr 2, 1950 in Los Angeles, California
Source: *ChPo S1; WhScrn 74, 77; WhoHol B*

Nash, George Frederick
American. Actor
b. 1873
d. Dec 31, 1944 in Amityville, New York
Source: *WhScrn 74, 77; WhoHol B*

Nash, Graham
[The Hollies; Crosby, Stills, Nash, and Young]
English. Musician, Singer
Hits "Suite: Judy Blue Eyes," "Marrakesh Express," "Wasted on the Way."
b. Feb 2, 1942 in Blackpool, England
Source: *BkPepl; ConMuA 80; IlEncRk; LilREn 78; RkOn 2; WhoAm 78; WhoRock 81*

Nash, John
English. Architect
b. 1752 in London, England
d. May 13, 1835 in Cowes, England
Source: *AtlBL; NewC*

Nash, N Richard
[Nathan Richard Nusbaum]
American. Author
b. Jun 7, 1913 in Philadelphia, Pennsylvania
Source: *CnMD; ConAu 85; IntMPA 75, 76, 77, 78, 79, 80, 81, 82; McGEWD; ModWD; NotNAT; WhoThe 77*

Nash, Ogden Frederick
American. Author
Wrote poem, *Candy is dandy, but liquor is quicker.*
b. Aug 19, 1902 in Rye, New York
d. May 19, 1971 in Baltimore, Maryland
Source: *AmAu&B; AmSCAP 66; AnCL; Au&Wr 71; AuBYP; BiE&WWA; BkCL; CasWL; ChPo, S1, S2; CnDAL; CnE&AP; CnMWL; ConAmA; ConAu 29R; ConAu P-1; ConP 70; CurBio 41, 71; DcLEL; EncMT; EncWL; LongCTC; ModAL; OxAmL; Pen AM; RAdv 1; REn; REnAL; SmATA 2; TwCA, SUP; TwCW; WebAB; WebE&AL; WhAm 5; WhoTwCL*

Nash, Paul
British. Artist, Designer
b. May 11, 1889
d. Jul 11, 1946 in London, England
Source: *CurBio 46*

Nash, Thomas
[Pasquil, pseud.]
English. Author, Dramatist
b. 1567 in Lowestoft, England
d. 1601 in Yarmouth, England
Source: *Alli; AtlBL; BbD; BiD&SB; BrAu; Chambr 1; CyWA; DcEnA; DcEnL; DcEuL; EvLB; NewC; OxEng; REn*

Nasser, Gamal Abdel
Egyptian. Premier
First president of Egypt, 1956-70.
b. Jan 15, 1918 in Beni Mor, Egypt
d. Sep 28, 1970 in Cairo, Egypt
Source: *CurBio 54, 70; NewYTBE 70; WhAm 5*

Nast, Conde
American. Publisher
President, publisher, *Vogue, House and Garden, Glamour,* etc.
b. Mar 26, 1874 in New York, New York
d. Jan 11, 1942 in New York, New York
Source: *AmAu&B; CurBio 42; WhAm 2; WorFshn*

Nast, Thomas
American. Cartoonist
b. Sep 27, 1840 in Landau, Germany
d. Dec 7, 1902 in Guayaquil, Ecuador
Source: *AmBi; ApCAB; ChPo; DcAmB; Drake; EarABI, SUP; EncAB-H; OxAmL; REn; REnAL; TwCBDA; WebAB; WhAm HA, 1, 4A; WhAmP*

Nastase, Ilie
Romanian. Tennis Player
b. Jul 19, 1946 in Bucharest, Romania
Source: *BkPepl; CelR 73; CurBio 74; NewYTBE 72; WhoAm 82*

Nathan, George Jean
American. Editor, Author, Critic
b. Feb 14, 1882 in Fort Wayne, Indiana
d. Apr 8, 1958 in New York, New York
Source: *AmAu&B; CnDAL; ConAmA; ConAmL; CurBio 45, 58; DcLEL; IndAu 1816; LongCTC; ModAL; OxAmL; OxEng; OxThe; Pen AM; REn; REnAL; TwCA, SUP; WebAB; WhAm 3*

Nathan, Robert
American. Author, Composer
b. Jan 2, 1894 in New York, New York
Source: *AmAu&B; AmNov; AmSCAP 66; Au&Wr 71; ChPo, S1; CnDAL; ConAmA; ConAmL; ConAu 13R; ConNov 72, 76; IntWW 74; LongCTC; OxAmL; REn; REnAL; SmATA 6; TwCA, SUP; WhoAm 74; WhoWest 74; WhoWorJ 72; WrDr 76*

Nation, Carry A(melia Moore)
American. Social Reformer
Proponent of temperance; known for using hatchet to smash saloons.
b. Nov 25, 1846 in Garrard County, Kentucky
d. Jun 9, 1911 in Leavenworth, Kansas
Source: *AmAu&B; AmBi; DcAmB; DcNAA; InWom; LongCTC; NotAW; OxAmL; WebAB; WhAm HA, 4*

Natwick, Mildred
American. Actress
b. Jun 19, 1908 in Baltimore, Maryland
Source: *BiE&WWA; FilmgC; InWom; IntMPA 75, 76, 77, 78, 79, 80, 81, 82; MotPP; MovMk; NotNAT; Vers A; WhoHol A; WhoThe 77*

Naudin, Emilio
Italian. Opera Singer
b. Oct 23, 1823 in Parma, Italy
d. May 5, 1890 in Bologna, Italy
Source: *NewEOp 71*

Naughton, David
American. Actor, Singer
b. 1951? in West Hartford, Connecticut
Source: *BioIn 12*

Navarra, Andre
French. Musician
b. 1911 in Biarritz, France
Source: *WhoMus 72*

Navarro, "Fats" (Theodore)
American. Jazz Musician
b. 1923
d. 1950
Source: *CmpEPM*

Navon, Yitzhak
Israeli. President
b. Apr 19, 1921 in Jerusalem, Palestine
Source: *BioIn 11; CurBio 82*

Navratilova, Martina
American. Tennis Player
Won 15 tournaments and $1.475 million, 1982.
b. Oct 10, 1956 in Prague, Czechoslovakia
Source: *BioIn 10; WhoAm 82*

Naylor, Bob
American. Cartoonist
b. Feb 15, 1910 in New York, New York
Source: *WorECom*

Nazareth
[Peter Agnew; Manny Charlton; Dan McCafferty; Darrell Sweet]
Scottish. Rock Group
Source: *ConMuA 80; IlEncRk; LilREn 78; RkOn 2; WhoRock 81*

Nazimova, Alla
Russian. Actress
b. Jun 4, 1879 in Yalta, Russia
d. Jul 13, 1945 in Hollywood, California
Source: *CurBio 45; DcAmB S3; FamA&A; Film 1; FilmgC; InWom; MotPP; MovMk; NotAW; OxFilm; OxThe; PlP&P; TwYS; WhAm 2; WhScrn 74, 77; WhoHol B; WhoStg 1908; WorEFlm*

Ne Win, U
[Shu Maung]
Burmese. President
b. 1911
Source: *NewCol 75*

Neagle, Dame Anna
[Marjorie Robertson]
English. Actress, Motion Picture Producer
b. Oct 20, 1904 in London, England
Source: *BiDFilm; BiE&WWA; CurBio 45; EncMT; FilmgC; InWom; IntMPA 75, 76, 77, 78, 79, 80, 81, 82; MotPP; MovMk; NotNAT; OxFilm; ThFT; Who 74; WhoHol A; WhoThe 77; WorEFlm*

Neal, James F
American. Lawyer
b. 1929
Source: *BioIn 11; WhoAm 82*

Neal, Larry (Lawrence P)
American. Poet, Dramatist
b. Sep 5, 1937 in Atlanta, Georgia
d. Jan 6, 1981 in Hamilton, New York
Source: *BlkAW; ConAu 81, 102; ConP 75; DrAP 75; LivgBAA; SelBAA; WhoBlA 77; WrDr 76, 80*

Neal, Patricia
American. Actress
Won 1963 Oscar for *Hud;* suffered stroke, 1965; returned, 1968, in *The Subject was Roses.*
b. Jan 20, 1926 in Packard, Kentucky
Source: *BiDFilm; BiE&WWA; BioNews 74; CelR 73; CurBio 64; FilmgC; InWom; IntMPA 75, 76, 77, 78, 79, 80, 81, 82; IntWW 74; MotPP; MovMk; NotNAT; OxFilm; WhoAm 74, 78, 78, 80, 82; WhoHol A; WhoThe 77; WhoWor 74; WorEFlm*

Nearing, Scott
American. Sociologist
b. Aug 6, 1883 in Morris Run, Pennsylvania
Source: *AmAu&B; AmLY; AmM&WS 73S; ChPo; ConAu 41R; CurBio 71; NewYTBE 71, 73; REnAL; WhoAm 74, 76, 78, 80, 82*

Nebel, "Long" John
American. Interviewer
b. Jun 11, 1911 in Chicago, Illinois
d. Apr 10, 1978 in New York, New York
Source: *CelR 73; WhAm 7*

Nebuchadnezzar I
Babylonian. King
b. 1146BC
d. 1123BC
Source: *NewC*

Necker, Jacques
French. Financier, Statesman
b. 1732 in Geneva, Switzerland
d. Apr 4, 1804 in Switzerland
Source: *DcEuL; McGEWB; OxFr; REn*

Nederlander, James Morton
American. Producer, Theater Owner
Owns theatres nationwide; has produced *Annie, Hello Dolly, Woman of the Year.*
b. Mar 21, 1922 in Detroit, Michigan
Source: *BiE&WWA; CelR 73; NewYTBS 81; NotNAT; WhoAm 76, 78, 80, 82; WhoThe 77, 81*

Needham, Paul M, Jr.
[The Hostages]
American. Former Hostage in Iran
b. 1951?
Source: *NewYTBS 81*

Neel, Alice Hartley
American. Artist
b. Jan 28, 1900 in Merion Square, Pennsylvania
Source: *BioIn 6, 7, 8, 10; CurBio 76; DcAmArt; WhoAm 74, 76, 78; WhoAmA 73, 76, 78; WhoAmW 75; WomArt*

Neel, (Louis) Boyd
English. Conductor
b. Jul 19, 1905 in London, England
d. Sep 30, 1981 in Toronto, ON
Source: *AnObit 1981; Baker 78; BioIn 1, 2, 3; CanWW 70, 79; CreCan 1; IntWW 74, 75, 76, 77, 78; NewYTBE 70; Who 74; WhoAm 76, 78, 80; WhoWor 74*

Nefertiti
Egyptian. Queen
b. 1390BC
d. 1360BC
Source: *InWom*

Neff, Hildegarde
[Hildegarde Knef]
German. Actress, Author
b. Dec 28, 1925 in Ulm, Germany
Source: *ConAu 45, 4NR; IntMPA 75, 76, 77, 78, 79, 80, 81, 82; MotPP; MovMk; OxFilm; WhoHol A*

Neff, Wallace
American. Architect
b. 1895 in La Mirada, California
Source: *AmArch 70; WhoAm 74, 76, 78; WhoWest 74*

Negri, Pola
[Appolonia Chalupez]
American. Actress
b. 1894 in Janowa, Poland
Source: *BiDFilm; Film 1; FilmgC; InWom; MotPP; MovMk; NewYTBE 70; OxFilm; ThFT; TwYS; WhoHol A; WorEFlm*

Negrin, Juan
Spanish. Physician, Politician
b. 1892? in Spain
d. Nov 14, 1956 in Paris, France
Source: *CurBio 45, 57*

Negulesco, Jean
American. Motion Picture Director
b. Feb 29, 1900 in Craiova, Romania
Source: *BiDFilm; CmMov; FilmgC; IntMPA 75, 76, 77, 78, 79, 80, 81, 81; MovMk; OxFilm; WomWMM; WorEFlm*

Nehemiah
Biblical Character
b. 400BC
Source: *DcOrL 3*

Nehemiah, Renaldo
"Skeets"
American. Football Player, Track Athlete
b. Mar 24, 1959 in Newark, New Jersey
Source: *BioIn 11*

Neher, Fred
American. Cartoonist
b. Sep 29, 1903 in Nappanee, Indiana
Source: *WhoAmA 73*

Nehru, Jawaharlal
Indian. Statesman
b. Nov 14, 1889 in Allahabad, India
d. May 27, 1964 in Allahabad, India
Source: *CasWL; ConAu 85; CurBio 41, 48, 64; DcLEL; LongCTC; OxEng; REn*

Neihardt, John Gneisenau
American. Author
b. Jan 8, 1881 in Sharpsburg, Illinois
d. Nov 3, 1973 in Columbia, Missouri
Source: *AmAu&B; AmLY; AnMV 1926; ChPo, S2; CnDAL; ConAmA; ConAmL; ConAu P-1; IntWW 74; OxAmL; REn; REnAL; TwCA, SUP; WebAB; WhAm 6; WhoMW 74*

Neill, A(lexander) S(utherland)
Scottish. Educator, Author
b. Oct 17, 1883 in Forfar, Scotland
d. Sep 24, 1973 in Suffolk, England
Source: *ConAu 45, 101; CurBio 61, 73; EvLB; LongCTC; NewYTBE 73; WhAm 6; WhoWor 74*

Neilson, William A
American. Educator
b. Mar 29, 1869 in Doune, Scotland
d. Feb 13, 1946 in Falls Village, Connecticut
Source: *AmAu&B; AmLY; CurBio 46; DcAmB S4; DcNAA; REnAL; TwCA, SUP; WhAm 2*

Neilson-Terry, Julia
English. Actress
b. Jun 12, 1858 in London, England
d. Nov 27, 1957 in London, England
Source: *NotNAT B*

Neiman, Abraham
American. Businessman, Philanthropist
b. 1875
d. 1970
Source: *NewYTBE 70*

Neiman, LeRoy
American. Artist
Known for paintings of athletes; collected in *Leroy Neiman Posters*, 1980.
b. Jun 8, 1926 in Saint Paul, Minnesota
Source: *WhoAm 82; WhoE 74*

Nekrasov, Nikolay Alexeyevich
Russian. Author
b. Dec 10, 1821 in Greshnevo, Russia
d. Jul 27, 1877? in Saint Petersburg, Russia
Source: *CasWL; EuAu; EvEuW; Pen EUR; REn*

Nelligan, Kate (Patricia Colleen)
Canadian. Actress
Starred in "Therese Raquin"; film roles *Dracula, Eye of the Needle.*
b. Mar 16, 1951 in London, ON
Source: *BioIn 10; NewYTBS 82; WhoThe 77, 81*

Nelson, "Baby Face" (George)
[Lester N Gillis]
American. Criminal
Member of John Dillinger's outlaw gang, 1930's.
b. Dec 6, 1908 in Chicago, Illinois
d. Nov 27, 1934 in Fox River Grove, Illinois
Source: *Blood*

Nelson, Barry
American. Actor
b. 1920 in San Francisco, California
Source: *BiE&WWA; FilmgC; IntMPA 75, 76, 77, 78, 79, 80, 81, 82; MotPP; MovMk; NotNAT; PlP&P A; WhoAm 74, 76, 78, 80, 82; WhoHol A; WhoThe 77*

Nelson, "Battling"
[Oscar Nielson]
American. Boxer
b. Jun 5, 1882 in Copenhagen, Denmark
d. Feb 7, 1954 in Chicago, Illinois
Source: *WhoBox 74*

Nelson, Cindy
American. Skier
b. Aug 19, 1955 in Lutsen, Minnesota
Source: *BioIn 11*

Nelson, David
American. Actor
Son of Ozzie and Harriet; appeared on their TV show, 1952-65.
b. Oct 24, 1936 in New York, New York
Source: *IntMPA 75, 76, 77, 78, 79, 80, 81, 82; WhoHol A*

Nelson, Ed
American. Actor
b. Dec 21, 1928 in New Orleans, Louisiana
Source: *FilmgC; WhoAm 82; WhoHol A*

Nelson, Gene
American. Actor, Dancer
b. Mar 24, 1920 in Seattle, Washington
Source: *CmMov; FilmgC; IntMPA 75, 76, 77, 78, 79, 80, 81, 82; MotPP; MovMk; PlP&P; WhoHol A; WhoThe 77*

Nelson, George
American. Architect
b. 1908 in Hartford, Connecticut
Source: *BioIn 5, 10; BnEnAmA; ConAu 81; EncMA; McGDA; WhoAm 74, 76, 78, 80, 82; WhoCon 73*

Nelson, Harriet
[Harriet Hilliard; Mrs. Ozzie Nelson]
American. Actress, Singer
Began career as singer in Ozzie Nelson's orchestra; starred on TV, 1952-65.
b. Jul 18, 1912 in Des Moines, Iowa
Source: *CurBio 49; FilmgC; InWom; IntMPA 75, 76, 77, 78, 79, 80, 81, 82; MotPP; ThFT; WhoAm 74, 76, 78, 80, 82; WhoHol A*

Nelson, Horatio Nelson, Viscount
English. Naval Commander
Defeated French fleet at Trafalgar, 1805; killed in battle.
b. Sep 29, 1758 in Burnham Thorpe, England
d. Oct 21, 1805
Source: *NewC; REn*

Nelson, Jimmy
American. Ventriloquist
b. 1928
Source: *BioIn 10*

Nelson, (John) Byron, Jr.
[Gold Dust Twins]
American. Golfer
Called "mechanical" golfer because play was so consistent; Hall of Fame, 1953.
b. Feb 4, 1912 in Fort Worth, Texas
Source: *BioIn 2, 4, 6, 11; WhoGolf*

Nelson, Larry Gene
American. Golfer
Won PGA Championship, 1981.
b. Sep 10, 1947 in Fort Payne, Alabama
Source: *BioIn 12; WhoAm 82*

Nelson, Ozzie (Oswald George)
American. Actor, Band Leader
Starred in TV series "The Adventures of Ozzie and Harriet," 1952-65.
b. Mar 20, 1906 in Jersey City, New Jersey
d. Jun 3, 1975 in Hollywood, California
Source: *ConAu 57, 93; CurBio 49, 75; FilmgC; IntMPA 75; MotPP; WhAm 6; WhScrn 77; WhoAm 74*

Nelson, Ralph
American. Researcher
b. Jun 19, 1927 in Minneapolis, Minnesota
Source: *AmM&WS 73P; ConAu 53; WhoAm 82*

Nelson, "Ricky" (Eric Hilliard)
American. Singer, Actor
Sold 35 million records before age 21.
b. May 8, 1940 in Teaneck, New Jersey
Source: *BkPepl; FilmgC; IntMPA 75, 76, 77, 78, 79, 80, 81, 82; MotPP; WhoAm 74, 76, 78, 80, 82; WhoHol A*

Nelson, Thomas, Jr.
American. Soldier
b. Dec 26, 1738 in Yorktown, Virginia
d. Jan 4, 1789 in Hanover County, Virginia
Source: *BiAuS; BiDrAC; TwCBDA; WhAmP*

Nelson, Wayne
see: Little River Band, The

Nelson, William Rockhill
American. Newspaper Editor
b. Mar 7, 1841 in Fort Wayne, Indiana
d. Apr 13, 1915
Source: *DcAmB; WhAm 1*

Nelson, Willie
American. Musician, Singer
Won Grammy, 1975, for "Blue Eyes Crying in the Rain."
b. Apr 30, 1933 in Abbott, Texas
Source: *EncFCWM 69; WhoAm 82*

Nelsova, Zara
[Sarah Nelson]
Canadian. Musician
b. Dec 24, 1924? in Winnipeg, MB
Source: *Baker 78; CreCan 2; WhoAm 74, 76, 78; WhoMus 72*

Nemec, Jan
Czech. Motion Picture Director
b. Jul 2, 1936 in Prague, Czechoslovakia
Source: *DcFM; FilmgC; OxFilm; WhoWor 74; WorEFlm*

Nemerov, Howard
American. Poet
b. Mar 1, 1920 in New York, New York
Source: *AmAu&B; AmWr; Au&Wr 71; CasWL; CnE&AP; ConAu 1R, 1NR; ConLC 2, 6, 9; ConNov 72, 76; ConP 70, 75; CroCAP; DrAF 76; DrAP 75; IntWW 74; ModAL, SUP; OxAmL; Pen AM; RAdv 1; REn; REnAL; TwCA SUP; WhoAm 74; WhoTwCL; WhoWor 74; WhoWorJ 72; WrDr 76*

Nemirovich-Danchenko, Vladimir I
Russian. Author, Dramatist, Producer
b. Dec 23, 1858 in Tiflis, Russia
d. Apr 25, 1943 in Moscow, U.S.S.R.
Source: *CasWL; DcRusL; ModWD; OxThe; PlP&P; REn*

Nenni, Pietro
Italian. Socialist Leader, Journalist
b. Feb 9, 1891 in Faenza, Italy
d. Jan 1, 1980 in Rome, Italy
Source: *CurBio 47; IntWW 74*

Nero
[Nero Claudius Caesar Germanicus]
Roman. Emperor
Known for persecuting Christians; started fire that destroyed Rome.
b. 37
d. 68
Source: *NewC; OxThe; Pen CL; PlP&P; REn*

Nero, Franco
Italian. Actor
b. 1941
Source: *FilmgC; WhoHol A*

Nero, Peter
American. Pianist
b. May 22, 1934 in New York, New York
Source: *CelR 73; WhoAm 74, 76, 78, 80, 82; WhoE 74*

Neruda, Pablo
[Neftali Ricardo Reyes Basualto]
Chilean. Poet, Diplomat, Author
b. Jul 12, 1904 in Parral, Chile
d. Sep 23, 1973 in Santiago, Chile
Source: *CasWL; CelR 73; CnMWL; ConAu 21R, 45; ConAu P-2; ConLC 1, 2, 5, 7, 9; CurBio 70, 73; DcSpL; EncWL; NewYTBE 71, 73; Pen AM; REn; TwCA SUP; TwCW; WhAm 6; WhoTwCL; WhoWor 74*

Nerval, Gerard de
French. Poet, Translator, Author
b. May 22, 1808 in Paris, France
d. Jan 25, 1855 in Paris, France
Source: *AtlBL; BbD; BiD&SB; CasWL; DcEuL; EuAu; EvEuW; OxFr; Pen EUR*

Nervi, Pier Luigi
Italian. Construction Engineer
b. Jun 21, 1891 in Sondrio, Italy
d. Jan 9, 1979 in Rome, Italy
Source: *CurBio 58, 79; EncMA; IntWW 75, 76, 77, 78; LinLib S; McGDA; McGEWB; WhoArch; WhoWor 74*

Nesbit, Edith
[Mrs. Hubert Bland]
English. Children's Author
b. Aug 19, 1858 in London, England
d. May 4, 1924
Source: *AuBYP; BioIn 3, 5, 6, 7, 8, 11; EvLB; NewC; TwCA, SUP*

Nesbit, Evelyn
American. Actress
b. 1885
d. Jan 18, 1967 in Santa Monica, California
Source: *Film 1; InWom; TwYS; WhScrn 74, 77; WhoHol B*

Nesbitt, Cathleen Mary
English. Actress
Originated stage role of Mrs. Higgins in *My Fair Lady,* 1956.
b. Nov 24, 1889 in Cheshire, England
d. Aug 2, 1982 in London, England
Source: *BiE&WWA; BioIn 4, 10, 11; CurBio 56, 82; FilmgC; MotPP; MovMk; NewYTBS 82; NotNAT, A; Who 74; WhoAmW 58; WhoHol A; WhoThe 72, 77*

Nesmith, Mike
[The Monkees]
American. Singer, Songwriter
Starred in TV series "The Monkees," 1966-69; always wore wool hat.
b. Dec 30, 1942 in Houston, Texas
Source: *EncPR&S; LilREn 78; WhoRock 81*

Ness, Eliot
American. FBI Agent
Portrayed by Robert Stack in TV series "The Untouchables," 1959-63.
b. Apr 19, 1903 in Chicago, Illinois
d. May 7, 1957
Source: *BioIn 1; WhAm 3*

Nessen, Ron
American. Journalist, Presidental Aide
b. May 25, 1934 in Rockville, Maryland
Source: *BioIn 10; CurBio 76; WhoAm 82*

Nessler, Victor E
German. Composer
b. Jan 28, 1841 in Baldenheim, Germany
d. May 28, 1890 in Strassburg, Germany
Source: *NewEOp 71; WebBD 80*

Nestingen, Ivan Arnold
American. Government Official
b. Sep 23, 1921 in Sparta, Wisconsin
d. Apr 24, 1978 in Washington, DC
Source: *BioIn 5, 6, 11; CurBio 62, 78; IntWW 74, 75, 76; WhoAm 74*

Nestle, Henri
Swiss. Candy Manufacturer
Original chocolate factory in Vevey, Switzerland.
b. 1814 in Germany
d. 1890
Source: *WebBD 80*

Nestorius
Syrian. Patriarch of Constantinople
d. 451
Source: *BioIn 4; WebBD 80*

Netanyahu, Yonatan
[Johnathan Netaniahu]
"Yoni"
Israeli. Army Officer
b. 1946 in New York
d. Jul 3, 1976 in Entebbe, Uganda
Source: *BioIn 12*

Nethersole, Olga
English. Actress
b. Jan 18, 1870 in London, England
d. Jan 9, 1951 in Bournemouth, England
Source: *FamA&A; InWom; OxThe; WhAm 3; WhoStg 1906, 1908*

Netsch, Walter Andrew, Jr.
American. Architect
b. Feb 23, 1920 in Chicago, Illinois
Source: *BioIn 9; WhoAm 74, 76, 78, 80; WhoWor 74*

Nettles, Graig
American. Baseball Player
b. Aug 20, 1944 in San Diego, California
Source: *BaseEn; BioIn 9, 11; WhoProB 73*

Nettleton, Lois
American. Actress
b. 1931 in Oak Park, Illinois
Source: *BiE&WWA; IntMPA 75, 76, 77, 78, 79, 80, 81, 82; NotNAT; WhoAm 74, 78, 80, 82; WhoHol A; WhoThe 77*

Neuendorff, Adolf
German. Conductor
b. Jun 13, 1843 in Hamburg, Germany
d. Dec 4, 1897 in New York, New York
Source: *NewEOp 71*

Neumann, Angelo
Austrian. Opera Singer
b. Aug 18, 1838 in Vienna, Austria
d. Dec 20, 1910 in Prague, Czechoslovakia
Source: *NewEOp 71*

Neumann, Robert Gerhard
American. Former Diplomat
b. Jan 2, 1916 in Vienna, Austria
Source: *AmM&WS 78S; ConAu 5R; IntWW 75, 76, 77, 78; IntYB 78, 79; USBiR 74; WhoAm 74, 76, 78, 80, 82; WhoAmP 73, 75, 77, 79; WhoGov 72, 75, 77; WhoWest 74, 76; WhoWor 74, 76*

Neurath, Constantin Freiherr von
[Konstantin von Neurath]
German. Nazi Criminal
b. Feb 2, 1873 in Klein Glattbach, Germany
d. Aug 14, 1956 in Enzweihingen, Germany (West)
Source: *BioIn 1, 3, 4; EncTR; NewCol 75; ObitOF 79; WhWW-II*

Neutra, Richard Joseph
American. Architect
b. Apr 8, 1892 in Vienna, Austria
d. Apr 16, 1970 in Wuppertal, Germany (West)
Source: *AmAu&B; ConAu 5R, 29R, 5NR; EncAB-H; WebAB; WhAm 5*

Nevada, Emma
[Emma Wixom]
American. Opera Singer
b. Feb 7, 1859 in Alpha, California
d. Jun 20, 1940 in Liverpool, England
Source: *AmWom; ApCAB; DcAmB S2; InWom; NotAW; TwCBDA; WhAm 5*

Nevelson, Louise Berliawsky
American. Artist
b. 1900 in Russia
Source: *CelR 73; CurBio 67; DcCAA 71; EncAB-H; InWom; IntWW 74; NewYTBE 71; WhoAm 74, 76, 78, 80, 82; WhoAmA 73; WhoAmW 77; WhoE 74; WhoWor 74*

Nevers, Ernie (Ernest A)
American. Football Player
b. Jun 11, 1903 in Willow River, Minnesota
d. 1976 in San Rafael, California
Source: *WhoFtbl 74*

Nevin, Ethelbert Woodbridge
American. Composer
b. Nov 25, 1862 in Edgeworth, Pennsylvania
d. Feb 17, 1901 in New Haven, Connecticut
Source: *AmBi; AmSCAP 66; DcAmB; OxAmL; REnAL; TwCBDA; WhAm 1*

Nevins, Allan
American. Journalist, Historian
b. May 20, 1890 in Camp Point, Illinois
d. Mar 5, 1971 in Menlo Park, California
Source: *AmAu&B; ConAu 5R, 29R; CurBio 68, 71; EncAB-H; LongCTC; NewYTBE 71; OxAmL; Pen AM; REn; REnAL; TwCA, SUP; WebAB; WhAm 5*

Nevski, Alexander, Saint
Russian. Hero
b. 1220?
d. 1263
Source: *WebBD 80*

Neway, Patricia
American. Opera Singer
b. Sep 30, 1919 in Brooklyn, New York
Source: *BiE&WWA; NotNAT; WhoMus 72; WhoThe 77*

Newberry, John Stoughton
American. Railroad Executive
b. Nov 18, 1826 in Sangerfield, New York
d. Jan 2, 1887 in Detroit, Michigan
Source: *ApCAB; BiDrAC; DcAmB; DcNAA; WhAm H*

Newbery, John
English. Publisher
Published children's books; *Mother Goose's Nursery Rhymes,* circa 1760.
b. 1713 in Berkshire, England
d. Dec 22, 1767 in London, England
Source: *Alli; BrAu; ChPo, S1; NewC; REn; REnAL; SmATA 20; WhoChL*

Newcomb, Simon
American. Astronomer
Wrote *Popular Astronomy,* 1878; *The Stars,* 1901.
b. Mar 12, 1835 in Wallace, NS
d. Jul 11, 1909 in Washington, DC
Source: *Alli SUP; AmAu; AmAu&B; AmBi; ApCAB; BbD; BiAuS; BiD&SB; BiDPara; DcAmAu; DcAmB; DcNAA; REnAL; TwCBDA; WebAB; WhAm 1*

Newcombe, Don(ald)
"Newk"
American. Baseball Player
b. Jun 14, 1926 in Madison, New Jersey
Source: *BaseEn; BioIn 10; CurBio 57; WhoProB 73*

Newcombe, John
"Newk"
Australian. Tennis Player
Won Wimbledon championship, 1967, 1970, 1971.
b. May 23, 1944 in Sydney, Australia
Source: *WhoWor 74*

Newcomen, Thomas
English. Inventor
Developed first practical steam engine.
b. Feb 24, 1663 in Dartmouth, England
d. Aug 5, 1729 in London, England
Source: *AsBiEn; BioIn 3, 6, 7, 9; DcAmB; McGEWB*

Newfield, Jack
American. Author, Editor
b. Feb 18, 1939 in New York, New York
Source: *AmAu&B; ConAu 21R; WhoAm 74*

Newhart, Bob (George Robert)
American. Comedian
Instant success first album, *The Button Down Mind of Bob Newhart,* 1960.
b. Sep 5, 1929 in Chicago, Illinois
Source: *BkPepl; CelR 73; CurBio 62; FilmgC; IntMPA 75, 76, 77, 78, 79, 80, 81, 82; WhoAm 74, 76, 78, 80, 82; WhoHol A; WhoWor 74*

Newhouse, Donald E
American. Publisher, Broadcasting Executive
b. 1929
Source: *BioIn 10*

Newhouse, Samuel Irving
American. Newspaper Publisher
Owned 31 newspapers; bought Booth Newspapers, Inc. for $305 million.
b. May 24, 1895 in New York, New York
d. Aug 29, 1979 in New York, New York
Source: *ConAu 89; CurBio 61, 79; IntWW 74; WhoAm 74; WhoE 74*

Newhouser, Harold (Hal)
"Prince Hal"
American. Baseball Player
Pitcher, 1939-55; MVP, 1944.
b. Nov 20, 1921 in Detroit, Michigan
Source: *BaseEn; BioIn 1, 2, 4, 5, 6; WhoProB 73*

Newley, Anthony
English. Actor, Singer, Songwriter
Wrote, directed, starred in *Stop the World, I Want to Get Off,* 1961-63.
b. Sep 24, 1931 in London, England
Source: *BiE&WWA; CelR 73; ConDr 73; CurBio 66; EncMT; FilmgC; IntMPA 75, 76, 77, 78, 78, 79, 80, 81, 82; MotPP; MovMk; NotNAT; OxFilm; Who 82; WhoAm 76, 78, 80, 82; WhoHol A; WhoThe 77; WhoWor 76*

Newman, Alfred
American. Composer, Conductor
b. Mar 17, 1901 in New Haven, Connecticut
d. Feb 17, 1970 in Hollywood, California
Source: *AmSCAP 66; CmMov; CurBio 43, 70; DcFM; FilmgC; NewYTBE 70; OxFilm; WhAm 5; WhScrn 74, 77; WorEFlm*

Newman, Arnold Abner
American. Photographer
b. Mar 3, 1918 in New York, New York
Source: *BioIn 2, 4, 7, 10, 11; CurBio 80; WhoAm 76, 78, 80, 82; WhoAmA 73, 76, 78*

Newman, Barnett
American. Artist
Best known for "Stations of the Cross" series, 1958-66.
b. Jan 29, 1905 in New York, New York
d. Jul 3, 1970 in New York, New York
Source: *CurBio 69, 70; NewCol 75*

Newman, Barry Foster
American. Actor
Starred in TV series "Petrocelli," 1974-76.
b. Nov 7, 1938 in Boston, Massachusetts
Source: *FilmgC; WhoAm 82; WhoHol A*

Newman, Edwin Harold
American. Author, TV Commentator
Won six Emmys; wrote *Strictly Speaking,* 1974; *Sunday Punch,* 1979.
b. Jan 25, 1919 in New York, New York
Source: *CelR 73; ConAu 69, 5NR; ConLC 14; CurBio 67; IntMPA 82; WhoAm 74, 76, 78, 80, 82; WhoE 74*

Newman, Ernest
English. Music Critic, Biographer
b. Nov 30, 1868 in Liverpool, England
d. Jul 7, 1959 in Tadworth, England
Source: *DcLEL; LongCTC; NewC; REn; TwCA, SUP; WhAm 3*

Newman, John Henry, Cardinal
English. Theologian, Author
b. Feb 21, 1801 in London, England
d. Aug 11, 1890 in Birmingham, England
Source: *Alli, SUP; AtlBL; BbD; BiD&SB; BrAu 19; CasWL; Chambr 3; ChPo, S1; CrtT 3; CyWA; DcEnA; DcEnL; DcEuL; DcLEL; EvLB; MouLC 4; NewC; OxEng; Pen ENG; PoChrch; REn; WebE&AL*

Newman, Mildred
American. Psychoanalyst, Author
b. 1920
Source: *BioIn 10, 11*

Newman, Paul
American. Actor
Starred in *The Sting,* 1973; *The Verdict,* 1982; races Formula One cars.
b. Jan 26, 1925 in Cleveland, Ohio
Source: *BiDFilm; BiE&WWA; BkPepl; CelR 73; CmMov; CurBio 59; FilmgC; IntMPA 75, 76, 77, 78, 79, 80, 81, 82; IntWW 74; MotPP; MovMk; NewYTBE 71; OxFilm; WhoAm 74, 76, 78, 80, 82; WhoHol A; WhoThe 77; WhoWor 74; WorEFlm*

Newman, Phyllis
American. Actress
b. 1935 in Jersey City, New Jersey
Source: *BiE&WWA; InWom; NotNAT; WhoHol A; WhoThe 77*

Newman, Randy
American. Singer, Songwriter
Album *Little Criminals,* featuring hit "Short People."
b. Nov 28, 1943 in Los Angeles, California
Source: *BiDAmM; BkPepl; CurBio 82; EncPR&S; IlEncRk; WhoAm 82*

Newmar, Julie
American. Dancer, Actress
Played Catwoman on TV series "Batman."
b. 1935 in Los Angeles, California
Source: *BiE&WWA; InWom; NotNAT; WhoAm 74*

Newquist, Roy
American. Author, Editor
b. Jul 25, 1925 in Ashland, Wisconsin
Source: *AmAu&B; ConAu 13R*

Newsom, "Bobo" (Louis Norman)
"Buck"
American. Baseball Player
b. Aug 11, 1907 in Hartsville, South Carolina
d. Dec 7, 1962 in Orlando, Florida
Source: *BaseEn; WhoProB 73*

Newsome, George
see: Climax Blues Band, The

Newton, Huey P
American. Political Leader
Founded, with Bobby Seale, Black Panther Party, 1966.
b. Feb 17, 1942 in New Orleans, Louisiana
Source: *CelR 73; CurBio 73; LivgBAA; NewYTBE 70; WhoBlA 75*

Newton, Sir Isaac
English. Philosopher, Mathematician
Developed reflecting telescope, 1668; law of universal gravitation.
b. Dec 25, 1642 in Woolsthorpe, England
d. Mar 20, 1727 in Kensington, England
Source: *Alli; BbD; BiD&SB; BrAu; CasWL; Chambr 2; CyWA; DcEnA; DcEnL; DcLEL; EvLB; NewC; OxEng; REn*

Newton, "Juice" (Judy Kay)
American. Singer
Sang "Angel of the Morning," "Loves Been a Little Hard on Me."
b. 1952?
Source: *BioIn 12*

Newton, Robert
English. Actor
b. Jun 1, 1905 in Shaftesbury, England
d. Mar 25, 1956 in Beverly Hills, California
Source: *BiDFilm; FilmgC; MovMk; OxFilm; Vers A; WhScrn 74, 77; WorEFlm*

Newton, Wayne
American. Singer
Yearly income from nightclub performances estimated at $10 million.
b. Apr 3, 1942 in Norfolk, Virginia
Source: *BkPepl; CelR 73; WhoAm 74, 76, 78, 80, 82; WhoHol A*

Newton-John, Olivia
English. Singer
Granddaughter of physicist Max Born; starred in *Grease* and *Xanadu.*
b. Sep 26, 1948 in Cambridge, England
Source: *BioNews 74; BkPepl; HerW; WhoAm 82*

Ney, Michel de la Moskova, Prince
French. Marshal
b. Jan 10, 1769 in Saarlouis, France
d. Dec 7, 1815 in Paris, France
Source: *OxFr; REn*

Ney, Richard
American. Actor, Investment Counselor
b. 1917
Source: *AuNews 1; FilmgC; IntMPA 82*

Neyland, Robert Reese
American. Football Coach, General
b. Feb 17, 1892 in Greenville, Texas
d. Mar 28, 1962 in New Orleans, Louisiana
Source: *WhAm 4; WhoFtbl 74*

Ngo dinh Diem
Vietnamese. President
b. 1901 in Quang Bihn, Annam
d. Nov 2, 1963
Source: *CurBio 55, 64*

Ngo dinh Nhu, Madame
Vietnamese. Politician
b. 1924
Source: *BioIn 9; IntWW 74*

Nguyen thi Binh, Madame
Vietnamese. Diplomat
b. 1927
Source: *WhoWor 74*

Niarchos, Stavros Spyros
Greek. Shipping Executive
Founded Niarchos Group, 1939; world's largest privately-owned fleet of tankers.
b. Jul 3, 1909 in Athens, Greece
Source: *CelR 73; CurBio 58; IntWW 74; NewYTBE 70; Who 74; WhoF&I 74; WhoWor 74*

Niblo, Fred
American. Actor
b. Jan 6, 1874 in York, Nebraska
d. Nov 11, 1948 in New Orleans, Louisiana
Source: *CmMov; DcFM; FilmgC; MovMk; OxFilm; TwYS; WorEFlm; WhScrn 74, 77; WhoHol B*

Nicholas I
Russian. Czar
b. 1796
d. 1855
Source: *BioIn 10; NewCol 75; WebBD 80; WhDW*

Nicholas II
[Nikolai Aleksandrovich Romanov]
Russian. Last Czar
b. 1868 in Tsarskoe Selo, Russia
d. Jul 19, 1918 in Ekaterinburg, U.S.S.R.
Source: *BioIn 10; NewCol 75; WebBD 80; WhDW; WhoModH*

Nicholas of Cusa
German. Churchman, Humanist
b. 1401? in Cusa, Germany
d. Aug 11, 1446 in Todi, Italy
Source: *AsBiEn; McGEWB; NewCol 75*

Nicholas, Saint
Bishop
d. Dec 6, 345?
Source: *NewC; REn*

Nicholas, Denise
American. Actress
b. in Detroit, Michigan
Source: *WhoHol A*

Nichols, Anne
American. Dramatist, Architect
b. Nov 26, 1891? in Dales Mill, Georgia
d. Sep 15, 1966 in New Jersey
Source: *AmAu&B; BiE&WWA; EvLB; InWom; LongCTC; McGEWD; ModWD; REn; REnAL; TwCW; WhAm 4*

Nichols, Beverly
English. Author, Composer, Dramatist
b. Sep 9, 1899 in Bristol, England
Source: *BioIn 1, 2, 3, 4, 6, 7, 8, 9, 10; IntAu&W 77; NewC*

Nichols, Bobby (Robert)
American. Golfer
b. Apr 14, 1936 in Louisville, Kentucky
Source: *BioIn 10; WhoGolf*

Nichols, Dale
American. Designer, Author
b. Jul 13, 1904 in David City, Nebraska
Source: *ConAu P-2; IlsCB 1744; WhE&EA; WhoAm 74, 82; WhoAmA 76, 78; WhoWor 74*

Nichols, Mike
[Michael Igor Peschkowsky]
American. Actor, Motion Picture Director
Teamed with Elaine May, late 1950's-60's.
b. Nov 6, 1931 in Berlin, Germany
Source: *BiE&WWA; BkPepl; CelR 73; CurBio 61; DcFM; FilmgC; IntMPA 75, 76, 77, 78, 79, 80, 81, 82; IntWW 74; MovMk; NotNAT; OxFilm; WebAB; WhoAm 82; WhoE 74; WhoHol A; WhoThe 77; WomWMM; WorEFlm*

Nichols, Peter
English. Dramatist
b. Jul 31, 1927 in Bristol, England
Source: *Au&Wr 71; BioIn 10; CnThe; ConAu 104; ConDr 73, 77; ConLC 5; DcLEL 1940; EncWT; McGEWD; ModBrL SUP; NewYTBS 74; WhoThe 72, 77; WorAu 1970; WrDr 76, 80*

Nichols, "Red" (Ernest Loring)
American. Musician
b. May 8, 1905 in Ogden, Utah
d. Jun 28, 1965 in Las Vegas, Nevada
Source: *AmSCAP 66; WhScrn 74, 77; WhoHol B; WhoJazz 72*

Nichols, Ruth Rowland
American. Pioneer Aviatrix
b. Feb 23, 1901 in New York, New York
d. Sep 25, 1960 in New York, New York
Source: *InWom; WhAm 4*

Nicholson, Ben
English. Artist
b. Apr 10, 1894 in Uxbridge, England
d. Feb 6, 1982 in London, England
Source: *BioIn 1, 2, 4, 5, 6, 8, 9, 11; ConArt; CurBio 58, 82; IntWW 74, 75, 76, 77, 78; McGDA; McGEWB; NewYTBS 82; WhoAm 74, 76, 78, 80, 82; WhoAmA 76, 78; WhoWor 74, 76*

Nicholson, Jack
American. Actor
Won 1975 Oscar for *One Flew Over the Cuckoo's Nest.*
b. Apr 22, 1937 in Neptune, New Jersey
Source: *BioNews 74; BkPepl; CelR 73; CurBio 74; FilmgC; IntMPA 75, 76, 77, 78, 79, 80, 81, 82; MotPP; MovMk; NewYTBS 74; OxFilm; WhoAm 78, 80, 82; WhoHol A*

Nichopoulos, George C
American. Elvis Presley's Physician
b. 1927
Source: *BioIn 12*

"Nick the Greek"
[Nicholas Andrea Dandolos]
American. Gambler
b. 1896
d. Dec 25, 1966 in Los Angeles, California
Source: *BioIn 3, 7, 8*

Nickerson, Albert L
American. Petroleum Executive
b. Jan 17, 1911 in Dedham, Massachusetts
Source: *CurBio 59; IntWW 74; Who 74; WhoAm 74, 76, 78, 80, 82*

Nicklaus, Jack
"Golden Bear"
American. Golfer
Has won over 20 major golf tournaments.
b. Jan 21, 1940 in Columbus, Ohio
Source: *BioNews 74; BkPepl; BusPN; CelR 73; CurBio 62; NewYTBE 70, 72, 73; NewYTBS 74; WebAB; Who 82; WhoAm 76, 78, 80, 82*

Nicks, "Stevie" (Stephanie)
[Fleetwood Mac]
American. Singer, Songwriter
First solo ablum was *Bella Donna,* 1981.
b. May 26, 1948 in Phoenix, California
Source: *BkPepl; WhoAm 80, 82*

Nicodemus
Biblical Character
Source: *NewCol 75; WebBD 80*

Nicolai, Carl Otto
German. Composer
b. Jun 9, 1810 in Konigsberg, Germany
d. May 11, 1849 in Berlin, Germany
Source: *NewEOp 71; OxMus*

Nicolay, John George
American. Biographer
b. Feb 26, 1832 in Essingen, Bavaria
d. Sep 26, 1901 in Washington, DC
Source: *Alli SUP; AmAu; AmAu&B; AmBi; BbD; BiD&SB; DcAmAu; DcAmB; DcNAA; OhA&B; OxAmL; REnAL; TwCBDA; WhAm 1; WhAmP*

Nicolet, Aurele
Swiss. Musician
b. 1926 in Neuchatel, Switzerland
Source: *WhoMus 72*

Nicolet, Jean
French. Explorer
First European to discover Lake Michigan and area of WI and MI, 1634.
b. 1598 in Cherbourg, France
d. Nov 1, 1642
Source: *DcAmB; REnAW; WebAB; WhAm H*

Nicolini
[Nicola Grimaldi]
Italian. Opera Singer
b. Apr 1673 in Naples, Italy
d. Jan 1, 1732 in Naples, Italy
Source: *NewEOp 71*

Nicoll, (John Ramsay) Allardyce
American. Drama Critic
Theatre historian; master of dramatic research.
b. Jun 28, 1894 in Glasgow, Scotland
d. Apr 17, 1976 in England
Source: *Au&Wr 71; BiE&WWA; ConAu 9R, 65, 5NR; LongCTC; NotNAT; OxThe; REn; TwCA; Who 74; TwCA SUP; WrDr 76; WhoThe 77*

Nicot, Jean
French. Diplomat, Scholar
b. 1530 in Nimes, France
d. May 5, 1600 in Paris, France
Source: *OxFr*

Nidetch, Jean
American. Health Service Executive
Founded Weight Watchers International, 1963; wrote *Weight Watchers Cookbook*, 1966.
b. Oct 12, 1923 in Brooklyn, New York
Source: *ConAu 89; CurBio 73; St&PR 75; WhoAm 76, 78, 80, 82; WhoAmW 77*

Niebuhr, Helmut Richard
American. Theologian
b. Sep 3, 1894 in Wright City, Missouri
d. Jul 5, 1962 in Greenfield, Massachusetts
Source: *AmAu&B; WhAm 4*

Niebuhr, Reinhold
American. Clergyman, Author
b. Jun 21, 1892 in Wright City, Missouri
d. Jun 1, 1971 in Stockbridge, Massachusetts
Source: *AmAu&B; AmWr; CasWL; ConAu 29R, 41R; CurBio 41, 51, 71; EncAB-H; LongCTC; ModAL; NewYTBE 71; OxAmL; REn; REnAL; TwCA, SUP; WebAB; WhAm 5*

Nielsen, Alice
American. Opera Singer
b. Jun 7, 1876 in Nashville, Tennessee
d. Mar 8, 1943 in New York, New York
Source: *CurBio 43; DcAmB S3; InWom; NotAW; WhAm 2; WhoStg 1906, 1908; WomWWA 14*

Nielsen, Arthur C
American. Marketing Research Analyst
Founded market research firm that conducts Nielsen TV ratings, 1923.
b. Sep 5, 1897 in Chicago, Illinois
d. Jun 1, 1980 in Chicago, Illinois
Source: *CelR 73; CurBio 51; St&PR 75; WhoAm 74; WhoF&I 74*

Nielsen, Carl August
Danish. Composer
b. Jun 9, 1864 in Norre-Lyndelse, Denmark
d. Oct 2, 1931 in Copenhagen, Denmark
Source: *DcCM*

Nielsen, Gertrude
American. Actress, Singer
b. 1918
d. May 27, 1975 in Hollywood, California
Source: *WhScrn 77*

Nielsen, Leslie
Canadian. Actor
Starred in *The Poseidon Adventure*, 1972; *Airplane*, 1980.
b. Feb 11, 1926 in Regina, SK
Source: *FilmgC; IntMPA 75, 76, 77, 78, 79, 80, 81, 82; MotPP; MovMk; WhoAm 82; WhoHol A*

Nielsen, Rick
see: Cheap Trick

Nieman, Lucius William
American. Newspaper Publisher
b. Dec 13, 1857 in Bear Creek, Wisconsin
d. Oct 1, 1935
Source: *DcAmB S1; WhAm 1*

Niemann, Albert
German. Opera Singer
b. Jan 15, 1831 in Erxleben, Germany
d. Jan 13, 1917 in Berlin, Germany
Source: *NewEOp 71*

Niemeyer, Oscar
Brazilian. Architect
b. Dec 15, 1907 in Rio de Janeiro, Brazil
Source: *CurBio 60; IntWW 74; Who 74*

Niemoller, Martin
German. Theologian
b. Jan 14, 1892 in Lippstadt, Germany
Source: *CurBio 43, 65; IntWW 74; LongCTC; OxGer; REn*

Niepce, Joseph Nicephore
French. Physician, Scientist
b. 1765
d. 1833
Source: *AsBiEn; BioIn 2, 8; DcFM; DcScB; NewCol 75*

Nietzsche, Friedrich Wilhelm
German. Philosopher, Poet
b. Oct 15, 1844 in Rocken, Germany
d. Aug 25, 1900 in Rocken, Germany
Source: *AtlBL; BiD&SB; CasWL; ClDMEL; CyWA; DcEuL; EncWL; EuAu; EvEuW; NewC; OxEng; OxGer; Pen EUR; RComWL; REn*

Nightingale, Florence
"Lady with a Lamp"
English. Nurse, Hospital Reformer
Founded nursing as profession; first woman to receive Order of Merit, 1907.
b. May 15, 1820 in Florence, Italy
d. Aug 13, 1910 in London, England
Source: *Alli, SUP; FilmgC; HerW; InWom; LongCTC; NewC; REn*

Nijinska, Bronislava
Russian. Ballerina, Choreographer
b. Jan 8, 1891 in Minsk, Russia
d. Feb 21, 1972 in Pacific Palisades, California
Source: *InWom; NewYTBE 72*

Nijinsky, Vaslav (Waslaw)
Russian. Dancer
b. Feb 28, 1890 in Kiev, Russia
d. Apr 8, 1950 in London, England
Source: *CurBio 40, 50; LongCTC; WhAm 4*

Nikisch, Arthur
Hungarian. Conductor
b. Oct 12, 1855 in Lebenyi Szent, Hungary
d. Jan 23, 1922 in Leipzig, Germany
Source: *NewEOp 71; OxMus*

Nikolaidi, Elena
Turkish. Opera Singer
b. Jun 13, 1909 in Smyrna, Turkey
Source: *InWom; WhoAm 74*

Nikolais, Alwin
American. Choreographer, Composer
b. Nov 25, 1912 in Southington, Connecticut
Source: *CelR 73; ConDr 73; CurBio 68; DcCM; NewYTBE 70; WhoAm 74, 76, 78, 80, 82*

Nikolayev, Andrian G
Russian. Cosmonaut
b. Sep 5, 1929 in Shorshely, U.S.S.R.
Source: *CurBio 64; IntWW 74; WhoWor 74*

Niles, John Jacob
American. Composer, Folklorist, Singer
b. Apr 28, 1892 in Louisville, Kentucky
d. Mar 1, 1980 in Lexington, Kentucky
Source: *AmAu&B; AmSCAP 66; AnObit 1980; Baker 78; BiDAmM; BioIn 1, 2, 5, 8; ConAu 41R, 97; CurBio 59, 80; DrAS 74E, 78E; EncFCWM 69; WhAm 7; WhoAm 74, 76, 78; WhoMus 72; WhoWor 74*

Nilsson, Anna Q
Swedish. Actress
b. Mar 30, 1888 in Ystad, Sweden
d. Feb 11, 1974 in Hemet, California
Source: *Film 1; FilmgC; MotPP; MovMk; NewYTBS 74; TwYS; WhScrn 77; WhoHol B*

Nilsson, Birgit
Swedish. Opera Singer
b. May 17, 1918 in West Karup, Sweden
Source: *CelR 73; CurBio 60; InWom; IntWW 74; NewYTBE 71, 72; Who 74; WhoAm 74, 76, 78, 80, 82; WhoHol A; WhoMus 72; WhoWor 74*

Nilsson, Christine
Swedish. Opera Singer
b. Aug 20, 1843 in Wexio, Sweden
d. Nov 22, 1921 in Stockholm, Sweden
Source: *ApCAB; InWom*

Nilsson, Kent
Swedish. Hockey Player
b. Aug 31, 1956 in Nynashamn, Sweden
Source: *HocReg*

Nilsson, Ulf
Swedish. Hockey Player
b. May 11, 1950 in Nynashamn, Sweden
Source: *BioIn 12; HocReg*

Nimeiry, Gaafar Mohammed al
Sudanese. President
b. Jan 1, 1930 in Wad Nubawi, Sudan
Source: *AfSS 78, 79; BioIn 10; CurBio 77; IntWW 78; IntYB 78, 79; MidE 78, 79; NewYTBE 73; NewYTBS 78; WhoWor 78; WorDWW*

Nimitz, Chester William
American. Naval Officer
Commanded Pacific Fleet, WW II; Japanese surrendered on his ship *Missouri,* 1945.
b. Feb 24, 1885 in Fredericksburg, Texas
d. Feb 20, 1966 in San Francisco, California
Source: *EncAB-H; WebAB; WhAm 4*

Nimmons, George Croll
American. Architect
b. Jul 8, 1865 in Wooster, Ohio
d. Jun 1947
Source: *WhAm 2*

Nimoy, Leonard
American. Actor
Played Mr. Spock on TV series "Star Trek," 1966-69.
b. Mar 26, 1931 in Boston, Massachusetts
Source: *ConAu 57; FilmgC; IntMPA 82; WhoAm 74, 76, 78, 80, 82; WhoHol A*

Nimzowitsch, Aron
Russian. Chess Player
b. 1886 in Latvia, Russia
d. 1935
Source: *BioIn 4, 10*

Nin, Anais
American. Author
Best known for diaries; wrote *A Spy in the House of Love,* 1954; *Delta of Venus,* 1977.
b. Feb 21, 1903 in Paris, France
d. Oct 14, 1977 in Los Angeles, California
Source: *AmAu&B; Au&Wr 71; ConAu 13R, 69; ConLC 1, 4, 8, 11, 14; ConNov 72, 76; DrAF 76; ModAL, SUP; OxAmL; RAdv 1; TwCA SUP; WrDr 76*

Nino, Pedro Alonzo
Spanish. Navigator of the Nina
b. 1468 in Monguer, Spain
d. 1505?
Source: *ApCAB; Drake*

Nitti, Francesco Saverio
Italian. Statesman
b. 1868
d. 1953
Source: *BioIn 3*

Nitty Gritty Dirt Band, The
[Ralph Barr; Chris Darrow; Jimmie Fadden; Jeff Hanna; Jim Ibbotson; Bruce Kunkel; John McEven; Leslie Thompson]
American. Musical Group
Source: *EncPR&S*

Niven, (James) David Graham
Scottish. Actor, Author
Won 1958 Oscar for *Separate Tables;* book *The Moon's A Balloon,* 1972, sold over four million copies.
b. Mar 1, 1910 in Kirriemuir, Scotland
Source: *BkPepl; CelR 73; ConAu 77; CurBio 57; IntMPA 75, 76, 77, 78, 79, 80, 81, 82; IntWW 75; MotPP; MovMk; OxFilm; Who 74; WhoAm 74, 76, 78, 80, 82; WhoHol A; WhoWor 74; WorEFlm; WrDr 76*

Nixon, Julie
see: Eisenhower, Julie Nixon

Nixon, Marni
American. Opera Singer
b. Feb 22, 1929 in Altadena, California
Source: *MotPP; WhoAm 74, 76, 78, 80, 82; WhoAmW 77; WhoHol; WhoMus 72*

Nixon, Patricia Ryan
American. Wife of Richard Nixon
b. Mar 16, 1912 in Ely, Nebraska
Source: *CurBio 70; NewYTBE 70*

Nixon, Richard Milhous
American. 37th US President
Watergate scandal lead to resignation, Aug 9, 1974.
b. Jan 9, 1913 in Yorba Linda, California
Source: *AmAu&B; BiDrAC; BiDrUSE; BioNews 74; BkPepl; CelR 73; ConAu 73; CurBio 48, 58, 69; EncAB-H; IntWW 74; NewYTBE 71, 72, 73; NewYTBS 74; WebAB; Who 82; WhoAm 74, 76, 78, 80, 82; WhoAmP 73; WhoE 74; WhoGov 72; WhoS&SW 73; WhoWest 74; WhoWor 74*

Nixon, Tricia
[Mrs. Edward Cox]
American. Daughter of Richard Nixon
b. Feb 21, 1946
Source: *NewYTBE 71*

Nizer, Louis
American. Lawyer, Author
b. Feb 6, 1902 in London, England
Source: *AmSCAP 66; BiE&WWA; CelR 73; ConAu 53; CurBio 55; IntMPA 75, 76, 77, 78, 79, 80, 81, 82; NewYTBE 71; NotNAT; St&PR 75; WebAB; WhoAm 74, 76, 78, 80, 82; WhoE 74; WhoWor 74; WhoWorJ 72; WrDr 76*

Nkomo, Joshua
South African. Politician
Minister of Home Affairs, 1980-81; without Portfolio, 1981--.
b. 1917 in Matopos, Rhodesia
Source: *BioIn 11; IntWW 74, 75, 76, 77, 78, 79, 80, 81; WhoModH*

Nkrumah, Kwame
Ghanaian. President
b. Sep 21, 1909 in British West Africa
d. Apr 27, 1972 in Conayry, Guinea
Source: *CurBio 53, 72; NewYTBE 72; WhAm 5*

Noah
Biblical Character
Source: *BioIn 10; NewCol 75*

Nobel, Alfred Bernhard
Swedish. Inventor, Philanthropist
Invented dynamite, 1866; willed funds for annual Nobel Prizes.
b. Oct 21, 1833 in Stockholm, Sweden
d. Dec 10, 1896 in San Remo, Italy
Source: *NewC; NewCol 75; REn*

Nobile, Umberto
Italian. Explorer, Airship Designer
b. Jan 21, 1885 in Naples, Italy
d. Jul 29, 1978 in Rome, Italy
Source: *BioIn 4, 8; ConAu 81; McGEWB*

Noble, Ray
English. Band Leader
b. 1908 in Brighton, England
d. 1978 in London, England
Source: *WhoHol A*

Noel, Cleo A
American. Ambassador to Sudan
b. Aug 6, 1918 in Oklahoma City, Oklahoma
d. Mar 1, 1973 in Khartoum, Sudan
Source: *WhAm 5*

Noffsinger, James P(hilip)
American. Educator
b. May 30, 1925 in Union City, Indiana
Source: *AmArch 70; DrAS 74H, 78H; IndAu 1917*

Nofziger, Lyn (Franklyn Curran)
American. Former Presidential Aide
b. Jun 8, 1924 in Bakersfield, California
Source: *BioIn 10, 11; CurBio 83; PolProf NF; WhoAmP 73, 75, 77*

Noguchi, Isamu
American. Sculptor, Landscape Designer
Works contributed to modern abstract art movement.
b. Nov 4, 1904 in Los Angeles, California
Source: *CelR 73; CurBio 43; DcCAA 71; IntWW 74; WebAB; WhoAm 74; WhoAmA 73; WhoWor 74; WomWMM*

Nolan, Bob
[Sons of the Pioneers]
American. Composer, Singer
b. 1908?
d. 1980 in Costa Mesa, California
Source: *BioIn 12*

Nolan, Doris
American. Actress
b. Jul 14, 1916 in New York, New York
Source: *FilmgC; ThFT; WhoHol A; WhoThe 77*

Nolan, Jeannette
American. Actress
b. Dec 30, 1911 in Los Angeles, California
Source: *FilmgC; WhoHol A*

Nolan, Jeannette Covert
American. Author
b. Mar 31, 1896 in Evansville, Indiana
d. Oct 12, 1974 in Indianapolis, Indiana
Source: *AmAu&B; Au&Wr 71; AuBYP; ConAu 5R, 53, 4NR; IndAu 1917; JBA 51; SmATA 2; WhAm 6; WhoAm 74*

Nolan, Kathy (Kathleen)
American. Actress
Former president of Screen Actors Guild; starred in "The Real McCoys," 1957-63.
b. Sep 27, 1933 in Saint Louis, Missouri
Source: *WhoAm 80; WhoHol A*

Nolan, Lloyd
American. Actor
b. Aug 11, 1902 in San Francisco, California
Source: *BiE&WWA; CmMov; CurBio 56; FilmgC; HolP 30; IntMPA 75, 76, 77, 78, 79, 80, 81, 82; MotPP; MovMk; NotNAT; WhoAm 74; WhoHol A; WhoThe 77; WhoWor 74; WorEFlm*

Noland, Kenneth Clifton
American. Artist
b. Apr 10, 1924 in Asheville, North Carolina
Source: *BioIn 6, 7, 8, 9, 11; BnEnAmA; CurBio 72; DcAmArt; McGDA; McGEWB; NewCol 75; WhoAm 76, 78, 80, 82*

Nolde, Emil
German. Artist
b. Aug 7, 1867 in Nolde, Germany
d. Apr 15, 1956 in Seebull, Sweden
Source: *AtlBL; OxGer; WhAm 4*

Noll, Chuck (Charles H)
American. Football Coach
b. Jan 5, 1932 in Cleveland, Ohio
Source: *BioIn 11; WhoFtbl 74*

Nolte, Henry R, Jr.
American. Automobile Executive
b. Mar 3, 1924 in New York, New York
Source: *St&PR 75; Ward 77*

Nolte, Nick
American. Actor
Played Tom Jordache on TV mini-series "Rich Man, Poor Man," 1976.
b. 1942 in Omaha, Nebraska
Source: *BkPepl; IntMPA 78, 79, 80, 81, 82; WhoAm 80, 82*

Nomura, Kichisaburo
Japanese. Admiral
b. Dec 1877 in Wakayama-Ken, Japan
d. May 8, 1964 in Tokyo, Japan
Source: *CurBio 41, 64; REn*

Nono, Luigi
Italian. Opera Composer
b. Jan 29, 1924 in Venice, Italy
Source: *DcCM; IntWW 74; WhoWor 74*

Noone, Jimmie
American. Jazz Musician
b. Apr 23, 1895 in Cut-Off, Louisiana
d. Apr 19, 1944 in Los Angeles, California
Source: *WhoJazz 72*

Nordhoff, Charles Bernard
American. Author, Traveler
b. Feb 1, 1887 in London, England
d. Apr 11, 1947 in Santa Barbara, California
Source: *AmAu&B; AmNov; AuBYP; CnDAL; CyWA; DcAmB S5; DcLEL; DcNAA; LongCTC; MnBBF; OxAmL*

Nordica, Lillian
[Lillian Norton]
American. Opera Singer
b. May 12, 1859 in Farmington, Maine
d. May 10, 1914 in Batavia, Indonesia
Source: *AmBi; ApCAB SUP; DcAmB; NotAW; TwCBDA; WebAB; WhAm 1; WhoStg 1906, 1908; WomWWA 14*

Nordli, Odvar
Norwegian. Prime Minister
b. Nov 3, 1927 in Stange, Norway
Source: *IntWW 74; WhoWor 78*

Norell, Norman
[Norman Levinson]
American. Costume Designer
b. Apr 20, 1900 in Noblesville, Indiana
d. Oct 25, 1972 in New York, New York
Source: *CurBio 64, 72; NewYTBE 72; WhAm 5; WorFshn*

Norena, Eide
[Kaja Hansen Eide]
Norwegian. Opera Singer
b. Apr 26, 1884 in Horten, Norway
d. Nov 19, 1968 in Switzerland
Source: *InWom*

Normand, Mabel
American. Actress
b. Nov 10, 1894 in Boston, Massachusetts
d. Feb 23, 1930 in Monrovia, California
Source: *Film 1; FilmgC; InWom; MotPP; MovMk; NotAW; OxFilm; TwYS; WhScrn 74, 77; WhoHol B; WomWMM; WorEFlm*

Norodom Sihanouk
Cambodian. Former King
b. Oct 31, 1922
Source: *BioIn 3, 4, 5, 6, 7, 8, 9, 10, 11; CurBio 54; IntWW 74; WhoWor 74*

Norris, Christopher
American. Actress
Appears on TV series "Trapper John, MD," 1979--.
b. Oct 7, 1943 in New York, New York
Source: *WhoHol A*

Norris, Frank(lin)
American. Author
Wrote *McTeague,* 1899; *The Pit,* 1903.
b. Mar 5, 1870 in Chicago, Illinois
d. Oct 25, 1902 in San Francisco, California
Source: *AmAu&B; AmBi; AmWr; AtlBL; BbD; BiD&SB; CasWL; Chambr 3; CnDAL; CrtT 3; CyWA; DcAmAu; DcAmB; DcBiA; DcLEL; DcNAA; EvLB; LongCTC; ModAL; OxAmL; OxEng; Pen AM; RAdv 1; REn; REnAL; TwCA, SUP; TwCBDA; TwCW; WebAB; WebE&AL; WhAm 1*

Norris, George William
American. Public Official
b. Jul 11, 1861 in Sandusky, Ohio
d. Sep 3, 1944 in McCook, Nebraska
Source: *BiDrAC; DcAmB S3; EncAB-H; OhA&B; WebAB; WhAm 2; WhAmP*

Norris, Paul
American. Cartoonist
b. Apr 26, 1914 in Greenville, Ohio
Source: *WorECom*

Norstad, Lauris
American. Air Force General
b. Mar 24, 1907 in Minneapolis, Minnesota
Source: *CurBio 48, 59; IntWW 74; St&PR 75; Who 74; WhoAm 74, 76, 78, 80, 82; WhoF&I 74; WhoWor 74*

North, Alex
American. Composer, Conductor
b. Dec 4, 1910 in Chester, Pennsylvania
Source: *AmSCAP 66; BiE&WWA; DcCM; FilmgC; IntMPA 75, 76, 77, 78, 79, 80, 81, 82; NotNAT; WhoAm 82; WorEFlm*

North, Frederick North, Baron
English. Prime Minister
b. Apr 13, 1732 in London, England
d. Aug 5, 1792 in London, England
Source: *BioIn 8, 9, 10; LinLib S; McGEWB; NewCol 75*

North, Jay
American. Actor
Played Dennis the Menance in TV series, 1959-63.
b. Aug 3, 1953 in North Hollywood, California
Source: *FilmgC; WhoHol A*

North, John Ringling
American. Circus Director
b. Aug 14, 1903 in Baraboo, Wisconsin
Source: *AmSCAP 66; CurBio 51; WhoAm 74, 76, 78, 80, 82*

North, Sheree
American. Actress
b. Jan 17, 1933 in Los Angeles, California
Source: *FilmgC; InWom; IntMPA 75, 76, 77, 78, 79, 80, 81, 82; MotPP; WhoHol A*

North, Sterling
American. Journalist, Author, Critic
b. Nov 4, 1906 in Edgerton, Wisconsin
d. Dec 21, 1974 in Whippany, New Jersey
Source: *AmAu&B; AmNov; Au&Wr 71; AuBYP; ConAu 5R, 53; CurBio 43, 75; NewYTBS 74; REnAL; SmATA 1; ThrBJA; TwCA, SUP; WhAm 6; WhoAm 74; WhoE 74*

Northcliffe, Alfred Charles William Harmsworth, Viscount
English. Newspaper Publisher
b. Jul 15, 1865 in Chapelizod, Ireland
d. Aug 14, 1922 in London, England
Source: *DcLEL; LongCTC; MnBBF; NewC; OxEng*

Northrop, John Knudsen
American. Aircraft Manufacturer
Founded Lockheed Aircraft, 1927; Northrop Aircraft, 1939.
b. Nov 10, 1895 in Newark, New Jersey
d. Feb 18, 1981 in Glendale, California
Source: *BioIn 1, 2, 11; CurBio 49, 81; IntYB 78, 79; NewYTBS 81; WebAB; WhAm 7; WhoAm 74*

Norton, Andre, pseud.
[Alice Mary Norton]
American. Author
b. Feb 17, 1912 in Cleveland, Ohio
Source: *AmAu&B; AuBYP; ConAu 1R, 2NR; CurBio 57; MorJA; OhA&B; SenS; SmATA 1; WorAu; WrDr 76*

Norton, Charles Eliot
American. Author, Educator
b. Nov 16, 1827 in Cambridge, Massachusetts
d. Oct 21, 1908 in Cambridge, Massachusetts
Source: *Alli, SUP; AmAu; AmAu&B; AmBi; ApCAB; BbD; BiD&SB; CarSB; Chambr 3; ChPo S1; CyAl 2; DcAmAu; DcAmB; DcNAA; EncAB-H; EvLB; LongCTC; OxAmL; Pen AM; REn; WebAB; WhAm 1*

Norton, Eleanor Holmes
American. Civic Leader
b. Jun 13, 1937 in Washington, DC
Source: *BioNews 75; NewYTBE 70*

Norton, Elliott
American. Drama Critic, Lecturer
b. May 17, 1903 in Boston, Massachusetts
Source: *BiE&WWA; CelR 73; WhoAm 74, 76, 78, 80, 82; WhoThe 72*

Norton, Jack
American. Actor
b. 1889 in New York, New York
d. Oct 15, 1958 in Saranac Lake, New York
Source: *FilmgC; MotPP; MovMk; Vers A; WhScrn 74, 77; WhoHol B*

Norton, Joshua Abraham
"Emperor Norton"
American. Eccentric
b. 1819
d. 1880
Source: *BioIn 10*

Norton, Ken(neth Howard)
American. Boxer
b. Aug 9, 1945 in Jacksonville, Illinois
Source: *BioIn 9, 10; WhoAm 80; WhoBox 74*

Norton-Taylor, Judy
American. Actress
Played Mary Ellen on "The Waltons."
b. Jan 29, 1958 in Santa Monica, California
Source: *BioIn 10, 11; WhoHol A*

Norvo, "Red" (Kenneth)
American. Jazz Musician
b. Mar 31, 1908 in Beardstown, Illinois
Source: *AmSCAP 66*

Norway, Nevil Shute
see: Shute, Nevil

Norwich, Alfred Duff Cooper, Viscount
English. Statesman, Author
b. Feb 22, 1890 in London, England
d. Jan 1, 1954 in Vigo, Spain
Source: *ChPo; CurBio 40, 54; DcLEL; EvLB; LongCTC; NewC; WhAm 3*

Norwich, Diana (Manners) Cooper, Viscountess
English. Actress
b. 1893
Source: *Au&Wr 71; InWom; LongCTC; NewC; Who 74*

Norworth, Jack
American. Actor
b. Jan 5, 1879 in Philadelphia, Pennsylvania
d. Sep 1, 1959 in Beverly Hills, California
Source: *AmSCAP 66; EncMT; OxThe; WhScrn 74, 77*

Nostradamus
[Michel de Notredame]
French. Astrologer, Physician
b. Dec 14, 1503 in Saint Remy, France
d. Jul 2, 1566 in Salon, France
Source: *NewC; OxFr; OxGer; REn*

Nott, John William Frederic
British. Defense Minister
Responsible for British military operations in Falkland Islands, 1982.
b. Feb 1, 1932 in London, England
Source: *IntYB 78, 79, 80, 81; NewYTBS 82; Who 74, 76, 78, 80, 82*

Nougues, Jean
French. Composer
b. Apr 25, 1875 in Bordeaux, France
d. Aug 28, 1932 in Paris, France
Source: *NewEOp 71*

Nourrit, Adolphe
French. Opera Singer
b. Mar 3, 1802 in Paris, France
d. Mar 8, 1839 in Naples, Italy
Source: *NewEOp 71*

Nouwen, Henri J M
Dutch. Priest, Author
b. Jan 24, 1932 in Nijerk, Netherlands
Source: *BioIn 5, 10, 11; ConAu 73*

Novaes, Guiomar
Brazilian. Musician
b. Feb 28, 1895 in Sao Paulo, Brazil
d. Mar 7, 1979 in Sao Paulo, Brazil
Source: *Baker 78; BiDAmM; BioIn 3, 4, 11; CurBio 53, 79; InWom; MusSN; NewYTBS 79; WhoAm 74; WhoAmW 66, 68, 70, 72, 74; WhoWor 74*

Novak, Kim (Marilyn)
American. Actress
Starred in *Vertigo,* 1959.
b. Feb 18, 1933 in Chicago, Illinois
Source: *CurBio 57; FilmgC; InWom; IntMPA 75, 76, 77, 78, 79, 80, 81, 82; MotPP; MovMk; OxFilm; WhoAm 74, 76, 78, 80, 82; WhoHol A; WorEFlm*

Novak, Robert
[Evans and Novak]
American. Journalist
b. Feb 26, 1931 in Joliet, Illinois
Source: *ConAu 13R; WhoAm 74, 76, 78, 80, 82*

Novak, Vitezslav
Czech. Composer
b. Dec 5, 1870 in Kamenitz, Bohemia
d. Jul 18, 1949 in Skutec, Czechoslovakia
Source: *DcCM*

Novalis
[Friedrich von Hardenberg]
German. Poet
b. May 2, 1772 in Halle, Germany
d. Mar 25, 1801 in Weissenfels, Germany
Source: *BbD; BiD&SB; CasWL; DcEnL; EuAu; EvEuW; OxEng; OxFr; OxGer; Pen EUR; REn*

Novarro, Ramon
Mexican. Actor
b. Feb 6, 1899 in Durango, Mexico
d. Oct 31, 1968 in Hollywood, California
Source: *CmMov; Film 1; FilmgC; MotPP; MovMk; OxFilm; TwYS; WhAm 5; WhScrn 74, 77; WorEFlm*

Novello, Ivor
[David Ivor Davies]
Welsh. Dramatist, Composer, Actor
b. Jan 15, 1893 in Cardiff, Wales
d. Mar 6, 1951 in London, England
Source: *BioIn 1, 2, 3, 4, 10; CnThe; DcLEL; EncMT; EncWT; EvLB; Film 2; FilmgC; LongCTC; McGEWD; ModWD; MotPP; NewC; NotNAT A, B; OxMus; OxThe; REn; TwCA SUP; TwCW; WhAm 4; WhE&EA; WhScrn 74, 77; WhThe; WhoHol B*

Novi, Carlo
see: Southside Johnny and the Asbury Jukes

Novotna, Jarmila
Czech. Opera Singer
b. Sep 23, 1907 in Prague, Czechoslovakia
Source: *CurBio 40; InWom; WhoAm 74; WhoMus 72; WhoWor 74*

Novotny, Antonin
Czech. Politician
b. Dec 10, 1904 in Prague, Czechoslovakia
d. Jan 28, 1975 in Prague, Czechoslovakia
Source: *CurBio 58; IntWW 74; WhAm 6*

Nowicki, Matthew
American. Architect
b. 1910 in Chitai, China
d. Aug 31, 1950 in Ityai el Barud, Egypt
Source: *BioIn 2, 3, 8, 10; EncMA; McGDA*

Nowlan, Phil
[Frank Phillips]
American. Comic Strip Creator
b. 1888 in Philadelphia, Pennsylvania
d. Feb 1, 1940 in Philadelphia, Pennsylvania
Source: *WorECom*

Noyes, Alfred
American. Author
b. Sep 16, 1880 in Staffordshire, England
d. Jun 28, 1958 in Philadelphia, Pennsylvania
Source: *BkC 6; CathA 1930; Chambr 3; ChPo, S1, S2; DcLEL; EvLB; LongCTC; ModBrL; NewC; OxEng; Pen ENG; REn; TwCA, SUP; TwCW; WhAm 3; WhoLA*

Noyes, Blanche Wilcox
American. Aviatrix, Actress
Co-designed twin motored plane, 1933.
b. Jun 23, 1900 in Cleveland, Ohio
d. 1981 in Washington, DC
Source: *BioIn 1, 5; InWom; WhoAm 74, 76; WhoAmW 58, 61, 66, 68, 70, 72, 74*

Noyes, David
American. Journalist, Businessman
b. 1898
d. Aug 7, 1981 in Los Angeles, California
Source: *BioIn 12; ConAu 104*

Noyes, Frank B
American. Newspaper Executive
b. Jul 7, 1863 in Washington, DC
d. Dec 1, 1948 in Washington, DC
Source: *DcAmB S4; WhAm 2*

Noyes, John Humphrey
American. Social Reformer
b. Sep 3, 1811 in Brattleboro, Vermont
d. Apr 13, 1886 in Niagara Falls, ON
Source: *Alli SUP; AmAu; AmAu&B; AmBi; ApCAB; BbD; BiD&SB; DcAmAu; DcAmB; EncAB-H; OxAmL; REn; REnAL; WebAB; WhAm H*

Noziere, Violette
French. Murderer
b. 1915
Source: *LookW*

Nu, U Thakin
Burmese. Socialist Premier
b. May 25, 1907
Source: *CurBio 51; DcOrL 2; IntWW 74; Pen CL; WhoWor 74*

Nuffield, William Richard Morris, Viscount
English. Automobile Manufacturer
b. Oct 10, 1877 in Worcester, England
d. Aug 22, 1963
Source: *BioIn 1, 2, 3, 4, 5, 6, 7, 8, 11; CurBio 41, 63*

Nugent, Edward
American. Actor
b. 1904 in New York, New York
Source: *TwYS; WhoHol A*

Nugent, Elliott
American. Actor, Dramatist
b. Sep 20, 1899 in Dover, Ohio
d. Aug 9, 1980 in New York, New York
Source: *AmAu&B; BiE&WWA; CnMD; ConAu 5R; ConDr 73, 77; CurBio 44, 80; Film 2; FilmgC; IntMPA 75, 76, 77, 78, 79; McGEWB; ModWD; MovMk; NotNAT; OhA&B; WhThe; WhoAm 74; WhoHol A; WhoThe 77; WhoWor 74; WorEFlm; WrDr 76*

Nugent, Luci Baines
see: Johnson, Luci Baines

Nugent, Nelle
American. Motion Picture Producer
b. Mar 24, 1939 in Jersey City, New Jersey
Source: *NewYTBS 81; WhoAm 82*

Nugent, Patrick
American. TV Executive
b. 1943
Source: *BioIn 7*

Nugent, Ted
[The Amboy Dukes]
"Motor City Mad Man"
American. Rock Singer
Wears earplugs while performing.
b. 1949 in Detroit, Michigan
Source: *BioIn 11; BkPepl; WhoAm 82*

Nuitter, Charles Louis
[Charles Louis Truinet]
French. Author, Musician, Librettist
b. Apr 24, 1828 in Paris, France
d. Feb 24, 1899 in Paris, France
Source: *NewEOp 71*

Nungesser, Charles
French. Aviator
b. 1892
d. 1927
Source: *BioIn 5, 8, 11; WhoMilH 76*

Nunn, Harold F
American. Shoe Manufacturer
b. Feb 25, 1915 in New York, New York
Source: *WhoF&I 74*

Nunn, Sam(uel Augustus, Jr.)
American. Senator
b. Sep 8, 1938 in Perry, Georgia
Source: *BioIn 9, 10, 11; CngDr 74; CurBio 80; IntWW 74; WhoAmP 73; WhoAmL 78*

Nunn, Trevor Robert
English. Theatrical Director
b. Jan 14, 1940 in Ipswich, England
Source: *CnThe; CurBio 80; IntWW 77, 78, 79; Who 74, 80; WhoThe 72, 77; WhoWor 74*

Nur el Hussein
[Lisa Halaby]
American. Wife of King Hussein
b. 1951?
Source: *BioIn 11*

Nureyev, Rudolf
Russian. Ballet Dancer
Defected from Soviet Union, 1961; partnered Margot Fonteyn.
b. Mar 17, 1938 in Irkutsk, U.S.S.R.
Source: *BioNews 74; BkPepl; CelR 73; CurBio 63; IntWW 74; NewYTBE 70; NewYTBS 74; Who 74; WhoAm 74; WhoHol A; WhoWor 74*

Nurmi, Paavo
Finnish. Track Athlete
b. Jun 13, 1897 in Turku, Finland
d. Oct 2, 1973 in Helsinki, Finland
Source: *NewYTBE 73; WhoTr&F 73*

Nuvolari, Tazio Giorgio
Italian. Auto Racer
b. 1892?
d. 1953
Source: *BioIn 3, 4, 5, 6, 8*

Nuyen, France
American. Actress
b. Jul 31, 1939 in Marseilles, France
Source: *BiE&WWA; FilmgC; InWom; MotPP; WhoAm 74; WhoHol A*

Nyad, Diana
American. Swimmer
First to swim from Bahamas to US, 1979.
b. Aug 22, 1949 in New York, New York
Source: *BioIn 10; CurBio 79*

Nye, Edgar Wilson (Bill)
American. Humorist, Author
b. Aug 25, 1850 in Shirley, Maine
d. Feb 22, 1896 in Arden, North Carolina
Source: *Alli SUP; AmAu; AmAu&B; AmBi; ApCAB; BbD; BiD&SB; ChPo S1, S2; CnDAL; DcAmAu; DcAmB; DcLEL; DcNAA; OxAmL; REnAL; TwCBDA; WhAm H; WisWr*

Nye, Gerald Prentice
American. Senator, Editor
b. Dec 19, 1892 in Hortonville, Wisconsin
d. Jul 17, 1971 in Washington, DC
Source: *BiDrAC; CurBio 41, 71; EncAB-H; NewYTBE 71; WhAm 5*

Nye, Louis
American. Comedian, Actor
Source: *WhoHol A*

Nye, Russel Blaine
American. Author, Educator
b. Feb 17, 1913 in Viola, Wisconsin
Source: *AmAu&B; Au&Wr 71; ConAu 1R, 4NR; CurBio 45; OxAmL; REnAL; TwCA SUP; WhoAm 74; WrDr 76*

Nyerere, Julius Kambarage
African. President
b. Mar 1922 in Butiama, Tanganyika
Source: *AfrA; CurBio 63; IntWW 74; Who 74; WhoGov 72; WhoWor 74*

Nyiregyhazi, Ervin
American. Musician
b. Jan 19, 1903 in Budapest, Hungary
Source:

Nykvist, Sven Vilhem
Swedish. Cinematographer
b. Dec 3, 1922 in Moheda, Sweden
Source: *DcFM; FilmEn; FilmgC; IntMPA 75, 76, 77, 78, 79, 80, 81; OxFilm; WhoAm 82; WorEFlm*

Nype, Russell
American. Actor
b. Apr 26, 1924 in Zion, Illinois
Source: *BiE&WWA; EncMT; NotNAT; WhoHol A; WhoThe 77*

Nyro, Laura
American. Singer, Composer
b. Oct 18, 1947 in Bronx, New York
Source: *CelR 73; RkOn; WhoAm 74, 76, 78, 80, 82*

Nystrom, Bob (Thor Robert)
Swedish. Hockey Player
b. Oct 10, 1952 in Stockholm, Sweden
Source: *HocReg; NewYTBS 75*

O

Oak Ridge Boys, The
[Duane Allen; Joe Bonsall; Bill Golden; Richard Sterban]
American. Singing Group
Hit song "Elvira," 1980.
Source: *WhoRock 81*

Oakie, Jack
[Lewis D Offield]
American. Actor
b. Nov 12, 1903 in Sedalia, Missouri
d. Feb 23, 1978 in Los Angeles, California
Source: *CmMov; FilmgC; HolP 30; IntMPA 75, 76, 77; MotPP; MovMk; TwYS; WhoHol A*

Oakes, Randi
American. Actress, Model
Starred in TV series "CHIPs."
b. 1952? in Randalia, Iowa
Source: *BioIn 12*

Oakey, Phil
see: Human League

Oakland, Simon
American. Actor
b. 1922 in New York, New York
Source: *FilmgC; IntMPA 75, 76, 77, 78, 79, 80, 81, 82; WhoAm 82; WhoHol A*

Oakley, Annie
[Mrs. Frank E Butler; Phoebe Anne Oakley Mozee]
American. Sharpshooter
Performed in Buffalo Bill's Wild West Show, 1885-1902.
b. Aug 13, 1860 in Darke County, Ohio
d. Nov 2, 1926 in Greenville, Ohio
Source: *DcAmB; Film 1; FilmgC; HerW; InWom; NotAW; REnAL; WebAB; WhAm HA, 4; WhScrn 77; WhoHol B*

Oakley, Don
American. Journalist
b. Nov 3, 1927 in Pittsburgh, Pennsylvania
Source: *ConAu 29R; SmATA 8*

Oates, John
[Hall and Oates]
American. Singer, Songwriter
Duo formed in 1967; hits "Rich Girl," 1977; "Maneater," 1982.
b. 1950 in New York, New York
Source: *IlEncRk; LilREn 78; WhoRock 81*

Oates, Joyce Carol
American. Author
b. Jun 16, 1938 in Lockport, New York
Source: *AmAu&B; AuNews 1; BioNews 74; CelR 73; ConAu 5R; ConLC 1, 2, 3, 6, 9, 11, 15; ConNov 72; DrAF 76; EncWL; ForWC 70; ModAL SUP; RAdv 1; WhoAm 74, 76, 78, 80, 82; WhoWor 74; WrDr 76*

Oates, Titus
English. Fabricator of Popish Plot
b. 1649 in Oakham, England
d. Jul 12, 1705 in London, England
Source: *Alli; NewC; REn*

Oates, Warren
American. Actor
Starred in *In the Heat of the Night,* 1967; *Stripes,* 1981.
b. Jul 5, 1928 in Depoy, Kentucky
d. Apr 3, 1982 in Hollywood Hills, California
Source: *BioIn 9; CmMov; FilmEn; FilmgC; IntMPA 75, 76, 77, 78, 79, 80, 81, 82; MovMk; NewYTBS 82; WhoAm 82; WhoHol A*

Obasanjo, Olusegun
Nigerian. Head of State
b. May 5, 1937 in Abeokuto, Nigeria
Source: *BioIn 11; WhoWor 78*

Obata, Gyo
American. Architect
b. Feb 28, 1923 in San Francisco, California
Source: *AmArch 70; WhoAm 74, 76, 78, 80, 82; WhoF&I 74; WhoWor 74*

Ober, Philip
American. Actor
Appeared in "I Love Lucy" with second wife, Vivian Vance.
b. Mar 23, 1902 in Fort Payne, Alabama
d. Sep 13, 1982 in Santa Monica, California
Source: *BiE&WWA; FilmgC; IntMPA 75, 76, 77, 78, 79, 80, 81, 82; NewYTBS 82; NotNAT; Vers A; WhThe; WhoHol A*

Oberon, Merle
American. Actress
b. Feb 19, 1911 in Hobart, Tasmania
d. Nov 23, 1979 in Los Angeles, California
Source: *CelR 73; CmMov; CurBio 41; FilmgC; InWom; IntMPA 77, 75; MotPP; MovMk; OxFilm; ThFT; Who 74; WhoAm 74; WhoHol A; WomWMM; WorEFlm*

Obolensky, Serge
Russian. Businessman
b. Oct 3, 1890 in Tsarskoe Selo, Russia
d. Sep 29, 1978 in Grosse Pointe, Michigan
Source: *BusPN; CelR 73; CurBio 59; NewYTBE 70; WhoAm 74*

Oboler, Arch
American. Dramatist
b. Dec 6, 1909 in Chicago, Illinois
Source: *AmAu&B; BiE&WWA; CnMD; CurBio 40; DcFM; FilmgC; IntMPA 75, 76, 77, 78, 79, 80, 81, 82; ModWD; NotNAT; REnAL; TwCA SUP; WhoAm 74; WorEFlm*

Obote, (Apollo) Milton
Ugandan. President
President, 1966-71; deposed by military coup; re-elected, 1980--.
b. 1924 in Akokoro, Uganda
Source: *CurBio 81; IntWW 77, 78, 79, 80, 81*

Obraztsova, Elena
Russian. Opera Singer
b. 1940
Source: *BioIn 11*

Obregon, Alvaro
Mexican. Statesman
b. Feb 17, 1880 in Alamos, Mexico
d. Jul 17, 1928 in San Angel, Mexico
Source: *REn*

O'Brian, Hugh
[Hugh Krampe]
American. Actor
b. Apr 19, 1930 in Rochester, New York
Source: *AmSCAP 66; BiE&WWA; CelR 73; CurBio 58; FilmgC; IntMPA 75, 76, 77, 78, 79, 80, 81, 82; MotPP; MovMk; WhoAm 74, 76, 78, 80, 82; WhoHol A; WhoThe 77*

O'Brian, Jack
American. Journalist
b. Aug 16, 1914 in Buffalo, New York
Source: *IntMPA 75, 76, 77, 78, 79, 80, 81, 82; WhoAm 82*

O'Brien, Conor Cruise
[Donat O'Donnell, pseud.]
Irish. Author, Diplomat
b. Nov 3, 1917 in Dublin, Ireland
Source: *ConAu 65; CurBio 67; IntWW 74; Who 74; WorAu; WrDr 76*

O'Brien, Edmond
American. Actor
b. Sep 10, 1915 in New York, New York
Source: *FilmgC; IntMPA 75, 76, 77, 78, 79, 80, 81, 82; MotPP; MovMk; OxFilm; WhoAm 74, 76, 78, 80, 82; WhoHol A; WorEFlm*

O'Brien, Edna
Irish. Author
b. Dec 15, 1931 in Tuamgraney, Ireland
Source: *CasWL; ConAu 1R; ConLC 3, 5, 8, 13; ConNov 72, 76; CurBio 80; NewC; TwCW; Who 74; WorAu; WrDr 76*

O'Brien, George
American. Actor
b. Apr 19, 1900 in San Francisco, California
Source: *CmMov; FilmgC; IntMPA 75, 76, 77, 78, 79, 80, 81, 82; MovMk; TwYS; WhoHol A; WorEFlm*

O'Brien, John J
American. Basketball Player, Executive
b. Nov 4, 1888 in Brooklyn, New York
d. Dec 9, 1967 in Rockville Centre, New York
Source: *BioIn 8, 9; WhoBbl 73*

O'Brien, Larry (Lawrence Francis)
American. NBA Commissioner
b. Jul 7, 1917 in Springfield, Massachusetts
Source: *BiDrUSE; ConAu 57; CurBio 61; IntWW 74; NewYTBE 70; WhoAm 74, 76, 78, 80, 82; WhoAmP 73; WhoS&SW 73; WrDr 76*

O'Brien, Margaret (Angela Maxine)
American. Actress
Won Oscar for *Meet Me in St. Louis,* 1944.
b. Jan 15, 1937 in San Diego, California
Source: *FilmgC; InWom; IntMPA 75, 76, 77, 78, 79, 80, 81, 82; MotPP; MovMk; WhoAm 74, 76, 78, 80, 82; WhoHol A; WorEFlm*

O'Brien, Parry
American. Track Athlete
b. Jan 28, 1932 in Santa Monica, California
Source: *WhoTr&F 73*

O'Brien, Pat (William Joseph Patrick)
American. Actor
Starred in *Knute Rockne-All American,* 1940.
b. Nov 11, 1899 in Milwaukee, Wisconsin
Source: *BiE&WWA; CurBio 66; FilmgC; IntMPA 75, 76, 77, 78, 79, 80, 81, 82; MotPP; MovMk; NotNAT; OxFilm; TwYS; WhoHol A*

O'Brien, Willis Harold
American. Animator
b. 1886 in Oakland, California
d. Nov 8, 1962 in Hollywood, California
Source: *BioIn 6; CmMov; EncSF; FanAl; FilmgC; ObitOF 79*

O'Brien-Moore, Erin
American. Actress
b. 1908 in Los Angeles, California
d. May 3, 1979 in Los Angeles, California
Source: *BioIn 11; NewYTBS 79; ThFT; WhThe; WhoHol A*

O'Callahan, Jack
[United States Olympic Hockey Team-1980]
American. Hockey Player
b. Jul 24, 1957 in Charleston, Massachusetts
Source: *HocReg*

Ocasek, Ric
see: Cars, The

O'Casey, Sean
Irish. Dramatist
b. Mar 30, 1880 in Dublin, Ireland
d. Sep 18, 1964 in Torquay, England
Source: *AtlBL; BiE&WWA; CasWL; Chambr 3; CnMD; CnMWL; CnThe; ConAu 89; ConLC 1, 5, 9, 11, 15; CroCD; CurBio 62, 64; CyWA; DcLEL; EncWL; EvLB; FilmgC; LongCTC; McGEWD; ModBrL, SUP; ModWD; NewC; NewYTBE 72; OxEng; OxThe; Pen ENG; PlP&P; RComWL; REn; REnWD; TwCA, SUP; TwCW; WebE&AL; WhAm 4; WhoTwCL*

Ochs, Adolph S, II
American. Newspaper Executive
b. Apr 14, 1885 in Chattanooga, Tennessee
d. May 1974
Source: *BioIn 10*

Ochs, Adolph Simon
American. Newspaper Publisher
b. Mar 12, 1858 in Cincinnati, Ohio
d. Apr 8, 1935 in Chattanooga, Tennessee
Source: *AmAu&B; AmBi; EncAB-H; OxAmL; REn; REnAL; WebAB; WhAm 1*

Ochs, Phil(ip David)
American. Singer, Political Activist
b. Dec 19, 1940 in El Paso, Texas
d. Apr 9, 1976 in Far Rockaway, New York
Source: *AmSCAP 66; ConAu 65; ConLC 17; EncFCWM 69; NewYTBE 71*

Ochsner, (Edward William) Alton
American. Surgeon, Teacher
b. May 4, 1896 in Kimball, South Dakota
d. Sep 24, 1981 in New Orleans, Louisiana
Source: *AmM&WS 73P, 79P; BioIn 1, 2, 3, 4, 7, 8; ConAu 17R; CurBio 66, 81; IntWW 76, 77, 78; WhoAm 78, 80; WhoS&SW 73, 75, 76*

Ochterveldt, Jacob Lucasz
Dutch. Artist
b. 1634
d. 1708
Source: *McGDA*

Ockham, William of
English. Philosopher
b. 1290? in Surrey, England
d. 1349? in Munich, Bavaria
Source: *Alli; BiD&SB; BrAu; CasWL; DcEnL; EvLB; NewC; NewCol 75; OxEng; REn*

O'Connell, Arthur
American. Actor
b. Mar 29, 1908 in New York, New York
d. May 19, 1981 in Los Angeles, California
Source: *BiE&WWA; FilmgC; IntMPA 75, 76, 77, 78, 79, 80, 81; MovMk; NewYTBS 81; NotNAT; WhAm 7; WhoAm 74, 76, 78, 80; WhoThe 77, 81*

O'Connell, Daniel
"The Liberator"
Irish. Political Leader
b. Aug 6, 1775 in Cahirsiveen, Ireland
d. May 15, 1847 in Genoa, Italy
Source: *Alli; BiD&SB; REn*

O'Connell, Helen
American. Singer
b. 1921 in Lima, Ohio
Source: *InWom; WhoHol A*

O'Connell, Hugh
American. Actor
b. Aug 4, 1898 in New York, New York
d. Jan 19, 1943 in Hollywood, California
Source: *CurBio 43; WhScrn 74, 77; WhoHol B*

O'Connor, Basil
American. Lawyer
b. Jan 8, 1892 in Taunton, Massachusetts
d. Mar 9, 1972 in Phoenix, Arizona
Source: *CurBio 44, 72; NewYTBE 72; WhAm 5*

O'Connor, Carroll
American. Actor
Star of "All in the Family," 1971--; won four Emmys.
b. Aug 2, 1924 in New York, New York
Source: *BioNews 74; BkPepl; CelR 73; CurBio 72; FilmgC; IntMPA 75, 76, 77, 78, 79, 80, 81, 82; MovMk; NewYTBE 71; WhoAm 82; WhoHol A*

O'Connor, Donald
American. Dancer, Singer, Actor
b. Aug 28, 1925 in Chicago, Illinois
Source: *AmSCAP 66; CmMov; CurBio 55; FilmgC; HolP 40; IntMPA 75, 76, 77, 78, 79, 80, 81, 82; MotPP; MovMk; OxFilm; WhoAm 74, 76, 78, 80, 82; WhoHol A; WorEFlm*

O'Connor, Edwin Greene
American. Author
Won Pulitzer Prize, 1962, for *The Edge of Sadness.*
b. Jul 29, 1918 in Providence, Rhode Island
d. Mar 23, 1968 in Boston, Massachusetts
Source: *AmAu&B; ConAu 25R, 93; ConLC 14; CurBio 63, 68; ModAL; OxAmL; Pen AM; REnAL; WhAm 5; WorAu*

O'Connor, Flannery
American. Author
b. Mar 25, 1925 in Savannah, Georgia
d. Aug 3, 1964 in Milledgeville, Georgia
Source: *AmAu&B; AmWr; ConAu 1R, 3NR; ConLC 1, 2, 3, 10, 13, 15; ConNov 76; CurBio 58, 65; EncWL; InWom; ModAL, SUP; OxAmL; Pen AM; RAdv 1; REn; REnAL; TwCW; WebE&AL; WhAm 4; WhoTwCL; WorAu*

O'Connor, Frank, pseud.
[Michael O'Donovan]
Irish. Author
Stories record realities of life in Ireland.
b. 1903 in Cork, Ireland
d. Mar 10, 1966 in Dublin, Ireland
Source: *AmAu&B; AtlBL; CasWL; ConAu 25R, 93; DcLEL; EvLB; LongCTC; ModBrL, SUP; NewC; OxEng; Pen ENG; RAdv 1; REn; TwCA SUP; WhAm 4*

O'Connor, Sandra Day
American. Supreme Court Justice
First woman Supreme Court justice; nominated by President Reagan, 1981.
b. Mar 26, 1930 in El Paso, Texas
Source: *AmBench 79; CurBio 82; WhoAm 82; WhoAmL 79; WhoAmP 73, 75, 77, 79; WhoAmW 74, 75, 79; WhoWest 78; WomPO 76*

O'Connor, Thomas Power
Irish. Journalist
b. Oct 5, 1848 in Athlone, Ireland
d. Nov 18, 1929
Source: *Alli SUP; DcLEL; LongCTC; NewC; OxEng*

O'Connor, Una
Irish. Actress
b. Oct 23, 1881 in Belfast, Northern Ireland
d. Feb 4, 1959 in New York, New York
Source: *FilmgC; MotPP; MovMk; ThFT; Vers A; WhScrn 74, 77; WhoHol B*

Octavia
Roman. Wife of Marc Antony
b. 69BC
d. 11BC
Source: *InWom; REn*

Octavius Caesar
see: Augustus

O'Dalaigh, Cearbhall
Irish. Jurist
b. Feb 12, 1911
d. Mar 21, 1978 in Sneem, Ireland
Source: *WhoWor 74*

O'Day, Anita
[Anita Colton]
American. Singer
b. Dec 18, 1919 in Chicago, Illinois
Source: *BiDAmM; BioIn 11; CmpEPM; EncJzS 70; InWom; WhoAmW 70, 72, 74; WhoHol A*

O'Day, Dawn
[Anne Shirley]
American. Actress, Journalist
b. 1918
Source: *FilmgC; MotPP; MovMk; ThFT; TwYS; WhoHol A*

Ode, Robert C
[The Hostages]
American. Former Hostage in Iran
b. Dec 10, 1915 in Illinois
Source: *NewYTBS 81; USBiR 74*

O'Dell, Scott
American. Author
Wrote *Island of the Blue Dolphins,* 1960; *The Black Pearl,* 1967.
b. May 23, 1903 in Los Angeles, California
Source: *AmAu&B; AmNov; AnCL; Au&ICB; AuBYP; BkCL; ChlLR 1; ConAu 61; MorJA; PiP; SenS; Str&VC; WhoAm 74, 76, 78, 80, 82; WhoWor 74*

Odets, Clifford
American. Dramatist
b. Jul 18, 1906 in Philadelphia, Pennsylvania
d. Aug 14, 1963 in Los Angeles, California
Source: *AmAu&B; CasWL; CnDAL; CnMD; CnMWL; CnThe; ConAu 85; ConLC 2; CroCD; CurBio 41, 63; CyWA; DcFM; DcLEL; EncWL; EvLB; FilmgC; LongCTC; McGEWD; ModAL; ModWD; OxAmL; OxEng; OxFilm; OxThe; Pen AM; PlP&P; REn; REnAL; REnWD; TwCA, SUP; TwCW; WebAB; WebE&AL; WhAm 4; WhoTwCL; WorEFlm*

Odetta
[Odetta Homes Felious Gordon]
American. Singer, Musician
b. Dec 31, 1930 in Birmingham, Alabama
Source: *InWom; WhoHol A; WhoWor 74*

Odlum, Floyd Bostwick
American. Financier
b. Mar 30, 1892 in Union City, Michigan
d. Jun 17, 1976
Source: *CurBio 41; IntWW 74; St&PR 75; WhoAm 74*

O'Doherty, Brian
Irish. Sculptor
b. 1934 in Ballaghaderreen, Ireland
Source: *WhoAmA 73*

O'Donnell, Cathy
American. Actress
b. Jul 6, 1925 in Siluria, Alabama
d. Apr 11, 1970 in Los Angeles, California
Source: *FilmgC; MotPP; WhScrn 74, 77; WhoHol B*

O'Donnell, Emmett
"Rosie"
American. Military Leader
b. Sep 15, 1906 in Brooklyn, New York
d. Dec 26, 1971 in McLean, Virginia
Source: *CurBio 48, 71; WhAm 5*

O'Donnell, Kenneth
American. Government Official
Best friend of John F Kennedy; wrote *Johnny We Hardly Knew Ye.*
b. Mar 4, 1924
d. Sep 9, 1977 in Boston, Massachusetts
Source: *ConAu 73*

O'Donnell, Peter
English. Author
b. Apr 11, 1920 in London, England
Source: *ScF&FL 1; TwCCr&M*

O'Donovan, Michael
see: O'Connor, Frank, pseud.

O'Driscoll, Martha
American. Actress
b. 1922 in Tulsa, Oklahoma
Source: *FilmgC; WhoHol A*

Oduber, Daniel
Costa Rican. President
b. Aug 25, 1921 in San Jose, Costa Rica
Source: *CurBio 77*

O'Dwyer, Paul
American. Lawyer, Politician
b. Jun 29, 1907 in Bohola, Ireland
Source: *ConAu 97; CurBio 69; NewYTBE 70*

O'Dwyer, Sloan Simpson
American. Wife of William O'Dwyer
b. 1917
Source: *BioIn 10*

O'Dwyer, William
American. Mayor, Diplomat
Mayor of NY City, 1946-50; ambassador to Mexico, 1950-52.
b. Jul 11, 1890 in Bohola, Ireland
d. Nov 24, 1964 in New York, New York
Source: *CurBio 41, 47, 65; WhAm 4*

Oenslager, Donald Mitchell
American. Scenic Designer
b. Mar 7, 1902 in Harrisburg, Pennsylvania
d. Jun 21, 1975 in Bedford, New York
Source: *BiE&WWA; ConAu 57, 61; CurBio 46; OxThe; PlP&P; WhAm 6; WhoAm 74; WhoAmA 73; WhoWor 74*

Oersted, Hans Christian
Danish. Physicist, Chemist
b. Aug 14, 1777 in Rudkobing, Denmark
d. Mar 9, 1851 in Copenhagen, Denmark
Source: *BioIn 2, 3, 8, 9; McGEWB*

Oerter, Al(fred A)
American. Track Athlete
Won gold medals in discus four consecutive Olympics, 1956, 1960, 1964, 1968.
b. Sep 19, 1936 in Astoria, New York
Source: *BioIn 8*

Oester, Ron(ald John)
American. Baseball Player
b. May 5, 1956 in Cincinnati, Ohio
Source: *BaseEn*

O'Faolain, Sean
Irish. Author
b. Feb 22, 1900 in Cork, Ireland
Source: *CasWL; CathA 1930; ConAu 61; ConLC 1, 7, 14; ConNov 72, 76; CyWA; DcLEL; EncWL; EvLB; IntWW 74; LongCTC; ModBrL, SUP; NewC; Pen ENG; RAdv 1; REn; TwCA, SUP; TwCW; WhoAm 74; WhoWor 74; WrDr 76*

Offenbach, Jacques
[Jacques Eberst]
French. Musician, Composer
b. Jun 20, 1819 in Cologne, Germany
d. Oct 4, 1880 in Paris, France
Source: *AtlBL; OxFr; PlP&P; REn*

O'Flaherty, Liam
Irish. Author
b. Aug 28, 1896 in County Galway, Ireland
Source: *CasWL; Chambr 3; ConAu 101; ConLC 5; ConNov 72, 76; CyWA; DcLEL; EncWL; EvLB; IntWW 74; LongCTC; ModBrL, SUP; NewC; OxEng; Pen ENG; REn; TwCA, SUP; TwCW; Who 74; WhoWor 74; WrDr 76*

Ogdon, John Andrew Howard
English. Musician, Composer
b. Jan 27, 1937
Source: *IntWW 74; Who 74; WhoMus 72; WhoWor 74*

Ogg, Oscar
American. Type Designer, Calligrapher
b. Dec 13, 1908 in Richmond, Virginia
d. Aug 10, 1971
Source: *ConAu 33R; ConAu P-1; NewYTBE 71; WhoGrA*

Ogilvie, Richard Buell
American. Former Governor
b. Feb 22, 1923 in Kansas City, Missouri
Source: *IntWW 74; WhoAm 74; WhoAmP 73; WhoGov 72; WhoMW 74*

Ogilvy, David Mackenzie
English. Advertising Executive
b. Jun 23, 1911 in West Horsley, England
Source: *CurBio 61; IntWW 74; Who 74; WhoAdv 72*

Ogilvy, Ian
British. Actor
b. Sep 30, 1943
Source: *FilmgC; WhoHol A*

Oglethorpe, James Edward
English. Colonizer
MP, 1722-54; founded GA, 1733.
b. Dec 22, 1696 in London, England
d. Jun 30, 1785 in Essex, England
Source: *AmBi; ApCAB; BiDSA; DcAmB; Drake; OxAmL; REnAL; TwCBDA; WebAB; WhAm H*

O'Grady, Sean
American. Boxer
b. Feb 10, 1959 in Oklahoma City, Oklahoma
Source: *BioIn 12; NewYTBS 77*

Oh, Sadaharu
Japanese. Baseball Player
b. May 5, 1940 in Tokyo, Japan
Source: *BioIn 11*

O'Hair, Madalyn Murray
American. Atheist, Lawyer
Founded United World Atheists, 1976.
b. Apr 13, 1919 in Pittsburgh, Pennsylvania
Source: *BioNews 75; ConAu 61; WhoAm 74, 76, 78, 80, 82; WhoRel 75*

O'Hanlon, Virginia
see: Douglas, Laura Virginia O'Hanlon

O'Hara, Fiske
American. Actor
b. May 1, 1878
d. Aug 2, 1945 in Hollywood, California
Source: *WhScrn 74, 77; WhoHol B*

O'Hara, Jill
American. Actress
b. Aug 23, 1947 in Warren, Pennsylvania
Source: *EncMT; WhoHol A*

O'Hara, John Henry
American. Author
b. Jan 31, 1905 in Pottsville, Pennsylvania
d. Apr 11, 1970 in Princeton, New Jersey
Source: *AmAu&B; AmNov; AmWr; BiE&WWA; CasWL; CnDAL; CnMD; ConAmA; ConAu 5R, 25R; ConLC 1, 2, 3, 6, 11; CurBio 41, 70; CyWA; DcLEL; EncWL; EvLB; FilmgC; LongCTC; ModAL, SUP; OxAmL; OxEng; Pen AM; RAdv 1; REn; REnAL; TwCA, SUP; TwCW; WebE&AL; WhAm 5; WhoTwCL; WorEFlm*

O'Hara, Mary
Irish. Singer, Musician
b. 1935?
Source: *BioIn 11*

O'Hara, Mary
[Mary O'Hara Alsop; Mary Sture-Vasa]
American. Author
Wrote *My Friend Flicka,* 1941.
b. Jul 10, 1885 in Cape May, New Jersey
d. Oct 15, 1980 in Chevy Chase, Maryland
Source: *AmAu&B; ConAu 9R, 104, 4NR; CurBio 44, 81; LinLib L; REn; REnAL; SmATA 2; TwCA SUP; TwCCW 78; WhoAm 74, 76, 78; WhoAmW 58, 61, 66, 68, 70, 72, 74; WrDr 80*

O'Hara, Maureen
[Maureen Fitzsimmons]
American. Actress
b. Aug 21, 1921 in Milltown, Ireland
Source: *CmMov; CurBio 53; FilmgC; InWom; IntMPA 75, 76, 77, 78, 79, 80, 81, 82; MotPP; MovMk; OxFilm; ThFT; WhoAm 74; WhoHol A; WomWMM; WorEFlm*

O'Hara, Patrick
[Irish Hunger Strikers]
"Patsy"
Irish. Jailed INLA Member
Died on 61st day of hunger strike.
b. 1957 in Londonderry, Northern Ireland
d. May 21, 1981 in Belfast, Northern Ireland
Source: *BioIn 12*

O'Herlihy, Dan
Irish. Actor
b. 1919 in Wexford, Ireland
Source: *FilmgC; IntMPA 75, 76, 77, 78, 79, 80, 81, 82; MovMk; WhoHol A*

O'Higgins, Bernardo
Chilean. Soldier, Statesman
b. Aug 20, 1778 in Chillan, Chile
d. Oct 24, 1842 in Lima, Peru
Source: *ApCAB; REn; WhAm H*

Ohira, Masayoshi
Japanese. Prime Minister
b. Mar 12, 1910 in Toyohama, Japan
d. Jun 11, 1980 in Tokyo, Japan
Source: *BioIn 10, 11; CurBio 64*

Ohm, Georg Simon
German. Physicist
b. Mar 16, 1787 in Erlangen, Germany
d. Jul 7, 1854 in Munich, Germany
Source: *REn*

Ohman, Jack
American. Political Cartoonist
b. 1960? in Saint Paul, Minnesota
Source: *BioIn 12*

O'Horgan, Tom
American. Director, Composer
b. May 3, 1926 in Chicago, Illinois
Source: *BioIn 8, 9, 11; CelR 73; CurBio 70; EncMT; EncWT; IntMPA 75, 76, 77, 78, 79; NewYTBE 72; NotNAT A; WhoAm 74, 78, 80, 82; WhoThe 77, 81; WhoWor 74*

Ohrbach, Nathan
American. Merchant
b. Aug 31, 1885 in Vienna, Austria
d. Nov 19, 1972 in New York, New York
Source: *NewYTBE 72; WhAm 5*

Oistrakh, David Fyodorovich
Russian. Musician
b. Oct 23, 1908 in Odessa, Russia
d. Oct 24, 1974 in Amsterdam, Netherlands
Source: *CurBio 56, 74; IntWW 74; NewYTBS 74; WhAm 6; Who 74; WhoMus 72; WhoWor 74*

Oistrakh, Igor Davidovich
Russian. Musician
b. Apr 27, 1931 in Odessa, U.S.S.R.
Source: *IntWW 74; Who 74; WhoMus 72; WhoWor 74*

O'Jays, The
[William Isles; Edward Levert; Robert Massey; William Powell; Sam Strain; Walter Williams]
American. Music Group
Source: *EncPR&S; RkOn*

Ojukwu, Chukwuemeka Odumegwu
Nigerian. Political Leader
b. 1933
Source: *BioIn 8, 9*

Okada, Kenzo
American. Artist
b. Sep 28, 1902 in Yokohama, Japan
d. Jul 25, 1982 in Tokyo, Japan
Source: *DcCAA 71, 77; FarE&A 78; IntWW 74, 75, 76, 77, 78, 79, 80, 81; McGDA; NewYTBS 82; PhDcTCA 77; WhoAm 74, 80, 82; WhoAmA 73, 76, 78, 80*

Okamoto, Kozo
Japanese. Terrorist
b. 1948
Source: *BioIn 9*

Okamura, Arthur
American. Artist
b. Feb 24, 1932 in Long Beach, California
Source: *DcCAA 71, 77; WhoAm 76, 78, 80, 82; WhoAmA 73, 76, 78, 80; WhoWor 74*

O'Keefe, Dennis
[Edward Vanes Flanagan, Jr.]
American. Actor
b. Mar 28, 1910 in Fort Madison, Iowa
d. Aug 31, 1968 in Santa Monica, California
Source: *FilmgC; HolP 40; MotPP; MovMk; WhAm 5; WhScrn 74, 77; WhoHol B*

O'Keefe, Walter
American. Author, Actor
b. Aug 18, 1900 in Hartford, Connecticut
Source: *AmSCAP 66*

O'Keeffe, Georgia
American. Artist
b. Nov 15, 1887 in Sun Prairie, Wisconsin
Source: *CelR 73; CurBio 41, 64; DcCAA 71; EncAB-H; REn; WebAB; Who 74; WhoAm 74; WhoAmA 73; WhoWest 74*

O'Keeffe, John
Irish. Dramatist
b. Jun 24, 1747 in Dublin, Ireland
d. Feb 4, 1833 in Southampton, England
Source: *BiD&SB; BrAu 19; DcLEL; NewC; OxEng; OxThe; PoIre*

Okun, Arthur Melvin
American. Economist
b. Nov 28, 1928 in Jersey City, New Jersey
d. Mar 23, 1980 in Washington, DC
Source: *AmEA 74; AmM&WS 73S, 78S; AnObit 1980; BioIn 8, 9, 10; ConAu 61, 97; CurBio 70, 80; IntWW 75, 76, 77, 78; PolProf J; WhoAm 74, 76, 78*

Okun, Milton
American. Composer
b. Dec 23, 1923 in New York, New York
Source: *AmSCAP 66; WhoE 74*

Olaf V
Norwegian. King
b. Jul 2, 1903 in Sandringham, England
Source: *BioIn 4, 6, 8, 10; CurBio 62*

Olaf, Pierre
French. Actor
b. Jul 14, 1928 in Cauderan, France
Source: *BiE&WWA; NotNAT; WhoHol A; WhoThe 77*

Oland, Warner
Swedish. Actor
b. Oct 3, 1880 in Umea, Sweden
d. Aug 5, 1938 in Stockholm, Sweden
Source: *CmMov; Film 1; FilmgC; MotPP; MovMk; TwYS; WhScrn 74, 77; WhoHol B*

Olatunji, Michael Babatunde
Nigerian. Author, Musician
b. in Nigeria
Source: *AuBYP*

Olcott, Chauncey (Chancellor)
American. Actor, Composer
b. Jul 21, 1860 in Buffalo, New York
d. Mar 18, 1932 in Monte Carlo, Monaco
Source: *AmAu&B; AmBi; AmSCAP 66; DcAmB; REnAL; WhAm 1; WhoStg 1906, 1908*

Olcott, Henry Steel
American. Author
b. Aug 2, 1832 in Orange, New Jersey
d. Feb 17, 1907 in Adyar, India
Source: *Alli, SUP; AmAu&B; AmBi; BiDPara; DcAmB; DcNAA; OhA&B; WhAm 1*

Olczewska, Maria
[Marie Berchtenbreitner]
German. Opera Singer
b. Aug 12, 1892 in Augsburg, Germany
d. May 17, 1969 in Baden-Baden, Germany (West)
Source: *NewEOp 71*

Oldenbourg, Zoe
French. Author
b. Mar 31, 1916 in Russia
Source: *EncWL; InWom; IntWW 74; REn; TwCW; WhoAm 82; WhoWor 74; WorAu*

Oldenburg, Claes Thure
American. Artist, Sculptor
Known for "soft" sculptures of ice cream cones, hamburgers, etc.
b. Jan 28, 1929 in Stockholm, Sweden
Source: *AmAu&B; CelR 73; ConDr 73; CurBio 70; DcCAA 71; IntWW 74; WebAB; WhoAm 74; WhoAmA 73; WhoE 74; WhoWor 74*

Older, Fremont
American. Journalist
b. Aug 30, 1856 in Appleton, Wisconsin
d. Mar 3, 1935 in Stockton, California
Source: *AmBi; DcAmB; DcNAA; WhAm 1; WhAmP; WhNAA*

Olderman, Murray
American. Cartoonist, Journalist
b. Mar 27, 1922 in New York, New York
Source: *ConAu 45, 1NR*

Oldfield, Barney (Berna Eli)
American. Auto Racer
First to travel a mile a minute, 1903.
b. Jan 29, 1878 in Wauseon, Ohio
d. Oct 4, 1946 in Beverly Hills, California
Source: *CurBio 46; DcAmB S4; Film 1; FilmgC; WebAB; WhScrn 74, 77; WhoHol B*

Oldfield, Brian
American. Track Athlete
b. Jun 1, 1945 in Elgin, Illinois
Source: *NewYTBE 73; WhoTr&F 73*

Oldfield, Sir Maurice
British. Head of MI6 Secret Service
b. Nov 6, 1915 in Bakewell, England
d. Mar 10, 1981 in England
Source: *AnObit 1980; BioIn 10, 11, 12; NewYTBS 81; Who 74*

Olds, Irving S
American. Corporation Executive
Secretary to Justice Oliver W Holmes, 1910-11; chairman, US Steel, 1940-52.
b. Jan 22, 1887 in Erie, Pennsylvania
d. Mar 4, 1963 in New York, New York
Source: *CurBio 48, 63; WhAm 4*

Olds, Ranson E(li)
American. Inventor
Built three-wheeled horseless carriage, 1886; founded Olds Motor Vehicle Co., 1896.
b. Jun 3, 1864 in Geneva, Ohio
d. Aug 26, 1950
Source: *WebAB; WhAm 3*

Olga
[Olga Erteszek]
American. Fashion Designer
b. in Krakow, Poland
Source: *InWom; WorFshn*

Oliphant, Laurence
English. Author
b. 1829 in Capetown, South Africa
d. Dec 23, 1888 in Twickenham, England
Source: *Alli, SUP; ApCAB; BbD; BiD&SB; BrAu 19; CasWL; Chambr 3; DcBiA; DcEnA; DcEnL; DcEuL; DcLEL; EvLB; NewC; OxEng; Pen ENG; REn*

Oliphant, Margaret
English. Author
b. Apr 4, 1828 in Musselburgh, Scotland
d. Jun 25, 1897 in Eton, England
Source: *Alli, SUP; BbD; BiD&SB; BrAu 19; CasWL; ChPo; DcBiA; DcEnA, AP; DcEnL; DcEuL; DcLEL; EvLB; InWom; NewC; OxEng; Pen ENG; REn*

Oliphant, Patrick Bruce
American. Editorial Cartoonist
b. Jul 24, 1935 in Adelaide, Australia
Source: *ConAu 101; WhoAm 74, 76, 78, 80, 82*

Olitski, Jules
American. Artist, Educator
b. Mar 27, 1922 in Snovsk, U.S.S.R.
Source: *CurBio 69; DcCAA 71; IntWW 74; WhoAm 74, 76, 78, 80, 82; WhoAmA 73; WhoWor 74*

Oliva, Tony (Antonio Pedro, Jr.)
Cuban. Baseball Player
b. Jul 20, 1940 in Pinar del Rio, Cuba
Source: *BaseEn; NewYTBE 73; WhoProB 73*

Oliver, Edith
American. Theatre Critic
b. Aug 11, 1913 in New York, New York
Source: *BiE&WWA; ChPo S2; NotNAT; WhoAm 74, 76, 78, 80, 82; WhoThe 77*

Oliver, Edna May
[Edna May Cox Nutter]
American. Actress
b. 1883 in Malden, Massachusetts
d. Nov 9, 1942 in Hollywood, California
Source: *CurBio 43; FilmgC; InWom; MotPP; MovMk; OxFilm; ThFT; TwYS; Vers A; WhAm 2; WhScrn 74, 77; WhoHol B; WorEFlm*

Oliver, James A(rthur)
American. Zoologist
b. Jan 1, 1914 in Caruthersville, Missouri
d. Dec 2, 1981 in New York, New York
Source: *BioIn 3, 5; CurBio 66, 82; WhoAm 74, 76, 78, 80; WhoE 74; WhoWor 74*

Oliver, Joe (Joseph)
American. Musician, Band Leader
b. May 11, 1885 in Abend, Louisiana
d. Apr 8, 1938 in Savannah, Georgia
Source: *DcAmB S2; WebAB; WhAm HA, 4*

Oliver, Sy (Melvin James)
American. Music Arranger, Composer
b. Dec 17, 1910 in Battle Creek, Michigan
Source: *WhoJazz 72*

Olivero, Magda (Maria Maddalena)
Italian. Opera Singer
b. Mar 25, 1914 in Saluzzo, Italy
Source: *Baker 78; BiDAmM; BioIn 8, 9, 11; CnOxOp 79; CurBio 80; NewEOp 71; NewYTBE 71; WhoAm 82; WhoOp 76*

Olivetti, Adriano
Italian. Typewriter Manufacturer
President, Olivetti and Co., 1938-60.
b. Apr 11, 1901 in Ivrea, Italy
d. Feb 28, 1960
Source: *CurBio 59, 60; WhAm 4*

Olivier, Sir Laurence Kerr Olivier
[Baron Olivier of Brighton]
English. Actor, Producer, Director
Won Oscars for *Henry I,* 1946, *Hamlet,* 1948.
b. May 22, 1907 in Dorking, England
Source: *BiE&WWA; BkPepl; CelR 73; CmMov; CurBio 46; DcFM; FamA&A; FilmgC; IntMPA 82; IntWW 74; MotPP; MovMk; NotNAT; OxFilm; OxThe; REn; Who 74; WhoAm 82; WhoHol A; WhoThe 77; WhoWor 74; WorEFlm*

Olmsted, Frederick Law
American. Landscape Architect
b. Apr 27, 1822 in Hartford, Connecticut
d. Aug 28, 1903 in Brookline, Massachusetts
Source: *Alli, SUP; AmAu; AmAu&B; AmBi; ApCAB; AtlBL; BbD; BiD&SB; CurBio 49, 58; CyAl 2; DcAmAu; DcAmB; DcNAA; Drake; EncAB-H; NewYTBE 72; OxAmL; REnAL; TwCBDA; WebAB; WhAm 1, 3*

Olsen, Harold G
American. Basketball Coach
Coach, Ohio State, 1922-46; won four conference titles.
b. May 12, 1895 in Rice Lake, Wisconsin
d. Oct 29, 1953
Source: *BioIn 3, 9*

Olsen, Merlin
American. Football Player, Actor
b. Sep 15, 1940 in Logan, Utah
Source: *BioIn 8; WhoAm 82; WhoFtbl 74*

Olsen, Ole
[Olsen and Johnson]
American. Comedian
b. Nov 6, 1892 in Peru, Indiana
d. Jan 26, 1963 in Albuquerque, New Mexico
Source: *EncMT; FilmgC; MovMk; WhScrn 74, 77; WhoCon 73; WhoHol B; WorEFlm*

Olsen and Johnson
see: Johnson, "Chic"; Olsen, Ole

Olson, Charles
American. Poet
b. Dec 27, 1910 in Worcester, Massachusetts
d. Jan 10, 1970
Source: *AmAu&B; CasWL; ConAu 25R; ConAu P-1; ConLC 1, 2, 5, 6, 9, 11; ConP 70, 75; CroCAP; ModAL SUP; OxAmL; Pen AM; RAdv 1; REnAL; TwCA SUP; WebE&AL; WhAm 5; WhoTwCL*

Olson, Nancy
American. Actress
b. Jul 14, 1928 in Milwaukee, Wisconsin
Source: *BiE&WWA; FilmgC; IntMPA 77, 75; NotNAT; WhoHol A*

O'Malley, J Pat
American. Actor
b. Mar 15, 1904 in Burnley, England
Source: *BiE&WWA; FilmgC; MovMk; NotNAT; WhoHol A*

O'Malley, Walter Francis
American. Baseball Executive, Lawyer
b. Oct 9, 1903 in New York, New York
d. Aug 9, 1979 in Rochester, Minnesota
Source: *BioIn 3, 4, 5, 6, 8, 11; CurBio 54, 79; NewYTBS 79; WhoAm 74, 76, 78; WhoProB 73*

Omar I
[Omar ibn al-Khattab]
Mohammedan Caliph
b. 581?
d. 644 in Medina, Saudi Arabia
Source: *BioIn 5, 8; NewC; NewCol 75*

Omar Khayyam
Persian. Poet, Astromomer
b. 1050 in Khurasan, Iran
d. 1123
Source: *BbD; BiD&SB; ChPo S1, S2; DcOrL 3; NewC*

O'Murphy, Louise
"La Morphise"
Irish. Mistress of Louis XV
b. 1737
d. 1814
Source: *BioIn 9*

Onassis, Aristotle Socrates
Greek. Shipping Executive
Founded oil tanker business, 1932; founded Olympic Airways, 1957; married Jackie Kennedy, 1968.
b. Jan 15, 1906 in Smyrna, Turkey
d. Mar 15, 1975 in Paris, France
Source: *BusPN; CelR 73; CurBio 63; IntWW 74; Who 74; WhoAm 74; WhoWor 74*

Onassis, Christina
"Chryso Mou"
Greek. Shipping Executive
Daughter of Aristotle Onassis; chief executive, Olympic Maritime Enterprises.
b. Dec 11, 1950 in New York, New York
Source: *BioIn 9, 10, 11; BkPepl; CurBio 76*

Onassis, Jacqueline Lee Bouvier Kennedy
American. Editor
Widow of John F Kennedy and Aristotle Onassis.
b. Jul 28, 1929 in Southampton, New York
Source: *BkPepl; CelR 73; CurBio 61; HerW; InWom; IntWW 74; NewYTBE 70; WhoAm 74, 76, 78, 80, 82; WhoAmW 77; WhoGov 72; WhoWor 74*

O'Neal, Patrick
American. Actor
b. Sep 26, 1927 in Ocala, Florida
Source: *FilmgC; IntMPA 75, 76, 77, 78, 79, 80, 81, 82; NotNAT; WhoHol A; WhoThe 77*

O'Neal, Ron
American. Actor
b. in Utica, New York
Source: *IntMPA 75, 76, 77, 78, 79, 80, 81, 82; NewYTBE 72; WhoHol A*

O'Neal, Ryan
American. Actor
Starred in TV series, "Peyton Place"; movie *Love Story,* 1970.
b. Apr 20, 1941 in Los Angeles, California
Source: *BkPepl; CelR 73; CurBio 73; FilmgC; IntMPA 75, 76, 77, 78, 79, 80, 81, 82; MovMk; NewYTBE 71; WhoAm 74, 76, 78, 80, 82; WhoHol A*

O'Neal, Tatum
American. Actress
Youngest Oscar winner in history for *Paper Moon,* 1973.
b. Nov 5, 1963 in Los Angeles, California
Source: *BkPepl; IntMPA 77, 78, 79, 80, 81, 82; MovMk; WhoAm 80, 82; WhoHol A*

Onegin, Sigrid
[Sigrid Hoffman]
Swedish. Opera Singer
b. Jun 1, 1891 in Stockholm, Sweden
d. Jun 16, 1943 in Magliasco, Switzerland
Source: *Baker 78; BioIn 4, 10; CnOxOp 79; EncOp; InWom; NewEOp 71; ObitOF 79; InWom*

O'Neil, James F(rancis)
American. Magazine Publisher
Published *American Legion,* 1950-78.
b. Jun 13, 1898 in Manchester, New Hampshire
d. Jul 28, 1981 in New York, New York
Source: *BioIn 1, 8; CurBio 47, 81; WhoAm 74, 76, 78, 80; WhoF&I 74, 75, 77, 79*

O'Neill, Eugene Gladstone
American. Dramatist
Won Pulitzer Prizes for *Beyond the Horizon, Anna Christie, A Long Day's Journey into Night.*
b. Oct 16, 1888 in New York, New York
d. Nov 27, 1953 in Boston, Massachusetts
Source: *AmAu&B; AmWr; AtlBL; AuNews 1; Chambr 3; CnDAL; CnMD; CnMWL; CnThe; ConAmA; ConAmL; CroCD; CyWA; DcLEL; EncAB-H; EncWL; EvLB; LongCTC; McGEWD; ModAL, SUP; ModWD; OxAmL; OxEng; OxThe; Pen AM; RComWL; REn; REnAL; REnWD; TwCA, SUP; TwCW; WebAB; WebE&AL; WhAm 3; WhoTwCL*

O'Neill, James
American. Actor
b. Oct 14, 1847 in County Kilkenny, Ireland
d. Aug 10, 1920 in New London, Connecticut
Source: *DcAmB; FamA&A; Film 1; FilmgC; OxAmL; REnAL; WhScrn 77; WhoStg 1906, 1908*

O'Neill, Jennifer
[Mrs. James Lederer]
American. Actress, Model
Starred in *The Summer of '42.*
b. Feb 20, 1949 in Rio de Janeiro, Brazil
Source: *MovMk; NewYTBE 71; WhoAm 82; WhoHol A*

O'Neill, Rose Cecil
American. Illustrator, Doll Designer
b. Jun 25, 1874 in Wilkes-Barre, Pennsylvania
d. Apr 6, 1944 in Springfield, Missouri
Source: *AmAu&B; ChPo, S2; DcAmB S3; DcNAA; NotAW; TwCA, SUP; WebAB*

O'Neill, Steve (Stephen Francis)
American. Baseball Player, Manager
b. Jul 6, 1891 in Minooka, Pennsylvania
d. Jan 26, 1962 in Cleveland, Ohio
Source: *WhoProB 73*

O'Neill, "Tip" (Thomas Philip)
American. Speaker of the House
Congressman from MA since 1952.
b. Dec 9, 1912 in Cambridge, Massachusetts
Source: *BiDrAC; CelR 73; CngDr 74; CurBio 74; NewYTBE 71; WhoAm 74, 76, 78, 80, 82; WhoAmP 73; WhoE 74; WhoGov 72*

Ongais, Danny
American. Auto Racer
b. May 21, 1942 in La Costa, California
Source: *BioIn 11; NewYTBS 78, 82*

Ono, Yoko
[Mrs. John Lennon]
Japanese. Artist, Musician
Married John Lennon, 1969; recorded, with husband, *Double Fantasy,* 1980.
b. Feb 18, 1933 in Tokyo, Japan
Source: *CelR 73; CurBio 72; WhoAm 74*

Onoda, Hiroo
Japanese. Lost Soldier of WW II
Surrendered, 1974; wrote *My 30 Year War in Luband Island,* 1975.
b. 1922? in Kinan, Japan
Source: *NewYTBS 74*

Ontkean, Michael
Actor
b. 1950 in Canada
Source: *IntMPA 82; WhoHol A*

Opatashu, David
American. Actor
b. Jan 30, 1918 in New York, New York
Source: *IntMPA 75, 76, 77, 78, 79, 80, 81, 82*

Opel, John Roberts
American. Chief Executive of IBM
Joined IBM, 1949; president, 1974-81; chief executive, 1981--.
b. Jan 5, 1925 in Kansas City, Missouri
Source: *IntWW 75, 76, 77, 78, 79, 80, 81; WhoAm 74, 76, 78, 80, 82; WhoE 79; WhoF&I 79*

Opel, Wilhelm von
German. Auto Manufacturer
b. 1871
d. 1948
Source: *BioIn 1*

Ophuls, Max
German. Motion Picture Director
b. May 6, 1902 in Saarbrucken, Germany
d. Mar 26, 1957 in Hamburg, Germany (West)
Source: *DcFM; FilmgC; MovMk; OxFilm; WorEFlm*

Oppenheim, James
American. Poet, Author
b. May 24, 1882 in Saint Paul, Minnesota
d. Aug 4, 1932 in New York, New York
Source: *AmAu&B; CasWL; ChPo, S1, S2; ConAmL; DcAmB; DcNAA; OxAmL; REn; REnAL; TwCA, SUP; WhAm 1; WhNAA*

Oppenheimer, Frank F
American. Physicist
b. Aug 14, 1912 in New York, New York
Source: *AmM&WS 73P*

Oppenheimer, Harry Frederick
South African. Industrialist
b. Oct 28, 1908 in Kimberley, South Africa
Source: *AfSS 78, 79; BioIn 4, 5, 6, 9, 10; IntWW 74, 75, 76, 77, 78; IntYB 78, 79; Who 74; WhoAm 74, 76, 78; WhoWor 74, 76, 78*

Oppenheimer, J(ulius) Robert
American. Physicist
b. Apr 22, 1904 in New York, New York
d. Feb 18, 1967 in Princeton, New Jersey
Source: *CurBio 45, 64, 67; EncAB-H; REnAL; WebAB*

Opper, Frederick Burr
American. Cartoonist
b. Jan 2, 1857 in Madison, Ohio
d. Aug 28, 1937 in New Rochelle, New York
Source: *Alli SUP; AmAu&B; AmBi; AuNews 1; ChPo; DcAmB S2; DcNAA; OhA&B; REnAL; TwCBDA; WhAm 1; WhNAA*

Orantes, Manuel
Spanish. Tennis Player
b. Feb 6, 1949 in Granada, Spain
Source: *BioIn 10; WhoWor 78*

Orange, Walter
[The Commodores]
"Clyde"
American. Musician, Singer
b. 1947 in Florida
Source: *BkPepl*

Orbach Jerry
American. Singer, Actor
b. Oct 20, 1935 in New York, New York
Source: *BiE&WWA; CelR 73; EncMT; NotNAT; WhoAm 82; WhoHol A; WhoThe 77*

Orbison, Roy
American. Singer, Musician
Songs include "Ooby-Dooby," 1956; "Crying," 1961.
b. Apr 23, 1936 in Wink, Texas
Source: *EncFCWM 69; WhoHol A*

Orczy, Emmuska, Baroness
[Emma Madgalena Rosalia Maria Josefa Barbara Orczy]
British. Author
b. Sep 23, 1865 in Tarna-Ors, Hungary
d. Nov 12, 1947 in London, England
Source: *AuBYP; BioIn 1, 5, 8; DcLEL; EncMys; EvLB; InWom; LongCTC; NewC; NotNAT B; ObitOF 79; REn; TwCA, SUP; TwCW; WhE&EA; WhLit; WhThe; WhoLA; WhoSpyF*

Ord, Edward Otho Cresap
American. Army Officer
b. Oct 18, 1818 in Cumberland, Maryland
d. Jul 22, 1883 in Havana, Cuba
Source: *AmBi; ApCAB; DcAmB; Drake; TwCBDA; WhAm H*

Orff, Carl
German. Composer
b. Jul 10, 1895 in Munich, Germany
d. Mar 29, 1982 in Munich, Germany (West)
Source: *Baker 78; CurBio 76, 82; DcCM; IntWW 74, 75, 76, 77, 78; NewEOp 71; NewYTBS 82; OxGer; OxMus; WhoWor 74, 76, 78*

Origen
Egyptian. Christian Philosopher, Scholar
b. 185 in Alexandria, Egypt
d. 254
Source: *BbD; BiD&SB; CasWL; OxEng; Pen CL; REn*

Orlando, Tony
[Michael Anthony Orlando Cassavitis; Tony Orlando and Dawn]
American. Singer
Sang "Tie a Yellow Ribbon Round the Old Oak Tree."
b. Apr 3, 1944 in New York, New York
Source: *BioNews 74; BkPepl; RkOn*

Orlando, Vittorio Emanuele
Italian. Jurist, Premier
b. May 19, 1860 in Palermo, Italy
d. Dec 1, 1952 in Rome, Italy
Source: *CurBio 44, 53; REn*

Orley, Bernard van
Flemish. Artist
b. 1491 in Brussels, Belgium
d. Jan 6, 1542 in Brussels, Belgium
Source: *NewCol 75*

Ormandy, Eugene
American. Conductor
Conductor, music director, Philadelphia Orchestra, 1936--.
b. Nov 18, 1899 in Budapest, Hungary
Source: *AmSCAP 66; BioNews 74; CelR 73; CurBio 41; IntWW 74; WebAB; Who 74; WhoAm 74; WhoE 74; WhoMus 72; WhoWor 74*

Ormsby Gore, Julian
English. Son of Lord Harlech
b. 1941
d. 1974 in London, England
Source: *BioIn 10*

O'Rourke, (Jim) James Henry
"Orator Jim"
American. Baseball Player
b. Aug 24, 1852 in Bridgeport, Connecticut
d. Jan 8, 1919 in Bridgeport, Connecticut
Source: *BaseEn; BioIn 7; WhoProB 73*

Orozco, Jose Clemente
Mexican. Muralist, Artist
b. Nov 23, 1883 in Zapotlan, Mexico
d. Sep 7, 1949 in Mexico City, Mexico
Source: *AtlBL; CurBio 40, 49; REn; WhAm 2*

Orozco, Romero Carlos
Mexican. Artist
b. 1898
Source: *BioIn 2, 5, 9*

Orpen, William
British. Artist
b. Nov 27, 1878 in Stillorgan, Ireland
d. Sep 29, 1931 in London, England
Source: *WhoLA*

Orr, Ben
see: Cars, The

Orr, Bobby (Robert Gordon)
"Our Moses"
Canadian. Hockey Player
Highest scoring defenseman ever; first to get 100 assists in season, 1970-71.
b. Mar 20, 1948 in Parry Sound, ON
Source: *CelR 73; CurBio 69; NewYTBE 71; WhoAm 82; WhoHcky 73*

Orr, Douglas William
American. Architect
b. Mar 25, 1892 in Meriden, Connecticut
d. Jul 29, 1966 in Stony Creek, Connecticut
Source: *BioIn 7, 10; NatCAB 54; ObitOF 79; WhAm 5*

Ortega, Francisco de
Spanish. Explorer
Source: *BioIn 9*

Ortega, Santos
American. Actor
b. 1899
d. 1976
Source: *BioIn 10*

Ortega y Gasset, Jose
Spanish. Philosopher
b. May 9, 1883 in Madrid, Spain
d. Oct 18, 1955 in Madrid, Spain
Source: *AtlBL; CasWL; ClDMEL; CnMWL; CyWA; DcSpL; EncWL; EvEuW; LongCTC; ModRL; OxEng; Pen EUR; REn; TwCA, SUP; TwCW; WhAm 3, 4*

Orton, Arthur
English. Imposter
b. 1834 in London, England
d. Apr 1, 1898 in London, England
Source: *NewC*

Orton, Joe (John Kingsley)
English. Dramatist
b. 1933 in Leicester, England
d. Aug 9, 1967 in London, England
Source: *CnThe; ConAu 25R, 85; ConLC 4, 13; LongCEL; McGEWD; ModWD; REnWD; WebE&AL*

Orwell, George, pseud.
[Eric Arthur Blair]
English. Author, Critic
Wrote *Animal Farm,* 1946; *1984,* 1949.
b. Jun 25, 1903 in Motihari, India
d. Jan 21, 1950 in London, England
Source: *AtlBL; CasWL; CnMWL; CyWA; DcLEL; EncWL; EvLB; LongCTC; ModBrL, SUP; NewC; OxEng; Pen ENG; RAdv 1; REn; TwCA, SUP; TwCW; WebE&AL; WhAm 4; WhoTwCL*

Orwell, Sonia
[Mrs. George Orwell]
English. Editor, Translator
b. 1919?
d. Dec 11, 1980 in London, England
Source: *BioIn 12*

Ory, "Kid" (Edward)
American. Musician
b. Dec 25, 1886 in LaPlace, Louisiana
d. Jan 23, 1973 in Honolulu, Hawaii
Source: *AmSCAP 66; ConAu 41R; NewYTBE 73; WhAm 5; WhScrn 77; WhoHol B; WhoJazz 72*

Osborne, Adam
American. Computer Executive
Produced Osborne 1 personal computer.
b. Mar 6, 1939 in Bangkok, Thailand
Source: *AmM&WS 73P; LElec*

Osborne, John Franklin
American. Editor, Journalist
b. Mar 15, 1907 in Corinth, Mississippi
d. May 2, 1981 in Washington, DC
Source: *BioIn 8, 9; ConAu 61; WhAm 7; WhoAm 74, 76, 78*

Osborne, John James
English. Dramatist, Author
b. Dec 12, 1929 in London, England
Source: *BiE&WWA; CasWL; CnMD; ConAu 13R; ConLC 1, 2, 5, 11; EncWL; IntMPA 82; IntWW 74; ModBrL; REnWD; TwCW; WebE&AL; WhoAm 82; WhoWor 74*

Osborne, Leone Neal
American. Children's Author
b. Sep 25, 1914 in Toledo, Oregon
Source: *ConAu 25R; SmATA 2*

Osbourne, "Ozzie" (John)
[Black Sabbath]
English. Rock Singer
b. Dec 3, 1949 in Birmingham, England
Source: *BioIn 12*

Osceola Nickanochee
American Indian. Seminole Leader
b. 1804 in Georgia
d. Jan 30, 1838 in Fort Moultrie, South Carolina
Source: *AmBi; ApCAB; DcAmB; WebAB; WhAm H*

Osceola, Joe Dan
American Indian. Seminole Chief
b. 1936
Source: *BioIn 9*

Osgood, Charles
[Charles Osgood Wood, III]
American. Broadcast Journalist, Author
b. Jan 8, 1933 in New York, New York
Source: *BioIn 10, 12; WhoAm 82*

Osgood, Frances Sargent Locke
American. Poet
b. Jun 18, 1811 in Boston, Massachusetts
d. May 12, 1850 in New York, New York
Source: *AmAu; AmAu&B; AmBi; ApCAB; BbD; BiD&SB; ChPo, S1; CnDAL; CyAl 2; DcAmAu; DcLEL; DcNAA; Drake; FemPA; InWom; NotAW; OxAmL; REnAL; TwCBDA; WhAm H*

O'Shea, Michael
American. Actor
b. 1906 in Connecticut
d. Dec 1973 in Dallas, Texas
Source: *AmBi; BiE&WWA; DcAmB; DcNAA; FilmgC; MotPP; NewYTBE 73; WhAm 1; WhScrn 77; WhoHol B*

O'Shea, Milo
Irish. Actor, Motion Picture Director
b. Jun 2, 1926 in Dublin, Ireland
Source: *CurBio 82; FilmgC; MovMk; NotNAT; WhoHol A*

O'Shea, Tessie
English. Comedienne, Singer
b. Mar 13, 1918 in Cardiff, Wales
Source: *FilmgC; WhoAm 74; WhoHol A*

O'Sheel, Shaemas
[Shaemas Shields, pseud.]
American. Author
b. Sep 19, 1886 in New York, New York
d. 1954
Source: *AmAu&B; ChPo; CnDAL; OxAmL; REnAL*

Osler, Sir William
Canadian. Physician, Educator
b. Jul 12, 1849 in Bondhead, ON
d. Dec 29, 1919 in Oxford, England
Source: *AmAu&B; AmBi; ApCAB; DcAmAu; DcAmB; DcLEL; DcNAA; OxEng; REnAL; WebAB; WhAm 1*

Osman I
Turkish. Founder of Ottoman Empire
b. 1259 in Bithynia
d. 1326
Source: *NewCol 75; WebBD 80*

Osmena, Sergio
Philippine. Political Leader
b. Sep 9, 1878 in Cebu, Philippines
d. Oct 19, 1961 in Manila, Philippines
Source: *CurBio 44, 61; WhAm 4*

Osmond, Donny (Donald Clark)
[The Osmonds]
American. Actor, Singer
b. Dec 9, 1958 in Ogden, Utah
Source: *BioIn 11; BkPepl; EncPR&S; IntMPA 82; RkOn; WhoAm 82*

Osmond, Ken
American. Actor
Played Eddie Haskell on "Leave it to Beaver," 1957-63.
Source: *NF*

Osmond, (Olive) Marie
[Mrs. Steve Craig; The Osmonds]
American. Actress, Singer
b. Oct 13, 1959 in Ogden, Utah
Source: *BioIn 11; BkPepl; EncPR&S; RkOn; WhoAm 82*

Osmonds, The
[Alan Osmond; Donny Osmond; Jay Osmond; Jimmy Osmond; Marie Osmond; Merrill Osmond; Wayne Osmond]
American. Singing Group
Source: *BioIn 10; EncPR&S; RkOn*

Ostade, Adriaen van
Dutch. Artist
b. Dec 10, 1610 in Haarlem, Netherlands
d. May 2, 1685 in Haarlem, Netherlands
Source: *AtlBL*

Ostenso, Martha
American. Author
b. Sep 17, 1900 in Bergen, Norway
d. Nov 24, 1963
Source: *AmAu&B; AmNov; CanNov; CanWr; ChPo S1; CnDAL; ConAmL; ConAu P-1; CreCan 1; InWom; MnnWr; OxAmL; OxCan; REnAL; TwCA, SUP; WhAm 4; WhNAA*

Osterwald, Bibi
American. Actress
b. Feb 3, 1920 in New Brunswick, New Jersey
Source: *BiE&WWA; ForWC 70; NotNAT; WhoAm 74, 76, 78, 80, 82; WhoHol A; WhoThe 77*

Ostrovsky, Aleksandr
Russian. Author
b. Apr 12, 1823 in Moscow, Russia
d. May 28, 1886 in Moscow, Russia
Source: *BiD&SB; CasWL; CnThe; EuAu; EvEuW; McGEWD; Pen EUR; REnWD*

Ostwald, Wilhelm
German. Chemist
b. Sep 2, 1853 in Riga, Russia
d. Apr 4, 1932 in Leipzig, Germany
Source: *AsBiEn; BioIn 1, 2, 3, 4, 6, 9; DcScB*

O'Sullivan, Maureen
American. Actress
b. May 17, 1911 in Boyle, Ireland
Source: *BiE&WWA; CmMov; FilmgC; InWom; IntMPA 75, 76, 77, 78, 79, 80, 81, 82; MotPP; MovMk; OxFilm; ThFT; WhoHol A; WhoThe 77; WorEFlm*

O'Sullivan, Timothy H
American. Photographer
b. 1840 in Ireland
d. Jan 14, 1882 in Staten Island, New York
Source: *BioIn 7; BnEnAmA; DcAmArt; NewCol 75; WebAB*

Oswald, Lee Harvey
American. Alleged Assassin of John Kennedy
Allegedly shot John Kennedy on Nov 22, 1963; killed two days later by Jack Ruby.
b. 1939 in New Orleans, Louisiana
d. Nov 24, 1963 in Dallas, Texas
Source: *BioIn 6, 7, 8, 9, 10, 11; Blood; NewCol 75*

Oswald, Marina Nikolaevna
[Marina Nikolaevna Pruskova]
Russian. Widow of Lee Harvey Oswald
b. 1941
Source: *InWom*

Oteri, Joseph Santo
American. Lawyer
b. Nov 7, 1930 in Boston, Massachusetts
Source: *WhoAm 78*

Otis, Elisha Graves
American. Inventor, Manufacturer
Developed first passenger elevator, 1857.
b. Aug 3, 1811 in Halifax, Vermont
d. Apr 8, 1861 in Yonkers, New York
Source: *AmBi; ApCAB; DcAmB; NewCol 75; WebAB; WhAm H*

Otis, James
American. Colonial Leader, Author
b. Feb 5, 1725 in West Barnstable, Massachusetts
d. May 23, 1783 in Andover, Massachusetts
Source: *Alli; AmAu; AmAu&B; AmBi; ApCAB; BiAuS; BiD&SB; CyAL 1; DcAmAu; DcAmB; DcLEL; DcNAA; Drake; EncAB-H; OxAmL; REnAL; TwCBDA; WebAB; WhAm H*

O'Toole, Peter Seamus
Irish. Actor
Starred in *Lawrence of Arabia*, 1962; *The Lion in Winter*, 1968.
b. Aug 2, 1933 in Connemara, Ireland
Source: *BkPepl; CelR 73; CurBio 68; FilmgC; IntMPA 75, 76, 77, 78, 79, 80, 81, 82; IntWW 74; MotPP; MovMk; NewC; NewYTBE 72; OxFilm; PlP&P; Who 82; WhoAm 82; WhoHol A; WhoThe 77; WhoWor 74; WorEFlm*

Ott, Mel(vin Thomas)
"Master Melvin"
American. Baseball Player, Manager
Played for NY Giants, 1926-47; manager, 1942-48; Hall of Fame, 1951.
b. Mar 2, 1909 in Gretna, Louisiana
d. Nov 21, 1958 in New Orleans, Louisiana
Source: *BaseEn; CurBio 41, 59; NewYTBE 70; WhoProB 73*

Ottaviani, Cardinal Alfredo
Italian. Church Official
b. Oct 29, 1890 in Rome, Italy
d. Aug 3, 1979 in Vatican City, Italy
Source: *BioIn 3, 6, 7, 8; CurBio 66, 79; IntWW 74, 75, 76, 77, 78; NewYTBS 79*

Otto, Nikolaus August
German. Engineer
Co-inventor of an internal combustion engine, 1867.
b. Jun 10, 1832 in Holzhausen, Germany
d. Jan 26, 1891 in Cologne, Germany
Source: *AsBiEn; NewCol 75; WebBD 80; WhDW*

Oughtred, William
English. Inventor, Mathematician
Invented slide rule, 1622; introduced multiplication sign, 1631.
b. Mar 5, 1575 in Eton, England
d. Jun 30, 1660 in Albury, England
Source: *Alli; AsBiEn; BioIn 2, 3; DcScB; WebBD 80*

Ouida, pseud.
[Marie Louise de la Ramee]
English. Author
b. Jan 1, 1839 in Bury St. Edmunds, England
d. Jan 25, 1908 in Viareggio, Italy
Source: *BbD; BiD&SB; BrAu 19; CasWL; Chambr 3; CyWA; DcBiA; DcEnA, AP; DcEnL; DcEuL; DcLEL; EvLB; HsB&A; InWom; JBA 34; LongCTC; NewC; OxEng; Pen ENG; REn*

Our Gang
[The Little Rascals; Matthew Beard ("Stymie"); Tommy Bond ("Butch"); Norman Chaney ("Chubby"); Joe Cobb ("Fat Joe"; "Wheezer"); Jackie Condon; Jackie Cooper; Mickey Daniels; Mickey Gubitosi; Scott Hastings; Darla Jean Hood; Allen Clayton Hoskins ("Farina"); Bobby Hutchins ("Wheezer"); Mary Ann Jackson; Dearwood Kaye ("Waldo"); Mary Kornman; Eugene Lee ("Porky"); "Spanky" McFarland (George Emmett); Dickie Moore; Carl Switzer ("Alfalfa"); Billy Thomas ("Buckwheat")]
Americans. Child Actors in Movie Serials
Source: *Film 2; HalFC 80*

Oursler, (Charles) Fulton
[Anthony Abbott]
American. Journalist, Author, Dramatist
b. Jan 22, 1893 in Baltimore, Maryland
d. May 24, 1952 in New York, New York
Source: *AmAu&B; AuBYP; CathA 1930; CurBio 42, 52; DcAmB S5; DcSpL; REn; REnAL; TwCA SUP; WhAm 3; WhNAA*

Oursler, William Charles
American. Author
b. Jul 12, 1913 in Baltimore, Maryland
Source: *WhoAm 74, 76, 78, 80, 82; WhoWor 74*

Ouspenskaya, Maria
Russian. Actress
b. Jul 29, 1876 in Tula, Russia
d. Dec 3, 1949 in Los Angeles, California
Source: *Film 1; FilmgC; InWom; MotPP; MovMk; PlP&P; ThFT; Vers A; WhScrn 74, 77; WhoHol B; WorEFlm*

Ouspensky, Petr D
see: Uspenskii, Petr D

Outcault, Richard Felton
American. Cartoonist
b. Jan 14, 1863 in Lancaster, Ohio
d. Sep 25, 1928 in Flushing, New York
Source: *AmAu&B; DcAmB; DcNAA; OhA&B; REnAL; WebAB; WhAm 1*

Outlaws, The
[Harvey Dalton Arnold; Billy Jones; Henry Paul; Hughie Thomasson; Monte Yoho]
American. Rock Group
Source: *ConMuA 80; IlEncRk*

Overgard, Bill
[Thomas William]
American. Cartoonist
b. Apr 30, 1926 in Los Angeles, California
Source: *WorECom*

Overman, Lynn
American. Actor
b. Sep 19, 1887 in Maryville, Missouri
d. Feb 19, 1943 in Santa Monica, California
Source: *CmMov; FilmgC; MovMk; NotNAT B; Vers B; WhScrn 74, 77; WhoHol B*

Overmyer, Robert F
American. Astronaut
b. Jul 14, 1936 in Lorain, Ohio
Source: *AmM&WS 73P; WhoS&SW 73; WhoWest 74*

Overstreet, Bonaro Wilkinson
American. Author
b. Oct 30, 1902 in Geyserville, California
Source: *AmAu&B; Au&Wr 71; InWom; WhNAA; WhoAm 74; WhoAmW 77; WhoS&SW 73; WhoWor 74*

Ovett, Steve
English. Track Athlete
Held world record in mile, 1981; broken by Sebastian Coe two days later.
b. Aug 9, 1955 in Brighton, England
Source: *BioIn 12*

Ovid
[Publius Ovidius Naso]
Roman. Poet
b. 43BC in Sulmona, Italy
d. 17AD in Tomi, Romania
Source: *AtlBL; BbD; BiD&SB; CasWL; DcEnL; DcEuL; NewC; OxEng; Pen CL; RComWL; REn*

Owen, Guy, Jr.
American. Author
b. Feb 24, 1925 in Clarkton, North Carolina
d. Jul 23, 1981 in Raleigh, North Carolina
Source: *AnObit 1981; ConAu 1R, 104, 3NR; ConNov 76; DrAF 76; DrAP 75; DrAS 78E; WhoS&SW 73; WrDr 76, 80*

Owen, (John) Reginald
English. Actor
b. Aug 5, 1887 in Wheathampstead, England
d. Nov 5, 1972 in Boise, Idaho
Source: *BiE&WWA; ConAu 37R; FilmgC; MotPP; MovMk; NewYTBE 72; PlP&P; Vers A; WhScrn 77; WhoHol B*

Owen, Lewis James
American. Educator
b. Apr 2, 1925 in Nanking, China
Source: *Alli; ConAu 29R; DrAS 74E; WhoAm 74, 76, 78, 80, 82*

Owen, "Mickey" (Arnold Malcolm)
American. Baseball Player, Sheriff
b. Apr 4, 1916 in Nixa, Missouri
Source: *BaseEn; WhoProB 73*

Owen, Richard Lee, II
American. Criminal, Jailhouse Lawyer
Self-taught lawyer who publishes *Criminal Law Review.*
b. 1946?
Source: *BioIn 12*

Owen, Robert
Welsh. Co-Operative Movement Pioneer
Wrote *New View of Society,* 1813; founded co-operative community of New Harmony, IN, 1825.
b. May 14, 1771 in Newtown, Wales
d. Nov 17, 1858 in Newtown, Wales
Source: *Alli, SUP; ApCAB; BiD&SB; BiDLA, SUP; BrAu 19; CasWL; ChPo; DcEnL; DcLEL; Drake; EvLB; NewC; OxAmL; OxEng; REn*

Owen, Robert Dale
American. Social Reformer, Author
b. Nov 8, 1801 in Glasgow, Scotland
d. Jun 24, 1877 in Lake George, New York
Source: *ChPo S2; CyAl 2; DcAmAu; DcAmB; DcEnL; DcNAA; IndAu 1816; REnAL; TwCBDA; WebAB; WhAm H*

Owen, Steve (Stephen Joseph)
American. Football Coach
b. Apr 21, 1898 in Oklahoma
d. May 17, 1964
Source: *BioIn 1, 6, 7, 8; CurBio 46, 64*

Owen, Wilfred
English. Poet
b. Mar 18, 1893 in Oswestry, England
d. Nov 4, 1918 in France
Source: *AtlBL; ChPo, S1, S2; CnE&AP; CnMWL; DcLEL; EncWL; EvLB; LongCTC; ModBrL, SUP; NewC; OxEng; Pen ENG; RAdv 1; REn; TwCA, SUP; TwCW; WebE&AL; WhoTwCL*

Owens, "Buck" (Alvis E, Jr.)
American. Singer, Musician
b. Aug 12, 1929 in Sherman, Texas
Source: *CelR 73; EncFCWM 69; WhoAm 82*

Owens, Jesse (James Cleveland)
American. Track Athlete
Won four gold medals, 1936 Olympics.
b. Sep 12, 1913 in Danville, Alabama
d. Mar 31, 1980 in Tucson, Arizona
Source: *BioNews 74; CurBio 56; St&PR 75; WebAB; WhoBlA 75*

Owens, Michael Joseph
American. Glass Manufacturer
Invented Owens automatic bottle machine, 1895.
b. Jan 1, 1859 in Mason County, Virginia
d. 1923 in Toledo, Ohio
Source: *BioIn 1, 7, 8; DcAmB; NatCAB; WhAm 1*

Owens, Rochelle
American. Dramatist, Poet
b. Apr 2, 1936 in Brooklyn, New York
Source: *ConAu 17R; ConDr 73; ConLC 8; ConP 70, 75; DrAP 75; ForWC 70; NatPD; NotNAT; PlP&P; WhoAm 74; WhoThe 77; WrDr 76*

Owens, Shirley Alston
see: Shirelles, The

Owens, Steve
American. Football Player
b. Dec 9, 1947 in Gore, Oklahoma
Source: *WhoAm 74; WhoFtbl 74*

Owings, Nathaniel Alexander
American. Architect
b. Feb 5, 1903 in Indianapolis, Indiana
Source: *BioIn 8, 9; ConAu 61; CurBio 71; IntWW 74, 75, 76, 77, 78; WhoAm 74, 76, 78, 80, 82; WhoF&I 74; WhoWest 74, 76, 78; WhoWor 74*

Oxford and Asquith, Henry Herbert Asquith, Earl
English. Statesman
b. Sep 12, 1852 in Morley, England
d. Feb 15, 1928
Source: *Alli SUP; McGEWB*

Oxnam, G(arfield) Bromley
American. Religious Leader
b. Aug 14, 1891 in Sonora, California
d. Mar 12, 1963 in White Plains, New York
Source: *BioIn 6; CurBio 44, 63; WhAm 4*

Oysher, Moishe
American. Actor, Singer
b. Mar 7, 1907 in Lipkon, Russia
d. Nov 27, 1958 in New Rochelle, New York
Source: *AmSCAP 66; WhScrn 74, 77; WhoHol B*

Oz, Frank
[Frank Richard Oznowicz]
American. Puppeteer
Performs voices of many of Muppet, Sesame Street characters.
b. May 24, 1944? in Hereford, England
Source: *WhoAm 80, 82*

Ozaki, Koyo, pseud.
[Ozaki Tokutaro]
Japanese. Author
b. Oct 1, 1868 in Tokyo, Japan
d. Oct 30, 1903 in Tokyo, Japan
Source: *CasWL; DcOrL 1*

Ozawa, Seiji
Japanese. Conductor
b. Sep 1, 1935 in Hoten, Japan
Source: *CurBio 68; IntWW 74; NewYTBE 70; WhoAm 74, 76, 78, 80, 82; WhoMus 72; WhoWest 74; WhoWor 74*

P

Paar, Jack
American. Entertainer
b. May 1, 1918 in Canton, Ohio
Source: *AmAu&B; CelR 73; CurBio 59; IntMPA 75, 76, 77, 78, 79, 80, 81, 82; IntWW 74; NewYTBE 73; WhoAm 74; WhoHol A; WhoWor 74*

Pablo Cruise
[Bud Cockrell; David Jenkins; Cory Lerios; Steve Price]
American. Rock Group
Source: *IlEncRk; RkOn*

Pabst, Frederick
American. Brewer
President, Pabst Brewing, 1889-1904.
b. Mar 28, 1836 in Saxony, Germany
d. 1904
Source: *NatCAB 3; WhAm 1*

Pabst, Georg W
Austrian. Motion Picture Director
b. 1885 in Vienna, Austria
d. May 29, 1967 in Vienna, Austria
Source: *DcFM; MovMk; OxFilm; TwYS; WhScrn 77*

Paca, William
American. Continental Congressman
b. Oct 31, 1740 in Abingdon, Maryland
d. Oct 13, 1799 in Abingdon, Maryland
Source: *AmBi; ApCAB; BiAuS; BiDrAC; BioIn 3, 7, 8, 9, 11; DcAmB; Drake; NatCAB 9; NewCol 75; TwCBDA; WhAm H; WhAmP*

Pacchierotti, Gasparo
Italian. Opera Singer
b. May 1740 in Fabriano, Italy
d. Oct 28, 1821 in Padua, Italy
Source: *NewEOp 71*

Pachelbel, Johann
German. Composer, Musician
b. Sep 1, 1653 in Nuremberg, Germany
d. Mar 3, 1706 in Nuremberg, Germany
Source: *Baker 78; BioIn 4, 7; McGEWB; OxMus*

Pacini, Giovanni
Italian. Composer
b. Feb 17, 1796 in Catania, Sicily
d. Dec 6, 1867 in Pescia, Italy
Source: *NewEOp 71; OxMus*

Pacino, Al(fredo James)
"The Male Garbo"
American. Actor
Starred in *The Godfather,* 1972; *Serpico,* 1974; *Cruising,* 1980.
b. Apr 25, 1940 in East Harlem, New York
Source: *BioNews 74; BkPepl; CelR 73; CurBio 74; FilmgC; IntMPA 75, 76, 77, 78, 79, 80, 81, 82; MovMk; NewYTBE 72; WhoAm 82; WhoHol A; WhoThe 77*

Paciorek, Tom (Thomas Marian)
American. Baseball Player
b. Nov 2, 1946 in Detroit, Michigan
Source: *BaseEn*

Packard, David
American. Government Official
b. Sep 7, 1912 in Pueblo, Colorado
Source: *AmM&WS 73P; IntWW 74; WhoAm 74, 76, 78, 80, 82; WhoAmP 73; WhoF&I 74; WhoWest 74; WhoWor 74*

Packard, Vance Oakley
American. Author, Journalist
b. May 22, 1914 in Granville Summit, Pennsylvania
Source: *AmAu&B; AuNews 1; BioNews 74; CelR 73; ConAu 9R; CurBio 58; IntWW 74; LongCTC; REnAL; Who 82; WhoAm 74, 76, 78, 80, 82; WhoE 74; WhoWor 74; WorAu; WrDr 76*

Packer, Alfred G
American. Cannibal
Murdered and ate five prospectors, 1873.
b. 1842 in Colorado
d. Apr 24, 1907 in Denver, Colorado
Source: *BioIn 2, 8, 11; Blood*

Packwood, Bob (Robert William)
American. Senator
b. Sep 11, 1932 in Portland, Oregon
Source: *AlmAP 78, 80; BiDrAC; BioIn 8, 9, 10, 11; CngDr 74, 77, 79; CurBio 81; IntWW 75, 76, 77, 78; WhoAm 74, 76, 78, 80, 82; WhoAmP 73, 75, 77, 79; WhoGov 72, 75, 77; WhoWest 74, 76, 78*

Paddleford, Clementine Haskin
American. Food Editor, Journalist
b. Sep 27, 1900 in Stockdale, Kansas
d. Nov 13, 1967 in New York, New York
Source: *ConAu 89; CurBio 58, 68; InWom; WhAm 4*

Paderewski, Ignace Jan
Polish. Concert Pianist, Statesman
b. Nov 18, 1860 in Kurilovka, Poland
d. Jun 29, 1941 in New York, New York
Source: *CurBio 41; FilmgC; REn; WhAm 1; WhScrn 74, 77; WhoHol B*

Padover, Saul Kussiel
American. Educator, Historian
b. Apr 13, 1905 in Vienna, Austria
d. Feb 22, 1981 in New York, New York
Source: *AmAu&B; AmM&WS 73S, 78S; BioIn 3; ConAu 49, 103; CurBio 52, 81; IntAu&W 77; REnAL; WhE&EA; WhNAA; WhoAm 74, 76, 78; WhoWor 74; WhoWorJ 72*

Paer, Ferdinando
Italian. Composer
b. Jun 1, 1771 in Parma, Italy
d. May 3, 1839 in Paris, France
Source: *NewEOp 71*

Paganini, Niccolo
Italian. Musician, Composer
b. Oct 27, 1782 in Genoa, Italy
d. May 27, 1840 in Nice, France
Source: *AtlBL; BioIn 1, 2, 3, 4, 5, 6, 7, 8, 9, 10, 11*

Page, Alan Cedric
American. Football Player, Lawyer
Defensive lineman, Minnesota Vikings, 1967-81; rookie of the year, 1967.
b. Aug 7, 1945 in Canton, Ohio
Source: *BioIn 10, 11; WhoAm 74, 76, 78, 80; WhoBlA 77; WhoFtbl 74*

Page, Charles Grafton
American. Inventor
Researcher in electromagnetism; developed electric locomotive.
b. Jan 25, 1812 in Salem, Massachusetts
d. May 5, 1868 in Washington, DC
Source: *Alli; ApCAB; BiDAmS; DcAmAu; DcAmB; DcNAA; Drake; NatCAB; WhAm H*

Page, Sir Frederick Handley
English. Aviation Pioneer
b. 1885
d. Apr 21, 1962 in London, England
Source: *BioIn 6, 7; WebBD 80*

Page, Geraldine
American. Actress
b. Nov 22, 1924 in Kirksville, Missouri
Source: *BiE&WWA; CelR 73; CurBio 53; FamA&A; FilmgC; InWom; IntMPA 75, 76, 77, 78, 79, 80, 81, 82; MotPP; MovMk; NotNAT; PlP&P; WhoAm 74, 76, 78, 80, 82; WhoAmW 77; WhoE 74; WhoHol A; WhoThe 77; WhoWor 74; WorEFlm*

Page, Greg
American. Boxer
b. 1958? in Louisville, Kentucky
Source: *BioIn 11*

Page, "Hot Lips" (Oran Thaddeus)
American. Jazz Musician
b. Jan 27, 1908 in Dallas, Texas
d. Nov 5, 1954 in New York, New York
Source: *DcAmB S5; WhoJazz 72*

Page, Jimmy (James Patrick)
[Led Zeppelin; Yardbirds]
English. Rock Musician
b. Jan 9, 1944 in Helston, England
Source: *WhoAm 80, 82*

Page, Joe (Joseph Francis)
"Fireman"; "The Gay Reliever"
American. Baseball Player
b. Oct 28, 1917 in Cherry Valley, Pennsylvania
d. Apr 21, 1980 in Latrobe, Pennsylvania
Source: *BaseEn; CurBio 50, 80; WhoProB 73*

Page, Patti
[Clara Ann Fowler]
American. Singer
b. Nov 8, 1927 in Clarence, Oklahoma
Source: *BioNews 74; CelR 73; CurBio 65; FilmgC; InWom; IntMPA 75, 76, 77, 78, 79, 80, 81, 82; WhoAm 74, 76, 78, 80, 82; WhoHol A*

Page, Thomas Nelson
American. Author
b. Apr 23, 1853 in Hanover County, Virginia
d. Nov 1, 1922 in Hanover County, Virginia
Source: *Alli SUP; AmAu; AmAu&B; AmBi; AmLY; ApCAB; BbD; BiD&SB; BiDSA; CarSB; CasWL; Chambr 3; ChPo; CnDAL; CyWA; DcAmAu; DcAmB; DcBiA; DcLEL; DcNAA; JBA 34; OxAmL; Pen AM; REn; REnAL; Str&VC; WebE&AL; WhAm 1*

Paget, Debra
[Debralee Griffin]
American. Actress
b. Aug 19, 1933 in Denver, Colorado
Source: *FilmgC; InWom; IntMPA 75, 76, 77, 78, 79, 80, 81, 82; MotPP; MovMk; WhoHol A*

Paget, Sir James
British. Surgeon
b. Jan 11, 1814
d. Dec 30, 1899
Source: *BioIn 1, 2, 5, 9*

Pagett, Nicola
English. Actress
b. Jun 15, 1945 in Cairo, Egypt
Source: *WhoThe 77*

Pagnol, Marcel Paul
French. Dramatist, Film Producer
b. Apr 18, 1895 in Aubagne, France
d. Apr 18, 1974 in Paris, France
Source: *BiE&WWA; CasWL; ClDMEL; CnMD; ConAu 49; CurBio 56, 74; DcFM; EncWL; EvEuW; FilmgC; McGEWD; ModWD; MovMk; NewYTBS 74; OxFilm; OxFr; Pen EUR; REn; TwCW; WhAm 6; Who 74; WhoWor 74; WorAu; WorEFlm*

Pahlevi, Farah Diba
Iranian. Former Empress
b. Oct 14, 1938
Source: *BioIn 5, 6, 8, 9, 10, 11; IntWW 74, 80*

Pahlevi, Mohammed Riza
[Shah of Iran]
Iranian. Deposed Shah
Shah of Iran, 1941-79; overthrown by Ayatollah Khomeini; died in exile.
b. Oct 26, 1919 in Teheran, Persia
d. Jul 27, 1980 in Cairo, Egypt
Source: *BioIn 1, 2, 3, 4, 5, 6, 7, 8, 9, 10, 11, 12; ConAu 106; CurBio 50, 80; IntWW 74; NewYTBS 74; WhoGov 72*

Pahlevi, Riza
Persian. Shah of Persia
b. 1877
d. 1944
Source: *BioIn 10*

Pahlevi, Riza Cyrus
Iranian. Self-Proclaimed Shah of Iran
b. Oct 1960
Source: *BioIn 12*

Pahlmann, William
American. Interior Decorator
b. Dec 12, 1906 in Pleasant Mound, Illinois
Source: *CurBio 64*

Paige, Janis
[Donna Mae Jaden]
American. Singer, Actress
b. Sep 16, 1923 in Tacoma, Washington
Source: *BiE&WWA; CurBio 59; EncMT; FilmgC; HolP 40; InWom; IntMPA 77, 75; MotPP; MovMk; NotNAT; WhoHol A; WhoThe 77*

Paige, Robert
American. Actor
b. 1910 in Indianapolis, Indiana
Source: *FilmgC; HolP 40; MotPP; WhoHol A*

Paige, "Satchel" (Leroy Robert)
American. Baseball Player
Said, "Don't look back...something might be gaining on you."
b. Jul 7, 1906 in Mobile, Alabama
d. Jun 8, 1982 in Kansas City, Missouri
Source: *BaseEn; BioIn 1, 3, 4, 5, 6, 7, 8, 9, 10, 11, 12; BioNews 74; CelR 73; CurBio 52, 82; NewYTBS 76, 82; WebAB; WhoAm 76, 78, 80, 82; WhoBlA 77; WhoProB 73*

Paine, Albert Bigelow
American. Author
b. Jul 10, 1861 in New Bedford, Massachusetts
d. Apr 9, 1937 in New Smyrna, Florida
Source: *AmAu&B; AmBi; BiD&SB; CarSB; ChPo, S1, S2; CnDAL; DcAmAu; DcAmB S2; DcNAA; JBA 34; OxAmL; REn; REnAL; TwCA; WhAm 1; WhNAA*

Paine, Robert Treat
American. Minister, Jurist
b. Mar 11, 1731 in Boston, Massachusetts
d. May 12, 1814 in Boston, Massachusetts
Source: *Alli; AmAu; AmAu&B; AmBi; ApCAB, SUP; BbD; BiAuS; BiD&SB; BiDrAC; ChPo; CnDAL; CyAL 1; DcAmAu; DcAmB; DcNAA; Drake; OxAmL; REnAL; TwCBDA; WebAB; WhAm H; WhAmP; WhoWest 74*

Paine, Thomas
American. Political Philosopher, Author
Advocated colonial independence in *Common Sense,* Jan, 1776.
b. Jan 29, 1737 in Thetford, England
d. Jun 8, 1809 in New York, New York
Source: *Alli; AmAu; AmAu&B; AmBi; ApCAB; AtlBL; BbD; BiD&SB; CasWL; Chambr 2; CnDAL; CrtT 3; CyAL 1; CyWA; DcAmAu; DcAmB; DcEnA; DcEnL; DcEuL; DcNAA; Drake; EncAB-H; EvLB; MouLC 2; OxAmL; OxEng; Pen AM, ENG; RComWL; REn; REnAL; TwCBDA; WebAB; WebE&AL; WhAm H; WhAmP*

Paine, Thomas Otten
American. Engineer, Government Official
b. Nov 9, 1921
Source: *AmM&WS 73P; CurBio 70; IntWW 74; St&PR 75; Who 74; WhoAm 74, 76, 78, 80, 82; WhoAmP 73*

Paisiello, Giovanni
Italian. Composer
b. May 8, 1740 in Taranto, Italy
d. Jun 5, 1816 in Naples, Italy
Source: *NewEOp 71*

Paisley, Ian Richard Kyle
Irish. Clergyman
b. Apr 6, 1926 in Armagh, Northern Ireland
Source: *CurBio 71; IntWW 74; NewYTBE 70; Who 74; WhoWor 74*

Pakula, Alan Jay
American. Motion Picture Director
Directed *Klute; All the President's Men; Sophie's Choice.*
b. Apr 7, 1928 in New York, New York
Source: *CurBio 80; IntMPA 82; NewYTBS 82; WhoAm 82*

Pal, George
American. Motion Picture Producer, Director
b. Feb 1, 1908 in Cegled, Hungary
d. May 2, 1980 in Beverly Hills, California
Source: *AnObit 1980; CmMov; FilmgC; WorEFlm*

Palance, Jack
American. Actor
b. Feb 18, 1920 in Lattimore Mines, Pennsylvania
Source: *CmMov; FilmgC; IntMPA 75, 76, 77, 78, 79, 80, 81, 82; MotPP; MovMk; OxFilm; WhoAm 82; WhoHol A; WhoWor 74; OxFilm; WorEFlm*

Palestrina, Giovanni
Italian. Composer
b. Dec 27, 1525 in Palestrina, Italy
d. Feb 2, 1594 in Rome, Italy
Source: *AtlBL; REn*

Palevsky, Max
American. Industrialist
b. Jul 24, 1924 in Chicago, Illinois
Source: *NewYTBE 72; St&PR 75; WhoAm 74, 76, 78, 80, 82; WhoAmP 73*

Paley, Barbara Cushing
"Babe"
American. Hostess, Philanthropist
b. 1915
d. Jul 6, 1978 in New York, New York
Source: *BioIn 2, 4, 5, 10, 11; InWom*

Paley, William Samuel
American. Radio, TV Executive
Founded CBS, 1928.
b. Sep 28, 1901 in Chicago, Illinois
Source: *CelR 73; CurBio 40, 51; IntMPA 75, 76, 77, 78, 79, 80, 81, 82; IntWW 74; St&PR 75; WhoAm 74, 76, 78, 80, 82; WhoAmA 73; WhoE 74; WhoF&I 74; WhoWor 74*

Palillo, Ron
American. Actor
Played a Sweathog on "Welcome Back, Kotter," 1975-79.
b. Apr 2, 1954 in New Haven, Connecticut
Source: *BioIn 11*

Palladio, Andrea
Italian. Architect
b. Nov 30, 1508 in Padua, Italy
d. Aug 19, 1580
Source: *AtlBL; OxThe; PlP&P; REn*

Pallandt, Nina, Baroness van
Danish. Singer
b. 1932
Source: *BioIn 9, 10*

Pallette, Eugene
American. Actor
b. Jul 8, 1889 in Winfield, Kansas
d. Sep 3, 1943 in Los Angeles, California
Source: *Film 1; FilmgC; MotPP; MovMk; OxFilm; TwYS; Vers A; WhScrn 74, 77; WhoHol B*

Palin, Michael
[Monty Python's Flying Circus]
British. Actor, Author
b. May 5, 1943
Source: *BioIn 10, 11*

Palligros, Tony
see: Southside Johnny and the Asbury Jukes

Palme, Olof
Swedish. Prime Minister
b. Jan 30, 1927 in Stockholm, Sweden
Source: *CurBio 70; IntWW 77*

Palmer, Alice Elvira Freeman
American. Educator
b. Feb 21, 1855 in Colesville, New York
d. Dec 6, 1902 in Paris, France
Source: *AmAu&B; AmBi; AmWom; ChPo, S1; DcAmB; DcNAA; HerW; InWom; NotAW; REnAL; TwCBDA; WebAB; WhAm 1*

Palmer, Arnold Daniel
American. Golfer
First million dollar winner in golf.
b. Sep 10, 1929 in Youngstown, Pennsylvania
Source: *Au&Wr 71; CelR 73; ConAu 85; CurBio 60; WebAB; WhoAm 74, 76, 78, 80, 82; WhoE 74; WhoWor 74*

Palmer, Austin Norman
American. Penman, Educator
b. 1859
d. 1927
Source: *WebBD 80*

Palmer, Betsy
American. Actress
b. Nov 1, 1926 in East Chicago, Indiana
Source: *BiE&WWA; FilmgC; InWom; IntMPA 75, 76, 77, 78, 79, 80, 81, 82; MotPP; NotNAT; WhoHol A; WhoThe 77*

Palmer, Bruce
see: Buffalo Springfield

Palmer, "Bud" (John S)
American. Sports Commentator
b. Sep 14, 1923 in Hollywood, California
Source: *CelR 73*

Palmer, Daniel David
American. Physician
Founded Palmer School of Chiropractic, Davenport, IA, 1898.
b. Mar 7, 1845 in Toronto, ON
d. Oct 20, 1913 in Los Angeles, California
Source: *AmBi; DcAmB; DcNAA; WebAB; WhAm HA, 4; WhoAm 74; WhoMW 74*

Palmer, Dave
see: Amboy Dukes, The

Palmer, Erastus Dow
American. Sculptor
b. Apr 2, 1817 in Pompey, New York
d. 1904 in Albany, New York
Source: *AmBi; ApCAB; DcAmB; Drake; TwCBDA; WhAm 1*

Palmer, Frederick
American. Correspondent, Author
b. Jan 29, 1873 in Pleasantville, Pennsylvania
d. Sep 2, 1958 in Charlottesville, Virginia
Source: *AmAu&B; DcAmAu; OxCan; REnAL; TwCA, SUP; WhAm 3; WhNAA*

Palmer, Jim (James Alvin)
American. Baseball Player
Pitcher, Baltimore Orioles, 1965--; led AL in most games won, 1975-77.
b. Oct 15, 1945 in New York, New York
Source: *BaseEn; BioIn 11; CurBio 80; WhoAm 82; WhoProB 73*

Palmer, Lilli
[Mrs. Carlos Thompson]
German. Actress, Author
Married to Rex Harrison, 1943-57.
b. May 24, 1914 in Posen, Germany
Source: *CurBio 51; FilmgC; InWom; IntMPA 75, 76, 77, 78, 79, 80, 81, 82; MotPP; MovMk; OxFilm; WhoAm 74, 76, 78, 80, 82; WhoHol A; WhoThe 77; WhoWor 74; WorEFlm*

Palmer, Nathaniel B
American. Sea Captain, Ship Designer
b. Aug 8, 1799 in Stonington, Connecticut
d. Jun 21, 1877 in San Francisco, California
Source: *AmBi; DcAmB; TwCBDA; WhAm H*

Palmer, Peter
American. Actor, Singer
b. Sep 20, 1931 in Milwaukee, Wisconsin
Source: *BiE&WWA; FilmgC; NotNAT; WhoHol A*

Palmer, Potter
American. Business Executive
b. May 20, 1826 in Albany County, New York
d. May 4, 1902 in Chicago, Illinois
Source: *ApCAB SUP; DcAmB; TwCBDA; WebAB; WhAm 1, 2*

Palmer, Robert
English. Rock Musician
Recent hit "Bad Case of Loving You," 1979.
b. 1949? in Batley, England
Source: *ConMuA 80; IlEncRk; WhoRock 81*

Palmer, William
English. Doctor, Murderer
b. 1824
d. 1856
Source: *BioIn 4*

Palmerston, Henry John Temple, Viscount
English. Statesman
b. Oct 20, 1784 in Broadlands, England
d. Oct 18, 1865 in Hertfordshire, England
Source: *Alli; REn; WhAm H; WhoModH*

Panama, Norman
American. Director, Producer, Author
b. Apr 21, 1914 in Chicago, Illinois
Source: *BiE&WWA; CmMov; ConAu 104; FilmgC; IntMPA 76, 77, 78, 79, 80, 81, 82; NotNAT; WorEFlm*

Panchen Lama X
Tibetan. Religious, Political Leader
b. 1937 in Chinghai, China
Source: *IntWW 74*

Pandit, Vijaya Lakshmi (Nehru)
Indian. Politician, Diplomat
b. Aug 18, 1900 in Allahabad, India
Source: *CurBio 46; HerW; InWom; IntWW 74; Who 74; WhoUN 75*

Pangborn, Franklin
American. Actor
b. 1894 in Newark, New Jersey
d. Jul 20, 1958 in Santa Monica, California
Source: *FilmgC; MovMk; Vers A; WhScrn 74, 77; WhoHol B*

Panizza, Ettore
Argentine. Conductor
b. Aug 12, 1875 in Buenos Aires, Argentina
d. Nov 29, 1967 in Milan, Italy
Source: *BiDAmM; NewEOp 71*

Pankhurst, Christabel, Dame
English. Suffragette
b. 1880 in Manchester, England
d. Feb 14, 1958 in Santa Monica, California
Source: *BioIn 4, 5, 8, 9, 11; HerW; InWom; LongCTC; WhoLA*

Pankhurst, Emmeline Goulden
English. Suffragette
b. Jul 14, 1858 in Manchester, England
d. Jun 14, 1928
Source: *BioIn 4, 6, 7, 8, 9, 10, 11; HerW; InWom; LongCTC; WhoModH*

Pankhurst, (Estelle) Sylvia
English. Suffragette
b. May 5, 1882 in Manchester, England
d. Sep 27, 1960 in Addis Ababa, Ethiopia
Source: *BioIn 5, 8, 9, 11; HerW; InWom*

Pannenberg, Wolfhart Ulrich
German. Theologian, Author
b. Oct 2, 1928 in Stettin, Germany
Source: *ConAu 25R*

Pannini, Giovanni Paolo
[Giovanni Paolo Panini]
Italian. Artist
b. 1691? in Piacenza, Italy
d. 1765 in Rome, Italy
Source: *BioIn 1, 2, 4; McGDA; NewCol 75*

Panov, Valery
Israeli. Ballet Dancer
Principal dancer, Maly Theatre of Opera and Ballet, 1957-63; wrote *To Dance,* 1978.
b. Mar 12, 1938 in Vilno, U.S.S.R.
Source: *BioNews 74; CurBio 74; WhoAm 82*

Panter-Downes, Mollie
English. Author, Journalist
b. Aug 25, 1906 in London, England
Source: *ConAu 101; LongCTC; NewC; TwCA, SUP; Who 74; WhoWor 74*

Pao, Sir Y(ue) K(ong)
Chinese. Shipping Executive
b. 1918 in Chekiang, China
Source: *BioIn 9, 10, 11; FarE&A 78, 79; IntWW 75, 76, 77, 78; NewYTBS 76*

Papadopoulos, George
Greek. Former Prime Minister
b. 1919 in Eleochorian, Greece
Source: *CurBio 70; NewYTBE 73; WhoGov 72; WhoWor 74*

Papandreou, Andreas George
Greek. Prime Minister
b. Feb 5, 1919 in Chios, Greece
Source: *BioIn 7, 8, 9, 11; ConAu 37R; CurBio 80; IntWW 74, 78; WhoAm 74; WhoWor 74, 78*

Papandreou, George
Greek. Political Leader
b. Feb 13, 1888 in Patras, Greece
d. Nov 1, 1968
Source: *BioIn 8; CurBio 44, 68*

Papanicolaou, George Nicholas
American. Physician, Cytologist
b. May 13, 1883 in Comi, Greece
d. Feb 19, 1962 in Miami, Florida
Source: *BioIn 2, 4, 5, 6, 8, 10; WhAm 4*

Papas, Irene
Greek. Actress
b. 1926 in Chiliomondion, Greece
Source: *CelR 73; FilmgC; IntMPA 75, 76, 77, 78, 79, 80, 81, 82; MotPP; MovMk; OxFilm; WhoAm 82; WhoHol A*

Papashvily, George
American. Humorist, Essayist, Sculptor
b. Aug 23, 1898 in Kobiankari, Russia
d. Mar 29, 1978 in Cambria, California
Source: *ConAu 77, 81; CurBio 45, 78; REnAL; SmATA 17; TwCA, SUP; WhoAmA 73*

Papen, Franz von
German. Diplomat, Soldier, Statesman
b. Oct 29, 1879 in Werl, Germany
d. May 2, 1969
Source: *CurBio 41, 69; REn*

Papi, Genarro
Italian. Conductor
b. Dec 21, 1886 in Naples, Italy
d. Nov 29, 1941 in New York, New York
Source: *NewEOp 71*

"Papillon"
see: Charriere, Henri

Papini, Giovanni
Italian. Author
b. Jan 9, 1881 in Florence, Italy
d. Jul 8, 1956 in Florence, Italy
Source: *CasWL; CathA 1930; ClDMEL; CnMWL; EncWL; EvEuW; LongCTC; Pen EUR; REn; TwCA; TwCW; WhoLA*

Papp, Joseph
American. Motion Picture Producer, Director
b. Jun 22, 1921 in Brooklyn, New York
Source: *BiE&WWA; CelR 73; CurBio 65; EncMT; NewYTBE 71, 72; NotNAT; OxThe; PlP&P A; WhoAm 74, 76, 78, 80, 82; WhoThe 77; WhoWor 74*

Pappas, Ike
American. Broadcast Journalist
Source: *NF*

Pappas, Irene
American. Public Relations Executive
b. May 22, 1919 in Butte, Montana
Source: *ForWC 70; WhoPubR 72; WhoWest 74*

Paracelsus, Philippus Aureolus
[Theophrastus B VonHohenheim]
Swiss. Alchemist, Physician
b. 1493 in Einsiedelin, Switzerland
d. 1541
Source: *CasWL; EuAu; EvEuW; NewC*

Paray, Paul
French. Conductor
b. May 24, 1886 in Treport, France
d. Oct 10, 1979 in Monte Carlo
Source: *WhAm 7; WhoAm 74*

Pare, Ambroise
French. Surgeon
b. 1510? in Laval, France
d. Dec 22, 1590 in Paris, France
Source: *AsBiEn; BiHiMed; BioIn 1, 2, 3, 4, 5, 6, 7, 8, 9; DcEuL; DcScB; McGEWB; NewCol 75; OxFr; REn*

Parent, Bernie (Bernard Marcel)
Canadian. Hockey Player
Goalie, Philadelphia Flyers, 1967-71, 1973-79.
b. Apr 3, 1945 in Montreal, PQ
Source: *NewYTBS 74; WhoHcky 73*

Pareto, Vilfredo
Italian. Literary Figure
b. Aug 15, 1848 in Paris, France
d. Aug 19, 1923 in Celigny, Switzerland
Source: *ClDMEL; REn; TwCA, SUP*

Pargeter, Edith Mary
see: Peters, Ellis, pseud.

Parisot, Aldo
Brazilian. Musician
b. 1920 in Natal, Brazil
Source: *BioIn 5, 6; WhoMus 72*

Park, Choong-Hoon
Korean. Politician
b. Jan 19, 1919 in Cheju, Korea
Source: *WhoWor 76*

Park, Chung Hee
Korean. General, Politician
President, 1963-79; was assassinated.
b. Sep 30, 1917 in Sosan Gun, Korea
d. Oct 26, 1979 in Seoul, Korea (South)
Source: *BioIn 9, 10, 11, 12; ConAu 61, 97; CurBio 69, 80; IntWW 74; WhoGov 72*

Park, (Douglas) Brad(ford)
Canadian. Hockey Player
Defenseman, NY Rangers, 1969-76; Boston Bruins, 1976--.
b. Jul 6, 1948 in Toronto, ON
Source: *BioIn 9, 10, 11; CurBio 76; WhoAm 82; WhoHcky 73*

Park, Mungo
Scottish. Explorer
b. Sep 10, 1771 in Scotland
d. 1806?
Source: *Alli; BbD; BiD&SB; BioIn 2, 3, 4, 6, 7, 8, 9, 10, 11; BrAu; Chambr 2; DcLEL; EvLB; LinLib L, S; NewC; NewCol 75; OxEng*

Park, Tongsun
Korean. Lobbyist
b. 1935?
Source: *BioIn 11*

Parker, Alan William
English. Motion Picture Director
Directed *Midnight Express, Fame,* Pink Floyd's *The Wall.*
b. Feb 14, 1944 in London, England
Source: *Who 82; WhoAm 82*

Parker, Bonnie
[Bonnie and Clyde]
American. Criminal
Faye Dunaway portrayed her in movie *Bonnie and Clyde,* 1968.
b. 1911 in Rowena, Texas
d. May 23, 1934 in Louisiana
Source: *BioIn 9; Blood*

Parker, Brant (Julian)
American. Cartoonist
b. Aug 26, 1920 in Los Angeles, California
Source: *WhoAm 82; WorECom*

Parker, "Buddy" (Raymond)
American. Football Coach
Coach, Detroit Lions, 1951-56; introduced two-minute offense.
b. Dec 16, 1913 in Kemp, Texas
d. Mar 22, 1982 in Kaufman, Texas
Source: *CurBio 55; NewYTBS 82; WhoFtbl 74*

Parker, Cecil
English. Actor
b. Sep 3, 1898 in Hastings, England
d. Apr 21, 1971 in Brighton, England
Source: *FilmgC; MovMk; NewYTBE 71; Vers B; WhScrn 74, 77; WhoHol B*

Parker, Charlie (Charles Christopher)
"Bird"; "Yardbird"
American. Jazz Musician
Alto-saxophonist; co-creator of bebop.
b. Aug 29, 1920 in Kansas City, Kansas
d. Mar 12, 1955 in New York, New York
Source: *DcAmB S5; WebAB; WhAm 4*

Parker, Daniel Francis
American. Sports Editor
b. Jul 1, 1893 in Waterbury, Connecticut
d. May 20, 1967 in Waterbury, Connecticut
Source: *WhAm 4*

Parker, Dorothy Rothschild
American. Author, Poet, Journalist
b. Aug 22, 1893 in West Bend, New Jersey
d. Jun 7, 1967 in New York, New York
Source: *AmAu&B; AmSCAP 66; BiE&WWA; CasWL; ChPo, S2; CnDAL; CnE&AP; ConAmA; ConAu 21R, 25R; ConAu P-2; ConLC 15; DcLEL; EvLB; LongCTC; ModAL; OxAmL; Pen AM; RAdv 1; REn; REnAL; TwCA, SUP; TwCW; WebAB; WhAm 4*

Parker, Eleanor
American. Actress
b. Jun 26, 1922 in Cedarville, Ohio
Source: *FilmgC; IntMPA 75, 76, 77, 78, 79, 80, 81, 82; MotPP; MovMk; WhoHol A; WorEFlm*

Parker, Fess
American. Actor
Played Davy Crockett and Daniel Boone in movies, on TV.
b. Aug 16, 1927 in Fort Worth, Texas
Source: *AmSCAP 66; FilmgC; IntMPA 75, 76, 77, 78, 79, 80, 81, 82; MotPP; WhoHol A*

Parker, Frank
American. Tennis Player
b. Jan 31, 1916 in Milwaukee, Wisconsin
Source: *BioIn 1; CurBio 48*

Parker, Graham
[Graham Parker and the Rumour]
English. Rock Musician
b. in London, England
Source: *ConMuA 80; IlEncRk*

Parker, Jameson
American. Actor
b. Nov 18, 1950 in Baltimore, Maryland
Source: *IntMPA 82*

Parker, Jean
[Mae Green]
American. Actress
b. 1915 in Deer Lodge, Montana
Source: *FilmgC; IntMPA 75; MotPP; MovMk; ThFT; WhoHol A*

Parker, Quannah
see: Quanah

Parker, Suzy
[Cecelia Parker]
American. Model
b. Oct 28, 1933 in San Antonio, Texas
Source: *FilmgC; InWom; IntMPA 75, 76, 77, 78, 79, 80, 81, 82; MovMk; WhoAm 82; WhoHol A*

Parker, Theodore
American. Religious Leader
b. Aug 24, 1810 in Lexington, Massachusetts
d. May 10, 1860 in Florence, Italy
Source: *Alli; AmAu; AmAu&B; AmBi; ApCAB; BbD; BiD&SB; CasWL; Chambr 3; CyAl 2; DcAmAu; DcAmB; DcEnL; DcLEL; DcNAA; Drake; EncAB-H; EvLB; OxAmL; REn; REnAL; TwCBDA; WebAB; WhAm H*

Parker, Thomas
English. Clergyman
b. Jun 8, 1595 in Wilts, England
d. Apr 24, 1677 in Newbury, Massachusetts
Source: *Alli; AmAu&B; ApCAB; DcAmAu; DcAmB; Drake; OxAmL; WhAm H*

Parker, Thomas Andrew
[Andreas Cornelius Van Kuijk]
"Colonel Tom"
American. Manager of Elvis Presley
b. 1910? in Breda, Netherlands
Source: *BioIn 5*

Parkhurst, Charles Henry
American. Clergyman
b. Apr 17, 1842 in Framingham, Massachusetts
d. Sep 8, 1933
Source: *Alli SUP; AmAu&B; AmBi; ApCAB; BbD; BiD&SB; DcAmAu; DcAmB; DcNAA; TwCBDA; WhAm 1*

Parkins, Barbara
Canadian. Actress
Starred in *Valley of the Dolls,* 1961; TV series *Peyton Place,* 1963-67.
b. May 22, 1942 in Vancouver, BC
Source: *FilmgC; WhoAm 82; WhoHol A*

Parkinson, C(yril) Northcote
English. Political Scientist
b. Jul 30, 1909 in Durham, England
Source: *ConAu 5R, 5NR; CurBio 40; IntWW 74; LongCTC; NewYTBE 71; RAdv 1; Who 74; WhoAm 74, 76, 78, 80, 82; WhoWor 74; WorAu*

Parkinson, James
English. Surgeon
b. Apr 11, 1755 in London, England
d. Dec 21, 1824 in London, England
Source: *BiHiMed; BioIn 3, 4, 7, 9; DcScB*

Parkman, Francis
American. Historian, Author
b. Sep 16, 1823 in Boston, Massachusetts
d. Nov 8, 1893 in Jamaica Plain, Massachusetts
Source: *Alli, SUP; AmAu; AmAu&B; AmBi; ApCAB; AtlBL; BbD; BbtC; BiD&SB; CasWL; CyAl 2; CyWA; DcAmAu; DcAmB; DcLEL; DcNAA; EncAB-H; EvLB; MouLC 4; OxAmL; OxCan; OxEng; Pen AM; REn; REnAL; TwCBDA; WebAB; WebE&AL; WhAm H*

Parks, Bert
American. Actor, Emcee
Hosted Miss America Pageant, 1954-79.
b. Dec 30, 1914 in Atlanta, Georgia
Source: *CurBio 73; IntMPA 75, 76, 77, 78, 79, 81, 82; WhoAm 74, 76, 78, 80, 82; WhoHol A*

Parks, Floyd Lavinius
American. Military Leader
b. Feb 9, 1896 in Louisville, Kentucky
d. Mar 10, 1959 in Washington, DC
Source: *BioIn 3, 5; WhAm 3*

Parks, Gordon Alexander Buchanan
American. Photographer, Author
b. Oct 30, 1912 in Fort Scott, Kansas
Source: *AfroAA; AmAu&B; AuNews 2; BlkAW; CelR 73; ConAu 41R; ConLC 1, 16; CurBio 68; IntMPA 75, 76, 77, 78, 79, 81, 82; LivgBAA; SmATA 8; WhoAm 74, 76, 78, 80, 82; WhoBlA 75; WhoE 74; WhoWor 74; WrDr 76*

Parks, Gordon, Jr.
American. Motion Picture Director
b. 1935? in Minneapolis, Minnesota
d. Apr 3, 1979 in Nairobi, Kenya
Source: *BioIn 11; DcBlPA; NewYTBS 79*

Parks, Larry
[Samuel Klausman]
American. Actor
b. Dec 3, 1914 in Olathe, Kansas
d. Apr 13, 1975 in Studio City, California
Source: *BiE&WWA; CmMov; FilmgC; HolP 40; IntMPA 75; MotPP; MovMk; WhScrn 77*

Parks, Lillian Rogers
American. White House Employee
Wrote *My Thirty Years Backstairs at the White House,* 1961; TV mini-series, 1979.
b. 1897?
Source: *BioIn 5, 8, 11*

Parks, Michael
American. Actor
b. Apr 4, 1938 in Corona, California
Source: *BioIn 7, 9; FilmEn; FilmgC; IntMPA 75, 76, 77, 78, 79, 80, 81; MotPP; WhoHol A*

Parks, Rosa Lee
American. Civil Rights Leader
Initiated bus boycott, Montgomery, AL, Dec 1, 1955.
b. Feb 4, 1913 in Tuskegee, Alabama
Source: *HerW; WhoBlA 75*

Parley, Peter, pseud.
see: Goodrich, Samuel Griswold

Parmenides
Greek. Philosopher
Founded Eleatic School; devised method of reasoned proof for assertions.
b. 515BC
Source: *BbD; BiD&SB; CasWL; NewC; Pen CL; REn*

Parmigiano
[Francesco Mazzola]
Italian. Artist
b. Jan 11, 1503 in Parma, Italy
d. Aug 24, 1540 in Casalmaggiore, Italy
Source: *AtlBL; NewCol 75*

Parnell, Charles Stewart
Irish. Nationalist Leader
Fought for Irish Home Rule.
b. 1846 in Avondale, Ireland
d. Oct 6, 1891 in Brighton, England
Source: *LongCTC; NewC; REn*

Parnis, Mollie
American. Fashion Designer
b. Mar 18, 1905 in New York, New York
Source: *CelR 73; CurBio 56; InWom; WhoAm 74; WorFshn*

Parr, Catherine
English. 6th Wife of Henry VIII
Married Henry, 1543.
b. 1512
d. 1548
Source: *Alli; BiDLA; DcEnL; InWom; REn*

Parr, Thomas
"Old Parr"
English. Centenarian
b. 1483 in Shropshire, England
d. Nov 14, 1635 in London, England
Source: *NewC*

Parrhasius
Greek. Artist
fl. 4th century BC in Ephesus, Greece
Source: *NewC*

Parrish, Anne
American. Author
b. Nov 12, 1888 in Colorado Springs, Colorado
d. Sep 5, 1957 in Danbury, Connecticut
Source: *AmAu&B; AmNov; CnDAL; ConAmL; EvLB; IlsBYP; IlsCB 1744, 1946; InWom; LongCTC; OxAmL; REnAL; TwCA, SUP; TwCW; WhAm 3; WhNAA*

Parrish, Maxfield
American. Artist
Student of Howard Pyle; known for original posters, book illustrations.
b. Jul 25, 1870 in Philadelphia, Pennsylvania
d. Mar 30, 1966 in Plainfield, New Hampshire
Source: *AmAu&B; ConICB; CurBio 65, 66; IlsBYP; IlsCB 1744; JBA 34, 51; OxAmL; REnAL; SmATA 14; TwCBDA; WebAB; WhAm 4*

Parry, Sir Charles Hubert Hastings
English. Composer, Musical Historian
b. Feb 27, 1848 in Bournemouth, England
d. Oct 7, 1918 in Little Hampton, England
Source: *Alli SUP; LongCTC; TwCA*

Parry, Sir William Edward
English. Explorer, Admiral
Discovered, named Meville Island and Barrow Strait.
b. 1790 in Bath, England
d. Jul 8, 1855
Source: *Alli; ApCAB; BrAu 19; DcLEL; Drake; OxEng; WhoStg 1908*

Parseghian, Ara Raoul
American. Football Coach, Sportscaster
Head coach, Notre Dame U, 1964-75.
b. May 10, 1923 in Akron, Ohio
Source: *BioNews 74; CurBio 68; WhoAm 82; WhoFtbl 74*

Parsons, Benny
American. Auto Racer
b. 1941
Source: *BioIn 10*

Parsons, Betty Pierson
American. Artist, Gallery Owner
b. Jan 31, 1900 in New York, New York
d. Jul 23, 1982 in Southold, New York
Source: *BioIn 6, 10, 11; NewYTBS 82; WhoAm 74, 76, 78, 80, 82; WhoAmA 73, 76, 78, 80; WhoAmW 58, 64, 66, 68, 70, 72, 74*

Parsons, Sir Charles Algernin
English. Inventor
Produced first practical steam turbine, 1884.
b. Jun 13, 1854 in London, England
d. Feb 11, 1931 in Kingston, Jamaica
Source: *NewCol 75; WhDW*

Parsons, Estelle
American. Actress
b. Nov 20, 1927 in Lynn, Massachusetts
Source: *BiE&WWA; CelR 73; FilmgC; IntMPA 75, 76, 77, 78, 79, 80, 81, 82; MovMk; NotNAT; WhoAm 74, 76, 78, 80, 82; WhoHol A; WhoThe 77*

Parsons, Gram
[Cecil Connor; The Byrds; The Flying Burrito Brothers]
American. Singer, Songwriter
b. Nov 5, 1946 in Winter Haven, Florida
d. Sep 19, 1973 in Joshua Tree, California
Source: *BioIn 10; ConMuA 80; EncPR&S; IlEncCM; IlEncRk; WhoRock 81*

Parsons, Louella Oettinger
American. Journalist
b. Aug 6, 1881 in Freeport, Illinois
d. Dec 9, 1972 in Santa Monica, California
Source: *ConAu 37R, 93; CurBio 40, 73; FilmgC; InWom; OxFilm; REnAL; WebAB; WhAm 5; WhScrn 77; WhoHol B; WorEFlm*

Partch, Harry
American. Composer
b. Jun 24, 1901 in Oakland, California
d. Sep 3, 1974 in San Diego, California
Source: *CurBio 65, 74; DcCM; NewYTBS 74; WhAm 6; WhoAm 74; WhoWest 74*

Partch, Virgil Franklin, II
American. Cartoonist
Created comic strip "Big George."
b. Oct 17, 1916 in St. Paul Island, Alaska
Source: *Au&Wr 71; CurBio 46; WhoAm 74, 76, 78, 80, 82; WhoAmA 73*

Parton, Dolly Rebecca
[Mrs. Carl Dean]
American. Singer, Songwriter, Actress
First gold record, 1978, for "Here You Come Again"; movie debut in *Nine to Five,* 1980.
b. Jan 19, 1946 in Sevierville, Tennessee
Source: *BkPepl; IntMPA 82; WhoAm 74, 76, 78, 80, 82*

Partridge, Bellamy
American. Biographer, Author
b. 1878 in Phelps, New York
d. Jul 5, 1960 in Bridgeport, Connecticut
Source: *AmAu&B; AmNov; REn; REnAL; TwCA, SUP; WhAm 4; WhNAA*

Partridge, Eric Honeywood
New Zealander. Lexicographer, Author
b. Feb 6, 1894 in Gisborne, New Zealand
d. Jun 1, 1979 in Devonshire, England
Source: *Au&Wr 71; ConAu 1R, 85, 3NR; CurBio 63, 79; DcLEL; EvLB; IntWW 74; LongCTC; NewC; TwCA SUP; Who 74; WhoE 74; WhoWor 74; WrDr 76*

Pasarell, Charlie
American. Tennis Player
b. Feb 12, 1944
Source: *BioIn 6*

Pascal, Blaise
French. Mathematician, Theologian
b. Jun 19, 1623 in Clermont, France
d. Aug 19, 1662 in Paris, France
Source: *AtlBL; BbD; BiD&SB; CasWL; CyWA; DcEuL; EuAu; EvEuW; NewC; OxEng; OxFr; Pen EUR; RComWL; REn*

Pascal, Gabriel
Hungarian. Motion Picture Producer
b. Jun 4, 1894 in Hungary
d. Jul 6, 1954 in New York, New York
Source: *CurBio 42, 54; FilmgC; OxFilm; WorEFlm*

Pascoli, Giovanni
Italian. Poet
b. Dec 31, 1855 in San Mauro, Italy
d. Apr 6, 1912 in Castelvecchio, Italy
Source: *CasWL; ClDMEL; EncWL; EuAu; EvEuW; OxEng; Pen EUR; REn; TwCW; WhoTwCL*

Pasdeloup, Jules Etienne
French. Conductor
b. Sep 15, 1819 in Paris, France
d. Aug 13, 1887 in Fontainebleau, France
Source: *Baker 78; BioIn 8; OxFr; OxMus*

Pasero, Tancredi
Italian. Opera Singer
b. Jan 11, 1893 in Turin, Italy
Source: *NewEOp 71*

Pasolini, Pier Paolo
Italian. Motion Picture Director
b. Mar 5, 1922 in Bologna, Italy
d. Nov 2, 1975 in Ostia, Italy
Source: *CasWL; ConAu 61, 93; CurBio 70; FilmgC; IntWW 74; OxFilm; Pen EUR; REn; TwCW; WhAm 6; WhScrn 77; WhoWor 74; WorAu; WorEFlm*

Pass, Joe
[Joseph Anthony Passalaqua]
American. Musician
b. Jan 13, 1929 in New Brunswick, New Jersey
Source: *BiDAmM; EncJzS 70; IlEncJ*

Passarella, Art
American. Actor, Baseball Umpire
b. 1910
d. Oct 1981 in Hemet, California
Source: *BioIn 11, 12; NewYTBS 81*

Pasta, Giuditta Negri
Italian. Opera Singer
b. Apr 9, 1798 in Saronno, Italy
d. Apr 1, 1865 in Como, Italy
Source: *NewEOp 71*

Pasternak, Boris Leonidovich
Russian. Author
Wrote *Doctor Zhivago,* 1957.
b. Feb 11, 1890 in Moscow, Russia
d. May 29, 1960 in Moscow, U.S.S.R.
Source: *AtlBL; CasWL; ChPo S1; ClDMEL; CnMWL; ConLC 7, 10, 18; CurBio 59, 60; DcRusL; EncWL; EvEuW; LongCTC; ModSL 1; OxEng; Pen EUR; RComWL; REn; TwCA SUP; TwCW; WhAm 4; WhoTwCL*

Pasternak, Joe (Joseph Vincent)
Hungarian. Motion Picture Producer
b. Sep 19, 1901 in Silagy, Romania
Source: *AmSCAP 66; CmMov; FilmgC; IntMPA 75, 76, 77, 78, 79, 80, 81, 82; WhoAm 74, 76, 78, 82; WhoWor 74; WorEFlm*

Pasteur, Louis
French. Chemist, Bacteriologist
Developed process of food sterilization--pasteurization.
b. Dec 27, 1822 in Dole, France
d. Sep 28, 1895
Source: *AsBiEn; BiHiMed; BioIn 1, 2, 3, 4, 5, 6, 7, 8, 9, 10, 11; DcScB; LinLib L; LongCEL; McGEWB; NewCol 75; OxFr; REn; WebBD 80*

Pastor, Tony (Antonio)
American. Actor, Theatre Manager
b. May 28, 1837 in New York, New York
d. Aug 26, 1908 in Elmhurst, New York
Source: *Alli; AmAu&B; DcAmB; DcNAA; FamA&A; OxAmL; OxThe; REn; REnAL; WebAB; WhoStg 1906, 1908*

Pastor, Tony
American. Band Leader
b. 1907 in Middletown, Connecticut
d. Oct 31, 1969 in New London, Connecticut
Source: *WhoHol B; WhoJazz 72*

Pastore, John Orlando
American. Senator
b. Mar 17, 1907 in Providence, Rhode Island
Source: *BiDrAC; CelR 73; CngDr 74; CurBio 53; IntWW 74; WhoAm 74; WhoAmP 73; WhoE 74; WhoGov 72; WhoWor 74*

Pastorini, Dan
American. Football Player
b. Dec 25, 1949 in Sonora, California
Source: *BioIn 11; WhoFtbl 74*

Patachou
French. Singer
b. 1918 in Paris, France
Source: *WhoHol A*

Patchen, Kenneth
American. Poet
b. Dec 13, 1911 in Niles, Ohio
d. Jan 8, 1972 in Palo Alto, California
Source: *AmAu&B; AmNov; Au&Wr 71; CasWL; ChPo, S1; CnDAL; ConAu 1R, 33R, 3NR; ConLC 1, 2, 18; ConNov 72; ConP 70, 75; DcLEL; ModAL; OhA&B; OxAmL; Pen AM; RAdv 1; REn; REnAL; TwCA, SUP; WebE&AL; WhAm 5; WhoTwCL*

Pater, Jean-Baptiste
French. Artist
b. 1695 in Valenciennes, France
d. 1736 in Paris, France
Source: *McGDA*

Pater, Walter Horatio
English. Author
b. Aug 5, 1839 in Shadwell, England
d. Jul 30, 1894 in Oxford, England
Source: *Alli SUP; AtlBL; BbD; BiD&SB; BrAu 19; CasWL; Chambr 3; ChPo, S1; CrtT 3; CyWA; DcBiA; DcEnA, AP; DcEuL; DcLEL; EvLB; MouLC 4; NewC; OxEng; Pen ENG; RAdv 1; REn; WebE&AL*

Paterno, Joseph V (Joe)
American. Football Coach
b. Dec 21, 1926 in Brooklyn, New York
Source: *BioIn 9, 10, 11; WhoE 74; WhoFtbl 74*

Paterson, Basil Alexander
American. Politician
b. Apr 27, 1926 in New York, New York
Source: *WhoAm 82; WhoAmP 73; WhoBlA 75*

Paterson, Tom
Canadian. Theatrical Director
b. Jun 20, 1920 in Stratford, ON
Source: *BioIn 11; CreCan 2*

Pathe, Charles
French. Film Pioneer
Introduced the newsreel, 1909 in France, 1910 in US.
b. Dec 25, 1863 in Chevry Cossigny, France
d. Dec 25, 1957 in Monte Carlo, Monaco
Source: *DcFM; FilmEn; FilmgC; OxFilm; WorEFlm*

Patino, Simon Iturri
"Tin King"
Bolivian. Industrialist, Diplomat
b. Jun 1, 1862 in Cochabamba, Bolivia
d. Apr 20, 1947 in Buenos Aires, Argentina
Source: *CurBio 42, 47*

Patman, (John Williams) Wright
American. Lawyer, Legislator
b. Aug 6, 1893 in Hughes Springs, Texas
d. Mar 7, 1976 in Bethesda, Maryland
Source: *BiDrAC; BioNews 74; CelR 73; CngDr 74; CurBio 46; WhAm 6; WhoAm 74; WhoAmP 73; WhoGov 72; WhoS&SW 73*

Patmore, Coventry Kersey Dighton
English. Poet
b. Jul 23, 1823 in Woodford, England
d. Nov 26, 1896 in Lymington, England
Source: *Alli, SUP; AtlBL; BbD; BiD&SB; BrAu 19; CasWL; Chambr 3; ChPo, S1, S2; CnE&AP; CrtT 3; DcEnA; DcEnL; DcEuL; DcLEL; EvLB; MouLC 4; NewC; OxEng; Pen ENG; REn; WebE&AL*

Paton, Alan Stewart
South African. Author, Politician
b. Jan 11, 1903 in Natal, South Africa
Source: *Au&Wr 71; AuBYP; CasWL; ConAu P-1; ConLC 4, 10; ConNov 72, 76; CurBio 52; CyWA; EncWL; IntWW 74; LongCTC; NewC; Pen ENG; REn; SmATA 11; TwCA SUP; TwCW; WebE&AL; Who 74; WhoTwCL; WhoWor 74; WrDr 76*

Patou, Jean
French. Fashion Designer
b. 1887
d. Mar 1936 in Paris, France
Source: *WhoFash; WorFshn*

Patrick, Saint
Irish. Patron Saint
b. 385
d. 461
Source: *Alli; CasWL; ChPo; EvLB; NewC; REn*

Patrick, Gail
[Margaret Fitzpatrick]
American. Actress
b. Jun 20, 1911 in Birmingham, Alabama
d. Jul 6, 1980 in Hollywood, California
Source: *AnObit 1980; BioIn 10, 11; FilmgC; HolP 30; MotPP; MovMk; ThFT; WhoHol A*

Patrick, John
American. Dramatist, Architect
b. May 17, 1905 in Louisville, Kentucky
Source: *AmAu&B; ConAu 89; OxAmL; Pen AM; REn; REnAL; WhoAm 74; WhoWor 74*

Patrick, Lee
American. Actress
Played Mrs. Topper in TV series "Topper"; Effie in *The Maltese Falcon.*
b. Nov 22, 1906 in New York, New York
d. Nov 21, 1982 in Laguna Hills, California
Source: *BiE&WWA; FilmgC; MotPP; MovMk; NewYTBS 82; NotNAT; Vers A; WhoHol A*

Patrick, Lester B
Canadian. Hockey Player
Hall of Fame, 1945; Patrick Division of NHL named for him, 1974.
b. Dec 30, 1883 in Drummondville, PQ
d. Jun 1, 1960 in Victoria, BC
Source: *BioIn 3, 5, 8, 9, 10, 11; WhoHcky 73*

Patrick, Lynn
Canadian. Hockey Player, Executive
b. 1919?
d. Jan 26, 1980 in Saint Louis, Missouri
Source: *BioIn 1*

Patrick, Ted
American. De-Programmer of Cult Members
b. 1930
Source: *BioIn 10*

Patrick, Van
American. Sportscaster
b. 1916 in Texas
d. Sep 29, 1974 in South Bend, Indiana
Source: *BioIn 10; BioNews 74*

Pattee, Fred Lewis
American. Educator
b. Mar 22, 1863 in Bristol, New Hampshire
d. May 6, 1950 in Winter Park, Florida
Source: *AmAu&B; CnDAL; DcAmAu; OxAmL; REn; REnAL; TwCA, SUP; TwCBDA; WhAm 3; WhNAA*

Patten, Gilbert
[Burt L Standish, pseud.]
American. Author
b. Oct 25, 1866 in Corinna, Maine
d. Jan 16, 1945 in Vista, California
Source: *AmAu&B; CurBio 45; DcAmB S3; DcNAA; OxAmL; REnAL; TwCA, SUP; WebAB; WhAm 2*

Patterson, Alicia
[Mrs. Harry F Guggenheim]
American. Editor, Publisher
Founded *Newsday* magazine with husband, 1940.
b. Oct 15, 1909 in Chicago, Illinois
d. Jul 2, 1963 in New York, New York
Source: *AmAu&B; ConAu 89; CurBio 55, 63; InWom; WhAm 4*

Patterson, Eleanor Medill
"Cissy"
American. Publisher
b. Nov 7, 1884 in Chicago, Illinois
d. Jul 24, 1948 in Marlboro, Maryland
Source: *AmAu&B; CurBio 40, 48; DcAmB S4; InWom; NotAW; WebAB; WhAm 2*

Patterson, Floyd
American. Boxer
Won Olympic gold medal, 1952; youngest ever to win heavywieght title, 1956,
b. Jan 4, 1935 in Waco, North Carolina
Source: *BioIn 3, 4, 5, 6, 7, 8, 9, 10, 11; CurBio 60; NewYTBE 70, 72; WhoBox 74*

Patterson, Joseph Medill
American. Publisher
b. Jan 6, 1879 in Chicago, Illinois
d. May 26, 1946 in New York, New York
Source: *AmAu&B; CurBio 42, 46; DcAmB S4; WhAm 2*

Patterson, Lorna
American. Actress
Plays Judy Benjamin on TV series, "Private Benjamn."
b. 1956 in Whittier, California
Source: *BioIn 12*

Patterson, Melody
American. Actress
Played Wrangler Jane on TV series, "F Troop," 1965-67.
b. 1947 in Los Angeles, California
Source: *WhoHol A*

Patterson, Neva
American. Actress
b. Feb 10, 1922 in Nevada, Iowa
Source: *BiE&WWA; NotNAT; WhoHol A; WhoThe 77*

Patterson, Tom (Harry Thomas)
Canadian. Founder of Stratford Festival
b. Jun 11, 1920 in Stratford, ON
Source: *BioIn 11; CreCan 2; WhoThe 72, 77, 81*

Patterson, William Allan
American. Aviation Pioneer
b. Oct 1, 1899 in Honolulu, Hawaii
d. Mar 7, 1980 in Glenview, Illinois
Source: *BioIn 1, 2, 8; CurBio 46*

Patti, Adelina Juana Maria
Italian. Opera Singer
b. Feb 10, 1843 in Madrid, Spain
d. Sep 27, 1919 in Brecknock, Wales
Source: *AmWom; ApCAB; Drake; InWom; NewC; NotAW; TwCBDA; WhAm 1; WhoStg 1908*

Patti, Carlotta
Italian. Singer, Music Teacher
b. Oct 30, 1835 in Florence, Italy
d. Jun 27, 1889 in Paris, France
Source: *ApCAB; Drake; InWom*

Patton, George Smith, Jr.
"Old Blood and Guts"
American. Army General
George C Scott portrayed him in movie *Patton,* 1970.
b. Nov 11, 1885 in San Gabriel, California
d. Dec 21, 1945 in Heidelberg, Germany
Source: *CurBio 43, 46; DcAmB S3; EncAB-H; REnAL; WebAB; WhAm 2*

Patton, George Smith, III
American. Army Officer
b. Dec 24, 1923 in Boston, Massachusetts
Source: *Who 76; WhoAm 82*

Patzak, Julius
Austrian. Opera Singer
b. Apr 9, 1898 in Vienna, Austria
d. Jan 26, 1974 in Rottach-Egern, Germany
Source: *NewYTBS 74; WhoMus 72*

Pauker, Ana
[Ana Rabinsohn]
Romanian. Political Leader
b. 1894 in Bucharest, Romania
d. Jun 1960 in Bucharest, Romania
Source: *CurBio 48; InWom; WhAm 4*

Paul VI, Pope
[Giovanni Battista Montini]
Italian. Roman Catholic Leader
Elected pope, June, 1963.
b. Sep 26, 1897 in Concesio, Italy
d. Aug 6, 1978 in Castel Gandolfo, Italy
Source: *CurBio 56, 63; WhoWor 74*

Paul, Saint
[Saul of Tarsus]
Biblical Character
b. in Tarsus, Asia
d. 64? in Rome, Italy
Source: *NewCol 75; REn*

Paul, Alan
see: Manhattan Transfer

Paul, Alice
American. Lawyer
b. Jan 11, 1885 in Moorestown, New Jersey
d. Jul 9, 1977 in Moorestown, New Jersey
Source: *BiCAW; CurBio 47; HerW; InWom; WebAB; WhoAmW 77; WomWWA 14*

Paul, Elliot Harold
American. Journalist
b. Feb 13, 1891 in Malden, Massachusetts
d. Apr 7, 1958 in Providence, Rhode Island
Source: *AmAu&B; CnDAL; ConAmL; CurBio 40, 58; EncMys; LongCTC; OxAmL; Pen AM; REn; REnAL; TwCA, SUP; WhAm 3*

Paul, Frank Rudolph
Austrian. Illustrator
b. 1884 in Vienna, Austria
d. Jun 29, 1963 in Teaneck, New Jersey
Source: *BioIn 6; EncSF; FanAl; WhoSciF*

Paul, Gabe (Gabriel)
American. Baseball Executive
President, Cleveland Indians, 1978--.
b. Jan 4, 1910 in Rochester, New York
Source: *WhoAm 74, 76, 78, 80, 82; WhoF&I 74; WhoProB 73*

Paul, Henry
see: Outlaws, The

Paul, Les
[Les Paul and Mary Ford; Lester William Polfus]
American. Musician, Inventor
Developed eight-track tape recorder.
b. Jun 9, 1916 in Waukesha, Wisconsin
Source: *BioIn 2, 3, 4, 5, 10, 11; WhoAm 82; WhoHol A*

Paul, Lester Warner
American. Physician, Educator
b. Dec 17, 1899 in Everly, Iowa
d. Nov 30, 1975
Source: *AmM&WS 73P; WhAm 7; WhoAm 74*

Paul, Oglesby
American. Physician
b. May 3, 1916 in Villanova, Pennsylvania
Source: *AmM&WS 73P; WhoAm 74*

Paul-Boncour, Joseph
French. Statesman
b. Aug 4, 1873 in Saint-Aignan, France
d. Mar 28, 1972
Source: *CurBio 45, 72; NewYTBE 72*

Paul Revere and the Raiders
[Charlie Coe; Joe Correrro; Mark Lindsay; Paul Revere; Freddy Weller]
American. Music Group
Source: *EncPR&S*

Pauley, Edwin Wendell
American. Oilman
b. Jan 7, 1903 in Indianapolis, Indiana
d. Jul 28, 1981 in Beverly Hills, California
Source: *BioIn 1, 5, 11; CurBio 45, 81; IntWW 74, 75, 76, 77, 78; WhoAm 74, 76, 78, 80; WhoAmP 75, 77, 79*

Pauley, (Margaret) Jane
[Mrs. Garry Trudeau]
American. Broadcast Journalist
Succeeded Barbara Walters on "The Today Show."
b. Oct 31, 1950 in Indianapolis, Indiana
Source: *BioIn 11; BkPepl; CurBio 80; IntMPA 82; WhoAm 82*

Pauling, Linus Carl
American. Chemist, Physicist
Won Nobel Prize for chemistry, 1954; Nobel Peace Prize, 1962.
b. Feb 28, 1901 in Portland, Oregon
Source: *AmAu&B; AmM&WS 73P; CelR 73; CurBio 49, 64; EncAB-H; IntWW 74; WebAB; Who 82; WhoAm 74, 76, 80, 82; WhoWor 74; WrDr 76*

Paulos, Jon
see: Buckinghams, The

Paulsen, Pat
American. Comedian
Regular on "The Smothers Brothers Show," 1966-68; ran for president, 1968.
b. 1930 in South Bend, Washington
Source: *WhoAm 74; WhoHol A*

Paulson, Donald Lowell
American. Surgeon
b. Sep 14, 1912 in Saint Paul, Minnesota
Source: *AmM&WS 73P; WhoAm 74*

Paulucci, Jeno Francisco
American. Business Executive
b. Jul 7, 1918 in Aurora, Minnesota
Source: *St&PR 75; WhoAm 74, 76, 78, 80, 82*

Paulus, Friedrich von
German. Field Marshal
b. 1890
d. Feb 1, 1957 in Dresden, Germany (West)
Source: *BioIn 1, 2, 4, 6, 10*

Paumgartner, Bernhard
Austrian. Musicologist, Composer
b. Nov 14, 1887 in Vienna, Austria
d. Jul 27, 1971 in Salzburg, Austria
Source: *NewYTBE 71; WhAm 5*

Paur, Emil
Austrian. Conductor
b. Aug 29, 1855 in Czernowitz, Austria
d. Jun 7, 1932 in Mistek, Moravia
Source: *WhAm 4*

Pavan, Marisa
[Marisa Pierangeli]
Italian. Actress
b. Jun 19, 1932 in Cagliara, Sardinia
Source: *FilmgC; IntMPA 75, 76, 77, 78, 79, 80, 81, 82; MotPP; WhoAm 74; WhoHol A*

Pavarotti, Luciano
Italian. Opera Singer, Actor
Best selling classical vocalist today; starred in *Yes, Giorgio,* 1982.
b. Oct 12, 1935 in Modena, Italy
Source: *BioIn 8, 9, 10, 11; CurBio 73; WhoAm 74, 76, 78, 80, 82; WhoMus 72*

Pavelich, Mark
[United States Olympic Hockey Team-1980]
American. Hockey Player
First American-born player to score five goals in NHL game, Feb 23, 1983.
b. Feb 28, 1958 in Eveleth, Minnesota
Source: *HocReg*

Pavese, Cesare
Italian. Author
b. Sep 9, 1908 in Cuneo, Italy
d. Aug 1950 in Turin, Italy
Source: *CasWL; CnMWL; EncWL; EvEuW; ModRL; OxEng; Pen EUR; REn; TwCA SUP; TwCW; WhoTwCL*

Pavlov, Ivan Petrovich
Russian. Physiologist
Discovered the conditioned reflex; won Nobel Prize, 1904.
b. Sep 14, 1849 in Ryazan, Russia
d. Feb 27, 1936 in Leningrad, U.S.S.R.
Source: *AsBiEn; BiHiMed; BioIn 1, 2, 3, 4, 5, 6, 7, 9, 10; DcScB; LongCTC; NewCol 75; WebBD 80*

Pavlova, Anna
Russian. Ballerina
Considered greatest ballerina of her time.
b. Jan 3, 1885 in Russia
d. Jan 23, 1931 in Netherlands
Source: *HerW; InWom; REn; WhScrn 74, 77; WhoHol B*

Paxinou, Katina
Greek. Actress
b. Dec 17, 1900 in Piraeus, Greece
d. Feb 22, 1973 in Athens, Greece
Source: *BiE&WWA; CurBio 43, 73; FilmgC; InWom; MotPP; MovMk; NewYTBE 73; OxFilm; OxThe; WhScrn 74; WhoHol B; WorEFlm*

Paxton, Sir Joseph
English. Architect
b. 1803
d. 1865
Source: *Alli*

Paxton, Tom (Thomas R)
American. Singer, Musician, Composer
b. Oct 31, 1937 in Chicago, Illinois
Source: *CurBio 82; EncFCWM 69; WhoAm 74, 76, 78, 80, 82*

Paycheck, Johnny
[Don Lytle]
American. Singer
Recorded "Take This Job and Shove It."
b. May 31, 1941 in Greenfield, Ohio
Source: *BiDAmM; EncFCWM 69; WhoAm 78, 80, 82; WhoRock 81*

Payne, Freda
American. Singer
b. Sep 19, 1945 in Detroit, Michigan
Source: *RkOn; WhoAm 74; WhoBlA 75*

Payne, John
American. Actor
b. 1912 in Roanoke, Virginia
Source: *CmMov; FilmgC; IntMPA 82; MovMk; WhoHol A; WorEFlm*

Payne, John Howard
American. Actor, Dramatist
b. Jun 9, 1791 in New York, New York
d. Apr 9, 1852 in Tunis, Tunisia
Source: *DcLEL; DcNAA; OxAmL; OxEng; OxThe; Pen AM; REn; REnAL; TwCBDA; WebAB; WhAm H*

Payne, Leon
American. Songwriter
b. Jun 15, 1917 in Alba, Texas
d. Sep 11, 1969 in San Antonio, Texas
Source: *EncFCWM 69*

Payne, Sidney
American. Sportswriter
b. 1930 in Bronx, New York
d. Dec 17, 1976 in Atlanta, Georgia
Source: *BioIn 11*

Payson, Joan Whitney
American. Philanthropist, Sportswoman
Principal owner, NY Mets, from their inception, 1962.
b. Feb 5, 1903 in New York, New York
d. Oct 4, 1975 in New York, New York
Source: *BioIn 6, 7, 8, 9, 10; CurBio 72, 75; NatCAB 58*

Payton, Lawrence
[The Four Tops]
American. Singer
With group, 1954--; first hit "Baby I Need Your Loving," 1964.
b. 1930? in Detroit, Michigan
Source: *IlEncRk; WhoRock 81*

Payton, Walter
"Sweetness"
American. Football Player
Running back, Chicago Bears, 1975--; MVP, 1978.
b. Jul 25, 1954 in Columbia, South Carolina
Source: *BioIn 11; WhoAm 80, 82; WhoBlA 77*

Paz, Octavio
Mexican. Poet, Critic
b. Mar 31, 1914 in Mexico City, Mexico
Source: *CasWL; CnMWL; ConAu 73; ConLC 3, 4, 6, 10; CurBio 74; DcCLAA; EncWL; IntWW 74; Pen AM; TwCW; Who 74; WhoAm 74; WhoTwCL; WhoWor 74; WorAu*

Paz Garcia, Policarpo
Honduran. President
b. 1933?
Source: *BioIn 12; WhoWor 74*

Peabody, Eddie
American. Musician
b. 1902
d. Nov 7, 1970 in Covington, Kentucky
Source: *WhoHol B*

Peabody, Elizabeth Palmer
American. Educator, Transcendentalist
Founded first kindergarten in US, 1861, in Boston.
b. May 16, 1804 in Billerica, Massachusetts
d. Jan 3, 1894 in Jamaica Plain, Massachusetts
Source: *Alli, SUP; AmAu; AmAu&B; AmBi; AmWom; ApCAB; BiD&SB; ChPo, S1; CnDAL; DcAmAu; DcAmB; DcNAA; Drake; InWom; NotAW; OxAmL; REnAL; TwCBDA; WebAB; WhAm H*

Peabody, George
American. Philanthropist, Merchant
b. Feb 18, 1795 in Peabody, Massachusetts
d. Nov 4, 1869 in London, England
Source: *AmBi; ApCAB; DcAmB; Drake; EncAB-H; TwCBDA; WebAB; WhAm H*

Peabody, Josephine Preston
American. Poet, Dramatist
b. May 30, 1874 in Brooklyn, New York
d. Dec 4, 1922
Source: *AmAu&B; AmBi; BiCAW; BiD&SB; CarSB; ChPo, S1; CnDAL; ConAmL; DcAmAu; DcAmB; DcNAA; EvLB; InWom; LongCTC; ModWD; NotAW; OxAmL; REnAL; TwCA; TwCBDA; WhAm 1; WomWWA 14*

Peace, Charles Frederick
English. Criminal
b. 1832
d. 1879
Source: *BioIn 6*

Peacock, Thomas Love
English. Author
b. Oct 18, 1785 in Weymouth, England
d. Jan 23, 1866 in Halliford, England
Source: *Alli; AtlBL; BbD; BiD&SB; BiDLA; BrAu 19; CasWL; Chambr 3; ChPo, S1, S2; CrtT 2; CyWA; DcBiA; DcEnA; DcEnL; DcEuL; DcLEL; EvLB; MouLC 3; NewC; OxEng; Pen ENG; RAdv 1; REn; WebE&AL*

Peale, Charles Willson
American. Artist
b. Apr 15, 1741 in Queen Annes County, Massachusetts
d. Feb 22, 1827 in Philadelphia, Pennsylvania
Source: *Alli; AmBi; ApCAB; AtlBL; BbD; BiD&SB; DcAmAu; DcAmB; DcNAA; Drake; EncAB-H; OxAmL; REn; TwCBDA; WebAB; WhAm H*

Peale, James
American. Artist
b. 1749 in Chestertown, Maryland
d. May 24, 1831 in Philadelphia, Pennsylvania
Source: *ApCAB; DcAmB; TwCBDA; WhAm H*

Peale, Norman Vincent
American. Clergyman
Wrote *The Power of Positive Thinking,* 1952.
b. May 31, 1898 in Bowersville, Ohio
Source: *AmAu&B; Au&Wr 71; AuBYP; AuNews 1; BioNews 74; CelR 73; ConAu 81; CurBio 46, 74; OhA&B; REnAL; SmATA 20; WebAB; WhoAm 74, 76, 78, 80, 82; WhoWor 74; WrDr 76*

Peale, Raphael
American. Artist
b. Feb 17, 1774 in Annapolis, Maryland
d. Mar 4, 1825
Source: *DcAmB; Drake; WhAm H*

Peale, Rembrandt
American. Artist
b. Feb 22, 1778 in Richboro, Pennsylvania
d. Oct 3, 1860
Source: *Alli; AmAu&B; AmBi; ApCAB; BiD&SB; DcAmAu; DcAmB; DcNAA; Drake; OxAmL; TwCBDA; WhAm H*

Peale, Titian Ramsay
American. Artist, Naturalist
b. Nov 17, 1799 in Philadelphia, Pennsylvania
d. Mar 13, 1885
Source: *ApCAB; DcAmB; DcNAA; WhAm H*

Pearce, Alice
American. Actress
b. 1917
d, Mar 3, 1966 in Los Angeles, California
Source: *BiE&WWA; FilmgC; InWom; MotPP; WhScrn 74, 77; WhoHol B*

Pearce, Charles S
American. Artist
b. Oct 13, 1851 in Boston, Massachusetts
d. May 1914
Source: *AmBi; ApCAB; DcAmB; TwCBDA; WhAm 1*

Pearl, Jack
American. Radio Entertainer
Popularized expression "Vas you dere, Sharlie?" on radio program, 1932-47.
b. Oct 29, 1895 in New York, New York
d. Dec 25, 1982 in New York, New York
Source: *BiE&WWA; EncMT; WhoHol A; WhoThe 77*

Pearl, Minnie
[Sarah Ophelia Colley Cannon]
American. Comedian
Trademark is straw hat with price tag hanging on it.
b. Oct 25, 1912 in Centerville, Tennessee
Source: *CelR 73; EncFCWM 69; WhoAm 74, 76, 78, 80, 82; WhoHol A*

Pears, Peter
English. Opera Singer
b. Jun 22, 1910 in Farnham, England
Source: *IntWW 74; NewYTBS 74; Who 74; WhoMus 72; WhoWor 74*

Pearse, Padraic (Patrick Henry)
Irish. Poet, Patriot
b. Nov 10, 1879 in Dublin, Ireland
d. May 3, 1916 in Dublin, Ireland
Source: *CasWL; ChPo; LongCTC; NewC; Pen ENG; REn; TwCA, SUP*

Pearson, David
American. Auto Racer
b. 1934
Source: *BioIn 8, 9, 10*

Pearson, Drew
American. Journalist
b. Dec 13, 1897 in Evanston, Illinois
d. Sep 1, 1969 in Washington, DC
Source: *AmAu&B; ConAu 5R, 25R; CurBio 41, 69; REnAL; TwCA SUP; WebAB; WhAm 5; WhScrn 77*

Pearson, Drew
American. Football Player
b. Jan 12, 1951 in Newark, New Jersey
Source: *WhoAm 78; WhoFtbl 74*

Pearson, Lester Bowles
Canadian. Prime Minister
Won Nobel Peace Prize, 1957, for helping to resolve Arab-Israeli war, 1956.
b. Apr 23, 1897 in Toronto, ON
d. Dec 27, 1972 in Toronto, ON
Source: *CanWW 70; ConAu 37R; CurBio 47, 63, 73; NewYTBE 72; OxCan SUP; WhAm 5*

Peart, Neil
see: Rush

Peary, Harold
"Great Gildersleeve"
American. Actor, Radio Entertainer
Source: *BioIn 10; WhoHol A*

Peary, Robert Edwin
American. Arctic Explorer
Led first expedition to reach N Pole, 1909.
b. May 6, 1856 in Cresson, Pennsylvania
d. Feb 20, 1920 in Washington, DC
Source: *AmAu&B; AmBi; BiD&SB; Chambr 3; DcAmAu; DcAmB; DcNAA; LongCTC; OxCan; REn; REnAL; TwCBDA; WebAB; WhAm 1*

Pease, James
American. Opera Singer
b. Jan 9, 1916 in Franklin, Indiana
d. Apr 26, 1967 in New York, New York
Source: *NewEOp 71*

Peattie, Donald Culross
American. Author, Naturalist
b. Jun 21, 1898 in Chicago, Illinois
d. Nov 16, 1964 in Santa Barbara, California
Source: *AmAu&B; AuBYP; ConAu 102; CurBio 40, 65; DcLEL; MnBBF; OxAmL; REnAL; TwCA, SUP; WhAm 4; WhNAA*

Peck, George Wilbur
American. Journalist, Humorist
b. Sep 28, 1840 in Henderson, New York
d. Apr 16, 1916
Source: *AmAu; AmAu&B; BbD; BiD&SB; CarSB; CnDAL; DcAmAu; DcAmB; DcNAA; OxAmL; Pen AM; REn; REnAL; TwCBDA; WhAm 1; WhAmP; WhoChL; WisWr*

Peck, Gregory
[Eldred Gregory Peck]
American. Actor
Won Oscar, 1962, for *To Kill a Mockingbird.*
b. Apr 5, 1916 in LaJolla, California
Source: *BiE&WWA; BkPepl; CelR 73; CmMov; CurBio 47; FilmgC; IntMPA 75, 76, 77, 78, 79, 80, 81, 82; IntWW 74; MotPP; MovMk; OxFilm; Who 82; WhoAm 74, 76, 78, 80, 82; WhoGov 72; WhoHol A; WhoThe 77; WhoWor 74; WorEFlm*

Peckinpah, (David) Sam(uel)
American. Director, Author
b. Feb 21, 1925 in Fresno, California
Source: *CelR 73; CmMov; CurBio 73; DcFM; FilmgC; IntMPA 75, 76, 77, 78, 79, 80, 81, 82; IntWW 74; MovMk; NewYTBE 71; OxFilm; WhoAm 82; WorEFlm*

Pecora, Ferdinand
American. Judge
b. Jan 6, 1882 in Nicosia, Italy
d. Dec 7, 1971 in New York, New York
Source: *NewYTBE 71; WhAm 5*

Pedro I
Brazilian. Emperor
b. Oct 12, 1798 in Lisbon, Portugal
d. Sep 24, 1834 in Lisbon, Portugal
Source: *NewCol 75; WebBD 80*

Pedro II
Brazilian. Emperor
b. Dec 2, 1825 in Rio de Janeiro, Brazil
d. Dec 5, 1891 in Paris, France
Source: *NewCol 75; WebBD 80*

Peel, Sir Robert
English. Statesman
b. Feb 5, 1788 in Lancashire, England
d. Jan 2, 1850 in England
Source: *Alli; REn*

Peele, George
English. Dramatist, Poet
b. 1558 in London, England
d. 1597 in London, England
Source: *Alli; AtlBL; BiD&SB; BrAu; CasWL; Chambr 1; ChPo S1; CnE&AP; CnThe; CroE&S; CrtT 1; CyWA; DcEnA; DcEnL; DcLEL; EvLB; McGEWD; MouLC 1; NewC; OxEng; OxThe; Pen ENG; PlP&P; REn; REnWD; WebE&AL*

Peerce, Alice Kaye
American. Civic Leader
Source: *WhoWorJ 72*

Peerce, Jan
American. Opera Singer
Leading tenor, NY Metropolitan Opera, 1941-66; wrote *Bluebird of Happiness,* 1976.
b. Jun 3, 1904 in New York, New York
Source: *CelR 73; CurBio 42; WhoAm 74, 76, 78, 80, 82; WhoHol A; WhoMus 72; WhoWor 74; WhoWorJ 72*

Peete, Calvin
American. Golfer
b. Jul 18, 1943 in Detroit, Michigan
Source: *NF*

Peeters, Pete(r)
Canadian. Hockey Player
b. Aug 1, 1957 in Edmonton, AB
Source: *HocReg*

Pegler, Westbrook
American. Journalist
b. Aug 2, 1894 in Minneapolis, Minnesota
d. Jun 24, 1969 in Tucson, Arizona
Source: *AmAu&B; ConAu 89, 103; CurBio 40, 69; OxAmL; WebAB; WhAm 5; WhScrn 77*

Pei, I(eoh) M(ing)
American. Architect
b. Apr 26, 1917 in Canton, China
Source: *CelR 73; CurBio 69; WhoAm 82*

Pei, Mario Andrew
Italian. Educator, Linguist
b. Feb 16, 1901 in Rome, Italy
d. Mar 2, 1978 in Glen Ridge, New Jersey
Source: *ConAu 5R, 77, 5NR; CurBio 68, 78; DrAS 74F; REnAL; TwCA SUP; WhoAm 74; WhoWor 74; WrDr 76*

Peirce, Benjamin
American. Astronomer, Mathematician
b. Apr 4, 1809 in Salem, Massachusetts
d. Oct 6, 1880
Source: *BioIn 5, 8; NewCol 75*

Peirce, Charles Sanders
American. Philosopher
b. Sep 10, 1839 in Cambridge, Massachusetts
d. Apr 19, 1914 in Milford, Pennsylvania
Source: *Alli SUP; AmAu; AmAu&B; AmBi; ApCAB; DcAmAu; DcAmB; DcNAA; EncAB-H; LongCTC; OxAmL; Pen AM; REn; REnAL; TwCBDA; WebAB; WebE&AL; WhAm 1*

Peirce, Waldo
American. Illustrator
b. Dec 17, 1884 in Bangor, Maine
d. Mar 8, 1970 in Seareport, Maine
Source: *CurBio 44, 70; DcCAA 71; IlsCB 1744; WhAm 5*

Pele
[Edson Arantes do Nascimento]
"Perola Negra"
Brazilian. Soccer Player
Scored 1,281 career goals; played with NY Cosmos, 1974-77 for $4.7 million.
b. Oct 23, 1940 in Tres Coracoes, Brazil
Source: *BioIn 10; BkPepl; CurBio 67; NewYTBE 71; WhoAm 82*

Pell, Claiborne
American. Politician
b. Nov 22, 1918 in New York, New York
Source: *BiDrAC; CngDr 74; ConAu 49; CurBio 72; IntWW 74; WhoAm 80, 82; WhoAmP 73; WhoE 74; WhoGov 72; WhoWor 74*

Pella, Giuseppe
Italian. Economist
b. Apr 18, 1902 in Rome, Italy
d. May 31, 1981 in Rome, Italy
Source: *BioIn 3; CurBio 53, 81; IntWW 74, 75, 76, 77, 78; IntYB 78, 79; NewYTBS 81*

Pelletier, Wilfred
Canadian. Conductor
b. Jun 20, 1896 in Montreal, PQ
d. Apr 9, 1982 in New York, New York
Source: *Baker 78; BiDAmM; BioIn 4, 7; CanWW 70, 79; CreCan 2; CurBio 44, 82; Who 74; WhoAm 74, 76, 78, 80, 82; WhoWor 74*

Pellicci, Derek
see: Little River Band, The

Pellico, Silvio
Italian. Author
b. Jun 25, 1788 in Saluzzo, Italy
d. Jan 31, 1854 in Turin, Italy
Source: *BiD&SB; CasWL; DcEuL; EuAu; EvEuW; McGEWD; Pen EUR; REn*

Pemberton, Brock
American. Motion Picture Producer, Director
b. Dec 14, 1885 in Leavenworth, Kansas
d. Mar 11, 1950 in New York, New York
Source: *CurBio 45, 50; DcAmB S4; WhAm 2; WhoHol B*

Pemberton, John Clifford
American. Military Leader
b. Dec 7, 1727 in Philadelphia, Pennsylvania
d. Jan 31, 1795 in Westphalia, Germany
Source: *ApCAB; BiDConf; DcAmB; NatCAB 10; TwCBDA; WebAB; WhAm H; WhoMilH 76*

Pemberton, John Stith
American. Inventor of Coca-Cola
b. Jul 8, 1831 in Knoxville, Georgia
d. Aug 1888
Source: *BioIn 12*

Penderecki, Krzysztof
Polish. Composer
b. Nov 23, 1933 in Debica, Poland
Source: *CurBio 71; DcCM; IntWW 74; WhoAm 82; WhoWor 74*

Pendergast, Thomas J
American. Political Leader
b. Jul 22, 1870
d. Jan 26, 1945 in Kansas City, Missouri
Source: *CurBio 45; DcAmB S3*

Pendergrass, Teddy (Theodore D)
American. Singer, Business Executive
Album *Life is a Song Worth Singing* was double platinum; paralyzed in car accident.
b. Mar 26, 1950 in Philadelphia, Pennsylvania
Source: *BioIn 11; WhoAm 82; WhoBlA 77*

Pendleton, Don
American. Author
b. Dec 12, 1927 in Little Rock, Arkansas
Source: *ConAu 33R; WhoMW 74*

Pendleton, Nat
American. Actor
b. Aug 9, 1899 in Davenport, Iowa
d. Oct 11, 1967 in San Diego, California
Source: *FilmgC; MotPP; MovMk; Vers A; WhScrn 74, 77; WhoHol B*

Penn, Arthur Heller
American. Theatre, Film Director
b. Sep 27, 1922 in Philadelphia, Pennsylvania
Source: *BiE&WWA; CelR 73; CurBio 72; DcFM; FilmgC; IntMPA 75, 76, 77, 78, 79, 80, 81, 82; IntWW 74; MovMk, ; NotNAT; OxFilm; WhoAm 82; WhoThe 77; WorEFlm*

Penn, Irving
American. Photographer
b. Jun 16, 1917 in Plainfield, Pennsylvania
Source: *CurBio 80; WhoAm 74, 76, 78, 80, 82*

Penn, John
American. Continental Congressman
Signed Declaration of Independence, 1776.
b. May 17, 1741 in Caroline County, Virginia
d. Sep 14, 1788 in Williamsburg, North Carolina
Source: *AmBi; ApCAB; DcAmB; Drake; TwCBDA; WhAm H; WhAmP*

Penn, William
English. Colonizer
Quaker who founded PA, 1682, based on religious, political freedom.
b. Oct 14, 1644 in London, England
d. Jul 30, 1718 in Ruscombe, England
Source: *Alli; AmAu&B; AmBi; ApCAB; BbD; BiD&SB; BrAu; CasWL; Chambr 2; DcAmB; DcEnL; DcEuL; DcLEL; Drake; EncAB-H; EvLB; OxAmL; OxEng; Pen AM; REn; REnAL; TwCBDA; WebAB; WhAm H; WhAmP*

Pennario, Leonard
American. Musician, Composer
b. Jul 9, 1924 in Buffalo, New York
Source: *AmSCAP 66; CurBio 59; WhoAm 74, 76, 78, 80, 82; WhoE 74; WhoMus 72; WhoWor 74*

Pennell, Joseph Stanley
American. Author
b. Jul 4, 1908 in Junction City, Kansas
d. Sep 26, 1963 in Seaside, Oregon
Source: *AmAu&B; CurBio 44; OxAmL; REnAL; TwCA SUP; WhAm 4*

Penner, Joe
[Joseph Pinter]
American. Comedian
Famous for phrase "Wanna buy a duck?"
b. Nov 11, 1904 in Budapest, Hungary
d. Jan 10, 1941 in Philadelphia, Pennsylvania
Source: *CurBio 41; FilmgC; MotPP; WhScrn 74, 77; WhoHol B*

Penney, J(ames) C(ash)
American. Merchant
b. Sep 16, 1875 in Hamilton, Missouri
d. Feb 12, 1971 in New York, New York
Source: *ConAu 29R; CurBio 47, 71; NewYTBE 71; WebAB; WhAm 5*

Pennington, Ann
American. Actress
b. 1893 in Camden, New Jersey
d. Nov 4, 1971 in New York, New York
Source: *BiE&WWA; EncMT; Film 1; NewYTBE 71; TwYS; WhScrn 74, 77; WhoHol B*

Pennington, John Selman
American. Journalist
b. 1924? in Andersonville, Georgia
d. Nov 23, 1980 in Saint Petersburg, Florida
Source: *ConAu 102*

Pennock, Her(bert Jefferis)
"The Knight of Kenneth Square"
American. Baseball Player
b. Feb 10, 1894 in Kennett Square, Pennsylvania
d. Jan 30, 1948 in New York, New York
Source: *BaseEn; WhoProB 73*

Pentifallo, Kenny
see: Southside Johnny and the Asbury Jukes

Pep, Willie
[William Papaleo]
American. Boxer
b. Sep 19, 1922 in Middletown, Connecticut
Source: *BioIn 1, 3, 4, 7, 10; WhoBox 74*

Pepinle Bref
French. Father of Charlemagne
b. 715
d. 768
Source: *OxFr*

Pepitone, Joe (Joseph Anthony)
"Pepi"
American. Baseball Player
b. Oct 9, 1940 in Brooklyn, New York
Source: *BaseEn; CurBio 73; NewYTBE 70, 71, 72; NewYTBS 74; WhoProB 73*

Peppard, George
American. Actor
b. Oct 1, 1928 in Detroit, Michigan
Source: *CelR 73; CurBio 65; FilmgC; IntMPA 75, 76, 77, 78, 79, 80, 81, 82; MotPP; MovMk; WhoAm 74, 76, 78, 80, 82; WhoHol A; WorEFlm*

Pepper, Art(hur Edward)
American. Jazz Musician
With Stan Kenton, 1943-52; narcotics problems curtailed career.
b. Sep 1, 1925 in Gardena, California
d. Jun 15, 1982 in Los Angeles, California
Source: *BiDAmM; CmpEPM; EncJzS 70; IlEncJ; NewYTBS 82*

Pepper, Claude Denson
American. Politician
US senator, 1936-51; congressman, 1963--; supports social reform.
b. Sep 8, 1900 in Dudleyville, Alabama
Source: *BiDrAC; CngDr 74; CurBio 41, 83; IntWW 74; WhoAm 74, 76, 78, 80, 82; WhoAmP 73; WhoGov 72; WhoS&SW 73*

Pepusch, Johann Christoph (John)
German. Composer
b. 1667 in Berlin, Germany
d. Jul 20, 1752 in London, England
Source: *NewEOp 71; OxMus*

Pepys, Samuel
English. Diarist, Naval Officer
Kept diary, 1660-69, detailing social, daily conditions of Restoration life.
b. Feb 23, 1633 in London, England
d. May 26, 1703 in Clapham, England
Source: *Alli; AtlBL; BbD; BiD&SB; BrAu; CasWL; Chambr 1; CroE&S; CrtT 2; CyWA; DcEnA; DcEnL; DcEuL; DcLEL; EvLB; LongCTC; MouLC 1; NewC; OxEng; OxThe; Pen ENG; PlP&P; RAdv 1; REn; WebE&AL*

Perahia, Murray
American. Pianist, Conductor
b. Apr 19, 1947 in New York, New York
Source: *Baker 78; BiDAmM; BioIn 9, 10; CurBio 82; WhoAm 78, 80, 82*

Percy, Charles Harting
American. Senator, Author
Wrote *Growing Old in the Country of the Young,* 1974.
b. Sep 27, 1919 in Pensacola, Florida
Source: *BiDrAC; BioNews 74; CelR 73; ConAu 65; CurBio 59; IntWW 74; WhoAm 74, 76, 78, 80, 82; WhoAmP 73; WhoGov 72; WhoMW 74; WhoWor 74*

Percy, Walker
American. Author
b. May 28, 1916 in Birmingham, Alabama
Source: *ConAu 1R, 1NR; ConLC 1, 2, 3, 6, 8, 14, 18; ConNov 72, 76; DrAF 76; EncWL; ModAL, SUP; OxAmL; RAdv 1; WebE&AL; WhoAm 74, 76, 78, 80, 82; WhoS&SW 73; WhoWor 74; WorAu; WrDr 76*

Pereira, Aristides
Cape Verdean. President
b. Nov 17, 1924 in Cape Verde
Source: *IntWW 74; WhoWor 78*

Pereira, William Leonard
American. Architect, City Planner
b. Apr 25, 1909 in Chicago, Illinois
Source: *AmArch 70; BioIn 1, 5, 6, 11; CurBio 79; IntWW 74, 75, 76, 77, 78; WhoAm 74, 76, 80, 82; WhoWor 74*

Perelman, S(idney) J(oseph)
American. Author, Humorist
b. Feb 1, 1904 in Brooklyn, New York
d. Oct 17, 1979 in New York, New York
Source: *AmAu&B; Au&Wr 71; AuNews 1, 2; BiE&WWA; BioNews 75; CelR 73; ConAu 73, 89; ConLC 1, 3, 5, 9, 15; CurBio 71; DcLEL; FilmgC; IntWW 74; LongCTC; McGEWD; NewYTBE 70, 72; NotNAT; OxAmL; Pen AM; RAdv 1; REn; REnAL; TwCA, SUP; TwCW; WebAB; WebE&AL; Who 74; WhoAm 74; WhoWor 74; WrDr 76*

Peres, Shimon
Israeli. Statesman
b. 1923 in Wolozyn, Poland
Source: *BioIn 10, 11; CurBio 76; WhoWor 74; WhoWorJ 72*

Peret, Benjamin
French. Author, Poet
b. 1899 in Nantes, France
d. 1959 in Paris, France
Source: *BioIn 10; OxFr; Pen EUR*

Peretti, Elsa
American. Jewelry Designer
b. May 1, 1940 in Florence, Italy
Source: *NewYTBS 74; WhoAm 82; WorFshn*

Peretz, Isaac Loeb
Polish. Author
b. May 18, 1851 in Zamoszcz, Poland
d. Apr 3, 1915 in Warsaw, Poland
Source: *CnMD; EuAu; McGEWD; OxThe; Pen EUR*

Perez, Leander Henry
American. Politician
b. 1891
d. Mar 19, 1969 in Belle Chasse, Louisiana
Source: *BioIn 8, 10, 11*

Perez, Tony (Atanasio Rigal)
Cuban. Baseball Player
b. May 14, 1942 in Camaguey, Cuba
Source: *BaseEn; BioIn 9, 11; WhoAm 82; WhoProB 73*

Perez de Cuellar, Javier
Peruvian. Secretary-General of UN
b. Jan 19, 1920 in Lima, Peru
Source: *BioIn 11; CurBio 82; IntWW 74, 75, 76, 77; IntWW 77, 78, 79; WhoAm 74, 76; WhoGov 72; WhoUN 75; WhoWor 74, 76, 78*

Perez de la Cova, Carlos
Venezuelan. Diplomat
b. Apr 27, 1904 in Caracas, Venezuela
Source: *IntWW 74*

Perez Galdos, Benito
Spanish. Author
b. May 10, 1843 in Canary Islands, Spain
d. Jan 4, 1920 in Madrid, Spain
Source: *AtlBL; BiD&SB; CasWL; ClDMEL; CnMD; CyWA; DcSpL; EncWL; EvEuW; McGEWD; ModRL; ModWD; OxThe; Pen EUR; REn; TwCA, SUP*

Perez Jimenez, Marcos
Venezuelan. Politician
b. Apr 25, 1914 in Tachira, Venezuela
Source: *CurBio 54; IntWW 74*

Pergolesi, Giovanni Battista
Italian. Composer
b. Jan 4, 1710 in Jesi, Italy
d. Mar 16, 1736 in Pozzuoli, Italy
Source: *AtlBL; OxMus; REn*

Peri, Jacopo
Italian. Composer
b. Aug 20, 1561 in Rome, Italy
d. Aug 12, 1633 in Florence, Italy
Source: *NewEOp 71; OxMus*

Pericles
Greek. Statesman
Led Democratic party, 460-429BC; called "The Periclean Age."
b. 495?BC
d. 429?BC in Athens, Greece
Source: *NewC; REn*

Perignon, Dominique Catherine
French. Field Marshal
b. 1754
d. 1818
Source: *OxFr*

Perkin, Sir William Henry
English. Chemist
b. Mar 12, 1838 in London, England
d. Jul 14, 1907 in Sudbury, England
Source: *AsBiEn; BioIn 1, 5; NewCol 75; WebBD 80*

Perkins, Al
see: Souther-Hillman-Furay Band, The

Perkins, Anthony
American. Actor
Son of Osgood Perkins; starred in *Psycho.*
b. Apr 14, 1932 in New York, New York
Source: *BkPepl; CurBio 60; FilmgC; IntMPA 75, 76, 77, 78, 79, 80, 81, 82; MotPP; MovMk; NewYTBE 72; NotNAT; OxFilm; WhoAm 74, 76, 78, 80, 82; WhoHol A; WhoThe 77; WorEFlm*

Perkins, Carl
American. Songwriter
b. Apr 9, 1932 in Jackson, Tennessee
Source: *BioIn 9, 11; ConAu 102; EncFCWM 69; WhoAm 82; WhoHol A*

Perkins, Frances
American. Government Official
First woman to serve in cabinet position; secretary of labor, 1933-45.
b. Apr 10, 1882 in Boston, Massachusetts
d. May 14, 1965 in New York, New York
Source: *BiDrUSE; CurBio 40, 65; EncAB-H; HerW; InWom; WebAB; WhAm 4; WhAmP; WomWWA 14*

Perkins, Jacob
American. Inventor
Inventions include machine for cutting, heading nails in one operation.
b. Jul 9, 1766 in Newburyport, Massachusetts
d. Jul 30, 1849 in London, England
Source: *AmBi; ApCAB; DcAmB; Drake; NatCAB 10; NewYHSD; WhAm H*

Perkins, Maxwell Evarts
American. Editor
Edited Thomas Wolfe's first novels: *Look Homeward Angel; Of Time and the River.*
b. Sep 20, 1884 in New York, New York
d. Jun 17, 1947 in Stamford, Connecticut
Source: *AmAu&B; BioIn 1, 2, 3, 6, 9, 11; NatCAB 37; REnAL*

Perkins, Millie
American. Actress
b. May 12, 1940 in New Jersey
Source: *FilmgC; MotPP; WhoHol A*

Perkins, Milo Randolph
American. Government Official
b. Jan 28, 1900 in Milwaukee, Wisconsin
d. Oct 26, 1972
Source: *BioIn 1; CurBio 42; WhAm 5*

Perkins, Osgood
American. Actor
b. 1892 in West Newton, Massachusetts
d. Sep 23, 1937 in Washington, DC
Source: *FamA&A; FilmgC; PlP&P; WhScrn 74, 77; WhoHol B*

Perkins, (Richard) Marlin
American. Naturalist
b. Mar 28, 1902 in Carthage, Missouri
Source: *ConAu 103; SmATA 21; WebAB; WhoAm 74*

Perkins, (Walter) Ray
American. Football Coach
b. Dec 6, 1941 in Olive, Mississippi
Source: *NewYTBS 79, 82*

Perky, Henry D
American. Cereal Manufacturer
Devised machine for shredding wheat kernels.
b. Dec 7, 1843 in Mount Holmes, Ohio
d. Jun 29, 1906 in Glencoe, Maryland
Source: *NatCAB 13, 24*

Perlea, Jonel
Romanian. Conductor, Educator
b. 1901
d. Jul 30, 1970
Source: *BioIn 2, 4, 9; NewYTBE 70; WhoMus 72*

Perlman, Itzhak
Israeli. Violinist
b. Aug 31, 1945 in Tel Aviv, Palestine
Source: *Who 82; WhoMus 72*

Perls, Frederick Salomon
German. Author, Psychiatrist
b. 1894 in Germany
d. Mar 14, 1970 in Chicago, Illinois
Source: *BioIn 8, 9, 10; ConAu 29R; NewYTBE 70*

Peron, Eva Duarte
[Mrs. Juan Peron]
"Evita"
Argentine. Political Figure
Co-governed with husband; play *Evita* based on her life.
b. May 7, 1919 in Los Toldos, Argentina
d. Jul 26, 1952 in Buenos Aires, Argentina
Source: *BioIn 9, 10, 11; CurBio 49, 52; InWom*

Peron, Isabel
[Mrs. Juan Peron]
Argentine. First Woman President
Succeeded husband as president, 1974-76; deposed in military coup.
b. Feb 4, 1931 in Las Rioja, Argentina
Source: *BioNews 74; CurBio 75; IntWW 74; NewYTBE 73; NewYTBS 74*

Peron, Juan
Argentine. President
Ruled, 1946-55, 1973-74.
b. Oct 8, 1895 in Lobos, Argentina
d. Jul 1, 1974 in Buenos Aires, Argentina
Source: *BioNews 74; ConAu 49; CurBio 44, 74; NewYTBS 74; WhAm 6; WhoWor 74*

Perot, (Henry) Ross
American. Philanthropist, Businessman
b. Jun 27, 1930 in Texarkana, Texas
Source: *BusPN; CurBio 71; IntWW 74; NewYTBE 71, 73; WhoAm 74; WhoS&SW 73*

Perpich, Rudy George
American. Governor of Minnesota
Former governor returned to office in 1982 elections.
b. Jun 27, 1928 in Carson Lake, Minnesota
Source: *AlmAP 78; AmCath 80; BiDrGov; IntWW 78, 79, 80, 81; WhoAm 74, 76, 78, 80, 82; WhoAmP 73, 75, 77, 79; WhoGov 72, 75, 77; WhoMW 74, 76, 78*

Perranoski, Ron(ald Peter)
American. Baseball Player
b. Apr 1, 1936 in Paterson, New Jersey
Source: *BaseEn; BioIn 7; WhoProB 73*

Perrault, Charles
French. Author, Poet
Known for his collection of fairy tales, 1697.
b. Jan 12, 1628 in Paris, France
d. May 16, 1703 in Paris, France
Source: *AnCL; BbD; BiD&SB; CarSB; CasWL; ChPo; DcEuL; EuAu; EvEuW; NewC; OxEng; OxFr; Pen EUR; REn; Str&VC; WhoChL*

Perrault, Claude
French. Physician, Architect
b. 1613
d. 1688
Source: *BioIn 10; NewCol 75; WhDW*

Perreault, Gilbert
Canadian. Hockey Player
b. Nov 13, 1950 in Victoriaville, PQ
Source: *BioIn 9, 10, 11; WhoHcky 73*

Perrin, Emile Cesare
French. Impresario
b. Jan 19, 1814 in Rouen, France
d. Oct 8, 1885 in Paris, France
Source: *NewEOp 71*

Perrine, Valerie
American. Actress
b. Sep 3, 1943 in Galveston, Texas
Source: *IntMPA 77, 78, 79, 80, 81, 82; NewYTBS 74; WhoAm 82; WhoHol A*

Perry, Antoinette
American. Actress, Director
Tony award is named for her.
b. Jun 27, 1888 in Denver, Colorado
d. Jun 28, 1946 in New York, New York
Source: *CurBio 46; DcAmB S4; InWom; NotAW; WhAm 2; WhScrn 74, 77; WhoHol B*

Perry, Bliss
American. Author, Educator
b. Nov 25, 1860 in Williamstown, Massachusetts
d. Feb 13, 1954 in Exeter, New Hampshire
Source: *AmAu&B; ApCAB SUP; BbD; BiD&SB; CnDAL; ConAmL; DcAmAu; DcAmB S5; LongCTC; OxAmL; REn; REnAL; TwCA, SUP; TwCBDA; WhAm 3*

Perry, Eleanor Bayer
[Oliver Weld Bayer, pseud.]
American. Screenwriter, Author
b. 1915? in Cleveland, Ohio
d. Mar 14, 1981 in New York, New York
Source: *AnObit 1981; ConAu 103; ConDr 73, 77A; IntMPA 75, 76, 77, 78, 79, 80, 81; NewYTBE 73; WhoAm 74, 76, 78, 80; WhoAmW 68, 70, 72, 74; WomWMM, B*

Perry, Frank
American. Motion Picture Director
b. 1930 in New York, New York
Source: *BioIn 9; CurBio 72; FilmEn; FilmgC; IntMPA 75, 76, 77, 78, 79, 80, 81; MovMk; WhoAm 74, 76, 78, 80, 82; WhoHol A*

Perry, Gaylord Jackson
American. Baseball Player
Over 300 victories; over 3,000 strikeouts; won Cy Young award in both leagues.
b. Sep 15, 1938 in Williamston, North Carolina
Source: *BaseEn; BioNews 74; CurBio 82; NewYTBE 72, 73; NewYTBS 74; WhoAm 74, 76, 78, 80, 82; WhoProB 73*

Perry, Guy
see: Motels, The

Perry, Matthew Calbraith, Commodore
American. Naval Officer
b. Apr 10, 1794 in Newport, Rhode Island
d. Mar 4, 1858 in New York, New York
Source: *Alli; AmBi; ApCAB; BiAuS; DcAmB; DcNAA; EncAB-H; OxAmL; REn; REnAL; TwCBDA; WebAB; WhAm H*

Perry, Nancy Ling
[S(ymbionese) L(iberation) A(rmy)]
American. Revolutionary
b. in Santa Rosa, California
d. May 24, 1974 in Los Angeles, California
Source: *BioIn 10*

Perry, Oliver Hazard, Admiral
American. Naval Officer
b. Aug 20, 1785 in South Kingstown, Rhode Island
d. Aug 23, 1819 in Angostura, Venezuela
Source: *Alli; AmBi; ApCAB; BbtC; DcAmB; Drake; EncAB-H; OxAmL; REn; REnAL; TwCBDA; WebAB; WhAm H*

Perry, Ralph Barton
American. Author, Educator
b. Jul 3, 1876 in Poultney, Vermont
d. Jan 22, 1957 in Boston, Massachusetts
Source: *AmAu&B; OxAmL; REnAL; TwCA, SUP; WhAm 3; WhNAA*

Perry, Steve
see: Journey

Persh, John
see: Rare Earth

Pershing, John J(oseph)
"Black Jack"
American. Army Commander
Won Pulitzer Prize, 1932, for *My Experiences in the World War.*
b. Sep 13, 1860 in Linn City, Missouri
d. Jul 15, 1948 in Washington, DC
Source: *AmAu&B; DcAmB S4; DcNAA; EncAB-H; OxAmL; REn; REnAL; WebAB; WhAm 2*

Persiani, Fanny
[Fanny Tacchinardi]
Italian. Opera Singer
b. Oct 4, 1812 in Rome, Italy
d. Nov 3, 1867 in Neuilly, France
Source: *InWom*

Persichetti, Vincent
American. Composer
b. Jun 6, 1915 in Philadelphia, Pennsylvania
Source: *AmSCAP 66; DcCM; WhoAm 74, 76, 78, 80, 82*

Persinger, Gregory A
[The Hostages]
American. Former Hostage in Iran
b. Dec 25, 1957
Source: *NewYTBS 81*

Persinger, Louis
American. Musician, Conductor
b. Feb 11, 1888 in Rochester, Illinois
d. Dec 31, 1966 in New York, New York
Source: *WhAm 4*

Persius
Roman. Satirist
b. Dec 4, 34? in Volaterrae, Italy
d. Nov 24, 62?
Source: *CasWL; NewC; OxEng; REn*

Persoff, Nehemiah
American. Actor
b. Aug 14, 1920 in Jerusalem, Palestine
Source: *BiE&WWA; FilmgC; IntMPA 75, 76, 77, 78, 79, 80, 81, 82; MotPP; NotNAT; WhoAm 74, 76, 78, 80, 82; WhoHol A; WhoThe 77; WhoWor 74*

Pertegaz, Manuel
Spanish. Fashion Designer
b. in Aragon, Spain
Source: *WorFshn*

Pertile, Aureliano
Italian. Opera Singer
b. Nov 9, 1885 in Montagnana, Italy
d. Jan 11, 1952 in Milan, Italy
Source: *NewEOp 71*

Pertini, Alessandro
Italian. President
b. Sep 25, 1896 in Stella, Italy
Source: *BioIn 11; NewYTBS 78*

Perugino
Italian. Artist
b. 1445 in Perugia, Italy
d. 1523 in Perugia, Italy
Source: *AtlBL; NewC*

Pestalozzi, Johann Heinrich
Swiss. Author, Philanthropist
b. Jan 12, 1746 in Zurich, Switzerland
d. Feb 17, 1827 in Aargau, Switzerland
Source: *BbD; BiD&SB; CasWL; DcEuL; EuAu; EvEuW; OxGer; Pen EUR; REn*

Petacci, Clara
Italian. Mistress of Mussolini
b. 1912
d. Apr 29, 1945 in Milan, Italy
Source: *BioIn 1, 2, 6*

Petain, Henri Phillippe
French. Military Leader, Statesman
Defended Verdun, 1916; premier, 1940, later headed Vichy govt.
b. Apr 24, 1856 in Cauchy a la Tour, France
d. Jul 23, 1951 in Island of Yeu
Source: *CurBio 40, 51; LongCTC; OxFr; REn*

Peter II
Yugoslav. King
b. Sep 6, 1923
d. Nov 4, 1970 in Los Angeles, California
Source: *BioIn 1, 3, 4, 5, 7, 8, 9, 10; CurBio 43, 70*

Peter, Saint
Biblical Character
d. 64?
Source: *NewCol 75*

Peter the Great
[Peter I]
Russian. Czar
b. May 30, 1672 in Moscow, Russia
d. Jan 28, 1725 in Saint Petersburg, Russia
Source: *CasWL; DcRusL; NewCol 75; REn; WebBD 80; WhoMilH 76*

Peter, Paul, and Mary
[Noel Paul Stookey; Mary Travers; Peter Yarrow]
American. Folk Singers
Won Grammy, 1963, for "Blowin' in the Wind"; group disbanded, 1971.
Source: *EncFCWM 69; IlEncRk*

Peter, Laurence Johnston
American. Educator, Author
b. Sep 16, 1919 in Vancouver, BC
Source: *AmM&WS 73S; ConAu 21R; LEduc 74; WhoAm 74, 76, 78, 80, 82*

Peter and Gordon
[Peter Asher; Gordon Waller]
English. Rock Duo
Source: *ConMuA 80; RkOn 2; WhoRock 81*

Peterik, Jim
see: Survivor

Peterkin, Julia Mood
American. Author
b. Oct 31, 1880 in Laurens County, South Carolina
d. Aug 10, 1961 in Orangeburg, South Carolina
Source: *AmAu&B; CnDAL; ConAmA; ConAu 102; LongCTC; OxAmL; REn; REnAL; TwCA, SUP; WhAm 4*

Peters, Audrey
American. Actress
b. in Maplewood, New Jersey
Source: *BioIn 10; BioNews 75; WhoHol A*

Peters, Bernadette
[Bernadette Lazzara]
American. Actress, Singer
b. Feb 28, 1948 in Queens, New York
Source: *BkPepl; EncMT; IntMPA 82; NotNAT; WhoAm 80, 82; WhoHol A; WhoThe 77*

Peters, Brandon
American. Actor
b. 1893 in Troy, New York
d. Feb 27, 1956 in New York, New York
Source: *BioIn 4; NotNAT B*

Peters, Brock
American. Actor, Singer
b. Jul 27, 1927 in New York, New York
Source: *BiE&WWA; FilmgC; IntMPA 75, 76, 77, 78, 79, 80, 81, 82; MotPP; MovMk; NotNAT; WhoAm 74, 76, 78, 80, 82; WhoBlA 75; WhoHol A; WomWMM*

Peters, Elizabeth, pseud.
see: Mertz, Barbara Louise Gross

Peters, Ellis, pseud.
[Edith Mary Pargeter]
English. Author
b. Sep 28, 1913 in Horsehay, England
Source: *Au&Wr 71; BioIn 10; ConAu 1R; IntAu&W 76, 77; LongCTC; ScF&FL 1, 2; TwCCr&M; WhE&EA; WhoWor 76; WorAu; WrDr 76, 80*

Peters, Frederick Emerson
American. Swindler
b. 1885 in New Salem, Ohio
d. Jul 29, 1959 in New Haven, Connecticut
Source: *BioIn 3, 5*

Peters, Jean
American. Actress
b. Oct 15, 1926 in Canton, Ohio
Source: *FilmgC; IntMPA 75; MotPP; MovMk; WhoHol A; WorEFlm*

Peters, Jon
American. Hairdresser, Producer
b. 1945
Source: *BioIn 10, 11; IntMPA 82*

Peters, Roberta
[Roberta Peterman]
American. Opera Singer
b. May 4, 1930 in New York, New York
Source: *CelR 73; CurBio 54; InWom; WhoAm 74, 76, 78, 80, 82; WhoE 74; WhoAmW 77; WhoHol A; WhoMus 72; WhoWor 74; WhoWorJ 72*

Peters, Susan
[Suzanne Carnahan]
American. Actress
b. Jul 3, 1921 in Spokane, Washington
d. Oct 23, 1952 in Visalia, California
Source: *FilmgC; MotPP; MovMk; WhScrn 74, 77; WhoHol B*

Peters, Svetlana
see: Stalina, Svetlana Alliluyeva

Petersen, Donald Eugene
American. Automobile Executive
President, Ford Motor Co., 1980--.
b. Sep 4, 1926 in Pipestone, Minnesota
Source: *WhoF&I 74, 75; WhoMW 74, 76, 78; WhoAm 78, 80, 82*

Peterson, Clarence
American. Businessman
b. Jul 14, 1904 in Martins Ferry, Ohio
Source: *St&PR 75; WhoAm 74; WhoF&I 74; WhoIns 75*

Peterson, Oscar (Emmauel)
Canadian. Jazz Musician
b. Aug 15, 1925 in Montreal, PQ
Source: *CanWW 70; CelR 73; CreCan 1; WhoAm 74, 76, 78, 80, 82; WhoWor 74*

Peterson, Roger Tory
American. Ornithologist
b. Aug 28, 1908 in Jamestown, New York
Source: *CelR 73; ConAu 1R, 1NR; CurBio 59; IntWW 74; NewYTBS 74; REnAL; TwCA SUP; WebAB; WhoAm 74, 76, 78, 80, 82; WhoWor 74*

Peterson, Ronnie
Swedish. Auto Racer
b. 1944
d. Sep 11, 1978 in Monza, Italy
Source: *BioIn 11*

Peterson, Virgilia
American. Critic
b. May 16, 1904 in New York, New York
d. Dec 24, 1966 in New York, New York
Source: *AmAu&B; ConAu 25R; CurBio 53, 67; InWom; WhAm 4; WorAu*

Petesson, Tom
see: Cheap Trick

Petipa, Marius
French. Dancer, Choreographer
b. Mar 11, 1822 in Marseilles, France
d. Jun 2, 1910 in Gurzuf, Russia
Source: *DcBiPP; WhDW*

Petit, Pascale
[Anne-Marie Petit]
French. Actress
b. Feb 27, 1938 in Paris, France
Source: *FilmEn; FilmgC; WhoHol A*

Petit, Roland
French. Dancer, Choreographer
b. Jan 13, 1924 in Villemomble, France
Source: *CurBio 52; IntWW 74; Who 74; WhoHol A; WhoThe 77; WhoWor 74*

Peto, John Frederick
American. Artist
b. May 21, 1854 in Philadelphia, Pennsylvania
d. Nov 23, 1907 in Island Heights, New Jersey
Source: *BioIn 2, 5; BnEnAmA; DcAmArt; McGDA; McGEWB; NewCol 75*

Petrarch, Francesco
Italian. Poet, Humorist
b. Jul 20, 1304 in Arezzo, Italy
d. Jul 19, 1374 in Arqua, Italy
Source: *AtlBL; BbD; BiD&SB; CasWL; CroE&S; CyWA; EuAu; EvEuW; NewC; OxEng; Pen EUR; RComWL; REn*

Petri, Elio
Italian. Film Director
Won Oscar, 1970, for *Invesitgation of a Citizen above Suspicion.*
b. Jan 29, 1929 in Rome, Italy
d. Nov 10, 1982 in Rome, Italy
Source: *DcFM; FilmEn; FilmgC; NewYTBS 82; WorEFlm*

Petrie, Sir Charles Alexander
English. Historian
b. Sep 28, 1895 in Liverpool, England
d. Dec 13, 1977 in London, England
Source: *Au&Wr 71; ConAu 17R; DcLEL; IntWW 74; TwCA SUP; Who 74; WhoWor 74*

Petrie, Sir (William Matthew) Flinders
English. Egyptologist
b. Jun 3, 1853 in Charlton, England
d. Jul 28, 1942 in Jerusalem, Palestine
Source: *BioIn 5, 6, 7, 8; DcScB; LongCTC; REn; WhoLA*

Petrillo, James Caesar
American. Union Leader
b. Mar 16, 1892 in Chicago, Illinois
Source: *CurBio 40; WhoF&I 74*

Petrocelli, Anthony
American. Fashion Designer
b. 1895
d. Mar 2, 1974 in New York, New York
Source: *NewYTBS 74*

Petrocelli, Rico (Americo Peter)
American. Baseball Player
b. Jun 27, 1943 in Brooklyn, New York
Source: *BaseEn; BioIn 9; WhoProB 73*

Petroff, Ossip
Russian. Opera Singer
b. Nov 15, 1807 in Elisavetgrad, Russia
d. Mar 14, 1878 in Saint Petersburg, Russia
Source: *NewEOp 71*

Petronius, Gaius
Roman. Author
Source: *CasWL; OxEng; RComWL*

Petrosian, Tigran Vartanovich
Russian. Chess Player
b. 1929 in U.S.S.R.
Source: *BioIn 8, 9, 10; IntWW 74*

Pettet, Joanna
American. Actress
b. 1945 in London, England
Source: *FilmgC; WhoHol A*

Pettiford, Oscar
American. Jazz Musician
b. Sep 30, 1922 in Okmulgee, Oklahoma
d. Sep 8, 1960 in Copenhagen, Denmark
Source: *WhoJazz 72*

Pettingill, Amos, pseud.
see: Harris, William Bliss

Pettit, William Thomas
American. Journalist
b. Apr 23, 1931 in Cincinnati, Ohio
Source: *WhoAm 74, 76, 78, 80, 82*

Petty, Richard
American. Auto Racer
Won Daytona 500 six times.
b. Jul 2, 1938 in Level Cross, North Carolina
Source: *BioIn 7, 8, 9, 10; BioNews 74; CelR 73; WhoAm 74, 76, 78, 80, 82*

Petty, Tom
[Tom Petty and the Heartbreakers]
American. Rock Musician
b. 1953 in Gainesville, Florida
Source: *BioIn 11; IlEncRk*

Peugeot, Rodolphe
French. Auto Executive
Former president, now director Societe Peugeot et Cie.
b. Apr 2, 1902 in Selancourt, France
Source: *IntWW 74, 75, 76, 77, 78, 79, 80, 81; WhoF&I 74; WhoWor 74*

Pevsner, Antoine
Russian. Artist
b. Jan 18, 1886 in Orel, Russia
d. Apr 12, 1962 in Paris, France
Source: *CurBio 59, 62; WhAm 4*

Pevsner, Sir Nikolaus
English. Architect, Art Historian
b. Jan 30, 1902 in Leipzig, Germany
Source: *Au&Wr 71; ConAu 9R; DcLEL; IntWW 74; LongCTC; Who 74; WhoWor 74; WorAu; WrDr 76*

Peyre, Henri Maurice
American. Author, Educator
b. Feb 21, 1901 in Paris, France
Source: *AmAu&B; Au&Wr 71; ConAu 5R, 3NR; DrAS 74F; WhoAm 82; WhoWor 74*

Peyrefitte, Roger
French. Author
b. Aug 17, 1907 in Castres, France
Source: *ConAu 65; EvEuW; IntWW 74; Pen EUR; REn; TwCW; Who 74; WhoWor 74; WorAu*

Pfeiffer, Jane Cahill
American. Corporation Executive
b. Sep 29, 1932 in Washington, DC
Source: *BioIn 11; CurBio 80; WhoAm 82*

Pfitzner, Hans
German. Composer
b. May 5, 1869 in Moscow, Russia
d. May 22, 1949 in Salzburg, Austria
Source: *DcCM; OxGer*

Pfizer, Charles
Drug Manufacturer
Source: *NF*

Pham van Dong
Vietnamese. Political Leader
b. Mar 1, 1906 in Quang Nam, Vietnam
Source: *CurBio 75; WhoWor 74*

Phelps, "Digger" (Richard)
American. Basketball Coach
b. Jul 4, 1941 in Beacon, New York
Source: *BioIn 10; WhoAm 82*

Phelps, Elizabeth Stuart
American. Children's Author
b. Aug 13, 1815 in Andover, Massachusetts
d. Nov 30, 1852
Source: *Alli; AmAu; AmAu&B; AmBi; ApCAB; BiDrLUS 70; CarSB; Chambr 3; CyAL 1; DcAmAu; DcNAA; Drake; InWom; OxAmL; REnAL; TwCBDA; WomWWA 14*

Phelps, Robert Eugene
American. Educator
b. Jul 15, 1924 in Kansas City, Missouri
Source: *LEduc 74; WhoE 74*

Phelps, William Lyon
American. Educator, Journalist
b. Jan 2, 1865 in New Haven, Connecticut
d. Aug 21, 1943 in New Haven, Connecticut
Source: *AmAu&B; ChPo, S1; CnDAL; ConAmL; CurBio 43; DcAmAu; DcAmB S3; DcNAA; EvLB; LongCTC; OxAmL; REnAL; TwCA, SUP; WhAm 2*

Phidias
Greek. Sculptor
b. 500BC in Athens, Greece
d. 432BC
Source: *AtlBL; REn*

Phil Napoleon and Memphis Six
Music Group
Source: *NF*

Philbrick, Herbert Arthur
American. Author, FBI Agent
b. May 11, 1915
Source: *CurBio 53*

Philby, Harold St. John Bridger
British. Explorer, Author
Advisor to King Ibn Saud of Saudi Arabia for 30 years.
b. 1885
d. Sep 30, 1960 in Beirut, Lebanon
Source: *NewCol 75; WebBD 80*

Philby, Kim (Harold Adrian Russell)
English. Traitor
b. 1912
Source: *NewCol 75; WebBD 80*

Philidor, Francois Andre
[Francois Danican]
French. Composer
b. Sep 7, 1726 in Dreux, France
d. Aug 24, 1795 in London, England
Source: *DcBiPP; NewEOp 71; OxFr*

Philip II
[Philip of Macedon]
Macedonian. Alexander the Great's Father
b. 382BC in Macedonia
d. 336BC
Source: *NewCol 75; WebBD 80*

Philip II
[Philip Augustus]
French. King
b. 1165
d. 1223
Source: *NewCol 75; WebBD 80*

Philip II
Spanish. King
b. 1527
d. 1598
Source: *BioIn 10; DcBiPP; NewCol 75; WebBD 80*

Philip V
Macedonian. King
b. 237BC
d. 179BC
Source: *BioIn 10; NewCol 75*

Philip VI
[Philip of Valois]
French. King
b. 1293
d. 1350
Source: *NewCol 75; WebBD 80*

Philip, Prince
[Duke of Edinburgh]
English. Husband of Elizabeth II
Became British citizen, 1947, renouncing Greek, Danish ties; married Elizabeth Nov 20, 1947.
b. Jun 10, 1921 in Corfu, Greece
Source: *BioIn 1, 2, 3, 5, 6, 7, 8, 9, 10, 11; CurBio 47; IntWW 74; WhoWor 74*

Philip, Saint
Biblical Character
Source: *NewCol 75; WebBD 80*

Philipe, Gerard
French. Actor, Motion Picture Director
b. Dec 4, 1922 in Cannes, France
d. Nov 27, 1959 in Paris, France
Source: *FilmgC; MotPP; MovMk; NotNAT; OxFilm; OxThe; WhScrn 74, 77; WhoHol; WorEFlm*

Philips, David Graham
[John Graham, pseud.]
American. Journalist, Author
b. Oct 31, 1867 in Madison, Indiana
d. Jan 24, 1911 in New York, New York
Source: *AmAu&B; CnDAL; DcLEL; DcNAA; IndAu 1816; LongCTC; OxAmL; REn; REnAL*

Phillips, Adelaide
English. Opera Singer
b. 1833 in Stratford, England
d. Oct 3, 1882 in Carlsbad, Bohemia
Source: *AmBi; Drake; InWom*

Phillips, Anthony
see: Genesis

Phillips, "Bum" (Oail Andrew)
American. Football Coach
b. Sep 29, 1923 in Orange, Texas
Source: *BioIn 10, 12; WhoAm 80, 82; WhoS&SW 78*

Phillips, John
[The Mamas and the Papas]
American. Singer
Founded group, 1965, in Virgin Islands; hit song "Monday, Monday."
b. Aug 30, 1935 in Parris Island, South Carolina
Source: *BioIn 7, 9, 11*

Phillips, Kevin Price
American. Journalist
b. Nov 30, 1940 in New York, New York
Source: *ConAu 65; WhoAm 76, 78, 80, 82; WhoAmP 73*

Phillips, (Laura) MacKenzie
American. Actress
Starred in *American Graffiti,* 1973; on TV series "One Day at a Time."
b. Nov 10, 1959 in Alexandria, Virginia
Source: *BioIn 10, 11; MovMk*

Phillips, Mark (Anthony Peter)
English. Husband of Princess Anne
b. Sep 22, 1948 in England
Source: *BioIn 9, 10, 11; NewYTBE 73; Who 74*

Phillips, Michelle Gillam
[The Mamas and the Papas]
American. Actress, Singer
b. Apr 6, 1944 in Long Beach, California
Source: *BioIn 7, 9, 11*

Phillips, Ricky
see: Babys, The

Phillips, Robin
English. Actor, Motin Picture Director
b. Feb 28, 1942 in Haslemere, England
Source: *BioIn 10; CanWW 79; WhoAm 78, 80, 82; WhoThe 77*

Phillips, Sian
Welsh. Actress
b. 1934 in Bettws, Wales
Source: *FilmgC; WhoHol A; WhoThe 77*

Phillips, Wendell
American. Author, Abolitionist
b. Nov 29, 1811 in Boston, Massachusetts
d. Feb 2, 1884 in Boston, Massachusetts
Source: *Alli; AmAu; AmAu&B; AmBi; ApCAB; BiD&SB; Chambr 3; ChPo; CyAl 2; DcAmAu; DcAmB; DcNAA; Drake; EncAB-H; OxAmL; REn; REnAL; TwCBDA; WebAB; WhAm H*

Phillpotts, Eden
English. Children's Author
b. Nov 4, 1862 in Mount Aber, India
d. Dec 29, 1960 in Exeter, England
Source: *BbD; BiD&SB; CarSB; Chambr 3; ConAu 93, 102; DcBiA; DcEnA AP; DcLEL; EncMys; EvLB; LongCTC; ModBrL; NewC; OxThe; REn; SmATA 24; TwCA, SUP; TwCW; WhAm 4; WhoChL; WhoLA*

Philo
Alexandrian. Philosopher
b. 20BC
d. 50AD
Source: *NewCol 75; WebBD 80*

Phryne
[Mnesarete]
Greek. Courtesan
b. 300BC
Source: *InWom; NewC; REn*

Phyfe, Duncan
Scottish. Cabinetmaker
b. 1768 in Inverness, Scotland
d. Aug 16, 1854 in New York, New York
Source: *AmBi; DcAmB; OxAmL; WebAB; WhAm H*

Piaf, Edith
French. Singer
b. Dec 1915 in Paris, France
d. Oct 11, 1963 in Paris, France
Source: *CurBio 50, 63; InWom; OxThe; WhAm 4; WhScrn 74, 77; WhoHol B*

Piaget, Jean
Swiss. Psychologist
Known for contributions to child psychology, intellectual development.
b. Aug 9, 1896 in Neuchatel, Switzerland
d. Sep 16, 1980 in Vienna, Austria
Source: *ConAu 21R, 101; CurBio 58, 80; IntWW 74; Who 74; WhoWor 74*

Piastro, Mishel
Russian. Conductor
b. Sep 1892 in Keatz, Russia
d. Apr 10, 1970 in New York, New York
Source: *NewYTBE 70; WhAm 5*

Piatigorsky, Gregor
Russian. Musician
b. Apr 17, 1903 in Ekaterinoslav, Russia
d. Aug 6, 1976 in Los Angeles, California
Source: *CelR 73; CurBio 45; Who 74; WhoAm 74; WhoMus 72; WhoWor 74*

Piave, Francesco Maria
Italian. Librettist
b. May 18, 1810 in Mureno, Italy
d. Mar 5, 1876 in Milan, Italy
Source: *NewEOp 71*

Piazza, Ben
American. Actor, Author
b. Jul 30, 1934 in Little Rock, Arkansas
Source: *BiE&WWA; ConAu 9R; FilmgC; MotPP; NotNAT; WhoHol A; WhoThe 77*

Piazza, Marguerite
American. Opera Singer, Actress
b. May 6, 1926 in New Orleans, Louisiana
Source: *BioNews 74; WhoAm 74, 76, 78, 80, 82*

Picabia, Francis
French. Author
b. Jan 22, 1879 in Paris, France
d. Nov 30, 1953 in Paris, France
Source: *AtlBL*

Picard, Charles Emile
French. Mathematician
b. 1856
d. 1941
Source: *WebBD 80*

Picard, Edmond
Belgian. Lawyer, Author
b. Dec 15, 1836 in Brussels, Belgium
d. Feb 19, 1924 in Belgium
Source: *CasWL; ClDMEL*

Picard, Raymond
French. Author, Critic
b. 1917
d. 1975
Source: *BioIn 10*

Picasso, Pablo
Spanish. Artist
Major works "Les Demoiselles d'Avignon," 1907; "Guernica," 1937.
b. Oct 25, 1881 in Malaga, Spain
d. Apr 9, 1973 in Mougins, France
Source: *BioNews 74; ConAu 41R; CurBio 43, 62, 73; DcFM; NewYTBE 71, 73; OxFr; REn; WhAm 5; WhScrn 77; WhoGrA*

Piccard, Auguste
Swiss. Physicist
b. Jan 28, 1884 in Basel, Switzerland
d. Mar 1, 1962 in Lausanne, Switzerland
Source: *CurBio 47, 62*

Piccard, Jacques
Swiss. Inventor, Explorer
Built bathyscoph; made deepest dive ever, 1960, to 35,800 feet.
b. Jul 28, 1922 in Brussels, Belgium
Source: *BioIn 7, 8, 9; ConAu 65; CurBio 65; IntWW 74; Who 74; WhoWor 74*

Piccard, Jeannette Ridlon
American. Balloonist, Episcopoal Priest
b. Jan 5, 1895 in Chicago, Illinois
d. May 17, 1981 in Minneapolis, Minnesota
Source: *BioIn 11; WhoAm 74, 76, 78, 80; WhoAmW 74; WhoRel 75, 77*

Piccaver, Alfred
English. Opera Singer
b. Feb 15, 1884 in Long Sutton, England
d. Sep 23, 1958 in Vienna, Austria
Source: *NewEOp 71*

Piccini, Nicola
Italian. Composer
b. Jan 16, 1725 in Bari, Italy
d. May 7, 1800 in Passy, France
Source: *Chambr 1; NewEOp 71; OxMus*

Piccolo, Brian
"Pic"
American. Football Player
Running back, Chicago, 1965-69; movie *Brian's Song,* 1973, based on life.
b. Oct 21, 1943 in Pittsfield, Massachusetts
d. Jun 16, 1970 in New York, New York
Source: *BioIn 8, 9; NewYTBE 70; WhoFtbl 74*

Pickens, Andrew
American. Military Leader
b. Sep 19, 1739 in Paxton, Pennsylvania
d. Aug 11, 1817 in Pendleton, South Carolina
Source: *AmBi; ApCAB; BiAuS; BiDrAC; DcAmB; Drake; TwCBDA; WhAm H*

Pickens, "Slim"
[Louis Bert Lindley]
American. Actor
b. Jun 29, 1919 in Kingsberg, California
Source: *FilmgC; IntMPA 75, 76, 77, 78, 79, 80, 81, 82; MovMk; Vers A; WhoHol A*

Pickering, Edward Charles
American. Astronomer
Directed Harvard Observatory, 1877-1919; devised meridian photometer.
b. Jul 19, 1846 in Boston, Massachusetts
d. Feb 3, 1919 in Cambridge, Massachusetts
Source: *Alli SUP; AmBi; ApCAB; BiDPara; DcAmAu; DcAmB; DcNAA; TwCBDA; WebAB; WhAm 1*

Pickering, William
English. Publisher
b. Apr 2, 1796 in London, England
d. Apr 27, 1854 in London, England
Source: *BioIn 9; NewC*

Pickering, William Henry
American. Astronomer
Predicted existence, location of ninth planet, 1919.
b. Feb 15, 1858 in Boston, Massachusetts
d. Jan 16, 1938 in Jamaica
Source: *AmBi; ApCAB; DcAmAu; DcNAA; WhAm 1; WhNAA*

Pickett, George Edward
American. Military Leader
Confederate general; "Pickett's charge" at Gettysburg disaster for South, 1863.
b. Jan 25, 1825 in Richmond, Virginia
d. Jul 30, 1875 in Norfolk, Virginia
Source: *AmBi; ApCAB; BiDConf; DcAmB; Drake; TwCBDA; WebAB; WhAm H*

Pickett, Wilson
American. Singer, Songwriter
b. Mar 18, 1941 in Prattville, Alabama
Source: *EncPR&S; IlEncRk; Rk100*

Pickford, Jack
[Jack Smith]
Canadian. Actor
b. Aug 18, 1896 in Toronto, ON
d. Jan 3, 1933 in Paris, France
Source: *FilmEn; Film 1, 2; FilmgC; NotNAT B; TwYS; WhScrn 74, 77*

Pickford, Mary
[Gladys Mary Smith]
"America's Sweetheart"
Canadian. Actress
Won Oscar, 1929, for *Coquette;* married to Douglas Fairbanks, Sr. and Buddy Rogers.
b. Apr 8, 1894 in Toronto, ON
d. May 29, 1979 in Santa Monica, California
Source: *BiDFilm; CanWW 70; CelR 73; CurBio 45; Film 1; FilmgC; InWom; IntMPA 75, 76, 77; IntWW 74; MotPP; MovMk; NewYTBE 71; OxFilm; PlP&P; ThFT; TwYS; WebAB; Who 74; WhoAm 74; WhoHol A; WhoThe 77; WhoWor 74; WomWMM; WorEFlm*

Pico della Mirandola, Giovanni
Italian. Philosopher
b. 1463 in Modena, Italy
d. 1494 in Florence, Italy
Source: *CasWL; DcEuL; EuAu; EvEuW; NewCol 75; WebBD 80*

Picon, Molly
American. Actress
b. Feb 28, 1898 in New York, New York
Source: *AmSCAP 66; BiE&WWA; CurBio 51; InWom; NotNAT; WhoAm 74; WhoHol A; WhoThe 77; WhoWor 74*

Picone, Evan
Fashion Designer
Source: *NF*

Pictet, Raoul-Pierre
Swiss. Chemist
Discovered liquefaction of oxygen; developed early refrigeration system.
b. Apr 4, 1846 in Geneva, Switzerland
d. Jul 27, 1929 in Paris, France
Source: *AsBiEn; DcScB*

Pidgeon, Walter
American. Actor
b. Sep 23, 1898 in Saint John, NB
Source: *BiDFilm; BiE&WWA; CanWW 70; CmMov; CurBio 42; FilmgC; IntMPA 75, 76, 77, 78, 79, 80, 81, 82; MotPP; MovMk; OxFilm; TwYS; WhoAm 74; WhoHol A; WhoThe 77; WorEFlm*

Piech, Paul Peter
American. Designer
b. 1921
Source: *BioIn 10*

Pieck, Wilhelm
German. Communist Leader
b. Jan 3, 1876 in Guben, Germany
d. Sep 7, 1960 in Berlin, Germany (East)
Source: *BioIn 1, 2, 3, 5, 11; CurBio 49, 60; WhAm 4*

Pierce, Edward Allen
American. Stockbroker
b. Aug 31, 1874 in Orrington, Maine
d. Dec 16, 1974 in New York, New York
Source: *BioIn 3, 10; ObitOF 79; WhAm 6*

Pierce, Franklin
American. 14th US President
b. Nov 23, 1804 in Hillsboro, New Hampshire
d. Oct 8, 1869 in Concord, New Hampshire
Source: *AmAu&B; AmBi; ApCAB; BiAuS; BiDrAC; BiDrUSE; DcAmB; Drake; EncAB-H; OxAmL; REnAL; TwCBDA; WebAB; WhAm H; WhAmP*

Pierce, Samuel Riley, Jr.
American. Government Official
b. Sep 8, 1922 in Glen Cove, New York
Source: *BioIn 5, 9, 11; CurBio 82; WhoAm 76, 78, 80, 82; WhoE 77, 79; WhoWor 76, 78*

Pierce, Webb
American. Singer
b. Aug 8, 1926 in West Monroe, Louisiana
Source: *EncFCWM 69*

Pierne, Gabriel
French. Composer
b. Aug 16, 1863 in Metz, France
d. Jul 17, 1937 in Ploujean, France
Source: *NewEOp 71; OxMus*

Pierodella Francesca
Italian. Artist
b. 1420 in Italy
d. Oct 12, 1492 in Italy
Source: *AtlBL*

Pierodi Cosimo
Italian. Artist
b. 1462 in Florence, Italy
d. 1521 in Florence, Italy
Source: *AtlBL*

Pierrot, George Francis
American. World Traveler, Author, Editor
b. Jan 11, 1898 in Chicago, Illinois
d. Feb 16, 1980 in Detroit, Michigan
Source: *AmAu&B; AuNews 2; ConAu 5R, 103; IntWW 74; WhNAA; WhoAm 74*

Pignatelli, Luciana, Princess
Italian. Fashion Designer
b. 1935
Source: *BioIn 7, 9*

Pike, Diana Kennedy
American. Wife of James A Pike
Source: *BioIn 8, 11*

Pike, Gary
[The Lettermen]
American. Singer
b. in Twin Falls, Idaho
Source: *EncPR&S; WhoRock 81*

Pike, James Albert
American. Episcopalean Bishop, Author
b. Feb 14, 1913 in Oklahoma City, Oklahoma
d. Sep 2, 1969 in Santa Barbara, California
Source: *AmAu&B; Au&Wr 71; ConAu 1R, 25R, 4NR; CurBio 57, 69; WhAm 5*

Pike, Jim
[The Lettermen]
American. Singer
b. in St. Louis, Missouri
Source: *EncPR&S; WhoRock 81*

Pike, Otis
American. Politician
b. Aug 31, 1921 in Riverhead, New York
Source: *BiDrAC; CngDr 74; WhoAm 74; WhoAmP 73; WhoE 74; WhoGov 72*

Pike, Robert L, pseud.
see: Fish, Robert Lloyd

Pike, Zebulon Montgomery
American. Army Officer, Explorer
Led expedition through Southwest, sighting peak named for him, 1806-07.
b. Feb 5, 1779 in Lamberton, New Jersey
d. Apr 27, 1813 in York, ON
Source: *Alli; AmAu&B; AmBi; ApCAB; BiAuS; BiDLA; CyAL 1; DcAmB; DcNAA; Drake; OxAmL; Pen AM; REnAL; TwCBDA; WebAB; WhAm H*

Pilate, Pontius
Roman. Procurator of Judaea
fl. 26 BC
Source: *NewCol 75; REn*

Pilkington, Francis M
Irish. Children's Author
b. Jun 16, 1907 in Dublin, Ireland
Source: *Alli; ConAu 25R; ConAu P-2; SmATA 4; WrDr 76*

Pillsbury, John Sargent
American. Flour Manufacturer
Joined Pillsbury Mills, Inc., 1900; chairman, 1932.
b. Dec 6, 1878 in Minneapolis, Minnesota
d. Jan 31, 1968 in West Palm Beach, Florida
Source: *BioIn 1, 8, 10; NewCol 75; WhAm 5*

Pillsbury, John Sargent, Jr.
American. Business Executive
b. Oct 28, 1912 in Minneapolis, Minnesota
Source: *St&PR 75; WhoAm 74, 76, 78, 80, 82; WhoF&I 74; WhoIns 75; WhoMW 74*

Pilou, Jeannette
Egyptian. Opera Singer
b. in Alexandria, Egypt
Source: *NewEOp 71*

Pilsudski, Jozef
Polish. General, Statesman
b. Dec 5, 1867 in Wilno, Poland
d. May 12, 1935
Source: *BioIn 2, 8, 9; NewCol 75; WebBD 80*

Pincay, Laffit, Jr.
American. Jockey
b. Dec 29, 1946 in Panama City, Panama
Source: *BioIn 9, 10; BioNews 75; NewYTBS 82*

Pinchback, Pinckney Benton Stewart
American. Politician, Lawyer
b. May 10, 1837 in Macon, Georgia
d. Dec 21, 1921 in Washington, DC
Source: *ApCAB; BioIn 5, 6, 8, 9, 10; DcAmB; TwCBDA; WhAm 1*

Pincherle, Alberto
see: Moravia, Alberto, pseud.

Pinchot, Gifford
American. Politician
b. Aug 11, 1865 in Simsbury, Connecticut
d. Oct 4, 1946 in New York, New York
Source: *AmAu&B; AmLY; CurBio 46; DcAmB S4; DcNAA; EncAB-H; REnAL; TwCBDA; WebAB; WhAm 2; WhNAA*

Pinckney, Charles Cotesworth
American. Statesman
b. Feb 25, 1746 in Charleston, South Carolina
d. Aug 16, 1825 in Charleston, South Carolina
Source: *AmBi; ApCAB; BiAuS; BiDSA; DcAmB; Drake; REn; REnAL; TwCBDA; WebAB; WhAm H; WhAmP*

Pincus, Gregory
American. Scientist, Physician, Engineer
b. Apr 9, 1903 in Woodbine, New Jersey
d. Aug 22, 1967 in Boston, Massachusetts
Source: *CurBio 66, 67; WhAm 4*

Pindar
Greek. Poet
Chief medium was choral lyric; set standard for triumphal ode.
b. 522?BC in Thebes, Greece
d. 442?BC
Source: *AtlBL; BbD; BiD&SB; CasWL; CyWA; DcEnL; NewC; OxEng; Pen CL; RComWL; REn*

Pindling, Lynden Oscar
Bahamian. Government Official
b. 1930 in Bahamas
Source: *CurBio 68; IntWW 74; NewYTBE 73; Who 74*

Pinel, Philippe
French. Physician
b. Apr 20, 1745 in Saint-Andre, France
d. Oct 26, 1826 in Paris, France
Source: *AsBiEn; McGEWB*

Pinero, Sir Arthur Wing
English. Dramatist
b. May 25, 1855 in Islington, England
d. Nov 23, 1934 in London, England
Source: *BbD; BiD&SB; BrAu 19; CasWL; Chambr 3; CnThe; CyWA; DcEnA, AP; DcLEL; EvLB; LongCTC; McGEWD; ModBrL; ModWD; NewC; OxEng; OxThe; Pen ENG; PIP&P; REn; REnWD; WebE&AL; WhScrn 77; WhoLA; WhoStg 1906, 1908*

Ping Lan
see: Chiang Ching

Pink Floyd
[Syd Barrett; Dave Gilmour; Nick Mason; Roger Waters; Rick Wright]
English. Rock Group
Source: *IlEncRk*

Pinkerton, Allan
American. Detective
Founded Pinkerton Detective Agency, 1850; secret service for US govt., 1861.
b. Aug 25, 1819 in Glasgow, Scotland
d. Jul 1, 1884 in Chicago, Illinois
Source: *Alli SUP; AmAu&B; AmBi; ApCAB; BiD&SB; DcAmAu; DcAmB; DcNAA; EncAB-H; EncMys; OxAmL; REnAL; TwCBDA; WebAB; WhAm H*

Pinkham, Lydia Estes
American. Medicine Manufacturer
Invented home remedy "Vegetable Compound," 1876.
b. Feb 19, 1819 in Lynn, Massachusetts
d. May 17, 1883 in Lynn, Massachusetts
Source: *AmBi; DcAmB; NotAW; WebAB; WhAm H*

Pinkney, William
American. Diplomat
b. Mar 17, 1764 in Annapolis, Maryland
d. Dec 25, 1822 in Washington, DC
Source: *Alli; AmBi; ApCAB; BiAuS; BiDSA; BiDrAC; BiDrUSE; CyAL 1; DcAmB; Drake; TwCBDA; WebAB; WhAm H; WhAmP*

Pinkwater, Manus
American. Author, Illustrator
b. Nov 15, 1941 in Memphis, Tennessee
Source: *ConAu 29R; SmATA 8*

Pinochet Ugarte, Augusto
Chilean. Chief of State
b. Nov 25, 1915 in Valparaiso, Chile
Source: *CurBio 74; NewYTBE 73*

Pinsent, Gordon Edward
Canadian. Actor, Writer
b. Jul 12, 1930 in Grand Falls, NF
Source: *CanWW 79; FilmgC; WhoHol A*

Pinter, Harold
English. Dramatist
Wrote *The Dumb Waiter,* 1957; screenplay *The French Lieutenant's Woman,* 1981.
b. Oct 10, 1930 in London, England
Source: *Au&Wr 71; BiE&WWA; CasWL; CelR 73; CnThe; ConAu 5R; ConDr 73; ConLC 1, 3, 6, 9, 11, 15; ConP 70; CroCD; DcFM; EncWL; FilmgC; IntWW 74; LongCTC; McGEWD; ModBrL, SUP; ModWD; NewC; NotNAT; OxFilm; OxThe; Pen ENG; RComWL; REn; REnWD; TwCW; WebE&AL; Who 82; WhoThe 77; WhoTwCL; WhoWor 74; WorAu; WorEFlm; WrDr 76*

Pinturicchio
Italian. Artist
b. 1454 in Perugia, Italy
d. Dec 11, 1513 in Siena, Italy
Source: *AtlBL*

Pinza, Ezio
[Fortunato Pinza]
American. Opera Singer
b. May 18, 1892 in Rome, Italy
d. May 9, 1957 in Stamford, Connecticut
Source: *CurBio 41, 53, 57; EncMT; FilmgC; PIP&P; WhAm 3; WhScrn 74, 77; WhoHol B*

Pio da Pietrelcina, Father (Francisco Forglone)
Italian. Monk, Clairvoyant
b. 1887
d. 1968
Source: *BioIn 8, 11*

Pious, Minerva
American. Radio Actress
Played Mrs. Nussbaum on radio show "Allen's Alley," 1933-49.
b. 1909 in Odessa, Russia
d. 1979 in New York, New York
Source: *BioIn 8, 11; What 2*

Piper, William Thomas
American. Airplane Manufacturer
Designed Piper Cub airplane, 1931.
b. Jan 8, 1881 in Knapps Creek, New York
d. Jan 15, 1970 in Lock Haven, Pennsylvania
Source: *BioIn 1, 2, 5, 7, 8, 9, 11; CurBio 46, 70; WhAm 5*

Pippin, Horace
American. Artist
b. Feb 22, 1888 in West Chester, Pennsylvania
d. Jul 6, 1946
Source: *AfroAA; CurBio 45, 47; DcAmB S4*

Piquet, Nelson
Brazilian. Auto Racer
b. Aug 17, 1952 in Brasilia, Brazil
Source: *BioIn 12*

Pirandello, Fausto
Italian. Artist
b. 1899
d. Nov 30, 1975 in Rome, Italy
Source: *BioIn 10*

Pirandello, Luigi
Italian. Author, Dramatist
b. Jun 28, 1867 in Agriegento, Sicily
d. Dec 10, 1936 in Rome, Italy
Source: *AtlBL; CasWL; ClDMEL; CnMD; CnMWL; CnThe; CyWA; DcEuL; EncWL; EvEuW; LongCTC; McGEWD; ModRL; ModWD; NewC; NewYTBE 73; OxEng; OxThe; Pen EUR; PlP&P, A; RComWL; REn; REnWD; TwCA, SUP; TwCW; WhoTwCL*

Piranesi, Giovanni Battista
Italian. Architect, Etcher
b. Oct 4, 1720 in Venice, Italy
d. Nov 1, 1778 in Rome, Italy
Source: *AtlBL; BioIn 1, 2, 6, 8, 9, 10, 11*

Pirelli, Alberto
Italian. Tire Manufacturer
b. Jul 28, 1882 in Milan, Italy
d. Oct 19, 1971
Source: *NewYTBE 71; WhAm 5*

Piro, Frank
"Killer Joe"
American. Dancer, Choreographer
b. 1920?
Source: *BioIn 4, 6, 7*

Pisano, Andrea
[Andrea da Pontedera]
Italian. Architect, Sculptor
b. 1290? in Pisa, Italy
d. 1348
Source: *AtlBL; REn*

Pisano, Antonio
[Pisanello]
Italian. Artist
b. 1395 in Pisa, Italy
d. 1455 in Rome, Italy
Source: *AtlBL; BioIn 9, 10*

Pisano, Giovanni
Italian. Architect
b. 1250
d. 1314
Source: *AtlBL*

Pisano, Nicola
Italian. Sculptor
b. 1220
d. 1283
Source: *AtlBL*

Pisier, Marie-France
French. Actress
b. May 1946 in Da Lat, Indochina
Source: *BioIn 11; FilmEn; IntMPA 82*

Pisis, Filippo de
Italian. Artist
b. 1896 in Ferrara, Italy
d. Apr 2, 1956 in Milan, Italy
Source: *BioIn 2, 4; McGDA*

Pissarro, Camille Jacob
French. Artist
b. Jul 10, 1831 in Saint Thomas, West Indies
d. Nov 13, 1903 in Paris, France
Source: *AtlBL; REn*

Piston, Walter
American. Musician, Composer
b. Jan 20, 1894 in Rockland, Maine
d. Nov 12, 1976 in Belmont, Massachusetts
Source: *CelR 73; ConAu 69; CurBio 48, 61; IntWW 74; OxAmL; REnAL; WebAB; Who 74; WhoAm 74; WhoMus 72; WhoWor 74*

Pitcairn, Robert
English. Midshipman
b. 1747?
d. 1770?
Source: *WebBD 80*

Pitcher, Molly
[Mary Ludwig Hays McCauley]
American. Revolutionary War Heroine
Earned nickname carrying water for soldiers in Battle of Monmouth, 1778.
b. Oct 13, 1750 in Trenton, New Jersey
d. Jan 22, 1832 in Carlisle, Pennsylvania
Source: *AmBi; DcAmB; InWom; NotAW; OxAmL; REn; TwCBDA; WebAB; WhAm H*

Pitkin, Walter Boughton
American. Author
b. Feb 6, 1878 in Ypsilanti, Michigan
d. Jan 25, 1953 in Palo Alto, California
Source: *AmAu&B; CurBio 41, 53; DcAmB S5; OxAmL; REnAL; TwCA, SUP; WebAB; WhAm 3*

Pitman, Isaac
English. Inventor
Invented phonographic shorthand, 1837.
b. Jan 4, 1813
d. Jan 12, 1897
Source: *Alli; DcEnL; LongCTC; OxEng*

Pitrone, Jean M
American. Author
b. Dec 20, 1920 in Ishpeming, Michigan
Source: *ConAu 17R; ForWC 70; SmATA 4; WrDr 76*

Pitt, Percy
English. Conductor
b. Jan 4, 1870 in London, England
d. Nov 23, 1932 in London, England
Source: *NewEOp 71*

Pitt, William
[Earl of Chatham]
"The Elder Pitt"; "The Great Commoner"
English. Statesman
Secretary of State, 1756-61, 1766-68.
b. Nov 15, 1708 in Westminster, England
d. May 11, 1778 in Hayes, England
Source: *Alli; Chambr 2; NewC; REn; WhAm H*

Pitt, William
"The Younger Pitt"
English. Prime Minister, Author
b. May 28, 1759 in Hayes, England
d. Jan 23, 1806 in Putney, England
Source: *Alli; ApCAB; NewC; REn*

Pitts, Zasu
American. Actress
b. Jan 3, 1900 in Parsons, Kansas
d. Jun 7, 1963 in Hollywood, California
Source: *BiDFilm; Film 1; FilmgC; InWom; MotPP; MovMk; OxFilm; ThFT; TwYS; Vers A; WhScrn 74, 77; WhoHol B; WorEFlm*

Pitz, Henry Clarence
American. Author
b. Jun 16, 1895 in Philadelphia, Pennsylvania
d. Nov 26, 1975 in Philadelphia, Pennsylvania
Source: *AmAu&B; ChPo; ConAu 9R, 69; ConICB; IlsBYP; IlsCB 1744, 1946, 1957; MorJA; SmATA 4; WhoAm 74; WhoAmA 73; WrDr 76*

Pius XII, Pope
[Eugenio Pacelli]
Italian. Pope
b. Mar 2, 1876 in Rome, Italy
d. Oct 9, 1958 in Rome, Italy
Source: *BioIn 10; CurBio 41, 50, 58; WebBD 80*

Pizarro, Francisco
Spanish. Conquerer
Defeated Incas; founded capital of Lima, Peru, 1535.
b. 1470 in Trujilo, Spain
d. Jun 26, 1541 in Lima, Peru
Source: *ApCAB; Drake; REn; WhAm H*

Pizzetti, Ildebrando
Italian. Composer
b. Sep 20, 1880 in Parma, Italy
d. Feb 13, 1968 in Rome, Italy
Source: *DcCM; DcFM; WhAm 4A; WorEFlm*

Place, Francis
English. Political Reformer
b. Oct 3, 1771
d. Jan 1, 1854
Source: *Alli; BrAu 19*

Placzek, Adolf K(urt)
American. Librarian
b. Mar 9, 1913 in Vienna, Austria
Source: *BiDrLUS 70; BioIn 5; DrAS 74H, 78H; WhoAm 74, 76, 78, 80, 82; WhoAmA 78*

Plain, Belva
American. Author
Wrote *Evergreen,* 1978; *Random Winds,* 1980.
b. 1918
Source: *ConAu 81; WrDr 82*

Planck, Max (Karl Ernst Ludwig)
German. Physicist
b. Apr 23, 1858 in Kiel, Germany
d. Oct 4, 1947 in Gottingen, Germany
Source: *OxGer; REn; WhAm 4*

Plancon, Pol-Henri
French. Opera Singer
b. Jun 12, 1854 in Fumay, France
d. Aug 11, 1914 in Paris, France
Source: *NewEOp 71*

Plank, Eddie (Edward Stewart)
"Gettysburg Eddie"
American. Baseball Player
b. Aug 31, 1875 in Gettysburg, Pennsylvania
d. Feb 24, 1926 in Gettysburg, Pennsylvania
Source: *BaseEn; WhoProB 73*

Planquette, Jean(-Robert)
French. Composer
b. Jul 31, 1848 in Paris, France
d. Jan 28, 1903 in Paris, France
Source: *NewEOp 71*

Plant, Robert Anthony
[Led Zeppelin]
English. Rock Singer
b. Aug 20, 1948 in Bromwich, England
Source: *BioIn 10; BkPepl; WhoAm 78, 80, 82*

Plante, (Joseph) Jacques
Canadian. Hockey Player
Goalie, Montreal Canadiens, 1952-63; first to wear mask in game.
b. Feb 17, 1929 in Shawinigan, PQ
Source: *BioIn 5, 8, 9, 10, 11; WhoHcky 73*

Plantin, Christophe
French. Printer
b. 1514
d. 1589
Source: *ChPo; OxFr*

Plasmatics, The
[John Beauvoir; Wes Beech; Neal Smith; Richie Stotts; Wendy O(rlean) Williams]
American. Punk Rock Group
Source: *NF*

Plath, Sylvia
[Victoria Lucas, pseud.]
American. Author, Poet
Wrote *The Bell Jar,* 1962.
b. Oct 27, 1932 in Boston, Massachusetts
d. Feb 11, 1963 in Devonshire, England
Source: *AmAu&B; CasWL; ConAu 21R; ConAu P-2; ConLC 1, 2, 3, 5, 9, 11, 14, 17; ConP 75; CroCAP; EncWL; LongCTC; ModAL SUP; NewYTBS 74; OxAmL; Pen AM; RAdv 1; TwCW; WebE&AL; WhAm 4; WhoTwCL; WorAu*

Plato
Greek. Philosopher, Author
Student of Socrates; wrote *The Republic.*
b. 427BC in Athens, Greece
d. 347BC in Athens, Greece
Source: *AtlBL; BbD; BiD&SB; CasWL; ChPo S1; CyWA; DcEnL; DcEuL; NewC; OxEng; OxThe; Pen CL; RComWL; REn*

Platt, Harry (Henry Barstow)
American. Chairman of Tiffany & Co.
Great-great grandson of Charles Tiffany; joined firm, 1947, chairman, 1981--.
b. in New York, New York
Source: *NewYTBS 81*

Platters, The
[David Lynch; Herb Reed; Paul Robi; Zola Taylor; Tony Williams]
American. Vocal Group
Source: *EncPR&S*

Plautus, Titus Maccius
Roman. Dramatist
b. 254BC in Sarsina, Italy
d. 184BC in Rome, Italy
Source: *OxThe; PlP&P*

Player, Gary Jim
South African. Golfer
Has won nine major tournaments.
b. Nov 1, 1935 in Johannesburg, South Africa
Source: *CelR 73; ConAu 101; CurBio 61; NewYTBS 74; Who 82; WhoAm 76, 78, 80, 82; WhoWor 74*

Pleasants, Henry
American. Music Critic, Author, Composer
b. May 23, 1884 in Radnor, Pennsylvania
d. Feb 7, 1963
Source: *ConAu 1R; WhAm 4; WhNAA*

Pleasence, Donald
English. Actor, Motion Picture Producer
b. Oct 5, 1919 in Worksop, England
Source: *BiE&WWA; CurBio 69; IntMPA 75, 76, 77, 78, 79, 80, 81, 82; IntWW 74; MotPP; MovMk; NotNAT; OxFilm; Who 82; WhoAm 82; WhoHol A*

Plekhanov, Georgi Valentinovich
Russian. Political Philosopher
b. Nov 26, 1857 in Tambov, Russia
d. May 30, 1918 in Leningrad, U.S.S.R.
Source: *CasWL; DcRusL*

Pleshette, John
American. Actor
Source: *WhoHol A*

Pleshette, Suzanne
[Mrs. Thomas Gallagher, III]
American. Actress
Played Emily Hartley on TV series "The Bob Newhart Show," 1972-78.
b. Jan 31, 1937 in New York, New York
Source: *FilmgC; InWom; IntMPA 75, 76, 77, 78, 79, 80, 81, 82; MotPP; MovMk; WhoAm 82; WhoHol A; WorEFlm*

Pletcher, "Stew" (Stuart)
American. Jazz Musician
b. Feb 21, 1907 in Chicago, Illinois
Source: *CmpEPM; WhoJazz 72*

Plimpton, Francis
American. Lawyer, Diplomat
b. Dec 7, 1900 in New York, New York
Source: *IntWW 74; NewYTBE 70; St&PR 75; WhoAm 74, 76, 78, 80, 82; WhoE 74; WhoUN 75; WhoWor 74*

Plimpton, George
American. Author
Wrote *Out of My League,* 1961; *Paper Lion,* 1966.
b. Mar 18, 1927 in New York, New York
Source: *AuNews 1; CelR 73; ConAu 21R; CurBio 69; NewYTBE 70; SmATA 10; WebAB; WhoAm 74, 76, 78, 80, 82; WhoHol A; WhoWor 74*

Plimsoll, Samuel
English. Politician, Social Reformer
b. 1824 in England
d. 1898
Source: *Alli SUP*

Pliny the Elder
[Gaius Plinius Secundus]
Roman. Scholar, Author
b. 23 in Como, Italy
d. Aug 24, 79 in Castellammare, Italy
Source: *AtlBL; BbD; BiD&SB; CasWL; NewC; OxEng; Pen CL; RComWL; REn*

Pliny the Younger
[Gaius Plinius Caecilius Secundus]
Roman. Orator, Statesman, Consul
b. 62 in Como, Italy
d. 114 in Bithynia, Asia Minor
Source: *AtlBL; BbD; BiD&SB; CasWL; NewC; OxEng; Pen CL; RComWL; REn*

Plisetskaya, Maya Mikhailovna
Russian. Ballerina
b. Nov 20, 1925 in Moscow, U.S.S.R.
Source: *CurBio 63; InWom; NewYTBS 74; WhoHol A*

Plishka, Paul Peter
American. Opera Singer
b. Aug 28, 1941 in Old Forge, Pennsylvania
Source: *Baker 78; BioIn 8, 9, 11; WhoAm 74; WhoOp 76*

Plomer, William Charles Franklyn
South African. Author
His opera *Gloriana* was performed during coronation of Queen Elizabeth, 1953.
b. Dec 10, 1903 in Pietersburg, South Africa
d. Sep 21, 1973 in England
Source: *Au&Wr 71; BlkAW; CasWL; Chambr 3; ConAu 21R; ConAu P-2; ConLC 4, 8; ConNov 72; ConP 70, 70, 75; DcLEL; EncWL; EvLB; LongCTC; ModBrL, SUP; NewC; Pen ENG; REn; SmATA 8; TwCA, SUP; TwCW; WebE&AL; WhoTwCL; WhoWor 74*

Plotinus
Egyptian. Philosopher
b. 205
d. 270
Source: *BiD&SB; CasWL; NewC; OxEng; Pen CL; RComWL; REn*

Plotkin, Jerry
[The Hostages]
American. Former Hostage in Iran
b. 1935? in New York, New York
Source: *NewYTBS 81*

Plotnik, Arthur
American. Author, Editor
b. Aug 1, 1937 in White Plains, New York
Source: *BiDrLUS 70*

Plowright, Joan
[Mrs. Laurence Olivier]
English. Actress
b. Oct 28, 1929 in Scunthorpe, England
Source: *BiE&WWA; CurBio 64; InWom; IntWW 74; NotNAT; OxThe; PlP&P; Who 74; WhoHol A; WhoThe 77; WhoWor 74*

Plumb, Charles
American. Comic Strip Creator
b. in San Gabriel, California
Source: *WorECom*

Plummer, Amanda
American. Actress
b. 1957? in New York
Source: *NewYTBS 81*

Plummer, (Arthur) Christopher
Canadian. Actor
Played Baron vonTrapp in *The Sound of Music,* 1965.
b. Dec 13, 1929 in Toronto, ON
Source: *BiE&WWA; CanWW 82; CelR 73; CreCan 2; CurBio 56; FilmgC; IntMPA 75, 76, 77, 78, 79, 80, 81, 82; IntWW 74; MotPP; MovMk; NotNAT; PlP&P; Who 82; WhoAm 74, 76, 78, 80, 82; WhoHol A; WhoThe 77; WhoWor 74; WorEFlm*

Plunkett, Jim (James William, Jr.)
American. Football Player
Won Heisman Trophy, 1970; quarterback, 1971--.
b. Dec 5, 1947 in San Jose, California
Source: *CelR 73; CurBio 71; NewYTBE 70, 71; WhoAm 74, 76, 78, 80, 82; WhoFtbl 74*

Plutarch
Greek. Biographer
b. 46 in Chaeronea, Greece
d. 120 in Chaeronea, Greece
Source: *AtlBL; BbD; BiD&SB; CasWL; CyWA; DcEnL; NewC; OxEng; Pen CL; RComWL; REn*

Pocahontas
[Matoaka; Mrs. John Rolfe]
American Indian. Princess
Daughter of Powhatan; supposedly saved life of Captain John Smith.
b. 1595 in Virginia
d. Mar 1617 in Gravesend, England
Source: *AmBi; DcAmB; DcNAA; Drake; EncAB-H; HerW; InWom; NewC; NotAW; OxAmL; REn; REnAL; WebAB; WhAm H*

Pocklington, Peter H
"Peter Puck"
Canadian. Sports Entrepreneur
Owner, Edmonton Oilers; chairman, Pocklington Financial Corp., Ltd.
b. Nov 18, 1941 in Regina, SK
Source: *WhoCan 80*

Poco
[Paul Cotton; Richie Furay; George Grantham; Jim Messina; Randy Meisner; Tim Schmit; Rusty Young]
American. Rock Group
Source: *ConMuA 80; LilREn 78; RkOn 2; WhoRock 81*

Podesta, Rossana
Italian. Actress
b. 1934? in Tripoli, Libya
Source: *BioIn 3; IntMPA 82*

Podgorny, Nikolai Viktorovich
Russian. Politician
President, USSR, 1965-77.
b. Feb 18, 1903 in Karlovka, Russia
d. Jan 10, 1983 in Kiev, U.S.S.R.
Source: *CurBio 66; IntWW 74, 75, 76, 77, 78, 79, 80, 81; IntYB 78, 79, 80, 81; WhoGov 72; WhoSocC 78; WhoWor 74, 76*

Podgwiski, Jeff
American. Boxer
b. 1954? in Las Vegas, Nevada
Source: *NF*

Podhoretz, Norman
American. Editor, Critic
b. Jan 16, 1930 in Brooklyn, New York
Source: *AmAu&B; Au&Wr 71; CelR 73; ConAu 9R; CurBio 68; NewYTBE 72; Pen AM; WhoAm 74; WhoWor 74; WhoWorJ 72; WorAu*

Podres, Johnny (John Joseph)
American. Baseball Player
b. Sep 30, 1932 in Witherbee, New York
Source: *BaseEn; WhoProB 73*

Poe, Edgar Allan
American. Poet, Author, Journalist
Wrote *The Raven,* 1845; *The Gold Bug,* 1843.
b. Jan 19, 1809 in Boston, Massachusetts
d. Oct 7, 1849 in Baltimore, Maryland
Source: *Alli; AmAu; AmAu&B; AmBi; AmWr; AnCL; ApCAB; AtlBL; BbD; BiD&SB; BiDSA; CasWL; Chambr 3; ChPo, S1, S2; CnDAL; CnE&AP; CrtT 3; CyAl 2; CyWA; DcAmAu; DcAmB; DcBiA; DcEnA; DcEnL; DcLEL; DcNAA; EncAB-H; EncMys; EvLB; FilmgC; MnBBF; MouLC 3; OxAmL; OxEng; Pen AM; RAdv 1; RComWL; REn; REnAL; Str&VC; TwCBDA; WebAB; WebE&AL; WhAm H*

Pogany, Willy
Hungarian. Illustrator
b. Aug 24, 1882 in Szeged, Hungary
d. Jul 30, 1955 in New York, New York
Source: *ChPo, S1, S2; ConICB; IlsCB 1744; JBA 34, 51; REn; WhAm 3*

Pogorelich, Ivo
Yugoslav. Musician
b. 1959 in Belgrade, Yugoslavia
Source: *BioIn 12*

Pogue, William R(eid)
American. Astronaut
With NASA 1966-75; piloted third Skylab mission.
b. Jan 23, 1930 in Okemah, Oklahoma
Source: *NewYTBE 73; WhoAm 74, 76, 78, 80, 82; WhoS&SW 73*

Pohl, Frederik
American. Editor, Author
b. Nov 26, 1919 in New York, New York
Source: *ConNov 72, 76; DrAF 76; Pen AM; WhoAm 74; WorAu; WrDr 76*

Poincare, Jules Henri
French. Mathematician
b. Apr 29, 1854 in Nancy, France
d. Jul 17, 1912 in Paris, France
Source: *AsBiEn; BioIn 3; DcScB; McGEWB; NewCol 75*

Poincare, Raymond
French. Statesman, Author
President, French Republic, 1913-20.
b. Aug 20, 1860 in Bar-le-Duc, France
d. Oct 15, 1934 in Paris, France
Source: *LinLib L, S; LongCTC; McGEWB; OxFr; REn*

Poinsett, Joel Roberts
American. Legislator, Diplomat
b. Mar 2, 1779 in Charleston, South Carolina
d. Dec 12, 1851 in Statesburg, South Carolina
Source: *AmBi; BioIn 1, 3, 6, 8, 10; DcAmAu; DcAmB; EncAB-H; NewCol 75; WebAB; WhAm H*

Pointer Sisters, The
[Anita Pointer; Bonnie Pointer; June Pointer; Ruth Pointer]
American. Vocal Group
Source: *BioIn 10*

Poiret, Paul
French. Couturier
b. Apr 20, 1879 in Paris, France
d. Apr 30, 1944 in Paris, France
Source: *BioIn 5, 9, 10; CurBio 44; ObitOF 79; WorFshn*

Poirier, Richard
American. Critic
b. Sep 9, 1925 in Gloucester, Massachusetts
Source: *AmAu&B; ConAu 1R; DrAS 74E; WhoAm 74, 76, 78, 80, 82; WhoE 74*

Poitier, Sidney
American. Actor, Motion Picture Director
First black actor to win Oscar, 1963, for *Lilies of the Field.*
b. Feb 20, 1924 in Miami, Florida
Source: *BiDFilm; BioNews 74; BkPepl; CelR 73; CurBio 59; FilmgC; IntMPA 75, 76, 77, 78, 79, 80, 81, 82; IntWW 74; MotPP; MovMk; NotNAT; OxFilm; Who 82; WhoAm 74, 76, 78, 80, 82; WhoBlA 75; WhoHol A; WhoThe 77; WhoWor 74*

Pol Pot
[Saloth Sar]
Cambodian. Former Premier
b. May 19, 1928?
Source: *BioIn 11; CurBio 80; FarE&A 79; IntWW 78; WhoSocC 78*

Polacco, Giorgio
Italian. Conductor
b. Apr 12, 1875 in Venice, Italy
d. Apr 30, 1960 in New York, New York
Source: *NewEOp 71*

Polanski, Roman
Polish. Motion Picture Director
Starred in *Rosemary's Baby,* 1968, *Chinatown,* 1974.
b. Aug 18, 1933 in Paris, France
Source: *BiDFilm; CelR 73; CurBio 69; DcFM; FilmgC; IntMPA 75, 76, 77, 78, 79, 80, 81, 82; IntWW 74; MovMk; NewYTBE 71, 73; OxFilm; WhoAm 74, 76, 78, 80, 82; WhoWest 74; WhoWor 74; WorEFlm*

Poli, Robert E
American. Former President of PATCO
Led air controllers strike, 1981.
b. Feb 27, 1936 in Pittsburgh, Pennsylvania
Source: *NewYTBS 81*

Police, The
[Stewart Copeland; Andy Summers; Gordon "Sting" Sumner]
British. Rock Group
First hit single, "Roxanne," 1978; two platinum albums.
Source: *ConMuA 80; IlEncRk; WhoRock 81*

Poling, Daniel A
American. Religious Leader
b. Nov 30, 1884 in Portland, Oregon
d. Feb 7, 1968 in Philadelphia, Pennsylvania
Source: *AmAu&B; ChPo; CurBio 43, 68; OhA&B; WhAm 5*

Politi, Leo
American. Author, Illustrator
b. 1908 in Fresno, California
Source: *Au&ICB; AuBYP; BkP; Cald 1938; CathA 1952; ConAu 17R; IlsBYP; IlsCB 1744, 1946, 1957; JBA 51; SmATA 1; Str&VC*

Politz, Alfred
American. Public Relations Executive
A founder of advertising research.
b. 1902? in Berlin, Germany
d. Nov 8, 1982 in Odessa, Florida
Source: *BioIn 1, 4, 11; NewYTBS 82; WhoAm 74, 78*

Polk, James K(nox)
American. 11th US President
Led US in war against Mexico, resulting in annexation of Southwest.
b. Nov 2, 1775 in Mecklenburg, North Carolina
d. Jun 15, 1849 in Nashville, Tennessee
Source: *Alli; AmAu&B; AmBi; ApCAB; BiAuS; BiDSA; BiDrAC; BiDrUSE; DcAmB; Drake; EncAB-H; OxAmL; REn; REnAL; TwCBDA; WebAB; WhAm H; WhAmP*

Polk, Ralph Lane
American. Publishing Company Executive
b. Jul 21, 1911 in Detroit, Michigan
Source: *WhoAm 78, 80*

Polk, Willis Jefferson
American. Architect
b. 1867 in Frankfort, Kentucky
d. 1924 in San Mateo, California
Source: *DcAmB; EncMA*

Pollack, Egon
Czech. Conductor
b. May 3, 1879 in Prague, Czechoslovakia
d. Jun 14, 1933 in Prague, Czechoslovakia
Source: *NewEOp 71*

Pollack, Sam
Canadian. Hockey Player, Executive
General manager, Montreal Canadians, 1967--.
b. Dec 15, 1925 in Montreal, PQ
Source: *WhoHcky 73*

Pollack, Sydney
American. Motion Picture Director
Directed *They Shoot Horses, Don't They,* 1969, *Absence of Malice,* 1981.
b. Jul 1, 1934 in South Bend, Indiana
Source: *BiDFilm; BioIn 10; FilmgC; FilmEn; IntMPA 76, 77, 78, 79, 80, 81; MovMk; NewYTBE 70; WhoAm 76, 78, 80; WhoWor 78; WorEFlm*

Pollaiuolo, Antonio
Italian. Artist
b. 1431 in Florence, Italy
d. 1498 in Rome, Italy
Source: *AtlBL; REn*

Pollard, Jack
Australian. Author
b. Jul 31, 1926 in Sydney, Australia
Source: *ConAu 29R*

Pollard, Michael J
American. Actor
b. May 30, 1939 in Passaic, New Jersey
Source: *BiE&WWA; FilmgC; MotPP; MovMk; WhoAm 74; WhoHol A*

Pollinger, Laurence Edward
English. Literary Agent
b. Apr 2, 1898
d. Apr 4, 1976
Source: *BioIn 10*

Pollock, Alex
American. Urban Designer
b. 1930
Source: *BioIn 10; BioNews 74*

Pollock, Channing
American. Author, Dramatist
b. Mar 4, 1880 in Washington, DC
d. Aug 17, 1946 in New York, New York
Source: *AmAu&B; AmLY; AmSCAP 66; CnDAL; CurBio 46; DcAmB S4; DcNAA; ModWD; OxAmL; REn; REnAL; TwCA, SUP; WhAm 2; WhNAA; WhoStg 1908*

Pollock, Jackson
American. Artist, Author
Founded "action painting" and Abstract Expressionism movement.
b. Jan 28, 1912 in Cody, Wyoming
d. Aug 11, 1956 in East Hampton, New York
Source: *AtlBL; BioNews 74; CurBio 56; DcCAA 71; EncAB-H; REn; WebAB; WhAm HA, 4*

Polo, Marco
see: Marco Polo

Polovchak, Walter
Russian. Defector
Granted political asylum in US after running away from home at age 13.
b. Oct 3, 1967? in U.S.S.R.
Source: *BioIn 12*

Polycletus The Elder
Greek. Sculptor
b. in Argos, Greece
Source: *NewCol 75*

Polygnotus
Greek. Artist
b. in Thaos, Greece
Source: *NewCol 75*

Polykoff, Shirley
American. Advertising Executive, Author
b. in Brooklyn, New York
Source: *ForWC 70; InWom; WhoE 74; WhoF&I 74*

Pompadour, Jeanne Antoinette Poisson
French. Mistress of Louis XV
b. Dec 29, 1721 in Paris, France
d. Apr 15, 1764 in Versailles, France
Source: *InWom; NewCol 75; WebBD 80*

Pompeia
Roman. 3rd Wife of Julius Caesar
Source: *InWom*

Pompey the Great
[Pompeius Magnus]
Roman. General, Statesman
b. 106BC
d. 48BC in Egypt
Source: *NewC; REn*

Pompidou, Georges Jean Raymond
French. President
Prime Minister, 1962-68; president, 1969-74.
b. Jul 5, 1911 in Cantal, France
d. Apr 2, 1974 in Paris, France
Source: *ConAu 49; CurBio 62, 74; NewYTBE 71, 73; WhAm 6; Who 74; WhoGov 72; WhoWor 74*

Ponce de Leon, Juan
Spanish. Explorer, Governor
Discovered FL, 1513, searching for legendary Fountain of Youth.
b. 1460 in Leon, Spain
d. 1521 in Florida
Source: *AmBi; ApCAB; DcAmB; Drake; REn; WebAB; WhAm H*

Ponchielli, Amilcare
Italian. Composer
b. Aug 31, 1834 in Paderno, Italy
d. Jan 16, 1886 in Milan, Italy
Source: *NewEOp 71*

Pons, Lily
French. Opera Singer
b. Apr 12, 1904 in Cannes, France
d. Feb 13, 1976 in Dallas, Texas
Source: *CurBio 44; FilmgC; InWom; ThFT; Who 74*

Ponselle, Carmela
[Carmela Ponzillo]
American. Opera Singer
b. Jun 7, 1892 in Schenectady, New York
d. 1977
Source: *BioIn 11; InWom*

Ponselle, Rosa
[Rose Ponzillo]
American. Opera Singer
b. Jan 22, 1894 in Meriden, Connecticut
d. May 25, 1981 in Stevenson, Maryland
Source: *Baker 78; BiDAmM; BioIn 1, 2, 3, 4, 5, 6, 7, 8, 10, 11; CnOxOp 79; EncOp; InWom; LibW; LinLib S; MusSN; NewCol 75; NewEOp 71; NewYTBE 72; NewYTBS 81; WhoAmW 70, 72, 74, 75; WhoMus 72*

Pontecorvo, Gillo
Italian. Motion Picture Director
b. 1919
Source: *BiDFilm; DcFM; FilmgC; OxFilm; WorEFlm*

Ponti, Carlo
Italian. Motion Picture Producer
Credited with discovering Sophia Loren, whom he later married.
b. Dec 11, 1913 in Milan, Italy
Source: *CelR 73; DcFM; FilmgC; IntMPA 75, 76, 77, 78, 79, 80, 81, 82; IntWW 74; OxFilm; WhoWor 74; WorEFlm*

Ponti, Gio(vanni)
Italian. Architect
b. Nov 18, 1891 in Milan, Italy
d. Sep 15, 1979 in Milan, Italy
Source: *BioIn 12; IntWW 74; WhoWor 74*

Pontiac
American Indian. Ottawa Chief
b. 1720
d. Apr 20, 1769 in Missouri
Source: *AmBi; ApCAB; DcAmB; Drake; EncAB-H; OxAmL; OxCan; REn; REnAL; WebAB; WhAm H*

Pontius Pilate
see: Pilate, Pontius

Pontormo, Jacopo da
[Jacopo Carrucci]
Italian. Artist
b. 1494 in Pontormo, Italy
d. Dec 1556 in Florence, Italy
Source: *McGEWB*

Ponty, Jean-Luc
French. Composer, Violinist
b. Sep 29, 1942 in Avranches, France
Source: *BioIn 11; ConMuA 80; EncJzS 70; IlEncJ; WhoAm 78, 80, 82; WhoRock 81; WhoWor 74*

Ponzi, Charles
American. Swindler
b. 1877
d. Jan 15, 1949 in Rio de Janeiro, Brazil
Source: *BioIn 1, 2, 3, 4, 9, 10*

Pool, David de Sola
English. Rabbi
b. 1885 in London, England
d. Dec 1, 1970 in New York, New York
Source: *AmAu&B; ConAu 29R; NewYTBE 70; WhAm 5; WhNAA*

Poole, Ernest
American. Journalist, Author
b. Jan 23, 1880 in Chicago, Illinois
d. Jan 10, 1950 in New York, New York
Source: *AmAu&B; AmLY; AmNov; CnDAL; ConAmA; ConAmL; DcAmB S4; DcLEL; OxAmL; REn; REnAL; TwCA, SUP; WhAm 2; WhNAA*

Poole, William Frederick
American. Librarian, Historian
b. Dec 24, 1821 in Peabody, Massachusetts
d. Mar 1, 1894 in Evanston, Illinois
Source: *AmBi; ApCAB; BioIn 1, 2, 3, 6, 10, 11; DcAmB; DcAmLiB; Drake; NatCAB 6; TwCBDA; WhAm H*

Poons, Lawrence (Larry)
American. Artist
b. Oct 1, 1937 in Tokyo, Japan
Source: *BioIn 9; WhoAm 82*

Poor, Henry Varnum
American. Artist
b. Sep 30, 1888 in Chapman, Kansas
d. Dec 8, 1970 in New York, New York
Source: *CurBio 42, 71; DcCAA 71; WhAm 5*

Pop, Iggy
[James Jewel Osterburg]
American. Rock Singer
b. 1947 in Ann Arbor, Michigan
Source: *ConMuA 80; IlEncRk; WhoRock 81*

Pope, Alexander
English. Poet
Wrote *The Rape of the Lock,* 1714 and *Moral Essays,* 1731-35.
b. May 21, 1688 in London, England
d. May 30, 1744 in Twickenham, England
Source: *Alli; AtlBL; BbD; BiD&SB; BrAu; CasWL; Chambr 2; ChPo, S1; CnE&AP; CrtT 2; CyWA; DcEnA; DcEnL; DcEuL; DcLEL; EvLB; MouLC 2; NewC; OxEng; Pen ENG; RAdv 1; RComWL; REn; WebE&AL*

Pope, Generoso
American. Publisher
b. 1927? in Italy
d. Apr 28, 1950 in New York, New York
Source: *BioIn 2, 8, 9*

Pope, John Russell
American. Architect
b. Apr 24, 1874 in New York, New York
d. Aug 27, 1937
Source: *AmBi; DcAmB S2; WhAm 1*

Popov, Aleksandr Stepanovich
Russian. Engineer
b. 1859
d. 1905
Source: *BioIn 2, 5, 6*

Popov, Dusko
"Tricycle"
British. Double Agent, Author
b. 1912? in Yugoslavia
d. Aug 21, 1981 in Opio, France
Source: *ASpks; BioIn 10, 11; BioNews 74*

Popov, Oleg Konstantinovich
Russian. Clown
b. Aug 3, 1930 in Moscow, U.S.S.R.
Source: *CurBio 64; IntWW 74; WhoWor 74*

Popovich, Pavel Romanovich
Russian. Cosmonaut
b. Oct 5, 1930
Source: *IntWW 74; WhoWor 74*

Porfirio, Jose de la Cruz
see: Diaz, Porfirio

Porpora, Niccolo
Italian. Teacher, Composer
b. Aug 19, 1686 in Naples, Italy
d. Feb 1766 in Naples, Italy
Source: *NewEOp 71*

Porritt, Sir Arthur Espie
New Zealander. Government Official
b. Aug 10, 1900
Source: *IntWW 74; Who 74; WhoGov 72*

Porsche, Ferdinand
Austrian. Automotive Engineer
Invented German Volkswagon.
b. 1875 in Maffersdorf, Bohemia
d. Jan 30, 1951 in Stuttgart, Germany (West)
Source: *BioIn 2, 5, 8, 11*

Porsche, Ferdinand
Austrian. Automotive Manufacturer
President of F Porsche K G, Stuttgart.
b. Sep 19, 1900 in Austria
Source: *WhoF&I 74; WhoWor 74*

Porter, Bernard H
American. Author
b. Feb 14, 1911 in Porter, Maine
Source: *WhoE 74*

Porter, Cole
American. Composer, Lyricist
Wrote musicals *Kiss Me, Kate; Can-Can; Silk Stockings;* song "Night and Day."
b. Jun 9, 1892 in Peru, Indiana
d. Oct 15, 1964 in Santa Monica, California
Source: *AmAu&B; AmSCAP 66; CmMov; ConAu 93; EncAB-H; EncMT; FilmgC; IndAu 1917; LongCTC; McGEWD; NewCBMT; OxFilm; REn; REnAL; WebAB; WhAm 4*

Porter, Darrell Ray
American. Baseball Player
b. Jan 17, 1952 in Joplin, Missouri
Source: *BaseEn; BioIn 12; WhoAm 82*

Porter, David Dixon
American. Military Leader
b. Jun 8, 1813 in Chester, Pennsylvania
d. Feb 13, 1891 in Washington, DC
Source: *Alli SUP; AmAu&B; AmBi; ApCAB; BiD&SB; DcAmAu; DcAmB; DcNAA; Drake; REnAL; TwCBDA; WebAB; WhAm H*

Porter, Edwin
American. Motion Picture Director
b. Apr 21, 1870 in Connellsville, Pennsylvania
d. Apr 30, 1941 in New York, New York
Source: *CmMov; CurBio 41; DcAmB S3; DcFM; FilmgC; OxFilm; REnAL; TwYS; WomWMM; WorEFlm*

Porter, Eleanor H
American. Author
b. Dec 19, 1868 in Littleton, New Hampshire
d. May 21, 1920
Source: *AmAu&B; AmLY; BioIn 1, 3, 8; CarSB; DcLEL; DcNAA; EvLB; LongCEL; OxAmL; REn; REnAL; TwCA, SUP; TwCW*

Porter, Eric
English. Actor
b. Apr 8, 1928 in London, England
Source: *FilmgC; IntWW 74; Who 74; WhoThe 77; WhoWor 74*
American. Artist
b. Jun 10, 1907 in Winnetka, Illinois
d. Sep 18, 1975 in Southampton, New York
Source: *BnEnAmA; ConAu 61; DcAmArt; DcCAA 71, 77; NewYTBS 75; ObitOF 79; WhAm 6; WhoAm 74; WhoAmA 73, 76, 78; WhoE 74*

Porter, Gene Stratton
American. Author, Naturalist
b. Aug 17, 1868 in Wabash County, Indiana
d. Dec 6, 1924 in Los Angeles, California
Source: *AmAu&B; AmBi; AmLY; CarSB; ChPo; CnDAL; DcAmB S1; DcLEL; DcNAA; EvLB; InWom; IndAu 1816; LongCTC; NotAW; OxAmL; Pen AM; REn; REnAL; TwCA, SUP; TwCW; WebAB; WhAm 1; WhoChL*

Porter, Hal
Australian. Author
b. Feb 16, 1911 in Victoria Park, Australia
Source: *Au&Wr 71; CasWL; ConAu 9R, 3NR; ConNov 72, 76; ConP 70, 75; NewC; WhoWor 74; WrDr 76*

Porter, Katherine Anne
American. Author
b. May 15, 1894 in Indian Creek, Texas
d. Sep 18, 1980 in Silver Spring, Maryland
Source: *AmAu&B; AmWr; AuNews 2; CasWL; CelR 73; CnDAL; CnMWL; ConAmA; ConAu 1R, 101, 1NR; ConLC 1, 3, 7, 10, 13, 15; ConNov 72, 76; CurBio 40, 63; CyWA; DcLEL; DrAF 76; EncWL; EvLB; ForWC 70; InWom; IntWW 74; LongCTC; ModAL, SUP; NewYTBE 70; OxAmL; OxEng; Pen AM; RAdv 1; REn; REnAL; TwCA, SUP; TwCW; WebAB; WebE&AL; Who 74; WhoAm 74; WhoAmW 77; WhoE 74; WhoTwCL; WhoWor 74; WrDr 76*

Porter, Nyree Dawn
New Zealander. Actress
b. 1940
Source: *FilmgC; WhoHol A*

Porter, Quincy
American. Composer
b. Feb 7, 1897 in New Haven, Connecticut
d. Nov 12, 1966 in New Haven, Connecticut
Source: *DcCM; WhAm 4*

Porter, Sylvia Field
American. Journalist, Author
Syndicated financial columnist; wrote *Sylvia Porter's New Money Book for the 80's,* 1979.
b. Jun 18, 1913 in Patchogue, New York
Source: *CelR 73; ConAu 81; CurBio 80; InWom; WhoAm 74, 76, 78, 80, 82; WhoE 74*

Porter, William Sydney
see: Henry, O, pseud.

Porter, William Trotter
American. Author
b. Dec 24, 1809 in Newburg, Vermont
d. Jul 19, 1858 in New York, New York
Source: *AmAu&B; ApCAB; DcAmB; DcNAA*

Portis, Charles
American. Author
b. Dec 28, 1933 in El Dorado, Arkansas
Source: *AmAu&B; ConAu 45, 1NR*

Portman, Eric
English. Actor
b. Jul 13, 1903 in Halifax, England
d. Dec 7, 1969 in Saint Veep, England
Source: *BiE&WWA; CurBio 57, 70; FilmgC; MotPP; PlP&P; WhScrn 74, 77; WhoHol B*

Portman, John Calvin
American. Architect
b. Dec 4, 1924 in Walhalla, South Carolina
Source: *NewYTBE 73; WhoAm 74, 76, 78, 80, 82; WhoS&SW 73*

Posell, Elsa Z
American. Author
b. in Russia
Source: *ConAu 1R, 4NR; SmATA 3*

Post, Charles William
American. Cereal Company Founder
Founded Postum Cereal Co., 1897; created Grape-Nuts cereal.
b. Oct 26, 1854 in Springfield, Illinois
d. May 9, 1914 in Santa Barbara, California
Source: *DcAmB; WebAB; WhAm 1; WorAl*

Post, Elizabeth Lindley
American. Author
Continues editing work of Emily Post, her husband's grandmother.
b. May 7, 1920 in Englewood, New Jersey
Source: *ConAu 49; WhoAm 82*

Post, Emily Price
American. Author, Journalist
Wrote definitive work on proper social behavior, *Etiquette,* 1922.
b. Oct 30, 1873 in Baltimore, Maryland
d. Sep 25, 1960 in New York, New York
Source: *AmAu&B; ConAu 89, 103; CurBio 41, 60; OxAmL; REn; REnAL; WebAB; WhAm 4*

Post, Wally (Walter Charles)
American. Baseball Player
With Cincinnati Reds, 1949-57, 1961-64; hit 210 home runs.
b. Jul 9, 1929 in Saint Wendelin, Ohio
d. Jan 7, 1982 in Saint Henry, Ohio
Source: *BaseEn; NewYTBS 82*

Post, Wiley
American. Aviator
Solo round the world flight, 1933; killed in crash with Will Rogers.
b. Nov 22, 1900 in Grand Saline, Texas
d. Aug 15, 1935 in Point Barrow, Alaska
Source: *AmBi; DcAmB S1; DcNAA; WebAB; WhAm 1; WhScrn 74, 77; WhoHol B*

Poston, Tom
American. Comedian, Actor
b. Oct 17, 1927 in Columbus, Ohio
Source: *BiE&WWA; CurBio 61; FilmgC; NotNAT; WhoAm 74, 76, 78, 80, 82; WhoHol A; WhoThe 77*

Pot, Pol
see: Pol Pot

Potemkin, Grigori Alexsandrovich
Russian. Field Marshall
b. 1739
d. 1791
Source: *NewCol 75; REn; WebBD 80*

Potofsky, Jacob Samuel
American. Labor Union Leader
b. Nov 16, 1894 in Radomisl, Russia
d. Aug 5, 1979 in New York, New York
Source: *BiDAmLL; CurBio 46, 79; NewYTBE 70, 72; NewYTBS 79; PolProf T; WhoAm 74; WhoGov 72, 75; WhoLab 76; WhoWor 74; WhoWorJ 72*

Potok, Chaim
American. Author, Editor
b. Feb 17, 1929 in New York, New York
Source: *AmAu&B; Au&Wr 71; AuNews 1, 2; BioNews 74; ConAu 17R; ConLC 2, 7, 14; DrAF 76; WhoAm 74, 76, 78, 80, 82; WhoE 74; WhoWor 74; WhoWorJ 72; WrDr 76*

Potter, (Helen) Beatrix
English. Illustrator, Author
Wrote *The Tale of Peter Rabbit,* 1902.
b. Jul 6, 1866
d. Dec 22, 1943 in Sawrey, England
Source: *AnCL; AuBYP; CarSB; CasWL; ChlLR 1; ChPo, S1, S2; CurBio 44; DcLEL; EvLB; FamAIYP; HerW; InWom; JBA 34, 51; LongCTC; NewC; OxEng; Pen ENG; REn; Str&VC; WhoChL; YABC 1*

Potter, Henry Codman
American. Social Reform Leader
b. Jun 25, 1834 in Schenectady, New York
d. Jul 21, 1908 in Cooperstown, New York
Source: *Alli SUP; AmAu&B; AmBi; ApCAB; BiD&SB; DcAmAu; DcAmB; DcNAA; TwCBDA; WebAB; WhAm 1*

Potter, Stephen
English. Author
b. Feb 1, 1900 in London, England
d. Dec 2, 1969 in London, England
Source: *AuBYP; ConAu 25R; DcLEL; EvLB; LongCTC; ModBrL; NewC; Pen ENG; RAdv 1; REn; TwCA SUP; TwCW; WhAm 5*

Potthast, Edward Henry
American. Artist
b. Jun 10, 1857 in Cincinnati, Ohio
d. Mar 9, 1927 in New York, New York
Source: *ArtsAmW; IlBEAAW; NatCAB 22; WhAm 1*

Potts, Nadia
English. Ballerina
With Toronto's National Ballet of Canada, 1966--.
b. Apr 20, 1948 in London, England
Source: *BioIn 11; CanWW 79; WhoAm 78, 80, 82*

Potvin, Denis Charles
Canadian. Hockey Player
b. Oct 29, 1953 in Hull, PQ
Source: *NewYTBE 73; NewYTBS 77; WhoAm 78, 80, 82*

Potzsch, Anett
German. Figure Skater
Won gold medal, 1980 Olympics.
b. 1961? in Germany (East)
Source: *NF*

Poulenc, Francis
[Les Six]
French. Composer
b. Jan 7, 1899 in Paris, France
d. Jan 30, 1963 in Paris, France
Source: *AtlBL; DcCM; DcFM; REn; WhAm 4*

Poulson, Norris
American. Mayor
Mayor of LA, 1953-61.
b. Jul 23, 1895 in Baker County, Oregon
d. Sep 25, 1982 in Orange, California
Source: *NewYTBS 82; PolProf E*

Poulter, Thomas Charles
American. Explorer
b. Mar 3, 1897 in Salem, Massachusetts
d. Jun 14, 1978 in Menlo Park, California
Source: *AmM&WS 73P; WhoAm 74; WhoWor 74*

Pound, Ezra Loomis
American. Poet, Critic
Indicted for treason, WW II; wrote *Cantos*, 1925-60.
b. Oct 30, 1885 in Hailey, Idaho
d. Nov 1, 1972 in Venice, Italy
Source: *AmAu&B; AmLY; AmWr; Au&Wr 71; CasWL; Chambr 3; ChPo; CnDAL; CnE&AP; CnMD; CnMWL; ConAmA; ConAmL; ConAu 5R, 37R; ConLC 1, 2, 3, 4, 5, 7, 10, 13, 18; CurBio 42, 63, 72; DcCM; DcLEL; EncAB-H; EncWL; EvLB; LongCTC; ModAL, SUP; NewYTBE 72; OxAmL; OxEng; Pen AM; RAdv 1; RComWL; REn; REnAL; SixAP; TwCA, SUP; TwCW; WebAB; WebE&AL; WhAm 5; WhoTwCL*

Pound, Louise
American. Educator
b. Jun 30, 1872 in Lincoln, Nebraska
d. Jun 17, 1958 in Lincoln, Nebraska
Source: *AmAu&B; OxAmL; REnAL; WhAm 3; WhNAA; WomWWA 14*

Pound, Roscoe
American. Educator
Dean, Harvard Law School, 1916-37; wrote on law philosophy, practice.
b. Oct 27, 1870 in Lincoln, Nebraska
d. Jul 1, 1964 in Cambridge, Massachusetts
Source: *AmAu&B; CurBio 47, 64; OxAmL; REnAL; WebAB; WhAm 4; WhNAA*

Poupeliniere, Alexandre-Jean-Joseph
French. Music Patron
b. 1692 in Paris, France
d. Dec 5, 1762 in Paris, France
Source: *NewEOp 71*

Poussin, Nicolas
French. Artist
b. Jun 1594 in Villers, France
d. Nov 19, 1665 in Rome, Italy
Source: *AtlBL; McGEWB; OxFr; REn*

Powell, Adam Clayton, Jr.
American. Congressman, Clergyman
Elected to Congress, 1945; expelled, 1967, for misuse of funds but relected same year.
b. Nov 29, 1908 in New Haven, Connecticut
d. Apr 4, 1972 in Miami, Florida
Source: *AmAu&B; ConAu 33R, 102; CurBio 42, 72; DcAmB S5; EncAB-H; NewYTBE 72; WebAB; WhAm 5; WhAmP*

Powell, Anthony Dymoke
English. Author
b. Dec 21, 1905 in London, England
Source: *ConAu 1R; ConLC 1; ConNov 72, 76; DcLEL; EncWL; EvLB; IntWW 74; LongCTC; ModBrL, SUP; NewC; NewYTBE 73; OxEng; Pen ENG; RAdv 1; REn; TwCA SUP; TwCW; WebE&AL; Who 74; WhoTwCL; WhoWor 74; WrDr 76*

Powell, Cecil F
British. Physicist, Educator
b. Dec 5, 1903 in Tonbridge, England
d. Aug 9, 1969 in Belluno, Italy
Source: *AsBiEn; DcScB; WhAm 5*

Powell, Dick
American. Actor
Starred in 1930's musicals, 1940's thrillers; TV series, 1956-62.
b. Nov 24, 1904 in Mountain View, Arkansas
d. Jan 2, 1963 in Hollywood, California
Source: *BiDFilm; CmMov; CurBio 48, 63; FilmgC; MotPP; MovMk; WhAm 4; WhScrn 74, 77; WhoHol B; WorEFlm*

Powell, Earl
"Bud"
American. Jazz Musician
b. Sep 27, 1924 in New York, New York
d. Aug 1, 1966 in Brooklyn, New York
Source: *BioIn 7, 8, 11; WhAm 4*

Powell, Eleanor
American. Dancer, Actress
Billed as "world's greatest tap dancer" while with MGM.
b. Nov 21, 1912 in Springfield, Massachusetts
d. Feb 11, 1982 in Beverly Hills, California
Source: *BiE&WWA; CmMov; EncMT; FilmgC; InWom; MotPP; MovMk; NewYTBS 82; OxFilm; ThFT; WhoHol A; WhoThe 77*

Powell, Gordon G
Australian. Author
b. Jan 22, 1911 in Victoria, Australia
Source: *Au&Wr 71; ConAu 1R; WrDr 76*

Powell, Jane
[Suzanne Burce]
American. Singer, Actress
In MGM musicals, 1940's-'50's including *Seven Brides for Seven Brothers,* 1954.
b. Apr 1, 1928 in Portland, Oregon
Source: *CmMov; CurBio 74; FilmgC; InWom; IntMPA 75, 76, 77, 78, 79, 80, 81, 82; MotPP; MovMk; WhoAm 74, 76, 78, 80, 82; WhoAmW 77; WhoHol A; WorEFlm*

Powell, Jody (Joseph Lester)
American. Former Presidential Aide
Press secretary for President Carter.
b. Sep 30, 1943 in Vienna, Georgia
Source: *BioIn 10; CurBio 77; WhoAm 74, 76, 78, 80, 82; WhoAmP 77; WhoGov 77*

Powell, (John) Enoch
English. Politician
b. Jun 16, 1912 in Birmingham, England
Source: *IntWW 74; Who 74; WhoWor 74; WrDr 76*

Powell, John Wesley
American. Ethnologist, Geologist
b. Mar 24, 1834 in Mount Morris, New York
d. Sep 23, 1902 in Haven, Maine
Source: *AmBi; ApCAB; BioIn 1, 2, 3, 4, 5, 6, 8, 9, 11; DcAmB; DcScB; EncAAH; EncAB-H; McGEWB; NatCAB 3; REnAW; TwCBDA; WebAB; WhAm 1*

Powell, Lawrence Clark
American. Author, Educator
b. Sep 3, 1906 in Washington
Source: *AmAu&B; AmEA 74; BiDrLUS 70; ChPo; ConAu 21R; CurBio 60; WhoAm 74; WorAu*

Powell, Lewis Franklin, Jr.
American. Supreme Court Justice
Appointed to bench by President Nixon, 1971.
b. Sep 19, 1907 in Suffolk, Virginia
Source: *CelR 73; CngDr 74; CurBio 65; DrAS 74P; IntWW 74; NewYTBE 71; St&PR 75; WebAB; Who 74; WhoAm 74, 76, 78, 80, 82; WhoAmP 73; WhoGov 72*

Powell, Maud
American. Musician
b. Aug 22, 1868 in Peru, Illinois
d. Jan 8, 1920 in Uniontown, Pennsylvania
Source: *AmBi; AmWom; DcAmB; InWom; NotAW; WhAm 1; WomWWA 14*

Powell, Michael
English. Motion Picture Director, Producer
b. Sep 30, 1905 in Canterbury, England
Source: *BiDFilm; CmMov; ConDr 73; DcFM; FilmgC; IntMPA 77, 75; MovMk; OxFilm; Who 74; WorEFlm*

Powell, Robert
English. Actor
Starred in TV epic *Jesus of Nazareth.*
b. Jun 1, 1944 in Salford, England
Source: *WhoThe 77, 81*

Powell, Teddy
American. Band Leader, Musician
b. Mar 1, 1906 in Oakland, California
Source: *AmSCAP 66; WhoJazz 72*

Powell, William
American. Actor
Starred in *The Thin Man,* 1934.
b. Jul 29, 1892 in Pittsburgh, Pennsylvania
Source: *BiDFilm; CmMov; CurBio 47; Film 1; FilmgC; IntMPA 75, 76, 77, 78, 78, 79, 80, 81, 82; MotPP; MovMk; OxFilm; TwYS; WhoHol A; WhoThe 77; WorEFlm*

Powell, William Henry
American. Artist
b. Feb 14, 1823 in New York, New York
d. Oct 6, 1879 in New York, New York
Source: *ApCAB; DcAmB; TwCBDA; WhAm H*

Power, Donald Clinton
American. Lawyer, Utilities Executive
b. Dec 25, 1899 in Paine Station, Ohio
d. Mar 11, 1979 in Galloway, Ohio
Source: *BioIn 3, 5, 10, 11; CurBio 60, 79; IntWW 74; IntYB 78, 79; NewYTBS 79; WhoWor 74, 76*

Power, Eugene Barnum
American. Microphotographer
b. Jun 4, 1905 in Traverse City, Michigan
Source: *St&PR 75; WhoAm 74, 76, 78, 80, 82; WhoGov 72*

Power, Frederick Tyrone Edmond
American. Actor
b. 1869 in London, England
d. Dec 30, 1931 in Hollywood, California
Source: *BioIn 9, 10; DcAmB; WhoHol B; WhoStg 1908*

Power, Jules
American. TV Producer
b. Oct 19, 1921 in Hammond, Indiana
Source: *Film 1; IndAu 1917; WhoAm 74, 76, 78, 80, 82; WhoGov 72*

Power, Thomas
American. Military Leader
b. Jun 18, 1905 in New York, New York
d. Dec 7, 1970 in Palm Springs, California
Source: *CurBio 58, 71; NewYTBE 70; WhAm 6*

Power, Tyrone
American. Actor
Handsome leading man better known for his looks than his talent.
b. May 15, 1914 in Cincinnati, Ohio
d. Nov 15, 1958 in Madrid, Spain
Source: *BiDFilm; CmMov; CurBio 50, 59; FilmgC; MotPP; MovMk; OxFilm; OxThe; WhAm 3; WhScrn 74, 77; WhoHol B; WorEFlm*

Powers, Anne
[Anne Powers Schwartz]
American. Author
b. May 7, 1913 in Cloquet, Minnesota
Source: *AmAu&B; Au&Wr 71; ConAu 1R, 1NR; MnnWr; SmATA 10; WhoAm 74, 76, 78, 80, 82; WrDr 76*

Powers, Dudley
American. Musician
b. Jun 25, 1911 in Moorhead, Minnesota
Source: *WhoAm 74, 76, 78, 80, 82*

Powers, Eugene
American. Actor
b. May 21, 1872 in Houlton, Maine
d. 1935
Source: *WhThe*

Powers, Francis Gary
American. Pilot
Plane shot down over USSR, 1960, imprisoned; exchanged for Soviet spy, 1962.
b. Aug 17, 1929 in Pound, Virginia
d. Aug 1, 1977 in Encino, California
Source: *BioIn 5, 6, 7, 8, 9, 10, 11; What 5; WorAl*

Powers, Hiram
American. Sculptor
b. Jul 29, 1805 in Woodstock, Vermont
d. Jun 27, 1873 in Florence, Italy
Source: *AmBi; ApCAB; BiAuS; DcAmB; Drake; EncAB-H; OxAmL; REnAL; TwCBDA; WebAB; WhAm H*

Powers, James Farl
American. Author
b. Jul 8, 1917 in Jacksonville, Illinois
Source: *AmAu&B; Au&Wr 71; CathA 1952; ConAu 1R, 2NR; ConLC 1, 4, 8; ConNov 72, 76; DrAF 76; ModAL; OxAmL; Pen AM; RAdv 1; REnAL; TwCA SUP; WebE&AL; WhoAm 74, 76, 78, 80, 82; WhoTwCL; WrDr 76*

Powers, John Robert
American. Owner of Modeling Agency
Founded model agency, 1921; modeling schools, 1929.
b. Sep 14, 1896 in Easton, Pennsylvania
d. Aug 19, 1977 in Glendale, California
Source: *CurBio 45; WhoAm 74*

Powers, Mala
American. Actress
b. Dec 29, 1921 in San Francisco, California
Source: *FilmgC; IntMPA 75, 76, 77; WhoAm 82; WhoAmW 77; WhoHol A; WomWMM*

Powers, Stefanie
American. Actress
Animal lover; established wildlife foundation in Africa in memory of William Holden.
b. Nov 12, 1942 in Hollywood, California
Source: *BioIn 7, 11; FilmgC; IntMPA 82; MotPP; MovMk; WhoAm 82; WhoHol A*

Powhatan
American Indian. Father of Pocahontas
b. 1550
d. Apr 1618
Source: *AmBi; ApCAB; DcAmB; Drake; WebAB; WhAm H*

Powys, John Cowper
English. Author, Essayist, Poet
b. Oct 8, 1872 in Shirley, England
d. Jun 17, 1963 in Wales
Source: *CasWL; ConAu 85; ConLC 7, 9, 15; CyWA; DcLEL; EncWL; EvLB; LongCTC; ModBrL, SUP; NewC; OxEng; Pen ENG; REn; TwCA, SUP; TwCW; WebE&AL; WhAm 4; WhNAA; WhoLA; WhoTwCL*

Powys, Llewelyn
English. Author, Essayist
b. Aug 13, 1884 in Dorchester, England
d. Dec 2, 1939 in Davos, Switzerland
Source: *CyWA; EvLB; LongCTC; NewC; OxEng; REn; TwCA, SUP*

Powys, Theodore Francis
English. Author
b. Dec 20, 1875 in Shirley, England
d. Nov 27, 1953 in Sturminster, England
Source: *CasWL; CyWA; DcLEL; EncWL; EvLB; LongCTC; ModBrL; NewC; OxEng; Pen ENG; REn; TwCA, SUP; TwCW; WebE&AL; WhoTwCL*

Prado Ugarteche, Manuel
Peruvian. Statesman
b. Apr 21, 1889
d. Aug 14, 1967
Source: *CurBio 42, 67; WhAm 4*

Praetorius, Michael
[Michael Schultheiss]
German. Composer, Musician
b. Feb 15, 1571 in Kreuzberg, Germany
d. Feb 15, 1621 in Wolfenbuttel, Germany
Source: *AtlBL; NewCol 75; WebBD 80*

Prang, Louis
Lithographer
Developed color printing; marketed first Christmas cards in England, US, 1875.
b. Mar 12, 1824 in Breslau, Germany
d. Jun 14, 1909 in Los Angeles, California
Source: *DcAmArt; DcAmB; DcNAA; NatCAB 11; NewYHSD; TwCBDA; WhAm 1*

Prasad, Ananda Shiva
American. Educator
b. Jan 1, 1928 in Buxar, India
Source: *AmM&WS 73P; WhoAm 74, 76, 78, 80, 82; WhoMW 74*

Prasad, Rajendra
Indian. Politician
b. Dec 3, 1884 in Bihar, India
d. Feb 28, 1963 in Patna, India
Source: *CurBio 50, 63; WhAm 4*

Pratella, Francesco Balilla
Italian. Composer
b. Feb 1, 1880 in Lugo di Romagna, Italy
d. May 18, 1955 in Ravenna, Italy
Source: *DcCM; WebBD 80*

Prater, Dave
see: Sam and Dave

Prather, Richard Scott
American. Author
b. Sep 9, 1921 in Santa Ana, California
Source: *ConAu 1R, 5NR; WhoWest 74*

Pratt, Bela Lyon
American. Sculptor
b. Dec 11, 1867 in Norwich, Connecticut
d. May 18, 1917
Source: *AmBi; ApCAB X; DcAmB; NatCAB 14; WhAm 1*

Pratt, Charles
American. Oilman, Philanthropist
b. Oct 2, 1830 in Watertown, Massachusetts
d. May 4, 1891 in New York, New York
Source: *AmBi; DcAmB; NatCAB 9, 26; TwCBDA; WhAm H*

Pratt, Edwin John
Canadian. Poet
b. Feb 4, 1883 in Western Bay, NF
d. Apr 26, 1964 in Toronto, ON
Source: *CanWr; CasWL; ChPo; ConAu 93; CreCan 2; DcLEL; EvLB; LongCTC; NewC; OxCan, SUP; OxEng; Pen ENG; REn; REnAL; TwCA SUP; WebE&AL; WhNAA*

Pratt, Fletcher
American. Author
b. Apr 25, 1897 in Buffalo, New York
d. Jun 10, 1956 in Long Branch, New Jersey
Source: *AmAu&B; AuBYP; CurBio 42, 56; REnAL; TwCA SUP; WhAm 3; WhNAA*

Pratt, Gerald Hillary
American. Surgeon, Educator, Author
b. Dec 15, 1903 in Montello, Wisconsin
d. Jan 31, 1979 in Pompano Beach, Florida
Source: *AmM&WS 73P; BioIn 11*

Pratt, Lawrence Arthur
American. Surgeon
b. Dec 20, 1907 in Paris, Illinois
Source: *WhoAm 74, 76, 78, 80, 82; WhoGov 72*

Praxiteles
Greek. Sculptor
b. 370?BC
d. 330?BC
Source: *AtlBL; NewC*

Praz, Mario
Italian. Scholar, Critic
Wrote *The Romantic Agony,* 1933.
b. Sep 6, 1896 in Rome, Italy
d. Mar 23, 1982 in Rome, Italy
Source: *CasWL; ConAu 101; IntWW 74, 75, 76, 77, 78, 79, 80, 81; LinLib L; NewYTBS 82; TwCA SUP; WhoWor 74, 76, 78*

Prefontaine, Steve Roland
American. Track Athlete
b. Jan 25, 1951 in Coos Bay, Oregon
d. May 30, 1975 in Eugene, Oregon
Source: *BioIn 9, 10; WhoTr&F 73*

Premice, Josephine
American. Actress, Singer, Dancer
b. Jul 21, 1926 in New York, New York
Source: *BiE&WWA; NotNAT*

Preminger, Otto
American. Motion Picture Director, Producer
Films include *Laura,* 1944; *Anatomy of a Murder,* 1959, *Exodus,* 1960.
b. Dec 5, 1906 in Vienna, Austria
Source: *BiDFilm; BiE&WWA; BioNews 74; CelR 73; CmMov; CurBio 59; FilmgC; IntMPA 75, 76, 77, 78, 79, 80, 81, 82; MovMk; NotNAT; OxFilm; WebAB; Who 82; WhoAm 74, 76, 78, 80, 82; WhoHol A; WhoWor 74; WorEFlm*

Prendergast, Maurice Brazil
[The Eight]
American. Artist
b. Oct 1861 in Boston, Massachusetts
d. Feb 1, 1924 in New York, New York
Source: *DcAmB; OxAmL; WhAm 1*

Prentice, George Denison
American. Journalist
b. Dec 18, 1802 in New London, Connecticut
d. Jan 22, 1870
Source: *Alli; AmAu; ApCAB; BbD; BiD&SB; BiDSA; ChPo, S1; CyAl 2; DcAmAu; DcNAA; Drake; OxAmL; REnAL; TwCBDA; WhAm H*

Prentiss, Paula
[Mrs. Richard Benjamin; Paula Ragusa]
American. Actress
Starred in *What's New,Pussycat?,* 1965; TV series with husband, *He and She,* 1967-68.
b. Mar 4, 1939 in San Antonio, Texas
Source: *BiDFilm; FilmgC; InWom; IntMPA 75, 76, 77, 78, 79, 80, 81, 82; MotPP; MovMk; NewYTBE 71; WhoHol A*

Prescott, Peter Sherwin
American. Book Critic
b. Jul 15, 1935 in New York, New York
Source: *ConAu 37R*

Prescott, Samuel
American. Revolutionary Patriot
b. Aug 19, 1751 in Concord, Massachusetts
d. 1777? in Halifax, NS
Source: *DcAmB; WebAB; WhAm H*

Prescott, William Hickling
American. Historian
b. May 4, 1796 in Salem, Massachusetts
d. Jan 28, 1859 in Boston, Massachusetts
Source: *Alli; AmAu; AmAu&B; AmBi; ApCAB; AtlBL; BbD; BiD&SB; Chambr 3; CyAL 1; CyWA; DcAmAu; DcAmB; DcEnA; DcEnL; DcLEL; DcNAA; DcSpL; Drake; EvLB; OxAmL; OxEng; Pen AM; REn; REnAL; TwCBDA; WebAB; WhAm H*

Presle, Micheline
[Micheline Chassagne]
French. Actress
b. Aug 22, 1922 in Paris, France
Source: *BiDFilm; FilmgC; IntMPA 75, 76, 77, 78, 79, 80, 81, 82; MotPP; MovMk; OxFilm; WhoHol A; WorEFlm*

Presley, Elvis Aron
"Elvis the Pelvis"
American. Singer, Actor
Rock 'n roll idol; hit songs include "Hound Dog", "Blue Suede Shoes."
b. Jan 8, 1935 in Tupelo, Mississippi
d. Aug 16, 1977 in Memphis, Tennessee
Source: *BiDFilm; CelR 73; CmMov; CurBio 59, 77; EncFCWM 69; FilmgC; IntMPA 77, 75; MotPP; MovMk; OxFilm; WebAB; WhoAm 74; WhoHol A; WhoWor 74; WorEFlm*

Presley, Lisa Marie
American. Daughter of Elvis Presley
b. Feb 1, 1968
Source: *BioIn 10*

Presley, Priscilla Ann Beaulieu
American. Former Wife of Elvis Presley
b. May 24, 1946 in Brooklyn, New York
Source: *BioIn 10*

Presnell, Harve
American. Actor, Opera Singer
b. 1933 in Modesto, California
Source: *FilmgC; MotPP; WhoHol A*

Press, Tamara
Russian. Track Athlete
b. May 10, 1937 in U.S.S.R.
Source: *WhoTr&F 73*

Presser, Theodore
American. Music Publisher
b. Jul 3, 1848 in Pittsburgh, Pennsylvania
d. Oct 27, 1925 in Philadelphia, Pennsylvania
Source: *DcAmB; DcNAA; WhAm 1*

Pressler, Larry
American. Senator
b. Mar 29, 1942 in Humboldt, South Dakota
Source: *AlmAP 78, 80; CngDr 77, 79; WhoAm 78, 80, 82; WhoAmP 75, 77, 79; WhoGov 75, 77; WhoMW 76, 78*

Preston, Billy
American. Singer, Musician, Songwriter
b. Sep 9, 1946 in Houston, Texas
Source: *EncPR&S; IlEncRk; WhoAm 82*

Preston, Rich(ard John)
Canadian. Hockey Player
b. May 22, 1952 in Regina, SK
Source: *HocReg*

Preston, Robert
[Robert Preston Meservey]
American. Actor
Starred in *The Music Man* on Broadway and film; *SOB,* 1981, *Victor/Victoria,* 1982.
b. Jun 8, 1918 in Newton Highlands, Massachusetts
Source: *BiE&WWA; CelR 73; CmMov; CurBio 58; EncMT; FamA&A; FilmgC; HolP 40; IntMPA 75, 76, 77, 78, 79, 80, 81, 82; MovMk; NotNAT; WhoAm 74, 76, 78, 80, 82; WhoE 74; WhoHol A; WhoThe 77; WhoWor 74; WorEFlm*

Prestopino, George
American. Artist
b. Jun 21, 1907 in New York, New York
Source: *CurBio 64; DcCAA 71, 77; McGDA; WhoAm 74, 76, 78, 80, 82*

Pretenders, The
[Martin Chambers; Pete Farndon; James Honeyman-Scott; Chrissie Hynde]
English. Rock Group
Source: *IlEncRk; NewWmR; WhoRock 81*

Pretorius, Marthinus Wessel
South African. President
First President of S African Republic, 1857-60, 1864-71.
b. 1819 in Graaff Reinet, South Africa
d. May 19, 1901 in Potchefstroom, South Africa
Source: *EncSoA*

Pretre, Georges
French. Opera Conductor
b. Aug 14, 1924 in Waziers, France
Source: *IntWW 74; WhoWor 74*

Previn, Andre
American. Composer, Pianist, Conductor
Won four Oscars; conductor, London Symphony, 1968-79; Pittsburgh Symphony, 1976--.
b. Apr 6, 1929 in Berlin, Germany
Source: *AmSCAP 66; BioNews 75; CelR 73; CmMov; CurBio 72; FilmgC; IntMPA 75, 76, 77, 78, 79, 80, 81, 82; IntWW 74; OxFilm; Who 82; WhoAm 74, 76, 78, 80, 82; WhoMus 72; WhoWor 74; WorEFlm*

Previn, Dory Langdon
American. Lyricist, Singer
b. Oct 22, 1925 in Rahway, New Jersey
Source: *AmSCAP 66; WhoAm 82*

Previtali, Fernando
Italian. Conductor
b. Feb 16, 1907 in Adria, Italy
Source: *WhoMus 72*

Prevost, Marcel
French. Author, Dramatist
b. May 1, 1862 in Paris, France
d. Apr 8, 1941 in Vianne, France
Source: *CasWL; ClDMEL; CurBio 41; EncWL; OxFr; TwCA, SUP*

Prevost d'Exiles, Antoine Francois, Abbe
French. Author, Journalist
b. Apr 1, 1697 in Hesdin, France
d. Nov 23, 1763 in Chantilly, France
Source: *Alli; AtlBL; BbD; BiD&SB; CasWL; CyWA; DcBiA; DcEuL; EuAu; EvEuW; NewC; OxEng; OxFr; Pen EUR; RComWL; REn*

Prey, Hermann
German. Opera Singer
b. Jul 11, 1929 in Berlin, Germany
Source: *CurBio 75; IntWW 74; WhoMus 72; WhoWor 74*

Price, Alan
[The Animals]
English. Singer, Songwriter
b. Apr 19, 1942 in Fairfield, England
Source: *EncPR&S; IlEncRk*

Price, Byron
American. Editor, Government Official
b. Mar 25, 1891 in Clearspring, Indiana
d. Aug 6, 1981 in Hendersonville, North Carolina
Source: *BioIn 1, 6; ConAu 104; CurBio 42, 81; IntWW 74, 75, 76, 77, 78; Who 74; WhoUN 75*

Price, Dennis
English. Actor
b. Jun 23, 1915 in Twyford, England
d. Oct 7, 1973 in Guernsey, England
Source: *BiE&WWA; FilmgC; MovMk; NewYTBE 73; OxFilm; WhScrn 77; WhoHol B*

Price, Garrett
American. Illustrator, Cartoonist
Best known for cover work for *New Yorker, Colliers* magazines.
b. 1896 in Bucyrus, Kansas
d. Apr 8, 1979 in Norwalk, Connecticut
Source: *ConAu 85; IlsBYP; IlsCB 1957*

Price, George
American. Cartoonist
b. Jun 9, 1901 in Coytesville, New Jersey
Source: *ConAu 103; NewYTBE 71; WhoAm 74, 76, 78, 80, 82; WhoAmA 73, 76, 78; WhoWor 74*

Price, Leontyne
American. Opera Singer
b. Feb 10, 1927 in Laurel, Mississippi
Source: *BiE&WWA; BioNews 74; CelR 73; CurBio 61; InWom; IntWW 74; NewYTBE 73; WebAB; Who 74; WhoAm 74, 76, 78, 80, 82; WhoAmW 77; WhoBlA 75; WhoMus 72; WhoWor 74*

Price, Ray
[Noble Ray Price]
"The Cherokee Cowboy"
American. Musician, Singer
b. Jan 12, 1926 in Perryville, Texas
Source: *EncFCWM 69; WhoAm 74, 76, 78, 80, 82*

Price, Roger
American. Comedian
b. Mar 6, 1920 in Charleston, West Virginia
Source: *ConAu 9R; IntMPA 75, 76, 77, 78, 79, 80, 81, 82; WhoAm 74*

Price, Sterling
American. Military Leader
b. Sep 11, 1809 in Virginia
d. Sep 29, 1867 in Saint Louis, Missouri
Source: *ApCAB; DcAmB; Drake; NewCol 75; WebBD 80*

Price, Steve
[Pablo Cruise]
American. Musician, Singer
Hit song "Love Will Find a Way," 1978.
Source: *IlEncRk; RkOn 2; WhoRock 81*

Price, Vincent
"Master of Menace"
American. Actor
Starred in horror films *House of Wax,* 1953; *Theatre of Blood,* 1973.
b. May 27, 1911 in Saint Louis, Missouri
Source: *BiDFilm; BiE&WWA; CelR 73; ConAu 89; CurBio 56; FilmgC; IntMPA 75, 76, 77, 78, 79, 80, 81, 82; MotPP; MovMk; NotNAT; OxFilm; WhoAm 74, 76, 78, 80, 82; WhoAmA 73; WhoGov 72; WhoHol A; WhoThe 77; WorEFlm*

Pride, Charley
"Country Charley"
American. Singer
Hits include "Kiss an Angel Good Morning."
b. Mar 8, 1938 in Sledge, Mississippi
Source: *BioNews 74; CelR 73; EncFCWM 69; WhoAm 74, 76, 78, 80, 82; WhoBlA 75*

Priesand, Sally Jane
American. Rabbi
b. Jun 27, 1946 in Cleveland, Ohio
Source: *NewYTBE 71; WhoAm 74, 76, 78, 80, 82; WhoRel 75*

Priest, Ivy (Maude) Baker
American. Treasurer of the United States
b. Sep 7, 1905 in Kimberley, Utah
d. Jun 23, 1975 in Santa Monica, California
Source: *CurBio 52; InWom; WhAm 6; WhoAm 74; WhoAmP 73; WhoGov 72; WhoWest 74*

Priestley, J(ohn) B(oynton)
English. Author, Dramatist
Wrote *Angel Pavement; Literature and Western Man; The Edwardians.*
b. Sep 13, 1894 in Bradford, England
Source: *Au&Wr 71; BiE&WWA; CasWL; Chambr 3; ChPo; CnMD; CnThe; ConAu 9R; ConDr 73; ConLC 2, 5, 9; ConNov 72, 76; CroCD; CyWA; DcLEL; EncMys; EncWL; EvLB; IntMPA 75, 76, 77, 78, 79, 80, 81, 82; IntWW 74; LongCTC; McGEWD; ModBrL, SUP; ModWD; NewC; NewYTBS 74; NotNAT; OxEng; OxThe; Pen ENG; REn; REnWD; TwCA, SUP; TwCW; WebE&AL; Who 74; WhoLA; WhoThe 77; WhoTwCL; WhoWor 74; WorEFlm; WrDr 76*

Priestley, Joseph
English. Clergyman, Chemist
b. Mar 13, 1733 in Fieldhead, England
d. Feb 6, 1804 in Northumberland, Pennsylvania
Source: *Alli; AmAu&B; AmBi; ApCAB; BiD&SB; BrAu; CasWL; Chambr 2; CyAl 2; DcAmAu; DcAmB; DcEnL; DcEuL; DcLEL; DcNAA; Drake; EvLB; NewC; OxAmL; OxEng; REn; TwCBDA; WhAm H*

Prigogine, Ilya
Russian. Chemist
b. Jan 25, 1917 in Moscow, Russia
Source: *IntWW 74; WhoAm 82; WhoWor 74*

Prima, Louis
American. Musician
b. Dec 7, 1912 in New Orleans, Louisiana
d. Aug 24, 1978 in New Orleans, Louisiana
Source: *AmSCAP 66; WhoAm 74; WhoHol A; WhoJazz 72*

Primaticcio, Francesco
Italian. Artist
b. 1503 in Bologna, Italy
d. Sep 1570 in Paris, France
Source: *REn*

Prime, Geoffrey Arthur
"Rowlands," code name
English. Spy
Convicted of spying for Soviets, 1968-81; sentenced to 35 years.
b. 1938? in Alton, England
Source: *NewYTBS 82*

Primo de Rivera, Jose A
Spanish. Founder of Facist Falange
b. 1903
d. 1936
Source: *DcBiPP*

Primrose, William
American. Musician
b. Aug 23, 1904 in Glasgow, Scotland
d. May 1, 1982 in Provo, Utah
Source: *CurBio 46; NewYTBS 82; Who 74; WhoAm 74; WhoMus 72*

Prin, Alice
[Kiki of Montparnasse]
French. Entertainer
b. 1901
d. Mar 23, 1953 in Paris, France
Source: *BioIn 1, 3, 7, 8, 9*

Prince, Hal (Harold Smith)
American. Theatrical Producer, Director
Plays include *Damn Yankees; West Side Story; Fiddler on the Roof; Cabaret.*
b. Jan 30, 1928 in New York, New York
Source: *BiE&WWA; BioNews 75; CelR 73; CurBio 71; EncMT; IntMPA 75, 76, 77, 78, 79, 80, 81, 82; NotNAT; WhoAm 74; WhoE 74; WhoThe 77; WhoWor 74*

Prince, Prairie
see: Tubes, The

Prince, William
American. Actor
b. Jan 26, 1913 in Nichols, New York
Source: *BiE&WWA; FilmgC; IntMPA 75, 76, 77, 78, 79, 80, 81, 82; WhoHol A; WhoThe 77*

Princess of Wales
see: Diana, Princess of Wales

Princip, Gavrilo
Serbian. Assassin
Assassinated Archduke Ferdinand and wife, 1914; sparked WW I.
b. 1893 in Sarajevo, Yugoslavia
d. Apr 30, 1918 in Prague, Czechoslovakia
Source: *REn*

Principal, Victoria
American. Actress
Plays Pamela Ewing on TV series "Dallas," 1978--.
b. Jan 3, 1944? in Fukuoka, Japan
Source: *WhoAm 80, 82; WhoHol A*

Pringle, Aileen
American. Actress
b. 1895 in San Francisco, California
Source: *Film 1; FilmgC; MotPP; MovMk; ThFT; TwYS; WhoHol A*

Pringle, Laurence
[Sean Edmund, pseud.]
American. Children's Author
b. Nov 26, 1935 in Rochester, New York
Source: *BiE&WWA; ConAu 29R; EncMT; InWom; OxFilm; OxThe; SmATA 4; WhoHol A; WhoThe 77*

Printemps, Yvonne
[Yvonne Wigniolle]
French. Actress, Singer
b. Jul 25, 1898 in Ermont, France
d. Jan 18, 1977 in Paris, France
Source: *BiE&WWA; BioIn 11; CnThe; EncMT; InWom; NewYTBS 77; OxFilm; OxThe; WhThe; WhoHol A*

Prinze, Freddie
American. Actor, Comedian
Starred in TV series *Chico and the Man,* 1974-77; suicide ruled accidental, 1983.
b. Jun 22, 1954 in New York, New York
d. Jan 28, 1977 in Los Angeles, California
Source: *BioIn 10, 11; CurBio 75, 77; IntMPA 77*

Prior, Matthew
English. Poet, Diplomat
b. Jul 21, 1664 in Winborne, England
d. Sep 18, 1721 in Cambridge, England
Source: *Alli; AtlBL; BbD; BiD&SB; BrAu; CasWL; Chambr 2; ChPo, S1; CnE&AP; CrtT 2; DcEnA; DcEnL; DcEuL; DcLEL; EvLB; NewC; OxEng; Pen ENG; REn; WebE&AL*

Priscilla of Boston
[Priscilla Kidder]
American. Bridal Gown Designer
b. Dec 14, 1916 in Quincy, Massachusetts
Source: *WorFshn*

Pritchard, John Michael
English. Conductor
b. Feb 5, 1921 in London, England
Source: *IntWW 74; Who 74; WhoMus 72; WhoWor 74*

Pritikin, Nathan
American. Inventor, Researcher
b. Aug 29, 1915 in Chicago, Illinois
Source: *ConAu 89; NewYTBS 79; WhoAm 82*

Procol Harum
[Gary Brooker; Matthew Fisher; Robert Harrison; David Knights; Keith Reid; Ray Royer; Robin Trower; Barry Wilson]
English. Rock Group
Source: *EncPR&S; IlEncRk*

Procter, Harley T
Soap Manufacturer
b. 1834?
d. 1907
Source: *BioIn 6, 7*

Procter, William Cooper
American. Manufacturer, Philanthropist
President, Procter and Gamble, 1907-30; instituted profit-sharing.
b. Aug 25, 1862 in Glendale, Ohio
d. May 2, 1934
Source: *DcAmB S1; WhAm 1*

Profaci, Joe
Criminal
b. 1898?
d. Jun 6, 1962 in Bay Shore, New York
Source: *Blood*

Profumo, John Dennis
English. Former Diplomat
b. Jan 30, 1915
Source: *BioIn 5, 6, 7, 8, 9, 10; CurBio 59; Who 74*

Prohaska, Felix
Austrian. Conductor
b. May 16, 1912 in Vienna, Austria
Source: *Baker 78*

Prokofiev, Sergei
Russian. Composer, Musician
b. Apr 23, 1891 in Sontsovka, Russia
d. Mar 5, 1953 in Moscow, U.S.S.R.
Source: *AnCL; AtlBL; CurBio 41, 53; DcCM; DcFM; OxFilm; REn; WhAm 3; WorEFlm*

Prokop, Eugen
Musician
Source: *NF*

Prokosch, Frederic
American. Author, Poet
b. May 17, 1908 in Madison, Wisconsin
Source: *CasWL; ConAu 73; ConLC 4; ConNov 72, 76; ConP 70, 75; DrAF 76; IntWW 74; LongCTC; OxAmL; Pen AM; REn; REnAL; SixAP; TwCA, SUP; Who 74; WrDr 76*

Pronovost, (Rene) Marcel
Canadian. Hockey Player, Coach
Defenseman, Detroit, 1950-65; Toronto, 1965-70.
b. Jun 15, 1930 in Lac-la-Tortue, PQ
Source: *WhoHcky 73*

Protagoras
Greek. Sophist
b. 490?BC in Abdera, Greece
d. 421?BC
Source: *NewCol 75; WebBD 80*

Protopopov, Ludmilla Evgenievna Belousova
[Mrs. Oleg Protopopov]
Russian. Figure Skater
b. Nov 22, 1935 in Ulyanousk, U.S.S.R.
Source: *BioIn 8*

Protopopov, Oleg Alekseevich
Russian. Figure Skater
b. Jul 16, 1932 in Leningrad, U.S.S.R.
Source: *BioIn 8*

Proudhon, Pierre Joseph
French. Anarchist, Author, Philosopher
b. Jan 15, 1809 in Besancon, France
d. Jan 16, 1865 in Paris, France
Source: *AtlBL; BbD; BiD&SB; CasWL; DcEuL; EuAu; OxFr; REn*

Proust, Marcel
French. Author
b. Jul 10, 1871 in Paris, France
d. Nov 18, 1922 in Paris, France
Source: *AtlBL; CasWL; ClDMEL; CnMWL; CyWA; DcEuL; EncWL; EvEuW; LongCTC; ModRL; NewC; OxEng; OxFr; Pen EUR; RComWL; REn; TwCA, SUP; TwCW; WhoTwCL*

Prouty, Jed
American. Actor
b. Apr 6, 1879 in Boston, Massachusetts
d. May 10, 1956 in New York, New York
Source: *FilmgC; MotPP; MovMk; TwYS; Vers A; WhScrn 74, 77; WhoHol B*

Provensen, Alice Rose Twitchell
American. Illustrator
b. Aug 14, 1918 in Chicago, Illinois
Source: *ChPo; ConAu 53, 5NR; IlsCB 1946, 1957; SmATA 9; ThrBJA; WhoAm 82; WhoChL; WhoE 74*

Provensen, Martin
American. Illustrator
b. Jul 10, 1916 in Chicago, Illinois
Source: *ConAu 53, 5NR; IlsCB 1946, 1957; SmATA 9; ThrBJA; WhoAm 82; WhoChL; WhoGrA*

Provine, Dorothy Michele
American. Actress, Dancer, Singer
b. Jan 20, 1937 in Deadwood, South Dakota
Source: *FilmgC; InWom; IntMPA 75, 76, 77, 78, 79, 80, 81, 82; MotPP; MovMk; WhoAm 74; WhoHol A*

Prowse, Juliet
American. Dancer, Actress
Film debut in *Can-Can,* 1960; TV series *Mona McClusky,* 1966.
b. 1936 in Bombay, India
Source: *FilmgC; InWom; MotPP; WhoAm 82; WhoHol A*

Proxmire, William
American. Politician
Senator, 1957--; awards "Golden Fleece" for beaucratic waste.
b. Nov 11, 1915 in Lake Forest, Illinois
Source: *BiDrAC; CelR 73; CngDr 74; ConAu 29R; CurBio 58; IntWW 74; NewYTBE 71, 73; WhoAm 74, 76, 78, 80, 82; WhoAmP 73; WhoGov 72; WhoMW 74; WhoWor 74; WrDr 76*

Prudden, Bonnie
American. Physiculturist
b. 1914?
Source: *BioIn 5*

Prudhon, Pierre
French. Artist
b. Apr 4, 1758 in Cluny, France
d. Feb 16, 1823 in Paris, France
Source: *McGEWB; NewCol 75; WebBD 80*

Pruitt, Greg(ory Donald)
American. Football Player
b. Aug 18, 1951 in Houston, Texas
Source: *BioIn 10; WhoAm 78, 80, 82; WhoBlA 75, 77; WhoFtbl 74*

Pryor, David Hampton
American. Politician
b. Aug 29, 1934 in Camden, Arkansas
Source: *BioIn 11; WhoAm 78, 80, 82*

Pryor, Nicholas
American. Actor
b. Jan 28, 1935 in Baltimore, Maryland
Source: *BiE&WWA; NotNAT; WhoHol A*

Pryor, Richard Franklin Lennox Thomas
American. Actor, Comedian
Films includes *Live on the Sunset Strip; Stir Crazy; The Toy.*
b. Dec 1, 1940 in Peoria, Illinois
Source: *BkPepl; FilmgC; IntMPA 82; MovMk; WhoAm 82; WhoHol A*

Pryor, Roger
American. Actor, TV Executive
b. Aug 27, 1901
d. Jan 31, 1974 in Puerto Vallarta, Mexico
Source: *FilmgC; HolP 30; Vers A; WhAm 6; WhScrn 74, 77*

Prysock, Arthur
American. Singer
b. 1929 in Spartanburg, South Carolina
Source: *BiDAmM*

Przhevalsky, Nikolai Mikhailovich
Russian. Geographer, Explorer
Traveled to Central China, 1870; Gobi Desert, 1884.
b. 1839
d. 1888
Source: *NewCol 75; WebBD 80*

Psalmanazar, George
French. Imposter
Posed as Formosan Christian; sent to Oxford to teach fictitious language, 1704.
b. 1679? in Languedoc, France
d. May 3, 1763 in London, England
Source: *Alli; BbD; BiD&SB; CasWL; Chambr 2; DcEnL; DcLEL; EvLB; OxEng*

Ptolemy
[Claudius Ptolemeaus]
Greek. Mathematician, Astronomer
Devised astronomical system whereby sun, planets revolved around Earth.
b. 150 in Alexandria, Egypt
Source: *BbD; BiD&SB; NewC; OxEng; Pen CL; REn*

Publius Horatius Cocles
Roman. Soldier
Source: *NewC*

Publius Vergilius Maro
see: Virgil

Pucci, Emilio Marchese di Barsento
Italian. Designer
b. Nov 20, 1914 in Naples, Italy
Source: *BioNews 74; CelR 73; CurBio 61; IntWW 74; WhoWor 74; WorFshn*

Puccini, Giacomo
Italian. Opera Composer
b. Dec 22, 1858 in Lucca, Italy
d. Nov 29, 1924 in Brussels, Belgium
Source: *AtlBL; OxAmL; PlP&P; REn*

Pudney, John Sleigh
English. Author, Dramatist
Wrote *Jacobson's Ladder,* 1938.
b. Jan 19, 1909 in Langley, England
d. Nov 10, 1977 in England
Source: *Au&Wr 71; ChPo; ConAu 9R, 77, 5NR; ConNov 72, 76; ConP 70, 75; IntWW 74; LongCTC; ModBrL; NewC; Pen ENG; SmATA 24; Who 74; WhoChL; WorAu; WrDr 76*

Pudovkin, Vsevolod
Russian. Motion Picture Director
b. Feb 6, 1893 in Penza, Russia
d. Jun 30, 1953 in Riga, U.S.S.R.
Source: *BiDFilm; DcFM; MovMk; OxFilm; REn; WhScrn 74, 77; WhoHol B; WorEFlm*

Puente, Tito
American. Orchestra Conductor, Arranger
b. Apr 20, 1923 in New York, New York
Source: *BioIn 11; WhoAm 82*

Pugachev, Yemelyan I
Russian. Posed as Peter III
b. 1741
d. 1775
Source: *BioIn 9; NewCol 75; WebBD 80*

Pulaski, Kazimierz
Polish. Nobleman, Patriot
b. Mar 4, 1747 in Winiary, Poland
d. Oct 11, 1779
Source: *AmBi; ApCAB; DcAmB; Drake; TwCBDA; WebAB; WhAm H*

Pulci, Luigi
Italian. Author
b. Aug 15, 1432 in Florence, Italy
d. Nov 1484 in Padua, Italy
Source: *BiD&SB; CasWL; DcEuL; EuAu; EvEuW; OxEng; Pen EUR; REn*

Pulitzer, Joseph
American. Editor, Publisher
Owner/publisher, St. Louis *Post-Dispatch,* New York *World;* endowed Pulitzer Prizes.
b. Apr 10, 1847 in Mako, Hungary
d. Oct 29, 1911 in Charleston, South Carolina
Source: *AmAu&B; AmBi; ApCAB; BiDrAC; CasWL; DcAmB; DcLEL; EncAB-H; EvLB; OxAmL; REn; REnAL; WebAB; WhAm 1*

Pulitzer, Joseph, II
American. Editor, Publisher
Editor/publisher, St. Louis *Post-Dispatch,* 1912-55.
b. Mar 21, 1885 in New York, New York
d. Mar 30, 1955 in Saint Louis, Missouri
Source: *AmAu&B; CurBio 54, 55; DcAmB S5; WhAm 3*

Pulitzer, Lilly
[Lillian McKim Rousseau]
American. Designer
b. in Palm Beach, Florida
Source: *WorFshn*

Pulitzer, "Peter" (Herbert, Jr.)
American. Publishing Heir
Grandson of Joseph Pulitzer; involved in divorce scandal with ex-wife, Roxanne, 1982.
b. 1930?
Source: *NF*

Pulitzer, Ralph
American. Publisher, Poet
b. Jun 11, 1879 in Saint Louis, Missouri
d. Jun 14, 1939 in New York, New York
Source: *AmAu&B; DcAmB S2; DcNAA; WhAm 1; WhNAA*

Pultizer, Roxanne
American. Ex-wife of Peter Pulitzer
Granted headline-making divorce, Dec, 1982.
b. 1952?
Source: *NF*

Pullein-Thompson, Diana
[Diana Fullein-Thompson Farr]
American. Children's Author
b. in Wimbledon, England
Source: *Au&Wr 71; ConAu 17R; SmATA 3; WhoChL; WrDr 76*

Pullman, George Mortimer
American. Inventor
Developed railroad sleeping car, 1864.
b. Mar 3, 1831 in Brocton, New York
d. Oct 19, 1897 in Chicago, Illinois
Source: *AmBi; ApCAB; DcAmB; EncAB-H; TwCBDA; WebAB; WhAm H*

Pully, B S
Comedian, Actor
b. 1910
d. Jan 6, 1972 in Philadelphia, Pennsylvania
Source: *WhScrn 77; WhoHol B*

Purcell, Henry
English. Composer
b. 1658 in London, England
d. Nov 21, 1695 in Westminster, England
Source: *Alli; AtlBL; NewC; REn*

Purcell, Sarah
[Sarah Pentecost]
American. TV Personality
Co-host of TV series "Real People."
b. 1948 in Richmond, Indiana
Source: *BioIn 12*

Purdom, Edmund
English. Actor
b. Dec 19, 1926 in Welwyn Garden, England
Source: *FilmgC; IntMPA 75, 76, 77, 78, 79, 80, 81, 82; MotPP; WhoHol A*

Purdy, James
American. Author
b. Jul 17, 1923 in Ohio
Source: *AmAu&B; Au&Wr 71; CasWL; ConAu 33R; ConLC 2, 4, 10; ConNov 76; DrAF 76; DrAP 75; IntWW 74; ModAL SUP; OxAmL; Pen AM; RAdv 1; REn; REnAL; TwCW; WebE&AL; WhoAm 74, 76, 78, 80, 82; WhoE 74; WhoTwCL; WhoWor 74; WorAu; WrDr 76*

Purdy, Ken(neth) William
American. Journalist
b. Apr 28, 1913 in Chicago, Illinois
d. Jun 7, 1972 in Wilton, Connecticut
Source: *Au&Wr 71; ConAu 29R; NewYTBE 72; WhAm 5; WhoAm 74*

Purdy, Susan Gold
American. Author, Illustrator
b. May 17, 1939 in New York, New York
Source: *AuBYP; ChPo, S1; ConAu 13R; ForWC 70; IlsCB 1957; SmATA 8; WhoAmW 77*

Purim, Flora
Brazilian. Singer
b. Mar 6, 1942 in Rio de Janeiro, Brazil
Source: *BioIn 10; WhoAm 82*

Purtell, William Arthur
American. Senator
b. May 6, 1897 in Hartford, Connecticut
d. May 31, 1978 in Hartford, Connecticut
Source: *BiDrAC; BioIn 4, 11; CurBio 56, 78; NewYTBS 78; ObitOF 79; WhoAmP 73, 75, 77*

Purviance, Edna
American. Actress
b. 1894 in Reno, Nevada
d. Jan 13, 1958 in Woodland Hills, California
Source: *Film 1; FilmgC; MotPP; MovMk; OxFilm; TwYS; WhScrn 74, 77; WhoHol B; WorEFlm*

Purvis, Melvin
American. FBI Agent
Credited with capturing or killing John Dillinger, Pretty Boy Floyd, etc.
b. 1903
d. Feb 29, 1960 in Florence, South Carolina
Source: *BioIn 5; Blood*

Pusey, Edward Bouverie
English. Author, Clergyman, Educator
b. Mar 22, 1800 in Pusey, England
d. Sep 14, 1882 in Ascot Priory, England
Source: *Alli, SUP; BbD; BiD&SB; BrAu 19; CasWL; Chambr 3; DcEnL; DcEuL; DcLEL; EvLB; NewC; OxEng; REn*

Pusey, Merlo John
American. Author, Editor
b. Feb 3, 1902 in Woodruff, Utah
Source: *AmAu&B; Au&Wr 71; ConAu 9R; CurBio 52; DrAS 74H; OxAmL; REnAL; TwCA SUP; WhoAm 74; WhoE 74; WrDr 76, 76*

Pusey, Nathan Marsh
American. Educator
b. Apr 4, 1907 in Council Bluffs, Iowa
Source: *CurBio 53; DrAS 74H; IntWW 74; LEduc 74; Who 74; WhoAm 74; WhoE 74; WhoWor 74*

Pushkin, Aleksandr Sergeyevich
Russian. Author, Poet
Introduced Russian Romanticism; wrote *Boris Godunov,* 1831.
b. Jun 6, 1799 in Moscow, Russia
d. Feb 10, 1837 in Saint Petersburg, Russia
Source: *AtlBL; BbD; BiD&SB; CasWL; ChPo S1; CnThe; CyWA; DcBiA; DcEuL; DcRusL; EuAu; EvEuW; McGEWD; NewC; OxEng; Pen EUR; RComWL; REn; REnWD*

Pusser, Buford
American. Sheriff
Exploits were basis for movie, *Walking Tall,* 1973.
b. 1937
d. Aug 21, 1974 in Adamsville, Tennessee
Source: *NewYTBS 74*

Putnam, Israel
American. General
b. Jan 7, 1718 in Salem, Massachusetts
d. May 29, 1790 in Brooklyn, Connecticut
Source: *AmBi; ApCAB; DcAmB; Drake; OxAmL; REn; REnAL; TwCBDA; WebAB; WhAm H*

Puvis de Chavannes, Pierre Cecile
French. Artist
b. Dec 14, 1824 in Lyons, France
d. Oct 10, 1898 in Paris, France
Source: *AtlBL; OxFr*

Puzo, Mario
American. Author
Won Oscars for screenplays of *The Godfather I, II* 1972, 1974.
b. Oct 15, 1920 in New York, New York
Source: *ConAu 65, 4NR; ConLC 1, 2, 6; ConNov 72, 76; DrAF 76; WhoAm 80, 82; WrDr 76*

Pye, Henry
British. Poet Laureate
b. 1745
d. 1813
Source: *Alli; Br&AmS; BrAu; Chambr 2; DcEnA; DcEnL; DcEuL; DcLEL; EvLB; NewC; OxEng; PoLE; REn*

Pyle, Denver
American. Actor
b. May 11, 1920 in Bethune, Colorado
Source: *FilmgC; MovMk; WhoAm 82; WhoHol A; WhoWest 74*

Pyle, Ernie (Ernest Taylor)
American. Journalist, War Correspondent
Won Pulitzer Prize, 1944, for WW II stories; killed on Ie Shima Island.
b. Aug 3, 1900 in Dana, Indiana
d. Apr 18, 1945
Source: *AmAu&B; CurBio 41, 45; DcAmB S3; DcNAA; IndAu 1917; TwCA SUP; WebAB; WhAm 2*

Pyle, Howard
American. Author, Illustrator
Wrote, illustrated juvenile tales *Story of King Arthur and His Knights,* 1903.
b. Mar 5, 1853 in Wilmington, Delaware
d. Nov 9, 1911 in Florence, Italy
Source: *Alli SUP; AmAu; AmAu&B; AmBi; AnCL; ApCAB; AuBYP; BbD; BiD&SB; CarSB; ChPo, S1, S2; DcAmAu; DcAmB; DcLEL; DcNAA; FamSYP; IlsBYP; JBA 34; OxAmL; REnAL; TwCBDA; WebAB; WhAm 1; WhoChL*

Pym, Barbara Mary Crampton
English. Author
b. Jun 2, 1913 in Oswestry, England
d. Jan 11, 1980 in England
Source: *Au&Wr 71; BioIn 12; ConAu 97; ConAu P-1; ConLC 13; WorAu 1970; WrDr 76, 80*

Pym, Francis Leslie
British. Foreign Secretary
b. Feb 13, 1922 in Abergavenny, Wales
Source: *CurBio 82; IntWW 74, 80; IntYB 78, 79; NewYTBS 82; Who 80*

Pynchon, Thomas
American. Author
b. May 8, 1937 in Glen Cove, New York
Source: *AmAu&B; CasWL; ConAu 21R; ConLC 2, 3, 6, 9, 11, 18; ConNov 72, 76; DrAF 76; EncWL; Pen AM; RAdv 1; WebE&AL; WhoAm 74, 76, 78, 80, 82; WorAu; WrDr 76*

Pyne, Joe
Entertainer
b. 1925 in Chester, Pennsylvania
d. Mar 23, 1970 in Hollywood, California
Source: *NewYTBE 70; WhScrn 74, 77; WhoHol B*

Pythagoras
Greek. Philosopher, Mathematician
Discovered principles of musical pitch.
b. 582BC in Samos, Greece
d. 507BC
Source: *BbD; BiD&SB; CasWL; NewC; Pen CL; REn*

Pytheas
Greek. Navigator, Geographer
Only fragments survive about voyages to Britain, N Europe.
b. in Massilia
Source: *NewC; Pen CL*

Q

Qadhafi, Mu'ammar al-
[Moamar al-Gaddafi; Muammar Khadafy]
Libyan. Political Leader
Led military coup against monarchy, 1969; president, Mar 1977--.
b. 1942 in Misurata, Libya
Source: *CurBio 73; IntWW 74, 75, 76, 77, 78, 79, 80, 81; IntYB 79, 80, 81; MidE 78, 79, 80; WhoGov 72*

Quabus bin Saud
[Qaboosbin Said]
Sultan of Muscat and Oman
b. Nov 18, 1940 in Oman
Source: *CurBio 78*

Quad, M, pseud.
[Charles Bertrand Lewis]
American. Journalist
b. Feb 15, 1842 in Liverpool, Ohio
d. Sep 21, 1924
Source: *Alli, SUP; AmAu; AmAu&B; BbD; BiD&SB; DcAmAu; DcAmB; DcNAA; HsB&A; OhA&B; OxAmL; REnAL; TwCBDA; WhAm 1*

Quaison-Sackey, Alex(ander)
Ghanaian. Diplomat
b. Aug 9, 1924 in Ghana
Source: *CurBio 66; IntWW 74; WhoUN 75*

Qualen, John Mandt
Entertainer
b. 1899 in Vancouver, BC
Source: *FilmgC; IntMPA 75, 76, 77, 78, 79, 80, 81, 82; MovMk; Vers A; WhoHol A; WhoWest 74*

Quanah
[Quannah Parker]
American. Indian Leader
b. 1845 in Texas
d. Feb 23, 1911 in Fort Sill, Oklahoma
Source: *NewCol 75; WebAB*

Quant, Mary
English. Cosmetic, Fashion Designer
Credited with starting Mod Look in London; also hot pants, body stockings.
b. Feb 11, 1934 in London, England
Source: *CurBio 68; InWom; IntWW 74; Who 82; WhoWor 74; WorFshn*

Quantrill, William Clarke
American. Confederate Commander
b. Jul 31, 1837 in Canal Dover, Ohio
d. Jun 6, 1865 in Louisville, Kentucky
Source: *AmAu&B; DcAmB; REnAL; WebAB; WhAm H*

Quarry, Jerry
American. Boxer
b. May 18, 1945 in Los Angeles, California
Source: *NewYTBS 74; WhoBox 74*

QuarterFlash
[Jack Charles; Rick DiGiallonardo; Rich Gooch; Marv Ross; Rindy Ross; Brian David Willis]
American. Rock Group
Source: *NF*

Quasimodo, Salvatore
Italian. Author
b. Aug 20, 1901 in Syracuse, Sicily
d. Jun 14, 1968 in Naples, Italy
Source: *CasWL; ConAu 25R; ConAu P-1; ConLC 10; CurBio 60, 68; EncWL; EvEuW; LongCTC; ModRL; Pen EUR; REn; TwCW; WhAm 5; WhoTwCL; WorAu*

Quatro, Suzi
American. Singer
b. Jun 3, 1950 in Detroit, Michigan
Source: *BioIn 10; BioNews 74; IlEncRk*

Quayle, Anna
English. Actress
b. Oct 6, 1936 in Birmingham, England
Source: *BiE&WWA; NotNAT; WhoHol A; WhoThe 77*

Quayle, Anthony
English. Actor, Motion Picture Director
b. Sep 7, 1913 in Lancashire, England
Source: *BiE&WWA; CelR 73; CurBio 71; FilmgC; IntMPA 75, 76, 77, 78, 79, 78, 79, 80, 81, 82; IntWW 74; MovMk; NewYTBE 71; NotNAT; OxThe; PlP&P; Who 74; WhoHol A; WhoThe 77; WhoWor 74*

Quayle, (James) Dan(forth)
American. Senator
b. Feb 4, 1947 in Indianapolis, Indiana
Source: *AlmAP 78, 80; CngDr 77, 79; WhoAm 78, 80, 82; WhoAmP 77, 79; WhoGov 77; WhoMW 78*

Queen
[John Deacon; Brian May; Freddie Mercury; Roger Taylor]
English. Rock Band
Source: *IlEncRk*

Queen, Ellery, pseud.
[Frederic Dannay; Manfred B Lee]
American. Author
Fictictious detective used as pseudonym for mystery novels.
Source: *AmAu&B; AuBYP; CelR 73; ConAu 1R, 1NR, 2NR; ConLC 3, 11; CurBio 40; DcLEL; EncMys; EvLB; IntWW 74; LongCTC; OxAmL; Pen AM; REn; REnAL; TwCA, SUP; TwCW; WebAB; Who 82; WhoWor 74; WrDr 76*

Queen, Richard I
[The Hostages]
American. Former Hostage in Iran
b. 1952?
Source: *BioIn 12*

Queensberry, John Sholto Douglas
[Marquis of Queensberry]
British. Originated Boxing Code
b. 1844
d. 1900
Source: *NewC; NewCol 75*

Queensberry, William Douglas, Duke
English. Vice Admiral of Scotland
b. 1724 in London, England
d. Dec 23, 1810
Source: *NewC; NewCol 75; WebBD 80*

Queeny, Edgar Monsanto
American. Chemical Executive
Monsanto Chemical Co., president 1928-43; chairman, 1943-60.
b. Sep 29, 1897 in Saint Louis, Missouri
d. Jul 7, 1968 in Saint Louis, Missouri
Source: *WhAm 5*

Queler, Eve Rabin
American. Conductor
b. 1931 in New York, New York
Source: *BioIn 9; WhoAm 82*

Quennell, Peter
English. Editor, Critic
b. Mar 1905
Source: *Au&Wr 71; ChPo S2; ConP 70; DcLEL; EvLB; IntWW 74; LongCTC; ModBrL; NewC; Pen ENG; RAdv 1; REn; TwCA, SUP; TwCW; Who 74; WrDr 76*

Quercia, Jacopo della
Italian. Sculptor
b. 1374
d. 1438
Source: *NewCol 75; WebBD 80*

Quesnay, Francois
French. Economist, Physician
b. Jun 4, 1694 in Merey, France
d. Dec 16, 1774 in Versailles, France
Source: *BbD; BiD&SB; BioIn 1, 7, 8; CasWL; DcEuL; EuAu; LinLib L, S; NewCol 75; OxFr; REn*

Quezon (y Molina), Manuel Luis
Philippine. President
b. Aug 19, 1878 in Baler, Philippines
d. Aug 1, 1944 in Saranac Lake, New York
Source: *BiDrAC; CurBio 40, 44; DcAmB S3; WhAm 2; WhAmP*

Quicksilver Messenger Service
[John Cipollina; Gary Duncan; Gregory Elmore; David Freiberg; Nicky Hopkins; Dino Valenti]
American. Music Group
Source: *IlEncRk; RkOn*

Quidor, John
American. Artist
b. Jan 26, 1801 in Tappan, New York
d. Dec 13, 1881 in Jersey City, New Jersey
Source: *AmBi; DcAmB; WhAm H*

Quilico, Louis
Canadian. Opera Singer
b. Jan 14, 1929 in Montreal, PQ
Source: *CanWW 82; CreCan 2; WhoAm 82*

Quill, Mike (Michael J)
Irish. Labor Leader
Organizer, president, Transport Workers Union, 1934-66.
b. Sep 8, 1905
d. Jan 28, 1966 in New York, New York
Source: *CurBio 41, 53, 66; WhAm 4*

Quillan, Eddie
American. Actor
b. Mar 31, 1907 in Philadelphia, Pennsylvania
Source: *FilmgC; IntMPA 75, 76, 77, 78, 79, 80, 81, 82; MovMk; TwYS; Vers A; WhoHol A*

Quiller-Couch, Sir Arthur Thomas
[Q, pseud.]
English. Critic, Journalist
b. Nov 21, 1863 in Cornwall, England
d. May 12, 1944 in Fowey, England
Source: *BbD; BiD&SB; CasWL; Chambr 3; ChPo, S1, S2; DcBiA; DcEnA, AP; DcLEL; EvLB; JBA 34; LongCTC; MnBBF; ModBrL; NewC; OxEng; Pen ENG; RAdv 1; REn; TwCA, SUP; TwCW; WhAm 2*

Quine, Richard
American. Actor
b. Nov 12, 1920 in Detroit, Michigan
Source: *AmSCAP 66; BiDFilm; CmMov; DcFM; FilmgC; IntMPA 75, 76, 77, 78, 79, 80, 81, 82; MovMk; OxFilm; WhoHol A; WorEFlm*

Quinlan, Karen Anne
American. Controversial Medical Patient
Comatose since 1975; parents won landmark court decision to remove life-support systems.
b. Mar 29, 1954
Source: *BioIn 10, 11, 12*

Quinlan, Kathleen
American. Actress
b. Nov 19, 1954 in Pasadena, California
Source: *BioIn 11; IntMPA 80, 81; NewYTBS 77*

Quinn, Anthony Rudolph Oaxaca
American. Actor, Author
Won Oscars for *Viva Zapata* and *Lust for Life.*
b. Apr 21, 1916 in Chihuahua, Mexico
Source: *BiDFilm; BkPepl; CelR 73; CmMov; CurBio 57; FilmgC; IntMPA 75, 76, 77, 78, 79, 80, 81, 82; IntWW 74; MotPP; MovMk; NewYTBE 70; OxFilm; WhoAm 74, 76, 78, 80, 82; WhoHol A; WhoThe 77; WhoWor 74; WorEFlm*

Quinn, Arthur Hobson
American. Teacher
b. 1875 in Philadelphia, Pennsylvania
d. 1960
Source: *AmAu&B; CathA 1930; DcAmAu; OxAmL; Pen AM; REnAL; TwCA, SUP; WhAm 4; WhNAA*

Quinn, Carmel
Irish. Singer
b. 1930
Source: *InWom*

Quinn, Edmond T
American. Sculptor
b. Dec 20, 1868 in Philadelphia, Pennsylvania
d. Sep 9, 1929 in New York, New York
Source: *AmBi; DcAmB; WebBD 80; WhAm 1*

Quinn, Jane Bryant
American. Journalist
b. Feb 5, 1939 in Niagara Falls, New York
Source: *WhoAm 78, 80, 82; WhoAmW 74, 75*

Quinn, (John Brian) Pat(rick)
Canadian. Hockey Player, Coach
b. Jan 29, 1943 in Hamilton, ON
Source: *WhoHcky 73*

Quinn, Sally
[Mrs. Ben Bradlee]
American. Journalist
b. Jul 1, 1941 in Savannah, Georgia
Source: *AuNews 2; ConAu 65; WhoAm 76, 78, 80, 82*

Quint, Bert
American. Broadcast Journalist
b. Sep 22, 1930 in New York, New York
Source: *ConAu 69*

Quintero, Jose
Panamanian. Showman
b. Oct 15, 1924 in Panama City, Panama
Source: *BiE&WWA; CurBio 54; NewYTBS 74; NotNAT; PlP&P, A; WhoAm 74, 76, 78, 80, 82; WhoE 74; WhoThe 77; WhoWor 74*

Quinteros, Adolfo
Mexican. Artist, Engraver
b. 1927
Source: *BioIn 9*

Quintilian Marcus Fabius
Roman. Rhetorician
b. 35 in Calagurris, Spain
d. 95
Source: *BbD; BiD&SB; CasWL; NewC; OxEng; RComWL; REn; WebBD 80*

Quintus Horatius Flaccus
see: Horace

Quisling, Vidkun
Norwegian. Traitor, Nazi Collaborator
b. Jul 18, 1887 in Fryesdal, Norway
d. Oct 24, 1945
Source: *CurBio 40, 46; LongCTC; NewCol 75; REn; WebBD 80*

Quoirez, Francoise
see: Sagan, Francoise, pseud.

R

Raab, Selwyn
American. Journalist, Author
Reporter, NY *Times,* 1974--.
b. Jun 26, 1934 in New York, New York
Source: *BioIn 10; ConAu 73; WhoAm 82*

Rabaud, Henri
French. Composer, Conductor
b. Nov 10, 1873 in Paris, France
d. Sep 11, 1949 in Paris, France
Source: *NewEOp 71; OxMus*

Rabbitt, Eddie (Edward Thomas)
American. Singer, Songwriter
Wrote over 300 songs including "Kentucky Rain."
b. Nov 27, 1941 in Brooklyn, New York
Source: *ConMuA 80; IlEncCM; WhoAm 80, 82*

Rabe, David William
American. Dramatist
b. Mar 10, 1940 in Dubuque, Iowa
Source: *BioIn 9, 10; ConAu 85; ConLC 4, 8; CurBio 73; NewYTBE 71; WhoAm 74, 76, 78, 80, 82*

Rabelais, Francois
[Alcofribas Nasier, pseud.]
French. Humorist, Satirist, Physician
Noted for ribald humor; wrote *Gargantua and Pantagruel.*
b. 1494 in Chinon, France
d. 1553 in Paris, France
Source: *AtlBL; BbD; BiD&SB; CasWL; CyWA; DcEnL; DcEuL; EuAu; EvEuW; NewC; OxEng; OxFr; Pen EUR; RComWL; REn*

Rabi, Isidor Isaac
Austrian. Scientist
b. Jul 29, 1898 in Rymahow, Austria
Source: *IntWW 74; WebAB; Who 74; WhoAm 76, 78, 80, 82; WhoWor 74, 74; WhoWorJ 72*

Rabin, Michael
American. Musician
b. May 2, 1936 in New York, New York
d. Jan 19, 1972 in New York, New York
Source: *NewYTBE 71, 72; WhAm 5*

Rabin, Yehuda L
Aircraft Company Executive
One of founders of Israeli Air Force.
b. 1917? in Russia
d. Jan 4, 1981 in New York, New York
Source: *NewYTBS 81*

Rabin, Yitzhak
Israeli. Statesman, Prime Minister
Ambassador to US, 1968-73; prime minister, 1974-77.
b. Mar 1, 1922 in Jerusalem, Palestine
Source: *CurBio 74; NewCol 75; WhoAm 74; WhoGov 72; WhoWor 74; WhoWorJ 72*

Rabinowitz, Solomon J
see: Aleichem, Shalom, pseud.

Rachel
Biblical Character
Source: *NewCol 75; WebBD 80*

Rachel
[Elisa(beth) Rachel Felix]
French. Actress
b. Feb 28, 1820 in Mumpf, Switzerland
d. Jan 3, 1858 in Cannes, France
Source: *BioIn 1, 3, 4, 5, 8, 9, 10, 11; CnThe; DcEuL; EncWT; FamA&A; InWom; NewCol 75; NotNAT A, B; OxFr; OxThe; PlP&P; REn*

Rachmaninoff, Sergei Vasilyevich
Russian. Composer, Musician, Conductor
Wrote symphonies, chamber music; familiar work, "Second Piano Concerto," 1901.
b. Apr 1, 1873 in Oneg, Russia
d. Mar 28, 1943 in Beverly Hills, California
Source: *AmSCAP 66; AtlBL; CurBio 43; DcAmB S3; NewCol 75; REn; WebBD 80; WhAm 2*

Racine, Jean Baptiste
French. Poet
b. Dec 1639 in Laferte-Milon, France
d. Apr 26, 1699 in Paris, France
Source: *AtlBL; BbD; BiD&SB; CasWL; CnThe; CyWA; DcEuL; EuAu; EvEuW; McGEWD; NewC; OxEng; OxFr; OxThe; Pen EUR; PlP&P; RComWL; REn; REnWD*

Rackham, Arthur
English. Illustrator
b. Sep 19, 1867
d. Sep 1939
Source: *CarSB; ChPo, S1, S2; ConICB; JBA 34, 51; LongCTC; Str&VC; WhoChL*

Radcliffe, Ann
English. Author
b. Jul 9, 1764 in London, England
d. Feb 7, 1823 in London, England
Source: *BbD; BiD&SB; BrAu, 19; CasWL; ChPo, S1; CrtT 2; CyWA; DcBiA; DcEnA; DcEuL; DcLEL; EncMys; EvLB; MouLC 2; NewC; OxEng; Pen ENG; RAdv 1; REn; WebE&AL*

Radek, Karl
Russian. Communist Leader
b. 1885 in Lvov, Poland
d. 1939?
Source: *NewCol 75; WebBD 80*

Rader, Dotson
American. Author
b. 1942 in Minnesota
Source: *CelR 73; ConAu 61; WhoAm 82*

Radford, Arthur William
American. Admiral
b. Feb 27, 1896 in Chicago, Illinois
d. Aug 17, 1973 in Washington, DC
Source: *CurBio 49, 73; NewYTBE 73; WhAm 6*

Radisson, Pierre Espirit
French. Explorer
Hudson Bay explorations led to formation of Hudson Bay Co. by English, 1670.
b. 1636 in Lyons, France
d. 1710
Source: *McGEWB; NewCol 75; WebAB; WhAm H*

Radner, Gilda
American. Actress, Comedienne
Original star of TV series "NBC's Saturday Night Live."
b. Jun 28, 1946 in Detroit, Michigan
Source: *BioIn 11; BkPepl; CurBio 80; IntMPA 82; WhoAm 80, 82*

Radziwill, (Caroline) Lee Bouvier, Princess
American. Sister of Jackie Onassis
Wrote childhood memoir, *One Special Summer,* with sister, Jacqueline Onassis.
b. Mar 3, 1933 in New York, New York
Source: *BkPepl; NewYTBS 74; WhoAm 74*

Rae, Charlotte
American. Actress
b. 1926 in Milwaukee, Wisconsin
Source: *BiE&WWA; NotNAT; WhoAm 82; WhoHol A; WhoThe 77*

Raeburn, Sir Henry
Scottish. Artist
b. Mar 4, 1756 in Stockbridge, Scotland
d. Jul 8, 1823 in Edinburgh, Scotland
Source: *AtlBL; NewC; REn*

Raeder, Erich
German. Nazi War Criminal
b. Apr 24, 1876
d. Nov 6, 1960 in Kiel, Germany (West)
Source: *CurBio 41, 61*

Raffaelinodel Garbo
[Raffaello Capponi]
Italian. Artist
b. 1466
d. 1524
Source: *WebBD 80*

Raffaello Sanzio d'Urbino
see: Raphael

Rafferty, "Chips"
[John Goffage]
Australian. Actor
b. 1909 in Australia
d. May 27, 1971 in Sydney, Australia
Source: *FilmgC; MovMk; NewYTBE 71; OxFilm; WhScrn 74, 77; WhoHol B*

Rafferty, Gerry
Scottish. Singer, Composer
b. 1945 in Scotland
Source: *IlEncRk*

Rafferty, Max(well Lewis, Jr.)
American. Educator, Author
b. May 7, 1917 in New Orleans, Louisiana
d. Jun 13, 1982 in Troy, Alabama
Source: *ConAu 1R, 1NR; CurBio 69, 82; LEduc 74; NewYTBS 82; WhoAm 74, 76, 78, 80, 82*

Raffin, Deborah
American. Actress, Model
b. Mar 13, 1953 in Los Angeles, California
Source: *IntMPA 75, 76, 77, 78, 79, 80, 81, 82*

Raffles, Sir Thomas Stamford
English. Colonial Administrator
b. 1781
d. 1826
Source: *Alli; BiDLA SUP; NewCol 75; WebBD 80*

Rafshoon, Gerald Monroe
American. Presidential Aide
Media director, President Carter's re-election campaign, 1980.
b. Jan 11, 1934 in New York, New York
Source: *CurBio 79; WhoAm 80, 82*

Raft, George
American. Actor
Played gangsters in *Scarface,* 1932; *Each Dawn I Die,* 1939.
b. Sep 26, 1895 in New York, New York
Source: *BiDFilm; BioNews 74; CmMov; FilmgC; IntMPA 75, 77; MotPP; MovMk; OxFilm; WhoHol A; WorEFlm*

Ragan, David
American. Editor, Author
b. Aug 26, 1925 in Jackson, Tennessee
Source: *ConAu 65; WhoAm 82*

Ragan, Regis
[The Hostages]
American. Former Hostage in Iran
b. 1942?
Source: *NewYTBS 81*

Raglan, Fitzroy James Henry Somerset, Baron
British. Field Marshal
b. Sep 30, 1788 in Badminton, England
d. Jun 28, 1855 in Sevastopol, Russia
Source: *NewCol 75; WebBD 80; WhoMilH 76*

Ragland, "Rags" (John Lee Morgan Beauregard)
American. Actor
b. Aug 23, 1906 in Louisville, Kentucky
d. Aug 20, 1946 in Hollywood, California
Source: *CurBio 46; FilmgC; MotPP; MovMk; Vers A; WhScrn 74, 77; WhoHol B*

Ragozina, Galina
Russian. Dancer
b. 1950
Source: *BioIn 10*

Rahman, Abdul, Prince
Indian. Malayan Prime Minister
b. Feb 8, 1903 in Alor Star, Malaya
d. Apr 1, 1960
Source: *WhAm 3*

Rahman, Mujibur, Sheik
Bangladeshi. President
b. 1920 in Bengal, India
d. Aug 15, 1975 in Dacca, Pakistan
Source: *CurBio 73; IntWW 74; Who 74; WhoWor 74*

Rahman, Ziaur
Bangladeshi. President
b. Jan 19, 1936 in Bogra, India
d. May 30, 1981 in Chittagong, Bangladesh
Source: *CurBio 81; IntWW 80; WorDWW*

Rahner, Karl
Austrian. Theologian
b. Mar 5, 1904 in Freiburg, Germany
Source: *BioIn 6, 7, 8, 9, 10; CurBio 70; LinLib L, S; McGEWB; NewYTBS 79; OxGer*

Raikes, Robert
English. Printer, Educator
b. 1735
d. 1811
Source: *BioIn 1, 3, 5, 6, 10; WebBD 80*

Raimu
[Jules Muraire]
French. Actor
b. Dec 17, 1883 in Toulon, France
d. Sep 20, 1946 in Paris, France
Source: *FilmEn; FilmgC; MotPP; MovMk; OxFilm; WhScrn 74, 77; WhoHol B; WorEFlm*

Raine, William MacLeod
Author
b. Jun 22, 1871 in London, England
d. Jul 25, 1954 in Denver, Colorado
Source: *AmAu&B; AmLY; EvLB; MnBBF; REnAL; TwCA, SUP; WhAm 3; WhNAA*

Rainer, Luise
Austrian. Actress
Won Oscars for *The Great Ziegfeld,* 1936; *The Good Earth,* 1937.
b. Jan 12, 1912 in Vienna, Austria
Source: *BiDFilm; FilmgC; InWom; MotPP; MovMk; OxFilm; ThFT; Who 74; WhoHol A; WhoThe 77; WorEFlm*

Raines, Cristina
American. Actress
b. 1952? in Manila, Philippines
Source: *BioIn 11; NewYTBS 78; WhoHol A*

Raines, Ella
American. Actress
b. Aug 6, 1921 in Snoquaimie, Massachusetts
Source: *FilmgC; HolP 40; InWom; IntMPA 75, 76, 77, 78, 79, 80, 81, 82; MotPP; MovMk; WhoHol A*

Raines, Tim(othy)
"Rock"
American. Baseball Player
b. Sep 16, 1959 in Sanford, Florida
Source: *BaseEn; BioIn 12*

Rainey, Joseph Hayne
American. Politician
b. Jun 21, 1832 in Georgetown, South Carolina
d. Aug 2, 1887 in Georgetown, South Carolina
Source: *ApCAB; BiAuS; BiDrAC; DcAmB; TwCBDA; WhAm H; WhAmP*

Rainey, "Ma" (Gertrude)
[Gertrude Malissa Nix Pridgett]
American. Singer
b. Apr 26, 1886 in Columbus, Georgia
d. Dec 22, 1939 in Columbus, Georgia
Source: *DcAmB S2; NotAW; WhAm 4; WhoJazz 72*

Rainier III, Prince
[Louis Henri Maxence Bertrand]
Monacan. Ruler
b. May 31, 1923 in Monaco
Source: *BioIn 10; IntWW 74; WhoGov 72; WhoWor 74*

Rains, Claude
American. Actor
Starred in *The Invisible Man,* 1933; *Casablanca,* 1942; *Notorious,* 1946.
b. Nov 9, 1889 in London, England
d. May 30, 1967 in Sandwich, New Hampshire
Source: *BiDFilm; BiE&WWA; CmMov; CurBio 49; FilmgC; MotPP; MovMk; OxFilm; WhAm 4; WhScrn 74, 77; WhoHol B; WorEFlm*

Raisa, Rosa
[Rose Burstein]
Polish. Opera Singer
b. May 30, 1893 in Bialystok, Poland
d. Sep 28, 1963 in Los Angeles, California
Source: *InWom; WhAm 4*

Raitt, Bonnie
American. Singer, Songwriter
b. Nov 8, 1949 in Los Angeles, California
Source: *BioIn 9, 10, 11, 12; BkPepl; IlEncRk; WhoAm 82*

Raitt, John Emmet
American. Singer
b. Jan 19, 1917 in Santa Ana, California
Source: *BiE&WWA; BioNews 74; EncMT; FilmgC; NotNAT; WhoAm 74, 76, 78, 80, 82; WhoHol A; WhoThe 77; WhoWest 74*

Rajai, Mohammed Ali
Iranian. President
b. 1933 in Quazin, Iran
d. Aug 30, 1981 in Teheran, Iran
Source: *NewYTBS 81*

Rakosi, Carl
American. Author
b. Nov 6, 1903 in Berlin, Germany
Source: *ConAu 25R; ConP 70, 75; DrAP 75; RAdv 1; WrDr 76*

Raleigh, Elizabeth Throckmorton
English. Wife of Sir Walter Raleigh
Source: *BioIn 4, 10*

Raleigh, Sir Walter
English. Courtier, Navigator, Historian
Favorite of Queen Elizabeth I; beheaded for treason against King James I.
b. 1552 in Devonshire, England
d. Oct 29, 1618 in London, England
Source: *Alli; ApCAB; AtlBL; BbD; BiD&SB; BrAu; CasWL; Chambr 1; ChPo, S1; CnE&AP; CroE&S; CrtT 1; DcEnA AP; DcEnL; DcEuL; DcLEL; Drake; EvLB; MouLC 1; NewC; NewCol 75; OxEng; Pen ENG; PlP&P; REn; REnAL; WebBD 80; WebE&AL; WhAm H*

Ralf, Torsten
Swedish. Opera Singer
b. Jan 2, 1901 in Malmo, Sweden
d. Apr 27, 1954 in Stockholm, Sweden
Source: *NewEOp 71*

Ralphs, Mick
see: Mott (the Hoople)

Ralston, Esther
American. Actress
b. 1902 in Bar Harbor, Maine
Source: *FilmgC; InWom; MotPP; MovMk; ThFT; TwYS; WhoAmW 77; WhoHol A; WomWMM*

Ralston, Vera
American. Actress
b. 1921 in Prague, Czechoslovakia
Source: *FilmgC; MotPP; MovMk; WhoHol A*

Rama IV
see: Mongkut

Rama IX
see: Bhumibal, Adulyadej, King

Rama, Swami
Indian. Teacher, Yogi
b. 1903
d. 1972
Source: *BioIn 10*

Rama Rau, Santha
Indian. Author
b. Jan 24, 1923 in Madras, India
Source: *AmAu&B; BiE&WWA; CelR 73; ConAu 1R; CurBio 45, 59; InWom; IntWW 74; NewC; Pen ENG; TwCW; Who 74; WhoWor 74; WorAu*

Ramakrishna, Sri
Indian. Yogi
b. 1834
d. 1886
Source: *NewCol 75*

Raman, Venkata
Indian. Physicist
b. Nov 7, 1888 in Madras, India
d. Nov 21, 1970
Source: *CurBio 48, 71*

Rambeau, Marjorie
American. Actress
b. Jul 15, 1889 in San Francisco, California
d. Jul 7, 1970 in Palm Springs, California
Source: *Film 1; FilmgC; InWom; MotPP; MovMk; NewYTBE 70; ThFT; TwYS; Vers B; WhScrn 74, 77; WhoHol B*

Rambert, Dame Marie
English. Ballet Company Director
b. Feb 20, 1888 in Warsaw, Poland
d. Jun 12, 1982 in London, England
Source: *BioIn 3, 4, 5, 6, 9; CurBio 81, 82; IntWW 74, 75, 76, 77, 78, 79, 80; NewYTBS 82; Who 74, 80; WhoThe 77; WhoWor 74, 76, 78*

Rameau, Jean-Philippe
French. Composer, Theorist
b. Sep 25, 1683 in Dijon, France
d. Sep 12, 1764 in Paris, France
Source: *NewEOp 71; OxMus*

Ramee, Marie Louise de la
see: Ouida, pseud.

Rameses II
Egyptian. King
Source: *NewCol 75; WebBD 80; WhDW*

Ramey, Samuel Edward
American. Opera Singer
b. Mar 28, 1942 in Colby, Kansas
Source: *CurBio 81; NewYTBS 77; WhoAm 82; WhoOp 76*

Ramirez, Raul
Mexican. Tennis Player
b. Jun 20, 1953 in Ensenada, Mexico
Source: *WhoAm 78, 80, 82*

Ramirez Sanchez, Ilitch
see: "Carlos"

Ramones, The
[Dee Dee Ramone; Joey Ramone, Johnny Ramone, Marky Ramone]
American. Rock Group
Source: *ConMuA 80; WhoRock 81*

Rampal, Jean-Pierre
French. Musician
b. Jul 1, 1922 in Marseilles, France
Source: *CurBio 70; IntWW 74; WhoAm 82; WhoMus 72; WhoWor 74*

Rampling, Charlotte
[Mrs. Jean-Michel Jarre]
English. Actress
Starred in *Georgy Girl; The Damned; The Night Porter;The Verdict.*
b. Feb 5, 1946 in Sturmer, England
Source: *FilmgC; IntMPA 75, 76, 77, 78, 79, 80, 81, 82; WhoHol A*

Ramsay, Allan
Scottish. Artist
b. 1713 in Edinburgh, Scotland
d. 1784
Source: *Alli; NewCol 75; REn*

Ramsbotham, Sir Peter
English. Diplomat
b. Oct 8, 1919 in London, England
Source: *BioIn 10, 11; IntWW 77*

Ramsey, Arthur Michael
English. Archbishop of Canterbury
Archbishop, 1961-74; president, World Council of Churches, 1961-68.
b. Nov 14, 1904 in Cambridge, England
Source: *CurBio 60; IntWW 74; NewCol 75; WebBD 80; Who 74; WhoWor 74; WrDr 76*

Ramsey, Mike (Michael Allen)
[United States Olympic Hockey Team-1980]
American. Hockey Player
b. Dec 3, 1960 in Minneapolis, Minnesota
Source: *HocReg*

Ramsey, William Morgan
Hymnist, Music Publisher
b. 1872
d. 1939
Source: *BioIn 9*

Rand, Ayn
American. Author
Novels reflect rational self-interest philosophy "objectivism"; *The Fountainhead,* 1943.
b. Feb 2, 1905 in Saint Petersburg, Russia
d. Mar 6, 1982 in New York, New York
Source: *AmAu&B; AmNov; CasWL; CelR 73; ConAu 13R; ConLC 3; ConNov 72, 76; EncSF; ForWC 70; InWom; IntAu&W 76, 77; NewYTBS 82; OxAmL; Pen AM; PolProf E; REn; REnAL; ScF&FL 1, 2; TwCA SUP; WebAB; WebE&AL; WhoAm 74, 76, 78, 80, 82; WhoAmW 58, 66, 68, 70, 72, 74, 75, 77; WhoSciF; WhoTwCL; WrDr 76, 80*

Rand, James Henry
American. Business Machine Manufacturer
Formed company that became Remington-Rand, 1926.
b. Nov 18, 1886 in North Tonawanda, New York
d. Jun 3, 1968 in Freeport, Bahamas
Source: *WhAm 5*

Rand, Paul
American. Designer
b. Aug 15, 1914 in New York, New York
Source: *AuBYP; ConAu 25R; IlsCB 1946, 1957; SmATA 6; ThrBJA; WhoAm 74, 76, 78, 80, 82; WhoAmA 73; WhoGrA*

Rand, Sally
[Helen Beck]
American. Fan Dancer
Exotic fan dance was sensation of 1933 Chicago World's Fair.
b. Jan 2, 1904 in Elkton, Missouri
d. Aug 31, 1979 in Glendora, California
Source: *FilmgC; InWom; TwYS; WebAB; WhoHol A*

Rand, Suzanne
[Monteith and Rand]
American. Actress, Comedienne
b. 1950 in Chicago, Illinois
Source: *BioIn 11*

Randall, Dudley
American. Poet
b. Jan 14, 1914 in Washington, DC
Source: *BiDrLUS 70; BlkAW; ConAu 25R; ConLC 1; ConP 70, 75; DrAP 75; LivgBAA; WhoMW 74; WrDr 76*

Randall, James Garfield
American. Historian, Author
b. Jun 24, 1881 in Indianapolis, Indiana
d. Feb 20, 1953 in Champaign, Illinois
Source: *AmAu&B; DcAmB S5; IndAu 1816; REnAL; TwCA SUP*

Randall, Samuel J
American. Government Official
b. Oct 10, 1828 in Philadelphia, Pennsylvania
d. Apr 13, 1890 in Washington, DC
Source: *AmBi; ApCAB; BiDrAC; DcAmB; EncAB-H; TwCBDA; WebAB; WhAm H; WhAmP*

Randall, Tony
American. Actor
Played Felix Unger in TV series "The Odd Couple," 1970-75.
b. Feb 26, 1924 in Tulsa, Oklahoma
Source: *BkPepl; CelR 73; CurBio 61; FilmgC; IntMPA 75, 76, 77, 78, 79, 80, 81, 82; MotPP; MovMk; NotNAT; WhoAm 74, 76, 78, 80, 82; WhoHol A; WhoWor 74; WorEFlm*

Randhawa, Mohinder Singh
Indian. Author
b. Feb 2, 1909 in Zira, India
Source: *ConAu 29R; WhoWor 74; WrDr 76*

Randolph, Asa Philip
American. Labor Leader
Organizer, president of Brotherhood of Sleeping Car Porters, 1925-68.
b. Apr 15, 1889 in Crescent City, Florida
d. May 16, 1979 in New York, New York
Source: *CelR 73; ConAu 85; CurBio 40, 51, 79; EbonySL 1; EncAB-H; IntWW 74, 78; SelBAA; WebAB; WhoAm 74, 76; WhoBlA 75; WhoLab 76*

Randolph, "Boots" (Homer Louis, III)
American. Saxophonist
Hit song "Yakety Sax," 1963.
b. in Paducah, Kentucky
Source: *IlEncCM; RkOn*

Randolph, Edmund Jennings
American. Statesman
b. Aug 10, 1753 in Williamsburg, Virginia
d. Sep 12, 1813 in Millwood, Virginia
Source: *Alli; AmBi; ApCAB; BiAuS; BiDSA; BiDrAC; BiDrUSE; DcAmB; Drake; EncAB-H; McGEWB; TwCBDA; WebAB; WhAm H; WhAmP*

Randolph, Jennings
American. Senator
b. Mar 8, 1902 in Salem, West Virginia
Source: *BioIn 6, 7, 8, 9, 10, 11; CurBio 62; IntWW 74; WhoAm 74; WhoAmP 73; WhoE 74*

Randolph, John
[Randolph of Roanoke]
American. Statesman
b. Jun 2, 1773 in Cawsons, Virginia
d. May 24, 1833 in Roanoke, Virginia
Source: *Alli; AmBi; ApCAB; BiAuS; BiD&SB; BiDLA; BiDrAC; CyAL 1; DcAmB; DcNAA; Drake; EncAB-H; REn; REnAL; TwCBDA; WebAB; WhAm H; WhAmP*

Randolph, Nancy, pseud.
[Julia McCarthy]
American. Journalist
b. 1897
d. 1974
Source: *InWom; WhoE 74*

Randolph, Peyton
American. Continental Congressman
b. Sep 1721 in Williamsburg, Virginia
d. Oct 22, 1775 in Williamsburg, Virginia
Source: *AmBi; ApCAB; BiAuS; BiDSA; BiDrAC; BiDrUSE; DcAmB; Drake; TwCBDA; WhAm H*

Randolph, Willie (William Larry, Jr.)
American. Baseball Player
b. Jul 6, 1954 in Holly Hill, South Carolina
Source: *BaseEn; NewYTBS 76, 77*

Rangel, Charles Bernard
American. Congressman
b. Jun 11, 1930 in Harlem, New York
Source: *BioIn 9, 10; NewYTBE 70, 71; NewYTBS 74; WhoAm 74, 76, 78, 80, 82; WhoAmP 73; WhoE 74*

Rank, J(oseph) Arthur
English. Motion Picture Executive
b. Dec 23, 1888 in Hull, England
d. Mar 29, 1972 in Winchester, England
Source: *CurBio 45, 72; DcFM; FilmgC; OxFilm; WhAm 5; WorEFlm*

Ranke, Leopold von
German. Author, Dramatist, Essayist
b. Dec 21, 1795 in Wiehe, Germany
d. May 23, 1886 in Berlin, Germany
Source: *BbD; BiD&SB; CasWL; DcEuL; EuAu; NewC; OxEng; OxGer; REn*

Rankin, Arthur
American. Actor
b. Aug 30, 1900 in New York, New York
d. Mar 23, 1947 in Hollywood, California
Source: *TwYS; WhScrn 74, 77; WhoHol B*

Rankin, Jeannette
American. Suffragist, Politician
First woman to serve in Congress, 1917-19.
b. Jul 11, 1880 in Missoula, Montana
d. May 18, 1973 in Carmel, California
Source: *BiDrAC; BioNews 75; ConAu 41R; EncAB-H; InWom; NewYTBE 72, 73; WebAB; WhAm 5; WhAmP*

Rankin, Judy Torluemke
American. Golfer
b. Feb 18, 1945 in Saint Louis, Missouri
Source: *BioIn 11; WhoGolf; WhoAm 78; WhoAmW 79*

Ransohoff, Martin
American. Motion Picture Producer
b. 1927 in New Orleans, Louisiana
Source: *FilmgC; IntMPA 75, 76, 77, 78, 79, 80, 81, 82; WhoAm 74, 76, 78, 80, 82*

Ransom, John Crowe
American. Author, Poet
b. Apr 30, 1888 in Pulaski, Tennessee
d. Jul 5, 1974 in Gambier, Ohio
Source: *AmAu&B; AmWr; CasWL; CelR 73; ChPo, S2; CnDAL; CnE&AP; CnMWL; ConAmA; ConAu 5R, 49; ConLC 2, 4, 5, 11; ConP 75; CurBio 64, 74; CyWA; DcLEL; EvLB; LongCTC; ModAL, SUP; NewYTBS 74; OhA&B; OxAmL; Pen AM; RAdv 1; REn; REnAL; SixAP; TwCA, SUP; TwCW; WebAB; WebE&AL; WhAm 6; WhoAm 74; WhoTwCL; WhoWor 74*

Ransome, Arthur Mitchell
English. Author, Poet
Wrote *Swallows and Amazons*, 1930, based on childhood memories.
b. Jan 18, 1884 in Leeds, England
d. Jun 3, 1967 in England
Source: *Alli SUP; AuBYP; CarSB; CasWL; ChPo; ConAu 73; DcLEL; EvLB; JBA 34, 51; LongCTC; NewC; Pen ENG; REn; SmATA 22; TwCA, SUP; WhoChL; WhoLA*

Rapacki, Adam
Polish. Government Official
b. Dec 24, 1909 in Lvov, Poland
d. Oct 10, 1970 in Warsaw, Poland
Source: *CurBio 58, 70; NewYTBE 70; WhAm 5*

Raphael
[Raffaello Sanzio d'Urbino]
Italian. Artist, Architect
Responsible for many paintings inside Vatican: *The School of Athens*.
b. Apr 6, 1483 in Urbino, Italy
d. 1520 in Rome, Italy
Source: *Alli; AtlBL; ChPo; McGEWB; NewC; REn*

Raphael, Frederic Michael
English. Author, Critic, Screenwriter
b. Aug 14, 1931 in Chicago, Illinois
Source: *Au&Wr 71; BioIn 8, 10; ConAu 1R; ConDr 73, 77A; ConLC 2, 14; ConNov 72, 76; DcLEL 1940; DrAF 76; FilmgC; IntAu&W 76, 77; IntMPA 75, 76, 77, 78, 79, 80, 81; ModBrL SUP; WhoAm 74, 76, 78, 80, 82; WhoWor 74; WorAu; WrDr 76, 80*

Raphaelson, Samson
American. Author, Screenwriter
b. Mar 30, 1896 in New York, New York
Source: *AmAu&B; BiE&WWA; BioIn 4; ConAu 65; FilmgC; IntMPA 75, 76, 77, 78, 79, 80, 81; McGEWD; NotNAT; REnAL; TwCA SUP; WhThe; WhoAm 78, 80, 82; WorEFlm*

Rapp, George
German. Theologist
b. Nov 1, 1757 in Iptingen, Germany
d. Aug 7, 1847 in Economy, Pennsylvania
Source: *AmBi; DcAmB; WhAm H*

Rare Earth
[Gil Bridges; Kenny James; John Persh; Rod Richards; Pete Rivera]
American. Rock Group
Source: *RkOn 2; WhoRock 81*

Rarebell, Herman
see: Scorpions

Rascals, The
[Eddie Brigati; Felix Cavaliere; Gene Cornish; Dino Danelli]
American. Rock Group
Source: *BiDAmM; ConMuA 80; LilREn 78; RkOn 2; WhoRock 81*

Rascoe, Burton
American. Journalist, Editor, Critic
b. Oct 22, 1892 in Fulton, Kentucky
d. Mar 19, 1957 in New York, New York
Source: *AmAu&B; OxAmL; REnAL; TwCA, SUP; WhAm 3*

Rashi
[Solomonben Isaac]
French. Hebrew Exegete of the Talmud
b. 1040
d. 1105
Source: *CasWL; EuAu; EvEuW*

Raskin, A(braham) H(enry)
Canadian. Journalist
b. Apr 26, 1911 in Edmonton, AB
Source: *ConAu 104; CurBio 78; WhoAm 74, 76, 78, 80, 82*

Raskin, Ellen
American. Children's Author, Illustrator
b. Mar 13, 1928 in Milwaukee, Wisconsin
Source: *BkP; ChlLR 1; ChPo, S1, S2; ConAu 25R; IlsBYP; IlsCB 1957; SmATA 2; ThrBJA; WhoAm 82*

Raskin, Judith
American. Opera Singer
b. Jun 21, 1928 in New York, New York
Source: *CurBio 64; InWom; WhoAm 74, 76, 78, 80, 82; WhoWor 74*

Raskob, John J
American. Businessman
b. Mar 19, 1879 in Lockport, New York
d. Oct 14, 1950 in Centreville, Maryland
Source: *DcAmB S4; WhAm 3*

Rasmussen, Knud Johan Victor
Danish. Arctic Explorer, Ethnologist
b. Jun 7, 1879 in Greenland
d. Dec 21, 1933
Source: *NewCol 75; OxCan; Pen EUR; REn; WebBD 80*

Raspberries, The
[Jim Bonfanti; Wally Bryson; Eric Carmen; David Smalley]
American. Rock Group
Source: *ConMuA 80; LilREn 78; RkOn 2; WhoRock 81*

Raspberry, William
American. Journalist
b. Oct 12, 1935 in Okalona, Mississippi
Source: *WhoAm 82; WhoBlA 75*

Rasputin, Grigori Efimovich
Russian. Monk
Known for strong influence in court of Czar Nicholas II; assassinated.
b. 1871 in Tobolsk, Russia
d. Dec 31, 1916 in Russia
Source: *LongCTC; NewCol 75; REn; WebBD 80; WorAl*

Ratelle, (Joseph Gilbert Yvon) Jean
Canadian. Hockey Player
b. Oct 3, 1940 in Lac St. Jean, PQ
Source: *WhoAm 74; WhoHcky 73*

Rathbone, Basil
English. Actor
Played Sherlock Holmes in series of 1930-40's films.
b. Jun 13, 1892 in Johannesburg, South Africa
d. Jul 21, 1967 in New York, New York
Source: *BiDFilm; BiE&WWA; CmMov; CurBio 51, 67; FamA&A; FilmgC; MotPP; MovMk; OxFilm; WhScrn 74, 77; WhoHol B; WorEFlm*

Rathbone, Monroe Jackson
American. Businessman
b. Mar 1, 1900 in Parkersburg, West Virginia
d. Aug 2, 1976 in Baton Rouge, Louisiana
Source: *CurBio 57; St&PR 75; Who 74; WhoAm 74; WhoWor 74*

Rathenau, Walter
German. Industrialist
b. 1867 in Berlin, Germany
d. Jun 24, 1922 in Berlin, Germany
Source: *McGEWB; REn; WhoModH*

Rather, Dan
American. Broadcast Journalist, Author
Wrote *The Palace Guard; The Camera Never Blinks;* anchor "The CBS Evening News."
b. Oct 31, 1931 in Wharton, Texas
Source: *AuNews 1; BioNews 74; BkPepl; ConAu 53; IntMPA 82; WhoAm 78, 80, 82*

Ratoff, Gregory
American. Actor
b. Apr 20, 1893 in Petrograd, Russia
d. Dec 14, 1960 in Solothurn, Switzerland
Source: *BiDFilm; CurBio 43, 61; FilmgC; MotPP; MovMk; Vers A; WhAm 4; WhScrn 74, 77; WhoHol B; WorEFlm*

Ratsirka, Didier
Malgasy Head of Government
b. Nov 4, 1936 in Madagascar
Source: *IntWW 74*

Rattigan, Terence Mervyn
English. Dramatist
b. Jun 10, 1911 in London, England
d. Nov 30, 1977 in Hamilton, Bermuda
Source: *Au&Wr 71; BiE&WWA; CasWL; CnMD; CnThe; ConAu 73, 85; ConLC 7; CroCD; CurBio 56, 78; DcLEL; EvLB; FilmgC; IntMPA 75, 76, 77; IntWW 74; LongCTC; McGEWD; ModBrL; ModWD; NewC; NotNAT; OxFilm; OxThe; Pen ENG; PlP&P; REn; TwCW; WebE&AL; Who 74; WhoThe 77; WhoTwCL; WhoWor 74; WorAu; WorEFlm; WrDr 76*

Rattner, Abraham
American. Artist, Printmaker
b. Jul 8, 1895 in Poughkeepsie, New York
d. Feb 14, 1978 in New York, New York
Source: *BioIn 1, 4, 5, 6, 11; BnEnAmA; ConArt; CurBio 48, 78; DcCAA 71, 77; McGDA; ObitOF 79; WhoAm 74, 76, 78; WhoAmA 73, 76; WhoWor 74*

Rau, Santha Rama
see: Rama Rau, Santha

Rausch, James Stevens
American. Bishop
b. Sep 4, 1928 in Albany, Minnesota
d. May 18, 1981 in Phoenix, Arizona
Source: *WhoAm 74, 76, 78, 80; WhoRel 75, 77*

Rauschenberg, Robert
American. Artist
Collages, called "combines," include *Gloria,* 1956; *Summer Rental III,* 1960.
b. Oct 22, 1925 in Port Arthur, Texas
Source: *CelR 73; ConDr 73; CurBio 65; DcCAA 71; EncAB-H; IntWW 74; WebAB; WhoAm 74; WhoAmA 73; WhoE 74; WhoWor 74*

Rauschenbusch, Walter
American. Theologian
b. Oct 4, 1861 in Rochester, New York
d. Jul 25, 1918 in Rochester, New York
Source: *AmAu&B; BioIn 2, 3, 4, 6, 7, 10; DcAmB; DcAmReB; DcNAA; EncAB-A; McGEWB; NatCAB 19; OxAmL; REnAL; WebAB; WhAm 1*

Ravaillac, Francois
French. Assassin of Henry IV
b. 1578 in Angouleme, France
d. 1610
Source: *OxFr; WebBD 80*

Ravel, Maurice Joseph
French. Composer
His work *Bolero,* 1928,theme for movie *10* , 1981.
b. Mar 7, 1875 in Ciboure, France
d. Dec 28, 1937 in Paris, France
Source: *AtlBL; DcCM; NewCol 75; OxFr; REn; WebBD 80; WorAl*

Rawlings, Jerry John
Ghanaian. Revolutionary Leader
b. Jun 22, 1947 in Accra, Ghana
Source: *AfSS 79; CurBio 82; NewYTBS 82*

Rawlings, Marjorie Kinnan
American. Author
Won 1939 Pulitzer Prize for *The Yearling.*
b. Aug 8, 1896 in Washington, DC
d. Dec 14, 1953 in Saint Augustine, Florida
Source: *AmAu&B; AmNov; CnDAL; CurBio 42, 54; CyWA; DcAmB S5; DcLEL; EvLB; InWom; LongCTC; ModAL; OxAmL; Pen AM; REn; REnAL; ThrBJA; TwCA, SUP; TwCW; WhAm 3; WorAl; YABC 1*

Rawlins, John A
American. Army Officer
b. Feb 13, 1831 in Galena, Illinois
d. Sep 6, 1869 in Washington, DC
Source: *AmBi; ApCAB; BiAuS; BiDrUSE; DcAmB; Drake; TwCBDA; WhAm H*

Rawlinson, Herbert
English. Actor
b. 1883 in Brighton, England
d. Jul 12, 1953 in Woodland Hills, California
Source: *CanWW 70; Film 1; MotPP; MovMk; TwYS; WhScrn 74, 77; WhoHol B*

Rawls, Betsy (Elizabeth Earle)
American. Golfer
b. May 4, 1928 in Spartanburg, South Carolina
Source: *WhoGolf*

Rawls, Lou
American. Singer
Has won four Grammys; has one platinum, six gold albums.
b. Dec 1, 1935 in Chicago, Illinois
Source: *BkPepl; CelR 73; WhoAm 74, 76, 78, 80, 82; WhoBlA 75; WhoHol A; WhoWest 74; WorAl*

Ray, Aldo
American. Actor
b. Sep 25, 1926 in Pen Argyl, Pennsylvania
Source: *BiDFilm; FilmgC; IntMPA 75, 76, 77, 78, 79, 80, 81, 82; MotPP; MovMk; OxFilm; WhoHol A; WorEFlm*

Ray, Charles
American. Actor
b. Mar 15, 1891 in Jacksonville, Illinois
d. Nov 23, 1943 in Los Angeles, California
Source: *CurBio 44; Film 1; FilmgC; MotPP; MovMk; TwYS; WhScrn 74, 77; WhoHol B*

Ray, Dixy Lee
American. Politician
Governor of WA, 1977-80.
b. Sep 3, 1914 in Tacoma, Washington
Source: *AmM&WS 73P; BioNews 74; CelR 73; CurBio 73; InWom; IntWW 74; NewYTBE 73; WhoAm 74, 76, 78, 80, 82; WorAl*

Ray, Elizabeth
American. Former Secretary to Wayne Hays
b. 1942
Source: *BioIn 10*

Ray, James Earl
American. Assassin of Martin Luther King
Convicted, sentenced to 99 years in prison.
b. 1928
Source: *BioIn 8, 9, 10; Blood*

Ray, Johnnie (John Alvin)
American. Singer
Sang hits "Cry," "The Little Cloud that Cried," 1951.
b. Jan 10, 1927 in Dallas, Oregon
Source: *AmSCAP 66; FilmgC; WhoHol A; WorAl*

Ray, Man
American. Artist, Photographer
Co-founded Dadaism, 1917; developed rayograph photographical technique.
b. Aug 27, 1890 in Philadelphia, Pennsylvania
d. Nov 18, 1976 in Paris, France
Source: *CurBio 65; DcFM; FilmgC; IntWW 74; NewYTBE 70, 72; OxFilm; REn; WebAB; WorAl*

Ray, Nicholas
[Raymond N Kienzle]
American. Motion Picture Director
b. Aug 7, 1911 in La Crosse, Wisconsin
d. 1979 in New York, New York
Source: *Alli; BiDFilm; DcFM; FilmgC; IntMPA 75, 77; MovMk; NewYTBE 72; OxFilm; WorEFlm*

Ray, Robert D
American. Politician
b. Sep 26, 1928 in Des Moines, Iowa
Source: *IntWW 74; WhoAm 74, 76, 78, 80, 82; WhoAmP 73; WhoGov 72; WhoMW 74*

Ray, Satyajit
Indian. Motion Picture Director
b. May 2, 1921 in Calcutta, India
Source: *BiDFilm; CurBio 61; DcFM; FilmgC; IntWW 74; MovMk; NewYTBE 73; OxFilm; Who 74; WhoWor 74; WorEFlm*

Rayburn, Gene
American. TV Game Show Host
b. Dec 17, 1917 in Christopher, Illinois
Source: *IntMPA 75, 76, 77, 78, 79, 80, 81, 82; WhoAm 74, 76, 78, 80, 82*

Rayburn, Sam(uel Taliaferro)
"Mr. Democrat"
American. Congressman
Speaker of House for periods from 1940-61.
b. Jan 6, 1882 in Roane County, Tennessee
d. Nov 16, 1961 in Bonham, Texas
Source: *CurBio 40, 49, 62; EncAB-H; NewCol 75; WebAB; WhAm 4; WhAmP; WorAl*

Raye, Martha
[Margaret Theresa Yvonne Reed]
American. Comedienne, Singer
Known for wide-mouthed zaniness; in films since 1936.
b. Aug 27, 1916 in Butte, Montana
Source: *BiE&WWA; BioNews 74; CelR 73; CurBio 63; EncMT; FilmgC; InWom; IntMPA 75, 76, 77, 78, 79, 80, 81, 82; NewYTBE 72; ThFT; WhoAm 74, 76, 78, 80, 82; WhoHol A; WhoThe 77; WorAl*

Raymond, Alex(ander Gillespie)
American. Cartoonist
b. Oct 2, 1909 in New Rochelle, New York
d. Sep 6, 1956 in Westport, Connecticut
Source: *WhAm 3*

Raymond, Gene
American. Actor
b. Aug 13, 1908 in New York, New York
Source: *BiE&WWA; FilmgC; HolP 30; IntMPA 75, 76, 77, 78, 79, 80, 81, 82; MotPP; MovMk; WhoAm 74, 76, 78, 80, 82; WhoHol A; WhoThe 77*

Raymond, Henry Jarvis
American. Congressman, Editor
b. Jan 24, 1820 in Lima, New York
d. Jun 18, 1869 in New York, New York
Source: *Alli; AmAu; AmAu&B; AmBi; ApCAB; BbD; BiD&SB; BiDrAC; CyAl 2; DcAmAu; DcAmB; DcNAA; Drake; OxAmL; REnAL; TwCBDA; WebAB; WhAm H; WhAmP*

Raymond, James C
American. Illustrator of "Blondie"
b. Feb 25, 1917 in Riverside, Connecticut
d. Oct 14, 1981 in Boynton Beach, Florida
Source: *BioIn 12; NewYTBS 81*

Rayner, Claire
English. Media Personality, Author
b. Jan 22, 1931 in England
Source: *Au&Wr 71; ConAu 21R; WrDr 76*

Rea, Gardner
American. Cartoonist
b. Aug 12, 1892 in Ironton, Ohio
d. Dec 27, 1966 in Long Island, New York
Source: *AmAu&B; ConAu 93; CurBio 46, 67; WhAm 4*

Read, George
American. Continental Congressman
b. Sep 18, 1733 in North East, Maryland
d. Sep 21, 1798 in New Castle, Delaware
Source: *Alli; AmBi; ApCAB; BiAuS; BiDrAC; DcAmB; Drake; TwCBDA; WebAB; WhAm H; WhAmP*

Read, Sir Herbert
English. Poet, Art Critic
b. Dec 4, 1893 in Kirbymoorside, England
d. Jun 12, 1968 in Malton, England
Source: *CasWL; ChPo; CnE&AP; ConAu 25R, 85; ConLC 4; CurBio 62, 68; DcLEL; EncWL; EvLB; LongCTC; ModBrL, SUP; NewC; OxEng; Pen ENG; RAdv 1; REn; TwCA, SUP; TwCW; WhAm 5; WhoLA; WhoTwCL*

Read, Piers Paul
English. Author
b. Mar 7, 1941 in Beaconsfield, England
Source: *Au&Wr 71; ConAu 25R; ConDr 73; ConLC 4, 10; ConNov 76; SmATA 21; Who 74; WhoAm 82; WrDr 76*

Read, Thomas Buchanan
American. Poet, Artist
b. Mar 12, 1822 in Corner Ketch, Pennsylvania
d. May 11, 1872 in New York, New York
Source: *Alli; AmAu; AmAu&B; AmBi; ApCAB; BbD; BiD&SB; Chambr 3; ChPo, S1; CnDAL; CyAl 2; DcAmAu; DcAmB; DcLEL; DcNAA; EvLB; OhA&B; OxAmL; REnAL; TwCBDA; WhAm H*

Reade, Charles
English. Author
b. Jun 8, 1814 in Ipsden, England
d. Apr 11, 1884 in London, England
Source: *Alli, SUP; AtlBL; BbD; BiD&SB; BrAu 19; CasWL; Chambr 3; CyWA; DcBiA; DcEnA; DcEnL; DcEuL; DcLEL; EvLB; HsB&A; MouLC 4; NewC; OxEng; OxThe; Pen ENG; RAdv 1; REn; WebE&AL*

Ready, William Bernard
Welsh. Educator, Librarian
b. Sep 16, 1914 in Cardiff, Wales
Source: *BiDrLUS 70; BkC 6; CanWW 70; CathA 1952; ConAu 25R; DrLC 69; WhoAm 74; WhoE 74; WrDr 76*

Reagan, Maureen
[Mrs. Dennis Revell]
American. Daughter of Ronald Reagan
b. Jan 4, 1941 in Los Angeles, California
Source: *BioIn 12*

Reagan, Michael
American. Son of Ronald Reagan, Businessman
b. Mar 18, 1946 in Los Angeles, California
Source: *BioIn 12*

Reagan, Nancy Davis
[Anne Frances Robbins]
American. Wife of Ronald Reagan
Appeared in high school play *First Lady,* 1939; last movie *Hellcats* with Ronald Reagan.
b. Jul 6, 1921 in New York, New York
Source: *BioNews 74; BkPepl; CurBio 82; NewYTBE 71; WhoAm 82; WhoAmW 77; WhoWest 74*

Reagan, Patricia
see: Davis, Patti

Reagan, Ronald Wilson
"Dutch"
American. 40th US President
Oldest man elected president; first divorced president.
b. Feb 6, 1911 in Tampico, Illinois
Source: *BiDFilm; BkPepl; CelR 73; ConAu 85; CurBio 49, 67, 82; EncAB-H; FilmgC; IntMPA 75, 76, 77, 78, 79, 80, 81, 82; IntWW 74; MotPP; MovMk; NewYTBE 70; NewYTBS 74; OxFilm; Who 82; WhoAm 76, 78, 80, 82; WhoAmP 73; WhoGov 72; WhoHol A; WhoWest 74; WhoWor 74; WorEFlm*

Reagan, Ronald Prescott
American. Son of Ronald Reagan, Dancer
b. May 20, 1958 in Los Angeles, California
Source: *BioIn 11, 12*

Reardon, John
American. Opera Singer, Actor
b. Apr 8, 1930
Source: *BiE&WWA; CurBio 74; NewYTBE 72; WhoAm 74, 76, 78, 80, 82; WhoE 74; WhoWor 74*

Reason, Rex
American. Actor
b. Nov 30, 1928 in Berlin, Germany
Source: *FilmgC; IntMPA 75, 76, 77, 78, 79, 80, 81, 82; WhoHol A*

Reasoner, Harry
American. Broadcast Journalist
Anchorman, "ABC Evening News," 1970-78; CBS news, 1956-70, 1978--; also on "60 Minutes."
b. Apr 17, 1923 in Dakota City, Iowa
Source: *AmAu&B; AuNews 1; BioNews 75; CelR 73; CurBio 66; IntMPA 75, 76, 77, 78, 79, 80, 81, 82; WhoAm 74, 76, 78, 80, 82; WhoE 74; WorAl*

Reber, Grote
American. Radio Astronomer
Built first radio telescope, 1937.
b. Dec 22, 1911 in Wheaton, Illinois
Source: *AsBiEn; WorAl*

Rebbot, Olivier
French. Photojournalist
b. 1949?
d. Feb 10, 1981 in Hialeah, Florida
Source: *NewYTBS 81*

Rebecca
Biblical Character
Source: *NewCol 75; WebBD 80*

Rebikov, Vladimir Ivanovich
Russian. Composer
b. May 31, 1866 in Krasnoyarsk, Russia
d. Dec 1, 1920 in Yalta, U.S.S.R.
Source: *BioIn 4; NewEOp 71; OxMus*

Rebozo, "Bebe" (Charles Gregory)
American. Real Estate Executive, Banker
Close friend of Richard Nixon; chairman, Key Biscayne Bank, 1964--.
b. Nov 17, 1912 in Tampa, Florida
Source: *WhoAm 74, 76, 78, 80, 82; WhoF&I 74; WhoS&SW 73; WorAl*

Recamier, (Jeanne Francoise) Julie(tte) Adelaide, Madame
French. Beauty and Social Figure
b. 1777
d. 1849
Source: *BioIn 2, 3, 4, 9, 10; NewCol 75*

Rechy, John Franklin
American. Author
b. Mar 10, 1934 in El Paso, Texas
Source: *AmAu&B; ConAu 5R; ConLC 1, 7, 14, 18; ConNov 72, 76; DrAF 76; Pen AM; WhoAm 74, 76, 78, 80, 82; WhoWor 74*

"Red Baron"
see: Richthofen, Manfred von, Baron

Red Cloud, Chief
American Indian. Leader of Oglala Sioux
b. 1822 in Nebraska
d. 1909 in Pine Ridge, South Dakota
Source: *NewCol 75; WebBD 80*

Redding, Otis
American. Singer, Songwriter
b. Sep 9, 1941 in Dawson, Georgia
d. Dec 10, 1967 in Madison, Wisconsin
Source: *WhAm 4A; WhScrn 77*

Reddy, Helen
"Queen of Housewife Rock"
Australian. Singer, Songwriter
Second single, "I Am Woman" became feminist movement theme song.
b. Oct 25, 1942 in Melbourne, Australia
Source: *BioNews 74; BkPepl; IntMPA 75, 76, 77, 78, 79, 80, 81, 82; NewYTBE 73; WhoAm 74, 76, 78, 80, 82; WhoHol A*

Reddy, N(eelam) Sanjiva
Indian. President
b. May 13, 1913 in Illure, India
Source: *CurBio 81; FarE&A 78, 79; IntWW 74, 75, 76, 77, 78, 79, 80; IntYB 79; NewYTBS 79; WhoWor 78*

Redenbacher, Orville
American. Popcorn Industry Executive
b. 1907 in Brazil, Indiana
Source: *BioIn 11*

Redfield, William
American. Football Player
b. Jan 26, 1927 in New York, New York
d. Aug 17, 1976 in New York, New York
Source: *BiE&WWA; FilmgC; WhoHol A; WhoThe 77*

Redford, Lola Van Wagenen
American. Wife of Robert Redford
b. 1938
Source: *BioIn 10*

Redford, Robert
[Charles Robert Redford, Jr.]
American. Actor, Director, Author
First movie *Barefoot in the Park,* 1963; won Oscar for directing *Ordinary People,* 1980.
b. Aug 18, 1937 in Santa Monica, California
Source: *BiDFilm 81; BioNews 74; BkPepl; CelR 73; CurBio 71, 82; FilmgC; IntMPA 75, 76, 77, 78, 79, 80, 81, 82; MotPP; MovMk; NewYTBS 74; OxFilm; WhoAm 74; WhoHol A; WorEFlm*

Redgrave, Lynn
English. Actress
Starred in *Georgy Girl,* 1967;TV series "House Calls."
b. Mar 8, 1943 in London, England
Source: *BioNews 74; CurBio 69; FilmgC; InWom; IntMPA 75, 76, 77, 78, 79, 80, 81, 82; MotPP; MovMk; NewYTBS 74; NotNAT; OxFilm; Who 82; WhoAm 82; WhoThe 77; WhoWor 74*

Redgrave, Corin
English. Actor
b. Jul 16, 1939 in London, England
Source: *CnThe; FilmEn; FilmgC; WhoHol A; WhoThe 72, 77*

Redgrave, Sir Michael Scudamore
English. Actor, Author
Starred in *The Quiet American,* 1958; *The Go-Between,* 1970.
b. Mar 20, 1908 in Bristol, England
Source: *Au&Wr 71; BiDFilm; BiE&WWA; BioNews 74; CmMov; CurBio 50; FilmgC; IntMPA 75, 76, 77, 78, 79, 80, 81, 82; IntWW 74; MotPP; MovMk; NotNAT; OxFilm; OxThe; PlP&P; Who 82; WhoE 74; WhoHol A; WhoThe 77; WhoWor 74; WorAl; WorEFlm*

Redgrave, Vanessa
English. Actress
Won 1977 Oscar for *Julia;* starred in *Blow-up; Camelot; Playing for Time.*
b. Jan 30, 1937 in London, England
Source: *BiDFilm; BkPepl; CelR 73; CurBio 66; FilmgC; InWom; IntMPA 75, 76, 77, 78, 79, 80, 81, 82; IntWW 74; MotPP; MovMk; OxFilm; OxThe; Who 82; WhoAm 82; WhoHol A; WhoThe 77; WhoWor 74; WorAl; WorEFlm*

Redhead, Hugh McCulloch
American. Advertising Executive
b. Jul 18, 1920 in Saint Louis, Missouri
d. 1975 in Detroit, Michigan
Source: *St&PR 75; WhoAdv 72*

Redi, Francesco
Italian. Author
b. Feb 18, 1626 in Arezzo, Italy
d. Mar 1, 1698 in Pisa, Italy
Source: *CasWL; DcEuL; EuAu; EvEuW; OxEng; Pen EUR*

Redman, Don
American. Jazz Musician
b. Jul 29, 1900 in Piedmont, West Virginia
d. Nov 30, 1964 in New York, New York
Source: *AmSCAP 66; WhoJazz 72*

Redman, Joyce
Irish. Actress
b. 1918 in County Mayo, Ireland
Source: *BiE&WWA; FilmgC; NotNAT; PlP&P; WhoHol A; WhoThe 77*

Redon, Odilon
French. Artist
b. Apr 22, 1840 in Bordeaux, France
d. Jul 6, 1916 in Paris, France
Source: *AtlBL; OxFr; REn*

Redpath, James
Canadian. Engineer
b. Jun 8, 1908 in Lethbridge, AB
Source: *CanWW 82; St&PR 75; WhoAm 74; WhoCan 73; WhoF&I 74; WhoWor 74*

Reed, Alan
[Teddy Bergman]
American. Actor
b. Aug 20, 1907 in New York, New York
d. Jun 14, 1977 in Los Angeles, California
Source: *AmSCAP 66; BioIn 11; IntMPA 75, 76, 77; NewYTBS 77; Vers A; WhAm 7; WhoAm 74, 76*

Reed, Betty Jane
American. Children's Author
b. Aug 6, 1921 in Pittsburgh, Pennsylvania
Source: *ConAu 29R; SmATA 4; WomPO 76*

Reed, Sir Carol
English. Motion Picture Producer
b. Dec 30, 1906 in London, England
d. Apr 25, 1976 in London, England
Source: *BiDFilm; CmMov; CurBio 50; DcFM; FilmgC; IntMPA 75; IntWW 74; MovMk; NewYTBE 70; OxFilm; Who 74; WhoThe 77; WhoWor 74; WorEFlm*

Reed, Dean
"The Frank Sinatra of Russia"
American. Singer
b. 1939? in Denver, Colorado
Source: *BioIn 8, 9, 11*

Reed, Donna
[Donna Mullenger]
American. Actress
Won 1953 Oscar for *From Here to Eternity;* TV series "The Donna Reed Show" 1958-66.
b. Jan 27, 1921 in Denison, Iowa
Source: *BiDFilm; FilmgC; InWom; IntMPA 75, 76, 77, 78, 79, 80, 81, 82; MotPP; MovMk; WhoAm 76, 76, 78, 80, 82; WhoHol A; WorEFlm*

Reed, Ed
American. Cartoonist
b. Dec 13, 1907 in Fort Towson, Oklahoma
Source: *WhoAm 74*

Reed, Eliot
see: Ambler, Eric, pseud.

Reed, Henry Hope
American. Critic, Educator
b. Jul 11, 1808 in Philadelphia, Pennsylvania
d. Sep 27, 1854
Source: *Alli; AmAu&B; ApCAB; CyAl 2; DcAmAu; DcAmB; DcNAA; Drake; EvLB; NatCAB 2; TwCBDA; WhAm H*

Reed, Ishmael
American. Author
b. Feb 22, 1938 in Chattanooga, Tennessee
Source: *AmAu&B; BlkAW; ConAu 25R; ConLC 2, 3, 5, 6, 11; ConNov 76; ConP 70, 75; DrAF 76; DrAP 75; LivgBAA; ModAL SUP; WhoAm 74, 76, 78, 80, 82*

Reed, Jerry
[Jerry Hubbard]
"The Alabama Wild Man"
American. Actor, Singer, Songwriter
Offbeat song "When You're Hot, You're Hot."
b. Mar 20, 1937 in Atlanta, Georgia
Source: *WhoAm 74, 76, 78, 80, 82*

Reed, John
American. Journalist, Communist Leader
Wrote account of 1917 Russian Revolution *Ten Days That Shook the World,* 1919.
b. Oct 22, 1887 in Portland, Oregon
d. Oct 19, 1920 in U.S.S.R.
Source: *AmAu&B; AmLY; DcAmB; DcNAA; LongCTC; ModAL; OxAmL; Pen AM; REn; REnAL; TwCA, SUP; WebAB; WhAm 1; WorAl*

Reed, John Shedd
American. Railway Executive
b. Jun 9, 1917 in Chicago, Illinois
Source: *WhoAm 78, 80, 82*

Reed, Oliver
English. Actor
b. Feb 13, 1938 in London, England
Source: *CelR 73; FilmgC; IntMPA 75, 76, 77, 78, 79, 80, 81, 82; MovMk; OxFilm; WhoHol A*

Reed, Peter Hugh
American. Critic, Author
b. 1892 in Maryland
d. Sep 25, 1969 in New York, New York
Source: *BioIn 8; IntMPA 82*

Reed, Rex
American. Movie Critic, Journalist
b. Oct 2, 1939 in Fort Worth, Texas
Source: *AuNews 1; BkPepl; CelR 73; ConAu 53; CurBio 72; NewYTBE 72; WhoAm 82; WhoE 74; WhoHol A; WrDr 76*

Reed, Robert
American. Actor
b. 1932 in Chicago, Illinois
Source: *WhoHol A*

Reed, Stanley Forman
American. Supreme Court Justice
Appointed by President Roosevelt, 1938-57.
b. Dec 31, 1884 in Maysville, Kentucky
d. Apr 2, 1980 in Huntington, New York
Source: *CngDr 74; CurBio 42, 80; DrAS 74P; NewCol 75; WebAB; WebBD 80; WhoGov 72*

Reed, Susan
American. Singer
b. 1927 in Columbia, South Carolina
Source: *EncFCWM 69; WhoHol A*

Reed, Walter
American. Army Surgeon, Bacteriologist
Yellow fever virus tracked to mosquito; Washington, DC hospital named for him.
b. Sep 13, 1851 in Gloucester County, Virginia
d. Nov 23, 1902 in Washington, DC
Source: *AmBi; DcAmB; EncAB-H; NewCol 75; REn; WebAB; WebBD 80; WhAm H; WorAl*

Reed, Willis
American. Basketball Player, Coach
Player, NY Knickerbockers, 1964-74; coach, 1977-79; rookie of year, 1965.
b. Jun 25, 1942 in Hico, Louisiana
Source: *CurBio 73; NewYTBE 70; NewYTBS 74; St&PR 75; WhoAm 74; WhoBbl 73; WhoBlA 75*

Reedy, George Edward
American. Journalist
b. Aug 5, 1917 in East Chicago, Indiana
Source: *ConAu 29R; IntWW 74; WhoAm 74, 76, 78, 80, 82*

Reems, Harry
[Herbert Streicher]
American. Actor, Author, Filmmaker
b. Aug 27, 1947 in New York, New York
Source: *BioIn 11; ConAu 61*

Rees, Ennis
American. Children's Author
b. Mar 17, 1925 in Newport News, Virginia
Source: *AuBYP; ChPo S1; ConAu 1R; DrAP 75; DrAS 74E; SmATA 3*

Rees, John
see: Men at Work

Rees, Roger
Welsh. Actor
Starred in *Nicholas Nickleby* in London, on Broadway, TV.
b. May 5, 1944 in Aberystwyth, Wales
Source: *WhoThe 77, 81*

Reese, Della
American. Singer, Actress
b. Jul 6, 1932 in Detroit, Michigan
Source: *BioNews 74; CurBio 71; InWom; WhoAm 74, 76, 78, 80, 82; WhoBlA 75; WhoHol A*

Reese, Don(ald Francis)
American. Football Player
Wrote 1982 SI article about drug abuse in NFL.
b. Sep 4, 1951 in Mobile, Alabama
Source: *FootReg*

Reese, Lizette Woodworth
American. Poet
b. Jan 9, 1856 in Waverly, Maryland
d. Dec 17, 1935
Source: *Alli SUP; AmAu&B; AmWom; AnCL; BiD&SB; BiDSA; ChPo, S2; CnDAL; ConAmA; ConAmL; DcAmAu; DcAmB S1; DcLEL; DcNAA; InWom; LongCTC; NotAW; OxAmL; REn; REnAL; TwCA, SUP; WhAm 1, 2*

Reese, Mason
American. Actor
b. 1967
Source: *BioIn 10, 11; BioNews 74; NewYTBE 73*

Reese, "Pee Wee" (Harold Henry)
"The Little Colonel"
American. Baseball Player
b. Jul 23, 1919 in Ekron, Kentucky
Source: *BaseEn; CurBio 50; WhoProB 73*

Reeve, Christopher
American. Actor
Starred in *Superman, I, II* 1978, 1980.
b. Sep 25, 1952 in New York, New York
Source: *BioIn 11, 12; CurBio 82; IntMPA 80, 82; WhoAm 82*

Reeves, George
[George Basselo]
American. Actor
Typecast in TV series "The Adventures of Superman."
b. 1914 in Ashland, Kentucky
d. Jun 16, 1959 in Beverly Hills, California
Source: *BioIn 5; FilmgC; MotPP; NotNAT B; WhScrn 74, 77; WhoHol B*

Reeves, Rosser
American. Advertising Executive
b. Sep 10, 1910 in Danville, Virginia
Source: *WhoAm 74, 76, 78, 80, 82; WhoE 74; WhoF&I 74*

Reeves, Steve
American. Actor
b. Jan 21, 1926 in Glasgow, Montana
Source: *FilmgC; IntMPA 75, 76, 77; MotPP; MovMk; WhoHol A; WorEFlm*

Regan, Donald Thomas
American. Government Official
Secretary of Treasury, 1981--.
b. Dec 21, 1918 in Cambridge, Massachusetts
Source: *CurBio 81; IntWW 74, 75, 76, 77, 78; St&PR 75; Who 82; WhoAm 76, 78, 80, 82; WhoE 74; WhoF&I 74, 75, 77, 79*

Regan, Phil
American. Actor, Singer
b. May 28, 1906 in Brooklyn, New York
Source: *IntMPA 75, 76, 78, 79, 80, 81, 82; WhoHol A*

Regan, Theodore M, Jr.
American. Advertising Executive
b. Jul 5, 1897 in Catawba, Kentucky
Source: *WhoAm 74*

Reger, Max
German. Composer
b. Mar 19, 1873 in Brand, Bavaria
d. May 11, 1916 in Leipzig, Germany
Source: *AtlBL; BioIn 1, 2, 3, 4, 5, 8, 9; NewCol 75; WebBD 80*

Regine
[Regina Zylberberg]
"Queen of the Night"
French. Nightclub Entrepreneur
Owns nightclubs bearing her name in NY, Paris.
b. Dec 26, 1929 in Etterbeck, Belgium
Source: *BioIn 10; CurBio 80*

Rehan, Ada
American. Actress
b. Apr 22, 1860 in Limerick, Ireland
d. Jan 8, 1916 in New York, New York
Source: *AmBi; AmWom; ApCAB; DcAmB; FamA&A; InWom; NotAW; OxAmL; OxThe; PlP&P; TwCBDA; WebAB; WhAm 1; WhoStg 1906, 1908; WomWWA 14*

Rehnquist, William Hubbs
American. Supreme Court Justice
b. Oct 1, 1924 in Milwaukee, Wisconsin
Source: *CelR 73; CngDr 74; CurBio 72; DrAS 74P; IntWW 74; NewYTBE 71; NewYTBS 74; WebAB; Who 74; WhoAm 74, 76, 78, 80, 82; WhoAmP 73; WhoGov 72; WhoS&SW 73*

Reich, Wilhelm
American. Psychoanalyst
b. Mar 24, 1897 in Austria
d. Nov 3, 1957 in Lewisburg, Pennsylvania
Source: *AmAu&B; NewYTBE 71; Pen AM; TwCA SUP; WhoTwCL*

Reichardt, Johann Friedrich
German. Composer, Conductor
b. Nov 25, 1752 in Konigsberg, Germany
d. Jun 27, 1814 in Giebichenstein, Germany
Source: *BioIn 1, 4; OxGer; WebBD 80*

Reichmann, Theodor
German. Opera Singer
b. Mar 15, 1848 in Rostock, Germany
d. May 22, 1903 in Marbach, Switzerland
Source: *NewEOp 71*

Reichstein, Tadeus
Swiss. Chemist
First to synthesize Vitamin C, 1933; shared Nobel Prize, 1950.
b. Jul 20, 1897 in Wloclawek, Poland
Source: *BioIn 2, 3, 5; CurBio 51; IntWW 74; NewCol 75; WebBD 80; Who 74; WhoWor 74; WhoWorJ 72; WorAl*

Reid, Beryl
English. Actress
b. Jun 17, 1920 in Hereford, England
Source: *FilmgC; WhoHol A; WhoThe 77*

Reid, Elliott
American. Actor
b. Jan 16, 1920 in New York, New York
Source: *BiE&WWA; MotPP; NotNAT; Vers A; WhoHol A*

Reid, Helen (Rogers)
[Mrs. Ogden Mills Reid]
American. Vice-President of NY Tribune
b. Nov 23, 1882 in Appleton, Wisconsin
d. Jul 27, 1970 in New York, New York
Source: *BiCAW; CurBio 41, 52, 70; ForWC 70; InWom; NewYTBE 70; WhAm 5; WomWWA 14*

Reid, Kate
English. Actress
b. Nov 4, 1930 in London, England
Source: *BiE&WWA; CanWW 70; CreCan 2; NotNAT; WhoAm 74, 76, 78, 80, 82; WhoHol A; WhoThe 77*

Reid, Ogden Mills
American. Newspaper Publisher
b. May 16, 1882 in New York, New York
d. Jan 3, 1947 in New York, New York
Source: *AmAu&B; DcAmB S4; WebAB; WhAm 2*

Reid, Wallace Eugene
American. Actor
b. Apr 15, 1891 in Saint Louis, Missouri
d. Jan 18, 1923 in Los Angeles, California
Source: *Film 1; FilmgC; MotPP; MovMk; St&PR 75; TwYS; WhScrn 74, 77; WhoHol B*

Reid, Whitelaw
American. Journalist
b. Oct 27, 1837 in Xenia, Ohio
d. Dec 15, 1912 in London, England
Source: *Alli; AmAu; AmAu&B; AmBi; ApCAB; BbD; BiD&SB; CyAl 2; DcAmAu; DcAmB; DcNAA; Drake; EncAB-H; OhA&B; OxAmL; REnAL; TwCBDA; WebAB; WhAm 1; Who 74; WhoAm 74; WhoF&I 74; WhoWor 74*

Reiffel, Leonard
American. Doctor, Journalist
b. Sep 30, 1927 in Chicago, Illinois
Source: *WhoAm 74, 76, 78, 80, 82*

Reik, Theodor
American. Psychoanalyst, Author
b. May 12, 1888 in Vienna, Austria
d. Dec 31, 1970 in New York, New York
Source: *AmAu&B; ConAu 5R, 25R, 5NR; REn; REnAL; TwCA SUP; WhAm 5; WhoWorJ 72*

Reilly, Charles Nelson
American. Actor, Comedian
b. Jan 13, 1931 in New York, New York
Source: *BiE&WWA; IntMPA 82; NotNAT; PlP&P A; WhoAm 74, 76, 78, 80, 82; WhoHol A; WhoThe 77*

Reiner, Carl
American. Actor, Author
Creator, writer, director "The Dick Van Dyke Show," 1961-66.
b. Mar 20, 1922 in New York, New York
Source: *BiE&WWA; CelR 73; CurBio 61; FilmgC; IntMPA 75, 76, 77, 78, 79, 80, 81, 82; MovMk; WhoAm 74, 76, 78, 80, 82; WhoHol A; WomWMM; WorAl*

Reiner, Fritz
Hungarian. Conductor
b. Dec 10, 1888 in Budapest, Hungary
d. Nov 15, 1963 in New York, New York
Source: *CurBio 41, 53, 64; WhAm 4; WhScrn 77*

Reiner, Rob
American. Actor, Motion Picture Director
Played Michael Stivic on "All in the Family," 1971-78; won two Emmys.
b. Mar 6, 1947 in New York, New York
Source: *BioIn 9, 11; WhoAm 78, 80, 82; WhoHol A*

Reinhardt, Ad(olph Frederick)
American. Artist
b. Dec 24, 1913 in Buffalo, New York
d. Aug 30, 1967
Source: *DcCAA 71; WhAm 4*

Reinhardt, Django (Jean Baptiste)
Belgian. Jazz Musician, Composer
b. Jan 23, 1910 in Liverchies, Belgium
d. May 16, 1953 in Fontainebleau, France
Source: *WhAm 4A*

Reinhardt, Max
[Max Goldman]
American. Motion Picture Director
b. Sep 9, 1873 in Baden, Austria
d. Oct 31, 1943 in New York, New York
Source: *CurBio 43; DcFM; FilmgC; LongCTC; OxFilm; OxGer; OxThe; PlP&P; REn; WhAm 2; WorEFlm*

Reinhart, Charles S
American. Artist
b. May 16, 1844 in Pittsburgh, Pennsylvania
d. Aug 30, 1896 in New York, New York
Source: *AmBi; ApCAB; ChPo; DcAmB; EarABI, SUP; TwCBDA; WhAm H*

Reinking, Ann
American. Dancer
b. Nov 10, 1949 in Seattle, Washington
Source: *BioIn 11; WhoAm 82; WhoThe 81*

Reisenberg, Nadia
Russian. Musician
b. Jul 14, 1904 in Vilna, Russia
Source: *InWom*

Reiser, Pete (Harold Patrick)
"Pistol Pete"
American. Baseball Player
Led NL in batting, 1941 with .343 average.
b. Mar 17, 1919 in Saint Louis, Missouri
d. Oct 25, 1981 in Palm Springs, California
Source: *BaseEn; BioIn 1, 6, 8, 10; NewYTBE 72, 73; NewYTBS 76; WhoProB 73*

Reiss, Albert
German. Opera Singer
b. Feb 22, 1870 in Berlin, Germany
d. Jun 20, 1940 in Nice, France
Source: *NewEOp 71*

Reisz, Karel
British. Motion Picture Director
b. 1926 in Czechoslovakia
Source: *BiDFilm; FilmgC; IntMPA 75, 76, 77, 78, 79, 80, 81, 82; IntWW 74; MovMk; OxFilm; WhoWor 74; WorEFlm*

Reitman, Ivan
Canadian. Motion Picture Director, Producer
b. 1946? in Komarmo, Czechoslovakia
Source: *BioIn 11*

Remarque, Erich Maria
[Erich Paul Remark]
American. Author
Wrote *All Quiet on the Western Front,* 1929.
b. Jun 22, 1898 in Osnabruck, Germany
d. Sep 25, 1970 in Locarno, Switzerland
Source: *AmAu&B; CasWL; ClDMEL; ConAu 29R, 77; EncWL; EvEuW; FilmgC; LongCTC; ModGL; OxEng; OxGer; Pen EUR; REn; REnAL; TwCA, SUP; TwCW; WhAm 5; WhScrn 77; WhoTwCL; WorAl*

Rembrandt (Harmenszoon van Rijn)
Dutch. Artist
Known for brilliant use of light, revealing portraits.
b. Jul 15, 1607 in Leyden, Netherlands
d. Oct 4, 1669 in Netherlands
Source: *AtlBL; BioIn 10; NewC; NewEOp 71; REn; WhDW; WorAl*

Remenyi, Eduard
Hungarian. Musician, Composer
b. Jul 17, 1830 in Heves, Hungary
d. May 15, 1898 in San Francisco, California
Source: *BiDAmM; OxMus*

Remick, Lee
[Mrs. William "Kip" Gowans]
American. Actress
Starred in *Days of Wine and Roses*, 1963.
b. Dec 14, 1935 in Boston, Massachusetts
Source: *BiDFilm; BkPepl; CurBio 66; FilmgC; InWom; IntMPA 75, 76, 77, 78, 79, 80, 81, 82; IntWW 74; MotPP; MovMk; NotNAT; OxFilm; WhoAm 74, 76, 78, 80, 82; WhoHol A; WorEFlm*

Remington, Eliphalet
American. Firearms Manufacturer
Manufactured the Remington rifle, 1828, with father.
b. Oct 27, 1793 in Suffield, Connecticut
d. Apr 4, 1889 in Silver Springs, Florida
Source: *AmBi; DcAmB; TwCBDA; WebAB; WhAm H; WorAl*

Remington, Frederic
American. Artist, Sculptor
Paintings, bronze sculptures depict the Old West.
b. Oct 4, 1861 in Canton, New York
d. Dec 26, 1909 in Ridgefield, Connecticut
Source: *AmAu; AmAu&B; AmBi; AtlBL; CnDAL; DcAmAu; DcAmB; DcLEL; DcNAA; EncAB-H; OxAmL; REn; REnAL; WebAB; WhAm 1; WhoFtbl 74; WorAl*

Remsen, Ira
American. Scientist, Physician, Engineer
b. Feb 10, 1846 in New York, New York
d. Mar 5, 1927 in Carmel, California
Source: *Alli SUP; AmAu&B; AmBi; ApCAB; BiDSA; DcAmAu; DcAmB; DcNAA; TwCBDA; WebAB; WhAm 1; WhNAA*

Remus
see: Romulus

Renaldo, Duncan
"The Cisco Kid"
American. Actor, Motion Picture Producer
b. Apr 23, 1904 in Camden, New Jersey
d. Sep 3, 1980 in Santa Barbara, California
Source: *FilmgC; IntMPA 75, 76, 77; MotPP; MovMk; WhoHol A; WhoWest 74*

Renan, (Joseph) Ernest
French. Historian, Philosopher, Author
b. Jan 27, 1823 in Treguier, France
d. Oct 2, 1892 in Paris, France
Source: *BbD; BiD&SB; CasWL; ClDMEL; DcEuL; EuAu; EvEuW; NewC; OxEng; OxFr; Pen EUR; RComWL; REn*

Renaud, Maurice
French. Opera Singer
b. Jul 24, 1861 in Bordeaux, France
d. Oct 16, 1933 in Paris, France
Source: *NewEOp 71*

Renault, Fernand
French. Auto Manufacturer
b. 1865 in Paris, France
d. 1909
Source: *NF*

Renault, Louis
French. Auto Manufacturer
b. 1877? in Paris, France
d. Oct 24, 1944 in Paris, France
Source: *BioIn 4, 8; CurBio 44*

Renault, Marcel
French. Auto Racer, Manufacturer
b. 1872 in Paris, France
d. 1903
Source: *NF*

Renault, Mary, pseud.
[Mary Challans]
English. Author
Wrote trilogy on Alexander the Great.
b. Sep 4, 1905 in London, England
Source: *Au&Wr 71; ConAu 81; ConLC 3; ConNov 72, 76; CurBio 59; InWom; IntWW 74; LongCTC; ModBrL SUP; NewC; RAdv 1; REn; SmATA 23; Who 74; WhoWor 74; WorAu; WrDr 76*

Renfro, Mel(vin Lacy)
American. Football Player
b. Dec 30, 1941 in Houston, Texas
Source: *WhoFtbl 74*

Reni, Guido
Italian. Artist
b. Nov 4, 1575 in Bologna, Italy
d. Aug 18, 1642 in Bologna, Italy
Source: *AtlBL; NewCol 75; REn; WebBD 80*

Renick, Marion Lewis
American. Children's Author
b. Mar 9, 1905 in Springfield, Ohio
Source: *AuBYP; ConAu 1R, 1NR; MorJA; OhA&B; SmATA 1*

Rennie, Michael
English. Actor
Played Harry Lime, in TV series "The Third Man," 1960.
b. Aug 29, 1909 in Bradford, England
d. Jun 10, 1971 in Harrogate, England
Source: *BiE&WWA; FilmgC; MotPP; MovMk; NewYTBE 71; WhScrn 74, 77; WhoHol B*

Renoir, Jean
French. Film Director, Screenwriter
b. Sep 15, 1894 in Paris, France
d. Feb 12, 1979 in Beverly Hills, California
Source: *Au&Wr 71; BiDFilm; CurBio 59; DcFM; FilmgC; IntMPA 75, 76, 77; IntWW 74; MovMk; OxFilm; REn; Who 74; WhoAm 74; WhoWor 74; WorEFlm*

Renoir, (Pierre) Auguste
French. Artist
Founder, leader of Impressionists; known for opulent nudes.
b. Feb 25, 1841 in Limoges, France
d. Dec 17, 1919 in Cagnes-sur-Mer, France
Source: *AtlBL; NewCol 75; OxFr; REn; WebBD 80; WorAl*

Rense, Paige
American. Magazine Editor
b. 1934? in Des Moines, Iowa
Source: *WhoWest 76*

Rentner, Maurice
Fashion Designer
b. 1889?
d. Jul 7, 1958 in New York, New York
Source: *BioIn 4, 5, 11*

Rentzel, Lance
"Bambi"
American. Football Player
b. Oct 14, 1943 in Flushing, New York
Source: *WhoFtbl 74*

Renwick, James
American. Architect
b. Nov 1, 1818 in Bloomingdale, New York
d. Jun 23, 1895 in New York, New York
Source: *AmBi; ApCAB; DcAmB; TwCBDA; WebAB; WhAm H*

REO Speedwagon
[Kevin Cronin; Neal Doughty; Alan Gratzer; Bruce Hall; Gary Richrath]
American. Rock Group
Source: *ConMuA 80; WhoRock 81*

Repin, Ilya Yefimovich
Russian. Artist
b. 1844
d. 1930
Source: *BioIn 2; NewCol 75; WebBD 80*

Repplier, Agnes
American. Essayist
b. Apr 1, 1858 in Philadelphia, Pennsylvania
d. Dec 15, 1950 in Philadelphia, Pennsylvania
Source: *Alli SUP; AmAu&B; ApCAB SUP; BiD&SB; CathA 1930; ChPo, S1; CnDAL; ConAmA; ConAmL; DcAmAu; DcAmB S4; DcLEL; InWom; LongCTC; NotAW; OxAmL; REn; REnAL; TwCA, SUP; TwCBDA; WhAm 3; WhNAA; WomWWA 14*

Repton, Humphry
English. Landscape Architect
b. 1752
d. 1818
Source: *BioIn 10*

Reshevsky, Samuel
American. Chess Player
b. Nov 26, 1911 in Ozorkow, Poland
Source: *CurBio 55; WhoAm 74, 76, 78, 80, 82*

Resnais, Alain
French. Motion Picture Producer
b. Jun 3, 1922 in Vannes, France
Source: *BiDFilm; ConLC 16; CurBio 65; FilmgC; IntMPA 82; IntWW 74; OxFilm; REn; WhoWor 74; WomWMM; WorEFlm*

Resnik, Muriel
American. Dramatist
b. Jun 25, 1903 in New York, New York
Source: *BiE&WWA; NotNAT*

Resnik, Regina
American. Opera Singer
b. Aug 20, 1922 in New York, New York
Source: *CelR 73; CurBio 56; InWom; IntWW 74; WhoAm 74, 76, 78, 80, 82; WhoMus 72; WhoWor 74; WhoWorJ 72*

Resor, Stanley Burnett
American. Advertising Executive
b. Apr 30, 1879 in Cincinnati, Ohio
d. Oct 29, 1962 in New York, New York
Source: *CurBio 49, 62; WhAm 4*

Resor, Stanley Rogers
American. Government Official
b. Dec 5, 1917 in New York, New York
Source: *CurBio 69; WhoAm 74; WhoGov 72*

Respighi, Ottorino
Italian. Composer, Musician
b. Jul 9, 1879 in Bologna, Italy
d. Apr 18, 1936 in Rome, Italy
Source: *OxMus; REn*

Reston, James Barrett
American. Journalist
b. Nov 3, 1909 in Clydebank, Scotland
Source: *AuNews 1, 2; CelR 73; ConAu 65; CurBio 43; IntWW 74; OhA&B; REnAL; St&PR 75; WebAB; WhoAm 74, 76, 78, 80, 82; WhoS&SW 73; WhoWor 74; WrDr 76*

Rethberg, Elizabeth
[Elizabeth Sattler]
German. Opera Singer
b. Sep 22, 1894 in Schwarzenburg, Germany
d. Jun 6, 1976 in Yorktown Heights, New York
Source: *NewEOp 71*

Reuben, David
American. Psychiatrist, Author
Wrote *Everything You Always Wanted to Know About Sex,* 1969.
b. Jul 29, 1933 in Chicago, Illinois
Source: *Au&Wr 71; AuNews 1; BioNews 74; CelR 73; ConAu 41R; WhoAm 82; WhoWest 74; WrDr 76*

Reulbach, Ed(ward Marvin)
"Big Ed"
American. Baseball Player
b. Dec 4, 1882 in Detroit, Michigan
d. Jul 17, 1961 in Glens Falls, New York
Source: *BaseEn; WhoProB 73*

Reutemann, Carlos
Argentine. Auto Racer
b. Apr 4, 1942 in Santa Fe, Argentina
Source: *NF*

Reuter, Ernst
German. Mayor of West Berlin
b. Jul 29, 1889 in Apenrade, Germany
d. Sep 29, 1953 in Berlin, Germany (West)
Source: *BioIn 1, 2, 3; CurBio 49, 53; ObitOF 79*

Reuter, Paul Julius
English. Founded Reuter's News Agency
b. 1816 in Kassel, Germany
d. 1899
Source: *REn*

Reuther, Roy
American. Labor Leader
b. 1909
d. Jan 10, 1968 in Detroit, Michigan
Source: *BioIn 8, 10*

Reuther, Walter Philip
American. Labor Leader
President, UAW, 1946-70.
b. Sep 1, 1907 in Wheeling, West Virginia
d. May 10, 1970 in Pellston, Michigan
Source: *AmAu&B; CurBio 41, 49, 70; EncAB-H; NewYTBE 70; WebAB; WhAm 5*

Revel, Jean Francois
French. Author, Philosopher
b. Jan 19, 1924 in Marseilles, France
Source: *CurBio 75; IntWW 74; NewYTBE 71; WhoWor 74*

Revels, Hiram R
American. Politician
b. Sep 1822 in Fayetteville, North Carolina
d. Mar 4, 1901 in Aberdeen, Mississippi
Source: *ApCAB; BiAuS; BiDrAC; DcAmB; TwCBDA; WebAB; WhAm H; WhAmP*

Reventlow, Lance
American. Auto Racer
b. 1936
d. Jul 25, 1972 in Colorado
Source: *BioIn 9; NewYTBE 72*

Revere, Anne
American. Actress
b. Jun 25, 1903 in New York, New York
d. 1972 in Aspen, Colorado
Source: *BiE&WWA; FilmgC; InWom; IntMPA 75, 77; MotPP; NotNAT; PlP&P; WhoHol A; WhoThe 77*

Revere, Paul
American. Patriot, Silversmith
Rode from Boston to Lexington, MA to warn of British attack, Apr 18, 1775.
b. Jan 1, 1735 in Boston, Massachusetts
d. May 10, 1818 in Boston, Massachusetts
Source: *AmBi; ApCAB; DcAmB; Drake; EarABI; EncAB-H; OxAmL; REn; REnAL; TwCBDA; WebAB; WhAm H; WorAl*

Revill, Clive Selsby
New Zealander. Actor
b. Apr 18, 1930 in Wellington, New Zealand
Source: *BiE&WWA; EncMT; FilmEn; FilmgC; IntMPA 77; WhoHol A; WhoThe 72, 77, 81*

Revillon Family
French. Furriers
Source: *WorFshn*

Revson, Charles Haskell
American. Founder of Revlon Cosmetics
Founded Revlon, Inc, 1932; president, 1932-62; chairman, 1962-75.
b. Oct 11, 1906 in Manchester, New Hampshire
d. Aug 24, 1975 in New York, New York
Source: *BusPN; CelR 73; St&PR 75; WhAm 6; WhoAm 74; WhoF&I 74; WhoWor 74*

Revson, Peter Jeffrey
American. Auto Racer, Revlon Heir
Nephew of Charles Revson; killed during practice for auto race.
b. Feb 27, 1939 in New York, New York
d. Mar 22, 1974 in Johannesburg, South Africa
Source: *BioNews 74; CelR 73*

Rexroth, Kenneth
American. Poet, Editor
Beat generation writer, 1950's; interested in mystical forms of experience.
b. Dec 22, 1905 in South Bend, Indiana
d. Jun 6, 1982 in Montecito, California
Source: *AmAu&B; CelR 73; ChPo, S3; CnE&AP; ConAu 5R; ConDr 73, 77; ConLC 1, 2, 6, 11; ConP 70, 75; CurBio 81, 82; DcLEL 1940; DrAP 75; EncWL; IndAu 1917; IntAu&W 76, 77; IntWW 74, 75, 76, 77, 78; IntWWP 77; ModAL, SUP; NewYTBS 82; OxAmL; Pen AM; RAdv 1; REn; REnAL; TwCA SUP; WebE&AL; WhoAm 74, 76, 78, 80, 82; WhoTwCL; WhoWest 74; WhoWor 74; WrDr 76, 80*

Rey, Alvino
[Alvin McGurney]
American. Band Leader, TV Producer
b. 1918 in Cleveland, Ohio
Source: *BiDAmM; BioIn 9*

Rey, Fernando
[Fernando Casado Arambillet]
Spanish. Actor
b. Sep 20, 1917 in LaCoruna, Spain
Source: *CurBio 79; FilmgC; MovMk*

Rey, Hans Augustus
American. Illustrator
b. Sep 16, 1898 in Hamburg, Germany
d. Aug 26, 1977 in Boston, Massachusetts
Source: *ConAu 5R, 73, 6NR; SmATA 1, 26; WhoAmA 73*

Reyer, (Louis) Ernest (Etienne)
French. Composer
b. Dec 1, 1823 in Marseilles, France
d. Jan 15, 1909 in Levandou, France
Source: *NewEOp 71*

Reyes, Alfonso
Mexican. Essayist
b. May 17, 1889 in Monterrey, Mexico
d. Dec 27, 1959 in Mexico City, Mexico
Source: *AtlBL; CasWL; CyWA; DcSpL; EncWL; Pen AM; REn; TwCW; WhAm 3; WhNAA; WorAu*

Reynaud, Paul
French. Politician
b. Oct 15, 1878 in Barcelonayye, France
d. Sep 21, 1966 in Neuilly, France
Source: *CurBio 40, 50, 66; WhAm 4*

Reynolds, Bobby (Robert)
American. Football Player
b. 1930 in Grand Island, Nebraska
Source: *BioIn 2; WhoFtbl 74*

Reynolds, Burt
American. Actor
First *Cosmopolitan* centerfold; first solid movie performance, *Deliverance,* 1972.
b. Feb 11, 1936 in Palm Beach, Florida
Source: *BkPepl; CelR 73; CurBio 73; FilmgC; IntMPA 75, 76, 77, 78, 79, 80, 81, 82; MotPP; MovMk; NewYTBE 72; WhoAm 74, 76, 78, 80, 82; WhoHol A*

Reynolds, Debbie (Marie Frances)
American. Actress, Singer
Starred in *The Unsinkable Molly Brown,* 1964; *Singing in the Rain,* 1952.
b. Apr 1, 1932 in El Paso, Texas
Source: *BiDFilm; BkPepl; CelR 73; CmMov; EncMT; FilmgC; InWom; IntMPA 75, 76, 77, 78, 79, 80, 81, 82; MovMk; OxFilm; WhoAm 74, 76, 78, 80, 82; WhoWest 74; WhoWor 74; WorEFlm*

Reynolds, Frank
American. Broadcast Journalist
b. Nov 29, 1923 in East Chicago, Illinois
Source: *WhoAm 74, 76, 78, 80, 82; WhoWor 74*

Reynolds, Jack (John Sumner)
"Hacksaw"
American. Football Player
b. Nov 22, 1947 in Cincinnati, Ohio
Source: *WhoAm 78, 80, 82*

Reynolds, Sir Joshua
English. Artist
Founded Literary Club, 1764.
b. Jul 16, 1723 in Plympton, England
d. Feb 23, 1792 in London, England
Source: *Alli; AtlBL; BbD; BiD&SB; CasWL; Chambr 2; ChPo, S1, S2; DcEnL; DcEuL; DcLEL; EvLB; NewC; OxEng; Pen ENG; REn*

Reynolds, Marjorie
American. Actress
b. Aug 12, 1921 in Buhl, Idaho
Source: *FilmgC; IntMPA 75, 76, 77, 78, 79, 80, 81, 82; MotPP; MovMk; WhoHol A*

Reynolds, Quentin
American. Journalist
b. Apr 11, 1902 in New York, New York
d. Mar 17, 1965 in California
Source: *AmAu&B; ConAu 73; CurBio 41, 65; IntWW 74; LongCTC; REnAL; St&PR 75; TwCA SUP; WhAm 4; WhScrn 77; WhoAm 74; WhoF&I 74; WhoWest 74*

Reynolds, Richard Joshua
American. Tobacco Executive
b. 1850
d. 1918
Source: *BioIn 1*

Reynolds, Ricky
see: Black Oak Arkansas

Reynolds, Robert Rice
American. Senator
b. Jun 18, 1884 in Asheville, North Carolina
d. Feb 13, 1963 in Asheville, North Carolina
Source: *BiDrAC; BioIn 6, 8; CurBio 40, 63; NatCAB 50; WhAm 4*

Reynolds, William
American. Actor
b. 1931 in Los Angeles, California
Source: *WhoHol A*

Reznicek, Emil von
Austrian. Composer
b. May 4, 1860 in Vienna, Austria
d. Aug 2, 1945 in Berlin, Germany
Source: *NewEOp 71; OxMus*

Rhee, Syngman
Korean. Statesman
First President of Korea, 1948-60; forced from offfice for political abuses.
b. Mar 26, 1875 in Hwanghai, Korea
d. Jul 19, 1965 in Honolulu, Hawaii
Source: *CurBio 47, 65; WhAm 4*

Rhine, J(oseph) B(anks)
American. Psychologist
b. Sep 29, 1895 in Waterloo, Pennsylvania
d. Feb 20, 1980 in Hillsboro, North Carolina
Source: *AmAu&B; AmM&WS 73S, 78S; AsBiEn; BiDPara; ConAu 5R, 93, 4NR; CurBio 49, 80; EncO&P 78; WebAB; Who 74; WhoAm 74, 76, 78; WhoWor 74*

Rhinelander, John Bassett
American. Government Official
b. Jun 18, 1933 in Boston, Massachusetts
Source: *WhoAm 74; WhoGov 72*

Rhodes, Cecil John
English. Administrator, Financier
b. Jul 5, 1853 in Bishop's Stortford, England
d. Mar 26, 1902 in Capetown, South Africa
Source: *LongCTC; NewC; REn*

Rhodes, "Dusty" (James Lamar)
American. Baseball Player
b. May 13, 1927 in Mathews, Alabama
Source: *BaseEn; BioIn 10; WhoProB 73*

Rhodes, Erik
[Ernest Rhoades Sharne]
American. Actor
b. Feb 10, 1906 in El Reno, Oklahoma
Source: *BiE&WWA; FilmgC; MovMk; NotNAT; PlP&P; WhoHol A*

Rhodes, Hari
American. Actor, Author
b. Apr 10, 1932 in Cincinnati, Ohio
Source: *BlkAW; ConAu 17R; WhoHol A*

Rhodes, James Allen
American. Governor of Ohio
b. Sep 13, 1909 in Jackson, Ohio
Source: *BioNews 75; CurBio 49; WhoAm 82; WhoAmP 73*

Rhodes, James Ford
American. Historian
b. May 1, 1848 in Cleveland, Ohio
d. Jan 22, 1927 in Brookline, Massachusetts
Source: *AmAu&B; AmBi; BiD&SB; Chambr 3; DcAmAu; DcAmB; DcNAA; EncAB-H; WhAm 1; WhNAA*

Rhodes, John Jacob
American. Politician
b. Sep 18, 1916 in Council Grove, Kansas
Source: *BiDrAC; CngDr 74; ConAu 103; NewYTBE 72, 73; WhoAm 74, 76, 78, 80, 82; WhoAmP 73; WhoGov 72; WhoWest 74*

Rhodes, Samuel
[The Julliard String Quartet]
American. Musician
b. Feb 13, 1941 in Long Beach, New York
Source: *WhoAm 74, 76, 78, 80, 82*

Rhys, Jean
English. Author
Wrote *After Leaving Mr. MacKenzie,* 1931; *Good Morning, Midnight,* 1939.
b. Aug 24, 1894 in Roseau, West Indies
d. May 14, 1979 in Exeter, England
Source: *CnMWL; ConAu 25R, 85; ConLC 2, 4, 6, 14; ConNov 72, 76; CurBio 72, 79; EncWL; IntAu&W 76, 77; LongCTC; ModBrL SUP; NewYTBS 78, 79; Pen ENG; Who 74; WhoTwCL; WorAu; WrDr 76, 80*

Ribbentrop, Joachim von
German. Nazi Diplomat
b. Apr 30, 1893 in Wesel, Germany
d. Oct 16, 1946 in Nuremberg, Germany
Source: *CurBio 41, 46; LongCTC; REn*

Ribera, Jusepe (Jose) de
"Lo Spagnoletto"
Spanish. Artist
b. Feb 17, 1590 in Jativa, Spain
d. Sep 2, 1652 in Naples, Italy
Source: *AtlBL; NewCol 75; WebBD 80*

Ribicoff, Abraham Alexander
American. Politician
b. Apr 9, 1910 in New Britain, Connecticut
Source: *BiDrAC; BiDrUSE; CelR 73; CngDr 74; CurBio 55; IntWW 74; WhoAm 74, 76, 78, 80, 82; WhoAmP 73; WhoE 74; WhoGov 72; WhoWor 74; WhoWorJ 72*

Ricardo, David
English. Author, Economist
b. Apr 19, 1772 in London, England
d. Sep 11, 1823 in Gatcomb Park, England
Source: *Alli; BbD; BiD&SB; BiDLA; BrAu 19; CasWL; Chambr 2; DcEnA; DcEnL; DcEuL; DcLEL; EvLB; NewC; OxEng; REn; WebE&AL*

Riccardo, John Joseph
American. Automotive Executive
President, Chrysler Corp., 1970-79.
b. Jul 2, 1924 in Little Falls, New York
Source: *WhoAm 78*

Ricci, Matteo
Italian. Missionary
b. 1552
d. 1610
Source: *NewCol 75; WebBD 80*

Ricci, Nina
[Marie Nielli]
French. Designer, Perfumer
Fashion house opened in 1932; signature perfume is *L'Air du Temps.*
b. 1883 in Turin, Italy
d. Nov 29, 1970 in Paris, France
Source: *NewYTBE 70; WhoFash; WorFshn*

Ricci, Ruggiero
American. Musician
b. Jul 24, 1920 in San Francisco, California
Source: *IntWW 74; WhoAm 74, 76, 78, 80, 82; WhoE 74; WhoMus 72; WhoWor 74*

Rice, Alice Caldwell Hegan
American. Author
b. Jan 11, 1870 in Shelbyville, Kentucky
d. Feb 10, 1942 in Louisville, Kentucky
Source: *AmAu&B; AmLY; BiDSA; CarSB; ChPo; CnDAL; ConAmL; DcAmAu; DcAmB S3; DcBiA; DcNAA; EvLB; InWom; LongCTC; NotAW; OxAmL; REn; REnAL; TwCA, SUP; TwCW; WhAm 1; WhNAA*

Rice, Anne
American. Author
Wrote *Interview with a Vampire, The Feast of All Saints.*
b. Oct 4, 1941 in New Orleans, Louisiana
Source: *ConAu 65; WrDr 80*

Rice, Cale Young
American. Poet, Author
b. Dec 7, 1872 in Dixon, Kentucky
d. Jan 23, 1943 in Louisville, Kentucky
Source: *AmAu&B; AmLY; BiDSA; ChPo, S1, S2; DcAmAu; DcNAA; LongCTC; REnAL; TwCA, SUP; WhAm 2; WhNAA*

Rice, Craig
American. Author
b. Jun 5, 1908 in Chicago, Illinois
d. Aug 28, 1957 in Los Angeles, California
Source: *EncMys; WhAm 3*

Rice, Elmer
[Elmer Leopold Reizenstein]
American. Dramatist
b. Sep 28, 1892 in New York, New York
d. May 8, 1967 in Southampton, England
Source: *AmAu&B; AmNov; AmSCAP 66; CasWL; CnDAL; CnMD; CnThe; ConAmA; ConAu 21R, 25R; ConAu P-2; ConLC 7; CyWA; DcLEL; EncWL; EvLB; FilmgC; LongCTC; McGEWD; ModAL; ModWD; OxAmL; OxEng; OxThe; Pen AM; REn; REnAL; REnWD; TwCA, SUP; TwCW; WebE&AL; WhAm 4; WhNAA; WhoTwCL*

Rice, (Henry) Grantland
American. Sportswriter, Poet
b. Nov 1, 1880 in Murfreesboro, Tennessee
d. Jul 13, 1954 in New York, New York
Source: *AmAu&B; BiDSA; ChPo, S1; CurBio 41, 54; DcAmB S5; REnAL; WebAB; WhAm 3; WhScrn 74, 77; WhoHol B*

Rice, Jim (James Edgar)
American. Baseball Player
b. Mar 8, 1953 in Anderson, South Carolina
Source: *BaseEn; BioIn 11*

Rice, "Sam" (Edgar Charles)
American. Baseball Player
b. Feb 20, 1892 in Morocco, Indiana
d. Oct 13, 1974 in Rossmoor, Maryland
Source: *BaseEn; NewYTBS 74; WhoProB 73*

Rice, Thomas Dartmouth
"Jim Crow"
American. Vaudeville Actor
b. May 20, 1808 in New York, New York
d. Sep 19, 1860 in New York, New York
Source: *AmAu&B; AmBi; ApCAB; BiDAmM; BioIn 3, 6, 11; DcAmB; Drake; EncAAH; FamA&A; NatCAB 11; NotNAT B; OxThe; PlP&P; REnAL; WebAB; WhAm H*

Rice, Tim(othy Miles Bindon)
English. Librettist
b. Nov 10, 1944 in Amersham, England
Source: *BioIn 9; ConAu 103; ConDr 73, 77D; LinLib L; NewYTBE 71; WhoAm 74, 76, 78, 80, 82; WhoThe 77; WhoWor 74, 76*

Rice-Davies, Mandy
English. Actress, Former Call Girl
b. 1944
Source: *BioIn 9, 10*

Rich, Adam
American. Actor
Played Nicholas Bradford on TV series "Eight is Enough."
b. Oct 12, 1968 in Brooklyn, New York
Source: *BioIn 11*

Rich, Adrienne
American. Poet
b. May 16, 1929 in Baltimore, Maryland
Source: *ConAu 9R; ConLC 3, 6; ConP 70, 75; CroCAP; DrAP 75; ModAL, SUP; Pen AM; RAdv 1; WorAu; WrDr 76*

Rich, "Buddy" (Bernard)
American. Jazz Musician
b. Jun 30, 1917 in New York, New York
Source: *CurBio 73; NewYTBS 74; WhoAm 74, 76, 78, 80, 82; WhoJazz 72*

Rich, Charlie (Charles Allan)
"The Silver Fox"
American. Musician, Singer
b. Dec 14, 1932 in Forrest City, Arkansas
Source: *BioNews 74; BkPepl; WhoAm 78, 80, 82*

Rich, Irene
American. Actress
b. Oct 13, 1897 in Buffalo, New York
Source: *Film 1; FilmgC; InWom; IntMPA 75, 76, 77, 78, 79, 80, 81, 82; MotPP; MovMk; ThFT; TwYS; WhoHol A*

Rich, Lee
American. President of Lorimar Productions
b. in Cleveland, Ohio
Source: *NewYTET; WhoAm 82*

Richard I
[Richard the Lionhearted]
English. King
Subject of many legends of chivalry; reigned, 1189-99.
b. Sep 8, 1157 in Oxford, England
d. Apr 6, 1199 in Chaluz, France
Source: *Alli; CasWL; McGEWB; NewC; NewCol 75; REn; WebBD 80; WorAl*

Richard II
English. King
b. 1367 in Bordeaux, France
d. 1400 in Leicester, England
Source: *NewCol 75; WebBD 80*

Richard III
English. King
b. Oct 2, 1452 in Fotheringay Castle, England
d. Aug 22, 1485 in Leicester, England
Source: *McGEWB; NewC; NewCol 75; REn; WebBD 80*

Richard, Duke of York
English. Nobleman
b. 1411
d. 1460 in Wakefield, England
Source: *Alli; NewCol 75*

Richard, Cliff
[Harry Roger Webb]
British. Singer
b. Oct 14, 1940 in Lucknow, India
Source: *ConMuA 80; IlEncRk; RkOn 2; WhoRock 81*

Richard, Gabriel
French. Priest, Educator, Printer
b. Oct 15, 1767 in Saintes, France
d. Sep 13, 1832 in Detroit, Michigan
Source: *ApCAB; BiAuS; BiDrAC; DcAmB; Drake; WhAm H*

Richard, Henri
"Pocket Rocket"
Canadian. Hockey Player
b. Feb 29, 1936 in Montreal, PQ
Source: *WhoAm 74; WhoHcky 73*

Richard, J(ames) R(odney)
American. Baseball Player
b. Mar 7, 1950 in Vienna, Louisiana
Source: *BaseEn; BioIn 11, 12; WhoAm 82; WhoProB 73*

Richard, Keith
[The Rolling Stones]
English. Musician, Singer
b. Dec 18, 1943 in Dartford, England
Source: *CelR 73; WhoAm 80, 82*

Richard, "Rocket" (Maurice Joseph Henri)
Canadian. Hockey Player
With Montreal Canadiens, 1942-60; scored 544 career goals.
b. Aug 4, 1921 in Montreal, PQ
Source: *CurBio 58; WorAl*

Richards, Ellen Henrietta Swallow
American. Chemist, Home Economist
b. Dec 3, 1842 in Dunstable, Massachusetts
d. 1911 in Jamaica Plain, Massachusetts
Source: *Alli SUP; AmBi; AmWom; ApCAB; DcAmAu; DcAmB; DcNAA; HerW; InWom; NotAW; TwCBDA; WhAm 1*

Richards, Ivor Armstrong
English. Literary Critic
b. Feb 26, 1893 in Sandbach, England
d. Sep 7, 1979 in Cambridge, England
Source: *AmAu&B; CasWL; Chambr 3; ConAu 41R, 89; ConP 75; DcLEL; DrAP 75; EncWL; EvLB; IntWW 74; LongCTC; ModBrL, SUP; NewC; OxAmL; OxEng; Pen ENG; RAdv 1; REn; TwCA, SUP; TwCW; WebAB; WebE&AL; Who 74; WhoAm 74; WhoLA; WrDr 76*

Richards, Rene
[Richard Raskind]
American. Tennis Player, Transsexual
b. Aug 19, 1934
Source: *BioIn 11*

Richards, Richard
American. Republican Party Official
Appointed GOP Chairman by President Reagan.
b. May 14, 1932 in Ogden, Utah
Source: *NewYTBS 81; WhoAmP 73, 75, 77, 79*

Richards, Rod
see: Rare Earth

Richards, Stanley
American. Dramatist, Author
b. Apr 23, 1918 in Brooklyn, New York
d. Jul 26, 1980 in New York, New York
Source: *ConAu 25R; IntMPA 75, 77; OxCan; WhoE 74*

Richards, William Trost
American. Artist
b. Nov 14, 1838 in Philadelphia, Pennsylvania
d. 1905 in Newport, Rhode Island
Source: *AmBi; ApCAB; DcAmB; EarABI; TwCBDA; WhAm 1*

Richardson, Bobby (Robert Clinton)
American. Baseball Player, Coach
b. Aug 19, 1935 in Sumter, South Carolina
Source: *BaseEn; CurBio 66; WhoProB 73*

Richardson, Dorothy Miller
English. Author
b. May 17, 1873 in Abingdon, England
d. Jun 17, 1957 in Beckenham, England
Source: *AmAu&B; CasWL; Chambr 3; CyWA; DcLEL; EncWL; EvLB; LongCTC; ModBrL, SUP; NewC; OxEng; Pen ENG; RAdv 1; REn; TwCA, SUP; TwCW; WebE&AL; WhoLA*

Richardson, Elliot Lee
American. Government Official
Govt. posts include Secretary of HEW, Defense, Commerce.
b. Jul 20, 1920 in Boston, Massachusetts
Source: *BiDrUSE; BioNews 74; CelR 73; IntWW 74; NewYTBE 72, 73; WhoAm 74; WhoAmP 73; WhoGov 72; WhoS&SW 73; WorAl*

Richardson, Henry Handel, pseud.
[Ethel Florence Lindsey Richardson; Henrietta Richardson Robertson]
Australian. Author
b. Jan 3, 1870 in Melbourne, Australia
d. Mar 20, 1946 in Hastings, England
Source: *CasWL; CyWA; DcLEL; EncWL; EvLB; LongCTC; NewC; OxEng; Pen ENG; REn; TwCA, SUP; TwCW; WebE&AL; WhoTwCL*

Richardson, Henry Hobson
American. Architect
b. Sep 29, 1838 in Saint James, Louisiana
d. Apr 27, 1886 in Brookline, Massachusetts
Source: *AmBi; DcAmB; EncAB-H; McGEWB; WebAB; WhAm H*

Richardson, Jack
American. Author, Dramatist
b. Feb 18, 1935 in New York, New York
Source: *AmAu&B; BiE&WWA; CnMD; CnThe; ConAu 5R; ConDr 73; CroCD; McGEWD; ModWD; NotNAT; Pen AM; REnWD; WorAu; WrDr 76*

Richardson, Lee
[Lee David Richard]
American. Actor
b. Sep 11, 1926 in Chicago, Illinois
Source: *BiE&WWA; NotNAT; WhoAm 82; WhoE 74*

Richardson, Sir Ralph David
English. Actor
b. Dec 19, 1902 in Cheltenham, England
Source: *BiDFilm; BiE&WWA; CelR 73; CurBio 50; FamA&A; FilmgC; IntMPA 75, 76, 77, 78, 79, 80, 81, 82; IntWW 74; MovMk; NotNAT; OxFilm; OxThe; Who 74; WhoThe 77; WhoWor 74; WorEFlm*

Richardson, Samuel
English. Author
b. 1689 in Derbyshire, England
d. Jul 4, 1761 in London, England
Source: *Alli; AtlBL; BbD; BiD&SB; BrAu; CasWL; Chambr 2; CrtT 2; CyWA; DcBiA; DcEnA, AP; DcEnL; DcEuL; DcLEL; EvLB; MouLC 2; NewC; OxEng; OxGer; Pen ENG; RAdv 1; REn; WebE&AL*

Richardson, S(tanley) D(ennis)
English. Author
b. Mar 28, 1925 in Spalding, England
Source: *ConAu 21R*

Richardson, Scovel
American. Judge
b. Feb 4, 1912 in Nashville, Tennessee
d. Mar 30, 1982 in New Rochelle, New York
Source: *NewYTBS 82; WhoAm 74, 76, 78, 80, 82; WhoBlA 75; WhoGov 72*

Richardson, Sid
American. Oil Magnate
b. Apr 25, 1891 in Athens, Texas
d. Sep 29, 1959
Source: *BioIn 3, 4, 5; WhAm 3, 4*

Richardson, Susan
American. Actress
Played Susan Bradford on TV series "Eight is Enough."
b. 1954
Source: *BioIn 11*

Richardson, Tony
English. Motion Picture Producer, Director
b. Jun 5, 1929 in Shipley, England
Source: *BiDFilm; BiE&WWA; CurBio 63; DcFM; FilmgC; IntMPA 75, 76, 77, 78, 79, 80, 81, 82; IntWW 74; MovMk; NewC; NotNAT; OxFilm; Who 74; WhoThe 77; WhoWor 74; WorEFlm*

Richelieu, Armand Jean du Plessis, Cardinal
[Jean du Plessis, Duc de Armand]
French. Statesman
Chief minister to Louis XIII; Roman catholic cardinal.
b. Sep 9, 1585 in Paris, France
d. Dec 4, 1642 in Paris, France
Source: *BiD&SB; BioIn 1, 2, 3, 4, 5, 6, 7, 8, 9, 10, 11; NewC; NewCol 75; OxFr; OxThe; REn; WorAl*

Richelieu, Louis Francois Armand de
French. Soldier, Diplomat
b. 1696
d. 1788
Source: *BioIn 7; WebBD 80*

Richie, Lionel
[The Commodores]
American. Singer
Sang hit "Truly," 1982; wrote "Lady," sung by Kenny Rogers.
b. 1950 in Tuskegee, Alabama
Source: *BioIn 12; BkPepl; WhoAm 82*

Richler, Mordecai
Canadian. Author
Wrote *The Apprenticeship of Duddy Kravitz,* 1959; filmed, 1974.
b. Jan 27, 1931 in Montreal, PQ
Source: *Au&Wr 71; AuNews 1; BioNews 75; CanWW 82; CanWr; CasWL; ConAu 65; ConLC 3, 5, 9, 13, 18; ConNov 72, 76; CreCan 1; EncWL; IntWW 74; OxCan, SUP; Pen ENG; REnAL; TwCW; WebE&AL; Who 74; WhoAm 82; WhoTwCL; WhoWor 74; WorAu; WrDr 76*

Richman, Charles
American. Actor
b. Jan 12, 1870 in Chicago, Illinois
d. Dec 1, 1940 in Bronx, New York
Source: *CurBio 41; Vers B; WhScrn 74, 77; WhoStg 1906, 1908*

Richman, Harry
American. Musician
b. Aug 10, 1895 in Cincinnati, Ohio
d. Nov 3, 1972 in Burbank, California
Source: *AmSCAP 66; BiE&WWA; EncMT; NewYTBE 72; WhScrn 77; WhoHol B; WhoWorJ 72*

Richrath, Gary
see: REO Speedwagon

Richter, Charles
American. Inventor
Invented Richter Scale, 1935, to determine severity of earthquakes.
b. Apr 26, 1900 in Hamilton, Ohio
Source: *AmM&WS 73P; CelR 73; NewYTBE 71; WhoAm 74, 76, 78, 80, 82; WhoWest 74*

Richter, Conrad Michael
American. Author
Won 1951 Pulitzer Prize for *The Town.*
b. Nov 13, 1890 in Pine Grove, Pennsylvania
d. Oct 30, 1968 in Pottsville, Pennsylvania
Source: *AmAu&B; AmNov; CnDAL; ConAu 5R, 25R; CurBio 51, 68; CyWA; DcLEL; ModAL; OxAmL; Pen AM; RAdv 1; REn; REnAL; SmATA 3; TwCA, SUP; WhAm 5; WhNAA*

Richter, Hans
Hungarian. Conductor
b. Apr 4, 1843 in Raab, Hungary
d. Dec 5, 1916 in Bayreuth, Germany
Source: *NewEOp 71; OxMus; WebBD 80*

Richter, Hans
German. Filmmaker
b. 1888 in Berlin, Germany
d. Feb 1, 1976 in Locarno, Switzerland
Source: *DcFM; FilmgC; MovMk; OxFilm; WorEFlm*

Richter, Jean Paul F
German. Author
b. Mar 21, 1763 in Wunsiedel, Bavaria
d. Nov 14, 1825 in Bayreuth, Germany
Source: *AtlBL; BiD&SB; DcBiA; REn*

Richter, Karl
German. Musician, Conductor
b. Oct 15, 1926 in Plauen, Germany
d. Feb 16, 1981 in Munich, Germany (West)
Source: *BioIn 2; IntWW 74, 75, 76, 77, 78; NewYTBS 81; WhoWor 74, 78*

Richter, Sviatoslav Theofilovich
Russian. Musician
b. 1915 in Zhitomir, Russia
Source: *CurBio 61; Who 74; WhoMus 72; WhoWor 74*

Richthofen, Manfred von, Baron
"The Red Baron"
German. World War I Aviator
Credited with shooting down 80 enemy aircraft; killed in action.
b. May 2, 1892 in Breslau, Germany
d. Apr 21, 1918 in France
Source: *BioIn 3, 4, 6, 7, 8, 9, 10; BioNews; Chambr 1; WorAl*

Richthofen Family
German. Authors
Source: *BioIn 10*

Rickenbacker, Eddie (Edward Vernon)
American. Aviator
Won Medal of Honor in WW I; head of Eastern Airlines, 1938-63.
b. Oct 8, 1890 in Columbus, Ohio
d. Jul 23, 1973 in Zurich, Switzerland
Source: *AmAu&B; ConAu 41R, 101; CurBio 40, 52, 73; OhA&B; WebAB; WhAm 5; WorAl*

Ricketts, Howard T
American. Scientist, Physician, Engineer
b. 1871 in Findlay, Ohio
d. May 3, 1910 in Mexico City, Mexico
Source: *DcAmB S1; DcNAA*

Rickey, George Warren
American. Sculptor
b. Jun 6, 1907 in South Bend, Indiana
Source: *BioIn 7, 8; BnEnAmA; CurBio 80; WhoAm 82*

Rickey, (Wesley) Branch
"The Mahatma"
American. Baseball Player, Manager
Signed Jackie Robinson, 1946, breaking color barrier.
b. Dec 20, 1881 in Stockdale, Ohio
d. Dec 9, 1965 in Columbia, Missouri
Source: *BaseEn; CurBio 45, 66; EncAB-H; WebAB; WhAm 4; WhoProB 73; WorAl*

Rickles, Don
American. Comedian
Well-known for comedy style based on insults.
b. May 8, 1926 in New York, New York
Source: *BioNews 75; CelR 73; FilmgC; WhoAm 74, 76, 78, 80, 82; WhoHol A*

Rickover, Hyman George
"Father of the Atomic Submarine"
American. Navy Admiral
Supervised construction of first nuclear submarine, *Nautilus,* 1947-54.
b. Jan 27, 1900 in Makow, Poland
Source: *AmAu&B; CelR 73; CurBio 53; IntWW 74; WebAB; WhoAm 74; WhoGov 72; WhoWor 74; WhoWorJ 72*

Rickword, (John) Edgell
English. Poet, Editor
b. Oct 22, 1898 in Colchester, England
d. Mar 15, 1982
Source: *BioIn 10; ConAu 101, 106*

Ricordi, Giovanni
Italian. Music Publisher
b. 1785
d. 1853
Source: *NewEOp 71; WebBD 80*

Ridder, Bernard Herman
American. Newspaper Publisher
b. Mar 20, 1883 in New York, New York
d. May 5, 1975 in West Palm Beach, Florida
Source: *St&PR 75; WhAm 6*

Riddle, Nelson
American. Musician, Composer
b. Jun 1, 1921 in Oradell, New Jersey
Source: *FilmgC; WhoAm 74, 76, 78, 80, 82*

Ride, Sally K
American. First Woman Astronaut
b. May 26, 1951 in Los Angeles, California
Source: *NF*

Ridgway, Matthew Bunker
American. General
b. Mar 3, 1895 in Fort Monroe, Virginia
Source: *IntWW 74; Who 74; WhoAm 74; WhoWor 74; WrDr 76*

Riding, Laura
[Laura Riding Jackson]
American. Poet, Critic
b. Jan 16, 1901 in New York, New York
Source: *AmAu&B; ChPo, S1; CnDAL; CnE&AP; ConAmA; ConAu 65; ConLC 3, 7; ConP 70; DcLEL; EvLB; InWom; IntWW 74; LongCTC; OxAmL; Pen AM; RAdv 1; REnAL; SixAP; TwCA, SUP; WhNAA; Who 74; WhoTwCL; WrDr 76*

Ridley, Gregory
see: Humble Pie

Riefenstahl, Leni
German. Actress, Motion Picture Director
b. Aug 22, 1902 in Berlin, Germany
Source: *BiDFilm; DcFM; FilmgC; OxFilm; WhoHol A; WhoWor 74; WorEFlm*

Riegger, Wallingford
American. Composer
b. Apr 29, 1885 in Albany, Georgia
d. Apr 2, 1961 in New York, New York
Source: *DcCM; WhAm 4*

Riegle, Donald Wayne, Jr.
American. Senator
b. Feb 4, 1938 in Flint, Michigan
Source: *BioIn 10; WhoAm 78, 80, 82*

Riel, Louis David
Canadian. Leader of Metis Rebellions
Led Indian rebellions against govt. land threats, 1870, 1885; hanged for treason.
b. Oct 23, 1844 in Saint Boniface, MB
d. Nov 16, 1885 in Regina, SK
Source: *ApCAB; BioIn 1, 3, 4, 5, 7, 8, 9, 10, 11; DcNAA; MacDCB 78; NewCol 75; REnAW; WhAm H*

Rienow, Robert
American. Educator
b. Dec 4, 1909 in Grafton, Wisconsin
Source: *AmM&WS 73S; ConAu 21R*

Riesel, Victor
American. Journalist, Commentator
b. 1917 in New York, New York
Source: *WhoAm 74; WhoGov 72; WhoWor 74*

Riessen, Marty (Martin Clare)
American. Tennis Player
b. Dec 4, 1941 in Hinsdale, Illinois
Source: *ConAu 41R; OfEnT*

Rigby, Bob
American. Soccer Player
b. Jul 3, 1951 in Ridley Park, Pennsylvania
Source: *AmEnS*

Rigby, Cathy
[Mrs. Tommy Mason]
American. Gymnast
b. 1952
Source: *BioIn 9, 10, 11; BioNews 74; HerW; NewYTBE 72*

Rigg, Diana
English. Actress
Played Emma Peel on TV series "The Avengers," 1965-68.
b. Jul 20, 1938 in Yorkshire, England
Source: *CelR 73; CurBio 74; FilmgC; IntMPA 75, 76, 77, 78, 79, 80, 81, 82; MotPP; PlP&P; Who 82; WhoHol A; WhoThe 77; WorAl*

Riggs, Bobby (Robert Larimore)
American. Tennis Player
Defeated by Billie Jean King in the "Match of the Century," 1973.
b. Feb 25, 1918 in Los Angeles, California
Source: *CurBio 49; NewYTBE 73; WorAl*

Riggs, Lynn
American. Dramatist
b. Aug 31, 1899 in Claremore, Oklahoma
d. Jun 30, 1954 in New York, New York
Source: *AmAu&B; CnDAL; CnMD; ConAmA; CyWA; McGEWD; ModWD; OxAmL; REn; REnAL; TwCA, SUP*

Righetti, Dave (David Allan)
American. Baseball Player
b. Nov 28, 1958 in San Jose, California
Source: *BaseEn; BioIn 11*

Righteous Brothers, The
[Bobby Hatfield; Bill Medley]
American. Vocal Group
Source: *EncPR&S*

Righter, Carroll
American. Astrologer
Hollywood columnist on astrology since 1939.
b. Feb 1, 1900 in Salem, New Jersey
Source: *CelR 73; CurBio 72*

Riis, Jacob August
American. Journalist, Writer
b. May 3, 1849 in Ribe, Denmark
d. May 26, 1914 in Barre, Massachusetts
Source: *AmAu&B; AmBi; BbD; BiD&SB; DcAmAu; DcAmB; DcNAA; EncAB-H; OxAmL; REn; REnAL; WebAB; WhAm 1*

Rikhoff, Jean
American. Children's Author
b. May 28, 1928 in Chicago, Illinois
Source: *ConAu 61; SmATA 9*

Riklis, Mishulam
American. Financier
b. Dec 2, 1924 in Istanbul, Turkey
Source: *BioIn 4, 5, 6, 7, 8, 9, 10, 11; CurBio 71; IntWW 74; WhoAm 74, 76, 78, 80, 82; WhoE 74; WhoF&I 74*

Riles, Wilson C
American. Educator
b. Jun 27, 1917 in Alexandria, Louisiana
Source: *CurBio 71; LEduc 74; NewYTBE 70; WhoAm 82; WhoAmP 73; WhoBlA 75; WhoWest 74*

Riley, Bridget
English. Artist
b. Apr 24, 1931 in London, England
Source: *IntWW 74; Who 74; WhoWor 74*

Riley, James
"Doc Middleton"
American. Outlaw
b. 1851
d. 1913
Source: *BioIn 10*

Riley, James Whitcomb
"Hoosier Poet"
American. Poet
Wrote poems *Little Orphant Annie; The Raggedy Man.*
b. Oct 7, 1849 in Greenfield, Indiana
d. Jul 22, 1916 in Indianapolis, Indiana
Source: *Alli SUP; AmAu; AmAu&B; AmBi; AmSCAP 66; BbD; BiD&SB; BlkAW; CarSB; CasWL; Chambr 3; ChPo, S1, S2; CnDAL; DcAmAu; DcAmB; DcEnA AP; DcLEL; DcNAA; EvLB; IndAu 1816; JBA 34; LongCTC; OxAmL; Pen AM; RAdv 1; REn; REnAL; Str&VC; WebAB; WorAl*

Riley, Jeannie C
[Jeannie C Stephenson]
American. Singer
b. Oct 19, 1945 in Anson, Texas
Source: *RkOn; WhoAm 82; WhoS&SW 73*

Rilke, Rainer Maria
German. Poet
b. Dec 4, 1876 in Prague, Czechoslovakia
d. Dec 29, 1926 in Muzot, Switzerland
Source: *AtlBL; CasWL; ClDMEL; CnMWL; CyWA; EncWL; EvEuW; LongCTC; ModGL; OxEng; Pen EUR; RComWL; REn; TwCA, SUP; TwCW; WhAm 4A; WhoTwCL*

Rillieux, Norbert
American. Engineer
b. 1806
d. 1894
Source: *BioIn 4, 6, 8, 9, 10, 11*

Rimbaud, (Jean Nicolas) Arthur
French. Poet
Wrote only from ages 16-19; great influence on Symbolist movement.
b. Oct 20, 1854 in Charlesville, France
d. Nov 10, 1891 in Marseilles, France
Source: *AtlBL; CasWL; ChPo; ClDMEL; CyWA; DcEuL; EuAu; EvEuW; LongCTC; ModRL; OxEng; OxFr; Pen EUR; RComWL; REn; WorAl*

Rimmer, William
American. Sculptor
b. Feb 20, 1816 in Liverpool, England
d. Aug 20, 1879 in Boston, Massachusetts
Source: *Alli SUP; AmBi; ApCAB; DcAmAu; DcAmB; OxAmL; REnAL; WebAB; WhAm H*

Rimsky-Korsakov, Nikolai
Russian. Composer
Wrote opera *The Snow Maiden,* 1881.
b. Mar 18, 1844 in Tikhvin, Russia
d. Jun 21, 1908 in Saint Petersburg, Russia
Source: *AtlBL; NewCol 75; REn; WorAl*

Rinaldi, Kathy
American. Tennis Player
b. 1967 in Stuart, Florida
Source: *BioIn 12*

Rindt, Jochen
Austrian. Auto Racer
b. Apr 18, 1942 in Germany
d. Sep 5, 1970 in Italy
Source: *BioIn 9, 10*

Rinehart, Frederick Roberts
American. Publisher
b. 1903 in Allegheny, Pennsylvania
d. Jun 15, 1981 in New York, New York
Source: *ConAu 104; NewYTBS 81*

Rinehart, Mary Roberts
American. Author, Dramatist
b. Aug 12, 1876 in Pittsburgh, Pennsylvania
d. Sep 22, 1958 in New York, New York
Source: *AmAu&B; AmNov; ConAmL; DcBiA; DcLEL; EncMys; EvLB; InWom; LongCTC; ModWD; OxAmL; Pen AM; REn; REnAL; TwCA, SUP; TwCW; WebAB; WhAm 3; WhNAA; WomWWA 14*

Rinehart, Stanley Marshall, Jr.
American. Publisher
President, Farrar and Rinehart, 1902-29, Rinehart and Co., Inc, 1929-60.
b. Aug 18, 1897 in Pittsburgh, Pennsylvania
d. Apr 26, 1969 in South Miami, Florida
Source: *ConAu 29R; CurBio 54; WhAm 5*

Rinehart, William H
American. Sculptor
b. Sep 13, 1825 in Union Bridge, Maryland
d. Oct 28, 1874 in Rome, Italy
Source: *AmBi; ApCAB; DcAmB; TwCBDA; WhAm H*

Ring, Blanche
American. Actress, Singer
b. Apr 24, 1872 in Boston, Massachusetts
d. Jan 13, 1961 in Santa Monica, California
Source: *EncMT; Film 1; InWom; WhAm 4; WhScrn 74, 77; WhoHol B; WhoStg 1908*

Ringer, Robert J
American. Author
b. 1938
Source: *BioIn 10; ConAu 81*

Ringling, Albert C
[Ringling Brothers]
American. Circus Owner
b. 1852
d. 1916
Source: *BioIn 1; WebBD 80*

Ringling, Alfred T
[Ringling Brothers]
American. Circus Owner
b. 1861
d. 1919
Source: *WebBD 80*

Ringling, Charles
[Ringling Brothers]
American. Circus Owner
b. Dec 2, 1863 in McGregor, Iowa
d. Dec 3, 1926 in Sarasota, Florida
Source: *DcAmB; WebAB; WhAm HA, 4*

Ringling, John
[Ringling Brothers]
American. Circus Owner
b. 1866 in Baraboo, Wisconsin
d. Dec 3, 1936 in Sarasota, Florida
Source: *WhAm 1*

Ringling, Otto
[Ringling Brothers]
American. Circus Owner
b. 1858
d. 1911
Source: *WebBD 80*

Ringo, John(ny)
American. Outlaw
Idealized figure of "gentleman outlaw."
b. 1844?
d. Jul 14, 1882
Source: *BioIn 11; REnAW*

Rinkoff, Barbara Jean
American. Children's Author
b. Jan 25, 1923 in New York, New York
d. Feb 18, 1975 in Mount Kisco, New York
Source: *AuBYP; ConAu 21R, 57; ConAu P-2; MorBMP; SmATA 46; WhAm 6*

Rinuccini, Ottavio
Italian. Poet, Librettist
b. Jan 20, 1562 in Florence, Italy
d. Mar 28, 1621 in Florence, Italy
Source: *BiD&SB; CasWL; EvEuW; REn*

Riopelle, Jean-Paul
Canadian. Artist
b. 1923 in Montreal, PQ
Source: *CanWW 70, 79; ConArt; CreCan 1; IntWW 74, 75, 76, 77, 78; McGDA; WhoAm 74; WhoWor 74*

Riordan, Bill
American. Manager of Jimmy Connors
b. 1925
Source: *BioIn 10, 11*

Rios Montt, Jose Efrain
Guatemalan. President
General who came to power in bloodless coup, Mar, 1982.
b. 1927?
Source: *WorDWW*

Riperton, Minnie
American. Singer
b. Nov 8, 1948 in Chicago, Illinois
d. Jul 12, 1979 in Los Angeles, California
Source: *BioIn 11; DcBlPA; NewYTBS 79; RkOn 2; WhoBlA 77; WhoRock 81*

Ripley, Elmer Horton
"Rip"
American. Basketball Player, Coach
b. 1891 in Staten Island, New York
d. Apr 29, 1982 in New York, New York
Source: *NewYTBS 82; WhoBbl 73*

Ripley, George
American. Author
Founded *The Dial, Harper's New Monthly Magazine.*
b. Oct 3, 1802 in Greenfield, Massachusetts
d. Jul 4, 1880 in New York, New York
Source: *Alli; AmAu; AmAu&B; AmBi; ApCAB; BiD&SB; CasWL; Chambr 3; CnDAL; CyAl 2; DcAmAu; DcAmB; DcEnL; DcLEL; DcNAA; EncAB-H; OxAmL; Pen AM; REn; REnAL; TwCBDA; WebAB; WhAm H; WorAl*

Ripley, Robert Leroy
American. Cartoonist, Author
First published *Believe it or Not* cartoons, 1918.
b. Dec 25, 1893 in Santa Rosa, California
d. May 27, 1949 in New York, New York
Source: *Alli; AmAu&B; ChPo S2; CurBio 45, 49; DcAmB S4; OxAmL; REnAL; WebAB; WhAm 2; WhScrn 74, 77; WhoHol B*

Rippy, Rodney Allen
American. Actor
b. 1968
Source: *BioIn 10, 11; WhoHol A*

Risdon, Elizabeth
American. Actress
b. Apr 26, 1888 in London, England
d. Dec 20, 1956 in Santa Monica, California
Source: *Film 1; FilmgC; MotPP; MovMk; ThFT; Vers A; WhScrn 74, 77; WhoHol B*

Ritaof Cascia, Saint
Italian. Religious Figure
b. 1381
d. 1457
Source: *BioIn 2, 3, 4, 6, 7, 10*

Ritchard, Cyril
Australian. Actor, Motion Picture Director
b. Dec 1, 1897 in Sydney, Australia
d. Dec 18, 1977 in Chicago, Illinois
Source: *BiE&WWA; ChPo; CurBio 57; EncMT; FilmgC; NewC; NotNAT; Who 74; WhoAm 74; WhoHol A; WhoThe 77; WhoWor 74*

Ritchie, Jean
American. Singer, Author
b. Dec 8, 1922 in Viper, Kentucky
Source: *AmSCAP 66; CurBio 59; EncFCWM 69; InWom*

Ritchie, Thomas
American. Journalist
b. Nov 5, 1778 in Tappahannock, Virginia
d. Dec 3, 1854 in Washington, DC
Source: *Alli; AmBi; ApCAB; BiAuS; DcAmB; Drake; WhAm H*

Ritchie-Calder, Peter Ritchie Ritchie-Calder, Baron
Scottish. Author, Journalist
b. Jul 1, 1906 in Forfar, Scotland
d. Jan 31, 1982
Source: *ConAu 4NR; IntAu&W 76, 77; IntWW 75, 76, 77, 78; NewYTBS 82; Who 74; WhoWor 74, 76, 78; WorAu; WrDr 76, 80*

Ritchie Blackmore's Rainbow
see: Blackmore, Ritchie

Ritchie Family, The
[Cheryl Mason Jacks; Gwendolyn Oliver; Cassandra Ann Wooten]
American. Vocal Group
Source: *BioIn 3; RkOn*

Ritola, Ville
Finnish. Track Athlete
Won five gold medals, 1924, 1928 Olympics.
b. Jan 18, 1896 in Peraseinajoki, Finland
d. Apr 24, 1982 in Helsinki, Finland
Source: *WhoTr&F 73*

Ritt, Martin
American. Motion Picture Director
b. Mar 2, 1920 in New York, New York
Source: *BiDFilm; BiE&WWA; BioNews 74; DcFM; FilmgC; IntMPA 75, 76, 77, 78, 79, 80, 81, 82; IntWW 74; MovMk; NotNAT; OxFilm; WhoAm 74, 76, 78, 80, 82; WhoHol A; WhoWor 74; WorEFlm*

Rittenhouse, David
American. Astronomer, Mathematician
b. Apr 5, 1732 in Germantown, Pennsylvania
d. Jun 26, 1796 in Philadelphia, Pennsylvania
Source: *Alli; AmBi; ApCAB; BiAuS; CyAL 1; DcAmB; Drake; EncAB-H; TwCBDA; WebAB; WhAm H*

Ritter, Blake
American. Singer, Actor
b. 1915
d. 1974
Source: *BioIn 10*

Ritter, John(athan Southworth)
American. Actor
Stars in TV series "Three's Company," 1977--; son of Tex Ritter.
b. Sep 17, 1948 in Burbank, California
Source: *BkPepl; CurBio 80; IntMPA 82; WhoAm 82; WhoHol A*

Ritter, Karl
German. Founded Modern Geography
b. Aug 17, 1779 in Germany
d. Sep 28, 1859
Source: *BioIn 5, 8; McGEWB; NewCol 75; WebBD 80*

Ritter, "Tex" (Woodward Maurice)
American. Singer, Actor
Singing cowboy in over 60 films; won Oscar, 1952, for *High Noon.*
b. Jan 12, 1907 in Murval, Texas
d. Jan 2, 1974 in Nashville, Tennessee
Source: *BioNews 74; EncFCWM 69; FilmgC; NewYTBE 70; NewYTBS 74; WhScrn 77; WhoHol B; WorAl*

Ritter, Thelma
American. Actress
b. Feb 14, 1905 in New York, New York
d. Feb 5, 1969 in New York, New York
Source: *BiDFilm; BiE&WWA; CurBio 57, 74; FilmgC; InWom; MotPP; MovMk; OxFilm; Vers A; WhAm 5; WhScrn 74, 77; WhoHol B; WorEFlm*

Ritz, Cesar
Swiss. Hotelkeeper, Restaurateur
b. 1850
d. 1918
Source: *BioIn 1, 9; WebBD 80*

Ritz Brothers
[Al Ritz; Harry Ritz; Jimmy Ritz]
American. Comedians
Source: *Film 1; FilmgC; MotPP; OxFilm; WhScrn 74, 77; WhoHol B*

Rivera, Chita
American. Singer, Dancer, Comedienne
b. Jan 23, 1933 in Washington, DC
Source: *BiE&WWA; EncMT; NotNAT; WhoAm 82; WhoHol A; WhoThe 77*

Rivera, Diego
Mexican. Artist
Painted murals depitcting peasants, workers; revived fresco technique.
b. Dec 8, 1886 in Guanajuato, Mexico
d. Nov 25, 1957 in Mexico City, Mexico
Source: *AtlBL; CurBio 48, 58; OxAmL; REn; WhAm 3; WorAl*

Rivera, Geraldo
American. Journalist, Lawyer
Correspondent on "20/20"; host "Goodnight America," 1974-78.
b. Jul 4, 1943 in Manhattan, New York
Source: *BioNews 74; CelR 73; IntMPA 82; NewYTBE 71; WhoAm 82; WhoE 74*

Rivera, Pete
see: Rare Earth

Rivers, Joan
[Mrs. Edgar Rosenberg]
American. Comedienne, Author, Director
Co-wrote, directed film *Rabbit Test,* 1977.
b. 1935 in New York, New York
Source: *BkPepl; CelR 73; CurBio 70; WhoAm 74, 76, 78, 80, 82; WhoHol A*

Rivers, Johnny
American. Singer
b. Nov 7, 1942 in New York, New York
Source: *WhoAm 74; WhoBlA 75*

Rivers, Larry
American. Artist
b. Aug 17, 1923 in New York, New York
Source: *CelR 73; CurBio 69; DcCAA 71; WhoAm 74, 76, 78, 80, 82; WhoAmA 73; WhoE 74; WhoWor 74*

Rivers, L(ucius) Mendel
American. Government Official
b. Sep 28, 1905 in Berkeley County, South Carolina
d. Dec 28, 1970 in Birmingham, Alabama
Source: *CurBio 71; NewYTBE 70; WhAm 5*

Rivlin, Alice Mitchell
American. Director of CBO
b. Mar 4, 1931 in Philadelphia, Pennsylvania
Source: *AmEA 74; AmM&WS 73S, 78S; BioIn 10, 11; ConAu 33R; NewYTBS 75; WhoAm 74, 76, 78, 80, 82; WhoAmP 77, 79; WhoAmW 66, 68, 70, 72, 74; WhoGov 77*

Rizal, Jose
Philippine. Patriot
b. 1861 in Calamba, Philippines
d. 1896 in Manila, Philippines
Source: *CasWL; DcOrL 2; NewCol 75; Pen CL; REn*

Rizzo, Frank L
American. Former Mayor of Philadelphia
b. Oct 23, 1920 in Philadelphia, Pennsylvania
Source: *CelR 73; CurBio 73; NewYTBE 71; WhoE 74; WhoGov 72*

Rizzuto, Phil(lip Francis)
"Scooter"
American. Baseball Player, Announcer
b. Sep 25, 1918 in New York, New York
Source: *BaseEn; CurBio 50; WhoAm 82; WhoProB 73*

Roa (y Garcia), Raul
Cuban. Author, Diplomat, Lawyer
b. Apr 18, 1907 in Havana, Cuba
d. Jul 6, 1982 in Havana, Cuba
Source: *BioIn 5, 7, 10; CurBio 73, 82; NewCol 75; NewYTBS 82*

Roach, Hal, Jr.
American. Motion Picture Director
b. 1892 in Elmira, New York
Source: *CmMov; DcFM; FilmgC; IntMPA 75, 76, 78, 80, ; OxFilm; WorEFlm*

Roach, Max(well)
American. Jazz Musician
b. 1925
Source: *BioIn 5, 8, 11; WhoAm 82*

Roark, Garland
American. Author
b. Jul 26, 1904
Source: *AmAu&B; AmNov; ConAu 1R, 1NR; REnAL; WhoS&SW 73*

Robards, Jason
American. Actor
b. Dec 31, 1892 in Hillsdale, Michigan
d. Apr 4, 1963 in Sherman Oaks, California
Source: *FilmgC; IntMPA 82; MotPP; MovMk; TwYS; WhScrn 74, 77; WhoHol B*

Robards, Jason, Jr.
American. Actor
b. Jul 22, 1922 in Chicago, Illinois
Source: *BiE&WWA; BkPepl; CelR 73; CurBio 59; FilmgC; IntMPA 75, 76, 77; MotPP; WhoAm 74, 76, 78, 80, 82; WhoWor 74*

Robb, Charles Spittal
American. Politician
Governor of VA, 1981--; husband of Lynda Bird Johnson.
b. Jun 26, 1939 in Phoenix, Arizona
Source: *WhoAm 82*

Robb, Lynda Bird
see: Johnson, Lynda Bird

Robbe-Grillet, Alain
French. Author, Lecturer
b. Aug 18, 1922 in Brest, France
Source: *Au&Wr 71; CasWL; CnMWL; ConAu 9R; ConLC 1, 2, 4, 6, 8, 10, 14; DcFM; EncWL; EvEuW; FilmgC; IntWW 74; ModRL; OxFilm; Pen EUR; REn; TwCW; Who 74; WhoTwCL; WhoWor 74; WorAu; WorEFlm*

Robbie, Joe (Joseph)
American. Football Team Owner, Lawyer
Founder, president of Miami Dolphins, 1965--.
b. Jul 7, 1916 in Sisseton, South Dakota
Source: *BioNews 74; WhoAm 74; WhoAmP 73; WhoFtbl 74; WhoMW 74; WhoS&SW 73*

Robbins, Frank
American. Cartoonist
b. Sep 9, 1917 in Boston, Massachusetts
Source: *IlsBYP; WhoAmA 73*

Robbins, Harold
American. Author
Wrote *The Carpetbaggers, The Adventurers, The Betsy.*
b. May 21, 1916 in New York, New York
Source: *AmAu&B; AmNov; BkPepl; ConAu 73; ConLC 5; CurBio 70; FilmgC; IntWW 74; TwCW; Who 74; WhoAm 74; WrDr 76*

Robbins, Jerome
American. Choreographer
NY City Ballet, 1949--; Won Tony, Oscar for *West Side Story.*
b. Oct 11, 1918 in New York, New York
Source: *BiE&WWA; CelR 73; CmMov; CurBio 47, 69; EncMT; FilmgC; IntWW 74; NewYTBS 74; NotNAT; OxFilm; PlP&P; WebAB; Who 74; WhoAm 82; WhoThe 77; WhoWor 74; WhoWorJ 72; WorEFlm*

Robbins, Marty
[Martin David Robinson]
American. Singer
Won Grammy, 1959 for "El Paso."
b. Sep 26, 1925 in Glendale, Arizona
d. Dec 8, 1982 in Nashville, Tennessee
Source: *BiDAmM; EncFCWM 69; IlEncCM; RkOn; WhoAm 76, 78, 80, 82; WorAl*

Roberge, Frank
American. Cartoonist
Source: *BioIn 4*

Robert I
[Robert the Bruce]
Scottish. King
b. 1274
d. Jun 1329 in Cardross, Scotland
Source: *BioIn 10; McGEWB; NewCol 75; WebBD 80*

Robert Guiscard
Norwegian. Emperor of Southern Italy
b. 1015
d. 1085
Source: *NewCol 75*

Robert, Hubert
French. Artist
b. 1733 in Paris, France
d. 1808 in Paris, France
Source: *BioIn 11; McGDA; NewCol 75; WebBD 80*

Robert, Paul
French. Lexicographer, Author
b. Oct 9, 1910 in Orleansville, Algeria
d. Aug 11, 1980 in Mougins, France
Source: *ConAu 101*

Roberti, Ercole
Italian. Artist
b. 1450? in Ferrara, Italy
d. 1496
Source: *McGDA*

Roberts, Sir Charles George Douglas
Canadian. Author
b. Jan 10, 1860 in Douglas, NB
d. Nov 26, 1943 in Toronto, ON
Source: *Alli SUP; ApCAB, SUP; BbD; BiD&SB; CanNov; CanWr; Chambr 3; ChPo, S1, S2; ConAmL; CreCan 2; CurBio 44; DcAmAu; DcBiA; DcNAA; EvLB; JBA 34; LongCTC; OxAmL; OxCan; OxEng; Pen ENG; REn; REnAL; TwCA, SUP; WebE&AL; WhAm 3*

Roberts, Edward Glenn
"Fireball"
American. Auto Racer
b. 1927 in Tavares, Florida
d. Jul 2, 1964 in Charlotte, North Carolina
Source: *BioIn 6; WebAB*

Roberts, Elizabeth Madox
American. Author
b. 1886 in Perryville, Kentucky
d. Mar 13, 1941 in Orlando, Florida
Source: *AmAu&B; BkCL; ChPo, S1; CnDAL; ConAmA; ConAmL; CurBio 41; CyWA; DcAmB S3; DcLEL; DcNAA; EncWL; InWom; LongCTC; ModAL; NotAW; OxAmL; Pen AM; REn; REnAL; Str&VC; TwCA, SUP; WebAB; WhAm 1*

Roberts, Eric
American. Actor
Starred in *King of the Gypsies, Raggedy Man.*
b. 1956 in Biloxi, Mississippi
Source: *BioIn 11*

Roberts, Estelle
English. Psychic
b. 1890
d. 1970
Source: *BioIn 5, 10*

Roberts, Frederick
British. Army Officer
b. 1832 in Cawnpore, India
d. 1914
Source: *NewCol 75; WebBD 80*

Roberts, Garry
see: Boomtown Rats

Roberts, Gene (Eugene Leslie, Jr.)
"The Frog"
American. Newspaper Editor
Executive editor, Philadelphia *Inquirer,* 1972--.
b. Jun 15, 1932 in Goldsboro, North Carolina
Source: *WhoAm 74, 76, 78, 80*

Roberts, Harold Selig
American. Author
b. Mar 14, 1911 in Zdunska-Wola, Poland
d. Feb 5, 1970
Source: *Au&Wr 71; ConAu 25R; ConAu P-2*

Roberts, Kenneth
American. Author
Wrote *Arundel, Rabble in Arms, Northwest Passage.*
b. Dec 8, 1885 in Kennebunk, Maine
d. Jul 21, 1957 in Kennebunkport, Maine
Source: *AmAu&B; AmNov; CasWL; CnDAL; ConAmA; DcLEL; EvLB; LongCTC; ModAL; OxAmL; OxCan; Pen AM; REn; REnAL; TwCA, SUP; TwCW; WhAm 3; WhNAA; WorAl*

Roberts, Oral
American. Evangelist
Founder, president, Oral Roberts U, Tulsa, OK, 1963--.
b. Jan 24, 1918 in Ada, Oklahoma
Source: *CelR 73; ConAu 41R; NewYTBE 73; WebAB; WhoAm 82; WhoRel 75; WorAl*

Roberts, Pernell
American. Actor
TV series roles in "Bonanza," 1959-65; "Trapper John, MD," 1979--.
b. May 18, in Waycross, Georgia
Source: *WhoAm 82; WhoHol A*

Roberts, Rachel
Welsh. Actress
Starred in *Saturday Night and Sunday Morning; This Sporting Life; O Lucky Man.*
b. Sep 20, 1927 in Llanelly, Wales
d. Nov 26, 1980 in Los Angeles, California
Source: *CelR 73; EncMT; FilmgC; IntMPA 77, 75; MotPP; NewYTBE 73; OxFilm; Who 74; WhoAm 74; WhoHol A; WhoThe 77; WhoWor 74*

Roberts, Robin Evan
American. Baseball Player
Pitcher who won 20 or more games, 1950-55.
b. Sep 30, 1926 in Philadelphia, Pennsylvania
Source: *BaseEn; CurBio 53; NewYTBS 74; WhoProB 73*

Roberts, Roy Allison
American. Journalist
b. Nov 25, 1887 in Muscotah, Kansas
d. Feb 23, 1967 in Kansas City, Missouri
Source: *BioIn 7; ConAu 89; WhAm 4*

Roberts, Tony (David Anthony)
American. Actor
b. Oct 22, 1939 in New York, New York
Source: *BioIn 11; NotNAT; WhoAm 82; WhoHol A; WhoThe 77*

Roberts, Xavier
American. Soft Sculpture Doll Designer
b. 1956?
Source: *BioIn 12*

Robertson, Brian
see: Thin Lizzy

Robertson, Charles Sammis
American. Investment Banker
b. 1904? in New York, New York
d. May 2, 1981 in Delray Beach, Florida
Source: *NewYTBS 81*

Robertson, Cliff
American. Actor
Won Oscar, 1969, for *Charley;* starred in *PT 109,* 1962.
b. Sep 9, 1925 in La Jolla, California
Source: *BiDFilm; BkPepl; CelR 73; CmMov; CurBio 69; FilmgC; IntMPA 75, 76, 77, 78, 79, 80, 81, 82; MotPP; MovMk; NewYTBE 72; WhoAm 74, 76, 78, 80, 82; WhoE 74; WhoHol A; WorEFlm*

Robertson, Dale
American. Actor
b. Jul 14, 1923 in Oklahoma City, Oklahoma
Source: *BiE&WWA; FilmgC; IntMPA 75, 76, 77, 78, 79, 80, 81, 82; MotPP; WhoHol A*

Robertson, Don
American. Author, Songwriter
b. Dec 5, 1922 in Peking, China
Source: *AmSCAP 66; ConAu 9R; EncFCWM 69*

Robertson, Oscar
"Big O"
American. Basketball Player
Guard, 1960-74; holds NBA record for career assists--9,887.
b. Nov 24, 1938 in Charlotte, Tennessee
Source: *CelR 73; CurBio 66; WhoAm 74; WhoBbl 73; WhoBlA 75; WorAl*

Robertson, Pat (Marion)
American. Broadcaster, Evangelist
b. 1930
Source: *BioIn 11*

Robertson, "Robbie" (Jaime)
[The Band]
Canadian. Rock Musician, Actor
b. Jul 5, 1944 in Toronto, ON
Source: *NF*

Robertson, William
Scottish. Author, Historian
b. Sep 19, 1721 in Borthwick, Scotland
d. Jun 11, 1793 in Edinburgh, Scotland
Source: *Alli; ApCAB; BbD; BiD&SB; BrAu; CasWL; DcEnA; DcEnL; DcEuL; DcLEL; Drake; EvLB; NewC; OxAmL; OxEng; Pen ENG; REn*

Robeson, Paul Leroy
American. Singer, Actor, Social Activist
Sang "Ol' Man River" in *Show Boat,* 1936.
b. Apr 9, 1898 in Princeton, New Jersey
d. Jan 23, 1976 in Philadelphia, Pennsylvania
Source: *BiE&WWA; BioNews 74; CelR 73; CurBio 41; EncMT; FilmgC; IntWW 74; MovMk; OxAmL; OxFilm; OxThe; PlP&P; REn; WhAm 6; Who 74; WhoAm 74; WhoBlA 75; WhoFtbl 74; WhoMus 72; WorAl*

Robespierre, Maximilien Francois de
"The Incorruptible"
French. Revolutionary
Led French Revolution; major figure in Reign of Terror.
b. May 6, 1758 in Arras, France
d. Jul 28, 1794 in Paris, France
Source: *DcEuL; NewC; NewCol 75; OxFr; REn; WebBD 80; WorAl*

Robey, Sir George
English. Music Hall Comedian, Actor
b. Sep 20, 1869 in London, England
d. Nov 29, 1954 in Saltdean, England
Source: *BioIn 4, 9; BioIn 3; CnThe; EncMT; EncWT; Film 1, 2; FilmgC; NewC; NotNAT A; ObitOF 79; OxFilm; OxThe; WhScrn 74, 77; WhThe; WhoHol B*

Robin Hood
English. Outlaw, Hero
Legendary 12th c. hero who robbed from rich to give to poor.
Source: *NewCol 75; REn; WebBD 80*

Robins, Elizabeth
American. Author
b. 1865 in Louisville, Kentucky
d. May 8, 1952 in Brighton, England
Source: *AmAu&B; BbD; BiDSA; Chambr 3; CnDAL; InWom; LongCTC; OhA&B; OxAmL; OxThe; REn; REnAL; TwCA, SUP; WhAm 5; WomWWA 14*

Robinson, Bill
"Bojangles"
American. Actor, Dancer
Tap dancer known for stairway dance, appearances in Shirley Temple films.
b. May 25, 1878 in Richmond, Virginia
d. Nov 25, 1949 in New York, New York
Source: *CurBio 41, 50; DcAmB S4; EncMT; FilmgC; MovMk; WebAB; WhAm 2; WhScrn 74, 77; WhoHol B; WorAl*

Robinson, Boardman
American. Artist, Illustrator
b. Sep 6, 1876 in Somerset, NS
d. Sep 5, 1952 in Stamford, Connecticut
Source: *AmAu&B; ChPo; CurBio 41, 52; DcAmB S5; DcCAA 71; IlsCB 1744; WhAm 3*

Robinson, Brooks Calbert, Jr.
American. Baseball Player, TV Commentator
With Baltimore Orioles, 1955-77; Hall of Fame, 1983.
b. May 18, 1937 in Little Rock, Arkansas
Source: *BaseEn; CelR 73; CurBio 73; WhoAm 74, 76, 78, 80, 82; WhoProB 73*

Robinson, David
see: Cars, The

Robinson, Earl Hawley
American. Composer, Singer
b. Jul 2, 1910 in Seattle, Washington
Source: *ConAu 45, 2NR; CurBio 45; EncFCWM 69; WhoAm 74, 76, 78, 80, 82; WhoWest 74*

Robinson, Edward G
[Emanuel Goldenberg]
American. Actor
Played gangsters in *Little Caesar, Brother Orchid, Key Largo;* won special Oscar, 1972.
b. Dec 12, 1893 in Bucharest, Romania
d. Jan 26, 1973 in Beverly Hills, California
Source: *BiDFilm; BiE&WWA; CmMov; ConAu 45; CurBio 50, 73; FilmgC; MotPP; MovMk; NewYTBE 72, 73; NewYTBS 74; OxFilm; WhAm 5; WhScrn 77; WhoHol B; WhoWorJ 72; WorAl; WorEFlm*

Robinson, Edwin Arlington
American. Poet
b. Dec 22, 1869 in Head Tide, Maine
d. Apr 6, 1935 in New York, New York
Source: *AmAu&B; AmBi; AmLY; AmWr; AnMV 1926; AtlBL; CasWL; Chambr 3; ChPo, S1, S2; CnDAL; CnE&AP; CnMWL; ConAmA; ConAmL; CyWA; DcAmAu; DcAmB S1; DcLEL; DcNAA; EncWL; EvLB; LongCTC; ModAL, SUP; OxAmL; OxEng; Pen AM; RAdv 1; REn; REnAL; SixAP; TwCA, SUP; TwCW; WebAB; WebE&AL; WhAm 1; WhNAA; WhoTwCL*

Robinson, (Esme Stuart) Lennox
Irish. Author, Dramatist
b. Oct 4, 1886 in Ireland
d. Oct 14, 1958 in Dublin, Ireland
Source: *CasWL; ChPo, S1; CnMD; CnThe; DcLEL; EncWL; EvLB; LongCTC; McGEWD; ModBrL; ModWD; NewC; OxEng; OxThe; REnWD; TwCA, SUP; WhAm 3*

Robinson, Forbes
English. Opera Singer
b. May 21, 1926 in Cheshire, England
Source: *IntWW 74; Who 74; WhoMus 72; WhoWor 74*

Robinson, Francis Arthur
American. Opera Manager
b. Apr 28, 1910 in Henderson, Kentucky
d. 1980 in New York, New York
Source: *WhoE 74*

Robinson, Frank
American. Baseball Player, Manager
NL rookie of year, 1956; manager, San Francisco Giants, 1981--.
b. Aug 31, 1935 in Beaumont, Texas
Source: *BaseEn; BioNews 74; CelR 73; CurBio 71; NewYTBS 74; WhoAm 74, 76, 78, 80, 82; WhoBlA 75; WhoProB 73*

Robinson, Henry Morton
American. Author, Poet
b. Sep 7, 1898 in Boston, Massachusetts
d. Jan 13, 1961 in New York, New York
Source: *AmAu&B; AmNov; CathA 1952; ChPo; CurBio 50, 61; REnAL; TwCA SUP; WhAm 4; WhNAA*

Robinson, Jackie (John Roosevelt)
American. Baseball Player
First black in ML with Brooklyn Dodgers, 1947-56; Hall of Fame, 1962.
b. Jan 31, 1919 in Cairo, Georgia
d. Oct 24, 1972 in Stamford, Connecticut
Source: *BaseEn; CurBio 47, 72; NewYTBE 71, 72; WhScrn 77; WhoHol B*

Robinson, James Harvey
American. Historian, Educator
b. Jun 29, 1863 in Bloomington, Illinois
d. Feb 16, 1936 in New York, New York
Source: *AmAu&B; AmBi; BiDAmEd; BioIn 1, 4; DcAmAu; DcAmB S2; DcNAA; LinLib L, S; McGEWB; NewCol 75; OxAmL; REnAL; TwCA, SUP; TwCBDA; WebAB; WhAm 1*

Robinson, Jay
American. Actor
b. Apr 14, 1930 in New York, New York
Source: *BiE&WWA; FilmgC; NotNAT; WhoHol A*

Robinson, Joan Mary Gale Thomas
English. Author
b. 1910 in Gerrards Cross, England
Source: *Au&Wr 71; ConAu 5R, 5NR; SmATA 7; WhoChL*

Robinson, Larry Clark
Canadian. Hockey Player
b. Jun 2, 1951 in Winchester, ON
Source: *HocReg*

Robinson, M(aurice) R(ichard)
American. Editor, Publisher
b. Dec 24, 1895 in Wilkinsburg, Pennsylvania
d. Feb 7, 1982 in Pelham, New York
Source: *BioIn 5, 6, 9; ChPo S1; CurBio 56, 82; NewYTBS 82; St&PR 75; WhoAm 74, 76, 78, 80, 82*

Robinson, Max C
American. Broadcast Journalist
b. May 1, 1939 in Richmond, Virginia
Source: *WhoAm 82; WhoBlA 75*

Robinson, Paul Minnich
American. Clergyman, Author
b. Jan 26, 1914 in Denver, Colorado
Source: *DrAS 74P; LEduc 74; WhoAm 74; WhoRel 75; WhoWor 74*

Robinson, Robert
British. Chemist
b. Sep 13, 1886 in Chesterfield, England
d. Feb 8, 1975 in Missenden, England
Source: *IntWW 74; WhAm 6; Who 74; WhoWor 74*

Robinson, "Smokey" (William, Jr.)
[Smokey Robinson and the Miracles]
American. Songwriter, Singer, Producer
b. Feb 19, 1940 in Detroit, Michigan
Source: *CurBio 80; DcBlPA; EncPR&S; PseudN; RkOn 2; WhoAm 78, 80, 82*

Robinson, "Sugar" Ray
[Walker Smith]
American. Boxer
Welterweight champ, 1946-51; five-time middleweight champ, 1951-60.
b. May 3, 1920 in Detroit, Michigan
Source: *CelR 73; CurBio 51; WebAB; WhoAm 74; WhoBlA 75; WhoHol A; WorAl*

Robison, Paula Judith
American. Musician
b. Jun 8, 1941 in Nashville, Tennessee
Source: *BioIn 10, 11; BioNews 74; CurBio 82; NewYTBE 73; NewYTBS 77; WhoAm 80, 82*

Robitscher, Jonas Bondi, Jr.
American. Psychiatrist, Author
b. Oct 28, 1920 in New York, New York
d. Mar 25, 1981 in Atlanta, Georgia
Source: *AmM&WS 79P; AnObit 1981; BiDrAPA 77; ConAu 21R; DrAS 78P; WhAm 7; WhoAm 76, 78, 80; WhoAmL 79*

Robson, Flora McKenzie
Welsh. Actress
b. Mar 28, 1902 in South Shields, Wales
Source: *BiE&WWA; CurBio 51; FilmgC; InWom; IntMPA 75, 76, 77, 78, 79, 80, 81, 82; IntWW 74; MotPP; MovMk; NotNAT; OxFilm; OxThe; PlP&P; ThFT; Vers A; Who 74; WhoHol A; WhoThe 77; WhoWor 74*

Robson, May
American. Actress
b. Apr 19, 1858 in Australia
d. Oct 20, 1942 in Beverly Hills, California
Source: *CurBio 42; DcAmB S3; Film 1; FilmgC; InWom; MotPP; MovMk; NotAW; OxFilm; PlP&P; ThFT; TwYS; Vers A; WhAm 2; WhNAA; WhScrn 74, 77; WhoHol B; WhoStg 1906, 1908*

Rocca, Lodovico
Italian. Opera Composer
b. Nov 29, 1895 in Turin, Italy
Source: *WhoMus 72*

Rochambeau, Jean Baptiste Donatien de Vimeur, Comte
French. General
b. Jul 1, 1725 in Vendome, France
d. May 10, 1807
Source: *AmBi; ApCAB; DcAmB; Drake; NewCol 75; REn; TwCBDA; WebAB; WebBD 80; WhAm H*

Rochberg, George
American. Composer, Educator
b. Jul 5, 1918 in Paterson, New Jersey
Source: *AmSCAP 66; DcCM; WhoAm 74, 76, 78, 80, 82; WhoWor 74*

Roche, John P
American. Author, Educator
b. May 7, 1923 in New York, New York
Source: *AmAu&B; AmM&WS 73S; ConAu 69; DrAS 74H; WhoAm 74, 76, 78, 80, 82; WhoE 74; WhoGov 72*

Roche, Kevin
American. Architect
b. Jun 14, 1922 in Dublin, Ireland
Source: *CurBio 70*

Rochefort, Henri
[Victor Henri Marquis de Rochefort-Lucay]
French. Journalist
b. 1830
d. 1913
Source: *NewCol 75; OxFr; WebBD 80*

"Rochester"
see: Anderson, Eddie

Rochester, Nathaniel
American. Merchant, Banker
Founded Rochester, NY, 1824.
b. Feb 21, 1752 in Virginia
d. May 17, 1831 in Rochester, New York
Source: *ApCAB; DcAmB; TwCBDA; WebBD 80; WhAm H*

Rock, Arthur
American. Businessman
b. Aug 19, 1926 in Rochester, New York
Source: *St&PR 75; WhoAm 74, 76, 78, 80, 82; WhoF&I 74*

Rock, John
American. Developed Birth Control Pill
Developed birth control pill, 1944; established first fertility clinic.
b. Mar 24, 1890 in Marlborough, Massachusetts
Source: *CelR 73; CurBio 64; IntWW 74; WhoAm 74*

Rock, Monti
American. Hairdresser, Singer
Source: *NewYTBE 71*

Rockefeller, Abby Aldrich
American. Philanthropist, Art Patron
b. Oct 26, 1874 in Providence, Rhode Island
d. Apr 15, 1948 in New York, New York
Source: *DcAmB S4; InWom; NotAW*

Rockefeller, "Bobo" (Barbara)
American. Wife of Winthrop Rockefeller
b. 1917
Source: *InWom*

Rockefeller, David
American. Banker
Son of John Rockefeller, Jr.; exec. with Chase National/Chase Manhatten Bank, 1948--.
b. Jun 12, 1915 in New York, New York
Source: *CelR 73; CurBio 59; IntWW 74; NewYTBE 70, 73; St&PR 75; Who 74; WhoAm 74, 76, 78, 80, 82; WhoAmA 73; WhoE 74; WhoF&I 74; WhoWor 74; WorAl*

Rockefeller, "Happy" (Margaretta Large)
American. Widow of Nelson Rockefeller
b. 1926
Source: *BioNews 74; InWom; NewYTBS 74; WhoAm 82; WhoAmW 77*

Rockefeller, John D(avison)
American. Oil Magnate
Founded Standard Oil of OH, 1870; U of Chicago, 1890; Rockefeller Foundation, 1913.
b. Jul 8, 1839 in Richford, New York
d. May 23, 1937 in Ormond Beach, Florida
Source: *AmBi; ApCAB SUP; ChPo S1; DcNAA; EncAB-H; OhA&B; REn; REnAL; WebAB; WhAm 1; WorAl*

Rockefeller, John D(avison), Jr.
American. Philanthropist
Helped to restore colonial Williamsburg, VA, 1926-60.
b. Jan 29, 1874 in Cleveland, Ohio
d. May 11, 1960 in Tucson, Arizona
Source: *CurBio 41, 60; OhA&B; WhAm 4; WorAl*

Rockefeller, John D(avison), III
American. Philanthropist
Head, Rockefeller Foundation, 1952-71.
b. Mar 21, 1906 in New York, New York
d. Jul 10, 1978 in Westchester County, New York
Source: *BiE&WWA; ConAu 77, 81; CurBio 53; IntWW 74; St&PR 75; Who 74; WhoAm 74; WhoAmA 73; WhoGov 72; WhoWor 74*

Rockefeller, John D(avison), IV
American. Politician
Governor of WV, 1977--.
b. Jun 18, 1937 in New York, New York
Source: *CelR 73; NewYTBE 70; WhoAm 74, 76, 78, 80, 82; WhoAmP 73; WhoE 74; WhoGov 72*

Rockefeller, Laurance Spelman
American. Conservationist, Businessman
b. May 26, 1910 in New York, New York
Source: *BusPN; CelR 73; IntWW 74; NewYTBE 70; St&PR 75; Who 74; WhoAm 74, 76, 78, 80, 82; WhoE 74; WhoF&I 74; WhoGov 72*

Rockefeller, Mary French
American. Government Official
b. May 1, 1910 in New York, New York
Source: *WhoAm 74, 76, 78, 80, 82*

Rockefeller, Michael Clark
American. Son of Nelson Rockefeller
b. 1938
d. 1961
Source: *BioIn 6, 9*

Rockefeller, Nelson A(ldrich)
American. Vice-President
Governor of NY, 1959-73; vice-president, 1974-76.
b. Jul 8, 1908 in Bar Harbor, Maine
d. Jan 26, 1979 in New York, New York
Source: *BioNews 74; CelR 73; CurBio 41, 51; EncAB-H; IntWW 74; NewYTBE 70, 73; NewYTBS 74; WebAB; Who 74; WhoAm 74; WhoAmA 73; WhoAmP 73; WhoE 74; WhoGov 72; WhoWor 74*

Rockefeller, Rodman C
American. Business Executive
b. 1932
Source: *St&PR 75; WhoAm 74; WhoF&I 74*

Rockefeller, Sharon Lee
American. Wife of John D Rockefeller, IV
b. 1945
Source: *BioIn 9*

Rockefeller, Winthrop
American. Politician
Governor of AR, 1967-71.
b. May 1, 1912 in New York, New York
d. Feb 22, 1973 in Palm Springs, California
Source: *BioNews 74; CurBio 59, 73; NewYTBE 73; WhAm 5, 6; WhoAm 74; WhoAmA 73; WhoF&I 74; WhoS&SW 73; WhoWor 74*

Rocker, Lee
see: Stray Cats

Rockets, The
[Donnie Backus; John "Bee" Badanjek; David Gilbert; Bobby Neil Haralson; Jim McCarty; Dennis Robbins]
American. Rock Group
Source: *NF*

Rockne, Knute Kenneth
American. Football Player, Coach
Coach at Notre Dame, 1918-31; five undefeated seasons.
b. Mar 4, 1888 in Voss, Norway
d. Mar 31, 1931 in Kansas
Source: *AmBi; DcAmB; IndAu 1917; WebAB; WhAm 1; WhoFtbl 74; WorAl*

Rockpile
[Billy Bremer; Dave Edmunds; Nick Lowe; Terry Williams]
British. Rock Group
Source: *NF*

Rockwell, "Doc" (George L)
American. Author, Comedian, Cartoonist
b. 1889 in Providence, Rhode Island
d. Mar 3, 1978 in Brunswick, Maine
Source: *BioIn 9*

Rockwell, George Lincoln
American. Nazi Party Leader
b. 1918
d. Aug 25, 1967 in Arlington, Virginia
Source: *BioIn 6, 7; WhDW*

Rockwell, Norman
American. Illustrator
Drew nostalgic covers for *The Saturday Evening Post.*
b. Feb 3, 1894 in New York, New York
d. Nov 8, 1978 in Stockbridge, Massachusetts
Source: *ConAu 81, 89; CurBio 45; IlsBYP; IlsCB 1744; NewYTBE 71; REn; REnAL; WebAB; WhoAm 74; WhoAmA 73; WhoGrA; WhoWor 74; WorAl*

Rodale, Jerome Irving
American. Author, Publisher
b. Aug 16, 1898 in New York, New York
d. Jun 7, 1971 in New York, New York
Source: *AmAu&B; ConAu 29R; NewYTBE 71; WhAm 5*

Roddenberry, Gene (Eugene Wesley)
American. Producer
Creator, producer of TV series "Star Trek," 1966-69.
b. Aug 19, 1921 in El Paso, Texas
Source: *FilmgC; WhoAm 80, 82; WhoSciF*

Rode, Jacques Pierre Joseph
French. Musician
b. Feb 16, 1774 in Bordeaux, France
d. Nov 25, 1830 in Chateau Bourbon, France
Source: *OxMus; WebBD 80*

Rodford, Jim
see: Argent

Rodgers, Bill (William Henry)
American. Runner
Won Boston Marathon, 1975, 1978-79; NY Marathon, 1976-79.
b. Dec 23, 1947 in Hartford, Connecticut
Source: *BioIn 11; CurBio 82; WhoAm 82*

Rodgers, Christopher Raymond Perry
American. Naval Officer
b. Nov 14, 1819 in Brooklyn, New York
d. Jan 8, 1892 in Washington, DC
Source: *Drake; NewCol 75; WhAm H*

Rodgers, Jimmie C
American. Singer, Songwriter
b. Sep 8, 1897 in Meridian, Mississippi
d. May 26, 1933 in New York, New York
Source: *AmSCAP 66; EncFCWM 69*

Rodgers, Jimmie F
American. Singer
Hits include "Kisses Sweeter than Wine"; "Honeycomb."
b. Sep 18, 1933 in Camas, Washington
Source: *EncFCWM 69*

Rodgers, John
American. Naval Officer
b. 1773 in Maryland
d. Aug 10, 1838 in Philadelphia, Pennsylvania
Source: *AmBi; ApCAB; DcAmB; Drake; NewCol 75; TwCBDA; WebAB; WebBD 80; WhAm H*

Rodgers, Mary
American. Composer, Author
b. Jan 11, 1931 in New York, New York
Source: *AmSCAP 66; BiE&WWA; ConAu 49; ConLC 12; EncMT; NewCBMT; NotNAT; SmATA 8; WhoAm 82*

Rodgers, Richard
[Rodgers and Hart; Rodgers and Hammerstein]
American. Composer
Won Pulitzer Prizes for *Oklahoma,* 1943; *South Pacific,* 1949.
b. Jul 28, 1902 in New York, New York
d. Dec 30, 1979 in New York, New York
Source: *AmSCAP 66; BiE&WWA; CmMov; ConAu 89; CurBio 40, 51; EncAB-H; EncMT; FilmgC; IntMPA 77, 75; IntWW 74; McGEWD; NewCBMT; NotNAT; OxAmL; OxFilm; PlP&P; REn; REnAL; WebAB; Who 74; WhoAm 74; WhoGov 72; WhoHol A; WhoMus 72; WhoThe 77; WhoWor 74; WhoWorJ 72; WorAl*

Rodilla, Simon
[Sam Rodia]
American. Architect
b. 1879
d. 1965
Source: *BioIn 10*

Rodin, (Francois) Auguste (Rene)
French. Sculptor
Works include "The Thinker," "Adam and Eve," "The Burghers of Calais."
b. Nov 12, 1840 in Paris, France
d. Nov 17, 1917 in Meudon, France
Source: *AtlBL; NewC; NewCol 75; OxFr; REn; WebBD 80; WorAl*

Rodino, Peter Wallace, Jr.
American. Politician
b. Jun 7, 1909 in Newark, New Jersey
Source: *BiDrAC; CngDr 74; CurBio 54; IntWW 74; NewYTBS 74, 74; WhoAm 74, 76, 78, 80, 82; WhoAmP 73; WhoE 74; WhoGov 72*

Rodman, Selden
American. Poet, Editor, Art Critic
b. Feb 19, 1909 in New York, New York
Source: *AmAu&B; ChPo; ConAu 5R, 5NR; OxAmL; REn; REnAL; SmATA 9; TwCA SUP; WhoAm 74; WhoAmA 73; WhoWor 74*

Rodney, Caesar
American. Politician
b. Oct 7, 1728 in Dover, Delaware
d. Jun 29, 1784 in Dover, Delaware
Source: *AmBi; ApCAB; BiAuS; BiDrAC; DcAmB; Drake; TwCBDA; WhAm H; WhAmP*

Rodney, George Brydges
English. Admiral
b. 1719
d. 1792
Source: *Alli; ApCAB; NewCol 75; REn; WebBD 80*

Rodnina, Irina
[Rodnina and Zaitsev; Mrs. Alexsander Zaitsev]
Russian. Figure Skater
b. 1949 in U.S.S.R.
Source: *BioIn 11*

Rodriguez, "Chi-Chi" (Juan)
Puerto Rican. Golfer
b. Oct 23, 1934 in Rio Piedras, Puerto Rico
Source: *CurBio 69; WhoGolf*

Rodriguez, Johnny
American. Musician
b. Dec 10, 1951 in Sabinal, Texas
Source: *BioIn 10; WhoAm 82*

Rodriguez, Tito
American. Actor, Singer, Band Leader
b. 1923
d. Feb 28, 1973 in New York, New York
Source: *WhScrn 77*

Rodzinski, Artur
Yugoslav. Conductor
b. Jan 2, 1894 in Split, Yugoslavia
d. Nov 27, 1958 in Boston, Massachusetts
Source: *CurBio 40, 59; WhAm 3*

Roe, Edward Payson
American. Clergyman, Author
b. Mar 7, 1838 in New Windsor, New York
d. Jul 19, 1888 in Cornwall, New York
Source: *Alli SUP; AmAu; AmAu&B; AmBi; ApCAB; BbD; BiD&SB; CarSB; Chambr 3; DcAmAu; DcAmB; DcLEL; DcNAA; MnBBF; OxAmL; REnAL; TwCBDA; WhAm H*

Roe, Tommy
American. Singer
b. May 9, 1942 in Atlanta, Georgia
Source: *RkOn; WhoRock 81*

Roebling, John Augustus
American. Designer of Brooklyn Bridge
Pioneered design, construction of suspension bridges.
b. Jun 12, 1806 in Muhlhausen, Germany
d. Jul 22, 1869 in New York, New York
Source: *AmBi; ApCAB; DcAmAu; DcAmB; DcNAA; Drake; EncAB-H; REn; TwCBDA; WebAB; WhAm H; WorAl*

Roebling, Washington Augustus
American. Builder of Brooklyn Bridge
Succeeded father as chief engineer on Brooklyn Bridge, 1869-83.
b. May 26, 1837 in Saxonburg, Pennsylvania
d. Jul 21, 1926 in Trenton, New Jersey
Source: *AmBi; ApCAB; DcAmAu; DcAmB; McGEWB; NatCAB 4, 26; REn; TwCBDA; WebAB; WhAm 1*

Roebuck, Alvah Curtis
American. Mail Order Merchant
Partner with Richard W Sears, 1887; sold shares, 1897.
b. 1864?
d. Jun 19, 1948 in Chicago, Illinois
Source: *BioIn 1, 2, 7, 10*

Roeder, David
[The Hostages]
American. Former Hostage in Iran
b. 1940?
Source: *BioIn 12; NewYTBS 81*

Roentgen, Wilhelm Konrad
German. Scientist
Discovered x-rays, 1895; won first Nobel Prize in Physics, 1901.
b. Mar 27, 1845 in Lennep, Prussia
d. Feb 10, 1923 in Munich, Germany
Source: *AsBiEn; LinLib S; McGEWB; NewCol 75; REn*

Roeser, Donald "Buck Dharma"
see: Blue Oyster Cult

Roessner, Elmer
American. Editor, Author
b. May 1, 1900 in Oakland, California
d. Apr 28, 1972
Source: *NewYTBE 72; WhAm 5*

Roethke, Theodore
American. Author
b. May 25, 1908 in Saginaw, Michigan
d. Aug 1, 1963 in Bainbridge Isle, Washington
Source: *AmAu&B; AmWr; AnCL; AtlBL; CasWL; ChPo, S1, S2; CnDAL; CnE&AP; ConAu 81; ConLC 1, 3, 8, 11; ConP 75; CroCAP; EncWL; LongCTC; ModAL, SUP; OxAmL; Pen AM; RAdv 1; REn; REnAL; TwCA SUP; TwCW; WebAB; WebE&AL; WhAm 4; WhoPNW; WhoTwCL*

Rogell, Albert S
American. Motion Picture Director, Producer
b. Aug 21, 1901 in Oklahoma City, Oklahoma
Source: *FilmgC; IntMPA 75, 76, 77, 78, 79; TwYS*

Rogers, Bill (William Charles)
American. Golfer
Won 1981 British Open.
b. Sep 10, 1951 in Waco, Texas
Source: *NewYTBS 81; WhoAm 82*

Rogers, Bruce
American. Book Designer
b. May 14, 1870 in Lafayette, Indiana
d. May 18, 1957 in New Fairfield, Connecticut
Source: *ChPo, S2; CurBio 46, 57; IndAu 1917; OxAmL; REnAL; WebAB; WhAm 3*

Rogers, Budd
American. Motion Picture Executive
b. Jun 4, 1891 in Boston, Massachusetts
d. 1975
Source: *IntMPA 75; St&PR 75*

Rogers, "Buddy" (Charles)
American. Actor
Starred in *Wings,* 1927, first picture to win Oscar; husband of Mary Pickford.
b. Aug 13, 1904 in Olathe, Kansas
Source: *FilmgC; IntMPA 75, 76, 77; MotPP; MovMk; TwYS; WhoHol A; WorAl*

Rogers, Carl Ransom
American. Psychologist
Wrote *On Becoming a Person,* 1961; *A Way of Being,* 1980.
b. Jan 8, 1902 in Oak Park, Illinois
Source: *AmM&WS 73S; ConAu 1R, 1NR; CurBio 62; WhoAm 76, 78, 80, 82; WhoWest 74*

Rogers, Fred
American. Educator, TV Performer
Producer, host of "Mister Rogers Neighborhood," 1965--.
b. Mar 20, 1928 in Latrobe, Pennsylvania
Source: *AmSCAP 66; CurBio 71; IntMPA 82; WhoAm 74, 76, 78, 80, 82; WhoE 74*

Rogers, George
American. Football Player
b. Dec 8, 1958 in Duluth, Georgia
Source: *NF*

Rogers, Ginger
[Virginia Katherine McNath]
American. Dancer, Actress
Won Oscar, 1940, for *Kitty Foyle;* frequent dance partner of Fred Astaire.
b. Jul 16, 1911 in Independence, Missouri
Source: *BiDFilm; BiE&WWA; BioNews 74; CelR 73; CmMov; CurBio 41, 67; EncMT; FilmgC; InWom; IntMPA 75, 76, 77, 78, 79, 80, 81, 82; IntWW 74; MotPP; MovMk; NewYTBE 72; OxFilm; ThFT; WhoAm 74, 76, 78, 80, 82; WhoHol A; WhoThe 77; WhoWor 74; WorAl; WorEFlm*

Rogers, Isaiah
American. Architect
b. Aug 17, 1800 in Marshfield, Massachusetts
d. Apr 13, 1869
Source: *BnEnAmA; DcAmB; McGDA; WhAm H*

Rogers, James Gamble
American. Architect
b. Mar 3, 1867 in Bryant Station, Kentucky
d. Oct 1, 1947
Source: *DcAmB S4; NewCol 75; WebBD 80; WhAm 2*

Rogers, John
American. Sculptor
b. Oct 30, 1829 in Salem, Massachusetts
d. Jul 26, 1904 in New Canaan, Connecticut
Source: *AmBi; ApCAB; DcAmB; Drake; NewCol 75; OxAmL; TwCBDA; WebAB; WebBD 80; WhAm 1*

Rogers, Karen
American. Jockey
b. 1962?
Source: *BioIn 12*

Rogers, Kenny (Kenneth Ray)
[Kenny Rogers and The First Edition]
American. Singer
b. Aug 21, 1938 in Houston, Texas
Source: *BioIn 11; BkPepl; ConAu 85; WhoAm 78, 80, 82*

Rogers, Mary Cecilia
American. Inspiration for Edgar Allan Poe
b. 1820
d. 1841
Source: *ApCAB; InWom*

Rogers, Randolph
American. Sculptor
b. Jul 6, 1825 in Waterloo, New York
d. Jan 15, 1892 in Rome, Italy
Source: *AmBi; ApCAB; DcAmB; TwCBDA; WhAm H*

Rogers, Rosemary
[Marina Mayson, pseud.]
American. Author
Wrote *Sweet Savage Love, Wicked Loving Lies, The Crowd Pleasers.*
b. Dec 7, 1933 in Panadura, Ceylon
Source: *ConAu 49, 3NR; WhoAm 82; WorAl; WrDr 76*

Rogers, Roy
[Leonard Slye]
"King of the Cowboys"
American. Actor, Singer
With *Sons of the Pioneers,* 1932-38; TV "The Roy Rogers Show," 1951-64.
b. Nov 5, 1912 in Cincinnati, Ohio
Source: *BkPepl; CmMov; EncFCWM 69; FilmgC; IntMPA 75, 76, 77, 78, 79, 80, 81, 82; MovMk; OxFilm; WhoAm 74, 76, 78, 80, 82; WorAl; WorEFlm*

Rogers, Samuel
English. Author
Known for friendships with Byron and Wordsworth than for poetry.
b. Jul 30, 1763 in London, England
d. Dec 18, 1855 in London, England
Source: *Alli; BbD; BiD&SB; BiDLA; BrAu 19; CasWL; ChPo, S1, S2; CrtT 2; DcEnA; DcEnL; DcEuL; DcLEL; EvLB; MouLC 3; NewC; OxEng; Pen ENG; REn; WebE&AL*

Rogers, "Shorty" (Milton M)
American. Jazz Musician
b. Apr 14, 1924 in Lee, Massachusetts
Source: *CmpEPM; WorAl*

Rogers, Thomas
American. Author
b. 1927
Source: *BioIn 8*

Rogers, Wayne
American. Actor
Played Trapper John in TV series "MASH."
b. Apr 7, 1933 in Birmingham, Alabama
Source: *BioNews 74; WhoAm 82; WhoHol A*

Rogers, Will(iam Penn Adair)
American. Actor, Lecturer, Humorist
"Comedy roper" in Ziegfield Follies from 1914; columnist, 1926-35.
b. Sep 5, 1879 in Oologah, Oklahoma
d. Aug 15, 1935 in Point Barrow, Alaska
Source: *AmAu&B; AmBi; BiDFilm; CnDAL; DcAmB S1; DcNAA; EncMT; Film 1; FilmgC; LongCTC; MotPP; MovMk; OxAmL; OxFilm; Pen AM; PlP&P; REn; REnAL; TwCA, SUP; TwYS; WebAB; WhAm 1; WhScrn 74, 77; WhoHol B; WorAl; WorEFlm*

Rogers, Will, Jr.
American. Actor, Lecturer, Humorist
Portrayed father in film *The Story of Will Rogers,* 1950.
b. Oct 12, 1912 in New York, New York
Source: *CurBio 53; IntMPA 75, 76, 77, 78, 79, 80, 81, 82; WhoHol A*

Rogers, William Pierce
American. Former Secretary of State
b. Jun 23, 1913 in Norfolk, New York
Source: *BiDrUSE; Who 74; WhoAm 74, 76, 78, 80, 82; WhoAmP 73; WhoGov 72; WhoS&SW 73*

Roget, Peter Mark
English. Lexicographer, Physician
Compiled *Thesaurus of English Words and Phrases,* 1852, still standard reference work.
b. Jan 18, 1779 in London, England
d. 1869
Source: *Alli; NewC; NewCol 75*

Roggeveen, Jacob
Dutch. Explorer, Navigator
b. 1659
d. 1729
Source: *BioIn 9*

Rohatyn, Fleix George
"Felix the Fixer"
American. Investment Banker
b. May 29, 1928 in Vienna, Austria
Source: *BioIn 9; BioIn 10; BioIn 11; CurBio 78; NewYTBE 72; NewYTBS 74, 75, 76; PolProf NF; St&PR 75; WhoAm 74, 76, 78, 80, 82*

Rohm, Ernst
German. Nazi Official
b. 1887
d. 1934
Source: *OxGer; REn*

Rohmer, Eric
French. Motion Picture Producer
b. Dec 1, 1920 in Nancy, France
Source: *BiDFilm; CelR 73; FilmgC; IntWW 74; MovMk; NewYTBE 71; OxFilm; WhoAm 82; WorEFlm*

Rohmer, Sax, pseud.
[Arthur Sarsfield Ward]
English. Author
b. 1883 in London, England
d. Jun 1, 1959 in London, England
Source: *ChPo; EncMys; EvLB; LongCTC; NewC; Pen ENG; TwCA, SUP; TwCW; WhoLA*

Rojankovsky, Feodor Stepanovich
Russian. Artist
b. Dec 24, 1891 in Mitava, Russia
d. Oct 21, 1970
Source: *AuBYP; BkP; Cald 1938; ChPo, S1; IlsBYP; IlsCB 1744, 1946, 1957; JBA 51; NewYTBE 70; WhAm 5; WhoChL*

Rojas, Fernando de
Spanish. Author
b. 1475 in Toledo, Spain
d. Apr 1541 in Talavera, Spain
Source: *CasWL; CyWA; DcEuL; DcSpL; EuAu; McGEWD; NewC; OxEng; OxThe; Pen EUR; REn*

Rojas Pinilla, Gustavo
Colombian. President
b. Mar 12, 1900 in Tunja, Colombia
d. Jan 17, 1975
Source: *CurBio 56; IntWW 74; NewYTBE 70; WhAm 6*

Rojas Zorrilla, Francisco de
Spanish. Dramatist
b. 1607 in Toledo, Spain
d. 1648 in Madrid, Spain
Source: *CasWL; DcSpL; EuAu; EvEuW; McGEWD; NewCol 75; OxThe; REn; WebBD 80*

Roker, Roxie
American. Actress
b. Aug 28, 1938? in Miami, Florida
Source: *BioIn 10; DcBlPA; NotNAT A; WhoAm 80, 82; WhoBlA 77*

Rokossovsky, Konstantin
Russian. General
b. Dec 21, 1896
d. Aug 3, 1968 in Moscow, U.S.S.R.
Source: *CurBio 44, 68; NewCol 75; WebBD 80*

Roland, Gilbert
American. Actor
b. Dec 11, 1905 in Juarez, Mexico
Source: *FilmgC; HolP 30; IntMPA 75, 76, 77, 78, 79, 80, 81, 82; MotPP; MovMk; TwYS; WhoAm 74, 76, 78, 80, 82; WhoHol A; WorEFlm*

Roland, Ruth
American. Actress
b. Aug 26, 1897 in San Francisco, California
d. Sep 22, 1937 in Los Angeles, California
Source: *Film 1; FilmgC; MotPP; TwYS; WhScrn 74, 77; WhoHol B*

Roland de la Porte, Henri-Horace
French. Artist
b. 1724 in Paris, France
d. 1793 in Paris, France
Source: *McGDA*

Roldos Aguilera, Jamie
Ecuadorean. President
b. Nov 5, 1940 in Guayaquil, Ecuador
d. May 24, 1981 in Andes Mountains, Ecuador
Source: *NewYTBS 79, 81*

Rolf, Ida
[Rolfing]
American. Physical Therapist
b. 1896
d. Mar 1979
Source: *BioIn 11*

Rolfe, Frederick William
see: Corvo, Baron, pseud.

Rolfe, John
English. Colonist, Married Pocahontas
Introduced tobacco cultivation to VA, 1612; married Pochontas, 1614.
b. 1585
d. 1622 in Bermuda Hundred, Virginia
Source: *AmBi; ApCAB SUP; DcAmB; EncAAH; EncAB-H; McGEWB; NewCol 75*

Rolfe, "Red" (Robert Abial)
American. Baseball Player, Manager
b. Oct 11, 1908 in Penacook, New Hampshire
d. Jul 8, 1969 in Gilford, New Hampshire
Source: *BaseEn; WhoProB 73*

Rolie, Gregg
see: Journey

Rolland, Duane
see: Molly Hatchet

Rolland, Romain
French. Author, Dramatist
b. Jan 29, 1866 in Clamecy, France
d. Dec 30, 1944 in Vezelay, France
Source: *CasWL; ClDMEL; CnMD; CnMWL; CurBio 43; CyWA; DcBiA; EncWL; EvEuW; LongCTC; McGEWD; ModRL; ModWD; NewC; OxEng; OxFr; Pen EUR; RComWL; REn; TwCA, SUP; TwCW; WhoTwCL*

Rolle, Esther
American. Actress
b. Nov 8, 1933? in Pompano Beach, Florida
Source: *BioNews 74; IntMPA 82; NewYTBS 74; NotNAT; WhoAm 82; WhoThe 77*

Roller, Alfred
Austrian. Scene Designer
b. Feb 10, 1864 in Vienna, Austria
d. Jun 21, 1935 in Vienna, Austria
Source: *NewEOp 71*

Rollin, Betty
American. Author, Television Journalist
With NBC News, 1971-80; wrote *First, You Cry,* 1976.
b. Jan 3, 1936 in New York, New York
Source: *ConAu 13R; ForWC 70; WhoAm 82*

Rolling Stones, The
[Mick Jagger; Brian Jones; Keith Richard; Mick Taylor; Charlie Watts; Ron Wood; Bill Wyman]
English. Rock Group
Group formed, 1962; first US single "Not Fade Away," 1964.
Source: *EncPR&S; RkOn; Rk100*

Rollini, Adrian
American. Musician
b. Jun 28, 1904 in New York, New York
d. May 15, 1956 in Homestead, Florida
Source: *WhoJazz 72*

Rollins, Carl Purington
American. Artist
b. Jan 7, 1880
d. Nov 20, 1960
Source: *CurBio 48, 61; OxAmL; WhAm 4*

Rollins, Howard E, Jr.
American. Actor
Played Coalhouse Walker, Jr., in *Ragtime.*
b. 1951 in Baltimore, Maryland
Source: *JohnWil 82*

Rollins, Kenny
"Fabulous Five"
American. Basketball Player
b. Sep 14, 1923 in Charleston, Missouri
Source: *WhoBbl 73*

Rollins, (Theodore) Sonny
American. Musician, Composer
b. Sep 7, 1930 in New York, New York
Source: *WhoAm 74, 76, 78, 80, 82; WhoE 74*

Rolls, Charles Stewart
English. Auto Manufacturer, Aviator
With F Royce formed Rolls-Royce Ltd, 1906.
b. Aug 27, 1877 in Hendre, England
d. Jul 12, 1910
Source: *WebBD 80; WorAl*

Roloff, Lester
American. Preacher
Radio ministry sponsored homes for rebellious children.
b. 1914?
d. Nov 1982 in Normangee, Texas
Source: *NF*

Rolvaag, Karl
American. Government Official
b. Jul 18, 1913 in Northfield, Minnesota
Source: *CurBio 64; WhoAm 74; WhoAmP 73*

Rolvaag, Ole Edvart
American. Author
b. Apr 22, 1876 in Helgeland, Norway
d. Nov 5, 1931 in Northfield, Minnesota
Source: *AmAu&B; AmBi; CasWL; CnDAL; ConAmA; CyWA; DcAmB; DcLEL; DcNAA; EncWL; EvLB; LongCTC; ModAL; OxAmL; Pen AM; REn; REnAL; TwCA, SUP; TwCW; WebAB; WebE&AL; WhAm 1; WhNAA*

Romains, Jules
French. Author, Philosopher
b. Aug 26, 1885 in Velay, France
d. Aug 14, 1972 in Paris, France
Source: *Au&Wr 71; CasWL; ClDMEL; CnMD; CnMWL; ConAu 85; EncWL; EvEuW; LongCTC; McGEWD; ModRL; ModWD; NewYTBE 72; OxEng; OxFr; OxThe; Pen EUR; REn; TwCA, SUP; TwCW; WhAm 5; WhoThe 77; WhoTwCL*

Roman, Ruth
American. Actress
b. Dec 23, 1924 in Boston, Massachusetts
Source: *FilmgC; IntMPA 75, 76, 77, 78, 79, 80, 81, 82; MotPP; MovMk; WhoHol A; WorEFlm*

Romani, Felice
Italian. Librettist
b. Jan 31, 1788 in Genoa, Italy
d. Jan 28, 1865 in Moneglia, Italy
Source: *OxThe*

Romano, John
American. Psychiatrist
b. Nov 20, 1908 in Milwaukee, Wisconsin
Source: *AmM&WS 73P; WhoAm 74, 76, 78, 80, 82*

Romano, Joseph
Israeli. Murdered Olympic Team Member
b. 1940? in Libya
d. Sep 5, 1972 in Munich, Germany (West)
Source: *BioIn 9*

Romano, Umberto
American. Artist, Educator
Noted for portraits of Martin Luther King, Jr. and John F Kennedy.
b. Feb 26, 1906 in Bracigliano, Italy
d. Sep 27, 1982 in New York, New York
Source: *CurBio 54, 82; NewYTBS 82; WhoAm 74, 76, 78, 80, 82; WhoAmA 73; WhoWor 74*

Romanoff, Mike
[Harry Gerguson]
American. Restaurateur
b. 1890 in Vilna, Lithuania
d. Sep 1, 1971 in Los Angeles, California
Source: *FilmgC; WhoHol B*

Romanov, Anastasia
Russian. Daughter of Czar Nicholas II
d. Jul 19, 1918 in Ekaterinburg, U.S.S.R.
Source: *NewCol 75*

Romanov, Nikolai Aleksandrovich
see: Nicholas II

Romantics, The
["Coz" (George) Canler; Rich Cole; Jimmy Marinos; Wally Palmer; Mike Skill]
American. Rock Group
Source: *NF*

Rombauer, Irma von Starkloff
American. Author
b. Oct 30, 1877 in Saint Louis, Missouri
d. Oct 14, 1962 in Saint Louis, Missouri
Source: *BioIn 2, 3, 6; CurBio 53, 62*

Romberg, Bernhard
German. Composer
b. Nov 11, 1767 in Dinklage, Germany
d. Aug 13, 1841 in Hamburg, Germany
Source: *Baker 78; OxMus*

Romberg, Sigmund
American. Composer
b. Jul 29, 1887 in Nagykanizsa, Hungary
d. Nov 9, 1951 in New York, New York
Source: *AmSCAP 66; CurBio 45, 51; DcAmB S5; EncMT; FilmgC; NewCBMT; PlP&P; WebAB; WhAm 3*

Rome, Harold Jacob
American. Composer
b. May 27, 1908 in Hartford, Connecticut
Source: *AmSCAP 66; BiE&WWA; CelR 73; CurBio 42; EncMT; NewCBMT; NotNAT; WhoAm 74, 76, 78, 80, 82; WhoAmA 73; WhoMus 72; WhoWor 74; WhoWorJ 72*

Romero, Carlos Humberto
Salvadoran. Former President
b. 1924 in Chalatenango, El Salvador
Source: *IntWW 78, 79, 80; IntYB 79, 81; WhoWor 78; WorDWW*

Romero, Cesar
American. Actor
b. Feb 15, 1907 in New York, New York
Source: *BiDFilm; FilmgC; HolP 30; IntMPA 75, 76, 77, 78, 79, 80, 81, 82; MotPP; MovMk; WhoHol A; WorEFlm*

Romero Barcelo, Carlos
Puerto Rican. Governor
b. Sep 4, 1952 in San Juan, Puerto Rico
Source: *CurBio 77; WhoAm 82*

Romero y Galdamez, Oscar Arnulfo
Salvadoran. Archbishop of San Salvador
Advocate of human rights; assassinated.
b. Aug 15, 1917 in Ciudad Barrios, El Salvador
d. Mar 24, 1980 in San Salvador, El Salvador
Source: *AnObit 1980; NewYTBS 80*

Romm, Mikhail
Russian. Motion Picture Director
b. 1901 in Irkutsk, Russia
d. Nov 1, 1971 in Moscow, U.S.S.R.
Source: *BiDFilm; DcFM; FilmgC; NewYTBE 71; OxFilm; WorEFlm*

Rommel, Erwin Johannes Eugin
"Desert Fox"
German. World War II General
Led German Afrika Korps in N Africa in WW II, 1941-43.
b. Nov 15, 1891 in Swabia, Germany
d. Jul 18, 1944 in Herrlingen, France
Source: *CurBio 42, 44; EncTR; McGEWB; NewCol 75; OxGer; REn; WhWW-II; WhoMilH 76*

Romney, George
English. Artist
b. Dec 15, 1734 in Lancashire, England
d. Nov 15, 1802 in Kendal, England
Source: *Alli; AtlBL; BkIE; NewC; NewCol 75; WebBD 80*

Romney, George Wilcken
American. Businessman, Politician
Governor of MI, 1962-69.
b. Jul 8, 1907 in Chihuahua, Mexico
Source: *BiDrUSE; CelR 73; CurBio 58; IntWW 74; Ward 77G; WhoAm 74, 76, 78, 80, 82; WhoAmP 73; WhoF&I 74; WhoGov 72; WhoMW 74; WhoWor 74*

Romney, Lenore la Fount
American. Wife of George Romney
b. in Logan, Vermont
Source: *WhoAmW 77*

Romney, Seymour Leonard
American. Physician, Educator
b. Jun 8, 1917 in New York, New York
Source: *WhoAm 74, 76, 78, 80, 82; WhoE 74*

Rompollo, Dominic
American. Fashion Designer
b. Jan 24, 1935 in Detroit, Michigan
Source: *WorFshn*

Romulo, Carlos Pena
Philippine. Statesman, Journalist
b. Apr 14, 1899 in Manila, Philippines
Source: *AmAu&B; BiDrAC; CathA 1930; ConAu 13R; CurBio 43, 57; IntWW 74; WhNAA; WhoUN 75; WhoWor 74*

Romulus
Roman. Founder and 1st King of Rome
Source: *CasWL; NewCol 75; WebBD 80*

Ronald, Sir Landon
English. Conductor
b. Jun 7, 1873 in London, England
d. Aug 14, 1938 in London, England
Source: *NewEOp 71; OxMus*

Ronan, William J
American. Public Official, Educator
b. Nov 8, 1912 in Buffalo, New York
Source: *AmM&WS 73S; CurBio 69; NewYTBE 70; NewYTBS 74; St&PR 75; WhoAm 74, 76, 78, 80, 82*

Roney, William Chapoton, Jr.
American. Stock Broker
Partner in William C Roney and Co, 1949--
b. Dec 19, 1924 in Detroit, Michigan
Source: *St&PR 75; WhoAm 74, 76, 78, 80, 82*

Ronne, Finn
American. Explorer, Geographer
b. Dec 20, 1899 in Horten, Norway
d. Jan 12, 1980 in Bethesda, Maryland
Source: *AmM&WS 73S; AnObit 1980; ConAu 1R, 97, 1NR; CurBio 48, 80; WhoAm 74; WhoWor 74*

Ronsard, Pierre de
French. Poet
b. Sep 11, 1524 in Vendomois, France
d. Dec 26, 1585 in Touraine, France
Source: *AtlBL; BbD; BiD&SB; CasWL; CyWA; DcEuL; EuAu; EvEuW; NewC; OxEng; OxFr; Pen EUR; RComWL; REn*

Ronstadt, Linda
American. Singer
Has six platinum albums; starred on Broadway in *The Pirates of Penzance,* 1981.
b. Jul 15, 1946 in Tucson, Arizona
Source: *BioIn 9, 10; BkPepl; EncPR&S; IlEncRk; WhoAm 82*

Ronzani, Gene
American. Football Player, Coach
b. 1909
d. 1975
Source: *BioIn 10*

Rooney, Andy (Andrew Aitken)
American. Writer, Producer
Regular commentator on "60 Minutes"; wrote *A Few Minutes with Andy Rooney.*
b. Jan 14, 1919 in Albany, New York
Source: *CurBio 82; NewYTET; WhoAm 78, 80, 82*

Rooney, Art(hur Joseph)
American. Football Team Owner
Chairman, Pittsburgh Steelers, 1933--.
b. Jan 27, 1901 in Coulterville, Pennsylvania
Source: *WhoAm 82; WhoFtbl 74*

Rooney, John (James)
American. Congressman
b. Nov 29, 1903 in Brooklyn, New York
d. Oct 26, 1975 in Washington, DC
Source: *BioIn 5, 7, 8, 9, 10, 11; CurBio 64, 76; WhoAm 74; WhoAmP 73; WhoE 74; WhoGov 72*

Rooney, Mickey
[Joe Yule, Jr.]
American. Actor
Played Andy Hardy in film series, 1937-46; on Broadway in *Sugar Babies.*
b. Sep 23, 1920 in Brooklyn, New York
Source: *AmSCAP 66; BiDFilm; BioNews 74; CelR 73; CmMov; CurBio 42, 65; FilmgC; IntMPA 75, 76, 77, 78, 79, 80, 81, 82; MotPP; MovMk; OxFilm; WhoAm 74, 76, 78, 80, 82; WhoHol A; WhoWor 74; WorAl; WorEFlm*

Rooney, Pat
American. Actor
b. Jul 4, 1880 in New York, New York
d. Sep 9, 1962 in New York, New York
Source: *AmSCAP 66; WhScrn 74, 77; WhoHol B*

Rooney, Pat B, Jr.
American. Motion Picture Producer
b. Nov 10, 1925
Source: *IntMPA 75, 77*

Roos, Frank John, Jr.
American. Author, Educator
b. Jan 10, 1903 in Chicago, Illinois
d. Feb 2, 1967
Source: *BioIn 8; OhA&B; WhAm 4*

Roosa, Stuart
American. Astronaut
Member of Apollo 14, March, 1971.
b. Aug 16, 1933 in Durango, Colorado
Source: *IntWW 74; NewYTBE 71; WhoAm 74, 76, 78, 80, 82; WhoS&SW 73; WhoWor 74*

Roose-Evans, James
English. Author, Theatrical Director
b. Nov 11, 1927 in London, England
Source: *ConAu 29R; WhoThe 77; WrDr 76*

Roosevelt, Anna Eleanor
see: Halsted, Anna Eleanor Roosevelt

Roosevelt, Anna Hall
American. Mother of Eleanor Roosevelt
b. 1863
d. 1892
Source: *BioIn 10*

Roosevelt, Edith Kermit
American. Wife of Theodore Roosevelt
b. Aug 16, 1861 in Norwich, Connecticut
d. Sep 30, 1948 in Oyster Bay, New York
Source: *ForWC 70; InWom; NotAW; TwCBDA; WhAm 2; WomWWA 14*

Roosevelt, Eleanor
"The First Lady of the World"
American. Wife of Franklin D Roosevelt
Married FDR, 1905; US delegate to UN, 1945-53, 1961.
b. Oct 11, 1884 in New York, New York
d. Nov 7, 1962 in New York, New York
Source: *AmAu&B; ConAu 89; CurBio 40, 49, 63; HerW; InWom; LongCTC; OxAmL; REn; REnAL; WebAB; WorAl*

Roosevelt, Elliot
American. Politician
Son of FDR; mayor of Miami Beach, FL, 1965-69.
b. Sep 23, 1910 in New York, New York
Source: *BioIn 10; WhoAm 74*

Roosevelt, Franklin Delano
American. 32nd US President
Served longest presidential term, 1933-45; stricken with polio, 1921.
b. Jan 30, 1882 in Hyde Park, New York
d. Apr 12, 1945 in Warm Springs, Georgia
Source: *AmAu&B; BiDrAC; BiDrUSE; CurBio 42, 45; DcNAA; EncAB-H; LongCTC; WebAB; WhAm 4A*

Roosevelt, Franklin Delano, Jr.
American. Politician
Congressman, 1949-53.
b. Aug 17, 1914 in Campobello, NB
Source: *BiDrAC; IntWW 74; WhoAm 74; WhoE 74; WhoGov 72*

Roosevelt, James
American. Mutual Fund Executive
Son of FDR; wrote several books about family *Affectionately, FDR; My Parents.*
b. Dec 23, 1907 in New York, New York
Source: *BiDrAC; CurBio 50; WhoAm 74, 76, 78, 80, 82; WhoAmP 73*

Roosevelt, John Aspinal
American. Investment Banker
b. Mar 13, 1916 in Washington, DC
d. Apr 27, 1981 in New York, New York
Source: *BioIn 1, 2, 3, 4; St&PR 75; WhoAm 74, 76, 78, 80*

Roosevelt, Kermit
American. Son of Theodore Roosevelt
Traveler; wrote *War in the Garden of Eden,* 1919.
b. Oct 10, 1889 in Oyster Bay, New York
d. Jun 4, 1943 in Alaska
Source: *AmAu&B; CurBio 43; DcAmB S3; DcNAA; REnAL; WhAm 2; WhNAA*

Roosevelt, Quentin
American. Son of Theodore Roosevelt
b. 1897
d. Jul 14, 1918
Source: *BioIn 1, 5*

Roosevelt, Sara Delano
American. Mother of Franklin Roosevelt
b. Sep 21, 1855
d. Sep 7, 1941 in Hyde Park, New York
Source: *CurBio 41; InWom*

Roosevelt, Theodore
American. 26th US President
Led "Rough Riders" in Cuba, 1898; president, 1901-09.
b. Oct 27, 1858 in New York, New York
d. Jan 6, 1919 in Sagamore Hill, New York
Source: *Alli SUP; AmAu&B; AmBi; AmLY; ApCAB, SUP; BbD; BiD&SB; BiDrAC; BiDrUSE; Br&AmS; Chambr 3; ChPo, S1, S2; DcAmAu; DcAmB; DcNAA; EncAB-H; EvLB; FilmgC; LongCTC; OxAmL; Pen AM; REn; REnAL; TwCBDA; WebAB; WhAm HA, 1, 4A; WhAmP; WorAl*

Root, Alan
British. Naturalist, Filmmaker
b. 1936 in London, England
Source: *BioIn 12*

Root, Elihu
American. Lawyer, Statesman
b. Feb 15, 1845 in Clinton, New York
d. Feb 7, 1937 in New York, New York
Source: *AmAu&B; AmBi; ApCAB, SUP; BiDrAC; DcAmB S2; DcNAA; EncAB-H; REnAL; TwCBDA; WebAB; WhAm 1; WhAmP*

Root, Jack
American. Boxer
b. May 26, 1876 in Austria
d. Jun 10, 1963 in Los Angeles, California
Source: *WhoBox 74*

Root, Joan
British. Naturalist, Filmmaker
b. 1936 in Nairobi, Kenya
Source: *BioIn 12*

Root, John Wellborn
American. Architect
b. Jul 14, 1887 in Chicago, Illinois
d. Oct 24, 1963
Source: *NewCol 75; WebBD 80; WhAm 4*

Rootes, William Edward Rootes, Baron
English. Business Executive
Chairman, Chrysler UK, 1967-73; director, Lucas Industries, 1973--.
b. Jun 14, 1917 in Loose, England
Source: *IntWW 74, 75, 76, 77, 78, 79, 80, 81; Who 74; WhoF&I 74, 75, 77; WhoWor 74*

Roper, Daniel C
American. Lawyer, Politician
b. Apr 1, 1867 in Marlboro, South Carolina
d. Apr 11, 1943 in Washington, DC
Source: *BiDrUSE; CurBio 43; DcAmB S3; WhAm 2*

Roper, Elmo Burns, Jr.
American. Marketing Consultant
b. Jul 31, 1900 in Hebron, Nebraska
d. Apr 30, 1971 in Norwalk, Connecticut
Source: *AmAu&B; CurBio 45, 71; NewYTBE 71*

Rorem, Ned
American. Composer
b. Oct 23, 1923 in Richmond, Indiana
Source: *AmAu&B; AmSCAP 66; ConAu 17R; CurBio 67; DcCM; IndAu 1917; WhoAm 74, 76, 78, 80, 82; WhoE 74; WhoMus 72; WhoWor 74*

Rorschach, Hermann
Swiss. Psychiatrist
b. Nov 8, 1884 in Zurich, Switzerland
d. Apr 2, 1922 in Herisau, Switzerland
Source: *AsBiEn; BioIn 5*

Rosa, Carl
German. Impresario
b. Mar 21, 1842 in Hamburg, Germany
d. Apr 30, 1889 in Paris, France
Source: *NewEOp 71*

Rosa, Salvator
Italian. Artist
b. Jul 1615 in Naples, Italy
d. Mar 15, 1673 in Rome, Italy
Source: *AtlBL; BbD; BiD&SB; DcEuL*

Rosand, Aaron
American. Musician
b. Mar 15, 1927 in Hammond, Indiana
Source: *WhoAm 74; WhoMus 72; WhoWorJ 72*

Rosay, Francoise
French. Actress
b. Apr 19, 1891 in Paris, France
d. Mar 28, 1974 in Paris, France
Source: *BiE&WWA; FilmgC; InWom; MotPP; MovMk; NewYTBS 74; OxFilm; WhScrn 77; Who 74; WhoHol B; WorEFlm*

Rosbaud, Hans
Austrian. Conductor
b. Jul 22, 1895 in Graz, Austria
d. Dec 30, 1962 in Lugano, Italy
Source: *WhAm 4*

Rose, Augustus Steele
American. Neurologist
b. Jul 14, 1907 in Fayetteville, North Carolina
Source: *AmM&WS 73P; DcNAA; WhoAm 74; WhoF&I 74*

Rose, Billy
[William S Rosenburg]
American. Theatrical Producer
Musicals included *Jumbo,* 1935; *Carmen Jones,* 1943; married to Fanny Brice.
b. Sep 6, 1899 in New York, New York
d. Feb 10, 1966 in Montego Bay, Jamaica
Source: *AmSCAP 66; BiE&WWA; ChPo S2; CurBio 40, 66; EncMT; WhAm 4; WorAl*

Rose, Carl
Cartoonist, Illustrator
b. 1903
d. Jun 21, 1971
Source: *ConAu 29R*

Rose, David
English. Musician
b. Jun 15, 1910 in London, England
Source: *AmSCAP 66; FilmgC; IntMPA 75, 77; WhoAm 74, 76, 78, 80, 82; WhoWorJ 72*

Rose, Felipe
see: Village People, The

Rose, Fred
American. Singer
b. Aug 24, 1897 in Evansville, Indiana
d. Dec 1, 1954 in Nashville, Tennessee
Source: *AmSCAP 66; EncFCWM 69*

Rose, George
English. Actor
b. Feb 19, 1920 in Bicester, England
Source: *BiE&WWA; FilmgC; MovMk; NotNAT; WhoHol A; WhoThe 77*

Rose, Helen
[Helen Bronberg]
American. Film, Fashion Designer
b. in Chicago, Illinois
Source: *ChPo S2; WhoAm 74; WorFshn*

Rose, Leonard
American. Musician
b. Jul 27, 1918 in Washington, DC
Source: *NewYTBE 71; WhoAm 74, 76, 78, 80, 82; WhoMus 72; WhoWor 74*

Rose, Murray
[Iain Murray Rose]
Australian. Swimmer
Won three gold medals, 1956 Olympics.
b. Jan 6, 1939 in Nairn, Scotland
Source: *BioIn 5, 6, 7, 10*

Rose, Pete(r Edward)
"Charlie Hustle"
American. Baseball Player
Has collected a NL record 3,869 hits through 1982.
b. Apr 14, 1941 in Cincinnati, Ohio
Source: *BaseEn; NewYTBE 73; WhoAm 82; WhoProB 73*

Rose, Vincent
American. Composer, Conductor
b. Jun 13, 1880 in Palermo, Italy
d. May 20, 1944 in Rockville Centre, New York
Source: *AmSCAP 66; BiDAmM; CmpEPM*

Rose-Marie
American. Comedienne, Singer
Played Sally Rogers on "The Dick Van Dyke Show," 1961-66.
b. in New York, New York
Source: *WhoHol A; WorAl*

Rosebery, Archibald Philip Primrose, Earl
British. Prime Minister
b. May 7, 1847 in London, England
d. May 21, 1929
Source: *BiD&SB; BioIn 2, 3, 5, 6, 8, 9, 10; Chambr 3; EvLB; LongCTC; NewCol 75; OxEng; WhoModH*

Roseboro, John H
"Gabby"
American. Baseball Player
b. May 13, 1933 in Ashland, Ohio
Source: *BaseEn; ConAu 102; WhoAm 74; WhoBlA 75, 77; WhoProB 73*

Rosecrans, William Starke
American. Army Officer, Diplomat
b. Sep 6, 1819 in Delaware County, Ohio
d. Mar 11, 1898 in Redondo Beach, California
Source: *AmBi; ApCAB; BiAuS; BiDrAC; DcAmB; Drake; TwCBDA; WebAB; WhAm H*

Rosen, Al(bert Leonard)
"Flip"
American. Baseball Player, Executive
With Cleveland Indians, 1947-56; general manager, Houston Astros, 1980--.
b. Mar 1, 1925 in Spartanburg, South Carolina
Source: *BaseEn; CurBio 54; WhoAm 82; WhoMus 72; WhoProB 73*

Rosen, Barry
[The Hostages]
American. Former Hostage in Iran
b. 1944?
Source: *NewYTBS 81*

Rosen, Nathaniel
American. Musician
b. 1948?
Source: *BioIn 11; WhoAm 82*

Rosen, Sheldon
American. Dramatist
b. Aug 26, 1943 in Bronx, New York
Source: *NatPD 81; OxCan SUP*

Rosen, Sidney
American. Children's Author
b. Jun 5, 1916 in Boston, Massachusetts
Source: *AmM&WS 73P; ConAu 9R; LEduc 74; SmATA 1; WrDr 76*

Rosenbach, Abraham Simon Wolf
American. Rare Book Dealer, Collector
b. Jul 22, 1876 in Philadelphia, Pennsylvania
d. Jul 1, 1952 in Philadelphia, Pennsylvania
Source: *AmAu&B; ChPo, S1, S2; DcAmB S5; LongCTC; OxAmL; REnAL; WebAB; WhAm 3*

Rosenberg, Alfred
German. Nazi Leader
b. Jan 12, 1893 in Reval, Russia
d. Oct 16, 1946 in Nuremberg, Germany
Source: *BioIn 1, 8, 9; CurBio 41, 46; EncTR; LongCTC; ObitOF 79; REn; WhWW-II*

Rosenberg, Anna Marie
American. Labor Relations Consultant
b. Jul 19, 1900 in Budapest, Hungary
Source: *CurBio 43, 51; InWom*

Rosenberg, Ethel Greenglass
American. Traitor
US communist convicted of giving secrets to USSR; first civilian executed for espionage.
b. Sep 28, 1915 in New York, New York
d. Jun 19, 1953 in Sing Sing, New York
Source: *DcAmB S5; InWom; WebAB; WhoAmW 77; WorAl*

Rosenberg, Hilding
Swedish. Opera Composer
b. Jun 21, 1892 in Bosjokloster, Sweden
Source: *DcCM*

Rosenberg, Issac
English. Poet
b. 1890 in Bristol, England
Source: *BioIn 1, 2, 7, 10, 11*

Rosenberg, Jakob
American. Curator, Art Historian
b. Sep 5, 1893 in Berlin, Germany
d. Apr 7, 1980 in Cambridge, Massachusetts
Source: *BioIn 10; ConAu 97*

Rosenberg, Julius
American. Traitor
With wife Ethel convicted of espionage; executed.
b. May 12, 1918 in New York, New York
d. Jun 19, 1953 in Sing Sing, New York
Source: *DcAmB S5; WebAB; WorAl*

Rosenberg, Richie
see: Southside Johnny and the Asbury Jukes

Rosenberg, Sharon
American. Author
b. Dec 14, 1942 in New York, New York
Source: *ConAu 57; SmATA 8*

Rosenbloom, Carroll D
American. Football Team Owner, Businessman
Owned LA Rams, Baltimore Colts; drowned while swimming.
b. Mar 5, 1907 in Baltimore, Maryland
d. Apr 2, 1979 in Miami, Florida
Source: *BioIn 7, 11; NewYTBS 79; WhoFtbl 74*

Rosenbloom, Georgia
[Georgia Frontiere]
"Madam Ram"
American. Football Team Owner
First woman owner of football team--LA Rams.
b. 1926 in Saint Louis, Missouri
Source: *NewYTBS 79*

Rosenbloom, Maxie
"Slapsie Maxie"
American. Boxer, Actor
b. Sep 6, 1906 in New York, New York
d. Mar 6, 1976 in South Pasadena, California
Source: *IntMPA 75; MotPP; MovMk; WhoBox 74*

Rosenfeld, Alvin Hirsch
American. Editor, Author
b. Apr 28, 1938 in Philadelphia, Pennsylvania
Source: *ConAu 49, 4NR; DrAS 74E*

Rosenfeld, Henry
American. Fashion Designer
b. May 17, 1911 in New York, New York
Source: *CurBio 48; WhoAm 74*

Rosenfeld, Paul
American. Music, Art Critic
b. May 4, 1890 in New York, New York
d. Jul 21, 1946 in New York, New York
Source: *AmAu&B; CnDAL; CurBio 46; DcAmB S4; DcNAA; OxAmL; REnAL; TwCA, SUP; WhAm 2*

Rosenkreutz, Christian
Founded Rosicrucian Society
Source: *WebBD 80*

Rosenquist, James Albert
American. Artist
b. Nov 29, 1933 in Grand Forks, North Dakota
Source: *CelR 73; CurBio 70; DcCAA 71; WhoAm 74; WhoE 74; WhoWor 74*

Rosenstein, Nettie
American. Designer, Philanthropist
b. Sep 26, 1893 in Vienna, Austria
d. Mar 13, 1980 in New York, New York
Source: *InWom; WhAm 7; WhoAm 74; WorFshn*

Rosenstock, Joseph
Polish. Conductor
b. Jan 27, 1895 in Krakow, Poland
Source: *CurBio 54; WhoMus 72; WhoWor 74; WhoWorJ 72*

Rosenthal, Abraham Michael
Canadian. Editor, Author
b. May 2, 1922 in Sault St. Marie, ON
Source: *AmAu&B; ConAu 21R; IntWW 74; WhoAm 74, 76, 78, 80, 82; WhoE 74; WhoF&I 74*

Rosenthal, Benjamin Stanley
American. Politician
Congressman from NY, 1962-82.
b. Jun 8, 1923 in New York, New York
d. Jan 4, 1983 in Washington, DC
Source: *AlmAP 78, 80; BiDrAC; CngDr 74, 77, 79, 81; WhoAm 74, 76, 78, 80, 82; WhoAmP 73, 75, 77, 79; WhoE 74, 75, 77, 79; WhoGov 72, 75, 77*

Rosenthal, Joe (Joseph J)
American. Photographer
b. Oct 9, 1911 in Washington, DC
Source: *ConAu 69; CurBio 45*

Rosenthal, Manuel
French. Conductor
b. 1904 in Paris, France
Source: *DcCM; WhoMus 72*

Rosenthal, Moriz
Polish. Musician
b. Dec 18, 1862 in Bemberg, Poland
d. Sep 3, 1946 in New York, New York
Source: *CurBio 46; NewCol 75; WebBD 80*

Rosenwald, Julius
American. Merchant, Philanthropist
b. Aug 12, 1862 in Springfield, Illinois
d. Jan 6, 1932 in Chicago, Illinois
Source: *AmBi; DcAmB; EncAB-H; WebAB; WhAm 1*

Rosewall, Ken
Australian. Tennis Player
b. Nov 2, 1934 in Sydney, Australia
Source: *CelR 73; CurBio 56*

Rosing, Vladimir
Russian. Opera Singer
b. Jan 23, 1890 in Saint Petersburg, Russia
d. Nov 24, 1963 in Los Angeles, California
Source: *WhAm 4*

Roskolenko, Harry
American. Author
b. Sep 21, 1907 in New York, New York
d. Jul 17, 1980 in New York, New York
Source: *ConAu 13R, 101; WrDr 76*

Rosovsky, Henry
American. College Dean, Economist
b. Sep 1, 1927 in Danzig, Germany
Source: *AmEA 74; AmM&WS 73S; WhoAm 74, 76, 78, 80, 82; WhoE 74*

Ross, Albion
American. Journalist
b. Apr 29, 1906 in Ashland, Wisconsin
Source: *DrAS 74E*

Ross, Barney
[Barnet David Rasofsky]
American. Boxer, Actor
b. Dec 23, 1907 in New York, New York
d. Jan 18, 1967 in Chicago, Illinois
Source: *WhScrn 74, 77; WhoBox 74; WhoHol B*

Ross, Betsy Griscom
American. Seamtress
Made first US flag at George Washington's request, 1776.
b. Jan 1, 1752 in Philadelphia, Pennsylvania
d. Jan 30, 1836 in Philadelphia, Pennsylvania
Source: *AmBi; ApCAB SUP; DcAmB; ForWC 70; HerW; InWom; NotAW; REnAL; WebAB; WhAm H; WorAl*

Ross, David
American. Actor, Poet
b. 1891 in New York, New York
d. Nov 12, 1975 in New York, New York
Source: *ChPo S2; ConAu 61, 65; WhAm 6; WhScrn 77; WhoAm 74*

Ross, David
American. Motion Picture Director, Producer
b. Jun 17, 1922 in Saint Paul, Minnesota
Source: *BiE&WWA*

Ross, Diana
[The Supremes]
American. Actress, Singer
Starred in *Lady Sings the Blues;* won Tony, 1977.
b. Mar 26, 1944 in Detroit, Michigan
Source: *BkPepl; CelR 73; CurBio 73; IntMPA 75, 76, 77, 78, 79, 80, 81, 82; MovMk; NewYTBE 72; WhoAm 74, 76, 78, 80, 82; WhoAmW 77; WhoBlA 75; WhoHol A; WhoWest 74*

Ross, George
American. Continental Congressman
b. Mar 10, 1730 in New Castle, Delaware
d. Jul 14, 1779 in Lancaster, Pennsylvania
Source: *AmBi; ApCAB; BiAuS; BiDrAC; DcAmB; Drake; TwCBDA; WhAm H; WhAmP*

Ross, Harold
American. Magazine Editor
b. Nov 6, 1892 in Aspen, Colorado
d. Dec 6, 1957 in Boston, Massachusetts
Source: *AmAu&B; CurBio 43, 52; DcAmB S5; LongCTC; REn; REnAL; WebAB; WhAm 3*

Ross, Herbert David
American. Motion Picture Director
b. May 13, 1927 in Brooklyn, New York
Source: *BiE&WWA; BioIn 4, 8, 11; CmMov; CurBio 80; FilmgC; IntMPA 75, 76, 77, 78, 79, 80, 81, 82; NotNAT; WhoAm 80, 82; WorEFlm*

Ross, Ishbel
American. Author
b. 1897 in Scotland
d. Sep 21, 1975 in New York, New York
Source: *AmAu&B; AmNov; ConAu 61, 93; ForWC 70; InWom*

Ross, Sir James Clark
Scottish. Explorer
Located north magnetic pole, 1831.
b. Apr 15, 1800 in Balsarroch, Scotland
d. Sep 21, 1862 in Aylsbury, Scotland
Source: *Alli; ApCAB; BrAu 19; DcLEL; NewC; NewCol 75; OxCan; OxEng*

Ross, Joe E
American. Comedian
d. Aug 13, 1982 in Los Angeles, California
Source: *WhoHol A*

Ross, John
[Kooweskoowe]
American. Cherokee Chief
b. Oct 2, 1790 in Lookout Mountain, Tennessee
d. Aug 1, 1866 in Washington, DC
Source: *BioIn 4, 5, 9, 11; NewCol 75*

Ross, Katharine
American. Actress
Starred in *The Graduate; Butch Cassidy and the Sundance Kid; The Stepford Wives.*
b. Jan 29, 1943 in Hollywood, California
Source: *FilmgC; IntMPA 75, 76, 77, 78, 79, 80, 81, 82; MotPP; MovMk; WhoAm 74, 76, 78, 80, 82; WhoHol A*

Ross, Lanny
American. Composer, Singer
b. Jan 19, 1906 in Seattle, Washington
Source: *AmSCAP 66; IntMPA 75, 76, 77, 78, 79, 80, 81, 82; WhoHol A*

Ross, Leonard Q, pseud.
see: Rosten, Leo Calvin

Ross, Lillian
American. Journalist, Author
b. Jun 8, 1927 in Syracuse, New Jersey
Source: *AmAu&B; ConAu 9R; RAdv 1; WhoAm 74; WorAu*

Ross, Marion
American. Actress
Plays Marion Cunningham on "Happy Days," 1974--.
b. Oct 25, 1936? in Albert Lea, Minnesota
Source: *BioIn 10; WhoAm 80, 82*

Ross, Nellie Tayloe
American. First Woman Governor in US
Governor of WY, 1925-27; first woman director of US Mint, 1933-53.
b. Nov 29, 1876 in Saint Joseph, Missouri
d. Dec 19, 1977 in Washington, DC
Source: *CurBio 40, 78; GoodHS; InWom; LibW; NewYTBS 77; WebAB; WhAmP; WorAl*

Ross, Sir Ronald
British. Scientist, Engineer, Physician
b. May 13, 1857 in Almora, India
d. Sep 16, 1932 in London, England
Source: *AsBiEn; LongCTC*

Ross, Roy G
American. Clergyman, Educator
b. 1898
d. Jan 8, 1978 in Pompano Beach, Florida
Source: *BioIn 11*

Ross, Ruth N
American. Journalist
b. in New York, New York
Source: *ForWC 70*

Rossant, James Stephan
American. Architect
b. Aug 17, 1928 in New York, New York
Source: *AmArch 70; WhoAm 78, 80, 82*

Rossellini, Isabella
[Mrs. Martin Scorsese]
Italian. Actress, Model
Daughter of Ingrid Bergman and Roberto Rossellini.
b. Jun 18, 1952 in Italy
Source: *NF*

Rossellini, Renzo
Italian. Opera Composer
b. Feb 2, 1908 in Rome, Italy
d. May 14, 1982 in Monte Carlo, Monaco
Source: *DcFM; IntWW 74; WhoHol A; WhoMus 72; WhoWor 74*

Rossellini, Roberto
Italian. Motion Picture Director
Directed *Open City, Stromboli;* second husband of Ingrid Bergman.
b. May 8, 1906 in Rome, Italy
d. Jun 3, 1977 in Rome, Italy
Source: *ConAu 69; CurBio 49; DcFM; FilmgC; IntMPA 75, 76, 77; IntWW 74; MovMk; NewYTBE 71; NewYTBS 74; OxFilm; REn; WhoWor 74; WorEFlm*

Rossen, Robert
American. Motion Picture Director, Producer
b. Mar 16, 1908 in New York, New York
d. Feb 18, 1966 in New York, New York
Source: *BiDFilm; CmMov; CurBio 50, 66; DcFM; FilmgC; MovMk; OxFilm; WhAm 4; WorEFlm*

Rossetti, Christina Georgina
English. Poet
b. Dec 5, 1830 in London, England
d. Dec 29, 1894 in London, England
Source: *Alli, SUP; AnCL; AtlBL; BbD; BiD&SB; BrAu 19; CarSB; CasWL; Chambr 3; ChPo, S1, S2; CnE&AP; CrtT 3; CyWA; DcEnA, AP; DcEnL; DcEuL; DcLEL; EvLB; InWom; JBA 34; MouLC 4; NewC; OxEng; Pen ENG; RAdv 1; REn; Str&VC; WebE&AL*

Rossetti, Dante Gabriel
English. Poet, Artist
b. May 12, 1828 in London, England
d. Apr 9, 1882 in Birchington, England
Source: *Alli; AtlBL; BbD; BiD&SB; BrAu 19; Chambr 3; ChPo, S1, S2; CnE&AP; CrtT 3; CyWA; DcEnA; DcEnL; DcLEL; EvLB; MouLC 4; NewC; OxEng; Pen ENG; RAdv 1; RComWL; REn; WebE&AL*

Rossetti, Gabriele Pasquale Giuseppe
Italian. Poet, Scholar
b. Feb 28, 1783 in Vasto, Italy
d. Apr 24, 1854 in London, England
Source: *Alli; BiD&SB; CasWL; DcEuL; EvEuW*

Rossetti, Gino (Louis A)
American. Architect
b. 1930
Source: *BioIn 10*

Rossetti, William Michael
English. Art Critic
b. Sep 25, 1829 in London, England
d. Feb 5, 1919
Source: *Alli, SUP; BiD&SB; BrAu 19; Chambr 3; ChPo, S1, S2; DcEnA, AP; DcEnL; DcEuL; DcLEL; EvLB; NewC; OxEng; REn*

Rossi, Gaetano
Italian. Librettist
b. 1780 in Verona, Italy
d. Jan 27, 1855 in Verona, Italy
Source: *NewEOp 71*

Rossi, Peter Henry
American. Educator
b. Dec 27, 1921 in New York, New York
Source: *AmAu&B; AmM&WS 73S; ConAu 1R, 4NR; WhoAm 74, 76, 78, 80, 82; WhoE 74*

Rossi-Lemeni, Nicola
Turkish. Opera Singer
b. Nov 6, 1920 in Constantinople, Turkey
Source: *WhoMus 72*

Rossini, Gioacchino Antonio
Italian. Opera Composer
b. Feb 29, 1792 in Pesaro, Italy
d. Nov 13, 1868 in Passy, France
Source: *AtlBL; NewCol 75; OxFr; WebBD 80*

Rossner, Judith
American. Author
Wrote *Looking for Mr. Goodbar,* 1975; filmed, 1977.
b. Mar 1, 1935 in New York, New York
Source: *ConAu 17R; ConLC 6, 9; DrAF 76; WhoAm 82; WrDr 76*

Rostand, Edmond Alexis
French. Dramatist
Wrote *Cyrano de Bergerac,* 1897.
b. Apr 1, 1868 in Marseilles, France
d. Dec 2, 1918 in Paris, France
Source: *AtlBL; BiD&SB; CasWL; ClDMEL; CnMD; CnThe; CyWA; EncWL; EvEuW; LongCTC; McGEWD; ModRL; ModWD; NewC; OxEng; OxFr; OxThe; Pen EUR; REn; REnWD; TwCA, SUP; WorAl*

Rosten, Leo Calvin
[Leonard Q Ross, pseud.]
American. Author, Political Scientist
b. Apr 11, 1908 in Lodz, Poland
Source: *AmAu&B; Au&Wr 71; ConAu 5R; ConNov 72, 76; CurBio 42; LongCTC; OxAmL; Pen AM; REn; REnAL; TwCA, SUP; WhNAA; Who 74; WhoAm 74, 76, 78, 80, 82; WhoWor 74; WhoWorJ 72; WrDr 76*

Rostenkowski, Daniel David
American. Congressman
b. Jan 2, 1928 in Chicago, Illinois
Source: *AlmAP 78, 80; BiDrAC; BioIn 11; CngDr 74, 77, 79; CurBio 82; WhoAm 74, 76, 78, 80, 82; WhoAmP 73, 75, 77, 79; WhoGov 72, 75, 77; WhoMW 74, 76, 78*

Rostow, Eugene Victor
American. Lawyer, Economist
Head, Arms Control, Disarmament Agency ousted by President Reagan over policy dispute, 1983.
b. Aug 25, 1913 in Brooklyn, New York
Source: *ConAu 5R; CurBio 61; DrAS 74P; IntWW 74; Who 74; WhoAm 74, 76, 78, 80, 82; WhoWor 74; WhoWorJ 72*

Rostow, Walt Whitman
American. Government Official
b. Oct 7, 1916 in New York, New York
Source: *AmAu&B; AmM&WS 73S; ConAu 13R; CurBio 61; DrAS 74H; EncAB-H; IntWW 74; Who 74; WhoAm 74, 76, 78, 80, 82; WhoAmP 73; WhoWor 74; WrDr 76*

Rostropovich, Mstislav Leopoldovich
Russian. Musician
b. Aug 12, 1927 in Baku, U.S.S.R.
Source: *CurBio 66; IntWW 74; Who 74; WhoAm 82; WhoMus 72; WhoWor 74*

Roswaenge, Helge
Danish. Opera Singer
b. Aug 29, 1897 in Copenhagen, Denmark
d. Aug 1972 in Denmark
Source: *WhScrn 77*

Roszak, Theodore
American. Sculptor
Designed 37-foot aluminum eagle for facade of US Embassy, London, 1960.
b. May 1, 1907 in Poznan, Poland
d. Sep 3, 1981 in New York, New York
Source: *AmAu&B; BioIn 1, 3, 4, 5; BnEnAmA; ConArt; CurBio 66, 81; DcAmArt; DcCAA 71, 77; WhoAm 74, 76, 78, 80; WhoAmA 73, 76, 78, 80; WhoWor 74, 76*

Roszak, Theodore
American. Historian, Author
b. 1933 in Chicago, Illinois
Source: *ConAu 77; CurBio 82; WhoAm 74, 76, 78, 80*

Rote, Kyle
American. Football Player, Sportscaster
With NY Giants, 1951-61.
b. Oct 27, 1928 in San Antonio, Texas
Source: *AmSCAP 66; ConAu 25R; CurBio 65; WhoFtbl 74*

Rote, Kyle, Jr.
American. Soccer Player
b. Dec 25, 1950 in Dallas, Texas
Source: *BioNews 74; NewYTBE 73; NewYTBS 74*

Roth, David Lee
see: Van Halen

Roth, Frank
American. Artist
b. Feb 22, 1936 in Boston, Massachusetts
Source: *DcCAA 71; WhoAm 74; WhoAmA 73*

Roth, Henry
American. Author
b. Feb 8, 1906 in Austria-Hungary
Source: *AmAu&B; CasWL; ConAu P-1; ConLC 2, 6; ConNov 72, 76; EncWL; ModAL; Pen AM; RAdv 1; WebE&AL; WhoAm 74, 76, 78, 80, 82; WhoTwCL; WhoWor 74; WorAu; WrDr 76*

Roth, Lillian
American. Singer
b. Dec 13, 1910 in Boston, Massachusetts
d. May 12, 1980 in New York, New York
Source: *BiE&WWA; ConAu 97; Film 1; FilmgC; MovMk; NotNAT; PlP&P; ThFT; WhoHol A; WhoThe 77*

Roth, Mark Stephan
American. Bowler
Has won 26 professional tournaments; leading money winner, 1977-78.
b. Apr 10, 1951 in Brooklyn, New York
Source: *BioIn 11; WhoAm 82*

Roth, Philip Milton
American. Author
b. Mar 19, 1933 in Newark, New Jersey
Source: *AmAu&B; CasWL; CelR 73; ConAu 1R, 1NR; ConLC 1, 2, 3, 4, 6, 9, 15; ConNov 72, 76; CurBio 70; DrAF 76; EncWL; IntWW 74; ModAL, SUP; NewYTBE 71; OxAmL; Pen AM; RAdv 1; REn; REnAL; TwCW; WebE&AL; WhoAm 74, 76, 78, 80, 82; WhoTwCL; WhoWor 74; WorAu; WrDr 76*

Roth, Richard Lynn
American. Advertising Executive
b. Jun 2, 1946 in Denver, Colorado
Source: *WhoMW 74*

Roth, William Victor, Jr.
American. Senator
b. Jul 22, 1921 in Great Falls, Montana
Source: *BioIn 9, 10; IntWW 74; WhoAm 74, 76, 78, 80, 82; WhoAmP 73; WhoE 74; WhoGov 72*

Roth, Wolfgang
American. Artist, Stage Designer
b. Feb 25, 1910 in Berlin, Germany
Source: *WhoAm 74*

Rothenberg, Jerome
American. Poet
b. Dec 11, 1931 in New York, New York
Source: *ConAu 45, 1NR; ConP 70, 75; CroCAP; DrAP 75; Pen AM; RAdv 1; WhoAm 82; WrDr 76*

Rothermere, Esmond Cecil Harmsworth, Viscount
English. Newspaper Publisher, Politician
b. May 29, 1898 in London, England
d. Jul 12, 1978 in London, England
Source: *BioIn 1, 11; ConAu 89; CurBio 48, 78; IntWW 74, 75, 76, 77, 78; IntYB 78; Who 74; WhoWor 74*

Rothermere, Harold Sidney Harmsworth
English. Journalist
b. 1868
d. Nov 26, 1940 in Hamilton, Bermuda
Source: *BioIn 2; NewCol 75; WebBD 80*

Rothier, Leon
French. Opera Singer
b. Dec 26, 1874 in Rheims, France
d. Dec 6, 1951 in New York, New York
Source: *WhAm 5*

Rothko, Mark
[Marcus Rothkovich]
American. Artist
Co-founded The Ten, an abstract expressionist group, 1935.
b. Sep 25, 1903 in Daugavpils, Russia
d. Feb 25, 1970 in New York, New York
Source: *AtlBL; CurBio 61, 70; DcCAA 71; EncAB-H; NewYTBE 70; WebAB; WhAm 5*

Rothmuller, Marko A
Yugoslav. Opera Singer
b. Dec 31, 1908 in Trnjani, Yugoslavia
Source: *WhoAm 74, 76, 78, 80, 82*

Rothschild, Edmond, Baron
French. Banker
b. 1845
d. 1934
Source: *BioIn 10*

Rothschild, Edmund Leopold de
English. Banker
President, N M Rothschild & Sons, 1975--.
b. Jan 16, 1916 in London, England
Source: *IntWW 74, 75, 76, 77, 78, 79, 80, 81; Who 74; WhoCan 73*

Rothschild, Guy Edouard Alphonse Paul de, Baron
French. Banker
With Banque Rothschild until govt. nationalization, 1981.
b. May 21, 1909 in Paris, France
Source: *CurBio 73; IntWW 74, 75, 76, 77, 78, 79, 80, 81; Who 74; WhoWor 74; WhoWorJ 72*

Rothschild, Leopold David
English. Banker
b. 1927
Source: *Who 74*

Rothschild, Lionel Nathan Rothschild, Baron
English. Banker, Member of Parliament
First Jewish member of Parliament, 1858-74; son of Nathan Mayer Rothschild.
b. Nov 22, 1808 in London, England
d. Jun 3, 1879
Source: *NewCol 75; WorAl*

Rothschild, Mayer Amschel
German. Financier
Founded Rothschild family financial dynasty, Frankfurt, Germany.
b. Feb 23, 1743 in Frankfurt, Germany
d. Sep 19, 1812
Source: *NewCol 75; WebBD 80; WhDW; WorAl*

Rothschild, Nathan Meyer
British. Banker
Opened British branch of family bank, 1805; son of Mayer Rothschild.
b. Sep 16, 1777 in Frankfurt, Germany
d. Jul 28, 1836
Source: *NewCol 75; WorAl*

Rothschild, Philippe, Baron
French. Vintner
b. 1902
Source: *NewYTBE 72*

Rothstein, Arnold
American. Gambler
Murdered in hotel room while playing cards, allegedly for reneging on bet.
b. 1882 in New York, New York
d. 1928
Source: *BioIn 9; NewCol 75*

Rothwell, Walter Henry
English. Conductor
b. Sep 22, 1872 in London, England
d. Mar 12, 1927 in Los Angeles, California
Source: *BiDAmM; NewEOp 71*

Rotten, Johnny
see: Sex Pistols

Rouault, Georges
French. Artist
b. May 27, 1871 in Paris, France
d. Feb 13, 1958 in Paris, France
Source: *AtlBL; CurBio 45, 58; NewCol 75; WebBD 80; WhAm 3*

Roudebush, Richard Lowell
American. Government Official
b. Jan 18, 1918 in Noblesville, Indiana
Source: *BiDrAC; NewYTBS 74; WhoAmP 73*

Roueche, Berton
American. Author
b. Apr 16, 1911 in Kansas City, Missouri
Source: *AmAu&B; ConAu 1R, 1NR; CurBio 59; DrAF 76; REnAL; WhoAm 74, 76, 78, 80, 82; WhoWor 74*

Rouget de Lisle, Claude Joseph
French. Songwriter
b. May 10, 1760 in Lons le Saulnier, France
d. Jun 20, 1836 in Choisy le Roi, France
Source: *BbD; BiD&SB; CasWL; DcEuL; EuAu; EvEuW; NewC; OxEng; OxFr; REn*

Roundfield, Dan(ny T)
American. Basketball Player
b. May 26, 1953 in Detroit, Michigan
Source: *OfNBA*

Roundtree, Richard
American. Actor
Starred in *Shaft*, 1971.
b. Sep 7, 1942 in New Rochelle, New York
Source: *CelR 73; FilmgC; IntMPA 75, 76, 77, 78, 79, 80, 81, 82; MovMk; NewYTBE 72; WhoAm 82; WhoBlA 75; WhoHol A*

Rounseville, Robert Field
American. Actor, Opera Singer
b. Mar 25, 1914 in Attleboro, Massachusetts
d. Aug 6, 1974 in New York, New York
Source: *BiE&WWA; EncMT; NewYTBS 74; WhAm 6; WhoAm 74; WhoHol B; WhoThe 77*

Rourke, Constance Mayfield
American. Author
b. Nov 14, 1885 in Cleveland, Ohio
d. Mar 23, 1941 in Grand Rapids, Michigan
Source: *AmAu&B; AnCL; CnDAL; ConAmA; CurBio 41; DcAmB S3; DcNAA; InWom; ModAL; MorJA; NotAW; OhA&B; OxAmL; Pen AM; REn; REnAL; TwCA, SUP; WhAm 1; YABC 1*

Rous, Peyton
American. Scientist, Physician, Engineer
b. Oct 5, 1879 in Baltimore, Maryland
d. Feb 16, 1970 in New York, New York
Source: *CurBio 67, 70; NewYTBE 70; WebAB; WhAm 5*

Rouse, James Wilson
American. Real Estate Developer
b. Apr 26, 1914 in Easton, Maryland
Source: *BioIn 11; CurBio 82; WhoAm 74; WhoF&I 75*

Roush, Edd J (Eddie)
American. Baseball Player
Forerunner of modern ball player; Hall of Fame, 1962.
b. May 8, 1893 in Oakland City, Indiana
Source: *BaseEn; WhoProB 73*

Rousseau, Henri
LeDouanier
French. Artist
b. May 21, 1844 in Laval, France
d. Sep 2, 1910 in Paris, France
Source: *AtlBL; NewCol 75; OxFr; REn; WebBD 80*

Rousseau, Jean Jacques
French. Philosopher, Author, Composer
Political theory involved submission of individual to general will.
b. Jun 28, 1712 in Geneva, Switzerland
d. Jul 2, 1778 in Ermenonville, France
Source: *AtlBL; BbD; BiD&SB; CasWL; ChPo S1, S2; CyWA; DcBiA; DcEnL; DcEuL; EuAu; EvEuW; NewC; OxEng; OxFr; OxGer; OxThe; Pen EUR; RAdv 1; RComWL; REn; WorAl*

Rousseau, (Pierre Etienne) Theodore
French. Artist
b. Apr 15, 1812 in Paris, France
d. Dec 22, 1867 in Barbizon, France
Source: *AtlBL; BioIn 4, 5, 7, 8, 9, 11; LinLib S; McGDA; McGEWB; NewCol 75; OxFr*

Roussel, Albert
French. Composer
b. Apr 5, 1869 in Tourcoing, France
d. Aug 23, 1937 in Royan, France
Source: *DcCM; NewCol 75; OxFr; WebBD 80*

Roux, Wilhelm
German. Scientist
Founded experimental embryology.
b. Jun 9, 1850 in Jena, Germany
d. Sep 15, 1924 in Halle, Germany
Source: *DcScB; InSci; NewCol 75; WebBD 80*

Roventini, Johnny
American. Philip Morris Trademark
b. 1913
Source: *BioIn 1, 7, 10; What 3*

Rovere, Richard Halworth
American. Author, Editor
b. May 5, 1915 in Jersey City, New Jersey
d. Nov 23, 1979 in Poughkeepsie, New York
Source: *AmAu&B; CelR 73; ConAu 49, 89, 3NR; OxAmL; REnAL; WhoAm 74; WhoWor 74*

Rowan, Carl Thomas
American. Diplomat, Journalist
b. Aug 11, 1925 in Ravenscraft, Tennessee
Source: *AmAu&B; ConAu 89; CurBio 58; LivgBAA; WhoAm 74, 76, 78, 80, 82; WhoAmP 73; WhoBlA 75; WhoS&SW 73; WhoWor 74*

Rowan, Dan
[Rowan and Martin]
American. Comedian
Creator, co-star of "Laugh-In," 1968-72.
b. Jul 2, 1922 in Beggs, Oklahoma
Source: *BioNews 74; CelR 73; CurBio 69; FilmgC; WhoAm 74; WhoHol A*

Rowan, Ford
American. Broadcast Journalist
b. May 31, 1943 in Houston, TX
Source: *ConAu 69; WhoAm 82*

Rowan and Martin
see: Rowan, Dan; Martin, Dick

Rowe, Nicholas
English. Poet
b. Jun 20, 1674 in Little Barford, England
d. Dec 6, 1718 in London, England
Source: *Alli; BbD; BiD&SB; BrAu; CasWL; Chambr 2; ChPo; CnThe; CrtT 2; DcEnA; DcEnL; DcEuL; DcLEL; EvLB; McGEWD; NewC; OxEng; OxThe; Pen ENG; PoLE; REn; REnWD; WebE&AL*

Rowen, Hobart
American. Journalist
b. Jul 31, 1918 in Burlington, Vermont
Source: *ConAu 9R; WhoAm 74, 76, 78, 80, 82; WhoF&I 74; WhoS&SW 73*

Rowlands, Gena
[Mrs. John Cassavetes]
American. Actress
b. Jun 19, 1936 in Cambria, Wisconsin
Source: *BiE&WWA; FilmgC; IntMPA 75, 76, 77, 78, 79, 80, 81, 82; MotPP; NotNAT; WhoAm 74, 76, 78, 80, 82; WhoHol A*

Rowlandson, Thomas
English. Caricaturist, Artist
b. Jul 1756 in London, England
d. Apr 22, 1827 in London, England
Source: *Alli; AtlBL; BiDLA; BkIE; ChPo, S2; NewC; REn*

Rowling, Wallace Edward
New Zealander. Politician
b. Nov 27, 1927
Source: *IntWW 74; Who 74*

Rowse, Alfred Leslie
English. Scholar, Biographer
b. Dec 4, 1903 in Saint Austell, England
Source: *ConAu 1R, 1NR; ConP 70, 75; LongCEL; ModBrL; NewC; TwCA SUP; WrDr 76*

Roxana
Wife of Alexander the Great
Married in 327; murdered along with her son Alexander IV.
d. 311?BC
Source: *NewCol 75; WebBD 80*

Roxon, Lillian
American. Journalist
b. 1933
d. Aug 9, 1973 in New York, New York
Source: *NewYTBE 70, 73*

Roxy Music
[Brian Eno; Bryan Ferry; John Gustafson; Eddie Jobson; Andrew MacKay; Phil Manzanera; Paul Thompson]
English. Rock Group
Source: *ConMuA 80; IlEncRk; LilREn 78; WhoRock 81*

Roy, Gabrielle
Canadian. Author
b. Mar 22, 1909 in Saint Boniface, MB
Source: *CanWW 82; CanWr; CasWL; CathA 1952; ConAu 53; CreCan 2; OxAmL; OxCan, SUP; Pen ENG; REn; REnAL; TwCA SUP; TwCW; WhoAm 82*

Roy, Mike (Michael)
American. Chef, Author
b. Jul 18, 1912 in Hanaford, North Dakota
d. Jun 26, 1976 in Los Angeles, California
Source: *ConAu 61, 65*

Roy, Ross
American. Advertising Executive
b. Jul 22, 1898 in ON
Source: *St&PR 75; WhoAdv 72; WhoAm 74, 76, 78, 80, 82*

Royal, Darrell
American. Football Coach
Source: *BioIn 8, 9, 10*

Royce, Sir Frederick Henry
English. Engineer, Automotive Pioneer
b. Mar 27, 1863 in Peterborough, England
d. Apr 22, 1933
Source: *WebBD 80; WorAl*

Royce, Josiah
American. Author
b. Nov 20, 1855 in Grass Valley, California
d. Sep 14, 1916 in Cambridge, Massachusetts
Source: *Alli SUP; AmAu&B; AmBi; ApCAB; BiD&SB; BiDPara; DcAmAu; DcAmB; DcLEL; DcNAA; EncAB-H; EvLB; OxAmL; Pen AM; REn; REnAL; TwCA, SUP; TwCBDA; WebAB; WebE&AL; WhAm 1*

Royer, William Blackburn, Jr.
[The Hostages]
American. Former Hostage in Iran
b. Oct 21, 1931 in Pennsylvania
Source: *NewYTBS 81; USBiR 74*

Royko, Mike
American. Author, Journalist
b. Sep 19, 1932 in Chicago, Illinois
Source: *ConAu 89; WhoAm 74, 76, 78, 80, 82; WhoMW 74*

Royle, Selena
American. Actress
b. 1904 in New York, New York
Source: *IntMPA 75, 76, 77, 78, 79, 80, 81, 82; Vers B; WhoHol A*

Royo, Aristides
Panamanian. Former President
President, 1978-82; resigned.
b. 1940
Source: *IntWW 80*

Royster, Vermont Connecticut
American. Newspaper Editor
b. Apr 30, 1914 in Raleigh, North Carolina
Source: *AmAu&B; AmM&WS 73S; ConAu 21R; CurBio 53; DrAS 74E; IntWW 74; WhoAm 74, 76, 78, 80, 82; WhoS&SW 73; WhoWor 74*

Rozanov, Vasili
Russian. Author
b. 1856 in Vetluga, Russia
d. 1919
Source: *CasWL; ClDMEL; DcRusL; EncWL; EuAu; EvEuW; ModSL 1; Pen EUR; REn*

Roze, Marie
[Marie Ponsen]
French. Opera Singer
b. Mar 2, 1846 in Paris, France
d. Jun 21, 1926 in Paris, France
Source: *InWom*

Rozelle, "Pete" (Alvin Ray)
American. Football Commissioner
Brought about merger of NFL and AFL, 1966.
b. Mar 1, 1926 in South Gate, California
Source: *CelR 73; CurBio 64; WhoAm 74, 76, 78, 80, 82; WhoFtbl 74*

Rozema, Dave (David Scott)
"Rosie"; "The Rose"
American. Baseball Player
b. Aug 5, 1956 in Grand Rapids, Michigan
Source: *BaseEn*

Rozhdestvensky, Gennadi Nikolaevich
Russian. Conductor
b. 1931 in Moscow, U.S.S.R.
Source: *IntWW 74; Who 74; WhoMus 72; WhoWor 74*

Rozsa, Miklos
American. Film Composer
b. Apr 18, 1907 in Budapest, Hungary
Source: *CmMov; DcCM; FilmgC; IntMPA 75, 76, 77, 78, 79, 80, 81, 82; OxFilm; WhoMus 72; WhoWor 74; WorEFlm*

Ruark, Robert Chester
American. Author
b. Dec 29, 1915 in Wilmington, North Carolina
d. Jul 1, 1965 in London, England
Source: *AmAu&B; ConAu 21R, 25R; ConAu P-2; LongCTC; REn; REnAL; WhAm 4; WhScrn 77*

Rubell, Steve
American. Discotheque Owner
Former owner of NY's Studio 54.
b. 1944?
Source: *BioIn 11*

Rubens, Alma
American. Actress
b. 1897 in San Francisco, California
d. Jan 23, 1931 in Los Angeles, California
Source: *Film 1; FilmgC; MotPP; MovMk; TwYS; WhScrn 74, 77; WhoHol B*

Rubens, Sir Peter Paul
Flemish. Artist
b. Jun 29, 1577 in Siegen, Prussia
d. May 30, 1640 in Antwerp, Belgium
Source: *AtlBL; ChPo; NewC; NewCol 75; REn; WorAl*

Rubicam, Raymond
American. Advertising Executive
b. Jun 16, 1892 in Brooklyn, New York
d. May 8, 1978 in Scottsdale, Arizona
Source: *CurBio 43; St&PR 75; WhoAm 74; WhoF&I 74; WhoWest 74*

Rubik, Erno
Hungarian. Educator, Creator of Rubik's Cube
b. 1944?
Source: *BioIn 12*

Rubin, Barbara Jo
American. Jockey
b. Nov 21, 1949 in Highland, Illinois
Source: *CurBio 69*

Rubin, Benny
American. Comedian
b. 1899 in New York, New York
Source: *TwYS; Vers A; WhoHol A*

Rubin, Jerry
[The Chicago 7]
American. Author, Activist
Director of business development at John Muir and Co.
b. Jul 14, 1938 in Cincinnati, Ohio
Source: *AmAu&B; ConAu 69*

Rubin, Reuven
Israeli. Artist
b. Nov 13, 1893 in Galati, Romania
d. Oct 13, 1974 in Tel Aviv, Israel
Source: *CurBio 43, 75; IntWW 74, 75; WhAm 6; WhoWor 74; WhoWorJ 72*

Rubin, Theodore Isaac
American. Psychoanalyst, Author
b. Apr 11, 1923 in Brooklyn, New York
Source: *AmM&WS 73P; BioIn 7, 9, 10; BioNews 74; CurBio 80; WhoAm 74, 76, 78, 80, 82; WhoWor 74*

Rubin, Vitaly
Russian. Author, Dissident
b. Sep 14, 1923 in Moscow, U.S.S.R.
d. Oct 18, 1981 in Beersheba, Israel
Source: *ConAu 69*

Rubini, Giovanni-Battista
Italian. Opera Singer
b. Apr 7, 1794 in Romano, Italy
d. Mar 2, 1854 in Romano, Italy
Source: *NewEOp 71*

Rubinstein, Anton Gregorovitch
Russian. Musician, Composer
b. Nov 28, 1829 in Kherson, Russia
d. Nov 20, 1894 in Peterhof, Russia
Source: *AtlBL; NewCol 75; OxMus; WebBD 80*

Rubinstein, Arthur
American. Pianist, Author
Wrote autobiographies *My Young Years* and *My Many Years.*
b. Jan 28, 1889 in Lodz, Poland
d. Dec 20, 1982 in Geneva, Switzerland
Source: *Baker 78; BiDAmM; CelR 73; IntWW 74, 75, 76, 77, 78, 79, 80, 81; LinLib S; NewYTBS 76; WebAB, 79; WhoAm 76, 78, 80, 82; WhoHol A; WhoMus 72; WhoWor 78; WhoWorJ 78; WorAl*

Rubinstein, Helena
American. Cosmetician
Founder, president of Helena Rubinstein, Inc.
b. 1870 in Cracow, Poland
d. Apr 1, 1965 in New York, New York
Source: *CurBio 43, 65; HerW; InWom; WhAm 4; WorAl*

Rubinstein, John
American. Actor
b. Dec 8, 1946 in Beverly Hills, California
Source: *BioIn 10; CelR 73; WhoAm 82; WhoHol A*

Rubinstein, S(amuel) Leonard
American. Author
b. Aug 20, 1922 in Salem, New Jersey
Source: *ConAu 45*

Rubinstein, Serge
Russian. Financier
b. 1908
d. 1955
Source: *BioIn 1, 3, 4, 6, 9*

Rubirosa, Porfirio
Dominican. President
b. 1909
d. Jul 5, 1965 in Paris, France
Source: *BioIn 10*

Rubloff, Arthur
American. Real Estate Executive
b. Jun 25, 1902 in Duluth, Minnesota
Source: *St&PR 75; WhoAm 74, 76, 78, 80, 82; WhoF&I 74*

Ruby, Harry
American. Songwriter
b. Jan 27, 1895 in New York, New York
d. Feb 23, 1974 in Woodland Hills, California
Source: *AmSCAP 66; BiE&WWA; BioIn 10; CmpEPM; EncMT; NewCBMT; NotNAT B; ObitOF 79; WhAm 6; WhThe*

Ruby, Jack
[Jacob Rubenstein]
American. Murderer
Killed Lee Harvey Oswald on TV, 1963.
b. 1911
d. Jan 3, 1967 in Dallas, Texas
Source: *BioIn 6, 7, 8, 9, 10, 11; WorAl*

Ruchlis, Hy(man)
American. Children's Author
b. Apr 6, 1913 in Brooklyn, New York
Source: *AuBYP; ConAu 1R, 2NR; SmATA 3*

Ruckelshaus, William Doyle
American. Government Official
b. Jul 24, 1934 in Indianapolis, Indiana
Source: *CurBio 71; IntWW 74; NewYTBE 70, 72, 73; WhoAm 74; WhoAmP 73; WhoE 74; WhoGov 72*

Ruckert, Friedrich
German. Poet, Orientalist
b. May 16, 1788 in Schweinfurt, Germany
d. Jan 31, 1866 in Neusess, Germany
Source: *BbD; BiD&SB; CasWL; DcEuL; EuAu; EvEuW; OxGer; Pen EUR; REn*

Rudd, Hughes Day
American. Journalist
b. Sep 14, 1921 in Wichita, Kansas
Source: *AmAu&B; ConAu 73; WhoAm 74, 76, 78, 80, 82*

Rudd, Paul
American. Actor
b. 1940 in Boston, Massachusetts
Source: *CurBio 77; WhoAm 82*

Rudd, Mark
American. Revolutionary
b. 1947?
Source: *BioIn 8, 9, 11*

Rudd, Phil
see: AC-DC

Ruddy, Al(bert Stotland)
Canadian. Motion Picture Producer
b. Mar 28, 1934 in Montreal, PQ
Source: *BioIn 9, 11; IntMPA 75, 76, 77, 78, 79, 80, 81, 82*

Rudel, Julius
Austrian. Conductor, Opera Manager
b. Mar 6, 1921 in Vienna, Austria
Source: *BiE&WWA; CelR 73; CurBio 65; NewYTBE 71; WhoAm 74, 76, 78, 80, 82; WhoE 74; WhoGov 72; WhoWor 74; WhoWorJ 72*

Ruder, Melvin
American. Editor
b. Jan 19, 1915 in Manning, North Dakota
Source: *St&PR 75; WhoAm 74, 76, 78, 80, 82; WhoWest 74*

Rudhyar, Dane
American. Author
b. Mar 23, 1895 in Paris, France
Source: *AmAu&B; ConAu 29R; DcCM; WhoAm 74, 76, 78, 80, 82; WrDr 76*

Rudkin, Margaret Fogarty
American. Bakery Executive
b. Sep 14, 1897 in New York, New York
d. Jun 1, 1967 in New Haven, Connecticut
Source: *CurBio 59, 67; InWom; WhAm 4*

Rudman, Warren Bruce
American. Senator
b. May 18, 1930 in Boston, Massachusetts
Source: *NewYTBS 79; WhoAm 82; WhoAmP 73, 75; WhoE 74, 75; WhoGov 72, 75, 77*

Rudolf II
Holy Roman Emperor
b. 1552
d. 1612
Source: *BioIn 9; NewCol 75; WebBD 80*

Rudolf of Hapsburg
Austrian. Crown Prince
b. 1858 in Laxenberg, Austria
d. Jan 30, 1889 in Mayerling, Austria
Source: *BioIn 9; NewCol 75; WebBD 80; WhoModH*

Rudolf, Max
German. Conductor
b. Jun 15, 1902 in Frankfurt, Germany
Source: *WhoAm 74, 76, 78, 80, 82; WhoWor 74*

Rudolph, Paul Marvin
American. Architect
b. Oct 23, 1918 in Elton, Kentucky
Source: *AmArch 70; CurBio 72; IntWW 74; WhoAm 74, 76, 78, 80, 82; WhoE 74; WhoWor 74*

Rudolph, Wilma Glodean
American. Track Athlete
Won three gold medals, 1960 Olympics.
b. Jun 23, 1940 in Saint Bethelem, Tennessee
Source: *CurBio 61; HerW; InWom; WhoTr&F 73; WorAl*

Ruffin, Clovis
American. Fashion Designer
b. in Clovis, New Mexico
Source: *WhoAm 82; WorFshn*

Ruffin, Jimmy
American. Singer
b. May 7, 1939 in Meridian, Mississippi
Source: *RkOn*

Ruffing, "Red" (Charles Herbert)
American. Baseball Player
Pitcher, 1924-47; 52 career shutouts; Hall of Fame, 1968.
b. May 5, 1905 in Granville, Illinois
Source: *BaseEn; CurBio 41; WhoProB 73*

Ruffo, Titta
[Ruffo Cafiero Titta]
Italian. Opera Singer
b. Jun 9, 1877 in Pisa, Italy
d. Jul 6, 1953 in Florence, Italy
Source: *NewEOp 71; WhScrn 74, 77*

Ruggles, Carl
American. Composer
b. Mar 11, 1876 in Marion, Massachusetts
d. Oct 24, 1971 in Bennington, Vermont
Source: *DcCM; NewYTBE 71; WhAm 5*

Ruggles, Charles
American. Actor
b. Feb 8, 1892 in Los Angeles, California
d. Dec 23, 1970 in Santa Monica, California
Source: *BiE&WWA; Film 1; MovMk; OxFilm; WhAm 5; WhScrn 74, 77; WorEFlm*

Rugolo, Pete
American. Jazz Musician
b. Dec 25, 1915 in Sicily, Italy
Source: *IntMPA 75, 76, 77, 78, 79, 80, 81, 82*

Ruhlmann, Francois
Belgian. Conductor
b. Jan 11, 1868 in Brussels, Belgium
d. Jun 8, 1948 in Paris, France
Source: *NewEOp 71*

Ruiz, Rosie
American. Disqualified Marathon Runner
Declared winner, then disqualified from Boston Marathon for cheating.
b. 1954?
Source: *NewYTBS 81*

Rukavishnikov, Nikolai Nikolayevich
Russian. Cosmonaut
b. 1932
Source: *BioIn 10*

Rukeyser, Louis
American. TV Commentator, Author
b. Jan 30, 1933 in New York, New York
Source: *ConAu 65*

Rukeyser, Merryle Stanley, Jr.
American. Television Executive
b. Apr 15, 1931 in New York, New York
Source: *BioIn 10; WhoAm 80*

Rukeyser, Muriel
American. Poet
b. Dec 15, 1913 in New York, New York
d. Feb 12, 1980 in New York, New York
Source: *AmAu&B; AuBYP; CasWL; ChPo, S1; CnDAL; ConAu 5R, 93; ConLC 6, 10, 15; ConP 70; CurBio 43; DcLEL; DrAP 75; DrAS 74E; ForWC 70; InWom; ModAL, SUP; OxAmL; Pen AM; RAdv 1; REn; REnAL; SixAP; TwCA, SUP; TwCW; WebE&AL; WhoAm 74; WhoWor 74; WrDr 76*

Rukeyser, William Simon
American. Magazine Editor
b. Jun 8, 1939 in New York, New York
Source: *ConAu 69; WhoAm 78, 80, 82*

Rule, Janice
American. Actress
b. Aug 15, 1931 in Norwood, Ohio
Source: *BiDFilm; BiE&WWA; FilmgC; InWom; IntMPA 75, 76, 77, 78, 79, 80, 81, 82; NotNAT; WhoThe 77*

Rumann, Sig
German. Actor
b. 1884 in Hamburg, Germany
d. Feb 14, 1967 in Julian, California
Source: *MovMk; WhoHol B*

Ruml, Beardsley
American. Business Executive
b. Nov 5, 1894 in Cedar Rapids, Iowa
d. Apr 18, 1960 in Danbury, Connecticut
Source: *CurBio 43, 60; EncAB-H; WhAm 3A*

Rumor, Mariano
Italian. Premier
b. Jun 16, 1915 in Vicenza, Italy
Source: *BioIn 8, 9; IntWW 74*

Rumsfeld, Donald
American. Government Official
b. Jul 9, 1932 in Chicago, Illinois
Source: *BiDrAC; BioNews 75; CurBio 70; IntWW 74; NewYTBE 70, 71; NewYTBS 74; WhoAm 74, 76, 78, 80, 82; WhoAmP 73; WhoGov 72; WhoS&SW 73; WhoWor 74*

Rundgren, Todd
American. Rock Musician, Singer
b. Jun 22, 1948 in Upper Darby, Pennsylvania
Source: *EncPR&S; IlEncRk; RkOn; WhoAm 82*

Rundstedt, Karl Rudolf Gerd von
German. World War II Field Marshal
b. Dec 12, 1875 in Aschersleben, Germany
d. Feb 24, 1953 in Hanover, Germany (West)
Source: *CurBio 41, 53; REn*

Runkle, Janice
American. Veterinarian
b. 1953 in Bloomfield Hills, Michigan
d. Jul 26, 1981 in Illinois
Source: *BioIn 12*

Runyon, (Alfred) Damon
American. Journalist, Author
b. Oct 4, 1884 in Manhattan, Kansas
d. Dec 10, 1946 in New York, New York
Source: *AmAu&B; CasWL; CnDAL; CnMWL; CurBio 42, 47; DcAmB S4; DcLEL; DcNAA; EncMys; FilmgC; LongCTC; ModAL; ModWD; OxAmL; Pen AM; PlP&P; REn; REnAL; TwCA, SUP; TwCW; WebAB; WebE&AL; WhAm 2; WhScrn 77; WhoHol B*

Rupp, Adolph F
American. Basketball Player, Coach
b. Sep 2, 1901 in Halstead, Kansas
d. Dec 10, 1977 in Lexington, Kentucky
Source: *WhoAm 74; WhoBbl 73; WhoS&SW 73*

Rush, Barbara
American. Actress
b. Jan 4, 1929 in Denver, Colorado
Source: *FilmgC; IntMPA 75, 76, 77, 78, 79, 80, 81, 82; MotPP; MovMk; WhoAm 74, 76, 78, 80, 82; WhoHol A; WorEFlm*

Rush, Benjamin
American. Physician
b. Dec 24, 1745 in Philadelphia, Pennsylvania
d. Apr 19, 1813 in Philadelphia, Pennsylvania
Source: *BioIn 10; WebAB*

Rush, Kenneth
American. Lawyer, Government Official
b. Jan 17, 1910 in Walla Walla, Washington
Source: *BioIn 4, 9, 10; BioNews; CurBio 75; IntWW 74; NewYTBE 71, 72; WhoAm 74, 76, 78, 80, 82; WhoAmP 73; WhoE 75; WhoGov 72; WhoWor 74*

Rush, Richard
American. Motion Picture Director, Producer
b. 1931?
Source: *FilmgC; IntMPA 79, 80, 81*

Rush, Tom
American. Singer, Songwriter
b. Feb 8, 1941 in Portsmouth, New Hampshire
Source: *BiDAmM; ConMuA 80; EncFCWM 69; WhoRock 81*

Rush, William
American. Sculptor
b. Jul 5, 1756 in Philadelphia, Pennsylvania
d. Jan 17, 1833 in Philadelphia, Pennsylvania
Source: *AmBi; ApCAB; DcAmB; OxAmL; TwCBDA; WebAB; WhAm H*

Rush, Willie
see: Southside Johnny and the Asbury Jukes

Rush
[Geddy Lee; Alex Liefson; Neil Peart; John Rutsey]
Canadian. Rock Group
Source: *ConMuA 80; LilREn 78; WhoRock 81*

Rusher, William Allen
American. Publisher
b. Jul 19, 1923 in Chicago, Illinois
Source: *ConAu 103; WhoAm 74, 76, 78, 80, 82; WhoE 74; WrDr 76*

Rushing, Jimmy
American. Jazz Musician
b. Aug 26, 1903 in Oklahoma City, Oklahoma
d. Jun 8, 1972 in New York, New York
Source: *NewYTBE 72; WhScrn 77; WhoJazz 72*

Rushmore, Robert
American. Author
b. Jul 7, 1926 in Tuxedo Park, New York
Source: *ConAu 25R; DrAF 76; SmATA 8*

Rusk, (David) Dean
American. Former Secretary of State
Secretary, 1961-69; defended US involvement in Vietnam.
b. Feb 9, 1909 in Cherokee County, Georgia
Source: *BiDrUSE; CelR 73; CurBio 49, 61; EncAB-H; IntWW 74; Who 82; WhoAm 74, 76, 78, 80, 82; WhoAmP 73; WhoGov 72; WhoWor 74*

Ruskin, John
English. Art Critic, Author
b. Feb 8, 1819 in London, England
d. Jan 20, 1900 in Coniston, England
Source: *Alli, SUP; AtlBL; BbD; BiD&SB; BrAu 19; CarSB; CasWL; Chambr 3; ChPo, S1, S2; CrtT 3; CyWA; DcEnA, AP; DcEnL; DcEuL; DcLEL; EvLB; FamSYP; MouLC 4; NewC; OxEng; Pen ENG; RComWL; REn; WebE&AL; WhoChL*

Ruskowski, Terry Wallace
Canadian. Hockey Player
b. Dec 31, 1954 in Prince Albert, SK
Source: *HocReg*

Russell, Andy
American. Singer
Source: *BioIn 10; CmpEPM*

Russell, Anna
English. Comedienne
b. Dec 27, 1911 in London, England
Source: *AmSCAP 66; BiE&WWA; CurBio 54; NewYTBS 74; NotNAT; OxThe; Who 74; WhoHol A; WhoWor 74*

Russell, Bertrand Arthur William
English. Mathematician, Philosopher
b. May 18, 1872 in Trelleck, England
d. Feb 2, 1970 in Wales
Source: *AtlBL; CasWL; Chambr 3; ConAu 25R; ConAu P-1; CurBio 40, 51, 70; DcLEL; EvLB; LongCTC; ModBrL; NewC; NewYTBE 70; OxEng; Pen ENG; REn; TwCA, SUP; TwCW; WebE&AL; WhAm 5; WhoLA*

Russell, Bill (William Felton)
American. Basketball Player, Coach
First black to coach in NBA, with Boston Celtics, 1965-69.
b. Feb 12, 1934 in Monroe, Louisiana
Source: *CelR 73; NewYTBE 73; WebAB; WhoAm 74, 76, 78, 80, 82; WhoBbl 73; WhoBlA 75; WorAl*

Russell, Charles Marion
American. Musician
b. Mar 19, 1864 in Saint Louis, Missouri
d. Oct 24, 1926
Source: *AmAu&B; DcNAA; NewCol 75; WhAm 1*

Russell, Charles Taze
American. Founded Jehovah's Witnesses
Founded the Russellites, 1878; became the Jehovah's Witnesses, 1931.
b. Feb 16, 1852 in Pittsburgh, Pennsylvania
d. Oct 31, 1916 in Pampa, Texas
Source: *AmAu&B; AmBi; ChPo S1; DcAmB; DcNAA; NewCol 75; WebAB; WhAm 1; WorAl*

Russell, Edward Frederick Langley, Baron of Liverpool
English. Military Jurist, Author
b. Apr 10, 1895 in Liverpool, England
d. Apr 8, 1981 in Hastings, England
Source: *Au&Wr 71; BioIn 5; ConAu 103; IntAu&W 77; WhoWor 74; WrDr 80*

Russell, Franklin Alexander
New Zealander. Author
b. Oct 9, 1926 in New Zealand
Source: *AmAu&B; AuBYP; ConAu 17R; SmATA 11; WhoAm 74, 76, 78, 80, 82; WrDr 76*

Russell, Gail
American. Actress
b. Sep 23, 1924 in Chicago, Illinois
d. Aug 26, 1961 in Los Angeles, California
Source: *FilmgC; HolP 40; MotPP; MovMk; WhScrn 74, 77; WhoHol B*

Russell, Henry
English. Impresario
b. Nov 14, 1871 in London, England
d. Oct 11, 1937 in London, England
Source: *NewEOp 71*

Russell, Jane
American. Actress
Better known for the buxom pinup poster accompaning 1943's *The Outlaw* than for film itself.
b. Jun 21, 1921 in Bemidji, Minnesota
Source: *BiDFilm; CelR 73; CmMov; FilmgC; InWom; IntMPA 75, 76, 77, 78, 79, 80, 81, 82; MotPP; MovMk; NewYTBE 71; OxFilm; WhoAm 74, 76, 78, 80, 82; WhoHol A; WorAl; WorEFlm*

Russell, Lord John
British. Author, Statesman
b. Aug 18, 1792 in London, England
d. May 28, 1878
Source: *Alli, SUP; BbD; BrAu 19; DcEnL; DcLEL; EvLB; NewC; OxEng*

Russell, Ken
English. Motion Picture Director
b. Jul 3, 1927 in Southampton, England
Source: *BiDFilm; CelR 73; FilmgC; IntMPA 75, 76, 77, 78, 79, 80, 81, 82; IntWW 74; OxFilm; Who 74; WhoAm 74, 76, 78, 80, 82; WhoWor 74; WorEFlm*

Russell, Kurt (Von Vogel)
American. Actor
b. Mar 17, 1951 in Springfield, Massachusetts
Source: *FilmgC; WhoAm 78, 80, 82; WhoHol A*

Russell, Leon
American. Rock Singer, Musician
b. Apr 2, 1941 in Lawton, Oklahoma
Source: *EncPR&S; IlEncRk; Rk100; WhoAm 78, 80, 82*

Russell, Lillian
[Helen Louise Leonard]
"The American Beauty"
American. Singer, Actress
In vaudeville and light opera including the Tony Pastor shows from 1880.
b. Dec 4, 1861 in Clinton, Iowa
d. Jun 6, 1922 in Pittsburgh, Pennsylvania
Source: *AmBi; AmWom; DcAmB; EncMT; FamA&A; InWom; NotAW; OxAmL; OxThe; PlP&P; REn; WebAB; WhAm 1; WhScrn 74, 77; WhoHol B; WhoStg 1906, 1908; WomWWA 14; WorAl*

Russell, Mark
[Mark Ruslander]
American. Comedian
b. Aug 23, 1932 in Buffalo, New York
Source: *BioIn 8; CurBio 81; WhoAm 82*

Russell, Nipsey
American. Comedian, Actor
Co-hosted "The Les Crane Show" on TV; first black regularly employed as MC on national TV.
b. 1924 in Atlanta, Georgia
Source: *CelR 73; WhoAm 82*

Russell, "Pee Wee" (Charles Ellsworth)
American. Jazz Musician
b. Mar 27, 1906 in Saint Louis, Missouri
d. Feb 15, 1969 in Alexandria, Virginia
Source: *AmSCAP 66; CurBio 44, 69; WhoHol B; WhoJazz 72*

Russell, Richard Brevard, Jr.
American. Politician
b. Nov 2, 1897 in Winder, Georgia
d. Jan 21, 1971 in Washington, DC
Source: *BiDrAC; CurBio 49, 71; EncAB-H; NewYTBE 71; WhAm 5; WhAmP*

Russell, Rosalind
American. Actress
Films include *His Girl Friday; My Sister Eileen; Picnic; Auntie Mame; Gypsy.*
b. Jun 4, 1911 in Waterbury, Connecticut
d. Nov 28, 1976 in Beverly Hills, California
Source: *BiDFilm; BiE&WWA; BioNews 75; CelR 73; CurBio 43; EncMT; FilmgC; InWom; IntMPA 77, 75; MotPP; MovMk; NewYTBE 71; NotNAT; OxFilm; ThFT; Who 74; WhoAm 74; WhoHol A; WhoThe 77; WomWMM; WorEFlm*

Russell, Solveig Paulson
American. Children's Author
b. Mar 1904 in Salt Lake City, Utah
Source: *AuBYP; ConAu 1R, 5NR; SmATA 3; WhoPNW*

Russell, Sir Sydney Gordon
British. Author, Industrial Designer
b. May 20, 1892 in London, England
Source: *Au&Wr 71; Who 74; WhoWor 74*

Russo, Anthony J
American. Engineer
b. 1937
Source: *BioIn 10*

Russwurm, John Brown
American. Journalist, Abolitionist
b. Oct 1, 1799 in Port Antonio, Jamaica
d. Jun 17, 1851 in Liberia
Source: *DcAmB; WebAB; WhAm H*

Rustin, Bayard
American. Civil Rights Activist
b. Mar 17, 1910 in West Chester, Pennsylvania
Source: *ConAu 53; CurBio 67; EncAB-H; LivgBAA; WhoAm 74, 76, 78, 80, 82; WhoBlA 75; WhoWor 74*

Rutgers, Henry
American. Soldier, Philanthropist
Queen's College changed it's name to Rutger's University in his honor.
b. Oct 7, 1745 in New York, New York
d. Feb 17, 1830 in New York, New York
Source: *AmBi; ApCAB; DcAmB; Drake; TwCBDA; WhAm H*

Ruth
Biblical Character
Source: *InWom*

Ruth, "Babe" (George Herman)
"The Bambino"; "The Sultan of Swat"
American. Baseball Player
With NY Yankees, 1920-34; held over 50 records at retirement; Hall of Fame, 1936.
b. Feb 6, 1895 in Baltimore, Maryland
d. Aug 16, 1948 in New York, New York
Source: *BaseEn; BioNews 74; CurBio 44, 48; DcAmB S4; EncAB-H; WebAB; WhScrn 74, 77; WhoHol B; WhoProB 73; WorAl*

Rutherford, Ann
Canadian. Actress
b. 1924 in Toronto, ON
Source: *FilmgC; IntMPA 75, 76, 77, 78, 79, 80, 81, 82; MotPP; MovMk; ThFT; WhoHol A*

Rutherford, Ernest
British. Physicist
b. Aug 30, 1871 in Spring Grove, New Zealand
d. Oct 19, 1937 in Cambridge, England
Source: *AsBiEn; McGEWB; WhDW*

Rutherford, Margaret
[Dame Margot Rutherford]
English. Actress
b. May 11, 1892 in London, England
d. May 22, 1972 in Chalfont, England
Source: *BiE&WWA; ConAu 33R; CurBio 64, 72; FilmgC; InWom; MotPP; MovMk; NewYTBE 72; OxFilm; OxThe; WhAm 5; WhScrn 77; WhoHol B*

Rutherford, Michael
see: Genesis

Rutherfurd, Lucy Page
[Lucy Page Mercer]
American. Friend of Franklin Roosevelt
With President Roosevelt at the time of his death.
b. 1891
d. 1948
Source: *BioIn 10*

Rutledge, Ann
American. Fiancee of Abraham Lincoln
Little fact to support claim to being Lincoln's fiancee; they were friends.
b. 1816 in New Salem, Illinois
d. 1835 in New Salem, Illinois
Source: *InWom; NewCol 75; NotAW; REn; WhAm H*

Rutledge, Edward
American. Revolutionary Patriot
b. Nov 23, 1749 in Charleston, South Carolina
d. Jan 23, 1800
Source: *AmBi; ApCAB; BiAuS; BiDSA; BiDrAC; DcAmB; Drake; TwCBDA; WhAm H; WhAmP*

Rutledge, John
American. Supreme Court Justice
b. Sep 1739 in Charleston, South Carolina
d. Jul 18, 1800 in Charleston, South Carolina
Source: *Alli; AmBi; ApCAB; BiAuS; BiDSA; BiDrAC; DcAmB; Drake; TwCBDA; WebAB; WhAm H*

Rutsey, John
see: Rush

Ruy Lopez de Segura
Spanish. Writer on Chess
b. 1530
Source: *OxEng*

Ruysdael, Jacob van
[Jacob van Ruisdael]
Dutch. Artist
b. 1628 in Haarlem, Netherlands
d. Mar 14, 1682 in Amsterdam, Netherlands
Source: *AtlBL; Chambr 1; OxAmL; REn; WebBD 80*

Ruzici, Virginia
Romanian. Tennis Player
b. Jan 31, 1955
Source: *OfEnT*

Ryan, Claude
Canadian. Journalist
b. Jan 26, 1925 in Montreal, PQ
Source: *CanWW 82; WhoAm 82; WhoE 74; WhoWor 74*

Ryan, Cornelius John
American. Journalist
b. Jun 5, 1920 in Dublin, Ireland
d. Nov 23, 1974 in New York, New York
Source: *CelR 73; ConAu 53, 69; ConLC 7; WhAm 6; Who 74; WhoAm 74; WhoE 74; WhoWor 74*

Ryan, Irene
American. Actress
"Granny Clampett" on TV series "Beverly Hillbillies," 1962-71.
b. Oct 17, 1903 in El Paso, Texas
d. Apr 26, 1973 in Santa Monica, California
Source: *FilmgC; MovMk; WhScrn 74, 77; WhoHol B*

Ryan, Leo Joseph
American. Politician
Congressman from California murdered by member of Jim Jones' Peoples Temple.
b. May 5, 1925 in Lincoln, Nebraska
d. Nov 19, 1978 in Jonestown, Guyana
Source: *CngDr 74; WhoAm 74; WhoAmP 73*

Ryan, (Lynn) Nolan
American. Baseball Player
Struck out record 383 batters, 1973; NY Mets, 1966-71; CA Angels, 1972-79; Houston Astros, 1980--.
b. Jan 31, 1947 in Refugio, Texas
Source: *BaseEn; CurBio 70; NewYTBE 70, 73; WhoAm 74, 76, 78, 80, 82; WorAl*

Ryan, Peggy
American. Actress
b. Aug 28, 1924 in Long Beach, California
Source: *FilmgC; HolP 40; IntMPA 75, 77; WhoHol A*

Ryan, Robert (Bushnell)
American. Actor
b. Nov 11, 1913 in Chicago, Illinois
d. Jul 11, 1973 in New York, New York
Source: *BiDFilm; BiE&WWA; CelR 73; CmMov; OxFilm; WhAm 5; WhoE 74; WorEFlm*

Ryan, Sylvester James
American. Judge
b. Sep 10, 1896 in New York, New York
d. Apr 10, 1981 in New York, New York
Source: *AmBench 79; WhoAm 74, 76; WhoAmL 79; WhoE 74; WhoGov 72*

Ryan, Thomas Fortune
American. Financier
b. Oct 17, 1851 in Lovingston, Virginia
d. Nov 23, 1928 in New York, New York
Source: *BioIn 1; DcAmB; EncAB-H; WebAB; WhAm 1*

Ryan, T(om) K
American. Cartoonist
b. Jun 6, 1926 in Anderson, Indiana
Source: *WhoAm 82; WorECom*

Ryan, Tommy
American. Boxer
b. Mar 31, 1870 in Redwood, New York
d. Aug 3, 1948 in Van Nuys, California
Source: *WhoBox 74*

Ryan, T(ubal) Claude
American. Aircraft Manufacturer
Founded company that built Lindbergh's "Spirit of St. Louis."
b. Jan 3, 1898 in Parsons, Kansas
d. Sep 11, 1982 in San Diego, California
Source: *CmCal; CurBio 43, 82; NewYTBS 82; WhoAm 74, 76, 78*

Rydell, Bobby
[Robert Ridarelli]
American. Singer
b. Apr 26, 1942 in Philadelphia, Pennsylvania
Source: *FilmgC; WhoHol A*

Ryder, Albert Pinkham
American. Artist
b. Mar 19, 1847 in New Bedford, Massachusetts
d. Mar 28, 1917 in Elmhurst, New York
Source: *AmBi; ApCAB; AtlBL; DcAmB; EncAB-H; OxAmL; REn; WebAB; WhAm 1*

Ryder, Alfred
American. Actor, Author
b. 1919 in New York, New York
Source: *BiE&WWA; MotPP; NotNAT; WhoHol A; WhoThe 77*

Ryder, James Arthur
American. Trucking Executive
President of Ryder System, Inc.
b. Jul 28, 1913 in Columbus, Ohio
Source: *St&PR 75; WhoAm 74; WhoF&I 74*

Ryder, Mitch
see: Mitch Ryder and the Detroit Wheels

Rylands, John
English. Merchant, Philanthropist
b. 1801
d. 1888
Source: *BioIn 10; WebBD 80*

Ryle, Gilbert
English. Philosopher, Editor
b. Aug 19, 1900 in England
d. Oct 6, 1976 in Yorkshire, England
Source: *ConAu 69, 73; LongCTC; OxEng; Who 74; WhoWor 74; WorAu; WrDr 76*

Rysanek, Leonie
Austrian. Opera Singer
b. Nov 12, 1926 in Vienna, Austria
Source: *CurBio 66; InWom; IntWW 74; WhoMus 72; WhoWor 74*

Ryskind, Morrie
American. Journalist, Dramatist
b. Oct 20, 1895 in New York, New York
Source: *AmAu&B; BiE&WWA; ConDr 73; EncMT; FilmgC; IntMPA 77, 75; ModWD; NewCBMT; NotNAT; WhNAA; WhoAm 82; WhoThe 77; WhoWorJ 72*

Ryun, Jim (James Ronald)
American. Track Athlete, Photographer
Held 1973 record for the mile, 3:5.1.
b. Apr 29, 1947 in Wichita, Kansas
Source: *BioNews 74; CelR 73; CurBio 68; NewCol 75; NewYTBE 72; WhoAm 82; WhoTr&F 73*

S

Saadi
[Muslihud-Din]
Persian. Poet
b. 1184? in Shiraz, Persia
d. 1291? in Shiraz, Persia
Source: *NewC*

Saarinen, Aline Bernstein
American. Art Critic, Author
b. Mar 25, 1914 in New York, New York
d. Jul 13, 1972 in New York, New York
Source: *AmAu&B; ConAu 37R; CurBio 56, 72; ForWC 70; InWom; NewYTBE 72; WhAm 5; WhoGov 72*

Saarinen, Eero
American. Architect
b. Aug 20, 1910 in Kyrkslatt, Finland
d. Sep 1, 1961 in Ann Arbor, Michigan
Source: *AtlBL; CurBio 49, 61; PlP&P; REn; WebAB; WhAm 4*

Saarinen, Eliel
Flemish. Architect
b. Aug 28, 1873 in Rantasalmi, Finland
d. Jul 1, 1950 in Bloomfield Hills, Michigan
Source: *CurBio 42, 50; WebAB; WhAm 3*

Sabah al-Ahmad al, Sheik
Kuwaiti. Premier
b. 1929?
Source: *BioIn 7*

Sabatini, Rafael
Italian. Author, Dramatist
b. Apr 29, 1875 in Jesi, Italy
d. Feb 13, 1950 in Aldenbogen, Switzerland
Source: *DcBiA; DcLEL; EvLB; FilmgC; LongCTC; NewC; REn; TwCA, SUP; TwCW; WhAm 2*

Sabich, "Spider" (Vladimir)
American. Skier
Two-time world champion skier accidentally killed by Claudine Longet.
b. 1943
d. Mar 21, 1976 in Aspen, Colorado
Source: *BioIn 10, 11*

Sabin, Albert Bruce
American. Microbiologist
b. Aug 26, 1906 in Bialystok, Russia
Source: *AmM&WS 73P; CelR 73; CurBio 58; IntWW 74; WebAB; Who 74; WhoWor 74; WhoWorJ 72*

Sablon, Jean
French. Actor, Motion Picture Director
b. 1909 in France
Source: *BiE&WWA*

Sabu
[Sabu Dastagir]
Indian. Actor
b. Mar 15, 1924 in Mysore, India
d. Dec 2, 1963 in Chatsworth, California
Source: *CmMov; FilmgC; HolP 40; MotPP; MovMk; OxFilm; WhScrn 74, 77; WhoHol B; WorEFlm*

Sacagawea
American Indian. Guide
Served as interpreter, guide on Lewis and Clark Expedition, 1804.
b. 1787?
d. Dec 2, 1812? in Fort Lisa, Nebraska
Source: *DcAmB; REnAW; WebAB; WhAm H*

Sacchini, Antonio
Italian. Composer
b. Jun 14, 1730 in Florence, Italy
d. Oct 6, 1786 in Paris, France
Source: *NewEOp 71; OxMus*

Sacco, Nicola
[Sacco and Vanzetti]
Italian. Political Activist, Anarchist
b. Apr 22, 1891 in Apulia, Italy
d. Aug 23, 1927 in Massachusetts
Source: *AmBi; DcAmB; WebAB; WhAm 4*

Sacco and Vanzetti
see: Sacco, Nicola; Vanzetti, Bartolomeo

Sacher, Paul
Swiss. Conductor
b. Apr 28, 1906 in Basel, Switzerland
Source: *IntWW 74; WhoMus 72; WhoWor 74*

Sacher-Masoch, Leopold von
Austrian. Author
b. Jan 27, 1836? in Lemberg, Austria
d. Mar 9, 1895
Source: *BbD; BiD&SB; EuAu; EvEuW; OxGer; REn*

Sachs, Eddy (Edward Julius)
American. Auto Racer
b. May 28, 1917 in Detroit, Michigan
d. May 30, 1964
Source: *BioIn 7*

Sachs, Hans
German. Dramatist, Poet, Composer
b. Nov 5, 1494 in Nurnberg, Germany
d. Jan 19, 1576
Source: *BbD; BiD&SB; CasWL; CnThe; CyWA; DcEuL; EuAu; EvEuW; McGEWD; NewC; OxEng; OxGer; OxThe; Pen EUR; REn; REnWD*

Sachs, Nelly
German. Poet
b. Oct 12, 1891 in Berlin, Germany
d. May 18, 1970 in Stockholm, Sweden
Source: *CasWL; ConAu 17R, 25R; ConAu P-2; ConLC 14; CurBio 67, 70; EncWL; InWom; ModGL; NewYTBE 70; OxGer; Pen EUR; TwCW; WhAm 5; WorAu*

Sachse, Leopold
German. Stage Director
b. Jan 5, 1880 in Berlin, Germany
d. Apr 4, 1961 in Englewood Cliffs, New Jersey
Source: *NewEOp 71*

Sack, Erna
"European Nightingale"
German. Opera Singer
b. 1903 in Germany
d. Mar 2, 1972
Source: *InWom; NewYTBE 72; WhScrn 77; WhoHol A*

Sackheim, Maxwell Byron
American. Advertising Executive
Co-founded Book of the Month Club, 1926.
b. Sep 25, 1890 in Kovna, Russia
d. Dec 2, 1982 in Largo, Florida
Source: *BioIn 2, 8, 10*

Sackler, Howard Oliver
American. Dramatist
Won Pulitzer Prize, 1969, for *The Great White Hope.*
b. Dec 19, 1927 in New York, New York
d. Oct 13, 1982 in Ibiza, Spain
Source: *ChPo S2; ConAu 61; ConDr 73, 77; ConLC 14; McGEWD; NewYTBS 82; NotNAT; PlP&P; WhoAm 74, 76, 78, 80, 82; WrDr 76, 80*

Sackville-West, Edward Charles
English. Author, Critic
b. Nov 13, 1901
d. 1965
Source: *CathA 1952; ChPo S2; DcLEL; EvLB; LongCTC; ModBrL; NewC; Pen ENG; REn; TwCA, SUP; TwCW*

Sackville-West, Victoria Mary
English. Poet, Author
b. Mar 9, 1892 in Knole Castle, England
d. Jun 2, 1962 in Kent, England
Source: *Chambr 3; ChPo; ConAu 93, 104; DcLEL; EncWL; EvLB; InWom; LongCTC; ModBrL; NewC; Pen ENG; RAdv 1; REn; TwCA, SUP; TwCW; WhAm 4; WhoLA*

Sadat, Anwar el
Egyptian. President
Shared 1979 Nobel Peace Prize with Menacham Begin; assassinated by Egyptian soldiers.
b. Dec 25, 1918 in Talah Maonufiya, Egypt
d. Oct 6, 1981 in Cairo, Egypt
Source: *BioIn 11; BioNews 75; BkPepl; ConAu 101, 104; CurBio 71, 81; IntYB 78, 79; LinLib S; NewCol 75; NewYTBE 70, 72; WhoGov 72; WhoWor 74, 76, 78*

Sadat, Jihan Raouf
Egyptian. Widow of Anwar el Sadat
b. 1933? in Cairo, Egypt
Source: *BioIn 10, 11; NewYTBS 78*

Sade, Marquis (Donatien) de
French. Hedonist, Author
b. Jun 2, 1740 in Paris, France
d. Dec 2, 1814
Source: *AtlBL; CasWL; EuAu; EvEuW; NewC; OxEng; OxFr; Pen EUR; REn*

Sadeh, Itzhak
Israeli. General
b. 1890?
d. Aug 20, 1952 in Petah Tikvah, Israel
Source: *BioIn 3; ObitOF 79*

Sadler, Barry
American. Singer
Wrote and sang "The Ballad of the Green Berets," 1966.
b. 1941 in Leadville, Colorado
Source: *BioIn 7, 9; RkOn*

Saerchinger, Cesar Victor Charles
American. Author, Radio Broadcaster
b. Oct 23, 1889 in Aachen, Germany
d. Oct 10, 1971
Source: *AmAu&B; ConAu 33R; CurBio 40; WebBD 80; WhAm 5*

Safdie, Moshe
Israeli. Architect
b. Jul 14, 1938 in Haifa, Palestine
Source: *CanWW 70; ConAu 69; CurBio 68; IntWW 74; WhoAm 74, 76, 78, 80, 82; WhoE 74; WhoWor 74*

Safer, Morley
Canadian. Broadcast Journalist
Vietnam correspondent, 1964-71; co-host of "60 Minutes," 1971--.
b. Nov 8, 1931 in Toronto, ON
Source: *ConAu 93; CurBio 80; IntMPA 82; WhoAm 74, 76, 78, 80, 82*

Saffir, Leonard
Editor, Publisher
b. 1930?
Source: *BioIn 11*

Safire, William L
American. Author, Journalist
b. Dec 17, 1929 in New York, New York
Source: *ConAu 17R; ConLC 10; CurBio 73; WhoAm 74, 76, 78, 80, 82; WhoGov 72; WhoS&SW 73*

Sagan, Carl Edward
American. Astronomer, Biologist
Won Pulitzer Prize, 1977, for *The Dragons of Eden.*
b. Nov 9, 1934 in New York, New York
Source: *AmM&WS 73P; ConAu 25R; CurBio 70; WhoAm 74, 76, 78, 80, 82*

Sagan, Francoise, pseud.
[Francoise Quoirez]
French. Author
b. Jun 21, 1935 in Cajarc, France
Source: *CasWL; ConAu 49; ConLC 3, 6, 9; CurBio 60; EncWL; EvEuW; FilmgC; InWom; IntWW 74; LongCTC; ModRL; Pen EUR; REn; TwCW; Who 74; WhoTwCL; WhoWor 74; WorAu*

Sage, Margaret Olivia
American. Philanthropist
b. Sep 8, 1828 in Syracuse, New York
d. Nov 4, 1918 in New York, New York
Source: *AmBi; DcAmB; InWom; NotAW; WebAB; WomWWA 14*

Sage, Russell
American. Financier
b. Aug 4, 1816 in Oneida County, New York
d. Nov 4, 1906 in New York, New York
Source: *AmBi; ApCAB; BiAuS; BiDrAC; DcAmB; TwCBDA; WebAB; WhAm 1*

Sager, Carole Bayer
[Mrs. Burt Bacharach]
American. Singer, Songwriter
Lyricist, with Marvin Hamlisch, *They're Playing Our Song,* 1979.
b. Mar 8, 1947 in New York, New York
Source: *BioIn 11; WhoAm 80, 82*

Sahl, Mort (Lyon)
American. Monologist, Satirist
b. May 11, 1927 in Montreal, PQ
Source: *BioNews 74; CurBio 60; FilmgC; WhoAm 82; WhoHol A*

Said bin Taimusr
Sultan of Muscat and Oman
b. Aug 13, 1910 in London, England
d. Oct 19, 1972 in London, England
Source: *BioIn 9; CurBio 78*

Saidenberg, Daniel
American. Musician, Conductor
b. Nov 12, 1906 in Winnipeg, MB
Source: *WhoAm 74, 76, 78, 80, 82; WhoAmA 73; WhoMus 72*

Sain, Johnny (John Franklin)
American. Baseball Player, Coach
b. Sep 15, 1918 in Havana, Arkansas
Source: *BaseEn; BioIn 1, 2, 3, 4, 6, 7, 8, 9, 10; WhoProB 73*

Saint, Eva Marie
American. Actress
b. Jul 4, 1924 in Newark, New Jersey
Source: *BiDFilm; BiE&WWA; BioNews 74; FilmgC; InWom; IntMPA 75, 76, 77, 78, 79, 80, 81, 82; MotPP; MovMk; WhoAm 74, 76, 78, 80, 82; WhoHol A; WhoWor 74; WorEFlm*

Saint Clair, Arthur
American. Military Leader
b. Mar 23, 1736 in Thurso, Scotland
d. Aug 31, 1818 in Ligonier, Pennsylvania
Source: *Alli; AmBi; ApCAB; BiAuS; BiDrAC; BiDrUSE; DcAmB; DcNAA; Drake; OhA&B; REnAL; TwCBDA; WebAB; WhAm H*

Saint Clair, James Draper
American. Lawyer
b. Apr 14, 1920 in Akron, Ohio
Source: *BioIn 10; NewYTBS 74; WhoAm 76, 78, 80, 82*

St. Clare
[Clara Schiffi]
Italian. Founder of the Poor Clares Order
b. 1194 in Assisi, Italy
d. 1253
Source: *WomAch 81*

Saint Cyr, Lillian
[Marie VanShaak]
American. Entertainer, Burlesque Queen
b. Jun 3, 1917 in Minneapolis, Minnesota
d. 1974 in New York, New York
Source: *BioIn 10; InWom; What 5*

Saint Denis, Ruth
American. Dancer, Choreographer
b. Jan 20, 1877 in Newark, New Jersey
d. Jun 21, 1968 in Los Angeles, California
Source: *CurBio 49, 68; InWom; WebAB; WhAm 5; WhScrn 74, 77; WhoHol B*

Saint-Exupery, Antoine
French. Author, Aviator
Wrote fable *The Little Prince,* 1943.
b. Jun 29, 1900 in Lyons, France
d. Jul 31, 1944 in France
Source: *AnCL; AtlBL; CasWL; ClDMEL; CnMWL; CurBio 40, 45; CyWA; EncWL; EvEuW; LongCTC; ModRL; OxFr; Pen EUR; REn; TwCA, SUP; TwCW; WhoTwCL*

Saint Gaudens, Augustus
American. Sculptor
b. Mar 1, 1848 in Dublin, Ireland
d. Aug 3, 1907 in Cornish, New Hampshire
Source: *AmAu&B; AmBi; ApCAB; AtlBL; DcAmB; EncAB-H; OxAmL; REn; REnAL; TwCBDA; WebAB; WhAm 1*

St. Genesius
Roman. Patron Saint of Actors
d. 286AD in Rome, Italy
Source: *NotNAT B*

Saint Georges, Jules
French. Author, Librettist
b. Nov 7, 1801 in Paris, France
d. Dec 23, 1875 in Paris, France
Source: *NewEOp 71*

St. Holmes, Derek
see: Amboy Dukes, The

Saint Jacques, Raymond
American. Actor
b. 1936?
Source: *FilmgC; IntMPA 75, 76, 77; MovMk; NewYTBE 73; WhoAm 74; WhoBlA 75; WhoHol A*

St. James, Lyn
American. Auto Racer
b. Mar 13, 1947 in Ohio
Source: *BioIn 12*

Saint James, Susan
American. Actress
Appeared in TV series "The Name of the Game"; "McMillan and Wife."
b. Aug 14, 1946 in Long Beach, California
Source: *FilmgC; IntMPA 75, 76, 77, 78, 79, 80, 81, 82; WhoAm 74; WhoHol A*

Saint John, Betta
American. Actress
b. 1929 in Hawthorne, California
Source: *FilmgC; IntMPA 75, 76, 77, 78, 79, 80, 81, 82; WhoHol A*

Saint John, Howard
American. Actor
b. 1905
d. Mar 13, 1974 in New York, New York
Source: *BiE&WWA; FilmgC; MovMk; WhScrn 77; WhoHol B*

St. John, J Hector, pseud.
see: Crevecoeur, Michel-Guillaume, Jean de

Saint John, Jill
[Jill Oppenheim]
American. Actress
b. Aug 9, 1940 in Los Angeles, California
Source: *CelR 73; FilmgC; InWom; MotPP; MovMk; WhoHol A*

Saint John, Robert
American. Journalist, Children's Author
b. Mar 9, 1902 in Chicago, Illinois
Source: *AmAu&B; ConAu 1R, 5NR; CurBio 42; WhoAm 74; WhoWor 74; WrDr 76*

Saint Johns, Adela Rogers
American. Author, Journalist
b. May 20, 1894 in Los Angeles, California
Source: *AuNews 1; CelR 73; ForWC 70; WhoAm 74; WrDr 76*

St. Laurent, Andre
"Ace"
Canadian. Hockey Player
b. Feb 16, 1953 in Rouyn Noranda, PQ
Source: *HocReg; PseudN*

Saint Laurent, Louis Stephen
Canadian. Political Leader
Prime Minister, Liberal Party, 1948-57.
b. Feb 1, 1882 in Compton, PQ
d. Jul 24, 1973 in Quebec City, PQ
Source: *CanWW 70; CurBio 48, 73; NewYTBE 73; OxCan; WhAm 5; WhoWor 74*

Saint Laurent, Yves Mathieu
French. Fashion Designer
Responsible for "chic beatnik" and "little boy look" of 1960's.
b. Aug 1, 1936 in Oran, Algeria
Source: *BkPepl; CelR 73; CurBio 64; IntWW 74; Who 82; WhoWor 74; WorFshn*

Saint-Saens, (Charles) Camille
French. Musician, Composer
b. Oct 9, 1835 in Paris, France
d. Dec 16, 1921 in Algiers, Morocco
Source: *AtlBL; OxFr; REn*

Saint-Simon, Claude-Henri de Rouvroy
French. Philosopher
b. Oct 17, 1760 in Paris, France
d. May 19, 1825 in Paris, France
Source: *ApCAB; BbD; BiD&SB; CasWL; DcEuL; EuAu; EvEuW; OxEng; OxFr; REn*

Saint-Subber, Arnold
American. Theatrical Producer
b. Feb 18, 1918 in Washington, DC
Source: *BiE&WWA; CelR 73; NotNAT; WhoThe 77*

Sainte-Beuve, Charles Augustin
French. Critic
b. Dec 23, 1804 in Boulogne, France
d. Oct 13, 1869 in Paris, France
Source: *AtlBL; BbD; BiD&SB; CasWL; CyWA; DcEnL; DcEuL; EuAu; EvEuW; NewC; OxEng; OxFr; OxThe; Pen EUR; RComWL; REn*

Sainte-Marie, "Buffy" (Beverly)
American Indian. Folk Singer, Composer
b. Feb 20, 1941 in Craven, SK
Source: *CurBio 69; EncFCWM 69; RkOn; WhoAm 74; WhoWor 74*

Saintsbury, George Edward Bateman
English. Author
b. Oct 10, 1845 in Southampton, England
d. Jan 28, 1933 in Bath, England
Source: *Alli SUP; AtlBL; BbD; BiD&SB; Chambr 3; ChPo, S2; DcEnA, AP; DcLEL; EvLB; LongCTC; ModBrL; NewC; OxEng; Pen ENG; RAdv 1; TwCA, SUP*

Saito, Yoshishige
Japanese. Artist
b. May 4, 1904 in Tokyo, Japan
Source: *ConArt; WhWW-II; WhoWor 74*

Sakall, S Z
"Cuddles"
Hungarian. Actor
b. Feb 2, 1884 in Budapest, Hungary
d. Feb 12, 1955 in Los Angeles, California
Source: *FilmgC; MotPP; MovMk; Vers A; WhScrn 74, 77; WhoHol B*

Sakharov, Andrei Dmitrievich
Russian. Physicist, Dissident
Led dissident movement in Soviet Union; won Nobel Peace Prize, 1975.
b. May 21, 1921 in Moscow, U.S.S.R.
Source: *CurBio 71; IntWW 74; NewYTBE 73; WhoWor 74*

Saki, pseud.
[Hector Hugh Munro]
Author
b. Dec 18, 1870 in Akyab, Burma
d. Nov 13, 1916 in Beaumont-Hamel, France
Source: *Alli SUP; AtlBL; CasWL; ChPo; CnMWL; CyWA; DcLEL; EvLB; LongCTC; ModBrL; NewC; OxEng; Pen ENG; RAdv 1; REn; TwCA, SUP; TwCW; WhoTwCL*

Saks, Gene
American. Theatrical Director
b. Nov 8, 1921 in New York, New York
Source: *BiE&WWA; FilmgC; IntMPA 75, 76, 77, 78, 79, 80, 81, 82; NotNAT; WhoAm 74; WhoHol A; WhoThe 77*

Saladin Yusuf ibn Ayyub
[Salah al-Din]
Sultan of Egypt and Syria
b. 1138
d. 1193
Source: *BioIn 1, 2, 4, 5, 6, 8, 9, 10, 11; NewC*

Saladino, John F
Interior Designer
Source: *BioIn 11*

Salam, Saeb
Lebanese. Premier
b. 1905 in Beirut, Lebanon
Source: *IntWW 74; WhoWor 74*

Salant, Richard S
American. Broadcasting Executive
b. Apr 14, 1914 in New York, New York
Source: *CurBio 61; IntMPA 75, 76, 77, 78, 79, 80, 81, 82; St&PR 75; WhoAm 74*

Salazar, Alberto
American. Marathon Runner
Won NY City Marathon, 1980, 1981; Boston Marathan, 1982.
b. Aug 7, 1957 in Havana, Cuba
Source: *NewYTBS 81*

Salazar, Antonio de Oliveira
Portuguese. Statesman
b. Apr 28, 1889 in Portugal
d. Jul 27, 1970 in Lisbon, Portugal
Source: *CurBio 41, 52, 70; NewYTBE 70*

Salem, Peter
American. Revolutionary Patriot
b. 1750
d. 1816
Source: *BioIn 7, 8, 9, 10*

Sale, Charles Partlow
"Chic"
American. Actor
b. 1885 in Huron, South Dakota
d. Nov 7, 1936 in Los Angeles, California
Source: *WhAm 1; WhScrn 74, 77*

Sales, Soupy
[Morton Supman]
American. TV Personality
Starred in "Soupy Sales Show," 1953-66; known for pie-throwing act.
b. Jan 8, 1930 in Wake Forest, North Carolina
Source: *AmSCAP 66; CurBio 67; FilmgC; MotPP; WhoHol A*

Salieri, Antonio
Italian. Conductor, Composer
b. Aug 18, 1750 in Legnano, Italy
d. May 7, 1825 in Vienna, Austria
Source: *BioIn 9; OxMus*

Salignac, Eustase Thomas
French. Opera Singer, Teacher
b. Mar 29, 1867 in Generac, France
d. 1945 in Paris, France
Source: *NewEOp 71*

Salinger, J(erome) D(avid)
American. Author
Wrote *Catcher in the Rye,* 1951.
b. Jan 1, 1919 in New York, New York
Source: *AmAu&B; AmWr; Au&Wr 71; CasWL; CelR 73; CnMWL; ConAu 5R; ConLC 1, 3, 8, 12; ConNov 72, 76; DrAF 76; EncAB-H; EncWL; IntWW 74; LongCTC; ModAL, SUP; OxAmL; Pen AM; RAdv 1; REn; REnAL; TwCA SUP; TwCW; WebAB; WebE&AL; Who 74; WhoAm 74, 76, 78, 80, 82; WhoTwCL; WhoWor 74; WrDr 76*

Salinger, Pierre Emil George
American. Journalist, Politician
Press secretary to John F Kennedy, 1961-63; author *America Held Hostage,* 1981.
b. Jun 14, 1925 in San Francisco, California
Source: *BiDrAC; ConAu 17R; CurBio 61; IntWW 74; Who 74; WhoAm 74, 76, 78, 80, 82; WhoAmP 73; WhoS&SW 73; WhoWor 74*

Salisbury, Harrison Evans
American. Journalist
b. Nov 14, 1908 in Minneapolis, Minnesota
Source: *AmAu&B; CelR 73; ConAu 1R, 3NR; CurBio 55, 82; IntWW 74; MnnWr; REnAL; Who 74; WhoAm 74, 76, 78, 80, 82; WhoE 74; WhoWor 74; WorAu; WrDr 76*

Salisbury, Robert Arthur Talbot, 3rd Marquess
British. Statesman
b. Feb 3, 1830 in Hatfield, England
d. Aug 1903 in Hatfield, England
Source: *BioIn 2, 3, 6, 8, 9, 10, 11; WhoModH*

Salk, Jonas Edward
American. Scientist, Immunologist
Discovered polio vaccine, 1953.
b. Oct 28, 1914 in New York, New York
Source: *AmM&WS 73P; BioNews 75; CelR 73; ConAu 49; CurBio 54; IntWW 74; LongCTC; WebAB; Who 74; WhoAm 74, 76, 78, 80, 82; WhoWor 74; WhoWorJ 72*

Salk, Lee
American. Psychologist, Author
b. Dec 27, 1926 in New York, New York
Source: *AuNews 1; BioIn 10, 11; ConAu 104; CurBio 79; WhoAm 82*

Salmi, Albert
American. Actor
b. 1928 in New York, New York
Source: *BiE&WWA; FilmgC; IntMPA 75, 76, 77, 78, 79, 80, 81, 82; NotNAT; WhoHol A*

Salome
Biblical Character
b. 14
d. 62
Source: *BioIn 2, 3, 4, 5; InWom*

Salomon, Charlotte
German. Artist
b. 1917 in Berlin, Germany
d. 1943 in Auschwitz, Poland
Source: *BioIn 12*

Salomon, Haym
American. Revolutionary Patriot
b. 1740 in Leszno, Poland
d. Jan 6, 1785 in Philadelphia, Pennsylvania
Source: *AmBi; ApCAB; DcAmB; WebAB; WhAm H; WhAmP*

Salt, Jennifer
American. Actress
b. Sep 4, 1944 in Los Angeles, California
Source: *FilmEn; WhoHol A*

Salt, Waldo
American. Screenwriter
b. Oct 18, 1914 in Chicago, Illinois
Source: *FilmEn; FilmgC; IntMPA 75, 76, 77, 78, 79, 80, 81, 82*

Saltonstall, Leverett
American. Politician
b. Sep 1, 1892 in Chestnut Hill, Massachusetts
d. Jun 17, 1979 in Dover, Massachusetts
Source: *BiDrAC; CurBio 44, 56, 79; NewYTBS 79; PolProf E; PolProf J; PolProf K; PolProf T; WhAmP; WhoAm 74, 76, 78; WhoAmL 78, 79; WhoAmP 73, 75, 77, 79*

Sam and Dave
[Sam Moore; Dave Prater]
American. Singing Duo
Source: *ConMuA 80; RkOn 2; WhoRock 81*

Sam the Sham and the Pharaohs
[Butch Gibson; David Martin; Jerry Patterson; Domingo Samudio; Ray Stinnet]
American. Rock Group
Source: *EncPR&S; RkOn*

Samaranch, Juan Antonio
Spanish. President of IOC
b. 1920?
Source: *NF*

Samaras, Lucas
American. Artist
b. Sep 14, 1936 in Kastoria, Greece
Source: *CurBio 72; DcCAA 71; WhoAm 82; WhoAmA 73*

Sammarco, Mario
Italian. Opera Singer
b. Dec 13, 1868 in Palermo, Sicily
d. Jan 24, 1930 in Milan, Italy
Source: *NewEOp 71*

Sample, Joe
see: Crusaders, The

Sample, Paul Starrett
American. Artist
b. Sep 14, 1896 in Louisville, Kentucky
d. Feb 26, 1974 in Norwich, Vermont
Source: *ArtsAmW; IlBEAAW; McGDA; WhAm 6; WhoAm 74; WhoAmA 73, 76, 78*

Sampson, Deborah
[Robert Shirtliff]
American. Continental Army Soldier
Spent three years in Continental Army disguised as a man.
b. Dec 17, 1760 in Massachusetts
d. 1827
Source: *AmBi; ApCAB; DcNAA; Drake; HerW; InWom; NotAW; OxAmL*

Sampson, Ralph
American. Basketball Player
Most sought-after college player in country; is 7'4" tall.
b. Jul 7, 1960 in Harrisonburg, Virginia
Source: *NewYTBS 82*

Sampson, William T
American. Military Leader
b. Feb 9, 1840 in Palmyra, New York
d. 1903
Source: *AmBi; ApCAB, SUP; TwCBDA; WhAm 1*

Samson
Biblical Character
Source: *BioIn 1, 2, 4, 6, 7, 8, 9, 10; NewCol 75*

Samsonov, Aleksandr Vasilievich
Russian. Military Officer
b. 1859
d. 1914 in Tannenberg, Prussia (East)
Source: *NewCol 75; WhoMilH 76*

Samstag, Nicholas
American. Advertiser, Promoter
b. Dec 25, 1903 in New York, New York
d. Mar 26, 1968
Source: *AuBYP; ConAu 5R, 25R*

Samuel
Biblical Character
Source: *BioIn 1, 2, 3, 4, 5, 6, 7, 8, 9, 10, 11; NewC*

Samuel, Maurice
American. Journalist, Author
b. Feb 8, 1895 in Macin, Romania
d. May 4, 1972 in New York, New York
Source: *AmAu&B; AmNov; ConAu 33R, 102; REnAL; TwCA SUP; WhAm 5; WhoWorJ 72*

Samuels, Ernest
American. Educator, Author
b. May 19, 1903 in Chicago, Illinois
Source: *AmAu&B; ConAu P-1; DrAS 74E; OxAmL; WhoAm 74, 76, 78, 80, 82; WhoWorJ 72; WorAu; WrDr 76*

Samuelson, Paul Anthony
American. Economist
Won Nobel Prize in Economics, 1970.
b. May 15, 1915 in Gary, Indiana
Source: *AmAu&B; AmM&WS 73S; CelR 73; ConAu 5R; CurBio 65; EncAB-H; IndAu 1917; IntWW 74; NewYTBE 70, 71; WebAB; Who 74; WhoAm 74; WhoE 74; WhoWor 74; WrDr 76*

San Juan, Olga
American. Actress
b. 1927 in New York, New York
Source: *FilmgC; WhoHol A*

San Martin, Jose de
Argentine. Revolutionary, Statesman
b. Feb 25, 1778 in Yapeyu, Argentina
d. Aug 17, 1850 in Boulogne, France
Source: *ApCAB; Drake; McGEWB; NewCol 75; REn*

Sanborn, Pitts
American. Music Critic, Author
b. Oct 19, 1878 in Port Huron, Michigan
d. Mar 7, 1941 in New York, New York
Source: *CurBio 41; DcNAA; TwCA*

Sanchez, Salvador
"Chava"
Mexican. Boxer
WBC featherweight champ, 1980-82.
b. Feb 5, 1959 in Santiago de Tianquistenco, Mexico
d. Aug 12, 1982 in Queretaro, Mexico
Source: *NewYTBS 82*

Sanchez Manduley, Celia
Cuban. Revolutionary
b. 1923
d. 1980
Source: *BioIn 7*

Sancho, Ignatius
Author, Poet
b. 1729
d. 1780
Source: *AfrA; Alli*

Sand, George, pseud.
[Amandine Aurore Lucie Dupin Dudevant]
French. Author
b. Sep 1, 1804 in Paris, France
d. Jun 8, 1876
Source: *AtlBL; BbD; BiD&SB; CasWL; CyWA; DcBiA; DcEnL; DcEuL; EuAu; EvEuW; InWom; OxEng; OxFr; Pen EUR; RComWL; REn*

Sand, Paul
American. Actor
b. Mar 5, 1941 in Los Angeles, California
Source: *NewYTBE 71; NotNAT; WhoHol A; WhoThe 77*

Sanda, Dominique
[Dominique Varaigne]
French. Actress
b. 1948 in Paris, France
Source: *BioIn 9, 10; CelR 73; FilmEn; FilmgC; MovMk; WhoHol A*

Sandburg, Carl August
American. Poet, Author
Won three Pulitzer Prizes in Poetry, 1918, 1940, 1951.
b. Jan 6, 1878 in Galesburg, Illinois
d. Jul 22, 1967 in Flat Rock, North Carolina
Source: *AmAu&B; AmSCAP 66; AmWr; AnCL; AtlBL; AuBYP; CasWL; Chambr 3; ChPo, S1, S2; CnDAL; CnE&AP; CnMWL; ConAmA; ConAmL; ConAu 5R, 25R; ConLC 1, 4, 10, 15; CurBio 40, 63, 67; CyWA; DcLEL; EncAB-H; EncFCWM 69; EncWL; EvLB; LongCTC; ModAL, SUP; OxAmL; OxEng; Pen AM; RAdv 1; REn; REnAL; SixAP; SmATA 8; Str&VC; TwCA, SUP; TwCW; WebAB; WebE&AL; WhAm 4; WhoTwCL; WisWr*

Sandburg, Helga
American. Children's Author
b. Nov 24, 1918 in Elmhurst, Illinois
Source: *ConAu 1R, 5NR; ConP 70; ForWC 70; SmATA 3; ThrBJA; WhoAm 74, 76, 78, 80, 82; WhoAmW 77*

Sande, Earl
American. Jockey
b. 1898 in Groton, South Dakota
d. Aug 18, 1968 in Jacksonville, Florida
Source: *DcBiPP*

Sander, Marty
see: Jay and the Americans

Sanderlin, George William
American. Children's Author
b. Feb 5, 1915 in Baltimore, Maryland
Source: *ConAu 13R; DrAS 74E; SmATA 4; WrDr 76*

Sanders, Bill (William Willard)
American. Editor, Cartoonist
b. 1933 in Tennessee
Source: *WorECom*

Sanders, "Colonel" (Harland David)
American. Restaurateur
Established Kentucky Fried Chicken franchise, using a secret recipe, at age 66.
b. Sep 9, 1890 in Henryville, Indiana
d. Dec 16, 1980
Source: *AnObit 1980; BusPN; CelR 73; ConAu 102; CurBio 73; NewYTBS 80; WhoAm 74; WhoS&SW 73*

Sanders, Doug(las)
American. Golfer
b. Jul 24, 1937 in Cedartown, Georgia
Source: *BioIn 10; WhoGolf*

Sanders, Ed Parish
"Black Hobart"
American. Author
b. Aug 17, 1939 in Kansas City, Missouri
Source: *AmAu&B; ConAu 13R; ConP 70, 75; DrAF 76; DrAP 75; DrAS 74P; Pen AM; WrDr 76*

Sanders, George
American. Actor
b. Jul 3, 1906 in Saint Petersburg, Russia
d. Apr 25, 1972 in Castelldefels, Spain
Source: *BiDFilm; CurBio 43, 72; FilmgC; MotPP; MovMk; NewYTBE 72; OxFilm; WhAm 5; WhScrn 77; WhoHol B; WorEFlm*

Sanders, Lawrence
American. Author
b. 1920 in New York, New York
Source: *BioIn 11; ConAu 81; EncSF; IntAu&W 76, 77; WhoAm 82*

Sanders, Marlene
American. Broadcast Journalist
b. Jan 10, 1931 in Cleveland, Ohio
Source: *ConAu 65; ForWC 70; WhoAm 82; WomWMM*

Sanders, Richard Kinard
American. Actor
Played Les Nessman on TV series "WKRP in Cincinnati," 1978-82.
b. Aug 23, 1940 in Harrisburg, Pennsylvania
Source: *WhoAm 80, 82*

Sanderson, Derek Michael
"Turk"
Canadian. Hockey Player
Center, 1967-78; won Calder Trophy, 1968; wrote autobiography *I've Got to Be Me.*
b. Jun 16, 1946 in Niagara Falls, ON
Source: *NewYTBE 70, 72, 73; NewYTBS 74; WhoHcky 73*

Sanderson, Ivan Terence
[Terence Roberts]
American. Zoologist, Author
b. Jan 30, 1911 in Edinburgh, Scotland
d. Feb 19, 1973
Source: *AmAu&B; AmM&WS 73P; AuBYP; ConAu 37R, 41R; IlsCB 1744, 1946; NewYTBE 73; REnAL; SmATA 6; TwCA, SUP*

Sanderson, Julia
[Julia Sackett]
American. Singer, Actress
b. Aug 22, 1887 in Springfield, Massachusetts
d. Jan 27, 1975 in Springfield, Massachusetts
Source: *BiE&WWA; EncMT; Film 1; InWom; WhAm 6; WhScrn 77; WhoStg 1908*

Sanderson, Sybil
American. Opera Singer
b. Dec 7, 1865 in Sacramento, California
d. May 15, 1903 in Paris, France
Source: *AmWom; InWom*

Sanderson, Thomas Cobden
English. Bookbinder, Printer
b. 1804
d. 1865
Source: *Alli; BiDLA*

Sandler and Young
[Tony Sandler; Ralph Young]
American. Singers
Source: *NF*

Sandow, Eugene
[Karl Frederick Mueller]
German. Weightlifter
b. 1867 in Konigsberg, Germany
d. Oct 14, 1925 in London, England
Source: *Film 1; WhScrn 77*

Sandoz, Mari
American. Author
b. 1900 in Sheridan County, Nebraska
d. Mar 10, 1966 in New York, New York
Source: *AmAu&B; AuBYP; CnDAL; ConAu 1R, 25R; InWom; OxAmL; REn; REnAL; SmATA 5; ThrBJA; TwCA, SUP; WhAm 4; WhNAA*

Sands, Bobby (Robert Gerard)
[Irish Hunger Strikers]
Irish. Jailed IRA Member, MP
Elected to Parliament while in prison for possession of weapons; died on 66th day of hunger strike.
b. Mar 9, 1954 in Belfast, Northern Ireland
d. May 5, 1981 in Belfast, Northern Ireland
Source: *AnObit 1981; BioIn 12; NewYTBS 81*

Sands, Diana Patricia
American. Actress
b. Aug 22, 1934 in New York, New York
d. Sep 21, 1973 in New York, New York
Source: *BiE&WWA; CelR 73; MotPP; NewYTBE 73; WhAm 6; WhScrn 77; WhoBlA 75; WhoHol B; WomWMM*

Sands, Dorothy
American. Actress, Motion Picture Director
b. Mar 5, 1893 in Cambridge, Massachusetts
d. Sep 11, 1980 in Croton-on-Hudson, New York
Source: *BiE&WWA; NotNAT; PlP&P; WhoAmW 58, 61; WhoThe 72, 77, 81*

Sands, Tommy
American. Singer
b. Aug 27, 1937 in Chicago, Illinois
Source: *FilmgC; IntMPA 75, 76, 77, 78, 79, 80, 81, 82; MotPP; WhoHol A*

Sandwich, Edward Montagu, Earl
British. Admiral
b. 1625
d. 1672
Source: *Alli*

Sandy, Gary
American. Actor
Played Andy Travis on TV series "WKRP in Cincinnati," 1978-82.
b. Dec 25, 1946? in Dayton, Ohio
Source: *BioIn 11; WhoAm 78, 80, 82*

Sandys, Duncan
English. Statesman
b. Jan 24, 1908
Source: *CurBio 52; Who 74; WhoWor 74*

Sandys, Sir Edwin
British. Statesman
One of founders of VA.
b. Dec 9, 1561
d. Oct 1629
Source: *ApCAB; BioIn 1, 3, 6; McGEWB; NewCol 75*

Saneev, Viktor
Russian. Track Athlete
b. Oct 3, 1945 in U.S.S.R.
Source: *WhoTr&F 73*

Sanford, Isabel Gwendolyn
American. Actress
Plays Louise Jefferson on TV series "The Jeffersons," 1974--.
b. Aug 29, 1933? in New York, New York
Source: *BioIn 10; WhoAm 74, 76, 78, 80, 82*

Sanford, Terry
American. Educator, Governor
b. Aug 20, 1917 in Laurinburg, North Carolina
Source: *ConAu 17R; CurBio 61; IntWW 74; LEduc 74; WhoAm 74, 76, 78, 80, 82; WhoAmP 73*

Sang, Samantha
Australian. Singer
b. Aug 5, 1953 in Melbourne, Australia
Source: *RkOn*

Sanger, Frederick
English. Molecular Biologist
b. Aug 13, 1918 in Rendcomb, England
Source: *AsBiEn; BioIn 5, 6, 8; CurBio 81; IntWW 74, 75, 76, 77, 78, 79, 80; McGEWB; Who 74; WhoWor 74, 76, 78*

Sanger, Margaret
[Margaret Higgins]
American. Nurse, Social Reformer
Founded National Birth Control League, 1914; wrote *Women, Morality, and Birth Control,* 1931.
b. Sep 14, 1883 in Corning, New York
d. Sep 6, 1966 in Tucson, Arizona
Source: *AmAu&B; ConAu 89; CurBio 44, 66; EncAB-H; HerW; LongCTC; OxAmL; WebAB; WhAm 4*

Sangster, Margaret Elizabeth
[Margaret Elizabeth Murson]
American. Author
b. Feb 22, 1838 in New Rochelle, New York
d. Jun 4, 1912 in Glen Ridge, New Jersey
Source: *Alli SUP; AmAu; AmAu&B; AmBi; AmWom; ApCAB; BbD; BiD&SB; ChPo, S1, S2; DcAmAu; DcAmB; DcNAA; InWom; NotAW; REnAL; TwCBDA; WhAm 1*

Sanguillen, Manny (Manuel DeJesus)
Panamanian. Baseball Player
b. Mar 21, 1944 in Colon, Panama
Source: *BaseEn; WhoProB 73*

Sann, Paul
American. Journalist
b. Mar 7, 1914 in Brooklyn, New York
Source: *AmAu&B; ConAu 13R, 5NR; WhoAm 74, 76, 78, 80, 82; WhoE 74*

Sansom, Odette Marie Celine
[Odette Marie Celine Churchill; Odette Marie Celine Hallowes]
British. Undercover Agent
b. Apr 28, 1912
Source: *BioIn 2, 3, 4, 7; EncE 75; InWom; IntWW 74, 75, 76, 77, 78; WhWW-II*

Sansom, William
English. Author
b. Jan 18, 1912 in London, England
d. Apr 20, 1976 in London, England
Source: *Au&Wr 71; CnMWL; ConAu 5R; ConLC 2, 6; ConNov 72, 76; EncWL; LongCTC; ModBrL, SUP; NewC; Pen ENG; RAdv 1; REn; TwCA SUP; TwCW; WhAm 7; Who 74; WhoWor 74; WrDr 76*

Sansovino, Andrea
[Andrea Andrea]
Italian. Artist
b. 1460 in Monte Sansavino, Italy
d. 1529
Source: *NewCol 75; OxArt*

Sansovino, Jacopo
[Jacopo Tatti]
Italian. Artist
b. 1486 in Florence, Italy
d. 1570
Source: *NewCol 75; OxArt*

Santa Anna, Antonio Lopez de
Mexican. Dictator, General
b. 1794 in Jalapa, Mexico
d. Jun 20, 1876 in Mexico City, Mexico
Source: *ApCAB; REn; REnAL; WhAm H*

Santana
[Jose Areas; David Brown; Michael Carabello; Ndugu Chancler; Tom Coster; Armando Pereza; Gregg Rolie; Carlos Santana; Michael Shrieve; Greg Walker]
American. Rock Group
Source: *IlEncRk; RkOn*

Santana, (Devadip) Carlos
[Santana]
Mexican. Musician
b. Jul 20, 1947 in Mexico
Source: *BioIn 11, 12; BkPepl; WhoAm 78, 80, 82*

Santander, Francisco de Paula
Colombian. Revolutionary, Politician
b. 1792
d. 1840
Source: *ApCAB; Drake*

Santayana, George
American. Philosopher, Essayist
b. Dec 16, 1863 in Madrid, Spain
d. Sep 26, 1952 in Rome, Italy
Source: *AmAu&B; AmWr; AtlBL; BiD&SB; CasWL; Chambr 3; ChPo, S1, S2; CnDAL; ConAmA; ConAmL; CurBio 44, 52; CyWA; DcAmAu; DcAmB S5; DcLEL; EncAB-H; EncWL; EvLB; LongCTC; ModAL, SUP; OxAmL; OxEng; Pen AM; REn; REnAL; TwCA, SUP; TwCBDA; TwCW; WebAB; WebE&AL; WhAm 3; WhoLA; WhoTwCL*

Santee, David
American. Figure Skater
b. Jul 22, 1957 in Park Ridge, Illinois
Source: *BioIn 12*

Santillana, Inigo Lopez de Mendoza
Spanish. Poet, Literary Patron
b. Aug 19, 1398 in Carrion, Spain
d. Mar 25, 1458 in Guadalajara, Spain
Source: *BbD; BiD&SB; CasWL; DcEuL; DcSpL; EuAu; EvEuW; Pen EUR; REn*

Santini Brothers
[Seven Santini Brothers]
Italian. Movers
Source: *NF*

Santos-Dumont, Alberto
Brazilian. Balloonist
b. 1873
d. 1932
Source: *REn*

Saperstein, Abraham
"Little Caesar"
American. Basketball Coach
Formed Harlem Globetrotters; Hall of Fame, 1970.
b. Jul 4, 1903 in London, England
d. Mar 15, 1966 in Chicago, Illinois
Source: *WhoBbl 73*

Saperton, David
American. Pianist, Music Teacher
b. 1890 in Pittsburgh, Pennsylvania
d. 1970
Source: *BioIn 10*

Sapir, Edward
American. Anthropologist, Author
b. Jan 26, 1884 in Louenburg, Germany
d. Feb 4, 1939 in New Haven, Connecticut
Source: *DcAmB S2; DcNAA; OxCan; REnAL; WebAB; WhAm 1*

Sapir, Pinchas
Israeli. Cabinet Member
b. 1909 in Suwalki, Poland
d. 1975 in Israel
Source: *WhoWor 74; WhoWorJ 72*

Sapir, Richard
American. Author
b. Jul 27, 1936 in New York, New York
Source: *ConAu 69*

Sappho
"The 10th Muse"
Greek. Poet
b. 612BC in Greece
d. in Sicily
Source: *AtlBL; BbD; BiD&SB; CasWL; CyWA; InWom; NewC; OxEng; Pen CL; RComWL; REn*

Saragat, Giuseppe
Italian. Politician
b. Sep 19, 1898
Source: *CurBio 56, 65; IntWW 74; Who 74; WhoGov 72; WhoWor 74*

Sarah
Biblical Character
Source: *BioIn 1, 2, 4, 5, 6, 7, 11; InWom*

Sarandon, Chris
American. Actor
Starred in *Dog Day Afternoon,* 1975.
b. Jul 24, 1942 in Beckley, West Virginia
Source: *NewYTBS 76; WhoHol A; WhoThe 81*

Sarandon, Susan Abigail
[Susan Tomaling]
American. Actress
b. Oct 4, 1946 in New York, New York
Source: *FilmEn; IntMPA 82; WhoAm 82; WhoHol A*

Sarasate, Pablo de
[Martin Meliton S y Navascuez]
Spanish. Musician, Composer
b. Mar 10, 1844 in Pamplona, Spain
d. Sep 20, 1908 in Biarritz, France
Source: *OxMus*

Sarasin, Jean Francois
French. Author
b. 1614
d. Dec 5, 1654
Source: *OxFr*

Sarazen, Gene
[Gene Saraceni]
American. Golfer
Invented the sand wedge, about 1930.
b. Feb 27, 1901 in Rye, New York
Source: *NewYTBE 72, 73; WebAB*

Sarbanes, Paul Spyros
American. Senator
b. Feb 3, 1933 in Salisbury, Maryland
Source: *AlmAP 78, 80; BioIn 10; CngDr 74, 77, 79; IntWW 77, 78; IntYB 78, 79; WhoAm 74, 76, 78, 80, 82; WhoAmP 73, 77, 79; WhoE 74, 75, 77, 79; WhoGov 72, 75, 77*

Sarcey, Francisque
French. Author, Critic
b. 1827
d. 1899
Source: *BbD; BiD&SB; ClDMEL; DcEuL; OxFr; OxThe*

Sardi, Vincent, Jr
American. Restauranteur
Owner, Sardi's restaurant, NY City.
b. Jul 23, 1915 in New York, New York
Source: *BiE&WWA; CelR 73; WhoAm 76, 78, 80, 82*

Sardi, Vincent, Sr.
American. Restauranteur
Opened Sardi's restaurant in Manhattan's theatre district, 1921.
b. Dec 23, 1885 in Canelli, Italy
d. Nov 19, 1969 in New York, New York
Source: *BioIn 3, 4, 8, 9; CurBio 57, 70*

Sardou, Victorien
French. Poet
b. Sep 7, 1831 in Paris, France
d. Nov 8, 1908 in Paris, France
Source: *AtlBL; BbD; BiD&SB; CasWL; ClDMEL; CnThe; DcEuL; EuAu; EvEuW; LongCTC; McGEWD; ModWD; NewC; OxFr; OxThe; Pen EUR; PlP&P; REn; REnWD; WhoStg 1908*

Sarett, Lew R
American. Poet
b. May 16, 1888 in Chicago, Illinois
d. Aug 17, 1954 in Gainesville, Florida
Source: *AmAu&B; AnMV 1926; ChPo, S1, S2; CnDAL; ConAmA; ConAmL; OxAmL; REn; REnAL; TwCA, SUP; WhAm 3; WhNAA*

Sarg, Tony (Anthony Frederick)
American. Marionette Maker
b. Apr 24, 1882 in Guatemala
d. Mar 7, 1942 in Nantucket, Massachusetts
Source: *AmAu&B; ChPo, S1, S2; ConICB; CurBio 42; DcAmB S3; DcNAA; JBA 34, 51; REnAL; WhAm 2; YABC 1*

Sargeant, Winthrop
American. Music Critic
b. Dec 10, 1903 in San Francisco, California
Source: *ConAu 29R; WhoAm 74, 76, 78, 80, 82; WhoWor 74; WrDr 76*

Sargent, Dick
American. Actor
b. Apr 19, 1933 in Carmel, California
Source: *FilmgC; IntMPA 82; WhoAm 74, 76, 78, 80, 82; WhoHol A*

Sargent, John Singer
American. Artist
b. Jan 12, 1856 in Florence, Italy
d. Apr 15, 1925 in London, England
Source: *AmBi; ApCAB; AtlBL; ChPo, S1; DcAmB; EncAB-H; LongCTC; OxAmL; REn; REnAL; TwCBDA; WebAB; WhAm 1*

Sargent, Sir Malcolm
English. Conductor
b. Apr 29, 1895 in Stamford, England
d. Oct 3, 1967 in London, England
Source: *CurBio 45, 68; WhScrn 77*

Sarkis, Elias
Lebanese. President
b. Jul 20, 1924 in Shibaniyah, Lebanon
Source: *CurBio 79*

Sarnoff, David
American. Head of RCA and NBC
b. Feb 27, 1891 in Minsk, Russia
d. Dec 12, 1971 in New York, New York
Source: *CurBio 40, 51, 72; EncAB-H; NewYTBE 70, 71; WebAB; WhAm 5; WhoWorJ 72*

Sarnoff, Dorothy
American. Author, Singer, Actress
b. May 25, 1919 in New York, New York
Source: *BiE&WWA; ConAu 33R; NotNAT; WhoWorJ 72*

Sarnoff, Robert W
American. Communications Executive
b. Jul 2, 1918 in New York, New York
Source: *BusPN; CelR 73; CurBio 56; IntMPA 75, 76, 77, 78, 79, 80, 81, 82; IntWW 74; St&PR 75; Who 74; WhoAm 74; WhoAmA 73; WhoE 74; WhoF&I 74; WhoGov 72; WhoWor 74*

Saroyan, William
American. Author, Dramatist
Won Pulitzer Prize, 1940, for *The Time of Your Life.*
b. Aug 31, 1908 in Fresno, California
d. May 18, 1981 in Fresno, California
Source: *AmAu&B; AmNov; Au&Wr 71; BiE&WWA; BioIn 2, 3, 4, 5, 6, 7, 8, 9, 10, 11; CasWL; CelR 73; CnDAL; CnMD; CnMWL; CnThe; ConAu 5R, 103; ConDr 73, 77; ConLC 1, 8, 11; ConNov 72, 76; CurBio 40, 72, 81; CyWA; DcLEL; DrAF 76; EncWL; EncWT; EvLB; FilmgC; IntAu&W 76, 77; IntWW 74, 75, 77, 78; LinLib L, S; LongCTC; McGEWB; McGEWD; ModAL, SUP; ModWD; NewYTBE 72; NewYTBS 75, 79; NotNAT; OxAmL; OxThe; Pen AM; PlP&P; RAdv 1; REn; REnAL; REnWD; TwCA, SUP; TwCW; WebAB; WebE&AL; WhAm 7; WhE&EA; Who 74; WhoAm 74, 76, 78, 80; WhoThe 72, 77; WhoTwCL; WhoWor 74; WrDr 76, 80*

Sarrazin, Michael
[Jacques Michel Andre Sarrazin]
Canadian. Actor
Starred in *The Reincarnation of Peter Proud,* 1975.
b. May 22, 1940 in Quebec City, PQ
Source: *FilmgC; IntMPA 75, 76, 77, 78, 79, 80, 81, 82; NewYTBE 70; WhoHol A*

Sarris, Andrew
American. Author
b. Oct 31, 1928 in Brooklyn, New York
Source: *AmAu&B; ConAu 21R; OxFilm; WhoAm 82; WhoE 74*

Sartain, John
American. Engraver
b. Oct 24, 1808 in London, England
d. Oct 25, 1897 in Philadelphia, Pennsylvania
Source: *Alli; AmAu&B; AmBi; ApCAB; DcAmAu; DcAmB; DcNAA; Drake; TwCBDA; WhAm H*

Sarti, Giuseppe
Italian. Composer
b. Dec 1, 1729 in Faenza, Italy
d. Jul 28, 1802 in Berlin, Germany
Source: *NewEOp 71; OxMus*

Sarto, Andrea del
[Andrea Domenico d'Agnolodi Francisco]
Italian. Artist
b. Jul 16, 1486 in Florence, Italy
d. Sep 29, 1531 in Florence, Italy
Source: *AtlBL; REn*

Sarton, May
American. Author, Poet
b. May 3, 1912 in Wondelgem, Belgium
Source: *AmAu&B; ConAu 1R, 1NR; ConNov 72, 76; ConP 70, 75; CurBio 82; DrAF 76; DrAP 75; DrAS 74E; ModAL, SUP; OxAmL; Pen AM; RAdv 1; REnAL; TwCA SUP; WhoAm 74, 76, 78, 80, 82; WhoWor 74; WrDr 76*

Sartre, Jean-Paul
French. Author, Dramatist
Exponent of 20th c. Existentialism; wrote *Being and Nothingness,* 1943.
b. Jun 21, 1905 in Paris, France
d. Apr 15, 1980 in Paris, France
Source: *Au&Wr 71; BiE&WWA; CasWL; CelR 73; ClDMEL; CnMD; CnMWL; CnThe; ConAu 9R, 97; ConLC 1, 4, 7, 9, 13, 18; CroCD; CurBio 47, 71; CyWA; EncWL; EvEuW; FilmgC; IntWW 74; LongCTC; McGEWD; ModRL; ModWD; NewYTBE 71; NotNAT; OxEng; OxFr; OxThe; Pen EUR; PlP&P; RComWL; REn; REnWD; TwCA SUP; TwCW; Who 74; WhoThe 77; WhoTwCL; WhoWor 74*

Sasser, Jim (James Ralph)
American. Senator
b. Sep 30, 1936 in Memphis, Tennessee
Source: *AlmAP 78, 80; CngDr 77, 79; WhoAm 78, 80, 82; WhoAmL 78; WhoAmP 77, 79; WhoGov 77; WhoS&SW 78*

Sassetta
[Stefano di Giovanni]
Italian. Artist
b. 1395? in Siena, Italy
d. 1450 in Siena, Italy
Source: *AtlBL; OxArt*

Sassoon, Siegfried
English. Poet
b. Sep 8, 1886 in Kent, England
d. Sep 1, 1967 in Wiltshire, England
Source: *AtlBL; Br&AmS; CasWL; Chambr 3; ChPo, S1, S2; CnE&AP; CnMWL; ConAu 25R, 104; CyWA; DcLEL; EvLB; LongCTC; ModBrL, SUP; NewC; OxEng; Pen ENG; RAdv 1; REn; TwCA, SUP; TwCW; WebE&AL; WhAm 4; WhoTwCL*

Sassoon, Vidal
English. Hairdresser
Founder, chairman, Vidal Sassoon, Inc.; wrote *A Year of Beauty and Health,* 1976.
b. Jan 17, 1928 in London, England
Source: *BioNews 74; BkPepl; CelR 73; ConAu 65; WhoAm 76, 78, 80, 82; WorFshn*

Sasway, Benjamin H
American. Draft Registration Resister
First person indicted for violation of Selective Service Act since draft revival, 1980.
b. 1961? in Vista, California
Source: *NewYTBS 82*

Sather, Glen Cameron
Canadian. Hockey Player, Executive
Coach, general manager, Edmonton Oilers, NHL, 1977--.
b. Sep 2, 1943 in High River, AB
Source: *NewYTBE 71; WhoHcky 73*

Satie, Erik
French. Composer
b. May 17, 1866 in Honfleur, France
d. Jul 1, 1925 in Paris, France
Source: *AtlBL; DcCM; OxFilm; REn; WhScrn 77; WorEFlm*

Sato, Eisaku
Japanese. Prime Minister
b. Mar 27, 1901 in Tabuse, Japan
d. Jun 3, 1975 in Tokyo, Japan
Source: *CurBio 65; IntWW 74; NewYTBS 74; WhAm 6; WhoGov 72; WhoWor 74*

Satovsky, Abraham
American. Lawyer
b. Oct 15, 1907 in Detroit, Michigan
Source: *WhoAm 82; WhoWorJ 72*

Sattler, Helen Roney
American. Children's Author
b. Mar 2, 1921 in Newton, Iowa
Source: *ConAu 33R; SmATA 4*

Saucier, Kevin Andrew
"Hot Sauce"
American. Baseball Player
b. Aug 9, 1956 in Pensacola, Florida
Source: *BaseEn*

Saud
Saudi. King
b. Jan 5, 1902 in Kuwait, Saudi Arabia
d. Feb 23, 1969 in Athens, Greece
Source: *BioIn 1, 3, 4, 5, 6, 7, 8, 9; CurBio 54, 69; NewCol 75*

Saudek, Robert
American. TV Executive
b. Apr 11, 1911 in Pittsburgh, Pennsylvania
Source: *St&PR 75; WhoWor 74*

Sauer, Emil von
German. Musician
b. Oct 8, 1862 in Hamburg, Germany
d. Apr 29, 1942 in Vienna, Austria
Source: *CurBio 42*

Sauer, William George
American. Physician
b. Jul 18, 1915 in Cincinnati, Ohio
Source: *AmM&WS 73P; WhoAm 74*

Saunders, Allen
American. Cartoonist
b. Mar 24, 1899 in Lebanon, Indiana
Source: *ConAu 69; WhoAm 82; WorECom*

Saunders, Charles E
Canadian. Scientist
b. Feb 2, 1867 in London, ON
d. Jul 25, 1937 in Toronto, ON
Source: *Alli; DcNAA*

Saunders, Lori
American. Actress
b. Oct 4, 1941 in Kansas City, Missouri
Source: *WhoHol A*

Saunders, Stuart T
American. Businessman
b. Jul 16, 1909 in McDowell, Wyoming
Source: *CurBio 66; IntWW 74; WhoAm 74; WhoE 74*

Saunders, William
Canadian. Agriculturist
b. Jun 13, 1836
d. Sep 13, 1914
Source: *DcNAA; WhNAA*

Saunders, William Laurence
American. Engineer, Inventor
Patented stone-cutting machines and drills.
b. Nov 1, 1856 in Columbus, Georgia
d. Jun 25, 1931 in Teneriffe, Canary Islands
Source: *DcAmB; DcNAA; NatCAB 14, 26; WhAm 1; WhNAA*

Saunderson, Nicholas
English. Mathematician
b. 1682
d. 1739
Source: *Alli*

Saura (Atares), Carlos
Spanish. Motion Picture Director, Writer
b. Jan 4, 1932 in Huesca, Spain
Source: *CurBio 78; NewYTBE 71; WorEFlm*

Sauter, Eddie (Edward Ernest)
American. Jazz Musician, Composer
b. Dec 2, 1914 in Brooklyn, New York
d. Apr 21, 1981 in Nyack, New York
Source: *AmSCAP 66; BiDAmM; CmpEPM; IlEncJ; WhAm 7; WhoJazz 72*

Savage, Edward
American. Artist
b. Nov 26, 1761 in Princeton, Massachusetts
d. Jul 6, 1817 in Princeton, Massachusetts
Source: *AmBi; ApCAB; BnEnAmA; DcAmArt; DcAmB; Drake; McGDA; NewYHSD; WhAm H*

Savage, Eugene Francis
American. Artist, Sculptor
b. Mar 29, 1883 in Covington, Indiana
Source: *WhoAm 76*

Savage, Henry Wilson
American. Impresario
b. Mar 21, 1859 in Alton, New Hampshire
d. Nov 29, 1927 in Boston, Massachusetts
Source: *DcAmB; EncMT; WhAm 1*

Savage, John
American. Journalist, Poet, Dramatist
b. Dec 13, 1828 in Dublin, Ireland
d. Sep 9, 1888 in Laurelside, Pennsylvania
Source: *Alli; AmAu; AmAu&B; ApCAB; BbD; BiD&SB; ChPo S1; CyAl 2; DcAmAu; DcAmB; DcNAA; Drake; PoIre; TwCBDA; WhAm H*

Savage, John
American. Actor
b. 1950? in Old Bethpage, New York
Source: *BioIn 11; IntMPA 80, 81, 82*

Savage, Richard
English. Poet
Reputation gained from biography by Samuel Johnson, friendship with Alexander Pope.
b. 1697
d. Aug 1, 1743 in Bristol, England
Source: *Alli; BbD; BrAu; CasWL; Chambr 2; ChPo, S1; DcEnA; DcEnL; DcEuL; EvLB; NewC; OxEng; Pen ENG; REn; WebE&AL*

Savage, Rick
see: Def Leppard

Savage, Robert Heath
American. Advertising Executive
b. Nov 24, 1929 in Chillicothe, Ohio
Source: *WhoAm 76, 78, 80, 82*

Savalas, "Telly" (Aristoteles)
American. Actor
First shaved head for role of Pontius Pilate in *The Greatest Story Ever Told*, 1965.
b. Jan 21, 1923 in Garden City, New York
Source: *BioNews 74; BkPepl; FilmgC; IntMPA 75, 76, 77, 78, 79, 80, 81, 82; MotPP; MovMk; NewYTBE 73; WhoAm 74, 76, 78, 80, 82; WhoHol A*

Savard, Denis
Canadian. Hockey Player
Center, Chicago Black Hawks, 1981--
b. Feb 4, 1961 in Pointe Gatineau, PQ
Source: *HocReg*

Savitch, Jessica Beth
American. Broadcast Journalist
With NBC News, 1977--; wrote *Anchorwoman,* 1982.
b. 1949 in Kennett Square, Pennsylvania
Source: *BioIn 11; CurBio 83; WhoAm 78, 80, 82*

Savitt, Jan
Russian. Band Leader
b. Sep 4, 1913 in Petrograd, Russia
d. Oct 4, 1948 in Sacramento, California
Source: *AmSCAP 66*

Savo, Jimmy
American. Actor, Comic
b. 1896 in Bronx, New York
d. Sep 6, 1960 in Teni, Italy
Source: *EncMT; PlP&P; WhScrn 74, 77; WhoHol B*

Savonarola, Girolamo
Italian. Religious Reformer
Preached against corruptions in secular life; burned at stake for heresy, 1498.
b. 1452 in Ferrara, Italy
d. May 23, 1498 in Florence, Italy
Source: *BbD; BiD&SB; CasWL; EuAu; EvEuW; NewC; Pen EUR; REn*

Sawallisch, Wolfgang
German. Conductor
b. Aug 26, 1923 in Munich, Germany
Source: *IntWW 74; WhoMus 72; WhoWor 74*

Sawatski, Carl Ernest
"Swats"
American. Baseball Player
b. Nov 4, 1927 in Shickshinny, Pennsylvania
Source: *BaseEn; WhoProB 73*

Sawchuk, Terry (Terrance Gordon)
American. Hockey Player
Had 103 career shutouts as goaltender, most in NHL history.
b. Dec 28, 1929 in Winnipeg, MB
d. May 31, 1970 in Mineola, New York
Source: *NewYTBE 70; WhoHcky 73*

Sawyer, Charles
American. Secretary of Commerce
b. Feb 10, 1887 in Cincinnati, Ohio
d. Apr 7, 1979 in Palm Beach, Florida
Source: *BioIn 1, 2, 3, 10; CurBio 79; WhoAm 74*

Sawyer, Diane K
American. Broadcast Journalist
b. Dec 22, 1946 in Glasgow, Kentucky
Source: *NewYTBS 81*

Sawyer, Ruth
American. Author
b. Aug 5, 1880 in Boston, Massachusetts
d. Jun 3, 1970
Source: *AmAu&B; AmLY; AnCL; AuBYP; BkCL; CarSB; ConAu 73; HerW; JBA 51; Newb 1922; TwCA, SUP; WhAm 5; WhNAA*

Sax, Adolphe
Belgian. Inventor
Developed the saxophone, 1842, and other instruments used by military bands.
b. Nov 6, 1814 in Dinant Meuse, Belgium
d. Feb 4, 1894 in Paris, France
Source: *Baker 78; WebBD 80; WhDW*

Sax, Charles Joseph
Belgian. Instrument Manufacturer
Made brass instruments at factory established in Brussels, 1815.
b. Feb 1, 1791 in Dinant-sur-Meuse, Belgium
d. Apr 26, 1865 in Paris, France
Source: *Baker 78; WebBD 80*

Saxbe, William Bart
American. Diplomat
b. Jun 25, 1916 in Mechanicsburg, Ohio
Source: *BiDrAC; BioNews 74; CngDr 74; CurBio 74; IntWW 74; NewYTBE 73; WhoAm 74, 76, 78, 80, 82; WhoAmP 73; WhoGov 72; WhoMW 74*

Saxe, Maurice
French. Marshal
b. 1696
d. 1750
Source: *OxFr; OxGer*

Saxon, Charles David
American. Cartoonist
b. Nov 13, 1920 in New York, New York
Source: *AmAu&B; WhoAm 74, 76, 78; WhoAmA 76, 78, 80*

Saxon, John
American. Actor
b. Aug 5, 1935 in Brooklyn, New York
Source: *FilmgC; IntMPA 75, 76, 77, 78, 79, 80, 81, 82; MotPP; MovMk; WhoHol A*

Sayao, Bidu
Brazilian. Opera Singer
b. May 11, 1902 in Rio de Janeiro, Brazil
Source: *CurBio 42; InWom*

Sayer, "Leo" (Gerald)
English. Singer
b. May 21, 1948 in Shoreham, England
Source: *BkPepl; IlEncRk; RkOn*

Sayers, Dorothy Leigh
English. Author
b. 1893 in Oxford, England
d. Dec 17, 1957 in Witham, England
Source: *CasWL; CnMD; ConAu 104; DcLEL; EncMys; EncWL; EvLB; InWom; LongCTC; ModBrL, SUP; ModWD; NewC; OxEng; Pen ENG; REn; TwCA, SUP; TwCW; WhAm 3*

Sayers, Gale Eugene
American. Football Player
Averaged five yards per carry with Chicago Bears, 1965-71; wrote *I Am Third,* 1970.
b. May 30, 1940 in Wichita, Kansas
Source: *NewYTBE 70, 72; WhoAm 74, 76, 78, 80, 82; WhoFtbl 74*

Sbriglia, Giovanni
Italian. Opera Singer, Teacher
b. Jun 23, 1832 in Naples, Italy
d. Feb 20, 1916 in Paris, France
Source: *NewEOp 71*

Scaasi, Arnold
American. Fashion Designer
b. May 8, 1931 in Montreal, PQ
Source: *CelR 73; WorFshn*

Scaggs, "Boz" (William Royce)
American. Musician, Singer
Won Grammy, 1976, for "Lowdown."
b. Jun 8, 1944 in Dallas, Texas
Source: *IlEncRk; RkOn; WhoAm 82*

Scala, Gia
English. Actress
b. Mar 3, 1934 in Liverpool, England
d. Apr 30, 1972 in Hollywood Hills, California
Source: *FilmgC; MotPP; MovMk; NewYTBE 72; WhScrn 77; WhoHol B*

Scalchi, Sofia
Italian. Opera Singer
b. Nov 29, 1850 in Turin, Italy
d. Aug 22, 1922 in Rome, Italy
Source: *InWom*

Scales, DeWayne Jay
American. Basketball Player
b. Dec 28, 1958 in Dallas, Texas
Source: *OfNBA*

Scali, John Alfred
American. Journalist, Diplomat
b. Apr 27, 1918 in Canton, Ohio
Source: *CelR 73; CurBio 73; IntWW 74; NewYTBE 71, 72; USBiR 74; WhoAm 74, 76, 78, 80, 82; WhoAmP 73; WhoS&SW 73; WhoUN 75; WhoWor 74*

Scanlon, Hugh Parr
English. Labor Union Leader
President, Amalgamated Union of Engineering Workers, 1968-78.
b. Oct 26, 1913 in Australia
Source: *IntWW 74; Who 74*

Scaria, Emil
Austrian. Opera Singer
b. Aug 18, 1838 in Graz, Austria
d. Jul 22, 1886 in Blasewitz, Germany
Source: *NewEOp 71*

Scarlatti, Alessandro
Italian. Composer
b. May 2, 1660 in Palermo, Sicily
d. Nov 24, 1725 in Naples, Italy
Source: *AtlBL; REn*

Scarlatti, Domenico Girolamo
Italian. Composer
b. Oct 26, 1685 in Naples, Italy
d. 1757 in Naples, Italy
Source: *AtlBL*

Scavullo, Francesco
American. Photographer
b. Jan 16, 1929 in Staten Island, New York
Source: *BioIn 10, 11; WhoAm 82*

Schaap, Dick (Richard J)
American. Journalist, Sports Commentator
b. Sep 27, 1934 in Brooklyn, New York
Source: *AmAu&B; ConAu 9R, 5NR; WhoE 74*

Schacht, Al(exander)
"Clown Prince of Baseball"
American. Baseball Player, Coach
b. Nov 11, 1892 in New York, New York
Source: *BaseEn; WhoProB 73*

Schacht, Hjalmar Horace Greeley
German. Financier
b. Jan 22, 1877 in Tingleff, Germany
d. Jun 4, 1970 in Munich, Germany (West)
Source: *CurBio 44, 70; REn*

Schachte, Henry Miner
American. Advertising Executive
b. Jan 12, 1913 in Pittsfield, Massachusetts
Source: *WhoAdv 72; WhoF&I 74; WhoWor 74*

Schadow, (Johann) Gottfried
German. Sculptor
b. 1764
d. 1850
Source: *BioIn 2, 6, 11; McGDA; NewCol 75*

Schaefer, Frederick M E
American. Brewer
b. 1891
d. 1976
Source: *St&PR 75*

Schaefer, "Germany" (Herman A)
American. Baseball Player
b. Feb 4, 1878 in Chicago, Illinois
d. May 16, 1919 in Saranac Lake, New York
Source: *BaseEn; BioIn 2, 3, 5; WhoProB 73*

Schaefer, Jack Warner
American. Author
Wrote *Shane,* 1949; *First Blood,* 1953.
b. Nov 19, 1907 in Cleveland, Ohio
Source: *AmAu&B; Au&Wr 71; AuBYP; ConAu 17R; ConAu P-1; IntMPA 75, 76, 77, 78, 79, 80, 81, 82; OhA&B; SmATA 3; ThrBJA; WhoAm 74, 76, 78, 80, 82; WhoWest 74*

Schaefer, Rudolph Jay
American. Brewery Executive
Chairman, F & M Schaefer Brewing Co., 1950-69.
b. Jul 9, 1900 in Larchmont, New York
d. Sep 2, 1982 in New York, New York
Source: *NewYTBS 82; St&PR 75; WhoAm 74*

Schaefer, Thomas E
[The Hostages]
American. Former Hostage in Iran
b. 1931?
Source: *NewYTBS 81*

Schaefer, William Donald
American. Mayor of Baltimore
b. Nov 2, 1921 in Baltimore, Maryland
Source: *WhoAm 78, 80, 82; WhoAmP 75, 77, 79; WhoGov 75, 77*

Schakne, Robert
American. Journalist
b. Aug 19, 1926 in New York, New York
Source: *ConAu 65*

Schalk, Franz
Austrian. Conductor
b. May 27, 1863 in Vienna, Austria
d. Sep 2, 1931 in Edlach, Austria
Source: *NewEOp 71*

Schally, Andrew Victor
American. Medical Research Scientist
b. Nov 30, 1926
Source: *AmM&WS 73P; WhoAm 74, 76, 78, 80, 82; WhoGov 72*

Schanberg, Sydney H
American. News Correspondent
b. Jan 17, 1934 in Clinton, Massachusetts
Source: *ConAu 69; WhoAm 82*

Scharfer, Swain
see: Box Tops, The

Schary, Dore
American. Film Producer, Dramatist
b. Aug 31, 1905 in Newark, New Jersey
d. Jul 7, 1980 in New York, New York
Source: *AmAu&B; BiDFilm; BiE&WWA; ConAu 1R, 101, 1NR; ConDr 73; CurBio 48; DcFM; FilmgC; ModWD; NatPD; NewYTBE 70; NotNAT; OxFilm; REnAL; WhoAm 74; WhoE 74; WhoThe 77; WhoWor 74; WhoWorJ 72; WorAu; WorEFlm; WrDr 76*

Schaudinn, Fritz Richard
German. Protozoologist
b. 1871
d. 1906
Source: *AsBiEn; BiHiMed; DcScB; NewCol 75; WebBD 80; WhDW*

Schauffler, Robert Haven
American. Poet, Essayist
b. Apr 8, 1879 in Brunn, Austria
d. Nov 24, 1964
Source: *AmAu&B; ChPo, S1, S2; OhA&B; REn; REnAL; TwCA, SUP; WhAm 4; WhNAA*

Schaufuss, Peter
Danish. Dancer
b. Apr 26, 1949 in Copenhagen, Denmark
Source: *BioIn 10, 11; CurBio 82; NewYTBS 75; WhoAm 78, 80, 82*

Schecter, Jerrold
American. Author, Journalist
b. Nov 27, 1932 in New York, New York
Source: *ConAu 25R*

Scheel, Walter
German. Diplomat
b. Jul 8, 1919 in Solingen, Germany
Source: *CurBio 71; IntWW 74; NewYTBS 74; Who 74; WhoWor 74*

Scheele, Karl Wilhelm
Swedish. Chemist
b. Dec 2, 1742
d. May 21, 1786
Source: *WhDW*

Scheer, Robert
American. Journalist
b. Apr 4, 1936 in New York, New York
Source: *AmAu&B*

Scheff, Frizi
Austrian. Opera Singer
b. Aug 30, 1879 in Vienna, Austria
d. Apr 8, 1954 in New York, New York
Source: *NewEOp 71*

Scheider, Roy Richard
American. Actor
Starred in *Jaws I, II* 1975, 1978; *All That Jazz,* 1979.
b. Oct 11, 1935 in Orange, New Jersey
Source: *FilmgC; IntMPA 75, 76, 77, 78, 79, 80, 81, 82; WhoAm 82; WhoHol A*

Scheidemann, Philipp
German. Social Democratic Leader
b. 1865
d. 1939 in Denmark
Source: *NewCol 75; REn*

Scheja, Staffan
Swedish. Musician
b. Apr 25, 1950 in Stockholm, Sweden
Source: *WhoWor 74*

Schell, Maria Margarethe
Austrian. Actress
b. 1926 in Vienna, Austria
Source: *CurBio 61; IntMPA 82*

Schell, Maximilian
Austrian. Actor
Won Oscar, 1961, for *Judgment at Nuremberg;* brother of Maria Schell.
b. Dec 8, 1930 in Vienna, Austria
Source: *BiE&WWA; CelR 73; CurBio 62; FilmgC; IntMPA 75, 76, 77, 78, 79, 80, 81, 82; IntWW 74; MotPP; MovMk; WhoAm 74, 76, 78, 80, 82; WhoHol A; WhoWor 74; WorEFlm*

Schell, Orville H
American. Journalist, Author
b. May 20, 1940 in New York, New York
Source: *AuBYP SUP; BioIn 11; ConAu 25R; SmATA 10*

Schelling, Ernest Henry
American. Musician, Composer, Conductor
b. Jul 26, 1876 in Belvidere, New Jersey
d. Dec 8, 1939 in New York, New York
Source: *AmBi; AmSCAP 66; CurBio 40; DcAmB S2; WhAm 1*

Schelling, Friedrich Wilhelm Joseph von
German. Philosopher
b. 1775 in Wurttemberg, Germany
d. 1854
Source: *BbD; BiD&SB; CasWL; DcEuL; EuAu; EvEuW; NewC; OxEng; OxGer; Pen EUR; REn*

Schembechler, "Bo" (Glenn Edward)
American. Football Coach
Head football coach, U of Michigan, 1969--.
b. Apr 1, 1929 in Barberton, Ohio
Source: *WhoAm 82; WhoFtbl 74*

Schenck, Joe (Joseph T)
American. Singer
b. 1892 in Brooklyn, New York
d. Jun 28, 1930 in Detroit, Michigan
Source: *WhScrn 74, 77; WhoHol B*

Schenck, Joseph M
American. Motion Picture Producer
b. 1878 in Russia
d. Oct 22, 1961 in Beverly Hills, California
Source: *FilmgC; OxFilm; WhAm 4*

Schenck, Nicholas M
Founder of MGM Studios
b. Nov 14, 1881 in Russia
d. Mar 3, 1969 in Miami Beach, Florida
Source: *BioIn 8; WhAm 5*

Schenck, Robert Cumming
American. Politician
b. Oct 4, 1809 in Franklin, Ohio
d. Mar 23, 1890 in Washington, DC
Source: *Alli SUP; AmBi; ApCAB; BiAuS; BiDrAC; DcAmB; Drake; OhA&B; TwCBDA; WhAm H; WhAmP*

Schenk, Ard
Dutch. Speed Skater
Won three gold medals, 1972 Olympics.
b. Sep 19, 1944 in Anna Paulowna, Netherlands
Source: *BioIn 10*

Schenkel, Chris(topher Eugene)
American. TV Sportscaster
b. 1924 in Bippus, Indiana
Source: *BioIn 6, 9, 10; BioNews 74; WhoAm 74, 76, 78, 80, 82*

Schenker, Rudolph
see: Scorpions

Schenker, Tillie Abramson
American. Librarian
b. Nov 12, 1910 in Baton Rouge, Louisiana
Source: *BiDrLUS 70; ForWC 70; WhoAm 74; WhoS&SW 73*

Scherchen, Hermann
German. Conductor
b. Jun 21, 1891 in Berlin, Germany
d. Jun 12, 1966 in Florence, Italy
Source: *WhAm 5*

Scherer, Ray(mond Lewis)
American. Communications Executive
b. Jun 7, 1919 in Fort Wayne, Indiana
Source: *WhoAm 74, 76, 78, 80, 82; WhoWor 74*

Scherman, Harry
American. Publisher, Author
b. Feb 1, 1887 in Montreal, PQ
d. Nov 12, 1969 in New York, New York
Source: *AmAu&B; CurBio 43, 63, 70; WhAm 5; WhoWorJ 72*

Scherman, Thomas K
American. Conductor
b. Feb 12, 1917 in New York, New York
d. May 14, 1979 in New York, New York
Source: *CurBio 54, 79; WhoWor 74, 74*

Scherr, Max
American. Lawyer, Newspaper Publisher
b. 1916?
d. 1981 in Berkeley, California
Source: *BioIn 8, 12*

Schiaparelli, (Elsa)
Italian. Fashion Designer
b. Sep 10, 1890 in Rome, Italy
d. Nov 14, 1973 in Paris, France
Source: *CelR 73; CurBio 40, 51, 74; InWom; NewYTBE 73; WhAm 6; Who 74; WhoWor 74; WorFshn*

Schiaparelli, Giovanni
Italian. Explorer, Scientist
Director, Milan Observatory, 1862-1900; discovered asteroid Hesperia, 1861.
b. Mar 14, 1835 in Savigliano, Italy
d. Jul 4, 1910 in Milan, Italy
Source: *AsBiEn; NewCol 75*

Schick, Bela
American. Scientist, Physician, Engineer
b. Jul 16, 1877 in Bolgar, Hungary
d. Dec 6, 1967 in New York, New York
Source: *CurBio 44, 68; WebAB; WhAm 4*

Schickel, Richard
American. Motion Picture Critic, Author
b. Feb 10, 1933 in Milwaukee, Wisconsin
Source: *AuNews 1; ConAu 1R, 1NR; WhoAm 74, 76, 78, 80, 82; WhoE 74; WrDr 76*

Schickele, Peter
American. Composer, Musician
b. Jul 17, 1935 in Ames, Iowa
Source: *AmSCAP 66; Baker 78; ConAu 85; CurBio 79; WhoAm 76, 78, 80, 82; WhoWor 74*

Schieffer, Bob
American. Broadcast Journalist
b. Feb 25, 1937 in Austin, Texas
Source: *ConAu 69; WhoAm 82*

Schiff, Dorothy
American. Publisher, Journalist
b. Mar 11, 1903 in New York, New York
Source: *AmAu&B; CelR 73; CurBio 45, 65; ForWC 70; InWom; IntWW 74; WhoAm 74; WhoAmW 77; WhoE 74; WhoWor 74; WhoWorJ 72*

Schiff, Jacob Henry
American. Philanthropist
b. 1847 in Frankfurt, Germany
d. Sep 25, 1920
Source: *AmBi; DcAmB; DcNAA; EncAB-H; WhAm 1*

Schifrin, Lalo Claudio
Argentine. Composer, Musician
b. Jun 21, 1932 in Buenos Aires, Argentina
Source: *IntMPA 75, 76, 77, 78, 79, 80, 81, 82; WorEFlm; WhoAm 74, 76, 78, 80, 82*

Schifter, Peter Mark
American. Motion Picture Director
b. 1950 in Westfield, New Jersey
Source: *BioIn 12*

Schikaneder, Johann Emanuel
Austrian. Producer, Actor, Librettist
b. Sep 1, 1748 in Straubing, Austria
d. Sep 21, 1812 in Vienna, Austria
Source: *BioIn 9; NewEOp 71; OxMus*

Schildkraut, Joseph
American. Actor
b. Mar 22, 1896 in Vienna, Austria
d. Jan 21, 1964 in New York, New York
Source: *BiE&WWA; CurBio 56, 64; FamA&A; FilmgC; MotPP; MovMk; TwYS; WhAm 4; WhScrn 74, 77; WhoHol B*

Schildkraut, Rudolph
American. Actor
b. 1865 in Turkey
d. Jul 30, 1930 in Los Angeles, California
Source: *Film 1; TwYS; WhScrn 74, 77; WhoHol B*

Schiller, (Johann Christoph) Friedrich von
German. Author
b. Nov 10, 1759 in Marbach, Germany
d. May 9, 1805 in Weimar, Germany
Source: *AtlBL; BbD; BiD&SB; CasWL; ChPo, S1, S2; CnThe; CyWA; DcEnL; DcEuL; EuAu; EvEuW; McGEWD; NewC; OxEng; OxFr; OxGer; OxThe; Pen EUR; RComWL; REn; REnWD*

Schillings, Max von
German. Conductor, Composer
b. Apr 19, 1868 in Duren, Germany
d. Jul 23, 1933 in Berlin, Germany
Source: *OxGer*

Schindler, Alexander (Monroe)
American. Rabbi
b. Oct 4, 1925 in Munich, Germany
Source: *NewYTBE 73; WhoAm 82; WhoE 74; WhoWorJ 72; WhoRel 75*

Schine, G(erard) David
American. Government Investigator
b. Sep 11, 1927 in Gloversville, New York
Source: *St&PR 75; WhoAm 74, 76, 78, 80, 82; WhoF&I 74; WhoWor 74*

Schipa, Tito
Italian. Opera Singer
b. Jan 2, 1889 in Lecce, Italy
d. Dec 16, 1965 in New York, New York
Source: *WhAm 4; WhScrn 74, 77; WhoHol B*

Schippers, Thomas
American. Conductor
b. Mar 9, 1930 in Kalamazoo, Michigan
d. Dec 16, 1977 in New York, New York
Source: *CelR 73; CurBio 70; IntWW 74; WhoAm 74; WhoMW 74; WhoMus 72; WhoWor 74*

Schirmer, Gustave
German. Music Publisher
b. Sep 19, 1829 in Konigsee, Germany
d. Aug 6, 1893 in Eisenach, Germany
Source: *DcAmB; WebAB; WhAm H*

Schirra, Wally (Walter Marty, Jr.)
American. Astronaut, Businessman
Pilot, Gemini 6, 1965; commander, Apollo 7, 1968.
b. Mar 12, 1923 in Hackensack, New Jersey
Source: *AmM&WS 73P; CurBio 66; IntWW 74, 75, 76, 77; WhoAm 74, 76, 78, 80, 82; WhoWor 74*

Schisgal, Murray
American. Dramatist
b. Nov 25, 1926 in Brooklyn, New York
Source: *AmAu&B; BiE&WWA; CelR 73; CnMD SUP; ConAu 21R; ConDr 73; ConLC 6; CroCD; CurBio 68; McGEWD; ModAL; ModWD; NotNAT; WhoAm 74, 76, 78, 80, 82; WhoThe 77; WhoWor 74; WorAu; WrDr 76*

Schlafly, Phyllis Stewart
American. Anti-Feminist, Author
National chairman, stop ERA, 1972--.
b. Aug 15, 1924 in Saint Louis, Missouri
Source: *AuNews 1; BioNews 74; ConAu 25R; CurBio 78; WhoAm 76, 78, 80, 82; WhoAmP 73*

Schlamme, Martha
Austrian. Singer
b. 1930 in Vienna, Austria
Source: *CurBio 64; InWom; WhoAm 74*

Schlegel, (Karl Wilhelm) Friedrich von
German. Critic
b. Mar 10, 1772 in Hannover, Germany
d. Jan 12, 1829 in Dresden, Germany
Source: *AtlBL; BiD&SB; CasWL; DcEuL; EuAu; NewC; OxEng; OxGer; REn; REnWD*

Schleicher, Kurt von
German. Soldier, Chancellor
b. 1882 in Brandenburg, Germany
d. 1934
Source: *BioIn 5; NewCol 75; REn; WebBD 80*

Schleiermacher, Friedrich Ernst Daniel
German. Theologian, Philosopher
b. Nov 21, 1768 in Breslau, Germany
d. Feb 12, 1834 in Berlin, Germany
Source: *BioIn 2, 7, 8, 9, 11; LinLib L; McGEWB*

Schlein, Miriam
American. Children's Author
b. Jun 6, 1926 in Brooklyn, New York
Source: *AuBYP; ConAu 1R, 2NR; CurBio 59; InWom; MorJA; SmATA 2*

Schlesinger, Arthur Meier, Jr.
American. Historian, Author, Educator
b. Oct 15, 1917 in Columbus, Ohio
Source: *AmAu&B; Au&Wr 71; AuNews 1; ConAu 1R, 1NR; CurBio 46; DrAS 74H; IntWW 74; OhA&B; OxAmL; Pen AM; REn; REnAL; Who 74; WhoAm 74; WhoGov 72; WhoWor 74; WrDr 76*

Schlesinger, James Rodney
American. Government Official
Secretary of Defense, 1973-75; Energy, 1977-79.
b. Feb 15, 1929 in New York, New York
Source: *AmM&WS 73S; CelR 73; CngDr 74; CurBio 73; IntWW 74; NewYTBE 71, 72; NewYTBS 74; Ward 77D; WhoAm 74, 76, 78, 80, 82; WhoAmP 73; WhoGov 72; WhoS&SW 73; WhoWor 74*

Schlesinger, John Richard
English. Motion Picture Director
b. Feb 16, 1926 in London, England
Source: *BiDFilm; CurBio 70; DcFM; FilmgC; IntMPA 77, 75; IntWW 74; MovMk; OxFilm; Who 74; WhoAm 82; WhoThe 77; WhoWor 74; WorEFlm*

Schley, Winfield Scott
American. Naval Officer
b. Oct 9, 1839 in Frederick County, Maryland
d. Oct 2, 1909 in New York, New York
Source: *Alli SUP; AmBi; ApCAB, SUP; BiDSA; DcAmAu; DcAmB; DcNAA; TwCBDA; WhAm 1*

Schlieffen, Alfred, Graf von
German. Field Marshal
b. 1833
d. 1913
Source: *NewCol 75; WebBD 80; WhoMilH 76*

Schliemann, Heinrich
German. Archaeologist, Traveler
b. Jan 6, 1822 in Neubuckow, Germany
d. Dec 26, 1890 in Naples, Italy
Source: *Alli SUP; AmBi; BbD; BiD&SB; NewC; OxGer; REn; WhAm H*

Schlumberger, Jean
French. Jewelry Designer
b. Jun 24, 1907 in Mulhouse, France
Source: *CelR 73; St&PR 75; WorFshn*

Schlusnus, Heinrich
German. Opera Singer
b. Aug 6, 1888 in Braubach, Germany
d. Jun 19, 1952 in Frankfurt, Germany (West)
Source: *NewEOp 71*

Schlussel, Mark Edward
American. Lawyer
b. Dec 14, 1940 in Detroit, Michigan
Source: *Who 76; WhoAm 82*

Schmedes, Erik
Danish. Opera Singer
b. Aug 6, 1866 in Gjentofte, Denmark
d. Mar 23, 1931 in Vienna, Austria
Source: *NewEOp 71*

Schmeling, Max(imilian)
German. Boxer
World heavyweight champ, 1930-32.
b. Sep 28, 1905 in Brandenburg, Germany
Source: *EncTR; WhoBox 74; WhoHol A*

Schmidt, Helmut
German. Former Chancellor
b. Dec 23, 1918 in Hamburg, Germany
Source: *CurBio 74; IntWW 74; NewYTBS 74; Who 74; WhoWor 74*

Schmidt, Joe (Joseph Paul)
American. Football Player, Coach
b. Jan 18, 1932 in Pittsburgh, Pennsylvania
Source: *BioIn 5, 6, 8; WhoFtbl 74*

Schmidt, Mike (Michael Jack)
American. Baseball Player
Infielder, Philadelphia, 1972--; MVP, 1980 World Series.
b. Sep 27, 1949 in Dayton, Ohio
Source: *BaseEn; NewYTBS 74; WhoAm 78, 80, 82*

Schmidt-Isserstedt, Hans
German. Conductor
b. May 5, 1900 in Berlin, Germany
d. May 28, 1973 in Hamburg, Germany (West)
Source: *NewYTBE 73; WhAm 6; WhoMus 72*

Schmidt, Tim
[The Eagles; Poco]
American. Rock Musician, Singer
Joined The Eagles, 1977, replacing Randy Meisner.
b. Oct 30, 1947 in Oakland, California
Source: *NF*

Schmitt, Bernadotte Everly
American. Historian, Educator, Editor
b. May 19, 1886 in Strasburg, Virginia
d. Mar 22, 1969 in Alexandria, Virginia
Source: *AmAu&B; ConAu 1R; CurBio 42, 69; OhA&B; OxAmL; TwCA, SUP; WhNAA*

Schmitt, Gladys
American. Author, Teacher, Editor
b. May 31, 1909 in Pittsburgh, Pennsylvania
d. Oct 3, 1972 in Pittsburgh, Pennsylvania
Source: *AmAu&B; AmNov; ConAu 1R, 37R, 2NR; CurBio 43, 72; InWom; OxAmL; REnAL; TwCA SUP; WhAm 5*

Schmitt, Harrison Hagan
American. Former Senator
Lost to Jeff Bingaman, 1982 election.
b. Jul 3, 1935 in Santa Rita, New Mexico
Source: *WhoAm 76, 78, 80, 82*

Schnabel, Artur
Austrian. Musician
b. Apr 17, 1882 in Lipnik, Austria
d. Aug 15, 1951 in Axenstein, Switzerland
Source: *CurBio 42, 51; DcAmB S5; REn; WhAm 3*

Schnabel, Karl Ulrich
Austrian. Musician
b. Aug 6, 1909 in Berlin, Germany
Source: *WhoAm 74, 76, 78, 80, 82; WhoMus 72*

Schneider, Alan
American. Motion Picture Director
b. Dec 12, 1917 in Kharkov, U.S.S.R.
Source: *BiE&WWA; CelR 73; CurBio 69; IntWW 74; NotNAT; WhoAm 74, 76, 78, 80, 82; WhoThe 77; WhoWor 74; WhoWorJ 72*

Schneider, Alexander
American. Musician
b. Oct 21, 1908 in Vilna, Russia
Source: *WhoAm 74, 76, 78, 80, 82; WhoWor 74*

Schneider, Bert
American. Motion Picture Producer
b. 1933?
Source: *NewYTBS 75; WhoAmA 76*

Schneider, Florian
see: Kraftwerk

Schneider, Herman
American. Children's Author
b. May 31, 1905 in Kreschov, Poland
Source: *Au&Wr 71; AuBYP; ConAu 29R; MorJA; SmATA 7*

Schneider, John
American. Actor, Singer
Plays Bo Duke on TV series "The Dukes of Hazard," 1979--
b. Apr 8, 1954
Source: *BioIn 12*

Schneider, Maria
French. Actress
b. Mar 27, 1952 in Paris, France
Source: *FilmEn; NewYTBE 73; MovMk; WhoHol A*

Schneider, Nina
American. Children's Author
b. Jan 29, 1913 in Antwerp, Belgium
Source: *Au&Wr 71; AuBYP; ConAu 29R; MorJA; SmATA 2*

Schneider, Richard Coy
American. Physician, Educator
b. May 29, 1913 in Newark, New Jersey
Source: *AmM&WS 73P; WhoAm 74, 76, 78, 80, 82; WhoWor 74*

Schneider, "Romy"
[Rosemarie Albach-Retty]
Austrian. Actress
Starred in *The Cardinal*, 1963.
b. Sep 23, 1938 in Vienna, Austria
d. May 29, 1982 in Paris, France
Source: *BiDFilm; CurBio 65, 82; FilmgC; InWom; IntMPA 75, 76, 77, 78, 79, 80, 81, 82; MotPP; MovMk; NewYTBS 82; WhoAm 74; WhoHol A; WhoWor 74; WorEFlm*

Schneiderhan, Walther
Austrian. Musician
b. 1901 in Vienna, Austria
Source: *WhoMus 72*

Schnitzer, Eduard
see: Emin Pasha

Schnitzler, Arthur
Austrian. Dramatist
b. May 15, 1862 in Vienna, Austria
d. Oct 21, 1931 in Vienna, Austria
Source: *AtlBL; CasWL; ClDMEL; CnMD; CnThe; EncWL; EvEuW; FilmgC; LongCTC; McGEWD; ModGL; ModWD; OxGer; OxThe; Pen EUR; REn; REnWD; TwCA, SUP; WhoLA*

Schnorr von Carolsfeld, Ludwig
German. Opera Singer
b. Jul 2, 1836 in Munich, Germany
d. Jul 21, 1865 in Dresden, Germany
Source: *NewEOp 71*

Schocken, Theodore
American. Publisher
President, Schocken Books, Inc., 1965-76.
b. Oct 8, 1914 in Zwickau, Germany
d. Mar 20, 1975 in White Plains, New York
Source: *ConAu 104; NewYTBS 75; WhAm 6; WhoAm 74; WhoWor 74; WhoWorJ 72*

Schoech, Othmar
Swiss. Composer, Conductor
b. Sep 1, 1886 in Brunnen, Switzerland
d. Mar 8, 1957 in Zurich, Switzerland
Source: *NewEOp 71; OxMus*

Schoeffler, Paul
German. Opera Singer
b. Sep 15, 1897 in Dresden, Germany
d. Nov 21, 1977 in Amersham, England
Source: *NewEOp 71*

Schoen-Rene, Anna
American. Singing Teacher
b. Jan 12, 1864 in Coblenz, Germany
d. Nov 13, 1942 in New York, New York
Source: *CurBio 43; DcNAA; InWom*

Schoenbach, Sol Israel
American. Musician
b. Mar 15, 1915 in New York, New York
Source: *WhoAm 74, 76, 78, 80, 82*

Schoenberg, Arnold
American. Composer
b. Sep 13, 1874 in Vienna, Austria
d. Jul 13, 1951 in Brentwood, California
Source: *AmSCAP 66; AtlBL; CurBio 42, 51; DcAmB S5; DcCM; EncAB-H; OxGer; REn; WebAB; WhAm 3*

Schoenbrun, David
American. Journalist
b. Mar 15, 1915 in New York, New York
Source: *AmAu&B; ConAu 49, 3NR; CurBio 60; WhoAm 74; WhoWor 74*

Schoendienst, "Red" (Albert Fred)
American. Baseball Player, Manager
Managed St. Louis Cardinals to 1967 World Championship.
b. Feb 2, 1923 in Germantown, Illinois
Source: *BaseEn; CurBio 64; WhoAm 74, 76, 78; WhoProB 73*

Schofield, John McAllister
American. Military Leader
b. Sep 29, 1831 in Gerry, New York
d. Mar 4, 1906 in Saint Augustine, Florida
Source: *AmBi; ApCAB; BiAuS; BiDrUSE; DcAmAu; DcAmB; DcNAA; Drake; TwCBDA; WebAB; WhAm 1*

Scholes, Percy Alfred
English. Musicologist, Author
b. Jul 1877 in Leeds, England
d. Aug 2, 1958 in Vevey, Switzerland
Source: *LongCTC; TwCA SUP; WhoLA*

Scholl, William M
"Doctor Scholl"
American. Podiatrist
Founder, president, Scholl Manufacturing Co., 1908-68.
b. Jun 22, 1882 in LaPorte, Indiana
d. Mar 30, 1968 in Chicago, Illinois
Source: *IndAu 1917; WhAm 5*

Schollander, Don(ald Arthur)
American. Swimmer
Won two gold medals, 1964 Olympics.
b. Apr 30, 1946 in Charlotte, North Carolina
Source: *BioIn 7, 8, 9, 10; CurBio 65*

Scholz, Tom
[Boston]
American. Rock Musician, Singer
b. Mar 10, 1947 in Toledo, Ohio
Source: *BkPepl*

Schon, Steve
see: Journey

Schonbein, Christian Friedrich
German. Chemist
Discovered ozone gas, 1840.
b. Oct 18, 1799 in Metzingen, Germany
d. Aug 29, 1868 in Sauersberg, Germany
Source: *AsBiEn; DcScB; NewCol 75*

Schonberg, Harold C
American. Music Critic, Journalist
b. Nov 29, 1915 in New York, New York
Source: *AmAu&B; IntWW 74; WhoAm 74, 76, 78, 80, 82; WhoE 74; WhoWor 74*

Schoneberg, Sheldon Clyde
American. Artist
b. Dec 3, 1926 in Chicago, Illinois
Source: *WhoWest 78*

Schonfield, Hugh
English. Author
b. May 17, 1901 in London, England
Source: *Au&Wr 71; ChPo; ConAu 9R; WrDr 76*

Schongauer, Martin
German. Artist, Engraver
b. 1450 in Colmar, Germany
d. Feb 2, 1491 in Breisach, Germany
Source: *AtlBL*

Schoolcraft, Henry Rowe
American. Explorer, Naturalist
Indian culture expert; wrote *The Myth of Hiawatha,* 1856, which inspired Longfellow's poem.
b. Mar 28, 1793 in Albany County, New York
d. Dec 10, 1864 in Washington, DC
Source: *Alli; AmAu; AmAu&B; AmBi; ApCAB; BbD; BiAuS; BiD&SB; CyAL 1; DcAmAu; DcAmB; DcNAA; Drake; EncAB-H; OxAmL; OxCan; REn; REnAL; TwCBDA; WebAB; WhAm H*

Schoonmaker, Frank
American. Author, Wine Authority
b. Aug 20, 1905 in Spearfish, South Dakota
d. Jan 11, 1976 in New York, New York
Source: *AmAu&B; ConAu 61*

Schopenhauer, Arthur
German. Philosopher, Author
b. Jan 22, 1788 in Danzig, Germany
d. Sep 20, 1860 in Frankfurt, Germany
Source: *AtlBL; BbD; BiD&SB; CasWL; CyWA; DcEuL; EuAu; EvEuW; NewC; OxEng; OxGer; Pen EUR; RComWL; REn*

Schorer, Mark
American. Author, Educator
b. May 17, 1908 in Sauk City, Wisconsin
d. Aug 11, 1977 in Oakland, California
Source: *AmAu&B; CnDAL; ConAu 5R, 73; ConNov 72, 76; DrAF 76; DrAS 74E; IntWW 74; OxAmL; Pen AM; REn; REnAL; TwCA SUP; WhoAm 74; WhoWor 74; WrDr 76*

Schorr, Daniel
American. Radio, TV Commentator
b. Aug 31, 1916 in New York, New York
Source: *ConAu 65; CurBio 59; WhoAm 74, 76, 78, 80, 82; WhoWor 74; WhoWorJ 72*

Schorr, Friedrich
Hungarian. Opera Singer
b. Sep 2, 1888 in Nagyvarad, Hungary
d. Aug 14, 1953 in Farmington, Connecticut
Source: *CurBio 42, 54*

Schott, Anton
German. Opera Singer
b. Jun 24, 1846 in Schloss, Bavaria
d. Jan 6, 1913 in Stuttgart, Germany
Source: *NewEOp 71*

Schoyer, (B) Preston
American. Author
b. Jun 13, 1912 in Pittsburgh, Pennsylvania
d. Mar 13, 1978 in Stratford, Connecticut
Source: *AmAu&B; AmNov; ConAu 77*

Schrader, Paul Joseph
American. Motion Picture Director, Writer
b. Jul 22, 1946 in Grand Rapids, Michigan
Source: *BioIn 10, 11; ConAu 37R; CurBio 81; WhoAm 82*

Schram, Emil
American. Businessman
b. Nov 23, 1893 in Peru, Indiana
Source: *CurBio 41, 53; Who 74; WhoAm 74*

Schramm, Tex(as Edward)
American. Football Executive
Dallas Cowboys, general manager, 1960--; president, 1966--.
b. Jun 2, 1920 in Los Angeles, California
Source: *WhoAm 82; WhoFtbl 74; WhoS&SW 73*

Schranz, Karl
Austrian. Skier
b. 1939?
Source: *BioIn 8, 9*

Schreiber, Avery
American. Actor, Comedian
b. Apr 9, 1935 in Chicago, Illinois
Source: *WhoAm 74; WhoHol A*

Schreiber, Hermann Otto Ludwig
Austrian. Historian, Author
b. May 4, 1920 in Wiener Nevstadt, Austria
Source: *Au&Wr 71; ConAu 25R; WrDr 76*

Schreker, Franz
German. Composer
b. Mar 23, 1878 in Monaco
d. Mar 21, 1934 in Berlin, Germany
Source: *NewEOp 71; OxMus*

Schreyer, Edward Richard
Canadian. Government Official
b. Dec 21, 1935 in Beausejour, MB
Source: *BioIn 11; CanWW 82; IntWW 77; WhoAm 82*

Schroder, Gerhard
[Gerhard Schroeder]
German. Politician, Lawyer
b. Sep 11, 1910 in Saarbrucken, Germany
Source: *CurBio 62; IntWW 74; WhoWor 74*

Schroder-Devrient, Wilhelmine
German. Opera Singer
b. Dec 6, 1804 in Hamburg, Germany
d. Jan 26, 1860 in Coburg, Germany
Source: *InWom*

Schroeder, Patricia Scott
[Mrs. James White Schroeder]
American. Congresswoman
b. Jul 30, 1940 in Portland, Oregon
Source: *AlmAP 78, 80; CngDr 74, 77, 79; CurBio 78; GoodHS; WhoAm 74, 76, 78, 80, 82; WhoAmP 73, 75, 77, 79; WhoAmW 72, 74, 75, 77, 79; WhoGov 75, 77; WhoWest 74, 76, 78; WomPO 76*

Schrum, Marion Margaret
American. Educator
b. Feb 1, 1924 in Bryant, Iowa
Source: *WhoAm 74, 76, 78, 80, 82*

Schubert, Franz Peter
Austrian. Composer
Wrote *The Unfinished Symphony,* published 1867.
b. Jan 31, 1797 in Vienna, Austria
d. Nov 19, 1828 in Vienna, Austria
Source: *AtlBL; NewC; OxGer; REn*

Schuch, Ernst von
Austrian. Conductor
b. Nov 23, 1846 in Graz, Austria
d. May 10, 1914 in Dresden, Germany
Source: *NewEOp 71*

Schulberg, Budd Wilson
American. Author, Journalist
b. Mar 27, 1914 in New York, New York
Source: *AmAu&B; AmNov; AmSCAP 66; BiE&WWA; CelR 73; CnDAL; ConAu 25R; ConDr 73; ConNov 72, 76; CurBio 41, 51; DcFM; DrAF 76; FilmgC; IntMPA 77, 75; IntWW 74; LongCTC; ModAL; NewYTBE 72; NotNAT; OxAmL; OxFilm; Pen AM; REn; REnAL; TwCA SUP; WebE&AL; WhoAm 74, 76, 78, 80, 82; WhoWor 74; WorEFlm; WrDr 76*

Schulberg, Stuart
Motion Picture Producer
b. 1922
d. Jun 1979
Source: *BioIn 11; NewYTET*

Schuller, Gunther
American. Composer, Conductor
b. Nov 22, 1925 in New York, New York
Source: *CurBio 64; DcCM; IntWW 74; LEduc 74; WebAB; WhoAm 74, 76, 78, 80, 82; WhoE 74; WhoWor 74; WrDr 76*

Schuller, Robert Harold
American. Evangelist, Author
b. Sep 16, 1926 in Alton, Iowa
Source: *BioIn 10, 11; ConAu 9R; CurBio 79; IntAu&W 77; WhoAm 82; WhoAmA 76, 78, 80; WhoRel 75; WrDr 76, 80*

Schullian, Dorothy May
American. Librarian, Historian
b. May 19, 1906 in Lakewood, Ohio
Source: *BiDrLUS 70; DrAS 74H; WhoAm 74, 76, 78, 80, 82*

Schultz, Dave (David William)
"The Hammer"
Canadian. Hockey Player
Holds NHL records, most penalty minutes in season (472), career (2,294).
b. Oct 14, 1949 in Waldheim, SK
Source: *NewYTBS 74, 75*

Schultz, Dutch
[Arthur Flegenheimer]
American. Gangster
b. Aug 6, 1900 in Bronx, New York
d. Oct 24, 1935 in Newark, New Jersey
Source: *Blood; DcAmB S1; WebAB*

Schultz, Harry D
American. Investment Consultant
b. Sep 11, 1923
Source: *ConAu 25R*

Schultze, Carl Edward
American. Cartoonist
b. May 25, 1866 in Lexington, Kentucky
d. Jan 18, 1939 in New York, New York
Source: *WorECom*

Schultze, Charles Louis
American. Economist
b. Dec 12, 1924 in Alexandria, Virginia
Source: *AmEA 74; BioIn 7, 8, 9, 11; CurBio 70; IntWW 74, 75, 76, 77, 78; IntYB 78, 79; NewYTBS 76, 77; PolProf J; WhoAm 74, 76, 78, 80; WhoAmP 77, 79; WhoE 77, 79; WhoGov 77*

Schulz, Charles Monroe
American. Cartoonist
Created "Peanuts" comic strip, 1950; won Emmy, 1966.
b. Nov 26, 1922 in Minneapolis, Minnesota
Source: *AmAu&B; AuBYP; BkPepl; CelR 73; CurBio 60; ConAu 9R; MnnWr; SmATA 10; ThrBJA; WhoAm 74, 76, 78, 80, 82; WhoAmA 73; WhoWor 74; WrDr 76*

Schulz, George J
American. Educator, Physicist
b. Apr 29, 1925 in Brno, Czechoslovakia
Source: *WhoAm 74; WhoE 74*

Schuman, Robert
French. Statesman, Political Economist
b. Jun 29, 1886 in Luxemburg
d. Sep 4, 1963 in Metz, France
Source: *CurBio 48, 63; WhAm 4*

Schuman, William Howard
American. Composer
b. Aug 4, 1910 in New York, New York
Source: *BiE&WWA; CurBio 42, 62; DcCM; EncAB-H; IntWW 74; REnAL; WebAB; WhoAm 74, 76, 78, 80, 82; WhoMus 72; WhoWor 74*

Schumann, Bliss
American. Sightseeing Guide
Source: *BioIn 10*

Schumann, Clara Josephine Wieck
German. Musician
b. Sep 13, 1819 in Leipzig, Germany
d. May 20, 1896 in Frankfurt, Germany
Source: *HerW; InWom*

Schumann, Elisabeth
German. Opera Singer
b. Jun 13, 1885 in Merseberg, Germany
d. Apr 23, 1952 in New York, New York
Source: *InWom*

Schumann, Henrietta
Musician
b. 1910
d. 1949
Source: *BioIn 2*

Schumann, Maurice
French. Author, Politician
b. Apr 10, 1911 in Paris, France
Source: *CurBio 70; IntWW 74; Who 74; WhoWor 74*

Schumann, Robert Alexander
German. Composer
Led Romantic movement; career as pianist ended due to hand injury.
b. Jun 8, 1810 in Zwickau, Germany
d. Jul 29, 1856 in Endenick, Germany
Source: *AtlBL; BbD; BiD&SB; OxGer; REn*

Schumann, Walter
American. Composer, Conductor
b. Oct 8, 1913 in New York, New York
d. Aug 21, 1958 in Minneapolis, Minnesota
Source: *AmSCAP 66*

Schumann-Heink, Ernestine Rossler
American. Opera Singer
b. Jun 15, 1861 in Lieben, Czechoslovakia
d. Nov 16, 1936 in Hollywood, California
Source: *AmBi; DcAmB S2; InWom; NotAW; REn; WebAB; WhAm 1; WhScrn 74, 77; WhoHol B; WomWWA 14*

Schumpeter, Joseph Alois
American. Economist
b. Feb 8, 1883 in Trest, Moravia
d. Jan 8, 1950 in Taconic, Connecticut
Source: *BioIn 2, 8, 10, 11; DcAmB S4; EncAB-H; McGEWB; NewCol 75; ObitOF 79; REnAL; WebAB; WhAm 2*

Schurz, Carl
American. Politician
b. Mar 2, 1829 in Cologne, Germany
d. May 14, 1906 in New York, New York
Source: *Alli, SUP; AmAu; AmAu&B; AmBi; ApCAB; BbD; BiAuS; BiDSA; BiDrAC; BiDrUSE; DcAmAu; DcAmB; DcNAA; Drake; EncAB-H; OxAmL; REnAL; TwCBDA; WebAB; WhAm 1; WhAmP; WisWr*

Schuschnigg, Kurt von
Austrian. Chancellor
b. Dec 14, 1897 in Riva, Italy
d. Nov 18, 1977 in Innsbruck, Austria
Source: *CathA 1952; IntWW 74; REn; Who 74; WhoWor 74*

Schuster, Max Lincoln
American. Publisher
Founded Simon and Schuster, with Richard Simon, 1924.
b. Mar 2, 1897 in Kalusz, Austria
d. Dec 20, 1970
Source: *AmAu&B; ConAu 29R; CurBio 41; REnAL; WhoWorJ 72*

Schutz, Heinrich
German. Composer
b. Oct 8, 1585 in Kostritz, Germany
d. Nov 6, 1672 in Dresden, Germany
Source: *AtlBL; OxGer; REn*

Schutz, Roger
Swiss. Clergyman
b. 1915?
Source: *BioIn 1*

Schutzendorf, Gustav
German. Opera Singer
b. 1883 in Cologne, Germany
d. Apr 27, 1937 in Berlin, Germany
Source: *NewEOp 71*

Schuyler, Phillip John
American. Statesman
b. Nov 20, 1773 in Albany, New York
d. Nov 18, 1804 in Albany, New York
Source: *AmBi; ApCAB; BiAuS; BiDrAC; DcAmB; Drake; McGEWB; NatCAB 1; TwCBDA; WebAB; WebAMB; WebBD 80; WhAm H*

Schwab, Charles Michael
American. Industrialist
b. Feb 18, 1862 in Williamsburg, Pennsylvania
d. Sep 18, 1939 in New York, New York
Source: *AmBi; DcAmB S2; EncAB-H; WebAB*

Schwartz, Alan Earl
American. Lawyer
b. Dec 21, 1925 in Detroit, Michigan
Source: *St&PR 75; WhoAm 74, 76, 78, 80, 82; WhoF&I 74; WhoWorJ 72*

Schwartz, Arthur
American. Songwriter
b. Nov 25, 1900 in Brooklyn, New York
Source: *AmSCAP 66; BiE&WWA; EncMT; FilmgC; IntMPA 75, 76, 77; NewCBMT; NotNAT; PlP&P; WhoThe 77*

Schwartz, Delmore
American. Author, Editor, Critic
b. Dec 8, 1913 in Brooklyn, New York
d. Jul 11, 1966 in New York, New York
Source: *AmAu&B; AtlBL; CasWL; CnDAL; CnE&AP; CnMWL; ConAu 17R, 25R; ConAu P-2; ConLC 2, 4, 10; CurBio 60, 66; EncWL; ModAL, SUP; OxAmL; Pen AM; RAdv 1; REn; REnAL; SixAP; TwCA, SUP; TwCW; WebE&AL; WhAm 4; WhoTwCL*

Schwartz, Maurice
American. Actor, Director, Producer
b. Jun 18, 1890 in Sedikov, Russia
d. May 10, 1960 in Tel Aviv, Israel
Source: *CurBio 56, 60; OxThe; WhAm 4; WhScrn 74, 77; WhoHol B*

Schwartz, Stephen L
American. Dramatist, Composer
b. Mar 6, 1948 in Roslyn, New York
Source: *CelR 73; ConAu 85; EncMT; NotNAT; SmATA 19; WhoAm 82; WhoThe 77*

Schwarz, Brinsley
see: Graham Parker and the Rumour

Schwarzenegger, Arnold
"Austrian Oak"
Austrian. Body Builder, Actor, Author
Five times Mr. Universe; six times Mr. Olympia.
b. Jul 30, 1947 in Graz, Austria
Source: *BioIn 10; ConAu 81; CurBio 79; NewYTBS 76*

Schwarzkopf, Elisabeth
German. Opera Singer
b. Dec 9, 1915 in Jarotschin, Poland
Source: *CurBio 55; InWom; IntWW 74; Who 74; WhoWor 74*

Schwatka, Frederik
American. Explorer, Naturalist
Explored AK's Yukon River, 1883-84; wrote *Nimrod of the North,* 1885.
b. Sep 29, 1849 in Galena, Illinois
d. Nov 2, 1892 in Portland, Oregon
Source: *AmBi; ApCAB; DcAmB; NatCAB; TwCBDA; WebBD 80; WhAm H*

Schweickart, Russell L
American. Astronaut
b. Oct 25, 1935 in Neptune, New Jersey
Source: *IntWW 74; WhoAm 74, 76, 78, 80, 82; WhoGov 72; WhoS&SW 73*

Schweiker, Richard Schultz
American. Government Official
Senator, 1969-80; secretary HHS, 1981-83.
b. Jun 1, 1926 in Norristown, Pennsylvania
Source: *BiDrAC; BioNews 74; CngDr 74; IntWW 74; WhoAm 74, 76, 78, 80, 82; WhoAmP 73; WhoE 74, 74; WhoGov 72*

Schweitzer, Albert
French. Medical Missionary, Musician
Won Nobel Peace Prize, 1954; wrote biography of Bach, 1905.
b. Jan 14, 1875 in Kaysersberg, Germany
d. Sep 4, 1965 in Lambarene, Gabon
Source: *ConAu 93; CurBio 48, 65; LongCTC; OxGer; REn; TwCA SUP; TwCW; WhAm 4*

Scipio, Publius Cornelius
Roman. General
d. 212BC
Source: *WebBD 80*

Scipio Africanus, Publius Cornelius
Roman. General
b. 234BC
d. 183BC
Source: *REn*

Scobie, Ronald Mackenzie
British. Army Officer
b. Jun 8, 1893
d. 1969
Source: *CurBio 45; WhWW-II*

Scofield, Paul
English. Actor
b. Jan 21, 1922 in Hurstpierpoint, England
Source: *BiE&WWA; CurBio 62; EncMT; FilmgC; IntMPA 82; IntWW 74; MotPP; MovMk; NotNAT; OxFilm; OxThe; PlP&P; Who 74; WhoHol A; WhoThe 77; WhoWor 74*

Scopas
Greek. Sculptor
Source: *NewCol 75; WebBD 80*

Scopes, John Thomas
American. Teacher
Tried for teaching theory of evolution against state law, 1925.
b. Jan 21, 1900 in Salem, Illinois
d. Oct 21, 1970 in Shreveport, Louisiana
Source: *ConAu 29R; NewYTBE 70*

Score, Herb(ert Jude)
American. Baseball Player
Pitcher; career ended when hit in eye by line drive, 1957.
b. Jun 7, 1933 in Rosedale, New York
Source: *BaseEn; BioIn 3, 4, 5, 6, 8, 11; WhoProB 73*

Scorel, Jan van
Dutch. Artist
b. 1495
d. 1562
Source: *NewCol 75; WebBD 80*

Scorpions
[Francis Buchholz; Matthias Jabs; Klaus Meine; Herman Rarebell; Rudolph Schenker]
German. Rock Group
Formed in 1971; first American tour, 1979-80.
Source: *IlEncRk*

Scorsese, Martin
American. Motion Picture Director, Writer
b. Nov 17, 1942 in Flushing, New York
Source: *IntMPA, 76, 77, 78, 79, 80, 81, 82; MovMk; WhoAm 74, 76, 78, 80, 82; WhoHol A*

Scott, Arleigh Winston
West Indian. Governor-General
b. Mar 27, 1900 in Barbados
Source: *IntWW 74; Who 74; WhoGov 72; WhoWor 74*

Scott, Austin
American. Educator
President of Rutgers U, 1891-1906.
b. Aug 10, 1848 in Maumee, Ohio
d. Aug 16, 1922 in Granville Centre, Massachusetts
Source: *DcAmB; TwCBDA; WhAm 1*

Scott, Austin W
American. Law Professor, Author
b. 1885 in New Brunswick, New Jersey
d. Apr 9, 1981 in Boston, Massachusetts
Source: *ConAu 103; NewYTBS 74*

Scott, Barbara Ann
Canadian. Figure Skater
Won gold medal, 1948 Olympics.
b. May 9, 1928 in Ottawa, ON
Source: *CanWW 70; CurBio 48; InWom*

Scott, Charles Wesly
[The Hostages]
American. Former Hostage in Iran
b. 1933?
Source: *NewYTBS 81*

Scott, Cyril
American. Actor
b. 1866 in Ireland
d. Aug 16, 1945 in Flushing, New York
Source: *Film 1; WhScrn 74, 77; WhoHol B; WhoStg 1906, 1908*

Scott, David Randolph
American. Astronaut
On flights of Gemini 8, 1966; Apollo 9, 1969; Apollo 15, 1971.
b. Jun 6, 1932 in San Antonio, Texas
Source: *CurBio 71; IntWW 74; NewYTBE 71; WhoAm 74, 76, 78, 80, 82; WhoS&SW 73; WhoWor 74, 76, 78, 80*

Scott, Dred
American. Slave
Sued for his freedom, 1846; lost Supreme Court decision, 1857.
b. 1795 in Southampton County, Virginia
d. Sep 17, 1858 in Saint Louis, Missouri
Source: *AmBi; DcAmB; EncAB-H; WhAm H*

Scott, Duncan Campbell
Canadian. Author, Poet
b. Aug 2, 1862 in Ottawa, ON
d. Dec 19, 1947 in Ottawa, ON
Source: *BiD&SB; CanNov; CanWr; CasWL; Chambr 3; ChPo, S1, S2; CreCan 2; DcLEL; DcNAA; EvLB; LongCTC; OxCan; Pen ENG; REn; REnAL; TwCA, SUP; WebE&AL*

Scott, Evelyn
[Elsie Dunn]
American. Author
b. Jan 17, 1893 in Clarksville, Tennessee
Source: *AmAu&B; CnDAL; ConAmA; ConAmL; ConAu 104; DcLEL; OxAmL; REnAL; TwCA, SUP; WhNAA*

Scott, George Campbell
American. Actor
First performer to refuse Oscar, 1970, for *Patton.*
b. Oct 18, 1927 in Wise, Virginia
Source: *BiDFilm; BiE&WWA; BkPepl; CelR 73; IntMPA 75, 76, 77, 78, 79, 80, 81, 82; NotNAT; OxFilm; WhoAm 82; WhoThe 77; WorEFlm*

Scott, Gordon
[Gordon M Werschkul]
American. Actor
b. Aug 3, 1927 in Portland, Oregon
Source: *FilmgC; IntMPA 75, 76, 77, 78, 79, 80, 81, 82; WhoHol A*

Scott, Hazel Dorothy
[Mrs. Adam Clayton Powell, Jr.]
American. Jazz Musician
b. Jun 11, 1920 in Port of Spain, Trinidad
d. Oct 2, 1981 in New York, New York
Source: *AmPS B; AmSCAP 66; AnObit 1981; BiDAmM; BioIn 6, 8, 10; CmpEPM; CurBio 43, 81; DcBlPA; InWom; WhoAmW 58; WhoHol A*

Scott, Hugh
American. Politician
b. Nov 11, 1900 in Fredericksburg, Virginia
Source: *CelR 73; IntWW 74; WhoAm 74, 76, 78, 80, 82; WhoAmP 73; WhoWor 74*

Scott, Ken
American. Textile, Fashion Designer
b. Nov 6, 1918 in Fort Wayne, Indiana
Source: *WhoHol A; WorFshn*

Scott, Lizabeth
[Emma Matzo]
American. Actress
b. 1922 in Scranton, Pennsylvania
Source: *FilmgC; IntMPA 75, 76, 77, 78, 79, 80, 81, 82; MotPP; MovMk; WhoAm 74, 76, 78, 80; WhoHol A; WorEFlm*

Scott, Martha Ellen
American. Actress
b. Sep 22, 1914 in Jamesport, Missouri
Source: *FilmgC; HolP 40; InWom; IntMPA 82; MovMk; WhoAm 74, 76, 78, 80, 82; WhoHol A; WhoThe 77*

Scott, Norman
American. Opera Singer
b. Nov 30, 1928 in New York, New York
d. Sep 22, 1968 in New York, New York
Source: *WhAm 5*

Scott, Pippa
American. Actress
b. 1935
Source: *BiE&WWA; FilmgC; MotPP; WhoHol A*

Scott, Randolph
American. Actor
b. Jan 23, 1903 in Orange County, Virginia
Source: *BiDFilm; CmMov; FilmgC; IntMPA 75, 76, 77, 78, 79, 80, 81, 82; MotPP; MovMk; OxFilm; WhoHol A; WorEFlm*

Scott, Raymond
American. Composer, Band Leader
b. Sep 10, 1909 in New York, New York
Source: *AmSCAP 66; CurBio 41; WhoJazz 72*

Scott, Robert Falcon
English. Explorer
Led expedition to S Pole, 1912, only to find Roald Amundsen had already been there.
b. Jun 6, 1868 in Devonport, England
d. Mar 1912 in South Pole
Source: *AnCL; AsBiEn; McGEWB; NewC; OxEng; REn*

Scott, Steve
American. Runner
b. 1956?
Source: *BioIn 12*

Scott, Thomas
American. Railroad Executive
b. Dec 28, 1823 in Fort Loudon, Pennsylvania
d. May 21, 1881 in Darby, Pennsylvania
Source: *AmBi; ApCAB; DcAmB; EncAB-H; TwCBDA; WhAm H*

Scott, Tony
American. Musician, Composer
b. Jun 17, 1921 in Morristown, New Jersey
Source: *WhoAm 74; WhoE 74*

Scott, Sir Walter
Scottish. Poet, Author, Historian
Father of historical novel, including *Ivanhoe,* 1820.
b. Aug 15, 1771 in Edinburgh, Scotland
d. Sep 21, 1832 in Abbotsford, Scotland
Source: *Alli; AnCL; AtlBL; BbD; BiD&SB; BiDLA, SUP; BrAu 19; CarSB; CasWL; Chambr 3; ChPo, S1, S2; CnE&AP; CrtT 2; CyWA; DcBiA; DcEnA, AP; DcEnL; DcEuL; DcLEL; EvLB; FamAYP; HsB&A; MnBBF; MouLC 3; NewC; OxEng; Pen ENG; PoChrch; RAdv 1; RComWL; REn; Str&VC; WebE&AL; WhoChL*

Scott, Walter
"Death Valley Scotty"
American. Adventurer
Built $2 million Moorish castle in Death Valley; tourist attraction today.
b. 1872
d. Jan 5, 1954 in Stovepipe Wells, California
Source: *DcAmB S5; WebAB*

Scott, Willard Herman
American. Weatherman
b. May 7, 1934 in Alexandria, Virginia
Source: *BioIn 12; WhoAm 82*

Scott, Winfield
American. General
b. Jun 13, 1786 in Petersburg, Virginia
d. May 29, 1866 in West Point, New York
Source: *Alli; AmAu&B; AmBi; ApCAB; BiAuS; BiDSA; DcAmAu; DcAmB; DcNAA; Drake; EncAB-H; REnAL; TwCBDA; WebAB; WhAm H*

Scott, Zachary
American. Actor
b. Feb 24, 1914 in Austin, Texas
d. Oct 3, 1965 in Austin, Texas
Source: *BiE&WWA; FilmgC; HolP 40; MotPP; MovMk; WhScrn 74, 77; WhoHol B*

Scotti, Antonio
Italian. Opera Singer
b. Jan 25, 1866 in Naples, Italy
d. Feb 26, 1936 in Naples, Italy
Source: *WhAm 1*

Scotto, Renata
Italian. Opera Singer
b. Feb 24, 1934 in Savona, Italy
Source: *IntWW 74; NewYTBE 72; WhoAm 82; WhoE 74; WhoMus 72; WhoWor 74*

Scottsboro Boys
[Olen Montgomery; Clarence Norris; Haywood Patterson; Ozie Powell; Willie Roberson; Charlie Weems; Eugene Williams; Andy Wright; Roy Wright]
American. Convicted Rapists
Charged and convicted of raping two girls in AL, 1931.
Source: *NewCol 75*

Scourby, Alexander
American. Actor
b. Nov 13, 1913 in Brooklyn, New York
Source: *BiE&WWA; CurBio 65; FilmgC; MotPP; MovMk; NotNAT; WhoE 74; WhoHol A; WhoThe 77*

Scranton, George Whitfield
American. Manufacturer
b. May 11, 1811 in Madison, Connecticut
d. Mar 24, 1861
Source: *AmBi; BiDrAC; DcAmB; NatCAB 9; WhoAmP 73*

Scranton, William Warren
American. Politician
b. Jul 19, 1917 in Madison, Connecticut
Source: *BiDrAC; BioNews 74; CurBio 64; IntWW 74; NewYTBE 70; St&PR 75; WhoAm 74, 76, 78, 80, 82*

Scriabin, Alexander Nicholaevich
[Alexsandr Scryabin]
Russian. Composer, Musician
b. Jan 6, 1872 in Moscow, Russia
d. Apr 27, 1915 in Moscow, Russia
Source: *AtlBL; DcCM; REn*

Scribner, Charles
American. Publisher
Founded Baker and Scribner Publishers, 1846; changed to Charles Scribner's Sons, 1878.
b. Feb 21, 1821 in New York, New York
d. Aug 26, 1871 in Lucerne, Switzerland
Source: *AmAu&B; AmBi; ApCAB; DcAmB; TwCBDA; WhAm H*

Scribner, Charles, Jr.
American. Publisher
Charles Scribner's Sons, president, 1952-77, chairman, 1977--.
b. Jul 13, 1921 in Quogue, New York
Source: *AmAu&B; ConAu 69; SmATA 13; St&PR 75; WhoAm 74, 76, 78, 80, 82; WhoF&I 74; WhoWor 74*

Scripps, Edward Wyllis
American. Newspaper Publisher
b. Jun 18, 1854 in Rushville, Illinois
d. Mar 12, 1926
Source: *AmAu&B; AmBi; DcAmB; EncAB-H; REnAL; WhAm 1*

Scripps, Robert Paine
American. Journalist
b. Oct 27, 1895 in San Diego, California
d. Mar 2, 1938
Source: *AmAu&B; AmBi; DcAmB S2; WhAm 1*

Scruggs, Earl
[Flatt and Scruggs]
American. Musician, Songwriter
Won Grammy, 1969, for "Foggy Mountain Breakdown."
b. Jan 6, 1924 in Flint Hill, North Carolina
Source: *EncFCWM 69; WhoAm 82; WhoAmP 73; WhoGov 72; WhoWor 74*

Scudery, Madeleine de
French. Author
b. 1607 in Le Havre, France
d. Jun 2, 1701 in Paris, France
Source: *BbD; BiD&SB; CasWL; CyWA; DcEuL; EvEuW; InWom; NewC; OxEng; OxFr; Pen EUR; REn*

Scully, Vince(nt Edward)
American. Sportscaster
b. Nov 29, 1927 in Bronx, New York
Source: *BioIn 4, 6, 9; WhoAm 78, 80, 82*

Seaborg, Glenn Theodore
American. Chemist, Government Official
b. Apr 19, 1912 in Ishpeming, Michigan
Source: *AmM&WS 73P; ConAu 49, 2NR; CurBio 48, 61; IntWW 74; St&PR 75; WebAB; Who 74; WhoAm 74, 76, 78, 80, 82; WhoAmP 73; WhoWor 74*

Seabury, Samuel
American. Anglican Bishop
b. Nov 30, 1729 in Groton, Connecticut
d. Feb 25, 1796 in New London, Connecticut
Source: *Alli; AmAu&B; AmBi; ApCAB; CnDAL; CyAL 1; DcAmAu; DcAmB; DcLEL; DcNAA; Drake; EncAB-H; OxAmL; REnAL; TwCBDA; WebAB; WhAm H*

Seaga, Edward Phillip George
Jamaican. Prime Minister
b. May 28, 1930 in Boston, Massachusetts
Source: *BioIn 12; CurBio 81*

Seagram, Joseph Edward Frowde
Canadian. Distiller
b. Aug 11, 1903 in Waterloo, ON
d. Nov 28, 1979 in Waterloo, ON
Source: *CanWW 70; St&PR 75; WhAm 7; WhoAm 74; WhoCan 73; WhoE 74; WhoF&I 74; WhoMW 74; WhoWor 74*

Seagram, Joseph William
Canadian. Distiller
b. Apr 16, 1907 in Toronto, ON
Source: *CanWW 70; WhoCan 73*

Seagrave, Gordon Stifler
American. Surgeon, Author
b. 1897 in Rangoon, Burma
d. Mar 28, 1965 in Namkham, Burma
Source: *CurBio 43, 65; OhA&B; WhAm 4*

Seale, Bobby G
American. Political Activist, Author
Co-founder, chairman, Black Panthers, 1966.
b. Oct 20, 1936 in Dallas, Texas
Source: *CelR 73; LivgBAA; NewYTBE 70; WhoBlA 75*

Seals, Jim (James)
[Seals and Crofts]
American. Singer, Songwriter
b. 1942 in Sindey, Texas
Source: *BkPepl; WhoAm 82*

Seals and Crofts
[Dash Crofts; Jim Seals]
American. Vocal, Instrumental Duo
Source: *BkPepl; EncPR&S; IlEncRk; RkOn*

Seaman, Elizabeth Cochrane
see: Bly, Nellie, pseud.

Searle, Ronald William Fordham
English. Artist, Editor, Author
b. Mar 3, 1920 in Cambridge, England
Source: *Au&Wr 71; ChPo S2; ConAu 9R; IlsBYP; IlsCB 1946; IntWW 74; NewC; Who 74; WhoAm 74, 76, 78, 80, 82; WhoGrA; WhoWor 74; WrDr 76*

Sears, Heather
English. Actress
b. 1935 in London, England
Source: *FilmgC; IntMPA 75, 76, 77, 78, 79, 80, 81, 82; MotPP; WhoHol A; WhoThe 77*

Sears, John Patrick
American. Lawyer
b. Jul 3, 1940 in Syracuse, New York
Source: *BioIn 8, 10, 11; WhoAm 82*

Sears, Richard Warren
American. Merchant
Issued first mail order catalog, 1887; Sears, Roebuck opened, 1893.
b. Dec 7, 1863 in Stewartville, Minnesota
d. Sep 28, 1914 in Waukesha, Wisconsin
Source: *AmBi; DcAmB; WebAB; WhAm 1*

Sears, Robert Richardson
American. Psychologist, Professor
b. Aug 31, 1908 in Palo Alto, California
Source: *AmAu&B; AmM&WS 73S; ConAu 17R; CurBio 52; WhoAm 74, 76, 78, 80, 82*

Seaton, Frederick Andrew
American. Newspaper Publisher
b. Dec 11, 1909 in Washington, DC
d. Jan 17, 1974 in Minneapolis, Minnesota
Source: *BiDrAC; BiDrUSE; ConAu 89; WhAm 1; WhoAmP 73; WhoGov 72*

Seaver, Tom (George Thomas)
American. Baseball Player
Pitcher, 1967--; has over 3,000 career strikeouts.
b. Nov 17, 1944 in Fresno, California
Source: *BaseEn; BkPepl; CelR 73; CurBio 70; NewYTBE 70; NewYTBS 74; WhoAm 74, 76, 78, 80, 82; WhoProB 73*

Sebastian, George
Hungarian. Conductor
b. Aug 17, 1903 in Budapest, Hungary
Source: *WhoWor 74*

Sebastian, John
[Lovin' Spoonful]
American. Singer
b. Mar 17, 1944 in New York, New York
Source: *WhoAm 74*

Sebelius, Keith George
American. Politician
Congressman from KS, 1969-81.
b. Sep 10, 1916 in Alamena, Kansas
d. Sep 5, 1982 in Norton, Kansas
Source: *BiDrAC; WhoAm 74, 76, 78, 80, 82; WhoAmL 79; WhoAmP 73, 75, 77, 79; WhoGov 72, 75, 77; WhoMW 76, 78, 80*

Seberg, Jean
American. Actress
Starred in *Paint Your Wagon,* 1969.
b. Nov 13, 1938 in Marshalltown, Iowa
d. Aug 31, 1979 in Paris, France
Source: *BiDFilm; CurBio 79; FilmgC; InWom; IntMPA 75, 76, 77; MovMk; OxFilm; WhoWor 74; WorEFlm*

Sebring, Jay
American. Hairstylist, Actor
Murdered, with Sharon Tate, by Charles Manson family.
b. Oct 10, 1933 in Alabama
d. Jul 8, 1969 in Los Angeles, California
Source: *WhScrn 77*

Secchi, Pietro Angelo
Italian. Explorer, Scientist
b. 1818
d. Feb 26, 1878
Source: *NewCol 75*

Secombe, Harry
Welsh. Actor, Comedian, Singer
b. Sep 8, 1921 in Swansea, Wales
Source: *ConAu 57; EncMT; FilmgC; IntMPA 75, 76, 77, 78, 79, 80, 81, 82; Who 74; WhoMus 72; WhoThe 77; WrDr 76*

Secord, Laura Ingersoll
Canadian. Loyalist Heroine
b. 1775 in Massachusetts
d. Oct 17, 1868 in Chippawa, ON
Source: *BioIn 10; ClbCR; MacDCB 78; NewCol 75; OxCan*

Secunda, (Holland) Arthur
American. Artist
b. Nov 12, 1927 in Jersey City, New Jersey
Source: *WhoAm 76, 78, 80, 82; WhoAmA 73, 76, 78*

Secunda, Sholom
Russian. Conductor
b. Aug 23, 1894 in Alexandria, Russia
d. Jun 13, 1974 in New York, New York
Source: *AmSCAP 66; ConAu 49; NewYTBS 74; WhAm 6; WhoAm 74; WhoMus 72; WhoWorJ 72*

Sedaka, Neil
American. Singer, Songwriter
Wrote songs "Breaking Up is Hard to Do," 1960; "Love Will Keep Us Together," 1975.
b. Mar 13, 1939 in Brooklyn, New York
Source: *BkPepl; ConAu 103; EncPR&S; IlEncRk; RkOn; WhoAm 82*

Sedgman, Frank (Francis Arthur)
Australian. Tennis Player
b. Oct 29, 1927 in Mont Albert, Australia
Source: *CurBio 51*

Sedgwick, Anne Douglas
American. Author
b. Mar 28, 1873 in Englewood, New Jersey
d. Jul 19, 1935
Source: *AmAu&B; AmBi; Chambr 3; CnDAL; ConAmA; ConAmL; DcAmB S1; DcLEL; DcNAA; EvLB; InWom; LongCTC; NotAW; OhA&B; OxAmL; REnAL; TwCA, SUP; WhAm 1; WomWWA 14*

Sedgwick, Catherine Maria
American. Author
b. Dec 28, 1789 in Stockbridge, Massachusetts
d. Jul 31, 1867 in West Roxbury, Massachusetts
Source: *Alli; AmWom; ApCAB; CarSB; ChPo; DcEnL; DcLEL; DcNAA*

Sedgwick, John
American. Army Officer
b. Sep 13, 1813 in Cornwall Hollow, Connecticut
d. May 9, 1864 in Spotsylvania, Virginia
Source: *Alli; AmBi; ApCAB; DcAmB; Drake; TwCBDA; WhAm H*

Sedny, Jules
Surinamese. Prime Minister
b. Sep 28, 1922 in Paramaribo, Surinam
Source: *IntWW 74*

Sedran, Barney
"Heavenly Twins"
American. Basketball Player
b. Jan 28, 1891 in New York, New York
d. Jan 14, 1969 in New York, New York
Source: *WhoBbl 73*

Seed, Jenny
South African. Author
b. May 18, 1930 in Capetown, South Africa
Source: *ConAu 21R; SmATA 8; WrDr 76*

Seefried, Irmgard Maria Theresia
German. Opera Singer
b. Oct 9, 1919 in Kongetvied, Germany
Source: *CurBio 56; InWom; IntWW 74; Who 74; WhoMus 72; WhoWor 74*

Seeger, Alan
American. Poet
Wrote "I Have a Rendevous with Death," 1916; killed in WW I.
b. Jun 22, 1888 in New York, New York
d. Jul 4, 1916 in Belloy en Senterre, France
Source: *AmAu&B; AmBi; Chambr 3; ChPo; CnDAL; DcAmB; DcLEL; DcNAA; EvLB; LongCTC; OxAmL; REn; REnAL; TwCA; TwCW; WhAm 4*

Seeger, Pete(r)
[The Weavers]
American. Folksinger, Songwriter
b. May 3, 1919 in New York, New York
Source: *BioNews 74; CelR 73; CurBio 63; EncFCWM 69; WebAB; WhoAm 74, 76, 78, 80, 82; WhoHol A; WhoWor 74*

Seeley, Blossom
American. Actress
b. 1892 in San Pablo, California
d. Apr 17, 1974 in New York, New York
Source: *BiE&WWA; NewYTBS 74; WhScrn 77; WhoHol B*

Seferiades, Giorgos Styljanou
Greek. Author, Diplomat
b. Feb 22, 1900
d. Sep 20, 1971 in Athens, Greece
Source: *ConAu 5R, 33R, 5NR*

Sefton, William
"Heavenly Twins"
American. Track Athlete
b. Jan 21, 1915
Source: *St&PR 75; WhoTr&F 73*

Segal, Alex
American. Motion Picture Director
b. Jul 1, 1915 in New York, New York
d. Aug 22, 1977 in Los Angeles, California
Source: *BiE&WWA; BioIn 3, 11; EncWT; FilmgC; IntMPA 75, 76, 77; NewYTBS 77; NewYTET; NotNAT; WhoAm 74, 76*

Segal, Erich Wolf
American. Author, Dramatist
Wrote *Love Story,* 1970; translated into 23 languages.
b. Jun 16, 1937 in Brooklyn, New York
Source: *AmAu&B; BkPepl; ConAu 25R; ConLC 3, 10; CurBio 71; DrAS 74F; NewYTBE 71; WhoAm 74, 76, 78, 80, 82; WhoE 74; WhoHol A; WhoWorJ 72; WrDr 76*

Segal, George
American. Sculptor
Known for life-size sculpture done in plaster.
b. Nov 26, 1924 in New York, New York
Source: *CelR 73; CurBio 72; DcCAA 71; WebAB; WhoAm 74; WhoAmA 73; WhoWor 74*

Segal, George
American. Actor
Starred in *A Touch of Class,* 1973.
b. Feb 13, 1934 in New York, New York
Source: *BiDFilm; BkPepl; FilmgC; IntMPA 75, 76, 77, 78, 79, 80, 81, 82; MotPP; MovMk; WhoAm 74, 76, 78, 80, 82; WhoHol A*

Segal, Lore Groszmann
American. Author
b. Mar 8, 1928 in Vienna, Austria
Source: *AmAu&B; ConAu 13R, 5NR; SmATA 4; WhoAm 74, 76, 78, 80, 82; WrDr 76*

Segal, Vivienne
American. Actress
b. 1897 in Philadelphia, Pennsylvania
Source: *BiE&WWA; EncMT; MotPP; NotNAT; ThFT; WhoHol A; WhoThe 77*

Segantini, Giovanni
Italian. Artist
b. 1858 in Italy
d. 1899
Source: *NewCol 75; WebBD 80*

Segar, Elzie Crisler
American. Comic Strip Creator
Created comic strip "Popeye," 1929.
b. Dec 8, 1894 in Chester, Illinois
d. Oct 13, 1938 in Santa Monica, California
Source: *DcNAA; WebAB*

Seger, Bob
[The Silver Bullet Band]
American. Rock Musician
Triple platinum albums: *Stranger in Town,* 1978; *Against the Wind,* 1980.
b. May 6, 1945 in Ann Arbor, Michigan
Source: *BioIn 11; IlEncRk; RkOn; WhoAm 80, 82*

Segni, Antonio
Italian. President
b. Feb 2, 1891
d. Dec 1, 1972 in Rome, Italy
Source: *CurBio 55, 73; NewYTBE 72; WhAm 5*

Segovia, Andres
Spanish. Musician
b. Feb 18, 1894 in Linares, Spain
Source: *CelR 73; CurBio 48, 64; IntWW 74; NewYTBE 73; Who 82; WhoAm 82; WhoMus 72; WhoWor 74*

Segre, Emilio
American. Scientist
b. Feb 1, 1905 in Tivoli, Italy
Source: *AmM&WS 73P; ConAu 33R; CurBio 60; IntWW 74; WebAB; Who 74; WhoAm 74, 76, 78, 80, 82; WhoWor 74; WhoWorJ 72; WrDr 76*

Segretti, Donald H
American. Lawyer, Watergate Participant
b. 1941
Source: *NewYTBE 73*

Segura, "Pancho" (Francisco)
Ecuadorean. Tennis Player
b. Jun 20, 1921 in Ecuador
Source: *CurBio 51; NewYTBE 71*

Seiberling, Frank Augustus
American. Businessman
b. Oct 6, 1859 in Western Star, Ohio
d. Aug 11, 1955 in Akron, Ohio
Source: *DcAmB S5; WhAm 3*

Seidel, Toscha
Russian. Musician
b. Nov 17, 1899 in Odessa, Russia
d. Nov 15, 1962 in California
Source: *WhAm 4*

Seidl, Anton
Hungarian. Conductor
b. May 7, 1850 in Budapest, Hungary
d. Mar 28, 1898 in New York, New York
Source: *ApCAB SUP; DcAmB; TwCBDA; WhAm H*

Seiss, Joseph Augustus
American. Pyramidologist
b. Mar 18, 1823 in Frederick County, Idaho
d. 1904 in Philadelphia, Pennsylvania
Source: *Alli, SUP; AmAu&B; ApCAB; BiDSA; ChPo; DcAmAu; DcAmB; DcNAA; Drake; TwCBDA; WhAm 1*

Selby, David
American. Actor
Starred in TV soap opera "Dark Shadows," 1966-71.
b. in Morganstown, West Virginia
Source: *IntMPA 75, 76, 77, 78, 79, 80, 81; WhoHol A*

Selby, Hubert, Jr.
American. Author
b. Jul 23, 1928 in New York, New York
Source: *AmAu&B; CasWL; ConAu 13R; ConLC 1, 2, 4; ConNov 72, 76; DrAF 76; ModAL SUP; WebE&AL; WhoAm 82; WrDr 76*

Selden, George Baldwin
American. Inventor
Developed gasoline engine, 1879; patented, 1895.
b. Sep 14, 1846 in Clarkon, New York
d. Jan 17, 1922 in Rochester, New York
Source: *DcAmB; LinLib S; NatCAB 20; WebAB; WhAm 4*

Selden, John
English. Jurist, Antiquary
b. Dec 10, 1584 in Salvington, England
d. Nov 30, 1654 in London, England
Source: *Alli; BiD&SB; BrAu; CasWL; Chambr 1; DcEnA; DcEnL; DcEuL; DcLEL; EvLB; NewC; OxEng; Pen ENG; REn; WebE&AL*

Seldes, George Henry
American. Journalist
b. Nov 16, 1890 in Alliance, New Jersey
Source: *AmAu&B; Au&Wr 71; ConAu 5R, 2NR; CurBio 41; OxAmL; REnAL; TwCA, SUP; WhNAA; WhoAm 74, 76, 78, 80, 82; WrDr 76*

Seldes, Gilbert Vivian
American. Critic, Author, Editor
b. Jan 3, 1893 in Alliance, New Jersey
d. Sep 29, 1970 in New York, New York
Source: *AmAu&B; Au&Wr 71; BiE&WWA; CnDAL; ConAu 5R, 29R; NewYTBE 70; OxAmL; OxFilm; Pen AM; REnAL; TwCA, SUP; WebAB; WhAm 5*

Seldes, Marian
American. Actress
b. Aug 23, 1928 in New York, New York
Source: *BiE&WWA; NotNAT; WhoAm 74, 76, 78, 80, 82; WhoE 74; WhoHol A; WhoThe 77*

Selfridge, Thomas Etholen
American. West Point Graduate
First fatality of powered airplane travel; Selfridge AFB, MI named for him.
b. 1882
d. Sep 17, 1908 in Fort Meyer, Virginia
Source: *BioIn 6; InSci*

Selkirk, Alexander
Scottish. Castaway Sailor
b. 1676 in Largo, Scotland
d. 1721
Source: *Alli; DcEuL; NewC; REn*

Selleck, Tom
American. Actor
Star of TV series "Magnum, P I"; appeared in Chaz commercials.
b. Jan 29, 1945 in Detroit, Michigan
Source: *BioIn 12; WhoAm 82; WhoHol A*

Sellers, Peter Richard Henry
English. Actor
Played Inspector Jacques Clouseau in *The Pink Panther* films, 1963-76.
b. Sep 8, 1925 in Southsea, England
d. Jul 24, 1980 in London, England
Source: *BiDFilm; CelR 73; CmMov; FilmgC; IntMPA 75, 76, 77; MovMk; OxFilm; Who 74; WhoWor 74; WorEFlm*

Sellinger, Frank J
American. Brewery Company Executive
b. 1914 in Philadelphia, Pennsylvania
Source: *WhoAm 80, 82*

Selmon, Lee Roy
American. Football Player
b. Oct 20, 1954 in Eufaula, Oklahoma
Source: *FootReg; WhoAm 82*

Selvon, Samuel Dirkson
West Indian. Author
b. May 20, 1923 in Trinidad
Source: *CasWL; ConNov 72, 76; LongCTC; WebE&AL; Who 74; WorAu; WrDr 76*

Selye, "Hans" (Hugo Bruno)
Canadian. Medical Researcher
Authority on stress; wrote *Stress without Distress,* 1974.
b. Jan 26, 1907 in Vienna, Austria
d. Oct 16, 1982 in Montreal, PQ
Source: *AmM&WS 73P, 76P, 79P; BioIn 2, 3, 4, 5, 6, 10, 11; CanWW 70, 79, 80; ConAu 5R; CurBio 53, 81, 83; IntAu&W 77; NewYTBS 82; WhoAm 74, 76, 78, 80, 82; WhoWor 74, 78; WrDr 76*

Selznick, David O(liver)
American. Motion Picture Producer
Won Oscar, 1939, for producing *Gone With the Wind.*
b. May 10, 1902 in Pittsburgh, Pennsylvania
d. Jun 22, 1965 in Hollywood, California
Source: *BiDFilm; CurBio 41, 65; DcFM; FilmgC; OxFilm; WebAB; WhAm 4; WorEFlm*

Selznick, Irene
American. Theatrical Producer
b. Apr 2, 1910 in New York, New York
Source: *BiE&WWA; InWom; NotNAT; WhoAm 74, 76, 78, 80, 82*

Sembrich, Marcella
[Marcelline Kochanska]
Polish. Opera Singer
b. Feb 18, 1858 in Wisniewczyk, Poland
d. Jan 11, 1935 in New York, New York
Source: *DcAmB S1; NewEOp 71; NotAW; WhAm 1*

Semenenko, Serge
Financier, Business Executive
b. 1930 in Russia
d. Apr 24, 1980
Source: *BioIn 6, 8; St&PR 75; WhAm 7; WhoAm 74; WhoE 74; WhoF&I 74*

Senanayake, Dudley
Ceylonese. Statesman
b. 1911
d. Apr 12, 1973 in Colombo, Sri Lanka
Source: *NewCol 75*

Sendak, Maurice Bernard
American. Author, Illustrator
Wrote, illustrated *Where the Wild Things Are,* 1963.
b. Jun 10, 1928 in Brooklyn, New York
Source: *AmAu&B; Au&ICB; AuBYP; BkP; ChlLR 1; ChPo, S1, S2; ConAu 5R; CurBio 68; FamAIYP; IlsBYP; IlsCB 1946, 1957; MorJA; NewYTBE 70, 73; PiP; SmATA 1; Str&VC; WhoAm 82; WrDr 76*

Sender, Ramon Jose
Spanish. Author
Considered finest novelist currently writing in Spanish.
b. Feb 3, 1902 in Alcolea de Cinca, Spain
Source: *AmAu&B; BioIn 1, 2, 3, 4, 8, 10; CasWL; ClDMEL; ConAu 5R; DcSpL; EncWL; EvEuW; IntAu&W 76, 77; IntWW 74, 75, 76, 77, 78, 79, 80; ModRL; REn; TwCA, SUP; TwCW; Who 74; WhoAm 74, 76*

Seneca, Lucius Annaeus, the Younger
Roman. Philosopher, Statesman
b. 4
d. 65
Source: *AtlBL; BbD; BiD&SB; CasWL; CnThe; CyWA; DcEnL; DcEuL; McGEWD; NewC; OxEng; Pen CL; RComWL; REn*

Senefelder, Aloys
German. Inventor
Invented lithography, 1796.
b. Nov 6, 1771 in Prague, Bohemia
d. Feb 26, 1834 in Munich, Germany
Source: *Chambr 1; DcAmB; NewCol 75*

Senesh, Hannah
Hungarian. Underground Leader
b. 1921
d. 1944
Source: *HerW; InWom; WhWW-II*

Senesino
Italian. Opera Singer
b. 1680 in Siena, Italy
d. 1750 in Siena, Italy
Source: *NewEOp 71*

Senghor, Leopold Sedar
Senegalese. Poet, Essayist
b. Oct 9, 1906 in Joal, Senegal
Source: *AfrA; CasWL; CurBio 62; EncWL; IntWW 74; Pen CL; RGAfL; TwCW; WhoGov 72; WhoTwCL; WhoWor 74; WorAu*

Sennacherib
Assyrian. King, Engineer
b. 705BC
d. 681BC
Source: *NewC; NewCol 75; WebBD 80*

Sennett, Mack
Canadian. Motion Picture Director, Producer
b. Jan 17, 1884 in Richmond, PQ
d. Nov 5, 1960 in Woodland Hills, California
Source: *BioNews 75; CmMov; DcFM; Film 1; FilmgC; MotPP; OxFilm; REn; REnAL; TwYS; WebAB; WhAm HA, 4; WhScrn 74, 77; WhoHol B; WorEFlm*

Senor Wences
Ventriloquist
Source: *WhoHol A*

Seper, Franjo
Yugoslav. Cardinal
Prefect, Sacred Congregation Doctrine of Faith, 1968-81.
b. Oct 2, 1905 in Osijek, Yugoslavia
d. Dec 31, 1981 in Rome, Italy
Source: *IntWW 74, 75, 76, 77, 78, 79, 80, 81; NewYTBS 81; WhoSocC 78; WhoWor 78*

Sequoya
[George Guess]
American Indian. Scholar
b. 1770? in Loudon County, Tennessee
d. 1843 in Tamaulipas, Mexico
Source: *AmBi; ApCAB; DcAmB; Drake; OxAmL; WebAB; WhAm H*

Serafin, Tullio
Italian. Opera Conductor
b. Dec 8, 1878 in Rottanova, Italy
d. Feb 2, 1968 in Rome, Italy
Source: *WhAm 4A*

Serban, Andrei George
Romanian. Motion Picture Director
b. Jun 21, 1943 in Bucharest, Romania
Source: *BioIn 11; CurBio 78; WhoAm 78, 80, 82*

Serkin, Peter A
American. Musician
b. Jul 24, 1947 in New York, New York
Source: *NewYTBE 73; WhoAm 74, 76, 78, 80, 82; WhoE 74; WhoMus 72; WhoWor 74*

Serkin, Rudolph
[Rudolf Serkin]
American. Musician
b. Mar 28, 1903 in Eger, Czechoslovakia
Source: *BiDAmM; CelR 73; WebBD 80; WhoAm 76, 78, 80, 82*

Serling, Rod
American. Author, Motion Picture Producer
Created TV series *Twilight Zone; Night Gallery.*
b. Dec 25, 1924 in Syracuse, New York
d. Jun 28, 1975 in Rochester, New York
Source: *AmAu&B; CelR 73; ConAu 57, 65; ConDr 73; CurBio 59; FilmgC; IntMPA 75; REnAL; WhAm 6; WhScrn 77; WhoAm 74; WhoWor 74; WorEFlm*

Serpico, Frank (Francisco Vincent)
American. Former Police Detective
Al Pacino starred in 1974 movie based on his life.
b. Apr 14, 1936 in New York, New York
Source: *BioIn 9; NewYTBE 71*

Serraillier, Ian Lucien
English. Children's Author
b. Sep 24, 1912 in London, England
Source: *Au&Wr 71; ChlLR 2; ChPo, S1, S2; ConAu 1R, 1NR; SmATA 1; ThrBJA; WrDr 76*

Serrault, Michel
French. Actor
b. 1928?
Source: *BioIn 12*

Sert, Jose Luis
Spanish. Architect
b. Jul 1, 1902 in Barcelona, Spain
Source: *AmAu&B; CurBio 74; IntWW 74; WhoAm 74, 76, 78, 80, 82*

Servan-Schreiber, Jean-Claude
French. Journalist
b. Apr 11, 1918 in Paris, France
Source: *ConAu 102; IntWW 74; WhoWor 74*

Service, John Stewart
Diplomat
b. 1909
Source: *BioIn 9*

Service, Robert William
Canadian. Author, Poet
b. Jan 16, 1874 in Preston, England
d. Sep 11, 1958 in Lancieux, France
Source: *CanNov; CanWr; CasWL; Chambr 3; ChPo, S1, S2; CnDAL; CnE&AP; CreCan 1; DcLEL; EvLB; LongCTC; NewC; OxAmL; OxCan; Pen ENG; REn; REnAL; TwCA, SUP; TwCW; WebE&AL; WhAm 3; WhNAA; WhoLA*

Sessions, Roger Huntington
American. Composer, Teacher
b. Dec 28, 1896 in Brooklyn, New York
Source: *AmAu&B; CelR 73; CurBio 75; DcCM; IntWW 74; OxAmL; REnAL; WebAB; WhoAm 74, 76, 78, 80, 82; WhoMus 72; WhoWor 74*

Seton, Anya Chase
American. Author
b. 1916 in New York, New York
Source: *AmAu&B; AmNov; Au&Wr 71; ConAu 17R; CurBio 53; InWom; LongCTC; OxAmL; Pen AM; REn; REnAL; SmATA 3; TwCA SUP; Who 74; WhoAm 74, 76, 78, 80, 82; WhoWor 74; WrDr 76*

Seton, Elizabeth Ann Bayley, Saint
[Mother Seton]
American. Religious Leader
b. Aug 28, 1774 in New York, New York
d. Jan 4, 1821 in Emmitsburg, Maryland
Source: *AmAu&B; AmBi; ApCAB; BioNews 75; DcAmAu; DcAmB; InWom; NotAW; TwCBDA; WebAB; WhAm H*

Seton, Ernest Thompson
Canadian. Naturalist, Author
b. Aug 14, 1860 in South Shields, England
d. Oct 23, 1946 in Santa Fe, New Mexico
Source: *AmAu&B; AmLY; CanWr; ChPo, S1; ConAmL; CreCan 2; DcAmB S4; DcNAA; EvLB; IlsCB 1744; JBA 34; LongCTC; OxAmL; OxCan; REn; REnAL; TwCA, SUP; TwCW; WhAm 2; WhNAA; WhoChL*

Setzer, Brian
see: Stray Cats

Seurat, Georges Pierre
French. Artist
Devised pointillist style of painting, tiny dots of color.
b. Dec 2, 1859 in Paris, France
d. Mar 29, 1891 in Paris, France
Source: *AtlBL; REn*

Seuss, Doctor, pseud.
[Theodore Seuss Geisel]
American. Author, Illustrator
Wrote *How The Grinch Stole Christmas*, 1957.
b. Mar 2, 1904 in Springfield, Massachusetts
Source: *AmAu&B; AmSCAP 66; Au&ICB; AuBYP; ChlLR 1; ChPo, S1, S2; ConAu 13R; FamAIYP; IlsCB 1744, 1946, 1957; REn; REnAL; SmATA 1; TwCA, SUP; WebAB; WhoAm 74; WhoWest 74; WhoWor 74*

Sevareid, (Arnold) Eric
American. Broadcast Journalist
With CBS News, 1939--; consultant, 1977--.
b. Nov 26, 1912 in Velva, North Dakota
Source: *AmAu&B; AuNews 1; CelR 73; ConAu 69; CurBio 42, 66; IntMPA 75, 76, 77, 78, 79, 80, 81, 82; IntWW 74; WhoWor 74*

Severini, Gino
Italian. Artist
b. 1883 in Italy
d. Feb 29, 1966 in Paris, France
Source: *BioIn 7; NewCol 75*

Severinsen, "Doc" (Carl H)
American. Musician, Band Leader
Musical director, "The Tonight Show," 1967--.
b. Jul 7, 1927 in Arlington, Oregon
Source: *AmSCAP 66; WhoAm 74, 76, 78, 80, 82; WhoE 74*

Severn, William Irving
American. Author
b. May 11, 1914 in Brooklyn, New York
Source: *ConAu 1R, 1NR; SmATA 1*

Sevier, John
American. Public Official
b. Sep 23, 1745 in New Market, Virginia
d. Sep 24, 1815 in Fort Decatur, Alabama
Source: *AmAu&B; AmBi; ApCAB; BiAuS; BiDrAC; BioIn 1, 3, 4, 5, 6, 10; DcAmB; Drake; EncAAH; McGEWB; NatCAB 3; NewCol 75; REn; REnAW; TwCBDA; WebAB; WebAMB; WhAm H; WhAmP*

Seville, David
[Ross Bagdasarian]
American. Singer
Wrote "The Chipmunk Song," 1958; led to animated TV series "The Alvin Show," 1960.
b. Jan 27, 1919 in Fresno, California
d. Jan 16, 1972 in Beverly Hills, California
Source: *AmSCAP 66; BiDAmM; EncPR&S; WhScrn 77; WhoHol B*

Sevitzky, Fabien
Russian. Conductor
b. Sep 30, 1893 in Volotchok, Russia
d. Feb 2, 1967 in Athens, Greece
Source: *AmSCAP 66; CurBio 46, 67; WhAm 4; WhoMus 72*

Sewall, Samuel
American. Jurist
b. Mar 28, 1652 in Bishopstoke, England
d. Jan 1, 1730 in Boston, Massachusetts
Source: *DcAmB; McGEWB; WebAB; WhAm H*

Seward, William Henry
American. Cabinet Member
b. May 16, 1801 in Florida, New York
d. Oct 10, 1872 in Auburn, New York
Source: *Alli; AmAu&B; AmBi; ApCAB; BbD; BiD&SB; BiDrAC; BiDrUSE; CyAl 2; DcAmAu; DcAmB; DcNAA; Drake; EncAB-H; REn; REnAL; TwCBDA; WebAB; WhAm H; WhAmP*

Sewell, Anna
English. Author
Wrote *Black Beauty,* 1877.
b. Mar 30, 1820 in Yarmouth, England
d. Apr 25, 1878 in Norwich, England
Source: *BrAu 19; CarSB; CasWL; DcLEL; EvLB; InWom; JBA 34; NewC; OxEng; REn; WhoChL*

Sex Pistols
[Paul Cook; Steve Jones; Johnny Rotten; Sid Vicious]
English. Punk Rock Group
Source: *ConMuA 80; IlEncRk; LilREn 78; WhoRock 81*

Sexton, Anne Harvey
American. Poet
b. Nov 9, 1928 in Newton, Massachusetts
d. Oct 4, 1974 in Weston, Massachusetts
Source: *AmAu&B; CasWL; ChPo S1; ConAu 1R, 53, 3NR; ConLC 2, 4, 6, 8, 10, 15; ConP 70; CroCAP; ModAL, SUP; Pen AM; RAdv 1; SmATA 10; WebE&AL; WhAm 6; WhoTwCL; WorAu*

Seymour, Anne Eckert
American. Actress
b. Sep 11, 1909 in New York, New York
Source: *BiE&WWA; FilmgC; MotPP; MovMk; NotNAT; WhoAm 82; WhoHol A*

Seymour, Charles
American. Educator, Historian
b. Jan 1, 1884 in New Haven, Connecticut
d. Aug 11, 1963 in Cape Cod, Massachusetts
Source: *AmAu&B; CurBio 41, 63; REnAL; WhAm 4; WhNAA*

Seymour, Dan
American. Advertising Executive
President, chairman, J Walter Thompson Co., 1964-74.
b. Jun 28, 1914 in New York, New York
d. Jul 27, 1982 in New York, New York
Source: *BioIn 6, 7, 8; NewYTBS 82; St&PR 75; WhoAdv 72; WhoAm 74, 76; WhoE 75; WhoF&I 74, 75*

Seymour, Dan
American. Actor
Appeared in films *Casablanca; Key Largo.*
b. Feb 22, 1915 in Chicago, Illinois
Source: *BioIn 4; FilmgC; IntMPA 75, 76, 77, 78, 79, 80, 81, 82; MotPP; MovMk; Vers A; WhoHol A*

Seymour, Jane
English. 3rd Wife of Henry VIII
Married Henry, 1536; mother of Edward VI.
b. 1509
d. Oct 24, 1537
Source: *InWom; NewCol 75; REn; WebBD 80*

Seymour, Jane
[Joyce Penelope Frankenberg]
English. Actress
Starred in TV mini-series, "East of Eden," 1980.
b. Feb 15, 1951 in Hillingdon, England
Source: *WhoAm 80, 82*

Seymour, Lynn
Canadian. Ballerina
b. Mar 8, 1939 in Wainwright, AB
Source: *CanWW 82; CreCan 2; Who 74; WhoAm 82; WhoWor 74*

Seyss-Inquart, Artur von
Austrian. Nazi Leader
b. Jul 2, 1892 in Stannern, Czechoslovakia
d. Oct 16, 1946 in Nuremberg, Germany
Source: *CurBio 41, 46; REn*

Sforza, Carlo
Italian. Author, Educator, Statesman
b. Sep 25, 1872 in Italy
d. Sep 4, 1952 in Rome, Italy
Source: *ClDMEL; CurBio 42, 52*

Sforza, Ludovico
[Duke of Milan]
Italian. Nobleman
b. 1451
d. 1508
Source: *NewCol 75; WebBD 80*

Sha Na Na
[Lenny Baker; John "Bowser" Bauman; Johnny Contrado; "Dennis" Frederick Greene; "Jocko" John; Dan McBride; "Chico" Dave Ryan; Tony Santini; "Screamin" Scott Simon; Donald York]
American. Rock Group
Source: *EncPR&S; RkOn*

Shackleton, Sir Ernest Henry
Irish. Explorer
Wrote *The Heart of the Antarctic,* 1909, which described expeditions.
b. Feb 15, 1874 in Kilkee, Ireland
d. Jan 5, 1922 in South Georgia, Antarctica
Source: *BioIn 2, 3, 4, 5, 6, 7, 8, 10, 11; LongCTC; REn*

Shadrach
[Meshach and Abednego]
Biblical Character
Source: *NewCol 75*

Shadwell, Thomas
English. Dramatist, Poet
b. 1642 in Norfolk, England
d. Nov 20, 1692 in London, England
Source: *Alli; AtlBL; BbD; BiD&SB; BrAu; CasWL; Chambr 1; CnThe; CrtT 2; DcEnA; DcEnL; DcEuL; DcLEL; EvLB; McGEWD; MouLC 1; NewC; OxEng; OxThe; Pen ENG; PoLE; REn; REnWD; WebE&AL*

Shaffer, Anthony
English. Author
b. May 15, 1926 in Liverpool, England
Source: *ConDr 73; WrDr 76*

Shaffer, Peter Levin
English. Dramatist
b. May 15, 1926 in Liverpool, England
Source: *Au&Wr 71; CnMD; CnThe; ConAu 25R; ConDr 73; ConLC 5, 14, 18; McGEWD; NewC; Pen ENG; REnWD; TwCW*

Shafran, Daniel
Russian. Musician
b. Feb 13, 1923 in Leningrad, U.S.S.R.
Source: *Baker 78*

Shafter, William Rufus
American. Military Leader
b. Oct 16, 1835 in Kalamazoo County, Michigan
d. Nov 12, 1906 in Bakersfield, California
Source: *AmBi; ApCAB SUP; DcAmB; TwCBDA; WebAB; WhAm 1*

Shaftesbury, Anthony Ashley Cooper, Earl
English. Philosopher, Statesman
b. Feb 26, 1671 in London, England
d. Feb 15, 1713 in Naples, Italy
Source: *BbD; BrAu; CasWL; DcEnA; DcEnL; DcEuL; DcLEL; EvLB; NewC; OxEng; Pen ENG; WebE&AL*

Shagari, Alhaji Shehu Usman Aliyu
Nigerian. President
b. Apr 1925 in Shagari, Nigeria
Source: *AfSS 78, 79; CurBio 80; IntWW 75, 76, 77; NewYTBS 79; WhoWor 74, 76*

Shah of Iran
see: Pahlevi, Mohammed Riza

Shah of Persia
see: Pahlevi, Riza

Shahn, Ben(jamin)
American. Artist
b. Sep 12, 1898 in Kaunas, Lithuania
d. Mar 14, 1969 in New York, New York
Source: *AtlBL; ConAu 89; CurBio 54, 69; DcCAA 71; EncAB-H; IlsCB 1957; OxAmL; REn; WebAB; WhAm 5; WhoGrA*

Shakespeare, William
[Bard of Avon]
English. Dramatist, Poet
Considered greatest dramatist ever; wrote 154 sonnets, 37 plays.
b. Apr 23, 1564 in Stratford-on-Avon, England
d. Apr 23, 1616 in Stratford-on-Avon, England
Source: *Alli; AnCL; AtlBL; BbD; BiD&SB; BrAu; CarSB; CasWL; Chambr 1, 2, 3; ChPo, S1, S2; CnE&AP; CnThe; CroE&S; CrtT 1; CyWA; DcEnA, AP; DcEnL; DcEuL; DcLEL; EvLB; FamAYP; FilmgC; McGEWD; MouLC 1; NewC; OxEng; OxFilm; OxFr; OxGer; OxThe; Pen ENG; RComWL; REn; REnWD; WebE&AL*

Shales, Tom (Thomas William)
American. Journalist
b. Nov 3, 1948 in Elgin, Illinois
Source: *BioIn 12; WhoAm 82*

Shalit, Gene
American. Movie Critic, Journalist
b. 1932 in New York, New York
Source: *BkPepl; IntMPA 77, 78, 79, 80, 81, 82*

Shamask, Ronaldus
Dutch. Fashion Designer
b. 1946
Source: *BioIn 12*

Shands, Alfred Rives, Jr.
American. Surgeon, Textbook Author
b. Jan 18, 1899 in Washington, DC
d. 1981 in Wilmington, Delaware
Source: *AmM&WS 73P, 76P, 79P; WhoAm 74, 76*

Shange, Ntozake
[Paulette L Williams]
American. Dramatist, Poet
b. Oct 18, 1948 in Trenton, New Jersey
Source: *ConAu 85; ConLC 8; CurBio 79; WhoAm 82*

Shankar, Ravi
Indian. Musician, Composer
Plays sitar; teacher of George Harrison, 1965.
b. Apr 7, 1920 in Benares, India
Source: *CelR 73; CurBio 68; IntWW 74; WhoHol A; WhoMus 72; WhoWor 74; WorEFlm*

Shankar, Uday
Indian. Dancer
b. 1901 in India
d. Sep 26, 1977 in Calcutta, India
Source: *DcFM; IntWW 74*

Shanker, Albert
American. Teacher, Union Leader
President, NY City United Federation of Teachers, 1964--.
b. Sep 14, 1928 in New York, New York
Source: *CurBio 69; LEduc 74; WhoAm 82; WhoE 74; WhoWorJ 72*

Shannon, William Vincent
American. Ambassador to Ireland
b. Aug 24, 1927 in Worcester, Massachusetts
Source: *ConAu 9R; CurBio 79; WhoAm 74, 76, 78, 80, 82*

Shannon, Willie
"The Cannon"
American. Boxer
b. 1952? in Portland, Oregon
Source: *NF*

Shapero, Nate S
American. Businessman
b. Sep 17, 1892 in Detroit, Michigan
d. Jan 23, 1980
Source: *WhAm 7; WhoAm 74; WhoWorJ 72*

Shapira, Amitzur
Israeli. Murdered Olympic Team Member
b. 1932?
d. Sep 5, 1972 in Munich, Germany (West)
Source: *BioIn 9*

Shapiro, Karl Jay
American. Poet, Critic
b. Nov 10, 1913 in Baltimore, Maryland
Source: *AmAu&B; AnCL; CasWL; CelR 73; ChPo, S2; CnDAL; CnE&AP; ConAu 1R, 1NR; ConLC 4, 15; ConP 70, 75; CroCAP; DcLEL; DrAF 76; DrAP 75; DrAS 74E; EncWL; EvLB; IntWW 74; ModAL, SUP; OxAmL; Pen AM; RAdv 1; REn; REnAL; SixAP; TwCA SUP; TwCW; WebAB; WebE&AL; WhoAm 74, 76, 78, 80, 82; WhoTwCL; WhoWest 74; WhoWor 74; WhoWorJ 72; WrDr 76*

Shapley, Harlow T
American. Astronomer
b. Nov 2, 1885 in Nashville, Missouri
d. Oct 20, 1972 in Boulder, Colorado
Source: *AmAu&B; AmM&WS 73P; ConAu 37R; CurBio 41, 52, 72; EncAB-H; REnAL; TwCA, SUP; WebAB; WhAm 5*

Shapp, Milton J
American. Governor of Pennsylvania
b. Jun 25, 1912 in Cleveland, Ohio
Source: *BioNews 74; CurBio 73; IntWW 74; WhoAm 74; WhoAmP 73; WhoE 74; WhoGov 72*

Sharer, Donald A
[The Hostages]
American. Former Hostage in Iran
b. 1941?
Source: *NewYTBS 81*

Sharett, Moshe
[Moshe Shertok]
Israeli. Government Official
b. Oct 3, 1894 in Kherson, Russia
d. Jul 7, 1965 in Jerusalem, Israel
Source: *CurBio 48, 65; WhAm 4*

Sharietmadari, Ayatollah Seyed
Iranian. Islamic Leader
b. 1902
Source: *BioIn 11*

Sharif, Omar
[Michael Shalhoub]
Egyptian. Actor
Starred in *Dr. Zhivago,* 1965; *Funny Girl,* 1968.
b. Oct 10, 1932 in Alexandria, Egypt
Source: *BiDFilm; BkPepl; CelR 73; CmMov; CurBio 70; FilmgC; IntMPA 75, 76, 77, 78, 79, 80, 81, 82; IntWW 74; MovMk; OxFilm; WhoWor 74; WhoAm 82; WorEFlm*

Sharkey, Jack (Joseph Paul)
American. Boxer
b. Oct 6, 1902 in Binghamton, New York
Source: *WhoBox 74*

Sharman, Bill (William Walton)
American. Basketball Executive
LA Lakers, coach, 1971-76, GM, 1976--; NBA coach of year, 1972.
b. May 25, 1926 in Abilene, Texas
Source: *WhoAm 78, 80, 82; WhoWest 80*

Sharmat, Marjorie Weinman
American. Children's Author
b. Nov 12, 1928 in Portland, Maine
Source: *ConAu 25R; SmATA 4; WrDr 76*

Sharon, Ariel
"Arik"
Israeli. Former Defense Minister
Forced to resign because of his role in the Beirut massacre.
b. 1928 in Kafr Malal, Palestine
Source: *CurBio 81; IntWW 75, 76, 77, 78; MidE 78, 79; NewYTBS 82*

Sharp, Granville
English. Philanthropist
b. 1735
d. 1813
Source: *BioIn 2, 6, 8, 9, 10; NewCol 75; WebBD 80*

Sharp, Margery
British. Author
b. 1905
Source: *Au&Wr 71; AuBYP; ConAu 21R; ConNov 72, 76; DcLEL; EvLB; LongCTC; NewC; RAdv 1; REn; SmATA 1; ThrBJA; TwCA, SUP; WrDr 76*

Sharp, William
[Fiona MacLeod, pseud.]
Scottish. Poet, Author
b. Sep 12, 1855 in Paisley, Scotland
d. Dec 12, 1905 in Sicily, Italy
Source: *Alli SUP; AnCL; BbD; BiD&SB; BrAu 19; CasWL; ChPo, S1, S2; DcBiA; DcEnA, AP; DcLEL; EvLB; LongCTC; NewC; OxEng; Pen ENG*

Sharp, Zerna A
American. Teacher
Originated *Dick and Jane* reader series for schools.
b. Aug 12, 1889 in Hillisburg, Indiana
d. Jun 17, 1981 in Frankfort, Indiana
Source: *ConAu 104; NewYTBS 81*

Shastri, Lal Badahur
Indian. Statesman
b. Oct 2, 1904 in Mughalsarai, India
d. Jan 11, 1966 in Tashkent, India
Source: *BioIn 7, 8, 9; CurBio 64, 66*

Shatner, William
American. Actor
Played James Kirk in TV series "Star Trek," 1966-69.
b. Mar 22, 1931 in Montreal, PQ
Source: *BioNews 74; CanWW 82; FilmgC; MotPP; MovMk; NotNAT; WhoAm 74, 76, 78, 80, 82; WhoHol A; WhoThe 77*

Shattuck, Arthur
American. Musician
b. Apr 19, 1881 in Neenah, Wisconsin
d. 1951
Source: *NatCAB 17; WhAm 3*

Shattuck, Roger Whitney
American. Author, Educator
b. Aug 20, 1923 in New York, New York
Source: *AmAu&B; Au&Wr 71; ConAu 5R; DrAP 75; DrAS 74F; WhoAm 74, 76, 78, 80, 82; WorAu; WrDr 76*

Shaughnessy, Clark Daniel
American. Football Coach
b. Mar 6, 1892 in Saint Cloud, Minnesota
d. May 15, 1970 in Santa Monica, California
Source: *NewYTBE 70; WhAm 5; WhoFtbl 74*

Shaver, Dorothy
American. Business Executive
b. Jul 29, 1897 in Center Point, Arkansas
d. Jun 28, 1959 in Hudson, New York
Source: *CurBio 46, 59; InWom; WhAm 3; WorFshn*

Shaver, Helen
Canadian. Actress
Source: *NF*

Shavers, Ernie
American. Boxer
b. Aug 31, 1945 in Garland, Alabama
Source: *BioIn 11, 12; NewYTBS 79; WhoBox 74*

Shaw, Albert
American. Editor
b. Jul 23, 1857 in Shandon, Ohio
d. Jun 25, 1947 in New York, New York
Source: *Alli SUP; AmAu&B; ApCAB; BbD; BiD&SB; DcAmAu; DcAmB S4; DcNAA; OhA&B; OxAmL; REnAL; TwCBDA; WhAm 2; WhNAA*

Shaw, Artie
[Arthur Arshowsky]
American. Musician
b. May 23, 1910 in New York, New York
Source: *AmSCAP 66; CelR 73; CurBio 41; WhoAm 74, 76, 78, 80, 82; WhoE 74; WhoHol A; WhoJazz 72; WhoWor 74*

Shaw, George Bernard
English. Dramatist, Critic
Greatest British dramatist since Shakespeare; wrote *Pygmalion,* 1913.
b. Jul 26, 1856 in Dublin, Ireland
d. Nov 2, 1950 in Ayot St. Lawrence, England
Source: *Alli SUP; AtlBL; BiD&SB; CasWL; Chambr 3; ChPo, S2; CnMD; CnMWL; CnThe; DcBiA; DcEnA AP; DcLEL; EncWL; EvLB; McGEWD; ModBrL, SUP; ModWD; NewC; OxEng; OxThe; Pen ENG; RComWL; REn; REnWD; TwCA, SUP; TwCW; WebE&AL; WhScrn 77; WhoStg 1906, 1908; WhoTwCL*

Shaw, Henry Wheeler
see: Billings, Josh, pseud.

Shaw, Irwin
American. Author, Dramatist
Wrote *Rich Man, Poor Man,* 1970.
b. Feb 27, 1913 in Brooklyn, New York
Source: *AmAu&B; AmNov; Au&Wr 71; AuNews 1; BiE&WWA; CelR 73; CnMD; CnThe; ConAu 13R; ConDr 73; ConLC 7; ConNov 72, 76; DrAF 76; EncWL; IntWW 74; LongCTC; McGEWD; ModAL; ModWD; NotNAT; OxAmL; Pen AM; RAdv 1; REn; REnAL; TwCA, SUP; TwCW; Who 74; WhoAm 74, 76, 78, 80, 82; WhoThe 77; WhoTwCL; WhoWor 74; WorEFlm; WrDr 76*

Shaw, Mary
American. Actress
b. 1860 in Boston, Massachusetts
d. May 18, 1929
Source: *DcAmB; InWom; PlP&P; WhAm 1; WhoStg 1906, 1908; WomWWA 14*

Shaw, Reta
American. Actress
b. 1912 in South Paris, Maine
d. Jan 8, 1982 in Encino, California
Source: *ForWC 70; WhoHol A*

Shaw, Robert
English. Actor, Dramatist, Author
Starred in *Jaws,* 1975.
b. Aug 9, 1927 in Lancashire, England
d. Aug 28, 1978 in Tourmakeady, Ireland
Source: *BiE&WWA; ConAu 1R, 81, 4NR; ConDr 73; ConLC 5; ConNov 72, 76; CroCD; FilmgC; IntMPA 75, 76, 77; McGEWD; MovMk; NotNAT; Who 74; WhoThe 77; WhoWor 74; WorAu; WrDr 76*

Shaw, Robert Gould
American. Military Officer
b. Oct 10, 1837 in Boston, Massachusetts
d. Jul 18, 1863 in Charleston, South Carolina
Source: *AmBi; BioIn 4, 5, 7, 10; Drake; EncAB-H; NatCAB 8; NewCol 75; TwCBDA; WebAMB; WhAm H*

Shaw, Robert Lawson
American. Conductor
b. Apr 30, 1916 in Red Bluff, California
Source: *BiDAmM; WebAB; WhoAm 76, 78, 80, 82*

Shaw, Wilbur
American. Auto Racer
b. Oct 31, 1902 in Shelbyville, Indiana
d. Oct 30, 1954 in Fort Wayne, Indiana
Source: *DcAmB S5; IndAu 1917*

Shawn, Dick
[Richard Schulefand]
American. Actor
b. Dec 1, 1929 in Buffalo, New York
Source: *FilmgC; IntMPA 75, 76, 77, 78, 79, 80, 81, 82; MotPP; MovMk; WhoHol A; WhoThe 77*

Shawn, Ted (Edwin Meyers)
American. Dancer
b. Oct 21, 1891 in Kansas City, Missouri
d. Jan 9, 1972 in Orlando, Florida
Source: *AmAu&B; ConAu X; CurBio 49, 72; NewYTBE 72; REnAL; WebAB; WhScrn 77; WhoHol B*

Shawn, William
American. Editor
b. Aug 31, 1907 in Chicago, Illinois
Source: *AmAu&B; CelR 73; IntWW 74; WhoAm 74, 76, 78, 80, 82; WhoWor 74*

Shays, Daniel
American. Revolutionary Soldier
Associated with 1786-87 rebellion, Springfield, MA.
b. 1747? in Hopkinton, Massachusetts
d. Sep 29, 1825 in Sparta, New York
Source: *AmBi; ApCAB; DcAmB; Drake; EncAB-H; REn; TwCBDA; WebAB; WhAm H*

Shazar, Zalman
Israeli. President
b. Nov 24, 1889 in Mir, Russia
d. Oct 5, 1974 in Jerusalem, Israel
Source: *ConAu 53, 101; CurBio 64, 74; NewYTBS 74; WhAm 6; WhoGov 72; WhoWor 74*

Shchedrin, Rodion Konstantinovich
Russian. Composer
b. Dec 16, 1932 in Moscow, U.S.S.R.
Source: *DcCM*

Shea, George Beverly
Canadian. Singer
b. Feb 1, 1909 in Winchester, ON
Source: *WhoAm 74, 76, 78, 80, 82; WhoMW 74; WhoRel 75*

Shea, John
American. Actor
b. Apr 14, 1949? in North Conway, New Hampshire
Source: *BioIn 12; NewYTBS 79*

Shea, William Alfred
American. Lawyer
b. Jun 21, 1907 in New York, New York
Source: *BioIn 7; CurBio 65; WhoAm 82; WhoMW 74; WhoRel 75*

Sheaffer, Walter A
American. Businessman
b. Jan 27, 1867 in Bloomfield, Iowa
d. Jun 19, 1946
Source: *WhAm 2*

Shean, Al
[Alfred Schoenberg]
American. Actor
b. 1868 in Dornum, Germany
d. Aug 12, 1949 in New York, New York
Source: *EncMT; FilmgC; WhScrn 74, 77; WhoHol B*

Shearer, Douglas
American. Movie Audio Engineer
b. 1899
d. Jan 5, 1971 in Culver City, California
Source: *FilmgC*

Shearer, Moira
Scottish. Dancer, Actress
b. Jan 17, 1926 in Dunfermline, Scotland
Source: *CurBio 50; FilmgC; InWom; MotPP; Who 74; WhoHol A; WhoThe 77; WhoWor 74*

Shearer, Norma
American. Actress
b. Aug 10, 1904 in Montreal, PQ
Source: *CanWW 70; CmMov; FilmgC; InWom; MotPP; MovMk; OxFilm; ThFT; TwYS; WhoHol A; WorEFlm*

Shearer, Taddeus Errington (Ted)
Artist, Cartoonist
b. Nov 1, 1919 in Jamaica
Source: *WhoAm 78; WorECom*

Sheares, Benjamin Henry
Singaporean. President
b. Aug 12, 1907 in Singapore
d. May 12, 1981 in Singapore
Source: *BioIn 10; FarE&A 78; IntWW 76, 77, 78; WhoWor 74, 76, 78, 80*

Shearing, George Albert
English. Musician
b. Aug 13, 1919 in London, England
Source: *CelR 73; CurBio 58; WhoAm 74, 76, 78, 80, 82; WhoHol A; WhoWest 74; WhoWor 74*

Sheba, Queen of
[Makeda]
Biblical queen who made visit to Solomon.
Source: *BioIn 1, 2, 3, 4, 5, 6, 7, 10; InWom*

Shedd, Charlie W
American. Author
b. Aug 8, 1915 in Cedar Rapids, Iowa
Source: *ConAu 17R*

Sheean, (James) Vincent
American. Journalist, Author
Covered world events from WW I to Korean War.
b. Dec 5, 1899 in Christian County, Illinois
d. Mar 15, 1975 in Arolo, Italy
Source: *AmAu&B; CnDAL; ConAmA; ConAu 61; CurBio 41, 75; NewYTBS 74; REn; REnAL; TwCA, SUP; WhAm 6; Who 74; WhoAm 74*

Sheed, Frank (Francis Joseph)
Australian. Author, Publisher
b. Mar 20, 1897 in Sydney, Australia
d. Nov 20, 1981 in Jersey City, New Jersey
Source: *Au&Wr 71; BioIn 1, 9, 10; CathA 1930; CurBio 81, 82; WhoAm 74*

Sheed, Wilfrid John Joseph
American. Author
b. Dec 27, 1930 in London, England
Source: *BioIn 10, 11; ConAu 65; ConLC 2, 4, 10; CurBio 81; WhoAm 82*

Sheehan, William Edward, Jr.
American. Radio, TV Executive
b. May 1925 in Boston, Massachusetts
Source: *WhoF&I 74*

Sheehy, Gail Henion
American. Journalist, Author
Wrote *Passages: Predictable Crisis of Adult Life*, 1976.
b. Nov 27, 1937 in Mamaroneck, New York
Source: *ConAu 49; ForWC 70; WhoAm 78, 80, 82*

Sheekman, Arthur
American. Screenwriter
b. Feb 5, 1901 in Chicago, Illinois
d. Jan 12, 1978 in Santa Monica, California
Source: *ConAu 73, 81; IntMPA 75, 76, 77*

Sheeler, Charles
American. Artist, Photographer
b. Jul 16, 1883 in Philadelphia, Pennsylvania
d. May 7, 1965 in Dobbs Ferry, New York
Source: *CurBio 50, 65; DcCAA 71; EncAB-H; WebAB; WhAm 4*

Sheen, Fulton John, Bishop
American. Religious Leader, Author
b. May 8, 1895 in El Paso, Illinois
d. Dec 10, 1979 in New York, New York
Source: *AmAu&B; ConAu 5R, 89, 5NR; CurBio 41, 51; IntWW 74; REnAL; TwCA SUP; WebAB; Who 74; WhoAm 74; WhoE 74; WhoHol A; WhoWor 74; WrDr 76*

Sheen, Martin
[Ramon Estevez]
American. Actor
b. Aug 3, 1940 in Dayton, Ohio
Source: *CurBio 77; IntMPA 75, 76, 77, 78, 79, 80, 81, 82; MovMk; NotNAT; WhoAm 82; WhoHol A; WhoThe 77*

Sheets, Millard Owen
American. Artist
b. Jun 24, 1907 in Pomona, California
Source: *DcCAA 71; WhAm 4; WhoAm 74; WhoAmA 73; WhoWest 74*

Shehu, Mehmet
"The Butcher"
Albanian. Politician
Prime Minister, 1954-81.
b. Jan 10, 1913 in Tirana, Albania
d. Dec 17, 1981 in Tirana, Albania
Source: *CurBio 58, 82; IntWW 74, 75, 76, 77, 78, 79, 80; NewYTBS 81; WhoSocC 78; WhoWor 74, 76, 78*

Sheil, Bernard James, Archbishop
American. Religious Leader
b. Feb 18, 1888 in Chicago, Illinois
d. Sep 13, 1969 in Tucson, Arizona
Source: *CurBio 68, 69; WhAm 5*

Sheinwold, Alfred
American. Bridge Expert, Author
b. Jan 26, 1912 in London, England
Source: *ConAu 61; WhoAm 74; WhoWor 74*

Sheldon, Sidney
American. Author
Wrote *The Other Side of Midnight,* 1973; *Rage of Angels,* 1980.
b. Feb 11, 1917 in Chicago, Illinois
Source: *AmSCAP 66; AuNews 1; BiE&WWA; BioNews 74; ConAu 29R; FilmgC; IntMPA 82; WhoAm 82*

Shelley, Mary Wollstonecraft
English. Author
Wrote *Frankenstein,* 1818.
b. Aug 30, 1797 in London, England
d. Feb 1, 1851 in Bournemouth, England
Source: *Alli; AtlBL; BbD; BiD&SB; BrAu 19; CasWL; Chambr 3; ChPo, S1; CyWA; DcBiA; DcEnA; DcEnL; DcEuL; DcLEL; EncMys; EvLB; FilmgC; HerW; InWom; MouLC 3; NewC; OxEng; Pen ENG; RAdv 1; REn; WebE&AL*

Shelley, Percy Bysshe
English. Poet
Romantic lyricist known for *Prometheus Unbound,* 1820.
b. Aug 4, 1792 in Field Place, England
d. Jul 8, 1822 in Viareggio, Italy
Source: *Alli; AtlBL; BbD; BiD&SB; BrAu 19; CasWL; Chambr 3; ChPo, S1, S2; CnE&AP; CnThe; CrtT 2; CyWA; DcEnA; DcEnL; DcEuL; DcLEL; EvLB; McGEWD; MouLC 2; NewC; OxEng; OxThe; Pen ENG; RAdv 1; RComWL; REn; REnWD; WebE&AL*

Shenker, Morris Abraham
American. Lawyer
b. Jan 10, 1907 in Kalius, Russia
Source: *BioIn 2, 8; WhoAm 82; WhoAmP 73*

Shepard, Alan Bartlett, Jr.
American. Astronaut
First American to travel in space, 1961.
b. Nov 18, 1923 in East Derry, New Hampshire
Source: *CelR 73; CurBio 61; IntWW 74; WhoAm 74, 76, 78, 80, 82; WhoS&SW 73; WhoWor 74*

Shepard, Odell
American. Author
b. Jul 22, 1884 in Rock Falls, Illinois
d. Jul 19, 1967 in New London, Connecticut
Source: *AmAu&B; ChPo; ConAu 5R, 25R, 3NR; OxAmL; OxCan; REnAL; TwCA, SUP; WhAm 4*

Shepard, Sam
[Samuel Shepard Rogers]
American. Author
b. Nov 5, 1943 in Fort Sheridan, Illinois
Source: *ConAu 69; ConDr 73; ConLC 6; CroCD; IntMPA 82; ModAL SUP; NatPD; NotNAT; WhoAm 74, 78, 80, 82; WhoThe 77; WrDr 76*

Shepherd, Cybill
American. Model, Actress
b. Feb 18, 1950 in Memphis, Tennessee
Source: *IntMPA 75, 76, 77, 78, 79, 80, 81, 82; MovMk; WhoAm 74, 78, 80, 82; WhoHol A; WomWMM*

Shepherd, Jean Parker
American. Actor, Author
b. Jul 26, 1929 in Chicago, Illinois
Source: *AuNews 2; CelR 73; ConAu 77; WhoAm 74*

Sheppard, Eugenia Benbow
American. Fashion Editor, Journalist
b. 1910 in Columbus, Ohio
Source: *CelR 73; InWom; WhoE 74; WorFshn*

Sheppard, Jack
English. Thief, Escape Artist
b. 1702
d. 1724 in London, England
Source: *BioIn 4, 7, 8; NewCol 75*

Sheppard, Sam(uel)
"Doctor Sam"
American. Osteopath, Accused Murderer
Accused of murdering wife, 1954.
b. 1923
d. Apr 6, 1970 in Columbus, Ohio
Source: *BioIn 7, 8*

Shera, Jesse Hauk
American. Librarian, Educator
b. Dec 8, 1903 in Oxford, Ohio
d. Mar 8, 1982 in Cleveland, Ohio
Source: *AmAu&B; BiDAmEd; ConAu 5R, 2NR; CurBio 64, 82; LEduc 74; WhoAm 74, 76, 78, 80, 82; WhoCon 73*

Sheraton, Thomas
English. Cabinet Maker
b. 1751 in Stockton, England
d. 1806 in London, England
Source: *Alli; NewC; OxEng*

Sheridan, Ann
[Clara Lou Sheridan]
American. Actress
b. Feb 21, 1915 in Denton, Texas
d. Jan 21, 1967 in Hollywood, California
Source: *BiDFilm; FilmgC; InWom; MotPP; MovMk; ThFT; WhAm 4; WhScrn 74, 77; WhoHol B; WorEFlm*

Sheridan, Philip Henry
American. General
b. Mar 6, 1831 in Albany, New York
d. Aug 5, 1888 in Nonquitt, Massachusetts
Source: *Alli SUP; AmAu&B; AmBi; ApCAB; BbD; BiD&SB; DcAmAu; DcAmB; DcNAA; Drake; EncAB-H; OhA&B; REn; REnAL; TwCBDA; WebAB; WhAm H*

Sheridan, Richard Brinsley
Irish. Dramatist, Orator
b. Oct 30, 1751 in Dublin, Ireland
d. Jul 7, 1816 in London, England
Source: *Alli; AtlBL; BbD; BiD&SB; BiDLA; BrAu; CasWL; Chambr 2; ChPo; CnThe; CrtT 2; CyWA; DcEnA; DcEnL; DcEuL; DcLEL; EvLB; McGEWD; MouLC 2; NewC; OxEng; OxThe; Pen ENG; PoIre; REn; REnWD; WebE&AL*

Sherman, Allan
American. Comedian
Known for satiric song, "Hello Muddah, Hello Faddah," 1963.
b. Nov 30, 1924 in Chicago, Illinois
d. Nov 20, 1973 in Los Angeles, California
Source: *AmSCAP 66; AuBYP; ChPo S1; ConAu 45; CurBio 66, 74; WhAm 6*

Sherman, Bobby
American. Singer, Actor
b. Jul 22, 1945 in Santa Monica, California
Source: *EncPR&S*

Sherman, Frank Dempster
American. Poet, Educator
b. May 6, 1860 in Peekskill, New York
d. Sep 19, 1916
Source: *Alli SUP; AmAu; AmAu&B; BbD; BiD&SB; ChPo, S1; CnDAL; DcAmAu; DcAmB; DcNAA; OxAmL; REn; REnAL; TwCBDA; WhAm 1*

Sherman, Lowell
American. Actor
b. Oct 11, 1885 in San Francisco, California
d. Dec 28, 1934 in Hollywood, California
Source: *BiDFilm; Film 1; FilmgC; MotPP; TwYS; WhScrn 74, 77; WhoHol B; WorEFlm*

Sherman, Roger
American. Statesman
b. Apr 19, 1721 in Newton, Massachusetts
d. Jul 23, 1793 in New Haven, Connecticut
Source: *AmBi; ApCAB; BiAuS; BiDrAC; DcAmB; Drake; EncAB-H; TwCBDA; WebAB; WhAm H; WhAmP*

Sherman, William Tecumseh
American. General
Said "War is Hell," 1880.
b. Feb 8, 1820 in Lancaster, Ohio
d. Feb 14, 1891 in New York, New York
Source: *Alli, SUP; AmAu&B; AmBi; BbD; BiD&SB; BiDrUSE; DcAmAu; DcAmB; DcNAA; EncAB-H; OhA&B; REn; REnAL; TwCBDA; WebAB; WhAm H*

Sherriff, Robert Cedric
English. Author, Dramatist
b. Jun 6, 1896 in Kingston, England
d. Nov 13, 1975
Source: *Au&Wr 71; Chambr 3; CnMD; CnThe; ConAu 61; ConDr 73; CroCD; CyWA; DcLEL; EvLB; LongCTC; McGEWD; ModBrL; ModWD; NewC; OxEng; Pen ENG; REn; TwCA, SUP; TwCW*

Sherrill, Henry Knox
American. Theologian
b. Nov 6, 1890 in Brooklyn, New York
d. May 12, 1980 in Boxford, Massachusetts
Source: *ConAu 97; CurBio 47; IntWW 74; Who 74; WhoAm 74; WhoWor 74*

Sherrill, Robert Glenn
American. Author
b. Dec 24, 1925 in Frogtown, Georgia
Source: *ConAu 21R; WhoS&SW 73*

Sherry, Larry (Lawrence)
American. Baseball Player
b. Jul 25, 1935 in Los Angeles, California
Source: *BaseEn; BioIn 5, 7; WhoProB 73*

Sherry, Louis
American. Chef, Restaurateur
b. 1856 in Saint Albans, Vermont
d. 1926
Source: *DcAmB*

Sherwood, Robert Emmet
American. Dramatist, Author
b. Apr 4, 1896 in New Rochelle, New York
d. Nov 14, 1955 in New York, New York
Source: *AmAu&B; CasWL; CnDAL; CnMD; DcLEL; OxAmL; Pen AM; TwCA, SUP; WebAB*

Sherwood, Roberta
American. Singer
b. 1913 in Saint Louis, Missouri
Source: *InWom; WhoHol A*

Shevchenko, Taras
Ukrainian. Poet
b. Mar 9, 1814 in Morintsy, Russia
d. Mar 10, 1861 in Russia
Source: *BbD; BiD&SB; CasWL; DcRusL; EuAu; Pen EUR*

Shields, Alexander
American. Fashion Designer
b. in San Francisco, California
Source: *WhoAm 82; WorFshn*

Shields, Brooke
[Christa Brooke Camille Shields]
"Brookie"
American. Model, Actress
Appeared on over 30 magazine covers, 1981.
b. May 31, 1965 in New York, New York
Source: *BioIn 11, 12; BkPepl; CurBio 82; IntMPA 82*

Shields, James
American. Politician
b. May 10, 1810 in Ireland
d. Jun 1, 1879 in Oregon
Source: *AmBi; ApCAB; BiAuS; BiDrAC; DcAmB; Drake; TwCBDA; WhAm H; WhAmP*

Shields, Larry
American. Musician
b. May 17, 1893 in New Orleans, Louisiana
d. Nov 22, 1953 in Hollywood, California
Source: *WhoJazz 72*

Shimkin, Leon
American. Publisher
b. Apr 7, 1907 in Brooklyn, New York
Source: *AmAu&B; CurBio 54; St&PR 75; WhoAm 74, 76, 78, 80, 82; WhoWorJ 72*

Shinburn, Max
[Jimmy Valentine]
American. Criminal
b. 1842
d. 1916
Source: *BioIn 8*

Shinn, Everett
American. Artist
b. Nov 7, 1876 in Woodstown, New Jersey
d. May 1, 1953 in New York, New York
Source: *ChPo, S2; CurBio 51, 53; DcAmB S5; DcCAA 71; IlsBYP; IlsCB 1744, 1946; WhAm 3*

Shipler, Guy Emery
American. Religious Leader
b. 1882?
d. Apr 18, 1968 in Arcadia, California
Source: *BioIn 8*

Shippen, Katherine Binney
American. Children's Author
b. Apr 1, 1892
d. Feb 20, 1980 in Suffern, New York
Source: *AnCL; AuBYP; ConAu 5R, 93; CurBio 54; MorJA; SmATA 1; Str&VC*

Shippen, Margaret
"Peggy"
American. Wife of Benedict Arnold
b. 1760 in Philadelphia, Pennsylvania
d. 1804
Source: *AmBi; BioIn 2, 3, 8, 9, 10, 11; InWom*

Shiras, George, Jr.
American. Supreme Court Justice
b. Jan 26, 1832 in Pittsburgh, Pennsylvania
d. Sep 2, 1924 in Pittsburgh, Pennsylvania
Source: *ApCAB SUP; DcAmB; TwCBDA; WebAB; WhAm 1*

Shire, Talia Rose Coppola
[Mrs. Jack Schwartzman]
American. Actress
Played Adrian in *Rocky* films.
b. Apr 25, 1946 in Jamaica, New York
Source: *IntMPA 82; NewYTBS 82; WhoAm 78, 80, 82; WhoHol A*

Shirelles, The
[Doris Kenner Jackson; Beverly Lee; Addie "Micki" Harris McFaddenShirley Alston Owens]
American. Singing Group
Hits include "Will You Love Me Tomorrow," 1961; "Soldier Boy," 1962.
Source: *BiDAmM; RkOn; WhoRock 81*

Shirer, William L(awrence)
American. Author, Journalist
b. Feb 23, 1904 in Chicago, Illinois
Source: *AmAu&B; Au&Wr 71; AuBYP; ConAu 9R; CurBio 41, 62; IntWW 74; OxAmL; REn; REnAL; TwCA SUP; WebAB; Who 74; WhoAm 74; WhoWor 74; WrDr 76*

Shirley, George Irving
American. Opera Singer
b. Apr 18, 1934 in Indianapolis, Indiana
Source: *BioNews 75; IntWW 74; NewYTBE 72; WhoAm 74, 76, 78, 80, 82; WhoBlA 75; WhoMus 72; WhoWor 74*

Shirley, James
English. Poet
b. 1596 in London, England
d. Oct 29, 1666 in London, England
Source: *Alli; AtlBL; BrAu; CasWL; Chambr 1; ChPo; CnE&AP; CnThe; CroE&S; CrtT 1; CyWA; DcEnA; DcEnL; DcEuL; DcLEL; EvLB; McGEWD; MouLC 1; NewC; OxEng; OxThe; Pen ENG; PlP&P; REn; REnWD; WebE&AL*

Shirley, Jerry
see: Humble Pie

Shirley-Quirk, John Stanton
American. Opera Singer
b. Aug 28, 1931
Source: *Who 74; WhoMus 72; WhoWor 74*

Shively, George Jenks
Author, Editor
b. 1893
d. Apr 11, 1980 in Bronxville, New York
Source: *ConAu 97*

Shoemaker, Vaughn Richard
American. Cartoonist
b. Aug 11, 1902 in Chicago, Illinois
Source: *AmAu&B; WhoAm 74, 76, 78, 80, 82; WhoAmA 73; WhoWor 74*

Shoemaker, Willie (William Lee)
American. Jockey
Has rode over 8,000 winning horses.
b. Aug 19, 1931 in Fabens, Texas
Source: *CelR 73; CurBio 66; NewYTBE 70, 73; WhoAm 82*

Sholes, Christopher Latham
American. Journalist, Printer
Invented typewriter, 1868.
b. Feb 14, 1819 in Mooresburg, Pennsylvania
d. Feb 17, 1890 in Milwaukee, Wisconsin
Source: *AmBi; ApCAB; DcAmB; WebAB; WhAm H*

Sholokhov, Mikhail Aleksandrovich
Russian. Author
b. May 24, 1905 in Kruzhilin, Russia
Source: *CasWL; ClDMEL; ConAu 101; CurBio 42, 60; CyWA; DcRusL; EncWL; EvEuW; IntWW 74; LongCTC; ModSL 1; Pen EUR; REn; TwCA, SUP; TwCW; Who 74; WhoTwCL; WhoWor 74*

Shor, "Toots" (Bernard)
American. Restaurateur
b. May 6, 1905 in Philadelphia, Pennsylvania
d. Jan 24, 1977 in New York, New York
Source: *BusPN; WhoAm 74*

Shore, Dinah
[Frances Rose Shore]
"Fannie"
American. Singer, Actress
Has won 10 Emmys; wrote *Someone's in the Kitchen with Dinah,* 1971.
b. Mar 1, 1917 in Winchester, Tennessee
Source: *BioNews 74; BkPepl; CelR 73; CurBio 42, 66; FilmgC; InWom; IntMPA 75, 76, 77, 78, 79, 80, 81, 82; MotPP; NewYTBE 72; WhoAm 74, 76, 78, 80, 82; WhoHol A*

Shore, Eddie
Canadian. Hockey Player
b. Nov 25, 1902 in Fort Qu'Appelle, SK
Source: *WhoHcky 73*

Shorr, Kehat
Israeli. Murdered Olympic Team Member
b. 1919? in Romania
d. Sep 5, 1972 in Munich, Germany (West)
Source: *NF*

Shorrock, Glenn
see: Little River Band, The

Short, Bobby
[Robert Waltrip Short]
American. Musician
b. Sep 15, 1926 in Danville, Illinois
Source: *CelR 73; CurBio 72; WhoAm 82; WhoBlA 75*

Shostakovich, Dmitri Dmitryevich
Russian. Composer
b. Sep 25, 1906 in Saint Petersburg, Russia
d. Aug 9, 1975 in Moscow, U.S.S.R.
Source: *CurBio 41; DcCM; DcFM; IntWW 74; NewYTBE 73; OxFilm; WhAm 6; Who 74; WhoMus 72; WhoWor 74; WorEFlm*

Shostakovich, Maksim
Russian. Conductor
b. 1939?
Source: *BioIn 7, 8*

Shotwell, Louisa R
American. Children's Author
b. 1902 in Chicago, Illinois
Source: *ConAu 1R, 4NR; MorBMP; SmATA 3; ThrBJA; WrDr 76*

Shrady, Henry M
American. Sculptor
b. Oct 24, 1871 in New York, New York
d. Apr 12, 1922 in Elmsford, New York
Source: *AmBi; DcAmB; TwCBDA; WhAm 1*

Shrapnel, Henry
English. Artillery Officer
b. 1761
d. 1842
Source: *WebBD 80*

Shrimpton, Jean Rosemary
English. Model
b. 1942 in High Wycombe, England
Source: *BioIn 7, 8; WhoHol A*

Shriner, Herb
American. TV Personality, Humorist
b. May 29, 1918 in Toledo, Ohio
d. Apr 23, 1970 in Delray Beach, Florida
Source: *AmSCAP 66; BiE&WWA; NewYTBE 70; WhAm 5; WhScrn 74, 77; WhoHol B*

Shriver, Eunice Mary Kennedy
[Mrs. Robert Sargent Shriver]
American. Civic Worker
Vice-president, Joseph P Kennedy, Jr. Foundation, 1950--.
b. 1921 in Brookline, Massachusetts
Source: *WhoAm 74, 76, 78, 80, 82; WhoAmW 77*

Shriver, Pam(ela Howard)
American. Tennis Player
b. Jul 4, 1962 in Baltimore, Maryland
Source: *BioIn 11; NewYTBS 82*

Shriver, (Robert) Sargent
American. Lawyer, Public Official
First director of Peace Corps, 1961-66.
b. Nov 9, 1915 in Westminster, Maryland
Source: *IntWW 74; NewYTBE 72; Who 82; WhoAm 76, 78, 80, 82; WhoAmP 73; WhoWor 74*

Shubert, Jacob J
American. Theatrical Manager, Producer
b. Aug 15, 1880 in Syracuse, New York
d. Dec 26, 1963 in New York, New York
Source: *EncAB-H; OxThe; PlP&P; WhAm 4*

Shubert, Lee
American. Theater Owner, Producer
b. Mar 15, 1875 in Syracuse, New York
d. Dec 25, 1953 in New York, New York
Source: *DcAmB S5; OxThe; PlP&P; WebAB; WhAm 3; WhoStg 1908*

Shukairy, Ahmed
Palestinian. Founder of PLO
b. 1908 in Acre, Palestine
d. Feb 26, 1980 in Amman, Jordan
Source: *AnObit 1980*

Shukshin, Vasilii Makarovich
Russian. Actor, Author, Director
b. 1929 in U.S.S.R.
d. Oct 2, 1974 in Caucasus, U.S.S.R.
Source: *BioIn 10, 11*

Shula, Don Francis
American. Football Coach
Co-owner, head coach, Miami Dolphins, 1970--
b. Jan 4, 1930 in Grand River, Ohio
Source: *BioNews 74; CelR 73; CurBio 74; NewYTBE 73; WhoAm 74, 76, 78, 80, 82; WhoS&SW 73*

Shulman, Irving
American. Author, Educator
b. May 21, 1913 in Brooklyn, New York
Source: *AmAu&B; AmNov; ConAu 1R; CurBio 56; SmATA 13; WhoAm 74; WhoE 74; WhoWorJ 72; WrDr 76*

Shulman, Max
American. Humorist
b. Mar 14, 1919 in Saint Paul, Minnesota
Source: *AmAu&B; AmNov; ConAu 89; CurBio 59; IntMPA 75, 76, 77, 78, 79, 80, 81, 82; NotNAT; St&PR 75; WhoAm 74; WhoE 74*

Shulman, Morton
Canadian. Author
b. Apr 2, 1925 in Toronto, ON
Source: *AmM&WS 73P; AuNews 1; ConAu 25R; WhoMW 74*

Shulsky, Sam
American. Financial Columnist
b. 1907?
d. Apr 21, 1982 in Silver Spring, Maryland
Source: *NF*

Shultz, George Pratt
American. Government Official
Secretary of State following Alexander Haig's resignation, 1982--.
b. Dec 13, 1920 in New York, New York
Source: *AmEA 74; AmM&WS 73S; BiDrUSE; CelR 73; CngDr 74; CurBio 69; IntWW 74; NewYTBE 70, 72, 73; Who 82; WhoAm 74; WhoAmP 73; WhoGov 72; WhoS&SW 73; WhoWor 74*

Shumlin, Herman Elliott
American. Theatrical Producer, Director
b. Dec 6, 1898 in Atwood, Colorado
d. Jun 14, 1979 in New York, New York
Source: *BiE&WWA; BioIn 11; CurBio 41, 79; FilmgC; NewYTBS 79; NotNAT; WhAm 7; WhoAm 74, 76, 78; WhoThe 77; WorEFlm*

Shuster, Alvin
American. Journalist
b. Jan 25, 1930 in Washington, DC
Source: *WhoAm 78*

Shuster, Frank
[Wayne and Shuster]
Canadian. Comedian
b. 1916
Source: *CreCan 2*

Shuster, Joe
American. Comic Strip Artist
b. Jul 10, 1914 in Toronto, ON
Source: *WorECom*

Shute, Nevil
[Nevil Shute Norway]
English. Author, Aeronautical Engineer
b. Jan 17, 1899 in Ealing, England
d. Jan 12, 1960 in Victoria, Australia
Source: *ConAu 93, 102; CurBio 42, 60; DcLEL; EvLB; FilmgC; LongCTC; ModBrL; NewC; Pen ENG; REn; TwCA, SUP; TwCW; WhAm 3, 4; WhoTwCL*

Shutt, Steve (Stephen John)
Canadian. Hockey Player
b. Jul 1, 1952 in Toronto, ON
Source: *HocReg; WhoAm 78, 80, 82*

Shutta, Ethel
American. Actress
b. Dec 1, 1896 in New York, New York
d. Feb 5, 1976
Source: *BioIn 9, 10; NewYTBE 71*

Shuttlesworth, Dorothy Edwards
American. Children's Author
b. 1907 in Brooklyn, New York
Source: *AuBYP; ConAu 1R, 4NR; ForWC 70; SmATA 3*

Shuttlesworth, Fred Lee
American. Clergyman, Civil Rights Leader
b. 1922
Source: *BioIn 7, 11*

Sibelius, Jean
Finnish. Composer
b. Dec 8, 1865 in Tavastehus, Finland
d. Sep 20, 1957 in Jarvenpaa, Finland
Source: *AtlBL; DcCM; REn; WhAm 3*

Sibley, Hiram
American. Businessman
b. Feb 6, 1807 in North Adams, Massachusetts
d. Jul 12, 1888 in Rochester, New York
Source: *AmBi; ApCAB; DcAmB; NatCAB 4; TwCBDA; WebAB; WhAm H*

Sickles, Daniel Edgar
American. Public Official, Soldier
b. Oct 20, 1825 in New York, New York
d. May 3, 1914 in New York, New York
Source: *AmBi; ApCAB; BiAuS; BiDrAC; DcAmB; Drake; TwCBDA; WebAB; WhAm 1; WhAmP*

Sickmann, Rodney Virgil
[The Hostages]
"Rocky"
American. Former Hostage in Iran
b. 1958?
Source: *BioIn 12; NewYTBS 81*

Siddal, Elizabeth Eleanor (Lizzie)
[Mrs. Dante Gabriel Rossetti]
English. Model, Artist
b. 1834 in Sheffield, England
d. Feb 10, 1862
Source: *BioIn 9, 10, 11; DcVicP; WomArt*

Siddons, Sarah Kemble
English. Actress
b. Jul 5, 1755 in Brecon, Wales
d. Jun 8, 1831 in London, England
Source: *ChPo S1; DcEuL; HerW; InWom; NewC; NewCol 75; OxThe; PlP&P; REn*

Sidey, Hugh Swanson
American. Author
b. Sep 3, 1927 in Greenfield, Iowa
Source: *WhoAm 74, 76, 78, 80, 82; WhoWor 74*

Sidgwick, Henry
English. Educator, Author
b. May 31, 1838 in Yorkshire, England
d. Aug 28, 1900 in Cambridge, England
Source: *Alli SUP; BbD; BiD&SB; BiDPara; BrAu 19; CasWL; Chambr 3; DcEnA, AP; DcEuL; DcLEL; EvLB; NewC; OxEng; Pen ENG*

Sidney, George
American. Motion Picture Director, Producer
b. Oct 4, 1916 in New York, New York
Source: *BiDFilm; CmMov; DcFM; FilmgC; IntMPA 75, 76, 77, 78, 79, 80, 81, 82; MovMk; WhoAm 74, 76, 78, 80, 82; WorEFlm*

Sidney, Sir Philip
English. Poet, Statesman
Wrote pastoral *Arcadia,* 1590, and over 100 sonnets.
b. Nov 30, 1554 in Kent, England
d. Oct 17, 1586 in Arnheim, Netherlands
Source: *Alli; AtlBL; BbD; BiD&SB; BrAu; CasWL; Chambr 1; ChPo, S2; CnE&AP; CroE&S; CrtT 1; CyWA; DcEnA; DcEnL; DcEuL; DcLEL; EvLB; MouLC 1; NewC; OxEng; Pen ENG; RAdv 1; REn; WebE&AL*

Sidney, Sylvia
[Sophia Kosow]
American. Actress
b. Aug 8, 1910 in New York, New York
Source: *BiDFilm; BiE&WWA; CelR 73; FilmgC; InWom; IntMPA 75, 76, 77, 78, 79, 80, 81, 82; MotPP; MovMk; NotNAT; OxFilm; ThFT; WhoAm 82; WhoHol A; WhoThe 77; WomWMM; WorEFlm*

Siegel, "Bugsy" (Benjamin)
American. Gangster
b. Feb 28, 1906 in Brooklyn, New York
d. Jun 20, 1947 in Beverly Hills, California
Source: *BioIn 1, 2, 8, 11; Blood*

Siegel, Janis
see: Manhattan Transfer

Siegel, Jerry
American. Cartoonist
b. Oct 17, 1914 in Cleveland, Ohio
Source: *BioIn 10; WorECom*

Siegel, Stanley E
American. Author, Educator
b. May 7, 1928 in Long Branch, New Jersey
Source: *ConAu 41R; WhoWorJ 72*

Siegmeister, Elie
American. Composer, Conductor
b. Jan 15, 1909 in New York, New York
Source: *AmAu&B; AmSCAP 66; AuBYP; BiE&WWA; ConAu 1R, 1NR; DcCM; NotNAT; WhoAm 74, 76, 78, 80, 82; WhoMus 72; WhoWorJ 72; WrDr 76*

Siemens, (Ernst) Werner von
German. Inventor, Industrialist
Developed electroplating process, 1841, and electric dynamo.
b. Dec 13, 1816 in Lenthe, Germany
d. Dec 6, 1892 in Berlin, Germany
Source: *BioIn 7; DcScB; NewCol 75*

Siemens, Sir William
English. Inventor, Physicist, Engineer
Developed open-hearth steelmaking process, 1861.
b. Apr 4, 1823 in Lenthe, Germany
d. Nov 18, 1883 in London, England
Source: *AsBiEn; NewCol 75; WebBD 80*

Sienkiewicz, Henryk
Polish. Author
b. May 5, 1846 in Okrzejska, Poland
d. Nov 15, 1916 in Vevey, Switzerland
Source: *AtlBL; BbD; BiD&SB; CasWL; ClDMEL; CyWA; DcBiA; DcEuL; EncWL; EuAu; EvEuW; LongCTC; ModSL 2; Pen EUR; REn*

Siepi, Cesare
Italian. Opera Singer
b. Feb 10, 1923 in Milan, Italy
Source: *BiE&WWA; CelR 73; CurBio 55; NewYTBE 71; WhoAm 74, 76, 78, 80, 82; WhoHol A; WhoMus 72; WhoWor 74*

Sigismond
Holy Roman Emperor
Source: *NewCol 75; WebBD 80*

Signac, Paul
French. Artist
b. Nov 11, 1863 in Paris, France
d. Aug 15, 1935 in Paris, France
Source: *AtlBL; BioIn 2, 3, 4, 5, 6, 8; REn*

Signorelli, Luca
Italian. Artist
b. 1441 in Cortona, Italy
d. Oct 16, 1523 in Cortona, Italy
Source: *AtlBL; BioIn 1, 5, 9; REn*

Signoret, Simone
[Simone Henrietta Charlotte Montand]
German. Actress
b. Mar 25, 1921 in Wiesbaden, Germany
Source: *BiDFilm; CelR 73; CurBio 60; FilmgC; InWom; IntMPA 75, 76, 77, 78, 79, 80, 81, 82; IntWW 74; MotPP; MovMk; OxFilm; Who 82; WhoAm 74, 76, 78, 80, 82; WhoHol A; WhoWor 74; WorEFlm*

Sigourney, Lydia Howard
American. Poet
b. Sep 1, 1791 in Norwich, Connecticut
d. Jun 10, 1865 in Hartford, Connecticut
Source: *AmBi; AmWom; ApCAB; BioIn 3, 4, 7, 9, 11; DcAmB; Drake; NatCAB 1; NotAW; TwCBDA; WebAB; WhAm H*

Sihanouk, Norodom
see: Norodom Sihanouk

Sikma, Jack Wayne
American. Basketball Player
b. Nov 14, 1955 in Kankakee, Illinois
Source: *OfNBA; WhoAm 82*

Sikorsky, Igor Ivanovich
American. Aeronautical Engineer
Developed first successful helicopter, 1939.
b. May 25, 1889 in Kiev, Russia
d. Oct 26, 1972 in Easton, Connecticut
Source: *AmAu&B; AmM&WS 73P; CurBio 40, 56, 72; NewYTBE 72; WebAB; WhAm 5*

Silas, Paul
American. Basketball Player, Coach
Head coach, San Diego Clippers, 1980--.
b. Jul 12, 1943 in Prescott, Arizona
Source: *OfNBA; WhoBbl 73*

Siles Zuazo, Hernan
Bolivian. Politician
President, 1956-60, 1982--.
b. Mar 19, 1914 in La Paz, Bolivia
Source: *CurBio 58; EncLatA; IntWW 74, 75, 76, 77, 78, 79, 80, 81; NewYTBS 82; WhoWor 74*

Silhouette, Etienne de
French. Tax Reformist
b. 1709
d. 1767
Source: *REn; WebBD 80*

Silk, Dave
[United States Olympic Hockey Team-1980]
American. Hockey Player
b. Jan 1, 1958 in Boston, Massachusetts
Source: *HocReg; NewYTBS 82*

Silk, George
American. Photographer, Journalist
b. Nov 17, 1916 in Levin, New Zealand
Source: *WhoAm 74, 76, 78, 80, 82*

Silkin, Jon
English. Poet
b. 1930 in London, England
Source: *BioIn 7, 10; ConAu 5R; ConLC 2, 6*

Silkwood, Karen
American. Nuclear Technician
Exposed to radiation on job; death raised suspicions.
b. 1946
d. Nov 13, 1974 in Oklahoma
Source: *BioIn 11*

Sill, Edward Rowland
American. Poet, Educator
b. Apr 29, 1841 in Windsor, Connecticut
d. Feb 27, 1887 in Cleveland, Ohio
Source: *Alli, SUP; AmAu; AmAu&B; AmBi; ApCAB; BiD&SB; Chambr 3; ChPo, S1, S2; CnDAL; DcAmAu; DcAmB; DcLEL; DcNAA; OhA&B; OxAmL; REn; REnAL; TwCBDA; WhAm H*

Sillanpaa, Frans E
Finnish. Author
b. Sep 16, 1888 in Hameenkyro, Finland
d. Jun 3, 1964 in Helsinki, Finland
Source: *CasWL; ConAu 93; CurBio 40, 64; EncWL; EvEuW; Pen EUR; REn; TwCA, SUP; TwCW; WhAm 4*

Silliman, Benjamin
American. Educator
b. Aug 8, 1779 in Trumbull, Connecticut
d. Nov 24, 1864 in New Haven, Connecticut
Source: *Alli; AmAu; AmBi; ApCAB; BbD; BbtC; CyAL 1; DcAmAu; DcAmB; DcNAA; Drake; OxCan; REnAL; TwCBDA; WebAB; WhAm H*

Silliphant, Stirling Dale
American. Screenwriter, Producer
b. Jan 16, 1918 in Detroit, Michigan
Source: *CmMov; ConAu 73; IntMPA 76, 77, 78, 79, 80, 81, 82; WhoAm 82*

Sillitoe, Alan
English. Author
b. Mar 4, 1928 in Nottinghamshire, England
Source: *Au&Wr 71; AuNews 1; ConAu 9R; ConLC 1, 3, 6; ConNov 72, 76; ConP 70, 75; EncWL; IntWW 74; LongCTC; ModBrL, SUP; NewC; Pen ENG; RAdv 1; REn; TwCW; WebE&AL; Who 74; WhoTwCL; WhoWor 74; WorAu; WrDr 76*

Sillman, Leonard
American. Producer, Actor, Author
b. May 9, 1908 in Detroit, Michigan
d. Jan 23, 1982 in New York, New York
Source: *BiE&WWA; EncMT; NewYTBS 82; NotNAT; WhoThe 72, 77*

Sills, Beverly
"Bubbles"
American. Opera Singer
b. May 25, 1929 in Brooklyn, New York
Source: *CelR 73; CurBio 69; IntWW 74; NewYTBE 71; Who 82; WhoAm 74, 76, 78, 80, 82; WhoAmW 77; WhoE 74; WhoGov 72; WhoMus 72; WhoWor 74*

Sills, Milton
American. Actor
b. Jan 10, 1882 in Chicago, Illinois
d. Sep 15, 1930 in Santa Barbara, California
Source: *DcAmB; DcNAA; Film 1; FilmgC; MovMk; TwYS; WhAm 1; WhScrn 74, 77; WhoHol B*

Silone, Ignazio
[Secondo Tranquilli]
Italian. Author
b. May 1, 1900 in Pescina, Italy
d. 1978 in Geneva, Switzerland
Source: *CasWL; ClDMEL; CnMD; CnMWL; ConAu 25R; ConAu P-2; ConLC 4; CyWA; EncWL; EvEuW; IntWW 74; LongCTC; ModRL; NewYTBE 72; Pen EUR; REn; TwCA, SUP; TwCW; Who 74; WhoTwCL; WhoWor 74*

Silver, Abba Hillel
American. Rabbi
b. Jan 28, 1893 in Lithuania
d. Nov 28, 1963 in Cleveland, Ohio
Source: *AmAu&B; ConAu 1R; CurBio 41, 63, 64; OhA&B; WhAm 4*

Silver, Eliezer
American. Religious Leader
b. 1881
d. 1968
Source: *BioIn 8*

Silver, Horace Ward Martin Tavares
American. Jazz Musician
b. Sep 28, 1928 in Norwalk, Connecticut
Source: *AmSCAP 66; WhoAm 74, 76, 78, 80, 82; WhoBlA 75; WhoE 74*

Silver Bullet Band, The
see: Seger, Bob

Silvera, Frank
American. Actor
b. 1914 in Kingston, Jamaica
d. Jun 11, 1970 in Pasadena, California
Source: *BiE&WWA; BlkAW; FilmgC; MovMk; NewYTBE 70; WhAm 5; WhScrn 74, 77; WhoHol B*

Silverberg, Robert
American. Author
b. in New York, New York
Source: *AmAu&B; AuBYP; ConAu 1R, 1NR; ConLC 7; SmATA 13; ThrBJA; WhoAm 74, 76, 78, 80, 82*

Silverheels, Jay
American. Actor
Played Tonto in *Lone Ranger* movies and TV series, 1948-61.
b. 1922 in ON
d. Mar 5, 1980 in Woodland Hills, California
Source: *FilmgC; WhoHol A*

Silverman, Fred
American. TV Executive
President, NBC, 1978-81.
b. Sep 13, 1937 in New York, New York
Source: *BioIn 9, 10, 11; CurBio 78; IntMPA 77, 78, 79, 80, 81, 82; WhoAm 74, 76, 78, 80, 82*

Silverman, Sime
American. Publisher
b. May 18, 1873 in Cortland, New York
d. Sep 22, 1933 in Los Angeles, California
Source: *AmAu&B; DcAmB; WebAB; WhAm HA, 4*

Silvers, Phil
[Philip Silversmith]
American. Comedian
Played Sergeant Bilko in TV series "You'll Never Get Rich," 1955-59.
b. May 11, 1911 in Brooklyn, New York
Source: *AmSCAP 66; BiE&WWA; CelR 73; CmMov; CurBio 57; EncMT; FilmgC; IntMPA 75, 76, 77, 78, 79, 80, 81, 82; MotPP; MovMk; NewYTBE 72; NotNAT; WhoAm 74, 76, 78, 80, 82; WhoHol A; WhoThe 77*

Silverstein, Alvin
American. Children's Author
b. Dec 30, 1933 in New York, New York
Source: *ConAu 49, 2NR; ConLC 17; SmATA 8*

Silverstein, Elliot
American. Motion Picture Producer
b. 1927 in Boston, Massachusetts
Source: *WorEFlm*

Silvia
Swedish. Queen
b. 1944
Source: *BioIn 10, 11*

Sim, Alastair
English. Actor, Motion Picture Producer
b. Oct 9, 1900 in Edinburgh, Scotland
d. Aug 19, 1976 in London, England
Source: *CmMov; FilmgC; IntMPA 75; MotPP; MovMk; Who 74; WhoHol A; WhoThe 77; WhoWor 74*

Simenon, Georges
[Georges Sim]
Belgian. Author
b. Feb 13, 1903 in Liege, Belgium
Source: *Au&Wr 71; CasWL; CnMWL; ConAu 85; ConLC 1, 2, 3, 8, 18; CurBio 70; EncMys; EncWL; EvEuW; FilmgC; IntWW 74; LongCTC; ModRL; OxEng; OxFr; Pen EUR; REn; REnAL; TwCA, SUP; TwCW; Who 74; WhoTwCL; WhoWor 74*

Simeon
Biblical Character
Source: *Alli; BioIn 5, 8; NewCol 75; WebBD 80*

Simeone, Harry
American. Composer
b. May 9, 1911 in Newark, New Jersey
Source: *AmSCAP 66*

Simic, Charles
American. Poet
b. May 9, 1938 in Belgrade, Yugoslavia
Source: *ConAu 29R; ConLC 6; ConP 75; DrAP 75; WhoAm 82; WrDr 76*

Simionato, Guilietta
Italian. Opera Singer
b. May 12, 1916 in Forli, Italy
Source: *BioIn 5, 11; CurBio 60; WhoMus 72*

Simionescu, Mariana
[Mrs. Bjorn Borg]
Romanian. Tennis Player
Source: *BioIn 12*

Simmel, Georg
German. Sociologist, Philosopher
b. Mar 1, 1858 in Berlin, Germany
d. Sep 26, 1918 in Strassburg, Germany
Source: *BioIn 4, 5, 7, 11; McGEWB; NewCol 75; TwCA SUP*

Simmer, Charlie (Charles Robert)
Canadian. Hockey Player
b. Mar 20, 1954 in Terrace Bay, ON
Source: *HocReg*

Simmons, Al(oysius Harry)
"Bucketfoot Al"
American. Baseball Player
b. May 22, 1903 in Milwaukee, Wisconsin
d. May 26, 1956 in Milwaukee, Wisconsin
Source: *BaseEn; BioIn 2, 3, 4, 5, 6, 7, 9, 10; WhoProB 73*

Simmons, Calvin
"Maestro Kid"
American. Conductor
Musical director, Oakland Symphony.
b. Apr 27, 1950 in San Francisco, California
d. Aug 21, 1982 in Connery Pond, New York
Source: *InB&W 80; NewYTBS 82; WhoBlA 77; WhoWest 80*

Simmons, Franklin
American. Sculptor
b. Jan 11, 1839 in Webster, Maine
d. Dec 8, 1913 in Rome, Italy
Source: *AmBi; ApCAB; DcAmB; TwCBDA; WhAm 1*

Simmons, Jean
English. Actress
Starred in *The Robe*, 1953.
b. Jan 31, 1929 in London, England
Source: *BiDFilm; BioNews 74; CelR 73; CmMov; CurBio 52; FilmgC; InWom; IntMPA 75, 76, 77, 78, 79, 80, 81, 82; MotPP; MovMk; OxFilm; Who 74; WhoAm 74, 76, 78, 80, 82; WhoHol A; WorEFlm*

Simmons, Richard
"The Clown Prince of Fitness"; "The Pied Piper of Pounds"
American. TV Personality, Author
Wrote *Never-Say-Diet-Book,* 1980.
b. Jul 12, 1948? in New Orleans, Louisiana
Source: *CurBio 82; NewYTBS 81*

Simms, Ginny (Virginia E)
American. Singer, Radio Personality
b. May 25, 1916 in San Antonio, Texas
Source: *FilmgC; InWom; MotPP*

Simms, Hilda
American. Actress
b. Apr 15, 1920 in Minneapolis, Minnesota
Source: *BiE&WWA; CurBio 44; InWom; NotNAT; WhoHol A; WhoThe 77*

Simms, Lu Ann
American. Actress
b. 1932
Source: *InWom*

Simms, Phil(ip)
American. Football Player
b. Nov 3, 1955 in Lebanon, Kentucky
Source: *NewYTBS 79*

Simms, William Gilmore
American. Author
b. Apr 17, 1806 in Charleston, South Carolina
d. Jun 11, 1870 in Charleston, South Carolina
Source: *Alli; AmAu; AmAu&B; AmBi; ApCAB; BbD; BiD&SB; BiDSA; CasWL; Chambr 3; ChPo, S1, S2; CnDAL; CyAl 2; CyWA; DcAmAu; DcAmB; DcBiA; DcEnL; DcLEL; DcNAA; Drake; EvLB; HsB&A, SUP; OxAmL; OxEng; Pen AM; REn; REnAL; TwCBDA; WebAB; WebE&AL; WhAm H, 3*

Simon, Saint
Apostle of Jesus
Source: *NewCol 75*

Simon, Abbey
American. Musician
b. Jan 8, 1922 in New York, New York
Source: *WhoAm 82; WhoMus 72*

Simon, Carly
American. Singer, Songwriter
Hits include "Anticipation," 1972; "Nobody Does It Better," 1977.
b. Jun 25, 1945 in New York, New York
Source: *BkPepl; CelR 73; HerW; NewYTBS 74; WhoAm 74, 76, 78, 80, 82*

Simon, Claude
French. Author
b. Oct 10, 1913 in Tananarive, Madagascar
Source: *CasWL; ConAu 89; ConLC 4; EncWL; IntWW 74; ModRL; Pen EUR; REn; TwCW; WhoTwCL; WhoWor 74*

Simon, Herbert Alexander
American. Psychologist, Professor
b. Jun 15, 1916 in Milwaukee, Wisconsin
Source: *AmM&WS 73S; ConAu 13R; IntWW 74; WhoAm 74, 76, 78, 80, 82; WhoWor 74*

Simon, Joe
American. Singer
b. Sep 2, 1943 in Simmesport, Louisiana
Source: *DcBlPA; RkOn 2; WhoRock 81*

Simon, John Ivan
American. Film, Drama Critic
b. May 12, 1925 in Subotica, Yugoslavia
Source: *BiE&WWA; ConAu 21R; NotNAT; WhoAm 82; WhoThe 77; WorAu*

Simon, John Alan
American. President of Discovery Films
b. 1950
Source: *BioIn 12*

Simon, (Marvin) Neil
"Doc"
American. Dramatist
Wrote *The Odd Couple,* 1965; *The Goodbye Girl,* 1977.
b. Jul 4, 1927 in New York, New York
Source: *AmAu&B; AuNews 1; BiE&WWA; BkPepl; CelR 73; CnThe; ConAu 21R; ConDr 73; ConLC 6, 11; CroCD; CurBio 68; EncMT; FilmgC; IntMPA 75, 76, 77, 78, 79, 80, 81, 82; IntWW 74; McGEWD; ModAL; ModWD; NewCBMT; NewYTBE 70, 71; NotNAT; PlP&P, A; WebAB; Who 74; WhoAm 74, 76, 78, 80, 82; WhoThe 77; WhoWor 74; WorAu; WrDr 76*

Simon, Norma Feldstein
American. Children's Author
Source: *AuBYP; ConAu 5R; ForWC 70; SmATA 3*

Simon, Norton
American. Business Executive
b. Feb 5, 1907 in Portland, Oregon
Source: *CelR 73; CurBio 68; IntWW 74; NewYTBE 70; NewYTBS 74; WhoAmA 73*

Simon, Paul
[Simon and Garfunkel]
American. Composer, Singer, Actor
Wrote screenplay, score, and starred in film *One-Trick Pony,* 1980.
b. Nov 5, 1942 in Newark, New Jersey
Source: *BkPepl; CelR 73; NewYTBE 72; WhoAm 74, 76, 78, 80, 82; WhoWor 74*

Simon, Richard Leo
American. Publisher
b. Mar 6, 1899 in New York, New York
d. Jul 29, 1960 in Stamford, Connecticut
Source: *AmAu&B; CurBio 41, 60; WhAm 4*

Simon, Simone
French. Actress
b. Apr 23, 1913 in Marseilles, France
Source: *BiDFilm; FilmgC; HolP 30; IntMPA 75, 76, 77; MotPP; MovMk; OxFilm; ThFT; WorEFlm*

Simon, William E(dward)
American. Government Official
Secretary of Treasury, 1974-77.
b. Nov 27, 1927 in Paterson, New Jersey
Source: *ConAu 81; CurBio 74; IntWW 74; NewYTBE 73; WhoAm 74, 76, 78, 80, 82; WhoAmP 73*

Simon and Garfunkel
[Arthur Garfunkel; Paul Simon]
American. Singing Duo
Have sold over 20 million albums and singles.
Source: *EncPR&S; RkOn*

Simone, Nina
[Eunice Wayman]
American. Singer, Composer, Musician
b. Feb 21, 1933 in Tryon, North Carolina
Source: *AmSCAP 66; BioNews 74; CelR 73; CurBio 68; InWom; WhoAm 74; WhoBlA 75*

Simoneau, Leopold
Canadian. Opera Singer
b. May 3, 1918 in Quebec City, PQ
Source: *CanWW 82; CreCan 1; WhoWor 74*

Simonetta
Italian. Author, Fashion Designer
b. 1922 in Rome, Italy
Source: *InWom; IntWW 74; WorFshn*

Simonon, Paul
see: Clash, The

Simons, Howard
American. Newspaper Editor
b. Jun 3, 1928 in Albany, New York
Source: *ConAu 65; WhoAm 74, 76, 78, 80, 82; WhoS&SW 73*

Simpson, Adele Smithline
American. Fashion Designer
b. Dec 8, 1903 in New York, New York
Source: *CelR 73; CurBio 70; InWom; WhoAm 74, 76, 78, 80, 82; WorFshn*

Simpson, Alan Kooi
American. Senator
b. Sep 2, 1936 in Denver, Colorado
Source: *AlmAP 80; CngDr 79; WhoAm 80, 82; WhoAmP 73, 75, 77, 79; WhoGov 75, 77*

Simpson, Sir James Young
Scottish. Obstetrician
b. Jun 7, 1811 in Scotland
d. May 6, 1870 in London, England
Source: *AsBiEn*

Simpson, Louis
[Louis Aston Marantz Simpson]
American. Author
b. Mar 27, 1923 in Kingston, Jamaica
Source: *ChPo, S1; CnE&AP; ConAu 1R, 1NR; ConLC 4, 7, 9; ConP 70; CroCAP; DrAF 76; DrAP 75; ModAL, SUP; OxAmL; Pen AM; RAdv 1; REn; REnAL; WebE&AL; WhoAm 74, 76, 78, 80, 82; WhoE 74; WhoTwCL; WhoWor 74; WorAu; WrDr 76*

Simpson, O(renthal) J(ames)
American. Football Player, Actor
Named NFL player of decade, 1970's; starred in *The Towering Inferno,* 1974.
b. Jul 9, 1947 in San Francisco, California
Source: *BkPepl; CelR 73; CurBio 69; NewYTBE 70, 73; St&PR 75; WhoAm 74, 76, 78, 80, 82; WhoFtbl 74; WhoHol A*

Simpson, Valerie
American. Singer, Songwriter, Musician
b. 1946
Source: *BioNews 74; CelR 73*

Simpson, Wallis Warfield
[Duchess of Windsor]
American. Wife of Edward VIII
The divorcee for whom Edward VIII abdicated his throne, 1936.
b. Jun 19, 1896 in Blue Ridge Summit, Pennsylvania
Source: *InWom; WebAB*

Simpson, William Hood
American. Army Officer
b. May 19, 1888 in Weatherford, Texas
d. Aug 15, 1980 in San Antonio, Texas
Source: *AnObit 1980; CurBio 45, 80*

Sims, Billy Ray
American. Football Player
b. Sep 18, 1955 in Saint Louis, Missouri
Source: *BioIn 11*

Sims, James Marion
American. Scientist, Physician, Engineer
b. Jan 25, 1813 in Lancaster County, Kentucky
d. Nov 13, 1883 in New York, New York
Source: *Alli, SUP; AmBi; ApCAB; BiDSA; DcAmAu; DcAmB; DcNAA; TwCBDA; WebAB; WhAm H*

Sims, William Sowden
American. Military Leader
b. Oct 15, 1858 in Port Hope, ON
d. Sep 25, 1936 in Boston, Massachusetts
Source: *AmBi; DcAmB S2; DcNAA; EncAB-H; OxAmL; WebAB; WhAm 1*

Sims, "Zoot" (John Haley)
American. Jazz Musician
b. Oct 29, 1925 in Inglewood, California
Source: *CmpEPM; WhoAm 82*

Sinatra, Barbara Marx Spencer
American. Wife of Frank Sinatra
b. 1926
Source: *BioIn 10*

Sinatra, Christina
American. Daughter of Frank Sinatra
b. 1948
Source: *BioIn 10*

Sinatra, Frank (Francis Albert)
"Ol' Blue Eyes"
American. Singer, Actor
Won Oscar, 1953, for *From Here to Eternity.*
b. Dec 12, 1915 in Hoboken, New Jersey
Source: *AmSCAP 66; BiDFilm; BioNews 74; BkPepl; CelR 73; CmMov; CurBio 43, 60; EncAB-H; FilmgC; IntMPA 75, 76, 77, 78, 79, 80, 81, 82; IntWW 74; MotPP; MovMk; OxFilm; WebAB; Who 82; WhoAm 76, 78, 80, 82; WhoHol A; WhoWor 74; WorEFlm*

Sinatra, Frank, Jr. (Francis Albert)
American. Singer, Son of Frank Sinatra
b. 1944 in Jersey City, New Jersey
Source: *WhoHol A*

Sinatra, Nancy
American. Singer, Daughter of Frank Sinatra
Recorded "Something Stupid," with father, 1969.
b. Jun 8, 1940 in Jersey City, New Jersey
Source: *CelR 73; FilmgC; WhoAm 74; WhoHol A*

Sinclair, Gordon
Canadian. Journalist, Radio Commentator
b. Jun 3, 1900 in Toronto, ON
Source: *AuNews 1; BioNews 74; CanWW 70, 81, 82*

Sinclair, Jo, pseud.
[Ruth Seid]
American. Author
b. Jul 1, 1913 in Brooklyn, New York
Source: *AmAu&B; AmNov; ConAu 5R; ConNov 72, 76; CurBio 46; InWom; OhA&B; TwCA SUP; WhoAm 74; WrDr 76*

Sinclair, Madge
American. Actress
Source: *WhoHol A*

Sinclair, Upton Beall
[Clarke Fitch; Frederick Garrison; Arthur Stirling, pseuds.]
American. Author
Novel *The Jungle,* 1906, led to reform of food inspection laws.
b. Sep 20, 1878 in Baltimore, Maryland
d. Nov 25, 1968 in Bound Brook, New Jersey
Source: *AmAu&B; AmNov; AuBYP; BiDPara; CasWL; Chambr 3; ChPo S1; CnDAL; ConAmA; ConAmL; ConAu 5R, 25R; ConLC 1, 11, 15; CurBio 62, 69; CyWA; DcAmAu; DcLEL; EncAB-H; EncWL; EvLB; LongCTC; ModAL; OxAmL; OxEng; OxFilm; Pen AM; RAdv 1; REn; REnAL; SmATA 9; TwCA, SUP; TwCW; WebAB; WebE&AL; WhNAA; WhoTwCL; WorEFlm*

Sinden, Donald
English. Actor
b. Oct 9, 1923 in Plymouth, England
Source: *FilmgC; IntMPA 75, 76, 77, 78, 79, 80, 81, 82; Who 74; WhoHol A; WhoThe 77*

Sinding, Christian
Norwegian. Composer
b. Jan 11, 1856 in Kongsberg, Norway
d. Dec 3, 1941 in Oslo, Norway
Source: *CurBio 42*

Sinfield, Pete
see: King Crimson

Singer, Burns James Hyman
American. Poet
b. Apr 29, 1928 in New York, New York
d. Sep 8, 1964 in Plymouth, England
Source: *ConAu 89, 102; ConP 75; WorAu*

Singer, Isaac Bashevis
[Isaac Warshofsky, pseud.]
American. Author
Won Nobel Prize, 1978.
b. Jul 14, 1904 in Radzymin, Poland
Source: *AmAu&B; AmWr; AnCL; Au&Wr 71; AuBYP; AuNews 1, 2; CasWL; CelR 73; ChlLR 1; ConAu 1R, 5NR; ConLC 1, 3, 6, 9, 11, 15; ConNov 72, 76; DrAF 76; EncWL; IntWW 74; ModAL SUP; MorBMP; NewYTBE 70, 72; Pen AM; SmATA 3; ThrBJA; TwCW; WebAB; WebE&AL; Who 82; WhoAm 76, 78, 80, 82; WhoE 74; WhoTwCL; WhoWor 74; WorAu; WrDr 76*

Singer, Isaac Merrit
American. Inventor
Manufactured first domestic sewing machine, 1851.
b. Oct 27, 1811 in Rensselaer, New York
d. Jul 23, 1875 in Torquay, England
Source: *AmBi; ApCAB; DcAmB; TwCBDA; WebAB; WhAm H*

Singer, Jane Sherrod
American. Author
b. May 26, 1917 in Wichita Falls, Texas
Source: *ConAu 25R; ForWC 70; SmATA 4; WhoAmW 77; WhoWest 74*

Singher, Martial
French. Opera Singer
b. Aug 14, 1904 in Oloron St. Marie, France
Source: *CurBio 47; WhoAm 74, 76, 78, 80, 82; WhoMus 72; WhoWest 74; WhoWor 74*

Singleton, Ken(neth Wayne)
American. Baseball Player
b. Jun 10, 1947 in New York, New York
Source: *BaseEn; BioIn 11; WhoProB 73*

Singleton, Penny
[Dorothy McNulty]
American. Actress
b. Sep 15, 1908 in Philadelphia, Pennsylvania
Source: *BioNews 74; BusPN; FilmgC; HolP 30; IntMPA 75, 76, 77, 78, 79, 80, 81, 82; MotPP; MovMk; ThFT; WhoHol A*

Singleton, "Zutty" (Arthur James)
American. Musician
b. May 14, 1898 in Bunkie, Louisiana
d. Jul 14, 1975 in New York, New York
Source: *WhScrn 77; WhoJazz 72*

Sinyavsky, Andrei
[Abram Terts, pseud.]
Russian. Author, Critic
b. Oct 8, 1925 in Moscow, U.S.S.R.
Source: *ConAu 85; ConLC 8; EncWL; Pen EUR; TwCW; WorAu*

Sipe, Brian Winfield
American. Football Player
b. Aug 8, 1949 in San Diego, California
Source: *BioIn 12; FootReg; WhoAm 82*

Siple, Paul Allman
American. Explorer, Geographer
Originated wind-chill index.
b. Dec 18, 1908 in Montpelier, Ohio
d. Nov 25, 1968 in Arlington, Virginia
Source: *AmAu&B; CurBio 57, 69; OhA&B; WhAm 5*

Siqueiros, David A
Mexican. Artist
Used air brushes to apply paint to outdoor murals.
b. Dec 29, 1896 in Chihuahua, Mexico
d. Jan 6, 1974 in Cuernavaca, Mexico
Source: *BioIn 1, 2, 4, 5, 6, 7, 8, 9, 10; CurBio 59, 74; NewCol 75; NewYTBS 74; WhAm 6; WhoAmA 73; WhoS&SW 73*

Sirhan, Sirhan Bishara
Jordanian. Assassin of Robert Kennedy
b. 1944?
Source: *BioIn 10; Blood*

Sirica, John Joseph
American. Judge
Presided over Watergate trial, 1973.
b. Mar 19, 1904 in Waterbury, Connecticut
Source: *CngDr 74; CurBio 74; IntWW 74; NewYTBE 73; WhoAm 74, 76, 78, 80, 82; WhoS&SW 73*

Sirk, Douglas
[Dietlef Sierck]
Danish. Motion Picture Director
b. Apr 26, 1900 in Skagen, Denmark
Source: *BiDFilm; DcFM; IntMPA 77, 78, 79, 80, 81; OxFilm; WorEFlm*

Sirluck, Ernest
Canadian. Educator
b. Apr 25, 1918 in Winkler, MB
Source: *CanWW 82; ConAu 25R; DrAS 74E; LEduc 74; WhoAm 74; WhoWor 74; WhoWorJ 72*

Sironi, Mario
Italian. Artist
b. May 12, 1885 in Tempio Pausania, Sardinia
d. Aug 13, 1961 in Milan, Italy
Source: *ConArt; McGDA; ObitOF 79*

Sisakyan, Norayr M
Russian. Scientist
b. 1907
d. 1966
Source: *BioIn 7*

Sisco, Joseph John
American. Government Official
b. Oct 31, 1919 in Chicago, Illinois
Source: *CurBio 72; IntWW 74; USBiR 74; WhoAm 74, 76, 78, 80, 82; WhoAmP 73; WhoGov 72; WhoS&SW 73*

Sisler, George Harold
"Gorgeous George"
American. Baseball Player
b. Mar 24, 1893 in Manchester, Ohio
d. Mar 26, 1973 in Richmond Heights, Missouri
Source: *BaseEn; BioIn 2, 3, 4, 5, 6, 7, 8, 9, 10; WhoProB 73*

Sisley, Alfred
French. Artist
b. Oct 30, 1839 in Paris, France
d. Jan 29, 1899 in Moret, France
Source: *AtlBL; REn*

Sissle, Noble
American. Conductor, Songwriter
b. Jul 10, 1889 in Indianapolis, Indiana
d. Dec 17, 1975 in Tampa, Florida
Source: *AmSCAP 66; BlkAW; EncMT; WhScrn 77; WhoJazz 72*

Sissman, L(ouis) E(dward)
American. Poet, Essayist
b. Jan 1, 1928 in Detroit, Michigan
d. Mar 10, 1976 in Boston, Massachusetts
Source: *ConAu 21R, 65; ConLC 9, 18; DrAP 75; WrDr 76*

Sisson, Charles Hubert
English. Poet
b. Apr 22, 1914 in Bristol, England
Source: *Au&Wr 71; ConAu 1R, 3NR; ConLC 8; ConP 70, 75; WhoTwCL; WrDr 76*

Sitting Bull
American Indian. Sioux Chief
Organized Indian forces at Battle of Little Bighorn, 1876.
b. 1831 in Grand River, South Dakota
d. Dec 15, 1890 in Grand River, South Dakota
Source: *AmBi; ApCAB; DcAmB; EncAB-H; FilmgC; WebAB; WhAm H*

Sittler, Darryl Glen
Canadian. Hockey Player
Only player to collect 10 points in one game, Feb 7, 1976.
b. Sep 18, 1950 in Kitchener, ON
Source: *BioIn 10; NewYTBS 76; WhoAm 78, 80, 82; WhoHcky 73*

Sitwell, Dame Edith
English. Poet, Critic, Author
b. 1887 in Scarborough, England
d. Dec 9, 1964 in London, England
Source: *AnCL; AtlBL; CasWL; Chambr 3; ChPo, S1, S2; ClDMEL; CnMWL; ConAu 9R; ConLC 2; DcLEL; EncWL; EvLB; InWom; LongCTC; ModBrL, SUP; NewC; OxEng; Pen ENG; RAdv 1; REn; TwCA, SUP; TwCW; WebE&AL; WhAm 4; WhoTwCL*

Sitwell, Sir Osbert
English. Author
b. Dec 6, 1892 in London, England
d. May 4, 1969 in Montagnana, Italy
Source: *CasWL; ConAu 21R, 25R; ConAu P-2; CurBio 65, 69; DcLEL; EncWL; EvLB; LongCTC; ModBrL, SUP; NewC; OxEng; Pen ENG; RAdv 1; REn; TwCA, SUP; TwCW; WhAm 5; WhoTwCL*

Sitwell, Sir Sacheverell
English. Author, Art Critic
b. Nov 15, 1897 in Scarborough, England
Source: *Au&Wr 71; Chambr 3; ChPo, S2; CnE&AP; ConAu 21R; ConP 70, 75; DcLEL; EncWL; EvLB; IntWW 74; LongCTC; ModBrL, SUP; NewC; OxEng; Pen ENG; REn; TwCA, SUP; TwCW; Who 74; WhoTwCL; WhoWor 74; WrDr 76*

Sjoberg, Alf
Swedish. Motion Picture Director
b. Jun 21, 1903 in Stockholm, Sweden
d. Apr 17, 1980 in Stockholm, Sweden
Source: *AnObit 1980; BiDFilm; DcFM; EncWT; FilmgC; IntWW 74, 75, 76, 77, 78; OxFilm; WhoWor 74, 76, 78*

Sjostrom, Victor
Swedish. Motion Picture Director
b. Sep 20, 1879 in Silbodal, Sweden
d. Jan 3, 1960 in Stockholm, Sweden
Source: *BiDFilm; DcFM; Film 1; FilmgC; MovMk; OxFilm; WhoHol B; WorEFlm*

Sjowall, Maj
Swedish. Author, Poet
b. Sep 25, 1935 in Stockholm, Sweden
Source: *ConAu 65; ConLC 7; EncMys; NewYTBE 71*

Skaggs, M B
American. Founder of Safeway Stores
b. 1888
d. May 8, 1976 in Oakland, California
Source: *BioIn 10*

Skaggs, Ricky
American. Musician, Singer
Won 1982 CMA awards for best male vocalist and newcomer of year.
b. 1954? in Kentucky
Source: *NF*

Skelly, Hal
American. Actor
b. 1891 in Allegheny, Pennsylvania
d. Jun 16, 1934 in West Cornwall, Connecticut
Source: *WhScrn 74, 77; WhoHol B*

Skelton, John
British. Poet
b. 1460?
d. Jun 21, 1529 in Westminster, England
Source: *Alli; AtlBL; BiD&SB; BrAu; CasWL; Chambr 1; ChPo, S1; CnE&AP; CroE&S; CrtT 1; DcEnL; DcEuL; DcLEL; EvLB; McGEWD; MouLC 1; NewC; OxEng; OxThe; Pen ENG; PoLE; RAdv 1; REn; WebE&AL*

Skelton, "Red" (Richard)
American. Comedian, Actor
Master of pantomime and slapstick comedy.
b. Jul 18, 1913 in Vincennes, Indiana
Source: *AmSCAP 66; CelR 73; CmMov; CurBio 47; FilmgC; IntMPA 75, 76, 77; MotPP; MovMk; WhoAm 74, 76, 78, 80, 82; WhoHol A*

Skelton, Robin
English. Poet
b. Oct 12, 1925 in Yorkshire, England
Source: *Au&Wr 71; AuNews 2; CanWW 70; ChPo S1; CnE&AP; ConAu 5R; ConLC 13; ConP 70; DrAP 75; DrAS 74E; OxCan SUP; Who 74; WhoWest 74; WorAu; WrDr 76*

Skerritt, Tom (Thomas Roy)
American. Actor
b. Aug 25, 1933 in Detroit, Michigan
Source: *WhoAm 80, 82; WhoHol A*

Skidmore, Louis
American. Architect
b. Apr 8, 1897 in Lawrenceburg, Indiana
d. Sep 27, 1962 in Winter Haven, Florida
Source: *CurBio 51, 62; WhAm 4, 5*

Skinner, B(urrhus) F(rederic)
American. Psychologist, Author
Leading exponent of Behaviorism; father of programmed instruction.
b. Mar 20, 1904 in Susquehanna, Pennsylvania
Source: *AmAu&B; AmM&WS 73S, 78S; Au&Wr 71; BiDAmEd; CelR 73; ConAu 9R; CurBio 64, 79; EncAB-H; EncSF; IntWW 74, 75, 76, 77, 78; McGEWB; WebAB; Who 82; WhoAm 76, 78, 80, 82; WhoWor 74; WorAu 1970; WrDr 76, 80*

Skinner, Cornelia Otis
American. Actress, Author
b. May 30, 1901 in Chicago, Illinois
d. Jul 9, 1979 in New York, New York
Source: *AmAu&B; BiE&WWA; CelR 73; ChPo; ConAu 17R, 89; CurBio 42, 64; DcLEL; EvLB; FilmgC; InWom; IntWW 74; LongCTC; NotNAT; OxAmL; Pen AM; REn; REnAL; SmATA 2; TwCA SUP; TwCW; Who 74; WhoAm 74; WhoHol A; WhoThe 77; WhoWor 74; WrDr 76*

Skinner, Otis
American. Actor
b. Jun 28, 1858 in Cambridge, Massachusetts
d. Jan 4, 1942 in New York, New York
Source: *AmAu&B; CurBio 42; DcAmB S3; DcNAA; FamA&A; Film 1; FilmgC; OxAmL; OxThe; PlP&P; REn; REnAL; TwYS; WebAB; WhAm 1; WhScrn 74, 77; WhoHol B*

Skipworth, Alison
American. Actress
b. Jul 25, 1870? in London, England
d. Jul 5, 1952 in New York, New York
Source: *FilmgC; MovMk; ThFT; Vers B; WhScrn 74, 77; WhoHol B; WhoStg 1908*

Skolsky, Sidney
American. Journalist
Hollywood gossip columnist since 1933.
b. May 5, 1905 in New York, New York
Source: *CelR 73; ConAu 103; IntMPA 76, 77, 78, 79, 80, 81, 82; WhoAm 74, 76, 78, 80, 82; WhoWorJ 72*

Skorpen, Liespel Moak
American. Children's Author
b. Jul 1, 1935 in Berlin, Germany
Source: *ConAu 25R; SmATA 3*

Skouras, Spyros Panagiotes
American. Motion Picture Producer
b. Mar 28, 1893 in Skourokhori, Greece
d. Aug 16, 1971 in Mamaroneck, New York
Source: *CurBio 43, 71; DcFM; FilmgC; NewYTBE 71; OxFilm; WebAB; WhAm 5; WorEFlm*

Skrowaczewski, Stanislaw
Polish. Composer, Conductor
b. Oct 3, 1923 in Lwow, Poland
Source: *CelR 73; CurBio 64; IntWW 74; WhoAm 74, 76, 78, 80, 82; WhoMW 74; WhoMus 72; WhoWor 74*

Skulnik, Menasha
Polish. Actor
b. May 15, 1898? in Warsaw, Poland
d. Jun 4, 1970 in New York, New York
Source: *BiE&WWA; NewYTBE 70; WhAm 5; WhScrn 77*

Skurzynski, Gloria
American. Author
b. Jul 6, 1930 in Duquesne, Pennsylvania
Source: *ConAu 33R; SmATA 8*

Slade, Bernard, pseud.
[Bernard Slade Newbound]
Canadian. Dramatist
b. May 2, 1930 in Saint Catherines, ON
Source: *ConAu 81; NewYTBS 75; WhoAm 82*

Slaughter, Enos Bradsher
"Country"
American. Baseball Player
Outfielder, 1938-59; lifetime batting average .300.
b. Apr 27, 1916 in Roxboro, North Carolina
Source: *BaseEn; WhoProB 73*

Slaughter, Frank G
American. Author, Surgeon
b. Feb 25, 1908 in Washington, DC
Source: *AmAu&B; AmNov; AuNews 2; ConAu 5R, 5NR; CurBio 42; LongCTC; Pen AM; REnAL; TwCA SUP; Who 74; WhoAm 74, 76, 78, 80, 82; WhoWor 74; WrDr 76*

Slavenska, Mia
Yugoslav. Dancer
b. Feb 20, 1916 in Slavonski-Brod, Yugoslavia
Source: *CurBio 54; InWom; WhoAm 74, 76, 78, 80, 82*

Slavin, Mark
Israeli. Murdered Olympic Team Member
b. 1954? in U.S.S.R.
d. Sep 5, 1972 in Munich, Germany (West)
Source: *BioIn 9*

Slavitt, David R
[Henry Sutton, pseud.]
American. Author
b. Mar 23, 1935 in White Plains, New York
Source: *ConAu 21R; ConLC 5, 14; ConNov 72, 76; ConP 70, 75; DrAF 76; DrAP 75; WrDr 76*

Slayton, Donald Kent
"Deke"
American. Astronaut
Flew on Apollo mission that docked with Russian Soyuz spaceship, 1975.
b. Mar 1, 1924 in Sparta, Wisconsin
Source: *AmM&WS 73P; CelR 73; IntWW 74; WhoAm 74, 76, 78, 80, 82; WhoGov 72; WhoS&SW 73; WhoWor 74*

Slenczynska, Ruth
American. Musician
b. Jan 15, 1925 in Sacramento, California
Source: *InWom; WhoAmW 77; WhoMus 72*

Slezak, Leo
Czech. Opera Singer
b. Aug 18, 1875? in Schonberg, Moravia
d. Jun 1, 1946 in Egern, Germany
Source: *WhAm 2; WhScrn 74, 77; WhoHol B*

Slezak, Walter
American. Actor
b. May 3, 1902 in Vienna, Austria
Source: *BiE&WWA; CelR 73; CmMov; CurBio 55; EncMT; FilmgC; IntMPA 75, 76, 77, 78, 79, 80, 81, 82; MotPP; MovMk; NotNAT; Vers A; WhoHol A; WhoThe 77; WhoWor 74*

Slick, Grace Wing
[Jefferson Airplane; Mrs. Skip Johnson; Grace Barnett Wing]
American. Singer
Lead vocalist, Jefferson Starship, 1966--.
b. Oct 30, 1943 in Chicago, Illinois
Source: *BkPepl; CelR 73; WhoAm 74, 76, 78, 80, 82*

Slim, William Joseph
English. Governor General of Australia
b. Aug 6, 1891 in Bristol, England
d. Dec 14, 1970 in London, England
Source: *CurBio 45, 71; WhAm 5*

Slim Jim Phantom (Jim McDonnell)
see: Stray Cats

Sliwa, Curtis
"The Rock"
American. Founder of Guardian Angels
b. Mar 26, 1954 in Brooklyn, New York
Source: *BioIn 12*

Sloan, Alfred Pritchard, Jr.
American. Industrialist
Founded Sloan-Kettering Institute for Cancer Research, 1945.
b. May 23, 1875 in New Haven, Connecticut
d. Feb 17, 1966 in New York, New York
Source: *CurBio 40, 66; WhAm 4*

Sloan, Hugh W
American. Former Presidential Aide
b. 1941
Source: *BioIn 10*

Sloan, John
American. Artist
b. Aug 2, 1871 in Lock Haven, Pennsylvania
d. Sep 8, 1951 in Hanover, New Hampshire
Source: *AtlBL; ChPo; DcAmB S5; DcCAA 71; EncAB-H; OxAmL; REn; REnAL; WebAB; WhAm 3*

Sloan, Samuel
American. Architect
b. 1815 in Chester County, Pennsylvania
d. Jul 19, 1884 in Raleigh, North Carolina
Source: *Alli; ApCAB X; BioIn 5; BnEnAmA; DcAmAu; DcNAA; Drake; NewYHSD*

Sloane, Eric
[Everard Jean Hinrichs]
American. Artist
b. 1905 in New York, New York
Source: *BioIn 8, 9, 10, 11; IlsCB 1957*

Sloane, Everett
American. Actor
b. Oct 1, 1909 in New York, New York
d. Aug 6, 1965 in Brentwood, California
Source: *BiDFilm; CurBio 57, 65; FilmgC; MotPP; MovMk; Vers A; WhScrn 74, 77; WhoHol B*

Sloane, John
Furniture Executive
b. 1883
d. 1971
Source: *BioIn 9*

Slobodkin, Louis
American. Sculptor, Author, Illustrator
b. Feb 19, 1903 in Albany, New York
d. May 8, 1975 in Miami Beach, Florida
Source: *AmAu&B; AuBYP; BkCL; BkP; Cald 1938; ChPo; ConAu 13R, 57; IlsBYP; IlsCB 1744, 1946, 1957; JBA 51; REnAL; SmATA 1; WhAm 6; WhoAm 74; WhoAmA 73; WhoWorJ 72*

Slobodkina, Esphyr
American. Author, Illustrator
b. 1909 in Siberia, Russia
Source: *AuBYP; ConAu 1R, 1NR; ForWC 70; IlsCB 1946; SmATA 1; ThrBJA*

Slocum, Joshua
American. Author, Sailor
b. Feb 20, 1844 in NS
d. 1910?
Source: *AmAu&B*

Slonimsky, Nicolas
American. Composer, Conductor, Musician
b. Apr 27, 1894 in Saint Petersburg, Russia
Source: *AmAu&B; AmSCAP 66; ConAu 17R; CurBio 55; DcCM; WhoAm 74, 76, 78, 80, 82; WhoMus 72; WhoWorJ 72; WrDr 76*

Slote, Alfred
American. Children's Author
b. Sep 11, 1926 in Brooklyn, New York
Source: *SmATA 8*

Slovik, Eddie (Edward Donald)
American. Army Deserter
Only American executed during WW II for desertion.
b. 1920 in Detroit, Michigan
d. Jan 31, 1945 in Sainte Marie Mines, France
Source: *BioIn 3, 9, 10*

Sluter, Claus
Dutch. Sculptor
b. 1350?
d. 1406? in Dijon, France
Source: *WebBD 80*

Sly and the Family Stone
[Gregg Errico; Lawence Graham, Jr.; Jerry Martini; Cynthia Robinson; Fred Stone; Rose Stone; Sly Stone]
American. Singing Group
Source: *EncPR&S; IlEncRk; RkOn*

Smallens, Alexander
Russian. Conductor
b. Jan 1, 1889 in Saint Petersburg, Russia
d. Nov 24, 1972 in Tucson, Arizona
Source: *CurBio 47, 73; NewYTBE 72; WhAm 5*

Smalley, David
see: Raspberries, The

Smalley, Roy Frederick, III
American. Baseball Player
b. Oct 25, 1952 in Los Angeles, California
Source: *BaseEn; NewYTBS 77; WhoAm 80, 82*

Smart, Christopher
English. Poet, Author
b. Apr 22, 1722 in Shipbourne, England
d. May 21, 1771 in Kings Bench, England
Source: *Alli; AtlBL; BiD&SB; BrAu; CasWL; Chambr 2; ChPo, S1; CnE&AP; CrtT 2; DcEnA; DcEnL; DcLEL; EvLB; MouLC 2; NewC; OxEng; Pen ENG; RAdv 1; REn; WebE&AL*

Smart, Jack Scott
American. Actor
b. 1903
d. Jan 15, 1960 in Springfield, Illinois
Source: *WhScrn 74, 77; WhoHol B*

Smathers, George Armistead
American. Government Official
b. Nov 14, 1913 in Atlantic City, New Jersey
Source: *BiDrAC; CurBio 54; IntWW 74; WhoAm 74; WhoAmP 73*

Smeal, Eleanor Marie Cutri
American. Feminist
President of NOW, 1977-82.
b. Jul 30, 1939 in Ashtabula, Ohio
Source: *BioIn 11; CurBio 80; NewYTBS 77; WhoAm 78, 80, 82; WhoAmW 79, 81*

Smedley, Agnes
American. Author, Journalist
b. 1894? in Missouri
d. May 6, 1950 in Oxford, England
Source: *AmAu&B; CurBio 44, 50; DcAmB S4; InWom; NotAW; TwCA, SUP; WhAm 3*

Smetana, Bedrich
Czech. Musician, Conductor, Composer
b. Mar 2, 1824 in Litomischl, Bohemia
d. May 12, 1884 in Prague, Czechoslovakia
Source: *AtlBL; REn*

Smith, Adam
Scottish. Economist
Laid foundation for classical economics with *An Inquiry into the Nature and Causes of the Wealth of Nations,* 1776.
b. Jun 5, 1723 in Kirkcaldy, Scotland
d. Jul 17, 1790 in Edinburgh, Scotland
Source: *Alli; BbD; BiD&SB; BrAu; CasWL; CyWA; DcEnA; DcEnL; DcEuL; DcLEL; EvLB; NewC; OxEng; Pen ENG; REn; WebE&AL*

Smith, Adrian
see: Iron Maiden

Smith, Alexander
Scottish. Poet, Essayist
b. Dec 31, 1830? in Kilmarnock, Scotland
d. Jan 5, 1867 in Wardie, Scotland
Source: *Alli; BbD; BiD&SB; BrAu 19; CasWL; Chambr 3; ChPo, S1, S2; DcEnA; DcEnL; DcEuL; DcLEL; EvLB; NewC; OxEng; Pen ENG; REn; WebE&AL*

Smith, Alexis
[Mrs. Craig Stevens]
American. Actress
b. Jun 8, 1921 in Penticton, BC
Source: *CelR 73; FilmgC; IntMPA 75, 76, 77, 78, 79, 80, 81, 82; MovMk; PlP&P; WhoAm 74, 76, 78, 80, 82; WhoHol A; WhoThe 77; WorEFlm*

Smith, Alfred Aloysius
see: Horn, Alfred Aloysius, pseud.

Smith, Alfred Emanuel
American. Political Leader
b. Dec 30, 1873 in New York, New York
d. Oct 4, 1944 in New York, New York
Source: *AmAu&B; CurBio 44; DcAmB S3; DcNAA; EncAB-H; OxAmL; REn; REnAL; WebAB; WhAm 2; WhAmP*

Smith, A(rthur) J(ames) M(arshall)
Canadian. Poet, Critic
b. Nov 8, 1902 in Montreal, PQ
d. Nov 21, 1980 in East Lansing, Michigan
Source: *BioIn 1, 4, 5; CanWr; ConAu 1R, 102; ConP 70, 75; CreCan 2; DcLEL 1940; DrAP 75; DrAS 74E, 78E; IntWWP 77; LongCTC; ModCmwL; OxCan, SUP; Pen ENG; REnAL; TwCA SUP; WebE&AL; WhoAm 76, 78, 80; WrDr 76, 80*

Smith, Asa
American. Soldier, Physician
b. 1836
d. 1901
Source: *BioIn 9*

Smith, Bessie
American. Singer, Songwriter
One of greatest Blues singers of 1920's.
b. Apr 15, 1894? in Chattanooga, Tennessee
d. Sep 26, 1937 in Clarksdale, Mississippi
Source: *DcAmB S2; HerW; InWom; NotAW; WebAB; WhAm HA, 4; WhScrn 77; WhoJazz 72*

Smith, Betty
[Betty Wehner]
American. Author
Wrote *A Tree Grows in Brooklyn,* 1943.
b. Dec 15, 1904 in Brooklyn, New York
d. Jan 17, 1972 in Shelton, Connecticut
Source: *AmAu&B; AmNov; CnDAL; ConAu 5R, 33R; CurBio 43, 72; CyWA; LongCTC; OxAmL; Pen AM; REn; REnAL; TwCA SUP; WhAm 5*

Smith, Bob
see: "Buffalo" Bob

Smith, "Bubba" (Charles Aaron)
American. Football Player
b. Feb 28, 1945 in Orange, Texas
Source: *BioIn 8, 9, 10, 11; WhoFtbl 74*

Smith, C Aubrey
English. Actor
b. Jul 21, 1863 in London, England
d. Dec 20, 1948 in Beverly Hills, California
Source: *Film 1; FilmgC; MotPP; MovMk; PlP&P; Vers A; WhScrn 74, 77; WhoHol B; WhoStg 1908*

Smith, Cecil Michener
American. Music Critic
b. 1906
d. 1956
Source: *BioIn 4*

Smith, Cecil
American. Polo Player
b. 1904?
Source: *BioIn 6, 11*

Smith, Chard Powers
American. Author, Lecturer
b. Nov 1, 1894 in Watertown, New York
d. Oct 31, 1977
Source: *AmAu&B; AmNov; AnMV 1926; ChPo S1; ConAu 5R, 73; OxAmL; REnAL; TwCA, SUP; WhAm 7; WhoAm 74; WrDr 76*

Smith, Charles
see: Kool and the Gang

Smith, Charles Edward Kingsford
see: Kingsford-Smith, Charles Edward

Smith, Charlie
American. Centenarian, Former Slave
b. 1842
d. 1979 in Bartow, Florida
Source: *BioIn 7, 8, 9, 10, 11*

Smith, Clarence
American. Jazz Musician
b. Jun 11, 1904 in Troy, Alabama
d. Mar 14, 1929 in Chicago, Illinois
Source: *WhoJazz 72*

Smith, Courtney Craig
American. Educator
b. Dec 20, 1916 in Winterset, Iowa
d. Jan 16, 1969 in Swarthmore, Pennsylvania
Source: *CurBio 59, 69*

Smith, Cyrus Rowlett
American. Airline Executive
President, American Airlines, 1934-42.
b. Sep 9, 1899 in Minerva, Texas
Source: *BiDrUSE; CurBio 45; IntWW 74; NewYTBE 73; WhoAm 74, 76, 78, 80, 82; WhoF&I 74*

Smith, David
American. Sculptor
b. Mar 9, 1906 in Decatur, Indiana
d. May 23, 1965 in Albany, New York
Source: *AtlBL; DcCAA 71; EncAB-H; WebAB; WhAm 4*

Smith, Dennis
American. Author
b. Sep 9, 1940 in New York, New York
Source: *ConAu 61; NewYTBE 72; WhoAm 82*

Smith, "Dodie" (Dorothy Gladys)
[C L Anthony, pseud.]
English. Dramatist, Author
b. 1896 in Whitefield, England
Source: *Au&Wr 71; Chambr 3; ConAu 33R; DcLEL; InWom; LongCTC; McGEWD; NewC; REn; SmATA 4; Who 74; WorAu; WrDr 76*

Smith, Donald Alexander
"Strathcona"
Scottish. Financier, Statesman
b. Aug 6, 1820 in Morayshire, Scotland
d. Jan 21, 1914
Source: *ApCAB; OxCan*

Smith, Edmund Kirby
American. Soldier
b. May 16, 1824 in Saint Augustine, Florida
d. Mar 8, 1893 in Sewanee, Tennessee
Source: *AmBi; ApCAB; BiDConf; DcAmB; Drake; TwCBDA; WhAm H*

Smith, Ethel
[Ethel Goldsmith]
American. Musician
b. Nov 22, 1910 in Pittsburgh, Pennsylvania
Source: *AmSCAP 66*

Smith, Frederick Wallace
American. Corporation Executive
Founded Federal Express, 1972.
b. Aug 11, 1944 in Marks, Mississippi
Source: *WhoAm 82*

Smith, Gerald Lyman Kenneth
American. Editor, Lecturer
b. Feb 27, 1898 in Pardeeville, Wisconsin
d. Apr 15, 1976 in Glendale, California
Source: *ConAu 65; CurBio 43, 76*

Smith, Gerrit
American. Philanthropist
b. Mar 6, 1797 in Utica, New York
d. Dec 28, 1874 in New York, New York
Source: *AmBi; ApCAB; BbD; BiD&SB; BiDrAC; DcAmAu; DcAmB; DcNAA; Drake; TwCBDA; WebAB; WhAm H*

Smith, Goldwin
English. Author
b. Aug 13, 1823 in Reading, England
d. Jun 7, 1910 in Toronto, ON
Source: *ApCAB; BbD; BiD&SB; BrAu 19; CanWr; Chambr 3; DcEnA, AP; DcEnL; DcEuL; DcLEL; DcNAA; EvLB; LongCTC; NewC; OxCan; OxEng; REn; REnAL; WhAm 1*

Smith, Harold
American. Boxing Promoter, Bank Embezzler
b. 1944?
Source: *NewYTBS 81*

Smith, H(arry) Allen
American. Author, Humorist
b. Dec 19, 1907? in McLeansboro, Illinois
d. Feb 23, 1976 in San Francisco, California
Source: *AmAu&B; AuNews 2; BiDrAC; CelR 73; ChPo; ConAu 5R, 65, 5NR; CurBio 42; LongCTC; REn; REnAL; TwCA SUP; WhAm 6; WhoAm 74; WhoAmP 73; WhoE 74; WhoGov 72; WrDr 76*

Smith, Hedrick Laurence
American. Journalist
b. Jul 9, 1933 in Kilmacolm, Scotland
Source: *ConAu 65; WhoAm 82; WhoS&SW 73*

Smith, Holland McTeire
"Howlin' Mad"
American. Military Leader
b. Apr 20, 1882 in Seale, Alabama
d. Jan 12, 1967 in San Diego, California
Source: *CurBio 45, 67; WhAm 4*

Smith, Horace
[Smith and Wesson]
American. Manufacturer, Inventor
Produced the first revolvers, 1857.
b. Oct 28, 1808 in Cheshire, Massachusetts
d. Jan 15, 1893
Source: *WhAm H*

Smith, Horton
"The Joplin Ghost"
American. Golfer
b. May 22, 1908 in Springfield, Missouri
d. Oct 15, 1963 in Detroit, Michigan
Source: *BioIn 6; WhoGolf*

Smith, Howard K(ingsbury)
American. Broadcast Journalist
b. May 12, 1914 in Ferriday, Louisiana
Source: *AmAu&B; CelR 73; ConAu 45, 2NR; CurBio 43; IntMPA 75, 76, 77, 78, 79, 80, 81, 82; IntWW 74; WhoAm 74, 76, 78, 80, 82; WhoS&SW 73; WhoWor 74; WrDr 76*

Smith, Howard Worth
American. Congressman
b. Feb 2, 1883 in Broad Run, Virginia
d. Oct 3, 1976 in Alexandria, Virginia
Source: *BiDrAC; WhAmP; WhoAm 74; WhoAmP 73*

Smith, Iain Crichton
Scottish. Poet
b. Jan 1, 1928 in Isle of Lewis, Scotland
Source: *CasWL; ChPo S2; ConAu 25R; ConNov 72, 76; ConP 70, 75; Pen ENG; WhoTwCL; WrDr 76*

Smith, Ian Douglas
Rhodesian. Former Prime Minister
b. Apr 8, 1919 in Seluwke, Rhodesia
Source: *CurBio 66; IntWW 74; Who 74; WhoGov 72; WhoWor 74*

Smith, Jaclyn
[Mrs. Tony Richmond]
American. Actress
Played Kelly Garrett on "Charlie's Angels," 1976-80.
b. Oct 26, 1948 in Houston, Texas
Source: *BkPepl; IntMPA 78, 79, 80, 81, 82; WhoAm 78, 80, 82*

Smith, James
American. Lawyer
b. 1713 in Northern Ireland
d. Jul 11, 1806 in York, Pennsylvania
Source: *AmBi; ApCAB; BiAuS; BiDrAC; DcAmAu; DcAmB; Drake; REnAL; WhAm H; WhAmP*

Smith, Jedediah Strong
American. Fur Trader, Western Explorer
Made first west to east crossing over Sierra Nevada, Great Salt Desert to Salt Lake, 1826-27.
b. Jan 6, 1799? in Bainbridge, New York
d. May 27, 1831
Source: *AmAu&B; AmBi; DcAmB; OxAmL; WebAB; WhAm H*

Smith, Jerome
see: K C and the Sunshine Band

Smith, Joe
[Joseph Seltzer; Smith and Dale]
American. Comedian
b. Feb 17, 1884 in New York, New York
d. Feb 22, 1981 in Englewood, New Jersey
Source: *AnObit 1981; BioIn 8, 9, 10; NewYTBS 81; WhoHol A*

Smith, Joe
American. Jazz Musician
b. Jun 1902 in Ohio
d. Dec 2, 1937 in New York, New York
Source: *CmpEPM; WhoJazz 72*

Smith, John
English. American Colonist
Leader of Jamestown, VA colony, 1607-09.
b. Jan 1580? in Willoughby, England
d. Jun 21, 1631 in London, England
Source: *Alli; AmAu; AmAu&B; AmBi; ApCAB; BiD&SB; CasWL; CnDAL; CyAL 1; DcAmAu; DcAmB; DcLEL; EncAB-H; EvLB; NewC; OxAmL; OxEng; Pen AM; REn; REnAL; WebAB; WebE&AL; WhAm H*

Smith, Joseph
American. Religious Leader
Founded Mormons, 1830; murdered by non-believers.
b. Dec 23, 1805 in Sharon, Vermont
d. Jun 27, 1844 in Carthage, Illinois
Source: *Alli; AmAu&B; AmBi; ApCAB; DcAmB; DcNAA; Drake; EncAB-H; OhA&B; OxAmL; REn; REnAL; WebAB; WhAm H*

Smith, Joseph Fielding
American. Religious Leader
b. Jul 19, 1876 in Salt Lake City, Utah
d. Jul 2, 1972 in Salt Lake City, Utah
Source: *ConAu 37R; WhAm 5*

Smith, Kate
[Kathryn Elizabeth Smith]
American. Singer
Known for her rendition of "God Bless America."
b. May 1, 1909 in Greenville, Virginia
Source: *BioNews 74; CurBio 40, 65; InWom; IntMPA 75, 76, 77, 78, 79, 80, 81, 82; ThFT; WebAB; WhoAm 74, 76, 78, 80, 82; WhoHol A*

Smith, Keely
American. Singer
b. Mar 9, 1932 in Norfolk, Virginia
Source: *AmSCAP 66; InWom; WhoAm 74; WhoHol A*

Smith, Kenneth Danforth
American. Museum Director, Author
b. Jan 8, 1902 in Danbury, Connecticut
Source: *ConAu 1NR; WhoAm 78*

Smith, Kent
American. Actor
b. Mar 19, 1907 in New York, New York
Source: *BiE&WWA; FilmgC; HolP 40; IntMPA 75, 76, 77, 78, 79, 80, 81, 82; MovMk; NotNAT; WhoHol A; WhoThe 77*

Smith, Kingsbury
see: Kingsbury-Smith, Joseph

Smith, Lillian
American. Author
b. Dec 12, 1897 in Jasper, Florida
d. Sep 28, 1966
Source: *AmAu&B; AmNov; CnDAL; ConAu 17R, 25R; ConAu P-2; LongCTC; OxAmL; REn; REnAL; TwCA SUP; WhAm 4*

Smith, Liz (Mary Elizabeth)
American. Journalist
b. Feb 2, 1923 in Fort Worth, Texas
Source: *ConAu 65; ForWC 70; WhoAm 82*

Smith, Loring
American. Actor
b. Nov 18, 1895 in Stratford, Connecticut
Source: *BiE&WWA; NotNAT; WhoHol A; WhoThe 77*

Smith, Madeline Hamilton
Scottish. Murderer
b. 1835
d. 1928
Source: *BioIn 2, 5, 10, 11; InWom*

Smith, Madolyn Story
American. Actress
b. 1957? in Albuquerque, New Mexico
Source: *BioIn 12*

Smith, Maggie
English. Actress
Won Oscars, 1969, 1978, for *The Prime of Miss Jean Brodie* and *California Suite.*
b. Dec 28, 1934 in Ilford, England
Source: *BiDFilm; CelR 73; CurBio 70; EncMT; FilmgC; IntMPA 75, 76, 77, 78, 79, 80, 81, 82; MotPP; MovMk; NewYTBE 70; PlP&P; Who 82; WhoAmW 77; WhoHol A; WhoThe 77; WhoWor 74*

Smith, Margaret Chase
American. Politician
Senator, 1948-72; served longer than any other woman.
b. Dec 14, 1897 in Skowhegan, Maine
Source: *ConAu 73; CurBio 45, 62; NewYTBE 70; WhoAm 74; WhoAmP 73; WhoAmW 77*

Smith, Marie D
American. Author
b. in Canton, Georgia
Source: *ConAu 13R; ForWC 70*

Smith, Martin Cruz
[Simon Quinn, pseud.]
American. Author
b. Nov 3, 1942 in Reading, Pennsylvania
Source: *ConAu 85; ScF&FL 1, 2*

Smith, Merriman
American. Journalist
b. Feb 10, 1913 in Savannah, Georgia
d. Apr 13, 1970 in Alexandria, Virginia
Source: *AmAu&B; ConAu 1R, 29R, 2NR; WhAm 5*

Smith, Oliver
American. Theatrical Producer, Designer
b. Feb 13, 1918 in Waupun, Wisconsin
Source: *BiE&WWA; CelR 73; CurBio 61; NotNAT; WhoAm 74, 76, 78, 80, 82; WhoE 74; WhoGov 72; WhoThe 77; WhoWor 74*

Smith, Patti
American. Singer, Poet
Hit single "Because the Night," written with Bruce Springsteen.
b. Dec 1946 in Chicago, Illinois
Source: *ConAu 93; ConLC 12; NewWmR*

Smith, Perry Edward
American. Murderer
b. 1928?
d. Apr 14, 1965
Source: *BioIn 7*

Smith, Pete
American. Motion Picture Producer, Narrator
b. Sep 4, 1892 in New York, New York
Source: *FilmgC; IntMPA 75, 76, 77*

Smith, "Red" (Walter Wellesley)
American. Journalist
b. Sep 25, 1905 in Green Bay, Wisconsin
d. Jan 15, 1982 in Stamford, Connecticut
Source: *CelR 73; ConAu 77; CurBio 59, 82; REnAL; WebAB; WhoAm 76, 78, 80, 82*

Smith, Rex
American. Actor, Singer
b. 1956? in Atlanta, Georgia
Source: *BioIn 12*

Smith, (Robert) Sidney
American. Cartoonist
b. Feb 13, 1877 in Bloomington, Illinois
d. Oct 20, 1935 in Harvard, Illinois
Source: *AmAu&B; DcAmB S1; DcNAA; WhAm 1, 4*

Smith, Robyn Caroline
[Mrs. Fred Astaire]
American. Jockey
First woman jockey to win major race.
b. Aug 14, 1944 in San Francisco, California
Source: *BioIn 9, 10, 11; WhoAm 82*

Smith, Roger
American. Actor
Husband, manager of Ann-Margaret.
b. Dec 18, 1932 in South Gate, California
Source: *FilmgC; IntMPA 75, 76, 77; MotPP; MovMk; WhoAm 82; WhoHol A*

Smith, Roger Bonham
American. Automotive Executive
Chairman, GM, 1981--.
b. Jul 12, 1925 in Columbus, Ohio
Source: *AutoN 79; Dun&B 79; Ward 77; WhoAm 74, 76, 78, 80, 82; WhoF&I 74*

Smith, Ronnie
see: K C and the Sunshine Band

Smith, Sammi
American. Singer
b. Aug 5, 1943 in Orange, California
Source: *RkOn*

Smith, Samuel Francis
American. Poet, Clergyman
b. Oct 21, 1808 in Boston, Massachusetts
d. Nov 16, 1895 in Boston, Massachusetts
Source: *Alli, SUP; AmAu; AmAu&B; AmBi; ApCAB; BiD&SB; ChPo, S1; CyAl 2; DcAmAu; DcAmB; DcLEL; DcNAA; Drake; EvLB; OxAmL; PoChrch; REn; TwCBDA; WebAB; WebE&AL; WhAm H*

Smith, Sheila Kaye
see: Kaye-Smith, Sheila

Smith, Stan(ley Roger)
American. Tennis Player
Winner of over 25 US singles, doubles titles.
b. Dec 14, 1946 in Pasadena, California
Source: *CelR 73; NewYTBE 73; WhoAm 82*

Smith, Steve
see: Journey

Smith, "Stevie" (Florence Margaret)
English. Poet
b. 1903 in Hull, England
d. Mar 7, 1971 in Ashburton, England
Source: *Au&Wr 71; CasWL; ConAu 29R; ConAu P-2; ConLC 3, 8; ConP 70, 75; DcLEL; LinLib L; LongCTC; ModBrL, SUP; WorAu*

Smith, Sydney
English. Clergyman, Essayist
b. Jun 3, 1771 in Woodford, England
d. Feb 22, 1845 in London, England
Source: *Alli; AtlBL; BbD; BiD&SB; BrAu 19; CasWL; DcEnA; DcEnL; DcEuL; DcLEL; EvLB; NewC; OxAmL; OxEng; Pen ENG; WebE&AL*

Smith, Sydney
British. Director of Drury Lane Theatre
b. 1887
d. Jul 9, 1935
Source: *WhoHol B*

Smith, Theobald
American. Pathologist
b. Jul 31, 1859 in Albany, New York
d. Dec 10, 1934
Source: *AmBi; DcAmB S1; DcNAA; EncAB-H; WebAB; WhAm 1*

Smith, Thorne
American. Author
b. 1892? in Annapolis, Maryland
d. Jun 21, 1934
Source: *AmAu&B; CnDAL; DcLEL; DcNAA; FilmgC; LongCTC; OxAmL; REn; REnAL; TwCA*

Smith, Tommie
American. Track Athlete
b. Jun 5, 1944 in Clarksville, Texas
Source: *BioIn 7, 11; WhoTr&F 73*

Smith, Tony
American. Sculptor
b. 1912 in Orange, New Jersey
d. Dec 26, 1980 in New York, New York
Source: *AnObit 1980; WhoAm 74; WhoAmA 73*

Smith, Walter Bedell
"Beetle"
American. General
b. Oct 5, 1895 in Indianapolis, Indiana
d. Aug 9, 1961 in Washington, DC
Source: *CurBio 44, 53, 61; IndAu 1917; REnAL; WebAB; WhAm 4*

Smith, Willi Donnell
American. Fashion Designer
b. Feb 29, 1948 in Philadelphia, Pennsylvania
Source: *WhoAm 82; WhoBlA 75; WorFshn*

Smith, William French
American. Government Official
US Attorney General, 1981--.
b. Aug 26, 1917 in Wilton, New Hampshire
Source: *CurBio 82; WhoAm 80, 82; WhoAmP 77, 79; WhoGov 75, 77*

Smith, William Jay
American. Children's Author
b. Apr 22, 1918 in Winnfield, Louisiana
Source: *BkCL; ChPo, S1, S2; ConAu 5R; ConLC 6; ConP 70, 75; DrAP 75; DrAS 74E; Pen AM; SmATA 2; WhoAm 74; WorAu; WrDr 76*

Smith, Willie
"Willie the Lion"
American. Singer, Composer
b. Nov 23, 1897 in Goshen, New York
d. Apr 18, 1973 in New York, New York
Source: *CmpEPM; WhoJazz 72*

Smith and Dale
see: Marks, Charles; Smith, Joe

Smith and Wesson
see: Smith, Horace; Wesson, Daniel Baird

Smith Brothers
English. Medicine Manufacturers
Source: *BioIn 9*

Smitherman, Geneva
American. Educator, Linguist, Author
b. Dec 10, 1940 in Brownsville, Tennessee
Source: *DrAS 74E, 78F; LEduc 74; WhoBlA 75, 77*

Smithers, Jan
American. Actress
Played Bailey on TV series "WKRP in Cincinnati," 1978-82.
b. 1950? in California
Source: *WhoHol A*

Smithson, Harriet Constance
Irish. Actress
b. Mar 18, 1800 in Ennis, Ireland
d. Mar 3, 1854
Source: *InWom; OxThe*

Smithson, James
American. Scientist
Left estate money for founding of Smithsonian Institution, 1826.
b. 1765 in Paris, France
d. Jun 29, 1829 in Genoa, Italy
Source: *Alli; ApCAB; DcScB; Drake; TwCBDA; WhAm H*

Smokey Robinson and the Miracles
see: Robinson, Smokey

Smollett, Tobias George
British. Author
b. Mar 1721 in Dalquhurn, Scotland
d. Sep 17, 1771 in Monte Nero, Italy
Source: *Alli; AtlBL; BbD; BiD&SB; BrAu; CasWL; Chambr 2; ChPo; CrtT 2; CyWA; DcBiA; DcEnA; DcEnL; DcEuL; DcLEL; EvLB; MouLC 2; NewC; OxEng; Pen ENG; RAdv 1; REn; WebE&AL*

Smothers, Dick (Richard)
[The Smothers Brothers]
American. Comedian, Singer
b. Nov 20, 1938 in New York, New York
Source: *CelR 73; CurBio 68; WhoAm 74; WhoHol A*

Smothers, Tommy (Thomas Bolyn, III)
[The Smothers Brothers]
American. Comedian, Singer
b. Feb 2, 1937 in New York, New York
Source: *CurBio 68; WhoAm 74; WhoHol A*

Smuts, Jan Christian
South African. Soldier, Statesman
b. May 24, 1870 in Capetown, South Africa
d. Sep 11, 1950 in Irene, South Africa
Source: *Chambr 3; CurBio 41, 50; LongCTC; OxEng; REn; WhAm 3*

Smyslov, Vasili Vasil'evich
Russian. Chess Player
b. Mar 23, 1921 in Moscow, U.S.S.R.
Source: *BioIn 3, 4, 5, 7, 8; CurBio 67*

Smythe, Conn
Canadian. Hockey Executive
b. Feb 1, 1895 in Toronto, ON
d. Nov 18, 1980 in Toronto, ON
Source: *BioIn 1, 2, 10; CanWW 70; ClbCR; WhoHcky 73*

Smythe, Daniel
see: Box Tops, The

Smythe, Reginald
English. Comic Strip Artist
b. 1917 in Hartlepool, England
Source: *AuNews 1*

Snead, Sam(uel Jackson)
"Slammin' Sammy"
American. Golfer
Won more than 100 championships; Hall of Fame, 1953.
b. May 27, 1912 in Hot Springs, Virginia
Source: *CurBio 49; NewYTBE 72; NewYTBS 74; WebAB; WhoGolf*

Sneider, Vernon John
American. Author
b. Oct 6, 1916 in Monroe, Michigan
d. May 1, 1981 in Monroe, Michigan
Source: *BioIn 3, 4; ConAu 5R, 103; CurBio 56, 81; IntAu&W 76, 77*

Snell, Peter George
New Zealander. Runner
b. Dec 17, 1938 in Opunake, New Zealand
Source: *CurBio 62; WhoTr&F 73*

Snepp, Frank
American. Former Intelligence Officer
b. 1941?
Source: *BioIn 11*

Sneva, Tom (Thomas Edsol)
American. Auto Racer
b. Jun 1, 1948 in Spokane, Washington
Source: *WhoAm 78*

Snider, "Duke" (Edwin Donald)
"The Silver Fox"
American. Baseball Player
Outfielder, 1947-64; Hall of Fame, 1980.
b. Sep 19, 1926 in Los Angeles, California
Source: *BaseEn; CurBio 56; WhoProB 73*

Snider, Paul
Canadian. Murderer
Husband of Dorothy Stratten; killed wife, himself in lover's quarrel.
b. 1951?
d. Aug 14, 1980 in Los Angeles, California
Source: *NF*

Snively, William Daniel, Jr.
American. Physician
b. Feb 9, 1911 in Rock Island, Illinois
Source: *AmM&WS 73P; WhoAm 74; WhoWor 74*

Snodgrass, W(illiam) D(eWitt)
American. Poet, Philologist
b. Jan 5, 1926 in Wilkinsburg, Pennsylvania
Source: *CasWL; ChPo, S1; ClDMEL; ConAu 1R; ConLC 2, 6, 10, 18; ConP 70; CroCAP; CurBio 60; DrAP 75; IntWW 74; ModAL, SUP; OxAmL; Pen AM; RAdv 1; REn; REnAL; WebE&AL; WhoAm 74; WhoTwCL; WhoWor 74; WorAu; WrDr 76*

Snodgress, Carrie
American. Actress
b. Oct 27, 1946 in Chicago, Illinois
Source: *CelR 73; IntMPA 75, 76, 77, 78, 79, 80, 81, 82; MovMk; NewYTBE 70; WhoHol A*

Snorri, Sturluson
Icelandic. Chieftain, Historian
b. 1178
d. 1241
Source: *NewCol 75*

Snow, Carmel White
American. Fashion Editor
b. Aug 21, 1887? in Dublin, Ireland
d. May 7, 1961 in New York, New York
Source: *InWom; WhAm 4; WorFshn*

Snow, Sir C(harles) P(ercy)
English. Scientist, Author
b. Oct 15, 1905 in Leicester, England
d. Jul 1, 1980 in London, England
Source: *Au&Wr 71; CasWL; ConAu 5R, 101; ConLC 1, 4, 6, 9, 13; ConNov 72, 76; CurBio 54, 61, 80; DcLEL; EncMys; EncWL; EvLB; IntWW 74; LongCTC; ModBrL, SUP; NewC; OxEng; Pen ENG; RAdv 1; REn; TwCA SUP; TwCW; WebE&AL; Who 74; WhoTwCL; WrDr 76*

Snow, Don
see: Squeeze

Snow, Dorothea Johnston
American. Children's Author
b. Apr 7, 1909 in McMinnville, Tennessee
Source: *ConAu 1R, 3NR; SmATA 9*

Snow, Edgar Parks
American. Journalist
b. Jul 19, 1905 in Kansas City, Missouri
d. Feb 15, 1972 in Eysins, Switzerland
Source: *AmAu&B; ConAu 33R, 81; CurBio 41, 72; REn; REnAL; TwCA, SUP; WhAm 5*

Snow, Hank
"The Singing Ranger"
American. Singer
b. May 9, 1914 in Liverpool, NS
Source: *EncFCWM 69; WhoAm 82*

Snow, Phoebe Laub
American. Singer
b. Jul 17, 1952 in New York, New York
Source: *BioIn 10; IlEncRk; WhoAm 82*

Snowdon, Earl of
see: Armstrong-Jones, Antony Charles Robert

Snyder, Gary Sherman
American. Poet
b. May 8, 1930 in San Francisco, California
Source: *AmAu&B; CasWL; ConAu 17R; ConLC 1, 2, 5; ConP 70, 75; CroCAP; DrAP 75; ModAL SUP; Pen AM; RAdv 1; REn; REnAL; WebE&AL; WhoAm 74, 76, 78, 80, 82; WhoE 74; WhoWor 74; WorAu; WrDr 76*

Snyder, James
see: "Jimmy the Greek"

Snyder, John Wesley
American. Banker
b. Jun 21, 1895 in Jonesboro, Arkansas
Source: *BiDrUSE; CurBio 45; IntWW 74; St&PR 75; Who 74; WhoAm 74, 76, 78, 80, 82; WhoAmP 73*

Snyder, Tom
American. Broadcast Journalist
b. May 12, 1936 in Milwaukee, Wisconsin
Source: *BkPepl; CurBio 80; IntMPA 77, 78, 79, 80, 81, 82; WhoAm 82*

Soames, (Arthur) Christopher (John)
[Baron of Fletching]
English. Government Official
b. Oct 12, 1920 in Penn, England
Source: *BioIn 5, 10; CurBio 81; IntWW 74, 75, 76, 77, 78; IntYB 78, 79; NewYTBS 79; Who 74; WhoWor 74, 76, 78*

Sobell, Morton
American. Convicted Rosenberg Accomplice
b. Apr 11, 1917 in New York, New York
Source: *ConAu 53; WrDr 76*

Sobhraj, Charles Gurmukh
see: Dumurq, Charles

Sobhuza II
"The Lion of Swaziland"
Swazi. King
Estimated to have had nearly 100 wives, 500 children.
b. Jul 22, 1899 in Swaziland
d. Aug 21, 1982 in Mbabane, Swaziland
Source: *AfSS 78, 79; BioIn 6, 8, 10, 11; CurBio 82; IntWW 74, 75, 76, 77, 78; NewCol 75; NewYTBS 82; WhoGov 72; WhoWor 74, 76, 78*

Sobol, Louis
American. Journalist, Author
b. Aug 10, 1896 in New Haven, Connecticut
d. Jan 19, 1948
Source: *AmAu&B; ConAu 29R; ConAu P-2; IntMPA 76, 77, 78, 79, 80, 81, 82; WhAm 2*

Sobrero, Ascanio
Italian. Chemist
Discovered nitroglycerine, 1847.
b. Oct 12, 1812 in Casale, Italy
d. May 26, 1888 in Turin, Italy
Source: *AsBiEn*

Soby, James Thrall
American. Art Critic, Editor
b. Dec 14, 1906 in Hartford, Connecticut
Source: *AmAu&B; ConAu 103; REnAL; TwCA SUP; WhoAm 74; WhoAmA 73*

Sockman, Ralph W
American. Religious Leader
b. Oct 1, 1889 in Mount Vernon, Ohio
d. Aug 29, 1970 in New York, New York
Source: *AmAu&B; ConAu 5R, 89; CurBio 70; OhA&B; WhAm 5; WhNAA*

Socrates
Greek. Philosopher
Viewed philosophy as necessary pursuit of all intelligent men; teacher of Plato.
b. 470?BC in Athens, Greece
d. 399?BC in Athens, Greece
Source: *AtlBL; BbD; BiD&SB; CasWL; ChPo S1; CyWA; NewC; OxEng; Pen CL; PlP&P; RComWL; REn*

Soderblom, Nathan
Swedish. Theologian
b. Jan 15, 1866
d. Jul 12, 1931
Source: *WhoLA*

Sodero, Cesare
Italian. Conductor
b. Aug 2, 1886 in Naples, Italy
d. Dec 16, 1947 in New York, New York
Source: *AmSCAP 66; CurBio 43, 48*

Soft Cell
[Marc Almond; Dave Ball]
British. Music Duo
Hit single remake of "Tainted Love," 1982.
Source: *NF*

Soglow, Otto
American. Comic Strip Artist
b. Dec 23, 1900 in New York, New York
d. Apr 3, 1975 in New York, New York
Source: *AmAu&B; ChPo; ConAu 57; CurBio 40; REnAL; WhAm 6; WhoAm 74; WhoAmA 73*

Sokolsky, George E
American. Journalist, Author
b. Sep 5, 1893 in Utica, New York
d. Dec 13, 1962 in Otis, Massachusetts
Source: *AmAu&B; ConAu 89; CurBio 41, 63; WhAm 4*

Soleri, Paolo
American. Architect
b. Jun 21, 1919 in Turin, Italy
Source: *CelR 73; CurBio 72; WhoAm 82; WhoAmA 73*

Solomon
Hebrew. King of Israel
b. 973?BC
d. 933?BC
Source: *DcOrL 3; NewC*

Solomon
English. Musician
b. Aug 9, 1902 in London, England
Source: *Who 74*

Solomon, Andy
see: Amboy Dukes, The

Solomon, Harold Charles
American. Tennis Player
b. Sep 17, 1952 in Washington, DC
Source: *OfEnT; WhoAm 82*

Solomon, Izler
American. Conductor
b. Jan 11, 1910 in Saint Paul, Minnesota
Source: *WhoAm 74; WhoMW 74; WhoMus 72; WhoWorJ 72*

Solomon, Neil
American. Scientist, State Official
b. Feb 27, 1932 in Pittsburgh, Pennsylvania
Source: *AmM&WS 73P; WhoAm 82; WhoE 74*

Solomon, Samuel J
American. Aviation Industrialist
b. Jul 11, 1899 in Washington, DC
d. Dec 8, 1977 in Bethesda, Maryland
Source: *St&PR 75; WhoAm 74*

Solotaroff, Theodore
American. Author
b. Oct 9, 1928 in Elizabeth, New Jersey
Source: *ConAu 9R; DrAF 76; WhoWorJ 72*

Soloviev, Sergei
Russian. Author
b. May 5, 1820 in Moscow, Russia
d. Oct 4, 1879
Source: *CasWL*

Solti, Sir Georg
English. Musician, Conductor
b. Oct 21, 1912 in Budapest, Hungary
Source: *BioNews 74; CelR 73; CurBio 64; IntWW 74; NewYTBE 71, 72; WhoAm 74, 76, 78, 80, 82; WhoMW 74; WhoMus 72; WhoWor 74*

Soltysik, Patricia
[S(ymbionese) L(iberation) A(rmy)]
"Mizmoon"
American. Revolutionary
b. 1949?
d. May 24, 1974 in Los Angeles, California
Source: *BioIn 10; GoodHS*

Solzhenitsyn, Aleksandr Isayevich
Russian. Author
Exiled to Siberia, 1953; won Nobel Prize, 1970.
b. Dec 11, 1918 in Kislovodsk, U.S.S.R.
Source: *AuNews 1; BioNews 74; CasWL; ConAu 25R, 69; ConLC 1, 2, 4, 7, 9, 10, 18; EncWL; IntWW 74; ModSL 1; NewYTBE 72; NewYTBS 74; Pen EUR; RComWL; REn; TwCW; Who 82; WhoAm 82; WhoTwCL; WorAu*

Somers, Brett
American. Actress
Source: *WhoHol A*

Somers, Suzanne
[Mrs. Alan Hamel; Suzanne Mahoney]
American. Actress
Starred in TV series "Three's Company," 1977-81.
b. Oct 16, 1946 in San Bruno, California
Source: *BioIn 11; BkPepl; IntMPA 82; WhoAm 78, 80, 82*

Somes, Michael
English. Dancer
b. Sep 28, 1917 in Horsley, England
Source: *CurBio 55; Who 74; WhoHol A; WhoThe 77; WhoWor 74*

Sommer, Elke
[Elke Schletze]
American. Actress
b. Nov 5, 1941? in Berlin, Germany
Source: *CelR 73; FilmgC; IntMPA 75, 76, 77, 78, 79, 80, 81, 82; MotPP; MovMk; WhoAm 82; WhoHol A*

Sommer, Frederick
American. Artist, Photographer
b. Sep 7, 1905 in Angri, Italy
Source: *BnEnAmA; WhoAm 82*

Sommers, Joanie
American. Singer
b. 1941
Source: *WhoHol A*

Somoza, Anastasio
Nicaraguan. President
b. Feb 1, 1896 in San Marcos, Nicaragua
d. Sep 29, 1956 in Managua, Nicaragua
Source: *CurBio 42, 56; WhAm 3*

Somoza Debayle, Anastasio
Nicaraguan. Former President
b. Dec 5, 1925 in Leon, Nicaragua
Source: *CurBio 78*

"Son of Sam"
see: Berkowitz, David

Sondergaard, Gale
American. Actress
b. 1899? in Litchfield, Minnesota
Source: *BiE&WWA; BioNews 74; FilmgC; IntMPA 75, 76, 77, 78, 79, 80, 81, 82; MotPP; MovMk; NotNAT; ThFT; Vers A; WhoAm 82; WhoHol A; WhoThe 77*

Sondheim, Stephen Joshua
American. Composer, Lyricist
b. Mar 22, 1930 in New York, New York
Source: *AmSCAP 66; BiE&WWA; BkPepl; ConAu 103; CurBio 73; EncMT; NatPD; NewCBMT; NotNAT; PlP&P, A; WhoAm 74, 76, 78, 80, 82; WhoThe 77*

Sonneck, Oscar George Theodore
American. Historian, Librarian, Musician
b. Oct 6, 1873 in Jersey City, New Jersey
d. Oct 30, 1928 in New York, New York
Source: *AmAu&B; Baker 78; BiDAmM; BioIn 1, 3; DcAmB; DcAmLiB; DcNAA; EncAAH; NatCAB 25; OxMus; REnAL; WhAm 1*

Sonnenfeldt, Helmut
American. Government Official
b. Sep 13, 1926 in Berlin, Germany
Source: *NewYTBE 73; USBiR 74; WhoAm 74, 76, 78, 80, 82; WhoAmP 73; WhoGov 72*

Sonny and Cher
[Sonny Bono; Cher]
American. Singing Group
Source: *RkOn*

Sons of the Pioneers
[Pat Brady; Roy Lanham; Rob Nolan; Lloyd Perryman; Rusty Richards; Roy Rogers; Tim Spencer; Dale Warren]
American. Vocal Group
Source: *EncFCWM 69*

Sontag, Henriette
German. Opera Singer
b. Jan 3, 1806 in Coblenz, Germany
d. Jun 17, 1854 in Mexico City, Mexico
Source: *ApCAB; InWom*

Sontag, Susan
American. Author, Critic
b. Jan 28, 1933 in New York, New York
Source: *AmAu&B; CelR 73; ConAu 17R; ConLC 1, 2; ConNov 72, 76; CurBio 69; DrAF 76; ModAL; OxFilm; Pen AM; RAdv 1; WhoAm 74, 76, 78, 80, 82; WhoE 74; WhoTwCL; WhoWor 74; WomWMM; WorAu; WrDr 76*

Sonzogno, Edoardo
Italian. Music Publisher
b. Apr 21, 1836 in Milan, Italy
d. Mar 14, 1920 in Milan, Italy
Source: *NewEOp 71*

Soo, Jack
[Goro Suzuki]
American. Actor
Played Yemana on TV series "Barney Miller," 1975-79.
b. 1916? in Oakland, California
d. Jan 11, 1979 in Los Angeles, California
Source: *MotPP; NewYTBS 79; WhoHol A*

Soong, T V
[Sung Tsu-Wen]
Chinese. Statesman
b. 1894 in Shanghai, China
d. Apr 25, 1971 in San Francisco, California
Source: *CurBio 41, 71; NewYTBE 71; WhAm 5*

Sophie
[Sophie Hass Gimbel]
American. Fashion Designer
b. in Houston, Texas
Source: *InWom; WorFshn*

Sophocles
Greek. Poet, Dramatist
Wrote *Antigone, Oepidus Rex,* circa 429 BC.
b. 496?BC in Colonus, Greece
d. 406?BC in Athens, Greece
Source: *AtlBL; BbD; BiD&SB; CasWL; ChPo S2; CnThe; CyWA; DcEnL; McGEWD; NewC; OxEng; OxThe; Pen CL; RComWL; REn; REnWD*

Sopwith, Thomas O M
English. Aeronautical Engineer
b. 1888
Source: *IntWW 74; Who 74; WhoWor 74*

Sor, Fernando
[Fernando Sors]
Spanish. Composer, Musician
b. Feb 13, 1778 in Barcelona, Spain
d. Jul 8, 1839 in Paris, France
Source: *Baker 78; BioIn 11; OxMus*

Sorensen, Ted (Theodore Chaikin)
American. Lawyer, Government Official
b. May 8, 1928 in Lincoln, Nebraska
Source: *AmAu&B; ConAu 45, 2NR; CurBio 61; WhoAm 74, 76, 78, 80, 82; WhoAmP 73; WhoWor 74*

Sorensen, Virginia
[Mrs. Alec Waugh]
American. Children's Author
b. Feb 17, 1912 in Provo, Utah
Source: *AmAu&B; AmNov; Au&Wr 71; AuBYP; ConAu 13R; CurBio 50; InWom; MorBMP; MorJA; SmATA 2; TwCA SUP; WhoAm 74, 76, 78, 80, 82; WhoWor 74; WrDr 76*

Sorge, Richard
German. Journalist, Spy
b. 1895
d. 1944
Source: *BioIn 2, 3, 4, 7, 8*

Soria, Dario
American. Opera Director, Record Executive
b. May 21, 1912 in Rome, Italy
d. Mar 28, 1980 in New York, New York
Source: *WhAm 7; WhoAm 74*

Sorvino, Paul
American. Actor
b. 1939 in New York, New York
Source: *IntMPA 78, 79, 80, 81, 82; WhoAm 82; WhoThe 77*

Sosnik, Harry
American. Conductor
b. Jul 13, 1906 in Chicago, Illinois
Source: *AmSCAP 66; St&PR 75; WhoAm 74, 76, 78, 80, 82*

Sostratus
Greek. Architect
Source: *WebBD 80*

Sotheby, John
English. Auctioneer, Cataloger
Founded Covent Gardens Auction Rooms, 1744.
d. 1807
Source: *WebBD 80*

Sotheby, Samuel Leigh
English. Auctioneer, Cataloger
b. 1805
d. 1861
Source: *WebBD 80*

Sothern, Ann
[Harriet Lake]
American. Actress
b. Jan 22, 1912? in Valley City, North Dakota
Source: *AmSCAP 66; CurBio 56; EncMT; FilmgC; InWom; IntMPA 82; MotPP; MovMk; OxFilm; ThFT; WhoAm 74, 76, 78, 80, 82; WhoHol A; WhoThe 77; WorEFlm*

Sothern, Edward Askew
English. Entertainer
b. Apr 1, 1826 in Liverpool, England
d. Jan 20, 1881 in London, England
Source: *Alli; AmBi; DcAmB; FamA&A; NewC; OxAmL; OxThe; REnAL; TwCBDA; WhAm H*

Sothern, Edward Hugh
American. Entertainer
b. Dec 6, 1859 in New Orleans, Louisiana
d. 1933 in New York, New York
Source: *AmAu&B; AmBi; ChPo; DcAmB; DcNAA; FamA&A; OxAmL; REn; REnAL; WhScrn 74*

Soul, David
American. Actor
Starred in TV shows "Here Come the Brides"; "Starsky and Hutch."
b. Aug 28, 1946 in Chicago, Illinois
Source: *IntMPA 82; WhoAm 80, 82; WhoHol A*

Soule, Olan
American. Actor
Source: *WhoHol A*

Soupault, Philippe
French. Poet, Author
b. Aug 2, 1897 in Chaville, France
Source: *CasWL; ClDMEL; EncWL; IntWW 74; ModRL; ModWD; OxFr; REn; WhoWor 74; WorAu*

Souphanouvong, Prince
Laotian. President
b. 1902
Source: *IntWW 74; WhoWor 74*

Sousa, John Philip
American. Bandmaster, Composer
Wrote 140 marches, including "Stars and Stripes Forever," 1897.
b. Nov 6, 1854 in Washington, DC
d. Mar 6, 1932 in Reading, Pennsylvania
Source: *AmAu&B; AmBi; AmSCAP 66; ApCAB SUP; AtlBL; DcAmAu; DcAmB; DcNAA; EncAB-H; EncMT; OxAmL; REn; REnAL; TwCBDA; WebAB; WhAm 1; WhoStg 1906, 1908*

Soustelle, Jacques
French. Scientist, Statesman
b. Feb 3, 1912 in Montpellier, France
Source: *CurBio 58; IntWW 74; Who 74; WhoWor 74*

South, Joe
American. Musician, Singer, Songwriter
Won two Grammys, 1969, for "Games People Play."
b. Feb 28, 1942 in Atlanta, Georgia
Source: *BioIn 8; RkOn; WhoRock 81*

Southall, Ivan Francis
Australian. Children's Author
b. Jun 8, 1921 in Canterbury, Australia
Source: *Au&Wr 71; AuBYP; ChlLR 2; ConAu 9R; SenS; SmATA 3; ThrBJA; WhoWor 74; WrDr 76*

Southampton, Henry Wriothesley, Earl
English. Statesman
b. Oct 6, 1573
d. Nov 10, 1624 in Netherlands
Source: *ApCAB; BioIn 7, 8, 11; LongCEL; NewC; REn*

Souther, J(ohn) D(avid)
[The Souther-Hillman-Furay Band]
American. Singer, Songwriter
b. in Detroit, Michigan
Source: *ConMuA 80; WhoRock 81*

Souther-Hillman-Furay Band, The
[Richie Furay; James Gordon; Paul Harris; Chris Hillman; Al Perkins; J(ohn) D(avid) Souther]
American. Rock Group
Source: *IlEncRk; LilREn 78; RkOn 2; WhoRock 81*

Southern, Terry
American. Author
b. May 1, 1924 in Alvarado, Texas
Source: *AmAu&B; CasWL; ConAu 1R, 1NR; ConDr 73; ConNov 72, 76; DrAF 76; Pen AM; WhoAm 74, 76, 78, 80, 82; WhoTwCL; WhoWor 74; WorAu; WrDr 76*

Southey, Robert
English. Poet, Author
One of "Lake Poets"; poet laurate, 1813-43.
b. Aug 12, 1774 in Bristol, England
d. Mar 21, 1843 in Keswick, England
Source: *Alli; AtlBL; BbD; BiD&SB; BiDLA; BrAu 19; CasWL; Chambr 3; ChPo, S1, S2; CnE&AP; CrtT 2; CyWA; DcEnA, AP; DcEnL; DcEuL; DcLEL; EvLB; MouLC 3; NewC; OxEng; Pen ENG; PoLE; REn; WebE&AL; WhoChL*

Southside Johnny and the Asbury Jukes
[Al Berger; Ricky Gazda; Kevin Kavanaugh; "Southside" Johnny Lyon; Eddie Manion; Carlo Novi; Tony Palligros; Kenny Pentifallo; Richie Rosenberg;Willie Rush]
American. Rock Group
Source: *ConMuA 80; RkOn 2; WhoRock 81*

Soutine, Chaim
French. Artist
b. 1894 in Smilovich, Russia
d. Aug 9, 1943 in Paris, France
Source: *AtlBL*

Souvanna Phouma, Prince
Laotian. Politician
b. Oct 7, 1901
Source: *BioIn 5, 6, 7, 8, 9, 10; CurBio 62; IntWW 74; WhoGov 72; WhoWor 74*

Souzay, Gerard
[Gerard Marcel Tisserand]
French. Opera Singer
b. Dec 8, 1920? in Angers, France
Source: *CurBio 66; IntWW 74; Who 74; WhoMus 72; WhoWor 74*

Sovern, Michael I(ra)
American. University Administrator
President, Columbia U, 1980--.
b. Dec 1, 1931 in Bronx, New York
Source: *BioIn 8, 10; CurBio 81; DrAS 74P, 78P; WhoAm 74, 76, 78, 80, 82; WhoAmL 78, 79; WhoE 74*

Sowell, Thomas
American. Economist
b. Jul 30, 1930 in Gastonia, North Carolina
Source: *AmEA 74; AmM&WS 73S, 78S; ConAu 41R; CurBio 81; WhoAm 76, 82; WhoBlA 75, 77*

Sowerby, Leo
American. Organist, Composer
b. May 1, 1895 in Grand Rapids, Michigan
d. Jul 7, 1968 in Port Clinton, Ohio
Source: *AmSCAP 66; DcCM; OxAmL; REnAL; WhAm 5*

Soyer, David
American. Musician
b. Feb 24, 1923 in Philadelphia, Pennsylvania
Source: *NewYTBE 71; WhoAm 82*

Soyer, Isaac
American. Artist
b. Apr 20, 1907 in Tambov, Russia
d. Jul 8, 1981 in New York, New York
Source: *BnEnAmA; CurBio 41, 81; McGDA; WhoAm 74, 76, 78*

Soyer, Moses
American. Artist
b. Dec 25, 1899 in Tambov, Russia
d. Sep 2, 1974 in New York, New York
Source: *CelR 73; CurBio 41, 74; DcCAA 71; NewYTBS 74; WhAm 6; WhoAm 74; WhoAmA 73*

Soyer, Raphael
American. Artist
b. Dec 25, 1899 in Tambov, Russia
Source: *ConAu 81; CurBio 41; DcCAA 71; NewYTBE 72; WhoAm 74, 76, 78, 80, 82; WhoAmA 73; WhoWorJ 72*

Soyinka, Wole (Akinwande Oluwole)
Nigerian. Author
b. Jul 13, 1934 in Abeokuta, Nigeria
Source: *CasWL; CnThe; ConAu 13R; ConDr 73; ConLC 3, 5; ConP 70, 75; IntWW 74; LongCTC; ModWD; Pen CL, ENG; REnWD; RGAfL; WebE&AL; WhoWor 74; WorAu; WrDr 76*

Spaak, Fernand Paul Jules
Belgian. Diplomat
b. Aug 8, 1923 in Forest, Belgium
d. Jul 1981 in Brussels, Belgium
Source: *IntWW 74, 75, 76, 77, 78; WhoWor 74, 76, 78*

Spaak, Paul-Henri
Belgian. Lawyer, Politician
b. Jan 25, 1899 in Schaerbeck, Belgium
d. Jul 31, 1972 in Brussels, Belgium
Source: *ConAu 37R; CurBio 45, 58, 72; NewYTBE 72; WhAm 5*

Spaatz, Carl Andrew
American. General
b. Jun 28, 1891 in Boyertown, Pennsylvania
d. Jul 14, 1974 in Washington, DC
Source: *ConAu 49; CurBio 42, 74; NewYTBS 74; WebAB; WhAm 6; Who 74*

Spacek, "Sissy" (Mary Elizabeth)
[Mrs. Jack Fiske]
American. Actress
Won Oscar, 1980, for *Coal Miner's Daughter*.
b. Dec 25, 1949 in Quitman, Texas
Source: *BkPepl; ConAu 77; CurBio 78; IntMPA 82; WhoAm 80, 82; WhoHol A*

Spaeth, Sigmund Gottfried
American. Musician, Author
b. Apr 10, 1885 in Philadelphia, Pennsylvania
d. Nov 12, 1965 in New York, New York
Source: *AmAu&B; AmSCAP 66; ChPo S1; ConAu 5R; CurBio 42, 66; REnAL; TwCA, SUP; WhAm 4; WhNAA*

Spahn, Warren Edward
American. Baseball Player
Won 363 games in career, 1942-64; Hall of Fame, 1972.
b. Apr 23, 1921 in Buffalo, New York
Source: *BaseEn; CelR 73; CurBio 62; WebAB; WhoAm 74; WhoProB 73*

Spalding, Albert
American. Musician
Composer of numerous works for violin and piano.
b. Aug 15, 1888 in Chicago, Illinois
d. May 26, 1953 in New York, New York
Source: *AmSCAP 66; CurBio 44, 53; DcAmB S5; WebAB; WhAm 3*

Spalding, Albert Goodwill
American. Baseball Player, Businessman
Founded A G Spalding, sporting goods manufacturing firm, 1876.
b. Sep 2, 1850 in Byron, Illinois
d. Sep 9, 1915 in Point Loma, California
Source: *DcAmB; DcNAA; WebAB; WhAm 1; WhoProB 73*

Spallanzani, Lazzaro
Italian. Explorer, Scientist
Disproved theory of spontaneous generation.
b. Jan 12, 1729 in Scandiano, Italy
d. Feb 11, 1799 in Pavia, Italy
Source: *NewCol 75*

Spanier, "Muggsy" (Francis Joseph)
American. Jazz Musician
b. Nov 9, 1906 in Chicago, Illinois
d. Feb 12, 1967 in Sausalito, California
Source: *WhScrn 74, 77; WhoHol B; WhoJazz 72*

Spargo, John
American. Author
b. Jan 31, 1876 in Cornwall, England
d. Aug 17, 1966 in Bennington, Vermont
Source: *AmAu&B; AmLY; ConAu 89; REnAL; WhAm 4; WhNAA*

Spark, Muriel Sarah
Scottish. Author
b. Feb 1, 1918 in Edinburgh, Scotland
Source: *Au&Wr 71; CasWL; ConAu 5R; ConLC 2, 3, 5, 8, 13, 18; ConNov 72, 76; ConP 70; EncWL; IntWW 74; LongCTC; ModBrL, SUP; NewC; Pen ENG; RAdv 1; REn; TwCW; WebE&AL; Who 74; WhoAm 82; WhoTwCL; WhoWor 74; WorAu; WrDr 76*

Sparkman, John Jackson
American. Government Official
b. Dec 20, 1899 in Morgan County, Alabama
Source: *BiDrAC; CngDr 74; CurBio 50; IntWW 74; Who 74; WhoAm 74; WhoAmP 73; WhoGov 72; WhoS&SW 73*

Sparks, Fred
English. Author
b. Apr 1939 in Colchester, England
Source: *ConAu 103*

Sparks, Jared
American. Editor, Historian
b. May 10, 1789 in Willington, Connecticut
d. Mar 14, 1866
Source: *Alli; AmAu; AmAu&B; AmBi; ApCAB; BiD&SB; CyAL 1; DcAmAu; DcAmB; DcNAA; Drake; EncAB-H; OxAmL; REn; REnAL; TwCBDA; WebAB; WhAm H*

Sparks, Ned
American. Actor
b. 1883 in Guelph, ON
d. Apr 2, 1957 in Apple Valley, California
Source: *Film 1; FilmgC; MotPP; MovMk; TwYS; Vers A; WhScrn 74, 77; WhoHol B*

Spartacus
Thracian. Slave, Gladiator
d. 71BC
Source: *REn*

Spassky, Boris Vasilievich
Russian. Chess Player, Journalist
World chess champion, 1969-72.
b. Jan 30, 1937 in Leningrad, U.S.S.R.
Source: *CurBio 72; IntWW 74*

Speaker, Tris(tram E)
"Spoke"; "The Grey Eagle"
American. Baseball Player
Had .344 lifetime batting average; Hall of Fame, 1937.
b. Apr 4, 1888 in Hubbard City, Texas
d. Dec 8, 1958 in Lake Whitney, Texas
Source: *BaseEn; BioIn 2, 3, 4, 5, 6, 7, 8, 9, 10; WhoProB 73*

Speakes, Larry Melvin
American. Deputy Press Secretary
b. Sep 13, 1939 in Cleveland, Mississippi
Source: *WhoAm 76, 78, 80, 82; WhoGov 75, 77*

Speaks, Oley
American. Composer
b. Jun 28, 1874 in Canal Winchester, Ohio
d. Aug 27, 1948 in New York, New York
Source: *AmSCAP 66; DcAmB S4; WhAm 2*

Spear, Roger Elliot
American. Investment Advisor
b. Sep 3, 1898 in Jamaica Plain, Massachusetts
d. Jul 16, 1976
Source: *WhAm 7; WhoAm 74*

Spear, Sammy
American. Band Leader
b. 1910 in Brooklyn, New York
d. Mar 11, 1975 in Miami, Florida
Source: *WhScrn 77*

Speare, Elizabeth George
American. Author
b. Nov 21, 1908 in Melrose, Massachusetts
Source: *AmAu&B; Au&Wr 71; AuBYP; ConAu 1R; CurBio 59; ForWC 70; InWom; MorBMP; MorJA; SmATA 5; WhoAm 74, 76, 78, 80, 82; WrDr 76*

Speck, Richard Franklin
American. Mass Murderer
Killed eight student nurses in Chicago, July 13-14, 1966.
b. Dec 6, 1941 in Kirkwood, Illinois
Source: *BioIn 7; Blood*

Specter, Arlen
American. Senator
b. Feb 12, 1930 in Russell, Kansas
Source: *BioIn 7; WhoAmP 73, 75, 77, 79; WhoE 74, 75*

Spector, Phil
American. Music Producer
b. Dec 25, 1940 in New York, New York
Source: *EncPR&S; IlEncRk; WhoAm 82*

Spectorsky, Auguste Compte
American. Editor, Author
b. Aug 13, 1910 in Paris, France
d. Jan 17, 1972 in Saint Croix, Virgin Islands
Source: *AmAu&B; ConAu 17R, 33R; ConAu P-2; CurBio 60, 72; NewYTBE 72; REnAL; WhAm 5*

Speer, Albert
German. Architect, Nazi Leader
b. Mar 19, 1905 in Mannheim, Germany
d. Sep 1, 1981 in London, England
Source: *BioIn 1, 2, 3, 8, 9, 10, 11; ConAu 65; CurBio 76, 81; EncTR; NewCol 75; WhWW-II*

Speicher, Eugene Edward
American. Artist
b. Apr 5, 1883 in Buffalo, New York
d. May 11, 1962 in Woodstock, New York
Source: *CurBio 47, 62; DcCAA 71; WhAm 4*

Speiser, Jerry
see: Men at Work

Speke, John Hanning
English. Explorer
Discovered Lake Tanganyika and Victoria Nyanza, 1858.
b. May 4, 1827 in Jordans, England
d. Sep 18, 1864 in Bath, England
Source: *Alli; BbD; BiD&SB; BrAu 19; DcLEL; EvLB; NewC; OxEng*

Spelling, Aaron
American. TV Producer
Produced "Charlie's Angels," "The Love Boat," "Fantasy Island."
b. Apr 22, 1925 in Dallas, Texas
Source: *IntMPA 77, 78, 79, 80, 81, 82; WhoAm 82; WhoHol A*

Spellman, Francis Joseph
American. Roman Catholic Cardinal
b. May 4, 1889 in Whitman, Massachusetts
d. Dec 2, 1967 in New York, New York
Source: *AmAu&B; CathA 1930; ChPo; CurBio 40, 47, 68; WhAm 4; WhNAA*

Spence, Sir Basil
English. Architect
b. Aug 13, 1907 in Bombay, India
Source: *Au&Wr 71; IntWW 74; Who 74; WhoWor 74*

Spencer, Lady Diana Frances
see: Diana, Princess of Wales

Spencer, Herbert
English. Philosopher
b. Apr 27, 1820 in Derby, England
d. Dec 8, 1903 in Brighton, England
Source: *Alli, SUP; BbD; BiD&SB; BrAu 19; CasWL; Chambr 3; DcEnA, AP; DcEnL; DcLEL; EvLB; NewC; OxEng; Pen ENG; REn; WebE&AL; WhAm H*

Spencer, Sir Stanley
British. Artist
b. 1891
d. Dec 14, 1959 in Buckinghamshire, England
Source: *NewCol 75; OxArt*

Spencer, William
American. Author
b. Jun 1, 1922 in Erie, Pennsylvania
Source: *AuBYP; ConAu 17R; SmATA 9; WrDr 76*

Spencer Davis Group, The
[Spencer Davis; Muff Winwood; Stevie Winwood; Pete York]
English. Rock Group
Source: *IlEncRk; WhoRock 81*

Spender, Stephen
English. Author, Journalist
b. Feb 28, 1909 in London, England
Source: *Au&Wr 71; CasWL; Chambr 3; ChPo, S2; CnE&AP; CnMD; CnMWL; ConAu 9R; ConLC 1, 2, 5, 10; ConP 70, 75; CurBio 40; CyWA; DcLEL; EncWL; EvLB; IntWW 74; LongCTC; ModBrL, SUP; ModWD; NewC; OxEng; Pen ENG; RAdv 1; REn; TwCA, SUP; TwCW; WebE&AL; Who 74; WhoTwCL; WhoWor 74; WrDr 76*

Spengler, Oswald
German. Philosopher
b. May 29, 1880 in Blankenburg, Germany
d. May 8, 1936 in Munich, Germany
Source: *CasWL; EvEuW; LongCTC; OxGer; REn; TwCA, SUP; TwCW*

Spenkelink, John Arthur
American. Murderer
Executed in electric chair.
b. 1949 in Buena Park, California
d. May 25, 1979 in Starke, Florida
Source: *BioIn 11, 12*

Spenser, Edmund
English. Poet
Developed Spenserian stanza used in allegorical epic *The Faerie Queen*, 1596.
b. 1552? in London, England
d. Jan 13, 1599 in Westminster, England
Source: *Alli; AtlBL; BbD; BiD&SB; BrAu; CasWL; Chambr 1; ChPo, S1, S2; CnE&AP; CroE&S; CrtT 1; CyWA; DcEnA; DcEnL; DcEuL; DcLEL; EvLB; MouLC 1; NewC; OxEng; Pen ENG; PoLE; RAdv 1; RComWL; REn; WebE&AL*

Speransky, Mikhail
Russian. Political Leader
b. 1772
d. 1839
Source: *NewCol 75; WebBD 80*

Sperling, Godfrey, Jr.
American. Children's Author
b. Sep 25, 1915 in Long Beach, California
Source: *WhoAm 74, 76, 78, 80, 82; WhoS&SW 73*

Sperry, Armstrong W
American. Artist
b. Nov 7, 1897 in New Haven, Connecticut
d. Apr 28, 1976 in Hanover, New Hampshire
Source: *AnCL; AuBYP; ConAu P-1; CurBio 41; IlsCB 1744, 1946; JBA 51; Newb 1922; SmATA 1, 27; Str&VC*

Sperry, Elmer Ambrose
American. Inventor
Invented gyrocompass and numerous electrical devices.
b. Oct 12, 1860 in Cortland, New York
d. Jun 10, 1930 in Brooklyn, New York
Source: *AmBi; DcAmB; EncAB-H; NewCol 75; WebAB; WhAm 1*

Spewack, Bella Cohen
American. Dramatist, Journalist
b. Mar 25, 1899 in Bucharest, Romania
Source: *AmAu&B; Au&Wr 71; BiE&WWA; ConDr 73; EncMT; InWom; IntMPA 75, 76, 77, 78, 79, 80, 81, 82; McGEWD; ModWD; NewCBMT; NotNAT; REn; REnAL; TwCA, SUP; WhoAm 74; WhoThe 77; WomWMM*

Spewack, Samuel
Russian. Dramatist
b. Sep 16, 1899 in Bachmut, Russia
d. Oct 14, 1971 in New York, New York
Source: *AmAu&B; Au&Wr 71; BiE&WWA; CnMD; ConAu 33R; McGEWD; ModWD; NewCBMT; NewYTBE 71; REn; REnAL; TwCA, SUP; WhAm 5*

Spiegel, Sam
American. Motion Picture Producer
b. Nov 11, 1904 in Jaroslau, Austria
Source: *BiDFilm; CelR 73; FilmgC; IntMPA 75, 76, 77, 78, 79, 80, 81, 82; OxFilm; WhoAm 82; WhoAmA 73; WhoWorJ 72; WorEFlm*

Spielberg, Steven
American. Motion Picture Director
Films include *Jaws*, 1975; *ET*, 1982.
b. Dec 18, 1947 in Cincinnati, Ohio
Source: *BkPepl; FilmgC; IntMPA 75, 76, 77, 78, 79, 80, 81, 82; WhoAm 80, 82*

Spier, Peter Edward
American. Artist, Author
b. Jun 6, 1927 in Amsterdam, Netherlands
Source: *BkP; ChPo S1, S2; ConAu 5R; IlsBYP; IlsCB 1946, 1957; SmATA 4; ThrBJA; WhoAm 74, 76, 78, 80, 82*

Spigelgass, Leonard
American. Dramatist
b. Nov 26, 1908 in New York, New York
Source: *ConAu 103; IntMPA 77, 78, 79, 80, 81, 82; NotNAT; WhoAm 74; WhoThe 77*

Spillane, Mickey (Frank Morrison)
American. Author
Known for Mike Hammer detective stories.
b. Mar 9, 1918 in Brooklyn, New York
Source: *AmAu&B; CelR 73; ConAu 25R; ConLC 3; EncMys; FilmgC; LongCTC; OxAmL; Pen AM; REn; TwCW; WebAB; WhoAm 82; WrDr 76*

Spilsbury, Sir Bernard Henry
English. Pathologist
b. 1877 in Leamington, England
d. Dec 17, 1947 in London, England
Source: *BioIn 1, 2, 5, 7, 10; LongCTC; ObitOF 79*

Spinks, Leon
American. Boxer
b. Jul 11, 1953 in Saint Louis, Missouri
Source: *BioIn 11*

Spinks, Michael
American. Boxer
b. Jul 29, 1956 in Saint Louis, Missouri
Source: *BioIn 12*

Spinoza, Baruch (Benedictus de)
Dutch. Philosopher
b. Nov 24, 1632 in Amsterdam, Netherlands
d. Feb 20, 1677 in The Hague, Netherlands
Source: *BbD; BiD&SB; CasWL; DcEuL; EvEuW; NewC; OxEng; Pen EUR; RComWL; REn*

Spitalny, Phil
American. Band Leader
b. Nov 7, 1890 in Odessa, Russia
d. Oct 11, 1970 in Miami, Florida
Source: *AmSCAP 66; What 3*

Spitta, (Julius August) Philipp
German. Author, Music Scholar
b. Dec 27, 1841 in Wechold, Germany
d. Apr 13, 1894 in Berlin, Germany
Source: *Baker 78; OxMus*

Spitz, Mark Andrew
American. Swimmer
First athlete to win seven gold medals in single Olympic games, 1972.
b. Feb 10, 1950 in Modesto, California
Source: *BioNews 74; CelR 73; CurBio 72; NewYTBE 72, 73; WhoAm 74*

Spitzer, Andre
Israeli. Murdered Olympic Team Member
b. 1945? in Romania
d. Sep 5, 1972 in Munich, Germany (West)
Source: *BioIn 9*

Spivak, Charlie
American. Band Leader, Musician
b. Feb 17, 1906 in New Haven, Connecticut
d. Mar 1, 1982 in Greenville, South Carolina
Source: *CmpEPM; NewYTBS 82; WhoJazz 72*

Spivak, Lawrence
American. TV Panelist, Producer
b. Jun 11, 1900 in Brooklyn, New York
Source: *CelR 73; CurBio 56; IntMPA 75, 76, 77, 78, 79, 80, 81, 82; WhoAm 82; WhoS&SW 73; WhoWorJ 72*

Spivakovsky, Tossy
Russian. Musician
b. Feb 4, 1907 in Odessa, Russia
Source: *IntWW 74; WhoWorJ 72*

Spock, Benjamin McLane
American. Pediatrician, Author
Wrote *Common Sense Book of Baby Care,* 1946; has sold over 11 million copies.
b. May 2, 1903 in New Haven, Connecticut
Source: *AmAu&B; Au&Wr 71; AuNews 1; BioNews 74; CelR 73; ConAu 21R; CurBio 56, 69; EncAB-H; IntWW 74; NewYTBE 72; REnAL; WebAB; Who 82; WhoAm 74, 76, 78, 80, 82; WhoAmP 73; WhoWor 74; WrDr 76*

Spode, Josiah
English. Potter
b. Jul 16, 1754
d. 1827
Source: *NewCol 75; WebBD 80*

Spohr, Louis Ludwig
German. Musician, Composer
b. Apr 5, 1784 in Brunswick, Germany
d. Oct 22, 1859 in Cassel, Germany
Source: *OxMus*

Spontini, Gasparo
Italian. Composer
b. Nov 14, 1774 in Majolati, Italy
d. Jan 24, 1851 in Majolati, Italy
Source: *NewEOp 71; OxMus*

Spooner, Bill
see: Tubes, The

Spooner, William Archibald
English. Educator
"Spoonerisms" are unconscious consonant transpositions.
b. Jul 22, 1844 in London, England
d. 1930
Source: *LongCTC; REn*

Spottswood, Stephen Gill, Bishop
American. Chairman of NAACP
b. Jul 18, 1897 in Boston, Massachusetts
d. Dec 1, 1974 in Washington, DC
Source: *CurBio 62, 75; NewYTBS 74; WhAm 6; WhoAm 74; WhoBlA 75; WhoS&SW 73; WhoWor 74*

Sprague, Frank Julian
American. Engineer
Constructed first major electric trolley system in US in Richmond, VA, 1887.
b. Jul 25, 1857 in Milford, Connecticut
d. Oct 25, 1934 in New York, New York
Source: *AmBi; ApCAB X; DcAmB S1; EncAB-H; McGEWB; NatCAB 3, 24; WebAB; WhAm 1*

Spreckels, Claus
"Sugar King"
German. Sugar Executive
b. Jul 9, 1828 in Lamstedt, Germany
d. Jan 10, 1908 in San Francisco, California
Source: *BioIn 7; DcAmB; WebAB; WhAm 1*

Springer, Axel Casar
German. Journalist
b. May 2, 1912 in Hamburg, Germany
Source: *CurBio 68; IntWW 74; WhoWor 74*

Springer, Ya'acov
Israeli. Murdered Olympic Team Member
b. 1920?
d. Sep 5, 1972 in Munich, Germany (West)
Source: *BioIn 9*

Springfield, Dusty
[Mary Isobel Catherine O'Brien]
English. Singer
b. Apr 16, 1939 in Hampstead, England
Source: *BiDAmM; EncPR&S; IlEncRk; RkOn*

Springfield, Rick (Richard)
Australian. Actor, Musician, Singer
Regular on TV soap opera "General Hospital"; sang "Jessie's Girl," 1981.
b. Aug 23, 1949 in Sydney, Australia
Source: *BioIn 12; RkOn 2*

Springsteen, Bruce
American. Singer, Songwriter
Wrote song, "Blinded By the Light."
b. Sep 23, 1949 in Freehold, New Jersey
Source: *BioIn 10, 11; ConLC 17; CurBio 78; IlEncRk; RkOn; WhoAm 82*

Sproul, Robert Gordon
American. Educator
b. May 22, 1891 in San Francisco, California
d. Sep 10, 1975 in Berkeley, California
Source: *CurBio 45, 75; WhAm 6; Who 74; WhoAm 74*

Spruance, Raymond Ames
American. Admiral, Statesman
b. Jul 3, 1886 in Baltimore, Maryland
d. Dec 13, 1969 in Pebble Beach, California
Source: *CurBio 44, 70; WebAB; WhAm 5*

Spychalski, Marian
Polish. Architect, Politician
b. Dec 6, 1906 in Lodz, Poland
Source: *IntWW 74*

Spyri, Johanna Heuser
Swiss. Author
Wrote *Heidi,* 1880.
b. Jun 12, 1827 in Hirzel, Switzerland
d. Jul 7, 1901 in Zurich, Switzerland
Source: *AnCL; AuBYP; CarSB; InWom; JBA 34, 51; OxGer; WhoChL*

Squanto
[Tisquantum]
American Indian. Guide, Interpreter
Taught Pilgrims wilderness survival.
b. 1585?
d. 1622 in Chatham Harbor, Massachusetts
Source: *AmBi; DcAmB; WebAB; WhAm H*

Spyropoulos, Jannis
Greek. Artist
b. Mar 12, 1912 in Pylos, Greece
Source: *IntWW 74, 75, 76, 77, 78; WhoWor 74, 78*

Squeeze
[John Bentley; Chris Difford; Gilson Lavis; Don Snow; Glenn Tilbrook]
British. Rock Group
Source: *IlEncRk*

Squibb, Edward Robinson
American. Manufacturer
Founded E R Squibb, 1858.
b. Jul 4, 1819 in Wilmington, Delaware
d. Oct 25, 1900 in Brooklyn, New York
Source: *Alli SUP; DcAmB; DcNAA; WebAB; WhAm H*

Stabile, Mariano
Italian. Opera Singer
b. May 12, 1888 in Palermo, Sicily
d. Jan 11, 1968 in Milan, Italy
Source: *NewEOp 71*

Stabler, Ken(neth Michael)
American. Football Player
b. Dec 25, 1945 in Foley, Alabama
Source: *WhoAm 80, 82; WhoFtbl 74*

Stacey, Thomas Charles Gerard
English. Author
b. Jan 11, 1930 in Bletchingley, England
Source: *Au&Wr 71; ConAu 9R*

Stack, Robert
American. Actor
Starred in TV series "The Untouchables," 1959-63.
b. Jan 13, 1919 in Los Angeles, California
Source: *BiDFilm; CelR 73; FilmgC; IntMPA 75, 76, 77, 78, 79, 80, 81, 82; MotPP; MovMk; WhoAm 74, 76, 78, 80*

Stacton, David Derek
American. Author
b. Apr 25, 1925 in Minden, Nevada
d. Jan 20, 1968 in Fredensborg, Sweden
Source: *AmAu&B; ConAu 5R, 25R*

Stacy, Hollis
American. Golfer
b. Mar 16, 1954 in Savannah, Georgia
Source: *BioIn 9, 11; WhoGolf*

Stacy, James
American. Actor
Source: *WhoHol A*

Stader, Maria
American. Opera Singer
b. 1915 in Budapest, Hungary
Source: *CurBio 58; InWom; WhoMus 72; WhoWor 74*

Stadler, Craig
"The Walrus"
American. Golfer
b. Jun 2, 1953 in San Diego, California
Source: *NewYTBS 82*

Stael, Nicolas de
French. Artist
b. 1914 in Saint Petersburg, Russia
d. Mar 22, 1955 in Antibes, France
Source: *AtlBL; McGDA; McGEWB*

Stael-Holstein, Anne Louise Germaine (Necker), Baroness
French. Author
b. Apr 22, 1766 in Paris, France
d. Jul 13, 1817 in Paris, France
Source: *AtlBL; BbD; BiD&SB; CasWL; CyWA; DcBiA; DcEuL; EvEuW; InWom; NewC; OxEng; OxFr; OxGer; Pen EUR*

Stafford, Jean
American. Author
b. Jul 1, 1915 in Covina, California
d. Mar 26, 1979 in White Plains, New York
Source: *AmAu&B; AmNov; CnDAL; ConAu 1R, 3NR; ConLC 4, 7; ConNov 72, 76; DrAF 76; EncWL; InWom; ModAL; OxAmL; Pen AM; RAdv 1; REn; REnAL; TwCA SUP; WhoAm 74; WhoE 74; WhoTwCL; WhoWor 74; WrDr 76*

Stafford, Jim
American. Singer, Songwriter
b. 1944 in Winter Haven, Florida
Source: *BioIn 10; RkOn*

Stafford, Jo
American. Singer
b. 1918 in Coalinga, California
Source: *InWom; WhoAm 74*

Stafford, Robert Theodore
American. Senator
b. Aug 8, 1913 in Rutland, Vermont
Source: *AlmAP 78, 80; BiDrAC; BioIn 5, 9, 10; CngDr 74, 77, 79; CurBio 60; NewYTBE 71; WhoAm 74, 76, 78, 80, 82; WhoAmL 79; WhoAmP 73, 75, 77, 79; WhoE 74, 75, 77, 79*

Stafford, Thomas P(atten)
American. Astronaut, General
Flew on Gemini VI, IX, and Apollo X flights.
b. Sep 17, 1930 in Weatherford, Oklahoma
Source: *AmM&WS 73P; IntWW 74; WhoAm 74, 76, 78, 80, 82; WhoS&SW 73; WhoWor 74*

Stafford, William Edgar
American. Author
b. Jan 17, 1914 in Hutchinson, Kansas
Source: *ChPo S1; ConAu 5R, 5NR; ConP 70, 75; CroCAP; DrAP 75; DrAS 74E; ModAL SUP; OxAmL; Pen AM; RAdv 1; WhoAm 74, 76, 78, 80, 82; WhoPNW; WorAu; WrDr 76*

Stagg, Amos Alonzo
American. Football Coach
Introduced huddle, several innovative plays still used today; Hall of Fame, 1951.
b. Aug 16, 1862 in West Orange, New Jersey
d. Mar 17, 1965 in Stockton, California
Source: *WebAB; WhAm 4; WhNAA; WhoBbl 73; WhoFtbl 74*

Stahl, Ben(jamin Albert)
American. Artist, Illustrator
b. Sep 7, 1910 in Chicago, Illinois
Source: *ConAu 29R; IlsBYP; IlsCB 1957; SmATA 5; WhoAm 74, 76, 78, 80, 82; WhoAmA 73; WhoS&SW 73*

Stahl, Lesley
American. Broadcast Journalist
b. Dec 16, 1941 in Lynn, Massachusetts
Source: *AuNews 2; BioIn 11; WhoAm 82*

Stalin, Joseph
[Iosif Visarionovich Stalin]
Russian. Chief of State
Succeeded Lenin; dictator, 1929-53.
b. Dec 21, 1879 in Tiflis, Russia
d. Mar 5, 1953 in Moscow, U.S.S.R.
Source: *CurBio 42, 53; DcRusL; REn; WhAm 3, 4*

Stalina, Svetlana Alliluyeva
[Svetlana Peters]
Russian. Daughter of Joseph Stalin
b. Feb 28, 1926 in Moscow, U.S.S.R.
Source: *CurBio 68; InWom; NewYTBE 73; WhoAm 74*

Stallings, Laurence
American. Author, Drama Critic
b. Nov 25, 1894 in Macon, Georgia
d. Feb 28, 1968
Source: *AmAu&B; BiE&WWA; CnDAL; ConAmA; ConAmL; ConAu 89; McGEWD; ModWD; OxAmL; Pen AM; REn; REnAL; TwCA, SUP; WhAm 4A*

Stallone, (Michael) Sylvester
American. Actor, Motion Picture Director
Best known for *Rocky* films, 1976, 1979, 1982.
b. Jul 6, 1946 in New York, New York
Source: *BioIn 11; BkPepl; ConAu 77; IntMPA 82*

Stambuliski, Aleksandr
[Alexandr Stamboliski]
Bulgarian. Premier
Leader of Peasant's Party; premier, 1920-23 until assassinated.
b. Mar 1, 1879
d. 1923
Source: *NewCol 75; WebBD 80*

Stamp, Terence
English. Actor
b. 1940? in London, England
Source: *FilmgC; IntMPA 75, 76, 77, 78, 79, 80, 81, 82; MotPP; MovMk; OxFilm; WhoHol A; WorEFlm*

Stander, Lionel
American. Actor
b. 1908 in New York, New York
Source: *BiE&WWA; FilmgC; IntMPA 75, 76, 77, 78, 79, 80, 81, 82; MotPP; MovMk; NewYTBE 71; NotNAT; Vers A; WhoHol A*

Standing, Guy
Entertainer
b. Sep 1, 1873 in London, England
d. Feb 24, 1937 in Los Angeles, California
Source: *FilmgC; MotPP; WhScrn 74, 77; WhoHol B; WhoStg 1906, 1908*

Standish, Burt L, pseud.
see: Patten, Gilbert

Standish, Miles
American. Pilgrim Colonist
Military leader, Plymouth Colony, 1620-25.
b. 1584 in Lancashire, England
d. Oct 3, 1656 in Duxbury, Massachusetts
Source: *AmBi; Drake; REn; REnAL; WebAB*

Stanford, (Amasa) Leland
American. Railroad, Government Official
b. Mar 9, 1824 in Watervliet, New York
d. Jun 21, 1893 in Palo Alto, California
Source: *AmBi; ApCAB; BiAuS; BiDrAC; BioIn 2, 3, 6, 7, 8, 9, 10, 11; DcAmB; Drake; EncAB-A; LinLib S; McGEWB; NatCAB 2; REnAW; TwCBDA; WebAB; WhAm H; WhAmP*

Stanford, Sally
[Mabel Janice Busby; Sally Gump]
American. Mayor of Sausalito
b. 1903 in Baker City, Oregon
d. Feb 2, 1982 in Greenbrae, California
Source: *BioIn 2, 10, 11; NewYTBS 82; WomPO 76*

Stang, Arnold
American. Comedian
b. Sep 28, 1925 in New York, New York
Source: *AmSCAP 66; BiE&WWA; IntMPA 75, 76, 77, 78, 79, 80, 81, 82; Vers A; WhoHol A; WhoWorJ 72*

Stangl, Franz Paul
Austrian. Nazi Criminal
b. 1908? in Austria
d. Jun 28, 1971 in Dusseldorf, Germany (West)
Source: *BioIn 7, 8, 9, 10; NewYTBE 71; WhWW-II*

Stanhope, Philip Dormer
see: Chesterfield, Philip Dormer, Earl

Stanislavsky, Konstantin Sergeyevich
Russian. Actor, Motion Picture Producer
b. Jan 17, 1863 in Moscow, Russia
d. Aug 7, 1938 in Moscow, U.S.S.R.
Source: *DcRusL; LongCTC; OxFilm; OxThe; REn*

Stanley, Frederick Arthur, Earl of Derby
[Lord Stanley of Preston]
English. Governor General of Canada
First awarded Stanley Cup to amateur hockey teams, 1893-1912, now to pros.
b. Jan 15, 1841 in England
d. Jun 14, 1908 in England
Source: *CelCen; WhoHcky 73*

Stanley, Sir Henry Morton
[Stanley and Livingstone]
English. Explorer, Journalist
Said "Dr. Livingstone I presume" after finding African explorer, 1871.
b. Jan 31, 1841 in Denbigh, Wales
d. May 10, 1904 in London, England
Source: *Alli SUP; AmAu&B; AmBi; BbD; BiD&SB; BrAu 19; CarSB; Chambr 3; DcAmAu; DcAmB; DcEnA, AP; EvLB; OxAmL; OxEng; REn; REnAL; WebAB; WhAm 1*

Stanley and Livingstone
see: Livingstone, David; Stanley, Sir Henry Morton

Stanley, Kim
American. Actress
b. Feb 11, 1925? in Tularosa, New Mexico
Source: *BiE&WWA; CurBio 55; FilmgC; InWom; MotPP; MovMk; NotNAT; WhoAm 74; WhoHol A; WhoThe 77*

Stans, Maurice Hubert
American. Former Government Official
b. Mar 22, 1908 in Shakopee, Minnesota
Source: *BiDFilm; CurBio 58; IntWW 74; NewYTBE 70, 71, 73, 74; WhoAm 74; WhoAmP 73; WhoS&SW 73*

Stanton, Edwin McMasters
American. Statesman
b. Dec 19, 1814 in Steubenville, Ohio
d. Dec 24, 1869 in Washington, DC
Source: *Alli; AmBi; ApCAB; BiAuS; BiDrUSE; DcAmB; Drake; EncAB-H; TwCBDA; WebAB; WhAm H*

Stanton, Elizabeth Cady
American. Feminist, Social Reformer
President, National Woman Suffrage Assn., 1868-70.
b. Nov 12, 1815 in Johnstown, New York
d. Oct 26, 1902 in New York, New York
Source: *Alli SUP; AmAu; AmAu&B; AmWom; ApCAB; BbD; BiCAW; BiD&SB; DcAmAu; DcAmB; DcNAA; EncAB-H; HerW; InWom; NotAW; OxAmL; REn; REnAL; TwCBDA; WebAB; WhAm 1; WhAmP*

Stanton, Frank
American. TV Executive, Author
b. Mar 20, 1908 in Muskegon, Michigan
Source: *AmM&WS 73S; BiE&WWA; CelR 73; CurBio 45, 65; IntMPA 75; IntWW 74; NewYTBE 71; St&PR 75; WhoAm 74; WhoE 74; WhoF&I 74; WhoGov 72*

Stanton, Frank Lebby
American. Poet, Journalist
b. Feb 22, 1857 in Charleston, South Carolina
d. Jan 7, 1927 in Atlanta, Georgia
Source: *AmAu&B; AmSCAP 66; BbD; BiDSA; ChPo; DcAmAu; DcAmB; DcNAA; OxAmL; WhAm 1*

Stanton, Henry Brewster
American. Reformer
b. 1805 in Griswold, Connecticut
d. Jan 14, 1887 in New York, New York
Source: *DcNAA*

Stanwyck, Barbara
[Ruby Stevens]
American. Actress
Starred in *Stella Dallas,* 1931; TV series "The Big Valley," 1965-69.
b. Jul 16, 1907 in Brooklyn, New York
Source: *BiDFilm; BiE&WWA; CelR 73; CmMov; CurBio 47; FilmgC; InWom; IntMPA 75, 76, 77, 78, 79, 80, 81, 82; MotPP; MovMk; OxFilm; ThFT; WhoAm 74; WhoHol A; WhoThe 77; WhoWor 74; WorEFlm*

Stapleton, Jean
[Mrs. William Putch]
American. Actress
Played Edith Bunker on TV series "All in the Family," 1971-79.
b. Jan 19, 1923 in New York, New York
Source: *BiE&WWA; BioNews 74; BkPepl; CelR 73; CurBio 72; IntMPA 75, 76, 77, 78, 79, 80, 81, 82; NewYTBE 71, 72; NotNAT; WhoAm 74; WhoAmW 77; WhoHol A; WhoThe 77; WhoWest 74*

Stapleton, Maureen
American. Actress
Won Tony, 1970, for *The Gingerbread Lady.*
b. Jun 21, 1925 in Troy, New York
Source: *BiE&WWA; BioNews 74; CelR 73; CurBio 59; FamA&A; FilmgC; InWom; IntMPA 75, 76, 77, 78, 79, 80, 81, 82; MotPP; MovMk; NewYTBE 71; NotNAT; WhoAm 74, 76, 78, 80, 82; WhoAmW 77; WhoHol A; WhoThe 77; WhoWor 74*

Stapleton, Ruth Carter
American. Sister of Jimmy Carter
b. Aug 7, 1929 in Archery, Georgia
Source: *BioIn 10; ConAu 81*

Starch, Daniel
American. Marketing Research Consultant
b. Mar 8, 1883 in La Crosse, Wisconsin
d. Feb 8, 1979
Source: *AmAu&B; AmM&WS 73S; ConAu 37R; CurBio 63; REnAL; WhAm 7; WhNAA; WhoAm 74*

Stare, Fredrick John
American. Nutritionist, Journalist
b. Apr 11, 1910 in Columbus, Wisconsin
Source: *AmM&WS 73P; WhoAm 74*

Stargell, Willie (Wilver Dornel)
"Pops"
American. Baseball Player
Outfielder, Pittsburgh, 1962-81; holds record for career strikeouts: 1,912.
b. Mar 4, 1941 in Earlsboro, Oklahoma
Source: *BaseEn; BioIn 9, 10, 11, 12; CurBio 80; WhoProB 73*

Stark, Abe
American. Municipal Official
b. Sep 28, 1894 in New York, New York
d. Jul 3, 1972 in New York, New York
Source: *NewYTBE 72; WhAm 5*

Stark, Harold Raynsford
American. Naval Officer
b. Nov 12, 1880 in Wilkes-Barre, Pennsylvania
d. Aug 20, 1972 in Washington, DC
Source: *CurBio 40, 72; NewYTBE 72; WhAm 5*

Stark, John
American. General
b. Aug 28, 1728 in Londonderry, New Hampshire
d. May 8, 1822 in Manchester, New Hampshire
Source: *Alli; AmBi; ApCAB; DcAmB; Drake; TwCBDA; WebAB; WhAm H*

Stark, "Koo" (Kathleen)
American. Actress
Involved in publicized romanace with Britain's Prince Andrew, 1982.
b. 1957? in New York, New York
Source: *NF*

Starker, Janos
Hungarian. Musician
b. Jul 5, 1924 in Budapest, Hungary
Source: *CurBio 63; IntWW 74; NewYTBE 72; Who 74; WhoAm 74; WhoMus 72*

Starkie, Walter Fitzwilliam
Irish. Literary Historian
b. Aug 9, 1894 in Killiney, Ireland
d. Nov 2, 1976 in Madrid, Spain
Source: *CathA 1930; ConAu 69, 77; CurBio 64; IntWW 74; LongCTC; NewC; TwCA, SUP; WhAm 7; Who 74; WhoAm 74; WhoMus 72*

Starkweather, Charles
American. Mass Murderer
Killed 11 people, 1958; executed, 1959.
b. 1940 in Lincoln, Nebraska
d. Jun 24, 1959 in Nebraska
Source: *BioIn 10; Blood*

Starr, Bart (Bryan B)
American. Football Player, Coach
Quarterback, Green Bay, 1956-71; Hall of Fame, 1977.
b. Jan 9, 1934 in Montgomery, Alabama
Source: *BioNews 75; CurBio 68; WhoAm 82; WhoFtbl 74*

Starr, Belle Shirley
American. Western Pioneer, Outlaw
Cattle rustler; harbored Jesse James, 1881.
b. Feb 5, 1848? in Carthage, Missouri
d. Feb 3, 1889 in Briartown, Oklahoma
Source: *InWom; NotAW; WhAm H*

Starr, Kay
American. Singer
b. 1924 in Doughtery, Oklahoma
Source: *BioIn 2; InWom*

Starr, Ringo
[The Beatles; Richard Starkey]
English. Singer, Musician
Solo performer, 1970--; starred in *Caveman,* 1981.
b. Jul 7, 1940 in Liverpool, England
Source: *BkPepl; CelR 73; CurBio 65; IntWW 74; MotPP; WhoAm 82; WhoHol A; WhoWor 74*

Starrett, (Charles) Vincent (Emerson)
American. Author, Critic
b. Oct 26, 1886 in Toronto, ON
d. Jan 4, 1974 in Chicago, Illinois
Source: *AmAu&B; AuBYP; ChPo; ConAu 45, 73; EncMys; NewYTBS 74; REn; REnAL; TwCA, SUP; WhAm 6*

Starzl, Thomas
American. Surgeon
b. Mar 11, 1926 in Le Mars, Iowa
Source: *AmM&WS 73P; WhoAm 74, 76, 78, 80, 82; WhoWest 74*

Stassen, Harold Edward
American. Lawyer, Politician
Governor of MN, 1938-45; youngest governor in US history.
b. Apr 13, 1907 in West St. Paul, Minnesota
Source: *AmAu&B; CurBio 40, 48; IntWW 74; WebAB; Who 74; WhoAm 74, 76, 78, 80, 82; WhoAmP 73*

Stastny, Anton
Czech. Hockey Player
b. Aug 9, 1959 in Bratislava, Czechoslovakia
Source: *NewYTBS 81*

Stastny, Marian
Czech. Hockey Player
b. Jan 8, 1953 in Bratislava, Czechoslovakia
Source: *NewYTBS 81*

Stastny, Peter
Czech. Hockey Player
Won Calder trophy, 1981; first non-North-American player honored.
b. Sep 18, 1956 in Bratislava, Czechoslovakia
Source: *NewYTBS 81*

Statler, Ellsworth Milton
American. Hotel Proprietor
Started Statler chain of hotels, Buffalo, NY, 1904.
b. Oct 26, 1863 in Somerset County, Pennsylvania
d. Apr 16, 1928 in New York, New York
Source: *DcAmB; WebAB; WhAm 1*

Statler Brothers
[Phillip Balsley; Lew C DeWitt; Don S Reid; Harold W Reid]
American. Singing Group
Source: *EncFCWM 69; RkOn*

Staub, "Rusty" (Daniel Joseph)
American. Baseball Player
Nicknamed by nurses at birth for hair color.
b. Apr 1, 1944 in New Orleans, Louisiana
Source: *BaseEn; BioIn 8, 9, 11; NewYTBE 72, 73; WhoAm 74, 76, 78; WhoProB 73*

Staubach, Roger Thomas
American. Football Player
Won Heisman Trophy, 1963; quarterback, Dallas, 1969-79.
b. Feb 5, 1942 in Cincinnati, Ohio
Source: *CelR 73; CurBio 72; NewYTBE 71, 72; WhoAm 74, 76, 78, 80, 82; WhoFtbl 74*

Stauffenberg, Claus (Schenk Graf) Von
[Klaus Graf Schenk von Stauffenberg]
German. Army Officer
b. Nov 15, 1907 in Upper Franconia, Germany
d. Jul 20, 1944 in Rastenburg, Germany
Source: *BioIn 2, 8, 10; EncTR; OxGer; WhWW-II*

Stauffer, Charles Albert
American. Publisher
b. Mar 23, 1880 in Sedgewick, Kansas
d. Dec 1970
Source: *WhAm 5*

Stavisky, Serge Alexandre
French. Swindler
b. 1886
d. 1934
Source: *REn*

Stavropoulos, George Peter
American. Fashion Designer
b. Jan 22, 1920 in Tripolis, Greece
Source: *WhoAm 82; WorFshn*

Stead, Christina Ellen
Australian. Author
b. Jul 17, 1902 in New South Wales, Australia
Source: *CasWL; ConAu 13R; ConLC 2, 5, 8; ConNov 72, 76; DcLEL; EvLB; LongCTC; RAdv 1; TwCA, SUP; TwCW; Who 74; WhoTwCL; WhoWor 74; WrDr 76*

Steber, Eleanor
American. Opera Singer
b. Jul 17, 1916 in Wheeling, West Virginia
Source: *CurBio 43; InWom; NewYTBE 73; WhoAm 74, 76, 78, 80, 82; WhoMus 72; WhoWor 74*

Stedman, Edmund Clarence
American. Author, Journalist
b. Oct 8, 1833 in Hartford, Connecticut
d. Jan 18, 1908
Source: *Alli, SUP; AmAu; AmAu&B; AmBi; ApCAB; BiD&SB; Chambr 3; ChPo, S1, S2; CnDAL; CyAl 2; DcAmAu; DcAmB; DcEnA AP; DcEnL; DcLEL; DcNAA; Drake; EvLB; OxAmL; OxCan; REn; REnAL; TwCBDA; WhAm 1*

Steegmuller, Francis
American. Biographer
b. Apr 3, 1906 in New Haven, Connecticut
Source: *AmAu&B; ChPo; ConAu 49, 2NR; ConNov 72, 76; REnAL; TwCA SUP; Who 74; WhoAm 74, 76, 78, 80, 82; WrDr 76*

Steel, Anthony
English. Actor
b. May 21, 1920 in London, England
Source: *FilmgC; IntMPA 75, 76, 77, 78, 79, 80, 81, 82*

Steele, Sir Richard
British. Essayist, Dramatist
b. Mar 1672 in Dublin, Ireland
d. Sep 1, 1729 in Carmarthen, Wales
Source: *AtlBL; CyWA*

Steele, Bob
American. Actor
b. 1907? in Oregon
Source: *FilmgC; TwYS; Vers A; WhoHol A*

Steele, Tommy
English. Actor
b. Dec 17, 1936 in London, England
Source: *EncMT; FilmgC; IntMPA 75, 76, 77, 78, 79, 80, 81, 82; MotPP; Who 74; WhoHol A; WhoThe 77*

Steelman, John R
American. Government Official
b. Jun 23, 1900 in Thornton, Arkansas
Source: *CurBio 41, 52*

Steely Dan
[Jeff Baxter; Walter Becker; Denny Dias; Donald Fagen; James Hodder; David Palmer]
American. Rock Group
Source: *IlEncRk; RkOn*

Steen, Jan
Dutch. Artist
b. 1626 in Leiden, Netherlands
d. Feb 3, 1679 in Leiden, Netherlands
Source: *AtlBL*

Steen, Roger
see: Tubes, The

Steenburgen, Mary
[Mrs. Malcolm McDowell]
American. Actress
Won Oscar, 1981, for *Melvin and Howard.*
b. 1953 in Little Rock, Arkansas
Source: *BioIn 12; JohnWil 81*

Stefansson, Vihjalmur
Canadian. Explorer, Ethnologist
Led Canadian Arctic Expedition, 1913-18; discovered new lands in Arctic archipelago.
b. Nov 3, 1879 in Arnes, MB
d. Aug 26, 1962 in Hanover, New Hampshire
Source: *CurBio 62; WebAB; WebBD 80; WorAl*

Steffani, Agostino
Italian. Composer
b. Jul 25, 1654 in Castelfranco, Italy
d. Feb 12, 1728 in Frankfurt, Germany
Source: *NewEOp 71; OxMus*

Steffens, Lincoln
American. Journalist
b. Apr 6, 1866 in San Francisco, California
d. Aug 9, 1936 in Carmel, California
Source: *AmAu&B; AmBi; DcAmB S2; LongCTC; ModAL; OxAmL; Pen AM; REn; REnAL; TwCA, SUP; WebAB; WebE&AL; WhAm 1*

Stegner, Wallace Earle
American. Author
b. Feb 18, 1909 in Lake Mills, Iowa
Source: *AmAu&B; AmNov; Au&Wr 71; AuNews 1; CnDAL; ConAu 1R, 1NR; ConLC 9; ConNov 72, 76; DrAF 76; DrAS 74E; ModAL; OxAmL; OxCan; Pen AM; RAdv 1; REn; REnAL; TwCA, SUP; WhNAA; WhoAm 74, 76, 78, 80, 82; WhoWest 74; WrDr 76*

Steichen, Edward Jean
American. Photographer, Artist
b. Mar 27, 1879 in Luxembourg
d. Mar 25, 1973 in West Redding, Connecticut
Source: *ConAu 41R; CurBio 42, 64, 73; NewYTBE 73; OxAmL; REn; REnAL; WebAB; WhAm 5; WhoE 74; WhoWor 74; WorFshn*

Steig, William
American. Author, Illustrator
Drawings featured in *The New Yorker;* wrote *The Lonely Ones; Small Fry.*
b. Nov 14, 1907 in New York, New York
Source: *AmAu&B; AuBYP; AuNews 1; ConAu 77; CurBio 44; IlsBYP; NewYTBE 72; REnAL; ThrBJA; WhoAm 74, 76, 78, 80, 82; WhoAmA 73; WhoE 74; WhoWor 74*

Steiger, Rod
American. Actor
Won Oscar, 1967, for *In the Heat of the Night.*
b. Apr 14, 1925 in Westhampton, New York
Source: *BiDFilm; BkPepl; CelR 73; CmMov; CurBio 65; FilmgC; IntMPA 75, 76, 77, 78, 79, 80, 81, 82; IntWW 74; MotPP; MovMk; OxFilm; WhoAm 74, 76, 78, 80, 82; WhoHol A; WhoWor 74; WorAl; WorEFlm*

Stein, Chris
see: Blondie

Stein, Clarence S
American. Architect, Town Planner
b. Jun 19, 1882 in Rochester, New York
d. Feb 7, 1975 in New York, New York
Source: *AmArch 70; IntWW 74; WhAm 7; WhoAm 74*

Stein, Gertrude
American. Author
Center of American expatriates in 1920's Paris; named the "Lost Generation."
b. Feb 3, 1874 in Allegheny, Pennsylvania
d. Jul 27, 1946 in Neuilly, France
Source: *AmAu&B; AmWr; AtlBL; CasWL; Chambr 3; ChPo S1; CnDAL; CnE&AP; CnMD; CnMWL; ConAmA; ConAmL; DcAmB S4; DcLEL; DcNAA; EncAB-H; EncWL; EvLB; HerW; InWom; LongCTC; ModAL, SUP; ModWD; NotAW; OxAmL; OxEng; Pen AM; RAdv 1; RComWL; REn; REnAL; SixAP; TwCA, SUP; TwCW; WebAB; WebE&AL; WhAm 2; WhNAA; WhoTwCL*

Stein, Herbert
American. Economist
b. Aug 27, 1916 in Detroit, Michigan
Source: *AmAu&B; AmEA 74; AmM&WS 73S; CurBio 73; IntWW 74; NewYTBE 71; WhoAm 74, 76, 78, 80, 82; WhoGov 72*

Stein, Horst
German. Opera Conductor
b. May 28, 1928 in Elberfeld, Germany
Source: *WhoMus 72; WhoWor 74*

Stein, Joseph
American. Dramatist, Librettist
b. May 30, 1912 in New York, New York
Source: *BiE&WWA; CanWW 70; ConAu 13R; ConDr 73; EncMT; IntMPA 82; NatPD; NewCBMT; NotNAT; WhoAm 82; WhoThe 77*

Stein, Jules Caesar
American. Record Company Executive
b. Apr 26, 1896 in South Bend, Indiana
d. Apr 29, 1981 in Los Angeles, California
Source: *BioIn 1, 7, 8, 10; CelR 73; CurBio 67, 81; IntMPA 75, 76, 77, 78, 79; NewYTBS 74; WhAm 7; WhoAm 74, 76, 78, 80; WhoF&I 74; WhoWest 74, 76*

Stein, Mark
[Vanilla Fudge]
American. Singer, Musician
b. Mar 1947 in Bayonne, New Jersey
Source: *NF*

Stein, Meridee
American. Theatrical Director
b. 1948?
Source: *BioIn 12*

Steinbeck, John Ernst
American. Author
Won 1962 Nobel Prize; wrote *The Grapes of Wrath; Of Mice and Men; East of Eden.*
b. Feb 27, 1902 in Salinas, California
d. Dec 20, 1968 in New York, New York
Source: *AmAu&B; AmNov; AmWr; BiE&WWA; CasWL; CnDAL; CnMD; CnMWL; CnThe; ConAmA; ConAu 1R, 25R, 1NR; ConLC 1, 5, 9, 13; CurBio 40, 63, 69; CyWA; DcLEL; EncAB-H; EncWL; EvLB; FilmgC; LongCTC; McGEWD; ModAL; ModWD; OxAmL; OxEng; OxFilm; OxThe; Pen AM; RAdv 1; RComWL; REn; REnAL; SmATA 9; TwCA, SUP; TwCW; WebAB; WebE&AL; WhAm 5; WhoTwCL*

Steinberg, David
Canadian. Author, Comedian
b. Aug 9, 1942 in Winnipeg, MB
Source: *CanWW 82; WhoAm 76, 78, 80, 82; WhoHol A*

Steinberg, Saul
American. Artist, Architect, Cartoonist
b. Jun 15, 1914 in Rimnicu-Sarat, Romania
Source: *AmAu&B; ConAu 89; CurBio 57; DcCAA 71; IntWW 74; OxAmL; REn; WebAB; WhoAm 74; WhoGrA; WhoWor 74*

Steinberg, Sigfrid Henry
British. Editor, Historian
b. Aug 3, 1899 in Goslar, Germany
d. Jan 28, 1969
Source: *BioIn 9; ConAu P-1*

Steinberg, William (Hans Wilhelm)
American. Conductor
b. Aug 1, 1899 in Cologne, Germany
d. May 16, 1978 in New York, New York
Source: *CelR 73; CurBio 40, 58; IntWW 74; Who 74; WhoAm 74; WhoE 74; WhoWor 74*

Steinbrenner, George Michael, III
American. Baseball Club Owner
Principal owner, NY Yankees, 1973--.
b. Jul 4, 1930 in Rocky River, Ohio
Source: *BioNews 74; BusPN; NewYTBE 73; St&PR 75; WhoAm 82; WhoF&I 74*

Steinem, Gloria
American. Feminist, Journalist
Co-founder, editor *Ms.* magazine, 1971--.
b. Mar 25, 1935 in Toledo, Ohio
Source: *AmAu&B; BioNews 74; BkPepl; CelR 73; ConAu 53; CurBio 72; ForWC 70; WhoAm 74, 76, 78, 80, 82; WhoAmW 77*

Steiner, Max
Austrian. Film Composer, Conductor
b. May 10, 1888 in Vienna, Austria
d. Dec 28, 1971 in Hollywood, California
Source: *CmMov; CurBio 43, 72; DcFM; FilmgC; OxFilm; WhAm 5; WorEFlm*

Steiner, Rudolf
Austrian. Philosopher
b. 1861
d. 1925
Source: *LongCTC; OxGer*

Steinitz, Wilhelm
German. Chess Player
b. May 17, 1836 in Prague, Czechoslovakia
d. Aug 12, 1900 in New York, New York
Source: *NewCol 75*

Steinman, David Barnard
American. Engineer, Bridge Designer
b. Jun 11, 1886 in New York, New York
d. Aug 22, 1960 in New York, New York
Source: *AmAu&B; WebAB; WhAm 4; WhNAA*

Steinmetz, Charles Proteus
American. Electrical Engineer
b. Apr 9, 1865 in Breslau, Germany
d. Oct 26, 1923 in Schenectady, New York
Source: *AmBi; DcAmAu; DcAmB; DcNAA; EncAB-H; WebAB; WhAm 1*

Steinway, Henry Engelhard
[Henry Engelhard Steinweg]
German. Piano Manufacturer
Founded Steinway and Sons piano manufacturers in NY, 1853.
b. Feb 15, 1797 in Wolfshagen, Germany
d. Nov 30, 1896 in New York, New York
Source: *AmBi; ApCAB; DcAmB; REn; WebAB; WhAm H; WorAl*

Stella, Frank Philip
American. Artist
Leader of "Minimal Art" movement; paintings emphasize shape and color.
b. May 12, 1936 in Malden, Massachusetts
Source: *CurBio 71; DcCAA 71; EncAB-H; IntWW 74; WebAB; WhoAm 82; WhoAmA 73*

Stella, Joseph
American. Artist
b. Jun 13, 1880 in Munra Lucano, Italy
d. Nov 5, 1946 in New York, New York
Source: *CurBio 46; DcAmB S4; DcCAA 71; REnAL; WhAm 2*

Stemkowski, Pete(r David)
Canadian. Hockey Player
b. Aug 25, 1943 in Winnipeg, MB
Source: *WhoHcky 73*

Stendhal
[Marie Henri Beyle]
French. Author, Critic
b. Jan 23, 1783 in Grenoble, France
d. Mar 23, 1842 in Paris, France
Source: *AtlBL; BiD&SB; CasWL; CyWA; DcBiA; DcEuL; EuAu; EvEuW; NewC; OxEng; OxFr; Pen EUR; RComWL; REn*

Stengel, "Casey" (Charles Dillon)
"The Old Professor"
American. Baseball Player, Manager
Manager, NY Yankees, 1949-60; won 10 pennants, 7 world championships.
b. Jul 30, 1891 in Kansas City, Missouri
d. Sep 29, 1975 in Glendale, California
Source: *BaseEn; CelR 73; CurBio 49, 75; NewYTBS 74; WebAB; WhAm 6; WhScrn 77; WhoAm 74; WhoE 74; WorAl*

Stenmark, Ingemar
Swedish. Skier
Won, World Cup Championship, 1976-78; two gold medals, 1980 Winter Olympics.
b. Mar 18, 1956 in Josesjo, Sweden
Source: *BioIn 11; CurBio 82; WorAl*

Stennis, John Cornelius
American. Politician
b. Aug 3, 1901 in Kemper County, Mississippi
Source: *BiDrAC; CngDr 74; CurBio 53; IntWW 74; WhoAm 74, 76, 78, 80, 82; WhoAmP 73; WhoGov 72; WhoS&SW 73*

Stephanie, Princess
[Stephanie Marie Elisabeth Grimaldi]
Monacan. Daughter of Grace Kelly
Youngest child of Prince Rainier, Princess Grace; injured in car crash that killed mother.
b. Feb 1, 1965
Source: *BioIn 12*

Stephen, John
American. Actor
b. 1912 in Buffalo, New York
d. Feb 13, 1966 in Los Angeles, California
Source: *WhScrn 77*

Stephen, Sir Leslie
English. Author, Critic
b. Nov 28, 1832 in London, England
d. Feb 22, 1904
Source: *McGEWB*

Stephens, Alexander Hamilton
American. Statesman
b. Feb 11, 1812 in Wilkes County, Georgia
d. Mar 4, 1883 in Atlanta, Georgia
Source: *Alli, SUP; AmAu&B; AmBi; ApCAB; BbD; BiAuS; BiD&SB; BiDConf; BiDSA; BiDrAC; DcAmAu; DcAmB; DcNAA; Drake; EncAB-H; REnAL; TwCBDA; WebAB; WhAm H; WhAmP*

Stephens, Helen
American. Track Athlete
b. Feb 3, 1918 in Fulton, Missouri
Source: *WhoTr&F 73*

Stephens, Henrietta Henkle
see: Buckmaster, Henrietta, pseud.

Stephens, James
British. Author
b. 1882 in Dublin, Ireland
d. Dec 26, 1950 in London, England
Source: *Alli SUP; AnCL; CarSB; CasWL; Chambr 3; ChPo, S1, S2; CnE&AP; CyWA; DcLEL; EncWL; EvLB; LongCTC; ModBrL, SUP; NewC; OxEng; Pen ENG; PoIre; RAdv 1; REn; Str&VC; TwCA, SUP; TwCW; WhAm 3*

Stephens, John Lloyd
American. Traveler, Author, Diplomat
b. Nov 28, 1805 in Shrewsbury, New Jersey
d. Oct 12, 1852
Source: *Alli; AmAu&B; AmBi; ApCAB; BbD; BiAuS; BiD&SB; CyAl 2; DcAmAu; DcAmB; DcNAA; Drake; OxAmL; REn; REnAL; TwCBDA; WhAm H*

Stephens, Robert
English. Actor
b. Jul 14, 1931 in Bristol, England
Source: *BioIn 9; CnThe; FilmEn; FilmgC; IntWW 74, 75, 76, 77, 78; Who 74; WhoHol A; WhoThe 72, 77; WhoWor 74*

Stephenson, George
English. Engineer, Inventor
Patented steam blast locomotive; developed railway system.
b. Jun 9, 1781 in Wylam, England
d. Aug 12, 1848 in Chesterfield, England
Source: *AsBiEn; McGEWB; NewCol 75; WebBD 80*

Stephenson, Henry
British. Actor
b. Apr 16, 1871 in West Indies
d. Apr 24, 1956 in San Francisco, California
Source: *CmMov; Film 1; FilmgC; MovMk; Vers A; WhScrn 74, 77; WhoHol B*

Stephenson, James
English. Actor
b. 1888 in Yorkshire, England
d. Jul 29, 1941 in Pacific Palisades, California
Source: *FilmgC; WhAm 2; WhScrn 74, 77*

Stephenson, Jan
American. Golfer
Rookie of year, 1974.
b. Dec 22, 1951 in Sydney, Australia
Source: *BioIn 11; NewYTBS 76, 81; WhoAm 78; WhoAmW 79; WhoGolf*

Stepheson, "Skip" (Charles Frederick)
American. TV Personality, Comedian
Co-host of TV series "Real People."
b. 1948? in Omaha, Nebraska
Source: *BioIn 12*

Stepinac, Alojzije, Cardinal
Yugoslav. Roman Catholic Prelate
b. May 8, 1898 in Croatia
d. Feb 10, 1960 in Krasic, Yugoslavia
Source: *BioIn 1, 2, 3, 5; CurBio 53, 60*

Steppenwolf
[George Biondo; Robert Cochran; Wayne Cook; Jerry Edmonton; JohnKay]
American. Rock Group
Source: *EncPR&S*

Steptoe, Patrick Christopher
English. Gynecologist
Developed in vitro fertilization with Robert Edwards--"the test tube baby."
b. 1913 in Oxford, England
Source: *BioIn 11; CurBio 79*

Sterban, Richard
see: Oak Ridge Boys, The

Sterling, Ford
American. Actor
b. Nov 3, 1880 in La Crosse, Wisconsin
d. Oct 13, 1939 in Los Angeles, California
Source: *Film 1; FilmgC; MovMk; TwYS; WhScrn 74, 77; WhoHol B*

Sterling, George
American. Poet
b. Dec 1, 1869 in Sag Harbor, New York
d. Nov 18, 1926 in San Francisco, California
Source: *AmAu&B; AnMV 1926; CasWL; ChPo, S1, S2; ConAmL; DcAmB; DcLEL; DcNAA; OxAmL; REn; REnAL; TwCA, SUP; WhAm 1*

Sterling, Jan
[Jan Sterling Andriance]
American. Actress
b. Apr 3, 1923 in New York, New York
Source: *BiE&WWA; FilmgC; InWom; IntMPA 75, 76, 77, 78, 79, 80, 81, 82; MovMk; NotNAT; WhoHol A; WhoThe 77*

Sterling, Robert
[William Sterling Hart]
American. Actor
b. Nov 13, 1917 in New Castle, Pennsylvania
Source: *BiE&WWA; FilmgC; IntMPA 75, 76, 77, 78, 79, 80, 81, 82; MotPP; WhoHol A*

Stern, Bert
American. Photographer
b. Oct 3, 1929 in New York, New York
Source: *WhoAm 74*

Stern, Bill (William)
American. Sportscaster
b. Jul 1, 1907 in Rochester, New York
d. Nov 19, 1971 in Rye, New York
Source: *IntMPA 75, 77; WhAm 5; WhScrn 74, 77; WhoHol B*

Stern, Carl (Leonard)
American. Broadcast Journalist
b. Aug 7, 1937 in New York, New York
Source: *ConAu 97; WhoAm 80*

Stern, Isaac
American. Violinist
b. Jul 21, 1920 in Kreminiecz, U.S.S.R.
Source: *CelR 73; CurBio 49; IntWW 74; NewYTBE 70; WebAB; Who 82; WhoAm 74, 76, 78, 80, 82; WhoE 74; WhoGov 72; WhoHol A; WhoMus 72; WhoWor 74; WhoWorJ 72*

Stern, James
Irish. Author
b. Dec 26, 1907 in Ireland
Source: *ConAu 25R; ConNov 72, 76; WorAu; WrDr 76*

Stern, Leonard Norman
American. Corporation Executive
b. Mar 28, 1938 in New York, New York
Source: *BioIn 10, 11; BusPN; WhoAm 74, 76, 78, 80, 82*

Stern, Max
American. Corporation Executive
Founded, Hartz Mountain Corp., 1932.
b. 1898
d. May 20, 1982 in New York, New York
Source: *BioIn 5, 10, 11; NewYTBS 82*

Stern, Richard Gustave
American. Author
b. Feb 25, 1928 in New York, New York
Source: *AmAu&B; ConAu 1R, 1NR; ConLC 4; ConNov 72, 76; DrAF 76; DrAS 74E; Pen AM; WhoAm 74, 76, 78, 80, 82; WhoWorJ 72; WorAu; WrDr 76*

Sterne, Laurence
[Mister Yorick, pseud.]
English. Author
b. Nov 24, 1713 in Clomnel, Ireland
d. Mar 18, 1768 in London, England
Source: *Alli; AtlBL; BbD; BiD&SB; BrAu; CasWL; Chambr 2; CrtT 2; CyWA; DcBiA; DcEnA; DcEnL; DcEuL; DcLEL; EvLB; MouLC 2; NewC; OxEng; OxGer; Pen ENG; PoIre; RAdv 1; RComWL; REn; WebE&AL*

Sterne, Maurice
American. Artist
b. Jul 13, 1878 in Libau, Russia
d. Jul 23, 1957
Source: *CurBio 43, 57; DcCAA 71; WhAm 3*

Sterrett, Cliff
American. Comic Strip Artist
b. Dec 12, 1883 in Fergus Falls, Minnesota
d. Dec 28, 1964
Source: *BioIn 7; WorECom*

Stetson, John Batterson
American. Hat Manufacturer
Formed John B Stetson Co., 1885; made wide-brimmed, high-crowned cowboy hats.
b. May 5, 1830 in Orange, New Jersey
d. Feb 18, 1906 in DeLand, Florida
Source: *AmBi; DcAmB; NewCol 75; TwCBDA; WebAB; WhAm 1*

Stettinius, Edward R, Jr.
American. Government Official
b. Oct 22, 1900 in Chicago, Illinois
d. Oct 31, 1949 in Greenwich, Connecticut
Source: *CurBio 40, 49; DcAmB S4; DcNAA; EncAB-H; WhAm 1, 2*

Steuben, Friedrich Wilhelm Ludolf Gerhard Augustin, Baron
German. Soldier
b. Sep 17, 1730 in Magdeburg, Prussia
d. Nov 28, 1794 in Remsen, New York
Source: *DcNAA; REnAL*

Stevens, Andrew
American. Actor
b. 1956? in Memphis, Tennessee
Source: *BioIn 11; IntMPA 82; WhoAm 82*

Stevens, Cat
[Stephen Demetri Georgiou; Yosef Islam]
English. Singer, Songwriter
Dropped out of music business, 1981; changed name, taught Koran.
b. Jul 21, 1948 in London, England
Source: *BioNews 74; NewYTBE 71; RkOn; WhoAm 74, 76, 78, 80, 82; WhoWorJ 72; WorAl*

Stevens, Connie
[Concetta Ingolia]
American. Actress, Singer
TV series "Hawaiian Eye," 1959-63; "Wendy and Me," 1964-65 with George Burns.
b. Aug 8, 1938 in Brooklyn, New York
Source: *FilmEn; InWom; IntMPA 75, 76, 77, 78, 79, 80, 81, 82; MotPP; WhoAm 74, 76, 78, 80, 82; WhoHol A; WomPO 76*

Stevens, Emily A
American. Actress
b. 1882 in New York
d. Jan 2, 1928 in New York, New York
Source: *DcAmB; Film 1; InWom; WhScrn 74, 77; WhoHol B*

Stevens, George
American. Motion Picture Director
b. Dec 18, 1904 in Oakland, California
d. Mar 8, 1975 in Lancaster, California
Source: *AmAu&B; BiDFilm; CelR 73; CmMov; CurBio 52; DcFM; Film 1; FilmgC; IntMPA 75; IntWW 74; MovMk; OxFilm; WhAm 6; WhScrn 77; Who 74; WhoAm 74; WhoWor 74; WorEFlm*

Stevens, Greer
South African. Tennis Player
b. Feb 15, 1957
Source: *OfEnT*

Stevens, Inger
[Inger Stensland]
American. Actress
Starred in "The Farmer's Daughter," 1963-66.
b. Oct 18, 1934 in Stockholm, Sweden
d. Apr 30, 1970 in Hollywood, California
Source: *BiE&WWA; FilmgC; InWom; MotPP; MovMk; NewYTBE 70; WhAm 5; WhScrn 74, 77; WhoHol B*

Stevens, John Frank
American. Civil Engineer
b. Apr 25, 1853 in West Gardiner, Maine
d. Jun 2, 1943 in Southern Pines, North Carolina
Source: *DcAmB S3; WhAm 4*

Stevens, John Paul
American. Supreme Court Justice
b. Apr 20, 1920 in Chicago, Illinois
Source: *AmBench 79; BioIn 9, 10, 11; CngDr 77, 79; CurBio 76; DrAS 78P; IntWW 76, 77, 78; LinLib S; NewYTBS 75; PolProf NF; WhoAm 74, 76, 78, 80, 82; WhoAmL 79; WhoGov 75, 77; WhoMW 74; WhoWor 74, 78*

Stevens, K T
[Gloria Wood]
American. Actress
b. in Hollywood, California
Source: *FilmgC; IntMPA 75, 76, 77, 78, 79, 80, 81, 82; WhoHol A; WhoThe 77*

Stevens, Kaye
American. Actress
b. 1935 in Pittsburgh, Pennsylvania
Source: *WhoHol A*

Stevens, Mark
[Richard Stevens]
American. Actor
b. Dec 13, 1922 in Cleveland, Ohio
Source: *IntMPA 75, 76, 77, 78, 79, 80, 81, 82; MotPP*

Stevens, Onslow
[Onslow Ford Stevenson]
American. Actor
b. Mar 29, 1906 in Los Angeles, California
d. Jan 5, 1977 in Van Nuys, California
Source: *BiE&WWA; BioIn 11; FilmgC; MovMk; NewYTBS 77; NotNAT; Vers A; WhoHol A; WhoThe 72*

Stevens, Ray
[Harold Ray Ragsdale]
American. Musician, Singer
b. Jan 24, 1939 in Clarksdale, Georgia
Source: *EncPR&S; WhoAm 78, 80, 82*

Stevens, Rise
American. Opera Singer
b. Jun 11, 1913 in New York, New York
Source: *CurBio 41; FilmgC; InWom; IntMPA 75; WhoAm 74, 76, 78, 80, 82; WhoAmW 77; WhoHol A*

Stevens, Shane
American. Author
b. Oct 8, 1941 in New York, New York
Source: *ConAu 21R; DrAF 76*

Stevens, Siaka Probyn
Sierra Leonean. Politician
First executive president, 1971--.
b. Aug 24, 1905 in Sierra Leone
Source: *AfSS 78, 79; IntWW 74, 75, 76, 77, 78; IntYB 78, 79; Who 74; WhoGov 72; WhoWor 74, 76, 78*

Stevens, Stella
[Estelle Egglestone]
American. Actress
b. Oct 1, 1938 in Hot Coffee, Mississippi
Source: *BiDFilm; FilmgC; IntMPA 75, 76, 77, 78, 79, 80, 81, 82; MotPP; NewYTBE 73; WhoAm 74; WhoHol A*

Stevens, Ted (Theodore Fulton)
American. Senator
b. Nov 18, 1923 in Indianapolis, Indiana
Source: *AlmAP 78, 80; BiDrAC; BioIn 8, 9, 10; CngDr 74, 77, 79; IntWW 74, 75, 76, 77, 78; WhoAm 74, 76, 78, 80, 82; WhoAmL 79; WhoAmP 73, 75, 77, 79; WhoGov 72, 75, 77; WhoWest 76, 78*

Stevens, Thaddeus
American. Abolitionist, Politician
b. Apr 4, 1792 in Danville, Vermont
d. Aug 11, 1868 in Washington, DC
Source: *AmBi; ApCAB; BiAuS; BiDrAC; DcAmB; Drake; EncAB-H; REn; REnAL; TwCBDA; WebAB; WhAm H; WhAmP*

Stevens, Wallace
American. Poet, Author
Won 1955 Pulitzer Prize in Poetry.
b. Oct 2, 1879 in Reading, Pennsylvania
d. Aug 2, 1955 in Hartford, Connecticut
Source: *AmAu&B; AmWr; AtlBL; CasWL; ChPo S2; CnDAL; CnE&AP; CnMWL; ConAmA; CyWA; DcAmB S5; DcLEL; EncAB-H; EncWL; LongCTC; ModAL, SUP; OxAmL; Pen AM; RAdv 1; REn; REnAL; SixAP; TwCA, SUP; TwCW; WebAB; WebE&AL; WhAm 3; WhoTwCL; WorAl*

Stevenson, Adlai Ewing
American. Lawyer, Politician
b. Oct 23, 1835 in Christian County, Kentucky
d. Jun 14, 1914 in Chicago, Illinois
Source: *AmBi; ApCAB SUP; BiDSA; BiDrAC; BiDrUSE; DcAmB; DcNAA; TwCBDA; WebAB; WhAm 1; WhAmP*

Stevenson, Adlai Ewing, Jr.
American. Diplomat, Politician
UN ambassador, 1961-65; lost to Eisenhower in presidential races, 1952, 1956.
b. Feb 5, 1900 in Los Angeles, California
d. Jul 14, 1965 in London, England
Source: *AmAu&B; ConAu P-1; CurBio 49, 61, 65; EncAB-H; OxAmL; REn; REnAL; WebAB; WhAm 4; WhAmP; WhScrn 77; WorAl*

Stevenson, Adlai Ewing, III
American. Politician, Lawyer
Senator from IL, 1970-81.
b. Oct 10, 1930 in Chicago, Illinois
Source: *BiDrAC; CurBio 74; WhoAm 74, 76, 78, 80, 82; WhoAmP 73; WhoGov 72; WhoMW 74*

Stevenson, Coke Robert
American. Governor of Texas
b. Mar 20, 1888 in Mason County, Texas
d. Jun 28, 1975 in San Angelo, Texas
Source: *BioIn 1, 10, 11; WhAm 6*

Stevenson, Edward A
American. Politician
b. Nov 9, 1907 in Jamaica
Source: *WhoAmP 73*

Stevenson, Janet
American. Author
b. Feb 4, 1913 in Chicago, Illinois
Source: *ConAu 13R; ForWC 70; SmATA 8*

Stevenson, McLean
American. Actor
Played Henry Blake on "MASH," 1972-75.
b. Nov 14, 1929? in Bloomington, Illinois
Source: *BioNews 74; CurBio 80; WhoAm 80; WhoHol A*

Stevenson, Parker
American. Actor
Starred in TV series "Hardy Boys Mysteries," 1978-79.
b. Jun 4, 1951? in Philadelphia, Pennsylvania
Source: *IntMPA 79, 80, 81, 82*

Stevenson, Robert Louis Balfour
Scottish. Author, Poet, Essayist
Wrote *Treasure Island; A Child's Garden of Verses; Dr. Jekyll and Mr. Hyde.*
b. Nov 13, 1850 in Edinburgh, Scotland
d. Nov 13, 1894 in Vailima, Samoa
Source: *Alli SUP; AnCL; ApCAB SUP; AtlBL; AuBYP; BbD; BiD&SB; BrAu 19; CarSB; CasWL; Chambr 3; ChPo, S1, S2; CrtT 3; CyWA; DcBiA; DcEnA, AP; DcEuL; DcLEL; EncMys; EvLB; FamAYP; FilmgC; JBA 34; MnBBF; MouLC 4; NewC; OxAmL; OxEng; Pen ENG; RAdv 1; REn; REnAL; Str&VC; WebE&AL; WhoChL; WorAl*

Stevenson, Teofilo
Cuban. Boxer
Won gold medals, heavyweight division, 1972, 1976 Olympics.
b. Mar 23, 1952 in Dlicias, Cuba
Source: *NewYTBS 82*

Steward, Emanuel
American. Boxing Trainer, Manager
b. Jul 7, 1944 in Bluefield, West Virginia
Source: *BioIn 12*

Stewart, Al
British. Singer
b. 1945 in Glasgow, Scotland
Source: *BioIn 11; IlEncRk; RkOn; WhoAm 82*

Stewart, Alexander Peter
American. Confederate Officer
b. Oct 2, 1821 in Rogersville, Tennessee
d. Aug 30, 1908
Source: *AmBi; ApCAB; BiDConf; DcAmB; TwCBDA; WhAm 1*

Stewart, Alexander Turney
American. Merchant
b. Oct 12, 1803 in Lisburn, Northern Ireland
d. Apr 10, 1876 in New York, New York
Source: *AmBi; ApCAB; BiAuS; DcAmB; Drake; EncAB-H; TwCBDA; WebAB; WhAm H*

Stewart, Andrew
American. Publishing Executive
b. Feb 8, 1938 in New York, New York
Source: *IntWW 74; Who 74; WhoAm 78, 80, 82*

Stewart, Anita
American. Actress
b. Feb 17, 1896 in Brooklyn, New York
d. May 4, 1961 in Beverly Hills, California
Source: *Film 1; FilmgC; TwYS; WhScrn 74, 77; WhoHol B*

Stewart, Donald Ogden
American. Author, Actor
b. Nov 30, 1894 in Columbus, Ohio
d. Aug 2, 1980 in London, England
Source: *AmAu&B; BiE&WWA; CarSB; ConAu 81, 101; CurBio 41; DcLEL; FilmgC; NotNAT; OhA&B; OxAmL; Pen AM; REnAL; TwCA, SUP; WhNAA; WhoAm 74; WhoThe 77; WorEFlm*

Stewart, Ellen
American. Theatrical Producer
b. Oct 7, 1931 in New Orleans, Louisiana
Source: *BioIn 8, 9, 10; CelR 73; NotNAT; PlP&P; WhThe*

Stewart, Eric
see: 10 CC

Stewart, George Rippey
American. Children's Author, Educator
b. May 31, 1895 in Sewickley, Pennsylvania
d. Aug 22, 1980 in San Francisco, California
Source: *AmAu&B; AmNov; ConAu 1R, 101, 3NR; CurBio 42, 80; EncSF; OxAmL; REnAL; ScF&FL 1, 2; SmATA 3; TwCA SUP; WhNAA; WhoAm 74; WrDr 76*

Stewart, Isabella
see: Gardner, Mrs. Jack

Stewart, Jackie (John Young)
Scottish. Auto Racer, Sports Commentator
b. Jun 11, 1939 in Scotland
Source: *BioIn 8, 9, 10, 11; Who 82*

Stewart, Jimmy (James)
American. Actor
Won 1940 Oscar for *The Philadelphia Story;* is a retired brigadier general.
b. May 20, 1908 in Indiana, Pennsylvania
Source: *BiDFilm; BiE&WWA; BkPepl; CelR 73; CmMov; IntMPA 82; IntWW 74; MovMk; OxFilm; WhoAm 82; WhoThe 77; WhoWor 74; WorEFlm*

Stewart, John Innes Mackintosh
[Michael Innes, pseud.]
Scottish. Author
b. Sep 30, 1906 in Edinburgh, Scotland
Source: *Au&Wr 71; ConAu 85; ConLC 7, 14; ConNov 72, 76; DcLEL; EncMys; EvLB; LongCTC; NewC; Pen ENG; REn; TwCA, SUP; TwCW; Who 74; WrDr 76*

Stewart, Mary Rainbow
English. Author
Wrote trilogy about Merlin and King Arthur.
b. Sep 17, 1916 in Sunderland, England
Source: *BioIn 9, 10, 11; ConAu 1R, 1NR; ConLC 8; EncMys; LongCEL; SmATA 12; TwCW; WhoAm 82; WrDr 76*

Stewart, Potter
American. Former Supreme Court Justice
Appointed by President Eisenhower, 1958-81; retired.
b. Jan 13, 1915 in Jackson, Michigan
Source: *CelR 73; CngDr 74; CurBio 59; DrAS 74P; IntWW 74; WebAB; Who 74; WhoAm 74, 76, 78, 80, 82; WhoAmP 73; WhoGov 72; WhoS&SW 73; WhoWor 74; WorAl*

Stewart, Rod(erick David)
Scottish. Singer
Singer with Jeff Beck Group, 1968-69; Faces, 1969-75; solo performer, 1975--.
b. Jan 10, 1945 in Glasgow, Scotland
Source: *BioIn 10; BkPepl; EncPR&S; IlEncRk; RkOn; Rk100; WhoAm 82; WorAl*

Stewart, "Slam" (Leroy)
American. Jazz Musician, Composer
b. Sep 21, 1914 in Englewood, New Jersey
Source: *WhoAm 82; WhoJazz 72*

Stewart, Thomas
[Thomas James Stewart Jr.]
American. Opera Singer
b. Aug 19, 1928 in San Saba, Texas
Source: *NewEOp 71; WhoAm 82*

Stich-Randall, Teresa
American. Opera Singer
b. Dec 24, 1927 in West Hartford, Connecticut
Source: *WhoAm 74; WhoMus 72; WhoWor 74*

Stickley, Gustav
[Gustav Stoeckel]
American. Editor, Publisher
b. Mar 9, 1858 in Osceola, Wisconsin
d. 1942
Source: *BioIn 3, 7, 11; NatCAB 14; WhAm 4*

Stickney, Dorothy
American. Actress
b. Jun 21, 1900 in Dickinson, North Dakota
Source: *BiE&WWA; CurBio 42; InWom; MotPP; NotNAT; WhoHol A; WhoThe 77*

Stiedry, Fritz
Austrian. Conductor
b. Oct 11, 1883 in Vienna, Austria
d. Aug 9, 1968 in Zurich, Switzerland
Source: *BiDAmM; NewEOp 71*

Stieglitz, Alfred
American. Photographer, Editor
b. Jan 1, 1864 in Hoboken, New Jersey
d. Jul 13, 1946 in New York, New York
Source: *AmAu&B; AtlBL; CurBio 40, 46; DcAmB S4; EncAB-H; OxAmL; REn; REnAL; WebAB; WhAm 2; WhNAA*

Stignani, Ebe
Italian. Opera Singer
b. Jul 10, 1907 in Naples, Italy
d. Oct 5, 1974
Source: *CurBio 49; InWom; WhAm 6*

Stigwood, Robert
Australian. Motion Picture Producer
b. Apr 16, 1934 in Adelaide, Australia
Source: *ConAu 102; CurBio 79; IntMPA 79, 80, 81*

Still, Andrew Taylor
American. Founder of Osteopathy
Believed disease derived from dislocation of vertebrae; remedy was manipulation.
b. Aug 6, 1828 in Jonesville, Virginia
d. Dec 12, 1917 in Kirksville, Missouri
Source: *AmBi; DcAmB; DcNAA; NewCol 75; WebAB; WhAm 1*

Still, Clyfford
American. Artist
Pioneer in use of mural sized canvas.
b. Oct 30, 1904 in Grandin, North Dakota
d. Jun 23, 1980 in Baltimore, Maryland
Source: *AnObit 1980; CelR 73; CurBio 71, 80; DcCAA 71; NewCol 75; NewYTBS 80; WhoAm 74, 76, 78, 80; WhoAmA 73, 76, 78, 80; WhoWor 74*

Still, William Grant
American. Composer
b. May 11, 1895 in Woodville, Mississippi
d. Dec 3, 1978 in Los Angeles, California
Source: *AmSCAP 66; Baker 78; BiDAmM; BioIn 1, 2, 3, 4, 6, 8, 9, 10, 11; CurBio 41, 79; DcCM; DcBlPA; EbonySL 1; McGEWB; NewCol 75; NewEOp 71; NewYTBS 78; ObitOF 79; OxMus; REnAL; SelBAA; WebAB; WhoAm 74, 76; WhoBlA 75, 77; WhoMus 72*

Stiller, Jerry
[Stiller and Meara]
American. Comedian, Actor
b. Jun 8, 1926? in New York, New York
Source: *BioNews 75; WhoAm 78, 80, 82; WhoHol A*

Stiller, Mauritz
Swedish. Motion Picture Director
b. Jul 17, 1883 in Helsinki, Finland
d. Nov 8, 1928 in Stockholm, Sweden
Source: *BiDFilm; DcFM; FilmgC; MovMk; OxFilm; TwYS; WhScrn 77; WorEFlm*

Stiller and Meara
see: Meara, Anne; Stiller, Jerry

Stillman, Irwin Maxwell
American. Physician, Diet Innovator
Wrote *The Doctor's Quick Weight-Loss Diet,* 1966.
b. Sep 11, 1895 in New York, New York
d. Aug 27, 1975 in Bal Harbour, Florida
Source: *BioIn 10; BioNews 74; ConAu 49, 61; NatCAB 59; NewYTBS 75*

Stills, Stephen
[Buffalo Springfield; Crosby, Stills, Nash, and Young]
American. Rock Musician, Singer, Songwriter
b. Jan 3, 1945 in Dallas, Texas
Source: *BkPepl; EncPR&S; IlEncRk*

Stilwell, Joseph Warren
"Vinegar Joe"
American. General
b. Mar 19, 1883 in Palatka, Florida
d. Oct 12, 1946 in San Francisco, California
Source: *CurBio 42, 46; DcAmB S4; EncAB-H; REnAL; WebAB; WhAm 2*

Stilwell, Richard
American. Opera Singer
b. May 6, 1942 in Saint Louis, Missouri
Source: *BioIn 9, 10, 11; WhoOp 76*

Stimson, Henry Lewis (Harry)
American. Government Official
b. Sep 21, 1867 in New York, New York
d. Oct 20, 1950 in Huntington, New York
Source: *BiDrUSE; CurBio 40, 50; DcAmB S4; EncAB-H; REnAL; WebAB; WhAm 3*

Stingley, Darryl
American. Former Football Player
New England Patriots, 1973-78; paralyzed during game, Aug 12, 1978.
b. Sep 18, 1951 in Chicago, Illinois
Source: *BioIn 11, 12; NewYTBS 78; WhoBlA 75, 77, 80*

Stips, Robert Jan
see: Golden Earring

Stirling, James
Scottish. Architect
b. Apr 22, 1926 in Glasgow, Scotland
Source: *IntWW 75, 76, 77, 78; WhoArch; WhoWor 78*

Stirling, Lord
American. Military Leader
b. 1726
d. 1783
Source: *Drake*

Stitt, "Sonny" (Edward)
American. Jazz Musician
b. Feb 2, 1924 in Boston, Massachusetts
d. Jul 22, 1982 in Washington, DC
Source: *BiDAmM; CmpEPM; DcBlPA; EncJzS 70; IlEncJ; NewYTBS 82; WhoAm 74, 76, 78, 80, 82*

Stix, Nathan
American. Merchant
b. 1899 in Cincinnati, Ohio
Source: *St&PR 75; WhoF&I 74*

Stock, Frederick A
German. Conductor
b. Nov 11, 1872 in Dulich, Germany
d. Oct 20, 1942 in Chicago, Illinois
Source: *CurBio 42; DcAmB S3; WhAm 2*

Stocker, Wally
see: Babys, The

Stockhausen, Karlheinz
German. Composer
b. Aug 28, 1928 in Modrath, Germany
Source: *CurBio 71; DcCM; IntWW 74; NewYTBE 71; Who 74; WhoMus 72; WhoWor 74*

Stockman, David Allen
American. Government Official
Director of OMB, 1981--.
b. Nov 10, 1946 in Fort Hood, Texas
Source: *AlmAP 78, 80; CngDr 77, 78; CurBio 81; WhoAm 78, 80, 82; WhoAmP 77, 79; WhoGov 77; WhoMW 78*

Stockton, Dave (David)
American. Golfer
b. Nov 2, 1941 in San Bernardino, California
Source: *NewYTBE 71; NewYTBS 74; WhoAm 82; WhoGolf*

Stockton, Dick
American. Tennis Player
b. 1951
Source: *BioIn 10; WhoAm 82*

Stockton, Frank (Francis Richard)
American. Author
b. Apr 5, 1834 in Philadelphia, Pennsylvania
d. Apr 20, 1902 in Washington, DC
Source: *Alli, SUP; AmAu; AmAu&B; AmBi; ApCAB; AuBYP; BbD; BiD&SB; CarSB; Chambr 3; CnDAL; CyAl 2; DcAmAu; DcAmB; DcBiA; DcEnA AP; DcLEL; DcNAA; EncMys; EvLB; FamSYP; JBA 34; LongCTC; OxAmL; OxEng; RAdv 1; REn; REnAL; TwCBDA; WebAB; WhAm 1*

Stockton, Richard
American. Continental Congressman
b. Oct 1, 1730 in Princeton, New Jersey
d. Feb 28, 1781 in Princeton, New York
Source: *AmBi; ApCAB; BiAuS; BiDrAC; DcAmB; Drake; TwCBDA; WhAm H*

Stockwell, Dean
American. Actor
b. Mar 5, 1936 in Hollywood, California
Source: *FilmgC; IntMPA 75, 76, 77, 78, 79, 80, 81, 82; MotPP; MovMk; WhoHol A*

Stockwell, Guy
American. Actor
b. 1938
Source: *FilmgC; WhoHol A*

Stoddard, Richard Henry
American. Poet
b. Jul 12, 1825 in Hingham, Massachusetts
d. May 12, 1903
Source: *Alli, SUP; AmAu; AmAu&B; AmBi; ApCAB; BbD; BiD&SB; Chambr 3; ChPo, S1; CnDAL; CyAl 2; DcAmAu; DcAmB; DcEnA AP; DcEnL; DcLEL; DcNAA; EvLB; OxAmL; REn; REnAL; TwCBDA; WhAm 1*

Stoessel, Albert
American. Conductor
b. Oct 11, 1894 in Saint Louis, Missouri
d. May 12, 1943 in New York, New York
Source: *AmSCAP 66; CurBio 43; DcAmB S3; WhAm 2*

Stoffels, Hendrickje
Dutch. Mistress, Model for Rembrandt
b. 1622
d. 1667
Source: *BioIn 9*

Stokely, Alfred Jehu
American. Food Company Executive
President, chief executive, Stokely Van Camp Inc.
b. Mar 26, 1916 in Newport, Tennessee
Source: *St&PR 75; WhoAm 74, 76, 78, 80, 82; WhoF&I 74; WhoWor 74*

Stoker, Bram
Irish. Author
b. 1847 in Dublin, Ireland
d. Apr 20, 1912
Source: *Alli SUP; CyWA; DcLEL; EncMys; EvLB; FilmgC; LongCTC; Pen ENG; REn; TwCA, SUP; WhoChL*

Stokes, Carl Burton
American. Former Mayor of Cleveland
b. Jun 21, 1927 in Cleveland, Ohio
Source: *CelR 73; CurBio 68; WhoAm 74, 76, 78, 80, 82; WhoAmP 73; WhoBlA 75; WhoWor 74*

Stokes, Donald Gresham Stokes, Baron
English. Automobile Executive
President, British Leyland, 1975--.
b. Mar 22, 1914 in London, England
Source: *IntWW 74; Who 74; WhoAm 74, 76, 78, 80, 82; WhoWor 74*

Stokowski, Leopold
American. Conductor, Musician
b. Apr 18, 1882 in London, England
d. Sep 13, 1977 in London, England
Source: *AmSCAP 66; BioNews 74; CelR 73; ChPo S2; CurBio 41, 53; FilmgC; NewYTBE 70; REn; WebAB; Who 74; WhoAm 74; WhoE 74; WhoHol A; WhoMus 72; WhoWor 74*

Stokowski, Olga Smaroff
American. Musician
b. Aug 8, 1882 in San Antonio, Texas
Source: *CurBio 46, 48; DcNAA; InWom; NotAW*

Stoltz, Rosine
[Victorine Noel]
French. Opera Singer
b. Feb 13, 1815 in Paris, France
d. Jul 28, 1903 in Paris, France
Source: *InWom*

Stolypin, Piotr Arkadevich
Russian. Political Leader
b. 1862 in Russia
d. Sep 14, 1911 in Kiev, Russia
Source: *BioIn 9, 10; NewCol 75*

Stolz, Robert
German. Composer
Wrote 2,000 songs, 50 operettas, music for films; won Oscars, 1941, 1944.
b. Aug 25, 1886 in Graz, Austria
d. Jun 27, 1975 in Berlin, Germany (West)
Source: *BiE&WWA; CurBio 43, 75; WhoMus 72; WhoWor 74*

Stolz, Teresa
[Teresina Stolzova]
Bohemian. Opera Singer
b. Jun 2, 1834 in Elbe Kosteletz, Bohemia
d. Aug 23, 1902 in Milan, Italy
Source: *InWom*

Stone, Carol
American. Entertainer
b. 1916 in New York, New York
Source: *BiE&WWA; InWom; WhoHol A; WhoThe 77*

Stone, Chuck (Charles Sumner)
American. Journalist, Author
b. Jul 21, 1924 in Saint Louis, Missouri
Source: *BlkAW; ConAu 77; LivgBAA*

Stone, Dorothy
American. Actress
b. 1905 in Bensonhurst, New York
d. Sep 24, 1974 in Montecito, California
Source: *BiE&WWA; WhScrn 77; WhoHol B; WhoMus 72*

Stone, Edward Durell
American. Architect
b. Mar 9, 1902 in Fayetteville, Arkansas
d. Aug 6, 1978 in New York, New York
Source: *BiE&WWA; CelR 73; IntWW 74; WebAB; WhoAm 74; WhoF&I 74; WhoWor 74*

Stone, Ezra (Chaim)
American. Actor, Motion Picture Director
b. Dec 2, 1917 in New Bedford, Massachusetts
Source: *AmAu&B; BiE&WWA; IntMPA 75, 76, 77, 78, 79, 80, 81, 82; NotNAT; WhoAm 74, 76, 78, 80, 82; WhoHol A*

Stone, Fred
American. Actor
b. Aug 19, 1873 in Denver, Colorado
d. Mar 6, 1959 in North Hollywood, California
Source: *EncMT; Film 1; TwYS; Vers A; WhAm 3; WhScrn 74, 77; WhoHol B*

Stone, George
American. Baseball Player
b. Jul 9, 1946 in Ruston, Louisiana
Source: *WhoProB 73*

Stone, Harlan Fiske
American. Supreme Court Justice
Associate justice, 1925-41; chief justice, 1941-46.
b. Oct 11, 1872 in Chesterfield, New Hampshire
d. Apr 22, 1946 in Washington, DC
Source: *BiDrUSE; CurBio 41, 46; DcAmB S4; EncAB-H; WebAB; WhAm 2; WorAl*

Stone, Harold J
American. Actor
b. 1911
Source: *FilmgC; WhoHol A*

Stone, Irving
American. Author
Wrote *Lust for Life; The Agony and the Ectasy; The Origin.*
b. Jul 14, 1903 in San Francisco, California
Source: *AmAu&B; AmNov; AuNews 1; ConAu 1R, 1NR; ConLC 7; ConNov 72, 76; DrAS 74E; IntWW 74; LongCTC; Pen AM; REn; REnAL; SmATA 3; TwCA, SUP; TwCW; WhNAA; WhoAm 74, 76, 78, 80, 82; WhoWor 74; WhoWorJ 72; WrDr 76*

Stone, I(sidor) F(einstein)
American. Journalist, Author
b. Dec 24, 1907 in Philadelphia, Pennsylvania
Source: *CelR 73; ConAu 61; CurBio 72; WhoAm 74; WhoWor 74*

Stone, Lewis
American. Actor
b. Nov 15, 1879 in Worcester, Massachusetts
d. Sep 11, 1953 in Los Angeles, California
Source: *Film 1; FilmgC; MovMk; TwYS; Vers B; WhAm 3; WhScrn 74, 77; WhoHol B*

Stone, Lucy
American. Feminist
b. Aug 13, 1818 in West Brookfield, Massachusetts
d. Oct 18, 1893 in Dorchester, Massachusetts
Source: *AmAu&B; AmBi; AmWom; ApCAB; BiD&SB; DcAmB; Drake; HerW; InWom; NotAW; OxAmL; REn; TwCBDA; WebAB; WhAm H; WhAmP*

Stone, Marvin Lawrence
American. Journalist
b. Feb 26, 1924 in Burlington, Vermont
Source: *ConAu 69; WhoAm 74, 76, 78, 80, 82; WhoWorJ 72*

Stone, Melville Elijah
American. Newspaper Publisher
b. Aug 22, 1848 in Hudson, Illinois
d. Feb 15, 1929 in New York, New York
Source: *AmAu&B; AmBi; ApCAB; ChPo S1; DcAmB; DcNAA; EncAB-H; REnAL; WebAB; WhAm 1*

Stone, Milburn
American. Actor
Played Doc Adams on "Gunsmoke," 1955-75; won Emmy, 1968.
b. Jul 5, 1904 in Burton, Kansas
d. Jun 12, 1980 in La Jolla, California
Source: *FilmgC; MotPP; WhoHol A*

Stone, Paula
American. Actress, Motion Picture Producer
b. Jan 20, 1916 in New York, New York
Source: *BiE&WWA; NotNAT; WhoHol A; WhoThe 77*

Stone, Richard Bernard (Dick)
American. Politician
b. Sep 22, 1928 in New York, New York
Source: *Who 74; WhoAmP 73; WhoGov 72*

Stone, Robert Anthony
American. Author
b. Aug 21, 1937 in New York, New York
Source: *AmAu&B; BioIn 10; ConAu 85; ConLC 5; DrAF 76; WhoAm 76, 78, 80, 82*

Stone, Sly
[Sylvester Stewart; Sly and the Family Stone]
American. Singer, Musician
b. Mar 15, 1944 in Dallas, Texas
Source: *BiDAmM; BioIn 10; RkOn*

Stone, Thomas
American. Lawyer
b. 1743 in Charles County, Maryland
d. Oct 5, 1787 in Alexandria, Virginia
Source: *AmBi; ApCAB; BiAuS; BiDrAC; DcAmB; Drake; TwCBDA; WhAm H; WhAmP*

Stone, W Clement
American. Businessman, Philanthropist
b. May 4, 1902 in Chicago, Illinois
Source: *Au&Wr 71; CurBio 72; St&PR 75; WhoAm 74, 76, 78, 80, 82; WhoAmP 73; WhoF&I 74; WhoIns 75; WhoMW 74*

Stoneham, Horace
American. Baseball Club Executive
President, San Francisco Giants, 1974.
b. 1904 in Newark, New Jersey
Source: *WhoAm 74*

Stoneman, George
American. General, Politician
b. Aug 8, 1822 in Busti, New York
d. Sep 5, 1894 in Buffalo, New York
Source: *AmBi; ApCAB; DcAmB; Drake; TwCBDA; WhAm H*

Stones, Dwight
American. Track Athlete
b. Dec 6, 1953 in Los Angeles, California
Source: *WhoTr&F 73*

Stookey, (Noel) Paul
[Peter, Paul, and Mary]
American. Singer, Songwriter
b. Nov 30, 1937 in Baltimore, Maryland
Source: *AmSCAP 66; EncFCWM 69; WhoAm 74, 76, 78, 80, 82*

Stoopnagle, Lemuel Q, Colonel
[Stoopnagle and Bud; F Chase Taylor]
American. Actor
b. Oct 4, 1897 in Buffalo, New York
d. May 29, 1950 in Boston, Massachusetts
Source: *WhScrn 77*

Stopes, Marie Charlotte Carmichael
English. Scientist
b. Oct 15, 1880
d. Oct 2, 1958 in Dorking, England
Source: *NewCol 75; WebBD 80*

Stoppard, Tom
British. Author
b. Jul 3, 1937 in Zlin, Czechoslovakia
Source: *Au&Wr 71; CnThe; ConAu 81; ConDr 73; ConLC 1, 3, 4, 5, 8, 15; CroCD; EncWL; IntWW 74; McGEWD; ModBrL SUP; ModWD; NotNAT; WebE&AL; Who 74; WhoAm 82; WhoThe 77; WhoTwCL; WrDr 76*

Storch, Larry
American. Actor, Comic
Starred on TV series "F Troop," 1965-67.
b. Jan 8, 1923 in New York, New York
Source: *BiE&WWA; MotPP; NotNAT; WhoHol A*

Storey, David Malcolm
English. Author, Playwright
Wrote *This Sporting Life*, 1960, filmed, 1963.
b. Jul 13, 1933 in Wakefield, England
Source: *CnThe; ConAu 81; ConDr 73, 77; ConNov 72, 76; CurBio 73; DcLEL 1940; EncWT; IntMPA, 75, 76, 77, 78, 79, 80, 81; LongCEL; LongCTC; ModBrL SUP; NotNAT; TwCW; Who 74, 82; WhoThe 72, 77, 81; WhoWor 74, 76, 78; WorAu; WrDr 76, 80*

Storm, Gale
[Josephine Cottle]
American. Actress
Starred in "My Little Margie," 1952-55; "The Gale Storm Show," 1956-62.
b. Apr 5, 1922 in Bloomington, Texas
Source: *FilmgC; HolP 40; InWom; IntMPA 75, 76, 77, 78, 79, 80, 81, 82; MotPP; MovMk; WhoHol A*

Story, Joseph
American. Supreme Court Justice
b. Sep 18, 1779 in Marblehead, Massachusetts
d. Sep 10, 1845 in Cambridge, Massachusetts
Source: *Alli; AmAu; AmAu&B; AmBi; ApCAB; BiAuS; BiD&SB; BiDrAC; CyAl 2; DcAmAu; DcAmB; DcEnL; DcNAA; Drake; EncAB-H; OxAmL; REnAL; TwCBDA; WebAB; WhAm H; WhAmP*

Story, William Wetmore
American. Sculptor, Author
b. Feb 12, 1819 in Salem, Massachusetts
d. Oct 7, 1895 in Vallombrosa, Italy
Source: *Alli, SUP; AmAu; AmAu&B; AmBi; ApCAB; BbD; BiD&SB; CasWL; Chambr 3; ChPo, S1; CyAl 2; DcAmAu; DcAmB; DcEnL; DcLEL; DcNAA; Drake; EvLB; OxAmL; REnAL; TwCBDA; WhAm H*

Stoss, Veit
German. Sculptor
b. 1445 in Nuremberg, Germany
d. 1533 in Nuremberg, Germany
Source: *NewCol 75; WebBD 80*

Stout, Rex Todhunter
American. Author
Founded Vanguard Press, 1926; created detective Nero Wolfe, 1934.
b. Dec 1, 1886 in Noblesville, Indiana
d. Oct 27, 1975 in Danbury, Connecticut
Source: *AmAu&B; AuNews 2; CasWL; CelR 73; ConAu 61; ConLC 3; ConNov 76; CurBio 46; EncMys; EvLB; IndAu 1917; LongCTC; OxAmL; Pen AM; REn; REnAL; TwCA, SUP; TwCW; WhAm 6; WhoAm 74; WorAl*

Stout, William Bushnell
American. Mechanical Engineer, Inventor
Built first commercial monoplane, 1919; gasoline driven passenger rail car, 1933.
b. Mar 16, 1880 in Quincy, Illinois
d. Mar 20, 1956
Source: *BioIn 2, 3, 4, 9; CurBio 57*

Stoutenburg, Adrien Pearl
[Pseudonym: Lace Kendall]
American. Children's Author
b. Dec 1, 1916 in Dafur, Minnesota
Source: *AmAu&B; Au&Wr 71; AuBYP; ChPo S2; ConAu 5R; ConP 70, 75; DrAP 75; MnnWr; SmATA 3; ThrBJA; WhoAm 74, 76, 78, 80, 82; WhoWest 74; WrDr 76*

Stove, Betty
Dutch. Tennis Player
b. Jun 24, 1945
Source: *OfEnT*

Stover, Russell
American. Candy Manufacturer
Perfected Eskimo Pie, 1921; president, Russell Stover Candies, 1925-43.
b. May 6, 1888 in Alton, Kansas
d. May 11, 1954 in Miami Beach, Florida
Source: *NatCAB 43*

Stow, (Julian) Randolph
Australian. Poet
b. Nov 28, 1935 in Geraldton, Australia
Source: *CasWL; ConAu 13R; ConNov 72, 76; ConP 70, 75; NewC; Pen ENG; TwCW; WebE&AL; Who 74; WorAu; WrDr 76*

Stowe, Harriet (Elizabeth) Beecher
American. Author
Wrote *Uncle Tom's Cabin,* 1852.
b. Jun 14, 1811 in Litchfield, Connecticut
d. Jul 1, 1896 in Hartford, Connecticut
Source: *Alli, SUP; AmAu; AmAu&B; AmBi; AtlBL; BbD; BiD&SB; CarSB; CasWL; Chambr 3; ChPo, S1, S2; CnDAL; CrtT 3; CyAl 2; CyWA; DcAmAu; DcBiA; DcEnA; DcEnL; DcLEL; DcNAA; EvLB; FilmgC; HerW; JBA 34; MouLC 4; NotAW; OhA&B; OxAmL; OxEng; Pen AM; RAdv 1; REn; REnAL; TwCBDA; WebAB; WebE&AL; WhAm H; WhAmP; WhoChL; YABC 1*

Stowe, Leland
American. Journalist
b. Nov 10, 1899 in Southbury, Connecticut
Source: *AmAu&B; ConAu 77; CurBio 40; REnAL; TwCA SUP; WhoAm 74, 76, 78, 80, 82; WhoWor 74*

Strabo
Greek. Geographer, Historian
b. 63?BC in Amasia, Pontus
d. 22AD
Source: *BbD; BiD&SB; CasWL; OxEng; Pen CL; REn*

Stracciari, Riccardo
Italian. Opera Singer
b. Jun 26, 1875 in Casalecchio, Italy
d. Oct 10, 1955 in Rome, Italy
Source: *NewEOp 71*

Strachey, (Giles) Lytton
English. Author, Biographer
b. Mar 1, 1880 in London, England
d. Jan 21, 1932 in Hungerford, England
Source: *AtlBL; CasWL; Chambr 3; CnMWL; CyWA; DcLEL; EncWL; EvLB; LongCTC; ModBrL; NewC; OxEng; Pen ENG; REn; TwCA, SUP; TwCW; WebE&AL; WhoLA; WhoTwCL*

Stradella, Alessandro
Italian. Opera Composer
b. 1642 in Naples, Italy
d. Feb 28, 1682 in Genoa, Italy
Source: *NewEOp 71; OxMus*

Stradivari, Antonio
[Antonius Stradivarius]
Italian. Violin Maker
Workmanship perfected violin; earliest known, 1666.
b. 1644 in Cremona, Italy
d. Dec 17, 1737 in Cremona, Italy
Source: *NewCol 75; OxMus; WebBD 80*

Straight, Beatrice Whitney
American. Actress, Motion Picture Producer
b. Aug 2, 1918 in Long Island, New York
Source: *BiE&WWA; ForWC 70; IntMPA 82; NotNAT; WhoAm 82; WhoAmW 77; WhoE 74; WhoHol A; WhoThe 77*

Strakosch, Maurice
Czech. Opera Impresario
b. Jan 15, 1825 in Butschowitz, Moravia
d. Oct 9, 1887 in Paris, France
Source: *ApCAB; WhAm H*

Strand, Mark
Canadian. Poet
b. Apr 11, 1934 in Summerside, PE
Source: *AmAu&B; ConAu 21R; ConLC 6, 18; ConP 70, 75; CroCAP; DrAP 75; RAdv 1; WhoAm 82; WhoE 74; WrDr 76*

Strasberg, Lee
American. Actor, Acting Teacher
Directed Actor's Studio, 1950-82; taught Stanislavsky acting method.
b. Nov 17, 1901 in Budzanow, Austria
d. Feb 17, 1982 in New York, New York
Source: *BiE&WWA; CelR 73; CnThe; ConAu 13R; CurBio 60, 82; EncWT; FilmgC; IntMPA 82; IntWW 74, 75, 76, 77, 78; NewYTBS 75, 82; NotNAT; PlP&P; WhoAm 74, 76, 78, 80; WhoE 77, 79; WhoHol A; WhoThe 72, 77; WhoWor 74*

Strasberg, Susan Elizabeth
American. Actress, Author
b. May 22, 1938 in New York, New York
Source: *BiE&WWA; CurBio 58; FilmgC; InWom; IntMPA 75, 76, 77, 78, 79, 80, 81, 82; MotPP; MovMk; NotNAT; WhoAm 74, 76, 78, 80, 82; WhoHol A*

Strasfogel, Ignace
Polish. Conductor
b. Jul 17, 1909 in Warsaw, Poland
Source: *WhoAm 74, 76, 78, 80, 82; WhoMus 72; WhoWor 74; WhoWorJ 72*

Stratas, Teresa
[Anastasia Strataki]
Canadian. Opera Singer
b. May 26, 1939 in Toronto, ON
Source: *CanWW 82; CreCan 2; WhoAm 74, 76, 78, 80, 82; WhoMus 72*

Stratemeyer, Edward L
American. Children's Author
Syndicate produced *The Rover Boys, Hardy Boys, Bobbsey Twins, Nancy Drew,* etc.
b. Oct 4, 1862 in Elizabeth, New Jersey
d. May 10, 1930 in Newark, New Jersey
Source: *AmAu&B; BiD&SB; CarSB; ConAu 21R; ConAu P-2; DcAmAu; EncMys; HsB&A; OxAmL; REn; REnAL; SmATA 1; TwCBDA; WebAB; WhAm 1*

Stratemeyer, George E
American. General
b. Nov 24, 1890 in Cincinnati, Ohio
d. Aug 9, 1969
Source: *CurBio 51, 69; WhAm 5*

Stratten, Dorothy
[Dorothy Hoogstratten; Mrs. Paul Snider]
Canadian. Actress, Model
Former Playboy centerfold shot to death by estranged husband.
b. Feb 28, 1960 in Vancouver, BC
d. Aug 14, 1980 in Los Angeles, California
Source: *BioIn 12*

Stratton, Dennis
see: Iron Maiden

Stratton, Monty Franklin Pierce
"Gander"
American. Baseball Player
Pitcher whose attempted comeback after losing leg in hunting accident was filmed, 1949.
b. May 21, 1912 in Celeste, Texas
d. Sep 29, 1982 in Greenville, Texas
Source: *BaseEn; NewYTBS 82; WhoProB 73*

Stratton, William R
American. Government Official
b. Jun 6, 1934 in Saint Paul, Minnesota
Source: *BioIn 10; WhoGov 75*

Straus, Isidor
American. Merchant, Philanthropist
b. Feb 6, 1845 in Otterberg, Germany
d. Apr 15, 1912
Source: *AmBi; BiDrAC; DcAmB; WebAB; WhAm 1*

Straus, Jack Isidor
American. Merchant
b. Jan 13, 1900 in New York, New York
Source: *CelR 73; CurBio 52; IntWW 74; St&PR 75; WhoAm 74, 76, 78, 80, 82; WhoF&I 74; WhoWorJ 72*

Straus, Nathan
American. Merchant, Philanthropist
b. Jan 31, 1848 in Otterberg, Germany
d. Jan 11, 1931 in New York, New York
Source: *AmBi; DcAmB; DcNAA; WebAB; WhAm 1*

Straus, Oscar
American. Lawyer, Diplomat
b. Dec 23, 1850 in Otterberg, Germany
d. May 3, 1926 in New York, New York
Source: *Alli SUP; AmAu&B; AmBi; ApCAB, SUP; BiD&SB; BiDSA; DcAmAu; DcAmB; DcNAA; REnAL; TwCBDA; WebAB; WhAm 1*

Straus, Oskar
Austrian. Composer
b. Apr 6, 1870 in Vienna, Austria
d. Jan 11, 1954 in Bad Ischl, Austria
Source: *Baker 78; BioIn 1, 2, 3, 4; CmpEPM; CurBio 44, 54; NotNAT B; ObitOF 79; OxMus; REn; WhAm 3; WhThe*

Straus, Roger W(illiams), Jr.
American. Publisher
Founder, president, Farrar, Straus & Co., 1945.
b. Jan 3, 1917 in New York, New York
Source: *AmM&WS 73P; BioIn 11; CurBio 80; WhoAm 82*

Strauss, Franz Josef
German. Politician
b. Sep 6, 1915 in Munich, Germany
Source: *CurBio 57; IntWW 74; Who 74; WhoWor 74*

Strauss, Johann, Sr.
Austrian. Composer, Conductor
b. Mar 14, 1804 in Vienna, Austria
d. Sep 25, 1849 in Vienna, Austria
Source: *NewCol 75; WebBD 80*

Strauss, Johann, Jr.
Austrian. Composer, Conductor, Violinist
Wrote *On the Beautiful Blue Danube,* 1864.
b. Oct 25, 1825 in Vienna, Austria
d. Jun 3, 1899 in Vienna, Austria
Source: *AtlBL; OxGer; REn*

Strauss, Joseph Baermann
American. Bridge Engineer
b. Jan 9, 1870 in Cincinnati, Ohio
d. May 16, 1938
Source: *BioIn 2, 4, 7*

Strauss, Levi
American. Clothing Manufacturer
Settled in San Francisco to manufacture denim pants 1850.
b. 1829?
d. 1902
Source: *WebAB*

Strauss, Lewis Lichtenstein
American. Author, Politician
b. Jan 31, 1896 in Charleston, West Virginia
d. Jan 21, 1974 in Brandy Station, Virginia
Source: *BiDrUSE; BioNews 74; ConAu 45; CurBio 47, 74; WhAm 6; Who 74; WhoWor 74*

Strauss, Peter
American. Actor
Won Emmy, 1979, for "The Jericho Mile"; starred in "Rich Man, Poor Man," 1976.
b. 1947 in Croton-on-Hudson, New York
Source: *IntMPA 77, 78, 79, 80, 81, 82; WhoAm 82; WhoHol A*

Strauss, Richard
German. Conductor, Composer
b. Jun 11, 1864 in Munich, Germany
d. Sep 8, 1949 in Garmisch, Germany (West)
Source: *AtlBL; CurBio 44, 49; DcCM; OxGer; REn; WhAm 2*

Strauss, Robert
American. Actor
b. Nov 8, 1913 in New York, New York
d. Feb 20, 1974 in New York, New York
Source: *BiE&WWA; BioNews 75; FilmgC; IntMPA 75; MovMk; Vers A; WhScrn 77*

Strauss, Robert
American. Presidential Aide
b. Oct 19, 1918 in Hamlin, Texas
Source: *CelR 73; WhoAm 82; WhoAmP 73*

Stravinsky, Igor Fedorovich
American. Composer
Ballet scores include *The Firebird; Petrouchka; The Rite of Spring.*
b. Jun 17, 1882 in Oranienbaum, Russia
d. Apr 6, 1971 in New York, New York
Source: *AmAu&B; AnCL; ConAu 29R; CurBio 40, 53, 71; DcCM; EncAB-H; REn; WebAB; WhAm 5*

Stravinsky, Vera de Bossett
Russian. Artist
Second wife of Igor Stravinsky, married, 1940.
b. Dec 25, 1888 in Saint Petersburg, Russia
d. Sep 17, 1982 in New York, New York
Source: *NewYTBE 71; NewYTBS 82*

Strawser, Neil Edward
American. Broadcast Journalist
b. Aug 16, 1927 in Rittman, Ohio
Source: *WhoAm 78, 80, 82*

Stray Cats
[Lee Rocker; Brian Setzer; Slim Jim Phantom (Jim McDonnell)]
American. Rock Band
Rockabilly group; first success in England; released album *Built for Speed,* 1982.
Source: *IlEncRk*

Strayhorn, Billy (William)
American. Jazz Musician
b. Nov 29, 1915 in Dayton, Ohio
d. May 31, 1967 in New York, New York
Source: *AmSCAP 66; WhoJazz 72*

Streep, Meryl (Mary Louise)
American. Actress
Won Oscar, 1980, for *Kramer Vs. Kramer;* Emmy, 1978, for "Holocaust."
b. Jun 22, 1949 in Summit, New Jersey
Source: *BioIn 11, 12; CurBio 80; IntMPA 82; NewYTBS 76, 79; WhoAm 80, 82*

Streeter, Edward
American. Humorist, Author
b. Aug 1, 1891 in New York, New York
d. Mar 31, 1976 in New York, New York
Source: *AmAu&B; Au&Wr 71; ConAu 1R, 65, 2NR; OxAmL; REnAL; WhNAA; WhoAm 74; WorAu*

Streich, Rita
German. Opera Singer
b. Dec 18, 1920 in Barnaul, U.S.S.R.
Source: *IntWW 74; WhoMus 72; WhoWor 74*

Streicher, Julius
German. Nazi War Criminal
b. Feb 12, 1885
d. Oct 16, 1946 in Nuremberg, Germany
Source: *CurBio 46; REn*

Streisand, Barbra Joan
American. Singer, Actress
Won Oscar, 1968, for *Funny Girl.*
b. Apr 24, 1942 in New York, New York
Source: *BiDFilm; BiE&WWA; BkPepl; CelR 73; CmMov; CurBio 64; EncMT; FilmgC; ForWC 70; InWom; IntMPA 75, 76, 77, 78, 80, 81, 82; IntWW 74; MotPP; MovMk; NewYTBE 73; NotNAT; OxFilm; PlP&P; WebAB; WhoAm 74, 76, 78, 80, 82; WhoE 74; WhoHol A; WhoThe 77; WhoWor 74; WomWMM*

Streithorst, Tom
American. Broadcast Journalist
b. 1932
d. Feb 19, 1981 in Palo Alto, California
Source: *ConAu 103*

Strepponi, Giuseppina
Italian. Opera Singer
b. Sep 18, 1815 in Lodi, Italy
d. Nov 15, 1897 in Busseto, Italy
Source: *InWom*

Stresemann, Gustav
German. Foreign Minister
b. May 10, 1878 in Berlin, Germany
d. Oct 3, 1929 in Berlin, Germany
Source: *McGEWB; OxGer; REn*

Stribling, Thomas Sigismund
American. Author
b. Mar 4, 1881 in Clinton, Tennessee
d. Jul 8, 1965 in Florence, Alabama
Source: *AmAu&B; CasWL; CnDAL; ConAmA; DcLEL; EncMys; EncWL; LongCTC; OxAmL; Pen AM; REn; TwCA; WhAm 4; WhNAA*

Stribling, Young (William Lawrence)
"Georgia Peach"
American. Boxer
b. Dec 26, 1904 in Bainbridge, Georgia
d. Oct 2, 1933 in Macon, Georgia
Source: *WhoBox 74*

Strindberg, (Johan) August
Swedish. Dramatist, Author
Developed realism, symbolism in work: *Miss Julie; The Ghost Sonata.*
b. Jan 22, 1849 in Stockholm, Sweden
d. May 14, 1912 in Stockholm, Sweden
Source: *AtlBL; BiD&SB; CnMD; CnThe; CyWA; DcEuL; EuAu; LongCTC; McGEWD; ModWD; NewC; NewYTBS 74; OxEng; OxGer; OxThe; Pen EUR; PlP&P A; RComWL; REn; REnWD; TwCA, SUP; WhoTwCL*

Stritch, Elaine
American. Actress, Singer
b. Feb 2, 1928 in Detroit, Michigan
Source: *BiE&WWA; CelR 73; EncMT; FilmgC; InWom; MotPP; NewYTBE 70; NotNAT; WhoHol A; WhoThe 77*

Strode, Hudson
American. Author, Educator, Lecturer
b. Oct 31, 1893 in Cairo, Illinois
d. Sep 22, 1976 in Tuscaloosa, Alabama
Source: *AmAu&B; ConAu 13R, 69; REnAL; TwCA, SUP; WhNAA; WhoAm 74*

Strode, Woody
American. Actor
b. 1914 in Los Angeles, California
Source: *CelR 73; CmMov; FilmgC; NewYTBE 71; WhoHol A*

Stroessner, Alfredo
Paraguayan. President
b. Nov 3, 1912 in Encarnacion, Paraguay
Source: *CurBio 58; IntWW 74; WhoGov 72; WhoWor 74*

Stromberg, Hunt
American. Motion Picture Producer
b. Jul 12, 1894 in Louisville, Kentucky
d. Aug 23, 1968 in Los Angeles, California
Source: *FilmgC; WhAm 5*

Strong, Anna Louise
American. Journalist
b. Nov 24, 1885 in Friend, Nebraska
d. Mar 29, 1970 in Peking, China
Source: *AmAu&B; ConAu 29R; CurBio 49, 70; InWom; NewYTBE 70; OhA&B; TwCA, SUP; WhAm 5; WhNAA; WomWWA 14*

Strong, Austin
American. Author
b. Jan 18, 1881 in San Francisco, California
d. Sep 17, 1952 in Nantucket, Massachusetts
Source: *AmAu&B; LongCTC; ModWD; OxAmL; REnAL; WhAm 3; WhNAA*

Strong, Ken
American. Football Player
b. Aug 6, 1906 in West Haven, Connecticut
Source: *WhoFtbl 74*

Strong, Philip Duffield
American. Author
b. 1899 in Keosauqua, Iowa
d. Apr 26, 1957
Source: *AmAu&B; AuBYP SUP; ConAmA*

Stronge, Sir (Charles) Norman (Lockhart)
Irish. Politician
b. Jul 23, 1894 in Bryansford, Northern Ireland
d. Jan 21, 1981 in Armagh, Northern Ireland
Source: *AnObit 1981; IntWW 74, 75, 76, 77, 78; Who 74; WhoWor 74, 76, 78*

Stroud, Robert Franklin
"Birdman of Alcatraz"
American. Orinthologist, Criminal
b. 1890 in Seattle, Washington
d. Nov 21, 1963 in Springfield, Missouri
Source: *BioIn 4, 6; WebAB*

Strougal, Lubomir
Czech. Government Official
b. Oct 19, 1924
Source: *IntWW 74; WhoGov 72; WhoWor 74*

Stroup, Thomas Bradley
American. Educator, Author
b. Dec 21, 1903 in Fletcher, North Carolina
Source: *ConAu 25R; DrAS 74E*

Strouse, Charles
American. Composer
b. Jun 7, 1928 in New York, New York
Source: *AmSCAP 66; BiE&WWA; EncMT; NewCBMT; NotNAT; WhoAm 74, 76, 78, 80, 82; WhoThe 77*

Strouse, Norman H
American. Advertising Executive
b. Nov 4, 1906 in Olympia, Washington
Source: *ChPo S1; CurBio 60; St&PR 75*

Strout, Richard Lee
American. Journalist
b. Mar 14, 1898 in Cohoes, New York
Source: *AmAu&B; ConAu 69; WhoAm 74*

Strudwick, Shepperd
American. Actor
Career began in 1928; over 200 roles in plays, movies, TV.
b. Sep 22, 1907 in Hillsboro, North Carolina
d. Jan 15, 1983 in New York, New York
Source: *BiE&WWA; FilmEn; FilmgC; IntMPA 75, 76, 77, 78, 79; MovMk; NotNAT; WhoAm 74, 76; WhoHol A; WhoThe 72, 77, 81*

Strummer, Joe
see: Clash, The

Struss, Karl
American. Cinematographer
Won first Oscar for cinematography, 1927.
b. Nov 30, 1886 in New York, New York
d. Dec 16, 1981 in Santa Monica, California
Source: *AnObit 1981; CmMov; FilmEn; FilmgC; IntMPA 75, 76, 77, 78, 79; WorEFlm*

Struther, Jan, pseud.
[Joyce Maxtone Graham]
English. Author
b. Jun 6, 1901 in London, England
d. Jul 20, 1953 in New York, New York
Source: *ChPo, S1, S2; CurBio 41; InWom; LongCTC; NewC; REn; TwCA, SUP; WhAm 3*

Struthers, Sally Anne
American. Actress
Played Gloria on "All in the Family," 1971-78; won two Emmys.
b. Jul 28, 1948 in Portland, Oregon
Source: *BkPepl; CelR 73; CurBio 74; IntMPA 82; NewYTBE 72; WhoAm 74, 76, 78, 80, 82; WhoHol A*

Strykent, Ron
see: Men at Work

Stuart, Chad
see: Chad and Jeremy

Stuart, Charles Edward
"Bonnie Prince Charlie"
English. Claimant to Throne
b. Dec 31, 1720 in Rome, Italy
d. Jan 31, 1788 in Rome, Italy
Source: *Alli; NewC; REn*

Stuart, Gilbert Charles
American. Artist
b. Dec 3, 1755 in North Kingstown, Rhode Island
d. Jul 9, 1828 in Boston, Massachusetts
Source: *AmBi; ApCAB; AtlBL; DcAmB; Drake; EncAB-H; OxAmL; REn; REnAL; TwCBDA; WebAB; WhAm H*

Stuart, James
English. Architect, Artist
b. 1713
d. 1788
Source: *Alli; NewCol 75; OxArt*

Stuart, "Jeb" (James Ewell Brown)
American. Confederate Army Officer
b. Feb 6, 1833 in Patrick County, Virginia
d. May 12, 1864 in Richmond, Virginia
Source: *AmBi; ApCAB; BiDConf; DcAmB; EncAB-H; TwCBDA; WebAB; WhAm H*

Stuart, Jesse Hilton
American. Author
Writes about KY mountains; *Head o' W-Hollow,* 1936.
b. Aug 8, 1907 in W-Hollow, Kentucky
Source: *AmAu&B; AmNov; Au&Wr 71; ChPo, S1; ConAu 5R; ConLC 1, 8, 11, 14; ConNov 72, 76; CyWA; OxAmL; RAdv 1; REn; REnAL; SixAP; SmATA 2; TwCA SUP; TwCW; WhoAm 74, 76, 78, 80, 82; WhoS&SW 73; WhoWor 74; WrDr 76*

Stuart, Lyle
American. Publisher
b. Aug 11, 1922 in Brooklyn, New York
Source: *CelR 73; ConAu 81; WhoAm 82*

Stuarti, Enzo
American. Singer
b. Mar 3, 1925 in Rome, Italy
Source: *AmSCAP 66*

Stubbs, George
English. Artist
b. 1724 in Liverpool, England
d. 1806
Source: *NewCol 75; OxArt*

Stubbs, Levi
[The Four Tops]
American. Singer
b. in Detroit, Michigan
Source: *NF*

Stuckey, Williamson
American. Businessman
b. 1909
d. Jan 7, 1977 in Eastman, Georgia
Source: *BioIn 11; NewYTBS 77*

Stuckgold, Grete Schmeidt
English. Opera Singer
b. Jul 6, 1895 in London, England
Source: *NewEOp 71*

Studebaker, Clement
American. Wagon Manufacturer
Formed wagon co., 1852; experimented with autos, 1897; major product, 1902.
b. Mar 12, 1831 in Pinetown, Pennsylvania
d. Nov 27, 1901 in South Bend, Indiana
Source: *DcAmB; WebAB; WhAm 1*

Studebaker, John Mohler
American. Automotive Pioneer
Joined brother's firm, 1858, president from 1901.
b. Oct 10, 1833 in Gettysburg, Pennsylvania
d. Mar 16, 1917
Source: *NatCAB 11; WhAm 1*

Stuhldreher, Harry A
[Four Horsemen of Notre Dame]
American. Football Player
b. Oct 14, 1901 in Massillon, Ohio
d. Jan 22, 1965 in Pittsburgh, Pennsylvania
Source: *OhA&B; WhoFtbl 74*

Stulberg, Louis
American. Union Leader
b. 1899
d. Dec 14, 1977 in New York, New York
Source: *WhoAm 74; WhoWorJ 72*

Sturgeon, Theodore Hamilton
American. Author
b. Feb 26, 1918 in Staten Island, New York
Source: *AmAu&B; ConAu 81; DrAF 76; Pen AM; REnAL; WhoAm 74; WorAu*

Sturgeon, William
English. Physicist
Developed the electromagnet.
b. May 22, 1783 in Whittington, England
d. Dec 4, 1850 in Prestwich, England
Source: *Alli; AsBiEn; DcScB*

Sturges, Preston
American. Screenwriter, Director
b. Aug 29, 1898 in Chicago, Illinois
d. Aug 6, 1959 in New York, New York
Source: *BiDFilm; CmMov; CurBio 41, 59; DcFM; FilmgC; ModWD; MovMk; OxFilm; REnAL; WhAm 3; WorEFlm*

Sturtzel, Howard Allison
American. Children's Author
b. Jun 25, 1894 in Minneapolis, Minnesota
Source: *ConAu 1R; SmATA 1*

Sturtzel, Jane Levington
American. Children's Author
b. Jun 22, 1903 in Detroit, Michigan
Source: *ConAu 1R; SmATA 1*

Stuyvesant, Peter (Petrus)
Dutch. Colonial Administrator
One-legged governor of New Amsterdam, now NY, 1647-64.
b. 1610 in Scherpenzeel, Netherlands
d. Feb 1672 in Manhattan, New York
Source: *AmBi; DcAmB; EncAB-H; REn; REnAL; WebAB; WhAm H*

Styne, Jule
English. Producer, Songwriter
b. Dec 31, 1905 in London, England
Source: *AmSCAP 66; BiE&WWA; CelR 73; EncMT; FilmgC; IntMPA 77, 78, 79, 80, 81, 82; NewCBMT; NotNAT; WhoAm 74, 76, 78, 80, 82; WhoThe 77; WhoWor 74*

Styron, William
American. Author
Won Pulitzer Prize, 1968, for *The Confessions of Nat Turner*.
b. Jun 11, 1925 in Newport News, Virginia
Source: *AmAu&B; AmWr; Au&Wr 71; CasWL; CelR 73; ConAu 5R; ConLC 1, 3, 5, 11, 15; ConNov 72, 76; DrAF 76; EncWL; IntWW 74; ModAL, SUP; OxAmL; Pen AM; RAdv 1; REn; REnAL; TwCW; WebE&AL; WhoAm 74; WhoE 74; WhoTwCL; WhoWor 74; WorAu; WrDr 76*

Suarez Gonzales, Adolfo
Spanish. Prime Minister
b. Sep 25, 1932 in Cebreros, Spain
Source: *CurBio 77*

Subic, Joseph, Jr.
[The Hostages]
American. Former Hostage in Iran
b. 1957?
Source: *NewYTBS 81*

Sublette, William L
American. Explorer, Naturalist
Established firm to transport people across Rocky Mts., 1823-30.
b. 1799 in Lincoln County, Kentucky
d. Jul 23, 1845 in Pittsburgh, Pennsylvania
Source: *DcAmB; WhAm H*

Sucre, Antonio J de
Venezuelan. Revolutionary
President of Bolivia, 1825-28.
b. 1795 in Cumana, Venezuela
d. Jun 4, 1830 in Pasto, Colombia
Source: *ApCAB; Drake; REn*

Sudermann, Hermann
German. Dramatist
b. Sep 30, 1857 in Matziken, Prussia (East)
d. Nov 21, 1928 in Berlin, Germany
Source: *BbD; BiD&SB; CasWL; ClDMEL; CnMD; CyWA; EvEuW; LongCTC; McGEWD; ModWD; NewC; OxEng; OxGer; OxThe; Pen EUR; REn; TwCA, SUP*

Sue, Eugene Joseph Marie
French. Author
b. Jan 20, 1804 in Paris, France
d. Aug 3, 1875 in Annecy, France
Source: *BbD; BiD&SB; CasWL; CyWA; DcBiA; DcEuL; EncMys; EuAu; EvEuW; NewC; OxEng; OxFr; OxThe; Pen EUR; REn*

Suetonius
Roman. Biographer
b. 69?
d. 140?
Source: *AtlBL; BiD&SB; CasWL; NewC; OxEng; REn*

Suggs, Louise
American. Golfer
b. Sep 7, 1923 in Lithia Springs, Georgia
Source: *CurBio 62; InWom*

Suharto, General
Indonesian. President
b. Jun 8, 1921 in Kemusa, Indonesia
Source: *BioIn 10; CurBio 67; FarE&A 78, 79; IntWW 74, 75, 76; IntWW 77, 78; LinLib S; WhoGov 72; WhoWor 74, 76*

Suhl, Yuri
American. Author
b. Jul 30, 1908 in Podhajce, Poland
Source: *ChlLR 2; ConAu 45; SmATA 8; WhoWorJ 72*

Sui, Wen Ti
Chinese. Nationalist Leader
b. 541
d. 604
Source: *NewCol 75*

Suk, Josef
Bohemian. Musician, Composer
b. Jan 4, 1874 in Krecovic, Bohemia
d. May 29, 1935 in Beneschau, Czechoslovakia
Source: *NewCol 75*

Sukarno, Achmed
Indonesian. President
b. Jun 1, 1901 in Surubaya, Indonesia
d. Jun 21, 1970 in Djakarta, Indonesia
Source: *WhAm 5*

Sukenik, Eliazer Lipa
Israeli. Archaeologist
b. 1889
d. Feb 28, 1953 in Jerusalem, Israel
Source: *BioIn 3; ObitOF 79*

Suleiman I
[Suleiman the Magnificent]
Turkish. Ottoman Sultan
b. 1496
d. 1566
Source: *NewCol 75; WebBD 80; WhDW*

Sulla, Lucius C
Roman. General, Dictator
b. 138BC
d. 78BC
Source: *REn*

Sullavan, Margaret
American. Actress
b. May 16, 1896 in Norfolk, Virginia
d. Jan 1, 1960 in New Haven, Connecticut
Source: *BiDFilm; CmMov; CurBio 44, 60; FilmgC; InWom; MotPP; MovMk; OxFilm; OxThe; ThFT; WhAm 3; WhScrn 74, 77; WhoHol B*

Sulley, Susanne
see: Human League

Sullivan, A(loysius) M(ichael)
American. Author
b. Aug 9, 1896 in Harrison, New Jersey
d. Jun 10, 1980 in Montclair, New Jersey
Source: *AnCL; BioIn 3; BkC 3; ConAu 97; ConAu P-2; CurBio 53, 80; Po&Wr 77; REnAL; WhAm 7; WhE&EA*

Sullivan, Anne
[Anne Sullivan Macy]
American. Teacher of Helen Keller
Teacher of Helen Keller, 1897; companion until 1936.
b. Apr 14, 1866 in Feeding Hills, Massachusetts
d. Oct 20, 1936 in Forest Hills, New York
Source: *AmBi; InWom; NotAW; WebAB*

Sullivan, Sir Arthur Seymour
[Gilbert and Sullivan]
English. Composer, Author
Composed "Onward, Christian Soldiers," 1871.
b. May 14, 1842 in London, England
d. Nov 22, 1900 in London, England
Source: *Alli; AtlBL; FilmgC; NewC; REn; REnWD*

Sullivan, Barry
[Patrick Barry]
American. Actor
b. Aug 12, 1912 in New York, New York
Source: *BiE&WWA; FilmgC; IntMPA 75, 76, 77, 78, 79, 80, 81, 82; MotPP; MovMk; NotNAT; WhoAm 82; WhoHol A*

Sullivan, Daniel P
American. FBI Agent
Helped track down John Dillinger and Barker-Karpis gang.
b. 1912 in Washington, DC
d. Jul 4, 1982 in Miami, Florida
Source: *NewYTBS 82*

Sullivan, Ed(ward Vincent)
American. Journalist, TV Emcee
"Toast of the Town" variety show evolved into "The Ed Sullivan Show," 1948-71.
b. Sep 28, 1902 in New York, New York
d. Oct 13, 1974 in New York, New York
Source: *CelR 73; ConAu 89; CurBio 52, 74; IntMPA 75; IntWW 74; NewYTBS 74; PlP&P; WebAB; WhAm 6; WhScrn 77; WhoAm 74; WhoHol B; WhoWor 74*

Sullivan, Francis Loftus
English. Actor
b. Jan 6, 1903 in London, England
d. Nov 19, 1956 in New York, New York
Source: *FilmgC; MotPP; NotNAT B; PlP&P; Vers A; WhScrn 74, 77; WhThe; WhoHol B*

Sullivan, Frank
American. Journalist, Humorist
b. Sep 22, 1892 in Saratoga, New York
d. Feb 19, 1976 in Saratoga, New York
Source: *AmAu&B; ConAu 25R, 65; ConAu P-2; LongCTC; REn; REnAL; TwCA, SUP; WhAm 6; WhoAm 74*

Sullivan, Frankie
see: Survivor

Sullivan, John
American. Revolutionary General
b. Feb 17, 1740 in Somersworth, New Hampshire
d. Jan 23, 1795 in Durham, North Carolina
Source: *Alli; AmBi; ApCAB; BiAuS; BiDrAC; DcAmB; Drake; REnAL; TwCBDA; WebAB; WhAm H; WhAmP*

Sullivan, John L(awrence)
"Boston Strong Boy"
American. Boxer
Last bare-knuckle heavyweight champ, 1882-92.
b. Oct 15, 1858 in Boston, Massachusetts
d. Feb 2, 1918 in Abingdon, Massachusetts
Source: *AmBi; DcAmB; DcNAA; REnAL; WebAB; WhAm H, 4; WhoBox 74*

Sullivan, Kathryn D
American. Astronaut
b. 1951? in New Jersey
Source: *BioIn 11*

Sullivan, Louis Henri
American. Architect
b. Sep 3, 1856 in Boston, Massachusetts
d. Apr 14, 1924 in Chicago, Illinois
Source: *AmAu&B; AmBi; AtlBL; DcAmB; DcNAA; EncAB-H; OxAmL; REn; REnAL; WebAB; WhAm 1*

Sullivan, Mark
American. Journalist, Publicist
b. Sep 10, 1874 in Avondale, Pennsylvania
d. Aug 13, 1952 in Avondale, Pennsylvania
Source: *AmAu&B; CathA 1952; DcAmB S5; OxAmL; REn; REnAL; TwCA, SUP; WhAm 3; WhNAA*

Sullivan, Maxine
American. Singer
b. May 13, 1911 in Pittsburgh, Pennsylvania
Source: *WhoJazz 72*

Sullivan, Walter Seager, Jr.
American. Journalist
b. Jan 12, 1918 in New York, New York
Source: *AmAu&B; ConAu 1R; CurBio 80; WhoAm 76, 78, 80, 82; WrDr 76, 80*

Sullivan, William Healy
American. Former Diplomat
b. Oct 12, 1922 in Cranston, Rhode Island
Source: *BioIn 9, 11; CurBio 79; IntWW 74, 75, 76, 77, 78; MidE 78, 79; NewYTBS 79; PolProf J; PolProf K; USBiR 74; WhoAm 76, 78; WhoAmP 77, 79; WhoGov 72, 75, 77; WhoWor 74, 76, 78*

Sully, Maximilien de Bethune, Duc
French. Statesman
b. 1560 in France
d. 1641 in France
Source: *BiD&SB; OxFr; REn*

Sully, Thomas
American. Artist
b. Jun 8, 1783 in Horncastle, England
d. Nov 5, 1872 in Philadelphia, Pennsylvania
Source: *Alli SUP; AmBi; ApCAB; ChPo; DcAmAu; DcAmB; Drake; EncAB-H; OxAmL; REn; TwCBDA; WebAB; WhAm H*

Sulzberger, Arthur Hays
American. Journalist
b. Sep 12, 1891 in New York, New York
d. Dec 11, 1968 in New York, New York
Source: *AmAu&B; ConAu 89; CurBio 43, 69; WebAB; WhAm 5*

Sulzberger, Arthur Ochs
American. Newspaper Executive
b. Feb 5, 1926 in New York, New York
Source: *CelR 73; CurBio 66; IntWW 74; Who 74; WhoAm 74, 76, 78, 80, 82; WhoE 74; WhoF&I 74; WhoWor 74*

Sulzberger, C(yrus) L(eon)
American. Journalist, Commentator
b. Oct 27, 1912 in New York, New York
Source: *Au&Wr 71; CelR 73; ConAu 53; CurBio 44; WhoAm 74, 76, 78, 80, 82; WhoWor 74*

Sumac, Yma
Peruvian. Singer
b. Sep 10, 1928 in Ichocan, Peru
Source: *CurBio 55; InWom; WhoHol A; WhoMus 72*

Summer, Donna
[LaDonna Andrea Gaines; Mrs. Bruce Sudano]
American. Singer
Disco hits include "Hot Stuff"; "Bad Girls"; "Last Dance."
b. Dec 31, 1948 in Boston, Massachusetts
Source: *BioIn 11; BkPepl; CurBio 79; RkOn; WhoAm 78, 80, 82; WhoBlA 77*

Summerfield, Arthur Ellsworth
American. Postmaster General
b. Mar 17, 1899 in Pinconning, Michigan
d. Apr 26, 1972 in West Palm Beach, Florida
Source: *BiDrUSE; CurBio 52, 72; NewYTBE 72; WhAm 5; Who 74*

Summers, Andy
see: Police, The

Summersby, Kay
[Kathleen McCarthy-Morrogh]
English. Secretary to Eisenhower
Wartime companion romantically linked to Eisenhower.
b. 1908 in County Cork, Ireland
d. Jan 20, 1975 in Southampton, England
Source: *BioIn 1, 7, 10, 11; BioNews 74*

Summerskill, Edith Clara, Baroness
English. Physician, Politician
b. Apr 19, 1901 in London, England
d. Feb 4, 1980 in London, England
Source: *BioIn 1, 2, 3, 4, 5, 6, 7, 8; CurBio 43, 63; IntWW 77*

Summerville, "Slim" (George J)
American. Comedian
b. 1896 in Albuquerque, New Mexico
d. Jan 6, 1946 in Laguna Beach, California
Source: *CurBio 46; Film 1; FilmgC; MotPP; MovMk; TwYS; WhScrn 74, 77; WhoHol B*

Sumner, Charles
American. Author
b. Jan 6, 1811 in Boston, Massachusetts
d. Mar 11, 1874 in Washington, DC
Source: *Alli, SUP; AmAu; AmAu&B; AmBi; ApCAB; BbD; BiAuS; BiD&SB; BiDrAC; CyAl 2; DcAmAu; DcAmB; EncAB-H; OxAmL; REn; REnAL; TwCBDA; WebAB; WhAm H; WhAmP*

Sumner, Edwin V
American. Army Officer
b. Jan 30, 1797 in Boston, Massachusetts
d. Mar 21, 1863
Source: *AmBi; ApCAB; DcAmB; Drake; TwCBDA; WhAm H*

Sumner, Gordon "Sting"
see: Police, The

Sumner, William Graham
American. Educator
b. Oct 30, 1840 in Paterson, New Jersey
d. Apr 12, 1910 in Englewood, New Jersey
Source: *Alli SUP; AmAu; AmAu&B; AmBi; ApCAB; BiD&SB; DcAmAu; DcAmB; EncAB-H; OxAmL; REn; REnAL; WebAB; WhAm 1*

Sumter, Thomas
American. Revolutionary General
b. Aug 14, 1734 in Hanover County, Virginia
d. Jun 1, 1832 in Stateburg, Virginia
Source: *AmBi; ApCAB; BiAuS; BiDrAC; DcAmB; Drake; TwCBDA; WebAB; WhAm H; WhAmP*

Sun Yat-Sen
[Sun Wen]
Chinese. Statesman, President
Planned 1911 revolution; head of S Chinese Republic, 1921.
b. Nov 12, 1866 in Macao, China
d. Mar 12, 1925
Source: *OxEng; REn; WorAl*

Sun Yat-Sen, Chingling Soong, Madame
[Ching-ling Sung Sun]
Chinese. Political Leader
b. 1890 in Shanghai, China
d. May 29, 1981 in Peking, China
Source: *BioIn 1, 4, 5, 9, 10; CurBio 44, 81; NewYTBS 81*

Sunay, Cevdet
Turkish. President
b. Feb 10, 1900 in Trabzon, Turkey
d. May 22, 1982 in Istanbul, Turkey
Source: *CurBio 69; IntWW 74, 75, 76, 77, 78; IntYB 78, 79; MidE 78, 79; WhoGov 72; WhoWor 78*

"Sundance Kid, The"
[Harry Longabaugh]
American. Outlaw
d. 1909?
Source: *BioIn 10; Blood*

Sunday, Billy (William Ashley)
American. Evangelist, Baseball Player
Conducted over 300 revivals with audience of 100 million.
b. Nov 18, 1862 in Ames, Iowa
d. Nov 6, 1935 in Chicago, Illinois
Source: *AmBi; DcAmB S1; DcNAA; LongCTC; WebAB; WhAm 1; WhoProB 73; WorAl*

Sundburg, Jim (James Howard)
American. Baseball Player
b. May 18, 1951 in Galesburg, Illinois
Source: *BaseEn*

Supertramp
[Bob C Benberg; Richard Davies; John Anthony Helliwell; Rodger Hodgson; Dougie Thompson]
English. Rock Band
Source: *IlEncRk; LilREn 78*

Supervia, Conchita
Spanish. Opera Singer
b. Dec 8, 1899 in Barcelona, Spain
d. Mar 30, 1936 in London, England
Source: *InWom*

Supremes, The
[Florence Ballard; Cindy Birdsong; Diana Ross; Jean Terrell; Mary Wilson]
American. Vocal Group
Detroit trio begun, 1962; hits "Stop in the Name of Love"; "Baby Love."
Source: *EncPR&S; Rk100*

Surratt, John H
American. Confederate Conspirator
b. 1844 in Maryland
d. 1916
Source: *BioIn 7; WhAm H*

Surratt, Mary Eugenia
American. Confederate Conspirator
b. May 1820 in Waterloo, Maryland
d. Jul 9, 1865 in Washington, DC
Source: *BioIn 1, 3, 6, 8, 9, 10; NatCAB 4; WebAB*

Surtees, John
British. Auto Racer
b. Feb 11, 1934
Source: *Who 74*

Survivor
[Dave Bickler; Marc Droubay; Stephan Ellis; Jim Peterik; Frankie Sullivan]
American. Rock Group
Number one hit "Eye of the Tiger," theme song from *Rocky III.*
Source: *NF*

Susann, Jacqueline
American. Author, Actress
Wrote *Valley of the Dolls; The Love Machine; Once is Not Enough.*
b. Aug 20, 1921 in Philadelphia, Pennsylvania
d. Sep 21, 1974 in New York, New York
Source: *AmAu&B; AuNews 1; CelR 73; ConAu 53, 65; ConLC 3; CurBio 72, 74; ForWC 70; NewYTBE 73; NewYTBS 74; WhAm 6; WhScrn 77; WhoAm 74; WhoHol B*

Suslov, Mikhail Andreevich
Russian. Politician
b. Nov 21, 1902 in Shakhovskol, Russia
d. Jan 26, 1982 in Moscow, U.S.S.R.
Source: *CurBio 57, 82; IntWW 74, 75, 76, 77, 78; IntYB 78, 79; NewYTBS 82; WhoSocC 78; WhoWor 74*

Suso, Heinrich
German. Mystic
b. 1300
d. 1366
Source: *DcEuL*

Susskind, David Howard
American. TV Producer
b. Dec 19, 1920 in Brookline, Massachusetts
Source: *BiE&WWA; BkPepl; CelR 73; CurBio 60; FilmgC; IntMPA 82; IntWW 74; NotNAT; WhoAm 74, 76, 78, 80, 82; WhoE 74; WhoWor 74; WhoWorJ 72*

Susskind, Walter
Czech. Conductor
b. May 1, 1913 in Prague, Czechoslovakia
d. Mar 25, 1980 in Berkeley, California
Source: *AnObit 1980; Baker 78; BioIn 2, 10; CanWW 70; CreCan 2; IntWW 74, 75, 76, 77, 78; WhAm 7; Who 74; WhoAm 74, 76, 78, 80; WhoMW 74; WhoMus 72; WhoWor 74, 76, 78, 80*

Suter, Bob
[United States Olympic Hockey Team-1980]
American. Hockey Player
Source: *BioIn 12*

Sutermeister, Heinrich
Swiss. Opera Composer
b. Aug 12, 1910 in Feuerthalen, Switzerland
Source: *DcCM; IntWW 74; WhoMus 72*

Sutherland, Donald
Canadian. Actor
Starred in *MASH,* 1970; *Invasion of the Body Snatchers,* 1978.
b. Jul 17, 1934 in Saint John, NB
Source: *BiDFilm; BkPepl; CanWW 82; CelR 73; FilmgC; IntMPA 76, 77, 78, 79, 80, 81, 82; MovMk; NewYTBE 70; WhoAm 74, 76, 78, 80, 82; WhoHol A; WomWMM*

Sutherland, Earl Wilbur, Jr.
American. Scientist, Physician, Engineer
b. Nov 19, 1915 in Burlingame, Kansas
d. Mar 9, 1974 in Miami, Florida
Source: *AmM&WS 73P; ConAu 49; NewYTBE 71; NewYTBS 74; WebAB; WhAm 6; Who 74; WhoAm 74; WhoS&SW 73; WhoWor 74*

Sutherland, Graham Vivian
English. Artist
b. Aug 24, 1903 in London, England
d. Feb 17, 1980 in London, England
Source: *AnObit 1980; CurBio 55, 80; IntWW 74; Who 74; WhoWor 74*

Sutherland, Joan
Australian. Opera Singer
b. Nov 7, 1929 in Sydney, Australia
Source: *CelR 73; CurBio 60; InWom; IntWW 74; NewYTBE 70; Who 74; WhoAm 74, 76, 78, 80, 82; WhoE 74; WhoLA; WhoMus 72; WhoWor 74*

Sutter, (Howard) Bruce
American. Baseball Player
Relief pitcher, 1976--; won Cy Young award, 1979.
b. Jan 8, 1953 in Lancaster, Pennsylvania
Source: *BaseEn; WhoAm 82*

Sutter, John Augustus
[Johann August Suter]
American. Pioneer, Gold Prospector
Discovery of gold on his land started 1848 CA gold rush.
b. Feb 15, 1803 in Kandern, Germany
d. Jun 18, 1880 in Washington, DC
Source: *AmAu&B; AmBi; ApCAB; DcAmB; OxAmL; WebAB; WhAm H*

Sutton, Horace (Ashley)
American. Author
b. May 17, 1919 in New York, New York
Source: *CelR 73; ConAu 13R; WhoAm 74, 76, 78, 80, 82; WhoWor 74*

Sutton, John
Actor
b. Oct 22, 1908 in Rawalpindi, India
d. 1963
Source: *FilmgC; IntMPA 75, 76, 77, 78, 79, 80, 81, 82; MovMk; WhScrn 74, 77; WhoHol A*

Sutton, Margaret Beebe
Children's Author
b. Jan 22, 1903
Source: *AuBYP; ConAu 1R; ForWC 70; SmATA 1*

Sutton, Willie (William Francis)
"The Actor"
American. Bank Robber
Stole $2 million in 35 years of bank robbing; disguises earned him nickname.
b. 1901
d. Nov 2, 1980 in Spring Hill, Florida
Source: *BioIn 2, 10; Blood*

Suvorov, Aleksandr V
Russian. Field Marshal
b. Nov 25, 1729
d. 1800
Source: *NewCol 75*

Suzman, Janet
South African. Actress
b. Feb 9, 1939 in Johannesburg, South Africa
Source: *CnThe; CurBio 76; FilmgC; IntWW 76, 78; WhoHol A; WhoThe 77, 81; WhoWor 74*

Suzuki, Daisetz Teitaro
Japanese. Buddhist Scholar
b. Oct 18, 1870 in Kanazawa, Japan
d. Jul 12, 1966
Source: *CurBio 58, 66*

Suzuki, Pat
American. Singer, Actress
b. 1931 in Cressy, California
Source: *CurBio 60; InWom; WhoAm 74; WhoHol A; WhoWor 74*

Suzuki, Zenko
Japanese. Prime Minister
b. 1911?
Source: *NF*

Svanholm, Set
Swedish. Opera Singer, Director
b. Sep 2, 1904 in Vasteras, Sweden
d. Oct 4, 1964 in Saltsjoe-Duvnaes, Sweden
Source: *CurBio 56, 64; WhAm 4*

Svensson, Robert
American. Advertising Executive
b. Aug 27, 1907 in Chicago, Illinois
Source: *WhoWest 74*

Sverdrup, Otto
Norwegian. Artic Explorer
Attempted to reach N Pole by way of Smith Sound, 1898-1902.
b. 1855
d. 1930
Source: *NewCol 75; OxCan*

Svetlanov, Evgeni Fyodorovich
[Yevgeny Svetlanov]
Russian. Composer, Conductor
b. 1928
Source: *IntWW 74; WhoWor 74*

Svetlova, Marina
Russian. Ballerina, Choreographer
b. May 3, 1922 in Paris, France
Source: *WhoAm 74, 76, 78, 80, 82; WhoAmW 77; WhoWor 74*

Svoboda, Ludvik
Czech. Communist Leader
b. Nov 25, 1895 in Horznatin, Czechoslovakia
d. 1979 in Prague, Czechoslovakia
Source: *IntWW 74; WhoGov 72; WhoWor 74*

Swados, Elizabeth A (Liz)
American. Author, Composer, Director
b. Feb 5, 1951 in Buffalo, New York
Source: *ConAu 97; ConLC 12; CurBio 79; NewYTBS 77, 78; WhoAm 78, 80, 82*

Swados, Harvey
American. Essayist, Author
b. Oct 28, 1920 in Buffalo, New York
Source: *AmAu&B; ConAu 5R, 37R; ConLC 5; ConNov 72; ModAL; OxAmL; Pen AM; REnAL; WhAm 5*

Swanberg, William Andrew
American. Author
b. Nov 23, 1907 in Saint Paul, Minnesota
Source: *Au&Wr 71; ConAu 5R; MnnWr; WhoAm 74, 76, 78, 80, 82; WorAu; WrDr 76*

Swann, Donald Ibrahim
Welsh. Musician, Composer, Lyricist
b. 1923 in Llanelly, Wales
Source: *Au&Wr 71; BiE&WWA; ConAu 25R; CurBio 70; IntWW 74; NotNAT; OxThe; Who 74; WhoMus 72; WhoThe 77; WhoWor 74; WrDr 76*

Swann, Lynn Curtis
American. Football Player
b. Mar 7, 1952 in Alcoa, Tennessee
Source: *WhoAm 82; WhoFtbl 74; WhoHol A*

Swann, Sir Michael Meredith
English. Educator
b. Mar 1, 1920 in Shortlands, England
Source: *IntWW 74; Who 74; WhoWor 74*

Swanson, Gloria May Josephine
[Josephine Swenson]
American. Actress
Starred in *Sunset Boulevard,* 1950.
b. Mar 27, 1899 in Chicago, Illinois
Source: *BiDFilm; BiE&WWA; CelR 73; Film 1; FilmgC; InWom; IntMPA 75, 76, 77, 78, 79, 80, 81, 82; MovMk; OxFilm; ThFT; Who 82; WhoAm 74, 76, 78, 80, 82; WhoHol A; WhoThe 77; WhoWor 74; WorAl; WorEFlm*

Swarthout, Gladys
American. Opera Singer
b. Dec 25, 1904 in Deepwater, Missouri
d. Jul 6, 1969 in La Ragnaia, Italy
Source: *CurBio 44, 69; FilmgC; InWom; ThFT; WhAm 5; WhScrn 74, 77; WhoHol B; WhoMus 72*

Swarthout, Glendon Fred
American. Author
b. Apr 8, 1918 in Pinckney, Michigan
Source: *ConAu 1R, 1NR; ConNov 72, 76; WhoAm 82; WhoWest 74; WrDr 76*

Swayne, Noah
American. Supreme Court Justice
b. Dec 7, 1804 in Frederick County, Virginia
d. Jun 8, 1884 in New York, New York
Source: *ApCAB; BiAuS; DcAmB; Drake; TwCBDA; WebAB; WhAm H*

Swayze, John Cameron, Sr.
American. Journalist
Does commercials for Timex watches.
b. Apr 4, 1906 in Wichita, Kansas
Source: *ConAu 102; IntMPA 76, 77, 78, 79, 80, 81, 82; WhoAm 82; WhoE 74; WorAl*

Swearingen, John Eldred
American. Corporation Executive
b. Sep 7, 1918 in Columbia, South Carolina
Source: *AmM&WS 73P, 79P; BioIn 6; CurBio 79; IntWW 74, 75, 76, 77, 78; WhoAm 74, 76, 78, 80, 82; WhoF&I 74, 75, 77, 79; WhoMW 74, 76, 78; WhoWor 74, 76, 78*

Swedenborg, Emanuel
Swedish. Scientist, Mystic
Religious works rejected traditional doctrines of original sin, eternal damnation.
b. Jan 29, 1688 in Stockholm, Sweden
d. Mar 29, 1772
Source: *BbD; BiD&SB; CasWL; CyWA; DcEuL; EuAu; EvEuW; NewC; OxEng; RComWL; REn; WorAl*

Sweelinck, Jan Pieterszoon
Dutch. Composer, Musician
b. 1562 in Amsterdam, Netherlands
d. Oct 16, 1621 in Amsterdam, Netherlands
Source: *AtlBL; Baker 78; BioIn 1, 4, 7; McGEWB; OxMus*

Sweet, Blanche
American. Actress
b. Jun 18, 1896 in Chicago, Illinois
Source: *BiE&WWA; Film 1; FilmgC; InWom; MotPP; MovMk; NotNAT; OxFilm; TwYS; WhoHol A*

Sweet, Darrell
see: Nazareth

Sweet, John Howard
Canadian. Publisher
b. Mar 21, 1907 in Emerson, MB
Source: *CanWW 82; WhoAm 74, 76, 78, 80, 82; WhoF&I 74; WhoS&SW 73; WhoWor 74*

Sweet, Rachel
American. Singer
Hit album *Fool Around;* single "Baby."
b. 1966 in Akron, Ohio
Source: *BioIn 12; NewWmR*

Swenson, Inga
American. Actress
b. Dec 29, 1932 in Omaha, Nebraska
Source: *BiE&WWA; EncMT; FilmgC; NotNAT; WhoAm 74; WhoHol A; WhoThe 77*

Swenson, May
American. Poet
b. May 28, 1919 in Logan, Utah
Source: *AmAu&B; AnCL; ChPo S1, S2; ConAu 5R; ConLC 4, 14; CroCAP; DrAP 75; RAdv 1; SmATA 15; WhoAm 74, 76, 78, 80, 82; WhoWor 74; WorAu; WrDr 76*

Swerling, Jo
American. Screenwriter, Dramatist
b. May 18, 1897 in Russia
Source: *BiE&WWA; FilmgC; IntMPA 75, 76, 77, 78, 79, 80, 81, 82; NotNAT; WorEFlm*

Swift, Elizabeth Ann
[The Hostages]
American. Former Hostage in Iran
b. Dec 3, 1940 in Washington, DC
Source: *BioIn 12; NewYTBS 81; USBiR 74; WhoGov 72*

Swift, Gustavus Franklin
American. Manufacturer
Developed refrigerated railroad cars to ship meats to market.
b. Jun 24, 1839 in Sandwich, Massachusetts
d. Mar 29, 1903 in Chicago, Illinois
Source: *AmBi; DcAmB; EncAB-H; WebAB; WhAm 1*

Swift, Jonathan
[Isaac Bickerstaff, pseud.]
English. Satirist, Author, Clergyman
Wrote *Gulliver's Travels,* 1726.
b. Nov 30, 1667 in Dublin, Ireland
d. Oct 19, 1745
Source: *AtlBL; BbD; BiD&SB; BrAu; CarSB; Chambr 2; ChPo, S1; CnE&AP; CrtT 2; CyWA; DcBiA; DcEnA, AP; DcEuL; DcLEL; EvLB; HsB&A; MouLC 2; NewC; OxEng; Pen ENG; PoIre; RAdv 1; RComWL; REn; WebE&AL; WhoChL; WorAl*

Swift, Kay
American. Lyricist, Songwriter
b. Apr 19, 1905 in New York, New York
Source: *AmSCAP 66; CmpEPM; EncMT; InWom*

Swigert, Jack (John Leonard, Jr.)
American. Astronaut, Congressman
Commanded Apollo 13; elected to Congress from CO, 1982; died before sworn in.
b. Aug 30, 1931 in Denver, Colorado
d. Dec 27, 1982 in Washington, DC
Source: *AmM&WS 73P, 79P; IntWW 74, 75, 76, 77; WhoAm 76, 78, 80, 82; WhoAmP 75, 77, 79; WhoGov 72, 75; WhoS&SW 73, 75, 76; WhoWor 78; WorDWW*

Swinburne, Algernon Charles
English. Poet, Dramatist, Critic
Wrote *Atalanta in Calydon,* 1865; *Poems and Ballads,* 1866.
b. Apr 5, 1837 in London, England
d. Apr 10, 1909 in London, England
Source: *Alli, SUP; AtlBL; BbD; BiD&SB; BrAu 19; CarSB; CasWL; Chambr 3; ChPo, S1, S2; CnE&AP; CrtT 3; CyWA; DcEnA, AP; DcEnL; DcEuL; DcLEL; EvLB; MouLC 4; NewC; OxEng; Pen ENG; RAdv 1; RComWL; REn; WebE&AL; WorAl*

Swinburne, Laurence
American. Author
b. Jul 2, 1924 in New York, New York
Source: *ConAu 61; SmATA 9*

Swing, Raymond Gram
American. News Commentator, Author
b. Mar 25, 1887 in Cortland, New York
d. Dec 22, 1968 in Washington, DC
Source: *AmAu&B; ConAu 89; CurBio 40, 69; LongCTC; OhA&B; TwCA SUP; WhAm 5*

Swinnerton, Frank Arthur
English. Author, Satirist
Associated with "Georgian" literary group.
b. Aug 12, 1884 in Wood Green, England
d. Nov 6, 1982 in Cranleigh, England
Source: *Chambr 3; ConNov 72, 76; CyWA; DcLEL; EvLB; IntAu&W 76, 77; IntWW 74, 75, 76, 77, 78, 79, 80, 81; LinLib L; LongCTC; ModBrL; NewYTBS 76, 82; Pen ENG; RAdv 1; REn; TwCA, SUP; TwCW; WhE&EA; Who 74; WhoLA; WhoWor 74, 76, 78; WrDr 76, 80*

Swinnerton, James Guilford
American. Comic Strip Artist
b. Nov 13, 1875 in Eureka, California
d. Sep 5, 1974 in Palm Springs, California
Source: *ConAu 93; NewYTBS 74; WhAm 6*

Swinton, Sir Ernest Dunlop
British. General
b. 1869
d. Jan 15, 1951 in Oxford, England
Source: *BioIn 2, 3, 9*

Swit, Loretta
American. Actress
Played Margaret Hoolihan in TV series "MASH" 1972-83.
b. Nov 4, 1943? in Passaic, New Jersey
Source: *BioNews 74; IntMPA 82; WhoAm 82; WhoHol A*

Switzer, Carl
[Our Gang]
"Alfalfa"
American. Actor
b. 1926
d. Jan 21, 1959 in Sepulveda, California
Source: *BioIn 5, 9; FilmgC; MotPP; NotNAT B; WhScrn 74, 77; WhoHol B*

Switzer, Katherine Virginia
American. Athlete, Public Relations Exec.
First woman to officially run in Boston Marathon, 1967.
b. Jan 5, 1947 in Amberg, Germany
Source: *NewYTBS 76; WhoAmW 77*

Swoboda, Henry
Czech. Conductor
b. 1897 in Prague, Czechoslovakia
Source: *WhoMus 72*

Swope, Gerard
American. Industrialist
President of General Electric Co., 1922-39, 1942-44.
b. Dec 1, 1872 in Saint Louis, Missouri
d. Nov 20, 1957 in New York, New York
Source: *BioIn 1, 4, 5, 6, 11; CurBio 41, 58; DcAmB S6; NatCAB 45; ObitOF 79; WebAB; WhAm 3*

Swope, Herbert Bayard
American. Journalist, Editor
b. Jan 5, 1882 in Saint Louis, Missouri
d. Jun 20, 1958 in Sands Point, New York
Source: *CurBio 44, 58; REn; REnAL; WebAB; WhAm 3*

Sydenham, Thomas
British. Scientist, Engineer, Physician
b. 1624
d. 1689
Source: *Alli*

Sykes, George
"Tardy George"
American. Military Leader
b. Oct 9, 1822 in Dover, Delaware
d. Feb 8, 1880 in Fort Brown, Texas
Source: *AmBi; ApCAB; BiDrAC; DcAmB; TwCBDA; WhAm H*

Sykes, Sir Mark
English. Statesman
b. 1879
d. 1919
Source: *BioIn 2, 10*

Sylvers, The
[Charmaine Sylver; Edmund Sylver; Foster Sylver; James Sylver; Joseph Sylver; Leon Sylver; Olympia-Ann Sylver]
American. Vocal Group
Source: *BioIn 11; RkOn*

Sylvester, Terry
see: Hollies, The

S(ymbionese) L(iberation) A(rmy)
[Angela Atwood; Donald David ("Cinque Mtume") DeFreeze; Emily ("Yolanda") Harris; William ("Teko") Harris; Russell ("Bo") Little; Nancy Ling Perry; Joseph ("Osceola") Romero; Kathy Soliah; Steven Soliah; Patricia ("Mizmoon")Soltysik; William ("Cujo") Wolfe]
American. Revolutionaries
Kidnapped Patricia Hearst, Feb, 1974.
Source: *NF*

Symington, (William) Stuart
American. Former Senator
b. Jun 26, 1901 in Amherst, Massachusetts
Source: *BiDrAC; BioIn 1, 2, 3, 4, 5, 6, 9, 10, 11; CelR 73; CngDr 74; CurBio 45, 56; IntWW 74, 75, 76, 77, 78; IntYB 78, 79; PolProf E; PolProf J; PolProf K; PolProf T; Who 74; WhoAm 74, 76; WhoAmP 73, 75, 77, 79; WhoGov 72, 75, 77; WhoMW 74, 76; WhoWor 74*

Symms, Steven Douglas
American. Senator
b. Apr 23, 1938 in Nampa, Idaho
Source: *AlmAP 78, 80; CngDr 74, 77, 79; WhoAm 74, 76, 78, 80, 82; WhoAmP 73, 75, 77, 79; WhoGov 75, 77; WhoWest 74, 76, 78*

Symon, Myles, pseud.
see: Follett, Ken(neth Martin)

Symonds, John Addington
English. Historian, Poet, Translator
b. Oct 5, 1840 in Bristol, England
d. Apr 19, 1893 in Rome, Italy
Source: *Alli, SUP; AtlBL; BbD; BiD&SB; BrAu 19; CasWL; ChPo, S1, S2; DcEnA; DcEuL; DcLEL; EvLB; MouLC 4; NewC; OxEng; Pen ENG; REn*

Symons, Arthur
Welsh. Author
b. Feb 28, 1865 in Milford Haven, Wales
d. Jan 22, 1945 in Wittersham, England
Source: *Alli SUP; AtlBL; BiD&SB; CasWL; Chambr 3; ChPo S1, S2; CnE&AP; DcEnA AP; DcLEL; EvLB; LongCTC; ModBrL; NewC; OxEng; Pen ENG; REn; TwCA, SUP; TwCW; WebE&AL*

Symons, Julian Gustave
English. Author, Critic
b. May 30, 1912 in London, England
Source: *ConAu 49, 3NR; ConLC 2, 14; ConNov 72, 76; ConP 70; EncMys; LongCTC; TwCA SUP; WhoAm 82*

Syms, Sylvia
English. Actress
b. 1934 in London, England
Source: *FilmgC; IntMPA 75, 76, 77, 78, 79, 80, 81, 82; MotPP; WhoHol A*

Synge, John Millington
Irish. Author, Dramatist
Wrote about peasants of W Ireland; *The Playboy of the Western World,* 1907.
b. Apr 16, 1871 in Dublin, Ireland
d. Mar 24, 1909 in Dublin, Ireland
Source: *AtlBL; CasWL; Chambr 3; ChPo S1; CnMD; CnMWL; CnThe; CyWA; DcEuL; DcLEL; EncWL; EvLB; LongCTC; McGEWD; ModBrL, SUP; ModWD; NewC; OxEng; OxThe; Pen ENG; PoIre; RComWL; REn; REnWD; TwCA; TwCW; WebE&AL; WhoTwCL; WorAl*

Szabo, Gabor
American. Musician
b. Mar 8, 1936 in Budapest, Hungary
d. Feb 26, 1982 in Budapest, Hungary
Source: *WhoAm 74, 76, 78, 80, 82; WhoWor 74*

Szabo, Violette Bushell
English. Spy
b. 1918
d. Jan 26, 1945 in Germany
Source: *BioIn 7, 8; InWom; WhWW-II*

Szasz, Thomas Stephen
American. Psychiatrist, Educator
b. Apr 15, 1920 in Budapest, Hungary
Source: *AmAu&B; AmM&WS 73S; ConAu 17R; CurBio 75; WhoAm 74, 76, 78, 80, 82; WhoWor 74; WrDr 76*

Szell, George
American. Conductor
b. Jun 7, 1897 in Budapest, Hungary
d. Jul 30, 1970 in Cleveland, Ohio
Source: *CurBio 45, 70; NewYTBE 70; WebAB*

Szenkar, Eugen
Hungarian. Opera Conductor
b. Apr 9, 1891 in Budapest, Hungary
Source: *NewEOp 71*

Szent-Gyorgyi, Albert von
American. Biochemist, Researcher
b. Sep 16, 1893 in Budapest, Hungary
Source: *AmM&WS 73P; CurBio 55; IntWW 74; WebAB; Who 74; WhoAm 74; WhoWor 74*

Szeryng, Henryk
Mexican. Musician
b. Sep 22, 1921? in Warsaw, Poland
Source: *CurBio 68; IntWW 74; Who 74; WhoAm 82; WhoMus 72; WhoS&SW 73; WhoWor 74*

Szewinska, Irena
Polish. Track Athlete
b. May 24, 1946 in Leningrad, U.S.S.R.
Source: *WhoTr&F 73*

Szigeti, Joseph
American. Musician
b. Sep 2, 1892 in Budapest, Hungary
d. Feb 20, 1973 in Lucerne, Switzerland
Source: *ConAu P-1; CurBio 40, 58, 73; NewYTBE 73; WhAm 5; WhScrn 77; WhoHol B; WhoMus 72*

Szilard, Leo
American. Scientist, Physician, Engineer
b. Feb 11, 1898 in Budapest, Hungary
d. May 30, 1964 in LaJolla, California
Source: *CurBio 47, 64; WebAB; WhAm 4*

Szoka, Edmund Casimir
American. Archbishop
Archbishop of Detroit, 1981--.
b. Sep 14, 1927 in Grand Rapids, Michigan
Source: *WhoAm 76, 78, 80; WhoRel 75, 77*

Szold, Henrietta
American. Zionist Leader
b. Dec 21, 1860 in Baltimore, Maryland
d. Feb 13, 1945 in Jerusalem, Palestine
Source: *CurBio 40, 45; DcAmB S3; HerW; InWom; NotAW; WhAm 2; WomWWA 14*

Szyk, Arthur
Polish. Artist
b. Jun 3, 1894 in Lodz, Poland
d. Sep 13, 1951 in New Canaan, Connecticut
Source: *ChPo; CurBio 46, 51; DcAmB S5; IlsBYP; IlsCB 1946; WhAm 3*

Szymanowski, Karol
Russian. Composer
b. Oct 6, 1882 in Timoshovka, Russia
d. Mar 29, 1937 in Lausanne, Switzerland
Source: *DcCM*

T

T. Rex
[Marc Bolan; Steven Currie; Mickey Finn; Jack Green; Bill Legend;Steven Peregrine Took]
English. Rock Group
Source: *RkOn 2; WhoRock 81*

Tabb, John B
American. Poet
b. Mar 22, 1845 in Amelia County, Virginia
d. 1909
Source: *AmAu; AmAu&B; AmBi; BiD&SB; BiDSA; Chambr 3; ChPo, S1; CnDAL; DcAmAu; DcAmB; DcLEL; DcNAA; EvLB; OxAmL; REnAL; WhAm 1*

Tabb, Mary Decker
[Mrs. Ron Tabb]
American. Track Athlete
Holds several indoor and outdoor running records.
b. 1958
Source: *BioIn 11; NewYTBS 82*

Tabbert, William
American. Actor, Singer
b. 1921
d. Oct 20, 1974 in Dallas, Texas
Source: *BiE&WWA; EncMT; NewYTBS 74*

Tabei, Junko
Japanese. Mountain Climber
First woman to climb to summit of Mt. Everest, 1975.
b. 1940 in Tokyo, Japan
Source: *GoodHS; WorAl*

Taber, Gladys Bagg
American. Journalist, Author
b. Apr 12, 1899 in Colorado Springs, Colorado
d. Mar 11, 1980 in Hyannis, Massachusetts
Source: *AmAu&B; AmNov; ConAu 5R, 97, 4NR; CurBio 52, 80; ForWC 70; WhoAm 74*

Tabor, Elizabeth Bonduel McCourt
"Baby Doe"
American. Adventurer, Frontierswoman
b. 1854
d. 1935
Source: *InWom; NewCol 75*

Tabori, Kristoffer
American. Actor
Son of actress Viveca Lindfors; TV series "Chicago Story," 1982.
b. Aug 4, 1952 in Los Angeles, California
Source: *NotNAT; WhoHol A*

Tacitus, Cornelius
[Gaius Tacitus; Publius Tacitus]
Roman. Historian, Orator
b. 55
d. 117
Source: *Alli; AtlBL; BbD; BiD&SB; CasWL; CyWA; DcEnL; NewC; OxEng; OxGer; Pen CL; RComWL; REn*

Taddei, Giuseppe
Italian. Opera Singer
b. Jun 26, 1916 in Genoa, Italy
Source: *WhoMus 72*

Taeuber-Arp, Sophie
Swiss. Artist
b. Jan 19, 1889 in Davos, Switzerland
d. Jan 13, 1943 in Zurich, Switzerland
Source: *ConArt; McGDA; WomArt*

Taft, Charles Phelps
American. Lawyer, Religious Leader
b. Sep 20, 1897
Source: *AmAu&B; Au&Wr 71; CurBio 45; IntWW 74; OhA&B; REnAL; Who 74; WhoAm 74, 76, 78, 82; WhoAmP 73; WhoGov 72*

Taft, Lorado
American. Sculptor
b. Apr 29, 1860 in Elmwood, Illinois
d. Oct 30, 1936
Source: *AmBi; AmLY; ApCAB, SUP; DcAmAu; DcAmB S2; DcNAA; OxAmL; REnAL; TwCBDA; WebAB; WhAm 1, 4A; WhNAA*

Taft, Robert A(lphonso)
American. Senator, Politician
b. Sep 8, 1889 in Cincinnati, Ohio
d. Jul 31, 1953 in New York, New York
Source: *BiDrAC; DcAmB S5; EncAB-H; OhA&B; REn; REnAL; WebAB; WhAm 3; WhAmP*

Taft, Robert Alphonso, Jr.
American. Senator
b. Feb 26, 1917 in Cincinnati, Ohio
Source: *BiDrAC; CelR 73; CngDr 74; IntWW 74; WhoAm 82*

Taft, William Howard
American. 27th US President
President, 1909-13; created Department of Labor, 1911.
b. Sep 15, 1857 in Cincinnati, Ohio
d. Mar 8, 1930 in Washington, DC
Source: *AmAu&B; AmBi; AmLY; ApCAB SUP; BiDrAC; BiDrUSE; DcAmB; DcNAA; EncAB-H; OhA&B; OxAmL; REnAL; TwCBDA; WebAB; WhAm 1; WhAmP; WorAl*

Tagliabue, Carlo
Italian. Opera Singer
b. Jan 13, 1898 in Como, Italy
d. Apr 5, 1978 in Monza, Italy
Source: *NewEOp 71*

Tagliavini, Ferruccio
Italian. Opera Singer
b. Aug 14, 1913 in Reggio Emilia, Italy
Source: *CurBio 47; WhoMus 72; WhoWor 74*

Taglioni, Marie
Italian. Ballet Dancer
b. 1804 in Stockholm, Sweden
d. 1884
Source: *NewCol 75; WebBD 80*

Tagore, Sir Rabindranath
[Ravindranath Thakur]
Indian. Poet
b. May 6, 1861 in Calcutta, India
d. Aug 7, 1941
Source: *CasWL; Chambr 3; ChPo, S1, S2; CnMD; CnThe; CurBio 41; DcLEL; DcOrL 2; EncWL; EvLB; LongCTC; McGEWD; ModWD; NewC; OxEng; Pen CL, ENG; REn; REnWD; TwCA, SUP; TwCW; WebE&AL; WhoTwCL*

Taine, Hippolyte Adolphe
French. Philosopher
b. Apr 21, 1828 in Vouziers, France
d. Mar 9, 1893 in Paris, France
Source: *AtlBL; BbD; BiD&SB; CasWL; ClDMEL; CyWA; DcEnL; DcEuL; EuAu; EvEuW; McGEWB; OxEng; OxFr; Pen EUR; REn*

Taishoff, Sol Joseph
American. Editor, Publisher
Co-founded *Broadcasting* magazine.
b. Oct 8, 1904 in Minsk, Russia
d. Aug 15, 1982 in Washington, DC
Source: *ConAu 73; NewYTBS 82; NewYTET; WhoAm 74, 76, 78, 80, 82; WhoF&I 74, 75, 77, 79; WhoS&SW 73; WhoWor 74, 76, 78; WhoWorJ 72*

Tait, Arthur Fitzwilliam
English. Artist
b. Aug 5, 1819 in Liverpool, England
d. 1905
Source: *ApCAB; BnEnAmA; DcAmArt; DcAmB; EarABI; IlBEAAW; NewYHSD; TwCBDA; WhAm 1*

Tajo, Italo
Italian. Opera Singer
b. Apr 15, 1915 in Pinerolo, Italy
Source: *NewEOp 71; WhoAm 82*

Takada, Kenzo
Japanese. Fashion Designer
Source: *WorFshn*

Taktakishvili, Otar Vasilevich
Russian. Composer
b. 1924
Source: *BioIn 9*

Tal, Mikhail
Russian. Chess Player
b. 1936
Source: *BioIn 11*

Talbot, Lyle
[Lysle Hollywood]
American. Actor
b. Feb 8, 1904 in Pittsburgh, Pennsylvania
Source: *FilmgC; IntMPA 75, 76, 77, 78, 79, 80, 81, 82; MovMk; Vers B; WhoAm 74; WhoHol A*

Talbot, Nita
American. Comedienne, Actress
b. 1930 in New York, New York
Source: *FilmgC; ForWC 70; InWom; WhoHol A*

Talbot, William Henry Fox
English. Photographer
b. Feb 11, 1800 in Lacock Abbey, England
d. Sep 17, 1877 in Lacock Abbey, England
Source: *Alli; AsBiEn; DcScB; NewCol 75*

Talese, Gay
American. Author, Journalist
Wrote *Honor Thy Father,* 1971; *Thy Neighbor's Wife,* 1980.
b. Feb 7, 1932 in Ocean City, New Jersey
Source: *ConAu 1R; WhoAm 74, 76, 78, 80, 82; WhoE 74; WhoWor 74*

Talking Heads, The
[David Byrne; Chris Frantz; Jerry Harrison; Christina Weymouth]
American. Rock Group
Source: *ConMuA 80; WhoRock 81*

Tallchief, Maria
American. Dancer
b. Jan 24, 1925 in Fairfax, Oklahoma
Source: *CurBio 51; HerW; InWom; WebAB; WhoAm 74, 76, 78, 80, 82; WhoHol A; WhoMus 72; WhoThe 77; WhoWor 74*

Talleyrand-Perigord, Charles Maurice
French. Statesman
b. Feb 13, 1754 in Paris, France
d. May 17, 1838 in Paris, France
Source: *BbD; BiD&SB; OxFr; REn; WhAm H*

Tallis, Thomas
[Thomas Tallys]
English. Organist, Composer
b. Nov 23, 1510 in Greenwich, England
d. 1585
Source: *Alli; AtlBL; NewCol 75*

Tallmadge, Thomas Eddy
American. Architect
Designed numerous churches; wrote *Architecture in America,* 1927.
b. Apr 24, 1876 in Washington, DC
d. Jan 1, 1940
Source: *DcNAA; WhAm 1; WhNAA*

Tallon, (Michael) Dale
Canadian. Hockey Player
b. Oct 19, 1950 in Rouyn Noranda, PQ
Source: *WhoHcky 73*

Talmadge, Constance
American. Actress, Comedienne
b. Apr 19, 1900? in Brooklyn, New York
d. Nov 23, 1973 in Los Angeles, California
Source: *Film 1; FilmgC; InWom; MotPP; MovMk; NewYTBE 73; OxFilm; TwYS; WhAm 6; WhScrn 77; WhoHol B; WorEFlm*

Talmadge, Eugene
American. Governor
b. Sep 23, 1884 in Forsyth, Georgia
d. Dec 21, 1946 in Atlanta, Georgia
Source: *CurBio 41, 47; DcAmB S4; WhAm 2*

Talmadge, Herman Eugene
American. Senator
b. Aug 9, 1913 in Telfair County, Georgia
Source: *BiDrAC; CngDr 74; CurBio 47; IntWW 74; WhoAm 74, 76, 78, 80, 82; WhoAmP 73; WhoGov 72*

Talmadge, Norma
American. Actress
b. May 26, 1897? in Jersey City, New Jersey
d. Dec 24, 1957 in Las Vegas, Nevada
Source: *BiDFilm; Film 1; FilmgC; InWom; MotPP; MovMk; OxFilm; ThFT; TwYS; WhAm 3; WhScrn 74, 77; WhoHol B; WorEFlm*

Talmadge, Thomas de Witt
American. Editor, Author, Clergyman
b. Jan 7, 1832 in Bound Brook, New Jersey
d. Apr 12, 1902
Source: *AmAu&B; NewCol 75*

Talman, William
American. Actor
b. Feb 4, 1915 in Detroit, Michigan
d. Aug 30, 1968 in Encino, California
Source: *FilmgC; MotPP; WhScrn 74, 77; WhoHol B*

Talvela, Martti Olavi
Finnish. Opera Singer
b. Feb 4, 1935 in Hiitola, Finland
Source: *IntWW 74; NewYTBS 74*

Tamagno, Francesco
Italian. Opera Singer
b. Dec 28, 1850 in Turin, Italy
d. Aug 31, 1905 in Varese, Italy
Source: *NewEOp 71*

Tamayo, Rufino
Mexican. Artist
b. Aug 26, 1899
Source: *CurBio 53; REn; WhoAm 74, 76, 78, 80, 82; WhoAmA 73; WhoS&SW 73; WhoWor 74*

Tamblyn, Russ
American. Actor
b. Dec 30, 1935 in Los Angeles, California
Source: *CmMov; FilmgC; IntMPA 75, 76, 77, 78, 79, 80, 81, 82; MotPP; MovMk; WhoHol A*

Tamburini, Antonio
Italian. Opera Singer
b. Mar 28, 1800 in Faenza, Italy
d. Nov 9, 1876 in Nice, France
Source: *NewEOp 71*

Tamerlane
[Timur]
"The Prince of Destruction"
Mongolian. Conquerer
Descendant of Genghis Khan; invaded Russia, Asia Minor.
b. 1336 in Kesh, Persia
d. 1405
Source: *BioIn 10; NewCol 75; WebBD 80*

Tamiroff, Akim
American. Actor
b. Oct 29, 1901 in Baku, Russia
d. Sep 17, 1972 in Palm Springs, California
Source: *BiDFilm; BiE&WWA; FilmgC; MotPP; MovMk; NewYTBE 72; OxFilm; Vers A; WhAm 5; WhScrn 77; WhoHol B; WorEFlm*

Tanaka, Kakuei
Japanese. Prime Minister
b. May 4, 1918
Source: *CurBio 72; IntWW 74; NewCol 75; NewYTBE 72; WhoWor 74*

Tanana, Frank Daryl
American. Baseball Player
b. Jul 3, 1953 in Detroit, Michigan
Source: *BaseEn; BioIn 11*

Tandy, Jessica
[Mrs. Hume Cronyn]
English. Actress
Won Tony, 1948, for *A Streetcar Named Desire*.
b. Jun 7, 1909 in London, England
Source: *BiE&WWA; CelR 73; CurBio 56; FilmgC; InWom; IntMPA 75, 76, 77, 78, 79, 80, 81, 82; MotPP; MovMk; NewYTBS 74; NotNAT; PlP&P; Who 74; WhoAm 74, 76, 78, 80, 82; WhoHol A; WhoThe 77; WhoWor 74*

Taney, Roger Brooke
American. Supreme Court Justice
b. Mar 17, 1777 in Calvert County, Maryland
d. Oct 12, 1864
Source: *Alli; AmBi; ApCAB; BiAuS; BiDSA; BiDrUSE; ChPo; DcAmB; Drake; EncAB-H; REn; REnAL; TwCBDA; WebAB; WhAm H*

Tange, Kenzo
American. Educator, Architect
b. Sep 4, 1913 in Osaka, Japan
Source: *IntWW 74; NewCol 75; WhoAm 82; WhoWor 74*

Tanguay, Eva
Canadian. Actress
b. Aug 1, 1878 in Marbleton, PQ
d. Jan 11, 1947 in Los Angeles, California
Source: *DcAmB S4; Film 1; InWom; NotAW; WhScrn 74, 77; WhoHol B; WhoStg 1908*

Tanguy, Yves
French. Artist
b. Jan 5, 1900 in Paris, France
d. Jan 15, 1955
Source: *DcCAA 71; NewCol 75; REn; WhAm 3*

Tannenbaum, Frank
American. Educator
b. Mar 1893 in Austria
d. Jun 1, 1969 in New York, New York
Source: *AmAu&B; ConAu 9R; NewCol 75; WhNAA*

Tanner, (Leonard) Roscoe, (III)
American. Tennis Player
b. Oct 15, 1951 in Lookout Mountain, Tennessee
Source: *BioIn 10; WhoAm 80, 82*

Tanner, Valno Alfred
Finnish. Statesman
b. Mar 12, 1881 in Helsinki, Finland
d. Apr 19, 1966 in Helsinki, Finland
Source: *BioIn 1, 4, 5, 7, 8; CurBio 60*

Tanny, Vic
Gymnasium Owner
b. 1912
Source: *BioIn 5*

Tao-chi
Chinese. Artist
b. 1630 in Wu-Chou, China
d. 1717?
Source: *McGDA*

Tappy, Eric
Swiss. Opera Singer
b. May 19, 1931 in Lausanne, Switzerland
Source: *WhoOp 76*

Tarbell, Ida Minerva
American. Author, Editor
b. Nov 5, 1857 in Erie County, Pennsylvania
d. Jan 6, 1944 in Bethel, Connecticut
Source: *AmAu&B; BiD&SB; CnDAL; CurBio 44; DcAmAu; DcAmB S3; DcLEL; DcNAA; EncAB-H; HerW; InWom; NotAW; OxAmL; REn; REnAL; TwCA, SUP; WebAB; WhAm 2; WhNAA; WomWWA 14*

Tarkenton, Fran(cis Asbury)
American. Football Player, TV Show Host
Quarterback, 1961-79; co-host, "That's Incredible."
b. Feb 3, 1940 in Richmond, Virginia
Source: *CelR 73; CurBio 69; NewYTBE 70, 71, 72; WhoAm 74, 76, 78, 80, 82; WhoFtbl 74*

Tarkington, Booth
American. Author, Dramatist
Won Pulitzer Prizes for *The Magnificent Ambersons,* 1919; *Alice Adams,* 1922.
b. Jul 29, 1869 in Indianapolis, Indiana
d. May 16, 1946 in Indianapolis, Indiana
Source: *AmAu&B; AtlBL; CarSB; ChPo S2; CnDAL; ConAmA; ConAmL; CurBio 46; CyWA; DcAmAu; DcAmB S4; DcLEL; DcNAA; FilmgC; JBA 34; LongCTC; McGEWD; ModAL; ModWD; OxAmL; OxEng; OxThe; Pen AM; REn; REnAL; TwCA, SUP; TwCW; WebAB; WebE&AL; WhAm 2; WhNAA; WhoChL; WorAl*

Tarnower, Herman
American. Cardiologist, Author
Wrote *The Complete Scarsdale Medical Diet,* 1979; murdered by longtime companion, Jean Harris.
b. Mar 18, 1910 in New York, New York
d. Mar 10, 1980 in Purchase, New York
Source: *BioIn 12; ConAu 89, 97*

Tartini, Giuseppe
Italian. Composer, Violinist
b. Apr 8, 1692 in Istria, Italy
d. Feb 26, 1770 in Padua, Italy
Source: *NewCol 75; REn; WebBD 80*

Tashman, Lilyan
American. Actress
b. Oct 23, 1899 in Brooklyn, New York
d. Mar 21, 1934 in New York, New York
Source: *FilmgC; MovMk; ThFT; TwYS; WhScrn 74, 77; WhoHol B*

Tasman, Abel Janszoon
Dutch. Explorer
Discovered Tasmania and New Zealand, 1642.
b. 1603
d. 1659
Source: *NewC; NewCol 75; REn; WebBD 80*

Tassell, Gustave
American. Designer
b. Feb 4, 1926 in Philadelphia, Pennsylvania
Source: *WhoAm 74; WorFshn*

Tasso, Torquato
Italian. Author
b. Mar 11, 1544 in Sorrento, Italy
d. Apr 25, 1595 in Rome, Italy
Source: *AtlBL; BbD; BiD&SB; CasWL; CnThe; CroE&S; CyWA; DcEuL; EuAu; EvEuW; McGEWD; NewC; OxEng; OxThe; Pen EUR; RComWL; REn; REnWD*

Taste of Honey
[Janice Marie Johnson; Hazel Payne]
American. Singing Duo
Source: *NF*

Tate, Allen
[John Orley]
American. Poet, Critic
b. Nov 19, 1899 in Winchester, Kentucky
d. Feb 9, 1979 in Nashville, Tennessee
Source: *AmAu&B; AmWr; Au&Wr 71; CasWL; CathA 1952; ChPo, S2; CnDAL; CnE&AP; ConAmA; ConAu 5R, 85; ConLC 2, 4, 6, 9, 11, 14; ConNov 72, 76; ConP 70, 75; DrAF 76; DrAP 75; DrAS 74E; EncWL; IntWW 74; LongCTC; ModAL, SUP; OxAmL; Pen AM; RAdv 1; REn; REnAL; SixAP; TwCA, SUP; TwCW; WebAB; WebE&AL; WhoAm 74; WhoS&SW 73; WhoTwCL; WhoWor 74; WrDr 76*

Tate, Nahum
British. Poet
b. 1652 in Dublin, Ireland
d. Aug 12, 1715 in London, England
Source: *Alli; AnCL; BrAu; CasWL; Chambr 2; ChPo; DcEnA; DcEnL; DcEuL; DcLEL; EvLB; NewC; OxEng; OxThe; Pen ENG; PoChrch; PoIre; PoLE; REn*

Tate, Sharon
[Mrs. Roman Polanski]
American. Actress
Murdered by Charles Manson family.
b. 1943 in Dallas, Texas
d. Aug 9, 1969 in Bel Air, California
Source: *FilmgC; MotPP; WhScrn 74, 77; WhoHol B*

Tati, Jacques
[Jacques Tatischeff]
French. Comedian, Motion Picture Director
Won Oscar, 1958, for *Mon Oncle;* inspired by Charlie Chaplin and Buster Keaton.
b. Oct 9, 1908 in Le Pecq, France
d. Nov 5, 1982 in Paris, France
Source: *BiDFilm; CurBio 61, 83; DcFM; FilmgC; IntWW 74, 75, 76, 77, 78, 79, 80, 81; MotPP; NewYTBS 82; OxFilm; Who 74; WhoHol A; WhoWor 74; WorEFlm*

Tatum, Art(hur)
American. Jazz Musician
b. Oct 13, 1910 in Toledo, Ohio
d. Nov 4, 1956 in Los Angeles, California
Source: *WebAB; WhAm 4; WhScrn 77; WhoJazz 72*

Tatum, Jack (John David)
"The Assassin"
American. Football Player
b. Nov 18, 1948 in Cherryville, North Carolina
Source: *BioIn 9, 10; WhoAm 78, 80; WhoBlA 77; WhoFtbl 74*

Tauber, Richard
Austrian. Opera Singer
b. May 16, 1892 in Linz, Austria
d. Jan 8, 1948 in London, England
Source: *EncMT; FilmgC; OxFilm; WhAm 2; WhScrn 74, 77; WhoHol B*

Taubes, Frederic
American. Artist
b. Apr 15, 1900 in Lwow, Poland
Source: *ConAu 17R, 104; CurBio 43; DcCAA 71; WhoAmA 73*

Taubman, (Hyman) Howard
American. Journalist, Author, Critic
b. Jul 4, 1907 in New York, New York
Source: *AmAu&B; BiE&WWA; CurBio 59; IntWW 74; NotNAT; WhoAm 74; WhoThe 77*

Taupin, Bernie
English. Lyricist
b. May 22, 1950 in Sleaford, England
Source: *EncPR&S; IlEncRk*

Taurog, Norman
American. Motion Picture Director
b. Feb 23, 1899 in Chicago, Illinois
d. Apr 7, 1981 in Rancho Mirage, California
Source: *CmMov; DcFM; Film 1; FilmgC; IntMPA 75, 76, 77, 78, 79; MovMk; TwYS; WhAm 7; WhoAm 74, 76, 78, 80; WorEFlm*

Taussig, Helen Brooke
American. Physician
b. May 24, 1898 in Cambridge, Massachusetts
Source: *AmM&WS 73P; CurBio 46, 66; InWom; WhoAm 74; WhoWor 74*

Tavoulareas, William Peter
"Tav"
American. President of Mobil Corporation
b. Nov 9, 1919 in Brooklyn, New York
Source: *IntWW 74, 75, 76, 77, 78; WhoAm 74, 76, 78, 80, 82; WhoE 74, 79; WhoF&I 74, 77, 79; WhoWor 74*

Tawney, Richard Henry
English. Economist, Author
b. Nov 30, 1880 in Calcutta, India
d. Jan 16, 1962
Source: *CasWL; ConAu 93; DcLEL; LongCTC; McGEWB; NewC; Pen; REn; TwCA, SUP*

Tayback, Vic
[Victor Tabback]
American. Actor
Plays Mel on TV series "Alice," 1976--.
b. Jan 6, 1929 in Brooklyn, New York
Source: *WhoAm 80, 82; WhoHol A*

Taylor, Arthur Robert
American. TV Executive
b. Jul 6, 1935 in Elizabeth, New Jersey
Source: *IntWW 74; WhoAm 74, 76, 78, 80, 82; WhoF&I 74*

Taylor, Bayard
American. Journalist
b. Jan 11, 1825 in Kennett Square, Pennsylvania
d. Dec 19, 1878 in Berlin, Germany
Source: *Alli, SUP; AmAu; AmAu&B; AmBi; ApCAB; BbD; BiD&SB; CasWL; Chambr 3; ChPo S1; CnDAL; CyAl 2; DcAmAu; DcAmB; DcBiA; DcEnA AP; DcEnL; DcLEL; DcNAA; EvLB; OxAmL; OxEng; Pen AM; REn; REnAL; TwCBDA; WebAB; WhAm H*

Taylor, Billy (William Edward)
American. Jazz Musician
b. Jul 24, 1921 in Greenville, North Carolina
Source: *NewYTBE 71; WhoAm 74, 76, 78, 80, 82*

Taylor, Dave
Canadian. Hockey Player
b. Dec 4, 1955 in Levack, ON
Source: *HocReg*

Taylor, Edward
American. Poet
b. 1642 in Coventry, England
d. 1729 in Westfield, Massachusetts
Source: *Alli; AmAu&B; AmBi; AmWr; ApCAB; AtlBL; CasWL; ChPo, S1; CnDAL; CnE&AP; CrtT 3; CyWA; DcAmB S1; DcLEL; OxAmL; OxEng; Pen AM; RAdv 1; REn; REnAL; WebAB; WebE&AL; WhAm H*

Taylor, Elizabeth
English. Actress
Won Oscars for *Butterfield 8,* 1960; *Who's Afraid of Virginia Woolf?* 1966.
b. Feb 27, 1932 in London, England
Source: *BiDFilm; BkPepl; CelR 73; FilmgC; InWom; IntMPA 75, 76, 77, 78, 79, 80, 81, 82; IntWW 74; MovMk; OxFilm; WebAB; Who 74; WhoAm 82; WhoE 74; WhoWor 74; WorAl; WorEFlm*

Taylor, Estelle
American. Actress
b. May 20, 1899 in Wilmington, Delaware
d. Apr 15, 1958 in Hollywood, California
Source: *BioIn 4; WhScrn 74*

Taylor, Frederick Winslow
American. Engineer, Inventor
Conducted first time-and-motion studies to improve efficiency, 1881.
b. Mar 20, 1856 in Germantown, Pennsylvania
d. Mar 21, 1915 in Philadelphia, Pennsylvania
Source: *AsBiEn; BioIn 2, 4, 5, 7, 8, 9, 10, 11; DcAmB; DcScB; EncAB-H; NewCol 75; WebAB; WhAm 1; WhoModH*

Taylor, George
American. Ironmaster, Patriot
b. 1716 in Northern Ireland
d. Feb 22, 1781 in Easton, Pennsylvania
Source: *AmBi; ApCAB; BiAuS; BiDrAC; DcAmB; Drake; TwCBDA; WhAm H; WhAmP*

Taylor, Graham
American. Clergyman, Sociologist
b. May 2, 1851 in Schenectady, New York
d. Sep 26, 1938
Source: *DcAmB S2; NatCAB 29; WhAm 1*

Taylor, Henry Junior
American. Journalist, Ambassador
b. Sep 2, 1902 in Chicago, Illinois
Source: *AmAu&B; CelR 73; ConAu 25R; ConAu P-2; IntWW 74; St&PR 75; WhoAm 74*

Taylor, J T
see: Kool and the Gang

Taylor, James Vernon
"Sweet Baby James"
American. Singer, Songwriter
Has nine gold albums, four platinum albums, three gold singles.
b. Mar 12, 1948 in Boston, Massachusetts
Source: *BkPepl; CelR 73; RkOn; WhoAm 82*

Taylor, Jeremy
British. Religious Leader
b. Aug 1613 in Cambridge, England
d. Aug 13, 1667 in Lisburn, Northern Ireland
Source: *Alli; BbD; BiD&SB; BrAu; CasWL; Chambr 1; ChPo, S1; CrtT 1; DcEnA; DcEnL; DcEuL; DcLEL; EvLB; MouLC 1; NewC; OxEng; Pen ENG; REn; WebE&AL*

Taylor, John Henry
English. Golfer
b. Mar 19, 1871 in Northam, England
d. Feb 10, 1963 in Northam, England
Source: *WhoGolf*

Taylor, (Joseph) Deems
American. Composer, Music Critic
b. Dec 22, 1885 in New York, New York
d. Jul 3, 1966 in New York, New York
Source: *AmAu&B; AmSCAP 66; ApCAB X; Baker 78; BiDAmM; BioIn 1, 3, 4, 5, 6, 7, 8, 11; ChPo S2; ConAu 89; CurBio 40, 66; DcCM; FilmgC; LinLib L, S; NewCol 75; NewEOp 71; NotNAT B; ObitOF 79; OxAmL; OxMus; REnAL; TwCA, SUP; WebAB; WhAm 4; WhScrn 77; WhThe*

Taylor, June
[June Taylor Dancers]
American. Choreographer, Dancer
b. 1918 in Chicago, Illinois
Source: *BiE&WWA; NotNAT*

Taylor, Kenneth Douglas
Canadian. Former Ambassador to Iran
Helped six Americans escape from Iran during hostage crisis.
b. Oct 5, 1934 in Calgary, AB
Source: *CanWW 81, 82; WhoAm 82*

Taylor, Kent
[Louis Weiss]
American. Actor
b. May 11, 1907 in Nashua, Iowa
Source: *FilmgC; IntMPA 75, 76, 77, 78, 79, 80, 81, 82; MovMk; WhoHol A*

Taylor, Laurette
[Laurette Cooney]
American. Actress
b. Apr 1, 1887? in New York, New York
d. Dec 7, 1946 in New York, New York
Source: *CurBio 45, 47; DcAmB S4; FamA&A; FilmgC; InWom; NotAW; OxThe; PlP&P; TwYS; WhAm 2; WhScrn 74, 77; WhoHol B*

Taylor, Maxwell Davenport
American. General
b. Aug 26, 1901 in Keytesville, Missouri
Source: *CurBio 46, 61; IntWW 74; Who 74; WhoAm 74, 76, 78, 80, 82; WhoWor 74*

Taylor, Mick
[The Rolling Stones]
English. Musician
b. 1948
Source: *CelR 73*

Taylor, Paul
American. Dancer, Choreographer
b. Jul 29, 1930 in Allegheny, New York
Source: *CurBio 64; WhoAm 74, 76, 78, 80, 82; WhoE 74; WhoWor 74*

Taylor, Phoebe Atwood
American. Author
b. May 18, 1910
d. Jan 9, 1976 in Boston, Massachusetts
Source: *ConAu 61; EncMys; TwCA, SUP*

Taylor, Robert
[Arlington Spangler Brugh]
American. Actor
b. Aug 5, 1911 in Filley, Nebraska
d. Jun 8, 1969 in Santa Monica, California
Source: *BiDFilm; CmMov; CurBio 52, 69; FilmgC; MotPP; MovMk; OxFilm; WhScrn 74, 77; WhoHol B; WorEFlm*

Taylor, Rod
Australian. Actor
b. Jan 11, 1930 in Sydney, Australia
Source: *CelR 73; FilmgC; IntMPA 75, 76, 77, 78, 79, 80, 81, 82; MotPP; MovMk; WhoAm 74, 76, 78, 80, 82; WhoHol A*

Taylor, Sam
"Sam the Man"
American. Jazz Musician
b. Jul 12, 1916 in Lexington, Tennessee
Source: *AmSCAP 66*

Taylor, Samuel (Albert)
American. Dramatist, Architect
b. Jun 13, 1912 in Chicago, Illinois
Source: *AmAu&B; BiE&WWA; ConAu 25R; ConDr 73; McGEWD; NotNAT; WhoAm 74, 76, 78, 80, 82; WhoThe 77; WrDr 76*

Taylor, Samuel Coleridge
see: Coleridge-Taylor, Samuel

Taylor, Sydney Brenner
American. Children's Author
Wrote *All-of-a-Kind Family* series.
b. 1904? in New York, New York
d. Feb 12, 1978 in Queens, New York
Source: *AuBYP; BkCL; ConAu 5R, 77, 4NR; MorBMP; MorJA; SmATA 1; WrDr 76*

Taylor, William Desmond
[William Cunningham Dean Tanner]
American. Motion Picture Director
b. Apr 26, 1877 in Ireland
d. Feb 2, 1922 in Hollywood, California
Source: *FilmEn; TwYS; WhScrn 74, 77; WhoHol B*

Taylor, Zachary
"Old Rough and Ready"
American. 12th US President
Hero of Mexican-American War, 1846-48; president, 1849-50.
b. Nov 24, 1784 in Orange County, Virginia
d. Jul 9, 1850 in Washington, DC
Source: *AmAu&B; AmBi; ApCAB; BiAuS; BiDSA; BiDrAC; BiDrUSE; DcAmB; Drake; EncAB-H; OxAmL; REnAL; TwCBDA; WebAB; WhAm H; WhAmP; WorAl*

Tchaikovsky, Peter Ilyich
[Petr Ilich Chaikovshy]
Russian. Composer
Known for classical ballet scores *Swan Lake; The Nutcracker; Sleeping Beauty.*
b. May 7, 1840 in Votiwsk, Russia
d. Nov 6, 1893 in Saint Petersburg, Russia
Source: *AtlBL; NewC; OxEng; REn; WorAl*

Tchelitchew, Pavel
American. Artist
b. Sep 21, 1898 in Russia
d. Jul 31, 1957 in Rome, Italy
Source: *ChPo; CurBio 43, 57; DcCAA 71*

Tcherepnin, Alexander
American. Pianist, Composer
b. Jan 20, 1899 in Saint Petersburg, Russia
d. Sep 29, 1977
Source: *DcCM; IntWW 74; WhAm 7; WhoAm 74; WhoMus 72; WhoWor 74*

Tcherepnin, Nicholas (Nicolai)
Russian. Composer
b. May 14, 1873 in Saint Petersburg, Russia
d. Jun 26, 1945 in Paris, France
Source: *NewEOp 71; OxMus*

Te, Chu
see: Chu Teh

Teagarden, Jack (Weldon John)
American. Jazz Musician
b. Aug 20, 1905 in Vernon, Texas
d. Jan 15, 1964 in New Orleans, Louisiana
Source: *WhAm 4; WhScrn 74, 77; WhoHol B; WhoJazz 72*

Teague, Walter Dorwin
American. Industrial Designer
b. Dec 18, 1883 in Decatur, Indiana
d. Dec 5, 1960 in Flemington, New Jersey
Source: *AmAu&B; ChPo S1; CurBio 42, 61; IndAu 1917; WhAm 4*

Teale, Edwin Way
American. Naturalist, Author
b. Jun 2, 1899 in Joliet, Illinois
d. Oct 18, 1980 in Norwich, Connecticut
Source: *AmAu&B; ConAu 1R, 102, 2NR; CurBio 61, 80; SmATA 7; Str&VC; ThrBJA; TwCA SUP; WhNAA; WhoAm 74; WhoWor 74; WrDr 76*

Teasdale, Sara
American. Author, Poet
b. Aug 8, 1884 in Saint Louis, Missouri
d. Jan 28, 1933 in New York, New York
Source: *AmAu&B; AmBi; AnCL; AnMV 1926; BiDSA; BkCL; CasWL; ChPo, S1, S2; CnDAL; ConAmA; ConAmL; DcAmB; DcLEL; DcNAA; EvLB; InWom; LongCTC; NotAW; OxAmL; RAdv 1; REn; REnAL; SixAP; Str&VC; TwCA, SUP; TwCW; WebAB; WhAm 1; WhNAA*

Tebaldi, Renata
Italian. Opera Singer
b. Feb 1, 1922 in Pesaro, Italy
Source: *CurBio 55; InWom; IntWW 74; NewYTBE 73; Who 74; WhoAm 74, 76, 78, 80, 82; WhoHol A; WhoMus 72; WhoWor 74*

Tebbel, John
American. Author, Educator
b. Nov 16, 1912 in Boyne City, Michigan
Source: *ConAu 85; CurBio 53; DrAS 74E; WhoAm 74, 76, 78, 80, 82*

Tebbetts, "Birdie" (George Robert)
American. Baseball Player, Manager
b. Nov 10, 1912 in Burlington, Vermont
Source: *BaseEn; WhoProB 73*

Tecumseh
[Tecumtha]
American Indian. Chief
Shawnee Indian chief, tried to unite tribes to resist westward expansion of whites.
b. Mar 1768 in Oldtown, Ohio
d. Oct 5, 1813 in Thamesville, ON
Source: *AmBi; ApCAB; DcAmB; EncAB-H; OxAmL; OxCan; REn; REnAL; WebAB; WhAm H; WorAl*

Tedder, Arthur William Tedder, Baron
English. Air Marshal
b. Jul 11, 1890
d. Jun 3, 1967 in Surrey, England
Source: *ConAu 25R; CurBio 43, 67; WhAm 4*

Teicher, Louis
[Ferrante and Teicher]
American. Pianist, Composer
Part of Ferrante and Teicher piano team, 1947--.
b. Aug 24, 1924 in Wilkes-Barre, Pennsylvania
Source: *AmSCAP 66; WhoAm 74, 76, 78, 80, 82*

Teichmann, Howard Miles
American. Dramatist
b. Jan 22, 1916 in Chicago, Illinois
Source: *BiE&WWA; ConAu 69; McGEWD; NatPD; NotNAT; WhoAm 82*

Teilhard de Chardin, Pierre
French. Priest, Anthropologist
b. May 1, 1881 in Auvergne, France
d. Apr 10, 1955 in New York, New York
Source: *CasWL; LongCTC; NewCol 75; WhAm HA, 4; WorAu*

Tekakwitha, Kateri
[Catherine Tegakovita]
"Lily of the Mohawks"
American Indian. Religious Figure
b. 1656 in New York
d. Apr 17, 1680 in Caughnawaga, PQ
Source: *BioIn 2, 3, 4, 5, 6, 7, 11; DcAmReB; InWom; LibW; MacDCB 78; NotAW; WebAB*

Tekere, Edgar Zivanai
Zimbabwean. Confessed Murderer
b. 1937?
Source: *BioIn 12*

Tekulve, Kent(on Charles)
American. Baseball Player
b. Mar 5, 1947 in Cincinnati, Ohio
Source: *BaseEn; NewYTBS 79; WhoAm 82*

Telemann, Georg Philipp
German. Opera Composer
b. Mar 14, 1681 in Magdeburg, Germany
d. Jun 25, 1767 in Hamburg, Germany
Source: *AtlBL*

Tell, Alma
American. Actress
b. 1892
d. Dec 30, 1937 in San Fernando, California
Source: *Film 1; TwYS; WhScrn 74, 77; WhoHol B*

Tell, William (Wilhelm)
Swiss. Legendary Patriot
In legend, shot an apple from son's head with arrow.
b. 1282
Source: *NewCol 75; OxGer*

Teller, Edward
American. Physicist
b. Jan 15, 1908 in Budapest, Hungary
Source: *AmAu&B; AmM&WS 73S; CelR 73; ConAu P-1; CurBio 54; EncAB-H; IntWW 74; WebAB; Who 74; WhoAm 74, 76, 78, 80, 82; WhoWor 74; WhoWorJ 72*

Teltscher, Eliot
American. Tennis Player
b. Mar 15, 1959 in Torrance, California
Source: *OfEnT*

Telva, Marion
American. Opera Singer
b. Sep 26, 1897 in Saint Louis, Missouri
d. Oct 23, 1962 in Norwalk, Connecticut
Source: *InWom; WhAm 4*

Tempest, Marie
English. Actress
b. Jul 15, 1864 in London, England
d. Oct 15, 1942 in London, England
Source: *CurBio 42; EncMT; FamA&A; Film 1; FilmgC; OxThe; PlP&P; REn; WhAm 2; WhScrn 74, 77; WhoHol B; WhoStg 1906, 1908*

Temple, Shirley
see: Black, Shirley Temple

Templeton, Alec
Welsh. Musician
b. Jul 4, 1910 in Cardiff, Wales
d. Mar 28, 1963 in Greenwich, Connecticut
Source: *AmSCAP 66; CurBio 40, 63; WhAm 4; WhoHol B*

Templeton, Fay
American. Actress
b. Dec 25, 1865 in Little Rock, Arkansas
d. Oct 3, 1939 in San Francisco, California
Source: *InWom; NotAW; WhAm 1; WhScrn 74, 77; WhoHol B; WhoStg 1906, 1908*

Templeton, Garry Lewis
"Jump Steady"; "Tempy"
American. Baseball Player
b. Mar 24, 1956 in Lockney, Texas
Source: *BaseEn*

Temptations, The
[Dennis Edwards; Melvin Franklin; Eddie Kendricks; Otis Williams;Paul Williams]
American. Vocal Group
Group formed in 1964; songs, "My Girl," "Just My Imagination."
Source: *BiDAmM; EncPR&S; IlEncRk; Rk100*

10 CC
[Paul Burgess; Lol Creme; Kevin Godley; Graham Gouldman; Eric Stewart]
English. Rock Group
Source: *ConMuA 80; LilREn 78; RkOn 2; WhoRock 81*

Teng, Hsiao-Ping
[Xiaoping Deng]
Chinese. Communist Leader
b. 1904 in Kuangan, China
Source: *BioIn 5, 9, 10, 11, 12; IntWW 74*

Tenggren, Gustaf
Swedish. Illustrator
b. Nov 3, 1896 in Sweden
d. Apr 6, 1970 in West Southport, Maine
Source: *IlsBYP; IlsCB 1744, 1946; MorJA; SmATA 18; WhAm 6*

Teniers, David, the Younger
Flemish. Artist
b. Dec 14, 1610 in Antwerp, Belgium
d. Apr 25, 1690 in Brussels, Belgium
Source: *AtlBL*

Tennant, Veronica
English. Ballerina
b. Jan 15, 1946 in London, England
Source: *BioIn 9, 11; CanWW 79; CreCan 1; WhoAm 78, 80, 82*

Tennenbaum, Silvia
American. Author
b. Mar 10, 1928 in Germany
Source: *ConAu 77*

Tenniel, Sir John
English. Illustrator, Artist
b. Feb 28, 1820
d. Feb 25, 1914
Source: *Alli; ChPo, S1, S2; IlsBYP; JBA 34, 51; LongCTC; NewC; REn; Str&VC; WhoChL*

Tennille, Toni
[Captain and Tennille]
American. Singer
Had 1975 hit "Love Will Keep Us Together," with husband Daryl Dragon.
b. May 8, 1943 in Montgomery, Alabama
Source: *BioIn 11; BkPepl; WorAl*

Tennyson, Alfred, Lord
English. Poet
Poet laureate, 1850-92; wrote *Idylls of the King,* 1884.
b. Aug 6, 1809 in Somersby, England
d. Oct 6, 1892 in Haslemere, England
Source: *Alli, SUP; AnCL; AtlBL; AuBYP; BbD; BiD&SB; BrAu 19; CasWL; Chambr 3; ChPo, S1, S2; CnE&AP; CnThe; CrtT 3; CyWA; DcEnA, AP; DcEnL; DcEuL; DcLEL; EvLB; McGEWD; MouLC 4; NewC; OxEng; OxThe; Pen ENG; PoLE; RAdv 1; RComWL; REn; REnWD; Str&VC; WebE&AL; WorAl*

Tenzing, Norgay
Mountaineer
b. 1914 in Tami, Nepal
Source: *CurBio 54*

Ter-Arutunian, Rouben
Russian. Scenic and Costume Designer
b. Jul 24, 1920 in Tiflis, U.S.S.R.
Source: *BiE&WWA; CurBio 63; NotNAT; WhoAm 74; WhoE 74; WhoThe 77; WhoWor 74*

Ter Borch, Gerard
Dutch. Artist
b. 1617 in Zwolle, Netherlands
d. Dec 8, 1681 in Deventer, Netherlands
Source: *BioIn 2; McGEWB*

Ter Horst, Jerald Franklin
American. Journalist
White House Press Secretary under President Ford, 1974.
b. Jul 11, 1922 in Grand Rapids, Michigan
Source: *AuNews 1; BioNews 74; NewYTBS 74; WhoAm 74, 76, 78, 80, 82*

Terbrugghen, Hendrick
Dutch. Artist
b. 1588
d. 1629
Source: *BioIn 5; NewCol 75; OxArt*

Terence
Roman. Dramatist, Poet
Wrote comic verse dramas *The Mother-in-Law; The Eunuch.*
b. 185?BC
d. 159BC
Source: *AtlBL; BbD; BiD&SB; CasWL; CnThe; CyWA; DcEnL; McGEWD; NewC; OxEng; OxThe; Pen CL; PlP&P; RComWL; REn; REnWD; WorAl*

Teresa, Mother
[Agnes Gonxha Bojaxhiu]
Nun, Missionary
Founded Missionaries of Charity, 1950; won Nobel Peace Prize, 1979.
b. Aug 27, 1910 in Skopje, Yugoslavia
Source: *BioIn 9, 10, 11; CurBio 73; Who 82*

Teresa, Saint
Spanish. Nun, Mystic
b. 1515 in Avila, Spain
d. 1582
Source: *DcEuL; NewC; REn*

Tereshkova-Nikolaeva, Valentina
Russian. Cosmonaut
b. Mar 6, 1937
Source: *IntWW 74; WhoWor 74*

Terhune, Albert Payson
American. Journalist, Author
b. Dec 21, 1872 in Newark, New Jersey
d. Feb 18, 1942 in Pompton Lakes, New Jersey
Source: *AmAu&B; AmLY; AuBYP; BiD&SB; ChPo; CnDAL; CurBio 42; DcAmAu; DcAmB S3; DcNAA; EvLB; JBA 34; OxAmL; REnAL; TwCA, SUP; WebAB; WhAm 2; WhNAA*

Terhune, Mary Virginia
American. Author
b. Dec 31, 1831 in Dennisville, Virginia
d. Jun 3, 1922
Source: *Alli, SUP; AmAu; AmAu&B; AmBi; AmWom; ApCAB; BbD; BiD&SB; BiDSA; CarSB; ChPo; CnDAL; CyAl 2; DcAmAu; DcAmB; DcNAA; Drake; InWom; LivgFWS; NotAW; OxAmL; REnAL; TwCBDA; WhAm 1; WomWWA 14*

Terkel, Studs (Louis)
American. Author, Journalist
Books based on tape-recorded interviews: *Hard Times; Working.*
b. May 16, 1912 in New York, New York
Source: *AmAu&B; AuNews 1; ConAu 57; CurBio 74; WhoAm 74, 76, 78, 80, 82; WhoMW 74; WrDr 76*

Ternina, Milka
Croatian. Opera Singer
b. Dec 19, 1863 in Belgisc, Croatia
d. May 18, 1941 in Zagreb, Croatia
Source: *InWom*

Terrell, Mary Church
American. Author, Educator
b. Sep 23, 1863 in Memphis, Tennessee
d. Jul 24, 1954 in Annapolis, Maryland
Source: *CurBio 42, 54; DcAmB S5; InWom; WhAm 3*

Terris, Norma
American. Actress
b. 1904 in Columbus, Kansas
Source: *EncMT; WhoHol A; WhoThe 77*

Terris, Susan
American. Children's Author
b. May 6, 1937 in Saint Louis, Missouri
Source: *ConAu 29R; SmATA 3; WrDr 76*

Terry, Alfred H
American. Military Leader
b. Nov 10, 1827 in Hartford, Connecticut
d. Dec 16, 1890 in New Haven, Connecticut
Source: *AmBi; ApCAB; DcAmB; Drake; NewCol 75; TwCBDA; WebAB; WebBD 80; WhAm H*

Terry, Dame Ellen Alicia
English. Actress
b. Feb 27, 1848 in Coventry, England
d. Jul 21, 1928 in Kent, England
Source: *FamA&A; Film 1; HerW; InWom; LongCTC; NewC; OxThe; PlP&P; REn; WhAm 1; WhScrn 74, 77; WhoStg 1906, 1908*

Terry, Luther Leonidas
American. Physician
Surgeon general, whose study revealed smoking hazardous to health, 1964.
b. Sep 15, 1911 in Red Level, Alabama
Source: *AmM&WS 73P; ConAu 33R; ConAu P-2; CurBio 61; IntWW 74; SmATA 11; WhoAm 74, 76, 78, 80, 82*

Terry, Megan
American. Dramatist
b. Jul 22, 1932 in Seattle, Washington
Source: *ConDr 73; CroCD; DrAP 75; NotNAT; PlP&P; WhoAm 82; WhoThe 77; WrDr 76*

Terry, Paul H
American. Cartoonist, Producer
b. Feb 19, 1887 in San Mateo, California
d. Oct 25, 1971 in New York, New York
Source: *DcFM; FilmgC; WorECom*

Terry, Walter
American. Dance Critic, Author
Dance critic, 1936-82; wrote 22 books.
b. May 14, 1913 in Brooklyn, New York
d. Oct 4, 1982 in New York, New York
Source: *AmAu&B; AuBYP; ConAu 21R; NewYTBS 82; SmATA 14; WhoAm 74, 76, 78, 80, 82*

Terry, Bill (William Harold)
"Memphis Bill"
American. Baseball Player, Manager
b. Oct 30, 1898 in Atlanta, Georgia
Source: *BaseEn; WhoProB 73*

Terry-Thomas
[Thomas Terry Hoar-Stevens]
English. Actor, Comedian
b. Jul 14, 1911 in London, England
Source: *FilmgC; IntMPA 77; MotPP; MovMk; Who 82; WhoHol A*

Teschemacher, Frank
American. Jazz Musician
b. Mar 14, 1906 in Kansas City, Missouri
d. Feb 29, 1932 in Chicago, Illinois
Source: *WhAm HA, 4; WhoJazz 72*

Teschemacher, Marguerite
German. Opera Singer
b. Mar 3, 1903 in Cologne, Germany
d. May 19, 1959 in Tegernsee, Germany
Source: *NewEOp 71*

Teshigahara, Hiroshi
Japanese. Motion Picture Director
b. 1927 in Tokyo, Japan
Source: *BiDFilm; DcFM; OxFilm; WorEFlm*

Tesla, Nikola
American. Electrical Engineer
Pioneer in high-tension electricity and radio transmission.
b. Jul 10, 1856 in Smiljan, Austria-Hungary
d. Jan 7, 1943 in New York, New York
Source: *AsBiEn; CurBio 43; DcAmB S3; DcNAA; DcScB; McGEWB; NewCol 75; WebAB; WhAm 2*

Tetrazzini, Luisa
Italian. Opera Singer
b. Jun 29, 1874 in Florence, Italy
d. Apr 28, 1940 in Milan, Italy
Source: *CurBio 40; InWom; WhAm 1*

Tex, Joe
[Joseph Arrington, Jr.]
American. Singer
Had 1964 hit "Hold On to What You've Got."
b. Aug 8, 1933 in Rogers, Texas
d. Aug 13, 1982 in Navasota, Texas
Source: *InB&W 80; RkOn 2; WhoBlA 77*

Tex and Jinx
[Jinx Falkenburg; Tex McCrary]
American. Radio Personalities
Source: *CurBio 53*

Tey, Josephine, pseud.
[Elizabeth Mackintosh]
Scottish. Author
b. 1897 in Inverness, Scotland
d. Feb 13, 1952
Source: *EncMys; LongCTC; NewC; Pen ENG; REn; TwCA SUP; TwCW*

Teyte, Dame Maggie
English. Opera Singer
b. Apr 17, 1888 in Wolverhampton, England
d. May 27, 1976 in London, England
Source: *CurBio 45; EncMT; InWom; Who 74*

Thackeray, William Makepeace
[George Savage Fitzboodle; Jeames; Mister Brown; Michael Angelo Titmarsh; Theophile Wagstaff; Charles James Yellowplush, pseuds.]
British. Author
Wrote satirical novel *Vanity Fair*, 1848.
b. Jul 18, 1811 in Calcutta, India
d. Dec 24, 1863 in London, England
Source: *Alli; AtlBL; BbD; BiD&SB; BrAu 19; CarSB; CasWL; Chambr 3; ChPo, S1, S2; CrtT 3; CyWA; DcBiA; DcEnA, AP; DcEnL; DcEuL; DcLEL; EvLB; FamSYP; HsB&A; MouLC 3; NewC; OxAmL; OxEng; Pen ENG; RAdv 1; RComWL; REn; WebE&AL; WhoChL; WorAl*

Thackrey, Russell I
American. Journalist
b. Dec 6, 1904 in Kansas City, Kansas
Source: *ConAu 37R; WhoAm 74*

Thalberg, Irving Grant
American. Motion Picture Producer
Head of MGM production under Louis Mayer, 1923-36.
b. May 30, 1899 in Brooklyn, New York
d. Sep 14, 1936 in Santa Monica, California
Source: *ConAu 41R; DcAmB S2; DcFM; FilmgC; OxFilm; WebAB; WhAm HA, 4; WorEFlm*

Thaddeus, Saint
see: Jude, Saint

Thales
Greek. Philosopher
Belief in rational rather than mythological approach to nature of universe.
b. 600BC
d. 540BC
Source: *BiD&SB; CasWL; NewC; Pen CL; REn; WorAl*

Thang, Ton Duc
[Ton Duc Thang]
Vietnamese. Government Official
b. Aug 20, 1888 in Long Xuyen Province, Vietnam
d. Mar 30, 1980 in Hanoi, Vietnam
Source: *AnObit 1980; BioIn 8, 9; IntWW 74; WhoWor 74, 76, 78*

Thani, Shiekh Khalifa Ben Hamad al
Qatari. Ruler
b. in Qatar
Source: *WhoWor 74*

Thant, U
Burmese. Statesman
Secretary-General, UN, 1962-72; focused on problems of Third World.
b. Jan 22, 1909 in Pantanaw, Burma
d. Nov 25, 1974 in New York, New York
Source: *CurBio 62, 75; IntWW 74; NewYTBS 74; WhAm 6; Who 74; WhoAm 74; WhoWor 74*

Tharp, Louise Hall
American. Children's Author
b. Jun 19, 1898 in Oneonta, New York
Source: *AmAu&B; Au&Wr 71; AuBYP; ChPo; ConAu 1R; CurBio 55; ForWC 70; InWom; MorJA; RAdv 1; SmATA 3; WhoAm 74; WorAu*

Tharp, Twyla
American. Choreographer, Dancer
Organized modern dance troupe, 1965--; wrote *Push Comes to Shove.*
b. Jul 1, 1941 in Portland, Indiana
Source: *BioIn 10; CurBio 75; WhoAm 78*

Thatcher, Margaret Hilda Roberts
English. Prime Minister
Leader of Conservative Party, 1975--; prime minister, May, 1979--.
b. Oct 13, 1925 in Grantham, England
Source: *IntWW 74; Who 74; WhoWor 74; WomPO 76*

Thaw, Harry Kendall
American. Murderer
Killed architect Stanford White in Madison Square Garden, 1906; ruled insane.
b. Feb 1, 1871 in Pittsburgh, Pennsylvania
d. Feb 22, 1947 in Miami Beach, Florida
Source: *Blood; DcAmB S4; EncACr; WorAl*

Thaxter, Phyllis
American. Actress
b. Nov 20, 1920 in Portland, Maine
Source: *BiE&WWA; FilmgC; IntMPA 75, 76, 77, 78, 79, 80, 81, 82; MotPP; MovMk; NotNAT; WhoHol A; WhoThe 77*

Thayendanegea
see: Brant, Joseph

Thayer, Abbott H
American. Artist
b. Aug 12, 1849 in Boston, Massachusetts
d. May 29, 1921 in Monadnock, New Hampshire
Source: *AmBi; ApCAB; DcAmB; WhAm 1*

Thayer, Ernest
American. Author
Wrote *Casey at the Bat,* 1888.
b. Aug 14, 1863 in Lawrence, Massachusetts
d. Aug 21, 1940
Source: *AuBYP; BioIn 1, 5, 6; ChPo S1; EvLB*

Thayer, George Chapman, Jr.
American. Author
b. Sep 18, 1933 in Philadelphia, Pennsylvania
d. Aug 13, 1973 in Washington, DC
Source: *ConAu 25R, 45; ConAu P-2; NewYTBE 73; WhAm 6*

Thayer, Sylvanus, General
"Man Who Made West Point"
American. Educator, Engineer
b. Jun 9, 1785 in Braintree, Massachusetts
d. Sep 7, 1872 in Braintree, Massachusetts
Source: *Alli; AmBi; ApCAB; DcAmAu; DcAmB; DcNAA; Drake; TwCBDA; WebAB; WhAm H*

Thayer, Tiffany Ellsworth
American. Author, Actor
b. Mar 1, 1902 in Freeport, Illinois
d. Aug 23, 1959 in Nantucket, Massachusetts
Source: *AmAu&B; TwCA, SUP; WhAm 3*

Thebom, Blanche
American. Opera Singer
b. Sep 19, 1919 in Monessen, Pennsylvania
d. 1976
Source: *BioIn 10, 11; BioNews 74; CurBio 48; InWom; WhoAm 74; WhoWor 74*

Theiler, Max
American. Scientist, Physician, Engineer
b. Jan 30, 1899 in Pretoria, South Africa
d. Aug 11, 1972 in New Haven, Connecticut
Source: *CurBio 52, 72; NewYTBE 72; WhAm 5*

Theismann, Joe (Joseph Robert)
American. Football Player
b. Sep 9, 1949 in New Brunswick, New Jersey
Source: *BioIn 9; WhoAm 80, 82; WhoFtbl 74*

Themistocles
Greek. Statesman, General
b. 527BC
d. 460BC
Source: *REn*

Theocritus
Greek. Poet
b. 310BC in Syracuse, Sicily
d. 250BC
Source: *BbD; BiD&SB; CasWL; ChPo; CyWA; DcEnL; NewC; OxEng; Pen CL; RComWL; REn*

Theodora
Roman. Consort of Justianian I
b. 508
d. 548
Source: *InWom; NewCol 75; PlP&P; REn*

Theodorakis, Mikis
Greek. Composer
b. Jul 29, 1925
Source: *CurBio 73; IntWW 74; OxFilm; WhoWor 74; WorEFlm*

Theodosius I
[Theodosius the Great]
Roman. Emperor
b. 346?
d. 395
Source: *BioIn 1, 6, 9; LinLib S; McGEWB; NewCol 75*

Theorell, (Axel) Hugh Teodor
Swedish. Biochemist
Won 1955 Nobel Prize for Medicine; pioneered enzyme research.
b. Jul 6, 1903 in Linkoping, Sweden
d. Aug 15, 1982 in Sweden
Source: *AsBiEn; CurBio 56; IntWW 74, 75, 76, 77, 78, 79, 80, 81; NewYTBS 82; WhoWor 74, 76, 78*

Theresa, Saint
Spanish. Seer, Psychic
b. 1515
d. 1582
Source: *NewC; NewCol 75; OxEng; REn*

Therese of Lisieux
[Marie Francoise-Therese Martin]
French. Saint
b. 1873 in Alencon, France
d. Sep 30, 1897 in Lisieux, France
Source: *InWom; NewCol 75; WhoModH*

Theroux, Paul Edward
American. Author
b. Apr 10, 1941 in Medford, Mississippi
Source: *Au&Wr 71; ConAu 33R; ConLC 5, 8, 11, 15; ConNov 72, 76; ConP 70; DrAF 76; WhoAm 82; WhoE 74; WrDr 76*

Thespis
Greek. Actor, Dramatist, Poet
fl. 6th century BC in Attica, Greece
Source: *CasWL; EncWT; Grk&L; LinLib L, S; NewCol 75; NotNAT B; OxThe; Pen CL; REn*

Thibault, Anatole
see: France, Anatole, pseud.

Thibault, Conrad
American. Singer
b. Nov 13, 1908 in Northbridge, Massachusetts
Source: *WhoAm 74, 76, 78, 80, 82*

Thiebaud, Wayne Morton
American. Artist
b. Nov 15, 1920 in Mesa, Arizona
Source: *ConArt; ConAu 45; DcAmArt; DcCAA 71, 77; WhoAm 74, 76, 78, 80, 82; WhoAmA 73, 76, 78; WhoWor 74, 76*

Thierry, Augustin
French. Historian
b. 1795 in Blois, France
d. 1856
Source: *DcEuL; OxFr*

Thiers, Adolphe
French. Statesman, Historian
b. Apr 15, 1797 in Marseilles, France
d. Sep 3, 1877 in Saint Germain, France
Source: *OxFr; WhoModH*

Thieu, Nguyen Van
Vietnamese. Statesman
President, Republic of Vietnam, 1967-75.
b. Apr 5, 1923 in French Indochina
Source: *CurBio 68; IntWW 74; NewYTBE 72; WhoGov 72; WhoWor 74*

Thill, Georges
French. Opera Singer
b. Dec 14, 1897 in Paris, France
Source: *NewEOp 71*

Thin Lizzy
[Eric Bell; Brian Downey; Scott Gorham; Phil Lynott; Garry Moore; Brian Robertson; Midge Ure]
Irish. Rock Group
Source: *ConMuA 80; IlEncRk; LilREn 78; RkOn 2; WhoRock 81*

Thinnes, Roy
American. Actor
b. Apr 6, 1936 in Chicago, Illinois
Source: *WhoAm 82; WhoHol A*

38 Special
[Don Barnes; Steve Brookins; Jeff Carlisi; Jack Grondin; Larry Junstrom; Donnie Van Zandt]
American. Rock Band
Source: *WhoRock 81*

Thoma, Hans
German. Artist, Lithographer
b. 1839
d. 1924
Source: *NewCol 75; OxArt; WebBD 80*

Thomas a Kempis
[Thomas Hamerken]
German. Theologian, Author
Wrote *The Imitation of Christ,* circa 1427.
b. 1380? in Kempen, Germany
d. Jul 25, 1471 in Agnietenberg, Netherlands
Source: *AtlBL; BioIn 1, 2, 5, 6, 7; CasWL; CyWA; DcEuL; EuAu; McGEWB; NewC; OxEng; OxGer; Pen EUR; RComWL; REn; WorAl*

Thomas, Saint
Biblical Character
Source: *NewC; REn*

Thomas, Billy
[Our Gang]
"Buckwheat"
American. Actor
Played Buckwheat in "Our Gang" comedies, 1934-44.
b. 1931
d. Oct 10, 1980 in Los Angeles, California
Source: *NewYTBS 80*

Thomas, B(illy) J(oe)
American. Singer
Hits include "Raindrops Keep Fallin' On My Head," "I Can't Help Believing."
b. Aug 7, 1942 in Houston, Texas
Source: *EncPR&S; WhoAm 82*

Thomas, Brandon
English. Actor, Dramatist
b. Dec 25, 1856 in Liverpool, England
d. Jun 19, 1914 in London, England
Source: *LongCTC; McGEWD; ModWD*

Thomas, Caitlin Macnamara
[Mrs. Dylan Thomas]
Welsh. Author
Source: *BioIn 4*

Thomas, Charles Allen
American. Chemist, Corporation Executive
Chairman, Monsanto Co., 1960-65.
b. Feb 15, 1900 in Scott County, Kentucky
d. Mar 30, 1982 in Albany, Georgia
Source: *AmM&WS 73P, 76P, 79P; BioIn 1, 2, 3, 4, 5; CurBio 50, 82; IntWW 74; IntYB 78, 79; NewYTBS 82; WhoAm 74, 76, 78, 80, 82; WhoWor 74, 76, 78*

Thomas, (Charles Louis) Ambroise
French. Opera Composer
b. Aug 5, 1811 in Metz, France
d. Feb 12, 1896 in Paris, France
Source: *NewCol 75; NewEOp 71; OxMus*

Thomas, Danny
[Amos Jacobs]
American. Actor, Comedian, Producer
Starred in "Make Room for Daddy," 1953-64.
b. Jan 6, 1914 in Deerfield, Michigan
Source: *BioNews 74; CelR 73; CurBio 59; FilmgC; IntMPA 75, 76, 77, 78, 79, 80, 81, 82; MotPP; WhoAm 74, 76, 78, 80, 82; WhoHol A*

Thomas, Dennis ("D T")
see: Kool and the Gang

Thomas, Dylan Marlais
Welsh. Author
Wrote *A Child's Christmas in Wales, Under Milk Wood,* 1954.
b. Oct 27, 1914 in Swansea, Wales
d. Nov 9, 1953 in New York, New York
Source: *AnCL; AtlBL; CasWL; ChPo, S1, S2; CnE&AP; CnMD; CnMWL; ConP 75; CyWA; DcLEL; EncWL; EvLB; LongCTC; McGEWD; ModBrL, SUP; ModWD; NewC; OxEng; Pen ENG; RAdv 1; RComWL; REn; TwCA, SUP; TwCW; WebE&AL; WhAm HA, 4; WhoTwCL*

Thomas, Edward
English. Poet, Author
b. Mar 3, 1878 in London, England
d. Apr 9, 1917 in Arras, France
Source: *AnCL; AtlBL; ChPo, S1, S2; CnE&AP; CnMWL; DcLEL; LongCTC; ModBrL, SUP; NewC; OxEng; Pen ENG; REn; TwCA, SUP; TwCW; WebE&AL; WhoTwCL*

Thomas, Elmer
American. Senator
b. Sep 8, 1876 in Greencastle, Indiana
d. Sep 19, 1965
Source: *CurBio 49, 65; WhAm 4*

Thomas, Franklin Augustine
American. Lawyer, Foundation Official
b. May 27, 1934 in Brooklyn, New York
Source: *CurBio 81; EbonySL 1; NewYTBS 79; WhoAm 76, 78, 80, 82; WhoBlA 75, 77*

Thomas, George Henry
American. General
b. Jul 31, 1816 in Southampton County, Virginia
d. Mar 28, 1870 in San Francisco, California
Source: *AmBi; ApCAB; DcAmB; Drake; EncAB-H; TwCBDA; WebAB; WhAm H*

Thomas, Gwyn
Welsh. Author
Wrote *Where Did I Put My Pity?, The Love Man, The Keep.*
b. Jul 6, 1913 in Porth, Wales
d. Apr 13, 1981 in Cardiff, Wales
Source: *BioIn 8, 10, 11; CasWL; ConAu 65, 103; ConDr 73, 77; ConNov 76; EncWT; Who 74; WhoThe 72, 77, 81; WorAu*

Thomas, Helen A
American. Journalist
b. Aug 4, 1920 in Winchester, Kentucky
Source: *BioNews 75; ConAu 101; WhoAm 74, 76, 78, 80, 82; WhoWor 74*

Thomas, Isaiah
American. Publisher
Founded American Antiquarian Society, 1812.
b. Jan 30, 1750 in Boston, Massachusetts
d. Apr 4, 1831 in Worcester, Massachusetts
Source: *Alli; AmAu; AmAu&B; AmBi; ApCAB; BiD&SB; ChPo S1; CyAL 1; DcAmAu; DcAmB; DcNAA; Drake; EarABI, SUP; OxAmL; REnAL; TwCBDA; WebAB; WhAm H*

Thomas, Isiah
"Pocket Magic"
American. Basketball Player
b. Apr 30, 1961 in Chicago, Illinois
Source: *BioIn 12; NewYTBS 81*

Thomas, James William Tudor
British. Surgeon
b. May 23, 1894
d. Jan 23, 1976 in Cardiff, Wales
Source: *Who 74*

Thomas, Jess
American. Opera Singer
b. Apr 8, 1927 in Hot Springs, South Dakota
Source: *CurBio 64; NewYTBE 71; WhoAm 74, 76, 78, 80, 82; WhoE 74; WhoWor 74; WhoMus 72*

Thomas, John Charles
American. Opera Singer
b. Sep 6, 1891 in Meyersdale, Pennsylvania
d. Dec 13, 1960 in Apple Valley, California
Source: *CurBio 43, 61; WhAm 4; WhScrn 74, 77; WhoHol B*

Thomas, Kurt
American. Gymnast
b. Mar 29, 1956 in Terre Haute, Indiana
Source: *BioIn 11, 12*

Thomas, Lowell Jackson
American. Author, Radio Commentator
Wrote *With Lawrence in Arabia,* 1924; hosted "High-Adventure," 1957-59.
b. Apr 6, 1892 in Woodington, Ohio
d. Aug 29, 1981 in Pawling, New York
Source: *AmAu&B; Au&Wr 71; AuBYP; AuNews 1, 2; BioIn 1, 2, 3, 4, 5, 7, 8, 10, 11; ConAu 45, 104, 3NR; CurBio 40, 52, 81; FilmgC; IntAu&W 77; IntMPA 75, 76, 77, 78, 79; JBA 34; LinLib L, S; NewYTBE 70; NewYTBS 78; NewYTET; OhA&B; TwCA, SUP; WebAB; WhE&EA; WhNAA; Who 74; WhoAm 74, 76, 78, 80; WhoHol A; WrDr 80*

Thomas, Lowell, Jr.
American. Author, TV Producer
b. Oct 6, 1923 in London, England
Source: *ConAu 85; IntMPA 82; SmATA 15; WhoAm 74, 76, 78, 80, 82; WhoAmP 73; WhoHol A; WhoWest 74*

Thomas, Marlo
[Mrs. Phil Donahue; Margaret Thomas]
American. Actress
Starred in "That Girl," 1966-71; won Emmy for "Free to Be...You and Me," 1977.
b. Nov 21, 1938 in Detroit, Michigan
Source: *BkPepl; CelR 73; IntMPA 75, 76, 77, 78, 79, 80, 81, 82; NewYTBE 73; WhoAm 74, 76, 78, 80, 82; WhoHol A*

Thomas, Michael Tilson
American. Conductor
b. Dec 21, 1944 in Hollywood, California
Source: *CelR 73; CurBio 71; NewYTBE 71; WhoAm 74; WhoE 74; WhoMus 72*

Thomas, Norman Mattoon
American. Author, Socialist Leader
b. Nov 20, 1884 in Marion, Ohio
d. Dec 19, 1968 in Huntington, New York
Source: *ConAu 25R, 101; CurBio 44, 62, 69; EncAB-H; OhA&B; OxAmL; Pen AM; REn; REnAL; WebAB; WhAm 5*

Thomas, Pinklon
American. Boxer
b. 1957? in Pontiac, Michigan
Source: *BioIn 12*

Thomas, Piri
American. Author
b. Sep 30, 1928 in New York, New York
Source: *ConAu 73; ConLC 17; DrAF 76; DrAP 75; WhoE 74; WrDr 76*

Thomas, Richard
American. Actor
Played John Boy in "The Waltons."
b. Jun 13, 1951 in New York, New York
Source: *FilmgC; IntMPA 75, 76, 77, 78, 79, 80, 81, 82*

Thomas, Ronald Stuart
Welsh. Poet
Bleak view of man in poetry, *The Stones of the Field,* 1946.
b. 1913 in Cardiff, Wales
Source: *BioIn 6, 10; ConAu 89; ConLC 6, 13*

Thomas, Seth
American. Clock Manufacturer
Founded Seth Thomas Clock Co., 1853.
b. Aug 19, 1785 in Wolcott, Connecticut
d. Jan 29, 1859 in Plymouth, Connecticut
Source: *AmBi; DcAmB; WebAB; WhAm H*

Thomas, Sidney Gilchrist
British. Inventor, Scientist
b. 1850
d. 1885
Source: *BioIn 2, 7*

Thomas, Theodore
German. Conductor
b. Oct 11, 1835 in Essen, Germany
d. Jan 4, 1905 in Chicago, Illinois
Source: *AmBi; ApCAB; DcAmB; DcNAA; OxAmL; REn; TwCBDA; WebAB; WhAm 1*

Thomasson, Hughie
see: Outlaws, The

Thomaz, Americo
[America R Tomas]
Portuguese. Politician
b. Nov 19, 1894 in Lisbon, Portugal
Source: *CurBio 58; IntWW 74; WhoWor 74*

Thomer, Banner
see: Molly Hatchet

Thompson, Bradbury
American. Graphic Designer
b. Mar 25, 1911 in Topeka, Kansas
Source: *WhoAmA 73; WhoGrA*

Thompson, Cecil
"Tiny"
Canadian. Hockey Player
Four time Vezina trophy winner as goalie for Boston Bruins, 1928-38.
b. May 31, 1905 in Sandon, BC
d. Feb 9, 1981 in Calgary, AB
Source: *WhoHcky 73*

Thompson, Chester
see: Genesis

Thompson, David
English. Explorer, Geographer
Discovered source of Mississippi River, 1798; Columbia River, 1807.
b. Apr 30, 1770 in London, England
d. Feb 10, 1857 in Montreal, PQ
Source: *DcAmB; McGEWB; REnAW; WebAB; WhAm H*

Thompson, David O'Neil
American. Basketball Player
Guard, Denver Nuggets, 1975--; MVP, all-star game, 1979.
b. Jul 13, 1954 in Shelby, North Carolina
Source: *BioIn 9; WhoAm 82; WhoBbl 73; WhoBlA 77*

Thompson, Dorothy
American. Journalist
b. Jul 9, 1894 in Lancaster, New York
d. Jan 31, 1961 in Lisbon, Portugal
Source: *ConAu 89; CurBio 40, 61; EncAB-H; EvLB; InWom; OxAmL; REn; REnAL; TwCA, SUP; WebAB; WhAm 4; WomPO 76*

Thompson, Francis Joseph
English. Poet, Essayist
b. Dec 18, 1859 in Preston, England
d. Nov 13, 1907 in London, England
Source: *AtlBL; BiD&SB; BrAu 19; CasWL; ChPo, S1, S2; CnE&AP; CrtT 3; DcEuL; DcLEL; EncWL; EvLB; LongCTC; MouLC 4; NewC; OxEng; Pen ENG; RAdv 1; REn; WebE&AL*

Thompson, Frank, Jr.
American. Congressman
b. Jul 26, 1918 in Trenton, New Jersey
Source: *BioIn 5, 8, 10, 11; CurBio 59; WhoAm 78*

Thompson, George Selden
American. Children's Author
b. May 14, 1929 in Hartford, Connecticut
Source: *AuBYP; ConAu 5R; SmATA 4*

Thompson, Hank
American. Singer, Musician, Band Leader
b. Sep 3, 1925 in Waco, Texas
Source: *AmSCAP 66; EncFCWM 69*

Thompson, Hunter S(tockton)
American. Journalist, Editor
b. Jul 18, 1939 in Louisville, Kentucky
Source: *ConAu 17R; ConLC 9; CurBio 81; IntAu&W 76, 77; NewYTBS 79; WhoAm 76, 78, 80, 82; WhoE 74*

Thompson, James Robert
American. Governor
b. May 8, 1936 in Chicago, Illinois
Source: *BioIn 9, 10, 11; CurBio 79; WhoAm 78, 80, 82*

Thompson, J(ames) Walter
American. Advertising Executive
b. Oct 28, 1847 in Pittsfield, Massachusetts
d. Oct 16, 1928 in New York, New York
Source: *BioIn 6, 7*

Thompson, John Taliaferro
American. Inventor
b. Dec 31, 1860 in Newport, Kentucky
d. Jun 21, 1940
Source: *CurBio 40; WhAm 1*

Thompson, Josiah
American. Author, Educator
b. Jan 17, 1935 in East Liverpool, Ohio
Source: *ConAu 41R; DrAS 74P; WhoAm 74; WhoE 74*

Thompson, Kay
American. Singer, Author
Wrote *Eloise,* 1955; *Eloise in Paris,* 1977.
b. Nov 9, 1913 in Saint Louis, Missouri
Source: *AmAu&B; AmSCAP 66; CelR 73; ChPo; CurBio 59; InWom; MotPP; WhoAm 74; WhoHol A*

Thompson, Marshall
[James Marshall Thompson]
American. Actor
b. Nov 27, 1926 in Peoria, Illinois
Source: *FilmgC; IntMPA 75, 76, 77, 78, 79, 80, 81, 82; MotPP; MovMk; WhoHol A*

Thompson, Mychal
American. Basketball Player
b. Jan 30, 1955 in Nassau, Bahamas
Source: *OfNBA*

Thompson, Oscar
American. Music Critic, Author
b. Aug 10, 1887 in Crawfordsville, Indiana
d. Jul 2, 1945 in New York, New York
Source: *AmAu&B; CurBio 45; DcAmB S3; DcNAA; IndAu 1917; WhAm 2; WhNAA*

Thompson, Paul
see: Roxy Music

Thompson, Randall
American. Composer
b. Apr 12, 1899 in New York, New York
Source: *AmM&WS 73P; AmSCAP 66; WhoAm 74, 76, 78, 80, 82; WhoWor 74*

Thompson, Sada Carolyn
American. Actress
Played Kate Lawrence in "Family," 1976-79.
b. Sep 27, 1929 in Des Moines, Iowa
Source: *BiE&WWA; BioNews 75; CurBio 73; IntMPA 82; NewYTBE 71; NotNAT; PlP&P A; WhoAm 74, 76, 78, 80, 82; WhoHol A; WhoThe 77*

Thompson, Thomas
American. Author
Wrote *Blood and Money* and *Serpentine.*
b. Oct 3, 1933 in Fort Worth, Texas
d. Oct 29, 1982 in Los Angeles, California
Source: *ConAu 65; NewYTBS 82; WrDr 80*

Thompson, Vivian Laubach
American. Children's Author
b. 1911 in Jersey City, New Jersey
Source: *AuBYP; ConAu 1R, 1NR; ForWC 70; SmATA 3; WrDr 76*

Thomson, Bobby (Robert Brown)
"The Staten Island Scot"
American. Baseball Player
Hit home run that won pennant for Giants, 1951.
b. Oct 25, 1923 in Glasgow, Scotland
Source: *BaseEn; WhoProB 73*

Thomson, George Paget
English. Physicist
b. May 3, 1892 in Cambridge, England
d. Sep 10, 1975 in Cambridge, England
Source: *ConAu 5R, 61, 4NR; CurBio 47, 75; IntWW 74; LongCTC; WhAm 6; Who 74; WhoLA; WhoWor 74*

Thomson, James
Scottish. Poet
b. Sep 11, 1700 in Ednam, Scotland
d. Aug 27, 1748 in Richmond, England
Source: *Alli; AtlBL; BbD; BiD&SB; BrAu; CasWL; ChPo, S1; CnE&AP; CrtT 2; DcEnA; DcEnL; DcEuL; DcLEL; EvLB; MouLC 2; NewC; OxEng; OxThe; Pen ENG; RAdv 1; REn; WebE&AL*

Thomson, James
[B V; Bysshe Vanolis, pseuds.]
Scottish. Poet, Essayist
b. Nov 23, 1834 in Scotland
d. Jun 3, 1882 in London, England
Source: *AtlBL; BbD; BiD&SB; BrAu 19; CasWL; CnE&AP; DcEnA; DcEuL; DcLEL; EvLB; Pen ENG*

Thomson, Meldrim, Jr.
American. Governor of New Hampshire
b. Mar 8, 1912 in Pittsburgh, Pennsylvania
Source: *AlmAP 78; CurBio 78; IntWW 77, 78; WhoAm 74, 76, 78; WhoAmP 73, 75, 77, 79; WhoE 77, 79; WhoGov 75, 77*

Thomson, Tom
Canadian. Artist
b. 1877 in Claremont, ON
d. Jul 8, 1917 in Canoe Lake, ON
Source: *BioIn 1, 2, 4, 8, 9, 10, 11; CreCan 1*

Thomson, Virgil Garnett
American. Composer, Musician, Critic
b. Nov 25, 1896 in Kansas City, Missouri
Source: *AmAu&B; AmSCAP 66; BiE&WWA; CelR 73; ConAu 41R; CurBio 40, 66; DcCM; EncAB-H; IntWW 74; NewYTBE 71, 72; NotNAT; OxFilm; REn; REnAL; TwCA, SUP; WebAB; WhoAm 74, 76, 78, 80, 82; WhoE 74; WhoMus 72; WhoWor 74*

Thomson of Fleet, Roy Herbert Thomson, Baron
British. Journalist
b. Jun 5, 1894
d. Aug 4, 1976 in London, England
Source: *CanWW 70; IntWW 74; Who 74*

Thon, William
American. Artist
b. Aug 8, 1906 in New York, New York
Source: *McGDA; WhoAm 74, 76, 78, 80, 82; WhoAmA 73, 76, 78*

Thor
[John Mikl]
Canadian. Rock Singer
Source: *BioIn 11*

Thorborg, Kerstin
Swedish. Opera Singer
b. May 19, 1896 in Hedemora, Sweden
d. Apr 12, 1970 in Falun, Sweden
Source: *CurBio 40; NewEOp 71; NewYTBE 70*

Thoreau, Henry David
American. Author
Wrote essay *Civil Disobedience,* 1849, book *Walden,* 1854.
b. Jul 12, 1817 in Concord, Massachusetts
d. May 6, 1862 in Concord, Massachusetts
Source: *Alli; AmAu; AmAu&B; AmBi; AmWr; AnCL; ApCAB; AtlBL; BbD; BbtC; BiD&SB; CasWL; Chambr 3; ChPo; CnDAL; CnE&AP; CrtT 3; CyAl 2; CyWA; DcAmAu; DcAmB; DcEnA; DcLEL; DcNAA; Drake; EncAB-H; EvLB; MouLC 3; OxAmL; OxCan; OxEng; Pen AM; RAdv 1; RComWL; REn; REnAL; TwCBDA; WebAB; WebE&AL; WhAm H*

Thorez, Maurice
French. Politician
b. Apr 28, 1900 in Noyelles Godault, France
d. Jul 11, 1964
Source: *CurBio 46, 64; WhAm 4*

Thornburgh, Richard Lewis
American. Governor
b. Jul 16, 1932 in Pittsburgh, Pennsylvania
Source: *WhoAm 82; WhoE 74; WhoGov 72*

Thorndike, Dame Sybil
English. Actress
b. Oct 24, 1882 in Gainsborough, England
d. Jun 6, 1976 in London, England
Source: *BiE&WWA; CurBio 53; FilmgC; InWom; IntWW 74; MotPP; MovMk; NewC; OxThe; PlP&P; REn; Who 74; WhoHol A; WhoThe 77; WhoWor 74*

Thorne, Jim
American. Author, Adventurer
First non-Mexican to make successful dive off Acapulco cliff, 1965.
b. 1922 in Milwaukee, Wisconsin
Source: *ConAu 1R, 1NR*

Thornell, Jack Randolph
American. Photographer
b. Aug 29, 1939 in Vicksburg, Mississippi
Source: *WhoAm 74, 76, 78, 80, 82; WhoS&SW 73*

Thornhill, Claude
American. Composer, Band Leader
b. Aug 10, 1908 in Terre Haute, Indiana
d. Jul 1, 1965 in Caldwell, New Jersey
Source: *AmSCAP 66; WhScrn 74, 77; WhoHol B; WhoJazz 72*

Thornton, Charles Bates
"Tex"
American. Businessman
b. Jul 22, 1913 in Haskell, Texas
d. Nov 24, 1981 in Holmby Hills, California
Source: *BioIn 6, 8, 9; CelR 73; CurBio 70, 82; Dun&B 79; IntWW 74, 75, 76, 77, 78; WhoAm 74, 76, 78, 80; WhoF&I 74, 75, 79; WhoWest 74, 76, 78; WhoWor 74*

Thorpe, Jim (James Francis)
American. Athlete
Only person to win Olympic gold medals decathlon, pentathlon, 1912.
b. May 28, 1888 in Shawnee, Oklahoma
d. Mar 28, 1953 in Lomita, California
Source: *CurBio 50, 53; DcAmB S5; EncAB-H; WebAB; WhAm 4; WhScrn 74, 77; WhoAmP 73; WhoFtbl 74; WhoHol B; WhoProB 73; WhoTr&F 73*

Thorpe, (John) Jeremy
English. Political Leader
b. Apr 29, 1929 in London, England
Source: *CurBio 74; IntWW 74; NewYTBS 74; Who 74; WhoWor 74*

Thornton, Matthew
American. Continental Congressman
b. 1714? in Ireland
d. Jun 24, 1803 in Newburyport, Massachusetts
Source: *Alli; AmBi; ApCAB; BiAuS; BiDrAC; BioIn 7, 8, 9; DcAmB; DcIrB; Drake; NatCAB 11; TwCBDA; WhAm H; WhAmP*

Thorvaldsen, Albert Bertel
[Bertel Thorwaldsen]
Danish. Sculptor
b. 1770 in Copenhagen, Denmark
d. 1844
Source: *NewCol 75; OxArt; WebBD 80*

Thou, Jacques Auguste de
French. Historian, Statesman
b. Oct 8, 1553
d. May 7, 1617
Source: *DcEuL; NewCol 75; OxFr; REn; WebBD 80*

Three Dog Night
[Michael Allsup; James Greenspoon; Daniel Hutton; Skip Konte; Charles Negron; Joseph Schermine; Floyd Sneed; Cory Wells]
Australian. Rock Group
Source: *BiDAmM; EncPR&S; IlEncRk*

Three Stooges, The
[Joe DeRita; Larry Fine; Curly Howard; Moe Howard; Shemp Howard]
American. Comedy Team
Performed in vaudeville, 1923; made 200 short films, 1934-58.
Source: *NF*

Threlkeld, Richard
American. Broadcast Journalist
b. Nov 30, 1937 in Cedar Rapids, Iowa
Source: *ConAu 65*

Throckmorton, Cleon
American. Scenic Designer
b. Oct 8, 1897 in Atlantic City, New Jersey
d. Oct 23, 1965
Source: *BiE&WWA; CurBio 43, 65; PlP&P; WhAm 4*

Thucydides
Greek. Historian
b. 460BC in Athens, Greece
d. 400BC
Source: *AtlBL; BbD; BiD&SB; CasWL; CyWA; DcEnL; NewC; OxEng; Pen CL; RComWL; REn*

Thulin, Ingrid
Swedish. Actress
b. Jan 27, 1929 in Solleftea, Sweden
Source: *BiDFilm; CelR 73; FilmgC; IntMPA 75, 76, 77, 78, 79, 80, 81, 82; IntWW 74; MotPP; MovMk; OxFilm; WhoHol A; WhoWor 74; WomWMM; WorEFlm*

Thum, Marcella
American. Children's Author
b. in St. Louis, Missouri
Source: *ConAu 9R; SmATA 3; WrDr 76*

Thurber, Charles
American. Inventor
Patented, 1843, hand printing machine that preceded typewriter.
b. Jan 2, 1803 in East Brookfield, Massachusetts
d. Nov 7, 1886 in Nashua, New Hampshire
Source: *DcAmB; WhAm H*

Thurber, James Grover
American. Humorist, Cartoonist, Author
Wrote *The Secret Life of Walter Middy.*
b. Dec 8, 1894 in Columbus, Ohio
d. Nov 2, 1961 in New York, New York
Source: *AmAu&B; AnCL; AtlBL; AuBYP; BkCL; CasWL; CnDAL; CnMWL; ConAmA; ConAu 73; ConLC 5, 11; CurBio 40, 60, 62; CyWA; DcLEL; EncWL; EvLB; FilmgC; LongCTC; McGEWD; ModAL; MorJA; OhA&B; OxAmL; OxEng; Pen AM; RAdv 1; REn; SmATA 13; TwCA, SUP; TwCW; WebAB; WebE&AL; WhoGrA; WhoTwCL*

Thurman, Howard
American. Clergyman, Educator, Author
b. Nov 18, 1900 in Daytona Beach, Florida
d. Apr 10, 1981 in San Francisco, California
Source: *BioIn 3, 4, 5, 7, 8, 11; BlkAW; CurBio 55, 81; EbonySL 1; LinLib L, S; LivgBAA; SelBAA; WhoAm 74, 76, 78; WhoBlA 75, 77; WhoRel 77*

Thurmond, (James) Strom
American. Senator
b. Dec 5, 1902 in Edgefield, South Carolina
Source: *BiDrAC; CelR 73; ConAu 89; IntWW 74; WebAB; WhoAm 74, 76, 78, 80, 82; WhoAmP 73; WhoGov 72; WhoS&SW 73; WhoWor 74*

Thurmond, Nate
American. Basketball Player
b. Jul 25, 1941 in Akron, Ohio
Source: *NewYTBS 76; OfNBA; WhoAm 74, 76, 78; WhoBbl 73; WhoBlA 75, 77, 80*

Thurston, Howard
American. Magician
b. Jul 20, 1869 in Columbus, Ohio
d. Apr 13, 1936
Source: *ChPo; DcAmB S2; DcNAA; OhA&B; WhAm 1*

Thyssen, Fritz
German. Industrialist
b. Nov 9, 1873
d. Feb 8, 1951 in Argentina
Source: *CurBio 40, 51*

Tiant, Luis Clemente
Cuban. Baseball Player
b. Nov 23, 1940 in Havana, Cuba
Source: *BaseEn; WhoAm 82; WhoProB 73*

Tibbets, Paul Warfield
American. Pilot
Piloted the *Enola Gay,* plane that dropped atomic bomb on Hiroshima.
b. 1915
Source: *BioIn 10, 11; WhWW-II*

Tibbett, Lawrence Mervil
American. Opera Singer
b. Nov 16, 1896 in Bakersfield, California
d. Jul 15, 1960 in New York, New York
Source: *CurBio 45, 60; FilmgC; WhAm 4; WhScrn 74, 77; WhoHol B*

Tiberius Julius Caesar Augustus
[Tiberius Claudius Nero]
Roman. Emperor
Second Roman Emperor, 14AD-37.
b. 42BC in Rome, Italy
d. 37AD in Capri
Source: *McGEWB; NewCol 75; REn*

Tiburzi, Bonni
American. Pilot
b. 1948?
Source: *BioIn 9*

Tichatschek, Joseph
German. Opera Singer
b. Jul 11, 1807 in Weckseldorf, Germany
d. Jan 18, 1886 in Dresden, Germany
Source: *NewEOp 71*

Tickner, Charlie
American. Figure Skater
b. Nov 13, 1953 in Oakland, California
Source: *BioIn 11, 12*

Tiede, Tom Robert
American. Journalist
b. Feb 24, 1937 in Huron, South Dakota
Source: *AmAu&B; ConAu 25R; WhoAm 74, 76, 78, 80, 82; WhoE 74*

Tiegs, Cheryl
[Mrs. Peter Beard]
American. Actress, Model
Highest paid model of 1970's.
b. Sep 25, 1947 in Alhambra, California
Source: *BioIn 11; BkPepl; CurBio 82; WhoAm 82*

Tiepolo, Giambattista (Giovanni Battista)
Italian. Artist
b. Mar 5, 1696 in Venice, Italy
d. Mar 27, 1770
Source: *AtlBL; McGEWB; REn; WebBD 80*

Tiepolo, Giovanni Domenico
Italian. Artist
b. 1727
d. 1804
Source: *BioIn 9; WebBD 80*

Tieri, Frank
"Funzi"; "Funzola"; "The Old Man"
Italian. Crime Boss
b. 1904 in Castel Gandolfo, Italy
d. Mar 29, 1981 in New York, New York
Source: *NewYTBS 81*

Tiernan, Robert Owens
American. Congressman, Lawyer
b. Feb 24, 1929 in Providence, Rhode Island
Source: *BiDrAC; CngDr 74; WhoAm 74; WhoAmP 73; WhoE 74; WhoGov 72*

Tierney, Gene
American. Actress
b. Nov 11, 1920 in Brooklyn, New York
Source: *BiDFilm; CmMov; FilmgC; InWom; IntMPA 75, 76, 77, 78, 79, 80, 81, 82; MotPP; MovMk; WhoHol A; WorEFlm*

Tietjen, Heinz
German. Conductor, Opera Producer
b. Jun 24, 1881 in Tangiers, Morocco
d. Nov 1, 1967 in Bayreuth, Germany
Source: *NewEOp 71*

Tietjens, Eunice
American. Poet, Author
b. Jul 29, 1884 in Chicago, Illinois
d. Sep 6, 1944
Source: *AmAu&B; ChPo, S1, S2; ConAmL; CurBio 44; DcLEL; DcNAA; InWom; JBA 34; NotAW; OxAmL; REn; REnAL; TwCA, SUP; WhAm 2; WhNAA*

Tiffany, Charles Lewis
American. Jeweler
b. Feb 15, 1812 in Killingly, Connecticut
d. Feb 18, 1902 in Yonkers, New York
Source: *AmBi; DcAmB; TwCBDA; WebAB; WhAm 1, 2*

Tiffany, Louis Comfort
American. Artist, Designer
b. Feb 18, 1848 in New York, New York
d. Jan 17, 1933 in New York, New York
Source: *AmBi; ApCAB; DcAmB; EncAB-H; REn; TwCBDA; WebAB; WhAm 1*

Tiffeau, Jacques Emile
French. Fashion Designer
b. Oct 11, 1927 in Chenevelles, France
Source: *WhoAm 74, 76, 78, 80, 82; WorFshn*

Tiffin, Pamela Kimberley
American. Model, Actress
b. Oct 13, 1942 in Oklahoma City, Oklahoma
Source: *FilmgC; ForWC 70; InWom; IntMPA 75, 76, 77, 78, 79, 80, 81, 82; MotPP; WhoAm 74; WhoHol A*

Tijuana Brass
see: Alpert, Herb

Tilbrook, Glenn
see: Squeeze

Tilden, Bill (William Tatem, Jr.)
"Big Bill"
American. Tennis Player
b. Feb 10, 1893 in Philadelphia, Pennsylvania
d. Jun 5, 1953 in Hollywood, California
Source: *DcAmB S5; WebAB; WhAm 4; WhScrn 74, 77; WhoHol B*

Tilden, Samuel Jones
American. Politician, Lawyer
b. Feb 9, 1814 in New Lebanon, New York
d. Aug 4, 1886 in Yonkers, New York
Source: *Alli SUP; AmAu&B; AmBi; ApCAB; BiAuS; DcAmAu; DcAmB; DcNAA; Drake; EncAB-H; REn; REnAL; TwCBDA; WebAB; WhAm H; WhAmP*

Tillich, Paul Johannes
German. Theologian
b. Aug 20, 1886 in Starzeddal, Germany
d. Oct 22, 1965 in Chicago, Illinois
Source: *AmAu&B; BioNews 74; ConAu 5R, 25R; CurBio 54, 65; EncAB-H; LongCTC; OxAmL; OxGer; REn; REnAL; TwCA SUP; WebAB; WhAm 4*

Tillis, James
"Quick"
American. Boxer
b. 1957? in Chicago, Illinois
Source: *BioIn 12*

Tillis, Mel(vin)
American. Singer, Songwriter
Has written over 450 songs; CMA entertainer of year, 1976.
b. Aug 8, 1932 in Pahokee, Florida
Source: *BkPepl; EncFCWM 69; WhoAm 82*

Tillstrom, Burr
American. Puppeteer
Created Kukla and Ollie, TV show "Kukla, Fran, and Ollie."
b. Oct 13, 1917 in Chicago, Illinois
Source: *AmSCAP 66; CelR 73; CurBio 51; IntMPA 75, 76, 77, 78, 79, 80, 81, 82; WebAB; WhoAm 74, 76, 78, 80, 82*

Tilton, Charlene
[Mrs. Johnny Lee]
American. Actress
Plays Lucy Ewing on "Dallas," 1978--.
b. 1960? in San Diego, California
Source: *BioIn 12*

Timerman, Jacobo
Argentine. Author, Journalist
b. Jan 6, 1923 in Bar, Russia
Source: *BioIn 11; CurBio 81; NewYTBS 79*

Timken, Henry
American. Inventor, Manufacturer
Patented Timken spring, 1977.
b. Aug 16, 1831 in Bremen, Germany
d. Mar 16, 1909 in San Diego, California
Source: *DcAmB; WhAm 4*

Timm, Barbara
American. Mother of Kevin Hermening
b. 1938?
Source: *BioIn 12*

Timoshenko, Semen
Russian. Army Commander
b. Feb 19, 1895 in Urmanka, Russia
d. Mar 31, 1970 in Moscow, U.S.S.R.
Source: *BioIn 1, 4, 6, 8, 9*

Timrod, Henry
American. Poet
b. Dec 8, 1828 in Charleston, South Carolina
d. Oct 6, 1867 in Columbia, South Carolina
Source: *Alli; AmAu; AmAu&B; AmBi; BiD&SB; BiDSA; CasWL; Chambr 3; ChPo, S1, S2; CnDAL; CyAL 1; DcAmAu; DcAmB; DcLEL; DcNAA; EvLB; OxAmL; Pen AM; REn; REnAL; TwCBDA; WebAB; WhAm H*

Tindenans, Leo
Belgian. Former Prime Minister
b. Apr 16, 1922 in Zwijndrecht, Belgium
Source: *CurBio 78*

Tinguely, Jean
Swiss. Sculptor
b. 1925
Source: *NewCol 75*

Tinker, Grant A
American. TV Producer, Head of NBC
President, Mary Tyler Moore Enterprises, 1970-81; head, NBC-TV, 1981--.
b. Jan 11, 1926 in Stamford, Connecticut
Source: *BioIn 10; CurBio 82; IntMPA 75, 76, 77, 78, 79, 80, 81, 82; NewYTET; WhoAm 78, 80, 82*

Tinker, Joe (Joseph Bert)
American. Baseball Player
Shortstop in famous double play combination of Tinker to Evers to Chance.
b. Jul 27, 1880 in Muscotah, Kansas
d. Jul 27, 1948 in Orlando, Florida
Source: *BaseEn; WhoProB 73*

Tinling, Ted
English. Fashion Designer
b. 1910?
Source: *BioIn 8, 11*

Tinney, Cal(vin Lawrence)
American. Journalist, Commentator
b. Feb 2, 1908 in Pontotoc County, Oklahoma
Source: *CurBio 43*

Tinney, Frank
American. Actor
b. Mar 29, 1878 in Philadelphia, Pennsylvania
d. Nov 27, 1940
Source: *CurBio 41; WhAm 1; WhoHol B*

Tintoretto
[Jacopo Robusti]
Italian. Artist
b. 1518 in Venice, Italy
d. May 31, 1594 in Venice, Italy
Source: *AtlBL; NewC; NewCol 75; REn; WebBD 80*

"Tiny Tim"
[Herbert Buckingham Khaury]
American. Entertainer
Married to Miss Vicki, 1969-74; one daughter, Tulip.
b. Apr 12, 1922 in New York, New York
Source: *BioNews 75; WhoAm 74; WhoHol A*

Tiomkin, Dimitri
American. Composer, Musician
b. May 10, 1899 in Saint Petersburg, Russia
d. Nov 11, 1979 in London, England
Source: *CelR 73; CmMov; DcFM; FilmgC; IntMPA 77, 75; IntWW 74; OxFilm; WebAB; WhoAm 74; WhoWor 74; WorEFlm*

Tippett, Sir Michael Kemp
English. Composer
b. Jan 2, 1905 in London, England
Source: *BioNews 74; CurBio 74; DcCM; IntWW 74; Who 74; WhoMus 72; WhoWor 74*

Tipton, Glenn
see: Judas Priest

Tirpitz, Alfred von
German. Admiral
b. 1849 in Kustrin, Germany
d. Mar 6, 1930
Source: *NewCol 75; OxGer; REn; WebBD 80*

Titian
[Tiziano Vecellio]
Italian. Artist
Works include "Assumption of the Virgin," 1518; "La Bella," 1537.
b. 1477 in Preve di Cadore, Italy
d. Aug 27, 1576 in Venice, Italy
Source: *AtlBL; McGEWB; NewC; NewCol 75; REn; WebBD 80*

Tito
[Josip Broz Tito]
Yugoslav. Chief of State
Premier, minister of defense, 1945-80; president, 1953-80.
b. May 25, 1892 in Kumrovec, Yugoslavia
d. May 4, 1980 in Ljublijana, Yugoslavia
Source: *BioIn 1, 10; ConAu 97; CurBio 43, 55; IntWW 74; NewCol 75; WebBD 80*

Titov, Gherman Stepanovich (Herman)
Russian. Astronaut
b. Sep 11, 1935 in Verkhneye, Russia
Source: *CurBio 62; IntWW 74; WhoWor 74*

Tittle, Y(elberton) A(braham)
American. Football Player
Quarterback, 1948-64.
b. Oct 24, 1926 in Marshall, Texas
Source: *CurBio 64; NewYTBE 70; WhoFtbl 74*

Titus
Roman. 2nd Flavian Emperor
b. 40 in Rome, Italy
d. 81
Source: *REn*

Tjader, Cal(len Radcliffe, Jr.)
American. Jazz Vibraphonist
Won 1981 Grammy for album *La Onda Va Bien.*
b. Jul 16, 1925 in Saint Louis, Missouri
d. May 5, 1982 in Philippines
Source: *CmpEPM; EncJzS 70; NewYTBS 82; WhoAm 74*

"Tobe"
see: Davis, "Tobe" Coller

Tobias, Andrew
American. Author, Business Executive
Wrote *The Funny Money Game,* 1971.
b. Apr 20, 1947 in New York, New York
Source: *BioIn 9, 10; ConAu 37R*

Tobias, Channing Heggie
American. Religious Leader
b. Feb 1, 1882 in Augusta, Georgia
d. Nov 5, 1961 in New York, New York
Source: *CurBio 45, 62; WhAm 4*

Tobias, George
American. Actor
b. 1905 in New York, New York
d. Feb 27, 1980 in Hollywood, California
Source: *BiE&WWA; FilmgC; IntMPA 75, 76, 77, 78, 79, 80; MotPP; MovMk; NotNAT; Vers A; WhoHol A*

Tobin, Daniel Joseph
American. Labor Leader
President, Teamsters, 1907-52.
b. Apr 1875 in County Clare, Ireland
d. Nov 14, 1955
Source: *DcAmB S5; NatCAB 42; WhAm 3*

Tobin, James
American. Economist
b. Mar 5, 1918 in Champaign, Illinois
Source: *AmEA 74; AmM&WS 73S, 78S; ConAu 53; IntAu&W 77; IntWW 74, 75, 76, 77, 78; PolProf K; WhoAm 74, 76, 78, 80, 82; WrDr 76, 80*

Toch, Ernst
Austrian. Composer, Musician
b. Dec 7, 1887 in Vienna, Austria
d. Oct 1, 1961 in Los Angeles, California
Source: *AmSCAP 66; DcCM; WhAm 4*

Tocqueville, Alexis, Comte de
French. Author
b. Jul 29, 1805 in Vernevil, France
d. Apr 16, 1859 in Cannes, France
Source: *AmBi; ApCAB; AtlBL; BbD; BiD&SB; CasWL; CnDAL; DcEuL; Drake; EuAu; NewC; NewCol 75; OxAmL; OxEng; OxFr; Pen AM; REn; REnAL; WebBD 80; WhAm H*

Todd, Ann
English. Actress
b. 1910 in Hartford, England
Source: *BiE&WWA; FilmgC; InWom; IntMPA 75, 76, 77, 78, 79, 80, 81, 82; MotPP; MovMk; OxFilm; Who 74; WhoHol A; WhoThe 77*

Todd, Mike (Michael)
[Avron Hirsch Goldbogen]
American. Film, Theatrical Producer
Married Elizabeth Taylor, 1957-58; killed in plane crash.
b. Jun 2, 1907 in Minneapolis, Minnesota
d. Mar 22, 1958 in Grants, Minnesota
Source: *CurBio 55, 58; DcFM; EncMT; FilmgC; OxFilm; WhAm 3*

Todd, Richard
Irish. Actor
b. Jun 11, 1919 in Dublin, Ireland
Source: *CmMov; CurBio 55; FilmgC; IntMPA 75, 76, 77, 78, 79, 80, 81, 82; MotPP; MovMk; Who 74; WhoAm 74; WhoHol A; WhoThe 77; WhoWor 74*

Todd, Richard
American. Football Player
Quarterback, NY Jets, 1976--.
b. Nov 19, 1953 in Birmingham, Alabama
Source: *CurBio 82; FootReg*

Todd, Sweeney
"Demon Barber of Fleet Street"
English. Murderer
Source: *NF*

Todd, Thelma
American. Actress
b. Jul 29, 1905 in Lawrence, Massachusetts
d. Dec 18, 1935 in Santa Monica, California
Source: *FilmgC; MotPP; MovMk; ThFT; TwYS; WhScrn 74, 77; WhoHol B*

Todman, William Selden
American. TV Producer
b. Jul 31, 1916 in New York, New York
d. 1979 in New York, New York
Source: *IntMPA 75, 76, 77; WhoAm 74*

Toffenetti, Dario Louis
Italian. Restaurateur
b. Jan 20, 1889 in Valdi Sole, Austria
d. Jan 16, 1962 in New York, New York
Source: *WhAm 4*

Toffler, Alvin
American. Author
Wrote *Future Shock,* 1970; *The Third Wave,* 1980.
b. Oct 4, 1928 in New York, New York
Source: *AmAu&B; ConAu 13R; WhoAm 74, 76, 78, 80, 82; WrDr 76*

Togliatti, Palmiro
[Ercole Ercoli]
Italian. Communist Party Leader
b. Mar 26, 1893 in Genoa, Italy
d. Aug 21, 1964
Source: *CurBio 47, 64; WhAm 4*

Togo, Heihachiro
Japanese. Admiral
b. 1847
d. 1934
Source: *NewCol 75; WebBD 80*

Tojo, Hideki (Eiki)
Japanese. WW II Premier, General
b. 1884 in Tokyo, Japan
d. Dec 23, 1948 in Tokyo, Japan
Source: *CurBio 41, 49; NewCol 75; REn; WebBD 80*

Tokatyan, Armand
Bulgarian. Opera Singer
b. Feb 12, 1899 in Plovdiv, Bulgaria
d. Jun 12, 1960 in Pasadena, California
Source: *BioIn 10; NewEOp 71*

Toklas, Alice B(abette)
American. Secretary to Gertrude Stein
b. Apr 30, 1877 in San Francisco, California
d. Mar 7, 1967 in Paris, France
Source: *AmAu&B; CnDAL; ConAu 25R, 81; LongCTC; OxAmL; REn*

Tokle, Torger
Norwegian. Skier
b. 1920?
d. 1945
Source: *BioIn 3, 5*

"Tokyo Rose"
[Iva Toguri d'Aquino]
American. Traitor
b. Jul 4, 1916 in Los Angeles, California
Source: *InWom; WhWW-II*

Toland, John Willard
American. Journalist, Author, Historian
b. Jun 29, 1912 in La Crosse, Wisconsin
Source: *AmAu&B; Au&Wr 71; ConAu 1R; WhoAm 74, 76, 78, 80, 82; WorAu; WrDr 76*

Tolbert, William Richard, Jr.
Liberian. President
b. May 13, 1913 in Bensonville, Liberia
d. Apr 12, 1980 in Monrovia, Liberia
Source: *CurBio 74, 80; IntWW 74; NewYTBE 72; WhoAm 74; WhoGov 72; WhoWor 74*

Toledano, Ralph de
American. Journalist, Author
b. Aug 17, 1916 in Tangiers, Morocco
Source: *AmAu&B; AuNews 1; ConAu 9R; CurBio 62; WhoAm 74, 76, 78, 80, 82; WrDr 76*

Toledo, Fernando Alvarez de
[Duke of Alva]
Spanish. General
b. 1508
d. 1582
Source: *ApCAB*

Toler, Sidney
American. Actor
b. Apr 28, 1874 in Warrensburg, Missouri
d. Feb 12, 1947 in Beverly Hills, California
Source: *DcNAA; FilmgC; MotPP; MovMk; WhScrn 74, 77; WhoHol B*

Tolkien, J(ohn) R(onald) R(euel)
English. Author
Wrote *The Hobbit*, 1938; *The Lord of the Rings*, 1954-56.
b. Jan 3, 1892 in Bloemfontein, South Africa
d. Sep 2, 1973 in Bournemouth, England
Source: *AnCL; Au&Wr 71; AuBYP; AuNews 1; CasWL; CelR 73; ChPo, S1, S2; CnMWL; ConAu 17R, 45; ConAu P-2; ConLC 1, 2, 3, 8, 12; ConNov 72, 76; CurBio 57, 67; DcLEL; EncWL; LongCTC; ModBrL, SUP; MorJA; NewC; OxEng; Pen ENG; RAdv 1; REn; SmATA 2; TwCW; WebE&AL; WhAm 6; WhoChL; WhoTwCL; WhoWor 74; WorAu*

Toller, Ernst
German. Poet, Dramatist
b. Dec 1, 1893 in Samotschin, Germany
d. May 22, 1939 in New York, New York
Source: *CasWL; ClDMEL; CnMD; CnMWL; CnThe; EncWL; EvEuW; LongCTC; McGEWD; ModGL; ModWD; OxEng; OxGer; OxThe; Pen EUR; REn; REnWD; TwCA, SUP; WhAm HA, 4; WhoTwCL*

Tolson, Clyde Anderson
American. Government Official
b. May 22, 1900 in Laredo, Missouri
d. Apr 14, 1975 in Washington, DC
Source: *WhAm 6; WhoAm 74; WhoGov 72; WhoS&SW 73*

Tolstoy, Aleksei Nikolavich
Russian. Author
b. 1882
d. Feb 23, 1945
Source: *BioIn 2, 4, 7, 10*

Tolstoy, Leo Nikolayevich
Russian. Author
Wrote *War and Peace*, 1865-69; *Anna Karenina*, 1875-77.
b. Aug 28, 1828 in Yasnaya Polyana, Russia
d. Nov 20, 1910 in Astapovo, Russia
Source: *AtlBL; ClDMEL; CnMD; CyWA; DcEuL; EuAu; FilmgC; LongCTC; McGEWD; ModWD; OxEng; OxThe; PlP&P; RComWL; REn; REnWD*

Tom Thumb, General
[Charles Sherwood Stratton]
American. Midget
b. Jan 4, 1838 in Bridgeport, Connecticut
d. Jul 15, 1883 in Middleboro, Massachusetts
Source: *AmBi; ApCAB; DcAmB; Drake; NewCol 75; WhAm H*

Tomasi di Lampedusa, Guiseppe
Italian. Author
b. Dec 23, 1896 in Palermo, Sicily
d. Jul 26, 1957 in Rome, Italy
Source: *CasWL; EvEuW; OxEng*

Tomasson, Helgi
Icelandic. Ballet Dancer
b. Oct 8, 1942 in Reykjavik, Iceland
Source: *CnOxB; CurBio 82; WhoAm 78, 80, 82; WhoE 79*

Tombalbaye, Nagarta Francois
Chadian. President
b. 1918
d. Apr 13, 1975 in Chad
Source: *WhAm 6; WhoWor 74*

Tomita, Kojiro Kenji
Author, Museum Curator
b. Mar 7, 1890
Source: *BioIn 5*

Tomjanovich, Rudy (Rudolph)
American. Basketball Player
Injured in fight with Kermit Washington, 1978; awarded $3 million in damages.
b. Apr 24, 1948 in Hamtramck, Michigan
Source: *BioIn 10; WhoAm 80; WhoBbl 73*

Tomkins, Calvin
American. Author
b. Dec 17, 1925 in Orange, New Jersey
Source: *ConAu 13R; WrDr 76*

Tomlin, "Lily" (Mary Jean)
American. Actress, Comedian
Starred in *Nashville*, 1975; *9 to 5*, 1980.
b. Sep 1, 1939 in Detroit, Michigan
Source: *BkPepl; ConLC 17; CurBio 73; IntMPA 77, 78, 79, 80, 81, 82; NewYTBE 70, 73; WhoAm 74, 76, 78, 80, 82; WhoHol A*

Tomlinson, Charles
English. Poet
b. 1927 in Stoke-on-Trent, England
Source: *BioIn 8, 10*

Tomlinson, Frank
British. Diplomat
b. Mar 21, 1912
Source: *IntWW 74; Who 74*

Tomlinson, Henry Major
English. Author
b. 1873 in London, England
d. Feb 5, 1958 in London, England
Source: *CyWA; DcLEL; EvLB; LongCTC; ModBrL; NewC; OxEng; Pen ENG; REn; REnAL; TwCA, SUP; TwCW*

Tomlinson, Jill
English. Children's Author
b. Dec 27, 1931 in Twickenham, England
d. 1976 in England
Source: *Au&Wr 71; ConAu 29R; ConAu P-2; SmATA 3, 24; WrDr 76*

Tompkins, Angel
American. Actress
b. 1943 in Albany, New York
Source: *ForWC 70; WhoHol A*

Tomseth, Victor Lloyd
[The Hostages]
American. Former Hostage in Iran
b. Apr 14, 1941 in OR
Source: *BioIn 12; NewYTBS 81; USBiR 74*

Ton-duc-thong
Vietnamese. President of North Vietnam
b. 1888
d. 1980 in Hanoi, Vietnam
Source: *BioIn 8, 9*

Tone, Franchot
American. Actor
b. Feb 27, 1905 in Niagara Falls, New York
d. Sep 18, 1968 in New York, New York
Source: *BiDFilm; BiE&WWA; CmMov; CurBio 40, 68; FilmgC; MotPP; MovMk; OxFilm; PlP&P; WhAm 5; WhScrn 74, 77; WhoHol B; WorEFlm*

Tone, Theobald Wolfe
Irish. Revolutionary
b. 1763
d. 1798
Source: *NewCol 75; WebBD 80*

Took, Steven Peregrine
see: T. Rex

Toombs, Robert Augustus
American. Statesman
b. Jul 2, 1810 in Wilkes County, Georgia
d. Dec 15, 1885 in Washington, Georgia
Source: *AmBi; ApCAB; BioIn 5, 7; DcAmB; Drake; NatCAB 4; NewCol 75; WebAB; WebBD 80; WhAm H*

Toomer, Jean
American. Author, Poet
b. Dec 26, 1894 in Washington, DC
d. Mar 30, 1967
Source: *AmAu&B; BlkAW; ConLC 1, 4, 13P; ModAL SUP; OxAmL; Pen AM; REnAL; WebE&AL; WorAu*

Toomey, Bill (William)
American. Track Athlete
Won gold medal in decathlon, 1968 Olympics.
b. Jan 10, 1939 in Philadelphia, Pennsylvania
Source: *WhoTr&F 73*

Toomey, Mary Rand
[Mrs. Bill Toomey]
American. Track Athlete
b. Feb 10, 1940
Source: *WhoTr&F 73*

Toomey, Regis
American. Actor
b. Aug 13, 1902 in Pittsburgh, Pennsylvania
Source: *FilmgC; IntMPA 75, 76, 77, 78, 79, 80, 81, 82; MotPP; MovMk; Vers A; WhoHol A*

Toon, Earl, Jr.
see: Kool and the Gang

Toon, Malcolm
American. Ambassador to USSR
b. Jul 4, 1916 in Troy, New York
Source: *CurBio 78; WhoAm 82*

Toorish, Bernard
see: Four Lads, The

Topol, Chaim
Israeli. Actor
b. Sep 9, 1935 in Tel Aviv, Palestine
Source: *FilmgC; NewYTBE 71; WhoHol A*

Topolski, Feliks
British. Artist
b. Aug 14, 1907 in Warsaw, Poland
Source: *IlsBYP; IlsCB 1946; IntWW 74; Who 74; WhoGrA; WhoWor 74*

Topping, Dan(iel Reid)
American. Baseball Executive
Owner, NY Yankees, 1945-66.
b. May 18, 1912 in Greenwich, Connecticut
d. May 18, 1974 in Miami, Florida
Source: *NewYTBS 74; WhAm 6*

Toren, Marta
Swedish. Actress
b. May 21, 1926 in Stockholm, Sweden
d. Feb 19, 1957 in Stockholm, Sweden
Source: *FilmgC; MotPP; WhScrn 74, 77; WhoHol B*

Torin, Sid
"Symphony Sid"
American. Disc Jockey
Source: *NewYTBE 72*

Tork, Peter
[The Monkees]
American. Singer, Musician
b. Feb 13, 1944 in Washington, DC
Source: *NF*

Torme, Mel(vin Howard)
["The Velvet Fog"]
American. Singer, Composer
Wrote "The Christmas Song."
b. Sep 13, 1925 in Chicago, Illinois
Source: *AmSCAP 66; CelR 73; FilmgC; IntMPA 75, 76, 77, 78, 79, 80, 81, 82; WhoAm 74, 76, 78, 80, 82; WhoHol A*

Torn, Rip
[Elmore Torn, Jr.]
American. Actor
b. Feb 6, 1931 in Temple, Texas
Source: *BiE&WWA; FilmgC; IntMPA 75, 76, 77, 78, 79, 80, 81, 82; MovMk; NotNAT; WhoAm 82; WhoHol A; WhoThe 77*

Torquemada, Tomas de
Spanish. Monk, Inquisitor
b. 1420 in Spain
d. 1498
Source: *NewC*

Torrance, Jack
[Fabulous Five]
American. Track Athlete
b. Jun 20, 1913 in Weathersby, Mississippi
d. Nov 10, 1970
Source: *WhoTr&F 73*

Torre, Joe (Joseph Paul)
American. Baseball Player, Manager
Led NL in batting, 1971; manager, Atlanta Braves, 1981--.
b. Jul 18, 1940 in Brooklyn, New York
Source: *BaseEn; CurBio 72; NewYTBE 71; NewYTBS 74; WhoAm 74, 76, 78, 80, 82; WhoProB 73*

Torre-Nilsson, Leopoldo
Argentine. Motion Picture Director
b. 1924
Source: *DcFM; FilmgC; IntWW 74; OxFilm; WorEFlm*

Torrence, Ernest
American. Actor, Opera Singer
b. Jun 16, 1878 in Edinburgh, Scotland
d. May 15, 1933 in New York, New York
Source: *FilmgC; MotPP; MovMk; TwYS; WhScrn 74, 77; WhoHol B*

Torrence, (Frederick) Ridgley
American. Dramatist, Poet
b. 1875 in Xenia, Ohio
d. Dec 25, 1950 in New York, New York
Source: *BioIn 8; WhAm 3*

Torresola, Griselio
Puerto Rican. Attempted Assassin of Truman
d. Nov 1, 1950
Source: *BioIn 8, 9, 10*

Torrey, Bill (William Arthur)
Canadian. Hockey Executive
GM, NY Islanders, 1972--.
b. Jun 23, 1934 in Montreal, PQ
Source: *NewYTBS 81; WhoAm 74, 76, 78, 80, 82; WhoE 79*

Torricelli, Evangelista
Italian. Scientist, Political Leader
Invented barometer, 1643, called Torricelli Tube.
b. Oct 15, 1608 in Piancaldoli, Italy
d. Oct 25, 1647 in Florence, Italy
Source: *NewC; NewCol 75*

Torrijos Herrera, Omar
Panamanian. General
b. Feb 13, 1929 in Santiago, Panama
d. Jul 31, 1981 in Panama
Source: *BioIn 9, 10, 11; BioNews 74; CurBio 73, 81; IntWW 74, 75, 76, 77, 78; IntYB 78, 79; NewYTBE 73; NewYTBS 77, 81; WhoWor 78*

Tors, Ivan
Hungarian. Motion Picture Producer, Director
b. Jun 12, 1916 in Budapest, Hungary
Source: *CelR 73; CurBio 69; FilmgC; IntMPA 75, 76, 77, 78, 79, 80, 81, 82; WhoAm 74, 78, 80, 82; WhoHol A*

Tortelier, Paul
French. Musician, Composer
b. Mar 21, 1914
Source: *Baker 78; IntWW 74, 75, 76, 77, 78; Who 74; WhoMus 72; WhoWor 74, 76, 78*

Toscanini, Arturo
Italian. Symphony Conductor
b. Mar 25, 1867 in Parma, Italy
d. Jan 16, 1957 in New York, New York
Source: *CurBio 42, 54, 57; REn; WebAB; WhAm 3; WhScrn 77*

Tosti, Francesco Paola
Italian. Composer
b. Apr 7, 1846 in Ortona, Italy
d. Dec 6, 1916 in Rome, Italy
Source: *OxMus; WebBD 80*

Totheroh, Dan
American. Dramatist
b. Jul 22, 1894 in Oakland, California
Source: *AmAu&B; CnDAL; CnMD; ConAmA; ModWD; OxAmL; Pen AM; REnAL; WhoThe 77*

Toto
[Bobby Kimball; Steve Lukather; David Paich; Jeff Porcaro]
American. Rock Group
Formed late 1970's; hits include "Rosanna," 1982, "Africa," 1983.
Source: *WhoRock 81*

Totter, Audrey
American. Actress
b. Dec 20, 1923? in Joliet, Illinois
Source: *FilmgC; IntMPA 75, 76, 77, 78, 79, 80, 81, 82; MotPP; MovMk; WhoHol A*

Tough, Dave
American. Jazz Musician
b. Apr 26, 1908 in Oak Park, Illinois
d. Dec 6, 1948 in Newark, New Jersey
Source: *BiDAmM; CmpEPM; IlEncJ; WhoJazz 72*

Touchy, Roger
American. Gangster
b. 1898 in Chicago, Illinois
d. Dec 17, 1959 in Chicago, Illinois
Source: *BioIn 5; Blood*

Toulouse-Lautrec (Monfa), (Henri Marie Raymond de)
French. Artist
Crippled by childhood fall; best known drawings of cabaret life in Paris.
b. Nov 24, 1864 in Albi, France
d. Sep 9, 1901 in Chateau de Malrome, France
Source: *AtlBL; NewCol 75; OxFr; REn; WebBD 80*

Toumanova, Tamara
Russian. Dancer
b. 1917
Source: *FilmgC; InWom; WhoHol A; WhoThe 77*

Toure, Sekou
Guinean. Dictator
b. Jan 9, 1922
Source: *CurBio 59; NewCol 75; WhoGov 72; WhoWor 74*

Tourel, Jennie
Canadian. Opera Singer
b. Jun 18, 1910 in Montreal, PQ
d. Nov 23, 1973 in New York, New York
Source: *BioNews 74; CurBio 47, 74; InWom; NewYTBE 73; WhAm 6; WhScrn 77; WhoHol B; WhoWor 74; WhoWorJ 72*

Tournachon, Gaspard-Felix
see: Nadar, pseud.

Tourneur, Cyril
English. Author
b. 1575
d. Feb 28, 1626
Source: *Alli; AtlBL; BiD&SB; BrAu; CasWL; Chambr 1; CnE&AP; CnThe; CroE&S; CrtT 1; CyWA; DcEnL; DcLEL; EvLB; McGEWD; MouLC 1; NewC; OxEng; OxThe; Pen ENG; REn; REnWD; WebE&AL*

Toussaint, Pierre
American. Black Leader
b. 1766
d. 1853
Source: *BioIn 9*

Toussaint l'Ouverture, Pierre Dominique
Haitian. General, Liberator
b. 1743 in Cape Francois, Haiti
d. 1803 in Fort-de-Joux, France
Source: *NewCol 75; REn; WebBD 80; WhAm H*

Tovey, Sir Donald Francis
English. Musicologist, Composer, Author
b. Jul 17, 1875 in Eton, England
d. Jul 10, 1940 in Edinburgh, Scotland
Source: *CurBio 40; EvLB; LongCTC; REn; TwCA SUP*

Tower, John Goodwin
American. Senator
b. Sep 29, 1925 in Houston, Texas
Source: *BiDrAC; BioIn 5, 6, 8, 9, 10, 11; CelR 73; CngDr 74; CurBio 68; IntWW 74; WhoAm 76, 78, 80, 82; WhoAmP 75, 77, 79; WhoGov 75, 77; WhoWor 78*

Towers, John Henry
American. Admiral
b. Jan 30, 1885 in Rome, Georgia
d. Apr 1, 1955 in Washington, DC
Source: *DcAmB S5; WebBD 80; WhAm 3*

Towne, Charles Hanson
American. Poet, Editor
b. Feb 2, 1877 in Louisville, Kentucky
d. Feb 28, 1949 in New York, New York
Source: *AmAu&B; AmSCAP 66; ChPo, S1, S2; DcAmB S4; DcNAA; OxCan; REnAL; TwCA, SUP; WhAm 2*

Townsend, Francis Everett
American. Social Reformer, Physician
b. Jan 13, 1867 in Livingston City, Illinois
d. Sep 1, 1960 in Los Angeles, California
Source: *WebAB; WhAm 4*

Townsend, George Alfred
American. Journalist, War Correspondent
b. Jan 30, 1841 in Georgetown, Delaware
d. Apr 15, 1914 in New York, New York
Source: *Alli, SUP; AmAu; AmAu&B; AmBi; ApCAB; BbD; BiD&SB; ChPo S1; DcAmAu; DcAmB; DcNAA; OxAmL; REnAL; TwCBDA; WhAm 1*

Townsend, Lynn Alfred
American. Automobile Executive
President, Chrysler Corp., 1961-66; board chairman, 1967-75.
b. May 12, 1919 in Flint, Michigan
Source: *BusPN; CurBio 66; IntWW 74, 75, 76, 77, 78, 79, 80; IntYB 78, 79, 80, 81; St&PR 75; WhoAm 74, 76, 78, 80; WhoF&I 74; WhoMW 74; WhoWor 74*

Townsend, Peter Wooldridge
English. Author
b. Nov 22, 1914 in Rangoon, Burma
Source: *Au&Wr 71; ConAu 29R; Who 74; WrDr 76*

Townsend, Willard Saxby
American. Labor Leader
President, United Transport Service Employees of America, 1940-57.
b. Dec 4, 1895 in Cincinnati, Ohio
d. Feb 3, 1957 in Chicago, Illinois
Source: *CurBio 48; WhAm 3*

Townshend, Peter
[The Who]
English. Rock Musician
b. May 19, 1945 in London, England
Source: *WhoAm 80*

Toye, Clive Roy
English. Soccer Executive
b. Nov 23, 1932 in Plymouth, England
Source: *WhoE 77, 79*

Toye, Geoffrey
English. Conductor, Opera Director
b. Feb 17, 1889 in Winchester, England
d. Jun 11, 1942 in London, England
Source: *NewEOp 71*

Toynbee, Arnold Joseph
English. Historian
b. Apr 14, 1889 in London, England
d. Oct 22, 1975 in York, England
Source: *Au&Wr 71; AuNews 2; CasWL; ConAu 5R, 61; CurBio 47; CyWA; DcLEL; EvLB; IntWW 74; LongCTC; NewC; OxEng; REn; TwCA, SUP; TwCW; WebE&AL; WhAm 6; Who 74; WhoAm 74; WhoLA; WhoWor 74*

Toynbee, (Theodore) Philip
English. Author, Critic, Journalist
Wrote *Tea with Mrs. Goodman,* 1947 and *The Garden to the Sea,* 1953.
b. Jun 25, 1916 in Oxford, England
d. Jun 15, 1981
Source: *AnObit 1981; ConAu 1R; ConNov 72, 76; ConP 70, 75, 80; LongCTC; ModBrL; Pen ENG; REn; TwCA SUP; TwCW*

Toyoda, Eiji
Japanese. Automobile Executive
President, Toyota Motor Co., 1967--.
b. Sep 12, 1913 in Kinjo, Japan
Source: *FarE&A 78, 79, 80; IntWW 74, 75, 76, 77, 78, 79, 80, 81; WhoAm 74, 76, 78, 80, 82; WhoWor 74, 78*

Tozzi, Giorgio
American. Opera Singer
b. Jan 8, 1923 in Chicago, Illinois
Source: *CelR 73; CurBio 61; WhoAm 74, 76, 78, 80, 82; WhoMus 72; WhoWor 74*

Trabert, Tony (Marion Anthony)
American. Tennis Player
b. Sep 16, 1930 in Cincinnati, Ohio
Source: *BioIn 2, 3, 4, 10; CurBio 54*

Tracy, Arthur
"The Street Singer"
American. Singer
b. Jun 25, 1903 in Kamenetz, Russia
Source: *BioIn 7, 10; What 1*

Tracy, Lee
American. Actor
b. Apr 4, 1898 in Atlanta, Georgia
d. Oct 18, 1968 in Santa Monica, California
Source: *BiE&WWA; FilmgC; HolP 30; MotPP; MovMk; WhAm 5; WhScrn 74, 77; WhoHol B*

Tracy, Spencer
American. Actor
Won Oscars for *Captains Courageous,* 1937; *Boy's Town,* 1938.
b. Apr 5, 1900 in Milwaukee, Wisconsin
d. Jun 10, 1967 in Beverly Hills, California
Source: *BiDFilm; BiE&WWA; CmMov; CurBio 43, 67; FilmgC; MotPP; MovMk; OxFilm; PlP&P; WebAB; WhAm 4; WhScrn 74, 77; WhoHol B; WorEFlm*

"Trader Vic"
see: Bergeron, Victor

Traetta, Tommaso
Italian. Composer
b. Mar 30, 1727 in Bitonto, Italy
d. Apr 6, 1779 in Venice, Italy
Source: *NewEOp 71*

Traffic
[Jim Capaldi; Dave Mason; Stevie Winwood; Chris Wood]
English. Rock Group
Source: *ConMuA 80; EncPR&S; IlEncRk; LilREn 78; WhoRock 81*

Traglia, Luigi, Cardinal
Italian. Ecclesiastic
b. Apr 3, 1896 in Albano Laziale, Italy
d. Nov 22, 1978 in Rome, Italy
Source: *IntWW 74; WhoWor 74*

Traikov, Georgi
Bulgarian. Politician
b. 1898 in Bulgaria
Source: *IntWW 74; NewCol 75; WhoGov 72; WhoWor 74*

Train, Russell Errol
American. Conservationist
b. Jun 4, 1920 in Washington, DC
Source: *CurBio 70; IntWW 74; NewYTBE 70; WhoAm 74, 76, 78, 80, 82; WhoAmP 73; WhoGov 72; WhoS&SW 73*

Trajan
[Marcus Ulpius Trajanus]
Roman. Emperor
b. 53? in Italica, Spain
d. 117 in Selinus, Cilicia
Source: *BioIn 5, 7, 8, 9, 11; McGEWB; NewC; NewCol 75; REn*

Trampler, Walter
American. Musician
b. Aug 25, 1915 in Munich, Germany
Source: *CurBio 71; WhoAm 74; WhoE 74; WhoMus 72; WhoWor 74*

Traphagen, Ethel Leigh
American. Fashion Designer
b. Oct 10, 1882 in New York, New York
d. Apr 29, 1963 in New York, New York
Source: *CurBio 48, 63; InWom*

Trapp, Maria Augusta von
Austrian. Singer, Author
Life story was inspiration for *The Sound of Music,* 1965.
b. Jan 26, 1905 in Vienna, Austria
Source: *AmAu&B; ConAu 81; CurBio 68; InWom; WhoAm 74, 76, 78, 80, 82; WhoE 74; WhoWor 74*

Trare, Moussa
Malian. President
b. Sep 25, 1936 in Kayes, Mali
Source: *IntWW 74; WhoGov 72; WhoWor 78*

Trask, Diana
Australian. Singer, Actress
Source: *BioIn 5*

Traubel, Helen
American. Opera Singer
b. Jun 20, 1899 in Saint Louis, Missouri
d. Jul 28, 1972 in Santa Monica, California
Source: *CurBio 40, 52, 72; FilmgC; InWom; NewYTBE 72; WhAm 5; WhScrn 77; WhoHol B*

Travanti, Daniel J(ohn)
American. Actor
Plays Captain Frank Furillo on "Hill Street Blues," 1980--.
b. Mar 7, 1940 in Kenosha, Wisconsin
Source: *BioIn 12*

Traven, B, pseud.
[Berick Traven Torsvan]
Mexican. Author
b. 1890?
d. Mar 27, 1969 in Mexico City, Mexico
Source: *AmAu&B; CasWL; CnMWL; ConAu 21R, 25R; ConAu P-2; ConLC 8, 11; EncWL; OxAmL; OxGer; Pen AM, EUR; REnAL; TwCA, SUP; WebE&AL; WhAm 5; WhoTwCL*

Travers, Ben
English. Dramatist, Author
b. Nov 12, 1886 in London, England
d. Dec 18, 1980 in London, England
Source: *Au&Wr 71; BiE&WWA; BioIn 4, 10, 11; ConAu 102; ConDr 73, 77; CroCD; EncWT; FilmgC; IntAu&W 76, 77; LongCTC; McGEWD; NotNAT, A; WhE&EA; Who 74; WhoThe 72, 77; WrDr 76, 80*

Travers, Bill
English. Actor, Producer, Director
b. 1922 in Newcastle, England
Source: *FilmgC; IntMPA 75, 76, 77, 78, 79, 80, 81, 82; MovMk; WhoHol A*

Travers, Mary
[Peter, Paul, and Mary]
American. Author, Composer, Singer
b. Nov 7, 1937 in Louisville, Kentucky
Source: *AmSCAP 66; EncFCWM 69; WhoAm 74; WhoWor 74*

Travers, P(amela) L(yndon)
Australian. Author
b. 1906 in Queensland, Australia
Source: *AnCL; AuBYP; BioIn 1, 2, 3, 4, 6, 7, 8, 9, 10, 11; ChILR 2; ConAu 33R; JBA 51; LinLib L; LongCTC; MorBMP; NewC; REn; ScF&FL 1; SmATA 4; TwCA, SUP; TwCCW 78; WhoChL; WhoWor 74; WrDr 80*

Travis, Merle
American. Musician
b. Nov 29, 1917 in Rosewood, Kentucky
Source: *EncFCWM 69*

Travis, Richard
American. Actor
b. Apr 17, 1913 in Carlsbad, New Mexico
Source: *FilmgC; IntMPA 75, 76, 77, 78, 79, 80, 81, 82; Vers B; WhoHol A*

Travolta, John
American. Actor, Singer
Starred in "Welcome Back Kotter," 1975-79; movies *Saturday Night Fever, Grease.*
b. Feb 18, 1954 in Englewood, New Jersey
Source: *BkPepl; CurBio 78; IntMPA 78, 79, 80, 81, 82; RkOn 2; WhoAm 78, 80, 82*

Traynor, "Pie" (Harold Joseph)
American. Baseball Player, Manager
Infielder, Pittsburgh, 1920-37; had 100 or more RBIs 7 times.
b. Nov 11, 1899 in Framingham, Massachusetts
d. Mar 16, 1972 in Pittsburgh, Pennsylvania
Source: *BaseEn; NewYTBE 72; WhoProB 73*

Treacher, Arthur
[Arthur Veary]
American. Actor
b. Jul 2, 1894 in Brighton, England
d. Dec 14, 1975 in Manhasset, New York
Source: *BiE&WWA; CelR 73; FilmgC; IntMPA 75; MotPP; MovMk; Vers B; WhScrn 77*

Treat, Lawrence
[Lawrence Arthur Goldstone]
American. Author
b. Dec 21, 1903 in New York, New York
Source: *ConAu 49; TwCCr&M; WhoAm 82*

Tree, Herbert Beerbohm
English. Actor, Manager
b. Dec 17, 1853 in Kensington, England
d. Jul 2, 1917 in London, England
Source: *FamA&A; Film 1; NewC; OxThe; WhAm 1; WhScrn 77; WhoHol B*

Tree, Marietta Endicott Peabody
American. Public Official
Served on Human Rights Committee, UN, 1961-64.
b. Apr 12, 1917 in Lawrence, Massachusetts
Source: *CurBio 61; WhoAm 76, 78, 80; WhoAmW 64, 66, 68, 70, 72, 74, 79; WhoWor 74*

Treece, Henry
English. Author, Poet, Dramatist
b. 1911 in Staffordshire, England
d. Jun 10, 1966 in Barton-on-Humber, England
Source: *AuBYP; ConAu 1R, 25R; EvLB; LongCEL; ModBrL; NewC; Pen ENG; REn; SmATA 2; TwCA SUP; TwCW; WhoChL*

Trefflich, Henry Herbert Frederick
American. Animal Dealer
b. Jan 9, 1908 in Hamburg, Germany
d. Jul 7, 1978 in Bound Brook, New Jersey
Source: *BioIn 2, 3, 11; ConAu 77; ConAu P-2; CurBio 53, 78; WhoAm 74, 76, 80*

Tregaskis, Richard William
American. Author
b. Nov 28, 1916 in Elizabeth, New Jersey
d. Aug 15, 1973 in Honolulu, Hawaii
Source: *AmAu&B; Au&Wr 71; ConAu 1R, 45, 2NR; CurBio 73; NewYTBE 73; SmATA 3; WhAm 6; WhoAm 74; WhoWor 74*

Treitschke, Heinrich Gotthard von
German. Historian
b. Sep 15, 1834 in Dresden, Germany
d. Apr 28, 1896 in Berlin, Germany
Source: *BiD&SB; BioIn 1, 4, 7, 9; CasWL; DcEuL; EuAu; McGEWB; OxGer; REn*

Trelawny, Edward John
English. Sailor, Adventurer
Wrote *Recollections of the Last Days of Shelley and Byron,* 1858.
b. Nov 13, 1792 in London, England
d. Aug 13, 1881 in Sompting, England
Source: *Alli; BiD&SB; BrAu 19; CasWL; DcAmAu; DcEnA; DcLEL; EvLB; OxEng; Pen ENG; REn*

Tremayne, Les
American. Actor
b. Apr 16, 1913 in London, England
Source: *FilmgC; IntMPA 75, 76, 77, 78, 79, 80, 81, 82; WhoAm 74, 76, 78, 80, 82; WhoHol A*

Trench, Richard Chenevix
Irish. Poet, Scholar
b. Sep 5, 1807 in Dublin, Ireland
d. Mar 28, 1886 in London, England
Source: *Alli, SUP; BbD; BiD&SB; BioIn 5; BrAu 19; Chambr 3; ChPo, S1, S2; DcEuL; DcLEL; EvLB; NewC; OxEng; PoIre; REn*

Trendle, George Washington
American. Radio, TV Producer
b. Jul 4, 1884 in Norwalk, Ohio
d. May 11, 1972 in Grosse Pointe, Michigan
Source: *BioIn 9; EncMys; NewYTBE 72; WhAm 5*

Treptow, Martin A
American. World War I Soldier
Ronald Reagan made reference to him in Inaugural speech, 1981.
b. 1894 in Bloomer, Wisconsin
d. Jul 28, 1918 in Chateau Thierry, France
Source: *BioIn 12*

Trethowan, Ian
English. Broadcasting Executive
b. Oct 20, 1922 in High Wycombe, England
Source: *IntWW 74; Who 74*

Tretyak, Vladislav
Russian. Hockey Player
Goalie, Soviet national hockey team.
b. Apr 25, 1952 in U.S.S.R.
Source: *NF*

Trevelyan, George Macaulay
English. Historian, Author
Known for dramatic histories of England.
b. Feb 16, 1876 in Stratford-on-Avon, England
d. Jul 21, 1962 in Cambridge, England
Source: *CasWL; Chambr 3; ConAu 89; DcLEL; EvLB; LongCTC; ModBrL; NewC; OxEng; Pen ENG; REn; TwCA, SUP; WebE&AL; WhAm 4; WhoLA*

Trevino, Elizabeth Borton de
American. Children's Author
b. Sep 2, 1904 in Bakersfield, California
Source: *AuBYP; ConAu 17R; SmATA 1; ThrBJA; WhoAm 74, 76, 78, 80, 82; WhoS&SW 73*

Trevino, Lee Buck
American. Golfer
SI sportsman of year, 1971.
b. Dec 1, 1939 in Dallas, Texas
Source: *CelR 73; CurBio 71; WebAB; WhoAm 74, 76, 78, 80, 82; WhoS&SW 73, 75, 76, 78, 80; WhoWor 74*

Trevithick, Richard
English. Inventor
Built first passenger steam train, 1801.
b. Apr 13, 1771 in Illogan, England
d. Apr 22, 1833 in Dartford, England
Source: *AsBiEn; BioIn 9; NewCol 75; WebBD 80; WhDW*

Trevor, Claire
American. Actress
b. 1909 in New York, New York
Source: *BiDFilm; CmMov; FilmgC; IntMPA 75, 76, 77, 78, 79, 80, 81, 82; MotPP; MovMk; OxFilm; ThFT; WhoAm 74; WhoHol A; WhoThe 77; WomWMM; WorEFlm*

Trevor, William
[William Trevor Cox]
Irish. Author, Dramatist
b. May 24, 1928 in Mitchelstown, Ireland
Source: *ConAu 9R, 4NR; ConDr 73; ConLC 9, 14; ConNov 72, 76; ModBrL SUP; TwCW; Who 74; WhoWor 74; WrDr 76*

Trevor-Roper, Hugh Redwald
English. Historian
b. Jan 15, 1914 in Glanton, England
Source: *ConAu 101; IntWW 74; LongCTC; REn; TwCA SUP; Who 74; WhoWor 74; WrDr 76*

Trifa, Valerian
Romanian. Archbishop, Alleged War Criminal
b. Jun 28, 1914 in Campeni, Romania
Source: *BioIn 11; WhoAm 82*

Trifonov, Yuri Valentinovich
Russian. Author
b. Aug 28, 1925 in Moscow, U.S.S.R.
d. Mar 21, 1981 in Moscow, U.S.S.R.
Source: *ConAu 103; WhoSocC 78*

Trigere, Pauline
American. Fashion Designer
b. Nov 4, 1912 in Paris, France
Source: *BioNews 74; CelR 73; CurBio 60; InWom; WhoAm 74, 76, 78, 80, 82; WorFshn*

Trillin, Calvin Marshall
American. Author
b. Dec 5, 1935 in Kansas City, Missouri
Source: *AuNews 1; ConAu 85; DrAF 76; WhoAm 82; WorFshn*

Trilling, Diana Rubin
American. Author, Literary Critic
b. Jul 21, 1905 in New York, New York
Source: *Au&Wr 71; ConAu 5R; ForWC 70; REnAL; WhoAm 82; WhoE 74; WhoWorJ 72*

Trilling, Lionel
American. Author, Critic
b. Jul 4, 1905 in New York, New York
d. Nov 5, 1975 in New York, New York
Source: *AmAu&B; AmNov; CasWL; CelR 73; CnDAL; ConAu 9R, 61; ConLC 9, 11; ConNov 72, 76; DcLEL; DrAS 74E; EncWL; IntWW 74; LongCTC; ModAL; OxAmL; Pen AM; RAdv 1; REn; REnAL; TwCA SUP; TwCW; WebAB; WhAm 6; Who 74; WhoAm 74; WhoE 74; WhoTwCL; WhoWor 74; WhoWorJ 72*

Trinidad, Francisco Flores Corky, Jr.
Philippine. Editorial Cartoonist
b. May 26, 1939 in Manila, Philippines
Source: *WhoAm 74*

Trintignant, Jean-Louis Xavier
French. Actor
b. Dec 11, 1930 in Polenc, France
Source: *BiDFilm; BioNews 74; CelR 73; FilmgC; IntMPA 75, 76, 77, 78, 79, 80, 81, 82; IntWW 74; MotPP; MovMk; OxFilm; WhoHol A; WhoWor 74; WorEFlm*

Tripp, Paul
American. Author, Actor, Producer
b. Feb 20, 1916 in New York, New York
Source: *AmSCAP 66; ConAu 21R; SmATA 8; WhoHol A*

Trippe, Juan Terry
American. Airline Executive
Founded Pan Am, 1928; had first transatlantic passenger service, 1939.
b. Jun 27, 1899 in Seabright, New Jersey
d. Apr 3, 1981 in New York, New York
Source: *BioIn 1, 2, 3, 4, 7, 8; CurBio 42, 55, 81; St&PR 75; WhAm 7; Who 74; WhoE 74; WhoF&I 74, 75, 77*

Tripucka, (Patrick) Kelly
American. Basketball Player
With Detroit Pistons, 1981--; scored 56 points in one game, Jan, 1983.
b. Feb 16, 1959 in Glen Ridge, New Jersey
Source: *BioIn 11; NewYTBS 78; OfNBA*

Tristano, Leonard Joseph
"Lennie"
American. Jazz Musician
b. Mar 19, 1919 in Chicago, Illinois
d. 1978 in Jamaica, New York
Source: *WhoE 74*

Triumph
[Rick Emmet; Mike Levine; Gil Moore]
Canadian. Rock Group
Source: *NF*

Troell, Jan
Swedish. Motion Picture Director
b. Jul 23, 1931 in Limhamn, Sweden
Source: *FilmEn; IntMPA 75, 76, 77, 78, 79, 80, 81, 82; MovMk; WorEFlm*

Trohan, Walter
American. Journalist
b. Jul 4, 1903 in Mount Carmel, Pennsylvania
Source: *ConAu 81; WhoAm 74, 76, 78, 80, 82*

Trollope, Anthony
English. Author
b. Apr 24, 1815 in London, England
d. Dec 6, 1882 in London, England
Source: *AtlBL; BbD; BiD&SB; Br&AmS; BrAu 19; CasWL; Chambr 3; ChPo S2; CrtT 3; CyWA; DcBiA; DcEnA; DcEnL; DcEuL; DcLEL; EvLB; HsB&A; MouLC 4; NewC; OxEng; Pen ENG; RAdv 1; REn; REnAL; WebE&AL*

Trollope, Frances
English. Author
b. Mar 10, 1780 in Bristol, England
d. Oct 6, 1863 in Florence, Italy
Source: *DcLEL; NewC; OxAmL*

Trotsky, Leon
[Lev Davidovitch Bronstein]
Russian. Communist Leader, Author
Organized 1917 revolution; banished, 1929, after power struggle with Stalin.
b. Nov 8, 1879 in Elisavetgrad, Russia
d. Aug 21, 1940 in Mexico City, Mexico
Source: *CasWL; CurBio 40; DcRusL; Film 1; LongCTC; REn; WhScrn 77; WhoHol B*

Trotta, Liz (Elizabeth)
American. Broadcast Journalist
b. Mar 28, 1937 in New Haven, Connecticut
Source: *WhoAm 74*

Trotter, John Scott
American. Musician
b. Jun 14, 1908 in Charlotte, North Carolina
d. Oct 29, 1975 in Los Angeles, California
Source: *AmSCAP 66; WhScrn 77*

Trottier, Bryan John
Canadian. Hockey Player
Scored NHL record six points in one period, Dec 23, 1978.
b. Jul 17, 1956 in Val Marie, SK
Source: *BioIn 11; NewYTBS 75, 78; WhoAm 80, 82*

Troup, Bobby (Robert William)
American. Singer, Songwriter, Musician
b. Oct 18, 1918 in Harrisburg, Pennsylvania
Source: *AmSCAP 66; WhoHol A*

Trout, Robert
American. Journalist, Commentator
b. Oct 15, 1908 in Wake County, North Carolina
Source: *CelR 73; CurBio 65; WhoAm 74*

Trowbridge, John Townsend
American. Journalist, Author
b. Sep 18, 1827 in Ogdensburg, New York
d. Feb 12, 1916 in Arlington, Massachusetts
Source: *Alli, SUP; AmAu; AmAu&B; AmBi; ApCAB; BbD; BiD&SB; CarSB; ChPo, S1; CyAl 2; CyWA; DcAmAu; DcAmB; DcBiA; DcEnL; DcLEL; DcNAA; Drake; OxAmL; REnAL; TwCBDA; WhAm 1*

Trower, Robin
[Procol Harum]
English. Musician
b. Mar 9, 1945 in London, England
Source: *EncPR&S; IlEncRk*

Troyanos, Tatiana
American. Opera Singer
b. Sep 12, 1938 in New York, New York
Source: *CurBio 79; NewYTBS 76; WhoAm 78, 80, 82; WhoMus 72; WhoOp 76*

Trudeau, Edward Livingston
American. Physician
b. Oct 5, 1848 in New York, New York
d. Nov 15, 1915
Source: *BioIn 1, 2, 3, 4, 5, 8, 9*

Trudeau, Garry (Garretson Beckman)
American. Cartoonist
Created comic strip "Doonesbury"; won Pulitzer Prize, 1975.
b. 1948 in New York, New York
Source: *AuNews 2; ConAu 81; CurBio 75; WhoAm 78, 80, 82; WorECom; WrDr 76, 80*

Trudeau, Margaret Joan Sinclair
[Mrs. Pierre Trudeau]
Canadian. Author, Socialite
Separated from husband, 1977; wrote *Beyond Reason,* 1979.
b. Sep 10, 1948 in Vancouver, BC
Source: *BioNews 74; BkPepl; ConAu 93*

Trudeau, Pierre Elliott
Canadian. Prime Minister
Liberal leader, 1968-79, 1980--.
b. Oct 18, 1919 in Montreal, PQ
Source: *CanWW 82; CelR 73; ConAu 45, 3NR; CurBio 68; IntWW 75, 76, 77, 78, 79, 80, 81; IntYB 78, 79, 80, 81; Who 82; WhoAm 78, 80, 82; WhoCan 73, 75, 77; WhoE 74, 75, 77, 79*

Truex, Ernest
American. Actor
b. Sep 19, 1889? in Kansas City, Missouri
d. Jun 27, 1973 in Fallbrook, California
Source: *BiE&WWA; CurBio 41, 73; EncMT; Film 1; FilmgC; MotPP; MovMk; TwYS; WhScrn 77; WhoHol B*

Truffaut, Francois
French. Motion Picture Director
b. Feb 6, 1932 in Paris, France
Source: *BiDFilm; ConAu 81; CurBio 69; DcFM; FilmgC; IntMPA 77, 78, 79, 80, 81, 82; MovMk; OxFilm; Who 82; WhoAm 82; WhoHol A; WorEFlm*

Trujillo (Molina), Rafael Leonidas
Dominican. Politician
b. Oct 24, 1891 in San Cristobal, Dominican Republic
d. May 30, 1961 in Ciudad Trujiool, Dominican Republic
Source: *CurBio 41, 61; WhAm 4*

Truly, Richard H
American. Astronaut
On second flight of space shuttle *Columbia,* 1982.
b. Nov 12, 1937 in Fayette, Mississippi
Source: *WhoS&SW 73; WhoWor 74; WorDWW*

Truman, Bess
[Elizabeth Virginia Wallace]
"The Boss"
American. Wife of Harry S Truman
b. Feb 13, 1885 in Independence, Missouri
d. Oct 18, 1982 in Kansas City, Missouri
Source: *CurBio 47, 83; InWom; NewYTBE 70, 72; NewYTBS 82; WhoAm 74, 76, 78, 80; WhoAmW 72, 74*

Truman, Harry S
"Give 'em Hell, Harry"
American. 33rd US President
Made decision to drop atomic bombs on Japan, 1945.
b. May 8, 1884 in Lamar, Missouri
d. Dec 26, 1972 in Kansas City, Missouri
Source: *AmAu&B; Au&Wr 71; BiDrAC; BiDrUSE; ConAu 37R; CurBio 42, 45, 73; EncAB-H; OxAmL; REn; REnAL; WebAB; WhAm 5; WhAmP; WhoGov 72*

Truman, (Mary) Margaret
[Mrs. Clifton Daniel, Jr.]
American. Author, Daughter of Harry Truman
Singer, 1947-54; wrote *Letters from Father,* 1981.
b. Feb 17, 1924 in Independence, Missouri
Source: *BioNews 74; CelR 73; CurBio 50; InWom; WhoAm 74, 76, 78, 80, 82*

Trumbauer, Frank(ie)
American. Composer, Conductor
b. May 30, 1901 in Carbondale, Illinois
d. Jun 11, 1956 in Kansas City, Missouri
Source: *AmSCAP 66; WhAm 4; WhoJazz 72*

Trumbauer, Horace
American. Architect
b. Dec 28, 1869 in Philadelphia, Pennsylvania
d. Sep 18, 1938 in Philadelphia, Pennsylvania
Source: *BioIn 4; BnEnAmA; DcAmB S2; NatCAB 28; WhAm HA, 4*

Trumbo, Dalton
American. Screenwriter, Author
b. Dec 9, 1905 in Montrose, Colorado
d. Sep 10, 1976 in Los Angeles, California
Source: *ConAu 21R, 69; ConDr 73; ConNov 72, 76; CurBio 41; DcFM; FilmgC; IntMPA 75; OxFilm; REnAL; TwCA, SUP; WhoAm 74; WorEFlm; WrDr 76*

Trumbull, Charles Gallaudet
American. Editor, Author
b. Feb 20, 1872 in Hartford, Connecticut
d. Jan 13, 1941 in Pasadena, California
Source: *AmAu&B; AmLY; DcNAA; WhAm 1; WhNAA*

Trumbull, John
American. Poet, Lawyer
b. Apr 24, 1750 in Watertown, Connecticut
d. May 11, 1831 in Detroit, Michigan
Source: *Alli; AmAu; AmAu&B; AmBi; ApCAB; BiAuS; BiD&SB; CasWL; ChPo, S1; CnDAL; CyAL 1; DcAmAu; DcAmB; DcEnL; DcLEL; DcNAA; Drake; EvLB; OxAmL; Pen AM; REn; REnAL; TwCBDA; WebAB; WebE&AL; WhAm H*

Trumbull, John
American. Artist
b. Jun 6, 1756 in Lebanon, Connecticut
d. Nov 10, 1843 in New York, New York
Source: *AmAu&B; AmBi; ApCAB; BiAuS; DcAmB; DcNAA; Drake; EncAB-H; OxAmL; TwCBDA; WebAB*

Trumbull, Jonathan
American. Merchant, Colonial Leader
b. Oct 12, 1710 in Lebanon, Connecticut
d. Aug 17, 1785 in Lebanon, Connecticut
Source: *Alli; AmBi; ApCAB; BiAuS; CyAL 1; DcAmB; Drake; OxAmL; REn; TwCBDA; WebAB; WhAm H*

Trumka, Richard Louis
American. Lawyer, Labor Union Official
President, UMW, 1982--; defeated Sam Church.
b. Jul 24, 1949 in Pennsylvania
Source: *NewYTBS 82*

Truth, Sojourner
[Isabella VanWagener]
American. Abolitionist, Feminist
Freed slave who advocated emanicpation, women's rights.
b. 1797 in Ulster County, New York
d. Nov 26, 1883 in Battle Creek, Michigan
Source: *AmBi; EncAB-H; HerW; InWom; NewCol 75; NotAW; WebAB*

Tryon, Dwight William
American. Artist
b. Aug 13, 1849 in Hartford, Connecticut
d. Jul 1, 1925
Source: *AmBi; ApCAB; DcAmB; TwCBDA; WhAm 1*

Tryon, Thomas
American. Author, Actor
Writes supernatural fiction: *The Other,* 1971; *Harvest Home,* 1973.
b. Jan 14, 1926 in Hartford, Connecticut
Source: *AuNews 1; BioNews 75; BkPepl; CelR 73; ConAu 29R; ConLC 3, 11; CurBio 77; IntMPA 82; WhoAm 76, 78, 80, 82; WrDr 76, 80*

Tsai, Gerald, Jr.
American. Business Executive
b. Mar 10, 1928 in Shanghai, China
Source: *St&PR 75; WhoAm 82; WhoE 74; WhoWor 74*

Ts'ai, Lun
Chinese. Inventor
Made paper from bamboo pulp, circa 105.
b. 50?AD in Kueiyang, China
d. 118?AD
Source: *AsBiEn; WebBD 80*

Tsatsos, Constantinos
Greek. President
b. Jul 1, 1899 in Athens, Greece
Source: *IntWW 74; WhoWor 78*

Tschaikovsky, Peter Ilyich
see: Tchaikovsky, Peter Ilyich

Tschirky, Oscar
"Oscar of the Waldorf"
American. Hotel Manager
b. Sep 28, 1866 in Locle, Switzerland
d. Nov 6, 1950
Source: *CurBio 47, 50; WhAm 3*

Tse-Tung, Mao
see: Mao Tse-Tung

Tsedenbal, Yumzahgin
Mongolian. Politician
b. Sep 17, 1916
Source: *BioIn 9; IntWW 74*

Tshombe, Moise
Congolese. Political Leader of Katanga
b. Nov 10, 1919 in Congo
d. Jun 29, 1969
Source: *CurBio 61, 69; NewCol 75*

Tsiolkovsky, Konstantin Eduardovich
Russian. Scientist
b. Sep 17, 1857
d. Sep 19, 1935
Source: *BioIn 10; NewCol 75*

Tsiranana, Philibert
African. Malagasy Republic Politician
b. Oct 18, 1912
d. Apr 16, 1978 in Tananarive, Madagascar
Source: *BioIn 11; IntWW 74; NewCol 75; WhoGov 72; WhoWor 74*

Tsongas, Paul Efthemios
American. Senator
b. Feb 14, 1941 in Lowell, Massachusetts
Source: *AlmAP 78, 80; BioIn 10, 11; CngDr 77, 79; CurBio 81; WhoAm 78, 80, 82; WhoAmP 75, 77, 79; WhoE 75, 77, 79; WhoGov 75, 77*

Tsu Hsi
see: Tz'u-Hsi

Tsvetayeva, Marina Ivanovna
Russian. Poet
b. Sep 26, 1892? in Moscow, Russia
d. Aug 31, 1941 in Yelabuga, U.S.S.R.
Source: *CasWL; ClDMEL; DcRusL; EvEuW; ModSL 1; Pen EUR; WorAu*

Tu, Fu
Chinese. Poet
b. 712 in Kung-Hsien, China
d. 777 in T'an-Chou, China
Source: *CasWL; DcOrL 1; Pen CL; REn*

Tubb, Ernie (Ernest)
"The Texas Troubadour"
American. Singer, Musician, Composer
b. Feb 9, 1914 in Crisp, Texas
Source: *EncFCWM 69*

Tubes, The
[Rich Anderson; Michael Cotten; Prairie Prince; Bill Spooner; Roger Steen; Fee Waybill; Vince Welnick]
American. Rock Group
Source: *ConMuA 80; IlEncRk; LilREn 78; WhoRock 81*

Tubman, Harriet Ross
"Moses of Her People"
American. Abolitionist, Liberator
Leader of Underground Railroad; helped over 300 slaves escape.
b. 1826 in Dorchester, Maryland
d. Mar 10, 1913 in Auburn, New York
Source: *AmBi; ApCAB; DcAmB; EncAB-H; HerW; InWom; NewCol 75; NotAW; REnAL; WebAB; WhAm HA; WhAmP*

Tubman, William Vacanarat Shadrach
Liberian. President
b. Nov 29, 1895 in Harper, Liberia
d. Jul 23, 1971 in Harper, Liberia
Source: *CurBio 55, 71; NewCol 75; WhAm 5; WhoGov 72*

Tucci, Gabriella
American. Opera Singer
b. Aug 4, 1932
Source: *WhoAm 74; WhoWor 74*

Tucci, Toni
American. Author
b. Oct 1, 1919 in Syracuse, New York
Source: *BioIn 12*

Tuchman, Barbara Wertheim
American. Historian
b. Jan 30, 1912 in New York, New York
Source: *AmAu&B; CelR 73; ConAu 1R, 3NR; CurBio 63; DrAS 74H; InWom; IntWW 74; OxAmL; WhoAm 74, 76, 78, 80, 82; WhoAmW 77; WhoE 74; WhoWor 74; WhoWorJ 72; WorAu; WrDr 76*

Tucker, Forrest Meredith
American. Actor
Starred in TV series "F-Troop," 1965-67.
b. Feb 2, 1919 in Plainfield, Indiana
Source: *BiE&WWA; BioNews 74; FilmgC; IntMPA 75, 76, 77, 78, 79, 80, 81, 82; MotPP; MovMk; WhoAm 74, 76, 78, 80, 82; WhoHol A*

Tucker, Larry
American. Author, Motion Picture Producer
Source: *WhoHol A*

Tucker, Lem(uel)
American. Broadcasting Executive
b. May 26, 1938 in Saginaw, Michigan
Source: *WhoAm 78, 80, 82; WhoE 74*

Tucker, Orrin
American. Band Leader
b. Feb 17, 1911 in Saint Louis, Missouri
Source: *AmSCAP 66*

Tucker, Preston Thomas
American. Auto Executive, Manufacturer
Developed rear engine car, 1940's.
b. Sep 21, 1903 in Capac, Michigan
d. Jan 7, 1956 in Ypsilanti, Michigan
Source: *BusPN; WhAm 3*

Tucker, Richard
[Reuben Tickel]
American. Opera Singer, Actor
Considered best operatic tenor, 1940's-50's.
b. Aug 28, 1913 in Brooklyn, New York
d. Jan 8, 1975 in Kalamazoo, Michigan
Source: *CelR 73; CurBio 56, 75; IntWW 74; NewYTBE 73; WhAm 6; WhScrn 77; WhoAm 74; WhoWor 74*

Tucker, Sophie
[Sophie Abuza]
American. Singer
Vaudeville performer billed as "last of the red-hot Mamas."
b. Jan 13, 1884 in Russia
d. Feb 9, 1966 in New York, New York
Source: *AmAu&B; BiE&WWA; CurBio 45, 66; EncMT; FilmgC; InWom; ThFT; WebAB; WhAm 4; WhScrn 74, 77; WhoHol B*

Tucker, Sterling
American. Urban League Director
b. Dec 21, 1923 in Akron, Ohio
Source: *LivgBAA; St&PR 75; WhoAm 82; WhoAmP 73; WhoGov 72*

Tucker, Tanya
American. Singer
First hit at age 14; millionaire by 16; hit song "Delta Dawn," 1973.
b. Oct 10, 1958 in Seminole, Texas
Source: *BioNews 75; WhoAm 82; WhoHol A; WhoRock 81*

Tucker, Tommy
"Little Tommy Tucker"
American. Band Leader
b. May 18, 1908 in Souris, North Dakota
Source: *AmSCAP 66; WhoAm 74; WhoMus 72*

Tucker, Vance Alan
American. Researcher
b. Apr 4, 1936 in Niagara Falls, New York
Source: *AmM&WS 73P, 76P, 79P*

Tuckwell, Barry Emmanuel
Australian. Musician
b. Mar 5, 1931 in Melbourne, Australia
Source: *BioIn 10; CurBio 79; NewYTBS 78; Who 79; WhoAm 82; WhoMus 72; WhoWor 76*

Tudor, Antony
English. Choreographer
b. Apr 4, 1908 in London, England
Source: *BiE&WWA; CurBio 45; WhoAm 74, 76, 78, 80, 82; WhoWor 74*

Tudor, Henry
see: Henry VII

Tufano, Denny
see: Buckinghams, The

Tuffin, Sally
English. Fashion Designer
b. in England
Source: *WorFshn*

Tufts, Sonny
American. Actor
b. 1911 in Boston, Massachusetts
d. Jun 5, 1970 in Santa Monica, California
Source: *FilmgC; HolP 40; MotPP; MovMk; NewYTBE 70; WhScrn 74, 77; WhoHol B*

Tugwell, Rexford Guy
American. Author, Political Scientist
b. Jul 10, 1891 in Sinclairville, New York
d. Jul 21, 1979 in Santa Barbara, California
Source: *AmAu&B; AmM&WS 73S; ConAu 85, 89; CurBio 41, 63, 79; EncAAH; EncAB-H; IntAu&W 76; IntWW 74, 75, 76, 77, 78; NewYTBE 70; NewYTBS 79; PolProf T; REnAL; WebAB; WhoAm 74, 76, 78; WhoWest 74, 76, 78; WhoWor 74, 78; WrDr 76, 80*

Tukhachevski, Mikhail N
Russian. Soviet Marshal
b. 1893 in Saint Petersburg, Russia
d. Jun 1937
Source: *NewCol 75; WebBD 80; WhoModH*

Tully, Alice
American. Singer, Philanthropist
Source: *BioIn 11; InWom; NewYTBS 77*

Tully, Tom
American. Actor
b. Aug 21, 1902 in Durango, California
Source: *FilmgC; IntMPA 75, 76, 77, 78, 79, 80, 81, 82; MotPP; MovMk; Vers A; WhoHol A*

Tune, Tommy (Thomas James)
American. Director, Choreographer
Won Tonys for *A Day in Hollywood/A Night in the Ukraine*, 1980; *Nine*, 1982.
b. Feb 28, 1939 in Wichita Falls, Texas
Source: *CurBio 83; NewYTBS 80; WhoAm 80, 82; WhoHol A; WhoThe 81; WorAl*

Tunis, Edwin Burdett
American. Children's Author
b. Dec 8, 1897 in New York
d. Aug 7, 1973
Source: *AuBYP; ChlLR 2; ConAu 5R, 45; IlsCB 1744, 1957; MorJA; SmATA 1; WhoAmA 73*

Tunnard, Christopher
Canadian. Architect
b. Jul 7, 1910 in Victoria, BC
d. Feb 14, 1979 in New Haven, Connecticut
Source: *AmAu&B; CurBio 59, 79; ConAu 5R; NewYTBS 79; WhoAm 74, 76, 78; WhoWor 74*

Tunney, "Gene" (James Joseph)
American. Boxer, Businessman
Beat Jack Dempsey, 1922, to become heavyweight champ; retired unbeaten.
b. May 25, 1898 in New York, New York
d. Nov 7, 1978 in Greenwich, Connecticut
Source: *AmAu&B; CelR 73; CurBio 40; IntWW 74; REnAL; WebAB; WhoAm 74; WhoBox 74*

Tunney, John Varick
American. Politician
b. Jun 26, 1934 in New York, New York
Source: *BiDrAC; CelR 73; CngDr 74; ConAu 61; CurBio 71; IntWW 74; NewYTBE 71; WhoAm 74, 76, 78, 80, 82; WhoAmP 73*

Tupac Amaru(, Jose Gabriel)
Inca Chief, National Hero
b. 1742
d. 1781
Source: *ApCAB*

Tura, Cosme
[Cosimo Tura]
Italian. Artist
b. 1430 in Ferrara, Italy
d. 1495 in Ferrara, Italy
Source: *AtlBL; NewCol 75; WebBD 80*

Turbay Ayala, Julio Cesar
Colombian. Former President
President, 1978-82.
b. Jun 18, 1916 in Bogota, Colombia
Source: *CurBio 79*

Turcotte, Ron
Canadian. Jockey
b. Jul 22, 1941 in Drummond, NB
Source: *CurBio 74*

Tureck, Rosalyn
American. Musician
b. Dec 14, 1914 in Chicago, Illinois
Source: *CurBio 59; InWom; IntWW 74; Who 74; WhoAm 74, 76, 78, 80, 82; WhoMus 72; WhoWor 74; WhoWorJ 72; WrDr 76*

Turenne, Henri D'Auvergne, Vicomte
French. Marshall
b. Sep 11, 1611
d. Jul 27, 1675
Source: *NewCol 75; OxFr; REn; WebBD 80*

Turgenev, Ivan Sergeevich
Russian. Author
b. Nov 9, 1818 in Orel, Russia
d. Sep 3, 1883 in Bougival, France
Source: *AtlBL; BbD; BiD&SB; CasWL; ClDMEL; CnThe; CyWA; DcBiA; DcEuL; DcRusL; EuAu; EvEuW; McGEWD; NewC; OxEng; Pen EUR; RComWL; REn; REnWD*

Turischeva, Ludmila
[Mrs. Valeri Borzov]
Russian. Gymnast
Won gold medals, 1968, 1972, 1976 Olympics.
b. Oct 7, 1952 in Grozny, U.S.S.R.
Source: *BioIn 11*

Turkle, Brinton Cassaday
American. Designer, Illustrator
b. Aug 15, 1915 in Alliance, Ohio
Source: *BkP; ChPo S2; ConAu 25R; FamAIYP; IlsBYP; IlsCB 1957; SmATA 2; ThrBJA*

Turkus, Burton B
"Mr. Arsenic"
American. Prosecutor
Cracked organized crime syndicate, Murder, Inc., 1940's.
b. 1902? in Brooklyn, New York
d. Nov 22, 1982 in New York, New York
Source: *NewYTBS 82; WhoAmL 79; WhoLab 76*

Turnbow, Donna
American. Gymnast
b. 1961
Source: *BioIn 10*

Turnbull, Agnes Sligh
American. Author
b. Oct 14, 1888 in New Alexandria, Pennsylvania
d. Jan 31, 1982 in Livingston, New Jersey
Source: *AmAu&B; AmNov; AuBYP; ConAu 1R, 2NR; InWom; NewYTBS 82; REnAL; TwCA, SUP; WhoAm 74, 76, 78, 80*

Turnbull, Collin M(acmillan)
English. Anthropologist
b. Nov 23, 1924 in Harrow, England
Source: *AmM&WS 73S; BioIn 7, 9, 10, 11; ConAu 1R; CurBio 80; WhoAm 82*

Turner, Claramae
American. Opera Singer
b. Oct 28, 1920 in Dinuba, California
Source: *BiE&WWA; WhoHol A*

Turner, Eva
English. Opera Singer
b. Mar 10, 1892 in Oldham, England
Source: *InWom; Who 74; WhoMus 72; WomPO 76*

Turner, Frederick Jackson
American. Historian
b. Nov 14, 1861 in Portage, Wisconsin
d. Mar 14, 1932 in Pasadena, California
Source: *AmAu&B; AmBi; CasWL; DcAmB; DcNAA; EncAB-H; EvLB; OxAmL; Pen AM; REn; REnAL; TwCA, SUP; WebAB; WebE&AL; WhAm 1; WisWr*

Turner, Glenn Wesley
American. Cosmetics Executive
b. 1925 in Columbia, South Carolina
Source: *BusPN; CelR 73; NewYTBE 72*

Turner, Henry McNeal
American. Religious Leader
b. Feb 1, 1834 in Abbeville, South Carolina
d. May 8, 1915
Source: *EncAB-H; McGEWB; WhAm 1; WhoColR*

Turner, Ike
[Ike and Tina Turner]
American. Singer
b. Nov 5, 1931 in Clarksdale, Mississippi
Source: *CelR 73; WhoHol A*

Turner, Joe
American. Jazz Musician
b. Nov 3, 1907 in Baltimore, Maryland
Source: *WhoJazz 72*

Turner, Joe
American. Singer
b. May 18, 1911 in Kansas City, Missouri
Source: *WhoJazz 72*

Turner, Joseph Mallord William
English. Artist
b. Apr 23, 1775 in London, England
d. Dec 19, 1851 in London, England
Source: *Alli; AtlBL; ChPo, S1; NewC; REn*

Turner, "Lana" (Julia Jean Mildred Frances)
"The Sweater Girl"
American. Actress
Allegedly discovered while drinking a soda at Schwab's Drugstore.
b. Feb 8, 1920 in Wallace, Idaho
Source: *BiDFilm; CelR 73; CmMov; CurBio 43; FilmgC; InWom; IntMPA 75, 76, 77, 78, 79, 80, 81, 82; MotPP; MovMk; NewYTBE 71; OxFilm; ThFT; WhoAm 74; WhoHol A; WorEFlm*

Turner, Morrie
American. Cartoonist, Children's Author
b. Dec 11, 1923 in Oakland, California
Source: *ConAu 29R*

Turner, Nat
American. Black Leader
Led only effective slave rebellion in US history, 1831.
b. Oct 2, 1800 in Southampton County, Virginia
d. Nov 11, 1831 in Jerusalem, Virginia
Source: *AmBi; ApCAB; DcAmB; EncAB-H; NewCol 75; WebAB; WebBD 80; WhAm H*

Turner, Roscoe Wilson
American. Aviator
b. Jun 13, 1905 in Marion, Illinois
d. 1970 in Indianapolis, Indiana
Source: *NewYTBE 70; WhoS&SW 73*

Turner, Stansfield
American. CIA Director
b. Dec 1, 1923 in Chicago, Illinois
Source: *WhoAm 74; WhoGov 72*

Turner, Ted (Robert Edward, III)
American. Sportsman, Businessman
Cable TV entrepreneur; owns Atlanta Braves and Hawks sports teams.
b. Nov 19, 1938 in Cincinnati, Ohio
Source: *NewYTBE 72; WhoAm 82*

Turner, Thomas Wyatt
American. Biologist, Civil Rights Leader
b. 1877
d. Apr 21, 1978 in Washington, DC
Source: *BioIn 11*

Turner, "Tina" (Annie Mae)
[Ike and Tina Turner]
American. Singer
Won Grammy, 1972, for "Proud Mary."
b. Nov 26, 1938 in Brownsville, Tennessee
Source: *CelR 73; WhoAm 82; WhoHol A*

Turnesa, Jim
American. Golfer
b. Dec 9, 1914 in Elmsford, New York
d. Aug 27, 1971 in Elmsford, New York
Source: *NewYTBE 71*

Turpin, Ben
American. Comedian
b. Sep 17, 1874 in New Orleans, Louisiana
d. Jul 1, 1940 in Santa Barbara, California
Source: *CurBio 40; DcAmB S2; Film 1; FilmgC; MotPP; MovMk; TwYS; WhAm HA, 4; WhScrn 74, 77; WhoHol B; WorEFlm*

Turpin, Dick (Richard)
English. Highwayman
b. 1706 in Essex, England
d. Apr 10, 1739 in York, England
Source: *FilmgC; NewC; REn*

Tushingham, Rita
English. Actress
b. Mar 14, 1942 in Liverpool, England
Source: *CurBio 65; FilmgC; InWom; IntMPA 75, 76, 77, 78, 79, 80, 81, 82; MotPP; MovMk; OxFilm; Who 74; WhoHol A; WhoThe 77; WhoWor 74; WorEFlm*

Tussaud, (Marie Gresholtz), Madame
Swiss. Wax Modeler
b. 1760 in Bern, Switzerland
d. 1850
Source: *InWom; NewCol 75; WebBD 80*

Tutankhamen
[Tut-Ankh-Amen]
Egyptian. King
b. 1358BC
d. 1340BC
Source: *DcBiPP; NewCol 75; WebBD 80*

Tuthill, Harry J
American. Cartoonist
b. 1886 in Chicago, Illinois
d. Jan 25, 1957 in Saint Louis, Missouri
Source: *WorECom*

Tuttle, Lurene
American. Actress
b. 1907
Source: *ForWC 70; Vers A; WhoHol A*

Tutuola, Amos
Nigerian. Author
b. Jun 1920 in Abeokuta, Nigeria
Source: *AfrA; Au&Wr 71; CasWL; CnMWL; ConAu 9R; ConLC 5, 14; ConNov 72, 76; IntWW 74; LongCTC; Pen CL, ENG; RGAfL; TwCW; WebE&AL; WorAu; WrDr 76*

Tuve, Merle Antony
American. Physicist
Scientific discoveries led to development of radar and nuclear energy.
b. Jun 27, 1901 in Canton, South Dakota
d. May 20, 1982 in Bethesda, Maryland
Source: *AmM&WS 76P, 79P; IntWW 74, 75, 76, 77, 78, 79, 80, 81; NewYTBS 82; WhoAm 74, 76, 78, 80; WhoGov 72; WhoWor 74*

Twachtman, John H
American. Artist
b. 1853 in Cincinnati, Ohio
d. 1902
Source: *AmBi; ApCAB; DcAmB; NewCol 75; WebBD 80*

Twain, Mark, pseud.
[Samuel Langhorne Clemens]
"The People's Author"
American. Author, Journalist
Wrote *Tom Sawyer*, 1876; *Huckleberry Finn*, 1885.
b. Nov 30, 1835 in Florida, Missouri
d. Apr 21, 1910 in Redding, Connecticut
Source: *Alli, SUP; AmAu; AmAu&B; AmBi; AmWr; AtlBL; AuBYP; BiD&SB; BiDPara; BiDSA; CasWL; Chambr 3; CnDAL; CrtT 3; CyWA; DcAmAu; DcAmB; DcEnA, AP; DcEnL; DcLEL; DcNAA; EncAB-H; EncMys; EncWL; EvLB; FamAYP; FilmgC; JBA 34; ModAL, SUP; OxAmL; OxEng; Pen AM; RAdv 1; RComWL; REn; REnAL; WebAB; WebE&AL; WhoChL; WhoTwCL*

Tweed, "Boss" (William Marcy)
American. Politician
b. Apr 3, 1823 in New York, New York
d. Apr 12, 1878 in New York, New York
Source: *AmBi; ApCAB; BiAuS; BiDrAC; DcAmB; EncAB-H; REn; WebAB; WhAm H; WhAmP*

Tweedsmuir, Baron
see: Buchan, Sir John

Twelvetrees, Helen
[Helen Jurgens]
American. Actress
b. Dec 25, 1908 in Brooklyn, New York
d. Feb 14, 1958 in Pennsylvania
Source: *FilmgC; HolP 30; MotPP; MovMk; ThFT; WhScrn 74, 77; WhoHol B*

Twiggy
[Leslie Hornby; Mrs. Michael Whitney]
English. Model
Ultra-thin model, 1966-76; starred in *The Boy Friend,* 1971.
b. Sep 19, 1949 in London, England
Source: *FilmgC; InWom; IntMPA 77, 78, 79, 80, 81, 82; WhoAm 82; WhoHol A*

Twining, Nathan F(arragut)
American. Air Force General
b. Oct 11, 1897 in Monroe, Wisconsin
d. Mar 29, 1982 in Lakeland Air Force Base, Texas
Source: *CurBio 53, 82; IntWW 74, 75, 76, 77, 78; PolProf E; NewYTBS 82; WhWW-II; Who 74; WhoAm 74, 76, 78; WhoWor 74*

Twitty, Conway
[Harold Jenkins]
"The High Priest of Country Music"
American. Singer, Songwriter
b. Sep 1, 1933 in Friars Point, Mississippi
Source: *BioNews 75; EncFCWM 69; WhoAm 82; WhoHol A*

Twombly, Cy
American. Artist
b. Apr 25, 1928 in Lexington, Virginia
Source: *BioIn 8, 11; ConArt; DcAmArt; DcCAA 71, 77; WhoAm 82; WhoAmA 73, 76, 78*

Tworkov, Jack
American. Artist
Leader of NY school of Abstract Expressionism.
b. 1900 in Biala, Poland
d. Sep 4, 1982 in Provincetown, Massachusetts
Source: *BnEnAmA; ConArt; CurBio 64, 82; DcCAA 71, 77; NewYTBS 82; PhDcTCA 77; WhoAm 74, 76, 78, 80, 82; WhoAmA 73, 76, 78, 80; WhoAmJ 80; WhoWor 74; WhoWorJ 72, 78*

Tydings, Millard Evelyn
American. Senator
b. Apr 6, 1890 in Havre de Grace, Maryland
d. Feb 9, 1961 in Havre de Grace, Maryland
Source: *BiDrAC; CurBio 45, 61; WhAm 4; WhAmP*

Tyler, Gus
American. Journalist
Source: *BioIn 10*

Tyler, John
American. 10th US President
First vice-president to become president due to death, 1841-45.
b. Mar 29, 1790 in Charles City, Virginia
d. Jan 18, 1862 in Richmond, Virginia
Source: *Alli; AmAu&B; AmBi; ApCAB; BiAuS; BiDConf; BiDrAC; BiDrUSE; DcAmB; Drake; EncAB-H; OxAmL; REn; REnAL; TwCBDA; WebAB; WhAm H; WhAmP*

Tyler, Parker
American. Poet, Critic
b. Mar 6, 1907 in New Orleans, Louisiana
d. Jul 24, 1974 in New York, New York
Source: *AmAu&B; ChPo; ConAu 5R, 49, 5NR; OxFilm; REnAL; TwCA SUP*

Tyler, Steve
[Aerosmith]
American. Rock Musician, Singer
b. Mar 26, 1948 in Boston, Massachusetts
Source: *BkPepl*

Tyler, Wat
English. Leader of Peasant Rebellion
d. 1381 in Smithfield, England
Source: *NewCol 75*

Tynan, Kenneth Peacock
English. Drama Critic, Author
b. Apr 2, 1927 in Birmingham, England
d. Jul 26, 1980 in Santa Monica, California
Source: *BiE&WWA; ConAu 13R, 101; CroCD; CurBio 63, 80; IntWW 74; LongCTC; ModBrL; NewC; NotNAT; Pen ENG; Who 74; WhoThe 77; WhoWor 74; WorAu; WrDr 76*

Tyndale, William
[William Hutchins; William Tindale]
English. Translator, Martyr
Translated New Testament into English, 1525; basis for King James version.
b. 1484? in Gloucester, England
d. Oct 6, 1536 in Antwerp, Belgium
Source: *Alli; BrAu; CasWL; Chambr 1; CroE&S; DcEnA; DcEnL; DcEuL; DcLEL; EvLB; NewC; NewCol 75; OxEng; Pen ENG; REn; WebBD 80; WebE&AL*

Tyndall, John
English. Physicist, Author
b. Aug 2, 1820
d. Dec 4, 1893
Source: *Alli, SUP; BbD; BiD&SB; BrAu 19; Chambr 3; DcEnA; DcEnL; EvLB; OxEng*

"Typhoid Mary"
[Mary Mallon]
American. Cook, Disease Carrier
Immune to typhoid fever, but carried virus during NY epidemics, 1904, 1914.
b. 1870
d. Nov 11, 1938 in New York, New York
Source: *InWom; WebAB*

Tyrell, Susan
American. Actress
b. 1946 in San Francisco, California
Source: *FilmEn; IntMPA 82; WhoHol A*

Tyrrell, Sir James
English. Courtier
d. 1502
Source: *BioIn 3, 11; NewC*

Tyrrell, Joseph Burr
Canadian. Geologist
b. Nov 1, 1858 in Weston, ON
d. Aug 26, 1957 in Toronto, ON
Source: *OxCan; WhNAA*

Tyson, Cicely
[Mrs. Miles Davis]
American. Actress
Won Emmy, 1973, for "The Autobiography of Miss Jane Pitman."
b. Dec 19, 1939 in New York, New York
Source: *IntMPA 82; MovMk; NewYTBE 72; NotNAT; WhoAm 82; WhoBlA 75; WhoHol A; WhoThe 77*

Tyus, Wyomia
American. Track Athlete
Won gold medals, 1964, 1968 Olympics.
b. Aug 29, 1945 in Griffin, Georgia
Source: *BioIn 10, 11; WhoBlA 77; WhoTr&F 73*

Tyzack, Margaret
British. Actress
b. 1933
Source: *WhoThe 72, 81*

Tzara, Tristan
French. Author, Poet
b. Apr 4, 1896 in Moinesti, Romania
d. Dec 24, 1963 in Paris, France
Source: *CasWL; EncWL; EvEuW; ModWD; OxFr; Pen EUR; REn; TwCW; WhoTwCL; WorAu*

Tz'u, Hsi
Chinese. Empress Dowager of China
b. 1835 in Peking, China
d. Nov 14, 1908
Source: *InWom; NewCol 75; WebBD 80*

U

Ubell, Earl
American. TV News Director
b. Jun 21, 1926 in Brooklyn, New York
Source: *ConAu 37R; SmATA 4; WhoAm 74, 76, 78, 80, 82*

Uccello, Paolo
[Paolo di Dono]
Italian. Artist
b. 1396 in Florence, Italy
d. Dec 10, 1475 in Florence, Italy
Source: *AtlBL; REn*

Udall, Mo(rris King)
American. Congressman
Sought Democratic presidential nomination, 1976.
b. Jun 15, 1922 in Saint Johns, Arizona
Source: *BiDrAC; BioNews 74; CngDr 74; ConAu 45; CurBio 69; WhoAm 74, 76, 78, 80, 82; WhoAmP 73; WhoGov 72; WhoWest 74*

Udall, Stewart Lee
American. Government Official
Secretary of Interior, 1961-69.
b. Jan 31, 1920 in Saint Johns, Arizona
Source: *AmAu&B; BiDrAC; ConAu 69; CurBio 61; IntWW 74; WhoAm 74, 76, 78, 80, 82*

Udet, Ernst
German. Aviator
b. Apr 26, 1896 in Frankfurt, Germany
d. Nov 17, 1941
Source: *BioIn 5, 8, 11; EncTR; ObitOF 79; WhWW-II; WhoMilH 76*

Udry, Janice May
American. Children's Author
b. Jun 14, 1928 in Jacksonville, Illinois
Source: *AuBYP; BkP; ConAu 5R; SmATA 4; ThrBJA*

Uemura, Naomi
Japanese. Adventurer
b. 1941
Source: *BioIn 11*

UFO
[Neil Carter; Paul Chapman; Phil Mogg; Andy Parker; Michael Schenker; Pete Way]
British. Rock Group
Source: *ConMuA 80; IlEncRk; LilREn 78*

Uggams, Leslie
American. Singer, Actress
Starred in TV mini-series "Roots"; "Backstairs at the White House."
b. May 25, 1943 in New York, New York
Source: *CelR 73; CurBio 67; EncMT; FilmgC; InWom; IntMPA 75, 76, 77, 78, 79, 80, 81, 82; NotNAT; WhoAm 74, 76, 78, 80, 82; WhoBlA 75; WhoHol A*

Uhde, Hermann
German. Opera Singer
b. Jul 20, 1914 in Bremen, Germany
d. Oct 10, 1965 in Copenhagen, Denmark
Source: *WhAm 4*

Uhlman, Wes(ley Carl)
American. Mayor, Lawyer
b. Mar 13, 1935 in Cashmere, Washington
Source: *WhoAm 74; WhoAmP 73; WhoGov 72; WhoWest 74*

Uhnak, Dorothy
American. Author
b. 1933 in New York, New York
Source: *AuNews 1; ConAu 81; EncMys; WrDr 76*

Ukrainka, Lesia
Russian. Poet
b. 1871 in Ukraine, Russia
d. 1913
Source: *NewCol 75*

Ulanova, Galina
Russian. Ballerina
b. 1910 in Saint Petersburg, Russia
Source: *CurBio 58; InWom; IntWW 74; Who 74; WhoHol A; WhoWor 74*

Ulbricht, Walter
German. Communist Leader
b. Jun 30, 1893 in Leipzig, Germany
d. Aug 1, 1973 in Berlin, Germany (East)
Source: *CurBio 52, 73; NewYTBE 73; OxGer; WhAm 5; WhoGov 72*

Ullman, Al(bert Conrad)
American. Congressman
b. Mar 9, 1914 in Great Falls, Montana
Source: *BiDrAC; BioNews 75; CngDr 74; NewYTBS 74; WhoAm 74, 76, 78, 80, 82; WhoAmP 73; WhoGov 72; WhoWest 74*

Ullman, James Ramsey
American. Author
Wrote books about mountaineering: *Kingdom of Everest,* 1947.
b. Nov 24, 1907 in New York, New York
d. Jun 20, 1971 in Boston, Massachusetts
Source: *AmAu&B; Au&Wr 71; AuBYP; ConAu 1R, 29R, 3NR; CurBio 45, 71; LongCTC; NewYTBE 71; REn; REnAL; SmATA 7; TwCA SUP; WhAm 5; WhNAA*

Ullman, Norm(man Victor Alexander)
Canadian. Hockey Player
b. Dec 26, 1935 in Provost, AB
Source: *WhoAm 74, 76; WhoHcky 73*

Ullmann, Liv Johanne
Norwegian. Actress
Star of Ingmar Bergman films; goodwill ambassador, UNICEF, 1980--.
b. Dec 16, 1939 in Tokyo, Japan
Source: *BiDFilm; BioNews 74; CelR 73; CurBio 73; IntMPA 75, 76, 77, 78, 79, 80, 81, 82; MovMk; NewYTBE 72; Who 82; WhoAm 82; WhoHol A*

Ulmer, James
"Blood"
American. Musician
b. 1942 in Saint Matthews, South Carolina
Source: *BioIn 12*

Ulreich, Nura Woodson
American. Illustrator
b. Dec 1899 in Kansas City, Missouri
d. 1950
Source: *IlsBYP; IlsCB 1744, 1946; InWom*

Ulric, Lenore
American. Actress
b. 1894 in New Ulm, Minnesota
d. Dec 30, 1970 in Orangeburg, New York
Source: *BiE&WWA; FamA&A; Film 1; FilmgC; InWom; MotPP; MovMk; NewYTBE 70; ThFT; TwYS; WhScrn 74, 77; WhoHol B*

Ultra-Violet
American. Actress
Source: *WhoHol A*

Ulvaeus, Bjorn
[ABBA]
Swedish. Singer, Musician
b. Apr 25, 1945 in Stockholm, Sweden
Source: *NF*

Umar ibn Al-Khattab
Islamic Religious Figure
b. 586
d. 644
Source: *NewCol 75*

Umberto II
see: Humbert II

Umeki, Miyoshi
Japanese. Singer, Actress
b. Apr 3, 1929 in Holdaido, Japan
Source: *FilmgC; InWom; MotPP; MovMk; WhoHol A*

Unamuno (y Jugo), Miguel de
Spanish. Philosopher, Author
b. Sep 29, 1864 in Bilbao, Spain
d. Dec 31, 1936 in Salamanca, Spain
Source: *AtlBL; CasWL; ClDMEL; CnMD; CnMWL; DcSpL; EncWL; EvEuW; LongCTC; McGEWD; ModRL; ModWD; OxEng; OxThe; Pen EUR; REn; TwCA, SUP; TwCW; WhoTwCL*

"Uncle Don"
see: Carney, Don

Underwood, John Thomas
American. Manufacturer
Introduced Underwood typewriter, 1897.
b. Apr 12, 1857 in London, England
d. Jul 2, 1937 in Wianno, Massachusetts
Source: *DcAmB S2; WhAm HA, 4*

Underwood, Oscar Wilder
American. Public Official
b. May 6, 1862 in Louisville, Kentucky
d. Jan 25, 1929 in Fairfax County, Virginia
Source: *AmBi; ApCAB SUP; BiDrAC; BioIn 4, 8; DcAmB; EncAAH; EncAB-H; NatCAB 12, 21; TwCBDA; WebAB; WhAm 1*

Undset, Sigrid
Norwegian. Author
b. May 20, 1882 in Kalundborg, Denmark
d. Jun 10, 1949 in Lillehammer, Norway
Source: *AtlBL; AuBYP; CasWL; CathA 1930; ClDMEL; CurBio 40, 49; CyWA; EncWL; EvEuW; InWom; LongCTC; OxEng; Pen EUR; REn; TwCA, SUP; TwCW; WhAm 2*

Ungaretti, Giuseppe
Italian. Poet
b. Feb 10, 1887 in Alexandria, Egypt
d. Jun 1, 1970
Source: *CasWL; ClDMEL; CnMWL; ConAu 21R, 25R; ConAu P-2; ConLC 7, 11, 15; EncWL; EvEuW; ModRL; NewYTBE 70; Pen EUR; REn; TwCW; WhoTwCL; WorAu*

Ungaro, Emanuel Matteotti
French. Fashion Designer
b. Feb 13, 1933 in Aix-en-Provence, France
Source: *BioIn 9; CurBio 80; WorFshn*

Unger, Caroline
Austrian. Opera Singer
b. Oct 28, 1803 in Vienna, Austria
d. Mar 23, 1877 in Florence, Italy
Source: *InWom*

Unger, Garry Douglas
Canadian. Hockey Player
Played in NHL record 914 consecutive games from 1968-79.
b. Dec 7, 1947 in Edmonton, AB
Source: *BioIn 10, 11; WhoAm 82; WhoHcky 73*

Unger, Irwin
American. Educator, Historian
b. May 2, 1927 in Brooklyn, New York
Source: *ConAu 9R; DrAS 74H; OxAmL; WhoAm 74, 76, 78, 80, 82*

Ungerer, Tomi (Jean Thomas)
French. Children's Author, Illustrator
b. Nov 28, 1931 in Strasbourg, France
Source: *AmAu&B; Au&Wr 71; AuBYP; BkP; ChPo; ConAu 41R; FamAIYP; IlsCB 1957; SmATA 5; ThrBJA; WhoAm 74, 76, 78, 80, 82; WhoGrA*

Unitas, Johnny (John Constantine)
American. Football Player
Named greatest quarterback of all time at 50th anniversary of NFL.
b. May 7, 1933 in Pittsburgh, Pennsylvania
Source: *BioNews 74; CelR 73; CurBio 62; NewYTBE 71; NewYTBS 74; WebAB; WhoAm 74, 76, 78, 80, 82; WhoFtbl 74*

United States Olympic Hockey Team-1980
[Bill (William) Baker; Neal Broten; Dave Christian; Steve Christoff; Jim Craig; Mike Eruzione; John Harrington; Steve Janaszak; Mark Johnson; Rob McClanahan; Ken Morrow; Jack O'Callahan; Mark Pavelich; Mike (Michael Allen) Ramsey; "Buzz" Schneider; Dave Silk; Eric Strobel; Bob Suter; Phil Verchota; MarkWells]
American.
Winners of gold medal at Lake Placid Olympics, 1980.
Source: *NF*

Unkelbach, Kurt
American. Children's Author
b. Nov 21, 1913 in New Britain, Connecticut
Source: *ConAu 25R; SmATA 4; WhoE 74*

Unruh, Howard B
American. Mass Murderer
Killed 13 people in 12 minutes in Camden, NJ, Jun 9, 1949.
b. 1921? in Camden, New Jersey
Source: *BioIn 2; Blood*

Unruh, Jesse Marvin
American. Politician
b. Sep 30, 1922 in Newton, Kansas
Source: *CurBio 69; WhoAm 74; WhoWest 74*

Unseld, Wes(ley)
American. Basketball Player
b. Mar 14, 1946 in Louisville, Kentucky
Source: *WhoBbl 73*

Unser, Al
American. Auto Racer
Won Indianapolis 500, 1970, 1971, 1978.
b. May 29, 1939 in Albuquerque, New Mexico
Source: *CelR 73; WhoAm 74, 76, 78, 80, 82*

Unser, Bobby
American. Auto Racer
Won Indianapolis 500, 1968, 1975.
b. Feb 20, 1924 in Albuquerque, New Mexico
Source: *CelR 73; NewYTBS 74; WhoAm 74, 76, 78, 80, 82*

Unsworth, Geoffrey
English. Cinematographer
b. 1914 in London, England
d. 1978
Source: *FilmEn; FilmgC; WorEFlm*

Untermeyer, Jean Starr
American. Author
b. Mar 13, 1886 in Zanesville, Ohio
d. Jul 27, 1970
Source: *AmAu&B; AnMV 1926; Au&Wr 71; ChPo, S2; CnDAL; ConAmL; ConAu 29R; ForWC 70; InWom; NewYTBE 70; OhA&B; OxAmL; REnAL; TwCA SUP; WhAm 5; WhNAA; WhoWorJ 72*

Untermeyer, Louis
American. Author, Editor
b. Oct 1, 1885 in New York, New York
d. Dec 18, 1977 in Newtown, Connecticut
Source: *AmAu&B; AmLY; AnCL; AnMV 1926; Au&Wr 71; AuBYP; CelR 73; Chambr 3; ChPo, S1, S2; CnDAL; ConAmA; ConAu 5R, 73; ConP 70, 75; CurBio 67; DcLEL; EvLB; IntWW 74; LongCTC; OxAmL; REn; REnAL; SmATA 2; TwCA, SUP; TwCW; WhNAA; Who 74; WhoAm 74; WhoWorJ 72; WrDr 76*

Unwin, Sir Stanley
English. Publisher, Author
b. Dec 19, 1884 in London, England
d. Oct 13, 1968 in London, England
Source: *ConAu 5R; CurBio 49, 68; LongCTC; WhAm 5*

Upchurch, John Jorden
American. Labor Leader
Founded Ancient Order of United Workmen, 1868, forerunner of fraternal societies.
b. Mar 26, 1820 in Franklin County, North Carolina
d. Jan 18, 1887 in Steelville, Missouri
Source: *DcAmB; WhAm H*

Updike, Daniel Berkeley
American. Printer, Publisher
b. 1860 in Providence, Rhode Island
d. Dec 28, 1941
Source: *CurBio 42; DcAmB S3; DcNAA; OxAmL; REnAL; WhAm 2*

Updike, John Hoyer
American. Author
Won Pulitzer Prize, 1981, for *Rabbit is Rich.*
b. Mar 18, 1932 in Shillington, Pennsylvania
Source: *AmAu&B; AmWr; AnCL; Au&Wr 71; AuBYP; CasWL; CelR 73; ChPo; ConAu 1R, 4NR; ConLC 1, 2, 3, 5, 7, 9, 13, 15; ConNov 72, 76; ConP 70, 75; CurBio 66; DrAF 76; EncAB-H; EncWL; IntWW 74; ModAL, SUP; OxAmL; Pen AM; RAdv 1; REn; REnAL; TwCW; WebAB; WebE&AL; Who 74; WhoAm 74, 76, 78, 80, 82; WhoTwCL; WhoWor 74; WorAu; WrDr 76*

Upjohn, Lawrence Northcote
American. Manufacturer
President, Upjohn Pharmaceuticals, 1930-44.
b. 1873
d. Jun 2, 1967 in Kalamazoo, Michigan
Source: *BioIn 9*

Upjohn, Richard
American. Architect
b. Jan 22, 1802 in Shaftesbury, England
d. Aug 17, 1878 in Garrison, New York
Source: *Alli; AmBi; ApCAB; DcAmB; OxAmL; TwCBDA; WebAB; WhAm H*

Uppman, Theodor
American. Opera Singer
b. Jan 12, 1920 in San Jose, California
Source: *WhoAm 74, 76, 78, 80, 82; WhoWor 74*

Upshaw, Gene (Eugene)
American. Football Player
President, NFL Players' Assn.
b. Aug 15, 1945 in Robstown, Texas
Source: *InB&W 80; WhoBlA 77; WhoFtbl 74*

Upshaw, William David
American. Author, Politician
b. Oct 15, 1866 in Newman, Georgia
d. Nov 21, 1952
Source: *BiDrAC; BioIn 3, 4; DcAmB S5; NatCAB 41; WhAm 3*

Upson, Ralph Hazlett
American. Aeronautical Engineer
b. Jun 21, 1888 in New York, New York
d. Aug 13, 1968
Source: *BioIn 10; NatCAB 54; WhAm 5*

Urban II, Pope
French. Launched Christian Crusades
b. 1042
d. 1099
Source: *NewCol 75*

Urban, Joseph Maria
Austrian. Scenic Designer
b. May 26, 1872 in Vienna, Austria
d. Jul 10, 1933 in New York, New York
Source: *AmBi; DcAmB; OxThe; WebAB; WhAm 1*

Ure, Mary
Scottish. Actress
b. Feb 18, 1933 in Glasgow, Scotland
d. Apr 3, 1975 in London, England
Source: *BiE&WWA; FilmgC; IntMPA 75; MotPP; MovMk; NewYTBE 72; PlP&P; WhAm 6; WhScrn 77; Who 74; WhoWor 74*

Ure, Midge
see: Thin Lizzy

U'Ren, William Simon
American. Statesman
b. Jan 10, 1859 in Lancaster, Wisconsin
d. Mar 8, 1949 in Portland, Oregon
Source: *DcAmB S4; WebAB; WhAm 4*

Urey, Harold Clayton
American. Chemist
b. May 29, 1893 in Walkerton, Indiana
Source: *AmM&WS 73P; CelR 73; ConAu 102; CurBio 41, 60; EncAB-H; IndAu 1917; IntWW 74; WebAB; Who 74; WhoAm 74; WhoWor 74*

Uriah Heep
[Mick Box, David Byron, Ken Hensley, Al Napier, Paul Newton]
English. Rock Group
Source: *EncPR&S; IlEncRk*

Urich, Robert
American. Actor
Starred in TV series "Vega$," 1978-80.
b. Dec 19, 1945? in Toronto, ON
Source: *IntMPA 82; WhoAm 80, 82*

Uris, Harold David
American. Philanthropist, Builder
b. May 26, 1905 in New York, New York
d. Mar 28, 1982 in Palm Beach, Florida
Source: *NewYTBS 82; WhoAm 74, 76*

Uris, Leon Marcus
American. Author
Wrote *Exodus,* 1958; *Trinity,* 1976.
b. Aug 3, 1924 in Baltimore, Maryland
Source: *AmAu&B; Au&Wr 71; AuNews 1, 2; CelR 73; ConAu 1R, 1NR; ConLC 7; ConNov 72, 76; CurBio 59; IntWW 74; REn; REnAL; TwCW; WebAB; WhoAm 74, 76, 78, 80, 82; WhoWor 74; WorAu; WrDr 76*

Urlus, Jacques
German. Opera Singer
b. Jan 9, 1867 in Hegenrath, Germany
d. Jun 6, 1935 in Noordwijk, Netherlands
Source: *NewEOp 71*

Urrutia Lleo, Manuel
Cuban. President, Judge
b. Dec 8, 1901 in Yaguajay, Cuba
d. Jul 5, 1981 in New York, New York
Source: *AnObit 1981; BioIn 5; CurBio 59, 81; NewYTBS 81*

Ursuleac, Viorica
Romanian. Opera Singer
b. Mar 26, 1899 in Czernowitz, Romania
Source: *NewEOp 71*

Urtain, Jose Manuel Ibar
Spanish. Boxer
b. May 14, 1943 in Spain
Source: *WhoBox 74*

Uspenskii, Petr D
[Petr D Ouspensky]
Russian. Author
b. 1878 in Moscow, Russia
d. 1947 in Virginia Water, England
Source: *BioIn 1; LongCTC; TwCA SUP*

Ussachevsky, Vladimir
Composer
b. Oct 21, 1911 in Hailar, China
Source: *DcCM; WhoAm 74; WhoWor 74*

Ussher, James
Irish. Prelate, Scholar
b. Jan 4, 1581 in Dublin, Ireland
d. Mar 21, 1656 in Reigate, England
Source: *Alli; BbD; BiD&SB; BrAu; Chambr 1; DcEnA; DcEnL; EvLB; NewC; OxEng; REn*

Ustinov, Peter Alexander
English. Dramatist, Actor
Won Oscar, 1949, for *Spartacus.*
b. Apr 16, 1921 in London, England
Source: *Au&Wr 71; AuNews 1; BiDFilm; BiE&WWA; BioNews 75; BkPepl; CelR 73; CmMov; CnMD; CnThe; ConAu 13R; ConDr 73; ConLC 1; CroCD; CurBio 55; FilmgC; IntMPA 75, 76, 77, 78, 79, 80, 81, 82; IntWW 74; LongCTC; McGEWD; ModBrL; ModWD; MotPP; MovMk; NotNAT; OxFilm; OxThe; PlP&P; TwCW; Who 82; WhoAm 74, 76, 78, 80, 82; WhoHol A; WhoThe 77; WhoUN 75; WhoWor 74; WorAu; WorEFlm; WrDr 76*

Ut, Huynh Cong
Vietnamese. Photojournalist
b. 1951 in Vietnam
Source: *WhoAm 74*

Utamaro, Kitagawa
Japanese. Artist
b. 1753
d. 1806
Source: *NewCol 75; OxArt*

Utley, (Clifton) Garrick
American. Journalist
b. Nov 19, 1939 in Chicago, Illinois
Source: *ConAu 69; WhoAm 82; WhoS&SW 73*

Utley, Freda
American. Journalist, Author
Wrote *Will the Middle East Go West,* 1957.
b. Jan 23, 1898 in London, England
d. Jan 21, 1978 in Washington, DC
Source: *AmAu&B; BioIn 1, 2, 5, 8, 11; ConAu 77, 81; CurBio 58, 78; InWom; NewYTBS 78; WhoAm 74, 76; WhoAmW 58, 64, 66, 68, 70, 72; WhoS&SW 73*

Utrillo, Maurice
French. Artist
Style based on modified form of Cubism.
b. Dec 25, 1883 in Paris, France
d. Nov 5, 1955 in Dax, France
Source: *AtlBL; CurBio 53, 56; OxFr; REn*

Uttley, Alice Jane Taylor
[Alison Uttley, pseud.]
English. Children's Author
b. Dec 17, 1884 in Derbyshire, England
d. May 7, 1976 in High Wycombe, England
Source: *ConAu 53, 65, 7NR; SmATA 3, 26*

Utzon, Joern
Danish. Architect
b. 1918
d. 1973
Source: *BioIn 10*

V

Vaccaro, Brenda
American. Actress
Starred in *Midnight Cowboy; Once Is Not Enough; Airport '77.*
b. Nov 18, 1939 in Brooklyn, New York
Source: *BiE&WWA; CelR 73; FilmgC; IntMPA 75, 76, 78, 79, 80, 81, 82; NotNAT; WhoAm 74, 76, 78, 80, 82; WhoHol A*

Vachon, Rogie (Rogatien Rosarie)
Canadian. Hockey Player
b. Sep 8, 1945 in Palmarolle, PQ
Source: *BioIn 11; WhoHcky 73*

Vadim, Roger
[Roger Vadim Piemiannikov]
French. Motion Picture Director
Former wives include Brigitte Bardot and Jane Fonda.
b. Jan 26, 1928 in Paris, France
Source: *BiDFilm; DcFM; FilmgC; IntWW 74; MovMk; NewYTBE 70; OxFilm; WhoHol A; WhoWor 74; WorEFlm*

Vail, Alfred Lewis
American. Manufacturer, Inventor
b. Sep 25, 1807 in Morristown, New Jersey
d. Jan 18, 1859 in Morristown, New Jersey
Source: *AmBi; ApCAB; DcAmB; NatCAB 4; TwCBDA; WebAB; WhAm H*

Vail, Theodore Newton
American. Businessman
b. Jul 16, 1845 in Carroll County, Ohio
d. Apr 25, 1920
Source: *AmBi; DcAmB; DcNAA; EncAB-H; OhA&B; WebAB; WhAm 1*

Valachi, Joe (Joseph M)
American. Mafia Informant
Hit man, turned informer to Justice Department, 1963.
b. Sep 22, 1904 in New York, New York
d. Apr 3, 1971 in El Paso, Texas
Source: *Blood; NewYTBE 71*

Valadon, Suzanne
French. Artist, Mother of Utrillo
b. 1869
d. 1938
Source: *BioIn 2, 4, 5, 10, 11*

Valdengo, Giuseppe
Italian. Opera Singer
b. May 24, 1920 in Turin, Italy
Source: *WhoWor 74*

Valente, Benita
American. Opera Singer
b. in Delano, California
Source: *NewYTBE 73; NewYTBS 75; WhoAm 78, 80, 82; WhoOp 76*

Valdes-Leal, Juan de
Spanish. Artist
b. 1622
d. 1690
Source: *NewCol 75; WebBD 80*

Valdez, Abelardo Lopez
American. Government Official
b. Aug 31, 1942 in Floresville, Texas
Source: *WhoAmP 77, 79; WhoGov 77*

Valens, Richie
[Richard Valenzuela]
American. Singer
b. May 13, 1941 in Pacoima, California
d. Feb 3, 1959 in Fargo, North Dakota
Source: *EncPR&S*

Valente, Caterina
French. Singer
b. Jan 14, 1931 in Paris, France
Source: *InWom; IntMPA 75, 76, 77, 78, 79, 80, 81, 82; WhoHol A*

Valenti, Jack Joseph
American. Film Executive, Statesman
Assistant to President Johnson, 1963-66; president, Motion Picture Assn., 1966--.
b. Sep 5, 1921 in Houston, Texas
Source: *BusPN; CelR 73; CurBio 68; FilmgC; IntMPA 75, 76, 77, 78, 79, 80, 81, 82; IntWW 74; WhoAm 74, 76, 78, 80, 82; WhoGov 72; WhoS&SW 73, 73; WhoWor 74*

Valentina
[Nicholaevna Sanina Schlee]
American. Fashion Designer
b. May 1, 1904 in Kiev, Russia
Source: *InWom; WorFshn*

Valentine, Jimmy
see: Shinburn, Max

Valentine, Karen
American. Actress
b. May 25, 1947 in Santa Rosa, California
Source: *BioIn 10*

Valentino
[Valentino Garavani]
Italian. Fashion Designer
b. May 11, 1932 in Milan, Italy
Source: *WhoAm 78; WhoFash; WorFshn*

Valentino, Francesco
[Francis Valentine Dinhaupt]
American. Opera Singer
b. Jan 6, 1907 in New York, New York
Source: *NewEOp 71*

Valentino, Rudolph
[Rodolfo d'Antonguella]
American. Actor
Starred in *The Sheik,* 1921; *Blood and Sand,* 1922.
b. May 6, 1895 in Castellaneta, Italy
d. Aug 23, 1926 in New York, New York
Source: *AmBi; BiDFilm; CmMov; DcNAA; Film 1; FilmgC; MotPP; MovMk; OxFilm; TwYS; WebAB; WhAm 1; WhScrn 74, 77; WhoHol B; WorEFlm*

Valenzuela, Fernando
[Fernando Anguamea]
"El Toro"
Mexican. Baseball Player
Pitcher, LA Dodgers, 1979--.
b. Nov 1, 1960 in Fundicion, Mexico
Source: *BaseEn; BioIn 12; CurBio 82; NewYTBS 81*

Valeriani, Richard Gerard
American. Broadcast Journalist
b. Aug 29, 1932 in Camden, New Jersey
Source: *ConAu 65; WhoAm 74, 76, 78, 80, 82; WhoS&SW 73*

Valerio, James Robert
American. Artist
b. Dec 2, 1938 in Chicago, Illinois
Source: *WhoAmA 78*

Valery, Paul Ambroise
French. Poet, Critic
b. Oct 30, 1871 in Sete, France
d. Jul 20, 1945 in Paris, France
Source: *AtlBL; CasWL; ChPo S2; ClDMEL; CnMD; CnMWL; CurBio 45; EncWL; EvEuW; LongCTC; ModRL; NewC; OxEng; OxFr; Pen EUR; REn; TwCA, SUP; TwCW; WhAm 4; WhoLA; WhoTwCL*

Vallee, "Rudy" (Herbert Prior)
American. Actor, Singer
Led band, the Connecticut Yankees; trademark is megaphone.
b. Jul 28, 1901 in Island Pond, Vermont
Source: *AmSCAP 66; BiE&WWA; ConAu 1R, 2NR; CurBio 47, 63; EncMT; FilmgC; IntMPA 75, 76, 77, 78, 79, 80, 81, 82; MotPP; MovMk; WebAB; WhoHol A*

Valleria, Alwina
[Alwina Schoening]
American. Opera Singer
b. Oct 12, 1848 in Baltimore, Maryland
d. Feb 17, 1925 in Nice, France
Source: *InWom*

Valletti, Cesare
Italian. Opera Singer
b. Dec 18, 1922 in Rome, Italy
Source: *WhoMus 72*

Valli, Alida
Italian. Actress
b. May 31, 1921 in Pola, Italy
Source: *FilmgC; IntMPA 77, 78, 79, 80, 81, 82; MovMk; OxFilm; WhoHol A; WorEFlm*

Valli, Frankie
[Francis Castelluccio; The Four Seasons]
American. Singer
Hits include "Sherry," "Big Girls Don't Cry," "My Eyes Adored You."
b. May 3, 1937 in Newark, New Jersey
Source: *BkPepl; IlEncRk; WhoAm 82*

Vallone, Raf
Italian. Actor
b. 1918 in Tropea, Italy
Source: *FilmgC; IntMPA 75, 76, 77, 78, 79, 80, 81, 82; MovMk; WhoHol A; WorEFlm*

Valory, Ross
see: Journey

Valtman, Edmund Siegfried
American. Cartoonist
b. May 31, 1914 in Tallinn, Russia
Source: *WhoAm 74; WhoAmA 73*

Van, Bobby
[Robert Van Stein]
American. Actor, Singer, Dancer
b. Dec 6, 1935 in New York, New York
d. Jul 31, 1980 in Los Angeles, California
Source: *EncMT; FilmgC; NotNAT; WhoHol A; WhoThe 77*

Van Allen, James Alfred
American. Physicist
b. Sep 7, 1914 in Mount Pleasant, Iowa
Source: *AmM&WS 73P; CelR 73; CurBio 59; IntWW 74; WebAB; Who 74; WhoAm 74, 76, 78, 80, 82; WhoWor 74*

VanAlstyne, Egbert Anson
American. Composer, Musician
b. Mar 5, 1882 in Chicago, Illinois
d. Jul 9, 1951 in Chicago, Illinois
Source: *AmPS; AmSCAP 66; BiDAmM; BioIn 2, 3, 4, 6, 10; CmpEPM; NotNAT; REnAL*

Van Andel, Jay
American. Business Executive
Co-founder, chairman of Amway Corp.
b. Jun 3, 1924 in Grand Rapids, Michigan
Source: *WhoAm 74, 76, 78, 80, 82; WhoF&I 74, 75; WhoMW 76, 78*

Van Arsdale, Dick (Richard Albert)
American. Basketball Player
b. Feb 22, 1943 in Indianapolis, Indiana
Source: *WhoAm 74; WhoBbl 73*

Van Arsdale, Tom (Thomas)
American. Basketball Player
b. Feb 22, 1943 in Indianapolis, Indiana
Source: *WhoBbl 73*

Van Beinum, Eduard
see: Beinum, Eduard Van

Van Brocklin, Norm(an Mack)
American. Football Player, Coach
Quarterback, 1949-60; head coach, Minnesota, 1961-66, Atlanta, 1968-73.
b. Mar 15, 1926 in Parade, South Dakota
Source: *WhoAm 74; WhoFtbl 74; WhoS&SW 73*

Van Buren, Abigail
[Pauline Esther Friedman; Mrs. Morton Phillips]
"Dear Abby"; "Popo"
American. Advice Columnist
Wrote *Dear Abby on Marriage,* 1962; twin sister of Ann Landers.
b. Jul 4, 1918 in Sioux City, Iowa
Source: *AmAu&B; CelR 73; ConAu 1R; CurBio 60; ForWC 70; InWom; WhoAm 74, 76, 78, 80, 82; WhoAmW 77*

Van Buren, Martin
American. 8th US President
President, 1836-40; lost 1840 election to William Henry Harrison.
b. Dec 5, 1782 in Kinderhook, New York
d. Jul 24, 1862 in Kinderhook, New York
Source: *Alli; AmAu&B; AmBi; ApCAB; BbD; BiAuS; BiD&SB; BiDrAC; BiDrUSE; DcAmAu; DcAmB; DcNAA; Drake; EncAB-H; OxAmL; REn; REnAL; TwCBDA; WebAB; WhAm H; WhAmP*

Van Camp, Gilbert C
American. Business Executive
President, Van Camp Packing Co, 1882-98.
b. Dec 25, 1817 in Brookline, Indiana
d. Apr 4, 1900 in Indianapolis, Indiana
Source: *NatCAB 28*

Vance, Clarence Arthur
"Dazzy"
American. Baseball Player
b. Mar 4, 1891 in Orient, Iowa
d. Feb 16, 1961 in Homosassa Springs, Florida
Source: *BaseEn; WhoProB 73*

Vance, Cyrus Roberts
American. Lawyer, Government Official
Secretary of State, 1977-80.
b. Mar 27, 1917 in Clarksburg, West Virginia
Source: *CurBio 62; IntWW 74; WhoAm 74, 76, 78, 80, 82; WhoAmP 73; WhoE 74; WhoGov 72*

Vance, Kenny
see: Jay and the Americans

Vance, Louis Joseph
American. Author
b. Sep 19, 1879 in Washington, DC
d. Dec 16, 1933
Source: *AmAu&B; AmBi; DcAmB S1; DcNAA; EncMys; LongCTC; TwCA; WhAm 1; WhNAA*

Vance, Vivian
American. Actress
Appeared in "I Love Lucy," 1951-59; "The Lucy Show," 1962-65.
b. 1912 in Cherryvale, Kansas
d. Aug 17, 1979 in Belvedere, California
Source: *BioIn 4, 7, 8, 10, 11; FilmgC; InWom; IntMPA 75, 77; MotPP; WhoAm 74*

Van Cleef, Lee
American. Actor
b. Jan 9, 1925 in Somerville, New Jersey
Source: *CmMov; FilmgC; IntMPA 75, 76, 77, 78, 79, 80, 81, 82; MotPP; MovMk; OxFilm; WhoAm 82; WhoHol A*

Van Cortlandt, Oloff Stevenszen
Dutch. Settler, Businessman
b. 1600 in Wijk, Netherlands
d. Apr 5, 1684 in New York, New York
Source: *ApCAB; DcAmB; WhAm H*

Van Cortlandt, Stephanus
American. First Mayor of New York City
b. 1643 in New York
d. Nov 25, 1700 in New York, New York
Source: *AmBi; ApCAB; DcAmB; TwCBDA; WebAB; WhAm H*

Vancouver, George
British. Explorer
Wrote *A Voyage of Discovery to the North Pacific Ocean and Round the World,* 1798.
b. 1757
d. Jun 10, 1798 in Petersham, England
Source: *Alli; ApCAB; BbD; BbtC; BiD&SB; BrAu; Drake; NewC; OxAmL; OxCan; OxEng; REn; WhAm H*

Vandegrift, Alexander Archer
American. General
b. Mar 13, 1887 in Charlottesville, Virginia
d. May 8, 1973 in Bethesda, Maryland
Source: *CurBio 43, 73; WebAB; WhAm 6*

Van Dellen, Theodore Robert
American. Physician, Educator
b. Aug 15, 1911 in Chicago, Illinois
Source: *AmM&WS 73P; WhoAm 74; WhoMW 74*

Vandenberg, Arthur Hendrick
American. Senator
b. Mar 22, 1884 in Grand Rapids, Michigan
d. Apr 18, 1951 in Grand Rapids, Michigan
Source: *AmAu&B; BiDrAC; CurBio 51; DcAmB S5; EncAB-H; WebAB; WhAm 3; WhAmP*

Vandenberg, Arthur Hendrick, Jr.
American. Senator, Presidential Aide
b. Jun 30, 1907 in Grand Rapids, Michigan
d. Jan 18, 1968 in Grand Rapids, Michigan
Source: *WhAm 4A*

Vandenberg, Hoyt Sanford
American. General
b. Jan 24, 1899 in Milwaukee, Wisconsin
d. Apr 2, 1954 in Washington, DC
Source: *CurBio 45, 54; DcAmB S5; WhAm 3*

Van Depoele, Charles Joseph
American. Inventor, Scientist
Held over 250 patents, including the electric railway, 1883.
b. Apr 27, 1846 in Lichtervelde, Belgium
d. Mar 18, 1892 in Lynn, Massachusetts
Source: *DcAmB; NatCAB 13; TwCBDA; WebAB; WhAm H*

Vanderbilt, Alfred G
English. Sportsman
b. Sep 22, 1912 in London, England
Source: *BioIn 1; CelR 73*

Vanderbilt, Amy
American. Etiquette Authority, Author
Wrote etiquette books: *Amy Vanderbilt's Complete Book of Etiquette,* 1952.
b. Jul 22, 1908 in Staten Island, New York
d. Dec 27, 1974 in New York, New York
Source: *AmAu&B; Au&Wr 71; CelR 73; ConAu 1R, 53, 3NR; CurBio 54, 75; NewYTBS 74; WhAm 6; WhoAm 74; WhoE 74*

Vanderbilt, Cornelius
American. Financier
b. May 27, 1794 in Staten Island, New York
d. Jan 4, 1877 in New York, New York
Source: *AmBi; ApCAB; DcAmB; Drake; EncAB-H; REn; REnAL; TwCBDA; WebAB; WhAm H*

Vanderbilt, Cornelius
American. Financier, Philanthropist
b. Nov 27, 1843 in Staten Island, New York
d. Sep 12, 1899 in New York, New York
Source: *ApCAB; DcAmB; TwCBDA; WebAB; WhAm 1*

Vanderbilt, Cornelius, Jr.
American. Journalist, Cinematographer
b. Apr 30, 1898 in New York, New York
d. Jul 7, 1974 in Miami Beach, Florida
Source: *AmAu&B; Au&Wr 71; AuNews 1; ConAu 49; ConAu P-1; WhAm 6; WhNAA*

Vanderbilt, Gloria Morgan
[Gloria Cooper]
American. Artist, Actress, Designer
TV movie *Little Gloria, Happy At Last,* 1982, based on her life.
b. Feb 20, 1924 in New York, New York
Source: *BiE&WWA; BioNews 74; CelR 73; ConAu 89; CurBio 72; ForWC 70; NotNAT; WhoAm 82; WhoAmW 77*

Vanderbilt, Harold Stirling
American. Yachtsman, Businessman
b. Jul 6, 1884 in Oakdale, New York
d. Jul 4, 1970 in Newport, Rhode Island
Source: *NewYTBE 70; WebAB; WhAm 5*

Vanderbilt, William Henry
American. Financier, Railroad Magnate
Succeeded father Cornelius as president, NY Central Railroad, 1877.
b. May 8, 1821 in New Brunswick, New Jersey
d. Dec 8, 1885 in New York, New York
Source: *AmBi; ApCAB; DcAmB; EncAB-H; TwCBDA; WebAB; WhAm H*

Vanderbilt, William Henry
American. Governor, Philanthropist
b. Nov 24, 1902 in New York, New York
d. Apr 14, 1981 in South Williamston, Massachusetts
Source: *NewYTBS 81; St&PR 75; WhoAm 74*

Vanderbilt, William Kissam
American. Sportsman, Businessman
b. Dec 12, 1849 in New York, New York
d. Jul 22, 1920 in Paris, France
Source: *ApCAB SUP; DcAmB; CurBio 44; WebAB; WhAm 1*

Vandercook, John Womack
American. Author, Broadcast Journalist
b. Apr 22, 1902 in London, England
d. Jan 6, 1963 in Delhi, New York
Source: *NotNAT B*

Vanderlyn, John
American. Artist
b. Oct 15, 1775 in Kingston, New York
d. Sep 23, 1852 in Kingston, New York
Source: *AmBi; ApCAB; BiAuS; DcAmB; Drake; OxAmL; TwCBDA; WebAB; WhAm H*

Vandermeer, Jan
see: Meer, Jan van der

Vander Meer, Johnny (John Samuel)
"Double No-Hit"; "The Dutch Master"
American. Baseball Player
b. Nov 2, 1914 in Prospect Park, New Jersey
Source: *BaseEn; WhoProB 73*

Van Der Post, Laurens
South African. Author
b. Dec 13, 1906 in Philioppis, South Africa
Source: *Au&Wr 71; CasWL; ConAu 5R; ConLC 5; ConNov 72, 76; DcLEL; IntWW 74; LongCTC; Pen ENG; REn; TwCW; Who 74; WhoAm 74; WhoWor 74; WorAu; WrDr 76*

Van der Weyden, Rogier
see: Weyden, Rogier van der

Van Devanter, Willis
American. Supreme Court Justice
b. Apr 17, 1859 in Marion, Indiana
d. Feb 8, 1941
Source: *CurBio 41; DcAmB S3; WebAB; WhAm 1*

Van De Velde, Emile
Belgian. Statesman
b. 1866
d. 1968
Source: *NewCol 75; WebBD 80*

Van Devere, Trish
[Patricia Dressel; Mrs. George C Scott]
American. Actress
Starred in *Where's Poppa?, Day of the Dolphin.*
b. Mar 9, 1945 in Englewood Cliffs, New Jersey
Source: *BioIn 9, 11; FilmEn*

Van Dine, S S, pseud.
[Willard Huntington Wright]
American. Author
b. Oct 15, 1888 in Charlottesville, Virginia
d. Apr 11, 1939 in New York, New York
Source: *AmAu&B; CnDAL; DcAmB S2; DcNAA; EncMys; EvLB; FilmgC; LongCTC; OxAmL; Pen AM; REnAL; TwCA, SUP; TwCW; WhAm 1; WhNAA*

Van Dongen, Kees
see: Dongen, Kees van

Van Doren, Carl Clinton
American. Critic, Biographer
b. Sep 10, 1885 in Hope, Illinois
d. Jul 18, 1950 in Torrington, Connecticut
Source: *AmAu&B; ChPo; CnDAL; ConAmA; ConAmL; DcAmB S4; DcLEL; EvLB; LongCTC; OxAmL; REn; REnAL; TwCA, SUP; TwCW; WebAB; WhAm 3*

Van Doren, Charles Lincoln
American. Educator, Editor
Vice-president, *Encyclopedia Britannica,* 1973-- 1973--.
b. Feb 12, 1926 in New York, New York
Source: *ConAu 5R, 4NR; DrAS 74E; WhoAm 82*

Van Doren, Dorothy Graffe
American. Author
b. May 2, 1896 in San Francisco, California
Source: *AmAu&B; AmNov; ConAu 1R; ForWC 70; InWom; REnAL; WhoAm 74*

Van Doren, Mamie
[Joan Lucille Olander]
American. Actress
b. Feb 6, 1933 in Rowena, South Dakota
Source: *FilmgC; InWom; IntMPA 75, 76, 77, 78, 79, 80, 81, 82; MotPP; MovMk; WhoHol A*

Van Doren, Mark
American. Poet, Critic, Author
b. Jun 13, 1894 in Hope, Illinois
d. Dec 10, 1972 in Torrington, Connecticut
Source: *AmAu&B; Au&Wr 71; BiE&WWA; CasWL; ChPo, S1, S2; CnDAL; CnE&AP; ConAmA; ConAu 1R, 37R, 3NR; ConLC 6, 10; ConNov 72; ConP 70; CurBio 40, 73; DcLEL; EvLB; LongCTC; ModAL, SUP; NewYTBE 72; OxAmL; Pen AM; RAdv 1; REn; REnAL; SixAP; TwCA, SUP; TwCW; WebAB; WhAm 5; WhNAA*

Van Druten, John William
English. Dramatist
b. Jun 1, 1901 in London, England
d. Dec 19, 1957 in Indio, California
Source: *Chambr 3; CnMD; CnThe; CurBio 44, 58; DcLEL; FilmgC; LongCTC; McGEWD; MnBBF; ModAL; ModBrL; ModWD; NewC; OxAmL; OxThe; Pen AM; PlP&P; REn; REnAL; TwCA, SUP; TwCW; WhAm 3*

Van Dusen, Henry Pitney
American. Clergyman, Educator
Helped found World Council of Churches, 1948.
b. Dec 11, 1897 in Philadelphia, Pennsylvania
d. Feb 13, 1975 in Belle Meade, New Jersey
Source: *AmAu&B; ConAu 1R, 57, 3NR; CurBio 50, 75; DrAS 74P; WhAm 6; WhNAA; WhoAm 74*

Van Dyck, Sir Anthony
Flemish. Artist
Court painter to Charles I of England; works include "Lamentation", "Iconography."
b. Mar 22, 1599 in Antwerp, Belgium
d. Dec 9, 1641
Source: *AtlBL; NewC; NewCol 75; REn; WebBD 80*

Van Dyke, Dick
American. Actor, Comedian
Starred in "The Dick Van Dyke Show," 1961-66; "The New Dick Van Dyke Show," 1971-74.
b. Dec 13, 1925 in West Plains, Missouri
Source: *CelR 73; CurBio 63; FilmgC; IntMPA 75, 76, 77, 78, 79, 80, 81, 82; MotPP; MovMk; WhoAm 74, 76, 78, 80, 82; WhoWest 74; WhoWor 74; WorEFlm*

Vandyke, Henry Jackson, Jr.
American. Clergyman, Poet, Educator
b. Nov 10, 1852 in Germantown, Pennsylvania
d. Apr 10, 1933 in Princeton, New Jersey
Source: *Alli SUP; AmAu&B; AmBi; ApCAB; BbD; BiD&SB; Chambr 3; ChPo, S1, S2; ConAmL; DcAmAu; DcAmB; DcNAA; EvLB; JBA 34; LongCTC; REnAL; Str&VC; TwCA, SUP; TwCBDA; WhAm 1; WhNAA*

Van Dyke, Jerry
American. Actor
b. 1932 in Danville, Illinois
Source: *MotPP; WhoHol A*

Van Dyke, W(oodbridge) S(trong)
American. Actor, Motion Picture Director
b. Mar 21, 1887 in San Diego, California
d. Feb 5, 1943 in Brentwood, California
Source: *BiDFilm; CmMov; DcFM; Film 1; FilmgC; MovMk; OxFilm; TwYS; WhScrn 77; WorEFlm*

Van Eyck, Hubert
Flemish. Artist
b. 1370
d. 1426
Source: *AtlBL; NewC; REn*

Van Eyck, Jan
Flemish. Artist
b. 1371 in Maeseyck, Netherlands
d. 1440
Source: *NewC; REn*

Van Fleet, James Alward
American. General
b. Mar 19, 1892 in Coytesville, New Jersey
Source: *WhoAm 74, 76, 78, 80, 82; WhoWor 74, 76*

Van Fleet, Jo
[Mrs. William Bales]
American. Actress
b. 1922 in Oakland, California
Source: *BiE&WWA; FilmgC; InWom; IntMPA 75, 76, 77, 78, 79, 80, 81, 82; MotPP; MovMk; NotNAT; Vers A; WhoAm 74, 76, 78, 80, 82; WhoHol A; WhoThe 77*

Vangelis
[Evangelos Papathanassiou]
Greek. Composer
Won Oscar for score of *Chariots of Fire,* 1982.
b. 1943 in Volos, Greece
Source: *IlEncRk*

Van Gogh, Vincent Willem
Dutch. Artist
Works include "Sunflowers," "Starry Night"; sold one painting during life.
b. Mar 30, 1853 in Groot Zundert, Netherlands
d. Jul 29, 1890 in Auvers, France
Source: *AtlBL; NewCol 75; OxFr; REn; WebBD 80*

Van Halen, Eddie (Edward)
[Van Halen]
American. Rock Musician
b. 1957? in Netherlands
Source: *BioIn 12*

Van Halen
[Michael Anthony; David Lee Roth; Alex Van Halen; Eddie Van Halen]
American. Rock Group
Source: *ConMuA 80; WhoRock 81*

Van Hamel, Martine
Canadian. Ballerina
Principal dancer, American Ballet Theatre, 1973--.
b. Nov 16, 1945 in Brussels, Belgium
Source: *BioIn 10; CreCan 2; CurBio 79; WhoAm 78, 80, 82*

Van Heusen, Jimmy (James)
American. Songwriter
b. Jan 26, 1913 in Syracuse, New York
Source: *AmSCAP 66; BiE&WWA; CelR 73; CurBio 70; FilmgC; IntMPA 75, 76, 77, 78, 79, 80, 81, 82; NotNAT; WhoAm 74; WhoThe 77*

Van Horne, Harriet
American. TV Critic, Journalist
b. May 17, 1920 in Syracuse, New York
Source: *CelR 73; CurBio 54; InWom*

Van Horne, Sir William Cornelius
American. Railroad Official
b. Feb 3, 1843 in Will County, Illinois
d. Sep 11, 1915
Source: *ApCAB; DcAmB; OxCan; WhAm 1*

Vanik, Charles Albert
American. Congressman
b. Apr 7, 1913 in Cleveland, Ohio
Source: *AlmAP 78, 80; BiDrAC; CngDr 74, 77, 79; PolProf J; PolProf NF; WhoAm 74, 76, 78, 80; WhoAmP 73, 75, 77; WhoGov 72, 75, 77; WhoMW 74, 76, 78*

Vanilla Fudge
[Carmine Appice; Tim Bogert; Vincent Martell; Mark Stein]
American. Rock Group
Source: *EncPR&S*

Van Itallie, Jean-Claude
American. Dramatist
b. May 23, 1936 in Brussels, Belgium
Source: *ConAu 45, 1NR; ConDr 73; CroCD; McGEWD; ModWD; NatPD; NotNAT; PlP&P; WhoAm 74; WhoThe 77; WhoWor 74; WrDr 76*

Van Lawick-Goodall, Baroness
see: Goodall, Jane

Van Leeuwenhoek, Anton
see: Leeuwenhoek, Anton van

Van Loon, Hendrik Willem
American. Journalist, Lecturer
b. Jan 14, 1882 in Rotterdam, Netherlands
d. Mar 10, 1944 in New York, New York
Source: *AmAu&B; AnCL; AuBYP; ChPo S2; ConAmA; ConAmL; CurBio 44; DcAmB S3; DcLEL; DcNAA; JBA 34; LongCTC; Newb 1922; OxAmL; REn; REnAL; TwCA, SUP; WhAm 2; WhNAA*

Van Meegeren, Hans
see: Meegeren, Hans van

Vannelli, Gino
Canadian. Singer, Songwriter
b. Jun 16, 1952 in Montreal, PQ
Source: *BioIn 11*

Van Nostrand, David
American. Publisher
b. Dec 5, 1811
d. Jun 14, 1886
Source: *AmAu&B; ApCAB; DcAmB*

Vanocur, Sander
American. Broadcast Journalist
b. Jan 8, 1928 in Cleveland, Ohio
Source: *CurBio 63; WhoAm 74; WhoHol A; WhoS&SW 73*

Van Paassen, Pierre
Canadian. Journalist, Author
b. Feb 7, 1895 in Goreum, Netherlands
d. Jan 8, 1968 in New York, New York
Source: *AmAu&B; CurBio 42, 68; REnAL; TwCA, SUP; WhAm 4A*

Van Patten, Dick
American. Actor
Appeared in "I Remember Mama," 1949-57; played Tom Bradford on "Eight Is Enough."
b. Dec 9, 1928 in Kew Gardens, New York
Source: *BiE&WWA; IntMPA 75, 76, 77, 78, 79, 80, 81, 82; NotNAT; WhoAm 82; WhoHol A; WhoThe 77*

Van Patten, Joyce
American. Actress
b. Mar 9, 1934 in New York, New York
Source: *BiE&WWA; FilmgC; NotNAT; WhoHol A; WhoThe 77*

Van Patten, Vince(nt)
American. Actor, Tennis Player
b. 1957?
Source: *BioIn 11*

Van Peebles, Melvin
American. Actor, Dramatist, Composer
b. 1932 in Chicago, Illinois
Source: *BlkAW; ConAu 85; ConLC 2; FilmgC; IntMPA 75, 76, 77, 78, 79, 80, 81, 82; LivgBAA; NewYTBE 72; NotNAT; PlP&P A; WhoBlA 75; WhoHol A; WhoThe 77*

Van Rensselaer, Stephen
American. Army Officer, Politician
b. Nov 1, 1764 in New York, New York
d. Jan 26, 1839 in Albany, New York
Source: *AmBi; ApCAB; BiAuS; BiDrAC; DcAmB; Drake; WebAB; WhAm H; WhAmP*

Van Rooy, Anton
Dutch. Opera Singer
b. Jan 1, 1870 in Rotterdam, Netherlands
d. Nov 28, 1932 in Munich, Germany
Source: *NewEOp 71*

Van Slyke, Helen Lenore Vogt
American. Author
b. Jul 9, 1919 in Washington, DC
d. Jul 3, 1979 in New York, New York
Source: *ConAu 37R, 89; WrDr 76*

Van Vechten, Carl
American. Author, Music Critic
b. Jun 17, 1880 in Cedar Rapids, Iowa
d. Dec 21, 1964 in New York, New York
Source: *AmAu&B; ConAmA; ConAmL; ConAu 89; CyWA; DcLEL; LongCTC; OxAmL; Pen AM; REn; REnAL; TwCA, SUP; WebE&AL; WhAm 4*

Van Vleck, John Hasbrouck
American. Physicist
b. Mar 13, 1899 in Middletown, Connecticut
d. Nov 28, 1980 in Cambridge, Massachusetts
Source: *AnObit 1980; IntWW 74; Who 74; WhoAm 74; WhoWor 74*

Van Vooren, Monique
American. Actress
b. Mar 17, 1938 in Brussels, Belgium
Source: *BiE&WWA; InWom; MotPP; WhoAm 74; WhoHol A*

Van Zandt, Marie
American. Opera Singer
b. Oct 8, 1861 in New York, New York
d. Dec 31, 1919 in Cannes, France
Source: *AmWom; ApCAB; InWom*

Van Zant, Ronnie (Ronald)
[Lynyrd Skynard]
American. Rock Musician
b. 1949
d. Oct 20, 1977 in Mississippi
Source: *BioIn 11*

Vanzetti, Bartolomeo
[Sacco and Vanzetti]
Italian. Political Radical
b. Jun 11, 1888 in Villafalletto, Italy
d. Aug 23, 1927 in Boston, Massachusetts
Source: *AmBi; DcAmB; REn; WebAB; WhAm 4*

Varda, Agnes
French. Screenwriter, Director
b. May 30, 1928 in Brussels, Belgium
Source: *BiDFilm; CurBio 70; DcFM; FilmgC; IntMPA 82; IntWW 74; OxFilm; WhoHol A; WhoWor 74; WomWMM; WorEFlm*

Vare, Glenna Collett
American. Golfer
b. Jun 20, 1903 in New Haven, Connecticut
Source: *InWom*

Varese, Edgar
American. Composer, Author
b. Dec 22, 1883 in Paris, France
d. Nov 6, 1965 in New York, New York
Source: *AtlBL; DcCM; WebAB; WhAm 4*

Varesi, Felice
French. Opera Singer
b. 1813 in Calais, France
d. Mar 13, 1889 in Milan, Italy
Source: *NewEOp 71*

Varga, Laszlo
Hungarian. Musician
b. 1924 in Budapest, Hungary
Source: *WhoMus 72*

Vargas, Alberto
[Joaquin Alberto Vargas y Chavez]
American. Artist
Created pinups for *Esquire* and *Playboy* magazines.
b. Feb 9, 1895 in Peru
d. Dec 30, 1982 in Los Angeles, California
Source: *BioIn 11*

Vargas, Getulio Dornelles
Brazilian. Lawyer, Political Leader
b. 1883 in Sao Borja, Brazil
d. Aug 24, 1954 in Rio de Janeiro, Brazil
Source: *CurBio 40, 51, 54; WhAm 3*

Varipapa, Andy
American. Bowler
b. 1894
Source: *BioIn 10*

Varley, F(rederick) H(orseman)
[Group of Seven]
Canadian. Artist
b. Jan 2, 1881 in Sheffield, England
d. Sep 8, 1969 in Toronto, ON
Source: *BioIn 11; CreCan 1; IlBEAAW; McGDA; WhoAmA 78*

Varnay, Astrid
Swedish. Opera Singer
b. Apr 25, 1918 in Stockholm, Sweden
Source: *CurBio 51; InWom; NewYTBS 74; WhoMus 72*

Varsi, Diane
American. Actress
b. 1938 in San Francisco, California
Source: *FilmgC; InWom; MotPP; MovMk; NewYTBE 72; WhoAm 74; WhoHol A*

Varviso, Silvio
Swiss. Conductor
b. Feb 26, 1924 in Zurich, Switzerland
Source: *WhoWor 74*

Vasarely, Victor
French. Artist
b. 1908 in Pecs, Hungary
Source: *CurBio 71; IntWW 74; WhoAm 74, 76, 78, 80, 82*

Vasari, Giorgio
Italian. Architect, Artist, Author
b. Jul 30, 1511 in Arezzo, Italy
d. Jun 27, 1574 in Florence, Italy
Source: *AtlBL; BiD&SB; CasWL; DcEuL; EuAu; NewC; OxEng; Pen EUR; REn*

Vashti
Persian. Queen
Source: *BioIn 9; NewCol 75; WebBD 80*

Vassallo, Jesse
American. Swimmer
b. 1961
Source: *BioIn 11*

Vassar, Matthew
English. Brewer, Merchant
Founded Vassar College, 1865.
b. Apr 29, 1792 in East Tuddingham, England
d. Jun 23, 1868 in Poughkeepsie, New York
Source: *AmBi; ApCAB; CyAl 2; DcAmB; NewCol 75; TwCBDA; WebAB; WebBD 80; WhAm H*

Vassilenko, Sergei
Russian. Composer
b. Mar 30, 1872 in Moscow, Russia
d. Mar 11, 1956 in Moscow, U.S.S.R.
Source: *NewEOp 71*

Vaughan, Agnes Carr
American. Author
b. Feb 1, 1887
Source: *ConAu P-1*

Vaughan, Bill (William Edward)
American. Journalist, Author
b. Oct 8, 1915 in Saint Louis, Missouri
d. Feb 26, 1977 in Kansas City, Kansas
Source: *ConAu 5R, 69; WhoAm 74; WhoMW 74*

Vaughan, Harry Hawkins
American. Major General
b. Nov 26, 1893 in Glasgow, Missouri
d. May 20, 1981 in Fort Belvoir, Virginia
Source: *BioIn 1, 2, 8, 11; CurBio 49, 81*

Vaughan, Henry
Welsh. Author
b. Apr 17, 1622 in Llansantfraed, Wales
d. Apr 23, 1695
Source: *Alli; AtlBL; BbD; BiD&SB; BrAu; CasWL; Chambr 1; ChPo, S2; CnE&AP; CroE&S; CrtT 1; DcEnA; DcEnL; DcEuL; DcLEL; EvLB; MouLC 1; NewC; OxEng; Pen ENG; RAdv 1; REn; WebE&AL*

Vaughan, Sarah
American. Singer
Sang with several orchestras, 1940's.
b. Mar 27, 1924 in Newark, New Jersey
Source: *BioNews 74; CelR 73; CurBio 57, 80; WhoAm 74, 76, 78, 80, 82; WhoBlA 75; WhoWor 74*

Vaughan Williams, Ralph
English. Composer
b. Oct 12, 1872 in Ampney, England
d. Aug 26, 1958 in London, England
Source: *AtlBL; CurBio 53, 58; DcCM; OxFilm; REn; WhAm 3*

Vaughn, Billy
American. Singer
b. Apr 12, 1919 in Glasgow, Kentucky
Source: *AmSCAP 66*

Vaughn, Joseph Floyd
"Arky"
American. Baseball Player
b. Mar 9, 1912 in Clifty, Arkansas
d. Aug 30, 1952 in Eagleville, California
Source: *BaseEn; WhoProB 73*

Vaughn, Robert
American. Actor
Played Napoleon Solo on "The Man from UNCLE," 1964-67.
b. Nov 22, 1932 in New York, New York
Source: *BioNews 74; CurBio 67; FilmgC; IntMPA 75, 76, 77, 78, 79, 80, 81, 82; MotPP; MovMk; WhoAm 74, 76, 78, 80, 82; WhoHol A; WorEFlm*

Vaux, Calvert
American. Landscape Architect
b. Dec 20, 1824 in London, England
d. Nov 19, 1895 in New York, New York
Source: *Alli; AmBi; ApCAB; DcAmAu; DcAmB; DcNAA; TwCBDA; WhAm H*

Veblen, Thorstein Bunde
American. Economist
b. Jul 30, 1857 in Manitowoc County, Wisconsin
d. Aug 3, 1929 in Palo Alto, California
Source: *AmAu&B; AmBi; DcAmAu; DcAmB; DcLEL; DcNAA; EncAB-H; EvLB; LongCTC; ModAL; OxAmL; Pen AM; REn; REnAL; TwCA, SUP; TwCW; WebAB; WebE&AL; WhAm 1; WhNAA; WhoTwCL*

Vedder, Elihu
American. Artist
b. Feb 26, 1836 in New York
d. Jan 29, 1923
Source: *AmAu&B; AmBi; AmLY; ApCAB; ChPo S1; DcAmB; DcNAA; Drake; EarABI, SUP; OxAmL; REnAL; TwCBDA; WhAm 1*

Veeck, Bill (William)
American. Baseball Executive
Former owner of Chicago White Sox, Milwaukee Brewers, Cleveland Indians.
b. Feb 9, 1914 in Chicago, Illinois
Source: *BioNews 74; CurBio 48; WebAB; WhoAm 74, 76, 78, 80, 82; WhoProB 73*

Vega (Carpio), Lope (Felix) de
Spanish. Dramatist, Poet
b. Nov 25, 1562? in Madrid, Spain
d. Aug 27, 1635 in Madrid, Spain
Source: *AtlBL; BbD; BiD&SB; CasWL; CnThe; CyWA; DcEuL; DcSpL; EuAu; EvEuW; McGEWD; NewC; OxEng; OxThe; Pen EUR; RComWL; REn; REnWD*

Veidt, Conrad
German. Actor
b. Jan 22, 1893 in Berlin, Germany
d. Apr 3, 1943 in Hollywood, California
Source: *BiDFilm; CurBio 43; Film 1; FilmgC; MotPP; MovMk; OxFilm; TwYS; WhScrn 74, 77; WhoHol B; WorEFlm*

Veil, Simone Annie Jacob
French. President of European Parliament
b. Jul 13, 1927 in Nice, France
Source: *CurBio 80; IntWW 75, 76, 77, 78; NewYTBS 74*

Velasco Alvarado, Juan
Peruvian. President
b. Jun 16, 1910 in Piura, Peru
d. Dec 24, 1977 in Lima, Peru
Source: *BioIn 8, 9, 11; CurBio 70, 78; IntWW 74, 75, 76, 77, 78; NewCol 75; NewYTBS 77; WhoGov 72; WhoWor 74, 76; WorDWW*

Velasco Ibarra, Jose Maria
Ecuadorean. President
b. Mar 19, 1893 in Quito, Ecuador
d. Mar 30, 1979 in Quito, Ecuador
Source: *BioIn 1, 3, 5, 8, 9, 11; CurBio 52, 79; IntWW 74, 75, 76, 77, 78; McGEWB; NewCol 75; NewYTBS 79; WhoGov 72*

Velazquez, Antonio Gonzalez
Spanish. Artist
b. 1723
d. 1794
Source: *BioIn 10*

Velazquez, Diego Rodriguez de Silva
Spanish. Artist
b. 1599 in Seville, Spain
d. Aug 6, 1660 in Madrid, Spain
Source: *AtlBL; NewC; NewCol 75; REn; WebBD 80*

Velde, Willem van de
Dutch. Artist
b. 1633 in Leyden, Netherlands
d. 1707 in London, England
Source: *McGDA; NewCol 75; WebBD 80*

Velez, Lupe
Mexican. Actress
b. Jul 18, 1908 in San Luis Potosi, Mexico
d. Dec 14, 1944
Source: *CurBio 45; FilmgC; InWom; MotPP; MovMk; ThFT; TwYS; WhScrn 74, 77; WhoHol B*

Velluti, Giovanni Battista
Italian. Opera Singer
b. Jan 28, 1780 in Monterone, Italy
d. Jan 22, 1861 in Sambruson, Italy
Source: *NewEOp 71; OxMus*

Velvet Underground, The
[John Cale; Sterling Morrison; Lou Reed; Marueen Tucker]
American. Rock Group
Source: *BiDAmM; EncPR&S; IlEncRk; Rk100*

Venizelos, Eleutherios
Greek. Statesman
b. Aug 23, 1864 in Mournies, Czechoslovakia
d. Mar 18, 1936 in Paris, France
Source: *McGEWB; WebBD 80; WhDW*

Ventura, Charlie
American. Jazz Musician
b. Dec 2, 1916 in Philadelphia, Pennsylvania
Source: *WhoJazz 72*

Ventures, The
[Bob Bogle; Johnny Durrill; Nokie Edwards; Howie Johnston; JerryMcGee; Mel Taylor; Don Wilson]
American. Vocal Group
Source: *EncPR&S; Rk100*

Venturi, Ken(neth)
American. Golfer
b. May 15, 1931 in San Francisco, California
Source: *BioIn 9, 10; WhoGolf*

Venuta, Benay
American. Actress, Singer
b. Jan 27, 1911 in San Francisco, California
Source: *BiE&WWA; NotNAT; WhoHol A; WhoThe 77*

Venuti, Joe (Giuseppe)
American. Jazz Musician
b. 1899 in Lecco, Italy
d. Aug 14, 1978 in Seattle, Washington
Source: *AmSCAP 66; WhoJazz 72*

Vera
[Vera Neumann]
American. Designer
Founded Vera Co., 1945.
b. Jul 24, 1910 in Stamford, Connecticut
Source: *WorFshn*

Vera-Ellen
[Vera-Ellen Rohe]
American. Dancer, Actress
b. Feb 16, 1926 in Cincinnati, Ohio
d. Aug 30, 1981 in Los Angeles, California
Source: *BioIn 11; CmMov; CmpEPM; CurBio 59, 81; FilmgC; InWom; MotPP; MovMk; WhoHol A; WorEFlm*

Verdi, Giuseppe
Italian. Opera Composer
Composed 27 operas, including *Rigoletto, La Traviata, Aida.*
b. Oct 10, 1813 in Le Roncole, Italy
d. Jan 27, 1901 in Milan, Italy
Source: *AtlBL; NewC; NewCol 75; REn; WebBD 80*

Verdon, Gwen (Gwyneth Evelyn)
American. Dancer, Actress
Won Tony award for *Can Can,* 1953; *Damn Yankees,* 1955; *Red Head,* 1958.
b. Jan 13, 1925 in Culver City, California
Source: *BiE&WWA; CelR 73; CurBio 60; EncMT; InWom; MotPP; NotNAT; WhoAm 74, 76, 78, 80, 82; WhoHol A; WhoThe 77*

Verdugo, Elena
American. Actress
b. 1926
Source: *FilmgC; InWom; MovMk; WhoHol A*

Verdy, Violette
[Nelly Guillerm]
French. Ballerina, Director
b. Dec 1, 1933 in Brittany, France
Source: *CurBio 80; WhoAm 82*

Vereen, Ben
American. Actor, Singer, Dancer
b. Oct 10, 1946 in Miami, Florida
Source: *CelR 73; EncMT; NewYTBE 72; NotNAT; WhoAm 82; WhoHol A; WhoThe 77*

Vereshchagin, Vasil
Russian. Artist
b. 1842
d. 1904
Source: *BioIn 9; NewCol 75; WebBD 80*

Verga, Giovanni
Italian. Author
b. Aug 31, 1840 in Catania, Sicily
d. Jan 27, 1922 in Catania, Sicily
Source: *AtlBL; BbD; BiD&SB; CasWL; ClDMEL; CnThe; CyWA; DcBiA; DcEuL; EncWL; EvEuW; LongCTC; McGEWD; ModRL; ModWD; OxEng; OxThe; Pen EUR; RComWL; REn; REnWD; TwCA SUP; WhoTwCL*

Verissimo, Erico Lopes
Brazilian. Author
b. Dec 17, 1905
Source: *CasWL; EncWL; IntWW 74; Pen AM; REn; TwCW; WhoWor 74; WorAu*

Verity, John
see: Argent

Verlaine, Paul Marie
French. Poet
b. Mar 30, 1844 in Metz, France
d. Jan 8, 1896 in Paris, France
Source: *AtlBL; BbD; BiD&SB; CasWL; ClDMEL; CyWA; DcEuL; EuAu; EvEuW; ModRL; NewC; OxEng; OxFr; Pen EUR; RComWL; REn*

Vermeer, Jan
Dutch. Artist
b. Oct 30, 1632 in Delft, Netherlands
d. Dec 15, 1675
Source: *AtlBL; NewC; NewCol 75; REn; WebBD 80*

Vermeil, Dick (Richard Albert)
American. Football Coach
Coach, Philadelphia Eagles, 1976-82.
b. Oct 30, 1936 in Calistoga, California
Source: *NewYTBS 81; WhoAm 82*

Verne, Jules
French. Author
Wrote *Twenty Thousand Leagues Under the Sea,* 1870; *Around the World in Eighty Days,* 1873.
b. Feb 8, 1828 in Nantes, France
d. Mar 24, 1905 in Amiens, France
Source: *AtlBL; AuBYP; BbD; BiD&SB; CarSB; CasWL; CyWA; DcBiA; DcEnL; DcEuL; EuAu; EvEuW; FilmgC; JBA 34, 51; LongCTC; MnBBF; NewC; OxEng; OxFr; Pen EUR; REn; WhoChL*

Vernier, Pierre
French. Mathematician
b. Aug 19, 1580 in Ornans, France
d. Sep 14, 1637 in Ornans, France
Source: *DcScB; WebBD 80*

Vernon, Sir Edward
"Old Grog"
English. Admiral
b. 1684
d. 1757
Source: *Alli; ApCAB; Drake; NewCol 75; WebBD 80*

Vernon, Jackie
American. Comedian
b. 1928 in New York, New York
Source: *WhoHol A*

Vernon, John
[Adolphus Vernon Agopsowicz]
Canadian. Actor
b. 1932 in Regina, SK
Source: *ClbCR; FilmgC; WhoHol A*

Veronese, Paolo
[Paolo Caliari]
Italian. Artist
b. 1528 in Verona, Italy
d. Apr 19, 1588
Source: *AtlBL; REn*

Veronica Giuliani, Saint
Italian. Nun
b. 1660
d. 1697
Source: *InWom; WebBD 80*

Veronis, John James
American. Publisher
b. Mar 6, 1928 in New Brunswick, New Jersey
Source: *WhoAm 82; WhoE 74; WhoF&I 74*

Verrazano, Giovanni da
Italian. Navigator, Explorer
Discovered mouth of Hudson River, 1524.
b. 1485? in Val di Greve, Italy
d. Nov 1528 in Puerto del Pico, Spain
Source: *AmBi; ApCAB; CnDAL; OxCan; REn; REnAL; WhAm H*

Verrett, Shirley
American. Opera Singer
b. May 31, 1933 in New Orleans, Louisiana
Source: *BioNews 75; CelR 73; InWom; IntWW 74; NewYTBS 74; WhoAm 74; WhoBlA 75; WhoE 74; WhoWor 74*

Verrill, Alpheus Hyatt
American. Archaeologist, Author
b. Jul 23, 1871 in New Haven, Connecticut
d. Nov 14, 1954 in Chiefland, Florida
Source: *AmAu&B; DcAmB S5; REnAL; WhAm 3; WhNAA*

Verrocchio, Andrea del
[Andrea di Michele di Francesco Cioni]
Italian. Artist
b. 1435 in Florence, Italy
d. Oct 7, 1488 in Venice, Italy
Source: *AtlBL; NewCol 75; REn; WebBD 80*

Verspronk, Johannes
Dutch. Artist
b. 1597 in Haarlem, Netherlands
d. 1662 in Haarlem, Netherlands
Source: *McGDA*

Vertes, Marcel
Hungarian. Artist
b. Aug 10, 1895 in Ujpest, Hungary
d. Oct 31, 1961 in Paris, France
Source: *CurBio 61, 62; WhAm 4; WhoGrA*

Veruschka
[Countess Vera VonLehndorff]
German. Model
b. 1943
Source: *BioIn 10*

Verwoerd, Hendrik F
South African. Prime Minister
b. Sep 8, 1901 in Amsterdam, Netherlands
d. Sep 6, 1966 in South Africa
Source: *BioIn 5, 6, 7, 8; CurBio 59, 67; WhAm 4*

Very, Jones
American. Author
b. Aug 28, 1813 in Salem, Massachusetts
d. May 8, 1880 in Salem, Massachusetts
Source: *Alli, SUP; AmAu; AmAu&B; AmBi; ApCAB; AtlBL; BiD&SB; CasWL; Chambr 3; ChPo, S1; CnDAL; CyAl 2; DcAmAu; DcAmB; DcLEL; DcNAA; Drake; EvLB; MouLC 3; OxAmL; Pen AM; REn; REnAL; WebAB; WebE&AL; WhAm H*

Vesalius, Andreas
Belgian. Scientist
b. Dec 31, 1514 in Brussels, Belgium
d. Oct 15, 1564 in Zante, Greece
Source: *AsBiEn; BiD&SB; McGEWB; REn*

Vesco, Robert Lee
American. Financier
b. Dec 4, 1935 in Detroit, Michigan
Source: *BioNews 74; BusPN; WhoE 74*

Vespasian
[Titus Flavius Vespasianus]
Roman. Emperor
b. 8BC in Reate, Italy
d. Jun 24, 79AD
Source: *Pen CL; REn*

Vespucci, Amerigo
[Americus Vespucius]
Italian. Navigator
America was named for him; discovered mouth of Rio de la Plata.
b. Mar 9, 1451 in Florence, Italy
d. Feb 22, 1512 in Seville, Spain
Source: *BbD; BiD&SB; Drake; NewC; OxAmL; REn; REnAL; TwCBDA; WebAB; WhAm H*

Vessey, John William, Jr.
American. Chairman of Joint Chiefs of Staff
b. Jun 29, 1922 in Minneapolis, Minnesota
Source: *WhoAm 82*

Vestris, Lucia Elizabeth
English. Opera Singer
b. 1787 in London, England
d. Aug 8, 1856 in London, England
Source: *InWom; OxThe*

Veyron-Lacroix, Robert
French. Musician
b. 1922 in Paris, France
Source: *WhoMus 72*

Viardot-Garcia, Pauline
French. Opera Singer
b. Jul 18, 1821 in Paris, France
d. May 18, 1910 in Paris, France
Source: *InWom*

Vicious, Sid
[John Simon Ritchie; The Sex Pistols]
English. Punk Rock Singer
b. 1957
d. Feb 2, 1979 in Greenwich Village, New York
Source: *BioIn 11*

Vickers, Edward
English. Steel Manufacturer
b. 1804
d. 1897
Source: *WebBD 80*

Vickers, Jon
Canadian. Opera Singer
b. Oct 29, 1926 in Prince Albert, SK
Source: *CanWW 82; CreCan 1; CurBio 61; IntWW 74; Who 74; WhoAm 74; WhoMus 72; WhoWor 74*

Vickers, Martha
[Martha MacVicar]
American. Actress
b. 1925
d. Nov 2, 1971 in Van Nuys, California
Source: *FilmgC; HolP 40; WhScrn 74, 77; WhoHol B*

Vickrey, Robert
American. Artist
b. Aug 20, 1926 in New York, New York
Source: *McGDA; WhoAm 82*

Vico, Giovanni Battista
Italian. Philosopher, Jurist
b. 1668
d. 1744
Source: *DcEuL; EuAu; LongCTC; NewCol 75; REn; WebBD 80*

Victor Emmanuel II
Italian. King
b. Mar 14, 1820 in Turin, Italy
d. Jan 9, 1878
Source: *NewCol 75; WebBD 80*

Victor Emmanuel III
Italian. King
b. 1869 in Naples, Italy
d. 1947
Source: *NewCol 75; WebBD 80*

Victor, Sally Josephs
American. Milliner, Designer
b. Feb 23, 1905 in Scranton, Pennsylvania
Source: *CurBio 54; InWom; WorFshn*

Victoria
English. Queen
Longest reign in British history, 1837-1901; married first cousin Prince Albert, 1840.
b. May 24, 1819 in London, England
d. Jan 22, 1901 in Isle of Wight, England
Source: *Alli, SUP; BbD; BiD&SB; ChPo; DcEnL; DcLEL; EvLB; HerW; NewC; OxEng; REn*

Vidal, "Gore" (Eugene)
American. Author, Dramatist
Wrote *Williwaw,* 1946; *Myra Breckinridge,* 1968.
b. Oct 3, 1925 in West Point, New York
Source: *AmAu&B; AmNov; AuNews 1; BiE&WWA; BioNews 74; BkPepl; CasWL; CelR 73; CnMD; ConAu 5R; ConDr 73; ConLC 2, 4, 6, 8, 10; ConNov 72, 76; CroCD; CurBio 65; DrAF 76; EncMys; EncWL; IntWW 74; LongCTC; McGEWD; ModWD; NotNAT; OxAmL; Pen AM; RAdv 1; REn; REnAL; TwCA SUP; TwCW; WebAB; WebE&AL; Who 82; WhoAm 74, 76, 78, 80, 82; WhoThe 77; WhoTwCL; WhoWor 74; WorEFlm; WrDr 76*

Videla, Jorge Rafael
Argentine. President
b. Aug 2, 1925 in Mercedes, Argentina
Source: *BioIn 10, 11; CurBio 78; IntWW 76, 77, 78; IntYB 78, 79; NewYTBS 75; WhoWor 76, 78*

Vidor, Florence
American. Actress
b. 1895
d. Nov 3, 1977 in Pacific Palisades, California
Source: *Film 1; FilmgC; MotPP; MovMk; TwYS; WhoHol A*

Vidor, King Wallis
American. Motion Picture Director
Directed *Hallelujah,* 1929; first Hollywood movie with all black cast.
b. Feb 8, 1894 in Galveston, Texas
d. Nov 1, 1982 in Paso Robles, California
Source: *BiDFilm; BkPepl; CmMov; CurBio 57, 83; Film 1; FilmgC; IntMPA 75, 76, 77, 78, 79, 80, 81, 82; IntWW 74; MovMk; NewYTBE 72; OxFilm; TwYS; Who 82; WhoAm 74, 76, 78, 80, 82; WhoWor 74; WorEFlm; WrDr 76*

Viereck, George Sylvester
American. Author, Editor
b. Dec 31, 1884 in Munich, Germany
d. Mar 18, 1962 in Holyoke, Massachusetts
Source: *AmAu&B; AmLY; CasWL; ChPo; CurBio 40, 62; OxAmL; REnAL; TwCA SUP; WhAm 4; WhNAA*

Viereck, Peter Robert Edwin
American. Poet, Educator
b. Aug 5, 1916 in New York, New York
Source: *AmAu&B; CnDAL; CnE&AP; ConAu 1R, 1NR; ConP 70, 75; CurBio 43; DrAP 75; DrAS 74E; IntWW 74; ModAL, SUP; OxAmL; Pen AM; RAdv 1; REn; REnAL; TwCA SUP; TwCW; WhoAm 74, 76, 78, 80, 82; WhoWor 74; WrDr 76*

Viertel, Peter
American. Author
b. Nov 16, 1920 in Dresden, Germany
Source: *AmAu&B; AmNov; ConAu 13R*

Vieuxtemps, Henri
Belgian. Musician, Composer
b. Feb 20, 1820 in Verviers, Belgium
d. Jun 6, 1881 in Mustapha, Algiers
Source: *NewCol 75; OxMus; WebBD 80*

Vigee-Lebrun, Elisabeth
French. Artist
b. 1755
d. 1842
Source: *NewCol 75; WebBD 80*

Vignola, Giacomo da
Italian. Architect
b. Oct 1, 1507 in Vignola, Italy
d. Jul 7, 1573 in Rome, Italy
Source: *AtlBL; NewCol 75; WebBD 80*

Vigny, Alfred, Comte de
French. Author
b. Mar 27, 1797 in Loches, France
d. Sep 17, 1863 in Paris, France
Source: *AtlBL; BbD; BiD&SB; CasWL; ChPo; CnThe; CyWA; DcBiA; DcEuL; EuAu; EvEuW; McGEWD; NewC; OxEng; OxFr; Pen EUR; RComWL; REn; REnWD*

Vigo, Jean
French. Motion Picture Director
b. 1905 in Paris, France
d. 1934
Source: *BiDFilm; DcFM; FilmgC; MovMk; OxFilm; WorEFlm*

Vigoda, Abe
American. Actor
Played Detective Fish on "Barney Miller," 1975-77.
b. Feb 24, 1921 in New York, New York
Source: *WhoAm 82; WhoHol A*

Viguerie, Richard A(rt)
"Godfather of the New Right"
American. Publisher
Founder of the *Conservative Digest,* 1975.
b. Sep 23, 1933 in Golden Acres, Texas
Source: *CurBio 83*

Vilas, Guillermo
Argentine. Tennis Player
b. Aug 17, 1952 in Mar del Plata, Argentina
Source: *BioIn 10, 11; CurBio 78*

Villa, Luz Corral de
"Dona Lucha"
Mexican. Widow of Pancho Villa
b. 1892 in Chihuahua, Mexico
d. Jul 6, 1981 in Chihuahua, Mexico
Source: *AnObit 1981; NewYTBS 81*

Villa, "Pancho" (Francisco)
[Doroteo Arango]
Mexican. Bandit, Revolutionary
b. Jun 5, 1878 in Rio Grande, Mexico
d. Jul 23, 1923 in Parral Chihahua, Mexico
Source: *REn; WhAm 4; WhoBox 74*

Villa-Lobos, Heitor
Brazilian. Composer
b. Mar 5, 1887 in Rio de Janeiro, Brazil
d. Nov 17, 1959 in Rio de Janeiro, Brazil
Source: *AtlBL; CurBio 45, 60; DcCM; REn; WhAm 3*

Village People, The
[Alex Briley; David Hodo; Glenn M Hughes; Randy Jones; Felipe Rose; Victor Willis]
American. Singing Group
Source: *ConMuA 80; WhoRock 81*

Villard, Helen Francis Garrison
American. Social Reformer
b. 1844 in Boston, Massachusetts
d. 1928 in Dobbs Ferry, New York
Source: *DcAmB; DcNAA*

Villard, Henry
American. Journalist, Businessman
b. Apr 10, 1835 in Speyer, Bavaria
d. Nov 12, 1900 in Dobbs Ferry, New York
Source: *AmAu&B; AmBi; ApCAB; DcAmB; DcNAA; EncAB-H; OhA&B; OxAmL; REnAL; TwCBDA; WebAB; WhAm H*

Villard, Oswald
American. Journalist
b. Mar 13, 1872 in Wiesbaden, Germany
d. Oct 1, 1949 in New York, New York
Source: *AmAu&B; CurBio 40, 49; DcAmB S4; DcNAA; EncAB-H; OxAmL; REn; REnAL; TwCA, SUP; WebAB; WhAm 2; WhNAA*

Villechaize, Herve Jean Pierre
French. Actor
Plays Tattoo on "Fantasy Island," 1978--.
b. Apr 23, 1943 in Paris, France
Source: *BioIn 11; IntMPA 82; WhoAm 82*

Villella, Edward Joseph
American. Ballet Dancer, Choreographer
Dancer, NY City Ballet, 1957--.
b. Oct 1, 1932 in Bayside, New York
Source: *BioNews 74; CelR 73; IntWW 74; WhoAm 74, 76, 78, 80, 82; WhoGov 72; WhoHol A; WhoWor 74*

Villeneuve, Gilles
Canadian. Auto Racer
Won six Grand Prix races.
b. 1952? in Berthierville, PQ
d. May 8, 1982 in Zolder, Belgium
Source: *BioIn 12*

Villiers, Alan John
Australian. Mariner, Author
b. Sep 23, 1903 in Melbourne, Australia
Source: *BioIn 1, 4, 7, 10, 11; ConAu 1NR; IntWW 74; SmATA 10; Who 74; WhoAm 74; WhoWor 74*

Villon, Francois
[Francois de Montcorbier; Francois Des Loges]
French. Poet
Wrote *Little Testament,* 1456; *Grand Testament,* 1461.
b. 1431? in Paris, France
d. 1463 in Paris, France
Source: *AtlBL; BbD; BiD&SB; CasWL; ChPo, S2; CyWA; DcEuL; EuAu; EvEuW; NewC; NewCol 75; OxEng; OxFr; Pen EUR; RComWL; REn*

Vinay, Ramon
Chilean. Opera Singer
b. Aug 31, 1912 in Chillan, Chile
Source: *NewEOp 71*

Vincennes, Francois Marie Bissot
[Sieur DeVincennes]
Canadian. Explorer
Established fort on Wabash River, 1731.
b. 1700 in Montreal, PQ
d. Mar 25, 1736
Source: *AmBi; DcAmB*

Vincent de Paul, Saint
French. Founder of Religious Order
b. Apr 24, 1581 in Pouy, France
d. Sep 27, 1660
Source: *NewCol 75; OxFr; WebBD 80*

Vincent, Jan-Michael
American. Actor
b. Jul 15, 1944 in Ventura, California
Source: *IntMPA 75, 76, 77, 78, 79, 80, 81, 82; WhoHol A*

Vinci, Leonardo da
see: Leonardo da Vinci

Vines, Ellsworth
American. Tennis Player
b. Sep 28, 1911
Source: *BioIn 1*

Vinson, Carl
American. Congressman
b. Nov 18, 1883 in Milledgeville, Georgia
d. Jun 1, 1981 in Milledgeville, Georgia
Source: *BiDrAC; BioIn 1, 2, 4, 5, 6, 7; CurBio 42, 81; PolProf J; PolProf K; PolProf T; WhAm 7; WhAmP*

Vinson, "Cleanhead" (Eddie)
American. Jazz Musician
b. Dec 18, 1917 in Houston, Texas
Source: *WhoJazz 72*

Vinson, Frederick Moore
American. Supreme Court Justice
b. Jan 22, 1890 in Louisa, Kentucky
d. Sep 8, 1953 in Washington, DC
Source: *BiDrAC; BiDrUSE; WebAB; WhAmP*

Vinson, Helen
American. Actress
b. Sep 17, 1907 in Beaumont, Texas
Source: *FilmgC; MovMk; ThFT; WhoHol A; WhoThe 77*

Vinton, Bobby (Stanley Robert)
American. Singer
Hits include "Blue Velvet"; had sold over 25 million records by 1974.
b. Apr 16, 1935 in Canonsburg, Pennsylvania
Source: *AmSCAP 66; BioNews 74; WhoAm 82; WhoHol A*

Viollet le Duc, Eugene Emmanuel
French. Architect
b. Jan 27, 1814 in Paris, France
d. Sep 17, 1879 in Lausanne, Switzerland
Source: *McGEWB; NewCol 75*

Viorst, Judith (Stahl)
American. Author, Poet
b. Feb 2, 1931 in Newark, New Jersey
Source: *ConAu 49, 2NR; SmATA 7; WhoAm 82; WhoS&SW 73*

Viotti, Giovanni Battista
Italian. Musician, Composer
b. May 23, 1753 in Vercelli, Italy
d. Mar 3, 1824 in London, England
Source: *OxMus*

Virchow, Rudolf
German. Pathologist, Political Leader
b. Oct 31, 1821 in Pomerania, Germany
d. Sep 5, 1905
Source: *AsBiEn; BiHiMed; WebBD 80*

Viren, Lasse
Finnish. Track Athlete
b. Jul 22, 1949
Source: *WhoTr&F 73*

Virgil
[Publius Vergilius Maro; Vergil]
Roman. Poet
Unfinished epic poem *Aeneid* was about the founding of Rome.
b. Oct 15, 70BC in Mantua, Gaul
d. Sep 21, 19BC in Brundisium, Italy
Source: *AtlBL; BbD; BiDLA; CasWL; DcBiA; DcEnL; DcEuL; NewC; OxEng; Pen CL; RComWL; REn*

Virgin, Craig
American. Runner
b. 1955?
Source: *BioIn 12*

Viscardi, Henry, Jr
American. Businessman
b. May 10, 1912 in New York, New York
Source: *ConAu 5R, 5NR; CurBio 54, 66; NewYTBE 72; WhoAm 74; WhoE 74*

Visconti, Luchino
Italian. Motion Picture Director
b. Nov 2, 1906 in Milan, Italy
d. Mar 17, 1976 in Rome, Italy
Source: *BiDFilm; CelR 73; ConAu 65, 81; ConLC 16; CurBio 65; DcFM; FilmgC; IntMPA 75; IntWW 74; OxFilm; OxThe; WhAm 6; Who 74; WhoWor 74; WorEFlm*

Vishinskii, Andrei
Russian. Jurist, Diplomat
b. Dec 10, 1883 in Odessa, Russia
d. Nov 22, 1954 in New York, New York
Source: *CurBio 44, 55; NewCol 75*

Vishnevskaya, Galina (Pavlovna)
Russian. Opera Singer
b. Oct 25, 1926 in Leningrad, U.S.S.R.
Source: *CurBio 66; InWom; IntWW 74; Who 74; WhoAm 82*

Vishnevsky, Alexander Alexandrovich
Russian. Surgeon
b. May 24, 1906 in Kazan, Russia
Source: *IntWW 74; WhoWor 74*

Vishniac, Roman
American. Microbiologist
b. Aug 19, 1897 in Saint Petersburg, Russia
Source: *CurBio 67*

Visscher, William Lightfoot
American. Actor, Poet
b. Nov 25, 1842 in Owingsville, Kentucky
d. Feb 10, 1924
Source: *AmAu&B; AmLY; DcNAA*

Vitale, Milly
Italian. Actress
b. Jul 16, 1938 in Rome, Italy
Source: *FilmgC; IntMPA 75, 76, 77, 78, 79, 80, 81, 82; WhoHol A*

Vitellius, Aulus
Roman. Emperor
b. 15
d. 69
Source: *NewCol 75; REn; WebBD 80*

Vitruvius
Roman. Architect
b. 70BC
d. 16BC
Source: *AtlBL; PlP&P; REn*

Vitti, Monica
Italian. Actress
b. 1933 in Rome, Italy
Source: *BiDFilm; FilmgC; MotPP; MovMk; OxFilm; WhoHol A; WorEFlm*

Vivaldi, Antonio
"The Red Priest"
Italian. Musician, Composer
b. 1675 in Venice, Italy
d. Jul 27, 1741 in Vienna, Austria
Source: *AtlBL; NewCol 75; REn; WebBD 80*

Vlaminck, Maurice de
French. Artist
b. Apr 4, 1876 in Paris, France
d. Oct 11, 1958 in Paris, France
Source: *AtlBL; NewCol 75; REn*

Vlieger, Simon Jacobsz de
Dutch. Artist
b. 1600 in Rotterdam, Netherlands
d. 1653 in Weesp, Netherlands
Source: *McGDA*

Voelker, John Donaldson
[Robert Traver, pseud.]
American. Judge, Author
b. Jun 29, 1903 in Ishpeming, Michigan
Source: *AmAu&B; ConAu 1R; ConNov 72, 76; WhoAm 74; WorAu; WrDr 76*

Voelker, Paul Frederick
American. College President, Author
b. Sep 30, 1875 in Evart, Michigan
Source: *WhAm 5; WhNAA*

Vogel, Mitch
American. Actor
b. 1956 in Alhambra, California
Source: *WhoHol A*

Vogl, Heinrich
German. Opera Singer
b. Jan 15, 1845 in Au, Germany
d. Apr 21, 1900 in Munich, Germany
Source: *NewEOp 71*

Vogues, The
[Charles Blasko; William Burkette; Hugh Geyer; Don Miller]
American. Vocal Group
Source: *EncPR&S*

Vohs, (Elinor) Joan
American. Actress
b. Jul 30, 1931 in Saint Albans, New York
Source: *IntMPA 75, 76, 77, 78, 79, 80, 81, 82*

Voight, Jon
American. Actor
Won Oscar, 1979, for *Coming Home.*
b. Dec 29, 1938 in Yonkers, New York
Source: *BioNews 74; BkPepl; CelR 73; CurBio 74; FilmgC; IntMPA 75, 76, 77, 78, 79, 80, 81, 82; MovMk; OxFilm; WhoAm 74; WhoHol A; WhoThe 77*

Voinovich, George Victor
American. Mayor of Cleveland
b. Jul 15, 1936 in Cleveland, Ohio
Source: *St&PR 75; WhoAm 80, 82; WhoAmP 73, 79*

Voit, Willard D
American. Rubber Company Executive
b. Nov 8, 1910 in Seattle, Washington
d. Feb 1980 in Newport Beach, California
Source: *St&PR 75; WhoAm 78*

Volcker, Paul Adolph
American. Federal Reserve System Chairman
b. Sep 5, 1927 in Cape May, New Jersey
Source: *CurBio 73; IntWW 74, 75, 76, 78; NewYTBS 75, 79; PolProf NF; WhoAm 74, 76, 78, 80, 82; WhoAmP 73, 75, 77, 79; WhoGov 72*

Volkov, Leon
American. Journalist
b. Jan 22, 1920
d. Jan 22, 1974 in Bethesda, Maryland
Source: *ConAu 45; NewYTBS 74*

Volkov, Vladislav
Russian. Cosmonaut
b. Nov 23, 1936
d. Jun 30, 1971 in New York, New York
Source: *NewYTBE 71; WhAm 5*

Vollbracht, Michaele J
American. Fashion Designer, Artist
b. Nov 17, 1947 in Quincy, Illinois
Source: *BioIn 11, 12*

Vollmer, Lula
American. Dramatist
b. 1898 in Keyser, North Carolina
d. May 2, 1955
Source: *AmAu&B; CnMD; ModWD; OxAmL; TwCA, SUP; WhAm 3; WhNAA*

Volner, Jill Wine
American. Lawyer
b. May 5, 1943 in Chicago, Illinois
Source: *BioNews 74; NewYTBE 73; WhoAm 74; WhoAmW 77*

Volney, (Constantin) Francois Chasseboeuf
French. Author
b. Feb 3, 1757 in Craon, France
d. Apr 25, 1820 in Paris, France
Source: *ApCAB; BbD; BbtC; BiD&SB; DcEuL; EuAu; OxFr*

Volpe, John Anthony
American. Diplomat
b. Dec 8, 1908 in Wakefield, Massachusetts
Source: *BiDrUSE; CelR 73; CurBio 62; IntWW 74; USBiR 74; WhoAm 74; WhoAmP 73; WhoF&I 74; WhoGov 72; WhoS&SW 73; WhoWor 74*

Volpi, Alfredo
Brazilian. Artist
b. 1895 in Lucca, Italy
Source: *McGDA*

Volstead, Andrew J
American. Legislator
b. 1860 in Goodhue County, Minnesota
d. Jan 20, 1947 in Granite Falls, Minnesota
Source: *BiDrAC; DcAmB S4; WhAm 2; WhAmP*

Volta, Alessandro
Italian. Physicist
The volt, a unit of electrical measurement, is named for him.
b. Feb 18, 1745 in Como, Italy
d. Mar 7, 1827
Source: *AsBiEn; DcScB; NewCol 75; WebBD 80*

Voltaire(, Francois Marie Arouet de)
French. Author, Philosopher
Wrote *Candide,* 1759.
b. Nov 21, 1694 in Paris, France
d. May 30, 1778 in Paris, France
Source: *AtlBL; BbD; BiD&SB; CasWL; CnThe; CyWA; DcBiA; DcEnL; DcEuL; EuAu; EvEuW; McGEWD; NewC; OxCan; OxEng; OxFr; OxGer; OxThe; Pen EUR*

VonBraun, Wernher
American. Space Scientist
Led development of V-2 missiles for Germany during WW II; directed rocket research in US.
b. Mar 23, 1912 in Wirsitz, Germany
d. Jun 1977 in Alexandria, Virginia
Source: *AmAu&B; AmM&WS 73P; AuBYP; ConAu 5R, 69; CurBio 52; IntWW 74; NewYTBE 70; WebAB; Who 74; WhoAm 74; WhoS&SW 73; WhoWor 74; WrDr 76*

Von Bulow, Claus
[Claus Borberg]
British. Alleged Attempted Murderer
Convicted, 1982, of injecting wife with insulin, resulting in irreversible coma.
b. 1926 in Denmark
Source: *BioIn 12*

VonBulow, Hans Guido
German. Musician, Conductor
b. Jan 8, 1830 in Dresden, Germany
d. Feb 12, 1894 in Cairo, Egypt
Source: *NewEOp 71*

Von Bulow, "Sunny" (Martha Sharp Crawford)
[Mrs. Claus Von Bulow]
American. Socialite, Coma Victim
Husband convicted, 1982, of trying to murder her with insulin injection.
b. 1932?
Source: *BioIn 12*

VonBunsen, Robert Wilhelm Eberhard
see: Bunsen, Robert Wilhelm Eberhard von

Von Carolsfeld, Ludwig Schnorr
see: Schnorr von Carolsfeld, Ludwig

VonCramm, Baron Gottfried
see: Cramm, Gottfried von, Baron

VonDaeniken, Erich
Swiss. Author
Wrote *Chariots of the Gods?, Unsolved Mysteries of the Past.*
b. Apr 14, 1935 in Zofingen, Switzerland
Source: *AuNews 1; BioNews 75; ConAu 37R*

VonDoderer, Heimito
Austrian. Author
b. Sep 5, 1896
d. Dec 23, 1966 in Vienna, Austria
Source: *CasWL; ConAu 25R; EncWL; EvEuW; ModGL; OxGer; Pen EUR; REn; TwCW; WhoTwCL; WorAu*

VonDohnanyi, Christoph
see: Dohnanyi, Christoph von

VonDohnanyi, Ernst
see: Dohnanyi, Ernst von

Von Eckardt, Wolf
German. Critic, Author
b. Mar 6, 1918 in Berlin, Germany
Source: *ConAu 5R; WhoAm 74, 76, 78, 80, 82*

Von Frisch, Karl
see: Frisch, Karl von

VonFurstenberg, Betsy
German. Actress
b. Aug 16, 1932 in Westphalia, Germany
Source: *BiE&WWA; CelR 73; InWom; MotPP; NotNAT; WhoAm 82; WhoHol A; WhoThe 77*

VonFurstenberg, Diane Halfin
see: Furstenberg, Diane Halfin von

VonFurstenberg, Egon
see: Furstenberg, Egon von

VonHardenberg, Friedrich
see: Novalis

VonHindenburg, Paul
see: Hindenburg, Paul von

VonHoesslin, Franz
see: Hoesslin, Franz von

VonHoffman, Nicholas
American. Journalist
b. Oct 16, 1929 in New York, New York
Source: *AmAu&B; ConAu 81; WhoAm 74, 76, 78, 80, 82; WhoS&SW 73*

VonKarajan, Herbert
see: Karajan, Herbert von

Von Karman, Theodore
American. Aeronautical Engineer
b. May 11, 1881 in Budapest, Hungary
d. May 7, 1963
Source: *WebAB; WhAm 4*

VonKleist, Heinrich
see: Kleist, Heinrich von

VonKlenau, Paul August
see: Klenau, Paul von

VonKotzebue, August Friedrich
see: Kotzebue, August Friedrich von

VonKrafft-Ebing, Richard
see: Krafft-Ebing, Richard von

VonLuckner, Count Felix
see: Luckner, Felix von, Count

VonMildenburg, Anna
see: Mildenburg, Anna von

VonMoltke, Helmuth James graf
see: Moltke, Helmuth James graf von

VonMoltke, Helmuth Karl Bernhard
see: Moltke, Helmuth Karl Bernhard von

VonMostenthal, Salomon Hermann
see: Mosenthal, Salomon Hermann von

VonMuenchhausen, Friedrich Ernst
see: Muenchhausen, Friedrich Ernst von

VonMunchhausen, Baron
see: Munchhausen, Baron von

Vonnegut, Kurt, Jr.
American. Author, Journalist
Wrote *Slaughterhouse Five,* 1969; *Breakfast of Champions,* 1973.
b. Nov 11, 1922 in Indianapolis, Indiana
Source: *AmAu&B; Au&Wr 71; AuNews 1; CasWL; CelR 73; ConAu 1R, 1NR; ConLC 1, 2, 3, 4, 5, 8, 12; ConNov 72, 76; CurBio 70; DrAF 76; EncAB-H; EncWL; IndAu 1917; IntWW 74; ModAL SUP; NatPD; NewYTBE 70, 71; Pen AM; RAdv 1; WebAB; WebE&AL; WhoAm 74, 76, 78, 80, 82; WhoTwCL; WhoWor 74; WorAu; WrDr 76*

Vonnegut, Mark
American. Author
b. May 11, 1947 in Chicago, Illinois
Source: *AuNews 2; ConAu 65*

Von Neumann, John
American. Mathematician
Helped develop atomic, hydrogen bombs.
b. Dec 28, 1903 in Budapest, Hungary
d. Feb 8, 1957 in Washington, DC
Source: *BioIn 3, 4, 5, 6, 7, 8, 11; CurBio 55, 57; DcAmB S6; EncAB-H; McGEWB; NatCAB 46; WebAB; WhAm 3*

Vonnoh, Robert W
American. Artist
b. Sep 17, 1858 in Hartford, Connecticut
d. Dec 28, 1933 in Lyme, Connecticut
Source: *AmBi; ApCAB; BnEnAmA; DcAmB; NatCAB 7*

VonOpel, Wilhelm
see: Opel, Wilhelm von

VonPapen, Franz
see: Papen, Franz von

VonPaulus, Friedrich
see: Paulus, Friedrich von

VonReznicek, Emil
see: Reznicek, Emil von

VonRibbentrop, Joachim
see: Ribbentrop, Joachim von

VonRundstedt, Karl Rudolph Gerd
see: Rundstedt, Karl Rudolph Gerd von

VonSacher-Masoch, Leopold
see: Sacher-Masoch, Leopold von

VonSauer, Emil
see: Sauer, Emil von

VonSchelling, Friedrich Wilhelm Joseph
see: Schelling, Friedrich Wilhelm Joseph von

VonSchmidt, Harold
American. Illustrator
b. May 19, 1893 in Alameda, California
d. Jun 3, 1982 in Westport, Connecticut
Source: *ArtsAmW; BioIn 9, 10; IlBEAAW; NewYTBS 82*

VonSchuch, Ernst
see: Schuch, Ernst von

VonSchuschnigg, Kurt
see: Schuschnigg, Kurt von

VonSeyss-Inquart, Arthur
see: Seyss-Inquart, Arthur von

VonStade, Frederica
American. Opera Singer
b. Jun 1, 1945 in Somerville, New Jersey
Source: *WhoAm 78, 80, 82*

VonSternberg, Josef
Austrian. Motion Picture Director
b. 1894 in Vienna, Austria
d. 1969
Source: *BiDFilm; DcFM; FilmgC; MovMk; OxFilm; TwYS; WhScrn 74, 77; WorEFlm*

VonSteuben, Friedrich
Prussian. American Revolutionary General
b. 1730 in Magdeburg, Prussia
d. 1794
Source: *WhAm H*

VonStroheim, Erich
German. Actor, Motion Picture Director
b. Sep 22, 1885 in Vienna, Austria
d. May 12, 1957 in Paris, France
Source: *BiDFilm; DcFM; Film 1; FilmgC; MotPP; MovMk; OxFilm; REn; TwYS; WebAB; WhAm 3; WhScrn 74, 77; WhoHol B; WorEFlm*

VonSydow, Max Carl Adolf
Swedish. Actor
b. Apr 10, 1929 in Lund, Sweden
Source: *BiDFilm; CelR 73; CurBio 67; FilmgC; IntMPA 75, 76, 77, 78, 79, 80, 81, 82; IntWW 74; MotPP; MovMk; OxFilm; WhoAm 82; WhoHol A; WhoWor 74; WorEFlm*

VonSzent-Gyorgyi, Albert
see: Szent-Gyorgyi, Albert von

Von Tilzer, Albert
American. Composer
b. Mar 29, 1878 in Indianapolis, Indiana
d. Oct 1, 1956 in Los Angeles, California
Source: *AmPS; AmSCAP 66; BiDAmM; BioIn 4, 6; CmpEPM; NotNAT B*

VonTilzer, Harry
[Harry Gumm]
American. Publisher, Songwriter
b. Jul 8, 1872 in Detroit, Michigan
d. Jan 10, 1946 in New York, New York
Source: *AmSCAP 66; CurBio 46; DcAmB S4; REnAL*

VonTirpitz, Alfred
see: Tirpitz, Alfred von

VonTrapp, Maria Augusta
see: Trapp, Maria Augusta von

Von Wangenheim, Chris
German. Fashion Photographer
b. 1942 in Breslau, Germany
d. Mar 9, 1981 in Saint Martin Island
Source: *ConAu 103; NewYTBS 81*

VonWeber, Carl Maria
see: Weber, Carl Maria von

VonWebern, Anton
see: Webern, Anton von

Von Welsbach, Carl Auer
see: Welsbach, Carl Auer von, Baron

Von Zell, Harry
American. Announcer
b. Jul 11, 1906 in Indianapolis, Indiana
d. Nov 21, 1981 in Woodland Hills, California
Source: *CurBio 44, 82; WhoHol A*

Von Zeppelin, Count Ferdinand
see: Zeppelin, Ferdinand von, Count

Voorhees, Donald
American. Conductor
b. Jul 26, 1903 in Allentown, Pennsylvania
Source: *CurBio 50; WhoAm 74*

Voroshilov, Kliment Efremovich
Russian. Soldier, Politician
b. Feb 3, 1881 in Ukraine, Russia
d. Dec 2, 1968 in Moscow, U.S.S.R.
Source: *CurBio 40, 70; WebBD 80*

Vorster, Balthazar Johannes
South African. Lawyer, Politician
b. Dec 13, 1915 in Jamestown, South Africa
Source: *CurBio 67; IntWW 74; Who 74; WhoGov 72; WhoWor 74*

Vos, Cornelis de
Flemish. Artist
b. 1584
d. 1651
Source: *NewCol 75; OxArt*

Vos, Martin de
Flemish. Artist
b. 1532
d. Dec 4, 1603
Source: *NewCol 75; OxArt*

Voskovec, George
Czech. Actor, Director, Dramatist
b. Jun 19, 1905 in Sazova, Czechoslovakia
d. Jul 1, 1981 in Pearblossom, California
Source: *BiE&WWA; BioIn 6, 11; FilmgC; MotPP; NotNAT; WhoHol A; WhoThe 77, 81*

Votipka, Thelma
American. Opera Singer
b. Dec 20, 1898 in Cleveland, Ohio
d. Oct 24, 1972
Source: *InWom; NewYTBE 72; WhAm 5*

Vouet, Simon
French. Artist
b. Jan 9, 1590
d. Jun 30, 1649
Source: *NewCol 75; OxArt*

Vought, Chance Milton
American. Aeronautical Engineer
b. Feb 26, 1890 in New York, New York
d. Jul 25, 1930 in Long Island, New York
Source: *DcAmB; WebAB; WhAm HA, 4*

Vreeland, Diana
American. Fashion Editor
b. 1903 in Paris, France
Source: *CelR 73; ForWC 70; InWom; WhoAm 74, 76, 78, 80, 82; WorFshn*

Vreeland, Thomas Reed, Jr.
American. Architect
b. 1925
Source: *AmArch 70*

Vronsky, Vitya
[Vronsky and Babin]
Musician
b. in Evpatoria, Russia
Source: *InWom; WhoAm 74*

Vronsky and Babin
see: Babin, Victor; Vronsky, Vitya

Vuillard, (Jean) Edouard
French. Artist
b. Nov 11, 1868 in Cuiseaux, France
d. Jun 21, 1940 in La Baule, France
Source: *AtlBL; McGEWB*

Vynnychenko, Volodymyr
Author
b. 1880 in Kherson, Russia
d. 1951 in Paris, France
Source: *ModSL 2; Pen EUR*

Vysotsky, Vladimir Semyonovich
Russian. Actor, Balladeer, Lyricist
b. 1938 in U.S.S.R.
d. Jul 25, 1980 in Moscow, U.S.S.R.
Source: *AnObit 1980; NewYTBE 70*

Vyvyan, Jennifer Brigit
English. Opera Singer
b. Mar 13, 1925 in Broadstairs, England
d. Apr 5, 1974 in London, England
Source: *InWom; Who 74; WhoHol B; WhoMus 72*

W

Waddell, "Rube" (George Edward)
American. Baseball Player
b. Oct 13, 1876 in Bradford, Pennsylvania
d. Apr 1, 1914 in San Antonio, Texas
Source: *BaseEn; BioIn 2, 3, 4, 5, 6, 7, 8, 9, 10; WhoProB 73*

Wade, Virginia
English. Tennis Player
Women's singles champ, Wimbledon, 1977.
b. Jul 10, 1945 in Bournemouth, England
Source: *BioIn 10, 11; CurBio 76*

Wade, Wallace
Football Coach
b. 1892
Source: *BioIn 10*

Wadsworth, James Jeremiah (Jerry)
American. Government Official
b. Jun 12, 1905 in Groveland, New York
Source: *ConAu 21R; CurBio 56; IntWW 74; WhoAm 74*

Wadsworth, James Samuel
American. General
b. Oct 30, 1807
d. May 8, 1864
Source: *AmBi; ApCAB; DcAmB; Drake; TwCBDA*

Waggoner, Lyle
American. Actor
b. Apr 13, 1935 in Kansas City, Kansas
Source: *IntMPA 75, 76, 77, 78, 79, 80, 81, 82; WhoAm 74*

Wagnalls, Adam Willis
American. Publisher
b. Sep 24, 1843 in Lithopolis, Ohio
d. Sep 3, 1924
Source: *AmAu&B; WhAm 1*

Wagner, Cosima Liszt
Hungarian. 2nd Wife of Richard Wagner
b. Dec 25, 1837 in Bellagio, Italy
d. Apr 1, 1930 in Bayreuth, Germany
Source: *InWom; NewCol 75; WebBD 80*

Wagner, (Helferich) Siegfried
German. Composer, Conductor
b. Jan 6, 1869 in Stiebschen, Switzerland
d. Aug 4, 1930 in Bayreuth, Germany
Source: *NewCol 75; NewEOp 71; WebBD 80*

Wagner, "Honus" (John Peter)
"The Flying Dutchman"
American. Baseball Player
One of first five elected to Hall of Fame, 1936; played 1897-1917.
b. Feb 24, 1874 in Carnegie, Pennsylvania
d. Dec 6, 1955 in Carnegie, Pennsylvania
Source: *BaseEn; DcAmB S5; WebAB; WhoProB 73*

Wagner, Lindsay
American. Actress
Starred in TV series the "Bionic Woman," 1976-78.
b. Jun 22, 1949 in Los Angeles, California
Source: *IntMPA 82; WhoAm 82; WhoHol A*

Wagner, Richard
[Wilhelm Richard Wagner]
German. Composer, Librettist, Poet
Opera themes derived from medieval legends; *Lohengrin; Tristan and Isolde.*
b. Mar 22, 1813 in Leipzig, Germany
d. Feb 13, 1883 in Venice, Italy
Source: *AtlBL; BbD; BiD&SB; CasWL; ClDMEL; EuAu; EvEuW; NewC; NewCol 75; OxEng; OxFr; OxGer; Pen EUR; REn; REnWD; WebBD 80*

Wagner, Robert
American. Senator
b. Jun 8, 1877 in Hesse-Nasseau, Germany
d. May 4, 1953 in New York, New York
Source: *BiDrAC; CurBio 41, 53; DcAmB S5; EncAB-H; WebAB; WhAm 3; WhAmP*

Wagner, Robert
"R J"
American. Actor
Starred in "It Takes a Thief"; "Switch"; "Hart to Hart"; husband of Natalie Wood.
b. Feb 10, 1930 in Detroit, Michigan
Source: *BkPepl; FilmgC; IntMPA 75, 76, 77, 78, 79, 80, 81, 82; MovMk; WhoAm 74, 76, 78, 80, 82; WorEFlm*

Wagner, Robert Ferdinand, Jr.
American. Lawyer, Former Mayor
b. Apr 20, 1910 in New York, New York
Source: *BiE&WWA; CurBio 54; IntWW 74; NewCol 75; WhoAm 74, 76, 78, 80, 82; WhoAmP 73; WhoE 74*

Wagner, Roger
American. Musician, Choral Director
b. Jan 16, 1914 in LePuy, France
Source: *AmSCAP 66; WhoAm 76, 78, 80, 82*

Wagner, Wieland Adolf Gottfried
German. Theatrical Director, Producer
b. Jan 5, 1917 in Bayreuth, Germany
d. Oct 16, 1966 in Munich, Germany (West)
Source: *WhAm 4*

Wagner, Wolfgang
German. Opera Designer, Producer
b. Aug 30, 1919 in Bayreuth, Germany
Source: *IntWW 74; WhoMus 72; WhoWor 74*

Wagner-Regeny, Rudolf
Romanian. Composer
b. Aug 28, 1903 in Regen, Romania
d. Sep 18, 1969 in Berlin, Germany
Source: *DcCM*

Wagoner, Porter
American. Singer
With Grand Ole Opry, 1957--; won three CMA awards with Dolly Parton.
b. Aug 12, 1927 in West Plains, Missouri
Source: *EncFCWM 69; IntMPA 75, 76, 77; WhoAm 74, 76, 78, 80, 82*

Wahloo, Per
Swedish. Journalist, Author
With wife Maj Sjowall wrote police procedure mysteries.
b. Aug 5, 1926 in Gothenburg, Sweden
d. Jun 22, 1975 in Malmo, Sweden
Source: *ConAu 57, 61; ConLC 7; EncMys; NewYTBE 71; WorAl*

Wain, Bea
American. Singer
b. Apr 30, 1917 in New York, New York
Source: *CmpEPM; IntMPA 75, 76, 77*

Wain, John Barrington
English. Author, Critic
b. Mar 14, 1925 in Stoke-on-Trent, England
Source: *Au&Wr 71; CasWL; ConAu 5R; ConLC 2, 11, 15; ConNov 72, 76; ConP 70, 75; EncWL; IntWW 74; LongCTC; ModBrL, SUP; NewC; Pen ENG; RAdv 1; REn; TwCW; Who 74; WhoTwCL; WhoWor 74; WorAu; WrDr 76*

Wainwright, James
American. Actor
b. Mar 5, 1938 in Danville, Illinois
Source: *WhoAm 76, 78, 80, 82; WhoHol A*

Wainwright, Jonathan Mayhew
American. General
b. Aug 23, 1883 in Walla Walla, Washington
d. Sep 2, 1953 in San Antonio, Texas
Source: *CurBio 42, 53; DcAmB S5; WhAm 3*

Waite, John
see: Babys, The

Waite, Morrison Remick
American. Supreme Court Justice
b. Nov 29, 1816 in Lyme, Connecticut
d. Mar 23, 1888 in Washington, DC
Source: *AmBi; ApCAB; BiAuS; DcAmB; EncAB-H; TwCBDA; WebAB; WhAm H*

Waite, Ralph
American. Actor
Played John Walton in TV series "The Waltons."
b. Jun 22, 1928 in White Plains, New York
Source: *WhoAm 82; WhoHol A*

Waitz, Grete
Norwegian. Runner
Won NY Marathon, 1978-80; holds six world records for distance.
b. Oct 1, 1953 in Oslo, Norway
Source: *CurBio 81*

Wajda, Andrzej
Polish. Film, Theatrical Director
Films include *Man of Marble* and *Man of Iron,* about the Solidarity labor movement.
b. Mar 6, 1926 in Suwalki, Poland
Source: *BiDFilm; ConAu 102; ConLC 16; CurBio 82; DcFM; FilmEn; FilmgC; IntMPA, 75, 76, 77, 78, 79, 80, 81; IntWW 74; MovMk; OxFilm; WhoSocC 78; WhoWor 74, 76, 78; WorEFlm*

Wakefield, Dan
American. Author
b. May 21, 1932 in Indianapolis, Indiana
Source: *AmAu&B; ConAu 21R; DrAF 76; IndAu 1917; WhoAm 74*

Wakefield, Ruth G
American. Creator of the Tollhouse Cookie
b. 1905?
d. 1977 in Plymouth, Massachusetts
Source: *BioIn 11*

Wakely, Jimmy
American. Actor, Singer, Songwriter
Starred in movie westerns, 1940's; had CBS radio show, 1952-57.
b. Feb 16, 1914 in Mineola, Arkansas
d. Sep 23, 1982 in Los Angeles, California
Source: *AmSCAP 66, 80; BiDAmM; CmpEPM; EncFCWM 69; IntMPA 75, 76, 77, 78, 79, 80, 81, 82; WhoHol A*

Wakeman, Frederic
American. Author
b. Dec 26, 1909 in Scranton, Kansas
Source: *AmAu&B; AmNov; CurBio 46; LongCTC; REn; REnAL; TwCA SUP; TwCW; WhoS&SW 73*

Wakeman, Rick
[Yes]
English. Musician
b. May 18, 1949 in London, England
Source: *BioIn 10; IlEncRk; WhoAm 82*

Wakoski, Diane
American. Poet
b. Aug 3, 1937 in Whittier, California
Source: *ConAu 13R; ConLC 2, 4, 7, 9, 11; ConP 70, 75; CroCAP; DrAP 75; ModAL SUP; Pen AM; RAdv 1; WhoAm 82; WrDr 76*

Waksman, Selman Abraham
American. Scientist, Physician, Engineer
b. Jul 2, 1888 in Priluka, Russia
d. Aug 16, 1973 in Hyannis, Massachusetts
Source: *BioIn 10; CurBio 46, 73; NewCol 75; WebAB*

Walbrook, Anton
German. Actor
b. Nov 19, 1900 in Vienna, Austria
d. Aug 9, 1967 in Munich, Germany (West)
Source: *BioIn 8, 9; WhScrn 74*

Walburn, Raymond
American. Actor
b. Sep 9, 1887 in Plymouth, Indiana
d. Jul 26, 1969 in New York, New York
Source: *FilmgC; MovMk; WhScrn 74, 77; WhoHol*

Walcott, "Jersey Joe"
[Arnold Raymond Cream]
American. Boxer
Heavyweight champ, 1951-52.
b. Jan 31, 1914 in Merchantville, New Jersey
Source: *CurBio 49; WhoBox 74; WorAl*

Wald, Jerry (Jerome Irving)
American. Motion Picture Producer
b. Sep 16, 1911 in New York, New York
d. Jul 13, 1962 in Beverly Hills, California
Source: *BioIn 1, 2, 3, 4, 5, 6, 9; ObitOF 79; WhAm 4*

Wald, Lillian D
American. Social Worker
b. Mar 10, 1867 in Cincinnati, Ohio
d. Sep 1, 1940 in Westport, Connecticut
Source: *AmAu&B; CurBio 40; DcAmB S2; DcNAA; EncAB-H; HerW; InWom; NotAW; OhA&B; WebAB; WhAm 1; WhNAA; WomWWA 14*

Walden, Robert
American. Actor
b. Sep 25, 1943 in New York, New York
Source: *WhoAm 82; WhoHol A*

Waldheim, Kurt
Austrian. Former UN Official
Secretary-general of UN, 1972-81.
b. Dec 21, 1918 in Woerdern, Austria
Source: *CelR 73; ConAu 89; CurBio 72; IntWW 74; NewYTBE 71; Who 82; WhoAm 74, 76, 78, 80, 82; WhoE 74; WhoGov 72; WhoUN 75; WhoWor 74*

Waldron, Charles D
American. Actor
b. Dec 23, 1875 in Waterford, New York
d. Mar 4, 1946 in Hollywood, California
Source: *Film 1; WhScrn 74, 77*

Waldock, Sir (Claud) Humphrey Meredith
British. UN Court of Justice President
b. Aug 13, 1904 in Colombo, Ceylon
d. Aug 15, 1981 in The Hague, Netherlands
Source: *IntWW 74, 75, 76, 77, 78; IntYB 78, 79; Who 74; WhoUN 75; WhoWor 74, 76, 78*

Wales, Princess of
see: Diana, Princess of Wales

Wales, Salem Howe
American. Journalist
b. Oct 4, 1825 in Wales, Massachusetts
d. 1902
Source: *ApCAB; WhAm 1*

Walesa, Lech
Polish. Solidarity Labor Movement Leader
Arrested in Aug, 1980 when martial law took effect; released Dec, 1982.
b. 1942 in Popow, Poland
Source: *BioIn 12; CurBio 81*

Waley, Arthur David
English. Author
b. Aug 19, 1889 in London, England
d. Jun 27, 1966
Source: *CasWL; ChPo, S1, S2; CnE&AP; CnMWL; ConAu 25R, 85; DcLEL; EvLB; LongCTC; NewC; OxEng; Pen ENG; REn; TwCA, SUP; TwCW*

Walgreen, Charles Rudolph
American. Founder of Drugstore Chain
Began Walgreens drugstores, 1916.
b. Oct 9, 1873 in Knox County, Illinois
d. Dec 11, 1939 in Chicago, Illinois
Source: *DcAmB S2; WebAB; WhAm 1*

Walgreen, Charles Rudolph, Jr.
American. Businessman
b. Mar 4, 1906 in Chicago, Illinois
Source: *IntWW 74; WhoAm 74; WhoF&I 74*

Walinsky, Adam
American. Lawyer
Source: *BioIn 7, 9, 10*

Walken, Christopher
American. Actor
Won Oscar, 1978, for *The Deer Hunter*.
b. Mar 31, 1943 in Astoria, New York
Source: *BioIn 11; FilmEn; IntMPA 81; NewYTBS 78; NotNAT; WhoAm 80, 82; WhoHol A; WhoThe 77*

Walker, Adam
English. Astronomer
b. 1766 in Kendal, England
d. 1821
Source: *Alli; BiDLA*

Walker, Clint
American. Actor
Star of TV series "Cheyenne," 1955-63.
b. May 30, 1927 in Hartford, Illinois
Source: *FilmgC; IntMPA 75, 76, 77, 78, 79, 80, 81, 82; MotPP; WhoHol A*

Walker, Daniel
American. Politician
b. Aug 6, 1922 in San Diego, California
Source: *IntWW 74; WhoAm 74; WhoMW 74*

Walker, Danton MacIntyre
American. Journalist
b. Jul 26, 1899 in Marietta, Georgia
d. Aug 8, 1960 in Hyannis, Massachusetts
Source: *AmAu&B; ConAu 93; REnAL; WhAm 4*

Walker, Edyth
American. Opera Singer
b. Mar 27, 1867 in Hopewell, New York
d. Feb 19, 1950 in New York, New York
Source: *NotAW*

Walker, Sir Emery
English. Type Designer, Printer
b. 1851
d. 1933
Source: *NewCol 75*

Walker, Ewell Doak, Jr.
"Doaker"
American. Football Player
b. Jan 1, 1927 in Dallas, Texas
Source: *WhoFtbl 74*

Walker, Frederick E
"Dixie"; "The Peepul's Cherce"
American. Baseball Player
Batted .306 over 18 seasons; won NL batting title, 1944.
b. Sep 24, 1910 in Villa Rica, Georgia
d. May 17, 1982 in Birmingham, Alabama
Source: *BaseEn; BioIn 1, 2, 3, 8; NewYTBS 82; WhoProB 73*

Walker, Harold Blake
American. Clergyman
b. May 7, 1904 in Denver, Colorado
Source: *ConAu 17R; WhoAm 74, 76, 78, 80, 82*

Walker, Henry Oliver
American. Artist
b. May 14, 1843 in Boston, Massachusetts
d. Jan 14, 1929 in Belmont, Massachusetts
Source: *AmBi; DcAmB; TwCBDA; WhAm 1*

Walker, Herschel
American. Football Player
Won Heisman Trophy, 1982; signed with New Jersey of USFL, Feb, 1983.
b. Mar 3, 1962 in Wrightsville, Georgia
Source: *NewYTBS 81*

Walker, Hiram
American. Liquor Manufacturer
b. Jul 4, 1816 in East Boston, Massachusetts
d. Jan 12, 1899 in Detroit, Michigan
Source: *MacDCB 78*

Walker, Jimmie
American. Actor, Comedian
b. 1948 in New York, New York
Source: *WhoHol A*

Walker, Jimmy (James John)
American. Mayor of New York City
b. Jun 19, 1881 in New York, New York
d. Nov 18, 1946 in New York, New York
Source: *AmSCAP 66; DcAmB S4; REn; REnAL; WebAB; WhAm 2*

Walker, Joseph Reddeford
American. Explorer, Naturalist
First white man to lead party across Sierra Nevadas.
b. Dec 13, 1798 in Virginia
d. Oct 27, 1876 in Ignacio Valley, California
Source: *ApCAB; DcAmB; WebAB; WhAm H*

Walker, Mary Edwards
American. First Woman Physician in US
Surgeon in Union Army; only woman to receive Medal of Honor, 1865.
b. Nov 26, 1832 in Oswego, New York
d. Feb 21, 1919
Source: *AmBi; AmWom; DcAmB; NatCAB 13; WebAMB; WhAm 1; WorAl*

Walker, Mickey
"Toy Bulldog"
American. Boxer, Artist
b. Jul 13, 1901 in Elizabeth, New Jersey
d. Apr 28, 1981 in Freehold, New Jersey
Source: *BioIn 4, 5, 6, 8, 10; WhoBox 74*

Walker, Mort
[Mortimer Walker Addison]
American. Comic Strip Artist
Created *Beetle Bailey,* 1950; *Hi and Lois,* 1954.
b. Sep 3, 1923 in El Dorado, Kansas
Source: *ConAu 49, 3NR; SmATA 8; WhoAm 74, 76, 78, 80, 82; WhoAmA 73; WhoE 74; WhoWor 74*

Walker, Nancy
[Anna Myrtle Swoyer]
American. Actress, Singer
b. May 10, 1921 in Philadelphia, Pennsylvania
Source: *BiE&WWA; BioNews 74; CurBio 65; EncMT; InWom; IntMPA 82; MotPP; MovMk; NotNAT; WhoAm 74, 76, 78, 80, 82; WhoHol A; WhoThe 77*

Walker, Ralph Thomas
American. Architect
b. Nov 28, 1889 in Waterbury, Connecticut
d. Jan 17, 1973
Source: *AmArch 70; CurBio 57, 73; WhoE 74*

Walker, Robert
American. Actor
Starred in *Strangers on a Train,* 1951.
b. Oct 13, 1914 in Salt Lake City, Utah
d. Aug 28, 1951 in Santa Monica, California
Source: *BiDFilm; FilmgC; MovMk; OxFilm; WhScrn 74, 77; WorEFlm*

Walker, Robert James
American. Legislator
b. Jul 23, 1801 in Northumberland, Pennsylvania
d. Nov 11, 1869 in Washington, DC
Source: *Alli; BiAuS; BiDSA; BiDrAC; BiDrUSE; DcAmAu; Drake; WhAm H; WhAmP*

Walker, Robert Miller
American. Educator
b. Dec 10, 1908 in Flushing, New York
Source: *WhoAm 74; WhoAmA 73*

Walker, Stanley
American. Journalist
b. Oct 21, 1898 in Lampasas, Texas
d. Nov 25, 1962 in Lampasas, Texas
Source: *AmAu&B; ConAu 93; CurBio 44, 63; REnAL; TexWr; WhAm 4*

Walker, "T-Bone" (Aaron)
"Daddy of the Blues"
American. Singer, Musician, Composer
b. May 28, 1910 in Linden, Texas
d. Mar 16, 1975 in Los Angeles, California
Source: *BiDAmM; BluesWW; EncJzS 70; IlEncJ; WhoJazz 72*

Walker, Wesley Darcel
American. Football Player
b. May 26, 1955 in San Bernardino, California
Source: *NewYTBS 78*

Walker, William
American. Adventurer
Overthrew Nicaraguan govt., president, 1856; captured, executed in Honduras.
b. May 8, 1824 in Nashville, Tennessee
d. Sep 12, 1860 in Honduras
Source: *Alli SUP; AmAu&B; AmBi; ApCAB; BiD&SB; BiDSA; DcAmAu; DcAmB; DcNAA; Drake; REnAL; WebAB; WhAm H*

Wall, Art(hur Johnathan), Jr.
American. Golfer
b. Nov 25, 1923 in Honesdale, Pennsylvania
Source: *BioIn 2, 5, 10; CurBio 59; WhoGolf*

Wallace, Alfred Russell
English. Engineer, Scientist, Physician
Proposed theory of evolution simultaneously, but independently, of Charles Darwin.
b. Jan 8, 1823 in Usk, England
d. Nov 7, 1913 in Broadstone, England
Source: *Alli, SUP; BbD; BiD&SB; BiDPara; BrAu 19; Chambr 3; DcEnA, AP; DcEnL; DcEuL; DcLEL; EvLB; NewC; OxEng; REn*

Wallace, Amy
American. Author
Wrote, with father *The People's Almanac Presents the Book of Lists,* 1977.
b. Jul 3, 1955 in Los Angeles, California
Source: *BioIn 11; ConAu 81*

Wallace, Chris
American. Broadcast Journalist
b. 1947?
Source: *BioIn 12*

Wallace, Cornelia Folsom
American. Former Wife of George Wallace
b. 1939
Source: *BioIn 10*

Wallace, DeWitt
American. Publisher
Founded *Reader's Digest,* 1922.
b. Nov 12, 1889 in Saint Paul, Minnesota
d. Mar 30, 1981 in Mount Kisco, New York
Source: *AmAu&B; BioIn 1, 2, 3, 4, 5, 6, 8; CelR 73; ConAu 103; CurBio 44, 56, 81; EncAB-H; IntWW 74, 75, 76, 77, 78; LinLib L, S; NewYTBS 81; St&PR 75; WebAB; WhAm 7; WhoAm 74, 76, 78, 80; WhoWor 74*

Wallace, Edgar
English. Author
b. Dec 1875 in Greenwich, England
d. Feb 10, 1932 in Hollywood, California
Source: *CasWL; DcLEL; EncMys; EvLB; FilmgC; LongCTC; MnBBF; ModBrL; NewC; OxEng; Pen ENG; REn; TwCA, SUP; TwCW; WhoTwCL; OxThe*

Wallace, Ed(ward Tatum)
American. Journalist
b. Aug 9, 1906
d. Oct 10, 1976 in New York, New York
Source: *BioIn 11; ConAu 69*

Wallace, George Corley
American. Politician
Governor of AL a record four times, 1963-66, 1971-79, 1983--.
b. Aug 25, 1919 in Clio, Alabama
Source: *CurBio 63; EncAB-H; IntWW 74; WebAB; WhoAm 74, 76, 78, 80, 82; WhoAmP 73; WhoGov 72; WhoS&SW 73; WhoWor 74*

Wallace, Henry Agard
American. Political Leader
b. Oct 7, 1888 in Adair County, Iowa
d. Nov 18, 1965 in Danbury, Connecticut
Source: *AmAu&B; BiDrAC; BiDrUSE; ConAu 89; CurBio 40, 47, 66; EncAB-H; REnAL; WebAB; WhAm 4; WhAmP; WhNAA*

Wallace, Horace Binney
American. Author, Critic
b. Feb 26, 1817
d. Dec 16, 1852 in Paris, France
Source: *Alli; AmAu&B; AmBi; ApCAB; BiD&SB; CyAl 2; DcAmAu; DcAmB; DcNAA; Drake; OxAmL; WhAm H*

Wallace, Irving
[Irving Wallechinsky]
American. Author
Wrote *The Chapman Report; The Word; The People's Almanac; The Book of Lists.*
b. Mar 19, 1916 in Chicago, Illinois
Source: *AmAu&B; Au&Wr 71; AuNews 1; BioNews 74; BkPepl; CelR 73; ConAu 1R, 1NR; ConLC 7, 13; IntMPA 75, 76, 77, 78, 79, 80, 81, 82; St&PR 75; TwCW; Who 74; WhoAm 74, 76, 78, 80, 82; WrDr 76*

Wallace, Lewis
American. Author
b. Apr 10, 1827 in Brookville, Indiana
d. Feb 15, 1905 in Crawfordsville, Indiana
Source: *Alli SUP; AmAu; AmAu&B; AmBi; BbD; BiD&SB; CarSB; CasWL; Chambr 3; ChPo; CnDAL; CyWA; DcAmAu; DcAmB; DcBiA; DcEnA AP; DcLEL; DcNAA; EncAB-H; EvLB; IndAu 1816; JBA 34; OxAmL; Pen AM; RAdv 1; REn; REnAL; WebAB; WhAm 1*

Wallace, Lila Bell Acheson
American. Publisher, Editor
b. Dec 25, 1889 in Virden, MB
Source: *AmAu&B; CanWW 70; CelR 73; CurBio 56; ForWC 70; InWom; WebAB; WhoAm 74; WhoE 74; WhoWor 74*

Wallace, Lurleen Burns
[Mrs. George Wallace]
American. Governor
Succeeded husband to become first woman governor of AL, 1967.
b. Sep 19, 1926 in Tuscaloosa, Alabama
d. May 7, 1968 in Montgomery, Alabama
Source: *CurBio 67, 68; InWom; WhAm 5*

Wallace, Mike (Myron Leon)
American. Broadcast Journalist
With CBS-TV, 1951--; co-host, "60 Minutes."
b. May 9, 1918 in Brookline, Massachusetts
Source: *BkPepl; ConAu 65; CurBio 57; IntMPA 75, 76, 77, 78, 79, 80, 81, 82; WhoAm 74, 76, 78, 80, 82; WhoE 74; WhoWorJ 72*

Wallach, Eli
American. Actor
b. Dec 7, 1915 in New York, New York
Source: *BiE&WWA; CelR 73; FilmgC; IntMPA 77, 78, 79, 80, 81, 82; MovMk; NotNAT; OxFilm; WhoAm 74; WhoThe 77; WhoWor 74; WhoWorJ 72; WorEFlm*

Wallack, James William
American. Actor, Manager
b. Aug 24, 1795 in London, England
d. Dec 25, 1864 in New York, New York
Source: *AmBi; ApCAB; DcAmB; Drake; FamA&A; OxThe; TwCBDA; WebAB; WhAm H*

Wallant, Edward Lewis
American. Author
b. Oct 19, 1926 in New Haven, Connecticut
d. Dec 5, 1962 in Norwalk, Connecticut
Source: *AmAu&B; ConAu 1R; ConLC 5; ConNov 76; EncWL; ModAL; OxAmL; Pen AM; WebE&AL; WhoTwCL; WorAu*

Wallechinsky, David
American. Author
b. Feb 5, 1948 in Los Angeles, California
Source: *ConAu 61*

Wallenberg, Marcus
Swedish. Banker
Business empire controlled one-third of all Swedish industry.
b. Oct 5, 1899 in Stockholm, Sweden
d. Sep 13, 1982 in Stockholm, Sweden
Source: *IntWW 74, 75, 76, 77, 78, 79, 80, 81; NewYTBS 77, 82; WhoWor 74, 76, 78*

Wallenberg, Raoul
Swedish. Diplomat, Underground Leader
b. 1912
d. 1947?
Source: *BioIn 1, 3, 4*

Wallenda, Karl
American. Circus Performer
Patriarch of famed high-wire troupe; killed in 100-foot fall.
b. 1905
d. Mar 22, 1978 in San Juan, Puerto Rico
Source: *BioIn 9, 10, 11*

Wallenstein, Alfred
American. Musician, Conductor
Director, LA Philharmonic, 1943-56.
b. Oct 7, 1898 in Chicago, Illinois
d. Feb 8, 1983 in New York, New York
Source: *Baker 78; BiDAmM; CurBio 40, 52, 83; WhoAm 74, 78, 78, 80, 82*

Waller, Edmund
English. Poet
b. Mar 3, 1606 in Coleshill, England
d. Oct 21, 1687 in Beaconsfield, England
Source: *Alli; AtlBL; BbD; BiD&SB; BrAu; CasWL; Chambr 1; ChPo, S1; CnE&AP; CroE&S; DcEnA; DcEnL; DcLEL; EvLB; MouLC 1; NewC; OxEng; Pen ENG; REn; WebE&AL*

Waller, "Fats" (Thomas Wright)
American. Jazz Musician, Composer
Began recording, 1934; composed "Ain't Misbehavin'"; "Honeysuckle Rose."
b. May 21, 1904 in New York, New York
d. Dec 15, 1943 in Kansas City, Missouri
Source: *AmSCAP 66; CurBio 42, 44; DcAmB S3; FilmgC; WhAm 4; WhScrn 74, 77; WhoHol B; WhoJazz 72; WorAl*

Waller, Fred(erick)
American. Inventor
Invented Cinerama, 1952; invented, patented first water ski.
b. Mar 10, 1886 in Brooklyn, New York
d. May 18, 1954 in Huntington, New York
Source: *CurBio 53, 54; DcFM; FilmgC*

Waller, Gordon
see: Peter and Gordon

Waller, Sir William
English. General, Member of Parliament
b. 1597
d. Sep 19, 1668
Source: *Alli; DcEnL*

Wallerstein, Lothar
Czech. Theatrical Director
b. Nov 6, 1882 in Prague, Czechoslovakia
d. Nov 13, 1949 in New Orleans, Louisiana
Source: *NewEOp 71*

Walley, Deborah
American. Actress
b. in Bridgeport, Connecticut
Source: *ForWC 70; MotPP; WhoHol A*

Wallington, Jimmy
American. Actor, Radio Announcer
b. Sep 15, 1907 in Rochester, New York
d. Dec 22, 1972 in Fairfax, Virginia
Source: *NewYTBE 72; WhScrn 77; WhoHol B*

Wallis, Sir Barnes Neville
English. Engineer
b. Sep 26, 1887 in Ripley, England
d. Oct 30, 1979 in England
Source: *BioIn 4, 9; IntWW 74, 75, 76, 77, 78; NewYTBS 79; WhWW-II; Who 74*

Wallis, Hal Brent
American. Motion Picture Producer
b. Sep 14, 1899 in Chicago, Illinois
Source: *BiDFilm; FilmgC; IntMPA 75, 76, 77, 78, 79, 80, 81, 82; OxFilm; WebAB; WhoAm 74, 76, 78, 80, 82; WhoWor 74; WorEFlm*

Wallis, Samuel
English. Navigator
Around the world voyage, 1766-68; discovered Easter Island, Tahiti.
b. Apr 23, 1728 in Fentonwoon, England
d. Jan 21, 1795 in London, England
Source: *ApCAB; DcNAB; OxShips; WebBD 80*

Wallis, Shani
English. Actress
b. Apr 16, 1933 in London, England
Source: *FilmgC; WhoHol A; WhoThe 77*

Wallmann, Margherita
Austrian. Motion Picture Producer
b. Jun 22, 1904 in Vienna, Austria
Source: *WhoMus 72*

Wallop, Malcom
American. Senator
b. Feb 27, 1933 in New York, New York
Source: *WhoAm 78; WhoAmP 73*

Wallraff, Gunter
German. Journalist, Author
b. 1942 in Cologne, Germany
Source: *BioIn 10, 11, 12*

Walmsley, Jon
American. Actor
b. 1956?
Source: *BioIn 11, 12; WhoHol A*

Waln, Nora
American. Journalist
b. Jun 4, 1895 in Grampian, Pennsylvania
d. Sep 27, 1964 in Madrid, Spain
Source: *AmAu&B; CurBio 40, 64; InWom; LongCTC; REnAL; TwCA, SUP; WhAm 4*

Walpole, Horace
[4th Earl of Orford]
English. Author
His work *The Castle of Otranto,* 1765, began fashion for Gothic novels.
b. Sep 24, 1717 in London, England
d. Mar 2, 1797 in London, England
Source: *Alli; AtlBL; BbD; BiD&SB; BrAu; CasWL; Chambr 2; ChPo, S2; CrtT 2; CyWA; DcBiA; DcEnA; DcEnL; DcEuL; DcLEL; EvLB; MouLC 2; NewC; OxEng; Pen ENG; RAdv 1; REn; WebE&AL; WorAl*

Walpole, Sir Hugh Seymour
English. Actor, Author
b. Mar 13, 1884 in Auckland, New Zealand
d. Jun 1, 1941 in Brackenburg, England
Source: *CasWL; Chambr 3; ChPo S2; CyWA; DcBiA; DcLEL; EvLB; FilmgC; LongCTC; MnBBF; ModBrL; NewC; OxEng; Pen ENG; REn; TwCA, SUP; TwCW; WebE&AL; WhScrn 74, 77; WhoChL; WhoLA; WhoTwCL; WorEFlm*

Walpole, Robert
[1st Earl of Orford]
English. Statesman
b. Aug 26, 1676 in Houghton, England
d. Mar 18, 1745 in Houghton, England
Source: *Alli; NewC; REn*

Walsh, Bill (William)
American. Football Coach
Coach, San Francisco 49ers, 1979--.
b. Nov 30, 1931 in Los Angeles, California
Source: *FootReg; WhoAm 82*

Walsh, James Edward
American. Bishop, Missionary
b. Apr 30, 1891? in Cumberland, Maryland
d. Jul 29, 1981 in Ossining, New York
Source: *BioIn 1, 5, 6, 9, 11; CathA 1930; WhoAm 74, 76, 78, 80*

Walsh, Joe (Joseph Fidler)
[The Eagles; The James Gang]
American. Musician, Singer
b. Nov 20, 1947 in Cleveland, Ohio
Source: *BioIn 11; RkOn; WhoAm 80, 82*

Walsh, Michael Patrick
American. Educator
President, Boston College, 1958-68; Fordham U, 1969-72.
b. Feb 28, 1912 in Boston, Massachusetts
d. Apr 23, 1982 in Boston, Massachusetts
Source: *AmCath 80; AmM&WS 76P, 79P; LEduc 74; NewYTBS 82; WhoE 74*

Walsh, Raoul
American. Actor, Motion Picture Director
b. Mar 11, 1887 in New York, New York
d. Dec 31, 1980 in Los Angeles, California
Source: *AnObit 1980; CmMov; DcFM; Film 1; IntMPA 75, 77; MovMk; OxFilm; TwYS; WorEFlm*

Walsh, Stella
[Stanislawa Walasiewicz]
Polish. Track Athlete
Won gold medal in 100 meter run, 1932 Olympics.
b. Apr 3, 1911 in Wierzchownia, Poland
d. Dec 4, 1980 in Cleveland, Ohio
Source: *AnObit 1980; BioIn 3, 5, 9, 11; GoodHS; InWom; WhoTr&F 73; WorAl*

Walsh, Thomas James
American. Lawyer, Senator
b. Jun 12, 1859 in Two Rivers, Wisconsin
d. Mar 2, 1933 in Wilson, North Carolina
Source: *AmBi; ApCAB X; BiDrAC; NatCAB 15, 24; WebAB; WhAm 1; WhAmP*

Walston, Ray
American. Actor, Motion Picture Director
Starred "My Favorite Martian," 1963-66; films *Damn Yankees; Paint Your Wagon.*
b. Nov 22, 1918 in New Orleans, Louisiana
Source: *BiE&WWA; FilmgC; IntMPA 75, 76, 77, 78, 79, 80, 81, 82; MotPP; MovMk; NotNAT; WhoAm 74, 76, 78, 80, 82; WhoHol A; WhoThe 77*

Waltari, Mika
Finnish. Critic, Author, Editor
b. Sep 19, 1908 in Helsinki, Finland
d. Aug 26, 1979 in Helsinki, Finland
Source: *Au&Wr 71; CasWL; ConAu 9R, 89; CurBio 50; EncWL; IntWW 74; Pen EUR; REn; TwCA SUP; Who 74; WhoWor 74*

Walter, Bruno
[Bruno Schlesinger]
American. Conductor
b. Sep 15, 1876 in Berlin, Germany
d. Feb 17, 1962 in Beverly Hills, California
Source: *CurBio 42, 62; REn; WebAB; WhAm 4*

Walter, Cyril
American. Musician, Composer
b. Sep 16, 1915 in Minneapolis, Minnesota
d. Aug 18, 1968 in New York, New York
Source: *AmSCAP 66; BiDAmM*

Walter, James Willis
American. Businessman
b. 1922 in Lewes, Delaware
Source: *WhoAm 74, 76, 78, 80, 82; WhoF&I 74; WhoWor 74*

Walter, Jessica
American. Actress
Won Emmy for "Amy Prentiss," 1974-75; films *Play Misty for Me,* 1971.
b. Jan 31, 1944 in Brooklyn, New York
Source: *FilmgC; IntMPA 75, 76, 77, 78, 79, 80, 81, 82; WhoAm 82; WhoHol A*

Walter, John
English. Newspaper Publisher
b. 1739
d. Nov 16, 1812
Source: *Alli; DcEnL; DcEuL; REn*

Walter, Marie Therese
French. Model, Mistress of Picasso
b. 1909?
d. 1977 in Antibes, France
Source: *BioIn 10*

Walters, Barbara
American. Broadcast Journalist
Co-host "The Today Show" 1963-76; "ABC World News Tonight," 1976--.
b. Sep 25, 1931 in Boston, Massachusetts
Source: *AuNews 2; BioNews 74; BkPepl; ConAu 65; CurBio 71; ForWC 70; IntMPA 77, 78, 79, 80, 81, 82; NewYTBE 72; WhoAm 74, 76, 78, 80, 82; WhoAmW 77*

Walters, "Bucky" (William Henry)
American. Baseball Player
b. Apr 19, 1910 in Philadelphia, Pennsylvania
Source: *BaseEn; WhoProB 73*

Walters, Charles
American. Film Director
Directed musicals *Easter Parade; The Unsinkable Molly Brown.*
b. Nov 17, 1903? in Pasadena, California
d. Aug 13, 1982 in Malibu, California
Source: *BiDFilm; CmMov; DcFM; EncMT; FilmgC; IntMPA 75, 76, 77, 78, 79, 80, 81, 82; MovMk; WhoAm 74, 76, 78, 80, 82; WorEFlm*

Walters, Henry
American. Businessman
b. Sep 26, 1848 in Baltimore, Maryland
d. Nov 30, 1931 in Baltimore, Maryland
Source: *DcAmB; WhAm 1*

Walters, Laurie
American. Actress
Source: *NF*

Walters, Lou
American. Nightclub Owner
b. 1897
d. 1977 in Miami, Florida
Source: *BioIn 11; NewYTBS 77*

Walthall, Henry B
American. Actor
b. Mar 16, 1878 in Shelby City, Alabama
d. Jun 17, 1936 in Monrovia, California
Source: *DcAmB S2; Film 1; FilmgC; MotPP; MovMk; OxFilm; TwYS; Vers B; WhScrn 74, 77; WhoHol B*

Walton, Bill
American. Basketball Player
Center, 1974--; NBA MVP, 1978.
b. Nov 5, 1952 in LaMesa, California
Source: *BioNews 74; NewYTBS 74; WhoAm 82; WhoBbl 73*

Walton, George
American. Jurist
b. 1741 in Farmville, Virginia
d. Feb 2, 1840 in College Hill, Georgia
Source: *AmBi; ApCAB; BiAuS; BiDSA; DcAmB; Drake; WhAm H*

Walton, Izaak
English. Biographer, Author
Wrote *Compleat Angler,* 1676; biographies of John Donne and George Herbert.
b. Aug 9, 1593 in Staffordshire, England
d. Dec 15, 1683 in Winchester, England
Source: *Alli; AtlBL; BbD; BiD&SB; BrAu; CarSB; Chambr 1; CroE&S; CyWA; DcEnA; DcEnL; DcEuL; DcLEL; EvLB; NewC; OxEng; Pen ENG; REn; WebE&AL*

Walton, Sir William Turner
English. Composer
b. Mar 29, 1902 in Oldham, England
Source: *CurBio 40; DcCM; DcFM; FilmgC; OxFilm; REn; Who 74; WhoAm 74, 76, 78, 80, 82; WhoMus 72; WhoWor 74*

Walton, William Turner
American. Artist
b. Aug 29, 1909 in Jacksonville, Florida
Source: *NewCol 75; WebBD 80; WhoAm 74; WhoGov 72*

Waltrip, Darrell (Lee)
American. Auto Racer
b. Feb 5, 1947 in Owensboro, Kentucky
Source: *BioIn 11; WhoAm 82*

Walworth, Sir William
English. Lord Mayor of London
d. 1385
Source: *WebBD 80*

Wambaugh, Joseph Aloysius
American. Author, Former Police Officer
Wrote *The New Centurions; The Blue Knight; The Choirboys;* with LA police 1960-74.
b. Jan 22, 1937 in East Pittsburgh, Pennsylvania
Source: *AuNews 1; ConAu 33R; ConLC 3, 18; CurBio 80; WhoAm 74, 76, 78, 80, 82; WrDr 76*

Wanamaker, John
American. Merchant
b. Jul 11, 1838 in Philadelphia, Pennsylvania
d. Dec 12, 1922 in Philadelphia, Pennsylvania
Source: *AmBi; ApCAB; BiDrUSE; ChPo S2; DcAmB; DcNAA; EncAB-H; REnAL; TwCBDA; WebAB; WhAm 1*

Wanamaker, John Rodman
American. Retail Executive
b. Jul 15, 1918 in Jenkintown, Pennsylvania
Source: *St&PR 75; WhoAm 74*

Wanamaker, Rodman
American. Merchant
b. 1863 in Philadelphia, Pennsylvania
d. Mar 9, 1928
Source: *WebBD 80; WhAm 1*

Wanamaker, Sam
American. Actor, Motion Picture Director
b. Jun 14, 1919 in Chicago, Illinois
Source: *BiE&WWA; FilmgC; IntMPA 75, 76, 77, 78, 79, 80, 81, 82; IntWW 74; MotPP; MovMk; NotNAT; Who 74; WhoHol A; WhoThe 77; WhoWor 74*

Waner, Paul Glee
"Big Poison"
American. Baseball Player
b. Apr 16, 1903 in Harrah, Oklahoma
d. Aug 29, 1965 in Sarasota, Florida
Source: *BaseEn; WhoProB 73*

Wang Shih-chieh
Chinese. Diplomat
b. Mar 10, 1891 in Hupeh, China
d. Apr 1981? in Taipei, Taiwan
Source: *BioIn 1; CurBio 45, 81*

Wang Hung-Wen
Chinese. Communist Leader
b. 1937 in China
Source: *IntWW 74; NewYTBE 73*

Wanger, Walter
American. Motion Picture Producer
b. Jul 11, 1894 in San Francisco, California
d. Nov 18, 1968 in New York, New York
Source: *BiDFilm; CmMov; CurBio 47, 69; DcFM; FilmgC; OxFilm; WorEFlm*

Wank, Roland A
American. Architect
b. Oct 2, 1898 in Budapest, Hungary
d. Apr 22, 1970 in New Rochelle, New York
Source: *CurBio 43, 70; NewYTBE 70; WhAm 5*

Wankel, Felix
German. Research Engineer
b. Aug 13, 1902 in Germany
Source: *IntWW 74; NewYTBE 72*

Warburg, Felix Moritz
American. Philanthropist, Banker
b. Jan 14, 1871 in Hamburg, Germany
d. Oct 20, 1937 in New York, New York
Source: *AmBi; DcAmB S2; WebBD 80; WhAm 1*

Warburg, Frederick Marcus
American. Investment Banker
b. Oct 14, 1897 in New York, New York
d. Jul 10, 1973
Source: *NewYTBE 73; WebBD 80; WhAm 6; WhoWorJ 72*

Warburg, James Paul
American. Businessman, Philanthropist
b. Aug 18, 1896 in Hamburg, Germany
d. Jun 3, 1969 in Greenwich, Connecticut
Source: *AmAu&B; AmSCAP 66; ConAu 21R, 25R; ConAu P-2; CurBio 48, 69; REnAL; TwCA SUP; WhAm 5*

Ward, (Aaron) Montgomery
American. Merchant
Founded Montgomery Ward and Co, the first mail-order house, 1872.
b. Feb 17, 1843 in Chatham, New Jersey
d. Dec 7, 1913 in Highland Park, Illinois
Source: *DcAmB; WebAB; WebBD 80; WhAm HA*

Ward, Artemus, pseud.
[Charles Farrar Browne]
American. Journalist, Humorist
b. Apr 26, 1834 in Waterford, Maine
d. Mar 6, 1867 in Southampton, England
Source: *Alli, SUP; AmAu; AmAu&B; AmBi; ApCAB; BbD; BiD&SB; CasWL; Chambr 3; ChPo; CnDAL; DcAmAu; DcAmB; DcEnA AP; DcEnL; DcLEL; DcNAA; Drake; EvLB; OhA&B; OxAmL; OxEng; Pen AM; REn; REnAL; TwCBDA; WebAB; WebE&AL; WhAm H*

Ward, Arthur Sarsfield
see: Rohmer, Sax, pseud.

Ward, Barbara Mary
English. Author, Economist
Wrote on political, economic affairs *India and the West,* 1961.
b. May 23, 1914 in York, England
d. May 31, 1981 in Lodsworth, England
Source: *AmM&WS 73S; BioIn 1, 2, 3, 4, 5; CathA 1930; ConAu 45, 103; CurBio 50, 77, 81; InWom; IntAu&W 77; IntWW 74, 75, 76, 77, 78; LinLib L, S; TwCA SUP; Who 74; WhoAm 74, 76, 78; WhoAmW 64, 66, 68, 70, 72, 75; WhoWor 74, 76, 78; WrDr 80*

Ward, Burt
American. Actor
Played Robin on TV series "Batman," 1966-68.
b. Jul 6, 1946 in Los Angeles, California
Source: *IntMPA 79, 80, 81, 82; WhoHol A*

Ward, Sir Deighton Harcourt Lisle
Governor General of Barbados
b. May 16, 1909 in Barbados
Source: *WhoWor 78, 80*

Ward, Douglas Turner
American. Actor, Dramatist
b. May 5, 1930 in Burnside, Louisiana
Source: *ConAu 81; ConDr 73; LivgBAA; NotNAT; PlP&P A; WhoAm 74; WhoBlA 75; WhoThe 77; WrDr 76*

Ward, Fannie
American. Actress
b. Nov 23, 1872 in Saint Louis, Missouri
d. Jan 27, 1952 in New York, New York
Source: *Film 1; InWom; MotPP; OxThe; TwYS; WhAm 3; WhScrn 74, 77; WhoHol B*

Ward, J(ohn) Q(uincy) A(dams)
American. Sculptor
b. Jun 29, 1830
d. 1910
Source: *Drake*

Ward, Lester Frank
American. Sociologist
b. Jun 18, 1841 in Joliet, Illinois
d. Apr 18, 1913 in Washington, DC
Source: *Alli SUP; AmAu; AmBi; ApCAB; DcAmAu; DcAmB; DcNAA; EncAB-H; OxAmL; REnAL; TwCBDA; WebAB; WhAm HA, 1*

Ward, Mary Jane
American. Author
b. Aug 27, 1905 in Fairmount, Indiana
Source: *AmAu&B; AmNov; CurBio 46; InWom; LongCTC; REnAL; TwCA SUP; WhNAA*

Ward, Paul W
American. Journalist
b. Oct 9, 1905 in Lorain, Ohio
d. Nov 24, 1976 in Chevy Chase, Maryland
Source: *ConAu 69; WhAm 7; WhoAm 74*

Ward, Phillip R
[The Hostages,]
American. Former Hostage in Iran
b. Mar 22, 1940
Source: *NewYTBS 81; USBiR 74*

Ward, Robert Eugene
American. Composer
b. Sep 13, 1917 in Cleveland, Ohio
Source: *DcCM; WhoAm 74; WhoS&SW 73; WhoWor 74*

Ward, Rodger
American. Auto Racer
Source: *BioIn 7, 11*

Ward, Simon
English. Actor
Portrayed Winston Churchill in film *Young Winston,* 1971.
b. Oct 19, 1941 in London, England
Source: *FilmgC; IntMPA 81; WhoThe 77*

Ward, William
see: Black Sabbath

Warden, Jack
American. Actor
b. Sep 18, 1920 in Newark, New Jersey
Source: *BiE&WWA; FilmgC; IntMPA 75, 76, 77, 78, 79, 80, 81, 82; MotPP; MovMk; NotNAT; WhoHol A*

Warfield, David
American. Actor
b. Nov 28, 1866
d. Jun 27, 1951 in New York, New York
Source: *DcAmB S5; FamA&A; OxAmL; OxThe; PlP&P; REn; REnAL; WhAm 3; WhoStg 1906, 1908*

Warfield, Paul Dryden
American. Football Player
Receiver, Cleveland Browns, 1964-69, 1974-77; Miami Dolphins, 1970-74.
b. Nov 28, 1942 in Warren, Ohio
Source: *NewYTBE 72; WhoAm 74; WhoBlA 75; WhoFtbl 74*

Warfield, William Caesar
American. Singer
b. Jan 22, 1920 in West Helena, Arkansas
Source: *BiE&WWA; NotNAT; WhoAm 74; WhoBlA 75; WhoHol A; WhoWor 74*

Warham, William
English. Prelate
b. 1450 in England
d. Aug 22, 1532 in England
Source: *NewCol 75; WebBD 80*

Warhol, Andy
[Andrew Warhola]
American. Artist, Author, Film Maker
Pop artist known for paintings of soup cans and celebrities; publishes *Interview* magazine, 1969--.
b. Aug 6, 1927 in McKeesport, Pennsylvania
Source: *AmAu&B; BiDFilm; BkPepl; ConAu 89; CurBio 68; DcCAA 71; EncAB-H; FilmgC; IntWW 74; OxFilm; WebAB; WhoAm 74; WhoAmA 73; WhoHol A; WhoWor 74; WorEFlm*

Waring, Fred M
American. Band Leader
Music conductor of The Pennsylvanians, 1923--.
b. Jun 9, 1900 in Tyrone, Pennsylvania
Source: *AmSCAP 66; BioNews 74; CurBio 40; IntMPA 75, 76, 77, 78, 79, 80, 81, 82; WhoAm 74; WhoHol A*

Warmerdam, Cornelius
American. Track Athlete
b. Jun 22, 1915 in Long Beach, California
Source: *BioNews 74; WhoTr&F 73*

Warneke, Lon(nie)
"The Arkansas Humming Bird"
American. Baseball Player, Umpire
b. Mar 28, 1909 in Mount Ida, Arkansas
d. Jun 23, 1976 in Hot Springs, Arkansas
Source: *BaseEn; WhoProB 73*

Warner, Albert
[Warner Brothers]
American. Motion Picture Executive
Co-founded Warner Brothers Pictures, Inc, 1923.
b. Jul 23, 1884 in Poland
d. Nov 26, 1967 in Miami Beach, Florida
Source: *BioIn 8, 10; NatCAB 54; WebAB; WhAm 4A; WorAl*

Warner, Charles Dudley
American. Editor, Author
b. Sep 12, 1829 in Plainfield, Massachusetts
d. Oct 20, 1900 in Hartford, Connecticut
Source: *Alli SUP; AmAu; AmAu&B; AmBi; ApCAB; BbD; BiD&SB; CasWL; Chambr 3; ChPo, S2; CnDAL; CyAl 2; DcAmAu; DcAmB; DcBiA; DcEnA AP; DcEnL; DcLEL; DcNAA; OxAmL; OxCan; Pen AM; REn; REnAL; TwCBDA; WebAB; WhAm 1*

Warner, David
English. Actor
Starred in *Morgan,* 1965; *Time After Time,* 1979; *Time Bandits,* 1980.
b. Jul 29, 1941 in Manchester, England
Source: *FilmgC; IntMPA 82; NewYTBE 71; OxFilm; WhoHol A; WhoThe 77*

Warner, Denis Ashton
Australian. Author, Journalist
b. Dec 12, 1917 in Hobart, Australia
Source: *ConAu 5R, 3NR; WhoWor 74*

Warner, Emily Howell
American. Pilot
First woman pilot for major US passenger airline (Frontier).
b. 1940 in Denver, Colorado
Source: *NF*

Warner, Harry Morris
[Warner Brothers]
American. Motion Picture Executive
Co-founder, president, Warner Brothers Pictures, Inc, 1923-56.
b. Dec 12, 1881 in Kraznashiltz, Poland
d. Jul 25, 1958 in Hollywood, California
Source: *CurBio 45, 58; DcFM; WebAB; WhAm 3*

Warner, Jack, Jr.
American. Motion Picture Executive
Organized Jack Warner Productions Inc, 1949.
b. Mar 27, 1916 in San Francisco, California
Source: *IntMPA 75, 76, 77, 78, 79, 80, 81, 82; WhoAm 82*

Warner, Jack Leonard
[Warner Brothers]
American. Motion Picture Executive
Introduced first film with soundtrack, 1926, with spoken sound, 1927.
b. Aug 2, 1892 in London, ON
d. Sep 9, 1978 in Los Angeles, California
Source: *CelR 73; CurBio 45; DcFM; FilmgC; IntMPA 75, 77; IntWW 74; WebAB; Who 74; WhoAm 74, 76, 78, 80; WhoHol A; WorAl*

Warner, John William
American. Senator
Senator from VA, 1979--; ex-husband of Elizabeth Taylor, 1976-82.
b. Feb 18, 1927 in Washington, DC
Source: *CngDr 74; WhoAm 74, 76, 78, 80, 82; WhoAmP 73; WorAl*

Warner, "Pop" (Glenn Scobey)
American. Football Coach
b. Apr 5, 1871 in Springville, New York
d. Sep 7, 1954 in Palo Alto, California
Source: *DcAmB S5; WebAB; WhAm 3; WhoFtbl 74*

Warner, Rawleigh, Jr.
American. Oil Executive
b. Feb 13, 1921 in Chicago, Illinois
Source: *WhoAm 78, 80, 82*

Warner, Roger Sherman, Jr.
American. Aircraft Engineer
b. 1908
d. Aug 3, 1976 in Washington, DC
Source: *BioIn 6*

Warner, Sam(uel Louis)
[Warner Brothers]
American. Motion Picture Executive
Formed Vitaphone Corp., 1927.
b. Aug 10, 1887 in Baltimore, Maryland
d. Oct 5, 1927 in Los Angeles, California
Source: *BioIn 1; NatCAB 21; WebAB*

Warner, Sylvia Townsend
English. Author
b. Dec 6, 1893 in Harrow, England
d. May 1, 1978 in Dorsetshire, England
Source: *ConAu 61, 77; ConLC 7; Who 74; WhoAmW 74; WhoWor 74*

Warnke, Paul Culliton
American. Lawyer, Government Official
Director, ACDA, 1977-78; chief US negotiator for SALT, 1977-78.
b. Jan 31, 1920 in Webster, Massachusetts
Source: *NewYTBE 72; WhoAm 74, 76, 78, 80, 82*

Warren, Austin
American. Critic, Author
b. Jul 4, 1899 in Waltham, Massachusetts
Source: *AmAu&B; ConAu 17R; REnAL; TwCA SUP; WhoAm 74*

Warren, Charles
American. Government Official
b. Apr 26, 1927 in Kansas City, Missouri
Source: *WhoAm 78; WhoAmP 73*

Warren, Earl
American. Supreme Court Justice
Chief Justice, 1953-69; headed investigation into assassination of John Kennedy.
b. Mar 19, 1891 in Los Angeles, California
d. Jul 9, 1974 in Washington, DC
Source: *BioNews 74; CelR 73; CngDr 74; ConAu 49; CurBio 44, 54, 74; EncAB-H; NewYTBS 74; REn; WebAB; WhAm 6; Who 74; WhoAm 74; WhoAmP 73; WhoGov 72; WhoWor 74*

Warren, Gerald Lee
American. Former Presidential Aide
b. Aug 17, 1930 in Hastings, Nebraska
Source: *BioIn 10, 11; WhoAm 78; WhoGov 72; WhoS&SW 73*

Warren, Harry
[Salvatore Guaragna]
American. Songwriter
b. Dec 24, 1893 in New York, New York
d. Sep 22, 1981 in Los Angeles, California
Source: *AmPS; AmSCAP 66; Baker 78; BiDAmM; BiE&WWA; BioIn 2, 4, 6, 9, 10, 11; CmpEPM; CurBio 43, 81; IntMPA 75, 76, 77, 78, 79, 80, 81, 82; NotNAT; OxFilm; WhoAm 74, 76*

Warren, Joseph
American. Physician, Soldier
b. Jun 11, 1741 in Roxbury, Massachusetts
d. Jun 17, 1775 in Charlestown, Massachusetts
Source: *Alli; AmBi; ApCAB; CyAL 1; DcAmB; DcNAA; Drake; TwCBDA; WebAB; WhAm H; WhoHol A*

Warren, Lavinia
American. Wife of Tom Thumb
b. 1841
d. 1919
Source: *InWom; NotAW*

Warren, Leonard
American. Opera Singer
b. Apr 21, 1911 in New York, New York
d. Mar 4, 1960 in New York, New York
Source: *CurBio 53, 60; WhAm 3; WhScrn 77*

Warren, Lesley Ann
American. Actress, Dancer
Starred in TV musical "Cinderella."
b. Aug 16, 1946 in New York, New York
Source: *WhoHol A*

Warren, Mercy Otis
American. Dramatist, Historian
b. Sep 14, 1728 in Barnstable, Massachusetts
d. Oct 19, 1814
Source: *Alli; AmAu; AmAu&B; BiD&SB; CnDAL; DcAmAu; DcNAA; OxAmL; REn; REnAL*

Warren, Michael
American. Actor
Plays Bobby Hill on TV series "Hill Street Blues."
b. 1946?
Source: *NF*

Warren, Robert Penn
American. Author, Poet, Critic
b. Apr 24, 1905 in Guthrie, Kentucky
Source: *AmAu&B; AmNov; AmWr; Au&Wr 71; AuNews 1; CasWL; CnDAL; CnE&AP; CnMD; ConAmA; ConAu 13R; ConLC 1, 4, 6, 8, 10, 13, 18; ConNov 72, 76; ConP 70, 75; CurBio 70; CyWA; DcLEL; DrAF 76; DrAP 75; EncWL; EvLB; FilmgC; IntWW 74; LongCTC; ModAL, SUP; ModWD; OxAmL; Pen AM; RAdv 1; RComWL; REn; REnAL; SixAP; TwCA, SUP; TwCW; WebAB; WebE&AL; WhNAA; Who 74; WhoAm 74, 76, 78, 80, 82; WhoTwCL; WhoWor 74; WrDr 76*

Warren, Rusty
Comedian
Source: *NF*

Warrington, Lewis
American. Naval Officer
b. Nov 3, 1782 in Williamsburg, Virginia
d. Oct 12, 1851 in Washington, DC
Source: *ApCAB; DcAmB; Drake; TwCBDA; WhAm H*

Warton, Joseph
English. Author
b. Apr 1722 in Dunsfold, England
d. Feb 23, 1800 in Wickham, England
Source: *Alli; BbD; BiD&SB; BrAu; CasWL; Chambr 2; ChPo; CnE&AP; DcEnL; DcEuL; DcLEL; EvLB; NewC; OxEng; Pen ENG; WebE&AL*

Warton, Thomas
English. Author
b. Jan 9, 1728 in Basingstake, England
d. May 21, 1790 in Oxford, England
Source: *Alli; BbD; BiD&SB; BrAu; CasWL; ChPo, S1; CnE&AP; DcEnA; DcEnL; DcEuL; DcLEL; EvLB; MouLC 2; NewC; OxEng; Pen ENG; PoLE; REn; WebE&AL*

Warwick, Dionne
American. Singer
Won Grammys 1969, 1970, 1980; hits "Alfie"; "Heartbreaker."
b. Dec 12, 1941 in East Orange, New Jersey
Source: *CurBio 69; WhoAm 74, 76, 78, 80, 82; WhoAmW 77; WhoBlA 75*

Warwick, Robert
American. Actor
b. Oct 9, 1876 in Sacramento, California
d. Jun 4, 1964 in Los Angeles, California
Source: *FilmgC; MotPP; MovMk; TwYS; WhScrn 74, 77; WhoHol B*

Washburn, Charles
American. Press Agent, Dramatist
b. 1890 in Chicago, Illinois
d. 1972 in Jersey City, New Jersey
Source: *NewYTBE 72*

Washington, Booker T(aliafero)
American. Educator, Author
Established Tuskegee Institute, 1881.
b. Apr 5, 1856 in Franklin County, Virginia
d. Nov 14, 1915 in Tuskegee, Alabama
Source: *AmAu&B; AmBi; ApCAB; BiD&SB; BiDSA; BlkAW; CasWL; Chambr 3; DcAmAu; DcAmB; DcLEL; DcNAA; EncAB-H; LongCTC; OxAmL; OxEng; Pen AM; REn; REnAL; TwCBDA; WebAB; WebE&AL; WhAm 1*

Washington, "Buck" (Ford Lee)
[Buck and Bubbles]
American. Jazz Pianist, Comedian
Formed comedy team with John Sublett, 1919-53.
b. Oct 16, 1903 in Louisville, Kentucky
d. Jan 31, 1955 in New York, New York
Source: *DcBlPA; WhoJazz 72*

Washington, Dinah
[Ruth Jones]
"Queen of the Blues"
American. Singer
Adapted blues style to pop songs; with Lionel Hampton's band, 1943-49.
b. Aug 29, 1924 in Tuscaloosa, Alabama
d. Dec 14, 1963 in Detroit, Michigan
Source: *InWom; WhScrn 77; WhoHol B; WorAl*

Washington, George
American. 1st US President
Commanded Continental Forces, 1775-83; president, 1789-97.
b. Feb 22, 1732 in Westmoreland, Virginia
d. Dec 14, 1799 in Mount Vernon, Virginia
Source: *Alli; AmAu&B; AmBi; ApCAB; BbD; BiAuS; BiD&SB; BiDSA; BiDrAC; BiDrUSE; Chambr 3; CyAL 1; DcAmAu; DcAmB; DcLEL; DcNAA; Drake; EncAB-H; FilmgC; OxAmL; OxCan; REn; REnAL; TwCBDA; WebAB; WhAm H; WhAmP; WorAl*

Washington, Grover, Jr.
American. Musician
b. Dec 12, 1943 in Buffalo, New York
Source: *WhoAm 78, 80, 82*

Washington, Harold
American. Mayor
Democratic mayor of Chicago, 1983--.
b. Apr 15, 1922 in Chicago, Illinois
Source: *CngDr 81; EbonySL 1; InB&W 80; NegAl 76; WhoAm 76; WhoAmP 73, 75, 77, 79; WhoBlA 75, 77*

Washington, Lawrence
American. Brother of George Washington
b. 1717
d. 1752
Source: *BioIn 11*

Washington, Martha Dandridge
American. Wife of George Washington
b. Jun 2, 1732 in Virginia
d. 1802
Source: *AmBi; AmWom; ApCAB; HerW; InWom; NewCol 75; NotAW; TwCBDA; WebBD 80; WhAm H*

Washington, Walter Edward
American. Former Mayor
b. Apr 15, 1915 in Dawson, Georgia
Source: *BioNews 74; CelR 73; CurBio 68; IntWW 74; WhoAm 74, 76, 78, 80, 82; WhoAmP 73; WhoBlA 75; WhoGov 72; WhoS&SW 73; WhoWor 74*

Wasserman, Dale
American. Dramatist
b. Nov 2, 1917 in Rhinelander, Wisconsin
Source: *AmAu&B; BiE&WWA; ConAu 49; ConDr 73; EncMT; IntMPA 75, 76, 77, 78, 79, 80, 81, 82; NotNAT; WhoAm 74, 76, 78, 80, 82; WrDr 76*

Wasserman, Lew(is Robert)
American. Motion Picture Executive
b. Mar 15, 1913 in Cleveland, Ohio
Source: *BioIn 10, 11; CelR 73; IntMPA 75, 76, 77, 78, 79, 80, 81, 82; WhoAm 82; WhoF&I 74*

Wassermann, August von
German. Physician
b. Feb 21, 1866 in Bamberg, Germany
d. Mar 15, 1925 in Berlin, Germany
Source: *AsBiEn; NewCol 75; WebBD 80*

Wassermann, Jakob
German. Author
b. Mar 10, 1873 in Nuremberg, Germany
d. Jan 1, 1934
Source: *CasWL; ClDMEL; CyWA; EncWL; EvEuW; ModGL; OxGer; Pen EUR; REn; TwCA, SUP; WhoLA*

Waterman, Lewis Edson
American. Inventor
b. Nov 20, 1837 in Decatur, New York
d. May 1, 1901 in Brooklyn, New York
Source: *AmBi; DcAmB; WebAB; WebBD 80; WhAm H*

Waters, Charlie (Charles Tutan)
American. Football Player
b. Sep 10, 1948 in Miami, Florida
Source: *FootReg*

Waters, Ethel
American. Singer, Actress
Starred in *Cabin in the Sky; Pinky;* sang in Billy Graham's crusades.
b. Oct 31, 1900 in Chester, Pennsylvania
d. Sep 1, 1977 in Chatsworth, California
Source: *BiE&WWA; ConAu 73, 81; CurBio 41, 51; EncMT; FamA&A; FilmgC; InWom; IntMPA 77, 75; MotPP; MovMk; NotNAT; OxThe; PlP&P; WebAB; WhoAm 74; WhoBlA 75; WhoHol A; WhoJazz 72; WhoThe 77; WorAl*

Waters, "Muddy"
[McKinley Morganfield]
American. Singer, Musician
b. Apr 4, 1915 in Rolling Fork, Mississippi
Source: *EncFCWM 69; WhoAm 74, 76, 78, 80, 82; WhoBlA 75*

Waterston, Sam(uel A)
American. Actor
b. Nov 15, 1940 in Cambridge, Massachusetts
Source: *IntMPA 75, 76, 77, 78, 79, 80, 81, 82; NewYTBE 72; NotNAT; WhoHol A; WhoThe 81*

Watkins, Ernest Shilston
English. Author, Lawyer
b. Jun 18, 1902 in Liverpool, England
Source: *CanWW 70; OxCan*

Watson, Bryan Joseph
"Bugsy"
Canadian. Hockey Player
Amassed 2,212 penalty minutes in 16-year career, second highest in NHL history.
b. Nov 14, 1942 in Bancroft, ON
Source: *BioIn 7; WhoHcky 73*

Watson, Charles
"Tex"
American. Member of Manson Cult
b. 1945?
Source: *BioIn 8, 10, 11; Blood*

Watson, "Doc" (Arthel)
American. Singer
b. Mar 2, 1923 in Deep Gap, North Carolina
Source: *EncFCWM 69*

Watson, Jack Hearn, Jr.
American. Lawyer, Government Official
b. Oct 24, 1938 in El Paso, Texas
Source: *BioIn 10, 11, 12; CurBio 80*

Watson, James Dewey
American. Biochemist
b. Apr 6, 1928 in Chicago, Illinois
Source: *AmAu&B; AmM&WS 73P, 76P, 79P; AsBiEn; BioIn 5, 6, 7, 8, 9; ConAu 25R; EncAB-H; IntWW 74, 75, 76, 77, 78; McGEWB; WebAB; Who 74; WhoAm 74, 76, 78, 80; WhoModH; WhoWor 74, 76, 78*

Watson, John Broadus
American. Psychologist
b. Jan 9, 1878 in Greenville, South Carolina
d. Sep 25, 1958
Source: *AsBiEn; BiDAmEd; EncAB-H; McGEWB; NatCAB 48; WebAB; WhAm 3*

Watson, Mark Skinner
American. Journalist
b. Jun 24, 1887 in Plattsburg, New York
d. Mar 25, 1966 in Baltimore, Maryland
Source: *ConAu 89; CurBio 46, 66; WhAm 4*

Watson, Thomas Edward
American. Politician
b. Sep 5, 1856 in Thomson, Georgia
d. Sep 26, 1922 in Washington, DC
Source: *CurBio 56; IntWW 74; St&PR 75; WhoAm 74; WhoE 74; WhoF&I 74; WhoGov 72; WhoWor 74*

Watson, Thomas J, Jr.
American. Business Executive
b. Jan 8, 1914 in Dayton, Ohio
Source: *WhoAm 74, 76, 78, 80, 82*

Watson, Thomas J, Sr.
American. Chairman of IBM Corporation
b. Feb 17, 1874 in Campbell, New York
d. Jun 19, 1956 in New York, New York
Source: *CurBio 40, 50, 56; EncAB-H; WebAB; WhAm 3*

Watson, Tom (Sturges)
American. Golfer
Won British Open, 1975, 1977; Masters, 1977, 1981; World Series of Golf, 1975, 1977, 1980.
b. Sep 4, 1949 in Kansas City, Missouri
Source: *BioIn 10; WhoAm 82; WhoGolf*

Watson-Watt, Robert
Scottish. Scientist, Engineer
b. Apr 13, 1892 in Brechin, Scotland
d. Dec 5, 1973 in Inverness, Scotland
Source: *Au&Wr 71; ConAu 45; ConAu P-1; CurBio 45, 74; NewYTBE 73; WhAm 6; Who 74*

Watt, Douglas (Benjamin)
American. Composer
b. Jan 20, 1914 in New York, New York
Source: *AmSCAP 66; NotNAT; WhoAm 74, 76, 78, 80, 82; WhoE 74*

Watt, George Willard
American. Chemist
b. Jan 8, 1911 in Bellaire, Ohio
d. Mar 29, 1980 in Austin, Texas
Source: *BioIn 10; WhoAm 78*

Watt, James
Scottish. Mechanical Engineer, Inventor
The watt, a unit of electrical power, was named for him.
b. Jan 19, 1736 in Greenock, Scotland
d. Aug 19, 1819
Source: *Alli; AsBiEn; BiDLA; DcScB; LongCEL; McGEWB; NewC; NewCol 75; WebBD 80*

Watt, James Gaius
American. Secretary of the Interior
Controversial for his environmental policies; appointed 1981--.
b. Jan 31, 1938 in Lusk, Wyoming
Source: *CurBio 82; WhoAm 76, 78, 80, 82; WhoAmP 73, 75, 77, 79; WhoGov 72, 75, 77*

Watt, Richard Martin
American. Author
b. Nov 10, 1930 in Berwyn, Illinois
Source: *ConAu 5R*

Watteau, Jean Antoine
French. Artist
b. Oct 10, 1684 in Valenciennes, France
d. Jul 18, 1721 in Nogent sur Marne, France
Source: *AtlBL; McGEWB; OxFr; REn*

Wattenberg, Ben J
American. Author
b. Aug 26, 1933 in New York, New York
Source: *BioIn 8; ConAu 57; WhoAm 76, 78, 80, 82; WrDr 80*

Watterson, Henry
American. Newspaper Editor
b. Feb 16, 1840 in Washington, DC
d. Dec 22, 1921 in Jacksonville, Florida
Source: *Alli SUP; AmAu&B; AmBi; ApCAB; BbD; BiD&SB; BiDConf; BiDSA; BiDrAC; DcAmAu; DcAmB; DcNAA; OxAmL; REnAL; TwCBDA; WebAB; WhAm 1; WhAmP*

Watts, Alan Wilson
American. Philosopher
b. Jan 6, 1915 in Chislehurst, England
d. Nov 16, 1973 in Mill Valley, California
Source: *AmAu&B; CelR 73; ConAu 41R, 45; CurBio 62, 74; NewYTBE 73; WebAB; WhAm 6; WhoAm 74; WhoWor 74; WomWMM; WorAu*

Watts, Andre
American. Musician
b. Jun 20, 1946 in Nuremberg, Germany
Source: *BioNews 75; CelR 73; CurBio 68; NewYTBE 71; WhoBlA 75; WhoE 74; WhoWor 74*

Watts, Charlie (Charles Robert)
[The Rolling Stones]
English. Rock Musician
b. Jun 2, 1941 in Islington, England
Source: *WhoAm 78, 80, 82*

Watts, George Frederic
English. Artist
b. 1817 in London, England
d. 1904 in London, England
Source: *BioIn 1, 3, 4, 6, 8, 10, 11; ChPo S2; DcVicP; LinLib S; McGDA*

Watts, Heather
American. Ballerina
With NY City Ballet, 1970--.
b. Sep 27, 1953 in Los Angeles, California
Source: *BioIn 12; WhoAm 82*

Watts, Isaac
English. Theologian, Hymnist
b. Jul 17, 1674 in Southampton, England
d. Nov 25, 1748 in Stoke Poges, England
Source: *Alli; AnCL; BbD; BiD&SB; BrAu; CarSB; CasWL; ChPo, S1, S2; CnE&AP; DcEnA; DcEnL; DcEuL; DcLEL; EvLB; NewC; OxEng; Pen ENG; PoChrch; REn; Str&VC; WebE&AL*

Watts, Pete
see: Mott (the Hoople)

Watts, Richard, Jr.
American. Drama Critic
b. Jan 12, 1898 in Parkersburg, West Virginia
d. Jan 2, 1981 in New York, New York
Source: *AmAu&B; BiE&WWA; ConAu 102; NotNAT; OxThe; WhoE 74; WhoThe 77*

Waugh, Alec (Alexander Raban)
English. Author
b. Jul 8, 1898 in London, England
d. Sep 3, 1981 in Tampa, Florida
Source: *Au&Wr 71; BioIn 4, 5, 6, 7, 8, 10; ConAu 17R, 104; ConNov 76; DcLEL; EvLB; IntAu&W 76, 77; IntWW 74, 75, 76, 77, 78; LongCTC; MnBBF; NewC; Pen ENG; RAdv 1; REn; TwCA, SUP; TwCW; WhE&EA; WhLit; Who 74; WhoWor 74, 76, 78; WrDr 76, 80*

Waugh, Auberon
English. Critic, Author
b. Nov 17, 1939 in Dulverton, England
Source: *Au&Wr 71; ConAu 45; ConLC 7; ConNov 76; DcLEL 1940; IntAu&W 76, 77; WrDr 80*

Waugh, Evelyn Arthur St. John
English. Author, Satirist
Wrote *Decline and Fall,* 1928; *Brideshead Revisited,* 1945.
b. Oct 1903 in London, England
d. Apr 10, 1966 in Taunton, England
Source: *AtlBL; CasWL; CathA 1930; CnMWL; ConAu 25R, 85; ConLC 1, 3; CyWA; DcLEL; EncWL; EvLB; LongCTC; ModBrL, SUP; NewC; NewYTBE 73; OxEng; Pen ENG; RAdv 1; REn; TwCA, SUP; TwCW; WebE&AL; WhAm 4; WhoTwCL; WomWMM; WorAl*

Waugh, Frederick Judd
American. Artist
b. Sep 13, 1861 in Bordentown, New Jersey
d. Sep 11, 1940
Source: *CurBio 40; DcAmB S2; WhAm 1*

Wauneka, Annie Dodge
American Indian. Navajo Leader
b. 1912
Source: *HerW*

Wavell, Archibald Percival Wavell, Earl
English. Field Marshal
b. May 5, 1883 in Colchester, England
d. May 24, 1950
Source: *ChPo S1; CurBio 41, 50; DcLEL; WhAm 3*

Waxman, Franz
German. Conductor, Composer
b. Dec 24, 1906 in Koenigsbutte, Germany
d. Feb 24, 1967 in Los Angeles, California
Source: *AmSCAP 66; CmMov; FilmgC; WhAm 4; WorEFlm*

Waybill, Fee
see: Tubes, The

Wayland, Francis
American. Clergyman, Educator
b. Mar 11, 1796 in New York, New York
d. Sep 30, 1865 in Providence, Rhode Island
Source: *Alli; AmAu&B; AmBi; ApCAB; BbD; BiD&SB; CyAL 1; DcAmAu; DcAmB; DcNAA; Drake; TwCBDA; WebAB; WhAm H*

Waymack, W(illiam) W(esley)
American. Editor, Civic Leader
b. Oct 18, 1888 in Savanna, Illinois
d. Nov 5, 1960 in Des Moines, Iowa
Source: *ConAu 93; CurBio 47, 61; WhAm 4*

Wayman, Dorothy
[Theodate Geoffrey, pseud.]
American. Author
b. Jan 7, 1893 in San Bernardino, California
d. Oct 27, 1975
Source: *AmAu&B; CathA 1952; ConAu 61; WhAm 6; WhNAA; WhoAm 74*

Wayne, Anthony
"Mad Anthony"
American. Soldier
b. Jan 1, 1745 in Waynesboro, Pennsylvania
d. Dec 15, 1796 in Erie, Pennsylvania
Source: *Alli; AmBi; ApCAB; BiAuS; BiDrAC; DcAmB; EncAB-H; REn; REnAL; TwCBDA; WebAB; WhAm H; WhAmP*

Wayne, David
[Wayne James McMeekan]
American. Actor
b. Jan 30, 1914 in Traverse City, Michigan
Source: *BiDFilm; BiE&WWA; CurBio 56; EncMT; FilmgC; IntMPA 75, 76, 77, 78, 79, 80, 81, 82; MotPP; MovMk; NotNAT, ; PlP&P; WhoHol A; WhoThe 77; WorEFlm*

Wayne, John
[Marion Michael Morrison]
American. Actor, Motion Picture Director
Won Oscar, 1968, for *True Grit;* awarded Congressional Medal, 1979.
b. May 26, 1907 in Winterset, Iowa
d. Jun 11, 1979 in Los Angeles, California
Source: *BiDFilm; BioNews 74; CmMov; ConAu 85; CurBio 51, 72; FilmgC; IntMPA 77, 75; IntWW 74; MotPP; MovMk; NewYTBE 73; OxFilm; WebAB; WhoAm 74; WhoHol A; WhoWor 74; WorEFlm*

Wayne, Johnny
[Wayne and Shuster]
Canadian. Comedian
b. 1918
Source: *CreCan 2*

Wayne, Paula
American. Actress
b. Nov 3, 1937 in Hobart, Oklahoma
Source: *BiE&WWA; NotNAT*

Wayne and Shuster
[Frank Shuster; Johnny Wayne]
Canadian. Comedy Team
Source: *NewYTET*

Weather Report
[Alejandro Acuna; Alphonso Johnson; Jaco Pastorius; Wayne Shorter; Chester Thompson; Norada Walden; Josef Zawainul]
American. Music Group
Source: *IlEncRk*

Weatherford, Teddy
American. Jazz Musician
b. Oct 11, 1903 in Bluefield, West Virginia
d. Apr 25, 1945 in Calcutta, India
Source: *WhoJazz 72*

Weathers, Felicia
American. Opera Singer
b. Aug 13, 1937 in Saint Louis, Missouri
Source: *WhoAm 74; WhoWor 74*

Weaver, Charley
see: Arquette, Cliff

Weaver, Dennis
American. Actor
Starred in TV series "Gunsmoke," 1955-64; "McCloud," 1970-77.
b. Jun 4, 1925 in Joplin, Missouri
Source: *FilmgC; IntMPA 75, 76, 77, 78, 79, 80, 81, 82; MotPP; MovMk; WhoAm 82; WhoHol A*

Weaver, "Doodles" (Winstead Sheffield Glendening Dixon)
American. Actor
Played hayseed comedic roles in over 60 films, 1930's-40's.
b. 1914 in Los Angeles, California
d. Jan 15, 1983 in Burbank, California
Source: *What 4; WhoHol A*

Weaver, Earl Sidney
American. Baseball Player, Manager
Manager, Baltimore Orioles, 1968-82; won four pennants, one World Series.
b. Aug 14, 1930 in Saint Louis, Missouri
Source: *BioIn 10; WhoAm 82; WhoProB 73*

Weaver, Fritz William
American. Actor
b. Jan 19, 1926 in Pittsburgh, Pennsylvania
Source: *BiE&WWA; BioIn 4, 7; CurBio 67; FilmgC; NotNAT; WhoAm 78; WhoHol A; WhoThe 77*

Weaver, James
see: K C and the Sunshine Band

Weaver, Mike (Michael Dwayne)
American. Boxer
Won 1980 WBA heavyweight title.
b. Jun 4, 1952 in Gatesville, Texas
Source: *NewYTBS 79; WhoAm 82*

Weaver, Robert Clifton
American. Former Cabinet Member
Secretary of HUD, 1966-69; first black US cabinet member.
b. Dec 29, 1907 in Washington, DC
Source: *AmM&WS 73S; BiDrUSE; ConAu 9R; CurBio 61; EncAB-H; IntWW 74; WebAB; WhoAm 74, 76, 78, 80, 82; WhoAmP 73; WhoBlA 75; WhoE 74*

Weaver, Sigourney
American. Actress
Starred in *Alien,* 1979; *Eyewitness,* 1981.
b. 1949 in New York, New York
Source: *BioIn 12; JohnWil 81*

Weaver, Thomas
American. Anthropologist, Author
b. May 1, 1929 in Greenville, New Mexico
Source: *AmM&WS 73S; ConAu 61; WhoAm 82; WhoWest 74*

Weavers, The
[Erik Darling; Lee Hays; Fred Hellerman; Bernie Krause; Pete Seeger]
American. Vocal, Instrumental Group
Source: *EncFCWM 69*

Webb, Beatrice Potter
English. Sociologist
b. Jan 22, 1858 in Gloucester, England
d. Apr 30, 1943 in Liphook, England
Source: *CurBio 43; DcLEL; EvLB; InWom; LongCTC; NewC; OxEng; TwCA, SUP*

Webb, "Chick" (William)
American. Jazz Musician
b. Feb 10, 1902 in Baltimore, Maryland
d. 1939 in Baltimore, Maryland
Source: *WhoJazz 72*

Webb, Clifton
[Webb Parmelee Hollenbeck]
American. Actor
b. Nov 19, 1891 in Indianapolis, Indiana
d. Oct 13, 1966 in Beverly Hills, California
Source: *BiDFilm; BiE&WWA; CurBio 43, 66; EncMT; FilmgC; MotPP; MovMk; WhAm 4; WhScrn 74, 77; WhoHol B; WorEFlm*

Webb, Del(bert Eugene)
American. Builder, Baseball Executive
b. May 17, 1899 in Fresno, California
d. Jul 4, 1974 in Rochester, New York
Source: *NewYTBS 74; WhAm 6*

Webb, Jack
American. Actor, Motion Picture Director
Played Sergeant Joe Friday on TV series "Dragnet," 1951-59, 1967-70.
b. Apr 2, 1920 in Santa Monica, California
d. Dec 23, 1982 in Los Angeles, California
Source: *CurBio 55; FilmgC; IntMPA 75, 76, 77, 78, 79, 80, 81, 82; MotPP; MovMk; OxFilm; WhoAm 74, 76, 78, 80, 82; WhoHol A; WhoWest 74; WorEFlm*

Webb, James Edwin
American. Lawyer
b. Oct 7, 1906 in Granville City, North Carolina
Source: *AmM&WS 73S; IntWW 74; WhoAm 74, 76, 78, 80, 82; WhoS&SW 73*

Webb, James H(enry)
American. Author
b. Feb 9, 1946 in Saint Joseph, Missouri
Source: *ConAu 81*

Webb, Jim
American. Composer
Wrote songs "Up, Up, and Away," 1967; "MacArthur Park," 1968; "Galveston," 1969.
b. Aug 15, 1946 in Elk City, Oklahoma
Source: *CelR 73*

Webb, Sidney James
[Baron Passfield]
English. Socialist Leader
b. Jul 13, 1859 in London, England
d. Oct 13, 1947 in Liphook, England
Source: *BbD; BiD&SB; DcLEL; EvLB; LongCTC; NewC; OxEng; TwCA, SUP*

Webb, Walter Prescott
American. Author
b. Apr 3, 1888 in Panola County, Texas
d. Mar 8, 1963 in Austin, Texas
Source: *AmAu&B; OxAmL; REnAL; TexWr; WhAm 4*

Webb, William Seward
American. Railroad Executive
b. Jan 31, 1851 in New York, New York
d. Oct 29, 1926
Source: *ApCAB SUP; DcAmAu; DcNAA; TwCBDA; WhAm 1*

Webber, Andrew Lloyd
American. Composer
Musicals include *Jesus Christ Superstar,* 1970; *Evita,* 1976; *Cats,* 1981.
b. Mar 22, 1948 in London, England
Source: *BioIn 9; CurBio 82; NewYTBE 71; WhoAm 82*

Weber, Adam
American. Conductor
b. 1854 in Cincinnati, Ohio
d. 1906
Source: *BiDAmM*

Weber, Carl Maria von
German. Composer
b. Nov 18, 1786 in Eutin, Germany
d. Jun 5, 1826 in London, England
Source: *AtlBL; NewCol 75; OxGer*

Weber, Dick
American. Bowler
Holds 19 PBA titles; bowled 16,300 games; Hall of Fame, 1970.
b. Dec 23, 1929 in Indianapolis, Indiana
Source: *CurBio 70; WhoWor 74*

Weber, Joseph M
[Weber and Fields]
American. Comedian
Formed comedy team with Lewis Fields, 1895-1904.
b. Aug 11, 1867 in New York, New York
d. May 10, 1942 in Los Angeles, California
Source: *CurBio 42; DcAmB S3; FamA&A; OxThe; REnAL; WhAm 2; WhoStg 1908*

Weber, Max
German. Sociologist, Author
b. Apr 21, 1864 in Erfurt, Germany
d. Jun 14, 1920 in Munich, Germany
Source: *CasWL; NewCol 75; OxGer; REn; TwCA SUP; WebBD 80*

Weber, Max
American. Artist, Author
b. Apr 18, 1881 in Bialystok, Russia
d. Oct 4, 1961 in Great Neck, New York
Source: *AmAu&B; AtlBL; REn; REnAL; WebAB; WhAm 4*

Weber, Robert Maxwell
American. Cartoonist
b. Apr 22, 1924 in Los Angeles, California
Source: *WhoAm 82; WorECar*

Weber, Wilhelm Eduard
German. Physicist
b. 1804
d. 1891
Source: *NewCol 75; WebBD 80*

Weber and Fields
[Lew Fields; Joseph Weber]
American. Comedy Team
Source: *OxThe; REn; WebBD 80*

Webern, Anton von
Austrian. Composer
b. Dec 3, 1883 in Vienna, Austria
d. Sep 15, 1945 in Mittersill, Austria
Source: *AtlBL; DcCM; NewCol 75; WebBD 80; WhAm 4*

Webster, Benjamin
English. Actor
b. 1864
d. 1947
Source: *OxThe*

Webster, Daniel
American. Lawyer, Statesman
Senator from MA, 1827-41, 1845-50; Secretary of State, 1841-43, 1850-52.
b. Jan 18, 1782 in Salisbury, New Hampshire
d. Oct 24, 1852 in Marshfield, Massachusetts
Source: *Alli; AmAu; AmAu&B; AmBi; ApCAB; BbD; BiAuS; BiD&SB; BiDrAC; BiDrUSE; Chambr 3; ChPo, S1; CyAL 1; DcAmAu; DcAmB; DcLEL; DcNAA; Drake; EncAB-H; EvLB; OxAmL; Pen AM; REn; REnAL; TwCBDA; WebAB; WhAm H; WhAmP*

Webster, Donald Blake
American. Author
b. Oct 14, 1933 in Rochester, New York
Source: *ConAu 37R*

Webster, H(arold) T(ucker)
American. Creator of Caspar Milquetoast
On staff of NY *Herald Tribune,* 1931-52.
b. Sep 21, 1885 in Parkersburg, West Virginia
d. Sep 22, 1952
Source: *AmAu&B; CurBio 45, 52; DcAmB S5; REnAL; WhAm 3*

Webster, John
English. Dramatist
Wrote *The White Devil,* 1612; *The Duchess of Malfi,* 1613.
b. 1580? in London, England
d. 1634?
Source: *AtlBL; BiD&SB; BrAu; CasWL; ChPo; CnE&AP; CnThe; CroE&S; CrtT 1; CyWA; DcEnA; DcEnL; DcEuL; DcLEL; EvLB; McGEWD; MouLC 1; NewC; OxEng; OxThe; Pen ENG; REn; REnWD; WebE&AL*

Webster, Margaret
American. Actress, Motion Picture Director
b. Mar 15, 1905 in New York, New York
d. Nov 13, 1972 in London, England
Source: *AmAu&B; BiE&WWA; ConAu 37R; CurBio 40, 50, 73; InWom; NewYTBE 72; OxThe; REn; WhAm 5; WhScrn 77; WhoThe 77*

Webster, Noah
American. Lexicographer, Author
Compiled *American Dictionary of the English Language,* 1828.
b. Oct 16, 1758 in West Hartford, Connecticut
d. May 28, 1843 in New Haven, Connecticut
Source: *Alli; AmAu; AmAu&B; AmBi; ApCAB; BbD; BiD&SB; CasWL; CnDAL; CyAL 1; DcAmAu; DcAmB; DcEnL; DcLEL; DcNAA; Drake; EncAB-H; EvLB; MouLC 3; OxAmL; OxEng; Pen AM; REn; REnAL; TwCBDA; WebAB; WebE&AL; WhAm H*

Webster, William Hedgcock
American. FBI Director, Judge
b. Mar 6, 1924 in Saint Louis, Missouri
Source: *WhoAm 74, 76, 78, 80, 82; WhoMW 74*

Wechsberg, Joseph
American. Author, Journalist
b. Aug 29, 1907 in Czechoslovakia
Source: *AmAu&B; Au&Wr 71; CurBio 55; OxAmL; REnAL; WhoAm 74, 76, 78, 80, 82; WhoMus 72; WhoWor 74*

Wechsler, David
American. Psychologist
b. Jan 12, 1896 in Lespede, Romania
d. May 1981 in New York, New York
Source: *AmM&WS 73S; ConAu 103; WhoAm 74, 76; WhoWorJ 72*

Wechsler, James Arthur
American. Author, Journalist
b. Oct 31, 1915 in New York, New York
Source: *AmAu&B; ConAu 101; IntWW 74; WhoAm 82; WhoE 74; WhoWor 74; WhoWorJ 72*

Weddell, James
British. Explorer
b. 1787
d. 1834
Source: *Alli*

Wedekind, Frank
German. Author
b. Jul 24, 1864 in Hannover, Germany
d. Mar 9, 1918 in Munich, Germany
Source: *AtlBL; CasWL; ClDMEL; CnMD; CnThe; CyWA; EncWL; EvEuW; LongCTC; McGEWD; ModGL; ModWD; OxGer; OxThe; Pen EUR; REn; REnWD; TwCA, SUP; TwCW; WhoTwCL*

Wedemeyer, Albert Coady
American. General, Industrialist
b. Jul 9, 1897 in Omaha, Nebraska
Source: *CurBio 45; WhoAm 82; WhoWor 74*

Wedgwood, Josiah
English. Potter
Began firm, 1759; invented translucent, unglazed semiporcelain called jasper ware.
b. Jul 12, 1730 in Burslem, England
d. Jan 3, 1795 in Etruria, England
Source: *Alli; NewC; NewCol 75; WorAl*

Wedgwood, Thomas
English. Potter, Photographer
b. 1771
d. 1805
Source: *BioIn 10*

Wedman, Scott Dean
American. Basketball Player
b. Jul 29, 1952 in Harper, Kansas
Source: *OfNBA*

Weed, Steven Andrew
American. Former Fiance of Patty Hearst
b. 1947
Source: *BioIn 10*

Weed, Thurlow
American. Journalist, Politician
b. Nov 15, 1797 in Cairo, New York
d. Nov 22, 1882 in New York, New York
Source: *Alli, SUP; AmAu&B; AmBi; ApCAB; BbD; BiD&SB; DcAmAu; DcAmB; DcNAA; Drake; EncAB-H; REnAL; TwCBDA; WebAB; WhAm H*

Weede, Robert
American. Opera Singer
b. 1903 in Baltimore, Maryland
d. Jul 10, 1972
Source: *BiE&WWA; CurBio 57, 72; EncMT; NewYTBE 72*

Weeks, Sinclair
American. Cabinet Member
b. Jun 15, 1893 in West Newton, Massachusetts
d. Jan 27, 1972 in Concord, Massachusetts
Source: *BiDrAC; BiDrUSE; CurBio 53, 72; NewYTBE 72; WhAm 5; WhAmP*

Weems, Ted (Wilfred Theodore)
American. Band Leader
b. 1900 in Pitcairn, Pennsylvania
d. May 6, 1963 in Tulsa, Oklahoma
Source: *AmSCAP 66; WhScrn 74, 77; WhoHol B*

Wegener, Alfred
German. Geophysicist
b. 1880
d. 1930
Source: *AsBiEn; BioIn 10; DcScB*

Wehrwein, Austin Carl
American. Journalist
b. Jan 12, 1916 in Austin, Texas
Source: *ConAu 77; WhoAm 74, 76, 78, 80, 82*

Weicker, Lowell Palmer, Jr.
American. Politician
Senator from CT, 1971--; member, Senate Watergate Committee, 1973-74.
b. May 16, 1931 in Paris, France
Source: *BiDrAC; CurBio 74; IntWW 74; WhoAm 74, 76, 78, 80, 82; WhoAmP 73; WhoE 74; WhoGov 72*

Weidenbaum, Murray Lew
American. Government Official, Economist
Chairman, Council of Economic Advisers, 1981--.
b. Feb 10, 1927 in Bronx, New York
Source: *AmEA 74; AmM&WS 73S, 78S; ConAu 37R; CurBio 82; IntWW 81; NewYTBS 81; WhoAm 74, 76, 78, 80, 82; WhoAmP 73, 75, 77, 79; WhoGov 72; WhoWorJ 78; WrDr 76, 80*

Weidman, Charles
American. Dancer
b. Jul 22, 1901 in Lincoln, Nebraska
d. Jul 15, 1975 in New York, New York
Source: *BiE&WWA; CurBio 42; WhAm 6; WhoAm 74*

Weidman, Jerome
American. Author
b. Apr 4, 1913 in New York, New York
Source: *AmAu&B; AmNov; Au&Wr 71; AuNews 2; BiE&WWA; CnDAL; ConAu 1R, 1NR; ConDr 73; ConLC 7; ConNov 72, 76; CurBio 42; DcLEL; DrAF 76; EncMT; LongCTC; NewCBMT; NotNAT; OxAmL; Pen AM; REn; REnAL; TwCA, SUP; WhNAA; WhoAm 74, 76, 78, 80, 82; WhoThe 77; WhoTwCL; WhoWorJ 72; WrDr 76*

Weil, Joseph R
"Yellow Kid"
American. Swindler
b. 1875?
d. Feb 26, 1976
Source: *BioIn 1, 4, 5, 10; EncACr*

Weil, Simone
French. Social Philosopher
b. Feb 3, 1909 in Paris, France
d. Aug 24, 1943 in Ashford, England
Source: *CnMWL; EvEuW; InWom; LongCTC; ModRL; OxFr; Pen EUR; REn; TwCA SUP; TwCW; WhoTwCL*

Weill, Claudia
American. Motion Picture Director
b. 1947 in New York, New York
Source: *BioIn 10, 11; FilmEn; NewYTBS 78; WhoAm 76, 78, 80, 82*

Weill, Kurt
American. Composer
Wrote *Threepenny Opera,* 1928; *Lost in the Stars,* 1949.
b. Mar 2, 1900 in Dessau, Germany
d. Apr 3, 1950 in New York, New York
Source: *AmSCAP 66; AtlBL; CurBio 41, 50; DcAmB S4; DcCM; EncMT; FilmgC; NewCBMT; OxFilm; OxGer; PlP&P; REn; WebAB; WhAm 3; WorAl; WorEFlm*

Wein, George Theodore
American. Musician, Producer
b. Oct 3, 1925 in Boston, Massachusetts
Source: *BioIn 7, 10; WhoAm 76, 78, 80, 82*

Weinberg, Chester
American. Fashion Designer
b. Sep 23, 1930 in New York, New York
Source: *WhoAm 82; WhoE 74; WorFshn*

Weinberg, Moshe
Israeli. Murdered Olympic Team Member
b. 1940?
d. Sep 5, 1972 in Munich, Germany (West)
Source: *BioIn 9*

Weinberger, Caspar Willard
"Cap the Knife"
American. Government Official
Secretary of HEW, 1973-75; Secretary of Defense, 1981--.
b. Aug 18, 1917 in San Francisco, California
Source: *CngDr 74; CurBio 73; IntWW 74; NewYTBE 72; WhoAm 74, 76, 78, 80, 82; WhoAmP 73; WhoF&I 74; WhoGov 72*

Weinberger, Jaromir
American. Composer
b. Jan 8, 1896 in Prague, Czechoslovakia
d. Aug 6, 1967 in Saint Petersburg, Florida
Source: *AmSCAP 66*

Weingarten, Violet
American. Journalist, Author
b. Feb 23, 1915 in San Francisco, California
Source: *ConAu 9R, 65; ForWC 70; SmATA 3*

Weingartner, Felix
Austrian. Conductor, Composer
b. Jun 2, 1863 in Zara, Austria
d. May 7, 1942 in Winterthur, Switzerland
Source: *CurBio 42; WhoLA*

Weinman, Adolph A
American. Sculptor
b. Dec 11, 1870 in Karlsruhe, Germany
d. Aug 8, 1952
Source: *WhAm 3*

Weinstein, Nathan Wallenstein
see: West, Nathanael, pseud.

Weintal, Edward
American. Diplomatic Correspondent
b. Mar 21, 1901 in Warsaw, Poland
d. Jan 24, 1973
Source: *ConAu 41R; NewYTBE 73; WhAm 5*

Weintraub, Jerry
American. Motion Picture Producer
b. 1937?
Source: *BioIn 11*

Weir, Bob (Robert Hall)
[The Grateful Dead]
American. Singer, Musician
b. Oct 16, 1949 in San Francisco, California
Source: *NF*

Weir, John F
American. Artist
b. Aug 28, 1841 in West Point, New York
d. Apr 8, 1926
Source: *AmBi; DcAmAu; DcAmB; DcNAA; EarABI SUP; TwCBDA; WhAm 1*

Weir, Julian Alden
American. Artist
b. Aug 30, 1852 in West Point, New York
d. Dec 8, 1919
Source: *AmBi; ApCAB; DcAmB; OxAmL; TwCBDA; WhAm 1*

Weir, Robert W
American. Artist
b. Jun 18, 1803 in New Rochelle, New York
d. May 1, 1889 in New York, New York
Source: *Alli; AmBi; ApCAB; BiAuS; DcAmB; Drake; EarABI, SUP; TwCBDA; WhAm H*

Weir, Walter
American. Advertising Executive
b. Mar 27, 1909 in Philadelphia, Pennsylvania
Source: *Alli SUP; ConAu 5R; WhoAm 74*

Weisgall, Hugo David
Czech. Composer
b. Oct 13, 1912 in Ivancice, Czechoslovakia
Source: *AmSCAP 66; DcCM; WhoAm 74, 76, 78, 80, 82; WhoMus 72; WhoWor 74; WhoWorJ 72*

Weiskopf, Tom Daniel
American. Golfer
Won British Open, World Series of Golf, Canadian Open, 1973.
b. Nov 9, 1942 in Massillon, Ohio
Source: *BioNews 74; CurBio 73; NewYTBE 73; WhoAm 82; WhoGolf*

Weiss, Carl Austin
American. Assassin
b. 1905
d. 1935
Source: *BioIn 10*

Weiss, Peter
Swedish. Dramatist
Wrote *Marat/Sade* ; won Tony, 1966.
b. Nov 8, 1916 in Nowawes, Germany
d. May 10, 1982 in Stockholm, Sweden
Source: *CasWL; CnThe; ConAu 45, 3NR; ConLC 3, 15; CroCD; CurBio 68; EncWL; EncWT; IntAu&W 76, 77; IntWW 74, 76, 77, 78; LinLib L; McGEWD; ModGL; NewYTBS 82; NotNAT; OxFilm; OxGer; Pen EUR; PlP&P, A; REnWD; TwCW; Who 74; WhoThe 72, 77; WhoWor 74; WorAu; WorEFlm*

Weiss, Theodore (Russell)
American. Poet, Editor
b. Dec 16, 1916 in Reading, Pennsylvania
Source: *ConAu 9R; ConLC 3, 8, 14; WhoAm 76, 78, 80, 82; WhoE 74; WhoWorJ 72*

Weissenberg, Alexis Sigismund
American. Musician
b. Jul 26, 1929 in Sofia, Bulgaria
Source: *BiDAmM; CurBio 78; MusSN; NewYTBE 71; WhoAm 74, 76, 78, 80, 82; WhoMus 72; WhoHrs 80; WhoWor 74*

Weissmuller, Johnny
American. Actor, Swimmer
Played Tarzan in 19 movies, 1934-48; won five gold medals in 1924, 1928 Olympics.
b. Jun 2, 1904 in Chicago, Illinois
Source: *FilmgC; IntMPA 75, 76, 77, 78, 79, 80, 81, 82; MotPP; MovMk; NewYTBE 72; OxFilm; WebAB; WhoHol A; WorEFlm*

Weitz, Bruce
American. Actor
Plays Mick Belker on "Hill Street Blues," 1981--.
b. 1943
Source: *NF*

Weitz, John
American. Fashion Designer
b. May 25, 1923 in Berlin, Germany
Source: *CelR 73; ConAu 29R; NewYTBE 72; WhoAm 82; WorFshn*

Weizman, Ezer
Israeli. Politician
b. 1924 in Tel Aviv, Palestine
Source: *BioIn 12; CurBio 79; IntWW 74*

Weizmann, Chaim
Israeli. Zionist Leader, Chemist
b. Nov 27, 1874 in Grodno, Russia
d. Nov 9, 1952 in Rehovot, Israel
Source: *CurBio 42, 48, 52; WhAm 4*

Welch, Bob
[Fleetwood Mac]
American. Rock Musician
b. Jul 31, 1946 in Los Angeles, California
Source: *BioIn 11*

Welch, Bob (Robert Lynn)
American. Baseball Player
b. Nov 3, 1956 in Detroit, Michigan
Source: *BaseEn; BioIn 12; NewYTBS 80*

Welch, Herbert
American. Religious Leader
b. Nov 7, 1862 in New York, New York
d. Apr 4, 1969 in New York, New York
Source: *ConAu P-1; OhA&B; WhAm 5*

Welch, John Francis, Jr.
American. Corporation Executive
b. Nov 19, 1935 in Peabody, Massachusetts
Source: *AmM&WS 79P; WhoAm 80, 82*

Welch, Joseph Nye
American. Lawyer, Actor
b. Oct 22, 1890 in Primghar, Iowa
d. Oct 6, 1960 in Hyannis, Massachusetts
Source: *CurBio 54, 60; WebAB; WhAm 4; WhScrn 74, 77*

Welch, Raquel
[Raquel Tejada; Mrs. Andre Weinfeld]
American. Actress, Model
Starred in *One Million BC*, 1967; on Broadway in *Woman of the Year*, 1982.
b. Sep 5, 1942 in Chicago, Illinois
Source: *BioNews 74; BkPepl; CelR 73; CurBio 71; FilmgC; IntMPA 75, 76, 77, 78, 79, 80, 81, 82; MotPP; MovMk; NewYTBE 72; WhoAm 74, 76, 78, 80, 82; WhoHol A; WorEFlm*

Welch, Robert Henry Winborne
American. Political Activist
Founder, president of John Birch Society, Indianapolis, 1958.
b. Dec 1, 1899 in Chowan County, North Carolina
Source: *CelR 73; St&PR 75; WebAB; WhoAm 74, 76, 78, 80, 82; WhoWor 74*

Welch, William Henry
American. Pathologist, Bacteriologist
b. Apr 8, 1850 in Bloomington, Illinois
d. Apr 30, 1934
Source: *AmAu&B; AmBi; ApCAB SUP; DcAmAu; DcAmB; DcNAA; EncAB-H; REnAL; WebAB; WhAm 1*

Weld, Tuesday (Susan Kerr)
American. Actress
Starred in *Return to Peyton Place; Looking for Mr. Goodbar.*
b. Aug 27, 1943 in New York, New York
Source: *BiDFilm; CelR 73; CurBio 74; FilmgC; InWom; IntMPA 75, 76, 77, 78, 79, 80, 81, 82; MotPP; MovMk; NewYTBE 71; WhoAm 82; WhoHol A; WorEFlm*

Weldon, Joan
American. Actress
b. Aug 5, 1933 in San Francisco, California
Source: *IntMPA 75, 76, 77, 78, 79, 80, 81, 82; WhoHol A*

Welitsch, Ljuba
Bulgarian. Opera Singer
b. Jul 10, 1913 in Borissova, Bulgaria
Source: *CurBio 49; InWom; NewYTBE 72; WhoMus 72*

Welk, Lawrence
American. Band Leader
Started band, 1927; "The Lawrence Welk Show," 1955--.
b. Mar 11, 1903 in Strasburg, North Dakota
Source: *AmSCAP 66; BioNews 74; CelR 73; CurBio 57; IntMPA 75, 76, 77, 78, 79, 80, 81, 82; WebAB; WhoAm 74, 76, 78, 80, 82; WhoMus 72*

Wellcome, Sir Henry
American. Chemical Manufacturer
b. 1854 in Wisconsin
d. 1936
Source: *WebBD 80*

Wellek, Rene
Author, Educator
b. Aug 22, 1903 in Vienna, Austria
Source: *AmAu&B; Au&Wr 71; ConAu 5R; DrAS 74; EncWL; NewYTBS 74; WhoAm 74, 76, 78, 80, 82; WhoWor 74; WorAu; WrDr 76*

Welles, (George) Orson
American. Actor, Director, Producer
Founder, Mercury Theater, 1937; starred in *Citizen Kane*, 1940.
b. May 6, 1915 in Kenosha, Wisconsin
Source: *AmAu&B; BiDFilm; BiE&WWA; BkPepl; CelR 73; CmMov; ConAu 93; ConDr 73; CurBio 41, 65; DcFM; EncAB-H; EncMT; FamA&A; FilmgC; IntMPA 75, 76, 77, 78, 79, 80, 81, 82; IntWW 74; MotPP; MovMk; NewYTBE 72; NotNAT; OxFilm; OxThe; PlP&P; REn; REnAL; WebAB; Who 74; WhoAm 74; WhoHol A; WhoThe 77; WhoWor 74; WorEFlm*

Welles, Gideon
American. Political Leader
b. Jul 1, 1802 in Glastonbury, Connecticut
d. Feb 11, 1878 in Hartford, Connecticut
Source: *Alli SUP; AmAu&B; AmBi; ApCAB; BiAuS; BiDrUSE; DcAmAu; DcAmB; DcNAA; Drake; EncAB-H; REn; REnAL; TwCBDA; WebAB; WhAm H*

Welles, Sumner
American. Diplomat, Author
b. Oct 14, 1892 in New York, New York
d. Sep 24, 1961 in Bernardsville, New Jersey
Source: *AmAu&B; CurBio 40, 61; EncAB-H; REnAL; TwCA SUP; WhAm 4*

Wellesley, Dorothy
English. Poet
b. 1889
d. 1956
Source: *Chambr 3; ChPo, S2; DcLEL; ModBrL; OxEng; REn*

Wellesz, Egon
Austrian. Opera Composer, Musicologist
b. Oct 21, 1885 in Vienna, Austria
d. Nov 9, 1974 in Oxford, England
Source: *Au&Wr 71; ConAu 53; DcCM; IntWW 74; NewYTBS 74; WhAm 6; Who 74; WhoMus 72; WhoWor 74*

Wellington, Arthur Wellesley, Duke
English. General, Statesman
b. May 1, 1769 in Dublin, Ireland
d. Sep 14, 1852
Source: *Alli; McGEWB; NewC; REn*

Wellman, Paul Iselin
American. Journalist, Author
b. Oct 14, 1898 in Enid, Oklahoma
d. Sep 17, 1966 in Los Angeles, California
Source: *AmAu&B; AmNov; Au&Wr 71; AuBYP; ConAu 1R, 25R; CurBio 49; REn; REnAL; SmATA 3; TwCA SUP; WhAm 4*

Wellman, Walter
American. Journalist
b. Nov 3, 1858 in Mentor, Ohio
d. Jan 31, 1934 in New York, New York
Source: *AmBi; DcAmB; DcNAA; OhA&B; TwCBDA; WebAB; WhAm 1*

Wellman, William Augustus
American. Motion Picture Director
b. 1896 in Brookline, Massachusetts
d. Dec 9, 1975 in Los Angeles, California
Source: *BiDFilm; CmMov; ConAu 61; CurBio 50; DcFM; Film 1; FilmgC; IntMPA 75; MovMk; OxFilm; TwYS; WhAm 6; WhScrn 77; WhoAm 74; WhoHol A; WhoWor 74; WorEFlm*

Wells, Henry
American. Express Company Executive
b. Dec 12, 1805 in Thetford, Vermont
d. Dec 10, 1878 in Glasgow, Scotland
Source: *AmBi; ApCAB; DcAmB; TwCBDA; WebAB; WhAm H*

Wells, H(erbert) G(eorge)
English. Author
Wrote *The Time Machine,* 1895; *The Invisible Man,* 1897; *The War of the Worlds,* 1898.
b. Sep 21, 1866 in Bromley, England
d. Aug 13, 1946 in London, England
Source: *AtlBL; BbD; BiD&SB; CasWL; Chambr 3; CnMWL; CurBio 46; CyWA; DcBiA; DcEnA AP; DcLEL; EncMys; EncWL; EvLB; FilmgC; LongCTC; MnBBF; ModBrL, SUP; NewC; OxEng; Pen ENG; PlP&P; RAdv 1; RComWL; REn; TwCA, SUP; TwCW; WebE&AL; WhAm 2; WhScrn 74, 77; WhoHol B; WhoLA; WhoTwCL*

Wells, Hubert George, pseud.
see: Ackerman, Forest J

Wells, Horace
American. Dentist
b. Jan 21, 1815 in Hartford, Vermont
d. Jan 24, 1848 in New York, New York
Source: *Alli; AmBi; ApCAB; DcAmB; DcNAA; Drake; TwCBDA; WebAB; WhAm H*

Wells, Kitty
[Muriel Deason]
American. Singer
b. Aug 30, 1919 in Nashville, Tennessee
Source: *EncFCWM 69; WhoAm 82*

Wells, Linton
American. Journalist, Radio Broadcaster
b. Apr 1, 1893 in Louisville, Kentucky
d. Jan 31, 1976 in Washington, DC
Source: *AmAu&B; ConAu 61, 97; WhAm 6; WhNAA; WhoAm 74*

Wells, Mary
American. Advertising Executive
b. 1928 in Youngstown, Ohio
Source: *CurBio 67; InWom; WhoE 74; WhoF&I 74; WhoWor 74*

Wells, Mary
American. Singer
Sang "Bye, Bye, Baby," 1961; "Two Lovers," 1962; "My Guy," 1964.
b. May 13, 1943 in Detroit, Michigan
Source: *EncPR&S*

Welnick, Vince
see: Tubes, The

Welsbach, Carl Auer von, Baron
Austrian. Chemist, Inventor
Discovered earth elements neodymium and praseodymium, 1885, lutetium, 1908.
b. Sep 1, 1858
d. Aug 4, 1929
Source: *NewCol 75; WebBD 80*

Welty, Eudora
American. Author
b. Apr 13, 1909 in Jackson, Mississippi
Source: *AmAu&B; AmNov; AmWr; CasWL; CelR 73; ChPo; CnDAL; ConAu 9R; ConLC 1, 2, 5; ConNov 72, 76; CurBio 42; CyWA; DrAF 76; EncWL; InWom; IntWW 74; LongCTC; ModAL, SUP; OxAmL; Pen AM; RAdv 1; REn; REnAL; TwCA SUP; WebAB; WebE&AL; Who 74; WhoAm 74, 76, 78, 80, 82; WhoTwCL; WhoWor 74; WrDr 76*

Wences, Senor
see: Senor Wences

Wenders, Wim
German. Motion Picture Director
b. 1945 in Dusseldorf, Germany
Source: *BioIn 10, 11; IntMPA 82*

Wengenroth, Stow
American. Lithographer
b. Jul 25, 1906 in New York, New York
d. Jan 22, 1978 in Gloucester, Massachusetts
Source: *ConAu 104; WhoAm 74; WhoAmA 73*

Wenner, Jann
American. Journalist, Publisher
b. Jan 7, 1947 in New York, New York
Source: *BioIn 11; ConAu 101; CurBio 80; WhoAm 82*

Wenner-Gren, Axel
Swedish. Industrialist
b. Jun 5, 1881 in Uddevalla, Sweden
d. Nov 24, 1961 in Stockholm, Sweden
Source: *CurBio 42, 62*

Wenrich, Percy
American. Composer, Musician
b. Jan 23, 1887 in Joplin, Missouri
d. Mar 17, 1952 in New York, New York
Source: *AmPS; AmSCAP 66, 80; BiDAmM; BioIn 2, 4, 6, 9; CmpEPM; NotNAT B*

Wenzel, Hanni
Liechtenstein. Skier
Source: *NF*

Werblin, "Sonny" (David Abraham)
American. Businessman
b. Mar 17, 1910 in Brooklyn, New York
Source: *CurBio 79; NewYTBS 79; WhoAm 74*

Werfel, Franz
Austrian. Author, Dramatist
b. Sep 10, 1890 in Prague, Bohemia
d. Aug 26, 1945 in Beverly Hills, California
Source: *CasWL; ClDMEL; CnMD; CnThe; CurBio 40, 45; CyWA; DcNAA; EncWL; EvEuW; LongCTC; McGEWD; ModGL; ModWD; OxGer; OxThe; Pen EUR; PlP&P; REn; REnWD; TwCA, SUP; TwCW; WhAm 2*

Werner, Oskar
[Oskar Josef Bschliessmayer]
Austrian. Actor
Starred in *Jules et Jim*, 1961; *Ship of Fools*, 1965; *Fahrenheit 451*, 1966.
b. Nov 13, 1922 in Vienna, Austria
Source: *BiDFilm; CelR 73; CurBio 66; FilmgC; IntMPA 75, 76, 77, 78, 79, 80, 81, 82; MotPP; MovMk; OxFilm; WhoAm 74, 76, 78, 80, 82; WhoHol A; WorEFlm*

Werner, Pierre
Luxembourg. Lawyer, Politician
b. Dec 29, 1913 in Saint-Andre, France
Source: *IntWW 74; WhoGov 72; WhoWor 74*

Werrenrath, Reinald
American. Singer, Conductor
b. Aug 7, 1883 in Brooklyn, New York
d. Sep 12, 1953 in Plattsburg, New York
Source: *BioIn 1, 3; WhAm 3*

Werth, Alexander
English. Journalist
b. Feb 4, 1901 in Russia
d. Mar 5, 1969 in Paris, France
Source: *ConAu 25R; ConAu P-1; CurBio 43, 69; WhAm 5*

Wertham, Fredric
German. Author, Psychiatrist
b. 1895 in Munich, Germany
d. Nov 18, 1981 in Kempton, Pennsylvania
Source: *AmAu&B; Au&Wr 71; BiDrAPA 77; BioIn 1, 2, 4; ConAu 5R; CurBio 49, 82; IntAu&W 76, 77; ScF&FL 1, 2; TwCA SUP; WhoAm 74, 76, 78; WhoWor 74*

Wertmuller, Lina von Eigg
Italian. Motion Picture Director
b. 1931 in Rome, Italy
Source: *IntMPA 82; MovMk; WomWMM*

Wescott, Glenway
American. Author
b. Apr 11, 1901 in Kewaskum, Wisconsin
Source: *AmAu&B; AmNov; CasWL; CnDAL; ConAmA; ConAmL; ConAu 13R; ConNov 72, 76; CyWA; DcLEL; LongCTC; ModAL; OxAmL; Pen AM; RAdv 1; REn; REnAL; TwCA, SUP; TwCW; WhoAm 74; WisWr; WrDr 76*

Wesendonck, Mathilde Luckemeyer
German. Friend of Wagner
b. 1828 in Traunblick, Austria
d. 1902
Source: *BioIn 3, 9; OxGer*

Wesker, Arnold
English. Dramatist
b. May 24, 1932 in London, England
Source: *Au&Wr 71; BiE&WWA; CasWL; CnMD; CnThe; ConAu 1R, 1NR; ConDr 73; ConLC 3, 5; CroCD; CurBio 62; EncWL; IntWW 74; LongCTC; McGEWD; ModBrL, SUP; ModWD; NewC; NotNAT; Pen ENG; REnWD; TwCW; WebE&AL; Who 74; WhoThe 77; WhoTwCL; WhoWor 74; WorAu; WrDr 76*

Wesley, John
English. Founder of Methodism
Formed at Oxford U, 1729; name derived from methodical devotion to study and religion.
b. Jun 28, 1703 in Lincoln, England
d. Mar 3, 1791 in London, England
Source: *Alli; ApCAB; AtlBL; BbD; BiD&SB; BrAu; CasWL; Chambr 2; ChPo, S1; DcEnA; DcEnL; DcEuL; DcLEL; Drake; EvLB; NewC; NewCol 75; OxEng; Pen ENG; PoChrch; RComWL; REn; WebE&AL*

Wesselmann, Tom
American. Artist
b. Feb 23, 1931 in Cincinnati, Ohio
Source: *DcCAA 71; IntWW 74; WhoAm 74; WhoAmA 73; WhoWor 74*

Wessinghage, Ellen
German. Track Athlete
b. 1948?
Source: *BioIn 11*

Wessinghage, Thomas
German. Track Athlete
b. 1952?
Source: *BioIn 11*

Wesson, Daniel Baird
[Smith and Wesson]
American. Firearms Manufacturer
With Horace Smith developed repeating action pistol, 1854; open cylinder revolver, 1857.
b. May 25, 1825 in Worcester, Massachusetts
d. 1906
Source: *DcAmB; WhAm 1*

West, Adam
American. Actor
Starred in TV series "Batman," 1965-68.
b. Sep 29, 1938 in Walla Walla, Washington
Source: *FilmgC; WhoHol A*

West, Benjamin
American. Artist
b. Oct 10, 1738 in Springfield, Pennsylvania
d. Mar 11, 1820 in London, England
Source: *Alli; AmBi; ApCAB; AtlBL; BiDLA; BkIE; DcAmB; Drake; EncAB-H; OxAmL; REn; TwCBDA; WebAB; WhAm H*

West, Dottie
[Dorothy Marie Marsh]
American. Singer
b. Oct 11, 1932 in McMinnville, Tennessee
Source: *BioIn 12; EncFCWM 69; WhoAm 74, 76, 78, 80, 82*

West, James Edward
American. Social Worker
First leader of US Boy Scouts, 1911.
b. May 16, 1876 in Washington, DC
d. May 15, 1948 in New Rochelle, New York
Source: *AmAu&B; DcAmB S4; WhAm 2*

West, Jerry
"Mr. Clutch"
American. Basketball Player, Coach
Guard, LA Lakers, 1960-74; coach, 1976-79.
b. May 28, 1938 in Cabin Creek, West Virginia
Source: *BioIn 5, 6, 8, 9, 10, 11; CelR 73; WhoAm 78; WhoBbl 73*

West, Jessamyn
American. Author
b. 1907 in Indiana
Source: *ConAu 9R; ConLC 7, 17; ConNov 72, 76; DrAF 76; InWom; IndAu 1917; OxAmL; REnAL; TwCA SUP; WhoAm 74, 76, 78, 80, 82; WrDr 76*

West, Mae
American. Actress
Described herself as "the first person to bring sex out in the open."
b. Aug 17, 1892 in Brooklyn, New York
d. Nov 22, 1980 in Hollywood, California
Source: *AmAu&B; BiDFilm; CelR 73; ConAu 89, 102; CurBio 67, 81; FamA&A; FilmgC; InWom; IntMPA 75, 76, 77, 78, 79, 80; IntWW 74; ModWD; MotPP; MovMk; NewYTBE 70; NotNAT; OxFilm; REnAL; ThFT; WebAB; WhoAm 74; WhoHol A; WhoThe 77; WhoWor 74; WomWMM; WorEFlm*

West, Morris Langlo
Australian. Author
b. Apr 26, 1916 in Melbourne, Australia
Source: *Au&Wr 71; ConAu 5R; ConLC 6; ConNov 72, 76; CurBio 66; IntWW 74; ModBrL; REn; TwCW; Who 74; WhoAm 82; WhoWor 76; WorAu; WrDr 76*

West, Nathanael, pseud.
[Nathan Wallenstein Weinstein]
American. Author
Wrote *Miss Lonelyhearts*, 1933; *The Day of the Locust*, 1939.
b. Oct 17, 1903 in New York, New York
d. Dec 22, 1940 in El Centro, California
Source: *AmAu&B; AmWr; AtlBL; CasWL; CnMWL; CurBio 41; CyWA; DcLEL; DcNAA; EncWL; FilmgC; LongCTC; ModAL, SUP; OxAmL; Pen AM; RAdv 1; REn; REnAL; TwCA, SUP; TwCW; WebAB; WebE&AL; WhAm 4; WhoTwCL*

West, Dame Rebecca, pseud.
[Cicily Isobel Fairfield]
Irish. Author, Journalist
Wrote *The Return of the Soldier*, 1918; *The Judge*, 1922.
b. Dec 21, 1892 in Kerry, Ireland
Source: *Au&Wr 71; CasWL; Chambr 3; ConAu 5R; ConLC 9, 7; ConNov 72, 76; CurBio 68; CyWA; DcLEL; EncWL; EvLB; InWom; IntWW 74; LongCTC; ModBrL, SUP; NewC; OxEng; Pen ENG; RAdv 1; REn; TwCA, SUP; TwCW; Who 74; WhoLA; WhoTwCL; WhoWor 74; WrDr 76*

Westermann, H(orace) C(lifford)
American. Sculptor
b. Dec 11, 1922 in Los Angeles, California
d. Nov 3, 1981 in Danbury, Connecticut
Source: *BioIn 5, 7, 8, 11; ConArt; DcCAA 71; WhoAm 74, 76, 78, 80; WhoAmA 73, 76, 78; WhoWor 74*

Westhead, Paul
American. Basketball Coach
b. Feb 21, 1939 in Malvern, Pennsylvania
Source: *OfNBA*

Westheimer, Irvin Ferdinand
American. Founder of Big Brothers
b. Sep 19, 1879 in Newark, New Jersey
d. Dec 29, 1980 in Cincinnati, Ohio
Source: *NewYTBS 81; WhoAm 74, 76, 78; WhoF&I 74, 75*

Westinghouse, George
American. Inventor, Manufacturer
Invented air brake and automatic railroad signals; held over 400 patents.
b. Oct 6, 1846 in Central Bridge, New York
d. Mar 12, 1914 in New York, New York
Source: *AmBi; DcAmB; EncAB-H; TwCBDA; WebAB; WhAm 1*

Westlake, Donald E(dwin)
American. Author
b. Jul 12, 1933 in New York, New York
Source: *AmAu&B; ConAu 17R; ConLC 7; EncMys; WhoAm 82*

Westley, Helen
American. Actress
b. Mar 28, 1879 in Brooklyn, New York
d. Dec 12, 1942 in Franklin County, New Jersey
Source: *CurBio 43; DcAmB S3; FilmgC; InWom; MovMk; NotAW; PlP&P; ThFT; Vers B; WhScrn 74, 77; WhoHol B*

Westmore, Perc(ival)
American. Cosmetician
b. Oct 29, 1904 in Canterbury, England
d. Sep 30, 1970
Source: *CurBio 45, 70; NewYTBE 70; WhoHol B*

Westmoreland, William Childs
American. General
Commanded US forces in Vietnam, 1964-68; Army chief of staff, 1968-72.
b. Mar 16, 1914 in Spartanburg, South Carolina
Source: *BioNews 74; EncAB-H; IntWW 74; WebAB; WhoAm 74; WhoGov 72; WhoWor 74*

Weston, Edward
American. Photographer
b. Mar 24, 1886 in Highland Park, Illinois
d. Jan 1, 1958 in Carmel, California
Source: *WhAm 3*

Weston, Edward F
American. Scientific Instrument Maker
b. Oct 24, 1879 in Newark, New Jersey
d. Jul 27, 1971
Source: *WhAm 5*

Westover, Russell
American. Comic Strip Creator
b. Aug 3, 1886 in Los Angeles, California
d. Mar 6, 1966 in San Rafael, California
Source: *WhAm 4*

Westphal, Paul Douglas
American. Basketball Player
b. Nov 30, 1950 in Torrance, California
Source: *WhoAm 80, 82; WhoBbl 73*

Westwood, Jean Miles
American. Political Leader
b. Nov 22, 1923 in Price, Utah
Source: *BioIn 9; WhoAmP 73; WhoAmW 74; WhoWest 74*

Wexler, Haskell
American. Motion Picture Director
b. 1926 in Chicago, Illinois
Source: *FilmgC; IntMPA 75, 76, 77, 78, 79, 80, 81, 82; NewYTBE 73; OxFilm; WhoAm 74, 76, 78, 80, 82; WorEFlm*

Wexley, John
American. Dramatist
b. 1907 in New York
Source: *AmAu&B; CnMD; ConAmA; ModWD; OxAmL; Pen AM; REn; REnAL; WhoThe 77*

Weyden, Rogier van der
[Roger de la Pasture]
Flemish. Artist
b. 1399 in Tournai, Belgium
d. Jun 16, 1464 in Brussels, Belgium
Source: *AtlBL; REn*

Weyerhaeuser, Frederick
American. Lumber Tycoon
b. Nov 21, 1834 in Mainz, Germany
d. Apr 4, 1914 in Pasadena, California
Source: *WebAB; WebBD 80; WhAm 1*

Weyerhaeuser, Frederick King
American. Lumber Executive
b. Jan 16, 1895 in Rock Island, Illinois
d. Oct 18, 1945 in Saint Paul, Minnesota
Source: *IntWW 74; St&PR 75; WhoAm 74*

Weygand, Maxime
French. General
Supreme allied commander, 1939, known for unsuccessful attempt to create new front.
b. Jan 21, 1867 in Brussels, Belgium
d. Jan 28, 1965 in Paris, France
Source: *CurBio 40, 65*

Weymouth, Christina
see: Talking Heads, The

Whale, James
English. Motion Picture Director
b. Jul 22, 1896 in Dudley, England
d. May 29, 1957 in California
Source: *BiDFilm; BioIn 4, 10, 11; CmMov; DcFM; FanAl; FilmgC; OxFilm; WhThe; WorEFlm*

Whalen, Grover
American. Merchant
b. Jun 2, 1886 in New York, New York
d. Apr 20, 1962 in New York, New York
Source: *WhAm 4*

Whalen, Michael
[Joseph Kenneth Shovlin]
American. Actor
b. 1902 in Wilkes-Barre, Pennsylvania
d. Apr 14, 1974 in Woodland Hills, California
Source: *FilmgC; MovMk; WhScrn 77; WhoHol B*

Wharton, Clifton Reginald, Jr.
American. University Chancellor
b. Sep 13, 1926 in Boston, Massachusetts
Source: *BioIn 8, 9, 10, 11; ConAu 41R; CurBio 58; WhoAm 74, 76, 78, 80, 82; WhoBlA 77*

Wharton, Edith
[Edith Newbold Jones]
American. Author
Won Pulitzer Prize, 1921, for *The Age of Innocence.*
b. Jan 24, 1862 in New York, New York
d. Aug 11, 1937 in Paris, France
Source: *AmAu&B; AmBi; AmWr; AtlBL; BiD&SB; CasWL; Chambr 3; CnDAL; ConAmA; ConAmL; CyWA; DcAmAu; DcAmB S2; DcBiA; DcLEL; DcNAA; EncAB-H; EncWL; EvLB; HerW; InWom; LongCTC; ModAL, SUP; NotAW; OxAmL; OxEng; Pen AM; RAdv 1; REn; REnAL; TwCA, SUP; TwCBDA; TwCW; WebAB; WebE&AL; WhAm 1; WhNAA; WhoTwCL; WomWWA 14*

Wharton, Joseph
American. Metallurgist
b. Mar 3, 1826 in Philadelphia, Pennsylvania
d. 1909
Source: *DcAmB; NatCAB 13; TwCBDA; WhAm 1*

Wheatley, Phillis
American. Poet
b. 1753 in Senegal
d. Dec 5, 1784 in Boston, Massachusetts
Source: *AfrA; Alli; AmAu; AmAu&B; AmBi; ApCAB; BlkAW; ChPo; ConAu 1R; DcAmAu; DcAmB; DcLEL; Drake; HerW; InWom; NotAW; OxAmL; OxEng; REn; REnAL; WebAB; WhAm H*

Wheatstone, Sir Charles
English. Scientist, Inventor
Anticipated Samuel Morse in invention of telegraph, 1837.
b. Feb 6, 1802 in Gloucester, England
d. Oct 19, 1875 in Paris, France
Source: *Alli, SUP; AsBiEn*

Wheeler, Bert
[Wheeler and Woolsey]
American. Comedian
b. 1895 in Paterson, New Jersey
d. Jan 18, 1968 in New York, New York
Source: *BiE&WWA; FilmgC; MovMk; WhScrn 74, 77; WhoHol B*

Wheeler, Burton Kendall
American. Senator
b. Feb 27, 1882 in Hudson, Massachusetts
d. Jan 6, 1975 in Washington, DC
Source: *BiDrAC; ConAu 53; CurBio 40, 75; WhAm 6; WhAmP; Who 74*

Wheeler, Earle G
American. Joint Chief of Staff
b. Jan 13, 1908 in Washington, DC
d. Dec 18, 1975 in Frederick, Maryland
Source: *CurBio 65; IntWW 74; WhAm 6; WhoAm 74*

Wheeler, Elmer P
American. Scientist
b. Feb 23, 1916 in Bow, New Hampshire
Source: *AmM&WS 73P*

Wheeler, Joseph
American. Military Leader
b. Sep 10, 1836 in Augusta, Georgia
d. Jan 25, 1906 in Brooklyn, New York
Source: *Alli SUP; AmBi; ApCAB; BiDConf; BiDSA; BiDrAC; ChPo S1; DcAmAu; DcAmB; DcNAA; TwCBDA; WebAB; WhAm 1; WhAmP*

Wheeler, Mortimer
British. Archeologist
b. Sep 10, 1890 in Edinburgh, Scotland
d. Jul 22, 1976 in Leatherhead, England
Source: *ConAu 65, 77; CurBio 56; IntWW 74; LongCTC; Who 74; WhoWor 74*

Wheeler, Roger Milton
American. Chairman of Telex Corporation
b. Feb 27, 1926 in Boston, Massachusetts
d. May 27, 1981 in Tulsa, Oklahoma
Source: *WhoAm 74, 76, 78, 80; WhoS&SW 73*

Wheeler, Schuyler Skaats
American. Inventor
Invented the electric fan.
b. May 17, 1860
d. 1923
Source: *BioIn 4; WebBD 80*

Wheeler and Woolsey
see: Wheeler, Bert; Woolsey, Robert

Wheelock, Eleazar
American. College Administrator
Founded Dartmouth College; served as first president, 1770-79.
b. Apr 22, 1711 in Windham, Connecticut
d. Apr 24, 1779
Source: *BioIn 1, 3, 9; WebBD 80*

Wheelock, John Hall
American. Poet
b. Sep 9, 1886 in Far Rockaway, New York
d. Mar 22, 1978 in New York, New York
Source: *AmAu&B; AmLY; AnMV 1926; Au&Wr 71; ChPo, S1, S2; CnDAL; ConAmA; ConAmL; ConAu 17R, 77; ConLC 14; ConP 70, 75; DcLEL; DrAP 75; IntWW 74; ModAL; OxAmL; RAdv 1; REn; REnAL; TwCA, SUP; WhNAA; WhoAm 74; WhoWor 74; WrDr 76*

Whiffen, Marcus
English. Author, Architectural Historian
b. Mar 4, 1916 in Ross, England
Source: *ConAu 61*

Whipple, George H
American. Pathologist
b. Aug 28, 1879 in Ashland, New Hampshire
d. Feb 1, 1976 in Rochester, New York
Source: *AmM&WS 73P; IntWW 74; WebAB; WhAm 6; Who 74; WhoAm 74; WhoWor 74*

Whipple, William
American. Continental Congressman
b. Jan 14, 1730 in Kittery, Maine
d. Nov 28, 1785 in Portsmouth, New Hampshire
Source: *AmBi; ApCAB; BiAuS; BiDrAC; DcAmB; Drake; WhAm H; WhAmP*

Whistler, Anna Matilda McNeill
"Whistler's Mother"
American. Mother of James Whistler
b. 1804
d. 1881
Source: *InWom*

Whistler, James Abbott McNeill
American. Artist, Author
Famous for *Arrangement in Gray and Black No.1: The Artist's Mother,* 1872 or "Whistler's Mother."
b. Jul 10, 1834 in Lowell, Massachusetts
d. Jul 17, 1903 in London, England
Source: *Alli SUP; AmAu; AmAu&B; AmBi; ApCAB; AtlBL; BiD&SB; Chambr 3; DcAmAu; DcAmB; DcLEL; DcNAA; EncAB-H; OxAmL; OxEng; REn; REnAL; TwCBDA; WebAB; WhAm 1*

Whitaker, John Francis
American. Sportscaster
b. May 18, 1924 in Philadelphia, Pennsylvania
Source: *WhoAm 76, 78, 80, 82*

Whitaker, Johnny
American. Actor
Played Jody on TV series "Family Affair," 1966-71.
b. 1959 in Van Nuys, California
Source: *WhoHol A*

Whitaker, Rogers E(rnest) M(alcolm)
[E M Frimbo, pseud.]
American. Author
b. Jan 15, 1899 in Arlington, Massachusetts
d. May 11, 1981 in New York, New York
Source: *BioIn 10; ConAu 103; NewYTBS 81*

White, Andrew Dickson
American. Founded Cornell University
b. Nov 7, 1832 in Ithaca, New York
d. Nov 4, 1918
Source: *BioIn 1, 2, 3, 5, 6, 7; WebBD 80*

White, Antonia
English. Author
Translated over 30 French works; wrote four novels.
b. Mar 31, 1899 in London, England
d. Apr 10, 1980 in London, England
Source: *AnObit 1980; Au&Wr 71; BkC 5; CathA 1952; ConAu 93, 104; ConNov 72, 76; IntAu&W 76; LongCTC; NewC; REn; Who 74; WorAu; WrDr 76, 80*

White, Barry
American. Singer
b. Sep 12, 1944 in Galveston, Texas
Source: *BioIn 10; BkPepl; IlEncRk; RkOn; WhoAm 82*

White, Betty
[Mrs. Allen Ludden]
American. Actress
Played Sue Ann Nevins on "The Mary Tyler Moore Show," 1970-77.
b. Jan 17, 1917 in Oak Park, Illinois
Source: *BioIn 4, 9; InWom; WhoAm 82; WhoHol A*

White, Byron Raymond
American. Supreme Court Justice
b. Jun 8, 1917 in Fort Collins, Colorado
Source: *CelR 73; CngDr 74; CurBio 62; DrAS 74P; IntWW 74; NewYTBE 72; WebAB; Who 74; WhoAm 82; WhoAmP 73; WhoFtbl 74; WhoGov 72; WhoS&SW 73; WhoWor 74*

White, Charles Raymond
American. Football Player
Won Heisman Trophy, 1979; Cleveland Browns, 1980--.
b. Jan 22, 1958 in Los Angeles, California
Source: *FootReg*

White, Chris(topher Taylor)
[The Zombies]
English. Singer
b. Mar 7, 1943 in Barnet, England
Source: *NF*

White, Dan(iel James)
American. Policeman, Accused Murderer
Murdered San Francisco mayor George Moscone, supervisor Harvey Milk, Dec, 1978.
b. 1946?
Source: *BioIn 11, 12*

White, Edward Douglass
American. Supreme Court Justice
Chief Justice, 1910-21.
b. Nov 3, 1845 in Lafourche, Louisiana
d. May 19, 1921 in Washington, DC
Source: *AmBi; ApCAB; BiDrAC; DcAmB; EncAB-H; TwCBDA; WebAB; WhAm 1; WhAmP*

White, Ed(ward Higgins, II)
American. Astronaut
b. Nov 14, 1930 in San Antonio, Texas
d. Jan 27, 1967 in Cape Canaveral, Florida
Source: *CurBio 65, 67; WhAm 4*

White, Ellen Gould Harmon
American. Founder of Seventh-Day Adventists
b. Nov 26, 1827 in Gorham, Maine
d. Jul 16, 1915 in Saint Helena, California
Source: *Alli SUP; BioIn 2, 3, 4, 5, 6, 7, 8, 9, 10, 11; DcAmAu; DcAmB; DcAmReB; DcNAA; GoodHS; InWom; LibW; NewCol 75; NotAW; WhAm HA, 4*

White, E(lwyn) B(rooks)
American. Author, Humorist
Wrote *Charlotte's Web*, 1952; *The Trumpet of the Swan*, 1970.
b. Jul 11, 1899 in Mount Vernon, New York
Source: *AmAu&B; Au&ICB; AuBYP; AuNews 2; BkCL; CelR 73; ChlLR 1; ChPo, S1, S2; CnDAL; ConAu 13R; ConLC 10; CurBio 60; DcLEL; EvLB; IntWW 74; LongCTC; ModAL; MorBMP; MorJA; OxAmL; Pen AM; PiP; RAdv 1; REn; REnAL; SmATA 4; TwCA, SUP; TwCW; WebAB; Who 74; WhoAm 74, 76, 78, 80, 82; WhoChL; WhoWor 74; WrDr 76*

White, George
American. Actor, Director, Producer
b. 1890 in Toronto, ON
d. Oct 11, 1968 in Los Angeles, California
Source: *BiE&WWA; EncMT; WhScrn 74, 77; WhoHol B*

White, James Laurie
"Deacon"
American. Baseball Player
b. Dec 7, 1847 in Canton, New York
d. Jul 7, 1939 in Aurora, Illinois
Source: *BaseEn; WhoProB 73*

White, Jesse
[Jesse Marc Weidenfeld]
American. Actor, Comedian
b. Jan 3, 1919 in Buffalo, New York
Source: *BiE&WWA; FilmgC; IntMPA 75, 76, 77, 78, 79, 80, 81, 82; MovMk; NotNAT; Vers A; WhoAm 82; WhoHol A*

White, "Jo Jo" (Joseph)
American. Basketball Player
b. Nov 16, 1946 in Saint Louis, Missouri
Source: *WhoBbl 73*

White, Josh(ua Daniel)
American. Folk Singer
b. Feb 11, 1908 in Greenville, South Carolina
d. Sep 5, 1969 in Manhasset, New York
Source: *AmSCAP 66; CurBio 44, 69; EncFCWM 69; WhAm 5*

White, Kevin Hagan
American. Mayor of Boston
b. Sep 25, 1929 in Boston, Massachusetts
Source: *CurBio 74; WhoAm 74, 76, 78, 80, 82; WhoAmP 73; WhoE 74; WhoGov 72; WhoWor 74*

White, Margaret Bourke
American. Photojournalist
b. Jun 14, 1906 in New York, New York
d. Aug 27, 1971 in Stamford, Connecticut
Source: *AmAu&B; ConAu 29R; ConAu P-1; CurBio 40, 71; HerW; InWom; NewYTBE 71; REn; REnAL; WebAB; WhAm 5; WhoAmW 77; WomPO 76*

White, Mark Wells, Jr.
American. Governor
State attorney general elected governor of TX, 1982.
b. Mar 17, 1940 in Henderson, Texas
Source: *WhoAm 78, 80, 82; WhoAmL 78, 79; WhoAmP 73, 75, 77, 79; WhoGov 77*

White, Patrick Victor Martindale
Australian. Author
b. May 28, 1912 in Hunter Valley, Australia
Source: *Au&Wr 71; CasWL; ConAu 81; ConDr 73; ConLC 3, 4, 5, 7, 9, 18; ConNov 72, 76; CurBio 74; DcLEL; EncWL; IntWW 74; LongCTC; NewC; NewYTBE 73; OxEng; Pen ENG; RAdv 1; REn; TwCA, SUP; WebE&AL; Who 74; WhoTwCL; WhoWor 74; WrDr 76*

White, Paul Dudley
American. Physician
b. Jun 6, 1886 in Roxbury, Massachusetts
d. Oct 31, 1973 in Boston, Massachusetts
Source: *AmM&WS 73P; ConAu 45; CurBio 55, 73; NewYTBE 73; WhAm 6; WhoAm 74; WhoE 74; WhoWor 74*

White, Pearl
American. Actress
b. Mar 4, 1889? in Greenridge, Missouri
d. Aug 4, 1938 in Paris, France
Source: *DcAmB S2; Film 1; FilmgC; InWom; MotPP; MovMk; NotAW; OxFilm; REnAL; TwYS; WhAm HA, 4; WhScrn 74, 77; WhoHol B; WorEFlm*

White, Randy Lee
American. Football Player
b. Jan 15, 1953 in Wilmington, Delaware
Source: *FootReg*

White, Richard Grant
American. Author, Critic
b. May 23, 1821 in New York, New York
d. Apr 8, 1885 in New York, New York
Source: *Alli, SUP; AmAu; AmAu&B; AmBi; ApCAB; BbD; BiD&SB; Chambr 3; CyAl 2; DcAmAu; DcAmB; DcEnL; DcNAA; EvLB; OxAmL; REnAL; TwCBDA; WhAm H*

White, Slappy
American. Comedian
Source: *WhoHol A*

White, Stan(ley Ray)
American. Football Player
First NFL player to sign contract with USFL team, 1983.
b. Oct 24, 1949 in Dover, Ohio
Source: *FootReg*

White, Stanford
American. Architect
Killed by Harry Thaw over alleged affair with Thaw's wife, showgirl Evelyn Nesbit.
b. Nov 9, 1853 in New York, New York
d. Jun 25, 1906 in New York, New York
Source: *AmBi; ApCAB; AtlBL; ChPo; DcAmB; EncAB-H; LongCTC; OxAmL; REnAL; TwCBDA; WebAB; WhAm 1*

White, Stewart Edward
American. Author
b. Mar 12, 1873 in Grand Rapids, Michigan
d. Sep 18, 1946 in San Francisco, California
Source: *AmAu&B; ArizL; BiDPara; CarSB; CnDAL; ConAmA; ConAmL; CurBio 46; DcAmAu; DcAmB S4; DcLEL; DcNAA; LongCTC; ObitOF 79; OxAmL; REnAL; TwCA, SUP; TwCBDA; WhAm 2; WhNAA*

White, T(erence) H(anbury)
Irish. Author
b. May 29, 1906 in Bombay, India
d. Jan 17, 1964 in Piraeus, Greece
Source: *CasWL; CnMWL; ConAu 73; DcLEL; LongCTC; ModBrL; OxEng; Pen ENG; RAdv 1; REn; SmATA 12; TwCA, SUP; TwCW; WhAm 4; WhoChL*

White, Theodore Harold
"Teddy"
American. Author
Wrote *The Making of the President,* 1960, 1964, 1968, 1972.
b. May 6, 1915 in Boston, Massachusetts
Source: *AmAu&B; Au&Wr 71; CelR 73; ConAu 1R, 3NR; CurBio 53; IntWW 74; OxAmL; REn; REnAL; WhoAm 74; WhoWor 74; WorAu; WrDr 76*

White, Walter Francis
American. Author, Civil Rights Leader
b. Jul 1, 1893 in Atlanta, Georgia
d. Mar 21, 1955 in New York, New York
Source: *AmAu&B; BlkAW; CurBio 42, 55; DcAmB S3; EncAB-H; REn; REnAL; TwCA, SUP; WebAB; WhAm 3; WhNAA*

White, Wilfrid Hyde
see: Hyde-White, Wilfrid

White, William Allen
American. Journalist, Editor, Author
b. Feb 10, 1868 in Emporia, Kansas
d. Jan 29, 1944 in Emporia, Kansas
Source: *AmAu&B; AmLY; ChPo, S1; CnDAL; CurBio 40, 44; DcAmAu; DcAmB S3; DcLEL; DcNAA; EncAB-H; LongCTC; OxAmL; REn; REnAL; TwCA, SUP; WebAB; WhAm 2; WhNAA*

White, William Lindsay
American. Editor, Publisher
b. Jun 17, 1900 in Emporia, Kansas
d. Jul 26, 1973 in Emporia, Kansas
Source: *AmAu&B; CnDAL; ConAu 41R, 101; OxAmL; REnAL; TwCA SUP; WhAm 6; WhoAm 74*

White, William Smith
American. Journalist
b. Feb 5, 1907 in DeLeon, Texas
Source: *AmAu&B; ConAu 5R; CurBio 55; IntWW 74; OxAmL; WhoAm 74, 76, 78, 80, 82; WhoS&SW 73*

Whitefield, George
English. Founded Calvinist Methodism
Joined Methodists, 1732; adapted Calvinist views to Methodism, 1741.
b. Dec 27, 1714 in Gloucester, England
d. Sep 30, 1770 in Newburyport, Massachusetts
Source: *Alli; AmAu&B; AmBi; ApCAB; BbD; BiD&SB; BiDSA; BrAu; Chambr 2; DcAmB; DcEnL; Drake; EncAB-H; NewC; OxAmL; OxEng; TwCBDA; WebE&AL; WhAm H*

Whitehead, Alfred North
English. Philosopher
Developed philosophy of organism which interrelated matter, space, time.
b. Feb 15, 1861 in Ramsgate, England
d. Dec 30, 1947 in Cambridge, Massachusetts
Source: *AmAu&B; Chambr 3; DcAmB S4; DcLEL; DcNAA; EncAB-H; LongCTC; NewC; OxAmL; OxEng; REn; REnAL; TwCA, SUP; WebAB; WhAm 2*

Whitehead, Don(ald Ford)
American. Journalist
b. Apr 8, 1908 in Inman, Virginia
d. Jan 12, 1981 in Knoxville, Tennessee
Source: *AmAu&B; BioIn 3, 5, 9; ConAu 9R, 102; CurBio 53, 81; SmATA 4; WhoAm 74, 76, 78, 80*

Whitehead, Edward
"Commander Whitehead"
English. Chairman of Schweppes Ltd.
b. May 20, 1908 in Hampshire, England
d. Apr 16, 1978 in Petersfield, England
Source: *CelR 73; CurBio 67, 78; Who 74*

Whitehead, Edwin C
American. Business Executive
b. Jun 1, 1919 in New York, New York
Source: *St&PR 75; WhoAm 74, 76, 78, 80, 82; WhoE 74; WhoF&I 74; WhoWor 74*

Whitehead, Robert
Canadian. Theatrical Producer
b. Mar 3, 1916 in Montreal, PQ
Source: *BiE&WWA; CanWW 82; NotNAT; PlP&P; WhoAm 74, 76, 78, 80, 82; WhoE 74; WhoThe 77*

Whitehead, William
British. Poet
b. 1715
d. 1785
Source: *Alli; BiD&SB; BrAu; ChPo, S1; DcEnA; DcEnL; DcEuL; DcLEL; EvLB; NewC; OxEng; PoLE*

Whitehill, Clarence Eugene
American. Opera Singer
b. Nov 5, 1871 in Marengo, Iowa
d. Dec 19, 1932 in New York, New York
Source: *AmBi; DcAmB; WhAm 1*

Whitelaw, Billie
English. Actress
b. Jun 6, 1932 in Coventry, England
Source: *FilmEn; FilmgC; IntMPA 75, 76, 77, 78, 79, 80, 81; Who 74; WhoHol A; WhoThe 77, 81*

Whiteman, Paul
"Pops"
American. Conductor
b. Mar 28, 1891 in Denver, Colorado
d. Dec 29, 1967 in Doylestown, Pennsylvania
Source: *BiE&WWA; CurBio 45, 68; FilmgC; WebAB; WhAm 4A; WhScrn 74, 77; WhoHol B; WhoJazz 72*

Whiting, George
American. Author, Singer
b. Aug 16, 1884 in Chicago, Illinois
d. Dec 18, 1943 in Bronx, New York
Source: *AmSCAP 66*

Whiting, Leonard
British. Actor
Film debut as Romeo in *Romeo and Juliet,* 1968.
b. 1950
Source: *BioIn 8, 9; FilmgC; MotPP; WhoHol A*

Whiting, Margaret
American. Singer
b. Jul 22, 1924 in Detroit, Michigan
Source: *CmpEPM; InWom; WhoHol A; WomPO 76*

Whiting, Richard Armstrong
American. Composer
b. Nov 12, 1891 in Peoria, Illinois
d. Feb 10, 1938 in Beverly Hills, California
Source: *AmSCAP 66; BioIn 4, 5, 6, 10; NatCAB 28*

Whitington, Dick (Richard)
English. Lord Mayor of London
b. 1358
d. 1423
Source: *NewCol 75*

Whitlam, Edward Gough
Australian. Former Prime Minister
b. Jul 11, 1916 in Melbourne, Australia
Source: *IntWW 74; NewYTBE 71; WhoWor 74*

Whitlock, Brand
American. Author, Diplomat
b. Mar 4, 1869 in Urbana, Ohio
d. May 24, 1934 in Cannes, France
Source: *AmAu&B; AmBi; DcAmAu; DcAmB; DcLEL; DcNAA; OhA&B; OxAmL; REnAL; TwCA; WebAB; WhAm 1*

Whitman, Alden
Canadian. Author, Journalist
b. Oct 27, 1913 in New Albany, NS
Source: *ConAu 17R; WhoE 74*

Whitman, Charles Joseph
American. Mass Murderer
Shooting spree on Texas U campus left 18 dead, 30 wounded.
b. 1941
d. Aug 1966 in Austin, Texas
Source: *BioIn 7*

Whitman, Marcus
American. Frontier Missionary
b. Sep 4, 1802 in Rushville, New York
d. Nov 29, 1847 in Oregon
Source: *AmAu&B; AmBi; ApCAB; DcAmB; OxAmL; TwCBDA; WebAB; WhAm H*

Whitman, Marina VonNeumann
American. Economist
b. Mar 6, 1936 in New York, New York
Source: *AmM&WS 73S, 78S; BioIn 9, 10, 11; ConAu 17R; CurBio 73; IntAu&W 77; IntWW 74, 75, 76, 77, 78; NewYTBE 72; WhoAm 74, 76, 78, 80, 82; WhoAmW 68, 70; WhoE 74, 75, 77; WrDr 76*

Whitman, Stuart
American. Actor
b. Feb 1, 1926 in San Francisco, California
Source: *FilmgC; IntMPA 75, 76, 77, 78, 79, 80, 81, 82; MotPP; MovMk; WhoHol A*

Whitman, Walt(er)
American. Poet, Essayist, Journalist
Used free verse style in *Leaves of Grass,* 1855.
b. May 31, 1819 in West Hills, New York
d. Mar 26, 1892 in Camden, New Jersey
Source: *Alli, SUP; AmAu; AmAu&B; AmBi; AmWr; AnCL; ApCAB; AtlBL; BbD; BiD&SB; CasWL; Chambr 3; ChPo, S1; CnDAL; CnE&AP; CrtT 3; CyWA; DcAmAu; DcAmB; DcEnA, AP; DcEnL; DcLEL; DcNAA; Drake; EncAB-H; EvLB; MouLC 4; OxAmL; OxCan; OxEng; Pen AM; RAdv 1; RComWL; REn; REnAL; Str&VC; TwCBDA; WebAB; WebE&AL; WhAm H*

Whitmire, Kathy
[Niederhofer, Kathryn Jean]
American. Mayor
First woman mayor of Houston, TX, 1981--.
b. Aug 15, 1946 in Houston, Texas
Source: *NewYTBS 81*

Whitmore, James Allen
American. Actor
b. Oct 1, 1921 in White Plains, New York
Source: *BiE&WWA; FilmgC; IntMPA 75, 76, 77, 78, 79, 80, 81, 82; MotPP; MovMk; WhoAm 74, 76, 78, 80, 82; WhoHol A; WhoThe 77*

Whitney, C(ornelius) V(anderbilt)
American. Businessman, Film Producer
b. Feb 20, 1899 in New York, New York
Source: *CelR 73; ConAu 85; IntWW 74; St&PR 75; WhoAm 74, 76, 78, 80, 82; WhoE 74*

Whitney, Mrs. Cornelius
[Mary Hosford]
American. Author
b. Dec 24, 1925 in Kansas City, Missouri
Source: *WhoAmW 74; WhoE 74*

Whitney, David, pseud.
see: Malick, Terence (Terry)

Whitney, Eli
American. Inventor
Invented cotton gin, 1793; first to use assembly line in industry, 1801.
b. Dec 8, 1765 in Westboro, Massachusetts
d. Jan 8, 1825 in New Haven, Connecticut
Source: *AmBi; ApCAB; DcAmB; Drake; EncAB-H; TwCBDA; WebAB; WhAm H, 1*

Whitney, Gertrude Vanderbilt
American. Sculptress, Art Patron
b. 1877 in New York, New York
d. Apr 18, 1942 in New York, New York
Source: *BiCAW; CurBio 42; DcAmB S3; InWom; NotAW; WhAm 2*

Whitney, Harry Payne
American. Banker, Sportsman
b. Apr 29, 1872 in New York, New York
d. Oct 26, 1930
Source: *DcAmB; WhAm 1*

Whitney, John Hay
"Jock"
American. Diplomat, Newspaper Publisher
b. Aug 17, 1904 in Ellsworth, Maine
d. Feb 8, 1982 in Manhasset, New York
Source: *CelR 73; CurBio 45, 82; IntWW 74, 75, 76, 77, 78; IntYB 78, 79; NewYTBS 82; WhoAm 74, 76, 78, 80, 82; WhoAmA 73, 76, 78; WhoGov 72, 75, 77; WhoWor 74*

Whitney, Phyllis Ayame
American. Author
b. Sep 9, 1903 in Yokohama, Japan
Source: *AmAu&B; AuBYP; AuNews 2; ConAu 1R, 3NR; CurBio 48; EncMys; ForWC 70; InWom; JBA 51; SmATA 1; WhoAm 74, 76, 78, 80, 82; WrDr 76*

Whitney, Richard
American. President of NY Stock Exchange
b. Aug 1, 1888 in Beverly, Massachusetts
d. Dec 5, 1974 in Far Hills, New Jersey
Source: *NewYTBS 74; WhAm 6*

Whitney, William Collins
American. Businessman, Philanthropist
b. Jul 5, 1841 in Conway, Massachusetts
d. Feb 2, 1904 in New York, New York
Source: *AmBi; ApCAB; BiDrUSE; DcAmB; DcNAA; EncAB-H; TwCBDA; WebAB; WhAm 1*

Whittemore, Arthur Austin
[Whittemore and Lowe]
American. Musician
b. Oct 23, 1916 in Vermillion, South Dakota
Source: *CurBio 54; WhoAm 74, 76, 78, 80, 82*

Whittemore and Lowe
see: Lowe, Jack W; Whittemore, Arthur Austin

Whittier, John Greenleaf
American. Poet, Essayist
b. Dec 17, 1807 in Haverhill, Massachusetts
d. Sep 7, 1905 in Hampton Falls, New Hampshire
Source: *Alli, SUP; AmAu; AmAu&B; AmBi; AnCL; ApCAB; AtlBL; BbD; BiD&SB; CarSB; CasWL; Chambr 3; ChPo, S1, S2; CnDAL; CrtT 3; CyAl 2; CyWA; DcAmAu; DcAmB; DcEnA; DcEnL; DcLEL; DcNAA; Drake; EncAB-H; EvLB; MouLC 4; OxAmL; OxEng; Pen AM; RAdv 1; REn; REnAL; Str&VC; TwCBDA; WebAB; WebE&AL; WhAm H*

Whitty, Dame May
English. Actress
b. Jun 19, 1865 in Liverpool, England
d. May 29, 1948 in Beverly Hills, California
Source: *CurBio 45, 48; Film 1; FilmgC; InWom; MotPP; MovMk; NewC; OxThe; ThFT; Vers A; WhScrn 74, 77; WhoHol B*

Whitworth, Kathy (Kathrynne Ann)
American. Golfer
Most victories in LPGA history; first woman to win over $1 million.
b. Sep 27, 1939 in Monahans, Texas
Source: *BioIn 7, 10, 11; CelR 73; CurBio 76; GoodHS; HerW; LibW; WhoAm 76, 78, 80, 82; WhoAmW 75, 77, 79; WhoGolf*

Who, The
[Roger Daltry; John Entwistle; Kenny Jones; Keith Moon; Peter Towshend]
English. Rock Group
Source: *EncPR&S; IlEncRk; RkOn*

Whorf, Richard
American. Actor
b. 1906 in Winthrop, Massachusetts
d. Dec 14, 1966 in Santa Monica, California
Source: *BiE&WWA; FilmgC; MovMk; PlP&P; WhAm 4; WhScrn 74, 77; WhoHol B*

Whyte, William Hollingsworth
American. Author
b. Oct 1, 1917 in West Chester, Pennsylvania
Source: *AmAu&B; Au&Wr 71; CelR 73; ConAu 9R; CurBio 59; IntWW 74; REnAL; WhoAm 74, 76, 78, 80, 82; WhoWor 74*

Wibberley, Leonard Patrick O'Connor
Irish. Author, Journalist
b. Apr 9, 1915 in Dublin, Ireland
Source: *AuBYP; ChPo; ConAu 5R, 3NR; EncMys; MorJA; REn; SmATA 2; WhoAm 82; WorAu*

Wicker, Tom (Thomas Grey)
American. Journalist, Correspondent
b. Jun 18, 1926 in Hamlet, North Carolina
Source: *AmAu&B; CelR 73; ConAu 65; CurBio 73; WhoAm 74, 76, 78, 80, 82; WhoS&SW 73; WhoWor 74; WrDr 76*

Widdemer, Margaret
American. Author
b. Sep 30, 1897? in Doylestown, Pennsylvania
d. Jul 31, 1978 in Gloversville, New York
Source: *AmAu&B; AmLY; AmNov; Au&Wr 71; ChPo, S1, S2; ConAmL; ConAu 5R, 77, 4NR; DcLEL; EvLB; InWom; IntWW 74; OxAmL; REn; REnAL; TwCA, SUP; TwCW; WhAm 7; WhNAA; WhoAm 74*

Widdoes, Kathleen
American. Actress
b. Mar 21, 1939 in Wilmington, Delaware
Source: *BiE&WWA; FilmgC; NewYTBE 73; NotNAT; WhoHol A; WhoThe 72, 77, 81*

Widener, George D
American. Businessman, Horse Breeder
b. Mar 11, 1889 in Philadelphia, Pennsylvania
Source: *NewYTBE 71; WhAm 5*

Widerberg, Bo
Swedish. Motion Picture Director
b. Jun 8, 1930 in Malmo, Sweden
Source: *BiDFilm; DcFM; FilmEn; FilmgC; IntWW 78; OxFilm; WorEFlm*

Widgery, Baron John Passmore
English. Lord Chief Justice
b. Jul 24, 1911 in Devonshire, England
d. Jul 25, 1981 in London, England
Source: *IntWW 78, 79; NewYTBS 81; Who 74*

Widmark, Richard
American. Actor
Starred in *Judgement at Nuremberg,* 1961; *Murder on the Orient Express,* 1974.
b. Dec 26, 1914 in Sunrise, Minnesota
Source: *BiDFilm; CmMov; CurBio 63; FilmgC; IntMPA 75, 76, 77, 78, 79, 80, 81, 82; MotPP; MovMk, ; NewYTBE 71; OxFilm; WhoAm 74, 76, 78, 80, 82; WhoHol A; WorEFlm*

Widor, Charles Marie Jean Albert
French. Composer
b. Feb 24, 1844 in Lyons, France
d. Mar 12, 1937 in Paris, France
Source: *Baker 78; BioIn 2, 4; OxMus*

Wiener, Norbert
American. Mathematician
b. Nov 26, 1894 in Columbia, Missouri
d. Mar 18, 1964 in Stockholm, Sweden
Source: *AmAu&B; CurBio 50, 64; EncAB-H; REnAL; WebAB; WhAm 4*

Wieniawski, Henri
Polish. Violinist, Composer
b. Jul 10, 1835 in Lublin, Poland
d. Apr 2, 1880 in Moscow, Russia
Source: *OxMus*

Wiese, Kurt
American. Author, Illustrator
b. Apr 22, 1887 in Minden, Germany
d. May 27, 1974
Source: *AmAu&B; AuBYP; ChPo; ConAu 9R, 49; ConICB; IlsCB 1744, 1946, 1957; JBA 34, 51; REnAL; SmATA 3*

Wiesel, Elie
American. Journalist, Author
b. Sep 30, 1928 in Sighet, Romania
Source: *AmAu&B; Au&Wr 71; AuNews 1; ConAu 5R; ConLC 3, 5, 11; CurBio 70; DrAF 76; EncWL; NewYTBE 73; WhoAm 74, 76, 78, 80, 82; WhoE 74; WhoWorJ 72; WorAu*

Wiesenthal, Simon
Austrian. Author, Nazi Hunter
b. Dec 31, 1908 in Buczacz, Poland
Source: *BioIn 6, 7, 9, 10, 11; ConAu 21R; CurBio 75; EncTR; IntAu&W 77; IntWW 74, 77, 78; WhoWor 74, 76, 78*

Wiggin, Kate Douglas
American. Author
b. Sep 28, 1856 in Philadelphia, Pennsylvania
d. Aug 24, 1923 in Harrow, England
Source: *Alli SUP; AmAu&B; AmBi; BbD; BiD&SB; CarSB; Chambr 3; ChPo, S1, S2; CnDAL; ConAmL; DcAmAu; DcAmB; DcLEL; DcNAA; EvLB; FamAYP; FamSYP; HerW; InWom; JBA 34; LongCTC; NotAW; OxAmL; REn; REnAL; TwCA, SUP; WebAB; WhAm 1; WhoChL; WomWWA 14; YABC 1*

Wiggins, Archibald Lee Manning
American. Businessman
b. Apr 9, 1891 in Durham, North Carolina
d. Jul 7, 1980 in Hartsville, South Carolina
Source: *IntWW 74; WhAm 7; WhoAm 74*

Wiggins, Charles Edward
American. Former Congressman
b. Dec 3, 1927 in El Monte, California
Source: *BioIn 12; BioNews; WhoAm 78; WhoAmP 73; WhoGov 72; WhoWest 74*

Wiggins, J(ames) R(ussell)
American. Journalist, Diplomat
b. Dec 4, 1903 in Luverne, Minnesota
Source: *AuNews 2; CurBio 69; IntWW 74; WhoAm 74, 76, 78, 80, 82; WhoWor 74*

Wigglesworth, Michael
American. Poet, Clergyman
b. Oct 18, 1631 in Yorkshire, England
d. May 27, 1705
Source: *Alli; AmAu&B; BiD&SB; CasWL; CnDAL; DcAmAu; DcNAA; OxAmL; OxEng; Pen AM; REn*

Wigle, Ernest Douglas
Canadian. Cardiologist, Educator
b. Oct 30, 1928 in Windsor, ON
Source: *WhoAm 76, 78, 80, 82*

Wilberforce, William
English. Abolitionist
b. Aug 24, 1759
d. Jul 29, 1833
Source: *Alli; BiD&SB; BiDLA; BrAu 19; Chambr 2; DcEnL; DcEuL; DcLEL; EvLB; NewC; OxEng*

Wilbur, Cornelia Burwell
American. Educator, Physician
b. Aug 26, 1908 in Cleveland, Ohio
Source: *WhoAm 74*

Wilbur, Richard Purdy
American. Author
b. Mar 1, 1921 in New York, New York
Source: *AmAu&B; Au&Wr 71; BiE&WWA; CasWL; ChPo S1, S2; CnDAL; CnE&AP; CnMWL; ConAu 1R, 2NR; ConLC 3, 6, 9, 14; ConP 70, 75; CroCAP; CurBio 66; DrAF 76; DrAP 75; DrAS 74E; EncWL; IntWW 74; ModAL, SUP; NotNAT; OxAmL; Pen AM; PlP&P; RAdv 1; REn; REnAL; SmATA 9; TwCA SUP; TwCW; WebE&AL; WhoAm 74, 76, 78, 80, 82; WhoE 74; WhoThe 77; WhoTwCL; WhoWor 74; WrDr 76*

Wilcock, John
English. Author, Newspaper Editor
b. 1927 in Shackhill, England
Source: *ConAu 1R, 2NR; NewYTBE 73; WhoAm 74, 76, 78, 80, 82*

Wilcox, Ella Wheeler
American. Poet
b. Nov 5, 1850 in Johnstown, Wisconsin
d. Oct 31, 1919 in Short Beach, Connecticut
Source: *Alli SUP; AmAu; AmAu&B; AmBi; AmLY; AmWom; BbD; BiD&SB; CasWL; Chambr 3; ChPo, S1, S2; DcAmAu; DcAmB; DcLEL; DcNAA; EvLB; InWom; LongCTC; NotAW; OxAmL; OxEng; Pen AM; REnAL; WebAB; WhAm 1; WisWr; WomWWA 14*

Wilcox, Herbert
British. Motion Picture Producer
b. Apr 19, 1891 in Cork, Ireland
d. May 15, 1977 in London, England
Source: *BioIn 8, 11; ConAu 57; CurBio 45, 77; DcFM; FilmgC; IntMPA 75, 76, 77; MovMk; NewYTBS 77; OxFilm; TwYS A; Who 74; WorEFlm*

Wilcox, Larry Dee
American. Actor
b. Aug 8, 1947 in San Diego, California
Source: *BioIn 12; WhoAm 78, 80, 82*

Wilcoxon, Henry
[Harry Wilcoxon]
British. Actor, Motion Picture Producer
b. 1905 in British West Indies
Source: *CmMov; FilmgC; IntMPA 75, 76, 77, 78, 79, 80, 81, 82; MotPP; MovMk; WhoHol A*

Wild, Earl
American. Musician, Composer
b. Nov 26, 1915 in Pittsburgh, Pennsylvania
Source: *IntWW 74*

Wild, Jack
English. Actor
b. Sep 30, 1952 in Manchester, England
Source: *FilmgC; IntMPA 77, 78, 79, 80, 81, 82; WhoHol A*

Wilde, Cornel
American. Actor, Producer, Director
b. Oct 13, 1918 in New York, New York
Source: *AmSCAP 66; BiDFilm; BiE&WWA; CmMov; FilmgC; IntMPA 75, 76, 77, 78, 79, 80, 81, 82; MotPP; WhoAm 74, 76, 78, 80, 82; WhoHol A; WhoWor 74; WorEFlm*

Wilde, Kim
British. Singer
Hit single "Kids in America," 1982.
b. 1962?
Source: *NewWmR*

Wilde, Oscar Fingal O'Flahertie Wills
Irish. Poet, Dramatist, Author
Wrote *The Importance of Being Earnest,* 1895; *Lady Windemere's Fan,* 1893.
b. Oct 16, 1856 in Dublin, Ireland
d. Nov 30, 1900 in Paris, France
Source: *Alli SUP; AtlBL; BbD; BiD&SB; BrAu 19; CarSB; CasWL; Chambr 3; ChPo, S2; CnE&AP; CnMD; CnThe; CrtT 3; CyWA; DcBiA; DcEnA AP; DcEuL; DcLEL; EncWL; EvLB; FilmgC; LongCTC; McGEWD; ModWD; MouLC 4; NewC; OxEng; OxFilm; OxFr; OxThe; Pen ENG; PlP&P; PoIre; RAdv 1; RComWL; REn; REnWD; WebE&AL; WhoChL*

Wilde, Patricia
Canadian. Ballerina
b. Jul 16, 1928 in Ottawa, ON
Source: *CanWW 70; CurBio 68; InWom; WhoAm 74, 76, 78, 80, 82; WhoWor 74*

Wilder, Alec (Alexander Lafayette Chew)
American. Composer
b. Feb 17, 1907 in Rochester, New York
d. Dec 24, 1980 in Gainesville, Florida
Source: *AuBYP; BiE&WWA; CurBio 80; WhoAm 74; WhoHol A; WhoWor 74*

Wilder, Billy
American. Author, Producer, Director
b. Jun 22, 1906 in Vienna, Austria
Source: *BiDFilm; BioNews 74; CelR 73; CmMov; ConDr 73; CurBio 51; DcFM; FilmgC; IntMPA 75, 76, 77, 78, 79, 80, 81, 82; IntWW 74; MovMk; OxFilm; WhoAm 74, 76, 78, 80, 82; WhoWest 74; WhoWor 74; WorEFlm*

Wilder, Brooks
American. Businessman, Lawyer
b. Oct 4, 1928 in Wheaton, Illinois
Source: *WhoAm 78*

Wilder, Gene
[Jerome Silberman]
American. Actor
Starred in *Blazing Saddles,* 1974; *Young Frankenstein,* 1974; *Stir Crazy,* 1980.
b. Jun 11, 1934 in Milwaukee, Wisconsin
Source: *BiE&WWA; CurBio 78; FilmgC; IntMPA 75, 76, 77, 78, 79, 80, 81, 82; MovMk; NotNAT; WhoAm 74, 76, 78, 80, 82; WhoHol A*

Wilder, Laura Ingalls
American. Author, Teacher, Editor
Wrote "Little House" children's classics which are basis for TV series.
b. Feb 7, 1867 in Pepin, Wisconsin
d. Jan 10, 1957 in Mansfield, Missouri
Source: *AnCL; AuBYP; BkCL; CasWL; ChlLR 2; ChPo S1; CurBio 48, 57; HerW; InWom; JBA 51; REnAL; Str&VC; WhAm 3; WhoChL*

Wilder, Robert Ingersoll
American. Author, Journalist
b. Jan 25, 1901 in Richmond, Virginia
d. Aug 22, 1974
Source: *AmAu&B; AmNov; Au&Wr 71; ConAu 13R, 53; LongCTC; TwCA SUP; WhAm 6; WhoAm 74*

Wilder, Thornton Niven
American. Author, Dramatist
Won Pulitzer Prizes for *The Bridge of San Luis Rey,* 1928; *Our Town,* 1938.
b. Apr 17, 1897 in Madison, Wisconsin
d. Dec 7, 1975 in Hamden, Connecticut
Source: *AmAu&B; AmNov; AmWr; Au&Wr 71; AuNews 2; CasWL; CelR 73; Chambr 3; CnDAL; CnMD; CnMWL; CnThe; ConAmA; ConAmL; ConAu 13R, 61; ConDr 73; ConICB; ConLC 1, 5, 6; ConNov 72; CroCD; CurBio 43, 71; CyWA; DcLEL; EncAB-H; EncWL; EvLB; FilmgC; IntWW 74; LongCTC; ModAL, SUP; ModWD; OxAmL; OxEng; OxThe; Pen AM; PiP; RAdv 1; RComWL; REn; REnAL; REnWD; TwCA, SUP; TwCW; WebAB; WebE&AL; WhAm 6; Who 74; WhoAm 74; WhoTwCL; WhoWor 74; WisWr; WorEFlm; WrDr 76*

Wilding, Michael
English. Actor
b. Jul 28, 1912 in Essex, England
d. Jul 9, 1979 in Chichester, England
Source: *FilmgC; IntMPA 75, 77; MotPP; MovMk; NewYTBS 79; OxFilm; Who 74; WhoHol A; WhoThe 77*

Wildmon, Donald Ellis
American. Minister
b. Jan 18, 1938 in Dumas, Mississippi
Source: *ConAu 61; WhoRel 77*

Wiley, George A
American. Professor, Civil Rights Leader
b. 1931
d. Aug 8, 1973 in Chesapeake Bay, Maryland
Source: *BioIn 10, 11*

Wiley, Harvey Washington
American. Pure Food Reformer, Chemist
b. Oct 18, 1844 in Kent, Indiana
d. Jun 30, 1930 in Washington, DC
Source: *AmBi; AmLY; ApCAB; DcAmAu; DcAmB; DcNAA; EncAB-H; IndAu 1816; TwCBDA; WebAB; WhAm 1; WhNAA*

Wiley, Lee
American. Jazz Musician
b. Oct 9, 1915 in Port Gibson, Oklahoma
Source: *AmSCAP 66; WhoJazz 72*

Wiley, William Bradford
American. Publisher
b. Nov 17, 1910 in Orange, New Jersey
Source: *BioIn 4; WhoAm 76, 78, 80, 82*

Wilhelm II
[William II]
German. Emperor
b. Jan 27, 1859 in Berlin, Germany
d. Jun 4, 1941 in Doorn, Netherlands
Source: *CurBio 41; NewCol 75*

Wilhelm, Hellmut
German. Scholar
b. Dec 10, 1905 in Tsingtao, China
Source: *ConAu 5R; DrAS 74H*

Wilhelm, (James) Hoyt
American. Baseball Player
Pitcher, 1952-72; famed for his knuckleball.
b. Jul 26, 1923 in Huntersville, North Carolina
Source: *BaseEn; CurBio 71; WhoProB 73*

Wilhelmina
[Wilhelmina Helena Pauline Maria]
Dutch. Queen
b. Aug 31, 1880 in The Hague, Netherlands
d. Nov 28, 1962 in Het Loo, Netherlands
Source: *CurBio 40, 63; InWom; WhAm 4*

Wilkens, Lenny (Leonard)
American. Basketball Player, Coach
b. Oct 28, 1937 in Brooklyn, New York
Source: *BioIn 8, 10, 11; WhoAm 82; WhoBbl 73*

Wilkes, Charles
American. Explorer, Naturalist
Round the world voyage, 1838-42; explored unknown parts of Antartica.
b. Apr 3, 1798 in New York, New York
d. Feb 8, 1877 in Washington, DC
Source: *Alli; AmAu&B; AmBi; ApCAB; BiD&SB; DcAmAu; DcAmB; DcNAA; EarABI; TwCBDA; WebAB; WhAm H*

Wilkes, Jamaal
[Jackson Keith Wilkes]
American. Basketball Player
NBA rookie of year, 1975.
b. May 2, 1953 in Berkeley, California
Source: *BioIn 12; OfNBA; WhoBlA 77*

Wilkes, John
English. Reformer, Libertarian
b. Oct 17, 1727 in London, England
d. Mar 2, 1797 in London, England
Source: *Alli; BrAu; CasWL; Chambr 2; DcEnA; DcEnL; EvLB; NewC; OxEng; REn; WebE&AL*

Wilkie, David
Scottish. Artist
b. Nov 18, 1785 in Cults, Scotland
d. Jun 1, 1841
Source: *Alli; ChPo, S1*

Wilkins, Dominique
American. Basketball Player
b. Jan 12, 1960 in Washington, North Carolina
Source: *NF*

Wilkins, Ernest H
American. Educator
b. Sep 14, 1880 in Newton Centre, Massachusetts
d. Jan 2, 1966
Source: *AmAu&B; OhA&B; WhAm 4; WhNAA*

Wilkins, Sir George Hubert
Australian. Explorer
Commanded submarine *Nautilus,* 1931.
b. Oct 31, 1888 in Mount Bryan, Australia
d. Dec 1, 1958
Source: *REn; WorAl*

Wilkins, Roy
American. Social Reformer, Editor
b. Aug 30, 1901 in Saint Louis, Missouri
d. Sep 8, 1981 in New York, New York
Source: *BioIn 2, 5, 6, 7, 8, 9, 10, 11; CelR 73; CivR 74; ConAu 104; CurBio 50, 64, 81; EbonySL 1; EncAB-H; IntWW 75, 76, 77, 78; McGEWB; PolProf E; PolProf J; PolProf K; PolProf NF; WebAB; WhoAm 74, 76, 78, 80; WhoAmP 73, 75, 77, 79; WhoBlA 75, 77; WhoWor 74, 76*

Wilkinson, Bud
American. Football Coach
b. Apr 23, 1916 in Minneapolis, Minnesota
Source: *CurBio 62*

Wilkinson, J Burke
American. Author
b. Aug 24, 1913 in New York, New York
Source: *ConAu 9R; SmATA 4; WhoAm 82; WrDr 76*

Will, George F
American. Editor
b. May 4, 1941 in Champaign, Illinois
Source: *BioIn 10; ConAu 77*

Willard, Archibald MacNeal
American. Artist
b. Aug 1836 in Bedford, Ohio
d. Oct 11, 1918 in Cleveland, Ohio
Source: *BioIn 11; NatCAB 24; NewYHSD; WhAm HA, 4*

Willard, Emma
American. Educator
b. Feb 23, 1787 in Berlin, Connecticut
d. Apr 15, 1870 in Troy, New York
Source: *Alli; AmAu; AmAu&B; AmBi; BiD&SB; ChPo S1; CyAl 2; DcAmAu; DcAmB; DcNAA; EncAB-H; InWom; NotAW; OxAmL; REn; REnAL; WebAB; WhAm H*

Willard, Frances E
American. Social Reformer
President, Women's Christian Temperance Union, 1879-98.
b. Sep 28, 1839 in Churchville, New York
d. Feb 18, 1898 in New York, New York
Source: *Alli SUP; AmAu; AmAu&B; AmBi; AmWom; ApCAB; BbD; BiD&SB; ChPo, S1; DcAmAu; DcAmB; DcNAA; Drake; EncAB-H; HerW; InWom; NotAW; OhA&B; OxAmL; REn; REnAL; TwCBDA; WebAB; WhAm H; WhAmP; WorAl*

Willard, Frank Henry
American. Cartoonist
b. Sep 21, 1893 in Chicago, Illinois
d. Jan 12, 1958 in Los Angeles, California
Source: *WhAm 3, 4*

Willard, Jess
American. Boxer
b. Dec 29, 1881 in Kansas
d. Dec 15, 1968 in Los Angeles, California
Source: *Film 1; WhScrn 77; WhoBox 74*

Willard, John Wesley
American. Chemist
Created "Willard's Water," banned by FDA.
b. Jun 23, 1907 in Davenport, Iowa
Source: *AmM&WS 73P, 76P, 79P*

Wille, Frank
American. Former Government Official
b. Feb 27, 1931 in New York, New York
Source: *BioIn 9; WhoAm 76, 78, 80, 82; WhoGov 72; WhoS&SW 73*

Wille, Lois Jean
American. Journalist
b. Sep 19, 1931 in Arlington Heights, Illinois
Source: *BioIn 7; WhoAm 82*

William I
[William the Lion]
Scottish. King
b. 1143
d. 1214
Source: *NewCol 75*

William II
see: Wilhelm II

William III
Dutch. Joint Sovereign of England
b. 1650 in The Hague, Netherlands
d. 1702
Source: *NewCol 75; WebBD 80*

William of Wales, Prince
[William Arthur Philip Louis]
English. Son of Charles and Diana
Second in line to British throne behind father, Prince Charles.
b. Jun 21, 1982 in London, England
Source: *NF*

William of Waynflete
English. Prelate
b. 1395
d. Aug 11, 1486
Source: *Alli; NewCol 75*

William the Conquerer
[William the Norman]
English. King
Conquered England, 1066, replacing English nobility with Norman followers.
b. 1027 in Falaise, France
d. 1087 in Rouen, France
Source: *NewC; REn; WorAl*

William, Warren
American. Actor
b. Dec 2, 1895 in Aitkin, Minnesota
d. Sep 24, 1948 in Encino, California
Source: *FilmgC; MotPP; MovMk; WhScrn 74, 77; WhoHol B*

Williams, Andy
[Howard Andrew Williams]
American. Singer
Williams Brothers Quartet, 1938-52; TV series 1962-67, 1969-71.
b. Dec 3, 1930 in Wall Lake, Iowa
Source: *BioNews 74; BkPepl; CelR 73; CurBio 60; WhoAm 74, 76, 78, 80, 82; WhoHol A*

Williams, Anson
American. Actor, Singer
b. 1949?
Source: *BioIn 11*

Williams, Barry
American. Actor
b. Sep 30, 1954 in Santa Monica, California
Source: *WhoAm 78; WhoHol A*

Williams, Ben Ames
American. Journalist, Author
b. Mar 7, 1889 in Macon, Mississippi
d. Feb 4, 1953 in Brookline, Massachusetts
Source: *AmAu&B; AmNov; CnDAL; DcAmB S5; OhA&B; OxAmL; TwCA, SUP; WhAm 3; WhNAA*

Williams, Bert (Egbert Austin)
American. Actor, Minstrel
b. 1876 in Bahamas
d. Mar 4, 1922 in New York, New York
Source: *AmAu&B; BlkAW; DcAmB; EncMT; FamA&A; Film 1; OxThe; REnAL; WebAB; WhAm 4; WhScrn 74, 77; WhoHol B*

Williams, Betty Smyth
Irish. Peace Activist
b. May 22, 1943 in Andersontown, Northern Ireland
Source: *BioIn 11, 12; CurBio 79*

Williams, Billy
American. Singer, Songwriter
b. 1910
d. Oct 12, 1972 in Chicago, Illinois
Source: *WhScrn 77*

Williams, Billy Dee
American. Actor
Starred in *Lady Sings the Blues,* 1972; *The Empire Strikes Back,* 1980.
b. Apr 6, 1937 in New York, New York
Source: *BiE&WWA; IntMPA 75, 76, 77, 78, 79, 80, 81, 82; WhoAm 82; WhoHol A; WhoThe 77*

Williams, Billy Leo
American. Baseball Player
b. Jun 15, 1938 in Whistler, Alabama
Source: *BaseEn; WhoAm 74; WhoBlA 75; WhoProB 73*

Williams, Charles
see: K C and the Sunshine Band

Williams, Cindy
[Mrs. Bill Hudson]
American. Actress
Starred in TV series "Laverne and Shirley," 1975--.
b. Aug 22, 1948 in Van Nuys, California
Source: *BkPepl; IntMPA 75, 76, 77, 78, 79, 80, 81, 82; MovMk; WhoAm 82; WhoHol A*

Williams, Clarence, III
American. Actor
b. Aug 21, 1939 in New York, New York
Source: *NotNAT; WhoHol A; WhoThe 77*

Williams, Cliff
see: AC-DC

Williams, "Cootie" (Charles Melvin)
American. Jazz Musician
b. Jul 24, 1908? in Mobile, Alabama
Source: *AmSCAP 66; WhoJazz 72*

Williams, Daniel Hale
American. Scientist, Engineer
b. Jan 18, 1858 in Hollidaysburg, Pennsylvania
d. Aug 4, 1931 in Idlewild, Michigan
Source: *DcAmB; WebAB; WhAm 1*

Williams, Delvin
American. Football Player
b. Apr 17, 1951 in Houston, Texas
Source: *FootReg; WhoBlA 77*

Williams, Dick (Richard Hirschfield)
American. Baseball Player, Manager
b. May 7, 1928 in Saint Louis, Missouri
Source: *BaseEn; BioIn 8, 10; CurBio 73; WhoAm 82; WhoProB 73*

Williams, Edward Bennett
American. Lawyer, Sports Team Owner
Owner, Baltimore Orioles; president, Washington Redskins.
b. May 31, 1920 in Hartford, Connecticut
Source: *BioIn 4, 5, 6, 7, 10, 11; CelR 73; ConAu 1R; CurBio 65; WebAB; WhoAm 76, 78, 80, 82; WhoF&I 74; WhoS&SW 73*

Williams, Eric Eustace
Trinidadian. Prime Minister
b. Sep 25, 1911 in Port of Spain, Trinidad
d. Mar 29, 1981 in Port of Spain, Trinidad
Source: *AnObit 1981; BioIn 4, 7, 8, 9, 10; ConAu 103; CurBio 66, 81; IntWW 74, 75, 76, 77, 78; WhoGov 72; WhoWor 74, 76, 78*

Williams, Esther
[Mrs. Fernando Lamas]
American. Actress, Swimmer
Starred in MGM aquatic musicals *Neptune's Daughter,* 1949; *Dangerous When Wet,* 1953.
b. Aug 8, 1923 in Los Angeles, California
Source: *BiDFilm; CmMov; CurBio 55; FilmgC; InWom; IntMPA 75, 76, 77, 78, 79, 80, 81, 82; MotPP; MovMk; OxFilm; WhoHol A; WorEFlm*

Williams, Garth Montgomery
American. Illustrator
Illustrator of children's books: "Little House" series and *Stuart Little,* 1945.
b. Apr 16, 1912 in New York, New York
Source: *AmAu&B; AuBYP; ChPo, S1; IlsCB 1744, 1946, 1957; MorJA; REnAL; Str&VC; WhoAm 74, 76, 78, 80, 82; WhoAmA 73*

Williams, (George) Emlyn
Welsh. Dramatist, Actor
b. Nov 26, 1905 in Mostyn, Wales
Source: *Au&Wr 71; BiE&WWA; CasWL; CnMD; CnThe; ConDr 73; CroCD; CurBio 41, 52; DcLEL; EncMys; EvLB; FamA&A; FilmgC; IntMPA 75, 76, 77, 78, 79, 80, 81, 82; IntWW 74; LongCTC; McGEWD; ModBrL; ModWD; MovMk; NewC; NotNAT; OxThe; Pen ENG; REn; TwCA, SUP; Who 82; WhoAm 74; WhoHol A; WhoThe 77; WhoWor 74; WorEFlm; WrDr 76*

Williams, Gus
American. Actor
b. Jul 19, 1847 in New York, New York
d. Jan 16, 1915 in Yonkers, New York
Source: *WhoStg 1906*

Williams, Gus
American. Basketball Player
b. Oct 10, 1953 in Mount Vernon, New York
Source: *BioIn 12; OfNBA*

Williams, "Hank" (Hiram)
"The Drifting Cowboy"
American. Singer, Actor
Composed country-western hits "Your Cheatin' Heart"; "Jambalaya."
b. Sep 15, 1923 in Georgiana, Alabama
d. Jan 1, 1953 in West Virginia
Source: *DcAmB S3; EncFCWM 69; WhScrn 74, 77; WhoHol B*

Williams, Hank, Jr.
American. Singer
b. May 26, 1949 in Shreveport, Louisiana
Source: *EncFCWM 69; WhoAm 82; WhoHol A*

Williams, Harrison Arlington, Jr.
American. Lawyer, Politician
b. Dec 10, 1919 in Plainfield, New Jersey
Source: *BiDrAC; CngDr 74; CurBio 60; IntWW 74; WhoAm 74, 76, 78, 80, 82; WhoAmP 73; WhoE 74; WhoGov 72*

Williams, Hosea Lorenzo
American. Civil Rights Leader
b. Jan 5, 1926 in Attapulgis, Georgia
Source: *BioIn 11; ConAu 49; WhoS&SW 73*

Williams, J(ames) R(obert)
American. Cartoonist
Created comic strip "Out Our Way, with the Willits."
b. Aug 18, 1888 in Halifax, NS
d. Jun 18, 1957 in Pasadena, California
Source: *WhAm 3; WorECom*

Williams, Jay
[Michael Delving, pseud.]
American. Children's Author
b. May 31, 1914 in Buffalo, New York
d. Jul 12, 1978 in London, England
Source: *ConAu 1R, 81, 2NR; CurBio 55; ObitOF 79; SmATA 3; WorAu; WrDr 76*

Williams, Joe
American. Singer
b. Dec 12, 1918 in Cordele, Georgia
Source: *BiDAmM; WhoAm 82*

Williams, John
Australian. Musician
b. Apr 24, 1941 in Melbourne, Australia
Source: *IntWW 74; Who 74; WhoAm 82; WhoMus 72*

Williams, John Towner
American. Composer
Conductor, Boston Pops, 1980--; won Oscars for scores of *Jaws,* 1975; *Star Wars,* 1977.
b. Feb 8, 1932 in Flushing, New York
Source: *IntMPA 82; WhoAm 76, 78, 80, 82; WhoMus 72*

Williams, Kit
British. Author, Artist
b. 1947 in Kent, England
Source: *NewYTBS 81*

Williams, Mary Lou
American. Jazz Composer, Musician
b. May 8, 1910 in Pittsburgh, Pennsylvania
d. May 28, 1981 in Durham, North Carolina
Source: *AmSCAP 66; BiDAmM; BioIn 2, 4, 6, 7, 9, 10, 11; CmpEPM; CurBio 66, 81; DcBlPA; EncJzS 70; IlEncJ; InWom; NewYTBS 81; WhoBlA 77; WhoJazz 72*

Williams, Mason
American. Composer, Musician, Author
Won Grammy, 1969, for "Classical Gas."
b. Aug 24, 1938 in Abilene, Texas
Source: *ConAu 25R; RkOn; WhoAm 74, 76, 78, 80, 82*

Williams, Milan
[The Commodores]
American. Musician, Singer
b. 1947 in Mississippi
Source: *BkPepl*

Williams, Paul
American. Architect
b. Feb 18, 1894 in Los Angeles, California
d. Jan 23, 1980 in Los Angeles, California
Source: *AfroAA; CurBio 41, 80; EbonySL 1; IntWW 74, 75, 76, 77, 78; WhoAm 74, 76; WhoBlA 75, 77*

Williams, Paul Hamilton
American. Singer, Composer
Won Oscar, 1976, for best song "Evergreen."
b. Sep 19, 1940 in Omaha, Nebraska
Source: *BkPepl; IntMPA 75, 76, 77, 78, 79, 80, 81, 82; RkOn; WhoAm 74, 76, 78, 80, 82; WhoHol A*

Williams, Robin
American. Comedian, Actor
Starred in "Mork and Mindy," 1978-81; won Grammy, 1979, for *Reality, What a Concept.*
b. Jul 21, 1952 in Chicago, Illinois
Source: *BioIn 11; BkPepl; IntMPA 82; WhoAm 78, 80, 82*

Williams, Roger
American. Clergyman
Founded RI colony and Providence, RI, 1636.
b. 1603? in London, England
d. 1683 in Providence, Rhode Island
Source: *Alli; AmAu; AmAu&B; AmBi; BbD; BiD&SB; CasWL; CnDAL; CyAL 1; DcAmAu; DcAmB; DcLEL; DcNAA; EncAB-H; IntMPA 82; OxAmL; Pen AM; REn; REnAL; WebAB; WebE&AL; WhAm H; WhAmP*

Williams, Roger
American. Pianist
b. Oct 1, 1926 in Omaha, Nebraska
Source: *AmSCAP 66; IntMPA 75, 77*

Williams, Roy
American. Mickey Mouse Club Host
Source: *BioIn 4*

Williams, Roy Lee
American. Labor Union Official
President of Teamsters, 1981--; convicted of bribery, 1982.
b. Mar 22, 1915 in Ottumwa, Iowa
Source: *BioIn 12; NewYTBS 81; WhoAm 82*

Williams, Samm-Art
American. Actor, Dramatist
b. 1946 in Burgaw, North Carolina
Source: *BioIn 12; NatPD 81*

Williams, Shirley
English. Politician
b. Jul 27, 1930 in London, England
Source: *CurBio 76; IntWW 78*

Williams, Simon
English. Actor
Source: *WhoHol A*

Williams, Ted (Theodore Samuel)
"The Splendid Splinter"; "The Thumper"
American. Baseball Player, Manager
Outfielder, Boston, 1939-60; manager, 1969-72; Hall of Fame, 1966.
b. Aug 30, 1918 in San Diego, California
Source: *BaseEn; CelR 73; CurBio 47; WebAB; WhoAm 82; WhoHol A; WhoProB 73; WhoS&SW 73*

Williams, "Tennessee" (Thomas Lanier)
American. Dramatist, Author
Won Pulitzer Prizes for *A Streetcar Named Desire,* 1947; *Cat on a Hot Tin Roof,* 1955.
b. Mar 26, 1911 in Columbus, Mississippi
d. Feb 24, 1983 in New York, New York
Source: *AmAu&B; AmSCAP 66; AmWr; Au&Wr 71; AuNews 1, 2; BiE&WWA; BioNews 74; BkPepl; CasWL; CelR 73; CnDAL; CnMD; CnMWL; CnThe; ConAu 5R; ConDr 73; ConLC 1, 2, 5, 7, 8, 11, 15, 19; ConNov 72, 76; CroCD; CurBio 40, 72, 83; DrAF 76; EncAB-H; EncWL; EvLB; FilmgC; IntMPA 75, 76, 77, 78, 79, 80, 81, 82; IntWW 74; LongCTC; McGEWD; ModAL, SUP; ModWD; NatPD; NewYTBS 83; NotNAT; OxAmL; OxEng; OxFilm; OxThe; Pen AM; RComWL; REn; REnAL; REnWD; TwCA SUP; TwCW; WebAB; WebE&AL; Who 82; WhoAm 74, 76, 78, 80, 82; WhoThe 77; WhoTwCL; WhoWor 74; WorEFlm; WrDr 76*

Williams, Tex
American. Singer, Songwriter, Band Leader
b. Aug 23, 1917 in Ramsey, Illinois
Source: *EncFCWM 69*

Williams, Treat
[Richard Treat Williams]
American. Actor
Starred in *Hair,* 1979; *Prince of the City,* 1981.
b. 1952? in Rowayton, Connecticut
Source: *IntMPA 81; NewYTBS 79*

Williams, Ursula Moray
English. Children's Author
b. Apr 19, 1911 in Petersfield, England
Source: *Au&Wr 71; ConAu 13R; SmATA 3*

Williams, Wayne Bertram
American. Murderer
Freelance photographer convicted of Atlanta's child killings, 1982.
b. May 27, 1958
Source: *BioIn 12; NewYTBS 81*

Williams, Wendy O(rlean)
[The Plasmatics]
American. Entertainer
b. 1946? in New York
Source: *BioIn 12; NewWmR*

Williams, William
American. Merchant, Jurist
b. Apr 23, 1731 in Lebanon, Connecticut
d. Aug 2, 1811 in Lebanon, Connecticut
Source: *AmBi; ApCAB; BiAuS; BiDrAC; DcAmB; Drake; TwCBDA; WhAm H; WhAmP*

Williams, William Carlos
American. Author, Poet
b. Sep 17, 1883 in Rutherford, New Jersey
d. Mar 4, 1963 in Rutherford, New Jersey
Source: *AmAu&B; AtlBL; CasWL; ConAu 89; ConLC 1, 2, 5, 9, 13; EvLB; LongCTC; REn; TwCA; WebAB*

Williamson, Nicol
Scottish. Actor
b. Sep 14, 1938 in Hamilton, Scotland
Source: *CelR 73; CurBio 70; FilmgC; IntMPA 82; MovMk; NotNAT; WhoAm 78, 80, 82; WhoHol A; WhoThe 77*

Williamson, Robin
[Incredible String Band]
Scottish. Singer
b. in Glasgow, Scotland
Source: *NF*

Willig, George
American. Climbed World Trade Center
b. 1950?
Source: *BioIn 11*

Willingham, Calder Baynard, Jr.
American. Dramatist
b. Dec 23, 1922 in Atlanta, Georgia
Source: *BiE&WWA; CnMD; ConAu 5R, 3NR; ConLC 5; ConNov 72, 76; DrAF 76; EncWL; NotNAT; REnAL; TwCA SUP; TwCW; WhoAm 74; WhoWor 74; WrDr 76*

Willis, Gordon
American. Cinematographer
Source: *BioIn 11; FilmEn; FilmgC; IntMPA 76, 77, 78, 79, 80, 81, 82; WhoAm 82*

Willis, Peter
see: Def Leppard

Willis, Nathaniel Parker
American. Journalist
b. Jan 20, 1806 in Portland, Maine
d. Jan 20, 1867 in Tarrytown, New York
Source: *Alli; AmAu; AmAu&B; AmBi; ApCAB; BbD; BiD&SB; CasWL; Chambr 3; ChPo, S1, S2; CnDAL; CyAl 2; DcAmAu; DcAmB; DcEnL; DcLEL; DcNAA; Drake; EvLB; McGEWD; OxAmL; OxCan; OxEng; OxThe; REn; REnAL; TwCBDA; WebAB; WhAm H*

Willis, Victor
see: Village People, The

Willkie, Wendell Lewis
American. Politician, Business Executive
Critic of New Deal programs; ran for president, 1940.
b. Feb 18, 1892 in Elwood, Indiana
d. Oct 8, 1944 in New York, New York
Source: *AmAu&B; ChPo S1; CurBio 40, 44; DcAmB S3; DcNAA; EncAB-H; IndAu 1917; OhA&B; OxAmL; REnAL; WebAB; WhAm 2; WhAmP*

Willmar 8
[Glennis Andresen; Doris Boshart; Sylvia Erickson; Jane Harguth;Teren Novotny; Shirley Solyntjes; Sandi Treml; Irene Wallin]
American. Protestors
Women employees of Citizens National Bank, Willmar, MN; staged strike, 1976, over sexual discrimination.
Source: *NF*

Wills, Bob
American. Singer
b. Mar 6, 1906 in Limestone County, Texas
d. May 13, 1975 in Fort Worth, Texas
Source: *EncFCWM 69; WhAm 6; WhScrn 77; WhoAm 74*

Wills, Chill
American. Actor
b. 1903 in Seagoville, Texas
d. Dec 15, 1978 in Encino, California
Source: *BioNews 74; FilmgC; IntMPA 75, 77; MotPP; MovMk; Vers A; WhoHol A*

Wills, Frank
American. Guard at Watergate Hotel
b. 1948?
Source: *BioIn 9, 10*

Wills, Garry
American. Author
b. May 22, 1934 in Atlanta, Georgia
Source: *AmAu&B; ConAu 1R, 1NR; CurBio 82; DrAS 74F; WhoAm 82; WhoE 74; WrDr 76*

Wills, Maury (Maurice Morning)
American. Baseball Player
Played with LA Dodgers 11 years; MVP, 1962.
b. Oct 2, 1932 in Washington, DC
Source: *BaseEn; CurBio 66; NewYTBE 72; WhoHol A; WhoProB 73*

Wills, Rick
see: Foreigner

Willson, Meredith
American. Band Leader, Composer
b. May 18, 1902 in Mason City, Iowa
Source: *AmAu&B; AmSCAP 66; BiE&WWA; ConAu 49; ConDr 73; CurBio 58; EncMT; NewCBMT; NotNAT; WhoAm 74, 76, 78, 80, 82; WhoMus 72*

Willys, John North
American. Industrialist
b. Oct 25, 1873 in Canandaigua, New York
d. Aug 26, 1935 in Riverdale, New York
Source: *DcAmB S1; WebAB; WhAm 1*

Wilmington 10, The
see: Chavis, Ben

Wilmot, David
American. Politician
Wrote *Wilmot Proviso,* 1846, prohibiting slavery in territory purchased from Mexico.
b. Jan 20, 1814 in Bethany, Pennsylvania
d. 1868
Source: *BioIn 7; NewCol 75*

Wilson, Al
American. Lyricist
b. May 24, 1906 in Providence, Rhode Island
d. Apr 25, 1951 in New York, New York
Source: *AmSCAP 66*

Wilson, Alexander
American. Explorer, Naturalist, Poet
Wrote *American Ornithology,* 1808-14, preceded Audubon's work by 20 yrs.
b. Jul 6, 1766 in Paisley, Scotland
d. Aug 23, 1813 in Philadelphia, Pennsylvania
Source: *Alli; AmAu; AmAu&B; AmBi; ApCAB; BiD&SB; ChPo, S1; CyAL 1; DcAmAu; DcAmB; DcEnL; DcNAA; Drake; EvLB; OxAmL; REnAL; TwCBDA; WebAB; WhAm H*

Wilson, Angus
English. Author
b. Aug 11, 1913 in Bexhill, England
Source: *Au&Wr 71; CasWL; ConAu 5R; ConLC 2, 3, 5; ConNov 72, 76; CurBio 59; EncWL; IntWW 74; LongCTC; ModBrL, SUP; NewC; Pen ENG; RAdv 1; REn; TwCA SUP; TwCW; WebE&AL; WhoTwCL; WrDr 76*

Wilson, Ann
[Heart]
Singer
b. 1951
Source: *NF*

Wilson, Brian Douglas
[The Beach Boys]
American. Singer, Songwriter
b. Jun 20, 1942 in Hawthorne, California
Source: *BkPepl; EncPR&S; IlEncRk; WhoAm 78, 80, 82*

Wilson, Carl Dean
[The Beach Boys]
American. Singer
b. Dec 21, 1946 in Hawthorne, California
Source: *BkPepl; EncPR&S; WhoAm 78, 80, 82*

Wilson, Charles Edward
American. Business Executive
b. Nov 18, 1886 in New York, New York
d. Jan 3, 1972 in Scarsdale, New York
Source: *CurBio 43, 51, 72; NewYTBE 72; WhAm 5*

Wilson, Charles Erwin
American. Cabinet Member
b. Jul 18, 1890 in Minerva, Ohio
d. Sep 26, 1961 in Norwood, Louisiana
Source: *CurBio 41, 50, 61*

Wilson, Colin Henry
English. Author
b. Jun 26, 1931 in Leicester, England
Source: *Au&Wr 71; CasWL; ConAu 1R, 1NR; ConLC 3, 14; ConNov 72, 76; IntWW 74; LongCTC; ModBrL, SUP; NewC; RAdv 1; REn; TwCW; Who 74; WhoAm 82; WhoWor 74; WorAu; WrDr 76*

Wilson, Demond
American. Actor
Starred in "Sanford and Son," 1972-77; "The New Odd Couple," 1982--.
b. Oct 13, 1946 in Valdosta, Georgia
Source: *WhoHol A*

Wilson, Dennis
[The Beach Boys]
American. Musician, Singer
b. Dec 1, 1941 in Hawthorne, California
Source: *BkPepl; EncPR&S; IlEncRk*

Wilson, Dolores
American. Singer
b. 1929 in Philadelphia, Pennsylvania
Source: *InWom*

Wilson, Don(ald Harlow)
American. Radio Announcer
b. Sep 1, 1900 in Lincoln, Nebraska
d. Apr 25, 1982 in Palm Springs, California
Source: *CurBio 44, 82; NewYTBS 82; WhoHol A*

Wilson, "Dooley" (Arthur)
American. Actor, Musician
Played Sam, the piano player, in *Casablanca,* 1943.
b. Apr 3, 1894 in Tyler, Texas
d. May 30, 1953 in Los Angeles, California
Source: *DcBlPA; FilmEn; FilmgC; HolP 40; WhScrn 74, 77; WhoHol B*

Wilson, Dorothy Clarke
American. Author
b. May 9, 1904 in Gardiner, Maine
Source: *AmAu&B; AmNov; Au&Wr 71; ConAu 1R; CurBio 51; ForWC 70; InWom; SmATA 16; WhoAm 74, 76, 78, 80, 82; WrDr 76*

Wilson, Earl
American. Journalist
b. May 3, 1907 in Rockford, Ohio
Source: *AmAu&B; AmSCAP 66; CelR 73; ConAu 69; REnAL; WhAmP; WhoAm 74, 76, 78, 80, 82; WhoE 74; WhoHol A*

Wilson, Edith Bolling Galt
American. Wife of Woodrow Wilson
b. 1872
d. Dec 28, 1961 in Washington, DC
Source: *InWom*

Wilson, Edmund
American. Author, Critic
b. May 8, 1895 in Red Bank, New Jersey
d. Jun 12, 1972 in Talcottville, New York
Source: *AmAu&B; AmWr; Au&Wr 71; CasWL; ChPo S1; CnDAL; CnMD; ConAmA; ConAu 1R, 37R, 1NR; ConLC 1, 2, 3, 8; ConNov 72; DcLEL; EncAB-H; EncWL; EvLB; LongCTC; ModAL, SUP; ModWD; OxAmL; OxCan; OxEng; Pen AM; RAdv 1; REn; REnAL; TwCA, SUP; TwCW; WebAB; WebE&AL; WhAm 5; WhoTwCL*

Wilson, Erica
English. Needlework Expert, Author
Wrote *Crewel Embroidery,* 1962; *Erica Wilson's Embroidery Book,* 1979.
b. 1929? in Shropshire, England
Source: *ConAu 53; NewYTBE 71*

Wilson, "Flip" (Clerow)
American. Actor, Comedian
Star of TV series "The Flip Wilson Show," 1970-74.
b. Dec 8, 1933 in Jersey City, New Jersey
Source: *BkPepl; CelR 73; CurBio 69; IntMPA 75, 76, 77, 78, 79, 80, 81, 82; WhoAm 74, 76, 78, 80, 82; WhoBlA 75; WhoHol A*

Wilson, Gahan
American. Author, Cartoonist
b. Feb 18, 1930 in Evanston, Illinois
Source: *ConAu 25R; IlsBYP; WhoAm 82*

Wilson, Harry E
"Lighthorse Harry"
American. Football Player
b. Aug 6, 1902 in Mingo Junction, Ohio
Source: *WhoFtbl 74*

Wilson, Hazel Hutchins
American. Children's Author
b. Apr 8, 1898 in Portland, Maine
Source: *AuBYP; ConAu 1R; SmATA 3; WrDr 76*

Wilson, Helen Dolan
American. Friend of John Patrick Cody
b. 1907? in Saint Louis, Missouri
Source: *BioIn 12*

Wilson, Henry Braid
American. Naval Officer
Commanded Atlantic Fleet, 1919-21.
b. Feb 23, 1861 in Camden, New Jersey
d. Jan 30, 1954 in New York, New York
Source: *WebAMB; WebBD 80; WhAm 3*

Wilson, Jack
see: Wovoka

Wilson, Jackie
American. Singer
b. Jun 9, 1932 in Detroit, Michigan
Source: *BiDAmM; EncPR&S*

Wilson, James
American. Supreme Court Justice
b. Sep 14, 1742 in Fifeshire, Scotland
d. Aug 21, 1798 in Edenton, North Carolina
Source: *AmBi; ApCAB X; BiAuS; BiDrAC; DcAmB; Drake; EncAB-H; McGEWB; NatCAB 1; TwCBDA; WebAB; WhAmP*

Wilson, (James) Harold
English. Statesman
b. Mar 11, 1916 in Huddersfield, England
Source: *ConAu 53; CurBio 63; NewYTBE 70, 72; NewYTBS 74; Who 74; WhoAm 74; WhoWor 74*

Wilson, John N
American. Composer, Conductor
b. Feb 9, 1909 in White Rock, California
Source: *AmSCAP 66*

Wilson, Julie
American. Actress
b. 1924 in Omaha, Nebraska
Source: *InWom; WhoHol A*

Wilson, Kemmons
American. Business Executive
b. Jan 5, 1913 in Osceola, Arkansas
Source: *CelR 73; CurBio 73; St&PR 75; WhoAm 74, 76, 78, 80, 82; WhoF&I 74; WhoS&SW 73*

Wilson, Lanford
American. Dramatist
Won Pulitzer Prize, 1980, for *Talley's Folley*.
b. Apr 13, 1937 in Lebanon, Missouri
Source: *BioIn 10, 11; ConAu 21R; ConLC 7, 14; CurBio 79; WhoAm 82*

Wilson, Lewis Robert
"Hack"
American. Baseball Player
b. Apr 26, 1900 in Ellwood City, Pennsylvania
d. Nov 23, 1948 in Baltimore, Maryland
Source: *BaseEn; WhoProB 73*

Wilson, Louis Hugh
American. Marine Corps Officer
b. Feb 11, 1920 in Brandon, Mississippi
Source: *BioIn 10; WhoAm 78*

Wilson, Lyle Campbell
American. Journalist
b. Aug 2, 1899 in Topeka, Kansas
d. May 23, 1967 in Stuart, Florida
Source: *WhAm 4*

Wilson, Malcolm
American. Former Governor of New York
b. Feb 26, 1914 in New York, New York
Source: *BioIn 5, 10; CurBio 74; WhoAm 82*

Wilson, Margaret
American. Author
b. Jan 16, 1882 in Traer, Iowa
Source: *AmAu&B; OxAmL; REnAL; TwCA*

Wilson, Marie (Katherine Elizabeth)
American. Actress
b. Aug 19, 1916 in Anaheim, California
d. Nov 23, 1972 in Hollywood Hills, California
Source: *FilmgC; InWom; MotPP; MovMk; NewYTBE 72; ThFT; WhScrn 77; WhoHol B*

Wilson, Mitchell
American. Author
b. Jul 17, 1913 in New York, New York
Source: *AmAu&B; AmNov; ConAu 1R, 41R, 3NR; ConNov 72; NewYTBE 72, 73; OxAmL*

Wilson, Nancy
American. Singer
b. Feb 20, 1937 in Chillicothe, Ohio
Source: *CelR 73; InWom; WhoAm 74, 76, 78, 80, 82; WhoBlA 75*

Wilson, Nancy
[Heart]
Singer, Musician
b. 1954
Source: *NF*

Wilson, Richard
American. Motion Picture Producer, Director
b. Dec 25, 1915 in McKeesport, Pennsylvania
Source: *FilmgC; IntMPA 75, 76, 77, 78, 79, 80, 81, 82; WorEFlm*

Wilson, Robert M
American. Dramatist, Producer
b. Oct 4, 1944 in Waco, Texas
Source: *ConArt; ConAu 49; ConDr 77; CurBio 79; NotNAT; WhoAm 76, 78, 80, 82; WrDr 76, 80*

Wilson, Samuel
American. Business Executive
b. Sep 16, 1766 in Arlington, Massachusetts
d. Jul 31, 1854 in Troy, New York
Source: *DcAmB; WebAB; WhAm H*

Wilson, Sandy (Alexander Galbraith)
American. Composer, Dramatist
b. May 19, 1924 in Sale, England
Source: *Au&Wr 71; BiE&WWA; ConDr 73; EncMT; NotNAT; Who 74; WhoThe 77; WrDr 76*

Wilson, Sarah
[Marchioness de Waldegrave]
English. Imposter
Escaped US indentured servitude to pose as sister of Queen Charlotte of England.
b. 1750 in Staffordshire, England
Source: *CarSB; InWom; NotAW*

Wilson, Sloan
American. Author
b. May 8, 1920 in Norwalk, Connecticut
Source: *AmAu&B; ConAu 1R, 1NR; ConNov 72, 76; CurBio 59; Pen AM; REnAL; WhoAm 74, 76, 78, 80, 82; WorAu; WrDr 76*

Wilson, Teddy (Theodore)
American. Musician
b. Nov 24, 1912 in Austin, Texas
Source: *AmSCAP 66; NewYTBS 74; WhoBlA 75; WhoHol A; WhoJazz 72*

Wilson, (Thomas) Woodrow
American. 28th US President
President, 1913-21; won 1919 Nobel Peace Prize.
b. Dec 28, 1856 in Staunton, Virginia
d. Feb 3, 1924 in Washington, DC
Source: *Alli SUP; AmAu&B; AmBi; AmLY; ApCAB; BbD; BiD&SB; BiDSA; BiDrAC; BiDrUSE; Chambr 3; DcAmAu; DcAmB; DcLEL; DcNAA; EncAB-H; EvLB; LongCTC; OxAmL; REn; REnAL; TwCBDA; WebAB; WhAm HA, 1; WhAmP; WorAl*

Wilson, Wesley
"Kid"
American. Musician, Singer
b. 1900
Source: *BiDAmM*

Wimsatt, William Kurtz, Jr.
American. Author, Critic, Educator
b. Nov 17, 1907 in Washington, DC
d. Dec 17, 1975 in New Haven, Connecticut
Source: *AmAu&B; CasWL; CathA 1930; ConAu 1R, 61, 3NR; ObitOF 79; Pen AM; WhoTwCL; WorAu; WrDr 76*

Winchell, Paul
American. Ventriloquist, Actor
b. Dec 21, 1922 in New York, New York
Source: *IntMPA 75, 76, 77, 78, 79, 80, 81, 82; WhoAm 74, 76, 78, 80, 82; WhoHol A*

Winchell, Walter
American. Journalist
Wrote syndicated gossip column; gossip radio program, 1930-50.
b. Apr 7, 1897 in New York, New York
d. Feb 20, 1972 in Los Angeles, California
Source: *AmAu&B; AmSCAP 66; ConAu 33R, 101; CurBio 43, 72; FilmgC; REnAL; WebAB; WhAm 5; WhScrn 77; WhoHol B*

Winchester, Jesse (James Ridout)
American. Singer, Songwriter
b. May 17, 1944 in Shreveport, Louisiana
Source: *BioIn 11; IlEncRk; WhoAm 82*

Winchester, Oliver Fisher
American. Industrialist
b. Nov 30, 1810 in Boston, Massachusetts
d. Dec 11, 1880 in New Haven, Connecticut
Source: *AmBi; ApCAB; DcAmB; WebAB; WhAm H*

Wind, Herbert Warren
American. Golf Authority, Author
b. Aug 11, 1916 in Brockton, Massachusetts
Source: *ConAu 1R; WhoAm 82*

Windgassen, Wolfgang Friedrich Hermann
German. Opera Singer
b. Jun 26, 1914 in Annemasse, Germany
Source: *IntWW 74; NewYTBS 74; WhAm 6; WhoWor 74*

Winding, Kai Chresten
American. Jazz Musician
b. May 18, 1922 in Aarhus, Denmark
Source: *AmSCAP 66; WhoAm 74*

Windom, William
American. Actor
Starred in "The Farmer's Daughter," 1962-65; "My World and Welcome to It," 1969-70.
b. Sep 28, 1923 in New York, New York
Source: *BiE&WWA; FilmgC; NotNAT; WhoAm 74, 76, 78, 80, 82*

Windsor, Duchess of
see: Simpson, Wallis Warfield

Windsor, Duke of
see: Edward VIII

Windsor, Claire
[Claire Viola Cronk]
American. Actress
b. Apr 14, 1897 in Coffee City, Kansas
d. Oct 24, 1972 in Los Angeles, California
Source: *Film 1; MovMk; NewYTBE 72; TwYS; WhScrn 77; WhoHol B*

Windsor, Marie
[Emily Marie Bertelson]
American. Actress
b. Dec 11, 1924 in Marysvale, Utah
Source: *FilmgC; IntMPA 75, 76, 77, 78, 79, 80, 81, 82; MotPP; MovMk; WhoHol A*

Winebrenner, John
American. Clergyman
b. Mar 25, 1797 in Walkerville, Maryland
d. Sep 12, 1860 in Harrisburg, Pennsylvania
Source: *AmBi; ApCAB; BiDSA; DcAmAu; DcAmB; DcNAA; Drake; WhAm H*

Winfield, Dave (David Mark)
American. Baseball Player
Joined Yankees, 1981, with $20 million, 10-year contract.
b. Oct 3, 1951 in Saint Paul, Minnesota
Source: *BaseEn; BioIn 11, 12; WhoAm 82*

Winfield, Paul Edward
American. Actor
b. May 22, 1941 in Los Angeles, California
Source: *MovMk; WhoAm 76, 78, 80, 82; WhoHol A*

Wingate, Orde Charles
English. WW II General
b. 1903 in India
d. Mar 24, 1944 in Assam, India
Source: *CurBio 44; WhoModH*

Wingert, Dick
American. Cartoonist
Source: *WorECom*

Wingler, Hans Maria
German. Author
b. Jan 5, 1920 in Constance, Germany
Source: *ConAu 29R*

Wings
see: McCartney, Paul

Winkelmann, Hermann
German. Opera Singer
b. Mar 8, 1849 in Brunswick, Germany
d. Jan 18, 1912 in Vienna, Austria
Source: *NewEOp 71*

Winkler, Henry Franklin
American. Actor
Plays "The Fonz" on TV series "Happy Days," 1974--.
b. Oct 30, 1945 in New York, New York
Source: *BkPepl; IntMPA 77, 78, 79, 80, 81, 82; WhoAm 82; WhoHol A*

Winkler, Irwin
American. Motion Picture Producer
b. May 28, 1931 in New York, New York
Source: *IntMPA 80, 81, 82; WhoAm 76*

Winner, Joseph Eastburn
American. Composer
b. 1837 in Philadelphia, Pennsylvania
d. 1918 in Philadelphia, Pennsylvania
Source: *BiDAmM*

Winninger, Charles
American. Actor
b. May 26, 1884 in Athens, Wisconsin
d. Jan 1969 in Palm Springs, California
Source: *BiE&WWA; EncMT; Film 1; FilmgC; MotPP; MovMk; PlP&P; Vers A; WhScrn 74, 77; WhoHol B*

Winograd, Arthur
American. Conductor
b. Apr 22, 1920 in New York, New York
Source: *WhoAm 74; WhoE 74*

Winpisinger, William Wayne
"Wimp"; "Wimpy"
American. Labor Union President
b. Dec 10, 1924 in Cleveland, Ohio
Source: *BioIn 11; CurBio 80; WhoAm 78, 80, 82; WhoE 79; WhoLab 76*

Winship, Elizabeth
American. Author
b. May 17, 1921 in Pittsfield, Massachusetts
Source: *ConAu 41R; WhoAmW 77*

Winslow, Edward
English. Leader of Plymouth Colony
Mayflower passenger who governed Plymouth Colony, 1633, 1636, 1644.
b. Oct 18, 1595 in Droitwich, England
d. May 8, 1655
Source: *Alli; AmAu; AmAu&B; AmBi; ApCAB; BiD&SB; DcAmAu; DcAmB; Drake; OxAmL; REnAL; TwCBDA; WebAB; WhAm H*

Winslow, Ola Elizabeth
American. Author, Educator
b. 1885 in Grant City, Missouri
d. Sep 27, 1977 in Damariscotta, Maine
Source: *ConAu 1R, 73, 3NR; DrAS 74H; OxAmL; REnAL; TwCA, SUP; WhoAm 74*

Winsor, Kathleen
American. Author
b. Oct 16, 1916 in Olivia, Minnesota
Source: *AmAu&B; AmNov; ConAu 97; CurBio 46; InWom; LongCTC; REn; REnAL; TwCW; WhoAm 74*

Winsten, Archer
American. Motion Picture Critic
b. Sep 18, 1904 in Seattle, Washington
Source: *IntMPA 75, 76, 77, 78, 79, 80, 81, 82; WhoAm 74*

Winston, Harry
American. Jeweler
b. Mar 1, 1896 in New York, New York
d. Dec 1978 in New York, New York
Source: *BlkAW; CurBio 65; WhoAm 74; WhoWor 74*

Winter, Edgar Holand
American. Rock Singer, Musician
b. Dec 28, 1946 in Beaumont, Texas
Source: *BkPepl; IlEncRk; RkOn; WhoAm 76, 78, 80, 82*

Winter, Edward
American. Actor
Source: *NF*

Winter, Johnny (John Dawson, III)
American. Rock Singer, Musician
b. Feb 23, 1944 in Beaumont, Texas
Source: *EncPR&S; IlEncRk; RkOn; WhoAm 76, 78, 80, 82*

Winter, Paul Theodore
American. Musician
b. Aug 31, 1939 in Altoona, Pennsylvania
Source: *WhoAm 76, 78, 80, 82; WhoMus 72*

Winter, William Forrest
American. Governor
b. Feb 21, 1923 in Grenada, Mississippi
Source: *WhoAm 76, 78, 80, 82; WhoAmP 73*

Winterhalter, Hugo
American. Band Leader
b. Aug 15, 1909 in Wilkes-Barre, Pennsylvania
d. Sep 17, 1973 in Greenwich, Connecticut
Source: *AmSCAP 66; NewYTBE 73*

Winterich, John Tracy
American. Author, Critic, Editor
b. May 25, 1891 in Middletown, Connecticut
d. Aug 15, 1970
Source: *AmAu&B; ChPo, S1, S2; ConAu 29R; OxAmL; REnAL; TwCA, SUP*

Winters, Jonathan
American. Comedian, Actor
Starred in TV series 1956-57, 1968-69, 1972-73.
b. Nov 11, 1925 in Dayton, Ohio
Source: *BkPepl; CelR 73; CurBio 65; FilmgC; IntMPA 75, 76, 77, 78, 79, 80, 81, 82; MotPP; MovMk; WhoAm 74, 76, 78, 80, 82; WhoHol A; WhoWest 74; WhoWor 74*

Winters, Shelley
[Shirley Schrift]
American. Actress
Won Oscars, 1959, for *The Diary of Anne Frank;* 1966, for *A Patch of Blue.*
b. Aug 18, 1922 in Saint Louis, Missouri
Source: *BiDFilm; BkPepl; CelR 73; FilmgC; InWom; IntMPA 75, 76, 77, 78, 79, 80, 81, 82; MovMk; NotNAT; OxFilm; WhoAm 74, 76, 78, 80, 82; WhoThe 77; WhoWor 74; WorEFlm*

Winthrop, John
English. Colonial Governor
Governor, MA Bay Colony, 1629-48.
b. Jan 12, 1588 in Suffolk, England
d. Mar 26, 1649 in Boston, Massachusetts
Source: *AmBi; ApCAB; DcAmB; Drake; EncAB-H; TwCBDA; WebAB; WhAm H*

Wintle, Justin Beecham
[Justin Beecham, pseud.]
English. Author
b. May 24, 1949 in London, England
Source: *ConAu 77*

Winwar, Frances (Francesca Vinciguerra)
American. Author, Literary Critic
b. May 3, 1900 in Taormina, Sicily
Source: *AmAu&B; Au&Wr 71; AuBYP; ConAu 89; OxAmL; REn; REnAL; TwCA, SUP; WhoAm 74, 76, 78, 80, 82*

Winwood, Estelle
[Estelle Goodwin]
English. Actress
b. Jan 24, 1883 in Lee, England
Source: *BiE&WWA; FamA&A; FilmEn; InWom; MovMk; NotNAT; Vers A; WhoHol A; WhoThe 77*

Winwood, Muff
see: Spencer David Group, The

Winwood, Steve (Stevie)
[Blind Faith; The Spencer Davis Group; Traffic]
English. Rock Musician, Singer
b. May 12, 1948 in Birmingham, England
Source: *ConMuA 80; IlEncRk; NewYTBS 81; WhoRock 81*

Wirtz, William Willard
American. Lawyer, Government Official
b. Mar 14, 1912 in Dekalb, Illinois
Source: *ConAu 101; IntWW 74; WhoAm 74, 76, 78, 80, 82*

Wisdom, Norman
English. Actor, Comedian
b. 1920 in London, England
Source: *EncMT; FilmgC; IntMPA 75, 76, 77, 78, 79, 81, 82; NotNAT; WhoHol A; WhoThe 77*

Wise, Isaac Mayer
Jewish Religious Leader
b. Mar 29, 1819 in Steingrub, Bohemia
d. Mar 26, 1900 in Cincinnati, Ohio
Source: *Alli, SUP; AmAu&B; AmBi; ApCAB; BiD&SB; DcAmAu; DcAmB; DcNAA; EncAB-H; OhA&B; REnAL; WebAB; WhAm H*

Wise, Robert
American. Motion Picture Director, Producer
b. Sep 10, 1914 in Winchester, Indiana
Source: *BiDFilm; CmMov; DcFM; FilmgC; IntMPA 75, 76, 77, 78, 79, 80, 81, 82; MovMk; OxFilm; WhoAm 74, 76, 78, 80, 82; WhoWest 74; WorEFlm*

Wise, Stephen Samuel
American. Religious Leader, Author
b. Mar 17, 1874 in Budapest, Hungary
d. Apr 19, 1949 in New York, New York
Source: *AmAu&B; CurBio 41, 49; DcAmB S4; EncAB-H; REnAL; WebAB; WhAm 2; WhNAA*

Wise, Thomas J
English. Bibliographer, Forger
b. Oct 7, 1859 in Gravesend, England
d. May 13, 1937 in London, England
Source: *CasWL; ChPo, S1, S2; DcLEL; EvLB; LongCTC; NewC; OxEng; TwCA, SUP*

Wise, William H
American. Author
b. Jul 21, 1923 in New York, New York
Source: *AuBYP; ChPo; ConAu 13R; SmATA 4*

Wise, Winifred E
American. Children's Author
b. in Fond du Lac, Wisconsin
Source: *AuBYP; ConAu 25R; ForWC 70; SmATA 2; WrDr 76*

Wiseman, Frederick
American. Documentary Filmmaker
b. Jan 1, 1930 in Boston, Massachusetts
Source: *BioIn 10, 11; CurBio 74; OxFilm; WhoAm 82*

Wiseman, Joseph
Canadian. Actor
b. 1918 in Montreal, PQ
Source: *BiE&WWA; FilmgC; IntMPA 75, 76, 77, 78, 79, 80, 81, 82; MotPP; NotNAT; WhoHol A; WhoThe 77; WhoWorJ 72*

Wiseman, Nicholas Patrick Stephen
British. Religious Leader
b. Aug 2, 1802 in Seville, Spain
d. Feb 15, 1865 in London, England
Source: *Alli; BbD; BiD&SB; BrAu 19; DcEnL; DcEuL; NewC; PoIre*

Wister, Owen
American. Author
b. Jul 14, 1860 in Germantown, Pennsylvania
d. Jul 21, 1938 in North Kingstown, Rhode Island
Source: *Alli SUP; AmAu&B; AmBi; AmLY; ArizL; BiD&SB; CarSB; CasWL; Chambr 3; ChPo, S2; CnDAL; ConAmA; ConAmL; CyWA; DcAmAu; DcAmB; DcLEL; DcNAA; EncAB-H; LongCTC; OxAmL; Pen AM; RAdv 1; REn; REnAL; TwCA, SUP; WebAB; WebE&AL; WhAm 1; WhNAA*

Withers, Bill
American. Singer, Songwriter
b. Jul 4, 1938 in Slab Fork, West Virginia
Source: *BioIn 9, 11; DcBlPA; EncJzS 70; NewYTBE 72; RkOn 2; WhoRock 81*

Withers, Googie
[Georgina McCallum]
British. Actress
b. Mar 12, 1917 in Karachi, Pakistan
Source: *FilmgC; IntMPA 75, 76, 77, 78, 79, 80, 81, 82; MovMk; OxFilm; Who 74; WhoHol A; WhoThe 77; WhoWor 74*

Withers, Jane
American. Actress
Child star of 1930's films; TV commercials as Josephine the Plumber.
b. 1926 in Atlanta, Georgia
Source: *FilmgC; HolP 30; InWom; IntMPA 75, 76, 77, 78, 79, 80, 81, 82; MotPP; MovMk; ThFT; WhoHol A*

Withers, Pick
see: Dire Straits

Witherspoon, Herbert
American. Opera Singer
b. Jul 21, 1873 in Buffalo, New York
d. May 10, 1935 in New York, New York
Source: *AmBi; DcAmB S1; WhAm 1*

Witherspoon, John
American. Educator, Religious Leader
b. Feb 5, 1723? in Gifford, Scotland
d. Nov 15, 1794 in Princeton, New Jersey
Source: *Alli; AmAu; AmAu&B; AmBi; ApCAB; BiAuS; BiD&SB; BiDrAC; CyAL 1; DcAmAu; DcAmB; DcEnL; DcNAA; Drake; OxAmL; REnAL; TwCBDA; WebAB; WhAm H; WhAmP*

Witte, Edwin Emil
American. Economist
b. Jan 4, 1887 in Jefferson County, Wisconsin
d. May 20, 1960
Source: *WhAm 4*

Witte, Erich
German. Opera Singer, Producer
b. Mar 19, 1911 in Bremen, Germany
Source: *NewEOp 71*

Witte, Sergei
Russian. Statesman
b. 1849 in Tiflis, Russia
d. Mar 12, 1915 in Saint Petersburg, Russia
Source: *McGEWB; REn*

Wittenmyer, Annie Turner
American. Social Reformer
b. Aug 26, 1827 in Sandy Springs, Ohio
d. Feb 2, 1900
Source: *AmWom; NatCAB 12; NotAW*

Wittgenstein, Ludwig
Austrian. Philosopher
b. Apr 26, 1889 in Vienna, Austria
d. Apr 29, 1951 in Cambridge, England
Source: *LongCTC; OxEng; OxGer; REn; WhAm 4; WorAu*

Wittgenstein, Paul
Austrian. Musician
b. 1887
d. 1961
Source: *OxMus*

Witz, Konrad
Swiss. Artist
b. 1400 in Rottweil, Germany
d. 1447 in Basel, Switzerland
Source: *AtlBL; NewCol 75*

Wodehouse, P(elham) G(renville)
English. Author
Created characters Bertie Wooster and Jeeves; *The Inimitable Jeeves,* 1924.
b. Oct 15, 1881 in Surrey, England
d. Feb 14, 1975 in New York, New York
Source: *AmAu&B; AmSCAP 66; Au&Wr 71; AuNews 2; BiE&WWA; CasWL; CelR 73; Chambr 3; ConAu 45, 57; ConDr 73; ConLC 2, 5, 10; ConNov 72, 76; CurBio 71; DcLEL; EncMT; EncWL; EvLB; IntWW 74; LongCTC; McGEWD; MnBBF; ModBrL, SUP; NewC; NewCBMT; OxEng; Pen ENG; PlP&P; RAdv 1; REn; SmATA 22; TwCA, SUP; TwCW; WebE&AL; WhAm 6; Who 74; WhoAm 74; WhoChL; WhoTwCL; WhoWor 74*

Woffington, Margaret
Irish. Actress
b. Oct 18, 1714
d. Mar 28, 1760
Source: *InWom; NewC*

Wohler, Friedrich
German. Chemist
b. Jul 31, 1800
d. Sep 23, 1882
Source: *WebBD 80*

Wojciechowicz, Alexander
American. Football Player
b. Aug 12, 1915 in South River, New Jersey
Source: *WhoFtbl 74*

Wojnilower, Albert M
American. Economist
b. 1926
Source: *AmEA 74; St&PR 75*

Wolcott, Oliver, Sr.
American. Jurist
b. Nov 26, 1726 in Windsor, Connecticut
d. Dec 1, 1797 in Litchfield, Connecticut
Source: *AmBi; ApCAB; BiAuS; BiDrAC; DcAmB; Drake; TwCBDA; WebAB; WhAmP*

Woldike, Mogens
Danish. Conductor
b. Jul 5, 1897 in Copenhagen, Denmark
Source: *WhoWor 74*

Wolf, Hugo
Austrian. Composer
b. Mar 13, 1860 in Windischgraez, Austria
d. Feb 22, 1903 in Vienna, Austria
Source: *AtlBL; OxGer*

Wolf, "Manny" (Emanuel L)
American. Motion Picture Executive
b. Mar 27, 1927 in Brooklyn, New York
Source: *IntMPA 77; St&PR 75; WhoAm 74, 76, 78, 80, 82; WhoE 74*

Wolf-Ferrari, Ermanno
German. Composer
b. Jan 12, 1876 in Venice, Italy
d. Jan 21, 1948 in Venice, Italy
Source: *NewEOp 71*

Wolfe, James
English. General
b. Jan 2, 1727 in Westerham, England
d. Sep 13, 1759 in Quebec, Canada
Source: *Alli; ApCAB; BbtC; Drake; OxCan; REn; WhAm H*

Wolfe, Thomas Clayton
American. Author
Wrote *Look Homeward, Angel,* 1929; *You Can't Go Home Again,* 1940.
b. Oct 3, 1900 in Asheville, North Carolina
d. Sep 15, 1938 in Baltimore, Maryland
Source: *AmAu&B; AmBi; AmSCAP 66; AmWr; AtlBL; CasWL; CnDAL; CnMD; CnMWL; ConAmA; CyWA; DcAmB S2; DcLEL; DcNAA; EncAB-H; EncWL; EvLB; LongCTC; ModAL; ModWD; OxAmL; OxEng; Pen AM; RAdv 1; REn; REnAL; TwCA, SUP; TwCW; WebAB; WebE&AL; WhAm 1; WhoTwCL*

Wolfe, Tom (Thomas Kennerly, Jr.)
American. Journalist, Author
Wrote *The Electric Kool-Aid Acid Test,* 1968; *The Right Stuff,* 1979.
b. Mar 2, 1931 in Richmond, Virginia
Source: *AmAu&B; AuNews 2; CelR 73; ConAu 13R; ConLC 1, 2, 9, 15; CurBio 71; Pen AM; WebE&AL; WhoAm 74, 76, 78, 80, 82; WhoTwCL; WhoWor 74*

Wolfe, William Lawton
[S(ymbionese) L(iberation) A(rmy)]
American. Revolutionary
b. 1952?
d. May 24, 1974 in Los Angeles, California
Source: *BioIn 10*

Wolfert, Ira
American. Journalist
b. Nov 1, 1908 in New York, New York
Source: *AmAu&B; AmNov; CurBio 43; OxAmL; TwCA SUP; WhoWorJ 72*

Wolff, Albert Louis
French. Conductor
b. Jan 19, 1884 in Paris, France
d. Feb 1970 in Paris, France
Source: *BioIn 9; NewEOp 71*

Wolff, Fritz
German. Opera Singer
b. Oct 28, 1894 in Munich, Germany
d. Jan 18, 1957 in Munich, Germany (West)
Source: *NewEOp 71*

Wolfgang, Myra K
American. Labor Leader
Helped organize Coalition of Labor Union Women, 1974.
b. 1914?
d. Apr 12, 1976 in Detroit, Michigan
Source: *WomPO 76*

Wolfington, Iggie
American. Actor
b. Oct 14, 1920 in Philadelphia, Pennsylvania
Source: *BiE&WWA; NotNAT; WhoHol A*

Wolfit, Sir Donald
English. Actor
b. Apr 20, 1902 in Newark, England
d. Feb 17, 1968 in London, England
Source: *CurBio 65, 68; FilmgC; MotPP; MovMk; OxFilm; OxThe; WhAm 4A, 5; WhScrn 74, 77; WhoHol B; WorEFlm*

"Wolfman Jack"
[Robert Smith]
American. Disc Jockey
b. Jan 21, 1938 in Brooklyn, New York
Source: *BioIn 10; BkPepl*

Wolfson, Louis Elwood
American. Industrialist
b. Jan 28, 1912 in Saint Louis, Missouri
Source: *IntWW 74; WhoWorJ 72*

Wolheim, Louis
American. Actor
b. Mar 23, 1880 in New York, New York
d. Feb 18, 1931 in Los Angeles, California
Source: *DcAmB S1; Film 1; FilmgC; MotPP; MovMk; OxThe; TwYS; WhScrn 74, 77; WhoHol B*

Wollstonecraft, Mary
see: Godwin, Mary Wollstonecraft

Wolper, David Lloyd
American. TV Producer
b. Jan 11, 1928 in New York, New York
Source: *FilmgC; IntMPA 75, 76, 77, 78, 79, 80, 81, 82; St&PR 75; WhoAm 74, 76, 78, 80, 82; WhoWest 74; WhoWor 74*

Wolsey, Thomas, Cardinal
English. Religious Figure
b. 1475 in Ipswich, England
d. Nov 29, 1530 in Leicester, England
Source: *Alli; McGEWB; NewC; REn*

Woltman, Frederick Enos
American. Journalist
b. Mar 16, 1905 in York, Pennsylvania
d. Mar 5, 1970 in Sarasota, Florida
Source: *ConAu 89; CurBio 47, 70; NewYTBE 70; WhAm 5*

Wonder, Stevie
[Steveland Morris Hardaway]
American. Singer, Musician
Albums *Innervision,* 1974; *Songs in the Key of Life,* 1977.
b. May 13, 1951 in Saginaw, Michigan
Source: *BioNews 74; BkPepl; NewYTBE 71; WhoAm 82; WhoBlA 75*

Wong, Anna May (Lu Tsong)
American. Actress
b. Jan 3, 1907 in Los Angeles, California
d. Feb 3, 1961 in Santa Monica, California
Source: *Film 1; FilmgC; HolP 30; InWom; MotPP; MovMk; ThFT; TwYS; WhScrn 74, 77; WhoHol B*

Wood, Arthur
see: Climax Blues Band, The

Wood, Chris
see: Traffic

Wood, Craig Ralph
American. Golfer
b. Nov 18, 1901 in Lake Placid, New York
d. May 8, 1968 in Palm Beach, Florida
Source: *WhoGolf*

Wood, Gar(field A)
American. Boat Racer
Powerboat champion of 1920's-30's with boat *Miss America.*
b. Dec 4, 1880 in Mapleton, Iowa
d. Jun 19, 1971 in Miami, Florida
Source: *BioNews 74; NewYTBE 71*

Wood, Grant
American. Artist
Depicted rural life in Midwest: *American Gothic,* 1930.
b. Feb 13, 1892 in Anamosa, Iowa
d. Feb 12, 1942 in Iowa City, Iowa
Source: *AtlBL; CurBio 40, 42; DcAmB S3; DcCAA 71; OxAmL; REn; WebAB; WhAm 1*

Wood, Guy B
American. Composer, Author
b. Jul 24, 1912 in Manchester, England
Source: *AmSCAP 66*

Wood, Mrs. Henry
English. Author
b. 1814
d. 1887
Source: *OxEng*

Wood, Sir Henry Joseph
English. Conductor, Composer
b. Mar 3, 1869 in London, England
d. Aug 19, 1944 in London, England
Source: *CurBio 44*

Wood, J Turtle
English. Archaeologist
d. 1890
Source: *Alli SUP*

Wood, James Rushmore
American. Surgeon
b. Sep 14, 1816 in Mamaroneck, New York
d. May 4, 1882 in New York, New York
Source: *AmBi; ApCAB; DcAmB; WebAB; WhAm H*

Wood, John Howland, Jr.
"Maximum John"
American. US District Court Judge
Appointed 1970-79; only federal judge assassinated in this century.
b. Mar 31, 1916 in Rockport, Texas
d. May 29, 1979 in San Antonio, Texas
Source: *BiDFedJ A; WhoAm 76, 78; WhoGov 75, 77*

Wood, Joseph
"Smokey Joe"
American. Baseball Player
b. Oct 25, 1889 in Kansas City, Missouri
Source: *BaseEn; WhoProB 73*

Wood, Leonard
American. Physician, General
b. Oct 9, 1860 in Winchester, New Hampshire
d. Aug 7, 1927 in Boston, Massachusetts
Source: *AmBi; AmLY; ApCAB SUP; DcAmB; DcNAA; EncAB-H; TwCBDA; WebAB; WhAm 1*

Wood, Natalie
[Natasha Gurdin; Mrs. Robert Wagner]
American. Actress
Starred in *Miracle on 34th Street,* 1946; *Rebel Without a Cause,* 1955; *West Side Story,* 1961.
b. Jul 20, 1939 in San Francisco, California
d. Nov 29, 1981 in Catalina Island, California
Source: *BiDFilm; BioIn 4, 5, 6, 7, 9, 10, 11; BkPepl; CurBio 62, 82; FilmgC; ForWC 70; GoodHS; InWom; IntMPA 76, 77, 78, 79, 80, 81, 82; MotPP; MovMk; OxFilm; WhoAm 74, 76, 78, 80; WhoAmW 66, 68, 70, 72, 74; WhoHol A; WorEFlm*

Wood, Peggy
American. Actress, Author
b. Feb 9, 1892 in New York, New York
d. Mar 18, 1978 in Stamford, Connecticut
Source: *BiE&WWA; CurBio 42, 53, 78; EncMT; FamA&A; Film 1; FilmgC; InWom; IntMPA 75, 77; MotPP; NotNAT; WhoE 74; WhoHol A; WhoThe 77*

Wood, Robert Elkington
American. Business Executive
b. Jun 13, 1879 in Kansas City, Missouri
d. Nov 6, 1969 in Lake Forest, Illinois
Source: *CurBio 41, 69; WebAB; WhAm 5*

Wood, Ron(ald)
[The Rolling Stones]
English. Rock Musician
b. Jun 1, 1947 in London, England
Source: *WhoAm 78, 80, 82*

Wood, Samuel Grosvenor
American. Actor, Motion Picture Director
b. Jul 10, 1884 in Philadelphia, Pennsylvania
d. Sep 22, 1949 in Hollywood, California
Source: *BiDFilm; CurBio 43, 49; DcFM; Film 1; FilmgC; MovMk; OxFilm; TwYS; WhScrn 74, 77; WhoHol B; WorEFlm*

Wood, Stuart
[Bay City Rollers]
"Woody"
Scottish. Musician, Singer
b. Feb 25, 1957 in Edinburgh, Scotland
Source: *BkPepl*

Wood, Wilbur Forrester
American. Baseball Player
b. Oct 22, 1941 in Cambridge, Massachusetts
Source: *BaseEn; BioIn 9; WhoAm 78; WhoProB 73*

Wood, Woodrow Johnson
American. Composer
b. Sep 29, 1918 in Richland Springs, Texas
Source: *AmSCAP 66*

Woodbridge, Frederick James Eugene
American. Educator
b. Mar 26, 1867 in Windsor, ON
d. Jun 1, 1940 in New York, New York
Source: *AmAu&B; CurBio 40; DcAmB S2; DcNAA; REnAL; WebAB; WhAm 1*

Woodbury, Woody
Comedian
Source: *NF*

Woodcock, Amos Walter Wright
American. Lawyer
b. Oct 29, 1883 in Salisbury, Maryland
d. Jan 17, 1964 in Salisbury, Maryland
Source: *WhAm 4*

Woodcock, Leonard Freel
American. Former Labor Union Official
President, UAW, 1970-77; ambassador to China, 1979-81.
b. Feb 15, 1911 in Providence, Rhode Island
Source: *CelR 73; CurBio 70; IntWW 74; NewYTBE 70; Ward 77C; WhoAm 74, 76, 78, 80, 82; WhoAmP 73; WhoMW 74*

Woode, William Henri
American. Musician
b. Sep 25, 1909 in Omaha, Nebraska
Source: *AmSCAP 66*

Wooden, John Robert
American. Basketball Player, Coach
Coached UCLA to 10 NCAA championships, 1948-75.
b. Oct 14, 1910 in Martinsville, Indiana
Source: *CelR 73; IndAu 1917; NewYTBE 72, 73; WhoAm 82; WhoBbl 73*

Woodhead, Cynthia
American. Swimmer
b. Feb 7, 1964 in Riverside, California
Source: *NF*

Woodhouse, Barbara Blackburn
British. TV Personality, Dog Trainer
Wrote *Dog Training My Way,* 1981; *No Bad Dogs: The Woodhouse Way,* 1982.
b. May 9, 1910 in Rathfarnham, Ireland
Source: *ConAu 5R*

Woodhull, Victoria Claflin
American. Author, Editor
b. Sep 23, 1838 in Homer, Ohio
d. Jun 10, 1927 in Norton Park, England
Source: *Alli SUP; AmAu; AmAu&B; AmBi; DcAmB; DcNAA; InWom; NotAW; OhA&B; OxAmL; REn; REnAL; WebAB; WhAm HA, 4; WhAmP*

Woodiwiss, Kathleen W
American. Author
b. Jun 3, 1939 in Alexandria, Louisiana
Source: *ConAu 89; WhoAm 82*

Woodruff, Judy Carline
American. Journalist, Author
NBC White House correspondent, 1977-82; reporter for "Today Show," 1982--.
b. Nov 20, 1946 in Tulsa, Oklahoma
Source: *ConAu 73; WhoAm 80, 82; WhoAmW 74, 75*

Woodruff, Maurice
English. Author
b. 1916
Source: *BioIn 7, 8*

Woodruff, Robert Winship
American. Beverage Manufacturer
b. 1889
Source: *BioIn 1, 2, 4, 7, 8, 11*

Woods, Donald
American. Actor, Realtor
b. Dec 2, 1904 in Brandon, MB
Source: *BiE&WWA; FilmgC; IntMPA 75, 76, 77, 78, 79, 80, 81, 82; MotPP; MovMk; NotNAT; WhoAm 74; WhoHol A*

Woods, Donald
South African. Journalist, Author
b. Dec 15, 1933 in Elliotdale, South Africa
Source: *BioIn 11; CurBio 82*

Woods, Granville T
American. Inventor
b. 1856
d. 1910
Source: *BioIn 6, 8, 9, 10*

Woods, James
American. Actor
b. Apr 18, 1947 in Vernal, Utah
Source: *BioIn 12; WhoHol A*

Woods, Paul
Canadian. Hockey Player
b. Apr 12, 1955 in Hespeler, ON
Source: *HocReg*

Woods, Rose Mary
American. Secretary to Richard Nixon
Executive secretary, 1969-75, who erased portions of Watergate tapes.
b. Dec 26, 1917 in Sebring, Ohio
Source: *BioIn 5, 8, 10, 12; BioNews; WhoAm 76, 78, 80, 82; WhoAmW 74; WhoGov 72; WhoS&SW 73*

Woods, Stuart
American. Author
b. Jan 9, 1938 in Manchester, Georgia
Source: *ConAu 93*

Woodson, Carter Godwin
American. Editor, Author
b. Dec 19, 1875 in New Canton, Virginia
d. Apr 3, 1950
Source: *AmAu&B; CurBio 44; DcAmB S4; EncAB-H; REnAL; WebAB; WhAm 3*

Woodsworth, James Shaver
Canadian. Clergyman, Politician
b. Jul 29, 1874 in Toronto, ON
d. Mar 21, 1942 in Vancouver, BC
Source: *DcNAA; OxCan*

Woodville, Richard Caton
American. Artist
b. 1825 in Baltimore, Maryland
d. 1855 in London, England
Source: *ApCAB; BnEnAmA; DcAmArt; DcBrBI; Drake; McGDA; NewYHSD*

Woodward, Bob (Robert Upshur)
American. Journalist
With Carl Bernstein uncovered Watergate scandal; wrote *All the President's Men,* 1974.
b. Mar 26, 1943 in Geneva, Illinois
Source: *AuNews 1; BioNews 74; BkPepl; ConAu 69; WhoAm 74, 76, 78, 80, 82*

Woodward, Joanne Gignilliat
[Mrs. Paul Newman]
American. Actress
Won Oscar, 1957, for *The Three Faces of Eve.*
b. Feb 27, 1930 in Thomasville, Georgia
Source: *BiDFilm; BkPepl; CelR 73; CurBio 58; FilmgC; InWom; IntMPA 75, 76, 77, 78, 79, 80, 81, 82; IntWW 74; MotPP; MovMk; OxFilm; WhoAm 74, 76, 78, 80, 82; WhoHol A; WhoWor 74; WorEFlm*

Woodward, William E
American. Author
b. Oct 2, 1874 in Ridge Spring, South Carolina
d. Sep 27, 1950 in Augusta, Georgia
Source: *AmAu&B; ConAmL; OxAmL; REn; REnAL; TwCA, SUP; WhAm 3; WhNAA*

Woodworth, Samuel
American. Journalist, Author
b. Jan 13, 1784 in Scituate, Massachusetts
d. Dec 9, 1842 in New York, New York
Source: *Alli; AmAu; AmAu&B; AmBi; ApCAB; BbD; BiD&SB; ChPo, S1; CyAL 1; DcAmAu; DcAmB; DcLEL; DcNAA; Drake; EvLB; McGEWD; OxAmL; OxThe; Pen AM; REnAL; TwCBDA; WhAm H*

Woody, Regina Llewellyn Jones
American. Children's Author
b. Jan 4, 1894 in Boston, Massachusetts
Source: *AuBYP; ConAu 5R, 3NR; ForWC 70; MorJA; SmATA 3; WhoE 74; WrDr 76*

Wooley, Sheb
American. Singer, Guitarist, Actor
b. Apr 10, 1921 in Erick, Oklahoma
Source: *AmSCAP 66; EncFCWM 69; WhoHol A*

Woolf, (Adeline) Virginia (Stephen)
English. Author, Critic
b. Jan 25, 1882 in London, England
d. Mar 28, 1941 in Lewes, England
Source: *AtlBL; CasWL; Chambr 3; CnMWL; CurBio 41; CyWA; DcLEL; EncWL; EvLB; InWom; LongCTC; ModBrL, SUP; NewC; OxEng; Pen ENG; RAdv 1; RComWL; REn; TwCA, SUP; TwCW; WebE&AL; WhoTwCL*

Woolf, Leonard Sidney
English. Author, Publisher
b. Nov 25, 1880 in London, England
d. Aug 14, 1969 in Rodmell, England
Source: *BioIn 4, 5, 6, 7, 8, 9, 10, 11, 12; ConAu 5R, 29R; CurBio 65, 69*

Woollcott, Alexander Humphreys
"Town Crier"
American. Author, Critic
b. Jan 19, 1887 in Phalanx, New Jersey
d. Jan 23, 1943 in New York, New York
Source: *AmAu&B; CasWL; ChPo, S1; CnDAL; ConAmA; DcAmB S3; DcLEL; DcNAA; EvLB; LongCTC; ModWD; OxAmL; OxThe; PlP&P; REn; REnAL; TwCA, SUP; WebAB; WhAm 2; WhScrn 74, 77; WhoHol B*

Woolley, Catherine (Jane Thayer)
American. Author
b. Aug 11, 1904 in Chicago, Illinois
Source: *ConAu 1R; SmATA 3; WhoAm 82*

Woolley, Monty (Edgar Montillion)
American. Actor
b. Aug 17, 1888 in New York, New York
d. May 6, 1962 in Albany, New York
Source: *CurBio 40, 63; EncMT; FilmgC; MotPP; MovMk; WhAm 4; WhScrn 74, 77; WhoHol B*

Woolman, John
American. Religious Leader
b. Oct 19, 1720 in Ancochs, New Jersey
d. Oct 7, 1772 in New York, New York
Source: *Alli; AmAu; AmAu&B; AmBi; ApCAB; BiD&SB; CasWL; CnDAL; CyAL 1; DcAmAu; DcAmB; Drake; EncAB-H; EvLB; OxAmL; OxEng; Pen AM; REn; REnAL; WebAB; WebE&AL; WhAm H*

Woolsey, Janette
American. Author
b. Dec 11, 1904 in Livingston, New York
Source: *AuBYP; ConAu 1R, 2NR; ForWC 70; SmATA 3*

Woolsey, Robert
[Wheeler and Woolsey]
American. Actor, Comedian
b. Aug 14, 1889 in Oakland, California
d. Oct 1938 in Malibu Beach, California
Source: *FilmgC; MovMk; WhScrn 74, 77*

Woolworth, Frank Winfield
American. Merchant
Founded F W Woolworth Co., 1879; sold only five and ten cent items.
b. Apr 13, 1852 in Rodman, New York
d. Apr 8, 1919 in Glen Cove, New York
Source: *AmBi; DcAmB; EncAB-H; WebAB; WhAm 1*

Wopat, Tom
American. Actor
Co-star of TV series "The Dukes of Hazzard," 1979--.
b. Sep 9, 1951 in Lodi, Wisconsin
Source: *BioIn 12*

Worcester, Joseph Emerson
American. Lexicographer
b. Aug 24, 1784 in Bedford, New Hampshire
d. Oct 27, 1865
Source: *BioIn 3, 6, 11; WebBD 80*

Worden, Alfred Merrill
American. Former Astronaut
With NASA, 1966-72; command module pilot of Apollo 15, 1971.
b. Feb 7, 1932 in Jackson, Michigan
Source: *IntWW 74; NewYTBE 71; WhoAm 74, 76, 78, 80, 82; WhoS&SW 73*

Worden, John Lorimer
American. Admiral
b. Mar 12, 1818 in Westchester County, New York
d. Oct 18, 1897 in Washington, DC
Source: *AmBi; ApCAB; DcAmB; Drake; TwCBDA; WhAm H*

Wordsworth, William
English. Poet
Poet laureate, 1843-50.
b. Apr 7, 1770 in Cockermouth, England
d. Apr 23, 1850 in Grasmere, England
Source: *Alli; AnCL; AtlBL; BbD; BiD&SB; BiDLA; BrAu 19; CasWL; Chambr 3; ChPo, S1, S2; CnE&AP; CrtT 2; CyWA; DcEnA; DcEnL; DcEuL; DcLEL; EvLB; MouLC 3; NewC; OxEng; Pen ENG; PoLE; RAdv 1; RComWL; REn; Str&VC; WebE&AL*

Worley, Jo Anne
American. Comedian, Actress, Singer
Starred on TV series "Laugh-In," 1968-73.
b. Sep 6, 1937 in Lowell, Indiana
Source: *NotNAT*

Worsley, "Gump" (Lorne)
Canadian. Hockey Player
Goalie, 1952-74; career average of 2.83 goals per game.
b. May 14, 1929 in Montreal, PQ
Source: *WhoHcky 73*

Worth, Charles Frederick
English. Fashion Designer
Founded House of Worth, Paris, 1858; began Parisian haute couture.
b. Oct 13, 1825 in Bourne, England
d. Mar 10, 1895 in Paris, France
Source: *WhoFash; WorAl; WorFshn*

Worth, Irene
American. Actress
b. Jun 23, 1916 in Nebraska
Source: *BiE&WWA; CurBio 68; FilmgC; InWom; IntMPA 82; IntWW 74; NotNAT; PlP&P; Who 74; WhoAm 74, 76, 78, 80, 82; WhoHol A; WhoThe 77; WhoWor 74*

Wortman, Denys
American. Cartoonist
b. May 1, 1887 in Saugerties, New York
d. Sep 20, 1958 in Massachusetts
Source: *WhAm 3*

Wortman, Sterling
American. Plant Geneticist
b. Apr 3, 1923 in Quinlan, Oklahoma
d. May 26, 1981 in Greenwich, Connecticut
Source: *WhoAm 78, 80; WhoWor 74*

Woss, Kurt
Austrian. Conductor
b. May 2, 1914 in Linz, Austria
Source: *Baker 78*

Wouk, Herman
American. Author, Dramatist
Wrote *The Caine Mutiny, The Winds of War,* 1971, *War and Remembrance,* 1978.
b. May 27, 1915 in New York, New York
Source: *AmAu&B; AmNov; Au&Wr 71; BiE&WWA; CnMD; ConAu 5R; ConLC 1, 9; ConNov 72, 76; CroCD; CurBio 52; EncWL; FilmgC; IntWW 74; LongCTC; ModAL; ModWD; NotNAT; OxAmL; Pen AM; REn; REnAL; TwCA SUP; TwCW; WebAB; Who 74; WhoAm 74, 76, 78, 80, 82; WhoWor 74; WhoWorJ 72; WrDr 76*

Wovoka
[Jack Wilson]
American. Religious Leader
b. 1856 in Esmeralda County, Nevada
d. Oct 1932 in Schurz, Nevada
Source: *DcAmB; WebAB; WhAm HA, 4*

Wozniak, Stephen
"Woz"
American. Co-founder of Apple Computer, Inc
Designed Apple II computer.
b. 1950?
Source: *LElec*

Wragge, Sidney
American. Designer
b. Mar 10, 1908 in New York, New York
d. Mar 28, 1978 in Boca Raton, Florida
Source: *WorFshn*

Wrangel, Ferdinand von, Baron
Russian. Explorer
Governor of Russian America (Alaska); promoted civilization of area, 1827-34.
b. 1795
d. 1870
Source: *Drake*

Wrangel, Pietr Nikolayevich
Russian. General
b. 1878
d. 1928
Source: *REn*

Wray, Fay
Canadian. Actress
Starred in *King Kong,* 1933.
b. Sep 10, 1907 in AB
Source: *CmMov; FilmgC; HolP 30; IntMPA 75, 76, 77, 78, 79, 80, 81, 82; MotPP; MovMk; OxFilm; ThFT; TwYS; WhoHol A*

Wren, Sir Christopher
English. Architect
Built 52 London churches; helped rebuild London after 1666 fire.
b. Oct 20, 1632 in Wiltshire, England
d. Feb 25, 1723 in London, England
Source: *Alli; AtlBL; NewC; OxThe; REn*

Wright, Adrian
see: Human League

Wright, Sir Almroth Edward
English. Physician, Researcher
b. 1861
d. Apr 30, 1947 in Buckinghamshire, England
Source: *BioIn 1, 2, 3, 5, 7, 10; NewCol 75*

Wright, Cobina
American. Journalist, Singer
b. 1921 in Lakeview, Oregon
d. Apr 9, 1970 in Hollywood, California
Source: *InWom; NewYTBE 70; WhAm 5; WhoHol A*

Wright, Frances
American. Reformer, Author
b. Sep 6, 1795 in Dundee, Scotland
d. Dec 13, 1852 in Cincinnati, Ohio
Source: *Alli; AmAu; AmAu&B; AmBi; DcAmB; Drake; EncAB-H; HerW; NotAW; OhA&B; OxAmL; WebAB; WhAm H; WhAmP; InWom*

Wright, Frank Lloyd
American. Architect
Known for prairie style houses: Fallingwater in Bear Run, PA.
b. Jun 8, 1869 in Richland Center, Wisconsin
d. Apr 9, 1959 in Phoenix, Arizona
Source: *AmAu&B; AtlBL; CurBio 41, 52, 59; DcLEL; EncAB-H; LongCTC; OxAmL; PlP&P; REn; REnAL; TwCA SUP; WebAB; WhAm 3*

Wright, (Frank) Lloyd (Jr.)
American. Architect
b. Mar 31, 1890 in Oak Park, Illinois
d. May 31, 1978 in Santa Monica, California
Source: *BioIn 10, 11; NewYTBS 78; ObitOF 79*

Wright, Gary
American. Rock Musician
b. Apr 26, 1943 in Englewood, New Jersey
Source: *IlEncRk; RkOn*

Wright, Harold Bell
American. Author, Minister
b. May 4, 1872 in Rome, New York
d. May 24, 1944 in La Jolla, California
Source: *AmAu&B; AmLY; ArizL; CurBio 44; DcAmB S3; DcLEL; DcNAA; EvLB; LongCTC; OxAmL; REnAL; TwCA, SUP; WebAB; WhAm 2; WhNAA*

Wright, Horatio G
American. Army Officer, Engineer
b. May 5, 1820 in Clinton, Connecticut
d. Jul 2, 1899 in Washington, DC
Source: *AmBi; ApCAB; DcAmB; TwCBDA; WhAm H*

Wright, James Arlington
American. Poet
b. Dec 13, 1927 in Martins Ferry, Ohio
d. Mar 25, 1980 in New York, New York
Source: *AuNews 2; BioIn 10; ConAu 49, 97, 4NR; ConLC 3, 5, 10; WhoAm 78*

Wright, James C(laud), Jr.
American. Congressman
b. Dec 22, 1922 in Fort Worth, Texas
Source: *BioIn 8, 11, 12; ConAu 49; CurBio 79; WhoAm 76, 78, 80, 82; WhoAmP 73; WhoS&SW 73*

Wright, John Joseph
American. Cardinal
b. Jul 18, 1909 in Boston, Massachusetts
d. Aug 10, 1979 in Cambridge, Massachusetts
Source: *ConAu 1R; CurBio 79; NewYTBS 79; WhoAm 74, 76, 78; WhoWor 74*

Wright, John Lloyd
American. Architect, Engineer
Son of Frank Lloyd Wright; established own practice, 1926.
b. Dec 12, 1892 in Oak Park, Illinois
d. Dec 20, 1972
Source: *BioIn 3, 4, 10; McGDA; WhAm 5*

Wright, Martha
American. Singer, Actress
b. Mar 23, 1926 in Seattle, Washington
Source: *CurBio 55; InWom*

Wright, Mickey
American. Golfer
b. Feb 14, 1935 in San Diego, California
Source: *CurBio 65; InWom*

Wright, Orville
[The Wright Brothers]
American. Inventor, Aviator
Designed engine and flew first flight in power-driven airplane, 1903.
b. Aug 19, 1871 in Dayton, Ohio
d. Jan 30, 1948 in Dayton, Ohio
Source: *CurBio 46, 48; DcAmB S4; EncAB-H; REn; REnAL; WebAB; WhAm 2*

Wright, Richard
American. Author, Social Scientist
b. Sep 4, 1908 in Natchez, Mississippi
d. Nov 28, 1960 in Paris, France
Source: *AmAu&B; AmNov; AmWr; BlkAW; CasWL; CnDAL; ConLC 1, 3, 4, 9, 14; ConNov 76; CurBio 40, 61; CyWA; DcLEL; EncAB-H; EncWL; EvLB; LongCTC; ModAL, SUP; OxAmL; Pen AM; RAdv 1; REn; REnAL; TwCA, SUP; TwCW; WebAB; WebE&AL; WhAm 4; WhoTwCL*

Wright, Russel
American. Industrial Designer
b. Apr 3, 1904 in Lebanon, Ohio
d. Dec 22, 1976 in New York, New York
Source: *BioIn 1, 2, 11; CurBio 77; WhoAm 74; WhoAmA 73*

Wright, Teresa
American. Actress
b. Oct 27, 1918 in New York, New York
Source: *BiDFilm; BiE&WWA; CurBio 43; FilmgC; HolP 40; InWom; IntMPA 75, 76, 77, 78, 79, 80, 81, 82; MotPP; MovMk; NotNAT; PlP&P; WhoHol A; WhoThe 77; WorEFlm*

Wright, Weaver, pseud.
see: Ackerman, Forest J

Wright, Wilbur
[The Wright Brothers]
American. Inventor, Aviator
Made first sustained, controlled flight in power-driven airplane, 1903.
b. Apr 16, 1867 in Millville, Indiana
d. May 30, 1912 in Dayton, Ohio
Source: *AmBi; DcAmB; REn; REnAL; WebAB; WhAm 1*

Wright, Willard Huntington
see: VanDine, S S, pseud.

Wrightson, Earl
American. Singer
b. 1916 in Baltimore, Maryland
Source: *BiDAmM*

Wrightson, Patricia
Australian. Author
b. Jun 19, 1921 in Lismore, Australia
Source: *AuBYP; ConAu 45, 3NR; SenS; SmATA 8*

Wrigley, Philip Knight
American. Chewing Gum Manufacturer
President, chairman, Wm Wrigley Jr Co, 1925-77; owner, Chicago Cubs, 1934-77.
b. Dec 5, 1894 in Chicago, Illinois
d. Apr 12, 1977 in Elkhorn, Wisconsin
Source: *CelR 73; St&PR 75; WhoAm 74; WhoF&I 74; WhoMW 74; WhoWor 74*

Wrigley, William
American. Corporation Executive
President, Wm Wrigley Jr Co, 1961--.
b. Jan 21, 1933 in Chicago, Illinois
Source: *WhoAm 76, 78, 80, 82; WhoF&I 74; WhoMW 74; WhoWor 74*

Wrigley, William, Jr
American. Founded Chewing Gum Company
Founded Wm Wrigley Jr Co, 1891; president until 1932.
b. Sep 3, 1861 in Philadelphia, Pennsylvania
d. Jan 26, 1932 in Phoenix, Arizona
Source: *ApCAB X; BioIn 1; DcAmB S1; NatCAB 23; WebAB; WhAm 1*

Wriston, Walter Bigelow
American. Banker
b. Aug 3, 1919 in Middleton, Colorado
Source: *BioIn 7, 9, 10, 11; CurBio 77; Dun&B 79; IntWW 74, 75, 76, 77, 78; IntYB 78, 79; PolProf NF; St&PR 75; WhoAm 74, 76, 78, 80, 82; WhoE 74, 77, 79; WhoF&I 74, 75, 79; WhoWor 74*

Wroth, Lawrence Councelman
American. Librarian, Historian
b. Jan 14, 1884
d. Dec 25, 1970
Source: *AmAu&B; ConAu 29R; NewYTBE 70; OxAmL; REnAL; WhNAA*

Wummer, John
American. Musician
b. 1899? in Philadelphia, Pennsylvania
d. Sep 6, 1977 in San Francisco, California
Source: *BioIn 11; NewYTBS 77*

Wunderlich, Fritz
German. Opera Singer
b. Sep 26, 1930 in Kusel, Germany
d. Sep 17, 1966 in Heidelberg, Germany (West)
Source: *WhAm 4; WhoMus 72*

Wurdemann, Audrey
American. Poet
b. Jan 1, 1911 in Seattle, Washington
d. May 18, 1960 in Miami, Florida
Source: *AmAu&B; ChPo; ConAmA; DcLEL; InWom; OxAmL; REn; REnAL; TwCA, SUP; WhAm 4; WhNAA*

Wurf, Jerry (Jerome)
American. Labor Union Official
President, AFSCME, 1964-81.
b. May 18, 1919 in New York, New York
d. Dec 10, 1981 in Washington, DC
Source: *BiDAmLL; BioIn 5, 9, 10; CurBio 79, 82; NewYTBS 74, 76, 79; PolProf J; PolProf NF; WhoAm 74, 76, 78, 80; WhoAmP 73, 75, 77, 79; WhoE 79; WhoLab 76; WhoS&SW 73, 75, 76*

Wurlitzer, Rudolph
American. Manufacturer
Introduced first automatically played, electric instruments, 1892.
b. Jan 31, 1831 in Schonesk, Germany
d. Jan 14, 1914 in Cincinnati, Ohio
Source: *NatCAB 16; WorAl*

Wurster, William
American. Architect
b. Oct 20, 1895 in Stockton, California
d. Sep 19, 1973
Source: *AmArch 70; CurBio 46, 73; WhAm 6; WhoAm 74; WhoGov 72; WhoWor 74*

Wyatt, Jane
American. Actress
Starred in TV series "Father Knows Best," 1954-62.
b. Aug 13, 1912 in Campgaw, New York
Source: *BiE&WWA; CurBio 57; FilmgC; HolP 30; InWom; IntMPA 75, 76, 77, 78, 79, 80, 81, 82; MotPP; MovMk; NotNAT; ThFT; WhoAm 74, 76, 78, 80, 82; WhoHol A; WhoThe 77*

Wyatt, Sir Thomas
English. Poet
b. 1503 in Kent, England
d. Oct 11, 1542 in Sherbourne, England
Source: *AtlBL; BbD; BiD&SB; BrAu; CasWL; Chambr 1; ChPo; CnE&AP; CroE&S; CrtT 1; DcEnA; DcEnL; DcEuL; DcLEL; EvLB; MouLC 1; NewC; OxEng; Pen ENG; RAdv 1; REn; WebE&AL*

Wycherley, Margaret
American. Actress
b. 1881 in London, England
d. Jun 6, 1966 in New York, New York
Source: *InWom; PlP&P*

Wycliffe, John
English. Philosopher, Author
b. Dec 31, 1320 in Richmond, England
d. 1384
Source: *Alli; AmAu&B; BiD&SB; BrAu; CasWL; Chambr 1; CrtT 1; DcEnA; DcEnL; DcLEL; EvLB; MouLC 1; NewC; OxEng; Pen ENG; RComWL; REn; WebE&AL*

Wyeth, Andrew
American. Artist
Painting, *Christina's World,* has sold over 300,000 reproductions.
b. Jul 12, 1917 in Chadds Ford, Pennsylvania
Source: *BkPepl; CelR 73; CurBio 55; DcCAA 71; EncAB-H; IntWW 74; OxAmL; REn; WebAB; Who 82; WhoAm 76, 78, 80, 82; WhoAmA 73; WhoE 74; WhoWor 74*

Wyeth, Henriette
American. Artist
b. Oct 22, 1907 in Wilmington, Delaware
Source: *WhoAmA 73*

Wyeth, Jamie (James Browning)
American. Artist
Called most commercially successful artist of his generation.
b. Jul 6, 1946 in Wilmington, Delaware
Source: *BioNews 75; BkPepl; CelR 73; WhoAm 74, 76, 78, 80, 82; WhoAmA 73*

Wyeth, N(ewell) C(onvers)
American. Illustrator, Muralist
Father of Andrew Wyeth; grandfather of Jamie Wyeth; illustrated popular children's novels.
b. Oct 22, 1882 in Needham, Massachusetts
d. Oct 19, 1945 in Chadds Ford, Pennsylvania
Source: *AmAu&B; ChPo, S2; ConICB; CurBio 45; DcAmB S3; IlsBYP; JBA 34, 51; REnAL; SmATA 17; WebAB; WhAm 2*

Wyler, Gretchen
American. Actress
b. 1932 in Oklahoma City, Oklahoma
Source: *BiE&WWA; ForWC 70; NotNAT; WhoHol A*

Wyler, William
American. Motion Picture Director, Producer
Won Oscars for *Mrs. Miniver,* 1942; *The Best Years of Our Lives,* 1946; *Ben Hur,* 1959.
b. Jul 1, 1902 in Mulhouse, Germany
d. Jul 28, 1981 in Beverly Hills, California
Source: *AnObit 1981; BioIn 1, 2, 5, 7, 10, 11; BioNews 74; CelR 73; CmMov; CurBio 51, 81; DcFM; FilmgC; IntMPA 76, 77, 78, 79; IntWW 75, 76, 77, 78; MovMk; OxFilm; TwYS; Who 74; WhoAm 76, 78, 80; WhoWor 74, 78; WorEFlm*

Wylie, Elinor Hoyt
American. Author
b. Sep 5, 1885 in Somerville, New Jersey
d. Dec 16, 1928 in New York, New York
Source: *AmAu&B; AmBi; AnCL; AtlBL; CasWL; Chambr 3; ChPo, S1, S2; CnDAL; CnE&AP; ConAmA; ConAmL; CyWA; DcAmB; DcLEL; DcNAA; EvLB; InWom; LongCTC; ModAL, SUP; NotAW; OxAmL; OxEng; Pen AM; RAdv 1; REn; REnAL; SixAP; Str&VC; TwCA, SUP; TwCW; WebAB; WhAm 1*

Wylie, Philip Gordon
American. Author
b. May 12, 1902 in Beverly, Massachusetts
d. Oct 25, 1971 in Miami, Florida
Source: *AmAu&B; AmNov; ChPo S2; CnDAL; ConAu 21R, 33R; ConNov 72; EncMys; EvLB; NewYTBE 71; REn; REnAL; TwCA, SUP; TwCW; WebAB; WhAm 5*

Wyman, Bill (William George)
[The Rolling Stones]
English. Rock Musician
b. Oct 24, 1941 in London, England
Source: *CelR 73; WhoAm 80, 82*

Wyman, Jane
[Sarah Jane Fulks]
American. Actress, 1st Wife of R Reagan
Won Oscar, 1948, for *Johnny Belinda;* star of TV series "Falcon Crest," 1982--.
b. Jan 4, 1914 in Saint Joseph, Missouri
Source: *BiDFilm; CmMov; CurBio 49; FilmgC; InWom; IntMPA 75, 76, 77, 78, 79, 80, 81, 82; MotPP; MovMk; ThFT; WhoAm 74; WhoHol A; WorEFlm*

Wyman, Willard Gordon
American. Military Leader
b. Mar 21, 1898 in Augusta, Maine
d. Mar 29, 1969 in Bethesda, Maryland
Source: *WhAm 5*

Wynette, Tammy
[Wynette Pugh]
American. Singer
CMA female vocalist of year, 1968, 69, 70; autobiography *Stand by Your Man,* 1979.
b. May 4, 1942 in Tupelo, Mississippi
Source: *BioNews 74; BkPepl; EncFCWM 69; WhoAm 74, 76, 78, 80, 82*

Wynn, Early
"Gus"
American. Baseball Player
b. Jan 6, 1920 in Hartford, Alabama
Source: *BaseEn; WhoProB 73*

Wynn, Ed
[Isiah Edwin Leopold]
American. Comedian
b. Nov 9, 1886 in Philadelphia, Pennsylvania
d. Jun 19, 1966 in Beverly Hills, California
Source: *AmSCAP 66; BiE&WWA; CurBio 45, 66; EncMT; FamA&A; FilmgC; MotPP; MovMk; WebAB; WhAm 4; WhScrn 74, 77; WhoHol B*

Wynn, Keenan
American. Actor
b. Jul 27, 1916 in New York, New York
Source: *BiE&WWA; BioNews 75; FilmgC; IntMPA 75, 76, 77, 78, 79, 80, 81, 82; MotPP; MovMk; WhoAm 74, 76, 78, 80, 82; WhoHol A*

Wynter, Dana
English. Actress
b. Jun 8, 1932 in London, England
Source: *FilmgC; InWom; IntMPA 75, 76, 77, 78, 79, 80, 81, 82; MotPP; MovMk; WhoAm 74, 76, 78, 80, 82; WhoHol A*

Wynyard, Diana
English. Actress
b. 1906 in London, England
d. May 13, 1964 in London, England
Source: *FilmgC; InWom; MotPP; MovMk; OxFilm; OxThe; ThFT; WhoHol B*

Wyss, Johann David
Swiss. Author
b. 1743 in Bern, Switzerland
d. 1818
Source: *CarSB; CasWL; OxGer; Str&VC; WhoChL*

Wyss, Johann Rudolf
Swiss. Author
b. Mar 13, 1782
d. Mar 21, 1830
Source: *BioIn 5, 8; WebBD 80*

Wyszynski, Stefan
Polish. Roman Catholic Cardinal
b. Aug 3, 1901 in Zuzela, Russia
d. May 28, 1981 in Warsaw, Poland
Source: *BioIn 3, 4, 5, 6, 7; CurBio 58, 81; IntWW 74, 75, 76, 77, 78; WhAm 7; WhoSocC 78; WhoWor 74, 78*

Wythe, George
American. Lawyer
b. 1726 in Elizabeth City, Virginia
d. Jun 8, 1806 in Richmond, Virginia
Source: *Alli; AmBi; ApCAB; BiDSA; BiDrAC; CyAL 1; DcAmAu; DcAmB; Drake; EncAB-H; TwCBDA; WebAB; WhAm H; WhAmP*

X

X
[D(on) J Bonebrake; John Doe; (Christine Cervenka) Exene; Billy Zoom]
American. Rock Group
Source: *NF*

Xenakis, Iannis
French. Composer
b. May 29, 1922 in Braila, Romania
Source: *Baker 78; DcCM; IntWW 74, 75, 76, 77, 78, 79, 80; McGEWB; NewYTBS 76; WhoAm 76, 78; WhoMus 72; WhoWor 74, 76, 78*

Xenophanes
Greek. Philosopher
Founded Eleatic philosophy.
b. 570BC
d. 480BC
Source: *BbD; BiD&SB; CasWL; NewC; OxEng; Pen CL*

Xenophon
Greek. Historian, Essayist
b. 434BC in Athens, Greece
d. 355BC
Source: *AtlBL; BbD; BiD&SB; CasWL; CyWA; DcEnL; NewC; OxEng; Pen CL; RComWL; REn*

Xerxes I
[Ahaseuerus]
Persian. King
b. 519BC
d. 465BC
Source: *WebBD 80*

Xuan Thuy
Vietnamese. Politician
Vice-chairman, Socialist Republic of Vietnam, 1976--.
b. Sep 2, 1912 in Hanoi, Vietnam
Source: *FarE&A 78, 79; IntWW 74, 75, 76, 77, 78, 79, 80, 81; WhoSocC 78*

Y

Yablonky, Ben
American. Journalist, Educator
b. Aug 26, 1911 in Chicago, Illinois
Source: *AmM&WS 73S; DrAS 74E*

Yablonski, Joseph
"Jock"
American. Labor Leader
Lost UMW presidency to Tony Boyle, 1969; Boyle convicted of his murder.
b. 1910 in Pittsburgh, Pennsylvania
d. Jan 5, 1969 in Clarksville, Pennsylvania
Source: *BioIn 8, 9, 10*

Yadin, Yigael
Israeli. Archaeologist
b. Mar 21, 1917
Source: *ConAu 9R; CurBio 66; IntWW 74; WhoAm 74; WhoWor 74; WhoWorJ 72*

Yahya Khan, Agha Muhammad
Pakistani. President
b. Feb 4, 1917 in Peshawar, Pakistan
d. Aug 8, 1980 in Rawalpindi, India
Source: *IntWW 74; NewYTBE 71; Who 74*

Yale, Elihu
American. Colonial Governor
b. Apr 5, 1649 in Boston, Massachusetts
d. Jul 8, 1721 in England
Source: *Alli; AmAu&B; AmBi; ApCAB; BioIn 8, 11; CyAL 1; DcAmB; Drake; LinLib S; NatCAB 1; TwCBDA; WhAm H*

Yale, Linus
American. Locksmith, Manufacturer
Developed lock for banker's safes, 1865; basic principal still used today.
b. Apr 4, 1821 in Salisbury, New York
d. Dec 25, 1868 in New York, New York
Source: *AmBi; ApCAB; DcAmB; WebAB; WhAm H*

Yalow, Rosalyn Sussman
American. Medical Researcher
b. Jul 19, 1921 in New York, New York
Source: *AmM&WS 73P; WhoAm 74, 76, 78, 80, 82*

Yamagughi, Paulo
Japanese. Sculptor
Source: *BioIn 9*

Yamamoto, Isoroku
Japanese. Admiral
b. Apr 4, 1884 in Nagaoka, Japan
d. May 1943
Source: *BioIn 10; WebBD 80*

Yamani, Ahmad Zaki, Sheik
Saudi. Cabinet Member
b. 1930
Source: *BioIn 10, 11; CurBio 75*

Yamasaki, Minoru
American. Architect
b. Dec 1, 1912 in Seattle, Washington
Source: *AmArch 70; CelR 73; IntWW 74; WebAB; WhoAm 74, 76, 78, 80, 82; WhoWor 74*

Yamashita, Tomoyuki
Japanese. General
b. 1888 in Kochi, Japan
d. Feb 23, 1946 in Luzon, Philippines
Source: *BioIn 10; WebBD 80*

Yancey, Jimmy (James Edward)
American. Jazz Musician
b. 1894? in Chicago, Illinois
d. Sep 17, 1951 in Chicago, Illinois
Source: *WhoJazz 72*

Yang, Chen Ning
American. Physicist
b. Sep 22, 1922 in Hofei, China
Source: *AmM&WS 73P; CurBio 58; IntWW 74; WebAB; Who 74; WhoAm 74, 76, 78, 80, 82*

Yankelovich, Daniel
American. Social Scientist
b. 1924 in Boston, Massachusetts
Source: *St&PR 75; WhoAm 74, 76, 78, 80, 82; WhoE 74*

Yarborough, Cale (William Caleb)
American. Auto Racer
b. Mar 27, 1940 in Timminsville, South Carolina
Source: *BioIn 8, 10, 11; BioNews 74; WhoAm 82*

Yarborough, Glenn
American. Singer
b. Jan 12, 1930 in Milwaukee, Wisconsin
Source: *EncFCWM 69*

Yarborough, Ralph Webster
American. Lawyer, Former Senator
b. Jun 8, 1903 in Chandler, Texas
Source: *BiDrAC; CurBio 60; IntWW 74; WhoAm 74, 76, 78, 80, 82; WhoAmP 73; WhoS&SW 73*

Yarbrough, Lee Roy
American. Auto Racer
b. 1938
Source: *BioIn 10*

Yardbirds
[Jeff Beck; Eric Clapton; Chris Dreja; James McCarty; Jimmy Page; Keith Relf; Paul Samwell-Smith; Anthony Sopham]
English. Rock Group
Source: *EncPR&S; IlEncRk; Rk100*

Yardley, Jonathan
American. Journalist
b. Oct 27, 1939 in Pittsburgh, Pennsylvania
Source: *ConAu 73; WhoAm 82; WhoS&SW 73*

Yarmon, Betty
American. Journalist
b. Nov 14, in Plainfield, New Jersey
Source: *ForWC 70; WhoAm 82*

Yarnell, Bruce
American. Actor
b. 1938 in Los Angeles, California
d. Nov 30, 1973 in California
Source: *NewYTBE 73; WhScrn 77; WhoHol B*

Yarnell, Harry E
American. Naval Officer
b. Oct 18, 1875 in Independence, Iowa
d. Jul 7, 1959 in Newport, Rhode Island
Source: *WhAm 3*

Yarrow, Peter
[Peter, Paul, and Mary]
American. Composer, Author, Folksinger
b. May 31, 1938 in New York, New York
Source: *AmSCAP 66; EncFCWM 69; WhoAm 74, 76, 78, 80, 82; WhoHol A*

Yastrzemski, Carl Michael
"Yaz"
American. Baseball Player
With Boston Red Sox, 1961--; won AL triple crown, 1967.
b. Aug 22, 1939 in Southampton, New York
Source: *BaseEn; CelR 73; CurBio 68; NewYTBE 70, 72; WhoAm 74, 76, 78, 80, 82; WhoProB 73*

Yates, Bill
American. Cartoonist
b. 1921?
Source: *BioIn 5*

Yates, Elizabeth
[Mrs. William McGreal]
American. Children's Author
b. Dec 6, 1905 in Buffalo, New York
Source: *AmAu&B; AmNov; Au&ICB; Au&Wr 71; AuBYP; ChPo; ConAu 1R, 13R; CurBio 48; InWom; JBA 51; MorBMP; Newb 1922; REnAL; SmATA 4; TwCA SUP; WhoAm 74, 76, 78, 80, 82; WhoProB 73*

Yates, Peter
English. Motion Picture Director
b. Jul 24, 1929 in Aldershot, England
Source: *FilmEn; IntMPA 80, 81, 82*

Yawkey, Thomas Austin
American. Baseball Executive
Owner, Boston Red Sox, 1933-76.
b. Feb 21, 1903 in Detroit, Michigan
d. Jul 9, 1976 in Boston, Massachusetts
Source: *CelR 73; WhoAm 76*

Yeager, Steve (Stephen Wayne)
American. Baseball Player
b. Nov 24, 1948 in Huntington, West Virginia
Source: *BaseEn*

Yeats, William Butler
Irish. Poet, Dramatist
Leader, Irish literary renaissance; founded Abbey Theater, Dublin.
b. Jun 13, 1865 in Dublin, Ireland
d. Jan 28, 1939 in Menton, France
Source: *Alli SUP; AnCL; ArizL; BbD; BiD&SB; CasWL; Chambr 3; ChPo, S1, S2; CnE&AP; CnMD; CnMWL; CnThe; CyWA; DcEnA, AP; DcLEL; EncWL; EvLB; LongCTC; McGEWD; ModBrL, SUP; ModWD; NewC; OxEng; OxThe; Pen ENG; PoIre; RAdv 1; RComWL; REn; REnWD; TwCA, SUP; TwCW; WebE&AL; WhoTwCL*

Yeend, Frances
American. Opera Singer
b. Jan 28, 1918 in Vancouver, Washington
Source: *WhoMus 72*

Yellen, Jack
American. Author, Songwriter
b. Jul 6, 1892 in Razcki, Poland
Source: *AmSCAP 66; BiE&WWA; NewCBMT; NotNAT*

Yeon, John
American. Architect
b. 1910 in Portland, Oregon
Source: *McGDA*

Yepes, Narcisco
Spanish. Musician
b. Nov 14, 1927 in Lorca, Spain
Source: *WhoWor 74*

Yepremian, Garo (Garabed S)
American. Football Player
b. Jun 2, 1944 in Larnaca, Cyprus
Source: *BioIn 10; WhoAm 82; WhoFtbl 74*

Yerby, Frank Garvin
American. Author
b. Sep 5, 1916 in Augusta, Georgia
Source: *AmAu&B; AmNov; Au&Wr 71; BlkAW; ConAu 9R; ConLC 1, 7; ConNov 72; CurBio 46; DcEnL; IntWW 74; LivgBAA; LongCTC; Pen AM; TwCA SUP; WebAB; Who 74; WhoAm 74, 76, 78, 80, 82; WhoBlA 75; WrDr 76*

Yes
[Jon Anderson; Steve Howe; Chris Squire; Rick Wakeman; Alan White]
English. Rock Group
Source: *EncPR&S; IlEncRk; Rk100*

Yesenin, Sergei Aleksandrovich
see: Esenin, Sergei Aleksandrovich

Yevtushenko, Yevgeni Alexandrovich
see: Evtushenko, Evgeniy Alexandrovich

Yezierska, Anzia
American. Author
b. 1885 in Sukovoly, Russia
d. Nov 21, 1970 in Ontario, California
Source: *AmAu&B; InWom; NewYTBE 70; OxAmL; REnAL; TwCA, SUP*

Yogananda, Paramahansa
Indian. Yogi Psychic
b. 1893
d. Mar 7, 1952 in Los Angeles, California
Source: *BioIn 1, 2, 3, 8, 9*

Yoho, Monte
see: Outlaws, The

Yonge, Charlotte Mary
English. Author
b. Aug 11, 1823 in Otterbourne, England
d. Mar 24, 1901 in Elderfield, England
Source: *Alli, SUP; BbD; BiD&SB; BrAu 19; CarSB; CasWL; Chambr 3; ChPo S1; DcBiA; DcEnA, AP; DcEnL; DcEuL; DcLEL; EvLB; FamSYP; InWom; JBA 34; NewC; OxEng; Pen ENG; REn; WhoChL*

York, David
American. Counselor, Founder of Toughlove
b. 1929? in Long Island, New York
Source: *BioIn 12*

York, Dick
[Richard Allen York]
American. Actor
Starred in TV series "Bewitched," 1964-72.
b. Sep 4, 1928 in Fort Wayne, Indiana
Source: *FilmgC; IntMPA 75, 76, 77, 78, 79, 80, 81, 82; MotPP; WhoHol A*

York, Edward Palmer
American. Architect
b. 1865 in Wellsville, New York
d. Dec 30, 1928
Source: *BioIn 2; BnEnAmA; WhAm 1*

York, Michael
[Michael York-Johnson]
English. Actor
Starred in *The Island of Dr. Moreau,* 1977.
b. Mar 27, 1942 in Fulmer, England
Source: *BkPepl; CelR 73; FilmgC; IntMPA 75, 76, 77, 78, 79, 80, 81, 82; MotPP; MovMk; OxFilm; WhoAm 82; WhoHol A*

York, Pete
see: Spencer Davis Group, The

York, Rudy (Rudolph Preston)
American. Baseball Player
First baseman, Detroit Tigers, 1937-45; hit 18 home runs in one month, 1937.
b. Aug 17, 1913 in Ragland, Alabama
d. Feb 5, 1970 in Rome, Georgia
Source: *BaseEn; BioIn 1, 4, 6; WhoProB 73*

York, Sergeant (Alvin Cullum)
American. Soldier
b. Dec 13, 1887 in Pall Mall, Tennessee
d. Dec 2, 1964 in Nashville, Tennessee
Source: *WebAB*

York, Susannah
English. Actress
Starred in *They Shoot Horses, Don't They?*, 1969.
b. Jan 9, 1941 in London, England
Source: *BiDFilm; CelR 73; FilmgC; IntMPA 75, 76, 77, 78, 79, 80, 81, 82; MotPP; MovMk; OxFilm; WhoAm 82; WhoHol A*

Yorty, Sam(uel William)
American. Public Official
Mayor, LA, 1961-73.
b. Oct 1, 1909 in Lincoln, Nebraska
Source: *BiDrAC; IntWW 74; WhoAm 74, 76, 78, 80, 82; WhoGov 72; WhoWor 74*

Yoshida, Shigeru
Japanese. Prime Minister
b. Sep 22, 1878 in Tokyo, Japan
d. Oct 20, 1967 in Oisi, Japan
Source: *Au&Wr 71; CurBio 46, 68; REn; WhAm 4A*

Yoshinobu
see: Hitotsubashi

Yost, Charles Woodruff
"The Gray Ghost"
American. Diplomat
One of founders of UN; chief American delegate, 1969-71.
b. Nov 6, 1907 in Watertown, New York
d. May 21, 1981 in Washington, DC
Source: *BioIn 4, 5, 8, 10; ConAu 9R, 104, 3NR; CurBio 59, 81; IntWW 74, 75, 76, 77, 78; PolProf K; Who 74; WhoAm 74, 76, 78; WhoGov 72, 75; WhoWor 74*

Yost, Fielding Harris
"Hurry Up"
American. Football Coach
Head coach, U of Michigan, 1901-25; won Rose Bowl, 1902.
b. Apr 30, 1871 in Fairview, West Virginia
d. Aug 20, 1946 in Ann Arbor, Michigan
Source: *BioIn 1, 4, 10; CurBio 46; DcAmB S4; WhAm 2; WhoFtbl 74*

Yost, Joseph Warren
American. Architect
b. Jun 15, 1847 in Clarington, Ohio
d. 1923
Source: *BioIn 3; NatCAB 13; WhAm 4*

Youmans, Vincent
American. Composer
b. Sep 27, 1898 in New York, New York
d. Apr 5, 1946 in Denver, Colorado
Source: *AmSCAP 66; CurBio 44, 46; DcAmB S4; EncMT; NewCBMT; PlP&P*

Young, Alan (Angus)
American. Comedian, Actor
b. Nov 19, 1919 in North Shields, England
Source: *CurBio 53; FilmgC; IntMPA 75, 76, 77, 78, 79, 80, 81, 82; WhoHol A*

Young, Angus
see: AC-DC

Young, Andrew
Scottish. Author
b. Apr 29, 1885 in Elgin, Scotland
d. Nov 26, 1971
Source: *Au&Wr 71; ChPo, S1, S2; CnE&AP; CnMWL; ConAu 5R; ConLC 5; ConP 70; DcLEL; EvLB; LongCTC; NewC; OxEng; Pen ENG; TwCW; WebE&AL; WhoTwCL; WorAu*

Young, Andrew J
American. Mayor of Atlanta
Ambassador to UN, 1977-79.
b. Mar 12, 1932 in New Orleans, Louisiana
Source: *BioNews 74; BkPepl; WhoAm 74, 76, 78, 80, 82; WhoAmP 73; WhoBlA 75*

Young, Art(hur Henry)
American. Cartoonist, Author
b. Jan 14, 1866 in Orangeville, Illinois
d. Dec 29, 1943 in Bethel, Connecticut
Source: *AmAu&B; CurBio 40, 44; DcAmB S3; DcNAA; OxAmL; REnAL; WhAm 2; WhNAA*

Young, Brigham
American. Mormon Leader
Led Mormons to Salt Lake City, 1846; governor of UT, 1850-58.
b. Jun 1, 1801 in Whitingham, Vermont
d. Aug 29, 1877 in Salt Lake City, Utah
Source: *AmAu&B; AmBi; ApCAB; BiAuS; DcAmB; Drake; EncAB-H; OxAmL; REn; REnAL; TwCBDA; WebAB; WhAm H*

Young, Burt
American. Actor, Screenwriter
b. Apr 30, 1940 in New York, New York
Source: *IntMPA 82; WhoAm 82; WhoHol A*

Young, Candy (Canzetta)
American. Track Athlete
b. 1963?
Source: *BioIn 12*

Young, Charles Augustus
American. Astronomer
Discovered solar reversing layer, 1870.
b. Dec 15, 1834 in Hanover, New Hampshire
d. Jan 4, 1908
Source: *AmBi; ApCAB; BiDAmEd; BioIn 1, 11; DcAmB; DcScB; NatCAB 6; TwCBDA; WhAm 1*

Young, "Chic" (Murat Bernard)
American. Cartoonist
Created comic strip "Blondie," 1930.
b. Jan 9, 1901
d. Mar 14, 1973 in Saint Petersburg, Florida
Source: *ConAu 41R; NewYTBE 73; WebAB; WhAm 5, 6; WhoAm 74*

Young, Clara Kimball
American. Actress
b. 1890 in Chicago, Illinois
d. Oct 15, 1960 in Woodland Hills, California
Source: *Film 2; FilmgC; MotPP; MovMk; OxFilm; TwYS; WhAm 4; WhScrn 74, 77; WhoHol B; WomWMM*

Young, Coleman A(lexander)
American. Mayor of Detroit
b. May 24, 1918 in Tuscaloosa, Alabama
Source: *BioNews 74; WhoAm 82; WhoAmP 73; WhoBlA 75*

Young, "Cy" (Denton True)
American. Baseball Player
Record 511 pitching victories; Hall of Fame, 1937.
b. Mar 29, 1867 in Gilmore, Ohio
d. Nov 4, 1955 in Peoli, Ohio
Source: *BaseEn; DcAmB S5; WebAB; WhAm HA, 4; WhoProB 73*

Young, Donna Caponi
see: Caponi, Donna

Young, Edward
English. Author
b. Jun 1683 in Upham, England
d. Apr 5, 1765 in Welwyn, England
Source: *Alli; AtlBL; BbD; BiD&SB; BrAu; CasWL; ChPo, S2; CnE&AP; CrtT 2; DcEnA; DcEnL; DcEuL; DcLEL; EvLB; MouLC 2; NewC; OxEng; OxFr; OxGer; Pen ENG; REn; WebE&AL*

Young, Faron
"The Sheriff"
American. Singer, Musician
b. Feb 25, 1932 in Shreveport, Louisiana
Source: *EncFCWM 69; WhoAm 82*

Young, Gig
[Bryon Barr]
American. Actor
b. Nov 4, 1913 in Saint Cloud, Minnesota
d. Oct 19, 1978 in New York, New York
Source: *BiE&WWA; CelR 73; FilmgC; HolP 40; IntMPA 77; MotPP; MovMk; NewYTBE 70; WhoAm 74; WhoHol A; WhoThe 77*

Young, James Webb
American. Advertising Executive
b. Jan 20, 1886 in Covington, Kentucky
d. Mar 1973 in Santa Fe, New Mexico
Source: *NewYTBE 73; WhAm 5; WhoF&I 74*

Young, Jimmy
American. Boxer
b. 1949 in Philadelphia, Pennsylvania
Source: *BioIn 10*

Young, John Watts
American. Astronaut
On maiden voyage of space shuttle *Columbia,* 1981.
b. Sep 24, 1930 in San Francisco, California
Source: *IntWW 74; WhoAm 74, 76, 78, 80, 82; WhoS&SW 73; WhoWor 74*

Young, Lester Willis
"Prez"
American. Jazz Musician
b. Aug 27, 1909 in Woodville, Mississippi
d. Mar 15, 1959 in New York, New York
Source: *AmSCAP 66; WhAm 5; WhoJazz 72*

Young, Loretta Gretchen
American. Actress
b. Jan 6, 1913 in Salt Lake City, Utah
Source: *BiDFilm; CelR 73; CurBio 48; Film 1; FilmgC; InWom; IntMPA 75, 76, 77, 78, 79, 80, 81, 82; MotPP; MovMk; OxFilm; ThFT; TwYS; WhoAm 74, 76, 78, 80, 82; WhoHol A; WorEFlm*

Young, Lyman
American. Cartoonist
b. in Chicago, Illinois
Source: *WorECom*

Young, Mahonri M
American. Sculptor
b. Aug 9, 1877 in Salt Lake City, Utah
d. Nov 2, 1957 in New York, New York
Source: *WhAm 3*

Young, Malcolm
see: AC-DC

Young, Margaret Ann Buckner
American. Children's Author
b. Mar 20, 1922 in Campbellsville, Kentucky
Source: *BkP; ChPo S1; ConAu 25R; LEduc 74; SmATA 2; WhoBlA 75; WhoE 74*

Young, Marian
[Martha Deane]
American. Radio Commentator
b. Nov 21, 1908 in Star Lake, New York
d. Dec 9, 1973 in New York
Source: *BiDrLUS 70; CelR 73; CurBio 52, 74; ForWC 70; InWom; NewYTBE 73; WhoAm 74*

Young, Neil
[Buffalo Springfield; Crosby, Stills, Nash, and Young]
Canadian. Musician
b. Nov 12, 1945 in Toronto, ON
Source: *CanWW 82; CurBio 80; WhoAm 82; WhoHol A*

Young, Ralph
[Sandler and Young]
American. Singer
Source: *CmpEPM*

Young, Robert George
American. Actor
Starred in TV series "Father Knows Best," 1954-62; "Marcus Welby, MD," 1969-76.
b. Feb 22, 1907 in Chicago, Illinois
Source: *BiDFilm; CelR 73; CmMov; FilmgC; IntMPA 75, 76, 77, 78, 79, 80, 81, 82; MovMk; OxFilm; WhoAm 82; WorEFlm*

Young, Roland
English. Actor
b. Nov 11, 1887 in London, England
d. Jun 5, 1953 in New York, New York
Source: *ChPo; FilmgC; MotPP; MovMk; OxFilm; PlP&P; Vers A; WhAm 3; WhScrn 74, 77; WhoHol B*

Young, Rusty
see: Poco

Young, Sheila
[Mrs. Jim Ochowicz]
American. Speed Skater, Cyclist
Won three medals in speed skating, 1976 Olympics.
b. Oct 14, 1950 in Birmingham, Michigan
Source: *BioIn 10, 11; CurBio 77*

Young, Stark
American. Author
b. Oct 11, 1881 in Como, Mississippi
d. Jan 6, 1963 in New York, New York
Source: *AmAu&B; CasWL; CnDAL; ConAmA; ConAmL; ConAu 89; CyWA; LongCTC; ModAL; OxAmL; OxThe; Pen AM; REnAL; TexWr; TwCA, SUP; WhAm 4; WhNAA*

Young, Stephen
Canadian. Actor
b. 1939 in Toronto, ON
Source: *FilmgC; WhoHol A*

Young, Terence
American. Actor
b. Jun 20, 1915 in Shanghai, China
Source: *BiDFilm; CmMov; FilmgC; IntMPA 75, 76, 77, 78, 79, 80, 81, 82; MovMk; OxFilm; WhoAm 74, 76, 78, 80, 82; WorEFlm*

Young, "Trummy" (James Osborne)
American. Jazz Musician
b. Jan 12, 1912 in Savannah, Georgia
Source: *WhoJazz 72*

Young, Victor
American. Composer, Conductor
b. Aug 8, 1900 in Chicago, Illinois
d. Nov 11, 1956 in Palm Springs, California
Source: *AmSCAP 66; CmMov; FilmgC; OxFilm; WhAm 3; WorEFlm*

Young, Whitney Moore, Jr.
American. Civil Rights Leader
Director, National Urban League, 1961-71; wrote *Beyond Racism,* 1969.
b. Jul 31, 1921 in Lincoln Ridge, Kentucky
d. Mar 11, 1971 in Lagos, Nigeria
Source: *ConAu P-1; CurBio 65, 71; EncAB-H; NewYTBE 70, 71; WebAB; WhAm 5*

Young Rascals, The
see: Rascals, The

Youngblood, (Herbert) Jack(son)
American. Football Player
b. Jan 26, 1950 in Jacksonville, Florida
Source: *WhoAm 78, 80, 82*

Youngdahl, Luther W
American. Governor, Judge
b. May 29, 1896 in Minneapolis, Minnesota
d. Jun 21, 1978 in Washington, DC
Source: *AmAu&B; CurBio 48; IntWW 74; MnnWr; WhoAm 74; WhoAmP 73; WhoS&SW 73; WhoGov 72*

Younger, (Thomas) Cole(man)
[The Younger Brothers]
American. Outlaw
b. Jan 15, 1844 in Jackson County, Missouri
d. Mar 21, 1916 in Jackson County, Missouri
Source: *BioIn 2, 4, 7, 8, 9, 10; DcAmB; NewCol 75; WebAB; WhAm H, 4*

Younger Brothers, The
[James Younger; Robert Younger; (Thomas) Cole(man) Younger]
American. Outlaws
Source: *BioIn 4, 6, 7, 8, 10; REnAW*

Youngman, Henny
American. Comedian
b. 1905 in London, England
Source: *CelR 73; WhoAm 82; WhoHol A*

Yount, Robin R
American. Baseball Player
Shortstop, Milwaukee Brewers, 1974--; MVP, 1982.
b. Sep 16, 1955 in Woodland Hills, California
Source: *BaseEn*

Yourcenar, Marguerite, pseud.
[Marguerite de Crayencour]
French. Author
Only woman ever admitted to Academie Francaise, 1980.
b. Jun 8, 1913 in Brussels, Belgium
Source: *BioIn 12; ConAu 69; CurBio 82; WhoAm 78, 80, 82; WorAu*

Youskevitch, Igor
Russian. Ballet Dancer
b. Mar 13, 1912 in Kiev, Russia
Source: *CurBio 56; WhoHol A; WhoWor 74*

Ysaye, Eugene
Belgian. Musician, Composer
b. Jul 16, 1858 in Liege, Belgium
d. May 13, 1931 in Brussels, Belgium
Source: *WhAm 1*

Yuan, Shih-Kai
Chinese. Dictator
b. 1859
d. 1916
Source: *NewCol 75*

Yukawa, Hideki
Japanese. Physicist
b. Jan 23, 1907 in Tokyo, Japan
d. Sep 8, 1981 in Kyoto, Japan
Source: *AsBiEn; BioIn 1, 2, 3; CurBio 50, 81; FarE&A 78, 79; IntWW 74, 75, 76, 77, 78; McGEWB; NewCol 75; WhoWor 74, 78*

Yung, Victor Sen
American. Actor
Played Hop Sing on TV series "Bonanza," 1959-73.
b. 1915 in San Francisco, California
d. Nov 9, 1980 in North Hollywood, California
Source: *WhoHol A*

Yunich, David Lawrence
American. Merchant
b. May 21, 1917 in Albany, New York
Source: *IntWW 74; NewYTBE 73; St&PR 75; WhoAm 74, 76, 78, 80, 82; WhoF&I 74*

Yurka, Blanche
American. Actress
b. 1887 in Saint Paul, Minnesota
d. Jun 6, 1974 in New York, New York
Source: *BiE&WWA; ConAu 9R; FamA&A; FilmgC; MotPP; MovMk; NewYTBS 74; ThFT; Vers A; WhAm 6; WhScrn 77; WhoHol B*

Z

ZZ Top
[Frank Beard; Billy Gibbons; Dusty Hill]
American. Rock Group
Source: *ConMuA 80; IlEncRk; LilREn 78; RkOn 2; WhoRock 81*

Zabach, Florian
American. Musician
b. Aug 15, 1921 in Chicago, Illinois
Source: *AmSCAP 66*

Zabaleta, Nicanor
Spanish. Musician
b. Jan 7, 1907 in San Sebastian, Spain
Source: *CurBio 71; WhoMus 72; WhoS&SW 73*

Zacchini, Edmondo
"Papa"
Italian. Human Cannonball, Circus Clown
b. 1894?
d. Oct 3, 1981 in Tampa, Florida
Source: *BioIn 12*

Zadkine, Ossip
Russian. Artist
b. Jul 14, 1890
d. Nov 25, 1967 in Paris, France
Source: *CurBio 57, 68; WhAm 4A*

Zaharias, Mildred
see: Didrikson, "Babe" (Mildred)

Zaharoff, Sir Basil
English. Financier
b. 1850 in Phanar, Turkey
d. 1936
Source: *WebBD 80*

Zaitsev, Alexsander
[Rodnina and Zaitsev]
Russian. Figure Skater
b. 1952
Source: *BioIn 11*

Zale, Tony
[Anthony Florian Zaleski]
American. Boxer
b. May 29, 1913 in Gary, Indiana
Source: *WhoBox 74*

Zaleski, August
Polish. Statesman
b. 1883
d. Apr 7, 1972 in London, England
Source: *WebBD 80*

Zamenhof, Ludwik Lazar
Polish. Linguist
Developed artificial language, Esperanto, 1887.
b. Dec 15, 1859 in Bialystok, Poland
d. Apr 14, 1917
Source: *BioIn 5; WebBD 80*

Zampa, Luigi
Italian. Motion Picture Director
b. 1905 in Rome, Italy
Source: *DcFM; FilmgC; IntMPA 75, 76, 77, 78, 79, 80, 81, 82; OxFilm; WorEFlm*

Zander, Robin
see: Cheap Trick

Zandonai, Riccardo
Italian. Composer
b. May 28, 1883 in Sacco, Italy
d. Jun 5, 1944 in Pesaro, Italy
Source: *CurBio 44*

Zane, Ebenezer
American. Boxer
b. Oct 7, 1747 in Berkeley County, Virginia
d. 1811
Source: *ApCAB; Drake; NatCAB 11*

Zanelli, Renato
[Renato Morales]
Chilean. Opera Singer
b. Apr 1, 1892 in Valparaiso, Chile
d. Mar 25, 1935 in Santiago, Chile
Source: *NewEOp 71*

Zangara, Giuseppe
American. Assassin
b. 1900 in Italy
d. 1933
Source: *BioIn 9*

Zangwill, Israel
English. Dramatist, Author
b. Feb 14, 1864 in London, England
d. Aug 1, 1926 in London, England
Source: *BbD; BiD&SB; Chambr 3; ChPo S2; CyWA; DcBiA; DcEnA AP; DcEuL; DcLEL; EncMys; EncWL; EvLB; LongCTC; ModWD; NewC; OxEng; OxThe; Pen ENG; TwCA; TwCW*

Zanuck, Darryl Francis
American. Film Producer, Executive
Founded 20th C. Pictures, 1933; produced *Grapes of Wrath,* 1940.
b. Sep 5, 1902 in Wahoo, Nebraska
d. Dec 22, 1979 in Palm Springs, California
Source: *BiDFilm; CelR 73; CmMov; ConAu 93; CurBio 41, 54, 80; DcFM; FilmgC; IntMPA 75, 76, 77; IntWW 74; OxFilm; WebAB; Who 74; WhoAm 74; WhoWor 74; WorEFlm*

Zanuck, Richard Darryl
American. Film Producer, Executive
Son of Darryl Zanuck; produced *The Sting,* 1973.
b. Dec 13, 1934 in Los Angeles, California
Source: *BkPepl; CelR 73; FilmgC; IntMPA 75, 76, 77, 78, 79, 80, 81, 82; OxFilm; St&PR 75; WhoAm 74, 76, 78, 80, 82*

Zao-Wou-Ki
French. Artist
b. 1921 in Peking, China
Source: *McGDA*

Zapata, Emiliano
Mexican. Revolutionary
b. 1879? in Anenecuilco, Mexico
d. Apr 10, 1919 in Chinameca, Mexico
Source: *McGEWB; REn*

Zapf, Hermann
German. Typographer
b. Nov 8, 1918 in Nuremberg, Germany
Source: *BioIn 6, 7; CurBio 65; WhoAm 82*

Zappa, Frank (Francis Vincent, Jr.)
[The Mothers of Invention]
American. Musician, Singer
Founded Mothers of Invention, 1964.
b. Dec 21, 1940 in Baltimore, Maryland
Source: *BioNews 74; CelR 73; NewYTBE 70; WhoAm 74, 76, 78, 80, 82; WhoHol A*

Zappa, Moon Unit
American. Daughter of Frank Zappa
Sings hit song "Valley Girl" written by father, 1982.
b. 1968?
Source: *NF*

Zass, Aleksandr
"Samson"
English. Strongman
b. 1887?
d. 1962
Source: *BioIn 6*

Zatopek, Emil
Czech. Track Athlete
b. Sep 19, 1922 in Koprivnice, Moravia
Source: *CurBio 53; WhoTr&F 73*

Zaturenska, Marya
[Mrs. Horace Gregory]
American. Poet
Won Pulitzer Prize, 1938, for *Cold Morning Sky.*
b. Sep 12, 1902 in Kiev, Russia
d. Jan 19, 1982 in Shelburne Falls, Massachusetts
Source: *ChPo, S3; CnDAL; ConAu 13R; ConLC 6, 11; ConP 70, 75; DrAP 75; ForWC 70; OxAmL; Pen AM; REn; REnAL; SixAP; TwCA, SUP; WhoAm 74, 76, 78; WhoAmW 68, 70, 72, 74, 75, 77; WrDr 76, 80*

Zayak, Elaine
American. Figure Skater
Won gold medal, 1982 world championship.
b. Apr 12, 1965 in Paramus, New Jersey
Source: *BioIn 12*

Zbyszko, Stanislaus
[Stanislaus Cyganiewicz]
Polish. Wrestler
b. 1879
d. 1967
Source: *BioIn 8*

Zeckendorf, William
American. Real Estate Executive
b. Jun 30, 1905 in Paris, Illinois
d. Oct 1, 1976 in New York, New York
Source: *St&PR 75*

Zeffirelli, Franco
Italian. Motion Picture Director
Pictures include *Taming of the Shrew,* 1966; *Romeo and Juliet,* 1968.
b. Feb 12, 1923 in Florence, Italy
Source: *BiE&WWA; CelR 73; CurBio 64; FilmgC; IntMPA 75, 76, 77, 78, 79, 80, 81, 82; IntWW 74; MovMk; NewYTBE 72; OxFilm; OxThe; Who 82; WhoAm 82; WhoHol A; WhoWor 74; WorEFlm*

Zeiss, Carl
German. Optical Manufacturer
b. 1816
d. 1888
Source: *WebBD 80*

Zeitlin, Zvi
Israeli. Musician
b. Feb 21, 1923 in Dubrowna, U.S.S.R.
Source: *WhoAm 82; WhoMus 72; WhoWorJ 72*

Zellerbach, William Joseph
American. Paper Industry Executive
President, Crown Zellerbach Corp., 1946--.
b. Sep 15, 1920 in San Francisco, California
Source: *IntWW 74; St&PR 75; WhoAm 74, 76, 78, 80, 82; WhoF&I 74*

Zemlinsky, Alexander
Austrian. Composer, Conductor
b. Oct 4, 1872 in Vienna, Austria
d. Mar 16, 1942 in New York, New York
Source: *CurBio 42; DcCM; WhAm 4A*

Zenatello, Giovanni
Italian. Opera Singer
b. Feb 22, 1876 in Verona, Italy
d. Feb 11, 1949 in New York, New York
Source: *BiDAmM; NewEOp 71*

Zenger, John Peter
German. Printer, Publisher, Journalist
b. 1697 in Germany
d. Jul 28, 1746 in New York, New York
Source: *Alli; AmAu; AmAu&B; AmBi; DcAmB; Drake; OxAmL; REn; REnAL; TwCBDA; WebAB; WhAm H*

Zeno of Citium
Greek. Philosopher
b. 334BC
d. 262BC
Source: *BiD&SB; CasWL; Pen CL; REn*

Zeno of Elea
Greek. Philosopher
b. 490BC
d. 430BC
Source: *NewCol 75; WebBD 80*

Zeno, Apostolo
Italian. Poet, Librettist
b. Dec 11, 1668 in Venice, Italy
d. Nov 11, 1750 in Venice, Italy
Source: *BiD&SB; CasWL; DcEuL; EvEuW; OxThe*

Zeppelin, Ferdinand von, Count
German. Soldier, Airship Designer
Built first rigid airship, 1900.
b. Jul 8, 1838 in Germany
d. Mar 8, 1917
Source: *BioIn 4, 7, 10; NewCol 75; REn*

Zerbe, Anthony
American. Actor
Won Emmy, 1976, for "Harry-O."
b. in Long Beach, California
Source: *BioIn 10; WhoAm 74, 76, 78, 80, 82*

Zerbe, Jerome
American. Photographer
b. Jul 24, 1904 in Euclid, Ohio
Source: *CelR 73; ConAu 17R; WhoAm 74*

Zernial, Gus Edward
"Ozark Ike"
American. Baseball Player
b. Jun 27, 1923 in Beaumont, Texas
Source: *BaseEn; BioIn 3; WhoProB 73*

Zetterling, Mai Elisabeth
Swedish. Actress, Motion Picture Director
b. May 24, 1925 in Sweden
Source: *Au&Wr 71; BiDFilm; FilmgC; IntMPA 75, 76, 77, 78, 79, 80, 81, 82; MovMk; NewYTBE 72; OxFilm; Who 74; WhoHol A; WhoThe 77; WomWMM; WorEFlm*

Zhao Ziyang
Chinese. Prime Minister
b. 1919 in Henan Province, China
Source: *FarE&A 79; IntWW 81*

Zhdanov, Andrei A
Russian. Communist Leader, General
b. 1896
d. Aug 31, 1948
Source: *REn; WhAm 2*

Zhivkov, Todor
Bulgarian. Politician
b. Sep 7, 1911 in Bulgaria
Source: *IntWW 74, 75, 76, 77, 78, 79, 80, 81; WhoWor 74*

Zhukov, Georgi Alexandrovich
Russian. Journalist, Politician
b. Apr 23, 1908 in Almazny, Russia
Source: *CurBio 60; IntWW 74; Who 74; WhoWor 74*

Zhukov, Georgi Konstantinovich
Russian. Military Leader
b. Dec 2, 1896 in Stelkovka, Russia
d. Jun 18, 1974 in Moscow, U.S.S.R.
Source: *CurBio 42, 55, 74; NewYTBS 74; WhAm 6; Who 74; WhoWor 74*

Zia-ul-Haq, Mohammad
[Mohammad Zia Al-Haq]
Pakistani. President
Established democratic government, Jul, 1977.
b. 1924 in Jullundur, India
Source: *BioIn 11; CurBio 80; FarE&A 78, 79; IntWW 78, 79, 80, 81; IntYB 79; NewYTBS 77*

Zieff, Howard
American. Motion Picture Director
Source: *IntMPA 77, 78, 79, 80, 81, 82; NewYTBE 73*

Ziegfeld, Flo(renz)
American. Producer
Produced lavish, musical revues, "Ziegfeld Follies," 1907-30.
b. Mar 21, 1867 in Chicago, Illinois
d. Jul 22, 1932 in Hollywood, California
Source: *AmBi; DcAmB; EncAB-H; EncMT; FilmgC; OxAmL; OxThe; PlP&P; REn; WebAB; WhAm 1*

Ziegler, Edward
American. Opera Manager
b. Mar 25, 1870 in Baltimore, Maryland
d. Oct 25, 1947 in New York, New York
Source: *AmAu&B; WhAm 2*

Ziegler, John Augustus, Jr.
American. Lawyer, Hockey Executive
President of NHL, 1977--.
b. Feb 9, 1934 in Grosse Pointe, Michigan
Source: *WhoAm 78, 80, 82*

Ziegler, Ron(ald Louis)
American. Public Official
Press secretary to Richard Nixon, 1969-74.
b. May 12, 1939 in Covington, Kentucky
Source: *BioNews 74; CurBio 71; IntWW 74; NewYTBE 71, 73; WhoAm 74, 76, 78, 80, 82; WhoAmP 73; WhoGov 72; WhoS&SW 73*

Ziff, William B
American. Publisher
b. Aug 1, 1898 in Chicago, Illinois
d. Dec 20, 1953 in New York, New York
Source: *AmAu&B; CurBio 46, 54; DcAmB S5; WhAm 3*

Zim, Herbert Spencer
American. Author, Educator
Writer of science books: *Life and Death,* 1970; *The Universe,* 1973.
b. Jul 12, 1909 in New York, New York
Source: *AmAu&B; Au&Wr 71; AuBYP; BkP; ChlLR 2; ConAu 13R; CurBio 56; JBA 51; SmATA 1; WhoAm 74, 76, 78, 80, 82*

Zimbalist, Efrem
American. Violinist, Musical Director
b. Apr 9, 1889 in Rostov, Russia
Source: *AmSCAP 66; CurBio 49; IntWW 74; Who 82; WhoWor 74*

Zimbalist, Efrem, Jr.
American. Actor, Composer
Played Lewis Erskine on TV series "The FBI," 1965-74.
b. Nov 30, 1923 in New York, New York
Source: *BiE&WWA; CelR 73; CurBio 60; FilmgC; IntMPA 75, 76, 77, 78, 79, 80, 81, 82; MovMk; NotNAT; WhoAm 82*

Zimmer, Don(ald William)
American. Baseball Player, Manager
b. Jan 17, 1931 in Cincinnati, Ohio
Source: *BaseEn; BioIn 5; WhoAm 82; WhoProB 73*

Zimmerman, Paul
American. Author
b. Oct 23, 1932 in Philadelphia, Pennsylvania
Source: *ConAu 25R*

Zindel, Paul
American. Author, Dramatist
b. May 15, 1936 in New York, New York
Source: *AuBYP; BioIn 9, 10, 11; CnThe; ConDr 73; ConLC 6; McGEWD; SmATA 16; WhoAm 82; WrDr 76*

Zingarelli, Nicola Antonio
Italian. Composer, Musician
b. Apr 4, 1752 in Naples, Italy
d. May 5, 1837 in Torre del Greco, Italy
Source: *Baker 78; OxMus*

Zinn, Howard
American. Historian
b. Aug 24, 1922 in New York, New York
Source: *AmAu&B; AmM&WS 73S; ConAu 1R, 2NR; DrAS 74H; WhoAm 74, 76, 78, 80, 82; WhoWor 74; WrDr 76*

Zinnemann, Fred
American. Motion Picture Director
b. Apr 25, 1907 in Vienna, Austria
Source: *BiDFilm; CmMov; CurBio 53; FilmgC; IntMPA 75, 76, 77, 78, 79, 80, 81, 82; IntWW 74; MovMk; OxFilm; Who 74; WhoAm 74, 76, 78, 80, 82; WhoWest 74; WhoWor 74; WorEFlm*

Zinoviev, Grigori
Russian. Political Leader
b. Sep 1883 in Elisavetgrad, Russia
d. Aug 25, 1936 in Moscow, U.S.S.R.
Source: *NewCol 75; WhoModH*

Ziolkowski, Korczak
American. Sculptor
Spent 35 years blasting Thunderhead Mt. creating monument to Crazy Horse.
b. Sep 6, 1908 in Boston, Massachusetts
d. Oct 20, 1982 in Sturgis, South Dakota
Source: *CelR 73; NewYTBS 82; WhoAm 76, 78, 80, 82; WhoAmA 73, 76, 78, 80; WhoPolA*

Zirato, Bruno
American. Concert Manager
b. Sep 27, 1884 in Calabria, Italy
d. Nov 28, 1972
Source: *CurBio 59, 73; NewYTBE 72; WhAm 5; WhoMus 72*

Zita
Italian. Empress of Austria
b. 1892 in Viareggio, Italy
d. 1922
Source: *InWom*

Zodiac Killer
American. Mass Murderer
Source: *EncACr*

Zoeller, "Fuzzy" (Frank Urban)
American. Golfer
b. Nov 11, 1951 in New Albany, Indiana
Source: *BioIn 11*

Zog I
[Ahmed Bey Zogu]
Albanian. King
b. 1895
d. Apr 9, 1961 in Suresnes, France
Source: *CurBio 44, 61*

Zola, Emile Edouard Charles
French. Author, Journalist
Leader of school of French naturalism; defended Dreyfus, 1898.
b. Apr 2, 1840 in Paris, France
d. Sep 29, 1902 in Paris, France
Source: *AtlBL; BbD; BiD&SB; CasWL; ClDMEL; CnThe; CyWA; DcBiA; DcEuL; EncWL; EuAu; EvEuW; FilmgC; McGEWD; ModWD; NewC; OxEng; OxFr; OxThe; Pen EUR; RComWL; REn; REnWD; WhoTwCL*

Zolotow, Charlotte Shapiro
American. Children's Author
b. Jun 26, 1915 in Norfolk, Virginia
Source: *AuBYP; BkP; ChlLR 2; ConAu 5R, 3NR; ForWC 70; MorJA; PiP; SmATA 1; WhoAmW 77; WrDr 76*

Zolotow, Maurice
American. Author
b. Nov 23, 1913 in New York, New York
Source: *AmAu&B; Au&Wr 71; ConAu 1R, 1NR; CurBio 57; REnAL; WhoAm 74, 76, 78, 80, 82; WhoWorJ 72; WrDr 76*

Zombies, The
[Rod Argent; Paul Atkinson; Colin Blunstone; Hugh Grundy; Chris Taylor White]
English. Rock Group
Source: *EncPR&S; IlEncRk*

Zorach, William
American. Artist
b. Feb 28, 1887 in Eurburg, Lithuania
d. Nov 15, 1967 in Bath, Maine
Source: *ConAu P-1; CurBio 43, 63, 67; DcCAA 71; WebAB; WhAm 4*

Zorina, Vera
[Eva Brigitta Hartwig]
German. Dancer, Actress
b. Jan 2, 1917 in Berlin, Germany
Source: *BiE&WWA; CurBio 41; EncMT; FilmgC; InWom; MotPP; MovMk; NotNAT; ThFT; WhoAm 74; WhoHol A; WhoThe 77*

Zorinsky, Edward
American. Senator
b. Nov 11, 1928 in Omaha, Nebraska
Source: *AlmAP 78, 80; CngDr 77, 79; WhoAm 78, 80, 82; WhoAmP 77, 79; WhoGov 75, 77*

Zorn, Anders Leonhard
Swedish. Artist
b. 1860 in Mora, Sweden
d. 1920
Source: *BioIn 1, 2, 5, 6; NewCol 75; OxArt; WebBD 80*

Zorn, Jim (John Eldon)
American. Football Player
b. Sep 24, 1947 in Garden City, Kansas
Source: *WhoAm 80*

Zoroaster
[Zarathustra]
Persian. Teacher, Prophet
b. 628BC
d. 551BC
Source: *BbD; CasWL; DcOrL 3; NewC; Pen CL; RComWL; REn*

Zorrilla, Francisco de Rojas
see: Rojas Zorilla, Francisco de

Zucco, George
English. Actor
b. Jan 11, 1886 in Manchester, England
d. May 28, 1960 in Hollywood, California
Source: *FilmgC; MovMk; Vers A; WhScrn 74, 77; WhoHol B*

Zuckerman, Ben
American. Fashion Designer, Manufacturer
b. Jul 29, 1890 in Romania
d. Aug 9, 1979 in New York, New York
Source: *WhAm 7; WorFshn*

Zuckmayer, Carl
German. Dramatist
b. Dec 27, 1896 in Nackenheim, Germany
d. Jan 18, 1977 in Visp, Switzerland
Source: *Au&Wr 71; CasWL; ClDMEL; CnMD; ConAu 69; ConLC 18; CroCD; EncWL; EvEuW; IntWW 74; McGEWD; ModGL; ModWD; OxGer; OxThe; Pen EUR; REn; REnWD; TwCW; WhoThe 77; WhoTwCL; WhoWor 74; WorEFlm*

Zuiderwijk, Cesar
see: Golden Earring

Zukerman, Pinchas
Israeli. Violinist
b. Jul 16, 1948 in Tel Aviv, Israel
Source: *IntWW 74, 75, 76, 77, 78, 79, 80, 81*

Zukofsky, Louis
American. Author
b. Jan 23, 1904 in New York, New York
d. May 12, 1978 in Port Jefferson, New York
Source: *AmAu&B; ConAu 9R, 77; ConLC 1, 2, 4, 7, 11, 18; ConP 70, 75; DrAF 76; DrAP 75; ModAL SUP; Pen AM; RAdv 1; WebE&AL; WhAm 7; WhoTwCL; WorAu; WrDr 76*

Zukor, Adolph
American. Film Producer, Executive
Founded Famous Players Lasky Corp., 1916; Paramount Pictures, 1927.
b. Jan 7, 1873 in Riese, Hungary
d. Jun 10, 1976 in Los Angeles, California
Source: *BusPN; CelR 73; CurBio 50; DcFM; FilmgC; IntMPA 75; IntWW 74; NewYTBE 73; OxFilm; WhAm 6; Who 74; WhoAm 74; WorEFlm*

Zumwalt, Elmo Russell, Jr.
American. Admiral
b. Nov 24, 1920 in San Francisco, California
Source: *IntWW 74; NewYTBE 70; WhoAm 74, 76, 78, 80, 82; WhoGov 72; WhoS&SW 73*

Zuppke, Robert C
American. Football Coach
b. Jul 12, 1879 in Berlin, Germany
d. Dec 22, 1957 in Champaign, Illinois
Source: *WhAm 3; WhoFtbl 74*

Zweig, Arnold
German. Author, Dramatist
b. Nov 10, 1887 in Prussia
d. Nov 26, 1968 in Berlin, Germany (East)
Source: *CasWL; ClDMEL; CnMD; CyWA; EncWL; EvEuW; LongCTC; ModGL; ModWD; OxEng; OxGer; Pen EUR; REn; TwCA, SUP; TwCW*

Zweig, Stefan
American. Author
b. Nov 28, 1881 in Vienna, Austria
d. Feb 22, 1942
Source: *CasWL; ClDMEL; CnMD; CnMWL; CurBio 42; EncWL; EvEuW; LongCTC; McGEWD; ModGL; ModWD; OxGer; Pen EUR; PlP&P; REn; REnWD; TwCA, SUP; TwCW; WhAm 2*

Zwerling, Israel
American. Educator
b. Jun 12, 1917 in New York, New York
Source: *AmM&WS 73P; WhoAm 74, 76, 78, 80, 82; WhoWorJ 72*

Zwicky, Fritz
Swiss. Astrophysicist
b. Feb 14, 1898 in Varna, Bulgaria
d. Feb 8, 1974
Source: *AmM&WS 73P; ConAu 49; CurBio 53, 74; NewYTBS 74; WhAm 6; WhoWor 74*

Zwingli, Huldreich
Swiss. Protestant Reformer
b. Jan 1, 1484 in Wildhause, Germany
d. Oct 10, 1531 in Kappel, Switzerland
Source: *CasWL; REn*

Zworykin, Vladimir K(osma)
American. Engineer, Physicist
b. Jul 30, 1889 in Mourom, Russia
d. Jul 29, 1982 in Princeton, New Jersey
Source: *AmM&WS 73P, 76P, 79P; AsBiEn; CurBio 49, 82; IntWW 74, 75, 76, 77, 78; McGEWB; NewYTBS 82; WebAB; WhoAm 74, 76, 78, 80; WhoWor 74, 78*

Zylis-Gara, Teresa
Polish. Opera Singer
b. Jan 23, 1937 in Vilna, Poland
Source: *NewEOp 71; NewYTBS 74*

&W	In Black and White
i	Index to Scientists
'om	Index to Women
Au	Indiana Authors and Their Books
u&W	International Authors and Writers Who's Who
MPA	International Motion Picture Almanac
VW	The International Who's Who
VWP	International Who's Who in Poetry
'B	The International Year Book and Statesmen's Who's Who
Fr	Joe Franklin's Encyclopedia of Comedians
	The Junior Book of Authors
nWil	John Willis' Screen World
uc	Leaders in Education
ec	Leaders in Electronics
W	Liberty's Women
En	Lillian Roxon's Rock Encyclopedia
Lib L	The Lincoln Library of Language Arts
Lib S	The Lincoln Library of Social Studies
BAA	Living Black American Authors
FWS	The Living Female Writers of the South
gCEL	Longman Companion to English Literature
gCTC	Longman Companion to Twentieth Century Literature
kW	Look for the Woman
hC	Lutheran Cyclopedia
M	The MGM Stock Company
DCB	The Macmillan Dictionary of Canadian Biography
GDA	McGraw-Hill Dictionary of Art
GEWB	The McGraw-Hill Encyclopedia of World Biography
GEWD	McGraw-Hill Encyclopedia of World Drama
GMS	McGraw-Hill Modern Scientists & Engineers
HR	Medal of Honor Recipients
BBF	The Men Behind Boys' Fiction
E	The Middle East and North Africa
nWr	Minnesota Writers
dAL	Modern American Literature
dBlW	Modern Black Writers
dBrL	Modern British Literature
dCmwL	Modern Commonwealth Literature
dFrL	Modern French Literature
dGL	Modern German Literature
dLAL	Modern Latin American Literature
dRL	Modern Romance Literatures
dSL	Modern Slavic Literatures
dWD	Modern World Drama
BMP	More Books by More People
JA	More Junior Authors
PP	Motion Picture Performers
uLC	Moulton's Library of Literary Criticism
Mk	The Movie Makers

MugS	Mug Shots
MusMk	The Music Makers
MusSN	Musicians since 1900
NamesHP	Names in the History of Psychology
NatCAB	The National Cyclopaedia of American Biography
NatPD	National Playwrights Directory
NegAl	Negro Almanac
NewC	The New Century Handbook of English Literature
NewCol	New Columbia Encyclopedia
NewCBMT	New Complete Book of the American Musical Theater
NewEOp	The New Encyclopedia of the Opera
NewGrD	The New Grove Dictionary of Music and Musicians
NewWmR	New Women in Rock
NewYHSD	The New-York Historical Society's Dictionary of Artists in America
NewYTBE	The New York Times Biographical Edition
NewYTBS	The New York Times Biographical Service
NewYTET	The New York Times Encyclopedia of Television
NewbC	Newbery and Caldecott Medal Books
Newb	Newbery Medal Books
NotAW	Notable American Women
NotNAT	Notable Names in the American Theatre
Novels	Novels and Novelists
ObitOF	Obituaries On File
ObitT	Obituaries from the Times
OfEnT	Official Encyclopedia of Tennis
OfNBA	Official NBA Register
OhA&B	Ohio Authors and Their Books
OxAmH	The Oxford Companion to American History
OxAmL	The Oxford Companion to American Literature
OxArt	The Oxford Companion to Art
OxCan	The Oxford Companion to Canadian History and Literature
OxDecA	The Oxford Companion to the Decorative Arts
OxEng	The Oxford Companion to English Literature
OxFilm	The Oxford Companion to Film
OxFr	The Oxford Companion to French Literature
OxGer	The Oxford Companion to German Literature
OxLaw	The Oxford Companion to Law
OxMus	The Oxford Companion to Music
OxShips	The Oxford Companion to Ships and the Sea
OxSpan	The Oxford Companion to Spanish Literature
OxThe	The Oxford Companion to the Theatre
Pen	The Penguin Companion to World Literature

PhDcTCA	Phaidon Dictionary of Twentieth Century Art
PiP	The Pied Pipers
PlP&P	Plays, Players, and Playwrights
PoChrch	The Poets of the Church
PoIre	The Poets of Ireland
PoLE	The Poets Laureate of England
Po&Wr	The Poets & Writers, Inc.
PolProf	Political Profiles
Pseud	Pseudonyms of Authors
PseudN	Pseudonyms and Nicknames Dictionary
PueRA	Puerto Rican Authors
RAdv	The Reader's Adviser
RComWL	The Reader's Companion to World Literature
REn	The Reader's Encyclopedia
REnAL	The Reader's Encyclopedia of American Literature
REnAW	The Reader's Encyclopedia of the American West
REnWD	The Reader's Encyclopedia of World Drama
RGAfL	A Reader's Guide to African Literature
RkOn	Rock On
Rk 100	Rock 100
ScF&FL	Science Fiction and Fantasy Literature
SelBAA	Selected Black American Authors
SenS	A Sense of Story
SixAP	Sixty American Poets, 1896-1944
SmATA	Something about the Author
St&PR	Standard and Poor's Register of Corporations, Directors and Executives
Str&VC	Story and Verse for Children
TexWr	Texas Writers of Today
ThFT	They Had Faces Then
ThrBJA	Third Book of Junior Authors
TwCA	Twentieth Century Authors
TwCBDA	The Twentieth Century Biographical Dictionary of Notable Americans
TwCCW	Twentieth-Century Children's Writers
TwCCr&M	Twentieth Century Crime and Mystery Writers
TwCLC	Twentieth-Century Literary Criticism
TwCW	Twentieth Century Writing
TwYS	Twenty Years of Silents
USBiR	United States. Department of State: The Biographic Register
Vers	The Versatiles
Ward	1977 Ward's Who's Who among U.S. Motor Vehicle Manufacturers
WebAB	Webster's American Biographies
WebAMB	Webster's American Military Biographies
WebBD	Webster's Biographical Dictionary
WebE&AL	Webster's New World Comp to English and American Literature
What	Whatever Became of . . .?
WhDW	Who Did What
WhAm	Who Was Who in America
WhAmP	Who Was Who in American Politics
WhE&EA	Who Was Who among Englis European Authors
WhFla	Who Was Who in Florida
WhJnl	Who Was Who in Journalism
WhLit	Who Was Who in Literature
WhNAA	Who Was Who among North American Authors
WhScrn	Who Was Who on Screen
WhThe	Who Was Who in the Theatr
WhWW-II	Who Was Who in World Wa
Who	Who's Who
WhoAdv	Who's Who in Advertising
WhoAm	Who's Who in America
WhoAmA	Who's Who in American Art
WhoAmJ	Who's Who in American Jew
WhoAmL	Who's Who in American Law
WhoAmP	Who's Who in American Poli
WhoAmW	Who's Who of American Wo
WhoArch	Who's Who in Architecture f 1400 to the Present Day
WhoArt	Who's Who in Art
WhoAtom	Who's Who in Atoms
WhoBbl	Who's Who in Basketball
WhoBlA	Who's Who among Black Americans
WhoBox	Who's Who in Boxing
WhoCan	Who's Who in Canada
WhoChL	The Who's Who of Children's Literature
WhoColR	Who's Who of the Colored Ra
WhoCon	Who's Who in Consulting
WhoE	Who's Who in the East
WhoFash	Who's Who in Fashion
WhoF&I	Who's Who in Finance and Industry
WhoFtbl	Who's Who in Football
WhoFr	Who's Who in France
WhoGolf	Who's Who in Golf
WhoGov	Who's Who in Government
WhoGrA	Who's Who in Graphic Art
WhoHcky	Who's Who in Hockey
WhoHol	Who's Who in Hollywood
WhoHr&F	Who's Who in Horror and Fa Fiction
WhoHrs	Who's Who of the Horrors an Other Fantasy Films
WhoIns	Who's Who in Insurance
WhoJazz	Who's Who of Jazz
WhoLab	Who's Who in Labor
WhoLA	Who's Who among Living Au of Older Nations
WhoMW	Who's Who in the Midwest
WhoMilH	Who's Who in Military Histor
WhoModH	Who's Who in Modern Histor 1860-1980